IN SIX VOLUMES, CAREFULLY REVISED AND CORRECTED

MATTHEW HENRY'S
COMMENTARY

ON THE WHOLE BIBLE

WHEREIN EACH CHAPTER, IS SUMMED UP IN ITS CONTENTS: THE SACRED TEXT
INSERTED AT LARGE IN DISTINCT PARAGRAPHS; EACH PARAGRAPH
REDUCED TO ITS PROPER HEADS: THE SENSE GIVEN,
AND LARGELY ILLUSTRATED

WITH

PRACTICAL REMARKS AND OBSERVATIONS

VOL. I.—GENESIS TO DEUTERONOMY

World Bible Publishers
Iowa Falls, Iowa

INTRODUCTION

By Charles G. Trumbull, Litt.D.

Matthew Henry digs deep down below the surface of God's Word; he sees truths hidden from most of us until he has shown them. He finds the most practical applications of God's wisdom to our everyday life; and applications, also, from the successes and failures of the men and women who live before us in the pages of the Bible.

So it is a rare spiritual treat to sit down with any part of Matthew Henry's Commentary open before us, and quietly read what he has written. Whether for sermon preparation, teaching a Sunday school class, leading a prayer meeting, light on a difficult passage, or for the enrichment of one's personal life, this truly great saint ministers to us unfailingly. The publishers have rendered a far-reaching service in continuing to make his Commentary available, and it is to be hoped that this new edition will introduce many of the present generation to treasures they have not yet known.

The Commentary is in constant use by the undersigned and other members of the editorial staff of *The Sunday School Times*, and one of the Associate Editors, Philip E. Howard, Jr. (*now Editor*) has expressed his personal indebtedness in an editorial review written for the *Times*, which follows:

"The apostolic Whitefield, whose labours and virtues inspired even the pen of Cowper, was trained, as a Christian and a preacher, by Mr. Henry's Commentary . . . he literally studied it on his knees; read it through four times; and to the close of life spoke of its author with profound veneration: ever calling him— the great Mr. Henry."

It was J. B. Williams who thus wrote of Whitefield's love for the Commentary. It will be remembered that George Whitefield was one of the early leaders of the Methodist Church, closely associated with John and Charles Wesley, and one of the greatest preachers of the Gospel of all time. Among the hymns that Cowper gave to the Church are those beginning, "There is a fountain filled with blood," "O for a closer walk with God," and "God moves in a mysterious way." Who can measure the blessing that these beautiful hymns have brought to Christians during the last century and a half? Who can trace the streams of blessing that began to flow out from Matthew Henry's Commentary two hundred years ago?

A valuable contribution was made to the literature of the present-day Christian Church when the Fleming H. Revell Company published its now well-known six-volume edition of the Commentary, carefully revised and corrected. It is of convenient size, each volume being about six by nine inches, and one and a half inches thick, and the text is clearly printed.

It is a monumental work, and one marvels at the industry and devotion of the author, who produced it, *besides forty-five other books and pamphlets,* in the midst of many duties as pastor, preacher, and father, during a lifetime of fifty-two years.

Matthew Henry's attitude toward the Scriptures may be seen in his own statement, where he sets forth "those great and sacred principles which I go upon, and am governed by, in this endeavour to explain and improve [make the best use of] these portions of holy writ; which endeavour I humbly offer to the service of those (and to those only I expect it will be acceptable) who agree with me in these six principles."

Mr. Henry then explains his principles in brief paragraphs. The headings are as follows:

I. That religion is the one thing useful.
II. That divine revelation is necessary to true religion.
III. That divine revelation is not now to be found or expected anywhere but in the Scriptures of the Old and New Testament, and there it is. . . . That *all scripture is given by inspiration of God* (2 Tim. 3: 16) and that holy men spake and wrote as they were moved by the Holy Ghost (2 Pet. 1: 21).
IV. That the Scriptures of the Old and New Testament were purposely designed for our learning.
V. That the holy Scriptures were not only designed for our learning, but are the settled standing rule of our faith and practice.
VI. That therefore it is the duty of all Christians diligently to search the Scriptures, and it is the office of ministers to guide and assist them therein.

The text of the whole Bible is given with the Commentary. Matthew Henry gives an introduction to each book, as well as a brief summary and outline at the head of each chapter; then follow the Scripture, a few verses at a time, and the notes on the text.

Following a well-known expository principle, Henry states, explains, and applies. In every passage of Scripture he finds lessons for daily living. The pages are full of such epigrammatic and refreshing sentences as the following:

"Carnal hearts are apt to think themselves as good as they should be, because perhaps, in some one particular instance, they are not so bad as they have been. Thus Micah retains his idols, but thinks himself happy in having a Levite to be his priest (Judges 17: 13)."

"Those that trust in God, and in his providence and promise, though they have great families and small incomes, can cheerfully hope that he who sends mouths will send meat. He who feeds the brood of the ravens will not starve the seed of the righteous."

"He [Moses] came down adorned with the best beauty; for *the skin of his face shone*, v. 29 [Exod. 34]. This time of his being in the mount, he heard only what he had heard before, but he saw more of the glory of God, which having with open face beheld, he was in some measure *changed into the same image, from glory to glory* (2 Cor. 3: 18)."

"See how much better Wisdom is than the precious onyx or the sapphire, for Wisdom was, from eternity, God's delight (Prov. 8: 30) and lay in his bosom, but the sapphires are the pavement under his feet; there let us put all the wealth of this world, and not in our hearts."

The Commentary is permeated with an atmosphere of deep love for the Word of God. It is full of kindly warning, sound counsel for everyday life, and comfort and good cheer. It is not alone a reference work for Bible students and Christian workers, but is valuable as a household book that may be read aloud at family prayers or during a quiet evening. Matthew Henry's biographer said of it, "To reckon the number of households in which the Exposition has for more than a century descended from father to son, with all the care of the most venerated heirloom, is impossible." The language of the notes is marked by simplicity and clearness, and since it is two hundred years old it comes to modern ears with just enough quaintness to make a pleasing and lasting impression.

The late Dr. Amos R. Wells, who owned a library of 24,000 volumes, in speaking of the Commentary to a friend said that there was nothing else like it, that he used it all the time, and that he got blessing from it each time he read it. All who know the Commentary bear testimony to the spiritual refreshment it invariably brings to the Christian's heart.

MEMOIRS
OF
MATTHEW HENRY
As Written by a Contemporary
S. PALMER

MOST readers of a work which has acquired such a degree of celebrity feel a desire to know something of the author; and that desire is increased in proportion as they find themselves interested in the work itself. It may therefore be presumed, that the users of Matthew Henry's Commentary, which has long been in high repute in the religious world, will wish for some information concerning the character and life of that excellent man. This is not merely an innocent, but a laudable, curiosity, which we are happy to have the present opportunity of gratifying, and we are persuaded that the more the author is known, the greater pleasure readers will feel in the use of his work.

Matthew Henry was the second son of the eminent minister of the gospel, Philip Henry. This his son was born October 28, in the same year, which also, he observes with pleasure in his diary, gave birth to many other ministers of his acquaintance, to whom God had appointed more peaceful days than their predecessors, whom their brethren, who hated them, had cast out. His birthplace was Broad-Oak, in Iscoid, Flintshire, within the parish of Malpal, which is in Cheshire, a district signalized in British annals for the famous monastery of Bangor. Hither his father removed but a fortnight before his birth, not being suffered any longer to continue in the place of his former ministry; and here the elder Henry spent the remainder of his days. Mr. Henry's mother was Katharine Matthews, the daughter and heiress of Daniel Matthews, a gentleman of an ancient family and a considerable estate, which, upon his death, came into the possession of Philip Henry, by which he was enabled to live in comfort after his ejectment, and not only to preach the gospel gratis, as he had opportunity, but likewise to relieve several of his necessitous brethren. But his wife proved to him a greater treasure, as she was a woman equally eminent for piety and every other endowment. Her son has done ample justice to her character in an excellent discourse occasioned by her death, on Prov. 31: 28: *Her children arise up, and call her blessed.*

The circumstances of Matthew's birth were rather remarkable. The birth was premature, and his mother's labour was so sudden that she was delivered before any assistance could be procured; and he was so weakly a child that no one expected him to live. He was therefore baptized the day after he was born by Mr. Holland, the minister of the parish, but without godfather or godmother; and his father desired the sign of the cross might not be used, but the minister said he durst not omit it.

When Matthew was about five years old he had the measles, by which his brother, who was a year older than himself, was cut off; a circumstance which deeply affected him, and which he noticed with great seriousness in a paper written on his thirteenth birthday, wherein he drew out a list of the mercies which he had received, with lively expressions of gratitude to the Author of them. He long continued weakly, subject to agues and other complaints; but he very early discovered a good mental capacity, and a thoughtful turn, so that it was remarked his childhood had less of vanity than that of most children, and that at an earlier period than is usual he put away childish things. He was able to read a chapter in the Bible distinctly when he was but about three years old, and was used to make pertinent remarks on what he read.

His first abiding convictions of religion, according to his own written account, in the paper above referred to, were wrought when he was ten years of age in consequence of a sermon preached by his excellent father on Psalm 51: 17: *The sacrifices of God are a broken spirit; a broken and a contrite heart, O God, thou wilt not despise.* "I think it was that," says Matthew, "that melted me; afterwards I began to enquire after Christ." He was early accustomed to make memorandums of the sermons which he heard, and of the effect they had upon his mind. From one of these papers, dated December 17, 1673, it appears that he heard a sermon on the signs of true grace, which put him upon the strict examination of himself by the rules which had been laid down; and, after opening his mind to his father, he was encouraged to draw a favourable conclusion respecting his spiritual state. He particularly mentions his repentance for sin, according to the Scripture account of it, in many passages which he transcribes; his solemn dedication of himself to God, according to the tenor of the Gospel covenant, and his love to God, as evidenced by his love to the people of God, whom he chose as his best companions; and his love to the Word of God, concerning which he expresses himself thus: "I esteem it above all; I desire it as the food of my soul; I greatly delight both in reading and hearing it; and my soul can witness subjection to it in some measure; I think I love the Word of God for the purity of it; I love the ministers and messengers of it; I rejoice in the good success of it; all which were given as marks of true love to the Word in a sermon I lately heard on Psalm 119: 140: *Thy word is very pure, therefore thy servant loveth it.*"

It seems that Matthew Henry had an inclination to the ministry from his childhood. This partly appeared in his fondness for imitating preaching, which he did with a degree of propriety and gravity beyond his years; as also in his frequent attendance at the private meetings of good people, with whom he would pray, and repeat sermons, and sometimes expound the Scriptures, to the surprise of all present. One of them once expressed to his father some concern lest his son should be too forward and fall into the snare of spiritual pride, to whom the good man replied, "Let him go on; he fears God and designs well, and I hope God will keep him and bless him."

Philip Henry was used generally to have some young student in his house, previous to his entrance on the ministry, who, while he was a pupil to Mr. Henry, acted as a tutor to the latter's children. One of these was William Turner, who was born in that neighbourhood, and afterwards was many years vicar of Walburton, in Sussex, and the author of a work in folio on the History of remarkable Providences. He lived with Mr. Henry at the time his son entered on his grammar, and was the person referred to by him in the papers quoted above as having initiated him into the Latin language; and it may be supposed, from his great piety and studious turn, that the tutor was in other respects useful to the boy. Matthew remained under his father's eye and tuition till he was about eighteen years of age, from which he enjoyed singular advantage for both literary and religious attainments to qualify him for the ministerial office; and he soon afforded ample proof that he had not enjoyed them in vain. As his constitution grew stronger with his growing years, his mind also improved in knowledge, grace, and holiness, so that he was richly furnished betimes for the important office to which he had devoted his life, and seemed not to need any further assistance than he had enjoyed, or might yet enjoy, under the tuition, and from the example, of such a father, who was not only an excellent scholar himself, but had an admirable method of communicating knowledge to others. He was desirous, however, that his son might enjoy some further advantages in his education at some more public seminary.

Philip Henry had been partial to a University, having himself passed some years at Christ Church, Oxford. But the sad alteration which had taken place in those seats of learning after the Restoration greatly altered his opinion, so that, to preserve his son from the snares and temptations to which he might have been exposed from the want of proper discipline, he determined upon sending him, in the year 1680, to an academy which was then kept at Islington by the learned and pious Thomas Doolittle, who trained up many young men for the ministry, and made a distinguished figure among the Protestant Dissenters. Here, among many other excellent young persons, Matthew enjoyed the society of Mr. Bury, who was from the same neighbourhood, and afterwards an eminent minister, who bore this honourable testimony to Matthew's character during the course of his studies: "I was never better pleased, when I was at Mr. Doolittle's, than when I was in young Mr. Henry's company. He had such a savour of religion always upon his spirit, was of such a cheerful temper, so diffusive of all knowledge, so ready in the Scriptures, so pertinent in all his petitions, so full and clear in all his performances, etc., that he was to me a most desirable friend, and I love heaven the better since he went thither." Mr. Bury observes, however, that "he had an almost inconceivable quickness in his speech, but that he afterwards happily corrected it, as well for his own sake as for the benefit of others."

How long Matthew continued with Mr. Doolittle is not quite certain. Such was the persecuting temper of the times, that Mr. Doolittle was obliged to leave Islington (upon which he removed to Battersea) and soon after to disperse his pupils into private families at Clapham, to which place it does not appear that Matthew Henry followed them. It is certain, however, that when he quitted this academy he returned to his father's house, where he pursued his studies with great assiduity. Among his papers is one dated Broad-Oak, 1682 (about which time it seems probable that he returned thither), which is a memorial of the mercies which he had received from the hand of God from his birth to that time, which was his birthday: it consists of twenty-six particulars, and discovers a lively spirit of devotion.

Matthew was now twenty years of age, and had made great improvement in all the branches of learning, which tended to fit him for appearing with great advantage under the ministerial character. But it does not appear that he had yet begun to exercise his talents in public. He was, however, frequently engaged in social exercises of devotion among the good people of his father's acquaintance who resorted to that house of prayer. His company was much coveted by them, and they were highly gratified by his visits, which he was ever ready to make to the meanest of them, when he was used to pray with them, and converse with great freedom, affection, and judgment, on their spiritual concerns.

As the times were dark, and the circumstances of dissenting ministers were very discouraging, Matthew had no prospect of a pastoral settlement with a congregation; he therefore, with the advice of friends, took up another and very different employment. Rowland Hunt, Esq. of Boreaton, who married the daughter of Lord Paget, and at whose house Philip Henry used to preach once a quarter, and administer the Lord's Supper, advised the father to enter his son in one of the Inns of court to study law. This was not to divert him from entering the ministry, but to find him some present employment which might hereafter be advantageous to him, not only in a temporal view, as he was heir to a handsome estate, but also as a minister. Accordingly, Matthew went to Gray's-Inn about the end of April, 1685.

Some of his friends discovered painful apprehensions lest this situation, and the connexions he might here form, should prove unfavourable to his religious interests, and, in the issue, divert him from the sacred office to which his former studies had been directed, and for which he discovered such peculiar qualifications. But their fears happily proved groundless; his heart was fully bent for God, and established with grace; so that he still maintained his stedfastness amidst all the temptations with which he was surrounded. He happily formed an acquaintance with several young gentlemen, then students of the law, who were exemplary for sobriety, diligence, and religion, who were glad to receive him as an intimate associate, and with whom a mutual friendship continued to the last. Here Matthew's diligence in study, his quick apprehension, his rapid proficiency, his tenacious memory, and his ready utterance, induced some of the profession to think that he would have been eminent in the practice of law had he applied himself to it as his business. But he felt himself under no temptation to relinquish the object of his first resolution, and he continually kept that in view, habituating himself to those exercises which might further his preparation for it. He heard the most celebrated preachers in town, among whom he seemed to be best pleased with Dr. Stillingfleet, at St. Andrew's, Holborn, for his serious, practical preaching; and with Dr. Tillotson, at Lawrence Jewry, for his admirable sermons against popery. He accustomed himself to take notes of what he heard, and he constantly sent a short scheme of the sermons to his father, to whom he generally wrote twice every week, giving him an account of all remarkable occurrences with great judgment, yet with all the caution and prudence which the difficulties of the times required.

During his residence in London, Matthew not only attended with constancy on the public worship of God, but promoted social prayer and religious conference with his particular friends, and he sometimes expounded the Scripture to them. When he was about to leave them, he delivered to them an excellent and affectionate discourse on 2 Thess. 2: 1: *By the coming of our Lord Jesus Christ, and our gathering together unto him*, recommending to himself and them the hope of that blessed meeting as their greatest comfort, now they were about to part. The letters which he wrote to his friends while he continued at Gray's-Inn discover the lively sense of divine things which he preserved upon his mind, of which an excellent one of great length was to his friend G. Illidge, of Nantwich, whose father's Memoirs were afterwards printed: from whence it appears how valuable a correspondent he was, and how much he aimed at useful-ness, in his letters as well as in his conversation.

But though his time was not unprofitably spent in London, Matthew sometimes complained of the want of the opportunities he had enjoyed in his father's house, his "Broad-Oak Sabbaths, and the heavenly manna" which he had tasted there, and expressed his earnest wish to return. Accordingly, in June, 1686, he went to Broad-Oak, and continued several months in the country, when he made it appear that his residence in London and his study of the law had been no way prejudicial to his religious temper or ministerial qualifications. He now began to preach frequently as a candidate for the ministry, and he everywhere met with great acceptance.

Matthew's great acceptance and success at the commencement of his ministry encouraged him to prosecute it with increasing ardour. He had occasion to take a journey to Chester, where some good people had heard of his fame, and desired him to preach to them one evening in a private house, liberty for public worship not being yet granted. He readily consented, and preached three evenings successively at different houses in the city. The specimen which these good people received of his talents excited in them an earnest desire to have him settle with them, having, about two years before, lost two aged and faithful ministers, and another in the city, Mr. Harvey being far advanced in years, and preaching very privately. Being encouraged by a prevailing report that government was disposed to grant indulgence to dissenters, some of them went, about the latter end of the year, to Broad-Oak, to express to Matthew their wishes for his continued services. He was then in the twenty-fifth year of his age. On consulting with his father, and thinking there was the voice of Providence in the affair, he gave them some encouragement to hope for a compliance with their invitation, if liberty should be granted, provided Mr. Harvey consented, and they would wait till his return from London, where he was going to reside some months. They expressed their readiness to receive him upon his own terms and in his own time.

On the 24th of January, 1687, he set out for London with the only son of his friend Mr. Hunt. The first material news he heard in London was that the king had granted indulgence to the dissenters, and had empowered certain gentlemen to give out licenses: the price of one for a single person was ten pounds; but if several joined, sixteen pounds; and eight persons might join in taking out one license.

Not many dissenters took out these licenses; but the disposition of the court being sufficiently understood, many began to meet publicly. About the end of February, Mr. Henry wrote to his father that Mr. Faldo, a Congregational minister, had preached both morning and afternoon, to many hundred people at Mr. Sclater's meeting in Moorfields. The people of Chester now reminded him of his engagements to them, the propriety of which he sometimes was ready to question, but he did not hesitate to fulfil them. The reverend and learned Mr. Woodcock came to him, and told him that he wished to engage him in a lecture which was set up chiefly for young persons; but thanking him for his respect, Matthew modestly declined the offer and said that his service was most wanted in the country, and might be most suitable there.

Matthew now began to think seriously on the business of ordination, and consulted some ministers about it, particularly Francis Tallents, of Salop, who had been some time in London, and James Owen, who was lately come up from Oswestry, both of whom had known him from his childhood, and they gave him all possible encouragement in this design. He viewed the ministerial office in so awful a light that he set himself to consider the engagement into which a person enters in his ordination with the greatest seriousness. He drew up, on this occasion, chiefly for his own use, a discourse on 1 Tim. 4: 15: *Give thyself wholly to them,* in which he stated the nature and several parts of the ministerial work, and what it is for a man to be *wholly in them* (as it is

in the Greek), and then proceeded thoroughly to examine his own heart with respect to his fitness for them. The paper is entitled "Serious Self-examination before Ordination," with this text prefixed: *Search me, O God, and know my heart, etc.* "It is worth while," says he, "for a man at such a time deliberately to ask himself, and conscientiously to answer, the six following questions: 1. What am I? 2. What have I done? 3. From what principles do I act in this undertaking? 4. What are the ends I aim at in it? 5. What do I want? 6. What are my purposes and resolutions for the future?" To each of these questions he gives a distinct answer, in several particulars, at a very considerable length, which fill more than four large folio pages. The whole discovers the utmost seriousness, humility, and conscientious regard to truth and duty.

A friend advised him to accept ordination from one of the bishops because of the king's declaration for liberty of conscience but which was really intended to promote popery. But Matthew decided against that step, and applied to ministers in London whom he knew to be favourably disposed towards him. He was ordained on the 9th of May, but where is not known: nor is there any certain record of a sermon or charge usually delivered on such occasions. The service was performed in private, and supposedly because of an excess of caution the ministers gave him only a brief testimonial of his ordination. The testimonial was signed by W. Wickens, Francis Tallents, Edward Lawrence, Nathanael Vincent, James Owen, and Richard Steele. However, of such importance was a regular certificate of Presbyterian ordination esteemed in those days that Matthew later applied to the ordainers then living for a certificate in form, which he received on December 17, 1702.

Soon after his ordination, Matthew hastened to Chester to enter on his pastoral charge. There he was joyfully received, especially because of the liberty which was now granted to dissenters, although the purpose of the king in granting it was sufficiently known. Matthew's first sermon, which was preached in an outbuilding, was on 1 Cor. 2: 2: *I determined not to know anything among you, save Jesus Christ, and him crucified.* It was said of Matthew that "they received him as an angel of God."

His situation at Chester proved highly agreeable to him, on account of the valuable society he met with there; and it was soon rendered the more so, as three of his sisters were providentially brought to reside in that place, in consequence of their being married to respectable and pious men, who belonged to his congregation (Mr. Radford, Mr. Holton, and Dr. Tilston), to whom he conducted himself with a truly fraternal affection. But a yet more agreeable and important circumstance was his entrance into the conjugal state with a lady who was possessed of every qualification to render that state happy. This was Katharine, daughter of John Hardware, of Moldsworth. On his first proposal, some obstacles lay in the way, but they were so completely removed that the match was as agreeable to her parents as it was to his, so that they came to reside at Chester, and they all lived together. But this pleasing scene, like many earthly ones, was of very short continuance; for within a year and a half Mrs. Henry was seized in childbed with the smallpox, and died, Feb. 14, 1689, though the child was spared.

It was no small alleviation of Matthew's grief that the child was spared. His good father came to visit him on the occasion, when he baptized the child in public, and the scene was peculiarly solemn and affecting. On presenting his child in baptism Matthew professed his faith and renewed his covenant in a most affecting manner, and then added, "Although my house be not so with God, yet he hath made with me an everlasting covenant, etc. I offer up this my child to the great God, a plant out of a dry ground, desiring it may be implanted into Christ."

Under this severe affliction, God strengthened his heart and his hands, so that he pursued his work with his usual diligence and vivacity. At length, a kind providence repaired his loss, and the mother of his deceased wife was the means of procuring him another. She recommended to him the daughter of Robert Warburton, Esq. of Grange, the son of Peter Warburton, Esq. serjeant-at-law, and one of the judges of the common pleas. He was a gentleman fond of retirement, who constantly had the Bible and Baxter's "Saint's Rest" on the table before him, and whose house was a sanctuary to the silenced ministers. Mr. Henry's marriage to this lady was consummated, July 8th, the same year, at Grange, when both his father and mother were present, who were greatly pleased with the new relation, and blessed God who had thus filled up the breach. Mr. and Mrs. Hardware now left Chester, and retired to an estate which they had in Wirral, but their affection for Matthew as a son continued.

From this time Matthew kept a regular diary of all material occurrences and transactions to the end of his life, a practice which he had lately recommended to his friends in a discourse on *Redeeming the Time.* From this diary of his the following part of his history is principally taken.—We shall now give some account of his family by this second marriage, and the manner in which he governed it.

In the space of twenty-two years he had nine children, eight of which were daughters. Three of them, namely, the first, second, and fourth, died in their infancy. The first of these children was born April 12, 1691, on which occasion Matthew made his will; but she died in about a year and a half. In his diary he makes many pious remarks on this event, and the night of her funeral he writes thus: "I have been this day doing a work I never did before—burying a child. A sad day's work! But my good friend, Mr. Lawrence, preached very seasonably and excellently, from Psalm 39: 9: *I was dumb, I opened not my mouth, because thou didst it.*"

On the birth of the fourth of these children, he writes, June 24, 1697, "This child has come into a world of tears," for his pious father, who had taken a pleasure in coming to baptize his grandchildren, (which he did in a peculiarly interesting manner) was now dead, and he was particularly affected at the recollection of that event, as it had happened the very same day of the month the preceding year. But, says Matthew, "God has set the one over against the other, that I may sing of mercy and judgment." But this child was taken away in less than a year and a half, upon which occasion Matthew writes, "My desire is to be sensible of the affliction, and yet patient under it. It is a smarting rod; God calls my sins to remembrance—the coldness of my love, my abuse of spiritual comforts." But he adds, " 'Tis a rod in the hand of my Father. I desire to see a father's authority, who may do what he will; and a father's love, who will do what is best. We resign the soul of the child to Him that gave it.—I am in deaths often; Lord, teach me how to die daily, etc."

On May 3, 1700, God was pleased to give Matthew a son. But the birth was attended with such uncommon danger to both mother and child that he mentions it as a miracle of mercy that their lives were spared. This child Matthew himself baptized, naming him Philip. (When this child was about a month old, he was so ill that there was but little hope of his life; and Mrs. Henry continued in such weakness, increased by her anxiety about her infant, that she, and all her friends, expected her speedy dissolution. But God mercifully interposed, and restored both her and her child.

We shall now notice Matthew's conduct in his family, which was in a great measure regulated by the example of his pious father, of whose house those who had access to it were ready to say, *This is no other than the house of God, and the gate of heaven*. Matthew was constant in the worship of God in his family, morning and evening, which nothing was suffered to prevent. He called all the members of it together as early in the morning as circumstances would permit; and he did not delay it to a late hour in the evening, lest drowsiness should prevent devotion. He was never tedious, but always full and comprehensive, performing much in a little time, which seldom exceeded half an hour. He began with a short invocation for assistance and acceptance. He then read a portion of Scripture (in the morning from the Old Testament, and from the New in the evening), giving a short exposition in a plain and familiar manner, so as to render it both intelligible and pleasant, and added practical reflections. To engage the greater attention, he used to examine some of his family how they understood, and what they remembered of what they had heard. After this, some part of a Psalm was constantly sung from a collection which he himself made, entitled, "Family Hymns," selected from different translations of the Psalms; and every one had a book to prevent the interruption occasioned by reading the lines. After singing, he prayed with great affection and propriety, noticing every particular case in his family, and not omitting the state of the nation and the Church. This variety prevented the service from being tedious, and his whole family attended it with pleasure. When the whole was ended, his children came to him for his blessing, which he gave with solemnity and affection.

Beside his stated family-worship, he occasionally kept family-fasts, as special circumstances required, when he sometimes called in the assistance of his friends, whose respective cases and trials were committed to God with his own.

On the Lord's Day he did not omit any part of his ordinary family-worship, but rising earlier on that day, after his private devotion he began it somewhat sooner. On returning from the public morning service, after he had dined, he sang a Psalm, offered a short prayer, and then retired till the time of the afternoon service. In the evening he usually repeated the substance of both his sermons in his family, when many of his neighbours came in: this he followed with singing and prayer, and concluded with singing two verses more, previous to the benediction. Before supper, he catechised the younger children: after supper, he sang the 136th Psalm, and catechised the elder children

vii

and servants; examined them as to what they remembered of the sermons, and concluded the day with prayer. Having a happy constitution of both body and mind, he went through all this service with constancy and comfort, besides all his ministerial work in public, which he performed without any assistance, and which we now proceed to notice.

After his public exposition was ended, he sang a second time, and prayed for about half an hour. After which he preached about an hour, then prayed, and usually concluded with singing the 117th Psalm. He pursued the same plan in the afternoon, excepting that he then expounded the New Testament, and at the close sang the 134th Psalm, or some verses of the 136th. In singing, he always made use of David's Psalms, or other Scripture-hymns, which he preferred to such as are wholly of human composition, the latter being generally liable to this exception: "that the fancy is too high, and the matter too low, and sometimes such as a wise and good man may not be able, with entire satisfaction, to offer up as a sacrifice to God." In this work of praise he took great delight, as appeared from the manner in which he engaged in it. In regard to public affairs, he was never guilty of profaning the worship of God by introducing anything obnoxious to government, or offensive to persons of any party; nor, on the other hand, by giving flattering titles to any description of men. The state of the reformed churches abroad was much upon his heart, and he was a fervent intercessor for those of them that suffered persecution for righteousness' sake. He shunned not to declared the whole counsel of God. He delighted in preaching Christ and the doctrines of free grace; but with equal zeal he preached up holiness in all its branches, constantly affirming it to be a *faithful saying, That they who believe in God should be careful to maintain good works*. He was indeed so practical a preacher, and sometimes used such a phraseology in treating on practical subjects, that some have censured him as being too legal; but he was no more of a legalist than the Apostle *James*, whom he knew well how to reconcile with the Apostle *Paul*.

It was a common custom with Mr. Henry to preach a series of sermons upon a particular subject, which sometimes took up several years. But he did not follow the practice of several old divines, who delivered a great number of discourses on the same text: his method was, to prevent the tediousness of such a practice, to fix upon different texts for all the different parts of the subject which he discussed. By thus treating the various branches of faith and practice in this connected view, as well as by his exposition of the Bible in course, his hearers had peculiar advantage for improving in Scripture knowledge above those whose ministers discourse only upon short detached passages: accordingly it was remarked that Mr. Henry's people in general greatly excelled in judgment and spiritual understanding.

Another part of Mr. Henry's constant work was CATECHISING, in which he engaged with peculiar delight, because of his affection to the young; and for which he was eminently qualified by his happy talent for adapting his instructions to the weakest capacities. The time set apart for this service was Saturday afternoon, when many besides the catechumens were used to attend. He usually spent about an hour in it, and both began and ended with prayer, in which his expressions were very plain and affectionate. He used the Assembly's Catechism with the elder children; but did not content himself with hearing them repeat the answers, but divided them into several short propositions, and put a distinct question to each, explaining every part in a familiar manner, and supporting it by a suitable text of Scripture. His method of catechising may be seen in the edition of the Assembly's Catechism which he published, entitled, "A Scripture Catechism in the Method of the Assembly's." A text of Scripture was annexed to the answer to every subordinate question, grounded on the general answer in that system, by which means children had a

viii

large collection of Scripture passages treasured up in their memories.

But we are informed that an excellent and judicious friend of Mr. Henry, "Mr. Charlton of Manchester, thinking even the Shorter Catechism of the Assembly too long for children, and some parts of it too abstruse, and quite above their capacity, desired and pressed Mr. Henry to draw up a shorter and plainer catechism for children very young," which accordingly he did; and in the collection of his works it is prefixed to the former. Its title is, "A plain Catechism for Children." To which is added, "Another for the Instruction of those who are to be admitted to the Lord's Supper."

The ordinance of the Lord's Supper Mr. Matthew Henry was used constantly to administer on the first Lord's Day in every month, not merely as this was customary in most other churches, but because it was in conformity with the practice of the Jews, who observed the beginnings of their months as holy, though he did not think their law about the new moons, etc., to be obligatory on Christians. In the manner of administering this ordinance he was particularly excellent, and is said herein to have excelled himself. On his lecture-days in the week before the sacrament he had a series of subjects adapted to that institution. And he followed his father's judgment and practice in encouraging young persons to come to the table of the Lord, to fulfil their baptismal covenant. Among his catechumens he marked those whom he looked upon as intelligent and serious, with this view: when he had a competent number of such in his eye, he appointed them separately to come to him, to converse with them about their spiritual state; and if he perceived good evidence of their real piety he recommended it to them to give themselves up to the Lord and His Church. For several Lord's Days he catechized them publicly concerning this ordinance, and the week preceding the administration he preached a sermon adapted to their circumstances, accompanied with suitable prayers for them, and then they were all received into the church together. This Philip Henry considered as the proper *confirmation*, or transition into a state of adult and complete church membership; and his son, in all that was material, adopted his method, in which he had much satisfaction from observing the great utility of it.

The other positive institution, that of BAPTISM, he administered with equal solemnity, and he always desired to have it in public, unless there was some peculiar reason against it. Mr. Henry had as little of the spirit of a sectarian about him as any man, and he lived in great friendship and affection with many good men who differed from him in regard to this controverted subject. But he was firm in his opinion about infant baptism, and thought it a matter of no small importance, though by no means one of the essentials of religion, as he considered it to be capable of being applied to very good purpose in a practical view, which was his grand object in his administration of it.

Visiting the sick Matthew Henry considered as an important part of ministerial duty, and he was diligent in the discharge of it. He never refused to attend the rich or the poor, when sent for, whether they were such as he knew, or strangers, whether resident in the town, or travellers, among whom were many passengers to or from Ireland; or whether they were persons of his own communion, or of the Established Church, among the latter of whom many desired his attendance in their illness. He often enquired of his friends whether they knew of any who were sick; and when the prayers of the congregation were desired, he requested that those who sent them would make themselves known, in order that he might properly attend to their cases. His prayers and conversation with sick persons were pertinent, affectionate, and useful. And if they recovered, he assisted them in their expressions of gratitude, reminded them of their sick-bed thoughts and promises, faithfully exhorting them to improve their renewed lives to the best purposes.

Matthew was also a great example of ministerial wisdom and fidelity in general. He carefully watched over his flock, and attended with diligence to the respective cases of individuals in it. When he heard an ill report of any, he would go to them, or send for them, and enquire impartially into the truth of the case. If he found the persons guilty, he would deal plainly and faithfully with them in his admonitions, and urge a speedy repentance, in which he was in most instances happily successful; and there were comparatively few whom he was obliged to cast out of his church. When any such case occurred, his diary shows how much his soul was grieved and what a discouragement it was to him in his ministerial labours. But his sorrow for such awful instances of apostasy was abundantly overbalanced by the joy he felt on the success of the ministry with the far greater part of his people, whom he saw growing up in wisdom and holiness, adorning the doctrine of God their Saviour, and strengthening the hands of their pastor.

But Mr. Henry's sphere of activity and attempts for usefulness were yet more extensive. Though his own flock was never neglected, he had a care for all the churches within his line, and readily lent his assistance to his brethren in all the adjacent parts, sometimes taking a compass of thirty miles, preaching every day in the week, but always returning home at the end of it. The towns and villages which lay near Chester enjoyed a large share of his labours, in several of which he had a monthly lecture. Besides attending stated meetings of ministers twice a year, he was frequently called upon to attend ordinations, to preach funeral sermons for his deceased brethren and other respectable persons at a distance: and he never refused complying with invitations to preach on any occasion when he was able to do it, the great strength of his constitution and the vigour of his mind rendering these uncommon exertions easy and pleasant to him.

He was used to take a yearly journey to Nantwich, Newcastle, etc., preaching wherever he came; and another into Lancashire, to preach at Manchester, Chowbent, Warrington, etc., where he was highly valued; but he performed all within the week, choosing to be at any labour or expense rather than not to be with his own people on the Lord's Day, from whom he was not absent on that day for ten years together, and on the first Sabbath in the month, but once, for twenty-four years, and that was when he was in London, after a long absence from it: for though he had many connexions in the metropolis, he rarely visited it, as he had no apprehension that his services were there needed so much as in the country, where they had been eminently useful in the revival of religion all around him, both among ministers and people, but particularly in his own congregation, where he had the pleasure of seeing the Redeemer's interest greatly to flourish, and many families rising up to call him blessed.

In the year 1700, Mr. Henry's congregation built a new meeting-house for him, which was decent, large, and commodious. On the first opening of it, August 8, he preached an appropriate and excellent sermon on Joshua 20: 22, 23: *The Lord God of gods, the Lord God of gods, he knows, and Israel he shall know, if it be in rebellion, or if it be in transgression against the Lord, that we have built an altar.*

After the building of this new meeting-house, the congregation much increased, especially by the accession of the greatest part of the people that had attended Mr. Harvey, who, in the year 1706, desisted from preaching in Chester on account of the declining state of his health and some difficulties about his place of worship, so that Mr. Henry's was now too strait for his hearers, and required a new gallery to be built. It was rather a singular circumstance that Mr. Harvey's congregation (according to the tradition still current at Chester) occupied this new gallery, and there continued by themselves. But it is presumed that those of them who had been church members united with Mr. Henry's church in the ordinance of the

Lord's Supper; for it appears that his church had considerably increased, so that he had at this time above three hundred and fifty communicants: and he had much comfort in them, as there was great unanimity among them, for which he expressed great thankfulness to God.

This being the case, it may appear a matter of surprise and lamentation that he should ever have quitted Chester, and accepted an invitation to a congregation in the vicinity of London. Of this great change, the cause and the consequences of it, an account shall now be given. He had received repeated invitations from congregations in or near London, before that which separated him from his friends at Chester, upon which he put an absolute negative without hesitation.

But after this (so lightly have dissenters been wont to view the evil of being *robbers of churches*) there was not a considerable vacancy in any London congregation, but Mr. Henry was thought of to fill it. Upon the death of Mr. Nathaniel Taylor, minister of Salters-hall, the people there had their eye upon Mr. Henry, but were discouraged from applying to him, at first, by the negative which he put upon the invitation from Hackney. However, after being disappointed in their expectations from Mr. Chorley of Norwich, and being much divided about an application to another minister, they unanimously agreed to make a vigorous effort to obtain Mr. Henry. Accordingly, letters were written to him by Mr. Howe, Mr. (afterwards Dr.) Williams, and Dr. Hamilton, urging this among other arguments, that by coming to this place he would unite both sides, between whom there had been some contests. These letters occasioned Mr. Henry some serious and uneasy thoughts, as appears from his diary, in which he expresses himself willing to be determined by the will of God, if he did but know it, whatever it might be. He afterwards takes notice that a dozen of his congregation had been with him to desire that he would not leave them, to whom he answered that he had once and again given a denial to this invitation, and that it was his present purpose not to leave them, though he could not tell what might happen hereafter.

In the review of this year, he takes particular notice of his invitation to Salters-hall as what surprised him; and he adds as follows: "I begged of God to keep me from being lifted up with pride by it. I sought of God the right way. Had I consulted my own fancy, which always had a kindness for London ever since I knew it, or the worldly advantage of my family, I had closed with it. And I was sometimes tempted to think it might open me a door of greater usefulness. I had also reason to think Mr. John Evans [then at Wrexham, afterwards Dr. Evans of London, author of 'The Christian Temper'] might have been had here, and might have been more acceptable to some, and more useful, than I. But I had not courage to break through the opposition of the affections of my friends here to me, and mine to them, nor to venture upon a new and unknown place and work, which I feared myself unfit for. I bless God, I am well satisfied in what I did in that matter. If it ever please God to call me from this place, I depend upon Him to make my way clear. Lord, lead me in a plain path!"

Hitherto Mr. Henry had enjoyed a great share of health, but in the year 1704 he had a very dangerous illness. As he was reading the Scripture on Lord's Day morning, August 27, he suddenly fainted away, but soon recovered so as to go on with his work. In the evening, however, feeling himself unwell, he writes, "A fever is coming upon me; let me be found ready whenever my Lord comes." He had a very restless night; but, having an appointment at Nantwich the next day, he went, and preached on Psalm 110: 3: "And then," says he, "I was well." The day following, he went to Haslington Chapel to preach the funeral sermon of Mr. Cope, an aged minister, who had spent some years there, and who had requested this of him. Mr. Egerton, the rector, gave his consent. But this, Mr. Henry remarks, was likely to be the last sermon preached there by a dissenter;

and it was like to have proved *his* last; for, on his return home, the fever came on with great violence, and confined him for more than three weeks.

It was soon after his recovery from this severe illness that he began his elaborate work on the Bible. A friend * has communicated the following passage, extracted from his diary, which Mr. Tong had overlooked, but which will appear to most readers both curious and interesting. "Nov. 12, 1704. This night, after many thoughts of heart, and many prayers concerning it, I began my Notes on the Old Testament. 'Tis not likely I should live to finish it; or, if I should, that it should be of [much] public service, for I am not *par negotiis*. Yet, in the strength of God, and I hope with a single eye to His glory, I set about it, that I may be endeavouring something, and spend my time to some good purpose; and let the Lord make what use He pleaseth of me. I go about it with fear and trembling, lest *I exercise myself in things too high for me*. The Lord help me to set about it with great humility."

In the year 1709, Mr. Henry received a letter, dated February 18, informing him that the congregation in which Mr. Howe and Mr. Spademan had been joint pastors, in SILVER-STREET (both of them now deceased) had chosen him to succeed the latter as co-pastor with Mr. Rosewell, and that some of them purposed to go down to Chester to treat with him on this business. He also received many letters from ministers and gentlemen, pressing his acceptance of this call with a view to his more extensive usefulness. Suffice it to say, he still remained immovable, "his affection for his people prevailing" (as he expressed it in his letter to Mr. Rosewell) "above his judgment, interest, and inclination."

After this, we might naturally have expected to find that Mr. Henry would have ended his days at Chester, and that no society would have attempted to remove him. But the congregation at Hackney being again vacant, by the death

* The Rev. Thomas Stedman, of St. Chad's, Shrewsbury.

xii

of the worthy Mr. Billio (who died of the small-pox in the year 1710), they determined upon renewing their application to Mr. Henry, which they did with increased importunity; and after a long negotiation, and repeated denials, they at length prevailed. As the best justification of his conduct in yielding to their desires, and as a further illustration of his integrity and piety, as well as his regard to his affectionate friends at Chester, the reader shall have the account of the transaction in his own words, extracted from his diary.

"About Midsummer, 1710, I had a letter from the congregation at Hackney, signifying that they had unanimously chosen me to be their minister; and that I should find them as the importunate widow, that would have no nay. I several times denied them. At length they wrote that some of them would come down hither, to prevent which (not being unwilling to take a London journey in the interval between my third and fourth volume) I wrote them word I would come up to them, and did so. Then I laid myself open to the temptation by increasing my acquaintance in the city. They followed me, after I came down again, with letters to me and the congregation. In October I wrote to them that if they would stay for me till next spring (which I was in hopes they would not have done) I would come up, and make a longer stay, for mutual trial. They wrote they would wait till then. In May, 1711, I went to them, and stayed till the end of July, and, before I parted with them signified my acceptance of their invitation, and my purpose to come to them, God willing, the next spring. However, I [should have] denied them but that Mr. Gunston, Mr. Smith, and some others, came to me from London, and begged me [not to refuse] for the sake of the public—which was the thing that turned the scales. By this determination I have brought upon myself more grief and care than I could have imagined, and have many a time wished it undone; but, having opened my mouth, I could not go back. I did with the utmost impartiality (if I know anything of myself) beg of God to incline my heart that way which would be most for His glory; and I trust I have a good conscience, willing to be found in the way of my duty. Wherein I have done amiss, the Lord forgive me for Jesus' sake, and make this change concerning the congregation to work together for good to it!"

Another paper, dated, Hackney, July 13, 1711, written after fervent prayer to God, contains the reasons which occurred to him why he should accept his invitation, which he wrote to be a satisfaction to him afterwards. The following is a brief epitome of them: "1. I am abundantly satisfied that it is lawful for ministers to remove, and in many cases expedient. 2. My invitation to Hackney is not only unanimous, but pressing; and, upon many weeks' trial, I do not perceive anything discouraging, but everything that promises comfort and usefulness. 3. There seems an intimation of Providence in the many calls I have had that way before. 4. There is manifestly a wider door of opportunity to do good opened to me at London than at Chester, which is my main inducement. 5. In drawing up and publishing my Exposition, it will be a great convenience to be near the press—also to have books at hand to consult and learned men to converse with for my own improvement. 6. I have followed Providence in this affair, and referred myself to its disposal. 7. I have asked the advice of many ministers and judicious Christians. 8. I have some reason to hope that my poor endeavours may be more useful to those to whom they are new. 9. I have not been without my discouragements at Chester, which have tempted me to think my work there in a great measure done; many have left us, and few been [of late] added. 10. I am not able to ride long journeys, as formerly, to preach, which last winter brought illness upon me, so that my services would be confined within the walls of Chester. 11. The congregation, though unwilling to part with me, have left the matter under their hands to my own conscience, etc."

The time now approached for Mr. Henry to fulfil his engagement with the people at Hackney, but the thought of leaving his friends at Chester proved a very severe trial to him, and pressed down his spirit beyond measure, as appears from many passages in his diary written about this time. On May 11, 1712, when he took his leave of his flock, he expounded the last chapter of Joshua in the morning, and of Matthew in the afternoon, and preached on 1 Thess. 4: 17, 18. After this service he writes. "A very sad day—I see I have been unkind to the congregation, who love me too well.— May 12. In much heaviness I set out in the coach for London, not knowing the things that shall befall me there. May 15. Came to London—But Lord, am I in my way? I look back with sorrow for leaving Chester; I look forward with fear; but unto thee, O Lord! do I look up."

On his first appearance as the minister in this congregation, in the morning he expounded Genesis 1, and in the afternoon Matthew 1, thus beginning, as it were, the world anew. He preached on Acts 16: 9: *Come over to Macedonia, and help us.* "O that good," says he, "may be done to precious souls! But I am sad in spirit, lamenting my departure from my friends in Chester. And yet if they be well provided for I shall be easy, whatever discouragements I may meet with here."

So many were the calls which Mr. Henry had to preach in and about London, and so ready was he to comply with them, that he sometimes appears in his diary to think that he needed an apology, and to excuse it to himself that he preached so often. After opening an evening lecture near Shadwell church, January 25, 1712, when his text was Psalm 73: 28, he writes thus: "I hope, through grace, I can say the reason why I am so much in my work is, because the love of Christ constrains me, and I find, by experience, it is good for me to draw near to God."

While he was thus laying himself out for the good of both old and young in and about London, Matthew Henry's heart lay much with his former congregation at Chester, which was still without a settled minister. Accordingly, he kept his promise to spend some Sabbaths with them every year. For these opportunities he gave God great thanks. But his uncommon exertions and his studious habits began to have an effect on his constitution, which not improbably tended to shorten his days.

At the beginning of 1714, his last year, Mr. Henry's mind appears from his diary to have been filled with dark apprehensions on account of public affairs. The bill which had passed for suppressing the schools of the dissenters he looked upon not only as a heavy grievance in itself, but as a prelude to further severities. On this occasion he preached an excellent discourse at Mr. Bush's meeting on 2 Chron. 20: 12: *Neither know we what to do, but our eyes are up unto thee.*

June 20th, which was the Sabbath, he spent at Chester, and it was the last he spent on earth: a remarkable circumstance that Providence should so order it that his last labours should be bestowed where they had begun, and where most of his days had been spent. It was also singular and pleasing that on his last two Sabbaths here he was directed to a subject so peculiarly adapted to the occasion, namely, that of the eternal Sabbath in heaven, on which he was so soon to enter; for on the preceding Lord's Day he had preached twice on Heb. 4: 9: *There remaineth a rest for the people of God,* which he considered, agreeably to the original, under the idea of a *Sabbath,* which he illustrated in a variety of particulars. On the Lord's Day following, he kept the same idea in view, while he dwelt on that solemn caution for the improvement of the subject—*Let us therefore fear, lest a promise being left us of entering into his rest, any of you should seem to come short of it.*

Matthew Henry was nearing the end of his remarkable ministry, for on his way back to London he fell ill, but persisted in continuing to Nantwich, where he had engaged to preach. He preached on Jer. 31: 18, and afterwards was so ill that he consented to being bled, and was put to bed in the home of Mr. Mottershed. While they were putting him to bed, he spoke of the excellence of spiritual comforts in a time of affliction, and blessed God that he enjoyed them. To his friend Mr. Illidge he addressed himself in these memorable words: "You have been used to take notice of the sayings of dying men. This is mine— That a life spent in the service of God, and communion with Him, is the most comfortable and pleasant life that one can live in the present world." On Tuesday, June 22, he expired. A near relation wrote of the occasion, "I believe it was most agreeable to him to have so short a passage from his work to his reward. And why should we envy him? It is glorious to die in the service of so great and good a Master, who, we are sure, will not let any of His servants lose by Him."

On Thursday, before the corpse was removed from Nantwich, Mr. Reynolds of Salop, preached an excellent sermon on the sad occasion, which was printed. Six ministers accompanied it to Chester, where they were met by eight of the clergy, ten coaches, and a great many persons on horseback. Many dissenting ministers followed the mourners, and a universal respect was paid to the deceased by persons of distinction of all denominations. He was buried in Trinity Church, in Chester, where several dear relatives had been laid before him. When the news of his death reached London, it occasioned universal lamentation: there was scarcely a pulpit among the dissenters in which notice was not taken of the breach made in the Church of God; almost every sermon was a funeral sermon for Mr. Henry; and many who were no friends to the nonconformists acknowledged that they had lost one who was a great support and honour to their interest. The sermon preached to his congregation at Hackney, July 11, 1714, was by his intimate friend, Mr. William Tong, on John 13: 36: *Whither I go thou canst not follow me now; but thou shalt follow me afterwards.*

AN

EXPOSITION,

WITH PRACTICAL OBSERVATIONS,

OF THE FIRST BOOK OF MOSES, CALLED

GENESIS.

WE have now before us the holy Bible, or *book*, for so *bible* signifies. We call it *the book*, by way of eminency; for it is incomparably the best book that ever was written, the book of books, shining like the sun in the firmament of learning, other valuable and useful books, like the moon and stars, borrowing their light from it. We call it the holy book, because it was written by holy men, and indited by the Holy Ghost; it is perfectly pure from all falsehood and corrupt intention; and the manifest tendency of it is to promote holiness among men. The great things of God's law and gospel are here *written* to us, that they might be reduced to a greater certainty, might spread further, remain longer, and be transmitted to distant places and ages more pure and entire than possibly they could be by report and tradition: and we shall have a great deal to answer for if these things which belong to our peace, being thus committed to us in black and white, be neglected by us as a strange and foreign thing, Hos. viii. 12. The scriptures, or writings of the several inspired penmen, from Moses down to St. John, in which divine light, like that of the morning, shone gradually (the sacred canon being now completed), are all put together in this blessed Bible, which, thanks be to God, we have in our hands, and they make as perfect a day as we are to expect on this side heaven. Every part was good, but all together very good. This is the *light that shines in a dark place* (2 Pet. i. 19), and a dark place indeed the world would be without the Bible.

We have before us that part of the Bible which we call the *Old Testament*, containing the acts and monuments of the church from the creation almost to the coming of Christ in the flesh, which was about four thousand years—the truths then revealed, the laws then enacted, the devotions then paid, the prophecies then given, and the events which concerned that distinguished body, so far as God saw fit to preserve to us the knowledge of them. This is called a *testament*, or *covenant* (Διαθήκη), because it was a settled declaration of the *will* of God concerning man in a federal way, and had its force from the designed death of the great testator, *the Lamb slain from the foundation of the world*, Rev. xiii. 8. It is called the *Old Testament*, with relation to the *New*, which does not cancel and supersede it, but crown and perfect it, by the bringing in of that better hope which was typified and foretold in it; the Old Testament still remains glorious, though the New far exceeds in glory, 2 Cor. iii. 9.

We have before us that part of the Old Testament which we call the *Pentateuch*, or five books of Moses, that servant of the Lord who excelled all the other prophets, and typified the great prophet. In our Saviour's distribution of the books of the Old Testament into the *law*, the *prophets*, and the *psalms*, or *Hagiographa*, these are the *law*; for they contain not only the laws given to Israel, in the last four, but the laws given to Adam, to Noah, and to Abraham, in the first. These five books were, for aught we know, the first that ever were written; for we have not the least mention of any *writing* in all the book of Genesis, nor till God bade Moses write (Exod. xvii. 14); and some think Moses himself never learned to write till God set him his copy in the writing of the Ten Commandments upon the tables of stone. However, we are sure these books are the most ancient writings now extant, and therefore best able to give us a satisfactory account of the most ancient things.

We have before us the first and longest of those five books, which we call *Genesis*, written, some think, when Moses was in Midian, for the instruction and comfort of his suffering brethren in Egypt: I rather think he wrote it in the wilderness, after he had been in the mount with God, where, probably, he received full and particular instructions for the writing of it. And, as he framed the tabernacle, so he did the more excellent and durable fabric of this book, exactly according to the pattern shown him in the mount, into which it is better to resolve the certainty of the things herein contained than into any tradition which possibly might be handed down from Adam to Methuselah, from him to Shem, from him to Abraham, and so to the family of Jacob. *Genesis* is a name borrowed from the Greek. It signifies the *original*, or *generation*: fitly is this book so called, for it is a history of originals—the creation of the world, the entrance of sin and death into it, the invention of arts, the rise of nations, and especially the planting of the church, and the state of it in its early days. It is also a history of generations—the generations of Adam, Noah, Abraham, &c., not endless, but useful genealogies. The beginning of the New Testament is called *Genesis* too (Matt. i. 1), Βίβλος γενέσεως, the book of the *genesis*, or *generation*, of Jesus Christ. Blessed be God for that book which shows us our remedy, as this opens our wound. Lord, open our eyes, that we may see the wondrous things both of thy law and gospel!

1

CHAP. I.

The foundation of all religion being laid in our relation to God as our Creator, it was fit that the book of divine revelations which was intended to be the guide, support, and rule, of religion in the world, should begin, as it does, with a plain and full account of the creation of the world—in answer to that first enquiry of a good conscience, "Where is God my Maker?" Job xxxv. 10. Concer g this the pagan philosophers wretchedly blundered, and be ne vain in their imaginations, some asserting the world's eternity and self-existence, others ascribing it to a fortuitous concourse of atoms: thus "the world by wisdom knew not God," but took a great deal of pains to lose him. The holy scripture therefore, designing by revealed religion to maintain and improve natural religion, to repair the decays of it and supply the defects of it, since the fall, for the reviving of the precepts of the law of nature, lays down, at first, this principle of the unclouded light of nature, That this world was, in the beginning of time, created by a Being of infinite wisdom and power, who was himself before all time and all worlds. The entrance into God's word gives this light, Ps. cxix. 130. The first verse of the Bible gives us a surer and better, a more satisfying and useful, knowledge of the origin of the universe, than all the volumes of the philosophers. The lively faith of humble Christians understands this matter better than the elevated fancy of the greatest wits, Heb. xi. 3. We have three things in this chapter:—I. A general idea given us of the work of creation, ver. 1, 2. II. A particular account of the several days' work, registered, as in a journal, distinctly and 'n order. The creation of the light the first day, ver. 3—5; of the firmament the second day, ver. 6—8; of the sea, the earth, and its fruits, the third day, ver. 9—13; of the lights of heaven the fourth day, ver. 14—19; of the fish and fowl the fifth day, ver. 20—23; of the beasts, ver. 24, 25; of man, ver. 26—28; and of food for both the sixth day, ver. 29, 30. III. The review and approbation of the whole work, ver. 31.

IN the beginning God created the heaven and the earth. 2 And the earth was without form, and void; and darkness *was* upon the face of the deep. And the Spirit of God moved upon the face of the waters.

In these verses we have the work of creation in its epitome and in its embryo.

I. In its epitome, *v.* 1, where we find, to our comfort, the first article of our creed, that *God the Father Almighty is the Maker of heaven and earth,* and as such we believe in him.

1. Observe, in this verse, four tnings :—

(1.) The effect produced—*the heaven and the earth,* that is, the world, including the whole frame and furniture of the universe, the *world and all things therein,* Acts xvii. 24. The world is a great house, consisting of upper and lower stories, the structure stately and magnificent, uniform and convenient, and every room well and wisely furnished. It is the visible part of the creation that Moses here designs to account for; therefore he mentions not the creation of angels. But as the earth has not only its surface adorned with grass and flowers, but also its bowels enriched with metals and precious stones (which partake more of its solid nature and are more valuable, though the creation of them is not mentioned here), so the heavens are not only beautified to our eye with glorious lamps which garnish its outside, of whose creation we here read, but they are within replenished with glorious beings, out of our sight, more celestial, and more surpassing them in worth and excellency than the gold or sapphires surpass the lilies of the field. In the visible world it is easy to observe, [1.] Great variety, several sorts of beings vastly differing in their nature and constitution from each other. *Lord, how manifold are thy works,* and all good! [2.] Great beauty. The azure sky and verdant earth are charming to the

eye of the curious spectator, much more the ornaments of both. How transcendent then must the beauty of the Creator be ! [3.] Great exactness and accuracy. To those that, with the help of microscopes, narrowly look into the works of nature, they appear far more fine than any of the works of art. [4.] Great power. It is not a lump of dead and inactive matter, but there is virtue, more or less, in every creature : the earth itself has a magnetic power. [5.] Great order, a mutual dependence of beings, an exact harmony of motions, and an admirable chain and connection of causes. [6.] Great mystery. There are phenomena in nature which cannot be solved, secrets which cannot be fathomed nor accounted for. But from what we see of heaven and earth we may easily enough infer the eternal power and Godhead of the great Creator, and may furnish ourselves with abundant matter for his praises. And let our make and place, as men, remind us of our duty as Christians, which is always to keep heaven in our eye and the earth under our feet.

(2.) The author and cause of this great work—GOD. The Hebrew word is *Elohim,* which bespeaks, [1.] The power of God the Creator. *El* signifies *the strong God;* and what less than almighty strength could bring all things out of nothing ? [2.] The plurality of persons in the Godhead, Father, Son, and Holy Ghost. This plural name of God, in Hebrew, which speaks of him as many though he is one, was to the Gentiles perhaps a savour of death unto death, hardening them in their idolatry; but it is to us a savour of life unto life, confirming our faith in the doctrine of the Trinity, which, though but darkly intimated in the Old Testament, is clearly revealed in the New. The Son of God, the eternal Word and Wisdom of the Father, was with him when he made the world (Prov. viii. 30), nay, we are often told that the world was made by him, and nothing made without him, John i. 3, 10 ; Eph. iii. 9 ; Col. i. 16 ; Heb. i. 2. O what high thoughts should this form in our minds of that great God whom we draw nigh to in religious worship, and that great Mediator in whose name we draw nigh !

(3.) The manner in which this work was effected : *God created it,* that is, made it out of nothing. There was not any pre-existent matter out of which the world was produced. The fish and fowl were indeed produced out of the waters and the beasts and man out of the earth ; but that earth and those waters were made out of nothing. By the ordinary power of nature, it is impossible that any thing should be made out of nothing ; no artificer can work, unless he has something to work on. But by the almighty power of God it is not only possible that something should be made of nothing (the God of nature is not subject to the laws of nature), but in the creation it is impossible it should be otherwise, for nothing is more injurious to the honour of the Eternal Mind than the supposition of eternal matter. Thus the excellency of the power is of God and all the glory is to him.

(4.) When this work was produced: *In the beginning*, that is, in the beginning of time, when that clock was first set a going: time began with the production of those beings that are measured by time. Before the beginning of time there was none but that Infinite Being that inhabits eternity. Should we ask why God made the world no sooner, we should but darken counsel by words without knowledge; for how could there be sooner or later in eternity? And he did make it in the beginning of time, according to his eternal counsels before all time. The Jewish Rabbies have a saying, that there were seven things which God created before the world, by which they only mean to express the excellency of these things:—The law, repentance, paradise, hell, the throne of glory, the house of the sanctuary, and the name of the Messiah. But to us it is enough to say, *In the beginning was the Word*, John i. 1.

2. Let us learn hence, (1.) That atheism is folly, and atheists are the greatest fools in nature; for they see there is a world that could not make itself, and yet they will not own there is a God that made it. Doubtless, they are without excuse, but the god of this world has blinded their minds. (2.) That God is sovereign Lord of all by an incontestable right. If he is the Creator, no doubt he is the owner and possessor of heaven and earth. (3.) That with God all things are possible, and therefore happy are the people that have him for their God, and whose help and hope stand in his name, Ps. cxxi. 2; cxxiv. 8. (4.) That the God we serve is worthy of, and yet is exalted far above, all blessing and praise, Neh. ix. 5, 6. If he made the world, he needs not our services, nor can be benefited by them (Acts xvii. 24, 25), and yet he justly requires them, and deserves our praise, Rev. iv. 11. If all is of him, all must be to him.

II. Here is the work of creation in its embryo, *v.* 2, where we have an account of the first matter and the first mover.

1. A chaos was the first matter. It is here called the earth (though the earth, properly taken, was not made till the third day *v.* 10), because it did most resemble that which afterwards was called *earth*, mere earth, destitute of its ornaments, such a heavy unwieldy mass was it; it is also called *the deep*, both for its vastness and because the waters which were afterwards separated from the earth were now mixed with it. This immense mass of matter was it out of which all bodies, even the firmament and visible heavens themselves, were afterwards produced by the power of the Eternal Word. The Creator could have made his work perfect at first, but by this gradual proceeding

he would show what is, ordinarily, the method of his providence and grace. Observe the description of this chaos. (1.) There was nothing in it desirable to be seen, for it was *without form and void*. *Tohu* and *Bohu*, confusion and emptiness; so these words are rendered, Isa. xxxiv. 11. It was shapeless, it was useless, it was without inhabitants, without ornaments, the shadow or rough draught of things to come, *and not the image of the things*, Heb. x. 1. The earth is almost reduced to the same condition again by the sin of man, under which the creation groans. See Jer. iv. 23, *I beheld the earth, and lo it was without form, and void.* To those who have their hearts in heaven this lower world, in comparison with that upper, still appears to be nothing but confusion and emptiness. There is no true beauty to be seen, no satisfying fulness to be enjoyed, in this earth, but in God only. (2.) If there had been any thing desirable to be seen, yet there was no light to see it by; for *darkness*, thick darkness, *was upon the face of the deep.* God did not create this darkness (as he is said to create the darkness of affliction, Isa. xlv. 7), for it was only the want of light, which yet could not be said to be wanted till something was made that might be seen by it; nor needs the want of it be much complained of, when there was nothing to be seen but confusion and emptiness. If the work of grace in the soul is a new creation, this chaos represents the state of an unregenerate graceless soul: *there* is disorder, confusion, and every evil work; it is empty of all good, for it is without God; it is dark, it is darkness itself. This is our condition by nature, till almighty grace effects a blessed change.

2. The Spirit of God was the first mover: He *moved upon the face of the waters.* When we consider the earth without form and void, methinks it is like the valley full of dead and dry bones. Can these live? Can this confused mass of matter be formed into a beautiful world? Yes, if a spirit of life from God enter into it, Ezek. xxxvii. 9. Now there is hope concerning this thing; for the Spirit of God begins to work, and, if he work, who or what shall hinder? God is said to make the world by his Spirit, Ps. xxxiii. 6; Job xxvi. 13; and by the same mighty worker the new creation is effected. He moved upon the face of the deep, as Elijah stretched himself upon the dead child,—as the *hen gathers her chickens under her wings*, and hovers over them, to warm and cherish them, Matt. xxiii. 37,—as the eagle stirs up her nest, and *flutters* over her young (it is the same word that is here used), Deut. xxxii. 11. Learn hence, That God is not only the author of all being, but the fountain of life and spring of motion. Dead matter would be for ever dead if he did not quicken it. And this makes it credible to us that God should raise the dead. That power which brought such a world as this out of confusion, emptiness, and darkness,

at the beginning of time, can, at the end of time, bring our vile bodies out of the grave, though it is *a land of darkness as darkness itself, and without any order* (Job x. 22), and can make them glorious bodies.

3 And God said, Let there be light : and there was light. 4 And God saw the light, that *it was* good : and God divided the light from the darkness. 5 And God called the light Day, and the darkness he called Night. And the evening and the morning were the first day.

We have here a further account of the first day's work, in which observe, 1. That the first of all visible beings which God created was light ; not that by it he himself might see to work (for the darkness and light are both alike to him), but that by it we might see his works and his glory in them, and might work our works while it is day. The works of Satan and his servants are works of darkness ; but he that doeth truth, and doeth good, cometh to the light, and coveteth it, *that his deeds may be made manifest*, John iii. 21. Light is the great beauty and blessing of the universe. Like the first-born, it does, of all visible beings, most resemble its great Parent in purity and power, brightness and beneficence ; it is of great affinity with a spirit, and is next to it ; though by it we see other things, and are sure that it is, yet we know not its nature, nor can describe what it is, or *by what way the light is parted*, Job xxxviii. 19, 24. By the sight of it let us be led to, and assisted in, the believing contemplation of him who is light, infinite and eternal light (1 John i. 5), and the *Father of lights* (Jam. i. 17), and who dwells in inaccessible light, 1 Tim. vi. 16. In the new creation, the first thing wrought in the soul is *light :* the blessed Spirit captivates the will and affections by enlightening the understanding, so coming into the heart by the door, like the good shepherd whose own the sheep are, while sin and Satan, like thieves and robbers, climb up some other way. Those that by sin were darkness by grace become light in the world. 2. That the light was made by the word of God's power. He said, Let *there be light ;* he willed and appointed it, and it was done immediately : *there was light,* such a copy as exactly answered the original idea in the Eternal Mind. · O the power of the word of God ! *He spoke, and it was done,* done really, effectually, and for perpetuity, not in show only, and to serve a present turn, for *he commanded, and it stood fast :* with him it was *dictum, factum—a word, and a world.* The word of God (that is, his will and the good pleasure of it) is quick and powerful. Christ is the Word, the essential eternal Word, and by him the light was produced, for *in him was light, and he is the true light,*

the light of the world, John i. 9 ; ix: 5. The divine light which shines in sanctified souls is wrought by the power of God, the power of his word and of the Spirit of wisdom and revelation, opening the understanding, scattering the mists of ignorance and mistake, and giving the knowledge of the glory of God in the face of Christ, as, at first, *God commanded the light to shine out of darkness,* 2 Cor. iv. 6. Darkness would have been perpetually upon the face of fallen man if the Son of God had not *come, and given us an understanding,* 1 John v. 20. 3. That the light which God willed, when it was produced, he approved of : *God saw the light that it was good.* It was exactly as he designed it, and it was fit to answer the end for which he designed it. It was useful and profitable ; the world, which now is a palace, would have been a dungeon without it. It was amiable and pleasant. *Truly the light is sweet* (Eccl. xi. 7) ; *it rejoiceth the heart,* Prov. xv. 30. What God commands he will approve and graciously accept ; he will be well pleased with the work of his own hands. That is good indeed which is so in the sight of God, for he sees not as man sees. If the light is good, how good is he that is the fountain of light, from whom we receive it, and to whom we owe all praise for it and all the services we do by it ! 4. That God *divided the light from the darkness,* so put them asunder as that they could never be joined together, or reconciled ; for *what fellowship has light with darkness?* 2 Cor. vi. 14. And yet he divided time between them, the day for light and the night for darkness, in a constant and regular succession to each other. Though the darkness was now scattered by the light, yet it was not condemned to a perpetual banishment, but takes its turn with the light, and has its place, because it has its use ; for, as the light of the morning befriends the business of the day, so the shadows of the evening befriend the repose of the night, and draw the curtains about us, that we may sleep the better. See Job vii. 2 God has thus divided time between light and darkness, because he would daily remind us that this is a world of mixtures and changes. In heaven there is perfect and perpetual light, and no darkness at all ; in hell, utter darkness, and no gleam of light. In that world between these two there is a great gulf fixed ; but, in this world, they are counterchanged, and we pass daily from one to another, that we may learn to expect the like vicissitudes in the providence of God, peace and trouble, joy and sorrow, and may set the one over-against the other, accommodating ourselves to both as we do to the light and darkness, bidding both welcome, and making the best of both. 5. That God divided them from each other by distinguishing names : *He called the light day, and the darkness he called night.* He gave them names, as the Lord of both ; for *the day is*

4

his, the night also is his, Ps. lxxiv. 16. He is the Lord of time, and will be so, till day and night shall come to an end, and the stream of time be swallowed up in the ocean of eternity. Let us acknowledge God in the constant succession of day and night, and consecrate both to his honour, by working for him every day and resting in him every night, and meditating in his law day and night. 6. That this was the first day's work, and a good day's work it was. *The evening and the morning were the first day.* The darkness of the evening was before the light of the morning, that it might serve for a foil to it, to set it off, and make it shine the brighter. This was not only the first day of the world, but the first day of the week. I observe it to the honour of that day, because the new world began on the first day of the week likewise, in the resurrection of Christ, as the light of the world, early in the morning. In him the day-spring from on high has visited the world; and happy are we, for ever happy, if that *day-star arise in our hearts.*

6 And God said, Let there be a firmament in the midst of the waters, and let it divide the waters from the waters. 7 And God made the firmament, and divided the waters which *were* under the firmament from the waters which *were* above the firmament: and it was so. 8 And God called the firmament Heaven. And the evening and the morning were the second day.

We have here an account of the second day's work, the creation of the firmament, in which observe, 1. The command of God concerning it: *Let there be a firmament,* an *expansion,* so the Hebrew word signifies, like a sheet spread, or a curtain drawn out. This includes all that is visible above the earth, between it and the third heavens: the air, its higher, middle, and lower, regions—the celestial globe, and all the spheres and orbs of light above: it reaches as high as the place where the stars are fixed, for that is called here the *firmament of heaven* (v. 14, 15), and as low as the place where the birds fly, for that also is called the *firmament of heaven,* v. 20. When God had made the light, he appointed the air to be the receptacle and vehicle of its beams, and to be as a medium of communication between the invisible and the visible world; for, though between heaven and earth there is an inconceivable distance, yet there is not an impassable gulf, as there is between heaven and hell. This firmament is not a wall of partition, but a way of intercourse. See Job xxvi. 7; xxxvii. 18; Ps. civ. 3; Amos ix. 6. 2. The creation of it. Lest it should seem as if God had only commanded it to be done, and some one else had

done it, he adds, *And God made the firmament.* What God requires of us he himself works in us, or it is not done. He that commands faith, holiness, and love, creates them by the power of his grace going along with his word, that he may have all the praise. *Lord, give what thou commandest, and then command what thou pleasest.* The firmament is said to be *the work of God's fingers,* Ps. viii. 3. Though the vastness of its extent declares it to be the work of his arm stretched out, yet the admirable fineness of its constitution shows that it is a curious piece of art, the work of his fingers. 3. The use and design of it—to *divide the waters from the waters,* that is, to distinguish between the waters that are wrapped up in the clouds and those that cover the sea, the waters in the air and those in the earth. See the difference between these two carefully observed, Deut. xi. 10, 11, where Canaan is upon this account preferred to Egypt, that Egypt was moistened and made fruitful with the waters that are under the firmament, but Canaan with waters from above, out of the firmament, even the dew of heaven, which tarrieth not *for the sons of men,* Mic. v. 7. God has, in the firmament of his power, chambers, store-chambers, whence he *watereth the earth,* Ps. civ. 13; lxv. 9, 10. He has also *treasures, or magazines, of snow and°hail, which he hath reserved against the day of battle and war,* Job xxxviii. 22, 23. O what a great God is he who has thus provided for the comfort of all that serve him and the confusion of all that hate him! It is good having him our friend, and bad having him our enemy. 4. The naming of it: *He called the firmament heaven.* It is the visible heaven, the pavement of the holy city; above the firmament God is said to have his throne (Ezek. i. 26), for he has prepared it in the heavens; the heavens therefore are said to rule, Dan. iv. 26. *Is not God in the height of heaven?* Job xxii. 12. Yes, he is, and we should be led by the contemplation of the heavens that are in our eye to consider *our Father who is in heaven.* The height of the heavens should remind us of God's supremacy and the infinite distance there is between us and him; the brightness of the heavens and their purity should remind us of his glory, and majesty, and perfect holiness; the vastness of the heavens, their encompassing of the earth, and the influence they have upon it, should remind us of his immensity and universal providence.

9 And God said, Let the waters under the heaven be gathered together unto one place, and let the dry *land* appear: and it was so. 10 And God called the dry *land* Earth; and the gathering together of the waters called he Seas: and God saw that *it was* good. 11 And God said, Let the

earth bring forth grass, the herb yielding seed, *and* the fruit tree yielding fruit after his kind, whose seed *is* in itself, upon the earth : and it was so. 12 And the earth brought forth grass, *and* herb yielding seed after his kind, and the tree yielding fruit, whose seed *was* in itself, after his kind : and God saw that *it was* good. 13 And the evening and the morning were the third day.

The third day's work is related in these verses—the forming of the sea and the dry land, and the making of the earth fruitful. Hitherto the power of the Creator had been exerted and employed about the upper part of the visible world; the light of heaven was kindled, and the firmament of heaven fixed : but now he descends to this lower world, the earth, which was designed for the children of men, designed both for their habitation and for their maintenance ; and here we have an account of the fitting of it for both, the building of their house and the spreading of their table. Observe,

I. How the earth was prepared to be a habitation for man, by the gathering of the waters together, and the making of the dry land to appear. Thus, instead of the confusion which there was (*v.* 2) when earth and water were mixed in one great mass, behold, now, there is order, by such a separation as rendered them both useful. God said, *Let it be so, and it was so ;* no sooner said than done. 1. The waters which had covered the earth were ordered to retire, and to gather into one place, namely, those hollows which were fitted and appointed for their reception and rest. The waters, thus cleared, thus collected, and thus lodged, in their proper place, he called *seas.* Though they are many, in distant regions, and washing several shores, yet, either above ground or under ground, they have communication with each other, and so they are one, and the common receptacle of waters, into which all the rivers flow, Eccl. i. 7. Waters and seas often, in scripture, signify troubles and afflictions, Ps. xlii. 7; lxix. 2, 14, 15. God's own people are not exempted from these in this world; but it is their comfort that they are only waters under the heaven (there are none in heaven), and that they are all in the place that God has appointed them and within the bounds that he has set for them. How the waters were gathered together at first, and how they are still bound and limited by the same Almighty hand that first confined them, are elegantly described, Ps. civ. 6—9, and are there mentioned as matter of praise. *Those that go down to the sea in ships* ought to acknowledge daily the wisdom, power, and goodness, of the Creator, in making the great waters serviceable to man for trade

and commerce ; and *those that tarry at home* must own themselves indebted to him that keeps the sea with bars and doors in its decreed place, and stays its proud waves, Job xxxviii. 10, 11. 2. The dry land was made to appear, and emerge out of the waters, and was called *earth,* and *given to the children of men.* The earth, it seems, was in being before ; but it was of no use, because it was under water. Thus many of God's gifts are received in vain, because they are buried ; make them to appear, and they become serviceable. We who, to this day, enjoy the benefit of the dry land (though, since this, it was once deluged, and dried again) must own our lves tenants to, and dependents upon, that God whose *hands formed the dry land,* Ps. xcv. 5 ; Jonah i. 9.

II. How the earth was furnished for the maintenance and support of man, *v.* 11, 12. Present provision was now made, by the immediate products of the upstart earth, which, in obedience to God's command, was no sooner made than it became fruitful, and brought forth grass for the cattle and herb for the service of man. Provision was likewise made for time to come, by the perpetuating of the several kinds of vegetables, which are numerous, various, and all curious, and every one *having its seed in itself after its kind,* that, during the continuance of man upon the earth, food might be fetched out of the earth for his use and benefit. *Lord, what is man, that he is thus visited and regarded*—that such care should be taken, and such provision made, for the support and preservation of those guilty and obnoxious lives which have been a thousand times forfeited ! Observe here, 1. That not only the earth is the Lord's, but *the fulness thereof,* and he is the rightful owner and sovereign disposer, not only of it, but of all its furniture. The earth was *emptiness* (*v.* 2), but now, by a word's speaking, it has become full of God's riches, and his they are still— *his corn and his wine, his wool and his flax,* Hos. ii. 9. Though the use of them is allowed to us, the property still remains in him, and to his service and honour they must be used. 2. That common providence is a continued creation, and in it *our Father worketh hitherto.* The earth still remains under the efficacy of this command, to bring forth grass, and herbs, and its annual products ; and though, being according to the common course of nature, these are not standing miracles, yet they are standing instances of the unwearied power and unexhausted goodness of the world's great Maker and Master. 3. That though God, ordinarily, makes use of the agency of second causes, according to their nature, yet he neither needs them nor is tied to them ; for, though the precious fruits of the earth are usually brought forth by the influences of the sun and moon (Deut. xxxiii. 14), yet here we find the earth bearing a great abundance of fruit, probably ripe fruit, before the sun and moon were made. 4. That it is good to provide things necessary before we have occasion to use them : before the beasts and man were made, here were grass and herbs prepared for them. God thus dealt wisely and graciously with man ; let not man then be foolish and unwise for himself. 5. That God must have the glory of all the benefit we receive from the products of the earth, either for food or physic. It is he that *hears the heavens when they hear the earth,* Hos. ii. 21, 22. And if we have, through grace, an interest in him who is the fountain, when the streams are dried up and the *fig-tree doth not blossom* we may rejoice in him.

14 And God said, Let there be lights in the firmament of the heaven to divide the day from the night; and let them be for signs, and for seasons, and for days, and years : 15 And let them be for lights in the firmament of the heaven to give light upon the earth : and it was so. 16 And God made two great lights; the greater light to rule the day, and the lesser light to rule the night : *he made* the stars also. 17 And God set them in the firmament of the heaven to give light upon the earth, 18 And to rule over the day and over the night, and to divide the light from the darkness : and God saw that *it was* good. 19 And the evening and the morning were the fourth day.

This is the history of the fourth day's work, the creating of the sun, moon, and stars, which are here accounted for, not as they are in themselves and in their own nature, to satisfy the curious, but as they are in relation to this earth, to which they serve as lights ; and this is enough to furnish us with matter for praise and thanksgiving. Holy Job mentions this as an instance of the glorious power of God, that *by the Spirit he hath garnished the heavens* (Job xxvi. 13); and here we have an account of that garniture which is not only so much the beauty of the upper world, but so much the blessing of this lower ; for though heaven is high, yet has it respect to this earth, and therefore should have respect from it. Of the creation of the lights of heaven we have an account,

I. In general, *v.* 14, 15, where we have 1. The command given concerning them : *Let there be lights in the firmament of heaven.* God had said, *Let there be light* (*v.* 3), and there was light; but this was, as it were, a chaos of light, scattered and confused : now it was collected and modelled, and made into several luminaries, and so rendered both more glorious and more serviceable. God is

the God of order, and not of confusion ; and, as he is light, so he is the Father and former of lights. Those lights were to be *in the firmament of heaven,* that vast expanse which encloses the earth, and is conspicuous to all; for *no man, when he has lighted a candle, puts it under a bushel, but on a candlestick* (Luke viii. 16), and a stately golden candlestick the firmament of heaven is, from which these candles give light *to all that are in the house.* The firmament itself is spoken of as having a brightness of its own (Dan. xii. 3), but this was not sufficient to give light to the earth ; and perhaps for this reason it is not expressly said of the second day's work, in which the firmament was made, that it was good, because, till it was adorned with these lights on the fourth day, it had not become serviceable to man. 2. The use they were intended to be of to this earth. (1.) They must be for the distinction of times, of day and night, summer and winter, which are interchanged by the motion of the sun, whose rising makes day, his setting night, his approach towards our tropic summer, his recess to the other winter : and thus, *under the sun,* there is *a season to every purpose,* Eccl. iii. 1. (2.) They must be for the direction of actions. They are for signs of the change of weather, that the husbandman may order his affairs with discretion, foreseeing, by the face of the sky, when second causes have begun to work, whether it will be fair or foul, Matt. xvi. 2, 3. They do also *give light upon the earth,* that we may *walk* (John xi. 9), and *work* (John ix. 4), according as the duty of every day requires. The lights of heaven do not shine for themselves, nor for the world of spirits above, who need them not; but they shine for us, for our pleasure and advantage. Lord, what is man, that he should be thus regarded ! Ps. viii. 3, 4. How ungrateful and inexcusable are we, if, when God has set up these lights for us to work by, we sleep, or play, or trifle away the time of business, and neglect the great work we were sent into the world about ! The lights of heaven are made to serve us, and they do it faithfully, and shine in their season, without fail : but we are set as lights in this world to serve God ; and do we in like manner answer the end of our creation ? No, we do not, our light does not shine before God as his lights shine before us, Matt. v. 14. We burn our Master's candles, but do not mind our Master's work.

II. In particular, *v.* 16—18.
1. Observe, The lights of heaven are the sun, moon, and stars ; and all these are the work of God's hands. (1.) The sun is the greatest light of all, more than a million times greater than the earth, and the most glorious and useful of all the lamps of heaven, a noble instance of the Creator's wisdom, power, and goodness, and an invaluable blessing to the creatures of this lower world. Let us learn from Ps. xix.

7

1—6 how to give unto God the glory due unto his name, as the Maker of the sun. (2.) The moon is a less light, and yet is here reckoned one of the greater lights, because though, in regard to its magnitude and borrowed light, it is inferior to many of the stars, yet, by virtue of its office, as ruler of the night, and in respect of its usefulness to the earth, it is more excellent than they. Those are most valuable that are most serviceable; and those are the greater lights, not that have the best gifts, but that humbly and faithfully do the most good with them. *Whosoever will be great among you, let him be your minister*, Matt. xx. 26. (3.) *He made the stars also*, which are here spoken of as they appear to vulgar eyes, without distinguishing between the planets and the fixed stars, or accounting for their number, nature, place, magnitude, motions, or influences; for the scriptures were written, not to gratify our curiosity and make us astronomers, but to lead us to God, and make us saints. Now these lights are said to *rule* (v. 16, 18); not that they have a supreme dominion, as God has, but they are deputy-governors, rulers under him. Here the less light, the moon, is said to rule *the night ;* but in Ps. cxxxvi. 9 the stars are mentioned as sharers in that government: *The moon and stars to rule by night.* No more is meant than that they *give light*, Jer. xxxi. 35. The best and most honourable way of ruling is by giving light and doing good: those command respect that live a useful life, and so shine as lights.

2. Learn from all this, (1.) The sin and folly of that ancient idolatry, the worshipping of the sun, moon, and stars, which, some think, took rise, or countenance at least, from some broken traditions in the patriarchal age concerning the rule and dominion of the lights of heaven. But the account here given of them plainly shows that they are both God's creatures and man's servants; and therefore it is both a great affront to God and a great reproach to ourselves to make deities of them and give them divine honours. See Deut. iv. 19. (2.) The duty and wisdom of daily worshipping that God who made all these things, and made them to be that to us which they are. The revolutions of the day and night oblige us to offer the solemn sacrifice of prayer and praise every morning and evening.

20 And God said, Let the waters bring forth abundantly the moving creature that hath life, and fowl *that* may fly above the earth in the open firmament of heaven. 21 And God created great whales, and every living creature that moveth, which the waters brought forth abundantly, after their kind, and every winged fowl after his kind: and God saw that *it was* good. 22 And God blessed them, saying,

Be fruitful, and multiply, and fill the waters in the seas, and let fowl multiply in the earth. 23 And the evening and the morning were the fifth day.

Each day, hitherto, has produced very noble and excellent beings, which we can never sufficiently admire; but we do not read of the creation of any living creature till the fifth day, of which these verses give us an account. The work of creation not only proceeded gradually from one thing to another, but rose and advanced gradually from that which was less excellent to that which was more so, teaching us to press towards perfection and endeavour that our last works may be our best works. It was on the fifth day that the fish and fowl were created, and both out of the waters. Though there is one kind of flesh of fishes, and another of birds, yet they were made together, and both out of the waters; for the power of the first Cause can produce very different effects from the same second causes. Observe, 1. The making of the fish and fowl, at first, v. 20, 21. God commanded them to be produced. He said, *Let the waters bring forth abundantly ;* not as if the waters had any productive power of their own, but, " Let them be brought into being, the fish in the waters and the fowl out of them." This command he himself executed: *God created great whales*, &c. Insects, which perhaps are as various and as numerous as any species of animals, and their structure as curious, were part of this day's work, some of them being allied to the fish and others to the fowl. Mr. Boyle (I remember) says he admires the Creator's wisdom and power as much in an ant as in an elephant. Notice is here taken of the various sorts of fish and fowl, each after their kind, and of the great numbers of both that were produced, for the waters brought forth abundantly; and particular mention is made of great whales, the largest of fishes, whose bulk and strength, exceeding that of any other animal, are remarkable proofs of the power and greatness of the Creator. The express notice here taken of the whale, above all the rest, seems sufficient to determine what animal is meant by the Leviathan, Job xli. 1. The curious formation of the bodies of animals, their different sizes, shapes, and natures, with the admirable powers of the sensitive life with which they are endued, when duly considered, serve, not only to silence and shame the objections of atheists and infidels, but to raise high thoughts and high praises of God in pious and devout souls, Ps. civ. 25, &c. 2. The blessing of them, in order to their continuance. Life is a wasting thing. Its strength is not the strength of stones. It is a candle that will burn out, if it be not first blown out; and therefore the wise Creator not only made the individuals, but provided

8

for the propagation of the several kinds: *God blessed them, saying, Be fruitful, and multiply,* v. 22. God will bless his own works, and not forsake them ; and *what he does shall be for a perpetuity*, Eccl. iii. 14. The power of God's providence preserves all things, as at first his creating power produced them. Fruitfulness is the effect of God's blessing and must be ascribed to it ; the multiplying of the fish and fowl, from year to year, is still the fruit of this blessing. Well, let us give to God the glory of the continuance of these creatures to this day for the benefit of man. See Job xii. 7, 9. It is a pity that fishing and fowling, recreations innocent in themselves, should ever be abused to divert any from God and their duty, while they are capable of being improved to lead us to the contemplation of the wisdom, power, and goodness, of him that made all these things, and to engage us to stand in awe of him, as the fish and fowl do of us.

24 And God said, Let the earth bring forth the living creature after his kind, cattle, and creeping thing, and beast of the earth after his kind: and it was so. 25 And God made the beast of the earth after his kind, and cattle after their kind, and every thing that creepeth upon the earth after his kind : and God saw that *it was* good.

We have here the first part of the sixth day's work. The sea was, the day before, replenished with its fish, and the air with its fowl; and this day were made the beasts of the earth, the cattle, and the creeping things that pertain to the earth. Here, as before, 1. *The Lord gave the word;* he said, *Let the earth bring forth*, not as if the earth had any such prolific virtue as to produce these animals, or as if God resigned his creating power to it; but, " Let these creatures now come into being upon the earth, and out of it, in their respective kinds, conformable to the ideas of them in the divine counsels concerning their creation." 2. He also did the work ; he made them all after their kind, not only of divers shapes, but of divers natures, manners, food, and fashions—some to be tame about the house, others to be wild in the fields—some living upon grass and herbs, others upon flesh—some harmless, and others ravenous—some bold, and others timorous—some for man's service, and not his sustenance, as the horse—others for his sustenance, and not his service, as the sheep—others for both, as the ox—and some for neither, as the wild beasts. In all this appears the manifold wisdom of the Creator.

26 And God said, Let us make man in our image, after our likeness : and let them have dominion over the fish of the sea, and over the fowl of

the air, and over the cattle, and over all the earth, and over every creeping thing that creepeth upon the earth. 27 So God created man in his *own* image, in the image of God created he him ; male and female created he them. 28 And God blessed them, and God said unto them, Be fruitful, and multiply, and replenish the earth, and subdue it : and have dominion over the fish of the sea, and over the fowl of the air, and over every living thing that moveth upon the earth.

We have here the second part of the sixth day's work, the creation of man, which we are, in a special manner, concerned to take notice of, that we may know ourselves. Observe, I. That man was made last of all the creatures, that it might not be suspected that he had been, any way, a helper to God in the creation of the world : that question must be for ever humbling and mortifying to him, *Where wast thou*, or any of thy kind, *when I laid the foundations of the earth ?* Job xxxviii 4. Yet it was both an honour and a favour to him that he was made last: an honour, for the method of the creation was to advance from that which was less perfect to that which was more so ; and a favour, for it was not fit he should be lodged in the palace designed for him till it was completely fitted up and furnished for his reception. Man, as soon as he was made, had the whole visible creation before him, both to contemplate and to take the comfort of. Man was made the same day that the beasts were, because his body was made of the same earth with theirs ; and, while he is in the body, he inhabits the same earth with them. God forbid that by indulging the body and the desires of it we should make ourselves like the beasts that perish !

II. That man's creation was a more signal and immediate act of divine wisdom and power than that of the other creatures. The narrative of it is introduced with something of solemnity, and a manifest distinction from the rest. Hitherto, it had been said, " Let there be light," and " Let there be a firmament," and " Let the earth, or waters, bring forth" such a thing ; but now the word of command is turned into a word of consultation, " *Let us make man*, for whose sake the rest of the creatures were made : this is a work we must take into our own hands." In the former he speaks as one having authority, in this as one having affection ; for his *delights were with the sons of men*, Prov. viii. 31. It should seem as if this were the work which he longed to be at ; as if he had said, " Having at last settled the preliminaries, let us now apply ourselves to the business, *Let us make man*." Man was to be a creature different from all that had been hitherto made. Flesh and spirit, heaven and earth, must be put together in him, and he must be allied to both worlds. And therefore God himself not only undertakes to make him, but is pleased so to express himself as if he called a council to consider of the making of him: *Let us make man.* The three persons of the Trinity, Father, Son, and Holy Ghost, consult about it and concur in it, because man, when he was made, was to be dedicated and devoted to Father, Son, and Holy Ghost. Into that great name we are, with good reason, baptized, for to that great name we owe our being, Let him rule man who said, *Let us make man.*

III. That man was made in. God's image and after his likeness, two words to express the same thing and making each other the more expressive; *image* and *likeness* denote the likest image, the nearest resemblance of any of the visible creatures. Man was not made in the likeness of any creature that went before him, but in the likeness of his Creator; yet still between God and man there is an infinite distance. Christ only is the *express* image of God's person, as the Son of his Father, having the same nature. It is only some of God's honour that is put upon man, who is God's image only as the shadow in the glass, or the king's impress upon the coin. God's image upon man consists in these three things :—1. In his nature and constitution, not those of his body (for God has not a body), but those of his soul. This honour indeed God has put upon the body of man, that the Word was made flesh, the Son of God was clothed with a body like ours and will shortly clothe ours with a glory like that of his. And this we may safely say, That he by whom God made the worlds, not only the great world, but man the little world, formed the human body, at the first, according to the platform he designed for himself in the fulness of time. But it is the soul, the great soul, of man, that does especially bear God's image. The soul is a spirit, an intelligent immortal spirit, an influencing active spirit, herein resembling God, the Father of Spirits, and the soul of the world. *The spirit of man is the candle of the Lord.* The soul of man, considered in its three noble faculties, understanding, will, and active power, is perhaps the brightest clearest looking-glass in nature, wherein to see God. 2. In his place and authority : *Let us make man in our image, and let him have dominion.* As he has the government of the inferior creatures, he is, as it were, God's representative, or viceroy, upon earth ; they are not capable of fearing and serving God, therefore God has appointed them to fear and serve man. Yet his government of himself by the freedom of his will has in it more of God's image than his government of the creatures. 3. In his purity and rectitude. God's image upon man consists in knowledge, righteousness, and true holiness, Eph. iv. 24 · Col. iii. 10.

10

He was upright, Eccl. vii. 29. He had an habitual conformity of all his natural powers to the whole will of God. His understanding saw divine things clearly and truly, and there were no errors nor mistakes in his knowledge. His will complied readily and universally with the will of God, without re luctancy or resistance. His affections were all regular, and he had no inordinate appetites or passions. His thoughts were easily brought and fixed to the best subjects, and there was no vanity nor ungovernableness in them. All the inferior powers were subject to the dictates and directions of the superior, without any mutiny or rebellion. Thus holy, thus happy, were our first parents, in having the image of God upon them. And this honour, put upon man at first, is a good reason why we should not speak ill one of another (Jam. iii. 9), nor do ill one to another (Gen. ix. 6), and a good reason why we should not debase ourselves to the service of sin, and why we should devote ourselves to God's service. But how art thou fallen, O son of the morning ! How is this image of God upon man defaced ! How small are the remains of it, and how great the ruins of it ! The Lord renew it upon our souls by his sanctifying grace !

IV. That man was made male and female, and blessed with the blessing of fruitfulness and increase. God said, *Let us make man,* and immediately it follows, *So God created man ;* he performed what he resolved. With us saying and doing are two things ; but they are not so with God. He created him male and female, Adam and Eve—Adam first, out of earth, and Eve out of his side, *ch.* ii. It should seem that of the rest of the creatures God made many couples, but of man *did not he make one ?* (Mal. ii. 15), though he had the residue of the Spirit, whence Christ gathers an argument against divorce, Matt. xix. 4, 5. Our first father, Adam, was confined to one wife ; and, if he had put her away, there was no other for him to marry, which plainly intimated that the bond of marriage was not to be dissolved at pleasure. Angels were not made male and female, for they were not to propagate their kind (Luke xx. 34—36) ; but man was made so, that the nature might be propagated and the race continued. Fires and candles, the luminaries of this lower world, because they waste, and go out, have a power to light more ; but it is not so with the lights of heaven : stars do not kindle stars. God made but one male and one female, that all the nations of men might know themselves to be made of one blood, descendants from one common stock, and might thereby be induced to love one another. God, having made them capable of transmitting the nature they had received, said to them, *Be fruitful, and multiply, and replenish the earth.* Here he gave them, 1. A large inheritance : *Replenish the earth ;* it is this that is bestowed upon the children of men.

They were made *to dwell upon the face of all the earth,* Acts xvii. 26. This is the place in which God has set man to be the servant of his providence in the government of the inferior creatures, and, as it were, the intelligence of this orb; to be the receiver of God's bounty, which other creatures live upon, but do not know it; to be likewise the collector of his praises in this lower world, and to pay them into the exchequer above (Ps. cxlv. 10); and, lastly, to be a probationer for a better state. 2. A numerous lasting family, to enjoy this inheritance, pronouncing a blessing upon them, in virtue of which their posterity should extend to the utmost corners of the earth and continue to the utmost period of time. Fruitfulness and increase depend upon the blessing of God: Obed-edom had eight sons, *for God blessed him,* 1 Chron. xxvi. 5. It is owing to this blessing, which God commanded at first, that the race of mankind is still in being, and that as *one generation passeth away another cometh.*

V. That God gave to man, when ne had made him, a dominion over the inferior creatures, *over the fish of the sea and over the fowl of the air.* Though man provides for neither, he has power over both, much more *over every living thing that moveth upon the earth,* which are more under his care and within his reach. God designed hereby to put an honour upon man, that he might find himself the more strongly obliged to bring honour to his Maker. This dominion is very much diminished and lost by the fall; yet God's providence continues so much of it to the children of men as is necessary to the safety and support of their lives, and God's grace has given to the saints a new and better title to the creature than that which was forfeited by sin; for all is ours if we are Christ's, 1 Cor. iii. 22.

29 And God said, Behold, I have given you every herb bearing seed, which *is* upon the face of all the earth, and every tree, in the which *is* the fruit of a tree yielding seed; to you it shall be for meat. 30 And to every beast of the earth, and to every fowl of the air, and to every thing that creepeth upon the earth, wherein *there is* life, I *have given* every green herb for meat: and it was so.

We have here the third part of the sixth day's work, which was not any new creation, but a gracious provision of food for all flesh, Ps. cxxxvi. 25. He that made man and beast thus took care to preserve both, Ps. xxxvi. 6. Here is,

I. Food provided for man, *v.* 29. Herbs and fruits must be his meat, including corn and all the products of the earth; these were allowed him, but (it should seem) not flesh, till after the flood, *ch.* ix. 3. And before the earth was deluged, much more before it was cursed for man's sake, its fruits, no doubt, were more pleasing to the taste and more strengthening and nourishing to the body than marrow and fatness, and all the portion of the king's meat, are now. See here, 1. That which should make us humble. As we were made out of the earth, so we are maintained out of it. Once indeed men did eat angels' food, bread from heaven; but they died (John vi. 49); it was to them but as food out of the earth, Ps. civ. 14. There is meat that endures to everlasting life; the Lord evermore give us this. 2. That which should make us thankful. The Lord is for the body; from him we receive all the supports and comforts of this life, and to him we must give thanks. He gives us all things richly to enjoy, not only for necessity, but plenty, dainties, and varieties, for ornament and delight. How much are we indebted! How careful should we be, as we live upon God's bounty, to live to his glory! 3. That which should make us temperate and content with our lot. Though Adam had dominion given him over fish and fowl, yet God confined him, in his food, to herbs and fruits; and he never complained of it. Though afterwards he coveted forbidden fruit, for the sake of the wisdom and knowledge he promised himself from it, yet we never read that he coveted forbidden flesh. If God give us food for our lives, let us not, with murmuring Israel, ask food for our lusts, Ps. lxxviii. 18; see Dan. i. 15.

II. Food provided for the beasts, *v.* 30. *Doth God take care for oxen?* Yes, certainly, he provides food convenient for them, and not for oxen only, which were used in his sacrifices and man's service, but even the young lions and the young ravens are the care of his providence; they ask and have their meat from God. Let us give to God the glory of his bounty to the inferior creatures, that are all fed, as it were, at his table, every day. He is a great housekeeper, a very rich and bountiful one, that satisfies the desire of every living thing. Let this encourage God's people to cast their care upon him, and not to be solicitous respecting what they shall eat and what they shall drink. He that provided for Adam without his care, and still provides for all the creatures without their care, will not let those that trust him want any good thing, Matt. vi. 26. He that feeds his birds will not starve his babes.

31 And God saw every thing that he had made, and, behold, it *was* very good. And the evening and the morning were the sixth day.

We have here the approbation and conclusion of the whole work of creation. As for God, his work is perfect; and if he begin he will also make an end, in providence and grace, as well as here in creation. Observe,

11

I. The review God took of his work: He saw *every thing that he had made.* So he does still; all the works of his hands are under his eye. He that made all sees all; he that made us sees us, Ps. cxxxix. 1—16. Omniscience cannot be separated from omnipotence. *Known unto God are all his works,* Acts xv. 18. But this was the Eternal Mind's solemn reflection upon the copies of its own wisdom and the products of its own power. God has hereby set us an example of reviewing our works. Having given us a power of reflection, he expects we should use that power, see our way (Jer. ii. 23), and think of it, Ps. cxix. 59. When we have finished a day's work, and are entering upon the rest of the night, we should commune with our own hearts about what we have been doing that day; so likewise when we have finished a week's work, and are entering upon the sabbath-rest, we should thus prepare to meet our God; and when we are finishing our life's work, and are entering upon our rest in the grave, that is a time to bring to remembrance, that we may die repenting, and so take leave of it.

II. The complacency God took in his work. When we come to review our works we find, to our shame, that much has been very bad; but, when God reviewed his, all was very good. He did not pronounce it good till he had seen it so, to teach us not to answer a matter before we hear it. The work of creation was a very good work. All that God made was well-made, and there was no flaw nor defect in it. 1. It was good. Good, for it is all agreeable to the mind of the Creator, just as he would have it to be; when the transcript came to be compared with the great original, it was found to be exact, no errata in it, not one misplaced stroke. Good, for it answers the end of its creation, and is fit for the purpose for which it was designed. Good, for it is serviceable to man, whom God had appointed lord of the visible creation. Good, for it is all for God's glory; there is that in the whole visible creation which is a demonstration of God's being and perfections, and which tends to beget, in the soul of man, a religious regard to him and veneration of him. 2. It was very good. Of each day's work (except the second) it was said that it was good, but now, it is very good. For, (1.) Now man was made, who was the chief of the ways of God, who was designed to be the visible image of the Creator's glory and the mouth of the creation in his praises. (2.) Now all was made; every part was good, but all together very good. The glory and goodness, the beauty and harmony, of God's works, both of providence and grace, as this of creation, will best appear when they are perfected. When the top-stone is brought forth we shall cry, *Grace, grace, unto it,* Zech. iv. 7. Therefore judge nothing before the time.

III. The time when this work was concluded: *The evening and the morning were the*

sixth day; so that in six days God made the world. We are not to think but that God could have made the world in an instant. He that said, *Let there be light, and there was light,* could have said, " Let there be a world," and there would have been a world, in a moment, in the twinkling of an eye, as at the resurrection, 1 Cor. xv. 52. But he did it in six days, that he might show himself a free-agent, doing his own work both in his own way and in his own time,—that his wisdom, power, and goodness, might appear to us, and be meditated upon by us, the more distinctly,—and that he might set us an example of working six days and resting the seventh; it is therefore made the reason of the fourth commandment. So much would the sabbath conduce to the keeping up of religion in the world that God had an eye to it in the timing of his creation. And now, as God reviewed his work, let us review our meditations upon it, and we shall find them very lame and defective, and our praises low and flat; let us therefore stir up ourselves, and all that is within us, to *worship him that made the heaven, earth, and sea, and the fountains of waters,* according to the tenour of the everlasting gospel, which is preached to every nation, Rev. xiv. 6, 7. All his works, in all places of his dominion, do bless him; and, therefore, *bless thou the Lord, O my soul!*

CHAP. II.

This chapter is an appendix to the history of the creation, more particularly explaining and enlarging upon that part of the history which relates immediately to man, the favourite of this lower world. We have in it, I. The institution and sanctification of the sabbath, which was made for man, to further his holiness and comfort, ver. 1–3. II. A more particular account of man's creation, as the centre and summary of the whole work, ver. 4–7. III. A description of the garden of Eden, and the placing of man in it under the obligations of a law and covenant, ver. 8—17. IV. The creation of the woman, her marriage to the man, and the institution of the ordinance of marriage, ver. 18, &c.

THUS the heavens and the earth were finished, and all the host of them. 2 And on the seventh day God ended his work which he had made; and he rested on the seventh day from all his work which he had made. 3 And God blessed the seventh day, and sanctified it; because that in it he had rested from all his work which God created and made.

We have here, I. The settlement of the kingdom of nature, in God's resting from the work of creation, v. 1, 2. Here observe, 1. The creatures made both in heaven and earth are the *hosts* or *armies* of them, which denotes them to be numerous, but marshalled, disciplined, and under command. How great is the sum of them! And yet every one knows and keeps his place. God uses them as his hosts for the defence of his people and the destruction of his enemies; for he is the Lord of hosts, of all these hosts, Dan. iv. 35. 2. The heavens and the earth are finished pieces, and so are all the creatures in them. So perfect is God's work that nothing can be added to it nor taken from it, Eccl. iii. 14. God that began to build showed himself well able to finish. 3. After the end of the first six days God ceased from all works of creation. He has so ended his work as that though, in his providence, he worketh hitherto (John v. 17), preserving and governing all the creatures, and particularly forming the spirit of man within him, yet he does not make any new species of creatures. In miracles, he has controlled and overruled nature, but never changed its settled course, nor repealed nor added to any of its establishments. 4. The eternal God, though infinitely happy in the enjoyment of himself, yet took a satisfaction in the work of his own hands. He did not rest, as one weary, but as one well-pleased with the instances of his own goodness and the manifestations of his own glory.

II. The commencement of the kingdom of grace, in the sanctification of the sabbath day, *v.* 3. He rested on that day, and took a complacency in his creatures, and then sanctified it, and appointed us, on that day, to rest and take a complacency in the Creator; and his rest is, in the fourth commandment, made a reason for ours, after six days' labour. Observe, 1. The solemn observance of one day in seven, as a day of holy rest and holy work, to God's honour, is the indispensable duty of all those to whom God has revealed his holy sabbaths. 2. The way of sabbath-sanctification is the good old way, Jer. vi. 16. Sabbaths are as ancient as the world; and I see no reason to doubt that the sabbath, being now instituted in innocency, was religiously observed by the people of God throughout the patriarchal age. 3. The sabbath of the Lord is truly honourable, and we have reason to honour it—honour it for the sake of its antiquity, its great Author, the sanctification of the first sabbath by the holy God himself, and by our first parents in innocency, in obedience to him. 4. The sabbath day is a blessed day, for God blessed it, and that which he blesses is blessed indeed. God has put an honour upon it, has appointed us, on that day, to bless him, and has promised, on that day, to meet us and bless us. 5. The sabbath day is a holy day, for God has sanctified it. He has separated and distinguished it from the rest of the days of the week, and he has consecrated it and set it apart to himself and his own service and honour. Though it is commonly taken for granted that the Christian sabbath we observe, reckoning from the creation, is not the seventh but the first day of the week, yet being a seventh day, and we, in it, celebrating the rest of God the Son, and the finishing of the work of our redemption, we may and ought to act faith upon this original institution of the sabbath day, and to commemorate the work of creation, to the honour of the great Creator, who is therefore worthy to receive, on that day, blessing, and honour, and praise, from all religious assemblies.

4 These *are* the generations of the heavens and of the earth when they were created, in the day that the LORD God made the earth and the heavens, 5 And every plant of the field before it was in the earth, and every herb of the field before it grew : for the LORD God had not caused it to rain upon the earth, and *there was* not a man to till the ground. 6 But there went up a mist from the earth, and watered the whole face of the ground. 7 And the LORD God formed man *of* the dust of the ground, and breathed into his nostrils the breath of life; and man became a living soul.

In these verses, I. Here is a name given to the Creator which we have not yet met with, and that is *Jehovah*—the LORD, in capital letters, which are constantly used in our English translation to intimate that in the original it is *Jehovah.* All along, in the first chapter, he was called *Elohim*—a God *of power ;* but now *Jehovah Elohim*—a God *of power and perfection,* a finishing God. As we find him known by his name Jehovah when he appeared to perform what he had promised (Exod. vi. 3), so now we have him known by that name, when he had perfected what he had begun. *Jehovah* is that great and incommunicable name of God which denotes his having his being of himself, and his giving being to all things; fitly therefore is he called by that name now that heaven and earth are finished.

II. Further notice taken of the production of plants and herbs, because they were made and appointed to be food for man, *v.* 5, 6. Here observe, 1. The earth did not bring forth its fruits of itself, by any innate virtue of its own but purely by the almighty power of God, which formed every plant and every herb before it grew in the earth. Thus grace in the soul, that plant of renown, grows not of itself in nature's soil, but is the work of God's own hands. 2. Rain also is the gift of God; it came not till *the Lord God caused it to rain.* If rain be wanted, it is God that withholds it; if rain come plentifully in its season, it is God that sends it; if it come in a distinguishing way, it is God that *causeth it to rain upon one city and not upon another,* Amos iv. 3. Though God, ordinarily, works by means, yet he is not tied to them, but when he pleases he can do his own work without them. As the plants were produced before the sun was made, so they were before there was either rain to water the earth or man to till it. Therefore though we must not tempt God in the neglect of means, yet we must trust God in the want of means. 4. Some way or other God will take care to water the plants that are of his

13

own planting. Though as yet there was no rain, God made a mist equivalent to a shower, and with it *watered the whole face of the ground.* Thus he chose to fulfil his purpose by the weakest means, *that the excellency of the power might be of God.* Divine grace descends like a mist, or silent dew, and waters the church without noise, Deut. xxxii. 2.

III. A more particular account of the creation of man, *v.* 7. Man is a little world, consisting of heaven and earth, soul and body. Now here we have an account of the origin of both and the putting of both together : let us seriously consider it, and say, to our Creator's praise, We are *fearfully and wonderfully made,* Ps. cxxxix. 14. Elihu, in the patriarchal age, refers to this history when he says (Job xxxiii. 6), *I also am formed out of the clay,* and (*v.* 4), *The breath of the Almighty hath given me life,* and (*ch.* xxxii. 8), *There is a spirit in man.* Observe then,

1. The mean origin, and yet the curious structure, of the body of man. (1.) The matter was despicable. He was made *of the dust of the ground,* a very unlikely thing to make a man of ; but the same infinite power that made the world of nothing made man, its master-piece, of next to nothing. He was made of the dust, the small dust, such as is upon the surface of the earth. Probably, not dry dust, but dust moistened with the mist that went up, *v.* 6. He was not made of gold-dust, powder of pearl, or diamond dust, but common dust, dust of the ground. Hence he is said to be of the earth, χοϊκὸς— *dusty,* 1 Cor. xv. 47. And we also are of the earth, for we are his offspring, and of the same mould. So near an affinity is there between the earth and our earthly parents that our mother's womb, out of which we were born, is called *the earth* (Ps. cxxxix. 15), and the earth, in which we must be buried, is called our *mother's womb,* Job i. 21. Our foundation is in the earth, Job iv. 19. Our fabric is earthly, and the fashioning of it like that of an earthen vessel, Job. x. 9. Our food is out of the earth, Job xxviii. 5. Our familiarity is with the earth, Job xvii. 14. Our fathers are in the earth, and our own final tendency is to it ; and what have we then to be proud of? (2.) Yet the Maker was great, and the make fine. The Lord God, the great fountain of being and power, formed man. Of the other creatures it is said that they were *created* and *made ;* but of man that he was *formed,* which denotes a gradual process in the work with great accuracy and exactness. To express the creation of this new thing, he takes a new word, a word (some think) borrowed from the potter's forming his vessel upon the wheel ; for we are the clay, and God the potter, Isa. lxiv. 8. The body of man is curiously wrought, Ps. cxxxix. 15, 16. *Materiam superabat opus—The workmanship exceeded the materials.* Let us present our bodies to God as living sacrifices (Rom. xii. 1),

as living temples (1 Cor. vi. 19), and then these vile bodies shall shortly be new-formed like Christ's glorious body, Phil. iii. 21.

2. The high origin and the admirable serviceableness of the soul of man. (1.) It takes its rise from the breath of heaven, and is produced by it. It was not made of earth, as the body was ; it is a pity then that it should cleave to the earth, and mind earthly things. It came immediately from God ; he gave it to be put into the body (Eccl. xii. 7), as afterwards he gave the tables of stone of his own writing to be put into the ark, and the *urim* of his own framing to be put into the breast-plate. Hence God is not only the former but the Father of spirits. Let the soul which God has breathed into us breathe after him ; and let it be for him, since it is from him. Into his hands let us commit our spirits, for from his hands we had them. (2.) It takes its lodging in a house of clay, and is the life and support of it. It is by it that man is a living soul, that is, a living man ; for the soul is the man. The body would be a worthless, useless, loathsome carcase, if the soul did not animate it. To God that gave us these souls we must shortly give an account of them, how we have employed them, used them, proportioned them, and disposed of them ; and if then it be found that we have lost them, though it were to gain the world, we shall be undone for ever. Since the extraction of the soul is so noble, and its nature and faculties are so excellent, let us not be of those fools that despise their own souls, by preferring their bodies before them, Prov. xv. 32. When our Lord Jesus anointed the blind man's eyes with clay perhaps he intimated that it was he who at first formed man out of the clay ; and when he *breathed on his disciples, saying, Receive you the Holy Ghost,* he intimated that it was he who at first breathed into man's nostrils the breath of life. He that made the soul is alone able to new-make it.

8 And the LORD God planted a garden eastward in Eden ; and there he put the man whom he had formed. 9 And out of the ground made the LORD God to grow every tree that is pleasant to the sight and good for food ; the tree of life also in the midst of the garden, and the tree of knowledge of good and evil. 10 And a river went out of Eden to water the garden ; and from thence it was parted, and became into four heads. 11 The name of the first *is* Pison : that *is* it which compasseth the whole land of Havilah, where *there is* gold ; 12 And the gold of that land *is* good ; there *is* bdellium and the onyx stone.

14

13 And the name of the second river *is* Gihon: the same *is* it that compasseth the whole land of Ethiopia. 14 And the name of the third river *is* Hiddekel: that *is* it which goeth toward the east of Assyria. And the fourth river *is* Euphrates. 15 And the Lord God took the man, and put him into the garden of Eden to dress it and to keep it.

Man consisting of body and soul, a body made out of the earth and a rational immortal soul the breath of heaven, we have, in these verses, the provision that was made for the happiness of both; he that made him took care to make him happy, if he could but have kept himself so and known when he was well off. That part of man by which he is allied to the world of sense was made happy; for he was put in the paradise of God: that part by which he is allied to the world of spirits was well provided for; for he was taken into covenant with God. Lord, what is man that he should be thus dignified —man that is a worm! Here we have,

I. A description of the garden of Eden, which was intended for the mansion and demesne of this great lord, the palace of this prince. The inspired penman, in this history, writing for the Jews first, and calculating his narratives for the infant state of the church, describes things by their outward sensible appearances, and leaves us, by further discoveries of the divine light, to be led into the understanding of the mysteries couched under them. Spiritual things were strong meat, which they could not yet bear; but he writes to them as unto carnal, 1 Cor. iii. 1. Therefore he does not so much insist upon the happiness of Adam's mind as upon that of his outward state. The Mosaic history, as well as the Mosaic law, has rather the patterns of heavenly things than the heavenly things themselves, Heb. ix. 23. Observe,

1. The place appointed for Adam's residence was a garden; not an ivory house nor a palace overlaid with gold, but a garden, furnished and adorned by nature, not by art. What little reason have men to be proud of stately and magnificent buildings, when it was the happiness of man in innocency that he needed none! As clothes came in with sin, so did houses. The heaven was the roof of Adam's house, and never was any roof so curiously ceiled and painted. The earth was his floor, and never was any floor so richly inlaid. The shadow of the trees was his retirement; under them were his dining-rooms, his lodging-rooms, and never were any rooms so finely hung as these: Solomon's, in all their glory, were not arrayed like them. The better we can accommodate ourselves to plain things, and the less we indulge our-

selves with those artificial delights which have been invented to gratify men's pride and luxury, the nearer we approach to a state of innocency. Nature is content with a little and that which is most natural, grace with less, but lust with nothing

2. The contrivance and furniture of this garden were the immediate work of God's wisdom and power. The Lord God planted this garden, that is, he *had* planted it—upon the third day, when the fruits of the earth were made. We may well suppose it to have been the most accomplished place for pleasure and delight that ever the sun saw, when the all-sufficient God himself designed it to be the present happiness of his beloved creature, man, in innocency, and a type and a figure of the happiness of the chosen remnant in glory. No delights can be agreeable nor satisfying to a soul but those that God himself has provided and appointed for it; no true paradise, but of God's planting. The light of our own fires, and the sparks of our own kindling, will soon leave us in the dark, Isa. l. 11. The whole earth was now a paradise compared with what it is since the fall and since the flood; the finest gardens in the world are a wilderness compared with what the whole face of the ground was before it was cursed for man's sake: yet that was not enough; God planted a garden for Adam. God's chosen ones shall have distinguishing favours shown them.

3. The situation of this garden was extremely sweet. It was in *Eden*, which signifies *delight* and *pleasure*. The place is here particularly pointed out by such marks and bounds as were sufficient, I suppose, when Moses wrote, to specify the place to those who knew that country; but now, it seems, the curious cannot satisfy themselves concerning it. Let it be our care to make sure a place in the heavenly paradise, and then we need not perplex ourselves with a search after the place of the earthly paradise. It is certain that, wherever it was, it had all desirable conveniences, and (which never any house nor garden on earth was) without any inconvenience. Beautiful for situation, the joy and glory of the whole earth, was this garden: doubtless it was earth in its highest perfection.

4. The trees with which this garden was planted. (1.) It had all the best and choicest trees in common with the rest of the ground. It was beautified and adorned with every tree that, for its height or breadth, its make or colour, its leaf or flower, was pleasant to the sight and charmed the eye; it was replenished and enriched with every tree that yielded fruit grateful to the taste and useful to the body, and so good for food. God, as a tender Father, consulted not only Adam's profit, but his pleasure; for there is a pleasure consistent with innocency, nay, there is a true and transcendent pleasure in innocency. God delights in the prosperity of his servants,

15

and would have them easy; it is owing to themselves if they be uneasy. When Providence puts us into an Eden of plenty and pleasure, we ought to *serve him with joyfulness and gladness of heart*, in the abundance of the good things he gives us. But, (2.) It had two extraordinary trees peculiar to itself; on earth there were not their like. [1.] There was the *tree of life in the midst of the garden*, which was not so much a memorandum to him of the fountain and author of his life, nor perhaps any natural means to preserve or prolong life; but it was chiefly intended to be a sign and seal to Adam, assuring him of the continuance of life and happiness, even to immortality and everlasting bliss, through the grace and favour of his Maker, upon condition of his perseverance in this state of innocency and obedience. Of this he might eat and live. Christ is now to us the tree of life (Rev. ii. 7,; xxii. 2), and the *bread of life*, John vi. 48, 53. [2.] There was *the tree of the knowledge of good and evil*, so called, not because it had any virtue in it to beget or increase useful knowledge (surely then it would not have been forbidden), but, *First*, Because there was an express positive revelation of the will of God concerning this tree, so that by it he might know moral good and evil. What is good? It is good not to eat of this tree. What is evil? It is evil to eat of this tree. The distinction between all other moral good and evil was written in the heart of man by nature; but this, which resulted from a positive law, was written upon this tree. *Secondly*, Because, in the event, it proved to give Adam an experimental knowledge of good by the loss of it and of evil by the sense of it. As the covenant of grace has in it, not only *Believe and be saved*, but also, *Believe not and be damned* (Mark xvi. 16), so the covenant of innocency had in it, not only "Do this and live," which was sealed and confirmed by the tree of life, but, "Fail and die," which Adam was assured of by this other tree: "Touch it at your peril;" so that, in these two trees, God set before him *good and evil, the blessing and the curse*, Deut. xxx. 19. These two trees were as two sacraments.

5. The rivers with which this garden was watered, *v.* 10—14. These four rivers (or one river branched into four streams) contributed much both to the pleasantness and the fruitfulness of this garden. The land of Sodom is said to be *well watered every where, as the garden of the Lord, ch.* xiii. 10. Observe, That which God plants he will take care to keep watered. The trees of righteousness are set by the rivers, Ps. i. 3. In the heavenly paradise there is a river infinitely surpassing these; for it is a river of the water of life, not coming out of Eden, as this, but proceeding out of the throne of God and of the Lamb (Rev. xxii. 1), a river that *makes glad the city of our God*, Ps. xlvi. 4. Hiddekel and Euphrates are rivers of Babylon, which

we read of elsewhere. By these the captive Jews sat down and *wept, when they remembered Sion* (Ps. cxxxvii. 1); but methinks they had much more reason to weep (and so have we) at the remembrance of Eden. Adam's paradise was their prison; such wretched work has sin made. Of the land of Havilah it is said (*v.* 12), *The gold of that land is good*, and *there is bdellium and the onyx-stone:* surely this is mentioned that the wealth of which the land of Havilah boasted might be as a foil to that which was the glory of the land of Eden. Havilah had gold, and spices, and precious stones; but Eden had that which was infinitely better, the tree of life, and communion with God. So we may say of the Africans and Indians: "They have the gold, but we have the gospel. The gold of their land is good, but the riches of ours are infinitely better."

II. The placing of man in this paradise of delight, *v.* 15, where observe,

1. How God put him in possession of it: *The Lord God took the man, and put him into the garden of Eden;* so *v.* 8, 15. Note here, (1.) Man was made *out* of paradise; for, after God had formed him, he put him into the garden: he was made of common clay, not of paradise-dust. He lived out of Eden before he lived in it, that he might see that all the comforts of his paradise-state were owing to God's free grace. He could not plead a tenant-right to the garden, for he was not born upon the premises, nor had any thing but what he received; all boasting was hereby for ever excluded. (2.) The same God that was the author of his being was the author of his bliss; the same hand that made him a living soul planted the tree of life for him, and settled him by it. He that made us is alone able to make us happy; he that is the former of our bodies and the Father of our spirits, he, and none but he, can effectually provide for the felicity of both. (3.) It adds much to the comfort of any condition if we have plainly seen God going before us and putting us into it. If we have not forced providence, but followed it, and taken the hints of direction it has given us, we may hope to find a paradise where otherwise we could not have expected it. See Ps. xlvii. 4.

2. How God appointed him business and employment. He put him there, not like Leviathan into the waters, to play therein, but to dress the garden and to keep it. Paradise itself was not a place of exemption from work. Note here, (1.) We were none of us sent into the world to be idle. He that made us these souls and bodies has given us something to work with; and he that gave us this earth for our habitation has made us something to work on. If a high extraction, or a great estate, or a large dominion, or perfect innocency, or a genius for pure contemplation, or a small family, could have given a man a writ of ease, Adam would not have been set to work; but he that gave us

16

being has given us business, to serve him and our generation, and to work out our salvation : if we do not mind our business, we are unworthy of our being and maintenance. (2.) Secular employments will very well consist with a state of innocency and a life of communion with God. The sons and heirs of heaven, while they are here in this world, have something to do about this earth, which must have its share of their time and thoughts; and, if they do it with an eye to God, they are as truly serving him in it as when they are upon their knees. (3.) The husband-man's calling is an ancient and honourable calling; it was needful even in paradise. The garden of Eden, though it needed not to be weeded (for thorns and thistles were not yet a nuisance), yet must be dressed and kept. Nature, even in its primitive state,' left room for the improvements of art and industry. It was a calling fit for a state of innocency, making provision for life, not for lust, and giving man an opportunity of admiring the Creator and acknowledging his providence : while his hands were about his trees, his heart might be with his God. (4.) There is a true pleasure in the business which God calls us to, and employs us in. Adam's work was so far from being an allay that it was an addition to the pleasures of paradise; he could not have been happy if he had been idle : it is still a law, He that will not work has no right to eat, 2 Thess. iii. 10; Prov. xxvii. 23.

III. The command which God gave to man in innocency, and the covenant he then took him into. Hitherto we have seen God as man's powerful Creator and his bountiful Benefactor ; now he appears as his Ruler and Lawgiver. God put him into the garden of Eden, not to live there as he might list, but to be under government. As we are not allowed to be idle in this world, and to do nothing, so we are not allowed to be wilful, and do what we please. When God had given man a dominion over the creatures, he would let him know that still he himself was under the government of his Creator.

16 And the LORD God commanded the man, saying, Of every tree of the garden thou mayest freely eat : 17 But of the tree of the knowledge of good and evil, thou shalt not eat of it : for in the day that thou eatest thereof thou shalt surely die.

Observe here, I. God's authority over man, as a creature that had reason and freedom of will. The Lord God commanded the man, who stood now as a public person, the father and representative of all mankind, to receive law, as he had lately received a nature, for himself and all his. God commanded all the creatures, according to their capacity ; the settled course of nature is a law, Ps. cxlviii. 6; civ. 9. The brute-creatures have their respective instincts; but man was made capable of performing reasonable service, and therefore received, not only the command of a Creator, but the command of a Prince and Master. Though Adam was a very great man, a very good man, and a very happy man, yet the Lord God commanded him; and the command was no disparagement to his greatness, no reproach to his goodness, nor any diminution at all to his happiness. Let us acknowledge God's right to rule us, and our own obligations to be ruled by him ; and never allow any will of our own in contradiction to, or competition with, the holy will of God.

II. The particular act of this authority, in prescribing to him what he should do, and upon what terms he should stand with his Creator. Here is,

1. A confirmation of his present happiness to him, in that grant, *Of every tree in the garden thou mayest freely eat.* This was not only an allowance of liberty to him, in taking the delicious fruits of paradise, as a recompence for his care and pains in dressing and keeping it (1 Cor. ix. 7, 10), but it was, withal, an assurance of life to him, immortal life, upon his obedience. For the tree of life being put *in the midst of the garden (v. 9),* as the heart and soul of it, doubtless God had an eye to that especially in this grant ; and therefore when, upon his revolt, this grant is recalled, no notice is taken of any tree of the garden as prohibited to him, except the tree of life *(ch. iii. 22),* of which it is there said he might have eaten and *lived for ever,* that is, never died, nor ever lost his happiness. " Continue holy as thou art, in conformity to thy Creator's will, and thou shalt continue happy as thou art in the enjoyment of thy Creator's favour, either in this paradise or in a better." Thus, upon condition of perfect personal and perpetual obedience, Adam was sure of paradise to himself and his heirs for ever.

2. A trial of his obedience, upon pain of the forfeiture of all his happiness : *"But of the* other tree which stood very near the tree of life (for they are both said to be *in the midst of the garden),* and which was called the *tree of knowledge, in the day thou eatest thereof, thou shalt surely die ;"* as if he had said, " Know, Adam, that thou art now upon thy good behaviour, thou art put into paradise upon trial ; be observant, be obedient, and thou art made for ever ; otherwise thou wilt be as miserable as now thou art happy." Here,

(1.) Adam is threatened with death in case of disobedience : *Dying thou shalt die,* denoting a sure and dreadful sentence, as, in the former part of this covenant, *eating thou shalt eat,* denotes a free and full grant. Observe, [1.] Even Adam, in innocency, was awed with a threatening ; fear is one of the handles of the soul, by which it is taken hold of and held. If he then needed this hedge,

17

much more do we now. [2.] The penalty threatened is death : *Thou shalt die,* that is, " Thou shalt be debarred from the tree of life, and all the good that is signified by it, all the happiness thou hast, either in possession or prospect ; and thou shalt become liable to death, and all the miseries that preface it and attend it." [3.] This was threatened as the immediate consequence of sin : *In the day thou eatest, thou shalt die,* that is, " Thou shalt become mortal and capable of dying ; the grant of immortality shall be recalled, and that defence shall depart from thee. Thou shalt become obnoxious to death, like a condemned malefactor that is dead in law" (only, because Adam was to be the root of mankind, he was reprieved) ; " nay, the harbingers and forerunners of death shall immediately seize thee, and thy life, thenceforward, shall be a dying life : and this, *surely ;* it is a settled rule, *the soul that sinneth, it shall die*

(2.) Adam is tried with a positive law, not to eat of the fruit *of the tree of knowledge.* Now it was very proper to make trial of his obedience by such a command as this, [1] Because the reason of it is fetched purely from the will of the Law-maker. Adam had in his nature an aversion to that which was evil in itself, and therefore he is tried in a thing which was evil only because it was forbidden ; and, being in a small thing, it was the more fit to prove his obedience by. [2.] Because the restraint of it is laid upon the desires of the flesh and of the mind, which, in the corrupt nature of man, are the two great fountains of sin. This prohibition checked both his appetite towards sensitive delights and his ambition of curious knowledge, that his body might be ruled by his soul and his soul by his God.

Thus easy, thus happy, was man in a state of innocency, having all that heart could wish to make him so. How good was God to him ! How many favours did he load him with ! How easy were the laws he gave him ! How kind the covenant he made with him ! Yet man, being in honour, understood not his own interest, but soon *became as the beasts that perish.*

18 And the LORD God said, *It is* not good that the man should be alone ; I will make him a help meet for him. 19 And out of the ground the LORD God formed every beast of the field, and every fowl of the air ; and brought *them* unto Adam to see what he would call them : and whatsoever Adam called every living creature, that *was* the name thereof. 20 And Adam gave names to all cattle, and to the fowl of the air, and to every beast of the field ; but for Adam

there was not found a help meet for him.

Here we have, I. An instance of the Creator's care of man and his fatherly concern for his comfort, *v.* 18. Though God had let him know that he was a subject, by giving him a command (*v.* 16, 17), yet here he lets him know also, for his encouragement in his obedience, that he was a friend, and a favourite, and one whose satisfaction he was tender of. Observe,

1. How God graciously pitied his solitude : *It is not good that man, this man, should be alone.* Though there was an upper world of angels and a lower world of brutes, and he between them, yet there being none of the same nature and rank of beings with himself, none that he could converse familiarly with, he might be truly said to be *alone.* Now he that made him knew both him and what was good for him, better than he did himself, and he said, " It is not good that he should continue thus alone." (1.) It is not for his comfort ; for man is a sociable creature. It is a pleasure to him to exchange knowledge and affection with those of his own kind, to inform and to be informed, to love and to be beloved. What God here says of the first man Solomon says of all men (Eccl. iv. 9, &c.), that *two are better than one, and woe to him that is alone.* If there were but one man in the world, what a melancholy man must he needs be ! Perfect solitude would turn a paradise into a desert, and a palace into a dungeon. Those therefore are foolish who are selfish and would be placed alone in the earth. (2.) It is not for the increase and continuance of his kind. God could have made a world of men at first, to replenish the earth, as he replenished heaven with a world of angels : but the place would have been too strait for the designed number of men to live together at once ; therefore God saw fit to make up that number by a succession of generations, which, as God had formed man, must be from two, and those male and female ; one will be ever one.

2. How God graciously resolved to provide society for him. The result of this reasoning concerning him was this kind resolution, *I will make a help-meet for him ;* a help *like* him (so some read it), one of the same nature and the same rank of beings ; a help *near* him (so others), one to cohabit with him, and to be always at hand ; a help *before* him (so others), one that he should look upon with pleasure and delight. Note hence, (1.) In our best state in this world we have need of one another's help ; for we are members one of another, and *the eye cannot say to the hand, I have no need of thee,* 1 Cor. xii. 21. We must therefore be glad to receive help from others, and give help to others, as there is occasion. (2.) It is God only who perfectly knows our wants, and is perfectly able to

supply them all, Phil. iv. 19. In him alone our help is, and from him are all our helpers. (3.) A suitable wife is a help-meet, and is from the Lord. The relation is then likely to be comfortable when meetness directs and determines the choice, and mutual helpfulness is the constant care and endeavour, 1 Cor. vii. 33, 34. (4.) Family-society, if it is agreeable, is a redress sufficient for the grievance of solitude. He that has a good God, a good heart, and a good wife, to converse with, and yet complains he wants conversation, would not have been easy and content in paradise; for Adam himself had no more: yet, even before Eve was created, we do not find that he complained of being alone, knowing that he *was not alone, for the Father was with him.* Those that are most satisfied in God and his favour are in the best way, and in the best frame, to receive the good things of this life, and shall be sure of them, as far as Infinite Wisdom sees good.

II. An instance of the creatures' subjection to man, and his dominion over them (v. 19, 20): *Every beast of the field and every fowl of the air God brought to Adam,* either by the ministry of angels, or by a special instinct, directing them to come to man as their master, teaching the ox betimes to know his owner. Thus God gave man livery and seisin of the fair estate he had granted him, and put him in possession of his dominion over the creatures. God brought them to him, that he might name them, and so might give, 1. A proof of his knowledge, as a creature endued with the faculties both of reason and speech, and so *taught more than the beasts of the earth and made wiser than the fowls of heaven,* Job xxxv. 11. And, 2. A proof of his power. It is an act of authority to impose names (Dan. i. 7), and of subjection to receive them. The inferior creatures did now, as it were, do homage to their prince at his inauguration, and swear fealty and allegiance to him. If Adam had continued faithful to his God, we may suppose the creatures themselves would so well have known and remembered the names Adam now gave them as to have come at his call, at any time, and answered to their names. God gave names to the day and night, to the firmament, to the earth, and to the sea; and he *calleth the stars by their names,* to show that he is the supreme Lord of these. But he gave Adam leave to name the beasts and fowls, as their subordinate lord; for, having made him in his own image, he thus put some of his honour upon him.

III. An instance of the creatures' insufficiency to be a happiness for man : *But* (among them all) *for Adam there was not found a help meet for him.* Some make these to be the words of Adam himself; observing all the creatures come to him by couples to be named, he thus intimates his desire to his Maker:— " Lord, these have all helps meet for them; but what shall I do? Here is never a one

for me." It is rather God's judgment upon the review. He brought them all together, to see if there were ever a suitable match for Adam in any of the numerous families of the inferior creatures; but there was none. Observe here, 1. The dignity and excellency of the human nature. On earth there was not its like, nor its peer to be found among all visible creatures; they were all looked over, but it could not be matched among them all. 2. The vanity of this world and the things of it; put them all together, and they will not make a help-meet for man. They will not suit the nature of his soul, nor supply its needs, nor satisfy its just desires, nor run parallel with its never-failing duration. God creates a new thing to be a help-meet for man—not so much the woman as the seed of the woman.

21 And the Lord God caused a deep sleep to fall upon Adam, and he slept : and he took one of his ribs, and closed up the flesh instead thereof; 22 And the rib, which the Lord God had taken from man, made he a woman, and brought her unto the man. 23 And Adam said, This *is* now bone of my bones, and flesh of my flesh : she shall be called Woman, because she was taken out of Man. 24 Therefore shall a man leave his father and his mother, and shall cleave unto his wife : and they shall be one flesh. 25 And they were both naked, the man and his wife, and were not ashamed.

Here we have, I. The making of the woman, to be a help-meet for Adam. This was done upon the sixth day, as was also the placing of Adam in paradise, though it is here mentioned after an account of the seventh day's rest; but what was said in general (*ch.* i. 27), that God made man male and female, is more distinctly related here. Observe, 1. That Adam was first formed, then Eve (1 Tim. ii. 13), and she was made of the man, and for the man (1 Cor. xi. 8, 9), all which are urged there as reasons for the humility, modesty, silence, and submissiveness, of that sex in general, and particularly the subjection and reverence which wives owe to their own husbands. Yet man being made last of the creatures, as the best and most excellent of all, Eve's being made after Adam, and out of him, puts an honour upon that sex, as the glory of the man, 1 Cor. xi. 7. If man is the head, she is the crown, a crown to her husband, the crown of the visible creation. The man was dust refined, but the woman was dust double-refined, one remove further from the earth. 2. That Adam slept while his wife was in making, that no room might be left to imagine that he had herein *directed* the Spirit of the Lord, or been his counsellor, Isa. xl. 13. He had been made sensible of his want of a meet help; but, God having undertaken to provide him one, he does not afflict himself with any care about it, but lies down and sleeps sweetly, as one that had cast all his care on God, with a cheerful resignation of himself and all his affairs to his Maker's will and wisdom. Jehovah-jireh, let the Lord provide when and whom he pleases. If we graciously rest in God, God will graciously work for us and work all for good. 3. That *God caused a sleep to fall on Adam,* and made it a deep sleep, that so the opening of his side might be no grievance to him; while he knows no sin, God will take care he shall feel no pain. When God, by his providence, does that to his people which is grievous to flesh and blood, he not only consults their happiness in the issue, but by his grace he can so quiet and compose their spirits as to make them easy under the sharpest operations. 4. That the woman was *made of a rib out of the side of Adam;* not made out of his head to rule over him, nor out of his feet to be trampled upon by him, but out of his side to be equal with him, under his arm to be protected, and near his heart to be beloved. Adam lost a rib, and without any diminution to his strength or comeliness (for, doubtless, the flesh was closed without a scar); but in lieu thereof he had a help meet for him, which abundantly made up his loss: what God takes away from his people he will, one way or other, restore with advantage. In this (as in many other things) Adam was a figure of him that was to come; for out of the side of Christ, the second Adam, his spouse the church was formed, when he slept the sleep, the deep sleep, of death upon the cross, in order to which his side was opened, and there came out blood and water, blood to purchase his church and water to purify it to himself. See Eph. v. 25, 26.

II. The marriage of the woman to Adam. Marriage is honourable, but this surely was the most honourable marriage that ever was, in which God himself had all along an immediate hand. Marriages (they say) are made in heaven: we are sure this was, for the man, the woman, the match, were all God's own work; he, by his power, made them *both,* and now, by his ordinance, made them *one.* This was a marriage made in perfect innocency, and so was never any marriage since, 1. God, as *her* Father, brought the woman to the man, as his second self, and a help-meet for him. When he had made her, he did not leave her to her own disposal; no, she was his child, and she must not marry without his consent. Those are likely to settle to their comfort who by faith and prayer, and a humble dependence upon providence, put themselves under a divine conduct. That wife that is of God's making by special grace, and of

God's bringing by special providence, is likely to prove a help-meet for a man. 2. From God, as *his* Father, Adam received her (v. 23): " *This is now bone of my bone.* Now I have what I wanted, and which all the creatures could not furnish me with, a help meet for me." God's gifts to us are to be received with a humble thankful acknowledgment of his wisdom in suiting them to us, and his favour in bestowing them on us. Probably she was revealed to Adam in a vision, when he was asleep, that this lovely creature, now presented to him, was a piece of himself, and was to be his companion and the wife of his covenant. Hence some have fetched an argument to prove that glorified saints in the heavenly paradise shall know one another. Further, in token of his acceptance of her, he gave her a name, not peculiar to her, but common to her sex: *She shall be called woman, Isha,* a *she-man,* differing from man in sex only, not in nature —made of man, and joined to man.

III. The institution of the ordinance of marriage, and the settling of the law of it, v. 24. The sabbath and marriage were two ordinances instituted in innocency, the former for the preservation of the church, the latter for the preservation of the world of mankind. It appears (by Matt. xix. 4, 5) that it was God himself who said here, " A man must leave all his relations, to cleave to his wife;" but whether he spoke it by Moses, the penman, or by Adam (who spoke, v. 23), is uncertain. It should seem, they are the words of Adam, in God's name, laying down this law to all his posterity. 1. See here how great the virtue of a divine ordinance is; the bonds of it are stronger even than those of nature. To whom can we be more firmly bound than to the fathers that begat us and the mothers that bore us? Yet the son must quit them, to be joined to his wife, and the daughter forget them, to cleave to her husband, Ps. xlv. 10, 11. 2. See how necessary it is that children should take their parents' consent along with them in their marriage, and how unjust those are to their parents, as well as undutiful, who marry without it; for they rob them of their right to them, and interest in them, and alienate it to another, fraudulently and unnaturally. 3. See what need there is both of prudence and prayer in the choice of this relation, which is so near and so lasting. That had need be well done which is to be done for life. 4. See how firm the bond of marriage is, not to be divided and weakened by having many wives (Mal. ii. 15) nor to be broken or cut off by divorce, for any cause but fornication, or voluntary desertion. 5. See how dear the affection ought to be between husband and wife, such as there is to our own bodies, Eph. v. 28. These two are one flesh; let them then be one soul.

IV. An evidence of the purity and innocency of that state wherein our first parents were created, *v.* 25. They were both naked. They needed no clothes for defence against cold nor heat, for neither could be injurious to them. They needed none for ornament. Solomon in all his glory was not arrayed like one of these. Nay, they needed none for decency; they were naked, and had no reason to be ashamed. *They knew not what shame was,* so the Chaldee reads it. Blushing is now the colour of virtue, but it was not then the colour of innocency. Those that had no sin in their conscience might well have no shame in their faces, though they had no clothes to their backs.

CHAP. III.

The story of this chapter is perhaps as sad a story (all things considered) as any we have in all the Bible. In the foregoing chapters we have had the pleasant view of the holiness and happiness of our first parents, the grace and favour of God, and the peace and beauty of the whole creation, all good, very good; but here the scene is altered. We have here an account of the sin and misery of our first parents, the wrath and curse of God against them, the peace of the creation disturbed, and its beauty stained and sullied, all bad, very bad. "How has the gold become dim, and the most fine gold changed!" O that our hearts were deeply affected with this record! For we are all nearly concerned in it; let it not be to us as a tale that is told. The general contents of this chapter we have, Rom. v. 12, "By one man sin entered into the world, and death by sin; and so death passed upon all men, for that all have sinned." More particularly, we have here, I. The innocent tempted, ver. 1—5. II. The tempted transgressing, ver. 6—8. III. The transgressors arraigned, ver. 9, 10. IV. Upon their arraignment, convicted, ver. 11—13. V. Upon their conviction, sentenced, ver. 14—19. VI. After sentence, reprieved, ver. 20, 21. VII. Notwithstanding their reprieve, execution in part done, ver. 22—24. And, were it not for the gracious intimations here given of redemption by the promised seed, they, and all their degenerate guilty race, would have been left to endless despair.

NOW the serpent was more subtle than any beast of the field which the Lord God had made. And he said unto the woman, Yea, hath God said, Ye shall not eat of every tree of the garden? 2 And the woman said unto the serpent, We may eat of the fruit of the trees of the garden: 3 But of the fruit of the tree which *is* in the midst of the garden, God hath said, Ye shall not eat of it, neither shall ye touch it, lest ye die. 4 And the serpent said unto the woman, Ye shall not surely die: 5 For God doth know that in the day ye eat thereof, then your eyes shall be opened, and ye shall be as gods, knowing good and evil.

We have here an account of the temptation with which Satan assaulted our first parents, to draw them into sin, and which proved fatal to them. Here observe,

I. The tempter, and that was the devil, in the shape and likeness of a serpent.

1. It is certain it was the devil that beguiled Eve. The devil and Satan is the old serpent (Rev. xii. 9), a malignant spirit, by creation an angel of light and an immediate attendant upon God's throne, but by sin become an apostate from his first state and a rebel against God's crown and dignity. Multitudes of the angels fell; but this that attacked our first parents was surely the prince of the devils, the ring-leader in the rebellion: no sooner was he a sinner than he was a Satan, no sooner a traitor than a tempter, as one enraged against God and his glory and envious of man and his happiness. He knew he could not destroy man but by debauching him. Balaam could not curse Israel, but he could tempt Israel, Rev. ii. 14. The game therefore which Satan had to play was to draw our first parents to sin, and so to separate between them and their God. Thus the devil was, from the beginning, a murderer, and the great mischief-maker. The whole race of mankind had here, as it were, but one neck, and at that Satan struck. The adversary and enemy is that wicked one.

2. It was the devil in the likeness of a serpent. Whether it was only the visible shape and appearance of a serpent (as some think those were of which we read, Exod. vii. 12), or whether it was a real living serpent, actuated and possessed by the devil, is not certain: by God's permission it might be either. The devil chose to act his part in a serpent, (1.) Because it is a specious creature, has a spotted dappled skin, and then went erect. Perhaps it was a flying serpent, which seemed to come from on high as a messenger from the upper world, one of the seraphim; for the fiery serpents were flying, Isa. xiv. 29. Many a dangerous temptation comes to us in gay fine colours that are but skin-deep, and seems to come from above; for Satan can seem an angel of light. And, (2.) Because it is a subtle creature; this is here taken notice of. Many instances are given of the subtlety of the serpent, both to do mischief and to secure himself in it when it is done. We are directed to be wise as serpents. But this serpent, as actuated by the devil, was no doubt more subtle than any other; for the devil, though he has lost the sanctity, retains the sagacity of an angel, and is wise to do evil. He knew of more advantage by making use of the serpent than we are aware of. Observe, There is not any thing by which the devil serves himself and his own interest more than by unsanctified subtlety. What Eve thought of this serpent speaking to her we are not likely to tell, when I believe she herself did not know what to think of it. At first, perhaps, she supposed it might be a good angel, and yet, afterwards, she might suspect something amiss. It is remarkable that the Gentile idolaters did many of them worship the devil in the shape and form of a serpent, thereby avowing their adherence to that apostate spirit, and wearing his colours.

II. The person tempted was the woman, now alone, and at a distance from her husband, but near the forbidden tree. It was the devil's subtlety, 1. To assault the weaker vessel with his temptations. Though perfect in her kind, yet we may suppose her inferior to Adam in knowledge, and strength, and presence of mind. Some think Eve received the command, not immediately from God, but at second hand by her husband, and therefore might the more easily be persuaded to discredit it. 2 It was his policy to enter into discourse with her when she was alone. Had she kept close to the side out of which she was lately taken, she would not have been so much exposed. There are many temptations to which solitude gives great advantage; but the communion of saints contributes much to their strength and safety. 3. He took advantage by finding her near the forbidden tree, and probably gazing upon the fruit of it, only to satisfy her curiosity. Those that would not eat the forbidden fruit must not come near the forbidden tree. *Avoid it, pass not by it,* Prov. iv. 15. 4. Satan tempted Eve, that by her he might tempt Adam; so he tempted Job by his wife, and Christ by Peter. It is his policy to send temptations by unsuspected hands, and theirs that have most interest in us and influence upon us.

III. The temptation itself, and the artificial management of it. We are often, in scripture, told of our danger by the temptations of Satan, his *devices* (2 Cor. ii. 11), his *depths* (Rev. ii. 24), his *wiles,* Eph. vi. 11. The greatest instances we have of them are in his tempting of the two Adams, here, and Matt. iv. In this he prevailed, but in that he was baffled. What he spoke *to* them, of whom he had no hold by any corruption in them, he speaks *in* us by our own deceitful hearts and their carnal reasonings; this makes his assaults on us less discernible, but not less dangerous. That which the devil aimed at was to persuade Eve to eat forbidden fruit; and, to do this, he took the same method that he does still. He questioned whether it was a sin or no, *v.* 1. He denied that there was any danger in it, *v.* 4. He suggested much advantage by it, *v.* 5. And these are his common topics.

1. He questioned whether it was a sin or no to eat of this tree, and whether really the fruit of it was forbidden. Observe,

(1.) *He said to the woman, Yea, hath God said, You shall not eat?* The first word intimated something said before, introducing this, and with which it is connected, perhaps some discourse Eve had with herself, which Satan took hold of, and grafted this question upon. In the chain of thoughts one thing strangely brings in another, and perhaps something bad at last. Observe here, [1.] He does not discover his design at first, but puts a question which seemed innocent: " I hear a piece of news, pray is it true? has God forbidden you to eat of this tree?" Thus he would begin a discourse, and draw her into a parley. Those that would be safe have need to be suspicious, and shy of talking with the tempter. [2.] He quotes the command fallaciously, as if it were a prohibition, not only of that tree, but of all. God had

said, *Of every tree you may eat, except one.* He, by aggravating the exception, endeavours to invalidate the concession : *Hath God said, You shall not eat of every tree?* The divine law cannot be reproached unless it be first misrepresented. [3.] He seems to speak it tauntingly, upbraiding the woman with her shyness of meddling with that tree; as if he had said, " You are so nice and cautious, and so very precise, because God has said, You shall not eat." The devil, as he is a liar, so he is a scoffer, from the beginning : and the scoffers of the last days are his children. [4.] That which he aimed at in the first onset was to take off her sense of the obligation of the command. " Surely you are mistaken, it cannot be that God should tie you out from this tree; he would not do so unreasonable a thing." See here, That it is the subtlety of Satan to blemish the reputation of the divine law as uncertain or unreasonable, and so to draw people to sin; and that it is therefore our wisdom to keep up a firm belief of, and a high respect for, the command of God. Has God said, " You shall not lie, nor take his name in vain, nor be drunk," &c.? " Yes, I am sure he has, and it is well said, and by his grace I will abide by it, whatever the tempter suggests to the contrary."

(2.) In answer to this question the woman gives him a plain and full account of the law they were under, *v.* 2, 3. Here observe, [1.] It was her weakness to enter into discourse with the serpent. She might have perceived by his question that he had no good design, and should therefore have started back with a *Get thee behind me, Satan, thou art an offence to me.* But her curiosity, and perhaps her surprise, to hear a serpent speak, led her into further talk with him. Note, It is a dangerous thing to treat with a temptation, which ought at first to be rejected with disdain and abhorrence. The garrison that sounds a parley is not far from being surrendered. Those that would be kept from harm must keep out of harm's way. See Prov. xiv. 7; xix. 27. [2.] It was her wisdom to take notice of the liberty God had granted them, in answer to his sly insinuation, as if God had put them into paradise only to tantalize them with the sight of fair but forbidden fruits. " Yea," says she, " we may eat of the fruit of the trees, thanks to our Maker, we have plenty and variety enough allowed us." Note, To prevent our being uneasy at the restraints of religion, it is good often to take a view of the liberties and comforts of it. [3.] It was an instance of her resolution that she adhered to the command, and faithfully repeated it, as of unquestionable certainty : " *God hath said,* I am confident he hath said it, You shall not eat of the fruit of this tree ;" and that which she adds, *Neither shall you touch it,* seems to have been with a good intention, not (as some think) tacitly to reflect upon the command as too strict *(Touch not, taste not handle not),* but to make a fence about it: "We must not eat, therefore we will not touch. It is forbidden in the highest degree, and the authority of the prohibition is sacred to us." [4.] She seems a little to waver about the threatening, and is not so particular and faithful in the repetition of that as of the precept. God had said, *In the day thou eatest thereof thou shalt surely die;* all she makes of that is, *Lest you die.* Note, Wavering faith and wavering resolutions give great advantage to the tempter.

2. He denies that there was any danger in it, insisting that, though it might be the transgressing of a precept, yet it would not be the incurring of a penalty: *You shall not surely die, v.* 4. " You shall not *dying die,*" so the word is, in direct contradiction to what God had said. Either, (1.) "It is not certain that you shall die," so some. "It is not so sure as you are made to believe it is." Thus Satan endeavours to shake that which he cannot overthrow, and invalidates the force of divine threatenings by questioning the certainty of them; and, when once it is supposed possible that there may be falsehood or fallacy in any word of God, a door is then opened to downright infidelity. Satan teaches men first to doubt and then to deny; he makes them sceptics first, and so by degrees makes them atheists. Or, (2.) "It is certain you shall not die," so some. He avers his contradiction with the same phrase of assurance that God had used in ratifying the threatening. He began to call the precept in question (*v.* 1), but, finding that the woman adhered to that, he quitted that battery, and made his second onset upon the threatening, where he perceived her to waver; for he is quick to spy all advantages, and to attack the wall where it is weakest : *You shall not surely die.* This was a lie, a downright lie; for,"[1.] It was contrary to the word of God, which we are sure is true. See 1 John ii. 21, 27. It was such a lie as gave the lie to God himself. [2.] It was contrary to his own knowledge. When he told them there was no danger in disobedience and rebellion he said that which he knew, by woeful experience, to be false. He had broken the law of his creation, and had found, to his cost, that he could not prosper in it; and yet he tells our first parents they shall not die. He concealed his own misery, that he might draw them into the like : thus he still deceives sinners into their own ruin. He tells them that, though they sin, they shall not die; and gains credit rather than God, who tells them, *The wages of sin is death.* Note, Hope of impunity is a great support to all iniquity, and impenitency in it. *I shall have peace, though I walk in the imagination of my heart,* Deut. xxix. 19.

3. He promises them advantage in it, *v.* 5. Here he follows his blow, and it was a blow at the root, a fatal blow to the tree we are branches of. He not only would undertake that they should be no losers by it, thus binding himself to save them from harm;

but (if they would be such fools as to venture upon the security of one that had himself become a bankrupt) he undertakes they shall be gainers by it, unspeakable gainers. He could not have persuaded them to run the hazard of ruining themselves if he had not suggested to them a great probability of bettering themselves.

(1.) He insinuates to them the great improvements they would make by eating of this fruit. And he suits the temptation to the pure state they were now in, proposing to them, not any carnal pleasures or gratifications, but intellectual delights and satisfactions. These were the baits with which he covered his hook. [1.] " *Your eyes shall be opened;* you shall have much more of the power and pleasure of contemplation than now you have ; you shall fetch a larger compass in your intellectual views, and see further into things than now you do." He speaks as if now they were but dim-sighted, and short-sighted, in comparison of what they would be then. [2.] " *You shall be as gods,* as *Elohim,* mighty gods; not only omniscient, but omnipotent too ;" or, "You shall be as God himself, equal to him, rivals with him ; you shall be sovereigns and no longer subjects, self-sufficient and no longer dependent." A most absurd suggestion ! As if it were possible for creatures of yesterday to be like their Creator that was from eternity. [3.] " You shall know *good and evil,* that is, every thing that is desirable to be known." To support this part of the temptation, he abuses the name given to this tree : it was intended to teach the practical knowledge of good and evil, that is, of duty and disobedience ; and it would prove the experimental knowledge of good and evil, that is, of happiness and misery. In these senses, the name of the tree was a warning to them not to eat of it ; but he perverts the sense of it, and wrests it to their destruction, as if this tree would give them a speculative notional knowledge of the natures, kinds, and originals, of good and evil. And, [4.] All this presently : " *In the day you eat thereof you* will find a sudden and immediate change for the better." Now in all these insinuations he aims to beget in them, *First,* Discontent with their present state, as if it were not so good as it might be, and should be. Note, No condition will of itself bring contentment, unless the mind be brought to it. Adam was not easy, no, not in paradise, nor the angels in their first state, Jude 6. *Secondly,* Ambition of preferment, as if they were fit to be gods. Satan had ruined himself by desiring to be like the Most High (Isa. xiv. 14), and therefore seeks to infect our first parents with the same desire, that he might ruin them too.

(2.) He insinuates to them that God had no good design upon them, in forbidding them this fruit: " *For God doth know* how much it will advance you ; and therefore, in envy and ill-will to you, he hath forbidden it :" as if he durst not let them eat of that tree because then they would know their own strength, and would not continue in an inferior state, but be able to cope with him ; or as if he grudged them the honour and happiness to which their eating of that tree would prefer them. Now, [1.] This was a great affront to God, and the highest indignity that could be done him, a reproach to his power, as if he feared his creatures, and much more a reproach to his goodness, as if he hated the work of his own hands and would not have those whom he has made to be made happy. Shall the best of men think it strange to be misrepresented and evil spoken of, when God himself is so ? Satan, as he is the accuser of the brethren before God, so he accuses God before the brethren ; thus he sows discord, and is the father of those that do so. [2.] It was a most dangerous snare to our first parents, as it tended to alienate their affections from God, and so to withdraw them from their allegiance to him. Thus still the devil draws people into his interest by suggesting to them hard thoughts of God, and false hopes of benefit and advantage by sin. Let us therefore, in opposition to him, always think well of God as the best good, and think ill of sin as the worst of evils: thus let us resist the devil, and he will flee from us.

6 And when the woman saw that the tree *was* good for food, and that it *was* pleasant to the eyes, and a tree to be desired to make *one* wise, she took of the fruit thereof, and did eat, and gave also unto her husband with her ; and he did eat. 7 And the eyes of them both were opened, and they knew that they *were* naked ; and they sewed fig leaves together, and made themselves aprons. 8 And they heard the voice of the LORD God walking in the garden in the cool of the day : and Adam and his wife hid themselves from the presence of the LORD God amongst the trees of the garden.

Here we see what Eve's parley with the tempter ended in. Satan, at length, gains his point, and the strong-hold is taken by his wiles. God tried the obedience of our first parents by forbidding them the tree of knowledge, and Satan does, as it were, join issue with God, and in that very thing undertakes to seduce them into a transgression; and here we find how he prevailed, God permitting it for wise and holy ends.

I. We have here the inducements that moved them to transgress. The woman, being deceived by the tempter's artful management, was ringleader in the transgression,

1 Tim. ii. 14. She was first in the fault; and it was the result of her consideration, or rather her inconsideration. 1. She saw no harm in this tree, more than in any of the rest. It was said of all the rest of the fruit-trees with which the garden of Eden was planted that they were *pleasant to the sight, and good for food, ch.* ii. 9. Now, in her eye, this was like all the rest. It seemed as good for food as any of them, and she saw nothing in the colour of its fruit that threatened death or danger ; it was as pleasant to the sight as any of them, and therefore, "What hurt could it do to them ? Why should this be forbidden them rather than any of the rest ?" Note, When there is thought to be no more harm in forbidden fruit than in other fruit sin lies at the door, and Satan soon carries the day. Nay, perhaps it seemed to her to be better for food, more grateful to the taste, and more nourishing to the body, than any of the rest, and to her eye it was more pleasant than any. We are often betrayed into snares by an inordinate desire to have our senses gratified. Or, if it had nothing in it more inviting than the rest, yet it was the more coveted because it was prohibited. Whether it was so in her or not, we find that in us (that is, in our flesh, in our corrupt nature) there dwells a strange spirit of contradiction. *Nitimur in vetitum—We desire what is prohibited.* 2. She imagined more virtue in this tree than in any of the rest, that it was a tree not only not to be dreaded, but *to be desired to make one wise,* and therein excelling all the rest of the trees. This she *saw,* that is, she perceived and understood it by what the devil had said to her ; and some think that she saw the serpent eat of that tree, and that he told her he thereby had gained the faculties of speech and reason, whence she inferred its power to make one wise, and was persuaded to think, " If it made a brute creature rational, why might it not make a rational creature divine ?" See here how the desire of unnecessary knowledge, under the mistaken notion of wisdom, proves hurtful and destructive to many. Our first parents, who knew so much, did not know this—that they knew enough. Christ is a tree to be desired to make one wise, Col. ii. 3 ; 1 Cor. i. 30. Let us, by faith, feed upon him, that we may be wise to salvation. In the heavenly paradise, the tree of knowledge will not be a forbidden tree ; for there we shall know as we are known. Let us therefore long to be there, and, in the mean time, not exercise ourselves in things too high or too deep for us, nor covet to be wise above what is written.

II. The steps of the transgression, not steps upward, but downward towards the pit— steps that take hold on hell. 1. She *saw.* She should have turned away her eyes from beholding vanity ; but she enters into temptation, by looking with pleasure on the forbidden fruit. Observe, A great deal of sin comes in at the eyes. At these windows Satan throws in those fiery darts which pierce and poison the heart. The eye affects the heart with guilt as well as grief. Let us therefore, with holy Job, make a covenant with our eyes, not to look on that which we are in danger of lusting after, Prov. xxiii. 31; Matt. v. 28. Let the fear of God be always to us for a covering of the eyes, *ch.* xx. 16. 2. *She took.* It was her own act and deed. The devil did not take it, and put it into her mouth, whether she would or no; but she herself took it. Satan may tempt, but he cannot force; may persuade us to cast ourselves down, but he cannot cast us down, Matt. iv. 6. Eve's taking was stealing, like Achan's taking the accursed thing, taking that to which she had no right. Surely she took it with a trembling hand. 3. She *did eat.* Perhaps she did not intend, when she looked, to take, nor, when she took, to eat; but this was the result. Note, The way of sin is down-hill; a man cannot stop himself when he will. The beginning of it is as the breaking forth of water, to which it is hard to say, " Hitherto thou shalt come and no further." Therefore it is our wisdom to suppress the first emotions of sin, and to leave it off before it be meddled with. *Obsta principiis—Nip mischief in the bud.* 4. She *gave also to her husband with her.* It is probable that he was not with her when she was tempted (surely, if he had, he would have interposed to prevent the sin), but came to her when she had eaten, and was prevailed upon by her to eat likewise; for it is easier to learn that which is bad than to teach that which is good. She gave it to him, persuading him with the same arguments that the serpent had used with her, adding this to all the rest, that she herself had eaten of it, and found it so far from being deadly that it was extremely pleasant and grateful. *Stolen waters are sweet.* She gave it to him, under colour of kindness—she would not eat these delicious morsels alone; but really it was the greatest unkindness she could do him. Or perhaps she gave it to him that, if it should prove hurtful, he might share with her in the misery, which indeed looks strangely unkind, and yet may, without difficulty, be supposed to enter into the heart of one that had eaten forbidden fruit. Note, Those that have themselves done ill are commonly willing to draw in others to do the same. As was the devil, so was Eve, no sooner a sinner than a tempter. 5. *He did eat*, overcome by his wife's importunity. It is needless to ask, " What would have been the consequence if Eve only had transgressed?" The wisdom of God, we are sure, would have decided the difficulty, according to equity; but, alas! the case was not so; Adam also did eat. " And what great harm if he did?" say the corrupt and carnal reasonings of a vain mind. What harm! Why, this act involved disbelief of God's word, together

with confidence in the devil's, discontent with his present state, pride in his own merits, and ambition of the honour which comes not from God, envy at God's perfections, and indulgence of the appetites of the body. In neglecting the tree of life of which he was allowed to eat, and eating of the tree of knowledge which was forbidden, he plainly showed a contempt of the favours God had bestowed on him, and a preference given to those God did not see fit for him. He would be both his own carver and his own master, would _have_ what he pleased and do what he pleased: his sin was, in one word, *disobedience* (Rom. v. 19), disobedience to a plain, easy, and express command, which probably he knew to be a command of trial. He sinned against great knowledge, against many mercies, against light and love, the clearest light and the dearest love that ever sinner sinned against. He had no corrupt nature within him to betray him; but had a freedom of will, not enslaved, and was in his full strength, not weakened or impaired. He turned aside quickly. Some think he fell the very day on which he was made; but I see not how to reconcile this with God's pronouncing all *very good* in the close of that day. Others suppose he fell on the sabbath day: the better day the worse deed. However, it is certain that he kept his integrity but a very little while: being in honour, he continued not. But the greatest aggravation of his sin was that he involved all his posterity in sin and ruin by it. God having told him that his race should replenish the earth, surely he could not but know that he stood as a public person, and that his disobedience would be fatal to all his seed; and, if so, it was certainly both the greatest treachery and the greatest cruelty that ever was. The human nature being lodged entirely in our first parents, henceforward it could not but be transmitted from them under an attainder of guilt, a stain of dishonour, and an hereditary disease of sin and corruption. And can we say, then, that Adam's sin had but little harm in it?

III. The immediate consequences of the transgression. Shame and fear seized the criminals, *ipso facto—in the fact itself;* these came into the world along with sin, and still attend it.

1. Shame seized them unseen, *v.* 7, where observe,

(1.) The strong convictions they fell under, in their own bosoms: *The eyes of them both were opened.* It is not meant of the eyes of the body; these were open before, as appears by this, that the sin came in at them. Jonathan's eyes were enlightened by eating forbidden fruit (1 Sam. xiv. 27), that is, he was refreshed and revived by it; but theirs were not so. Nor is it meant of any advances made hereby in true knowledge; but the eyes of their consciences were opened, their hearts smote them for what they had done. Now,

25

when it was too late, they saw the folly of eating forbidden fruit. They saw the happiness they had fallen from, and the misery they had fallen into. They saw a loving God provoked, his grace and favour forfeited, his likeness and image lost, dominion over the creatures gone. They saw their natures corrupted and depraved, and felt a disorder in their own spirits of which they had never before been conscious. They saw a law in their members warring against the law of their minds, and captivating them both to sin and wrath. They saw, as Balaam, when *his eyes were opened* (Num. xxii. 31), the angel of the Lord standing in the way, and his sword drawn in his hand; and perhaps they saw the serpent that had abused them insulting over them. The text tells us that they saw *that they were naked*, that is, [1.] That they were stripped, deprived of all the honours and joys of their paradise-state, and exposed to all the miseries that might justly be expected from an angry God. They were disarmed; their defence had departed from them. [2.] That they were shamed, for ever shamed, before God and angels. They saw themselves disrobed of all their ornaments and ensigns of honour, degraded from their dignity and disgraced in the highest degree, laid open to the contempt and reproach of heaven, and earth, and their own consciences. Now see here, *First*, What a dishonour and disquietment sin is; it makes mischief wherever it is 'admitted, sets men against themselves, disturbs their peace, and destroys all their comforts. Sooner or later, it will have shame, either the shame of true repentance, which ends in glory, or that shame and everlasting contempt to which the wicked shall rise at the great day. Sin is a reproach to any people. *Secondly*, What a deceiver Satan is. He told our first parents, when he tempted them, that their eyes should be opened; and so they were, but not as they understood it; they were opened to their shame and grief, not to their honour nor advantage. Therefore, when he speaks fair, believe him not. The most malicious mischievous liars often excuse themselves with this, that they only equivocate; but God will not so excuse them.

(2.) The sorry shift they made to palliate these convictions, and to arm themselves against them: *They sewed*, or platted, *fig-leaves together ;* and to cover, at least, part of their shame from one another, they *made themselves aprons*. See here what is commonly the folly of those that have sinned. [1.] That they are more solicitous to save their credit before men than to obtain their pardon from God ; they are backward to confess their sin, and very desirous to conceal it, as much as may be. *I have sinned, yet honour me.* [2.] That the excuses men make, to cover and extenuate their sins, are vain and frivolous. Like the aprons of fig-leaves, they make the matter never the better, but the

worse ; the shame, thus hidden, becomes more shameful. Yet thus we are all apt to *cover our transgressions as Adam*, Job xxxi. 33.

2. Fear seized them immediately upon their eating the forbidden fruit, *v.* 8. Observe here, (1.) What was the cause and occasion of their fear : They *heard the voice of the Lord God walking in the garden in the cool of the day*. It was the approach of the Judge that put them into a fright; and yet he came in such a manner as made it formidable only to guilty consciences. It is supposed that he came in a human shape, and that he who judged the world now was the same that shall judge the world at the last day, even *that man whom God has ordained*. He appeared to them now (it should seem) in no other similitude than that in which they had seen him when he put them into paradise ; for he came to convince and humble them, not to amaze and terrify them. He came into the garden, not descending immediately from heaven in their view, as afterwards on mount Sinai (making either thick darkness his pavilion or the flaming fire his chariot), but he came into the garden, as one that was still willing to be familiar with them. He came walking, not running, not riding upon the wings of the wind, but walking deliberately, as one slow to anger, teaching us, when we are ever so much provoked, not to be hot nor hasty, but to speak and act considerately and not rashly. He came in the cool of the day, not in the night, when all fears are doubly fearful, nor in the heat of day, for he came not in the heat of his anger. *Fury is not in him*, Isa. xxvii. 4. Nor did he come suddenly upon them; but they heard his voice at some distance, giving them notice of his coming, and probably it was a still small voice, like that in which he came to enquire after Elijah. Some think they heard him discoursing with himself concerning the sin of Adam, and the judgment now to be passed upon him, perhaps as he did concerning Israel, Hos. xi. 8, 9, *How shall I give thee up ?* Or, rather, they heard him calling for them, and coming towards them. (2.) What was the effect and evidence of their fear : *They hid themselves from the presence of the Lord God*—a sad change! Before they had sinned, if they had heard the voice of the Lord God coming towards them, they would have run to meet him, and with a humble joy welcomed his gracious visits. But, now that it was otherwise, God had become a terror to them, and then no marvel that they had become a terror to themselves, and were full of confusion. Their own consciences accused them, and set their sin before them in its proper colours. Their fig-leaves failed them, and would do them no service. God had come forth against them as an enemy, and the whole creation was at war with them ; and as yet they knew not of any mediator between them and an angry God, so that nothing remained but a

certain fearful looking for of judgment. In this fright they hid themselves among the bushes; having offended, they fled for the same. Knowing themselves guilty, they durst not stand a trial, but absconded, and fled from justice. See here, [1.] The falsehood of the tempter, and the frauds and fallacies of his temptations. He promised them they should be safe, but now they cannot so much as think themselves so; he said they should not die, and yet now they are forced to fly for their lives; he promised them they should be advanced, but they see themselves abased—never did they seem so little as now; he promised them they should be knowing, but they see themselves at a loss, and know not so much as where to hide themselves; he promised them they should be as gods, great, and bold, and daring, but they are as criminals discovered, trembling, pale, and anxious to escape: they would not be subjects, and so they are prisoners [2.] The folly of sinners, to think it either possible or desirable to hide themselves from God: can they conceal themselves from the Father of lights? Ps. cxxxix. 7, &c.; Jer. xxiii. 24. Will they withdraw themselves from the fountain of life, who alone can give help and happiness? Jon. ii. 8. [3.] The fear that attends sin. All that amazing fear of God's appearances, the accusations of conscience, the approaches of trouble, the assaults of inferior creatures, and the arrests of death, which is common among men, is the effect of sin. Adam and Eve, who were partners in the sin, were sharers in the shame and fear that attended it; and though hand joined in hand (hands so lately joined in marriage), yet could they not animate nor fortify one another: miserable comforters they had become to each other!

9 And the LORD God called unto Adam, and said unto him, Where *art* thou? 10 And he said, I heard thy voice in the garden, and I was afraid, because I *was* naked; and I hid myself.

We have here the arraignment of these deserters before the righteous Judge of heaven and earth, who, though he is not tied to observe formalities, yet proceeds against them with all possible fairness, that he may be justified when he speaks. Observe here,

I. The startling question with which God pursued Adam and arrested him: *Where art thou?* Not as if God did not know where he was; but thus he would enter the process against him. "Come, where is this foolish man?" Some make it a bemoaning question: "Poor Adam, what has become of thee?" "Alas for thee!" (so some read it) "How art thou fallen, Lucifer, son of the morning! Thou that wast my friend and favourite, whom I had done so much for, and would have done so much more for; hast thou now

forsaken me, and ruined thyself? Has it come to this?" It is rather an upbraiding question, in order to his conviction and humiliation: *Where art thou?* Not, In what *place?* but, In what *condition?* "Is this all thou hast gotten by eating forbidden fruit? Thou that wouldest vie with me, dost thou now fly from me?" Note, 1. Those who by sin have gone astray from God should seriously consider where they are; they are afar off from all good, in the midst of their enemies, in bondage to Satan, and in the high road to utter ruin. This enquiry after Adam may be looked upon as a gracious pursuit, in kindness to him, and in order to his recovery If God had not called to him, to reclaim him, his condition would have been as desperate as that of fallen angels; this lost sheep would have wandered endlessly, if the good Shepherd had not sought after him, to bring him back, and, in order to that, reminded him where he was, where he should not be, and where he could not be either happy or easy. Note, 2. If sinners will but consider where they are, they will not rest till they return to God.

II. The trembling answer which Adam gave to this question: *I heard thy voice in the garden, and I was afraid, v.* 10. He does not own his guilt, and yet in effect confesses it by owning his shame and fear; but it is the common fault and folly of those that have done an ill thing, when they are questioned about it, to acknowledge no more than what is so manifest that they cannot deny it. Adam was afraid, because he was naked; not only unarmed, and therefore afraid to contend with God, but unclothed, and therefore afraid so much as to appear before him. We have reason to be afraid of approaching to God if we be not clothed and fenced with the righteousness of Christ, for nothing but this will be armour of proof and cover the shame of our nakedness. Let us therefore *put on the Lord Jesus Christ*, and then draw near with humble boldness.

11 And he said, Who told thee that thou *wast* naked? Hast thou eaten of the tree, whereof I commanded thee that thou shouldest not eat? 12 And the man said, The woman whom thou gavest *to be* with me, she gave me of the tree, and I did eat. 13 And the LORD God said unto the woman, What *is* this *that* thou hast done? And the woman said, The serpent beguiled me, and I did eat.

We have here the offenders found guilty by their own confession, and yet endeavouring to excuse and extenuate their fault. They could not confess and justify what they had done, but they confess and palliate it. Observe,

I. How their confession was extorted from

them. God put it to the man: *Who told thee that thou wast naked? v.* 11. "How camest thou to be sensible of thy nakedness as thy shame?" *Hast thou eaten of the forbidden tree?* Note, Though God knows all our sins, yet he will know them from us, and requires from us an ingenuous confession of them; not that he may be informed, but that we may be humbled. In this examination, God reminds him of the command he had given him: "I commanded thee not to eat of it, I thy Maker, I thy Master, I thy benefactor; I commanded thee to the contrary." Sin appears most plain and most sinful in the glass of the commandment, therefore God here sets it before Adam; and in it we should see our faces. The question put to the woman was, *What is this that thou hast done? v.* 13. "Wilt thou also own thy fault, and make confession of it? And wilt thou see what an evil thing it was?" Note, It concerns those who have eaten forbidden fruit themselves, and especially those who have enticed others to eat it likewise, seriously to consider what they have done. In eating forbidden fruit, we have offended a great and gracious God, broken a just and righteous law, violated a sacred and most solemn covenant, and wronged our own precious souls by forfeiting God's favour and exposing ourselves to his wrath and curse: in enticing others to eat of it, we do the devil's work, make ourselves guilty of other men's sins, and accessory to their ruin. *What is this that we have done?*

II. How their crime was extenuated by them in their confession. It was to no purpose to plead *not guilty* The show of their countenances testified against them; therefore they become their own accusers: "*I did eat,*" says the man, "And so did I," says the woman; for when God judges he will overcome. But these do not look like penitent confessions; for instead of aggravating the sin, and taking shame to themselves, they excuse the sin, and lay the shame and blame on others. 1. Adam lays all the blame upon his wife. "She gave me of the tree, and pressed me to eat of it, which I did, only to oblige her"—a frivolous excuse. He ought to have taught her, not to have been taught by her; and it was no hard matter to determine which of the two he must be ruled by, his God or his wife. Learn, hence, never to be brought to sin by that which will not bring us off in the judgment; let not that bear us up in the commission which will not bear us out in the trial; let us therefore never be overcome by importunity to act against our consciences, nor ever displease God, to please the best friend we have in the world. But this is not the worst of it. He not only lays the blame upon his wife, but expresses it so as tacitly to reflect on God himself: "It is the woman whom thou gavest me, and gavest to be with me as my companion, my guide, and my acquaintance; she

gave me of the tree, else I had not·eaten of it." Thus he insinuates that God was accessory to his sin: he gave him the woman, and she gave him the fruit; so that he seemed to have it at but one remove from God's own hand. Note, There is a strange proneness in those that are tempted to say that they are tempted of God, as if our abusing God's gifts would excuse our violation of God's laws. God gives us riches, honours, and relations, that we may serve him cheerfully in the enjoyment of them; but, if we take occasion from them to sin against him, instead of blaming Providence for putting us into such a condition, we must blame ourselves for perverting the gracious designs of Providence therein. 2. Eve lays all the blame upon the serpent: *The serpent beguiled me.* Sin is a brat that nobody is willing to own, a sign that it is a scandalous thing. Those that are willing enough to take the pleasure and profit of sin are backward enough to take the blame and shame of it. "The serpent, that subtle creature of thy making, which thou didst permit to come into paradise to us, he beguiled me," or *made me to err;* for our sins are our errors. Learn hence, (1.) That Satan's temptations are all beguilings, his arguments are all fallacies, his allurements are all cheats; when he speaks fair, believe him not. Sin deceives us, and, by deceiving, cheats us. It is by the *deceitfulness of sin* that the heart is hardened. See Rom. vii. 11; Heb. iii. 13. (2.) That though Satan's subtlety drew us into sin, yet it will not justify us in sin: though he is the tempter, we are the sinners; and indeed it is our own lust that draws us aside and entices us, Jam. i. 14. Let it not therefore lessen our sorrow and humiliation for sin that we are beguiled into it; but rather let it increase our self-indignation that we should suffer ourselves to be beguiled by a known cheat and a sworn enemy. Well, this is all the prisoners at the bar have to say why sentence should not be passed and execution awarded, according to law; and this *all* is next to nothing, in some respects worse than nothing.

14 And the LORD God said unto the serpent, Because thou hast done this, thou *art* cursed above all cattle, and above every beast of the field; upon thy belly shalt thou go, and dust shalt thou eat all the days of thy life: 15 And I will put enmity between thee and the woman, and between thy seed and her seed; it shall bruise thy head, and thou shalt bruise his heel.

The prisoners being found guilty by their own confession, besides the personal and infallible knowledge of the Judge, and nothing material being offered in arrest of judgment,

God immediately proceeds to pass sentence; and, in these verses, he begins (where the sin began) with the serpent. God did not examine the serpent, nor ask him what he had done nor why he did it; but immediately sentenced him, 1. Because he was already convicted of rebellion against God, and his malice and wickedness were notorious, not found by secret search, but openly avowed and declared as Sodom's. 2. Because he was to be for ever excluded from all hope of pardon; and why should any thing be said to convince and humble him who was to find no place for repentance? His wound was not searched, because it was not to be cured. Some think the condition of the fallen angels was not declared desperate and helpless, until now that they had seduced man into the rebellion.

I. The sentence passed upon the tempter may be considered as lighting upon the serpent, the brute-creature which Satan made use of, which was, as the rest, made for the service of man, but was now abused to his hurt. Therefore, to testify a displeasure against sin, and a jealousy for the injured honour of Adam and Eve, God fastens a curse and reproach upon the serpent, and makes it to groan, being burdened. See Rom. viii. 20. The devil's instruments must share in the devil's punishments. Thus the bodies of the wicked, though only instruments of unrighteousness, shall partake of everlasting torments with the soul, the principal agent. Even the ox that killed a man must be stoned, Exod. xxi. 28, 29. See here how God hates sin, and especially how much displeased he is with those who entice others into sin. It is a perpetual brand upon Jeroboam's name *that he made Israel to sin.* Now, 1. The serpent is here laid under the curse of God: *Thou art cursed above all cattle.* Even the creeping things, when God made them, were blessed of him (*ch.* i. 22), but sin turned the blessing into a curse. *The serpent was more subtle than any beast of the field* (*v.* 1), and here, *cursed above every beast of the field.* Unsanctified subtlety often proves a great curse to a man; and the more crafty men are to do evil the more mischief they do, and, consequently, they shall receive the greater damnation. Subtle tempters are the most accursed creatures under the sun. 2. He is here laid under man's reproach and enmity. (1.) He is to be for ever looked upon as a vile and despicable creature, and a proper object of scorn and contempt: " *Upon thy belly thou shalt go,* no longer upon .feet, or half erect, but thou shalt crawl along, thy belly cleaving to the earth," an expression of a very abject miserable condition, Ps. xliv. 25; "and thou shalt not avoid eating dust with thy meat." His crime was that he tempted Eve to eat that which she should not; his punishment was that he was necessitated to eat that which he would not: *Dust thou shalt eat* This

denotes not only a base and despicable condition, but a mean and pitiful spirit; it is said of those whose courage has departed from them that they *lick the dust like a serpent,* Mic. vii. 17. How sad it is that the serpent's curse should be the covetous worldling's choice, whose character it is that he *pants after the dust of the earth !* Amos ii. 7. These choose their own delusions, and so shall their doom be. (2.) He is to be for ever looked upon as a venomous noxious creature, and a proper object of hatred and detestation: *I will put enmity between thee and the woman.* The inferior creatures being made for man, it was a curse upon any of them to be turned against man and man against them; and this is part of the serpent's curse. The serpent is hurtful to man, and often bruises his heel, because it can reach no higher; nay, notice is taken of his biting the horses' heels, *ch.* xlix. 17. But man is victorious over the serpent, and bruises his head, that is, gives him a mortal wound, aiming to destroy the whole generation of vipers. It is the effect of this curse upon the serpent that, though that creature is subtle and very dangerous, yet it prevails not (as it would if God gave it commission) to the destruction of mankind. This sentence pronounced upon the serpent is much fortified by that promise of God to his people, *Thou shalt tread upon the lion and the adder* (Ps. xci. 13), and that of Christ to his disciples, *They shall take up serpents* (Mark xvi. 18), witness Paul, who was unhurt by the viper that fastened upon his hand. Observe here, The serpent and the woman had just now been very familiar and friendly in discourse about the forbidden fruit, and a wonderful agreement there was between them; but here they are irreconcilably set at variance. Note, Sinful friendships justly end in mortal feuds: those that unite in wickedness will not unite long.

II. This sentence may be considered as levelled at the devil, who only made use of the serpent as his vehicle in this appearance, but was himself the principal agent. He that spoke through the serpent's mouth is here struck at through the serpent's side, and is principally intended in the sentence, which, like the pillar of cloud and fire, has a dark side towards the devil and a bright side towards our first parents and their seed. Great things are contained in these words.

1. A perpetual reproach is here fastened upon that great enemy both to God and man. Under the cover of the serpent, he is here sentenced to be, (1.) Degraded and accursed of God. It is supposed that the sin which turned angels into devils was pride, which is here justly punished by a great variety of mortifications couched under the mean circumstances of a serpent crawling on his belly and licking the dust. *How art thou fallen, O Lucifer !* He that would be above God, and would head a rebellion

against him, is justly exposed here to contempt and lies to be trodden on; a man's pride will bring him low, and God will humble those that will not humble themselves. (2.) Detested and abhorred of all mankind. Even those that are really seduced into his interest yet profess a hatred and abhorrence of him; and all that are born of God make it their constant care to keep themselves, that this wicked one touch them not, 1 John v. 18. He is here condemned to a state of war and irreconcilable enmity. (3.) Destroyed and ruined at last by *the great Redeemer,* signified by the breaking of his head. His subtle politics shall all be baffled, his usurped power shall be entirely crushed, and he shall be for ever a captive to the injured honour of divine sovereignty. By being told of this now he was tormented before the time.

2. A perpetual quarrel is here commenced between the kingdom of God and the kingdom of the devil among men; war is proclaimed between the seed of the woman and the seed of the serpent. That war in heaven between Michael and the dragon began now, Rev. xii. 7. It is the fruit of this enmity, (1.) That there is a continual conflict between grace and corruption in the hearts of God's people. Satan, by their corruptions, assaults them, buffets them, sifts them, and seeks to devour them; they, by the exercise of their graces, resist him, wrestle with him, quench his fiery darts, force him to flee from them. Heaven and hell can never be reconciled, nor light and darkness; no more can Satan and a sanctified soul, for these are contrary the one to the other. (2.) That there is likewise a continual struggle between the wicked and the godly in this world. Those that love God account those their enemies that hate him, Ps. cxxxix. 21, 22. And all the rage and malice of persecutors against the people of God are the fruit of this enmity, which will continue while there is a godly man on this side heaven, and a wicked man on this side hell. *Marvel not therefore if the world hate you,* 1 John iii. 13.

3. A gracious promise is here made of Christ, as the deliverer of fallen man from the power of Satan. Though what was said was addressed to the serpent, yet it was said in the hearing of our first parents, who, doubtless, took the hints of grace here given them, and saw a door of hope opened to them, else the following sentence upon themselves would have overwhelmed them. Here was the dawning of the gospel day. No sooner was the wound given than the remedy was provided and revealed. Here, *in the head of the book,* as the word is (Heb. x. 7), in the beginning of the Bible, it is written of Christ, that he should *do the will of God.* By faith in this promise, we have reason to think, our first parents, and the patriarchs before the flood, were justified and saved and to this promise, and the

benefit of it, instantly serving God day and night, they hoped to come. Notice is here given them of three things concerning Christ:—(1.) His incarnation, that he should be *the seed of the woman,* the seed of *that* woman; therefore his genealogy (Luke iii.) goes so high as to show him to be the son of Adam, but God does the woman the honour to call him rather her seed, because she it was whom the devil had beguiled, and on whom Adam had laid the blame; herein God magnifies his grace, in that, though the woman was first in the transgression, yet she shall be saved by childbearing (as some read it), that is, by the promised seed who shall descend from her, 1 Tim. ii. 15. He was likewise to be the seed of a woman only, of a virgin, that he might not be tainted with the corruption of our nature; he was sent forth, *made of a woman* (Gal. iv. 4), that this promise might be fulfilled. It is a great encouragement to sinners that their Saviour *is the seed of the woman, bone of our bone,* Heb. ii. 11, 14. Man is therefore sinful and unclean, because he is *born of a woman* (Job xxv. 4), and therefore *his days are full of trouble,* Job xiv. 1. But the seed of the woman was made sin and a curse for us, so saving us from both. (2.) His sufferings and death, pointed at in Satan's *bruising his heel,* that is, his human nature. Satan tempted Christ in the wilderness, to draw him into sin; and some think it was Satan that terrified Christ in his agony, to drive him to despair. It was the devil that put it into the heart of Judas to betray Christ, of Peter to deny him, of the chief priests to prosecute him, of the false witnesses to accuse him, and of Pilate to condemn him, aiming in all this, by destroying the Saviour, to ruin the salvation; but, on the contrary, it was by death that Christ *destroyed him that had the power of death,* Heb. ii. 14. Christ's heel was bruised when his feet were pierced and nailed to the cross, and Christ's sufferings are continued in the sufferings of the saints for his name. The devil tempts them, casts them into prison, persecutes and slays them, and so bruises the heel of Christ, who is afflicted in their afflictions. But, while the heel is bruised on earth, it is well that the head is safe in heaven. (3.) His victory over Satan thereby. Satan had now trampled upon the woman, and insulted over her; but the seed of the woman should be raised up in the fulness of time to avenge her quarrel, and to trample upon him, to spoil him, to lead him captive, and to *triumph over him,* Col. ii. 15. *He shall bruise his head,* that is, he shall destroy all his politics and all his powers, and give a total overthrow to his kingdom and interest. Christ baffled Satan's temptations, rescued souls out of his hands, cast him out of the bodies of people, dispossessed the strong man armed, and divided his spoil: by his death, he gave a fatal and incurable blow to the devil's kingdom, a wound to the head of this beast, that can never be healed. As his gospel gets ground, *Satan falls* (Luke x. 18) and is *bound*, Rev. xx. 2. By his grace, he treads Satan under his people's feet (Rom. xvi. 20) and will shortly cast him into the lake of fire, Rev. xx. 10. And the devil's perpetual overthrow will be the complete and everlasting joy and glory of the chosen remnant.

16 Unto the woman he said, I will greatly multiply thy sorrow and thy conception ; in sorrow thou shalt bring forth children ; and thy desire *shall be* to thy husband, and he shall rule over thee.

We have here the sentence passed upon the woman for her sin. Two things she is condemned to : a state of sorrow, and a state of subjection, proper punishments of a sin in which she had gratified her pleasure and her pride.

I. She is here put into a state of sorrow, one particular of which only is specified, that in bringing forth children ; but it includes all those impressions of grief and fear which the mind of that tender sex is most apt to receive, and all the common calamities which they are liable to. Note, Sin brought sorrow into the world ; it was this that made the world a vale of tears, brought showers of trouble upon our heads, and opened springs of sorrows in our hearts, and so deluged the world : had we known no guilt, we should have known no grief. The pains of child-bearing, which are great to a proverb, a scripture proverb, are the effect of sin ; every pang and every groan of the travailing woman speak aloud the fatal consequences of sin : this comes of eating forbidden fruit. Observe, 1. The sorrows are here said to be multiplied, *greatly multiplied.* All the sorrows of this present time are so ; many are the calamities which human life is liable to, of various kinds, and often repeated, the clouds returning after the rain, and no marvel that our sorrows are multiplied when our sins are : both are innumerable evils. The sorrows of child-bearing are multiplied ; for they include, not only the travailing throes, but the indispositions before (it is sorrow from the conception), and the nursing toils and vexations after ; and after all, if the children prove wicked and foolish, they are, more than ever, the heaviness of her that bore them. Thus are the sorrows multiplied ; as one grief is over, another succeeds in this world. 2. It is God that multiplies our sorrows : *I will do it.* God, as a righteous Judge, does it, which ought to silence us under all our sorrows ; as many as they are, we have deserved them all, and more : nay, God, as a tender Father, does it for our necessary correction, that we may be humbled for sin, and weaned from

the world by all our sorrows ; and the good we get by them, with the comfort we have under them, will abundantly balance our sorrows, how greatly soever they are multiplied.

II. She is here put into a state of subjection. The whole sex, which by creation was equal with man, is, for sin, made inferior, and forbidden to *usurp authority,* 1 Tim. ii. 11, 12. The wife particularly is hereby put under the dominion of her husband, and is not *sui juris—at her own disposal,* of which see an instance in that law, Num. xxx. 6—8, where the husband is empowered, if he please, to disannul the vows made by the wife. This sentence amounts only to that command, *Wives, be in subjection to your own husbands ;* but the entrance of sin has made that duty a punishment, which otherwise it would not have been. If man had not sinned, he would always have ruled with wisdom and love ; and, if the woman had not sinned, she would always have obeyed with humility and meekness ; and then the dominion would have been no grievance : but our own sin and folly make our yoke heavy. If Eve had not eaten forbidden fruit herself, and tempted her husband to eat it, she would never have complained of her subjection ; therefore it ought never to be complained of, though harsh ; but sin must be complained of, that made it so. Those wives who not only despise and disobey their husbands, but domineer over them, do not consider that they not only violate a divine law, but thwart a divine sentence.

III. Observe here how mercy is mixed with wrath in this sentence. The woman shall have sorrow, but it shall be in bringing forth children, and the sorrow shall be *forgotten for joy that a child is born,* John xvi. 21. She shall be subject, but it shall be to her own husband that loves her, not to a stranger, or an enemy : the sentence was not a curse, to bring her to ruin, but a chastisement, to bring her to repentance. It was well that enmity was not put between the man and the woman, as there was between the serpent and the woman.

17 And unto Adam he said, Because thou hast hearkened unto the voice of thy wife, and hast eaten of the tree, of which I commanded thee, saying, Thou shalt not eat of it : cursed *is* the ground for thy sake ; in sorrow shalt thou eat *of* it all the days of thy life ; 18 Thorns also and thistles shall it bring forth to thee ; and thou shalt eat the herb of the field ; 19 In the sweat of thy face shalt thou eat bread, till thou return unto the ground ; for out of it wast thou taken : for dust thou *art,* and unto dust shalt thou return.

We have here the sentence passed upon Adam, which is prefaced with a recital of his crime : ·*Because thou hast hearkened to the voice of thy wife, v.* 17. He excused the fault, by laying it on his wife : *She gave it me.* But God does not admit the excuse. She could but tempt him, she could not force him ; though it was her fault to persuade him to eat, it was his fault to hearken to her. Thus men's frivolous pleas will, in the day of God's judgment, not only be overruled, but turned against them, and made the grounds of their sentence. *Out of thine own mouth will I judge thee.* Observe,

I. God put marks of his displeasure on Adam in three instances :—

1. His habitation is, by this sentence, cursed : *Cursed is the ground for thy sake ;* and the effect of that curse is, *Thorns and thistles shall it bring forth unto thee.* It is here intimated that his habitation·should be changed; he should no longer dwell in a distinguished, blessed, paradise, but should be removed to common ground, and that cursed. The ground, or earth, is here put for the whole visible creation, which, by the sin of man, is made subject to vanity, the several parts of it being not so serviceable to man's comfort and happiness as they were designed to be when they were made, and would have been if he had not sinned. God gave the earth to the children of men, designing it to be a comfortable dwelling to them. But sin has altered the property of it. It is now cursed for man's sin ; that is, it is a dishonourable habitation, it bespeaks man mean, that his foundation is in the dust; it is a dry and barren habitation, its spontaneous productions are now weeds and briers, something nauseous or noxious ; what good fruits it produces must be extorted from it by the ingenuity and industry of man. Fruitfulness was its blessing, for man's service (*ch.* i. 11, 29), and now barrenness was its curse, for man's punishment. It is not what it was in the day it was created. Sin turned a fruitful land into barrenness ; and man, having become as the wild ass's colt, has the wild ass's lot, *the wilderness for his habitation,* and *the barren land his dwelling,* Job xxxix. 6; Ps. lxviii. 6. Had not this curse been in part removed, for aught I know, the earth would have been for ever barren, and never produced any thing but thorns and thistles. The ground is *cursed,* that is, doomed to destruction at the end of time, when the earth, and *all the works that are therein, shall be burnt up* for the sin of man, the measure of whose iniquity will then be full, 2 Pet. iii. 7, 10. But observe a mixture of mercy in this sentence. (1.) Adam himself is not cursed, as the serpent was (*v.* 14), but only the ground for his sake. God had blessings in him, even the holy seed : *Destroy it not, for that blessing is in it,* Isa. lxv. 8. And he had blessings in store for him; therefore he is not directly and immediately cursed, but, as it were, at

32

second hand. (2.) He is yet above ground. The earth does not open and swallow him up ; only it is not what it was : as he continues alive, notwithstanding his degeneracy from his primitive purity and rectitude, so the earth continues to be his habitation, notwithstanding its degeneracy from its primitive beauty and fruitfulness. (3.) This curse upon the earth, which cut off all expectations of a happiness in things below, might direct and quicken him to look for bliss and satisfaction only in things above.

2. His employments and enjoyments are all embittered to him.

(1.) His business shall henceforth become a toil to him, and he shall go on with it *in the sweat of his face, v.* 19. His business, before he sinned, was a constant pleasure to him . the garden was then dressed without any uneasy labour, and kept without any uneasy care ; but now his labour shall be a weariness and shall waste his body ; his care shall be a torment and shall afflict his mind. The curse upon the ground which made it barren, and produced thorns and thistles, made his employment about it much more difficult and toilsome. If Adam had not sinned, he had not sweated. Observe here, [1.] That labour is our duty, which we must.faithfully perform ; we are bound to work, not as creatures only, but as criminals ; it is part of our sentence, which idleness daringly defies. [2.] That uneasiness and weariness with labour are our just punishment, which we must patiently submit to, and not complain of, since they are less than our iniquity deserves. Let not us, by inordinate care and labour, make our punishment heavier than God has made it ; but rather study to lighten our burden, and wipe off our sweat, by eyeing Providence in all and expecting rest shortly.

(2.) His food shall henceforth become (in comparison with what it had been) unpleasant to him. [1.] The matter of his food is changed ; he must now eat the herb of the field, and must no longer be feasted with the delicacies of the garden of Eden. Having by sin made himself like the beasts that perish, he is justly turned to be a fellow-commoner with them, and to *eat grass as oxen, till he know that the heavens do rule.* [2.] There is a change in the manner of his eating it : *In sorrow* (*v.* 17) and *in the sweat of his face* (*v.* 19) he must eat of it. Adam could not but eat in sorrow all the days of his life, remembering the forbidden fruit he had eaten, and the guilt and shame he had contracted by it. Observe, *First,* That human life is exposed to many miseries and calamities, which very much embitter the poor remains of its pleasures and delights. Some never eat with pleasure (Job xxi. 25), through sickness or melancholy ; all, even the best, have cause to eat with sorrow for sin ; and all, even the happiest in this world, have some allays to their joy : troops of diseases, disasters, and deaths, in various shapes, entered the world with sin, and still ravage it. Secondly, That the righteousness of God is to be acknowledged in all the sad consequences of sin. *Wherefore then should a living man complain?* Yet, in this part of the sentence, there is also a mixture of mercy. He shall sweat, but his toil shall make his rest the more welcome when he returns to his earth, as to his bed; he shall grieve, but he shall not starve; he shall have sorrow, but in that sorrow he shall eat bread, which shall strengthen his heart under his sorrows. He is not sentenced to eat dust as the serpent, only to eat the herb of the field.

3. His life also is but short. Considering how full of trouble his days are, it is in favour to him that they are few; yet death being dreadful to nature (yea, even though life be unpleasant) *that* concludes the sentence. " *Thou shalt return to the ground out of which thou wast taken;* thy body, that part of thee which was taken out of the ground, shall return to it again; for *dust thou art.*" This points either to the first original of his body; it was made *of the dust,* nay, it was *made dust,* and was still so; so that there needed no more than to recal the grant of immortality, and to withdraw the power which was put forth to support it, and then he would, of course, *return to dust.* Or to the present corruption and degeneracy of his mind: *Dust thou art,* that is, " Thy precious soul is now lost and buried in the dust of the body and the mire of the flesh; it was made spiritual and heavenly, but it has become carnal and earthly." His doom is therefore read: " *To dust thou shalt return.* Thy body shall be forsaken by thy soul, and become itself a lump of dust; and then it shall be lodged in the grave, the proper place for it, and mingle itself with the dust of the earth," *our dust,* Ps. civ. 29. *Earth to earth, dust to dust.* Observe here, (1.) That man is a mean frail creature, *little* as dust, the small dust of the balance—*light* as dust, altogether lighter than vanity—*weak* as dust, and of no consistency. Our strength is not the strength of stones; he that made us considers it, and *remembers that we are dust,* Ps. ciii. 14. Man is, indeed the *chief part of the dust of the world* (Prov. viii. 26), but still he is dust. (2.) That he is a mortal dying creature, and hastening to the grave. Dust may be raised, for a time, into a little cloud, and may seem considerable while it is held up by the wind that raised it; but, when the force of that is spent, it falls again, and returns to the earth out of which it was raised. Such a thing is man; a great man is but a great mass of dust, and must return to his earth. (3.) That sin brought death into the world. If Adam had not sinned, he would not have died, Rom. v. 12. God entrusted Adam with a spark of immortality, which he, by a patient continuance in well-doing, might have blown up into an everlasting flame; but he foolishly blew it out by wilful sin: and now

death is *the wages of sin, and sin is the sting of death.*

II. We must not go off from this sentence upon our first parents, which we are all so nearly concerned in, and feel from, to this day, till we have considered two things:—

1. How fitly the sad consequences of sin upon the soul of Adam and his sinful race were represented and figured out by this sentence, and perhaps were more intended in it than we are aware of. Though that misery only is mentioned which affected the body, yet that was a pattern of spiritual miseries, the curse that entered into the soul. (1.) The pains of a woman in travail represent the terrors and pangs of a guilty conscience, awakened to a sense of sin; from the conception of lust, these sorrows are greatly multiplied, and, sooner or later, will come upon the sinner like pain upon a woman in travail, which cannot be avoided. (2.) The state of subjection to which the woman was reduced represents that loss of spiritual liberty and freedom of will which is the effect of sin. The dominion of sin in the soul is compared to that of a husband (Rom. vii. 1—5), the sinner's desire is towards it, for he is fond of his slavery, and it rules over him. (3.) The curse of barrenness which was brought upon the earth, and its produce of briars and thorns, are a fit representation of the barrenness of a corrupt and sinful soul in that which is good and its fruitfulness in evil. It is all overgrown with thorns, and nettles cover the face of it; and therefore it is *nigh unto cursing,* Heb. vi. 8. (4.) The toil and sweat bespeak the difficulty which, through the infirmity of the flesh, man labours under, in the service of God and the work of religion, so hard has it now become to *enter into the kingdom of heaven.* Blessed be God, it is not impossible. (5.) The embittering of his food to him bespeaks the soul's want of the comfort of God's favour, which is life, and the bread of life. (6.) The soul, like the body, returns to the dust of this world; its tendency is that way; it has an earthy taint, John iii. 31.

2. How admirably the satisfaction our Lord Jesus made by his death and sufferings answered to the sentence here passed upon our first parents. (1.) Did travailing pains come in with sin? We read of the *travail of Christ's soul* (Isa. liii. 11); and the pains of death he was held by are called ὠδῖναι (Acts ii. 24), *the pains of a woman in travail.* (2.) Did subjection come in with sin? Christ was made under the law, Gal. iv. 4. (3.) Did the curse come in with sin? Christ was made a curse for us, died a cursed death, Gal. iii 13. (4.) Did thorns come in with sin? He was crowned with thorns for us. (5.) Did sweat come in with sin? He for us did sweat as it were great drops of blood. (6.) Did sorrow come in with sin? He was a man of sorrows, his soul was, in his agony, exceedingly sorrowful. (7.) Did death come in with sin? He became obedient unto death. Thus

is the plaster as wide as the wound. Blessed be God for Jesus Christ!

20 And Adam called his wife's name Eve; because she was the mother of all living.

God having named the man, and called him *Adam*, which signifies *red earth*, Adam, in further token of dominion, named the woman, and called her *Eve*, that is, *life*. Adam bears the name of the dying body, Eve that of the living soul. The reason of the name is here given (some think, by Moses the historian, others, by Adam himself): *Because she was* (that is, was to be) *the mother of all living*. He had before called her *Ishah—woman*, as a wife; here he calls her *Evah—life*, as a mother. Now, 1. If this was done by divine direction, it was an instance of God's favour, and, like the new naming of Abraham and Sarah, it was a seal of the covenant, and an assurance to them that, notwithstanding their sin and his displeasure against them for it, he had not reversed that blessing wherewith he had blessed them: *Be fruitful and multiply*. It was likewise a confirmation of the promise now made, that the seed of the woman, of this woman, should break the serpent's head. 2. If Adam did it of himself, it was an instance of his faith in the word of God. Doubtless it was not done, as some have suspected, in contempt or defiance of the curse, but rather in a humble confidence and dependence upon the blessing. (1.) The blessing of a reprieve, admiring the patience of God, that he should spare such sinners to be the parents of all living, and that he did not immediately shut up those fountains of the human life and nature, because they could send forth no other than polluted, poisoned, streams. (2.) The blessing of a Redeemer, the promised seed, to whom Adam had an eye, in calling his wife *Eve—life;* for he should be the life of all the living, and in him all the families of the earth should be blessed, in hope of which he thus triumphs.

21 Unto Adam also and to his wife did the LORD God make coats of skins, and clothed them.

We have here a further instance of God's care concerning our first parents, notwithstanding their sin. Though he corrects his disobedient children, and puts them under the marks of his displeasure, yet he does not disinherit them, but, like a tender father, provides the herb of the field for their food and *coats of skins* for their clothing. Thus the father provided for the returning prodigal, Luke xv. 22, 23. If the Lord had been pleased to kill them, he would not have done this for them. Observe, 1. That clothes came in with sin. We should have had no occasion for them, either for defence or decency, if sin had not made us naked, to our shame. Little reason therefore we have to be proud of our clothes, which are but the

34

badges of our poverty and infamy. 2. That when God made clothes for our first parents he made them warm and strong, but coarse and very plain: not robes of scarlet, but coats of skin. Their clothes were made, not of silk and satin, but plain skins; not trimmed, nor embroidered, none of the ornaments which the daughters of Sion afterwards invented, and prided themselves in. Let the poor, that are meanly clad, learn hence not to complain: having food and a covering, let them be content; they are as well done to as Adam and Eve were. And let the rich, that are finely clad, learn hence not to make the putting on of apparel their adorning, 1 Pet. iii. 3. 3. That God is to be acknowledged with thankfulness, not only in giving us food, but in giving us clothes also, *ch.* xxviii. 20. The wool and the flax are his, as well as *the corn and the wine*, Hos. ii. 9. 4. These coats of skin had a significancy. The beasts whose skins they were must be slain, slain before their eyes, to show them what death is, and (as it is Eccl. iii. 18) that they may see that they themselves were beasts, mortal and dying. It is supposed that they were slain, not for food, but for sacrifice, to typify the great sacrifice, which, in the latter end of the world, should be offered once for all. Thus the first thing that died was a sacrifice, or Christ in a figure, who is therefore said to be the *Lamb slain from the foundation of the world*. These sacrifices were divided between God and man, in token of reconciliation: the flesh was offered to God, a whole burnt-offering; the skins were given to man for clothing, signifying that, Jesus Christ having offered himself to God a sacrifice of a sweet-smelling savour, we are to clothe ourselves with his righteousness as with a garment, that the shame of our nakedness may not appear. Adam and Eve made for themselves aprons of fig-leaves, a covering too narrow for them to *wrap themselves in*, Isa. xxviii. 20. Such are all the rags of our own righteousness. But God made them coats of skins, large, and strong, and durable, and fit for them; such is the righteousness of Christ. Therefore *put on the Lord Jesus Christ*.

22 And the LORD God said, Behold, the man is become as one of us, to know good and evil: and now, lest he put forth his hand, and take also of the tree of life, and eat, and live for ever: 23 Therefore the LORD God sent him forth from the garden of Eden, to till the ground from whence he was taken. 24 So he drove out the man; and he placed at the east of the garden of Eden cherubims, and a flaming sword which turned every way, to keep the way of the tree of life.

Sentence being passed upon the offenders,

we have here execution, in part, done upon them immediately. Observe here,

I. How they were justly disgraced and shamed before God and the holy angels, by the ironical upbraiding of them with the issue of their enterprise: "*Behold, the man has become as one of us, to know good and evil!* A goodly god he makes! Does he not? See what he has got, what preferments, what advantages, by eating forbidden fruit!" This was said to awaken and humble them, and to bring them to a sense of their sin and folly, and to repentance for it, that, seeing themselves thus wretchedly deceived by following the devil's counsel, they might henceforth pursue the happiness God should offer in the way he should prescribe. God thus *fills their faces with shame, that they may seek his name*, Ps. lxxxiii. 16. He puts them to this confusion, in order to their conversion. True penitents will thus upbraid themselves: " What fruit have I now by sin? Rom. vi. 21. Have I gained what I foolishly promised myself in a sinful way? No, no, it never proved what it pretended to, but the contrary."

II. How they were justly discarded, and shut out of paradise, which was a part of the sentence implied in that, *Thou shalt eat the herb of the field*. Here we have,

1. The reason God gave why he shut man out of paradise; not only because he had put forth his hand, and taken of the tree of knowledge, which was his sin, but lest he should again put forth his hand, and take also of the tree of life (now forbidden him by the divine sentence, as before the tree of knowledge was forbidden by the law), and should dare to eat of that tree, and so profane a divine sacrament and defy a divine sentence, and yet flatter himself with a conceit that thereby he should live for ever. Observe, (1.) There is a foolish proneness in those that have rendered themselves unworthy of the substance of Christian privileges to catch at the signs and shadows of them. Many that like not the terms of the covenant, yet, for their reputation's sake, are fond of the seals of it. (2.) It is not only justice, but kindness, to such, to be denied them; for, by usurping that to which they have no title, they affront God and make their sin the more heinous, and by building their hopes upon a wrong foundation they render their conversion the more difficult and their ruin the more deplorable.

2. The method God took, in giving him this bill of divorce, and expelling and excluding him from this garden of pleasure. He turned him out, and kept him out.

(1.) He turned him out, from the garden to the common. This is twice mentioned: *He sent him forth* (*v.* 23), and then *he drove him out, v.* 24. God bade him go out, told him that that was no place for him, he should no longer occupy and enjoy that garden; but he liked the place too well to be willing to part with it, and therefore God *drove him out*, made him go out, whether he would or no.

This signified the exclusion of him, and all his guilty race, from that communion with God which was the bliss and glory of paradise. The tokens of God's favour to him and his delight in the sons of men, which he had in his innocent estate, were now suspended; the communications of his grace were withheld, and Adam became weak, and like other men, as Samson when the *Spirit of the Lord had departed from him*. His acquaintance with God was lessened and lost, and that correspondence which had been settled between man and his Maker was interrupted and broken off. He was driven out, as one unworthy of this honour and incapable of this service. Thus he and all mankind, by the fall, forfeited and lost communion with God. But whither did he send him when he turned him out of Eden? He might justly have chased him out of the world (Job xviii. 18), but he only chased him out of the garden. He might justly have cast him down to hell, as he did the angels that sinned when he shut them out from the heavenly paradise, 2 Pet. ii. 4. But man was only sent to till the ground out of which he was taken. He was sent to a place of toil, not to a place of torment. He was sent to the ground, not to the grave,—to the work-house, not to the dungeon, not to the prison-house,—to hold the plough, not to drag the chain. His tilling the ground would be recompensed by his eating of its fruits; and his converse with the earth whence he was taken was improvable to good purposes, to keep him humble, and to remind him of his latter end. Observe, then, that though our first parents were excluded from the privileges of their state of innocency, yet they were not abandoned to despair, God's thoughts of love designing them for a second state of probation upon new terms.

(2.) He kept him out, and forbade him all hopes of a re-entry; for he *placed at the east of the garden of Eden* a detachment of *cherubim*, God's hosts, armed with a dreadful and irresistible power, represented by flaming swords which turned every way, on that side the garden which lay next to the place whither Adam was sent, to keep the way that led to the tree of life, so that he could neither steal nor force an entry; for who can make a pass against an angel on his guard or gain a pass made good by such a force? Now this intimated to Adam, [1.] That God was displeased with him. Though he had mercy in store for him, yet at present he was angry with him, was turned to be his enemy and fought against him, for here was a sword drawn (Num. xxii. 23); and he was to him a consuming fire, for it was a flaming sword. [2.] That the angels were at war with him; no peace with the heavenly hosts, while he was in rebellion against their Lord and ours. [3.] That the way to the tree of life was shut up, namely, that way which, at first, he was put into, the way of spotless innocency. I is not said that the cherubim were set to keep him and his for ever from the tree of life (thanks be to God, there is a paradise set before us, and a tree of life in the midst of it, which we rejoice in the hopes of); but they were set to keep that way of the tree of life which hitherto they had been in ; that is, it was henceforward in vain for him and his to expect righteousness, life, and happiness, by virtue of the first covenant, for it was irreparably broken, and could never be pleaded, nor any benefit taken by it. The command of that covenant being broken, the curse of it is in full force; it leaves no room for repentance, but we are all undone if we be judged by that covenant. God revealed this to Adam, not to drive him to despair, but to oblige and quicken him to look for life and happiness in the promised seed, by whom the flaming sword is removed. God and his angels are reconciled to us, and a new and living way into the holiest is consecrated and laid open for us.

CHAP. IV.

In this chapter we have both the world and the church in a family, in a little family, in Adam's family, and a specimen given of the character and state of both in after-ages, nay, in all ages, to the end of time. As all mankind were represented in Adam, so that great distinction of mankind into saints and sinners, godly and wicked, the children of God and the children of the wicked one, was here represented in Cain and Abel, and an early instance is given of the enmity which was lately put between the seed of the woman and the seed of the serpent. We have here, I. The birth, names, and callings, of Cain and Abel, ver. 1, 2. II. Their religion, and different success in it, ver. 3, 4, and part of ver. 5. III. Cain's anger at God, and the reproof of him for that anger, ver. 5—7. IV. Cain's murder of his brother, and the process against him for that murder. The murder committed, ver. 8. The proceedings against him. 1. His arraignment, ver. 9, former part. 2. His plea, ver. 9, latter part. 3. His conviction, ver. 10. 4. The sentence passed upon him, ver. 11, 12. 5. His complaint against the sentence, ver. 13, 14. 6. The ratification of the sentence, ver. 15. 7. The execution of the sentence, ver. 15, 16. V. The family and posterity of Cain, ver. 17—24. VI. The birth of another son and grandson of Adam, ver. 25, 26.

AND Adam knew Eve his wife; and she conceived, and bare Cain, and said, I have gotten a man from the LORD. 2 And she again bare his brother Abel. And Abel was a keeper of sheep, but Cain was a tiller of the ground.

Adam and Eve had many sons and daughters, *ch.* v. 4. But Cain and Abel seem to have been the two eldest. Some think they were twins, and, as Esau and Jacob, the elder hated and the younger loved. Though God had cast our first parents out of paradise, he did not write them childless ; but, to show that he had other blessings in store for them, he preserved to them the benefit of that first blessing of increase. Though they were sinners, nay, though they felt the humiliation and sorrow of penitents, they did not write themselves comfortless, having the promise of a Saviour to support themselves with. We have here,

I. The names of their two sons. 1. *Cain* signifies *possession;* for Eve, when she bore him, said with joy, and thankfulness, and great expectation, *I have gotten a man from the* LORD. Observe, Children are God's gifts, and he must be acknowledged in the

building up of our families. It doubles and sanctifies our comfort in them when we see them coming to us from the hand of God, who will not forsake the works and gifts of his own hand. Though Eve bore him with the sorrows that were the consequence of sin, yet she did not lose the sense of the mercy in her pains. Comforts, though alloyed, are more than we deserve; and therefore our complaints must not drown our thanksgivings. Many suppose that Eve had a conceit that this son was the promised seed, and that therefore she thus triumphed in him, as her words may be read, *I have gotten a man, the* LORD, God-man. If so, she was wretchedly mistaken, as Samuel, when he said, *Surely the* LORD's *anointed is before me,* 1 Sam. xvi. 6. When children are born, who can foresee what they will prove? He that was thought to be *a man, the* LORD, or at least a man from the LORD, and for his service as priest of the family, became an enemy to the LORD. The less we expect from creatures, the more tolerable will disappointments be. 2. *Abel* signifies *vanity.* When she thought she had obtained the promised seed in Cain, she was so taken up with that possession that another son was as vanity to her. To those who have an interest in Christ, and make him their all, other things are as nothing at all. It intimates likewise that the longer we live in this world the more we may see of the vanity of it. What, at first, we are fond of, as a possession, afterwards we see cause to be dead to, as a trifle. The name given to this son is put upon the whole race, Ps. xxxix. 5. Every man is at his best estate *Abel—vanity.* Let us labour to see both ourselves and others so. *Childhood and youth are vanity.*

II. The employments of Cain and Abel. Observe, 1. They both had a calling. Though they were heirs apparent to the world, their birth noble and their possessions large, yet they were not brought up in idleness. God gave their father a calling, even in innocency, and he gave them one. Note, It is the will of God that we should every one of us have something to do in this world. Parents ought to bring up their children to business. " Give them a Bible and a calling (said good Mr. Dod), and God be with them." 2. Their employments were different, that they might trade and exchange with one another, as there was occasion. The members of the body politic have need one of another, and mutual love is helped by mutual commerce. 3. Their employments belonged to the husbandman's calling, their father's profession—a needful calling, for *the king himself is served of the field,* but a laborious calling, which required constant care and attendance. It is now looked upon as a mean calling ; the *poor of the land* serve for *vine-dressers and husbandmen,* Jer. lii. 16. But the calling was far from being a dishonour to them ; rather, they were an honour to it. 4. It should seem, by the order of the story, that Abel, though the younger brother, yet entered first into his calling, and probably his example drew in Cain. 5. Abel chose that employment which most befriended contemplation and devotion, for to these a pastoral life has been looked upon as being peculiarly favourable. Moses and David kept sheep, and in their solitudes conversed with God. Note, That calling or condition of life is best for us, and to be chosen by us, which is best for our souls, that which least exposes us to sin and gives us most opportunity of serving and enjoying God.

3 And in process of time it came to pass, that Cain brought of the fruit of the ground an offering unto the LORD. 4 And Abel, he also brought of the firstlings of his flock and of the fat thereof. And the LORD had respect unto Abel and to his offering: 5 But unto Cain and to his offering he had not respect. And Cain was very wroth, and his countenance fell.

Here we have, I. The devotions of Cain and Abel. *In process of time*, when they had made some improvement in their respective callings (Heb. *At the end of days*, either at the end of the year, when they kept their feast of in-gathering or perhaps an annual fast in remembrance of the fall, or at the end of the days of the week, the seventh day, which was the sabbath)—at some set time, Cain and Abel brought to Adam, as the priest of the family, each of them *an offering to the Lord*, for the doing of which we have reason to think there was a divine appointment given to Adam, as a token of God's favour to him and his thoughts of love towards him and his, notwithstanding their apostasy. God would thus try Adam's faith in the promise and his obedience to the remedial law; he would thus settle a correspondence again between heaven and earth, and give *shadows of good things to come.* Observe here, 1. That the religious worship of God is no novel invention, but an ancient institution. It is that which was *from the beginning* (1 John i. 1); it is the *good old way*, Jer. vi. 16. The city of our God is indeed that joyous city whose antiquity is of ancient days, Isa. xxiii. 7. Truth got the start of error, and piety of profaneness. 2. That it is a good thing for children to be well taught when they are young, and trained up betimes in religious services, that when they come to be capable of acting for themselves they may, of their own accord, *bring an offering to God.* In this *nurture of the Lord* parents must bring up their children, *ch.* xviii. 19; Eph. vi. 4. 3. That we should every one of us honour God with what we have, according as he has prospered us. Ac-

cording as their employments and possessions were, so they brought their offering. See 1 Cor. xvi. 1, 2. *Our merchandize and our hire*, whatever they are, must be *holiness to the Lord*, Isa. xxiii. 18. He must have his dues of it in works of piety and charity, the support of religion and the relief of the poor. Thus we must now bring our offering with an upright heart; *and with such sacrifices God is well pleased.* 4. That hypocrites and evil doers may be found going as far as the best of God's people in the external services of religion. Cain brought an offering with Abel; nay, Cain's offering is mentioned first, as if he were the more forward of the two. A hypocrite may possibly hear as many sermons, say as many prayers, and give as much alms, as a good Christian, and yet, for want of sincerity, come short of acceptance with God. The Pharisee and the publican went to the temple to pray, Luke xviii. 10.

II. The different success of their devotions. That which is to be aimed at in all acts of religion is God's acceptance: we speed well if we attain this, but in vain do we worship if we miss of it, 2 Cor. v. 9. Perhaps, to a stander-by, the sacrifices of Cain and Abel would have seemed both alike good. Adam accepted them both, but God, *who sees not as man sees*, did not. God had *respect to Abel and to his offering*, and showed well his acceptance of it, probably by fire from heaven; but to *Cain and his offering he had not respect.* We are sure there was a good reason for this difference; the Governor of the world, though an absolute sovereign, does not act arbitrarily in dispensing his smiles and frowns.

1. There was a difference in the characters of the persons offering. Cain was a wicked man, led a bad life, under the reigning power of the world and the flesh; and therefore his sacrifice was an *abomination to the Lord* (Prov. xv. 8), *a vain oblation*, Isa. i. 13. God had no respect to Cain himself, and therefore no respect to his offering, as the manner of the expression intimates. But Abel was a righteous man; he is called *righteous Abel* (Matt. xxiii. 35); his heart was upright and his life was pious; he was one of those whom God's countenance beholds (Ps. xi. 7) and whose prayer is therefore his delight, Prov. xv. 8. God had respect to him as a holy man, and therefore to his offering as a holy offering. The tree must be good, else the fruit cannot be pleasing to the heart-searching God.

2. There was a difference in the offerings they brought. It is expressly said (Heb. xi. 4), Abel's was a *more excellent sacrifice* than Cain's: either, (1.) In the nature of it. Cain's was only a sacrifice of acknowledgment offered to the Creator; the meat-offerings of the fruit of the ground were no more, and, for aught I know, they might be offered in innocency. But Abel brought a sacrifice

37

of atonement, the blood whereof was shed in order to remission, thereby owning himself a sinner, deprecating God's wrath, and imploring his favour in a Mediator. Or, (2.) In the qualities of the offering. Cain brought *of the fruit of the ground*, any thing that came next to hand, what he had not occasion for himself or what was not marketable. But Abel was curious in the choice of his offering : not the lame, nor the lean, nor the refuse, but the *firstlings of the flock*—the best he had, *and the fat thereof*—the best of those best. Hence the Hebrew doctors give it for a general rule that every thing that is for the name of the good God must be the goodliest and best. It is fit that he who is the first and best should have the first and best of our time, strength, and service.

3. The great difference was this, that Abel offered in faith, and Cain did not. There was a difference in the principle upon which they went. Abel offered with an eye to God's will as his rule, and God's glory as his end, and in dependence upon the promise of a Redeemer; but Cain did what he did only for company's sake, or to save his credit, not in faith, and so it turned into sin to him. Abel was a penitent believer, like the publican that went away justified : Cain was unhumbled; his confidence was within himself; he was like the Pharisee who glorified himself, but was not so much as justified before God.

III. Cain's displeasure at the difference God made between his sacrifice and Abel's. Cain was very wroth, which presently appeared in his very looks, for his countenance fell, which bespeaks not so much his grief and discontent as his malice and rage. His sullen churlish countenance, and a downlook, betrayed his passionate resentments : he carried ill-nature in his face, and *the show of his countenance witnessed against him.* This anger bespeaks, 1. His enmity to God, and the indignation he had conceived against him for making such a difference between his offering and his brother's. He should have been angry at himself for his own infidelity and hypocrisy, by which he had forfeited God's acceptance; and his countenance should have fallen in repentance and holy shame, as the publican's, who *would not lift up so much as his eyes to heaven*, Luke xviii. 13. But, instead of this, he flies out against God, as if he were partial and unfair in distributing his smiles and frowns, and as if he had done him a deal of wrong. Note, It is a certain sign of an unhumbled heart to quarrel with those rebukes which we have, by our own sin, brought upon ourselves. *The foolishness of man perverteth his way*, and then, to make bad worse, *his heart fretteth against the Lord*, Prov. xix. 3. 2. His envy of his brother, who had the honour to be publicly owned. Though his brother had no thought of having any slur put upon him, nor did now insult over him to provoke him, yet he conceived a hatred of him as an

enemy, or, which is equivalent, a rival. Note, (1.) It is common for those who have rendered themselves unworthy of God's favour by their presumptuous sins to have indignation against those who are dignified and distinguished by it. The Pharisees walked in this way of Cain, when they *neither entered into the kingdom of God themselves* nor *suffered those that were entering to go in*, Luke xi. 52. Their eye is evil, because their master's eye and the eye of their fellow-servants are good. (2.) Envy is a sin that commonly carries with it both its own discovery, in the paleness of the looks, and its own punishment, in the rottenness of the bones.

6 And the LORD said unto Cain, Why art thou wroth? and why is thy countenance fallen? 7 If thou doest well, shalt thou not be accepted? and if thou doest not well, sin lieth at the door. And unto thee *shall be* his desire, and thou shalt rule over him.

God is here reasoning with Cain, to convince him of the sin and folly of his anger and discontent, and to bring him into a good temper again, that further mischief might be prevented. It is an instance of God's patience and condescending goodness that he would deal thus tenderly with so bad a man, in so bad an affair. *He is not willing that any should perish, but that all should come to repentance.* Thus the father of the prodigal argued the case with the elder son (Luke xv. 28, &c.), and God with those Israelites who said, *The way of the Lord is not equal*, Ezek. xviii. 25.

I. God puts Cain himself upon enquiring into the cause of his discontent, and considering whether it were indeed a just cause: *Why is thy countenance fallen?* Observe, 1. That God takes notice of all our sinful passions and discontents. There is not an angry look, an envious look, nor a fretful look, that escapes his observing eye. 2. That most of our sinful heats and disquietudes would soon vanish before a strict and impartial enquiry into the cause of them. "*Why am I wroth?* Is there a real cause, a just cause, a proportionable cause, for it? Why am I so soon angry? Why so very angry, and so implacable?"

II. To reduce Cain to his right mind again, it is here made evident to him,

1. That he had no reason to be angry at God, for that he had proceeded according to the settled and invariable rules of government suited to a state of probation. He sets before men life and death, the blessing and the curse, and then *renders to them according to their works*, and differences them according as they difference themselves—so shall their doom be. The rules are just, and therefore his ways, according to those rules, must needs be equal, and he will be justified when he speaks
38

(1.) God sets before Cain life and a blessing: " *If thou doest well, shalt thou not be accepted?* No doubt thou shalt, nay, thou knowest thou shalt ;" either, [1.] " If thou hadst done well, as thy brother did, thou shouldst have been accepted, as he was." *God is no respecter of persons,* hates nothing that he has made, denies his favour to none but those who have forfeited it, and is an enemy to none but those who by sin have made him their enemy: so that if we come short of acceptance with him we must thank ourselves, the fault is wholly our own ; if we had done our duty, we should not have missed of his mercy. This will justify God in the destruction of sinners, and will aggravate their ruin ; there is not a damned sinner in hell, but, if he had done well, as he might have done, had been a glorious saint in heaven. Every mouth will shortly be stopped with this. Or, [2.] " If now thou do well, if thou repent of thy sin, reform thy heart and life, and bring thy sacrifice in a better manner, if thou not only do that which is good but do it well, thou shalt yet be accepted, thy sin shall be pardoned, thy comfort and honour restored, and all shall be well." See here the effect of a Mediator's interposal between God and man ; we do not stand upon the footing of the first covenant, which left no room for repentance, but God has come upon new terms with us. Though we have offended, if we repent and return, we shall find mercy. See how early the gospel was preached, and the benefit of it here offered even to one of the chief of sinners.

(2.) He sets before him death and a curse : But *if not well,* that is, " Seeing thou didst not do well, didst not offer in faith and in a right manner, *sin lies at the door*," that is, " sin was imputed to thee, and thou wast frowned upon and rejected as a sinner. So high a charge had not been laid at thy door, if thou hadst not brought it upon thyself, by not doing well." Or, as it is commonly taken, " If now thou wilt not do well, if thou persist in this wrath, and, instead of humbling thyself before God, harden thyself against him, *sin lies at the door,*" that is, [1.] Further sin. " Now that anger is in thy heart, murder is at the door." The way of sin is down-hill, and men go from bad to worse. Those who do not sacrifice well, but are careless and remiss in their devotion to God, expose themselves to the worst temptations ; and perhaps the most scandalous sin lies at the door. Those who do not keep God's ordinances are in danger of committing all abominations, Lev. xviii. 30. Or, [2.] The punishment of sin. So near akin are sin and punishment that the same word in Hebrew signifies both. If sin be harboured in the house, the curse waits at the door, like a bailiff, ready to arrest the sinner whenever he looks out. It lies as if it slept, but it lies at the door where it will be soon awaked, and then it will appear that the damnation slumbered not. Sin will *find thee out,* Num. xxxii. 23. Yet some choose to understand this also as an intimation of mercy. " If thou doest not well, *sin* (that is, *the sin-offering),* lies at the door, and thou mayest take the benefit of it." The same word signifies *sin* and *a sacrifice for sin.* " Though thou hast not done well, yet do not despair ; the remedy is at hand ; the propitiation is not far to seek ; lay hold on it, and the iniquity of thy holy things shall be forgiven thee." Christ, the great sin-offering, is said to *stand at the door,* Rev. iii. 20. And those well deserve to perish in their sins that will not go to the door for an interest in the sin-offering. All this considered, Cain had no reason to be angry at God, but at himself only.

2. That he had no reason to be angry at his brother : " *Unto thee shall be his desire,* he shall continue his respect to thee as an elder brother, and thou, as the first-born, shalt rule over him as much as ever." God's acceptance of Abel's offering did not transfer the birth-right to him (which Cain was jealous of), nor put upon him that excellency of dignity and of power which is said to belong to it, *ch.* xlix. 3. God did not so intend it ; Abel did not so interpret it ; there was no danger of its being improved to Cain's prejudice ; why then should he be so much exasperated ? Observe here, (1.) That the difference which God's grace makes does not alter the distinctions which God's providence makes, but preserves them, and obliges us to do the duty which results from them : believing servants must be obedient to unbelieving masters. Dominion is not founded in grace, nor will religion warrant disloyalty or disrespect in any relation. (2.) That the jealousies which civil powers have sometimes conceived of the true worshippers of God as dangerous to their government, enemies to Cæsar, and hurtful to kings and provinces (on which suspicion persecutors have grounded their rage against them) are very unjust and unreasonable. Whatever may be the case with some who call themselves Christians, it is certain that *Christians indeed* are the best subjects, and the quiet in the land ; their desire is towards their governors, and these shall rule over them.

8 And Cain talked with Abel his brother : and it came to pass, when they were in the field, that Cain rose up against Abel his brother, and slew him.

We have here the progress of Cain's anger, and the issue of it in Abel's murder, which may be considered two ways :—

I. As Cain's sin ; and a scarlet, crimson, sin it was, a sin of the first magnitude, a sin against the light and law of nature, and which the consciences even of bad men have startled at. See in it, 1. The sad effects of sin's entrance into the world and into the hearts of men. See what a root of bitterness the corrupt nature is, which bears this gall and wormwood. Adam's eating forbidden fruit seemed but a little sin, but it opened the door to the greatest. 2. A fruit of the enmity which is in the seed of the serpent against the seed of the woman. As Abel leads the van in the *noble army of martyrs* (Matt. xxiii. 35), so Cain stands in the front of the ignoble army of persecutors, Jude 11. So early did he that was after the flesh *persecute him that was after the Spirit ; and so it is now,* more or less (Gal. iv. 29), and so it will be till the war shall end in the eternal salvation of all the saints and the eternal perdition of all that hate them. 3. See also what comes of *envy, hatred, malice, and all uncharitableness ;* if they be indulged and cherished in the soul, they are in danger of involving men in the horrid guilt of murder itself. Rash anger is heart-murder, Matt. v. 21, 22. Much more is malice so ; he that hates his brother is already a murderer before God ; and, if God leave him to himself, he wants nothing but an opportunity to render him a murderer before the world. Many were the aggravations of Cain's sin. (1.) It was his brother, his own brother, that he murdered, his own mother's son (Ps. l. 20), whom he ought to have loved, his younger brother, whom he ought to have protected. (2.) He was a good brother, one who had never done him any wrong, nor given him the least provocation in word or deed, but one whose desire had been always towards him, and who had been, in all instances, dutiful and respectful to him. (3.) He had fair warning given him, before, of this. God himself had told him what would come of it, yet he persisted in his barbarous design. (4.) It should seem that he covered it with a show of friendship and kindness : *He talked with Abel his brother,* freely and familiarly, lest Abel should suspect danger, and keep out of his reach. Thus Joab kissed Abner, and then killed him. Thus Absalom feasted his brother Amnon and then killed him. According to the Septuagint [a Greek version of the Old Testament, supposed to have been translated by seventy-two Jews, at the desire of Ptolemy Philadelphus, above 200 years before Christ], Cain said to Abel, *Let us go into the field ;* if so, we are sure Abel did not understand it (according to the modern sense) as a challenge, else he would not have accepted it, but as a brotherly invitation to go together to their work. The Chaldee paraphrast adds that Cain, when they were in discourse in the field, maintained that there was no judgment to come, no future state, no rewards and punishments in the other world, and that when Abel spoke in defence of the truth Cain took that occasion to fall upon him. However, (5.) That which the scripture tells us was the reason why he slew him was a sufficient aggravation of the murder; it was *because his own works*

were *evil and his brother's righteous,* so that herein he showed himself to be *of that wicked one* (1 John iii. 12), a *child of the devil,* as being *an enemy to all righteousness,* even in his own brother, and, in this, employed immediately by the destroyer. Nay, (6.) In killing his brother, he directly struck at God himself ; for God's accepting Abel was the provocation pretended, and for this very reason he hated Abel, because God loved him. (7.) The murder of Abel was the more inhuman because there were now so few men in the world to replenish it. The life of a man is precious at any time ; but it was in a special manner precious now, and could ill be spared.

II. As Abel's suffering. Death reigned ever since Adam sinned, but we read not of any taken captive by him till now ; and now, 1. The first that dies is a saint, one that was accepted and beloved of God, to show that, though the promised seed was so far to destroy him that had the power of death as to save believers from its sting, yet still they should be exposed to its stroke. The first that went to the grave went to heaven. God would secure to himself the first-fruits, the first-born to the dead, that first opened the womb into another world. Let this take off the terror of death, that it was betimes the lot of God's chosen, which alters the property of it. Nay, 2. The first that dies is a martyr, and dies for his religion ; and of such it may more truly be said than of soldiers, that they die on the bed of honour. Abel's death has not only no curse in it, but it has a crown in it ; so admirably well is the property of death altered that it is not only rendered innocent and inoffensive to those that die in Christ, but honourable and glorious to those that die for him. Let us not think it strange concerning the fiery trial, nor shrink if we be called to resist unto blood ; for we know there is a crown of life for all that are faithful unto death.

9 And the Lord said unto Cain, Where *is* Abel thy brother ? And he said, I know not : *Am* I my brother's keeper ? 10 And he said, What hast thou done ? the voice of thy brother's blood crieth unto me from the ground. 11 And now *art* thou cursed from the earth, which hath opened her mouth to receive thy brother's blood from thy hand ; 12 When thou tillest the ground, it shall not henceforth yield unto thee her strength ; a fugitive and a vagabond shalt thou be in the earth.

We have here a full account of the trial and condemnation of the first murderer. Civil courts of judicature not being yet erected for this purpose, as they were afterwards (*ch.* ix. 6), God himself sits Judge ; for he is the God to whom vengeance belongs, and who will be sure to make inquisition for blood, especially the blood of saints. Observe,

I. The arraignment of Cain: *The Lord said unto Cain, Where is Abel thy brother?* Some think Cain was thus examined the next sabbath after the murder was committed, when *the sons of God came,* as usual, *to present themselves before the Lord,* in a religious assembly, and Abel was missing, whose place did not use to be empty; for the God of heaven takes notice who is present at and who is absent from public ordinances. Cain is asked, not only because there is just cause to suspect him, he having discovered a malice against Abel and having been last with him, but because God knew him to be guilty; yet he asks him, that he may draw from him a confession of his crime, for those who would be justified before God must accuse themselves, and the penitent will do so.

II. Cain's plea: he pleads *not guilty,* and adds rebellion to his sin. For, 1. He endeavours to cover a deliberate murder with a deliberate lie: *I know not.* He knew well enough what had become of Abel, and yet had the impudence to deny it. Thus, in Cain, the devil was both a murderer and a liar from the beginning. See how sinners' minds are blinded, and their hearts hardened by the deceitfulness of sin: those are strangely blind that think it possible to conceal their sins from a God that sees all, and those are strangely hard that think it desirable to conceal them from a God who pardons those only that confess. 2. He impudently charges his Judge with folly and injustice, in putting this question to him: *Am I my brother's keeper?* He should have humbled himself, and have said, *Am not I my brother's murderer?* But he flies in the face of God himself, as if he had asked him an impertinent question, to which he was no way obliged to give an answer: "*Am I my brother's keeper?* Surely he is old enough to take care of himself, nor did I ever take any charge of him." Some think he reflects on God and his providence, as if he had said, "Art not thou his keeper? If he be missing, on thee be the blame, and not on me, who never undertook to keep him." Note, A charitable concern for our brethren, as their keepers, is a great duty, which is strictly required of us, but is generally neglected by us. Those who are unconcerned in the affairs of their brethren, and take no care, when they have opportunity, to prevent their hurt in their bodies, goods, or good name, especially in their souls, do, in effect, speak Cain's language. See Lev. xix. 17; Phil. ii. 4.

III. The conviction of Cain, *v.* 10. God gave no direct answer to his question, but rejected his plea as false and frivolous: "*What hast thou done?* Thou makest a light matter of it; but hast thou considered what an evil thing it is, how deep the stain, how heavy the burden, of this guilt is? Thou thinkest to conceal it, but it is to no pur-

pose, the evidence against thee is clear and incontestable: *The voice of thy brother's blood cries.*" He speaks as if the blood itself were both witness and prosecutor, because God's own knowledge testified against him and God's own justice demanded satisfaction Observe here, 1. Murder is a crying sin, none more so. Blood calls for blood, the blood of the murdered for the blood of the murderer; it cries in the dying words of Zechariah (2 Chron. xxiv. 22), *The Lord look upon it, and require it;* or in those of the souls under the altar (Rev. vi. 10), *How long, Lord, holy, and true?* The patient sufferers cried for pardon *(Father, forgive them),* but their blood cries for vengeance. Though they hold their peace, their blood has a loud and constant cry, to which the ear of the righteous God is always open. 2. The blood is said to cry from the ground, the earth, which is said *to open her mouth to receive his brother's blood from his hand, v.* 11. The earth did, as it were, blush to see her own face stained with such blood, and therefore opened her mouth to hide that which she could not hinder. When the heaven revealed Cain's iniquity, the earth also rose up against him (Job xx. 27), and groaned on being thus made *subject to vanity,* Rom. viii. 20, 22. Cain, it is likely, buried the blood and the body, to conceal his crime; but "murder will out." He did not bury them so deep but the cry of them reached heaven. 3. In the original the word is plural, thy brother's *bloods,* not only his blood, but the blood of all those that might have descended from him; or the blood of all the seed of the woman, who should, in like manner, seal the truth with their blood. Christ puts all on one score (Matt. xxiii. 35); or because account was kept of every drop of blood shed. How well is it for us that the blood of Christ speaks better things than that of Abel! Heb. xii. 24. Abel's blood cried for vengeance, Christ's blood cries for pardon.

IV. The sentence passed upon Cain: *And now art thou cursed from the earth, v.* 11. Observe here,

1. He is cursed, separated to all evil, laid under the wrath of God, as it is revealed from heaven against all ungodliness and unrighteousness of men, Rom. i. 18. Who knows the extent and weight of a divine curse, how far it reaches, how deep it pierces? God's pronouncing a man cursed makes him so; for those whom he curses are cursed indeed. The curse for Adam's disobedience terminated on the ground: *Cursed is the ground for thy sake;* but that for Cain's rebellion fell immediately upon himself: *Thou art cursed;* for God had mercy in store for Adam, but none for Cain. We have all deserved this curse, and it is only in Christ that believers are saved from it and inherit the blessing, Gal. iii. 10, 13.

2. He is cursed from the earth. Thence the cry came up to God, thence the curse

came up to Cain. God could have taken vengeance by an immediate stroke from heaven, by the sword of an angel, or by a thunderbolt; but he chose to make the earth the avenger of blood, to continue him upon the earth, and not immediately to cut him off, and yet to make even this his curse. The earth is always near us, we cannot fly from it; so that, if this is made the executioner of divine wrath, our punishment is unavoidable: it is sin, that is, the punishment of sin, lying at the door. Cain found his punishment where he chose his portion and set his heart. Two things we expect from the earth, and by this curse both are denied to Cain and taken from him: *sustenance* and *settlement.* (1.) Sustenance out of the earth is here withheld from him. It is a curse upon him in his enjoyments, and particularly in his calling: *When thou tillest the ground, it shall not henceforth yield unto thee its strength.* Note, Every creature is to us what God makes it, a comfort or a cross, a blessing or a curse. If the earth yield not her strength to us, we must therein acknowledge God's righteousness; for we have not yielded our strength to him. The ground was cursed before to Adam, but it was now doubly cursed to Cain. That part of it which fell to his share, and of which he had the occupation, was made unfruitful and uncomfortable to him by the blood of Abel. Note, The wickedness of the wicked brings a curse upon all they do and all they have (Deut. xxviii. 15, &c.), and this curse embitters all they have and disappoints them in all they do. (2.) Settlement on the earth is here denied him: *A fugitive and a vagabond shalt thou be in the earth.* By this he was condemned, [1.] To perpetual disgrace and reproach among men. It should be ever looked upon as a scandalous thing to harbour him, converse with him, or show him any countenance. And justly was a man that had divested himself of all humanity abhorred and abandoned by all mankind, and made infamous. [2.] To perpetual disquietude and horror in his own mind. His own guilty conscience should haunt him wherever he went, and make him *Magor-missabib,* a *terror round about.* What rest can those find, what settlement, that carry their own disturbance with them in their bosoms wherever they go? Those must needs be fugitives that are thus tossed. There is not a more restless fugitive upon earth than he that is continually pursued by his own guilt, nor a viler vagabond than he that is at the beck of his own lusts.

This was the sentence passed upon Cain; and even in this there was mercy mixed, inasmuch as he was not immediately cut off, but had space given him to repent; for God is long-suffering to us-ward, not willing that any should perish.

13 And Cain said unto the LORD, My punishment *is* greater than I can

bear. 14 Behold, thou hast driven me out this day from the face of the earth; and from thy face shall I be hid; and I shall be a fugitive and a vagabond in the earth; and it shall come to pass, *that* every one that findeth me shall slay me. 15 And the LORD said unto him, Therefore whosoever slayeth Cain, vengeance shall be taken on him sevenfold. And the LORD set a mark upon Cain, lest any finding him should kill him.

We have here a further account of the proceedings against Cain.

I. Here is Cain's complaint of the sentence passed upon him, as hard and severe. Some make him to speak the language of despair, and read it, *My iniquity is greater than that it may be forgiven;* and so what he says is a reproach and affront to the mercy of God, which those only shall have the benefit of that hope in it. There is forgiveness with the God of pardons for the greatest sins and sinners; but those forfeit it who despair of it. Just now Cain made nothing of his sin, but now he is in the other extreme: Satan drives his vassals from presumption to despair. We cannot think too ill of sin, provided we do not think it unpardonable. But Cain seems rather to speak the language of indignation: *My punishment is greater than I can bear;* and so what he says is a reproach and affront to the justice of God, and a complaint, not of the greatness of his sin, but of the extremity of his punishment, as if this were disproportionable to his merits. Instead of justifying God in the sentence, he condemns him, not accepting the punishment of his iniquity, but quarrelling with it. Note, Impenitent unhumbled hearts are therefore not reclaimed by God's rebukes because they think themselves wronged by them; and it is an evidence of great hardness to be more concerned about our sufferings than about our sins. Pharaoh's care was concerning this death only, not this sin (Exod. x. 17); so was Cain's here. He is a living man, and yet complains of the punishment of his sin, Lam. iii. 39. He thinks himself rigorously dealt with when really he is favourably treated; and he cries out of wrong when he has more reason to wonder that he is out of hell. Woe unto him that thus strives with his Maker, and enters into judgment with his Judge. Now, to justify this complaint, Cain descants upon the sentence. 1. He sees himself excluded by it from the favour of his God, and concludes that, being cursed, he is hidden from God's face, which is indeed the true nature of God's curse; damned sinners find it so, to whom it is said, *Depart from me you cursed.* Those are cursed indeed that are for ever shut out from God's love and care and from all hopes of his grace. 2. He sees himself expelled from all the comforts of this life, and concludes that, being a fugitive, he is, in effect, *driven out this day from the face of the earth.* As good have no place on earth as not have a settled place. Better rest in the grave than not rest at all. 3. He sees himself excommunicated by it, and cut off from the church, and forbidden to attend on public ordinances. His hands being full of blood, he must *bring no more vain oblations,* Isa. i. 13, 15. Perhaps this he means when he complains that he is *driven out from the face of the earth ;* for being shut out of the church, which none had yet deserted, he was *hidden from God's face,* being not admitted to come *with the sons of God to present himself before the Lord.* 4. He sees himself exposed by it to the hatred and ill-will of all mankind : *It shall come to pass that every one that finds me shall slay me.* Wherever he wanders, he goes in peril of his life, at least he thinks so; and, like a man in debt, thinks every one he meets a bailiff. There were none alive but his near relations ; yet even of them he is justly afraid who had himself been so barbarous to his brother. Some read it, *Whatsoever* finds me shall slay me ; not only, " Whosoever among men," but, " Whatsoever among all the creatures." Seeing himself thrown out of God's protection, he sees the whole creation armed against him. Note, Unpardoned guilt fills men with continual terrors, Prov. xxviii. 1 ; Job. xv. 20, 21 ; Ps. liii. 5. It is better to fear and not sin than to sin and then fear. Dr. Lightfoot thinks this word of Cain should be read as a wish : *Now, therefore, let it be that any that find me may kill me.* Being bitter in soul, he *longs for death, but it comes not* (Job iii. 20—22), as those under spiritual torments do, Rev. ix. 5, 6.

II. Here is God's confirmation of the sentence ; for when he judges he will overcome, *v.* 15. Observe, 1. How Cain is protected in wrath by this declaration, notified, we may suppose, to all that little world which was then in being : *Whosoever slayeth Cain, vengeance shall be taken on him seven-fold,* because thereby the sentence he was under (that he should be a fugitive and a vagabond) would be defeated. Condemned prisoners are under the special protection of the law ; those that are appointed sacrifices to public justice must not be sacrificed to private revenge. God having said in Cain's case, *Vengeance is mine, I will repay,* it would have been a daring usurpation for any man to take the sword out of God's hand, a contempt put upon an express declaration of God's mind, and therefore avenged sevenfold. Note, God has wise and holy ends in protecting and prolonging the lives even of very wicked men. God deals with some according to that prayer, *Slay them not, lest my people forget ; scatter them by thy power,* Ps. lix. 11. Had Cain been slain immediately, he would have been forgotten (Eccl. viii. 10); but now he lives a more fearful and lasting

monument of God's justice, hanged in chains, as it were. 2. How he is marked in wrath : *The Lord set a mark upon Cain,* to distinguish him from the rest of mankind and to notify that he was the man that murdered his brother, whom nobody must hurt, but every body must hoot at. God stigmatized him (as some malefactors are burnt in the cheek), and put upon him such a visible and indelible mark of infamy and disgrace as would make all wise people shun him, so that he could not be otherwise than a fugitive and a vagabond, and the off-scouring of all things.

16 And Cain went out from the presence of the LORD, and dwelt in the land of Nod, on the east of Eden. 17 And Cain knew his wife ; and she conceived, and bare Enoch : and he builded a city, and called the name of the city, after the name of his son, Enoch. 18 And unto Enoch was born Irad : and Irad begat Mehujael : and Mehujael begat Methusael : and Methusael begat Lamech.

We have here a further account of Cain, and what became of him after he was rejected of God.

I. He tamely submitted to that part of his sentence by which he was hidden from God's face ; for (*v.* 16) *he went out from the presence of the Lord,* that is, he willingly renounced God and religion, and was content to forego its privileges, so that he might not be under its precepts. He forsook Adam's family and altar, and cast off all pretensions to the fear of God, and never came among good people, nor attended on God's ordinances, any more. Note, Hypocritical professors, that have dissembled and trifled with God Almighty, are justly left to themselves, to do something that is grossly scandalous, and so to throw off that form of godliness to which they have been a reproach, and under colour of which they have denied the power of it. Cain went out now from the presence of the Lord, and we never find that he came into it again, to his comfort. Hell is *destruction from the presence of the Lord,* 2 Thess. i. 9. It is a perpetual banishment from the fountain of all good. This is the choice of sinners ; and so shall their doom be, to their eternal confusion.

II. He endeavoured to confront that part of the sentence by which he was made a fugitive and a vagabond ; for,

1. He chose his land. He went and *dwelt on the east of Eden,* somewhere distant from the place where Adam and his religious family resided, distinguishing himself and his accursed generation from the holy seed, his camp from the *camp of the saints and the beloved city,* Rev. xx. 9. On the east of Eden, the cherubim were, with the flaming sword, *ch.* iii. 24. There he chose his lot, as if to defy the terrors of the Lord. But his at-

43

tempt to settle was in vain; for the land he dwelt in was to him *the land of Nod* (that is, of *shaking* or *trembling),* because of the continual restlessness and uneasiness of his own spirit. Note, Those that depart from God cannot find rest any where else. After Cain went out from the presence of the Lord, he never rested. Those that shut themselves out of heaven abandon themselves to a perpetual trembling. " *Return therefore to thy rest, O my soul,* to thy rest in God; else thou art for ever restless."

2. He built a city for a habitation, *v.* 17. *He was building a city,* so some read it, ever building it, but, a curse being upon him and the work of his hands, he could not finish it. Or, as we read it, he *built a city,* in token of a fixed separation from the church of God, to which he had no thoughts of ever returning. This city was to be the head-quarters of the apostasy. Observe here, (1.) Cain's defiance of the divine sentence. God said he should be a *fugitive and a vagabond.* Had he repented and humbled himself, this curse might have been turned into a blessing, as that of the tribe of Levi was, that they should be *divided in Jacob and scattered in Israel;* but his impenitent unhumbled heart walking contrary to God, and resolving to fix in spite of heaven, that which might have been a blessing was turned into a curse. (2.) See what was Cain's choice, after he had forsaken God; he pitched upon a settlement in this world, as his rest for ever. Those who looked for the heavenly city chose, while on earth, to dwell in tabernacles; but Cain, as one that minded not *that* city, built himself one on earth. Those that are cursed of God are apt to seek their settlement and satisfaction here below, Ps. xvii. 14. (3.) See what method Cain took to defend himself against the terrors with which he was perpetually haunted. He undertook this building, to divert his thoughts from the consideration of his own misery, and to drown the clamours of a guilty conscience with the noise of axes and hammers. Thus many baffle their convictions by thrusting themselves into a hurry of worldly business. (4.) See how wicked people often get the start of God's people, and out-go them in outward prosperity. Cain and his cursed race dwell in a city, while Adam and his blessed family dwell in tents. We cannot judge of *love or hatred by all that is before us,* Eccl. ix. 1, 2.

3. His family also was built up. Here is an account of his posterity, at least the heirs of his family, for seven generations. His son was *Enoch,* of the same name, but not of the same character, with that holy man that *walked with God, ch.* v. 22. Good men and bad may bear the same names: but God can distinguish between Judas Iscariot and Judas *not* Iscariot, John xiv. 22. The names of more of his posterity are mentioned, and but just mentioned; not as those of the holy seed (*ch.* v.), where we have three verses con-

cerning each, whereas here we have three or four in one verse. They are numbered in haste, as not valued or delighted in, in comparison with God's chosen.

19 And Lamech took unto him two wives : the name of the one *was* Adah, and the name of the other Zillah. 20 And Adah bare Jabal : he was the father of such as dwell in tents, and *of such as have* cattle. 21 And his brother's name *was* Jubal : he was the father of all such as handle the harp and organ. 22 And Zillah, she also bare Tubal-cain, an instructor of every artificer in brass and iron : and the sister of Tubal-cain *was* Naamah.

We have here some particulars concerning Lamech, the seventh from Adam in the line of Cain. Observe,

I. His marrying two wives. It was one of the degenerate race of Cain who first transgressed that original law of marriage that two only should be one flesh. Hitherto one man had but one wife at a time; but Lamech took two. *From the beginning it was not so.* Mal. ii. 15; Matt. xix. 5. See here, 1. Those who desert God's church and ordinances lay themselves open to all manner of temptation. 2. When a bad custom is begun by bad men sometimes men of better characters are, through unwariness, drawn in to follow them. Jacob, David, and many others, who were otherwise good men, were afterwards ensnared in this sin which Lamech begun.

II. His happiness in his children, notwithstanding this. Though he sinned, in marrying two wives, yet he was blessed with children by both, and those such as lived to be famous in their generation, not for their piety, no mention is made of this (for aught that appears they were the heathen of that age), but for their ingenuity. They were not only themselves men of business, but men that were serviceable to the world, and eminent for the invention, or at least the improvement, of some useful arts. 1. Jabal was a famous shepherd; he delighted much in keeping cattle himself, and was so happy in devising methods of doing it to the best advantage, and instructing others in them, that the shepherds of those times, nay, the shepherds of after-times, called him *father ;* or perhaps, his children after him being brought up to the same employment, the family was a family of shepherds. 2. Jubal was a famous musician, and particularly an organist, and the first that gave rules for the noble art or science of music. When Jabal had set them in a way to be rich, Jubal put them in a way to be merry. Those that spend their days in wealth will not be without the timbrel and harp, Job xxi. 12, 13. From his name, *Jubal,* probably the jubilee-trumpet was so called; for the best music was that which proclaimed liberty and redemption. Jabal was their Pan and Jubal their Apollo. 3. Tubal Cain was a famous smith, who greatly improved the art of working in brass and iron, for the service both of war and husbandry. He was their Vulcan. See here, (1.) That worldly things are the only things that carnal wicked people set their hearts upon and are most ingenious and industrious about. So it was with this impious race of cursed Cain. Here were a father of shepherds and a father of musicians, but not a father of the faithful. Here was one to teach in brass and iron, but none to teach the good knowledge of the Lord. Here were devices how to be rich, and how to be mighty, and how to be merry, but nothing of God, nor of his fear and service, among them. Present things fill the heads of most people. (2.) That even those who are destitute of the knowledge and grace of God may be endued with many excellent and useful accomplishments, which may make them famous and serviceable in their generation. Common gifts are given to bad men, while God chooses to himself the foolish things of the world.

23 And Lamech said unto his wives, Adah and Zillah, hear my voice; ye wives of Lamech, hearken unto my speech: for I have slain a man to my wounding, and a young man to my hurt: 24 If Cain shall be avenged sevenfold, truly Lamech seventy and sevenfold.

By this speech of Lamech, which is here recorded, and probably was much talked of in those times, he further appears to have been a wicked man, as Cain's accursed race generally were. Observe, 1. How haughtily and imperiously he speaks to his wives, as one that expected a mighty regard and observance: *Hear my voice, you wives of Lamech.* No marvel that he who had broken one law of marriage, by taking two wives, broke another, which obliged him to be kind and tender to those he had taken, and to give honour to the wife as to the weaker vessel. Those are not always the most careful to do their own duty that are highest in their demands of respect from others, and most frequent in calling upon their relations to know their place and do their duty. 2. How bloody and barbarous he was to all about him: *I have slain,* or (as it is in the margin) *I would slay a man in my wound, and a young man in my hurt.* He owns himself a man of a fierce and cruel disposition, that would lay about him without mercy, and kill all that stood in his way; be it a man, or a young man, nay, though he himself were in danger to be wounded and hurt in the conflict. Some think, because (v. 24) he compares himself with Cain, that he had murdered some

of the holy seed, the true worshippers of God, and that he acknowledged this to be the wounding of his conscience and the hurt of his soul; and yet that, like Cain, he continued impenitent, trembling and yet unhumbled. Or his wives, knowing what manner of spirit he was of, how apt both to give and to resent provocation, were afraid lest somebody or other would be the death of him. "Never fear," says he, "I defy any man to set upon me; whosoever does, let me alone to make my part good with him; I will slay him, be he a man or a young man." Note, It is a common thing for fierce and bloody men to *glory in their shame* (Phil. iii. 19), as if it were both their safety and their honour that they care not how many lives are sacrificed to their angry resentments, nor how much they are hated, provided they may be feared. *Oderint, dum metuant—Let them hate, provided they fear.* 3. How impiously he presumes even upon God's protection in his wicked way, v. 24. He had heard that *Cain should be avenged seven-fold* (v. 15), that is, that if any man should dare to kill Cain he should be severely reckoned with and punished for so doing, though Cain deserved to die a thousand deaths for the murder of his brother, and hence he infers that if any one should kill him for the murders he had committed God would much more avenge his death. As if the special care God took to prolong and secure the life of Cain, for special reasons peculiar to his case (and indeed for his sorer punishment, as the beings of the damned are continued) were designed as a protection to all murderers. Thus Lamech perversely argues, "If God provided for the safety of Cain, much more for mine, who, though I have slain many, yet never slew my own brother, and upon no provocation, as he did." Note, The reprieve of some sinners, and the patience God exercises towards them, are often abused to the hardening of others in the like sinful ways, Eccl. viii. 11. But, though justice strike some slowly, others cannot therefore be sure but that they may be taken away with a swift destruction. Or, if God should bear long with those who thus presume upon his forbearance, they do but hereby treasure up unto themselves *wrath against the day of wrath.*

Now this is all we have upon record in scripture concerning the family and posterity of cursed Cain, till we find them all cut off and perishing in the universal deluge.

25 And Adam knew his wife again; and she bare a son, and called his name Seth: For God, *said she,* hath appointed me another seed instead of Abel, whom Cain slew. 26 And to Seth, to him also there was born a son; and he called his name Enos: then began men to call upon the name of the LORD.

45

This is the first mention of Adam in the story of this chapter. No question, the murder of Abel, and the impenitence and apostasy of Cain, were a very great grief to him and Eve, and the more because their own wickedness did now correct them and their backslidings did reprove them. Their folly had given sin and death entrance into the world; and now they smarted by it, being, by means thereof, deprived of *both their sons in one day, ch.* xxvii. 45. When parents are grieved by their children's wickedness they should take occasion thence to lament that corruption of nature which was derived from them, and which is the root of bitterness. But here we have that which was a relief to our first parents in their affliction.

I. God gave them to see the re-building of their family, which was sorely shaken and weakened by that sad event. For, 1. They saw their seed, *another seed instead of Abel, v.* 25. Observe God's kindness and tenderness towards his people, in his providential dealings with them; when he takes away one comfort from them, he gives them another instead of it, which may prove a greater blessing to them than that was in which they thought their lives were bound up. This other seed was he in whom the church was to be built up and perpetuated, and he comes instead of Abel, for the succession of confessors is the revival of the martyrs and as it were the resurrection of God's slain witnesses. Thus we are *baptized for the dead* (1 Cor. xv. 29), that is, we are, by baptism, admitted into the church, for or instead of those who by death, especially by martyrdom, are removed out of it; and we fill up their room. Those who slay God's servants hope by this means to wear out the saints of the Most High; but they will be deceived. Christ shall still see his seed; God can out of stones raise up children for him, and make the blood of the martyrs the seed of the church, whose lands, we are sure, shall never be lost for want of heirs. This son, by a prophetic spirit, they called *Seth* (that is, *set, settled,* or *placed),* because, in his seed, mankind should continue to the end of time, and from him the Messiah should descend. While Cain, the head of the apostasy, is made a wanderer, Seth, from whom the true church was to come, is one fixed. In Christ and his church is the only true settlement. 2. They saw their seed's seed, *v.* 26. *To Seth was born a son called Enos,* that general name for all men, which bespeaks the weakness, frailty, and misery, of man's state. The best men are most sensible of these, both in themselves and their children. We are never so settled but we must remind ourselves that we are frail.

II. God gave them to see the reviving of religion in their family: *Then began men to call upon the name of the Lord, v.* 26. It is small comfort to a good man to see his children's children, if he do not, withal, see peace upon Israel, and those that come of him

46

walking in the truth. Doubtless God's name was called upon before, but now, 1. The worshippers of God began to stir up themselves to do more in religion than they had done; perhaps not more than had been done at first, but more than had been done of late, since the defection of Cain. Now men began to worship God, not only in their closets and families, but in public and solemn assemblies. Or now there was so great a reformation in religion that it was, as it were, a new beginning of it. *Then* may refer, not to the birth of Enos, but to the whole foregoing story: *then,* when men saw in Cain and Lamech the sad effects of sin by the workings of natural conscience,—when they saw God's judgments upon sin and sinners,—*then* they were so much the more lively and resolute in religion. The worse others are the better we should be, and the more zealous. 2. The worshippers of God began to distinguish themselves. The margin reads it, *Then began men to be called by the name of the Lord,* or to call themselves by it. Now that Cain and those that had deserted religion had built a city, and begun to declare for impiety and irreligion, and called themselves the *sons of men,* those that adhered to God began to declare for him and his worship, and called themselves the *sons of God.* Now began the distinction between professors and profane, which has been kept up ever since, and will be while the world stands.

CHAP. V.

This chapter is the only authentic history extant of the first age of the world from the creation to the flood, containing (according to the verity of the Hebrew text) 1656 years, as may easily be computed by the ages of the patriarchs, before they begat that son through whom the line went down to Noah. This is none of those which the apostle calls "endless genealogies" (1 Tim. i. 4), for Christ, who was the end of the Old-Testament law, was also the end of the Old-Testament genealogies; towards him they looked, and in him they centred. The genealogy here recorded is inserted briefly in the pedigree of our Saviour (Luke iii. 36—38), and is of great use to show that Christ was the " seed of the woman" that was promised. We have here an account, I. Concerning Adam, ver. 1—5. II. Seth, ver. 6—8. III. Enos, ver. 9—11. IV. Cainan, ver. 12—14. V. Mahalaleel, ver. 15—17. VI. Jared, ver. 18—20. VII. Enoch, ver. 21—24. VIII. Methuselah, ver. 25—27. IX. Lamech and his son Noah, ver. 28—32. All scripture, being given by inspiration of God, is profitable, though not all alike profitable.

THIS *is* the book of the generations of Adam. In the day that God created man, in the likeness of God made he him; *2* Male and female created he them; and blessed them, and called their name Adam, in the day when they were created. *3* And Adam lived a hundred and thirty years, and begat *a son* in his own likeness after his image; and called his name Seth: *4* And the days of Adam after he had begotten Seth were eight hundred years: and he begat sons and daughters: *5* And all the days that Adam lived were nine hundred and thirty years: and he died.

The first words of the chapter are the title or argument of the whole chapter: it is *the book of the generations of Adam ;* it is the list or catalogue of the posterity of Adam, not of all, but only of the *holy seed who were the substance thereof* (Isa. vi. 13), and *of whom, as concerning the flesh, Christ came* (Rom. ix. 5), the names, ages, and deaths, of those that were the successors of the first Adam in the custody of the promise, and the ancestors of the second Adam. The genealogy begins with Adam himself. Here is,

I. His creation, *v.* 1, 2, where we have a brief rehearsal of what was before at large related concerning the creation of man. This is what we have need frequently to hear of and carefully to acquaint ourselves with. Observe here, 1. That *God created man.* Man is not his own maker, therefore he must not be his own master; but the Author of his being must be the director of his motions and the centre of them. 2. That there was a day in which God created man. He was not from eternity, but of yesterday; he was not the first-born, but the junior of the creation. 3. That God made him in his own likeness, righteous and holy, and therefore, undoubtedly, happy. Man's nature resembled the divine nature more than that of any of the creatures of this lower world. 4. That God created them male and female (*v.* 2), for their mutual comfort as well as for the preservation and increase of their kind. Adam and Eve were both made immediately by the hand of God, both made in God's likeness; and therefore between the sexes there is not that great distance and inequality which some imagine. 5. That God blessed them. It is usual for parents to bless their children; so God, the common Father, blessed his. But earthly parents can only beg a blessing; it is God's prerogative to command it. It refers chiefly to the blessing of increase, not excluding other blessings. 6. That he *called their name Adam. Adam* signifies *earth, red earth.* Now, (1.) God gave him this name. Adam had himself named the rest of the creatures, but he must not choose his own name, lest he should assume some glorious pompous title. But God gave him a name which would be a continual memorandum to him of the meanness of his original, and oblige him to *look unto the rock whence he was hewn and the hole of the pit whence he was digged,* Isa. li. 1. Those have little reason to be proud who are so near akin to dust. (2.) He gave this name both to the man and to the woman. Being at first one by nature, and afterwards one by marriage, it was fit they should both have the same name, in token of their union. The woman is *of the earth earthy* as well as the man.

II. The birth of his son *Seth, v.* 3. He was born in the hundred and thirtieth year of Adam's life; and probably the murder of Abel was not long before. Many other sons and daughters were born to Adam, besides Cain and Abel, before this; but no notice is taken of them, because an honourable mention must be made of his name only in whose loins Christ and the church were. But that which is most observable here concerning Seth is that Adam begat him *in his own likeness, after his image.* Adam was made in the image of God; but, when he was fallen and corrupt, he begat a son in his own image, sinful and defiled, frail, mortal, and miserable, like himself; not only a *man* like himself, consisting of body and soul, but a *sinner* like himself, guilty and obnoxious, degenerate and corrupt. Even the man after God's own heart owns himself *conceived and born in sin,* Ps. li. 5. This was Adam's own likeness, the reverse of that divine likeness in which Adam was made; but, having lost it himself, he could not convey it to his seed. Note, Grace does not run in the blood, but corruption does. A sinner begets a sinner, but a saint does not beget a saint.

III. His age and death. He lived, in all, nine hundred and thirty years, and then he died, according to the sentence passed upon him, *To dust thou shalt return.* Though he did not die in the day he ate forbidden fruit, yet in that very day he became mortal. Then he began to die; his whole life afterwards was but a reprieve, a forfeited condemned life ; nay, it was a wasting dying life: he was not only like a criminal sentenced, but as one already crucified, that dies slowly and by degrees.

6 And Seth lived a hundred and five years, and begat Enos : 7 And Seth lived after he begat Enos eight hundred and seven years, and begat sons and daughters : 8 And all the days of Seth were nine hundred and twelve years : and he died. 9 And Enos lived ninety years, and begat Cainan : 10 And Enos lived after he begat Cainan eight hundred and fifteen years, and begat sons and daughters : 11 And all the days of Enos were nine hundred and five years : and he died. 12 And Cainan lived seventy years, and begat Mahalaleel : 13 And Cainan lived after he begat Mahalaleel eight hundred and forty years, and begat sons and daughters. 14 And all the days of Cainan were nine hundred and ten years : and he died. 15 And Mahalaleel lived sixty and five years, and begat Jared : 16 And Mahalaleel lived after he begat Jared eight hundred and thirty years, and begat sons and daughters : 17 And all the days of Mahalaleel were eight hundred

ninety and five years : and he died.
18 And Jared lived a hundred
sixty and two years, and he begat
Enoch : 19 And Jared lived after
he begat Enoch eight hundred years,
and begat sons and daughters : 20
And all the days of Jared were nine
hundred sixty and two years : and
he died.

We have here all that the Holy Ghost
thought fit to leave upon record concerning
five of the patriarchs before the flood, Seth,
Enos, Cainan, Mahalaleel, and Jared. There
is nothing observable concerning any of these
particularly, though we have reason to think
they were men of eminence, both for prudence
and piety, in their day : but in general,

I. Observe how largely and expressly their
generations are recorded. This matter, one
would think, might have been delivered in
fewer words; but it is certain that there is
not one idle word in God's books, whatever
there is in men's. It is thus plainly set down,
1. To make it easy and intelligible to the
meanest capacity. When we are informed
how old they were when they begat such a
son, and how many years they lived afterwards, a very little skill in arithmetic will
enable a man to tell how long they lived in
all; yet the Holy Ghost sets down the sum
total, for the sake of those that have not even
so much skill as this. 2. To show the pleasure God takes in the names of his people.
We found Cain's generation numbered in
haste (*ch.* iv. 18), but this account of the holy
seed is enlarged upon, and given in words at
length, and not in figures; we are told how
long those lived that lived in God's fear, and
when those died that died in his favour; but
as for others it is no matter. *The memory of
the just is blessed, but the name of the wicked
shall rot.*

II. Their life is reckoned by days (*v.* 8):
All the days of Seth, and so of the rest, which
intimates the shortness of the life of man
when it is at the longest, and the quick revolution of our times on earth. If they
reckoned by days, surely we must reckon by
hours, or rather make that our frequent
prayer (Ps. xc.12), *Teach us to number our days.*

III. Concerning each of them, except
Enoch, it is said, *and he died.* It is implied
in the numbering of the years of their life
that their life, when those years were numbered and finished, came to an end; and yet
it is still repeated, *and he died,* to show that
death passed upon all men without exception,
and that it is good for us particularly to observe and improve the deaths of others for
our own edification. Such a one was a strong
healthful man, but he died; such a one was
a great and rich man, but he died; such a
one was a wise politic man, but he died; such
a one was a very good man, perhaps a very
useful man, but he died, &c.

IV. That which is especially observable is
that they all lived very long; not one of them
died till he had seen the revolution of almost
eight hundred years, and some of them lived
much longer, a great while for an immortal
soul to be imprisoned in a house of clay.
The present life surely was not to them such
a burden as commonly it is now, else they
would have been weary of it; nor was the
future life so clearly revealed then as it is
now under the gospel, else they would have
been impatient to remove to it : long life to
the pious patriarchs was a blessing and made
them blessings. 1. Some natural causes may
be assigned for their long life in those first
ages of the world. It is very probable that
the earth was more fruitful, that the productions of it were more strengthening, that the
air was more healthful, and that the influences
of the heavenly bodies were more benign,
before the flood, than afterwards. Though
man was driven out of paradise, yet the earth
itself was then paradisiacal—a garden in
comparison with its present wilderness-state .
and some think that their great knowledge
of the creatures, and of their usefulness both
for food and medicine, together with their
sobriety and temperance, contributed much
to it; yet we do not find that those who were
intemperate, as many were (Luke xvii. 27),
were as short-lived as intemperate men generally are now. 2. It must chiefly be resolved
into the power and providence of God. He
prolonged their lives, both for the more
speedy replenishing of the earth and for the
more effectual preservation of the knowledge
of God and religion, then, when there was
no written word, but tradition was the channel of its conveyance. All the patriarchs
here, except Noah, were born before Adam
died; so that from him they might receive a
full and satisfactory account of the creation,
paradise, the fall, the promise, and those divine precepts which concerned religious worship and a religious life : and, if any mistake
arose, they might have recourse to him while
he lived, as to an oracle, for the rectifying of
it, and after his death to Methuselah, and
others, that had conversed with him : so great
was the care of Almighty God to preserve in
his church the knowledge of his will and the
purity of his worship.

21 And Enoch lived sixty and five
years, and begat Methuselah : 22
And Enoch walked with God after
he begat Methuselah three hundred
years, and begat sons and daughters :
23 And all the days of Enoch were
three hundred sixty and five years :
24 And Enoch walked with God :
and he *was* not ; for God took him.

The accounts here run on for several generations without any thing remarkable, or any
variation but of the names and numbers ; but
at length there comes in one that must not

be passed over so, of whom special notice must be taken, and that is *Enoch*, the seventh from Adam: the rest, we may suppose, did virtuously, but he excelled them all, and was the brightest star of the patriarchal age. It is but little that is recorded concerning him; but this little is enough to make his name great, greater than the name of the other Enoch, who had a city called by his name. Here are two things concerning him:—

I. His gracious conversation in this world, which is twice spoken of: *Enoch walked with God after he begat Methuselah* (v. 22), and again, *Enoch walked with God, v.* 24. Observe,

1. The nature of his religion and the scope and tenour of his conversation: he *walked with God*, which denotes, (1.) True religion; what is godliness, but walking with God? The ungodly and profane are without God in the world, they walk contrary to him: but the godly walk with God, which presupposes reconciliation to God, for two cannot *walk together except they be agreed* (Amos iii. 3), and includes all the parts and instances of a godly, righteous, and sober life. To walk with God is to set God always before us, and to act as those that are always under his eye. It is to live a life of communion with God both in ordinances and providences. It is to make God's word our rule and his glory our end in all our actions. It is to make it our constant care and endeavour in every thing to please God, and in nothing to offend him. It is to comply with his will, to concur with his designs, and to be workers together with him. It is to be *followers of him as dear children*. (2.) Eminent religion. He was entirely dead to this world, and did not only walk after God, as all good men do, but he walked with God, as if he were in heaven already. He lived above the rate, not only of other men, but of other saints: not only good in bad times, but the best in good times. (3.) Activity in promoting religion among others. Executing the priest's office is called *walking before God*, 1 Sam. ii. 30, 35, and see Zech. iii. 7. Enoch, it should seem, was a priest of the most high God, and like Noah, who is likewise said to walk with God, he was a preacher of righteousness, and prophesied of Christ's second coming. Jude 14, *Behold, the Lord cometh with his holy myriads.* Now the Holy Spirit, instead of saying, Enoch *lived*, says, Enoch *walked with God;* for it is the life of a good man to walk with God. This was, [1.] The business of Enoch's life, his constant care and work; while others lived to themselves and the world, he lived to God. [2.] It was the joy and support of his life. Communion with God was to him better than life itself. *To me to live is Christ*, Phil. i. 21.

2. The date of his religion. It is said (v. 21), *he lived sixty-five years, and begat Methuselah;* but (v. 22) *he walked with God after he begat Methuselah*, which intimates that he did not begin to be eminent for piety

till about that time; at first he walked but as other men. Great saints arrive at their eminence by degrees.

3. The continuance of his religion: he walked with God *three hundred years*, as long as he continued in this world. The hypocrite will not pray always; but the real saint that acts from a principle, and makes religion his choice, will persevere to the end, and walk with God while he lives, as one that hopes to live for ever with him, Ps. civ. 33.

II. His glorious removal to a better world. As he did not live like the rest, so he did not die like the rest (v. 24): *He was not, for God took him;* that is, as it is explained (Heb. xi. 5), *He was translated that he should not see death, and was not found, because God had translated him.* Observe,

1. When he was thus translated. (1.) What time of his life. It was when he had lived but three hundred and sixty-five years (a year of years), which, as men's ages went then, was in the midst of his days; for there was none of the patriarchs before the flood that did not more than double that age. But why did God take him so soon? Surely, because the world, which had now grown corrupt, was not worthy of him, or because he was so much above the world, and so weary of it, as to desire a speedy removal out of it, or because his work was done, and done the sooner for his minding it so closely. Note, God often takes those soonest whom he loves best, and the time they lose on earth is gained in heaven, to their unspeakable advantage. (2.) What time of the world. It was when all the patriarchs mentioned in this chapter were living, except Adam, who died fifty-seven years before, and Noah, who was born sixty-nine years after; those two had sensible confirmations to their faith other ways, but to all the rest, who were or might have been witnesses of Enoch's translation, it was a sensible encouragement to their faith and hope concerning a future state.

2. How his removal is expressed: *He was not, for God took him.* (1.) He was not any longer in this world; it was not the period of his being, but of his being here: he was *not found*, so the apostle explains it from the LXX.; not found by his friends, who sought him as the sons of the prophets sought Elijah (2 Kings ii. 17); not found by his enemies, who, some think, were in quest of him, to put him to death in their rage against him for his eminent piety. It appears by his prophecy that there were then many ungodly sinners, who spoke hard speeches, and probably did hard things too, against God's people (Jude 15), but God hid Enoch from them, not under heaven, but in heaven. (2.) God took him body and soul to himself in the heavenly paradise, by the ministry of angels, as afterwards he took Elijah. He was changed, as those saints will be that shall be found alive at Christ's second coming. Whenever a good man dies God takes him,

49

fetches him hence, and receives him to himself. The apostle adds concerning Enoch that, *before his translation, he had this testimony, that he pleased God,* and this was the good report he obtained. Note, [1.] Walking with God pleases God. [2.] We cannot walk with God so as to please him, but by faith. [3.] God himself will put an honour upon those that by faith walk with him so as to please him. He will own them now, and witness for them before angels and men at the great day. Those that have not this testimony before the translation, yet shall have it afterwards. [4.] Those whose conversation in the world is truly holy shall find their removal out of it truly happy. Enoch's translation was not only an evidence to faith of the reality of a future state, and of the possibility of the body's existing in glory in that state; but it was an encouragement to the hope of all that walk with God that they shall be for ever with him: signal piety shall be crowned with signal honours.

25 And Methuselah lived a hundred eighty and seven years, and begat Lamech : 26 And Methuselah lived after he begat Lamech seven hundred eighty and two years, and begat sons and daughters : 27 And all the days of Methuselah were nine hundred sixty and nine years : and he died.

Concerning Methuselah observe, 1. The signification of his name, which some think was prophetical, his father Enoch being a prophet. *Methuselah* signifies, *he dies,* or, *there is a dart,* or, *a sending forth,* namely, of the deluge, which came the very year that Methuselah died. If indeed his name was so intended and so explained, it was fair warning to a careless world, a long time before the judgment came. However, this is observable, that the longest liver that ever was carried death in his name, that he might be reminded of its coming surely, though it came slowly. 2. His age : he lived nine hundred and sixty-nine years, the longest we read of that ever any man lived on earth ; and yet he died. The longest liver must die at last. Neither youth nor age will discharge from that war, for that is the end of all men : none can challenge life by long prescription, nor make that a plea against the arrests of death. It is commonly supposed that Methuselah died a little before the flood ; the Jewish writers say, " seven days before," referring to *ch.* vii. 10, and that he was taken away from the evil to come, which goes upon this presumption, which is generally received, that all the patriarchs mentioned in this chapter were holy good men. I am loth to offer any surmise to the contrary ; and yet I see not that this can be any more inferred from their enrollment here among the ancestors of Christ than that all those kings of

Judah were so whose names are recorded in his genealogy, many of whom, we are sure, were much otherwise : and, if this be questioned, it may be suggested as probable that Methuselah was himself drowned with the rest of the world ; for it is certain that he died that year.

28 And Lamech lived a hundred eighty and two years, and begat a son : 29 And he called his name Noah, saying, This *same* shall comfort us concerning our work and toil of our hands, because of the ground which the LORD hath cursed. 30 And Lamech lived after he begat Noah five hundred ninety and five years, and begat sons and daughters : 31 And all the days of Lamech were seven hundred seventy and seven years : and he died. 32 And Noah was five hundred years old : and Noah begat Shem, Ham, and Japheth.

Here we have the first mention of Noah, of whom we shall read much in the following chapters. Observe,

I. His name, with the reason of it : *Noah* signifies *rest ;* his parents gave him that name, with a prospect of his being a more than ordinary blessing to his generation : *This same shall comfort us concerning our work and toil of our hands, because of the ground which the Lord hath cursed.* Herein,1. Lamech's complaint of the calamitous state of human life. By the entrance of sin, and the entail of the curse for sin, our condition has become very miserable : our whole life is spent in labour, and our time filled up with continual toil. God having cursed the ground, it is as much as some can do, with the utmost care and pains, to fetch a hard livelihood out of it. He speaks as one fatigued with the business of this life, and grudging that so many thoughts and precious minutes, which otherwise might have been much better employed, are unavoidably spent for the support of the body. 2. His comfortable hopes of some relief by the birth of this son : *This same shall comfort us,* which denotes not only the desire and expectation which parents generally have concerning their children (that, when they grow up, they will be comforts to them and helpers in their business, though they often prove otherwise), but an apprehension and prospect of something more. Very probably there were some prophecies that went before of him, as a person that should be wonderfully serviceable to his generation, which they so understood as to conclude that he was the promised seed, the Messiah that should come ; and then it intimates that a covenant-interest in Christ as ours, and the believing expectation of his coming, furnish us with the best and surest comforts, both in reference to the wrath and curse of God which we have deserved and to the toils and troubles of this present time of which we are often complaining. "Is Christ ours? Is heaven ours? *This same shall comfort us.*"

II. His children, Shem, Ham, and Japheth. These Noah begat (the eldest of these) when he was 500 years old. It should seem that Japheth was the eldest (*ch.* x. 21), but Shem is put first because on him the covenant was entailed, as appears by *ch.* ix. 26, where God is called the *Lord God of Shem.* To him, it is probable, the birth-right was given, and from him, it is certain, both Christ the head, and the church the body, were to descend. Therefore he is called *Shem*, which signifies a *name*, because in his posterity the name of God should always remain, till he should come out of his loins whose name is above every name; so that in putting Shem first Christ was, in effect, put first, who in all things must have the pre-eminence.

CHAP. VI.

The most remarkable thing we have upon record concerning the old world is the destruction of it by the universal deluge, the account of which commences in this chapter, wherein we have, I. The abounding iniquity of that wicked world, ver. 1—5, and ver. 11, 12. II. The righteous God's just resentment of that abounding iniquity, and his holy resolution to punish it, ver. 6, 7. III. The special favour of God to his servant Noah. 1. In the character given of him, ver. 8 —10. 2. In the communication of God's purpose to him, ver. 13, 17. 3. In the directions he gave him to make an ark for his own safety, ver. 14–16. 4. In the employing of him for the preservation of the rest of the creatures, ver. 18—21. Lastly, Noah's obedience to the instructions given him, ver. 22. And this concerning the old world is written for our admonition, upon whom the ends of the new world have come.

AND it came to pass, when men began to multiply on the face of the earth, and daughters were born unto them, 2 That the sons of God saw the daughters of men that they *were* fair; and they took them wives of all which they chose.

For the glory of God's justice, and for warning to a wicked world, before the history of the ruin of the old world, we have a full account of its degeneracy, its apostasy from God and rebellion against him. The destroying of it was an act, not of absolute sovereignty, but of necessary justice, for the maintaining of the honour of God's government. Now here we have an account of two things which occasioned the wickedness of the old world:—1. The increase of mankind: *Men began to multiply upon the face of the earth.* This was the effect of the blessing (*ch.* i. 28), and yet man's corruption so abused and perverted this blessing that it was turned into a curse. Thus sin takes occasion by the mercies of God to be the more exceedingly sinful. Prov. xxix. 16, *When the wicked are multiplied, transgression increaseth.* The more sinners the more sin; and the multitude of offenders emboldens men. Infectious diseases are most destructive in populous cities; and sin is a spreading leprosy. Thus in the New-Testament church, *when the number of the disciples was m ltiplied, there arose a*

murmuring (Acts vi. 1), and we read of a nation that was multiplied, not to the increase of their joy, Isa. ix. 3. Numerous families need to be well-governed, lest they become wicked families. 2. Mixed marriages (*v.* 2): *The sons of God* (that is, the professors of religion, who were called by the name of the Lord, and called upon that name), *married the daughters of men*, that is, those that were profane, and strangers to God and godliness. The posterity of Seth did not keep by themselves, as they ought to have done, both for the preservation of their own purity and in detestation of the apostasy. They intermingled themselves with the excommunicated race of Cain: *They took them wives of all that they chose.* But what was amiss in these marriages? (1.) They chose only by the eye: *They saw that they were fair*, which was all they looked at. (2.) They followed the choice which their own corrupt affections made: they took *all that they chose*, without advice and consideration. But, (3.) That which proved of such bad consequence to them was that they *married strange wives, were unequally yoked with unbelievers*, 2 Cor. vi. 14. This was forbidden to Israel, Deut. vii. 3, 4. It was the unhappy occasion of Solomon's apostasy (1 Kings xi. 1—4), and was of bad consequence to the Jews after their return out of Babylon, Ezra ix. 1, 2. Note, Professors of religion, in marrying both themselves and their children, should make conscience of keeping within the bounds of profession. The bad will sooner debauch the good than the good reform the bad. Those that profess themselves the children of God must not marry without his consent, which they have not if they join in affinity with his enemies.

3 And the LORD said, My spirit shall not always strive with man, for that he also *is* flesh: yet his days shall be a hundred and twenty years.

This comes in here as a token of God's displeasure at those who married strange wives; he threatens to withdraw from them his Spirit, whom they had grieved by such marriages, contrary to their convictions: fleshly lusts are often punished with spiritual judgments, the sorest of all judgments. Or as another occasion of the great wickedness of the old world; the Spirit of the Lord, being provoked by their resistance of his motions, ceased to strive with them, and then all religion was soon lost among them. This he warns them of before, that they might not further vex his Holy Spirit, but by their prayers might stay him with them. Observe in this verse,

I. God's resolution not always to strive with man by his Spirit. The Spirit then strove by Noah's preaching (1 Pet. iii. 19, 20) and by inward checks, but it was in vain with the most of men; therefore, says God, *He shall not always strive.* Note, 1. The blessed Spirit strives with sinners, by the convictions and admonitions of conscience, to turn them from sin to God. 2. If the Spirit be resisted, quenched, and striven against, though he strive long, he will not strive always, Hos. iv. 17. 3. Those are ripening apace for ruin whom the Spirit of grace has left off striving with.

II. The reason of this resolution: *For that he also is flesh,* that is, incurably corrupt, and carnal, and sensual, so that it is labour lost to strive with him. Can the Ethiopian change his skin? *He also,* that is, All, one as well as another, they have all sunk into the mire of flesh. Note, 1. It is the corrupt nature, and the inclination of the soul towards the flesh, that oppose the Spirit's strivings and render them ineffectual. 2. When a sinner has long adhered to that interest, and sided with the flesh against the Spirit, the Spirit justly withdraws his agency, and strives no more. None lose the Spirit's strivings but those that have first forfeited them.

III. A reprieve granted, notwithstanding: *Yet his days shall be one hundred and twenty years;* so long I will defer the judgment they deserve, and give them space to prevent it by their repentance and reformation. Justice said, *Cut them down;* but mercy interceded, *Lord, let them alone this year also;* and so far mercy prevailed, that a reprieve was obtained for six-score years. Note, The time of God's patience and forbearance towards provoking sinners is sometimes long, but always limited: reprieves are not pardons; though God bear a great while, he will not bear always.

4 There were giants in the earth in those days; and also after that, when the sons of God came in unto the daughters of men, and they bare *children* to them, the same *became* mighty men which *were* of old, men of renown. 5 And GOD saw that the wickedness of man *was* great in the earth, and *that* every imagination of the thoughts of his heart *was* only evil continually.

We have here a further account of the corruption of the old world. When the *sons of God* had matched with the *daughters of men,* though it was very displeasing to God, yet he did not immediately cut them off, but waited to see what would be the issue of these marriages, and which side the children would take after; and it proved (as usually it does), that they took after the worst side. Here is,

I. The temptation they were under to oppress and do violence. They were *giants,* and they were *men of renown;* they became too hard for all about them, and carried all before them, 1. With their great bulk, as

the sons of Anak, Num. xiii. 33. 2. With their great name, as the king of Assyria, Isa. xxxvii. 11. These made them the *terror of the mighty in the land of the living;* and, thus armed, they daringly insulted the rights of all their neighbours and trampled upon all that is just and sacred. Note, Those that have so much power over others as to be able to oppress them have seldom so much power over themselves as not to oppress; great might is a very great snare to many. This degenerate race slighted the honour their ancestors had obtained by virtue and religion, and made themselves a great name by that which was the perpetual ruin of their good name.

II. The charge exhibited and proved against them, *v.* 5. The evidence produced was incontestable. God saw it, and that was instead of a thousand witnesses. God sees all the wickedness that is among the children of men; it cannot be concealed from him now, and, if it be not repented of, it shall not be concealed by him shortly. Now what did God take notice of? 1. He observed all the streams of sin that flowed along in men's lives, and the breadth and depth of those streams: He *saw that the wickedness of man was great in the earth.* Observe the connection of this with what goes before: the oppressors were *mighty men and men of renown;* and, *then, God saw that the wickedness of man was great.* Note, The wickedness of a people is great indeed when the most notorious sinners are men of renown among them. Things are bad when bad men are not only honoured notwithstanding their wickedness, but honoured for their wickedness, and the vilest men exalted. Wickedness is then great when great men are wicked. Their wickedness was great, that is, abundance of sin was committed in all places, by all sorts of people; and such sin as was in its own nature most gross, and heinous, and provoking; it was committed daringly, and with a defiance of heaven, nor was any care taken by those that had power in their hands to restrain and punish it. This God saw. Note, All the sins of sinners are known to God the Judge. Those that are most conversant in the world, though they see much wickedness in it, yet they see but little of that which is; but God sees all, and judges aright concerning it, how great it is, nor can he be deceived in his judgment. 2. He observed the fountain of sin that was in men's hearts. Any one might see that *the wickedness of man was great,* for they declared their sin as Sodom; but God's eye went further: He saw that every imagi-*nation of the thoughts of his heart was only evil continually*—a sad sight, and very offensive to God's holy eye! This was the bitter root, the corrupt spring: all the violence and oppression, all the luxury and wantonness, that were in the world, proceeded from the corruption of nature; lust conceived them,

52

Jam. i. 15. See Matt. xv. 19. (1.) The heart was naught; it was deceitful and desperately wicked. The principles were corrupt, and the habits and dispositions evil. (2.) The thoughts of the heart were so. Thought is sometimes taken for the settled judgment or opinion, and this was bribed, and biased, and misled; sometimes it signifies the workings of the fancy, and these were always either vain or vile, either weaving the spider's web or hatching the cockatrice's egg. (3.) The imagination of the thoughts of the heart was so, that is, their designs and devices were wicked. They did not do evil through mere carelessness, as those that walk at all adventures, not heeding what they do; but they did evil deliberately and designedly, contriving how to do mischief. It was bad indeed; for it was only evil, continually evil, and every imagination was so. There was no good to be found among them, no, not at any time: the stream of sin was full, and strong, and constant; and God saw it; see Ps. xiv. 1—3.

6 And it repented the LORD that he had made man on the earth, and it grieved him at his heart. 7 And the LORD said, I will destroy man whom I have created from the face of the earth; both man, and beast, and the creeping thing, and the fowls of the air; for it repenteth me that I have made them.

Here is, I. God's resentment of man's wickedness. He did not see it as an unconcerned spectator, but as one injured and affronted by it; he saw it as a tender father sees the folly and stubbornness of a rebellious and disobedient child, which not only angers him, but grieves him, and makes him wish he had been written childless. The expressions here used are very strange: *It repented the Lord that he had made man upon the earth*, that he had made a creature of such noble powers and faculties, and had put him on this earth, which he built and furnished on purpose to be a convenient, comfortable, habitation for him; *and it grieved him at his heart.* These are expressions after the manner of men, and must be understood so as not to reflect upon the honour of God's immutability or felicity. 1. This language does not imply any passion or uneasiness in God (nothing can create disturbance to the Eternal Mind), but it expresses his just and holy displeasure against sin and sinners, against sin as odious to his holiness and against sinners as obnoxious to his justice. He is pressed by the sins of his creatures (Amos ii. 13), wearied (Isa. xliii. 24), broken (Ezek. vi. 9), grieved (Ps. xcv. 10), and here *grieved to the heart*, as men are when they are wronged and abused by those they have been very kind to, and therefore repent of their kind-

ness, and wish they had never fostered that snake in their bosom which now hisses in their face and stings them to the heart. Does God thus hate sin? And shall not we hate it? Has our sin grieved him to the heart? And shall not we be grieved and pricked to the heart for it? O that this consideration may humble us and shame us, and that we may look on him whom we have thus grieved, and mourn! Zech. xii. 10. 2. It does not imply any change of God's mind; for *he is in one mind, and who can turn him?* ·With him *there is no variableness.* But it expresses a change of his way. When God had made man upright, *he rested and was refreshed* (Exod. xxxi. 17), and his way towards him was such as showed he was pleased with the work of his own hands; but, now that man had apostatized, he could not do otherwise than show himself displeased; so that the change was in man, not in God. God repented that he had made man; but we never find him repenting that he redeemed man (though that was a work of much greater expense), because special and effectual grace is given to secure the great ends of redemption; so that those *gifts and callings are without repentance,* Rom. xi. 29.

II. God's resolution to destroy man for his wickedness, v. 7. Observe, 1. When God repented that he had made man, he resolved to destroy man. Thus those that truly repent of sin will resolve, in the strength of God's grace, to mortify sin and to destroy it, and so to undo what they have done amiss. We do but mock God in saying that we are sorry for our sin, and that it grieves us to the heart, if we continue to indulge it. In vain do we ˉpretend a change of our mind if we do not evidence it by a change of our way. 2. He resolves to destroy man. The original word is very significant: *I will wipe off man from the earth* (so some), as dirt or filth is wiped off from a place which should be clean, and is thrown to the dunghill, the proper place for it. See 2 Kings xxi. 13. Those that are the spots of the places they live in are justly wiped away by the judgments of God. *I will blot out man from the earth* (so others), as those lines which displease the author are blotted out of a book, or as the name of a citizen is blotted out of the rolls of the freemen, when he is dead or disfranchised. 3. He speaks of man as his own creature even when he resolves upon his ruin: *Man whom I have created.* "Though I have created him, this shall not excuse him," Isa. xxvii. 11. *He that made him will not save him;* he that is our Creator, if he be not our ruler, will be our destroyer. Or, "Because I have created him, and he has been so undutiful and ungrateful to his Creator, therefore I will destroy him:" those forfeit their lives that do not answer the end of their living. 4. Even the brute-creatures were to be involved in this destruction—*Beasts, and creeping things, and the fowls of the air.* These were made for man, and therefore must be destroyed with man ; for it follows : *It repenteth me that I have made them ;* for the end of their creation also was frustrated. They were made that man might serve and honour God with them ; and therefore were destroyed because he had served his lusts with them, and made them subject to vanity. 5. God took up this resolution concerning man after his Spirit had been long striving with him in vain. None are ruined by the justice of God but those that hate to be reformed by the grace of God.

8 But Noah found grace in the eyes of the LORD. 9 These *are* the generations of Noah : Noah was a just man *and* perfect in his generations, *and* Noah walked with God. 10 And Noah begat three sons, Shem, Ham, and Japheth.

We have here Noah distinguished from the rest of the world, and a peculiar mark of honour put upon him. 1. When God was displeased with the rest of the world, he favoured Noah : *But Noah found grace in the eyes of the Lord, v.* 8. This vindicates God's justice in his displeasure against the world, and shows that he had strictly examined the character of every person in it before he pronounced it universally corrupt; for, there being one good man, he found him out, and smiled upon him. It also magnifies his grace towards Noah that he was made a vessel of God's mercy when all mankind besides had become the generation of his wrath : distinguishing favours bring under peculiarly strong obligations. Probably Noah did not find favour in the eyes of men ; they hated and persecuted him, because both by his life and preaching he *condemned the world.* But *he found grace in the eyes of the Lord,* and this was honour and comfort enough. God made more account of Noah than of all the world besides, and this made him greater and more truly honourable than all the giants that were in those days, who became mighty men and men of renown. Let this be the summit of our ambition, to *find grace in the eyes of the Lord ;* herein let us labour, that, present or absent, we may be accepted of him, 2 Cor. v. 9. Those are highly favoured whom God favours. 2. When the rest of the world was corrupt and wicked, Noah kept his integrity : *These are the generations of Noah* (this is the account we have to give of him), *Noah was a just man, v.* 9. This character of Noah comes in here either, (1.) As the reason of God's favour to him ; his singular piety qualified him for singular tokens of God's loving-kindness. Those that would find grace in the eyes of the Lord must be as Noah was and do as Noah did ; God loves those that love him : or, (2.)

As the effect of God's favour to him. It was God's good-will to him that produced this good work in him. He was a very good man, but he was no better than the grace of God made him, 1 Cor. xv. 10. Now observe his character. [1.] He *was a just man,* that is, justified before God by faith in the promised seed ; for he was an *heir of the righteousness which is by faith,* Heb. xi. 7. He was sanctified, and had right principles and dispositions implanted in him; and he was righteous in his conversation, one that made conscience of rendering to all their due, to God his due and to men theirs. Note, None but a downright honest man can find favour with God. That conversation which will be pleasing to God must be governed by *simplicity and godly sincerity,* not by *fleshly wisdom,* 2 Cor. i. 12. God has sometimes chosen the foolish things of the world, but he never chose the knavish things of it. [2.] He was *perfect,* not with a sinless perfection, but a perfection of sincerity ; and it is well for us that by virtue of the covenant of grace, upon the score of Christ's righteousness, sincerity is accepted as our gospel perfection. [3.] He *walked with God,* as Enoch had done before him. He was not only honest, but devout : he *walked,* that is, he acted with God, as one always under his eye. He lived a life of communion with God ; it was his constant care to conform himself to the will of God, to please him, and to approve himself to him. Note, God looks down upon those with an eye of favour who sincerely look up to him with an eye of faith. But, [4.] That which crowns his character is that thus he was, and thus he did, *in his generation,* in that corrupt degenerate age in which his lot was cast. It is easy to be religious when religion is in fashion ; but it is an evidence of strong faith and resolution to swim against a stream to heaven, and to appear for God when no one else appears for him : so Noah did, and it is upon record, to his immortal honour.

11 The earth also was corrupt before God, and the earth was filled with violence. 12 And God looked upon the earth, and, behold, it was corrupt; for all flesh had corrupted his way upon the earth.

The wickedness of that generation is here again spoken of, either as a foil to Noah's piety—he was just and perfect, when all the earth was corrupt ; or as a further justification of God's resolution to destroy the world, which he was now about to communicate to his servant Noah. 1. All kinds of sin was found among them, for it is said (*v.* 11) that the earth was, (1.) *Corrupt before God,* that is, in the matters of God's worship ; either they had other gods before him, or they worshipped him by images, or they were corrupt and wicked in despite and contempt of God, daring him and defying him to his face. (2.) *The earth was also filled with violence* and injustice towards men. There was no order nor regular government; no man was safe in the possession of that which he had the most clear and incontestable right to, no, not the most innocent life; there was nothing but murders, rapes, and rapine. Note, Wickedness, as it is the shame of human nature, so it is the ruin of human society. Take away conscience and the fear of God, and men become beasts and devils to one another, like the fishes of the sea, where the greater devour the less. Sin fills the earth with violence, and so turns the world into a wilderness, into a cock-pit. 2. The proof and evidence of it were undeniable; for *God looked upon the earth*, and was himself an eye-witness of the corruption that was in it, of which before, *v.* 5. The righteous Judge in all his judgments proceeds upon the infallible certainty of his own omniscience, Ps. xxxiii. 13. 3. That which most aggravated the matter was the universal spreading of the contagion: *All flesh had corrupted his way.* It was not some particular nations or cities that were thus wicked, but the whole world of mankind were so; there was none that did good, no, not one besides Noah. Note, When wickedness has become general and universal ruin is not far off; while there is a remnant of praying people in a nation, to empty the measure as it fills, judgments may be kept off a great while; but when all hands are at work to pull down the fences by sin, and none stand in the gap to make up the breach, what can be expected but an inundation of wrath?

13 And God said unto Noah, The end of all flesh is come before me; for the earth is filled with violence through them; and, behold, I will destroy them with the earth. 14 Make thee an ark of gopher wood; rooms shalt thou make in the ark, and shalt pitch it within and without with pitch. 15 And this *is the fashion* which thou shalt make it *of:* The length of the ark *shall be* three hundred cubits, the breadth of it fifty cubits, and the height of it thirty cubits. 16 A window shalt thou make to the ark, and in a cubit shalt thou finish it above; and the door of the ark shalt thou set in the side thereof; *with* lower, second, and third *stories* shalt thou make it. 17 And, behold, I, even I, do bring a flood of waters upon the earth, to destroy all flesh, wherein *is* the breath of life, from under heaven; *and* every

thing that *is* in the earth shall die. 18 But with thee will I establish my covenant; and thou shalt come into the ark, thou, and thy sons, and thy wife, and thy sons' wives with thee. 19 And of every living thing of all flesh, two of every *sort* shalt thou bring into the ark, to keep *them* alive with thee; they shall be male and female. 20 Of fowls after their kind, and of cattle after their kind, of every creeping thing of the earth after his kind, two of every *sort* shall come unto thee, to keep *them* alive. 21 And take thou unto thee of all food that is eaten, and thou shalt gather *it* to thee; and it shall be for food for thee, and for them.

Here it appears indeed that Noah *found grace in the eyes of the Lord.* God's favour to him was plainly intimated in what he said of him, *v.* 8—10, where his name is mentioned five times in five lines, when once might have served to make the sense clear, as if the Holy Ghost took a pleasure in perpetuating his memory; but it appears much more in what he says to him in these verses — the informations and instructions here given him.

I. God here makes Noah the *man of his counsel*, communicating to him his purpose to destroy this wicked world by water. As, afterwards, he told Abraham his resolution concerning Sodom (*ch.* xviii. 17, *Shall I hide from Abraham?*) so here "Shall I hide from Noah the thing that I do, seeing that he shall *become a great nation?*" Note, *The secret of the Lord is with those that fear him* (Ps. xxv. 14); it was with *his servants the prophets* (Amos iii. 7), by a spirit of revelation, informing them particularly of his purposes; it is with all believers by a spirit of wisdom and faith, enabling them to understand and apply the general declarations of the written word, and the warnings there given. Now,

1. God told Noah, in general, that he would destroy the world (*v.* 13): *The end of all flesh has come before me; I will destroy them;* that is, the ruin of this wicked world is decreed and determined; *it has come*, that is, it will come surely, and come quickly. Noah, it is likely, in preaching to his neighbours, had warned them, in general, of the wrath of God that they would bring upon themselves by their wickedness, and now God seconds his endeavours by a particular denunciation of wrath, that Noah might try whether this would work upon them. Hence observe, (1.) That God *confirmeth the words of his messengers*, Isa. xliv. 26. (2.) That *to him that has*, and uses what he has for the good of others, *more shall be given*, more full instructions.

2. He told him, particularly, that he would destroy the world by a flood of waters : *And behold, I, even I, do bring a flood of waters upon the earth, v.* 17. God could have destroyed all mankind by the sword of an angel, a flaming sword turning every way, as he destroyed all the first-born of the Egyptians and the camp of the Assyrians ; and then there needed no more than to set a mark upon Noah and his family for their preservation. But God chose to do it by a *flood of waters,* which should drown the world. The reasons, we may be sure, were wise and just, though to us unknown. God has many arrows in his quiver, and he may use which he please : as he chooses the rod with which he will correct his children, so he chooses the sword with which he will cut off his enemies. Observe the manner of expression: *"I, even I, do bring a flood ;* I that am infinite in power, and therefore *can* do it, infinite in justice, and therefore *will* do it." (1.) It intimates the certainty of the judgment : *I, even I,* will do it. That cannot but be done effectually which God himself undertakes the doing of. See Job xi. 10. (2.) It intimates the tendency of it to God's glory and the honour of his justice. Thus he will be magnified and exalted in the earth, and all the world shall be made to know that he is the God *to whom vengeance belongs :* methinks the expression here is somewhat like that, Isa. i. 24, *Ah, I will ease me of mine adversaries.*

II. God here makes Noah the *man of his covenant,* another Hebrew periphrasis of a friend (*v.* 18) : *But with thee will I establish my covenant.* 1. The covenant of providence, that the course of nature shall be continued to the end of time, notwithstanding the interruption which the flood would give to it. This promise was immediately made to Noah and his sons, *ch.* ix. 8, &c. They were as trustees for all this part of the creation, and a great honour was thereby put upon him and his. 2. The covenant of grace, that God would be to him a God and that out of his seed God would take to himself a people. Note, (1.) When God makes a covenant, he establishes it, he makes it sure, he makes it good ; his are everlasting covenants. (2.) The covenant of grace has in it the recompence of singular services, and the fountain and foundation of all distinguishing favours ; we need desire no more, either to make up our losses for God or to make up a happiness for us in God, than to have his covenant established with us.

III. God here makes Noah a monument of sparing mercy, by putting him in a way to secure himself in the approaching deluge, that he might not perish with the rest of the world : *I will destroy them,* says God, *with the earth, v.* 13. " But *make thee an ark ;* I will take care to preserve thee alive." Note, Singular piety shall be recompensed with distinguishing salvations, which are in

a special manner obliging. This will add much to the honour and happiness of glorified saints, that they shall be saved when the greatest part of the world is left to perish. Now,

1. God directs Noah to *make an ark, v.* 14—16. This ark was like the hulk of a ship, fitted not to sail upon the waters (there was no occasion for that, when there should be no shore to sail to), but to float upon the waters, waiting for their fall. God could have secured Noah by the ministration of angels, without putting him to any care, or pains, or trouble, himself ; but he chose to employ him in making that which was to be the means of his preservation, both for the trial of his faith and obedience and to teach us that none shall be saved by Christ but those only that *work out their salvation.* We cannot do it without God, and he will not without us. Both the providence of God, and the grace of God, own and crown the endeavours of the obedient and diligent. God gave him very particular instructions concerning this building, which could not but be admirably well fitted for the purpose when Infinite Wisdom itself was the architect. (1.) It must be made of *gopher-wood.* Noah, doubtless, knew what sort of wood that was, though we now do not, whether cedar, or cypress, or what other. (2.) He must make it three stories high within. (3.) He must divide it into cabins, with partitions, places fitted for the several sorts of creatures, so as to lose no room. (4.) Exact dimensions were given him, that he might make it proportionable, and might have room enough in it to answer the intention and no more. Note, Those that work for God must take their measures from him and carefully observe them. Note, further, It is fit that he who appoints us our habitation should fix the bounds and limits of it. (5.) He must *pitch it within and without*—without, to shed off the rain, and to prevent the water from soaking in—within, to take away the bad smell of the beasts when kept close. Observe, God does not bid him paint it, but pitch it. If God gives us habitations that are safe, and warm, and wholesome, we are bound to be thankful, though they are not magnificent or nice. (6.) He must make a little window towards the top, to let in light, and (some think) that through that window he might behold the desolations to be made in the earth. (7.) He must make a door in the side of it, by which to go in and out.

2. God promises Noah that he and his shall be preserved alive in the ark (*v.* 18) : *Thou shalt come into the ark.* Note, What we do in obedience to God, we ourselves are likely to have the comfort and benefit of. *If thou be wise, thou shalt be wise for thyself.* Nor was he himself only saved in the ark, but *his wife, and his sons, and his sons' wives.* Observe, (1.) The care of good parents ; they are solicitous not only for their own salva-

tion, but for the salvation of their families, and especially their children. (2.) The happiness of those children that have godly parents. Their parents' piety often procures them temporal salvation, as here; and it furthers them in the way to eternal salvation, if they improve the benefit of it.

IV. God here makes Noah a great blessing to the world, and herein makes him an eminent type of the Messiah, though not the Messiah himself, as his parents expected, *ch.* v. 29. 1. God made him a preacher to the men of that generation. As a watchman, he received the word from God's mouth, that he might give them warning, Ezek. iii. 17. Thus, *while the long-suffering of God waited,* by his Spirit in Noah, he *preached to* the old world, who, when Peter wrote, were *spirits in prison* (1 Pet. iii. 18—20), and herein he was a type of Christ, who, in a land and age wherein all flesh had corrupted their way, went about preaching repentance and warning men of a deluge of wrath coming. 2. God made him a saviour to the inferior creatures, to keep the several kinds of them from perishing and being lost in the deluge, *v.* 19—21. This was a great honour put upon him, that not only in him the race of mankind should be kept up, and that from him should proceed a new world, the church, the soul of the world, and Messiah, the head of that church, but that he should be instrumental to preserve the inferior creatures, and so mankind should in him acquire a new title to them and their service. (1.) He was to provide shelter for them, that they might not be drowned. *Two of every sort, male and female,* he must take with him into the ark; and lest he should make any difficulty of gathering them together, and getting them in, God promises (*v.* 20) that they shall of their own accord come to him. He that makes the ox to know his owner and his crib then made him know his preserver and his ark. (2.) He was to provide sustenance for them, that they might not be starved, *v.* 21. He must victual his ship according to the number of his crew, that great family which he had now the charge of, and according to the time appointed for his confinement. Herein also he was a type of Christ, to whom it is owing that the world stands, by whom all things consist, and who preserves mankind from being totally cut off and ruined by sin; in him the holy seed is saved alive, and the creation rescued from the vanity under which it groans. Noah saved those whom he was to rule, so does Christ, Heb. v. 9.

22 Thus did Noah; according to all that God commanded him, so did he.

Noah's care and diligence in building the ark may be considered, 1. As an effect of his faith in the word of God. God had told him he would shortly drown the world; he believed it, feared the threatened deluge, and,

in that fear, prepared the ark. Note, We ought to mix faith with the revelation God has made of his wrath against all ungodliness and unrighteousness of men; the threatenings of the word are not false alarms. Much might have been objected against the credibility of this warning given to Noah. "Who could believe that the wise God, who made the world, should so soon unmake it again, that he who had drawn the waters off the dry land (*ch.* i. 9, 10) should cause them to cover it again? How would this be reconciled with the mercy of God, which is over all his works, especially that the innocent creatures should die for man's sin? Whence could water be had sufficient to deluge the world? And, if it must be so, why should notice be given of it to Noah only?" But Noah's faith triumphed over all these corrupt reasonings. 2. As an act of obedience to the command of God. Had he consulted with flesh and blood, many objections would have been raised against it. To rear a building, such a one as he never saw, so large, and of such exact dimensions, would put him upon a great deal of care, and labour, and expense. It would be a work of time; the vision was for a great while to come. His neighbours would ridicule him for his credulity, and he would be the song of the drunkards; his building would be called *Noah's folly.* If the worst came to the worst, as we say, each would fare as well as his neighbours. But these, and a thousand such objections, Noah by faith got over. His obedience was ready and resolute: *Thus did Noah,* willingly and cheerfully, without murmuring and disputing. God says, *Do this,* and he does it. It was also punctual and persevering: he did all exactly according to the instructions given him, and, having begun to build, did not leave off till he had finished it; so did he, and so must we do. 3. As an instance of wisdom for himself, thus to provide for his own safety. He feared the deluge, and therefore prepared the ark. Note, When God gives warning of approaching judgments, it is our wisdom and duty to provide accordingly. See Exod. ix. 20, 21; Ezek. iii. 18. We must prepare to meet the Lord in his judgments on earth, flee to his name as a strong tower (Prov. xviii. 10), enter into our chambers (Isa. xxvi. 20, 21), especially prepare to meet him at death and in the judgment of the great day, build upon Christ the Rock (Matt. vii. 24), go into Christ the Ark. 4. As intended for warning to a careless world; and it was fair warning of the deluge coming. Every blow of his axes and hammers was a call to repentance, a call to them to prepare arks too. But, since by it he could not convince the world, by it he condemned the world, Heb. xi. 7.

CHAP. VII.

In this chapter we have the performance of what was foretold in the foregoing chapter, both concerning the destruction of the old world and the salvation of Noah; for we may be sure that no word of God shall fall to the ground. There we left Noah busy about his ark, and full of care to get it finished in time, while the rest of his neighbours were laughing at him for his pains. Now here we see what was the end thereof, the end of his care and of their carelessness. And this famous period of the old world gives us some idea of the state of things when the world that now is shall be destroyed by fire, as that was by water. See 2 Pet. iii. 6, 7. We have, in this chapter, I. God's gracious call to Noah to come into the ark (ver. 1), and to bring the creatures that were to be preserved alive along with him (ver. 2, 3), in consideration of the deluge at hand, ver. 4. II. Noah's obedience to this heavenly vision, ver. 5. When he was six hundred years old, he came with his family into the ark (ver. 6, 7), and brought the creatures along with him (ver. 8, 9), an account of which is repeated (ver. 13—16), to which is added God's tender care to shut him in. III. The coming of the threatened deluge (ver. 10); the causes of it (ver. 11, 12); the prevalency of it, ver. 17—20. IV. The dreadful desolations that were made by it in the death of every living creature upon earth, except those that were in the ark, ver. 21—23. V. The continuance of it in full sea, before it began to ebb, one hundred and fifty days, ver. 24.

AND the LORD said unto Noah, Come thou and all thy house into the ark; for thee have I seen righteous before me in this generation. 2 Of every clean beast thou shalt take to thee by sevens, the male and his female: and of beasts that *are* not clean by two, the male and his female. 3 Of fowls also of the air by sevens, the male and the female; to keep seed alive upon the face of all the earth. 4 For yet seven days, and I will cause it to rain upon the earth forty days and forty nights; and every living substance that I have made will I destroy from off the face of the earth.

Here is, I. A gracious invitation of Noah and his family into a place of safety, now that the flood of waters was coming, v. 1.

1. The call itself is very kind, like that of a tender father to his children, to come in doors, when he sees night or a storm coming: *Come thou, and all thy house,* that small family that thou hast, *into the ark.* Observe, (1.) Noah did not go into the ark till God bade him; though he knew it was designed for his place of refuge, yet he waited for a renewed command, and had it. It is very comfortable to follow the calls of Providence, and to see God going before us in every step we take. (2.) God does not bid him *go* into the ark, but *come* into it, implying that God would go with him, would lead him into it, accompany him in it, and in due time bring him safely out of it. Note, Wherever we are, it is very desirable to have the presence of God with us, for this is all in all to the comfort of every condition. It was this that made Noah's ark, which was a prison, to be to him not only a refuge, but a palace. (3.) Noah had taken a great deal of pains to build the ark, and now he was himself preserved alive in it. Note, What we do in obedience to the command of God, and in faith, we ourselves shall certainly have the comfort of, first or last. (4.) Not he only, but his house also, his wife and children, are called with him into the ark. Note, It is good to belong to

the family of a godly man; it is safe and comfortable to dwell under such a shadow. One of Noah's sons was Ham, who proved afterwards a bad man, yet he was saved in the ark, which intimates, [1.] That wicked children often fare the better for the sake of their godly parents. [2.] That there is a mixture of bad with good in the best societies on earth, and we are not to think it strange. In Noah's family there was a Ham, and in Christ's family there was a Judas. There is no perfect purity on this side heaven. (5.) This call to Noah was a type of the call which the gospel gives to poor sinners. Christ is an ark already prepared, in whom alone we can be safe when death and judgment come. Now the burden of the song is, "Come, come;" the word says, "Come;" ministers say, "Come;" the Spirit says, "Come, come into the ark."

2. The reason for this invitation is a very honourable testimony to Noah's integrity: *For thee have I seen righteous before me in this generation.* Observe, (1.) Those are righteous indeed that are righteous before God, that have not only the form of godliness by which they appear righteous before men, who may easily be imposed upon, but the power of it by which they approve themselves to God, who searches the heart, and cannot be deceived in men's characters. (2.) God takes notice of and is pleased with those that are righteous before him: *Thee have I seen.* In a world of wicked people God could see one righteous Noah; that single grain of wheat could not be lost, no, not in so great a heap of chaff. *The Lord knows those that are his.* (3.) God, that is a witness to, will shortly be a witness for, his people's integrity; he that sees it will proclaim it before angels and men, to their immortal honour. Those that obtain mercy to be righteous shall obtain witness that they are righteous. (4.) God is, in a special manner, pleased with those that are good in bad times and places. Noah was therefore illustriously righteous, because he was so in that wicked and adulterous generation. (5.) Those that keep themselves pure in times of common iniquity God will keep safe in times of common calamity; those that partake not with others in their sins shall not partake with them in their plagues; those that are better than others are, even in this life, safer than others, and it is better with them.

II. Here are necessary orders given concerning the brute-creatures that were to be preserved alive with Noah in the ark, v. 2, 3. They were not capable of receiving the warning and directions themselves, as man was, who herein is taught *more than the beasts of the earth, and made wiser than the fowls of heaven*—that he is endued with the power of foresight; therefore man is charged with the care of them: being under his dominion, they must be under his protection; and, though he could not secure every individual,

58

yet he must carefully preserve every species, that no tribe, no, not the least considerable, might entirely perish out of the creation. Observe in this, 1. God's care for man, for his comfort and benefit. We do not find that Noah was solicitous of himself about this matter; but God consults our happiness more than we do ourselves. Though God saw that the old world was very provoking, and foresaw that the new one would be little better, yet he would preserve the brute creatures for man's use. *Doth God take care for oxen?* 1 Cor. ix. 9. Or was it not rather for man's sake that this care was taken? 2. Even the unclean beasts, which were least valuable and profitable, were preserved alive in the ark; for God's tender mercies are over all his works, and not over those only that are of most eminence and use. 3. Yet more of the clean were preserved than of the unclean. (1.) Because the clean were most for the service of man; and therefore, in favour to him, more of them were preserved and are still propagated. Thanks be to God, there are not herds of lions as there are of oxen, nor flocks of tigers as there are of sheep. (2.) Because the clean were for sacrifice to God; and therefore, in honour to him, more of them were preserved, three couple for breed, and the odd seventh for sacrifice, *ch.* viii. 20. God gives us six for one in earthly things, as in the distribution of the days of the week, that in spiritual things we should be all for him. What is devoted to God's honour, and used in his service, is particularly blessed and increased.

III. Here is notice given of the now imminent approach of the flood: *Yet seven days, and I will cause it to rain, v.* 4. 1. " It shall be seven days *yet,* before I do it." After the hundred and twenty years had expired, God grants them a reprieve of seven days longer, both to show how slow he is to anger and that punishing work is his strange work, and also to give them some further space for repentance: but all in vain; these seven days were trifled away, after all the rest; they continued secure and sensual until the day that the flood came. 2. "It shall be *but* seven days." While Noah told them of the judgment at a distance, they were tempted to put off their repentance, because the vision was for a great while to come; but now he is ordered to tell them that it is at the door, that they have but one week more to turn them in, but one sabbath more to improve, to see if that will now, at last, awaken them to consider the things that belong to their peace, which otherwise will soon be hidden from their eyes. But it is common for those that have been careless of their souls during the years of their health, when they have looked upon death at a distance, to be as careless during the days, the seven days, of their sickness, when they see it approaching, their hearts being hardened by the deceitfulness of sin.

5 And Noah did according unto all that the Lord commanded him. 6 And Noah *was* six hundred years old when the flood of waters was upon the earth. 7 And Noah went in, and his sons, and his wife, and his sons' wives with him, into the ark, because of the waters of the flood. 8 Of clean beasts, and of beasts that *are* not clean, and of fowls, and of every thing that creepeth upon the earth, 9 There went in two and two unto Noah into the ark, the male and the female, as God had commanded Noah. 10 And it came to pass after seven days, that the waters of the flood were upon the earth.

Here is Noah's ready obedience to the commands that God gave him. Observe, 1. He went into the ark, upon notice that the flood would come after seven days, though probably as yet there appeared no visible sign of its approach, no cloud arising that threatened it, nothing done towards it, but all continued serene and clear; for, as he prepared the ark by faith in the warning given that the flood would come, so he went into it by faith in this warning that it would come quickly, though he did not see that the second causes had yet begun to work. In every step he took, he walked by faith, and not by sense. During these seven days, it is likely, he was settling himself and his family in the ark, and distributing the creatures into their several apartments. This was the conclusion of that visible sermon which he had long been preaching to his careless neighbours, and which, one would think, might have awakened them; but, not obtaining that desired end, it left their blood upon their own heads. 2. He took all his family along with him, his wife, to be his companion and comfort (though it should seem that, after this, he had no children by her), his sons, and his sons' wives, that by them not only his family, but the world of mankind, might be built up. Observe, Though men were to be reduced to so small a number, and it would be very desirable to have the world speedily repeopled, yet Noah's sons were each of them to have but one wife, which strengthens the arguments against having many wives; for from the beginning of this new world it was not so: as, at first, God made, so now he kept alive, but one woman for one man. See Matt. xix. 4, 8. 3. The brute creatures readily went in with him. The same hand that at first brought them to Adam to be named now brought them to Noah to be preserved. The ox now knew his owner, and the ass his protector's crib, nay, even the wildest creatures flocked to it; but man had become more brutish than the brutes themselves, and did not know, did not consider, Isa. i. 3

11 In the six hundredth year of Noah's life, in the second month, the seventeenth day of the month, the same day were all the fountains of the great deep broken up, and the windows of heaven were opened. 12 And the rain was upon the earth forty days and forty nights.

Here is, I. The date of this great event; this is carefully recorded, for the greater certainty of the story.

1. It was in the 600th year of Noah's life, which, by computation, appears to be 1656 years from the creation. The years of the old world are reckoned, not by the reigns of the giants, but by the lives of the patriarchs; saints are of more account with God than princes. *The righteous shall be had in everlasting remembrance.* Noah was now a very old man, even as men's years went then. Note, (1.) The longer we live in this world the more we see of the miseries and calamities of it; it is therefore spoken of as the privilege of those that die young that their *eyes shall not see the evil* which is coming, 2 Kings xxii. 20. (2.) Sometimes God exercises his old servants with extraordinary trials of obedient patience. The oldest of Christ's soldiers must not promise themselves a discharge from their warfare till death discharge them. Still they must gird on their harness, and not boast as though they had put it off. As the year of the deluge is recorded, so,

2. We are told that it was in the *second month, the seventeenth day of the month,* which is reckoned to be about the beginning of November; so that Noah had had a harvest just before, from which to victual his ark.

II. The second causes that concurred to this deluge. Observe,

1. In the self-same day that Noah was fixed in the ark, the inundation began. Note, (1.) Desolating judgments come not till God has provided for the security of his own people; see *ch.* xix. 22, I can *do nothing till thou be come thither:* and we find (Rev. vii. 3) that the winds are held till the servants of God are sealed. (2.) When good men are removed judgments are not far off; for they are *taken away from the evil to come,* Isa. lvii. 1. When they are called into the chambers, hidden in the grave, hidden in heaven, then God is *coming out of his place to punish,* Isa. xxvi. 20, 21.

2. See what was done on that day, that fatal day to the world of the ungodly. (1.) The *fountains of the great deep were broken up.* Perhaps there needed no new creation of waters; what were already made to be, in the common course of providence, blessings to the earth, were now, by an extraordinary act of divine power, made the ruin of it. God

has laid up the deep in storehouses (Ps. xxxiii. 7), and now he broke up those stores. As our bodies have in themselves those humours which, when God pleases, become the seeds and springs of mortal diseases, so the earth had in its bowels those waters which, at God's command, sprang up and flooded it. God had, in the creation, set *bars and doors* to the waters of *the sea,* that they *might not return to cover the earth* (Ps. civ. 9; Job xxxviii. 9—11); and now he only removed those ancient land-marks, mounds, and fences, and the waters of the sea returned to cover the earth, as they had done at first, *ch.* i. 9. Note, All the creatures are ready to fight against sinful man, and any of them is able to be the instrument of his ruin, if God do but take off the restraints by which they are held in during the day of God's patience. (2.) *The windows of heaven were opened,* and *the waters which were above the firmament* were poured out upon the world; those treasures which God had *reserved against the time of trouble, the day of battle and war,* Job xxxviii. 22, 23. The rain, which ordinarily descends in drops, then came down in streams, or *spouts,* as they call them in the Indies, where clouds have been often known to *burst,* as they express it there, when the rain descends in a much more violent torrent than we have ever seen in the greatest shower. We read (Job xxvi. 8) that *God binds up the waters in his thick clouds,* and the *cloud is not rent under them;* but now the bond was loosed, the cloud was rent, and such rains descended as were never known before nor since, in such abundance and of such continuance: the thick cloud was not, as ordinarily it is, wearied with waterings (Job xxxvii. 11), that is, soon spent and exhausted; but still the clouds returned after the rain, and the divine power brought in fresh recruits. It rained, without intermission or abatement, *forty days and forty nights (v.* 12), and that upon the whole earth at once, not, as sometimes, *upon one city and not upon another.* God made the world in six days, but he was forty days in destroying it; for he is slow to anger: but, though the destruction came slowly and gradually, yet it came effectually.

3. Now learn from this, (1.) That all the creatures are at God's disposal, and that he makes what use he pleases of them, whether *for correction, or for his land, or for mercy,* as Elihu speaks of the rain, Job xxxvii. 12, 13. (2.) That God often makes that which *should be for our welfare to become a trap,* Ps. lxix. 22. That which usually is a comfort and benefit to us becomes, when God pleases, a scourge and a plague to us. Nothing is more needful nor useful than water, both the springs of the earth and the showers of heaven; and yet now nothing was more hurtful, nothing more destructive: every creature is to us what God makes it. (3.) That it is impossible to escape the righteous judgments of God

when they come against sinners with commission; for God can arm both heaven and earth against them; see Job xx. 27. God can surround men with the messengers of his wrath, so that, if they look upwards, it is with horror and amazement, if they look to the earth, *behold, trouble and darkness,* Isa. viii. 21, 22. Who then is able to stand before God, when he is angry? (4.) In this destruction of the old world by water God gave a specimen of the final destruction of the world that now is by fire. We find the apostle setting the one of these over against the other, 2 Pet. iii. 6, 7. As there are waters under the earth, so Ætna, Vesuvius, and other volcanoes, proclaim to the world that there are subterraneous fires too; and fire often falls from heaven, many desolations are made by lightning; so that, when the time predetermined comes, between these two fires the earth and all the works therein shall be burnt up, as the flood was brought upon the old world out of the fountains of the great deep and through the windows of heaven.

13 In the selfsame day entered Noah, and Shem, and Ham, and Japheth, the sons of Noah, and Noah's wife, and the three wives of his sons with them, into the ark; 14 They, and every beast after his kind, and all the cattle after their kind, and every creeping thing that creepeth upon the earth after his kind, and every fowl after his kind, every bird of every sort. 15 And they went in unto Noah into the ark, two and two of all flesh, wherein *is* the breath of life. 16 And they that went in, went in male and female of all flesh, as God had commanded him: and the LORD shut him in.

Here is repeated what was related before of Noah's entrance into the ark, with his family and the creatures that were marked for preservation. Now,

I. It is thus repeated for the honour of Noah, whose faith and obedience herein shone so brightly, by which he obtained a good report, and who herein appeared so great a favourite of Heaven and so great a blessing to this earth.

II. Notice is here taken of the beasts going in *each after his kind,* according to the phrase used in the history of the creation (*ch.* i. 21—25), to intimate that just as many kinds as were created at first were saved now, and no more; and that this preservation was as a new creation: a life remarkably protected is, as it were, a new life.

III. Though all enmities and hostilities between the creatures ceased for the present, and ravenous creatures were not only so mild and manageable as that the *wolf and the lamb*

lay down together, but so strangely altered as that the *lion did eat straw like an ox* (Isa. xi. 6, 7), yet, when this occasion was over, the restraint was taken off, and they were still of the same kind as ever; for the ark did not alter their constitution. Hypocrites in the church, that externally conform to the laws of that ark, may yet be unchanged, and then it will appear, one time or other, what kind they are after.

IV. It is added (and the circumstance deserves our notice), *The Lord shut him in, v.* 16. As Noah continued his obedience to God, so God continued his care of Noah: and here it appeared to be a very distinguishing care; for the shutting of this door set up a partition wall between him and all the world besides. God shut the door, 1. To secure him, and keep him safe in the ark. The door must be shut very *close,* lest the waters should break in and sink the ark, and very *fast,* lest any without should break it down. Thus God made up Noah, as he *makes up his jewels,* Mal. iii. 17. 2. To exclude all others, and keep them for ever out. Hitherto the door of the ark stood open, and if any, even during the last seven days, had repented and believed, for aught I know they might have been welcomed into the ark; but now the door was shut, and they were cut off from all hopes of admittance: for God *shutteth, and none can open.*

V. There is much of our gospel duty and privilege to be seen in Noah's preservation in the ark. The apostle makes it a type of our baptism, that is, our Christianity, 1 Pet. iii. 20, 21. Observe then, 1. It is our great duty, in obedience to the gospel call, by a lively faith in Christ, to come into that way of salvation which God has provided for poor sinners. When Noah came into the ark, he quitted his own house and lands; so must we quit our own righteousness and our worldly possessions, whenever they come into competition with Christ. Noah must, for a while, submit to the confinements and inconveniences of the ark, in order to his preservation for a new world; so those that come into Christ to be saved by him must deny themselves, both in sufferings and services. 2. Those that come into the ark themselves should bring as many as they can in with them, by good instructions, by persuasions, and by a good example. *What knowest thou, O man, but thou mayest thus save thy wife* (1 Cor. vii. 16), as Noah did his? There is room enough in Christ for all comers. 3. Those that by faith come into Christ, the ark, shall by the power of God be shut in, and kept as in a strong-hold *by the power of God,* 1 Pet. i. 5. God put Adam into paradise, but he did not shut him in, and so he threw himself out; but when he put Noah into the ark he shut him in, and so when he brings a soul to Christ he ensures its salvation: it is not in our own keeping, but in the Mediator's hand. 4. The door of mercy will shortly be shut against those that now make light of it. Now, *knock und it shall be opened ;* but the time will come when it shall not, Luke xiii. 25.

17 And the flood was forty days upon the earth; and the waters increased, and bare up the ark, and it was lift up above the earth. 18 And the waters prevailed, and were increased greatly upon the earth; and the ark went upon the face of the waters. 19 And the waters prevailed exceedingly upon the earth; and all the high hills, that *were* under the whole heaven, were covered. 20 Fifteen cubits upward did the waters prevail; and the mountains were covered.

We are here told,

I. How long the flood was increasing—*forty days, v. 17.* The profane world, who believed not that it would come, probably when it came flattered themselves with hopes that it would soon abate and never come to extremity; but still it increased, it prevailed. Note, 1. When God judges he will overcome. If he begin, he will make an end; his way is perfect, both in judgment and mercy. 2. The gradual approaches and advances of God's judgments, which are designed to bring sinners to repentance, are often abused to the hardening of them in their presumption.

II. To what degree they increased: they rose so high that not only the low flat countries were deluged, but to make sure work, and that none might escape, the tops of the highest mountains were overflowed—*fifteen cubits,* that is, seven yards and a half; so that *in vain was salvation hoped for from hills or mountains,* Jer. iii. 23   None of God's creatures are so high but his power can overtop them; and he will make them know that wherein they deal proudly he is above them. Perhaps the tops of the mountains were washed down by the strength of the waters, which helped much towards the prevailing of the waters above them; for it is said (Job xii. 15), *He sends out the waters,* and they not only overflow, but overturn, the earth. Thus the refuge of lies was swept away, and the waters overflowed the hiding-place of those sinners (Isa. xxviii. 17), and in vain they fly to them for safety, Rev. vi. 16. Now the mountains departed, and the hills were removed, and nothing stood a man in stead but the *covenant of peace,* Isa. liv. 10. There is no place on earth so high as to set men out of the reach of God's judgments, Jer. xlix. 16 ; Obad. iii. 4. God's hand will *find out all his enemies,* Ps. xxi. 8. Observe how exactly they are fathomed *(fifteen cubits),* not by Noah's plummet, but by his knowledge who *weighs the waters by measure,* Job xxviii. 25.

III. What became of Noah's ark when the waters thus increased : *It was lifted up above the earth (v. 17), and went upon the face of the*

waters, *v.* 18. When all other buildings were demolished by the waters, and buried under them, the ark alone subsisted. Observe,

1. The waters which broke down every thing else bore up the ark. That which to unbelievers is a savour of death unto death is to the faithful a savour of life unto life.

2. The more the waters increased the higher the ark was lifted up towards heaven. Thus sanctified afflictions are spiritual promotions; and as troubles abound consolations much more abound.

21 And all flesh died that moved upon the earth, both of fowl, and of cattle, and of beast, and of every creeping thing that creepeth upon the earth, and every man: 22 All in whose nostrils *was* the breath of life, of all that *was* in the dry *land,* died. 23 And every living substance was destroyed which was upon the face of the ground, both man, and cattle, and the creeping things, and the fowl of the heaven ; and they were destroyed from the earth : and Noah only remained *alive,* and they that *were* with him in the ark. 24 And the waters prevailed upon the earth a hundred and fifty days.

Here is, I. The general destruction of all flesh by the waters of the flood. *Come, and see the desolations which God makes in the earth* (Ps. xlvi. 8), and how he lays heaps upon heaps. Never did death triumph, from its first entrance unto this day, as it did then. Come, and see Death upon his pale horse, and hell following with him, Rev. vi. 7, 8.

1. All the cattle, fowl, and creeping things, died, except the few that were in the ark. Observe how this is repeated : *All flesh died, v.* 21. *All in whose nostrils was the breath of life, of all that was on the dry land, v. 22. Every living substance, v. 23.* And why so ? Man only had done wickedly, and justly is God's hand against him ; but *these sheep, what have they done ?* I answer, (1.) We are sure God did them no wrong. He is the sovereign Lord of all life, for he is the sole fountain and author of it. He that made them as he pleased might unmake them when he pleased ; and who shall say unto him, *What doest thou ?* May he not do what he will with his own, which were created for his pleasure ? (2.) God did admirably serve the purposes of his own glory by their destruction, as well as by their creation. Herein his holiness and justice were greatly magnified ; by this it appears that he hates sin, and is highly displeased with sinners, when even the inferior creatures, because they are the servants of man and part of his possession, and because they have been abused to be the servants of sin, are destroyed with him. This

makes the judgment the more remarkable, the more dreadful, and, consequently, the more expressive of God's wrath and vengeance. The destruction of the creatures was their deliverance from the bondage of corruption, which deliverance the whole creation now groans after, Rom. viii. 21, 22. It was likewise an instance of God's wisdom. As the creatures were made for man when he was made, so they were multiplied for him when he was multiplied; and therefore, now that mankind was reduced to so small a number, it was fit that the beasts should proportionably be reduced, otherwise they would have had the dominion, and would have replenished the earth, and the remnant of mankind that was left would have been overpowered by them. See how God considered this in another case, Exod. xxiii. 29, *Lest the beast of the field multiply against thee.*

2. All the men, women, and children, that were in the world (except what were in the ark) died. *Every man* (*v.* 21 and *v.* 23), and perhaps they were as many as are now upon the face of the earth, if not more. Now, (1.) We may easily imagine what terror and consternation seized on them when they saw themselves surrounded. Our Saviour tells us that till the very day that the flood came they were *eating and drinking* (Luke xvii. 26, 27); they were drowned in security and sensuality before they were drowned in those waters, crying *Peace, peace,* to themselves, deaf and blind to all divine warnings. In this posture death surprised them, as 1 Sam. xxx. 16, 17. But O what an amazement were they in then! Now they see and feel that which they would not believe and fear, and are convinced of their folly when it is too late; now they find no place for repentance, though they seek it carefully with tears. (2.) We may suppose that they tried all ways and means possible for their preservation, but all in vain. Some climb to the tops of trees or mountains, and spin out their terrors there awhile. But the flood reaches them, at last, and they are forced to die with the more deliberation. Some, it is likely, cling to the ark, and now hope that this may be their safety which they had so long made their sport. Perhaps some get to the top of the ark, and hope to shift for themselves there; but either they perish there for want of food, or, by a speedier despatch, a dash of rain washes them off that deck. Others, it may be, hoped to prevail with Noah for admission into the ark, and pleaded old acquaintance, *Have we not eaten and drunk in thy presence? Hast thou not taught in our streets?* "Yes," might Noah say, "that I have, many a time, to little purpose. *I called but you refused; you set at nought all my counsel* (Prov. i. 24, 25), and now it is not in my power to help you: God has shut the door, and I cannot open it." Thus it will be at the great day. Neither climbing high in an outward profession, nor claiming relation to good people,

will bring men to heaven, Matt. vii. 22; xxv. 8, 9. Those that are not found in Christ, the ark, are certainly undone, undone for ever; salvation itself cannot save them. See Isa. x. 3. (3.) We may suppose that some of those that perished in the deluge had themselves assisted Noah, or were employed by him, in the building of the ark, and yet were not so wise as by repentance to secure themselves a place in it. Thus wicked ministers, though they may have been instrumental to help others to heaven, will themselves be thrust down to hell.

Let us now pause awhile and consider this tremendous judgment! Let our hearts meditate terror, the terror of this destruction. Let us see, and say, *It is a fearful thing to fall into the hands of the living God; who can stand before him when he is angry?* Let us see, and say, *It is an evil thing, and a bitter, to depart from God.* The sin of sinners will, without repentance, be their ruin, first or last; if God be true, it will. *Though hand join in hand, yet the wicked shall not go unpunished,* The righteous God knows how to bring a flood upon the world of the ungodly, 2 Pet. ii. 5. Eliphaz appeals to this story as a standing warning to a careless world (Job xxii. 15, 16), *Hast thou marked the old way, which wicked men have trodden, who were cut down out of time,* and sent into eternity, *whose foundation was overflown with the flood?*

II. The special preservation of Noah and his family : *Noah only remained alive, and those that were with him in the ark, v.* 23. Observe, 1. Noah lives. When all about him were monuments of justice, thousands falling on his right hand and ten thousands on his left, he was a monument of mercy. Only with his eyes might he *behold and see the reward of the wicked,* Ps. xci. 7, 8. *In the floods of great waters, they did not come nigh him,* Ps. xxxii. 6. We have reason to think that, while the long-suffering of God waited, Noah not only preached to, but prayed for, that wicked world, and would have turned away the wrath; but his prayers return into his own bosom, and are answered only in his own escape, which is plainly referred to, Ezek. xiv. 14, *Noah, Daniel, and Job, shall but deliver their own souls.* A mark of honour shall be set on intercessors. 2. He but lives. Noah remains alive, and this is all; he is, in effect, buried alive—cooped up in a close place, alarmed with the terrors of the descending rain, the increasing flood, and the shrieks and outcries of his perishing neighbours, his heart overwhelmed with melancholy thoughts of the desolations made. But he comforts himself with this, that he is in the way of duty and in the way of deliverance. And we are taught (Jer. xlv. 4, 5) that when desolating judgments are abroad we must not seek great nor pleasant things to ourselves, but reckon it an unspeakable favour if we have our lives given us for a prey.

CHAP. VIII.

In the close of the foregoing chapter we left the world in ruins and the church in straits; but in this chapter we have the repair of the one and the enlargement of the other. Now the scene alters, and another face of things begins to be presented to us, and the brighter side of that cloud which there appeared so black and dark; for, though God contend long, he will not contend for ever, nor be always wrath. We have here, I. The earth made anew by the recess of the waters, and the appearing of the dry land, now a second time, and both gradual. 1. The increase of the waters is stayed, ver. 1, 2. 2. They begin sensibly to abate, ver. 3. 3. After sixteen days' ebbing, the ark rests, ver. 4. 4. After sixty days' ebbing, the tops of the mountains appeared above water, ver, 5. 5. After forty days' ebbing, and twenty days before the mountains appeared, Noah began to send out his spies, a raven and a dove, to gain intelligence, ver. 6—12. 6. Two months after the appearing of the tops of the mountains, the waters had gone, and the face of the earth was dry (ver. 13), though not dried so as to be fit for man till almost two months after, ver. 14. II. Man placed anew upon the earth, in which, 1. Noah's discharge and departure out of the ark, ver. 15—19. 2. His sacrifice of praise, which he offered to God upon his enlargement, ver. 20. 3. God's acceptance of his sacrifice, and the promise he made thereupon not to drown the world again, ver. 21, 22. And thus, at length, mercy rejoices against judgment.

A ND God remembered Noah, and every living thing, and all the cattle that *was* with him in the ark: and God made a wind to pass over the earth, and the waters assuaged.

2 The fountains also of the deep and the windows of heaven were stopped, and the rain from heaven was restrained; 3 And the waters returned from off the earth continually: and after the end of the hundred and fifty days the waters were abated.

Here is, I. An act of God's grace: *God remembered Noah and every living thing.* This is an expression after the manner of men; for not any of his creatures (Luke xii. 6), much less any of his people, are forgotten of God, Isa. xlix. 15, 16. But, 1. The whole race of mankind, except Noah and his family, was now extinguished, and driven into the land of forgetfulness, to be remembered no more; so that God's remembering Noah was the return of his mercy to mankind, of whom he would not make a full end. It is a strange expression, Ezek. v. 13, *When I have accomplished my fury in them, I will be comforted.* The demands of divine justice had been answered by the ruin of those sinners; he had eased him of his adversaries (Isa. i. 24), and now his spirit was quieted (Zech. vi. 8), and *he remembered Noah and every living thing.* He remembered mercy in wrath (Hab. iii. 2), remembered the days of old (Isa. lxiii. 11), remembered the holy seed, and then remembered Noah. 2. Noah himself, though one that had found grace in the eyes of the Lord, yet seemed to be forgotten in the ark, and perhaps began to think himself so; for we do not find that God had told him how long he should be confined and when he should be released. Very good men have sometimes been ready to conclude themselves forgotten of God, especially when their afflictions have been unusually grievous and long. Perhaps Noah, though a great believer, yet when he found the flood continuing so long after it might reasonably be presumed to have done

its work, was tempted to fear lest he that shut him in would keep him in, and began to expostulate. *How long wilt thou forget me?* But at length God returned in mercy to him, and this is expressed by remembering him. Note, Those that remember God shall certainly be remembered by him, how desolate and disconsolate soever their condition may be. He will appoint them a set time and remember them, Job xiv. 13. 3 With Noah, God remembered every living thing; for, though his delight is especially in the sons of men, yet he rejoices in all his works, and hates nothing that he has made. He takes special care, not only of his people's persons, but of their possessions—of them and all that belongs to them. He considered the cattle of Nineveh, Jon. iv. 11.

II. An act of God's power over wind and water, both of which are at his beck, though neither of them is under man's control. Observe,

1. He commanded the wind, and said to that, *Go,* and it went, in order to the carrying off of the flood: *God made a wind to pass over the earth.* See here, (1.) What was God's remembrance of Noah: it was his relieving him. Note, Those whom God remembers he remembers effectually, for good; he remembers us to save us, that we may remember him to serve him. (2.) What a sovereign dominion God has over the winds. He has them in his fist (Prov. xxx. 4) and brings them out of his treasuries, Ps. cxxxv. 7. He sends them when, and whither, and for what purposes, he pleases. Even stormy winds fulfil his word, Ps. cxlviii. 8. It should seem, while the waters increased, there was no wind; for that would have added to the toss of the ark; but now God sent a wind, when it would not be so troublesome. Probably, it was a north wind, for that drives away rain. However, it was a drying wind, such a wind as God sent to divide the Red Sea before Israel, Exod. xiv. 21.

2. He remanded the waters, and said to them, *Come,* and they came. (1.) He took away the cause. He sealed up the springs of those waters, *the fountains of the great deep, and the windows of heaven.* Note, [1.] As God has a key to open, so he has a key to shut up again, and to stay the progress of judgments by stopping the causes of them: and the same hand that brings the desolation must bring the deliverance; to that hand therefore our eye must ever be. He that wounds is alone able to heal. See Job xii. 14, 15. [2.] When afflictions have done the work for which they are sent, whether killing work or curing work, they shall be removed. God's word shall not return void, Isa. lv. 10, 11. (2.) Then the effect ceased; not all at once, but by degrees: *The waters abated* (*v.* 1), *returned from off the earth continually,* Heb. they were *going and returning* (*v.* 3), which denotes a gradual departure.

The heat of the sun exhaled much, and perhaps the subterraneous caverns soaked in more. Note, As the earth was not drowned in a day, so it was not dried in a day. In the creation, it was but one day's work to clear the earth from the waters that covered it, and to make it dry land; nay, it was but half a day's work, *ch.* i. 9, 10. But, the work of creation being finished, this work of providence was effected by the concurring influence of second causes, yet thus enforced by the almighty power of God. God usually works deliverance for his people gradually, that the day of small things may not be despised, nor the day of great things despaired of, Zech. iv. 10. See Prov. iv. 18.

4 And the ark rested in the seventh month, on the seventeenth day of the month, upon the mountains of Ararat.

5 And the waters decreased continually until the tenth month: in the tenth *month*, on the first *day* of the month, were the tops of the mountains seen.

Here we have the effects and evidences of the ebbing of the waters. 1. The ark rested. This was some satisfaction to Noah, to feel the house he was in upon firm ground, and no longer movable. It rested upon a mountain, whither it was directed, not by Noah's prudence (he did not steer it), but by the wise and gracious providence of God, that it might rest the sooner. Note, God has times and places of rest for his people after their tossings; and many a time he provides for their seasonable and comfortable settlement without their own contrivance and quite beyond their own foresight. The ark of the church, though sometimes tossed with tempests and not comforted (Isa. liv. 11), yet has its rests, Acts ix. 31. 2. The tops of the mountains were seen, like little islands, appearing above the water. We must suppose that they were seen by Noah and his sons; for there were none besides to see them. It is probable that they had looked through the window of the ark every day, like the longing mariners, after a tedious voyage, to see if they could discover land, or as the prophet's servant (1 Kings xviii. 43, 44), and at length they spy ground, and enter the day of the discovery in their journal. They felt ground above forty days before they saw it, according to Dr. Lightfoot's computation, whence he infers that, if the waters decreased proportionably, the ark drew eleven cubits in water.

6 And it came to pass at the end of forty days, that Noah opened the window of the ark which he had made: 7 And he sent forth a raven, which went forth to and fro, until the waters were dried up from off the

earth. 8 Also he sent forth a dove from him, to see if the waters were abated from off the face of the ground; 9 But the dove found no rest for the sole of her foot, and she returned unto him into the ark, for the waters *were* on the face of the whole earth: then he put forth his hand, and took her, and pulled her in unto him into the ark. 10 And he stayed yet other seven days; and again he sent forth the dove out of the ark; 11 And the dove came in to him in the evening; and, lo, in her mouth *was* an olive leaf plucked off: so Noah knew that the waters were abated from off the earth. 12 And he stayed yet other seven days; and sent forth the dove; which returned not again unto him any more.

We have here an account of the spies which Noah sent forth to bring him intelligence from abroad, a raven and a dove. Observe here,

I. That though God had told Noah particularly when the flood would come, even to a day (*ch.* vii. 4), yet he did not give him a particular account by revelation at what times, and by what steps, it should *go away*, 1. Because the knowledge of the former was necessary to his preparing the ark, and settling himself in it; but the knowledge of the latter would serve only to gratify his curiosity, and the concealing of it from him would be the needful exercise of his faith and patience. And, 2. He could not foresee the flood, but by revelation; but he might, by ordinary means, discover the decrease of it, and therefore God was pleased to leave him to the use of them.

II. That though Noah by faith expected his enlargement, and by patience waited for it, yet he was inquisitive concerning it, as one that thought it long to be thus confined. Note, Desires of release out of trouble, earnest expectations of it, and enquiries concerning its advances towards us, will very well consist with the sincerity of faith and patience. *He that believes does not make haste* to run before God, but he does make haste to go forth to meet him, Isa. xxviii. 16. Particularly, 1. Noah sent forth a raven through the window of the ark, which went forth, as the Hebrew phrase is, *going forth and returning*, that is, flying about, and feeding on the carcases that floated, but returning to the ark for rest; probably not in it, but upon it. This gave Noah little satisfaction; therefore, 2. He sent forth a dove, which returned the first time with no good news, but probably wet and dirty; but, the second time, she brought an olive-leaf in her

65

bill, which appeared to be first plucked off, a plain indication that now the trees, the fruit-trees, began to appear above water. Note here, (1.) That Noah sent forth the dove the second time seven days after the first time, and the third time was after seven days too ; and probably the first sending of her out was seven days after the sending forth of the raven. This intimates that it was done on the sabbath day, which, it should seem, Noah religiously observed in the ark. Having kept the sabbath in a solemn assembly of his little church, he then expected special blessings from heaven, and enquired concerning them. Having directed his prayer, he looked up, Ps. v. 3. (2.) The dove is an emblem of a gracious soul, which finding no rest for its foot, no solid peace or satisfaction in this world, this deluged defiling world, returns to Christ as to its ark, as to its Noah. The carnal heart, like the raven, takes up with the world, and feeds on the carrions it finds there ; *but return thou to thy rest, O my soul,* to thy Noah, so the word is, Ps. cxvi. 7. *O that I had wings like a dove,* to flee to him ! Ps. lv. 6. And as Noah put forth his hand, and took the dove, and pulled her in to him, into the ark, so Christ will graciously preserve, and help, and welcome, those that fly to him for rest. (3.) The olive-branch, which was an emblem of peace, was brought, not by the raven, a bird of prey, nor by a gay and proud peacock, but by a mild, patient, humble, dove. It is a dove-like disposition that brings into the soul earnests of rest and joy. (4.) Some make these things an allegory. The law was first sent forth like the raven, but brought no tidings of the assuaging of the waters of God's wrath, with which the world of mankind was deluged ; therefore, in the fulness of time, God sent forth his gospel, as the dove, in the likeness of which the Holy Spirit descended, and this presents us with an olive-branch and brings in a better hope.

13 And it came to pass in the six hundredth and first year, in the first *month,* the first *day* of the month, the waters were dried up from off the earth : and Noah removed the covering of the ark, and looked, and, behold, the face of the ground was dry. 14 And in the second month, on the seven and twentieth day of the month, was the earth dried.

Here is, 1. The ground dry (*v* 13), that is, all the water carried off it, which, upon the first day of the first month (a joyful new-year's-day it was), Noah was himself an eye-witness of. He *removed the covering of the ark,* not the whole covering, but so much as would suffice to give him a prospect of the earth about it ; and a most comfortable prospect he had. For behold, behold and

66

wonder, *the face of the ground was dry.* Note, (1.) It is a great mercy to see ground about us. Noah was more sensible of it than we are ; for mercies restored are much more affecting than mercies continued. (2.) The divine power which now renewed the face of the earth can renew the face of an afflicted troubled soul and of a distressed persecuted church. He can make dry ground to appear even where it seemed to have been lost and forgotten, Ps. xviii. 16. 2. The ground dried (*v.* 14), so as to be a fit habitation for Noah. Observe, Though Noah saw the ground dry the first day of the first month, yet God would not suffer him to go out of the ark till the twenty-seventh day of the second month. Perhaps Noah, being somewhat weary of his restraint, would have quitted the ark at first ; but God, in kindness to him, ordered him to stay so much longer. Note, God consults our benefit rather than our desires ; for he knows what is good for us better than we do for ourselves, and how long it is fit our restraints should continue and desired mercies should be delayed. We would go out of the ark before the ground is dried : and perhaps, if the door be shut, are ready to remove the covering, and to climb up some other way ; but we should be satisfied that God's time of showing mercy is certainly the best time, when the mercy is ripe for us and we are ready for it.

15 And God spake unto Noah, saying, 16 Go forth of the ark, thou, and thy wife, and thy sons, and thy sons' wives with thee. 17 Bring forth with thee every living thing that *is* with thee, of all flesh, *both* of fowl, and of cattle, and of every creeping thing that creepeth upon the earth ; that they may breed abundantly in the earth, and be fruitful, and multiply upon the earth. 18 And Noah went forth, and his sons, and his wife, and his sons' wives with him : 19 Every beast, every creeping thing, and every fowl, *and* whatsoever creepeth upon the earth, after their kinds, went forth out of the ark.

Here is, I. Noah's dismission out of the ark, *v.* 15—17. Observe, 1. Noah did not stir till God bade him. As he had a command to go into the ark (*ch.* vii. 1), so, how tedious soever his confinement there was, he would wait for a command to go out of it again. Note, We must in all our ways acknowledge God, and set him before us in all our removes. Those only go under God's protection that follow God's direction and submit to his government. Those that steadily adhere to God's word as their rule, and are guided by his grace as their principle, and take hints from his providence to assist them in their application of general directions to particular cases, may in faith see him guiding their motions in their march through this wilderness. 2. Though God detained him long, yet at last he gave him his discharge; for *the vision is for an appointed time, and at the end it shall speak,* it shall speak truth (Hab. ii. 3), it shall not lie. 3. God had said, *Come into the ark,* which intimated that God went in with him; now he says, not, *Come forth,* but, *Go forth,* which intimates that God, who went in with him, staid with him all the while, till he sent him out safely; for he has said, *I will not leave thee.* 4. Some observe that, when they were ordered into the ark, the men and the women were mentioned separately (*ch.* vi. 18): *Thou, and thy sons, and thy wife, and thy sons' wives;* hence they infer that, during the time of mourning, they were apart, and their wives apart, Zech. xii. 12. But now God did as it were new-marry them, sending out Noah and his wife together, and his sons and their wives together, that they might be fruitful and multiply. 5. Noah was ordered to bring the creatures out with him, that having taken the care of feeding them so long, and been at so much pains about them, he might have the honour of leading them forth by their armies, and receiving their homage.

II. Noah's departure when he had his dismission. As he would not go out without leave, so he would not, out of fear or humour, stay in when he had leave, but was in all points observant of the heavenly vision. Though he had been now a full year and ten days a prisoner in the ark, yet when he found himself preserved there, not only for a new life, but for a new world, he saw no reason to complain of his long confinement. Now observe, 1. Noah and his family came out alive, though one of them was a wicked Ham, whom, though he escaped the flood, God's justice could have taken away by some other stroke. But they are all alive. Note, When families have been long continued together, and no breaches made among them, it must be looked upon as a distinguishing favour, and attributed to the Lord's mercies. 2. Noah brought out all the creatures that went in with him, except the raven and the dove, which, probably, were ready to meet their mates at their coming out. Noah was able to give a very good account of his charge; for of all that were given to him he had lost none, but was faithful to him that appointed him, *pro hac vice—on this occasion,* high steward of his household.

20 And Noah builded an altar unto the LORD; and took of every clean beast, and of every clean fowl, and offered burnt offerings on the altar. 21 And the LORD smelled a sweet savour; and the LORD said in his heart, I will not again curse the ground any more for man's sake; for the imagination of man's heart *is* evil from his youth; neither will I again smite any more every thing living, as I have done. 22 While the earth remaineth, seedtime and harvest, and cold and heat, and summer and winter, and day and night shall not cease.

Here is, I. Noah's thankful acknowledgment of God's favour to him, in completing the mercy of his deliverance, *v.* 20. 1. He *built an altar.* Hitherto he had done nothing without particular instructions and commands from God. He had a particular call into the ark, and another out of it; but, altars and sacrifices being already of divine institution for religious worship, he did not stay for a particular command thus to express his thankfulness. Those that have received mercy from God should be forward in returning thanks, and do it *not of constraint, but willingly.* God is pleased with free-will offerings, and praises that wait for him. Noah was now turned out into a cold and desolate world, where, one would have thought, his first care would have been to build a house for himself; but, behold, he begins with an altar for God: God, that is the first, must be first served; and he begins well that begins with God. 2. He offered a sacrifice upon his altar, *of every clean beast, and of every clean fowl*—one, the odd seventh that we read of, *ch.* vii. 2, 3: Here observe, (1.) He offered only those that were clean; for it is not enough that we sacrifice, but we must sacrifice that which God appoints, according to the law of sacrifice, and not a corrupt thing. (2.) Though his stock of cattle was so small, and that rescued from ruin at so great an expense of care and pains, yet he did not grudge to give God his dues out of it. He might have said, "Have I but seven sheep to begin the world with, and must one of these seven be killed and burnt for sacrifice? Were it not better to defer it till we have greater plenty?" No, to prove the sincerity of his love and gratitude, he cheerfully gives the seventh to his God, as an acknowledgment that all was his, and owing to him. Serving God with our little is the way to make it more; and we must never think that wasted with which God is honoured. (3.) See here the antiquity of religion: the first thing we find done in the new world was an act of worship, Jer. vi. 16. We are now to express our thankfulness, not by burnt-offerings, but by the sacrifices of praise and the sacrifices of righteousness, by pious devotions and a pious conversation.

II. God's gracious acceptance of Noah's thankfulness. It was a settled rule in the patriarchal age: *If thou doest well, shalt thou not be accepted?* Noah was so. For, 1. God was well pleased with the performance, *v.* 21. He *smelt a sweet savour,* or, as it is in the Hebrew, *a savour of rest,* from it. As, when he had made the world at first on the seventh day, he rested and was refreshed, so, now that he had new-made it, in the sacrifice of the seventh he rested. He was well pleased with Noah's pious zeal, and these hopeful beginnings of the new world, as men are with fragrant and agreeable smells ; though his offering was small, it was according to his ability, and God accepted it. Having caused his anger to rest upon the world of sinners, he here caused his love to rest upon this little remnant of believers.

2. Hereupon, he took up a resolution never to drown the world again. Herein he had an eye, not so much to Noah's sacrifice as to Christ's sacrifice of himself, which was typified and represented by it, and which was indeed an *offering of a sweet-smelling savour,* Eph. v. 2. Good security is here given, and that which may be relied upon,

(1.) That this judgment should never be repeated. Noah might think, " To what purpose should the world be repaired, when, in all probability, for the wickedness of it, it will quickly be in like manner ruined again?" "No," says God, " it never shall." It was said (*ch.* vi. 6), *It repented the Lord that he had made man ;* now here he speaks as if it repented him that he had destroyed man : neither means a change of his mind, but both a change of his way. *It repented him concerning his servants,* Deut. xxxii. 36. Two ways this resolve is expressed :—[1.] *I will not again curse the ground,* Heb. *I will not add to curse the ground any more.* God had cursed the ground upon the first entrance of sin (*ch.* iii. 17), when he drowned it he added to that curse ; but now he determines not to add to it any more. [2.] *Neither will I again smite any more every living thing ;* that is, it was determined that whatever ruin God might bring upon particular persons, or families, or countries, he would never again destroy the whole world till the day shall come when time shall be no more. But the reason of this resolve is very surprising, for it seems the same in effect with the reason given for the destruction of the world : *Because the imagination of man's heart is evil from his youth,* ch. vi. 5. But there is this difference—there it is said, *The imagination of man's heart is evil continually,* that is, " his actual transgressions continually cry against him ;" here it is said, It is evil *from his youth or childhood.* It is bred in the bone ; he brought it into the world with him ; he was shapen and conceived in it. Now, one would think it should follow, " Therefore that guilty race shall be wholly extinguished, and *I will make a full end.*" No, "Therefore I will no more take this severe method ; for," *First,* " He is rather to be pitied, for it is all the effect of sin dwelling in him ; and it is but what might be expected from such a degenerate race : he is called a *transgressor*

from the womb, and therefore it is not strange that he deals so very treacherously," Isa. xlviii. 8. Thus God *remembers that he is flesh,* corrupt and sinful, Ps. lxxviii. 39. *Secondly,* " He will be utterly ruined ; for, if he be dealt with according to his deserts, one flood must succeed another till all be destroyed." See here, 1. That outward judgments, though they may terrify and restrain men, yet cannot of themselves sanctify and renew them ; the grace of God must work with those judgments. Man's nature .was as sinful after the deluge as it had been before. 2. That God's goodness takes occasion from man's sinfulness to magnify itself the more ; his reasons of mercy are all drawn from himself, not from any thing in us.

(2.) That the course of nature should never be discontinued (*v.* 22) : " *While the earth remaineth,* and man upon it, there shall be *summer and winter* (not all winter as had been this last year), *day and night,*" not all night, as probably it was while the rain was descending. Here, [1.] It is plainly intimated that this earth is not to remain always ; it, and all the works in it, must shortly be burnt up ; and we look for *new heavens and a new earth,* when all these things must be dissolved. But, [2.] As long as it does remain God's providence will carefully preserve the regular succession of times and seasons, and cause each to know its place. To this we owe it that the world stands, and the wheel of nature keeps its track. See here how changeable the times are and yet how unchangeable. *First,* The course of nature always changing. As it is with the times, so it is with the events of time, they are subject to vicissitudes—*day and night, summer and winter,* counterchanged. In heaven and hell it is not so, but on earth *God hath set the one over against the other. Secondly,* Yet never changed. It is constant in this inconstancy. These seasons have never ceased, nor shall cease, while the sun continues such a steady measurer of time and the moon such a *faithful witness in heaven.* This is *God's covenant of the day and of the night,* the stability of which is mentioned for the confirming of our faith in the covenant of grace, which is no less inviolable, Jer. xxxiii. 20, 21. We see God's promises to the creatures made good, and thence may infer that his promises to all believers shall be so.

CHAP. IX.

AND God blessed Noah and his sons, and said unto them, Be fruitful, and multiply, and replenish the earth. 2 And the fear of you and the dread of you shall be upon every beast of the earth, and upon every fowl of the air, upon all that moveth *upon* the earth, and upon all the fishes of the sea; into your hand are they delivered. 3 Every moving thing that liveth shall be meat for you; even as the green herb have I given you all things. 4 But flesh with the life thereof, *which is* the blood thereof, shall ye not eat. 5 And surely your blood of your lives will I require; at the hand of every beast will I require it, and at the hand of man; at the hand of every man's brother will I require the life of man. 6 Whoso sheddeth man's blood, by man shall his blood be shed: for in the image of God made he man. 7 And you, be ye fruitful, and multiply; bring forth abundantly in the earth, and multiply therein.

We read, in the close of the foregoing chapter, the very kind things which God said in his heart, concerning the remnant of mankind which was now left to be the seed of a new world. Now here we have these kind things *spoken to them.* In general, *God blessed Noah and his sons* (v. 1), that is, he assured them of his good-will to them and his gracious intentions concerning them. This follows from what he said in his heart. Note, All God's promises of good flow from his purposes of love and the counsels of his own will. See Eph. i. 11; iii. 11, and compare Jer. xxix. 11. *I know the thoughts that I think towards you.* We read (*ch.* viii. 20) how *Noah blessed God,* by his altar and sacrifice. Now here we find God blessing Noah. Note, God will graciously bless (that is, do well for) those who sincerely bless (that is, speak well of) him. Those that are truly thankful for the mercies they have received take the readiest way to have them confirmed and continued to them.

Now here we have the *Magna Charta*— the great charter of this new kingdom of nature which was now to be erected, and incorporated, the former charter having been forfeited and seized.

I. The grants of this charter are kind and gracious to men. Here is,

1. A grant of lands of vast extent, and a promise of a great increase of men to occupy and enjoy them. The first blessing is here renewed: *Be fruitful, and multiply, and replenish the earth* (v. 1), and repeated (v. 7), for the race of mankind was, as it were, to begin again. Now, (1.) God sets the whole earth before them, tells them it is all their own, *while it remains,* to them and their heirs. Note, The earth God has given to the children of men, for a possession and habitation, Ps. cxv. 16. Though it is not a paradise, but a wilderness rather; yet it is better than we deserve. Blessed be God, it is not hell. (2.) He gives them a blessing, by the force and virtue of which mankind should be both multiplied and perpetuated upon earth, so that in a little time all the habitable parts of the earth should be more or less inhabited; and, though one generation should pass away, yet another generation should come, while the world stands, so that the stream of the human race should be supplied with a constant succession, and run parallel with the current of time, till both should be delivered up together into the ocean of eternity. Though death should still reign, and the Lord would still be known by his judgments, yet the earth should never again be dispeopled as now it was, but still replenished, Acts xvii. 24—26.

2. A grant of power over the inferior creatures, v. 2. He grants, (1.) A title to them: *Into your hands they are delivered,* for your use and benefit. (2.) A dominion over them, without which the title would avail little: *The fear of you and the dread of you shall be upon every beast.* This revives a former grant (*ch.* i. 28), only with this difference, that man in innocence ruled by love, fallen man rules by fear. Now this grant remains in force, and thus far we have still the benefit of it, [1.] That those creatures which are any way useful to us are reclaimed, and we use them either for service or food, or both, as they are capable. The horse and ox patiently submit to the bridle and yoke, and the sheep is dumb both before the shearer and before the butcher; for the fear and dread of man are upon them. [2.] Those creatures that are any way hurtful to us are restrained, so that, though now and then man may be hurt by some of them, they do not combine together to rise up in rebellion against man, else God could by these destroy the world as effectually as he did by a deluge; it is one of God's sore judgments, Ezek. xiv. 21. What is it that keeps wolves out of our towns, and lions out of our streets, and confines them to the wilderness, but this fear and dread? Nay, some have been tamed, Jas. iii. 7.

3. A grant of maintenance and subsistence: *Every moving thing that liveth shall be meat for you,* v. 3. Hitherto, most think, man had been confined to feed only upon the products of the earth, fruits, herbs, and roots, and all sorts of corn and milk; so was the first grant, *ch.* i. 29. But the flood having perhaps washed away much of the virtue of the earth, and so rendered its fruits less pleas-

ing and less nourishing, God now enlarged the grant, and allowed man to eat flesh, which perhaps man himself never thought of, till now that God directed him to it, nor had any more desire to than a sheep has to suck blood like a wolf. But now man is allowed to feed upon flesh, as freely and safely as upon the green herb. Now here see, (1.) That God is a good Master, and provides, not only that we may live, but that we may live comfortably, in his service; not for necessity only, but for delight. (2.) That every *creature of God is good,* and nothing to be refused, 1 Tim. iv. 4. Afterwards some meats that were proper enough for food were prohibited by the ceremonial law; but from the beginning, it seems, it was not so, and therefore is not so under the gospel.

II. The precepts and provisos of this charter are no less kind and gracious, and instances of God's good-will to man. The Jewish doctors speak so often of the seven precepts of Noah, or of the sons of Noah, which they say were to be observed by all nations, that it may not be amiss to set them down. The first against the worship of idols. The second against blasphemy, and requiring to bless the name of God. The third against murder. The fourth against incest and all uncleanness. The fifth against theft and rapine. The sixth requiring the administration of justice. The seventh against eating of flesh with the life. These the Jews required the observance of from the *proselytes of the gate.* But the precepts here given all concern the life of man.

1. Man must not prejudice his own life by eating that food which is unwholesome and prejudicial to his health (*v.* 4): "*Flesh with the life thereof, which is the blood thereof* (that is, raw flesh), shall you not eat, as the beasts of prey do." It was necessary to add this limitation to the grant of liberty to eat flesh, lest, instead of nourishing their bodies by it, they should destroy them. God would hereby show, (1.) That though they were lords of the creatures, yet they were subjects to the Creator, and under the restraints of his law. (2.) That they must not be greedy and hasty in taking their food, but stay the preparing of it; not like Saul's soldiers (1 Sam. xiv. 32), nor *riotous eaters of flesh,* Prov. xxiii. 20. (3.) That they must not be barbarous and cruel to the inferior creatures. They must be lords, but not tyrants; they might kill them for their profit, but not torment them for their pleasure, nor tear away the member of a creature while it was yet alive, and eat that. (4.) That during the continuance of the law of sacrifices, in which the blood made *atonement for the soul* (Lev. xvii. 11), signifying that the life of the sacrifice was accepted for the life of the sinner, blood must not be looked upon as a common thing, but must be *poured out before the Lord* (2 Sam. xxiii. 16), either upon his altar or upon his earth. But, now that the great and true sacrifice has

been offered, the obligation of the law ceases with the reason of it.

2. Man must not take away his own life : *Your blood of your lives will I require, v.* 5. Our lives are not so our own as that we may quit them at our own pleasure, but they are God's, and we must resign them at his pleasure; if we in any way hasten our own deaths, we are accountable to God for it.

3. The beasts must not be suffered to hurt the life of man : *At the hand of every beast will I require it.* To show how tender God was of the life of man, though he had lately made such destruction of lives, he will have the beast put to death that kills a man. This was confirmed by the law of Moses (Exod. xxi. 28), and I think it would not be unsafe to observe it still. Thus God showed his hatred of the sin of murder, that men might hate it the more, and not only punish, but prevent it. And see Job v. 23.

4. Wilful murderers must be put to death. This is the sin which is here designed to be restrained by the terror of punishment. (1.) God will punish murderers : *At the hand of every man's brother will I require the life of man,* that is, "I will avenge the blood of the murdered upon the murderer." 2 Chron. xxiv. 22. When God requires the life of a man at the hand of him that took it away unjustly, the murderer cannot render that, and therefore must render his own in lieu of it, which is the only way left of making restitution. Note, The righteous God will certainly make inquisition for blood, though men cannot or do not. One time or other, in this world or in the next, he will both discover concealed murders, which are hidden from man's eye, and punish avowed and justified murders, which are too great for man's hand. (2.) The magistrate must punish murderers (*v.* 6): *Whoso sheddeth man's blood,* whether upon a sudden provocation or having premeditated it (for rash anger is heart-murder as well as malice prepense, Matt. v. 21, 22), *by man shall his blood be shed,* that is, by the magistrate, or whoever is appointed or allowed to be the avenger of blood. There are those who are ministers of God for this purpose, to be a protection to the innocent, by being a terror to the malicious and evildoers, and they must not *bear the sword in vain,* Rom. xiii. 4. Before the flood, as it should seem by the story of Cain, God took the punishment of murder into his own hands; but now he committed this judgment to men, to masters of families at first, and afterwards to the heads of countries, who ought to be faithful to the trust reposed in them. Note, Wilful murder ought always to be punished with death. It is a sin *which the Lord would not pardon* in a prince (2 Kings xxiv. 3, 4), and which therefore a prince should not pardon in a subject. To this law there is a reason annexed: *For in the image of God made he man* at first. Man is a creature dear to his Creator, and therefore

ought to be so to us. God put honour upon him, let not us then put contempt upon him. Such remains of God's image are still even upon fallen man as that he who unjustly kills a man defaces the image of God and does dishonour to him. When God allowed men to kill their beasts, yet he forbade them to kill their slaves; for these are of a much more noble and excellent nature, not only God's creatures, but his image, Jam. iii. 9. All men have something of the image of God upon them; but magistrates have, besides, the image of his power, and the saints the image of his holiness, and therefore those who shed the blood of princes or saints incur a double guilt.

8 And God spake unto Noah, and to his sons with him, saying, 9 And I, behold, I establish my covenant with you, and with your seed after you; 10 And with every living creature that *is* with you, of the fowl, of the cattle, and of every beast of the earth with you; from all that go out of the ark, to every beast of the earth. 11 And I will establish my covenant with you; neither shall all flesh be cut off any more by the waters of a flood; neither shall there any more be a flood to destroy the earth.

Here is, I. The general establishment of God's covenant with this new world, and the extent of that covenant, *v.* 9, 10. Here observe, 1. That God is graciously pleased to deal with man in the way of a covenant, wherein God greatly magnifies his condescending favour, and greatly encourages man's duty and obedience, as a reasonable and gainful service. 2. That all God's covenants with man are of his own making: *I, behold, I.* It is thus expressed both to raise our admiration—" Behold, and wonder, that though God be high yet he has this respect to man," and to confirm our assurances of the validity of the covenant—" Behold and see, I make it; I that am faithful and able to make it good." 3. That God's covenants are established more firmly than the pillars of heaven or the foundations of the earth, and cannot be disannulled. 4. That God's covenants are made with the covenanters and with their seed; the promise is to them and their children. 5. That those may be taken into covenant with God, and receive the benefits of it, who yet are not capable of re-stipulating, or giving their own consent. For this covenant is made with *every living creature, every beast of the earth.* II. The particular intention of this covenant. It was designed to secure the world from another deluge: *There shall not any more be a flood.* God had drowned the world once, and still it was as filthy and provoking

as ever, and God foresaw the wickedness of it, and yet promised he would never drown it any more; for he deals not with us according to our sins. It is owing to God's goodness and faithfulness, not to any reformation of the world, that it has not often been deluged, and that it is not deluged now. As the old world was ruined to be a monument of justice, so this world remains to this day, a monument of mercy, according to the oath of God, that the waters of Noah should no more return to cover the earth, Isa. liv. 9. This promise of God keeps the sea and clouds in their decreed place, and *sets them gates and bars; hitherto they shall come,* Job xxxviii. 10, 11. If the sea should flow but for a few days, as it ·does twice every day for a few hours, what desolation would it make! And how destructive would the clouds be, if such showers as we have sometimes seen were continued long! But God, by flowing seas and sweeping rains, shows what he could do in wrath; and yet, by preserving the earth from being deluged between both, shows what he can do in mercy and will do in truth. Let us give him the glory of his mercy in promising and of his truth in performing. This promise does not hinder, 1. But that God may bring other wasting judgments upon mankind; for, though he has here bound himself not to use this arrow any more, yet he has other ˚arrows in his quiver. 2. Nor but that he may destroy particular places and countries by the inundations of the sea or rivers. 3. Nor will the destruction of the world at the last day by fire be any breach of his promise. Sin which drowned the old world will burn this.

12 And God said, This *is* the token of the covenant which I make between me and you and every living creature that *is* with you, for perpetual generations: 13 I do set my bow in the cloud, and it shall be for a token of a covenant between me and the earth. 14 And it shall come to pass, when I bring a cloud over the earth, that the bow shall be seen in the cloud: 15 And I will remember my covenant, which *is* between me and you and every living creature of all flesh; and the waters shall no more become a flood to destroy all flesh. 16 And the bow shall be in the cloud; and I will look upon it, that I may remember the everlasting covenant between God and every living creature of all flesh that *is* upon the earth. 17 And God said unto Noah, This *is* the token of the covenant, which I have established be-

tween me and all flesh that *is* upon the earth.

Articles of agreement among men are usually sealed, that the covenants may be the more solemn, and the performances of the covenants the more sure, to mutual satisfaction. God therefore, being *willing more abundantly to show to the heirs of promise the immutability of his councils*, has confirmed his covenant by a seal (Heb. vi. 17), which makes the foundations we build on stand sure, 2 Tim. ii. 19. The seal of this covenant of nature was natural enough; it was the *rainbow*, which, it is likely, was seen in the clouds before, when second causes concurred, but was never a seal of the covenant till now that it was made so by a divine institution. Now, concerning this seal of the covenant, observe, 1. This seal is affixed with repeated assurances of the truth of that promise of which it was designed to be the ratification: *I do set my bow in the cloud* (*v.* 13); it *shall be seen in the cloud* (*v.* 14), that the eye may affect the heart and confirm the faith; and it shall be *the token of the covenant.*(*v.* 12, 13), *and I will remember my covenant, that the waters shall no more become a flood, v.* 15. Nay, as if the Eternal Mind needed a memorandum, *I will look upon it, that I may remember the everlasting covenant, v.* 16. Thus here is line upon line, that we might have sure and strong consolation who have laid hold of this hope. 2. The rainbow appears when the clouds are most disposed to wet, and returns after the rain; when we have most reason to fear the rain prevailing, then God shows this seal of the promise that it shall not prevail. Thus God obviates òur fears with such encouragements as are both suitable and seasonable. 3. The thicker the cloud the brighter the bow in the cloud. Thus, as threatening afflictions abound, encouraging consolations much more abound, 2 Cor. i. 5. 4. The rainbow appears when one part of the sky is clear, which intimates mercy remembered in the midst of wrath; and the clouds are hemmed as it were with the rainbow, that they may not overspread the heavens, for the bow is coloured rain or the edges of a cloud gilded. 5. The rainbow is the reflection of the beams of the sun, which intimates that all the glory and significancy of the seals of he covenant are derived from Christ the Sun of righteousness, who is also described with a *rainbow about his throne* (Rev. iv. 3), and a *rainbow upon his head* (Rev. x. 1), which intimates, not only his majesty, but his mediatorship. 6. The rainbow has fiery colours in it, to signify that though God will not again drown the world, yet, when the mystery of God shall be finished, the world shall be consumed by fire. 7. A bow bespeaks terror, but this bow has neither string nor arrow, as the bow ordained against the persecutors has (Ps.

vii. 12, 13), and a bow alone will do little execution. It is a bow, but it is directed upwards, not towards the earth; for the seals of the covenant were intended to comfort, not to terrify. 8. As God looks upon the bow, that he may remember the covenant, so should we, that we also may be ever mindful of the covenant, with faith and thankfulness.

18 And the sons of Noah, that went forth of the ark, were Shem, and Ham, and Japheth: and Ham *is* the father of Canaan. 19 These *are* the three sons of Noah: and of them was the whole earth overspread. 20 And Noah began *to be* a husbandman, and he planted a vineyard: 21 And he drank of the wine, and was drunken; and he was uncovered within his tent. 22 And Ham, the father of Canaan, saw the nakedness of his father, and told his two brethren without. 23 And Shem and Japheth took a garment, and laid *it* upon both their shoulders, and went backward, and covered the nakedness of their father; and their faces *were* backward, and they saw not their father's nakedness.

Here is, I. Noah's family and employment. The names of his sons are again mentioned (*v.* 18, 19) as those from whom the whole earth was overspread, by which it appears that Noah, after the flood, had no more children: all the world came from these three. Note, God, when he pleases, can make *a little one to become a thousand*, and greatly increase the latter end of those whose beginning was small. Such are the power and efficacy of a divine blessing. The business Noah applied himself to was that of *a husbandman*, Heb. *a man of the earth*, that is, a man dealing in the earth, that kept ground in his hand, and occupied it. We are all naturally men of the earth, made of it, living on it, and hastening to it: many are sinfully so, addicted to earthly things. Noah was by his calling led to trade in the fruits of the earth. He *began to be a husbandman*, that is, some time after his departure out of the ark, he returned to his old employment, from which he had been diverted by the building of the ark first, and probably afterwards by the building of a house on dry land for himself and family. For this good while he had been a carpenter, but now he began again to be a husbandman. Observe, Though Noah was a great man and a good man, an old man and a rich man, a man greatly favoured by heaven and honoured on earth, yet he would not live an idle life, nor think the husbandman's calling

72

below him. Note, Though God by his providence may take us off from our callings for a time, yet when the occasion is over we ought with humility and industry to apply ourselves to them again, and, in the calling wherein we are called, faithfully to *abide with God*, 1 Cor. vii. 24.

II. Noah's sin and shame: *He planted a vineyard;* and, when he had gathered his vintage, probably he appointed a day of mirth and feasting in his family, and had his sons and their children with him, to rejoice with him in the increase of his house as well as in the increase of his vineyard; and we may suppose he prefaced his feast with a sacrifice to the honour of God. If this was omitted, it was just with God to leave him to himself, that he who did not begin with God might end with the beasts; but we charitably hope that it was not: and perhaps he appointed this feast with a design, at the close of it, to bless his sons, as *Isaac, ch.* xxvii. 3, 4, *That I may eat, and that my soul may bless thee.* At this feast he *drank of the wine ;* for who planteth a vineyard and *eateth not of the fruit of it ?* But he drank too liberally, more than his head at this age would bear, for he was *drunk.* We have reason to think he was never drunk before nor after ; observe how he came now to be overtaken in this fault. It was his sin, and a great sin, so much the worse for its being so soon after a great deliverance ; but God left him to himself, as he did Hezekiah (2 Chron. xxxii. 31), and has left this miscarriage of his upon record, to teach us, 1. That the fairest copy that ever mere man wrote since the fall had its blots and false strokes. It was said of Noah that he was *perfect in his generations* (ch. vi. 9), but this shows that it is meant of sincerity, not a sinless perfection. 2. That sometimes those who, with watchfulness and resolution, have, by the grace of God, kept their integrity in the midst of temptation, have, through security, and carelessness, and neglect of the grace of God, been surprised into sin, when the hour of temptation has been over. Noah, who had kept sober in drunken company, is now drunk in sober company. *Let him that thinks he stands take heed.* 3. That we have need to be very careful, when we use God's good creatures plentifully, lest we use them to excess. Christ's disciples must take heed lest at any time *their hearts be overcharged,* Luke xxi. 34. Now the consequence of Noah's sin was shame. He was *uncovered within his tent,* made naked to his shame, as Adam when he had eaten forbidden fruit. Yet Adam sought concealment ; Noah is so destitute of thought and reason that he seeks no covering. This was a fruit of the vine that Noah did not think of. Observe here the great evil of the sin of drunkenness. (1.) It discovers men. What infirmities they have, they betray when they are drunk, and what secrets they are entrusted with are then

easily got out of them. Drunken porters keep open gates. (2.) It disgraces men, and exposes them to contempt. As it shows them, so it shames them. Men say and do that when drunk which when they are sober they would blush at the thoughts of, Hab. ii 15, 16.

III. Ham's impudence and impiety: He *saw the nakedness of his father, and told his two brethren, v.* 22. To see it accidentally and involuntarily would not have been a crime ; but, 1. He pleased himself with the sight, *as the Edomites looked upon the day of their brother* (Obad. 12), pleased, and insulting. Perhaps Ham had sometimes been himself drunk, and reproved for it by his good father, whom he was therefore pleased to see thus overcome. Note, It is common for those who walk in false ways themselves to rejoice at the false steps which they sometimes see others make. But charity rejoices not in iniquity, nor can true penitents that are sorry for their own sins rejoice in the sins of others. 2. *He told his two brethren without (in the street,* as the word is), in a scornful deriding manner, that his father might seem vile unto them. It is very wrong, (1.) To make a jest of sin (Prov. xiv. 9), and to be puffed up with that for which we should rather mourn, 1 Cor. v. 2. And, (2.) To publish the faults of any, especially of parents, whom it is our duty to honour. Noah was not only a good man, but had been a good father to him; and this was a most base disingenuous requital to him for his tenderness. Ham is here called the *father of Canaan,* which intimates that he who was himself a father should have been more respectful to him that was his father.

IV. The pious care of Shem and Japheth to cover their poor father's shame, *v.* 23. They not only would not see it themselves, but provided that no one else might see it, herein setting us an example of charity with reference to other men's sin and shame ; we must not only not say, *A confederacy,* with those that proclaim it, but we must be careful to conceal it, or at least to make the best of it, so doing as we would be done by. 1. There is a mantle of love to be thrown over the faults of all, 1 Pet. iv. 8. 2. Besides this, there is a robe of reverence to be thrown over the faults of parents and other superiors.

24 And Noah awoke from his wine, and knew what his younger son had done unto him. 25 And he said, Cursed *be* Canaan ; a servant of servants shall he be unto his brethren. 26 And he said, Blessed *be* the LORD God of Shem ; and Canaan shall be his servant. 27 God shall enlarge Japheth, and he shall dwell in the tents of Shem ; and Canaan shall be his servant.

Here, I. Noah comes to himself: He awoke from his wine. Sleep cured him, and, we may suppose, so cured him that he never relapsed into that sin afterwards. Those that sleep as Noah did should awake as he did, and not as that drunkard (Prov. xxiii. 35) who says when he awakes, *I will seek it yet again.*

II. The spirit of prophecy comes upon him, and, like dying Jacob, he tells his sons what shall befal them, ch. xlix. 1.

1. He pronounces a curse on Canaan the son of Ham (v. 25), in whom Ham is himself cursed, either because this son of his was now more guilty than the rest, or because the posterity of this son was afterwards to be rooted out of their land, to make room for Israel. And Moses here records it for the animating of Israel in the wars of Canaan; though the Canaanites were a formidable people, yet they were of old an accursed people, and doomed to ruin. The particular curse is, *A servant of servants* (that is, the meanest and most despicable servant) *shall he be,* even *to his brethren.* Those who by birth were his equals shall by conquest be his lords. This certainly points at the victories obtained by Israel over the Canaanites, by which they were all either put to the sword or put under tribute (Josh. ix. 23; Judg. i. 28, 30, 33, 35), which happened not till about 800 years after this. Note, (1.) God often visits the iniquity of the fathers upon the children, especially when the children inherit the fathers' wicked dispositions, and imitate the fathers' wicked practices, and do nothing to cut off the entail of the curse. (2.) Disgrace is justly put upon those that put disgrace upon others, especially that dishonour and grieve their own parents. An undutiful child that mocks at his parents is *no more worthy to be called a son,* but deserves to be *made as a hired servant,* nay, as *a servant of servants,* among his brethren. (3.) Though divine curses operate slowly, yet, first or last, they will take effect. The Canaanites were under a curse of slavery, and yet, for a great while, had the dominion; for a family, a people, a person, may lie under the curse of God, and yet may long prosper in the world, till the measure of their iniquity, like that of the Canaanites, be full. Many are marked for ruin that are not yet ripe for ruin. Therefore, *Let not thy heart envy sinners.*

2. He entails a blessing upon Shem and Japheth.

(1.) He blesses Shem, or rather blesses God for him, yet so that it entitles him to the greatest honour and happiness imaginable, v. 26. Observe, [1.] He calls the Lord *the God of Shem;* and happy, thrice happy, is that people whose God is the LORD, Ps. cxliv. 15. All blessings are included in this. This was the blessing conferred on Abraham and his seed; the God of heaven was not ashamed to be called their God, Heb. xi.

16. Shem is sufficiently recompensed for his respect to his father by this, that the Lord himself puts this honour upon him, *to be his God,* which is a sufficient recompence for all our services and all our sufferings for his name. [2.] He gives to God the glory of that good work which Shem had done, and, instead of blessing and praising him that was the instrument, he blesses and praises God that was the author. Note, The glory of all that is at any time well done, by ourselves or others, must be humbly and thankfully transmitted to God, who works all our good works in us and for us. When we see men's good works we should glorify, not them, but *our Father,* Matt. v. 16. Thus David, in effect, blessed Abigail, when he *blessed God* that sent her (1 Sam. xxv. 32, 33), for it is an honour and a favour to be employed for God and used by him in doing good. [3.] He foresees and foretels that God's gracious dealings with Shem and his family would be such as would evidence to all the world that he was the God of Shem, on which behalf thanksgivings would by many be rendered to him: *Blessed be the Lord God of Shem.* [4.] It is intimated that the church should be built up and continued in the posterity of Shem; for of him came the Jews, who were, for a great while, the only professing people God had in the world. [5.] Some think reference is here had to Christ, who was the Lord God that, in his human nature, should descend from the loins of Shem; for of him, as concerning the flesh, Christ came. [6.] Canaan is particularly enslaved to him: *He shall be his servant.* Note, Those that have the Lord for their God shall have as much of the honour and power of this world as he sees good for them.

(2.) He blesses Japheth, and, in him, *the isles of the Gentiles,* which were peopled by his seed: *God shall enlarge Japheth, and he shall dwell in the tents of Shem, v.* 27. Now, [1.] Some make this to belong wholly to Japheth, and to denote either, *First,* His outward prosperity, that his seed should be so numerous and so victorious that they should be masters of the tents of Shem, which was fulfilled when the people of the Jews, the most eminent of Shem's race, were tributaries to the Grecians first and afterwards to the Romans, both of Japheth's seed. Note, Outward prosperity is no infallible mark of the true church: the tents of Shem are not always the tents of the conqueror. Or, *Secondly,* It denotes the conversion of the Gentiles, and the bringing of them into the church; and then we should read it, *God shall persuade Japheth* (for so the word signifies), and then, being so persuaded, *he shall dwell in the tents of Shem,* that is, Jews and Gentiles shall be united together in the gospel fold. After many of the Gentiles shall have been proselyted to the Jewish religion, both shall be one in Christ (Eph.

74

ii. 14, 15), and the Christian church, mostly made up of the Gentiles, shall succeed the Jews in the privileges of church-membership; the latter having first cast themselves out by their unbelief, the Gentiles shall dwell in their tents, Rom. xi 11, &c. Note, It is God only that can bring those again into the church who have separated themselves from it. It is the power of God that makes the gospel of Christ effectual to salvation, Rom. i. 16. And again, Souls are brought into the church, not by force, but by persuasion, Ps. cx. 3. They are drawn by the cords of a man, and persuaded by reason to be religious. [2.] Others divide this between Japheth and Shem, Shem having not been directly blessed, *v.* 26. *First,* Japheth has the blessing of the earth beneath : *God shall enlarge Japheth,* enlarge his seed, enlarge his border. Japheth's posterity peopled all Europe, a great part of Asia, and perhaps America. Note, God is to be acknowledged in all our enlargements. It is he that enlarges the coast and enlarges the heart. And again, many dwell in large tents that do not dwell in God's tents, as Japheth did. *Secondly,* Shem has the blessing of heaven above: *He shall* (that is, God shall) *dwell in the tents of Shem,* that is, "From his loins *Christ shall come,* and in his seed the *church shall be continued.*" The birth-right was now to be divided between Shem and Japheth, Ham being utterly discarded. In the principality which they equally share Canaan shall be servant to both. The double portion is given to Japheth, whom God shall enlarge; but the priesthood is given to Shem, for *God shall dwell in the tents of Shem:* and certainly we are more happy if we have God dwelling in our tents than if we had there all the silver and gold in the world. It is better to dwell in tents with God than in palaces without him. In Salem, where is God's tabernacle, there is more satisfaction than in all the isles of the Gentiles. *Thirdly,* They both have dominion over Canaan: *Canaan shall be servant to them;* so some read it. When Japheth joins with Shem, Canaan falls before them both. When strangers become friends, enemies become servants.

28 And Noah lived after the flood three hundred and fifty years. 29 And all the days of Noah were nine hundred and fifty years : and he died.

Here see, 1. How God prolonged the life of Noah; he lived 950 years, twenty more than Adam and but nineteen less than Methuselah : this long life was a further reward of his signal piety, and a great blessing to the world, to which no doubt he continued a *preacher of righteousness,* with this advantage, that now all he preached to were his own children. 2. How God put a period to his life at last. Though he lived long, yet he died, having probably first seen many

that descended from him dead before him. Noah lived to see two worlds, but, being an heir of the righteousness which is by faith, when he died he went to see a better than either.

CHAP. X.

This chapter shows more particularly what was said in general (ch. ix. 19), concerning the three sons of Noah, that "of them was the whole earth overspread;" and the fruit of that blessing (ch. ix. 1, 7), "replenish the earth." It is the only certain account extant of the origin of nations; and yet perhaps there is no nation but that of the Jews that can be confident from which of these seventy fountains (for so many there are here) it derives its streams. Through the want of early records, the mixtures of people, the revolutions of nations, and distance of time, the knowledge of the lineal descent of the present inhabitants of the earth is lost; nor were any genealogies preserved but those of the Jews, for the sake of the Messiah, only in this chapter we have a brief account, I. Of the posterity of Japheth, ver. 2—5. II. The posterity of Ham (ver. 6—20), and in this particular notice is taken of Nimrod, ver. 8—10. III. The posterity of Shem, ver. 21, &c.

NOW these *are* the generations of the sons of Noah, Shem, Ham, and Japheth : and unto them were sons born after the flood. 2 The sons of Japheth; Gomer, and Magog, and Madai, and Javan, and Tubal, and Meshech, and Tiras. 3 And the sons of Gomer; Ashkenaz, and Riphath, and Togarmah. 4 And the sons of Javan; Elishah, and Tarshish, Kittim, and Dodanim. 5 By these were the isles of the Gentiles divided in their lands; every one after his tongue, after their families, in their nations.

Moses begins with Japheth's family, either because he was the eldest, or because his family lay remotest from Israel and had least concern with them at the time when Moses wrote, and therefore he mentions that race very briefly, hastening to give an account of the posterity of Ham, who were Israel's enemies, and of Shem, who were Israel's ancestors; for it is the church that the scripture is designed to be the history of, and of the nations of the world only as they were some way or other related to Israel and interested in the affairs of Israel. Observe, 1. Notice is taken that the sons of Noah had sons born to them after the flood, to repair and rebuild the world of mankind which the flood had ruined. He that had killed now makes alive. 2. The posterity of Japheth were allotted to the isles of the Gentiles (*v.* 5), which were solemnly, by lot, after a survey, divided among them, and probably this island of ours among the rest; all places beyond the sea from Judea are called *isles* (Jer. xxv. 22), and this directs us to understand that promise (Isa. xlii. 4), *the isles shall wait for his law,* of the conversion of the Gentiles to the faith of Christ.

6 And the sons of Ham; Cush, and Mizraim, and Phut, and Canaan. 7 And the sons of Cush; Seba, and Havilah, and Sabtah, and Raamah, and Sabtechah : and the sons of

Raamah; Shebah, and Dedan. 8 And Cush begat Nimrod: he began to be a mighty one in the earth. 9 He was a mighty hunter before the LORD: wherefore it is said; Even as Nimrod the mighty hunter before the LORD. 10 And the beginning of his kingdom was Babel, and Erech, and Accad, and Calneh, in the land of Shinar. 11 Out of that land went forth Asshur, and builded Nineveh, and the city Rehoboth, and Calah, 12 And Resen between Nineveh and Calah: the same *is* a great city. 13 And Mizraim begat Ludim, and Anamim, and Lehabim, and Naphtuhim, 14 And Pathrusim, and Casluhim, (out of whom came Philistim,) and Caphtorim.

That which is observable and improvable in these verses is the account here given of Nimrod, v. 8—10. He is here represented as a great man in his day : *He began to be a mighty one in the earth,* that is, whereas those that went before him were content to stand upon the same level with their neighbours, and though every man bore rule in his own house yet no man pretended any further, Nimrod's aspiring mind could not rest here ; he was resolved to tower above his neighbours, not only to be eminent among them, but to lord it over them. The same spirit that actuated the giants before the flood (who became *mighty men, and men of renown, ch.* vi. 4), now revived in him, so soon was that tremendous judgment which the pride and tyranny of those mighty men brought upon the world forgotten. Note, There are some in whom ambition and affectation of dominion seem to be bred in the bone; such there have been and will be, notwithstanding the wrath of God often revealed from heaven against them. Nothing on this side hell will humble and break the proud spirits of some men, in this like Lucifer, Isa. xiv. 14, 15. Now,

I. Nimrod was a great hunter ; with this he began, and for this became famous to a proverb. Every great hunter is, in remembrance of him, called a *Nimrod.* 1. Some think he did good with his hunting, served his country by ridding it of the wild beasts which infested it, and so insinuated himself into the affections of his neighbours, and got to be their prince. Those that exercise authority either are, or at least would be called, *benefactors,* Luke xxii. 25. 2. Others think that under pretence of hunting he gathered men under his command, in pursuit of another game he had to play, which was to make himself master of the country and to bring them into subjection. He was
76

a *mighty hunter,* that is, he was a violent invader of his neighbours' rights and properties, and a persecutor of innocent men, carrying all before him, and endeavouring to make all his own by force and violence. He thought himself a mighty prince, but *before the Lord* (that is, in God's account) he was but a *mighty hunter.* Note, Great conquerors are but great hunters. Alexander and Cesar would not make such a figure in scripture-history as they do in common history; the former is represented in prophecy but as a he-goat pushing, Dan. viii. 5. Nimrod was a mighty hunter *against* the Lord, so the LXX.; that is, (1.) He set up idolatry, as Jeroboam did, for the confirming of his usurped dominion. That he might set up a new government, he set up a new religion upon the ruin of the primitive constitution of both. *Babel was the mother of harlots.* Or, (2.) He carried on his oppression and violence in defiance of God himself, daring Heaven with his impieties, as if he and his huntsmen could out-brave the Almighty, and were a match for the Lord of hosts and all his armies. *As if it were a small thing to weary men, he thinks to weary my God also,* Isa. vii. 13.

II. Nimrod was a great ruler : *The beginning of his kingdom was Babel, v.* 10. Some way or other, by arts or arms, he got into power, either being chosen to it or forcing his way to.it; and so laid the foundations of a monarchy, which was afterwards a head of gold, and the terror of the mighty, and bade fair to be universal. It does not appear that he had any right to rule by birth ; but either his fitness for government recommended him, as some think, to an election, or by power and policy he advanced gradually, and perhaps insensibly, into the throne. See the antiquity of civil government, and particularly that form of it which lodges the sovereignty in a single person. If Nimrod and his neighbours began, other nations soon learned to incorporate under one head for their common safety and welfare, which, however it began, proved so great a blessing to the world that things were reckoned to go ill indeed when there *was no king in Israel.*

III. Nimrod was a great builder. Probably he was architect in the building of Babel, and there he began his kingdom; but, when his project to rule all the sons of Noah was baffled by the confusion of tongues, *out of that land he went forth into Assyria* (so the margin reads it, *v.* 11) *and built Nineveh,* &c., that, having built these cities, he might command them and rule over them. Observe, in Nimrod, the nature of ambition. 1. It is boundless. Much would have more, and still cries, *Give, give.* 2. It is restless. Nimrod, when he had four cities under his command, could not be content till he had four more. 3. It is expensive. Nimrod will rather be at the charge of rearing cities than not have the honour of ruling them. The spirit of building is the common effect of a spirit of pride. 4. It is daring, and will stick at nothing. Nimrod's name signifies rebellion, which (if indeed he did abuse his power to the oppression of his neighbours) teaches us that tyrants to men are rebels to God, and their *rebellion is as the sin of witchcraft.*

15 And Canaan begat Sidon his firstborn, and Heth, 16 And the Jebusite, and the Amorite, and the Girgasite, 17 And the Hivite, and the Arkite, and the Sinite, 18 And the Arvadite, and the Zemarite, and the Hamathite : and afterward were the families of the Canaanites spread abroad. 19 And the border of the Canaanites was from Sidon, as thou comest to Gerar, unto Gaza; as thou goest, unto Sodom, and Gomorrah, and Admah, and Zeboim, even unto Lasha. 20 These *are* the sons of Ham, after their families, after their tongues, in their countries, *and* in their nations.

Observe here, 1. The account of the posterity of Canaan, of the families and nations that descended from him, and of the land they possessed, is more particular than of any other in this chapter, because these were the nations that were to be subdued before Israel, and their land was in process of time to become the holy land, *Immanuel's land ;* and this God had an eye to when, in the mean time, he cast the lot of that accursed devoted race in that spot of ground which he had selected for his own people ; this Moses takes notice of, Deut. xxxii. 8, *When the Most High divided to the nations their inheritance, he set the bounds of the people according to the number of the children of Israel.* 2. By this account it appears that the posterity of Canaan were numerous, and rich, and very pleasantly situated; and yet Canaan was under a curse, a divine curse, and not a curse causeless. Note, Those that are under the curse of God may yet perhaps thrive and prosper greatly in this world ; for we cannot know love or hatred, the blessing or the curse, by what is before us, but by what is within us, Eccl. ix. 1. The curse of God always works really and always terribly : but perhaps it is a secret curse, a curse to the soul, and does not work visibly, or a slow curse, and does not work immediately ; but sinners are by it reserved for, and bound over to, a day of wrath. Canaan here has a better land than either Shem or Japheth, and yet they have a better lot, for they inherit the blessing.

21 Unto Shem also, the father of all the children of Eber, the brother

of Japheth the elder, even to him were *children* born. 22 The children of Shem ; Elam, and Asshur, and Arphaxad, and Lud, and Aram. 23 And the children of Aram ; Uz, and Hul, and Gether, and Mash. 24 And Arphaxad begat Salah ; and Salah begat Eber. 25 And unto Eber were born two sons : the name of one *was* Peleg ; for in his days was the earth divided ; and his brother's name *was* Joktan. 26 And Joktan begat Almodad, and Sheleph, and Hazarmaveth, and Jerah, 27 And Hadoram, and Uzal, and Diklah, 28 And Obal, and Abimael, and Sheba, 29 And Ophir, and Havilah, and Jobab : all these *were* the sons of Joktan. 30 And their dwelling was from Mesha, as thou goest, unto Sephar a mount of the east. 31 These *are* the sons of Shem, after their families, after their tongues, in their lands, after their nations. 32 These *are* the families of the sons of Noah, after their generations, in their nations : and by these were the nations divided in the earth after the flood.

Two things especially are observable in this account of the posterity of Shem :—
I. The description of Shem, *v.* 21. We have not only his name, *Shem,* which signifies *a name,* but two titles to distinguish him by :—
1. He was *the father of all the children of Eber.* Eber was his great grandson ; but why should he be called the father of all *his* children, rather than of all Arphaxad's, or Salah's, &c.? Probably because Abraham and his seed, God's covenant-people, not only descended from Heber, but from him were called *Hebrews; ch.* xiv. 13, *Abram the Hebrew.* Paul looked upon it as his privilege that he was a *Hebrew of the Hebrews,* Phil. iii. 5. Eber himself, we may suppose, was a man eminent for religion in a time of general apostasy, and a great example of piety to his family ; and, the holy tongue being commonly called from him the *Hebrew,* it is probable that he retained it in his family, in the confusion of Babel, as a special token of God's favour to him ; and from him the professors of religion were called *the children of Eber.* Now, when the inspired penman would give Shem an honourable title, he calls him *the father of the Hebrews.* Though, when Moses wrote this, they were a poor despised people, bond-slaves in Egypt, yet, being God's people, it was an honour to a man to be akin to them. As Ham, though he had many sons, is disowned by being called *the father of Canaan,* on whose seed

the *curse* was entailed (*ch.* ix. 22), so Shem, though he had many sons, is dignified with the title of *the father of Eber*, on whose seed the blessing was entailed. Note, A family of saints is more truly honourable than a family of nobles, Shem's holy seed than Ham's royal seed, Jacob's twelve patriarchs than Ishmael's twelve princes, *ch.* xvii. 20. Goodness is true greatness.

2. He was *the brother of Japheth the elder*, by which it appears that, though Shem is commonly put first, he was not Noah's first-born, but Japheth was older. But why should this also be put as part of Shem's title and description, that he *was the brother of Japheth*, since it had been, in effect, said often before? And was he not as much brother to Ham? Probably this was intended to signify the union of the Gentiles with the Jews in the church. The sacred historian had mentioned it as Shem's honour that he was the father of the Hebrews; but, lest Japheth's seed should therefore be looked upon as for ever shut out from the church, he here reminds us that he *was the brother of Japheth*, not in birth only, but in blessing; for *Japheth was to dwell in the tents of Shem*. Note, (1.) Those are brethren in the best manner that are so by grace, and that meet in the covenant of God and in the communion of saints. (2.) God, in dispensing his grace, does not go by seniority, but the younger sometimes gets the start of the elder in coming into the church; *so the last shall be first and the first last*.

II. The reason of the name of Peleg (*v.* 25): Because *in his days* (that is, about the time of his birth, when his name was given him), *was the earth divided* among the children of men that were to inhabit it; either when Noah divided it by an orderly distribution of it, as Joshua divided the land of Canaan by lot, or when, upon their refusal to comply with that division, God, in justice, divided them by the confusion of tongues: whichsoever of these was the occasion, pious Heber saw cause to perpetuate the remembrance of it in the name of his son; and justly may our sons be called by the same name, for in our days, in another sense, is the earth, the church, most wretchedly divided.

CHAP. XI.

AND the whole earth was of one language, and of one speech. 2 And it came to pass, as they journeyed from the east, that they found a plain in the land of Shinar; and they dwelt there. 3 And they said one to another, Go to, let us

make brick, and burn them thoroughly. And they had brick for stone, and slime had they for mortar. 4 And they said, Go to, let us build us a city and a tower, whose top *may reach* unto heaven; and let us make us a name, lest we be scattered abroad upon the face of the whole earth.

The close of the foregoing chapter tells us that *by* the sons of Noah, or *among* the sons of Noah, *the nations were divided in the earth after the flood*, that is, were distinguished into several tribes or colonies; and, the places they had hitherto lived in together having grown too strait for them, it was either appointed by Noah, or agreed upon among his sons, which way each several tribe or colony should steer its course, beginning with the countries that were next them, and designing to proceed further and further, and to remove to a greater distance from each other, as the increase of their several companies should require. Thus was the matter well settled, one hundred years after the flood, about the time of Peleg's birth; but the sons of men, it should seem, were loth to disperse into distant places; they thought the more the merrier and the safer, and therefore they contrived to keep together, and were *slack to go to possess the land which the Lord God of their fathers had given them* (Josh. xviii. 3), thinking themselves wiser than either God or Noah. Now here we have,

I. The advantages which befriended their design of keeping together, 1. They were all of *one language, v.* 1. If there were any different languages before the flood, yet Noah's only, which it is likely was the same with Adam's, was preserved through the flood, and continued after it. Now, while they all understood one another, they would be the more likely to love one another, and the more capable of helping one another, and the less inclinable to separate one from another. 2. They found a very convenient commodious place to settle in (*v.* 2), *a plain in the land of Shinar*, a spacious plain, able to *contain* them all, and a *fruitful* plain, able, according as their present numbers were, to support them all, though perhaps they had not considered what room there would be for them when their numbers should be increased. Note, Inviting accommodations, for the present, often prove too strong temptations to the neglect of both duty and interest, as it respects futurity.

II. The method they took to bind themselves to one another, and to settle together in one body. Instead of coveting to enlarge their borders by a peaceful departure under the divine protection, they contrived to fortify them, and, as those that were resolved to wage war with Heaven, they put themselves into a posture of defence. Their unanimous resolution is, *Let us build ourselves a city and a tower.* It is observable that the first builders of cities, both in the old world (*ch.* iv. 17), and in the new world here, were not men of the best character and reputation: tents served God's subjects to dwell in; cities were first built by those that were rebels against him and revolters from him. Observe here,

1. How they excited and encouraged one another to set about this work. They said, *Go to, let us make brick* (*v.* 3), and again, (*v.* 4), *Go to, let us build ourselves a city;* by mutual excitements they made one another more daring and resolute. Note, Great things may be brought to pass when the undertakers are numerous and unanimous, and stir up one another. Let us learn to provoke one another to love and to good works, as sinners stir up and encourage one another to wicked works. See Ps. cxxii. 1; Isa. ii. 3, 5; Jer. l. 5.

2. What materials they used in their building. The country, being plain, yielded neither stone nor mortar, yet this did not discourage them from their undertaking, but they made brick to serve instead of stone, and slime or pitch instead of mortar. See here, (1.) What shift those will make that are resolute in their purposes: were we but thus zealously affected in a good thing, we should not stop our work so often as we do, under pretence that we want conveniences for carrying it on. (2.) What a difference there is between men's building and God's; when men build their Babel, brick and slime are their best materials; but, when God builds his Jerusalem, he lays even the *foundations of it with sapphires, and all its borders with pleasant stones,* Isa. liv. 11, 12; Rev. xxi. 19.

3. For what ends they built. Some think they intended hereby to secure themselves against the waters of another flood. God had told them indeed that he would not again drown the world; but they would trust to a tower of their own making, rather than to a promise of God's making or an ark of his appointing. If, however, they had had this in their eye, they would have chosen to build their tower upon a mountain rather than upon a plain, but three things, it seems, they aimed at in building this tower:—

(1.) It seems designed for an affront to God himself; for they would build a tower *whose top might reach to heaven,* which bespeaks a defiance of God, or at least a rivalship with him. They would be *like the Most High,* or would come as near him as they could, not in holiness but in height. They forgot their place, and, scorning to creep on the earth, resolved to climb to heaven, not by the door or ladder, but some other way.

(2.) They hoped hereby to make themselves a name; they would do something to be talked of now, and to give posterity to know that there had been such men as they in the world. Rather than die and leave no memorandum behind them, they would leave this monument of their pride, and ambition,

and folly. Note, [1.] Affectation of honour and a name among men commonly inspires with a strange ardour for great and difficult undertakings, and often betrays to that which is evil and offensive to God. [2.] It is just with God to bury those names in the dust which are raised by sin. These Babel-builders put themselves to a great deal of foolish expense to make themselves a name; but they could not gain even this point, for we do not find in any history the name of so much as one of these Babel-builders. Philo Judæus says, They engraved every one his name upon a brick, *in perpetuam rei memoriam—as a perpetual memorial;* yet neither did this serve their purpose.

(3.) They did it to prevent their dispersion: *Lest we be scattered abroad upon the face of the earth.* "It was done" (says Josephus) "in disobedience to that command (*ch.* ix. 1), *Replenish the earth.*" God orders them to disperse. "No," say they, "we will not, we will live and die together." In order hereunto, they engage themselves and one another in this vast undertaking. That they might unite in one glorious empire, they resolve to build this city and tower, to be the metropolis of their kingdom and the centre of their unity. It is probable that the band of ambitious Nimrod was in all this. He could not content himself with the command of a particular colony, but aimed at universal monarchy, in order to which, under pretence of uniting for their common safety, he contrives to keep them in one body, that, having them all under his eye, he might not fail to have them under his power. See the daring presumption of these sinners. Here is, [1.] A bold opposition to God: "You shall be scattered," says God. "But we will not," say they. *Woe unto him that thus strives with his Maker.* [2.] A bold competition with God. It is God's prerogative to be universal monarch, Lord of all, and King of kings; the man that aims at it offers to step into the throne of God, who will not give his glory to another.

5 And the LORD came down to see the city and the tower, which the children of men builded. 6 And the LORD said, Behold, the people *is* one, and they have all one language; and this they begin to do: and now nothing will be restrained from them, which they have imagined to do. 7 Go to, let us go down, and there confound their language, that they may not understand one another's speech. 8 So the LORD scattered them abroad from thence upon the face of all the earth: and they left off to build the city. 9 Therefore is the name of it called Babel; because

79

the LORD did there confound the language of all the earth: and from thence did the LORD scatter them abroad upon the face of all the earth.

We have here the quashing of the project of the Babel-builders, and the turning of the counsel of those froward men headlong, that God's counsel might stand in spite of them. Here is,

I. The cognizance God took of the design that was on foot: *The Lord came down to see the city, v. 5.* It is an expression after the manner of men; he knew it as clearly and fully as men know that which they come to the place to view. Observe, 1. Before he gave judgment upon their cause, he enquired into it; for God is incontestably just and fair in all his proceedings against sin and sinners, and condemns none unheard. 2. It is spoken of as an act of condescension in God to take notice even of this building, which the undertakers were ·so proud of; for he humbles himself to behold the transactions, even the most considerable ones, of this lower world, Ps. cxiii. 6. 3. It is said to be *the tower which the children of men built,* which intimates, (1.) Their weakness and frailty as men. It was a very foolish thing for the children of men, worms of the earth, to defy Heaven, and to provoke the Lord to jealousy. *Are they stronger than he?* (2.) Their sinfulness and obnoxiousness. They were the sons of *Adam,* so it is in· the Hebrew; nay, of that Adam, that sinful disobedient Adam, whose children are by nature children of disobedience, children that are corrupters. (3.) Their distinction from the children of God, the professors of religion, from whom these daring builders had separated themselves, and built this tower to support and perpetuate the separation. Pious Eber is not found among this ungodly crew; for he and his are called the children of God, and therefore their souls come not into the secret, nor unite themselves to the assembly, of these children of men.

II. The counsels and resolves of the Eternal God concerning this matter; he did not come down merely as a spectator, but as a judge, as a prince, to *look upon these proud men, and abase them,* Job xl. 11—14. Observe,

1. He suffered them to proceed a good way in their enterprise before he put a stop to it, that they might have space to repent, and, if they had so much consideration left, might be ashamed of it and weary of it themselves; and if not that their disappointment might be the more shameful, and every one that passed by might laugh at them, saying, *These men began to build, and were not able to finish,* that so the works of their hands, from which they promised themselves immortal honour, might turn to their perpetual reproach. Note, God has wise and holy ends in permitting the enemies of his glory to carry on their impious projects a great way, and to prosper long in their enterprises.

80

2. When they had, with much care and toil, made some considerable progress in their building, then God determined to break their measures and disperse them. Observe,

(1.) The righteousness of God, which appears in the considerations upon which he proceeded in this resolution, *v.* 6. Two things he considered :—[1.] Their oneness, as a reason why they must be scattered: *" Behold, the people are one, and they have all one language.* If they continue one, much of the earth will be left uninhabited; the power of their prince will soon be exorbitant; wickedness and profaneness will be insufferably rampant, for they will strengthen one another's hands in it; and, which is worst of all, there will be an overbalance to the church, and these children of men, if thus incorporated, will swallow up the little remnant of God's children." Therefore it is decreed that they must not be one. Note, Unity is policy, but it is not the infallible mark of a true church; yet, while the builders of Babel, though of different families, dispositions, and interests, were thus unanimous in opposing God, what a pity is it, and what a shame, that the builders of Sion, though united in one common head and Spirit, should be divided, as they are, in serving God! But marvel not at the matter. Christ came not to send peace. [2.] Their obstinacy: *Now nothing will be restrained from them;* and this is a reason why they must be crossed and thwarted in their design. God had tried, by his commands and admonitions, to bring them off from this project, but in vain; therefore he must take another course with them. See here, *First,* The sinfulness of sin, and the wilfulness of sinners; ever since Adam would not be restrained from the forbidden tree, his unsanctified seed have been impatient of restraint and ready to rebel against it. *Secondly,* See the necessity of God's judgments upon earth, to keep the world in some order and to tie the hands of those that will not be checked by law.

(2.) The wisdom and mercy of God in the methods that were taken for the defeating of this enterprise (*v.* 7): *Go to, let us go down, and there confound their language.* This was not spoken to the angels, as if God needed either their advice or their assistance, but God speaks it to himself, or the Father to the Son and Holy Ghost. They said, *Go to, let us make brick,* and *Go to, let us build a tower,* animating one another to the attempt; and now God says, *Go to, let us confound their language;* for, if men stir up themselves to sin, God will stir up himself to take vengeance, Isa. lix. 17, 18. Now observe here, [1.] The mercy of God, in moderating the penalty, and not making it proportionable to the offence; for *he deals not with us according to our sins.* He does not say, *" Let us go down now in thunder and lightning, and consume those rebels in a moment;"* or, " Let the earth open, and swallow up them and their building, and let those go down quickly into hell who are climbing to heaven the wrong way." No; only, " *Let us go down, and scatter them.*" They deserved death, but are only banished or transported; for the patience of God is very great towards a provoking world. Punishments are chiefly reserved for the future state. God's judgments on sinners in this life, compared with those which are reserved, are little more than restraints. [2.] The wisdom of God, in pitching upon an effectual expedient to stay proceedings, which was the confounding of their language, that they might not understand one another's speech, nor could they well join hands when their tongues were divided; so that this would be a very proper method both for taking them off from their building (for, if they could not understand one another, they could not help one another) and also for disposing them to scatter; for, when they could not understand one another, they could not take pleasure in one another. Note, God has various means, and effectual ones, to baffle and defeat the projects of proud men that set themselves against him, and particularly to divide them among themselves, either by dividing their spirits (Judg. ix. 23), or by dividing their tongues, as David prays, Ps. lv. 9. III. The execution of these counsels of God, to the blasting and defeating of the counsels of men, *v.* 8, 9. God made them know *whose word should stand, his or theirs,* as the expression is, Jer. xliv. 28. Notwithstanding their oneness and obstinacy, God was too hard for them, and wherein they dealt proudly he was above them; for *who ever hardened his heart against him and prospered?* Three things were done:—

1. Their language was confounded. God, who, when he made man, taught him to speak, and put words into his mouth fit to express the conceptions of his mind by, now caused these builders to forget their former language, and to speak and understand a new one, which yet was common to those of the same tribe or family, but not to others: those of one colony could converse together, but not with those of another. Now, (1.) This was a great miracle, and a proof of the power which God has upon the minds and tongues of men, which he turns as the rivers of water. (2.) This was a great judgment upon these builders; for, being thus deprived of the knowledge of the ancient and holy tongue, they had become incapable of communicating with the true church, in which it was retained, and probably it contributed much to their loss of the knowledge of the true God. (3.) We all suffer by it, to this day. In all the inconveniences we sustain by the diversity of languages, and all the pains and trouble we are at to learn the languages we have occasion for, we smart for the rebellion of our ancestors at Babel. Nay, and those unhappy controversies which are strifes of words, and

arise from our misunderstanding one another's language, for aught I know are owing to this confusion of tongues. (4.) The project of some to frame a universal character, in order to a universal language, how desirable soever it may seem, is yet, I think, but a vain thing to attempt; for it is to strive against a divine sentence, by which the languages of the nations will be divided while the world stands. (5.) We may here lament the loss of the universal use of the Hebrew tongue, which from this time was the vulgar language of the Hebrews only, and continued so till the captivity in Babylon, where, even among them, it was exchanged for the Syriac. (6.) As the confounding of tongues divided the children of men and scattered them abroad, so the gift of tongues, bestowed upon the apostles (Acts ii.), contributed greatly to the gathering together of the children of God, who were scattered abroad, and the uniting of them in Christ, that with one mind and one mouth they might glorify God, Rom. xv. 6.

2. Their building was stopped: *They left off to build the city.* This was the effect of the confusion of their tongues; for it not only incapacitated them for helping one another, but probably struck such a damp upon their spirits that they could not proceed, since they saw, in this, the hand of the Lord gone out against them. Note, (1.) It is wisdom to leave off that which we see God fights against. (2.) God is able to blast and bring to nought all the devices and designs of Babel-builders. He sits in heaven, and laughs at the counsels of the kings of the earth against him and his anointed; and will force them to confess that there is no wisdom nor counsel against the Lord, Prov. xxi. 30; Isa. viii. 9, 10.

3. The builders were scattered abroad upon the face of the whole earth, *v.* 8, 9. They departed in companies, after their families, and after their tongues (*ch.* x. 5, 20, 31), to the several countries and places allotted to them in the division that had been made, which they knew before, but would not go to take possession of till now that they were forced to it. Observe here, (1.) The very thing which they feared came upon them That dispersion which they sought to evade by an act of rebellion they by this act brought upon themselves; for we are most likely to fall into that trouble which we seek to evade by indirect and sinful methods. (2.) It was God's work : *The Lord scattered them.* God's hand is to be acknowledged in all scattering providences; if the family be scattered, relations scattered, churches scattered, it is the Lord's doing. (3.) Though they were as firmly in league with one another as could be, yet the Lord scattered them; for no man can keep together what God will put asunder (4.) Thus God justly took vengeance on them for their oneness in that presumptuous attempt to build their tower. Shameful dispersions are the just punishment of sinful

unions. Simeon and Levi, who had been brethren in iniquity, were divided in Jacob, *ch.* xlix. 5, 7 ; Ps. lxxxiii. 3—13. (5.) They left behind them a perpetual memorandum of their reproach, in the name given to the place . It was called *Babel, confusion.* Those that aim at a great name commonly come off with a *bad* name. (6.) The children of men were now finally scattered, and never did, nor ever will, come all together again, till the great day, when the Son of man shall sit upon the throne of his glory, and all nations shall be gathered before him, Matt. xxv. 31, 32.

10 These *are* the generations of Shem: Shem *was* a hundred years old, and begat Arphaxad two years after the flood : 11 And Shem lived after he begat Arphaxad five hundred years, and begat sons and daughters. 12 And Arphaxad lived five and thirty years, and begat Salah : 13 And Arphaxad lived after he begat Salah four hundred and three years, and begat sons and daughters. 14 And Salah lived thirty years, and begat Eber : 15 And Salah lived after he begat Eber four hundred and three years, and begat sons and daughters. 16 And Eber lived four and thirty years, and begat Peleg : 17 And Eber lived after he beget Peleg four hundred and thirty years, and begat sons and daughters. 18 And Peleg lived thirty years, and begat Reu : 19 And Peleg lived after he begat Reu two hundred and nine years, and begat sons and daughters. 20 And Reu lived two and thirty years, and begat Serug : 21 And Reu lived after he begat Serug two hundred and seven years, and begat sons and daughters. 22 And Serug lived thirty years, and begat Nahor : 23 And Serug lived after he begat Nahor two hundred years, and begat sons and daughters. 24 And Nahor lived nine and twenty years, and begat Terah : 25 And Nahor lived after he begat Terah a hundred and nineteen years, and begat sons and daughters. 26 And Terah lived seventy years, and begat Abram, Nahor, and Haran.

We have here a genealogy, not an endless genealogy, for here it ends in Abram, the friend of God, and leads further to Christ, the promised seed, who was the son of Abram, and from Abram the genealogy of Christ is

reckoned (Matt. i. 1, &c.); so that put *ch.* v., *ch.* xi., and Matt. i., together, and you have such an entire genealogy of Jesus Christ as cannot be produced, for aught I know, concerning any person in the world, out of his line, and at such a distance from the fountain-head. And, laying these three genealogies together, we shall find that twice ten, and thrice fourteen, generations or descents, passed between the first and second Adam, making it clear concerning Christ that he was not only the Son of Abraham, but the Son of man, and the seed of the woman. Observe here, 1. Nothing is left upon record concerning those of this line but their names and ages, the Holy Ghost seeming to hasten through them to the story of Abram. How little do we know of those that have gone before us in this world, even those that lived in the same places where we live, as we likewise know little of those that are our contemporaries in distant places! we have enough to do to mind the work of our own day, and let God alone to *require that which is past,* Eccl. iii. 15. 2. There was an observable gradual decrease in the years of their lives. Shem reached to 600 years, which yet fell short of the age of the patriarchs before the flood ; the next three came short of 500 ; the next three did not reach to 300 ; after them we read not of any that attained to 200, except Terah ; and, not many ages after this, Moses reckoned seventy, or eighty, to be the utmost men ordinarily arrive at. When the earth began to be replenished, men's lives began to shorten ; so that the decrease is to be imputed to the wise disposal of Providence, rather than to any decay of nature. For the elect's sake, men's days are shortened ; and, being evil, it is well they are few, and *attain not to the years of the lives of our fathers,* *ch.* xlvii. 9. 3. Eber, from whom the Hebrews were denominated, was the longest-lived of any that was born after the flood, which perhaps was the reward of his singular piety and strict adherence to the ways of God.

27 Now these *are* the generations of Terah : Terah begat Abram, Nahor, and Haran ; and Haran begat Lot. 28 And Haran died before his father Terah in the land of his nativity, in Ur of the Chaldees. 29 And Abram and Nahor took them wives : the name of Abram's wife *was* Sarai ; and the name of Nahor's wife, Milcah, the daughter of Haran, the father of Milcah, and the father of Iscah. 30 But Sarai was barren ; she *had* no child. 31 And Terah took Abram his son, and Lot the son of Haran his son's son, and Sarai his daughter in law, his son Abram's wife ; and they went forth with them from Ur,

of the Chaldees, to go into the land of Canaan ; and they came unto Haran, and dwelt there. 32 And the days of Terah were two hundred and five years : and Terah died in Haran.

Here begins the story of Abram, whose name is famous, henceforward, in both Testaments. We have here,

I. His country : *Ur of the Chaldees.* This was the land of his nativity, an idolatrous country, where even the children of Eber themselves had degenerated. Note, Those who are, through grace, heirs of the land of promise, ought to remember what was the land of their nativity, what was their corrupt and sinful state by nature, the rock out of which they were hewn.

II. His relations, mentioned for his sake, and because of their interest in the following story. 1. His father was *Terah*, of whom it is said (Josh. xxiv. 2) that he served other gods, on the other side of the flood, so early did idolatry gain footing in the world, and so hard is it even for those that have some good principles to swim against the stream. Though it is said (*v.* 26) that when Terah was seventy years old he begat Abram, Nahor, and Haran (which seems to tell us that Abram was the eldest son of Terah, and was born in his seventieth year), yet, by comparing *v.* 32, which makes Terah to die in his 205*th* year, with Acts vii. 4 (where it is said that Abram removed from Haran when his father was dead), and with *ch.* xii. 4 (where it is said that he was but seventy-five years old when he removed from Haran), it appears that he was born in the 130*th* year of Terah, and probably was his youngest son ; for, in God's choices, the last are often first and the first last. We have, 2. Some account of his brethren. (1.) *Nahor*, out of whose family both Isaac and Jacob had their wives. (2.) *Haran*, the father of Lot, of whom it is here said (*v.* 28) *that he died before his father Terah.* Note, Children cannot be sure that they shall survive their parents ; for death does not go by seniority, taking the eldest first. *The shadow of death is without any order,* Job x. 22. It is likewise said that he died *in Ur of the Chaldees,* before the happy removal of the family out of that idolatrous country. Note, It concerns us to hasten out of our natural state, lest death surprise us in it. 3. His wife was *Sarai,* who, some think, was the same with Iscah, the daughter of Haran. Abram himself says of her that she was the daughter of his father, but not the daughter of his mother, *ch.* xx. 12. She was ten years younger than Abram.

III. His departure out of Ur of the Chaldees, with his father Terah, his nephew Lot, and the rest of his family, in obedience to the call of God, of which we shall read more, *ch.* xii. 1, &c. This chapter leaves them in Haran, or Charran, a place about mid-way between Ur and Canaan, where they dwelt

till Terah's head was laid, probably because the old man was unable, through the infirmities of age, to proceed in his journey. Many reach to Charran, and yet fall short of Canaan ; they are not far from the kingdom of God, and yet never come thither.

CHAP. XII.

The pedigree and family of Abram we had an account of in the foregoing chapter; here the Holy Ghost enters upon his story, and henceforward Abram and his seed are almost the only subject of the sacred history. In this chapter we have, I. God's call of Abram to the land of Canaan, ver. 1—3. II. Abram's obedience to this call, ver. 4, 5. III. His welcome to the land of Canaan, ver. 6—9. IV. His journey to Egypt, with an account of what happened there. Abram's flight and fault, ver. 10—13. Sarai's danger and deliverance, ver. 14—20.

NOW the LORD had said unto Abram, Get thee out of thy country, and from thy kindred, and from thy father's house, unto a land that I will show thee : 2 And I will make of thee a great nation, and I will bless thee, and make thy name great ; and thou shalt be a blessing : 3 And I will bless them that bless thee, and curse him that curseth thee : and in thee shall all families of the earth be blessed.

We have here the call by which Abram was removed out of the land of his nativity into the land of promise, which was designed both to try his faith and obedience and also to separate him and set him apart for God, and for special services and favours which were further designed. The circumstances of this call we may be somewhat helped to the knowledge of from Stephen's speech, Acts vii. 2, where we are told, 1. That the God of glory appeared to him to give him this call, appeared in such displays of his glory as left Abram no room to doubt the divine authority of this call. God spoke to him afterwards in divers manners ; but this first time, when the correspondence was to be settled, he appeared to him as *the God of glory,* and spoke to him. 2. That this call was given him in Mesopotamia, before he dwelt in Charran ; therefore we rightly read it, The Lord had *said unto Abram,* namely, in Ur of the Chaldees ; and, in obedience to this call, as Stephen further relates the story (Acts vii. 4), *he came out of the land of the Chaldeans, and dwelt in Charran, or Haran, about five years, and thence, when his father was dead,* by a fresh command, pursuant to the former, God removed him into the land of Canaan. Some think that Haran was in Chaldea, and so was still a part of Abram's country, or that Abram, having staid there five years, began to call it his country, and to take root there, till God let him know this was not the place he was intended for. Note; If God loves us, and has mercy in store for us, he will not suffer us to take up our rest any where short of Canaan, but will graciously repeat his calls, till the good work begun be performed, and our souls repose in

God only. In the call itself we have a precept and a promise.

I. A trying precept: *Get thee out of thy country, v.* 1. Now,

1. By this precept he was tried whether he loved his native soil and dearest friends, and whether he could willingly leave all, to go along with God. His country had become idolatrous, his kindred and his father's house were a constant temptation to him, and he could not continue with them without danger of being infected by them; therefore, *Get thee out,* לֶךְ־לְךָ—*Vade tibi, Get thee gone,* with all speed,*escape for thy life,look not behind thee, ch.* xix. 17. Note, Those that are in a sinful state are concerned to make all possible haste out of it. *Get out for thyself* (so some read it), that is, for thy own good. Note, Those who leave their sins, and turn to God, will themselves be unspeakable gainers by the change, Prov. ix. 12. This command which God gave to Abram is much the same with the gospel call by which all the spiritual seed of faithful Abram are brought into covenant with God. For, (1.) Natural affection must give way to divine grace. Our country is dear to us, our kindred dearer, and our father's house dearest of all; and yet they must all be hated (Luke xiv. 26), that is, we must love them less than Christ, hate them in comparison with him, and, whenever any of these come in competition with him, they must be postponed, and the preference given to the will and honour of the Lord Jesus. (2.) Sin, and all the occasions of it, must be forsaken, and particularly bad company; we must abandon all the idols of iniquity which have been set up in our hearts, and get out of the way of temptation, plucking out even a right eye that leads us to sin (Matt. v. 29), willingly parting with that which is dearest to us, when we cannot keep it without hazard of our integrity. Those that resolve to keep the commandments of God must quit the society of evil doers, Ps. cxix. 115; Acts ii. 40. (3.) The world, and all our enjoyments in it, must be looked upon with a holy indifference and contempt; we must no longer look upon it as our country, or home, but as our inn, and must accordingly sit loose to it and live above it, get out of it in affection.

2. By this precept he was tried whether he could trust God further than he saw him; for he must leave his own country, to go to a *land that God would show him.* He does not say, "It is a land that I will give thee," but merely, "a land that I will show thee." Nor does he tell him what land it was, nor what kind of land; but he must follow God with an implicit faith, and take God's word for it, in the general, though he had no particular securities given him that he should be no loser by leaving his country, to follow God. Note, Those that will deal with God must deal upon trust; we must quit the things that are seen for things that are not seen, and submit to the sufferings of this present time in hopes of a glory that is yet to be revealed (Rom. viii. 18); for *it doth not yet appear what we shall be* (1 John iii. 2), any more than it did to Abram, when God called him to a land he would show him, so teaching him to live in a continual dependence upon his direction, and with his eye ever towards him.

II. Here is an encouraging promise, nay, it is a complication of promises, many, and exceedingly great and precious. Note, All God's precepts are attended with promises to the obedient. When he makes himself known to us as a commander he makes himself known also as a rewarder: if we obey the command, God will not fail to perform the promise. Here are six promises:—

1. *I will make of thee a great nation.* When God took him from his own people, he promised to make him the head of another; he cut him off from being the branch of a wild olive, to make him the root of a good olive. This promise was, (1.) A great relief to Abram's burden; for he had now no child. Note, God knows how to suit his favours to the wants and necessities of his children. He that has a plaster for every sore will provide one for that first which is most painful. (2.) A great trial to Abram's faith; for his wife had been long barren, so that, if he believe, it must be against hope, and his faith must build purely upon that power which *can out of stones raise up children unto Abraham,* and make them a great nation. Note, [1.] God makes nations: by him they are *born at once* (Isa. lxvi. 8), and he speaks, to build and plant them, Jer. xviii. 9. And, [2.] If a nation be made great in wealth and power, it is God that makes it great. [3.] God can raise great nations out of dry ground, and can make *a little one to be a thousand.*

2. *I will bless thee,* either particularly with the blessing of fruitfulness and increase, as he had blessed Adam and Noah, or, in general, " *I will bless thee* with all manner of blessings, both of the upper and the nether springs. Leave thy father's house, and I will give thee a father's blessing, better than that of thy progenitors." Note, Obedient believers will be sure to inherit the blessing.

3. *I will make thy name great.* By deserting his country, he lost his name there. " Care not for that," says God, " but trust me, and I will make thee a greater name than ever thou couldst have had there." Having no child, he feared he should have no name; but God will make him a great nation, and so make him a great name. Note, (1.) God is the fountain of honour, and from him promotion comes, 1 Sam. ii. 8. (2.) The name of obedient believers shall certainly be celebrated and made great. The best report is that which the elders obtained by faith, Heb. xi. 2.

4. *Thou shalt be a blessing;* that is, (1.) " Thy happiness shall be a sample of happiness, so that those who would bless their

friends shall only pray that God would make them like Abram;" as Ruth iv. 11. Note, God's dealings with obedient believers are so kind and gracious that we need not desire for ourselves or our friends to be any better dealt with: to have God for our friend is blessedness enough. (2.) " Thy life shall be a blessing to the places where thou shalt sojourn." Note, Good men are the blessings of their country, and it is their unspeakable honour and happiness to be made so.

5. *I will bless those that bless thee and curse him that curseth thee.* This made it a kind of a league, offensive and defensive, between God and Abram. Abram heartily espoused God's cause, and here God promises to interest himself in his. (1.) He promises to be a friend to his friends, to take kindnesses shown to him as done to himself, and to recompense them accordingly. God will take care that none be losers, in the long run, by any service done for his people; even a cup of cold water shall be rewarded. (2.) He promises to appear against his enemies. There were those that hated and cursed even Abram himself; but, while their causeless curses could not hurt Abram, God's righteous curse would certainly overtake and ruin them, Num. xxiv. 9. This is a good reason why we should bless those that curse us, because it is enough that God *will* curse them, Ps. xxxviii. 13—15.

6. *In thee shall all the families of the earth be blessed.* This was the promise that crowned all the rest; for it points at the Messiah, in whom *all the promises are yea and amen.* Note, (1.) Jesus Christ is the great blessing of the world, the greatest that ever the world was blessed with. He is a family blessing, by him salvation is brought to the house (Luke xix. 9); when we reckon up our family blessings, let us put Christ in the *imprimis—the first place,* as the blessing of blessings. But how are all the families of the earth blessed in Christ, when so many are strangers to him? *Answer,* [1.] All that are blessed are blessed in him, Acts iv. 12. [2.] All that believe, of what family soever they be, shall be blessed in him. [3.] Some of all the families of the earth are blessed in him. [4.] There are some blessings which all the families of the earth are blessed with in Christ; for the gospel salvation is a *common salvation,* Jude 3. (2.) It is a great honour to be related to Christ; this made Abram's name great, that the Messiah was to descend from his loins, much more than that he should be the father of many nations. It was Abram's honour to be his father by nature; it will be ours to be his brethren by grace, Matt. xii. 50.

4 So Abram departed, as the LORD had spoken unto him; and Lot went with him: and Abram *was* seventy and five years old when he departed out of Haran. 5 And Abram took

Sarai his wife, and Lot his brother's son, and all their substance that they had gathered, and the souls that they had gotten in Haran; and they went forth to go into the land of Canaan; and into the land of Canaan they came.

Here is, I. Abraham's removal out of his country, out of Ur first and afterwards out of Haran, in compliance with the call of God: *So Abram departed;* he was not disobedient to the heavenly vision, but did as he was bidden, not conferring with flesh and blood, Gal. i. 15, 16. His obedience was speedy and without delay, submissive and without dispute; for he *went out, not knowing whither he went* (Heb. xi. 8), but knowing whom he followed and under whose direction he went. Thus God *called him to his foot,* Isa. xli. 2.

II. His age when he removed: he was *seventy-five years old,* an age when he should rather have had rest and settlement; but, if God will have him to begin the world again now in his old age, he will submit. Here is an instance of an old convert.

III. The company and cargo that he took with him.

1. He took his wife, and his nephew Lot, with him; not by force and against their wills, but by persuasion. Sarai, his wife, would be sure to go with him; God had joined them together, and nothing should put them asunder. If Abram leave all, to follow God, Sarai will leave all, to follow Abram, though neither of them knew whither. And it was a mercy to Abram to have such a companion in his travels, a help meet for him. Note, It is very comfortable when husband and wife agree to go together in the way to heaven. Lot also, his kinsman, was influenced by Abram's good example, who was perhaps his guardian after the death of his father, and he was willing to go along with him too. Note, Those that go to Canaan need not go alone; for, though few find the strait gate, blessed be God, some do; and it is our wisdom to go with those with whom God is (Zech. viii. 23), wherever they go.

2. They took all their effects with them— *all their substance* and movable goods, *that they had gathered.* For, (1.) With themselves they would give up their all, to be at God's disposal, would keep back no part of the price, but venture all in one bottom, knowing it was a good bottom. (2.) They would furnish themselves with that which was requisite, both for the service of God and the supply of their family, in the country whither they were going. To have thrown away his substance, because God had promised to bless him, would have been to tempt God, not to trust him. (3.) They would not be under any temptation to return; therefore they leave not a hoof behind, lest that should make them *mindful of the country from which they came out.*

3. They took with them the *souls that they had gotten*, that is, (1.) The servants they had bought, which were part of their substance, but are called *souls*, to remind masters that their poor servants have souls, precious souls, which they ought to take care of and provide food convenient for. (2.) The proselytes they had made, and persuaded to attend the worship of the true God, and to go with them to Canaan: the souls which (as one of the rabbin expresses it) they had *gathered under the wings of the divine Majesty.* Note, Those who serve and follow God themselves should do all they can to bring others to serve and follow him too. These souls they are said to have *gained.* We must reckon ourselves true gainers if we can but win souls to Christ.

IV. Here is their happy arrival at their journey's end: *They went forth to go into the land of Canaan;* so they did before (*ch.* xi. 31), and then took up short, but now they held on their way, and, by the good hand of their God upon them, to the land of Canaan they came, where by a fresh revelation they were told that this was the land God promised to show them. They were not discouraged by the difficulties they met with in their way, nor diverted by the delights they met with, but *pressed forward.* Note, 1. Those that set out for heaven must persevere to the end, still reaching forth to those things that are before. 2. That which we undertake in obedience to God's command, and a humble attendance upon his providence, will certainly succeed, and end with comfort at last.

6 And Abram passed through the land unto the place of Sichem, unto the plain of Moreh. And the Canaanite *was* then in the land. 7 And the Lord appeared unto Abram, and said, Unto thy seed will I give this land: and there builded he an altar unto the Lord, who appeared unto him. 8 And he removed from thence unto a mountain on the east of Beth-el, and pitched his tent, *having* Beth-el on the west, and Hai on the east: and there he builded an altar unto the Lord, and called upon the name of the Lord. 9 And Abram journeyed, going on still toward the south.

One would have expected that Abram having had such an extraordinary call to Canaan some great event should have followed upon his arrival there, that he should have been introduced with all possible marks of honour and respect, and that the kings of Canaan should immediately have surrendered their crowns to him, and done him homage. But no; he comes not with observation, little notice is taken of him, for

still God will have him to live by faith, and to look upon Canaan, even when he was in it, as a land of promise; therefore observe here,

I. How little comfort he had in the land he came to; for, 1. He had it not to himself: *The Canaanite was then in the land.* He found the country peopled and possessed by Canaanites, who were likely to be but bad neighbours and worse landlords; and, for aught that appears, he could not have ground to pitch his tent on but by their permission. Thus the accursed Canaanites seemed to be in better circumstances than blessed Abram. Note, The children of this world have commonly more of it than God's children. 2. He had not a settlement in it. He *passed through the land, v.* 6. He *removed to a mountain, v.* 8. He *journeyed, going on still, v.* 9. Observe here, (1.) Sometimes it is the lot of good men to be unsettled, and obliged often to remove their habitation. Holy David had his wanderings, his flittings, Ps. lvi. 8. (2.) Our removes in this world are often into various conditions. Abram sojourned, first in a plain (*v.* 6), then in a mountain, *v.* 8. God has set the one over-against the other. (3.) All good people must look upon themselves as strangers and sojourners in this world, and by faith sit loose to it as a strange country. So Abram did, Heb. xi. 8—14. (4.) While we are here in this present state, we must be journeying, and going on still from strength to strength, as having not yet attained.

II. How much comfort he had in the God he followed; when he could have little satisfaction in converse with the Canaanites whom he found there, he had abundance of pleasure in communion with that God who brought him thither, and did not leave him. Communion with God is kept up by the word and by prayer, and by these, according to the methods of that dispensation, Abram's communion with God was kept up in the land of his pilgrimage.

1. God appeared to Abram, probably in a vision, and spoke to him good words and comfortable words: *Unto thy seed will I give this land.* Note, (1.) No place nor condition of life can shut us out from the comfort of God's gracious visits. Abram is a sojourner, unsettled among Canaanites; and yet here also he meets with him that lives and sees him. Enemies may part us and our tents, us and our altars, but not us and our God. Nay, (2.) With respect to those that faithfully follow God in a way of duty, though he lead them from their friends, he will himself make up that loss by his gracious appearances to them. (3.) God's promises are sure and satisfying to all those who conscientiously observe and obey his precepts; and those who, in compliance with God's call, leave or lose any thing that is dear to them, shall be sure of something else abundantly better in lieu of it. Abram had left

86

the *land of his nativity:* "Well," says God, "I will give thee this land," Matt. xix. 29. (4.) God reveals himself and his favours to his people by degrees; before he had promised to *show* him this land, now to *give* it to him: as grace is growing, so is comfort. (5.) It is comfortable to have land of God's giving, not by providence only, but by promise. (6.) Mercies to the children are mercies to the parents. "I will give it, not to thee, but to thy seed;" it is a grant in reversion to his seed, which yet, it should seem, Abram understood also as a grant to himself of a better land in reversion, of which this was a type; for he looked for a heavenly country, Heb. xi. 16.

2. Abram attended on God in his instituted ordinances. He *built an altar unto the Lord who appeared to him, and called on the name of the Lord, v. 7, 8.* Now consider this, (1.) As done upon a special occasion. When God appeared to him, then and there he built an altar, with an eye to the God who appeared to him. Thus he returned God's visit, and kept up his correspondence with heaven, as one that resolved it should not fail on his side; thus he acknowledged, with thankfulness, God's kindness to him in making him that gracious visit and promise; and thus he testified his confidence in and dependence upon the word which God had spoken. Note, An active believer can heartily bless God for a promise the performance of which he does not yet see, and build an altar to the honour of God who appears to him, though he does not yet appear for him. (2.) As his constant practice, whithersoever he removed. As soon as Abram had got to Canaan, though he was but a stranger and sojourner there, yet he set up, and kept up, the worship of God in his family; and wherever he had a tent God had an altar, and that an altar sanctified by prayer. For he not only minded the ceremonial part of religion, the offering of sacrifice, but made conscience of the natural duty of seeking to his God, and calling on his name, that spiritual sacrifice with which God is well pleased. He preached concerning the name of the Lord, that is, he instructed his family and neighbours in the knowledge of the true God and his holy religion. The *souls he had gotten in Haran,* being discipled, must be further taught. Note, Those that would approve themselves the children of faithful Abram, and would inherit the blessing of Abram, must make conscience of keeping up the solemn worship of God, particularly in their families, according to the example of Abram. The way of family worship is a good old way, is no novel invention, but the ancient usage of all the saints. Abram was very rich and had a numerous family, was now unsettled and in the midst of enemies, and yet, wherever he pitched his tent, he built an altar. Wherever we go, let us not fail to take our religion along with us.

10 And there was a famine in the land: and Abram went down into Egypt to sojourn there; for the famine *was* grievous in the land. 11 And it came to pass, when he was come near to enter into Egypt, that he said unto Sarai his wife, Behold now, I know that thou *art* a fair woman to look upon: 12 Therefore it shall come to pass, when the Egyptians shall see thee, that they shall say, This *is* his wife: and they will kill me, but they will save thee alive. 13 Say, I pray thee, thou *art* my sister: that it may be well with me for thy sake; and my soul shall live because of thee.

Here is, I. A famine in the land of Canaan, *a grievous famine.* That fruitful land was turned into barrenness, not only to punish the iniquity of the Canaanites who dwelt therein, but to exercise the faith of Abram who sojourned therein; and a very sore trial it was; it tried what he would think, 1. Of God that brought him thither, whether he would not be ready to say with his murmuring seed that he was brought forth to be *killed with hunger,* Exod. xvi. 3. Nothing short of a strong faith could keep up good thoughts of God under such a providence. 2. Of the land of promise, whether he would think the grant of it worth the accepting, and a valuable consideration for the relinquishing of his own country, when, for aught that now appeared, it was a land that *ate up the inhabitants.* Now he was tried whether he could preserve an unshaken confidence that the God who brought him to Canaan would maintain him there, and whether he could rejoice in him as the God of his salvation when the fig-tree did not blossom, Hab. iii. 17, 18. Note, (1.) Strong faith is commonly exercised with divers temptations, that it may be *found to praise, and honour, and glory,* 1 Pet. i. 6, 7. (2.) It pleases God sometimes to try those with great afflictions who are but young beginners in religion. (3.) It is possible for a man to be in the way of duty, and in the way to happiness, and yet meet with great troubles and disappointments.

II. Abram's removal into Egypt, upon occasion of this famine. See how wisely God provides that there should be plenty in one place when there was scarcity in another, that, as members of the great body, we may not say to one another, *I have no need of you.* God's providence took care there should be a supply in Egypt, and Abram's prudence made use of the opportunity; for we tempt God, and do not trust him, if, in the time of distress, we use not the means he has graciously provided for our preservation: We must not expect needless miracles. But that which is especially observable here, to the praise of Abram, is that he did not offer to return, upon this occasion, to the country from which he came out, nor so much as towards it. The land of his nativity lay north-east from Canaan; and therefore, when he must, for a time, quit Canaan, he chooses to go to Egypt, which lay south-west, the contrary way, that he might not so much as seem to look back. See Heb. xi. 15, 16. Further observe, When he went down into Egypt, it was to sojourn there, not to dwell there. Note, 1. Though Providence, for a time, may cast us into bad places, yet we ought to tarry there no longer than needs must; we may *sojourn* where we may not *settle.* 2. A good man, while he is on this side heaven, wherever he is, is but a sojourner.

III. A great fault which Abram was guilty of, in denying his wife, and pretending that she was his sister. The scripture is impartial in relating the misdeeds of the most celebrated saints, which are recorded, not for our imitation, but for our admonition, that he *who thinks he stands may take heed lest he fall.* 1. His fault was dissembling his relation to Sarai, equivocating concerning it, and teaching his wife, and probably all his attendants, to do so too. What he said was, in a sense, true (*ch.* xx. 12), but with a purpose to deceive; he so concealed a further truth as in effect to deny it, and to expose thereby both his wife and the Egyptians to sin. 2. That which was at the bottom of it was a jealous timorous fancy he had that some of the Egyptians would be so charmed with the beauty of Sarai (Egypt producing few such beauties) that, if they should know he was her husband, they would find some way or other to take him off, that they might marry her. He presumes they would rather be guilty of murder than adultery, such a heinous crime was it then accounted and such a sacred regard was paid to the marriage bond; hence he infers, without any good reason, *They will kill me.* Note, The fear of man brings a snare, and many are driven to sin by the dread of death, Luke xii. 4, 5. The grace Abram was most eminent for was faith; and yet he thus fell through unbelief and distrust of the divine Providence, even *after God had appeared to him twice.* Alas! what will become of the willows, when the cedars are thus shaken?

14 And it came to pass, that, when Abram was come into Egypt, the Egyptians beheld the woman that she *was* very fair. 15 The princes also of Pharaoh saw her, and commended her before Pharaoh: and the woman was taken into Pharaoh's house. 16 And he entreated Abram well for her sake: and he had sheep and

oxen, and he asses, and menservants, and maidservants, and she asses, and camels. 17 And the LORD plagued Pharaoh and his house with great plagues because of Sarai Abram's wife. 18 And Pharaoh called Abram, and said, What *is* this *that* thou hast done unto me? why didst thou not tell me that she *was* thy wife? 19 Why saidst thou, She *is* my sister? so I might have taken her to me to wife: now therefore behold thy wife, take *her,* and go thy way. 20 And Pharaoh commanded *his* men concerning him: and they sent him away, and his wife, and all that he had.

Here is, I. The danger Sarai was in of having her chastity violated by the king of Egypt: and without doubt the peril of sin is the greatest peril we can be in. *Pharaoh's princes* (his pimps rather) *saw her, and,* observing what a comely woman she was, they *commended her before Pharaoh,* not for that which was really her praise—her virtue and modesty, her faith and piety (these were no excellencies in their eyes), but for her beauty, which they thought too good for the embraces of a subject. They recommended her to the king, and she was presently taken into Pharaoh's house, as Esther into the seraglio of Ahasuerus (Esth. ii. 8), in order to her being taken into his bed. Now we must not look upon Sarai as standing fair for preferment, but as entering into temptation; and the occasions of it were her own beauty (which is a snare to many) and Abram's equivocation, which is a sin that commonly is an inlet to much sin. While Sarai was in this danger, Abram fared the better for her sake. Pharaoh gave him sheep, oxen, &c. (*v.* 16), to gain his consent, that he might the more readily prevail with her whom he supposed to be his sister. We cannot think that Abram expected this when he came down into Egypt, much less that he had an eye to it when he denied his wife; but God brought good out of evil. And thus the wealth of the sinner proves, in some way or other, to be laid up for the just. II. The deliverance of Sarai from this danger. For if God did not deliver us, many a time, by prerogative, out of those straits and distresses which we bring ourselves into by our own sin and folly, and which therefore we could not expect any deliverance from by promise, we should soon be ruined, nay, we should have been ruined long before this. He deals not with us according to our deserts.

1. God chastised Pharaoh, and so prevented the progress of his sin. Note, Those are happy chastisements that hinder us in a sinful way, and effectually bring us to our duty, and particularly to the duty of restoring that

which we have wrongfully taken and detained. Observe, Not Pharaoh only, but his house, was plagued, probably those princes especially that had commended Sarai to Pharaoh. Note, Partners in sin are justly made partners in the punishment. Those that serve others' lusts must expect to share in their plagues. We are not told particularly what these plagues were; but doubtless there was something in the plagues themselves, or some explication added to them, sufficient to convince them that it was for Sarai's sake that they were thus plagued.

2. Pharaoh reproved Abram, and then dismissed him with respect.

(1.) The reproof was calm, but very just: *What is this that thou hast done?* What an improper thing! How unbecoming a wise and good man! Note, If those that profess religion do that which is unfair and disingenuous, especially if they say that which borders upon a lie, they must expect to hear of it, and have reason to thank those that will tell them of it. We find a prophet of the Lord justly reproved and upbraided by a heathen ship-master, Jon. i. 6. Pharaoh reasons with him: *Why didst thou not tell me that she was thy wife?* intimating that, if he had known this, he would not have taken her into his house. Note, It is a fault too common among good people to entertain suspicions of others beyond what there is cause for. We have often found more of virtue, honour, and conscience, in some people than we thought they possessed; and it ought to be a pleasure to us to be thus disappointed, as Abram was here, who found Pharaoh to be a better man than he expected. Charity teaches us to hope the best.

(2.) The dismission was kind and very generous. He restored him his wife without offering any injury to her honour: *Behold thy wife, take her, v.* 19. Note, Those that would prevent sin must remove the temptation, or get out of the way of it. He also sent him away in peace, and was so far from any design to kill him, as he apprehended, that he took particular care of him. Note, We often perplex and ensnare ourselves with fears which soon appear to have been altogether groundless. We often fear where no fear is. We fear the *fury of the oppressor, as though he were ready to destroy,* when really there is no danger, Isa. li. 13. It would have been more for Abram's credit and comfort to have told the truth at first; for, after all, *honesty is the best policy.* Nay, it is said (*v.* 20), *Pharaoh commanded his men concerning him,* that is, [1.] He charged them not to injure him in any thing. Note, It is not enough for those in authority to do no hurt themselves, but they must restrain their servants, and those about them, from doing hurt. Or, [2.] He appointed them, when Abram was disposed to return home, after the famine, to conduct him safely out of the country, as his convoy. Probably he

was alarmed by the plagues (*v.* 17), and inferred from them that Abram was a particular favourite of Heaven, and therefore, through fear of their return, took special care he should receive no injury in his country. Note, God has often raised up friends for his people, by making men know that it is at their peril if they hurt them. It is a dangerous thing to offend Christ's little ones. Matt. xviii. 6. To this passage, among others, the Psalmist refers, Ps. cv. 13—15, *He reproved kings for their sakes, saying, Touch not my anointed.* Perhaps, if Pharaoh had not *sent him away,* he would have been tempted to stay in Egypt and to forget the land of promise. Note, Sometimes God makes use of the enemies of his people to convince them, and remind them, that this world is not their rest, but that they must think of departing.

Lastly, Observe a resemblance between this deliverance of Abram out of Egypt and the deliverance of his seed thence: 430 years after Abram went into Egypt on occasion of a famine they went thither on occasion of a famine also; he was fetched out with great plagues on Pharaoh, so were they; as Abram was dismissed by Pharaoh, and enriched with the spoil of the Egyptians, so were they. For God's care of his people is the same *yesterday, to-day, and for ever.*

CHAP. XIII.

In this chapter we have a further account concerning Abram. I. In general, of his condition and behaviour in the land of promise, which was now the land of his pilgrimage. 1. His removes, ver. 1, 3, 4, 18. 2. His riches, ver. 2. 3. His devotion, ver. 4, 18. II. A particular account of a quarrel that happened between him and Lot. 1. The unhappy occasion of their strife, ver. 5, 6. 2. The parties concerned in the strife, with the aggravation of it, ver. 7. III. The making up of the quarrel, by the prudence of Abram, ver. 8, 9. IV. Lot's departure from Abram to the plain of Sodom, ver. 10—13. V. God's appearance to Abram, to confirm the promise of the land of Canaan to him, ver. 14, &c.

AND Abram went up out of Egypt, he, and his wife, and all that he had, and Lot with him, into the south. 2 And Abram *was* very rich in cattle, in silver, and in gold. 3 And he went on his journeys from the south even to Beth-el, unto the place where his tent had been at the beginning, between Beth-el and Hai; 4 Unto the place of the altar, which he had made there at the first: and there Abram called on the name of the LORD.

I. Here is Abram's return out of Egypt, *v.* 1. He came himself and brought all his with him back again to Canaan. Note, Though there may be occasion to go sometimes into places of temptation, yet we must hasten out of them as soon as possible. See Ruth i. 6.

II. His wealth: *He was very rich, v.* 2. He was very *heavy,* so the Hebrew word signifies; for *riches are a burden,* and those that *will be rich do but load themselves with thick clay,* Hab. ii. 6. There is a burden of care in getting them, fear in keeping them, temptation in using them, guilt in abusing them, sorrow in losing them, and a burden of account, at last, to be given up concerning them. Great possessions do but make men heavy and unwieldy. Abram was not only rich in faith and good works, and in the promises, but he was *rich in cattle, and in silver and gold.* Note, 1. God, in his providence, sometimes makes good men rich men, and teaches them how to abound, as well as how to suffer want. 2. The riches of good men are the fruits of God's blessing. God had said to Abram, *I will bless thee;* and that blessing made him rich without sorrow, Prov. x. 22. 3. True piety will very well consist with great prosperity. Though it is hard for a rich man to get to heaven, yet it is not impossible, Mark x. 23, 24. Abram was very rich and yet very religious. Nay, as piety is a friend to outward prosperity (1 Tim. iv. 8), so outward prosperity, if well-managed, is an ornament to piety, and furnishes an opportunity of doing so much the more good.

III. His removal to Beth-el, *v.* 3, 4. Thither he went, not only because there he had formerly had his tent, and he was willing to go among his old acquaintance, but because there he had formerly had his altar: and, though the altar was gone (probably he himself having taken it down, when he left the place, lest it should be polluted by the idolatrous Canaanites), yet he *came to the place of the altar,* either to revive the remembrance of the sweet communion he had had with God in that place, or perhaps to pay the vows he had there made to God when he undertook his journey into Egypt. Long afterwards God sent Jacob to this same place on that errand (*ch.* xxxv. 1), *Go up to Beth-el, where thou vowedst the vow.* We have need to be reminded, and should take all occasions to remind ourselves, of our solemn vows; and perhaps the place where they were made may help to bring them afresh to mind, and it may therefore do us good to visit it.

IV. His devotion there. His altar was gone, so that he could not offer sacrifice; but *he called on the name of the Lord,* as he had done, *ch.* xii. 8. Note, 1. All God's people are praying people. You may as soon find a living man without breath as a living Christian without prayer. 2. Those that would approve themselves upright with their God must be constant and persevering in the services of religion. Abram did not leave his religion behind him in Egypt, as many do in their travels. 3. When we cannot do *what we would* we must make conscience of doing *what we can* in the acts of devotion. When we want an altar, let us not be wanting in prayer, but, wherever we are, call on the name of the Lord.

5 And Lot also, which went with Abram, had flocks, and herds, and

tents. 6 And the land was not able to bear them, that they might dwell together: for their substance was great, so that they could not dwell together. 7 And there was a strife between the herdmen of Abram's cattle, and the herdmen of Lot's cattle: and the Canaanite and the Perizzite dwelled then in the land. 8 And Abram said unto Lot, Let there be no strife, I pray thee, between me and thee, and between my herdmen and thy herdmen; for we *be* brethren. 9 *Is* not the whole land before thee? separate thyself, I pray thee, from me: if *thou wilt take* the left hand, then I will go to the right; or if *thou depart* to the right hand, then I will go to the left.

We have here an unhappy falling out between Abram and Lot, who had hitherto been inseparable companions (see *v.* 1, and *ch.* xii. 4), but now parted.

I. The occasion of their quarrel was their riches. We read (*v.* 2) how rich Abram was; now here we are told (*v.* 5) that *Lot, who went with Abram,* was rich too; and therefore God blessed him with riches because he went with Abram. Note, 1. It is good being in good company, and going with those with whom God is, Zech. viii. 23. 2. Those that are partners with God's people in their obedience and sufferings shall be sharers with them in their joys and comforts, Isa. lxvi. 10. Now, they both being very rich, *the land was not able to bear them, that they might dwell* comfortably and peaceably together. So that their riches may be considered, (1.) As setting them at a distance one from another. Because the place was too strait for them, and they had not room for their stock, it was necessary they should live asunder. Note, Every comfort in this world has its cross attending it. Business is a comfort; but it has this inconvenience in it, that it allows us not the society of those we love so often, nor so long, as we could wish. (2.) As setting them at variance one with another. Note, Riches are often an occasion of strife and contention among relations and neighbours. This is one of those *foolish and hurtful lusts which those that will be rich fall into,* 1 Tim. vi. 9. Riches not only afford matter for contention, and are the things most commonly striven about, but they also stir up a spirit of contention, by making people proud and covetous. *Meum* and *tuum*—*Mine* and *thine,* are the great make-bates of the world. Poverty and travail, wants and wanderings, could not separate between Abram and Lot; but riches did. Friends are soon lost; but God is a friend from whose love neither the height of prosperity nor the depth of adversity shall separate us.

II. The immediate instruments of the quarrel were their servants. The strife began between *the herdsmen of Abram's cattle and the herdsmen of Lot's cattle*, v. 7. They strove, it is probable, which should have the better pasture or the better water ; and both interested their masters in the quarrel. Note, Bad servants often make a great deal of mischief in families, by their pride and passion, their lying, slandering, and tale-bearing. It is a very wicked thing for servants to do ill offices between relations and neighbours, and to sow discord ; those that do so are the devil's agents and their masters' worst enemies.

III. The aggravation of the quarrel was that *the Canaanite and the Perizzite dwelt then in the land ;* this made the quarrel, 1. Very dangerous. If Abram and Lot cannot agree to feed their flocks together, it is well if the common enemy do not come upon them and plunder them both. Note, The division of families and churches often proves the ruin of them. 2. Very scandalous. No doubt the eyes of all the neighbours were upon them, especially because of the singularity of their religion, and the extraordinary sanctity they professed; and notice would soon be taken of this quarrel, and improvement made of it, to their reproach, by the Canaanites and Perizzites. Note, The quarrels of professors are the reproach of profession, and give occasion, as much as any thing, to ;the enemies of the Lord to blaspheme.

IV. The making up of this quarrel was very happy. It is best to preserve the peace, that it be not broken ; but the next best is, if differences do happen, with all speed to accommodate them, and quench the fire that has broken out. The motion for staying this strife was made by Abram, though he was the senior and superior relation, v. 8.

1. His petition for peace was very affectionate : *Let there be no strife, I pray thee.* Abram here shows himself to be a man, (1.) Of a cool spirit, that had the command of his passion, and knew how to turn away wrath with a soft answer. Those that would keep the peace must never render railing for railing. (2.) Of a condescending spirit ; he was willing to beseech even his inferior to be at peace, and made the first overture of reconciliation. Conquerors reckon it their glory to give peace by power ; and it is no less so to give peace by the meekness of wisdom. Note, The people of God should always approve themselves a peaceable people ; whatever others are for, they must be for peace.

2. His plea for peace was very cogent. (1.) " Let there be no strife *between me and thee.* Let the Canaanites and Perizzites contend about trifles ; but let not thee and me fall out, who know better things, and look for a better country." Note, Professors of religion should, of all others, be careful to avoid contention. *You shall not be so,* Luke xxii. 26. *We have no such custom,* 1 Cor. xi. 16. " Let there be no strife *between me and thee,* who have lived together and loved one another so long." Note, The remembrance of old friendships should quickly put an end to new quarrels which at any time happen. (2.) Let it be remembered that *we are brethren,* Heb. *we are men brethren ;* a double argument. [1.] We are men ; and, as men, we are mortal creatures—we may die to-morrow, and are concerned to be found in peace. We are rational creatures, and should be ruled by reason. We are men, and not brutes, men, and not children ; we are sociable creatures, let us be so to the uttermost. [2.] We are brethren. Men of the same nature, of the same kindred and family, of the same religion, companions in obedience, companions in patience. Note, The consideration of our relation to each other, as brethren, should always prevail to moderate our passions, and either to prevent or put an end to our contentions. Brethren should love as brethren.

3. His proposal for peace was very fair. Many who profess to be for peace yet will do nothing towards it ; but Abram hereby approved himself a real friend to peace that he proposed an unexceptionable expedient for the preserving of it : *Is not the whole land before thee ? v.* 9. As if he had said, " Why should we quarrel for room, while there is room enough for us both ?" (1.) He concludes that they must part, and is very desirous that they should part friends : *Separate thyself, I pray thee, from me.* What could be expressed more affectionately ? He does not expel him, and force him away, but advises that he should separate himself. Nor does he charge him to depart, but humbly desires him to withdraw. Note, Those that have power to command, yet sometimes, for love's sake, and peace' sake, should rather beseech, as Paul besought Philemon, *v.* 8, 9. When the great God condescends to beseech us, we may well afford to beseech one another, to *be reconciled,* 2 Cor. v. 20. (2.) He offers him a sufficient share of the land they were in. Though God had promised Abram to give this land to his seed (*ch.* xii. 7), and it does not appear that ever any such promise was made to Lot, which Abram might have insisted on, to the total exclusion of Lot, yet he allows him to come in partner with him, and tenders an equal share to one that had not an equal right, and will not make God's promise to patronise his quarrel, nor, under the protection of that, put any hardship on his kinsman. (3.) He gives him his choice, and offers to take up with him his leavings : *If thou wilt take the left hand, I will go to the right.* There was all the reason in the world that Abram should choose first ; yet he recedes from his right. Note, It is a noble conquest to be willing to yield for peace' sake ; it is the conquest of ourselves, and our own pride and passion, Matt. v.

39, 40. It is not only the punctilios of honour, but even interest itself, that in many cases must be sacrificed to peace.

10 And Lot lifted up his eyes, and beheld all the plain of Jordan, that it *was* well watered every where, before the LORD destroyed Sodom and Gomorrah, *even* as the garden of the LORD, like the land of Egypt, as thou comest unto Zoar. 11 Then Lot chose him all·the plain of Jordan ; and Lot journeyed east : and they separated themselves the one from the other. 12 Abram dwelled in the land of Canaan, and Lot dwelled in the cities of the plain, and pitched *his* tent toward Sodom. ·13 But the men of Sodom *were* wicked and sinners before the LORD exceedingly.

We have here the choice that Lot made when he parted from Abram. Upon this occasion, one would have expected, 1. That he should have expressed an unwillingness to part from Abram, and that, at least, he should have done it with reluctancy. 2. That he should have been so civil as to have remitted the choice back again to Abram. But we find not any instance of deference or respect to his uncle in the whole management. Abram having offered him the choice, without compliment he accepted it, and made his election. Passion and selfishness make men rude. Now, in the choice which Lot made, we may observe,

I. How much he had an eye to the goodness of the land. He *beheld all the plain of Jordan*, the flat country in which Sodom stood, that it was admirably *well watered every where* (and perhaps the strife had been about water, which made him particularly fond of that convenience), and so *Lot chose all that plain, v.* 10, 11. That valley, which was like the garden of Eden itself, now yielded him a most pleasant prospect. It was, in his eye, beautiful for situation, the joy of the whole earth ; and therefore he doubted not but that it would yield him a comfortable settlement, and that in such a fruitful soil he should certainly thrive, and grow very rich : and this was all he looked at. But what came of it ? Why, the next news we hear of him is that he is in the briars among them, he and his carried captive. While he lived among them, he vexed his righteous soul with their conversation, and never had a good day with them, till, at last, God fired the town over his head, and forced him to the mountain for safety who chose the plain for wealth and pleasure. Note, Sensual choices are sinful choices, and seldom speed well. Those who in choosing relations, callings, dwellings, or settlements, are guided and governed by the lusts of the flesh, the lusts of the eye, or the

pride of life, and consult not the interests of their souls and their religion, cannot expect God's presence with them, nor his blessing upon them, but are commonly disappointed even in that which they principally aimed at, and miss of that which they promised themselves satisfaction in. In all our choices this principle should overrule us, That that is best for us which is best for our souls.

II. How little he considered the wickedness of the inhabitants : *But the men of Sodom were wicked, v.* 13. Note, 1. Though all are sinners, yet some are greater sinners than others. The men of Sodom were sinners of the first magnitude, *sinners before the Lord*, that is, impudent daring sinners ; they were so to a proverb. Hence we read of those that *declare their sin as Sodom, they hide it not*, Isa. iii. 9. 2. That some sinners are the worse for living in a good land. So the Sodomites were : for this was the iniquity of Sodom, *pride, fulness of bread, and abundance of idleness ;* and all these were supported by the great plenty their country afforded, Ezek. xvi. 49. Thus *the prosperity of fools destroys them.* 3. That God often gives great plenty to great sinners. Filthy Sodomites dwell in a city, in a fruitful plain, while faithful Abram and his pious family dwell in tents upon the barren mountains. 4. When wickedness has come to the height, ruin is not far off. Abounding sins are sure presages of approaching judgments. Now Lot's coming to dwell among the Sodomites may be considered, (1.) As a great mercy to them, and a likely means of bringing them to repentance ; for now they had a prophet among them and a preacher of righteousness, and, if they had hearkened to him, they might have been reformed, and the ruin prevented. Note, God sends preachers, before he sends destroyers ; for he is not *willing that any should perish.* (2.) As a great affliction to Lot, who was not only grieved to see their wickedness (2 Pet. ii. 7, 8), but was molested and persecuted by them, because he would not do as they did. Note, It has often been the vexatious lot of good men to live among wicked neighbours, to *sojourn in Mesech* (Ps. cxx. 5), and it cannot but be the more grievous, if, as Lot here, they have brought it upon themselves by an unadvised choice.

14 And the LORD said unto Abram, after that Lot was separated from him, Lift up now thine eyes, and look from the place where thou art northward, and southward, and eastward, and westward : 15 For all the land which thou seest, to thee will I give it, and to thy seed for ever. 16 And I will make thy seed as the dust of the earth : so that if a man can number the dust of the earth, *then* shall thy seed also be numbered. 17 Arise,

walk through the land in the length of it and in the breadth of it; for I will give it unto thee. 18 Then Abram removed *his* tent, and came and dwelt in the plain of Mamre, which *is* in Hebron, and built there an altar unto the LORD.

We have here an account of a gracious visit which God paid to Abram, to confirm the promise to him and his. Observe,

I. When it was that God renewed and ratified the promise: *After that Lot was separated from him,* that is, 1. After the quarrel was over; for those are best prepared for the visits of divine grace whose spirits are calm and sedate, and not ruffled with any passion. 2. After Abram's humble self-denying condescensions to Lot for the preserving of peace. It was then that God came to him with this token of his favour. Note, God will abundantly make up in spiritual peace what we lose for the preservation of neighbourly peace. When Abram had willingly offered Lot one-half of his right, God came, and confirmed the whole to him. 3. After he had lost the comfortable society of his kinsman, by whose departure his hands were weakened and his heart was saddened, then God came to him with these good words and comfortable words. Note, Communion with God may, at any time, serve to make up the want of conversation with our friends; when our relations are separated from us, yet God is not. 4. After Lot had chosen that pleasant fruitful vale, and had gone to take possession of it, lest Abram should be tempted to envy him and to repent that he had given him the choice, God comes to him, and assures him that what he had should remain to him and *his heirs for ever;* so that, though Lot perhaps had the better land, yet Abram had the better *title.* Lot had the paradise, such as it was, but Abram had the promise; and the event soon made it appear that, however it seemed now, Abram had really the better part. See Job xxii. 20. God owned Abram after his strife with Lot, as the churches owned Paul after his strife with Barnabas, Acts xv. 39, 40.

II. The promises themselves with which God now comforted and enriched Abram. Two things he assures him of—a good land, and a numerous issue to enjoy it.

1. Here is the grant of a good land, a land famous above all lands, for it was to be the holy land, and Immanuel's land; this is the land here spoken of. (1.) God here shows Abram the land, as he had promised (*ch.* xii. 1), and afterwards he showed it to Moses from the top of Pisgah. *Lot had lifted up his eyes and beheld the plain of Jordan* (*v.* 10), and he had gone to enjoy what he saw: "Come," says God to Abram, "*now lift thou up thy eyes, and look, and see thy own.*" Note, That which God has to show us is infinitely

better and more desirable than any thing that the world has to offer to our view. The prospects of an eye of faith are much more rich and beautiful than those of an eye of sense. Those for whom the heavenly Canaan is designed in the other world have sometimes, by faith, a comfortable prospect of it in their present state; for we look at the *things that are not seen,* as real, though distant. (2.) He secures this land to him and his seed for ever (*v.* 15): *To thee will I give it;* and again (*v.* 17), *I will give it unto thee;* every repetition of the promise is a ratification of it. *To thee and thy seed,* not to Lot and his seed; they were not to have their inheritance in this land, and therefore Providence so ordered it that Lot should be separated from Abram first, and then the grant should be confirmed to him and his seed. Thus God often brings good out of evil, and makes men's sins and follies subservient to his own wise and holy counsels. *To thee and thy seed*—to thee to sojourn in as a stranger, to thy seed to dwell and rule in as proprietors. *To thee,* that is, *to thy seed.* The granting of it to him and his for ever intimates that it was typical of the heavenly Canaan, which is given to the spiritual seed of Abram for ever, Heb. xi. 14. (3.) He gives him livery and seisin of it, though it was a reversion: "*Arise, walk through the land, v.* 17. Enter, and take possession, survey the parcels, and it will appear better than upon a distant prospect.*" Note, God is willing more abundantly to show to the heirs of promise the immutability of his covenant, and the inestimable worth of covenant blessings. *Go, walk about Sion,* Ps. xlviii. 12.

2. Here is the promise of a numerous issue to replenish this good land, so that it should never be lost for want of heirs (*v.* 16): *I will make thy seed as the dust of the earth,* that is, "They shall increase incredibly, and, take them altogether, they shall be such a great multitude as no man can number." They were so in Solomon's time, 1 Kings iv. 20, *Judah and Israel were many as the sand which is by the sea in multitude.* This God here gives him the promise of. Note, The same God that provides the inheritance provides the heirs. He that has prepared the holy land prepares the holy seed; he that gives glory gives grace to make meet for glory.

Lastly, We are told what Abram did when God had thus confirmed the promise to him, *v.* 18. 1. He *removed his tent.* God bade him *walk through the land,* that is, "Do not think of fixing in it, but expect to be always unsettled, and walking through it to a better Canaan:" in compliance with God's will herein, *he removes his tent,* conforming himself to the condition of a pilgrim. 2. He *built there an altar,* in token of his thankfulness to God for the kind visit he had paid him. Note, When God meets us with gracious promises, he expects that we should attend him with our humble praises.

CHAP. XIV.

We have four things in the story of this chapter. I. A war with the king of Sodom and his allies, ver. 1—11. II. The captivity of Lot in that war, ver. 12. III. Abram's rescue of Lot from that captivity, with the victory he obtained over the conquerors, ver. 13—16. IV. Abram's return from the expedition (ver. 17), with an account of what passed, 1. Between him and the king of Salem, ver. 18—20. 2. Between him and the king of Sodom, ver. 21—24. So that here we have that promise to Abram in part fulfilled, that God would make his name great.

AND it came to pass in the days of Amraphel king of Shinar, Arioch king of Ellasar, Chedorlaomer king of Elam, and Tidal, king of nations; 2 *That these* made war with Bera king of Sodom, and with Birsha king of Gomorrah, Shinab king of Admah, and Shemeber king of Zeboiim, and the king of Bela, which is Zoar. 3 All these were joined together in the vale of Siddim, which is the salt sea. 4 Twelve years they served Chedorlaomer, and in the thirteenth year they rebelled. 5 And in the fourteenth year came Chedorlaomer, and the kings that *were* with him, and smote the Rephaims in Ashteroth Karnaim, and the Zuzims in Ham, and the Emims in Shaveh Kiriathaim, 6 And the Horites in their mount Seir, unto El-paran, which *is* by the wilderness. 7 And they returned, and came to En-mishpat, which *is* Kadesh, and smote all the country of the Amalekites, and also the Amorites, that dwelt in Hazezontamar. 8 And there went out the king of Sodom, and the king of Gomorrah, and the king of Admah, and the king of Zeboiim, and the king of Bela (the same *is* Zoar;) and they joined battle with them in the vale of Siddim; 9 With Chedorlaomer the king of Elam, and with Tidal king of nations, and Amraphel king of Shinar, and Arioch king of Ellasar; four kings with five. 10 And the vale of Siddim *was full of* slimepits; and the kings of Sodom and Gomorrah fled, and fell there; and they that remained fled to the mountain. 11 And they took all the goods of Sodom and Gomorrah, and all their victuals, and went their way. 12 And they took Lot, Abram's brother's son, who dwelt in Sodom, and his goods, and departed.

We have here an account of the first war that ever we read of in scripture, which

(though the wars of the nations make the greatest figure in history) we should not have had the history of if Abram and Lot had not been concerned in it. Now, concerning this war, we may observe,

I. The parties engaged in it. The invaders were four kings, two of them no less than kings of Shinar and Elam (that is, Chaldea and Persia), yet probably not the sovereign princes of those great kingdoms in their own persons, but either officers under them, or rather the heads and leaders of some colonies which came out of those great nations, and settled themselves near Sodom, but retained the names of the countries from which they had their origin. The invaded were the kings of five cities that lay near together in the plain of Jordan, namely, Sodom, Gomorrah, Admah, Zeboiim, and Zoar. Four of them are named, but not the fifth, the king of Zoar or Bela, either because he was much more mean and inconsiderable or because he was much more wicked and inglorious than the rest, and worthy to be forgotten.

II. The occasion of this war was the revolt of the five kings from under the government of Chedorlaomer. Twelve years they served him. Small joy they had of their fruitful land, while thus they were tributaries to a foreign power, and could not call what they had their own. Rich countries are a desirable prey, and idle luxurious countries are an easy prey, to growing greatness. The Sodomites were the posterity of Canaan whom Noah had pronounced a servant to Shem, from whom Elam descended; thus soon did that prophecy begin to be fulfilled. In the thirteenth year, beginning to be weary of their subjection, they rebelled, denied their tribute, and attempted to shake off the yoke and retrieve their ancient liberties. In the fourteenth year, after some pause and preparation, Chedorlaomer, in conjunction with his allies, set himself to chastise and reduce the rebels, and, since he could not have it otherwise, to fetch his tribute from them on the point of his sword. Note, Pride, covetousness, and ambition, are the lusts from which wars and fightings come. To these insatiable idols the blood of thousands has been sacrificed.

III. The progress and success of the war. The four kings laid the neighbouring countries waste and enriched themselves with the spoil of them (*v.* 5—7), upon the alarm of which it had been the wisdom of the king of Sodom to submit, and desire conditions of peace; for how could he grapple with an enemy thus flushed with victory? But he would rather venture the utmost extremity than yield, and it sped accordingly. *Quos Deus destruet eos dementat—Those whom God means to destroy he delivers up to infatuation.* 1. The forces of the king of Sodom and his allies were routed; and, it should seem, many of them perished in the slime-pits who had escaped the sword, *v.* 10. In all places we are surrounded with deaths of various kinds, especially in the field of battle. 2. The cities were plundered, *v.* 11. All the goods of Sodom, and particularly their stores and provisions of victuals, were carried off by the conquerors. Note, When men abuse the gifts of a bountiful providence to gluttony and excess, it is just with God, and his usual way, by some judgment or other to strip them of that which they have so abused, Hos. ii. 8, 9. 3. Lot was carried captive, *v.* 12. They took Lot among the rest, and his goods. Now Lot may here be considered, (1.) As sharing with his neighbours in this common calamity. Though he was himself a righteous man, and (which is here expressly noticed) Abram's brother's son, yet he was involved with the rest in this trouble. Note, *All things come alike to all,* Eccl. ix. 2. The best of men cannot promise themselves an exemption from the greatest troubles in this life; neither our own piety nor our relation to those that are the favourites of heaven will be our security, when God's judgments are abroad. Note, further, Many an honest man fares the worse for his wicked neighbours. It is therefore our wisdom to separate ourselves, or at least to distinguish ourselves, from them (2 Cor. vi. 17), and so deliver ourselves, Rev. xviii. 4. (2.) As smarting for the foolish choice he made of a settlement here. This is plainly intimated when it is said, *They took Abram's brother's son, who dwelt in Sodom.* So near a relation of Abram should have been a companion and disciple of Abram, and should have abode by his tents; but, if he choose to dwell in Sodom, he must thank himself if he share in Sodom's calamities. Note, When we go out of the way of our duty we put ourselves from under God's protection, and cannot expect that the choices which are made by our lusts should issue to our comfort. Particular mention is made of their taking Lot's *goods,* those goods which had occasioned his contest with Abram and his separation from him. Note, It is just with God to deprive us of those enjoyments by which we have suffered ourselves to be deprived of our enjoyment of him.

13 And there came one that had escaped, and told Abram the Hebrew; for he dwelt in the plain of Mamre the Amorite, brother of Eshcol, and brother of Aner: and these *were* confederate with Abram. 14 And when Abram heard that his brother was taken captive, he armed his trained *servants,* born in his own house, three hundred and eighteen, and pursued *them* unto Dan. 15 And he divided himself against them, he and his servants, by night, and smote them, and pursued them unto Hobah, which *is*

on the left hand of Damascus. 16 And he brought back all the goods, and also brought again his brother Lot, and his goods, and the women also, and the people.

We have here an account of the only military action we ever find Abram engaged in, and this he was prompted to, not by his avarice or ambition, but purely by a principle of charity; it was not to enrich himself, but to help his friend. Never was any military expedition undertaken, prosecuted, and finished, more honourably than this of Abram's. Here we have,

I. The tidings brought him of his kinsman's distress. Providence so ordered it that he now sojourned not far off, that he might be a very present help. 1. He is here called *Abram the Hebrew,* that is, the son and follower of Heber, in whose family the profession of the true religion was kept up in that degenerate age. Abram herein acted like a Hebrew—in a manner not unworthy the name and character of a religious professor. 2. The tidings were brought by one that had escaped with his life for a prey. Probably he was a Sodomite, and as bad as the worst of them; yet knowing Abram's relation to Lot, and concern for him, he implores his help, and hopes to speed for Lot's sake. Note, The worst of men, in the day of their trouble, will be glad to claim acquaintance with those that are wise and good, and so get an interest in them. The rich man in hell called Abram *Father;* and the foolish virgins made court to the wise for a share of their oil.

II. The preparations he made for this expedition. The cause was plainly good, his call to engage in it was clear, and therefore, with all speed, he *armed his trained servants, born in his house,* to the number of *three hundred and eighteen*—a great family, but a small army, about as many as Gideon's that routed the Midianites, Judg. vii. 7. He drew out his *trained* servants, or his *catechised* servants, not only instructed in the art of war, which was then far short of the perfection which later and worse ages have improved it to, but instructed in the principles of religion; for Abram commanded his household to keep the way of the Lord. This shows that Abram was, 1. A great man, who had so many servants depending upon him, and employed by him, which was not only his strength and honour, but gave him a great opportunity of doing good, which is all that is truly valuable and desirable in great places and great estates. 2. A good man, who not only served God himself, but instructed all about him in the service of God. Note, Those that have great families have not only many bodies, but many souls besides their own, to take care of and provide for. Those that would be found the followers of Abram must see that their servants be catechised servants. 3. A wise man for, though he was a man of peace, yet he disciplined his servants for war, not knowing what occasion he might have, some time or other, so to employ them. Note, Though our holy religion teaches us to be for peace, yet it does not forbid us to provide for war.

III. His allies and confederates in this expedition. He prevailed with his neighbours, *Aner, Eshcol, and Mamre* (with whom he kept up a fair correspondence) to go along with him. It was his prudence thus to strengthen his own troops with their auxiliary forces; and probably they saw themselves concerned, in interest, to act, as they could, against this formidable power, lest their own turn should be next. Note, 1. It is our wisdom and duty to behave ourselves so respectfully and obligingly towards all men as that, whenever there is occasion, they may be willing and ready to do us a kindness. 2. Those who depend on God's help, yet, in times of distress, ought to make use of men's help, as Providence offers it; else they tempt God.

IV. His courage and conduct were very remarkable. 1. There was a great deal of bravery in the enterprise itself, considering the disadvantages he lay under. What could one family of husbandmen and shepherds do against the armies of four princes, who now came fresh from blood and victory? It was not a vanquished, but a victorious army, that he was to pursue; nor was he constrained by necessity to this daring attempt, but moved to it by generosity; so that, all things considered, it was, for aught I know, as great an instance of true courage as ever Alexander or Cesar was celebrated for. Note, Religion tends to make men, not cowardly, but truly valiant. The righteous is bold as a lion. The true Christian is the true hero. 2. There was a great deal of policy in the management of it. Abram was no stranger to the stratagems of war: He *divided himself,* as Gideon did his little army (Judg. vii. 16), that he might come upon the enemy from several quarters at once, and so make his few seem a great many; he made his attack by night, that he might surprise them. Note, Honest policy is a good friend both to our safety and to our usefulness. The serpent's head (provided it be nothing akin to the old serpent) may well become a good Christian's body, especially if it have a dove's eye in it, Matt. x. 16.

V. His success was very considerable, *v.* 15, 16. He defeated his enemies, and rescued his friends; and we do not find that he sustained any loss. Note, Those that venture in a good cause, with a good heart, are under the special protection of a good God, and have reason to hope for a good issue. Again, It is all one with the Lord *to save by many or by few,* 1 Sam. xiv. 6. Observe,

1. He rescued his kinsman; twice here he is called his *brother Lot.* The remembrance of the relation that was between them, both by nature and grace, made him forget the little quarrel that had been between them, in which Lot had by no means acted well towards Abram. Justly might Abram have upbraided Lot with his folly in quarrelling with him and removing from him, and have told him that he was well enough served, he might have known when he was well off; but, in the charitable breast of pious Abram, it is all forgiven and forgotten, and he takes this opportunity to give a real proof of the sincerity of his reconciliation. Note, (1.) We ought to be ready, whenever it is in the power of our hands, to succour and relieve those that are in distress, especially our relations and friends. *A brother is born for adversity,* Prov. xvii. 17. A friend in need is a friend indeed. (2.) Though others have been wanting in their duty to us, yet we must not therefore deny our duty to them. Some have said that they can more easily forgive their enemies than their friends; but we shall see ourselves obliged to forgive both if we consider, not only that our God, when we were enemies, reconciled us, but also that he *passeth by the transgression of the remnant of his heritage,* Mic. vii. 18.

2. He rescued the rest of the captives, for Lot's sake, though they were strangers to him and such as he was under no obligation to at all; nay, though they were Sodomites, sinners before the Lord exceedingly, and though, probably, he might have recovered Lot alone by ransom, yet he brought back all the women, and the people, and their goods, *v.* 16. Note, As we have opportunity we must do good to all men. Our charity must be extensive, as opportunity offers itself. Wherever God gives life, we must not grudge the help we can give to support it. God does good to the just and unjust, and so must we, Matt. v. 45. This victory which Abram obtained over the kings the prophet seems to refer to, Isa. xli. 2, *Who raised up the righteous man from the east, and made him rule over kings?* And some suggest that, as before he had a title to this land by grant, so now by conquest.

17 And the king of Sodom went out to meet him after his return from the slaughter of Chedorlaomer, and of the kings that *were* with him, at the valley of Shaveh, which *is* the king's dale. 18 And Melchizedek king of Salem brought forth bread and wine: and he *was* the priest of the most high God. 19 And he blessed him, and said, Blessed *be* Abram of the most high God, possessor of heaven and earth: 20 And blessed be the most high God, which hath delivered thine enemies into thy hand. And he gave him tithes of all.

This paragraph begins with the mention of the respect which the king of Sodom paid to

Abram, at his return from the slaughter of the kings; but, before a particular account is given of this, the story of Melchizedek is briefly related, concerning whom observe,

I. Who he was. He was *king of Salem* and *priest of the most high God;* and other glorious things are said of him, Heb. vii. 1, &c. 1. The rabbin, and most of our rabbinical writers, conclude that Melchizedek was Shem the son of Noah, who was king and priest to those that descended from him, according to the patriarchal model. But this is not at all probable; for why should his name be changed? And how came he to settle in Canaan? 2. Many Christian writers have thought that this was an appearance of the Son of God himself, our Lord Jesus, known to Abram, at this time, by this name, as, afterwards, Hagar called him by another name, *ch.* xvi. 13. He appeared to him as a righteous king, owning a righteous cause, and giving peace. It is difficult to imagine that any mere man should be said to *be without father, without mother, and without descent, having neither beginning of days nor end of life,* Heb. vii. 3. It is witnessed of Melchizedek that he liveth, and that he abideth a priest continually (*v.* 3, 8); nay (*v.* 13, 14), the apostle makes him of whom these things are spoken to be our Lord who sprang out of Judah. It is likewise difficult to think that any mere man should, at this time, be greater than Abram in the things of God, that Christ should be a priest after the order of any mere man, and that any human priesthood should so far excel that of Aaron as it is certain that Melchizedek's did. 3. The most commonly received opinion is that Melchizedek was a Canaanitish prince, that reigned in Salem, and kept up the true religion there; but, if so, why his name should occur here only in all the story of Abram, and why Abram should have altars of his own and not attend the altars of his neighbour Melchizedek who was greater than he, seem unaccountable. Mr. Gregory of Oxford tells us that the *Arabic Catena,* which he builds much upon the authority of, gives this account of Melchizedek, That he was the son of Heraclim, the son of Peleg, the son of Eber, and that his mother's name was Salathiel, the daughter of Gomer, the son of Japheth, the son of Noah.

II. What he did. 1. He *brought forth bread and wine,* for the refreshment of Abram and his soldiers, and in congratulation of their victory. This he did as a king, teaching us to do good and to communicate, and to be given to hospitality, according to our ability; and representing the spiritual provisions of strength and comfort which Christ has laid up for us in the covenant of grace for our refreshment, when we are wearied with our spiritual conflicts. 2. As priest of the most high God, he blessed Abram, which we may suppose a greater refreshment to Abram than his bread and wine were. Thus God, having raised up his Son Jesus, has

sent him to bless us, as one having authority; and those whom he blesses are blessed indeed. Christ went to heaven when he was blessing his disciples (Luke xxiv. 51); for this is what he ever lives to do.

III. What he said, *v.* 19, 20. Two things were said by him:—1. He blessed Abram from God: *Blessed be Abram, blessed of the most high God, v.* 19. Observe the titles he here gives to God, which are very glorious. (1.) *The most high God,* which bespeaks his absolute perfections in himself and his sovereign dominion over all the creatures; he is King of kings. Note, It will greatly help both our faith and our reverence in prayer to eye God as the most high God, and to call him so. (2.) *Possessor of heaven and earth,* that is, rightful owner, and sovereign Lord, of all the creatures, because he made them. This bespeaks him a great God, and greatly to be praised (Ps. xxiv. 1), and those a happy people who have an interest in his favour and love. 2. He blessed God for Abram (*v.* 20): and *blessed be the most high God.* Note, (1.) In all our prayers, we must praise God, and join hallelujahs with all our hosannahs. These are the spiritual sacrifices we must offer up daily, and upon particular occasions. (2.) God, as the most high God, must have the glory of all our victories, Exod. xvii. 15; 1 Sam. vii. 10, 12; Judg. v. 1, 2; 2 Chron. xx. 21. In them he shows himself higher than our enemies (Exod. xviii. 11), and higher than we; for without him we could do nothing. (3.) We ought to give thanks for others' mercies as for our own, triumphing with those that triumph. (4.) Jesus Christ, our great high priest, is the Mediator both of our prayers and praises, and not only offers up ours, but his own for us. See Luke x. 21.

IV. What was done to him : *Abram gave him tithes of all,* that is, of the spoils, Heb. vii. 4. This may be looked upon, 1. As a gratuity presented to Melchizedek, by way of return for his tokens of respect. Note, Those that receive kindness should show kindness. Gratitude is one of nature's laws. 2. As an offering vowed and dedicated to the most high God, and therefore put into the hands of Melchizedek his priest. Note, (1.) When we have received some signal mercy from God, it is very fit that we should express our thankfulness by some special act of pious charity. God must always have his dues out of our substance, especially when, by any particular providence, he has either preserved or increased it to us. (2.) That the tenth of our increase is a very fit proportion to be set apart for the honour of God and the service of his sanctuary. (3.) That Jesus Christ, our great Melchizedek, is to have homage done him, and to be humbly acknowledged by every one of us as our king and priest; and not only the tithe of all, but all we have, must be surrendered and given up to him.

21 And the king of Sodom said unto

Abram, Give me the persons, and take the goods to thyself. 22 And Abram said to the king of Sodom, I have lift up mine hand unto the LORD, the most high God, the possessor of heaven and earth, 23 That I will not *take* from a thread even to a shoelatchet, and that I will not take any thing that *is* thine, lest thou shouldest say, I have made Abram rich: 24 Save only that which the young men have eaten, and the portion of the men which went with me, Aner, Eshcol, and Mamre; let them take their portion.

We have here an account of what passed between Abram and the king of Sodom, who succeeded him that fell in the battle (*v.* 10), and thought himself obliged to do this honour to Abram, in return for the good services he had done him. Here is,

I. The king of Sodom's grateful offer to Abram (*v.* 21): *Give me the soul, and take thou the substance;* so the Hebrew reads it. Here he fairly begs the persons, but as freely bestows the goods on Abram. Note, 1. Where a right is dubious and divided, it is wisdom to compound the matter by mutual concessions rather than to contend. The king of Sodom had an original right both to the persons and to the goods, and it would bear a debate whether Abram's acquired right by rescue would supersede his title and extinguish it; but, to prevent all quarrels, the king of Sodom makes this fair proposal. 2. Gratitude teaches us to recompense to the utmost of our power those that have undergone fatigues, run hazards, and been at expense for our service and benefit. *Who goes a warfare at his own charges?* 1 Cor. ix. 7. Soldiers purchase their pay dearer than any labourers, and are well worthy of it, because they expose their lives.

II. Abram's generous refusal of this offer. He not only resigned the persons to him, who, being delivered out of the hand of their enemies, ought to have served Abram, but he restored all the goods too. He would not take *from a thread to a shoe-latchet,* not the least thing that had ever belonged to the king of Sodom or any of his. Note, A lively faith enables a man to look upon the wealth of this world with a holy contempt, 1 John v. 4. What are all the ornaments and delights of sense to one that has God and heaven ever in his eye? He resolves even to a thread and a shoe-latchet; for a tender conscience fears offending in a small matter. Now,

1. Abram ratifies this resolution with a solemn oath: *I have lifted up my hand to the Lord that I will not take any thing, v.* 22. Here observe, (1.) The titles he gives to God,

The most high God, the possessor of heaven and earth, the same that Melchizedek had just now used, *v.* 19. Note, It is good to learn of others how to order our speech concerning God, and to imitate those who speak well in divine things. This improvement we are to make of the conversation of devout good men, we must learn to speak after them. (2.) The ceremony used in this oath: *I have lifted up my hand.* In religious swearing we appeal to God's knowledge of our truth and sincerity and imprecate his wrath if we swear falsely, and the *lifting up of the hand* is very significant and expressive of both. (3.) The matter of the oath, namely, that he would not take any reward from the king of Sodom, was lawful, but what he was not antecedently obliged to. [1.] Probably Abram vowed, before he went to the battle, that, if God would give him success, he would, for the glory of God and the credit of his profession, so far deny himself and his own right as to take nothing of the spoils to himself. Note, The vows we have made when we are in pursuit of a mercy must be carefully and conscientiously kept when we have obtained the mercy, though they were made against our interest. A citizen of Zion, if he has sworn, whether it be to God or man, though it prove to *his own hurt, yet he changeth not,* Ps. xv. 4. Or, [2.] Perhaps Abram, now when he saw cause to refuse the offer made him, at the same time confirmed his refusal with this oath, to prevent further importunity. Note, *First,* There may be good reason sometimes why we should debar ourselves of that which is our undoubted right, as St. Paul, 1 Cor. viii. 13; ix. 12. *Secondly,* That strong resolutions are of good use to put by the force of temptations.

2. He backs his refusal with a good reason: *Lest thou shouldest say, I have made Abram rich,* which would reflect reproach, (1.) Upon the promise and covenant of God, as if they would not have enriched Abram without the spoils of Sodom. And, [2.] Upon the piety and charity of Abram, as if all he had in his eye, when he undertook that hazardous expedition, was to enrich himself. Note, [1.] We must be very careful that we give no occasion to others to say things that look mean or mercenary, or that savours of covetousness and self-seeking. Probably Abram knew the king of Sodom to be a proud and scornful man, and one that would be apt to turn such a thing as this to his reproach afterwards, though most unreasonably. When we have to do with such men, we have need to act with particular caution.

3. He limits his refusal with a double proviso, *v.* 24. In making vows, we ought carefully to insert the necessary exceptions, that we may not afterwards say before the angel, *It was an error,* Eccl. v. 6. Abram here

excepts, (1.) The food of his soldiers; they were worthy of their meat while they trod out the corn. This would give no colour to the king of Sodom to say that he had enriched Abram. (2.) The shares of his allies and confederates: *Let them take their portion.* Note, Those who are strict in restraining their own liberty yet ought not to impose those restraints upon the liberties of others, nor to judge of them accordingly. We must not make ourselves the standard to measure others by. A good man will deny himself that liberty which he will not deny another, contrary to the practice of the Pharisees, Matt. xxiii. 4. There was not the same reason why Aner, Eshcol, and Mamre, should quit their right, that there was why Abram should. They did not make the profession that he made, nor were they, as he was, under the obligation of a vow. They had not the hopes that Abram had of a portion in the other world, and therefore, by all means, *let them take their portion* of this.

CHAP. XV.

In this chapter we have a solemn treaty between God and Abram concerning a covenant that was to be established between them. In the former chapter we had Abram in the field with kings; here we find him in the mount with God; and, though there he looked great, yet, methinks, here he looks much greater: that honour have the great men of the world, but "this honour have all the saints." The covenant to be settled between God and Abram was a covenant of promises; accordingly, here is, I. A general assurance of God's kindness and good-will to Abram, ver. 1. II A particular declaration of the purposes of his love concerning him, in two things:—1. That he would give him a numerous issue, ver. 2—6. 2. That he would give him Canaan for an inheritance, ver. 7—21. Either an estate without an heir, or an heir without an estate, would have been but a half comfort to Abram. But God ensures both to him; and that which made these two, the promised seed and the promised land, comforts indeed to this great believer was that they were both typical of those two invaluable blessings, Christ and heaven; and so, we have reason to think, Abram eyed them.

AFTER these things the word of the Lord came unto Abram in a vision, saying, Fear not, Abram: I *am* thy shield, *and* thy exceeding great reward.

Observe here, I. The time when God made this treaty with Abram: *After these things.* 1. After that famous act of generous charity which Abram had done, in rescuing his friends and neighbours out of distress, and that, *not for price nor reward.* After this, God made him this gracious visit. Note, Those that show favour to men shall find favour with God. 2. After that victory which he had obtained over four kings. Lest Abram should be too much elevated and pleased with that, God comes to him, to tell him he had better things in store for him. Note, A believing converse with spiritual blessings is an excellent means to keep us from being too much taken up with temporal enjoyments. The gifts of common providence are not comparable to those of covenant love.

II. The manner in which God conversed with Abram: *The word of the Lord came unto Abram* (that is, God manifested himself and his will to Abram) *in a vision,* which supposes Abram awake, and some visible

appearance of the Shechinah, or some sensible token of the presence of the divine glory. Note, The methods of divine revelation are adapted to our state in a world of sense.

III. The gracious assurance God gave him of his favour to him.

1. He called him by name—*Abram,* which was a great honour to him, and made his name great, and was also a great encouragement and assistance to his faith. Note, God's good word does us good when it is spoken by his Spirit to us in particular, and brought to our hearts. The word says, *Ho, every one* (Isa. lv. 1), the Spirit says, *Ho, such a one.*

2. He cautioned him against being disquieted and confounded: *Fear not, Abram.* Abram might fear lest the four kings he had routed should rally again, and fall upon him to his ruin: "No," says God, "Fear not. Fear not their revenges, nor thy neighbour's envy; I will take care of thee." Note, (1.) Where there is great faith, yet there may be many fears, 2 Cor. vii. 5. (2.) God takes cognizance of his people's fears though ever so secret, and *knows their souls,* Ps. xxxi. 7. (3.) It is the will of God that his people should not give way to prevailing fears, whatever happens. Let the sinners in Sion be afraid, but fear not, Abram.

3. He assured him of safety and happiness, that he should for ever be, (1.) As safe as God himself could keep him: *I am thy shield,* or, somewhat more emphatically, *I am a shield to thee,* present with thee, actually caring for thee. See 1 Chron. xvii. 24. Not only the God of Israel, but a God to Israel. Note, The consideration of this, that God himself is, and will be, a shield to his people to secure them from all destructive evils, a shield ready to them and a shield round about them, should be sufficient to silence all their perplexing tormenting fears. (2.) As happy as God himself could make him: *I will be thy exceedingly great reward;* not only thy rewarder, but thy reward. Abram had generously refused the rewards which the king of Sodom offered him, and here God comes) and tells him he shall be no loser by it. Note, [1.] The rewards of believing obedience and self-denial are exceedingly great, 1 Cor. ii. 9. [2.] God himself is the chosen and promised felicity of holy souls—chosen in this world, promised in a better. He is the *portion of their inheritance and their cup.*

2 And Abram said, Lord God, what wilt thou give me, seeing I go childless, and the steward of my house *is* this Eliezer of Damascus? 3 And Abram said, Behold, to me thou hast given no seed: and, lo, one born in my house is mine heir. 4 And, behold, the word of the Lord *came* unto him, saying, This shall not be thine heir; but he that shall come

forth out of thine own bowels shall be thine heir. 5 And he brought him forth abroad, and said, Look now toward heaven, and tell the stars, if thou be able to number them : and he said unto him, So shall thy seed be. 6 And he believed in the LORD; and he counted it to him for righteousness.

We have here the assurance given to Abram of a numerous offspring which should descend from him, in which observe,

I. Abram's repeated complaint, *v.* 2, 3. This was that which gave occasion to this promise. The great affliction that sat heavy upon Abram was the want of a child ; and the complaint of this he here *pours out before the Lord, and shows before him his trouble,* Ps. cxlii. 2. Note, Though we must never complain of God, yet we have leave to complain to him, and to be large and particular in the statement of our grievances ; and it is some ease to a burdened spirit to open its case to a faithful and compassionate friend : such a friend God is, whose ear is always open. Now his complaint is four-fold:—1. That he had no child (*v.* 3): *Behold, to me thou hast given no seed;* not only no son, but *no seed ;* if he had had a daughter, from her the promised Messiah might have come, who was to be the seed of the woman; but he had neither son nor daughter. He seems to lay an emphasis on that, *to me.* His neighbours were full of children, his servants had children born in his house. " But *to me,*" he complains, " thou hast given none ;" and yet God had told him he should be a favourite above all. Note, Those that are written childless must see God writing them so. Again, God often withholds those temporal comforts from his own children which he gives plentifully to others that are strangers to him. 2. That he was never likely to have any, intimated in that, *I go,* or " *I am going, childless,* going into years, going down the hill apace ; nay, I am going out of the world, going the way of all the earth. *I die childless,*" so the LXX. " I leave the world, and leave no child behind me." 3. That his servants were for the present and were likely to be to him instead of sons. While he lived, *the steward of his house was Eliezer of Damascus ;* to him he committed the care of his family and estate, who might be faithful, but only as a servant, not as a son. When he died, *one born in his house would be his heir,* and would bear rule over all that for which he had laboured, Eccl. ii. 18, 19, 21. God had already told him that he would make of him *a great nation* (*ch.* xii. 2), and his *seed as the dust of the earth* (*ch.* xiii. 16); but he had left him in doubt whether it should be his seed begotten or his seed adopted, by a son of his loins or only a son of his house. "Now, Lord," says Abram, " if it be only an adopted son,

100

it must be one of my servants, which will reflect disgrace upon the promised seed, that is to descend from him." Note, While promised mercies are delayed our unbelief and impatience are apt to conclude them denied. 4. That the want of a son was so great a trouble to him that it took away the comfort of all his enjoyments : " *Lord, what wilt thou give me ?* All is nothing to me, if I have not a son." Now, (1.) If we suppose that Abram looked no further than a temporal comfort, this complaint was culpable. God had, by his providence, given him some good things, and more by his promise ; and yet Abram makes no account of them, because he has not a son. It did very ill become the father of the faithful to say, *What wilt thou give me, seeing I go childless,* immediately after God had said, *I am thy shield, and thy exceedingly great reward.* Note, Those do not rightly value the advantages of their covenant-relation to God and interest in him who do not think them sufficient to balance the want of any creature-comfort whatever. But, (2.) If we suppose that Abram, herein, had an eye to the promised seed, the importunity of his desire was very commendable : all was nothing to him, if he had not the earnest of that great blessing, and an assurance of his relation to the Messiah, of which God had already encouraged him to maintain the expectation. He has wealth, and victory, and honour ; but, while he is kept in the dark about the main matter, it is all nothing to him. Note, Till we have some comfortable evidence of our interest in Christ and the new covenant, we should not rest satisfied with any thing else. "This, and the other, I have ; but what will all this avail me, if I go Christless ?" Yet thus far the complaint was culpable, that there was some diffidence of the promise at the bottom of it, and a weariness of waiting God's time. Note, True believers sometimes find it hard to reconcile God's promises and his providences, when they seem to disagree.

II. God's gracious answer to this complaint. To the first part of the complaint (*v.* 2) God gave no immediate answer, because there was something of fretfulness in it ; but, when he renews his address somewhat more calmly (*v.* 3), God answered him graciously. Note, If we continue instant in prayer, and yet pray with a humble submission to the divine will, we shall not seek in vain. 1. God gave him an express promise of a son, *v.* 4. This that is born in thy house *shall not be thy heir,* as thou fearest, but one that shall *come forth out of thy own bowels shall be thy heir.* Note, (1.) God makes heirs ; he says, "This shall not, and this shall ;" and whatever men devise and design, in settling their estates, God's counsel shall stand. (2.) God is often better to us than our own fears, and gives the mercy we had long despaired of. **2. To** affect him the more with this promise, he took him out, and showed him the stars (this vision being early in the morning, before day), and then tells him, *So shall thy seed be, v.* 5. (1.) So numerous; the stars seem innumerable to a common eye : Abram feared he should have no child at all, but God assured him that the descendants from his loins should be so many as not to be numbered. (2.) So illustrious, resembling the stars in splendour ; for to *them pertained the glory,* Rom. ix. 4. Abram's seed, according to his flesh, were like the dust of the earth (*ch.* xiii 16), but his spiritual seed are like the stars of heaven, not only numerous, but glorious, and very precious.

III. Abram's firm belief of the promise God now made him, and God's favourable acceptance of his faith, *v.* 6. 1. He *believed in the Lord,* that is, he believed the truth of that promise which God had now made him, resting upon the irresistible power and the inviolable faithfulness of him that made it. *Hath he spoken, and shall he not make it good?* Note, Those who would have the comfort of the promises must mix faith with the promises. See how the apostle magnifies this faith of Abram, and makes it a standing example, Rom. iv. 19—21. *He was not weak in faith; he staggered not at the promise; he was strong in faith; he was fully persuaded.* The Lord work such a faith in every one of us! Some think that his believing in the Lord respected, not only the Lord promising, but the Lord promised, the Lord Jesus, the Mediator of the new covenant. He *believed in him,* that is, received and embraced the divine revelation concerning him, and *rejoiced to see his day,* though at so great a distance, John viii. 56. 2. *God counted it to him for righteousness;* that is, upon the score of this he was accepted of God, and, as the rest of the patriarchs, by faith he *obtained witness that he was righteous,* Heb. xi. 4. This is urged in the New Testament to prove that we are justified by faith without the works of the law (Rom. iv. 3; Gal. iii. 6); for Abram was so justified while he was yet uncircumcised. If Abram, that was so rich in good works, was not justified by them, but by his faith, much less can we, that are so poor in them. This faith, which was imputed to Abram for righteousness, had lately struggled with unbelief (*v.* 2), and, coming off a conqueror, it was thus crowned, thus honoured. Note, A fiducial practical acceptance of, and dependence upon, God's promise of grace and glory, in and through Christ, is that which, according to the tenour of the new covenant, gives us a right to all the blessings contained in that promise. All believers are justified as Abram was, and it was his faith that was *counted to him for righteousness.*

7 And he said unto him, I *am* the LORD that brought thee out of Ur of

the Chaldees, to give thee this land to inherit it. 8 And he said, Lord GOD, whereby shall I know that I shall inherit it? 9 And he said unto him, Take me a heifer of three years old, and a she goat of three years old, and a ram of three years old, and a turtle dove, and a young pigeon. 10 And he took unto him all these, and divided them in the midst, and laid each piece one against another: but the birds divided he not. 11 And when the fowls came down upon the carcases, Abram drove them away.

We have here the assurance given to Abram of the land of Canaan for an inheritance.

I. God declares his purpose concerning it, *v.* 7. Observe here, Abram made no complaint in this matter, as he had done for the want of a child. Note, Those that are sure of an interest in the promised seed will see no reason to doubt of a title to the promised land. If Christ is ours, heaven is ours. Observe again, When he believed the former promise (*v.* 6) then God explained and ratified this to him. Note, To him that has (improves what he has) more shall be given. Three things God here reminds Abram of, for his encouragement concerning the promise of this good land :—

1. What God is in himself: *I am the Lord* Jehovah; and therefore, (1.) " I may give it to thee, for I am sovereign Lord of all, and have a right to dispose of the whole earth." (2.) " I can give it to thee, whatever opposition may be made, though by the sons of Anak." God never promises more than he is able to perform, as men often do. (3.) " I will make good my promise to thee." Jehovah is *not a man that he should lie.*

2. What he had done for Abram. He had brought him out of Ur of the Chaldees, *out of the fire of the Chaldees,* so some, that is, either from their idolatries (for the Chaldeans worshipped the fire), or from their persecutions. The Jewish writers have a tradition that Abram was cast into a fiery furnace for refusing to worship idols, and was miraculously delivered. It is rather a place of that name. Thence God brought him by an effectual call, brought him with a gracious violence, snatched him as a brand out of the burning. This was, (1.) A special mercy : " I brought thee, and left others, thousands, to perish there." *God called him alone,* Isa. li. 2. (2.) A spiritual mercy, a mercy to his soul, a deliverance from sin and its fatal consequences. If God save our souls, we shall want nothing that is good for us. (3.) A fresh mercy, lately bestowed, and therefore should be the more affecting,

as that in the preface to the commandments, *I am the Lord that brought thee out of Egypt lately.* (4.) A foundation mercy, the beginning of mercy, peculiar mercy to Abram, and therefore a pledge and earnest of further mercy, Isa. lxvi. 9. Observe how God speaks of it as that which he gloried in : *I am the Lord that brought thee out.* He glories in it as an act both of power and grace ; compare Isa. xxix. 22, where he glories in it, long afterwards. *Thus saith the Lord who redeemed* Abraham, redeemed him from sin.

3. What he intended to do yet further for him : " *I brought thee* hither, on purpose *to give thee this land to inherit it,* not only to possess it, but to possess it as an inheritance, which is the sweetest and surest title." Note, (1.) The providence of God has secret but gracious designs in all its various dispensations towards good people ; we cannot conceive the projects of Providence, till the event shows them in all their mercy and glory. (2.) The great thing God designs in all his dealings with his people is to bring them safely to heaven. They are *chosen to salvation* (2 Thess. ii. 13), *called to the kingdom* (1 Thess. ii. 12), *begotten to the inheritance* (1 Pet. i. 3, 4), and by all *made meet* for it, Col. i. 12, 13 ; 2 Cor. iv. 17.

II. Abram desires a sign : *Whereby shall I know that I shall inherit it ? v.* 8. This did not proceed from distrust of God's power or promise, as that of Zacharias ; but he desired this, 1. For the strengthening and confirming of his own faith ; he believed (*v.* 6), but here he prays, *Lord, help me against my unbelief. Now* he believed, but he desired a sign to be treasured up against an hour of temptation, not knowing how his faith might, by some event or other, be shocked and tried. Note, We all need, and should desire, helps from heaven for the confirming of our faith, and should improve sacraments, which are instituted signs, for that purpose. See Judg. vi. 36—40 ; 2 Kings xx. 8—10 ; Isa. vii. 11, 12. 2. For the ratifying of the promise to his posterity, that they also might be brought to believe it. Note, Those that are satisfied themselves should desire that others also may be satisfied of the truth of God's promises. John sent his disciples to Christ, not so much for his own satisfaction as for theirs, Matt. xi. 2, 3. Canaan was a type of heaven. Note, It is a very desirable thing to know that we shall inherit the heavenly Canaan, that is, to be confirmed in our belief of the truth of that happiness, and to have the evidences of our title to it more and more cleared up to us.

III. God directs Abram to make preparations for a sacrifice, intending by that to give him a sign, and Abram makes preparation accordingly (*v.* 9—11): *Take me a heifer,* &c. Perhaps Abram expected some extraordinary sign from heaven ; but God gives him a sign upon a sacrifice. Note,

Those that would receive the assurances of God's favour, and would have their faith confirmed, must attend instituted ordinances, and expect to meet with God in them. Observe, 1. God appointed that each of the beasts used for this service should be three years old, because then they were at their full growth and strength : God must be served with the best we have, for he is the best. 2. We do not read that God gave Abram particular directions how to manage these beasts and fowls, knowing that he was so well versed in the law and custom of sacrifices that he needed not any particular directions ; or perhaps instructions were given him, which he carefully observed, though they are not recorded : at least it was intimated to him that they must be prepared for the solemnity of ratifying a covenant ; and he well knew the manner of preparing them. 3. Abram took as God appointed him, though as yet he knew not how these things should become a sign to him. This was not the first instance of Abram's implicit obedience. He divided the beasts in the midst, according to the ceremony used in confirming covenants, Jer. xxxiv. 18, 19, where it is said, They cut *the calf in twain, and passed between the parts.* 4. Abram, having prepared according to God's appointment, now set himself to wait for the sign God might give him by these, like the prophet upon his watch-tower, Hab. ii. 1. While God's appearing to own his sacrifice was deferred, Abram continued waiting, and his expectations were raised by the delay ; when *the fowls came down upon the carcases* to prey upon them, as common and neglected things, *Abram drove them away* (*v.* 11), believing that the vision would, at the end, *speak, and not lie.* Note, A very watchful eye must be kept upon our spiritual sacrifices, that nothing be suffered to prey upon them and render them unfit for God's acceptance. When vain thoughts, like these fowls, come down upon our sacrifices, we must drive them away, and not suffer them to lodge within us, but *attend on God without distraction.*

12 And when the sun was going down, a deep sleep fell upon Abram ; and, lo, a horror of great darkness fell upon him. 13 And he said unto Abram, Know of a surety that thy seed shall be a stranger in a land *that is* not their's, and shall serve them ; and they shall afflict them four hundred years ; 14 And also that nation, whom they shall serve, will I judge : and afterward shall they come out with great substance. 15 And thou shalt go to thy fathers in peace ; thou shalt be buried in a good old

age. 16 But in the fourth generation they shall come hither again : for the iniquity of the Amorites *is* not yet full.

We have here a full and particular discovery made to Abram of God's purposes concerning his seed. Observe,

I. The time when God came to him with this discovery : *When the sun was going down,* or *declining,* about the time of the *evening oblation,* 1 Kings xviii. 36 ; Dan. ix. 21. Early in the morning, before day, while the stars were yet to be seen, God had given him orders concerning the sacrifices (*v.* 5), and we may suppose it was, at least, his morning's work to prepare them and set them in order ; when he had done this, he abode by them, praying and waiting till towards evening. Note, God often keeps his people long in expectation of the comforts he designs them, for the confirmation of their faith ; but though the answers of prayer, and the performance of promises, come slowly, yet they come surely. *At evening time it shall be light.*

II. The preparatives for this discovery. 1. *A deep sleep fell upon Abram,* not a common sleep through weariness or carelessness, but a divine ecstacy, like that which the *Lord God caused to fall upon Adam* (*ch.* ii. 21), that, being hereby wholly taken off from the view of things sensible, he might be wholly taken up with the contemplation of things spiritual. The doors of the body were locked up, that the soul might be private and retired, and might act the more freely and like itself. 2. With this sleep, *a horror of great darkness fell upon him.* How sudden a change ! But just before we had him solacing himself in the comforts of God's covenant, and in communion with him ; and here a *horror of great darkness* falls upon him. Note, The children of light do not always walk in the light, but sometimes clouds and darkness are round about them. This great darkness, which brought horror with it, was designed, (1.) To strike an awe upon the spirit of Abram, and to possess him with a holy reverence, that the familiarity to which God was pleased to admit him might not breed contempt. Note, Holy fear prepares the soul for holy joy ; the spirit of bondage makes way for the spirit of adoption. God wounds first, and then heals ; humbles first, and then lifts up, Isa. vi. 5, 6, &c. (2.) To be a specimen of the methods of God's dealings with his seed. They must first be in the horror and darkness of Egyptian slavery, and then enter with joy into the good land ; and therefore he must have the foretaste of their sufferings, before he had the foresight of their happiness. (3.) To be an indication of the nature of that covenant of peculiarity which God was now about to make with Abram. The Old-Testament dispensation, which was founded on that covenant, was a dispensation, [1.] Of dark-

ness and obscurity, 2 Cor. iii. 13, 14. [2.] Of dread and horror, Heb. xii. 18, &c.

III. The prediction itself. Several things are here foretold.

1. The suffering state of Abram's seed for a long time, *v.* 13. Let not Abram flatter himself with the hopes of nothing but honour and prosperity in his family ; no, he must know, of a surety, that which he was loth to believe, that the promised seed should be a persecuted seed. Note, God sends the worst first ; we must first suffer, and then reign. He also lets us know the worst before it comes, that when it comes it may not be a surprise to us, John xvi. 4. Now we have here,

(1.) The particulars of their sufferings. [1.] They shall be strangers ; so they were, first in Canaan (Ps. cv. 12) and afterwards in Egypt ; before they were lords of their own land they were strangers in a strange land. The inconveniences of an unsettled state make a happy settlement the more welcome. Thus the heirs of heaven are first strangers on earth, a land that is not theirs. [2.] They shall be servants ; so they were to the Egyptians, Exod. i. 13. See how that which was the doom of the Canaanites (*ch.* ix. 25) proves the distress of Abram's seed : they are made to serve, but with this difference, the Canaanites under a curse, the Hebrews under a blessing ; and the *upright shall have dominion in the morning,* Ps. xlix. 14. [3.] They shall be sufferers. Those whom they serve shall afflict them ; see Exod. i. 11. Note, Those that are blessed and beloved of God are often sorely afflicted by wicked men ; and God foresees it, and takes cognizance of it.

(2.) The continuance of their sufferings —*four hundred years.* This persecution began with mocking, when Ishmael, the son of an Egyptian, persecuted Isaac, who was *born after the Spirit,* ch. xxi. 9 ; Gal. iv. 29. It continued in loathing ; for it was an abomination to the Egyptians to eat bread with the Hebrews, *ch.* xliii. 32 ; and it came at last to murder, the basest of murders, that of their new-born children ; so that, more or less, it continued 400 years, though, in extremity, not so many. This was a long time, but a limited time.

2. The judgment of the enemies of Abram's seed : *That nation whom they shall serve,* even the Egyptians, *will I judge,* *v.* 14. This points at the plagues of Egypt, by which God not only constrained the Egyptians to release Israel, but punished them for all the hardships they had put upon them. Note, (1.) Though God may suffer persecutors and oppressors to trample upon his people a great while, yet he will certainly reckon with them at last ; for his *day is coming,* Ps. xxxvii. 12, 13. (2.) The punishing of persecutors is the judging of them; it is a righteous thing with God, and a particular act of justice, to recompense tribulations to those that trouble his people. The

judging of the church's enemies is God's work: *I will judge.* God can do it, for he is the Lord ; he will do it, for he is his people's God, and he has said, *Vengeance is mine, I will repay.* To him therefore we must leave it, to be done in his way and time.

3. The deliverance of Abram's seed out of Egypt. That great event is here foretold: *Afterwards shall they come out with great substance.* It is here promised, (1.) That they should be enlarged: *Afterwards they shall come out ;* that is, either after they have been afflicted 400 years, when the days of their servitude are fulfilled, or after the Egyptians are judged and plagued, then they may expect deliverance. Note, The destruction of oppressors is the redemption of the oppressed ; they will not let God's people go till they are forced to it. (2.) That they should be enriched: *They shall come out with great substance ;* this was fulfilled, Exod. xii. 35, 36. God took care they should have, not only a good land to go to, but a good stock to carry with them.

4. Their happy settlement in Canaan, *v.* 16. They shall not only come out of Egypt, but *they shall come hither again,* hither to the land of Canaan, wherein thou now art. The discontinuance of their possession shall be no defeasance of their right : we must not reckon those comforts lost for ever that are intermitted for a time. The reason why they must not have the land of promise in possession till the fourth generation was because *the iniquity of the Amorites was not yet full.* Israel cannot be possessed of Canaan till the Amorites be dispossessed ; and they are not yet ripe for ruin. The righteous God has determined that they shall not be cut off till they have persisted in sin so long, and arrived at such a pitch of wickedness, that there may appear some equitable proportion between their sin and their ruin; and therefore, till it come to that, the seed of Abram must be kept out of possession. Note, (1.) The measure of sin fills gradually. Those that continue impenitent in wicked ways are treasuring up unto themselves wrath. (2.) Some people's measure of sin fills slowly. The Sodomites, who were sinners before the Lord exceedingly, soon filled their measure ; so did the Jews, who were, in profession, near to God. But the iniquity of the Amorites was long in the filling up. (3.) That this is the reason of the prosperity of wicked people ; the measure of their sins is not yet full. The wicked *live, become old, and are mighty in power,* while God is *laying up their iniquity for their children,* Job xxi. 7, 19. See Matt. xxiii. 32 ; Deut. xxxii. 34.

5. Abram's peaceful quiet death and burial, before these things should come to pass, *v.* 15. As he should not live to see that good land in the possession of his family, but must die, as he lived, a stranger in it, so, to balance this, he should not live to see the troubles that should come upon his seed,

much less to share in them. This is promised to Josiah, 2 Kings xxii. 20. Note, Good men are sometimes greatly favoured by being *taken away from the evil to come,* Isa. lvii. 1. Let this satisfy Abram, that, for his part, (1.) He shall *go to his fathers in peace.* Note, [1.] Even the friends and favourites of Heaven are not exempted from the stroke of death. Are we greater than our father Abram, who is dead? John viii. 53. [2.] Good men die willingly ; they are not fetched, they are not forced, but they go ; their soul is not required, as the rich fool's (Luke xii. 20), but cheerfully resigned : they would not live always. [3.] At death we go to our fathers, to all our fathers that have gone before us to the state of the dead (Job xxi. 32, 33), to our godly fathers that have gone before us to the state of the blessed, Heb. xii. 23. The former thought helps to take off the terror of death, the latter puts comfort into it. [4.] Whenever a godly man dies, he dies in peace. If the way be piety, the end is peace, Ps. xxxvii. 37. Outward peace, to the last, is promised to Abram, peace and truth in his days, whatever should come afterwards (2 Kings xx. 19) ; peace with God, and everlasting peace, are sure to all the seed.

(2.) He shall be *buried in a good old age.* Perhaps mention is made of his burial here, where the land of Canaan is promised him, because a burying place was the first possession he had in it. He shall not only die in peace, but die in honour, die, and be buried decently ; not only die in peace, but die in season, Job v. 26. Note, [1.] Old age is a blessing. It is promised in the fifth commandment; it is pleasing to nature ; and it affords a great opportunity for usefulness. [2.] Especially, if it be a good old age. Theirs may be called a good old age, *First,* That are old and healthful, not loaded with such distempers as make them weary of life. *Secondly,* That are old and holy, old disciples (Acts xxi. 16), whose hoary head is *found in the way of righteousness* (Prov. xvi. 31), old and useful, old and exemplary for godliness; theirs is indeed a good old age.

17 And it came to pass, that, when the sun went down, and it was dark, behold a smoking furnace, and a burning lamp that passed between those pieces. 18 In the same day the LORD made a covenant with Abram, saying, Unto thy seed have I given this land, from the river of Egypt unto the great river, the river Euphrates : 19 The Kenites, and the Kenizzites, and the Kadmonites, 20 And the Hittites, and the Perizzites, and the Rephaims, 21 And the Amorites, and the Canaanites, and the Girgashites, and the Jebusites.

Here is, I. The covenant ratified (*v.* 17); the sign which Abram desired was given, at length, when the sun had gone down, so that it was dark; for that was a dark dispensation.

1. The *smoking furnace* signified the affliction of his seed in Egypt. They were there in the *iron furnace* (Deut. iv. 20), the *furnace of affliction* (Isa. xlviii. 10), labouring in the very fire. They were there in the smoke, their eyes darkened, that they could not see to the end of their troubles, and themselves at a loss to conceive what God would do with them. Clouds and darkness were round about them.

2. The *burning lamp* denotes comfort in this affliction; and this God showed to Abram, at the same time that he showed him the *smoking furnace.* (1.) Light denotes deliverance out of the furnace; their salvation was as *a lamp that burneth,* Isa. lxii. 1. When God came down to deliver them, he appeared in a bush that *burned, and was not consumed,* Exod. iii. 2. (2.) The lamp denotes direction in the smoke. God's word was their lamp: this word to Abram was so, it was a light shining in a dark place. Perhaps this burning lamp prefigured the pillar of cloud and fire, which led them out of Egypt, in which God was. (3.) The burning lamp denotes the destruction of their enemies who kept them so long in the furnace. See Zech. xii. 6. The same cloud that enlightened the Israelites troubled and burned the Egyptians.

3. The passing of these between the pieces was the confirming of the covenant God now made with him, that he might have strong consolation, being fully persuaded that what God promised he would certainly perform. It is probable that the furnace and lamp, which passed between the pieces, burnt and consumed them, and so completed the sacrifice, and testified God's acceptance of it, as of Gideon's (Judg. vi. 21), Manoah's (Judg. xiii.19,20), and Solomon's, 2 Chron.vii. 1. So it intimates, (1.) That God's covenants with man are made by sacrifice (Ps. l. 5), by Christ, the great sacrifice: no agreement without atonement. (2.) God's acceptance of our spiritual sacrifices is a token for good and an earnest of further favours. See Judg. xiii. 23. And by this we may know that he accepts our sacrifices if he kindle in our souls a holy fire of pious and devout affections in them.

II. The covenant repeated and explained: *In that same day,* that day never to be forgotten, *the Lord made a covenant with Abram,* that is, gave a promise to Abram, saying, *Unto thy seed have I given this land, v.* 18. Here is,

1. A rehearsal of the grant. He had said before, *To thy seed will I give this land, ch.* xii. 7; xiii. 15. But here he says, *I have given it;* that is, (1.) I have given the promise of it, the charter is sealed and delivered, and cannot be disannulled. Note, God's

promises are God's gifts, and are so to be accounted. (2.) The possession is as sure, in due time, as if it were now actually delivered to them. What God has promised is as sure as if it were already done; hence, it is said, *He that believes hath everlasting life* (John iii. 36), for he shall as surely go to heaven as if he were there already.

2. A recital of the particulars granted, such as is usual in the grants of lands. He specifies the boundaries of the land intended hereby to be granted, *v.* 18. And then, for the greater certainty, as is usual in such cases, he mentions in whose tenure and occupation these lands now were. Ten several nations, or tribes, are here spoken of (*v.* 19—21) that must be cast out, to make room for the *seed of Abram.* They were not possessed of all these countries when God brought them into Canaan. The bounds are fixed much narrower, Num. xxxiv. 2, 3, &c. But, (1.) In David's time, and Solomon's, their jurisdiction extended to the utmost of these limits, 2 Chron. ix. 26. (2.) It was their own fault that they were not sooner and longer in possession of all these territories. They forfeited their right by their sins, and by their own sloth and cowardice kept themselves out of possession. (3.) The land granted is here described in its utmost extent because it was to be a type of the heavenly inheritance, where there is room enough: in our father's house are many mansions. The present occupants are named, because their number, and strength, and long prescription, should be no hindrance to the accomplishment of this promise in its season, and to magnify God's love to Abram and his seed, in giving to that one nation the possessions of many nations. so precious were they in his sight, and so honourable, Isa. xliii. 4

CHAP. XVI.

Hagar is the person mostly concerned in the story of this chapter, an obscure Egyptian woman, whose name and story we never should have heard of if Providence had not brought her into the family of Abram. Probably she was one of those maid-servants whom the king of Egypt, among other gifts, bestowed upon Abram, ch. xii. 16. Concerning her, we have four things in this chapter:—1 Her marriage to Abram her master, ver. 1—3. II. Her mis behaviour towards Sarai her mistress, ver. 4—6. III. Her discourse with an angel that met her in her flight, ver. 7—14. IV. Her delivery of a son, ver. 15, 16.

NOW Sarai Abram's wife bare him no children: and she had a handmaid, an Egyptian, whose name *was* Hagar. 2 And Sarai said unto Abram, Behold now, the LORD hath restrained me from bearing: I pray thee, go in unto my maid; it may be that I may obtain children by her. And Abram hearkened to the voice of Sarai. 3 And Sarai Abram's wife took Hagar her maid the Egyptian, after Abram had dwelt ten years in the land of Canaan, and gave her to her husband Abram to be his wife.

We have here the marriage of Abram to Hagar, who was his secondary wife. Herein, though some excuse may be made for him, he cannot be justified, for *from the beginning it was not so ;* and, when it was so, it seems to have proceeded from an irregular desire to build up families for the speedier peopling of the world and the church. Certainly it must not be so now. Christ has reduced this matter to the first institution, and makes the marriage union to be between one man and one woman only. Now,

I. The maker of this match (would one think it?) was Sarai herself: she said to Abram, *I pray thee, go in unto my maid, v.* 2. Note, 1. It is the policy of Satan to tempt us by our nearest and dearest relations, or those friends that we have an opinion of and an affection for. The temptation is most dangerous when it is sent by a hand that is least suspected : it is our wisdom therefore to consider, not so much who speaks as what is spoken. 2. God's commands consult our comfort and honour much better than our own contrivances do. It would have been much more for Sarai's interest if Abram had kept to the rule of God's law instead of being guided by her foolish projects; but we often do ill for ourselves.

II. The inducement to it was Sarai's barrenness.

1. *Sarai bare Abram no children.* She was very fair (*ch.* xii. 14), was a very agreeable dutiful wife, and a sharer with him in his large possessions ; and yet written childless. Note, (1.) God dispenses his gifts variously, loading us with benefits, but not overloading us : some cross or other is appointed to be an alloy to great enjoyments. (2.)' The mercy of children is often given to the poor and denied to the rich, given to the wicked and denied to good people, though the rich have most to leave them and good people would take most care of their education. God does herein as it has pleased him.

2. She owned God's providence in this affliction : *The Lord hath restrained me from bearing.* Note, (1.) As, where children are, it is God that gives them (*ch.* xxxiii. 5), so where they are wanted it is he that withholds them, *ch.* xxx. 2. This evil is of the Lord. (2.) It becomes us to acknowledge this, that we may bear it, and improve it, as an affliction of his ordering for wise and holy ends.

3. She used this as an argument with Abram to marry his maid ; and he was prevailed upon by this argument to do it. Note, (1.) When our hearts are too much set upon any creature-comfort, we are easily put upon the use of indirect methods for the obtaining of it. Inordinate desires commonly produce irregular endeavours. If our wishes be not kept in a submission to God's providence, our pursuits will scarcely be kept under the restraints of his precepts. (2.) It is for want of a firm dependence upon God's promise, and a patient waiting for God's time, that we

go out of the way of our duty to catch at expected mercy. *He that believes does not make haste.*

4. Abram's compliance with Sarai's proposal, we have reason to think, was from an earnest desire of the promised seed, on whom the covenant should be entailed, God had told him that his heir should be a son of his body, but had not yet told him that it should be a son by Sarai; therefore he thought, " Why not by Hagar, since Sarai herself proposed it ?" Note, (1.) Foul temptations may have very fair pretences, and be coloured with that which is very plausible. (2.) Fleshly wisdom, as it anticipates God's time of mercy, so it puts us out of God's way. (3.) This would be happily prevented if we would ask counsel of God by the word and by prayer, before we attempt that which is important and suspicious. Herein Abram was wanting ; he married without God's consent. *This persuasion came not of him that called him.*

4 And he went in unto Hagar, and she conceived : and when she saw that she had conceived, her mistress was despised in her eyes. **5** And Sarai said unto Abram, My wrong *be* upon thee : I have given my maid into thy bosom ; and when she saw that she had conceived, I was despised in her eyes : the LORD judge between me and thee. **6** · But Abram said unto Sarai, Behold, thy maid *is* in thy hand ; do to her as it pleaseth thee. And when Sarai dealt hardly with her, she fled from her face.

We have here the immediate bad consequences of Abram's unhappy marriage to Hagar. A great deal of mischief it made quickly. When we do not well both sin and trouble lie at the door ; and we may thank ourselves for the guilt and grief that follow us when we go out of the way of our duty. See it in this story.

I. Sarai is despised, and thereby provoked and put into a passion, *v.* 4. Hagar no sooner perceives herself with child by her master than she looks scornfully upon her mistress, upbraids her perhaps with her barrenness, insults over her, to make her to fret (as 1 Sam. i. 6), and boasts of the prospect she had of bringing an heir to Abram, to that good land, and to the promise. Now she thinks herself a better woman than Sarai, more favoured by Heaven, and likely to be better beloved by Abram ; and therefore she will not submit as she has done Note, 1. Mean and servile spirits, when favoured and advanced either by God or man, are apt to grow haughty and insolent, and to forget their place and origin. See Prov. xxix. 21 ; xxx. 21—23. It is a hard thing to bear honour aright. 2. We justly suffer by those whom we have sinfully indulged, and it is a righteous thing with God to make those instruments of our trouble whom we have made instruments of our sin, and to ensnare us in our own evil counsels : this stone will return upon him that rolleth it.

II. Abram is clamoured upon, and cannot be easy while Sarai is out of humour; she upbraids him vehemently, and very unjustly charges him with the injury (*v.* 5) : *My wrong be upon thee*, with a most unreasonable jealousy suspecting that he countenanced Hagar's insolence; and, as one not willing to hear what Abram had to say for the rectifying of the mistake and the clearing of himself, she rashly appeals to God in the case : *The Lord judge between me and thee;* as if Abram had refused to right her. Thus does Sarai, in her passion, speak *as one of the foolish women speaketh.* Note, 1. It is an absurdity which passionate people are often guilty of to quarrel with others for that of which they themselves must bear the blame. Sarai could not but own that she had given her maid to Abram, and yet she cries out, *My wrong be upon thee,* when she should have said, *What a fool was I to do so!* That is never said wisely which pride and anger have the inditing of; when passion is upon the throne, reason is out of doors, and is neither heard nor spoken. 2. Those are not always in the right who are most loud and forward in appealing to God. Rash and bold imprecations are commonly evidences of guilt and a bad cause.

III. Hagar is afflicted, and driven from the house, *v.* 6. Observe, 1. Abram's meekness resigns the matter of the maid-servant to Sarai, whose proper province it was to rule that part of the family : *Thy maid is in thy hand.* Though she was his wife, he would not countenance nor protect her in any thing that was disrespectful to Sarai, for whom he still retained the same affection that ever he had. Note, Those who would keep up peace and love must return soft answers to hard accusations. Husbands and wives particularly should agree, and endeavour not to be both angry together. *Yielding pacifies great. offences.* See Prov. xv. 1. 2. Sarai's passion will be revenged upon Hagar : *She dealt hardly with her,* not only confining her to her usual place and work as a servant, but probably making her to serve with rigour. Note, God takes notice of, and is displeased with, the hardships which harsh masters unreasonably put upon their servants. They ought to forbear threatening, with Job's thought, *Did not he that made me make him?* Job xxxi. 15. 3. Hagar's pride cannot bear it, her high spirit having become impatient of rebuke : *She fled from her face.* She not only avoided her wrath for the present, as David did Saul's, but she totally deserted her service, and ran away from the house, forgetting, (1.) What wrong she hereby did to her mistress, whose servant she was, and to her master, whose wife she was. Note, Pride will hardly be restrained by *any* bonds

of duty, no, not by *many.* (2.) That she herself had first given the provocation, by despising her mistress. Note, Those that suffer for their faults ought to bear their sufferings patiently, 1 Pet. ii. 20.

7 And the angel of the LORD found her by a fountain of water in the wilderness, by the fountain in the way to Shur. 8 And he said, Hagar, Sarai's maid, whence camest thou? and whither wilt thou go? And she said, I flee from the face of my mistress Sarai. 9 And the angel of the LORD said unto her, Return to thy mistress, and submit thyself under her hands.

Here is the first mention we have in scripture of an angel's appearance. Hagar was a type of the law, which was *given by the disposition of angels ; but the world to come is not put in subjection to them,* Heb. ii. 5. Observe, I. How the angel arrested her in her flight, *v.* 7. It should seem, she was making towards her own country ; for she was in the way to Shur, which lay towards Egypt. It were well if our afflictions would make us think of our home, the better country. But Hagar was now out of her place, and out of the way of her duty, and going further astray, when the angel found her. Note, 1. It is a great mercy to be stopped in a sinful way either by conscience or by Providence. 2. God suffers those that are out of the way to wander awhile, that when they see their folly, and what a loss they have brought themselves to, they may be the better disposed to return. Hagar was not stopped till she was in the wilderness, and had sat down, weary enough, and glad of clear water to refresh herself with. God brings us into a wilderness, and there meets us, Hos. ii. 14.

II. How he examined her, *v.* 8. Observe, 1. He called her *Hagar, Sarai's maid,* (1.) As a check to her pride. Though she was Abram's wife, and, as such, was obliged to return, yet he calls her *Sarai's maid,* to humble her. Note, Though civility teaches us to call others by their highest titles, yet humility and wisdom teach us to call ourselves by the lowest. (2.) As a rebuke to her flight. Sarai's maid ought to be in Sarai's tent, and not wandering in the wilderness and sauntering by a fountain of water. Note, It is good for us often to call to mind what our place and relation are. See Eccl. x. 4. 2. The questions the angel put to her were proper and very pertinent. (1.) " *Whence comest thou?* " Consider that thou art running away both from the duty thou wast bound to and the privileges thou wast blessed with in Abram's tent." Note, It is a great advantage to live in a religious family, which those ought to consider who have that advantage, yet upon every slight inducement are forward to quit it. (2.) " *Whither wilt thou go?* Thou art running thyself into sin, in Egypt" (if she return to that people, she wil. return to their gods), "and into danger, in the wilderness," through which she must travel, Deut. viii. 15. Note, Those who are forsaking God and their duty would do well to remember not only *whence they have fallen,* but *whither they are falling.* See Jer. ii. 18, *What hast thou to do* (with Hagar) in the way of Egypt? John vi. 68.

3. Her answer was honest, and a fair confession : *I flee from the face of my mistress.* In this, (1.) She acknowledges her fault in fleeing from her mistress, and yet, (2.) Excuses it, that it was *from the face,* or displeasure, of her mistress. Note, Children and servants must be treated with mildness and gentleness, lest we provoke them to take any irregular courses and so become accessory to their sins, which will condemn us, though it will not justify them.

4. How he sent her back, with suitable and compassionate counsel : " *Return to thy mistress, and submit thyself under her hand, v.* 9. Go home, and humble thyself for what thou hast done amiss, and beg pardon, and resolve for the future to behave thyself better." He makes no question but she would be welcome, though it does not appear that Abram sent after her. Note, Those that have gone away from their place and duty, when they are convinced of their error, must hasten their return and reformation, how mortifying soever it may be.

10 And the angel of the LORD said unto her, I will multiply thy seed exceedingly, that it shall not be numbered for multitude. 11 And the angel of the LORD said unto her, Behold, thou *art* with child, and shalt bear a son, and shalt call his name Ishmael; because the LORD hath heard thy affliction. 12 And he will be a wild man; his hand *will be* against every man, and every man's hand against him ; and he shall dwell in the presence of all his brethren. 13 And she called the name of the LORD that spake unto her, Thou God seest me : for she said, Have I also here looked after him that seeth me ? 14 Wherefore the well was called Beer-lahai-roi; behold, *it is* between Kadesh and Bered.

We may suppose that the angel having given Hagar that good counsel (*v.* 9) to *return to her mistress* she immediately promised to do so, and was setting her face homeward ; and then the angel went on to encourage her with an assurance of the mercy God had in store for her and her seed : for

God will meet those with mercy that are returning to their duty. *I said, I will confess, and thou forgavest,* Ps. xxxii. 5. Here is,

I. A prediction concerning her posterity given her for her comfort in her present distress. Notice is taken of her condition : *Behold, thou art with child ;* and therefore this is not a fit place for thee to be in. Note, It is a great comfort to women with child to think that they are under the particular cognizance and care of the divine Providence. God graciously considers their case and suits supports to it. Now, 1. The angel assures her of a safe delivery, and that of a *son,* which Abram desired. This fright and ramble of hers might have destroyed her hope of an offspring ; but God dealt not with her according to her folly : *Thou shalt bear a son.* She was saved in child-bearing, not only by providence, but by promise. 2. He names her child, which was an honour both to her and it : Call him *Ishmael, God will hear ;* and the reason is, because the Lord has heard ; he has, and therefore he will. Note, The experience we have had of God's seasonable kindness to us in distress should encourage us to hope for similar help in similar exigencies, Ps. x. 17. He has *heard thy affliction, v.* 11. Note, Even where there is little cry of devotion, the God of pity sometimes graciously hears the cry of affliction. Tears speak as well as prayers. This speaks comfort to the afflicted, that God not only sees what their afflictions are, but hears what they say. Note, further, Seasonable succours, in a day of affliction, ought always to be remembered with thankfulness to God. Such a time, in such a strait, *the Lord heard the voice of my affliction, and helped me.* See Deut. xxvi. 7 ; Ps. xxxi. 22.

3. He promises her a numerous offspring, (*v.* 10) : *I will multiply thy seed exceedingly,* Heb. *multiplying, I will multiply it,* that is, multiply it in every age, so as to perpetuate it. It is supposed that the Turks at this day descend from Ishmael ; and they are a great people. This was in pursuance of the promise made to Abram : *I will make thy seed as the dust of the earth,* ch. xiii. 16. Note, Many that are children of godly parents have, for their sakes, a very large share of outward common blessings, though, like Ishmael, they are not taken into covenant : many are multiplied that are not sanctified. 4. He gives a character of the child she should bear, which, however it may seem to us, perhaps was not very disagreeable to her (*v.* 12) : *He will be a wild man ; a wild ass of a man* (so the word is), rude, and bold, and fearing no man—untamed, untractable, living at large, and impatient of service and restraint. Note, The children of the bondwoman, who are out of covenant with God, are, as they were born, like the wild ass's colt ; it is grace that reclaims men, civilizes them, and makes them wise, and good for something. It is foretold, (1.) That he should live in strife,

and in a state of war: *His hand against every man*—this is his *sin; and every man's hand against him*—this is his *punishment.* Note, Those that have turbulent spirits have commonly troublesome lives; those that are provoking, vexatious, and injurious to others, must expect to be repaid in their own coin. He that has his hand and tongue against every man shall have every man's hand and tongue against him, and he has no reason to complain of it. And yet, (2.) That he should live in safety, and hold his own against all the world: *He shall dwell in the presence of all his brethren;* though threatened and insulted by all his neighbours, yet he shall keep his ground, and for Abram's sake, more than his own, shall be able to make his part good with them. Accordingly we read (*ch.* xxv. 18), that he *died*, as he lived, *in the presence of all his brethren.* Note, Many that are much exposed by their own imprudence are yet strangely preserved by the divine Providence, so much better is God to them than they deserve, when they not only forfeit their lives by sin, but hazard them.

II. Hagar's pious reflection upon this gracious appearance of God to her, *v.* 13, 14. Observe in what she said,

1. Her awful adoration of God's omniscience and providence, with application of it to herself: *She called the name of the Lord that spoke unto her,* that is, thus she made confession of his name, this she said to his praise, *Thou God seest me:* this should be, with her, his name for ever, and this his memorial, by which she will know him and remember him while she lives, *Thou God seest me.* Note, (1.) The God with whom we have to do is a seeing God, an all-seeing God. *God is* (as the ancients expressed it) *all eye.* (2.) We ought to acknowledge this with application to ourselves. He that sees all sees me, as David (Ps. cxxxix. 1), O Lord, *thou hast searched me, and known me.* (3.) A believing regard to God, as a God that sees us, will be of great use to us in our returns to him. It is a proper word for a penitent:— [1.] "Thou seest my sin and folly." I have *sinned before thee,* says the prodigal; *in thy sight,* says David. [2.] "Thou seest my sorrow and affliction;" this Hagar especially refers to. When we have brought ourselves into distress by our own folly, yet God has not forsaken us. [3.] "Thou seest the sincerity and seriousness of my return and repentance. Thou seest my secret mournings for sin, and secret motions towards thee." [4.] "Thou seest me, if in any instance I depart from thee," Ps. xliv. 20, 21. This thought should always restrain us from sin and excite us to duty: *Thou God seest me.*

2. Her humble admiration of God's favour to her: "*Have I here also looked after him that seeth me?* Have I here *seen the back parts* of him that seeth me?" so it might be read, for the word is much the same with that, Exod. xxxiii. 23. She saw not *face to face,* but as *through a glass darkly,* 1 Cor. xiii. 12. Probably she knew not who it was that talked with her, till he was departing (as Judg. vi. 21, 22; xiii. 21), and then she looked after him, with a reflection like that of the two disciples, Luke xxiv. 31, 32. Or, *Have I here seen him that sees me?* Note, (1.) The communion which holy souls have with God consists in their having an eye of faith towards him, as a God that has an eye of favour towards them. The intercourse is kept up by the eye. (2.) The privilege of our communion with God is to be looked upon with wonder and admiration, [1.] Considering what we are who are admitted to this favour. "Have I? I that am so mean, I that am so vile?" 2 Sam. vii. 18. [2.] Considering the place where we are thus favoured—"*here* also? Not only in Abram's tent and at his altar, but *here* also, in this wilderness? Here, where I never expected it, where I was out of the way of my duty? *Lord, how is it?*" John xiv. 22. Some make the answer to this question to be negative, and so look upon it as a penitent reflection: "*Have I here also,* in my distress and affliction, *looked after God?* No, I was as careless and unmindful of him as ever I used to be; and yet he has thus visited and regarded me:" for God often anticipates us with his favours, and is found of those that seek him not, Isa. lxv. 1.

III. The name which this gave to the place: *Beer-lahai-roi, The well of him that liveth and seeth me, v.* 14. It is probable that Hagar put this name upon it; and it was retained long after, *in perpetuam rei memoriam—a lasting memorial of this event.* This was the place where the God of glory manifested the special cognizance and care he took of a poor woman in distress. Note, 1. He that is all-seeing is ever-living; he lives and sees us. 2. Those that are graciously admitted into communion with God, and receive seasonable comforts from him, should tell others what he has done for their souls, that they also may be encouraged to seek him and trust in him. 3. God's gracious manifestations of himself to us are to be had in everlasting remembrance by us, and should never be forgotten.

15 And Hagar bare Abram a son: and Abram called his son's name, which Hagar bare, Ishmael. 16 And Abram *was* fourscore and six years old, when Hagar bare Ishmael to Abram.

It is here taken for granted, though not expressly recorded, that Hagar did as the angel commanded her, returning to her mistress and submitting herself; and then, in the fulness of time, she brought forth her son. Note, Those who obey divine precepts shall have the comfort of divine promises. This was the son of the bond-woman that was *born after the flesh* (Gal. iv. 23), repre-

senting the unbelieving Jews, *v.* 25.   Note,
1. Many who can call Abraham father are
yet *born after the flesh*, Matt. iii. 9.   2. The
carnal seed in the church are sooner brought
forth than the spiritual.   It is an easier thing
to persuade men to assume the form of godliness than to submit to the power of godliness.

CHAP. XVII.

This chapter contains articles of agreement covenanted and concluded upon between the great Jehovah, the Father of mercies,
on the one part, and pious Abram, the father of the faithful, on
the other part.   Abram is therefore called " the friend of God,"
not only because he was the man of his counsel, but because he
was the man of his covenant; both these secrets were with him.
Mention was made of this covenant (ch. xv. 18), but here it is
particularly drawn up, and put into the form of a covenant, that
Abram might have strong consolation.   Here are, I. The circumstances of the making of this covenant, the time and manner
(ver. 1), and the posture Abram was in, ver. 3.   II. The covenant itself.   In the general scope of it, ver. 1.   And, afterwards,
in the particular instances.   1. That he should be the father of
many nations (ver. 4, 6), and, in token of this, his name was
changed, ver. 5.   2. That God would be a God to him and his
seed, and would give them the land of Canaan, ver 7, 8.   And
the seal of this part of the covenant was circumcision, ver. 9—14.
3. That he should have a son by Sarai, and, in token thereof,
her name was changed, ver. 15, 16.   This promise Abram received, ver. 17.   And his request for Ishmael (ver. 18) was answered, abundantly to his satisfaction, ver. 19—22.   III. The
circumcision of Abram and his family, according to God's appointment, ver. 23, &c.

AND when Abram was ninety
years old and nine, the LORD
appeared to Abram, and said unto
him, I *am* the Almighty God ; walk
before me, and be thou perfect.   2
And I will make my covenant between me and thee, and will multiply
thee exceedingly.   3 And Abram fell
on his face : and God talked with
him, saying,

Here is, I. The time when God made Abram
this gracious visit : *When he was ninety-nine
years old*, full thirteen years after the birth of
Ishmael.   1. So long, it should seem, God's
extraordinary appearances to Abram were
intermitted ; and all the communion he had
with God was only in the usual way of ordinances and providences.   Note, There are
some special comforts which are not the
daily bread, no, not of the best saints, but
they are favoured with them now and then.
On this side heaven they have convenient
food, but not a continual feast.   2. So long
the promise of Isaac was deferred.   (1.) Perhaps to correct Abram's over-hasty marrying
of Hagar.   Note, The comforts we sinfully
anticipate are justly delayed.   (2.) That
Abram and Sarai being so far stricken in age
God's power, in this matter, might be the
more magnified, and their faith the more
tried.   See Deut. xxxii. 36 ; John xi. 6, 15.
(3.) That a child so long waited for might be
an *Isaac, a son indeed*, Isa. liv. 1.

II. The way in which God made this covenant with him : *The Lord appeared to Abram*,
in the *shechinah*, some visible display of God's
immediate glorious presence with him.   Note,
God first makes himself known to us, and
gives us a sight of him by faith, and then
takes us into his covenant.

III. The posture Abram put himself into
110

upon this occasion : *He fell on his face while
God talked with him, v.* 3.   1. As one overcome by the brightness of the divine glory,
and unable to bear the sight of it, though he
had seen it several times before.   Daniel and
John did likewise, though they were also acquainted with the visions of the Almighty,
Dan. viii. 17 ; x. 9, 15 ; Rev. i. 17.   Or, 2.
As one ashamed of himself, and blushing to
think of the honours done to one so unworthy.   He looks upon himself with humility, and upon God with reverence, and, in
token of both, *falls on his face*, putting himself into a posture of adoration.   Note, (1.)
God graciously condescends to talk with
those whom he takes into covenant and
communion with himself.   He talks with
them by his *word*, Prov. vi. 22.   He talks
with them by his *Spirit*, John xiv. 26.   This
honour have all his saints.   (2.) Those that
are admitted into fellowship with God are,
and must be, very humble and very reverent
in their approaches to him.   If we say we
have fellowship with him, and the familiarity
breeds contempt, we deceive ourselves.   (3.)
Those that would receive comfort from God
must set themselves to give glory to God and
to worship at his footstool.

IV. The general scope and summary of
the covenant laid down as the foundation on
which all the rest was built ; it is no other
than the covenant of grace still made with
all believers in Jesus Christ, *v.* 1.   Observe
here,
1. What we may expect to find God to us :
I am the Almighty God.   By this name he
chose to make himself known to Abram
rather than by his name *Jehovah*, Exod. vi. 3.
He used it to Jacob, *ch.* xxxv. 11.   They
called him by this name, *ch.* xxviii. 3 ; xliii.
14 ; xlviii. 3.   It is the name of God that is
mostly used throughout the book of Job,
at least in the *discourses* of that book.
After Moses, *Jehovah* is more frequently
used, and this, *El-shaddai*, very rarely ; it
bespeaks the almighty power of God, either,
(1.) As an avenger, from שׁדד *he laid
waste*, so some ; and they think God took
this title from the destruction of the old
world.   This is countenanced by Isa. xiii. 6,
and Joel i. 15.   Or, (2.) As a benefactor, שׁ
for אשׁר *who*, and י *sufficient*.   He is a God
that is enough ; or, as our old English translation reads it here very significantly, *I am
God all-sufficient*.   Note, The God with whom
we have to do is a God *that is enough*.   [1.]
He is enough in himself ; he is self-sufficient ;
he has every thing, and he needs not any
thing.   [2.] He is enough to us, if we be in
covenant with him : we have all in him, and
we have enough in him, enough to satisfy
our most enlarged desires, enough to supply
the defect of every thing else, and to secure
to us a happiness for our immortal souls.
See Ps. xvi. 5, 6 ; lxxiii. 25.
2. What God requires that we should be
to him.   The covenant is mutual : *Walk be-*

fore me, and be thou perfect, that is, upright and sincere; for herein the covenant of grace is well-ordered that sincerity is our gospel perfection. Observe, (1.) That to be religious is to walk before God in our integrity; it is to set God always before us, and to think, and speak, and act, in every thing, as those that are always under his eye. It is to have a constant regard to his word as our rule and to his glory as our end in all our actions, and to be continually in his fear. It is to be *inward with him,* in all the duties of religious worship, for in them particularly we walk before God (1 Sam. ii. 30), and to be *entire for him,* in all holy conversation. I know no religion but sincerity. (2.) That upright walking with God is the condition of our interest in his all-sufficiency. If we neglect him, or dissemble with him, we forfeit the benefit and comfort of our relation to him. (3.) A continual regard to God's all-sufficiency will have a great influence upon our upright walking with him.

4 As for me, behold, my covenant *is* with thee, and thou shalt be a father of many nations. 5 Neither shall thy name any more be called Abram, but thy name shall be Abraham; for a father of many nations have I made thee. 6 And I will make thee exceeding fruitful, and I will make nations of thee, and kings shall come out of thee.

The promise here is introduced with solemnity : "*As for me,*" says the great God, "behold, behold and admire it, behold and be assured of it, my covenant is with thee;" as before (*v.* 2), *I will make my covenant.* Note, The covenant of grace is a covenant of God's own making; this he glories in *(as for me),* and so may we. Now here,

I. It is promised to Abraham that he should be a *father of many nations;* that is, 1. That his seed after the flesh should be very numerous, both in Isaac and Ishmael, as well as in the sons of Keturah : something extraordinary is doubtless included in this promise, and we may suppose that the event answered to it, and that there have been, and are, more of the children of men descended from Abraham than from any one man at an equal distance with him from Noah, the common root. 2. That all believers in every age should be looked upon as his spiritual seed, and that he should be called, not only the *friend of God,* but the *father of the faithful.* In this sense the apostle directs us to understand this promise, Rom. iv. 16, 17. He is the father of those in every nation that by faith enter into covenant with God, and (as the Jewish writers express it) *are gathered under the wings of the divine Majesty.*

II. In token of this his name was changed from *Abram, a high father,* to *Abraham, the father of a multitude.* This was, 1. To put an honour upon him. It is spoken of as the glory of the church that she shall be *called by a new name, which the mouth of the Lord shall name,* Isa. lxii. 2. Princes dignify their favourites by conferring new titles upon them; thus was Abraham dignified by him that is indeed the fountain of honour. All believers have a new name, Rev. ii. 17. Some think it added to the honour of Abraham's new name that a letter of the name *Jehovah* was inserted into it, as it was a disgrace to Jeconiah to have the first syllable of his name cut off, because it was the same with the first syllable of that sacred name, Jer. xxii. 28. Believers are named from Christ, Eph. iii. 15. 2. To encourage and confirm the faith of Abraham. While he was childless perhaps even his own name was sometimes an occasion of grief to him : why should he be called a high father who was not a father at all ? But now that God had promised him a numerous issue, and had given him a name which signified so much, that name was his joy. Note, God calls things that are not as though they were. It is the apostle's observation upon this very thing, Rom. iv. 17. He called Abraham *the father of a multitude* because he should prove to be so in due time, though as yet he had but one child.

7 And I will establish my covenant between me and thee and thy seed after thee in their generations for an everlasting covenant, to be a God unto thee, and to thy seed after thee. 8 And I will give unto thee, and to thy seed after thee, the land wherein thou art a stranger, all the land of Canaan, for an everlasting possession; and I will be their God. 9 And God said unto Abraham, Thou shalt keep my covenant therefore, thou, and thy seed after thee in their generations. 10 This *is* my covenant, which ye shall keep, between me and you and thy seed after thee; Every man child among you shall be circumcised. 11 And ye shall circumcise the flesh oɪ your foreskin; and it shall be a token of the covenant betwixt me and you. 12 And he that is eight days old shall be circumcised among you, every man child in your generations, he that is born in the house, or bought with money of any stranger, which *is* not of thy seed. 13 He that is born in thy house, and he that is bought with thy money, must needs

be circumcised: and my covenant shall be in your flesh for an everlasting covenant. 14 And the uncircumcised man child whose flesh of his foreskin is not circumcised, that soul shall be cut off from his people; he hath broken my covenant.

Here is, I. The continuance of the covenant, intimated in three things:—1. It is established; not to be altered nor revoked. It is fixed, it is ratified, it is made as firm as the divine power and truth can make it. 2. It is entailed; it is a covenant, not with Abraham only (then it would die with him), but with his seed after him, not only his seed after the flesh, but his spiritual seed. 3. It is everlasting in the evangelical sense and meaning of it. The covenant of grace is everlasting. It is from everlasting in the counsels of it, and to everlasting in the consequences of it; and the external administration of it is transmitted with the seal of it to the seed of believers, and the internal administration of it by the Spirit to Christ's seed in every age.

II. The contents of the covenant: it is a covenant of promises, exceedingly great and precious promises. Here are two which indeed are all-sufficient:—1. That God would be their God, *v.* 7, 8. All the privileges of the covenant, all its joys and all its hopes, are summed up in this. A man needs desire no more than this to make him happy. What God is himself, that he will be to his people: his wisdom theirs, to guide and counsel them; his power theirs, to protect and support them; his goodness theirs, to supply and comfort them. What faithful worshippers can expect from the God they serve believers shall find in God as theirs. This is enough, yet not all. 2. That Canaan should be their everlasting possession, *v.* 8. God had before promised this land to Abraham and his seed, *ch.* xv. 18. But here, where it is promised for an everlasting possession, surely it must be looked upon as a type of heaven's happiness, that everlasting rest which remains for the people of God, Heb. iv. 9. This is that better country to which Abraham had an eye, and the grant of which was that which answered to the vast extent and compass of that promise, that God would be to them a God; so that, if God had not prepared and designed this, he would have been ashamed to be called their God, Heb. xi. 16. As the land of Canaan was secured to the seed of Abraham according to the flesh, so heaven is secured to all his spiritual seed, by a covenant, and for a possession, truly everlasting. The offer of this eternal life is made in the word, and confirmed by the sacraments, to all that are under the external administration of the covenant; and the earnest of it is given to all believers, Eph. i. 14. Canaan is here said

to be the land wherein Abraham was a stranger; and the heavenly Canaan is a land to which we are strangers, for it does not yet appear what we shall be.

III. The token of the covenant, and that is circumcision, for the sake of which the covenant is itself called the *covenant of circumcision*, Acts vii. 8. It is here said to be the covenant which Abraham and his seed must keep, as a copy or counterpart, *v.* 9, 10. It is called a sign and seal (Rom. iv. 11), for it was, 1. A confirmation to Abraham and his seed of those promises which were God's part of the covenant, assuring them that they should be fulfilled, that in due time Canaan should be theirs: and the continuance of this ordinance, after Canaan was theirs, intimates that these promises looked further to another Canaan, which they must still be in expectation of. See Heb. iv. 8. 2. An obligation upon Abraham and his seed to that duty which was their part of the covenant; not only to the duty of accepting the covenant and consenting to it, and putting away the corruption of the flesh (which were more immediately and primarily signified by circumcision), but, in general, to the observance of all God's commands, as they should at any time hereafter be intimated and made known to them; for circumcision made men *debtors to do the whole law*, Gal. v. 3. Those who will have God to be to them a God must consent and resolve to be to him a people. Now, (1.) Circumcision was a bloody ordinance; for all things by the law were purged with blood, Heb. ix. 22. See Exod. xxiv. 8. But, the blood of Christ being shed, all bloody ordinances are now abolished; circumcision therefore gives way to baptism. (2.) It was peculiar to the males, though the women were also included in the covenant, for the man is the head of the woman. In our kingdom, the oath of allegiance is required only from men. Some think that the blood of the males only was shed in circumcision because respect was had in it to Jesus Christ and his blood. (3.) It was the flesh of the foreskin that was to be cut off, because it is by ordinary generation that sin is propagated, and with an eye to the promised seed, who was to come from the loins of Abraham. Christ having not yet offered himself for us, God would have man to enter into covenant by the offering of some part of his own body, and no part could be better spared. It is a secret part of the body; for the true circumcision is that of the heart: this honour God put upon an uncomely part, 1 Cor. xii. 23, 24. (4.) The ordinance was to be administered to children when they were eight days old, and not sooner, that they might gather some strength, to be able to undergo the pain of it, and that at least one sabbath might pass over them. (5.) The children of the strangers, of whom the master of the family was the true domestic owner, were to

112

be circumcised (*v.* 12, 13), which looked favourably upon the Gentiles, who should in due time be brought into the family of Abraham, by faith. See Gal. iii. 14. (6.) The religious observance of this institution was required under a very severe penalty, *v.* 14. The contempt of circumcision was a contempt of the covenant; if the parents did not circumcise their children, it was at their peril, as in the case of Moses, Exod. iv. 24, 25. With respect to those that were not circumcised in their infancy, if, when they grew up, they did not themselves come under this ordinance, God would surely reckon with them. If they cut not off the flesh of their foreskin, God would cut them off from their people. It is a dangerous thing to make light of divine institutions, and to live in the neglect of them.

15 And God said unto Abraham, As for Sarai thy wife, thou shalt not call her name Sarai, but Sarah *shall* her name *be.* 16 And I will bless her, and give thee a son also of her: yea, I will bless her, and she shall be *a mother* of nations; kings of people shall be of her. 17 Then Abraham fell upon his face, and laughed, and said in his heart, Shall *a child* be born unto him that is a hundred years old? and shall Sarah, that is ninety years old, bear? 18 And Abraham said unto God, O that Ishmael might live before thee! 19 And God said, Sarah thy wife shall bear thee a son indeed; and thou shalt call his name Isaac: and I will establish my covenant with him for an everlasting covenant, *and* with his seed after him. 20 And as for Ishmael, I have heard thee: Behold, I have blessed him, and will make him fruitful, and will multiply him exceedingly; twelve princes shall he beget, and I will make him a great nation. 21 But my covenant will I establish with Isaac, which Sarah shall bear unto thee at this set time in the next year. 22 And he left off talking with him, and God went up from Abraham.

Here is, I. The promise made to Abraham of a son by *Sarai,* that son in whom the promise made to him should be fulfilled, that he should be the father of many nations; for *she also shall be a mother of nations, and kings of people shall be of her, v.* 16. Note, 1. God reveals the purposes of his good-will to his people by degrees. God had told

Abraham long before that he should have a son, but never till now that he should have a son by *Sarai.* 2. The blessing of the Lord makes fruitful, and adds no sorrow with it, no such sorrow as was in Hagar's case. " I will bless her with the blessing of fruitfulness, and then thou shalt have a son of her." 3. Civil government and order are a great blessing to the church. It is promised, not only that *people,* but *kings of people,* should be of her; not a headless rout, but a well-modelled well-governed society.

II. The ratification of this promise was the change of *Sarai's* name into *Sarah* (*v.* 15), the same letter being added to her name that was to Abraham's, and for the same reasons. *Sarai* signifies *my princess,* as if her honour were confined to one family only. *Sarah* signifies *a princess*—namely, of *multitudes,* or signifying that from her should come the Messiah the prince, even the prince of the kings of the earth.

III. Abraham's joyful, thankful, entertainment of this gracious promise, *v.* 17. Upon this occasion he expressed, 1. Great humility: He *fell on his face.* Note, The more honours and favours God confers upon us the lower we should be in our own eyes, and the more reverent and submissive before God. 2. Great joy: He *laughed.* It was a laughter of delight, not of distrust. Note, Even the promises of a holy God, as well as his performances, are the joys of holy souls; there is the joy of faith as well as the joy of fruition. Now it was that Abraham rejoiced to see Christ's day. Now he saw it and was glad (John viii. 56); for, as he saw heaven in the promise of Canaan, so he saw Christ in the promise of Isaac. 3. Great admiration: *Shall a child be born to him that is a hundred years old?* He does not here speak of it as at all doubtful (for we are sure that *he staggered not at the promise,* Rom. iv. 20), but as very wonderful and that which could not be effected but by the almighty power of God, and as very *kind,* and a favour which was the more affecting and obliging for this, that it was extremely surprising, Ps. cxxvi. 1, 2.

IV. Abraham's prayer for Ishmael: *O that Ishmael might live before thee! v.* 18. This he speaks, not as desiring that Ishmael might be preferred before the son he should have by Sarah; but, dreading lest he should be abandoned and forsaken of God, he puts up this petition on his behalf. Now that God is talking with him he thinks he has a very fair opportunity to speak a good word for Ishmael, and he will not let it slip. Note, 1. Though we ought not to prescribe to God, yet he gives us leave, in prayer, to be humbly free with him, and particular in making known our requests, Phil. iv. 6. Whatever is the matter of our care and fear should be spread before God in prayer. 2. It is the duty of parents to pray for their children, for all their children, as Job, who

113

offered burnt-offerings according to the number of them all, Job i. 5. Abraham would not have it thought that, when God promised him a son by Sarah, which he so much desired, then his son by Hagar was forgotten; no, still he bears him upon his heart, and shows a concern for him. The prospect of further favours must not make us unmindful of former favours. 3. The great thing we should desire of God for our children is that they may live before him, that is, that they may be kept in covenant with him, and may have grace to walk before him in their uprightness. Spiritual blessings are the best blessings, and those for which we should be most earnest with God, both for ourselves and others. Those live well that live before God.

V. God's answer to his prayer; and it is an answer of peace. Abraham could not say that he sought God's face in vain.

1. Common blessings are secured to Ishmael (*v.* 20): *As for Ishmael,* whom thou art in so much care about, *I have heard thee;* he shall find favour for thy sake; *I have blessed him,* that is, I have many blessings in store for him. (1.) His posterity shall be numerous: *I will multiply him exceedingly,* more than his neighbours. This is the fruit of the blessing, as that, *ch.* i. 28. (2.) They shall be considerable: *Twelve princes shall he beget.* We may charitably hope that spiritual blessings also were bestowed upon him, though the visible church was not brought out of his loins and the covenant was not lodged in his family. Note, Great plenty of outward good things is often given to those children of godly parents who are born after the flesh, for their parents' sake.

2. Covenant blessings are reserved for Isaac, and appropriated to him, *v.* 19, 21. If Abraham, in his prayer for Ishmael, meant that he would have the covenant made with him, and the promised seed to come from him, then God did not answer him in the letter, but in that which was equivalent, nay, which was every way better. (1.) God repeats to him the promise of a son by Sarah: *She shall bear thee a son indeed.* Note, Even true believers need to have God's promises doubled and repeated to them, that they may have strong consolation, Heb. vi. 18. Again, Children of the promise are children indeed. (2.) He names that child—calls him *Isaac, laughter,* because Abraham rejoiced in spirit when this son was promised him. Note, If God's promises be our joy, his mercies promised shall in due time be our *exceeding* joy. Christ will be laughter to those that look for him; those that now rejoice in hope shall shortly rejoice in having that which they hope for: this is laughter that is not mad. (3.) He entails the covenant upon that child: *I will establish my covenant with him.* Note, God takes whom he pleases into covenant with himself, according to the good pleasure of his will. See Rom. ix. 8, 18. Thus was the covenant settled between God and Abra-

ham, with its several limitations and remainders, and then the conference ended: *God left off talking with him,* and the vision disappeared, *God went up from Abraham.* Note, Our communion with God here is broken and interrupted; in heaven it will be a continual and everlasting feast.

23 And Abraham took Ishmael his son, and all that were born in his house, and all that were bought with his money, every male among the men of Abraham's house; and circumcised the flesh of their foreskin in the selfsame day, as God had said unto him. 24 And Abraham *was* ninety years old and nine, when he was circumcised in the flesh of his foreskin. 25 And Ishmael his son *was* thirteen years old, when he was circumcised in the flesh of his foreskin. 26 In the selfsame day was Abraham circumcised, and Ishmael his son. 27 And all the men of his house, born in the house, and bought with money of the stranger, were circumcised with him.

We have here Abraham's obedience to the law of circumcision. He himself and all his family were circumcised, so receiving the token of the covenant and distinguishing themselves from other families, that had no part nor lot in the matter. 1. It was an implicit obedience: He did *as God had said to him,* and did not ask why or wherefore. God's will was not only a law to him, but a reason; he did it because God told him. 2. It was a speedy obedience: *In the self-same day, v.* 23, 26. Sincere obedience is not dilatory, Ps. cxix. 60. While the command is yet sounding in our ears, and the sense of duty is fresh, it is good to apply ourselves to it immediately, lest we deceive ourselves by putting it off to a more convenient season. 3. It was a universal obedience: He did not circumcise his family and excuse himself, but set them an example; nor did he take the comfort of the seal of the covenant to himself only, but desired that all his might share with him in it. This is a good example to masters of families; they and their houses must serve the Lord. Though God's covenant was not established with Ishmael, yet he was circumcised; for children of believing parents, as such, have a right to the privileges of the visible church, and the seals of the covenant, whatever they may prove afterwards. Ishmael is blessed, and therefore circumcised. 4. Abraham did this though much might be objected against it. Though circumcision was painful,—though to grown men it was shameful,—though, while they were sore and unfit for action, their enemies might take advantage against them, as Simeon and Levi did against the Shechemites,—though Abraham was ninety-nine years old, and had been justified and accepted of God long since,—though so strange a thing done religiously might be turned to his reproach by the Canaanite and the Perizzite that dwelt then in the land,—yet God's command was sufficient to answer these and a thousand such objections : what God requires we must do, not *conferring with flesh and blood.*

CHAP. XVIII.

We have an account in this chapter of another interview between God and Abraham, probably within a few days after the former, as the reward of his cheerful obedience to the law of circumcision. Here is, I. The kind visit which God made him, and the kind entertainment which he gave to that visit, ver. 1—8. II. The matters discoursed of between them. 1. The purposes of God's love concerning Sarah, ver. 9—15. 2. The purposes of God's wrath concerning Sodom. (1.) The discovery God made to Abraham of his design to destroy Sodom, ver. 16—22. (2.) The intercession Abraham made for Sodom, ver. 23, &c.

AND the Lord appeared unto him in the plains of Mamre : and he sat in the tent-door in the heat of the day ; 2 And he lift up his eyes and looked, and, lo, three men stood by him : and when he saw *them,* he ran to meet them from the tent-door, and bowed himself toward the ground, 3 And said, My Lord, if now I have found favour in thy sight, pass not away, I pray thee, from thy servant : 4 Let a little water, I pray you, be fetched, and wash your feet, and rest yourselves under the tree : 5 And I will fetch a morsel of bread, and comfort ye your hearts ; after that ye shall pass on : for therefore are ye come to your servant. And they said, So do, as thou hast said. 6 And Abraham hastened into the tent unto Sarah, and said, Make ready quickly three measures of fine meal, knead *it,* and make cakes upon the hearth. 7 And Abraham ran unto the herd, and fetched a calf tender and good, and gave *it* unto a young man ; and he hasted to dress it. 8 And he took butter, and milk, and the calf which he had dressed, and set *it* before them ; and he stood by them under the tree, and they did eat.

This appearance of God to Abraham seems to have had in it more of freedom and familiarity, and less of grandeur and majesty, than those we have hitherto read of ; and therefore more resembles that great visit which, in the fulness of time, the Son of God was to make to the world, when the Word would be made flesh, and appear as one of us. Observe here,

I. How Abraham expected strangers, and how richly his expectations were answered (*v.* 1): *He sat in the tent-door, in the heat of the day ;* not so much to repose or divert himself as to seek an opportunity of doing good, by giving entertainment to strangers and travellers, there being perhaps no inns to accommodate them. Note, 1. We are likely to have the most comfort of those good works to which we are most free and forward. 2. God graciously visits those in whom he has first raised the expectation of him, and manifests himself to those that wait for him. When Abraham was thus sitting, he saw three men coming towards him. These three men were three spiritual heavenly beings, now assuming human bodies, that they might be visible to Abraham, and conversable with him. Some think that they were all created angels, others that one of them was the Son of God, the angel of the covenant, whom Abraham distinguished from the rest (*v.* 3), and who is called *Jehovah, v.* 13. The apostle improves this for the encouragement of hospitality, Heb. xiii. 2. Those that have been forward to entertain strangers have entertained angels, to their unspeakable honour and satisfaction. Where, upon a prudent and impartial judgment, we see no cause to suspect ill, charity teaches us to hope well and to show kindness accordingly. It is better to feed five drones, or wasps, than to starve one bee.

II. How Abraham entertained those strangers, and how kindly his entertainment was accepted. The Holy Ghost takes particular notice of the very free and affectionate welcome Abraham gave to the strangers. 1. He was very complaisant and respectful to them. Forgetting his age and gravity, he *ran to meet them* in the most obliging manner, and with all due courtesy *bowed himself towards the ground,* though as yet he knew nothing of them but that they appeared graceful respectable men. Note, Religion does not destroy, but improve, good manners, and teaches us to honour all men. Decent civility is a great ornament to piety. 2. He was very earnest and importunate for their stay, and took it as a great favour, *v.* 3, 4. Note, (1.) It becomes those whom God has blessed with plenty to be liberal and open-hearted in their entertainments, according to their ability, and (not in compliment, but cordially) to bid their friends welcome. We should take a pleasure in showing kindness to any ; for both God and man love a cheerful giver. Who would *eat the bread of him that has an evil eye ?* Prov. xxiii. 6, 7. (2.) Those that would have communion with God must earnestly desire it and pray for it. God is a guest worth entreating. 3. His entertainment, though it was very free, was yet plain and homely, and there was nothing in it of the gaiety and niceness of our times. His dining-room was an arbour under a tree ; no rich table-linen, no side-board set with plate. His feast was a joint or two of veal, and some cakes baked on the hearth, and both hastily dressed up. Here were no dainties, no varieties, no forced-meats, no sweet-meats, but good, plain, wholesome food, though Abraham was very rich and his guests were very honourable. Note, We ought not to be curious in our diet. Let us be thankful for food convenient, though it be homely and common; and not be desirous of dainties, for they are deceitful meat to those that love them and set their hearts upon them. 4. He and his wife were both of them very attentive and busy, in accommodating their guests with the best they had. Sarah herself is cook and baker; Abraham runs to fetch the calf, brings out the milk and butter, and thinks it not below him to wait at table, that he might show how heartily welcome his guests were. Note, (1.) Those that have real merit need not take state upon them, nor are their prudent condescensions any disparagement to them. (2.) Hearty friendship will stoop to any thing but sin. Christ himself has taught us to wash one another's feet, in humble love. Those that thus abase themselves shall be exalted. Here Abraham's faith showed itself in good works; and so must ours, else it is dead, Jam. ii. 21, 26. The father of the faithful was famous for charity, and generosity, and good housekeeping; and we must learn of him to *do good and to communicate.* Job did not eat his morsel alone, Job xxxi. 17.

9 And they said unto him, Where *is* Sarah thy wife? And he said, Behold, in the tent. 10 And he said, I will certainly return unto thee according to the time of life; and, lo, Sarah thy wife shall have a son. And Sarah heard *it* in the tent-door, which *was* behind him. 11 Now Abraham and Sarah *were* old *and* well stricken in age; *and* it ceased to be with Sarah after the manner of women. 12 Therefore Sarah laughed within herself, saying, After I am waxed old shall I have pleasure, my lord being old also? 13 And the LORD said unto Abraham, Wherefore did Sarah laugh, saying, Shall I of a surety bear a child, which am old? 14 Is any thing too hard for the LORD? At the time appointed I will return unto thee, according to the time of life, and Sarah shall have a son. 15 Then Sarah denied, saying, I laughed not; for she was afraid. And he said, Nay; but thou didst laugh.

These heavenly guests (being sent to confirm the promise lately made to Abraham, that he should have a son by Sarah), while

they are receiving Abraham's kind entertainment, thus return his kindness. He receives angels, and has angels' rewards, a gracious message from heaven, Matt. x. 41.

I. Care is taken that Sarah should be within hearing. She must conceive by faith, and therefore the promise must be made to her, Heb. xi. 11. It was the modest usage of that time that the women did not sit at meat with men, at least not with strangers, but confined themselves to their own apartments; therefore Sarah is here out of sight: but she must not be out of hearing. The angels enquire (*v.* 9), *Where is Sarah thy wife?* By naming her, they gave intimation enough to Abraham that, though they seemed strangers, yet they very well knew him and his family. By enquiring after her, they showed a friendly kind concern for the family and relations of one whom they found respectful to them. It is a piece of common civility, which ought to proceed from a principle of Christian love, and then it is sanctified. And, by speaking of her (she overhearing it), they drew her to listen to what was further to be said. *Where is Sarah thy wife?* say the angels. "*Behold in the tent,*" says Abraham. "Where should she be else? There she is in her place, as she uses to be, and is now within call." Note, 1. The daughters of Sarah must learn of her to be *chaste, keepers at home,* Tit. ii. 5. There is nothing got by gadding. 2. Those are most likely to receive comfort from God and his promises that are in their place and in the way of their duty, Luke ii. 8.

II. The promise is then renewed and ratified, that she should have a son (*v.* 10): "*I will certainly return unto thee,* and visit thee next time with the performance, as now I do with the promise." God will return to those that bid him welcome, that entertain his visits: "I will return thy kindness, *Sarah thy wife shall have a son;*" it is repeated again, *v.* 14. Thus the promises of the Messiah were often repeated in the Old Testament, for the strengthening of the faith of God's people. We are slow of heart to believe, and therefore have need of line upon line to the same purport. This is that word of promise which the apostle quotes (Rom. ix. 9) as that by the virtue of which Isaac was born. Note, 1. The same blessings which others have from common providence believers have from the promise, which makes them very sweet and very sure. 2. The spiritual seed of Abraham owe their life, and joy, and hope, and all, to the promise. They are born by the word of God, 1 Pet. i. 23.

III. Sarah thinks this too good news to be true, and therefore cannot as yet find in her heart to believe it: *Sarah laughed within herself, v.* 12. It was not a pleasing laughter of faith, like Abraham's (*ch.* xvii. 17), but it was a laughter of doubting and mistrust. Note, The same thing may be done from very different principles, of which God only, who knows the heart, can judge. The great objection which Sarah could not get over was her age : " *I am waxed old*, and past childbearing in the course of nature, especially having been hitherto barren, and (which magnifies the difficulty) *my lord is old also.*" Observe here, 1. Sarah calls Abraham her *lord ;* it was the only good word in this saying, and the Holy Ghost takes notice of it to her honour, and recommends it to the imitation of all Christian wives. 1 Pet. iii. 6, *Sarah obeyed Abraham, calling him lord,* in token of respect and subjection. Thus must the wife reverence her husband, Eph. v. 33. And thus must we be apt to take notice of what is spoken decently and well, to the honour of those that speak it, though it may be mixed with that which is amiss, over which we should cast a mantle of love. 2. Human improbability often sets up in contradiction to the divine promise. The objections of sense are very apt to stumble and puzzle the weak faith even of true believers. It is hard to cleave to the first Cause, when second causes frown. 3. Even where there is true faith, yet there are often sore conflicts with unbelief, Sarah could say, *Lord, I believe* (Heb. xi. 11), and yet must say, *Lord, help my unbelief.*

IV. The angel reproves the indecent expressions of her distrust, *v.* 13, 14. Observe, 1. Though Sarah was now most kindly and generously entertaining these angels, yet, when she did amiss, they reproved her for it, as Christ reproved Martha in her own house, Luke x. 40, 41. If our friends be kind to us, we must not therefore be so unkind to them as to suffer sin upon them. 2. God gave this reproof to Sarah by Abraham her husband. To him he said, *Why did Sarah laugh ?* perhaps because he had not told her of the promise which had been given him some time before to this purport, and which, if he had communicated it to her with its ratifications, would have prevented her from being so surprised now. Or Abraham was told of it that he might tell her of it. Mutual reproof, when there is occasion for it, is one of the duties of the conjugal relation. 3. The reproof itself is plain, and backed with a good reason : *Wherefore did Sarah laugh ?* Note, It is good to enquire into the reason of our laughter, that it may not be the laughter of the fool, Eccl. vii. 6. " Wherefore did I laugh ?" Again, Our unbelief and distrust are a great offence to the God of heaven. He justly takes it ill to have the objections of sense set up in contradiction to his promise, as Luke i. 18. 4. Here is a question asked which is enough to answer all the cavils of flesh and blood : *Is any thing too hard for the Lord ?* (Heb. *too wonderful*), that is, (1.) Is any thing so secret as to escape his cognizance ? No, not Sarah's laughing, though it was only *within herself.* Or, (2.) Is any thing so difficult as to exceed his power ? No, not the giving of a child to Sarah in her old age.

V. Sarah foolishly endeavours to conceal her fault (*v.* 15): *She denied, saying, I did not laugh,* thinking nobody could contradict her : she told this lie, because *she was afraid ;* but it was in vain to attempt concealing it from an all-seeing eye ; she was told, to her shame, *Thou didst laugh.* Now, 1. There seems to be in Sarah a retraction of her distrust. Now she perceived, by laying circumstances together, that it was a divine promise which had been made concerning her, she renounced all doubting distrustful thoughts about it. But, 2. There was withal a sinful attempt to cover a sin with a lie. It is a shame to do amiss, but a greater shame to deny it ; for thereby we add iniquity to our iniquity. Fear of a rebuke often betrays us into this snare. See Isa. lvii. 11, *Whom hast thou feared, that thou hast lied ?* But we deceive ourselves if we think to impose upon God ; he can and will bring truth to light, to our shame. *He that covers his sin cannot prosper,* for the day is coming which will discover it.

16 And the men rose up from thence, and looked toward Sodom : and Abraham went with them to bring them on the way. 17 And the LORD said, Shall I hide from Abraham that thing which I do ; 18 Seeing that Abraham shall surely become a great and mighty nation, and all the nations of the earth shall be blessed in him ? 19 For I know him, that he will command his children and his household after him, and they shall keep the way of the LORD, to do justice and judgment ; that the LORD may bring upon Abraham that which he hath spoken of him. 20 And the LORD said, Because the cry of Sodom and Gomorrah is great, and because their sin is very grievous ; 21 I will go down now, and see whether they have done altogether according to the cry of it, which is come unto me ; and if not, I will know. 22 And the men turned their faces from thence, and went toward Sodom : but Abraham stood yet before the LORD.

The messengers from heaven had now despatched one part of their business, which was an errand of grace to Abraham and Sarah, and which they delivered first ; but now they have before them work of another nature. Sodom is to be destroyed, and they must do it, *ch.* xix. 13. Note, As with the Lord there is mercy, so he is the God to whom vengeance belongs. Pursuant to their commission, we here find, 1. That *they looked towards Sodom* (*v.* 16) ; they set their faces against it in wrath, as God is said to look unto the host of the Egyptians, Exod. xiv. 24. Note, Though

117

God has long seemed to connive at sinners, from which they have inferred that the Lord does not see, does not regard, yet, when the day of his wrath comes, he will look towards them. 2. That they *went towards Sodom* (*v.* 22), and accordingly we find two of them at Sodom, *ch.* xix. 1. Whether the third was the Lord, before whom Abraham yet stood, and to whom he drew near (*v.* 23), as most think, or whether the third left them before they came to Sodom, and the Lord before whom Abraham stood was the *shechinah*, or that appearance of the divine glory which Abraham had formerly seen and conversed with, is uncertain. However, we have here, I. The honour Abraham did to his guests : *He went with them to bring them on the way,* as one that was loth to part with such good company, and was desirous to pay his utmost respects to them. This is a piece of civility proper to be shown to our friends ; but it must be done as the apostle directs (3 John 6), *after a godly sort.*
II. The honour they did to him ; for those that honour God he will honour. God communicated to Abraham his purpose to destroy Sodom, and not only so, but entered into a free conference with him about it. Having taken him, more closely than before, into covenant with himself (*ch.* xvii.), he here admits him into more intimate communion with himself than ever, as the man of his counsel. Observe here,
1. God's friendly thoughts concerning Abraham, *v.* 17—19, where we have his resolution to make known to Abraham his purpose concerning Sodom, with the reasons of it. If Abraham had not brought them on their way, perhaps he would not have been thus favoured ; but he that loves to walk with wise men shall be wise, Prov. xiii. 20. See how God is pleased to argue with himself : *Shall I hide from Abraham* (or, as some read it, *Am I concealing from Abraham) that thing which I do ?* " Can I go about such a thing, and not tell Abraham ?" Thus does God, in his counsels, express himself, after the manner of men, with deliberation. But why must Abraham be of the cabinet-council? The Jews suggest that because God had granted the land of Canaan to Abraham and his seed therefore he would not destroy those cities which were a part of that land, without his knowledge and consent. But God here gives two other reasons :—
(1.) Abraham must know, for he is a friend and a favourite, and one that God has a particular kindness for and great things in store for. He is to become a great nation ; and not only so, but in the Messiah, who is to come from his loins, *All nations of the earth shall be blessed.* Note, *The secret of the Lord is with those that fear him,* Ps. xxv. 14 ; Prov. iii. 32. Those who by faith live a life of communion with God cannot but know more of his mind than other people, though not with a prophetical, yet with a prudential 118

practical knowledge. They have a better insight than others into what is present (Hos. xiv. 9 ; Ps. cvii. 43), and a better foresight of what is to come, at least so much as suffices for their guidance and for their comfort.
(2.) Abraham must know, for he will teach his household : *I know Abraham very well, that he will command his children and his household after him, v.* 19. Consider this, [1.] As a very bright part of Abraham's character and example. He not only prayed with his family, but he taught them as a man of knowledge, nay, he commanded them as a man in authority, and was prophet and king, as well as priest, in his own house. Observe, *First,* God having made the covenant with him and his seed, and his household being circumcised pursuant to that, he was very careful to teach and rule them well. Those that expect family blessings must make conscience of family duty. If our children be the Lord's, they must be nursed for him ; if they wear his livery, they must be trained up in his work. *Secondly,* Abraham took care not only of his children, but of his household ; his servants were catechised servants. Masters of families should instruct and inspect the manners of all under their roof. The poorest servants have precious souls that must be looked after. *Thirdly,* Abraham made it his care and business to promote practical religion in his family. He did not fill their heads with matters of nice speculation, or doubtful disputation ; but he taught them to keep *the way of the Lord, and to do judgment and justice,* that is, to be serious and devout in the worship of God and to be honest in their dealings with all men. *Fourthly,* Abraham, herein, had an eye to posterity, and was in care not only that his household should keep the way of the Lord, but that his household after him, should keep the way of the Lord, that religion might flourish in his family when he was in his grave. *Fifthly,* His doing this was the fulfilling of the conditions of the promises which God had made him. Those only can expect the benefit of the promises that make conscience of their duty. [2.] As the reason why God would make known to him his purpose concerning Sodom, because he was communicative of his knowledge, and improved it for the benefit of those that were under his charge. Note, To him that hath shall be given, Matt. xiii. 12 ; xxv. 29. Those that make a good use of their knowledge shall know more.
2. God's friendly talk with Abraham, in which he makes known to him his purpose concerning Sodom, and allows him a liberty of application to him about that matter. (1.) He tells him of the evidence there was against Sodom : *The cry of Sodom is great, v.* 20. Note, Some sins, and the sins of some sinners, cry aloud to heaven for vengeance. The iniquity of Sodom was crying iniquity, that is, it was so very provoking that it even urged God to punish. (2.) The enquiry he

would make upon this evidence: *I will go down now and see*, v. 21. Not as if there were any thing concerning which God is in doubt, or in the dark; but he is pleased thus to express himself after the manner of men, [1.] To show the incontestable equity of all his judicial proceedings. Men are apt to suggest that his way is not equal; but let them know that his judgments are the result of an eternal counsel, and are never rash or sudden resolves. He never punishes upon report, or common fame, or the information of others, but upon his own certain and infallible knowledge. [2.] To give example to magistrates, and those in authority, with the utmost care and diligence to enquire into the merits of a cause, before they give judgment upon it. [3.] Perhaps the decree is here spoken of as not yet peremptory, that room and encouragement might be given to Abraham to make intercession for them. Thus God looked if there were any to intercede, Isa. lix. 16.

23 And Abraham drew near, and said, Wilt thou also destroy the righteous with the wicked? 24 Peradventure there be fifty righteous within the city: wilt thou also destroy and not spare the place for the fifty righteous that *are* therein? 25 That be far from thee to do after this manner, to slay the righteous with the wicked: and that the righteous should be as the wicked, that be far from thee: Shall not the Judge of all the earth do right? 26 And the Lord said, If I find in Sodom fifty righteous within the city, then I will spare all the place for their sakes. 27 And Abraham answered and said, Behold now, I have taken upon me to speak unto the Lord, which *am but* dust and ashes: 28 Peradventure there shall lack five of the fifty righteous: wilt thou destroy all the city for *lack of* five? And he said, If I find there forty and five, I will not destroy *it*. 29 And he spake unto him yet again, and said, Peradventure there shall be forty found there. And he said, I will not do *it* for forty's sake 30 And he said *unto him*, Oh let not the Lord be angry, and I will speak: Peradventure there shall thirty be found there. And he said, I will not do *it*, if I find thirty there. 31 And he said, Behold now, I have taken upon me to speak unto the Lord: Peradventure there shall be twenty

found there. And he said, I will not destroy *it* for twenty's sake. 32 And he said, Oh let not the Lord be angry, and I will speak yet but this once: Peradventure ten shall be found there. And he said, I will not destroy *it* for ten's sake. 33 And the Lord went his way, as soon as he had left communing with Abraham: and Abraham returned unto his place.

Communion with God is kept up by the word and by prayer. In the word God speaks to us; in prayer we speak to him. God had revealed to Abraham his purposes concerning Sodom; now from this Abraham takes occasion to speak to God on Sodom's behalf. Note, God's word then does us good when it furnishes us with matter for prayer and excites us to it. When God has spoken to us, we must consider what we have to say to him upon it. Observe,

I. The solemnity of Abraham's address to God on this occasion: *Abraham drew near*, v. 23. The expression intimates, 1. A holy concern: *He engaged his heart* to approach to God, Jer. xxx. 21. "Shall Sodom be destroyed, and I not speak one good word for it?" 2. A holy confidence: He drew near *with an assurance of faith*, drew near *as a prince*, Job xxxi. 37. Note, When we address ourselves to the duty of prayer, we ought to remember that we are drawing near to God, that we may be filled with a reverence of him, Lev. x. 3.

II. The general scope of this prayer. It is the first solemn prayer we have upon record in the Bible; and it is a prayer for the sparing of Sodom. Abraham, no doubt, greatly abhorred the wickedness of the Sodomites; he would not have lived among them, as Lot did, if they would have given him the best estate in their country; and yet he prayed earnestly for them. Note, Though sin is to be hated, sinners are to be pitied and prayed for. God delights not in their death, nor should we desire, but deprecate, the woeful day. 1. He begins with a prayer that the righteous among them might be spared, and not involved in the common calamity, having an eye particularly to just Lot, whose disingenuous carriage towards him he had long since forgiven and forgotten, witness his friendly zeal to rescue him before by his sword and now by his prayers. 2. He improves this into a petition that all might be spared for the sake of the righteous that were among them, God himself countenancing this request, and in effect putting him upon it by his answer to his first address, v. 26. Note, We must pray, not only for ourselves, but for others also; for we are members of the same body, at least of the same body of mankind. *All we are brethren.*

III. The particular graces eminent in this prayer.

119

1. Here is great faith; and it is the prayer of faith that is the prevailing prayer. His faith pleads with God, orders the cause, and fills his mouth with arguments. He acts faith especially upon the righteousness of God, and is very confident, (1.) That God will not *destroy the righteous with the wicked*, v. 23. No, *that be far from thee*, v. 25. We must never entertain any thought that derogates from the honour of God's righteousness. See Rom. iii. 5, 6. Note, [1.] The righteous are mingled with the wicked in this world. Among the best there are, commonly, some bad, and among the worst some good: even in Sodom, one Lot. [2.] Though the righteous be among the wicked, yet the righteous God will not, certainly he will not, destroy the righteous with the wicked. Though in this world they may be involved in the same common calamities, yet in the great day a distinction will be made. (2.) That the righteous shall not *be as the wicked*, v. 25. Though they may suffer with them, yet they do not suffer like them. Common calamities are quite another thing to the righteous than what they are to the wicked, Isa. xxvii. 7. (3.) That *the Judge of all the earth will do right;* undoubtedly he will, because he is the Judge of all the earth; it is the apostle's argument, Rom. iii. 5, 6. Note, [1.] God is the Judge of all the earth; he gives charge to all, takes cognizance of all, and will pass sentence upon all. [2.] That God Almighty never did nor ever will do any wrong to any of the creatures, either by withholding that which is right or by exacting more than is right, Job xxxiv. 10, 11.

2. Here is great humility. (1.) A deep sense of his own unworthiness (v. 27): *Behold now, I have taken upon me to speak unto the Lord, who am but dust and ashes;* and again, v. 31. He speaks as one amazed at his own boldness, and the liberty God graciously allowed him, considering God's greatness—he is *the Lord;* and his own meanness—*but dust and ashes.* Note, [1.] The greatest of men, the most considerable and deserving, are but dust and ashes, mean and vile before God, despicable, frail, and dying. [2.] Whenever we draw near to God, it becomes us reverently to acknowledge the vast distance that there is between us and God. He is the Lord of glory, we are worms of the earth. [3.] The access we have to the throne of grace, and the freedom of speech allowed us, are just matter of humble wonder, 2 Sam. vii. 18. (2.) An awful dread of God's displeasure: *O let not the Lord be angry* (v. 30), and again, v. 32. Note, [1.] The importunity which believers use in their addresses to God is such that, if they were dealing with a man like themselves, they could not but fear that he would be angry with them. But he with whom we have to do is *God and not man;* and, however he may seem, is not really

120

angry with the prayers of the upright (Ps. lxxx. 4), for they are *his delight* (Prov. xv. 8), and he is pleased when he is wrestled with. [2.] That even when we receive special tokens of the divine favour we ought to be jealous over ourselves, lest we make ourselves obnoxious to the divine displeasure; and therefore we must bring the Mediator with us in the arms of our faith, to atone for *the iniquity of our holy things.*

3. Here is great charity. (1.) A charitable opinion of Sodom's character: as bad as it was, he thought there were several good people in it. It becomes us to hope the best of the worst places. Of the two it is better to err in that extreme. (2.) A charitable desire of Sodom's welfare: he used all his interest at the throne of grace for mercy for them. We never find him thus earnest in pleading with God for himself and his family, as here for Sodom.

4. Here are great boldness and believing confidence. (1.) He took the liberty to pitch upon a certain number of righteous ones which he supposed might be in Sodom. Suppose there be fifty, v. 24. (2.) He advanced upon God's concessions, again and again. As God granted much, he still begged more, with the hope of gaining his point. (3.) He brought the terms as low as he could for shame (having prevailed for mercy if there were but ten righteous ones in five cities), and perhaps so low that he concluded they would have been spared.

IV. The success of the prayer. He that thus wrestled prevailed wonderfully; as a prince he had power with God: it was but ask and have. 1. God's general good-will appears in this, that he consented to spare the wicked for the sake of the righteous. See how swift God is to show mercy; he even seeks a reason for it. See what great blessings good people are to any place, and how little those befriend themselves that hate and persecute them. 2. His particular favour to Abraham appeared in this, that he did not leave off granting till Abraham left off asking. Such is the power of prayer. Why then did Abraham leave off asking, when he had prevailed so far as to get the place spared if there were but ten righteous in it? Either, (1.) Because he owned that it deserved to be destroyed if there were not so many; *as the dresser of the vineyard,* who consented that the barren tree should be cut down if one year's trial more did not make it fruitful, Luke xiii. 9. Or, (2.) Because God restrained his spirit from asking any further. When God has determined the ruin of a place, he forbids it to be prayed for, Jer. vii. 16; xi. 14; xiv. 11.

V. Here is the breaking up of the conference, v. 33. 1. *The Lord went his way.* The visions of God must not be constant in this world, where it is by faith only that we are to set God before us. God did not go away till Abraham had said all he had to say; for he is never weary of hearing prayer, Isa. lix. 1. 2. *Abraham returned unto his place*, not puffed up with the honour done him, nor by these extraordinary interviews taken off from the ordinary course of duty. He returned to his place to observe what the event would be; and it proved that his prayer was heard, and yet Sodom was not spared, because there were not ten righteous in it. We cannot expect too little from man nor too much from God.

CHAP. XIX.

The contents of this chapter we have, 2 Pet. ii. 6—8, where we find that "God, turning the cities of Sodom and Gomorrah into ashes, condemned them with an overthrow, and delivered just Lot." It is the history of Sodom's ruin, and Lot's rescue from that ruin. We read (ch. xviii.) of God's coming to take a view of the present state of Sodom, what its wickedness was, and what righteous persons there were in it: now here we have the result of that enquiry. I. It was found, upon trial, that Lot was very good (ver. 1—3), and it did not appear that there was any more of the same character. II. It was found that the Sodomites were very wicked and vile, ver. 4—11. III. Special care was therefore taken for the securing of Lot and his family, in a place of safety, ver. 12—23. IV. Mercy having rejoiced therein, justice shows itself in the ruin of Sodom and the death of Lot's wife (ver. 24—26), with a general repetition of the story, ver. 27—29. V. A foul sin that Lot was guilty of, in committing incest with his two daughters, ver. 30, &c.

AND there came two angels to Sodom at even; and Lot sat in the gate of Sodom: and Lot seeing *them* rose up to meet them; and he bowed himself with his face toward the ground; 2 And he said, Behold now, my lords, turn in, I pray you, into your servant's house, and tarry all night, and wash your feet, and ye shall rise up early, and go on your ways. And they said, Nay; but we will abide in the street all night. 3 And he pressed upon them greatly; and they turned in unto him, and entered into his house; and he made them a feast, and did bake unleavened bread, and they did eat.

These angels, it is likely, were two of the three that had just before been with Abraham, the two created angels that were sent to execute God's purpose concerning Sodom. Observe here, 1. There was but one good man in Sodom, and these heavenly messengers soon found him out. Wherever we are, we should enquire out those of the place that live in the fear of God, and should choose to associate ourselves with them. Matt. x. 11, *Enquire who is worthy, and there abide.* Those of the same country, when they are in a foreign country, love to be together. 2. Lot sufficiently distinguished himself from the rest of his neighbours, at this time, which plainly set a mark upon him. He that did not act like the rest must not fare like the rest. (1.) Lot sat in the gate of Sodom at even. When the rest, it is likely, were tippling and drinking, he sat alone, waiting for an opportunity to do good. (2.) He was extremely respectful to men whose mien and aspect were sober and serious, though

they did not come in state. He bowed himself to the ground, when he met them, as if, upon the first view, he discerned something divine in them. (3.) He was hospitable, and very free and generous in his invitations and entertainments. He courted these strangers to his house, and to the best accommodations he had, and gave them all the evidences that he could of his sincerity; for, [1.] When the angels, to try whether he was hearty in the invitation, declined the acceptance of it, at first (which is the common usage of modesty, and no reproach at all to truth and honesty), their refusal did but make him more importunate; for he *pressed upon them greatly* (v.3), partly because he would by no means have them to expose themselves to the inconveniences and perils of lodging in the street of Sodom, and partly because he was desirous of their company and converse. He had not seen two such honest faces in Sodom this great while. Note, Those that live in bad places should know how to value the society of those that are wise and good, and earnestly desire it. [2.] When the angels accepted his invitation, he treated them nobly; he made a feast for them, and thought it well-bestowed on such guests. Note, Good people should be (with prudence) generous people.

4 But before they lay down, the men of the city, *even* the men of Sodom, compassed the house round, both old and young, all the people from every quarter: 5 And they called unto Lot, and said unto him, Where *are* the men which came in to thee this night? bring them out unto us, that we may know them. 6 And Lot went out at the door unto them, and shut the door after him, 7 And said, I pray you, brethren, do not so wickedly. 8 Behold now, I have two daughters which have not known man; let me, I pray you, bring them out unto you, and do ye to them as *is* good in your eyes: only unto these men do nothing; for therefore came they under the shadow of my roof. 9 And they said, Stand back. And they said *again*, This one *fellow* came in to sojourn, and he will needs be a judge: now will we deal worse with thee, than with them. And they pressed sore upon the man, *even* Lot, and came near to break the door. 10 But the men put forth their hand, and pulled Lot into the house to them, and shut to the door. 11 And they smote the men that *were* at the

door of the house with blindness, both small and great : so that they wearied themselves to find the door.

Now it appeared, beyond contradiction, that the cry of Sodom was no louder than there was cause for. This night's work was enough to fill the measure. For we find here, I. That they were all wicked, *v.* 4. Wickedness had become universal, and they were unanimous in any vile design. Here were old and young, and all from every quarter, engaged in this riot; the old were not past it, and the young had soon come up to it. Either they had no magistrates to keep the peace, and protect the peaceable, or their magistrates were themselves aiding and abetting. Note, When the disease of sin has become epidemical, it is fatal to any place, Isa. i. 5—7.

II. That they had arrived at the highest pitch of wickedness ; they were *sinners before the Lord exceedingly* (*ch.* xiii. 13) ; for, 1. It was the most unnatural and abominable wickedness that they were now set upon, a sin that still bears their name, and is called *Sodomy.* They were carried headlong by those vile affections (Rom. i. 26, 27), which are worse than brutish, and the eternal reproach of the human nature, and which cannot be thought of without horror by those that have the least spark of virtue and any remains of natural light and conscience. Note, Those that allow themselves in unnatural uncleanness are marked for the vengeance of eternal fire. See Jude 7. 2. They were not ashamed to own it, and to prosecute their design by force and arms. The practice would have been bad enough if it had been carried on by intrigue and wheedling ; but they proclaimed war with virtue, and bade open defiance to it. Hence daring sinners are said to *declare their sin as Sodom,* Isa. iii. 9. Note, Those that have become impudent in sin generally prove impenitent in sin ; and it will be their ruin. Those have hard hearts indeed that sin with a high hand, Jer. vi. 15. 3. When Lot interposed, with all the mildness imaginable, to check the rage and fury of their lust, they were most insolently rude and abusive to him. He ventured himself among them, *v.* 6. He spoke civilly to them, called them *brethren* (*v.* 7), and begged of them not to do so wickedly ; and, being greatly disturbed at their vile attempt, he unadvisedly and unjustifiably offered to prostitute his two daughters to them, *v.* 8. It is true, of two evils we must choose the less ; but of two sins we must choose neither, nor ever do evil that good may come of it. He reasoned with them, pleaded the laws of hospitality and the protection of his house which his guests were entitled to ; but he might as well have offered reason to a roaring lion and a raging bear as to these head-strong sinners, who were governed only by lust and passion. Lot's arguing with them does but exasperate
122

them ; and, to complete their wickedness, and fill up the measure of it, they fall foul upon him. (1.) They ridicule him, charge him with the absurdity of pretending to be a magistrate, when he was not so much as a free-man of their city, *v.* 9. Note, It is common for a reprover to be unjustly upbraided as a usurper ; and, while offering the kindness of a friend, to be charged with assuming the authority of a judge : as if a man might not speak reason without taking too much upon him. (2.) They threaten him, and lay violent hands upon him ; and the good man is in danger of being pulled in pieces by this outrageous rabble. Note, [1.] Those that hate to be reformed hate those that reprove them, though with ever so much tenderness. Presumptuous sinners do by their consciences as the Sodomites did by Lot, baffle their checks, stifle their accusations, press hard upon them, till they have seared them and quite stopped their mouths, and so made themselves ripe for ruin. [2.] Abuses offered to God's messengers and to faithful reprovers soon fill the measure of a people's wickedness, and bring destruction without remedy. See Prov. xxix. 1, and 2 Chron. xxxvi. 16. If reproofs remedy not, there is no remedy. See 2 Chron. xxv. 16.

III. That nothing less than the power of an angel could save a good man out of their wicked hands. It was now past dispute what Sodom's character was and what course must be taken with it, and therefore the angels immediately give a specimen of what they further intended. 1. They rescue Lot, *v.* 10. Note, He that watereth shall be watered also himself. Lot was solicitous to protect them, and now they take effectual care for his safety, in return for his kindness. Note further, Angels are employed for the special preservation of those that expose themselves to danger by well-doing. The saints, at death, are pulled like Lot into a house of perfect safety, and the door shut for ever against those that pursue them. 2. They chastise the insolence of the Sodomites : *They smote them with blindness, v.* 11. This was designed, (1.) To put an end to their attempt, and disable them from pursuing it. Justly were those struck blind who had been deaf to reason. Violent persecutors are often infatuated, so that they cannot push on their malicious designs against God's messengers, Job v. 14, 15. Yet these Sodomites, after they were struck blind, continued seeking the door, to break it down, till they were tired. No judgments will, of themselves, change the corrupt natures and purposes of wicked men. If their minds had not been blinded as well as their bodies, they would have said, as the magicians, *This is the finger of God,* and would have submitted. (2.) It was to be an earnest of their utter ruin, the next day. When God, in a way of righteous judgment, blinds men, their condition is already desperate, Rom. xi. 8, 9

12 And the men said unto Lot, Hast thou any here besides? son in law, and thy sons, and thy daughters, and whatsoever thou hast in the city, bring *them* out of this place : 13 For we will destroy this place, because the cry of them is waxen great before the face of the LORD ; and the LORD hath sent us to destroy it. 14 And Lot went out, and spake unto his sons in law, which married his daughters, and said, Up, get you out of this place ; for the LORD will destroy this city. But he seemed as one that mocked unto his sons in law.

We have here the preparation for Lot's deliverance.

I. Notice is given him of the approach of Sodom's ruin : *We will destroy this place, v.* 13. Note, The holy angels are ministers of God's wrath for the destruction of sinners, as well as of his mercy for the preservation and deliverance of his people. In this sense, the good angels become *evil angels,* Ps. lxxviii. 49.

II. He is directed to give notice to his friends and relations, that they, if they would, might be saved with him (*v.* 12): "*Hast thou here any besides,* that thou art concerned for? If thou hast, go tell them what is coming." Now this implies, 1. The command of a great duty, which was to do all he could for the salvation of those about him, to snatch them as brands out of the fire. Note, Those who through grace are themselves delivered out of a sinful state should do what they can for the deliverance of others, especially their relations. 2. The offer of great favour. They do not ask whether he knew any righteous ones in the city fit to be spared: no, they knew there were none ; but they ask what relations he had there, that, whether righteous or unrighteous, they might be saved with him. Note, Bad people often fare the better in this world for the sake of their good relations. It is good being akin to a godly man.

III. He applies himself accordingly to his sons-in-law, *v.* 14. Observe, 1. The fair warning that Lot gave them : *Up, get you out of this place.* The manner of expression is startling and quickening. It was no time to trifle when the destruction was just at the door. They had not forty days to repent in, as the Ninevites had. Now or never they must make their escape. At midnight this cry was made. Such as this is our call to the unconverted, to turn and live. 2. The slight they put upon this warning : *He seemed to them as one that mocked.* They thought, perhaps, that the assault which the Sodomites had just now made upon his house had disturbed his head, and put him into such a fright that he knew not what he said ; or they thought that he was not in earnest with

them. Those who lived a merry life, and made a jest of every thing, made a jest of this warning, and so they perished in the overthrow. Thus many who are warned of the misery and danger they are in by sin make a light matter of it, and think their ministers do but jest with them ; such will perish with their blood upon their own heads.

15 And when the morning arose, then the angels hastened Lot, saying, Arise, take thy wife, and thy two daughters, which are here ; lest thou be consumed in the iniquity of the city. 16 And while he lingered, the men laid hold upon his hand, and upon the hand of his wife, and upon the hand of his two daughters ; the LORD being merciful unto him : and they brought him forth, and set him without the city. 17 And it came to pass, when they had brought them forth abroad, that he said, Escape for thy life ; look not behind thee, neither stay thou in all the plain ; escape to the mountain, lest thou be consumed. 18 And Lot said unto them, Oh, not so, my Lord : 19 Behold now, thy servant hath found grace in thy sight, and thou hast magnified thy mercy, which thou hast showed unto me in saving my life ; and I cannot escape to the mountain, lest some evil take me, and I die : 20 Behold now, this city *is* near to flee unto, and it *is* a little one : Oh, let me escape thither, (*is* it not a little one?) and my soul shall live. 21 And he said unto him, See, I have accepted thee concerning this thing also, that I will not overthrow this city, for the which thou hast spoken. 22 Haste thee, escape thither ; for I cannot do any thing till thou be come thither. Therefore the name of the city was called Zoar. 23 The sun was risen upon the earth when Lot entered into Zoar.

Here is, I. The rescue of Lot out of Sodom. Though there were not ten righteous men in Sodom, for whose sakes it might be spared, yet that one righteous man that was among them delivered his own soul, Ezek. xiv. 14. Early in the morning his own guests, in kindness to him, turned him out of doors, and his family with him, *v.* 15. His daughters that were married perished with their unbelieving husbands ; but those that continued with him were preserved with him. Observe,

1. With what a gracious violence Lot was brought out of Sodom, *v.* 16. It seems, though he did not make a jest of the warning given, as his sons-in-law did, yet he lingered, he trifled, he did not make so much haste as the case required. Thus many that are under some convictions about the misery of their spiritual state, and the necessity of a change, yet defer that needful work, and foolishly linger. Lot did so, and it might have been fatal to him if the angels had not *laid hold of his hand, and brought him forth,* and saved him with fear, Jude 23. Herein it is said, *The Lord was merciful to him ;.* otherwise he might justly have left him to perish, since he was so loth to depart. Note, (1.) The salvation of the most righteous men must be attributed to God's mercy, not to their own merit. We are saved by grace. (2.) God's power also must be acknowledged in the bringing of souls out of a sinful state. If God had not brought us forth, we had never come forth. (3.) If God had not been merciful to us, our lingering had been our ruin.
2. With what a gracious vehemence he was urged to make the best of his way, when he was *brought forth, v.* 17. (1.) He must still apprehend himself in danger of being consumed, and be quickened by the law of self-preservation to flee for his life. Note, A holy fear and trembling are found necessary to the working out of our salvation. (2.) He must therefore mind his business with the utmost care and diligence. He must not hanker after Sodom: *Look not behind thee.* He must not loiter by the way: *Stay not in all the plain ;* for it would all be made one dead sea. He must not take up short of the place of refuge appointed him : *Escape to the mountain.* Such as these are the commands given to those who through grace are delivered out of a sinful state. [1.] Return not to sin and Satan, for that is looking back to Sodom. [2.] Rest not in self and the world, for that is staying in the plain. And, [3.] Reach towards Christ and heaven, for that is escaping to the mountain, short of which we must not take up.
II. The fixing of a place of refuge for him. The mountain was first appointed for him to flee to, but, 1. He begged for a city of refuge, one of the five that lay together, called *Bela, ch.* xiv. 2, 18—20. It was Lot's weakness to think a city of his own choosing safer than the mountain of God's appointing. And he argued against himself when he pleaded, *Thou hast magnified thy mercy in saving my life, and I cannot escape to the mountain ;* for could not he that plucked him out of Sodom, when he lingered, carry him safely to the mountain, though he began to tire ? Could not he that saved him from greater evils save him from the less ? He insists much in his petition upon the smallness of the place : *It is a little one, is it not?* therefore, it was to be hoped, not so bad as the rest. This gave a new name to the place ; it was called *Zoar,*

a *little one.* Intercessions for little ones are worthy to be remembered. 2. God granted him his request, though there was much infirmity in it, *v.* 21, 22. See what favour God showed to a true saint, though weak. (1.) Zoar was spared, to gratify him. Though his intercession for it was not, as Abraham's for Sodom, from a principle of generous charity, but merely from self-interest, yet God granted him his request, to show how much the fervent prayer of a righteous man avails. (2.) Sodom's ruin was suspended till he was safe : *I cannot do any thing till thou shalt have come thither.* Note, The very presence of good men in a place helps to keep off judgments. See what care God takes for the preservation of his people. The winds are held till God's servants are sealed, Rev. vii. 3 ; Ezek. ix. 4.
III. It is taken notice of that the sun had risen when Lot entered into Zoar ; for when a good man comes into a place he brings light along with him, or should do.

24 Then the LORD rained upon Sodom and upon Gomorrah brimstone and fire from the LORD out of heaven ; 25 And he overthrew those cities, and all the plain, and all the inhabitants of the cities, and that which grew upon the ground.

Then, when Lot had got safely into Zoar, then this ruin came ; for good men are taken away from the evil to come. *Then,* when the sun had risen bright and clear, promising a fair day, then this storm arose, to show that it was not from natural causes. Concerning this destruction observe, 1. God was the immediate author of it. It was destruction from the Almighty : *The Lord rained—from the Lord* (*v.* 24), that is, God from himself, by his own immediate power, and not in the common course of nature. Or, God the Son from God the Father ; for the Father has committed all judgment to the Son. Note, He that is the Saviour will be the destroyer of those that reject the salvation. 2. It was a strange punishment, Job xxxi. 3. Never was the like before nor since. Hell was rained from heaven upon them. *Fire, and brimstone, and a horrible tempest, were the portion of their cup* (Ps. xi. 6); not a flash of lightning, which is destructive enough when God gives it commission, but a shower of lightning. Brimstone was scattered upon their habitation (Job xviii. 15), and then the fire soon fastened upon them. God could have drowned them, as he did the old world; but he would show that he has many arrows in his quiver, fire as well as water. 3. It was a judgment that laid all waste : *It overthrew the cities,* and destroyed all the inhabitants of them, the plain, and all that grew upon the ground, *v.* 25. It was an utter ruin, and irreparable. That fruitful valley remains to this day a great lake, or dead sea ; it is called

124

the Salt Sea, Num. xxxiv. 12. Travellers say that it is about thirty miles long and ten miles broad; it has no living creature in it; it is not moved by the wind; the smell of it is offensive; things do not easily sink in it. The Greeks call it *Asphaltites,* from a sort of pitch which it casts up. Jordan falls into it, and is lost there. 4. It was a punishment that answered to their sin. Burning lusts against nature were justly punished with this preternatural burning. Those that went after strange flesh were destroyed by strange fire, Jude 7. They persecuted the angels with their rabble, and made Lot afraid; and now God persecuted them with his tempest, and made them afraid with his storm, Ps. lxxxiii. 15. 5. It was designed for a standing revelation of the wrath of God against sin and sinners in all ages. It is, accordingly, often referred to in the scripture, and made a pattern of the ruin of Israel (Deut. xxix. 23), of Babylon (Isa. xiii. 19), of Edom (Jer. xlix. 18), of Moab and Ammon, Zeph. ii. 9. Nay, it was typical of *the vengeance of eternal fire* (Jude 7), and the ruin of all *that live ungodly* (2 Pet. ii. 6), especially that despise the gospel, Matt. x. 15. It is in allusion to this destruction that the place of the damned is often represented by a lake that burns, as Sodom did, with fire and brimstone. Let us learn from it, (1.) The evil of sin, and the hurtful nature of it. Iniquity tends to ruin. (2.) The terrors of the Lord. See what a fearful thing it is to fall into the hands of the living God!

26 But his wife looked back from behind him, and she became a pillar of salt.

This also is written for our admonition. Our Saviour refers to it (Luke xvii. 32), *Remember Lot's wife.* As by the example of Sodom the wicked are warned to turn from their wickedness, so by the example of Lot's wife the righteous are warned not to turn from their righteousness. See Ezek. iii. 18, 20. We have here,

I. The sin of Lot's wife: *She looked back from behind him.* This seemed a small thing, but we are sure, by the punishment of it, that it was a great sin, and exceedingly sinful. 1. She disobeyed an express command, and so sinned after the similitude of Adam's transgression, which ruined us all. 2. Unbelief was at the bottom of it; she questioned whether Sodom would be destroyed, and thought she might still have been safe in it. 3. She looked back upon her neighbours whom she had left behind with more concern than was fit, now that their day of grace was over, and divine justice was glorifying itself in their ruin. See Isa. lxvi. 24. 4. Probably she hankered after her house and goods in Sodom, and was loth to leave them. Christ intimates this to be her sin (Luke xvii. 31, 32); she too much regarded her *stuff.* 5 Her looking back evinced an incli-

nation to go back; and therefore our Saviour uses it as a warning against apostasy from our Christian profession. We have all renounced the world and the flesh, and have set our faces heaven-ward; we are in the plain, upon our probation; and it is at our peril if we return into the interests we profess to have abandoned. Drawing back is to perdition, and looking back is towards it. *Let us therefore fear,* Heb. iv. 1.

II. The punishment of Lot's wife for this sin. She was struck dead in the place; yet her body did not fall down, but stood fixed and erect like a pillar, or monument, not liable to waste nor decay, as human bodies exposed to the air are, but metamorphosed into a metallic substance which would last perpetually. Come, behold the goodness and severity of God (Rom. xi. 22), towards Lot, who went forward, goodness; towards his wife, who looked back, severity. Though she was nearly related to a righteous man, though better than her neighbours, and though a monument of distinguishing mercy in her deliverance out of Sodom, yet God did not connive at her disobedience; for great privileges will not secure us from the wrath of God if we do not carefully and faithfully improve them. This pillar of salt should season us. Since it is such a dangerous thing to look back, let us always press forward, Phil. iii. 13, 14.

27 And Abraham gat up early in the morning to the place where he stood before the LORD: **28** And he looked toward Sodom and Gomorrah, and toward all the land of the plain, and beheld, and, lo, the smoke of the country went up as the smoke of a furnace. **29** And it came to pass, when God destroyed the cities of the plain, that God remembered Abraham, and sent Lot out of the midst of the overthrow, when he overthrew the cities in the which Lot dwelt.

Our communion with God consists in our gracious regard to him and his gracious regard to us; we have here therefore one communion that was between God and Abraham, in the event concerning Sodom, as before in the consultation concerning it, for communion with God is to be kept up in providences as well as in ordinances.

I. Here is Abraham's pious regard to God in this event, in two things:—1. A careful expectation of the event, *v.* 27. *He got up early* to look towards Sodom; and, to intimate that his design herein was to see what became of his prayers, he went to the very place where he had stood before the Lord, and set himself there, as upon his watch tower, Hab. ii. 1. Note, When we have prayed we must look after our prayers, and observe the success of them. We must direct our prayer as a letter, and then look up for an answer, direct our prayer as an arrow, and then look up to see whether it reach the mark, Ps. v. 3. Our enquiries after news must be in expectation of an answer to our prayers. 2. An awful observation of it: *He looked towards Sodom* (*v.* 28), not as Lot's wife did, tacitly reflecting upon the divine severity, but humbly adoring it and acquiescing in it. Thus the saints, when they see the smoke of Babylon's torment rising up for ever (like Sodom's here), will say again and again, *Alleluia*, Rev. xix. 3. Those that have, in the day of grace, most earnestly interceded for sinners, will, in the day of judgment, be content to see them perish, and will glorify God in their destruction.

II. Here is God's favourable regard to Abraham, *v.* 29. As before, when Abraham prayed for Ishmael, God heard him for Isaac, so now, when he prayed for Sodom, he heard him for Lot. *He remembered Abraham, and, for his sake, sent Lot out of the overthrow.* Note, 1. God will certainly give an answer of peace to the prayer of faith, in his own way and time; though, for a while, it seem to be forgotten, yet, sooner or later, it will appear to be remembered. 2. The relations and friends of godly people fare the better for their interest in God and intercessions with him; it was out of respect to Abraham that Lot was rescued: perhaps this word encouraged Moses long afterwards to pray (Exod. xxxii. 13), *Lord, remember Abraham;* and see Isa. lxiii. 11.

30 And Lot went up out of Zoar, and dwelt in the mountain, and his two daughters with him; for he feared to dwell in Zoar: and he dwelt in a cave, he and his two daughters. 31 And the firstborn said unto the younger, Our father *is* old, and *there is* not a man in the earth to come in unto us after the manner of all the earth: 32 Come, let us make our father drink wine, and we will lie with him, that we may preserve seed of our father. 33 And they made their father drink wine that night: and the firstborn went in, and lay with her father; and he perceived not when she lay down, nor when she arose. 34 And it came to pass on the morrow, that the firstborn said unto the younger, Behold, I lay yesternight with my father: let us make him drink wine this night also; and go thou in, *and* lie with him, that we may preserve seed of our father. 35 And they made their father drink wine that night also; and the younger

arose, and lay with him; and he perceived not when she lay down, nor when she arose. 36 Thus were both the daughters of Lot with child by their father. 37 And the firstborn bare a son, and called his name Moab: the same *is* the father of the Moabites unto this day. 38 And the younger, she also bare a son, and called his name Ben-ammi: the same *is* the father of the children of Ammon unto this day.

Here is, I. The great trouble and distress that Lot was brought into after his deliverance, *v.* 30. 1. He was frightened out of Zoar, durst not dwell there; probably because he was conscious to himself that it was a refuge of his own choosing and that herein he had foolishly prescribed to God, and therefore he could not but distrust his safety in it; or because he found it as wicked as Sodom, and therefore concluded it could not long survive it; or perhaps he observed the rise and increase of those waters which after the conflagration, perhaps from Jordan, began to overflow the plain, and which, mixing with the ruins, by degrees made the Dead Sea; in those waters he concluded Zoar must needs perish (though it had escaped the fire) because it stood upon the same flat. Note, Settlements and shelters of our own choosing, and in which we do not follow God, commonly prove uneasy to us. 2. He was forced to betake himself to the mountain, and to take up with a cave for his habitation there. Methinks it was strange that he did not return to Abraham, and put himself under his protection, to whom he had once and again owed his safety: but the truth is there are some good men that are not wise enough to know what is best for themselves. Observe, (1.) He was now glad to go to the mountain, the place which God had appointed for his shelter. Note, It is well if disappointment in our way drive us at last to God's way. (2.) He that, awhile ago, could not find room enough for himself and his stock in the whole land, but must jostle with Abraham, and get as far from him as he could, is now confined to a hole in a hill, where he has scarcely room to turn himself, and there he is solitary and trembling. Note, It is just with God to reduce those to poverty and restraint who have abused their liberty and plenty. See also in Lot what those bring themselves to, at last, that forsake the communion of saints for secular advantages; they will be beaten with their own rod.

II. The great sin that Lot and his daughters were guilty of, when they were in this desolate place. It is a sad story.

1. His daughters laid a very wicked plot to bring him to sin; and theirs was, doubtless, the greater guilt. They contrived, under pretence of cheering up the spirits of

their father in his present condition, to make him drunk, and then to lie with him, *v.* 31, 32. (1.) Some think that their pretence was plausible. Their father had no sons, they had no husbands, nor knew they where to have any of the holy seed, or, if they had children by others, their father's name would not be preserved in them. Some think that they had the Messiah in their eye, who, they hoped, might descend from their father; for he came from Terah's elder son, was separated from the rest of Shem's posterity as well as Abraham, and was now signally delivered out of Sodom. Their mother, and the rest of the family, were gone; they might not marry with the cursed Canaanites; and therefore they supposed that the end they aimed at, and the extremity they were brought to, would excuse the irregularity. Thus the learned Monsieur Allix. Note, Good intentions are often abused to patronise bad actions. But, (2.) Whatever their pretence was, it is certain that their project was very wicked and vile, and an impudent affront to the very light and law of nature. Note, [1.] The sight of God's most tremendous judgments upon sinners will not of itself, without the grace of God, restrain evil hearts from evil practices: one would wonder how the fire of lust could possibly kindle upon those, who had so lately been the eye-witnesses of Sodom's flames. [2.] Solitude has its temptations as well as company, and particularly to uncleanness. When Joseph was alone with his mistress he was in danger, *ch.* xxxix. 11. Relations that dwell together, especially if solitary, have need carefully to watch even against the least evil thought of this kind, lest Satan get an advantage.

2. Lot himself, by his own folly and unwariness, was wretchedly overcome, and suffered himself so far to be imposed upon by his own children as, two nights together, to be drunk, and to commit incest, *v.* 33, &c. *Lord, what is man!* What are the best of men, when God leaves them to themselves! See here, (1.) The peril of security. Lot, who not only kept himself sober and chaste in Sodom, but was a constant mourner for the wickedness of the place and a witness against it, was yet, in the mountain, where he was alone, and as he thought quite out of the way of temptation, shamefully overtaken. Let him therefore that thinks he stands, stands high and stands firm, *take heed lest he fall.* No mountain, on this side the holy hill above, can set us out of the reach of Satan's fiery darts. (2.) The peril of drunkenness. It is not only a great sin itself, but it is the inlet of many sins; it may prove the inlet of the worst and most unnatural sins, which may be a perpetual wound and dishonour. Excellently does Mr. Herbert describe it,

"He that is druuken may his mother kill
Big with his sister." ————

A man may do that without reluctance, when

he is drunk, which, when he is sober, he could not think of without horror. (3.) The peril of temptation from our dearest relations and friends, whom we love, and esteem, and expect kindness from. Lot, whose temperance and chastity were impregnable against the batteries of foreign force, was surprised into sin and shame by the base treachery of his own daughters: we must dread a snare wherever we are, and be always upon our guard.

3. In the close we have an account of the birth of the two sons, or grandsons (call them which you will), of Lot, Moab and Ammon, the fathers of two nations, neighbours to Israel, and which we often read of in the Old Testament; both together are called *the children of Lot,* Ps. lxxxiii. 8. Note, Though prosperous births may attend incestuous conceptions, yet they are so far from justifying them that they rather perpetuate the reproach of them and entail infamy upon posterity; yet the tribe of Judah, of which our Lord sprang, descended from such a birth, and Ruth, a Moabitess, has a name in his genealogy, Matt. i. 3, 5.

Lastly, Observe that, after this, we never read any more of Lot, nor what became of him: no doubt he repented of his sin, and was pardoned; but from the silence of the scripture concerning him henceforward we may learn that drunkenness, as it makes men forgetful, so it makes them forgotten; and many a name, which otherwise might have been remembered with respect, is buried by it in contempt and oblivion.

CHAP. XX.

We are here returning to the story of Abraham; yet that part of it which is here recorded is not to his honour. The fairest marbles have their flaws, and, while there are spots in the sun, we must not expect any thing spotless under it. The scripture, it should be remarked, is impartial in relating the blemishes even of its most celebrated characters. We have here, I. Abraham's sin in denying his wife, and Abimelech's sin thereupon in taking her, ver. 1, 2. II. God's discourse with Abimelech in a dream, upon this occasion, wherein he shows him his error (ver. 3), accepts his plea (ver. 4—6), and directs him to make restitution, ver. 7. III. Abimelech's discourse with Abraham, wherein he chides him for the cheat he had put upon him (ver. 8—10), and Abraham excuses it as well as he can, ver. 11—13. IV. The good issue of the story, in which Abimelech restores Abraham his wife (ver. 14—16), and Abraham, by prayer, prevails with God for the removal of the judgment Abimelech was under, ver. 17, 18.

AND Abraham journeyed from thence toward the south country, and dwelled between Kadesh and Shur, and sojourned in Gerar. 2 And Abraham said of Sarah his wife, She *is* my sister: and Abimelech king of Gerar sent, and took Sarah.

Here is, 1. Abraham's removal from Mamre, where he had lived nearly twenty years, into the country of the Philistines: *He sojourned in Gerar, v.* 1. We are not told upon what occasion he removed, whether terrified by the destruction of Sodom, or because the country round was for the present prejudiced by it, or, as some of the Jewish writers say, because he was grieved at Lot's incest with his daughters, and the reproach which the Canaanites cast upon him and his religion, for his kinsman's sake : doubtless there was some good cause for his removal. Note, In a world where we are strangers and pilgrims we cannot expect to be always in the same place. Again, Wherever we are, we must look upon ourselves but as sojourners. 2. His sin in denying his wife, as before (*ch.* xii. 13), which was not only in itself such an equivocation as bordered upon a lie, and which, if admitted as lawful, would be the ruin of human converse and an inlet to all falsehood, but was also an exposing of the chastity and honour of his wife, of which he ought to have been the protector. But, besides this, it had here a two-fold aggravation :—(1.) He had been guilty of this same sin before, and had been reproved for it, and convinced of the folly of the suggestion which induced him to it ; yet he returns to it. Note, It is possible that a good man may, not only fall into sin, but relapse into the same sin, through the surprise and strength of temptation and the infirmity of the flesh. Let backsliders repent then, but not despair, Jer. iii. 22. (2.) Sarah, as it should seem, was now with child of the promised seed, or, at least, in expectation of being so quickly, according to the word of God ; he ought therefore to have taken particular care of her now, as Judg. xiii. 4. 3. The peril that Sarah was brought into by this means : *The king of Gerar sent, and took her* to his house, in order to the taking of her to his bed. Note, The sin of one often occasions the sin of others ; he that breaks the hedge of God's commandments opens a gap to he knows not how many ; the beginning of sin is as the letting forth of water.

3 But God came to Abimelech in a dream by night, and said to him, Behold, thou *art but* a dead man, for the woman which thou hast taken ; for she *is* a man's wife. 4 But Abimelech had not come near her : and he said, LORD, wilt thou slay also a righteous nation ? 5 Said he not unto me, She *is* my sister ? and she, even she herself said, He *is* my brother : in the integrity of my heart and innocency of my hands have I done this. 6 And God said unto him in a dream, Yea, I know that thou didst this in the integrity of thy heart ; for I also withheld thee from sinning against me : therefore suffered I thee not to touch her. 7 Now therefore restore the man *his* wife ; for he *is* a prophet, and he shall pray for thee, and thou shalt live : and if thou restore *her* not, know thou that thou shalt surely die, thou, and all that *are* thine.

It appears by this that God revealed him-

self by dreams (which evidenced themselves to be divine and supernatural) not only to his servants the prophets, but even to those who were out of the pale of the church and covenant ; but then, usually, it was with some regard to God's own people as in Pharaoh's dream, to Joseph, in Nebuchadnezzar's, to Daniel, and here, in Abimelech's, to Abraham and Sarah, for he reproved this king for their sake, Ps. cv. 14, 15.

I. God gives him notice of his danger (*v.* 3), his danger of *sin*, telling him that the woman is a man's wife, so that if he take her he will wrong her husband ; his danger of death for this sin : *Thou art a dead man ;* and God's saying so of a man makes him so. Note, Every wilful sinner ought to be told that he is a dead man, as the condemned malefactor, and the patient whose disease is mortal, are said to be so. If thou art a bad man, certainly thou art a dead man.

II. He pleads ignorance that Abraham and Sarah had agreed to impose upon him, and not to let him know that they were any more than brother and sister, *v.* 6. See what confidence a man may have towards God when his heart condemns him not, 1 John iii. 21. If our consciences witness to our integrity, and that, however we may have been cheated into a snare, we have not knowingly and wittingly sinned against God, it will be our rejoicing in the day of evil. He pleads with God as Abraham had done, *ch.* xviii. 23. *Wilt thou slay a righteous nation ? v.* 4. Not such a nation as Sodom, which was indeed justly destroyed, but a nation which, in this matter, was innocent.

III. God gives a very full answer to what he had said.

1. He allows his plea, and admits that what he did he did in the integrity of his heart : *Yea, I know it, v.* 6. Note, It is matter of comfort to those that are honest that God knows their honesty, and will acknowledge it, though perhaps men that are prejudiced against them either cannot be convinced of it or will not own that they are.

2. He lets him know that he was kept from proceeding in the sin merely by the good hand of God upon him : *I withheld thee from sinning against me.* Abimelech was hereby kept from doing wrong, Abraham from suffering wrong, and Sarah from both. Note, (1.) There is a great deal of sin devised and designed that is never executed. As bad as things are in the world, they are not so bad as the devil and wicked men would have them. (2.) It is God that restrains men from doing the ill they would do. It is not from him that there is sin, but it is from him that there is not more sin, either by his influence upon men's minds, checking their inclination to sin, or by his providence, taking away the opportunity to sin. (3.) It is a great mercy to be hindered from committing sin ; of this God must have the glory, whoever is the instrument, 1 Sam. xxv. 32, 33.

3. He charges him to make restitution : Now *therefore,* now that thou art better informed, *restore the man his wife, v.* 7. Note, Ignorance will excuse no longer than it continues. If we have entered upon a wrong course through ignorance this will not excuse our knowingly persisting in it, Lev. v. 3—5. The reasons why he must be just and kind to Abraham are, (1.) Because *he is a prophet,* near and dear to God, for whom God does in a particular manner concern himself. God highly resents the injuries done to his prophets, and takes them as done to himself. (2.) Being a prophet, *he shall pray for thee;* this is a prophet's reward, and a good reward it is. It is intimated that there was great efficacy in the prayers of a prophet, and that good men should be ready to help those with their prayers that stand in need of them, and should make, at least, this return for the kindnesses that are done them. Abraham was accessory to Abimelech's trouble, and therefore was obliged in justice to pray for him. (3.) It is at thy peril if thou do not restore her : *Know thou that thou shalt surely die.* Note, He that does wrong, whoever he is, prince or peasant, shall certainly receive for the wrong which he has done, unless he repent and make restitution, Col. iii. 25. No injustice can be made passable with God, no, not by Cæsar's image stamped upon it.

8 Therefore Abimelech rose early in the morning, and called all his servants, and told all these things in their ears : and the men were sore afraid. 9 Then Abimelech called Abraham, and said unto him, What hast thou done unto us ? and what have I offended thee, that thou hast brought on me and on my kingdom a great sin ? thou hast done deeds unto me that ought not to be done. 10 And Abimelech said unto Abraham, What sawest thou, that thou hast done this thing ? 11 And Abraham said, Because I thought, Surely the fear of God *is* not in this place ; and they will slay me for my wife's sake. 12 And yet indeed *she is* my sister ; she *is* the daughter of my father, but not the daughter of my mother ; and she became my wife. 13 And it came to pass, when God caused me to wander from my father's house, that I said unto her, This *is* thy kindness which thou shalt show unto me ; at every place whither we shall come, say of me, He *is* my brother.

Abimelech, being thus warned of God in a

dream, takes the warning, and, as one truly afraid of sin and its consequences, he rises early to obey the directions given him.

I. He has a caution for his servants, *v.* 8. Abraham himself could not be more careful than he was to command his household in this matter. Note, Those whom God has convinced of sin and danger ought to tell others what God has done for their souls, that they also may be awakened and brought to a like holy fear.

II. He has a chiding for Abraham. Observe,

1. The serious reproof which Abimelech gave to Abraham, *v.* 9, 10. His reasoning with Abraham upon this occasion was very strong, and yet very mild. Nothing could be said better ; he does not reproach him, nor insult over him, does not say, " Is this your profession ? I see, though you will not swear, you will lie. If these be prophets, I will beg to be freed from the sight of them :" but he fairly represents the injury Abraham had done him, and calmly signifies his resentment of it. (1.) He calls that sin which he now found he had been in danger of a great sin. Note, Even the light of nature teaches men that the sin of adultery is a very great sin : be it observed, to the shame of many who call themselves Christians, and yet make a light matter of it. (2.) He looks upon it that both himself and his kingdom would have been exposed to the wrath of God if he had been guilty of this sin, though ignorantly. Note, The sins of kings often prove the plagues of kingdoms ; rulers should therefore, for their people's sake, dread sin. (3.) He charges Abraham with doing that which was not justifiable, in disowning his marriage. This he speaks of justly, and yet tenderly ; he does not call him a liar and cheat, but tells him he had done *deeds that ought not to be done.* Note, Equivocation and dissimulation, however they may be palliated, are very bad things, and by no means to be admitted in any case. (4.) He takes it as a very great injury to himself and his family that Abraham had thus exposed them to sin : " *What have I offended thee ?* If I had been thy worst enemy, thou couldst not have done me a worse turn, nor taken a more effectual course to be revenged on me." Note, We ought to reckon that those do us the greatest unkindness in the world that any way tempt us or expose us to sin, though they may pretend friendship, and offer that which is grateful enough to the corrupt nature. (5.) He challenges him to assign a cause for his suspecting them as a dangerous people for an honest man to live among: " *What sawest thou, that thou hast done this thing ? v.* 10. What reason hadst thou to think that if we had known her to be thy wife thou wouldst have been exposed to any danger by it ?" Note, A suspicion of our goodness is justly reckoned a greater affront than a slight upon our greatness.

2. The poor excuse that Abraham made for himself.

(1.) He pleaded the bad opinion he had of the place, *v.* 11. He thought within himself (though he could not give any good reason for his thinking so), " *Surely the fear of God is not in this place,* and then they will slay me." [1.] Little good is to be expected where no fear of God is. See Ps. xxxvi. 1. [2.] There are many places and persons that have more of the fear of God in them than we think they have : perhaps they are not called by our dividing name, they do not wear our badges, they do not tie themselves to that which we have an opinion of; and therefore we conclude they have not the fear of God in their hearts, which is very injurious both to Christ and Christians, and makes us obnoxious to God's judgment, Matt. vii 1. [3.]. Uncharitableness and censoriousness are sins that are the cause of many other sins. When men have once persuaded themselves concerning such and such that they have not the fear of God, they think this will justify them in the most unjust and unchristian practices towards them. Men would not do ill if they did not first think ill.

(2.) He excused it from the guilt of a downright lie by making it out that, in a sense, she was his sister, *v.* 12. Some think she was own sister to Lot, who is called his *brother Lot* (*ch.* xiv. 16), though he was *his nephew ;* so Sarah is called his *sister.* But those to whom he said, *She is my sister,* understood that she was so his sister as not to be capable of being his wife ; so that it was an equivocation, with an intent to deceive.

(3.) He clears himself from the imputation of an affront designed to Abimelech in it by alleging that it had been his practice before, according to an agreement between him and his wife, when they first became sojourners (*v.* 13) : " *When God caused me to wander from my father's house,* then we settled this matter." Note, [1.] God is to be acknowledged in all our wanderings. [2.] Those that travel abroad, and converse much with strangers, as they have need of the wisdom of the serpent, so it is requisite that that wisdom be ever tempered with the innocence of the dove. It may, for aught I know, be suggested that God denied to Abraham and Sarah the blessing of children so long to punish them for this sinful compact which they had made to deny one another ; if they will not own their marriage, why should God own it ? But we may suppose that, after this reproof which Abimelech gave them, they agreed never to do so again, and then presently we read (*ch.* xxi. 1, 2) that *Sarah conceived.*

14 And Abimelech took sheep, and oxen, and menservants, and womenservants, and gave *them* unto Abraham, and restored him Sarah his wife. 15 And Abimelech said, Behold, my

land *is* before thee : dwell where it pleaseth thee. 16 And unto Sarah he said, Behold, I have given thy brother a thousand *pieces* of silver : behold, he *is* to thee a covering of the eyes, unto all that *are* with thee, and with all *other :* thus she was reproved. 17 So Abraham prayed unto God : and God healed Abimelech, and his wife, and his maidservants ; and they bare *children.* 18 For the LORD had fast closed up all the wombs of the house of Abimelech, because of Sarah Abraham's wife.

Here is, I. The kindness of a prince which Abimelech showed to Abraham. See how unjust Abraham's jealousies were. He fancied that if they knew that Sarah was his wife they would kill him ; but, when they did know it, instead of killing him they were kind to him, frightened at least to be so by the divine rebukes they were under. 1. He gives him his royal licence to dwell where he pleased in his country, courting his stay because he saw that God was with him, *v.* 15. 2. He gives him his royal gifts (*v.* 14), *sheep and oxen,* and (*v.* 16) *a thousand pieces of silver.* This he gave when he restored Sarah, either, [1.] By way of satisfaction for the wrong he had offered to do, in taking her to his house : when the Philistines restored the ark, being plagued for detaining it, they sent a present with it. The law appointed that when restitution was made something should be added to it, Lev. vi. 5. Or, [2.] To engage Abraham's prayers for him ; not as if prayers should be bought and sold, but we should endeavour to be kind to those of whose spiritual things we reap, 1 Cor. ix. 11. Note, It is our wisdom to get and keep an interest with those that have an interest in heaven, and to make those our friends who are the friends of God. [3.] He gives to Sarah good instruction, tells her that her husband (her *brother* he calls him, to upbraid her with calling him so) must be to her for *a covering of the eyes,* that is, she must look at no other, nor desire to be looked at by any other. Note, Yoke-fellows must be to each other for a covering of the eyes. The marriage-covenant is a covenant with the eyes, like Job's, *ch.* xxxi. 1.

II. The kindness of a prophet which Abraham showed to Abimelech : he *prayed for him, v.* 17, 18. This honour God would put upon Abraham that, though Abimelech had restored Sarah, yet the judgment he was under should be removed upon the prayer of Abraham, and not before. Thus God healed Miriam, when Moses, whom she had most affronted, prayed for her (Num. xii. 13), and was reconciled to Job's friends when Job, whom they had grieved, prayed for them

(Job xlii. 8—10), and so did, as it were, give it under his hand that he was reconciled to them. Note, The prayers of good men may be a kindness to great men, and ought to be valued.

CHAP. XXI.

In this chapter we have, I. Isaac, the child of promise born into Abraham's family, ver. 1—8. II. Ishmael, the son of the bond-woman, cast out of it, ver. 9—21. III. Abraham's league with his neighbour Abimelech, ver. 22—32. IV. His devotion to his God, ver. 33.

AND the LORD visited Sarah as he had said, and the LORD did unto Sarah as he had spoken. 2 For Sarah conceived, and bare Abraham a son in his old age, at the set time of which God had spoken to him. 3 And Abraham called the name of his son that was born unto him, whom Sarah bare to him, Isaac. 4 And Abraham circumcised his son Isaac being eight days old, as God had commanded him. 5 And Abraham was a hundred years old, when his son Isaac was born unto him. 6 And Sarah said, God hath made me to laugh, *so that* all that hear will laugh with me. 7 And she said, Who would have said unto Abraham, that Sarah should have given children suck? for I have borne *him* a son in his old age. 8 And the child grew, and was weaned : and Abraham made a great feast the *same* day that Isaac was weaned.

Long-looked-for comes at last. The vision concerning the promised seed is for an appointed time, and now, at the end, it speaks, and does not lie ; few under the Old Testament were brought into the world with such expectation as Isaac was, not for the sake of any great personal eminence at which he was to arrive, but because he was to be, in this very thing, a type of Christ, that seed which the holy God had so long promised and holy men so long expected. In this account of the first days of Isaac we may observe,

I. The fulfilling of God's promise in the conception and birth of Isaac, *v.* 1, 2. Note, God's providences look best and brightest when they are compared with his word, and when we observe how God, in them all, acts as he has said, as he has spoken. 1. Isaac was born according to the promise. The Lord visited Sarah in mercy, as he had said. Note, No word of God shall fall to the ground ; for he is faithful that has promised, and God's faithfulness is the stay and support of his people's faith. He was born *at the set time of which God had spoken, v.* 2. Note, God is always punctual to his time ; though his promised mercies come not at the time we set, they will certainly come at

the time he sets, and that is the best time. 2. He was born by virtue of the promise : *Sarah by faith received strength to conceive* Heb. xi. 11. God therefore by promise gave that strength. It was not by the power of common providence, but by the power of a special promise, that Isaac was born. A sentence of death was, as it were, passed upon the second causes : Abraham was old, and Sarah old, and both as good as dead ; and then the word of God took place. Note, True believers, by virtue of God's promises, are enabled to do that which is above the power of human nature, for *by them they partake of a divine nature,* 2 Pet. i. 4.

II. Abraham's obedience to God's precept concerning Isaac.

1. He named him, as God commanded him, *v.* 3. God directed him to a name for a memorial, *Isaac, laughter ;* and Abraham, whose office it was, gave him that name, though he might have designed him some other name of a more pompous signification. Note, It is fit that the luxuriancy of human invention should always yield to the sovereignty and plainness of divine institution ; yet there was good reason for the name, for, (1.) When Abraham received the promise of him he laughed for joy, *ch.* xvii. 17. Note, When the sun of comfort has risen upon the soul it is good to remember how welcome the dawning of the day was, and with what exultation we embraced the promise. (2.) When Sarah received the promise she laughed with distrust and diffidence. Note, When God gives us the mercies we began to despair of we ought to remember with sorrow and shame our sinful distrusts of God's power and promise, when we were in pursuit of them. (3.) Isaac was himself, afterwards, laughed at by Ishmael (*v.* 9), and perhaps his name bade him expect it. Note, God's favourites are often the world's laughing-stocks. (4.) The promise which he was not only the son, but the heir of, was to be the joy of all the saints in all ages, and that which would fill their mouths with laughter.

2. He circumcised him, *v.* 4. The covenant being established with him, the seal of the covenant was administered to him ; and though a bloody ordinance, and he a darling, yet it must not be omitted, no, nor deferred beyond the eighth day. God had kept time in performing the promise, and therefore Abraham must keep time in obeying the precept.

III. The impressions which this mercy made upon Sarah.

1. It filled her with joy (*v.* 6) : "*God has made me to laugh ;* he has given me both cause to rejoice and a heart to rejoice" Thus the mother of our Lord, Luke i. 46, 47. Note, (1.) God bestows mercies upon his people to encourage their joy in his work and service ; and, whatever is the matter of

our joy, God must be acknowledged as the author of it, unless it be the *laughter of the fool.* (2.) When mercies have been long deferred they are the more welcome when they come. (3.) It adds to the comfort of any mercy to have our friends rejoice with us in it: *All that hear will laugh with me ;* for laughing is catching. See Luke i. 58. Others would rejoice in this instance of God's power and goodness, and be encouraged to trust in him. See Ps. cxix. 74.

2. It filled her with wonder, *v.* 7. Observe here, (1.) What it was she thought so wonderful: That *Sarah should give children suck,* that she should, not only bear a child, but be so strong and hearty at that age as to give it suck. Note, Mothers, if they be able, ought to be nurses to their own children. Sarah was a person of quality, was aged; nursing might be thought prejudicial to herself, or to the child, or to both; she had choice of nurses, no doubt, in her own family: and yet she would do her duty in this matter; and her daughters the good wives are while they thus *do well,* 1 Pet. iii. 5, 6. See Lam. iv. 3. (2.) How she expressed her wonder: *" Who would have said it?"* The thing was so highly improbable, so near to impossible, that if any one but God had said it we could not have believed it." Note, God's favours to his covenant-people are such as surpass both their own and others' thoughts and expectations. Who could imagine that God should do so much for those that deserve so little, nay, for those that deserve so ill? See Eph. iii. 20 ; 2 Sam. vii. 18, 19. Who would have said that God should send his Son to die for us, his Spirit to sanctify us, his angels to attend us? Who would have said that such great sins should be pardoned, such mean services accepted, and such worthless worms taken into covenant and communion with the great and holy God?

IV. A short account of Isaac's infancy: *The child grew, v.* 8. Special notice is taken of this, though a thing of course, to intimate that the children of the promise are growing children. See Luke i. 80; ii. 40. Those that are born of God shall increase more and more with the increase of God, Col. ii. 19. He grew so as not always to need milk, but was able to bear strong meat, and then he was weaned. See Heb. v. 13, 14. And then it was that Abraham made a great feast for his friends and neighbours, in thankfulness to God for his mercy to him. He made this feast, not on the day that Isaac was born, that would have been too great a disturbance to Sarah ; nor on the day that he was circumcised, that would have been too great a diversion from the ordinance; but on the day that he was weaned, because God's blessing upon the nursing of children, and the preservation of them through the perils of the infant age, are signal instances of the care and tenderness of the divine pro-

132

vidence, which ought to be acknowledged, to its praise. See Ps. xxii. 9, 10; Hos. xi. 1.

9 And Sarah saw the son of Hagar the Egyptian, which she had borne unto Abraham, mocking. 10 Wherefore she said unto Abraham, Cast out this bondwoman and her son : for the son of this bondwoman shall not be heir with my son, *even* with Isaac. 11 And the thing was very grievous in Abraham's sight because of his son. 12 And God said unto Abraham, Let it not be grievous in thy sight because of the lad, and because of thy bondwoman ; in all that Sarah hath said unto thee, hearken unto her voice ; for in Isaac shall thy seed be called. 13 And also of the son of the bondwoman will I make a nation, because he *is* thy seed.

The casting out of Ishmael is here considered of, and resolved on.

I. Ishmael himself gave the occasion by some affronts he gave to Isaac his little brother, some think on the day that Abraham made the feast for joy that Isaac was safely weaned, which the Jews say was not till he was three years old, others say five. Sarah herself was an eye-witness of the abuse : she *saw the son of the Egyptian mocking (v.* 9), mocking Isaac, no doubt, for it is said, with reference to this (Gal. iv. 29), that *he that was born after the flesh persecuted him that was born after the Spirit.* Ishmael is here called the *son of the Egyptian,* because, as some think, the 400 years' affliction of the seed of Abraham by the Egyptians began now, and was to be dated hence, *ch.* xv. 13. She saw him *playing with Isaac,* so the LXX., and, in play, *mocking him.* Ishmael was fourteen years older than Isaac; and, when children are together, the elder should be careful and tender of the younger : but it argued a very base and sordid disposition in Ishmael to be abusive to a child that was no way a match for him. Note, 1. God takes notice of what children say and do in their play, and will reckon with them if they say or do amiss, though their parents do not. 2. Mocking is a great sin, and very provoking to God. 3. There is a rooted remaining enmity in the seed of the serpent against the seed of the woman. The children of promise must expect to be mocked. This is persecution, which those that will live godly must count upon. 4. None are rejected and cast out from God but those who have first deserved it. Ishmael is continued in Abraham's family till he becomes a disturbance, grief, and scandal to it.

II. Sarah made the motion: *Cast out this bond-woman, v.* 10. This seems to be spoken in some heat, yet it is quoted (Gal. iv. 30) as if it had been spoken by a spirit of prophecy; and it is the sentence passed on all hypocrites and carnal people, though they have a place and a name in the visible church. All that are born after the flesh and not born again, that rest in the law and reject the gospel promise, shall certainly be cast out. It is made to point particularly at the rejection of the unbelieving Jews, who, though they were the seed of Abraham, yet, because they submitted not to the gospel covenant, were unchurched and disfranchised: and that which, above any thing, provoked God to cast them off was their mocking and persecuting the gospel church, God's Isaac, in its infancy, 1 Thess. ii. 16. Note, There are many who are familiarly conversant with the children of God in this world, and yet shall not partake with them in the inheritance of sons. Ishmael might be Isaac's play-fellow and school-fellow, yet not his fellow-heir.

III. Abraham was averse to it: *The thing was very grievous in Abraham's sight, v.* 11. 1. It grieved him that Ishmael had given such a provocation. Note, Children ought to consider that the more their parents love them the more they are grieved at their misconduct, and particularly at their quarrels among themselves. 2. It grieved him that Sarah insisted upon such a punishment. "Might it not suffice to correct him? would nothing less serve than to expel him?" Note, Even the needful extremities which must be used with wicked and incorrigible children are very grievous to tender parents, who cannot thus afflict willingly.

IV. God determined it, *v.* 12, 13. We may well suppose Abraham to be greatly agitated about this matter, loth to displease Sarah, and yet loth to expel Ishmael; in this difficulty God tells him what his will is, and then he is satisfied. Note, A good man desires no more in doubtful cases than to know his duty, and what God would have him do; and, when he is clear in this, he is, or should be, easy. To make Abraham so, God sets this matter before him in a true light, and shows him, 1. That the casting out of Ishmael was necessary to the establishment of Isaac in the rights and privileges of the covenant: *In Isaac shall thy seed be called.* Both Christ and the church must descend from Abraham through the loins of Isaac; this is the entail of the promise upon Isaac, and is quoted by the apostle (Rom. ix. 7) to show that not all who came from Abraham's loins were the heirs of Abraham's covenant. Isaac, the promised son, must be the father of the promised seed; therefore, "Away with Ishmael, send him far enough, lest he corrupt the manners or attempt to invade the rights of Isaac." It will be his security to have his rival banished. The covenant seed of Abraham must be a peculiar people, a people by themselves, from the

very first, distinguished, not mingled with those that were out of covenant; for this reason Ishmael must be separated. Abraham was *called alone,* and so must Isaac be. See Isa. li. 2. It is probable that Sarah little thought of this (John xi. 51), but God took what she said, and turned it into an oracle, as afterwards, *ch.* xxvii. 10. 2. That the casting out of Ishmael should not be his ruin, *v.* 13. He shall be a *nation, because he is thy seed.* We are not sure that it was his eternal ruin. It is presumption to say that all those who are left out of the external dispensation of God's covenant, are therefore excluded from all his mercies: those may be saved who are not thus honoured. However, we are sure it was not his temporal ruin. Though he was chased out of the church, he was not *chased out of the world. I will make him a nation.* Note, (1.) Nations are of God's making: he founds them, he forms them, he fixes them. (2.) Many are full of the blessings of God's providence that are strangers to the blessings of his covenant. (3.) The children of this world often fare the better, as to outward things, for their relation to the children of God.

14 And Abraham rose up early in the morning, and took bread, and a bottle of water, and gave *it* unto Hagar, putting *it* on her shoulder, and the child, and sent her away: and she departed, and wandered in the wilderness of Beer-sheba. 15 And the water was spent in the bottle, and she cast the child under one of the shrubs. 16 And she went, and sat her down over against *him* a good way off, as it were a bowshot: for she said, Let me not see the death of the child. And she sat over against *him,* and lift up her voice, and wept. 17 And God heard the voice of the lad; and the angel of God called to Hagar out of heaven, and said unto her, What aileth thee, Hagar? fear not; for God hath heard the voice of the lad where he *is.* 18 Arise, lift up the lad, and hold him in thine hand; for I will make him a great nation. 19 And God opened her eyes, and she saw a well of water; and she went, and filled the bottle with water, and gave the lad drink. 20 And God was with the lad; and he grew, and dwelt in the wilderness, and became an archer. 21 And he dwelt in the wilderness of Paran and his mother took him a wife out of the land of Egypt.

Here is, I. The casting out of the bondwoman and her son from the family of Abraham, *v.* 14. Abraham's obedience to the divine command in this matter was speedy—*early in the morning*, we may suppose immediately after he had, in the night's visions, received orders to do this. It was also submissive; it was contrary to his judgment, at least to his own inclination, to do it; yet as soon as he perceives that it is the mind of God he makes no objections, but silently does as he is bidden, as one trained up to an implicit obedience. In sending them away without any attendants, on foot, and slenderly provided for, it is probable that he observed the directions given him. If Hagar and Ishmael had conducted themselves well in Abraham's family, they might have continued there; but they threw themselves out by their own pride and insolence, which were thus justly chastised. Note, By abusing our privileges we forfeit them. Those that know not when they are well off, in such a desirable place as Abraham's family, deserve to be cashiered, and to be made to know the worth of mercies by the want of them.

II. Their wandering in the wilderness, missing their way to the place Abraham designed them for a settlement.

1. They were reduced to great distress there. Their provisions were spent, and Ishmael was sick. He that used to be full fed in Abraham's house, where he waxed fat and kicked, now fainted and sunk, when he was brought to short allowance. Hagar is in tears, and sufficiently mortified. Now she wishes for the crumbs she had wasted and made light of at her master's table. Like one under the power of the spirit of bondage, she despairs of relief, counts upon nothing but *the death of the child* (*v.* 15, 16), though God had told her, before he was born, that he should live to be a man, a great man. We are apt to forget former promises, when present providences seem to contradict them; for we live by sense.

2. In this distress, God graciously appeared for their relief: he heard *the voice of the lad, v.* 17. We read not of a word he said; but his sighs, and groans, and calamitous state, cried aloud in the ears of mercy. An angel was sent to comfort Hagar, and it was not the first time that she had met with God's comforts in a wilderness; she had thankfully acknowledged the former kind visit which God made her in such a case (*ch.* xvi. 13), and therefore God now visited her again with seasonable succours. (1.) The angel assures her of the cognizance God took of her distress: *God has heard the voice of the lad where he is*, though he is in a wilderness (for, wherever we are, there is a way open heaven-ward); therefore *lift up the lad, and hold him in thy hand, v.* 18. Note, God's readiness to help us when we are in trouble must not slacken, but quicken, our endeavours to help ourselves. (2.) He repeats the promise concerning her son, that he should

be *a great nation*, as a reason why she should bestir herself to help him. Note, It should engage our care and pains about children and young people to consider that we know not what God has designed them for, nor what great use Providence may make of them. (3.) He directs her to a present supply (*v.* 19): *He opened her eyes* (which were swollen and almost blinded with weeping), and then *she saw a well of water*. Note, Many that have reason enough to be comforted go mourning from day to day, because they do not see the reason they have for comfort. There is a well of water by them in the covenant of grace, but they are not aware of it; they have not the benefit of it, till the same God that opened their eyes to see their wound opens them to see their remedy, John xvi. 6, 7. Now the apostle tells us that those things concerning Hagar and Ishmael are ἀλληγορούμενα (Gal. iv. 24), they are to be allegorized; this then will serve to illustrate the folly, [1.] Of those who, like the unbelieving Jews, seek for righteousness by the law and the carnal ordinances of it, and not by the promise made in Christ, thereby running themselves into a wilderness of want and despair. Their comforts are soon exhausted, and if God save them not by his special prerogative, and by a miracle of mercy open their eyes and undeceive them, they are undone. [2.] Of those who seek for satisfaction and happiness in the world and the things of it. Those that forsake the comforts of the covenant and communion with God, and choose their portion in this earth, take up with a bottle of water, poor and slender provision, and that soon spent; they wander endlessly in pursuit of satisfaction, and, at length, sit down short of it.

III. The settlement of Ishmael, at last, in the wilderness of Paran (*v.* 20, 21), a wild place, fittest for a wild man; and such a one he was, *ch.* xvi. 12. Those that are born after the flesh take up with the wilderness of this world, while the children of the promise aim at the heavenly Canaan, and cannot be at rest till they are there. Observe, 1. He had some tokens of God's presence: *God was with the lad;* his outward prosperity was owing to this. 2. By trade he was an archer, which intimates that craft was his excellency and sport his business: rejected Esau was a cunning hunter. 3. He matched among his mother's relations; she took him a wife out of Egypt: as great an archer as he was, he did not think he could take his aim well, in the business of marriage, if he proceeded without his mother's advice and consent.

22 And it came to pass at that time, that Abimelech and Phichol the chief captain of his host spake unto Abraham, saying, God *is* with thee in all that thou doest: 23 Now therefore swear unto me here by God that

thou wilt not deal falsely with me, nor with my son, nor with my son's son: *but* according to the kindness that I have done unto thee, thou shalt do unto me, and to the land wherein thou hast sojourned. 24 And Abraham said, I will swear. 25 And Abraham reproved Abimelech because of a well of water, which Abimelech's servants had violently taken away. 26 And Abimelech said, I wot not who hath done this thing: neither didst thou tell me, neither yet heard I *of it*, but to day. 27 And Abraham took sheep and oxen, and gave them unto Abimelech; and both of them made a covenant. 28 And Abraham set seven ewe lambs of the flock by themselves. 29 And Abimelech said unto Abraham, What *mean* these seven ewe lambs which thou hast set by themselves? 30 And he said, For *these* seven ewe lambs shalt thou take of my hand, that they may be a witness unto me, that I have digged this well. 31 Wherefore he called that place Beersheba; because there they sware both of them. 32 Thus they made a covenant at Beer-sheba: then Abimelech rose up, and Phichol the chief captain of his host, and they returned into the land of the Philistines.

We have here an account of the treaty between Abimelech and Abraham, in which appears the accomplishment of that promise (*ch.* xii. 2) that God would *make his name great.* His friendship is valued, is courted, though a stranger, though a tenant at will to the Canaanites and Perizzites.

I. The league is proposed by Abimelech, and Phichol his prime-minister of state and general of his army.

1. The inducement to it was God's favour to Abraham (*v.* 22): " *God is with thee in all that thou doest,* and we cannot but take notice of it." Note, (1.) God in his providence sometimes shows his people such tokens for good that their neighbours cannot but take notice of it, Ps. lxxxvi. 17. Their affairs do so visibly prosper, and they have such remarkable success in their undertakings, that a confession is extorted from all about them of God's presence with them. (2.) It is good being in favour with those that are in favour with God, and having an interest in those that have an interest in heaven, Zech. viii. 23. *We will go with you, for we have heard that God is with you.* We do well for ourselves if we have fellowship with those that have fellowship with God, 1 John i. 3.

2. The tenour of it was, in general, that there should be a firm and constant friendship between the two families, which should not upon any account be violated. This bond of friendship must be strengthened by the bond of an oath, in which the true God was appealed to, both as a witness of their sincerity and an avenger in case either side were treacherous, *v.* 23. Observe, (1.) He desires the entail of this league upon his posterity and the extension of it to his people. He would have his son, and his son's son, and his land likewise, to have the benefit of it. Good men should secure an alliance and communion with the favourites of Heaven, not for themselves only, but for theirs also. (2.) He reminds Abraham of the fair treatment he had found among them: *According to the kindness I have done unto thee.* As those that have received kindness must return it, so those that have shown kindness may expect it.

II. It is consented to by Abraham, with a particular clause inserted about a well. In Abraham's part of this transaction observe,

1. He was ready to enter into this league with Abimelech, finding him to be a man of honour and conscience, and that had the fear of God before his eyes: *I will swear,* v. 24. Note, (1.) Religion does not make men morose and unconversable; I am sure it ought not. We must not, under colour of shunning bad company, be sour to all company, and jealous of every body. (2.) An honest mind does not startle at giving assurances: if Abraham say that he will be true to Abimelech, he is not afraid to swear it; an oath is for confirmation.

2. He prudently settled the matter concerning a well, about which Abimelech's servants had quarrelled with him. Wells of water, it seems, were choice goods in that country: thanks be to God, that they are not so scarce in ours. (1.) Abraham mildly told Abimelech of it, v 25. Note, If our brother trespass against us, we must, with the meekness of wisdom, tell him his fault, that the matter may be fairly accommodated and an end made of it, Matt. xviii. 15. (2.) He acquiesced in Abimelech's justification of himself in this matter: *I wot not who has done this thing,* v. 26. Many are suspected of injustice and unkindness that are perfectly innocent, and we ought to be glad when they clear themselves. The faults of servants must not be imputed to their masters, unless they know of them and justify them; and no more can be expected from an honest man than that he be ready to do right as soon as he knows that he has done wrong. (3.) He took care to have his title to the well cleared and confirmed, to prevent any disputes or quarrels for the future, v. 30. It is justice, as well as wisdom, to do thus, *in perpetuam rei memoriam—that the circumstance may be perpetually remembered.*

3. He made a very handsome present to Abimelech, v. 27. It was not any thing curious or

fine that he presented to him, but that which was valuable and useful—*sheep and oxen*, in gratitude for Abimelech's kindness to him, and in token of hearty friendship between them. The interchanging of kind offices is the improving of love : that which is mine is my friend's.

4. He ratified the covenant by an oath, and registered it by giving a new name to the place (*v.* 31), *Beer-sheba*, the *well of the oath*, in remembrance of the covenant they swore to, that they might be ever mindful of it ; or *the well of seven*, in remembrance of the seven lambs given to Abimelech, as a consideration for his confirming Abraham's title to that well. Note, Bargains made must be remembered, that we may make them good, and may not break our word through oversight.

33 And *Abraham* planted a grove in Beer-sheba, and called there on the name of the LORD, the everlasting God. 34 And Abraham sojourned in the Philistines' land many days.

Observe, 1. Abraham, having got into a good neighbourhood, knew when he was well off, and continued a great while there. There he planted a grove for a shade to his tent, or perhaps an orchard of fruit-trees ; and there, though we cannot say he settled, for God would have him, while he lived, to be a stranger and a pilgrim, yet he sojourned many days, as many as would consist with his character, as Abraham the *Hebrew*, or *passenger*. 2. There he made, not only a constant practice, but an open profession, of his religion : *There he called on the name of the Lord, the everlasting God*, probably in the grove he planted, which was his oratory or house of prayer. Christ prayed 'in a garden, on a mountain. (1.) Abraham kept up public worship, to which, probably, his neighbours resorted, that they might join with him. Note, Good men should not only retain their goodness wherever they go, but do all they can to propagate it, and make others good. (2.) In calling on the Lord, we must eye him as *the everlasting God, the God of the world*, so some. Though God had made himself known to Abraham as his God in particular, and in covenant with him, yet he forgets not to give glory to him as the Lord of all : *The everlasting God*, who was, before all worlds, and will be, when time and days shall be no more. See Isa. xl. 28.

CHAP. XXII.

We have here the famous story of Abraham's offering up his son Isaac, that is, his offering to offer him, which is justly looked upon as one of the wonders of the church. Here is, I. The strange command which God gave to Abraham concerning it, ver. 1, 2. II. Abraham's strange obedience to this command, ver. 3—10. III. The strange issue of this trial. 1. The sacrificing of Isaac was countermanded, ver. 11, 12. 2. Another sacrifice was provided, ver. 13, 14. 3. The covenant was renewed with Abraham hereupon, ver. 15—19. Lastly, an account of some of Abraham's relations, ver. 20, &c.

AND it came to pass after these things that God did tempt Abraham, and said unto him, Abraham : and he said, Behold, *here* I *am.* 2

And he said, Take now thy son, thine only *son* Isaac, whom thou lovest, and get thee into the land of Moriah ; and offer him there for a burnt offering upon one of the mountains which I will tell thee of.

Here is the trial of Abraham's faith, whether it continued so strong, so vigorous, so victorious, after a long settlement in communion with God, as it was at first, when by it he left his country : then it was made to appear that he loved God better than his father ; now that he loved him better than his son. Observe here,

I. The time when Abraham was thus tried (*v.* 1) : *After these things*, after all the other exercises he had had, all the hardships and difficulties he had gone through. Now, perhaps, he was beginning to think the storms had all blown over ; but, after all, this encounter comes, which is sharper than any yet. Note, Many former trials will not supersede nor secure us from further trials ; we have not yet put off the harness, 1 Kings xx. 11. See Ps. xxx. 6, 7.

II. The author of the trial : *God* tempted him, not to draw him to sin, so Satan tempts (if Abraham had sacrificed Isaac, he would not have sinned, his orders would have justified him, and borne him out), but to discover his graces, how strong they were, that they might be *found to praise, and honour, and glory*, 1 Pet. i. 7. Thus God tempted Job, that he might appear not only a good man, but a great man. *God did tempt Abraham ;* he did *lift up Abraham*, so some read it ; as a scholar that improves well is lifted up, when he is put into a higher form. Note, Strong faith is often exercised with strong trials and put upon hard services.

III. The trial itself. God appeared to him as he had formerly done, called him by name, *Abraham*, that name which had been given him in ratification of the promise. Abraham, like a good servant, readily answered, " Here am I ; what says my Lord unto his servant ?" Probably he expected some renewed promise like those, *ch.* xv. 1, and xvii. 1. But, to his great amazement, that which God has to say to him is, in short, *Abraham, Go kill thy son ;* and this command is given him in such aggravating language as makes the temptation abundantly more grievous. When God speaks, Abraham, no doubt, takes notice of every word, and listens attentively to it ; and every word here is a sword in his bones : the trial is steeled with trying phrases. Is it any pleasure to the Almighty that he should afflict ? No, it is not ; yet, when Abraham's faith is to be tried, God seems to take pleasure in the aggravation of the trial, *v.* 2. Observe,

1. The person to be offered. (1.) " *Take thy son*, not thy bullocks and thy lambs ;" how willingly would Abraham have parted with them by thousands to redeem Isaac !

"No, *I will take no bullock out of thy house,* Ps. l. 9. I must have thy son : not thy servant, no, not the steward of thy house, that shall not serve the turn; I must have thy son." Jephthah, in pursuance of a vow, offered a daughter ; but Abraham must offer his son, in whom the family was to be built up. "Lord, let it be an adopted son ;" "No, (2.) *Thy only son;* thy only son by *Sarah.*" Ishmael was lately cast out, to the grief of Abraham ; and now Isaac only was left, and must he go too ? Yes, (3.) "Take *Isaac,* him, by name, *thy laughter,* that *son indeed,*" ch. xvii. 19. Not "Send for Ishmael back, and offer him ;" no, it must be Isaac. "But, Lord, I love Isaac, he is to me as my own soul. Ishmael is not, and wilt thou take Isaac also ? All this is against me :" Yea, (4.) That son *whom thou lovest.* It was a trial of Abraham's love to God, and therefore it must be in a beloved son, and that string must be touched most upon : in the Hebrew it is expressed more emphatically, and, I think, might very well be read thus : *Take now that son of thine, that only one of thine, whom thou lovest, that Isaac.* God's command must overrule all these considerations.

2. The place : *In the land of Moriah,* three days' journey off ; so that he might have time to consider it, and, if he did it, must do it deliberately, that it might be a service the more reasonable and the more honourable.

3. The manner : *Offer him for a burnt-offering.* He must not only kill his son, but kill him as a sacrifice, kill him devoutly, kill him by rule, kill him with all that pomp and ceremony, with all that sedateness and composure of mind, with which he used to offer his burnt-offerings.

3 And Abraham rose up early in the morning, and saddled his ass, and took two of his young men with him, and Isaac his son, and clave the wood for the burnt offering, and rose up, and went unto the place of which God had told him. 4 Then on the third day Abraham lifted up his eyes, and saw the place afar off. 5 And Abraham said unto his young men, Abide ye here with the ass ; and I and the lad will go yonder and worship, and come again to you. 6 And Abraham took the wood of the burnt offering, and laid *it* upon Isaac his son ; and he took the fire in his hand, and a knife ; and they went both of them together. 7 And Isaac spake unto Abraham his father, and said, My father : and he said, Here *am* I, my son. And he said, Behold the fire and the wood : but where *is* the lamb for a burnt offering ? 8 And Abraham said, My son,

God will provide himself a lamb for a burnt offering : so they went both of them together. 9 And they came to the place which God had told him of ; and Abraham built an altar there, and laid the wood in order, and bound Isaac his son, and laid him on the altar upon the wood. 10 And Abraham stretched forth his hand, and took the knife to slay his son.

We have here Abraham's obedience to this severe command. *Being tried, he offered up Isaac,* Heb. xi. 17. Observe,

I. The difficulties which he broke through in this act of obedience. Much might have been objected against it ; as, 1. It seemed directly against an antecedent law of God, which forbids murder, under a severe penalty, *ch.* ix. 5, 6. Now can the unchangeable God contradict himself ? He that hates robbery for burnt-offering (Isa. lxi. 8) cannot delight in murder for it. 2. How would it consist with natural affection to his own son ? It would be not only murder, but the worst of murders. Cannot Abraham be obedient but he must be unnatural ? If God insist upon a human sacrifice, is there none but Isaac to be the offering, and none but Abraham to be the offerer ? Must the father of the faithful be the monster of all fathers ? 3. God gave him no reason for it. When Ishmael was to be cast out, a just cause was assigned, which satisfied Abraham ; but here Isaac must die, and Abraham must kill him, and neither the one nor the other must know why or wherefore. If Isaac had been to die a martyr for the truth, or his life had been the ransom of some other life more precious, it would have been another matter ; or if he had died as a criminal, a rebel against God or his parents, as in the case of the idolater (Deut. xiii. 8, 9), or the stubborn son (Deut. xxi. 18, 19), it might have passed as a sacrifice to justice. But the case is not so : he is a dutiful, obedient, hopeful, son. "Lord, what profit is there in his blood ?" 4. How would this consist with the promise ? Was it not said that in *Isaac shall thy seed be called ?* But what comes of that seed, if this pregnant bud be broken off so soon ? 5. How should he ever look Sarah in the face again ? With what face can he return to her and his family with the blood of Isaac sprinkled on his garments and staining all his raiment ? *" Surely a bloody husband hast thou been to me "* would Sarah say (as Exod. iv. 25, 26), and it would be likely to alienate her affections for ever both from him and from his God. 6. What would the Egyptians say, and the Canaanites and the Perizzites who dwelt then in the land ? It would be an eternal reproach to Abraham, and to his altars. "Welcome nature, if this be grace." These and many similar objections might have been made ; but he was infallibly assured that it was indeed a command of God and not a delusion, and this was sufficient to answer them all. Note, God's commands must not be disputed, but obeyed; we must not consult with flesh and blood about them (Gal. i. 15, 16), but with a gracious obstinacy persist in our obedience to them.

II. The several steps of obedience, all which help to magnify it, and to show that he was guided by prudence, and governed by faith, in the whole transaction.

1. He rises early, *v.* 3. Probably the command was given in the visions of the night, and early the next morning he set himself about the execution of it—did not delay, did not demur, did not take time to deliberate; for the command was peremptory, and would not admit a debate. Note, Those that do the will of God heartily will do it speedily; while we delay, time is lost and the heart hardened.

2. He gets things ready for a sacrifice, and, as if he himself had been a Gibeonite, it should seem, with his own hands he cleaves the wood for the burnt-offering, that it might not be to seek when the sacrifice was to be offered. Spiritual sacrifices must thus be prepared for.

3. It is very probable that he said nothing about it to Sarah. This is a journey which she must know nothing of, lest she prevent it. There is so much in our own hearts to hinder our progress in duty that we have need, as much as may be, to keep out of the way of other hindrances.

4. He carefully looked about him, to discover the place appointed for this sacrifice, to which God had promised by some sign to direct him. Probably the direction was given by an appearance of the divine glory in the place, some pillar of fire reaching from heaven to earth, visible at a distance, and to which he pointed when he said (*v.* 5), " We will go yonder, where you see the light, and worship."

5. He left his servants at some distance off (*v.* 5), lest they should interpose, and create him some disturbance in his strange oblation; for Isaac was, no doubt, the darling of the whole family. Thus, when Christ was entering upon his agony in the garden, he took only three of his disciples with him, and left the rest at the garden door. Note, It is our wisdom and duty, when we are going to worship God, to lay aside all those thoughts and cares which may divert us from the service, leave them at the bottom of the hill, that we may attend on the Lord without distraction.

6. He obliged Isaac to carry the wood (both to try his obedience in a smaller matter first, and that he might typify Christ, who carried his own cross, John xix. 17), while he himself, though he knew what he did, with a steady and undaunted resolution carried the fatal knife and fire, *v.* 6. Note, Those that through grace are resolved upon the substance of any service or suffering for

God must overlook the little circumstances which make it doubly difficult to flesh and blood.

7. Without any ruffle or disorder, he talks it over with Isaac, as if it had been but a common sacrifice that he was going to offer, *v.* 7, 8.

(1.) It was a very affecting question that Isaac asked him, as they were going together: *My father,* said Isaac; it was a melting word, which, one would think, would strike deeper into the breast of Abraham than his knife could into the breast of Isaac. He might have said, or thought, at least, " Call me not thy father who am now to be thy murderer; can a father be so barbarous, so perfectly lost to all the tenderness of a father?" Yet he keeps his temper, and keeps his countenance, to admiration; he calmly waits for his son's question, and this is it: *Behold the fire and the wood, but where is the lamb?* See how expert Isaac was in the law and custom of sacrifices. This it is to be well-catechised: this is, [1.] A trying question to Abraham. How could he endure to think that Isaac was himself the lamb? So it is, but Abraham, as yet, dares not tell him so. Where God knows the faith to be armour of proof, he will laugh at *the trial of the innocent,* Job ix. 23. [2.] It is a teaching question to us all, that, when we are going to worship God, we should seriously consider whether we have every thing ready, especially the lamb for a burnt-offering. Behold, the fire is ready, the Spirit's assistance and God's acceptance; the wood is ready, the instituted ordinances designed to kindle our affections (which indeed, without the Spirit, are but like wood without fire, but the Spirit works by them); *all things are now ready,* but where is the lamb? Where is the heart? Is that ready to be offered up to God, to ascend to him as a burnt-offering?

(2.) It was a very prudent answer which Abraham gave him: *My son, God will provide himself a lamb.* This was the language, either, [1.] Of his obedience. " We must offer the lamb which God has appointed now to be offered ;" thus giving him this general rule of submission to the divine will, to prepare him for the application of it to himself very quickly. Or, [2.] Of his faith. Whether he meant it so or not, this proved to be the meaning of it; a sacrifice was provided instead of Isaac. Thus, *First,* Christ, the great sacrifice of atonement, was of God's providing; when none in heaven or earth could have found a lamb for that burnt-offering, God himself found the ransom, Ps. lxxxix. 20. *Secondly,* All our sacrifices of acknowledgment are of God's providing too. It is he that prepares the heart, Ps. x. 17. The broken and contrite spirit is a sacrifice of God (Ps. li. 17), of his providing.

8. With the same resolution and composedness of mind, after many thoughts of heart, he applies himself to the completing

of this sacrifice, *v.* 9, 10. He goes on with a holy wilfulness, after many a weary step, and with a heavy heart he arrives at length at the fatal place, builds the altar (an altar of earth, we may suppose, the saddest that ever he built, and he had built many a one), lays the wood in order for his Isaac's funeral pile, and now tells him the amazing news : "Isaac, thou art the lamb which God has provided." Isaac, for aught that appears, is as willing as Abraham ; we do not find that he raised any objection against it, that he petitioned for his life, that he attempted to make his escape, much less that he struggled with his aged father, or made any resist- ance : Abraham does it, God will have it done, and Isaac has learnt to submit to both, Abraham no doubt comforting him with the same hopes with which he himself by faith was comforted. Yet it is necessary that a sacrifice be bound. The great sacrifice, which in the fulness of time was to be offered up, must be bound, and therefore so must Isaac. But with what heart could tender Abraham tie those guiltless hands, which perhaps had often been lifted up to ask his blessing, and stretched out to em- brace him, and were now the more straitly bound with the cords of love and duty! However, it must be done. Having bound him, he lays him upon the altar, and his hand upon the head of his sacrifice ; and now, we may suppose, with floods of tears, he gives, and takes, the final farewell of a parting kiss : perhaps he takes another for Sarah from her dying son. This being done, he resolutely forgets the bowels of a father, and puts on the awful gravity of a sacrificer. With a fixed heart, and an eye lifted up to heaven, he takes the knife, and stretches out his hand to give the fatal cut to Isaac's throat. Be astonished, O heavens ! at this ; and wonder, O earth ! Here is an act of faith and obedience, which deserves to be a spec- tacle to God, angels, and men. Abraham's darling, Sarah's laughter, the church's hope, the heir of promise, lies ready to bleed and die by his own father's hand, who never shrinks at the doing of it. Now this obe- dience of Abraham in offering up Isaac is a lively representation, (1.) Of the love of God to us, in delivering up his only-begotten Son to suffer and die for us, as a sacrifice. It *pleased the Lord* himself to *bruise him.* See Isa. liii. 10; Zech. xiii. 7. Abraham was obliged, both in duty and gratitude, to part with Isaac, and parted with him to a friend ; but God was under no obligations to us, for we were enemies. (2.) Of our duty to God, in return for that love. We must tread in the steps of this faith of Abraham. God, by his word, calls us to part with all for Christ, —all our sins, though they have been as a right hand, or a right eye, or an Isaac—all those things that are competitors and rivals with Christ for the sovereignty of the heart (Lu. xiv. 26); and we must cheerfully let

them all go. God, by his providence, which is truly the voice of God, calls us to part with an Isaac sometimes, and we must do it with a cheerful resignation and submission to his holy will, 1 Sam. iii. 18.

11 And the angel of the LORD called unto him out of heaven, and said, Abraham, Abraham : and he said, Here *am* I. 12 And he said, Lay not thine hand upon the lad, neither do thou any thing unto him : for now I know that thou fearest God, seeing thou hast not withheld thy son, thine only *son* from me. 13 And Abraham lifted up his eyes, and looked, and behold behind *him* a ram caught in a thicket by his horns : and Abraham went and took the ram, and offered him up for a burnt offering in the stead of his son. 14 And Abraham called the name of that place Jehovah- jireh : as it is said *to* this day, In the mount of the LORD it shall be seen.

Hitherto this story has been very melan- choly, and seemed to hasten towards a most tragical period ; but here the sky suddenly clears up, the sun breaks out, and a bright and pleasant scene opens. The same hand that had wounded and cast down here heals and lifts up ; for, though he cause grief, he will have compassion. *The angel of the Lord,* that is, God himself, the eternal Word, the angel of the covenant, who was to be the great Redeemer and comforter, he interposed, and gave a happy issue to this trial.

I. Isaac is rescued, *v.* 11, 12. The com- mand to offer him was intended only for trial, and it appearing, upon trial, that Abraham did indeed love God better than he loved Isaac, the end of the command was answered ; and therefore the order is countermanded, with- out any reflection at all upon the unchange- ableness of the divine counsels : *Lay not thy hand upon the lad.* Note, 1.Our creature-com- forts are most likely to be continued to us when we are most willing to resign them up to God's will. 2. God's time to help and re- lieve his people is when they are brought to the greatest extremity. The more imminent the danger is, and the nearer to be put in execution, the more wonderful and the more welcome is the deliverance.

II. Abraham is not only approved, but ap- plauded. He obtains an honourable testi- mony that he is righteous : *Now know I that thou fearest God.* God knew it before, but now Abraham had given a most memorable evidence of it. He needed do no more ; what he had done was sufficient to prove the religious regard he had to God and his au- thority. Note, 1. When God, by his provi- dence, hinders the performance of our sincere intentions in his services, he graciously accepts the will for the deed, and the honest endeavour, though it come short of finishing. 2. The best evidence of our fearing God is our being willing to serve and honour him with that which is dearest to us, and to part with all to him or for him.

III. Another sacrifice is provided instead of Isaac, *v.* 13. Now that the altar was built, and the wood laid in order, it was necessary that something should be offered. For, 1. God must be acknowledged with thankfulness for the deliverance of Isaac; and the sooner the better, when here is an altar ready. 2. Abraham's words must be made good: *God will provide himself a lamb.* God will not disappoint those expectations of his people which are of his own raising; but according to their faith it is to them. *Thou shalt decree a thing, and it shall be established.* 3. Reference must be had to the promised Messiah, the blessed seed. (1.) Christ was sacrificed in our stead, as this ram instead of Isaac, and his death was our discharge. "*Here am I* (said he), *let these go their way.*" (2.) Though that blessed seed was lately promised, and now typified by Isaac, yet the offering of him up should be suspended till the latter end of the world: and in the mean time the sacrifice of beasts should be accepted, as this ram was, as a pledge of that expiation which should one day be made by that great sacrifice. And it is observable that the temple, the place of sacrifice, was afterwards built upon this mount Moriah (2 Chron. iii. 1); and mount Calvary, where Christ was crucified, was not far off.

IV. A new name is given to the place, to the honour of God, and for the encouragement of all believers, to the end of the world, cheerfully to trust in God in the way of obedience: *Jehovah-jireh, The Lord will provide* (*v.* 14), probably alluding to what he had said (*v.* 8), *God will provide himself a lamb.* It was not owing to any contrivance of Abraham, nor was it in answer to his prayer, though he was a distinguished intercessor; but it was purely the Lord's doing. Let it be recorded for the generations to come, 1. That *the Lord will see;* he will always have his eye upon his people in their straits and distresses, that he may come in with seasonable succour in the critical juncture. 2. That he will *be seen,* be seen *in the mount,* in the greatest perplexities of his people. He will not only manifest, but magnify, his wisdom, power, and goodness, in their deliverance. Where God sees and provides, he should be seen and praised. And, perhaps, it may refer to God *manifest in the flesh.*

15 And the angel of the LORD called unto Abraham out of heaven the second time, 16 And said, By myself have I sworn, saith the LORD, for because thou hast done this thing, and

140

hast not withheld thy son, thine only son: 17 That in blessing I will bless thee, and in multiplying I will multiply thy seed as the stars of the heaven, and as the sand which *is* upon the sea shore; and thy seed shall possess the gate of his enemies; 18 And in thy seed shall all the nations of the earth be blessed; because thou hast obeyed my voice. 19 So Abraham returned unto his young men, and they rose up and went together to Beersheba; and Abraham dwelt at Beersheba.

Abraham's obedience was graciously accepted; but this was not all: here we have it recompensed, abundantly recompensed, before he stirred from the place; probably while the ram he had sacrificed was yet burning God sent him this gracious message, renewed and ratified his covenant with him, All covenants were made by sacrifice, so was this by the typical sacrifices of Isaac and the ram. Very high expressions of God's favour to Abraham are employed in this confirmation of the covenant with him, expressions exceeding any he had yet been blessed with. Note, Extraordinary services shall be crowned with extraordinary honours and comforts; and favours in the promise, though not yet performed, ought to be accounted real and valuable recompences. Observe, 1. God is pleased to make mention of Abraham's obedience as the consideration of the covenant; and he speaks of it with an encomium: *Because thou hast done this thing, and hast not withheld thy son, thine only son, v.* 16. He lays a strong emphasis on this, and (*v.* 18) praises it as an act of obedience: in it thou hast *obeyed my voice,* and to obey is better than sacrifice. Not that this was a proportionable consideration, but God graciously put this honour upon that by which Abraham had honoured him. 2. God now confirmed the promise with an oath. It was said and sealed before; but now it is sworn: *By myself have I sworn;* for he could swear by no greater, Heb. vi. 13. Thus he interposed himself by an oath, as the apostle expresses it, Heb. vi. 17. He did (to speak with reverence) even pawn his own life and being upon it *(As I live),* that by all those immutable things, in which it was impossible for God to lie, he and his might have strong consolation. Note, If we exercise faith, God will encourage it. Improve the promises, and God will ratify them. 3. The particular promise here renewed is that of a numerous offspring: *Multiplying, I will multiply thee, v.* 17. Note, Those that are willing to part with any thing for God shall have it made up to them with unspeakable advantage. Abraham has but one son, and is willing to part with that one, in obedience to God. "Well," said God, "thou shalt be recompensed with thousands and millions." What a figure does the seed of Abraham make in history! How numerous, how illustrious, were his known descendants, who, to this day, triumph in this, that they have Abraham to their father! Thus he received a thousand-fold in this life, Matt. xix. 29. 4. The promise, doubtless, points at the Messiah, and the grace of the gospel. This is the oath sworn to our father Abraham, which Zacharias refers to, Luke i. 73, &c. And so here is a promise, (1.) Of the great blessing of the Spirit: *In blessing, I will bless thee,* namely, with that best of blessings the gift of the Holy Ghost; the promise of the Spirit was that blessing of Abraham which was to come upon the Gentiles through Jesus Christ, Gal. iii. 14. (2.) Of the increase of the church, that believers, his spiritual seed, should be numerous as the stars of heaven. (3.) Of spiritual victories: *Thy seed shall possess the gate of his enemies.* Believers, by their faith, overcome the world, and triumph over all the powers of darkness, and are more than conquerors. Probably Zacharias refers to this part of the oath (Luke i. 74), *That we, being delivered out of the hand of our enemies, might serve him without fear.* But the crown of all is the last promise. (4.) Of the incarnation of Christ: *In thy seed,* one particular person that shall descend from thee (for he speaks not of many, but of one, as the apostle observes, Gal. iii. 16), *shall all the nations of the earth be blessed,* or shall *bless themselves,* as the phrase is, Isa. lxv. 16. In him all may be happy if they will, and all that belong to him shall be so, and shall think themselves so. Christ is the great blessing of the world. Abraham was ready to give up his son for a sacrifice to the honour of God, and, on that occasion, God promised to give his Son a sacrifice for the salvation of man.

20 And it came to pass after these things, that it was told Abraham, saying, Behold, Milcah, she hath also borne children unto thy brother Nahor; 21 Huz his first born, and Buz his brother, and Kemuel the father of Aram, 22 And Chesed, and Hazo, and Pildash, and Jidlaph, and Bethuel. 23 And Bethuel begat Rebekah: these eight Milcah did bear to Nahor, Abraham's brother. 24 And his concubine, whose name *was* Reumah, she bare also Tebah, and Gaham, and Thahash, and Maachah.

This is recorded here, 1. To show that though Abraham saw his own family highly dignified with peculiar privileges, admitted into covenant, and blessed with the entail of the promise, yet he did not look with con-

tempt and disdain upon his relations, but was glad to hear of the increase and prosperity of their families. 2. To make way for the following story of the marriage of Isaac to Rebekah, a daughter of this family.

CHAP. XXIII.

Here is, I. Abraham a mourner for the death of Sarah, ver. 1, 2. II. Abraham a purchaser of a burying-place for Sarah. 1. The purchase humbly proposed by Abraham, ver. 3, 4. 2. Fairly treated of, and agreed to, with a great deal of mutual civility and respect, ver. 5—16. 3. The purchase-money paid, ver. 16. 4. The premises conveyed and secured to Abraham, ver. 17, 18, 20. 5. Sarah's funeral, ver. 19.

AND Sarah was a hundred and seven and twenty years old: *these were* the years of the life of Sarah. 2 And Sarah died in Kirjath-arba; the same *is* Hebron in the land of Canaan: and Abraham came to mourn for Sarah, and to weep for her.

We have here, 1. Sarah's age, *v.* 1. Almost forty years before, she had called herself old, *ch.* xviii. 12. Old people will die never the sooner, but may die the better, for reckoning themselves old. 2. Her death, *v.* 2. The longest liver must die at last. Abraham and Sarah had lived comfortably together many years; but death parts those whom nothing else could part. The special friends and favourites of Heaven are not exempted from the stroke of death. She died in the land of Canaan, where she had been above sixty years a sojourner. 3. Abraham's mourning for her; and he was a true mourner. He did not only perform the ceremonies of mourning according to the custom of those times, as the mourners that go about the streets, but he did sincerely lament the great loss he had of a good wife, and gave proof of the constancy of his affection to her to the last. Two words are used: he came both to *mourn* and to *weep.* His sorrow was not counterfeit, but real. He came to her tent, and sat down by the corpse, there to pay the tribute of his tears, that his eye might affect his heart, and that he might pay the greater respect to the memory of her that was gone. Note, It is not only lawful, but it is a duty, to lament the death of our near relations, both in compliance with the providence of God, who thus calls to weeping and mourning, and in honour to those to whom honour is due. Tears are a tribute due to our deceased friends. When the body is sown, it must be watered. But we must not sorrow as those that have no hope; for we have a good hope through grace both concerning them and concerning ourselves.

3 And Abraham stood up from before his dead, and spake unto the sons of Heth, saying, 4 I *am* a stranger and a sojourner with you: give me a possession of a buryingplace with you, that I may bury my dead out of my sight. 5 And the children of Heth

answered Abraham, saying unto him, 6 Hear us, my lord: thou *art* a mighty prince among us: in the choice of our sepulchres bury thy dead; none of us shall withhold from thee his sepulchre, but that thou mayest bury thy dead. 7 And Abraham stood up, and bowed himself to the people of the land, *even* to the children of Heth. 8 And he communed with them, saying, If it be your mind that I should bury my dead out of my sight; hear me, and intreat for me to Ephron the son of Zohar, 9 That he may give me the cave of Machpelah, which he hath, which *is* in the end of his field; for as much money as it is worth he shall give it me for a possession of a buryingplace amongst you. 10 And Ephron dwelt among the children of Heth: and Ephron the Hittite answered Abraham in the audience of the children of Heth, *even* of all that went in at the gate of his city, saying, 11 Nay, my lord, hear me: the field give I thee, and the cave that *is* therein, I give it thee; in the presence of the sons of my people give I it thee: bury thy dead. 12 And Abraham bowed down himself before the people of the land. 13 And he spake unto Ephron in the audience of the people of the land, saying, But if thou *wilt give it*, I pray thee, hear me: I will give thee money for the field; take *it* of me, and I will bury my dead there. 14 And Ephron answered Abraham, saying unto him, 15 My lord, hearken unto me: the land *is worth* four hundred shekels of silver; what *is* that betwixt me and thee? bury therefore thy dead.

Here is, I. The humble request which Abraham made to his neighbours, the Hittites, for a burying-place among them, *v.* 3, 4. It was strange he had this to do now; but we are to impute it rather to God's providence than to his improvidence, as appears Acts vii. 5, where it is said, *God gave him no inheritance in Canaan.* It were well if all those who take care to provide burying-places for their bodies after death were as careful to provide a resting-place for their souls. Observe here, 1. The convenient diversion which this affair gave, for the present, to Abraham's grief: He *stood up from before his dead.* Those that find themselves

in danger of over-grieving for their dead relations, and are entering into that temptation, must take heed of poring upon their loss and of sitting alone and melancholy. There must be a time of standing up from before their dead, and ceasing to mourn. For, thanks be to God, our happiness is not bound up in the life of any creature. Care of the funeral may, as here, be improved to divert grief for the death at first, when it is most in danger of tyrannizing. Weeping must not hinder sowing. 2. The argument he used with the children of Heth, which was this: "*I am a stranger and a sojourner with you,* therefore I am unprovided, and must become a humble suitor to you for a burying-place." This was one occasion which Abraham took to confess that he was a stranger and a pilgrim upon earth; he was not ashamed to own it thus publicly, Heb. xi. 13. Note, The death of our relations should effectually remind us that we are not at home in this world. When they are gone, say, "We are going." 3. His uneasiness till this affair was settled, intimated in that word, *that I may bury my dead out of my sight.* Note, Death will make those unpleasant to our sight who while they lived were the desire of our eyes. The countenance that was fresh and lively becomes pale and ghastly, and fit to be removed into land of darkness. While she was in his sight, it renewed his grief, which he would prevent.

II. The generous offer which the children of Heth made to him, *v.* 5, 6. They compliment him, 1. With a title of respect: *Thou art a prince of God among us,* so the word is; not only great, but good. He called himself a stranger and a sojourner; they call him a great prince; for those that humble themselves shall be exalted. God had promised to make Abraham's name great. 2. With a tender of the best of their burying-places. Note, Even the light of nature teaches us to be civil and respectful towards all, though they be strangers and sojourners. The noble generosity of these Canaanites shames and condemns the closeness, and selfishness, and ill-humour, of many that call themselves Israelites. Observe, These Canaanites would be glad to mingle their dust with Abraham's and to have their last end like his.

III. The particular proposal which Abraham made to them, *v.* 7—9. He returns them his thanks for their kind offer with all possible decency and respect; though a great man, an old man, and now a mourner, yet he stands up, and bows himself humbly before them, *v.* 7. Note, Religion teaches good manners; and those abuse it that place it in rudeness and clownishness. He then pitches upon the place he thinks most convenient, namely, the cave of Machpelah, which probably lay near him, and had not yet been used for a burying-place. The present owner was *Ephron.* Abraham cannot pretend to any interest in him, but he desires that they would improve theirs with him to get the purchase of that cave, and the field in which it was. Note, A moderate desire to obtain that which is convenient for us, by fair and honest means, is not such a coveting of that which is our neighbour's as is forbidden in the tenth commandment.

IV. The present which Ephron made to Abraham of his field : *The field give I thee, v.* 10, 11. Abraham thought he must be entreated to sell it ; but, upon the first mention of it, without entreaty, Ephron freely gives it. Some men have more generosity than they are thought to have. Abraham, no doubt, had taken all occasions to oblige his neighbours, and do them any service that lay in his power ; and now they return his kindness : for *he that watereth shall be watered also himself.* Note, If those that profess religion adorn their profession by eminent civility and serviceableness to all, they shall find it will redound to their own comfort and advantage, as well as to the glory of God.

V. Abraham's modest and sincere refusal of Ephron's kind offer, *v.* 12, 13. Abundance of thanks he returns him for it (*v.* 12), makes his obeisance to him before the people of the land, that they might respect Ephron the more for the respect they saw Abraham give him (1 Sam. xv. 30), but resolves to give him money for the field, even the full value of it. It was not in pride that Abraham refused the gift, or because he scorned to be beholden to Ephron ; but, 1. In justice. Abraham was rich in silver and gold (*ch.* xiii. 2) and was able to pay for the field, and therefore would not take advantage of Ephron's generosity. Note, Honesty, as well as honour, forbids us to sponge upon our neighbours and to impose upon those that are free. Job reflected upon it with comfort, when he was poor, that he had not *eaten the fruits of his land without money,* Job xxxi. 39. 2. In prudence. He would pay for it lest Ephron, when this good humour was over, should upbraid him with it, and say, *I have made Abraham rich (ch.* xiv. 23), or lest the next heir should question Abraham's title (because that grant was made without any consideration), and claim back the field. Thus David afterwards refused Araunah's offer, 2 Sam. xxiv. 24. We know not what affronts we may hereafter receive from those that are now most kind and generous.

VI. The price of the land fixed by Ephron but not insisted on : *The land is worth four hundred shekels of silver* (about fifty pounds of our money), *but what is that between me and thee? v.* 14, 15. He would rather oblige his friend than have so much money in his pocket. Herein Ephron discovers, 1. A great contempt of worldly wealth. " What is that between me and thee ? It is a small

matter, not worth speaking of." Many a one would have said, " It is a deal of money ; it will go far in a child's portion." But Ephron says, " What is that?" Note, It is an excellent thing for people to have low and mean thoughts of all the wealth of this world ; it is that which is not, and in the abundance of which a man's life does not consist, Luke xii. 15. 2. Great courtesy, and obligingness to his friend and neighbour. Ephron was not jealous of Abraham as a resident foreigner, nor envious at him as a man likely to thrive and grow rich. He bore him no ill-will for his singularity in religion, but was much kinder to him than most people now-a-days are to their own brothers : *What is that between me and thee?* Note, No little thing should occasion demurs and differences between true friends. When we are tempted to be hot in resenting affronts, high in demanding our rights, or hard in denying a kindness, we should answer the temptation with this question : " What is that between me and my friend ? "

16 And Abraham hearkened unto Ephron ; and Abraham weighed to Ephron the silver, which he had named in the audience of the sons of Heth, four hundred shekels of silver, current *money* with the merchant. 17 And the field of Ephron, which *was* in Machpelah, which *was* before Mamre, the field, and the cave which *was* therein, and all the trees that *were* in the field, that *were* in all the borders round about, were made sure 18 Unto Abraham for a possession in the presence of the children of Heth, before all that went in at the gate of his city. 19 And after this, Abraham buried Sarah his wife in the cave of the field of Machpelah before Mamre : the same *is* Hebron in the land of Canaan. 20 And the field, and the cave that *is* therein, were made sure unto Abraham for a possession of a buryingplace by the sons of Heth.

We have here the conclusion of the treaty between Abraham and Ephron about the burying-place. The bargain was publicly made before all the neighbours, *in the presence and audience of the sons of Heth, v.* 16, 17. Note, Prudence, as well as justice, directs us to be fair, and open, and above-board, in our dealings. Fraudulent contracts hate the light, and choose to be clandestine ; but those that design honestly in their bargains care not who are witnesses to them. Our law countenances sales made in market-overt, and by deed enrolled. Observe, 1. Abraham, without fraud, covin, or further delay, pays

the money, *v.* 16. He pays it readily, without hesitation,—pays it in full, without diminution,—and pays it by weight, current
money with the merchant, without deceit.
See how anciently money was used for the
help of commerce; and see how honestly
money should be paid where it is due. Observe, Though all the land of Canaan was
Abraham's by promise, yet, the time of his
possessing not having come, what he had
now occasion for he bought and paid for.
Note, Dominion is not founded in grace. The
saints' title to an eternal inheritance does not
entitle them to the possessions of this world,
nor justify them in doing wrong. 2. Ephron
honestly and fairly makes him a good title to
the land, *v.* 17, 18, 20. The field, with all
its appurtenances, is conveyed to Abraham
and his heirs for ever, in open court, not by
writing (it does not appear that writing was
then used), but by such a public solemn declaration before witnesses as was sufficient to
pass it. Note, As that which is bought must
be honestly paid for, so that which is sold
must be honestly delivered and secured. 3.
Abraham, thereupon, takes possession, and
buries Sarah in the cave or vault (whether
framed by nature or art is not certain) which
was in the purchased field. It is probable
that Abraham had buried servants out of his
family since he came to Canaan, but the graves
of the common people (2 Kings xxiii. 6) might
suffice for them; now that Sarah was dead a
peculiar place must be found for her remains.
It is worth noting, (1.) That a burying-place
was the first spot of ground Abraham possessed in Canaan. Note, When we are entering into the world it is good to think of our
going out of it; for, as soon as we are born,
we begin to die. (2.) That it was the only
piece of land he ever possessed, though the
country was all his own in reversion. Those
that have least of this earth find a grave in it.
Abraham provided, not cities, as Cain and
Nimrod, but a sepulchre, [1.] To be a constant memorandum of death to himself and
his posterity, that he and they might learn
to die daily. This sepulchre is said to be
at the end of the field (*v.* 9); for, whatever our
possessions are, there is a sepulchre at the end
of them. [2.] To be a token of his belief
and expectation of the resurrection; for why
should such care be taken of the body if it
be thrown away for ever, and must not rise
again? Abraham, in this, said plainly that
he sought a better country, that is, a heavenly. Abraham is content to be still flitting,
while he lives, but secures a place where,
when he dies his flesh may rest in hope.

CHAP. XXIV.

Marriages and funerals are the changes of families, and the common
news among the inhabitants of the villages. In the foregoing
chapter we had Abraham burying his wife, here we have him
marrying his son. These stories concerning his family, with
their minute circumstances, are largely related, while the histories
of the kingdoms of the world then in being, with their revolutions, are buried in silence; for the Lord knows those that are
his. The subjoining of Isaac's marriage to Sarah's funeral (with
a particular reference to it, ver. 67) shows us 'that as " one generation passes away another generation comes;" and thus the
entail both of the human nature, and of the covenant, is pre-

served. Here is, I. Abraham's care about the marrying of his
son, and the charge he gave to his servant about it, ver. 1—9.
II. His servant's journey into Abraham's country, to seek a wife
for his young master among his own relations, ver. 10—14. III.
The kind providence which brought him acquainted with Rebekah, whose father was Isaac's cousin-german, ver. 15—28. IV.
The treaty of marriage with her relations, ver. 29—49. V. Their
consent obtained, ver. 50—60. VI. The happy meeting and mar
riage between Isaac and Rebekah, ver. 61, &c.

AND Abraham was old, *and* well
stricken in age : and the Lord
had blessed Abraham in all things. 2
And Abraham said unto his eldest
servant of his house, that ruled over
all that he had, Put, I pray thee, thy
hand under my thigh : 3 And I will
make thee swear by the Lord, the
God of heaven, and the God of the
earth, that thou shalt not take a wife
unto my son of the daughters of the
Canaanites, among whom I dwell :
4 But thou shalt go unto my country,
and to my kindred, and take a wife
unto my son Isaac. 5 And the servant said unto him, Peradventure the
woman will not be willing to follow
me unto this land : must I needs bring
thy son again unto the land from
whence thou camest? 6 And Abraham said unto him, Beware thou that
thou bring not my son thither again.
7 The Lord God of heaven, which
took me from my father's house, and
from the land of my kindred, and
which spake unto me, and that sware
unto me, saying, Unto thy seed will
I give this land; he shall send his
angel before thee, and thou shalt take
a wife unto my son from thence. 8
And if the woman will not be willing
to follow thee, then thou shalt be clear
from this my oath : only bring not
my son thither again. 9 And the servant put his hand under the thigh of
Abraham his master, and sware to
him concerning that matter.

Three things we may observe here concerning Abraham :—
I. The care he took of a good son, to get
him married, well married. It was high time
to think of it now, for Isaac was about forty
years old, and it had been customary with his
ancestors to marry at thirty, or sooner, *ch.* xi.
14, 18, 22, 24. Abraham believed the promise of the building up of his family, and
therefore did not make haste ; not more haste
than good speed. Two considerations moved
him to think of it now (*v.* 1):—1. That he
himself was likely to leave the world quickly,
for he was *old, and well-stricken in age,* and
it would be a satisfaction to him to see his
son settled before he died ; and, 2. That he

had a good estate to leave behind him, for *the Lord had blessed him in all things;* and the blessing of the Lord makes rich. See how much religion and piety befriend outward prosperity. Now Abraham's pious care concerning his son was, (1.) That he should not marry a daughter of Canaan, but one of his kindred. He saw that the Canaanites were degenerating into great wickedness, and knew by revelation that they were designed for ruin, and therefore he would not marry his son among them, lest they should be either a snare to his soul, or at least a blot to his name. (2.) That yet he should not leave the land of Canaan, to go himself among his kindred, not even for the purpose of choosing a wife, lest he should be tempted to settle there. This caution is given *v.* 6, and repeated, *v.* 8. "*Bring not my son thither again,*" whatever comes of it. Let him rather want a wife than expose himself to that temptation." Note, Parents, in disposing of their children, should carefully consult the welfare of their souls, and their furtherance in the way to heaven. Those who through grace have escaped the corruption that is in the world through lust, and have brought up their children accordingly, should take heed of doing any thing by which they may be again entangled therein and overcome, 2 Pet. ii. 20. Beware that you bring them not thither again, Heb. xi. 15.

II. The charge he gave to a good servant, probably Eliezer of Damascus, one of whose conduct, fidelity, and affection to him and his family, he had had long experience. He trusted him with this great affair, and not Isaac himself, because he would not have Isaac go at all into that country, but marry there by proxy; and no proxy so fit as this *steward of his house.* This matter is settled between the master and the servant with a great deal of care and solemnity. 1. The servant must be bound by an oath to do his utmost to get a wife for Isaac from among his relations, *v.* 2—4. Abraham swears him to it, both for his own satisfaction and for the engagement of his servant to all possible care and diligence in this matter. Thus God swears his servants to their work, that, having sworn, they may perform it. Honour is here done to the eternal God; for he it is that is sworn by, to whom alone these appeals ought to be made. And some think honour is done to the covenant of circumcision by the ceremony here used of *putting his hand under his thigh.* Note, Swearing being an ordinance not peculiar to the church, but common to mankind, is to be performed by such signs as are the appointments and common usages of our country, for binding the person sworn. 2. He must be clear of this oath if, when he had done his utmost, he could not prevail. This proviso the servant prudently inserted (*v.* 5), putting the case that the woman would not follow him; and Abraham allowed the exception, *v.* 8. Note,

Oaths are to be taken with great caution, and the matter sworn to should be rightly understood and limited, because it is a *snare to devour that which is holy, and, after vows, to make the enquiry* which should have been made before.

III. The confidence he put in a good God, who, he doubts not, will give his servant success in this undertaking, *v.* 7. He remembers that God had wonderfully brought him out of the land of his nativity, by the effectual call of his grace; and therefore doubts not but he will succeed him in his care not to bring his son thither again. He remembers also the promise God had made and confirmed to him that he would give Canaan to his seed, and thence infers that God would own him in his endeavours to match his son, not among those devoted nations, but to one that was fit to be the mother of such a seed. "Fear not therefore; he shall send his angel before thee to make thy way prosperous." Note, 1. Those that carefully keep in the way of duty, and govern themselves by the principles of their religion in their designs and undertakings, have good reason to expect prosperity and success in them. God will cause that to issue in our comfort in which we sincerely aim at his glory. 2. God's promises, and our own experiences, are sufficient to encourage our dependence upon God, and our expectations from him, in all the affairs of this life. 3. God's angels are ministering spirits, sent forth, not only for the protection, but for the guidance, of the heirs of promise, Heb. i. 14. "*He shall send his angel before thee,* and then thou wilt speed well."

10 And the servant took ten camels of the camels of his master, and departed; for all the goods of his master *were* in his hand: and he arose, and went to Mesopotamia, unto the city of Nahor. 11 And he made his camels to kneel down without the city by a well of water at the time of the evening, *even* the time that women go out to draw *water.* 12 And he said, O LORD God of my master Abraham, I pray thee, send me good speed this day, and show kindness unto my master Abraham. 13 Behold, I stand *here* by the well of water; and the daughters of the men of the city come out to draw water: 14 And let it come to pass, that the damsel to whom I shall say, Let down thy pitcher, I pray thee, that I may drink; and she shall say, Drink, and I will give thy camels drink also: *let the same be* she *that* thou hast appointed for thy ser-

145

vant Isaac; and thereby shall I know that thou hast showed kindness unto my master. 15 And it came to pass, before he had done speaking, that, behold, Rebekah came out, who was born to Bethuel, son of Milcah, the wife of Nahor, Abraham's brother, with her pitcher upon her shoulder. 16 And the damsel *was* very fair to look upon, a virgin, neither had any man known her: and she went down to the well, and filled her pitcher, and came up. 17 And the servant ran to meet her, and said, Let me, I pray thee, drink a little water of thy pitcher. 18 And she said, Drink, my lord : and she hasted, and let down her pitcher upon her hand, and gave him drink. 19 And when she had done giving him drink, she said, I will draw *water* for thy camels also, until they have done drinking. 20 And she hasted, and emptied her pitcher into the trough, and ran again unto the well to draw *water*, and drew for all his camels. 21 And the man wondering at her held his peace, to wit whether the LORD had made his journey prosperous or not. 22 And it came to pass, as the camels had done drinking, that the man took a golden earring of half a shekel weight, and two bracelets for her hands of ten *shekels* weight of gold ; 23 And said, Whose daughter *art* thou? tell me, I pray thee : is there room *in* thy father's house for us to lodge in? 24 And she said unto him, I *am* the daughter of Bethuel the son of Milcah, which she bare unto Nahor 25 She said moreover unto him, We have both straw and provender enough, and room to lodge in. 26 And the man bowed down his head, and worshipped the LORD. 27 And he said, Blessed *be* the LORD God of my master Abraham, who hath not left destitute my master of his mercy and his truth : I *being* in the way, the LORD led me to the house of my master's brethren. 28 And the damsel ran, and told *them of* her mother's house these things.

Abraham's servant now begins to make a figure in this story ; and, though he is not named, yet much is here recorded to his honour, and for an example to all servants,

who shall be honoured if, by faithfully serving God and their masters, they adorn the doctrine of Christ (compare Prov. xxvii. 18 with Titus ii. 10); for there is no respect of persons with God, Col. iii. 24, 25. A good servant that makes conscience of the duty of his place, and does it in the fear of God, though he make not a figure in the world nor have praise of men, yet shall be owned and accepted of God and have praise of him. Observe here,

I. How faithful Abraham's servant approved himself to his master. Having received his charge, he with all expedition set out on his journey, with an equipage suitable to the object of his negociation (*v.* 10), *and he had all the goods of his master*, that is, in a schedule or particular account of them, *in his hand*, to show to those with whom he was to treat ; for, from first to last, he consulted his master's honour. Isaac being a type of Christ, some make this fetching of a wife for him to signify the espousing of the church by the agency of his servants the ministers. The church is the bride, the Lamb's wife, Rev. xxi. 9. Christ is the bridegroom, and ministers are the friends of the bridegroom (John iii. 29), whose work it is to persuade souls to consent to him, 2 Cor. xi. 2. The spouse of Christ must not be of the Canaanites, but of his own kindred, born again from above. Ministers, like Abraham's servant, must lay out themselves with the utmost wisdom and care to serve their master's interest herein.

II. How devoutly he acknowledged God in this affair, like one of that happy household which Abraham had *commanded to keep the way of the Lord*, &c., *ch.* xviii. 19. He arrived early in the evening (after many days' journeying) at the place of his destination, and reposed himself by a well of water, to consider how he might manage his business for the best. And,

1. He acknowledges God by a particular prayer (*v.* 12—14), wherein, (1.) He petitions for prosperity and good success in this affair : *Send me good speed, this day*. Note, We have leave to be particular in recommending our affairs to the conduct and care of divine Providence. Those that would have good speed must pray for it. *This day, in this affair ;* thus we must, in all our ways, acknowledge God, Prov. iii. 6. And, if we thus look up to God in every undertaking which we are in care about, we shall have the comfort of having done our duty, whatever the issue be. (2.) He pleads God's covenant with his master Abraham : *O God of my master Abraham, show kindness to him*. Note, As the children of good parents, so the servants of good masters, have peculiar encouragement in the prayers they offer to God for prosperity and success. (3.) He proposes a sign (*v.* 14), not by it to limit God, nor with a design to proceed no further if he were not gratified in it ; but it is a prayer, [1.] That God would provide a good wife for his young

master, and this was a good prayer. He knew that *a prudent wife is from the Lord* (Prov. xix. 14), and therefore that for this he will be enquired of He desires that his master's wife might be a humble and industrious woman, bred up to care and labour, and willing to put her hand to any work that was to be done; and that she might be of a courteous disposition, and charitable to strangers. When he came to seek a wife for his master, he did not go to the playhouse or the park, and pray that he might meet one there, but to *the well of water,* expecting to find one there well employed. [2.] That he would please to make his way, in this matter, plain and clear before him, by the concurrence of minute circumstances in his favour. Note, *First,* It is the comfort, as well as the belief, of a good man, that God's providence extends itself to the smallest occurrences and admirably serves its own purposes by them. Our times are in God's hand; not only events themselves, but the times of them. *Secondly,* It is our wisdom, in all our affairs, to follow Providence, and folly to force it. *Thirdly,* It is very desirable, and that which we may lawfully pray for, while in the general we set God's will before us as our rule, that he will, by hints of providence, direct us in the way of our duty, and give us indications what his mind is. Thus he guides his people with his eye (Ps. xxxii. 8), and leads them in a plain path, Ps. xxvii. 11.

2. God owns him by a particular providence. He decreed the thing, and it was established to him, Job xxii. 28. According to his faith, so was it unto him. The answer to this prayer was, (1.) Speedy—*before he had made an end of speaking* (v. 15), as it is written (Isa. lxv. 24), *While they are yet speaking, I will hear.* Though we are backward to pray, God is forward to hear prayer. (2.) Satisfactory: the first that came to draw water was, and did, in every thing, according to his own heart. [1.] She was so well qualified that in all respects she answered the characters he wished for in the woman that was to be his master's wife, handsome and healthful, humble and industrious, very courteous and obliging to a stranger, and having all the marks of a good disposition. When she came to the well (v. 16), she went down and *filled her pitcher, and came up to* go home with it. She did not stand to gaze upon the strange man and his camels, but minded her business, and would not have been diverted from it but by an opportunity of doing good. She did not curiously nor confidently enter into discourse with him, but modestly answered him, with all the decorum that became her sex. What a degenerate age do we live in, in which appear all the instances of pride, luxury, and laziness, the reverse of Rebekah's character, whose daughters few are! Those instances of goodness which were then in honour are now in contempt. [2.] Providence so ordered it that

she did that which exactly answered to his sign, and was wonderfully the counterpart of his proposal: she not only gave him drink, but, which was more than could have been expected, she offered her services to give his camels drink, which was the very sign he proposed. Note, *First,* God, in his providence, does sometimes wonderfully own the prayer of faith, and gratify the innocent desires of his praying people, even in little things, that he may show the extent of his care, and may encourage them at all times to seek to him and trust in him; yet we must take heed of being over-bold in prescribing to God, lest the event should weaken our faith rather than strengthen it. *Secondly,* It is good to take all opportunities of showing a humble, courteous, charitable, disposition, because, some time or other, it may turn more to our honour and benefit than we think of; some hereby have entertained angels, and Rebekah hereby, quite beyond her expectation at this time, was brought into the line of Christ and the covenant. *Thirdly,* There may be a great deal of obliging kindness in that which costs but little : our Saviour has promised a reward for a cup of cold water, Matt. x. 42. *Fourthly,* The concurrence of providences and their minute circumstances, for the furtherance of our success in any business, ought to be particularly observed, with wonder and thankfulness, to the glory of God : *The man wondered, v.* 21. We have been wanting to ourselves, both in duty and in comfort, by neglecting to observe Providence. [3.] Upon enquiry he found, to his great satisfaction, that she was a near relation to his master, and that the family she was of was considerable, and able to give him entertainment, v. 23—25. Note, Providence sometimes wonderfully directs those that by faith and prayer seek direction from heaven in the choice of suitable yoke-fellows : happy marriages those are likely to be that are made in the fear of God; and these, we are sure, are made in heaven.

3. He acknowledges God in a particular thanksgiving. He first paid his respects to Rebekah, in gratitude for her civility (v. 22), obliging her with such ornaments and attire as a maid, especially a bride, cannot forget (Jer. ii. 32), which yet, we should think, ill suited the *pitcher of water ;* but the ear-rings and bracelets she sometimes wore did not make her think herself above the labours of a virtuous woman (Prov. xxxi. 13), who *works willingly with her hands ;* nor the services of a child, who, while *under age, differs nothing from a servant,* Gal. iv. 1. Having done this, he turns his wonder (v. 21) into worshipping: *Blessed be the Lord God of my master Abraham, v.* 26, 27. Observe here, (1.) He had prayed for good speed (v. 12), and now that he had sped well he gives thanks. Note, What we win by prayer we must wear with praise ; for mercies in answer to prayer lay us under particular obligations.

(2.) He had as yet but a comfortable prospect of mercy, and was not certain what the issue might prove; yet he gives thanks. Note, When God's favours are coming towards us we must meet them with our praises. (3.) He blesses God for success when he was negociating for his master. Note, We should be thankful for our friend's mercies as for our own. (4.) He gives thanks that, being in the way, at a loss what course to steer, the Lord had led him. Note, In doubtful cases, it is very comfortable to see God leading us, as he led Israel in the wilderness by the pillar of cloud and fire. (5.) He thinks himself very happy, and owns God in it, that he was led to the *house of his master's brethren*, those of them that had come out of Ur of the Chaldees, though they had not come to Canaan, but remained in Haran. They were not idolaters, but worshippers of the true God, and inclinable to the religion of Abraham's family. Note, God is to be acknowledged in providing suitable yoke-fellows, especially such as are agreeable in religion. (6.) He acknowledges that God, herein, had not left his master *destitute of his mercy and truth.* God had promised to build up Abraham's family, yet it seemed destitute of the benefit of that promise; but now Providence is working towards the accomplishing of it. Note, [1.] God's faithful ones, how destitute soever they may be of worldly comforts, shall never be left destitute of God's mercy and truth; for God's mercy is an inexhaustible fountain, and his truth an inviolable foundation. [2.] It adds much to the comfort of any blessing to see in it the continuance of God's mercy and truth.

29 And Rebekah had a brother, and his name *was* Laban: and Laban ran out unto the man, unto the well. 30 And it came to pass, when he saw the earring and bracelets upon his sister's hands, and when he heard the words of Rebekah his sister, saying, Thus spake the man unto me; that he came unto the man; and, behold, he stood by the camels at the well. 31 And he said, Come in, thou blessed of the LORD; wherefore standest thou without? for I have prepared the house, and room for the camels. 32 And the man came into the house: and he ungirded his camels, and gave straw and provender for the camels, and water to wash his feet, and the men's feet that *were.* with him. 33 And there was set *meat* before him to eat: but he said, I will not eat, until I have told mine errand. And he said, Speak on. 34 And he said, I *am* Abraham's servant. 35 And the

LORD hath blessed my master greatly; and he is become great: and he hath given him flocks, and herds, and silver, and gold, and menservants, and maidservants, and camels, and asses. 36 And Sarah my master's wife bare a son to my master when she was old: and unto him hath he given all that he hath. 37 And my master made me swear, saying, Thou shalt not take a wife to my son of the daughters or the Canaanites, in whose land I dwell: 38 But thou shalt go unto my father's house, and to my kindred, and take a wife unto my son. 39 And I said unto my master, Peradventure the woman will not follow me. 40 And he said unto me, The LORD, before whom I walk, will send his angel with thee, and prosper thy way; and thou shalt take a wife for my son of my kindred, and of my father's house: 41 Then shalt thou be clear from *this* my oath, when thou comest to my kindred; and if they give not thee *one*, thou shalt be clear from my oath. 42 And I came this day unto the well, and said, O LORD God of my master Abraham, if now thou do prosper my way which I go: 43 Behold, I stand by the well of water; and it shall come to pass, that when the virgin cometh forth to draw *water*, and I say to her, Give me, I pray thee, a little water of thy pitcher to drink; 44 And she say to me, Both drink thou, and I will also draw for thy camels: *let* the same *be* the woman whom the LORD hath appointed out for my master's son. 45 And before I had done speaking in mine heart, behold, Rebekah came forth with her pitcher on her shoulder; and she went down unto the well, and drew *water:* and I said unto her, Let me drink, I pray thee. 46 And she made haste, and let down her pitcher from her *shoulder*, and said, Drink, and I will give thy camels drink also: so I drank, and she made the camels drink also. 47 And I asked her, and said, Whose daughter *art* thou? And she said, The daughter of Bethuel, Nahor's son, whom Milcah bare unto him: and I put the earring upon her face, and the bracelets upon her hands.

48 And I bowed down my head, and worshipped the LORD, and blessed the LORD God of my master Abraham, which had led me in the right way to take my master's brother's daughter unto his son. 49 And now if ye will deal kindly and truly with my master, tell me: and if not, tell me; that I may turn to the right hand, or to the left. 50 Then Laban and Bethuel answered and said, The thing proceedeth from the LORD: we cannot speak unto thee-bad or good. 51 Behold, Rebekah *is* before thee, take *her*, and go, and let her be thy master's son's wife, as the LORD hath spoken. 52 And it came to pass, that, when Abraham's servant heard their words, he worshipped the LORD, *bowing himself* to the earth. 53 And the servant brought forth jewels of silver, and jewels of gold, and raiment, and gave *them* to Rebekah : he gave also to her brother and to her mother precious things.

We have here the making up of the marriage between Isaac and Rebekah. It is related very largely and particularly, even to the minute circumstances, which, we should think, might have been spared, while other things of great moment and mystery (as the story of Melchizedek) are related in few words. Thus God conceals that which is curious from the wise and prudent, reveals to babes that which is common and level to their capacity (Matt. xi. 25), and rules and *saves the world by the foolishness of preaching*, 1 Cor. i. 21. Thus also we are directed to take notice of God's providence in the little common occurrences of human life, and in them also to exercise our own prudence and other graces; for the scripture was not intended for the use of philosophers and statesmen only, but to make us all wise and virtuous in the conduct of ourselves and families. Here is,

I. The very kind reception given to Abraham's servant by Rebekah's relations. Her brother Laban went to invite and conduct him in, but not till he saw the *ear-rings and the bracelets upon his sister's hands, v.* 30. "O," thinks Laban, "here is a man that there is something to be got by, a man that is rich and generous; we will be sure to bid him welcome!" We know so much of Laban's character, by the following story, as to think that he would not have been so free of his entertainment if he had not hoped to be well paid for it, as he was, *v.* 53. Note, *A man's gift maketh room for him* (Prov. xviii. 16), *which way soever it turneth, it prospereth,*

Prov. xvii. 8. 1. The invitation was kind : *Come in, thou blessed of the Lord, v.* 31. They saw he was rich, and therefore pronounced him *blessed of the Lord ;* or, perhaps, because they heard from Rebekah (*v.* 28) of the gracious words which proceeded out of his mouth, they concluded him a good man, and therefore *blessed of the Lord*. Note, Those that are blessed of God should be welcome to us. It is good owning those whom God owns. 2. The entertainment was kind, *v.* 32, 33. Both the house and stable were well furnished, and Abraham's servant was invited to the free use of both. Particular care was taken of the camels ; for a *good man regardeth the life of his beast*, Prov. xii. 10. If the ox knows his owner to serve him, the owner should know his ox to provide for him that which is fitting for him.

II. The full account which he gave them of his errand, and the court he made to them for their consent respecting Rebekah. Observe,

1. How intent he was upon his business ; though he had come off a journey, and come to a good house, he would *not eat, till he had told his errand, v.* 33. Note, The doing of our work, and the fulfilling of our trusts, either for God or man, should be preferred by us before our necessary food: it was our Saviour's meat and drink, John iv. 34.

2. How ingenious he was in the management of it ; he approved himself, in this matter, both a prudent man and a man of integrity, faithful to his master by whom he was trusted, and just to those with whom he now treated.

(1.) He gives a short account of the state of his master's family, *v.* 34—36. He was welcome before, but we may suppose him doubly welcome when he said, *I am Abraham's servant*. Abraham's name, no doubt, was well known among them and respected, and we may suppose them not altogether ignorant of his state, for Abraham knew theirs, *ch.* xxii. 20—24. Two things he suggests, to recommend his proposal :—[1.] That his master Abraham, through the blessing of God, had a very good estate ; and, [2.] That he had settled it all upon Isaac, for whom he was now a suitor.

(2.) He tells them the charge his master had given him, to fetch a wife for his son from among his kindred, with the reason of it, *v.* 37, 38. Thus he insinuates a pleasing hint, that, though Abraham had removed to a country at so great a distance, yet he still retained the remembrance of his relations that he had left behind, and a respect for them. The highest degrees of divine affection must not divest us of natural affection. He likewise obviates an objection, That, if Isaac were deserving, he needed not send so far off for a wife : why did he not marry nearer home ? "For a good reason," says he; "my master's son must not match with a Canaanite." He further recommends his proposal, [1.] From the faith his master had that it would succeed, *v.* 40. Abraham took encouragement from the testimony of his conscience that he *walked before God* in a regular course of holy living, and thence inferred that God would prosper him; probably he refers to that covenant which God had made with him (*ch.* xvii. 1), *I am God, all-sufficient, walk before me.* Therefore, says he, *the God before whom I walk will send his angel.* Note, While we make conscience of our part of the covenant, we may take the comfort of God's part of it; and we should learn to apply general promises to particular cases, as there is occasion. [2.] From the care he himself had taken to preserve their liberty of giving or refusing their consent, as they should see cause, without incurring the guilt of perjury (*v.* 39—41), which showed him, in general, to be a cautious man, and particularly careful that their consent might not be forced, but be either free or not at all. (3.) He relates to them the wonderful concurrence of providences, to countenance and further the proposal, plainly showing the finger of God in it. [1.] He tells them how he had prayed for direction by a sign, *v.* 42—44. Note, It is good dealing with those who by prayer take God along with them in their dealings. [2.] How God had answered his prayer in the very letter of it. Though he did but *speak in his heart* (*v.* 45), which perhaps he mentions, lest it should be suspected that Rebekah had overheard his prayer and designedly humoured it. "No," says he, "I spoke *it in my heart*, so that none heard it but God, to whom thoughts are words, and from him the answer came," *v.* 46, 47. [3.] How he had immediately acknowledged God's goodness to him therein, *leading him,* as he here expresses it, *in the right way.* Note, God's way is always the *right way* (Ps. cvii. 7), and those are well led whom he leads.

(4.) He fairly refers the matter to their consideration, and waits their decision (*v.* 49): "*If you will deal kindly and truly with my master,* well and good: if you will be sincerely kind, you will accept the proposal, and I have what I came for; if not, do not hold me in suspense." Note, Those who deal fairly have reason to expect fair dealing.

(5.) They freely and cheerfully close with the proposal upon a very good principle (*v.* 50): "*The thing proceedeth from the Lord,* Providence smiles upon it, and we have nothing to say against it." They do not object distance of place, Abraham's forsaking them, or his having no land in possession, but personal estate only: they do not question the truth of what this man said; but, [1.] They trust much to his integrity. It were well if honesty did so universally prevail among men that it might be as much an act of prudence as it is of good nature to take a man's word. [2.] They trust more to God's providence, and therefore by silence give consent, because it appears to be directed

150

and disposed by Infinite Wisdom. Note, A marriage is then likely to be comfortable when it appears to proceed from the Lord.

(6.) Abraham's servant makes a thankful acknowledgment of the good success he had met with, [1.] To God: *He worshipped the Lord, v.* 52. Observe, *First,* As his good success went on, he went on to bless God. Those that *pray without ceasing* should *in every thing give thanks,* and own God in every step of mercy. *Secondly,* God sent his angel before him, and so gave him success, *v.* 7, 40. But when he has the desired success, he worships God, not the angel. Whatever benefit we have by the ministration of angels, all the glory must be given to the Lord of the angels, Rev. xxii. 9. [2.] He pays his respects to the family also, and particularly to the bride, *v.* 53. He presented her, and her mother, and brother, with many precious things, both to give a real proof of his master's riches and generosity and in gratitude for their civility to him, and further to ingratiate himself with them.

54 And they did eat and drink, he and the men that *were* with him, and tarried all night; and they rose up in the morning, and he said, Send me away unto my master. 55 And her brother and her mother said, Let the damsel abide with us *a few* days, at the least ten; after that she shall go. 56 And he said unto them, Hinder me not, seeing the LORD hath prospered my way; send me away that I may go to my master. 57 And they said, We will call the damsel, and enquire at her mouth. 58 And they called Rebekah, and said unto her, Wilt thou go with this man? And she said, I will go. 59 And they sent away Rebekah their sister, and her nurse, and Abraham's servant, and his men. 60 And they blessed Rebekah, and said unto her, Thou *art* our sister, be thou *the mother* of thousands of millions, and let thy seed possess the gate of those which hate them. 61 And Rebekah arose, and her damsels, and they rode upon the camels, and followed the man: and the servant took Rebekah, and went his way.

Rebekah is here taking leave of her father's house; and 1. Abraham's servant presses for a dismission. Though he and his company were very welcome, and very cheerful there, yet he said, *Send me away* (*v.* 54), and again, *v.* 56. He knew his master would expect him home with some impatience; he had business to do at home which wanted **him,** and therefore, as one that preferred his work before his pleasure, he was for hastening home. Note, Lingering and loitering no way become a wise and good man; when we have despatched our business abroad we must not delay our return to our business at home, nor be longer from it than needs must; for as a bird that *wanders from her nest so is he that wanders from his place,* Prov. xxvii. 8. 2. Rebekah's relations, from natural affection and according to the usual expression of kindness in that case, solicit for her stay some time among them, *v.* 55. They could not think of parting with her on a sudden, especially as she was about to remove so far off and it was not likely that they would ever see one another again: *Let her stay a few days, at least ten,* which makes it as reasonable a request as the reading in the margin seems to make it unreasonable, *a year,* or *at least ten months.* They had consented to the marriage, and yet were loth to part with her. Note, It is an instance of the vanity of this world that there is nothing in it so agreeable but it has its alloy. *Nulla est sincera voluptas—There is no unmingled pleasure.* They were pleased that they had matched a daughter of their family so well, and yet, when it came to the last, it was with great reluctance that they sent her away. 3. Rebekah herself determined the matter. To her they appealed, as it was fit they should (*v.* 57): *Call the damsel* (who had retired to her apartment with a modest silence) and *enquire at her mouth.* Note, As children ought not to marry without their parents' consent, so parents ought not to marry them without their own. Before the matter is resolved on, "Ask at the damsel's mouth;" she is a party principally concerned, and therefore ought to be principally consulted. Rebekah consented, not only to go, but to go immediately: *I will go, v.* 58. We may hope that the notice she had taken of the servant's piety and devotion gave her such an idea of the prevalence of religion and godliness in the family she was to go to as made her desirous to hasten thither, and willing to forget her own people and her father's house, where religion had not so much the ascendant. 4. Hereupon she is sent away with Abraham's servant; not, as we may suppose, the very next day after, but very quickly: her friends see that she has a good heart on it, and so they dismiss her, (1.) With suitable attendants— her *nurse* (*v.* 59), her *damsels, v.* 61. It seems, then, that when she went to the well for water it was not because she had not servants at command, but because she took a pleasure in works of humble industry. Now that she was going among strangers, it was fit she should take those with her with whom she was acquainted. Here is nothing said of her portion. Her personal merits were a portion in her, she needed none with her, nor did that ever come into the treaty of marriage. (2.) With hearty good wishes: *They blessed Re-*

bekah, v. 60. Note, When our relations are entering into a new condition, we ought by prayer to recommend them to the blessing and grace of God. Now that she was going to be a wife, they prayed that she might be a mother both of a numerous and of a victorious progeny. Perhaps Abraham's servant had told them of the promise God had lately made to his master, which, it is likely, Abraham acquainted his household with, that God *would multiply his seed as the stars of heaven, and that they should possess the gate of their enemies* (*ch.* xxii. 17), to which promise they had an eye in this blessing, *Be thou the mother* of that seed.

62 And Isaac came from the way of the well Lahai-roi; for he dwelt in the south country. 63 And Isaac went out to meditate in the field at the eventide: and he lifted up his eyes, and saw, and, behold, the camels *were* coming. 64 And Rebekah lifted up her eyes, and when she saw Isaac, she lighted off the camel. 65 For she *had* said unto the servant, What man *is* this that walketh in the field to meet us? And the servant *had* said, It *is* my master: therefore she took a veil, and covered herself. 66 And the servant told Isaac all things that he had done. 67 And Isaac brought her into his mother Sarah's tent, and took Rebekah, and she became his wife; and he loved her: and Isaac was comforted after his mother's *death.*

Isaac and Rebekah are, at length, happily brought together. Observe,

I. Isaac was well employed when he met Rebekah: *He went out to meditate,* or pray, *in the field, at the even-tide, v.* 62, 63. Some think he expected the return of his servants about this time, and went out on purpose to meet them. But, it should seem, he went out on another errand, to take the advantage of a silent evening and a solitary field for meditation and prayer, those divine exercises by which we converse with God and our own hearts. Note, 1. Holy souls love retirement. It will do us good to be often left alone, walking alone and sitting alone; and, if we have the art of improving solitude, we shall find we are never less alone than when alone. 2. Meditation and prayer ought to be both our business and our delight when we are alone; while we have a God, a Christ, and a heaven, to acquaint ourselves with, and to secure our interest in, we need not want matter either for meditation or prayer, which, if they go together, will mutually befriend each other. 3. Our walks in the field are then truly pleasant when in them we apply ourselves to meditation and prayer. We there have a free and open prospect of the heavens above us and the earth around us, and the host and riches of both, by the view of which we should be led to the contemplation of the Maker and owner of all. 4. The exercises of devotion should be the refreshment and entertainment of the evening, to relieve us from the fatigue occasioned by the care and business of the day, and to prepare us for the repose and sleep of the night. 5. Merciful providences are then doubly comfortable when they find us well employed and in the way of our duty. Some think Isaac was now praying for good success in this affair that was depending, and meditating upon that which was proper to encourage his hope in God concerning it; and now, when he sets himself, as it were, upon his watchtower, to see what God would answer him, as the prophet (Hab. ii. 1), *he sees the camels coming.* Sometimes God sends in the mercy prayed for immediately, Acts xii. 12.

II. Rebekah behaved herself very becomingly, when she met Isaac: understanding who he was, she *alighted off her camel* (*v.* 64), and *took a veil, and covered herself* (*v.* 65), in token of humility, modesty, and subjection. She did not reproach Isaac for not coming himself to fetch her, or, at least, to meet her a day's journey or two, did not complain of the tediousness of her journey, or the difficulty of leaving her relations, to come into a strange place; but, having seen Providence going before her in the affair, she accommodates herself with cheerfulness to her new relation. Those that by faith are espoused to Christ, and would be presented as chaste virgins to him, must, in conformity to his example, humble themselves, as Rebekah, who alighted when she saw Isaac on foot, and must put themselves into subjection to him who is their head (Eph. v. 24), as Rebekah, signifying it by the veil she put on, 1 Cor. xi. 10.

III. They were brought together (probably after some further acquaintance), to their mutual comfort, *v.* 67. Observe here, 1. What an affectionate son he was to his mother: it was about three years since her death, and yet he was not, till now, comforted concerning it; the wound which that affliction gave to his tender spirit bled so long, and was never healed till God brought him into this new relation. Thus crosses and comforts are balances to each other (Eccl. vii. 14), and help to keep the scale even. 2. What an affectionate husband he was to his wife. Note, Those that have approved themselves well in one relation, it may be hoped, will do so in another: *She became his wife, and he loved her;* there was all the reason in the world why he should, for so *ought men to love their wives even as themselves.* The duty of the relation is then done, and the comfort of the relation is then enjoyed, when mutual love governs; for *there the Lord commands the blessing.*
152

CHAP. XXV.

The sacred historian, in this chapter, I. Takes his leave of Abraham, with an account, 1. Of his children by another wife, ver. 1—4. 2. Of his last will and testament, ver. 5, 6. 3. Of his age, death, and burial, ver. 7—10. II. He takes his leave of Ishmael, with a short account, 1. Of his children, ver. 12—16. 2. Of his age and death, ver. 17, 18. III. He enters upon the history of Isaac. 1. His prosperity, ver. 11. 2. The conception and birth of his two sons, with the oracle of God concerning them, ver. 19—26. 3. Their different characters, ver. 27, 28. 4. Esau's selling his birthright to Jacob, ver. 29—34.

THEN again Abraham took a wife, and her name *was* Keturah. 2 And she bare him Zimran, and Jokshan, and Medan, and Midian, and Ishbak, and Shuah. 3 And Jokshan begat Sheba, and Dedan. And the sons of Dedan were Asshurim, and Letushim, and Leummim. 4 And the sons of Midian; Ephah, and Epher, and Hanoch, and Abidah, and Eldaah. All these were the children of Keturah. 5 And Abraham gave all that he had unto Isaac. 6 But unto the sons of the concubines, which Abraham had, Abraham gave gifts, and sent them away from Isaac his son, while he yet lived, eastward, unto the east country. 7 And these *are* the days of the years of Abraham's life which he lived, a hundred threescore and fifteen years. 8 Then Abraham gave up the ghost, and died in a good old age, an old man, and full of *years;* and was gathered to his people. 9 And his sons Isaac and Ishmael buried him in the cave of Machpelah, in the field of Ephron the son of Zohar the Hittite, which *is* before Mamre; 10 The field which Abraham purchased of the sons of Heth : there was Abraham buried, and Sarah his wife.

Abraham lived, after the marriage of Isaac, thirty-five years, and all that is recorded concerning him during that time lies here in a very few verses. We hear no more of God's extraordinary appearances to him or trials of him; for all the days, even of the best and greatest saints, are not eminent days, some slide on silently, and neither come nor go with observation; such were these last days of Abraham. We have here,

I. An account of his children by Keturah, another wife whom he married after the death of Sarah. He had buried Sarah and married Isaac, the two dear companions of his life, and was now solitary. He wanted a nurse, his family wanted a governess, and it was not good for him to be thus alone. He therefore marries Keturah, probably the chief of his maid-servants, born in his house or bought with money. Marriage is not forbidden to old age. By her he had six sons, in whom the promise made to Abraham concerning the great increase of his posterity was in part fulfilled, which, it is likely, he had an eye to in this marriage. The strength he received by the promise still remained in him, to show how much the virtue of the promise exceeds the power of nature.

II. The disposition which Abraham made of his estate, *v.* 5, 6. After the birth of these sons, he set his house in order, with prudence and justice. 1. He made Isaac his heir, as he was bound to do, in justice to Sarah his first and principal wife, and to Rebekah who married Isaac upon the assurance of it, *ch.* xxiv. 36. In this *all*, which he settled upon Isaac, are perhaps included the promise of the land of Canaan, and the entail of the covenant. Or, God having already made him the heir of the promise, Abraham therefore made him heir of his estate. Our affection and gifts should attend God's. 2. He gave portions to the rest of his children, both to Ishmael, though at first he was sent empty away, and to his sons by Keturah. It was justice to provide for them; parents that do not imitate him in this are worse than infidels. It was prudence to settle them in places distant from Isaac, that they might not pretend to divide the inheritance with him, nor be in any way a care or expense to him. Observe, He did this *while he yet lived*, lest it should not be done, or not so well done, afterwards. Note, In many cases it is wisdom for men to make their own hands their executors, and what they find to do to do it while they live, as far as they can. These *sons of the concubines* were sent into the country that lay east from Canaan, and their posterity were called *the children of the east*, famous for their numbers, Judg. vi. 5, 33. Their great increase was the fruit of the promise made to Abraham, that God would multiply his seed. God, in dispensing his blessings, does as Abraham did ; common blessings he gives to the children of this world, as to the sons of the bond-woman, but covenant-blessings he reserves for the heirs of promise. All that he has is theirs, for they are his Isaacs, from whom the rest shall be for ever separated.

III. The age and death of Abraham, *v.* 7, 8. He lived 175 years, just 100 years after he came to Canaan ; so long he was a sojourner in a strange country. Though he lived long and lived well, though he did good and could ill be spared, yet he died at last. Observe how his death is here described. 1. He *gave up the ghost.* His life was not extorted from him, but he cheerfully resigned it ; into the hands of the Father of spirits he committed his spirit. 2. He *died in a good old age, an old man ;* so God had promised him. His death was his discharge from the burdens of his age : an old man would not *so* live always. It was also the crown of the glory of his old age. 3. He was *full of years*, or full of *life* (as it might be supplied), including all the conveniences and comforts of life. He did

not live till the world was weary of him, but till he was weary of the world ; he had had enough of it, and desired no more. *Vixi quantum satis est—I have lived long enough.* A good man, though he should not die old, dies full of days, satisfied with living here, and longing to live in a better place. 4. He *was gathered to his people.* His body was gathered to the congregation of the dead, and his soul to the congregation of the blessed. Note, Death gathers us to our people. Those that are our people while we live, whether the people of God or the children of this world, are the people to whom death will gather us.

IV. His burial, *v.* 9, 10. Here is nothing recorded of the pomp or ceremony of his funeral ; only we are told, 1. Who buried him : *His sons Isaac and Ishmael.* It was the last office of respect they had to pay to their good father. Some distance there had formerly been between Isaac and Ishmael ; but it seems either that Abraham had himself brought them together while he lived, or at least that his death reconciled them. 2. Where they buried him : in his own burying-place, which he had purchased, and in which he had buried Sarah. Note, Those that in life have been very dear to each other may not only innocently, but laudably, desire to be buried together, that in their deaths they may not be divided, and in token of their hopes of rising together.

11 And it came to pass after the death of Abraham, that God blessed his son Isaac ; and Isaac dwelt by the well Lahai-roi. 12 Now these *are* the generations of Ishmael, Abraham's son, whom Hagar the Egyptian, Sarah's handmaid, bare unto Abraham : 13 And these *are* the names of the sons of Ishmael, by their names, according to their generations : the firstborn of Ishmael, Nebajoth ; and Kedar, and Adbeel, and Mibsam, 14 And Mishma, and Dumah, and Massa, 15 Hadar, and Tema, Jetur, Naphish, and Kedemah : 16 These *are* the sons of Ishmael, and these *are* their names, by their towns, and by their castles ; twelve princes according to their nations. 17 And these *are* the years of the life of Ishmael, a hundred and thirty and seven years : and he gave up the ghost and died ; and was gathered unto his people. 18 And they dwelt from Havilah unto Shur, that *is* before Egypt, as thou goest toward Assyria : *and* he died in the presence of all his brethren.

Immediately after the account of Abraham's death, Moses begins the story of Isaac (*v.* 11), and tells us where he dwelt and how remarkably God blessed him. Note, The blessing of Abraham did not die with him, but survived to all the children of the promise. But he presently digresses from the story of Isaac, to give a short account of Ishmael, forasmuch as he also was a son of Abraham, and God had made some promises concerning him, which it was requisite we should know the accomplishment of. Observe here what is said, 1. Concerning his children. He had twelve sons, *twelve princes* they are called (*v.* 16), heads of families, which in process of time became nations, distinct tribes, numerous and very considerable. They peopled a very large continent, that lay between Egypt and Assyria, called *Arabia.* The names of his twelve sons are recorded. Midian and Kedar we often read of in scripture. And some very good expositors have taken notice of the signification of those three names which are put together (*v.* 14), as containing good advice to us all, *Mishma, Dumah,* and *Massa,* that is, *hear, keep silence,* and *bear;* we have them together in the same order, Jam. i. 19, *Be swift to hear, slow to speak, slow to wrath.* The posterity of Ishmael had not only tents in the fields, wherein they grew rich in times of peace; but they had towns and castles (*v.* 16), wherein they fortified themselves in time of war. Now the number and strength of this family were the fruit of the promise made to Hagar concerning Ishmael (*ch.* xvi. 10), and to Abraham, *ch.* xvii. 20 and xxi. 13. Note, Many that are strangers to the covenants of promise are yet blessed with outward prosperity for the sake of their godly ancestors. *Wealth and riches shall be in their house.* 2. Concerning himself. Here is an account of his age: He *lived* 137 *years* (*v.* 17), which is recorded to show the efficacy of Abraham's prayer for him (*ch.* xvii. 18), *O that Ishmael might live before thee!* Here is also an account of his death; he too *was gathered to his people;* but it is not said that he was *full of days,* though he lived to so great an age: he was not so weary of the world, nor so willing to leave it, as his good father was. Those words, *he fell in the presence of all his brethren,* whether they mean, as we take them, *he died,* or, as others, *his lot fell,* are designed to show the fulfilling of that word to Hagar (*ch.* xvi. 12), *He shall dwell in the presence of all his brethren,* that is, he shall flourish and be eminent among them, and shall hold his own to the last. Or he died with his friends about him, which is comfortable.

19 And these *are* the generations of Isaac, Abraham's son : Abraham begat Isaac : 20 And Isaac was forty years old when he took Rebekah to wife, the daughter of Bethuel the Syrian of Padan-aram, the sister to Laban the Syrian. 21 And Isaac in-

treated the LORD for his wife, because she *was* barren : and the LORD was intreated of him, and Rebekah his wife conceived. 22 And the children struggled together within her; and she said, If *it be* so, why *am* I thus ? And she went to inquire of the LORD. 23 And the LORD said unto her, Two nations *are* in thy womb, and two manner of people shall be separated from thy bowels; and *the one* people shall be stronger than *the other* people; and the elder shall serve the younger. 24 And when her days to be delivered were fulfilled, behold, *there were* twins in her womb. 25 And the first came out red, all over like a hairy garment; and they called his name Esau. 26 And after that came his brother out, and his hand took hold on Esau's heel; and his name was called Jacob : and Isaac *was* threescore years old when she bare them. 27 And the boys grew : and Esau was a cunning hunter, a man of the field ; and Jacob *was* a plain man, dwelling in tents. 28 And Isaac loved Esau, because he did eat of *his* venison : but Rebekah loved Jacob.

We have here an account of the birth of Jacob and Esau, the twin sons of Isaac and Rebekah : their entrance into the world was (which is not usual) one of the most considerable parts of their story ; nor is much related concerning Isaac but what had reference to his father while he lived and to his sons afterwards. For Isaac seems not to have been a man of action, nor much tried, but to have spent his days in quietness and silence. Now concerning Jacob and Esau we are here told,

I. That they were prayed for. Their parents, after they had been long childless, obtained them by prayer, *v.* 20, 21. *Isaac was forty years old when he was married;* though he was an only son, and the person from whom the promised seed was to come, yet he made no haste to marry. He was sixty years old when his sons were born (*v.* 26), so that, after he was married, he had no child for twenty years. Note, Though the accomplishment of God's promise is always sure, yet it is often slow, and seems to be crossed and contradicted by Providence, that the faith of believers may be tried, their patience exercised, and mercies long waited for may be the more welcome when they come. While this mercy was delayed, Isaac did not approach to a handmaid's bed, as Abraham had done, and Jacob afterwards; for he loved

Rebekah, *ch.* xxiv. 67. But, 1. He prayed: he entreated the Lord for his wife. Though God had promised to multiply his family, he prayed for its increase; for God's promises must not supersede, but encourage, our prayers, and be improved as the ground of our faith. Though he had prayed for this mercy very often, and had continued his supplication many years, and it was not granted, yet he did not leave off praying for it; for men ought always to pray, and not to faint (Luke xviii. 1), to pray without ceasing, and knock till the door be opened. He prayed *for* his wife; some read it *with* his wife. Note, Husbands and wives should pray together, which is intimated in the apostle's caution, that their *prayers be not hindered,* 1 Pet. iii. 7. The Jews have a tradition that Isaac, at length, took his wife with him to mount Moriah, where God had promised that he would multiply Abraham's seed (*ch.* xxii. 17), and there, in his prayer with her and for her, pleaded the promise made in that very place. 2. God heard his prayer, and was entreated of him. Note, Children are the gift of God. Those that continue instant in prayer, as Isaac did, shall find, at last, that they did not *seek in vain,* Isa. xlv. 19.

II. That they were prophesied of before they were born, and great mysteries were wrapped up in the prophecies which went before of them, *v.* 22, 23. Long had Isaac prayed for a son; and now his wife is with child of two, to recompense him for his long waiting. Thus God often outdoes our prayers, and gives more than we are able to ask or think. Now Rebekah being with child of these two sons, observe here,

1. How she was perplexed in her mind concerning her present case : *The children struggled together within her.* The commotion she felt was altogether extraordinary and made her very uneasy. Whether she was apprehensive that the birth would be her death, or whether she was weary of the intestine tumult, or whether she suspected it to be an ill omen, it seems she was ready to wish that either she had not been with child or that she might die immediately, and not bring forth such a struggling brood : *If it be so,* or, *since it is so, Why am I thus?* Before, the want of children was her trouble, now, the struggle of the children is no less so. Note, (1.) The comforts we are most desirous of are sometimes found to bring along with them more occasion of trouble and uneasiness than we thought of; vanity being written upon all things under the sun, God thus teaches us to read it. (2.) We are too apt to be discontented with our comforts, because of the uneasiness that attends them. We know not when we are pleased; we know neither how to want nor how to abound. This struggle between Jacob and Esau in the womb represents the struggle that is maintained between the kingdom of God and the kingdom of Satan, [1.] In

the world. The seed of the woman and the seed of the serpent have been contending ever since the enmity was put between them (*ch.* iii. 15), and this has occasioned a constant uneasiness among men. Christ himself came *to send fire on earth, and this division,* Luke xii. 49, 51. But let not this be an offence to us. A holy war is better than the peace of the devil's palace. [2.] In the hearts of believers. No sooner is Christ formed in the soul than immediately there begins a conflict between the flesh and spirit, Gal. v. 17. The stream is not turned without a mighty struggle, which yet ought not to discourage us. It is better to have a conflict with sin than tamely to submit to it.

2. What course she took for her relief: *She went to enquire of the Lord.* Some think Melchizedek was now consulted as an oracle, or perhaps some *Urim* or *Teraphim* were now used to enquire of God by, as afterwards in the breast-plate of judgment. Note, The word and prayer, by both which we now enquire of the Lord, give great relief to those that are upon any account perplexed. It is a great relief to the mind to spread our case before the Lord, and ask counsel at his mouth. *Go into the sanctuary,* Ps. lxxiii. 17.

3. The information given her, upon her enquiry, which expounded the mystery : *Two nations are in thy womb, v.* 23. She was now pregnant, not only with two children, but two nations, which should not only in their manners and dispositions greatly differ from each other, but in their interests clash and contend with each other; and the issue of the contest should be that the elder should serve the younger, which was fulfilled in the subjection of the Edomites, for many ages, to the house of David, till they revolted, 2 Chron. xxi. 8. Observe here, (1.) God is a free agent in dispensing his grace; it is his prerogative to make a difference between those who have not as yet themselves done either good or evil. This the apostle infers hence, Rom. ix. 12. (2.) In the struggle between grace and corruption in the soul, grace, the younger, shall certainly get the upper hand at last.

III. That when they were born there was a great difference between them, which served to confirm what had been foretold (*v.* 23), was a presage of the accomplishment of it, and served greatly to illustrate the type.

1. There was a great difference in their bodies, *v.* 25. Esau, when he was born, was rough and hairy, as if he had been already a grown man, whence he had his name *Esau, made,* reared already. This was an indication of a very strong constitution, and gave cause to expect that he would be a very robust, daring, active man. But Jacob was smooth and tender as other children. Note, (1.) The difference of men's capacities, and consequently of their condition in the world, arises very much from the difference of their natural constitution; some are plainly designed by nature for activity and honour,

others as manifestly marked for obscurity. This instance of the divine sovereignty in the kingdom of providence may perhaps help to reconcile us to the doctrine of the divine sovereignty in the kingdom of grace. (2.) It is God's usual way to choose the weak things of the world, and to pass by the mighty, 1 Cor. i. 26, 27.

2. There was a manifest contest in their births. Esau, the stronger, came forth first; but Jacob's hand *took hold of his heel*, v. 26. This signified, (1.) Jacob's pursuit of the birthright and blessing; from the first, he reached forth to catch hold of it, and, if possible, to prevent his brother. (2.) His prevailing for it at last, that, in process of time, he should undermine his brother, and gain his point. This passage is referred to (Hos. xii. 8), and hence he had his name, *Jacob, a supplanter.*

3. They were very unlike in the temper of their minds, and the way of living they chose, v. 27. They soon appeared to be of very different dispositions. (1.) Esau was a man for this world. He was a man addicted to his sports, for he was a hunter; and a man who knew how to live by his wits, for he was a cunning hunter. Recreation was his business; he studied the art of it, and spent all his time in it. He never loved a book, nor cared for being within doors; but he was a man of the field, like Nimrod and Ishmael, all for the game, and never well but when he was upon the stretch in pursuit of it: in short, he set up for a gentleman and a soldier. (2.) Jacob was a man for the other world. He was not cut out for a statesman, nor did he affect to look great, but he was *a plain man, dwelling in tents*, an honest man that always meant well, and dealt fairly, that preferred the true delights of solitude and retirement to all the pretended pleasure of busy noisy sports: he dwelt in tents, [1.] As a shepherd. He was attached to that safe and silent employment of keeping sheep, to which also he bred up his children, *ch.* xlvi. 34. Or, [2.] As a student. He frequented the tents of Melchizedek, or Heber, as some understand it, to be taught by them divine things. And this was that son of Isaac on whom the covenant was entailed.

4. Their interest in the affections of their parents was likewise different. They had but these two children, and, it seems, one was the father's darling and the other the mother's, v. 28. (1.) Isaac, though he was not a stirring man himself (for when he went into the fields he went to meditate and pray, not to hunt), yet loved to have his son active. Esau knew how to please him, and showed a great respect for him, by treating him often with venison, which gained him the affections of the good old man, and won upon him more than one would have thought. (2.) Rebekah was mindful of the oracle of God, which had given the preference to Jacob, and therefore she preferred him in her love.

And, if it be lawful for parents to make a difference between their children upon any account, doubtless Rebekah was in the right, that loved him whom God loved.

29 And Jacob sod pottage : and Esau came from the field, and he *was* faint : 30 And Esau said to Jacob, Feed me, I pray thee, with that same red *pottage;* for I *am* faint : therefore was his name called Edom. 31 And Jacob said, Sell me this day thy birthright. 32 And Esau said, Behold, I *am* at the point to die: and what profit shall this birthright do to me ? 33 And Jacob said, Swear to me this day; and he sware unto him : and he sold his birthright unto Jacob. 34 Then Jacob gave Esau bread and pottage of lentiles ; and he did eat and drink, and rose up, and went his way : thus Esau despised *his* birthright.

We have here a bargain made between Jacob and Esau about the birthright, which was Esau's by providence but Jacob's by promise. It was a spiritual privilege, including the excellency of dignity and the excellency of power, as well as the double portion, *ch.* xlix. 3. It seemed to be such a birthright as had then the blessing annexed to it, and the entail of the promise. Now see,

I. Jacob's pious desire of the birthright, which yet he sought to obtain by indirect courses, not agreeable to his character as a plain man. It was not out of pride or ambition that he coveted the birthright, but with an eye to spiritual blessings, which he had got well acquainted with in his tents, while Esau had lost the scent of them in the field. For this he is to be commended, that he coveted earnestly the best gifts; yet in this he cannot be justified, that he took advantage of his brother's necessity to make him a very hard bargain (v. 31) : *Sell me this day thy birthright.* Probably there had formerly been some communication between them about this matter, and then it was not so great a surprise upon Esau as here it seems to be; and, it may be, Esau had sometimes spoken slightly of the birthright and its appurtenances, which encouraged Jacob to make this proposal to him. And, if so, Jacob is, in some measure, excusable in what he did to gain his point. Note, Plain men that have their conversation in simplicity and godly sincerity, and without worldly wisdom, are often found wisest of all for their souls and eternity. Those are wise indeed that are wise for another world. Jacob's wisdom appeared in two things :—1. He chose the fittest time, took the opportunity when it offered itself, and did not let it slip. 2. Having made the bargain, he made it sure, and got it confirmed by Esau's oath : *Swear to me this day, v. 33.* He took Esau when he was in the mind, and would not leave him a power of revocation. In a case of this nature, it is good to be sure.

II. Esau's profane contempt of the birthright, and the foolish sale he made of it. He is called *profane Esau* for it (Heb. xii. 16), because *for one morsel of meat he sold his birthright,* as dear a morsel as ever was eaten since the forbidden fruit; and he lived to regret it when it was too late. Never was there such a foolish bargain as this which Esau now made; and yet he valued himself upon his policy, and had the reputation of a cunning man, and perhaps had often bantered his brother Jacob as a weak and simple man. Note, There are those that are penny-wise and pound-foolish, cunning hunters that can out-wit others and draw them into their snares, and yet are themselves imposed upon by Satan's wiles and led captive by him at his will. Again, God often chooses the foolish things of the world, by them to confound the wise. Plain Jacob makes a fool of cunning Esau. Observe the instances of Esau's folly.

1. His appetite was very strong, *v.* 29, 30. Poor Jacob had got some bread and pottage (*v.* 34) for his dinner, and was sitting down to it contentedly enough, without venison, when Esau came from hunting, hungry and weary, and perhaps had caught nothing. And now Jacob's pottage pleased his eye better than ever his game had done. Give me (says he) some of *that red, that red,* as it is in the original; it suited his own colour (*v.* 25), and, in reproach to him for this, he was ever afterwards called *Edom, red.* Nay, it should seem, he was so faint that he could not feed himself, nor had he a servant at hand to help him, but entreats his brother to feed him. Note, (1.) Those that addict themselves to sport *weary themselves for very vanity,* Hab. ii. 13. They might do the most needful business, and gain the greatest advantages, with half the pains they take, and half the perils they run into, in pursuit of their foolish pleasures. (2.) Those that work with quietness are more constantly and comfortably provided for than those that hunt with noise: bread is not always to the wise, but those that trust in the Lord and do good, verily they shall be fed, fed with daily bread; not as Esau, sometimes feasting and sometimes fainting. (3.) The gratifying of the sensual appetite is that which ruins thousands of precious souls: surely, if Esau was hungry and faint, he might have got a meal's meat cheaper than at the expense of his birthright; but he was unaccountably fond of the colour of this pottage, and could not deny himself the satisfaction of a mess of it, whatever it cost him. Never better can come of it, when men's *hearts walk after their eyes* (Job xxxi. 7), and when they serve their own bellies: therefore look not thou upon the wine, or, as Esau, upon the pottage,

when it is red, when it gives that colour in the cup, in the dish, which is most inviting, Prov. xxiii. 31. If we use ourselves to deny ourselves, we break the force of most temptations.

2. His reasoning was very weak (*v.* 32): *Behold, I am at the point to die;* and, if he were, would nothing serve to keep him alive but this pottage? If the famine were now in the land (*ch.* xxvi. 1), as Dr. Lightfoot conjectures, we cannot suppose Isaac so poor, or Rebekah so bad a house-keeper, but that he might have been supplied with food convenient, other ways, and might have saved his birthright: but his appetite has the mastery of him; he is in a longing condition, nothing will please him but this *red* this *red pottage,* and, to palliate his desire, he pretends he is at the point to die. If it had been so, was it not better for him to die in honour than to live in disgrace, to die under a blessing than to live under a curse? The birthright was typical of spiritual privileges, those of the church of the first-born. Esau was now tried how he would value them, and he shows himself sensible only of present grievances; may he but get relief against them, he cares not for his birthright. Better principled was Naboth, who would lose his life rather than sell his vineyard, because his part in the earthly Canaan signified his part in the heavenly, 1 Kings xxi. 3. (1.) If we look on Esau's birthright as only a temporal advantage, what he said had something of truth in it, namely, that our worldly enjoyments, even those we are most fond of, will stand us in no stead in a dying hour (Ps. xlix. 6—8); they will not put by the stroke of death, nor ease the pangs nor remove the sting: yet Esau, who set up for a gentleman, should have had a greater and more noble spirit than to sell even such an honour so cheaply. (2.) But, being of a spiritual nature, his undervaluing it was the greatest profaneness imaginable. Note, It is egregious folly to part with our interest in God, and Christ, and heaven, for the riches, honours, and pleasures, of this world, as bad a bargain as his that sold a birthright for a dish of broth.

3. Repentance was hidden from his eyes (*v.* 34): *He did eat and drink,* pleased his palate, satisfied his cravings, congratulated himself on the good meal's meat he had had, and then carelessly rose up and went his way, without any serious reflections upon the bad bargain he had made, or any show of regret. Thus Esau despised his birthright; he used no means at all to get the bargain revoked, made no appeal to his father about it, nor proposed to his brother to compound the matter; but the bargain which his necessity had made (supposing it were so) his profaneness confirmed *ex post facto—after the deed;* and by his subsequent neglect and contempt he did, as it were, acknowledge a fine, and by justifying himself in what he

had done he put the bargain past recal. Note, People are ruined, not so much by doing what is amiss, as by doing it and not repenting of it, doing it and standing to it.

CHAP. XXVI.

In this chapter we have, I. Isaac in adversity, by reason of a famine in the land, which, 1. Obliges him to change his quarters, ver. 1. But, 2. God visits him with direction and comfort, ver. 2—5. 3. He foolishly denies his wife, being in distress, and is reproved for it by Abimelech, ver. 6—11. II. Isaac in prosperity, by the blessing of God upon him, ver. 12—14. And, 1. The Philistines were envious at him, ver. 14—17. 2. He continued industrious in his business, ver. 18—23. 3. God appeared to him, and encouraged him, and he devoutly acknowledged God, ver. 24, 25. 4. The Philistines, at length, made court to him, and made a covenant with him, ver. 26—33. 5. The disagreeable marriage of his son Esau was an alloy to the comfort of his prosperity, ver. 34, 35.

AND there was a famine in the land, beside the first famine that was in the days of Abraham. And Isaac went unto Abimelech king of the Philistines unto Gerar. 2 And the LORD appeared unto him, and said, Go not down into Egypt; dwell in the land which I shall tell thee of: 3 Sojourn in this land, and I will be with thee, and will bless thee; for unto thee, and unto thy seed, I will give all these countries, and I will perform the oath which I sware unto Abraham thy father; 4 And I will make thy seed to multiply as the stars of heaven, and will give unto thy seed all these countries; and in thy seed shall all the nations of the earth be blessed; 5 Because that Abraham obeyed my voice, and kept my charge, my commandments, my statutes, and my laws.

Here, I. God tried Isaac by his providence. Isaac had been trained up in a believing dependence upon the divine grant of the land of Canaan to him and his heirs; yet now there is *a famine in the land*, v. 1. What shall he think of the promise when the promised land will not find him bread? Is such a grant worth accepting, upon such terms, and after so long a time? Yes, Isaac will still cleave to the covenant; and the less valuable Canaan in itself seems to be the better he is taught to value it, 1. As a token of God's everlasting kindness to him; and, 2. As a type of heaven's everlasting blessedness. Note, The intrinsic worth of God's promises cannot be lessened in a believer's eye by any cross providences.

II. He directed him under this trial by his word. Isaac finds himself straitened by the scarcity of provisions. Somewhere he must go for supply; it should seem, he set out for Egypt, whither his father went in the like strait, but he takes Gerar in his way, full of thoughts, no doubt, which way he had best steer his course, till God graciously appeared to him, and determined him, abundantly to his satisfaction. 1. God bade him stay where he was, and *not go down into*

158

Egypt: Sojourn in this land, v. 2, 3. There was a famine in Jacob's days, and God bade him *go down into Egypt* (ch. xlvi. 3, 4), a famine in *Isaac's* days, and God bade him *not to go down*, a famine in Abraham's days, and God left him to his liberty, directing him neither way. This variety in the divine procedure (considering that Egypt was always a place of trial and exercise to God's people) some ground upon the different characters of these three patriarchs. Abraham was a man of very high attainments, and intimate communion with God; and to him all places and conditions were alike. Isaac was a very good man, but not cut out for hardship; therefore he is forbidden to go to Egypt. Jacob was inured to difficulties, strong and patient; and therefore he must go down into Egypt, that *the trial of his faith might be to praise, and honour, and glory.* Thus God proportions his people's trials to their strength. 2. He promised to be *with him, and bless him,* v. 3. As we may go any where with comfort when God's blessing goes with us, so we may stay any where contentedly if that blessing rest upon us. 3. He renewed the covenant with him, which had so often been made with Abraham,' repeating and ratifying the promises of the land of Canaan, a numerous issue, and the Messiah, v. 3, 4. Note, Those that must live by faith have need often to review, and repeat to themselves, the promises they are to live upon, especially when they are called to any instance of suffering or self-denial. 4. He recommended to him the good example of his father's obedience, as that which had preserved the entail of the covenant in his family (v. 5): " *Abraham obeyed my voice ;* do thou do so too, and the promise shall be sure to thee." Abraham's obedience is here celebrated, to his honour; for by it he obtained a good report both with God and men. A great variety of words is here used to express the divine will, to which Abraham was obedient *(my voice, my charge, my commandments, my statutes, and my laws),* which may intimate that Abraham's obedience was universal; he obeyed the original laws of nature, the revealed laws of divine worship, particularly that of circumcision, and all the extraordinary precepts God gave him, as that of quitting his country, and that (which some think is more especially referred to) of the offering up of his son, which Isaac himself had reason enough to remember. Note, Those only shall have the benefit and comfort of God's covenant with their godly parents that tread in the steps of their obedience.

6 And Isaac dwelt in Gerar: 7 And the men of the place asked *him* of his wife; and he said, She *is* my sister: for he feared to say, She *is* my wife; lest, *said he,* the men of the place should kill me for Rebekah; be-

cause she *was* fair to look upon. 8 And it came to pass, when he had been there a long time, that Abimelech king of the Philistines looked out at a window, and saw, and, behold, Isaac *was* sporting with Rebekah his wife. 9 And Abimelech called Isaac, and said, Behold, of a surety she *is* thy wife: and how saidst thou, She *is* my sister? And Isaac said unto him, Because I said, Lest I die for her. 10 And Abimelech said, What *is* this thou hast done unto us? one of the people might lightly have lien with thy wife, and thou shouldest have brought guiltiness upon us. 11 And Abimelech charged all *his* people, saying, He that toucheth this man or his wife shall surely be put to death.

Isaac had now laid aside all thoughts of going into Egypt, and, in obedience to the heavenly vision, sets up his staff in Gerar, the country in which he was born (*v.* 6), yet there he enters into temptation, the same temptation that his good father had been once and again surprised and overcome by, namely, to deny his wife, and to give out that she was his sister. Observe,

I. How he sinned, *v.* 7. Because his wife was handsome, he fancied the Philistines would find some way or other to take him off, that some of them might marry her; and therefore she must pass for his sister. It is an unaccountable thing that both these great and good men should be guilty of so strange a piece of dissimulation, by which they so much exposed both their own and their wives' reputation. But we see, 1. That very good men have sometimes been guilty of very great faults and follies. Let those therefore that stand take heed lest they fall, and those that have fallen not despair of being helped up again. 2. That there is an aptness in us to imitate even the weaknesses and infirmities of those we have a value for. We have need therefore to keep our foot, lest, while we aim to tread in the steps of good men, we sometimes tread in their by-steps.

II. How he was detected, and the cheat discovered, by the king himself. Abimelech (not the same that was in Abraham's days, *ch.* xx., for this was nearly 100 years after that, but this was the common name of the Philistine kings, as Cæsar of the Roman emperors) saw Isaac more familiar and pleasant with Rebekah than he knew he would be with his sister (*v.* 8): he saw him sporting with her, or *laughing ;* it is the same word with that from which Isaac had his name. He was *rejoicing with the wife of his youth*, Prov. v. 18. It becomes those in that relation to be pleasant with one another, as those that are pleased with one another.

Nowhere may a man more allow himself to be innocently merry than with his own wife and children. Abimelech charged him with the fraud (*v.* 9), showed him how frivolous his excuse was and what might have been the bad consequences of it (*v.* 10), and then, to convince him how groundless and unjust his jealousy of them was, took him and his family under his particular protection, forbidding any injury to be done to him or his wife upon pain of death, *v.* 11. Note, 1. A lying tongue is but for a moment. Truth is the daughter of time; and, in time, it will out. 2. One sin is often the inlet to many, and therefore the beginnings of sin ought to be avoided. 3. The sins of professors shame them before those that are without. 4. God can make those that are incensed against his people, though there may be some colour of cause for it, to know that it is at their peril if they do them any hurt. See Ps. cv. 14, 15.

12 Then Isaac sowed in that land, and received in the same year a hundredfold: and the Lord blessed him: 13 And the man waxed great, and went forward, and grew until he became very great: 14 For he had possession of flocks, and possession of herds, and great store of servants: and the Philistines envied him. 15 For all the wells which his father's servants had digged in the days of Abraham his father, the Philistines had stopped them, and filled them with earth. 16 And Abimelech said unto Isaac, Go from us; for thou art much mightier than we. 17 And Isaac departed thence, and pitched his tent in the valley of Gerar, and dwelt there. 18 And Isaac digged again the wells of water, which they had digged in the days of Abraham his father; for the Philistines had stopped them after the death of Abraham: and he called their names after the names by which his father had called them. 19 And Isaac's servants digged in the valley, and found there a well of springing water. 20 And the herdmen of Gerar did strive with Isaac's herdmen, saying, The water *is* our's: and he called the name of the well Esek; because they strove with him. 21 And they digged another well, and strove for that also: and he called the name of it Sitnah. 22 And he removed from thence, and digged another well; and for that they strove not: and he called the name of it Rehoboth; and he said, For now

the LORD hath made room for us, and we shall be fruitful in the land. 23 And he went up from thence to Beersheba. 24 And the LORD appeared unto him the same night, and said, I *am* the God of Abraham thy father: fear not, for I *am* with thee, and will bless thee, and multiply thy seed for my servant Abraham's sake. 25 And he builded an altar there, and called upon the name of the LORD, and pitched his tent there: and there Isaac's servants digged a well.

Here we have,

I. The tokens of God's good-will to Isaac. He *blessed him,* and prospered him, and made all that he had to thrive under his hands. 1. His corn multiplied strangely, *v.* 12. He had no land of his own, but took land of the Philistines, and sowed it ; and (be it observed for the encouragement of poor tenants, that occupy other people's lands, and are honest and industrious) God blessed him with a great increase. He reaped *a hundred fold ;* and there seems to be an emphasis laid upon the time : it was that *same year* when there was a famine in the land ; while others scarcely reaped at all, he reaped thus plentifully. See Isa. lxv. 13, *My servants shall eat, but you shall be hungry,* Ps. xxxvii. 19, *In the days of famine they shall be satisfied.* 2. His cattle also increased, *v.* 14. And then, 3. He had *great store of servants,* whom he employed and maintained. Note, *As goods are increased those are increased that eat them,* Eccl. v. 11.

II. The tokens of the Philistines' ill-will to him. They *envied him, v.* 14. It is an instance, 1. Of the vanity of the world that the more men have of it the more they are envied, and exposed to censure and injury. *Who can stand before envy ?* Prov. xxvii. 4. See Eccl. iv. 4. 2. Of the corruption of nature ; for that is a bad principle indeed which makes men *grieve at the good of others,* as if it must needs be ill with me because it is well with my neighbour. (1.) They had already shown their ill-will to his family, by stopping up the wells which his father had digged, *v.* 15. This was spitefully done. Because they had not flocks of their own to water at these wells, they would not leave them for the use of others ; so absurd a thing is malice. And it was perfidiously done, contrary to the covenant of friendship they had made with Abraham, *ch.* xxi. 31, 32. No bonds will hold ill-nature. (2.) They expelled him out of their country, *v.* 16, 17. The king of Gerar began to look upon him with a jealous eye. Isaac's house was like a court, and his riches and retinue eclipsed Abimelech's ; and therefore he must go further off. They were weary of his neighbourhood,

because they saw that the Lord blessed him; whereas, for that reason, they should the rather have courted his stay, that they also might be blessed for his sake. Isaac does not insist upon the bargain he had made with them for the lands he held, nor upon his occupying and improving them, nor does he offer to contest with them by force, though he had become very great, but very peaceably departs thence further from the royal city, and perhaps to a part of the country less fruitful. Note, We should deny ourselves both in our rights and in our conveniences, rather than quarrel : a wise and a good man will rather retire into obscurity, like Isaac here into a valley, than sit high to be the butt of envy and ill-will.

III. His constancy and continuance in his business still.

1. He kept up his husbandry, and continued industrious to find wells of water, and to fit them for his use, *v.* 18, &c. Though he had grown very rich, yet he was as solicitous as ever about the state of his flocks, and still looked well to his herds ; when men grow great, they must take heed of thinking themselves too big and too high for their business. Though he was driven from the conveniences he had had, and could not follow his husbandry with the same ease and advantage as before, yet he set himself to make the best of the country he had come into, which it is every man's prudence to do. Observe,

(1.) He opened the wells that his father had digged (*v.* 18), and out of respect to his father called them by the same names that he had given them. Note, In our searches after truth, that fountain of living water, it is good to make use of the discoveries of former ages, which have been clouded by the corruptions of later times. Enquire for the old way, the wells which our fathers digged, which the adversaries of truth have stopped up : *Ask thy elders, and they shall teach thee.*

(2.) His servants dug new wells, *v.* 19. Note, Though we must use the light of former ages, it does not therefore follow that we must rest in it, and make no advances. We must still be building upon their foundation, *running to and fro, that knowledge may be increased,* Dan. xii. 4.

(3.) In digging his wells he met with much opposition, *v.* 20, 21. Those that open the fountains of truth must expect contradiction. The first two wells which they dug were called *Esek* and *Sitnah, contention* and *hatred.* See here, [1.] What is the nature of worldly things ; they are make-bates and occasions of strife. [2.] What is often the lot even of the most quiet and peaceable men in this world ; those that avoid striving yet cannot avoid being striven with, Ps. cxx. 7. In this sense, Jeremiah was a *man of contention* (Jer. xv. 10), and Christ himself, though he is the prince of peace. [3.] What a mercy it is to have plenty of water, to have it

160

without striving for it. The more common this mercy is the more reason we have to be thankful for it.

(4.) At length he removed to a quiet settlement, cleaving to his peaceable principle, rather to fly than fight, and unwilling to dwell with those that hated peace, Ps. cxx. 6. He preferred quietness to victory. *He dug a well, and for this they strove not, v.* 22. Note, Those that follow peace, sooner or later, shall find peace ; those that study to be quiet seldom fail of being so. How unlike was Isaac to his brother Ishmael, who, right or wrong, would hold what he had, against all the world! *ch.* xvi. 12. And which of these would we be found the followers of? This well they called *Rehoboth, enlargements,* room enough : in the two former wells we may see what the earth is, *straitness* and *strife ;* men cannot thrive, for the throng of their neighbours. This well shows us what heaven is ; it is *enlargement* and *peace,* room enough there, for there are many mansions.

2. He continued firm to his religion, and kept up his communion with God. (1.) God graciously appeared to him, *v.* 24. When the Philistines expelled him, forced him to remove from place to place, and gave him continual molestation, then God visited him, and gave him fresh assurances of his favour. Note, When men are found false and unkind, we may comfort ourselves that God is faithful and gracious ; and his time to show himself so is when we are most disappointed in our expectations from men. When Isaac had come to Beer-sheba (*v.* 23) it is probable that it troubled him to think of his unsettled condition, and that he could not be suffered to stay long in a place ; and, in the multitude of these thoughts within him, that same night that he came weary and uneasy to Beer-sheba God brought him his comforts to delight his soul. Probably he was apprehensive that the Philistines would not let him rest there : *Fear not,* says God to him, *I am with thee, and will bless thee.* Those may remove with comfort that are sure of God's presence with them wherever they go. (2.) He was not wanting in his returns of duty tô God ; for *there he built an altar, and called upon the name of the Lord, v.* 25. Note, [1.] Wherever we go, we must take our religion along with us. Probably Isaac's altars and his religious worship gave offence to the Philistines, and provoked them to be the more troublesome to him ; yet he kept up his duty, whatever ill-will he might be exposed to by it. [2.] The comforts and encouragements God gives us by his word should excite and quicken us to every exercise of devotion by which God may be honoured and our intercourse with heaven maintained.

26 Then Abimelech went to him from Gerar, and Ahuzzath one of his friends, and Phichol the chief captain of his army. 27 And Isaac said unto them, Wherefore come ye to me, seeing ye hate me, and have sent me away from you? 28 And they said, We saw certainly that the LORD was with thee : and we said, Let there be now an oath betwixt us, *even* betwixt us and thee, and let us make a covenant with thee ; 29 That thou wilt do us no hurt, as we have not touched thee, and as we have done unto thee nothing but good, and have sent thee away in peace : thou *art* now the blessed of the LORD. 30 And he made them a feast, and they did eat and drink; 31 And they rose up betimes in the morning, and sware one to another : and Isaac sent them away, and they departed from him in peace. 32 And it came to pass the same day, that Isaac's servants came, and told him concerning the well which they had digged, and said unto him, We have found water. 33 And he called it Shebah : therefore the name of the city *is* Beer-sheba unto this day.

We have here the contests that had been between Isaac and the Philistines issuing in a happy peace and reconciliation.

I. Abimelech pays a friendly visit to Isaac, in token of the respect he had for him, *v.* 26. Note, *When a man's ways please the Lord he makes even his enemies to be at peace with him,* Prov. xvi. 7. King's hearts are in his hands, and when he pleases he can turn them to favour his people.

II. Isaac prudently and cautiously questions his sincerity in this visit, *v.* 27. Note, In settling friendships and correspondences, there is need of the wisdom of the serpent, as well as the innocence of the dove ; nor is it any transgression of the law of meekness and love plainly to signify our strong perception of injuries received, and to stand upon our guard in dealing with those that have acted unfairly.

III. Abimelech professes his sincerity, in this address to Isaac, and earnestly courts his friendship, *v.* 28, 29. Some suggest that Abimelech pressed for this league with him because he feared lest Isaac, growing rich, should, some time or other, avenge himself upon them for the injuries he had received. However, he professes to do it rather from a principle of love. 1. He makes the best of their behaviour towards him. Isaac complained they had *hated him, and sent him away.* No, said Abimelech, *we sent thee away in peace.* They turned him off from the land he held of them ; but they suffered him to take away his stock, and all his effects, with him. Note, The lessening of injuries is necessary to the preserving of friendship; for the aggravating of them exasperates and widens breaches. The unkindness done to us might have been worse. 2. He acknowledges the tokens of God's favour to him, and makes this the ground of their desire to be in league with him : *The Lord is with thee, and thou art the blessed of the Lord.* As if he had said, "Be persuaded to overlook and pass by the injuries offered thee; for God has abundantly made up to thee the damage thou receivedst." Note, Those whom God blesses and favours have reason enough to forgive those who hate them, since the worst enemy they have cannot do them any real hurt. Or, "For this reason we desire thy friendship, because *God is with thee.*" Note, It is good to be in covenant and communion with those who are in covenant and communion with God, 1 John i. 3; Zech. viii. 23. 3. He assures him that their present address to him was the result of mature deliberation : *We said, Let there be an oath between us.* Whatever some of his peevish envious subjects might mean otherwise, he and his prime-ministers of state, whom he had now brought with him, designed no other than a cordial friendship. Perhaps Abimelech had received, by tradition, the warning God gave to his predecessor not to hurt Abraham (*ch.* xx. 7), and this made him stand in such awe of Isaac, who appeared to be as much the favourite of Heaven as Abraham was.

IV. Isaac entertains him and his company, and enters into a league of friendship with him, *v.* 30, 31. Here see how generous the good man was, 1. In giving : *He made them a feast,* and bade them welcome. (2.) In forgiving. He did not insist upon the unkindnesses they had done him, but freely entered into a covenant of friendship with them, and bound himself never to do them any injury. Note, Religion teaches us to be neighbourly, and, as much as in us lies, to *live peaceably with all men.*

V. Providence smiled upon what Isaac did; for the same day that he made this covenant with Abimelech his servants brought him the tidings of a well of water they had found, *v.* 32, 33. He did not insist upon the restitution of the wells which the Philistines had unjustly taken from him, lest this should break off the treaty, but sat down silent under the injury; and, to recompense him for this, immediately he is enriched with a new well, which, because it suited so well to the occurence of the day, he called by an old name, *Beer-sheba, The well of the oath.*

34 And Esau was forty years old when he took to wife Judith the daughter of Beeri the Hittite, and Bashemath the daughter of Elon the Hittite : 35 Which were a grief of mind unto Isaac and to Rebekah.

Here is, 1. Esau's foolish marriage—foolish,

some think, in marrying two wives together, for which perhaps he is called a *fornicator* (Heb. xii. 16), or rather in marrying Canaanites, who were strangers to the blessing of Abraham, and subject to the curse of Noah, for which he is called *profane;* for hereby he intimated that he neither desired the blessing nor dreaded the curse of God. 2. The grief and trouble it created to his tender parents. (1.) It grieved them that he married without asking, or at least without taking, their advice and consent : see whose steps those children tread in who either contemn or contradict their parents in disposing of themselves. (2.) It grieved them that he married the daughters of Hittites, who had no religion among them; for Isaac remembered his father's care concerning him, that he should by no means marry a Canaanite. (3.) It should seem, the wives he married were provoking in their conduct towards Isaac and Rebekah; those children have little reason to expect the blessing of God who do that which is a grief of mind to their good parents.

CHAP. XXVII.

In this chapter we return to the typical story of the struggle between Esau and Jacob. Esau had profanely sold the birthright to Jacob; but Esau hopes he shall be never the poorer, nor Jacob the richer, for that bargain, while he preserves his interest in his father's affections, and so secures the blessing. Here therefore we find how he was justly punished for his contempt of the birthright (of which he foolishly deprived himself) with the loss of the blessing, of which Jacob fraudulently deprives him. Thus this story is explained, Heb. xii. 16, 17, " Because he sold the birthright, when he would have inherited the blessing he was rejected." For those that make light of the name and profession of religion, and throw them away for a trifle, thereby forfeit the powers and privileges of it. We have here, I. Isaac's purpose to entail the blessing upon Esau, ver. 1—5. II. Rebekah's plot to procure it for Jacob, ver. 6—17. III. Jacob's successful management of the plot, and his obtaining the blessing, ver. 18—29. IV. Esau's resentment of this, in which, 1. His great importunity with his father to obtain a blessing, ver. 30—40. 2. His great enmity to his brother for defrauding him of the first blessing, ver. 41, &c.

AND it came to pass, that when Isaac was old, and his eyes were dim, so that he could not see, he called Esau his eldest son, and said unto him, My son : and he said unto him, Behold, *here am* I. 2 And he said, Behold now, I am old, I know not the day of my death : 3 Now therefore take, I pray thee, thy weapons, thy quiver and thy bow, and go out to the field, and take me *some* venison ; 4 And make me savoury meat, such as I love, and bring *it* to me, that I may eat; that my soul may bless thee before I die. 5 And Rebekah heard when Isaac spake to Esau his son. And Esau went to the field to hunt *for* venison, *and* to bring *it.*

Here is, I. Isaac's design to make his will, and to declare Esau his heir. The promise of the Messiah and the land of Canaan was a great trust, first committed to Abraham, inclusive and typical of spiritual and eternal blessings; this, by divine direction, he transmitted to Isaac. Isaac, being now old, and not knowing, or not understanding, or not duly considering, the divine oracle concerning his two sons, that the elder should serve the younger, resolves to entail all the honour and power that were wrapped up in the promise upon Esau his eldest son. In this he was governed more by natural affection, and the common method of settlements, than he ought to have been, if he knew (as it is probable he did) the intimations God had given of his mind in this matter. Note, We are very apt to take our measures rather from our own reason than from divine revelation, and thereby often miss our way; we think the wise and learned, the mighty and noble, should inherit the promise; but God sees not as man sees. See 1 Sam. xvi. 6, 7.

II. The directions he gave to Esau, pursuant to this design. He calls him to him, *v.* 1. For Esau, though married, had not yet removed; and, though he had greatly grieved his parents by his marriage, yet they had not expelled him, but it seems were pretty well reconciled to him, and made the best of it. Note, Parents that are justly offended at their children yet must not be implacable towards them.

1. He tells him upon what considerations he resolved to do this now (*v.* 2): "*I am old,* and therefore must die shortly, yet *I know not the day of my death,* nor when I must die; I will therefore do that at this time which must be done,some time." Note, (1.) Old people should be reminded by the growing infirmities of age to do quickly, and with all the little might they have, what their hand finds to do. See Josh. xiii. 1. (2.) The consideration of the uncertainty of the time of our departure out of the world (about which God has wisely kept us in the dark) should quicken us to do the work of the day in its day. The heart and the house should both be set, and kept, in order, because *at such an hour as we think not the Son of man comes;* because we *know not the day of our death,* we are concerned to mind the business of life.

2. He bids him to get things ready for the solemnity of executing his last will and testament, by which he designed to make him his heir, *v.* 3, 4. Esau must go a hunting, and bring some venison, which his father will eat of, and then bless him. In this he designed, not so much the refreshment of his own spirits, that he might give the blessing in a lively manner, as it is commonly taken, but rather the receiving of a fresh instance of his son's filial duty and affection to him, before he bestowed this favour upon him. Perhaps Esau, since he had married, had brought his venison to his wives, and seldom to his father, as formerly (*ch.* xxv. 28), and therefore Isaac, before he would bless him, would have him show this piece of respect to him. Note, It is fit, if the *less be blessed of the greater,* that the greater should be served and honoured by the less He says, *That my soul may*

bless thee before I die. Note, (1.) Prayer is the work of the soul, and not of the lips only; as the soul must be employed in blessing God (Ps. ciii. 1), so it must be in blessing ourselves and others: the blessing will not come to the heart if it do not come from the heart. (2.) The work of life must be done before we die, for it cannot be done afterwards (Eccl. ix. 10); and it is very desirable, when we come to die, to have nothing else to do but to die. Isaac lived above forty years after this; let none therefore think that they shall die the sooner for making their wills and getting ready for death.

6 And Rebekah spake unto Jacob her son, saying, Behold, I heard thy father speak unto Esau thy brother, saying, 7 Bring me venison, and make me savoury meat, that I may eat, and bless thee before the LORD before my death. 8 Now therefore, my son, obey my voice according to that which I command thee. 9 Go now to the flock, and fetch me from thence two good kids of the goats; and I will make them savoury meat for thy father, such as he loveth : 10 And thou shalt bring *it* to thy father, that he may eat, and that he may bless thee before his death. 11 And Jacob said to Rebekah his mother, Behold, Esau my brother *is* a hairy man, and I *am* a smooth man : 12 My father peradventure will feel me, and I shall seem to him as a deceiver; and I shall bring a curse upon me, and not a blessing. 13 And his mother said unto him, Upon me *be* thy curse, my son : only obey my voice, and go fetch me *them.* 14 And he went, and fetched, and brought *them* to his mother : and his mother made savoury meat, such as his father loved. 15 And Rebekah took goodly raiment of her eldest son Esau, which *were* with her in the house, and put them upon Jacob her younger son : 16 And she put the skins of the kids of the goats upon his hands, and upon the smooth of his neck : 17 And she gave the savoury meat and the bread, which she had prepared, into the hand of her son Jacob.

Rebekah is here contriving to procure for Jacob the blessing which was designed for Esau ; and here,

I. The end was good, for she was directed in this intention by the oracle of God, by which she had been governed in dispensing her affections. God had said it should be so, that the elder should *serve the younger ;* and therefore Rebekah resolves it shall be so, and cannot bear to see her husband designing to thwart the oracle of God. But,

II. The means were bad, and no way justifiable. If it was not a wrong to Esau to deprive him of the blessing (he himself having forfeited it by selling the birthright), yet it was a wrong to Isaac, taking advantage of his infirmity, to impose upon him; it was a wrong to Jacob too, whom she taught to deceive, by putting a lie into his mouth, or at least by putting one into his right hand. It would likewise expose him to endless scruples about the blessing, if he should obtain it thus fraudulently, whether it would stand him or his in any stead, especially if his father should revoke it, upon the discovery of the cheat, and plead, as he might, that it was nulled by an *error personæ—a mistake of the person.* He himself also was aware of the danger, lest (*v.* 12), if he should miss of the blessing, as he might probably have done, he should bring upon himself his father's curse, which he dreaded above any thing; besides, he laid himself open to that divine curse which is pronounced upon him that *causeth the blind to wander out of the way,* Deut. xxvii. 18. If Rebekah, when she heard Isaac promise the blessing to Esau, had gone, at his return from hunting, to Isaac, and, with humility and seriousness, put him in remembrance of that which God had said concerning their sons,—if she further had shown him how Esau had forfeited the blessing both by selling his birthright and by marrying strange wives, it is probable that Isaac would have been prevailed upon knowingly and wittingly to confer the blessing upon Jacob, and needed not thus to have been cheated into it. This would have been honourable and laudable, and would have looked well in the history; but God left her to herself, to take this indirect course, that he might have the glory of bringing good out of evil, and of serving his own purposes by the sins and follies of men, and that we might have the satisfaction of knowing that, though there is so much wickedness and deceit in the world, God governs it according to his will, to his own praise. See Job xii. 16, *With him are strength and wisdom, the deceived and the deceiver are his.* Isaac had lost the sense of seeing, which, in this case, could not have been imposed upon, Providence having so admirably well ordered the difference of features that no two faces are exactly alike: conversation and commerce could scarcely be maintained if there were not such a variety. Therefore she endeavours to deceive, 1. His sense of tasting, by dressing some choice pieces of kid, seasoning them, serving them up, so as to make him believe they were venison : this it was no hard matter to do. See the folly of those that are nice and cu-

rious in their appetite, and take a pride in humouring it. It is easy to impose upon them with that which they pretend to despise and dislike, so little perhaps does it differ from that to which they give a decided preference. Solomon tells us that dainties are *deceitful meat ;* for it is possible for us to be deceived by them in more ways than one, Prov. xxiii. 32. 2. His sense of feeling and smelling. She put Esau's clothes upon Jacob, his best clothes, which, it might be supposed, Esau would put on, in token of joy and respect to his father, when he was to receive the blessing. Isaac knew these, by the stuff, shape, and smell, to be Esau's. If we would obtain a blessing from our heavenly Father, we must come for it in the garments of our elder brother, clothed with his righteousness, who is the first-born among many brethren. Lest the smoothness and softness of Jacob's hands and neck should betray him, she covered them, and probably part of his face, with the skins of the kids that were newly killed, *v.* 16. Esau was rough indeed when nothing less than these would serve to make Jacob like him. Those that affect to seem rough and rugged in their carriage put the beast upon the man, and really shame themselves, by thus disguising themselves. And, *lastly,* it was a very rash word which Rebekah spoke, when Jacob objected the danger of a curse : *Upon me be thy curse, my son, v.* 13. Christ indeed, who is mighty to save, because mighty to bear, has said, *Upon me be the curse, only obey my voice ;* he has borne the burden of the curse, the curse of the law, for all those that will take upon them the yoke of the command, the command of the gospel. But it is too daring for any creature to say, *Upon me be the curse,* unless it be that curse causeless which we are sure *shall not come,* Prov. xxvi. 2.

18 And he came unto his father, and said, My father: and he said, Here *am* I ; who *art* thou, my son? 19 And Jacob said unto his father, I *am* Esau thy firstborn; I have done according as thou badest me : arise, I pray thee, sit and eat of my venison, that thy soul may bless me. 20 And Isaac said unto his son, How *is it* that thou hast found *it* so quickly, my son ? And he said, Because the LORD thy God brought *it* to me. 21 And Isaac said unto Jacob, Come near, I pray thee, that I may feel thee, my son, whether thou *be* my very son Esau or not. 22 And Jacob went near unto Isaac his father; and he felt him, and said, The voice *is* Jacob's voice, but the hands *are* the hands of Esau. 23 And he discerned him not,

because his hands were hairy, as his brother Esau's hands : so he blessed him. 24 And he said, *Art* thou my very son Esau? And he said, I *am.* 25 And he said, Bring *it* near to me, and I will eat of my son's venison, that my soul may bless thee. And he brought *it* near to him, and he did eat : and he brought him wine, and he drank. 26 And his father Isaac said unto him, Come near now, and kiss me, my son. 27 And he came near, and kissed him : and he smelled the smell of his raiment, and blessed him, and said, See, the smell of my son *is* as the smell of a field which the Lord hath blessed : 28 Therefore God give thee of the dew of heaven, and the fatness of the earth, and plenty of corn and wine : 29 Let people serve thee, and nations bow down to thee : be lord over thy brethren, and let thy mother's sons bow down to thee : cursed *be* every one that curseth thee, and blessed *be* he that blesseth thee.

Observe here, I. The art and assurance with which Jacob managed this intrigue. Who would have thought that this plain man could have played his part so well in a design of this nature? His mother having put him in the way of it, and encouraged him in it, he dexterously applied himself to those methods which he had never accustomed himself to, but had always conceived an abhorrence of. Note, Lying is soon learnt. The psalmist speaks of those who, *as soon as they are born, speak lies,* Ps. lviii. 3 ; Jer. ix. 5. I wonder how honest Jacob could so readily turn his tongue to say (*v.* 19), *I am Esau thy first-born ;* nor do I see how the endeavour of some to bring him off with that equivocation, *I am made thy first-born,* namely by purchase, does him any service ; for when his father asked him (*v.* 24), *Art thou my very son Esau?* he said, *I am.* How could he say, *I have done as thou badest me,* when he had received no command from his father, but was doing as his mother bade him? How could he say, *Eat of my venison,* when he knew it came, not from the field, but from the fold? But especially I wonder how he could have the assurance to father it upon God, and to use his name in the cheat (*v.* 20): *The Lord thy God brought it to me.* Is this Jacob? Is this Israel indeed, without guile? It is certainly written, not for our imitation, but for our admonition. *Let him that thinks he stands take heed lest he fall.* Good men have sometimes failed in the exercise of those graces for which they have been most eminent.

II. The success of this management. Jacob with some difficulty gained his point, and obtained the blessing.
1. Isaac was at first dissatisfied, and would have discovered the fraud if he could have trusted his own ears ; for *the voice was Jacob's voice, v.* 22. Providence has ordered a strange variety of voices as well as faces, which is also of use to prevent our being imposed upon ; and the voice is a thing not easily disguised nor counterfeited. This may be alluded to to illustrate the character of a hypocrite. His voice is Jacob's voice, but his hands are Esau's. He speaks the language of a saint, but does the works of a sinner ; but the judgment will be, as here, by the hands.
2. At length he yielded to the power of the cheat, *because the hands were hairy* (*v.* 23), not considering how easy it was to counterfeit that circumstance ; and now Jacob carries it on dexterously, sets his venison before his father, and waits at table very officiously, till dinner is done, and the blessing comes to be pronounced in the close of this solemn feast. That which in some small degree extenuates the crime of Rebekah and Jacob is that the fraud was intended, not so much to hasten the fulfilling, as to prevent the thwarting, of the oracle of God: the blessing was just going to be put upon the wrong head, and they thought it was time to bestir themselves. Now let us see how Isaac gave Jacob his blessing, *v.* 26—29. (1.) He embraced him, in token of a particular affection to him. Those that are blessed of God are kissed with the kisses of his mouth, and they do, by love and loyalty, *kiss the Son,* Ps. ii. 12. (2.) He praised him. *He smelt the smell of his raiment, and said, See, the smell of my son is as the smell of a field which the Lord hath blessed,* that is, like that of the most fragrant flowers and spices. It appeared that God had blessed him, and therefore Isaac would bless him. (3.) He prayed for him, and therein prophesied concerning him. It is the duty of parents to pray for their children, and to bless them in the name of the Lord. And thus, as well as by their baptism, to do what they can to preserve and perpetuate the entail of the covenant in their families. But this was an extraordinary blessing ; and Providence so ordered it that Isaac should bestow it upon Jacob ignorantly and by mistake, that it might appear he was beholden to God for it, and not to Isaac. Three things Jacob is here blessed with :—[1.] Plenty (*v.* 28), heaven and earth concurring to make him rich. [2.] Power (*v.* 29), particularly dominion over his brethren, namely, Esau and his posterity. [3.] Prevalency with God, and a great interest in Heaven : " *Cursed be every one that curseth thee and blessed be he that blesseth thee.* Let God be a friend to all thy friends, and an enemy to all thy enemies." More is certainly comprised in this blessing than appears *prima facie*—at first sight. It must amount

to an entail of the promise of the Messiah, and of the church; this was, in the patriarchal dialect, *the blessing:* something spiritual, doubtless, is included in it. *First,* That from him should come the Messiah, who should have a sovereign dominion on earth. It was that top-branch of his family which people should serve and nations bow down to. See Num. xxiv. 19, *Out of Jacob shall come he that shall have dominion,* the *star* and *sceptre,* *v.* 17. Jacob's dominion over Esau was to be only typical of this, *ch.* xlix. 10. *Secondly,* That from him should come the church, which should be particularly owned and favoured by Heaven. It was part of the blessing of Abraham, when he was first called to be the father of the faithful (*ch.* xii. 3), *I will bless those that bless thee;* therefore, when Isaac afterwards confirmed the blessing to Jacob, he called it *the blessing of Abraham, ch.* xxviii. 4. Balaam explains this too, Num. xxiv. 9. Note, It is the best and most desirable blessing to stand in relation to Christ and his church, and to be interested in Christ's power and the church's favours.

30 And it came to pass, as soon as Isaac had made an end of blessing Jacob, and Jacob was yet scarce gone out from the presence of Isaac his father, that Esau his brother came in from his hunting. 31 And he also had made savoury meat, and brought it unto his father, and said unto his father, Let my father arise, and eat of his son's venison, that thy soul may bless me. 32 And Isaac his father said unto him, Who *art* thou? And he said, I *am* thy son, thy firstborn Esau. 33 And Isaac trembled very exceedingly, and said, Who? where *is* he that hath taken venison, and brought *it* me, and I have eaten of all before thou camest and have blessed him? yea, *and* he shall be blessed. 34 And when Esau heard the words of his father, he cried with a great and exceeding bitter cry, and said unto his father, Bless me, *even* me also, O my father. 35 And he said, Thy brother came with subtlety, and hath taken away thy blessing. 36 And he said, Is not he rightly named Jacob? for he hath supplanted me these two times: he took away my birthright; and, behold, now he hath taken away my blessing. And he said, Hast thou not reserved a blessing for me? 37 And Isaac answered and said unto Esau, Behold, I have made him thy lord, and all his bre-
166

thren have I given to him for servants; and with corn and wine have I sustained him: and what shall I do now unto thee, my son? 38 And Esau said unto his father, Hast thou but one blessing, my father? bless me, *even* me also, O my father. And Esau lifted up his voice, and wept. 39 And Isaac his father answered and said unto him, Behold, thy dwelling shall be the fatness of the earth, and of the dew of heaven from above; 40 And by thy sword shalt thou live, and shalt serve thy brother; and it shall come to pass when thou shalt have the dominion, that thou shalt break his yoke from off thy neck.

Here is, I. The covenant-blessing denied to Esau. He that made so light of the birthright *would now have inherited the blessing, but he was rejected, and found no place of repentance* in his father, *though he sought it carefully with tears,* Heb. xii. 17. Observe, 1. How carefully he sought it. He prepared the savoury meat, as his father had directed him, and then begged the blessing which his father had encouraged him to expect, *v.* 31. When he understood that Jacob had obtained it surreptitiously, he *cried with a great and exceedingly bitter cry, v.* 34. No man could have laid the disappointment more to heart than he did; he made his father's tent to ring with his grief, and again (*v.* 38) *lifted up his voice and wept.* Note, The day is coming when those that now make light of the blessings of the covenant, and sell their title to them for a thing of nought, will in vain be importunate for them. Those that will not so much as ask and seek now will knock shortly, and cry, Lord, Lord. Slighters of Christ will then be humble suitors to him. 2. How he was rejected. Isaac, when first made sensible of the imposition that had been practised on him, *trembled exceedingly, v.* 33. Those that follow the choice of their own affections, rather than the dictates of the divine will, involve themselves in such perplexities as these. But he soon recovers himself, and ratifies the blessing he had given to Jacob: *I have blessed him, and he shall be blessed;* he might, upon very plausible grounds, have recalled it, but now, at last, he is sensible that he was in an error when he designed it for Esau. Either himself recollecting the divine oracle, or rather having found himself more than ordinarily filled with the Holy Ghost when he gave the blessing to Jacob, he perceived that God did, as it were, say Amen to it. Now, (1.) Jacob was hereby confirmed in his possession of the blessing, and abundantly satisfied of the validity of it, though he obtained it fraudulently; hence too he had reason to hope that God graciously overlooked and pardoned his misconduct. (2.) Isaac hereby acquiesced in the will of God, though it contradicted his own expectation and affection. He had a mind to give Esau the blessing, but, when he perceived the will of God was otherwise, he submitted; and this he did *by faith* (Heb. xi. 20), as Abraham before him, when he had solicited for Ishmael. May not God do what he will with his own? (3.) Esau hereby was cut off from the expectation of that special blessing which he thought to have preserved to himself when he sold his birthright. We, by this instance, are taught, [1.] That *it is not of him that willeth, nor of him that runneth, but of God that showeth mercy*, Rom. ix. 16. The apostle seems to allude to this story. Esau had a good will to the blessing, and ran for it; but God that showed mercy designed it for Jacob, *that the purpose of God according to election might stand, v.* 11. The Jews, like Esau, hunted *after the law of righteousness* (*v.* 31), yet missed of the blessing of righteousness, *because they sought it by the works of the law* (*v.* 32); while the Gentiles, who, like Jacob, sought it by faith in the oracle of God, obtained it by force, with that violence which the kingdom of heaven suffers. See Matt. xi. 12. [2.] That those who undervalue their spiritual birthright, and can afford to sell it for a morsel of meat, forfeit spiritual blessings, and it is just with God to deny them those favours they were careless of. Those that will part with their wisdom and grace, with their faith and a good conscience, for the honours, wealth, or pleasures, of this world, however they may pretend a zeal for the blessing, have already judged themselves unworthy of it, and so shall their doom be. [3.] That those who lift up hands in wrath lift them up in vain. Esau, instead of repenting of his own folly, reproached his brother, unjustly charged him with taking away the birthright which he had fairly sold to him (*v.* 36), and conceived malice against him for what he had now done, *v.* 41. Those are not likely to speed in prayer who turn those resentments upon their brethren which they should turn upon themselves, and lay the blame of their miscarriages upon others, when they should take shame to themselves. [4.] That those who seek not till it is too late will be rejected. This was the ruin of Esau, he did not come in time. As there is an accepted time, a time when God will be found, so there is a time when he will not answer those that call upon him, because they neglected the appointed season. See Prov. i. 28. The time of God's patience and our probation will not last always; the day of grace will come to an end, and the door will be shut. Then many that now despise the blessing will seek it carefully; for then they will know how to value it, and will see themselves undone, for ever undone, without it, but to no purpose, Luke xiii. 25—27 O that we would there-

fore, in this our day, *know the things that belong to our peace!*

II. Here is a common blessing bestowed upon Esau.

1. This he desired: *Bless me also, v.* 34. *Hast thou not reserved a blessing for me? v.* 36. Note, (1.) The worst of men know how to wish well to themselves; and even those who profanely sell their birthright seem piously to desire the blessing. Faint desires of happiness, without a right choice of the end and a right use of the means, deceive many into their own ruin. Multitudes go to hell with their mouths full of good wishes. The desire of the slothful and unbelieving kills them. Many will seek to enter in, as Esau, who shall not be able, because they do not strive, Luke xiii. 24. (2.) It is the folly of most men that they are willing to take up with any good (Ps. iv. 6), as Esau here, who desired but a second-rate blessing, a- blessing separated from the birthright. Profane hearts think any blessing as good as that from God's oracle: *Hast thou but one?* As if he had said, " I will take up with any: though I have not the blessing of the church, yet let me have some blessing."

2. This he had; and let him make his best of it, *v.* 39, 40.

(1.) It was a good thing, and better than he deserved. It was promised him, [1.] That he should have a competent livelihood— *the fatness of the earth, and the dew of heaven.* Note, Those that come short of the blessings of the covenant may yet have a very good share of outward blessings. God gives good ground and good weather to many that reject his covenant, and have no part nor lot in it. [2.] That by degrees he should recover his liberty. If Jacob must rule (*v.* 29), Esau must serve; but he has this to comfort him, he shall *live by his sword.* He shall serve, but he shall not starve; and, at length, after much skirmishing, he shall break the yoke of bondage, and wear the marks of freedom. This was fulfilled (2 Kings viii. 20, 22) when the Edomites revolted.

(2.) Yet it was far short of Jacob's blessing. For him God had reserved some better thing. [1.] In Jacob's blessing *the dew of heaven* is put first, as that which he most valued, and desired, and depended upon; in Esau's *the fatness of the earth* is put first, for it was this that he had the first and principal regard to. [2.] Esau has these, but Jacob has them from God's hand: *God give thee the dew of heaven, v.* 28. It was enough to Esau to have the possession; but Jacob desired it by promise, and to have it from covenant-love. [3.] Jacob shall have dominion over his brethren: hence the Israelites often ruled over the Edomites. Esau shall have dominion, that is, he shall gain some power and interest, but shall never have dominion over his brother: we never find that the Jews were sold into the hands of the Edomites, or that they oppressed them. But the great difference in

167

that there is nothing in Esau's blessing that points at Christ, nothing that brings him or his into the church and covenant of God, without which the fatness of the earth, and the plunder of the field, will stand him in little stead. Thus Isaac by faith blessed them both according as their lot should be. Some observe that Jacob was blessed with a *kiss* (*v.* 27), so was not Esau.

41 And Esau hated Jacob because of the blessing wherewith his father blessed him: and Esau said in his heart, The days of mourning for my father are at hand; then will I slay my brother Jacob. 42 And these words of Esau her elder son were told to Rebekah: and she sent and called Jacob her younger son, and said unto him, Behold, thy brother Esau, as touching thee, doth comfort himself, *purposing* to kill thee. 43 Now therefore, my son, obey my voice; and arise, flee thou to Laban my brother to Haran; 44 And tarry with him a few days, until thy brother's fury turn away; 45 Until thy brother's anger turn away from thee, and he forget *that* which thou hast done to him: then I will send, and fetch thee from thence: why should I be deprived also of you both in one day? 46 And Rebekah said to Isaac, I am weary of my life because of the daughters of Heth: if Jacob take a wife of the daughters of Heth, such as these *which are* of the daughters of the land, what good shall my life do me?

Here is, I. The malice Esau bore to Jacob upon account of the blessing which he had obtained, *v.* 41. Thus he went in the way of Cain, who slew his brother because he had gained that acceptance with God of which he had rendered himself unworthy. Esau's hatred of Jacob was, 1. A causeless hatred. He hated him for no other reason but because his father blessed him and God loved him. Note, The happiness of saints is the envy of sinners. Whom Heaven blesses, hell curses. 2. It was a cruel hatred. Nothing less would satisfy him than to slay his brother. It is the blood of the saints that persecutors thirst after: *I will slay my brother.* How could he say that word without horror? How could he call him *brother*, and yet vow his death? Note, The rage of persecutors will not be tied up by any bonds, no, not the strongest and most sacred. 3. It was a politic hatred. He expected his father would soon die, and then titles must be tried and interests contested between the brothers, which would give him

168

a fair opportunity for revenge. He thinks it not enough to *live by his sword himself* (*v.* 40), unless his brother die by it. He is loth to grieve his father while he lives, and therefore puts off the intended murder till his death, not caring how much he then grieved his surviving mother. Note, (1.) Those are bad children to whom their good parents are a burden, and who, upon any account, long for the days of mourning for them. (2.) Bad men are long held in by external restraints from doing the mischief they would do, and so their wicked purposes come to nought. (3.) Those who think to defeat God's purposes will undoubtedly be disappointed themselves. Esau aimed to prevent Jacob, or his seed, from having the dominion, by taking away his life before he was married; but who can disannul what God has spoken? Men may fret at God's counsels, but cannot change them.

II. The method Rebekah took to prevent the mischief.

1. She gave Jacob warning of his danger, and advised him to withdraw for a while, and shift for his own safety. She tells him what she heard of Esau's design, that he comforted himself with the hope of an opportunity to kill his brother, *v.* 42. Would one think that such a bloody barbarous thought as this could be a comfort to a man? If Esau could have kept his design to himself his mother would not have suspected it; but men's impudence in sin is often their infatuation; and they cannot accomplish their wickedness because their rage is too violent to be concealed, and a bird of the air carries the voice. Observe here, (1.) What Rebekah feared—lest she *should be deprived of them both in one* day (*v.* 45), deprived, not only of the murdered, but of the murderer, who either by the magistrate, or by the immediate hand of God, would be sacrificed to justice, which she herself must acquiesce in, and not obstruct: or, if not so, yet thenceforward she would be deprived of all joy and comfort in him. Those that are lost to virtue are in a manner lost to all their friends. With what pleasure can a child be looked upon that can be looked upon as no other than a child of the devil? (2.) What Rebekah hoped—that, if Jacob for a while kept out of sight, the affront which his brother resented so fiercely would by degrees go out of mind. The strength of passions is weakened and taken off by the distances both of time and place. She promised herself that his brother's anger would turn away. Note, Yielding pacifies great offences; and even those that have a good cause, and God on their side, must yet use this with other prudent expedients for their own preservation.

2. She impressed Isaac with an apprehension of the necessity of Jacob's going among her relations upon another account, which was to take a wife, *v.* 46. She would not tell him of Esau's wicked design against the life of Jacob, lest it should trouble him; but pru-

dently took another way to gain her point. Isaac was as uneasy as she was at Esau's being unequally yoked with Hittites ; and therefore, with a very good colour of reason, she moves to have Jacob married to one that was better principled. Note, One miscarriage should serve as a warning to prevent another ; those are careless indeed that stumble twice at the same stone. Yet Rebekah seems to have expressed herself somewhat too warmly in the matter, when she said, *What good will my life do me if Jacob marry a Canaanite?* Thanks be to God, all our comfort is not lodged in one hand ; we may do the work of life, and enjoy the comforts of life, though every thing do not fall out to our mind, and though our relations be not in all respects agreeable to us. Perhaps Rebekah spoke with this concern because she saw it necessary, for the quickening of Isaac, to give speedy orders in this matter. Observe, Though Jacob was himself very towardly, and well fixed in his religion, yet he had need to be put out of the way of temptation. Even he was in danger both of following the bad example of his brother and of being drawn into a snare by it. We must not presume too far upon the wisdom and resolution, no, not of those children that are most hopeful and promising ; but care must be taken to keep them out of harm's way.

CHAP. XXVIII.

We have here, I. Jacob parting with his parents, to go to Padanaram ; the charge his father gave him (ver. 1, 2), the blessing he sent him away with (ver. 3, 4), his obedience to the orders given him (ver. 5, 10), and the influence this had upon Esau, ver. 6—9. II. Jacob meeting with God, and his communion with h.m by the way. And there, 1. his vision of the ladder, ver. 11, 12. 2. The gracious promises God made him, ver. 13—15. 3. The impression this made upon him, ver. 16.—19. 4. The vow he made to God, upon this occasion, ver. 20, &c.

AND Isaac called Jacob, and blessed him, and charged him, and said unto him, Thou shalt not take a wife of the daughters of Canaan. 2 Arise, go to Padan-aram, to the house of Bethuel thy mother's father ; and take thee a wife from thence of the daughters of Laban thy mother's brother. 3 And God Almighty bless thee, and make thee fruitful, and multiply thee, that thou mayest be a multitude of people ; 4 And give thee the blessing of Abraham, to thee, and to thy seed with thee ; that thou mayest inherit the land wherein thou art a stranger, which God gave unto Abraham. 5 And Isaac sent away Jacob : and he went to Padan-aram unto Laban, son of Bethuel the Syrian, the brother of Rebekah, Jacob's and Esau's mother.

Jacob had no sooner obtained the blessing than immediately he was forced to flee from his country ; and, as if it were not enough

that he was a stranger and sojourner there, he must go to be more so, and no better than an exile, in another country. Now *Jacob fled into Syria*, Hos. xii. 12. He was blessed with plenty of corn and wine, and yet he went away poor, was blessed with government, and yet went out to service, a hard service. This was, 1. Perhaps to correct him for his dealing fraudulently with his father. The blessing shall be confirmed to him, and yet he shall smart for the indirect course he took to obtain it. While there is such an alloy as there is of sin in our duties, we must expect an alloy of trouble in our comforts. However, 2. It was to teach us that those who inherit the blessing must expect persecution ; those who have peace in Christ shall have tribulation in the world, John xvi. 33. Being told of this before, we must not think it strange, and, being assured of a recompence hereafter, we must not think it hard. We may observe, likewise, that God's providences often seem to contradict his promises, and to go cross to them ; and yet, when the mystery of God shall be finished, we shall see that all was for the best, and that cross providences did but render the promises and the accomplishment of them the more illustrious. Now Jacob is here dismissed by his father,

I. With a solemn charge : *He blessed him, and charged him, v.* 1, 2. Note, Those that have the blessing must keep the charge annexed to it, and not think to separate what God has joined. The charge is like that in 2 Cor. vi. 14, *Be not unequally yoked with unbelievers ;* and all that inherit the promises of the remission of sins, and the gift of the Holy Ghost, must keep this charge, which follows those promises, *Save yourselves from this untoward generation,* Acts ii. 38—40. Those that are entitled to peculiar favours must be a peculiar people. If Jacob be an heir of promise, he must *not take a wife of the daughters of Canaan ;* those that profess religion should not marry those that are irreligious.

II. With a solemn blessing, *v.* 3, 4. He had before blessed him unwittingly ; now he does it designedly, for the greater encouragement of Jacob in that melancholy condition to which he was now removing. This blessing is more express and full than the former ; it is an entail of the blessing of Abraham, that blessing which was poured on the head of Abraham like the anointing oil, thence to run down to his chosen seed, as the skirts of his garments. It is a gospel blessing, the blessing of church-privileges, that is the blessing of Abraham, which comes upon the Gentiles through faith, Gal. iii. 14. It is a blessing from God Almighty, by which name God appeared to the patriarchs, Exod. vi. 3. Those are blessed indeed whom God Almighty blesses ; for he commands and effects the blessing. Two great promises Abraham was blessed with, and Isaac here entails them both upon Jacob.

169

1. The promise of heirs: *God make thee fruitful, and multiply thee, v.* 3. (1.) Through his loins should descend from Abraham that people who should be numerous as the stars of heaven, and the sand of the sea, and who should increase more than the rest of the nations, so as to be *an assembly of people*, as the margin reads it. And never was such a multitude of people so often gathered into one assembly as the tribes of Israel were in the wilderness, and afterwards. (2.) Through his loins should descend from Abraham that person in whom all the families of the earth should be blessed, and to whom the gathering of the people should be. Jacob had in him a multitude of people indeed, for all things in heaven and earth are united in Christ (Eph. i. 10), all centre in him, that corn of wheat, which, falling to the ground, produced much fruit, John xii. 24.

2. The promise of an inheritance for those heirs: *That thou mayest inherit the land of thy sojournings, v.* 4. Canaan was hereby entailed upon the seed of Jacob, exclusive of the seed of Esau. Isaac was now sending Jacob away into a distant country, to settle there for some time; and, lest this should look like disinheriting him, he here confirms the settlement of it upon him, that he might be assured that the discontinuance of his possession should be no defeasance of his right. Observe, He is here told that he should inherit the land wherein he sojourned. Those that are sojourners now shall be heirs for ever: and, even now, those do most inherit the earth (though they do not inherit most of it) that are most like strangers in it. Those have the best enjoyment of present things that sit most loose to them! This promise looks as high as heaven, of which Canaan was a type. This was the better country, which Jacob, with the other patriarchs, had in his eye, when he confessed himself a stranger and pilgrim upon the earth, Heb. xi. 13.

Jacob, having taken leave of his father, was hastened away with all speed, lest his brother should find an opportunity to do him a mischief, and away he went to Padan-aram, *v.* 5. How unlike was his taking a wife thence to his father's! Isaac had servants and camels sent to fetch his; Jacob must go himself, go alone, and go afoot, to fetch his: he must go too in a fright from his father's house, not knowing when he might return. Note, If God, in his providence, disable us, we must be content, though we cannot keep up the state and grandeur of our ancestors. We should be more in care to maintain their piety than to maintain their dignity, and to be as good as they were than to be as great. Rebekah is here called *Jacob's and Esau's mother.* Jacob is named first, not only because he had always been his mother's darling, but because he was now made his father's heir, and Esau was, in this sense, set aside. Note, The time will come when piety will have precedency, whatever it has now.

6 When Esau saw that Isaac had blessed Jacob, and sent him away to Padan-aram, to take him a wife from thence; and that as he blessed him he gave him a charge, saying, Thou shalt not take a wife of the daughters of Canaan; 7 And that Jacob obeyed his father and his mother, and was gone to Padan-aram; 8 And Esau seeing that the daughters of Canaan pleased not Isaac his father; 9 Then went Esau unto Ishmael, and took unto the wives which he had Mahalath the daughter of Ishmael Abraham's son, the sister of Nebajoth, to be his wife.

This passage concerning Esau comes in in the midst of Jacob's story, either, 1. To show the influence of a good example. Esau, though the greater man, now begins to think Jacob the better man, and disdains not to take him for his pattern in this particular instance of marrying with a daughter of Abraham. The elder children should give to the younger an example of tractableness and obedience; it is bad if they do not: but it is some alleviation if they take the example of it from them, as Esau here did from Jacob. Or, 2. To show the folly of an after-wit. Esau did well, but he did it when it was too late. He *saw that the daughters of Canaan pleased not his father*, and he might have seen that long ago if he had consulted his father's judgment as much as he did his palate. And how did he now mend the matter? Why, truly, so as to make bad worse. (1.) He married a daughter of Ishmael, the son of the bond-woman, who was cast out, and was not to inherit with Isaac and his seed, thus joining with a family which God had rejected, and seeking to strengthen his own pretensions by the aid of another pretender. (2.) He took a third wife, while, for aught that appears, his other two were neither dead nor divorced. (3.) He did it only to please his father, not to please God. Now that Jacob was sent into a far country Esau would be all in all at home, and he hoped so to humour his father as to prevail with him to make a new will, and entail the promise upon him, revoking the settlement lately made upon Jacob. And thus, [1.] He was wise when it was too late, like Israel that would venture when the decree had gone forth against them (Num. xiv. 40), and the foolish virgins, Matt. xxv. 11. [2.] He rested in a partial reformation, and thought, by pleasing his parents in one thing, to atone for all his other miscarriages. It is not said that when he saw how obedient Jacob was, and how willing to please his parents, he repented of his malicious design against him: no, it appeared afterwards that he persisted in that, and retained his malice. Note, Carnal hearts are apt to think themselves as good as they should be, because perhaps, in some one particular instance, they are not so bad as they have been. Thus Micah retains his idols, but thinks himself happy in having a Levite to be his priest, Judg. xvii. 13.

10 And Jacob went out from Beersheba, and went toward Haran. 11 And he lighted upon a certain place, and tarried there all night, because the sun was set; and he took of the stones of that place, and put *them for* his pillows, and lay down in that place to sleep. 12 And he dreamed, and behold a ladder set up on the earth, and the top of it reached to heaven: and behold the angels of God ascending and descending on it. 13 And, behold, the LORD stood above it, and said, I *am* the LORD God of Abraham thy father, and the God of Isaac: the land whereon thou liest, to thee will I give it, and to thy seed; 14 And thy seed shall be as the dust of the earth, and thou shalt spread abroad to the west, and to the east, and to the north, and to the south: and in thee and in thy seed shall all the families of the earth be blessed. 15 And, behold, I *am* with thee, and will keep thee in all *places* whither thou goest, and will bring thee again into this land; for I will not leave thee, until I have done *that* which I have spoken to thee of.

We have here Jacob upon his journey towards Syria, in a very desolate condition, like one that was sent to seek his fortune; but we find that, though he was alone, yet he was not alone, for *the Father was with him,* John xvi. 32. If what is here recorded happened (as it should seem it did) the first night, he had made a long day's journey from Beersheba to Bethel, above forty miles. Providence brought him to a convenient place, probably shaded with trees, to rest himself in that night; and there he had,

I. A hard lodging (*v.* 11), the *stones for his pillows,* and the heavens for his canopy and curtains. As the usage then was, perhaps this was not so bad as it seems now to us; but we should think, 1. He lay very cold, the cold ground for his bed, and, which one would suppose made the matter worse, a cold stone for his pillow, and in the cold air. 2. Very uneasy. If his bones were sore with his day's journey, his night's rest would but make them sorer. 3. Very much exposed. He forgot that he was fleeing for

his life; for had his brother, in his rage, pursued, or sent a murderer after him, here he lay ready to be sacrificed, and destitute of shelter and defence. We cannot think it was by reason of his poverty that he was so ill accommodated, but, (1.) It was owing to the plainness and simplicity of those times, when men did not take so much state, and consult their ease so much, as in these later times of softness and effeminacy. (2.) Jacob had been particularly used to hardships, as a plain man dwelling in tents; and, designing now to go to service, he was the more willing to inure himself to them; and, as it proved, it was well, *ch.* xxxi. 40. (3.) His comfort in the divine blessing, and his confidence in the divine protection, made him easy, even when he lay thus exposed; being sure that his God made him to dwell in safety, he could lie down and sleep upon a stone.

II. In his hard lodging he had a pleasant dream. Any Israelite indeed would be willing to take up with Jacob's pillow, provided he might but have Jacob's dream. Then, and there, he *heard the words of God, and saw the visions of the Almighty.* It was the best night's sleep he ever had in his life. Note, God's time to visit his people with his comforts is when they are most destitute of other comforts, and other comforters; when afflictions in the way of duty (as these were) do abound, then shall consolations so much the more abound. Now observe here,

1. The encouraging vision Jacob saw, *v.* 12. He saw a ladder which reached from earth to heaven, the angels ascending and descending upon it, and God himself at the head of it. Now this represents the two things that are very comfortable to good people at all times, and in all conditions:—(1.) The providence of God, by which there is a constant correspondence kept up between heaven and earth. The counsels of heaven are executed on earth, and the actions and affairs of this earth are all known in heaven and judged there. Providence does its work gradually, and by steps. Angels are employed as ministering spirits, to serve all the purposes and designs of Providence, and the wisdom of God is at the upper end of the ladder, directing all the motions of second causes to the glory of the first Cause. The angels are active spirits, continually ascending and descending; they rest not, day nor night, from service, according to the posts assigned them. They ascend, to give account of what they have done, and to receive orders; and then descend, to execute the orders they have received. Thus we should always abound in the work of the Lord, that we may do it as the angels do it, Ps. ciii. 20, 21. This vision gave very seasonable comfort to Jacob, letting him know that he had both a good guide and a good guard, in his going out and coming in,—that, though he was made to wander from his father's house, yet still he was the care of a kind Providence, and the charge of the holy

angels. This is comfort enough, though we should not admit the notion which some have, that the tutelar angels of Canaan were ascending, having guarded Jacob out of their land, and the angels of Syria descending to take him into their custody. Jacob was now the type and representative of the whole church, with the guardianship of which the angels are entrusted. (2.) The mediation of Christ. He is this ladder, the foot on earth in his human nature, the top in heaven in his divine nature: or the former in his humiliation, the latter in his exaltation. All the intercourse between heaven and earth, since the fall, is by this ladder. Christ is the way; all God's favours come to us, and all our services go to him, by Christ. If God dwell with us, and we with him, it is by Christ. We have no way of getting to heaven, but by this ladder; if we climb up any other way we are thieves and robbers. To this vision our Saviour alludes when he speaks of the angels of God *ascending and descending upon the Son of man* (John i. 51); for the kind offices the angels do us, and the benefits we receive by their ministration, are all owing to Christ, who has reconciled things on earth and things in heaven (Col. i. 20), and made them all meet in himself, Eph. i. 10.

2. The encouraging words Jacob heard. God now brought him into the wilderness, and spoke comfortably to him, spoke from the head of the ladder; for all the glad tidings we receive from heaven come through Jesus Christ.

(1.) The former promises made to his father were repeated and ratified to him, *v.* 13, 14. In general, God intimated to him that he would be the same to him that he had been to Abraham and Isaac. Those that tread in the steps of their godly parents are interested in their covenant and entitled to their privileges. Particularly, [1.] The land of Canaan is settled upon him, *the land whereon thou liest;* as if by his lying so contentedly upon the bare ground he had taken livery and seisin of the whole land. [2.] It is promised him that his posterity should multiply exceedingly as the dust of the earth—that, though he seemed now to be plucked off as a withered branch, yet he should become a flourishing tree, that should send out his boughs unto the sea. These were the blessings with which his father had blessed him (*v.* 3, 4), and God here said Amen to them, that he might have strong consolation. [3.] It is added that the Messiah should come from his loins, in whom all the families of the earth should be blessed. Christ is the great blessing of the world. All that are blessed, whatever family they are of, are blessed in him, and none of any family are excluded from blessedness in him, but those that exclude themselves.

(2.) Fresh promises were made him, accommodated to his present condition, *v.* 15. [1.] Jacob was apprehensive of danger from
172

his brother Esau; but God promises to keep him. Note, Those are safe whom God protects, whoever pursues them. [2.] He had now a long journey before him, had to travel alone, in an unknown road, to an unknown country; but, *behold, I am with thee,* says God. Note, Wherever we are, we are safe, and may be easy, if we have God's favourable presence with us. [3.] He knew not, but God foresaw, what hardships he should meet with in his uncle's service, and therefore promises to preserve him in all places. Note, God knows how to give his people graces and comforts accommodated to the events that shall be, as well as to those that are. [4.] He was now going as an exile into a place far distant, but God promises him to bring him back again to this land. Note, He that preserves his people's going out will also take care of their coming in, Ps. cxxi. 8. [5.] He seemed to be forsaken of all his friends, but God here gives him this assurance, *I will not leave thee.* Note, Whom God loves he never leaves. This promise is sure to all the seed, Heb. xiii. 5. [6.] Providences seemed to contradict the promises; he is therefore assured of the performance of them in their season: All shall *be done that I have spoken to thee of.* Note, Saying and doing are not two things with God, whatever they are with us.

16 And Jacob awaked out of his sleep, and he said, Surely the LORD is in this place; and I knew *it* not. 17 And he was afraid, and said, How dreadful *is* this place! this *is* none other but the house of God, and this *is* the gate of heaven. 18 And Jacob rose up early in the morning, and took the stone that he had put *for* his pillows, and set it up *for* a pillar, and poured oil upon the top of it. 19 And he called the name of that place Beth-el: but the name of that city *was called* Luz at the first. 20 And Jacob vowed a vow, saying, If God will be with me, and will keep me in this way that I go, and will give me bread to eat, and raiment to put on, 21 So that I come again to my father's house in peace; then shall the LORD be my God: 22 And this stone, which I have set *for* a pillar, shall be God's house: and of all that thou shalt give me I will surely give the tenth unto thee.

God manifested himself and his favour to Jacob when he was asleep and purely passive; for the Spirit, like the wind, blows when and where he listeth, and God's grace, like the dew, tarrieth not for the sons of men, Mic. v. 7. But Jacob applied himself to the improvement of the visit God had made him when he was awake; and we may well think he awaked, as the prophet did (Jer. xxxi. 26), and behold his sleep was sweet to him. Here is much of Jacob's devotion on this occasion.

I. He expressed a great surprise at the tokens he had of God's special presence with him in that place: *Surely the Lord is in this place and I knew it not, v.* 16. Note, 1. God's manifestations of himself to his people carry their own evidence along with them. God can give undeniable demonstrations of his presence, such as give abundant satisfaction to the souls of the faithful that God is with them of a truth, satisfaction not communicable to others, but convincing to themselves. 2. We sometimes meet with God where we little thought of meeting with him. He is where we did not think he had been, is found where we asked not for him. No place excludes divine visits (*ch.* xvi. 13, *here also*); wherever we are, in the city or in the desert, in the house or in the field, in the shop or in the street, we may keep up our intercourse with Heaven if it be not our own fault.

II. It struck an awe upon him (*v.* 17): *He was afraid;* so far was he from being puffed up, and exalted above measure, with the abundance of the revelations (2 Cor. xii. 7), that he was afraid. Note, The more we see of God the more cause we see for holy trembling and blushing before him. Those to whom God is pleased to manifest himself are thereby laid, and kept, very low in their own eyes, and see cause to fear even the Lord and his goodness, Hos. iii. 5. He said, *How dreadful is this place!* that is, "The appearance of God in this place is never to be thought of, but with a holy awe and reverence. I shall have a respect for this place, and remember it by this token, as long as I live:" not that he thought the place itself any nearer the divine visions than other places; but what he saw there at this time was, as it were, *the house of God,* the residence of the divine Majesty, and *the gate of heaven,* that is, the general rendezvous of the inhabitants of the upper world, as the meetings of a city were in their gates; or the angels ascending and descending were like travellers passing and re-passing through the gates of a city. Note, 1. God is in a special manner present where his grace is revealed and where his covenants are published and sealed, as of old by the ministry of angels, so now by instituted ordinances, Matt. xxviii. 20. 2. Where God meets us with his special presence we ought to meet him with the most humble reverence, remembering his justice and holiness, and our own meanness and vileness.

III. He took care to preserve the memorial of it two ways: 1. He set up the stone for a pillar (*v.* 18); not as if he thought the visions of his head were any way owing to

the stone on which it lay, but thus he would mark the place against he came back, and erect a lasting monument of God's favour to him, and because he had not time now to build an altar here, as Abraham did in the places where God appeared to him, *ch.* xii. 7. He therefore *poured oil on the top of this stone,* which probably was the ceremony then used in dedicating their altars, as an earnest of his building an altar when he should have conveniences for it, as afterwards he did, in gratitude to God for this vision, *ch.* xxxv. 7. Note, Grants of mercy call for returns of duty, and the sweet communion we have with God ought ever to be remembered. 2. He gave a new name to the place, *v.* 19. It had been called *Luz, an almond-tree;* but he will have it henceforward called *Beth-el, the house of God.* This gracious appearance of God to him put a greater honour upon it, and made it more remarkable, than all the almond-trees that flourished there. This is that Beth-el where, long after, it is said, *God found Jacob, and there* (in what he said to him) *he spoke with us,* Hos. xii. 4. In process of time, this *Beth-el, the house of God,* became *Beth-aven, a house of vanity* and iniquity, when Jeroboam set up one of his calves there.

IV. He made a solemn vow upon this occasion, *v.* 20—22. By religious vows we give glory to God, own our dependence upon him, and lay a bond upon our own souls to engage and quicken our obedience to him. Jacob was now in fear and distress; and it is seasonable to make vows in times of trouble, or when we are in pursuit of any special mercy, Jon. i. 16; Ps. lxvi. 13, 14; 1 Sam. i. 11; Num. xxi. 1—3. Jacob had now had a gracious visit from heaven. God had renewed his covenant with him, and the covenant is mutual. When God ratifies his promises to us, it is proper for us to repeat our promises to him. Now in this vow observe, 1. Jacob's faith. God had said (*v.* 15), *I am with thee, and will keep thee.* Jacob takes hold of this, and infers, "*Seeing God will be with me, and will keep me,* as he hath said, and (which is implied in that promise) will provide comfortably for me,—and seeing he has promised to *bring me again to this land,* that is, *to the house of my father,* whom I hope to find alive at my return *in peace*" (so unlike was he to Esau who longed for the days of mourning for his father),—" I depend upon it." Note, God's promises are to be the guide and measure of our desires and expectations. 2. Jacob's modesty and great moderation in his desires. He will cheerfully content himself with bread to eat, and raiment to put on; and, though God's promise had now made him heir to a very great estate, yet he indents not for soft clothing and dainty meat. Agur's wish is his, *Feed me with food convenient for me;* and see 1 Tim. vi. 8. Nature is content with a little, and grace with less. Those that have most have, in effect, no more for themselves than food and raiment; of the overplus they have only either the keeping or the giving, not the enjoyment: if God give us more, we are bound to be thankful, and to use it for him; if he give us but this, we are bound to be content, and cheerfully to enjoy him in it. 3. Jacob's piety, and his regard to God, which appear here, (1.) In what he desired, that God would be with him and keep him. Note, We need desire no more to make us easy and happy, wherever we are, than to have God's presence with us and to be under his protection. It is comfortable, in a journey, to have a guide in an unknown way, a guard in a dangerous way, to be well carried, well provided for, and to have good company in any way; and those that have God with them have all this in the best manner. (2.) In what he designed. His resolution is, [1.] In general, to cleave to the Lord, as his God in covenant: *Then shall the Lord be my God.* Not as if he would disown him and cast him off if he should want food and raiment; no, though he slay us, we must cleave to him; but " then I will rejoice in him as my God; then I will more strongly engage myself to abide with him." Note, Every mercy we receive from God should be improved as an additional obligation upon us to walk closely with him as our God. [2.] In particular, that he would perform some special acts of devotion, in token of his gratitude. *First,* "This pillar shall keep possession here till I come back in peace, and then it shall be God's house," that is, " an altar shall be erected here to the honour of God." *Secondly,* "The house of God shall not be unfurnished, nor his altar without a sacrifice: *Of all that thou shalt give me I will surely give the tenth unto thee,* to be spent either upon God's altars or upon his poor," both which are his receivers in the world. Probably it was according to some general instructions received from heaven that Abraham and Jacob offered the tenth of their acquisitions to God. Note, 1. God must be honoured with our estates, and must have his dues out of them. When we receive more than ordinary mercy from God we should study to give some signal instances of gratitude to him. 2. The tenth is a very fit proportion to be devoted to God and employed for him, though, as circumstances vary, it may be more or less, as God prospers us, 1 Cor. xvi. 2; 2 Cor. ix. 7.

CHAP. XXIX.

This chapter gives us an account of God's providences concerning Jacob, pursuant to the promises made to him in the foregoing chapter. 1. How he was brought in safety to his journey's end, and directed to his relations there, who bade him welcome, ver. 1—14. II. How he was comfortably disposed of in marriage, ver. 15—30. III. How his family was built up in the birth of four sons, ver. 31—35. The affairs of princes and mighty nations that were then in being are not recorded in the book of God, but are left to be buried in oblivion; while these small domestic concerns of holy Jacob are particularly recorded with their minute circumstances, that they may be in everlasting remembrance. For "the memory of the just is blessed."

THEN Jacob went on his journey, and came into the land of the people of the east. 2 And he looked,

and behold a well in the field, and, lo, there *were* three flocks of sheep lying by it; for out of that well they watered the flocks: and a great stone *was* upon the well's mouth. 3 And thither were all the flocks gathered: and they rolled the stone from the well's mouth, and watered the sheep, and put the stone again upon the well's mouth in his place. 4 And Jacob said unto them, My brethren, whence *be* ye? And they said, Of Haran *are* we. 5 And he said unto them, Know ye Laban the son of Nahor? And they said, We know *him.* 6 And he said unto them, *Is* he well? And they said, *He is* well: and, behold, Rachel his daughter cometh with the sheep. 7 And he said, Lo, *it is* yet high day, neither *is it* time that the cattle should be gathered together: water ye the sheep, and go *and* feed *them.* 8 And they said, We cannot, until all the flocks be gathered together, and *till* they roll the stone from the well's mouth; then we water the sheep.

All the stages of Israel's march to Canaan are distinctly noticed, but no particular journal is kept of Jacob's expedition further than Beth-el; no, he had no more such happy nights as he had at Beth-el, no more such visions of the Almighty. That was intended for a feast; he must not expect it to be his daily bread. But, 1. We are here told how cheerfully he proceeded in his journey after the sweet communion he had with God at Beth-el: *Then Jacob lifted up his feet;* so the margin reads it, *v.* 1. Then he went on with cheerfulness and alacrity, not burdened with his cares, nor cramped with his fears, being assured of God's gracious presence with him. Note, After the visions we have had of God, and the vows we have made to him in solemn ordinances, we should run the way of his commandments with enlarged hearts, Heb. xii. 1. 2. How happily he arrived at his journey's end. Providence brought him to the very field where his uncle's flocks were to be watered, and there he met with Rachel, who was to be his wife. Observe, (1.) The divine Providence is to be acknowledged in all the little circumstances which concur to make a journey, or other undertaking, comfortable and successful. If, when we are at a loss, we meet seasonably with those that can direct us—if we meet with a disaster, and those are at hand that will help us—we must not say that it was by chance, nor that fortune therein favoured us, but that it was by Providence, and that God therein favoured us. Our ways are ways of pleasantness, if we continually acknowledge God in them. (2.) Those that have flocks must look well to them, and be diligent to know their state, Prov. xxvii. 23. What is here said of the constant care of the shepherds concerning their sheep (v. 2, 3, 7, 8) may serve to illustrate the tender concern which our Lord Jesus, the great Shepherd of the sheep, has for his flock, the church ; for he is the good Shepherd, that knows his sheep, and is known of them, John x. 14. The stone at the well's mouth, which is so often mentioned here, was either to secure their property in it (for water was scarce, it was not there *usus communis aquarum—for every one's use),* or it was to save the well from receiving damage from the heat of the sun, or from any spiteful hand, or to prevent the lambs of the flock from being drowned in it. (3.) Separate interests should not take us from joint and mutual help ; when all the shepherds came together with their flocks, then, like loving neighbours, at watering-time, they watered their flocks together. (4.) It becomes us to speak civilly and respectfully to strangers. Though Jacob was no courtier, but a plain man, dwelling in tents, and a stranger to compliment, yet he addresses himself very obligingly to the people he met with, and calls them his *brethren, v.* 4. The law of kindness in the tongue has a commanding power, Prov. xxxi. 26. Some think he calls them brethren because they were of the same trade, shepherds like him. Though he was now upon his preferment, he was not ashamed of his occupation. . (5.) Those that show respect have usually respect shown to them. As Jacob was civil to these strangers, so he found them civil to him. When he undertook to teach them how to despatch their business (v. 7), they did not bid him meddle with his own concerns and let them alone ; but, though he was a stranger, they gave him the reason of their delay, v. 8. Those that are neighbourly and friendly shall have neighbourly and friendly usage.

9 And while he yet spake with them, Rachel came with her father's sheep : for she kept them. 10 And it came to pass, when Jacob saw Rachel the daughter of Laban his mother's brother, and the sheep of Laban his mother's brother, that Jacob went near, and rolled the stone from the well's mouth, and watered the flock of Laban his mother's brother. 11 And Jacob kissed Rachel, and lifted up his voice, and wept. 12 And Jacob told Rachel that he *was* her father's brother, and that he *was* Rebekah's son : and she ran and told her father. 13 And it came to pass, when Laban heard the tidings of Jacob his sister's

son, that he ran to meet him, and embraced him, and kissed him, and brought him to his house. And he told Laban all these things. 14 And Laban said to him, Surely thou *art* my bone and my flesh. And he abode with him the space of a month.

Here we see, 1. Rachel's humility and industry : *She kept her father's sheep (v.* 9), that is, she took the care of them, having servants under her that were employed about them. Rachel's name signifies *a sheep.* Note, Honest useful labour is that which nobody needs be ashamed of, nor ought it to be a hindrance to any one's preferment. 2. Jacob's tenderness and affection. When he understood that this was his kinswoman (probably he had heard of her name before), knowing what his errand was into that country, we may suppose it struck his mind immediately that this must be his wife. Being already smitten with her ingenuous comely face (though it was probably sun-burnt, and she was in the homely dress of a shepherdess), he is wonderfully officious, and anxious to serve her (v. 10), and addresses himself to her with tears of joy and kisses of love, v. 11. She runs with all haste to tell her father ; for she will by no means entertain her kinsman's address without her father's knowledge and approbation, v. 12. These mutual respects, at their first interview, were good presages of their being a happy couple. 3. Providence made that which seemed contingent and fortuitous to give speedy satisfaction to Jacob's mind, as soon as ever he came to the place which he was bound for. Abraham's servant, when he came upon a similar errand, met with similar encouragment. Thus God guides his people with his eye, Ps. xxxii. 8. It is a groundless conceit which some of the Jewish writers have, that Jacob, when he kissed Rachel, wept because he had been set upon in his journey by Eliphaz the eldest son of Esau, at the command of his father, and robbed of all his money and jewels, which his mother had given him when she sent him away. It was plain that it was his passion for Rachel, and the surprise of this happy meeting, that drew these tears from his eyes 4. Laban, though none of the best-humoured men, bade him welcome, was satisfied in the account he gave of himself, and of the reason of his coming in such poor circumstances. While we avoid the extreme, on the one hand, of being foolishly credulous, we must take heed of falling into the other extreme, of being uncharitably jealous and suspicious. Laban owned him for his kinsman : *Thou art my bone and my flesh, v.* 14. Note, Those are hard-hearted indeed that are unkind to their relations, and that *hide themselves from their own flesh,* Isa. lviii. 7.

15 And Laban said unto Jacob, Be-

175

cause thou *art* my brother, shouldest thou therefore serve me for nought? tell me, what *shall* thy wages *be?* 16 And Laban had two daughters: the name of the elder *was* Leah, and the name of the younger *was* Rachel. 17 Leah *was* tender eyed; but Rachel was beautiful and well favoured. 18 And Jacob loved Rachel; and said, I will serve thee seven years for Rachel thy younger daughter. 19 And Laban said, *It is* better that I give her to thee, than that I should give her to another man: abide with me. 20 And Jacob served seven years for Rachel; and they seemed unto him *but* a few days, for the love he had to her. 21 And Jacob said unto Laban, Give *me* my wife, for my days are fulfilled, that I may go in unto her. 22 And Laban gathered together all the men of the place, and made a feast. 23 And it came to pass in the evening, that he took Leah his daughter, and brought her to him; and he went in unto her. 24 And Laban gave unto his daughter Leah Zilpah his maid *for* a handmaid. 25 And it came to pass, that in the morning, behold, it *was* Leah: and he said to Laban, What *is* this thou hast done unto me? did not I serve with thee for Rachel? wherefore then hast thou beguiled me? 26 And Laban said, It must not be so done in our country, to give the younger before the firstborn. 27 Fulfil her week, and we will give thee this also for the service which thou shalt serve with me yet seven other years. 28 And Jacob did so, and fulfilled her week: and he gave him Rachel his daughter to wife also. 29 And Laban gave to Rachel his daughter Bilhah his handmaid to be her maid. 30 And he went in also unto Rachel, and he loved also Rachel more than Leah, and served with him yet seven other years.

Here is, I. The fair contract made between Laban and Jacob, during the month that Jacob spent there as a guest, *v.* 14. It seems he was not idle, nor did he spend his time in sport and pastime; but like a man of business, though he had no stock of his own, he applied himself to serve his uncle, as he had begun (*v.* 10) when he *watered his flock.*

Note, Wherever we are, it is good to be employing ourselves in some useful business, which will turn to a good account to ourselves or others. Laban, it seems, was so taken with Jacob's ingenuity and industry about his flocks that he was desirous he should continue with him, and very fairly reasons thus: "*Because thou art my brother, shouldst thou therefore serve me for nought?* *v.* 15. No, what reason for that?" If Jacob be so respectful to his uncle as to give him his service without demanding any consideration for it, yet Laban will not be so unjust to his nephew as to take advantage either of his necessity or of his good-nature. Note, Inferior relations must not be imposed upon; if it be their duty to serve us, it is our duty to reward them. Now Jacob had a fair opportunity to make known to Laban the affection he had for his daughter Rachel; and, having no worldly goods in his hand with which to endow her, he promises him seven years' service, upon condition that, at the end of the seven years, he would bestow her upon him for his wife. It appears by computation that Jacob was now seventy-seven years old when he bound himself apprentice for a wife, *and for a wife he kept sheep,* Hos. xii. 12. His posterity are there reminded of it long afterwards, as an instance of the meanness of their origin: probably Rachel was young, and scarcely marriageable, when Jacob first came, which made him the more willing to stay for her till his seven years' service had expired.

II. Jacob's honest performance of his part of the bargain, *v.* 20. He served seven years for Rachel. If Rachel still continued to keep her father's sheep (as she did, *v.* 9), his innocent and religious conversation with her, while they kept the flocks, could not but increase their mutual acquaintance and affection (Solomon's song of love is a pastoral); if she now left it off, his easing her of that care was very obliging. Jacob honestly served out his seven years, and did not forfeit his indentures, though he was old; nay, he served them cheerfully: *They seemed to him but a few days, for the love he had to her,* as if there were more his desire to earn her than to have her. Note, Love makes long and hard services short and easy; hence we read of *the labour of love,* Heb. vi. 10. If we know how to value the happiness of heaven, the sufferings of this present time will be as nothing to us in comparison of it. An age of work will be but as a few days to those that love God and long for Christ's appearing.

III. The base cheat which Laban put upon him when he was out of his time: he put Leah into his arms instead of Rachel, *v.* 23. This was Laban's sin; he wronged both Jacob and Rachel, whose affections, doubtless, were engaged to each other, and, if (as some say) Leah was herein no better than an adulteress, it was no small wrong to her too. But it was Jacob's affliction, a damp to the mirth of the marriage-feast, when in the morning behold it was Leah, v. 25. It is easy to observe here how Jacob was paid in his own coin. He had cheated his own father when he pretended to be Esau, and now his father-in-law cheated him. Herein, how unrighteous soever Laban was, the Lord was righteous; as Judges i. 7. Even the righteous, if they take a false step, are sometimes thus recompensed on the earth. Many that are not, like Jacob, disappointed in the person, soon find themselves, as much to their grief, disappointed in the character. The choice of that relation therefore, on both sides, ought to be made with good advice and consideration, that, if there should be a disappointment, it may not be aggravated by a consciousness of mismanagement.

IV. The excuse and atonement Laban made for the cheat. 1. The excuse was frivolous: *It must not be so done in our country, v. 26.* We have reason to think there was no such custom of his country as he pretends; only he banters Jacob with it, and laughs at his mistake. Note, Those that can do wickedly and then think to turn it off with a jest, though they may deceive themselves and others, will find at last that God is not mocked. But if there had been such a custom, and he had resolved to observe it, he should have told Jacob so when he undertook to serve him for his younger daughter. Note, As saith the proverb of the ancients, *Wickedness proceeds from the wicked*, 1 Sam. xxiv. 13. Those that deal with treacherous men must expect to be dealt treacherously with. 2. His compounding the matter did but make bad worse: *We will give thee this also, v. 27.* Hereby he drew Jacob into the sin, and snare, and disquiet, of multiplying wives, which remains a blot in his escutcheon, and will be so to the end of the world. Honest Jacob did not design it, but to have kept as true to Rachel as his father had done to Rebekah. He that had lived without a wife to the eighty-fourth year of his age could then have been very well content with one; but Laban, to dispose of his two daughters without portions, and to get seven years' service more out of Jacob, thus imposes upon him, and draws him into such a strait by his fraud, that (the matter not being yet settled, as it was afterwards by the divine law, Lev. xviii. 18, and more fully since by our Saviour, Matt. xix. 5) he had some colourable reasons for marrying them both. He could not refuse Rachel, for he had espoused her; still less could he refuse Leah, for he had married her; and therefore Jacob must *be content, and take two talents*, 2 Kings v. 23. Note, One sin is commonly the inlet of another. Those that go in by one door of wickedness seldom find their way out but by another. The polygamy of the patriarchs was, in some measure, excusable in them, because, though there was a reason against it as ancient as Adam's marriage (Mal. ii. 15), yet there was no express

command against it; it was in them a sin of ignorance. It was not the product of any sinful lust, but for the building up of the church, which was the good that Providence brought out of it; but it will by no means justify the like practice now, when God's will is plainly made known, that one man and one woman only must be joined together, 1 Cor. vii. 2. The having of many wives suits well enough with the carnal sensual spirit of the Mahomedan imposture, which allows it; but we have not so learned Christ. Dr. Lightfoot makes Leah and Rachel to be figures of the two churches, the Jews under the law and the Gentiles under the gospel: the younger the more beautiful, and more in the thoughts of Christ when he came in the form of a servant; but the other, like Leah, first embraced: yet in this the allegory does not hold, that the Gentiles, the younger, were more fruitful, Gal. iv. 27.

31 And when the Lord saw that Leah *was* hated, he opened her womb: but Rachel *was* barren. 32 And Leah conceived, and bare a son, and she called his name Reuben: for she said, Surely the Lord hath looked upon my affliction; now therefore my husband will love me. 33 And she conceived again, and bare a son; and said, Because the Lord hath heard that I *was* hated, he hath therefore given me this *son* also: and she called his name Simeon. 34 And she conceived again, and bare a son; and said, Now this time will my husband be joined unto me, because I have borne him three sons: therefore was his name called Levi. 35 And she conceived again, and bare a son: and she said, Now will I praise the Lord: therefore she called his name Judah; and left bearing.

We have here the birth of four of Jacob's sons, all by Leah. Observe, 1. That Leah, who was less beloved, was blessed with children, when Rachel was denied that blessing, v. 31. See how Providence, in dispensing its gifts, observes a proportion, to keep the balance even, setting crosses and comforts one over-against another, that none may be either too much elevated or too much depressed. Rachel wants children, but she is blessed with her husband's love; Leah wants that, but she is fruitful. Thus it was between Elkana's two wives (1. Sam. i. 5); for the Lord is wise and righteous. *When the Lord saw that Leah was hated*, that is, loved less than Rachel, in which sense it is required that we hate father and mother, in comparison with Christ (Luke xiv. 26), then the Lord granted her a child, which was a rebuke

177

to Jacob, for making so great a difference between those that he was equally related to,— a check to Rachel, who perhaps insulted over her sister upon that account,—and a comfort to Leah, that she might not be overwhelmed with the contempt put upon her: thus *God giveth abundant honour to that which lacked,* 1 Cor. xii. 24. 2. The names she gave her children were expressive of her respectful regards both to God and to her husband. (1.) She appears very ambitious of her husband's love: she reckoned the want of it her affliction (*v.* 32); not upbraiding him with it as his fault, nor reproaching him for it, and so making herself uneasy to him, but laying it to heart as her grief, which yet she had reason to bear with the more patience because she herself was consenting to the fraud by which she became his wife; and we may well bear that trouble with patience which we bring upon ourselves by our own sin and folly. She promised herself that the children she bore him would gain her the interest she desired in his affections. She called her first-born *Reuben (see a son),* with this pleasant thought, *Now will my husband love me;* and her third son *Levi (joined),* with this expectation, *Now will my husband be joined unto me, v.* 34. Mutual affection is both the duty and comfort of that relation; and yoke-fellows should study to recommend themselves to each other, 1 Cor. vii. 33, 34. (2.) She thankfully acknowledges the kind providence of God in it: *The Lord hath looked upon my affliction, v.* 32. "*The Lord hath heard,* that is, taken notice of it, *that I was hated* (for our afflictions, as they are before God's eyes, so they have a cry in his ears), *he has therefore given me this son.*" Note, Whatever we have that contributes either to our support and comfort under our afflictions or to our deliverance from them, God must be owned in it, especially his pity and tender mercy. Her fourth she called *Judah (praise),* saying, *Now will I praise the Lord, v.* 35. And this was he of whom, as concerning the flesh, Christ came. Note, [1.] Whatever is the matter of our rejoicing ought to be the matter of our thanksgiving. Fresh favours should quicken us to praise God for former favours. *Now will I praise the Lord* more and better than I have done. [2.] All our praises must centre in Christ, both as the matter of them and as the Mediator of them. He descended from him whose name was praise, for he is our praise. Is Christ formed in my heart? *Now will I praise the Lord.*

CHAP. XXX.

In this chapter we have an account of the increase, I. Of Jacob's family. Eight children more we find registered in this chapter; Dan and Naphtali by Bilhah, Rachel's maid, ver. 1—8. Gad and Asher by Zilpah, Leah's maid, ver. 9—13. Issachar, Zebulun, and Dinah, by Leah, ver. 14—21. And, last of all, Joseph, by Rachel, ver. 22—24. II. Of Jacob's estate. He makes a new bargain with Laban, ver. 25—34. And in the six years' further service he did to Laban God wonderfully blessed him, so that his stock of cattle became very considerable, ver. 35—43. Herein was fulfilled the blessing with which Isaac dismissed him (ch. xxviii. 3), "God make thee fruitful, and multiply thee." Even these small matters concerning Jacob's house and field, though they seem inconsiderable, are improvable for our learning. For

the scriptures were written, not for princes and statesmen, to instruct them in politics; but for all people, even the meanest, to direct them in their families and callings: yet some things are here recorded concerning Jacob, not for imitation, but for admonition.

AND when Rachel saw that she bare Jacob no children, Rachel envied her sister; and said unto Jacob, Give me children, or else I die. 2 And Jacob's anger was kindled against Rachel: and he said, *Am* I in God's stead, who hath withheld from thee the fruit of the womb? 3 And she said, Behold my maid Bilhah, go in unto her; and she shall bear upon my knees, that I may also have children by her. 4 And she gave him Bilhah her handmaid to wife: and Jacob went in unto her. 5 And Bilhah conceived, and bare Jacob a son. 6 And Rachel said, God hath judged me, and hath also heard my voice, and hath given me a son: therefore called she his name Dan. 7 And Bilhah Rachel's maid conceived again, and bare Jacob a second son. 8 And Rachel said, With great wrestlings have I wrestled with my sister, and I have prevailed: and she called his name Naphtali. 9 When Leah saw that she had left bearing, she took Zilpah her maid, and gave her Jacob to wife. 10 And Zilpah Leah's maid bare Jacob a son. 11 And Leah said, A troop cometh: and she called his name Gad. 12 And Zilpah Leah's maid bare Jacob a second son. 13 And Leah said, Happy am I, for the daughters will call me blessed: and she called his name Asher.

We have here the bad consequences of that strange marriage which Jacob made with the two sisters. Here is,

I. An unhappy disagreement between him and Rachel (*v.* 1, 2), occasioned, not so much by her own barrenness as by her sister's fruitfulness. Rebekah, the only wife of Isaac, was long childless, and yet we find no uneasiness between her and Isaac; but here, because Leah bears children, Rachel cannot live peaceably with Jacob.

1. Rachel frets. She *envied her sister, v.* 1. Envy is grieving at the good of another, than which no sin is more offensive to God, nor more injurious to our neighbour and ourselves. She considered not that it was God that made the difference, and that though, in this single instance, her sister was preferred before her, yet in other things she had the advantage. Let us carefully watch against all the risings and workings of this passion in our minds. Let not our eye be evil to

178

wards any of our fellow-servants because our master's is good. But this was not all; she said to Jacob, *Give me children, or else I die.* Note, We are very apt to err in our desires of temporal mercies, as Rachel here. (1.) One child would not content her; but, because Leah has more than one, she must have more too: *Give me children.* (2.) Her heart is inordinately set upon it, and, if she have not what she would have, she will throw away her life, and all the comforts of it. " Give them to me, or *else I die,*" that is, " I shall fret myself to death; the want of this satisfaction will shorten my days." Some think she threatens Jacob to lay violent hands upon herself, if she could not obtain this mercy. (3.) She did not apply to God by prayer, but to Jacob only, forgetting that *children are a heritage of the Lord,* Ps. cxxvii. 3. We wrong both God and ourselves when our eye is more to men, the instruments of our crosses and comforts, than to God the author. Observe a difference between Rachel's asking for this mercy and Hannah's, 1 Sam. i. 10, &c. Rachel envied; Hannah wept. Rachel must have children, and she died of the second; Hannah prayed for one child, and she had four more. Rachel is importunate and peremptory; Hannah is submissive and devout. *If thou wilt give me a child, I will give him to the Lord.* Let Hannah be imitated, and not Rachel; and let our desires be always under the direction and control of reason and religion.

2. Jacob chides, and most justly. He loved Rachel, and therefore reproved her for what she said amiss, *v.* 2. Note, Faithful reproofs are products and instances of true affection, Ps. cxli. 5; Prov. xxvii. 5, 6. Job reproved his wife when she spoke the language of the foolish women, Job ii. 10. See 1 Cor. vii. 16. He was angry, not at the person, but at the sin; he expressed himself so as to show his displeasure. Note, Sometimes it is requisite that a reproof should be given warm, like a medical potion; not too hot, lest it scald the patient; yet not cold, lest it prove ineffectual. It was a very grave and pious reply which Jacob gave to Rachel's peevish demand: *Am I in God's stead?* The Chaldee paraphrases it well, *Dost thou ask sons of me? Oughtest thou not to ask them from before the Lord?* The Arabic reads it, " *Am I above God?* can I give thee that which God denies thee?" This was said like a plain man. Observe, (1.) He acknowledges the hand of God in the affliction which he was a sharer with her in: He *hath withheld the fruit of the womb.* Note, Whatever we want, it is God that withholds it, a sovereign Lord, most wise, holy, and just, that may do what he will with his own, and is debtor to no man, that never did, nor ever can do, any wrong to any of his creatures. The keys of the clouds, of the heart, of the grave, and of the womb, are four keys which God has in his hand, and which (the rabbin say) he entrusts neither with angels

nor seraphim. See Rev. iii. 7. Job xi. 10; xii. 14. (2.) He acknowledges his own inability to alter what God had appointed: " *Am I in God's stead?* What! dost thou make a god of me?" *Deos qui rogat ille facit—He to whom we offer supplications is to us a god.* Note, [1.] There is no creature that is, or can be, to us, in God's stead. God may be to us instead of any creature, as the sun instead of the moon and stars; but the moon and all the stars will not be to us instead of the sun. No creature's wisdom, power, and love, will be to us instead of God's. [2.] It is therefore our sin and folly to place any creature in God's stead, and to place that confidence in any creature which is to be placed in God only.

II. An unhappy agreement between him and the two handmaids.

1. At the persuasion of Rachel, he took Bilhah her handmaid to wife, that, according to the usage of those times, his children by her might be adopted and owned as her mistress's children, *v.* 3, &c. She would rather have children by reputation than none at all, children that she might fancy to be her own, and call her own, though they were not so. One would think her own sister's children were nearer akin to her than her maid's, and she might with more satisfaction have made them her own if she had so pleased; but (so natural is it for us all to be fond of power) children that she had a right to rule were more desirable to her than children that she had more reason to love; and, as an early instance of her dominion over the children born in her apartment, she takes a pleasure in giving them names that carry in them nothing but marks of emulation with her sister, as if she had overcome her, (1.) At law. She calls the first son of her handmaid *Dan (judgment),* saying, " God hath judged me" (*v.* 6), that is, "given sentence in my favour." (2.) In battle. She calls the next *Naphtali (wrestlings),* saying, *I have wrestled with my sister, and have prevailed* (*v.* 8); as if all Jacob's sons must be born men of contention. See what roots of bitterness envy and strife are, and what mischief they make among relations.

2. At the persuasion of Leah, he took Zilpah her handmaid to wife also, *v.* 9. Rachel had done that absurd and preposterous thing of giving her maid to her husband, in emulation with Leah; and now Leah (because she missed one year in bearing children) does the same, to be even with her, or rather to keep before her. See the power of jealousy and rivalship, and admire the wisdom of the divine appointment, which unites one man and one woman only; for *God hath called us to peace* and purity, 1 Cor. vii. 15. Two sons Zilpah bore to Jacob, whom Leah looked upon herself as entitled to, in token of which she called one *Gad* (*v.* 11), promising herself a little *troop* of children; and children are the militia of a family, they fill the quiver, Ps. cxxvii. 4, 5. The other she called *Asher*

179

(happy), thinking herself happy in him, and promising herself that her neighbours would think so too: *The daughters will call me blessed,* **v. 13.** Note, It is an instance of the vanity of the world, and the foolishness bound up in our hearts, that most people value themselves and govern themselves more by reputation than either by reason or religion; they think themselves blessed if the daughters do but call them so. There was much amiss in the contest and competition between these two sisters, yet God brought good out of this evil; for, the time being now at hand when the seed of Abraham must begin to increase and multiply, thus Jacob's family was replenished with twelve sons, heads of the thousands of Israel, from whom the celebrated twelve tribes descended and were named.

14 And Reuben went in the days of wheat harvest, and found mandrakes in the field, and brought them unto his mother Leah. Then Rachel said to Leah, Give me, I pray thee, of thy son's mandrakes. 15 And she said unto her, *Is it* a small matter that thou hast taken my husband? and wouldest thou take away my son's mandrakes also? And Rachel said, Therefore he shall lie with thee to night for thy son's mandrakes. 16 And Jacob came out of the field in the evening, and Leah went out to meet him, and said, Thou must come in unto me; for surely I have hired thee with my son's mandrakes. And he lay with her that night. 17 And God hearkened unto Leah, and she conceived, and bare Jacob the fifth son. 18 And Leah said, God hath given me my hire, because I have given my maiden to my husband: and she called his name Issachar. 19 And Leah conceived again, and bare Jacob the sixth son. 20 And Leah said, God hath endued me *with* a good dowry; now will my husband dwell with me, because I have borne him six sons: and she called his name Zebulun. 21 And afterwards she bare a daughter, and called her name Dinah. 22 And God remembered Rachel, and God hearkened to her, and opened her womb. 23 And she conceived, and bare a son; and said, God hath taken away my reproach: 24 And she called his name Joseph; and said, the Lord shall add to me another son.

Here is, I. Leah fruitful again, after she had, for some time, left off bearing. Jacob,

it should seem, associated more with Rachel than with Leah. The law of Moses supposes it a common case that, if a man had two wives, one would be beloved and the other hated, Deut. xxi. 15. But at length Rachel's strong passions betrayed her into a bargain with Leah that Jacob should return to her apartment. Reuben, a little lad, five or six years old, playing in the field, found *mandrakes, dudaim.* It is uncertain what they were, the critics are not agreed about them; we are sure they were some rarities, either fruits or flowers that were very pleasant to the smell, Cant. vii. 13. Note, The God of nature has provided, not only for our necessities, but for our delights; there are products of the earth in the exposed fields, as well as in the planted protected gardens, that are very valuable and useful. How plentifully is nature's house furnished and her table spread! Her precious fruits offer themselves to be gathered by the hands of little children. It is a laudable custom of the devout Jews, when they find pleasure, suppose in eating an apple, to lift up their hearts, and say, "Blessed be he that made this fruit pleasant!" Or, in smelling a flower, "Blessed be he that made this flower sweet." Some think these mandrakes were jessamine flowers. Whatever they were, Rachel could not see them in Leah's hands, where the child had placed them, but she must covet them. She cannot bear the want of these pretty flowers, but will purchase them at any rate. Note, There may be great sin and folly in the inordinate desire of a small thing. Leah takes this advantage (as Jacob had of Esau's coveting his red pottage) to obtain that which was justly due to her, but to which Rachel would not otherwise have consented. Note, Strong passions often thwart one another, and those cannot but be continually uneasy that are hurried on by them. Leah is overjoyed that she shall have her husband's company again, that her family might yet further be built up, which is the blessing she desires and devoutly prays for, as is intimated, v. 17, where it is said, *God hearkened unto Leah.* The learned bishop Patrick very well suggests here that the true reason of this contest between Jacob's wives for his company, and their giving him their maids to be his wives, was the earnest desire they had to fulfil the promise made to Abraham (and now lately renewed to Jacob), that his seed should be as the stars of heaven for multitude, and that in one seed of his, the Messiah, all the nations of the earth should be blessed. And he thinks it would have been below the dignity of this sacred history to take such particular notice of these things if there had not been some such great consideration in them. Leah was now blessed with two sons; the first she called *Issachar (a hire),* reckoning herself well repaid for her mandrakes, nay (which is a strange construction of the providence) rewarded for giving her maid to her husband. Note, We abuse God's mercy when we reckon that his favours countenance and patronize our follies. The other she called *Zebulun (dwelling)*, owning God's bounty to her : *God has endowed me with a good dowry, v.* 20. Jacob had not endowed her when he married her, nor had he wherewithal in possession ; but she reckons a family of children not a bill of charges, but a good dowry, Ps. cxiii. 9. She promises herself more of her husband's company now that she had borne him six sons, and that, in love to his children at least, he would often visit her lodgings. Mention is made (*v.* 21) of the birth of a daughter, *Dinah*, because of the following story concerning her, *ch.* xxxiv. Perhaps Jacob had other daughters, though their names are not registered.

II. Rachel fruitful at last (*v.* 22): *God remembered Rachel*, whom he seemed to have forgotten, and *hearkened to her* whose prayers had been long denied ; and then she bore a son. Note, As God justly denies the mercy we have been inordinately desirous of, so sometimes he graciously grants, at length, that which we have long waited for. He corrects our folly, and yet considers our frame, and does not contend for ever. Rachel called her son *Joseph*, which in Hebrew is akin to two words of a contrary signification, *Asaph (abstulit), He has taken away my reproach*, as if the greatest mercy she had in this son was that she had saved her credit ; and *Jasaph (addidit), The Lord shall add to me another son*, which may be looked upon either as the language of her inordinate desire (she scarcely knows how to be thankful for one unless she may be sure of another), or of her faith—she takes this mercy as an earnest of further mercy. "Has God given me his grace ? I may call it Joseph, and say, He shall add more grace ! Has he given me his joy ? I may call it Joseph, and say, He will give me more joy. Has he begun, and shall he not make an end ?"

25 And it came to pass, when Rachel had borne Joseph, that Jacob said unto Laban, Send me away, that I may go unto mine own place, and to my country. 26 Give *me* my wives and my children, for whom I have served thee, and let me go : for thou knowest my service which I have done thee. 27 And Laban said unto him, I pray thee, if I have found favour in thine eyes, *tarry : for* I have learned by experience that the LORD hath blessed me for thy sake. 28 And he said, Appoint me thy wages, and I will give *it*. 29 And he said unto him, Thou knowest how I have served thee, and how thy cattle was with me. 30 For *it was* little which thou hadst before I *came*, and it is *now* increased

unto a multitude ; and the LORD hath blessed thee since my coming : and now when shall I provide for mine own house also ? 31 And he said, What shall I give thee ? And Jacob said, Thou shalt not give me any thing: if thou wilt do this thing for me, I will again feed *and* keep thy flock: 32 I will pass through all thy flock to day, removing from thence all the speckled and spotted cattle, and all the brown cattle among the sheep, and the spotted and speckled among the goats : and *of such* shall be my hire. 33 So shall my righteousness answer for me in time to come, when it shall come for my hire before thy face : every one that *is* not speckled and spotted among the goats, and brown among the sheep, that shall be counted stolen with me. 34 And Laban said, Behold, I would it might be according to thy word. 35 And he removed that day the he goats that were ringstraked and spotted, and all the she goats that were speckled and spotted, *and* every one that had *some* white in it, and all the brown among the sheep, and gave *them* into the hand of his sons. 36 And he set three days' journey betwixt himself and Jacob: and Jacob fed the rest of Laban's flocks.

We have here,

I. Jacob's thoughts of home. He faithfully served his time out with Laban, even his second apprenticeship, though he was an old man, had a large family to provide for, and it was high time for him to set up for himself. Though Laban's service was hard, and he had cheated him in the first bargain he had made, yet Jacob honestly performs his engagements. Note, A good man, though he swear to his own hurt, will not change. And though others have deceived us this will not justify us in deceiving them. Our rule is to do as we *would be* done by, not as we *are* done by. Jacob's term having expired, he begs leave to be gone, *v.* 25. Observe, 1. He retained his affection for the land of Canaan, not only because it was the land of his nativity, and his father and mother were there, whom he longed to see, but because it was the land of promise ; and, in token of his dependence upon the promise of it, though he sojourn in Haran he can by no means think of settling there. Thus should we be affected towards our heavenly country, looking upon ourselves as strangers here, viewing the heavenly country as our home, and longing to be there, as soon as the days of our service upon earth are numbered and finished.

We must not think of taking root here, for this is not our place and country, Heb. xiii. 14. 2. He was desirous to go to Canaan, though he had a great family to take with him, and no provision yet made for them. He had got wives and children with Laban, but nothing else ; yet he does not solicit Laban to give him either a portion with his wives or the maintenance of some of his children. No, all his request is, *Give me my wives and my children, and send me away, v. 25, 26.* Note, Those that trust in God, in his providence and promise, though they have great families and small incomes, can cheerfully hope that he who sends mouths will send meat. He who feeds the brood of the ravens will not starve the seed of the righteous.

II. Laban's desire of his stay, *v. 27.* In love to himself, not to Jacob or to his wives or children, Laban endeavours to persuade him to continue his chief shepherd, entreating him, by the regard he bore him, not to leave him : *If I have found favour in thy eyes, tarry.* Note, Churlish selfish men know how to give good words when it is to serve their own ends. Laban found that his stock had wonderfully increased with Jacob's good management, and he owns it, with very good expressions of respect both to God and Jacob : *I have learned by experience that the Lord has blessed me for thy sake.* Observe, 1. Laban's learning : *I have learned by experience.* Note, There is many a profitable good lesson to be learned by experience. We are very unapt scholars if we have not learned by experience the evil of sin, the treachery of our own hearts, the vanity of the world, the goodness of God, the gains of godliness, and the like. 2. Laban's lesson. He owns, (1.) That his prosperity was owing to God's blessing : *The Lord has blessed me.* Note, worldly men, who choose their portion in this life, are often blessed with an abundance of this world's goods. Common blessings are given plentifully to many that have no title to covenant-blessings. (3.) That Jacob's piety had brought that blessing upon him : *The Lord has blessed me,* not for my own sake (let not such a man as Laban, that lives without God in the world, *think that he shall receive any thing of the Lord,* Jam. i. 7), but *for thy sake.* Note, [1.] Good men are blessings to the places where they live, even where they live meanly and obscurely, as Jacob in the field, and Joseph in the prison, *ch.* xxxix. 23. [2.] God often blesses bad men with outward mercies for the sake of their godly relations, though it is seldom that they have either the wit to see it or the grace to own it, as Laban did here.

III. The new bargain they came upon. Laban's craft and covetousness took advantage of Jacob's plainness, honesty, and goodnature ; and, perceiving that Jacob began to be won upon by his fair speeches, instead of making him a generous offer and bidding

182

high, as he ought to have done, all things considered, he puts it upon him to make his demands (*v.* 28): *Appoint me thy wages,* knowing he would be very modest in them, and would ask less than he could for shame offer. Jacob accordingly makes a proposal to him, in which,

1. He shows what reason he had to insist upon so much, considering, (1.) That Laban was bound in gratitude to do well for him, because he had served him not only faithfully, but very successfully, *v.* 30. Yet here observe how he speaks, like himself, very modestly. Laban had said, *The Lord has blessed me for thy sake :* Jacob will not say so, but, *The Lord has blessed thee since my coming.* Note, Humble saints take more pleasure in doing good than in hearing of it again. (2.) That he himself was bound in duty to take care of his own family : *Now, when shall I provide for my own house also ?* Note, Faith and charity, though they are excellent things, must not take us off from making necessary provisions for our own support, and the support of our families. We must, like Jacob, *trust in the Lord and do good,* and yet we must, like him, provide for our own houses also ; he that does not the latter *is worse than an infidel,* 1 Tim. v. 8.

2. He is willing to refer himself to the providence of God, which, he knew, extends itself to the smallest things, even the colour of the cattle ; and he will be content to have for his wages the sheep and goats of such and such a colour, speckled, spotted, and brown, which should hereafter be brought forth, *v.* 32, 33. This, he thinks, will be a most effectual way both to prevent Laban's cheating him and to secure himself from being suspected of cheating Laban. Some think he chose this colour because in Canaan it was generally most desired and delighted in ; their shepherds in Canaan are called *Nekohim* (Amos i. 1), the word here used for *speckled ;* and Laban was willing to consent to this bargain because he thought if the few he had that were now speckled and spotted were separated from the rest, which by agreement was to be done immediately, the body of the flock which Jacob was to tend, being of one colour, either all black or all white, would produce few or none of mixed colours, and so he should have Jacob's service for nothing, or next to nothing. According to this bargain, those few that were partycoloured were separated, and put into the hands of Laban's sons, and sent three days' journey off; so great was Laban's jealousy lest any of them should mix with the rest of the flock, to the advantage of Jacob. And now a fine bargain Jacob has made for himself ! Is this his providing for his own house, to put it upon such an uncertainty ? If these cattle bring forth, as usually cattle do, young ones of the same colour with themselves, he must still serve for nothing, and be a drudge and a beggar all the days of his

life; but he knows whom he has trusted, and the event showed, (1.) That he took the best way that could be taken with Laban, who otherwise would certainly have been too hard for him. And, (2.) That it was not in vain to rely upon the divine providence, which owns and blesses honest humble diligence. Those that find men whom they deal with unjust and unkind shall not find God so, but, some way or other, he will recompense the injured, and be a good pay-master to those that commit their cause to him.

37 And Jacob took him rods of green poplar, and of the hazel and chesnut tree; and pilled white strakes in them, and made the white appear which *was* in the rods. 38 And he set the rods which he had pilled before the flocks in the gutters in the watering troughs when the flocks came to drink, that they should conceive when they came to drink. 39 And the flocks conceived before the rods, and brought forth cattle ringstraked, speckled, and spotted. 40 And Jacob did separate the lambs, and set the faces of the flocks toward the ringstraked, and all the brown in the flock of Laban; and he put his own flocks by themselves, and put them not unto Laban's cattle. 41 And it came to pass, whensoever the stronger cattle did conceive, that Jacob laid the rods before the eyes of the cattle in the gutters, that they might conceive among the rods. 42 But when the cattle were feeble, he put *them* not in: so the feebler were Laban's, and the stronger Jacob's. 43 And the man increased exceedingly, and had much cattle, and maidservants, and menservants, and camels, and asses.

Here is Jacob's honest policy to make his bargain more advantageous to himself than it was likely to be. If he had not taken some course to help himself, it would have been a bad bargain indeed, which he knew Laban would never consider, or rather would be well pleased to see him a loser by, so little did Laban consult any one's interest but his own. Now Jacob's contrivances were, 1. To set peeled sticks before the cattle where they were watered, that, looking much at those unusual party-coloured sticks, by the power of imagination they might bring forth young ones in like manner party-coloured, *v.* 37—39. Probably this custom was commonly used by the shepherds of Canaan, who coveted to have their cattle of this motley colour. Note, It becomes a man to be master of his trade, whatever it is, and to be not only industrious, but ingenious in it, and to be versed in all its lawful arts and mysteries; for what is a man but his trade? There is a discretion which God teaches the husbandman (as plain a trade as that is), and which he ought to learn, Isa. xxviii. 26. 2. When he began to have a stock of ring-straked and brown, he contrived to set them first, and to put the faces of the rest towards them, with the same design as in the former contrivance; but would not let his own, that were motley-coloured, look at Laban's that were of one colour, *v.* 40. Strong impressions, it seems, are made by the eye, with which therefore we have need to make a covenant. 3. When he found that his project succeeded, through the special blessing of God upon it, he contrived, by using it only with the stronger cattle, to secure to himself those that were most valuable, leaving the feebler to Laban, *v.* 41, 42. Thus *Jacob increased exceedingly* (*v.* 43), and grew very rich in a little time. This success of his policy, it is true, was not sufficient to justify it, if there had been any thing fraudulent or unjust in it, which we are sure there was not, for he did it by divine direction (*ch.* xxxi. 12); nor was there any thing in the thing itself but the honest improvement of a fair bargain, which the divine providence wonderfully prospered, both in justice to Jacob whom Laban had wronged and dealt hardly with and in pursuance of the particular promises made to him of the tokens of the divine favour. Note, Those who, while their beginning is small, are humble and honest, contented and industrious, are in a likely way to see their latter end greatly increasing. He that is faithful in a little shall be entrusted with more. He that is faithful in that which is another man's shall be entrusted with something of his own. Jacob, who had been a just servant, became a rich master.

CHAP. XXXI.

Jacob was a very honest good man, a man of great devotion and integrity, yet he had more trouble and vexation than any of the patriarchs. He left his father's house in a fright, went to his uncle's in distress, very hard usage he met with there, and now is going back surrounded with fears. Here is, I. His resolution to return, ver. 1—16. II. His clandestine departure, ver. 17—21. III. Laban's pursuit of him in displeasure, ver. 22—25. IV. The hot words that passed between them, ver. 26—42. V. Their amicable agreement at last, ver. 43, &c.

AND he heard the words of Laban's sons, saying, Jacob hath taken away all that *was* our father's; and of *that* which *was* our father's hath he gotten all this glory. 2 And Jacob beheld the countenance of Laban, and, behold, it *was* not toward him as before. 3 And the LORD said unto Jacob, Return unto the land of thy fathers, and to thy kindred; and I will be with thee. 4 And Jacob sent and called Rachel and Leah to the field unto his flock, 5 And said unto them, I see your father's countenance, that it *is* not toward me as before; but the God of my father hath been with me. 6 And ye know that with all my power I have served your father. 7 And your father hath deceived me, and changed my wages ten times; but God suffered him not to hurt me. 8 If he said thus, The speckled shall be thy wages; then all the cattle bare speckled: and if he said thus, The ringstraked shall be thy hire; then bare all the cattle ringstraked. 9 Thus God hath taken away the cattle of your father, and given *them* to me. 10 And it came to pass at the time that the cattle conceived, that I lifted up mine eyes, and saw in a dream, and, behold, the rams which leaped upon the cattle *were* ringstraked, speckled, and grisled. 11 And the angel of God spake unto me in a dream, *saying*, Jacob: And I said, Here *am* I. 12 And he said, Lift up now thine eyes, and see, all the rams which leap upon the cattle *are* ringstraked, speckled, and grisled: for I have seen all that Laban doeth unto thee. 13 I *am* the God of Beth-el, where thou anointedst the pillar, *and* where thou vowedst a vow unto me: now arise, get thee out from this land, and return unto the land of thy kindred. 14 And Rachel and Leah answered and said unto him, *Is there* yet any portion or inheritance for us in our father's house? 15 Are we not counted of him strangers? for he hath sold us, and hath quite devoured also our money. 16 For all the riches which God hath taken from our father, that *is* our's, and our children's: now then, whatsoever God hath said unto thee, do.

Jacob is here taking up a resolution immediately to quit his uncle's service, to take what he had and go back to Canaan. This resolution he took up upon a just provocation, by divine direction, and with the advice and consent of his wives.

I. Upon a just provocation; for Laban and his sons had become very cross and ill-natured towards him, so that he could not stay among them with safety or satisfaction.

1. Laban's sons showed their ill-will in what they said, *v.* 1. It should seem they

said it in Jacob's hearing, with a design to vex him. The last chapter began with Rachel's envying Leah; this begins with Laban's sons envying Jacob. Observe, (1.) How greatly they magnify Jacob's prosperity: *He has gotten all this glory.* And what was this glory that they made so much ado about? It was a parcel of brown sheep and speckled goats (and perhaps the fine colours made them seem more glorious), and some camels and asses, and such like trading; and this was *all this glory.* Note, Riches are glorious things in the eyes of carnal people, while to all those that are conversant with heavenly things they have no glory in comparison with the glory which excelleth. Men's over-valuing worldly wealth is that fundamental error which is the root of covetousness, envy, and all evil. (2.) How basely they reflect upon Jacob's fidelity, as if what he had he had not gotten honestly: *Jacob has taken away all that was our father's.* Not all, surely. What had become of those cattle which were committed to the custody of Laban's sons, and sent *three days' journey* off? *ch.* xxx. 35, 36. They mean all that was committed to him; but, speaking invidiously, they express themselves thus generally. Note, [1.] Those that are ever so careful to keep a good conscience cannot always be sure of a good name. [2.] This is one of the vanities and vexations which attend outward prosperity, that it makes a man to be envied of his neighbours (Eccl. iv. 4), and *who can stand before envy?* Prov. xxvii. 4. Whom Heaven blesses hell curses, and all its children on earth.

2. Laban himself said little, but his countenance was not towards Jacob as it used to be; and Jacob could not but take notice of it, *v.* 2, 5. He was but a churl at the best, but now he was more churlish than formerly. Note, Envy is a sin that often appears in the countenance; hence we read of an *evil eye,* Prov. xxiii. 6. Sour looks may do a great deal towards the ruin of peace and love in a family, and the making of those uneasy of whose comfort we ought to be tender. Laban's angry countenance lost him the greatest blessing his family ever had, and justly.

II. By divine direction and under the convoy of a promise: *The Lord said unto Jacob, Return, and I will be with thee, v.* 3. Though Jacob had met with very hard usage here, yet he would not quit his place till God bade him. He came thither by orders from Heaven, and there he would stay till he was ordered back. Note, It is our duty to set ourselves, and it will be our comfort to see ourselves, under God's guidance, both in our going out and in our coming in. The direction he had from Heaven is more fully related in the account he gives of it to his wives (*v.* 10—13), where he tells them of a dream he had about the cattle, and the wonderful increase of those of his colour; and how the angel of God, in that dream (for I suppose the dream spoken of *v.* 10 and that *v.* 11 to be the same), took notice of the workings of his fancy in his sleep, and instructed him, so that it was not by chance, nor by his own policy, that he obtained that great advantage; but, 1. By the providence of God, who had taken notice of the hardships Laban had put upon him, and took this way to recompense him : " *For I have seen all that Laban doeth unto thee,* and herein I have an eye to that." Note, There is more of equity in the distributions of the divine providence than we are aware of, and by them the injured are recompensed really, though perhaps insensibly. Nor was it only by the justice of providence that Jacob was thus enriched, but, 2. In performance of the promise intimated in what is said *v.* 13, *I am the God of Beth-el.* This was the place where the covenant was renewed with him. Note, Worldly prosperity and success are doubly sweet and comfortable when we see them flowing, not from common providence, but from covenant-love, *to perform the mercy promised*—when we have them from God as *the God of Beth-el,* from those promises of the life which now is that belong to godliness. Jacob, even when he had this hopeful prospect of growing rich with Laban, must think of returning. When the world begins to smile upon us we must remember it is not our home. *Now arise* (*v.* 13) *and return,* (1.) To thy devotions in Canaan, the solemnities of which had perhaps been much intermitted while he was with Laban. The times of this servitude God had winked at; but now, " Return to the place where thou anointedst the pillar and vowedst the vow. Now that thou beginnest to grow rich it is time to think of an altar and sacrifices again." (2.) To thy comforts in Canaan : *Return to the land of thy kindred.* He was here among his near kindred ; but those only he must look upon as his kindred in the best sense, the kindred he must live and die with, to whom pertained the covenant. Note, The heirs of Canaan must never reckon themselves at home till they come thither, however they may seem to take root here.

III. With the knowledge and consent of his wives. Observe,

1. He sent for Rachel and Leah to him to the field (*v.* 4), that he might confer with them more privately, or because one would not come to the other's apartment and he would willingly talk with them together, or because he had work to do in the field which he would not leave. Note, Husbands that love their wives will communicate their purposes and intentions to them. Where there is a mutual affection there will be a mutual confidence. And the prudence of the wife should engage the heart of her husband to trust in her, Prov. xxxi. 11. Jacob told his wives, (1.) How faithfully he had served their father, *v.* 6. Note, If others do not do their duty to us, yet we shall have the comfort of having done ours to them. (2.) How unfaithfully their father had dealt with him, *v.* 7. He would never keep to any bargain that he made with him, but, after the first year, still as he saw Providence favour Jacob with the colour agreed on, every half year of the remaining five he changed it for some other colour, which made it ten times ; as if he thought not only to deceive Jacob, but the divine Providence, which manifestly smiled upon him. Note, Those that deal honestly are not always honestly dealt with. (3.) How God had owned him notwithstanding. He had protected him from Laban's ill-will : *God suffered him not to hurt me.* Note, Those that keep close to God shall be kept safely by him. He had also provided plentifully for him, notwithstanding Laban's design to ruin him : *God has taken away the cattle of your father, and given them to me, v.* 9. Thus the righteous God paid Jacob for his hard service out of Laban's estate ; as afterwards he paid the seed of Jacob for their serving the Egyptians, with their spoils. Note, God is not unrighteous to forget his people's work and labour of love, though men be so, Heb. vi. 10. Providence has ways of making those honest in the event that are not so in their design. Note, further, *The wealth of the sinner is laid up for the just,* Prov. xiii. 22. (4.) He told them of the command God had given him, in a dream, to return to his own country (*v.* 13), that they might not suspect his resolution to arise from inconstancy, or any disaffection to their country or family, but might see it to proceed from a principle of obedience to his God, and dependence on him.

2. His wives cheerfully consented to his resolution. They also brought forward their grievances, complaining that their father had been not only unkind, but unjust, to them (*v.* 14—16), that he looked upon them as strangers, and was without natural affection towards them ; and, whereas Jacob had looked upon the wealth which God had transferred from Laban to him as his wages, they looked upon it as their portions ; so that, both ways, God forced Laban to pay his debts, both to his servant and to his daughters. So then it seemed, (1.) They were weary of their own people and their father's house, and could easily forget them. Note, This good use we should make of the unkind usage we meet with from the world, we should sit the more loose to it, and be willing to leave it and desirous to be at home. (2.) They were willing to go along with their husband, and put themselves with him under the divine direction : *Whatsoever God hath said unto thee do.* Note, Those wives that are their husband's meet helps will never be their hindrances in doing that to which God calls them.

17 Then Jacob rose up, and set his sons and his wives upon camels ; 18

And he carried away all his cattle, and all his goods which he had gotten, the cattle of his getting, which he had gotten in Padan-aram, for to go to Isaac his father in the land of Canaan. 19 And Laban went to shear his sheep: and Rachel had stolen the images that *were* her father's. 20 And Jacob stole away unawares to Laban the Syrian, in that he told him not that he fled. 21 So he fled with all that he had; and he rose up, and passed over the river, and set his face *toward* the mount Gilead. 22 And it was told Laban on the third day that Jacob was fled. 23 And he took his brethren with him, and pursued after him seven days' journey; and they overtook him in the mount Gilead. 24 And God came to Laban the Syrian in a dream by night, and said unto him, Take heed that thou speak not to Jacob either good or bad.

Here is, I. Jacob's flight from Laban. We may suppose he had been long considering of it, and casting about in his mind respecting it; but when now, at last, God had given him positive orders to go, he made no delay, nor was he disobedient to the heavenly vision. The first opportunity that offered itself he laid hold of, when Laban was shearing his sheep (*v.* 19), that part of his flock which was in the hands of his sons three days' journey off. Now, 1. It is certain that it was lawful for Jacob to leave his service suddenly, without giving a quarter's warning. It was not only justified by the particular instructions God gave him, but warranted by the fundamental law of self-preservation, which directs us, when we are in danger, to shift for our own safety, as far as we can do it without wronging our consciences. 2. It was his prudence to steal away unawares to Laban, lest, if Laban had known, he should have hindered him or plundered him. 3. It was honestly done to take no more than his own with him, the *cattle of his getting, v.* 18. He took what Providence gave him, and was content with that, and would not take the repair of his damages into his own hands. Yet Rachel was not so honest as her husband; she *stole her father's images* (*v.* 19) and carried them away with her. The Hebrew calls them *teraphim.* Some think they were only little representations of the ancestors of the family, in statues or pictures, which Rachael had a particular fondness for, and was desirous to have with her, now that she was going into another country. It should rather seem that they were images for a religious use, *penates, household-gods,* either worshipped or consulted

as oracles; and we are willing to hope (with bishop Patrick) that she took them away not out of covetousness of the rich metal they were made of, much less for her own use, or out of any superstitious fear lest Laban, by consulting his *teraphim,* might know which way they had gone (Jacob, no doubt, dwelt with his wives as a man of knowledge, and they were better taught than so), but out of a design hereby to convince her father of the folly of his regard to those as gods which could not secure themselves, Isa. xlvi. 1, 2.

II. Laban's pursuit of Jacob. Tidings were brought him, on the third day, that Jacob had fled; he immediately raises the whole clan, takes his brethren, that is, the relations of his family, that were all in his interests, and pursues Jacob (as Pharaoh and his Egyptians afterwards pursued the seed of Jacob), to bring him back into bondage again, or with design to strip him of what he had. Seven days' journey he marched in pursuit of him, *v.* 23. He would not have taken half the pains to have visited his best friends. But the truth is bad men will do more to serve their sinful passions than good men will to serve their just affections, and are more vehement in their anger than in their love. Well, at length Laban overtook him, and the very night before he came up with him God interposed in the quarrel, rebuked Laban and sheltered Jacob, charging Laban not to *speak unto him either good or bad* (*v.* 24), that is, to say nothing against his going on with his journey, for that it proceeded from the Lord. The same Hebraism we have, *ch.* xxiv. 50. Laban, during his seven days' march, had been full of rage against Jacob, and was now full of hopes that his lust should be satisfied upon him (Exod. xv. 9); but God comes to him, and with one word ties his hands, though he does not turn his heart. Note, 1. In a dream, and in slumberings upon the bed, God has ways of opening the *ears of men, and sealing their instruction,* Job xxxiii. 15, 16. Thus he admonishes men by their consciences, in secret whispers, which the man of wisdom will hear and heed. 2. The safety of good men is very much owing to the hold God has of the consciences of bad men and the access he has to them. 3. God sometimes appears wonderfully for the deliverance of his people when they are upon the very brink of ruin. The Jews were saved from Haman's plot when the king's decree drew near to be put in execution, Esth. ix. 1.

25 Then Laban overtook Jacob. Now Jacob had pitched his tent in the mount: and Laban with his brethren pitched in the mount of Gilead. 26 And Laban said to Jacob, What hast thou done, that thou hast stolen away unawares to me, and carried away my daughters, as captives *taken* with the

186

sword? 27 Wherefore didst thou flee away secretly, and steal away from me; and didst not tell me, that I might have sent thee away with mirth, and with songs, with tabret, and with harp? 28 And hast not suffered me to kiss my sons and my daughters? thou hast now done foolishly in *so* doing. 29 It is in the power of my hand to do you hurt: but the God of your father spake unto me yesternight, saying, Take thou heed that thou speak not to Jacob either good or bad. 30 And now, *though* thou wouldest needs be gone, because thou sore longedst after thy father's house, *yet* wherefore hast thou stolen my gods? 31 And Jacob answered and said to Laban, Because I was afraid: for I said, Peradventure thou wouldest take by force thy daughters from me. 32 With whomsoever thou findest thy gods, let him not live: before our brethren discern thou what *is* thine with me, and take *it* to thee. For Jacob knew not that Rachel had stolen them. 33 And Laban went into Jacob's tent, and into Leah's tent, and into the two maidservants' tents; but he found *them* not. Then went he out of Leah's tent, and entered into Rachel's tent. 34 Now Rachel had taken the images, and put them in the camel's furniture, and sat upon them. And Laban searched all the tent, but found *them* not. 35 And she said to her father, Let it not displease my lord that I cannot rise up before thee; for the custom of women *is* upon me. And he searched, but found not the images.

We have here the reasoning, not to say the rallying, that took place between Laban and Jacob at their meeting, in that mountain which was afterwards called *Gilead, v.* 25. Here is,

I The high charge which Laban exhibited against him. He accuses him,

1. As a renegade that had unjustly deserted his service. To represent Jacob as a criminal, he will have it thought that he intended kindness to his daughters (*v.* 27, 28), that he would have dismissed them with all the marks of love and honour that could be, that he would have made a solemn business of it, would have kissed his little grandchildren (and that was all he would have given them), and, according to the foolish custom of the country, would have sent them

away *with mirth, and with songs, with tabret, and with harp:* not as Rebekah was sent away out of the same family, above 120 years before, with prayers and blessings (*ch* xxiv. 60), but with sport and merriment, which was a sign that religion had very much decayed in the family, and that they had lost their seriousness. However, he pretends they would have been treated with respect at parting. Note, It is common for bad men, when they are disappointed in their malicious projects, to pretend that they designed nothing but what was kind and fair. When they cannot do the mischief they intended, they are loth it should be thought that they ever did intend it. When they have not done what they should have done they come off with this excuse, that they would have done it. Men may thus be deceived, but God cannot. He likewise suggests that Jacob had some bad design in stealing away thus (*v.* 26), that he took his wives away as captives. Note, Those that mean ill themselves are most apt to put the worst construction upon what others do innocently. The insinuating and the aggravating of faults are the artifices of a designing malice, and those must be represented (though never so unjustly) as intending ill against whom ill is intended. Upon the whole matter, (1.) He boasts of his own power (*v.* 29): *It is in the power of my hand to do you hurt.* He supposes that he had both right on his side (*a good action,* as we say, against Jacob) and *strength* on his side, either to avenge the wrong or recover the right. Note, Bad people commonly value themselves much upon their power to do hurt, whereas a power to do good is much more valuable. Those that will do nothing to make themselves amiable love to be thought formidable. And yet, (2.) He owns himself under the check and restraint of God's power; and, though it redounds much to the credit and comfort of Jacob, he cannot avoid telling him the caution God had given him the night before in a dream, *Speak not to Jacob good nor bad.* Note, As God has all wicked instruments in a chain, so when he pleases he can make them sensible of it, and force them to own it to his praise, as protector of the good, as Balaam did. Or we may look upon this as an instance of some conscientious regard felt by Laban for God's express prohibitions. As bad as he was he durst not injure one whom he saw to be the particular care of Heaven. Note, A great deal of mischief would be prevented if men would but attend to the caveats which their own consciences give them in slumberings upon the bed, and regard the voice of God in them.

2. As a thief, *v.* 30. Rather than own that he had given him any colour of provocation to depart, he is willing to impute it to a foolish fondness for his father's house, which made him that he would needs be gone; but then (says he) *wherefore hast thou*

stolen my gods? Foolish man! to call those his gods that could be stolen! Could he expect protection from those that could neither resist nor discover their invaders? Happy are those who have the Lord for their God, for they have a God that they cannot be robbed of. Enemies may steal our goods, but not our God. Here Laban lays to Jacob's charge things that he knew not, the common distress of oppressed innocency.

II. Jacob's apology for himself. Those that commit their cause to God, yet are not forbidden to plead it themselves with meekness and fear. 1. As to the charge of stealing away his own wives he clears himself by giving the true reason why he went away unknown to Laban, v. 31. He feared lest Laban would by force take away his daughters, and so oblige him, by the bond of his affection to his wives, to continue in his service. Note, Those that are unjust in the least, it may be suspected, will be unjust also in much, Luke xvi. 10. If Laban deceive Jacob in his wages, it is likely he will make no conscience of robbing him of his wives, and putting those asunder whom God has joined together. What may not be feared from men that have no principle of honesty? 2. As to the charge of stealing Laban's gods he pleads not guilty, v. 32. He not only did not take them himself (he was not so fond of them), but he did not know that they were taken. Yet perhaps he spoke too hastily and inconsiderately when he said, "Whoever has taken them, *let him not live ;*" upon this he might reflect with some bitterness when, not long after, Rachel who had taken them died suddenly in travail. How just soever we think ourselves to be, it is best to forbear imprecations, lest they fall heavier than we imagine.

III. The diligent search Laban made for his gods (v. 33—35), partly out of hatred to Jacob, whom he would gladly have an occasion to quarrel with, partly out of love to his idols, which he was loth to part with. We do not find that he searched Jacob's flocks for stolen cattle; but he searched his furniture for stolen gods. He was of Micah's mind, *You have taken away my gods, and what have I more?* Judg. xviii. 24. Were the worshippers of false gods so set upon their idols? did they thus walk in the name of their gods? And shall not we be as solicitous in our enquiries after the true God? When he has justly departed from us, how carefully should we ask, *Where is God my Maker?* *O that I knew where I might find him!* Job xxiii. 3. Laban, after all his searches, missed of finding his gods, and was baffled in his enquiry with a sham; but our God will not only be found of those that seek him, but they shall find him their bountiful rewarder.

36 And Jacob was wroth, and chode with Laban : and Jacob answered and

said to Laban, What *is* my trespass ? what *is* my sin, that thou hast so hotly pursued after me? 37 Whereas thou hast searched all my stuff, what hast thou found of all thy household stuff? set *it* here before my brethren and thy brethren, that they may judge betwixt us both. 38 This twenty years *have* I *been* with thee; thy ewes and thy she goats have not cast their young, and the rams of thy flock have I not eaten. 39 That which was torn *of beasts* I brought not unto thee; I bare the loss of it; of my hand didst thou require it, *whether* stolen by day, or stolen by night. 40 *Thus* I was; in the day the drought consumed me, and the frost by night; and my sleep departed from mine eyes. 41 Thus have I been twenty years in thy house; I served thee fourteen years for thy two daughters, and six years for thy cattle : and thou hast changed my wages ten times. 42 Except the God of my father, the God of Abraham, and the fear of Isaac, had been with me, surely thou hadst sent me away now empty. God hath seen mine affliction and the labour of my hands, and rebuked *thee* yesternight.

See in these verses,

I. The power of provocation. Jacob's natural temper was mild and calm, and grace had improved it ; he was a smooth man, and a plain man ; and yet Laban's unreasonable carriage towards him put him into a heat that transported him into some vehemence, v. 36, 37. His chiding with Laban, though it may admit of some excuse, was not justifiable, nor is it written for our imitation. Grievous words stir up anger, and commonly do but make bad worse. It is a very great affront to one that bears an honest mind to be charged with dishonesty, and yet even this we must learn to bear with patience, committing our cause to God.

II. The comfort of a good conscience. This was Jacob's rejoicing, that when Laban accused him his own conscience acquitted him, and witnessed for him that he had been in all things willing and careful to live honestly, Heb. xiii. 18. Note, Those that in any employment have dealt faithfully, if they cannot obtain the credit of it with men, yet shall have the comfort of it in their own bosoms.

III. The character of a good servant, and particularly of a faithful shepherd. Jacob had approved himself such a one, v. 38—40. 1. He was very careful, so that, through his oversight or neglect, the ewes did not cast their young. His piety also procured a blessing upon his master's effects that were under his hands. Note, Servants should take no less care of what they are entrusted with for their masters than if they were entitled to it as their own. 2. He was very honest, and took none of that for his own eating which was not allowed him. He contented himself with mean fare, and coveted not to feast upon the rams of the flock. Note, Servants must not be dainty in their food, nor covet what is forbidden them, but in that, and other instances, show all good fidelity. 3. He was very laborious, *v.* 40. He stuck to his business, all weathers; and bore both heat and cold with invincible patience. Note, Men of business, that intend to make something of it, must resolve to endure hardness. Jacob is here an example to ministers; they also are shepherds, of whom it is required that they be true to their trust and willing to take pains.

IV. The character of a hard master. Laban had been such a one to Jacob. Those are bad masters, 1. Who exact from their servants that which is unjust, by obliging them to make good that which is not damaged by any default of theirs. This Laban did, *v.* 39. Nay, if there has been a neglect, yet it is unjust to punish above the proportion of the fault. That may be an inconsiderable damage to the master which would go near to ruin a poor servant. 2. Those also are bad masters who deny to their servants that which is just and equal. This Laban did, *v.* 41. It was unreasonable for him to make Jacob serve for his daughters, when he had in reversion so great an estate secured to him by the promise of God himself; as it was also to give him his daughters without portions, when it was in the power of his hands to do well for them. Thus he robbed the poor because he was poor, as he did also by changing his wages.

V. The care of providence for the protection of injured innocence, *v.* 42. God took cognizance of the wrong done to Jacob, and repaid him whom Laban would otherwise have sent empty away, and rebuked Laban, who otherwise would have swallowed him up. Note, God is the patron of the oppressed; and those who are wronged and yet not ruined, cast down and yet not destroyed, must acknowledge him in their preservation and give him the glory of it. Observe, 1. Jacob speaks of God as the God of his father, intimating that he thought himself unworthy to be thus regarded, but was beloved for the father's sake. 2. He calls him the God of Abraham, and the fear of Isaac; for Abraham was dead, and had gone to that world where perfect love casts out fear; but Isaac was yet alive, sanctifying the Lord in his heart, as his fear and his dread

43 And Laban answered and said

unto Jacob, *These* daughters *are* my daughters, and *these* children *are* my children, and *these* cattle *are* my cattle, and all that thou seest *is* mine: and what can I do this day unto these my daughters, or unto their children which they have borne? 44 Now therefore come thou, let us make a covenant, I and thou; and let it be for a witness between me and thee. 45 And Jacob took a stone, and set it up *for* a pillar. 46 And Jacob said unto his brethren, Gather stones; and they took stones, and made a heap: and they did eat there upon the heap. 47 And Laban called it Jegar-sahadutha: but Jacob called it Galeed. 48 And Laban said, This heap *is* a witness between me and thee this day. Therefore was the name of it called Galeed; 49 And Mizpah; for he said, The LORD watch between me and thee, when we are absent one from another. 50 If thou shalt afflict my daughters, or if thou shalt take *other* wives beside my daughters, no man *is* with us; see, God *is* witness betwixt me and thee. 51 And Laban said to Jacob, Behold this heap, and behold *this* pillar, which I have cast betwixt me and thee; 52 This heap *be* witness, and *this* pillar *be* witness, that I will not pass over this heap to thee, and that thou shalt not pass over this heap and this pillar unto me, for harm. 53 The God of Abraham, and the God of Nahor, the God of their father, judge betwixt us. And Jacob sware by the fear of his father Isaac. 54 Then Jacob offered sacrifice upon the mount, and called his brethren to eat bread: and they did eat bread, and tarried all night in the mount. 55 And early in the morning Laban rose up, and kissed his sons and his daughters, and blessed them: and Laban departed, and returned unto his place.

We have here the compromising of the matter between Laban and Jacob. Laban had nothing to say in reply to Jacob's remonstrance: he could neither justify himself nor condemn Jacob, but was convicted by his own conscience of the wrong he had done him; and therefore desires to hear no more of the matter He is not willing to own himself in a fault, nor to ask Jacob's forgiveness, and make him satisfaction, as he ought to have done. But,

I. He turns it off with a profession of kindness for Jacob's wives and children (*v.* 43): *These daughters are my daughters.* When he cannot excuse what he has done, he does, in effect, own what he should have done; he should have treated them as his own, but he had counted them as strangers, *v.* 15. Note, It is common for those who are without natural affection to pretend much to it when it will serve a turn. Or perhaps Laban said this in a vain-glorious way, as one that loved to talk big, and use great swelling words of vanity: " All that thou seest is mine." It was not so, it was all Jacob's, and he had paid dearly for it; yet Jacob let him have his saying, perceiving him coming into a better humour. Note, Property lies near the hearts of worldly people. They love to boast of it, " This is mine, and the other is mine," as Nabal, 1 Sam. xxv. 11, *my bread and my water.*

II. He proposes a covenant of friendship between them, to which Jacob readily agrees, without insisting upon Laban's submission, much less his restitution. Note, When quarrels happen, we should be willing to be friends again upon any terms : peace and love are such valuable jewels that we can scarcely buy them too dearly. Better sit down losers than go on in strife. Now observe here,

1. The substance of this covenant. Jacob left it wholly to Laban to settle it. The tenour of it was, (1.) That Jacob should be a good husband to his wives, that he should not afflict them, nor marry other wives besides them, *v.* 50. Jacob had never given him any cause to suspect that he would be any other than a kind husband; yet, as if he had, he was willing to come under this engagement. Though Laban had afflicted them himself, yet he will bind Jacob that he shall not afflict them. Note, Those that are injurious themselves are commonly most jealous of others, and those that do not do their own duty are most peremptory in demanding duty from others. (2.) That he should never be a bad neighbour to Laban, *v.* 52. It was agreed that no act of hostility should ever pass between them, that Jacob should forgive and forget all the wrongs he had received and not remember them against Laban or his family in after-times. Note, We may resent an injury which yet we may not revenge.

2. The ceremony of this covenant. It was made and ratified with great solemnity, according to the usages of those times. (1.) A pillar was erected (*v.* 45), and a heap of stones raised (*v.* 46), to perpetuate the memory of the thing, the way of recording agreements by writing being then either not known or not used. (2.) A sacrifice was offered (*v.* 54), a sacrifice of peace-offerings. Note, Our peace with God is that which puts true comfort into our peace with our friends. If parties contend, the reconciliation of both

190

to him will facilitate their reconciliation one to another. (3.) They did eat bread together (*v.* 46), jointly partaking of the feast upon the sacrifice, *v.* 54. This was in token of a hearty reconciliation. Covenants of friendship were anciently ratified by the parties eating and drinking together. It was in the nature of a love-feast. (4.) They solemnly appealed to God concerning their sincerity herein, [1.] As a witness (*v.* 49): *The Lord watch between me and thee,* that is, " The Lord take cognizance of every thing that shall be done on either side in violation of this league. When we are out of one another's sight, let this be a restraint upon us, that wherever we are we are under God's eye." This appeal is convertible into a prayer. Friends at a distance from each other may take the comfort of this, that when they cannot know or succour one another God watches between them, and has his eye on them both. [2.] As a Judge, *v.* 53. *The God of Abraham* (from whom Jacob descended), *and the God of Nahor* (from whom Laban descended), *the God of their father* (the common ancestor, from whom they both descended), *judge betwixt us.* God's relation to them is thus expressed to intimate that they worshipped one and the same God, upon which consideration there ought to be no enmity between them. Note, Those that have one God should have one heart: those that agree in religion should strive to agree in every thing else. God is Judge between contending parties, and he will judge righteously; whoever does wrong, it is at his peril. (5.) They gave a new name to the place, *v.* 47, 48. Laban called it in Syriac, and Jacob in Hebrew, *the heap of witness;* and (*v.* 49) it was called *Mizpah, a watch-tower.* Posterity being included in the league, care was taken that thus the memory of it should be preserved. These names are applicable to the seals of the gospel covenant, which are witnesses to us if we be faithful, but witnesses against us if we be false. The name Jacob gave this heap *(Galeed)* stuck by it, not the name Laban gave it. In all this rencounter, Laban was noisy and full of words, affecting to say much; Jacob was silent, and said little. When Laban appealed to God under many titles, Jacob only *swore by the fear of his father Isaac,* that is, the God whom his father Isaac feared, who had never served other gods, as Abraham and Nahor had done. Two words of Jacob's were more memorable than all Laban's speeches and vain repetitions : *for the words of wise men are heard in quiet, more than the cry of him that ruleth among fools,* Eccl. ix. 17.

Lastly, After all this angry parley, they part friends, *v.* 55. Laban very affectionately *kissed his sons and his daughters, and blessed them,* and then went back in peace. Note, God is often better to us than our fears, and strangely overrules the spirits of men in our favour, beyond what we could have expected; for it is not in vain to trust in him.

CHAP. XXXII.

We have here Jacob still upon his journey towards Canaan. Never did so many memorable things occur in any march as in this of Jacob's little family. By the way he meets, I. With good tidings from his God, ver. 1, 2. II. With bad tidings from his brother, to whom he sent a message to notify his return, ver. 3—6. In his distress, 1. He divides his company, ver. 7, 8. 2. He makes his prayer to God, ver. 9—12. *3. He sends a present to his brother, ver. 13—23. 4. He wrestles with the angel, ver. 24—32.

AND Jacob went on his way, and the angels of God met him. 2 And when Jacob saw them, he said, This *is* God's host: and he called the name of that place Mahanaim.

Jacob, having got clear of Laban, pursues his journey homewards towards Canaan: when God has helped us through difficulties we should go on our way heaven-ward with so much the more cheerfulness and resolution. Now, 1. Here is Jacob's convoy in his journey (*v.* 1): *The angels of God met him*, in a visible appearance, whether in a vision by day or in a dream by night, as when he saw them upon the ladder (*ch.* xxviii. 12), is uncertain. Note, Those that keep in a good way have always a good guard; angels themselves are ministering spirits for their safety, Heb. i. 14. Where Jacob pitched his tents, they pitched theirs about him, Ps. xxxiv. 7. They met him, to bid him welcome to Canaan again; a more honourable reception this was than ever any prince had, that was met by the magistrates of a city in their formalities. They met him to congratulate him on his arrival, as well as on his escape from Laban; for they have pleasure in the prosperity of God's servants. They had invisibly attended him all along, but now they appeared to him, because he had greater dangers before him than those he had hitherto encountered. Note, When God designs his people for extraordinary trials, he prepares them by extraordinary comforts. We should think it had been more seasonable for these angels to have appeared to him amidst the perplexity and agitation occasioned first by Laban, and afterwards by Esau, than in this calm and quiet interval, when he saw not himself in any imminent peril; but God will have us, when we are in peace, to provide for trouble, and, when trouble comes, to live upon former observations and experiences; for *we walk by faith, not by sight.* God's people, at death, are returning to Canaan, to their Father's house; and then the angels of God will meet them, to congratulate them on the happy finishing of their servitude, and to carry them to their rest. 2. The comfortable notice he took of this convoy, *v.* 2. *This is God's host*, and therefore, (1.) It is a powerful host; very great is he that is thus attended, and very safe that is thus guarded. (2.) God must have the praise of this protection: "This I may thank God for, for it is his host." A good man may with an eye of faith see the same that Jacob saw with his

bodily eyes, by believing that promise (Ps. xci. 11), *He shall give his angels charge over thee.* What need have we to dispute whether every particular saint has a guardian angel, when we are sure he has a guard of angels about him? To preserve the remembrance of this favour, Jacob gave a name to the place from it, *Mahanaim, two hosts*, or *two camps.* That is, say some of the rabbin, one host of the guardian angels of Mesopotamia, who conducted Jacob thence, and delivered him safely to the other host of the angels of Canaan, who met him upon the borders where he now was. Rather, they appeared to him in two hosts, one on either side, or one in the front and the other in the rear, to protect him from Laban behind and Esau before, that they might be a complete guard. Thus he is *compassed* with God's favour. Perhaps in allusion to this the church is called *Mahanaim, two armies*, Cant. vi. 13. Here were Jacob's family, which made one army, representing the church militant and itinerant on earth; and the angels, another army, representing the church triumphant and at rest in heaven.

3 And Jacob sent messengers before him to Esau his brother unto the land of Seir, the country of Edom. 4 And he commanded them, saying, Thus shall ye speak unto my lord Esau; Thy servant Jacob saith thus, I have sojourned with Laban, and stayed there until now: 5 And I have oxen, and asses, flocks, and menservants, and womenservants: and I have sent to tell my lord, that I may find grace in thy sight. 6 And the messengers returned to Jacob, saying, We came to thy brother Esau, and also he cometh to meet thee, and four hundred men with him. 7 Then Jacob was greatly afraid and distressed: and he divided the people that *was* with him, and the flocks, and herds, and the camels, into two bands; 8 And said, If Esau come to the one company, and smite it, then the other company which is left shall escape.

Now that Jacob was re-entering Canaan God, by the vision of angels, reminded him of the friends he had when he left it, and thence he takes occasion to remind himself of the enemies he had, particularly Esau. It is probable that Rebekah had sent him word of Esau's settlement in Seir, and of the continuance of his enmity to him. What shall poor Jacob do? He longs to see his father, and yet he dreads to see his brother. He rejoices to see Canaan again, and yet cannot but rejoice with trembling because of Esau.

I. He sends a very kind and humble

message to Esau. It does not appear that his way lay through Esau's country, or that he needed to ask his leave for a passage; but his way lay near it, and he would not go by him without paying him the respect due to a brother, a twin-brother, an only brother, an elder brother, a brother offended. Note, 1. Though our relations fail in their duty to us, yet we must make conscience of doing our duty to them. 2. It is a piece of friendship and brotherly love to acquaint our friends with our condition, and enquire into theirs. Acts of civility may help to slay enmities. Jacob's messsge to him is very obliging, *v.* 4, 5. (1.) He calls Esau his lord, himself his servant, to intimate that he did not insist upon the prerogatives of the birthright and blessing he had obtained for himself, but left it to God to fulfil his own purpose in his seed. Note, *Yielding pacifies great offences,* Eccl x. 4. We must not refuse to speak in a respectful and submissive manner to those that are ever so unjustly exasperated against it. (2.) He gives him a short account of himself, that he was not a fugitive and a vagabond, but, though long absent, had had a certain dwelling-place, with his own relations: *I have sojourned with Laban, and staid there till now;* and that he was not a beggar, nor did he come home, as the prodigal son, destitute of necessaries and likely to be a charge to his relations; no, *I have oxen and asses.* This he knew would (if any thing) recommend him to Esau's good opinion. And, (3.) He courts his favour: *I have sent, that I might find grace in thy sight.* Note, It is no disparagement to those that have the better cause to become petitioners for reconciliation, and to sue for peace as well as right.

II. He receives a very formidable account of Esau's warlike preparations against him (*v.* 6), not a word, but a blow, a very coarse return to his kind message, and a sorry welcome home to a poor brother: *He comes to meet thee, and four hundred men with him.* He is now weary of waiting for the days of mourning for his good father, and even before they come he resolves to slay his brother. 1. He remembers the old quarrel, and will now be avenged on him for the birthright and blessing, and, if possible, defeat Jacob's expectations from both. Note, Malice harboured will last long, and find an occasion to break out with violence a great while after the provocations given. Angry men have good memories. 2. He envies Jacob what little estate he had, and, though he himself was now possessed of a much better, yet nothing will serve him but to feed his eyes upon Jacob's ruin, and fill his fields with Jacob's spoils. Perhaps the account Jacob sent him of his wealth did but provoke him the more. 3. He concludes it easy to destroy him, now that he was upon the road, a poor weary traveller, unfixed, and (as he thinks) unguarded. Those that have the serpent's poison have commonly the serpent's policy, to

take the first and fairest opportunity that offers itself for revenge. 4. He resolves to do it suddenly, and before Jacob had come to his father, lest he should interpose and mediate between them. Esau was one of those that hated peace; when Jacob speaks, speaks peaceably, *he* is for war, Ps. cxx. 6, 7. Out he marches, spurred on with rage, and intent on blood and murders; four hundred men he had with him, probably such as used to hunt with him, armed, no doubt, rough and cruel like their leader, ready to execute the word of command though ever so barbarous, and now breathing nothing but threatenings and slaughter. The tenth part of these were enough to cut off poor Jacob, and his guiltless helpless family, root and branch. No marvel therefore that it follows (*v.* 7), *then Jacob was greatly afraid and distressed,* perhaps the more so from having scarcely recovered the fright Laban had put him in. Note, Many are the troubles of the righteous in this world, and sometimes the end of one is but the beginning of another. The clouds return after the rain. Jacob, though a man of great faith, yet was now greatly afraid. Note, A lively apprehension of danger, and a quickening fear arising from it, may very well consist with a humble confidence in God's power and promise. Christ himself, in his agony, was sorely amazed. III. He puts himself into the best posture of defence that his present circumstances will admit. It was absurd to think of making resistance, all his contrivance is to make an escape, *v.* 7, 8. He thinks it prudent not to venture all in one bottom, and therefore divides what he had into two companies, that, if one were smitten, the other might escape. Like a tender careful master of a family, he is more solicitous for their safety than for his own. He divided his company, not as Abraham (*ch.* xiv. 15), for fight, but for flight.

9 And Jacob said, O God of my father Abraham, and God of my father Isaac, the LORD which saidst unto me, Return unto thy country, and to thy kindred, and I will deal well with thee : 10 I am not worthy of the least of all the mercies, and of all the truth, which thou hast showed unto thy servant; for with my staff I passed over this Jordan ; and now I am become two bands. 11 Deliver me, I pray thee, from the hand of my brother, from the hand of Esau : for I fear him, lest he will come and smite me, *and* the mother with the children. 12 And thou saidst, I will surely do thee good, and make thy seed as the sand of the sea, which cannot be numbered for multitude.

Our rule is to call upon God in the time of

trouble; we have here an example to this rule, and the success encourages us to follow this example. It was now a time of Jacob's trouble, but he shall be saved out of it; and here we have him praying for that salvation, Jer. xxx. 7. In his distress he sought the Lord, and he heard him. Note, Times of fear should be times of prayer; whatever frightens us should drive us to our knees, to our God. Jacob had lately seen his guard of angels, but, in this distress, he applied to God, not to them; he knew they were his fellow-servants, Rev. xxii. 9. Nor did he consult Laban's *teraphim;* it was enough for him that he had a God to go to. To him he addresses himself with all possible solemnity, so running for safety into the name of the Lord, *as a strong tower,* Prov. xviii. 10. This prayer is the more remarkable because it won him the honour of being an *Israel, a prince with God,* and the father of the praying remnant, who are hence called *the seed of Jacob,* to whom he never said, *Seek you me in vain.* Now it is worth while to enquire what there was extraordinary in this prayer, that it should gain the petitioner all this honour.

I. The request itself is one, and very express: *Deliver me from the hand of my brother, v.* 11. Though there was no human probability on his side, yet he believed the power of God could rescue him as a lamb out of the bloody jaws of the lion. Note, 1. We have leave to be particular in our addresses to God, to mention the particular straits and difficulties we are in; for the God with whom we have to do is one we may be free with: *we have liberty of speech (παρρησία)* at the throne of grace. 2. When our brethren aim to be our destroyers, it is our comfort that we have a Father to whom we may apply as our deliverer.

II. The pleas are many, and very powerful; never was cause better ordered, Job xxiii. 4. He offers up his request with great faith, fervency, and humility. How earnestly does he beg! *Deliver me, I pray thee, v.* 11. His fear made him importunate. With what holy logic does he argue! With what divine eloquence does he plead! Here is a noble copy to write after.

1. He addresses himself to God as the God of his fathers, *v.* 9. Such was the humble self-denying sense he had of his own unworthiness that he did not call God his own God, but a God in covenant with his ancestors: *O God of my father Abraham, and God of my father Isaac;* and this he could the better plead because the covenant, by divine designation, was entailed upon him. Note, God's covenant with our fathers may be a comfort to us when we are in distress. It has often been so to the Lord's people, Ps. xxii. 4, 5. Being born in God's house, we are taken under his special protection.

2. He produces his warrant: *Thou saidst unto me, Return unto thy country.* He did not rashly leave his place with Laban, nor undertake this journey out of a fickle humour,

or a foolish fondness for his native country, but in obedience to God's command. Note, (1.) We may be in the way of our duty, and yet may meet with trouble and distress in that way. As prosperity will not prove us in the right, so cross events will not prove us in the wrong; we may be going whither God calls us, and yet may think our way hedged up with thorns. (2.) We may comfortably trust God with our safety, while we carefully keep to our duty. If God be our guide, he will be our guard.

3. He humbly acknowledges his own unworthiness to receive any favour from God (*v.* 10): *I am not worthy;* it is an unusual plea. Some would think he should have pleaded that what was now in danger was his own, against all the world, and that he had earned it dear enough; no, he pleads, *Lord, I am not worthy of it.* Note, Self-denial and self-abasement well become us in all our addresses to the throne of grace. Christ never commended any of his petitioners so much as him who said, *Lord, I am not worthy* (Matt. viii. 8), and her who said, *Truth, Lord, yet the dogs eat of the crumbs which fall from their master's table,* Matt. xv. 27. Now observe here, (1.) How magnificently and honourably he speaks of the mercies of God to him. We have here, *mercies,* in the plural number, an inexhaustible spring, and innumerable streams; *mercies and truth,* that is, past mercies given according to the promise, and further mercies secured by the promise. Note, What is laid up in God's truth, as well as what is laid out in God's mercies, is the matter both of the comforts and the praises of active believers. Nay, observe, it is *all* the mercies, and *all* the truth; the manner of expression is copious, and intimates that his heart was full of God's goodness. (2.) How meanly and humbly he speaks of himself, disclaiming all thought of his own merit: "*I am not worthy of the least of all thy mercies,* much less am I worthy of so great a favour as this I am now suing for." Jacob was a considerable man, and, upon many accounts, very deserving, and, in treating with Laban, had justly insisted on his merits, but not before God. *I am less than all thy mercies;* so the word is. Note, The best and greatest of men are utterly unworthy of the least favour from God, and must be ready to own it upon all occasions. It was the excellent Mr. Herbert's motto, *Less than the least of all God's mercies.* Those are best prepared for the greatest mercies that see themselves unworthy of the least.

4. He thankfully owns God's goodness to him in his banishment, and how much it had outdone his expectations: "*With my staff I passed over this Jordan,* poor and desolate, like a forlorn and despised pilgrim;" he had no guides, no companions, no attendants, no conveniences for travel, but his staff only, nothing else to stay himself upon; "*and now I have become two bands,* now I am surrounded with a numerous and comfortable retinue of

children and servants:" though it was his distress that had now obliged him to divide his family into two bands, yet he makes use of that for the magnifying of the mercy of his increase. Note, (1.) The increase of our families is then comfortable indeed to us when we see God's mercies, and his truth, in it. (2.) Those whose latter end greatly increases ought, with humility and thankfulness, to remember how small their beginning was. Jacob pleads, "Lord, thou didst keep me when I went out with only my staff, and had but one life to lose; wilt thou not keep me now that so many are embarked with me?"

5. He urges the extremity of the peril he was in: *Lord, deliver me from Esau, for I fear him, v.* 11. The people of God have not been shy of telling God their fears; for they know he takes cognizance of them, and considers them. The fear that quickens prayer is itself pleadable. It was not a robber, but a murderer, that he was afraid of; nor was it his own life only that lay at stake, but the mothers' and the children's, that had left their native soil to go along with him. Note, Natural affection may furnish us with allowable acceptable pleas in prayer.

6. He insists especially upon the promise God had made him (*v.* 9): *Thou saidst, I will deal well with thee,* and again, in the close (*v.* 12): *Thou saidst, I will surely do thee good.* Note, (1.) The best we can say to God in prayer is what he has said to us. God's promises, as they are the surest guide of our desires in prayer, and furnish us with the best petitions, so they are the firmest ground of our hopes, and furnish us with the best pleas. "Lord, thou saidst thus and thus; and wilt thou not be as good as thy word, the word upon which thou hast *caused me to hope?*" Ps. cxix. 49. (2.) The most general promises are applicable to particular cases. "Thou saidst, *I will do thee good;* Lord, do me good in this matter." He pleads also a particular promise, that of *the multiplying of his seed.* "Lord, what will become of that promise, if they be all cut off?" Note, [1.] There are promises to the families of good people, which are improvable in prayer for family-mercies, ordinary and extraordinary, *ch.* xvii. 7; Ps. cxii. 2; cii. 28. [2.] The world's threatenings should drive us to God's promises.

13 And he lodged there that same night; and took of that which came to his hand a present for Esau his brother; 14 Two hundred she goats, and twenty he goats, two hundred ewes, and twenty rams, 15 Thirty milch camels with their colts, forty kine, and ten bulls, twenty she asses, and ten foals. 16 And he delivered *them* into the hand of his servants, every drove by themselves; and said unto his servants, Pass over before me, and put

194

a space betwixt drove and drove. 17 And he commanded the foremost, saying, When Esau my brother meeteth thee, and asketh thee, saying, Whose *art* thou? and whither goest thou? and whose *are* these before thee? 18 Then thou shalt say, *They be* thy servant Jacob's; it *is* a present sent unto my lord Esau: and, behold, also he *is* behind us. 19 And so commanded he the second, and the third, and all that followed the droves, saying, On this manner shall ye speak unto Esau, when ye find him. 20 And say ye moreover, Behold, thy servant Jacob *is* behind us. For he said, I will appease him with the present that goeth before me, and afterward I will see his face; peradventure he will accept of me. 21 So went the present over before him: and himself lodged that night in the company. 22 And he rose up that night, and took his two wives, and his two womenservants, and his eleven sons, and passed over the ford Jabbok. 23 And he took them, and sent them over the brook, and sent over that he had.

Jacob, having piously made God his friend by a prayer, is here prudently endeavouring to make Esau his friend by a present. He had prayed to God to deliver him from the hand of Esau, for he feared him; but neither did his fear sink into such a despair as dispirits for the use of means, nor did his prayer make him presume upon God's mercy, without the use of means. Note, When we have prayed to God for any mercy, we must second our prayers with our endeavours; else, instead of trusting God, we tempt him; we must so depend upon God's providence as to make use of our own prudence. "Help thyself, and God will help thee;" God answers our prayers by teaching us to order our affairs with discretion. To pacify Esau,

I. Jacob sent him a very noble present, not of jewels or fine garments (he had them not), but of cattle, to the number of 580 in all, *v.* 13—15. Now, 1. It was an evidence of the great increase with which God had blessed Jacob that he could spare such a number of cattle out of his stock. 2. It was an evidence of his wisdom that he would willingly part with some, to secure the rest; some men's covetousness loses them more than ever it gained them, and, by grudging a little expense, they expose themselves to great damage; *skin for skin, and all that a man has,* if he be a wise man, *he will give for his life.* 3. It was a present that he thought would be acceptable to Esau, who had traded so much in hunting wild beasts that perhaps he was but ill furnished with tame cattle with which to stock his new conquests. And we may suppose that the mixed colours of Jacob's cattle, ring-straked, speckled, and spotted, would please Esau's fancy. 4. He promised himself that by this present he should gain Esau's favour; for a gift commonly *prospers, which way soever it turns* (Prov. xvii. 8), *and makes room for a man* (Prov. xviii. 16); nay, *it pacifies anger and strong wrath,* Prov. xxi. 14. Note, [1.] We must not despair of reconciling ourselves even to those that have been most exasperated against us; we ought not to judge men unappeasable, till we have tried to appease them. [2.] Peace and love, though purchased dearly, will prove a good bargain to the purchaser. Many a morose ill-natured man would have said, in Jacob's case, "Esau has vowed my death without cause, and he shall never be a farthing the better for me; I will see him far enough before I will send him a present:" but Jacob forgives and forgets.

II. He sent him a very humble message, which he ordered his servants to deliver in the best manner, *v.* 17, 18. They must call Esau their *lord,* and Jacob his *servant;* they must tell him the cattle they had was a small present which Jacob had sent him, as a specimen of his acquisitions while he was abroad. The cattle he sent were to be disposed of in several droves, and the servants that attended each drove were to deliver the same message, that the present might appear the more valuable, and his submission, so often repeated, might be the more likely to influence Esau. They must especially take care to tell him that Jacob was coming after (*v.* 18—20), that he might not suspect he had fled through fear. Note, A friendly confidence in men's goodness may help to prevent the mischief designed us by their badness: if Jacob will seem not to be afraid of Esau, Esau, it may be hoped, will not be a terror to Jacob.

24 And Jacob was left alone; and there wrestled a man with him until the breaking of the day. 25 And when he saw that he prevailed not against him, he touched the hollow of his thigh; and the hollow of Jacob's thigh was out of joint, as he wrestled with him. 26 And he said, Let me go, for the day breaketh. And he said, I will not let thee go, except thou bless me. 27 And he said unto him, What *is* thy name? And he said, Jacob. 28 And he said, Thy name shall be called no more Jacob, but Israel: for as a prince hast thou power with God and with men, and hast prevailed. 29 And Jacob asked *him,* and said, Tell *me,* I pray thee, thy name. And he

said, Wherefore *is* it *that* thou dost ask after my name? And he blessed him there. 30 And Jacob called the name of the place Peniel: for I have seen God face to face, and my life is preserved. 31 And as he passed over Penuel the sun rose upon him, and he halted upon his thigh. 32 Therefore the children of Israel eat not *of* the sinew which shrank, which *is* upon the hollow of the thigh, unto this day: because he touched the hollow of Jacob's thigh in the sinew that shrank.

We have here the remarkable story of Jacob's wrestling with the angel and prevailing, which is referred to, Hos. xii. 4. Very early in the morning, a great while before day, Jacob had helped his wives and his children over the river, and he desired to be private, and was left alone, that he might again more fully spread his cares and fears before God in prayer. Note, We ought to continue instant in prayer, always to pray and not to faint: frequency and importunity in prayer prepare us for mercy. While Jacob was earnest in prayer, *stirring up himself to take hold on God,* an angel takes hold on him. Some think this was a created angel, the *angel of his presence* (Isa. lxiii. 9), one of those that *always behold the face of our Father* and attend on the *shechinah,* or the divine Majesty, which probably Jacob had also in view. Others think it was Michael our prince, the eternal Word, the angel of the covenant, who is indeed the Lord of the angels, who often appeared in a human shape before he assumed the human nature for a perpetuity; whichsoever it was, we are sure *God's name was in him,* Exod. xxiii. 21. Observe,

I. How Jacob and this angel engaged, *v.* 24. It was a single combat, hand to hand; they had neither of them any seconds. Jacob was now full of care and fear about the interview he expected, next day, with his brother, and, to aggravate the trial, God himself seemed to come forth against him as an enemy, to oppose his entrance into the land of promise, and to dispute the pass with him, not suffering him to follow his wives and children whom he had sent before. Note, Strong believers must expect divers temptations, and strong ones. We are told by the prophet (Hos. xii. 4) how *Jacob wrestled:* he *wept, and made supplication;* prayers and tears were his weapons. It was not only a corporal, but a spiritual, wrestling, by the vigorous actings of faith and holy desire; and thus all the spiritual seed of Jacob, that pray in praying, still wrestle with God.

II. What was the success of the engagement. 1. Jacob kept his ground; though the struggle continued long, the angel *prevailed not against him* (*v.* 25), that is, this discouragement did not shake his faith, nor silence his prayer. It was not in his own strength that he wrestled, nor by his own strength that he prevailed, but in and by strength derived from Heaven. That of Job illustrates this (Job xxiii. 6), *Will he plead against me with his great power?* No (had the angel done so, Jacob had been crushed), *but he will put strength in me;* and by that *strength Jacob had power over the angel,* Hos. xii. 4. Note, We cannot prevail with God but in his own strength. It is his Spirit that intercedes in us, and *helps our infirmities,* Rom. viii. 26. 2. The angel put out Jacob's thigh, to show him what he could do, and that it was God he was wrestling with, for no man could disjoint his thigh with a touch. Some think that Jacob felt little or no pain from this hurt; it is probable that he did not, for he did not so much as halt till the struggle was over (v. 31), and, if so, this was an evidence of a divine touch indeed, which wounded and healed at the same time. Jacob prevailed, and yet had his thigh put out. Note, Wrestling believers may obtain glorious victories, and yet come off with broken bones; for *when they are weak then are they strong,* weak in themselves, but strong in Christ, 2 Cor. xii. 10. Our honours and comforts in this world have their alloys. 3. The angel, by an admirable condescension, mildly requests Jacob to let him go (v. 26), as God said to Moses (Exod. xxxii. 10), *Let me alone.* Could not a mighty angel get clear of Jacob's grapples? He could; but thus he would put an honour on Jacob's faith and prayer, and further try his constancy. *The king is held in the galleries* (Cant. vii. 5); *I held him* (says the spouse) *and would not let him go,* Cant. iii. 4. The reason the angel gives why he would be gone is *because the day breaks,* and therefore he would not any longer detain Jacob, who had business to do, a journey to go, a family to look after, which, especially in this critical juncture, called for his attendance. Note, Every thing is beautiful in its season; even the business of religion, and the comforts of communion with God, must sometimes give way to the necessary affairs of this life: God *will have mercy, and not sacrifice.* 4. Jacob persists in his holy importunity: *I will not let thee go, except thou bless me;* whatever becomes of his family and journey, he resolves to make the best he can of this opportunity, and not to lose the advantage of his victory: he does not mean to wrestle all night for nothing, but humbly resolves he will have a blessing, and rather shall all his bones be put out of joint than he will go away without one. The credit of a conquest will do him no good without the comfort of a blessing. In begging this blessing he owns his inferiority, though he seemed to have the upper hand in the struggle; for *the less is blessed of the better.* Note, Those that would have the blessing of Christ must be in good earnest, and be importunate for it, as those

196

that resolve to have no denial. It is the fervent prayer that is the effectual prayer. 5. The angel puts a perpetual mark of honour upon him, by changing his name (v. 27, 28): " Thou art a brave combatant" (says the angel), " a man of heroic resolution; what is thy name?" " Jacob," says he, *a supplanter;* so *Jacob* signifies: " Well," says the angel, " be thou never so called any more; henceforth thou shalt be celebrated, not for craft and artful management, but for true valour; thou shalt be called *Israel, a prince with God,* a name greater than those of the great men of the earth." He is a prince indeed that is a prince with God, and those are truly honourable that are mighty in prayer, Israels, Israelites indeed. Jacob is here knighted in the field, as it were, and has a title of honour given him by him that is the fountain of honour, which will remain, to his praise, to the end of time. Yet this was not all; having power with God, he shall have power with men too. Having prevailed for a blessing from heaven, he shall, no doubt, prevail for Esau's favour. Note, Whatever enemies we have, if we can but make God our friend, we are well off; those that by faith have power in heaven have thereby as much power on earth as they have occasion for. 6. He dismisses him with a blessing, v. 29. Jacob desired to know the angel's name, that he might, according to his capacity, do him honour, Judg. xiii. 17. But that request was denied, that he might not be too proud of his conquest, nor think he had the angel at such an advantage as to oblige him to what he pleased. No, " *Wherefore dost thou ask after my name?* What good will it do thee to know that?" The discovery of that was reserved for his death-bed, upon which he was taught to call him *Shiloh.* But, instead of telling him his name, he gave him his blessing, which was the thing he wrestled for: *He blessed him there,* repeated and ratified the blessing formerly given him. Note, Spiritual blessings, which secure our felicity, are better and much more desirable than fine notions which satisfy our curiosity. An interest in the angel's blessing is better than an acquaintance with his name. The tree of life is better than the tree of knowledge. Thus Jacob carried his point; a blessing he wrestled for, and a blessing he had; nor did ever any of his praying seed seek in vain. See how wonderfully God condescends to countenance and crown importunate prayer: those that resolve, though God slay them, yet to trust in him, will, at length, be more than conquerors. 7. Jacob gives a new name to the place; he calls it *Peniel,* the *face of God* (v. 30), because there he had seen the appearance of God, and obtained the favour of God. Observe, The name he gives to the place preserves and perpetuates, not the honour of his valour or victory, but only the honour of God's free grace. He does not say, " In this place I wrestled with God, and prevailed;" but, " In this place I saw God face to face, and my life was preserved;" not, " It was my praise that I came off a conqueror, but it was God's mercy that I escaped with my life." Note, It becomes those whom God honours to take shame to themselves, and to admire the condescensions of his grace to them. Thus David did, after God had sent him a gracious message (2 Sam. vii. 18), *Who am I, O Lord God?* 8. The memorandum Jacob carried of this in his bones : *He halted on his thigh* (v. 31); some think he continued to do so to his dying-day ; and, if he did, he had no reason to complain, for the honour and comfort he obtained by this struggle were abundantly sufficient to countervail the damage, though he went limping to his grave. He had no reason to look upon it as his reproach thus *to bear in his body the marks of the Lord Jesus* (Gal. vi. 17); yet it might serve, like Paul's thorn in the flesh, to keep him from being lifted up with the abundance of the revelations. Notice is taken of the sun's rising upon him when he passed over *Penuel ;* for it is sun-rise with that soul that has communion with God. The inspired penman mentions a traditional custom which the seed of Jacob had, in remembrance of this, never to eat of that sinew, or muscle, in any beast, by which the hip-bone is fixed in its cup: thus they preserved the memorial of this story, and gave occasion to their children to enquire concerning it ; they also did honour to the memory of Jacob. And this use we may still make of it, to acknowledge the mercy of God, and our obligations to Jesus Christ, that we may now keep up our communion with God, in faith, hope, and love, without peril either of life or limb.

CHAP. XXXIII.

We read, in the former chapter, how Jacob had power with God, and prevailed ; here we find what power he had with men too, and how his brother Esau was mollified, and, on a sudden, reconciled to him ; for so it is written, Prov. xvi. 7, " When a man's ways please the Lord, he maketh even his enemies to be at peace with him." Here is, I. A very friendly meeting between Jacob and Esau, ver. 1—4. II. Their conference at their meeting, in which they vie with each other in civil and kind expressions. Their discourse is, 1. About Jacob's family, ver. 5—7. 2. About the present he had sent, ver. 8—11. 3. About the progress of their journey, ver. 12—15. III. Jacob's settlement in Canaan, his house, ground, and altar, ver. 16—20.

AND Jacob lifted up his eyes, and looked, and, behold, Esau came, and with him four hundred men. And he divided the children unto Leah, and unto Rachel, and unto the two handmaids. 2 And he put the handmaids and their children foremost, and Leah and her children after, and Rachel and Joseph hindermost. 3 And he passed over before them, and bowed himself to the ground seven times, until he came near to his brother. 4 And Esau ran to meet him, and embraced him, and fell on his neck, and kissed him : and they wept.

Here, I. Jacob discovered Esau's approach, v. 1. Some think that his lifting up his eyes denotes his cheerfulness and confidence, in opposition to a dejected countenance; having by prayer committed his case to God, he went on his way, *and his countenance was no more sad,* 1 Sam. i. 18. Note, Those that have cast their care upon God may look before them with satisfaction and composure of mind, cheerfully expecting the issue, whatever it may be ; come what will, nothing can come amiss to him whose heart is fixed, trusting in God. Jacob sets himself upon his watch-tower to see what answer God will give to his prayers, Hab. ii. 1.

II. He put his family into the best order he could to receive him, whether he should come as a friend or as an enemy, consulting their decency if he came as a friend and their safety if he came as an enemy, v. 1, 2. Observe what a different figure these two brothers made. Esau is attended with a guard of 400 men, and looks big ; Jacob is followed by a cumbersome train of women and children that are his care, and he looks tender and solicitous for their safety; and yet Jacob had the birthright, and was to have the dominion, and was every way the better man. Note, It is no disparagement to very great and good men to give a personal attendance to their families, and to their family affairs. Jacob, at the head of his household, set a better example than Esau at the head of his regiment.

III. At their meeting, the expressions of kindness were interchanged in the best manner that could be between them.

1. Jacob bowed to Esau, v. 3. Though he feared Esau as an enemy, yet he did obeisance to him as an elder brother, knowing and remembering perhaps that when Abel was preferred in God's acceptance before his elder brother Cain, yet God undertook for him to Cain that he should not be wanting in the duty and respect owing by a younger brother. *Unto thee shall be his desire, and thou shalt rule over him,* ch. iv. 7. Note, (1.) The way to recover peace where it has been broken is to do our duty, and pay our respects, upon all occasions, as if it had never been broken. It is the remembering and repeating of matters that separates friends and perpetuates the separation. (2.) A humble submissive carriage goes a great way towards the turning away of wrath. Many preserve themselves by humbling themselves: the bullet flies over him that stoops.

2. Esau embraced Jacob (v. 4): *He ran to meet him,* not in passion, but in love; and, as one heartily reconciled to him, he received him with all the endearments imaginable, *embraced him, fell on his neck, and kissed him.* Some think that when Esau came out to meet Jacob it was with no bad design, but that he brought his 400 men only for state, that he might pay so much the greater respect to his returning brother. It is certain

that Jacob understood the report of his messengers otherwise, *ch.* xxxii: 5, 6. Jacob was a man of prudence and fortitude, and we cannot suppose him to admit of a groundless fear to such a degree as he did this, nor that the Spirit of God would stir him up to pray such a prayer as he did for deliverance from a merely imaginary danger: and, if there was not some wonderful change wrought upon the spirit of Esau at this time, I see not how wrestling Jacob could be said to obtain such power with men as to denominate him a *prince.* Note, (1.) God has the hearts of all men in his hands, and can turn them when and how he pleases, by a secret, silent, but resistless power. He can, of a sudden, convert enemies into friends, as he did two Sauls, one by restraining grace (1 Sam. xxvi. 21, 25), the other by renewing grace, Acts ix. 21, 22. (2.) It is not in vain to trust in God, and to call upon him in the day of trouble; those that do so often find the issue much better than they expected.

3. They both wept. Jacob wept for joy, to be thus kindly received by his brother whom he had feared; and Esau perhaps wept for grief and shame, to think of the bad design he had conceived against his brother, which he found himself strangely and unaccountably prevented from executing.

5 And he lifted up his eyes, and saw the women and the children; and said, Who *are* those with thee? And he said, The children which God hath graciously given thy servant. 6 Then the handmaidens came near, they and their children, and they bowed themselves. 7 And Leah also with her children came near, and bowed themselves: and after came Joseph near and Rachel, and they bowed themselves. 8 And he said, What *meanest* thou by all this drove which I met? And he said, *These are* to find grace in the sight of my lord. 9 And Esau said, I have enough, my brother; keep that thou hast unto thyself. 10 And Jacob said, Nay, I pray thee, if now I have found grace in thy sight, then receive my present at my hand: for therefore I have seen thy face, as though I had seen the face of God, and thou wast pleased with me. 11 Take, I pray thee, my blessing that is brought to thee; because God hath dealt graciously with me, and because I have enough. And he urged him, and he took *it.* 12 And he said, Let us take our journey, and let us go, and I will go before thee. 13 And he

said unto him, My lord knoweth that the children *are* tender, and the flocks and herds with young *are* with me: and if men should overdrive them one day, all the flock will die. 14 Let my lord, I pray thee, pass over before his servant: and I will lead on softly, according as the cattle that goeth before me and the children be able to endure, until I come unto my lord unto Seir. 15 And Esau said, Let me now leave with thee *some* of the folk that *are* with me. And he said, What needeth it? let me find grace in the sight of my lord.

We have here the discourse between the two brothers at their meeting, which is very free and friendly, without the least intimation of the old quarrel. It was the best way to say nothing of it. They converse, I. About Jacob's retinue, *v.* 5—7. Eleven or twelve little ones, the eldest of them not fourteen years old, followed Jacob closely: *Who are these?* says Esau. Jacob had sent him an account of the increase of his estate (*ch.* xxxii. 5), but made no mention of his children; perhaps because he would not expose them to his rage if he should meet him as an enemy, or would please him with the unexpected sight if he should meet him as a friend: Esau therefore had reason to ask, *Who are those with thee?* to which common question Jacob returns a serious answer, such as became his character: They are *the children which God hath graciously given thy servant.* It had been a sufficient answer to the question, and fit enough to be given to profane Esau, if he had only said, "They are my children;" but then Jacob would not have spoken like himself, like a man whose eyes were ever towards the Lord. Note, It becomes us not only to do common actions, but to speak of them, *after a godly sort,* 3 John 6. Jacob speaks of his children, 1. As God's gifts; they are a *heritage of the Lord,* Ps. cxxviii. 3; cxii. 9; cvii. 41. 2. As choice gifts; he hath graciously given them. Though they were many, and now much his care, and as yet but slenderly provided for, yet he accounts them great blessings. His wives and children, hereupon, come up in order, and pay their duty to Esau, as he had done before them (*v.* 6, 7); for it becomes the family to show respect to those to whom the master of the family shows respect.

II. About the present he had sent him.

1. Esau modestly refused it because he had enough, and did not need it, *v.* 9. Note, Those who wish to be considered men of honour will not *seem* to be mercenary in their friendship: whatever influence Jacob's present had upon Esau to pacify him, he would not have it thought that it had any, and therefore he refused it. His reason is *I have*

enough, I have *much* (so the word is), so much that he was not willing to take any thing that was his brother's. Note, (1.) Many that come short of spiritual blessings, and are out of covenant, yet have much of this world's wealth. Esau had what was promised him, the fatness of the earth and a livelihood by his sword. (2.) It is a good thing for those that have much to know that they have enough, though they have not so much as some others have. Even Esau can say, *I have enough.* (3.) Those that are content with what they have must show it by not coveting what others have. Esau bids Jacob keep what he had to himself, supposing he had more need of it. Esau, for his part, needs it not, either to supply him, for he was rich, or to pacify him, for he was reconciled : we should take heed lest at any time our covetousness impose upon the courtesy of others, and meanly take advantage of their generosity.

2. Jacob affectionately urges him to accept it, and prevails, *v.* 10, 11. Jacob sent it, through fear (*ch.* xxxii. 20), but, the fear being over, he now importunes his acceptance of it for love, to show that he desired his brother's friendship, and did not merely dread his wrath ; two things he urges :—(1.) The satisfaction he had in his brother's favour, of which he thought himself bound to make this thankful acknowledgment. It is a very high compliment that he passes upon him : *I have seen thy face, as though I had seen the face of God,* that is, "I have seen thee reconciled to me, and at peace with me, as I desire to see God reconciled." Or the meaning is that Jacob saw God's favour to him in Esau's : it was a token for good to him that God had accepted his prayers. Note, Creature-comforts are comforts indeed to us when they are granted as answers to prayer, and are tokens of our acceptance with God. Again, It is matter of great joy to those that are of a peaceable and affectionate disposition to recover the friendship of those relations with whom they have been at variance. (2.) The competency he had of this world's goods: *God has dealt graciously with me.* Note, If what we have in this world increase under our hands, we must take notice of it with thankfulness, to the glory of God, and own that therein he has dealt graciously with us, better than we deserve. It is he that gives *power to get wealth,* Deut. viii. 18. He adds, "And *I have enough ;* I have *all,*" so the word is. Esau's enough was much, but Jacob's enough was all. Note, A godly man, though he have but little in the world, yet may truly say, "I have all," [1.] Because he has the God of all, and has all in him; all is yours if you be Christ's, 1 Cor. iii. 22. [2.] Because he has the comfort of all. *I have all, and abound,* Phil. iv. 18. He that has much would have more ; but he that thinks he has all is sure he has enough. He has all in prospect; he will have all shortly, when he comes to heaven :

upon this principle Jacob urged Esau, and he took his present. Note, It is an excellent thing when men's religion makes them generous, free-hearted, and open-handed, scorning to do a thing that is paltry and sneaking.

III. About the progress of their journey. 1. Esau offers himself to be his guide and companion, in token of sincere reconciliation, *v.* 12. We never find that Jacob and Esau were so sociable with one another, and so affectionate, as they were now. Note, As for God his work is perfect. He made Esau, not only not an enemy, but a friend. This bone that had been broken, being well set, became stronger than ever. Esau has become fond of Jacob's company, courts him to Mount Seir : let us never despair of any, nor distrust God in whose hand all hearts are. Yet Jacob saw cause modestly to refuse this offer (*v.* 13, 14), wherein he shows a tender concern for his own family and flocks, like a good shepherd and a good father. He must consider the children, and the flocks with young, and not lead the one, nor drive the other, too fast. This prudence and tenderness of Jacob ought to be imitated by those that have the care and charge of young people in the things of God. They must not be over-driven, at first, by heavy tasks in religious services, but led, as they can bear, having their work made as easy to them as possible. Christ, the good Shepherd, does so, Isa. xl. 11. Now Jacob will not desire Esau to slacken his pace, nor force his family to quicken theirs, nor leave them, to keep company with his brother, as many would have done, that love any society better than their own house ; but he desires Esau to march before, and promises to follow him leisurely, as he could get forward. Note, It is an unreasonable thing to tie others to our rate ; we may come with comfort, at last, to the same journey's end, though we do not journey together, either in the same path or with the same pace. There may be those with whom we cannot fall in and yet with whom we need not fall out by the way. Jacob intimates to him that it was his present design to come to him to Mount Seir ; and we may presume he did so, after he had settled his family and concerns elsewhere, though that visit is not recorded. Note, When we have happily recovered peace with our friends we must take care to cultivate it, and not to be behind-hand with them in civilities. 2. Esau offers some of his men to be his guard and convoy, *v.* 15. He saw Jacob but poorly attended, no servants but his husbandmen and shepherds, no pages or footmen ; and therefore, thinking he was as desirous as himself (if he could afford it) to take state upon him, and look great, he would needs lend him some of his retinue, to attend upon him, that he might appear like Esau's brother ; but Jacob humbly refuses his offer, only desiring he would not take it amiss that he did not accept it : *What needeth it?* (1.) Jacob is humble, and needs it not for state; he desires not to make a fair show in the flesh, by encumbering himself with a needless retinue. Note, It is the vanity of pomp and grandeur that they are attended with a great deal of which it may be said, *What needeth it?* (2.) Jacob is under the divine protection, and needs it not for safety. Note, Those are sufficiently guarded that have God for their guard and are under a convoy of his hosts, as Jacob was. Those need not be beholden to an arm of flesh that have God for their arm every morning. Jacob adds, "Only *let me find grace in the sight of my lord;* having thy favour, I have all I need, all I desire from thee." If Jacob thus valued the good-will of a brother, much more reason have we to reckon that we have enough if we have the good-will of our God.

16 So Esau returned that day on his way unto Seir. 17 And Jacob journeyed to Succoth, and built him a house, and made booths for his cattle: therefore the name of the place is called Succoth. 18 And Jacob came to Shalem a city of Shechem, which *is* in the land of Canaan, when he came from Padan-aram; and pitched his tent before the city. 19 And he bought a parcel of a field, where he had spread his tent, at the hand of the children of Hamor, Shechem's father, for a hundred pieces of money. 20 And he erected there an altar, and. called it El-elohe-Israel.

Here, 1. Jacob comes to Succoth. Having in a friendly manner parted with Esau, who had gone to his own country (*v.* 16), he comes to a place where, it should seem, he rested for some time, set up booths for his cattle, and other conveniences for himself and family. The place was afterwards known by the name of Succoth, a city in the tribe of Gad, on the other side Jordan (it signifies *booths*), that when his posterity afterwards dwelt in houses of stone, they might remember that *the Syrian ready to perish* was their father, who was glad of booths (Deut. xxvi. 5); such was the rock whence they were hewn. 2. He comes to Shechem; we read it, to *Shalem, a city of Shechem;* the critics generally incline to read it appellatively: *he came safely, or in peace, to the city of Shechem.* After a perilous journey, in which he had met with many difficulties, he came safely, at last, into Canaan. Note, Diseases and dangers should teach us how to value health and safety, and should help to enlarge our hearts in thankfulness, when our going out and coming in have been signally preserved. Here, (1.) He buys a field, *v.* 19. Though the land of Canaan was his by promise, yet

the time for taking possession not having yet come, he is content to pay for his own, to prevent disputes with the present occupants. Note, Dominion is not founded in grace. Those that have heaven on free-cost must not expect to have earth so. (2.) He builds an altar, *v.* 20. [1.] In thankfulness to God, for the good hand of his providence over him. He did not content himself with verbal acknowledgments of God's favour to him, but made real ones. [2.] That he might keep up religion, and the worship of God, in his family. Note, Where we have a tent God must have an altar, where we have a house he must have a church in it. He dedicated this altar to the honour of *El-elohe-Israel—God, the God of Israel,* to the honour of God, in general, the only living and true God, the best of beings and first of causes; and to the honour of the God of Israel, as a God in covenant with him. Note, In our worship of God we must be guided and governed by the joint-discoveries both of natural and revealed religion. God had lately called him by the name of *Israel,* and now he calls God *the God of Israel;* though he is styled *a prince with God,* God shall still be a prince with him, his Lord and his God. Note, Our honours then become honours indeed to us when they are consecrated to God's honour; Israel's God is Israel's glory.

CHAP. XXXIV.

At this chapter begins the story of Jacob's afflictions in his children, which were very great, and are recorded to show, 1. The vanity of this world. That which is dearest to us may prove our greatest vexation, and we may meet with the greatest crosses in those things of which we said, "This same shall comfort us." 2. The common griefs of good people. Jacob's children were circumcised, were well taught, and prayed for, and had very good examples set them; yet some of them proved very untoward. "The race is not to the swift, nor the battle to the strong." Grace does not run in the blood, and yet the interrupting of the entail of grace does not cut off the entail of profession and visible church-privileges: nay, Jacob's sons, though they were his grief in some things, yet were all taken into covenant with God. In this chapter we have, I. Dinah debauched, ver. 1—5. II. A treaty of marriage between her and Shechem who had defiled her, ver. 6—19. III. The circumcision of the Shechemites, pursuant to that treaty, ver. 20—24. IV. The perfidious and bloody revenge which Simeon and Levi took upon them, ver. 25—31.

AND Dinah the daughter of Leah, which she bare unto Jacob, went out to see the daughters of the land. 2 And when Shechem the son of Hamor the Hivite, prince of the country, saw her, he took her, and lay with her, and defiled her. 3 And his soul clave unto Dinah the daughter of Jacob, and he loved the damsel, and spake kindly unto the damsel. 4 And Shechem spake unto his father Hamor, saying, Get me this damsel to wife. 5 And Jacob heard that he had defiled Dinah his daughter: now his sons were with his cattle in the field: and Jacob held his peace until they were come.

Dinah was, for aught that appears, Jacob's only daughter, and we may suppose her therefore the mother's fondling and the darling of the family, and yet she proves neither a joy nor a credit to them; for those children seldom prove either the best or the happiest that are most indulged. She is reckoned now but fifteen or sixteen years of age when she here occasioned so much mischief. Observe, 1. Her vain curiosity, which exposed her. She went out, perhaps unknown to her father, but by the connivance of her mother, *to see the daughters of the land* (v. 1); probably it was at a ball, or on some public day. Being an only daughter, she thought herself solitary at home, having none of her own age and sex to converse with; and therefore she must needs go abroad to divert herself, to keep off melancholy, and to accomplish herself by conversation better than she could in her father's tents. Note, It is a very good thing for children to love home; it is parents' wisdom to make it easy to them, and children's duty then to be easy in it. Her pretence was *to see the daughters of the land*, to see how they dressed, and how they danced, and what was fashionable among them. She went to *see*, yet that was not all, she went to be *seen* too; she went to see the daughters of the land, but, it may be, with some thoughts of the sons of the land too. I doubt she went to get an acquaintance with those Canaanites, and to learn their way. Note, The pride and vanity of young people betray them into many snares. 2. The loss of her honour by this means (v. 2): *Shechem, the prince of the country*, but a slave to his own lusts, took her, and lay with her, it should seem, not so much by force as by surprise. Note, Great men think they may do any thing; and what more mischievous than untaught and ungoverned youth? See what came of Dinah's gadding: young women must learn to be *chaste, keepers at home;* these properties are put together, Tit. ii. 5, for those that are not keepers at home expose their chastity. Dinah went abroad to look about her; but, if she had looked about her as she ought, she would not have fallen into this snare. Note, The beginning of sin is as the letting forth of water. How great a matter does a little fire kindle! We should therefore carefully avoid all occasions of sin and approaches to it. 3. The court Shechem made to her, after he had defiled her. This was fair and commendable, and made the best of what was bad; he loved her (not as Amnon, 2 Sam. xiii. 15), and he engaged his father to make a match for him with her, v. 4. 4. The tidings brought to poor Jacob, v. 5. As soon as his children grew up they began to be a grief to him. Let not godly parents, that are lamenting the miscarriages of their children, think their case singular or unprecedented. The good man *held his peace*, as one astonished, that knows not what to say: or he said nothing, for fear of saying amiss, as David (Ps. xxxix. 1, 2); he smothered his resentments, lest, if

he had suffered them to break out, they should have transported him into any indecencies. Or, it should seem, he had left the management of his affairs very much (too much I doubt) to his sons, and he would do nothing without them: or, at least, he knew they would make him uneasy if he did, they having shown themselves, of late, upon all occasions, bold, forward, and assuming. Note, Things never go well when the authority of a parent runs low in a family. Let every man *bear rule in his own house, and have his children in subjection with all gravity.*

6 And Hamor the father of Shechem went out unto Jacob to commune with him. 7 And the sons of Jacob came out of the field when they heard *it:* and the men were grieved, and they were very wroth, because he had wrought folly in Israel in lying with Jacob's daughter; which thing ought not to be done. 8 And Hamor communed with them, saying, The soul of my son Shechem longeth for your daughter: I pray you give her him to wife. 9 And make ye marriages with us, *and* give your daughters unto us, and take our daughters unto you. 10 And ye shall dwell with us: and the land shall be before you; dwell and trade ye therein, and get you possessions therein. 11 And Shechem said unto her father and unto her brethren, Let me find grace in your eyes, and what ye shall say unto me I will give. 12 Ask me never so much dowry and gift, and I will give according as ye shall say unto me: but give me the damsel to wife. 13 And the sons of Jacob answered Shechem and Hamor his father deceitfully, and said, because he had defiled Dinah their sister: 14 And they said unto them, We cannot do this thing, to give our sister to one that is uncircumcised; for that *were* a reproach unto us: 15 But in this will we consent unto you: If ye will be as we *be*, that every male of you be circumcised; 16 Then will we give our daughters unto you, and we will take your daughters to us, and we will dwell with you, and we will become one people. 17 But if ye will not hearken unto us, to be circumcised; then will we take our daughter, and we will be gone.

Jacob's sons, when they heard of the injury done to Dinah, showed a very great resentment of it, influenced perhaps rather by jealousy for the honour of their family than by a sense of virtue. Many are concerned at the shamefulness of sin that never lay to heart the sinfulness of it. It is here called *folly in Israel* (*v.* 7), according to the language of after-times; for Israel was not yet a people, but a family only. Note, 1. Uncleanness is folly; for it sacrifices the favour of God, peace of conscience, and all the soul can pretend to that is sacred and honourable, to a base and brutish lust. 2. This folly is most shameful in *Israel*, in a family of Israel, where God is known and worshipped, as he was in Jacob's tents, by the name of *the God of Israel*. Folly in Israel is scandalous indeed. 3. It is a good thing to have sin stamped with a bad name : uncleanness is here proverbially called *folly in Israel*, 2 Sam. xiii. 12. Dinah is here called *Jacob's daughter*, for warning to all the daughters of Israel, that they betray not themselves to this folly.

Hamor came to treat with Jacob himself, but he turns him over to his sons; and here we have a particular account of the treaty, in which, it is a shame to say, the Canaanites were more honest than the Israelites.

I. Hamor and Shechem fairly propose this match, in order to a coalition in trade. Shechem is deeply in love with Dinah; he will have her upon any terms, *v.* 11, 12. His father not only consents, but solicits for him, and gravely insists upon the advantages that would follow from the union of the families, *v.* 9, 10. He shows no jealousy of Jacob, though he was a stranger, but rather an earnest desire to settle a correspondence with him and his family, making him that generous offer, *The land shall be before you, trade you therein.*

II. Jacob's sons basely pretend to insist upon a coalition in religion, when really they designed nothing less. If Jacob had taken the management of this affair into his own hands, it is probable that he and Hamor would soon have concluded it; but Jacob's sons meditate only revenge, and a strange project they have for the compassing of it—the Shechemites must be circumcised; not to make them holy (they never intended that), but to make them sore, that they might become an easier prey to their sword. 1. The pretence was specious. " It is the honour of Jacob's family that they carry about with them the token of God's covenant with them ; and it will be a reproach to those that are thus dignified and distinguished to enter into such a strict alliance with those that are *uncircumcised* (*v.* 14); and therefore, *if you will be circumcised, then we will become one people with you*," *v.* 15, 16. Had they been sincere herein their proposal of these terms would have had in it something commendable ; for Israelites should not inter-marry with Canaanites, professors with pro-

202

fane ; it is a great sin, or at least the cause and inlet of a great deal, and has often been of pernicious consequence. The interest we have in any persons, and the hold we have of them, should be wisely improved by us, to bring them to the love and practice of religion *(He that winneth souls is wise);* but then we must not, like Jacob's sons, think it enough to persuade them to submit to the external rites of religion, but must endeavour to convince them of its reasonableness, and to bring them acquainted with the power of it. 2. The intention was malicious, as appears by the sequel of the story; all they aimed at was to prepare them for the day of slaughter. Note, Bloody designs have often been covered, and carried on, with a pretence of religion; thus they have been accomplished most plausibly and most securely; but this dissembled piety is, doubtless, double iniquity. Religion is never more injured, nor are God's sacraments more profaned, than when they are thus used for a cloak of maliciousness. Nay, if Jacob's sons had not had this bloody design, I do not see how they could justify their offering the sacred sign of circumcision, the seal of God's covenant, to these devoted Canaanites, who had no part nor lot in the matter. Those had no right to the seal that had no right to the promise. *It is not meet to take the children's bread, and cast it to dogs :* but Jacob's sons valued not this, while they could make it serve their turn.

18 And their words pleased Hamor, and Shechem Hamor's son. 19 And the young man deferred not to do the thing, because he had delight in Jacob's daughter : and he *was* more honourable than all the house of his father. 20 And Hamor and Shechem his son came unto the gate of their city, and communed with the men of their city, saying, 21 These men *are* peaceable with us ; therefore let them dwell in the land, and trade therein ; for the land, behold, *it is* large enough for them ; let us take their daughters to us for wives, and let us give them our daughters. 22 Only herein will the men consent unto us for to dwell with us, to be one people, if every male among us be circumcised, as they *are* circumcised. 23 *Shall* not their cattle and their substance and every beast of their's *be* our's ? only let us consent unto them, and they will dwell with us. 24 And unto Hamor and unto Shechem his son hearkened all that went out of the gate of his city ;

and every male was circumcised, all that went out of the gate of his city.

Here, 1. Hamor and Shechem gave consent themselves to be circumcised, *v.* 18, 19. To this perhaps they were moved, not only by the strong desire they had to bring about this match, but by what they might have heard of the sacred and honourable intentions of this sign, in the family of Abraham, which, it is probable, they had some confused notions of, and of the promises confirmed by it, which made them the more desirous to incorporate with the family of Jacob, Zech. viii. 23. Note, Many who know little of religion, yet know so much of it as makes them willing to join themselves with those that are religious. Again, If a man would take upon him a form of religion to gain a good wife, much more should we embrace the power of it to gain the favour of a good God, even circumcise our hearts to love him, and, as Shechem here, *not defer to do the thing.* 2. They gained the consent of the men of their city, Jacob's sons requiring that they also should be circumcised. (1.) They themselves had great influence upon them by their command and example. Note, Religion would greatly prevail if those in authority, who, like Shechem, are more honourable than their neighbours, would appear forward and zealous for it. (2.) They urged an argument which was very cogent (*v.* 23), *Shall not their cattle and their substance be ours?* They observed that Jacob's sons were industrious thriving people, and promised themselves and their neighbours advantage by an alliance with them; it would improve ground and trade, and bring money into their country. Now, [1.] It was bad enough to marry upon this principle: yet we see covetousness the greatest matchmaker in the world, and nothing designed so much, with many, as the laying of house to house, and field to field, without regard had to any other consideration. [2.] It was worse to be circumcised upon this principle. The Shechemites will embrace the religion of Jacob's family only in hopes of interesting themselves thereby in the riches of that family. Thus there are many with whom gain is godliness, and who are more governed and influenced by their secular interest than by any principle of their religion.

25 And it came to pass on the third day, when they were sore, that two of the sons of Jacob, Simeon and Levi, Dinah's brethren, took each man his sword, and came upon the city boldly, and slew all the males. 26 And they slew Hamor and Shechem his son with the edge of the sword, and took Dinah out of Shechem's house, and went out. 27 The sons of Jacob came upon the slain, and spoiled the city,

because they had defiled their sister. 28 They took their sheep, and their oxen, and their asses, and that which *was* in the city, and that which *was* in the field, 29 And all their wealth, and all their little ones, and their wives took they captive, and spoiled even all that *was* in the house. 30 And Jacob said to Simeon and Levi, Ye have troubled me to make me to stink among the inhabitants of the land, among the Canaanites and the Perizzites: and I *being* few in number, they shall gather themselves together against me, and slay me; and I shall be destroyed, I and my house. 31 And they said, Should he deal with our sister as with a harlot?

Here we have Simeon and Levi, two of Jacob's sons, young men not much above twenty years old, cutting the throats of the Shechemites, and thereby breaking the heart of their good father.

I. Here is the barbarous murder of the Shechemites. Jacob himself was used to the sheep-hook, but his sons had got swords by their sides, as if they had been the seed of Esau, who was to live by his sword; we have them here,

1. Slaying the inhabitants of Shechem—*all the males*, Hamor and Shechem particularly, with whom they had been treating in a friendly manner but the other day, yet with a design upon their lives. Some think that all Jacob's sons, when they wheedled the Shechemites to be circumcised, designed to take advantage of their soreness, and to rescue Dinah from among them; but that Simeon and Levi, not content with that, would themselves avenge the injury—and they did it with a witness. Now, (1.) It cannot be denied but that God was righteous in it. Had the Shechemites been circumcised in obedience to any command of God, their circumcision would have been their protection; but when they submitted to that sacred rite only to serve a turn, to please their prince and to enrich themselves, it was just with God to bring this upon them. Note, As nothing secures us better than true religion, so nothing exposes us more than religion only pretended to. (2.) But Simeon and Levi were most unrighteous. [1.] It was true that Shechem had *wrought folly against Israel*, in defiling Dinah; but it ought to have been considered how far Dinah herself had been accessory to it. Had Shechem abused her in her own mother's tent, it would have been another matter; but she went upon his ground, and perhaps by her indecent carriage had struck the spark which began the fire: when we are severe upon the sinner we ought to consider

who was the tempter. [2.] It was true that Shechem had done ill; but he was endeavouring to atone for it, and was as honest and honourable, *ex post facto—after the deed*, as the case would admit: it was not the case of the Levite's concubine that was abused to death; nor does he justify what he has done, but courts a reconciliation upon any terms. [3.] It was true that Shechem had done ill; but what was that to all the Shechemites? Does one man sin, and will they be wroth with all the town? Must the innocent fall with the guilty? This was barbarous indeed. [4.] But that which above all aggravated the cruelty was the most perfidious treachery that was in it. The Shechemites had submitted to their conditions, and had done that upon which they had promised to become one people with them (*v.* 16); yet they act as sworn enemies to those to whom they had lately become sworn friends, making as light of their covenant as they did of the laws of humanity. And are these the sons of Israel? *Cursed be their anger, for it was fierce.* [5.] This also added to the crime, that they made a holy ordinance of God subservient to their wicked design, so making that odious; as if it were not enough for them to shame themselves and their family, they bring a reproach upon that honourable badge of their religion; justly would it be called a bloody ordinance.

2. Seizing the prey of Shechem, and plundering the town. They rescued Dinah (*v.* 26), and, if that was all they came for, they might have done that without blood, as appears by their own showing (*v.* 17); but they aimed at the spoil; and, though Simeon and Levi only were the murderers, yet it is intimated that others of the sons of Jacob *came upon the slain and spoiled the city* (*v.* 27), and so became accessory to the murder. In them it was manifest injustice; yet here we may observe the righteousness of God. The Shechemites were willing to gratify the sons of Jacob by submitting to the penance of circumcision, upon this principle, *Shall not their cattle and their substance be ours?* (*v.* 23), and see what was the issue; instead of making themselves masters of the wealth of Jacob's family, Jacob's family become masters of their wealth. Note, Those who unjustly grasp at that which is another's justly lose that which is their own.

II. Here is Jacob's resentment of this bloody deed of Simeon and Levi, *v.* 30. Two things he bitterly complains of :—1. The reproach they had brought upon him thereby: *You have troubled me*, put me into a disorder, for you have made me *to stink among the inhabitants of the land*, that is, "You have rendered me and my family odious among them. What will they say of us and our religion? We shall be looked upon as the most perfidious barbarous people in the world." Note, The gross misconduct of wicked children is the grief and shame of their godly parents. Children should be the

joy of their parents; but wicked children are their trouble, sadden their hearts, break their spirits, and make them go mourning from day to day. Children should be an ornament to their parents; but wicked children are their reproach, and are as dead flies in the pot of ointment: but let such children know that, if they repent not, the grief they have caused to their parents, and the damage religion has sustained in its reputation through them, will come into the account and be reckoned for. 2. The ruin they had exposed him to. What could be expected, but that the Canaanites, who were numerous and formidable, would confederate against him, and he and his little family would become an easy prey to them? *I shall be destroyed, I and my house.* If all the Shechemites must be destroyed for the offence of one, why not all the Israelites for the offence of two? Jacob knew indeed that God had promised to preserve and perpetuate his house; but he might justly fear that these vile practices of his children would amount to a forfeiture, and cut off the entail. Note, When sin is in the house, there is reason to fear ruin at the door. The tender parents foresee those bad consequences of sin which the wicked children have no dread of. One would think this should have made them to relent, and they should have humbled themselves to their good father, and begged his pardon; but, instead of this, they justify themselves, and give him this insolent reply, *Should he deal with our sister as with a harlot?* No, he should not; but, if he do, must they be their own avengers? Will nothing less than so many lives, and the ruin of a whole city, serve to atone for an abuse done to one foolish girl? By their question they tacitly reflect upon their father, as if he would have been content to let them deal with his daughter as with a harlot. Note, It is common for those who run into one extreme to reproach and censure those who keep the mean as if they ran into the other. Those who condemn the rigour of revenge shall be misrepresented, as if they countenanced and justified the offence.

CHAP. XXXV.

In this chapter we have three communions and three funerals. I. Three communions between God and Jacob. 1. God ordered Jacob to Beth-el; and, in obedience to that order, he purged his house of idols, and prepared for that journey, ver. 1—5. 2. Jacob built an altar at Beth-el, to the honour of God that had appeared to him, and in performance of his vow, ver. 6, 7. 3. God appeared to him again, and confirmed the change of his name and the covenant with him (ver. 9—13), of which appearance Jacob made a grateful acknowledgment, ver. 14, 15. II. Three funerals. 1. Deborah's, ver. 8. 2. Rachel's, ver. 16—20. 3. Isaac's, ver. 27—29. Here is also Reuben's incest (ver. 22), and an account of Jacob's sons, ver. 23—26.

AND God said unto Jacob, Arise, go up to Beth-el, and dwell there: and make there an altar unto God, that appeared unto thee when thou fleddest from the face of Esau thy brother. 2 Then Jacob said unto his household, and to all that *were* with him, Put away the strange gods that *are* among you, and be clean, and change your garments : 3 And let us arise, and go up to Beth-el; and I will make there an altar unto God, who answered me in the day of my distress, and was with me in the way which I went. 4 And they gave unto Jacob all the strange gods which *were* in their hand, and *all their* earrings which *were* in their ears ; and Jacob hid them under the oak which *was* by Shechem. 5 And they journeyed: and the terror of God was upon the cities that *were* round about them, and they did not pursue after the sons of Jacob.

Here, I. God reminds Jacob of his vow at Beth-el, and sends him thither to perform it, *v.* 1. Jacob had said in the day of his distress, *If I come again in peace, this stone shall be God's house, ch.* xxviii. 22. God had performed his part of the bargain, and had given Jacob more than bread to eat and raiment to put on—he had got an estate, and had become two bands ; but, it should seem, he had forgotten his vow, or at least had too long deferred the performance of it. Seven or eight years it was now since he came to Canaan ; he had purchased ground there, and had built an altar in remembrance of God's last appearance to him when he called him *Israel* (*ch.* xxxiii. 19, 20) ; but still Beth-el is forgotten. Note, Time is apt to wear out the sense of mercies and the impressions made upon us by them ; it should not be so, but so it is. God had exercised Jacob with a very sore affliction in his family (*ch.* xxxiv.), to see if this would bring his vow to his remembrance, and put him upon the performance of it, but it had not this effect; therefore God comes himself and puts him in mind of it: *Arise, go to Beth-el.* Note, 1. As many as God loves he will remind of neglected duties, one way or other, by conscience or by providences. 2. When we have vowed a vow to God, it is best not to defer the payment of it (Eccles. v. 4), yet better late than never. God bade him go to Beth-el and dwell there, that is, not only go himself, but take his family with him, that they might join with him in his devotions. Note, In Beth-el, the house of God, we should desire to dwell, Ps. xxvii. 4. That should be our home, not our inn. God reminds him not expressly of his vow, but of the occasion of it : *When thou fleddest from the face of Esau.* Note, The remembrance of former afflictions should bring to mind the workings of our souls under them, Ps. lxvi. 13, 14.

II. Jacob commands his household to prepare for this solemnity; not only for the journey and remove, but for the religious services that were to be performed, *v.* 2, 3.

Note, 1. Before solemn ordinances, there must be solemn preparation. *Wash you, make you clean, and then come, and let us reason together,* Isa. i. 16—18. 2. Masters of families should use their authority for the promoting of religion in their families. Not only we, but our houses also, should serve the Lord, Josh. xxiv. 15. Observe the commands he gives his household, like Abraham, *ch.* xviii. 19. (1.) They must *put away the strange gods.* Strange gods in Jacob's family! Strange things indeed! Could such a family, that was taught the good knowledge of the Lord, admit them? Could such a master, to whom God had appeared twice, and oftener, connive at them? Doubtless this was his infirmity. Note, Those that are good themselves cannot always have those about them so good as they should be. In those families where there is a face of religion, and an altar to God, yet many times there is much amiss, and more strange gods than one would suspect. In Jacob's family, Rachel had her teraphim, which, it is to be feared, she secretly made some superstitious use of. The captives of Shechem brought their gods along with them, and perhaps Jacob's sons took some with the plunder. However they came by them, now they must *put them away.* (2.) They must be clean, and *change their garments ;* they must observe a due decorum, and make the best appearance they could. Simeon and Levi had their hands full of blood, it concerned them particularly to wash, and to put off their garments that were so stained. These were but ceremonies, signifying the purification and change of the heart. What are clean clothes, and new clothes, without a clean heart, and a new heart? Dr. Lightfoot, by their *being clean,* or *washing* themselves, understands Jacob's admission of the proselytes of Shechem and Syria into his religion by baptism, because circumcision had become odious. 3. They must go with him to Bethel, *v.* 3. Note, Masters of families, when they go up to the house of God, should bring their families with them.

III. His family surrendered all they had that was idolatrous or superstitious, *v.* 4. Perhaps, if Jacob had called for them sooner, they would sooner have parted with them, being convicted by their own consciences of the vanity of them. Note, Sometimes attempts for reformation succeed better than one could have expected, and people are not so obstinate against them as we feared. Jacob's servants, and even the retainers of his family, gave him all the strange gods, and the ear-rings they wore, either as charms or to the honour of their gods; they parted with all. Note, Reformation is not sincere if it be not universal. We hope they parted with them cheerfully, and without reluctance, as Ephraim did, when he said, *What have I to do any more with idols?* (Hos. xiv. 8), or that people that said to their idols, *Get you hence,* Isa. xxx. 22. Jacob took care to bury their

205

images, we may suppose in some place unknown to them, that they might not afterwards find them and return to them. Note, We must be wholly separated from our sins, as we are from those that are dead and buried ɔut of our sight, cast them *to the moles and the bats,* Isa. ii. 20.

IV. He removes without molestation from Shechem to Bethel, *v.* 5. *The terror of God was upon the cities.* Though the Canaanites were much exasperated against the sons of Jacob for their barbarous usage of the Shechemites, yet they were so restrained by a divine power that they could not take this fair opportunity, which now offered itself, when they were upon their march, to avenge their neighbours' quarrel. Note, The way of duty is the way of safety. While there was sin in Jacob's house, he was afraid of his neighbours; but now that the strange gods were put away, and they were all going together to Bethel, his neighbours were afraid of him. When we are about God's work, we are under special protection. God is with us, while we are with him; and, if he be for us, who can be against us? See Exod. xxxiv. 24, *No man shall desire thy land, when thou goest up to appear before the Lord.* God governs the world more by secret terrors on men's minds than we are aware of.

6 So Jacob came to Luz, which *is* in the land of Canaan, that *is,* Beth-el, he and all the people that *were* with him. 7 And he built there an altar, and called the place El-beth-el: because there God appeared unto him, when he fled from the face of his brother. 8 But Deborah Rebekah's nurse died, and she was buried beneath Beth-el under an oak: and the name of it was called Allon-bachuth. 9 And God appeared unto Jacob again, when he came out of Padan-aram, and blessed him. 10 And God said unto him, Thy name *is* Jacob: thy name shall not be called any more Jacob, but Israel shall be thy name: and he called his name Israel. 11 And God said unto him, I *am* God Almighty: be fruitful and multiply; a nation and a company of nations shall be of thee, and kings shall come out of thy loins; 12 And the land which I gave Abraham and Isaac, to thee I will give it, and to thy seed after thee will I give the land. 13 And God went up from him in the place where he talked with him. 14 And Jacob set up a pillar in the place where he talked with him, *even* a pillar of stone · and he poured

206

a drink offering thereon, and he poured oil thereon. 15 And Jacob called the name of the place where God spake with him, Beth-el.

Jacob and his retinue having safely arrived at Bethel, we are here told what passed there.

I. There he built an altar (*v.* 7), and no doubt offered sacrifice upon it, perhaps the tenth of his cattle, according to his vow, *I will give the tenth unto thee.* With these sacrifices he joined praises for former mercies, particularly that which the sight of the place brought afresh to his remembrance; and he added prayers for the continuance of God's favour to him and his family. And he called the place (that is, *the altar) El-beth-el, the God of Bethel.* As, when he made a thankful acknowledgment of the honour God had lately done him in calling him *Israel,* he worshipped God by the name of *El-elohe Israel;* so, now that he was making a grateful recognition of God's former favour to him at Bethel, he worships God by the name of *El-beth-el, the God of Bethel,* because there God appeared to him. Note, The comfort which the saints have in holy ordinances is not so much from *Bethel, the house of God,* as from *El-beth-el, the God of the house.* The ordinances are but empty things if we do not meet with God in them.

II. There he buried Deborah, Rebekah's nurse, *v.* 8. We have reason to think that Jacob, after he came to Canaan, while his family dwelt near Shechem, went himself (it is likely, often) to visit his father Isaac at Hebron. Rebekah probably was dead, but her old nurse (of whom mention is made *ch.* xxiv. 59) survived her, and Jacob took her to his family, to be a companion to his wives, her country-women, and an instructor to his children; while they were at Bethel, she died, and died lamented, so much lamented that the oak under which she was buried was called *Allon-bachuth, the oak of weeping.* Note, 1. Old servants in a family, that have in their time been faithful and useful, ought to be respected. Honour was done to this nurse, at her death, by Jacob's family, though she was not related to them, and though she was aged. Former services, in such a case, must be remembered. 2. We do not know where death may meet us; perhaps at Beth-el, the house of God. Therefore let us be always ready. 3. Family-afflictions may come even when family-reformation and religion are on foot. Therefore rejoice with trembling.

III. There God appeared to him (*v.* 9), to own his altar, to answer to the name by which he had called him, *The God of Bethel* (*v.* 7), and to comfort him under his affliction, *v.* 8. Note, God will appear to those in a way of grace that attend on him in a way of duty. Here, 1. He confirmed the change of his name, *v.* 10. It was done before by the angel that wrestled with him (*ch.* xxxii. 28), and here it was ratified by the divine Majesty, or *Shechinah*, that appeared to him. There it was to encourage him against the fear of Esau, here against the fear of the Canaanites. Who can be too hard for Israel, a prince with God? It is below those who are thus dignified to droop and despond. 2. He renewed and ratified the covenant with him, by the name *El-shaddai. I am God Almighty, God all-sufficient* (*v.* 11), able to make good the promise in due time, and to support thee and provide for thee in the mean time. Two things are promised him which we have met with often before :—(1.) That he should be the father of a great nation, great in number —*a company of nations shall be of thee* (every tribe of Israel was a nation, and all the twelve a company of nations), great in honour and power—*kings shall come out of thy loins.* (2.) That he should be the master of a good land (*v.* 12), described by the grantees, Abraham and Isaac, to whom it was promised, not by the occupants, the Canaanites in whose possession it now was. The land that was given to Abraham and Isaac is here entailed on Jacob and his seed. He shall not have children without an estate, which is often the case of the poor, nor an estate without children, which is often the grief of the rich; but both. These two promises had a spiritual signification, of which we may suppose Jacob himself had some notion, though not so clear and distinct as we now have; for, without doubt, Christ is the promised seed, and heaven is the promised land; the former is the foundation, and the latter the top-stone, of all God's favours. 3. He then went up from him, or *from over him*, in some visible display of glory, which had hovered over him while he talked with him, *v.* 13. Note, The sweetest communions the saints have with God in this world are short and transient, and soon have an end. Our vision of God in heaven will be everlasting; there we shall be ever with the Lord; it is not so here.

IV. There Jacob erected a memorial of this, *v.* 14. 1. He set up a pillar. When he was going to Padan-aram, he set up for a pillar that stone on which he had laid his head. This was agreeable enough to his low condition and his hasty flight; but now he took time to erect one more stately, more distinguishable and durable, probably placing that stone in it. In token of his intending it for a sacred memorial of his communion with God, he poured oil and the other ingredients of a drink-offering upon it. His vow was, *This stone shall be God's house,* that is, shall be set up for his honour, as houses to the praise of their builders; and here he performs it, transferring it to God by anointing it. 2. He confirmed the name he had formerly given to the place (*v.* 15), *Beth-el, the house of God.* Yet this very place afterwards lost the honour of its name, and became *Beth-aven, a house of iniquity ;* for here it was that Jeroboam set up one of his calves.

It is impossible for the best men to entail upon a place so much as the profession and form of religion.

16 And they journeyed from Bethel; and there was but a little way to come to Ephrath: and Rachel travailed, and she had hard labour. 17 And it came to pass, when she was in hard labour, that the midwife said unto her, Fear not; thou shalt have this son also. 18 And it came to pass, as her soul was in departing, (for she died) that she called his name Ben-oni: but his father called him Benjamin. 19 And Rachel died, and was buried in the way to Ephrath, which *is* Bethlehem. 20 And Jacob set a pillar upon her grave: that *is* the pillar of Rachel's grave unto this day.

We have here the story of the death of Rachel, the beloved wife of Jacob. 1. She fell in travail by the way, not able to reach to Bethlehem, the next town, though they were near it; so suddenly does pain sometimes come upon a woman in travail, which she cannot escape, or put off. We may suppose Jacob had soon a tent up, convenient enough for her reception. 2. Her pains were violent. She had hard labour, harder than usual: this was the effect of sin, *ch.* iii. 16. Note, Human life begins with sorrow, and the roses of its joy are surrounded with thorns 3. The midwife encouraged her, *v.* 17. No doubt she had her midwife with her, ready at hand, yet that would not secure her. Rachel had said, when she bore Joseph, *God shall add another son,* which now the midwife remembers, and tells her her words were made good. Yet this did not avail to keep up her spirits; unless God command away fear, no one else can. He only says as one having authority, *Fear not.* We are apt, in extreme perils, to comfort ourselves and our friends with the hopes of a temporal deliverance, in which we may be disappointed; we had better found our comforts on that which cannot fail us, the hope of eternal life. 4. Her travail was to the life of the child, but to her own death. Note, Though the pains and perils of childbearing were introduced by sin, yet they have sometimes been fatal to very holy women, who, though not saved in childbearing, are saved through it with an everlasting salvation. Rachel had passionately said, *Give me children, or else I die ;* and now that she had children (for this was her second) she died. Her dying is here called *the departing of her soul.* Note, The death of the body is but the departure of the soul to the world of spirits. 5. Her dying lips called her new-born son *Ben-oni, The son of my sorrow.* And many a son, not born in such hard labour, yet proves the son of his parent's sorrow, and the heaviness of her that bore him. Children are enough the sorrow of their poor mothers in the breeding, bearing, and nursing of them; they should therefore, when they grow up, study to be their joy, and so, if possible, to make them some amends. But Jacob, because he would not renew the sorrowful remembrance of the mother's death every time he called his son by his name, changed his name, and called him *Benjamin, The son of my right hand;* that is, "very dear to me, set on my right hand for a blessing, the support of my age, like the staff in my right hand." 6. Jacob buried her near the place where she died. As she died in child-bed, it was convenient to bury her quickly; and therefore he did not bring her to the burying-place of his family. If the soul be at rest after death, it matters little where the body lies. In the place where the tree falls, there let it be. No mention is made of the mourning that was at her death, because that might easily be taken for granted. Jacob, no doubt, was a true mourner. Note, Great afflictions sometimes befal us immediately after great comforts. Lest Jacob should be lifted up with the visions of the Almighty with which he was honoured, this was sent as a thorn in the flesh to humble him. Those that enjoy the favours peculiar to the children of God must yet expect the troubles that are common to the children of men. Deborah, who, had she lived, would have been a comfort to Rachel in her extremity, died but a little before. Note, When death comes into a family, it often strikes double. God by it speaks once, yea, twice. The Jewish writers say, "The death of Deborah and Rachel was to expiate the murder of the Shechemites, occasioned by Dinah, a daughter of the family." 7. Jacob set up a pillar upon her grave, so that it was known, long after, to be Rachel's sepulchre (1 Sam. x. 2), and Providence so ordered it that this place afterwards fell in the lot of Benjamin. Jacob set up a pillar in remembrance of his joys (*v.* 14), and here he sets up one in remembrance of his sorrows; for, as it may be of use to ourselves to keep both in mind, so it may be of use to others to transmit the memorials of both: the church, long afterwards, owned that what God said to Jacob at Bethel, both by his word and by his rod, he intended for their instruction (Hos. xii. 4), *There he spake with us.*

21 And Israel journeyed, and spread his tent beyond the tower of Edar. 22 And it came to pass, when Israel dwelt in that land, that Reuben went and lay with Bilhah his father's concubine: and Israel heard *it*. Now the sons of Jacob were twelve: 23 The sons of Leah; Reuben, Jacob's firstborn, and Simeon, and Levi, and Ju-

dah, and Issachar, and Zebulun: 24 The sons of Rachel; Joseph, and Benjamin: 25 And the sons of Bilhah, Rachel's handmaid; Dan, and Naphtali: 26 And the sons of Zilpah, Leah's handmaid; Gad, and Asher: these *are* the sons of Jacob, which were born to him in Padan-aram. 27 And Jacob came unto Isaac his father unto Mamre, unto the city of Arbah, which *is* Hebron, where Abraham and Isaac sojourned. 28 And the days of Isaac were a hundred and fourscore years. 29 And Isaac gave up the ghost, and died, and was gathered unto his people, *being* old and full of days: and his sons Esau and Jacob buried him.

Here is, 1. Jacob's removal, *v.* 21. He also, as his fathers, sojourned in the land of promise as in a strange country, and was not long in a place. Immediately after the story of Rachel's death he is here called *Israel* (*v.* 21, 22), and not often so afterwards: the Jews say, "The historian does him this honour here because he bore that affliction with such admirable patience and submission to Providence." Note, Those are Israels indeed, princes with God, that support the government of their own passions. He that has this rule over his own spirit is better than the mighty. Israel, a prince with God, yet dwells in tents; the city is reserved for him in the other world. 2. The sin of Reuben. A piece of abominable wickedness it was that he was guilty of (*v.* 22), that very sin which the apostle says (1 Cor. v. 1) is not so much as named among the Gentiles, *that one should have his father's wife.* It is said to have been *when Israel dwelt in that land;* as if he were then absent from his family, which might be the unhappy occasion of these disorders. Though perhaps Bilhah was the greater criminal, and it is probable was abandoned by Jacob for it, yet Reuben's crime was so provoking that, for it, he lost his birthright and blessing, *ch.* xlix. 4. The first-born is not always the best, nor the most promising. This was Reuben's sin, but it was Jacob's affliction; and what a sore affliction it was is intimated in a little compass, *and Israel heard it.* No more is said—that is enough; he heard it with the utmost grief and shame, horror and displeasure. Reuben thought to conceal it, that his father should never hear of it; but those that promise themselves secresy in sin are generally disappointed; a bird of the air carries the voice. 3. A complete list of the sons of Jacob, now that Benjamin the youngest was born. This is the first time we have the names of these heads of the twelve tribes together; afterwards we find them very often spoken of and enumerated, even to the end of the Bible, Rev. vii. 4; xxi. 12.　4. The visit which Jacob made to his father Isaac at Hebron. We may suppose he had visited him before since his return, for he *sorely longed after his father's house;* but never, till now, brought his family to settle with him, or near him, *v.* 27. Probably he did this now upon the death of Rebekah, by which Isaac was left solitary, and not disposed to marry again.　5. The age and death of Isaac are here recorded, though it appears, by computation, that he died not till many years after Joseph was sold into Egypt, and much about the time that he was preferred there.　Isaac, a mild quiet man, lived the longest of all the patriarchs, for he was 180 years old; Abraham was but 175.　Isaac lived about forty years after he had made his will, *ch.* xxvii. 2. We shall not die an hour the sooner, but abundantly the better, for our timely setting our heart and house in order.　Particular notice is taken of the amicable agreement of Esau and Jacob, in solemnizing their father's funeral (*v.* 29), to show how wonderfully God had changed Esau's mind since he vowed his brother's murder immediately after his father's death, *ch.* xxvii. 41.　Note, God has many ways of preventing bad men from doing the mischief they intended; he can either tie their hands or turn their hearts.

CHAP. XXXVI.

In this chapter we have an account of the posterity of Esau, who, from him, were called Edomites, that Esau who sold his birthright, and lost his blessing, and was not loved of God as Jacob was.　Here is a brief register kept of his family for some generations.　1. Because he was the son of Isaac, for whose sake this honour is put upon him.　2. Because the Edomites were neighbours to Israel, and their genealogy would be of use to give light to the following stories of what passed between them.　3. It is to show the performance of the promise to Abraham, that he should be "the father of many nations," and of that answer which Rebekah had from the oracle she consulted, "Two nations are in thy womb," and of the blessing of Isaac, "Thy dwelling shall be the fatness of the earth."　We have here, I. Esau's wives, ver. 1—5.　II. His remove to mount Seir, ver. 6—8.　III. The names of his sons, ver. 9—14.　IV. The dukes who descended of his sons, ver. 15—19.　V. The dukes of the Horites, ver. 20—30.　VI. The kings and dukes of Edom, ver. 31—43.　Little more is recorded than their names, because the history of those that were out of the church (though perhaps it might have been serviceable in politics) would have been of little use in divinity. It is in the church that the memorable instances are found of special grace, and special providence; for that is the enclosure, the rest is common. This chapter is abridged, 1 Chron. i. 35, &c.

NOW these *are* the generations of Esau, who *is* Edom.　2 Esau took his wives of the daughters of Canaan; Adah the daughter of Elon the Hittite, and Aholibamah the daughter of Anah the daughter of Zibeon the Hivite; 3 And Bashemath Ishmael's daughter, sister of Nebajoth.　4 And Adah bare to Esau Eliphaz; and Bashemath bare Reuel; 5 And Aholibamah bare Jeush, and Jaalam, and Korah: these *are* the sons of Esau, which were born unto him in the land of Canaan.　6 And Esau took his wives, and his sons, and his daughters, and all the persons of his house, and

his cattle, and all his beasts, and all his substance, which he had got in the land of Canaan; and went into the country from the face of his brother Jacob.　7 For their riches were more than that they might dwell together; and the land wherein they were strangers could not bear them because of their cattle.　8 Thus dwelt Esau in mount Seir: Esau *is* Edom.

Observe here, 1. Concerning Esau himself, *v.* 1.　He is called *Edom* (and again, *v.* 8), that name by which was perpetuated the remembrance of the foolish bargain he made, when he sold his birthright for *that red, that red pottage.* The very mention of that name is enough to intimate the reason why his family is turned off with such a short account.　Note, If men do a wrong thing they must thank themselves, when it is, long afterwards, remembered against them to their reproach.　2. Concerning his wives, and the children they bore him in the land of Canaan. He had three wives, and, by them all, but five sons: many a one has more by one wife. God in his providence often disappoints those who take indirect courses to build up a family; yet here the promise prevailed, and Esau's family was built up.　3. Concerning his removal to mount Seir, which was the country God had given him for a possession, when he reserved Canaan for the seed of Jacob.　God owns it, long afterwards: *I gave to Esau mount Seir* (Deut. ii. 5; Josh. xxiv. 4), which was the reason why the Edomites must not be disturbed in their possession. Those that have not a right by promise, such as Jacob had, to Canaan, may have a very good title by providence to their estates, such as Esau had to mount Seir.　Esau had begun to settle among his wives' relations, in Seir, before Jacob came from Padan-aram, *ch.* xxxii. 3.　Isaac, it is likely, had sent him thither (as Abraham in his life-time had sent the sons of the concubines from Isaac his son into the east country, *ch.* xxv. 6), that Jacob might have the clearer way made for him to the possession of the promised land.　During the life of Isaac, however, Esau had probably still some effects remaining in Canaan; but, after his death, he wholly withdrew to mount Seir, took with him what came to his share of his father's personal estate, and left Canaan to Jacob, not only because he had the promise of it, but because Esau perceived that if they should continue to thrive as they had begun there would not be room for both. *Thus dwelt Esau in Mount Seir, v.* 8.　Note, Whatever opposition may be made, God's word will be accomplished, and even those that have opposed it will see themselves, some time or other, under a necessity of yielding to it, and acquiescing in it.　Esau had struggled for Canaan, but now he tamely retires to mount Seir; for God's counsels shall certainly stand, concerning the times before appointed, and the bounds of our habitation.

9 And these *are* the generations of Esau the father of the Edomites in mount Seir : 10 These *are* the names of Esau's sons; Eliphaz the son of Adah the wife of Esau, Reuel the son of Bashemath the wife of Esau. 11 And the sons of Eliphaz were Teman, Omar, Zepho, and Gatam, and Kenaz. 12 And Timna was concubine to Eliphaz Esau's son; and she bare to Eliphaz Amalek : these *were* the sons of Adah Esau's wife. 13 And these *are* the sons of Reuel; Nahath, and Zerah, Shammah, and Mizzah : these were the sons of Bashemath Esau's wife. 14 And these were the sons of Aholibamah, the daughter of Anah the daughter of Zibeon, Esau's wife : and she bare to Esau Jeush, and Jaalam, and Korah. 15 These *were* dukes of the sons of Esau : the sons of Eliphaz the firstborn *son* of Esau ; duke Teman, duke Omar, duke Zepho, duke Kenaz, 16 Duke Korah, duke Gatam, *and* duke Amalek : these *are* the dukes *that came* of Eliphaz in the land of Edom ; these *were* the sons of Adah. 17 And these *are* the sons of Reuel Esau's son ; duke Nahath, duke Zerah, duke Shammah, duke Mizzah : these *are* the dukes *that came* of Reuel in the land of Edom ; these *are* the sons of Bashemath Esau's wife. 18 And these *are* the sons of Aholibamah Esau's wife ; duke Jeush, duke Jaalam, duke Korah : these *were* the dukes *that came* of Aholibamah the daughter of Anah, Esau's wife. 19 These *are* the sons of Esau, who *is* Edom, and these *are* their dukes.

Observe here, 1. That only the names of Esau's sons and grandsons are recorded, only their names, not their history ; for it is the church that Moses preserves the records of, not the record of those that are without. Those elders that lived by faith alone obtained a good report. It is Sion that produces the men of renown, not Seir, Ps. lxxxvii. 5. Nor does the genealogy go any further than the third and fourth generation ; the very names of all after are buried in oblivion. It is only the pedigree of the Israelites, who were to be the heirs of Canaan, and of whom were to come the promised seed, and the holy seed, that is drawn out to any length, as far as there was occasion for it, even of

all the tribes till Canaan was divided among them, and of the royal line till Christ came. 2. That these sons and grandsons of Esau are called *dukes, v.* 15—19. Probably they were military commanders, dukes, or captains, that had soldiers under them ; for Esau and his family lived *by the sword, ch.* xxvii. 40. Note, Titles of honour have been more ancient out of the church than in it. Esau's sons were dukes when Jacob's sons were but plain shepherds, *ch.* xlvii. 3. This is not a reason why such titles should not be used among Christians ; but it is a reason why men should not overvalue themselves, or others, for the sake of them. There is an honour that comes from God, and a name in his house that is infinitely more valuable. Edomites may be dukes with men, but Israelites indeed are made to our God kings and priests. 3. We may suppose those dukes had numerous families of children and servants, that were their dukedoms. God promised to multiply Jacob, and to enrich him ; yet Esau increases, and is enriched first. Note, It is no new thing for the men of this world to be full of children, and to have their bellies too *filled with hidden treasure,* Ps. xvii. 14. God's promise to Jacob began to work late, but the effect of it remained longer, and it had its complete accomplishment in the spiritual Israel.

20 These *are* the sons of Seir the Horite, who inhabited the land ; Lotan, and Shobal, and Zibeon, and Anah, 21 And Dishon, and Ezer, and Dishan : these *are* the dukes of the Horites, the children of Seir in the land of Edom. 22 And the children of Lotan were Hori and Hemam ; and Lotan's sister *was* Timna. 23 And the children of Shobal *were* these ; Alvan, and Manahath, and Ebal, Shepho, and Onam. 24 And these *are* the children of Zibeon ; both Ajah, and Anah : this *was that* Anah that found the mules in the wilderness, as he fed the asses of Zibeon his father. 25 And the children of Anah *were* these ; Dishon, and Aholibamah the daughter of Anah. 26 And these *are* the children of Dishon ; Hemdan, and Eshban, and Ithran, and Cheran. 27 The children of Ezer *are* these ; Bilhan, and Zaavan, and Akan. 28 The children of Dishan *are* these ; Uz, and Aran. 29 These *are* the dukes *that came* of the Horites ; duke Lotan, duke Shobal, duke Zibeon, duke Anah, 30 Duke Dishon, duke Ezer, duke Dishan : these *are* the dukes *that came* of

Hori, among their dukes in the land of Seir.

In the midst of this genealogy of the Edomites here is inserted the genealogy of the Horites, those Canaanites, or Hittites (compare *ch.* xxvi. 34), that were the natives of Mount Seir. Mention is made of them, *ch.* xiv. 6, and of their interest in Mount Seir, before the Edomites took possession of it, Deut. ii. 12, 22. This comes in here, not only to give light to the story, but to be a standing reflection upon the Edomites for intermarrying with them, by which, it is probable, they learned their way, and corrupted themselves. Esau having sold his birthright, and lost his blessing, and entered into alliance with the Hittites, his posterity and the sons of Seir are here reckoned together. Note, Those that treacherously desert God's church are justly numbered with those that were never in it; apostate Edomites stand on the same ground with accursed Horites. Particular notice is taken of one Anah who fed the asses of Zibeon his father (*v.* 24), and yet is called *duke Anah, v.* 29. Note, Those that expect to rise high should begin low. An honourable descent should not keep men from an honest employment, nor a mean employment hinder any man's preferment. This Anah was not only industrious in his business, but ingenious too, and successful; for he found *mules,* or (as some read it) *waters, hot-baths,* in the wilderness. Those that are diligent in their business sometimes find more advantages than they expected.

31 And these *are* the kings that reigned in the land of Edom, before there reigned any king over the children of Israel. 32 And Bela the son of Beor reigned in Edom : and the name of his city *was* Dinhabah. 33 And Bela died, and Jobab the son of Zerah of Bozrah reigned in his stead. 34 And Jobab died, and Husham of the land of Temani reigned in his stead. 35 And Husham died, and Hadad the son of Bedad, who smote Midian in the field of Moab, reigned in his stead : and the name of his city *was* Avith. 36 And Hadad died, and Samlah of Masrekah reigned in his stead. 37 And Samlah died, and Saul of Rehoboth *by* the river reigned in his stead. 38 And Saul died, and Baal-hanan the son of Achbor reigned in his stead. 39 And Baal-hanan the son of Achbor died, and Hadar reigned in his stead : and the name of his city *was* Pau ; and his wife's name *was* Mehetabel, the daughter of Matred, the daughter

of Mezahab. 40 And these *are* the names of the dukes *that came* of Esau, according to their families, after their places, by their names ; duke Timnah, duke Alvah, duke Jetheth, 41 Duke Aholibamah, duke Elah, duke Pinon, 42 Duke Kenaz, duke Teman, duke Mibzar, 43 Duke Magdiel, duke Iram : these *be* the dukes of Edom, according to their habitations in the land of their possession : he *is* Esau the father of the Edomites.

By degrees, it seems, the Edomites wormed out the Horites, obtained full possession of the country, and had a goverment of their own. 1. They were ruled by kings, who governed the whole country, and seem to have come to the throne by election, and not by lineal descent; so bishop Patrick observes. These kings reigned in *Edom before there reigned any king over the children of Israel,* that is, before Moses's time, for *he was king in Jeshurun, v.* 3. God had lately promised *Jacob that kings should come out of his loins* (*ch.* xxxv. 11), yet Esau's blood becomes royal long before any of Jacob's did. Note, In external prosperity and honour, the children of the covenant are often cast behind, and those that are out of covenant get the start. The triumphing of the wicked may be quick, but it is short ; soon ripe, and as soon rotten : but the products of the promise, though they are slow, are sure and lasting ; *at the end it shall speak, and not lie.* We may suppose it was a great trial to the faith of God's Israel to hear of the pomp and power of the kings of Edom, while they were bond-slaves in Egypt ; but those that look for great things from God must be content to wait for them; God's time is the best time. 2. They were afterwards governed by dukes, again here named, who, I suppose, ruled all at the same time in several places in the country. Either they set up this form of government in conformity to the Horites, who had used it (*v.* 29), or God's providence reduced them to it, as some conjecture, to correct them for their unkindness to Israel, in refusing them a passage through their country, Num. xx. 18. Note, When power is abused, it is just with God to weaken it, by turning it into divers channels. *For the transgression of a land, many are the princes thereof.* Sin brought Edom from kings to dukes, from crowns to coronets. We read of the dukes of Edom (Exod. xv. 15), yet, long afterwards, of their kings again. 3. Mount Seir is called *the land of their possession, v.* 43. While the Israelites dwelt in the house of bondage, and their Canaan was only the land of promise, the Edomites dwelt in their own habitations, and Seir was in their possession. Note, The children of this world have their all in hand, and nothing in hope (Luke xvi. 25); *while* the children of God have their all in hope, and next to nothing in hand. But, all things considered, it is better to have Canaan in promise than mount Seir in possession.

CHAP. XXXVII.

At this chapter begins the story of Joseph, who, in every subsequent chapter but one to the end of this book, makes the greatest figure. He was Jacob's eldest son by his beloved wife Rachel, born, as many eminent men were, of a mother that had been long barren. His story is so remarkably divided between his humiliation and his exaltation that we cannot avoid seeing something of Christ in it, who was first humbled and then exalted, and, in many instances, so as to answer the type of Joseph. It also shows the lot of Christians, who must through many tribulations enter into the kingdom. In this chapter we have, I. The malice his brethren bore against him. They hated him, 1. Because he informed his father of their wickedness, ver. 1, 2. 2. Because his father loved him, ver. 3. 4. 3. Because he dreamed of his dominion over them, ver. 5—11. II. The mischiefs his brethren designed and did to him. 1. The kind visit he made them gave an opportunity, ver. 12—17. 2. They designed to slay him, but determined to starve him, ver. 18—24. 3. They changed their purpose, and sold him for a slave, ver. 25—28. 4. They made their father believe that he was torn in pieces, ver. 29—35. 5. He was sold into Egypt to Potiphar, ver. 36. And all this was working together for good.

AND Jacob dwelt in the land wherein his father was a stranger, in the land of Canaan. 2 These *are* the generations of Jacob. Joseph, *being* seventeen years old, was feeding the flock with his brethren; and the lad *was* with the sons of Bilhah, and with the sons of Zilpah, his father's wives: and Joseph brought unto his father their evil report. 3 Now Israel loved Joseph more than all his children, because he *was* the son of his old age: and he made him a coat of *many* colours. 4 And when his brethren saw that their father loved him more than all his brethren, they hated him, and could not speak peaceably unto him.

Moses has no more to say of the Edomites, unless as they happen to fall in Israel's way; but now applies himself closely to the story of Jacob's family: *These are the generations of Jacob*. His is not a bare barren genealogy as that of Esau (*ch*. xxxvi. 1), but a memorable useful history. Here is, 1. Jacob a sojourner with his father Isaac, who was yet living, *v*. 1. We shall never be at home, till we come to heaven. 2. Joseph a shepherd, *feeding the flock with his brethren, v*. 2. Though he was his father's darling, yet he was not brought up in idleness or delicacy. Those do not truly love their children that do not inure them to business, and labour, and mortification. The fondling of children is with good reason commonly called the spoiling of them. Those that are trained up to do nothing are likely to be good for nothing. 3. Joseph beloved by his father (*v*. 3), partly for his dear mother's sake that was dead, and partly for his own sake, because he was the greatest comfort of his old age; probably he waited on him, and was more observant of him than the rest of his sons; he was the *son of the ancient* so some; that is, when he was a child, he was as grave and

discreet as if he had been an old man, a child, but not childish. Jacob proclaimed his affection to him by dressing him finer than the rest of his children: He *made him a coat of divers colours*, which probably was significant of further honours intended him. Note, Though those children are happy that have that in them which justly recommends them to their parents' particular love, yet it is the prudence of parents not to make a difference between one child and another, unless there be a great and manifest cause given for it by the children's dutifulness or undutifulness; paternal government must be impartial, and managed with a steady hand. 4. Joseph hated by his brethren, (1.) Because his father loved him; when parents make a difference, children soon take notice of it, and it often occasions feuds and quarrels in families. (2.) Because he *brought to his father their evil report*. Jacob's sons did that, when they were from under his eye, which they durst not have done if they had been at home with him; but Joseph gave his father an account of their bad carriage, that he might reprove and restrain them; not as a malicious tale-bearer, to sow discord, but as a faithful brother, who, when he durst not admonish them himself, represented their faults to one that had authority to admonish them. Note, [1.] It is common for friendly monitors to be looked upon as enemies. Those that hate to be reformed hate those that would reform them, Prov. ix. 8. [2.] It is common for those that are beloved of God to be hated by the world; whom Heaven blesses, hell curses. To those to whom God speaks comfortably wicked men will not speak peaceably. It is said here of Joseph, *the lad was with the sons of Bilhah;* some read it, and he was *servant to them,* they made him their drudge.

5 And Joseph dreamed a dream, and he told *it* his brethren: and they hated him yet the more. 6 And he said unto them, Hear, I pray you, this dream which I have dreamed: 7 For, behold, we *were* binding sheaves in the field, and, lo, my sheaf arose, and also stood upright; and, behold, your sheaves stood round about, and made obeisance to my sheaf. 8 And his brethren said to him, Shalt thou indeed reign over us? or shalt thou indeed have dominion over us? And they hated him yet the more for his dreams, and for his words. 9 And he dreamed yet another dream, and told it his brethren, and said, Behold, I have dreamed a dream more; and, behold, the sun and the moon and the eleven stars made obeisance to me. 10 And he told *it* to his father, and

to his brethren: and his father rebuked him, and said unto him, What *is* this dream that thou hast dreamed? Shall I and thy mother and thy brethren indeed come to bow down ourselves to thee to the earth? 11 And his brethren envied him; but his father observed the saying.

Here, I. Joseph relates the prophetical dreams he had, *v.* 6, 7, 9, 10. Though he was now very young (about seventeen years old), yet he was pious and devout, and well-inclined, and this fitted him for God's gracious discoveries of himself to him. Joseph had a great deal of trouble before him, and therefore God gave him betimes this prospect of his advancement, to support and comfort him under the long and grievous troubles with which he was to be exercised. Thus Christ had a *joy set before him,* and so have Christians. Note, God has ways of preparing his people beforehand for the trials which they cannot foresee, but which he has an eye to in the comforts with which he furnishes them. His dreams were, 1. That his brethren's sheaves all bowed to his, intimating upon what occasion they should be brought to do homage to him, namely, in seeking to him for corn; their empty sheaves should bow to his full one. 2. That the sun, and moon, and eleven stars, did obeisance to him, *v.* 9. Joseph was more of a prophet than a politician, else he would have kept this to himself, when he could not but know that his brethren did already hate him and that this would but the more exasperate them. But, if he told it in his simplicity, yet God directed it for the mortification of his brethren. Observe, Joseph dreamed of his preferment, but he did not dream of his imprisonment. Thus many young people, when they are setting out in the world, think of nothing but prosperity and pleasure, and never dream of trouble.

II. His brethren take it very ill, and are more and more enraged against him (*v.* 8): *Shalt thou indeed reign over us?* See here, 1. How truly they interpreted his dream, that he should reign over them. Those become the expositors of his dream who were enemies to the accomplishment of it, as in Gideon's story (Judg. vii. 13, 14); they perceived that he spoke of them, Matt. xxi. 45. The event exactly answered to this interpretation, *ch.* xlii. 6, &c. 2. How scornfully they resented it: " *Shalt thou,* who art but one, *reign over us,* who are many? Thou, who art the youngest, over us who are older?" Note, The reign and dominion of Jesus Christ, our Joseph, have been, and are, despised and striven against by a carnal and unbelieving world, who cannot endure to think that this man should reign over them. The dominion also of the upright, in the morning of the resurrection, is thought of with the utmost disdain.

III. His father gives him a gentle rebuke for it, yet observes the saying, *v.* 10, 11. Probably he checked him for it, to lessen the offence which his brethren would be apt to take at it; yet he took notice of it more than he seemed to do: he insinuated that it was but an idle dream, because his mother was brought in, who had been dead some time since; whereas *the sun, moon, and eleven stars,* signify no more than the whole family that should have a dependence upon him, and be glad to be beholden to him. Note, The faith of God's people in God's promises is often sorely shaken by their misunderstanding the promises and then suggesting the improbabilities that attend the performance; but God is doing his own work, and will do it, whether we understand him aright or no. Jacob, like Mary (Luke ii. 51), kept these things in his heart, and no doubt remembered them long afterwards, when the event answered to the prediction.

12 And his brethren went to feed their father's flock in Shechem. 13 And Israel said unto Joseph, Do not thy brethren feed *the flock* in Shechem? come, and I will send thee unto them. And he said to him, Here *am I.* 14 And he said to him, Go, I pray thee, see whether it be well with thy brethren, and well with the flocks; and bring me word again. So he sent him out of the vale of Hebron, and he came to Shechem. 15 And a certain man found him, and, behold, *he was* wandering in the field: and the man asked him, saying, What seekest thou? 16 And he said, I seek my brethren: tell me, I pray thee, where they feed *their flocks.* 17 And the man said, They are departed hence; for I heard them say, Let us go to Dothan. And Joseph went after his brethren, and found them in Dothan. 18 And when they saw him afar off, even before he came near unto them, they conspired against him to slay him. 19 And they said one to another, Behold, this dreamer cometh. 20 Come now therefore, and let us slay him, and cast him into some pit, and we will say, Some evil beast hath devoured him: and we shall see what will become of his dreams. 21 And Reuben heard *it,* and he delivered him out of their hands; and said, Let us not kill him. 22 And Reuben said unto them, Shed no blood, *but* cast him into this pit

that *is* in the wilderness, and lay no hand upon him ; that he might rid him out of their hands, to deliver him to his father again.

Here is, I. The kind visit which Joseph, in obedience to his father's command, made to his brethren, who were feeding the flock at Shechem, many miles off. Some suggest that they went thither on purpose, expecting that Joseph would be sent to see them, and that then they should have an opportunity to do him a mischief. However, Joseph and his father had both of them more of the innocence of the dove than of the wisdom of the serpent, else he had never come thus into the hands of those that hated him : but God designed it all for good. See in Joseph an instance, 1. Of dutifulness to his father. Though he was his father's darling, yet he was made, and was willing to be, his father's servant. How readily does he wait his father's orders ! *Here am I, v.* 13. Note, Those children that are best beloved by their parents should be most obedient to their parents ; and then their love is well-bestowed and well-returned. 2. Of kindness to his brethren. Though he knew they hated him and envied him, yet he made no objections against his father's commands, either from the distance of the place or the danger of the journey, but cheerfully embraced the opportunity of showing his respect to his brethren. Note, It is a very good lesson, though it is learnt with difficulty and rarely practised, *to love those that hate us :* if our relations do not their duty to us, yet we must not be wanting in our duty to them. This is thank-worthy. Joseph was sent by his father to Shechem, to see whether his brethren were well there, and whether the country had not risen upon them and destroyed them, in revenge of their barbarous murder of the Shechemites some years before. But Joseph, not finding them there, went to Dothan, which showed that he undertook this journey, not only in obedience to his father (for then he might have returned when he missed them at Shechem, having done what his father told him), but out of love to his brethren, and therefore he sought diligently till he found them. Thus let brotherly love continue, and let us give proofs of it.

II. The bloody and malicious plot of his brethren against him, who rendered good for evil, and, for his love, were his adversaries. Observe, 1. How deliberate they were in the contrivance of this mischief : when they *saw him afar off, they conspired against him, v.* 18. It was not in a heat, or upon a sudden provocation, that they thought to slay him, but from malice prepense, and in cold blood. Note, Whosoever hateth his brother is a murderer ; for he will be one if he have an opportunity, 1 John iii. 15. Malice is a most mischievous thing, and is in danger of making bloody work where it is harboured and

214

indulged. The more there is of a project and contrivance in a sin the worse it is ; it is bad to do evil, but worse to devise it. 2. How cruel they were in their design ; nothing less than his blood would satisfy them : *Come, and let us slay him, v.* 20. Note, The old enmity hunts for the precious life. It is the *blood-thirsty* that *hate the upright* (Prov. xxix. 10), and it is the blood of the saints that the harlot is drunk with. 3. How scornfully they reproached him for his dreams (*v.* 19) : *This dreamer cometh ;* and (*v.* 20), *We shall see what will become of his dreams.* This shows what it was that fretted and enraged them. They could not endure to think of doing homage to him ; this was what they were plotting to prevent by the murder of him. Note, Men that fret and rage at God's counsels are impiously aiming to defeat them ; but they imagine a vain thing, Ps. ii. 1—3. God's counsels will stand. 4. How they agreed to keep one another's counsel, and to cover the murder with a lie : *We will say, Some evil beast hath devoured him ;* whereas in thus consulting to devour him they proved themselves worse than the most evil beasts ; for evil beasts prey not on those of their own kind, but they were tearing a piece of themselves.

III. Reuben's project to deliver him, *v.* 21, 22. Note, God can raise up friends for his people, even among their enemies ; for he has all hearts in his hands. Reuben, of all the brothers, had most reason to be jealous of Joseph, for he was the first-born, and so entitled to those distinguishing favours which Jacob was conferring on Joseph ; yet he proves his best friend. Reuben's temper seems to have been soft and effeminate, which had betrayed him to the sin of uncleanness ; while the temper of the next two brothers, Simeon and Levi, was fierce, which betrayed them to the sin of murder, a sin which Reuben startled at the thought of. Note, Our natural constitution should be guarded against those sins to which it is most inclinable, and improved (as Reuben's here) against those sins to which it is most averse. Reuben made a proposal which they thought would effectually answer their intention of destroying Joseph, and yet which he designed should answer his intention of rescuing Joseph out of their hands and restoring him to his father, probably hoping thereby to recover his father's favour, which he had lately lost ; but God overruled all to serve his own purpose of making Joseph an instrument to save much people alive. Joseph was here a type of Christ. Though he was the beloved Son of his Father, and hated by a wicked world, yet the Father sent him out of his bosom to visit us in great humility and love. He came from heaven to earth, to seek and save us ; yet then malicious plots were laid against him. He came to his own, and his own not only received him not, but consulted against him : *This is the heir, come let us kill him ; Crucify him, crucify him.* This he submitted to, in pursuance of his design to redeem and save us.

23 And it came to pass, when Joseph was come unto his brethren, that they stript Joseph out of his coat, *his* coat of *many* colours that *was* on him; 24 And they took him, and cast him into a pit: and the pit *was* empty, *there was* no water in it. 25 And they sat down to eat bread: and they lifted up their eyes and looked, and, behold, a company of Ishmeelites came from Gilead with their camels bearing spicery and balm and myrrh, going to carry *it* down to Egypt. 26 And Judah said unto his brethren, What profit *is it* if we slay our brother, and conceal his blood? 27 Come, and let us sell him to the Ishmeelites, and let not our hand be upon him; for he *is* our brother *and* our flesh. And his brethren were content. 28 Then there passed by Midianites merchantmen; and they drew and lifted up Joseph out of the pit, and sold Joseph to the Ishmeelites for twenty *pieces* of silver: and they brought Joseph into Egypt. 29 And Reuben returned unto the pit; and, behold, Joseph *was* not in the pit; and he rent his clothes. 30 And he returned unto his brethren, and said, the child *is* not; and I, whither shall I go?

We have here the execution of their plot against Joseph. 1. They stripped him, each striving to seize the envied coat of many colours, *v.* 23. Thus, in imagination, they degraded him from the birthright, of which perhaps this was the badge, grieving him, affronting their father, and making themselves sport, while they insulted over him. "Now, Joseph, where is the fine coat?" Thus our Lord Jesus was stripped of his seamless coat, and thus his suffering saints have first been industriously divested of their privileges and honours, and then made the off-scouring of all things. 2. They went about to starve him, throwing him into a dry pit, to perish there with hunger and cold, so cruel were their tender mercies, *v.* 24. Note, Where envy reigns pity is banished, and humanity itself is forgotten, Prov. xxvii. 4. So full of deadly poison is malice that the more barbarous any thing is the more grateful it is. Now Joseph begged for his life, in *the anguish of his soul* (*ch.* xlii. 21), entreated, by all imaginable endearments, that they would be content with his coat and spare his life. He pleads innocence, relation, affection, submission; he weeps and makes supplication, but all in vain. Reuben alone

relents and intercedes for him, *ch.* xlii. 22. But he cannot prevail to save Joseph from the horrible pit, in which they resolve he shall die by degrees, and be buried alive. Is this he to whom his brethren must do homage? Note, God's providences often seem to contradict his purposes, even when they are serving them, and working at a distance towards the accomplishment of them. 3. They slighted him when he was in distress, and were not grieved for the affliction of Joseph; for when he was pining away in the pit, bemoaning his own misery, and with a languishing cry calling to them for pity, they *sat down to eat bread, v.* 25. (1.) They felt no remorse of conscience for the sin; if they had, it would have spoiled their appetite for their meat, and the relish of it. Note, A great force put upon conscience commonly stupifies it, and for the time deprives it both of sense and speech. Daring sinners are secure ones. But the consciences of Joseph's brethren, though asleep now, were roused long afterwards, *ch.* xlii. 21. (2.) They were now pleased to think how they were freed from the fear of their brother's dominion over them, and that, on the contrary, they had turned the wheel upon him. They made merry over him, as the persecutors over the two witnesses that had tormented them, Rev. xi. 10. Note, Those that oppose God's counsels may possibly prevail so far as to think they have gained their point, and yet be deceived. 4. They sold him. A caravan of merchants very opportunely passed by (Providence so ordering it), and Judah made the motion that they should sell Joseph to them, to be carried far enough off into Egypt, where, in all probability, he would be lost, and never heard of more. (1.) Judah proposed it in compassion to Joseph (*v.* 26): "*What profit is it if we slay our brother?* it will be less guilt, and more gain, to sell him." Note, When we are tempted to sin, we should consider the unprofitableness of it. It is what there is nothing to be got by. (2.) They acquiesced in it, because they thought that if he were sold for a slave he would never be a lord; if sold into Egypt he would never be their lord; yet all this was working towards it. Note, The wrath of man shall praise God, and the remainder of wrath he will restrain, Ps. lxxvi. 10. Joseph's brethren were wonderfully restrained from murdering him, and their selling him was as wonderfully turned to God's praise. As Joseph was sold by the contrivance of Judah for twenty pieces of silver, so was our Lord Jesus for thirty, and by one of the same name too, *Judas.* Reuben (it seems) had gone away from his brethren, when they sold Joseph, intending to come round some other way to the pit, and to help Joseph out of it, and return him safely to his father. This was a kind project, but, if it had taken effect, what had become of God's purpose concerning his preferment in Egypt? Note, There are many devices in man's heart, many devices of the enemies of God's people to destroy them and of their friends to help them, which perhaps are both disappointed, as these were; but the counsel of the Lord, that shall stand. Reuben thought himself undone, because the child was sold : *I, whither shall I go ?* v. 30. He being the eldest, his father would expect from him an account of Joseph; but, as it proved, they would all have been undone if he had not been sold.

31 And they took Joseph's coat, and killed a kid of the goats, and dipped the coat in the blood ; 32 And they sent the coat of *many* colours, and they brought *it* to their father ; and said, This have we found : know now whether it *be* thy son's coat or no. 33 And he knew it, and said, *It is* my son's coat; an evil beast hath devoured him ; Joseph is without doubt rent in pieces. 34 And Jacob rent his clothes, and put sackcloth upon his loins, and mourned for his son many days. 35 And all his sons and all his daughters rose up to comfort him ; but he refused to be comforted ; and he said, For I will go down into the grave unto my son mourning. Thus his father wept for him. 36 And the Midianites sold him into Egypt unto Potiphar, an officer of Pharaoh's, *and* captain of the guard.

I. Joseph would soon be missed, great enquiry would be made for him, and therefore his brethren have a further design, to make the world believe that Joseph was torn in pieces by a wild beast ; and this they did, 1. To clear themselves, that they might not be suspected to have done him any mischief. Note, We have all learned of Adam to cover our transgression, Job xxxi. 33. When the devil has taught men to commit one sin, he then teaches them to conceal it with another, theft and murder with lying and perjury; but he that covers his sin shall not prosper long. Joseph's brethren kept their own and one another's counsel for some time, but their villany came to light at last, and it is here published to the world, and the remembrance of it transmitted to every age. 2. To grieve their good father. It seems designed by them on purpose to be revenged upon him for his distinguishing love of Joseph. It was contrived on purpose to create the utmost vexation to him. They sent him Joseph's coat of many colours, with one colour more than it had had, a bloody colour, v. 32. They pretended they had found it in the fields, and Jacob himself must be scornfully asked, *Is this thy son's coat ?* Now the badge of his honour is the discovery of his fate; and it is rashly inferred from the bloody coat that *Joseph, without doubt, is rent in pieces.* Love is always apt to fear the worst concerning the person beloved ; there is a love that casteth out fear, but that is a perfect love. Now let those that know the heart of a parent suppose the agonies of poor Jacob, and put their souls into his soul's stead. How strongly does he represent to himself the direful idea of Joseph's misery ! Sleeping or waking, he imagines he sees the wild beast setting upon Joseph, thinks he hears his piteous shrieks when the lion roared against him, makes himself tremble and grow chill, many a time, when he fancies how the beast sucked his blood, tore him limb from limb, and left no remains of him, but the coat of many colours, to carry the tidings. And no doubt it added no little to the grief that he had exposed him, by sending him, and sending him all alone, on this dangerous journey, which proved so fatal to him. This cuts him to the heart, and he is ready to look upon himself as an accessory to the death of his son. Now, (1.) Endeavours were used to comfort him. His sons basely pretended to do it (v. 35); but miserable hypocritical comforters were they all. Had they really desired to comfort him, they might easily have done it, by telling him the truth, "Joseph is alive, he is indeed sold into Egypt, but it will be an easy thing to send thither and ransom him." This would have *loosened his sackloth, and girded him with gladness* presently. I wonder their countenances did not betray their guilt, and with what face they could pretend to condole with Jacob on the death of Joseph, when they knew he was alive. Note, The heart is strangely hardened by the deceitfulness of sin. But, (2.) It was all in vain : *Jacob refused to be comforted, v.* 35. He was an obstinate mourner, resolved to go down to the grave mourning. It was not a sudden transport of passion, like that of David, *Would God I had died for thee, my son, my son !* But, like Job, he hardened himself in sorrow. Note, [1.] Great affection to any creature does but prepare for so much the greater affliction, when it is either removed from us or embittered to us. Inordinate love commonly ends in immoderate grief; as much as the sway of the pendulum throws one way, so much it will throw the other way. [2.] Those consult neither the comfort of their souls nor the credit of their religion that are determined in their sorrow upon any occasion whatsoever. We must never say, "We will go to our grave mourning," because we know not what joyful days Providence may yet reserve for us, and it is our wisdom and duty to accommodate ourselves to Providence. [3.] We often perplex ourselves with imaginary troubles. We fancy things worse than they are, and then afflict ourselves more than we need. Sometimes there needs no more to comfort us than to undeceive us : it is good to hope the best.

II. The Ishmaelites and Midianites having bought Joseph only to make their market of him, here we have him sold again (with gain enough to the merchants, no doubt) to Potiphar, *v.* 36. Jacob was lamenting the loss of his life; had he known all he would have lamented, though not so passionately, the loss of his liberty. Shall Jacob's free-born son exchange the best robe of his family for the livery of an Egyptian lord, and all the marks of servitude? How soon was the land of Egypt made a house of bondage to the seed of Jacob! Note, It is the wisdom of parents not to bring up their children too delicately, because they know not to what hardships and mortifications Providence may reduce them before they die. Jacob little thought that ever his beloved Joseph would be thus bought and sold for a servant.

CHAP. XXXVIII.

This chapter gives us an account of Judah and his family, and such an account it is that one would wonder that, of all Jacob's sons, our Lord should spring out of Judah, Heb. vii. 14. If we were to form a character of him by this story, we should not say, "Judah, thou art he whom thy brethren shall praise," ch. xlix. 8. But God will show that his choice is of grace and not of merit, and that Christ came into the world to save sinners, even the chief, and is not ashamed, upon their repentance, to be allied to them, also that the worth and worthiness of Jesus Christ are personal, of himself, and not derived from his ancestors. Humbling himself to be " made in the likeness of sinful flesh," he was pleased to descend from some that were infamous. How little reason had the Jews, who were so called from this Judah, to boast, as they did, that they were not born of fornication! John viii. 41. We have, in this chapter, I. Judah's marriage and issue, and the untimely death of his two eldest sons, ver. 1—11. II. Judah's incest with his daughter-in-law Tamar, without his knowing it, ver. 12—23. III. His confusion, when it was discovered, ver. 24—26. IV. The birth of his twin sons, in whom his family was built up, ver. 27, &c.

AND it came to pass at that time, that Judah went down from his brethren, and turned in to a certain Adullamite, whose name *was* Hirah. 2 And Judah saw there a daughter of a certain Canaanite, whose name *was* Shuah; and he took her, and went in unto her. 3 And she conceived, and bare a son; and he called his name Er. 4 And she conceived again, and bare a son; and she called his name Onan. 5 And she yet again conceived, and bare a son; and called his name Shelah: and he was at Chezib, when she bare him. 6 And Judah took a wife for Er his firstborn, whose name *was* Tamar. 7 And Er, Judah's first-born, was wicked in the sight of the Lord; and the Lord slew him. 8 And Judah said unto Onan, Go in unto thy brother's wife, and marry her, and raise up seed to thy brother. 9 And Onan knew that the seed should not be his; and it came to pass, when he went in unto his brother's wife, that he spilled *it* on the ground, lest that he should give seed to his brother. 10 And the thing which he did

displeased the Lord: wherefore he slew him also. 11 Then said Judah to Tamar his daughter in law, Remain a widow at thy father's house, till Shelah my son be grown: for he said, Lest peradventure he die also, as his brethren *did*. And Tamar went and dwelt in her father's house.

Here is, 1. Judah's foolish friendship with a Canaanite-man. He went down from his brethren, and withdrew for a time from their society and his father's family, and got to be intimately acquainted with one Hirah, an Adullamite, *v.* 1. It is computed that he was now not much above fifteen or sixteen years of age, an easy prey to the tempter. Note, When young people that have been well educated begin to change their company, they will soon change their manners, and lose their good education. Those that go down from their brethren, that despise and forsake the society of the seed of Israel, and pick up Canaanites for their companions, are going down the hill apace. It is of great consequence to young people to choose proper associates; for these they will imitate, study to recommend themselves to, and, by their opinion of them, value themselves: an error in this choice is often fatal. 2. His foolish marriage with a Canaanite-woman, a match made, not by his father, who, it should seem, was not consulted, but by his new friend Hirah, *v.* 2. Many have been drawn into marriages scandalous and pernicious to themselves and their families by keeping bad company, and growing familiar with bad people: one wicked league entangles men in another. Let young people be admonished by this to take their good parents for their best friends, and to be advised by them, and not by flatterers, who wheedle them, to make a prey of them. 3. His children by this Canaanite, and his disposal of them. Three sons he had by her, Er, Onan, and Shelah. It is probable that she embraced the worship of the God of Israel, at least in profession, but, for aught that appears, there was little of the fear of God in the family. Judah married too young, and very rashly; he also married his sons too young, when they had neither wit nor grace to govern themselves, and the consequences were very bad. (1.) His first-born, *Er*, was notoriously wicked; he was so *in the sight of the Lord*, that is, in defiance of God and his law; or, if perhaps he was not wicked in the sight of the world, he was so in the sight of God, to whom all men's wickedness is open; and what came of it? Why, God cut him off presently (*v.* 7): *The Lord slew him.* Note, Sometimes God makes quick work with sinners, and takes them away in his wrath, when they are but just setting out in a wicked course of life. (2.) The next son, *Onan*, was, according to the ancient usage, married to the widow, to preserve the name of his deceased brother that died childless. Though God had taken away his life for his wickedness, yet they were solicitous to preserve his memory; and their disappointment therein, through Onan's sin, was a further punishment of his wickedness. The custom of marrying the brother's widow was afterwards made one of the laws of Moses, Deut. xxv. 5. Onan, though he consented to marry the widow, yet, to the great abuse of his own body, of the wife that he had married, and of the memory of his brother that was gone, he refused to raise up seed unto his brother, as he was in duty bound. This was so much the worse because the Messiah was to descend from Judah, and, had he not been guilty of this wickedness, he might have had the honour of being one of his ancestors. Note, Those sins that dishonour the body and defile it are very displeasing to God and evidences of vile affections. (3.) *Shelah,* the third son, was reserved for the widow (*v.* 11), yet with a design that he should not marry so young as his brothers had done, *lest he die also.* Some think that Judah never intended to marry Shelah to Tamar, but unjustly suspected her to have been the death of her two former husbands (whereas it was their own wickedness that slew them), and then sent her to her father's house, with a charge to remain a widow. If so, it was an inexcusable piece of prevarication that he was guilty of. However, Tamar acquiesced for the present, and waited the issue.

12 And in process of time the daughter of Shuah Judah's wife died; and Judah was comforted, and went up unto his sheepshearers to Timnath, he and his friend Hirah the Adullamite. 13 And it was told Tamar, saying, Behold thy father in law goeth up to Timnath to shear his sheep. 14 And she put her widow's garments off from her, and covered her with a veil, and wrapped herself, and sat in an open place, which *is* by the way to Timnath; for she saw that Shelah was grown, and she was not given unto him to wife. 15 When Judah saw her, he thought her *to be* an harlot; because she had covered her face. 16 And he turned unto her by the way, and said, Go to, I pray thee, let me come in unto thee; (for he knew not that she *was* his daughter in law.) And she said, What wilt thou give me, that thou mayest come in unto me? 17 And he said, I will send *thee* a kid from the flock. And she said, Wilt thou give *me* a pledge, till thou

send *it?* 18 And he said, What pledge shall I give thee? And she said, Thy signet, and thy bracelets, and thy staff that *is* in thine hand. And he gave *it* her, and came in unto her, and she conceived by him. 19 And she arose, and went away, and laid by her veil from her, and put on the garments of her widowhood. 20 And Judah sent the kid by the hand of his friend the Adullamite, to receive *his* pledge from the woman's hand: but he found her not. 21 Then he asked the men of that place, saying, Where *is* the harlot, that *was* openly by the way side? And they said, There was no harlot in this *place.* 22 And he returned to Judah, and said, I cannot find her, and also the men of the place said, *that* there was no harlot in this *place.* 23 And Judah said, Let her take *it* to her, lest we be shamed: behold, I sent this kid, and thou hast not found her.

It is a very ill-favoured story that, is here told concerning Judah; one would not have expected such folly in Israel. Judah had buried his wife; and widowers have need to stand upon their guard with the utmost caution and resolution against all fleshly lusts He was unjust to his daughter-in-law, either through negligence or design, in not giving her his surviving son, and this exposed her to temptation.

I. Tamar wickedly prostituted herself as a harlot to Judah, that, if the son might not, the father might raise up seed to the deceased. Some excuse this by suggesting that, though she was a Canaanite, yet she had embraced the true religion, and believed the promise made to Abraham and his seed, particularly that of the Messiah, who was to descend from the loins of Judah, and that she was therefore thus earnestly desirous to have a child by one of that family that she might have the honour, or at least stand fair for the honour, of being the mother of the Messiah. And, if this was indeed her desire, it had its success; she is one of the four women particularly named in the genealogy of Christ, Matt. i. 3. Her sinful practice was pardoned, and her good intention was accepted, which magnifies the grace of God, but can by no means be admitted to justify or encourage the like. Bishop Patrick thinks it probable that she hoped Shelah, who was by right her husband, might have come along with his father, and that he might have been allured to her embraces. There was a great deal of plot and contrivance in Tamar's sin. 1. She took an opportunity for it, when Judah had a time of mirth and feasting with his sheep-shearers. Note, Times of jollity often prove times of temptation, particularly to the sin of uncleanness; when men are fed to the full, the reins are apt to be let loose. 2. She exposed herself as a harlot *in an open place, v.* 14. Those that are, and would be, chaste, must be *keepers at home,* Tit. ii. 5. It should seem, it was the custom of harlots, in those times, to cover their faces, that, though they were not ashamed, yet they might seem to be so. The sin of uncleanness did not then go so barefaced as it does now.

II. Judah was taken in the snare, and though it was ignorantly that he was guilty of incest with his daughter-in-law (not knowing who she was), yet he was wilfully guilty of fornication: whoever she was, he knew she was not his wife, and therefore not to be touched. Nor was his sin capable, in the least, of such a charitable excuse as some make for Tamar, that though the action was bad the intention possibly might be good. Observe, 1. Judah's sin began in the eye (*v.* 15): *He saw her.* Note, Those have eyes, and hearts too, full of adultery (as it is 2 Pet. ii. 14), that catch at every bait that presents itself to them and are as tinder to every spark. We have need to make a covenant with our eyes, and to turn them from beholding vanity, lest the eye infect the heart. 2. It added to the scandal that the hire of a harlot (than which nothing is more infamous) was demanded, offered, and accepted—*a kid from the flock,* a goodly price at which her chastity and honour were valued! Nay, had the consideration been thousands of rams, and ten thousand rivers of oil, it had not been a valuable consideration. The favour of God, the purity of the soul, the peace of conscience, and the hope of heaven, are too precious to be exposed to sale at any such rates; the Topaz of Ethiopia cannot equal them: what are those profited that lose their souls to gain the world? 3. It turned to the reproach of Judah that he left his jewels in pawn for a kid. Note, Fleshly lusts are not only brutish, but sottish, and ruining to men's secular interests. It is plain that whoredom, as well as wine, and new wine, takes away the heart first, else it would never take away the signet and the bracelets.

III. He lost his jewels by the bargain; he sent the kid, according to his promise, to redeem his pawn, but the supposed harlot could not be found. He sent it by his friend (who was indeed his *back-friend,* because he was aiding and abetting in his evil deeds) the Adullamite, who came back without the pledge. It is a good account (if it be but true) of any place which they here gave, *there is no harlot in this place;* for such sinners are the scandals and plagues of any place. Judah sits down content to lose his signet and his bracelets, and forbids his friend to make any further enquiry after them, giving this reason, *lest we be shamed,*

v. 23. Either, 1. Lest his sin should come to be known publicly, and be talked of. Fornication and uncleanness have ever been looked upon as scandalous things and the reproach and shame of those that are convicted of them. Nothing will make those blush that are not ashamed of these. 2. Lest he should be laughed at as a fool for trusting a strumpet with his signet and his bracelets. He expresses no concern about the sin, to get that pardoned, only about the shame, to prevent that. Note, There are many who are more solicitous to preserve their reputation with men than to secure the favour of God and a good conscience; *lest we be shamed* goes further with them than *lest we be damned.*

24 And it came to pass about three months after, that it was told Judah, saying, Tamar thy daughter in law hath played the harlot; and also, behold, she *is* with child by whoredom. And Judah said, Bring her forth, and let her be burnt. 25 When she *was* brought forth, she sent to her father in law, saying, By the man, whose these *are, am* I with child: and she said, Discern, I pray thee, whose *are* these, the signet, and bracelets, and staff. 26 And Judah acknowledged *them,* and said, She hath been more righteous than I; because that I gave her not to Shelah my son. And he knew her again no more. 27 And it came to pass in the time of her travail, that, behold, twins *were* in her womb. 28 And it came to pass, when she travailed, that *the one* put out *his* hand: and the midwife took and bound upon his hand a scarlet thread, saying, This came out first. 29 And it came to pass, as he drew back his hand, that, behold, his brother came out: and she said, How hast thou broken forth? *this* breach *be* upon thee: therefore his name was called Pharez. 30 And afterward came out his brother, that had the scarlet thread upon his hand: and his name was called Zarah.

Here is, I. Judah's rigour against Tamar, when he heard she was an adulteress. She was, in the eye of the law, Shelah's wife, and therefore her being with child by another was looked upon as an injury and reproach to Judah's family: *Bring her forth therefore,* says Judah, the master of the family, and *let her be burnt;* not burnt to death, but burnt in the cheek or forehead, stigmatized for a harlot. This seems probable, *v.* 24.

Note, It is a common thing for men to be severe against those very sins in others in which yet they allow themselves; and so, in judging others, they condemn themselves, Rom. ii. 1; xiv. 22. If he designed that she should be burnt to death, perhaps, under pretence of zeal against the sin, he was contriving how to get rid of his daughter-in-law, being loth to marry Shelah to her. Note, It is a common thing, but a very bad thing, to cover malice against men's persons with a show of zeal against their vices.

II. Judah's shame, when it was made to appear that he was the adulterer. She produced *the ring and the bracelets* in court, which justified the fathering of the child upon Judah, *v.* 25, 26. Note, The wickedness that has been most secretly committed, and most industriously concealed, yet sometimes is strangely brought to light, to the shame and confusion of those who have said, *No eye sees.* A bird of the air may carry the voice; however, there is a discovering day coming, when all will be laid open. Some of the Jewish writers observe that as Judah had said to his father, *See, is this thy son's coat?* (*ch.* xxxvii. 32) so it was now said to him, " See, are these thy signet and bracelets?" Judah, being convicted by his own conscience, 1. Confesses his sin: *She has been more righteous than I.* He owns that a perpetual mark of infamy should be fastened rather upon him, who had been so much accessory to it. Note, Those offenders ought to be treated with the greatest tenderness to whom we have any way given occasion of offending. If servants purloin, and their masters, by withholding from them what is due, tempt them to it, they ought to forgive them. 2. He never returned to it again: *He knew her again no more.* Note, Those do not truly repent of their sins that do not forsake them.

III. The building up of Judah's family hereby, notwithstanding, in the birth of Pharez and Zarah, from whom descended the most considerable families of the illustrious tribe of Judah. It should seem, the birth was hard to the mother, by which she was corrected for her sin. The children also, like Jacob and Esau, struggled for the birthright, and Pharez obtained it, who is ever named first, and from him Christ descended. He had his name from his breaking forth before his brother: *This breach be upon thee,* which is applicable to those that sow discord, and create distance, between brethren. The Jews, as Zarah, bade fair for the birthright, and were marked with a scarlet thread, as those that came out first; but the Gentiles, like Pharez, as a son of violence, got the start of them, by that violence which the kingdom of heaven suffers, and attained to the righteousness of which the Jews came short. Yet, when the fulness of time is come, all Israel shall be saved. Both these sons are named in the genealogy of

220

our Saviour (Matt. i. 3), to perpetuate the story, as an instance of the humiliation of our Lord Jesus. Some observe that the four eldest sons of Jacob fell under very foul guilt, Reuben and Judah under the guilt of incest, Simeon and Levi under that of murder; yet they were patriarchs, and from Levi descended the priests, from Judah the kings and Messiah. Thus they became examples of repentance, and monuments of pardoning mercy.

CHAP. XXXIX.

At this chapter we return to the story of Joseph. We have him here, I. A servant, a slave in Potiphar's house (ver. 1), and yet there greatly honoured and favoured, 1. By the providence of God, which made him, in effect, a master, ver. 2—6. 2. By the grace of God, which made him more than a conqueror over a strong temptation to uncleanness, ver. 7—12. II. We have him here a sufferer, falsely accused (ver. 13—18), imprisoned (ver. 19, 20), and yet his imprisonment made both honourable and comfortable by the tokens of God's special presence with him, ver. 21—23. And herein Joseph was a type of Christ, " who took upon him the form of a servant," and yet then did that which made it evident that " God was with him," who was tempted by Satan, but overcame the temptation, who was falsely accused and bound, and yet had all things committed to his hand.

AND Joseph was brought down to Egypt; and Potiphar, an officer of Pharaoh, captain of the guard, an Egyptian, bought him of the hands of the Ishmeelites, which had brought him down thither. 2 And the LORD was with Joseph, and he was a prosperous man; and he was in the house of his master the Egyptian. 3 And his master saw that the LORD *was* with him, and that the LORD made all that he did to prosper in his hand. 4 And Joseph found grace in his sight, and he served him : and he made him overseer over his house, and all *that* he had he put into his hand. 5 And it came to pass from the time *that* he had made him overseer in his house, and over all that he had, that the LORD blessed the Egyptian's house for Joseph's sake; and the blessing of the LORD was upon all that he had in the house, and in the field. 6 And he left all that he had in Joseph's hand; and he knew not aught he had, save the bread which he did eat. And Joseph was *a* goodly *person*, and well favoured.

Here is, I. Joseph bought (*v.* 1), and he that bought him, whatever he gave for him, had a good bargain of him; it was better than the merchandise of silver. The Jews have a proverb, " If the world did but know the worth of good men, they would hedge them about with pearls." He was sold to an officer of Pharaoh, with whom he might get acquainted with public persons and public business, and so be fitted for the preferment for which he was designed. Note, 1. What

God intends men for he will be sure, some way or other, to qualify them for. 2. Providence is to be acknowledged in the disposal even of poor servants and in their settlements, and therein may perhaps be working towards something great and important.

II. Joseph blessed, wonderfully blessed, even in the house of his servitude.

1. God prospered him, *v.* 2, 3. Perhaps the affairs of Potiphar's family had remarkably gone backward before; but, upon Joseph's coming into it, a discernible turn was given to them, and the face and posture of them altered on a sudden. Though, at first, we may suppose that his hand was put to the meanest services, even in those appeared his ingenuity and industry; a particular blessing of Heaven attended him, which, as he rose in his employment, became more and more discernible. Note. (1.) Those that have wisdom and grace have that which cannot be taken away from them, whatever else they are robbed of. Joseph's brethren had stripped him of his coat of many colours, but they could not strip him of his virtue and prudence. (2.) Those that can separate us from all our friends, yet cannot deprive us of the gracious presence of our God. When Joseph had none of 'all his relations with him, he had his God with him, even in the house of the Egyptian. Joseph was separated from his brethren, but not from his God; banished from his father's house, but *the Lord was with him,* and this comforted him. (3.) It is God's presence with us that makes all we do prosperous. Those that would prosper must therefore make God their friend; and those that do prosper must therefore give God the praise.

2. His master preferred him, by degrees made him steward of his household, *v.* 4. Note, (1.) Industry and honesty are the surest and safest way both of rising and thriving : *Seest thou a man* prudent, and faithful, and *diligent in his business?* He shall *stand before kings* at length, and not always *before mean men.* (2.) It is the wisdom of those that are in any sort of authority to countenance and employ those with whom it appears that the presence of God is, Ps. ci. 6. Potiphar knew what he did when he put all into the hands of Joseph; for he knew it would prosper better there than in his own hand. (3.) He that is faithful in a few things stands fair for being made ruler over many things, Matt. xxv. 21. Christ goes by this rule with his servants. (4.) It is a great ease to a master to have those employed under him that are trusty. Potiphar was so well satisfied with Joseph's conduct that *he knew not aught he had, save the bread which he did eat, v.* 6. The servant had all the care and trouble of the estate; the master had only the enjoyment of it : an example not to be imitated by any master, unless he could be sure that he had one in all respects like Joseph for a servant.

3. God favoured his master for his sake (*v.* 5) : *He blessed the Egyptian's house,* though he was an Egyptian, a stranger to the true God, *for Joseph's sake;* and he himself, like Laban, soon learned it by experience, *ch.* xxx. 27. Note, (1.) Good men are the blessings of the places where they live; even good servants may be so, though mean, and lightly esteemed. (2.) The prosperity of the wicked is, one way or other, for the sake of the godly. Here was a wicked family blessed for the sake of one good servant in it.

7 And it came to pass after these things, that his master's wife cast her eyes upon Joseph; and she said, Lie with me. 8 But he refused, and said unto his master's wife, Behold, my master wotteth not what *is* with me in the house, and he hath committed all that he hath to my hand; 9 *There is* none greater in this house than I; neither hath he kept back any thing from me but thee, because thou *art* his wife : how then can I do this great wickedness, and sin against God? 10 And it came to pass, as she spake to Joseph day by day, that he hearkened not unto her, to lie by her, *or* to be with her. 11 And it came to pass about this time, that *Joseph* went into the house to do his business; and *there was* none of the men of the house there within. 12 And she caught him by his garment, saying, Lie with me : and he left his garment in her hand, and fled, and got him out.

Here is, I. A most shameful instance of impudence and immodesty in Joseph's mistress, the shame and scandal of her sex, perfectly lost to all virtue and honour, and not to be mentioned, nor thought of, without the utmost indignation. It was well that she was an Egyptian; for we must have shared in the confusion if such folly had been found in Israel. Observe,

1. Her sin began in the eye : She *cast her eyes upon Joseph* (*v.* 7), who *was a goodly person, and well-favoured, v.* 6. Note, (1.) Remarkable beauty, either of men or women, often proves a dangerous snare both to themselves and others, which forbids pride in it and commands constant watchfulness against the temptation that attends it; favour is deceitful — deceiving. (2.) We have great need to make a covenant with our eyes (Job xxxi. 1), lest the eye infect the heart. Joseph's mistress had a husband that ought to have been to her for a covering of the eyes from all others, *ch.* xx. 16.

2 She was daring and shameless in the

sin. With an impudent face, and a harlot's forehead, she said, *Lie with me*, having already, by her wanton looks and unchaste desires, committed adultery with him in her heart. Note, Where the unclean spirit gets possession and dominion in a soul, it is as with the possessed of the devils (Luke viii. 27, 29), the clothes of modesty are thrown off and the bands and fetters of shame are broken in pieces. When lust has got head, it will stick at nothing, blush at nothing; decency, and reputation, and conscience, are all sacrificed to that Baal-peor. 3. She was urgent and violent in the temptation. Often she had been denied with the strongest reasons, and yet as often renewed her vile solicitations. She *spoke to him day by day*, *v*. 10. Now this was, (1.) Great wickedness in her, and showed her heart fully set to do evil. (2.) A great temptation to Joseph. The hand of Satan, no doubt, was in it, who, when he found he could not overcome him with troubles and the frowns of the world (for in them he still held fast his integrity), assaulted him with soft and charming pleasures, which have ruined more than the former, and have slain their ten-thousands.

II. Here is a most illustrious instance of virtue and resolved chastity in Joseph, who, by the grace of God, was enabled to resist and overcome this temptation ; and, all things considered, his escape was, for aught I know, as great an instance of the divine power as the deliverance of the three children out of the fiery furnace.

1. The temptation he was assaulted with was very strong. Never was a more violent onset made upon the fort of chastity than this recorded here. (1.) The sin he was tempted to was uncleanness, which considering his youth, his beauty, his single state, and his plentiful living at the table of a ruler, was a sin which, one would think, might most easily beset him and betray him. (2.) The tempter was his mistress, a person of quality, whom it was his place to obey and his interest to oblige, whose favour would contribute more than any thing to his preferment, and by whose means he might arrive at the highest honours of the court. On the other hand, it was at his utmost peril if he slighted her, and made her his enemy. (3.) Opportunity makes a thief, makes an adulterer, and that favoured the temptation. The tempter was in the house with him ; his business led him to be, without any suspicion, where she was; none of the family were within (*v*. 11); there appeared no danger of its being ever discovered, or, if it should be suspected, his mistress would protect him. (4.) To all this was added importunity, frequent constant importunity, to such a degree that, at last, she laid violent hands on him.

2. His resistance of the temptation was very brave, and the victory truly honourable. The almighty grace of God enabled him to overcome this assault of the enemy,

(1.) By strength of reason; and, wherever right reason may be heard, religion no doubt will carry the day. He argues from the respect he owed both to God and his master, *v*. 8, 9. [1.] He would not wrong his master, nor do such an irreparable injury to his honour. He considers, and urges, how kind his master had been to him, what a confidence he had reposed in him, in how many instances he had befriended him, for which he abhorred the thought of making such an ungrateful return. Note, We are bound in honour, as well as justice and gratitude, not in any thing to injure those that have a good opinion of us and place a trust in us, how secretly soever it may be done. See how he argues (*v*. 9) : "*There is none greater in this house than I*, therefore I will not do it." Note, Those that are great, instead of being proud of their greatness, should use it as an argument against sin. "Is none greater than I ? Then I will scorn to do a wicked thing ; it is below me to serve a base lust ; I will not disparage myself so much." [2.] He would not offend his God. This is the chief argument with which he strengthens his aversion to the sin. *How can I do this?* not only, How shall I ? or, How dare I ? but, *How can I ? Id possumus, quod jure possumus—We can do that which we can do lawfully*. It is good to shut out sin with the strongest bar, even that of an impossibility. He that is born of God cannot sin, 1 John iii. 9. Three arguments Joseph urges upon himself. *First*, He considers who he was that was tempted. "*I ;* others may perhaps take their liberty, but *I* cannot. *I* that am an Israelite in covenant with God, that profess religion, and relation to him : it is next to impossible for me to do so." *Secondly*, What the sin was to which he was tempted : *This great wickedness.* Others might look upon it as a small matter, a peccadillo, a trick of youth ; but Joseph had another idea of it. In general, when at any time we are tempted to sin, we must consider the great wickedness there is in it, let sin appear sin (Rom. vii. 13), call it by its own name, and never go about to lessen it. Particularly let the sin of uncleanness always be looked upon as great wickedness, as an exceedingly sinful sin, that wars against the soul as much as any other. *Thirdly*, Against whom he was tempted to sin—*against God ;* not only, "How shall I do it, and sin against my master, my mistress, myself, my own body and soul; but against God ?" Note, Gracious souls look upon this as the worst thing in sin that it is against God, against his nature and his dominion, against his love and his design. Those that love God do for this reason hate sin.

(2.) By stedfastness of resolution. The grace of God enabled him to overcome the temptation by avoiding the tempter. [1.] He *hearkened not to her*, so much as to be with her, *v*. 10. Note, Those that would be

222

kept from harm must keep themselves out of harm's way. *Avoid it, pass not by it.* Nay, [2.] When she laid hold of him, he *left his garment in her hand, v.* 12. He would not stay so much as to parley with the temptation, but flew out from it with the utmost abhorrence; he left his garment, as one escaping for his life. Note, It is better to lose a good coat than a good conscience.

13 And it came to pass, when she saw that he had left his garment in her hand, and was fled forth, 14 That she called unto the men of her house, and spake unto them, saying, See, he hath brought in a Hebrew unto us to mock us; he came in unto me to lie with me, and I cried with a loud voice : 15 And it came to pass, when he heard that I lifted up my voice and cried, that he left his garment with me, and fled, and got him out. 16 And she laid up his garment by her, until his lord came home. 17 And she spake unto him according to these words, saying, The Hebrew servant, which thou hast brought unto us, came in unto me to mock me : 18 And it came to pass, as I lifted up my voice and cried, that he left his garment with me, and fled out.

Joseph's mistress, having tried in vain to make him a criminal, now endeavours to represent him as one ; so to be revenged on him for his virtue. Now was her love turned into the utmost rage and malice, and she pretends she cannot endure the sight of him whom awhile ago she could not endure out of her sight. Chaste and holy love will continue, though slighted ; but sinful love, like Amnon's to Tamar, is easily changed into sinful hatred. 1. She accused him to his fellow servants (*v.* 13—15) and gave him a bad name among them. Probably they envied him his interest in their master's favour, and his authority in the house ; and perhaps found themselves aggrieved sometimes by his fidelity, which prevented their purloining ; and therefore they were glad to hear any thing that might tend to his disgrace, and, if there was room for it, incensed their mistress yet more against him. Observe, When she speaks of her husband, she does not call him her husband, or her lord, but only *he ;* for she had forgotten the covenant of her God, that was between them. Thus the adulteress (Prov. vii. 19) calls her husband *the good man.* Note, Innocence itself cannot secure a man's reputation. Not every one that keeps a good conscience can keep a good name. 2. She accused him to his master, who had power in his hand to punish him, which his fellow-servants had

not, *v.* 17, 18. Observe, (1.) What an improbable story she tells, producing his garment as an evidence that he had offered violence to her, which was a plain indication that she had offered violence to him. Note, Those that have broken the bonds of modesty will never be held by the bonds of truth. No marvel that she who had impudence enough to say, *Lie with me,* had front enough to say, "He would have lien with me." Had the lie been told to conceal her own crime it would have been bad enough, yet, in some degree, excusable ; but it was told to be revenged upon his virtue, a most malicious lie. And yet, (2.) She manages it so as to incense her husband against him, reflecting upon him for bringing this Hebrew servant among them, perhaps at first against her mind, because he was a Hebrew. Note, It is no new thing for the best of men to be falsely accused of the worst of crimes by those who themselves are the worst of criminals. As this matter was represented, one would have thought chaste Joseph a very bad man and his wanton mistress a virtuous woman ; it is well that there is a day of discovery coming, in which all shall appear in their true characters. This was not the first time that Joseph's coat was made use of as a false witness concerning him ; his father had been deceived by it before, now his master.

19 And it came to pass, when his master heard the words of his wife, which she spake unto him, saying, After this manner did thy servant to me ; that his wrath was kindled. 20 And Joseph's master took him, and put him into the prison, a place where the king's prisoners *were* bound : and he was there in the prison. 21 But the Lord was with Joseph, and showed him mercy, and gave him favour in the sight of the keeper of the prison. 22 And the keeper of the prison committed to Joseph's hand all the prisoners that *were* in the prison ; and whatsoever they did there, he was the doer *of it.* 23 The keeper of the prison looked not to any thing *that was* under his hand ; because the Lord was with him, and *that* which he did, the Lord made *it* to prosper.

Here is, 1. Joseph wronged by his master. He believed the accusation, and either Joseph durst not make his defence by telling the truth, as it would reflect too much upon his mistress, or his master would not hear it, or would not believe it, and there is no remedy, he is condemned to perpetual imprisonment, *v.* 19, 20. God restrained his wrath, else he had put him to death ; and that wrath which imprisoned him God made to turn to his praise, in order to which Providence so disposed that he should be shut up among the king's prisoners, the state-prisoners. Potiphar, it is likely, chose that prison because it was the worst; for there the iron entered into the soul (Ps. cv. 18), but God designed to pave the way to his enlargement. He was committed to the king's prison, that he might thence be preferred to the king's person. Note, Many an action of false imprisonment will, in the great day, be found to lie against the enemies and persecutors of God's people. Our Lord Jesus, like Joseph here, was bound, and numbered with the transgressors. 2. Joseph owned and righted by his God, who is, and will be, the just and powerful patron of oppressed innocence. Joseph was at a distance from all his friends and relations, had not them with him to comfort him, or to minister to him, or to mediate for him ; but *the Lord was with Joseph, and showed him mercy, v.* 21. Note, (1.) God despises not his prisoners, Ps. lxix. 33. No gates nor bars can shut out his gracious presence from his people ; for he has promised that he will never leave them. (2.) Those that have a good conscience in a prison have a good God there. Integrity and uprightness qualify us for the divine favour, wherever we are. Joseph is not long a prisoner before he becomes a little ruler even in the prison, which is to be attributed, under God, [1.] To the keeper's favour. God *gave him favour in the sight of the keeper of the prison.* Note, God can raise up friends for his people even where they little expect to find them, and can *make them to be pitied* even of those that carry them captive, Ps. cvi. 46. [2.] To Joseph's fitness for business. The keeper saw that God was with him, and that every thing prospered under his hand ; and therefore entrusted him with the management of the affairs of the prison, *v.* 22, 23. Note, Wisdom and virtue will shine in the narrowest spheres. A good man will do good wherever he is, and will be a blessing even in bonds and banishment; for the Spirit of the Lord is not bound nor banished, witness St. Paul, Phil. i. 12, 13.

CHAP. XL.

In this chapter things are working, though slowly, towards Joseph's advancement. I. Two of Pharaoh's servants are committed to prison, and there to Joseph's care, and so become witnesses of his extraordinary conduct, ver. 1—4. II. They dreamed each of them a dream, which Joseph interpreted (ver. 5—19), and the event verified the interpretation (ver. 20—22), and so they became witnesses of his extraordinary skill. III. Joseph recommends his case to one of them, whose preferment he foresaw (ver. 14, 15), but in vain, ver. 23.

AND it came to pass after these things, *that* the butler of the king of Egypt and *his* baker had offended their lord the king of Egypt. 2 And Pharaoh was wroth against two *of* his officers, against the chief of the butlers, and against the chief of the bakers. 3 And he put them in ward in the house of the captain of the

guard, into the prison, the place where Joseph *was* bound. 4 And the captain of the guard charged Joseph with them, and he served them : and they continued a season in ward.

We should not have had this story of Pharaoh's butler and baker recorded in scripture if it had not been serviceable to Joseph's preferment. The world stands for the sake of the church, and is governed for its good. Observe, 1. Two of the great officers of Pharaoh's court, having offended the king, are committed to prison. Note, High places are slippery places ; nothing more uncertain than the favour of princes. Those that make God's favour their happiness, and his service their business, will find him a better Master than Pharaoh was, and not so extreme to mark what they do amiss. Many conjectures there are concerning the offence of these servants of Pharaoh ; some make it no less than an attempt to take away his life, others no more than the casual lighting of a fly into his cup and a little sand into his bread. Whatever it was, Providence by this means brought them into the prison where Joseph was. 2. The *captain of the guard* himself, who was Potiphar, charged Joseph with them (*v.* 4), which intimates that he began now to be reconciled to him, and perhaps to be convinced of his innocence, though he durst not release him for fear of disobliging his wife. John Baptist must lose his head, to please Herodias.

5 And they dreamed a dream both of them, each man his dream in one night, each man according to the interpretation of his dream, the butler and the baker of the king of Egypt, which *were* bound in the prison. 6 And Joseph came in unto them in the morning, and looked upon them, and, behold, they *were* sad. 7 And he asked Pharaoh's officers that *were* with him in the ward of his lord's house, saying, Wherefore look ye *so* sadly to day ? 8 And they said unto him, We have dreamed a dream, and *there is* no interpreter of it. And Joseph said unto them, *Do* not interpretations *belong* to God ? tell me *them,* I pray you. 9 And the chief butler told his dream to Joseph, and said to him, In my dream, behold, a vine *was* before me; 10 And in the vine *were* three branches : and it *was* as though it budded, *and* her blossoms shot forth; and the clusters thereof brought forth ripe grapes : 11 And Pharaoh's cup *was* in my hand : and I took the grapes, and

pressed them into Pharaoh's cup, and I gave the cup into Pharaoh's hand. 12 And Joseph said unto him, This *is* the interpretation of it: The three branches *are* three days: 13 Yet within three days shall Pharaoh lift up thine head, and restore thee unto thy place: and thou shalt deliver Pharaoh's cup into his hand, after the former manner when thou wast his butler. 14 But think on me when it shall be well with thee, and show kindness, I pray thee, unto me, and make mention of me unto Pharaoh, and bring me out of this house: 15 For indeed I was stolen away out of the land of the Hebrews: and here also have I done nothing that they should put me into the dungeon. 16 When the chief baker saw that the interpretation was good, he said unto Joseph, I also *was* in my dream, and, behold, *I had* three white baskets on my head: 17 And in the uppermost basket *there was* of all manner of bakemeats for Pharaoh; and the birds did eat them out of the basket upon my head. 18 And Joseph answered and said, This *is* the interpretation thereof: The three baskets *are* three days: 19 Yet within three days shall Pharaoh lift up thy head from off thee, and shall hang thee on a tree; and the birds shall eat thy flesh from off thee.

Observe, I. The special providence of God, which filled the heads of these two prisoners with unusual dreams, such as made extraordinary impressions upon them, and carried with them evidences of a divine origin, both in one night. Note, God has immediate access to the spirits of men, which he can make serviceable to his own purposes whenever he pleases, quite beyond the intention of those concerned. To him all hearts are open, and anciently he spoke not only to his own people, but to others, in dreams, Job xxxiii. 15. Things to come were thus foretold, but very obscurely.

II. The impression which was made upon these prisoners by their dreams (*v.* 6): They *were sad.* It was not the prison that made them sad (they were pretty well used to that, and perhaps lived jovially there), but the dream. Note, God has more ways than one to sadden the spirits of those that are to be made sad. Those sinners that are hardy enough under outward troubles, and will not yield to them, yet God can find out a way to punish; he can take off their wheels, by

wounding their spirits, and laying loads upon them.

III. Joseph's great tenderness and compassion towards them. He enquired with concern, *Wherefore look you so sadly to-day? v.* 7. Joseph was their keeper, and in that office he was mild. Note, It becomes us to take cognizance of the sorrows even of those that are under our check. Joseph was their companion in tribulation, he was now a prisoner with them, and had been a dreamer too. Note, Communion in sufferings helps to work compassion towards those that do suffer. Let us learn hence, 1. To concern ourselves in the sorrows and troubles of others, and to enquire into the reason of the sadness of our brethren's countenances; we should be often considering the tears of the oppressed, Eccl. iv. 1. It is some relief to those that are in trouble to be taken notice of. 2. To enquire into the causes of our own sorrow, " Wherefore do I look so sadly? Is there a reason? Is it a good reason? Is there not a reason for comfort sufficient to balance it, whatever it is? *Why art thou cast down, O my soul?''*

IV. The dreams themselves, and the interpretation of them. That which troubled these prisoners was that being confined they could not have recourse to the diviners of Egypt who pretended to interpret dreams: *There is no interpreter* here in the prison, *v.* 8. Note, There are interpreters which those that are in prison and sorrow should wish to have with them, to instruct them in the meaning and design of Providence (Elihu alludes to such, when he says, If *there be an interpreter, one among a thousand, to show unto man his uprightness,* Job xxxiii. 23, 24), interpreters to guide their consciences, not to satisfy their curiosity. Joseph hereupon directed them which way to look: *Do not interpretations belong to God?* He means the God whom he worshipped, to the knowledge of whom he endeavours hereby to lead them. Note, It is God's prerogative to foretel things to come, Isa. xlvi. 10. He must therefore have the praise of all the gifts of foresight which men have, ordinary or extraordinary. Joseph premises a caveat against his own praise, and is careful to transmit the glory to God, as Daniel, *ch.* ii. 30. Joseph suggests, " If interpretations belong to God, he is a free agent, and may communicate the power to whom he pleases, and therefore tell me your dreams.'' Now, 1. The chief butler's dream was a happy presage of his enlargement, and re-advancement, within three days; and so Joseph explained it to him, *v.* 12, 13. Probably it had been usual with him to press the full-ripe grapes immediately into Pharaoh's cup, the simplicity of that age not being acquainted with the modern arts of making the wine fine. Observe, Joseph foretold the chief butler's deliverance, but he did not foresee his own. He had long before dreamt of his own honour, and the obeisance which his brethren should do to him, with the remembrance of which he must now support himself, without any new or fresh discoveries. The visions that are for the comfort of God's saints are for a great while to come, and relate to things that are very far off, while the foresights of others, like this recorded here, look but three days before them. 2. The chief baker's dream portended his ignominious death, *v.* 18, 19. The happy interpretation of the other's dream encouraged him to relate his. Thus hypocrites, when they hear good things promised to good Christians, would put in for a share, though they have no part nor lot in the matter. It was not Joseph's fault that he brought him no better tidings. Ministers are but interpreters, they cannot make the thing otherwise than it is; if therefore they deal faithfully, and their message prove unpleasing, it is not their fault. Bad dreams cannot expect a good interpretation.

V. The improvement Joseph made of this opportunity to get a friend at court, *v.* 14, 15. He modestly bespoke the favour of the chief butler, whose preferment he foretold: *But think of me when it shall be well with thee.* Though the respect paid to Joseph made the prison as easy to him as a prison could be, yet none can blame him for being desirous of liberty. See here, 1. What a modest representation he makes of his own case, *v.* 15. He does not reflect upon his brethren that sold him; he only says, *I was stolen out of the land of the Hebrews,* that is, unjustly sent thence, no matter where the fault was. Nor does he reflect on the wrong done him in this imprisonment by his mistress that was his prosecutrix, and his master that was his judge; but mildly avers his own innocence: *Here have I done nothing that they should put me into the dungeon.* Note, When we are called to vindicate ourselves we should carefully avoid, as much as may be, speaking ill of others. Let us be content to prove ourselves innocent, and not be fond of upbraiding others with their guilt. 2. What a modest request he makes to the chief butler: "Only, *think of me.* Pray do me a kindness, if it lie in your way." And his particular petition is, *Bring me out of this house.* . He does not say, "Bring me into Pharaoh's house, get me a place at court." No, he begs for enlargement, not preferment. Note, Providence sometimes designs the greatest honours for those that least covet or expect them.

20 And it came to pass the third day, *which was* Pharaoh's birthday, that he made a feast unto all his servants: and he lifted up the head of the chief butler and of the chief baker among his servants. 21 And he restored the chief butler unto his butlership again; and he gave the cup into Pharaoh's hand: 22 But he hanged the chief baker: as Joseph had inter-

226

preted to them. 23 Yet did not the chief butler remember Joseph, but forgat him.

Here is, 1. The verifying of Joseph's interpretation of the dreams, on the very day prefixed. The chief butler and baker were both advanced, one to his office, the other to the gallows, and both at the three days' end. Note, Very great changes, both for the better and for the worse, often happen in a very little time, so sudden are the revolutions of the wheel of nature. The occasion of giving judgment severally upon their case was the solemnizing of Pharaoh's birth-day, on which, all his servants' being obliged by custom to attend him, these two came to be enquired after, and the cause of their commitment looked into. The solemnizing of the birth-days of princes has been an ancient piece of respect done them; and if it be not abused, as Jeroboam's was (Hos. vii. 5), and Herod's (Mark vi. 21), is a usage innocent enough: and we may all profitably take notice of our birth-days, with thankfulness for the mercies of our birth, sorrow for the sinfulness of it, and an expectation of the day of our death as better than the day of our birth. On Pharaoh's birth-day he lifted up the head of these two prisoners, that is, arraigned and tried them (when Naboth was tried he was *set on high* among the people, 1 Kings xxi. 9), and *he restored the chief butler,* and *hanged the chief baker.* If the butler was innocent and the baker guilty, we must own the equity of Providence in clearing up the innocency of the innocent, and making the sin of the guilty to find him out. If both were either equally innocent or equally guilty, it is an instance of the arbitrariness of such great princes as pride themselves in that power which Nebuchadnezzar set up for (Dan. v. 19, *whom he would he slew, and whom he would he kept alive),* forgetting that there is a higher than they, to whom they are accountable. 2. The disappointing of Joseph's expectation from the chief butler: He *remembered not Joseph, but forgot him, v.* 23. (1.) See here an instance of base ingratitude: Joseph had deserved well at his hands, had ministered to him, sympathized with him, helped him to a favourable interpretation of his dream, had recommended himself to him as an extraordinary person upon all accounts; and yet he forgot him. We must not think it strange if in this world we have hatred shown us for our love, and slights for our respects. (2.) See how apt those that are themselves at ease are to forget others in distress. Perhaps it is in allusion to this story that the prophet speaks of those that *drink wine in bowls, and are not grieved for the affliction of Joseph,* Amos vi. 6. Let us learn hence to cease from man. Joseph perhaps depended too much upon his interest in the chief butler, and promised himself too much from him; he learned by his disappointment to trust in

God only. We cannot expect too little from man nor too much from God.

Some observe the resemblance between Joseph and Christ in this story. Joseph's fellow-sufferers were like the two thieves that were crucified with Christ—the one saved, the other condemned. (It is Dr. Lightfoot's remark, from Mr. Broughton). One of these, when Joseph said to him, *Remember me when it shall be well with thee*, forgot him; but one of those, when he said to Christ, *Remember me when thou comest into thy kingdom*, was not forgotten. We justly blame the chief butler's ingratitude to Joseph, yet we conduct ourselves much more disingenuously towards the Lord Jesus. Joseph had but foretold the chief butler's enlargement, but Christ wrought out ours, mediated with the King of kings for us; yet we forget him, though often reminded of him, though we have promised never to forget him: thus ill do we requite him, like foolish people and unwise.

CHAP. XLI.

Two things Providence is here bringing about:—I. The advancement of Joseph. II. The maintenance of Jacob and his family in a time of famine; for the eyes of the Lord run to and fro through the earth, and direct the affairs of the children of men for the benefit of those few whose hearts are upright with him. In order to these, we have here, 1. Pharaoh's dreams, ver. 1—8. 2. The recommendation of Joseph to him for an interpreter, ver. 9—13. 3. The interpretation of the dreams, and the prediction of seven years of plenty and seven years of famine in Egypt, with the prudent advice given to Pharaoh thereupon, ver. 14—36. 4. The preferment of Joseph to a place of the highest power and trust in Egypt, ver. 37—45. 5. The accomplishment of Joseph's prediction, and his fidelity to his trust, ver. 46, &c.

AND it came to pass at the end of two full years, that Pharaoh dreamed: and, behold, he stood by the river. 2 And, behold, there came up out of the river seven well favoured kine and fatfleshed; and they fed in a meadow. 3 And, behold, seven other kine came up after them out of the river, ill favoured and leanfleshed; and stood by the *other* kine upon the brink of the river. 4 And the ill favoured and leanfleshed kine did eat up the seven well favoured and fat kine. So Pharaoh awoke. 5 And he slept and dreamed the second time: and, behold, seven ears of corn came up upon one stalk, rank and good. 6 And, behold, seven thin ears and blasted with the east wind sprung up after them. 7 And the seven thin ears devoured the seven rank and full ears. And Pharaoh awoke, and, behold, *it was* a dream. 8 And it came to pass in the morning that his spirit was troubled; and he sent and called for all the magicians of Egypt, and all the wise men thereof: and Pharaoh told them his dreams; but *there was* none that could interpret them unto Pharaoh.

Observe, 1. The delay of Joseph's enlargement. It was not till *the end of two full years* (*v.* 1); so long he waited after he had entrusted the chief butler with his case and began to have some prospect of relief. Note, We have need of patience, not only bearing, but waiting, patience. Joseph lay in prison until the time that his word came, Ps. cv. 19. There is a time set for the deliverance of God's people; that time will come, though it seem to tarry; and, when it comes, it will appear to have been the best time, and therefore we ought to wait for it (Hab. ii. 3), and not think two full years too long to continue waiting. 2. The means of Joseph's enlargement, which were Pharaoh's dreams, here related. If we were to look upon them as ordinary dreams, we might observe from them the follies and absurdities of a roving working fancy, how it represents to itself tame cows as beasts of prey (nay, more ravenous than any, eating up those of their own kind), and ears of corn as devouring one another. Surely in the multitude of dreams, nay, even in one dream, there are divers vanities, Eccl. v. 7. Now that God no longer speaks to us in that way, I think it is no matter how little we either heed them or tell them. Foolish dreams related can make no better than foolish talk. But these dreams which Pharaoh dreamed carried their own evidence with them that they were sent of God; and therefore, when he awoke, his spirit was troubled, *v.* 8. It cannot but put us into a concern to receive any extraordinary message from heaven, because we are conscious to ourselves that we have no reason to expect any good tidings thence. His magicians were puzzled, the rules of their art failed them: these dreams of Pharaoh, it seems, did not fall within the compass of them, so that they could not offer at the interpretation of them. This was to make Joseph's performance by the Spirit of God the more admirable. Human reason, prudence, and foresight, must be nonplussed, that divine revelation may appear the more glorious in the contrivance of our redemption, 1 Cor. ii. 13, 14. Compare with this story, Dan. ii. 27; iv. 7; v. 8. Joseph's own dreams were the occasion of his troubles, and now Pharaoh's dreams were the occasion of his enlargement.

9 Then spake the chief butler unto Pharaoh, saying, I do remember my faults this day: 10 Pharaoh was wroth with his servants, and put me in ward in the captain of the guard's house, *both* me and the chief baker: 11 And we dreamed a dream in one night, I and he; we dreamed each man according to the interpretation of his dream. 12 And *there was* there with us a young man, a Hebrew, servant to the captain of the guard; and we told

him, and he interpreted to us our dreams ; to each man according to his dream he did interpret. 13 And it came to pass, as he interpreted to us, so it was ; me he restored unto mine office, and him he hanged. 14 Then Pharaoh sent and called Joseph, and they brought him hastily out of the dungeon : and he shaved *himself*, and changed his raiment, and came in unto Pharaoh. 15 And Pharaoh said unto Joseph, I have dreamed a dream, and *there is* none that can interpret it : and I have heard say of thee, *that* thou canst understand a dream to interpret it. 16 And Joseph answered Pharaoh, saying, *It is* not in me : God shall give Pharaoh an answer of peace.

Here is, 1. The recommending of Joseph to Pharaoh for an interpreter. The chief butler did it more in compliment to Pharaoh, to oblige him, than in gratitude to Joseph, or in compassion for his case. He makes a fair confession (*v.* 9) : " *I remember my faults this day*, in forgetting Joseph." Note, It is best to remember our duty, and to do it in its time ; but, if we have neglected that, it is next best to remember our faults, and repent of them, and do our duty at last ; better late than never. Some think he means his faults against Pharaoh, for which he was imprisoned ; and then he would insinuate that, though Pharaoh had forgiven him, he had not forgiven himself. The story he had to tell was, in short, That there was an obscure young man in the king's prison, who had very properly interpreted his dream, and the chief baker's (the event corresponding in each with the interpretation), and that he would recommend him to the king his master for an interpreter. Note, God's time for the enlargement of his people will appear at last to be the fittest time. If the chief butler had at first used his interest for Joseph's enlargement, and had obtained it, it is probable that upon his release he would have gone back to *the land of the Hebrews* again, which he spoke of so feelingly (*ch.* xl. 15), and then he would neither have been so blessed himself, nor such a blessing to his family, as afterwards he proved. But staying two years longer, and coming out now upon this occasion, at last, to interpret the king's dreams, way was made for his very great preferment. Those that patiently wait for God shall be paid for their waiting, not only principal but interest, Lam. iii. 26. 2. The introducing of Joseph to Pharaoh. The king's business requires haste. Joseph is sent for out of the dungeon with all speed ; Pharaoh's order discharged him both from his imprisonment and from his servitude, and made him a candidate for some of the highest trusts at court. The

king can scarcely allow him time, but that decency required it, to shave himself, and to change his raiment, *v.* 14. It is done with all possible expedition, and Joseph is brought in, perhaps almost as much surprised as Peter was, Acts xii. 9. So suddenly is his captivity brought back that he is as one that dreams, Ps. cxxvi. 1. Pharaoh immediately, without enquiring who or whence he was, tells him his business, that he expected he should interpret his dream, *v.* 15. To which, Joseph makes him a very modest decent reply (*v.* 16), in which, (1.) He gives honour to God. " It is not in me, God must give it." Note, Great gifts appear most graceful and illustrious when those that have them use them humbly, and take not the praise of them to themselves, but give it to God. To such God gives more grace. (2.) He shows respect to Pharaoh, and hearty good-will to him and his government, in supposing that the interpretation would be an answer of peace. Note, Those that consult God's oracles may expect an answer of peace. If Joseph be made the interpreter, hope the best.

17 And Pharaoh said unto Joseph, In my dream, behold, I stood upon the bank of the river ; 18 And, behold, there came up out of the river seven kine, fat-fleshed and well favoured ; and they fed in a meadow : 19 And, behold, seven other kine came up after them, poor and very ill favoured and lean-fleshed, such as I never saw in all the land of Egypt for badness : 20 And the lean and the ill favoured kine did eat up the first seven fat kine : 21 And when they had eaten them up, it could not be known that they had eaten them ; but they *were* still ill favoured, as at the beginning. So I awoke. 22 And I saw in my dream, and, behold, seven ears came up in one stalk, full and good : 23 And, behold, seven ears, withered, thin, *and* blasted with the east wind, sprung up after them : 24 And the thin ears devoured the seven good ears : and ,I told *this* unto the magicians ; but *there was* none that could declare *it* to me. 25 And Joseph said unto Pharaoh, The dream of Pharaoh *is* one : God hath showed Pharaoh what he *is* about to do. 26 The seven good kine *are* seven years ; and the seven good ears *are* seven years : the dream *is* one. 27 And the seven thin and ill favoured kine that came up after them *are* seven years ; and the seven empty ears

blasted with the east wind shall be seven years of famine. 28 This *is* the thing which I have spoken unto Pharaoh : What God *is* about to do he showeth unto Pharaoh. 29 Behold, there come seven years of great plenty throughout all the land of Egypt : 30 And there shall arise after them seven years of famine ; and all the plenty shall be forgotten in the land of Egypt ; and the famine shall consume the land ; 31 And the plenty shall not be known in the land by reason of that famine following ; for it *shall be* very grievous. 32 And for that the dream was doubled unto Pharaoh twice ; *it is* because the thing *is* established by God, and God will shortly bring it to pass.

Here, I. Pharaoh relates his dream. He dreamt that he stood upon the bank of the river Nile, and saw the kine, both the fat ones and the lean ones, come out of the river. For the kingdom of Egypt had no rain, as appears, Zech. xiv. 18, but the plenty of the year depended upon the overflowing of the river, and it was about one certain time of the year that it overflowed. If it rose to fifteen or sixteen cubits, there was plenty ; if to twelve or thirteen only, or under, there was scarcity. See how many ways Providence has of dispensing its gifts ; yet, whatever the second causes are, our dependence is still the same upon the first Cause, who makes every creature that to us that it is, be it rain or river.

II. Joseph interprets his dream, and tells him that it signified seven years of plenty now immediately to ensue, which should be succeeded by as many years of famine. Observe, 1. The two dreams signified the same thing, but the repetition was to denote the certainty, the nearness, and the importance, of the event, *v.* 32. Thus God has often shown *the immutability of his counsel by two immutable things,* Heb. vi. 17, 18. The covenant is sealed with two sacraments ; and in the one of them there are both bread and wine, wherein the dream is one, and yet it is doubled, for the thing is certain. 2. Yet the two dreams had a distinct reference to the two things wherein we most experience plenty and scarcity, namely, grass and corn. The plenty and scarcity of grass for the cattle were signified by the fat kine and the lean ones ; the plenty and scarcity of herb for the service of man by the full ears and the thin ones. 3. See what changes the comforts of this life are subject to. After great plenty may come great scarcity ; how strong soever we may think our mountain stands, if God speak the word, it will soon be moved. We cannot be sure that *to-morrow shall be as this day,* next year as this, and *much more abund-*

ant, Isa. lvi. 12. We must learn how to want, as well as how to abound. 4. See the goodness of God in sending the seven years of plenty before those of famine, that provision might be made accordingly. Thus he *sets the one over-against the other,* Eccl. vii. 14. With what wonderful wisdom has Providence, that great housekeeper, ordered the affairs of this numerous family from the beginning hitherto ! Great variety of seasons there have been, and the produce of the earth is sometimes more and sometimes less ; yet, take one time with another, what was miraculous concerning the manna is ordinarily verified in the common course of Providence, *He that gathers much has nothing over, and he that gathers little has no lack,* Exod. xvi. 18. 5. See the perishing nature of our worldly enjoyments. The great increase of the years of plenty was quite lost and swallowed up in the years of famine ; and the overplus of it, which seemed very much, yet did but just serve to keep men alive, *v.* 29—31. *Meats for the belly, and the belly for meats, but God shall destroy both it and them,* 1 Cor. vi. 13. There is bread which *endures to everlasting life,* which shall not be forgotten, and which it is worth while to labour for, John vi. 27. Those that make the things of this world their good things will find but little pleasure in remembering that they have received them, Luke xvi. 25. 6. Observe, God revealed this beforehand to Pharaoh, who, as king of Egypt, was to be the father of his country, and to make prudent provision for them. Magistrates are called *shepherds,* whose care it must be, not only to rule, but to feed.

33 Now therefore let Pharaoh look out a man discreet and wise, and set him over the land of Egypt. 34 Let Pharaoh do *this,* and let him appoint officers over the land, and take up the fifth part of the land of Egypt in the seven plenteous years. 35 And let them gather all the food of those good years that come, and lay up corn under the hand of Pharaoh, and, let them keep food in the cities. 36 And that food shall be for store to the land against the seven years of famine, which shall be in the land of Egypt ; that the land perish not through the famine. 37 And the thing was good in the eyes of Pharaoh, and in the eyes of all his servants. 38 And Pharaoh said unto his servants, Can we find such a one as this *is,* a man in whom the Spirit of God *is ?* 39 And Pharaoh said unto Joseph, Forasmuch as God hath showed thee all this, *there is* none so discreet and wise as thou

art : 40 Thou shalt be over my house, and according unto thy word shall all my people be ruled: only in the throne will I be greater than thou. 41 And Pharaoh said unto Joseph, See, I have set thee over all the land of Egypt. 42 And Pharaoh took off his ring from his hand, and put it upon Joseph's hand, and arrayed him in vestures of fine linen, and put a gold chain about his neck ; 43 And he made him to ride in the second chariot which he had ; and they cried before him, Bow the knee : and he made him *ruler* over all the land of Egypt. 44 And Pharaoh said unto Joseph, I *am* Pharaoh, and without thee shall no man lift up his hand or foot in all the land of Egypt. 45 And Pharaoh called Joseph's name Zaphnath-paaneah ; and he gave him to wife Asenath the daughter of Poti-pherah priest of On. And Joseph went out over *all* the land of Egypt.

Here is, I. The good advice that Joseph gave to Pharaoh, which was, 1. That in the years of plenty he should lay up for the years of famine, buy up corn when it was cheap, that he might both enrich himself and supply the country when it would be dear and scarce. Note, Fair warning should always be followed with good counsel. Therefore the prudent man foresees the evil, that he may hide himself. God has in his word told us of a day of trial and exigence before us, when we shall need all the grace we can get, and all little enough, "Now, therefore, provide accordingly." Note, further, Times of gathering must be diligently improved, because there will come a time of spending. Let us go to the ant, and learn of her this wisdom, Prov. vi. 6—8. 2. Because that which is everybody's work commonly proves nobody's work, he advises Pharaoh to appoint officers who should make it their business, and to select some one person to preside in the affair, *v.* 33. Probably, if Joseph had not advised this, it would not have been done ; Pharaoh's counsellors could no more improve the dream than his magicians interpret it; therefore it is said of him (Ps. cv. 22) that he *taught the senators wisdom.* Hence we may justly infer with Solomon (Eccl. iv. 13), *Better is a poor and a wise child than an old and foolish king.*

II. The great honour that Pharaoh did to Joseph. 1. He gave him an honourable testimony: He is *a man in whom the Spirit of God is ;* and this puts a great excellency upon any man ; such men ought to be valued, *v.* 38. He is a nonsuch for prudence:

There is none so discreet and wise as thou art, v. 39. Now he is abundantly recompensed for the disgrace that had been done him ; and his righteousness is as the morning-light, Ps. xxxvii. 6. 2. He put him into an honourable office ; not only employed him to buy up corn, but made him prime-minister of state, comptroller of the household—*Thou shalt be over my house,* chief justice of the kingdom—*according to thy word shall all my people be ruled,* or *armed,* as some read it, and then it bespeaks him general of the forces. His commission was very ample : *I have set thee over all the land of Egypt* (v. 41); *without thee shall no man lift up his hand or foot* (v. 44); all the affairs of the kingdom must pass through his hand. Nay (v. 40), *only in the throne will I be greater than thou.* Note, It is the wisdom of princes to prefer those, and the happiness of people to have those preferred, to places of power and trust, in whom the Spirit of God is. It is probable that there were those about the court who opposed Joseph's preferment, which occasioned Pharaoh so often to repeat the grant, and with that solemn sanction (v. 44), *I am Pharaoh.* When the proposal was made that there should be a corn-master-general nominated, it is said (v. 37), *Pharaoh's servants were all pleased* with the proposal, each hoping for the place ; but when Pharaoh said to them, "Joseph shall be the man," we do not read that they made him any answer, being uneasy at it, and acquiescing only because they could not help it. Joseph had enemies, no doubt, archers that shot at him, and hated him (ch. xlix. 23), as Daniel, ch. vi. 4. 3. He put upon him all the marks of honour imaginable, to recommend him to the esteem and respect of the people as the king's favourite, and one whom he delighted to honour. (1.) He gave him his own ring, as a ratification of his commission, and in token of peculiar favour ; or it was like delivering him the great seal. (2.) He put fine clothes upon him, instead of his prison garments. For those that are in kings' palaces must wear soft clothing ; he that, in the morning, was dragging his fetters of iron, before night was adorned with a chain of gold. (3.) He made him *ride in the second chariot* to his own, and ordered all to do homage to him : "*Bow the knee,* as to Pharaoh himself." (4.) He gave him a new name, to show his authority over him, and yet such a name as bespoke the value he had for him, *Zaphnath-paaneah—A revealer of secrets.* (5.) He married him honourably to a prince's daughter. Where God had been liberal in giving wisdom and other merits, Pharaoh was not sparing in conferring honours. Now this preferment of Joseph was, [1.] An abundant recompence for his innocent and patient suffering, a lasting instance of the equity and goodness of Providence, and an encouragement to all good people to trust in a good God. [2.] It was typical of the exaltation of Christ, that great *revealer of secrets* (John i. 18), or, as some translate Joseph's new name, the *Saviour of the world.* The brightest glories of the upper world are put upon him, the highest trust is lodged in his hand, and all power is given to him both in heaven and earth. He is gatherer, keeper, and disposer, of all the stores of divine grace, and chief ruler of the kingdom of God among men. The work of ministers is to cry before him, "*Bow the knee; kiss the Son.*"

46 And Joseph *was* thirty years old when he stood before Pharaoh king of Egypt. And Joseph went out from the presence of Pharaoh, and went throughout all the land of Egypt. 47 And in the seven plenteous years the earth brought forth by handfuls. 48 And he gathered up all the food of the seven years, which were in the land of Egypt, and laid up the food in the cities : the food of the field, which *was* round about every city, laid he up in the same. 49 And Joseph gathered corn as the sand of the sea, very much, until he left numbering; for it *was* without number. 50 And unto Joseph were born two sons before the years of famine came, which Asenath the daughter of Poti-pherah priest of On bare unto him. 51 And Joseph called the name of the firstborn Manasseh : For God, *said he,* hath made me forget all my toil, and all my father's house. 52 And the name of the second called he Ephraim : For God hath caused me to be fruitful in the land of my affliction. 53 And the seven years of plenteousness, that was in the land of Egypt, were ended. 54 And the seven years of dearth began to come, according as Joseph had said : and the dearth was in all lands ; but in all the land of Egypt there was bread. 55 And when all the land of Egypt was famished, the people cried to Pharaoh for bread : and Pharaoh said unto all the Egyptians, Go unto Joseph ; what he saith to you, do. 56 And the famine was over all the face of the earth : and Joseph opened all the storehouses, and sold unto the Egyptians; and the famine waxed sore in the land of Egypt. 57 And all countries came into Egypt to Joseph for to buy *corn ;*

because that the famine was *so* sore in all lands.

Observe here, I. The building of Joseph's family in the birth of two sons, Manasseh and Ephraim, v. 50—52. In the names he gave them, he owned the divine Providence giving this happy turn to his affairs, 1. He was made to forget his misery, Job xi. 16. We should bear our afflictions when they are present as those that know not but Providence may so outweigh them by aftercomforts as that we may even forget them when they are past. But could he be so unnatural as to *forget all his father's house ?* He means the unkindness he received from his brethren, or perhaps the wealth and honour he expected from his father, with the birthright. The robes he now wore made him forget the coat of divers colours which he wore in his father's house. 2. He was made *fruitful in the land of his affliction.* It had been the land of his affliction, and in some sense it was still so, for it was not Canaan, the land of promise. His distance from his father was still his affliction. Note, Light is sometimes sown for the righteous in a barren and unlikely soil; and yet if God sow it, and water it, it will come up again. The afflictions of the saints promote their fruitfulness. *Ephraim* signifies *fruitfulness,* and *Manasseh forgetfulness,* for these two often go together ; when Jeshurun waxed fat, he forgot God his Maker.

II. The accomplishment of Joseph's predictions. Pharaoh had great confidence in the truth of them, perhaps finding in his own mind, beyond what another person could, an exact correspondence between them and his dreams, as between the key and the lock; and the event showed that he was not deceived. The seven plenteous years came (*v.* 47), and, at length, they were ended, *v.* 53. Note, We ought to foresee the approaching period of the days both of our prosperity and of our opportunity, and therefore must not be secure in the enjoyment of our prosperity nor slothful in the improvement of our opportunity ; years of plenty will end, therefore, Whatever thy hand finds to do do it ; and gather in gathering time. *The morning cometh and also the night* (Isa. xxi. 12), plenty and also the famine. *The seven years of dearth began to come, v.* 54. See what changes of condition we are liable to in this world, and what need we have to be joyful in a day of prosperity and in a day of adversity to consider, Eccl. vii. 14. This famine, it seems, was not only in Egypt, but in other lands, in *all lands,* that is, all the neighbouring countries ; *fruitful lands* are soon *turned into barrenness for the iniquity of those that dwell therein,* Ps. cvii. 34. It is here said that *in the land of Egypt there was bread,* meaning probably, not only that which Joseph had bought up for the king, but that which private persons, by his example, and upon the public notice of this prediction, as well as by the rules of common prudence, had laid up.

III. The performance of Joseph's trust. He was found faithful to it, as a steward ought to be. 1. He was diligent in laying up, while the plenty lasted, *v.* 48, 49. He that thus gathers is a wise son. 2. He was prudent and careful in giving out, when the famine came, and kept the markets low by furnishing them at reasonable rates out of his stores. The people in distress cried to Pharaoh, as that woman to the king of Israel (2 Kings vi. 26), *Help, my lord, O king:* he sent them to his treasurer, *Go to Joseph.* Thus God in the gospel directs those that apply to him for mercy and grace to *go to the Lord Jesus*, in whom all fulness dwells; and, *What he saith to you, do.* Joseph, no doubt, with wisdom and justice fixed the price of the corn he sold, so that Pharaoh, whose money had bought it up, might have a reasonable profit, and yet the country might not be oppressed, nor advantage taken of their prevailing necessity; while he that withholdeth corn when it is dear, in hopes it will yet grow dearer, though people perish for want of it, has many a curse for so doing (and it is not a curse causeless), *blessings shall be upon the head of him that* thus *selleth it,* Prov. xi. 26. And let the price be determined by that golden rule of justice, to do as we would be done by.

CHAP. XLII.

We had, in the foregoing chapter, the fulfilling of the dreams which Joseph had interpreted: in this and the following chapters we have the fulfilling of the dreams which Joseph himself had dreamed, that his father's family should do homage to him. The story is very largely and particularly related of what passed between Joseph and his brethren, not only because it is an entertaining story, and probably was much talked of, both among the Israelites and among the Egyptians, but because it is very instructive, and it gave occasion for the removal of Jacob's family into Egypt, on which so many great events afterwards depended. We have, in this chapter, I. The humble application of Jacob's sons to Joseph to buy corn, ver. 1—6. II. The fright Joseph put them into, for their trial, ver. 7—20. III. The conviction they were now under of their sin concerning Joseph long before, ver. 21—24. IV. Their return to Canaan with corn, and the great distress their good father was in upon hearing the account of their expedition, ver. 25, &c.

NOW when Jacob saw that there was corn in Egypt, Jacob said unto his sons, Why do ye look one upon another? 2 And he said, Behold, I have heard that there is corn in Egypt: get you down thither, and buy for us from thence; that we may live, and not die. 3 And Joseph's ten brethren went down to buy corn in Egypt. 4 But Benjamin, Joseph's brother, Jacob sent not with his brethren; for he said, Lest peradventure mischief befal him. 5 And the sons of Israel came to buy *corn* among those that came: for the famine was in the land of Canaan. 6 And Joseph *was* the governor over the land,

and he *it was* that sold to all the people of the land: and Joseph's brethren came, and bowed down themselves before him *with* their faces to the earth.

Though Jacob's sons were all married, and had families of their own, yet, it should seem, they were still incorporated in one society, under the conduct and presidency of their father Jacob. We have here,

I. The orders he gave them to go and buy corn in Egypt, *v.* 1, 2. Observe, 1. The famine was grievous in the land of Canaan. It is observable that all the three patriarchs, to whom Canaan was the land of promise, met with famine in that land, which was not only to try their faith, whether they could trust God though he should slay them, though he should starve them, but to teach them to seek the better country, that is, the heavenly, Heb. xi. 14—16. We have need of something to wean us from this world, and make us long for a better. 2. Still, when there was famine in Canaan, there was corn in Egypt. Thus Providence orders it, that one place should be a succour and supply to another; for we are all brethren. The Egyptians, the seed of accursed Ham, have plenty, when God's blessed Israel want: thus God, in dispensing common favours, often crosses hands. Yet observe, The plenty Egypt now had was owing, under God, to Joseph's prudence and care: if his brethren had not sold him into Egypt, but respected him according to his merits, who knows but he might have done the same thing for Jacob's family which now he had done for Pharaoh, and the Egyptians might then have come to them to buy corn? but those who drive away from among them wise and good men know not what they do. 3. *Jacob saw that there was corn in Egypt;* he saw the corn that his neighbours had bought there and brought home. It is a spur to exertion to see where supplies are to be had, and to see others supplied. Shall others get food for their souls, and shall we starve while it is to be had? 4. He reproved his sons for delaying to provide corn for their families. *Why do you look one upon another?* Note, When we are in trouble and want, it is folly for us to stand looking upon one another, that is, to stand desponding and despairing, as if there were no hope, no help,—to stand disputing either which shall have the honour of going first or which shall have the safety of coming last,—to stand deliberating and debating what we shall do, and doing nothing,—to stand dreaming under a spirit of slumber, as if we had nothing to do, and to stand delaying, as if we had time at command. Let it never be said, "We left that to be done to-morrow which we could as well have done to-day." 5. He quickened them to go to Egypt: *Get you down thither.* Masters of families must not only pray for daily bread for their families, and food convenient, but must lay out themselves with care and industry to provide it.

II. Their obedience to these orders, *v.* 3. They *went down to buy corn;* they did not send their servants, but very prudently went themselves, to lay out their own money. Let none think themselves too great nor too good to take pains. Masters of families should see with their own eyes, and take heed of leaving too much to servants. Only Benjamin went not with them, for he was his father's darling. To Egypt they came, among others, and, having a considerable cargo of corn to buy, they were brought before Joseph himself, who probably expected they would come; and, according to the laws of courtesy, *they bowed down themselves before him, v.* 6. Now their empty sheaves did obeisance to his full one. Compare this with Isa. lx. 14 and Rev. iii. 9.

7 And Joseph saw his brethren, and he knew them, but made himself strange unto them, and spake roughly unto them; and he said unto them, Whence come ye? And they said, From the land of Canaan to buy food. 8 And Joseph knew his brethren, but they knew not him. 9 And Joseph remembered the dreams which he dreamed of them, and said unto them, Ye *are* spies; to see the nakedness of the land ye are come. 10 And they said unto him, Nay, my lord, but to buy food are thy servants come. 11 We *are* all one man's sons; we *are* true *men,* thy servants are no spies. 12 And he said unto them, Nay, but to see the nakedness of the land ye are come. 13 And they said, Thy servants *are* twelve brethren, the sons of one man in the land of Canaan; and, behold, the youngest *is* this day with our father, and one *is* not. 14 And Joseph said unto them, That *is* it that I spake unto you, saying, Ye *are* spies: 15 Hereby ye shall be proved: By the life of Pharaoh ye shall not go forth hence, except your youngest brother come hither. 16 Send one of you, and let him fetch your brother, and ye shall be kept in prison, that your words may be proved, whether *there be any* truth in you: or else by the life of Pharaoh surely ye *are* spies. 17 And he put them all together into ward three days. 18 And Joseph said unto them the third day, This do, and live; *for* I fear

God: 19 If ye *be* true *men,* let one of your brethren be bound in the house of your prison: go ye, carry corn for the famine of your houses: 20 But bring your youngest brother unto me; so shall your words be verified, and ye shall not die. And they did so.

We may well wonder that Joseph, during the twenty years that he had now been in Egypt, especially during the last seven years that he had been in power there, never sent to his father to acquaint him with his circumstances; nay, it is strange that he who so often *went throughout all the land of Egypt* (ch. xli. 45, 46) never made an excursion to Canaan, to visit his aged father, when he was in the borders of Egypt, that lay next to Canaan. Perhaps it would not have been above three or four days' journey for him in his chariot. It is a probable conjecture that his whole management of himself in this affair was by special direction from Heaven, that the purpose of God concerning Jacob and his family might be accomplished. When Joseph's brethren came, he knew them by many a satisfactory token, but they knew not him, little thinking to find him there, *v.* 8. He *remembered the dreams* (v. 9), but they had forgotten them. The laying up of God's oracles in our hearts will be of excellent use to us in all our conduct. Joseph had an eye to his dreams, which he knew to be divine, in his carriage towards his brethren, and aimed at the accomplishment of them and the bringing of his brethren to repentance for their former sins; and both these points were gained.

I. He showed himself very rigorous and harsh with them. The very manner of his speaking, considering the post he was in, was enough to frighten them; for *he spoke roughly to them, v.* 7. He charged them with bad designs against the government (*v.* 9), treated them as dangerous persons, saying, *You are spies,* and protesting *by the life of Pharaoh* that they were so, *v.* 16. Some make this an oath, others make it no more than a vehement asseveration, like that, *as thy soul liveth;* however it was more than yea, yea, and nay, nay, and therefore came of evil. Note, Bad words are soon learned by converse with those that use them, but not so soon unlearned. Joseph, by being much at court, got the courtier's oath, *By the life of Pharaoh,* perhaps designing hereby to confirm his brethren in their belief that he was an Egyptian, and not an Israelite. They knew this was not the language of a son of Abraham. When Peter would prove himself no disciple of Christ, he cursed and swore. Now why was Joseph thus hard upon his brethren? We may be sure it was not from a spirit of revenge, that he might now trample upon those who had formerly trampled upon him; he was not a man of that temper. But, 1. It was to enrich his own dreams, and complete the accomplishment of them. 2. It was to bring them to repentance. 3. It was to get out of them an account of the state of their family, which he longed to know: they would have discovered him if he had asked as a friend, therefore he asks as a judge. Not seeing his brother Benjamin with them, perhaps he began to suspect that they had made away with him too, and therefore gives them occasion to speak of their father and brother. Note, God in his providence sometimes seems harsh with those he loves, and speaks roughly to those for whom yet he has great mercy in store.

II. They, hereupon, were very submissive. They spoke to him with all the respect imaginable: *Nay, my lord* (v. 10)—a great change since they said, *Behold, this dreamer comes.* They very modestly deny the charge: *We are no spies.* They tell him their business, that they came to buy food, a justifiable errand, and the same that many strangers came to Egypt upon at this time. They undertake to give a particular account of themselves and their family (v. 13), and this was what they wanted.

III. He clapped them all up in prison for three days, v. 17. Thus God deals with the souls he designs for special comfort and honour; he first humbles them, and terrifies them, and brings them under a spirit of bondage, and then binds up their wounds by the Spirit of adoption.

IV. He concluded with them, at last, that one of them should be left as a hostage, and the rest should go home and fetch Benjamin. It was a very encouraging word he said to them (v. 18): *I fear God;* as if he had said, "You may assure yourselves I will do you no wrong; I dare not, for I know that, high as I am, there is one higher than I." Note, With those that fear God we have reason to expect fair dealing. The fear of God will be a check upon those that are in power, to restrain them from abusing their power to oppression and tyranny. Those that have no one else to stand in awe of ought to stand in awe of their own consciences. See Neh. v. 15, *So did not I, because of the fear of God.*

21 And they said one to another, We *are* verily guilty concerning our brother, in that we saw the anguish of his soul, when he besought us, and we would not hear; therefore is this distress come upon us. 22 And Reuben answered them, saying, Spake I not unto you, saying, Do not sin against the child; and ye would not hear? therefore, behold, also his blood is required. 23 And they knew not that Joseph understood *them;* for he spake unto them by an interpreter.

234

24 And he turned himself about from them, and wept; and returned to them again, and communed with them, and took from them Simeon, and bound him before their eyes. 25 Then Joseph commanded to fill their sacks with corn, and to restore every man's money into his sack, and to give them provision for the way: and thus did he unto them. 26 And they laded their asses with the corn, and departed thence. 27 And as one of them opened his sack to give his ass provender in the inn, he espied his money; for, behold, it *was* in his sack's mouth. 28 And he said unto his brethren, My money is restored; and, lo, *it is* even in my sack: and their heart failed *them*, and they were afraid, saying one to another, What *is* this *that* God hath done unto us?

Here is, I. The penitent reflection Joseph's brethren made upon the wrong they had formerly done to him, v. 21. They talked the matter over in the Hebrew tongue, not suspecting that Joseph, whom they took for a native of Egypt, understood them, much less that he was the person they spoke of.

1. They remembered with regret the barbarous cruelty wherewith they persecuted him: *We are verily guilty concerning our brother.* We do not read that they said this during their three days' imprisonment; but now, when the matter had come to some issue and they saw themselves still embarrassed, now they began to relent. Perhaps Joseph's mention of *the fear of God* (v. 18) put them upon consideration and extorted this reflection. Now see here, (1.) The office of conscience; it is a remembrancer, to bring to mind things long since said and done, to show us wherein we have erred, though it was long ago, as the reflection here mentioned was above twenty years after the sin was committed. As time will not wear out the guilt of sin, so it will not blot out the records of conscience; when the guilt of this sin of Joseph's brethren was fresh they made light of it, and sat down to eat bread; but now, long afterwards, their consciences reminded them of it. (2.) The benefit of afflictions; they often prove the happy and effectual means of awakening conscience, and bringing sin to our remembrance, Job xiii. 26. (3.) The evil of guilt concerning our brethren; of all their sins, it was this that conscience now reproached them for. Whenever we think we have wrong done us, we ought to remember the wrong we have done to others, Eccl. vii. 21, 22.

2. Reuben alone remembered, with comfort, that he had been an advocate for his

brother, and had done what he could to prevent the mischief they did him (*v.* 22): *Spoke I not unto you, saying, Do not sin against the child?* Note, (1.) It is an aggravation of any sin that it was committed against admonitions. (2.) When we come to share with others in their calamities, it will be a comfort to us if we have the testimony of our consciences for us that we did not share with them in their iniquities, but, in our places, witnessed against them. This shall be our rejoicing in the day of evil, and shall take out the sting.

II. Joseph's tenderness towards them upon this occasion. He retired from them to weep, *v.* 24. Though his reason directed that he should still carry himself as a stranger to them, because they were not as yet humbled enough, yet natural affection could not but work, for he was a man of a tender spirit. This represents the tender mercies of our God towards repenting sinners. See Jer. xxxi. 20, *Since I spoke against him I do earnestly remember him still.* See Judg. x. 16.

III. The imprisonment of Simeon, *v.* 24. He chose him for the hostage probably because he remembered him to have been his most bitter enemy, or because he observed him now to be least humbled and concerned; he bound him *before their eyes* to affect them all; or perhaps it is intimated that, though he bound him with some severity before them, yet afterwards, when they were gone, he took off his bonds.

IV. The dismission of the rest of them. They came for corn, and corn they had; and not only so, but every man had his money restored in his sack's mouth. Thus Christ, our Joseph, gives out supplies without money and without price. Therefore the poor are invited to buy, Rev. iii. 17, 18. This put them into great consternation (*v.* 28): *Their heart failed them, and they were afraid, saying one to another, What is this that God hath done to us?*

1. It was really a merciful event; for I hope they had no wrong done to them when they had their money given them back, but a kindness; yet they were thus terrified by it. Note, (1.) Guilty consciences are apt to take good providences in a bad sense, and to put wrong constructions even upon those things that make for them. They flee when none pursues. (2.) Wealth sometimes brings as much care along with it as want does, and more too. If they had been robbed of their money, they could not have been worse frightened than they were now when they found their money in their sacks. Thus whose ground brought forth plentifully said, *What shall I do?* Luke xii. 17.

2. Yet in their circumstances it was very amazing. They knew that the Egyptians abhorred a Hebrew (*ch.* xliii. 32), and therefore, since they could not expect to receive any kindness from them, they concluded that this was done with a design to pick a

quarrel with them, and the rather because the man, the lord of the land, had charged them as spies. Their own consciences also were awake, and their sins set in order before them; and this put them into confusion. Note, (1.) When men's spirits are sinking every thing helps to sink them. (2.) When the events of Providence concerning us are surprising it is good to enquire what it is that God has done and is doing with us, and to consider the operation of his hands.

29 And they came unto Jacob their father unto the land of Canaan, and told him all that befel unto them; saying, 30 The man, *who is* the lord of the land, spake roughly to us, and took us for spies of the country. 31 And we said unto him, We *are* true *men;* we are no spies: 32 We *be* twelve brethren, sons of our father; one *is* not, and the youngest *is* this day with our father in the land of Canaan. 33 And the man, the lord of the country, said unto us, Hereby shall I know that ye *are* true *men;* leave one of your brethren *here* with me, and take *food for* the famine of your households, and be gone: 34 And bring your youngest brother unto me: then shall I know that ye *are* no spies, but *that* ye *are* true *men: so* will I deliver you your brother, and ye shall traffic in the land. 35 And it came to pass as they emptied their sacks, that, behold, every man's bundle of money *was* in his sack: and when *both* they and their father saw the bundles of money, they were afraid. 36 And Jacob their father said unto them, Me have ye bereaved *of my children:* Joseph *is* not, and Simeon *is* not, and ye will take Benjamin *away:* all these things are against me. 37 And Reuben spake unto his father, saying, Slay my two sons, if I bring him not to thee: deliver him into my hand, and I will bring him to thee again. 38 And he said, My son shall not go down with you; for his brother is dead, and he is left alone: if mischief befal him by the way in the which ye go, then shall ye bring down my gray hairs with sorrow to the grave.

Here is, 1. The report which Jacob's sons made to their father of the great distress they had been in in Egypt; how they had been suspected, and threatened, and obliged

235

to leave Simeon a prisoner there, till they should bring Benjamin with them thither. Who would have thought of this when they left home? When we go abroad we should consider how many sad accidents, that we little think of, may befal us before we return home. *We know not what a day may bring forth ;* we ought therefore to be always ready for the worst. 2. The deep impression this made upon the good man. The very bundles of money which Joseph returned, in kindness to his father, frightened him (*v.* 35); for he concluded it Was done with some mischievous design, or perhaps suspected his own sons to have committed some offence, and so to have run themselves into a *præmunire—a penalty,* which is intimated in what he says (*v.* 36): *Me have you bereaved.* He seems to lay the fault upon them; knowing their characters, he feared they had provoked the Egyptians, and perhaps forcibly, or fraudulently, brought home their money. Jacob is here much out of temper. (1.) He has very melancholy apprehensions concerning the present state of his family: *Joseph is not, and Simeon is not ;* whereas Joseph was in honour and Simeon in the way to it. Note, We often perplex ourselves with our own mistakes, even in matters of fact. True griefs may arise from false intelligence and suppositions, 2 Sam. xiii. 31. Jacob gives up Joseph for gone, and Simeon and Benjamin as being in danger; and he concludes, *All these things are against me.* It proved otherwise, that all these were for him, were working together for his good and the good of his family: yet here he thinks them all against him. Note, Through our ignorance and mistake, and the weakness of our faith, we often apprehend that to be against us which is really for us. We are afflicted in body, estate, name, and relations; and we think all these things are against us, whereas these are really working for us the weight of glory. (2.) He is at present resolved that Benjamin shall not go down. Reuben will undertake to bring him back in safety (*v.* 37), not so much as putting in, *If the Lord will,* nor excepting the common disasters of travellers ; but he foolishly bids Jacob slay his two sons (which, it is likely, he was very proud of) if he brought him not back ; as if the death of two grandsons could satisfy Jacob for the death of a son. No, Jacob's present thoughts are, *My son shall not go down with you.* He plainly intimates a distrust of them, remembering that he never saw Joseph since he had been with them ; therefore, " Benjamin shall not go with you, by the way in which you go, for *you will bring down my gray hairs with sorrow to the grave.*" Note, It is bad with a family when children conduct themselves so ill that their parents know not how to trust them.

CHAP. XLIII.

Here the story of Joseph's brethren is carried on, and verv particularly related. I. Their melancholy parting with their father Jacob in Canaan, ver. 1--14. II. Their pleasant meeting with

236

AND the famine *was* sore in the land. 2 And it came to pass, when they had eaten up the corn which they had brought out of Egypt, their father said unto them, Go again, buy us a little food. 3 And Judah spake unto him, saying, The man did solemnly protest unto us, saying, Ye shall not see my face, except your brother *be* with you. 4 If thou wilt send our brother with us, we will go down and buy thee food : 5 But if thou wilt not send *him,* we will not go down : for the man said unto us, Ye shall not see my face, except your brother *be* with you. 6 And Israel said, Wherefore dealt ye *so* ill with me, *as* to tell the man whether ye had yet a brother? 7 And they said, The man asked us straitly of our state, and of our kindred, saying, *Is* your father yet alive? have ye *another* brother? and we told him according to the tenor of these words: could we certainly know that he would say, Bring your brother down? 8 And Judah said unto Israel his father, Send the lad with me, and we will arise and go ; that we may live, and not die, both we, and thou, *and* also our little ones. 9 I will be surety for him; of my hand shalt thou require him : if I bring him not unto thee, and set him before thee, then let me bear the blame for ever : 10 For except we had lingered, surely now we had returned this second time.

Here, 1. Jacob urges his sons to go and buy more corn in Egypt, *v.* 1, 2. The famine continued ; and the corn they had bought was all spent, for it is meat that perisheth. Jacob, as a good master of a family, is in care to provide for those of his own house food convenient ; and shall not God provide for his children, for *the household of faith?* Jacob bids them go again and buy a *little* food ; now, in time of scarcity, a little must suffice, for nature is content with a little. 2. Judah urges him to consent that Benjamin should go down with them, how much soever it went against his feelings and previous determination. Note, It is not at all inconsistent with the honour and duty which children owe their parents humbly and modestly to advise them, and, as occasion is, to reason with them. *Plead with your mother, plead,* Hos. ii. 2. (1.) He insists upon the absolute necessity they were under of bringing Benjamin with them, of which he, who was a witness to all that had passed in Egypt, was a more competent judge than Jacob could be. Joseph's protestation (*v.* 3) may be alluded to to show upon what terms we must draw nigh to God; unless we bring Christ along with us in the arms of our faith, we cannot see the face of God with comfort. (2.) He engages to take all possible care of him, and to do his utmost for his safety, *v.* 8, 9. Judah's conscience had lately smitten him for what he had done a great while ago against Joseph (*ch.* xlii. 21); and, as an evidence of the truth of his repentance, he is ready to undertake, as far as a man could do it, for Benjamin's security. He will not only not wrong him, but will do all he can to protect him. This is restitution, as far as the case will admit; when he knew not how he could restore Joseph, he would make some amends for the irreparable injury he had done him by doubling his care concerning Benjamin.

11 And their father Israel said unto them, If *it must be* so now, do this; take of the best fruits in the land in your vessels, and carry down the man a present, a little balm, and a little honey, spices, and myrrh, nuts, and almonds: 12 And take double money in your hand;· and the money that was brought again in the mouth of your sacks, carry *it* again in your hand; peradventure it *was* an oversight: 13 Take also your brother, and arise, go again unto the man: 14 And God Almighty give you mercy before the man, that he may send away your other brother, and Benjamin. If I be bereaved *of my children,* I am bereaved.

Observe here, I. Jacob's persuasibleness. He would be ruled by reason, though they were his inferiors that urged it. He saw the necessity of the case; and, since there was no remedy, he consented to yield to the necessity (*v.* 11): "*If it must be so now, take your brother.*" If no corn can be had but upon those terms, we may as well expose him to the perils of the journey as suffer ourselves and families, and Benjamin amongst the rest, to perish for want of bread." *Skin for skin, and all that a man has,* even a Benjamin, the dearest of all, *will he give for his life.* No death so dreadful as that by famine, Lam. iv. 9. Jacob had said (*ch.* xlii. 38), *My son shall not go down;* but now he is over-persuaded to consent. Note, It is no fault, but our wisdom and duty, to alter our purposes and resolutions when there is a good reason for our so doing. Constancy is a virtue, but

obstinacy is not. It is God's prerogative not to repent, and to make unchangeable resolves.

II. Jacob's prudence and justice, which appeared in three things:—1. He sent back the money which they had found in the sacks' mouths, with this discreet construction of it, *Peradventure it was an oversight.* Note, Honesty obliges us to make restitution, not only of that which comes to us by our own fault, but of that which comes to us by the mistakes of others. Though we get it by oversight, if we keep it when the oversight is discovered, it is kept by deceit. In the stating of accounts, errors must be excepted, even those that make for us as well as those that make against us. Jacob's words furnish us with a favourable construction to put upon that which we are tempted to resent as an injury and affront; pass it by, and say, *Peradventure it was an oversight.* 2. He sent double money, as much again as they took the time before, upon supposition that the price of corn might have risen,—or that if it should be insisted upon they might pay a ransom for Simeon, or his prison-fees,—or to show a generous spirit, that they might be the more likely to find generous treatment with *the man, the lord of the land.* 3. He sent a present of such things as the land afforded, and as were scarce in Egypt—*balm and honey,* &c. (*v.* 11), the commodities that Canaan exported, *ch.* xxxvii. 25. Note, (1.) Providence dispenses its gifts variously. Some countries produce one commodity, others another, that commerce may be preserved. (2.) Honey and spice will never make up the want of bread-corn. The famine was sore in Canaan, and yet they had balm and myrrh, &c. We may live well enough upon plain food without dainties; but we cannot live upon dainties without plain food. Let us thank God that that which is most needful and useful is generally most cheap and common. (3.) A *gift in secret pacifies wrath,* Prov. xxi. 14. Jacob's sons were unjustly accused as spies, yet Jacob was willing to be at the expense of a present, to pacify the accuser. Sometimes we must not think it too much to buy peace even where we may justly demand it, and insist upon it as our right.

III. Jacob's piety appearing in his prayer: *God Almighty give you mercy before the man! v.* 14. Jacob had formerly turned an angry brother into a kind one with a present and a prayer; and here he betakes himself to the same tried method, and it sped well. Note, Those that would find mercy with men must seek it of God, who has all hearts in his hands, and turns them as he pleases.

IV. Jacob's patience. He concludes all with this: "*If I be bereaved of my children, I am bereaved;* if I must part with them thus one after another, I must acquiesce, and say, *The will of the Lord be done.*" Note, It is our wisdom to reconcile ourselves to the sorest afflictions, and make the best of them; for there is nothing got by striving with our Maker, 2 Sam. xv. 25, 26.

15 And the men took the present, and they took double money in their hand, and Benjamin; and rose up, and went down to Egypt, and stood before Joseph. 16 And when Joseph saw Benjamin with them, he said to the ruler of his house, Bring *these* men home, and slay, and make ready; for *these* men shall dine with me at noon. 17 And the man did as Joseph bade; and the man brought the men into Joseph's house. 18 And the men were afraid, because they were brought into Joseph's house; and they said, Because of the money that was returned in our sacks at the first time are we brought in; that he may seek occasion against us, and fall upon us, and take us for bondmen, and our asses. 19 And they came near to the steward of Joseph's house, and they communed with him at the door of the house, 20 And said, O sir, we came indeed down at the first time to buy food: 21 And it came to pass, when we came to the inn, that we opened our sacks, and, behold, *every* man's money *was* in the mouth of his sack, our money in full weight: and we have brought it again in our hand. 22 And other money have we brought down in our hands to buy food: we cannot tell who put our money in our sacks. 23 And he said, Peace *be* to you, fear not: your God, and the God of your father, hath given you treasure in your sacks: I had your money. And he brought Simeon out unto them. 24 And the man brought the men into Joseph's house, and gave *them* water, and they washed their feet; and he gave their asses provender. 25 And they made ready the present against Joseph came at noon: for they heard that they should eat bread there.

Jacob's sons, having got leave to take Benjamin with them, were observant of the orders their father had given them, and went down the second time into Egypt to buy corn. If we should ever know what a famine of the word means, let us not think it much to travel as far for spiritual food as they did for corporal food. Now here we have an ac-

238

count of what passed between them and Joseph's steward, who, some conjecture, was in the secret, and knew them to be Joseph's brethren, and helped to humour the thing; I rather think not, because no man was permitted to be present when Joseph afterwards made himself known to them, *ch.* xlv. 1. Observe, 1. Joseph's steward has orders from his master (who was busy selling corn, and receiving money) to take them to his house, and make ready for their entertainment. Though Joseph saw Benjamin there, he would not leave his work at working-time, nor trust another with it. Note, Business must take place of civility in its season. Our needful employments must not be neglected, no, not to pay respect to our friends. 2. Even this frightened them: *They were afraid, because they were brought into Joseph's house, v.* 18. The just challenges of their own consciences, and Joseph's violent suspicions of them, forbade them to expect any favour, and suggested to them that this was done with a bad design upon them. Note, Those that are guilty and timorous are apt to make the worst of every thing. Now they thought they should be reckoned with about the money in the sacks' mouths, and should be charged as cheats, and men not fit to be dealt with, who had taken advantage of the hurry of the market to carry off their corn unpaid for. They therefore laid the case before the steward, that he, being apprized of it, might stand between them and danger; and, as a substantial proof of their honesty, before they were charged with taking back their money they produced it. Note, Integrity and uprightness will preserve us, and will clear themselves as the light of the morning. 3. The steward encouraged them (*v.* 23): *Peace be to you, fear not;* though he knew not what his master drove at, yet he was aware these were men whom he meant no harm to, while he thus amused them; and therefore he directs them to look at the divine Providence in the return of their money: *Your God, and the God of your father, has given you treasure in your sacks.* Observe, (1.) Hereby he shows that he had no suspicion at all of dishonesty in them: for of what we get by deceit we cannot say, "God gives it to us." (2.) Hereby he silences their further enquiry about it. "Ask not how it came thither; Providence brought it to you, and let that satisfy you." (3.) It appears by what he said that, by his good master's instructions, he was brought to the knowledge of the true God, the God of the Hebrews. It may justly be expected that those who are servants in religious families should take all fit occasions to speak of God and his providence with reverence and seriousness. (4.) He directs them to look up to God, and acknowledge his providence in the good bargain they had. We must own ourselves indebted to God, as *our God and the God of our fathers* (a God in covenant with us and them) for all our successes and advantages, and the kindnesses of our friends; for every creature is that to us, and no more, which God makes it to be. The steward encouraged them, not only in words but in deeds; for he made very much of them till his master came, v. 24.

26 And when Joseph came home, they brought him the present which *was* in their hand into the house, and bowed themselves to him to the earth. 27 And he asked them of *their* welfare, and said, *Is* your father well, the old man of whom ye spake? *Is* he yet alive? 28 And they answered, Thy servant our father *is* in good health, he *is* yet alive. And they bowed down their heads, and made obeisance. 29 And he lifted up his eyes, and saw his brother Benjamin, his mother's son, and said, *Is* this your younger brother, of whom ye spake unto me? And he said, God be gracious unto thee, my son. 30 And Joseph made haste; for his bowels did yearn upon his brother: and he sought *where* to weep; and he entered into *his* chamber, and wept there. 31 And he washed his face, and went out, and refrained himself, and said, Set on bread. 32 And they set on for him by himself, and for them by themselves, and for the Egyptians, which did eat with him, by themselves: because the Egyptians might not eat bread with the Hebrews; for that *is* an abomination unto the Egyptians. 33 And they sat before him, the firstborn according to his birthright, and the youngest according to his youth: and the men marvelled one at another. 34 And he took *and sent* messes unto them from before him: but Benjamin's mess was five times so much as any of their's. And they drank, and were merry with him.

Here is, I. The great respect that Joseph's brethren paid to him. When they brought him the present, *they bowed themselves before him* (v. 26); and again, when they gave him an account of their father's health, *they made obeisance*, and called him, *Thy servant our father*, v. 28. Thus were Joseph's dreams fulfilled more and more: and even the father, by the sons, *bowed before him*, according to the dream, ch. xxxvii. 10. Probably Jacob had directed them, if they had occasion to speak of him to *the man, the lord of the land*, to call him *his servant.*

II. The great kindness that Joseph showed to them, while they little thought it was a brotherly kindness. Here is,

1. His kind enquiry concerning Jacob: *Is he yet alive?*—a very fit question to be asked concerning any, especially concerning old people; for we are dying daily: it is strange that we are *yet alive.* Jacob had said many years before, *I will go to the grave to my son ;* but *he is yet alive :* we must not die when we will.

2. The kind notice he took of Benjamin, his own brother. (1.) He put up a prayer for him: *God be gracious unto thee, my son*, v. 29. Joseph's favour, though he was the lord of the land, would do him little good, unless God were gracious to him. Many seek the ruler's favour, but Joseph directs him to seek the favour of the ruler of rulers. (2.) He shed some tears for him, v. 30. His natural affection to his brother, his joy to see him, his concern at seeing him and the rest of them in distress for bread, and the remembrance of his own griefs since he last saw him, produced a great agitation in him, which perhaps was the more uneasy because he endeavoured to stifle and suppress it; but he was forced to retire into his closet, there to give vent to his feelings by tears. Note, [1.] Tears of tenderness and affection are no disparagement at all, even to great and wise men. [2.] Gracious weepers should not proclaim their tears. *My soul shall weep in secret*, says the prophet, Jer. xiii. 17. *Peter went out and wept bitterly.* See Matt. xxvi. 75.

3. His kind entertainment of them all. When his weeping had subsided so that he could refrain himself, he sat down to dinner with them, treated them nobly, and yet contrived every thing to amuse them.

(1.) He ordered three tables to be spread, one for his brethren, another for the Egyptians that dined with him (for so different were their customs that they did not care to eat together), another for himself, who durst not own himself a Hebrew, and yet would not sit with the Egyptians. See here an instance, [1.] Of hospitality and good house-keeping, which are very commendable, according as the ability is. [2.] Of compliance with people's humours, even whimsical ones, as bishop Patrick calls this of the Egyptians not eating with the Hebrews. Though Joseph was the lord of the land, and orders were given that all people should obey him, yet he would not force the Egyptians to eat with the Hebrews, against their minds, but let them enjoy their humours. Spirits truly generous hate to impose. [3.] Of the early distance between Jews and Gentiles; one table would not hold them.

(2.) He placed his brethren according to their seniority (v. 33), as if he *could certainly divine.* Some think they placed themselves so, according to their custom; but, if so, I see not why such particular notice is taken of it, especially as a thing they marvelled at.

(3.) He gave them a very plentiful entertainment, sent messes to them from his own table, *v.* 34. This was the more generous in him, and the more obliging to them, because of the present scarcity of provisions. In a day of famine, it is enough to be fed; but here they were feasted. Perhaps they had not had such a good dinner for many months. It is said, *They drank and were merry ;* their cares and fears were now over, and they ate their bread with joy, concluding they were now upon good terms with the man, the lord of the land. If God accept our works, *our present,* we have reason to be cheerful. Yet when we sit, as they here did, to eat with a ruler, we should consider what is before us, and not indulge our appetite, nor be desirous of dainties, Prov. xxiii. 1—3. Joseph gave them to understand that Benjamin was his favourite; for his mess was *five times as much as any of theirs,* not as if he would have him eat so much more than the rest, for then he must eat more than would do him good (and it is no act of friendship, but rather an injury and unkindness, to press any either to eat or drink to excess), but thus he would testify his particular respect for him, that he might try whether his brethren would envy Benjamin his larger messes, as formerly they had envied himself his finer coat. And it must be our rule, in such cases, to be content with what we have, and not to grieve at what others have.

CHAP. XLIV.

Joseph, having entertained his brethren, dismissed them; but here we have them brought back in a greater fright than any they had been in yet. Observe, I. What method he took both to humble them further and also to try their affection to his brother Benjamin, by which he would be able to judge of the sincerity of their repentance for what they had done against himself, of which he was desirous to be satisfied before he manifested his reconciliation to them. This he contrived to do by bringing Benjamin into distress, ver. 1—17. II. The good success of the experiment; he found them all heartily concerned, and Judah particularly, both for the safety of Benjamin and for the comfort of their aged father, ver. 18, &c.

AND he commanded the steward of his house, saying, Fill the men's sacks *with* food, as much as they can carry, and put every man's money in his sack's mouth. 2 And put my cup, the silver cup, in the sack's mouth of the youngest, and his corn money. And he did according to the word that Joseph had spoken. 3 As soon as the morning was light, the men were sent away, they and their asses. 4 *And* when they were gone out of the city, *and* not *yet* far off, Joseph said unto his steward, Up, follow after the men; and when thou dost overtake them, say unto them, Wherefore have ye rewarded evil for good? 5 *Is* not this *it* in which my lord drinketh, and whereby indeed he divineth? ye have done evil in so doing. 6 And he overtook them, and he spake unto them these same words.

7 And they said unto him, Wherefore saith my lord these words? God forbid that thy servants should do according to this thing: 8 Behold, the money, which we found in our sacks' mouths, we brought again unto thee out of the land of Canaan: how then should we steal out of thy lord's house silver or gold? 9 With whomsoever of thy servants it be found, both let him die, and we also will be my lord's bondmen. 10 And he said, Now also *let* it *be* according unto your words: he with whom it is found shall be my servant; and ye shall be blameless. 11 Then they speedily took down every man his sack to the ground, and opened every man his sack. 12 And he searched, *and* began at the eldest, and left at the youngest: and the cup was found in Benjamin's sack. 13 Then they rent their clothes, and laded every man his ass, and returned to the city. 14 And Judah and his brethren came to Joseph's house; for he *was* yet there: and they fell before him on the ground. 15 And Joseph said unto them, What deed *is* this that ye have done? wot ye not that such a man as I can certainly divine? 16 And Judah said, What shall we say unto my lord? what shall we speak? or how shall we clear ourselves? God hath found out the iniquity of thy servants: behold, we *are* my lord's servants, both we, and *he* also with whom the cup is found. 17 And he said, God forbid that I should do so: *but* the man in whose hand the cup is found, he shall be my servant; and as for you, get you up in peace unto your father.

Joseph heaps further kindnesses upon his brethren, fills their sacks, returns their money, and sends them away full of gladness; but he also exercises them with further trials. Our God thus humbles those whom he loves and loads with benefits. Joseph ordered his steward to put a fine silver cup which he had (and which, it is likely, was used at his table when they dined with him) into Benjamin's sack's mouth, that it might seem as if he had stolen it from the table, and put it there himself, after his corn was delivered to him. If Benjamin had stolen it, it had been the basest piece of dishonesty and ingratitude that could be and if Joseph, by ordering it to be put there, had designed really to take advantage against him, it had been in him most horrid cruelty and oppression; but it proved, in the issue, that there was no harm done, nor any designed, on either side. Observe,

I. How the pretended criminals were pursued and arrested, on suspicion of having stolen a silver cup. The steward charged them with ingratitude—rewarding evil for good; and with folly, in taking away a cup of daily use, and which therefore would soon be missed, and diligent search made for it; for so it may be read: *Is not this it in which my lord drinketh* (as having a particular fondness for it), *and for which he would search thoroughly? v.* 5. Or, " By which, leaving it carelessly at your table, he would make trial whether you were honest men or no."

II. How they pleaded for themselves. They solemnly protested their innocence, and detestation of so base a thing (*v.* 7), urged it as an instance of their honesty that they had brought their money back (*v.* 8), and offered to submit to the severest punishment if they should be found guilty, *v.* 9, 10.

III. How the theft was fastened upon Benjamin. In his sack the cup was found to whom Joseph had been particularly kind. Benjamin, no doubt, was ready to deny, upon oath, the taking of the cup, and we may suppose him as little liable to suspicion as any of them; but it is in vain to confront such notorious evidence: the cup is found in his custody; they dare not arraign Joseph's justice, nor so much as suggest that perhaps he that had put their money in their sacks' mouths had put the cup there; but they throw themselves upon Joseph's mercy. And,

IV. Here is their humble submission, *v.* 16. 1. They acknowledge the righteousness of God: *God hath found out the iniquity of thy servants,* perhaps referring to the injury they had formerly done to Joseph, for which they thought God was now reckoning with them. Note, Even in those afflictions wherein we apprehend ourselves wronged by men yet we must own that God is righteous, and finds out our iniquity. 2. They surrender themselves prisoners to Joseph : *We are my lord's servants.* Now Joseph's dreams were accomplished to the utmost. Their bowing so often, and doing homage, might be looked upon but as a compliment, and no more than what other strangers did ; but the construction they themselves, in their pride, had put upon his dreams was, *Shalt thou have dominion over us?* (*ch.* xxxvii. 8), and in this sense it is now at length fulfilled ; they own themselves his vassals. Since they did invidiously so understand it, so it shall be fulfilled in them.

V. Joseph, with an air of justice, gives sentence that Benjamin only should be kept in bondage, and the rest should be dismissed; for why should any suffer but the guilty ?

Perhaps Joseph intended hereby to try Benjamin's temper, whether he could bear such a hardship as this with the calmness and composure of mind that became a wise and good man : in short, whether he was indeed his own brother, in *spirit* as well as *blood :* for Joseph himself had been falsely accused, and had suffered hard things in consequence, and yet kept possession of his own soul. However, it is plain he intended hereby to try the affection of his brethren to Benjamin and to their father. If they had gone away contentedly, and left Benjamin in bonds, no doubt Joseph would soon have released and promoted him, and sent notice to Jacob, and would have left the rest of his brethren justly to suffer for their hard-heartedness ; but they proved to be better affected to Benjamin than he feared. Note, We cannot judge what men are by what they have been formerly, nor what they will do by what they have done : age and experience may make men wiser and better. Those that had sold Joseph would not now abandon Benjamin. The worst may mend in time.

18 Then Judah came near unto him, and said, Oh my lord, let thy servant, I pray thee, speak a word in my lord's ears, and let not thine anger burn against thy servant : for thou *art* even as Pharaoh. 19 My lord asked his servants, saying, Have ye a father, or a brother ? 20 And we said unto my lord, We have a father, an old man, and a child of his old age, a little one; and his brother is dead, and he alone is left of his mother, and his father loveth him. 21 And thou saidst unto thy servants, Bring him down unto me, that I may set mine eyes upon him. 22 And we said unto my lord, The lad cannot leave his father : for *if* he should leave his father, *his father* would die. 23 And thou saidst unto thy servants, Except your youngest brother come down with you, ye shall see my face no more. 24 And it came to pass when we came up unto thy servant my father, we told him the words of my lord. 25 And our father said, Go again, *and* buy us a little food. 26 And we said, We cannot go down : if our youngest brother be with us, then will we go down : for we may not see the man's face, except our youngest brother *be* with us. 27 And thy servant my father said unto us, Ye know that my wife bare me two *sons :* 28 And the one went

241

out from me, and I said, Surely he is torn in pieces; and I saw him not since: 29 And if ye take this also from me, and mischief befall him, ye shall bring down my gray hairs with sorrow to the grave. 30 Now therefore when I come to thy servant my father, and the lad *be* not with us; seeing that his life is bound up in the lad's life; 31 It shall come to pass, when he seeth that the lad *is* not *with us*, that he will die: and thy servants shall bring down the gray hairs of thy servant our father with sorrow to the grave. 32 For thy servant became surety for the lad unto my father, saying, If I bring him not unto thee, then I shall bear the blame to my father for ever. 33 Now therefore, I pray thee, let thy servant abide instead of the lad a bondman to my lord; and let the lad go up with his brethren. 34 For how shall I go up to my father, and the lad *be* not with me? lest peradventure I see the evil that shall come on my father.

We have here a most ingenious and pathetic speech which Judah made to Joseph on Benjamin's behalf, to obtain his discharge from the sentence passed upon him. Perhaps Judah was a better friend to Benjamin than the rest were, and more solicitous to bring him off; or he thought himself under greater obligations to attempt it than the rest, because he had passed his word to his father for his safe return; or the rest chose him for their spokesman, because he was a man of better sense, and better spirit, and had a greater command of language than any of them. His address, as it is here recorded, is so very natural and so expressive of his present feelings that we cannot but suppose Moses, who wrote it so long after, to have written it under the special direction of him that made man's mouth.

I. A great deal of unaffected art, and unstudied unforced rhetoric, there is in this speech. 1. He addresses himself to Joseph with a great deal of respect and deference, calls him his *lord*, himself and his brethren his *servants*, begs his patient hearing, and ascribes sovereign authority to him: " *Thou art even as Pharaoh,* one whose favour we desire and whose wrath we dread as we do Pharaoh's." Religion does not destroy good manners, and it is prudence to speak respectfully to those at whose mercy we lie: titles of honour to those that are entitled to them are not flattering titles. 2. He represented Benjamin as one well worthy of his compassionate consideration (*v.* 20); he was *a little*

one, compared with the rest of them; the youngest, not acquainted with the world, nor ever inured to hardship, having always been brought up tenderly with his father. It made the case the more pitiable that he alone was left of his mother, and his brother was dead, namely, *Joseph.* Little did Judah think what a tender point he touched upon now. Judah knew that Joseph was sold, and therefore had reason enough to think that he was alive; at least he could not be sure that he was dead: but they had made their father believe he was dead; and now they had told that lie so long that they had forgotten the truth, and begun to believe the lie themselves. 3. He urged it very closely that Joseph had himself constrained them to bring Benjamin with them, had expressed a desire to see him (*v.* 21), and had forbidden them his presence unless they brought Benjamin with them (*v.* 23, 26), all which intimated that he designed him some kindness; and must he be brought with so much difficulty to the preferment of a perpetual slavery? Was he not brought to Egypt, in obedience, purely in obedience, to the command of Joseph? and would he not show him some mercy? Some observe that Jacob's sons, in reasoning with their father, had said, *We will not go down unless Benjamin go with us* (*ch.* xliii. 5); but that when Judah comes to relate the story he expresses it more decently: " *We cannot go down* with any expectation to speed well." Indecent words spoken in haste to our superiors should be recalled and amended. 4. The great argument he insisted upon was the insupportable grief it would be to his aged father if Benjamin should be left behind in servitude: *His father loveth him, v.* 20. This they had pleaded against Joseph's insisting on his coming down (*v.* 22): " *If he should leave his father, his father would die;* much more if now he be left behind, never more to return to him." This the old man, of whom they spoke, had pleaded against his going down: *If mischief befal him, you shall bring down my gray hairs,* that crown of glory, *with sorrow to the grave, v.* 29. This therefore Judah presses with a great deal of earnestness: " *His life is bound up in the lad's life* (*v.* 30); when he sees that the lad is not with us, he will faint away, and die immediately (*v.* 31), or will abandon himself to such a degree of sorrow as will, in a few days, make an end of him." And, *lastly,* Judah pleads that, for his part, he could not bear to see this: *Let me not see the evil that shall come on my father, v.* 34. Note, It is the duty of children to be very tender of their parents' comfort, and to be afraid of every thing that may be an occasion of grief to them. Thus the love that descended first must again ascend, and something must be done towards a recompence for their care. 5. Judah, in honour to the justice of Joseph's sentence, and to show his sincerity in this plea, offers himself to become a bondsman instead of Benjamin, *v.* 33. Thus the law would be satisfied; Joseph would be no loser (for we may suppose Judah a more able-bodied man than Benjamin, and fitter for service); and Jacob would better bear the loss of him than of Benjamin. Now, so far was he from grieving at his father's particular fondness for Benjamin, that he was himself willing to be a bondman to indulge it.

Now, had Joseph been, as Judah supposed him, an utter stranger to the family, yet even common humanity could not but be wrought upon by such powerful reasonings as these; for nothing could be said more moving, more tender; it was enough to melt a heart of stone. But to Joseph, who was nearer akin to Benjamin than Judah himself was, and who, at this time, felt a greater affection both for him and his aged father than Judah did, nothing could be more pleasingly nor more happily said. Neither Jacob nor Benjamin needed an intercessor with Joseph; for he himself loved them.

II. Upon the whole matter let us take notice, 1. How prudently Judah suppressed all mention of the crime that was charged upon Benjamin. Had he said any thing by way of acknowledgment of it, he would have reflected on Benjamin's honesty, and seemed too forward to suspect that; had he said any thing by way of denial of it, he would have reflected on Joseph's justice, and the sentence he had passed: therefore he wholly waives that head, and appeals to Joseph's pity. Compare with this that of Job, in humbling himself before God (Job ix. 15), *Though I were righteous, yet would I not answer;* I would not argue, but petition; *I would make supplication to my Judge.* 2. What good reason dying Jacob had to say, *Judah, thou art he whom thy brethren shall praise* (ch. xlix. 8), for he excelled them all in boldness, wisdom, eloquence, and especially tenderness for their father and family. 3. Judah's faithful adherence to Benjamin, now in his distress, was recompensed long after by the constant adherence of the tribe of Benjamin to the tribe of Judah, when all the other ten tribes deserted it. 4. How fitly does the apostle, when he is discoursing of the mediation of Christ, observe, that *our Lord sprang out of Judah* (Heb. vii. 14); for, like his father Judah, he not only *made intercession for the transgressors,* but he became a surety for them, as it follows there (*v.* 22), testifying therein a very tender concern both for his father and for his brethren.

CHAP. XLV.

It is a pity that this chapter and the foregoing should be parted, and read asunder. There we had Judah's intercession for Benjamin, with which, we may suppose, the rest of his brethren signified their concurrence; Joseph let him go on without interruption, heard all he had to say, and then answered it all in one word, "I am Joseph." Now he found his brethren humbled for their sins, mindful of himself (for Judah had mentioned him twice in his speech), respectful to their father, and very tender of their brother Benjamin; now they were ripe for the comfort he designed them, by making himself known to them, the story of which we have in this chapter. It was to Joseph's brethren

as clear shining after rain, nay, it was to them as life from the dead. Here is, I. Joseph's discovery of himself to his brethren, and his discourse with them upon that occasion, ver. 1—15. II. The orders Pharaoh, hereupon, gave to fetch Jacob and his family down to Egypt, and Joseph's despatch of his brethren, accordingly, back to his father with those orders, ver. 16—24. III. The joyful tidings of this brought to Jacob, ver. 25, &c.

THEN Joseph could not refrain himself before all them that stood by him; and he cried, Cause every man to go out from me. And there stood no man with him, while Joseph made himself known unto his brethren. 2 And he wept aloud: and the Egyptians and the house of Pharaoh heard. 3 And Joseph said unto his brethren, I *am* Joseph; doth my father yet live? And his brethren could not answer him; for they were troubled at his presence. 4 And Joseph said unto his brethren, Come near to me, I pray you. And they came near. And he said, I *am* Joseph your brother, whom ye sold into Egypt. 5 Now therefore be not grieved, nor angry with yourselves, that ye sold me hither: for God did send me before you to preserve life. 6 For these two years *hath* the famine *been* in the land: and yet *there are* five years, in the which *there shall* neither *be* earing nor harvest. 7 And God sent me before you to preserve you a posterity in the earth, and to save your lives by a great deliverance. 8 So now *it was* not you *that* sent me hither, but God: and he hath made me a father to Pharaoh, and lord of all his house, and a ruler throughout all the land of Egypt. 9 Haste ye, and go up to my father, and say unto him, Thus saith thy son Joseph, God hath made me lord of all Egypt: come down unto me, tarry not: 10 And thou shalt dwell in the land of Goshen, and thou shalt be near unto me, thou, and thy children, and thy children's children, and thy flocks, and thy herds, and all that thou hast: 11 And there will I nourish thee; for yet *there are* five years of famine; lest thou, and thy household, and all that thou hast, come to poverty. 12 And, behold, your eyes see, and the eyes of my brother Benjamin, that *it is* my mouth that speaketh unto you. 13 And ye shall tell my father of all my glory in Egypt, and of all that ye have seen; and ye shall haste and bring down my father hither. 14 And he fell upon his brother Benjamin's neck, and wept; and Benjamin wept upon his neck. 15 Moreover he kissed all his brethren, and wept upon them: and after that his brethren talked with him.

Judah and his brethren were waiting for an answer, and could not but be amazed to discover, instead of the gravity of a judge, the natural affection of a father or brother. I. Joseph ordered all his attendants to withdraw, *v.* 1. The private conversations of friends are the most free. When Joseph would put on love he puts off state, and it was not fit his servants should be witnesses of this. Thus Christ graciously manifests himself and his loving-kindness to his people, out of the sight and hearing of the world. II. Tears were the preface or introduction to his discourse, *v.* 2. He had dammed up this stream a great while, and with much ado : but now it swelled so high that he could no longer contain, but *he wept aloud,* so that those whom he had forbidden to see him could not but hear him. These were tears of tenderness and strong affection, and with these he threw off that austerity with which he had hitherto carried himself towards his brethren ; for he could bear it no longer. This represents the divine compassion towards returning penitents, as much as that of the father of the prodigal, Luke xv. 20 ; Hos. xiv. 8, 9. III. He very abruptly (as one uneasy till it was out) tells them who he was : *I am Joseph.* They knew him only by his Egyptian name, *Zaphnath-paaneah,* his Hebrew name being lost and forgotten in Egypt ; but now he teaches them to call him by that : *I am Joseph ;* nay, that they might not suspect it was another of the same name, he explains himself (*v.* 4): *I am Joseph, your brother.* This would both humble them yet more for their sin in selling him, and would encourage them to hope for kind treatment. Thus when Christ would convince Paul he said, *I am Jesus ;* and when he would comfort his disciples he said, *It is I, be not afraid.* This word, at first, startled Joseph's brethren ; they started back through fear, or at least stood still astonished ; but Joseph called kindly and familiarly to them : *Come near, I pray you.* Thus when Christ manifests himself to his people he encourages them to draw near to him with a true heart. Perhaps, being about to speak of their selling him, he would not speak aloud, lest the Egyptians should overhear, and it should make the Hebrews to be yet more an abomination to them ; therefore he would have them come near, that he might whisper with them, which, now that the tide of his passion was a little over, he was able to do, whereas at first he could not but cry out. IV. He endeavours to assuage their grief

for the injuries they had done him, by showing them that whatever they designed God meant it for good, and had brought much good out of it (*v.* 5): *Be not grieved, nor angry with yourselves.* Sinners must grieve, and be angry with themselves, for their sins ; yea, though God by his power brings good out of them, for no thanks are due to the sinner for this : but true penitents should be greatly affected when they see God thus bringing good out of evil, *meat out of the eater.* Though we must not with this consideration extenuate our own sins and so take off the edge of our repentance, yet it may be well thus to extenuate the sins of others and so take off the edge of our angry resentments. Thus Joseph does here ; his brethren needed not to fear that he would avenge upon them an injury which God's providence had made to turn so much to his advantage and that of his family. Now he tells them how long the famine was likely to last—*five years ;* yet (*v.* 6) what a capacity he was in of being kind to his relations and friends, which is the greatest satisfaction that wealth and power can give to a good man, *v.* 8. See what a favourable colour he puts upon the injury they had done him : *God sent me before you, v.* 5, 7. Note, 1. God's Israel is the particular care of God's providence. Joseph reckoned that his advancement was not so much designed to save a whole kingdom of Egyptians as to preserve a small family of Israelites : *for the Lord's portion is his people ;* whatever becomes of others, they shall be secured. 2. Providence looks a great way forward, and has a long reach. Even long before the years of plenty, Providence was preparing for the supply of Jacob's house in the years of famine. The psalmist praises God for this (Ps. cv. 17): *He sent a man before them, even Joseph.* God sees his work from the beginning to the end, but we do not, Eccl. iii. 11. How admirable are the projects of providence ! How remote its tendencies ! What wheels are there within wheels, and yet all directed by the eyes in the wheels, and the spirit of the living creature ! Let us therefore judge nothing before the time. 3. God often works by contraries. The envy and contention of brethren threaten the ruin of families, yet, in this instance, they prove the occasion of preserving Jacob's family. Joseph could never have been *the shepherd and stone of Israel* if his brethren had not shot at him, and hated him ; even those that had wickedly sold Joseph into Egypt yet themselves reaped the benefit of the good God brought out of it ; as those that put Christ to death were many of them saved by his death. 4. God must have all the glory of the seasonable preservations of his people, by what way soever they are effected. *It was not you that sent me hither, but God, v.* 8. As, on the one hand, they must not fret at it, because it ended so well, so on the other hand they must not be proud of it, because it was God's doing, and not theirs. They designed, by selling him into Egypt, to defeat his dreams, but God thereby designed to accomplish them. Isa. x. 7, *Howbeit he meaneth not so.*

V. He promises to take care of his father and all the family during the rest of the years of famine. 1. He desires that his father may speedily be made glad with the tidings of his life and dignity. His brethren must hasten to Canaan, and must inform Jacob that his son Joseph was *lord of all Egypt* (*v.* 9): they must tell him of all his glory there, *v.* 13. He knew it would be a refreshing oil to his hoary head and a sovereign cordial to his spirits. If any thing would make him young again, this would. He desires them to give themselves, and take with them to their father, all possible satisfaction of the truth of these surprising tidings: *Your eyes see that it is my mouth, v.* 12. If they would recollect themselves, they might remember something of his features, speech, &c., and be satisfied. 2. He is very earnest that his father and all his family should come to him to Egypt: *Come down unto me, tarry not, v.* 9. He allots his dwelling in Goshen, that part of Egypt which lay towards Canaan, that they might be mindful of the country from which they were to come out, *v.* 10. He promises to provide for him: *I will nourish thee, v.* 11. Note, It is the duty of children, if the necessity of their parents do at any time require it, to support and supply them to the utmost of their ability; and *Corban* will never excuse them, Mark vii. 11. This is showing piety at home, 1 Tim. v. 4. Our Lord Jesus being, like Joseph, exalted to the highest honours and powers of the upper world, it is his will that all that are his should be with him where he is, John xvii. 24. This is his commandment, that we be with him now in faith and hope, and a heavenly conversation; and this is his promise, that we shall be for ever with him.

VI. Endearments were interchanged between him and his brethren. He began with the youngest, his own brother Benjamin, who was but about a year old when Joseph was separated from his brethren; they wept on each other's neck (*v.* 14), perhaps to think of their mother Rachel, who died in travail of Benjamin. Rachel, in her husband Jacob, had been lately weeping for her children, because, in his apprehension, they were not—Joseph gone, and Benjamin going; and now they were weeping for her, because she was not. After he had embraced Benjamin, he, in like manner, caressed them all (*v.* 15); and then *his brethren talked with him* freely and familiarly of all the affairs of their father's house. After the tokens of true reconciliation follow the instances of a sweet communion.

16 And the fame thereof was heard in Pharaoh's house, saying, Joseph's brethren are come: and it pleased Pharaoh well, and his servants. 17 And Pharaoh said unto Joseph, Say unto thy brethren, This do ye; lade your beasts, and go, get you unto the land of Canaan; 18 And take your father and your households, and come unto me: and I will give you the good of the land of Egypt, and ye shall eat the fat of the land. 19 Now thou art commanded, this do ye; take you wagons out of the land of Egypt for your little ones, and for your wives, and bring your father, and come. 20 Also regard not your stuff; for the good of all the land of Egypt *is* your's. 21 And the children of Israel did so: and Joseph gave them wagons, according to the commandment of Pharaoh, and gave them provision for the way. 22 To all of them he gave each man changes of raiment; but to Benjamin he gave three hundred *pieces* of silver, and five changes of raiment. 23 And to his father he sent after this *manner;* ten asses laden with the good things of Egypt, and ten she asses laden with corn and bread and meat for his father by the way. 24 So he sent his brethren away, and they departed: and he said unto them, See that ye fall not out by the way.

Here is, 1. The kindness of Pharaoh to Joseph, and to his relations for his sake: he bade his brethren welcome (*v.* 16), though it was a time of scarcity, and they were likely to be a charge to him. Nay, because it pleased Pharaoh, it pleased his servants too, at least they pretended to be pleased because Pharaoh was. He engaged Joseph to send for his father down to Egypt, and promised to furnish them with all conveniences both for his removal thither and his settlement there If the good of all the land of Egypt (as it was now better stocked than any other land, thanks to Joseph, under God) would suffice him, he was welcome to it all, it was all his own, even *the fat of the land* (*v.* 18), so that they need not *regard their stuff, v.* 20. What they had in Canaan he reckoned but stuff, in comparison with what he had for them in Egypt; and therefore if they should be constrained to leave some of that behind them, let them not be discontented; Egypt would afford them enough to make up the losses of their removal. Thus those for whom Christ intends shares in his heavenly glory ought not to regard the stuff of this world: The best of its enjoyments are but stuff, but lumber; we cannot make sure of it while we are here, much less can we carry it away with us; let us not therefore be solicitous about it, nor set our eyes or hearts upon it. There are better things reserved for us in that blessed land whither our Joseph has gone to prepare a place.

II. The kindness of Joseph to his father and brethren. Pharaoh was respectful to Joseph, in gratitude, because he had been an instrument of much good to him and his kingdom, not only preserving it from the common calamity, but helping to make it considerable among the nations; for all their neighbours would say, " Surely the Egyptians are a wise and an understanding people, that are so well stocked in a time of scarcity." For this reason Pharaoh never thought any thing too much that he could do for Joseph. Note, There is a gratitude owing even to inferiors; and when any have shown us kindness we should study to requite it, not only to them, but to their relations. And Joseph likewise was respectful to his father and brethren in duty, because they were his near relations, though his brethren had been his enemies, and his father long a stranger. 1. He furnished them for necessity, v. 21. He gave them waggons and provisions for the way, both going and coming; for we never find that Jacob was very rich, and, at this time, when the famine prevailed, we may suppose he was rather poor. 2. He furnished them for ornament and delight. To his brethren he gave two suits apiece of good clothes, to Benjamin five suits, and money besides in his pocket, v. 22. To his father he sent a very handsome present of the varieties of Egypt, v. 23. Note, Those that are wealthy should be generous, and devise liberal things; what is an abundance good for, but to do good with it? 3. He dismissed them with a seasonable caution: *See that you fall not out by the way,* v. 24. He knew they were but too apt to be quarrelsome; and what had lately passed, which revived the remembrance of what they had done formerly against their brother, might give them occasion to quarrel. Joseph had observed them to contend about it, *ch.* xlii. 22. To one they would say, " It was you that first upbraided him with his dreams;" to another, " It was you that said, Let us kill him;" to another, " It was you that stripped him of his fine coat;" to another, " It was you that threw him into the pit," &c. Now Joseph, having forgiven them all, lays this obligation upon them, not to upbraid one another. This charge our Lord Jesus has given in us, *that we love one another,* that we live in peace, that whatever occurs, or whatever former occurrences are remembered, we fall not out. For, (1.) We are brethren, we have all one Father. (2.) We are his brethren, and we shame our relation to him *who is our peace,* if we fall out. (3.) We are guilty, *verily guilty,* and, instead of quarrelling with

one another, have a great deal of reason to fall out with ourselves. (4.) We are, or hope to be, forgiven of God whom we have all offended, and therefore should be ready to forgive one another. (5.) We are *by the way,* a way that lies through the land of Egypt, where we have many eyes upon us, that seek occasion and advantage against us, a way that leads to Canaan, where we hope to be for ever in perfect peace.

25 And they went up out of Egypt, and came into the land of Canaan unto Jacob their father, 26 And told him, saying, Joseph *is* yet alive, and he *is* governor over all the land of Egypt. And Jacob's heart fainted, for he believed them not. 27 And they told him all the words of Joseph, which he had said unto them: and when he saw the wagons which Joseph had sent to carry him, the spirit of Jacob their father revived: 28 And Israel said, *It is* enough; Joseph my son *is* yet alive: I will go and see him before I die.

We have here the good news brought to Jacob. 1. The relation of it, at first, sunk his spirits. When, without any preamble, his sons came in, crying, *Joseph is yet alive,* each striving which should first proclaim it, perhaps he thought they bantered him, and the affront grieved him; or the very mention of Joseph's name revived his sorrow, so that his heart fainted, v. 26. It was a good while before he came to himself. He was in such care and fear about the rest of them that at this time it would have been joy enough to him to hear that Simeon was released, and that Benjamin had come safely home (for he had been ready to despair concerning both these); but to hear that *Joseph is alive* is too good news to be true; he faints, for he believes it not. Note, We faint, because we do not believe; David himself had fainted if he had not believed, Ps. xxvii. 13. 2. The confirmation of it, by degrees, revived his spirit. Jacob had easily believed his sons formerly when they told him, *Joseph is dead;* but he can hardly believe them now that they tell him, *Joseph is alive.* Weak and tender spirits are influenced more by fear than hope, and are more apt to receive impressions that are discouraging than those that are encouraging. But at length Jacob is convinced of the truth of the story, especially when he sees the waggons which were sent to carry him (for seeing is believing), then his *spirit revived.* Death is as the waggons which are sent to fetch us to Christ: the very sight of it approaching should revive us. Now Jacob is called Israel (*v.* 28), for he begins to recover his wonted vigour. (1.) It pleases him to think that Joseph is alive. He says nothing of Joseph's glory, of which they told him; it

246

was enough to him that Joseph was alive. Note, Those that would be content with less degrees of comfort are best prepared for greater. (2.) It pleases him to think of going to see him. Though he was old, and the journey long, yet he would go to see Joseph, because Joseph's business would not permit him to come to see him. Observe, He says, " *I will go and see him,*" not, " I will go and live with him ;" Jacob was old, and did not expect to live long ; " But I will go and see him *before I die,* and then let me depart in peace ; let my eyes be refreshed with this sight before they are closed, and then it is *enough,* I need no more to make me happy in this world." Note, It is good for us all to make death familiar to us, and to speak of it as near, that we may think how little we have to do before we die, that we may do it with all our might, and may enjoy our comforts as those that must quickly die, and leave them.

CHAP. XLVI.

Jacob is here removing to Egypt in his old age, forced thither by a famine, and invited thither by a son. Here, I. God sends him thither, ver. 1—4. II. All his family goes with him, ver. 5—27. III. Joseph bids him welcome, ver. 28—34.

AND Israel took his journey with all that he had, and came to Beer-sheba, and offered sacrifices unto the God of his father Isaac. 2 And God spake unto Israel in the visions of the night, and said, Jacob, Jacob. And he said, Here *am* I. 3 And he said, I *am* God, the God of thy father : fear not to go down into Egypt ; for I will there make of thee a great nation : 4 I will go down with thee into Egypt ; and I will also surely bring thee up *again :* and Joseph shall put his hand upon thine eyes.

The divine precept is, *In all thy ways acknowledge God ;* and the promise annexed to it is, *He sha'l direct thy paths.* Jacob has here a very great concern before him, not only a journey, but a removal, to settle in another country, a change which was very surprising to him (for he never had any other thoughts than to live and die in Canaan), and which would be of great consequence to his family for a long time to come. Now here we are told,

I. How he acknowledged God in this way. He *came to Beersheba,* from Hebron, where he now dwelt ; and there *he offered sacrifices to the God of his father Isaac, v.* 1. He chose that place, in remembrance of the communion which his father and grandfather had with God in that place. Abraham called on God there (*ch.* xxi. 33), so did Isaac (*ch.* xxvi. 25), and therefore Jacob made it the place of his devotion, the rather because it lay in his way. In his devotion, 1. He had an eye to God as the God of his father Isaac, that is, a God in covenant with him ; for by Isaac the cove-

nant was entailed upon him. God had forbidden Isaac to go down to Egypt when there was a famine in Canaan (*ch.* xxvi. 2), which perhaps Jacob calls to mind when he consults God as the God of his father Isaac, with this thought, " Lord, though I am very desirous to see Joseph, yet if thou forbid me to go down to Egypt, as thou didst my father Isaac, I will submit, and very contentedly stay where I am." 2. He *offered sacrifices,* extraordinary sacrifices, besides those at his stated times ; these sacrifices were offered, (1.) By way of thanksgiving for the late blessed change of the face of his family, for the good news he had received concerning Joseph, and for the hopes he had of seeing him. Note, We should give God thanks for the beginnings of mercy, though they are not yet perfected ; and this is a decent way of begging further mercy. (2.) By way of petition for the presence of God with him in his intended journey ; he desired by these sacrifices to make his peace with God, to obtain the forgiveness of sin, that he might take no guilt along with him in this journey, for that is a bad companion. By Christ, the great sacrifice, we must reconcile ourselves to God, and offer up our requests to him. (3.) By way of consultation. The heathen consulted their oracles by sacrifice. Jacob would not go till he had asked God's leave : " Shall I go down to Egypt, or back to Hebron ?" Such must be our enquiries in doubtful cases ; and, though we cannot expect immediate answers from heaven, yet, if we diligently attend to the directions of the word, conscience, and providence, we shall find it is not in vain to ask counsel of God.

II. How God directed his paths : *In the visions of the night* (probably the very next night after he had offered his sacrifices, as 2 Chron. i. 7) *God spoke unto him, v.* 2. Note, Those who desire to keep up communion with God shall find that it never fails on his side. If we speak to him as we ought, he will not fail to speak to us. God called him by name, by his old name, *Jacob, Jacob,* to remind him of his low estate ; his present fears did scarcely become an Israel. Jacob, like one well acquainted with the visions of the Almighty, and ready to obey them, answers, " *Here am I,* ready to receive orders :" and what has God to say to him ?

1. He renews the covenant with him : *I am God, the God of thy father* (v. 3) ; that is, " I am what thou ownest me to be : thou shalt find me a God, a divine wisdom and power engaged for thee ; and thou shalt find me the God of thy father, true to the covenant made with him."

2. He encourages him to make this removal of his family : *Fear not to go down into Egypt.* It seems, though Jacob, upon the first intelligence of Joseph's life and glory in Egypt, resolved, without any hesitation, *I will go and see him ;* yet, upon second thoughts, he saw some difficulties in it, which

he knew not well how to get over. Note, Even those changes that seem to have in them the greatest joys and hopes, yet have an alloy of cares and fears, *Nulla est sincera voluptas* — *There is no unmingled pleasure.* We must always rejoice with trembling. Jacob had many careful thoughts about this journey, which God took notice of. (1.) He was old, 130 years old ; and it is mentioned as one of the infirmities of old people that they are *afraid of that which is high, and fears are in the way,* Eccl. xii. 5. It was a long journey, and Jacob was unfit for travel, and perhaps remembered that his beloved Rachel died in a journey. (2.) He feared lest his sons should be tainted with the idolatry of Egypt, and forget the God of their fathers, or enamoured with the pleasures of Egypt, and forget the land of promise. (3.) Probably he thought of what God had said to Abraham concerning the bondage and affliction of his seed (*ch.* xv. 13), and was apprehensive that his removal to Egypt would issue in that. Present satisfactions should not take us off from the consideration and prospect of future inconveniences, which possibly may arise from what now appears most promising. (4.) He could not think of laying his bones in Egypt. But, whatever his discouragements were, this was enough to answer them all, *Fear not to go down into Egypt.*

3. He promises him comfort in the removal. (1.)That he should multiply in Egypt: " *I will there,* where thou fearest that thy family will sink and be lost, *make it a great nation.* That is the place Infinite Wisdom has chosen for the accomplishment of that promise." (2.) That he should have God's presence with him : *I will go down with thee into Egypt.* Note, Those that go whither God sends them shall certainly have God with them, and that is enough to secure them wherever they are and to silence their fears ; we may safely venture even into Egypt if God go down with us. (3.) That neither he nor his should be lost in Egypt: *I will surely bring thee up again.* Though Jacob died in Egypt, yet this promise was fulfilled, [1.] In the bringing up of his body, to be buried in Canaan, about which, it appears, he was very solicitous, *ch.* xlix. 29, 32. [2.] In the bringing up of his seed to be settled in Canaan. Whatever low or darksome valley we are called into at any time, we may be confident, if God go down with us into it, that he will surely bring us up again. If he go with us down to death, he will surely bring us up again to glory. (4.) That living and dying, his beloved Joseph should be a comfort to him : *Joseph shall put his hand upon thine eyes.* This is a promise that Joseph should live as long as he lived, that he should be with him at his death, and close his eyes with all possible tenderness and respect, as the dearest relations used to do. Probably Jacob, in the multitude of his thoughts within

him, had been wishing that Joseph might do this last office of love for him : *Ille meos oculos comprimat—Let him close my eyes ;* and God thus answered him in the letter of his desire. Thus God sometimes gratifies the innocent wishes of his people, and makes not only their death happy, but the very circumstances of it agreeable.

5 And Jacob rose up from Beersheba : and the sons of Israel carried Jacob their father, and their little ones, and their wives, in the wagons which Pharaoh had sent to carry him. 6 And they took their cattle, and their goods,which they had gotten in the land of Canaan, and came into Egypt, Jacob, and all his seed with him : 7 His sons, and his sons' sons with him, his daughters, and his sons' daughters, and all his seed brought he with him into Egypt. 8 And these *are* the names of the children of Israel, which came into Egypt, Jacob and his sons : Reuben, Jacob's firstborn. 9 And the sons of Reuben ; Hanoch, and Phallu, and Hezron, and Carmi. 10 And the sons of Simeon ; Jemuel, and Jamin, and Ohad, and Jachin, and Zohar, and Shaul the son of a Canaanitish woman. 11 And the sons of Levi ; Gershon, Kohath, and Merari. 12 And the sons of Judah ; Er, and Onan, and Shelah, and Pharez, and Zarah : but Er and Onan died in the land of Canaan. And the sons of Pharez were Hezron and Hamul. 13 And the sons of Issachar ; Tola, and Phuvah, and Job, and Shimron. 14 And the sons of Zebulun ; Sered, and Elon, and Jahleel. 15 These *be* the sons of Leah, which she bare unto Jacob in Padanaram, with his daughter Dinah: all the souls of his sons and his daughters *were* thirty and three. 16 And the sons of Gad ; Ziphion, and Haggi, Shuni, and Ezbon, Eri, and Arodi, and Areli. 17 And the sons of Asher ; Jimnah, and Ishuah, and Isui, and Beriah, and Serah their sister : and the sons of Beriah ; Heber, and Malchiel. 18 These *are* the sons of Zilpah, whom Laban gave to Leah his daughter, and these she bare unto Jacob, *even* sixteen souls. 19 The sons of Rachel Jacob's wife ; Joseph, and Benjamin. 20 And unto Joseph in

the land of Egypt were born Manasseh and Ephraim, which Asenath the daughter of Poti-pherah priest of On bare unto him. 21 And the sons of Benjamin *were* Belah, and Becher, and Ashbel, Gera, and Naaman, Ehi, and Rosh, Muppim, and Huppim, and Ard. 22 These *are* the sons of Rachel, which were born to Jacob: all the souls *were* fourteen. 23 And the sons of Dan; Hushim. 24 And the sons of Naphtali; Jahzeel, and Guni, and Jezer, and Shillem. 25 These *are* the sons of Bilhah, which Laban gave unto Rachel his daughter, and she bare these unto Jacob: all the souls *were* seven. 26 All the souls that came with Jacob into Egypt, which came out of his loins, besides Jacob's sons' wives, all the souls *were* threescore and six; 27 And the sons of Joseph, which were born him in Egypt, *were* two souls: all the souls of the house of Jacob, which came into Egypt, *were* threescore and ten.

Old Jacob is here flitting. Little did he think of ever leaving Canaan; he expected, no doubt, *to die in his nest,* and to leave his seed in actual possession of the promised land: but Providence orders it otherwise. Note, Those that think themselves well settled may yet be unsettled in a little time. Even old people, who think of no other removal than that to the grave (which Jacob had much upon his heart, *ch.* xxxvii. 35; xlii. 38), sometimes live to see great changes in their family. It is good to be ready, not only for the grave, but for whatever may happen betwixt us and the grave. Observe, 1. How Jacob was conveyed; not in a chariot, though chariots were then used, but in a waggon, *v.* 5. Jacob had the character of a plain man, who did not affect any thing stately or magnificent; his son rode in a chariot (*ch.* xli. 43), but a waggon would serve him. 2. The removal of what he had with him. (1.) His effects (*v.* 6), *cattle and goods;* these he took with him that he might not wholly be beholden to Pharaoh for a livelihood, and that it might not afterwards be said of them "that they came beggars to Egypt." (2.) His family, *all his seed, v.* 7. It is probable that they had continued to live together in common with their father; and therefore when he went they all went, which perhaps they were the more willing to do, because, though they had heard that the land of Canaan was promised them, yet, to this day, they had none of it in possession. We have here a particular account of the names of Jacob's family, *his sons' sons,* most of whom are afterwards men-

tioned as heads of houses in the several tribes. See Num. xxvi. 5, &c. Bishop Patrick observes that Issachar called his eldest son *Tola,* which signifies a *worm,* probably because when he was born he was a very little weak child, a worm, and no man, not likely to live; and yet there sprang from him a very numerous offspring, 1 Chron. vii. 2. Note, Living and dying do not go by probability. The whole number that went down into Egypt was sixty-six (*v.* 26), to which add Joseph and his two sons, who were there before, and Jacob himself, the head of the family, and you have the number of seventy, *v.* 27. The LXX. make them seventy-five, and Stephen follows them (Acts vii. 14), the reason of which we leave to the conjecture of the critics; but let us observe, [1.] Masters of families ought to take care of all under their charge, and to provide for those of their own house food convenient both for body and soul. When Jacob himself removed to a land of plenty, he would not leave any of his children behind him to starve in a barren land. [2.] Though the accomplishment of promises is always sure, yet it is often slow. It was now 215 years since God had promised Abraham to make of him a great nation (*ch.* xii. 2); and yet that branch of his seed on which the promise was entailed had increased only to seventy, of which this particular account is kept, that the power of God in multiplying these seventy to so vast a multitude, even in Egypt, may appear the more illustrious. When God pleases, *a little one shall become a thousand,* Isa. lx. 22.

28 And he sent Judah before him unto Joseph, to direct his face unto Goshen; and they came into the land of Goshen. 29 And Joseph made ready his chariot, and went up to meet Israel his father, to Goshen, and presented himself unto him; and he fell on his neck, and wept on his neck a good while. 30 And Israel said unto Joseph, Now let me die, since I have seen thy face, because thou *art* yet alive. 31 And Joseph said unto his brethren, and unto his father's house, I will go up, and show Pharaoh, and say unto him, My brethren, and my father's house, which *were* in the land of Canaan, are come unto me; 32 And the men *are* shepherds, for their trade hath been to feed cattle; and they have brought their flocks, and their herds, and all that they have. 33 And it shall come to pass, when Pharaoh shall call you, and shall say, What *is* your occupation? 34 That ye shall say, Thy servants' trade hath been

about cattle from our youth even until now, both we, *and* also our fathers : that ye may dwell in the land of Goshen ; for every shepherd *is* an abomination unto the Egyptians.

We have here, I. The joyful meeting between Jacob and his son Joseph, in which observe,

1. Jacob's prudence in sending Judah before him to Joseph, to give him notice of his arrival in Goshen. This was a piece of respect owing to the government, under the protection of which these strangers had come to put themselves, *v.* 28. We should be very careful not to give offence to any, especially not to the higher powers.

2. Joseph's filial respect to him. He went in his chariot to meet him, and, in the interview, showed, (1.) How much he honoured him : *He presented himself unto him.* Note, It is the duty of children to reverence their parents, yea, though Providence, as to outward condition, has advanced them above their parents. (2.) How much he loved him. Time did not wear out the sense of his obligations, but his tears which he shed abundantly upon his father's neck, for joy to see him, were real indications of the sincere and strong affection he had for him. See how near sorrow and joy are to each other in this world, when tears serve for the expression of both. In the other world weeping will be restrained to sorrow only ; in heaven there is perfect joy, but no tears of joy : all tears, even those, shall there be wiped away, because the joys there are, as no joys are here, without any alloy. When Joseph embraced Benjamin he *wept upon his neck,* but when he embraced his father he *wept upon his neck a good while ;* his brother Benjamin was dear, but his father Jacob must be dearer.

3. Jacob's great satisfaction in this meeting: *Now let me die, v.* 30. Not but that it was further desirable to live with Joseph, and to see his honour and usefulness ; but he had so much pleasure and satisfaction in this first meeting that he thought it too much to desire or expect any more in this world, where our comforts must always be imperfect. Jacob wished to die immediately, and lived seventeen years longer, which, as our lives go now, is a considerable part of a man's age. Note, Death will not always come just when we call for it, whether in a passion of sorrow or in a passion of joy. Our times are in God's hand, and not in our own ; we must die just when God pleases, and not either just when we are surfeited with the pleasures of life or just when we are overwhelmed with its griefs.

II. Joseph's prudent care concerning his brethren's settlement. It was justice to Pharaoh to let him know that such a colony had come to settle in his dominions. Note,

If others repose a confidence in us, we must not be so base and disingenuous as to abuse it by imposing upon them. If Jacob and his family should come to be a charge to the Egyptians, yet it should never be said that they came among them clandestinely and by stealth. Thus Joseph took care to pay his respects to Pharaoh, *v.* 31. But how shall he dispose of his brethren ? Time was when they were contriving to get rid of him ; now he is contriving to settle them to their satisfaction and advantage : this is rendering good for evil. Now, 1. He would have them to live by themselves, separate as much as might be from the Egyptians, *in the land of Goshen,* which lay nearest to Canaan, and which perhaps was more thinly peopled by the Egyptians, and well furnished with pastures for cattle. He desired they might live separately, that they might be in the less danger both of being infected by the vices of the Egyptians and of being insulted by the malice of the Egyptians. Shepherds, it seems, *were an abomination to the Egyptians,* that is, they looked upon them with contempt, and scorned to converse with them ; and he would not send for his brethren to Egypt to be trampled upon. And yet, 2. He would have them to continue shepherds, and not to be ashamed to own that as their occupation before Pharaoh. He could have employed them under himself in the corn-trade, or perhaps, by his interest in the king, might have procured places for them at court or in the army, and some of them, at least, were deserving enough ; but such preferments would have exposed them to the envy of the Egyptians, and would have tempted them to forget Canaan and the promise made unto their fathers ; therefore he contrives to continue them in their old employment. Note, (1.) An honest calling is no disparagement, nor ought we to account it so either in ourselves or in our relations, but rather reckon it a shame to be idle, or to have nothing to do. (2.) It is generally best for people to abide in the callings that they have been bred to, and used to, 1 Cor. vii. 24. Whatever employment or condition God, in his providence, has allotted for us, let us accommodate ourselves to it, and satisfy ourselves with it, and *not mind high things.* It is better to be the credit of a mean post than the shame of a high one.

CHAP. XLVII.

In this chapter we have instances, I. Of Joseph's kindness and affection to his relations, presenting his brethren first and then his father to Pharaoh (ver. 1—10), settling them in Goshen, and providing for them there (ver. 11, 12), and paying his respects to his father when he sent for him, ver. 27—31. II. Of Joseph's justice between prince and people in a very critical affair, selling Pharaoh's corn to his subjects with reasonable profits to Pharaoh, and yet without any wrong to them, ver. 13, &c. Thus he approved himself wise and good, both in his private and in his public capacity.

THEN Joseph came and told Pharaoh, and said, My father and my brethren, and their flocks, and their herds, and all that they have, are come out of the land of Canaan; and, behold, they *are* in the land of Goshen. 2 And he took some of his brethren, *even* five men, and presented them unto Pharaoh. 3 And Pharaoh said unto his brethren, What *is* your occupation? And they said unto Pharaoh, Thy servants *are* shepherds, both we, *and* also our fathers. 4 They said moreover unto Pharaoh, For to sojourn in the land are we come; for thy servants have no pasture for their flocks; for the famine *is* sore in the land of Canaan: now therefore, we pray thee, let thy servants dwell in the land of Goshen. 5 And Pharaoh spake unto Joseph, saying, Thy father and thy brethren are come unto thee: 6 The land of Egypt *is* before thee; in the best of the land make thy father and brethren to dwell; in the land of Goshen let them dwell: and if thou knowest *any* men of activity among them, then make them rulers over my cattle. 7 And Joseph brought in Jacob his father, and set him before Pharaoh: and Jacob blessed Pharaoh. 8 And Pharaoh said unto Jacob, How old *art* thou? 9 And Jacob said unto Pharaoh, The days of the years of my pilgrimage *are* a hundred and thirty years: few and evil have the days of the years of my life been, and have not attained unto the days of the years of the life of my fathers in the days of their pilgrimage. 10 And Jacob blessed Pharaoh, and went out from before Pharaoh. 11 And Joseph placed his father and his brethren, and gave them a possession in the land of Egypt, in the best of the land, in the land of Rameses, as Pharaoh had commanded. 12 And Joseph nourished his father, and his brethren, and all his father's household, with bread, according to *their* families.

Here is, I. The respect which Joseph, as a subject, showed to his prince. Though he was his favourite, and prime-minister of state, and had had particular orders from him to send for his father down to Egypt, yet he would not suffer him to settle till he had given notice of it to Pharaoh, *v.* 1. Christ, our Joseph, disposes of his followers in his kingdom as it is prepared of his Father, saying, *It is not mine to give,* Matt. xx. 23.

II. The respect which Joseph, as a brother, showed to his brethren, notwithstanding all the unkindness he had formerly received from them.

1. Though he was a great man, and they were comparatively mean and despicable, especially in Egypt, yet he owned them. Let those that are rich and great in the world learn hence not to overlook nor despise their poor relations. Every branch of the tree is not a top branch; but, because it is a lower branch, is it therefore not of the tree? Our Lord Jesus, like Joseph here, is not *ashamed to call us brethren.*

2. They being strangers and no courtiers, he introduced some of them to Pharaoh, *to kiss his hand,* as we say, intending thereby to put an honour upon them among the Egyptians. Thus Christ presents his brethren in the court of heaven, and improves his interest for them, though in themselves unworthy and *an abomination to the Egyptians.* Being presented to Pharaoh, according to the instructions which Joseph had given them, they tell him, (1.) What was their business—that they were shepherds, *v.* 3. Pharaoh asked them (and Joseph knew it would be one of his first questions, *ch.* xlvi. 33), *What is your occupation?* He takes it for granted they had something to do, else Egypt should be no place for them, no harbour for idle vagrants. If they would not work, they should not eat of his bread in this time of scarcity. Note, All that have a place in the world should have an employment in it according to their capacity, some occupation or other, mental or manual. Those that need not work for their bread must yet have something to do, to keep them from idleness. Again, Magistrates should enquire into the occupation of their subjects, as those that have the care of the public welfare; for idle people are as drones in the hive, unprofitable burdens of the commonwealth. (2.) What was their business in Egypt—to sojourn in the land (*v.* 4), not to settle there for ever, only to sojourn there for a time, while the famine so prevailed in Canaan, which lay high, that it was not habitable for shepherds, the grass being burnt up much more than in Egypt, which lay low, and where the corn chiefly failed, while there was tolerably good pasture.

3. He obtained for them a grant of a settlement in the land of Goshen, *v.* 5, 6. This was an instance of Pharaoh's gratitude to Joseph; because he had been such a blessing to him and his kingdom, he would be kind to his relations, purely for his sake. He offered them preferment as shepherds over his cattle, provided they were men of activity; for it is the man who is diligent in his business that shall stand before kings. And, whatever our profession or employment is, we should aim to be excellent in it, and to prove ourselves ingenious and industrious.

III. The respect Joseph, as a son, showed to his father.

1. He presented him to Pharaoh, *v.* 7. And here,

(1.) Pharaoh asks Jacob a common question: *How old art thou? v.* 8. A question usually put to old men, for it is natural to us to admire old age and to reverence it (Lev. xix. 32), as it is very unnatural and unbecoming to despise it, Isa. iii. 5. Jacob's countenance, no doubt, showed him to be very old, for he had been a man of labour and sorrow; in Egypt people were not so long-lived as in Canaan, and therefore Pharaoh looks upon Jacob with wonder; he was as a show in his court. When we are reflecting upon ourselves, this should come into the account, "How old are we?"

(2.) Jacob gives Pharaoh an uncommon answer, *v.* 9. He speaks as becomes a patriarch, with an air of seriousness, for the instruction of Pharaoh. Though our speech be not always of grace, yet it must thus be always with grace. Observe here, [1.] He calls his life *a pilgrimage,* looking upon himself as a stranger in this world, and a traveller towards another world : this earth his inn, not his home. To this the apostle refers (Heb. xi. 13), *They confessed that they were strangers and pilgrims.* He not only reckoned himself a pilgrim now that he was in Egypt, a strange country in which he never was before; but his life, even in the land of his nativity, was a pilgrimage, and those who so reckon it can the better bear the inconvenience of banishment from their native soil; they are but pilgrims still, and so they were always. [2.] He reckons his life by *days ;* for, even so, it is soon reckoned, and we are not sure of the continuance of it for a day to an end, but may be turned out of this tabernacle at less than an hour's warning. Let us therefore number our days (Ps. xc. 12), and measure them, Ps. xxxix. 4. [3.] The character he gives of them is, *First,* That they were few. Though he had now lived 130 years, they seemed to him but a few days, in comparison with the days of eternity, the eternal God, and the eternal state, in which a thousand years (longer than ever any man lived) are but as one day. *Secondly,* That they were evil. This is true concerning man in general, *he is of few days, and full of trouble* (Job xiv. 1); and, since his days are evil, it is well they are few. Jacob's life, particularly, had been made up of evil days; and the pleasantest days of his life were yet before him. *Thirdly,* That they were short of the days of his fathers, not so many, not so pleasant, as their days. Old age came sooner upon him than it had done upon some of his ancestors. As the young man should not be proud of his strength or beauty, so the old man should not be proud of his age, and the crown of his hoary hairs, though others justly reverence it; for those who are accounted very old attain not to the years of

the patriarchs. The hoary head is a crown of glory only when it is found in the way of righteousness.

(3.) Jacob both addresses himself to Pharaoh and takes leave of him with a blessing (*v.* 7): *Jacob blessed Pharaoh,* and again, *v.* 10, which was not only an act of civility (he paid him respect and returned him thanks for his kindness), but an act of piety—he prayed for him, as one having the authority of a prophet and a patriarch. Though in worldly wealth Pharaoh was the greater, yet, in interest with God, Jacob was the greater; he was God's anointed, Ps. cv. 15. And a patriarch's blessing was not a thing to be despised, no, not by a potent prince. Darius valued the prayers of the church for himself and for his sons, Ezra vi. 10. Pharaoh kindly received Jacob, and, whether in the name of a prophet or no, thus he had a prophet's reward, which sufficiently recompensed him, not only for his courteous converse with him, but for all the other kindnesses he showed to him and his.

2. He provided well for him and his, *placed him in Goshen* (*v.* 11), *nourished him* and all his with food convenient for them, *v.* 12. This bespeaks, not only Joseph a good man, who took this tender care of his poor relations, but God a good God, who raised him up for this purpose, and put him into a capacity of doing it, as Esther came to the kingdom for such a time as this. What God here did for Jacob he has, in effect, promised to do for all his, that serve him and trust in him. Ps. xxxvii. 19, *In the days of famine they shall be satisfied.*

13 And *there was* no bread in all the land; for the famine *was* very sore, so that the land of Egypt and *all* the land of Canaan fainted by reason of the famine. 14 And Joseph gathered up all the money that was found in the land of Egypt, and in the land of Canaan, for the corn which they bought : and Joseph brought the money into Pharaoh's house. 15 And when money failed in the land of Egypt, and in the land of Canaan, all the Egyptians came unto Joseph, and said, Give us bread : for why should we die in thy presence ? for the money faileth. 16 And Joseph said, Give your cattle; and I will give you for your cattle, if money fail. 17 And they brought their cattle unto Joseph : and Joseph gave them bread *in exchange* for horses, and for the flocks, and for the cattle of the herds, and for the asses : and he fed them with bread for all their cattle for that year. 18 When that year was ended, they came

unto him the second year, and said unto him, We will not hide *it* from my lord, how that our money is spent; my lord also hath our herds of cattle; there is not aught left in the sight of my lord, but our bodies, and our lands: 19 Wherefore shall we die before thine eyes, both we and our land? buy us and our land for bread, and we and our land will be servants unto Pharaoh: and give *us* seed, that we may live, and not die, that the land be not desolate. 20 And Joseph bought all the land of Egypt for Pharaoh; for the Egyptians sold every man his field, because the famine prevailed over them: so the land became Pharaoh's. 21 And as for the people, he removed them to cities from *one* end of the borders of Egypt even to the *other* end thereof. 22 Only the land of the priests bought he not; for the priests had a portion *assigned them* of Pharaoh, and did eat their portion which Pharaoh gave them: wherefore they sold not their lands. 23 Then Joseph said unto the people, Behold, I have bought you this day and your land for Pharaoh: lo, *here is* seed for you, and ye shall sow the land. 24 And it shall come to pass in the increase, that ye shall give the fifth *part* unto Pharaoh, and four parts shall be your own, for seed of the field, and for your food, and for them of your households, and for food for your little ones. 25 And they said, Thou hast saved our lives: let us find grace in the sight of my lord, and we will be Pharaoh's servants. 26 And Joseph made it a law over the land of Egypt unto this day, *that* Pharaoh should have the fifth *part;* except the land of the priests only, *which* became not Pharaoh's.

Care being taken of Jacob and his family, the preservation of which was especially designed by Providence in Joseph's advancement, an account is now given of the saving of the kingdom of Egypt too from ruin; for God is King of nations as well as King of saints, and provideth food for all flesh. Joseph now returns to the management of that great trust which Pharaoh had lodged in his hand. It would have been pleasing enough to him to have gone and lived with his father

and brethren in Goshen; but his employment would not permit it. When he had seen his father, and seen him well settled, he applied himself as closely as ever to the execution of his office. Note, Even natural affection must give way to necessary business. Parents and children must be content to be absent one from another, when it is necessary, on either side, for the service of God or their generation. In Joseph's transactions with the Egyptians observe,

I. The great extremity that Egypt, and the parts adjacent, were reduced to by the famine. There was no bread, and they *fainted* (*v.* 13), they were ready to die, *v.* 15, 19. 1. See here what a dependence we have upon God's providence. If its usual favours are suspended but for a while, we die, we perish, we all perish. All our wealth would not keep us from starving if the rain of heaven were but withheld for two or three years. See how much we lie at God's mercy, and let us keep ourselves always in his love. 2. See how much we smart by our own improvidence. If all the Egyptians had done for themselves in the seven years of plenty as Joseph did for Pharaoh, they had not been now in these straits; but they regarded not the warning they had of the years of famine, concluding that to-morrow shall be as this day, next year as this, and much more abundant. Note, Because man knows not his time (his time of gathering when he has it) therefore his misery is great upon him when the spending time comes, Eccl. viii. 6, 7. 3. See how early God put a difference between the Egyptians and the Israelites, as afterwards in the plagues, Exod. viii. 22; ix. 4, 26; x. 23. Jacob and his family, though strangers, were plentifully fed on free cost, while the Egyptians were dying for want. See Isa. lxv. 13, *My servants shall eat, but you shall be hungry. Happy art thou, O Israel.* Whoever wants, God's children shall not, Ps. xxxiv. 10.

II. The price they had come up to, for their supply, in this exigency. 1. They parted with all their money which they had hoarded up, *v.* 14. Silver and gold would not feed them; they must have corn. All the money of the kingdom was by this means brought into the exchequer. 2. When the money failed, they parted with all their cattle, those for labour, as the horses and asses, and those for food, as the flocks and the herds, *v.* 17. By this it should seem that we may better live upon bread without flesh than upon flesh without bread. We may suppose they parted the more easily with their cattle because they had little or no grass for them; and now Pharaoh saw in reality what he had before seen in vision, nothing but lean kine. 3. When they had sold their stocks off their land, it was easy to persuade themselves (rather than starve) to sell their land too; for what good would that do them, when they had neither corn to sow it nor cattle to eat of it? They therefore sold that next, for a further supply of corn. 4. When their land was sold, so that they had nothing to live on, they must of course sell themselves, that they might live purely upon their labour, and hold their lands by the base tenure of villanage, at the courtesy of the crown. Note, *Skin for skin, and all that a man hath,* even liberty and property (those darling twins), *will he give for his life;* for life is sweet. There are few (though perhaps there are some) who would even dare to die rather than live in slavery, and dependence on an arbitrary power. And perhaps there are those who, in that case, could die by the sword, in a heat, who yet could not deliberately die by famine, which is much worse, Lam. iv. 9. Now it was a great mercy to the Egyptians that, in this distress, they could have corn at any rate ; if they had all died for hunger, their lands perhaps would have escheated to the crown of course, for want of heirs; they therefore resolved to make the best of bad.

III. The method which Joseph took to accommodate the matter between prince and people, so that the prince might have his just advantage, and yet the people not be quite ruined. 1. For their lands, he needed not come to any bargain with them while the years of famine lasted ; but when these were over (for God will not contend for ever, nor will he be always wroth) he came to an agreement, which it seems both sides were pleased with, that the people should occupy and enjoy the lands, as he thought fit to assign them, and should have seed to sow them with out of the king's stores, for their own proper use and behoof, yielding and paying only a fifth part of the yearly profits as a chief rent to the crown. This became a standing law, *v.* 26. And it was a very good bargain to have food for their lands, when otherwise they and theirs must have starved, and then to have their lands again upon such easy terms. Note, Those ministers of state are worthy of double honour, both for wisdom and integrity, that keep the balance even between prince and people, so that liberty and property may not intrench upon prerogative, nor the prerogative bear hard upon liberty and property: in the multitude of such counsellers there is safety. If afterwards the Egyptians thought it hard to pay so great a duty to the king out of their lands, they must remember, not only how just, but how kind, the first imposing of it was. They might thankfully pay a fifth where all was due. It is observable how faithful Joseph was to him that appointed him. He did not put the money into his own pocket, nor entail the lands upon his own family ; but converted both entirely to Pharaoh's use ; and therefore we do not find that his posterity went out of Egypt any richer than the rest of their poor brethren. Those in public trusts, if they raise great estates, must take heed that it be not at the expense of a good conscience, which is much

more valuable. 2. For their persons, he removed them to cities, *v.* 21. He transplanted them, to show Pharaoh's sovereign power over them, and that they might, in time, forget their titles to their lands, and be the more easily reconciled to their new condition of servitude. The Jewish writers say, " He removed them thus from their former habitations because they reproached his brethren as strangers, to silence which reproach they were all made, in effect, strangers." See what changes a little time may make with a people, and how soon God can empty those from vessel to vessel who had settled upon their lees. How hard soever this seems to have been upon them, they themselves were at this time sensible of it as a very great kindness, and were thankful they were not worse used : *Thou hast saved our lives, v.* 25. Note, There is good reason that the Saviour of our lives should be the Master of our lives. " Thou hast saved us ; do what thou wilt with us."

IV. The reservation he made in favour of the priests. They were maintained on free cost, so that they needed not to sell their lands, *v.* 22. *All people will thus walk in the name of their God ;* they will be kind to those that attend the public service of their God, and that minister to them in holy things ; and we should, in like manner, honour our God, by esteeming his ministers highly in love for their work's sake.

27 And Israel dwelt in the land of Egypt, in the country of Goshen ; and they had possessions therein, and grew, and multiplied exceedingly. 28 And Jacob lived in the land of Egypt seventeen years : so the whole age of Jacob was a hundred forty and seven years. 29 And the time drew nigh that Israel must die : and he called his son Joseph, and said unto him, If now I have found grace in thy sight, put, I pray thee, thy hand under my thigh, and deal kindly and truly with me ; bury me not, I pray thee, in Egypt : 30 But I will lie with my fathers, and thou shalt carry me out of Egypt, and bury me in their buryingplace. And he said, I will do as thou hast said. 31 And he said, Swear unto me. And he sware unto him. And Israel bowed himself upon the bed's head.

Observe, 1. The comfort Jacob lived in (*v.* 27, 28) ; while the Egyptians were impoverished in their own land, Jacob was replenished in a strange land. He lived seventeen years after he came into Egypt, far beyond his own expectation. Seventeen years he had nourished Joseph (for so old he was when he was sold from him, *ch.* xxxvii. 2), and now, by way of requital, seventeen years Joseph nourished him. Observe how kindly Providence ordered Jacob's affairs, that when he was old, and least able to bear care or fatigue, he had least occasion for it, being well provided for by his son without his own forecast. Thus God considers the frame of his people. 2. The care Jacob died in. At last *the time drew nigh that Israel must die, v.* 29. Israel, a prince with God, that had power over the angel and prevailed, yet must yield to death. There is no remedy, he *must die:* it is appointed for all men, therefore for him; and there is no discharge in that war. Joseph supplied him with bread, that he might not die by famine; but this did not secure him from dying by age or sickness. He died by degrees; his candle was not blown out, but gradually burnt down to the socket, so that he saw, at some distance, the time drawing nigh. Note, It is an improvable advantage to see the approach of death before we feel its arrests, that we may be quickened to do what our hand finds to do with all our might: however, it is not far from any of us. Now Jacob's care, as he saw the day approaching, was about his burial, not the pomp of it (he was no way solicitous about that), but the place of it. (1.) He would be buried in Canaan. This he resolved on, not from mere humour, because Canaan was the land of his nativity, but in faith, because it was the land of promise (which he desired thus, as it were, to keep possession of, till the time should come when his posterity should be masters of it), and because it was a type of heaven, that better country which he that said these things declared plainly that he was in expectation of, Heb. xi. 14. He aimed at a good land, which would be his rest and bliss on the other side death. (2.) He would have Joseph sworn to bring him thither to be buried (*v.* 29, 31), that Joseph, being under such a solemn obligation to do it, might have that to answer to the objections which otherwise might have been made against it, and for the greater satisfaction of Jacob now in his dying minutes. Nothing will better help to make a death-bed easy than the certain prospect of a rest in Canaan after death. (3.) When this was done *Israel bowed himself upon the bed's head,* yielding himself, as it were, to the stroke of death (" Now let it come, and it shall be welcome"), or worshipping God, as it is explained, Heb. xi. 21, giving God thanks for all his favours, and particularly for this, that Joseph was ready, not only to put his hand upon his eyes to close them, but under his thigh to give him the satisfaction he desired concerning his burial. Thus those that go down to the dust should, with humble thankfulness, bow before God, the God of their mercies, Ps. xxii. 29.

CHAP. XLVIII.

The time drawing nigh that Israel must die, having, in the former chapter, given order about his burial, in this he takes leave of his grand-children by Joseph, and in the next of all his children. Thus Jacob's dying words are recorded, because he then spoke by a spirit of prophecy; Abraham's and Isaac's are not. God's gifts and graces shine forth much more in some saints than in others upon their death-beds. The Spirit, like the wind, blows where it listeth. In this chapter, I. Joseph, hearing of his father's sickness, goes to visit him, and takes his two sons with him, ver. 1, 2. II. Jacob solemnly adopts his two sons, and takes them for his own, ver. 3–7. III. He blesses them, ver. 8–16. IV. He explains and justifies the crossing of his hands in blessing them, ver. 17–20. V. He leaves a particular legacy to Joseph, ver. 21, 22.

AND it came to pass after these things, that *one* told Joseph, Behold, thy father *is* sick: and he took with him his two sons, Manasseh and Ephraim. 2 And *one* told Jacob, and said, Behold, thy son Joseph cometh unto thee: and Israel strengthened himself, and sat upon the bed. 3 And Jacob said unto Joseph, God Almighty appeared unto me at Luz in the land of Canaan, and blessed me, 4 And said unto me, Behold, I will make thee fruitful, and multiply thee, and I will make of thee a multitude of people; and will give this land to thy seed after thee *for* an everlasting possession. 5 And now thy two sons, Ephraim and Manasseh, which were born unto thee in the land of Egypt before I came unto thee into Egypt, *are* mine; as Reuben and Simeon, they shall be mine. 6 And thy issue, which thou begettest after them, shall be thine, *and* shall be called after the name of their brethren in their inheritance. 7 And as for me, when I came from Padan, Rachel died by me in the land of Canaan in the way, when yet *there was* but a little way to come unto Ephrath: and I buried her there in the way of Ephrath; the same *is* Beth-lehem.

Here, I. Joseph, upon notice of his father's illness, goes to see him; though a man of honour and business, yet he will not fail to show this due respect to his aged father, *v.* 1. Visiting the sick, to whom we lie under obligations, or may have opportunity of doing good, either for body or soul, is our duty. The sick bed is a proper place both for giving comfort and counsel to others and receiving instruction ourselves. Joseph took his two sons with him, that they might receive their dying grandfather's blessing, and that what they might see in him, and hear from him, might make an abiding impression upon them. Note, 1. It is good to acquaint young people that are coming into the world with the aged servants of God that are going out of it, whose dying testimony to the goodness of God, and the pleasantness of wisdom's ways, may be a great encouragement to the rising generation. Manasseh and Ephraim (I dare say) would never forget what passed at this time. 2. Pious parents are desirous of a blessing, not only for themselves, but for their children. "O that they may live before God!" Joseph had been, above all his brethren, kind to his father, and therefore had reason to expect particular favour from him.

II. Jacob, upon notice of his son's visit, prepared himself as well as he could to entertain him, *v.* 2. He did what he could to rouse his spirits, and to stir up the gift that was in him; what little was left of bodily strength he put forth to the utmost, and *sat upon the bed.* Note, It is very good for sick and aged people to be as lively and cheerful as they can, that they may not faint in the day of adversity. *Strengthen thyself*, as Jacob here, and God will strengthen thee; hearten thyself and help thyself, and God will help and hearten thee. Let the spirit sustain the infirmity.

III. In recompence to Joseph for all his attentions to him, he adopted his two sons. In this charter of adoption there is, 1. A particular recital of God's promise to him, to which this had reference: "*God blessed me (v.* 3), and let that blessing be entailed upon them." God had promised him two things, a numerous issue, and Canaan for an inheritance (*v.* 4); and Joseph's sons, pursuant hereunto, should each of them multiply into a tribe, and each of them have a distinct lot in Canaan, equal with Jacob's own sons. See how he blessed them by faith in that which God had said to him, Heb. xi. 21. Note, In all our prayers, both for ourselves and for our children, we ought to have a particular eye to, and remembrance of, God's promises to us. 2. An express reception of Joseph's sons into his family: "*Thy sons are mine (v.* 5), not only my grandchildren, but as my own children." Though they were born in Egypt, and their father was then separated from his brethren, which might seem to have cut them off from the heritage of the Lord, yet Jacob takes them in, and owns them for visible church members. He explains this at *v.* 16, *Let my name be named upon them, and the name of my fathers;* as if he had said, "Let them not succeed their father in his power and grandeur here in Egypt, but let them succeed me in the inheritance of the promise made to Abraham," which Jacob looked upon as much more valuable and honourable, and would have them to prize and covet accordingly. Thus the aged dying patriarch teaches these young persons, now that they were of age (being about twenty-one years old), not to look upon Egypt as their home, nor to incorporate themselves with the Egyptians, but to take their lot with the people of God, as Moses afterwards
256

in the like temptation, Heb. xi. 24—26. And because it would be a piece of self-denial in them, who stood so fair for preferment in Egypt, to adhere to the despised Hebrews, to encourage them he constitutes each of them the head of a tribe. Note, Those are worthy of double honour who, through God's grace, break through the temptations of worldly wealth and preferment, to embrace religion in disgrace and poverty. Jacob will have Ephraim and Manasseh to believe that it is better to be low and in the church than high and out of it, to be called by the name of poor Jacob than to be called by the name of rich Joseph. 3. A proviso inserted concerning the children he might afterwards have; they should not be accounted heads of tribes, as Ephraim and Manasseh were, but should fall in with either the one or the other of their brethren, *v.* 6. It does not appear that Joseph had any more children; however, it was Jacob's prudence to give this direction, for the preventing of contest and mismanagement. Note, In making settlements, it is good to take advice, and to provide for what may happen, while we cannot foresee what will happen. Our prudence must attend God's providence. 4. Mention is made of the death and burial of Rachel, Joseph's mother, and Jacob's best beloved wife (*v.* 7), referring to that story, *ch.* xxxv. 19. Note, (1.) When we come to die ourselves, it is good to call to mind the death of our dear relations and friends, that have gone before us, to make death and the grave the more familiar to us. See Num. xxvii. 13. Those that were to us as our own souls are dead and buried; and shall we think it much to follow them in the same path? (2.) The removal of dear relations from us is an affliction the remembrance of which cannot but abide with us a great while. Strong affections in the enjoyment cause long afflictions in the loss.

8 And Israel beheld Joseph's sons, and said, Who *are* these? 9 And Joseph said unto his father, They *are* my sons, whom God hath given me in this *place.* And he said, Bring them, I pray thee, unto me, and I will bless them. 10 Now the eyes of Israel were dim for age, *so that* he could not see. And he brought them near unto him; and he kissed them, and embraced them. 11 And Israel said unto Joseph, I had not thought to see thy face: and, lo, God hath showed me also thy seed. 12 And Joseph brought them out from between his knees, and he bowed himself with his face to the earth. 13 And Joseph took them both, Ephraim in his

right hand toward Israel's left hand, and Manasseh in his left hand toward Israel's right hand, and brought *them* near unto him. 14 And Israel stretched out his right hand, and laid *it* upon Ephraim's head, who *was* the younger, and his left hand upon Manasseh's head, guiding his hands wittingly ; for Manasseh *was* the firstborn. 15 And he blessed Joseph, and said, God, before whom my fathers Abraham and Isaac did walk, the God which fed me all my life long unto this day, 16 The Angel which redeemed me from all evil, bless the lads ; and let my name be named on them, and the name of my fathers Abraham and Isaac ; and let them grow into a multitude in the midst of the earth. 17 And when Joseph saw that his father laid his right hand upon the head of Ephraim, it displeased him : and he held up his father's hand, to remove it from Ephraim's head unto Manasseh's head. 18 And Joseph said unto his father, Not so, my father : for this *is* the firstborn ; put thy right hand upon his head. 19 And his father refused, and said, I know *it*, my son, I know *it :* he also shall become a people, and he also shall be great : but truly his younger brother shall be greater than he, and his seed shall become a multitude of nations. 20 And he blessed them that day, saying, In thee shall Israel bless, saying, God make thee as Ephraim, and as Manasseh : and he set Ephraim before Manasseh. 21 And Israel said unto Joseph, Behold, I die : but God shall be with you, and bring you again unto the land of your fathers. 22 Moreover I have given to thee one portion above thy brethren, which I took out of the hand of the Amorite with my sword and with my bow.

Here is, I. The blessing with which Jacob blessed the two sons of Joseph, which is the more remarkable because the apostle makes such particular mention of it (Heb. xi. 21), while he says nothing of the blessing which Jacob pronounced on the rest of his sons, though that also was done in faith. Observe here,

1. Jacob was blind for age, *v.* 10. It is one of the common infirmities of old age. *Those that look out at the windows are darkened*, Eccl. xii. 3. It is folly to *walk in the*

sight of our eyes, and to suffer our hearts to go after them, while we know death will shortly close them, and we do not know but some accident between us and death may darken them. Jacob, like his father before him, when he was old, was dim-sighted. Note, (1.) Those that have the honour of age must therewith be content to take the burden of it. (2.) The eye of faith may be very clear even when the eye of the body is very much clouded.

2. Jacob was very fond of Joseph's sons : *He kissed them and embraced them, v.* 10. It is common for old people to have a very particular affection for their grand-children, perhaps more than they had for their own children when they were little, which Solomon gives a reason for (Prov. xvii. 6), *Children's children are the crown of old men.* With what satisfaction does Jacob say here (*v.* 11), *I had not thought to see thy face* (having many years given him up for lost), *and, lo, God has shown me also thy seed !* See here, (1.) How these two good men own God in their comforts. Joseph says (*v.* 9), *They are my sons whom God has given me*, and, to magnify the favour, he adds, " *In this place* of my banishment, slavery, and imprisonment." Jacob says here, *God has shown me thy seed.* Our comforts are then doubly sweet to us when we see them coming from God's hand. (2.) How often God, in his merciful providences, outdoes our expectations, and thus greatly magnifies his favours. He not only prevents our fears, but exceeds our hopes. We may apply this to the promise which is made to us and to our children. We could not have thought that we should have been taken into covenant with God ourselves, considering how guilty and corrupt we are ; and yet, lo, he has shown us our seed also in covenant with him.

3. Before he entails his blessing, he recounts his experiences of God's goodness to him. He had spoken (*v.* 3) of God's appearing to him. The particular visits of his grace, and the special communion we have sometimes had with him, ought never to be forgotten. But (*v.* 15, 16) he mentions the constant care which the divine Providence had taken of him all his days. (1.) He had *fed him all his life long unto this day, v.* 15. Note, As long as we have lived in this world we have had continual experience of God's goodness to us, in providing for the support of our natural life. Our bodies have called for daily food, and no little has gone to feed us, yet we have never wanted food convenient. He that has fed us *all our life long* surely will not fail us at last. (2.) He had by his angel *redeemed him from all evil, v.* 16. A great deal of hardship he had known in his time, but God had graciously kept him from the evil of his troubles. Now that he was dying he looked upon himself as *redeemed from all evil*, and bidding an everlasting farewell to sin and sorrow. Christ, the Angel of the covenant, is he that redeems us from

all evil, 2 Tim. iv. 18. Note, [1.] It becomes the servants of God, when they are old and dying, to witness for our God that they have found him gracious. [2.] Our experiences of God's goodness to us are improvable, both for the encouragement of others to serve God, and for encouragement to us in blessing them and praying for them.

4. When he confers the blessing and name of Abraham and Isaac upon them he recommends the pattern and example of Abraham and Isaac to them, *v.* 15. He calls God the *God before whom his fathers Abraham and Isaac walked,* that is, in whom they believed, whom they observed and obeyed, and with whom they kept up communion in instituted ordinances, according to the condition of the covenant. *Walk before me, ch.* xvii. 1. Note, (1.) Those that would inherit the blessing of their godly ancestors, and have the benefit of God's covenant with them, must tread in the steps of their piety. (2.) It should recommend religion and the service of God to us that God was the God of our fathers, and that they had satisfaction in walking before him.

5. In blessing them, he *crossed hands.* Joseph placed them so as that Jacob's right hand should be put on the head of Manasseh the elder, *v.* 12, 13. But Jacob would put it on the head of Ephraim the younger, *v.* 14. This displeased Joseph, who was willing to support the reputation of his first-born, and would therefore have removed his father's hands, *v.* 17, 18. But Jacob gave him to understand that he knew what he did, and that he did it not by mistake, nor in a humour, nor from a partial affection to one more than the other, but from a spirit of prophecy, and in compliance with the divine counsels. Manasseh should be great, but truly Ephraim should be greater. When the tribes were mustered in the wilderness, Ephraim was more numerous than Manasseh, and had the standard of that squadron (Num. i. 32, 33, 35; ii. 18, 20), and is named first, Ps. lxxx. 2. Joshua was of that tribe, so was Jeroboam. The tribe of Manasseh was divided, one half on one side Jordan, the other half on the other side, which made it the less powerful and considerable. In the foresight of this, *Jacob crossed hands.* Note, (1.) God, in bestowing his blessings upon his people, gives more to some than to others, more gifts, graces, and comforts, and more of the good things of this life. (2.) He often gives most to those that are least likely. He chooses the weak things of the world ; raises the poor out of the dust. Grace observes not the order of nature, nor does God prefer those whom we think fittest to be preferred, but as it pleases him. It is observable how often God, by the distinguishing favours of his covenant, advanced the younger above the elder, Abel above Cain, Shem above Japheth, Abraham above Nahor and Haran, Isaac above Ishmael, Jacob above Esau; Judah and Joseph were preferred before

Reuben, Moses before Aaron, David and Solomon before their elder brethren. See 1 Sam. xvi. 7. He tied the Jews to observe the birthright (Deut. xxi. 17), but he never tied himself to observe it. Some make this typical of the preference given to the Gentiles above the Jews; the Gentile converts were much more numerous than those of the Jews. See Gal. iv. 27. Thus free grace becomes more illustrious.

II. The particular tokens of his favour to Joseph. 1. He left with him the promise of their return out of Egypt, as a sacred trust: *I die, but God shall be with you, and bring you again, v.* 21. Accordingly, Joseph, when he died, left it with his brethren, *ch.* l. 24. This assurance was given them, and carefully preserved among them, that they might neither love Egypt too much when it favoured them, nor fear it too much when it frowned upon them. These words of Jacob furnish us with comfort in reference to the death of our friends : *They die ;* but God shall be with us, and his gracious presence is sufficient to make up the loss : they leave us, but he will never fail us. Further, He will bring us to the land of our fathers, the heavenly Canaan, whither our godly fathers have gone before us. If God be with us while we stay behind in this world, and will receive us shortly to be with those that have gone before to a better world, we ought not to sorrow as those that have no hope. 2. He bestowed one portion upon him above his brethren, *v.* 22. The lands bequeathed are described to be those which he *took out of the hand of the Amorite with his sword, and with his bow.* He purchased them first (Josh. xxiv. 32), and, it seems, was afterwards disseized of them by the Amorites, but retook them by the sword, repelling force by force, and recovering his right by violence when he could not otherwise recover it. These lands he settled upon Joseph; mention is made of this grant, John iv. 5. Pursuant to it, this parcel of ground was given to the tribe of Ephraim as their right, and the lot was never cast upon it ; and in it Joseph's bones were buried, which perhaps Jacob had an eye to as much as to any thing in this settlement. Note, It may sometimes be both just and prudent to give some children portions above the rest; but a grave is that which we can most count upon as our own in this earth.

CHAP. XLIX.

This chapter is a prophecy ; the likest to it we have yet met with was that of Noah, ch. ix. 25, &c. Jacob is here upon his death-bed, making his will. He put it off till now, because dying men's words are apt to make deep impressions, and to be remembered long : what he said here, he could not say when he would, but as the Spirit gave him utterance, who chose this time, that divine strength might be perfected in his weakness. The twelve sons of Jacob were, in their day, men of renown, but the twelve tribes of Israel, which descended and were denominated from them, were much more renowned ; we find their names upon the gates of the New Jerusalem, Rev. xxi. 12. In the prospect of this their dying father says something remarkable of each son, or of the tribe that bore his name. I. The preface, ver. 1, 2. II. The prediction concerning each tribe, ver. 3—28. III. The charge repeated concerning his burial, ver. 29—32. IV. His death, ver. 33.

AND Jacob called unto his sons, and said, Gather yourselves together, that I may tell you *that* which shall befal you in the last days. 2 Gather yourselves together, and hear, ye sons of Jacob; and hearken unto Israel your father. 3 Reuben, thou *art* my firstborn, my might, and the beginning of my strength, the excellency of dignity, and the excellency of power: 4 Unstable as water, thou shalt not excel; because thou wentest up to thy father's bed; then defiledst thou *it:* he went up to my couch.

Here is, I. The preface to the prophecy, in which, 1. The congregation is called together (v. 2): *Gather yourselves together;* let them all be sent for from their several employments, to see their father die, and to hear his dying words. It was a comfort to Jacob, now that he was dying, to see all his children about him, and none missing, though he had sometimes thought himself bereaved. It was of use to them to attend him in his last moments, that they might learn of him how to die, as well as how to live: what he said to each he said in the hearing of all the rest; for we may profit by the reproofs, counsels, and comforts, that are principally intended for others. His calling upon them once and again to gather together intimated both a precept to them to unite in love, (to keep together, not to mingle with the Egyptians, not to forsake the assembling of themselves together,) and a prediction that they should not be separated from each other, as Abraham's sons and Isaac's were, but should be incorporated, and all make one people. 2. A general idea is given of the intended discourse (v. 1): *That I may tell you that which shall befal you* (not your persons, but your posterity) *in the latter days;* this prediction would be of use to those that came after them, for the confirming of their faith and the guiding of their way, on their return to Canaan, and their settlement there. We cannot tell our children what shall befal them or their families in this world; but we can tell them, from the word of God, what will befal them in the last day of all, according as they conduct themselves in this world. 3. Attention is demanded (v. 2): "*Hearken to Israel your father;* let Israel, that has prevailed with God, prevail with you." Note, Children must diligently hearken to what their godly parents say, particularly when they are dying. *Hear, you children, the instruction of a father,* which carries with it both authority and affection, Prov. iv. 1.

II. The prophecy concerning Reuben. He begins with him (v. 3, 4), for he was the firstborn; but by committing uncleanness with his father's wife, to the great reproach of the family to which he ought to have been an ornament, he forfeited the prerogatives of the birthright; and his dying father here so-

lemnly degrades him, though he does not disown nor disinherit him: he shall have all the privileges of a son, but not of a firstborn. We have reason to think Reuben had repented of his sin, and it was pardoned; yet it was a necessary piece of justice, in detestation of the villany, and for warning to others, to put this mark of disgrace upon him. Now according to the method of degrading, 1. Jacob here puts upon him the ornaments of the birthright (v. 3), that he and all his brethren might see what he had forfeited, and, in that, might see the evil of the sin: as the firstborn, he was his father's joy, almost his pride, being *the beginning of his strength.* How welcome he was to his parents his name bespeaks, *Reuben, See a son.* To him belonged the excellency of dignity above his brethren, and some power over them. Christ Jesus is the firstborn among many brethren, and to him, of right, belong the most excellent power and dignity: his church also, through him, is a church of firstborn. 2. He then strips him of these ornaments (v. 4), lifts him up, that he may cast him down, by that one word, "*Thou shalt not excel;* a being thou shalt have as a tribe, but not an excellency." No judge, prophet, nor prince, is found of that tribe, nor any person of renown except Dathan and Abiram, who were noted for their impious rebellion against Moses. That tribe, as not aiming to excel, meanly chose a settlement on the other side Jordan. Reuben himself seems to have lost all that influence upon his brethren to which his birthright entitled him; for *when he spoke unto them they would not hear, ch.* xlii. 22. Those that have not understanding and spirit to support the honours and privileges of their birth will soon lose them, and retain only the name of them. The character fastened upon Reuben, for which he is laid under this mark of infamy, is that he was *unstable as water.* (1.) His virtue was unstable; he had not the government of himself and his own appetites: sometimes he would be very regular and orderly, but at other times he deviated into the wildest courses. Note, Instability is the ruin of men's excellency. Men do not thrive because they do not fix. (2.) His honour consequently was unstable; it departed from him, vanished into smoke, and became as water spilt upon the ground. Note, Those that throw away their virtue must not expect to save their reputation. Jacob charges him particularly with the sin for which he was thus disgraced: *Thou wentest up to thy father's bed.* It was forty years ago that he had been guilty of this sin, yet now it is remembered against him. Note, As time will not of itself wear off the guilt of any sin from the conscience, so there are some sins whose stains it will not wipe off from the good name, especially seventh-commandment sins. Reuben's sin left an indelible mark of infamy upon his family, a dishonour that was a wound not to be healed without a scar, Prov. vi. 32, 33. Let us never do evil, and then we need not fear being told of it.

5 Simeon and Levi *are* brethren; instruments of cruelty *are in* their habitations. 6 O my soul, come not thou into their secret; unto their assembly, mine honour, be not thou united: for in their anger they slew a man, and in their selfwill they digged down a wall. 7 Cursed *be* their anger, for *it was* fierce; and their wrath, for it was cruel: I will divide them in Jacob, and scatter them in Israel.

These were next in age to Reuben, and they also had been a grief and shame to Jacob, when they treacherously and barbarously destroyed the Shechemites, which he here remembers against them. Children should be afraid of incurring their parents' just displeasure, lest they fare the worse for it long afterwards, and, when they would inherit the blessing, be rejected. Observe, 1. The character of Simeon and Levi: they were brethren in disposition; but, unlike their father, they were passionate and revengeful, fierce and uncontrollable; their swords, which should have been only weapons of defence, were (as the margin reads it, *v.* 5) *weapons of violence*, to do wrong to others, not to save themselves from wrong. Note, It is no new thing for the temper of children to differ very much from that of their parents. We need not think this strange: it was so in Jacob's family. It is not in the power of parents, no, not by education, to form the dispositions of their children; Jacob bred his sons to every thing that was mild and quiet, and yet they proved to be thus furious. 2. A proof of this is the murder of the Shechemites, which Jacob deeply resented at the time (*ch.* xxxiv. 30) and still continued to resent. They slew a man, Shechem himself, and many others; and, to effect that, they digged down a wall, broke the houses, to plunder them, and murder the inhabitants. Note, The best governors cannot always restrain those under their charge from committing the worst villanies. And when two in a family are mischievous they commonly make one another so much the worse, and it were wisdom to part them. Simeon and Levi, it is probable, were most active in the wrong done to Joseph, to which some think Jacob has here some reference; for in their anger they would have slain *that man*. Observe what a mischievous thing self-will is in young people: Simeon and Levi would not be advised by their aged and experienced father; no, they would be governed by their own passion rather than by his prudence. Young people would better consult their own interests if they would less indulge their own will. 3. Jacob's protestation against

this barbarous act of theirs: *O my soul, come not thou into their secret.* Hereby he professes not only his abhorrence of such practices in general, but his innocence particularly in that matter. Perhaps he had been suspected as, under-hand, aiding and abetting; he therefore thus solemnly expresses his detestation of the fact, that he might not die under that suspicion. Note, Our soul is our honour; by its powers and faculties we are distinguished from, and dignified above, the beasts that perish. Note, further, We ought, from our hearts, to detest and abhor all society and confederacy with bloody and mischievous men. We must not be ambitious of coming into their secret, or knowing the depths of Satan. 4. His abhorrence of those brutish lusts that led them to this wickedness: *Cursed be their anger.* He does not curse their persons, but their lusts. Note, (1.) Anger is the cause and original of a great deal of sin, and exposes us to the curse of God, and his judgment, Matt. v. 22. (2.) We ought always, in the expressions of our zeal, carefully to distinguish between the sinner and the sin, so as not to love nor bless the sin for the sake of the person, nor to hate nor curse the person for the sake of the sin. 5. A token of displeasure which he foretels their posterity should lie under for this : *I will divide them.* The Levites were scattered throughout all the tribes, and Simeon's lot lay not together, and was so strait that many of the tribe were forced to disperse themselves in quest of settlements and subsistence. This curse was afterwards turned into a blessing to Levites; but the Simeonites, for Zimri's sin (Num. xxv. 14), had it bound on. Note, Shameful dispersions are the just punishment of sinful unions and confederacies.

8 Judah, thou *art he* whom thy brethren shall praise: thy hand *shall be* in the neck of thine enemies; thy father's children shall bow down before thee. 9 Judah *is* a lion's whelp: from the prey, my son, thou art gone up: he stooped down, he couched as a lion, and as an old lion; who shall rouse him up? 10 The sceptre shall not depart from Judah, nor a lawgiver from between his feet, until Shiloh come; and unto him *shall* the gathering of the people *be.* 11 Binding his foal unto the vine, and his ass's colt unto the choice vine; he washed his garments in wine, and his clothes in the blood of grapes: 12 His eyes *shall be* red with wine, and his teeth white with milk.

Glorious things are here said of Judah. The mention of the crimes of the three elder of his sons had not so put the dying patri-arch out of humour but that he had a bless-ing ready for Judah, to whom blessings belonged. Judah's name signifies *praise,* in allusion to which he says, *Thou art he whom thy brethren shall praise, v.* 8. God was praised for him (*ch.* xxix. 35), praised by him, and praised in him; and therefore his brethren shall praise him. Note, Those that are to God for a praise shall be the praise of their brethren. It is prophesied that, 1. The tribe of Judah should be victorious and successful in war: *Thy hand shall be in the neck of thy enemies.* This was fulfilled in David, Ps. xviii. 40. 2. It should be superior to the rest of the tribes; not only in itself more numerous and illustrious, but having a dominion over them: *Thy father's children shall bow down before thee.* Judah was the lawgiver, Ps. lx. 7. That tribe led the van through the wilderness, and in the conquest of Canaan, Judg. i. 2. The prerogatives of the birthright which Reuben had for-feited, the excellency of dignity and power, were thus conferred upon Judah. Observe, "Thy brethren shall bow down before thee, and yet shall praise thee, reckoning them-selves happy in having so wise and bold a commander." Note, Honour and power are then a blessing to those that have them when they are not grudged and envied, but praised and applauded, and cheerfully sub-mitted to. 3. It should be a strong and courageous tribe, and so qualified for com-mand and conquest: *Judah is a lion's whelp, v.* 9. The lion is the king of beasts, the terror of the forest when he roars; when he seizes his prey, none can resist him; when he goes up from the prey, none dare pursue him to revenge it. By this it is foretold that the tribe of Judah should become very formida-ble, and should not only obtain great victo-ries, but should peaceably and quietly enjoy what was obtained by those victories—that they should make war, not for the sake of war, but for the sake of peace. Judah is compared, not to a lion *rampant,* always tear-ing, always raging, always ranging; but to a lion *couchant,* enjoying the satisfaction of his power and success, without creating vexa-tion to others: this is to be truly great. 4. It should be the royal tribe, and the tribe from which Messiah the Prince should come: *The sceptre shall not depart from Judah, till Shiloh come, v.* 10. Jacob here foresees and foretels, (1.) That the sceptre should come into the tribe of Judah, which was fulfilled in David, on whose family the crown was en-tailed. (2.) That Shiloh should be of this tribe —his seed, that promised seed, in whom the earth should be blessed: *that peaceable and prosperous one,* or *the Saviour,* so others translate it, he shall come of Judah. Thus dying Jacob, at a great distance, saw Christ's day, and it was his comfort and support on his death-bed. (3.) That after the coming of the sceptre into the tribe of Judah it should

continue in that tribe, at least a government of their own, till the coming of the Messiah, in whom, as the king of the church, and the great high priest, it was fit that both the priesthood and the royalty should determine. Till the captivity, all along from David's time, the sceptre was in Judah, and subse-quently the governors of Judea were of that tribe, or of the Levites that adhered to it (which was equivalent), till Judea became a province of the Roman empire, just at the time of our Saviour's birth, and was at that time taxed as one of the provinces, Luke ii. 1. And at the time of his death the Jews expressly owned, *We have no king but Cæsar.* Hence it is undeniably inferred against the Jews that our Lord Jesus is he that should come, and that we are to look for no other; for he came exactly at the time appointed. Many excellent pens have been admirably well employed in ex-plaining and illustrating this famous pro-phecy of Christ. 5. It should be a very fruit-ful tribe, especially that it should abound with milk for babes, and wine to make glad the heart of strong men (*v.* 11, 12)—vines so common in the hedge-rows and so strong that they should tie their asses to them, and so fruitful that they should load their asses from them—wine as plentiful as water, so that the men of that tribe should be very healthful and lively, their eyes brisk and sparkling, their teeth white. Much of what is here said concerning Judah is to be ap-plied to our Lord Jesus. (1.) He is the ruler of all his father's children, and the conqueror of all his father's enemies; and he it is that is the praise of all the saints. (2.) He is *the lion of the tribe of Judah,* as he is called with reference to this prophecy (Rev. v. 5), who, having spoiled principalities and powers, went up a conqueror, and couched so as none can stir him up, when he sat down on the right hand of the Father. (3.) To him belongs the sceptre; he is the *law-giver,* and *to him shall the gathering of the people be,* as the desire of all nations (Hag. ii. 7), who, being lifted up from the earth, should draw all men unto him (John xii. 32), and in whom the children of God that are scattered abroad should meet as the centre of their unity, John xi. 52. (4.) In him there is plenty of all that which is nourishing and refreshing to the soul, and which maintains and cheers the divine life in it; in him we may have wine and milk, the riches of Judah's tribe, without money and without price, Isa. lv. 1.

13 Zebulun shall dwell at the haven of the sea; and he *shall be* for a haven of ships; and his border *shall be* unto Zidon. 14 Issachar *is* a strong ass couching down between two bur-dens: 15 And he saw that rest *was* good, and the land that *it was* pleasant;

and bowed his shoulder to bear, and became a servant unto tribute. 16 Dan shall judge his people, as one of the tribes of Israel. 17 Dan shall be a serpent by the way, an adder in the path, that biteth the horse heels, so that his rider shall fall backward. 18 I have waited for thy salvation, O LORD. 19 Gad, a troop shall overcome him : but he shall overcome at the last. 20 Out of Asher his bread *shall be* fat, and he shall yield royal dainties. 21 Naphtali *is* a hind let loose : he giveth goodly words.

Here we have Jacob's prophecy concerning six of his sons.

I. Concerning Zebulun (*v.* 13), that his posterity should have their lot upon the sea-coast, and should be merchants, and mariners, and traders at sea. This was fulfilled when, two or three hundred years after, the land of Canaan was divided by lot, and the *border of Zebulun went up towards the sea,* Josh. xix. 11. Had they chosen their lot themselves, or Joshua appointed it, we might have supposed it done with design to make Jacob's words good ; but, being done by lot, it appears that it was divinely disposed, and Jacob divinely inspired. Note, The lot of God's providence exactly agrees with the plan of God's counsel, like a true copy with the original. If prophecy says, *Zebulun shall be a haven of ships,* Providence will so plant him. Note, 1. God appoints the bounds of our habitation. 2. It is our wisdom and duty to accommodate ourselves to our lot and to improve it. If Zebulun dwell at the haven of the sea, let him be for a haven of ships.

II. Concerning Issachar, *v.* 14, 15. 1. That the men of that tribe should be strong and industrious, fit for labour and inclined to labour, particularly the toil of husbandry, like the ass, that patiently carries his burden, and, by using himself to it, makes it the easier. Issachar submitted to two burdens, tillage and tribute. It was a tribe that took pains, and, thriving thereby, was called upon for rents and taxes. 2. That they should be encouraged in their labour by the goodness of the land that should fall to their lot. (1.) *He saw that rest* at home *was good.* Note, The labour of the husbandman is really rest, in comparison with that of soldiers and seamen, whose hurries and perils are such that those who tarry at home in the most constant service have no reason to envy them. (2.) *He saw that the land was pleasant,* yielding not only pleasant prospects to charm the eye of the curious, but pleasant fruits to recompense his toils. Many are the pleasures of a country life, abundantly sufficient to balance the inconveniences of it, if we can

but persuade ourselves to think so. Issachar, in prospect of advantage, *bowed his shoulders to bear :* let us, with an eye of faith, see the heavenly rest to be good, and that land of promise to be pleasant ; and this will make our present services easy, and encourage us to bow our shoulder to them.

III. Concerning Dan, *v.* 16, 17. What is said concerning Dan has reference either, 1. To that tribe in general, that though Dan was one of the sons of the concubines yet he should be a tribe governed by judges of his own as well as other tribes, and should, by art, and policy, and surprise, gain advantages against his enemies, like a serpent suddenly biting the heel of the traveller. Note, In God's spiritual Israel there is no distinction made of *bond or free,* Col. iii. 11. Dan shall be incorporated by as good a charter as any of the other tribes. Note, also, Some, like Dan, may excel in the subtlety of the serpent, as others, like Judah, in the courage of the lion ; and both may do good service to the cause of God against the Canaanites. Or it may refer, 2. To Samson, who was of that tribe, and judged Israel, that is, delivered them out of the hands of the Philistines, not as the other judges, by fighting them in the field, but by the vexations and annoyances he gave them underhand : when he pulled the house down under the Philistines that were upon the roof of it, he made the horse throw his rider.

Thus was Jacob going on with his discourse ; but now, being almost spent with speaking, and ready to faint and die away, he relieves himself with those words which come in as a parenthesis (*v.* 18), *I have waited for thy salvation, O Lord !* as those that are fainting are helped by taking a spoonful of a cordial, or smelling at a bottle of spirits ; or, if he must break off here, and his breath will not serve him to finish what he intended, with these words he pours out his soul into the bosom of his God, and even breathes it out. Note, The pious ejaculations of a warm and lively devotion, though sometimes they may be incoherent, are not therefore to be censured as impertinent ; that may be uttered affectionately which does not come in methodically. It is no absurdity, when we are speaking to men, to lift up our hearts to God. The salvation he waited for was *Christ,* the promised seed, whom he had spoken of, *v.* 10. Now that he was going to be gathered to his people, he breathes after him to whom the gathering of the people shall be. The salvation he waited for was also *heaven,* the better country, which he declared plainly that he sought (Heb. xi. 13, 14), and continued seeking, now that he was in Egypt. Now that he is going to enjoy the salvation he comforts himself with this, that he had waited for the salvation. Note, It is the character of a living saint that he waits for the salvation of the Lord. Christ, as our way to heaven, is to be waited on ;

and heaven, as our rest in Christ, is to be waited for. Again, It is the comfort of a dying saint thus to have waited for the salvation of the Lord; for then he shall have what he has been waiting for: long-looked-for will come.

IV. Concerning Gad, *v.* 19. He alludes to his name, which signifies a *troop*, foresees the character of that tribe, that it should be a warlike tribe, and so we find (1 Chron. xii. 8); the *Gadites were men of war fit for the battle.* He foresees that the situation of that tribe on the other side Jordan would expose it to the incursions of its neighbours, the Moabites and Ammonites; and, that they might not be proud of their strength and valour, he foretels that the troops of their enemies should, in many skirmishes, overcome them; yet, that they might not be discouraged by their defeats, he assures them that they should *overcome at the last,* which was fulfilled when, in Saul's time and David's, the Moabites and Ammonites were wholly subdued: see 1 Chron. v. 18, &c. Note, The cause of God and his people, though it may seem for a time to be baffled and run down, will yet be victorious at last. *Vincimur in prælio, sed non in bello— We are foiled in a battle, but not in a campaign.* Grace in the soul is often foiled in its conflicts, troops of corruption overcome it, but the cause is God's, and grace will in the issue come off conqueror, yea, *more than conqueror,* Rom. viii. 37.

V. Concerning Asher (*v.* 20), that it should be a very rich tribe, replenished not only with bread for necessity, but with fatness, with *dainties, royal dainties* (for the king himself is *served of the field,* Eccl. v. 9), and these exported out of Asher to other tribes, perhaps to other lands. Note, The God of nature has provided for us not only necessaries but dainties, that we might call him a bountiful benefactor; yet, whereas all places are competently furnished with necessaries, only some places afford dainties. Corn is more common than spices. Were the supports of luxury as universal as the supports of life, the world would be worse than it is, and that it needs not be.

VI. Concerning Naphtali (*v.* 21), a tribe that carries struggles in its name; it signifies *wrestling,* and the blessing entailed upon it signifies prevailing; it is *a hind let loose.* Though we find not this prediction so fully answered in the event as some of the rest, yet, no doubt, it proved true that those of this tribe were, 1. As the loving hind (for that is her epithet, Prov. v. 19), friendly and obliging to one another and to other tribes; their converse remarkably kind and endearing. 2. As the loosened hind, zealous for their liberty. 3. As the swift hind (Ps. xviii. 33), quick in despatch of business; and perhaps, 4. As the trembling hind, timorous in times of public danger. It is rare that those that are most amiable to their friends are most formidable to their enemies. 5. That

they should be affable and courteous, their language refined, and they complaisant, *giving goodly words.* Note, Among God's Israel there is to be found a great variety of dispositions, contrary to each other, yet all contributing to the beauty and strength of the body, Judah like a lion, Issachar like an ass, Dan like a serpent, Naphtali like a hind. Let not those of different tempers and gifts censure one another, nor envy one another, any more than those of different statures and complexions.

22 Joseph *is* a fruitful bough, *even* a fruitful bough by a well; *whose* branches run over the wall: 23 The archers have sorely grieved him, and shot *at him,* and hated him: 24 But his bow abode in strength, and the arms of his hands were made strong by the hands of the mighty *God* of Jacob; (from thence *is* the shepherd, the stone of Israel:) 25 *Even* by the God of thy father, who shall help thee; and by the Almighty, who shall bless thee with blessings of heaven above, blessings of the deep that lieth under, blessings of the breasts, and of the womb: 26 The blessings of thy father have prevailed above the blessings of my progenitors unto the utmost bound of the everlasting hills: they shall be on the head of Joseph, and on the crown of the head of him that was separate from his brethren. 27 Benjamin shall ravin *as* a wolf: in the morning he shall devour the prey, and at night he shall divide the spoil.

He closes with the blessings of his best beloved sons, Joseph and Benjamin; with these he will breathe his last.

I. The blessing of Joseph, which is very large and full. He is compared (*v.* 22) to *a fruitful bough,* or young tree; for God had made him fruitful in the land of his affliction; he owned it, *ch.* xli. 52. His two sons were as branches of a vine, or other spreading plant, *running over the wall.* Note, God can make those fruitful, great comforts to themselves and others, who have been looked upon as dry and withered. More is recorded in the history concerning Joseph than concerning any other of Jacob's sons; and therefore what Jacob says of him is historical as well as prophetical. Observe,

1. The providences of God concerning Joseph, *v.* 23, 24. These are mentioned to the glory of God, and for the encouragement of Jacob's faith and hope, that God had blessings in store for his seed. Here observe (1.) Joseph's straits and troubles, *v.* 23. Though he now lived at ease and in honour,

Jacob reminds him of the difficulties he had formerly waded through. He had had many enemies, here called *archers*, being skilful to do mischief, masters of their art of persecution. They hated him : there persecution begins. They shot their poisonous darts at him, and thus they sorely grieved him. His brethren, in his father's house, were very spiteful towards him, mocked him, stripped him, threatened him, sold him, thought they had been the death of him. His mistress, in the house of Potiphar, sorely grieved him, and shot at him, when she impudently assaulted his chastity (temptations are fiery darts, thorns in the flesh, sorely grievous to gracious souls); when she prevailed not in this, she hated him, and shot at him by her false accusations, arrows against which there is little fence but the hold God has in the consciences of the worst of men. Doubtless he had enemies in the court of Pharaoh, that envied his preferment, and sought to undermine him. (2.) Joseph's strength and support under all these troubles (*v.* 24): *His bow abode in strength*, that is, his faith did not fail, but he kept his ground, and came off a conqueror. The *arms of his hands were made strong*, that is, his other graces did their part, his wisdom, courage, and patience, which are better than weapons of war. In short, he maintained both his integrity and his comfort through all his trials; he bore all his burdens with an invincible resolution, and did not sink under them, nor do any thing unbecoming him. (3.) The spring and fountain of this strength; it was *by the hands of the mighty God*, who was therefore able to strengthen him, and *the God of Jacob*, a God in covenant with him, and therefore engaged to help him. All our strength for the resisting of temptations, and the bearing of afflictions, comes from God : his grace is sufficient, and his strength is perfected in our weakness. (4.) The state of honour and usefulness to which he was subsequently advanced: *Thence* (from this strange method of providence) he became the *shepherd and stone*, the feeder and supporter, *of* God's *Israel*, Jacob and his family. Herein Joseph was a type, [1.] Of Christ ; he was shot at and hated, but borne up under his sufferings (Isa. l. 7—9), and was afterwards advanced to be *the shepherd and stone*. [2.] Of the church in general, and particular believers ; hell shoots its arrows against the saints, but Heaven protects and strengthens them, and will crown them.

2. The promises of God to Joseph. See how these are connected with the former : *Even by the God of thy father Jacob, who shall help thee, v.* 25. Note, Our experiences of God's power and goodness in strengthening us hitherto are our encouragements still to hope for help from him; he that has helped us will help : we may build much upon our *Eben-ezers.* See what Joseph may expect from *the Almighty*, even *the God of his father.* (i.) He shall help thee in difficulties and dan-

gers which may yet be before thee, help thy seed in their wars. Joshua came from him, who commanded in chief in the wars of Canaan. (2.) He shall bless thee ; and he only blesses indeed. Jacob prays for a blessing upon Joseph, but the God of Jacob commands the blessing. Observe the blessings conferred on Joseph. [1.] Various and abundant blessings : *Blessings of heaven above* (rain in its season, and fair weather in its season, and the benign influences of the heavenly bodies); *blessings of the deep that lieth under* this earth, which, compared with the upper world, is but a great deep, with subterraneous mines and springs. Spiritual blessings are blessings of heaven above, which we ought to desire and seek for in the first place, and to which we must give the preference ; while temporal blessings, those of this earth, must lie under in our account and esteem. *Blessings of the womb and the breasts* are given when children are safely born and comfortably nursed. In the word of God, by which we are born again, and nourished up (1 Pet. i. 23 ; ii. 2), there are to the new man blessings both of the womb and the breasts. [2.] Eminent and transcendent blessings, which *prevail above the blessings of my progenitors, v.* 26. His father Isaac had but one blessing, and, when he had given that to Jacob, he was at a loss for a blessing to bestow upon Esau; but Jacob had a blessing for each of his twelve sons, and now, at the latter end, a copious one for Joseph. The great blessing entailed upon that family was increase, which did not so immediately and so signally follow the blessings which Abraham and Isaac gave to their sons as it followed the blessing which Jacob gave to his ; for, soon after his death, they multiplied exceedingly. [3.] Durable and extensive blessings: *Unto the utmost bounds of the everlasting hills,* including all the productions of the most fruitful hills, and lasting as long as they last, Isa. liv. 10. Note, the blessings of the everlasting God include the riches of the everlasting hills, and much more. Well, of these blessings it is here said, *They shall be,* so it is a promise, or, *Let them be,* so it is a prayer, *on the head of Joseph,* to which let them be as a crown to adorn it and a helmet to protect it. Joseph *was separated from his brethren* (so we read it) for a time ; yet, as others read it, *he was a Nazarite among his brethren,* better and more excellent than they. Note, It is no new thing for the best men to meet with the worst usage, for Nazarites among their brethren to be cast out and separated from their brethren; but the blessing of God will make it up to them.

II. The blessing of Benjamin (*v.* 27): *He shall raven as a wolf;* it is plain by this that Jacob was guided in what he said by a spirit of prophecy, and not by natural affection ; else he would have spoken with more tenderness of his beloved son Benjamin, concerning whom he only foresees and foretels this, that his posterity should be a warlike tribe, strong and daring, and that they should enrich themselves with the spoils of their enemies—that they should be active and busy in the world, and a tribe as much feared by their neighbours as any other : *In the morning, he shall devour the prey,* which he seized and divided over night. Or, in the first times of Israel, they shall be noted for activity, though many of them left-handed, Judg. iii. 15; xx. 16. Ehud the second judge, and Saul the first king, were of this tribe ; and so also in the last times Esther and Mordecai, by whom the enemies of the Jews were destroyed, were of this tribe. The Benjamites ravened like wolves when they desperately espoused the cause of the men of Gibeah, those men of Belial, Judg. xx. 14. Blessed Paul was of this tribe (Rom. xi. 1; Phil. iii. 5); and he did, in the morning of his day, devour the prey as a persecutor, but, in the evening, divided the spoil as a preacher. Note, God can serve his own purposes by the different tempers of men ; *the deceived and the deceiver are his.*

28 All these *are* the twelve tribes of Israel : and this *is it* that their father spake unto them, and blessed them; every one according to his blessing he blessed them. 29 And he charged them, and said unto them, I am to be gathered unto my people : bury me with my fathers in the cave that *is* in the field of Ephron the Hittite, 30 In the cave that *is* in the field of Machpelah, which *is* before Mamre, in the land of Canaan, which Abraham bought with the field of Ephron the Hittite for a possession of a buryingplace. 31 There they buried Abraham and Sarah his wife; there they buried Isaac and Rebekah his wife; and there I buried Leah. 32 The purchase of the field and of the cave that *is* therein *was* from the children of Heth. 33 And when Jacob had made an end of commanding his sons, he gathered up his feet into the bed, and yielded up the ghost, and was gathered unto his people.

Here is, I. The summing up of the blessings of Jacob's sons, *v.* 28. Though Reuben, Simeon, and Levi were put under the marks of their father's displeasure, yet he is said to *bless them every one according to his blessing;* for none of them were rejected as Esau was. Note, Whatever rebukes of God's word or providence we are under at any time, yet, as long as we have an interest in God's covenant, a place and a name among his people, and good hopes of a share in the heavenly Canaan, we must account ourselves blessed.

II. The solemn charge Jacob gave them concerning his burial, which is a repetition of what he had before given to Joseph. See how he speaks of death, now that he is dying : *I am to be gathered unto my people, v.* 29. Note, It is good to represent death to ourselves under the most desirable images, that the terror of it may be taken off. Though it separates us from our children and our people in this world, it gathers us to our fathers and to our people in the other world. Perhaps Jacob uses this expression concerning death as a reason why his sons should bury him in Canaan ; for, says he, " *I am to be gathered unto my people,* my soul must go to *the spirits of just men made perfect :* and therefore bury me with my fathers, Abraham and Isaac, and their wives," *v.* 31. Observe, 1. His heart was very much upon it, not so much from a natural affection to his native soil as from a principle of faith in the promise of God, that Canaan should be the inheritance of his seed in due time. Thus he would keep up in his sons a remembrance of the promised land, and not only would have their acquaintance with it renewed by a journey thither on that occasion, but their desire towards it and their expectation of it preserved. 2. He is very particular in describing the place both by the situation of it and by the purchase Abraham had made of it for a burying-place, *v.* 30, 32. He was afraid lest his sons, after seventeen years' sojourning in Egypt, had forgotten Canaan, and even the burying-place of their ancestors there, or lest the Canaanites should dispute his title to it; and therefore he specifies it thus largely, and the purchase of it, even when he lies a-dying, not only to prevent mistakes, but to show how mindful he was of that country. Note, It is, and should be, a great pleasure to dying saints to fix their thoughts upon the heavenly Canaan, and the rest they hope for there after death.

III. The death of Jacob, *v.* 33. When he had finished both his blessing and his charge (both which are included in the commanding of his sons), and so had finished his testimony, he addressed himself to his dying work. 1. He put himself into a posture for dying ; having before seated himself upon the bed-side, to bless his sons (the spirit of prophecy bringing fresh oil to his expiring lamp, Dan. x. 19), when that work was done, *he gathered up his feet into the bed,* that he might lie along, not only as one patiently submitting to the stroke, but as one cheerfully composing himself to rest, now that he was weary. *I will lay me down, and sleep.* 2. He freely resigned his spirit into the hand of God, the Father of spirits : *He yielded up the ghost.* 3. His separated soul went to the assembly of the souls of the faithful, which, after they are delivered from the burden of the flesh, are in joy and felicity : he was *gathered to his people.* Note, If God's people be our people, death will gather us to them.

CHAP. L.

Here is, 1. The preparation for Jacob's funeral, ver. 1—6. II. The funeral itself, ver. 7—14. III. The settling of a good understanding between Joseph and his brethren after the death of Jacob, ver. 15—21. IV. The age and death of Joseph, ver. 22—26. Thus the book of Genesis, which began with the origin of light and life, ends with nothing but death and darkness; so sad a change has sin made.

AND Joseph fell upon his father's face, and wept upon him, and kissed him. 2 And Joseph commanded his servants the physicians to embalm his father: and the physicians embalmed Israel. 3 And forty days were fulfilled for him; for so are fulfilled the days of those which are embalmed: and the Egyptians mourned for him threescore and ten days. 4 And when the days of his mourning were past, Joseph spake unto the house of Pharaoh, saying, If now I have found grace in your eyes, speak, I pray you, in the ears of Pharaoh, saying, 5 My father made me swear, saying, Lo, I die: in my grave which I have digged for me in the land of Canaan, there shalt thou bury me. Now therefore let me go up, I pray thee, and bury my father, and I will come again. 6 And Pharaoh said, Go up, and bury thy father, according as he made thee swear.

Joseph is here paying his last respects to his deceased father. 1. With tears and kisses, and all the tender expressions of a filial affection, he takes leave of the deserted body, *v.* 1. Though Jacob was old and decrepit, and must needs die in the course of nature—though he was poor comparatively, and a constant charge to his son Joseph, yet such an affection he had for a loving father, and so sensible was he of the loss of a prudent, pious, praying father, that he could not part with him without floods of tears. Note, As it is an honour to die lamented, so it is the duty of survivors to lament the death of those who have been useful in their day, though for some time they may have survived their usefulness. The departed soul is out of the reach of our tears and kisses, but with them it is proper to show our respect to the poor body, of which we look for a glorious and joyful resurrection. Thus Joseph showed his faith in God, and love to his father, by kissing his pale and cold lips, and so giving an affectionate farewell. Probably the rest of Jacob's sons did the same, much moved, no doubt, with his dying words. 2. He ordered the body to be embalmed (*v.* 2), not only because he died in Egypt, and that was the manner of the Egyptians, but because he was to be carried to Canaan, which would be a work of time, and therefore it was necessary the body should be preserved as well as it might be from putrefaction. See how vile our bodies are, when the soul has forsaken them; without a great deal of art, and pains, and care, they will, in a very little time, become noisome. If the body have been dead four days, by that time it is offensive. 3. He observed the ceremony of solemn mourning for him, *v.* 3. Forty days were taken up in embalming the body, which the Egyptians (they say) had an art of doing so curiously as to preserve the very features of the face unchanged; all this time, and thirty days more, seventy in all, they either confined themselves and sat solitary, or, when they went out, appeared in the habit of close mourners, according to the decent custom of the country. Even the Egyptians, many of them, out of the great respect they had for Joseph (whose good offices done for the king and country were now fresh in remembrance), put themselves into mourning for his father: as with us, when the court goes into mourning, those of the best quality do so too. About ten weeks was the court of Egypt in mourning for Jacob. Note, What they did in state, we should do in sincerity, *weep with those that weep*, and mourn with those that mourn, as being ourselves also in the body. 4. He asked and obtained leave of Pharaoh to go to Canaan, thither to attend the funeral of his father, *v.* 4—6. (1.) It was a piece of necessary respect to Pharaoh that he would not go without leave; for we may suppose that, though his charge about the corn was long since over, yet he continued a prime-minister of state, and therefore would not be so long absent from his business without licence. (2.) He observed a decorum, in employing some of the royal family, or some of the officers of the household, to intercede for this licence, either because it was not proper for him in the days of his mourning to come into the presence-chamber, or because he would not presume too much upon his own interest. Note, Modesty is a great ornament to dignity. (3.) He pleaded the obligation his father had laid upon him, by an oath, to bury him in Canaan, *v.* 5. It was not from pride or humour, but from his regard to an indispensable duty, that he desired it. All nations reckon that oaths must be performed, and the will of the dead must be observed. (4.) He promised to return: *I will come again.* When we return to our own houses from burying the bodies of our relations, we say, "We have left them behind;" but, if their souls have gone to our heavenly Father's house, we may say with more reason, "They have left us behind." (5.) He obtained leave (*v.* 6): *Go and bury thy father.* Pharaoh was willing his business should stand still so long; but the service of Christ is more needful, and therefore he would not allow one that had work to do for him to go first and bury his father; no, *Let the dead bury their dead,* Matt. viii. 22.

7 And Joseph went up to bury his father: and with him went up all the servants of Pharaoh, the elders of his house, and all the elders of the land of Egypt, 8 And all the house of Joseph, and his brethren, and his father's house: only their little ones, and their flocks, and their herds, they left in the land of Goshen. 9 And there went up with him both chariots and horsemen: and it was a very great company. 10 And they came to the threshingfloor of Atad, which *is* beyond Jordan, and there they mourned with a great and very sore lamentation: and he made a mourning for his father seven days. 11 And when the inhabitants of the land, the Canaanites, saw the mourning in the floor of Atad, they said, This *is* a grievous mourning to the Egyptians: wherefore the name of it was called Abelmizraim, which *is* beyond Jordan. 12 And his sons did unto him according as he commanded them: 13 For his sons carried him into the land of Canaan, and buried him in the cave of the field of Machpelah, which Abraham bought with the field for a possession of a buryingplace of Ephron the Hittite, before Mamre. 14 And Joseph returned into Egypt, he, and his brethren, and all that went up with him to bury his father, after he had buried his father.

We have here an account of Jacob's funeral. Of the funerals of the kings of Judah, usually, no more is said than this, *They were buried with their fathers in the city of David:* but the funeral of the patriarch Jacob is more largely and fully described, to show how much better God was to him than he expected (he had spoken more than once of dying for grief, and going to the grave bereaved of his children, but, behold, he dies in honour, and is followed to the grave by all his children), and also because his orders concerning his burial were given and observed in faith, and in expectation both of the earthly and of the heavenly Canaan. Now, 1. It was a stately funeral. He was attended to the grave, not only by his own family, but by the courtiers, and all the great men of the kingdom, who, in token of their gratitude to Joseph, showed this respect to his father for his sake, and did him honour at his death. Though the Egyptians had had an antipathy to the Hebrews, and had looked upon them with disdain (*ch* xliii. 32),

yet now, that they were better acquainted with them, they began to have a respect for them. Good old Jacob had conducted himself so well among them as to gain universal esteem. Note, Professors of religion should endeavour, by wisdom and love, to remove the prejudices which many may have conceived against them because they do not know them. There went abundance of chariots and horsemen, not only to attend them a little way, but to go through with them. Note, The decent solemnities of funerals, according to a man's situation, are very commendable; and we must not say of them, *To what purpose is this waste?* See Acts viii. 2; Luke vii. 12. 2. It was a sorrowful funeral (*v.* 10, 11); standers-by took notice of it as a grievous mourning. Note, The death of good men is a great loss to any place, and ought to be greatly lamented. Stephen dies a martyr, and yet devout men make great lamentations for him. The solemn mourning for Jacob gave a name to the place, *Abel-Mizraim, the mourning of the Egyptians,* which served for a testimony against the next generation of the Egyptians, who oppressed the posterity of this Jacob to whom their ancestors showed such respect.

15 And when Joseph's brethren saw that their father was dead, they said, Joseph will peradventure hate us, and will certainly requite us all the evil which we did unto him. 16 And they sent a messenger unto Joseph, saying, Thy father did command before he died, saying, 17 So shall ye say unto Joseph, Forgive, I pray thee now, the trespass of thy brethren, and their sin; for they did unto thee evil: and now, we pray thee, forgive the trespass of the servants of the God of thy father. And Joseph wept when they spake unto him. 18 And his brethren also went and fell down before his face; and they said, Behold, we *be* thy servants. 19 And Joseph said unto them, Fear not: for *am* I in the place of God? 20 But as for you, ye thought evil against me; *but* God meant it unto good, to bring to pass, as *it is* this day, to save much people alive. 21 Now therefore fear ye not: I will nourish you, and your little ones. And he comforted them, and spake kindly unto them.

We have here the settling of a good correspondence between Joseph and his brethren, now that their father was dead. Joseph was at court, in the royal city; his brethren were in Goshen, remote in the

267

country; yet the keeping up of a good understanding, and a good affection, between them, would be both his honour and their interest. Note, When Providence has removed the parents by death, the best methods ought to be taken, not only for the preventing of quarrels among the children (which often happen about the dividing of the estate), but for the preserving of acquaintance and love, that unity may continue even when that centre of unity is taken away.

I. Joseph's brethren humbly make their court to him for his favour. 1. They began to be jealous of Joseph, not that he had given them any cause to be so, but the consciousness of guilt, and of their own inability in such a case to forgive and forget, made them suspicious of the sincerity and constancy of Joseph's favour (v. 15): *Joseph will peradventure hate us.* While their father lived, they thought themselves safe under his shadow; but now that he was dead they feared the worst from Joseph. Note, A guilty conscience exposes men to continual frights, even where no fear is, and makes them suspicious of every body, as Cain, *ch.* iv. 14. Those that would be fearless must keep themselves guiltless. If our heart reproach us not, then have we confidence both towards God and man. 2. They humbled themselves before him, confessed their fault, and begged his pardon. They did it by proxy (v. 17); they did it in person, v. 18. Now that the sun and moon had set, the eleven stars did homage to Joseph, for the further accomplishment of his dream. They speak of their former offence with fresh regret: *Forgive the trespass.* They throw themselves at Joseph's feet, and refer themselves to his mercy: *We are thy servants.* Thus we must bewail the sins we committed long ago, even those which we hope through grace are forgiven; and, when we pray to God for pardon, we must promise to be his servants. 3. They pleaded their relation to Jacob and to Jacob's God. (1.) To Jacob, urging that he directed them to make this submission, rather because he questioned whether they would do their duty in humbling themselves than because he questioned whether Joseph would do his duty in forgiving them; nor could he reasonably expect Joseph's kindness to them unless they thus qualified themselves for it (v. 16): *Thy father did command.* Thus, in humbling ourselves to Christ by faith and repentance, we may plead that it is the command of his Father, and our Father, that we do so. (2.) To Jacob's God. They plead (v. 17), *We are the servants of the God of thy father;* not only children of the same Jacob, but worshippers of the same Jehovah. Note, Though we must be ready to forgive all that are any way injurious to us, yet we must especially take heed of bearing malice towards any that are the servants of the God

of our father: such we should always treat with a peculiar tenderness; for we and they have the same Master.

II. Joseph, with a great deal of compassion, confirms his reconciliation and affection to them; his compassion appears, *v.* 17. *He wept when they spoke to him.* These were tears of sorrow for their suspicion of him, and tears of tenderness upon their submission. In his reply, 1. He directs them to look up to God in their repentance (v. 19): *Am I in the place of God?* He, in his great humility, thought they showed him too much respect, as if all their happiness were bound up in his favour, and said to them, in effect, as Peter to Cornelius, " *Stand up, I myself also am a man.* Make your peace with God, and then you will find it an easy matter to make your peace with me." Note, When we ask forgiveness of those whom we have offended we must take heed of putting them in the place of God, by dreading their wrath and soliciting their favour more than God's. " Am I in the place of God, to whom alone vengeance belongs? No, I will leave you to his mercy." Those that avenge themselves step into the place of God, Rom. xii. 19. 2. He extenuates their fault, from the consideration of the great good which God wonderfully brought out of it, which, though it should not make them the less sorry for their sin, yet might make him the more willing to forgive it (v. 20): *You thought evil* (to disappoint the dreams), *but God meant it unto good,* in order to the fulfilling of the dreams, and the making of Joseph a greater blessing to his family than otherwise he could have been. Note, When God makes use of men's agency for the performance of his counsels, it is common for him to mean one thing and them another, even the* quite contrary, but God's counsel shall stand. See Isa. x. 7. Again, God often brings good out of evil, and promotes the designs of his providence even by the sins of men; not that he is the author of sin, far be it from us to think so; but this infinite wisdom so overrules events, and directs the chain of them, that, in the issue, that ends in his praise which in its own nature had a direct tendency to his dishonour; as the putting of Christ to death, Acts ii. 23. This does not make sin the less sinful, nor sinners the less punishable, but it redounds greatly to the glory of God's wisdom. 3. He assures them of the continuance of his kindness to them : *Fear not; I will nourish you,* v. 21. See what an excellent spirit Joseph was of, and learn of him to render good for evil. He did not tell them they were upon their good behaviour, and he would be kind to them if he saw they conducted themselves well; no, he would not thus hold them in suspense, nor seem jealous of them, though they had been suspicious of him : *He comforted them,* and, to banish all their fears, *he spoke kindly to them.* **Note,**

Broken spirits must be bound up and encouraged. Those we love and forgive we must not only do well for but speak kindly to.

22 And Joseph dwelt in Egypt, he, and his father's house: and Joseph lived a hundred and ten years. 23 And Joseph saw Ephraim's children of the third *generation:* the children also of Machir the son of Manasseh were brought up upon Joseph's knees. 24 And Joseph said unto his brethren, I die: and God will surely visit you, and bring you out of this land unto the land which he sware to Abraham, to Isaac, and to Jacob. 25 And Joseph took an oath of the children of Israel, saying, God will surely visit you, and ye shall carry up my bones from hence. 26 So Joseph died, *being* a hundred and ten years old: and they embalmed him, and he was put in a coffin in Egypt.

Here is, I. The prolonging of Joseph's life in Egypt: he lived to be *a hundred and ten years old, v.* 22. Having honoured his father, his days were long in the land which, for the present, God had given him; and it was a great mercy to his relations that God continued him so long, a support and comfort to them.

II. The building up of Joseph's family: he lived to see his great-grand-children by both his sons (*v.* 23), and probably he saw his two sons solemnly owned as heads of distinct tribes, equal to any of his brethren. It contributes much to the comfort of aged parents if they see their posterity in a flourishing condition, especially if with it they see peace upon Israel, Ps. cxxviii. 6.

III. The last will and testament of Joseph published in the presence of his brethren, when he saw his death approaching. Those that were properly his brethren perhaps were some of them dead before him, as several of them were older than he; but to those of them who yet survived, and to the sons of those who were gone, who stood up in their fathers' stead, he said this. 1. He comforted them with the assurance of their return to Canaan in due time: *I die, but God will surely visit you, v.* 24. To this purport Jacob had spoken to him, *ch.* xlviii.

21. Thus must we comfort others with the same comforts with which we ourselves have been comforted of God, and encourage them to rest on those promises which have been our support. Joseph was, under God, both the protector and the benefactor of his brethren; and what would become of them now that he was dying? Why, let this be their comfort, *God will surely visit you.* Note, God's gracious visits will serve to make up the loss of our best friends. They die; but we may live, and live comfortably, if we have the favour and presence of God with us. He bids them be confident: *God will bring you out of this land,* and therefore, (1.) They must not hope to settle there, nor look upon it as their rest for ever; they must set their hearts upon the land of promise, and call that their home. (2.) They must not fear sinking, and being ruined there; probably he foresaw the ill usage they would meet with there after his death, and therefore gives them this word of encouragement: " *God will bring you* in triumph *out of this land* at last." Herein he has an eye to the promise, *ch.* xv. 13, 14, and, in God's name, assures them of the performance of it. 2. For a confession of his own faith, and a confirmation of theirs, he charges them to keep him unburied till that day, that glorious day, should come, when they should be settled in the land of promise, *v.* 25. He makes them promise him with an oath that they would bury him in Canaan. In Egypt they buried their great men very honourably and with abundance of pomp; but Joseph prefers **a** significant burial in Canaan, and that deferred too almost 200 years, before a magnificent one in Egypt. Thus Joseph, by faith in the doctrine of the resurrection and the promise of Canaan, gave *commandment concerning his bones,* Heb. xi. 22. He dies in Egypt; but lays his bones at stake that God will surely visit Israel, and bring them to Canaan.

IV. The death of Joseph, and the reservation of his body for a burial in Canaan, *v.* 26. He was *put in a coffin in Egypt,* but not buried till his children had received their inheritance in Canaan, Josh. xxiv. 32. Note, 1. If the separate soul, at death, do but return to its rest with God, the matter is not great though the deserted body find not at all, or not quickly, its rest in the grave. 2. Yet care ought to be taken of the dead bodies of the saints, in the belief of their resurrection; for there is a covenant with the dust, which shall be remembered, and a commandment is given concerning the bones.

AN

EXPOSITION,

WITH PRACTICAL OBSERVATIONS,

OF THE SECOND BOOK OF MOSES, CALLED

EXODUS.

MOSES (the *servant of the Lord* in writing for him as well as in acting for him—with the pen of God as well as with the rod of God in his hand) having, in the first book of his history, preserved and transmitted the records of the church, while it existed in private families, comes, in this second book, to give us an account of its growth into a great nation ; and, as the former furnishes us with the best economics, so this with the best politics. The beginning of the former book shows us how God formed the world for himself ; the beginning of this shows us how he formed Israel for himself, and both to show forth his praise, Isa. xliii. 21. There we have the creation of the world in history, here the redemption of the world in type. The Greek translators called this book *Exodus* (which signifies a *departure* or *going out*) because it begins with the story of the going out of the children of Israel from Egypt. Some allude to the names of this and the foregoing book, and observe that immediately after *Genesis*, which signifies the *beginning* or *original*, follows *Exodus*, which signifies *a departure* ; for a time to be born is immediately succeeded by a time to die. No sooner have we made our entrance into the world than we must think of making our exit, and going out of the world. When we begin to live we begin to die. The forming of Israel into a people was a new creation. As the earth was, in the beginning, first fetched from under water, and then beautified and replenished, so Israel was first by an almighty power made to emerge out of Egyptian slavery, and then enriched with God's law and tabernacle. This book gives us, I. The accomplishment of the promises made before to Abraham (*ch.* i.—xix.), and then, II. The establishment of the ordinances which were afterwards observed by Israel, *ch.* xx.—xl. Moses, in this book, begins, like Cæsar, to write his own Commentaries ; nay, a greater, a far greater, than Cæsar is here. But henceforward the penman is himself the hero, and gives us the history of those things of which he was himself an eye and ear-witness, *et quorum pars magna fuit—and in which he bore a conspicuous part.* There are more types of Christ in this book than perhaps in any other book of the Old Testament ; for Moses wrote of him, John v. 46. The way of man's reconciliation to God, and coming into covenant and communion with him by a Mediator, is here variously represented ; and it is of great use to us for the illustration of the New Testament, now that we have that to assist us in the explication of the Old.

CHAP. I.

We have here, I. God's kindness to Israel, in multiplying them exceedingly, ver. 1—7. II. The Egyptians' wickedness to them, 1. Oppressing and enslaving them, ver. 8—14. 2. Murdering their children, ver. 15—22. Thus whom the court of heaven blessed the country of Egypt cursed, and for that reason.

NOW these *are* the names of the children of Israel, which came into Egypt ; every man and his houshold came with Jacob. 2 Reuben, Simeon, Levi, and Judah, 3 Issachar, Zebulun, and Benjamin, 4 Dan, and Naphtali, Gad, and Asher. 5 And all the souls that came out of the loins of Jacob were seventy souls : for Joseph was in Egypt *already.* 6 And Joseph died, and all his brethren, and all that generation. 7 And the children of Israel were fruitful, and increased abundantly, and multiplied, and waxed exceeding mighty ; and the land was filled with them.

In these verses we have, 1. A recital of the names of the *twelve patriarchs*, as they are called, Acts vii. 8. Their names are often repeated in scripture, that they may not sound uncouth to us, as other hard names, but that, by their occurring so frequently, they may become familiar to us ; and to show how precious God's spiritual Israel are to him, and how much he delights in them. 2. The account which was kept of the number of Jacob's family, when they went down into Egypt ; they were in all *seventy souls* (*v.* 5). according to the computation we had, Gen. xlvi. 27. This was just the number of nations by which the earth was peopled, according to the account given, Gen. x. *For*

270

when the Most High separated the sons of Adam, he set the bounds of the people according to the number of the children of Israel, as Moses observes, Deut. xxxii. 8. Notice is here taken of this that their increase in Egypt might appear the more wonderful. Note, It is good for those whose latter end greatly increases often to remember how small their beginning was, Job viii. 7. 3. The death of Joseph, *v.* 6. *All that generation* by degrees wore off. Perhaps all Jacob's sons died much about the same time; for there was not more than seven years' difference in age between the eldest and the youngest of them, except Benjamin; and, when death comes into a family, sometimes it makes a full end in a little time. When Joseph, the stay of the family, died, the rest went off apace. Note, We must look upon ourselves and our bre- thren, and all we converse with, as dying and hastening out of the world. This generation passeth away, as that did which went before. 4. The strange increase of Israel in Egypt, *v.* 7. Here are four words used to express it: They *were fruitful,* and *increased abund- antly,* like fishes or insects, so that they *multiplied;* and, being generally healthful and strong, they *waxed exceedingly mighty,* so that they began almost to outnumber the natives, for the land was in all places filled with them, at least Goshen, their own allot- ment. Observe, (1.) Though, no doubt, they increased considerably before, yet, it should seem, it was not till after the death of Joseph that it began to be taken notice of as extraor- dinary. Thus, when they lost the benefit of his protection, God made their numbers their defence, and they became better able° than they had been to shift for themselves. If God continue our friends and relations to us while we most need them, and remove them when they can be better spared, let us own that he is wise, and not complain that he is hard upon us. After the death of Christ, our Joseph, his gospel Israel began most remark- ably to increase: and his death had an in- fluence upon it; it was like the sowing of a corn of wheat, which, if it die, bringeth forth much fruit, John xii. 24. (2.) This wonder- ful increase was the fulfilment of the promise long before made unto the fathers. From the call of Abraham, when God first told him he would make of him a great nation, to the de- liverance of his seed out of Egypt, it was 430 years, during the first 215 of which they were increased but to seventy, but, in the latter half, those seventy multiplied to 600,000 fighting men. Note, [1.] Sometimes God's providences may seem for a great while to thwart his promises, and to go counter to them, that his people's faith may be tried, and his own power the more magnified. [2.] Though the performance of God's promises is sometimes slow, yet it is always sure; *at the end it shall speak, and not lie,* Hab. ii. 3.

8 Now there arose up a new king

over Egypt, which knew not Joseph. 9 And he said unto his people, Be- hold, the people of the children of Is- rael *are* more and mightier than we: 10 Come on, let us deal wisely with them; lest they multiply, and it come to pass, that, when there falleth out any war, they join also unto our enemies, and fight against us, and *so* get them up out of the land. 11 Therefore they did set over them taskmasters to afflict them with their burdens. And they built for Pharaoh treasure cities, Pi- thom and Raamses. 12 But the more they afflicted them, the more they multiplied and grew. And they were grieved because of the children of Is- rael. 13 And the Egyptians made the children of Israel to serve with rigour: 14 And they made their lives bitter with hard bondage, in mortar, and in brick, and in all manner of service in the field: all their service, wherein they made them serve, *was* with rigour.

The land of Egypt here, at length, becomes to Israel a house of bondage, though hitherto it had been a happy shelter and settlement for them. Note, The place of our satisfaction may soon become the place of our affliction, and that may prove the greatest cross to us of which we said, *This same shall comfort us.* Those may prove our sworn enemies whose parents were our faithful friends; nay, the same persons that loved us may possibly turn to hate us: therefore cease from man, and say not concerning any place on this side heaven, *This is my rest for ever.* Observe here,

I. The obligations they lay under to Israel upon Joseph's account were forgotten: *There arose a new king,* after several successions in Joseph's time, *who knew not Joseph, v.* 8. All that knew him loved him, and were kind to his relations for his sake; but when he was dead he was soon forgotten, and the remem- brance of the good offices he had done was either not retained or not regarded, nor had it any influence upon their councils. Note, The best and the most useful and acceptable services done to men are seldom remembered, so as to be recompensed to those that did them, in the notice taken either of their memory, or of their posterity, after their death, Eccl. ix. 5, 15. Therefore our great care should be to serve God, and please him, who is not unrighteous, whatever men are, to forget our work and labour of love, Heb. vi. 10. If we work for men only, our works, at furthest, will die with us; if for God, they will follow us, Rev. xiv. 13. This king of Egypt knew not Joseph; and after him arose one that had the impudence to say, *I know* not the Lord, ch. v. 2. Note, Those that are unmindful of their other benefactors, it is to be feared, will forget the supreme benefactor, 1 John iv. 20.

II. Reasons of state were suggested for their dealing hardly with Israel, v. 9, 10. 1. They are represented as more and mightier than the Egyptians; certainly they were not so, but the king of Egypt, when he resolved to oppress them, would have them thought so, and looked on as a formidable body. 2. Hence it is inferred that if care were not taken to keep them under they would become dangerous to the government, and in time of war would side with their enemies and revolt from their allegiance to the crown of Egypt. Note, It has been the policy of persecutors to represent God's Israel as a dangerous people, *hurtful to kings and provinces*, not fit to be trusted, nay, not fit to be tolerated, that they may have some pretence for the barbarous treatment they design them, Ezra iv. 12, &c.; Esth. iii. 8. Observe, The thing they feared was lest they should *get them up out of the land*, probably having heard them speak of the promise made to their fathers that they should settle in Canaan. Note, The policies of the church's enemies aim to defeat the promises of the church's God, but in vain; God's counsels shall stand. 3. It is therefore proposed that a course be taken to prevent their increase: *Come on, let us deal wisely with them, lest they multiply.* Note, (1.) The growth of Israel is the grief of Egypt, and that against which the powers and policies of hell are levelled. (2.) When men deal wickedly, it is common for them to imagine that they deal wisely; but the folly of sin will, at last, be manifested before all men.

III The method they took to suppress them, and check their growth, v. 11, 13, 14. The Israelites behaved themselves so peaceably and inoffensively that they could not find any occasion of making war upon them, and weakening them by that means: and therefore, 1. They took care to keep them poor, by charging them with heavy taxes, which, some think, is included in the *burdens* with which they afflicted them. 2. By this means they took an effectual course to make them slaves. The Israelites, it should seem, were much more industrious laborious people than the Egyptians, and therefore Pharaoh took care to find them work, both in building (they built him *treasure-cities*), and in husbandry, even *all manner of service in the field:* and this was exacted from them with the utmost rigour and severity. Here are many expressions used, to affect us with the condition of God's people. They had *taskmasters* set over them, who were directed, not only to burden them, but, as much as might be, *to afflict them with their burdens*, and contrive how to make them grievous. They not only made them serve, which was sufficient for Pharaoh's profit, but they made them *serve with rigour*, so that their lives became bitter to them, intending hereby, (1.) To break their spirits, and rob them of every thing in them that was ingenuous and generous. (2.) To ruin their health and shorten their days, and so diminish their numbers. (3.) To discourage them from marrying, since their children would be born to slavery. (4.) To oblige them to desert the Hebrews, and incorporate themselves with the Egyptians. Thus he hoped to cut off the name of Israel, that it might be no more in remembrance. And it is to be feared that the oppression they were under had this bad effect upon them, that it brought over many of them to join with the Egyptians in their idolatrous worship; for we read (Josh. xxiv. 14) that they served other gods in Egypt; and, though it is not mentioned here in this history, yet we find (Ezek. xx. 8) that God had threatened to destroy them for it, even while they were in the land of Egypt: however, they were kept a distinct body, unmingled with the Egyptians, and by their other customs separated from them, which was *the Lord's doing, and marvellous.*

IV. The wonderful increase of the Israelites, notwithstanding the oppressions they groaned under (v. 12): *The more they afflicted them the more they multiplied*, sorely to the grief and vexation of the Egyptians. Note, 1. Times of affliction have often been the church's growing times, *Sub pondere crescit—Being pressed, it grows.* Christianity spread most when it was persecuted: the blood of the martyrs was the seed of the church. 2. Those that take counsel against the Lord and his Israel do but imagine a vain thing (Ps. ii. 1), and create so much the greater vexation to themselves: hell and earth cannot diminish those whom Heaven will increase.

15 And the king of Egypt spake to the Hebrew midwives, of which the name of the one *was* Shiphrah, and the name of the other Puah: 16 And he said, When ye do the office of a midwife to the Hebrew women, and see *them* upon the stools; if it *be* a son, then ye shall kill him: but if it *be* a daughter, then she shall live. 17 But the midwives feared God, and did not as the king of Egypt commanded them, but saved the men children alive. 18 And the king of Egypt called for the midwives, and said unto them, Why have ye done this thing, and have saved the men children alive? 19 And the midwives said unto Pharaoh, Because the Hebrew women *are* not as the Egyptian women; for they *are* lively, and are delivered ere the midwives come in unto them. 20 Therefore God dealt well with the mid-

wives : and the people multiplied, and waxed very mighty. 21 And it came to pass, because the midwives feared God, that he made them houses. 22 And Pharaoh charged all his people, saying, Every son that is born ye shall cast into the river, and every daughter ye shall save alive.

The Egyptians' indignation at Israel's increase, notwithstanding the many hardships they put upon them, drove them at length to the most barbarous and inhuman methods of suppressing them, by the murder of their children. It was strange that they did not rather pick quarrels with the grown men, against whom they might perhaps find some occasion : to be thus bloody towards the infants, whom all must own to be innocents, was a sin which they had no cloak for. Note, 1. There is more cruelty in the corrupt heart of man than one would imagine, Rom. iii. 15, 16. The enmity that is in the seed of the serpent against the seed of the woman divests men of humanity itself, and makes them forget all pity. One would not think it possible that ever men should be so barbarous and blood-thirsty as the persecutors of God's people have been, Rev. xvii. 6. 2. Even confessed innocence is no defence against the old enmity. What blood so guiltless as that of a child new-born ? Yet that is prodigally shed like water, and sucked with delight like milk or honey. Pharaoh and Herod sufficiently proved themselves agents for that *great red dragon, who stood to devour the man-child as soon as it was born*, Rev. xii. 3, 4. Pilate delivered Christ to be crucified, after he had confessed that he found no fault in him. It is well for us that, though man can kill the body, this is all he can do. Two bloody edicts are here signed for the destruction of all the male children that were born to the Hebrews.

I. The midwives were commanded to murder them. Observe, 1. The orders given them, *v.* 15, 16. It added much to the barbarity of the intended executions that the *midwives* were appointed to be the executioners ; for it was to make them, not only bloody, but perfidious, and to oblige them to betray a trust, and to destroy those whom they undertook to save and help. Could he think that their sex would admit such cruelty, and their employment such base treachery ? Note, Those who are themselves barbarous think to find, or make, others as barbarous. Pharaoh's project was secretly to engage the midwives to stifle the men-children as soon as they were born, and then to lay it upon the difficulty of the birth, or some mischance common in that case, Job iii. 11. The two midwives he tampered with in order hereunto are here named ; and perhaps, at this time, which was above eighty years before their going out of Egypt, those two might suffice for all the Hebrew women, at least so many of them as lay near the court, as it is plain by *ch.* ii. 5, 6, many of them did, and of them he was most jealous. They are called *Hebrew midwives*, probably not because they were themselves Hebrews (for surely Pharaoh could never expect they should be so barbarous to those of their own nation), but because they were generally made use of by the Hebrews ; and, being Egyptians, he hoped to prevail with them. 2. Their pious disobedience to this impious command, *v.* 17. *They feared God*, regarded his law, and dreaded his wrath more than Pharaoh's, and therefore saved the men-children alive. Note, If men's commands be any way contrary to the commands of God, we must obey God and not man, Acts iv. 19 ; v. 29. No power on earth can warrant us, much less oblige us, to sin against God, our chief Lord. Again, Where the fear of God rules in the heart, it will preserve it from the snare which the inordinate fear of man brings. 3. Their justifying themselves in this disobedience, when they were charged with it as a crime, *v.* 18. They gave a reason for it, which, it seems, God's gracious promise furnished them with— that they came too late to do it, for generally the children were born before they came, *v.* 19. I see no reason we have to doubt the truth of this ; it is plain that the Hebrews were now under an extraordinary blessing of increase, which may well be supposed to have this effect, that the women had very quick and easy labour, and, the mothers and children being both lively, they seldom needed the help of midwives : this these midwives took notice of, and, concluding it to be the finger of God, were thereby emboldened to disobey the king, in favour of those whom Heaven thus favoured, and with this justified themselves before Pharaoh, when he called them to an account for it. Some of the ancient Jews expound it thus, *Ere the midwife comes to them they pray to their Father in heaven, and he answereth them, and they do bring forth*. Note, God is a readier help to his people in distress than any other helpers are, and often anticipates them with the blessings of his goodness ; such deliverances lay them under peculiarly strong obligations. 4. The recompence God gave them for their tenderness towards his people : *He dealt well with them, v.* 20. Note, God will be behindhand with none for any kindness done to his people, taking it as done to himself. In particular, *he made them houses* (*v.* 21), built them up into families, blessed their children, and prospered them in all they did. Note, The services done for God's Israel are often repaid in kind. The midwives kept up the Israelites' houses, and, in recompence for it, *God made them houses*. Observe, The recompence has relation to the principle upon which they went : *Because they feared God, he made them houses*. Note, Religion and piety are good friends to outward prosperity :

the fear of God in a house will help to build it up and establish it. Dr. Lightfoot's notion of it is, That, for their piety, they were married to Israelites, and Hebrew families were built up by them.

II. When this project did not take effect, Pharaoh gave public orders to all his people to drown all the male children of the Hebrews, *v.* 22. We may suppose it was made highly penal for any to know of the birth of a son to an Israelite, and not to give information to those who were appointed to throw him into the river. Note, The enemies of the church have been restless in their endeavours to *wear out the saints of the Most High,* Dan. vii. 25. But *he that sits in heaven shall laugh at them.* See Ps. ii. 4.

CHAP. II.

This chapter begins the story of Moses, that man of renown, famed for his intimate acquaintance with Heaven and his eminent usefulness on earth, and the most remarkable type of Christ, as a prophet, saviour, lawgiver, and mediator, in all the Old Testament. The Jews have a book among them of the life of Moses, which tells a great many stories concerning him, which we have reason to think are mere fictions; what he has recorded concerning himself is what we may rely upon, for we know that his record is true; and it is what we may be satisfied with, for it is what Infinite Wisdom thought fit to preserve and transmit to us. In this chapter we have, I. The perils of his birth and infancy, ver. 1—4. II. His preservation through those perils, and the preferment of his childhood and youth, ver. 5—10. III. The pious choice of his riper years, which was to own the people of God. 1. He offered them his service at present, if they would accept it, ver. 11—14. 2. He retired, that he might reserve himself for further service hereafter, ver. 15—22. IV. The dawning of the day of Israel's deliverance, ver. 23, &c.

A ND there went a man of the house of Levi, and took *to wife* a daughter of Levi. 2 And the woman conceived, and bare a son: and when she saw him that he *was a* goodly *child,* she hid him three months. 3 And when she could not longer hide him, she took for him an ark of bulrushes, and daubed it with slime and with pitch, and put the child therein; and she laid *it* in the flags by the river's brink. 4 And his sister stood afar off, to wit what would be done to him.

Moses was a Levite, both by father and mother. Jacob left Levi under marks of disgrace (Gen. xlix. 5); and yet, soon after, Moses appears a descendant from him, that he might typify Christ, who came in the likeness of sinful flesh and was made a curse for us. This tribe began to be distinguished from the rest by the birth of Moses, as afterwards it became remarkable in many other instances. Observe, concerning this newborn infant,

I. How he was hidden. It seems to have been just at the time of his birth that the cruel law was made for the murder of all the male children of the Hebrews; and many, no doubt, perished by the execution of it. The parents of Moses had Miriam and Aaron, both older than he, born to them before this edict came out, and had nursed them without that peril: but those that begin in the world in peace know not what troubles they may meet with before they have got through it. Pro-
274

bably the mother of Moses was full of anxiety in the expectation of his birth, now that this edict was in force, and was ready to say, *Blessed are the barren that never bore,* Luke xxiii. 29. Better so than bring forth children to the murderer, Hos. ix. 13. Yet this child proves the glory of his father's house. Thus that which is most our fear often proves, in the issue, most our joy. Observe the beauty of providence: just at the time when Pharaoh's cruelty rose to this height the deliverer was born, though he did not appear for many years after. Note, When men are projecting the church's ruin God is preparing for its salvation. Moses, who was afterwards to bring Israel out of this house of bondage, was himself in danger of falling a sacrifice to the fury of the oppressor, God so ordering it that, being afterwards told of this, he might be the more animated with a holy zeal for the deliverance of his brethren out of the hands of such bloody men. 1. His parents observed him to be a *goodly child,* more than ordinarily beautiful; he was *fair to God,* Acts vii. 20. They fancied he had a lustre in his countenance that was something more than human, and was a specimen of the shining of his face afterwards, Exod. xxxiv. 29. Note, God sometimes gives early earnests of his gifts, and manifests himself betimes in those for whom and by whom he designs to do great things. Thus he put an early strength into Samson (Judge xiii. 24, 25), an early forwardness into Samuel (1 Sam. ii. 18), wrought an early deliverance for David (1 Sam. xvii. 37), and began betimes with Timothy, 2 Tim. iii. 15. 2. Therefore they were the more solicitous for his preservation, because they looked upon this as an indication of some kind purpose of God concerning him, and a happy omen of something great. Note, A lively active faith can take encouragement from the least intimation of the divine favour; a merciful hint of Providence will encourage those whose spirits make diligent search, *Three months* they hid him in some private apartment of their own house, though probably with the hazard of their own lives, had he been discovered. Herein Moses was a type of Christ, who, in his infancy, was forced to abscond, and in Egypt too (Matt. ii. 13), and was wonderfully preserved, when many innocents were butchered. It is said (Heb. xi. 23) that the parents of Moses *hid him by faith;* some think they had a special revelation to them that the deliverer should spring from their loins; however they had the general promise of Israel's preservation, which they acted faith upon, and in that faith hid their child, not being afraid of the penalty annexed to the king's commandment. Note, Faith in God's promise is so far from superseding that it rather excites and quickens to the use of lawful means for the obtaining of mercy. Duty is ours, events are God's. Again, Faith in God will set us above the ensnaring fear of man.

II. How he was exposed. At three months' end, probably when the searchers came about to look for concealed children, so that they could not hide him any longer (their faith perhaps beginning now to fail), they put him in an ark of bulrushes by the *river's brink* (*v.* 3), and set his little sister at some distance to watch what would become of him, and into whose hands he would fall, *v.* 4. God put it into their hearts to do this, to bring about his own purposes, that Moses might by this means be brought into the hands of Pharaoh's daughter, and that by his deliverance from this imminent danger a specimen might be given of the deliverance of God's church, which now lay thus exposed. Note, 1. God takes special care of the outcasts of Israel (Ps. cxlvii. 2); they are *his* outcasts, Isa. xvi. 4. Moses seemed quite abandoned by his friends; his own mother durst not own him: but now the Lord took him up and protected him, Ps. xxvii. 10. 2. In times of extreme difficulty it is good to venture upon the providence of God. Thus to have exposed their child while they might have preserved it, would have been to tempt Providence; but, when they could not, it was to trust to Providence. "Nothing venture, nothing win." *If I perish, I perish.*

5 And the daughter of Pharaoh came down to wash *herself* at the river; and her maidens walked along by the river's side; and when she saw the ark among the flags, she sent her maid to fetch it. 6 And when she had opened *it*, she saw the child: and, behold, the babe wept. And she had compassion on him, and said, This *is* one of the Hebrews' children. 7 Then said his sister to Pharaoh's daughter, Shall I go and call to thee a nurse of the Hebrew women, that she may nurse the child for thee? 8 And Pharaoh's daughter said to her, Go. And the maid went and called the child's mother. 9 And Pharaoh's daughter said unto her, Take this child away, and nurse it for me, and I will give *thee* thy wages. And the woman took the child, and nursed it. 10 And the child grew, and she brought him unto Pharaoh's daughter, and he became her son. And she called his name Moses: and she said, Because I drew him out of the water.

Here is, I. Moses saved from perishing. Come see the place where that great man lay when he was a little child; he lay in a bulrush-basket by the river's side. Had he been left to lie there, he must have perished in a little time with hunger, if he had not

been sooner washed into the river or devoured by a crocodile. Had he fallen into any other hands than those he did fall into, either they would not, or durst not, have done otherwise than have thrown him straightway into the river; but Providence brings no less a person thither than Pharaoh's daughter, just at that juncture, guides her to the place where this poor forlorn infant lay, and inclines her heart to pity it, which she dares do when none else durst. Never did poor child cry so seasonably, so happily, as this did: *The babe wept*, which moved the compassion of the princess, as no doubt his beauty did, *v.* 5, 6. Note, 1. Those are hard-hearted indeed that have not a tender compassion for helpless infancy. How pathetically does God represent his compassion for the Israelites in general considered in this pitiable state! Ezek. xvi. 5, 6. 2. It is very commendable in persons of quality to take cognizance of the distresses of the meanest, and to be helpful and charitable to them. 3. God's care of us in our infancy ought to be often made mention of by us to his praise. Though we were not thus exposed (that we were not was God's mercy) yet many were the perils we were surrounded with in our infancy, out of which the Lord delivered us, Ps. xxii. 9, 10. 4. God often raises up friends for his people even among their enemies. Pharaoh cruelly seeks Israel's destruction, but his own daughter charitably compassionates a Hebrew child, and not only so, but, beyond her intention, preserves Israel's deliverer. *O Lord, how wonderful are thy counsels!*

II. Moses well provided with a good nurse, no worse than his own dear mother, *v.* 7—9. Pharaoh's daughter thinks it convenient that he should have a Hebrew nurse (pity that so fair a child should be suckled by a sable Moor), and the sister of Moses, with art and good management, introduces the mother into the place of a nurse, to the great advantage of the child; for mothers are the best nurses, and those who receive the blessings of the breasts with those of the womb are not just if they give them not to those for whose sake they received them: it was also an unspeakable satisfaction to the mother, who received her son as life from the dead, and now could enjoy him without fear. The transport of her joy, upon this happy turn, we may suppose sufficient to betray her to be the true mother (had there been any suspicion of it) to a less discerning eye than that of Solomon, 1 Kings iii. 27.

III. Moses preferred to be the son of Pharaoh's daughter (*v.* 10), his parents herein perhaps not only yielding to necessity, having nursed him *for her*, but too much pleased with the honour thereby done to their son; for the smiles of the world are stronger temptations than its frowns, and more difficult to resist. The tradition of the Jews is that Pharaoh's daughter had no child of her own, and that she was the only child of her father, so that when he was adopted for her son he stood fair for the crown: however it is certain he stood fair for the best preferments of the court in due time, and in the mean time had the advantage of the best education and improvements of the court, with the help of which, having a great genius, he became master of all the lawful learning of the Egyptians, Acts vii. 22. Note, 1. Providence pleases itself sometimes in raising the poor out of the dust, to set them among princes, Ps. cxiii. 7, 8. Many who, by their birth, seem marked for obscurity and poverty, by surprising events of Providence are brought to sit at the upper end of the world, to make men know that *the heavens do rule.* 2. Those whom God designs for great services he finds out ways to qualify and prepare beforehand. Moses, by having his education in a court, is the fitter to be a prince and *king in Jeshurun;* by having his education in a learned court (for such the Egyptian then was) is the fitter to be an historian; and by having his education in the court of Egypt is the fitter to be employed, in the name of God, as an ambassador to that court.

IV. Moses named. The Jews tell us that his father, at his circumcision, called him *Joachim,* but Pharaoh's daughter called him *Moses, Drawn out of the water,* so it signifies in the Egyptian language. The calling of the Jewish lawgiver by an Egyptian name is a happy omen to the Gentile world, and gives hopes of that day when it shall be said, *Blessed be Egypt my people,* Isa. xix. 25. And his tuition at court was an earnest of the performance of that promise, Isa. xlix. 23, *Kings shall be thy nursing fathers, and queens thy nursing mothers.*

11 And it came to pass in those days, when Moses was grown, that he went out unto his brethren, and looked on their burdens: and he spied an Egyptian smiting a Hebrew, one of his brethren. 12 And he looked this way and that way, and when he saw that *there was* no man, he slew the Egyptian, and hid him in the sand. 13 And when he went out the second day, behold, two men of the Hebrews strove together: and he said to him that did the wrong, Wherefore smitest thou thy fellow? 14 And he said, Who made thee a prince and a judge over us? intendest thou to kill me, as thou killedst the Egyptian? And Moses feared, and said, Surely this thing is known. 15 Now when Pharaoh heard this thing, he sought to slay Moses. But Moses fled from the face of Pharaoh, and dwelt in the land of Midian: and he sat down by a well.

Moses had now passed the first forty years of his life in the court of Pharaoh, preparing himself for business; and now it was time for him to enter upon action, and,

I. He boldly owns and espouses the cause of God's people: *When Moses was grown he went out unto his brethren, and looked on their burdens, v. 11.* The best exposition of these words we have from an inspired pen, Heb. xi. 24—26, where we are told that by this he expressed, 1. His holy contempt of the honours and pleasures of the Egyptian court; he *refused to be called the son of Pharaoh's daughter,* for *he went out.* The temptation was indeed very strong. He had a fair opportunity (as we say) to make his fortune, and to have been serviceable to Israel too, with his interest at court. He was obliged, in gratitude as well as interest, to Pharaoh's daughter, and yet he obtained a glorious victory by faith over his temptation. He reckoned it much more his honour and advantage to be a son of Abraham than to be the son of Pharaoh's daughter. 2. His tender concern for his poor brethren in bondage, with whom (though he might easily have avoided it) he *chose to suffer affliction;* he looked on their burdens as one that not only pitied them, but was resolved to venture with them, and, if occasion were, to venture for them.

II. He gives a specimen of the great things he was afterwards to do for God and his Israel in two little instances, related particularly by Stephen (Acts vii. 23, &c.) with design to show how their fathers had *always resisted the Holy Ghost* (v. 51), even in Moses himself, when he first appeared as their deliverer, wilfully shutting their eyes against this day-break of their enlargement. He found himself, no doubt, under a divine direction and impulse in what he did, and that he was in an extraordinary manner called of God to do it. Now observe,

1. Moses was afterwards to be employed in plaguing the Egyptians for the wrongs they had done to God's Israel; and, as a specimen of that, he killed the Egyptian who smote the Hebrew (v. 11, 12); probably it was one of the Egyptian taskmasters, whom he found abusing his Hebrew slave, a relation (as some think) of Moses, a man of the same tribe. It was by special warrant from Heaven (which makes not a precedent in ordinary cases) that Moses slew the Egyptian, and rescued his oppressed brother. The Jews' tradition is that he did not slay him with any weapon, but, as Peter slew Ananias and Sapphira, with the word of his mouth. His *hiding him in the sand* signified that hereafter Pharaoh and all his Egyptians should, under the control of the rod of Moses, be buried in the sand of the Red Sea. His taking care to execute this justice privately, when no man saw, was a piece of needful prudence and caution, it being but an assay; and perhaps his faith was as yet

weak, and what he did was with some hesitation. Those who come to be of great faith, yet began with a little, and at first spoke tremblingly.

2. Moses was afterwards to be employed in governing Israel, and, as a specimen of this, we have him here trying to end a controversy between two Hebrews, in which he is forced (as he did afterwards for forty years) to suffer their manners. Observe here,

(1.) The unhappy quarrel which Moses observed between two Hebrews, *v.* 13. It does not appear what was the occasion; but, whatever it was, it was certainly very unseasonable for Hebrews to strive with one another when they were all oppressed and ruled with rigour by the Egyptians. Had they not beating enough from the Egyptians, but they must beat one another? Note, [1.] Even sufferings in common do not always unite God's professing people to one another, so much as one might reasonably expect. [2.] When God raises up instruments of salvation for the church they will find enough to do, not only with oppressing Egyptians, to restrain them, but with quarrelsome Israelites, to reconcile them.

(2.) The way he took of dealing with them; he marked him that caused the division, that did the wrong, and mildly reasoned with him: *Wherefore smitest thou thy fellow?* The injurious Egyptian was killed, the injurious Hebrew was only reprimanded; for what the former did was from a rooted malice, what the latter did we may suppose was only upon a sudden provocation. The wise God makes, and, according to his example, all wise governors make, a difference between one offender and another, according to the several qualities of the same offence. Moses endeavoured to make them friends, a good office; thus we find Christ often reproving his disciples' strifes (Luke ix. 46, &c.; xxii. 24, &c.), for he was a prophet like unto Moses, a healing prophet, a peacemaker, who visited his brethren with a design to slay all enmities. The reproof Moses gave on this occasion may still be of use, *Wherefore smitest thou thy fellow?* Note, Smiting our fellows is bad in any, especially in Hebrews, smiting with tongue or hand, either in a way of persecution or in a way of strife and contention. Consider the person thou smitest; it is thy fellow, thy fellow-creature, thy fellow-christian, it is thy fellow-servant, thy fellow-sufferer. Consider the cause, *Wherefore smitest?* Perhaps it is for no cause at all, or no just cause, or none worth speaking of.

(3.) The ill success of his attempt (*v.* 14): *He said, Who made thee a prince?* He that did the wrong thus quarrelled with Moses; the injured party, it should seem, was inclinable enough to peace, but the wrong-doer was thus touchy. Note, It is a sign of guilt to be impatient of reproof; and it is often easier to persuade the injured to bear the

trouble of taking wrong than the injurious to bear the conviction of having *done wrong,* 1 Cor. vi. 7, 8. It was a very wise and mild reproof which Moses gave to this quarrelsome Hebrew, but he could not bear it, he kicked against the pricks (Acts ix. 5), and crossed questions with his reprover. [1.] He challenges his authority: *Who made thee a prince?* A man needs no great authority for the giving of a friendly reproof, it is an act of kindness; yet this man needs will interpret it an act of dominion, and represents his reprover as imperious and assuming. Thus when people dislike good discourse, or a seasonable admonition, they will call it *preaching,* as if a man could not speak a word for God and against sin but he took too much upon him. Yet Moses was indeed a prince and a judge, and knew it, and thought the Hebrews would have understood it, and struck in with him; but they stood in their own light, and *thrust him away,* Acts vii. 25, 27. [2.] He upbraids him with what he had done in killing the Egyptian: *Intendest thou to kill me?* See what base constructions malice puts upon the best words and actions. Moses, for reproving him, is immediately charged with a design to kill him. An attempt upon his sin was interpreted an attempt upon his life; and his having killed the Egyptian was thought sufficient to justify the suspicion; as if Moses made no difference between an Egyptian and a Hebrew. If Moses, to right an injured Hebrew, had put his life in his hand, and slain an Egyptian, he ought therefore to have submitted to him, not only as a friend to the Hebrews, but as a friend that had more than ordinary power and zeal. But he throws that in his teeth as a crime which was bravely done, and was intended as a specimen of the promised deliverance; if the Hebrews had taken the hint, and come in to Moses as their head and captain, it is probable that they would have been delivered now; but, despising their deliverer, their deliverance was justly deferred, and their bondage prolonged forty years, as afterwards their despising Canaan kept them out of it forty years more. *I would, and you would not.* Note, Men know not what they do, nor what enemies they are to their own interest, when they resist and despise faithful reproofs and reprovers. When the Hebrews strove with Moses, God sent him away into Midian, and they never heard of him for forty years; thus the things that belonged to their peace were hidden from their eyes, because they knew not the day of their visitation. As to Moses, we may look on it as a great damp and discouragement to him. He was now *choosing to suffer affliction with the people of God,* and embracing *the reproach of Christ;* and now, at his first setting out, to meet with this affliction and reproach from them was a very sore trial of his resolution. He might have said, "If this be the spirit of the Hebrews, I will go to court again, and be the son of Pharaoh's daughter." Note, *First,* We must take heed of being prejudiced against the ways and people of God by the follies and peevishness of some particular persons that profess religion. *Secondly,* It is no new thing for the church's best friends to meet with a great deal of opposition and discouragement in their healing, saving attempts, even from their own mother's children ; Christ himself was set at nought by the builders, and is still rejected by those he would save.

(4.) The flight of Moses to Midian, in consequence. The affront given him thus far proved a kindness to him; it gave him to understand that his killing the Egyptian was discovered, and so he had time to make his escape, otherwise the wrath of Pharaoh might have surprised him and taken him off. Note, God can overrule even the strife of tongues, so as, one way or other, to bring good to his people out of it. Information was brought to Pharaoh (and it is well if it was not brought by the Hebrew himself whom Moses reproved) of his killing the Egyptian; warrants are presently out for the apprehending of Moses, which obliged him to shift for his own safety, by flying into the land of Midian, *v.* 15. [1.] Moses did this out of a prudent care of his own life. If this be his forsaking of Egypt which the apostle refers to as done by faith (Heb. xi. 27), it teaches us that when we are at any time in trouble and danger for doing our duty the grace of faith will be of good use to us in taking proper methods for our own preservation. Yet there it is said, *He feared not the wrath of the king ;* here it is said he *feared, v.* 14. He did not fear with a fear of diffidence and amazement, which weakens and has torment, but with a fear of diligence, which quickened him to take that way which Providence opened to him for his own preservation. [2.] God ordered it for wise and holy ends. Things were not yet ripe for Israel's deliverance : the measure of Egypt's iniquity was not yet full; the Hebrews were not sufficiently humbled, nor were they yet increased to such a multitude as God designed ; Moses is to be further fitted for the service, and therefore is directed to withdraw for the present, till the time to favour Israel, even the set time, should come. God guided Moses to Midian because the Midianites were of the seed of Abraham, and retained the worship of the true God among them, so that he might have not only a safe but a comfortable settlement among them. And through this country he was afterwards to lead Israel, with which (that he might do it the better) he now had opportunity of making himself acquainted. Hither he came, and sat down by a well, tired and thoughtful, at a loss, and waiting to see which way Providence would direct him. It was a great change with him,

278

since he was but the other day at ease in Pharaoh's court : thus God tried his faith, and it was found to praise and honour.

16 Now the priest of Midian had seven daughters : and they came and drew *water,* and filled the troughs to water their father's flock. 17 And the shepherds came and drove them away: but Moses stood up and helped them, and watered their flock. 18 And when they came to Reuel their father, he said, How *is it that* ye are come so soon to day ? 19 And they said, An Egyptian delivered us out of the hand of the shepherds, and also drew *water* enough for us, and watered the flock. 20 And he said unto his daughters, And where *is* he ? why *is* it *that* ye have left the man ? call him, that he may eat bread. 21 And Moses was content to dwell with the man : and he gave Moses Zipporah his daughter. 22 And she bare *him* a son, and he called his name Gershom : for he said, I have been a stranger in a strange land.

Moses here gains a settlement in Midian, just as his father Jacob had gained one in Syria, Gen. xxix. 2, &c. And both these instances should encourage us to trust Providence, and to follow it. Events that seem inconsiderable, and purely accidental, afterwards appear to have been designed by the wisdom of God for very good purposes, and of great consequence to his people. A casual transient occurrence has sometimes occasioned the greatest and happiest turns of a man's life. Observe,

I. Concerning the seven daughters of Reuel the priest or prince of Midian. 1. They were humble, and very industrious, according as the employment of the country was : they *drew water for their father's flock, v.* 16. If their father was a prince, it teaches us that even those who are honourably born, and are of quality and distinction in their country, should yet apply themselves to some useful business, and what their hand finds to do do it with all their might. Idleness can be no one's honour. If their father was a priest, it teaches us that ministers' children should, in a special manner, be examples of humility and industry. 2. They were modest, and would not ask this strange Egyptian to come home with them (though handsome and a great courtier), till their father sent for him. Modesty is the ornament of woman.

II. Concerning Moses. He was taken for an Egyptian (*v.* 19); and strangers must be content to be the subjects of mistake; but it is observable, 1. How ready he was to help Reuel's daughters to water their flocks. Though bred in learning and at court, yet he knew how to turn his hand to such an office as this when there was occasion ; nor had he learned of the Egyptians to despise shepherds. Note, Those that have had a liberal education yet should not be strangers to servile work, because they know not what necessity Providence may put them in of working for themselves, or what opportunity Providence may give them of being serviceable to others. These young women, it seems, met with some opposition in their employment, more than they and their servants could conquer ; the shepherds of some neighbouring prince, as some think, or some idle fellows that called themselves shepherds, *drove away their flocks ;* but Moses, though melancholy and in distress, *stood up and helped them,* not only to get clear of the shepherds, but, when that was done, to water the flocks. This he did, not only in complaisance to the daughters of Reuel (though that also did very well become him), but because, wherever he was, as occasion offered itself, (1.) He loved to be doing justice, and appearing in the defence of such as he saw injured, which every man ought to do as far as it is in the power of his hand to do it. (2.) He loved to be doing good. Wherever the Providence of God casts us we should desire and endeavour to be useful ; and, when we cannot do the good we would, we must be ready to do the good we can. And he that is faithful in a little shall be entrusted with more. 2. How well he was paid for his serviceableness. When the young women acquainted their father with the kindnesses they had received from this stranger, he sent to invite him to his house, and made much of him, *v.* 20. Thus God will recompense the kindnesses which are at any time shown to his children ; they shall in no wise lose their reward. Moses soon recommended himself to the esteem and good affection of this prince of Midian, who took him into his house, and, in process of time, married one of his daughters to him (*v.* 21), by whom he had a son, whom he called *Gershom, a stranger there* (*v.* 22), that if ever God should give him a home of his own he might keep in remembrance the land in which he had been a stranger. Now this settlement of Moses in Midian was designed by Providence, (1.) To shelter him for the present. God will find hiding-places for his people in the day of their distress ; nay, he will himself be to them a little sanctuary, and will secure them, either under heaven or in heaven. But, (2.) It was also designed to prepare him for the great services he was further designed for. His manner of life in Midian, where he kept the flock of his father-in-law (having none of his own to keep), would be of use to him, [1.] To inure him to hardship and poverty, that he might learn how to want as well as how to abound. Those whom God intends to exalt he first humbles. [2.] To inure him to contempla-

tion and devotion. Egypt accomplished him as a scholar, a gentleman, a statesman, a soldier, all which accomplishments would be afterwards of use to him ; but yet he lacked one thing, in which the court of Egypt could not befriend him. He that was to do all by divine revelation must know, by a long experience, what it was to live a life of communion with God ; and in this he would be greatly furthered by the solitude and retirement of a shepherd's life in Midian. By the former he was prepared to rule in Jeshurun, but by the latter he was prepared to converse with God in Mount Horeb, near which mount he had spent much of his time. Those that know what it is to be alone with God in holy exercises are acquainted with better delights than ever Moses tasted in the court of Pharaoh.

23 And it came to pass in process of time, that the king of Egypt died : and the children of Israel sighed by reason of the bondage, and they cried, and their cry came up unto God by reason of the bondage. 24 And God heard their groaning, and God remembered his covenant with Abraham, with Isaac, and with Jacob. 25 And God looked upon the children of Israel, and God had respect unto *them.*

Here is, 1. The continuance of the Israelites' bondage in Egypt, *v.* 23. Probably the murdering of their infants did not continue; this part of their affliction attended only the period immediately connected with the birth of Moses, and served to signalize it. The Egyptians now were content with their increase, finding that Egypt was enriched by their labour ; so that they might have them for slaves, they cared not how many they were. On this therefore they were intent, to keep them all at work, and make the best hand they could of their labour. When one Pharaoh died, another rose up in his place that was governed by the same maxims, and was as cruel to Israel as his predecessors. If there was sometimes a little relaxation, yet it presently revived again with as much rigour as ever ; and probably, as the more Israel were oppressed the more they multiplied, so the more they multiplied the more they were oppressed. Note, Sometimes God suffers the rod of the wicked to lie very long and very heavily on the lot of the righteous. If Moses, in Midian, at any time began to think how much better his condition might have been had he staid among the courtiers, he must of himself think this also, how much worse it would have been if he had had his lot with his brethren : it was a great degradation to him to be keeping sheep in Midian, but better so than making brick in Egypt. The consideration of our brethren's afflictions would help to reconcile us to our own. 2. The preface to their deliverance at last. (1.) *They cried, v.* 23. Now, at last, they began to think of God under their troubles, and to return to him from the idols they had served, Ezek. xx. 8. Hitherto they had fretted at the instruments of their trouble, but God was not in all their thoughts. Thus *hypocrites in heart heap up wrath; they cry not when he binds them*, Job xxxvi. 13. But before God unbound them he put it into their hearts to cry unto him, as it is explained, Num. xx. 16. Note, It is a good sign that God is coming towards us with deliverance when he inclines and enables us to cry to him for it. (2.) *God heard, v.* 24, 25. The name of God is here emphatically prefixed to four different expressions of a kind intention towards them. [1.] *God heard their groaning;* that is, he made it to appear that he took notice of their complaints. The groans of the oppressed cry aloud in the ears of the righteous God, to whom vengeance belongs, especially the groans of God's spiritual Israel; he knows the burdens they groan under and the blessings they groan after, and that the blessed Spirit, by these groanings, makes intercession in them. [2.] *God remembered his covenant*, which he seemed to have forgotten, but of which he is ever mindful. This God had an eye to, and not to any merit of theirs, in what he did for them. See Lev. xxvi. 42. (3.) *God looked upon the children of Israel.* Moses looked upon them and pitied them (*v.* 11); but now God looked upon them and helped them. (4.) *God had a respect unto them*, a favourable respect to them as his own. The frequent repetition of the name of God here intimates that now we are to expect something great, *Opus Deo dignum—A work worthy of God.* His eyes, which run to and fro through the earth, are now fixed upon Israel, to show himself strong, to show himself a God in their behalf.

CHAP. III.

As prophecy had ceased for many ages before the coming of Christ, that the revival and perfection of it in that great prophet might be the more remarkable, so vision had ceased (for aught that appears) among the patriarchs for some ages before the coming of Moses, that God's appearances to him for Israel's salvation might be the more welcome; and in this chapter we have God's first appearance to him in the bush and the conference between God and Moses in that vision. Here is, I. The discovery God was pleased to make of his glory to Moses at the bush, to which Moses was forbidden to approach too near, ver. 1—5. II. A general declaration of God's grace and good-will to his people, who were beloved for their fathers' sakes, ver. 6. III. A particular notification of God's purpose concerning the deliverance of Israel out of Egypt. 1. He assures Moses it should now be done, ver. 7—9. 2. He gives him a commission to act in it as his ambassador both to Pharaoh (ver. 10) and to Israel, ver. 16. 3. He answers the objection Moses made of his own unworthiness, ver. 11, 12. 4. He gives him full instructions what to say both to Pharaoh and to Israel, ver. 13—18. 5. He tells him beforehand what the issue would be, ver. 19, &c.

NOW Moses kept the flock of Jethro his father in law, the priest of Midian: and he led the flock to the backside of the desert, and came to the mountain of God, *even* to Horeb. 2 And the angel of the LORD appeared unto him in a flame of fire out of the midst of a bush: and he

looked, and, behold, the bush burned with fire, and the bush *was* not consumed. 3 And Moses said, I will now turn aside, and see this great sight, why the bush is not burnt. 4 And when the LORD saw that he turned aside to see, God called unto him out of the midst of the bush, and said, Moses, Moses. And he said, Here *am* I. 5 And he said, Draw not nigh hither: put off thy shoes from off thy feet, for the place whereon thou standest *is* holy ground. 6 Moreover he said, I *am* the God of thy father, the God of Abraham, the God of Isaac, and the God of Jacob. And Moses hid his face; for he was afraid to look upon God.

The years of the life of Moses are remarkably divided into three forties: the first forty he spent as a prince in Pharaoh's court, the second a shepherd in Midian, the third a king in Jeshurun; so changeable is the life of men, especially the life of good men. He had now finished his second forty, when he received his commission to bring Israel out of Egypt. Note, Sometimes it is long before God calls his servants out to that work which of old he designed them for, and has been graciously preparing them for. Moses was born to be Israel's deliverer, and yet not a word is said of it to him till he is eighty years of age. Now observe,

I. How this appearance of God to him found him employed. He was keeping the flock (tending sheep) near mount Horeb, *v.* 1. This was a poor employment for a man of his parts and education, yet he rests satisfied with it, and thus learns meekness and contentment to a high degree, for which he is more celebrated in sacred writ than for all his other learning. Note, 1. In the calling to which we are called we should abide, and not be given to change. 2. Even those that are qualified for great employments and services must not think it strange if they be confined to obscurity; it was the lot of Moses before them, who foresaw nothing to the contrary but that he should die, as he had lived a great while, a poor despicable shepherd. Let those that think themselves buried alive be content to shine like lamps in their sepulchres, and wait till God's time come for setting them on a candlestick. Thus employed Moses was, when he was honoured with this vision. Note, (1.) God will encourage industry. The shepherds were keeping their flocks when they received the tidings of our Saviour's birth, Luke ii. 8. Satan loves to find us idle; God is well pleased when he finds us employed. (2.) Retirement is a good friend to our communion with God. When we are alone, the Father is with us.

Moses saw more of God in a desert than ever he had seen in Pharaoh's court.

II. What the appearance was. To his great surprise he saw a bush burning, when he perceived no fire either from earth or heaven to kindle it, and, which was more strange, it did not consume, v. 2. It was an angel of the Lord that appeared to him; some think, a created angel, who speaks in the language of him that sent him; others, the second person, the angel of the covenant, who is himself Jehovah. It was an extraordinary manifestation of the divine presence and glory; what was visible was produced by the ministry of an angel, but he heard God in it speaking to him. 1. He saw a flame of fire; *for our God is a consuming fire.* When Israel's deliverance out of Egypt was promised to Abraham, he saw a burning lamp, which signified the light of joy which that deliverance should cause (Gen. xv. 17); but now it shines brighter, as a flame of fire, for God in that deliverance brought terror and destruction to his enemies, light and heat to his people, and displayed his glory before all. See Isa. x. 17. 2. This fire was not in a tall and stately cedar, but in a bush, *a thorny bush,* so the word signifies; for God chooses the weak and despised things of the world (such as Moses, now a poor shepherd), with them to confound the wise; he delights to beautify and crown the humble. 3. *The bush burned,* and yet *was not consumed,* an emblem of the church now in bondage in Egypt, burning in the brick-kilns, yet not consumed; perplexed, but not in despair; cast down, but not destroyed.

III. The curiosity Moses had to enquire into this extraordinary sight: *I will turn aside and see, v. 3.* He speaks as one inquisitive and bold in his enquiry; whatever it was, he would, if possible, know the meaning of it. Note, Things revealed belong to us, and we ought diligently to enquire into them.

IV. The invitation he had to draw near, yet with a caution not to come too near, nor rashly.

1. God gave him a gracious call, to which he returned a ready answer, v. 4. When God saw that he took notice of the burning bush, and turned aside to see it, and left his business to attend it, then God called to him. If he had carelessly neglected it as an *ignis fatuus—a deceiving meteor,* a thing not worth taking notice of, it is probable that God would have departed, and said nothing to him; but, when he turned aside, God called to him. Note, Those that would have communion with God must attend upon him, and approach to him, in those ordinances wherein he is pleased to manifest himself, and his power and glory, though it be in a bush; they must come to the treasure, though in an earthen vessel. Those that seek God diligently shall find him, and find him their bountiful rewarder. *Draw nigh to God, and he will draw nigh to you.* God called him by name, *Moses, Moses.* This

which he heard could not but surprise him much more than what he saw. The word of the Lord always went along with the glory of the Lord, for every divine vision was designed for divine revelation, Job iv. 16, &c.; xxxiii. 14—16. Divine calls are then effectual, (1.) When the Spirit of God makes them particular, and calls us by name. The word calls, Ho, every one! The Spirit, by the application of that, calls, Ho, such a one! *I know thee by name,* Exod. xxxiii. 12. (2.) When we return an obedient answer to them, as Moses here, "*Here am I, what saith my Lord unto his servant? Here am I,* not only to hear what is said, but to do what I am bidden."

2. God gave him a needful caution against rashness and irreverence in his approach, (1.) He must keep his distance; draw near, but not too near; so near as to hear, but not so near as to pry. His conscience must be satisfied, but not his curiosity; and care must be taken that familiarity do not breed contempt. Note, In all our approaches to God, we ought to be deeply affected with the infinite distance there is between us and God, Eccl. v. 2. Or this may be taken as proper to the Old-Testament dispensation, which was a dispensation of darkness, bondage, and terror, from which the gospel happily frees us, giving us boldness to enter into the holiest, and inviting us to draw near. (2.) He must express his reverence, and his readiness to obey: *Put off thy shoes from off thy feet,* as a servant. Putting off the shoe was then what putting off the hat is now, a token of respect and submission. "The ground, for the present, is *holy ground,* made so by this special manifestation of the divine presence, during the continuance of which it must retain this character; therefore tread not on that ground with soiled shoes." *Keep thy foot,* Eccl. v. 1. Note, We ought to approach to God with a solemn pause and preparation; and, though bodily exercise alone profits little, yet we ought to glorify God with our bodies, and to express our inward reverence by a grave and reverent behaviour in the worship of God, carefully avoiding every thing that looks light, and rude, and unbecoming the awfulness of the service.

V. The solemn declaration God made of his name, by which he would be known to Moses: *I am the God of thy father, v. 6.* 1. He lets him know that it is God who speaks to him, to engage his reverence and attention, his faith and obedience; for this is enough to command all these: *I am the Lord.* Let us always hear the word *as the word of God,* 1 Thess. ii. 13. 2. He will be known as the God of his father, his pious father Amram, and the God of Abraham, Isaac, and Jacob, his ancestors, and the ancestors of all Israel, for whom God was now about to appear. By this God designed, (1.) To instruct Moses in the knowledge of another world, and to strengthen his belief of a future state. Thus it is interpreted by our Lord Jesus, the best expositor of scripture, who from this proves that the dead are raised, against the Sadducees. *Moses, says he, showed it at the bush* (Luke xx. 37), that is, God there showed it to him, and in him to us, Matt. xxii. 31, &c. Abraham was dead, and yet God is the God of Abraham; therefore Abraham's soul lives, to which God stands in relation; and, to make his soul completely happy, his body must live again in due time. This promise made unto the fathers, that God would be their God, must include a future happiness; for he never did any thing for them in this world sufficient to answer to the vast extent and compass of that great word, but, having prepared for them a city, he is not ashamed to be called their God, Heb. xi. 16; and see Acts xxvi. 6, 7; xxiv. 15. (2.) To assure Moses of the fulfilment of all those particular promises made to the fathers. He may confidently expect this, for by these words it appears that God remembered his covenant, *ch.* ii. 24. Note, [1.] God's covenant-relation to us as our God is the best support in the worst of times, and a great encouragement to our faith in particular promises. [2.] When we are conscious to ourselves of our own great unworthiness we may take comfort from God's relation to our fathers, 2 Chron. xx. 6.

VI. The solemn impression this made upon Moses: He *hid his face*, as one both ashamed and afraid to look upon God. Now that he knew it was a divine light his eyes were dazzled with it; he was not afraid of a burning bush till he perceived that God was in it. Yea, though God called himself *the God of his father*, and a God in covenant with him, yet he was afraid. Note, 1. The more we see of God the more cause we shall see to worship him with reverence and godly fear. 2. Even the manifestations of God's grace and covenant-love should increase our humble reverence of him.

7 And the LORD said, I have surely seen the affliction of my people which *are* in Egypt, and have heard their cry by reason of their taskmasters; for I know their sorrows; 8 And I am come down to deliver them out of the hand of the Egyptians, and to bring them up out of that land unto a good land and a large, unto a land flowing with milk and honey; unto the place of the Canaanites, and the Hittites, and the Amorites, and the Perizzites, and the Hivites, and the Jebusites. 9 Now therefore, behold, the cry of the children of Israel is come unto me: and I have also seen the oppression wherewith the Egyptians oppress them. 10 Come now therefore, and I will send thee unto Pharaoh, that

thou mayest bring forth my people the children of Israel out of Egypt.

Now that Moses had put off his shoes (for, no doubt, he observed the orders given him, *v.* 5), and covered his face, God enters upon the particular business that was now to be concerted, which was the bringing of Israel out of Egypt. Now, after forty years of Israel's bondage and Moses's banishment, when we may suppose both he and they began to despair, they of being delivered and he of delivering them, at length, the time has come, even the year of the redeemed. Note, God often comes for the salvation of his people when they have done looking for him. *Shall he find faith?* Luke xviii. 8.

Here is, I. The notice God takes of the afflictions of Israel (*v.* 7, 9): *Seeing I have seen*, not only, *I have surely seen*, but I have strictly observed and considered the matter. Three things God took cognizance of:—1. *Their sorrows, v.* 7. It is likely they were not permitted to make a remonstrance of their grievances to Pharaoh, nor to seek relief against their task-masters in any of his courts, nor scarcely durst complain to one another; but God observed their tears. Note, Even the secret sorrows of God's people are known to him. 2. Their cry: *I have heard their cry (v.* 7), *it has come unto me, v.* 9. Note, God is not deaf to the cries of his afflicted people. 3. The tyranny of their persecutors: *I have seen the oppression, v.* 9. Note, As the poorest of the oppressed are not below God's cognizance, so the highest and greatest of their oppressors are not above his check, but he will surely visit for these things.

II. The promise God makes of their speedy deliverance and enlargement: *I have come down to deliver them, v.* 8. 1. It denotes his resolution to deliver them, and that his heart was upon it, so that it should be done speedily and effectually, and by methods out of the common road of providence: when God does something very extraordinary he is said to *come down* to do it, as Isa. lxiv. 1. 2. This deliverance was typical of our redemption by Christ, in which the eternal Word did indeed come down from heaven to deliver us: it was his errand into the world. He promises also their happy settlement in the land of Canaan, that they should exchange bondage for liberty, poverty for plenty, labour for rest, and the precarious condition of tenants at will for the ease and honour of lords proprietors. Note, Whom God by his grace delivers out of a spiritual Egypt he will bring to a heavenly Canaan.

III. The commission he gives to Moses in order hereunto, *v.* 10. He is not only sent as a prophet to Israel, to assure them that they should speedily be delivered (even that would have been a great favour), but he is sent as an ambassador to Pharaoh, to treat with him, or rather as a herald at arms, to demand their discharge, and to denounce war in case of refusal; and he is sent as a prince to Israel, to conduct and command them. Thus is he taken from *following the ewes great with young,* to a pastoral office much more noble, as David, Ps. lxxviii. 71. Note, God is the fountain of power, and the powers that be are ordained of him as he pleases. The same hand that now fetched a shepherd out of a desert, to be the planter of a Jewish church, afterwards fetched fishermen from their ships, to be the planters of the Christian church, *That the excellency of the power might be of God.*

11 And Moses said unto God, Who *am* I, that I should go unto Pharaoh, and that I should bring forth the children of Israel out of Egypt? 12 And he said, Certainly I will be with thee; and this *shall be* a token unto thee, that I have sent thee: When thou hast brought forth the people out of Egypt, ye shall serve God upon this mountain. 13 And Moses said unto God, Behold, *when* I come unto the children of Israel, and shall say unto them, The God of your fathers hath sent me unto you; and they shall say to me, What *is* his name? what shall I say unto them? 14 And God said unto Moses, I AM THAT I AM: And he said, Thus shalt thou say unto the children of Israel, I AM hath sent me unto you. 15 And God said moreover unto Moses, Thus shalt thou say unto the children of Israel, The Lord God of your fathers, the God of Abraham, the God of Isaac, and the God of Jacob, hath sent me unto you: this *is* my name for ever, and this *is* my memorial unto all generations.

God, having spoken to Moses, allows him also a liberty of speech, which he here improves; and,

I. He objects his own insufficiency for the service he was called to (v. 11): *Who am I?* He thinks himself unworthy of the honour, and not *par negotio—equal to the task.* He thinks he wants courage, and therefore cannot go to Pharaoh, to make a demand which might cost the demandant his head: he thinks he wants skill, and therefore cannot bring forth the children of Israel out of Egypt; they are unarmed, undisciplined, quite dispirited, utterly unable to help themselves; it is morally impossible to bring them out. 1. Moses was incomparably the fittest of any man living for this work, eminent for learning, wisdom, experience, valour, faith, holiness; and yet he says, *Who am I?* Note, The more fit any person is for service commonly the less opinion he has of himself: see Judg. ix. 8, &c.

2. The difficulties of the work were indeed very great, enough to startle the courage and stagger the faith of Moses himself. Note, Even wise and faithful instruments may be much discouraged at the difficulties that lie in the way of the church's salvation. 3. Moses had formerly been very courageous when he slew the Egyptian, but now his heart failed him; for good men are not always alike bold and zealous. 4. Yet Moses is the man that does it at last; for God gives grace to the lowly. Modest beginnings are very good presages.

II. God answers this objection, v. 12. 1. He promises him his presence: *Certainly I will be with thee,* and that is enough. Note, Those that are weak in themselves may yet do wonders, being strong in the Lord and in the power of his might; and those that are most diffident of themselves may be most confident in God. God's presence puts an honour upon the worthless, wisdom and strength into the weak and foolish, makes the greatest difficulties dwindle to nothing, and is enough to answer all objections. 2. He assures him of success, and that the Israelites should serve God upon this mountain. Note, (1.) Those deliverances are most valuable which open to us a door of liberty to serve God. (2.) If God gives us opportunity and a heart to serve him, it is a happy and encouraging earnest of further favours designed us.

III. He begs instructions for the executing of his commission, and has them, thoroughly to furnish him. He desires to know by what name God would at this time make himself known, v. 13.

1. He supposes the children of Israel would ask him, *What is his name?* This they would ask either, (1.) To perplex Moses: he foresaw difficulty, not only in dealing with Pharaoh, to make him willing to part with them, but in dealing with them, to make them willing to remove. They would be scrupulous and apt to cavil, would bid him produce his commission, and probably this would be the trial: "Does he know the name of God? Has he the watch-word?" Once he was asked, *Who made thee a judge?* Then he had not his answer ready, and he would not be nonplussed so again, but would be able to tell in whose name he came. Or, (2.) For their own information. It is to be feared that they had grown very ignorant in Egypt, by reason of their hard bondage, want of teachers, and loss of the sabbath, so that they needed to be told the first principles of the oracles of God. Or this question, *What is his name?* amounted to an enquiry into the nature of the dispensation they were now to expect: "How will God in it be known to us, and what may we depend upon from him?"

2. He desires instructions what answer to give them: "*What shall I say to them?* What name shall I vouch to them for the proof of my authority? I must have something great

283

and extraordinary to say to them; what must it be? If I must go, let me have full instructions, that I may not run in vain." Note, (1.) It highly concerns those who speak to people in the name of God to be well prepared beforehand. (2.) Those who would know what to say must go to God, to the word of his grace and to the throne of his grace, for instructions, Ezek. ii. 7; iii. 4, 10, 17. (3.) Whenever we have any thing to do with God, it is desirable to know, and our duty to consider, what is his name.

IV. God readily gives him full instructions in this matter. Two names God would now be known by:—

1. A name that denotes what he is in himself (v. 14): *I am that I am.* This explains his name *Jehovah*, and signifies, (1.) That he is self-existent; he has his being of himself, and has no dependence upon any other: the greatest and best man in the world must say, By the grace of God *I am what I am;* but God says absolutely—and it is more than any creature, man or angel, can say—*I am that I am.* Being self-existent, he cannot but be self-sufficient, and therefore all-sufficient, and the inexhaustible fountain of being and bliss. (2.) That he is eternal and unchangeable, and always the same, yesterday, to-day, and for ever; he will be what he will be and what he is; see Rev. i. 8. (3.) That we cannot by searching find him out. This is such a name as checks all bold and curious enquiries concerning God, and in effect says, *Ask not after my name, seeing it is secret,* Judg. xiii. 18; Prov. xxx. 4. Do we ask what is God? Let it suffice us to know that he is what he is, what he ever was, and ever will be. *How little a portion is heard of him!* Job xxvi. 14. (4.) That he is faithful and true to all his promises, unchangeable in his word as well as in his nature, and not a man that he should lie. Let Israel know this, *I AM hath sent me unto you.*

2. A name that denotes what he is to his people. Lest that name *I AM* should amuse and puzzle them, he is further directed to make use of another name of God more familiar and intelligible : *The Lord God of your fathers hath sent me unto you (v.* 15) : Thus God had made himself known to him (v. 6), and thus he must make him known to them, (1.) That he might revive among them the religion of their fathers, which, it is to be feared, was much decayed and almost lost. This was necessary to prepare them for deliverance, Ps. lxxx. 19. (2.) That he might raise their expectations of the speedy performance of the promises made unto their fathers. Abraham, Isaac, and Jacob, are particularly named, because with Abraham the covenant was first made, and with Isaac and Jacob often expressly renewed; and these three were distinguished from their brethren, and chosen to be the trustees of the covenant, when their brethren were rejected. God will have this to be his name for ever, and it has

been, is, and will be, his name, by which his worshippers know him, and distinguish him from all false gods; see 1 Kings xviii. 36. Note, God's covenant-relation to his people is what he will be ever mindful of, what he glories in, and what he will have us never forget, but give him the glory of: if he will have this to be his memorial unto all generations, we have all the reason in the world to make it so with us, for it is a precious memorial.

16 Go, and gather the elders of Israel together, and say unto them, The LORD God of your fathers, the God of Abraham, of Isaac, and of Jacob, appeared unto me, saying, I have surely visited you, and *seen* that which is done to you in Egypt: 17 And I have said, I will bring you up out of the affliction of Egypt unto the land of the Canaanites, and the Hittites, and the Amorites, and the Perizzites, and the Hivites, and the Jebusites, unto a land flowing with milk and honey. 18 And they shall hearken to thy voice: and thou shalt come, thou and the elders of Israel, unto the king of Egypt, and ye shall say unto him, The LORD God of the Hebrews hath met with us: and now let us go, we beseech thee, three days' journey into the wilderness, that we may sacrifice to the LORD our God. 19 And I am sure that the king of Egypt will not let you go, no, not by a mighty hand. 20 And I will stretch out my hand, and smite Egypt with all my wonders which I will do in the midst thereof: and after that he will let you go. 21 And I will give this people favour in the sight of the Egyptians: and it shall come to pass, that, when ye go, ye shall not go empty: 22 But every woman shall borrow of her neighbour, and of her that sojourneth in her house, jewels of silver, and jewels of gold, and raiment: and ye shall put *them* upon your sons, and upon your daughters; and ye shall spoil the Egyptians.

Moses is here more particularly instructed in his work, and informed beforehand of his success. 1. He must deal with the elders of Israel, and raise their expectations of a speedy removal to Canaan, v. 16, 17. He must repeat to them what God had said to him, as a faithful ambassador. Note, That which ministers have received of the Lord they must deliver to his people, and keep back nothing that is profitable. Lay an emphasis on that, *v.* 17 : "*I have said, I will bring you up ;* this is enough to satisfy them, *I have said it :*" hath he spoken, and will he not make it good? With us saying and doing are two things, but they are not so with God, for he is in one mind and who can turn him? "I have said it, and all the world cannot gainsay it. My counsel shall stand." His success with the elders of Israel would be good; so he is told (*v.* 18): *They shall hearken to thy voice,* and not thrust thee away as they did forty years ago. He who, by his grace, inclines the heart, and opens the ear, could say beforehand, *They shall hearken to thy voice,* having determined to make them willing in this day of power. 2. He must deal with the king of Egypt (*v.* 18), he and the elders of Israel, and in this they must not begin with a demand, but with a humble petition ; that gentle and submissive method must be first tried, even with one who, it was certain, would not be wrought upon by it : *We beseech thee, let us go.* Moreover, they must only beg leave of Pharaoh to go as far as Mount Sinai to worship God, and say nothing to him of going quite away to Canaan; the latter would have been immediately rejected, but the former was a very modest and reasonable request, and his denying it was utterly inexcusable and justified them in the total deserting of his kingdom. If he would not give them leave to go and sacrifice at Sinai, justly did they go without leave to settle in Canaan. Note, The calls and commands which God sends to sinners are so highly reasonable in themselves, and delivered to them in such a gentle winning way, that the mouth of the disobedient must needs be for ever stopped. As to his success with Pharaoh, Moses is here told, (1.) That petitions, and persuasions, and humble remonstrances, would not prevail with him, no, nor a mighty hand stretched out in signs and wonders: *I am sure he will not let you go, v.* 19. Note, God sends his messengers to those whose hardness and obstinacy he certainly knows and foresees, that it may appear he would have them turn and live. (2.) That plagues should compel him to it : *I will smite Egypt,* and then he will *let you go, v.* 20. Note, Those will certainly be broken by the power of God's hand that will not bow to the power of his word ; we may be sure that *when God judges he will overcome.* (3.) That his people should be more kind to them, and furnish them at their departure with abundance of plate and jewels, to their great enriching : *I will give this people favour in the sight of the Egyptians, v.* 21, 22. Note, [1.] God sometimes makes the enemies of his people, not only to be at peace with them, but to be kind to them. [2.] God has many ways of balancing accounts between the injured and the injurious, of righting the oppressed, and compelling those that have done wrong to make restitution ; for he sits in the throne judging right.

This chapter, I. Continues and concludes God's discourse with Moses at the bush concerning this great affair of bringing Israel out of Egypt. 1. Moses objects the people's unbelief (ver. 1), and God answers that objection by giving him a power to work miracles, (1.) To turn his rod into a serpent, and then into a rod again, ver. 2—5. (2.) To make his hand leprous, and then whole again, ver. 6—8. (3.) To turn the water into blood, ver. 9. 2. Moses objects his own slowness of speech (ver. 10), and begs to be excused (ver. 13) ; but God answers this objection, (1.) By promising him his presence, ver. 11, 12. (2.) By joining Aaron in commission with him, ver. 14—16. (3.) By putting an honour upon the very staff in his hand, ver. 17. II. It begins Moses's execution of his commission. 1. He obtains leave of his father-in-law to return into Egypt, ver. 18. 2. He receives further instructions and encouragements from God, ver. 19, 21—23. 3. He hastens his departure, and takes his family with him, ver. 20. 4. He meets with some difficulty in the way about the circumcising of his son, ver. 24—26. 5. He has the satisfaction of meeting his brother Aaron, ver. 27, 28. 6. He produces his commission before the elders of Israel, to their great joy, ver. 29—31. And thus the wheels were set a going towards that great deliverance.

AND Moses answered and said, But, behold, they will not believe me, nor hearken unto my voice: for they will say, The LORD hath not appeared unto thee. 2 And the LORD said unto him, What *is* that in thine hand? And he said, A rod. 3 And he said, Cast it on the ground. And he cast it on the ground, and it became a serpent; and Moses fled from before it. 4 And the LORD said unto Moses, Put forth thine hand, and take it by the tail. And he put forth his hand, and caught it, and it became a rod in his hand : 5 That they may believe that the LORD God of their fathers, the God of Abraham, the God of Isaac, and the God of Jacob, hath appeared unto thee. 6 And the LORD said furthermore unto him, Put now thine hand into thy bosom. And he put his hand into his bosom: and when he took it out, behold, his hand *was* leprous as snow. 7 And he said, Put thine hand into thy bosom again. And he put his hand into his bosom again; and plucked it out of his bosom, and, behold, it was turned again as his *other* flesh. 8 And it shall come to pass, if they will not believe thee, neither hearken to the voice of the first sign, that they will believe the voice of the latter sign. 9 And it shall come to pass, if they will not believe also these two signs, neither hearken unto thy voice, that thou shalt take of the water of the river, and pour *it* upon the dry *land:* and the water which thou takest out of the river shall become blood upon the dry *land.*

It was a very great honour that Moses was called to when God commissioned him to bring Israel out of Egypt; yet he is with difficulty persuaded to accept the commission, and does it at last with great reluctance, which we should rather impute to a humble diffidence of himself and his own sufficiency than to any unbelieving distrust of God and his word and power. Note, Those whom God designs for preferment he clothes with humility ; the most fit for service are the least forward.

I. Moses objects that in all probability the people would not *hearken to his voice* (v. 1), that is, they would not take his bare word, unless he showed them some sign, which he had not been yet instructed to do. This objection cannot be justified, because it contradicts what God had said (*ch.* iii. 18), They *shall hearken to thy voice.* If God says, *They will,* does it become Moses to say, *They will not ?* Surely he means, " Perhaps they will not at first, or some of them will not." If there should be some gainsayers among them who would question his commission, how should he deal with them ? And what course should he take to convince them? He remembered how they had once rejected him, and feared it would be so again. Note, 1. Present discouragements often arise from former disappointments. 2. Wise and good men have sometimes a worse opinion of people than they deserve. Moses said (v. 1), They *will not believe me ;* and yet he was happily mistaken, for it is said (v. 31), The *people believed;* but then the signs which God appointed in answer to this objection were first wrought in their sight.

II. God empowers him to work miracles, directs him to three particularly, two of which were now immediately wrought for his own satisfaction. Note, True miracles are the most convincing external proofs of a divine mission attested by them. Therefore our Saviour often appealed to his works (as John v. 36), and Nicodemus owns himself convinced by them, John iii. 2. And here Moses, having a special commission given him as a judge and lawgiver to Israel, has this seal affixed to his commission, and comes supported by these credentials.

1. The rod in his hand is made the subject of a miracle, a double miracle : it is but thrown out of his hand and it becomes a serpent; he resumes it and it becomes a rod again, v. 2—4. Now, (1.) Here was a divine power manifested in the change itself, that a dry stick should be turned into a living serpent, a lively one, so formidable a one that Moses himself, on whom, it should seem, it turned in some threatening manner, *fled from before it,* though we may suppose, in that desert, serpents were no strange things to him ; but what was produced miraculously was always the best and strongest of the kind, as the water turned to wine: and, then, that this living serpent should be turned into a dry stick again, this was the Lord's doing. (2.) Here was an honour put upon Moses, that this change was wrought upon his throwing it down and taking it up, without

286

any spell, or charm, or incantation : nis being empowered thus to act under God, out of the common course of nature and providence, was a demonstration of his authority, under God, to settle a new dispensation of the kingdom of grace. We cannot imagine that the God of truth would delegate such a power as this to an impostor. (3.) There was a significancy in the miracle itself. Pharaoh had turned the rod of Israel into a serpent, representing them as dangerous (*ch.* i. 10), causing their belly to cleave to the dust, and seeking their ruin ; but now they should be turned into a rod again : or, thus Pharaoh had turned the rod of government into the serpent of oppression, from which Moses had himself fled into Midian ; but by the agency of Moses the scene was altered again. (4.) There was a direct tendency in it to convince the children of Israel that Moses was indeed sent of God to do what he did, v. 5. Miracles were for signs to those that believed not, 1 Cor. xiv. 22.

2. His hand itself is next made the subject of a miracle. He puts it once into his bosom, and takes it out leprous ; he puts it again into the same place, and takes it out well, v. 6, 7. This signified, (1.) That Moses, by the power of God, should bring sore diseases upon Egypt, and that, at his prayer, they should be removed. (2.) That whereas the Israelites in Egypt had become leprous, polluted by sin, and almost consumed by oppression (a leper is *as one dead,* Num. xii. 12), by being taken into the bosom of Moses they should be cleansed and cured, and have all their grievances redressed. (3.) That Moses was not to work miracles by his own power, nor for his own praise, but by the power of God and for his glory ; the leprous hand of Moses does for ever exclude boasting. Now it was supposed that, if the former sign did not convince, this latter would. Note, God is willing more abundantly to show the truth of his word, and is not sparing in his proofs ; the multitude and variety of the miracles corroborate the evidence.

3. He is directed, when he shall come to Egypt, to turn some of the water of the river into blood, v. 9. This was done, at first, as a sign, but, not gaining due credit with Pharaoh, the whole river was afterwards turned into blood, and then it became a plague. He is ordered to work this miracle in case they would not be convinced by the other two. Note, Unbelief shall be left inexcusable, and convicted of a wilful obstinacy. As to the people of Israel, God had said (*ch.* iii. 18), They *shall hearken ;* yet he appoints these miracles to be wrought for their conviction, for he that has ordained the end has ordained the means.

10 And Moses said unto the LORD, O my Lord, I *am* not eloquent, neither heretofore, nor since thou hast spoken unto thy servant : but I *am* slow of

speech, and of a slow tongue. 11 And the LORD said unto him, Who hath made man's mouth? or who maketh the dumb, or deaf, or the seeing, or the blind? have not I the LORD? 12 Now therefore go, and I will be with thy mouth, and teach thee what thou shalt say. 13 And he said, O my Lord, send, I pray thee, by the hand *of him whom* thou wilt send. 14 And the anger of the LORD was kindled against Moses, and he said, *Is* not Aaron the Levite thy brother? I know that he can speak well. And also, behold, he cometh forth to meet thee : and when he seeth thee, he will be glad in his heart. 15 And thou shalt speak unto him, and put words in his mouth: and I will be with thy mouth, and with his mouth, and will teach you what ye shall do. 16 And he shall be thy spokesman unto the people : and he shall be, *even* he shall be to thee instead of a mouth, and thou shalt be to him instead of God. 17 And thou shalt take this rod in thine hand, wherewith thou shalt do signs.

Moses still continues backward to the service for which God had designed him, even to a fault; for now we can no longer impute it to his humility and modesty, but must own that there was too much of cowardice, slothfulness, and unbelief in it. Observe here,

I. How Moses endeavours to excuse himself from the work.

1. He pleads that he was no good spokesman: *O my Lord! I am not eloquent, v.* 10. He was a great philosopher, statesman, and divine, and yet no orator ; a man of a clear head, great thought, and solid judgment, but had not a voluble tongue, or ready utterance, and therefore he thought himself unfit to speak before great men about great affairs, and in danger of being run down by the Egyptians. Observe, (1.) We must not judge of men by the readiness and fluency of their discourse. Moses was *mighty in word* (Acts vii. 22), and yet not eloquent : what he said was strong and nervous, and to the purpose, and distilled as the dew (Deut. xxxii. 2), though he did not deliver himself with that readiness, ease, and elegance, that some do, who have not the tenth part of his sense. St. Paul's speech was contemptible, 2 Cor. x. 10. A great deal of wisdom and true worth is concealed by a slow tongue. (2.) God is pleased sometimes to make choice of those as his messengers who have fewest of the advantages of art or nature, that his grace in them may appear the more glorious.

Christ's disciples were no orators, till the Spirit made them such.

2. When this plea was overruled, and all his excuses were answered, he begged that God would send somebody else on this errand and leave him to keep sheep in Midian (*v.* 13) : " Send by any hand but mine ; thou canst certainly find one much more fit." Note, An unwilling mind will take up with a sorry excuse rather than none, and is willing to devolve those services upon others that have any thing of difficulty or danger in them.

II. How God condescends to answer all his excuses. Though *the anger of the Lord was kindled against him* (*v.* 14), yet he continued to reason with him, till he had overcome him. Note, Even self-diffidence, when it either hinders us from duty or clogs us in duty, or when it discourages our dependence upon the grace of God—is very displeasing to him. God justly resents our backwardness to serve him, and has reason to take it ill ; for he is such a benefactor as is before-hand with us, and such a rewarder as will not be behind-hand with us. Note further, God is justly displeased with those whom yet he does not reject : he vouchsafes to reason the case even with his froward children, and overcomes them, as he did Moses here, with grace and kindness.

1. To balance the weakness of Moses, he here reminds him of his own power, *v.* 11. (1.) His power in that concerning which Moses made the objection : *Who has made man's mouth ? Have not I the Lord ?* Moses knew that God made man, but he must be reminded now that God made man's mouth. An eye to God as Creator would help us over a great many of the difficulties which lie in the way of our duty, Ps. cxxiv. 8. God, as the author of nature, has given us the power and faculty of speaking ; and from him, as the fountain of gifts and graces, comes the faculty of speaking well, the *mouth and wisdom* (Luke xxi. 15), the *tongue of the learned* (Isa. l. 4); he *pours grace into the lips,* Ps. xlv. 2. (2.) His power in general over the other faculties. Who but God *makes the dumb and the deaf, the seeing and the blind ?* [1.] The perfections of our faculties are his work, he makes the *seeing :* he formed the eye (Ps. xciv. 9); he opens the understanding, the eye of the mind, Luke xxiv. 45. [2.] Their imperfections are from him too ; he makes the *dumb,* and *deaf,* and *blind.* Is there any evil of this kind, and the Lord has not done it ? No doubt he has, and always in wisdom and righteousness, and for his own glory, John ix. 3. Pharaoh and the Egyptians were made deaf and blind spiritually, as Isa. vi. 9, 10. But God knew how to manage them, and get himself honour upon them.

2. To encourage him in this great undertaking, he repeats the promise of his presence, not only in general, *I will be with thee* (*ch.*

iii. 12), but in particular, "*I will be with thy mouth*, so that the imperfection in thy speech shall be no prejudice to thy message." It does not appear that God did immediately remove the infirmity, whatever it was; but he did that which was equivalent, he taught him what to say, and then let the matter recommend itself: if others spoke more gracefully, none spoke more powerfully. Note, Those whom God employs to speak for him ought to depend upon him for instructions, and *it shall be given them what they shall speak*, Matt. x. 19.

3. He joins Aaron in commission with him. He promises that Aaron shall meet him opportunely, and that he will be glad to see him, they having not seen one another (it is likely) for many years, *v.* 14. He directs him to make use of Aaron as his spokesman, *v.* 16. God might have laid Moses wholly aside, for his backwardness to be employed; but he considered his frame, and ordered him an assistant. Observe, (1.) Two are better than one, Eccl. iv. 9. God will have his two witnesses (Rev. xi. 3), that out of their mouths every word may be established. (2.) Aaron was the brother of Moses, divine wisdom so ordering it, that their natural affection one to another might strengthen their union in the joint execution of their commission. Christ sent his disciples two and two, and some of the couples were brothers. (3.) Aaron was the elder brother, and yet he was willing to be employed under Moses in this affair, because God would have it so. (4.) Aaron could speak well, and yet was far inferior to Moses in wisdom. God dispenses his gifts variously to the children of men, that we may see our need one of another, and each may contribute something to the good of the body, 1 Cor. xii. 21. The tongue of Aaron, with the head and heart of Moses, would make one completely fit for this embassy. (5.) God promises, *I will be with thy mouth, and with his mouth*. Even Aaron, that could speak well, yet could not speak to purpose unless God was with his mouth; without the constant aids of divine grace the best gifts will fail.

4. He bids him take the rod with him in his hand (*v.* 17), to intimate that he must bring about his undertaking rather by acting than by speaking; the signs he should work with this rod might abundantly supply the want of eloquence; one miracle would do him better service than all the rhetoric in the world. *Take this rod*, the rod he carried as a shepherd, that he might not be ashamed of that mean condition out of which God called him. This rod must be his staff of authority, and must be to him instead both of sword and sceptre.

18 And Moses went and returned to Jethro his father in law, and said unto him, Let me go, I pray thee, and return unto my brethren which *are* in

Egypt, and see whether they be yet alive. And Jethro said to Moses, Go in peace. 19 And the LORD said unto Moses in Midian, Go, return into Egypt: for all the men are dead which sought thy life. 20 And Moses took his wife and his sons, and set them upon an ass, and he returned to the land of Egypt: and Moses took the rod of God in his hand. 21 And the LORD said unto Moses, When thou goest to return into Egypt, see that thou do all those wonders before Pharaoh, which I have put in thine hand: but I will harden his heart, that he shall not let the people go. 22 And thou shalt say unto Pharaoh, Thus saith the LORD, Israel *is* my son, *even* my firstborn: 23 And I say unto thee, Let my son go, that he may serve me: and if thou refuse to let him go, behold, I will slay thy son, *even* thy firstborn.

Here, I. Moses obtains leave of his father-in-law to return into Egypt, *v.* 18. His father-in-law had been kind to him when he was a stranger, and therefore he would not be so uncivil as to leave his family, nor so unjust as to leave his service, without giving him notice. Note, The honour of being admitted into communion with God, and of being employed for him, does not exempt us from the duties of our relations and callings in this world. Moses said nothing to his father-in-law (for aught that appears) of the glorious manifestation of God to him; such favours we are to be thankful for to God, but not to boast of before men.

II. He receives from God further encouragements and directions in his work. After God had appeared to him in the bush to settle a correspondence, it should seem, he often spoke to him, as there was occasion, with less overwhelming solemnity. And, 1. He assures Moses that the coasts were clear. Whatever new enemies he might make by his undertaking, his old enemies were *all dead, all that sought his life*, *v.* 19. Perhaps some secret fear of falling into their hands was at the bottom of Moses's backwardness to go to Egypt, though he was not willing to own it, but pleaded unworthiness, insufficiency, want of elocution, &c. Note, God knows all the temptations his people lie under, and how to arm them against their secret fears, Ps. cxlii. 3. 2. He orders him to do the miracles, not only before the elders of Israel, but before Pharaoh, *v.* 21. There were some alive perhaps in the court of Pharaoh who remembered Moses when he was the son of Pharaoh's daughter, and had many a time called him a fool for deserting the honours of that relation; but he is now sent back to court, clad with greater powers than Pharaoh's daughter could have advanced him to, so that it might appear he was no loser by his choice: this wonder-working rod did more adorn the hand of Moses than the sceptre of Egypt could have done. Note, Those that look with contempt upon worldly honours shall be recompensed with the honour that cometh from God, which is the true honour. 3. That Pharaoh's obstinacy might be no surprise nor discouragement to him, God tells him before that he would *harden his heart.* Pharaoh had hardened his own heart against the groans and cries of the oppressed Israelites, and shut up the bowels of his compassion from them; and now God, in a way of righteous judgment, hardens his heart against the conviction of the miracles, and the terror of the plagues. Note, Ministers must expect with many to labour in vain: we must not think it strange if we meet with those who will not be wrought upon by the strongest arguments and fairest reasonings; yet our judgment is with the Lord. 4. Words are put into his mouth with which to address Pharaoh, *v.* 22, 23. God had promised him (*v.* 12), *I will teach thee what thou shalt say;* and here he does teach him. (1.) He must deliver his message in the name of the great Jehovah: *Thus saith the Lord;* this is the first time *that* preface is used by any man which afterwards is used so frequently by all the prophets: whether Pharaoh will hear, or whether he will forbear, Moses must tell him, *Thus saith the Lord.* (2.) He must let Pharaoh know Israel's relation to God, and God's concern for Israel. *Is Israel a servant? is he a home-born slave?* Jer. ii. 14. "No, *Israel is my son, my firstborn, precious in my sight, honourable,* and dear to me, not to be thus insulted and abused." (3.) He must demand a discharge for them: "*Let my son go;* not only my servant whom thou hast no right to detain, but my son whose liberty and honour I am very jealous for. It is my son, my son that serves me, and therefore must be spared, must be pleaded for," Mal. iii. 17. (4.) He must threaten Pharaoh with the death of the first-born of Egypt, in case of a refusal: *I will slay thy son, even thy firstborn.* As men deal with God's people, let them expect to be themselves dealt with; with the froward he will wrestle.

III. Moses addresses himself to this expedition. When God had assured him (*v.* 19) that the men were dead who sought his life, immediately it follows (*v.* 20), *he took his wife, and his sons,* and set out for Egypt. Note, Though corruption may object much against the services God calls us to, yet grace will get the upper hand, and will be obedient to the heavenly vision.

24 And it came to pass by the way in the inn, that the LORD met him,

and sought to kill him. 25 Then Zipporah took a sharp stone, and cut off the foreskin of her son, and cast *it* at his feet, and said, Surely a bloody husband *art* thou to me. 26 So he let him go: then she said, A bloody husband *thou art,* because of the circumcision. 27 And the LORD said to Aaron, Go into the wilderness to meet Moses. And he went, and met him in the mount of God, and kissed him. 28 And Moses told Aaron all the words of the LORD who had sent him, and all the signs which he had commanded him. 29 And Moses and Aaron went and gathered together all the elders of the children of Israel: 30 And Aaron spake all the words which the LORD had spoken unto Moses, and did the signs in the sight of the people. 31 And the people believed: and when they heard that the LORD had visited the children of Israel, and that he had looked upon their affliction, then they bowed their heads and worshipped.

Moses is here going to Egypt, and we are told,

I. How God met him in anger, *v.* 24—26. This is a very difficult passage of story; much has been written, and excellently written, to make it intelligible; we will try to make it improving. Here is,

1. The sin of Moses, which was neglecting to circumcise his son. This was probably the effect of his being unequally yoked with a Midianite, who was too indulgent of her child, while Moses was too indulgent of her. Note, (1.) We have need to watch carefully over our own hearts, lest fondness for any relation prevail above our love to God, and take us off from our duty to him. It is charged upon Eli that he *honoured his sons more than God* (1 Sam. ii. 29); and see Matt. x. 37. (2.) Even good men are apt to cool in their zeal for God and duty when they have long been deprived of the society of the faithful: solitude has its advantages, but they seldom counterbalance the loss of Christian communion.

2. God's displeasure against him. He met him, and, probably by a sword in an angel's hand, sought to kill him. This was a great change; very lately God was conversing with him, and lodging a trust in him, as a friend; and now he is coming forth against him as an enemy. Note, (1.) Omissions are sins, and must come into judgment, and particularly the contempt and neglect of the seals of the covenant; for it is a sign that we undervalue the promises of the covenant, and are displeased with the conditions of it.

He that has made a bargain, and is not willing to seal and ratify it, one may justly suspect, neither likes it nor designs to stand to it. (2.) God takes notice of, and is much displeased with, the sins of his own people. If they neglect their duty, let them expect to hear of it by their consciences, and perhaps to feel from it by cross providences: for this cause many are sick and weak, as some think Moses was here.

3. The speedy performance of the duty for the neglect of which God had now a controversy with him. His son must be circumcised; Moses is unable to circumcise him; therefore, in this case of necessity, Zipporah does it, whether with passionate words (expressing her dislike of the ordinance itself, or at least the administration of it to so young a child, and in a journey), as to me it seems, or with proper words—solemnly expressing the espousal of the child to God by the covenant of circumcision (as some read it) or her thankfulness to God for sparing her husband, giving him a new life, and thereby giving her, as it were, a new marriage to him, upon her circumcising her son (as others read it)—I cannot determine: but we learn, (1.) That when God discovers to us what is amiss in our lives we must give all diligence to amend it speedily, and particularly return to the duties we have neglected. (2.) The putting away of our sins is indispensably necessary to the removal of God's judgments. This is the voice of every rod, it calls us to return to him that smites us.

4. The release of Moses thereupon: *So he let him go ;* the distemper went off, the destroying angel withdrew, and all was well: only Zipporah cannot forget the fright she was in, but will unreasonably call Moses *a bloody husband,* because he obliged her to circumcise the child; and, upon this occasion (it is probable), he sent them back to his father-in-law, that they might not create him any further uneasiness. Note, (1.) When we return to God in a way of duty he will return to us in a way of mercy; take away the cause, and the effect will cease. (2.) We must resolve to bear it patiently, if our zeal for God and his institutions be misinterpreted and discouraged by some that should understand themselves, and us, and their duty, better, as David's zeal was misinterpreted by Michal; but if this be to be vile, if this be to be bloody, we must be yet more so. (3.) When we have any special service to do for God we should remove as far from us as we can that which is likely to be our hindrance. *Let the dead bury their dead, but follow thou me.*

II. How Aaron met him in love, *v.* 27, 28. 1. God sent Aaron to meet him, and directed him where to find him, in the wilderness that lay towards Midian. Note, The providence of God is to be acknowledged in the comfortable meeting of relations and friends. 2. Aaron made so much haste, in obedience to his God, and in love to his brother, that he

met him *in the mount of God,* the place where God had met with him. 3. They embraced one another with mutual endearments. The more they saw of God's immediate direction in bringing them together the more pleasant their interview was : they *kissed,* not only in token of brotherly affection, but as a pledge of their hearty concurrence in the work to which they were jointly called. 4. Moses informed his brother of the commission he had received, with all the instructions and credentials affixed to it, *v.* 28. Note, What we know of God we should communicate for the benefit of others; and those that are fellow-servants to God in the same work should use a mutual freedom, and endeavour rightly and fully to understand one another.

III. How the elders of Israel met him in faith and obedience. When Moses and Aaron first opened their commission in Egypt, said what they were ordered to say, and, to confirm it, did what they were ordered to do, they met with a better reception than they promised themselves, *v.* 29—31. 1. The Israelites gave credit to them : *The people believed,* as God had foretold (*ch.* iii. 18), knowing that no man could do those works that they did, unless God were with him. They gave glory to God: *They bowed their heads and worshipped,* therein expressing not only their humble thankfulness to God, who had raised them up and sent them a deliverer, but also their cheerful readiness to observe orders, and pursue the methods of their deliverance.

CHAP. V.

Moses and Aaron are here dealing with Pharaoh, to get leave of him to go and worship in the wilderness. I. They demand leave in the name of God (ver. 1), and he answers their demand with a defiance of God, ver. 2. II. They beg leave in the name of Israel (ver. 3), and he answers their request with further orders to oppress Israel, ver. 4 - 9. These cruel orders were, 1. Executed by the task-masters, ver. 10—14. 2. Complained of to Pharaoh, but in vain, ver. 15—19. 3. Complained of by the people to Moses (ver. 20, 21), and by him to God, ver. 22, 23.

AND afterward Moses and Aaron went in, and told Pharaoh, Thus saith the LORD God of Israel, Let my people go, that they may hold a feast unto me in the wilderness. 2 And Pharaoh said, Who *is* the LORD, that I should obey his voice to let Israel go ? I know not the LORD, neither will I let Israel go.

Moses and Aaron, having delivered their message to the elders of Israel, with whom they found good acceptance, are now to deal with Pharaoh, to whom they come in peril of their lives—*Moses* particularly, who perhaps was out-lawed for killing the Egyptian forty years before, so that if any of the old courtiers should happen to remember that against him now it might cost him his head. Their message itself was displeasing, and touched Pharaoh both in his honour and in his profit, two tender points; yet these faithful ambassadors boldly deliver it, whether he will hear or whether he will forbear.

I. Their demand is piously bold: *Thus saith the Lord God of Israel, Let my people go, v.* 1. Moses, in treating with the elders of Israel, is directed to call God *the God of their fathers;* but, in treating with Pharaoh, they call him *the God of Israel,* and it is the first time we find him called so in scripture: he is called *the God of Israel,* the *person* (Gen. xxxiii. 20); but here it is Israel, the *people.* They are just beginning to be formed into a people when God is called their God. Moses, it is likely, was directed to call him so, at least it might be inferred from *ch.* iv. 22, *Israel is my son.* In this great name they deliver their message: *Let my people go.* 1. They were God's people, and therefore Pharaoh ought not to detain them in bondage. Note, God will own his own people, though ever so poor and despicable, and will find a time to plead their cause. "The Israelites are slaves in Egypt, but they are my people," says God, "and I will not suffer them to be always trampled upon." See Isa. lii. 4, 5. 2. He expected services and sacrifices from them, and therefore they must have leave to go where they could freely exercise their religion, without giving offence to, or receiving offence from, the Egyptians. Note, God delivers his people out of the hand of their enemies, that they may serve him, and serve him cheerfully, that they may hold a feast to him, which they may do, while they have his favour and presence, even in a wilderness, a dry and barren land.

II. Pharaoh's answer is impiously bold: *Who is the Lord, that I should obey his voice? v.* 2. Being summoned to surrender, he thus hangs out the flag of defiance, hectors Moses and the God that sends him, and peremptorily refuses to let Israel go; he will not treat about it, nor so much as bear the mention of it. Observe, 1. How scornfully he speaks of the God of Israel: "*Who is Jehovah?* I neither know him nor care for him, neither value him nor fear him:" it is a hard name that he never heard of before, but he resolves it shall be no bug-bear to him. Israel was now a despised oppressed people, looked on as the tail of the nation, and, by the character they bore, Pharaoh makes his estimate of their God, and concludes that he made no better a figure among the gods than his people did among the nations. Note, Hardened persecutors are more malicious against God himself than they are against his people. See Isa. xxxvii. 23. Again, Ignorance and contempt of God are at the bottom of all the wickedness that is in the world. Men know not the Lord, or have very low and mean thoughts of him, and therefore they obey not his voice, nor will let any thing go for him. 2. How proudly he speaks of himself: "*That I should obey his voice;* I, the king of Egypt, a great people, obey the God of Israel, a poor enslaved people? Shall I, that rule the Israel of God, obey the God of Israel? No, it is below me;

I scorn to answer his summons." Note, Those are the children of pride that are the *children of disobedience,* Job xli. 34; Eph. v 6. Proud men think themselves too good to stoop even to God himself, and would not be under control, Jer. xliii. 2. Here is the core of the controversy: God must rule, but man will not be ruled. " I will have my will done," says God: " But I will do my own will," says the sinner. 3. How resolutely he denies the demand: *Neither will I let Israel go.* Note, Of all sinners none are so obstinate, nor so hardly persuaded to leave their sin, as persecutors are.

3 And they said, The God of the Hebrews hath met with us: let us go, we pray thee, three days' journey into the desert, and sacrifice unto the LORD our God; lest he fall upon us with pestilence, or with the sword. 4 And the king of Egypt said unto them, Wherefore do ye, Moses and Aaron, let the people from their works? get you unto your burdens. 5 And Pharaoh said, Behold, the people of the land now *are* many, and ye make them rest from their burdens. 6 And Pharaoh commanded the same day the taskmasters of the people, and their officers, saying, 7 Ye shall no more give the people straw to make brick, as heretofore: let them go and gather straw for themselves. 8 And the tale of the bricks, which they did make heretofore, ye shall lay upon them; ye shall not diminish *aught* thereof: for they *be* idle; therefore they cry, saying, Let us go *and* sacrifice to our God. 9 Let there more work be laid upon the men, that they may labour therein; and let them not regard vain words.

Finding that Pharaoh had no veneration at all for God, Moses and Aaron next try whether he had any compassion for Israel, and become humble suitors to him for leave to go and sacrifice, but in vain.

I. Their request is very humble and modest, *v.* 3. They make no complaint of the rigour they were ruled with. They plead that the journey they designed was not a project formed among themselves, but that their God had met with them, and called them to it. They beg with all submission: *We pray thee.* The poor useth entreaties; though God may summon princes that oppress, it becomes us to beseech and make supplication to them. What they ask is very reasonable, only for a short vacation, while they went three days' journey into the desert, and that on a good errand, and unexceptionable: " *We will sacrifice unto the Lord our God,* as other people do to theirs;" and, *lastly,* they give a very good reason, " Lest, if we quite cast off his worship, he fall upon us with one judgment or other, and then Pharaoh will lose his vassals."

II. Pharaoh's denial of their request is very barbarous and unreasonable, v. 4—9.

1. His suggestions were very unreasonable. (1.) That the people were idle, and that therefore they talked of going to sacrifice. The cities they built for Pharaoh, and the other fruit of their labours, were witnesses for them that they were not idle; yet he thus basely misrepresents them, that he might have a pretence to increase their burdens. (2.) That Moses and Aaron made them idle with vain words, v. 9. God's words are here called vain words; and those that called them to the best and most needful business are accused of making them idle. Note, The malice of Satan has often represented the service and worship of God as fit employment for those only that have nothing else to do, and the business only of the idle; whereas indeed it is the indispensable duty of those that are most busy in the world.

2. His resolutions hereupon were most barbarous. (1.) Moses and Aaron themselves must get to *their burdens* (v. 4); they are Israelites, and, however God had distinguished them from the rest, Pharaoh makes no difference: they must share in the common slavery of their nation. Persecutors have always taken a particular pleasure in putting contempt and hardship upon the ministers of the churches. (2.) The usual tale of bricks must be exacted, without the usual allowance of straw to mix with the clay, or to burn the bricks with, that thus more work might be laid upon the men, which if they performed, they would be broken with labour; and, if not, they would be exposed to punishment.

10 And the taskmasters of the people went out, and their officers, and they spake to the people, saying, Thus saith Pharaoh, I will not give you straw. 11 Go ye, get you straw where ye can find it: yet not aught of your work shall be diminished. 12 So the people were scattered abroad throughout all the land of Egypt to gather stubble instead of straw. 13 And the taskmasters hasted *them*, saying, Fulfil your works, *your* daily tasks, as when there was straw. 14 And the officers of the children of Israel, which Pharaoh's taskmasters had set over them, were beaten, *and* demanded, Wherefore have ye not fulfilled your task in

making brick both yesterday and to day, as heretofore?

Pharaoh's orders are here put in execution; straw is denied, and yet the work not diminished. 1. The Egyptian task-masters were very severe. Pharaoh having decreed unrighteous decrees, the task-masters were ready to write the grievousness that he had prescribed, Isa. x. 1. Cruel princes will never want cruel instruments to be employed under them, who will justify them in that which is most unreasonable. These task-masters insisted upon the daily tasks, as when there was straw, v. 13. See what need we have to pray that *we may be delivered from unreasonable and wicked men,* 2 Thess. iii. 2. The enmity of the serpent's seed against the seed of the woman is such as breaks through all the laws of reason, honour, humanity, and common justice. 2. The people hereby were dispersed throughout all the land of Egypt, to gather stubble, v. 12. By this means Pharaoh's unjust and barbarous usage of them came to be known to all the kingdom, and perhaps caused them to be pitied by their neighbours, and made Pharaoh's government less acceptable even to his own subjects: good-will is never got by persecution. 3. The Israelite-officers were used with particular harshness, v. 14. Those that were the fathers of the houses of Israel paid dearly for their honour; for from them immediately the service was exacted, and they were beaten when it was not performed. See here, (1.) What a miserable thing slavery is, and what reason we have to be thankful to God that we are a free people, and not oppressed. Liberty and property are valuable jewels in the eyes of those whose services and possessions lie at the mercy of an arbitrary power. (2.) What disappointments we often meet with after the raising of our expectations. The Israelites were now lately encouraged to hope for enlargement, but behold greater distresses. This teaches us always to rejoice with trembling. (3.) What strange steps God sometimes takes in delivering his people; he often brings them to the utmost straits when he is just ready to appear for them. The lowest ebbs go before the highest tides; and very cloudy mornings commonly introduce the fairest days, Deut. xxxii. 36. God's time to help is when things are at the worst; and Providence verifies the paradox, *The worse the better.*

15 Then the officers of the children of Israel came and cried unto Pharaoh, saying, Wherefore dealest thou thus with thy servants? 16 There is no straw given unto thy servants, and they say to us, Make brick: and, behold, thy servants *are* beaten; but the fault *is* in thine own people. 17 But he said, Ye *are* idle, *ye are* idle:

therefore ye say, Let us go *and* do sacrifice to the Lord. 18 Go therefore now, *and* work; for there shall no straw be given you, yet shall ye deliver the tale of bricks. 19 And the officers of the children of Israel did see *that* they *were* in evil *case*, after it was said, Ye shall not minish *aught* from your bricks of your daily task. 20 And they met Moses and Aaron, who stood in the way, as they came forth from Pharaoh: 21 And they said unto them, The Lord look upon you, and judge; because ye have made our savour to be abhorred in the eyes of Pharaoh, and in the eyes of his servants, to put a sword in their hand to slay us. 22 And Moses returned unto the Lord, and said, Lord, wherefore hast thou *so* evil entreated this people? why *is* it *that* thou hast sent me? 23 For since I came to Pharaoh to speak in thy name, he hath done evil to this people; neither hast thou delivered thy people at all.

It was a great strait that the head-workmen were in, when they must either abuse those that were under them or be abused by those that were over them; yet, it should seem, rather than they would tyrannize, they would be tyrannized over; and they were so. In this evil case (*v.* 19), observe,

I. How justly they complained to Pharaoh: They *came and cried unto Pharaoh, v.* 15. Whither should they go with a remonstrance of their grievances but to the supreme power, which is ordained for the protection of the injured? As bad as Pharaoh was his oppressed subjects had liberty to complain to him; there was no law against petitioning: it was a very modest, but moving, representation that they made of their condition (*v.* 16): *Thy servants are beaten* (severely enough, no doubt, when things were in such a ferment), and yet *the fault is in thy own people,* the task-masters, who deny us what is necessary for carrying on our work. Note, It is common for those to be most rigorous in blaming others who are most blameworthy themselves. But what did they get by this complaint? It did but make bad worse. 1. Pharaoh taunted them (*v.* 17); when they were almost killed with working, he told them they were idle: they underwent the fatigue of industry, and yet lay under the imputation of slothfulness, while nothing appeared to ground the charge upon but this, that they said, *Let us go and do sacrifice.* Note, It is common for the best actions to be mentioned under the worst names; holy diligence in the best business is censured by many as a culpable carelessness

in the business of the world. It is well for us that men are not to be our judges, but a God who knows what the principles are on which we act. Those that are diligent in doing sacrifice to the Lord will, with God, escape the doom of the slothful servant, though, with men, they do not. 2. He bound on their burdens : *Go now and work, v.* 18. Note, Wickedness proceedeth from the wicked; what can be expected from unrighteous men but more unrighteousness?

II. How unjustly they complained of Moses and Aaron : *The Lord look upon you, and judge, v.* 21. This was not fair. Moses and Aaron had given sufficient evidence of their hearty good-will to the liberties of Israel; and yet, because things succeed not immediately as they hoped, they are reproached as accessaries to their slavery. They should have humbled themselves before God, and taken to themselves the shame of their sin, which turned away good things from them ; but, instead of this, they fly in the face of their best friends, and quarrel with the instruments of their deliverance, because of some little difficulties and obstructions they met with in effecting it. Note, Those that are called out to public service for God and their generation must expect to be tried, not only by the malicious threats of proud enemies, but by the unjust and unkind censures of unthinking friends, who judge only by outward appearance and look but a little way before them. Now what did Moses do in this strait? It grieved him to the heart that the event did not answer, but rather contradict, his expectation; and their upbraidings were very cutting, and like a sword in his bones; but, 1. He returned to the Lord (*v.* 22), to acquaint him with it, and to represent the case to him: he knew that what he had said and done was by divine direction; and therefore what blame is laid upon him for it he considers as reflecting upon God, and, like Hezekiah, spreads it before him as interested in the cause, and appeals to him. Compare this with Jer. xx. 7—9. Note, When we find ourselves, at any time, perplexed and embarrassed in the way of our duty, we ought to have recourse to God, and lay open our case before him by faithful and fervent prayer. If we retreat, let us retreat to him, and no further. 2. He expostulated with him, *v.* 22, 23. He knew not how to reconcile the providence with the promise and the commission which he had received. " Is this God's coming down to deliver Israel? Must I, who hoped to be a blessing to them, become a scourge to them? By this attempt to get them out of the pit, they are but sunk the deeper into it." Now he asks, (1.) *Wherefore hast thou so evil entreated this people?* Note, Even when God is coming towards his people in ways of mercy, he sometimes takes such methods as that they may think themselves but ill treated. The instruments of deliverance, when they aim to help, are found to hinder, and that becomes a trap which, it was hoped, would have been for their welfare, God suffering it to be so that we may learn to cease from man, and may come off from a dependence upon second causes. Note, further, When the people of God think themselves ill treated, they should go to God by prayer, and plead with him, and that is the way to have better treatment in God's good time. (2.) *Why is it thou hast sent me?* Thus, [1.] He complains of his ill success: " Pharaoh has done evil to this people, and not one step seems to be taken towards their deliverance." Note, It cannot but sit very heavily upon the spirits of those whom God employs for him to see that their labour does no good, and much more to see that it does hurt eventually, though not designedly. It is uncomfortable to a good minister to perceive that his endeavours for men's conviction and conversion do but exasperate their corruptions, confirm their prejudices, harden their hearts, and seal them up under unbelief. This makes them go in the bitterness of their souls, as the prophet, Ezek. iii. 14. Or, [2.] He enquires what was further to be done: *Why hast thou sent me?* that is, " What other method shall I take in pursuance of my commission?" Note, Disappointments in our work must not drive us from our God, but still we must consider why we are sent.

CHAP. VI.

Much ado there was to bring Moses to his work, and when the ice was broken, some difficulty having occurred in carrying it on, there was no less ado to put him forward in it. Witness this chapter, in which, I. God satisfies Moses himself in an answer to his complaints in the close of the foregoing chapter, ver. 1. II. He gives him fuller instructions than had yet been given him what to say to the children of Israel, for their satisfaction (ver. 2–8), but to little purpose, ver. 9. III. He sends him again to Pharaoh, ver. 10, 11. But Moses objects against that (ver. 12), upon which a very strict charge is given to him and his brother to execute their commission with vigour, ver. 13. IV. Here is an abstract of the genealogy of the tribes of Reuben and Simeon, to introduce that of Levi, that the pedigree of Moses and Aaron might be cleared (ver. 14–25), and then the chapter concludes with a repetition of so much of the preceding story as was necessary to make way for the following chapter.

THEN the LORD said unto Moses, Now shalt thou see what I will do to Pharaoh: for with a strong hand shall he let them go, and with a strong hand shall he drive them out of his land. 2 And God spake unto Moses, and said unto him, I *am* the LORD: 3 And I appeared unto Abraham, unto Isaac, and unto Jacob, by *the name of* God Almighty, but by my name JEHOVAH was I not known to them. 4 And I have also established my covenant with them, to give them the land of Canaan, the land of their pilgrimage, wherein they were strangers. 5 And I have also heard the groaning of the children of Israel, whom the Egyptians keep in bondage; and I have remembered my covenant. 6

294

Wherefore say unto the children of Israel, I *am* the LORD, and I will bring you out from under the burdens of the Egyptians, and I will rid you out of their bondage, and I will redeem you with a stretched out arm, and with great judgments: 7 And I will take you to me for a people, and I will be to you a God: and ye shall know that I *am* the LORD your God, which bringeth you out from under the burdens of the Egyptians. 8 And I will bring you in unto the land, concerning the which I did swear to give it to Abraham, to Isaac, and to Jacob; and I will give it you for an heritage: I *am* the LORD. 9 And Moses spake so unto the children of Israel: but they hearkened not unto Moses for anguish of spirit, and for cruel bondage.

Here, I. God silences Moses's complaints with the assurance of success in this negociation, repeating the promise made him in *ch.* iii. 20, *After that, he will let you go.* When Moses was at his wit's end, wishing he had staid in Midian, rather than have come to Egypt to make bad worse—when he was quite at a loss what to do—*Then the Lord said unto Moses*, for the quieting of his mind, " *Now shalt thou see what I will do to Pharaoh* (v. 1); now shalt thou see what I will do to Pharaoh; now that the affair has come to a crisis, things are as bad as they can be, Pharaoh is in the height of pride and Israel in the depth of misery, now is my time to appear." See Ps. xii. 5, *Now will I arise.* Note, Man's extremity is God's opportunity of helping and saving. Moses had been expecting what God would do; but now he shall see what he will do, shall see his day at length, Job xxiv. 1. Moses had been trying what he could do, and could effect nothing. " Well," says God, " now thou shalt see what I will do; let me alone to deal with this proud man," Job xl. 12, 13. Note, Then the deliverance of God's church will be accomplished, when God takes the work into his own hands. *With a strong hand*, that is, being forced to it by a strong hand, *he shall let them go.* Note, As some are brought to their duty by the strong hand of God's grace, who are made willing in the day of his power, so others by the strong hand of his justice, breaking those that would not bend.

II. He gives him further instructions, that both he and the people of Israel might be encouraged to hope for a glorious issue of this affair. Take comfort,

1. From God's name, Jehovah, *v.* 2, 3. He begins with this, *I am Jehovah*, the same with, *I am that I am*, the fountain of being, and blessedness, and infinite perfection. The patriarchs knew this name, but they did not

know him in this matter by that which this name signifies. God would now be known by his name *Jehovah*, that is, (1.) A God performing what he had promised, and so inspiring confidence in his promises. (2.) A God perfecting what he had begun, and finishing his own work. In the history of the creation, God is never called Jehovah till the heavens and the earth were finished, Gen. ii. 4. When the salvation of the saints is completed in eternal life, then he will be known by his name Jehovah (Rev. xxii. 13); in the mean time they shall find him, for their strength and support, *El-shaddai, a God all-sufficient,* a God that is enough and will be so, Mic. vii. 20.

2. From his covenant: *I have established my covenant, v.* 4. Note, The covenants God makes he establishes ; they are made as firm as the power and truth of God can make them. We may venture our all upon this bottom.

3. From his compassions (*v.* 5): *I have heard the groaning of the children of Israel ;* he means their groaning on occasion of the late hardships put upon them. Note, God takes notice of the increase of his people's calamities, and observes how their enemies grow upon them.

4. From his present resolutions, *v.* 6—8. Here is line upon line, to assure them that they should be brought triumphantly out of Egypt (*v.* 6), and should be put in possession of the land of Canaan (*v.* 8): *I will bring you out. I will rid you. I will redeem you. I will bring you into the land of Canaan, and I will give it to you.* Let man take the shame of his unbelief, which needs such repetitions; and let God have the glory of his condescending grace, which gives us such repeated assurances for our satisfaction.

5. From his gracious intentions in all these, which were great, and worthy of him, *v.* 7. (1.) He intended their happiness : *I will take you to me for a people,* a peculiar people, and *I will be to you a God ;* more than this we need not ask, we cannot have, to make us happy. (2.) He intended his own glory : *You shall know that I am the Lord.* God will attain his own ends, nor shall we come short of them if we make them our chief end too. Now, one would think, these good words, and comfortable words, should have revived the drooping Israelites, and caused them to forget their misery; but, on the contrary, their miseries made them regardless of God's promises (*v.* 9): *They hearkened not unto Moses for anguish of spirit.* That is, [1.] They were so taken up with their troubles that they did not heed him. [2.] They were so cast down with their late disappointment that they did not believe him. [3.] They had such a dread of Pharaoh's power and wrath that they durst not themselves move in the least towards their deliverance. Note, *First,* Disconsolate spirits often put from them the comforts they are entitled to, and stand in their own light. See Isa. xxviii. 12. *Se-*

condly, Strong passions oppose strong consolations. By indulging ourselves in discontent and fretfulness, we deprive ourselves of the comfort we might have both from God's word and from his providence, and must thank ourselves if we go comfortless.

10 And the LORD spake unto Moses, saying, 11 Go in, speak unto Pharaoh king of Egypt, that he let the children of Israel go out of his land. 12 And Moses spake before the LORD, saying, Behold, the children of Israel have not hearkened unto me ; how then shall Pharaoh hear me, who *am* of uncircumcised lips ? 13 And the LORD spake unto Moses and unto Aaron, and gave them a charge unto the children of Israel, and unto Pharaoh king of Egypt, to bring the children of Israel out of the land of Egypt.

Here, I. God sends Moses the second time to Pharaoh (*v.* 11) upon the same errand as before, to command him, at his peril, that he *let the children of Israel go.* Note, God repeats his precepts before he begins his punishments. Those that have often been called in vain to leave their sins must yet be called again and again, whether they will hear or whether they will forbear, Ezek. iii. 11. God is said to *hew* sinners by his prophets (Hos. vi. 5), which denotes the repetition of the strokes. *How often would I have gathered you ?*

II. Moses makes objections, as one discouraged, and willing to give up the cause, *v.* 12. He pleads, 1. The unlikelihood of Pharaoh's hearing : " *Behold the children of Israel have not hearkened unto me ;* they give no heed, no credit, to what I have said ; how then can I expect that Pharaoh should hear me ? If the anguish of their spirit makes them deaf to that which would compose and comfort them, much more will the anger of his spirit, his pride and insolence, make him deaf to that which will but exasperate and provoke him." If God's professing people hear not his messengers, how can it be thought that his professed enemy should ? Note, The frowardness and untractableness of those that are called Christians greatly discourage ministers, and make them ready to despair of success in dealing with those that are atheistical and profane. We would be instrumental to unite Israelites, to refine and purify them, to comfort and pacify them ; but, if they hearken not to us, how shall we prevail with those in whom we cannot pretend to such an interest ? But with God all things are possible. 2. He pleads the unreadiness and infirmity of his own speaking : *I am of uncircumcised lips ;* it is repeated, *v.* 30. He was conscious to himself that he had not the gift of utterance, had no command of language ; his talent did not lie that way. To this objection God had given a sufficient answer before, and therefore he ought not to have insisted upon it, for the sufficiency of grace can supply tĥe defects of nature at any time. Note, Though our infirmities ought to humble us, yet they ought not to discourage us from doing our best in any service we have to do for God. His strength is made perfect in our weakness.

III. God again joins Aaron in commission with Moses, and puts an end to the dispute by interposing his own authority, and giving them both a solemn charge, upon their allegiance to their great Lord, to execute it with all possible expedition and fidelity. When Moses repeats his baffled arguments, he shall be argued with no longer, but God gives him a charge, and Aaron with him, both to the children of Israel and to Pharaoh, *v.* 13. Note, God's authority is sufficient to answer all objections, and binds us to obedience, without murmuring or disputing, Phil. ii. 14. Moses himself has need to be charged, and so has Timothy, 1 Tim. vi. 13; 2 Tim. iv. 1.

14 These *be* the heads of their fathers' houses: The sons of Reuben the firstborn of Israel; Hanoch, and Pallu, Hezron, and Carmi: these *be* the families of Reuben. 15 And the sons of Simeon; Jemuel, and Jamin, and Ohad, and Jachin, and Zohar, and Shaul the son of a Canaanitish woman: these *are* the families of Simeon. 16 And these *are* the names of the sons of Levi according to their generations; Gershon, and Kohath, and Merari: and the years of the life of Levi *were* a hundred thirty and seven years. 17 The sons of Gershon; Libni, and Shimi, according to their families. 18 And the sons of Kohath; Amram, and Izhar, and Hebron, and Uzziel: and the years of the life of Kohath *were* a hundred thirty and three years. 19 And the sons of Merari; Mahali and Mushi: these *are* the families of Levi according to their generations. 20 And Amram took him Jochebed his father's sister to wife; and she bare him Aaron and Moses: and the years of the life of Amram *were* a hundred and thirty and seven years. 21 And the sons of Izhar; Korah, and Nepheg, and Zithri. 22 And the sons of Uzziel; Mishael, and Elzaphan, and Zithri. 23 And Aaron took him Elisheba, daughter of Amminadab, sister of Naashon, to wife; and she bare him Nadab, and

Abihu, Eleazar, and Ithamar. 24 And the sons of Korah; Assir, and Elkanah, and Abiasaph; these *are* the families of the Korhites. 25 And Eleazar Aaron's son took him *one* of the daughters of Putiel to wife; and she bare him Phinehas: these *are* the heads of the fathers of the Levites according to their families. 26 These *are* that Aaron and Moses, to whom the LORD said, Bring out the children of Israel from the land of Egypt according to their armies. 27 These *are* they which spake to Pharaoh king of Egypt, to bring out the children of Israel from Egypt: these *are* that Moses and Aaron. 28 And it came to pass on the day *when* the LORD spake unto Moses in the land of Egypt, 29 That the LORD spake unto Moses, saying, I *am* the LORD: speak thou unto Pharaoh king of Egypt all that I say unto thee. 30 And Moses said before the LORD, Behold, I *am* of uncircumcised lips, and how shall Pharaoh hearken unto me?

I. We have here a genealogy, not an endless one, such as the apostle condemns (1 Tim. i. 4), for it ends in those two great patriots Moses and Aaron, and comes in here to show that they were Israelites, bone of their bone and flesh of their flesh whom they were sent to deliver, raised up unto them of their brethren, as Christ also should be, who was to be the prophet and priest, the Redeemer and lawgiver, of the people of Israel, and whose genealogy also, like this, was to be carefully preserved. The heads of the houses of three of the tribes are here named, agreeing with the accounts we had, Gen. xlvi. Dr. Lightfoot thinks that Reuben, Simeon, and Levi, are thus dignified here by themselves for this reason, because they were left under marks of infamy by their dying father, Reuben for his incest and Simeon and Levi for their murder of the Shechemites; and therefore Moses would put this particular honour upon them, to magnify God's mercy in their repentance and remission, as a pattern to those that should afterwards believe: the two former seem rather to be mentioned only for the sake of a third, which was Levi, from whom Moses and Aaron descended, and all the priests of the Jewish church. Thus was the tribe of Levi distinguished betimes. Observe here, 1. That Kohath, from whom Moses and Aaron, and all the priests, derived their pedigree, was a younger son of Levi, *v.* 16. Note, The grants of God's favours do not go by seniority of age and priority of birth, but the divine sovereignty often prefers the younger before the elder, so crossing hands. 2. That the ages of Levi, Kohath, and Amram, the father, grandfather, and great grandfather, of Moses, are here recorded ; they all lived to a great age, Levi to 137, Kohath to 133, and Amram to 137. Moses himself came much short of them, and fixed seventy or eighty for the ordinary stretch of human life (Ps. xc. 10) ; for now that God's Israel was multiplied and had become a great nation, and divine revelation was by the hand of Moses committed to writing and no longer trusted to tradition, the two great reasons for the long lives of the patriarchs had ceased, and therefore henceforward fewer years must serve men. 3. That Aaron married Elisheba (the same name with that of the wife of Zecharias, Elizabeth, as Miriam is the same with Mary), daughter of Amminadab, one of the chief of the fathers of the tribe of Judah ; for the tribes of Levi and Judah often intermarried, v. 23. 4. It must not be omitted that Moses has recorded the marriage of his father Amram with Jochebed his own aunt (v. 20); and it appears by Num. xxvi. 59 that it must be taken strictly for his father's own sister, at least by the half blood. This marriage was afterwards forbidden as incestuous (Lev. xviii. 12), which might be looked upon as a blot upon his family, though before that law ; yet Moses does not conceal it, for he sought not his own praise, but wrote with a sincere regard to truth, whether it smiled or frowned upon him. 5. He concludes it with a particular mark of honour on the persons he is writing of, though he himself was one of them, v. 26, 27. These are *that Moses and Aaron* whom God pitched upon to be his plenipotentiaries in this treaty. These were those to whom *God spoke* (v. 26), and who *spoke to Pharaoh* on Israel's behalf, v. 27. Note, Communion with God and serviceableness to his church are things that, above any other, put true honour upon men. Those are great indeed with whom God converses and whom he employs in his service. Such were that Moses and Aaron ; and something of this honour have all his saints, who are made to our God kings and priests.

II. In the close of the chapter Moses returns to his narrative, from which he had broken off somewhat abruptly (v. 13), and repeats, 1. The charge God had given him to deliver his message to Pharaoh (v. 29): *Speak all that I say unto thee,* as a faithful ambassador. Note, Those that go on God's errand must not shun to declare *the whole counsel of God.* 2. His objection against it, v. 30. Note, Those that have at any time spoken unadvisedly with their lips ought often to reflect upon it with regret, as Moses seems to do here.

CHAP. VII.

In this chapter, I. The dispute between God and Moses finishes, and Moses applies himself to the execution of his commission, in obedience to God's command, ver. 1—7. II. The dispute between Moses and Pharaoh begins, and a famous trial of skill

it was. Moses, in God's name, demands Israel's release ; Pharaoh denies it. The contest is between the power of the great God and the power of a proud prince ; and it will be found, in the issue, that when God judgeth he will overcome. 1. Moses confirms the demand he had made to Pharaoh, by a miracle, turning his rod into a serpent ; but Pharaoh hardens his heart against this conviction, ver. 8—13. 2. He chastises his disobedience by a plague, the first of the ten, turning the waters into blood ; but Pharaoh hardens his heart against this correction, ver. 14, &c.

AND the Lord said unto Moses, See, I have made thee a god to Pharaoh : and Aaron thy brother shall be thy prophet. 2 Thou shalt speak all that I command thee : and Aaron thy brother shall speak unto Pharaoh, that he send the children of Israel out of his land. 3 And I will harden Pharaoh's heart, and multiply my signs and my wonders in the land of Egypt. 4 But Pharaoh shall not hearken unto you, that I may lay my hand upon Egypt, and bring forth mine armies, *and* my people the children of Israel, out of the land of Egypt by great judgments. 5 And the Egyptians shall know that I *am* the Lord, when I stretch forth mine hand upon Egypt, and bring out the children of Israel from among them. 6 And Moses and Aaron did as the Lord commanded them, so did they. 7 And Moses *was* fourscore years old, and Aaron fourscore and three years old, when they spake unto Pharaoh.

Here, I. God encourages Moses to go to Pharaoh, and at last silences all his discouragements. 1. He clothes him with great power and authority (v. 1): *I have made thee a god to Pharaoh ;* that is, my representative in this affair, as magistrates are called *gods,* because they are God's vicegerents. He was authorized to speak and act in God's name and stead, and, under the divine direction, was endued with a divine power to do that which is above the ordinary power of nature, and invested with a divine authority to demand obedience from a sovereign prince and punish disobedience. Moses was a god, but he was only a *made* god, not essentially one by nature ; he was no god but by commission. He was a god, but he was a god only to Pharaoh ; the living and true God is a God to all the world. It is an instance of God's condescension, and an evidence that his thoughts towards us are thoughts of peace, that when he treats with men he treats by men, whose terror shall not make us afraid. 2. He again nominates him an assistant, his brother Aaron, who was not a man of uncircumcised lips, but a notable spokesman : " He shall be *thy prophet,*" that is, " he shall speak from thee to Pharaoh, as prophets do from God to the children of men. Thou shalt, as a god, inflict and remove the plagues, and Aaron, as a prophet, shall denounce them, and threaten Pharaoh with them." 3. He tells him the worst of it, that Pharaoh would not hearken to him, and yet the work should be done at last, Israel should be delivered and God therein would be glorified, *v.* 4, 5. The Egyptians, who would not know the Lord, should be made to know him. Note, It is, and ought to be, satisfaction enough to God's messengers that, whatever contradiction and opposition may be given them, thus far they shall gain their point, that God will be glorified in the success of their embassy, and all his chosen Israel will be saved, and then they have no reason to say that they have laboured in vain. See here, (1.) How God glorifies himself; he makes people know that he is Jehovah. Israel is made to know it by the performance of his promises to them (*ch.* vi. 3), and the Egyptians are made to know it by the pouring out of his wrath upon them. Thus God's name is exalted both in those that are saved and in those that perish. (2.) What method he takes to do this: he humbles the proud, and exalts the poor, Luke i. 51, 52. If God stretch out his hand to sinners in vain, he will at last stretch out his hand upon them; and who can bear the weight of it?

II. Moses and Aaron apply themselves to their work without further objection: *They did as the Lord commanded them, v.* 6. Their obedience, all things considered, was well worthy to be celebrated, as it is by the Psalmist (Ps. cv. 28), *They rebelled not against his word,* namely, Moses and Aaron, whom he mentions, *v.* 26. Thus Jonah, though at first he was very averse, at length went to Nineveh. Notice is taken of the age of Moses and Aaron when they undertook this glorious service. Aaron the elder (and yet the inferior in office) was eighty-three, Moses was eighty; both of them men of great gravity and experience, whose age was venerable, and whose years might teach wisdom, *v.* 7. Joseph, who was to be only a servant to Pharaoh, was preferred at thirty years old; but Moses, who was to be a god to Pharaoh, was not so dignified until he was eighty years old. It was fit that he should long wait for such an honour, and be long in preparing for such a service.

8 And the Lord spake unto Moses and unto Aaron, saying, 9 When Pharaoh shall speak unto you, saying, Show a miracle for you: then thou shalt say unto Aaron, Take thy rod, and cast *it* before Pharaoh, *and* it shall become a serpent. 10 And Moses and Aaron went in unto Pharaoh, and they did so as the Lord had commanded: and Aaron cast down his rod before Pharaoh, and before his servants, and it became a serpent. 11 Then Pharaoh also called the wise men and the sorcerers: now the magicians of Egypt, they also did in like manner with their enchantments. 12 For they cast down every man his rod, and they became serpents: but Aaron's rod swallowed up their rods. 13 And he hardened Pharaoh's heart, that he hearkened not unto them; as the Lord had said.

The first time that Moses made his application to Pharaoh, he produced his instructions only; now he is directed to produce his credentials, and does accordingly. 1. It is taken for granted that Pharaoh would challenge these demandants to work a miracle, that, by a performance evidently above the power of nature, they might prove their commission from the God of nature. Pharaoh will say, *Show a miracle;* not with any desire to be convinced, but with the hope that none will be wrought, and then he would have some colour for his infidelity. 2. Orders are therefore given to turn the rod into a serpent, according to the instructions, *ch.* iv. 3. The same rod that was to give the signal of the other miracles is now itself the subject of a miracle, to put a reputation upon it. Aaron cast his rod to the ground, and instantly it became a serpent, *v.* 10. This was proper, not only to affect Pharaoh with wonder, but to strike a terror upon him. Serpents are hurtful dreadful animals; the very sight of one, thus miraculously produced, might have softened his heart into a fear of that God by whose power it was produced. This first miracle, though it was not a plague, yet amounted to the threatening of a plague. If it made not Pharaoh feel, it made him fear; and this is God's method of dealing with sinners—he comes upon them gradually. 3. This miracle, though too plain to be denied, is enervated, and the conviction of it taken off, by the magicians' imitation of it, *v.* 11, 12. Moses had been originally instructed in the learning of the Egyptians, and was suspected to have improved himself in magical arts in his long retirement; the magicians are therefore sent for, to vie with him. And some think those of that profession had a particular spite against the Hebrews ever since Joseph put them all to shame, by interpreting a dream which they could make nothing of, in remembrance of which slur put on their predecessors these magicians withstood Moses, as it is explained, 2 Tim. iii. 8. Their rods became serpents, real serpents; some think, by the power of God, beyond their intention or expectation, for the hardening of Pharaoh's heart; others think, by the power of evil angels, artfully substituting serpents in the room of the rods, God permitting the delusion to be wrought for wise and holy ends, that those might believe a lie who received not the truth: and herein the Lord was righ-

298

teous. Yet this might have helped to frighten Pharaoh into a compliance with the demands of Moses, that he might be freed from these dreadful unaccountable phenomena, with which he saw himself on all sides surrounded. But to the seed of the serpent these serpents were no amazement. Note, God suffers the lying spirit to do strange things, that the faith of some may be tried and manifested (Deut. xiii. 3; 1 Cor. xi. 19), that the infidelity of others may be confirmed, and that he who is filthy may be filthy still, 2 Cor. iv. 4. 4. Yet, in this contest, Moses plainly gains the victory. The serpent which Aaron's rod was turned into swallowed up the others, which was sufficient to have convinced Pharaoh on which side the right lay. Note, Great is the truth, and will prevail. The cause of God will undoubtedly triumph at last over all competition and contradiction, and will reign alone, Dan. ii. 44. But Pharaoh was not wrought upon by this. The magicians having produced serpents, he had this to say, that the case between them and Moses was disputable; and the very appearance of an opposition to truth, and the least head made against it, serve those for a justification of their infidelity who are prejudiced against the light and love of it.

14 And the LORD said unto Moses, Pharaoh's heart *is* hardened, he refuseth to let the people go. 15 Get thee unto Pharaoh in the morning; lo, he goeth out unto the water; and thou shalt stand by the river's brink against he come; and the rod which was turned to a serpent shalt thou take in thine hand. 16 And thou shalt say unto him, The LORD God of the Hebrews hath sent me unto thee, saying, Let my people go, that they may serve me in the wilderness : and, behold, hitherto thou wouldest not hear. 17 Thus saith the LORD, In this thou shalt know that I *am* the LORD : behold, I will smite with the rod that *is* in mine hand upon the waters which *are* in the river, and they shall be turned to blood. 18 And the fish that *is* in the river shall die, and the river shall stink; and the Egyptians shall loathe to drink of the water of the river. 19 And the LORD spake unto Moses, Say unto Aaron, Take thy rod, and stretch out thine hand upon the waters of Egypt, upon their streams, upon their rivers, and upon their ponds, and upon all their pools of water, that they may become blood; and *that* there may be blood throughout all the land of Egypt, both in *vessels of* wood, and in *vessels of* stone. 20 And Moses and Aaron did so, as the LORD commanded ; and he lifted up the rod, and smote the waters that *were* in the river, in the sight of Pharaoh, and in the sight of his servants; and all the waters that *were* in the river were turned to blood. 21 And the fish that *was* in the river died; and the river stank, and the Egyptians could not drink of the water of the river; and there was blood throughout all the land of Egypt. 22 And the magicians of Egypt did so with their enchantments : and Pharaoh's heart was hardened, neither did he hearken unto them; as the LORD had said. 23 And Pharaoh turned and went into his house, neither did he set his heart to this also. 24 And all the Egyptians digged round about the river for water to drink; for they could not drink of the water of the river. 25 And seven days were fulfilled, after that the LORD had smitten the river.

Here is the first of the ten plagues, the turning of the water into blood, which was, 1. A dreadful plague, and very grievous. The very sight of such vast rolling streams of blood, pure blood no doubt, florid and high-coloured, could not but strike a horror upon people : much more afflictive were the consequences of it. Nothing more common than water : so wisely has Providence ordered it, and so kindly, that that which is so needful and serviceable to the comfort of human life should be cheap, and almost every where to be had; but now the Egyptians must either drink blood, or die for thirst. Fish was much of their food (Num. xi. 5), but the changing of the waters was the death of the fish; it was a pestilence in that element (*v.* 21): *The fish died.* In the general deluge they escaped, because perhaps they had not then contributed so much to the luxury of man as they have since ; but in this particular judgment they perished (Ps. cv. 29) : *He slew their fish ;* and when another destruction of Egypt, long afterwards, is threatened, the disappointment of those that make sluices and ponds for fish is particularly noticed, Isa. xix. 10. Egypt was a pleasant land, but the noisome stench of dead fish and blood, which by degrees would grow putrid, now rendered it very unpleasant. 2. It was a righteous plague, and justly inflicted upon the Egyptians. For, (1.) Nilus, the river of Egypt, was their idol; they and their land derived so much benefit from it that they served and worshipped it more than the

Creator. The true fountain of the Nile being unknown to them, they paid all their devotions to its streams : here therefore God punished them, and turned that into blood which they had turned into a god. Note, That creature which we idolize God justly removes from us, or embitters to us. He makes that a scourge to us which we make a competitor with him. (2.) They had stained the river with the blood of the Hebrews' children, and now God made that river all bloody. Thus he gave them blood to drink, for they were worthy, Rev. xvi. 6. Note, Never any thirsted after blood, but, sooner or later, they had enough of it. 3. It was a significant plague. Egypt had a great dependence upon their river (Zech. xiv. 18), so that in smiting the river they were warned of the destruction of all the productions of their country, till it came at last to their first-born ; and this red river proved a direful omen of the ruin of Pharaoh and all his forces in the Red Sea. This plague of Egypt is alluded to in the prediction of the ruin of the enemies of the New-Testament church, Rev. xvi. 3, 4. But there the sea, as well as the rivers and fountains of water, is turned into blood ; for spiritual judgments reach further, and strike deeper, than temporal judgments do. And, *lastly,* let me observe in general concerning this plague that one of the first miracles Moses wrought was turning water into blood, but one of the first miracles our Lord Jesus wrought was turning water into wine ; for the law was given by Moses, and it was a dispensation of death and terror ; but grace and truth, which, like wine, make glad the heart, came by Jesus Christ. Observe,

I. Moses is directed to give Pharaoh warning of this plague. "Pharaoh's heart is hardened (*v.* 14), therefore go and try what this will do to soften it," *v.* 15. Moses perhaps may not be admitted into Pharaoh's presence-chamber, or the room of state where he used to give audience to ambassadors ; and therefore he is directed to meet him by the river's brink, whither God foresaw he would come in the morning, either for the pleasure of a morning's walk or to pay his morning devotions to the river : for thus all people will walk, every one in the name of his god ; they will not fail to worship their god every morning. There Moses must be ready to give him a new summons to surrender, and, in case of a refusal, to tell him of the judgment that was coming upon that very river on the banks of which they were now standing. Notice is thus given him of it beforehand, that they might have no colour to say it was a chance, or to attribute it to any other cause, but that it might appear to be done by the power of the God of the Hebrews, and as a punishment upon him for his obstinacy. Moses is expressly ordered to take the rod with him, that Pharaoh might be alarmed at the sight of that rod which had

so lately triumphed over the rods of the magicians. Now learn hence, 1. That the judgments of God are all known to himself beforehand. He knows what he will do in wrath as well as in mercy. Every consumption is a consumption determined, Isa. x. 23. 2. That men cannot escape the alarms of God's wrath, because they cannot go out of the hearing of their own consciences : he that made their hearts can make his sword to approach them. 3. That God warns before he wounds ; for he is *long-suffering, not willing that any should perish, but that all should come to repentance.*

II. Aaron (who carried the mace) is directed to summon the plague by smiting the river with his rod, *v.* 19, 20. It was done in the sight of Pharaoh and his attendants ; for God's true miracles were not performed, as Satan's lying wonders were, by those that peeped and muttered : truth seeks no corners. An amazing change was immediately wrought ; all the waters, not only in the rivers, but in all their ponds, were turned into blood. 1. See here the almighty power of God. Every creature is that to us which he makes it to be, water or blood. 2. See the mutability of all things under the sun, and what changes we may meet with in them. That which is water to-day may be blood to-morrow ; what is always vain may soon become vexatious. A river, at the best, is transient ; but divine justice can quickly make it malignant. 3. See what mischievous work sin makes. If the things that have been our comforts prove our crosses, we must thank ourselves : it is sin that turns our waters into blood.

III. Pharaoh endeavours to confront the miracle, because he resolves not to humble himself under the plague. He sends for the magicians, and, by God's permission, they ape the miracle with their enchantments (*v.* 22), and this serves Pharaoh for an excuse not to set his heart to this also (*v.* 23), and a pitiful excuse it was. Could they have turned the river of blood into water again, this would have been something to the purpose ; then they would have proved their power, and Pharaoh would have been obliged to them as his benefactors. But for them, when there was such scarcity of water, to turn more of it into blood, only to show their art, plainly intimates that the design of the devil is only to delude his devotees and amuse them, not to do them any real kindness, but to keep them from doing a real kindness to themselves by repenting and returning to their God.

IV. The Egyptians, in the mean time, are seeking for relief against the plague, digging round about the river for water to drink, *v.* 24. Probably they found some, with much ado, God remembering mercy in the midst of wrath ; for he is full of compassion, and would not let the subjects smart too much for the obstinacy of their prince.

V. The plague continued seven days (*v.* 25), and, in all that time, Pharaoh's proud heart would not let him so much as desire Moses to intercede for the removal of it. Thus the hypocrites in heart heap up wrath; *they cry not when he binds them* (Job xxxvi. 13); and then no wonder that his anger is not turned away, but his hand is stretched out still.

CHAP. VIII.

Three more of the plagues of Egypt are related in this chapter, I. That of the frogs, which is, 1. Threatened, ver. 1—4. 2. Inflicted, ver. 5, 6. 3. Mimicked by the magicians, ver. 7. 4. Removed, at the humble request of Pharaoh (ver. 8—14), who yet hardens his heart, and, notwithstanding his promise while the plague was upon him (ver. 8), refuses to let Israel go, ver. 15. II. The plague of lice (ver. 16, 17), by which, 1. The magicians were baffled (ver. 18, 19), and yet, 2. Pharaoh was hardened, ver. 19. III. That of flies. 1. Pharaoh is warned of it before (ver. 20, 21), and told that the land of Goshen should be exempt from this plague, ver. 22, 23. 2. The plague is brought, ver. 24. 3. Pharaoh treats with Moses about the release of Israel, and humbles himself, ver. 25—29. 4. The plague is thereupon removed (ver. 31), and Pharaoh's heart hardened, ver. 32.

AND the Lord spake unto Moses, Go unto Pharaoh, and say unto him, Thus saith the Lord, Let my people go, that they may serve me. 2 And if thou refuse to let *them* go, behold, I will smite all thy borders with frogs: 3 And the river shall bring forth frogs abundantly, which shall go up and come into thine house, and into thy bedchamber, and upon thy bed, and into the house of thy servants, and upon thy people, and into thine ovens, and into thy kneadingtroughs: 4 And the frogs shall come up both on thee, and upon thy people, and upon all thy servants. 5 And the Lord spake unto Moses, Say unto Aaron, Stretch forth thine hand with thy rod over the streams, over the rivers, and over the ponds, and cause frogs to come up upon the land of Egypt. 6 And Aaron stretched out his hand over the waters of Egypt; and the frogs came up, and covered the land of Egypt. 7 And the magicians did so with their enchantments, and brought up frogs upon the land of Egypt. 8 Then Pharaoh called for Moses and Aaron, and said, Intreat the Lord, that he may take away the frogs from me, and from my people; and I will let the people go, that they may do sacrifice unto the Lord. 9 And Moses said unto Pharaoh, Glory over me: when shall I intreat for thee, and for thy servants, and for thy people, to destroy the frogs from thee and thy houses, *that* they may remain in the river only? 10 And he said, To morrow. And he said, *Be it* according to

thy word: that thou mayest know that *there is* none like unto the Lord our God. 11 And the frogs shall depart from thee, and from thy houses, and from thy servants, and from thy people; they shall remain in the river only. 12 And Moses and Aaron went out from Pharaoh: and Moses cried unto the Lord because of the frogs which he had brought against Pharaoh. 13 And the Lord did according to the word of Moses; and the frogs died out of the houses, out of the villages, and out of the fields. 14 And they gathered them together upon heaps: and the land stank. 15 But when Pharaoh saw that there was respite, he hardened his heart, and hearkened not unto them; as the Lord had said.

Pharaoh is here first threatened and then plagued with frogs, as afterwards, in this chapter, with lice and flies, little despicable inconsiderable animals, and yet by their vast numbers rendered sore plagues to the Egyptians. God could have plagued them with lions, or bears, or wolves, or with vultures or other birds of prey; but he chose to do it by these contemptible instruments. 1. That he might magnify his own power. He is Lord of the hosts of the whole creation, has them all at his beck, and makes what use he pleases of them. Some have thought that the power of God is shown as much in the making of an ant as in the making of an elephant; so is his providence in serving his own purposes by the least creatures as effectually as by the strongest, that the excellency of the power, in judgment as well as mercy, may be of God, and not of the creature. See what reason we have to stand in awe of this God, who, when he pleases, can arm the smallest parts of the creation against us. If God be our enemy, all the creatures are at war with us. 2. That he might humble Pharaoh's pride, and chastise his insolence. What a mortification must it needs be to this haughty monarch to see himself brought to his knees, and forced to submit, by such despicable means! Every child is, ordinarily, able to deal with those invaders, and can triumph over them; yet now so numerous were their troops, and so vigorous their assaults, that Pharaoh, with all his chariots and horsemen, could make no head against them. Thus he *poureth contempt upon princes* that offer contempt to him and his sovereignty, and makes those who will not own him above them to know that, when he pleases, he can make the meanest creature to insult them and trample upon them. As to the plague of frogs we may observe,

I. How it was threatened. Moses, no doubt, attended the divine Majesty daily for fresh instructions, and (perhaps while the river was yet blood) he is here directed to give notice to Pharaoh of another judgment coming upon him, in case he continue obstinate : *If thou refuse to let them go,* it is at thy peril, *v.* 1, 2. Note, God does not punish men for sin unless they persist in it. *If he turn not, he will whet his sword* (Ps. vii. 12), which implies favour *if he turn.* So here, *If thou refuse, I will smite thy borders,* intimating that if Pharaoh complied the controversy should immediately be dropped. The plague threatened, in case of refusal, was formidably extensive. Frogs were to make such an inroad upon them as should make them uneasy in their houses, in their beds, and at their tables ; they should not be able to eat, nor drink, nor sleep in quietness, but, wherever they were, should be infested by them, *v.* 3, 4. Note, 1. God's curse upon a man will pursue him wherever he goes, and lie heavily upon him whatever he does. See Deut. xxviii. 16, &c. 2. There is no avoiding divine judgments when they invade with commission.

II. How it was inflicted. Pharaoh not regarding the alarm, nor being at all inclined to yield to the summons, Aaron is ordered to draw out the forces, and with his outstretched arm and rod to give the signal of battle. *Dictum factum—No sooner said than done;* the host is mustered, and, under the direction and command of an invisible power, shoals of frogs invade the land, and the Egyptians, with all their art and all their might, cannot check their progress, nor so much as give them a diversion. Compare this with that prophecy of an army of locusts and caterpillars, Joel ii. 2, &c. ; and see Isa. xxxiv. 16, 17. Frogs came up, at the divine call, and *covered the land.* Note, God has many ways of disquieting those that live at ease.

III. How the magicians were permitted to imitate it, *v.* 7. They also brought up frogs, but could not remove those that God sent. The unclean spirits which came *out of the mouth of the dragon* are said to be like frogs, which go forth to the kings of the earth, to deceive them (Rev. xvi. 13), which probably alludes to these frogs, for it follows the account of the turning of the waters into blood. The dragon, like the magicians, intended by them to deceive, but God intended by them to destroy those that would be deceived.

IV. How Pharaoh relented under this plague : it was the first time he did so, *v.* 8. He begs of Moses to intercede for the removal of the frogs, and promises fair that he will let the people go. He that a little while ago had spoken with the utmost disdain both of God and Moses is now glad to be beholden to the mercy of God and the prayers of Moses. Note, Those that bid defiance to God and prayer in a day of extremity will, first or last, be made to see their need of both, and will cry, *Lord, Lord,* Matt. vii. 22. Those

that have bantered prayer have been brought to beg it, as the rich man that had scorned Lazarus courted him for a drop of water.

V. How Moses fixes the time with Pharaoh, and then prevails with God by prayer for the removal of the frogs. Moses, to show that his performances had no dependence upon the conjunctions or oppositions of the planets, or the luckiness of any one hour more than another, bids Pharaoh name his time. *Nullum occurrit tempus regi—No time fixed on by the king shall be objected to, v.* 9. *Have thou this honour over me,* tell me *against when I shall entreat for thee.* This was designed for Pharaoh's conviction, that, if his eyes were not opened by the plague, they might by the removal of it. So various are the methods God takes to bring men to repentance. Pharaoh sets the time for *to-morrow, v.* 10. And why not immediately ? Was he so fond of his guests that he would have them stay another night with him ? No, but probably he hoped that they would go away of themselves, and then he should get clear of the plague without being obliged either to God or Moses. However, Moses joins issue with him upon it : *" Be it according to thy word,* it shall be done just when thou wouldst have it done, *that thou mayest know that,* whatever the magicians pretend to, *there is none like unto the Lord our God.* None has such a command as he has over all the creatures, nor is any one so ready to forgive those that humble themselves before him." Note, The great design both of judgments and mercies is to convince us that there is none like the Lord our God, none so wise, so mighty, so good, no enemy so formidable, no friend so desirable, so valuable. Moses, hereupon, applies to God, prays earnestly to him, to remand the frogs, *v.* 12. Note, We must pray for our enemies and persecutors, even the worst, as Christ did. In answer to the prayer of Moses, the frogs that came up one day perished the next, or the next but one. They all died (*v.* 13), and, that it might appear that they were real frogs, their dead bodies were left to be raked together in heaps, so that the smell of them became offensive, *v.* 14. Note, The great Sovereign of the world makes what use he pleases of the lives and deaths of his creatures ; and he that gives a being, to serve one purpose, may, without wrong to his justice, call for it again immediately, to serve another purpose.

VI. What was the issue of this plague (*v.* 15): *When Pharaoh saw there was a respite,* without considering either what he had lately felt or what he had reason to fear, he hardened his heart. Note, 1. Till the heart is renewed by the grace of God, the impressions made by the force of affliction do not abide ; the convictions wear off, and the promises that were extorted are forgotten. Till the disposition of the air is changed, what thaws in the sun will freeze again in the shade. 2. God's patience is shamefully abused by impenitent sinners. The respite he gives them, to lead them to repentance, they are hardened by; and while he graciously allows them a truce, in order to the making of their peace, they take that opportunity to rally again the baffled forces of an obstinate infidelity. See Eccl. viii. 11; Ps. lxxviii. 34, &c.

16 And the LORD said unto Moses, Say unto Aaron, Stretch out thy rod, and smite the dust of the land, that it may become lice throughout all the land of Egypt. 17 And they did so; for Aaron stretched out his hand with his rod, and smote the dust of the earth, and it became lice in man, and in beast; all the dust of the land became lice throughout all the land of Egypt. 18 And the magicians did so with their enchantments to bring forth lice, but they could not: so there were lice upon man, and upon beast. 19 Then the magicians said unto Pharaoh, This *is* the finger of God: and Pharaoh's heart was hardened, and he hearkened not unto them; as the LORD had said.

Here is a short account of the plague of lice. It does not appear that any warning was given of it before. Pharaoh's abuse of the respite granted to him might have been a sufficient warning to him to expect another plague: for if the removal of an affliction harden us, and so we lose the benefit of it, we may conclude it goes away with a purpose to return or to make room for a worse. Observe,

I. How this plague of lice was inflicted on the Egyptians, *v.* 16, 17. The frogs were produced out of the waters, but these lice out of *the dust of the earth :* for out of any part of the creation God can fetch a scourge, with which to correct those that rebel against him. He has many arrows in his quiver. Even the dust of the earth obeys him. "*Fear not then, thou worm Jacob,* for God can use thee as a threshing instrument, if he please," Isa. xli. 14, 15. These lice, no doubt, were extremely vexatious, as well as scandalous, to the Egyptians. Though they had respite, they had respite but awhile, Rev. xi. 14. The second woe was past, but behold the third woe came very quickly.

II. How the magicians were baffled by it, *v.* 18. They attempted to imitate it, but they could not. When they failed in this, it should seem they attempted to remove it; for it follows, *So there were lice upon man and beast,* in spite of them. This forced them to confess themselves overpowered: *This is the finger of God (v.* 19); that is, "This check and restraint put upon us must needs be from a divine power." Note, 1. God has

the devil in a chain, and limits him both as a deceiver and as a destroyer; *hitherto he shall come, but no further.* The devil's agents, when God permitted them, could do great things; but when he laid an embargo upon them, though but with his finger, they could do nothing. The magicians' inability, in this less instance, showed whence they had their ability in the former instances which seemed greater, and that they had no power against Moses but what was given them from above. 2. Sooner or later God will extort, even from his enemies, an acknowledgment of his own sovereignty and over-ruling power. It is certain they must all (as we say) knock under at last, as Julian the apostate did, when his dying lips confessed, *Thou hast overcome me, O thou Galilean!* God will not only be too hard for all opposers, but will force them to own it.

III. How Pharaoh, notwithstanding this, was made more and more obstinate (*v.* 19); even those that had deceived him now said enough to undeceive him, and yet he grew more and more obstinate. Even the miracles and the judgments were to him a savour of death unto death. Note, Those that are not made better by God's word and providences are commonly made worse by them.

20 And the LORD said unto Moses, Rise up early in the morning, and stand before Pharaoh; lo, he cometh forth to the water; and say unto him, Thus saith the LORD, Let my people go, that they may serve me. 21 Else, if thou wilt not let my people go, behold, I will send swarms *of flies* upon thee, and upon thy servants, and upon thy people, and into thy houses: and the houses of the Egyptians shall be full of swarms *of flies,* and also the ground whereon they *are.* 22 And I will sever in that day the land of Goshen, in which my people dwell, that no swarms *of flies* shall be there; to the end thou mayest know that I *am* the LORD in the midst of the earth. 23 And I will put a division between my people and thy people: to morrow shall this sign be. 24 And the LORD did so; and there came a grievous swarm *of flies* into the house of Pharaoh, and *into* his servants' houses, and into all the land of Egypt: the land was corrupted by reason of the swarm *of flies.* 25 And Pharaoh called for Moses and for Aaron, and said, Go ye, sacrifice to your God in the land. 26 And Moses said, It is not meet so to do; for we shall sacrifice

the abomination of the Egyptians to the LORD our God: lo, shall we sacrifice the abomination of the Egyptians before their eyes, and will they not stone us? 27 We will go three days' journey into the wilderness, and sacrifice to the LORD our God, as he shall command us. 28 And Pharaoh said, I will let you go, that ye may sacrifice to the LORD your God in the wilderness; only ye shall not go very far away: intreat for me. 29 And Moses said, Behold, I go out from thee, and I will intreat the LORD that the swarms *of flies* may depart from Pharaoh, from his servants, and from his people, to morrow: but let not Pharaoh deal deceitfully any more in not letting the people go to sacrifice to the LORD. 30 And Moses went out from Pharaoh, and intreated the LORD. 31 And the LORD did according to the word of Moses; and he removed the swarms *of flies* from Pharaoh, from his servants, and from his people; there remained not one. 32 And Pharaoh hardened his heart at this time also, neither would he let the people go.

Here is the story of the plague of flies, in which we are told,

I. How it was threatened, like that of frogs, before it was inflicted. Moses is directed (*v.* 20) to rise early in the morning, to meet Pharaoh when he came forth to the water, and there to repeat his demands. Note, 1. Those that would bring great things to pass for God and their generation must rise early, and redeem time in the morning. Pharaoh was early up at his superstitious devotions to the river; and shall we be for more sleep and more slumber when any service is to be done which would pass well in our account in the great day? 2. Those that would approve themselves God's faithful servants must not be afraid of the face of man. Moses must *stand before Pharaoh*, proud as he was, and tell him that which was in the highest degree humbling, must challenge him (if he refused to release his captives) to engage with an army of flies, which would obey God's orders if Pharaoh would not. See a similar threatening, Isa. vii. 18, *The Lord will hiss* (or whistle) *for the fly and the bee*, to come and serve his purposes.

II. How the Egyptians and the Hebrews were to be remarkably distinguished in this plague, *v.* 22, 23. It is probable that this distinction had not been so manifest and observable in any of the foregoing plagues as it

was to be in this. Thus, as the plague of lice was made more convincing than any before it, by its running the magicians aground, so was this, by the distinction made between the Egyptians and the Hebrews. Pharaoh must be made to know that *God is the Lord in the midst of the earth;* and by this it will be known beyond dispute. 1. Swarms of flies, which seem to us to fly at random, shall be manifestly under the conduct of an intelligent mind, while they are above the direction of any man. "Hither they shall go," says Moses, "and thither they shall not come;" and the performance is punctually according to this appointment, and both, compared, amount to a demonstration that he that said it and he that did it was the same, even a Being of infinite power and wisdom. 2. The servants and worshippers of the great Jehovah shall be preserved from sharing in the common calamities of the place they live in, so that the plague which annoys all their neighbours shall not approach them; and this shall be an incontestable proof that God is *the Lord in the midst of the earth.* Put both these together, and it appears that *the eyes of the Lord run to and fro through the earth*, and through the air too, to direct that which to us seems most casual, to serve some great and designed end, that he may *show himself strong on the behalf of those whose hearts are upright with him*, 2 Chron. xvi. 9. Observe how it is repeated: *I will put a division between my people and thy people, v.* 23. Note, The Lord knows those that are his, and will make it appear, perhaps in this world, certainly in the other, that he has set them apart for himself. A day will come when you shall *return and discern between the righteous and the wicked* (Mal. iii. 18), *the sheep and the goats* (Matt. xxv. 32; Ezek. xxxiv. 17), though now intermixed.

III. How it was inflicted, the day after it was threatened: *There came a grievous swarm of flies* (*v.* 24), flies of divers sorts, and such as devoured them, Ps. lxxviii. 45. The prince of the power of the air has gloried in being *Beelzebub—the god of flies;* but here it is proved that even in *that* he is a pretender and a usurper, for even with swarms of flies God fights against his kingdom and prevails.

IV. How Pharaoh, upon this attack, sounded a parley, and entered into a treaty with Moses and Aaron about a surrender of his captives: but observe with what reluctance he yields.

1. He is content they should sacrifice to their God, provided they would do it in the land of Egypt, *v.* 25. Note, God can extort a toleration of his worship, even from those that are really enemies to it. Pharaoh, under the smart of the rod, is content they should do sacrifice, and will allow liberty of conscience to God's Israel, even in his own land. But Moses will not accept his concession; he cannot do it, *v.* 26. It would be an abomination to God should they offer the Egyp-

tian sacrifices, and an abomination to the Egyptians should they offer to God their own sacrifices, as they ought; so that they could not sacrifice in the land without incurring the displeasure either of their God or of their task-masters; therefore he insists: *We will go three days' journey into the wilderness*, v. 27. Note, Those that would offer an acceptable sacrifice to God must, (1.) Separate themselves from the wicked and profane; for we cannot have fellowship both with the Father of lights and with the works of darkness, both with Christ and with Belial, 2 Cor. vi. 14, &c.; Ps. xxvi. 4, 6. (2.) They must retire from the distractions of the world, and get as far as may be from the noise of it. Israel cannot keep the feast of the Lord either among the brick-kilns or among the flesh-pots of Egypt; no, *We will go into the wilderness*, Hos. ii. 14; Cant. vii. 11. (3.) They must observe the divine appointment: "We will sacrifice as God shall command us, and not otherwise." Though they were in the utmost degree of slavery to Pharaoh, yet, in the worship of God, they must observe his commands and not Pharaoh's.

2. When this proposal is rejected, he consents for them to go into the wilderness, provided they do not go *very far away*, not so far but that he might fetch them back again, v. 28. It is probable he had heard of their design upon Canaan, and suspected that if once they left Egypt they would never come back again; and therefore, when he is forced to consent that they shall go (the swarms of flies buzzing the necessity in his ears), yet he is not willing that they should go out of his reach. Thus some sinners who, in a pang of conviction, part with their sins, yet are loth they should go very far away; for, when the fright is over, they will return to them again. We observe here a struggle between Pharaoh's convictions and his corruptions; his convictions said, "Let them go;" his corruptions said, "Yet not very far away:" but he sided with his corruptions against his convictions, and this was his ruin. This proposal Moses so far accepted as that he promised the removal of this plague upon it, v. 29. See here, (1.) How ready God is to accept sinners' submissions. Pharaoh does but say, *Entreat for me* (though it is with regret that he humbles so far), and Moses promises immediately, *I will entreat the Lord for thee*, that Pharaoh might see what the design of the plague was, not to bring him to ruin, but to bring him to repentance. With what pleasure did God say (1 Kings xxi. 29), *Seest thou how Ahab humbles himself?* (2.) What need we have to be admonished that we be sincere in our submission: *But let not Pharaoh deal deceitfully any more.* Those that deal deceitfully are justly suspected, and must be cautioned not to return again to folly, after God has once more spoken peace. *Be not deceived, God is not mocked;* if we think to put a cheat upon God by a counterfeit repentance, and a fraudulent surrender of ourselves to him, we shall prove, in the end, to have put a fatal cheat upon our own souls.

Lastly, The issue of all was that God graciously removed the plague (v. 30, 31), but Pharaoh perfidiously returned to his hardness, and *would not let the people go*, v. 32. His pride would not let him part with such a flower of his crown as his dominion over Israel was, nor his covetousness with such a branch of his revenue as their labours were. Note, Reigning lusts break through the strongest bonds, and make men impudently presumptuous and scandalously perfidious. Let not sin therefore reign; for, if it do, it will betray and hurry us to the grossest absurdities.

CHAP. IX.

In this chapter we have an account of three more of the plagues of Egypt. I. Murrain among the cattle, which was fatal to them, ver. 1—7. II. Boils upon man and beast, ver. 8—12. III. Hail, with thunder and lightning. 1. Warning is given of this plague, ver. 13—21. 2. It is inflicted, to their great terror, ver. 22—26. 3. Pharaoh, in a fright, renews his treaty with Moses, but instantly breaks his word, ver. 27, &c.

THEN the Lord said unto Moses, Go in unto Pharaoh, and tell him, Thus saith the Lord God of the Hebrews, Let my people go, that they may serve me. 2 For if thou refuse to let *them* go, and wilt hold them still, 3 Behold, the hand of the Lord is upon thy cattle which *is* in the field, upon the horses, upon the asses, upon the camels, upon the oxen, and upon the sheep: *there shall be* a very grievous murrain. 4 And the Lord shall sever between the cattle of Israel and the cattle of Egypt: and there shall nothing die of all *that is* the children's of Israel. 5 And the Lord appointed a set time, saying, To morrow the Lord shall do this thing in the land. 6 And the Lord did that thing on the morrow, and all the cattle of Egypt died: but of the cattle of the children of Israel died not one. 7 And Pharaoh sent, and, behold, there was not one of the cattle of the Israelites dead. And the heart of Pharaoh was hardened, and he did not let the people go.

Here is, I. Warning given of another plague, namely, the murrain of beasts. When Pharaoh's heart was hardened, after he had seemed to relent under the former plague, then Moses is sent to tell him there is another coming, to try what that would do towards reviving the impressions of the former plagues. Thus is the wrath of God revealed from heaven, both in his word and in his works, *against all ungodliness and unrighteousness of men.*

1. Moses puts Pharaoh in a very fair way to prevent it: *Let my people go, v.* 1. This was still the demand. God will have Israel released; Pharaoh opposes it, and the trial is, *whose word shall stand.* See how jealous God is for his people. When *the year of his redeemed has come,* he will *give Egypt for their ransom;* that kingdom shall be ruined, rather than Israel shall not be delivered. See how reasonable God's demands are. Whatever he calls for, it is but *his own:* They are my people, therefore let them go. 2. He describes the plague that should come, if he refused, *v.* 2, 3. *The hand of the Lord* immediately, without the stretching out of Aaron's hand, *is upon the cattle,* many of which, some of all kinds, should die by a sort of pestilence. This was greatly to the loss of the owners: they had made Israel poor, and now God would make them poor. Note, The hand of God is to be acknowledged even in the sickness and death of cattle, or other damage sustained in them; for a *sparrow falls not to the ground without our Father.* 3. As an evidence of the special hand of God in it, and of his particular favour to his own people, he foretels that none of their cattle should die, though they breathed in the same air and drank of the same water with the Egyptians' cattle: *The Lord shall sever, v.* 4. Note, When God's judgments are abroad, though they may fall both on the righteous and the wicked, yet God makes such a distinction that they are not the same to the one that they are to the other. See Isa. xxvii. 7. The providence of God is to be acknowledged with thankfulness in the life of the cattle, for he preserveth man and beast, Ps. xxxvi. 6. 4. To make the warning the more remarkable, the time is fixed (*v.* 5): *To-morrow* it shall be done. We know not what any day will bring forth, and therefore we cannot say what we will do to-morrow, but it is not so with God.

II. The plague itself inflicted. The cattle died, *v.* 6. Note, The creature is made subject to vanity by the sin of man, being liable, according to its capacity, both to serve his wickedness and to share in his punishment, as in the universal deluge, Rom. viii. 20, 22. Pharaoh and the Egyptians sinned; but the *sheep, what had they done?* Yet they are plagued. See Jer. xii. 4, For the *wickedness of the land, the beasts are consumed.* The Egyptians afterwards, and (some think) now, worshipped their cattle; it was among them that the Israelites learned to make a god of a calf: in this therefore the plague here spoken of meets with them. Note, What we make an idol of it is just with God to remove from us, or embitter to us. See Isa. xix. 1.

III. The distinction put between the cattle of the Egyptians and the Israelites' cattle, according to the word of God: Not *one of the cattle of the Israelites died, v.* 6, 7. Does God take care for oxen? Yes, he does; his providence extends itself to the meanest of his creatures. But it is written also for our

306

sakes, that, trusting in God, and making him our refuge, we may not be *afraid of the pestilence that walketh in darkness,* no, not though *thousands fall at our side,* Ps. xci. 6, 7. Pharaoh sent to see if the cattle of the Israelites were infected, not to satisfy his conscience, but only to gratify his curiosity, or with design, by way of reprisal, to repair his own losses out of their stocks; and, having no good design in the enquiry, the report brought to him made no impression upon him, but, on the contrary, his heart was hardened. Note, To those that are wilfully blind, even those methods of conviction which are ordained to life prove a savour of death unto death.

8 And the Lord said unto Moses and unto Aaron, Take to you handfuls of ashes of the furnace, and let Moses sprinkle it toward the heaven in the sight of Pharaoh. 9 And it shall become small dust in all the land of Egypt, and shall be a boil breaking forth *with* blains upon man, and upon beast, throughout all the land of Egypt. 10 And they took ashes of the furnace, and stood before Pharaoh; and Moses sprinkled it up toward heaven; and it became a boil breaking forth *with* blains upon man, and upon beast. 11 And the magicians could not stand before Moses because of the boils; for the boil was upon the magicians, and upon all the Egyptians. 12 And the Lord hardened the heart of Pharaoh, and he hearkened not unto them; as the Lord had spoken unto Moses.

Observe here, concerning the plague of boils and blains,

I. When they were not wrought upon by the death of their cattle, God sent a plague that seized their own bodies, and touched them to the quick. If less judgments do not do their work, God will send greater. Let us therefore humble ourselves under the mighty hand of God, and go forth to meet him in the way of his judgments, that his anger may be turned away from us.

II. The signal by which this plague was summoned was the sprinkling of warm ashes from the *furnace, towards heaven* (*v.* 8, 10), which was to signify the heating of the air with such an infection as should produce in the bodies of the Egyptians sore boils, which would be both noisome and painful. Immediately upon the scattering of the ashes, a scalding dew came down out of the air, which blistered wherever it fell. Note, Sometimes God shows men their sin in their punishment; they had oppressed Israel in the furnaces, and now the ashes of the furnace are made as much a terror to them as ever their task-masters had been to the Israelites.

III. The plague itself was very grievous— a common eruption would be so, especially to the nice and delicate, but these eruptions were inflammations, like Job's. This is afterwards called the *botch of Egypt* (Deut. xxviii. 27), as if it were some new disease, never heard of before, and known ever after by that name. Note, Sores in the body are to be looked upon as the punishments of sin, and to be hearkened to as calls to repentance.

IV. The magicians themselves were struck with these boils, *v.* 11. 1. Thus they were punished, (1.) For helping to harden Pharaoh's heart, as Elymas for seeking to *pervert the right ways of the Lord;* God will severely reckon with those that strengthen the hands of the wicked in their wickedness. (2.) For pretending to imitate the former plagues, and making themselves and Pharaoh sport with them. Those that would produce lice shall, against their wills, produce boils. Note, It is ill jesting with God's judgments, and more dangerous than playing with fire. *Be you not mockers, lest your bands be made strong.* 2. Thus they were shamed in the presence of their admirers. How weak were their enchantments, which could not so much as secure themselves! The devil can give no protection to those that are in confederacy with him. 3. Thus they were driven from the field. Their power was restrained before (*ch.* viii. 18), but they continued to confront Moses, and confirm Pharaoh in his unbelief, till now, at length, they were forced to retreat, and could not stand before Moses, to which the apostle refers (2 Tim. iii. 9) when he says that their *folly was made manifest unto all men.*

V. Pharaoh continued obstinate, for now *the Lord hardened* his heart, *v.* 12. Before, he had hardened his own heart, and resisted the grace of God; and now God justly gave him up to his own heart's lusts, to a reprobate mind, and strong delusions, permitting Satan to blind and harden him, and ordering every thing, henceforward, so as to make him more and more obstinate. Note, Wilful hardness is commonly punished with judicial hardness. If men shut their eyes against the light, it is just with God to close their eyes. Let us dread this as the sorest judgment a man can be under on this side hell.

13 And the LORD said unto Moses, Rise up early in the morning, and stand before Pharaoh, and say unto him, Thus saith the LORD God of the Hebrews, Let my people go, that they may serve me. 14 For I will at this time send all my plagues upon thine heart, and upon thy servants, and upon thy people; that thou mayest know that *there is* none like me in all the earth. 15 For now I will stretch

out my hand, that I may smite thee and thy people with pestilence; and thou shalt be cut off from the earth. 16 And in very deed for this *cause* have I raised thee up, for to show *in* thee my power; and that my name may be declared throughout all the earth. 17 As yet exaltest thou thyself against my people, that thou wilt not let them go? 18 Behold, to morrow about this time I will cause it to rain a very grievous hail, such as hath not been in Egypt since the foundation thereof even until now. 19 Send therefore now, *and* gather thy cattle, and all that thou hast in the field; *for upon* every man and beast which shall be found in the field, and shall not be brought home, the hail shall come down upon them, and they shall die. 20 He that feared the word of the LORD among the servants of Pharaoh made his servants and his cattle flee into the houses: 21 And he that regarded not the word of the LORD left his servants and his cattle in the field.

Here is, I. A general declaration of the wrath of God against Pharaoh for his obstinacy. Though God has hardened his heart (*v.* 12), yet Moses must repeat his applications to him; God suspends his grace and yet demands obedience, to punish him for requiring bricks of the children of Israel when he denied them straw. God would likewise show forth a pattern of long-suffering, and how he waits to be gracious to a *rebellious and gainsaying people.* Six times the demand had been made in vain, yet Moses must make it the seventh time: *Let my people go, v.* 13. A most dreadful message Moses is here ordered to deliver to him, whether he will hear or whether he will forbear. 1. He must tell him that he is marked for ruin, that he now stands as the butt at which God would shoot all the arrows of his wrath, *v.* 14, 15. "Now I will send *all my plagues.*" Now that no place is found for repentance in Pharaoh, nothing can prevent his utter destruction, for that only would have prevented it. Now that God begins to *harden his heart,* his case is desperate. "I will send my plagues *upon thy heart,* not only temporal plagues upon thy body, but spiritual plagues upon thy soul." Note, God can send plagues upon the heart, either by making it senseless or by making it hopeless—and these are the worst plagues. Pharaoh must now expect no respite, no cessation of arms, but to be followed with plague upon plague, till he is utterly consumed. Note. When God judges he will overcome; none ever hardened his heart against him and prospered. 2. He must tell him that he is to remain in history a standing monument of the justice and power of God's wrath (v. 16): "*For this cause have I raised thee up* to the throne at this time, and made thee to stand the shock of the plagues hitherto, *to show in thee my power.*" Providence ordered it so that Moses should have a man of such a fierce and stubborn spirit as he was to deal with; and every thing was so managed in this transaction as to make it a most signal and memorable instance of the power God has to humble and bring down the proudest of his enemies. Every thing concurred to signalize this, that God's name (that is, his incontestable sovereignty, his irresistible power, and his inflexible justice) might be declared throughout all the earth, not only to all places, but through all ages while the earth remains. Note, God sometimes raises up very bad men to honour and power, spares them long, and suffers them to grow insufferably insolent, that he may be so much the more glorified in their destruction at last. See how the neighbouring nations, at that time, improved the ruin of Pharaoh to the glory of God. Jethro said upon it, *Now know I that the Lord is greater than all gods, ch.* xviii. 11. The apostle illustrates the doctrine of God's sovereignty with this instance, Rom. ix. 17. To justify God in these resolutions, Moses is directed to ask him (v. 17), *As yet exaltest thou thyself against my people?* Pharaoh was a great king; God's people were poor shepherds at the best, and now poor slaves; and yet Pharaoh shall be ruined if he exalt himself against them, for it is considered as exalting himself against God. This was not the first time that God reproved kings for their sakes, and let them know that he would not suffer his people to be trampled upon and insulted, no, not by the most powerful of them.

II. A particular prediction of the plague of hail (v. 18), and a gracious advice to Pharaoh and his people to send for their servants and cattle out of the field, that they might be sheltered from the hail, v. 19. Note, When God's justice threatens ruin his mercy, at the same time, shows us a way of escape from it, so unwilling is he that any should perish. See here what care God took, not only to distinguish between Egyptians and Israelites, but between some Egyptians and others. If Pharaoh will not yield, and so prevent the judgment itself, yet an opportunity is given to those that have any dread of God and his word to save themselves from sharing in the judgment. Note, Those that will take warning may take shelter; and those that will not may thank themselves if they fall by the overflowing scourge, and the hail which will *sweep away the refuge of lies,* Isa. xxviii. 17. See the different effect of this warning. 1.

Some believed the things that were spoken, and they feared, and housed their servants and cattle (v. 20), like Noah (Heb. xi. 7), and it was their wisdom. Even among the servants of Pharaoh there were some that trembled at God's word; and shall not the sons of Israel dread it? But, 2. Others believed not: though, whatever plague Moses had hitherto foretold, the event exactly answered to the prediction; and though, if they had had any reason to question this, it would have been no great damage to them to have kept their cattle in the house for one day, and so, supposing it a doubtful case, to have chosen the surer side; yet they were so foolhardy as in defiance to the truth of Moses, and the power of God (of both which they had already had experience enough, to their cost), to leave their cattle in the field, Pharaoh himself, it is probable, giving them an example of the presumption, v. 21. Note, Obstinate infidelity, which is deaf to the fairest warnings and the wisest counsels, leaves the blood of those that perish upon their own heads.

22 And the Lord said unto Moses, Stretch forth thine hand toward heaven, that there may be hail in all the land of Egypt, upon man, and upon beast, and upon every herb of the field, throughout the land of Egypt. 23 And Moses stretched forth his rod toward heaven: and the Lord sent thunder and hail, and the fire ran along upon the ground; and the Lord rained hail upon the land of Egypt. 24 So there was hail, and fire mingled with the hail, very grievous, such as there was none like it in all the land of Egypt since it became a nation. 25 And the hail smote throughout all the land of Egypt all that *was* in the field, both man and beast; and the hail smote every herb of the field, and brake every tree of the field. 26 Only in the land of Goshen, where the children of Israel *were,* was there no hail. 27 And Pharaoh sent, and called for Moses and Aaron, and said unto them, I have sinned this time: the Lord *is* righteous, and I and my people *are* wicked. 28 Intreat the Lord (for *it is* enough) that there be no *more* mighty thunderings and hail; and I will let you go, and ye shall stay no longer. 29 And Moses said unto him, As soon as I am gone out of the city, I will spread abroad my hands unto the Lord; *and* the thunder shall

cease, neither shall there be any more hail; that thou mayest know how that the earth *is* the LORD's. 30 But as for thee and thy servants, I know that ye will not yet fear the LORD God. 31 And the flax and the barley was smitten: for the barley *was* in the ear, and the flax *was* bolled. 32 But the wheat and the rye were not smitten: for they *were* not grown up. 33 And Moses went out of the city from Pharaoh, and spread abroad his hands unto the LORD: and the thunders and hail ceased, and the rain was not poured upon the earth. 34 And when Pharaoh saw that the rain and the hail and the thunders were ceased, he sinned yet more, and hardened his heart, he and his servants. 35 And the heart of Pharaoh was hardened, neither would he let the children of Israel go; as the LORD had spoken by Moses.

The threatened plague of hail is here summoned by the powerful hand and rod of Moses (v. 22, 23), and it obeys the summons, or rather the divine command; for *fire and hail fulfil God's word*, Ps. cxlviii. 8. And here we are told,

I. What desolations it made upon the earth. The thunder, and fire from heaven (or lightning), made it both the more dreadful and the more destroying, v. 23, 24. Note, God makes the clouds, not only his store-houses whence he drops fatness on his people, but his magazines whence, when he pleases, he can draw out a most formidable train of artillery, with which to destroy his enemies. He himself speaks of the *treasures of hail which he hath reserved against the day of battle and war*, Job xxxviii. 22, 23. Woeful havoc this hail made in the land of Egypt. It killed both men and cattle, and battered down, not only the herbs, but the trees, v. 25. The corn that was aboveground was destroyed, and that only preserved which as yet had not come up, v. 31, 32. Note, God has many ways of *taking away the corn in the season thereof* (Hos. ii. 9), either by a secret blasting, or a noisy hail. In this plague the *hot thunderbolts*, as well as the hail, are said to destroy *their flocks*, Ps. lxxviii. 47, 48; and see Ps. cv. 32, 33. Perhaps David alludes to this when, describing God's glorious appearances for the discomfiture of his enemies, he speaks of the hail-stones and coals of fire he threw among them, Ps. xviii. 12, 13. And there is a plain reference to it on the pouring out of the seventh vial, Rev. xvi. 21. Notice is here taken (v. 26) of the land of Goshen's being preserved from receiving any damage by this plague. God has the directing of the pregnant clouds, and causes it to rain or hail on one city and not on another, either in mercy or in judgment.

II. What a consternation it put Pharaoh in. See what effect it had upon him, 1. He humbled himself to Moses in the language of a penitent, v. 27, 28. No man could have spoken better. He owns himself on the wrong side in his contest with the God of the Hebrews: " *I have sinned* in standing it out so long." He owns the equity of God's proceedings against him: *The Lord is righteous*, and must be justified when he speaks, though he speak in thunder and lightning. He condemns himself and his land: " *I and my people are wicked*, and deserve what is brought upon us." He begs the prayers of Moses: " *Entreat the Lord* for me, that this direful plague may be removed." And, *lastly*, he promises to yield up his prisoners: *I will let you go.* What could one desire more? And yet his heart was hardened all this while. Note, The terror of the rod often extorts penitent acknowledgments from those who have no penitent affections; under the surprise and smart of affliction, they start up, and say that which is pertinent enough, not because they are deeply affected, but because they know that they should be and that *it is meet to be said.* 2. Moses, hereupon, becomes an intercessor for him with God. Though he had all the reason in the world to think that he would immediately repent of his repentance, and told him so (v. 30), yet he promises to be his friend in the court of heaven. Note, Even those whom we have little hopes of, yet we should continue to pray for, and to admonish, 1 Sam. xii. 23. Observe, (1.) The place Moses chose for his intercession. He went *out of the city* (v. 33), not only for privacy in his communion with God, but to show that he durst venture abroad into the field, notwithstanding the hail and lightning which kept Pharaoh and his servants within-doors, knowing that every hail-stone had its direction from his God, who meant him no hurt. Note, Peace with God makes men thunder-proof, for thunder is the voice of their Father. (2.) The gesture: He *spread abroad his hands unto the Lord*—an outward expression of earnest desire and humble expectation. Those that come to God for mercy must stand ready to receive it. (3.) The end Moses aimed at in interceding for him: *That thou mayest know*, and be convinced, *that the earth is the Lord's* (v. 29), that is, that God has a sovereign dominion over all the creatures, that they all are ruled by him, and therefore that thou oughtest to be so. See what various methods God uses to bring men to their proper senses. Judgments are sent, judgments removed, and all for the same end, to make men know that the Lord reigns. (4.) The success of it. [1.] He prevailed with God, v. 33. But, [2.] He could not prevail with Pharaoh : *He sinned yet more, and hardened his heart, v.* 34, 35. The prayer of Moses opened and shut heaven, like Elias's (Jam. v. 17, 18), and such is the power of God's two witnesses (Rev. xi. 6) ; yet neither Moses nor Elias, nor those two witnesses, could subdue the hard hearts of men. Pharaoh was frightened into a compliance by the judgment, but, when it was over, his convictions vanished, and his fair promises were forgotten. Note, Little credit is to be given to confessions upon the rack. Note also, Those that are not bettered by judgments and mercies are commonly made worse.

CHAP. X.

The eighth and ninth of the plagues of Egypt, that of locusts and that of darkness, are recorded in this chapter. I. Concerning the plague of locusts, 1. God instructs Moses in the meaning of these amazing dispensations of his providence, ver. 1, 2. *2. He threatens the locusts, ver.* 3—6. *3. Pharaoh, at the persuasion of his servants, is willing to treat again with Moses (ver.* 7—9), *but they cannot agree, ver.* 10, 11. *4. The locusts come, ver.* 12—15. *5. Pharaoh cries Peccavi—I have offended (ver.* 16, 17), *whereupon Moses prays for the removal of the plague, and it is done; but Pharaoh's heart is still hardened, ver.* 18—20. II. *Concerning the plague of darkness,* 1. *It is inflicted, ver.* 21—23. *2. Pharaoh again treats with Moses about a surrender, but the treaty breaks off in a heat, ver.* 24, &c.

AND the LORD said unto Moses, Go in unto Pharaoh : for I have hardened his heart, and the heart of his servants, that I might show these my signs before him : 2 And that thou mayest tell in the ears of thy son, and of thy son's son, what things I have wrought in Egypt, and my signs which I have done among them ; that ye may know how that I *am* the LORD. 3 And Moses and Aaron came in unto Pharaoh, and said unto him, Thus saith the LORD God of the Hebrews, How long wilt thou refuse to humble thyself before me ? let my people go, that they may serve me. 4 Else, if thou refuse to let my people go, behold, to morrow will I bring the locusts into thy coast : 5 And they shall cover the face of the earth, that one cannot be able to see the earth : and they shall eat the residue of that which is escaped, which remaineth unto you from the hail, and shall eat every tree which groweth for you out of the field : 6 And they shall fill thy houses, and the houses of all thy servants, and the houses of all the Egyptians ; which neither thy fathers, nor thy fathers' fathers have seen, since the day that they were upon the earth unto this day. And he turned himself, and went out from Pharaoh. 7 And Pharaoh's servants said unto him,

How long shall this man be a snare unto us ? let the men go, that they may serve the LORD their God : knowest thou not yet that Egypt is destroyed ? 8 And Moses and Aaron were brought again unto Pharaoh : and he said unto them, Go, serve the LORD your God : *but* who *are* they that shall go ? 9 And Moses said, We will go with our young and with our old, with our sons and with our daughters, with our flocks and with our herds will we go ; for we *must hold* a feast unto the LORD. 10 And he said unto them, Let the LORD be so with you, as I will let you go, and your little ones : look *to it ;* for evil *is* before you. 11 Not so : go now ye *that are* men, and serve the LORD ; for that ye did desire. And they were driven out from Pharaoh's presence.

Here, I. Moses is instructed. We may well suppose that he, for his part, was much astonished both at Pharaoh's obstinacy and at God's severity, and could not but be compassionately concerned for the desolations of Egypt, and at a loss to conceive what this contest would come to at last. Now here God tells him what he designed, not only Israel's release, but the magnifying of his own name : *That thou mayest tell* in thy writings, which shall continue to the world's end, *what I have wrought in Egypt, v.* 1, 2. The ten plagues of Egypt must be inflicted, that they may be recorded for the generations to come as undeniable proofs, 1. Of God's overruling power in the kingdom of nature, his dominion over all the creatures, and his authority to use them either as servants to his justice or sufferers by it, according to the counsel of his will. 2. Of God's victorious power over the kingdom of Satan, to restrain the malice and chastise the insolence of his and his church's enemies. These plagues are standing monuments of the greatness of God, the happiness of the church, and the sinfulness of sin, and standing monitors to the children of men in all ages not to *provoke the Lord to jealousy* nor to *strive with their Maker.* The benefit of these instructions to the world sufficiently balances the expense.

II. Pharaoh is reproved (*v.* 3): *Thus saith the Lord God of the* poor, despised, persecuted, Hebrews, *How long wilt thou refuse to humble thyself before me ?* Note, It is justly expected from the greatest of men that they humble themselves before the great God, and it is at their peril if they refuse to do it. This has more than once been God's quarrel with princes. Belshazzar did not humble his heart, Dan. v. 22. Zedekiah humbled

not himself before Jeremiah, 2 Chron. xxxvi.
12. Those that will not humble themselves
God will humble. Pharaoh had sometimes
pretended to humble himself, but no account
was made of it, because he was neither sincere nor constant in it.

III. The plague of locusts is threatened,
v. 4—6. The hail had broken down the
fruits of the earth, but these locusts should
come and devour them : and not only so,
but they should fill their houses, whereas the
former inroads of these insects had been confined to their lands. This should be much
worse than all the calamities of that kind
which had ever been known. Moses, when
he had delivered his message, not expecting
any better answer than he had formerly,
turned himself and went out from Pharaoh, *v.*
6. Thus Christ appointed his disciples to
depart from those who would not receive
them, and to *shake off the dust of their feet for
a testimony against them ;* and ruin is not far
off from those who are thus justly abandoned
by the Lord's messengers, 1 Sam. xv. 27, &c.

IV. Pharaoh's attendants, his ministers of
state, or privy-counsellers, interpose, to persuade him to come to some terms with Moses,
v. 7. They, as in duty bound, represent to
him the deplorable condition of the kingdom
(Egypt is destroyed), and advise him by all
means to release his prisoners *(Let the men
go) ;* for Moses, they found, would be a
snare to them till it was done, and it were
better to consent at first than to be compelled
at last. The Israelites had become a burdensome stone to the Egyptians, and now, at
length, the princes of Egypt were willing to
be rid of them, Zech. xii. 3. Note, It is a
thing to be regretted (and prevented, if
possible) that a whole nation should be
ruined for the pride and obstinacy of its
princes, *Salus populi suprema lex—To consult the welfare of the people is the first of
laws.*

V. A new treaty is, hereupon, set on foot
between Pharaoh and Moses, in which Pharaoh consents for the Israelites to go into
the wilderness to do sacrifice ; but the matter
in dispute was who should go, *v.* 8. 1.
Moses insists that they should take their
whole families, and all their effects, along
with them, *v.* 9. Note, Those that serve
God must serve him with all they have.
Moses pleads, " We must hold a feast, therefore we must have our families to feast with,
and our flocks and herds to feast upon, to
the honour of God." 2. Pharaoh will by no
means grant this : he will allow the men to
go, pretending that this was all they desired,
though this matter was never yet mentioned
in any of the former treaties ; but, for the
little ones, he resolves to keep them as hos-
tages, to oblige them to return, *v.* 10, 11. In
a great passion he curses them, and threatens
that, if they offer to remove their little ones,
they will do it at their peril. Note, Satan does
all he can to hinder those that serve God them-

selves from bringing their children in to serve
him. He is a sworn enemy to early piety,
knowing how destructive it is to the interests of
his kingdom : whatever would hinder us from
engaging our children to the utmost in God's
service, we have reason to suspect the hand
of Satan in it. 3 The treaty, hereupon,
breaks off abruptly ; those that before went
out from Pharaoh's presence (*v.* 6) were now
driven out. Those will quickly hear their
doom that cannot bear to hear their duty.
See 2 Chron. xxv. 16. *Quos Deus destruet
eos dementat—Whom God intends to destroy
he delivers up to infatuation.* Never was man
so infatuated to his own ruin as Pharaoh was.

12 And the Lord said unto Moses,
Stretch out thine hand over the land
of Egypt for the locusts, that they
may come up upon the land of Egypt,
and eat every herb of the land, *even*
all that the hail hath left. 13 And
Moses stretched forth his rod over the
land of Egypt, and the Lord brought
an east wind upon the land all that
day, and all *that* night ; *and* when it
was morning the east wind brought
the locusts. 14 And the locusts went
up over all the land of Egypt, and
rested in all the coasts of Egypt : very
grievous *were they ;* before them there
were no such locusts as they, neither
after them shall be such. 15 For they
covered the face of the whole earth,
so that the land was darkened ; and
they did eat every herb of the land,
and all the fruit of the trees which the
hail had left : and there remained not
any green thing in the trees, or in the
herbs of the field, through all the land
of Egypt. 16 Then Pharaoh called
for Moses and Aaron in haste ; and he
said, I have sinned against the Lord
your God, and against you. 17 Now
therefore forgive, I pray thee, my sin
only this once, and intreat the Lord
your God, that he may take away from
me this death only. 18 And he went
out from Pharaoh, and intreated the
Lord. 19 And the Lord turned a
mighty strong west wind, which took
away the locusts, and cast them into
the Red sea ; there remained not one
locust in all the coasts of Egypt. 20
But the Lord hardened Pharaoh's
heart, so that he would not let the
children of Israel go.

Here is, I. The invasion of the land by

the locusts—*God's great army,* Joel ii. 11. God bids *Moses stretch out his hand* (*v.* 12), to beckon them, as it were (for they came at a call), and he *stretched forth his rod, v.* 13. Compare *ch.* ix. 22, 23. Moses ascribes it to the stretching out, not of his own hand, but of the *rod of God,* the instituted sign of God's presence with him. The locusts obey the summons, and fly upon the wings of the wind, the east wind, and *caterpillars without number,* as we are told, Ps. cv. 34, 35. A formidable army of horse and foot might more easily have been resisted than this host of insects. Who then is able to stand before the great God?

II. The desolations they made in it (*v.* 15): They *covered the face of the earth,* and *ate up the fruit* of it. The earth God has *given to the children of men;* yet, when God pleases, he can disturb their possession and send locusts and caterpillars to force them out. Herbs grow *for the service of man;* yet, when God pleases, those contemptible insects shall not only be fellow-commoners with him, but shall plunder him, and eat the bread out of his mouth. Let our labour be, not for the habitation and meat which thus lie exposed, but for those which *endure to eternal life,* which cannot be thus invaded, nor thus corrupted.

III. Pharaoh's admission, hereupon, *v.* 16, 17. He had driven Moses and Aaron from him (*v.* 11), telling them (it is likely) he would have no more to do with them. But now he calls for them again in all haste, and makes court to them with as much respect as before he had dismissed them with disdain. Note, The day will come when those who set at nought their counsellers, and despise all their reproofs, will be glad to make an interest in them and engage them to intercede on their behalf. The foolish virgins court the wise to *give them of their oil;* and see Ps. cxli. 6. 1. Pharaoh confesses his fault: *I have sinned against the Lord your God, and against you.* He now sees his own folly in the slights and affronts he had put on God and his ambassadors, and *seems,* at least, to repent of it. When God convinces men of sin, and humbles them for it, their contempt of God's ministers, and the word of the Lord in their mouths, will certainly come into the account, and lie heavily upon their consciences. Some think that when Pharaoh said, "The LORD *your* God," he did in effect say, "The LORD shall not be *my* God." Many treat with God as a potent enemy, whom they are willing not to be at war with, but care not for treating with him as their rightful prince, to whom they are willing to submit with loyal affection. True penitents lament sin as committed against God, even their own God, to whom they stand obliged. 2. He begs pardon, not of God, as penitents ought, but of Moses, which was more excusable in him, because, by a special commission, Moses was made a *god*

to Pharaoh, and *whosoever sins he remitted* they were forgiven; when he prays, *Forgive this once,* he, in effect, promises not to offend in like manner any more, yet seems loth to express that promise, nor does he say any thing particularly of letting the people go. Note, Counterfeit repentance commonly cheats men with general promises and is loth to covenant against particular sins. 3. He entreats Moses and Aaron to pray for him. There are those who, in distress, implore the help of other persons' prayers, but have no mind to pray for themselves, showing thereby that they have no true love to God, nor any delight in communion with him. Pharaoh desires their prayers *that this death* only might be taken away, not *this sin:* he deprecates the plague of locusts, not the plague of a hard heart, which yet was much the more dangerous.

IV. The removal of the judgment, upon the prayer of Moses, *v.* 18, 19. This was, 1. As great an instance of the power of God as the judgment itself. An east wind brought the locusts, and now a west wind carried them off. Note, Whatever point of the compass the wind is in, it is fulfilling God's word, and turns about by his counsel. The *wind bloweth where it listeth,* as it respects any control of ours; not so as it respects the control of God: he *directeth it under the whole heaven.* 2. It was as great a proof of the authority of Moses, and as firm a ratification of his commission and his interest in that God who both *makes peace* and *creates evil,* Isa. xlv. 7. Nay, hereby he not only commanded the respect, but recommended himself to the good affections of the Egyptians, inasmuch as, while the judgment came in obedience to his summons, the removal of it was in answer to his prayers. He never desired the woeful day, though he threatened it. His commission indeed ran against Egypt, but his intercession was for it, which was a good reason why they should love him, though they feared him. 3. It was also as strong an argument for their repentance as the judgment itself; for by this it appeared that God is ready to forgive, and swift to show mercy. If he turn away a particular judgment, as he did often from Pharaoh, or defer it, as in Ahab's case, upon the profession of repentance and the outward tokens of humiliation, what will he do if we be sincere, and how welcome will true penitents be to him! O that this goodness of God might lead us to repentance!

V. Pharaoh's return to his impious resolution again not to let the people go (*v.* 20), through the righteous hand of God upon him, hardening his heart, and confirming him in his obstinacy. Note, Those that have often baffled their convictions, and stood it out against them, forfeit the benefit of them, and are justly given up to those lusts of their own hearts which (how strong soever their convictions) prove too strong for them.

21 And the LORD said unto Moses, Stretch out thine hand toward heaven, that there may be darkness over the land of Egypt, even darkness *which* may be felt. 22 And Moses stretched forth his hand toward heaven; and there was a thick darkness in all the land of Egypt three days: 23 They saw not one another, neither rose any from his place for three days: but all the children of Israel had light in their dwellings. 24 And Pharaoh called unto Moses, and said, Go ye, serve the LORD; only let your flocks and your herds be stayed: let your little ones also go with you. 25 And Moses said, Thou must give us also sacrifices and burnt offerings, that we may sacrifice unto the LORD our God. 26 Our cattle also shall go with us; there shall not a hoof be left behind; for thereof must we take to serve the LORD our God; and we know not with what we must serve the LORD, until we come thither. 27 But the LORD hardened Pharaoh's heart, and he would not let them go. 28 And Pharaoh said unto him, Get thee from me, take heed to thyself, see my face no more; for in *that* day thou seest my face thou shalt die. 29 And Moses said, Thou hast spoken well, I will see thy face again no more.

Here is, I. The plague of darkness brought upon Egypt, and a most dreadful plague it was, and therefore is put first of the ten in Ps. cv. 28, though it was one of the last; and in the destruction of the spiritual Egypt it is produced by the fifth vial, which is poured out upon the *seat of the beast*, Rev. xvi. 10. *His kingdom was full of darkness.* Observe particularly concerning this plague, 1. That it was a total darkness. We have reason to think, not only that the lights of heaven were clouded, but that all their fires and candles were put' out by the damps or clammy vapours which were the cause of this darkness; for it is said (*v.* 23), They *saw not one another.* It is threatened to the wicked (Job xviii. 5, 6) that the *spark of his fire shall not shine* (even *the sparks of his own kindling*, as they are called, Isa. l. 11), and that the *light shall be dark in his tabernacle.* Hell is *utter darkness.* The light of *a candle shall shine no more at all in thee*, Rev. xviii. 23. 2. That it was darkness which *might be felt* (*v.* 21), felt in its *causes* by their fingers' ends (so thick were the fogs), felt in its *effects*, some think, by their eyes, which were pricked with pain, and made the more sore

by their rubbing them. Great pain is spoken of as the effect of that darkness, Rev. xvi. 10, which alludes to this. 3. No doubt it astonished and terrified them. The cloud of locusts, which had *darkened the land* (*v.* 15), was nothing to this. The tradition of the Jews is that in this darkness they were terrified by the apparitions of evil spirits, or rather by dreadful sounds and murmurs which they made, or (which is no less frightful) by the horrors of their own consciences; and this is the plague which some think is intended (for, otherwise, it is not mentioned at all there) Ps. lxxviii. 49, *He poured upon them the fierceness of his anger, by sending evil angels among them;* for to those to whom the devil has been a deceiver he will, at length, be a terror. 4. It continued three days, *six nights* (says bishop Hall) *in one;* so long they were imprisoned by those chains of darkness, and the most lightsome palaces were perfect dungeons. No *man rose from his place, v.* 23. They were all confined to their houses; and such a terror seized them that few of them had the courage to go from the chair to the bed, or from the bed to the chair. Thus were they *silent in darkness*, 1 Sam. ii. 9. Now Pharaoh had time to consider, if he would have improved it. Spiritual darkness is spiritual bondage; while Satan blinds men's eyes that they see not, he binds their hands and feet that they work not for God, nor move towards heaven. They *sit in darkness.* 5. It was a righteous thing with God thus to punish them. Pharaoh and his people had rebelled against the light of God's word, which Moses spoke to them; justly therefore are they punished with darkness, for they loved it and chose it rather. The blindness of their minds brings upon them this darkness of the air. Never was mind so blinded as Pharaoh's, never was air so darkened as Egypt's. The Egyptians by their cruelty would have extinguished the lamp of Israel, and quenched their coal; justly therefore does God put out their lights. Compare it with the punishment of the Sodomites, Gen. xix. 11. Let us dread the consequences of sin; if three days' darkness was so dreadful, what will everlasting darkness be? 6. The children of Israel, at the same time, had *light in their dwellings* (*v.* 23), not only in the land of Goshen, where most of them dwelt, but in the habitations of those who were dispersed among the Egyptians: for that some of them were thus dispersed appears from the distinction afterwards appointed to be put on their door-posts, *ch.* xii. 7. This is an instance, (1.) Of the power of God above the ordinary power of nature. We must not think that we share in common mercies as a matter of course, and therefore that we owe no thanks to God for them; he could distinguish, and withhold that from us which he grants to others. He does indeed ordinarily make his sun to shine on the just and the unjust; but he could make a difference, and we must own ourselves indebted to his mercy that he does not. (2.) Of the particular favour he bears to his people: they *walk in the light* when others *wander* endlessly *in thick darkness ;* wherever there is an Israelite indeed, though in this dark world, there is light, there is a *child of light,* one for whom *light is sown,* and whom the *day-spring from on high visits.* When God made this difference between the Israelites and the Egyptians, who would not have preferred the poorest cottage of an Israelite to the finest palace of an Egyptian? There is still a real difference, though not so discernible a one, between the house of the wicked, which is under a curse, and the habitation of the just, which is blessed, Prov. iii. 33. We should believe in that difference, and govern ourselves accordingly. Upon Ps. cv. 28, *He sent darkness and made it dark, and they rebelled not against his word,* some ground a conjecture that, during these three days of darkness, the Israelites were circumcised, in order to their celebrating the passover which was now approaching, and that the command which authorized this was the word against which they rebelled not; for their circumcision, when they entered Canaan, is spoken of as a second general circumcision, Josh. v. 2. During these three days of darkness to the Egyptians, if God had so pleased, the Israelites, by the light which they had, might have made their escape, and without asking leave of Pharaoh; but God would bring them out *with a high hand,* and not by stealth, nor in haste, Isa. lii. 12.

II. Here is the impression made upon Pharaoh by this plague, much like that of the foregoing plagues. 1. It awakened him so far that he renewed the treaty with Moses and Aaron, and now, at length, consented that they should take their little ones with them, only he would have their cattle left in pawn, *v.* 24. It is common for sinners thus to bargain with God Almighty. Some sins they will leave, but not all; they will leave their sins for a time, but they will not bid them a final farewell; they will allow him some share in their hearts, but the world and the flesh must share with him: thus they mock God, but they deceive themselves. Moses resolves not to abate in his terms: *Our cattle shall go with us, v.* 26. Note, The terms of reconciliation are so fixed that though men dispute them ever so long they cannot possibly alter them, nor bring them lower. We must come up to the demands of God's will, for we cannot expect he should condescend to the provisos of our lusts. God's messengers must always be bound up by that rule (Jer. xv. 19), *Let them return unto thee, but return not thou unto them.* Moses gives a very good reason why they must take their cattle with them ; they must go to do sacrifice, and therefore they must take wherewithal. What numbers and kinds of sacrifices would be required they did not yet know, and therefore they must take all

they had. Note, With ourselves, and our children, we must devote all our worldly possessions to the service of God, because we know not what use God will make of what we have, nor in what way we may be called upon to honour God with it. 2. Yet it exasperated him so far that, when he might not make his own terms, he broke off the conference abruptly, and took up a resolution to treat no more. Wrath now came upon him to the utmost, and he became outrageous beyond all bounds, *v.* 28. Moses is dismissed in anger, forbidden the court upon pain of death, forbidden so much as to meet Pharaoh any more, as he had been used to do, by the river's side: *In that day thou seest my face, thou shalt die.* Prodigious madness! Had he not found that Moses could plague him without seeing his face? Or had he forgotten how often he had sent for Moses as his physician to heal him and ease him of his plagues? and must he now be bidden to come near him no more? Impotent malice! To threaten him with death who was armed with such a power, and at whose mercy he had so often laid himself. What will not hardness of heart and contempt of God's word and commandments bring men to? Moses takes him at his word (*v.* 29): *I will see thy face no more,* that is, " after this time ;" for this conference did not break off till *ch.* xi. 8, when Moses went out *in a great anger,* and told Pharaoh how soon he would change his mind, and his proud spirit would come down, which was fulfilled (*ch.* xii. 31), when Pharaoh became a humble supplicant to Moses to depart. So that, after this interview, Moses came no more, till he was sent for. Note, When men drive God's word from them he justly permits their delusions, and answers them according to the multitude of their idols. When the Gadarenes desired Christ to depart, he presently left them.

CHAP. XI.

Pharaoh had told Moses to get out of his presence (ch. x. 28), and Moses had promised this should be the last time he would trouble him, yet he resolves to say out what he had to say, before he left him ; accordingly, we have in this chapter, I. The instructions God had given to Moses, which he was now to pursue (ver. 1, 2), together with the interest Israel and Moses had in the esteem of the Egyptians, ver. 3. II. The last message Moses delivered to Pharaoh, concerning the death of the firstborn, ver. 4—8. III. A repetition of the prediction of Pharaoh's hardening his heart (ver. 9), and the event answering to it, ver. 10.

AND the LORD said unto Moses, Yet will I bring one plague *more* upon Pharaoh, and upon Egypt; afterwards he will let you go hence: when he shall let *you* go, he shall surely thrust you out hence altogether. 2 Speak now in the ears of the people, and let every man borrow of his neighbour, and every woman of her neighbour, jewels of silver, and jewels of gold. 3 And the LORD gave the people favour in the sight of the Egyptians. Moreover the man Moses *was* very great in the land of Egypt, in the sight of Pharaoh's servants, and in the sight of the people.

Here is, I. The high favour Moses and Israel were in with God. 1. Moses was a favourite of Heaven, for God will not hide from him the thing he will do. God not only makes him his messenger to deliver his errands, but communicates to him his purpose (as the man of his counsel) that he would bring one plague more, and but one, upon Pharaoh, by which he would complete the deliverance of Israel, *v.* 1. Moses longed to see an end of this dreadful work, to see Egypt no more plagued and Israel no more oppressed : " Well," says God, " now it is near an end ; the warfare shall shortly be accomplished; the point gained ; Pharaoh shall be forced to own himself conquered, and to give up the cause." After all the rest of the plagues, God says, *I will bring one more.* Thus, after all the judgments executed upon sinners in this world, still there is one more reserved to be brought on them in the other world, which will completely humble those whom nothing else would humble. 2. The Israelites were favourites of Heaven; for God himself espouses their injured cause, and takes care to see them paid for all their pains in serving the Egyptians. This was the last day of their servitude ; they were about to go away, and their masters, who had abused them in their work, would now have defrauded them of their wages, and have sent them away empty; while the poor Israelites were so fond of liberty that they would be satisfied with that, without pay, and would rejoice to get that upon any terms: but he that *executeth righteousness and judgment for the oppressed* provided that the labourers should not lose their hire, and ordered them to demand it now at their departure (*v.* 2), *in jewels of silver and jewels of gold,* to prepare for which God, by the plagues, had now made the Egyptians as willing to part with them upon any terms as, before, the Egyptians, by their severities, had made them willing to go upon any terms. Though the patient Israelites were content to lose their wages, yet God would not let them go without them. Note, One way or other, God will give redress to the injured, who in a humble silence commit their cause to him; and he will see to it that none be losers at last by their patient suffering any more than by their services.

II. The high favour Moses and Israel were in with the Egyptians, *v.* 3. 1. Even the people that had been hated and despised now came to be respected ; the wonders wrought on their behalf put an honour upon them and made them considerable. How great do they become for whom God thus fights ! Thus *the Lord gave them favour* in the sight of the Egyptians, by making it appear how much he favoured them : he also changed

the spirit of the Egyptians towards them, and made them to be pitied of their oppressors, Ps. cvi 46. 2. *The man Moses was very great.* How could it be otherwise when they saw what power he was clothed with, and what wonders were wrought by his hand ? Thus the apostles, though otherwise despicable men, came to be magnified, Acts v. 13. Those that honour God he will honour; and with respect to those that approve themselves faithful to him, how meanly soever they may pass through this world, there is a day coming when they will look great, very great, in the eyes of all the world, even theirs who now look upon them with the utmost contempt. Observe, Though Pharaoh hated Moses, there were those of Pharaoh's servants that respected him. Thus in Cæsar's household, even Nero's, there were some that had an esteem for blessed Paul, Phil. i. 13.

4 And Moses said, Thus saith the Lord, About midnight will I go out into the midst of Egypt : 5 And all the firstborn in the land of Egypt shall die, from the firstborn of Pharaoh that sitteth upon his throne, even unto the firstborn of the maidservant that *is* behind the mill; and all the firstborn of beasts. 6 And there shall be a great cry throughout all the land of Egypt, such as there was none like it, nor shall be like it any more. 7 But against any of the children of Israel shall not a dog move his tongue, against man or beast : that ye may know how that the Lord doth put a difference between the Egyptians and Israel. 8 And all these thy servants shall come down unto me, and bow down themselves unto me, saying, Get thee out, and all the people that follow thee : and after that I will go out. And he went out from Pharaoh in a great anger. 9 And the Lord said unto Moses, Pharaoh shall not hearken unto you; that my wonders may be multiplied in the land of Egypt. 10 And Moses and Aaron did all these wonders before Pharaoh : and the Lord hardened Pharaoh's heart, so that he would not let the children of Israel go out of his land.

Warning is here given to Pharaoh of the last and conquering plague which was now to be inflicted. This was the *death of all the first-born in* Egypt at once, which had been first threatened (*ch.* iv. 23, *I will slay thy son, thy first-born*), but is last executed ; less judgments were tried, which, if they had done the work, would have prevented this.

315

See how slow God is to wrath, and how willing to be met with in the way of his judgments, and to have his anger turned away, and particularly how precious the lives of men are in his eyes: if the death of their cattle had humbled and reformed them, their children would have been spared; but, if men will not improve the gradual advances of divine judgments, they must thank themselves if they find, in the issue, that the worst was reserved for the last. 1. The plague itself is here particularly foretold, *v.* 4—6. The time is fixed—about midnight, the very next midnight, the dead time of the night; when they were all asleep, all their first-born should sleep the sleep of death, not silently and insensibly, so as not to be discovered till morning, but so as to rouse the families at midnight to stand by and see them die. The extent of this plague is described, *v.* 5. The prince that was to succeed in the throne was not too high to be reached by it, nor were the slaves at the mill too low to be taken notice of. Moses and Aaron were not ordered to summon this plague; no, *I will go out, saith the Lord, v.* 4. *It is a fearful thing to fall into the hands of the living God;* what is hell but this? 2. The special protection which the children of Israel should be under, and the manifest difference that should be put between them and the Egyptians. While angels drew their swords against the Egyptians, there should not so much as a dog bark at any of the children of Israel, *v.* 7. An earnest was hereby given of the difference which shall be put in the great day between God's people and his enemies: did men know what a difference God puts, and will put to eternity, between those that serve him and those that serve him not, religion would not seem to them such an indifferent thing as they make it, nor would they act in it with so much indifference as they do. 3. The humble submission which Pharaoh's servants should make to Moses, and how submissively they should request him to go (*v.* 8): *They shall come down, and bow themselves.* Note, The proud enemies of God and his Israel shall be made to fall under at last (Rev. iii. 9), and shall be found liars to them, Deut. xxxiii. 29. When Moses had thus delivered his message, it is said, *He went out from Pharaoh in a great anger,* though he was the meekest of all the men of the earth. Probably he expected that the very threatening of the death of the first-born would have induced Pharaoh to comply, especially as Pharaoh had complied so far already, and had seen how exactly all Moses's predictions hitherto were fulfilled. But it had not that effect; his proud heart would not yield, no, not to save all the first-born of his kingdom: no marvel that men are not deterred from vicious courses by the prospects given them of eternal misery in the other world, when the imminent peril they run of the loss of all that is dear to

216

them in this world will not frighten them. Moses, hereupon, was provoked to a holy indignation, being grieved (as our Saviour afterwards) for the *hardness of his heart,* Mark iii. 5. Note, It is a great vexation to the spirits of good ministers to see people deaf to all the fair warnings given them, and running headlong upon ruin, notwithstanding all the kind methods taken to prevent it. Thus Ezekiel went in *the bitterness of his spirit* (Ezek. iii. 14), because God had told him that the house of Israel would not hearken to him, *v.* 7. To be angry at nothing but sin is the way not to sin in anger. Moses, having thus adverted to the disturbance which Pharaoh's obstinacy gave him, (1.) Reflects upon the previous notice God had given him of this (*v.* 9): *The Lord said unto Moses, Pharaoh shall not hearken to you.* The scripture has foretold the incredulity of those who should hear the gospel, that it might not be a surprise nor stumbling-block to us, John xii. 37, 38; Rom. x. 16. Let us think never the worse of the gospel of Christ for the slights men generally put upon it, for we were told before what cold entertainment it would meet with. (2.) He recapitulates all he had said before to this purport (*v.* 10), that Moses did all these wonders, as they are here related, before Pharaoh (he himself was an eye-witness of them), and yet he could not prevail, which was a certain sign that God himself had, in a way of righteous judgment, hardened his heart. Thus the Jews' rejection of the gospel of Christ was so gross an absurdity that it might easily be inferred from it that God *had given them the spirit of slumber,* Rom. xi. 8.

CHAP. XII.

This chapter gives an account of one of the most memorable ordinances, and one of the most memorable providences, of all that are recorded in the Old Testament. I. Not one of all the ordinances of the Jewish church was more eminent than that of the passover, nor is any one more frequently mentioned in the New Testament; and we have here an account of the institution of it. The ordinance consisted of three parts:—1. The killing and eating of the paschal Lamb, ver. 1—6, 8—11. 2. The sprinkling of the blood upon the door-posts, spoken of as a distinct thing (Heb. xi. 28), and peculiar to this first passover (ver. 7), with the reason for it, ver. 13. 3. The feast of unleavened bread for seven days following; this points rather at what was to be done afterwards, in the observance of this ordinance, ver. 14—20. This institution is communicated to the people, and they are instructed in the observance, (1.) Of this first passover, ver. 21—23. (2.) Of the after passovers, ver. 24—27. And the Israelites' obedience to these orders, ver. 28. II. Not one of all the providences of God concerning the Jewish church was more illustrious, or is more frequently mentioned, than the deliverance of the children of Israel out of Egypt. 1. The firstborn of the Egyptians are slain, ver. 29, 30. 2. Orders are given immediately for their discharge, ver. 31—33. 3. They begin their march. (1.) Loaded with their own effects, ver. 34. (2.) Enriched with the spoils of Egypt, ver. 35, 36. (3.) Attended with a mixed multitude, ver. 37, 38. (4.) Put to their shifts for present supply, ver. 39. The event is dated, ver. 40—42. Lastly, A recapitulation in the close, [1.] Of this memorable ordinance, with some additions, ver. 43—49. [2.] Of this memorable providence, ver. 50, 51.

A ND the Lord spake unto Moses and Aaron in the land of Egypt, saying, 2 This month *shall be* unto you the beginning of months: it *shall be* the first month of the year to you. 3 Speak ye unto all the congregation of Israel, saying, In the tenth *day* of this month they shall take to them every man a lamb, according to the house of *their* fathers, a lamb for a house: 4 And if the household be too little for the lamb, let him and his neighbour next unto his house take *it* according to the number of the souls; every man according to his eating shall make your count for the lamb. 5 Your lamb shall be without blemish, a male of the first year: ye shall take *it* out from the sheep, or from the goats: 6 And ye shall keep it up until the fourteenth day of the same month: and the whole assembly of the congregation of Israel shall kill it in the evening. 7 And they shall take of the blood, and strike *it* on the two side posts and on the upper door post of the houses, wherein they shall eat it. 8 And they shall eat the flesh in that night, roast with fire, and unleavened bread; *and* with bitter *herbs* they shall eat it. 9 Eat not of it raw, nor sodden at all with water, but roast *with* fire; his head with his legs, and with the purtenance thereof. 10 And ye shall let nothing of it remain until the morning; and that which remaineth of it until the morning ye shall burn with fire. 11 And thus shall ye eat it; *with* your loins girded, your shoes on your feet, and your staff in your hand; and ye shall eat it in haste: it *is* the LORD's passover. 12 For I will pass through the land of Egypt this night, and will smite all the firstborn in the land of Egypt, both man and beast; and against all the gods of Egypt I will execute judgment: I *am* the LORD. 13 And the blood shall be to you for a token upon the houses where ye *are:* and when I see the blood, I will pass over you, and the plague shall not be upon you to destroy *you*, when I smite the land of Egypt. 14 And this day shall be unto you for a memorial; and ye shall keep it a feast to the LORD throughout your generations; ye shall keep it a feast by an ordinance for ever. 15 Seven days shall ye eat unleavened bread; even the first day ye shall put away leaven out of your houses: for whosoever eateth leavened bread from

the first day until the seventh day, that soul shall be cut off from Israel. 16 And in the first day *there shall be* a holy convocation, and in the seventh day there shall be a holy convocation to you; no manner of work shall be done in them, save *that* which every man must eat, that only may be done of you. 17 And ye shall observe *the feast of* unleavened bread; for in this selfsame day have I brought your armies out of the land of Egypt: therefore shall ye observe this day in your generations by an ordinance for ever. 18 In the first *month*, on the fourteenth day of the month at even, ye shall eat unleavened bread, until the one and twentieth day of the month at even. 19 Seven days shall there be no leaven found in your houses: for whosoever eateth that which is leavened, even that soul shall be cut off from the congregation of Israel, whether he be a stranger, or born in the land. 20 Ye shall eat nothing leavened; in all your habitations shall ye eat unleavened bread.

Moses and Aaron here *receive of the Lord* what they were afterwards to *deliver to the people* concerning the ordinance of the passover, to which is prefixed an order for a new style to be observed in their months (*v.* 1, 2): *This shall be to you the beginning of months.* They had hitherto begun their year from the middle of September, but henceforward they were to begin it from the middle of March, at least in all their ecclesiastical computations. Note, It is good to begin the day, and begin the year, and especially to begin our lives, with God. This new calculation began the year with the spring, which *reneweth the face of the earth*, and was used as a figure of the coming of Christ, Cant. ii. 11, 12. We may suppose that, while Moses was bringing the ten plagues upon the Egyptians, he was directing the Israelites to prepare for their departure at an hour's warning. Probably he had by degrees brought them near together from their dispersions, for they are here called *the congregation of Israel* (*v.* 3), and to them as a congregation orders are here sent. Their amazement and hurry, it is easy to suppose, were great; yet now they must apply themselves to the observance of a sacred rite, to the honour of God. Note, When our heads are fullest of care, and our hands of business, yet we must not forget our religion, nor suffer ourselves to be indisposed for acts of devotion.

I. God appointed that on the night wherein they were to go out of Egypt they should, in each of their families, *kill a lamb*, or that two or three families, if they were small, should join for a lamb. The lamb was to be got ready four days before, and that afternoon they were to *kill it* (v. 6) as a sacrifice; not strictly, for it was not offered *upon the altar*, but as a religious ceremony, acknowledging God's goodness to them, not only in preserving them from, but in delivering them by, the plagues inflicted on the Egyptians. See the antiquity of family-religion; and see the convenience of the joining of small families together for religious worship, that it may be made the more solemn.

II. The lamb so slain they were to eat, roasted (we may suppose, in its several quarters), with unleavened bread and bitter herbs, because they were to eat it *in haste* (v. 11), and to leave none of it until the morning; for God would have them to depend upon him for their daily bread, and not to take thought for the morrow. He that led them would feed them.

III. Before they ate the flesh of the lamb, they were to sprinkle the blood upon the door-posts, *v.* 7. By this their houses were to be distinguished from the houses of the Egyptians, and so their first-born secured from the sword of the destroying angel, v. 12, 13. Dreadful work was to be made this night in Egypt; all the first-born both of man and beast were to be slain, and judgment executed upon the gods of Egypt. Moses does not mention the fulfilment, in this chapter, yet he speaks of it Num. xxxiii. 4. It is very probable that the idols which the Egyptians worshipped were destroyed, those of metal melted, those of wood consumed, and those of stone broken to pieces, whence Jethro infers (*ch.* xviii. 11), *The Lord is greater than all gods.* The same angel that destroyed their first-born demolished their idols, which were no less dear to them. For the protection of Israel from this plague they were ordered to sprinkle the blood of the lamb upon the door-posts, their doing which would be accepted as an instance of their faith in the divine warnings and their obedience to the divine precepts. Note, 1. In times of common calamity God will secure his own people, and set a mark upon them; they shall be hidden either in heaven or under heaven, preserved either from the stroke of judgments or at least from the sting of them. 2. The blood of sprinkling is the saint's security in times of common calamity; it is this that marks them for God, pacifies conscience, and gives them boldness of access to the throne of grace, and so becomes a wall of protection round them and a wall of partition between them and the children of this world.

IV. This was to be annually observed as a feast of the Lord in their generations, to which the *feast of unleavened bread* was annexed, during which, for seven days, they were to eat no bread but what was unleavened, in remembrance of their being confined to such bread, of necessity, for many days after they came out of Egypt, v. 14—20. The appointment is inculcated for their better direction, and that they might not mistake concerning it, and to awaken those who perhaps in Egypt had grown generally very stupid and careless in the matters of religion to a diligent observance of the institution. Now, without doubt, there was much of the gospel in this ordinance; it is often referred to in the New Testament, and, in it, to us is *the gospel preached*, and *not to them only*, who *could not stedfastly look to the end of these things*, Heb. iv. 2; 2 Cor. iii. 13.

1. The paschal lamb was typical. Christ is *our Passover*, 1 Cor. v. 7. (1.) It was to be a *lamb;* and Christ is *the Lamb of God* (John i. 29), often in the Revelation called the *Lamb*, meek and innocent as a lamb, dumb before the shearers, before the butchers. (2.) It was to be a *male of the first year* (v. 5), in its prime; Christ offered up himself in the midst of his days, not in infancy with the babes of Bethlehem. It denotes the strength and sufficiency of the Lord Jesus, on whom our help was laid. (3.) It was to be *without blemish* (v. 5), denoting the purity of the Lord Jesus, a Lamb *without spot*, 1 Pet. i. 19. The judge that condemned him (as if his trial were only like the scrutiny that was made concerning the sacrifices, whether they were without blemish or no) pronounced him innocent. (4.) It was to be set apart four days before (v. 3. 6), denoting the designation of the Lord Jesus to be a Saviour, both in the purpose and in the promise. It is very observable that as Christ was crucified at the passover, so he solemnly entered into Jerusalem four days before, the very day that the paschal lamb was set apart. (5.) It was to be *slain*, and *roasted with fire* (v. 6—9), denoting the exquisite sufferings of the Lord Jesus, even unto death, the death of the cross. The wrath of God is as fire, and Christ was made a curse for us. (6.) It was to be killed by the whole congregation between the two evenings, that is, between three o'clock and six. Christ suffered in the *end of the world* (Heb. ix. 26), by the hand of the Jews, the whole multitude of them (Luke xxiii. 18), and for the good of all his spiritual Israel. (7.) Not *a bone of it must be broken* (v. 46), which is expressly said to be fulfilled in Christ (John xix. 33, 36), denoting the unbroken strength of the Lord Jesus.

2. The sprinkling of the blood was typical. (1.) It was not enough that the blood of the lamb was shed, but it must be sprinkled, denoting the application of the merits of Christ's death to our souls; we must *receive the atonement*, Rom. v. 11. (2.) It was to be sprinkled with *a bunch of hyssop* (v. 22) *dipped in the basin.* The everlasting covenant, like the basin, is the conservatory of this blood, the benefits and privileges purchased by it are laid up for us there; faith is the bunch of

hyssop by which we apply the promises to ourselves and the benefits of the blood of Christ laid up in them. (3.) It was to be sprinkled upon the *door-posts*, denoting the open profession we are to make of faith in Christ, and obedience to him, as those that are not ashamed to own our dependence upon him. The mark of the beast may be received on the forehead or in the right hand, but the seal of the *Lamb* is always *in the forehead*, Rev. vii. 3. There is a back-way to hell, but no back-way to heaven; no, the only way to this is a high-way, Isa. xxxv. 8. (4.) It was to be sprinkled upon the *lintel* and the *side-posts*, but not upon the *threshold* (*v.* 7), which cautions us to take heed of trampling under foot the blood of the covenant, Heb. x. 29. It is precious blood, and must be precious to us. (5.) The blood, thus sprinkled, was a means of the preservation of the Israelites from the destroying angel, who had nothing to do where the blood was. If the blood of Christ be sprinkled upon our consciences, it will be our protection from the wrath of God, the curse of the law, and the damnation of hell, Rom. viii. 1.

3. The solemnly eating of the lamb was typical of our gospel-duty to Christ. (1.) The paschal lamb was killed, not to be looked upon only, but to be fed upon; so we must by faith make Christ ours, as we do that which we eat, and we must receive spiritual strength and nourishment from him, as from our food, and have delight and satisfaction in him, as we have in eating and drinking when we are hungry or thirsty: see John vi. 53—55. (2.) It was to be all eaten; those that by faith feed upon Christ must feed upon a whole Christ; they must take Christ and his yoke, Christ and his cross, as well as Christ and his crown. *Is Christ divided?* Those that gather much of Christ will have nothing over. (3.) It was to be eaten immediately, not deferred till morning, *v.* 10. *To-day* Christ is offered, and is to be accepted while it is called to-day, before we sleep the sleep of death. (4.) It was to be eaten *with bitter herbs* (*v.* 8), in remembrance of the bitterness of their bondage in Egypt. We must feed upon Christ with sorrow and brokenness of heart, in remembrance of sin; this will give an admirable relish to the paschal lamb. Christ will be sweet to us if sin be bitter. (5.) It was to be eaten in a departing posture (*v.* 11); when we feed upon Christ by faith we must absolutely forsake the rule and dominion of sin, shake off Pharaoh's yoke; and we must sit loose to the world, and every thing in it, forsake all for Christ, and reckon it no bad bargain, Heb. xiii. 13, 14.

4. The feast of unleavened bread was typical of the Christian life, 1 Cor. v. 7, 8. Having received Christ Jesus the Lord, (1.) We must keep a feast in holy joy, continually delighting ourselves in Christ Jesus; no *manner of work must be done* (*v.* 16), no care admitted or indulged, inconsistent with, or pre-

judicial to, this holy joy: if true believers have not a continual feast, it is their own fault. (2.) It must be a feast of unleavened bread, kept in charity, without the leaven of malice, and in sincerity, without the leaven of hypocrisy. The law was very strict as to the passover, and the Jews were so in their usages, that no leaven should be *found in their houses*, *v.* 19. All the old leaven of sin must be put far from us, with the utmost caution and abhorrence, if we would keep the feast of a holy life to the honour of Christ. (3.) It was by an *ordinance for ever* (*v.* 17); as long as we live, we must continue feeding upon Christ and rejoicing in him, always making thankful mention of the great things he has done for us.

21 Then Moses called for all the elders of Israel, and said unto them, Draw out and take you a lamb according to your families, and kill the passover. 22 And ye shall take a bunch of hyssop, and dip *it* in the blood that *is* in the bason, and strike the lintel and the two side posts with the blood that *is* in the bason; and none of you shall go out at the door of his house until the morning. 23 For the LORD will pass through to smite the Egyptians; and when he seeth the blood upon the lintel, and on the two side posts, the LORD will pass over the door, and will not suffer the destroyer to come in unto your houses to smite *you*. 24 And ye shall observe this thing for an ordinance to thee and to thy sons for ever. 25 And it shall come to pass, when ye be come to the land which the LORD will give you, according as he hath promised, that ye shall keep this service. 26 And it shall come to pass, when your children shall say unto you, What mean ye by this service? 27 That ye shall say, It *is* the sacrifice of the LORD's passover, who passed over the houses of the children of Israel in Egypt, when he smote the Egyptians, and delivered our houses. And the people bowed the head and worshipped. 28 And the children of Israel went away, and did as the LORD had commanded Moses and Aaron, so did they.

I. Moses is here, as a faithful steward in God's house, teaching the children of Israel to *observe all things which God had commanded him ;* and no doubt he gave the instructions as largely as he received them, though they are not so largely recorded. It is here added,

1. That this night, when the first-born

were to be destroyed, no Israelite must *stir out of doors till morning*, that is, till towards morning, when they would be called to march out of Egypt, *v.* 22. Not but that the destroying angel could have known an Israelite from an Egyptian in the street; but God would intimate to them that their safety was owing to the *blood of sprinkling ;* if they put themselves from under the protection of that, it was at their peril. Those whom God has marked for himself must not mingle with evil doers: see Isa. xxvi. 20, 21. They must not go out of the doors, lest they should straggle and be out of the way when they should be summoned to depart: they must stay within, to *wait for the salvation of the Lord,* and it is good to do so.

2. That hereafter they should carefully teach their children the meaning of this service, *v.* 26, 27. Observe,

(1.) The question which the children would ask concerning this solemnity (which they would soon take notice of in the family): *"What mean you by this service?"* What is the meaning of all this care and exactness about eating this lamb, and this unleavened bread, more than about common food? Why such a difference between this meal and other meals?" Note, [1.] It is a good thing to see children inquisitive about the things of God; it is to be hoped that those who are careful to ask for the way will find it. Christ himself, when a child, *heard and asked questions,* Luke ii. 46. [2.] It concerns us all rightly to understand the meaning of those holy ordinances wherein we worship God, what is the nature and what the end of them, what is signified and what intended, what is the duty expected from us in them and what are the advantages to be expected by us. Every ordinance has a meaning; some ordinances, as sacraments, have not their meaning so plain and obvious as others have; therefore we are concerned to search, that we may not offer *the blind for sacrifice,* but may do a reasonable service. If either we are ignorant of, or mistake about, the meaning of holy ordinances, we can neither please God nor profit ourselves.

(2.) The answer which the parents were to return to this question (*v.* 27): *You shall say, It is the sacrifice of the Lord's passover,* that is, "By the killing and sacrificing of this lamb, we keep in remembrance the work of wonder and grace which God did for our fathers, when," [1.] "To make way for our deliverance out of bondage, he slew the firstborn of the Egyptians, so compelling them to sign our discharge;" and, [2.] "Though there were *with us, even with us, sins against the Lord our God,* for which the destroying angel, when he was abroad doing execution, might justly have destroyed our first-born too, yet God graciously appointed and accepted the family-sacrifice of a lamb, instead of the first-born, as, of old, the ram instead of Isaac, and in every house where the lamb

was slain the first-born were saved." The repetition of this solemnity in the return of every year was designed, *First,* To look backward as a memorial, that in it they might remember what great things God had done for them and their fathers. The word *pesach* signifies a *leap,* or *transition ;* it is a passing over; for the destroying angel passed over the houses of the Israelites, and did not destroy their first-born. When God brings utter ruin upon his people he says, *I will not pass by them any more* (Amos vii. 8; viii. 2), intimating how often he had passed by them, as now when the destroying angel passed over their houses. Note, 1. Distinguishing mercies lay under peculiar obligations. When *a thousand fall at our side, and ten thousand at our right hand,* and yet we are preserved, and have our lives given us for a prey, this should greatly affect us, Ps. xci. 7. In war or pestilence, if the arrow of death have passed by us, passed over us, hit the next to us and just missed us, we must not say it was by chance that we were preserved, but by the special providence of our God. 2. Old mercies to ourselves, or to our fathers, must not be forgotten, but be had in everlasting remembrance, that God may be praised, our faith in him encouraged, and our hearts enlarged in his service. *Secondly,* It was designed to look forward as an earnest of the great sacrifice of the Lamb of God in the fulness of time, instead of us and our first-born. We were obnoxious to the sword of the destroying angel, but *Christ our passover was sacrificed for us,* his death was our life, and thus he was the *Lamb slain from the foundation of the world,* from the foundation of the Jewish church: Moses kept the passover by faith in Christ, for Christ was *the end of the law for righteousness.*

II. The people received these instructions with reverence and ready obedience. 1. They *bowed the head and worshipped* (*v.* 27): they hereby signified their submission to this institution as a law, and their thankfulness for it as a favour and privilege. Note, When God gives law to us, we must give honour to him; when he speaks, we must *bow our heads and worship.* 2. They *went away and did* as they were commanded, *v.* 23. Here was none of that discontent and murmuring among them which we read of, *ch.* v. 20, 21. The plagues of Egypt had done them good, and raised their expectations of a glorious deliverance, which before they despaired of; and now they went forth to meet it in the way appointed. Note, The perfecting of God's mercies to us must be waited for in a humble observance of his institutions.

29 And it came to pass, that at midnight the Lord smote all the firstborn in the land of Egypt, from the firstborn of Pharaoh that sat on his throne unto the firstborn of the cap-

tive that *was* in the dungeon; and all the firstborn of cattle. 30 And Pharaoh rose up in the night, he, and all his servants, and all the Egyptians; and there was a great cry in Egypt; for *there was* not a house where *there was* not one dead. 31 And he called for Moses and Aaron by night, and said, Rise up, *and* get you forth from among my people, both ye and the children of Israel; and go, serve the Lord, as ye have said. 32 Also take your flocks and your herds, as ye have said, and be gone; and bless me also. 33 And the Egyptians were urgent upon the people, that they might send them out of the land in haste; for they said, We *be* all dead *men*. 34 And the people took their dough before it was leavened, their kneadingtroughs being bound up in their clothes upon their shoulders. 35 And the children of Israel did according to the word of Moses; and they borrowed of the Egyptians jewels of silver, and jewels of gold, and raiment: 36 And the Lord gave the people favour in the sight of the Egyptians, so that they lent unto them *such things as they required.* And they spoiled the Egyptians.

Here we have, I. The Egyptians' sons, even their first-born, slain, *v.* 29, 30. If Pharaoh would have taken the warning which was given him of this plague, and would thereupon have released Israel, what a great many dear and valuable lives might have been preserved! But see what obstinate infidelity brings upon men. Observe, 1. The time when this blow was given: It was *at midnight,* which added to the terror of it. The three preceding nights were made dreadful by the additional plague of darkness, which might be felt, and doubtless disturbed their repose; and now, when they hoped for one quiet night's rest, at midnight was the alarm given. When the destroying angel drew his sword against Jerusalem, it was in the day-time (2 Sam. xxiv. 15), which made it the less frightful; but the destruction of Egypt was by a *pestilence walking in darkness,* Ps. xci. 6. Shortly there will be an alarming cry at midnight, *Behold, the bridegroom cometh.* 2. On whom the plague fastened—on *their first-born,* the joy and hope of their respective families. They had slain the Hebrews' children, and now God slew theirs. Thus he visits the iniquity of the fathers upon the children; and he is *not unrighteous who taketh vengeance.* 3. How

far it reached—from the throne to the dungeon. Prince and peasant stand upon the same level before God's judgments, for there is no respect of persons with him; see Job xxxiv. 19, 20. Now the *slain of the Lord were many; multitudes, multitudes,* fall in this *valley of decision,* when the controversy between God and Pharaoh was to be determined. 4. What an outcry was made upon it: *There was a great cry in Egypt,* universal lamentation for their *only* son (with many), and with all for their *first-born.* If any be suddenly taken ill in the night, we are wont to call up neighbours; but the Egyptians could have no help, no comfort, from their neighbours, all being involved in the same calamity. Let us learn hence, (1.) To tremble before God, and to be *afraid of his judgments,* Ps. cxix. 120. Who is able to stand before him, or dares resist him? (2.) To be thankful to God for the daily preservation of ourselves and our families: lying so much exposed, we have reason to say, "It is of the Lord's mercies that we are not consumed."

II. God's sons, even his first-born, released; this judgment conquered Pharaoh, and obliged him to *surrender at discretion,* without capitulating. Men had better come up to God's terms at first, for he will never come down to theirs, let them object as long as they will. Now Pharaoh's pride is abased, and he yields to all that Moses had insisted on: *Serve the Lord as you have said* (*v.* 31), and *take your flocks as you have said, v.* 32. Note, God's word will stand, and we shall get nothing by disputing it, or delaying to submit to it. Hitherto the Israelites were not permitted to depart, but now things had come to the last extremity, in consequence of which, 1. They are commanded to depart: *Rise up, and get you forth, v.* 31. Pharaoh had told Moses he should *see his face no more;* but now he sent for him. Those will seek God early in their distress who before had set him at defiance. Such a fright he was now in that he gave orders by night for their discharge, fearing lest, if he delayed any longer, he himself should fall next; and that he sent them out, not as men hated (as the pagan historians have represented this matter), but as men feared, is plainly discovered by his humble request to them (*v.* 32): "*Bless me also;* let me have your prayers, that I may not be plagued for what is past, when you are gone." Note, Those that are enemies to God's church are enemies to themselves, and, sooner or later, they will be made to see it. 2. They are hired to depart by the Egyptians; they cried out (*v.* 33), *We be all dead men.* Note, When death comes into our houses, it is seasonable for us to think of our own mortality. Are our relations dead? It is easy to infer thence that we are dying, and, in effect, already dead men. Upon this consideration they were urgent with the Israel ites to be gone, which gave great advantage to the Israelites in borrowing their jewels, *v.* 35, 36. When the Egyptians urged them to be gone, it was easy for them to say that the Egyptians had kept them poor, that they could not undertake such a journey with empty purses, but that, if they would give them wherewithal to bear their charges, they would be gone. And this the divine Providence designed in suffering things to come to this extremity, that they, becoming formidable to the Egyptians, might have what they would, for asking; the Lord also, by the influence he has on the minds of people, inclined the hearts of the Egyptians to furnish them with what they desired, they probably intending thereby to *make atonement,* that the plagues might be stayed, as the Philistines, when they returned the ark, sent a present with it for a trespass-offering, having an eye to this precedent, 1 Sam. vi. 3, 6. The Israelites might receive and keep what they thus borrowed, or rather required, of the Egyptians, (1.) As justly as servants receive wages from their masters for work done, and sue for it if it be detained. (2.) As justly as conquerors take the spoils of their enemies whom they have subdued; Pharaoh was in rebellion against the *God of the Hebrews,* by which all that he had was forfeited. (3.) As justly as subjects receive the estates granted to them by their prince. God is the sovereign proprietor of the earth, and the fulness thereof; and, if he take from one and give to another, who may say unto him, *What doest thou?* It was by God's special order and appointment that the Israelites did what they did, which was sufficient to justify them, and bear them out; but what they did will by no means authorize others (who cannot pretend to any such warrant) to do the same. Let us remember, [1.] That the King of kings can do no wrong. [2.] That he will do right to those whom men injure, Ps. cxlvi. 7. Hence it is that the *wealth of the sinner* often proves to be *laid up for the just,* Prov. xiii. 22; Job xxvii. 16, 17.

37 And the children of Israel journeyed from Rameses to Succoth, about six hundred thousand on foot *that were* men, beside children. 38 And a mixed multitude went up also with them; and flocks, and herds, *even* very much cattle. 39 And they baked unleavened cakes of the dough which they brought forth out of Egypt, for it was not leavened; because they were thrust out of Egypt, and could not tarry, neither had they prepared for themselves any victual. 40 Now the sojourning of the children of Israel, who dwelt in Egypt, *was* four hundred

and thirty years. 41 And it came to pass at the end of the four hundred and thirty years, even the selfsame day it came to pass, that all the hosts of the LORD went out from the land of Egypt. 42 It *is* a night to be much observed unto the LORD for bringing them out from the land of Egypt: this *is* that night of the LORD to be observed of all the children of Israel in their generations.

Here is the departure of the children of Israel out of Egypt; having obtained their dismission, they set forward without delay, and did not defer to a more convenient season. Pharaoh was now in a good mind; but they had reason to think he would not long continue so, and therefore it was no time to linger. We have here an account, 1. Of their number, about 600,000 men (*v.* 37), besides women and children, which, I think, we cannot suppose to make less than 1,200,000 more. What a vast increase was this, to arise from seventy souls in little more than 200 years' time! See the power and efficacy of that blessing, when God commands it, *Be fruitful and multiply.* This was typical of the multitudes that were brought into the gospel church when it was first founded; *so mightily grew the word of God, and prevailed.* 2. Of their retinue (*v.* 38): *A mixed multitude went up with them,* hangers on to that great family, some perhaps willing to leave their country, because it was laid waste by the plagues, and to seek their fortune, as we say, with the Israelites; others went out of curiosity, to see the solemnities of Israel's sacrifice to their God, which had been so much talked of, and expecting to see some glorious appearances of their God to them in the wilderness, having seen such glorious appearances of their God for them in the field of Zoan, Ps. lxxviii. 12. Probably the greatest part of this mixed multitude were but a rude unthinking mob, that followed the crowd they knew not why; we afterwards find that they proved a snare to them (Num. xi. 4), and it is probable that when, soon afterwards, they understood that the children of Israel were to continue forty years in the wilderness, they quitted them, and returned to Egypt. Note, There were always those among the Israelites that were not Israelites, and there are still hypocrites in the church, who make a deal of mischief, but will be shaken off at last. 3. Of their effects. They had with them *flocks and herds,* even *very much cattle.* This is taken notice of because it was long before Pharaoh would give them leave to remove their effects, which were chiefly cattle, Gen. xlvi. 32. 4. Of the provision made for the camp, which was very poor and slender. They brought some dough with them out of Egypt in their knapsacks, *v.* 34.

They had prepared to bake, the next day, in order to their removal, understanding it was very near; but, being hastened away sooner than they thought of, by some hours, they took the dough as it was, unleavened; when they came to Succoth, their first stage, they baked unleavened cakes, and, though these were of course insipid, yet the liberty they were brought into made this the most joyful meal they had ever eaten in their lives. Note, The servants of God must not be slaves to their appetites, nor solicitous to wind up all the delights of sense to their highest pitch. We should be willing to take up with dry bread, nay, with unleavened bread, rather than neglect or delay any service we have to do for God, as those whose meat and drink it is to do his will. 5. Of the date of this great event: it was just 430 years from the promise made to Abraham (as the apostle explains it, Gal. iii. 17) at his first coming into Canaan, during all which time *the children of Israel*, that is, the Hebrews, the distinguished chosen seed, were sojourners in a land that was not theirs, either Canaan or Egypt. So long the promise God made to Abraham of a settlement lay dormant and unfulfilled, but now, at length, it revived, and things began to work towards the accomplishment of it. The first day of the march of Abraham's seed towards Canaan was just 430 years (it should seem to a day) from the promise made to Abraham Gen. xii. 2, *I will make of thee a great nation.* See how punctual God is to his time; though his promises be not performed quickly, they will be accomplished in their season. 6. Of the memorableness of it: *It is a night to be much observed, v. 42.* (1.) The providences of that first night were very observable; memorable was the destruction of the Egyptians, and the deliverance of the Israelites by it; God herein made himself taken notice of. (2.) The ordinances of that night, in the annual return of it, were to be carefully observed: *This is that night of the Lord*, that remarkable night, to be celebrated in all generations. Note, The great things God does for his people are not to be a nine days' wonder, as we say, but the remembrance of them is to be perpetuated throughout all ages, especially the work of our redemption by Christ. This first passover-night was a night of the Lord *much to be observed;* but the last passover-night, in which Christ was betrayed (and in which the passover, with the rest of the ceremonial institutions, was superseded and abolished), was a night of the Lord *much more to be observed,* when a yoke heavier than that of Egypt was broken from off our necks, and a land better than that of Canaan set before us. That was a temporal deliverance to be celebrated *in their generation;* this is an eternal redemption to be celebrated in the praises of glorious saints, *world without end.*

43 And the Lord said unto Moses and Aaron, This *is* the ordinance or the passover: There shall no stranger eat thereof: 44 But every man's servant that is bought for money, when thou hast circumcised him, then shall he eat thereof. 45 A foreigner and a hired servant shall not eat thereof. 46 In one house shall it be eaten; thou shalt not carry forth aught of the flesh abroad out of the house; neither shall ye break a bone thereof. 47 All the congregation of Israel shall keep it. 48 And when a stranger shall sojourn with thee, and will keep the passover to the Lord, let all his males be circumcised, and then let him come near and keep it; and he shall be as one that is born in the land: for no uncircumcised person shall eat thereof. 49 One law shall be to him that is homeborn, and unto the stranger that sojourneth among you. 50 Thus did all the children of Israel; as the Lord commanded Moses and Aaron, so did they. 51 And it came to pass the selfsame day, *that* the Lord did bring the children of Israel out of the land of Egypt by their armies.

Some further precepts are here given concerning the passover, as it should be observed in times to come.

I. *All the congregation of Israel must keep it, v. 47.* All that share in God's mercies should join in thankful praises for them. Though it was observed in families apart, yet it is looked upon as the act of the whole congregation; for the smaller communities constituted the greater. The New-Testament passover, the Lord's supper, ought not to be neglected by any who are capable of celebrating it. He is unworthy the name of an Israelite that can contentedly neglect the commemoration of so great a deliverance. 1. No stranger that was uncircumcised might be admitted to eat of it, *v.* 43, 45, 48. None might sit at the table but those that came in by the door; nor may any now approach to the improving ordinance of the Lord's supper who have not first submitted to the initiating ordinance of baptism. We must be born again by the word ere we can be nourished by it. Nor shall any partake of the benefit of Christ's sacrifice, or feast upon it, who are not first circumcised in heart, Col. ii. 11. 2. Any stranger that was circumcised might be welcome to eat of the passover, even *servants, v.* 44. If, by circumcision, they would make themselves debtors to the law in its burdens, they were welcome to share in the joy of its solemn feasts, and not otherwise. Only it is intimated (*v.* 48) that those who were masters of families must not only be circumcised themselves, but have all their males circumcised too. If in sincerity, and with that zeal which the thing requires and deserves, we give up ourselves to God, we shall, with ourselves, give up all we have to him, and do our utmost that all ours may be his too. Here is an early indication of favour to the poor Gentiles, that the stranger, if circumcised, stands upon the same level with the home-born Israelite. *One law* for both, *v.* 49. This was a mortification to the Jews, and taught them that it was their dedication to God, not their descent from Abraham, that entitled them to their privileges. A sincere proselyte was as welcome to the passover as a native Israelite, Isa. lvi. 6, 7.

II. *In one house shall it be eaten* (*v.* 46), for good-fellowship' sake, that they might rejoice together, and edify one another in the eating of it. None of it must be carried to another place, nor left to another time; for God would not have them so taken up with care about their departure as to be indisposed to take the comfort of it, but to leave Egypt, and enter upon a wilderness, with cheerfulness, and, in token of that, to eat a good hearty meal. The papists' carrying their consecrated host from house to house is not only superstitious in itself, but contrary to this typical law of the passover, which directed that no part of the lamb should be carried abroad.

The chapter concludes with a repetition of the whole matter, that the children of Israel did as they were bidden, and God did for them as he promised (*v.* 50, 51); for he will certainly be the author of salvation to those that obey him.

CHAP. XIII.

In this chapter we have, I. The commands God gave to Israel, 1. To sanctify all their firstborn to him, ver. 1, 2. 2. To be sure to remember their deliverance out of Egypt (ver. 3, 4), and, in remembrance of it, to keep the feast of unleavened bread, ver. 5—7. 3. To transmit the knowledge of it with all possible care to their children, ver. 8—10. 4. To set apart unto God the firstlings of their cattle (ver. 11—13), and to explain that also to their children, ver. 14—16. II. The care God took of Israel, when he had brought them out of Egypt. 1. Choosing their way for them, ver. 17, 18. 2. Guiding them in the way, ver. 20—22. And III. Their care of Joseph's bones, ver. 19.

AND the Lord spake unto Moses, saying, 2 Sanctify unto me all the firstborn, whatsoever openeth the womb among the children of Israel, *both* of man and of beast: it *is* mine. 3 And Moses said unto the people, Remember this day, in which ye came out from Egypt, out of the house of bondage; for by strength of hand the LORD brought you out from this *place:* there shall no leavened bread be eaten. 4 This day came ye out in the month Abib. 5 And it shall be when the

LORD shall bring thee into the land of the Canaanites, and the Hittites, and the Amorites, and the Hivites, and the Jebusites, which he sware unto thy fathers to give thee, a land flowing with milk and honey, that thou shalt keep this service in this month. 6 Seven days thou shalt eat unleavened bread, and in the seventh day *shall be* a feast to the LORD. 7 Unleavened bread shall be eaten seven days; and there shall no leavened bread be seen with thee, neither shall there be leaven seen with thee in all thy quarters. 8 And thou shalt show thy son in that day, saying, *This is done* because of that which the LORD did unto me when I came forth out of Egypt. 9 And it shall be for a sign unto thee upon thine hand, and for a memorial between thine eyes, that the LORD's law may be in thy mouth: for with a strong hand hath the LORD brought thee out of Egypt. 10 Thou shalt therefore keep this ordinance in his season from year to year.

Care is here taken to perpetuate the remembrance,

I. Of the preservation of Israel's firstborn, when the firstborn of the Egyptians were slain. In memory of that distinguishing favour, and in gratitude for it, the firstborn, in all ages, were to be consecrated to God, as his peculiars (*v.* 2), and to be redeemed, *v.* 13. God, who by the right of creation is proprietor and sovereign of all the creatures, here lays claim in particular to the firstborn of the Israelites, by right of protection: *Sanctify to me all the firstborn.* The parents were not to look upon themselves as interested in their firstborn, till they had first solemnly presented them to God, recognised his title to them, and received them back, at a certain rate, from him again. Note, 1. That which is by special distinguishing mercy spared to us should in a peculiar manner be dedicated to God's honour; at least some grateful acknowledgment, in works of piety and charity, should be made, when our lives, or the lives of our children, have been given us for a prey. 2. God, who is the first and best, should have the first and best, and to him we should resign that which is most dear to us, and most valuable. The firstborn were the joy and hope of their families. Therefore *they shall be mine,* says God. By this it will appear that we love God best (as we ought) if we are willing to part with that to him which we love best in this world. 3. It is the *church of the firstborn* that is sanctified to God, Heb. xii. 23. Christ is the *firstborn among many brethren* (Rom. viii. 29), and, by virtue of their union with him, all that are born again, and born from above, are accounted as firstborn. There is an *excellency of dignity and power* belonging to them ; and, *if children, then heirs.*

II. The remembrance of their coming out of Egypt must also be perpetuated : " *Remember this day, v.* 3. Remember it by a good token, as the most remarkable day of your lives, the birthday of your nation, or the day of its coming of age, to be no longer under the rod." Thus the day of Christ's resurrection is to be remembered, for in it we were raised up with Christ out of death's *house of bondage.* The scripture tells us not expressly what day of the *year* Christ rose (as Moses told the Israelites what day of the year they were brought out of Egypt, that they might remember it yearly), but very particularly what day of the *week* it was, plainly intimating that, as the more valuable deliverance, and of greater importance, it should be remembered *weekly.* Remember it, for *by strength of hand the Lord brought you out.* Note, The more of God and his power appears in any deliverance, the more memorable it is. Now, that it might be remembered,

1. They must be sure to *keep the feast of unleavened bread, v.* 5—7. It was not enough that they remembered it, but they must celebrate the memorial of it in that way which God had appointed, and use the instituted means of preserving the remembrance of it. So, under the gospel, we must not only remember Christ, but *do this in remembrance* of him. Observe, How strict the prohibition of leaven is (v. 7) ; not only no leaven must be eaten, but none must be seen, no, not in all their quarters. Accordingly, the Jews' usage was, before the feast of the passover, to cast all the leavened bread out of their houses : they burnt it, or buried it, or broke it small and scattered it in the wind ; they searched diligently with lighted candles in all the corners of their houses, lest any leaven should remain. The care and strictness enjoined in this matter were designed, (1.) To make the feast the more solemn, and consequently the more taken notice of by their children, who would ask, " Why is so much ado made ?" (2.) To teach us how solicitous we should be to put away from us all sin, 1 Cor. v. 7.

2. They must instruct their children in the meaning of it, and relate to them the story of their deliverance out of Egypt, *v.* 8. Note, (1.) Care must be taken betimes to instruct children in the knowledge of God. Here is an ancient law for catechising. (2.) It is particularly of great use to acquaint children betimes with the stories of the scripture, and to make them familiar to them. (3.) It is a debt we owe to the honour of God, and to the benefit of our children's souls, to tell them of the great works God has done for his

church, both those which we have seen with our eyes done in our day and which we have heard with our ears and our fathers have told us : *Thou shalt show thy son in that day* (the day of the feast) these things. When they were celebrating the ordinance, they must explain it. *Every thing is beautiful in its season.* The passover is appointed *for a sign, and for a memorial,* that *the Lord's law may be in thy mouth.* Note, We must retain the remembrance of God's works, that we may remain under the influence of God's law. And those that have God's law in their heart should have it in their mouth, and be often speaking of it, the more to affect themselves and to instruct others.

11 And it shall be when the LORD shall bring thee into the land of the Canaanites, as he sware unto thee and to thy fathers, and shall give it thee, 12 That thou shalt set apart unto the LORD all that openeth the matrix, and every firstling that cometh of a beast which thou hast ; the males *shall be* the LORD's. 13 And every firstling of an ass thou shalt redeem with a lamb ; and if thou wilt not redeem it, then thou shalt break his neck : and all the firstborn of man among thy children shalt thou redeem. 14 And it shall be when thy son asketh thee in time to come, saying, What *is* this ? that thou shalt say unto him, By strength of hand the LORD brought us out from Egypt, from the house of bondage : 15 And it came to pass, when Pharaoh would hardly let us go, that the LORD slew all the firstborn in the land of Egypt, both the firstborn of man, and the firstborn of beast : therefore I sacrifice to the LORD all that openeth the matrix, being males ; but all the firstborn of my children I redeem. 16 And it shall be for a token upon thine hand, and for frontlets between thine eyes : for by strength of hand the LORD brought us forth out of Egypt.

Here we have,

I. Further directions concerning the dedicating of their firstborn to God. 1. The firstlings of their cattle were to be dedicated to God, as part of their possessions. Those of clean beasts—calves, lambs, and kids—if males, were to be sacrificed, Exod. xxii. 30 ; Num. xviii. 17, 18. Those of unclean beasts, as colts, were to be redeemed with a lamb, or knocked on the head. For whatsoever is unclean (as we all are by nature), if it be not redeemed, will be destroyed, *v.* 11, 13. 2 The firstborn of their children were to be redeemed, and by no means sacrificed, as the Gentiles sacrificed their children to Moloch. The price of the redemption of the firstborn was fixed by the law (Num. xviii. 16) at *five shekels.* We were all obnoxious to the wrath and curse of God ; by the blood of Christ we are redeemed, that we may be joined to the *church of the firstborn.* They were to redeem their children, as well as the firstlings of the unclean beasts, for our children are by nature polluted. *Who can bring a clean thing out of an unclean ?*

II. Further directions concerning the catechising of their children, and all those of the rising generation, from time to time, in this matter. It is supposed that, when they saw all the firstlings thus devoted, they would ask the meaning of it, and their parents and teachers must tell them (*v.* 14—16) that God's special propriety in their firstborn, and all their firstlings, was founded in his special preservation of them from the sword of the destroying angel. Being thus delivered, they must serve him. Note, 1. Children should be directed and encouraged to ask their parents questions concerning the things of God, a practice which would be perhaps of all others the most profitable way of catechising ; and parents must furnish themselves with useful knowledge, that they may be ready always to give an answer to their enquiries. If ever the *knowledge of God cover the earth,* as the waters do the sea, the fountains of family-instruction must first be broken up. 2. We should all be able to show cause for what we do in religion. As sacraments are sanctified by the word, so they must be explained and understood by it. God's service is reasonable, and it is then acceptable when we perform it intelligently, knowing what we do and why we do it. 3. It must be observed how often it is said in this chapter that *by strength of hand* (*v.* 3, 14, 16), *with a strong hand* (*v.* 9), the Lord brought them out of Egypt. The more opposition is given to the accomplishment of God's purposes the more is his power magnified therein. It is a strong hand that conquers hard hearts. Sometimes God is said to work deliverance *not by might nor power* (Zech. iv. 6), not by such visible displays of his power as that recorded here. 4. Their posterity that should be born in Canaan are directed to say, *The Lord brought us out of Egypt,* *v.* 14, 16. Mercies to our fathers are mercies to us ; we reap the benefit of them, and therefore must keep up a grateful remembrance of them. We stand upon the bottom of former deliverances, and were in the loins of our ancestors when they were delivered. Much more reason have we to say that in the death and resurrection of Jesus Christ we were redeemed.

17 And it came to pass, when Pha-
326

raoh had let the people go, that God led them not *through* the way of the land of the Philistines, although that *was* near; for God said, Lest peradventure the people repent when they see war, and they return to Egypt : 18 But God led the people about, *through* the way of the wilderness of the Red sea : and the children of Israel went up harnessed out of the land of Egypt. 19 And Moses took the bones of Joseph with him : for he had straitly sworn the children of Israel, saying, God will surely visit you ; and ye shall carry up my bones away hence with you. 20 And they took their journey from Succoth, and encamped in Etham, in the edge of the wilderness. 21 And the LORD went before them by day in a pillar of a cloud, to lead them the way ; and by night in a pillar of fire, to give them light ; to go by day and night : 22 He took not away the pillar of the cloud by day, nor the pillar of fire by night, *from* before the people.

Here is, I. The choice God made of their way, *v.* 17, 18. He was their guide. Moses gave them direction but as he received it from the Lord. Note, The way of man is not in himself, Jer. x. 23. He may *devise his way,* and design it ; but, after all, it is God that *directs his steps,* Prov. xvi. 9. Man proposes, but God disposes, and in his disposal we must acquiesce, and set ourselves to follow providence. There were two ways from Egypt to Canaan. One was a short cut from the north of Egypt to the south of Canaan, perhaps about four or five days' journey ; the other was much further about, through the wilderness, and that was the way in which God chose to lead his people Israel, *v.* 18. 1. There were many reasons why God led them *through the way of the wilderness of the Red Sea.* The Egyptians were to be drowned in the Red Sea. The Israelites were to be humbled and proved in the wilderness, Deut. viii. 2. God had given it to Moses for a sign (*ch.* iii. 12), *You shall serve God in this mountain.* They had again and again told Pharaoh that they must go *three days' journey into the wilderness to do sacrifice,* and therefore it was requisite that they should bend their march that way, else they would justly have been exclaimed against as notorious dissemblers. Before they entered the lists with their enemies, matters must be settled between them and their God, laws must be given, ordinances instituted, covenants sealed, and the original contract ratified, for the doing of which it was necessary that they should retire into the solitudes of a wilderness, the only closet for such a crowd; the high road would be no proper place for these transactions. It is said (Deut. xxxii. 10), *He led them about,* some hundreds of miles about, and yet (Ps. cvii. 7), *He led them forth by the right way.* God's way is the right way, though it seem *about.* If we think he leads not his people the nearest way, yet we may be sure he leads them the best way, and so it will appear when we come to our journey's end. *Judge nothing before the time.* 2. There was one reason why God did not lead them the nearest way, which would have brought them after a few days' march to *the land of the Philistines* (for it was that part of Canaan that lay next to Egypt), namely, because they were not as yet fit for war, much less for war with the Philistines, *v.* 17. Their spirits were broken with slavery; it was not easy for them to turn their hands of a sudden from the trowel to the sword. The Philistines were formidable enemies, too fierce to be encountered by raw recruits; it was more suitable that they should begin with the Amalekites, and be prepared for the wars of Canaan by experiencing the difficulties of the wilderness. Note, God proportions his people's trials to their strength, and will *not suffer them to be tempted above what they are able,* 1 Cor. x. 13. That promise, if compared with the foregoing verses, will seem to refer to this event, as an instance of it. *God knows our frame,* and considers our weakness and faint-heartedness, and by less trials will prepare us for greater. God is said to bring Israel out of Egypt as the eagle *brings up her young ones* (Deut. xxxii. 11), teaching them by degrees to fly. Orders being thus given which way they should go, we are told, (1.) That they went up themselves, not as a confused rout, but in good order, rank and file: they *went up harnessed, v.* 18. They went up by *five in a rank* (so some), in *five squadrons,* so others. They marched like an army with banners, which added much to their strength and honour. (2.) That they took the *bones of Joseph* along with them (*v.* 19), and probably the bones of the rest of Jacob's sons, unless (as some think) they had been privately carried to Canaan (Acts vii. 16), severally as they died. Joseph had particularly appointed that his bones should be carried up when God should visit them (Gen. l. 25, 26), so that their carrying up his bones was not only a performance of the oath their fathers had sworn to Joseph, but an acknowledgment of the performance of God's promise to them by Joseph that he would visit them and bring them out of the land of Egypt, and an encouragement to their faith and hope that he would fulfil the other part of the promise, which was to bring them to Canaan, in expectation of which they carried these bones with them while they wandered in the desert.

They might think, "Joseph's bones must rest at last, and then we shall." Moses is said to take these bones with him. Moses was now a very great man; so had Joseph been in his day, yet he was now but a box full of dry bones; this was all that remained of him in this world, which might serve for a monitor to Moses to remember his mortality. *I have said, You are gods;* it was said so to Moses expressly (*ch.* vii. 1); *but you shall die like men.*

II. Here is the guidance they were blessed with in the way: *The Lord went before them in a pillar, v.* 21, 22. In the first two stages it was enough that God directed Moses whither to march : he knew the country and the road well enough; but now that they had come *to the edge of the wilderness* (*v.* 20) they would have occasion for a guide; and a very good guide they had, one that was infinitely wise, kind, and faithful : *The Lord went before them,* the *shechinah* (or appearance of the divine Majesty, which was typical of Christ) or a previous manifestation of the eternal Word, which, in the fulness of time, was to be *made flesh,* and *dwell among us.* Christ was with the church in the wilderness, 1 Cor. x. 9. Now *their King passed before them, even the Lord on the head of them,* Mic. ii. 13. Note, Those whom God brings into a wilderness he will not leave nor lose there, but will take care to lead them through it; and we may well think it was a very great satisfaction to Moses and the pious Israelites to be sure that they were under divine guidance. Those needed not to fear missing their way who were thus led, nor being lost who were thus directed; those needed not to fear being benighted who were thus illuminated, nor being robbed who were thus protected. Those who make the glory of God their end, and the word of God their rule, the Spirit of God the guide of their affections, and the providence of God the guide of their affairs, may be confident that *the Lord goes before them,* as truly as he went before Israel in the wilderness, though not so sensibly; we must live by faith. 1. They had sensible evidences of God's going before them. They all saw an appearance from heaven of a pillar, which in the bright day appeared cloudy, and in the dark night appeared fiery. We commonly see that that which is a flame in the night is a smoke in the day; so was this. God gave them this ocular demonstration of his presence, in compassion to the infirmity of their faith, and in compliance with that infant state of the church, which needed to be thus lisped to in their own language; but blessed are *those that have not seen and yet have believed* God's gracious presence with them, according to his promise. 2. They had sensible effects of God's going before them in this pillar. For, (1.) It led the way in that vast howling wilderness, in which there was no road, no track, no way-mark, of which they had no

maps, through which they had no guides.
When they marched, this pillar went before
them, at the rate that they could follow, and
appointed the place of their encampment, as
Infinite Wisdom saw fit, which both eased
them from care, and secured them from
danger, both in moving and in resting. (2.) It
sheltered them by day from the heat, which, at
some times of the year, was extreme. (3.)
It gave them light by night when they had
occasion for it, and at all times made their
camp pleasant and the wilderness they were
in less frightful.

III. These were constant standing miracles (*v.* 22): He *took not away the pillar of
cloud;* no, not when they seemed to have
less occasion for it, travelling through inhabited countries, no, not when they murmured
and were provoking; it never left them, till
it brought them to the borders of Canaan.
It was a cloud which the wind could not
scatter. This favour is acknowledged with
thankfulness long afterwards, Neh. ix. 19;
Ps. lxxviii. 14. There was something spiritual in this pillar of cloud and fire. 1. The
children of Israel were baptized unto Moses
in this cloud, which, some think, distilled
dew upon them, 1 Cor. x. 2. By coming
under this cloud, they signified their putting
themselves under the divine guidance and
command by the ministry of Moses. Protection draws allegiance; this cloud was the
badge of God's protection, and so became the
bond of their allegiance. Thus they were
initiated, and admitted under that government, now when they were entering upon
the wilderness. 2. Some make this cloud a
type of Christ. The cloud of his human
nature was a veil to the light and fire of his
divine nature; we find him (Rev. x. 1)
*clothed with a cloud, and his feet as pillars of
fire.* Christ is our way, the light of our way
and the guide of it. 3. It signifies the special guidance and protection which the church
of Christ is under in this world. God himself is the keeper of Israel, and he *neither
slumbers nor sleeps,* Ps. cxxi. 4; Isa. xxvii. 3.
There is a defence created, not only on Sion's
assemblies, but on every dwelling-place in
Sion. See Isa. iv. 5, 6. Nay, every Israelite
indeed is hidden under the shadow of God's
wings (Ps. xvii. 8); angels, whose ministry was
made use of in this cloud, are employed for
their good, and pitch their tents about them.
*Happy art thou, O Israel! who is like unto
thee, O people?*

CHAP. XIV.

The departure of the children of Israel out of Egypt (which was
indeed the birth of the Jewish church) is made yet more memorable by further works of wonder, which were wrought immediately upon it. Witness the records of this chapter, the contents
whereof, together with a key to it, we have, Heb. xi. 29. "They
passed through the Red Sea as by dry land, which the Egyptians
assaying to do were drowned;" and this they did by faith, which
intimates that there was something typical and spiritual in it.
Here is, I. The extreme distress and danger that Israel was in
at the Red Sea. 1. Notice was given of it to Moses before, ver.
1—4. 2. The cause of it was Pharaoh's violent pursuit of them,
ver. 5—9. 3. Israel was in a great consternation upon it, ver.
10—12. 4. Moses endeavours to encourage them, ver. 13, 14. II.
The wonderful deliverance that God wrought for them out of this
distress. 1. Moses is instructed concerning it, ver. 15—18. 2.

Lines that could not be forced are set between the camp of Israel
and Pharaoh's camp, ver. 19, 20. 3. By the divine power the Red
Sea is divided (ver. 21), and is made, (1.) A lane to the Israelites,
who marched safely through it, ver. 22, 29. But, (2.) To the
Egyptians it was made, [1.] An ambush into which they were
drawn, ver. 23—25. And, [2.] A grave in which they were all
buried, ver. 26—28. III. The impressions this made upon the
Israelites, ver. 30, 31.

AND the LORD spake unto Moses,
saying, 2 Speak unto the children of Israel, that they turn and encamp before Pi-hahiroth, between
Migdol and the sea, over against Baal-
zephon: before it shall ye encamp by
the sea. 3 For Pharaoh will say of
the children of Israel, They *are* entangled in the land, the wilderness
hath shut them in. 4 And I will
harden Pharaoh's heart, that he shall
follow after them; and I will be honoured upon Pharaoh, and upon all
his host; that the Egyptians may
know that I *am* the LORD. And they
did so. 5 And it was told the king of
Egypt that the people fled: and the
heart of Pharaoh and of his servants
was turned against the people, and they
said, Why have we done this, that we
have let Israel go from serving us? 6
And he made ready his chariot, and
took his people with him: 7 And he
took six hundred chosen chariots, and
all the chariots of Egypt, and captains
over every one of them. 8 And the
LORD hardened the heart of Pharaoh
king of Egypt, and he pursued after
the children of Israel: and the children of Israel went out with a high
hand. 9 But the Egyptians pursued
after them, all the horses *and* chariots
of Pharaoh, and his horsemen, and his
army, and overtook them encamping
by the sea, beside Pi-hahiroth, before
Baal-zephon.

We have here,

I. Instructions given to Moses concerning
Israel's motions and encampments, which were
so very surprising that if Moses had not had
express orders about them before they would
scarcely have been persuaded to follow the
pillar of cloud and fire. That therefore there
might be no scruple nor dissatisfaction about
it, Moses is told before, 1. Whither they
must go, *v.* 1, 2. They had got to the edge
of the wilderness (*ch.* xiii. 20), and a stage or
two more would have brought them to Horeb,
the place appointed for their serving God;
but, instead of going forward, they are ordered to turn short off, on the right hand
from Canaan, and to march towards the Red
Sea. Where they were, at Etham, there
was no sea in their way to obstruct their

passage: but God himself orders them into straits, which might give them an assurance that when his purposes were served he would without fail bring them out of those straits. Note, God sometimes raises difficulties in the way of the salvation of his people, that he may have the glory of subduing them, and helping his people over them. 2. What God designed in these strange orders. Moses would have yielded an implicit obedience, though God had given him no reason; but shall he hide from Moses the thing that he does? No, Moses shall know, (1.) That Pharaoh has a design to ruin Israel, *v.* 3. (2.) That therefore God has a design to ruin Pharaoh, and he takes this way to effect it, *v.* 4. Pharaoh's sagacity would conclude that Israel was entangled in the wilderness and so would become an easy prey to him; and, that he might be the more apt to think so, God orders them into yet greater entanglements; also, by turning them so much out of their road, he amazes him yet more, and gives him further occasion to suppose that they were in a state of embarrassment and danger. And thus (says God) *I will be honoured upon Pharaoh.* Note, [1.] All men being made for the honour of their Maker, those whom he is not honoured by he will be honoured upon. [2.] What seems to tend to the church's ruin is often overruled to the ruin of the church's enemies, whose pride and malice are fed by Providence, that they may be ripened for destruction.

II. Pharaoh's pursuit of Israel, in which, while he gratifies his own malice and revenge, he is furthering the accomplishment of God's counsels concerning him. *It was told him that the people fled, v.* 5. Such a fright was he in, when he gave them leave to go, that when the fright was a little over he either forgot, or would not own, that they departed with his consent, and therefore was willing that it should be represented to him as a revolt from their allegiance. Thus what may easily be justified is easily condemned, by putting false colours upon it. · Now, hereupon,

1. He reflects upon it with regret that he had connived at their departure. He and his servants, though it was with the greatest reason in the world that they had let Israel go, yet were now angry with themselves for it: *Why have we done thus?* (1.) It vexed them that Israel had their liberty, that they had lost the profit of their labours, and the pleasure of chastising them. It is meat and drink to proud persecutors to trample upon the saints of the Most High, and say to their souls, *Bow down, that we may go over;* and therefore it vexes them to have their hands tied. Note, The liberty of God's people is a heavy grievance to their enemies, Esth. v. 12, 13; Acts v. 17, 33. (2.) It aggravated the vexation that they themselves had consented to it, thinking now that they might have hindered it, and that they needed not to have yielded, though they had stood it out to the

last extremity. Thus God makes men's envy and rage against his people a torment to themselves, Ps. cxii. 10. It was well done to let Israel go, and what they would have reflected on with comfort if they had done it from an honest principle; but, doing it by constraint, they called themselves a thousand fools for doing it, and passionately wished it undone again. Note, It is very common, but very absurd and criminal, for people to repent of their good deeds; their justice and charity, and even their repentance, are repented of. See an instance somewhat like this, Jer. xxxiv. 10, 11.

2. He resolves, if possible, either to reduce them or to be revenged on them; in order to this, he levies an army, musters all his force of chariots and horsemen, *v.* 17, 18 (for, it should seem, he took no foot with him, because the king's business required haste), and thus he doubts not but he shall re-enslave them, *v.* 6, 7. It is easy to imagine what a rage Pharaoh was now in, roaring like a lion disappointed of his prey, how his proud heart aggravated the affront, swelled with indignation, scorned to be baffled, longed to be revenged: and now all the plagues are as it they had never been. He has quite forgotten the sorrowful funerals of his firstborn, and can think of nothing but making Israel feel his resentments; now he thinks he can be too hard for God himself; for, otherwise, could he have hoped to conquer a people so dear to him? God gave him up to these passions of his own heart, and so hardened it. It is said (*v.* 8), The children of Israel went out with *a high hand,* that is, with a great deal of courage and bravery, triumphing in their release, and resolved to break through the difficulties that lay in their way. *But the Egyptians* (*v.* 9) *pursued after them.* Note, Those that in good earnest set their faces heaven-ward, and will live godly in Christ Jesus, must expect to be set upon by Satan's temptations and terrors. He will not tamely part with any out of his service, nor go out without raging, Mark ix. 26.

10 And when Pharaoh drew nigh, the children of Israel lifted up their eyes, and, behold, the Egyptians marched after them; and they were sore afraid : and the children of Israel cried out unto the LORD. 11 And they said unto Moses, Because *there were* no graves in Egypt, hast thou taken us away to die in the wilderness? wherefore hast thou dealt thus with us, to carry us forth out of Egypt? 12 *Is* not this the word that we did tell thee in Egypt, saying, Let us alone, that we may serve the Egyptians? For *it had been* better for us to serve the Egyptians, than that we should die in

the wilderness. 13 And Moses said unto the people, Fear ye not, stand still, and see the salvation of the LORD, which he will show to you to day : for the Egyptians whom ye have seen to day, ye shall see them again no more for ever. 14 The LORD shall fight for you, and ye shall hold your peace.

We have here, I. The fright that the children of Israel were in when they perceived that Pharaoh pursued them, *v.* 10. They knew very well the strength and rage of the enemy, and their own weakness ; numerous indeed they were, but all on foot, unarmed, undisciplined, disquieted by long servitude, and (which was worst of all) now penned up by the situation of their camp, so that they could not make their escape. On the one hand was Pi-hahiroth, a range of craggy rocks impassable ; on the other hand were Migdol and Baalzephon, which, some think, were forts and garrisons upon the frontiers of Egypt; before them was the sea ; behind them were the Egyptians : so that there was no way open for them but upwards, and thence their deliverance came. Note, We may be in the way of our duty, following God and hastening towards heaven, and yet may be in great straits, *troubled on every side,* 2 Cor. iv. 8. In this distress, no marvel that the children of Israel were sorely afraid ; their father Jacob was so in a like case (Gen. xxxii. 7); when without are fightings, it cannot be otherwise but that within are fears : what therefore was the fruit of this fear ? According as that was, the fear was good or evil. 1. Some of them cried out unto the Lord ; their fear set them a praying, and that was a good effect of it. God brings us into straits that he may bring us to our knees. 2. Others of them cried out against Moses ; their fear set them a murmuring, *v.* 11, 12. They give up themselves for lost ; and as if God's arm were shortened all of a sudden, and he were not as able to work miracles to-day as he was yesterday, they despair of deliverance, and can count upon nothing but *dying in the wilderness.* How inexcusable was their distrust ! Did they not see themselves under the guidance and protection of a pillar from heaven ? And can almighty power fail them, or infinite goodness be false to them ? Yet this was not the worst ; they quarrel with Moses for bringing them out of Egypt, and, in quarrelling with him, fly in the face of God himself, and provoke him to wrath whose favour was now the only succour they had to flee to. As the Egyptians were angry with themselves for the best deed they ever did, so the Israelites were angry with God for the greatest kindness that was ever done them ; so gross are the absurdities of unbelief. They here express, (1.) A sordid contempt of liberty, preferring servitude before

it, only because it was attended with some difficulties. A generous spirit would have said, " If the worst come to the worst," as we say, " it is better to die in the field of honour than to live in the chains of slavery ;" nay, under God's conduct, they could not miscarry, and therefore they might say, " Better live God's freemen in the open air of a wilderness than the Egyptians' bondmen in the smoke of the brick-kilns." But because, for the present, they are a little embarrassed, they are angry that they were not left buried alive in their house of bondage. (2.) Base ingratitude to Moses, who had been the faithful instrument of their deliverance. They condemn him, as if he had dealt hardly and unkindly with them, whereas it was evident, beyond dispute, that whatever he did, and however it issued, it was by direction from their God, and with design for their good. What they had said in a former ferment (when they hearkened not to Moses for anguish of spirit), they repeat and justify in this : *We said in Egypt, Let us alone ;* and it was ill-said, yet more excusable, because then they had not had so much experience as they had now of God's wonderful appearances in their favour. But they had as soon forgotten the miracles of mercy as the Egyptians had forgotten the miracles of wrath ; and they, as well as the Egyptians, hardened their hearts, at last, to their own ruin ; as Egypt after ten plagues, so Israel after ten provocations, of which this was the first (Num. xiv. 22), were sentenced to die in the wilderness.

II. The seasonable encouragement that Moses gave them in this distress, *v.* 13, 14. He answered not these fools according to their folly. God bore with the provocation they gave to him, and did not (as he might justly have done) choose their delusions, and bring their fears upon them ; and therefore Moses might well afford to pass by the affront they put upon him. Instead of chiding them, he comforts them, and with an admirable presence and composure of mind, not disheartened either by the threatenings of Egypt or the tremblings of Israel, stills their murmuring, with the assurance of a speedy and complete deliverance : *Fear you not.* Note, It is our duty and interest, when we cannot get out of our troubles, yet to get above our fears, so that they may only serve to quicken our prayers and endeavours, but may not prevail to silence our faith and hope. 1. He assures them that God would deliver them, that he would undertake their deliverance, and that he would effect it in the utter ruin of their pursuers : *The Lord shall fight for you.* This Moses was confident of himself, and would have them to be so, though as yet he knew not how or which way it would be brought to pass. God had assured him that Pharaoh and his host should be ruined, and he comforts them with the same comforts wherewith he had been comforted. 2. He directs them to leave it to God, in a silent expectation of the event: "*Stand still,* and think not to save yourselves either by fighting or flying; wait God's orders, and observe them; be not contriving what course to take, but follow your leader; wait God's appearances, and take notice of them, that you may see how foolish you are to distrust them. Compose yourselves, by an entire confidence in God, into a peaceful prospect of the great salvation God is now about to work for you. Hold your peace; you need not so much as give a shout against the enemy, as Josh. vi. 16. The work shall be done without any concurrence of yours." Note, (1.) If God himself bring his people into straits, he will himself discover a way to bring them out again. (2.) In times of great difficulty and great expectation, it is our wisdom to keep our spirits calm, quiet, and sedate; for then we are in the best frame both to do our own work and to *consider the work of God. Your strength is to sit still* (Isa. xxx. 7), *for the Egyptians shall help in vain,* and threaten to hurt in vain.

15 And the LORD said unto Moses, Wherefore criest thou unto me? speak unto the children of Israel, that they go forward: 16 But lift thou up thy rod, and stretch out thine hand over the sea, and divide it: and the children of Israel shall go on dry *ground* through the midst of the sea. 17 And I, behold, I will harden the hearts of the Egyptians, and they shall follow them: and I will get me honour upon Pharaoh, and upon all his host, upon his chariots, and upon his horsemen. 18 And the Egyptians shall know that I *am* the LORD, when I have gotten me honour upon Pharaoh, upon his chariots, and upon his horsemen. 19 And the angel of God, which went before the camp of Israel, removed and went behind them; and the pillar of the cloud went from before their face, and stood behind them: 20 And it came between the camp of the Egyptians and the camp of Israel; and it was a cloud and darkness *to them,* but it gave light by night *to these:* so that the one came not near the other all the night.

We have here,

I. Direction given to Israel's leader.

1. What he must do himself. He must, for the present, leave off praying, and apply himself to his business (*v.* 15): *Wherefore criest thou unto me?* Moses, though he was

assured of a good issue to the present distress, yet did not neglect prayer. We read not of one word he said in prayer, but he lifted up to God his heart, the language of which God well understood and took notice of. Moses's silent prayers of faith prevailed more with God than Israel's loud outcries of fear, *v.* 10. Note, (1.) Praying, if of the right kind, is *crying to God,* which denotes it to be the language both of a natural and of an importunate desire. (2.) There may be true crying to God by prayer where the voice is not heard, as Hannah's, 1 Sam. i. 13. But is God displeased with Moses for praying? No, he asks this question, *Wherefore cryest thou unto me?* [1.] To satisfy his faith. "Wherefore shouldst thou press thy petition any further, when it is already granted? enough is said; speak no more of this matter: *I have accepted thy prayer,*" so the Chaldee explains it. [2.] To quicken his diligence. Moses had something else to do besides praying; he was to command the hosts of Israel, and it was now requisite that he should be at his post. *Every thing is beautiful in its season.*

2. What he must order Israel to do. *Speak to them, that they go forward.* Some think that Moses had prayed, not so much for their deliverance (he was assured of that) as for the pardon of their murmurings, and that God's ordering them to go forward was an intimation of the pardon. There is no going forward with any comfort but in the sense of our reconciliation to God. Moses had bidden them stand still, and expect orders from God; and now orders are given. They thought they must have been directed either to the right hand or to the left. "No," says God, "speak to them to go forward, directly to the sea-side;" as if there had lain a fleet of transport-ships ready for them to embark in. Note, When we are in the way of our duty, though we meet with difficulties, we must go forward, and not stand in mute astonishment; we must mind present work and then leave the event to God, use means and trust him with the issue.

3. What he might expect God to do. Let the children of Israel go as far as they can upon dry ground, and then God will divide the sea, and open a passage for them through it, *v.* 16—18. God designs, not only to deliver the Israelites, but to destroy the Egyptians; and the plan of his counsels is accordingly. (1.) He will show favour to Israel; the waters shall be divided for them to pass through, *v.* 16. The same power could have congealed the waters for them to pass over; but Infinite Wisdom chose rather to divide the waters for them to pass through; for that way of salvation is always pitched upon which is most humbling. Thus it is said, with reference to this (Isa. lxiii. 13, 14), *He led them through the deep, as a beast goes down into the valley,* and thus *made himself a glorious name.* (2.) He will get him honour

upon Pharaoh. if the due rent of honour be not paid to the great landlord, by and from whom we have and hold our beings and comforts, he will distrain for it, and recover it. God will be a loser by no man. In order to this, it is threatened : *I, behold I, will harden Pharaoh's heart, v.* 17. The manner of expression is observable: *I, behold I, will do it.* "I, that may do it;" so it is the language of his sovereignty. We may not contribute to the hardening of any man's heart, nor withhold any thing that we can do towards the softening of it ; but God's grace is his own, *he hath mercy on whom he will have mercy, and whom he will he hardeneth.* "I, that can do it;" so it is the language of his power ; none but the Almighty can make the heart soft (Job xxiii. 16), nor can any other being make it hard. "I, that will do it ;" for it is the language of his justice ; it is a righteous thing with God to put those under the impressions of his wrath who have long resisted the influences of his grace. It is spoken in a way of triumph over this obstinate and presumptuous rebel: "*I, even I,* will take an effectual course to humble him ; he shall break that would not bend." It is an expression like that (Isa. i. 24), *Ah, I will ease me of my adversaries.*

II. A guard set upon Israel's camp where it now lay most exposed, which was *in the rear, v.* 19, 20. *The angel of God,* whose ministry was made use of in the pillar of cloud and fire, went from *before the camp of Israel,* where they did not now need a guide (there was no danger of missing their way through the sea, nor needed they any other word of command than to go forward), and it came behind them, where now they needed a guard (the Egyptians being just ready to seize the hindmost of them), and so was a wall of partition between them. There it was of use to the Israelites, not only to protect them, but to light them through the sea, and, at the same time, it confounded the Egyptians, so that they lost sight of their prey just when they were ready to lay hands on it. The word and providence of God have a black and dark side towards sin and sinners, but a bright and pleasant side towards those that are Israelites indeed. That which is a savour of life unto life to some is a savour of death unto death to others. This was not the first time that he who in the beginning divided between light and darkness (Gen. i. 4), and still forms both (Isa. xlv. 7), had, at the same time, allotted darkness to the Egyptians and light to the Israelites, a specimen of the endless distinction which will be made between the inheritance of the saints in light and that utter darkness which for ever will be the portion of hypocrites. God will separate between the precious and the vile.

21 And Moses stretched out his hand over the sea ; and the LORD

332

caused the sea to go *back* by a strong east wind all that night, and made the sea dry *land,* and the waters were divided. 22 And the children of Israel went into the midst of the sea upon the dry *ground :* and the waters *were* a wall unto them, on their right hand, and on their left. 23 And the Egyptians pursued, and went in after them to the midst of the sea, *even* all Pharaoh's horses, his chariots, and his horsemen. 24 And it came to pass, that in the morning watch the LORD looked unto the host of the Egyptians through the pillar of fire and of the cloud, and troubled the host of the Egyptians, 25 And took off their chariot wheels, that they drave them heavily: so that the Egyptians said, Let us flee from the face of Israel ; for the LORD fighteth for them against the Egyptians. 26 And the LORD said unto Moses, Stretch out thine hand over the sea, that the waters may come again upon the Egyptians, upon their chariots, and upon their horsemen. 27 And Moses stretched forth his hand over the sea, and the sea returned to his strength when the morning appeared ; and the Egyptians fled against it ; and the LORD overthrew the Egyptians in the midst of the sea. 28 And the waters returned, and covered the chariots, and the horsemen, *and* all the host of Pharaoh that came into the sea after them ; there remained not so much as one of them. 29 But the children of Israel walked upon dry *land* in the midst of the sea ; and the waters *were* a wall unto them on their right hand, and on their left. 30 Thus the LORD saved Israel that day out of the hand of the Egyptians ; and Israel saw the Egyptians dead upon the sea shore. 31 And Israel saw that great work which the LORD did upon the Egyptians : and the people feared the LORD, and believed the LORD, and his servant Moses.

We have here the history of that work of wonder which is so often mentioned both in the Old and New Testament, the dividing of the Red Sea before the children of Israel. It was the terror of the Canaanites (Josh. ii.

9, 10), the praise and triumph of the Israelites, Ps. cxiv. 3; cvi. 9; cxxxvi. 13, 14. It was a type of baptism, 1 Cor. x. 1, 2. Israel's passage through it was typical of the conversion of souls (Isa. xi. 15), and the Egyptians' perdition in it was typical of the final ruin of all impenitent sinners, Rev. xx. 14. Here we have,

I. An instance of God's almighty power in the kingdom of nature, in dividing the sea, and opening a passage through the waters. It was a bay, or gulf, or arm of the sea, two or three leagues over, which was divided, v. 21. The instituted sign made use of was Moses's stretching out his hand over it, to signify that it was done in answer to his prayer, for the confirmation of his mission, and in favour to the people whom he led. The natural sign was a strong east wind, signifying that it was done by the power of God, whom the winds and the seas obey. If there be any passage in the book of Job which has reference to the miracles wrought for Israel's deliverance out of Egypt, it is that in Job xxvi. 12, He divideth the sea with his power, and by his understanding he smiteth through Rahab (so the word is), that is, Egypt. Note, God can bring his people through the greatest difficulties, and force a way where he does not find it. The God of nature has not tied himself to its laws, but, when he pleases, dispenses with them, and then the fire does not burn, nor the water flow.

II. An instance of his wonderful favour to his Israel. They went through the sea to the opposite shore (for I cannot suppose, with some, that they fetched a compass, and came out again on the same side, v. 22. They walked upon dry land in the midst of the sea, v. 29. And the pillar of cloud, that glory of the Lord, being their rearward (Isa. lviii. 8), that the Egyptians might not charge them in the flank, the waters were a wall to them (it is twice mentioned) on their right hand and on their left. Moses and Aaron, it is probable, ventured first into this untrodden path, and then all Israel after them; and this march through the paths of the great waters would make their march afterwards, through the wilderness, less formidable. Those who had followed God through the sea needed not to fear following him whithersoever he led them. This march through the sea was in the night, and not a moon-shiny night, for it was seven days after the full moon, so that they had no light but what they had from the pillar of cloud and fire. This made it the more awful; but where God leads us he will light us; while we follow his conduct, we shall not want his comforts.

This was done, and recorded, in order to encourage God's people in all ages to trust in him in the greatest straits. What cannot he do who did this? What will not he do for those that fear and love him who did this for these murmuring unbelieving Israelites, who yet were beloved for their fathers' sake, and

for the sake of a remnant among them? We find the saints, long afterwards, making themselves sharers in the triumphs of this march (Ps. lxvi. 6): They went through the flood on foot; there did we rejoice in him: and see how this work of wonder is improved, Ps. lxxvii. 11, 16, 19.

III. An instance of his just and righteous wrath upon his and his people's enemies, the Egyptians. Observe here, 1. How they were infatuated. In the heat of their pursuit, they went after the Israelites into the midst of the sea, v. 23. "Why," thought they, "may not we venture where Israel did?" Once or twice, the magicians of Egypt had done what Moses did, with their enchantments; Pharaoh remembered this, but forgot how they were nonplussed at last. They were more advantageously provided with chariots and horses, while the Israelites were on foot. If Pharaoh had said, I know not the Lord; and by this it appeared he did not, else he would not have ventured thus. None so bold as those that are blind. Rage against Israel made them thus daring and inconsiderate: they had long hardened their own hearts; and now God hardened them to their ruin, and hid from their eyes the things that belonged to their peace and safety. Surely in vain is the net spread in the sight of any bird (Prov. i. 17); yet so blind were the Egyptians that they hastened to the snare, Prov. vii. 23. Note, The ruin of sinners is brought on by their own presumption, which hurries them headlong into the pit. They are self-destroyers. 2. How they were troubled and perplexed, v. 24, 25. For some hours they marched through the divided waters as safely and triumphantly as Israel did, not doubting but that, in a little time, they should gain their point. But, in the morning watch, the Lord looked upon the host of the Egyptians, and troubled them. Something or other they saw or heard from the pillar of cloud and fire, which put them into great consternation, and gave them an apprehension of their ruin before it was brought upon them. Now it appeared that the triumphing of the wicked is short, and that God has ways to frighten sinners into despair, before he plunges them into destruction. He cuts off the spirit of princes, and is terrible to the kings of the earth. (1.) They had hectored and boasted as if the day were their own; but now they were troubled and dismayed, struck with a panic-fear. (2.) They had driven furiously; but now they drove heavily, and found themselves plunged and embarrassed at every step; the way grew deep, their hearts grew sad, their wheels dropped off, and the axle-trees failed. Thus can God check the violence of those that are in pursuit of his people. (3.) They had been flying upon the back of Israel, as the hawk upon the trembling dove; but now they cried, Let us flee from the face of Israel, which had become to them like a torch of fire in a sheaf, Zech. xii. 6. Israel has

333

now, all of a sudden, become as much a terror to them as they had been to Israel. They might have let Israel alone and would not; now they would flee from the face of Israel and cannot. Men will not be convinced, till it is too late, that those who meddle with God's people meddle to their own hurt; when the Lord shall come with ten thousands of his saints, to execute judgment, the mighty men will in vain seek to shelter themselves under rocks and mountains *from the face of Israel* and Israel's King, Rev. vi. 15. Compare with this story, Job xxvii. 20, &c. 3. How they were all drowned. As soon as ever the children of Israel had got safely to the shore, Moses was ordered to *stretch out his hand over the sea*, and thereby give a signal to the waters to close again, as before, upon the word of command, they had *opened to the right and the left, v.* 29. He did so, and immediately the waters returned to their place, and overwhelmed all the host of the Egyptians, *v.* 27, 28. Pharaoh and his servants, who had hardened one another in sin, now fell together, and not one escaped. An ancient tradition says that Pharaoh's magicians, Jannes and Jambres, perished with the rest, as Balaam with the Midianites whom he had seduced, Num. xxxi. 8. And now, (1.) God avenged upon the Egyptians the blood of the firstborn whom they had drowned: and the principal is repaid with interest, it is recompensed double, full-grown Egyptians for new-born Israelites; thus the Lord is righteous, and precious is his people's blood in his sight, Ps. lxxii. 14. (2.) God reckoned with Pharaoh for all his proud and insolent conduct towards Moses his ambassador. Mocking the messengers of the Lord, and playing the fool with them, bring ruin without remedy. Now God *got him honour upon Pharaoh,* looking upon that proud man, and abasing him, Job xl. 12. Come and see the desolations he made, and write it, not in water, but with an iron pen in the rock for ever. Here lies that bloody tyrant who bade defiance to his Maker, to his demands, threatenings, and judgments; a rebel to God, and a slave to his own barbarous passions; perfectly lost to humanity, virtue, and all true honour; here he lies, buried in the deep, a perpetual monument of divine justice. Here he went down to the pit, though he was the terror of the mighty in the land of the living. This is Pharaoh and all his multitude, Ezek. xxxi. 18.

IV. Here is the notice which the Israelites took of this wonderful work which God wrought for them, and the good impressions which it made upon them for the present.

1. They saw the Egyptians dead upon the sands, *v.* 30. Providence so ordered it that the next tide threw up the dead bodies, (1.) For the greater disgrace of the Egyptians. Now the beasts and birds of prey were called to *eat the flesh of the captains and mighty men,* Rev. xix. 17, 18. The Egyptians were very nice and curious in embalming and preserving

the bodies of their great men, but here the utmost contempt is poured upon all the grandees of Egypt; see how they lie, heaps upon heaps, as dung upon the face of the earth. (2.) For the greater triumph of the Israelites, and to affect them the more with their deliverance; for the eye affects the heart. See Isa. lxvi. 24, *They shall go forth, and look upon the carcases of the men that have transgressed against me.* Probably they stripped the slain, and, having borrowed jewels of their neighbours before, which (the Egyptians having by this hostile pursuit of them broken their faith with them) henceforward they were not under any obligation to restore, they now got arms from them, which, some think, they were not before provided with. Thus, when God broke the heads of Leviathan in pieces, *he gave him to be meat to the people inhabiting the wilderness,* Ps. lxxiv. 14.

2. The sight of this great work greatly affected them, and now they *feared the Lord, and believed the Lord, and his servant Moses, v.* 31. Now they were ashamed of their distrusts and murmurings, and, in the good mind they were in, they would never again despair of help from Heaven, no, not in the greatest straits; they would never again quarrel with Moses, nor talk of returning to Egypt. They were now baptized unto Moses in the sea, 1 Cor. x. 2. This great work which God wrought for them by the ministry of Moses bound them effectually to follow his directions, under God. This confirmed their faith in the promises that were yet to be fulfilled; and, being brought thus triumphantly out of Egypt, they did not doubt that they should be in Canaan shortly, having such a God to trust to, and such a mediator between him and them. O that there had been such a heart in them as now there seemed to be! Sensible mercies, when they are fresh, make sensible impressions; but with many these impressions soon wear off: while they see God's works, and feel the benefit of them, they fear him and trust in him; but they soon forget his works, and then they slight him. How well were it for us if we were always in as good a frame as we are in sometimes!

CHAP. XV.

THEN sang Moses and the children of Israel this song unto the Lord, and spake, saying, I will sing unto the Lord, for he hath triumphed gloriously: the horse and his rider hath he thrown into the sea. 2 The Lord is my strength and song, and he is become my salvation: he *is* my God, and I will prepare him a habitation; my father's God, and I will exalt him.

3 The Lord *is* a man of war : the Lord *is* his name. 4 Pharaoh's chariots and his host hath he cast into the sea : his chosen captains also are drowned in the Red sea. 5 The depths have covered them : they sank into the bottom as a stone. 6 Thy right hand, O Lord, is become glorious in power: thy right hand, O Lord, hath dashed in pieces the enemy. 7 And in the greatness of thine excellency thou hast overthrown them that rose up against thee: thou sentest forth thy wrath, *which* consumed them as stubble. 8 And with the blast of thy nostrils the waters were gathered together, the floods stood upright as a heap, *and* the depths were congealed in the heart of the sea. 9 The enemy said, I will pursue, I will overtake, I will divide the spoil; my lust shall be satisfied upon them; I will draw my sword, my hand shall destroy them. 10 Thou didst blow with thy wind, the sea covered them : they sank as lead in the mighty waters. 11 Who *is* like unto thee, O Lord, among the gods ? who *is* like thee, glorious in holiness, fearful *in* praises, doing wonders? 12 Thou stretchedst out thy right hand, the earth swallowed them. 13 Thou in thy mercy hast led forth the people *which* thou hast redeemed : ᴸ hast guided *them* in thy strength unto thy holy habitation. 14 The people shall hear, *and* be afraid : sorrow shall take hold on the inhabitants of Palestina. 15 Then the dukes of Edom shall be amazed; the mighty men of Moab, trembling shall take hold upon them; all the inhabitants of Canaan shall melt away. 16 Fear and dread shall fall upon them; by the greatness of thine arm they shall be *as* still as a stone ; till thy people pass over, O Lord, till the people pass over, *which* thou hast purchased. 17 Thou shalt bring them in, and plant them in the mountain of thine inheritance, *in* the place, O Lord, *which* thou hast made for thee to dwell in, *in* the Sanctuary, O Lord, *which* thy hands have established. 18 The Lord shall reign for ever and ever. 19 For the horse of Pharaoh went in with his chariots and with his horsemen into the sea, and the Lord brought again the waters of the sea upon them; but the children of Israel went on dry *land* in the midst of the sea. 20 And Miriam the prophetess, the sister of Aaron, took a timbrel in her hand; and all the women went out after her with timbrels and with dances. 21 And Miriam answered them, Sing ye to the Lord, for he hath triumphed gloriously; the horse and his rider hath he thrown into the sea.

Having read how that complete victory of Israel over the Egyptians was obtained, here we are told how it was celebrated ; those that were to hold their peace while the deliverance was in working (*ch.* xiv. 14) must not hold their peace now that it was wrought; the less they had to do then the more they had to do now. If God accomplishes deliverance by his own immediate power, it redounds so much the more to his glory. Moses, no doubt by divine inspiration, indited this song, and delivered it to the children of Israel, to be sung before they stirred from the place where they saw the Egyptians dead upon the shore. Observe, 1. They expressed their joy in God, and thankfulness to him, by singing ; it is almost natural to us thus to give vent to our joy and the exultations of our spirit. By this instance it appears that the singing of psalms, as an act of religious worship, was used in the church of Christ before the giving of the ceremonial law, and therefore was no part of it, nor abolished with it. Singing is as much the language of holy joy as praying is of holy desire. 2. Moses, who had gone before them through the sea, goes before them in the song, and composes it for them. Note, Those that are active in public services should not be neuters in public praises. 3. When the mercy was fresh, and they were much affected with it, then they sang this song. Note, When we have received special mercy from God, we ought to be quick and speedy in our returns of praise to him, before time and the deceitfulness of our own hearts efface the good impressions that have been made. David sang his triumphant song in the day that the Lord delivered him, 2 Sam. xxii. 1. *Bis dat qui cito dat—He gives twice who gives quickly.* 4. When they *believed the Lord* (*ch.* xiv. 31) then they sang this song : it was a song of faith ; this connection is observed (Ps. cvi. 12): *Then believed they his words, they sang his praise.* If with the heart man believes, thus confession must be made. Here is,

I. The song itself; and,

1. We may observe respecting this song, that it is, (1.) An ancient song, the most ancient that we know of. (2.) A most admirable composition, the style lofty and magnificent, the images lively and proper, and the whole

very moving. (3.) It is a holy song, consecrated to the honour of God, and intended to exalt his name and celebrate his praise, and his only, not in the least to magnify any man: holiness to the Lord is engraven on it, and to him they made melody in the singing of it. (4.) It is a typical song. The triumphs of the gospel church, in the downfal of its enemies, are expresssed in the song of Moses and the song of the Lamb put together, which are said to be sung upon a sea of glass, as this was upon the Red Sea, Rev. xv. 2, 3.

2. Let us observe what Moses chiefly aims at in this song.

(1.) He gives glory to God, and triumphs in him; this is first in his intention (v. 1): *I will sing unto the Lord.* Note, All our joy must terminate in God, and all our praises be offered up to him, the Father of lights and Father of mercies, *for he hath triumphed.* Note, All that love God triumph in his triumphs; what is his honour should be our joy. Israel rejoiced in God, [1.] As their own God, and therefore their *strength, song,* and *salvation, v.* 2. Happy therefore the people whose God is the Lord; they need no more to make them happy. They have work to do, temptations to grapple with, and afflictions to bear, and are weak in themselves; but he strengthens them: his grace is their strength. They are often in sorrow, upon many accounts, but in him they have comfort, he is *their song ;* sin, and death, and hell, threaten them, but he is, and will be, *their salvation :* See Isa. xii. 2. [2.] *As their fathers' God.* This they take notice of, because, being conscious to themselves of their own unworthiness and provocations, they had reason to think that what God had now done for them was for their *fathers' sake,* Deut. iv. 37. Note, The children of the covenant ought to improve their fathers' relation to God as their God for comfort, for caution, and for quickening. [3.] As a God of infinite power (v. 3): *The Lord is a man of war,* that is, well able to deal with all those that strive with their Maker, and will certainly be too hard for them. [4.] As a God of matchless and incomparable perfection, *v.* 11. This is expressed, *First,* More generally : *Who is like unto thee, O Lord, among the gods !* This is pure praise, and a high expression of humble adoration.—It is a challenge to all other gods to compare with him : " Let them stand forth, and pretend their utmost ; none of them dare make the comparison." Egypt was notorious for the multitude of its gods, but the *God of the Hebrews* was too hard for them and baffled them all, Num. xxxviii. 4; Deut. xxxii. 23--39. The princes and potentates of the world are called *gods,* but they are feeble and mortal, none of them all comparable to Jehovah, the almighty and eternal God. — It is a confession of his infinite perfection, as transcendent and unparalleled. Note, God is to be worshipped and adored as a being of such

336

infinite perfection that there is none like him, nor any to be compared with him, as one that in all things has and must have the pre-eminence, Ps. lxxxix. 6. *Secondly,* More particularly, 1. *He is glorious in holiness ;* his holiness is his glory. It is that attribute which angels adore, Isa. vi. 3 His holiness appeared in the destruction of Pharaoh, his hatred of sin, and his wrath against obstinate sinners. It appeared in the deliverance of Israel, his delight in the holy seed, and his faithfulness to his own promise. God is *rich in mercy*—this is his treasure, *glorious in holiness*—this is his honour. Let us always give thanks at the remembrance of his holiness. 2. *He is fearful in praises.* That which is the matter of our praise, though it is joyful to the servants of God, is dreadful and very terrible to his enemies, Ps. lxvi. 1—3. Or it directs us in the manner of our praising God ; we should praise him with a humble holy awe, and *serve the Lord with fear.* Even our spiritual joy and triumph must be balanced with a religious fear. 3. He is *doing wonders,* wondrous to all, being above all power and out of the common course of nature ; especially wondrous to us, in whose favour they are wrought, who are so unworthy that we had little reason to expect them. They were wonders of power and wonders of grace ; in both God was to be humbly adored.

(2.) He describes the deliverance they were now triumphing in, because the song was intended, not only to express and excite their thankfulness for the present, but to preserve and perpetuate the remembrance of this work of wonder to after-ages. Two things were to be taken notice of :—

[1.] The destruction of the enemy ; the waters were divided, *v.* 8. *The floods stood upright as a heap.* Pharaoh and all his hosts were buried in the waters. *The horse and his rider* could not escape (*v.* 1), the *chariots,* and the *chosen captains* (*v.* 4); they themselves went into the sea, and they were overwhelmed, *v.* 19. *The depths, the sea, covered them,* and the proud waters went over the proud sinners ; they *sank like a stone, like lead* (*v.* 5. 10), under the weight of their own guilt and God's wrath. Their sin had made them hard like a stone, and now they justly sink like a stone. Nay, *the earth itself swallowed them* (*v.* 12); their dead bodies sank into the sands upon which they were thrown up, which sucked them in. Those whom the Creator fights against the whole creation is at war with. All this was the Lord's doing, and his only. It was an act of his power : *Thy right hand, O Lord,* not ours, *has dashed in pieces the enemy, v.* 6. It was with *the blast of thy nostrils* (*v.* 8), and *thy wind* (*v.* 10), and the *stretching out of thy right hand, v.* 12. It was an instance of his transcendent power—in *the greatness of thy excellency ;* and it was the execution of his justice : *Thou sentest forth thy wrath, v.* 7. This destruction of the Egyptians was made the more remarkable by their pride and insolence, and their strange assurance of success: *The enemy said, I will pursue, v. 9.* Here is, *First*, Great confidence. When they pursue, they do not question but they shall overtake; and, when they overtake, they do not question but they shall overcome, and obtain so decisive a victory as to *divide the spoil.* Note, It is common for men to be most elevated with the hope of success when they are upon the brink of ruin, which makes their ruin so much the sorer. See Isa. xxxvii. 24, 25. *Secondly,* Great cruelty—nothing but killing, and slaying, and destroying, and this will satisfy his lust; and a barbarous lust that is which so much blood must be the satisfaction of. Note, It is a cruel hatred with which the church is hated; its enemies are bloody men. This is taken notice of here to show, 1. That God resists the proud, and delights to humble those who lift up themselves; he that says, " I will, and I will, whether God will or no," shall be made to know that wherein he deals proudly God is above him. 2. That those who thirst for blood shall have enough of it. Those who love to be destroying shall he destroyed; for we know who has said, *Vengeance is mine, I will repay.*

[2.] The protection and guidance of Israel (*v.* 13): *Thou in thy mercy hast led forth the people,* led them forth out of the bondage of Egypt, led them forth out of the perils of the Red Sea, *v.* 19. *But the children of Israel went on dry land.* Note, The destruction of the wicked serves for a foil to set off the salvation of Israel, and to make it the more illustrious, Isa. xlv. 13—15.

(3.) He sets himself to improve this wonderful appearance of God for them. [1.] In order to quicken them to serve God: in consideration of this, *I will prepare him a habitation, v.* 2. God having preserved them, and prepared a covert for them under which they had been safe and easy, they resolve to spare no cost nor pains for the erecting of a tabernacle to his honour, and there they will exalt him, and mention, to his praise, the honour he had got upon Pharaoh. God had now exalted them, making them great and high, and therefore they will exalt him, by speaking of his infinite height and grandeur. Note, Our constant endeavour should be, by praising his name and serving his interests, to exalt God; and it is an advancement to us to be so employed. [2.] In order to encourage them to trust in God. So confident is this Psalmist of the happy issue of the salvation which was so gloriously begun that he looks upon it as in effect finished already: " *Thou hast guided them to thy holy habitation, v.* 13. Thou hast thus put them into the way to it, and wilt in due time bring them to the end of that way," for God's work is perfect; or, " *Thou hast guided them* to attend thy holy habitation in heaven with their praises." Note, Those whom God takes under his di-

rection he will guide to his holy habitation, in faith now, and in fruition shortly. Two ways this great deliverance was encouraging:— *First,* It was such an instance of God's power as would terrify their enemies, and quite dishearten them, *v.* 14—16. The very report of the overthrow of the Egyptians would be more than half the overthrow of all their other enemies; it would sink their spirits, which would go far towards the sinking of their powers and interests; the Philistines, Moabites, Edomites, and Canaanites (with each of which nations Israel was to grapple), would be alarmed by it, would be quite dispirited, and would conclude it was in vain to fight against Israel, when a God of such power fought for them. It had this effect; the Edomites were afraid of them (Deut. ii. 4), so were the Moabites (Num. xxii. 3), and the Canaanites, Josh. ii. 9, 10; v. 1. Thus God sent his fear before them (*ch.* xxiii. 27), and cut off the spirit of princes. *Secondly,* It was such a beginning of God's favour to them as gave them an earnest of the perfection of his kindness. This was but in order to something further: *Thou shalt bring them in, v.* 17. If he thus *bring them out of Egypt,* notwithstanding their unworthiness, and the difficulties that lay in the way of their escape, doubtless he will bring them into Canaan; for has he begun (*so* begun), and will he not make an end? Note, Our experiences of God's power and favour should be improved for the support of our expectations· " Thou *hast,* therefore, not only thou *canst,* but we trust thou *wilt,*" is good arguing. *Thou wilt plant them in the place which thou hast made for thee to dwell in.* Note, It is good dwelling where God dwells, in his church on earth (Ps. xxvii. 4), in his church in heaven, John xvii. 24. Where he says, " This is my rest for ever," we should say, " Let it be ours." *Lastly,* The great ground of the encouragement which they draw from this work of wonder is, *The Lord shall reign for ever and ever, v.* 18. They had now seen an end of Pharaoh's reign; but time itself shall not put a period to Jehovah's reign, which, like himself, is eternal, and not subject to change. Note, It is the unspeakable comfort of all God's faithful subjects, not only that he does reign universally and with an incontestable sovereignty, but that he will reign eternally, and there shall be no end of his dominion.

II. The solemn singing of this song, *v.* 20, 21. Miriam (or Mary, it is the same name) presided in an assembly of the women, who (according to the softness of their sex, and the common usage of those times for expressing joy, with timbrels and dances) sang this song. Moses led the psalm, and gave it out for the men, and then Miriam for the women. Famous victories were wont to be applauded by the daughters of Israel (1 Sam. xviii. 6, 7); so was this. When God brought Israel out of Egypt, it is said (Micah vi. 4), *He sent before them Moses, Aaron, and Miriam.*

though we read not of any thing memorable that Miriam did but this. But those are to be reckoned great blessings to a people who assist them, and go before them, in praising God.

22 So Moses brought Israel from the Red sea, and they went out into the wilderness of Shur; and they went three days in the wilderness, and found no water. 23 And when they came to Marah, they could not drink of the waters of Marah, for they *were* bitter: therefore the name of it was called Marah. 24 And the people murmured against Moses, saying, What shall we drink? 25 And he cried unto the LORD; and the LORD showed him a tree, *which* when he had cast into the waters, the waters were made sweet: there he made for them a statute and an ordinance, and there he proved them, 26 And said, If thou wilt diligently hearken to the voice of the LORD thy God, and wilt do that which is right in his sight, and wilt give ear to his commandments, and keep all his statutes, I will put none of these diseases upon thee, which I have brought upon the Egyptians: for I *am* the LORD that healeth thee. 27 And they came to Elim, where *were* twelve wells of water, and threescore and ten palm-trees: and they encamped there by the waters.

It should seem, it was with some difficulty that Moses prevailed with Israel to leave that triumphant shore on which they sang the foregoing song. They were so taken up with the sight, or with the song, or with the spoiling of the dead bodies, that they cared not to go forward, but Moses with much ado brought them from the Red Sea into a wilderness. The pleasures of our way to Canaan must not retard our progress, but quicken it, though we have a wilderness before us. Now here we are told,

I. That in the wilderness of Shur they had no water, *v.* 22. This was a sore trial to the young travellers, and a diminution to their joy; thus God would train them up to difficulties. David, in a dry and thirsty land where no water is, reaches forth towards God, Ps. lxiii. 1.

II. That at Marah they had water, but it was bitter, so that though they had been three days without water they could not drink it, because it was extremely unpleasant to the taste or was likely to be prejudicial to their health, or was so brackish that it rather increased their thirst than quenched it, *v.* 23. Note, God can embitter that to us from which we promise ourselves most satisfaction, and

338

often does so in the wilderness of this world, that our wants and disappointments in the creature may drive us to the Creator, in whose favour alone true comfort is to be had. Now in this distress, 1. The people fretted and quarrelled with Moses, as if he had done ill by them. *What shall we drink?* is all their clamour, *v.* 24. Note, The greatest joys and hopes are soon turned into the greatest griefs and fears with those that live by sense only, and not by faith. 2. Moses prayed: *He cried unto the Lord, v.* 25. The complaints which they brought to him he brought to God, on whom, notwithstanding his elevation, Moses owned a constant dependence. Note, It is the greatest relief of the cares of magistrates and ministers, when those under their charge make them uneasy, that they may have recourse to God by prayer: he is the guide of the church's guides; and to him, as the Chief Shepherd, the under-shepherds must upon all occasions apply. 3. God provided graciously for them. He directed Moses to a tree, which he cast into the waters, in consequence of which, all of a sudden, they were made sweet. Some think this wood had a peculiar virtue in it for this purpose, because it is said, *God showed him the tree.* God is to be acknowledged, not only in the creating of things useful for man, but in discovering their usefulness. Or perhaps this was only a sign, and not at all a means, of the cure, any more than the brazen serpent, or Elisha's casting one cruse full of salt into the waters of Jericho. Some make this tree typical of the cross of Christ, which sweetens the bitter waters of affliction to all the faithful, and enables them to rejoice in tribulation. The Jews' tradition is that the wood of this tree was itself bitter, yet it sweetened the waters of Marah; the bitterness of Christ's sufferings and death alters the property of ours. 4. Upon this occasion, God came upon terms with them, and plainly told them, now that they had got clear of the Egyptians, and had entered into the wilderness, that they were upon their good behaviour, and that according as they carried themselves so it would be well or ill with them: *There he made a statute and an ordinance,* and settled matters with them. *There he proved them,* that is, there he put them upon the trial, admitted them as probationers for his favour. In short, he tells them, *v.* 26, (1.) What he expected from them, and that was, in one word, obedience. They must diligently *hearken to his voice, and give ear to his commandments,* that they might know their duty, and not transgress through ignorance; and they must take care in every thing to do that which was right in God's sight, and to *keep all his statutes.* They must not think, now that they were delivered from their bondage in Egypt, that they had no lord over them, but were their own masters; no, therefore they must look upon themselves as God's servants, because he had *loosed their bonds*, Ps. cxvi. 16; Luke i. 74, 75. (2.) What they might then expect from him: *I will put none of these diseases upon thee*, that is, "I will not bring upon thee any of the plagues of Egypt." This intimates that, if they were rebellious and disobedient, the very plagues which they had seen inflicted upon their enemies should be brought upon them; so it is threatened, Deut. xxviii. 60. God's judgments upon Egypt, as they were mercies to Israel, opening the way to their deliverance, so they were warnings to Israel, and designed to awe them into obedience. Let not the Israelites think, because God had thus highly honoured them in the great things he had done for them, and had proclaimed them to all the world his favourites, that therefore he would connive at their sins and let them do as they would. No, God is no respecter of persons; a rebellious Israelite shall fare no better than a rebellious Egyptian; and so they found, to their cost, before they got to Canaan. "But, if thou wilt be obedient, thou shalt be safe and happy;" the threatening is implied only, but the promise is expressed: "*I am the Lord that healeth thee*, and will take care of thy comfort wherever thou goest." Note, God is the great physician. If we be kept well, it is he that keeps us; if we be made well, it is he that restores us; he is our life, and the length of our days

III. That at Elim they had good water, and enough of it, *v.* 27. Though God may, for a time, order his people to encamp by the waters of Marah, yet that shall not always be their lot. See how changeable our condition is in this world, from better to worse, from worse to better. Let us therefore learn both how to be abased and how to abound, to rejoice as though we rejoiced not when we are full, and to weep as though we wept not when we are emptied. Here were twelve wells for their supply, one for every tribe, that they might not strive for water, as their fathers had sometimes done; and, for their pleasure, there were seventy palm-trees, under the shadow of which their great men might repose themselves. Note, God can find places of refreshment for his people even in the wilderness of this world, wells in the valley of Baca, lest they should faint in their mind with perpetual fatigue: yet, whatever our delights may be in the land of our pilgrimage, we must remember that we do but encamp by them for a time, that here we have no continuing city.

CHAP. XVI.

This chapter gives us an account of the victualling of the camp of Israel. I. Their complaint for want of bread, ver. 1—3. II. The notice God gave them beforehand of the provision he intended to make for them, ver. 4—12. III. The sending of the manna, ver. 13—15. IV. The laws and orders concerning the manna. 1. That they should gather it daily for their daily bread, ver. 16—21. 2. That they should gather a double portion on the sixth day, ver. 22—26. 3. That they should expect none on the seventh day, ver. 27—31. 4. That they should preserve a pot of it for a memorial, ver. 32, &c.

A ND they took their journey from Elim, and all the congregation of the children of Israel came unto the wilderness of Sin, which *is* between Elim and Sinai, on the fifteenth day of the second month after their departing out of the land of Egypt. 2 And the whole congregation of the children of Israel murmured against Moses and Aaron in the wilderness: 3 And the children of Israel said unto them, Would to God we had died by the hand of the Lord in the land of Egypt, when we sat by the flesh pots, *and* when we did eat bread to the full; for ye have brought us forth into this wilderness, to kill this whole assembly with hunger. 4 Then said the Lord unto Moses, Behold, I will rain bread from heaven for you; and the people shall go out and gather a certain rate every day, that I may prove them, whether they will walk in my law, or no. 5 And it shall come to pass, that on the sixth day they shall prepare *that* which they bring in; and it shall be twice as much as they gather daily. 6 And Moses and Aaron said unto all the children of Israel, At even, then ye shall know that the Lord hath brought you out from the land of Egypt: 7 And in the morning, then ye shall see the glory of the Lord; for that he heareth your murmurings against the Lord: and what *are we*, that ye murmur against us? 8 And Moses said, *This shall be*, when the Lord shall give you in the evening flesh to eat, and in the morning bread to the full; for that the Lord heareth your murmurings which ye murmur against him: and what *are* we? your murmurings *are* not against us, but against the Lord. 9 And Moses spake unto Aaron, Say unto all the congregation of the children of Israel, Come near before the Lord: for he hath heard your murmurings. 10 And it came to pass, as Aaron spake unto the whole congregation of the children of Israel, that they looked toward the wilderness, and, behold, the glory of the Lord appeared in the cloud. 11 And the Lord spake unto Moses, saying, 12 I have heard the murmurings of the children of Israel: speak unto them, saying, At even ye shall eat flesh, and in the morning ye shall be filled with bread ; and ye shall know that I *am* the LORD your God.

The host of Israel, it seems, took along with them out of Egypt, when they came thence on the fifteenth day of the first month, a month's provisions, which, by the fifteenth day of the second month, was all spent ; and here we have,

I. Their discontent and murmuring upon that occasion, *v.* 2, 3. The whole congregation, the greatest part of them, joined in this mutiny ; it was not immediately against God that they murmured, but (which was equivalent) against Moses and Aaron, God's vicegerents among them. 1. They count upon being killed in the wilderness—nothing less, at the first appearance of disaster. If the Lord had been pleased to kill them, he could easily have done that in the Red Sea ; but then he preserved them, and now could as easily provide for them. It argues great distrust of God, and of his power and goodness, in every distress and appearance of danger to despair of life, and to talk of nothing but being speedily killed. 2. They invidiously charge Moses with a design to starve them when he brought them out of Egypt ; whereas what he had done was both by order from God and with a design to promote their welfare. Note, It is no new thing for the greatest kindnesses to be misinterpreted and basely represented as the greatest injuries. The worst colours are sometimes put upon the best actions. Nay, 3. They so far undervalue their deliverance that they wish they had died in Egypt, nay, and died by the hand of the Lord too, that is, by some of the plagues which cut off the Egyptians, as if it were not the hand of the Lord, but of Moses only, that brought them into this hungry wilderness. It is common for people to say of that pain, or sickness, or sore, of which they see not the second causes, " It is what pleases God," as if that were not so likewise which comes by the hand of man, or some visible accident. Prodigious madness! They would rather die by the fleshpots of Egypt, where they found themselves with provision, than live under the guidance of the heavenly pillar in a wilderness and be provided for by the hand of God ! they pronounce it better to have fallen in the destruction of God's enemies than to bear the fatherly discipline of his children ! We cannot suppose that they had any great plenty in Egypt, how largely soever they now talk of the flesh-pots ; nor could they fear dying for want in the wilderness, while they had their flocks and herds with them. But discontent magnifies what is past, and vilifies what is present, without regard to truth or reason. None talk more absurdly than murmurers. Their impatience, ingratitude, and distrust of God, were so much the worse in that they had lately received such miraculous

340

favours, and convincing proofs both that God could help them in the greatest exigences and that really he had mercy in store for them. See how *soon they forgot his works, and provoked him at the sea, even at the Red Sea,* Ps. cvi. 7—13. Note, Experiences of God's mercies greatly aggravate our distrusts and murmurings.

II. The care God graciously took for their supply. Justly he might have said, " I will rain fire and brimstone upon these murmurers, and consume them ;" but, quite contrary, he promises to rain bread upon them. Observe,

1. How God makes known to Moses his kind intentions, that he might not be uneasy at their murmurings, nor be tempted to wish he had let them alone in Egypt. (1.) He takes notice of the people's complaints : *I have heard the murmurings of the children of Israel, v.* 12. As a God of pity, he took cognizance of their necessity, which was the occasion of their murmuring ; as a just and holy God, he took cognizance of their base and unworthy reflections upon his servant Moses, and was much displeased with them. Note, When we begin to fret and be uneasy, we ought to consider that God hears all our murmurings, though silent, and only the murmurings of the heart. Princes, parents, masters, do not hear all the murmurs of their inferiors against them, and it is well they do not, for perhaps they could not bear it ; but God hears, and yet bears. We must not think, because God does not immediately take vengeance on men for their sins, that therefore he does not take notice of them ; no, he hears the murmurings of Israel, and is grieved with this generation, and yet continues his care of them, as the tender parent of the froward child. (2.) He promises them a speedy, sufficient, and constant supply, *v.* 4. Man being made out of the earth, his Maker has wisely ordered him food out of the earth, Ps. civ. 14. But the people of Israel, typifying the church of the first-born that are written in heaven, and born from above, and being themselves immediately under the direction and government of heaven, receiving their charters, laws, and commissions, from heaven, from heaven also received their food : their law being given by the disposition of angels, they did also eat angels' food. See what God designed in making this provision for them : *That I may prove them, whether they will walk in my law or no.* [1.] Thus he tried whether they would trust him, and walk in the law of faith or no, whether they could live from hand to mouth, and (though now uneasy because their provisions were spent) could rest satisfied with the bread of the day in its day, and depend upon God for fresh supplies to-morrow. [2.] Thus he tried whether they would serve him, and be always faithful to so good a Master, that provided so well for his servants ; and hereby he made it appear to all the world, in the issue, what an ungrateful

people they were, whom nothing could affect with a sense of obligation. Let *favour be shown* to them, yet *will they not learn righteousness,* Isa. xxvi. 10.

2. How Moses made known these intentions to Israel, as God ordered him. Here Aaron was his prophet, as he had been to Pharaoh. Moses directed Aaron what to *speak to the congregation of Israel* (v. 9); and some think that, while Aaron was giving a public summons to the congregation to *come near before the Lord,* Moses retired to pray, and that the appearance of the glory of the Lord (v. 10) was in answer to his prayer. They are called to come near, as Isa. i. 18, *Come, and let us reason together.* Note, God condescends to give even murmurers a fair hearing; and shall we then despise the cause of our inferiors when they contend with us? Job xxxi. 13. (1.) He convinces them of the evil of their murmurings. They thought they reflected only upon Moses and Aaron, but here they are told that God was struck at through their sides. This is much insisted on (v. 7, 8): " *Your murmurings are not against us,* then we would have been silent, but *against the Lord;* it was he that led you into these straits, and not we." Note, When we murmur against those who are instruments of any uneasiness to us, whether justly or unjustly, we should do well to consider how much we reflect upon God by it; men are but God's hand. Those that quarrel with the reproofs and convictions of the word, and are angry with their ministers when they are touched in a tender part, know not what they do, for therein they strive with their Maker. Let this for ever stop the mouth of murmuring, that it is daring impiety to murmur at God, because he is God; and gross absurdity to murmur at men, because they are but men. (2.) He assures them of the supply of their wants, that since they had harped upon the flesh-pots so much they should for once have flesh in abundance that evening, and bread the next morning, and so on every day thenceforward, v. 8, 12. Many there are of whom we say that they are better fed than taught; but the Israelites were thus fed, that they might be taught. *He led him about, he instructed him* (Deut. xxxii. 10); and, as to this instance, see Deut. viii. 3, *He fed thee with manna, that thou mightest know that man doth not live by bread only.* And, besides this, here are two things mentioned, which he intended to teach them by sending them manna:—[1.] *By this you shall know that the Lord hath brought you out from the land of Egypt,* v. 6. That they were brought out of Egypt was plain enough; but so strangely sottish and short-sighted were they that they said it was Moses that brought them out, v. 3. Now God sent them manna, to prove that it was no less than infinite power and goodness that brought them out, and this could perfect what was begun. If Moses only had brought them out of Egypt, he could not thus have fed them; they must therefore own that that was the Lord's doing, because this was so, and both were marvellous in their eyes; yet, long afterwards, they needed to be told that *Moses gave them not this bread from heaven,* John vi. 32. [2.] *By this you shall know that I am the Lord your God,* v. 12. This gave proof of his power as the Lord, and his particular favour to them as their God. When God plagued the Egyptians, it was to make them know that he was the Lord; when he provided for the Israelites, it was to make them know that he was their God.

3. How God himself manifested his glory, to still the murmurings of the people, and to put a reputation upon Moses and Aaron, v. 10. While Aaron was speaking, *the glory of the Lord appeared in the cloud.* The cloud itself, one would think, was enough both to strike an awe upon them and to give encouragement to them; yet, in a few days, it had grown so familiar to them that it made no impression upon them, unless it shone with an unusual brightness. Note, What God's ministers say to us is then likely to do us good when the glory of God shines in with it upon our souls.

13 And it came to pass, that at even the quails came up, and covered the camp: and in the morning the dew lay round about the host. 14 And when the dew that lay was gone up, behold, upon the face of the wilderness *there lay* a small round thing, *as* small as the hoar frost on the ground. 15 And when the children of Israel saw *it,* they said one to another, It *is* manna: for they wist not what it *was.* And Moses said unto them, This *is* the bread which the LORD hath given you to eat. 16 This *is* the thing which the LORD hath commanded, Gather of it every man according to his eating, an omer for every man, *according to* the number of your persons; take ye every man for *them* which *are* in his tents. 17 And the children of Israel did so, and gathered, some more, some less. 18 And when they did mete *it* with an omer, he that gathered much had nothing over, and he that gathered little had no lack; they gathered every man according to his eating. 19 And Moses said, Let no man leave of it till the morning. 20 Notwithstanding they hearkened not unto Moses; but some of them left of it until the morning, and it bred worms, and stank:

and Moses was wroth with them. 21
And they gathered it every morning,
every man according to his eating:
and when the sun waxed hot, it melted.

Now they begin to be provided for by the
immediate hand of God.

I. He makes them a feast, at night, of delicate fowl, *feathered fowl* (Ps. lxxviii. 27),
therefore not *locusts*, as some think; quails,
or pheasants, or some wild fowl, came up,
and covered the camp, so tame that they
might take up as many of them as they
pleased. Note, God gives us of the good
things of this life, not only for necessity, but
for delight, that we may not only serve him,
but serve him cheerfully.

II. Next morning he rained manna upon
them, which was to be continued to them
for their daily bread. 1. That which was
provided for them was manna, which descended from the clouds, so that, in some
sense, they might be said to live upon the
air. It came down in dew that melted, and
yet was itself of such a consistency as to
serve for nourishing strengthening food,
without any thing else. They called it *manna, manhu*, "What is this?" Either, "What
a poor thing this is!" despising it: or, "What
a strange thing this is!" admiring it: or, "It
is a portion, no matter what it is; it is that
which our God has allotted us, and we will
take it and be thankful," *v.* 14, 15. It was
pleasant food; the Jews say that it was pa-
latable to all, however varied their tastes. It
was wholesome food, light of digestion, and
very necessary (Dr. Grew says) to cleanse
them from disorders with which he thinks it
probable that they were, in the time of their
bondage, more or less infected, which disorders a luxurious diet would have made
contagious. By this spare and plain diet we
are all taught a lesson of temperance, and
forbidden to desire dainties and varieties. 2.
They were to gather it every morning (*v.* 21),
the portion of a day in his day, v. 4. Thus
they must live upon daily providence, as the
fowls of the air, of which it is said, *That
which thou givest them they gather* (Ps. civ.
28); not to-day for to-morrow: *let the morrow take thought for the things of itself.* To
this daily raining and gathering of manna
our Saviour seems to allude when he teaches
us to pray, *Give us this day our daily bread.*
We are hereby taught, (1.) Prudence and
diligence in providing food convenient for
ourselves and our household. What God
graciously gives we must industriously gather; with quietness working, and eating
our own bread, not the bread either of idleness or deceit. God's bounty leaves room
for man's duty; it did so even when manna
was rained: they must not eat till they have
gathered. (2.) Contentment and satisfaction
with a sufficiency. They must gather, *every
man according to his eating;* enough is as
good as a feast, and more than enough is as
342

bad as a surfeit. Those that have most
have, for themselves, but food, and raiment,
and mirth; and those that have least generally have these: so that *he who gathers much
has nothing over, and he who gathers little has
no lack.* There is not so great a disproportion between one and another in the comforts
and enjoyments of the things of this life as
there is in the property and possession of
the things themselves. (3.) Dependence
upon Providence: *Let no man leave till morning* (*v.* 19), but let them learn to go to bed
and sleep quietly, though they have not a
bit of bread in their tent, nor in all their
camp, trusting that God, with the following
day, will bring them their daily bread." It
was surer and safer in God's store-house
than in their own, and would thence come
to them sweeter and fresher. Read with
this, Matt. vi. 25, *Take no thought for your
life,* &c. See here the folly of hoarding.
The manna that was laid up by some (who
thought themselves wiser and better ma-
nagers than their neighbours, and who would
provide in case it should fail next day), putrefied, and bred worms, and became good
for nothing. Note, That proves to be most
wasted which is covetously and distrustfully
spared. Those riches are corrupted, Jam. v. 2,
3. Let us set ourselves to think, [1.] Of that
great power of God which fed Israel in the
wilderness, and made miracles their daily
bread. What cannot this God do, who prepared a table in the wilderness, and furnished it richly even for those who questioned whether he could or no? Ps. lxxviii.
19, 20. Never was there such a market of
provisions as this, where so many hundred
thousand men were daily furnished, without
money and without price. Never was there
such an open house kept as God kept in the
wilderness for forty years together, nor such
free and plentiful entertainment given. The
feast which Ahasuerus made, to show the
riches of his kingdom, and the *honour of his
majesty,* was nothing to this, Est. i. 4. It is
said (*v.* 21), *When the sun waxed hot, it melted;*
as if what was left were drawn up by the heat
of the sun into the air to be the seed of the
next day's harvest, and so from day to day.
[2.] Of that constant providence of God
which *gives food to all flesh, for his mercy
endures for ever,* Ps. cxxxvi. 25. He is a
great house-keeper that provides for all the
creatures. The same wisdom, power, and
goodness that now brought food daily out of
the clouds, are employed in the constant
course of nature, bringing food yearly out
of the earth, and giving us all things richly
to enjoy.

22 And it came to pass, *that* on the
sixth day they gathered twice as much
bread, two omers for one *man:* and all
the rulers of the congregation came
and told Moses. 23 And he said unto

them, This *is that* which the LORD hath said, To morrow *is* the rest of the holy sabbath unto the LORD : bake *that* which ye will bake *to day*, and seethe that ye will seethe ; and that which remaineth over lay up for you to be kept until the morning. 24 And they laid it up till the morning, as Moses bade : and it did not stink, neither was there any worm therein. 25 And Moses said, Eat that to day ; for to day *is* a sabbath unto the LORD : to day ye shall not find it in the field. 26 Six days ye shall gather it ; but on the seventh day, *which is* the sabbath, in it there shall be none. 27 And it came to pass, *that* there went out *some* of the people on the seventh day for to gather, and they found none. 28 And the LORD said unto Moses, How long refuse ye to keep my commandments and my laws ? 29 See, for that the LORD hath given you the sabbath, therefore he giveth you on the sixth day the bread of two days ; abide ye every man in his place, let no man go out of his place on the seventh day. 30 So the people rested on the seventh day. 31 And the house of Israel called the name thereof Manna : and it *was* like coriander seed, white ; and the taste of it *was* like wafers *made* with honey.

We have here, 1. A plain intimation of the observing of a *seventh day sabbath,* not only before the giving of the law upon Mount Sinai, but before the bringing of Israel out of Egypt, and therefore, *from the beginning,* Gen. ii. 3. If the sabbath had now been first instituted, how could Moses have understood what God said to him (*v.* 5), concerning a double portion to be gathered on the sixth day, without making any express mention of the sabbath ? And how could the people so readily take the hint (*v.* 22), even to the surprise of the rulers, before Moses had declared that it was done with a regard to the sabbath, if they had not had some knowledge of the sabbath before ? The setting apart of one day in seven for holy work, and, in order to that, for holy rest, was a divine appointment ever since God created man upon the earth, and the most ancient of positive laws. The way of sabbath-sanctification is the good old way. 2. The double provision which God made for the Israelites, and which they were to make for themselves, on the sixth day : God gave them *on the sixth day the bread of two days, v.* 29. Appointing them

to rest on the seventh day, he took care that they should be no losers by it ; and none ever will be losers by serving God. On that day they were to fetch in enough for two days, and to prepare it, *v.* 23. The law was very strict, that they must bake and seeth, the day before, and not on the sabbath day. This does not now make it unlawful for us to dress meat on the Lord's day, but directs us to contrive our family affairs so that they may hinder us as little as possible in the work of the sabbath. Works of necessity, no doubt, are to be done on that day ; but it is desirable to have as little as may be to do of things necessary to the life that now is, that we may apply ourselves the more closely to the one thing needful. That which they kept for their food on the sabbath day did not putrefy, *v.* 24. When they kept it in opposition to a command (*v.* 20) it stank ; when they kept it in obedience to a command it was sweet and good ; for every thing is sanctified by the *word of God and prayer.* 3. The intermission of the manna on the seventh day. God did not send it then, and therefore they must not expect it, nor go out to gather, *v.* 25, 26. This showed that it was not produced by natural causes, and that it was designed for a confirmation of the divine authority of the law which was to be given by Moses. Thus God took an effectual course to make them *remember the sabbath day ;* they could not forget it, nor the day of preparation for it. Some, it seems, went out on the seventh day, expecting to find manna (*v.* 27) ; but they found none, for those that will find must seek in the appointed time : seek the Lord *while he may be found.* God, upon this occasion, said to Moses, *How long refuse you to keep my commandments ? v.* 28. Why did he say this to Moses ? He was not disobedient. No, but he was the ruler of a disobedient people, and God charges it upon him that he might the more warmly charge it upon them, and might take care that their disobedience should not be through any neglect or default of his. It was for going out to seek for manna on the seventh day that they were thus reproved. Note, (1.) Disobedience, even in a small matter, is very provoking. (2.) God is jealous for the honour of his sabbaths. If walking out on the sabbath to seek for food was thus reproved, walking out on that day purely to find our own pleasure cannot be justified.

32 And Moses said, This *is* the thing which the LORD commandeth, Fill an omer of it to be kept for your generations ; that they may see the bread wherewith I have fed you in the wilderness, when I brought you forth from the land of Egypt. 33 And Moses said unto Aaron, Take a pot, and put an omer full of manna therein,

and lay it up before the LORD, to be kept for your generations. 34 As the LORD commanded Moses, so Aaron laid it up before the Testimony, to be kept. 35 And the children of Israel did eat manna forty years, until they came to a land inhabited; they did eat manna, until they came unto the borders of the land of Canaan. 36 Now an omer *is* the tenth *part* of an ephah.

God having provided manna to be his people's food in the wilderness, and to be to them a continual feast, we are here told, 1. How the memory of it was preserved. An omer of this manna was laid up in *a golden pot*, as we are told (Heb. ix. 4), and kept *before the testimony*, or the ark, when it was afterwards made, *v.* 32—34. The preservation of this manna from waste and corruption was a standing miracle, and therefore the more proper memorial of this miraculous food. "Posterity shall *see the bread*," says God, "*wherewith I have fed you in the wilderness*," see what sort of food it was, and how much each man's daily proportion of it was, that it may appear they were neither kept to hard fare nor to short allowance, and then judge between God and Israel, whether they had any cause given them to murmur and find fault with their provisions, and whether they and their seed after them had not a great deal of reason gratefully to own God's goodness to them. Note, Eaten bread must not be forgotten. God's miracles and mercies are to be had in everlasting remembrance, for our encouragement to trust in him at all times. 2. How the mercy of it was continued as long as they had occasion for it. The manna never ceased till they came to the borders of Canaan, where there was bread enough and to spare, *v.* 35. See how constant the care of Providence is; seed-time and harvest fail not, while the earth remains. Israel was very provoking in the wilderness, yet the manna never failed them: thus still God causes his rain to fall on the just and unjust. The manna is called *spiritual meat* (1 Cor. x. 3), because it was typical of spiritual blessings in heavenly things. Christ himself is the true manna, the bread of life, of which this was a figure, John vi. 49—51. The word of God is the manna by which our souls are nourished, Matt. iv. 4. The comforts of the Spirit are hidden manna, Rev. ii. 17. These come from heaven, as the manna did, and are the support and comfort of the divine life in the soul, while we are in the wilderness of this world. It is food for *Israelites*, for those only that follow the pillar of cloud and fire. It is to be *gathered ;* Christ in the word is to be applied to the soul, and the means of grace are to be used. We must every one of us gather for ourselves, and gather in the morning of

our days, the morning of our opportunities, which if we let slip, it may be too late to gather. The manna they gathered must not be hoarded up, but eaten ; those that have received Christ must by faith live upon him, and not receive his grace in vain. There was manna enough for all, enough for each, and none had too much ; so in Christ there is a complete sufficiency, and no superfluity. But those that did eat manna hungered again, died at last, and with many of them God was not well-pleased; whereas those that feed on Christ by faith shall never hunger, and shall die no more, and with them God will be for ever well pleased. The Lord evermore give us this bread !

CHAP. XVII.

Two passages of story are recorded in this chapter, I. The watering of the host of Israel, 1. In the wilderness they wanted water, ver. 1. 2. In their want they chided Moses, ver. 2, 3. 3. Moses cried to God, ver. 4. 4. God ordered him to smite the rock, and fetch water out of that; Moses did so, ver. 5, 6. 5. The place named from it, ver. 7. II. The defeating of the host of Amalek. 1. The victory obtained by the prayer of Moses, ver. 8—12. 2. By the sword of Joshua, ver. 13. 3. A record kept of it, ver. 14, 16. And these things which happened to them are written for our instruction in our spiritual journey and warfare

AND all the congregation of the children of Israel journeyed from the wilderness of Sin, after their journeys, according to the commandment of the LORD, and pitched in Rephidim : and *there was* no water for the people to drink. 2 Wherefore the people did chide with Moses, and said, Give us water that we may drink. And Moses said unto them, Why chide ye with me ? wherefore do ye tempt the LORD ? 3 And the people thirsted there for water; and the people murmured against Moses, and said, Wherefore *is* this *that* thou hast brought us up out of Egypt, to kill us and our children and our cattle with thirst. 4 And Moses cried unto the LORD, saying, What shall I do unto this people ? they be almost ready to stone me. 5 And the LORD said unto Moses, Go on before the people, and take with thee of the elders of Israel ; and thy rod, wherewith thou smotest the river, take in thine hand, and go. 6 Behold, I will stand before thee there upon the rock in Horeb ; and thou shalt smite the rock, and there shall come water out of it, that the people may drink. And Moses did so in the sight of the elders of Israel. 7 And he called the name of the place Massah, and Meribah, because of the chiding of the children of Israel, and because they tempted the LORD, saying, Is the LORD among us, or not?

Here is, I. The strait that the children of Israel were in for want of water; once before they were in the like distress, and now, a second time, *v.* 1. They journeyed *according to the commandment of the Lord,* led by the pillar of cloud and fire, and yet they came to a place where there was no water for them to drink. Note, We may be in the way of our duty, and yet may meet with troubles, which Providence brings us into for the trial of our faith, and that God may be glorified in our relief. II. Their discontent and distrust in this strait. It is said (*v.* 3), They *thirsted there for water.* If they had no water to drink, they must needs thirst; but this intimates, not only that they wanted water and felt the inconvenience of that want, but that their passion sharpened their appetites and they were violent and impatient in their desire; their thirst made them outrageous. Natural desires, and those that are most craving, have need to be kept under the check and control of religion and reason. See what was the language of this inordinate desire. 1. They challenged Moses to supply them (*v.* 2): *Give us water, that we may drink,* demanding it as a debt, and strongly suspecting that he was not able to discharge it. Because they were supplied with bread, they insist upon it that they must be supplied with water too; and indeed to those that by faith and prayer live a life of dependence upon God one favour is an earnest of another, and may be humbly pleaded; but the unthankful and unbelieving have reason to think that the abuse of former favours is the forfeiture of further favours: *Let not them think that they shall receive any thing* (Jam. i. 7), yet they are ready to demand every thing. 2. They quarrelled with him for bringing them out of Egypt, as if, instead of delivering them, he designed to murder them, than which nothing could be more base and invidious, *v.* 3. Many that have not only designed well, but done well, for their generation, have had their best services thus misconstrued, and their patience thereby tried, by unthinking unthankful people. To such a degree their malice against Moses rose that they were *almost ready to stone him, v.* 4. *Many good works he had shown them;* and for which of these would they stone him? John x. 32. Ungoverned passions, provoked by the crossing of unbridled appetites, sometimes make men guilty of the greatest absurdities, and act like madmen, that cast firebrands, arrows, and death, among their best friends. 3. They began to question whether God were with them or not: They *tempted the Lord, saying, " Is the Lord among us or not? v.* 7. Is Jehovah among us by that name by which he made himself known to us in Egypt?" They question his essential presence—whether there was a God

or not; his common providence—whether that God governed the world; and his special promise—whether he would be as good as his word to them. This is called their *tempting God,* which signifies, not only a distrust of God in general, but a distrust of him after they had received such proofs of his power and goodness, for the confirmation of his promise. They do, in effect, suppose that Moses was an impostor, Aaron a deceiver, the pillar of cloud and fire a mere sham and illusion, which imposed upon their senses, that long series of miracles which had rescued them, served them, and fed them, a chain of cheats, and the promise of Canaan a banter upon them; it was all so, if *the Lord was not among them.* Note, It is a great provocation to God for us to question his presence, providence, or promise, especially for his Israel to do it, who are so peculiarly bound to trust him.

III. The course that Moses took, when he was thus set upon, and insulted. 1. He reproved the murmurers (*v.* 2): *Why chide you with me?* Observe how mildly he answered them; it was well that he was a man of extraordinary meekness, else their tumultuous conduct would have made him lose the possession of himself: it is folly to answer passion with passion, for that makes bad worse; but *soft answers turn away wrath.* He showed them whom their murmurings reflected upon, and that the reproaches they cast on him fell on God himself: *You tempt the Lord;* that is, " By distrusting his power, you try his patience, and so provoke his wrath." 2. He made his complaint to God (*v.* 4): *Moses cried unto the Lord.* This servant came, and showed his Lord all these things, Luke xiv. 21. When men unjustly censure us and quarrel with us, it will be a great relief to us to go to God, and by prayer lay the case before him and leave it with him: if men will not hear us, God will; if their bad conduct towards us ruffle our spirits, God's consolations will compose them. Moses begs of God to direct him what he should do, for he was utterly at a loss; he could not of himself either supply their want or pacify their tumult; God only could do it. He pleads his own peril: " *They are almost ready to stone me;* Lord, if thou hast any regard to the life of thy poor servant, interpose now."

IV. God's gracious appearance for their relief, *v.* 5, 6. He orders Moses to go on before the people, and venture himself in his post, though they spoke of stoning him. He must take his rod with him, not (as God might justly have ordered) to summon some plague or other to chastise them for their distrust and murmuring, but to fetch water for their supply. O the wonderful patience and forbearance of God towards provoking sinners! He loads those with benefits that make him to serve with their sins, maintains those that are at war with him, and reaches out the hand of his bounty to those that lift up the heel against him. Thus he teaches us, if our enemy hunger, to feed him, and if he thirst, as Israel did now, *to give him drink*, Rom. xii. 20; Matt. v. 44, 45. Will he fail those that trust him, when he was so liberal even to those that tempted him? If God had only shown Moses a fountain of water in the wilderness, as he did Hagar not far hence (Gen. xxi. 19), that would have been a great favour; but that he might show his power as well as his pity, and make it a miracle of mercy, he gave them water out of a rock. He directed Moses whither to go, and appointed him to take some of the elders of Israel with him, to be witnesses of what was done, that they might themselves be satisfied, and might satisfy others, of the certainty of God's presence with them. He promised to meet him there in the cloud of glory (to encourage him), and ordered him to smite the rock; Moses obeyed, and immediately water came out of the rock in great abundance, which ran throughout the camp in streams and rivers (Ps. lxxviii. 15, 16), and followed them wherever they went in that wilderness: it is called *a fountain of waters*, Ps. cxiv. 8. God showed the care he took of his people in giving them water when they wanted it; he showed his power in fetching the water out of a rock; and he put an honour upon Moses in appointing the water to flow out upon his smiting the rock. This fair water, that came out of the rock, is called *honey and oil* (Deut. xxxii. 13), because the people's thirst made it doubly pleasant; coming when they were in extreme want, it was like honey and oil to them. It is probable that the people digged canals for the conveyance of it, and pools for the reception of it, in like manner as, long afterwards, passing through the valley of Baca, they made it a well, Ps. lxxxiv. 6; Num. xxi. 18. Let this direct us to live in a dependence, 1. Upon God's providence, even in the greatest straits and difficulties. God can open fountains for our supply where we least expect them, *waters in the wilderness* (Isa. xliii. 20), because he makes a *way in the wilderness, v.* 19. Those who, in this wilderness, keep to God's way, may trust him to provide for them. While we follow the pillar of cloud and fire, surely goodness and mercy shall follow us, like the water out of the rock. 2. Upon Christ's grace: *That rock was Christ,* 1 Cor. x. 4. The graces and comforts of the Spirit are compared to *rivers of living water,* John vii. 38, 39; iv. 14. These flow from Christ, who is the rock smitten by the law of Moses, for he was made under the law. Nothing will supply the needs, and satisfy the desires, of a soul, but water out of this rock, this fountain opened. The pleasures of sense are puddle-water; spiritual delights are rock-water, so pure, so clear, so refreshing—rivers of pleasure.

V. A new name was, upon this occasion,

given to the place, preserving the remembrance, not of the mercy of their supply (the water that followed them was sufficient to do that), but of the sin of their murmuring—*Massah, temptation*, because they tempted God; *Meribah, strife*, because they chid with Moses, *v.* 7. There was thus a remembrance kept of sin, both for the disgrace of the sinners themselves (sin leaves a blot upon the name) and for warning to their seed to take heed of sinning after the similitude of their transgression.

8 Then came Amalek, and fought with Israel in Rephidim. 9 And Moses said unto Joshua, Choose us out men, and go out, fight with Amalek: to morrow I will stand on the top of the hill with the rod of God in mine hand. 10 So Joshua did as Moses had said to him, and fought with Amalek: and Moses, Aaron, and Hur went up to the top of the hill. 11 And it came to pass, when Moses held up his hand, that Israel prevailed: and when he let down his hand, Amalek prevailed. 12 But Moses' hands *were* heavy; and they took a stone, and put *it* under him, and he sat thereon; and Aaron and Hur stayed up his hands, the one on the one side, and the other on the other side; and his hands were steady until the going down of the sun. 13 And Joshua discomfited Amalek and his people with the edge of the sword. 14 And the LORD said unto Moses, Write this *for* a memorial in a book, and rehearse *it* in the ears of Joshua: for I will utterly put out the remembrance of Amalek from under heaven. 15 And Moses built an altar, and called the name of it Jehovah-nissi: 16 For he said, Because the LORD hath sworn *that* the LORD *will have* war with Amalek from generation to generation.

We have here the story of the war with Amalek, which, we may suppose, was the first that was recorded in the *book of the wars of the Lord*, Num. xxi. 14. Amalek was the first of the nations that Israel fought with, Num. xxiv. 20. Observe,

I. Amalek's attempt: They *came out, and fought with Israel, v.* 8. The Amalekites were the posterity of Esau, who hated Jacob because of the birthright and blessing, and this was an effort of the hereditary enmity, a malice that ran in the blood, and perhaps was now exasperated by the working of the promise towards an accomplishment. Consider this, 1. As Israel's affliction. They had been quarrelling with Moses (v. 2), and now God sends Amalekites to quarrel with them; wars abroad are the just punishment of strifes and discontents at home. 2. As Amalek's sin; so it is reckoned, Deut. xxv. 17, 18. They did not boldly front them as a generous enemy, but without any provocation given by Israel, or challenge given to them, basely fell upon their rear, and smote those that were faint and feeble and could neither make resistance nor escape. Herein they bade defiance to that power which had so lately ruined the Egyptians; but in vain did they attack a camp guarded and victualled by miracles: verily they knew not what they did.

II. Israel's engagement with Amalek, in their own necessary defence against the aggressors. Observe,

1. The post assigned to Joshua, of whom this is the first mention: he is nominated commander-in-chief in this expedition, that he might be trained up to the services he was designed for after the death of Moses, and be a *man of war from his youth.* He is ordered to draw out a detachment of choice men from the thousands of Israel and to drive back the Amalekites, *v.* 9. When the Egyptians pursued them Israel must stand still and see what God would do; but now it was required that they should bestir themselves. Note, God is to be trusted in the use of means.

2. The post assumed by Moses: *I will stand on the top of the hill with the rod of God in my hand, v.* 9. See how God qualifies his people for, and calls them to, various services for the good of his church: Joshua fights, Moses prays, and both minister to Israel. Moses went up to the top of the hill, and placed himself, probably, so as to be seen by Israel; there he held up *the rod of God in his·hand,* that wonder-working rod which had summoned the plagues of Egypt, and under which Israel had passed out of the house of bondage. This rod Moses held up to Israel, to animate them; the rod 'was held up as the banner to encourage the soldiers, who might look up, and say, "Yonder is the rod, and yonder the hand that used it, when such glorious things were wrought for us." Note, It tends much to the encouragement of faith to reflect upon the great things God has done for us, and review the monuments of his favours. Moses also held up this rod to God, by way of appeal to him: "Is not the battle the Lord's? Is not he able to help, and engaged to help? Witness this rod, the voice of which, thus held up, is (Isa. li. 9, 10), *Put on strength, O arm of the Lord; art not thou it that hath cut Rahab?"* Moses was not only a standard-bearer, but an intercessor, pleading with God for success and victory. Note, When the host goes forth against the enemy earnest prayers should be made to the God of hosts for his

presence with them. It is here the praying legion that proves the thundering legion. There, in Salem, in Sion where prayers were made, there the victory was won, *there broke he the arrows of the bow,* Ps. lxxvi. 2, 3. Observe, (1.) How Moses was tired (v. 12): *His hands were heavy.* The strongest arm will fail with being long extended; it is God only whose hand is *stretched out still.* We do not find that Joshua's hands were heavy in fighting, but Moses's hands were heavy in praying. The more spiritual any service is the more apt we are to fail and flag in it. Praying work, if done with due intenseness of mind and vigour of affection, will be found hard work, and, though *the spirit be willing, the flesh will be weak.* Our great Intercessor in heaven faints not, nor is he weary, though he attends continually to this very thing. (2.) What influence the rod of Moses had upon the battle (v. 11): *When Moses held up his hand* in prayer (so the Chaldee explains it) *Israel prevailed,* but, *when he let down his hand* from prayer, *Amalek prevailed.* To convince Israel that the hand of Moses (with whom they had just now been chiding) contributed more to their safety than their own hands, his rod than their sword, the success rises and falls as Moses lifts up or lets down his hands. It seems, the scale wavered for some time, before it turned on Israel's side. Even the best cause must expect disappointments as an alloy to its successes; though the battle be the Lord's, Amalek may prevail for a time. The reason was, Moses let down his hands. Note, The church's cause is, commonly, more or less successful according as the church's friends are more or less strong in faith and fervent in prayer. (3.) The care that was taken for the support of Moses. When he could not stand any longer he sat down, not in a chair of state, but upon a stone (v. 12); when he could not hold up his hands, he would have them held up. Moses, the man of God, is glad of the assistance of Aaron his brother, and Hur, who, some think, was his brother-in-law, the husband of Miriam. We should not be shy either of asking help from others or giving help to others, for we are members one of another. Moses's hands, thus stayed, were *steady till the going down of the sun;* and, though it was with much·ado that he held out, yet his willing mind was accepted. No doubt it was a great encouragement to the people to see Joshua before them in the field of battle and Moses above them upon the top of the hill: Christ is both to us—our Joshua, the captain of our salvation who fights our battles, and our Moses, who, in the upper world, ever lives making intercession, that our faith fail not.

III. The defeat of Amalek. Victory had hovered awhile between the camps; sometimes Israel prevailed and sometimes Amalek, but Israel carried the day, v. 13. Though Joshua fought with great disadvantages—

his soldiers undisciplined, ill-armed, long inured to servitude, and apt to murmur; yet by them God wrought a great salvation, and made Amalek pay dearly for his insolence. Note, Weapons formed against God's Israel cannot prosper long, and shall be broken at last. The cause of God and his Israel will be victorious. Though God gave the victory, yet it is said, *Joshua discomfited Amalek,* because Joshua was a type of Christ, and of the same name, and in him it is that we are more than conquerors. It was his arm alone that spoiled principalities and powers, and routed all their force.

IV. The trophies of this victory set up. 1. Moses took care that God should have the glory of it (*v.* 15); instead of setting up a triumphal arch, to the honour of Joshua (though it had been a laudable policy to put marks of honour upon him), he builds an altar to the honour of God, and we may suppose it was not an altar without sacrifice; but that which is most carefully recorded is the inscription upon the altar, *Jehovah-nissi—The Lord is my banner,* which probably refers to the lifting up of the rod of God as a banner in this action. The presence and power of Jehovah were the banner under which they enlisted, by which they were animated and kept together, and therefore which they erected in the day of their triumph. In the name of our God we must always lift up our banners, Ps. xx. 5. It is fit that he who does all the work should have all the praise. 2. God took care that posterity should have the comfort and benefit of it: "*Write this for a memorial,* not in loose papers, but in a book, *write it,* and then *rehearse it in the ears of Joshua,* let him be entrusted with this memorial, to transmit it to the generations to come." Moses must now begin to keep a diary or journal of occurrences; it is the first mention of writing that we find in scripture, and perhaps the command was not given till after the writing of the law upon the tables of stone: "Write it *in perpetuam rei memoriam—that the event may be had in perpetual remembrance;* that which is written remains. (1.) "Write what has been done, what Amalek has done against Israel; write in gall their bitter hatred, write in blood their cruel attempts, let them never be forgotten, nor yet what God has done for Israel in saving them from Amalek. Let ages to come know that God fights for his people, and *he that touches them touches the apple of his eye.*" (2.) Write what shall be done. [1.] That in process of time Amalek shall be totally ruined and rooted out (*v.* 14), that he shall be remembered only in history." Amalek would have cut off the name of Israel, that it might be no more in remembrance (Ps. lxxxiii. 4, 7); and therefore God not only disappoints him in this, but cuts off his name. "Write it for the encouragement of Israel, whenever the Amalekites are an annoyance to them,

that Israel will at last undoubtedly triumph in the fall of Amalek." This sentence was executed in part by Saul (1 Sam. xv.), and completely by David (*ch.* xxx.; 2 Sam. i. 1; viii. 12); after his time we never read so much as of the name of Amalek. [2.] This in the mean time God would have a continual controversy with him (*v.* 16): *Because his hand is upon the throne of the Lord,* that is, against the camp of Israel in which the Lord ruled, which was the *place of his sanctuary,* and is therefore called a *glorious high throne from the beginning* (Jer. xvii. 12); therefore the Lord will have *war with Amalek from generation to generation.* This was written for direction to Israel never to make any league with the Amalekites, but to look upon them as irreconcilable enemies, doomed to ruin. Amalek's destruction was typical of the destruction of all the enemies of Christ and his kingdom. Whoever *make war with the Lamb, the Lamb will overcome them.*

CHAP. XVIII.

This chapter is concerning Moses himself, and the affairs of his own family. I. Jethro his father-in-law brings to him his wife and children, ver. 1—6. II. Moses entertains his father-in-law with great respect (ver. 7), with good discourse (ver. 8—11), with a sacrifice and a feast, ver. 12. III. Jethro advises him about the management of his business as a judge in Israel, to take inferior judges in to his assistance (ver. 13—23), and Moses, after some time, takes his counsel (ver. 24—26), and so they part, ver. 27.

WHEN Jethro, the priest of Midian, Moses' father in law, heard of all that God had done for Moses, and for Israel his people, *and* that the Lord had brought Israel out of Egypt; 2 Then Jethro, Moses' father in law, took Zipporah, Moses' wife, after he had sent her back, 3 And her two sons; of which the name of the one *was* Gershom; for he said, I have been an alien in a strange land: 4 And the name of the other *was* Eliezer; for the God of my father, *said he, was* mine help, and delivered me from the sword of Pharaoh: 5 And Jethro, Moses' father in law, came with his sons and his wife unto Moses into the wilderness, where he encamped at the mount of God: 6 And he said unto Moses, I thy father in law Jethro am come unto thee, and thy wife, and her two sons with her.

This incident may very well be allowed to have happened as it is placed here, before the giving of the law, and not, as some place it, in connection with what is recorded, Num. x. 11, 29, &c. Sacrifices were offered before; in these mentioned here (*v.* 12) it is observable that *Jethro* is said to take them, not *Aaron.* And as to Jethro's advising Moses to constitute judges under him, though it is intimated (*v.* 13) that the occasion of his giving that advice was *on the morrow*, yet it does not follow but that Moses's settlement of that affair might be some time after, when the law was given, as it is placed, Deut. i. 9. It is plain that Jethro himself would not have him make this alteration in the government till he had received instructions from God about it (*v.* 23), which he did not till some time after. Jethro comes,

I. To congratulate the happiness of Israel, and particularly the honour of Moses his son-in-law; and now Jethro thinks himself well paid for all the kindness he had shown to Moses in his distress, and his daughter better matched than he could have expected. Jethro could not but hear what all the country rang of, the glorious appearances of God for his people Israel (*v.* 1); and he comes to enquire, and inform himself more fully thereof (see Ps. cxi. 2), and to rejoice with them, as one that had a true respect both for them and for their God. Though he, as a Midianite, was not to share with them in the promised land, yet he shared with them in the joy of their deliverance We may thus make the comforts of others our own, by taking pleasure, as God does, in the *prosperity of the righteous.*

II. To bring Moses's wife and children to him. It seems, he had sent them back, probably from the inn where his wife's aversion to the circumcision of her son had like to have cost him his life (*ch.* iv. 25); fearing lest they should prove a further hindrance, he sent them home to his father-in-law. He foresaw what discouragements he was likely to meet with in the court of Pharaoh, and therefore would not take any with him in his own family. He was of that tribe that said to his father, *I have not known him*, when service was to be done for God, Deut. xxxiii. 9. Thus Christ's disciples, when they were to go upon an expedition not much unlike that of Moses, were to forsake *wife and children*, Matt. xix. 29. But though there might be a reason for the separation that was between Moses and his wife for a time, yet they must come together again, as soon as ever they could with any convenience. It is the law of the relation. *You husbands, dwell with your wives*, 1 Pet. iii. 7. Jethro, we may suppose, was glad of his daughter's company, and fond of her children, yet he would not keep her from her husband, nor them from their father, *v.* 5, 6. Moses must have his family with him, that while he ruled the church of God he might set a good example of prudence in family-government, 1 Tim. iii. 5. Moses had now a great deal both of honour and care put upon him, and it was fit that his wife should be with him to share with him in both. Notice is taken of the significant names of his two sons. 1. The eldest was called *Gershom* (*v.* 3), *a stranger*, Moses designing thereby, not only a memorial of his own condition, but a memorandum to his son of his condition also:

for we are all strangers upon earth, as all our fathers were. Moses had a great uncle almost of the same name, *Gershon, a stranger*; for though he was born in Canaan (Gen. xlvi. 11), yet even there the patriarchs confessed themselves strangers. 2. The other he called *Eliezer* (*v.* 4), *My God a help*, as we translate it; it looks back to his deliverance from Pharaoh, when he made his escape, after the slaying of the Egyptian; but, if this was (as some think) the son that was circumcised at the inn as he was going, I would rather translate it so as to look forward, which the original will bear, *The Lord is my help, and will deliver me* from the sword of Pharaoh, which he had reason to expect would be drawn against him when he was going to fetch Israel out of bondage. Note, When we are undertaking any difficult service for God and our generation, it is good for us to encourage ourselves in God as our help: he that has delivered does and will deliver.

7 And Moses went out to meet his father in law, and did obeisance, and kissed him; and they asked each other of *their* welfare; and they came into the tent. 8 And Moses told his father in law all that the LORD had done unto Pharaoh and to the Egyptians for Israel's sake, *and* all the travail that had come upon them by the way, and *how* the LORD delivered them. 9 And Jethro rejoiced for all the goodness which the LORD had done to Israel, whom he had delivered out of the hand of the Egyptians. 10 And Jethro said, Blessed *be* the LORD, who hath delivered you out of the hand of the Egyptians, and out of the hand of Pharaoh, who hath delivered the people from under the hand of the Egyptians. 11 Now I know that the LORD *is* greater than all gods: for in the thing wherein they dealt proudly *he was* above them. 12 And Jethro, Moses' father in law, took a burnt offering and sacrifices for God: and Aaron came, and all the elders of Israel, to eat bread with Moses' father in law before God.

Observe here, I. The kind greeting that took place between Moses and his father-in-law, *v.* 7. Though Moses was a prophet of the Lord, a great prophet, and king in Jeshurun, yet he showed a very humble respect to his father-in-law. However God in his providence is pleased to advance us, we must make conscience of giving honour to whom honour is due, and never look with disdain upon our poor relations. Those that stand high in the favour of God are not thereby discharged from the duty they owe to men, nor will that justify them in a stately haughty carriage. Moses went out to meet Jethro, did *homage to him, and kissed him.* Religion does not destroy good manners. *They asked each other of their welfare.* Even the kind How-do-you-do's that pass between them are taken notice of, as the expressions and improvements of mutual love and friendship.

II. The narrative that Moses gave his father-in-law of the great things God had done for Israel, *v.* 8. This was one thing Jethro came for, to know more fully and particularly what he had heard the general report of. Note, Conversation concerning *God's wondrous works* is profitable conversation; it is *good, and to the use of edifying,* Ps. cv. 2. Compare Ps. cxlv. 11, 12. Asking and telling news, and discoursing of it, are not only an allowable entertainment of conversation, but are capable of being turned to a very good account, by taking notice of God's providence, and the operations and tendencies of that providence, in all occurrences.

III. The impressions this narrative made upon Jethro. 1. He congratulated God's Israel: *Jethro rejoiced, v.* 9. He not only rejoiced in the honour done to his son-in-law, but in *all the goodness done to Israel, v.* 9. Note, Public blessings are the joy of public spirits. While the Israelites were themselves murmuring, notwithstanding all God's goodness to them, here was a Midianite rejoicing. This was not the only time that the faith of the Gentiles shamed the unbelief of the Jews; see Matt. viii. 10. Standers-by were more affected with the favours God had shown to Israel than those were that received them. 2. He gave the glory to Israel's God (*v.* 10): "*Blessed be Jehovah*" (for by that name he is now known), "*who hath delivered you,* Moses and Aaron, *out of the hand of Pharaoh,* so that though he designed your death he could not effect it, and by your ministry has *delivered the people.*" Note, Whatever we have the joy of God must have the praise of. 3. His faith was hereby confirmed, and he took this occasion to make a solemn profession of it: *Now know I that Jehovah is greater than all gods, v.* 11. Observe, (1.) The matter of his faith : that the God of Israel is greater than all pretenders, all false and counterfeit-deities, that usurp divine honours; he silences them, subdues them, and is too hard for them all, and therefore is himself the only *living and true God.* He is also higher than all princes and potentates (who are called gods), and has both an incontestable authority over them and an irresistible power to control and over-rule them; he manages them all as he pleases, and gets honour upon them, how great soever they are. (2.) The confirmation and improvement of his faith : *Now know I;* he knew it

before, but now he knew it better; his faith grew up to a full assurance, upon this fresh evidence. Those obstinately shut their eyes against the clearest light who do not know that *the Lord is greater than all gods.* (3.) The ground and reason upon which he built it : *For wherein they dealt proudly,* the magicians, and the idols which the Egyptians worshipped, or Pharaoh and his grandees (they both opposed God and set up in competition with him), *he was above them.* The magicians were baffled, the idols shaken, Pharaoh humbled, his powers broken, and, in spite of all their confederacies, God's Israel was rescued out of their hands. Note, Sooner or later, God will show himself above those that by their proud dealings contest with him. He that *exalts himself* against God *shall be abased.*

IV. The expressions of their joy and thankfulness. They had communion with each other both in a feast and in a sacrifice, *v.* 12. Jethro, being hearty in Israel's interests, was cheerfully admitted, though a Midianite, into fellowship with Moses and the elders of Israel, *forasmuch as he also was a son of Abraham,* though of a younger house. 1. They joined in a sacrifice of thanksgiving : *Jethro took burnt offerings for God,* and probably offered them himself, for he was a priest in Midian, and a worshipper of the true God, and the priesthood was not yet settled in Israel. Note, Mutual friendship is sanctified by joint-worship. It is a very good thing for relations and friends, when they come together, to join in the spiritual sacrifice of prayer and praise, as those that meet in Christ the centre of unity. 2. They joined in a feast of rejoicing, a feast upon the sacrifice. Moses, upon this occasion, invited his relations and friends to an entertainment in his own tent, a laudable usage among friends, and which Christ himself, not only warranted, but recommended, by his acceptance of such invitations. This was a temperate feast : *They did eat bread ;* this bread, we may suppose, was manna. Jethro must see and taste that bread from heaven, and, though a Gentile, is as welcome to it as any Israelite ; the Gentiles still are so to Christ the bread of life. It was a feast kept after a godly sort : *They did eat bread before God,* soberly, thankfully, in the fear of God ; and their table-talk was such as became saints. Thus we must eat and drink to the glory of God, behaving ourselves at our tables as those who believe that God's eye is upon us.

13 And it came to pass on the morrow, that Moses sat to judge the people : and the people stood by Moses from the morning unto the evening. 14 And when Moses' father in law saw all that he did to the people, he said, What *is* this thing that thou

doest to the people? why sittest thou thyself alone, and all the people stand by thee from morning unto even? 15 And Moses said unto his father in law, Because the people come unto me to enquire of God: 16 When they have a matter, they come unto me; and I judge between one and another, and I do make *them* know the statutes of God, and his laws. 17 And Moses' father in law said unto him, The thing that thou doest *is* not good. 18 Thou wilt surely wear away, both thou, and this people that *is* with thee: for this thing *is* too heavy for thee; thou art not able to perform it thyself alone. 19 Hearken now unto my voice, I will give thee counsel, and God shall be with thee: Be thou for the people, to God-ward, that thou mayest bring the causes unto God: 20 And thou shalt teach them ordinances and laws, and shalt show them the way wherein they must walk, and the work that they must do. 21 Moreover thou shalt provide out of all the people able men, such as fear God, men of truth, hating covetousness; and place *such* over them, *to be* rulers of thousands, *and* rulers of hundreds, rulers of fifties, and rulers of tens: 22 And let them judge the people at all seasons: and it shall be, *that* every great matter they shall bring unto thee, but every small matter they shall judge: so shall it be easier for thyself, and they shall bear *the burden* with thee. 23 If thou shalt do this thing, and God command thee *so*, then thou shalt be able to endure, and all this people shall also go to their place in peace. 24 So Moses hearkened to the voice of his father in law, and did all that he had said. 25 And Moses chose able men out of all Israel, and made them heads over the people, rulers of thousands, rulers of hundreds, rulers of fifties, and rulers of tens. 26 And they judged the people at all seasons: the hard causes they brought unto Moses, but every small matter they judged themselves. 27 And Moses let his father in law depart; and he went his way into his own land.

Here is, I. The great zeal and industry of Moses as a magistrate.

1. Having been employed to redeem Israel out of the house of bondage, herein he is a further type of Christ, that he is employed as a lawgiver and a judge among them. (1.) He was to answer enquiries, to acquaint them with the will of God in doubtful cases, and to explain the laws of God that were already given them, concerning the sabbath, the manna, &c., beside the laws of nature, relating both to piety and equity, v. 15. *They came to enquire of God;* and happy it was for them that they had such an oracle to consult: we are ready to wish, many a time, that we had some such certain way of knowing God's mind when we are at a loss what to do. Moses was faithful both to him that appointed him and to those that consulted him, and made them *know the statutes of God and his laws, v.* 16. His business was, not to make laws, but to make known God's laws; his place was but that of a servant. (2.) He was to decide controversies, and determine matters in variance, judging between a man and his fellow, *v.* 16. And, if the people were as quarrelsome one with another as they were with God, no doubt he had a great many causes brought before him, and the more because their trials put them to no expense, nor was the law costly to them. When a quarrel happened in Egypt, and Moses would have reconciled the contenders, they asked, *Who made thee a prince and a judge?* But now it was past dispute that God had made him one; and they humbly attend him whom they had then proudly rejected.

2. Such was the business Moses was called to, and it appears that he did it, (1.) With great consideration, which, some think, is intimated in his posture: he *sat* to judge (*v.* 13), composed and sedate. (2.) With great condescension to the people, who stood *by him, v.* 14. He was very easy of access; the meanest Israelite was welcome himself to bring his cause before him. (3.) With great constancy and closeness of application. [1.] Though Jethro, his father-in-law, was with him, which might have given him a good pretence for a vacation (he might have adjourned the court for that day, or at least have shortened it), yet he sat, even the next day after his coming, *from morning till evening.* Note, Necessary business must always take place of ceremonious attentions. It is too great a compliment to our friends to prefer the enjoyment of their company before our duty to God, which ought to be done, while yet the other is not left undone. [2.] Though Moses was advanced to great honour, yet he did not therefore take his ease and throw upon others the burden of care and business; no, he thought his preferment, instead of discharging him from service, made it more obligatory upon him. Those think of themselves above what is meet who think it below them to do good. It is the honour even of angels themselves to be serviceable. [3.] Though the people had been provoking to

351

him, and were ready to stone him (*ch.* xvii. 4), yet still he made himself the servant of all. Note, Though others fail in their duty to us, yet we must not therefore neglect ours to them. [4.] Though he was an old man, yet he kept to his business from morning to night, and made it his meat and drink to do it. God had given him great strength both of body and mind, which enabled him to go through a great deal of work with ease and pleasure; and, for the encouragement of others to spend and be spent in the service of God, it proved that after all his labours his natural force was not diminished. Those that wait on the Lord and his service shall renew their strength

II. The great prudence and consideration of Jethro as a friend.

1. He disliked the method that Moses took, and was so free with him as to tell him so, *v.* 14, 17, 18. He thought it was too much business for Moses to undertake alone, that it would be a prejudice to his health and too great a fatigue to him, and also that it would make the administration of justice tiresome to the people; and therefore he tells him plainly, *It is not good.* Note, There may be over-doing even in well-doing, and therefore our zeal must always be governed by discretion, that our good may not be evil spoken of. Wisdom is profitable to direct, that we may neither content ourselves with less than our duty nor over-task ourselves with that which is beyond our strength.

2. He advised him to such a model of government as would better answer the intention, which was, (1.) That he should reserve to himself all applications to God (*v.* 19): *Be thou for them to God-ward;* that was an honour in which it was not fit any other should share with him, Num. xii. 6—8. Also whatever concerned the whole congregation in general must pass through his hand, *v.* 20. But, (2.) That he should appoint judges in the several tribes and families, who should try causes between man and man, and determine them, which would be done with less noise, and more despatch, than in the general assembly wherein Moses himself presided. Thus they must be governed as a nation by a king as supreme, and inferior magistrates sent and commissioned by him, 1 Pet. ii. 13, 14. Thus many hands would make light work, causes would be sooner heard, and the people eased by having justice thus brought to their tent-doors. Yet, (3.) An appeal might lie, if there were just cause for it, from these inferior courts to Moses himself; at least if the judges were themselves at a loss: *Every great matter they shall bring unto thee, v.* 22. Thus that great man would be the more serviceable by being employed only in great matters. Note, Those whose gifts and stations are most eminent may yet be greatly furthered in their work by the assistance of those that are every way their inferiors, whom therefore they should not despise. The

head has need of the hands and feet, 1 Cor. xii. 21. Great men should not only study to be useful themselves, but contrive how to make others useful, according as their capacity is. Such is Jethro's advice, by which it appears that though Moses excelled him in prophecy he excelled Moses in politics; yet,

3. He adds two qualifications to his counsel:—(1.) That great care should be taken in the choice of the persons who should be admitted into this trust (*v.* 21); they must be *able men,* &c. It was requisite that they should be men of the very best character, [1.] For judgment and resolution—*able men,* men of good sense, that understood business, and bold men, that would not be daunted by frowns or clamours. Clear heads and stout hearts make good judges. [2.] For piety and religion—*such as fear God,* as believe there is a God above them, whose eye is upon them, to whom they are accountable, and of whose judgment they stand in awe. Conscientious men, that dare not do a base thing, though they could do it ever so secretly and securely. The fear of God is that principle which will best fortify a man against all temptations to injustice, Neh. v. 15; Gen. xlii. 18. [3.] For integrity and honesty—*men of truth,* whose word one may take, and whose fidelity one may rely upon, who would not for a world tell a lie, betray a trust, or act an insidious part. [4.] For noble and generous contempt of worldly wealth—*hating covetousness,* not only not seeking bribes nor aiming to enrich themselves, but abhorring the thought of it; he is fit to be a magistrate, and he alone, who *despiseth the gain of oppressions, and shaketh his hands from the holding of bribes,* Isa. xxxiii. 15. (2.) That he should attend God's direction in the case (*v.* 23): *If thou shalt do this thing, and God command thee so.* Jethro knew that Moses had a better counsellor than he was, and to his counsel he refers him. Note, Advice must be given with a humble submission to the word and providence of God, which must always overrule.

Now Moses did not despise this advice because it came from one not acquainted, as he was, with the words of God and the visions of the Almighty; but he *hearkened to the voice of his father-in-law, v.* 24. When he came to consider the thing, he saw the reasonableness of what his father-in-law proposed and resolved to put it in practice, which he did soon afterwards, when he had received directions from God in the matter. Note, Those are not so wise as they would be thought to be who think themselves too wise to be counselled; for *a wise man* (one who is truly so) *will hear, and will increase learning,* and not slight good counsel, though given by an inferior. Moses did not leave the election of the magistrates to the people, who had already done enough to prove themselves unfit for such a trust; but he chose them, and appointed them, some for greater, others for less divisions, the less probably subordinate to the greater. We have reason to value government as a very great mercy, and to thank God for laws and magistrates, so that we are not like *the fishes of the sea, where the greater devour the less.*

III. Jethro's return to his own land, *v.* 27. No doubt he took home with him the improvements he had made in the knowledge of God, and communicated them to his neighbours for their instruction. It is supposed that the Kenites (mentioned 1 Sam. xv. 6) were the posterity of Jethro (compare Judg. i. 16), and they are there taken under special protection, for the kindness their ancestor here showed to Israel. The good-will shown to God's people, even in the smallest instances, shall in no wise lose its reward, but shall be recompensed, at furthest, in the resurrection.

CHAP. XIX.

This chapter introduces the solemnity of the giving of the law upon mount Sinai, which was one of the most striking appearances of the divine glory that ever was in this lower world. We have here, I. The circumstances of time and place, ver. 1, 2. II. The covenant between God and Israel settled in general. The gracious proposal God made to them (ver. 3—6), and their consent to the proposal, ver. 7, 8. III. Notice given three days before of God's design to give the law out of a thick cloud, ver. 9. Orders given to prepare the people to receive the law, ver. 10—13), and care taken to execute those orders, ver. 14, 15. IV. A terrible appearance of God's glory upon mount Sinai, ver. 16—20. V. Silence proclaimed, and strict charges given to the people to observe decorum while God spoke to them, ver. 21, &c.

IN the third month, when the children of Israel were gone forth out of the land of Egypt, the same day came they *into* the wilderness of Sinai. 2 For they were departed from Rephidim, and were come *to* the desert of Sinai, and had pitched in the wilderness; and there Israel camped before the mount. 3 And Moses went up unto God, and the Lord called unto him out of the mountain, saying, Thus shalt thou say to the house of Jacob, and tell the children of Israel; 4 Ye have seen what I did unto the Egyptians, and *how* I bare you on eagles' wings, and brought you unto myself. 5 Now therefore, if ye will obey my voice indeed, and keep my covenant, then ye shall be a peculiar treasure unto me above all people : for all the earth *is* mine : 6 And ye shall be unto me a kingdom of priests, and a holy nation. These *are* the words which thou shalt speak unto the children of Israel. 7 And Moses came and called for the elders of the people, and laid before their faces all these words which the Lord commanded him. 8 And all the people answered together, and said, All that the Lord hath spoken we will do. And Moses returned the words of the people unto the Lord.

Here is, I. The date of that great charter by which Israel was incorporated. 1. The time when it bears date (*v.* 1)—*in the third month* after they came out of Egypt. It is computed that the law was given just fifty days after their coming out of Egypt, in remembrance of which the feast of Pentecost was observed the fiftieth day after the passover, and in compliance with which the Spirit was poured out upon the apostles at the feast of Pentecost, fifty days after the death of Christ. In Egypt they had spoken of a three days' journey into the wilderness to the place of their sacrifice (*ch.* v. 3), but it proved to be almost a two months' journey; so often are we out in the calculation of times, and things prove longer in the doing than we expected. 2. The place whence it bears date—from *mount Sinai,* a place which nature, not art, had made eminent and conspicuous, for it was the highest in all that range of mountains. Thus God put contempt upon cities, and palaces, and magnificent structures, setting up his pavilion on the top of a high mountain, in a waste and barren desert, there to carry on this treaty. It is called *Sinai,* from the multitude of thorny bushes that overspread it.

II. The charter itself. Moses was called up to the mountain (on the top of which God had pitched his tent, and at the foot of which Israel had pitched theirs), and was employed as the mediator, or rather no more than the messenger of the covenant : *Thus shalt thou say to the house of Jacob, and tell the children of Israel, v.* 3. Here the learned bishop Patrick observes that the people are called by the names both of *Jacob* and *Israel,* to remind them that those who had lately been as low as Jacob when he went to Padan-aram had now grown as great as God made him when he came thence (justly enriched with the spoils of him that had oppressed him) and was called *Israel.* Now observe, 1. That the maker, and first mover, of the covenant, is God himself. Nothing was said nor done by this stupid unthinking people themselves towards this settlement; no motion made, no petition put up for God's favour, but this blessed charter was granted *ex mero motu—purely out of God's own good-will.* Note, In all our dealings with God, free grace anticipates us with the blessings of goodness, and all our comfort is owing, not to our knowing God, but rather to our being *known of him,* Gal. iv. 9. *We love him,* visit him, and covenant with him, *because he first loved us,* visited us, and covenanted with us. God is the Alpha, and therefore must be the Omega. 2. That the matter of the covenant is not only just and unexceptionable, and such as puts no hardship upon them, but kind and gracious, and such as gives them the greatest privileges and advantages imaginable. (1.) He reminds them of what he had done for them, *v.* 4. He had righted them, and avenged them upon their persecutors and oppressors : " *You have seen what I did unto the Egyptians,*

353

how many lives were sacrificed to Israel's honour and interests:" he had given them unparalleled instances of his favour to them, and his care of them: *I bore you on eagles' wings,* a high expression of the wonderful tenderness God had shown for them. It is explained, Deut. xxxii. 11, 12. It denotes great speed. God not only came upon the wing for their deliverance (when the set time was come, he rode on a cherub, and did fly), but he hastened them out, as it were, upon the wing. He did it also with great ease, with the strength as well as with the swiftness of an eagle: those that faint not, nor are weary, are said to *mount up with wings as eagles,* Isa. xl. 31. Especially, it denotes God's particular care of them and affection to them. Even Egypt, that iron furnace, was the nest in which these young ones were hatched, where they were first formed as the embryo of a nation; when, by the increase of their numbers, they grew to some maturity, they were carried out of that nest. Other birds carry their young in their talons, but the eagle (they say) upon her wings, so that even those archers who shoot flying cannot hurt the young ones, unless they first shoot through the old one. Thus, in the Red Sea, the pillar of cloud and fire, the token of God's presence, interposed itself between the Israelites and their pursuers (lines of defence which could not be forced, a wall which could not be penetrated): yet this was not all; their way so paved, so guarded, was glorious, but their end much more so: *I brought you unto myself.* They were brought not only into a state of liberty and honour, but into covenant and communion with God. This, this was the glory of their deliverance, as it is of ours by Christ, that he died, *the just for the unjust, that he might bring us to God.* This God aims at in all the gracious methods of his providence and grace, to bring us back to himself, from whom we have revolted, and to bring us home to himself, in whom alone we can be happy. He appeals to themselves, and their own observation and experience, for the truth of what is here insisted on: *You have seen what I did;* so that they could not disbelieve God, unless they would first disbelieve their own eyes. They saw how all that was done was purely the Lord's doing. It was not they that reached towards God, but it was he that brought them to himself. Some have well observed that the *Old-Testament church* is said to be borne upon eagles' wings, denoting the power of that dispensation, which was carried on with *a high hand and an out-stretched arm;* but the *New-Testament church* is said to be gathered by the Lord Jesus, *as a hen gathers her chickens under her wings* (Matt. xxiii. 37), denoting the grace and compassion of that dispensation, and the admirable condescension and humiliation of the Redeemer. (2.) He tells them plainly what he expected and required from them in one word, obedience (*v.* 5), that they should *obey his voice indeed and keep his covenant.* Being thus saved by him, that which he insisted upon was that they should be ruled by him. The reasonableness of this demand is, long after, pleaded with them, that *in the day he brought them out of the land of Egypt* this was the condition of the covenant, *Obey my voice* (Jer. vii. 23); and this he is said to protest earnestly to them, Jer. xi. 4, 7. Only obey *indeed,* not in profession and promise only, not in pretence, but in sincerity. God had shown them real favours, and therefore required real obedience. (3.) He assures them of the honour he would put upon them, and the kindness he would show them, in case they did thus keep his covenant (*v.* 5, 6): *Then you shall be a peculiar treasure to me.* He does not specify any one particular favour, as giving them the land of Canaan, or the like, but expresses it in that which was inclusive of all happiness, that he would be to them a God in covenant, and they should be to him a people. [1.] God here asserts his sovereignty over, and propriety in, the whole visible creation: *All the earth is mine.* Therefore he needed them not; he that had so vast a dominion was great enough, and happy enough, without concerning himself for so small a demesne as Israel was. All nations on the earth being his, he might choose which he pleased for his peculiar, and act in a way of sovereignty. [2.] He appropriates Israel to himself, *First,* As a people dear unto him. *You shall be a peculiar treasure;* not that God was enriched by them, as a man is by his treasure, but he was pleased to value and esteem them as a man does his treasure; they were *precious in his sight and honourable* (Isa. xliii. 4); he *set his love upon them* (Deut. vii. 7), took them under his special care and protection, as a treasure that is kept under lock and key. He looked upon the rest of the world but as trash and lumber in comparison with them. By giving them divine revelation, instituted ordinances, and promises inclusive of eternal life, by sending his prophets among them, and pouring out his Spirit upon them, he distinguished them from, and dignified them above, all people. And this honour have all the saints; they are unto God a *peculiar people* (Tit. ii. 14), his when he *makes up his jewels. Secondly,* As a people devoted to him, to his honour and service (*v.* 6), a *kingdom of priests,* a *holy nation.* All the Israelites, if compared with other people, were priests unto God, so near were they to him (Ps. cxlviii. 14), so much employed in his immediate service, and such intimate communion they had with him. When they were first made a free people it was that they might *sacrifice to the Lord their God,* as *priests:* they were under God's immediate government, and the tendency of the laws given them was to distinguish them from others, and engage them for God as a holy nation. Thus all believers are, through Christ, made to our God kings and priests (Rev. i. 6), *a chosen generation, a royal priesthood,* 1 Pet. ii. 9.

III. Israel's acceptance of this charter, and consent to the conditions of it. 1. Moses faithfully delivered God's message to them (*v.* 7): He *laid before their faces all those words;* he not only explained to them what God had given him in charge, but he put it to their choice whether they would accept these promises upon these terms or no. His laying it to their faces denotes his laying it to their consciences. 2. They readily agreed to the covenant proposed. They would oblige themselves to obey the voice of God, and take it as a great favour to be made a kingdom of priests to him. They answered together as one man, *nemine contradicente—without a dissentient voice* (*v* 8): *All that the Lord hath spoken we will do.* Thus they strike the bargain, accepting the Lord to be to them a God, and giving up themselves to be to him a people. O that there had been such a heart in them! 3. Moses, as a mediator, returned the words of the people to God, *v.* 8. Thus Christ, the Mediator between us and God, as a prophet reveals God's will to us, his precepts and promises, and then as a priest offers up to God our spiritual sacrifices, not only of prayer and praise, but of devout affections and pious resolutions, the work of his own Spirit in us. Thus he is that blessed *days-man who lays his hand upon us both.*

9 And the LORD said unto Moses, Lo, I come unto thee in a thick cloud, that the people may hear when I speak with thee, and believe thee for ever. And Moses told the words of the people unto the LORD. 10 And the LORD said unto Moses, Go unto the people, and sanctify them to day and to morrow, and let them wash their clothes, 11 And be ready against the third day: for the third day the LORD will come down in the sight of all the people upon mount Sinai. 12 And thou shalt set bounds unto the people round about, saying, Take heed to yourselves, *that ye* go *not* up into the mount, or touch the border of it: whosoever toucheth the mount shall be surely put to death: 13 There shall not a hand touch it, but he shall surely be stoned, or shot through; whether *it be* beast or man, it shall not live: when the trumpet soundeth long, they shall come up to the mount. 14 And Moses went down from the mount unto the people, and sanctified the people; and they washed their clothes. 15 And he said unto the

people, Be ready against the third day: come not at *your* wives.

Here, I. God intimates to Moses his purpose of coming down upon mount Sinai, in some visible appearance of his glory, in *a thick cloud* (*v.* 9); for he said that he would *dwell in the thick darkness* (2 Chron. vi. 1), and make this his pavilion (Ps. xviii. 11), *holding back the face of his throne* when he set it upon *mount Sinai, and spreading a cloud upon it,* Job xxvi. 9. This thick cloud was to prohibit curious enquiries into things secret, and to command an awful adoration of that which was revealed. God would come down *in the sight of all the people* (*v.* 11); though they should see no manner of similitude, yet they should see so much as would convince them that God was among them of a truth. And so high was the top of mount Sinai that it is supposed that not only the camp of Israel, but even the countries about, might discern some extraordinary appearance of glory upon it, which would strike a terror upon them. It seems also to have been particularly intended to put an honour upon Moses: *That they may hear when I speak with thee, and believe thee for ever, v.* 9. Thus the correspondence was to be first settled by a sensible appearance of the divine glory, which was afterwards to be carried on more silently by the ministry of Moses. In like manner, the Holy Ghost descended visibly upon Christ at his baptism, and all that were present heard God speak to him (Matt. iii. 17), that afterwards, without the repetition of such visible tokens, they might believe him. So likewise the Spirit descended in cloven tongues upon the apostles (Acts ii. 3), that they might be believed. Observe, When the people had declared themselves willing to obey the voice of God, then God promised they should hear his voice; for, if any man be resolved to *do his will, he shall know it,* John vii. 17.

II. He orders Moses to make preparation for this great solemnity, giving him two days' time for it.

1. He must *sanctify the people* (*v.* 10), as Job, before this, sent and *sanctified his sons,* Job i. 5. He must raise their expectation by giving them notice what God would do, and assist their preparation by directing them what they must do. " *Sanctify them,*" that is, " Call them off from their worldly business, and call them to religious exercises, meditation and prayer, that they may receive the law from God's mouth with reverence and devotion. *Let them be ready,*" *v.* 11. Note, When we are to attend upon God in solemn ordinances it concerns us to sanctify ourselves, and to get ready beforehand. Wandering thoughts must be gathered in, impure affections abandoned, disquieting passions suppressed, nay, and all cares about secular business, for the present, dismissed and laid by, that our hearts may be *engaged to approach unto God.* Two things particu-

larly were prescribed as signs and instances of their preparation :—(1.) In token of their cleansing themselves from all sinful pollutions, that they might be holy to God, they must *wash their clothes* (v. 10), and they did so (v. 14); not that God regards our clothes; but while they were washing their clothes he would have them think of washing their souls by repentance from the sins they had contracted in Egypt and since their deliverance. It becomes us to appear in clean clothes when we wait upon great men; so clean hearts are required in our attendance on the great God, who sees them as plainly as men see our clothes. This is absolutely necessary to our acceptably worshipping God. See Ps. xxvi. 6; Isa. i. 16—18; Heb. x. 22. (2.) In token of their devoting themselves entirely to religious exercises, upon this occasion, they must abstain even from lawful enjoyments during these three days, and not *come at their wives, v.* 15. See 1 Cor. vii. 5.

2. He must *set bounds about the mountain, v.* 12, 13. Probably he drew a line, or ditch, round at the foot of the hill, which none were to pass upon pain of death. This was to intimate, (1.) That humble awful reverence which ought to possess the minds of all those that worship God. We are mean creatures before a great Creator, vile sinners before a holy righteous Judge; and therefore a godly fear and shame well become us, Heb. xii. 28; Ps. ii. 11. (2.) The distance at which worshippers were kept, under that dispensation, which we ought to take notice of, that we may the more value our privilege under the gospel, having *boldness to enter into the holiest by the blood of Jesus,* Heb. x. 19.

3. He must order the people to attend upon the summons that should be given (v. 13): "*When the trumpet soundeth long* then let them take their places at the foot of the mount, and so sit down at God's feet," as it is explained, Deut. xxxiii. 3. Never was so great a congregation called together, and preached to, at once, as this was here. No one man's voice could have reached so many, but the voice of God did.

16 And it came to pass on the third day in the morning, that there were thunders and lightnings, and a thick cloud upon the mount, and the voice of the trumpet exceeding loud; so that all the people that *was* in the camp trembled. 17 And Moses brought forth the people out of the camp to meet with God; and they stood at the nether part of the mount. 18 And mount Sinai was altogether on a smoke, because the LORD descended upon it in fire: and the smoke thereof ascended as the smoke of a furnace, and the whole mount quaked greatly. 19 And when the voice of the trumpet sounded long, and waxed louder and louder, Moses spake, and God answered him by a voice. 20 And the LORD came down upon mount Sinai, on the top of the mount: and the LORD called Moses *up* to the top of the mount; and Moses went up. 21 And the LORD said unto Moses, Go down, charge the people, lest they break through unto the LORD to gaze, and many of them perish. 22 And let the priests also, which come near to the LORD, sanctify themselves, lest the LORD break forth upon them. 23 And Moses said unto the LORD, The people cannot come up to mount Sinai: for thou chargedst us, saying, Set bounds about the mount, and sanctify it. 24 And the LORD said unto him, Away, get thee down, and thou shalt come up, thou, and Aaron with thee: but let not the priests and the people break through to come up unto the LORD, lest he break forth upon them. 25 So Moses went down unto the people and spake unto them.

Now, at length, comes that memorable day, that terrible day of the Lord, that day of judgment, in which *Israel heard the voice of the Lord God* speaking to them *out of the midst of the fire, and lived,* Deut. iv. 33. Never was there such a sermon preached, before nor since, as this which was here preached to the church in the wilderness. For,

I. The preacher was God himself (v. 18): *The Lord descended in fire,* and (v. 20), *The Lord came down upon mount Sinai.* The *shechinah,* or glory of the Lord, appeared in the sight of all the people; he *shone forth from mount Paran with ten thousands of his saints* (Deut. xxxiii. 2), that is, attended, as the divine Majesty always is, by a multitude of the holy angels, who were both to grace the solemnity and to assist at it. Hence the law is said to be given *by the disposition of angels,* Acts vii. 53.

II. The pulpit (or throne rather) was mount Sinai, hung with a *thick cloud* (v. 16), covered with *smoke* (v. 18), and made to *quake* greatly. Now it was that the earth *trembled at the presence of the Lord,* and the *mountains skipped like rams* (Ps. cxiv. 4, 7), that Sinai itself, though rough and rocky, *melted from before the Lord God of Israel,* Judg. v. 5. Now it was that the *mountains saw him, and trembled* (Hab. iii. 10), and were witnesses against a hard-hearted un-

356

moved people, whom nothing would influence.

III. The congregation was called together by the *sound of a trumpet, exceedingly loud* (v. 16), and *waxing louder and louder, v. 19.* This was done by the ministry of the angels, and we read of trumpets sounded by angels, Rev. viii. 6. It was the *sound of the trumpet that made all the people tremble,* as those who knew their own guilt, and who had reason to expect that the sound of this trumpet was to them the *alarm of war.*

IV. Moses brought the hearers to the place of meeting, v. 17. He that had led them out of the bondage of Egypt now led them to receive the law from God's mouth. Public persons are indeed public blessings when they lay out themselves in their places to promote the public worship of God. Moses, at the head of an assembly worshipping God, was as truly great as Moses at the head of an army in the field.

V. The introductions to the service were *thunders and lightnings, v. 16.* These were designed to strike an awe upon the people, and to raise and engage their attention. Were they asleep? The thunders would awaken them. Were they looking another way? The lightnings would engage them to turn their faces towards him that spoke to them. Thunder and lightning have natural causes, but the scripture directs us in a particular manner to take notice of the power of God, and his terror, in them. Thunder is the voice of God, and lightning the fire of God, proper to engage the senses of sight and hearing, those senses by which we receive so much of our information.

VI. Moses is God's minister, who is spoken to, to command silence, and keep the congregation in order: *Moses spoke, v.* 19. Some think it was now that he said, *I exceedingly fear and quake* (Heb. xii. 21); but God stilled his fear by his distinguishing favour to him, in calling him up to the top of the mount (v. 20), by which also he tried his faith and courage. No sooner had Moses got up a little way towards the top of the mount than he was sent down again to keep the people from *breaking through to gaze, v.* 21. Even the priests or princes, the heads of the houses of their fathers, who officiated *for* their respective families, and therefore are said to *come near to the Lord* at other times, must now keep their distance, and conduct themselves with a great deal of caution. Moses pleads that they needed not to have any further orders given them, effectual care being taken already to prevent any intrusions, *v.* 23. But God, who knew their wilfulness and presumption, and what was now in the hearts of some of them, hastens him down with this in charge, that neither the priests nor the people should offer to force the lines that were set, to *come up unto the Lord,* but Moses and Aaron only, the men whom God delighted to honour. Observe,

1. What it was that God forbade them—breaking through to gaze; enough was provided to awaken their consciences, but they were not allowed to gratify their vain curiosity. They might see, but not gaze. Some of them, probably, were desirous to see some similitude, that they might know how to make an image of God, which he took care to prevent, for they *saw no manner of similitude,* Deut. iv. 5. Note, In divine things we must not covet to know more than God would have us know; and he has allowed us as much as is good for us. A desire of forbidden knowledge was the ruin of our first parents. Those that would be wise above what is written, and intrude into those things which they have not seen, need this admonition, that they *break not through to gaze.* 2. Under what penalty it was forbidden: *Lest the Lord break forth upon them* (v. 22—24), and *many of them perish.* Note, (1.) The restraints and warnings of the divine law are all intended for our good, and to keep us out of that danger into which we should otherwise, by our own folly, run ourselves. (2.) It is at our peril if we break the bounds that God has set us, and intrude upon that which he has not allowed us; the Bethshemites and Uzzah paid dearly for their presumption. And, even when we are called to approach God, we must remember that he is in heaven and we upon earth, and therefore it behoves us to exercise reverence and godly fear.

CHAP. XX.

All things being prepared for the solemn promulgation of the divine law, we have, in this chapter, I. The ten commandments, as God himself spoke them upon mount Sinai (ver. 1—17), as remarkable a portion of scripture as any in the Old Testament. II. The impressions made upon the people thereby, ver. 18—21. III. Some particular instructions which God gave privately to Moses, to be by him communicated to the people, relating to his worship, ver. 22, &c.

AND God spake all these words, saying, 2 I *am* the LORD thy God, which have brought thee out of the land of Egypt, out of the house of bondage. 3 Thou shalt have no other gods before me. 4 Thou shalt not make unto thee any graven image, or any likeness *of any thing* that *is* in heaven above, or that *is* in the earth beneath, or that *is* in the water under the earth: 5 Thou shalt not bow down thyself to them, nor serve them: for I the LORD thy God *am* a jealous God, visiting the iniquity of the fathers upon the children unto the third and fourth *generation* of them that hate me; 6 And shewing mercy unto thousands of them that love me, and keep my commandments. 7 Thou shalt not take the name of the LORD thy God in vain; for the LORD will not hold him guiltless that taketh his

357

name in vain. 8 Remember the sabbath day, to keep it holy. 9 Six days shalt thou labour, and do all thy work: 10 But the seventh day *is* the sabbath of the LORD thy God : *in it* thou shalt not do any work, thou, nor thy son, nor thy daughter, thy manservant, nor thy maidservant, nor thy cattle, nor thy stranger that *is* within thy gates : 11 For *in* six days the LORD made heaven and earth, the sea, and all that in them *is*, and rested the seventh day : wherefore the LORD blessed the sabbath day, and hallowed it.

Here is, I. The preface of the law-writer, Moses : *God spoke all these words, v. 1.* The law of the ten commandments is, 1. A law of God's making. They are enjoined by the infinite eternal Majesty of heaven and earth. And *where the word of the King* of kings *is surely there is power.* 2. It is a law of his own speaking. God has many ways of speaking to the children of men (Job xxxiii. 14); *once, yea twice*—by his Spirit, by conscience, by providences, by his voice, all which we ought carefully to attend to; but he never spoke, at any time, upon any occasion, as he spoke the ten commandments, which therefore we ought to hear with the *more earnest heed.* They were not only spoken audibly (so he owned the Redeemer by a voice from heaven, Matt. iii. 17), but with a great deal of dreadful pomp. This law God had given to man before (it was written in his heart by nature); but sin had so defaced that writing that it was necessary, in this manner, to revive the knowledge of it.

II. The preface of the Law-maker : *I am the Lord thy God, v. 2.* Herein, 1. God asserts his own authority to enact this law in general : " I am the Lord who command thee all that follows." 2. He proposes himself as the sole object of that religious worship which is enjoined in the first four of the commandments. They are here bound to obedience by a threefold cord, which, one would think, could not *easily be broken.* (1.) Because God is ˙the Lord—Jehovah, self-existent, independent, eternal, and the fountain of all being and power ; therefore he has an incontestable right to command us. He that gives being may give law ; and therefore he is able to bear us out in our obedience, to reward it, and to punish our disobedience. (2.) He was their God, a God in covenant with them, their God by their own consent ; and, if they would not keep his commandments, who would ? He had laid himself under obligations to them by promise, and therefore might justly lay his obligations on them by precept. Though that covenant of peculiarity is now no more, yet there is another, by virtue of which all that are baptized are taken into relation to him as their God, 358

and are therefore unjust, unfaithful, and very ungrateful, if they obey him not. (3.) He had *brought them out of the land of Egypt ;* therefore they were bound in gratitude to obey him, because he had done them so great a kindness, had brought them out of a grievous slavery into a glorious liberty. They themselves had been eye-witnesses of the great things God had done in order to their deliverance, and could not but have observed that every circumstance of it heightened their obligation. They were now enjoying the blessed fruits of their deliverance, and in expectation of a speedy settlement in Canaan ; and could they think any thing too much to do for him that had done so much for them ? Nay, by redeeming them, he acquired a further right to rule them ; they owed their service to him to whom they owed their freedom, and whose they were by purchase. And thus Christ, having rescued us out of the bondage of sin, is entitled to the best service we can do him, Luke i. 74. Having loosed our bonds, he has bound us to obey him, Ps. cxvi. 16.

III. The law itself. The first four of the ten commandments, which concern our duty to God (commonly called *the first table*), we have in these verses. It was fit that those should be put first, because man had a Maker to love before he had a neighbour to love ; and justice and charity are acceptable acts of obedience to God only when they flow from the principles of piety. It cannot be expected that he should be true to his brother who is false to his God. Now our duty to God is, in one word, to worship him, that is, to give to him the glory due to his name, the inward worship of our affections, the outward worship of solemn address and attendance. This is spoken of as the sum and substance of the everlasting gospel. Rev. xiv. 7, *Worship God.*

1. The first commandment concerns the object of our worship, Jehovah, and him only (*v.* 3): *Thou shalt have no other gods before me.* The Egyptians, and other neighbouring nations, had many gods, the creatures of their own fancy, strange gods, *new gods ;* this law was prefixed because of that transgression, and, Jehovah being the God of Israel, they must entirely cleave to him, and not be for any other, either of their own invention or borrowed from their neighbours. This was the sin they were most in danger of now that the world was so overspread with polytheism, which yet could not be rooted out effectually but by the gospel of Christ. The sin against this commandment which *we* are most in danger of is giving the glory and honour to any creature which are due to God only. Pride makes a god of self, covetousness makes a god of money, sensuality makes a god of the belly ; whatever is esteemed or loved, feared or served, delighted in or depended on, more than God, that (whatever it is) we do in effect make a

god of. This prohibition includes a precept which is the foundation of the whole law, that we take the Lord for our God, acknowledge that he is God, accept him for ours, adore him with admiration and humble reverence, and set our affections entirely upon him. In the last words, *before me*, it is intimated, (1.) That we cannot have any other God but he will certainly know it. There is none besides him but what is before him. Idolaters covet secresy; but *shall not God search this out?* (2.) That it is very provoking to him; it is a sin that dares him to his face, which he cannot, which he will not, overlook, nor connive at. See Ps. xliv. 20, 21.

2. The second commandment concerns the ordinances of worship, or the way in which God will be worshipped, which it is fit that he himself should have the appointing of. Here is,

(1.) The prohibition: we are here forbidden to worship even the true God by images, *v.* 4, 5. [1.] The Jews (at least after the captivity) thought themselves forbidden by this commandment to make any image or picture whatsoever. Hence the very images which the Roman armies had in their ensigns are called *an abomination* to them (Matt. xxiv. 15), especially when they were set up *in the holy place.* It is certain that it forbids making any image of God (for *to whom can we liken him?* Isa. xl. 18, 15), or the image of any creature for a religious use. It is called the changing of the truth of God into a lie (Rom. i. 25), for an image is a teacher of lies; it insinuates to us that God has a body, whereas he is an infinite spirit, Hab. ii. 18. It also forbids us to make images of God in our fancies, as if he were a man as we are. Our religious worship must be governed by the power of faith, not by the power of imagination. They must not make such images or pictures as the heathen worshipped, lest they also should be tempted to worship them. Those who would be kept from sin must keep themselves from the occasions of it. [2.] They must not *bow down to them* occasionally, that is, show any sign of respect or honour to them, much less serve them constantly, by sacrifice or incense, or any other act of religious worship. When they paid their devotion to the true God, they must not have any image before them, for the directing, exciting, or assisting of their devotion. Though the worship was designed to terminate in God, it would not please him if it came to him through an image. The best and most ancient lawgivers among the heathen forbade the setting up of images in their temples. This practice was forbidden in Rome by Numa, a pagan prince; yet commanded in Rome by the pope, a Christian bishop, but, in this, anti-christian. The use of images in the church of Rome, at this day, is so plainly contrary to the letter of this command, and so impossible to be reconciled

to it, that in all their catechisms and books of devotion, which they put into the hands of the people, they leave out this commandment, joining the reason of it to the first; and so the third commandment they call the second, the fourth the third, &c.; only, to make up the number ten, they divide the tenth into two. Thus have they committed two great evils, in which they persist, and from which they hate to be reformed; they take away from God's word, and add to his worship.

(2.) The reasons to enforce this prohibition (*v.* 5, 6), which are, [1.] God's jealousy in the matters of his worship: "*I the Lord* Jehovah, and *thy God, am a jealous God*, especially in things of this nature." This intimates the care he has of his own institutions, his hatred of idolatry and all false worship, his displeasure against idolaters, and that he resents every thing in his worship that looks like, or leads to, idolatry. Jealousy is quicksighted. Idolatry being spiritual adultery, as it is very often represented in scripture, the displeasure of God against it is fitly called *jealousy*. If God is jealous herein, we should be so, afraid of offering any worship to God otherwise than as he has appointed in his word. [2.] The punishment of idolaters. God looks upon them as haters of him, though they perhaps pretend love to him; he will *visit their iniquity*, that is, he will very severely punish it, not only as a breach of his law, but as an affront to his majesty, a violation of the covenant, and a blow at the root of all religion. He will *visit it upon the children*, that is, this being a sin for which churches shall be unchurched and a bill of divorce given them, the children shall be cast out of covenant and communion together with the parents, as with the parents the children were at first taken in. Or he will bring such judgments upon a people as shall be the total ruin of families. If idolaters live to be old, so as to see their children of the third or fourth generation, it shall be the vexation of their eyes, and the breaking of their hearts, to see them fall by the sword, carried captive, and enslaved. Nor is it an unrighteous thing with God (if the parents died in their iniquity, and the children tread in their steps, and keep up false worships, because they received them by tradition from their fathers), when the measure is full, and God comes by his judgments to reckon with them, to bring into the account the idolatries their fathers were guilty of. Though he bear long with an idolatrous people, he will not bear always, but by the fourth generation, at furthest, he will begin to visit. Children are dear to their parents; therefore, to deter men from idolatry, and to show how much God is displeased with it, not only a brand of infamy is by it entailed upon families, but the judgments of God may for it be executed upon the poor children when the parents are dead and gone. [3.] The favour God would show to his faithful worshippers: *Keeping mercy for thousands* of persons, thousands of generations *of those that love me, and keep my commandments.* This intimates that the second commandment, though, in the letter of it, is only a prohibition of false worships, yet includes a precept of worshipping God in all those ordinances which he has instituted. As the first commandment requires the inward worship of love, desire, joy, hope, and admiration, so the second requires the outward worship of prayer and praise, and solemn attendance on God's word. Note, *First,* Those that truly love God will make it their constant care and endeavour to keep his commandments, particularly those that relate to his worship. Those that love God, and keep those commandments, shall receive grace to keep his other commandments. Gospel worship will have a good influence upon all manner of gospel obedience. *Secondly,* God has mercy in store for such. Even they need mercy, and cannot plead merit; and mercy they shall find with God, merciful protection in their obedience and a merciful recompence of it. *Thirdly,* This mercy shall extend to thousands, much further than the wrath threatened to those that hate him, for that reaches but to the third or fourth generation. The streams of mercy run now as full, as free, and as fresh, as ever.

3. The third commandment concerns the manner of our worship, that it be done with all possible reverence and seriousness, *v.* 7. We have here,

(1.) A strict prohibition: *Thou shalt not take the name of the Lord thy God in vain.* It is supposed that, having taken Jehovah for their God, they would make mention of his name (for thus *all people will walk every one in the name of his god);* this command gives a needful caution not to mention it in vain, and it is still as needful as ever. We take God's name in vain, [1.] By hypocrisy, making a profession of God's name, but not living up to that profession. Those that name the name of Christ, but do not depart from iniquity, as that name binds them to do, name it in vain; their worship is vain (Matt. xv. 7—9), their oblations are vain (Isa. i. 11, 13), their religion is vain, Jam. i. 26. [2.] By covenant-breaking; if we make promises to God, binding our souls with those bonds to that which is good, and yet perform not to the Lord our vows, we take his name in vain (Matt. v. 33), it is folly, and God *has no pleasure in fools* (Eccl. v. 4), nor will he be *mocked,* Gal. vi. 7. [3.] By rash swearing, mentioning the name of God, or any of his attributes, in the form of an oath, without any just occasion for it, or due application of mind to it, but as a by-word, to no purpose at all, or to no good purpose. [4.] By false swearing, which, some think, is chiefly intended in the letter of the commandment; so it was expounded by those of old time. *Thou shalt not forswear thyself,* Matt. v. 33. One part of the religious

regard the Jews were taught to pay to their God was to *swear by his name,* Deut. x. 20. But they affronted him, instead of doing him honour, if they called him to be witness to a lie. [5.] By using the name of God lightly and carelessly, and without any regard to its awful significancy. The profanation of the forms of devotion is forbidden, as well as the profanation of the forms of swearing; as also the profanation of any of those things whereby God makes himself known, his word, or any of his institutions; when they are either turned into charms and spells, or into jest and sport, the name of God is taken in vain.

(2.) A severe penalty: *The Lord will not hold him guiltless;* magistrates, who punish other offences, may not think themselves concerned to take notice of this, because it does not immediately offer injury either to private property or the public peace; but God, who is jealous for his honour, will not thus connive at it. The sinner may perhaps hold himself guiltless, and think there is no harm in it, and that God will never call him to an account for it. To obviate this suggestion, the threatening is thus expressed, God will *not hold him guiltless,* as he hopes he will; but more is implied, namely, that God will himself be the avenger of those that take his name in vain, and they will find it a fearful thing to fall into the hands of the living God.

4. The fourth commandment concerns the time of worship. God is to be served and honoured daily, but one day in seven is to be particularly dedicated to his honour and spent in his service. Here is,

(1.) The command itself (*v.* 8): *Remember the sabbath day to keep it holy;* and (*v.* 10), *In it thou shalt do no manner of work.* It is taken for granted that the sabbath was instituted before; we read of God's blessing and sanctifying a seventh day from the beginning (Gen. ii. 3), so that this was not the enacting of a new law, but the reviving of an old law. [1.] They are told what is the day they must religiously observe—*a seventh, after six days' labour;* whether this was the seventh by computation from the first seventh, or from the day of their coming out of Egypt, or both, is not certain: now the precise day was notified to them (*ch.* xvi. 23), and from this they were to observe the seventh. [2.] How it must be observed. *First,* As a day of rest; they were to do no manner of work on this day in their callings or worldly business. *Secondly,* As a holy day, set apart to the honour of the holy God, and to be spent in holy exercises. God, by blessing it, had made it holy; they, by solemnly blessing him, must keep it holy, and not alienate it to any other purpose than that for which the difference between it and other days was instituted. [3.] Who must observe it: *Thou, and thy son, and thy daughter;* the wife is not mentioned, because she is supposed to be one with the husband and present with him, and, if he sanctify the sabbath, it is taken for granted that she will join with him; but the rest of the family are specified. Children and servants must keep the sabbath, according to their age and capacity: in this, as in other instances of religion, it is expected that masters of families should take care, not only to serve the Lord themselves, but that their houses also should serve him, at least that it may not be through their neglect if they do not, Josh. xxiv. 15. Even the proselyted strangers must observe a difference between this day and other days, which, if it laid some restraint upon them then, yet proved a happy indication of God's gracious purpose, in process of time, to bring the Gentiles into the church, that they might share in the benefit of sabbaths. Compare Isa. lvi. 6, 7. God takes notice of what we do, particularly what we do on sabbath days, though we should be where we are strangers. [4.] A particular memorandum put upon this duty: *Remember it*. It is intimated that the sabbath was instituted and observed before; but in their bondage in Egypt they had lost their computation, or were restrained by their taskmasters, or, through a great degeneracy and indifference in religion, they had let fall the observance of it, and therefore it was requisite they should be reminded of it. Note, Neglected duties remain duties still, notwithstanding our neglect. It also intimates that we are both apt to forget it and concerned to remember it. Some think it denotes the preparation we are to make for the sabbath; we must think of it before it comes, that, when it does come, we may keep it holy, and do the duty of it.

(2.) The reasons of this command. [1.] We have time enough for ourselves on the other six days: *Six days must thou labour.* Time enough we have to serve ourselves in those six days, on the seventh day let us serve God; and time enough to tire ourselves, on the seventh it will be a kindness to us to be obliged to rest. [2.] This is God's day: it is the *sabbath of the Lord thy God*, not only instituted by him, but consecrated to him. It is sacrilege to alienate it; the sanctification of it is a debt. [3.] It is designed for a memorial of the creation of the world, and therefore to be observed to the glory of the Creator, as an engagement upon ourselves to serve him and an encouragement to us to trust in him who made heaven and earth. By the sanctification of the sabbath, the Jews declared that they worshipped the God that made the world, and so distinguished themselves from all other nations, who worshipped gods which they themselves made. [4.] God has given us an example of rest, after six days' work: he *rested the seventh day*, took a complacency in himself, and *rejoiced in the work of his hand*, to teach us, on that day, to take a complacency in him, and to give him the glory of his works, Ps.

xcii. 4. The sabbath began in the finishing of the work of creation, so will the everlasting sabbath in the finishing of the work of providence and redemption; and we observe the weekly sabbath in expectation of that, as well as in remembrance of the former, in both conforming ourselves to him we worship. [5.] He has himself *blessed the sabbath day and sanctified it.* He has put an honour upon it by setting it apart for himself; it is the holy of the Lord and honourable: and he has put blessings into it, which he has encouraged us to expect from him in the religious observance of that day. It is *the day which the Lord hath made,* let not us do what we can to unmake it. He has blessed, honoured, and sanctified it, let not us profane it, dishonour it, and level that with common time which God's blessing has thus dignified and distinguished.

12 Honour thy father and thy mother: that thy days may be long upon the land which the Lord thy God giveth thee. 13 Thou shalt not kill. 14 Thou shalt not commit adultery. 15 Thou shalt not steal. 16 Thou shalt not bear false witness against thy neighbour. 17 Thou shalt not covet thy neighbour's house, thou shalt not covet thy neighbour's wife, nor his manservant, nor his maidservant, nor his ox, nor his ass, nor any thing that *is* thy neighbour's.

We have here the laws of the second table, as they are commonly called, the last six of the ten commandments, comprehending our duty to ourselves and to one another, and constituting a comment upon the second great commandment, *Thou shalt love thy neighbour as thyself.* As religion towards God is an essential branch of universal righteousness, so righteousness towards men is an essential branch of true religion. Godliness and honesty must go together.

I. The fifth commandment concerns the duties we owe to our relations; those of children to their parents are alone specified: *Honour thy father and thy mother,* which includes, 1. A decent respect to their persons, an inward esteem of them outwardly expressed upon all occasions in our conduct towards them. *Fear them* (Lev. xix. 3), *give them reverence,* Heb. xii. 9. The contrary to this is mocking at them and despising them, Prov. xxx. 17. 2. Obedience to their lawful commands; so it is expounded (Eph. vi. 1—3): "*Children, obey your parents,* come when they call you, go where they send you, do what they bid you, refrain from what they forbid you; and this, as children, cheerfully, and from a principle of love. Though you have said, "We will not," yet afterwards repent and obey, Matt. xxi. 29. 3. Submission to their rebukes, instructions, and corrections;

not only to the good and gentle, but also to the froward, out of conscience towards God. 4. Disposing of themselves with the advice, direction, and consent, of parents, not alienating their property, but with their approbation. 5. Endeavouring, in every thing, to be the comfort of their parents, and to make their old age easy to them, maintaining them if they stand in need of support, which our Saviour makes to be particularly intended in this commandment, Matt. xv. 4—6. The reason annexed to this commandment is a promise: *That thy days may be long in the land which the Lord thy God giveth thee.* Having mentioned, in the preface to the commandments, his bringing them out of Egypt as a reason for their obedience, he here, in the beginning of the second table, mentions his bringing them into Canaan, as another reason; that good land they must have upon their thoughts and in their eye, now that they were in the wilderness. They must also remember, when they came to that land, that they were upon their good behaviour, and that, if they did not conduct themselves well, their days should be shortened in that land, both the days of particular persons who should be cut off from it, and the days of their nation which should be removed out of it. But here a long life in that good land is promised particularly to obedient children. Those that do their duty to their parents are most likely to have the comfort of that which their parents gather for them and leave to them; those that support their parents shall find that God, the common Father, will support them. This promise is expounded (Eph. vi. 3), *That it may be well with thee, and thou mayest live long on the earth.* Those who, in conscience towards God, keep this and the rest of God's commandments, may be sure that it shall be well with them, and that they shall live as long on earth as Infinite Wisdom sees good for them, and that what they may seem to be cut short of on earth shall be abundantly made up in eternal life, the heavenly Canaan which God will give them.

II. The sixth commandment concerns our own and our neighbour's life (v. 13): " *Thou shalt not kill;* thou shalt not do any thing hurtful or injurious to the health, ease, and life, of thy own body, or any other person's unjustly." This is one of the laws of nature, and was strongly enforced by the precepts given to Noah and his sons, Gen. ix. 5, 6. It does not forbid killing in lawful war, or in our own necessary defence, nor the magistrate's putting offenders to death, for those things tend to the preserving of life; but it forbids all malice and hatred to the person of any (for *he that hateth his brother is a murderer)*, and all personal revenge arising therefrom; also all rash anger upon sudden provocations, and hurt said or done, or aimed to be done, in passion: of this our Saviour expounds this commandment, Matt. v. 22. And, as that which is worst of all, it forbids

persecution, laying wait for the blood of the innocent and excellent ones of the earth.

III. The seventh commandment concerns our own and our neighbour's chastity: *Thou shalt not commit adultery, v.* 14. This is put before the sixth by our Saviour (Mark x. 19): *Do not commit adultery, do not kill;* for our chastity should be as dear to us as our lives, and we should be as much afraid of that which defiles the body as of that which destroys it. This commandment forbids all acts of uncleanness, with all those fleshly lusts which produce those acts and war against the soul, and all those practices which cherish and excite those fleshly lusts, as looking, in order to lust, which, Christ tells us, is forbidden in this commandment, Matt. v. 28.

IV. The eighth commandment concerns our own and our neighbour's wealth, estate, and goods: *Thou shalt not steal, v.* 15. Though God had lately allowed and appointed them to spoil the Egyptians in a way of just reprisal, yet he did not intend that it should be drawn into a precedent and that they should be allowed thus to spoil one another. This command forbids us to rob ourselves of what we have by sinful spending, or of the use and comfort of it by sinful sparing, and to rob others by removing the ancient landmarks, invading our neighbour's rights, taking his goods from his person, or house, or field, forcibly or clandestinely, over-reaching in bargains, not restoring what is borrowed or found, withholding just debts, rents, or wages, and (which is worst of all) to rob the public in the coin or revenue, or that which is dedicated to the service of religion.

V. The ninth commandment concerns our own and our neighbour's good name: *Thou shalt not bear false witness, v.* 16. This forbids, 1. Speaking falsely in any matter, lying, equivocating, and any way devising and designing to deceive our neighbour. 2. Speaking unjustly against our neighbour, to the prejudice of his reputation; and (which involves the guilt of both), 3. Bearing false witness against him, laying to his charge things that he knows not, either judicially, upon oath (by which the third commandment, and the sixth or eighth, as well as this, are broken), or extrajudicially, in common converse, slandering, backbiting, tale-bearing, aggravating what is done amiss and making it worse than it is, and any way endeavouring to raise our own reputation upon the ruin of our neighbour's.

VI. The tenth commandment strikes at the root: *Thou shalt not covet, v.* 17. The foregoing commands implicitly forbid all desire of doing that which will be an injury to our neighbour; this forbids all inordinate desire of having that which will be a gratification to ourselves. "O that such a man's house were mine! Such a man's wife mine! Such a man's estate mine!" This is certainly the language of discontent at our own lot, and envy at our neighbour's; and these are the sins principally forbidden here. St. Paul, when the grace of God caused the scales to fall from his eyes, perceived that this law, *Thou shalt not covet*, forbade all those irregular appetites and desires which are the first-born of the corrupt nature, the first risings of the sin that dwelleth in us, and the beginnings of all the sin that is committed by us: this is that lust which, he says, he had not known the evil of, if this commandment, when it came to his conscience in the power of it, had not shown it to him, Rom. vii. 7. God give us all to see our face in the glass of this law, and to lay our hearts under the government of it!

18 And all the people saw the thunderings, and the lightnings, and the noise of the trumpet, and the mountain smoking: and when the people saw *it*, they removed, and stood afar off. 19 And they said unto Moses, Speak thou with us, and we will hear: but let not God speak with us, lest we die. 20 And Moses said unto the people, Fear not: for God is come to prove you, and that his fear may be before your faces, that ye sin not. 21 And the people stood afar off, and Moses drew near unto the thick darkness where God *was*.

I. The extraordinary terror with which the law was given. Never was any thing delivered with such awful pomp; every word was accented, and every sentence paused, with thunder and lightning, much louder and brighter, no doubt, than ordinary. And why was the law given in this dreadful manner, and with all this tremendous ceremony? 1. It was designed (once for all) to give a sensible discovery of the glorious majesty of God, for the assistance of our faith concerning it, that, *knowing the terror of the Lord*, we may be persuaded to live in his fear. 2. It was a specimen of the terrors of the general judgment, in which sinners will be called to an account for the breach of this law: the archangel's trumpet will then sound an alarm, to give notice of the Judge's coming, and a *fire shall devour before him.* 3. It was an indication of the terror of those convictions which the law brings into conscience, to prepare the soul for the comforts of the gospel. Thus was the law given by Moses in such a way as might startle, affright, and humble men, that the *grace and truth which came by Jesus Christ* might be the more welcome. The apostle largely describes this instance of the terror of that dispensation, as a foil to set off our privileges, as Christians, in the light, liberty, and joy, of the New-Testament dispensation, Heb. xii. 18, &c.

II. The impression which this made, for the present, upon the people; they must have had stupid hearts indeed, if this had not affected them. 1. *They removed, and stood afar off*, v. 18. Before God began to speak, they were thrusting forward to gaze (*ch.* xix. 21); but now they were effectually cured of their presumption, and taught to keep their distance. 2. *They entreated that the word should not be so spoken to them any more* (Heb. xii. 19), but begged that God would speak to them by Moses, *v.* 19. Hereby they obliged themselves to acquiesce in the mediation of Moses, they themselves nominating him as a fit person to deal between them and God, and promising to hearken to him as to God's messenger; hereby also they teach us to acquiesce in that method which Infinite Wisdom takes, of speaking to us by men like ourselves, whose *terror shall not make us afraid, nor their hand be heavy upon us.* Once God tried the expedient of speaking to the children of men immediately, but it was found that they could not bear it; it rather drove men from God than brought them to him, and, as it proved in the issue, though it terrified them, it did not deter them from idolatry, for soon after this they worshipped the golden calf. Let us therefore rest satisfied with the instructions given us by the scriptures and the ministry; for, if we believe not them, neither should we be persuaded though God should speak to us in thunder and lightning, as he did from Mount Sinai: here that matter was determined.

III. The encouragement Moses gave them, by explaining the design of God in his terror (*v.* 20): *Fear not*, that is, "Think not that the thunder and fire are designed to consume you," which was the thing they feared (*v.* 19, *lest we die);* thunder and lightning constituted one of the plagues of Egypt, but Moses would not have them think they were sent to them on the same errand on which they were sent to the Egyptians: no, they were intended, 1. To prove them, to try how they would like dealing with God immediately, without a mediator, and so to convince them how admirably well God had chosen for them, in putting Moses into that office. Ever since Adam fled, upon hearing God's voice in the garden, sinful man could not bear either to speak to God or hear from him immediately. 2. To keep them to their duty, and prevent their sinning against God. He encourages them, saying, *Fear not*, and yet tells them that God thus spoke to them, *that his fear might be before their face.* We must not fear with amazement—with that fear which has torment, which only works upon the fancy for the present, sets us a trembling, genders to bondage, betrays us to Satan, and alienates us from God; but we must always have in our minds a reverence of God's majesty, a dread of his displeasure, and an obedient regard to his sovereign authority over us: this fear will quicken us to our duty and make us circumspect in our walking. Thus *stand in awe, and sin not,* Ps. iv. 4.

IV. The progress of their communion with God by the mediation of Moses, *v.* 21. While the people continued to stand afar off, conscious of guilt and afraid of God's wrath, *Moses drew near unto the thick darkness; he was made to draw near,* so the word is: Moses, of himself, durst not have ventured into the thick darkness, if God had not called him, and encouraged him, and, as some of the rabbies suppose, sent an angel to take him by the hand, and lead him up. Thus it is said of the great Mediator, *I will cause him to draw near* (Jer xxx. 21), and by him it is that we also are intro luced, Eph. iii. 12.

22 And the LORD said unto Moses, Thus thou shalt say unto the children of Israel, Ye have seen that I have talked with you from heaven. 23 Ye shall not make with me gods of silver, neither shall ye make unto you gods of gold. 24 An altar of earth thou shalt make unto me, and shalt sacrifice thereon thy burnt offerings, and thy peace offerings, thy sheep, and thine oxen : in all places where I record my name I will come unto thee, and I will bless thee. 25 And if thou wilt make me an altar of stone, thou shalt not build it of hewn stone : for if thou lift up thy tool upon it, thou hast polluted it. 26 Neither shalt thou go up by steps unto mine altar, that thy nakedness be not discovered thereon.

Moses having gone into *the thick darkness, where God was,* God there spoke in his hearing only, privately and without terror, all that follows hence to the end of *ch.* xxiii., which is mostly an exposition of the ten commandments ; and he was to transmit it by word of mouth first, and afterwards in writing, to the people. The laws in these verses related to God's worship.

I. They are here forbidden to make images for worship (*v.* 22, 23) : *You have seen that I have talked with you from heaven* (such was his wonderful condescension, much more than for some mighty prince to talk familiarly with a company of poor beggars); now *you shall not make gods of silver.*

1. This repetition of the second commandment comes in here, either, (1.) As pointing to that which God had chiefly in view in giving them this law in this manner, that is, their peculiar addictedness to idolatry, and the peculiar sinfulness of that crime. Ten commandments God had given them, but Moses is ordered to inculcate upon them especially the first two. They must not forget any of them, but they must be sure to remember those. Or, (2.) As pointing to that which might properly be inferred from God's speaking to them as he had done. He

had given them sufficient demonstration or his presence among them ; they needed not to make images of him, as if he were absent. Besides, they had only seen that he talked with them ; they had seen no manner of similitude, so that they could not make any image of God ; and his manifesting himself to them only by a voice plainly showed them that they must not make any such image, but keep up their communion with God by his word, and not otherwise.

2. Two arguments are here hinted against image-worship :—(1.) That thereby they would affront God, intimated in that, *You shall not make with me gods.* Though they pretended to worship them but as representations of God, yet really they made them rivals with God, which he would not endure. (2.) That thereby they would abuse themselves, intimated in that, "*You shall not make unto you gods;* while you think by them to assist your devotion, you will really corrupt it, and put a cheat upon yourselves." At first, it should seem, they made their images for worship of gold and silver, pretending, by the richness of those metals, to honour God, and, by the brightness of them, to affect themselves with his glory ; but, even in these, they *changed the truth of God into a lie,* and so, by degrees, were justly given up to such strong delusions as to worship images of wood or stone.

II. They are here directed in making altars for worship: it is meant of occasional altars, such as they reared now in the wilderness, before the tabernacle was erected, and afterwards upon special emergencies, for present use, such as Gideon built (Judg. vi. 24), Manoah (Judg. xiii 19), Samuel (1 Sam. vii. 17), and many others. We may suppose, now that the people of Israel were so much affected, as it appears they were, with this glorious discovery which God had made of himself to them, that many of them would incline, in this pang of devotion, to offer sacrifice to God ; and, it being necessary to a sacrifice that there be an altar, they are here appointed,

1. To make their altars very plain, either of *earth* or of *unhewn stone, v.* 24, 25. That they might not be tempted to think of a graven image, they must not so much as hew into shape the stones that they made their altars of, but pile them up as they were, in the rough. This rule being prescribed before the establishment of the ceremonial law, which appointed altars much more costly, intimates that, after the period of that law, plainness should be accepted as the best ornament of the external services of religion, and that gospel-worship should not be performed with external pomp and gaiety. The beauty of holiness needs no paint, nor do th oe do any service to the spouse of Christ that dress her in the attire of a harlot, as the church of Rome does : an *altar of earth* does best.

2. To make their altars very low (**v.** 26),

so that they might not go up by steps to them. That the higher the altar was, and the nearer heaven, the more acceptable the sacrifice was, was a foolish fancy of the heathen, who therefore chose high places; in opposition to this, and to show that it is the elevation of the heart, not of the sacrifice, that God looks at, they were here ordered to make their altars low. We may suppose that the altars they reared in the wilderness, and other occasional altars, were designed only for the sacrifice of one beast at a time; but the altar in Solomon's temple, which was to be made much longer and broader, that it might contain many sacrifices at once, was made ten cubits high, that the height might bear a decent proportion to the length and breadth; and to that it was requisite they should go up by steps, which yet, no doubt, were so contrived as to prevent the inconvenience here spoken of, the *discovering of their nakedness* thereon.

III. They are here assured of God's gracious acceptance of their devotions, wherever they were paid according to his will (*v.* 24): *In all places where I record my name,* or where my name is recorded (that is, where I am worshipped in sincerity), *I will come unto thee, and I will bless thee.* Afterwards, God chose one particular place wherein to record his name: but that being taken away now under the gospel, when men are encouraged to pray every where, this promise revives in its full extent, that, wherever God's people meet in his name to worship him, he will be *in the midst of them,* he will honour them with his presence, and reward them with the gifts of his grace; there he will come unto them, and will bless them, and more than this we need not desire for the beautifying of our solemn assemblies.

CHAP. XXI.

The laws recorded in this chapter relate to the fifth and sixth commandments; and though they are not accommodated to our constitution, especially in point of servitude, nor are the penalties annexed binding on us, yet they are of great use for the explanation of the moral law, and the rules of natural justice. Here are several enlargements, I. Upon the fifth commandment, which concerns particular relations 1. The duty of masters towards their servants, their men-servants (ver. 2—6), and maid-servants, ver. 7—11. 2. The punishment of disobedient children that strike their parents (ver. 15), or curse them, ver. 17. II. Upon the sixth commandment, which forbids all violence offered to the person of a man. Here is, 1. Concerning murder, ver. 12—14. 2. Man-stealing, ver. 16. 3. Assault and battery, ver. 18, 19. 4. Correcting a servant, ver. 20, 21. 5. Hurting a woman with child, ver. 22, 23. 6. The law of retaliation, ver. 24, 25. 7. Maiming a servant, ver. 26, 27. 8. An ox goring, ver. 28—32. 9. Damage by opening a pit, ver. 33, 34. 10. Cattle fighting, ver. 35, 36.

N OW these *are* the judgments which thou shalt set before them. 2 If thou buy a Hebrew servant, six years he shall serve: and in the seventh he shall go out free for nothing. 3 If he came in by himself, he shall go out by himself: if he were married, then his wife shall go out with him. 4 If his master have given him a wife, and she have borne him sons or daughters; the wife and her children shall

be her master's, and he shall go out by himself. 5 And if the servant shall plainly say, I love my master, my wife, and my children; I will not go out free: 6 Then his master shall bring him unto the judges; he shall also bring him to the door, or unto the door post; and his master shall bore his ear through with an awl; and he shall serve him for ever. 7 And if a man sell his daughter to be a maidservant, she shall not go out as the menservants do. 8 If she please not her master, who hath betrothed her to himself, then shall he let her be redeemed: to sell her unto a strange nation he shall have no power, seeing he hath dealt deceitfully with her. 9 And if he have betrothed her unto his son, he shall deal with her after the manner of daughters. 10 If he take him another *wife;* her food, her raiment, and her duty of marriage, shall he not diminish. 11 And if he do not these three unto her, then shall she go out free without money.

The first verse is the general title of the laws contained in this and the two following chapters, some of them relating to the religious worship of God, but most of them relating to matters between man and man. Their government being purely a Theocracy, that which in other states is to be settled by human prudence was directed among them by a divine appointment, so that the constitution of their government was peculiarly adapted to make them happy. These laws are called *judgments,* because they are framed in infinite wisdom and equity, and because their magistrates were to give judgment according to them. God delivered them privately to Moses, and he was to communicate them to the people. In the doubtful cases that had hitherto occurred, Moses had particularly enquired of God for them, as appeared, *ch.* xviii. 15; but now God gave him statutes in general by which to determine particular cases, which likewise he must apply to other like cases that might happen, which, falling under the same reason, fell under the same rule. He begins with the laws concerning servants, commanding mercy and moderation towards them. The Israelites had lately been servants themselves; and now that they had become, not only their own masters, but masters of servants too, lest they should abuse their servants, as they themselves had been abused and ruled with rigour by the Egyptian task-masters, provision was made by these laws for the mild and gentle usage of servants. Note, If those who have had power over us have been injurious to us this will not in the least excuse us if we be in like manner injurious to those who are under our power, but will rather aggravate our crime, because, in that case, we may the more easily put our souls into their soul's stead. Here is,

I. A law concerning men-servants, sold, either by themselves or their parents, through poverty, or by the judges, for their crimes; even those of the latter sort (if Hebrews) were to continue in slavery but seven years at the most, in which time it was taken for granted that they would sufficiently have smarted for their folly or offence. At the seven years' end the servant should either go out free (v. 2, 3), or his servitude should thenceforward be his choice, v. 5, 6. If he had a wife given him by his master, and children, he might either leave them and go out free himself, or, if he had such a kindness for them that he would rather tarry with them in bondage than go out at liberty without them, he was to have his ear bored through to the door-post and serve till the death of his master, or the year of jubilee.

1. By this law God taught, (1.) The Hebrew servants generosity, and a noble love of liberty, for they were the Lord's freemen; a mark of disgrace must be put upon him who refused liberty when he might have it, though he refused it upon considerations otherwise laudable enough. Thus Christians, being *bought with a price, and called unto liberty*, must not be the servants of men, nor of the lusts of men, 1 Cor. vii. 23. There is a free and princely spirit that much helps to uphold a Christian, Ps. li. 12. He likewise taught, (2.) The Hebrew masters not to trample upon their poor servants, knowing, not only that they had been by birth upon a level with them, but that, in a few years, they would be so again. Thus Christian masters must look with respect on believing servants, Philem. 16.

2. This law will be further useful to us, (1.) To illustrate the right God has to the children of believing parents, as such, and the place they have in his church. They are by baptism enrolled among his servants, because they are *born in his house*, for they are therefore *born unto him*, Ezek. xvi. 20. David owns himself God's servant, as he was *the son of his handmaid* (Ps. cxvi. 16), and therefore entitled to protection, Ps. lxxxvi. 16. (2.) To explain the obligation which the great Redeemer laid upon himself to prosecute the work of our salvation, for he says (Ps. xl. 6), *My ears hast thou opened*, which seems to allude to this law. He loved his Father, and his captive spouse, and the children that were given him, and would not go out free from his undertaking, but engaged to serve in it for ever, Isa. xlii. 1, 4. Much more reason have we thus to engage ourselves to serve God for ever; we have all the reason in the world to love our Master and his work,

366

and to have our ears bored to his door-posts, as those who desire not to go out free from his service, but to be found more and more free to it, and in it, Ps. lxxxiv. 10.

II. Concerning maid-servants, whom their parents, through extreme poverty, had sold, when they were very young, to such as they hoped would marry them when they grew up; if they did not, yet they must not sell them to strangers, but rather study how to make them amends for the disappointment; if they did, they must maintain them handsomely, v. 7—11. Thus did God provide for the comfort and reputation of the daughters of Israel, and has taught husbands to *give honour to their wives* (be their extraction ever so mean) as to the *weaker vessels*, 1 Pet. iii. 7.

12 He that smiteth a man, so that he die, shall be surely put to death. 13 And if a man lie not in wait, but God deliver *him* into his hand; then I will appoint thee a place whither he shall flee. 14 But if a man come presumptuously upon his neighbour, to slay him with guile; thou shalt take him from mine altar, that he may die. 15 And he that smiteth his father, or his mother, shall be surely put to death. 16 And he that stealeth a man, and selleth him, or if he be found in his hand, he shall surely be put to death. 17 And he that curseth his father, or his mother, shall surely be put to death. 18 And if men strive together, and one smite another with a stone, or with *his* fist, and he die not, but keepeth *his* bed: 19 If he rise again, and walk abroad upon his staff, then shall he that smote *him* be quit: only he shall pay *for* the loss of his time, and shall cause *him* to be thoroughly healed. 20 And if a man smite his servant, or his maid, with a rod, and he die under his hand; he shall be surely punished. 21 Notwithstanding if he continue a day or two, he shall not be punished: for he *is* his money.

Here is, I. A law concerning murder. He had lately said, *Thou shalt not kill;* here he provides, 1. For the punishing of wilful murder (v. 12): *He that smiteth a man,* whether upon a sudden passion or in malice prepense, *so that he die,* the government must take care that the murderer be *put to death,* according to that ancient law (Gen. ix. 6), *Whoso sheddeth man's blood, by man shall his blood be shed.* God, who by his providence gives and maintains life, thus by his law protects it; so that mercy shown to a wilful murderer is real cruelty to all mankind besides: such a one, God here says, shall be taken even *from his altar* (v. 14), to which he might flee for protection; and, if God will not shelter him, let him *flee to the pit, and let no man stay him.* 2. For the relief of such as killed by accident, *per infortunium*—*by misfortune,* or *chance-medley,* as our law expresses it, when a man, in doing a lawful act, without intent of hurt to any, happens to kill another, or, as it is here described, *God delivers him into his hand;* for nothing comes to pass by chance; what seems to us purely casual is ordered by the divine Providence, for wise and holy ends secret to us. In this case God provided cities of refuge for the protection of those whose infelicity it was, but not their fault, to occasion the death of another, v. 13. With us, who know no avengers of blood but the magistrates, the law itself is a sufficient sanctuary for those whose minds are innocent, though their hands are guilty, and there needs no other.

II. Concerning rebellious children. It is here made a capital crime, to be punished with death, for children either, 1. To strike their parents (v. 15) so as either to draw blood or to make the place struck black and blue. Or, 2. To curse their parents (v. 17), if they profaned any name of God in doing it, as the rabbies say. Note, The undutiful behaviour of children towards their parents is a very great provocation to God our common Father; and, if men do not punish it, he will. Those are perfectly lost to all virtue, and abandoned to all wickedness, that have broken through the bonds of filial reverence and duty to such a degree as in word or action to abuse their own parents. What yoke will those bear that have shaken off this? Let children take heed of entertaining in their minds any such thought or passions towards their parents as savour of undutifulness and contempt; for the righteous God searches the heart.

III. Here is a law against man-stealing (v. 16): *He that steals a man* (that is, a person, man, woman, or child), with design to sell him to the Gentiles (for no Israelite would buy him), was adjudged to death by this statute, which is ratified by the apostle (1 Tim. i. 10), where *men-stealers* are reckoned among those wicked ones against whom laws must be made by Christian princes.

IV. Care is here taken that satisfaction be made for hurt done to a person, though death do not ensue, v. 18, 19. He that did the hurt must be accountable for damages, and pay, not only for the cure, but for the loss of time, to which the Jews add that he must likewise give some recompence both for the pain and for the blemish, if there were any.

V. Direction is given what should be done if a servant died by his master's correction. This servant must not be an Israelite, but a Gentile slave, as the negroes to our planters; and it is supposed that he smite him with a rod, and not with any thing that was likely to give a mortal wound; yet, if he died under his hand, he should be punished for his cruelty, at the discretion of the judges, upon consideration of circumstances, v. 20. But, if he continued a day or two after the correction given, the master was supposed to suffer enough by losing his servant, v. 21. Our law makes the death of a servant, by his master's reasonable beating of him, but *chance-medley.* Yet let all masters take heed of tyrannizing over their servants; the gospel teaches them even to forbear and moderate threatenings (Eph. vi. 9), considering with holy Job, *What shall I do, when God riseth up?* Job xxxi. 13—15.

22 If men strive, and hurt a woman with child, so that her fruit depart *from her,* and yet no mischief follow: he shall be surely punished, according as the woman's husband will lay upon him; and he shall pay as the judges *determine.* 23 And if *any* mischief follow, then thou shalt give life for life, 24 Eye for eye, tooth for tooth, hand for hand, foot for foot, 25 Burning for burning, wound for wound, stripe for stripe. 26 And if a man smite the eye of his servant, or the eye of his maid, that it perish; he shall let him go free for his eye's sake. 27 And if he smite out his manservant's tooth, or his maidservant's tooth; he shall let him go free for his tooth's sake. 28 If an ox gore a man or a woman, that they die: then the ox shall be surely stoned, and his flesh shall not be eaten: but the owner of the ox *shall be* quit. 29 But if the ox were wont to push with his horn in time past, and it hath been testified to his owner, and he hath not kept him in, but that he hath killed a man or a woman; the ox shall be stoned, and his owner also shall be put to death. 30 If there be laid on him a sum of money, then he shall give for the ransom of his life whatsoever is laid upon him. 31 Whether he have gored a son, or have gored a daughter, according to this judgment shall it be done unto him. 32 If the ox shall push a manservant or a maidservant; he shall give unto their master thirty shekels of silver, and the ox shall be stoned. 33 And if a man shall open a pit, or if a man shall dig a pit, and not cover it, and an ox or

367

an ass fall therein; 34 The owner of the pit shall make *it* good, *and* give money unto the owner of them; and the dead *beast* shall be his. 35 And if one man's ox hurt another's, that he die; then they shall sell the live ox, and divide the money of it; and the dead ox also they shall divide. 36 Or if it be known that the ox hath used to push in time past, and his owner hath not kept him in; he shall surely pay ox for ox; and the dead shall be his own.

Observe here,

I. The particular care which the law took of women with child, that no hurt should be done them which might occasion their miscarrying. The law of nature obliges us to be very tender in that case, lest the tree and fruit be destroyed together, *v.* 22, 23. Women with child, who are thus taken under the special protection of the law of God, if they live in his fear, may still believe themselves under the special protection of the providence of God, and hope that they shall be saved in child-bearing. On this occasion comes in that general law of retaliation which our Saviour refers to, Matt. v. 38, *An eye for an eye.* Now, 1. The execution of this law is not hereby put into the hands of private persons, as if every man might avenge himself, which would introduce universal confusion, and make men like the fishes of the sea. The tradition of the elders seems to have put this corrupt gloss upon it, in opposition to which our Saviour commands us to forgive injuries, and not to meditate revenge, Matt. v. 39. 2. God often executes it in the course of his providence, making the punishment, in many cases, to answer to the sin, as Judg. i. 7; Isa. xxxiii. 1; Hab. ii. 13; Matt. xxvi. 52. 3. Magistrates ought to have an eye to this rule in punishing offenders, and doing right to those that are injured. Consideration must be had of the nature, quality, and degree of the wrong done, that reparation may be made to the party injured, and others deterred from doing the like; either *an eye* shall go *for an eye,* or the forfeited eye shall be redeemed by a sum of money. Note, He that does wrong must expect one way or other to receive *according to the wrong he has done,* Col. iii. 25. God sometimes brings men's violent dealings upon their own heads (Ps. vii. 16); and magistrates are in this the ministers of his justice, that they are *avengers* (Rom. xiii. 4), and they shall not bear the sword in vain.

II. The care God took of servants. If their masters maimed them, though it was only striking out a tooth, that should be their discharge, *v.* 26, 27. This was intended, 1. To prevent their being abused; masters would be careful not to offer them any violence, lest they should lose their service. 2. To comfort them if they were abused; the loss of a limb

should be the gaining of their liberty, which would do something towards balancing both the pain and disgrace they underwent. Nay,

III. *Does God take care for oxen?* Yes, it appears by the following laws in this chapter that he does, *for our sakes,* 1 Cor. ix. 9, 10. The Israelites are here directed what to do,

1. In case of hurt done by oxen, or any other brute-creature; for the law, doubtless, was designed to extend to all parallel cases. (1.) As an instance of God's care of the life of man (though forfeited a thousand times into the hands of divine justice), and in token of his detestation of the sin of murder. If an ox killed any man, woman, or child, the ox was to be *stoned* (*v.* 28); and, because the greatest honour of the inferior creatures is to be serviceable to man, the criminal is denied that honour: his *flesh shall not be eaten.* Thus God would keep up in the minds of his people a rooted abhorrence of the sin of murder and every thing that was barbarous. (2.) To make men careful that none of their cattle might do hurt, but that, by all means possible, mischief might be prevented. If the owner of the beast knew that he was mischievous, he must answer for the hurt done, and, according as the circumstances of the case proved him to be more or less accessory, he must either be *put to death* or ransom his life with a sum of money, *v.* 29—32. Some of our ancient books make this felony, by the common law of England, and give this reason, "The owner, by suffering his beast to go at liberty when he knew it to be mischievous, shows that he was very willing that hurt should be done." Note, It is not enough for us not to do mischief ourselves, but we must take care that no mischief be done by those whom it is in our power to restrain, whether man or beast.

2. In case of hurt done to oxen, or other cattle. (1.) If they fall into a pit, and perish there, he that opened the pit must make good the loss, *v.* 33, 34. Note, We must take heed not only of doing that which will be hurtful, but of doing that which may be so. It is not enough not to design and devise mischief, but we must contrive to prevent mischief, else we become accessory to our neighbours' damage. Mischief done in malice is the great transgression; but mischief done through negligence, and for want of due care and consideration, is not without fault, but ought to be reflected upon with great regret, according as the degree of the mischief is: especially we must be careful that we do nothing to make ourselves accessory to the sins of others, by laying an occasion of offence in our brother's way, Rom. xiv. 13. (2.) If cattle fight, and one kill another, the owners shall equally share in the loss, *v.* 35. Only if the beast that had done the harm was known to the owner to have been mischievous he shall answer for the damage, because he ought either to have killed him or kept him up, *v.* 36. The determinations of

these cases carry with them the evidence of their own equity, and give such rules of justice as were then, and are still, in use, for the decision of similar controversies that arise between man and man. But I conjecture that these cases might be specified, rather than others (though some of them seem minute), because they were then cases in fact actually depending before Moses; for in the wilderness where they lay closely encamped, and had their flocks and herds among them, such mischiefs as these last mentioned were likely enough to occur. That which we are taught by these laws is that we should be very careful to do no wrong, either directly or indirectly; and that, if we have done wrong, we must be very willing to make satisfaction, and desirous that nobody may lose by us.

CHAP. XXII.

The laws of this chapter relate, I. To the eighth commandment, concerning theft (ver. 1—4), trespass by cattle (ver. 5), damage by fire (ver. 6), trusts (ver. 7—13), borrowing cattle (ver. 14, 15), or money, ver. 25—27. II. To the seventh commandment. Against fornication (ver. 16, 17), bestiality, ver. 19. III. To the first table, forbidding witchcraft (ver. 18), idolatry, ver. 20. Commanding to offer the firstfruits, ver. 29, 30. IV. To the poor, ver. 21—24. V. To the civil government, ver. 28. VI. To the peculiarity of the Jewish nation, ver. 31.

IF a man shall steal an ox, or a sheep, and kill it, or sell it; he shall restore five oxen for an ox, and four sheep for a sheep. 2 If a thief be found breaking up, and be smitten that he die, *there shall* no blood *be shed* for him. 3 If the sun be risen upon him, *there shall be* blood *shed* for him; *for* he should make full restitution; if he have nothing, then he shall be sold for his theft. 4 If the theft be certainly found in his hand alive, whether it be ox, or ass, or sheep; he shall restore double. 5 If a man shall cause a field or vineyard to be eaten, and shall put in his beast, and shall feed in another man's field; of the best of his own field, and of the best of his own vineyard, shall he make restitution. 6 If fire break out, and catch in thorns, so that the stacks of corn, or the standing corn, or the field, be consumed *therewith;* he that kindled the fire shall surely make restitution.

Here are the laws,

I. Concerning theft, which are these:—1. If a man steal any cattle (in which the wealth of those times chiefly consisted), and they be found in his custody, he must restore double, *v.* 4. Thus he must both satisfy for the wrong and suffer for the crime. But it was afterwards provided that if the thief were touched in conscience, and voluntarily confessed it, before it was discovered or enquired into by any other, then he should only make

restitution of what he had stolen, and add to it a fifth part, Lev. vi. 4, 5. 2. If he had killed or sold the sheep or ox he had stolen, and thereby persisted in his crime, he must restore *five oxen for an ox, and four sheep for a sheep* (*v.* 1), more for an ox than for a sheep because the owner, besides all the other profit, lost the daily labour of his ox. This law teaches us that fraud and injustice, so far from enriching men, will impoverish them: if we unjustly get and keep that which is another's, it will not only waste itself, but it will consume that which is our own. 3. If he was not able to make restitution, he must be sold for a slave, *v.* 3. The court of judgment was to do it, and it is probable that the person robbed had the money. Thus with us, in some cases, felons are transported into plantations where alone Englishmen know what slavery is. 4. If a thief broke a house in the night, and was killed in the doing of it, his blood was upon his own head, and must not be required at the hand of him that shed it, *v.* 2. As he that does an unlawful act bears the blame of the mischief that follows to others, so likewise of that which follows to himself. A man's house is his castle, and God's law, as well as man's, sets a guard upon it; he that assaults it does so at his peril. Yet, if it was in the day-time that the thief was killed, he that killed him must be accountable for it (*v.* 3), unless it was in the necessary defence of his own life. Note, We ought to be tender of the lives even of bad men; the magistrate must afford us redress, and we must not avenge ourselves.

II. Concerning trespass, *v.* 5. He that wilfully put his cattle into his neighbour's field must make restitution of the best of his own. Our law makes a much greater difference between this and other thefts than the law of Moses did. The Jews hence observed it as a general rule that restitution must always be made of the best, and that no man should keep any cattle that were likely to trespass upon his neighbours or do them any damage. We should be more careful not to do wrong than not to suffer wrong, because to suffer wrong is only an affliction, but to do wrong is a sin, and sin is always worse than affliction.

III. Concerning damage done by fire, *v.* 6. He that designed only the burning of thorns might become accessory to the burning of corn, and should not be held guiltless. Men of hot and eager spirits should take heed, lest, while they pretend only to pluck up the tares, they root out the wheat also. If the fire did mischief, he that kindled it must answer for it, though it could not be proved that he designed the mischief. Men must suffer for their carelessness, as well as for their malice. We must take heed of beginning strife; for, though it seem but little, we know not how great a matter it may kindle, the blame of which we must bear, if, with the madman, we cast fire-brands, arrows, and death, and pretend we mean no harm. It will make us very careful of ourselves, if we consider that we are accountable, not only for the hurt we do, but for the hurt we occasion through inadvertency.

7 If a man shall deliver unto his neighbour money or stuff to keep, and it be stolen out of the man's house; if the thief be found let him pay double. 8 If the thief be not found, then the master of the house shall be brought unto the judges, *to see* whether he have put his hand unto his neighbour's goods. 9 For all manner of trespass, *whether it be* for ox, for ass, for sheep, for raiment, *or* for any manner of lost thing, which *another* challengeth to be his, the cause of both parties shall come before the judges; *and* whom the judges shall condemn, he shall pay double unto his neighbour. 10 If a man deliver unto his neighbour an ass, or an ox, or a sheep, or any beast, to keep; and it die, or be hurt, or driven away, no man seeing *it :* 11 *Then* shall an oath of the LORD be between them both, that he hath not put his hand unto his neighbour's goods; and the owner of it shall accept *thereof,* and he shall not make *it* good. 12 And if it be stolen from him, he shall make restitution unto the owner thereof. 13 If it be torn in pieces, *then* let him bring it *for* witness, *and* he shall not make good that which was torn. 14 And if a man borrow *aught* of his neighbour, and it be hurt, or die, the owner thereof *being* not with it, he shall surely make *it* good. 15 *But* if the owner thereof *be* with it, he shall not make *it* good: if it *be* a hired *thing,* it came for his hire.

These laws are,

I. Concerning trusts, *v.* 7—13. If a man deliver goods, suppose to a carrier to be conveyed, or to a warehouse-keeper to be preserved, or cattle to a farmer to be fed, upon a valuable consideration, and if a special confidence be reposed in the person they are lodged with, in case these goods be stolen or lost, perish or be damaged, if it appear that it was not by any fault of the trustee, the owner must stand to the loss, otherwise he that has been false to his trust must be compelled to make satisfaction. The trustee must aver his innocence upon oath before the judges, if the case was such as afforded no other proof, and they were to determine the

matter according as it appeared. This teaches us, 1. That we ought to be very careful of every thing we are entrusted with, as careful of it, though it be another's, as if it were our own. It is unjust and base, and that which all the world cries shame on, to betray a trust. 2. That there is such a general failing of truth and justice upon earth as gives too much occasion to suspect men's honesty whenever it is their interest to be dishonest. 3. That *an oath for confirmation is an end of strife,* Heb. vi. 16. It is called an *oath for the Lord* (*v.* 11), because to him the appeal is made, not only as to a witness of truth, but as to an avenger of wrong and falsehood. Those that had offered injury to their neighbour by doing any unjust thing, yet, it might be hoped, had not so far debauched their consciences as to profane an oath of the Lord, and call the God of truth to be witness to a lie: perjury is a sin which natural conscience startles at as much as any other. The religion of an oath is very ancient, and a plain indication of the universal belief of a God, and a providence, and a judgment to come. 4. That magistracy is an ordinance of God, designed, among other intentions, to assist men both in discovering rights disputed and recovering rights denied; and great respect ought to be paid to the determination of the judges. 5. That there is no reason why a man should suffer for that which he could not help: masters should consider this, in dealing with their servants, and not rebuke that as a fault which was a mischance, and which they themselves, had they been in their servants' places, could not have prevented.

II. Concerning loans, *v.* 14, 15. If a man (suppose) lent his team to his neighbour, if the owner was with it, or was to receive profit for the loan of it, whatever harm befel the cattle the owner must stand to the loss of: but if the owner was so kind to the borrower as to lend it to him gratis, and put such a confidence in him as to trust it from under his own eye, then, if any harm happened, the borrower must make it good. Let us learn hence to be very careful not to abuse any thing that is lent us; it is not only unjust, but base and disingenuous, inasmuch as it is rendering evil for good; we should much rather choose to lose ourselves than that any should sustain loss by their kindness to us. *Alas, master! for it was borrowed,* 2 Kings vi.5.

16 And if a man entice a maid that is not betrothed, and lie with her, he shall surely endow her to be his wife. 17 If her father utterly refuse to give her unto him, he shall pay money according to the dowry of virgins. 18 Thou shalt not suffer a witch to live. 19 Whosoever lieth with a beast shall surely be put to death. 20 He that sacrificeth unto *any* god, save unto the

LORD only, he shall be utterly destroyed. 21 Thou shalt neither vex a stranger, nor oppress him: for ye were strangers in the land of Egypt. 22 Ye shall not afflict any widow, or fatherless child. 23 If thou afflict them in any wise, and they cry at all unto me, I will surely hear their cry; 24 And my wrath shall wax hot, and I will kill you with the sword; and your wives shall be widows, and your children fatherless.

Here is, I. A law that he who debauched a yuung woman should be obliged to marry her, *v.* 16, 17. If she was betrothed to another, it was death to debauch her (Deut. xxii. 23, 24); but the law here mentioned respects her as single. But, if the father refused her to him, he was to give satisfaction in money for the injury and disgrace he had done her. This law puts an honour upon marriage and shows likewise how improper a thing it is that children should marry without their parents' consent: even here, where the divine law appointed the marriage, both as a punishment to him that had done wrong and a recompence to her that had suffered wrong, yet there was an express reservation for the father's power; if he denied his consent, it must be no marriage.

II. A law which makes witchcraft a capital crime, *v.* 18. Witchcraft not only gives that honour to the devil which is due to God alone, but bids defiance to the divine Providence, wages war with God's government, and puts his work into the devil's hand, expecting him to do good and evil, and so making him indeed *the god of this world;* justly therefore was it punished with death, especially among a people that were blessed with a divine revelation, and cared for by divine Providence above any people under the sun. By our law, consulting, covenanting with, invocating, or employing, any evil spirit, to any intent whatsoever, and exercising any enchantment, charm, or sorcery, whereby hurt shall be done to any person whatsoever, is made felony, without benefit of clergy; also pretending to tell where goods lost or stolen may be found, or the like, is an iniquity punishable by the judge, and the second offence with death. The justice of our law herein is supported by the law of God recorded here.

III. Unnatural abominations are here made capital; such beasts in the shape of men as are guilty of them are unfit to live (*v.* 19): *Whosoever lies with a beast shall die.*

IV. Idolatry is also made capital, *v.* 20. God having declared himself jealous in this matter, the civil powers must be jealous in it too, and utterly destroy those persons, families, and places of Israel, that worshipped any god, save the Lord: this law might have prevented the woeful apostasies of the Jewish nation in after times, if those that should have executed it had not been ringleaders in the breach of it.

V. A caution against oppression. Because those who were empowered to punish other crimes were themselves most in danger of this, God takes the punishing of it into his own hands.

1. Strangers must not be abused (*v.* 21), not wronged in judgment by the magistrates, not imposed upon in contracts, nor must any advantage be taken of their ignorance or necessity; no, nor must they be taunted, trampled upon, treated with contempt, or upbraided with being strangers; for all these were vexations, and would discourage strangers from coming to live among them, or would strengthen their prejudices against their religion, to which, by all kind and gentle methods, they should endeavour to proselyte them. The reason given why they should be kind to strangers is, "*You were strangers in Egypt,* and knew what it was to be vexed and oppressed there." Note, (1.) Humanity is one of the laws of religion, and obliges us particularly to be tender of those that lie most under disadvantages and discouragements, and to extend our compassionate concern to strangers, and those to whom we are not under the obligations of alliance or acquaintance. Those that are strangers to us are known to God, and he preserves them, Ps. cxlvi. 9. (2.) Those that profess religion should study to oblige strangers, that they may thereby recommend religion to their good opinion, and take heed of doing any thing that may tempt them to think ill of it or its professors, 1 Pet. ii. 12. (3.) Those that have themselves been in poverty and distress, if Providence enrich and enlarge them, ought to show a particular tenderness towards those that are now in such circumstances as they were in formerly, doing now by them as they then wished to be done by.

2. Widows and fatherless must not be abused (*v.* 22): *You shall not afflict them,* that is, "You shall comfort and assist them, and be ready upon all occasions to show them kindness" In making just demands from them, their condition must be considered, who have lost those that should deal for them, and protect them; they are supposed to be unversed in business, destitute of advice, timorous, and of a tender spirit, and therefore must be treated with kindness and compassion; no advantage must be taken against them, nor any hardship put upon them, from which a husband or a father would have sheltered them. For, (1.) God takes particular cognizance of their case, *v.* 23. Having no one else to complain and appea. to, they will *cry unto God,* and he will be sure *to hear them;* for his law and his providence are guardians to the widows and fatherless, and if men do not pity them, and will not

hear them, he will.   Note, It is a great comfort to those who are injured and oppressed
by men that they have a God to go to who
will do more than *give them the heuring;* and
it ought to be a terror to those who are oppressive that they have the cry of the poor
against them, which God will hear.   Nay,
(2.) He will severely reckon with those
that do oppress them.   Though they escape
punishments from men, God's righteous
judgments will pursue and overtake them,
v. 24.   Men that have a sense of justice
and honour will espouse the injured cause of
the weak and helpless; and shall not the
righteous God do it?   Observe the equity of
the sentence here passed upon those that oppress the widows and fatherless : their wives
shall become widows, and their children
fatherless; and the Lord is known by these
judgments, which he sometimes excutes still.

25 If thou lend money to *any of*
my people *that is* poor by thee, thou
shalt not be to him as a usurer, neither shalt thou lay upon him usury.
26 If thou at all take thy neighbour's
raiment to pledge, thou shalt deliver it
unto him by that the sun goeth down:
27 For that *is* his covering only, it *is*
his raiment for his skin: wherein shall
he sleep? and it shall come to pass,
when he crieth unto me, that I will
hear; for I *am* gracious.   28 Thou
shalt not revile the gods, nor curse
the ruler of thy people.   29 Thou
shalt not delay *to offer* the first of thy
ripe fruits, and of thy liquors: the
firstborn of thy sons shalt thou give
unto me.   30 Likewise shalt thou do
with thine oxen, *and* with thy sheep :
seven days it shall be with his dam ;
on the eighth day thou shall give it
me.   31 And ye shall be holy men
unto me : neither shall ye eat *any*
flesh *that is* torn of beasts in the field;
ye shall cast it to the dogs.

Here is, I. A law against extortion in lending.   1. They must not receive use for money
from any that borrowed for necessity (*v.* 25),
as in that case, Neh. v. 5, 7.   And such provision the law made for the preservation of
estates to their families by the year of jubilee
that a people who had little concern in trade
could not be supposed to borrow money but
for necessity, and therefore it is generally forbidden among themselves; but to a stranger,
whom yet they might not oppress, they were
allowed to lend upon usury: this law, therefore, in the strictness of it, seems to have
been peculiar to the Jewish state; but, in the
equity of it, it obliges us to show mercy to
those of whom we might take advantage, and

to be content to share, in loss as well as profit,
with those we lend to, if Providence cross
them; and, upon this condition, it seems as
lawful to receive interest for my money,
which another takes pains with and improves,
but runs the hazard of, in trade, as it is to
receive rent for my land, which another takes
pains with and improves, but runs the hazard
of, in husbandry.   2. They must not take a
poor man's bed-clothes in pawn; but, if they
did, must restore them by bed-time, *v.* 26, 27.
Those who lie soft and warm themselves
should consider the hard and cold lodgings
of many poor people, and not do any thing
to make bad worse, or to add affliction to the
afflicted.

II. A law against the contempt of authority
(*v.* 28): *Thou shalt not revile the gods,* that is,
the *judges* and *magistrates,* for their executing
these laws; they must do their duty, whoever suffer by it.   Magistrates ought not to
fear the reproach of men, nor their revilings,
but to despise them as long as they keep a
good conscience; but those that do revile
them for their being a terror to evil works
and workers reflect upon God himself, and
will have a great deal to answer for another
day.   We find those under a black character,
and a heavy doom, that *despise dominion, and
speak evil of dignities,* Jude 8.   Princes and
magistrates are our fathers, whom the fifth
commandment obliges us to honour and forbids us to revile.   St. Paul applies this law
to himself, and owns that he ought not to
speak evil of the ruler of his people; no, not
though the ruler was then his most unrighteous persecutor, Acts xxiii. 5; see Eccl. x. 20.

III. A law concerning the offering of their
first-fruits to God, *v.* 29, 30.   It was appointed
before (*ch.* xiii.), and it is here repeated : *The
firstborn of thy sons shalt thou give unto me;*
and much more reason have we to give ourselves, and all we have, to God, who *spared
not his own Son, but delivered him up for us
all.*   The first ripe of their corn they must
not delay to offer.   There is danger, if we
delay our duty, lest we wholly omit it; and
by slipping the first opportunity, in expectation of another, we suffer Satan to cheat us
of all our time.   Let not young people delay
to offer to God the first-fruits of their time
and strength, lest their delays come, at last,
to be denials, through the deceitfulness of
sin, and the more convenient season they
promise themselves never arrive.   Yet it is
provided that the firstlings of their cattle
should not be dedicated to God till they were
past seven days old, for then they began to
be good for something.   Note, God is the
first and best, and therefore must have the
first and best.

IV. A distinction put between the Jews
and all other people : *You shall be holy men
unto me;* and one mark of that honourable
distinction is appointed in their diet, which
was, that they should not *eat any flesh that
was torn of beasts* (*v.* 31), not only because it

was unwholesome, but because it was paltry, and base, and covetous, and a thing below those who were holy men unto God, to eat the leavings of the beasts of prey. We that are sanctified to God must not be curious in our diet; but we must be conscientious, not feeding ourselves without fear, but eating and drinking by rule, the rule of sobriety, to the glory of God.

CHAP. XXIII.

This chapter continues and concludes the acts that passed in the first session (if I may so call it) upon mount Sinai. Here are, 1. Some laws of universal obligation, relating especially to the ninth commandment, against bearing false witness (ver. 1), and giving false judgment, ver. 2, 3, 6—8. Also a law of doing good to our enemies (ver. 4, 5), and not oppressing strangers, ver. 9. II. Some laws peculiar to the Jews. The sabbatical year (ver. 10, 11), the three annual feasts (ver. 14—17), with some laws pertaining thereto. III. Gracious promises of the completing of the mercy God had begun for them, upon condition of their obedience. That God would conduct them through the wilderness (ver. 20—24), that he would prosper all they had (ver. 25, 26), that he would put them in possession of Canaan, ver. 27—31. But they must not mingle themselves with the nations, ver. 32, 33.

THOU shalt not raise a false report: put not thine hand with the wicked to be an unrighteous witness. 2 Thou shalt not follow a multitude to *do* evil; neither shalt thou speak in a cause to decline after many to wrest *judgment:* 3 Neither shalt thou countenance a poor man in his cause. 4 If thou meet thine enemy's ox or his ass going astray, thou shalt surely bring it back to him again. 5 If thou see the ass of him that hateth thee, lying under his burden, and wouldest forbear to help him, thou shalt surely help with him. 6 Thou shalt not wrest the judgment of thy poor in his cause. 7 Keep thee far from a false matter; and the innocent and righteous slay thou not: for I will not justify the wicked. 8 And thou shalt take no gift: for the gift blindeth the wise, and perverteth the words of the righteous. 9 Also thou shalt not oppress a stranger: for ye know the heart of a stranger, seeing ye were strangers in the land of Egypt.

Here are, I. Cautions concerning judicial proceedings; it was not enough that they had good laws, better than ever any nation had, but care must be taken for the due administration of justice according to those laws.

1. The witnesses are here cautioned that they neither occasion an innocent man to be indicted, by raising a false report of him and setting common fame against him, nor assist in the prosecution of an innocent man, or one whom they do not know to be guilty, by *putting their hand* in swearing as witnesses against him, *v.* 1. Bearing false witness against a man, in a matter that touches his life, has in it all the guilt of lying, perjury,

malice, theft, murder, with the additional stains of colouring all with a pretence of justice and involving many others in the same guilt. There is scarcely any one act of wickedness that a man can possibly be guilty of which has in it a greater complication of villanies than this has. Yet the former part of this caution is to be extended, not only to judicial proceedings, but to common conversation; so that slandering and backbiting are a species of falsewitness-bearing. A man's reputation lies as much at the mercy of every company as his estate or life does at the mercy of a judge or jury; so that he who raises, or knowingly spreads, a false report against his neighbour, especially if the report be made to wise and good men whose esteem one would desire to enjoy, sins as much against the laws of truth, justice, and charity, as a false witness does—with this further mischief, that he leaves it not in the power of the person injured to obtain redress. That which we translate, Thou shalt not *raise*, the margin reads, Thou shalt not *receive* a false report; for sometimes the receiver, in this case, is as bad as the thief; and a backbiting tongue would not do so much mischief as it does if it were not countenanced. Sometimes we cannot avoid hearing a false report, but we must not receive it, that is, we must not hear it with pleasure and delight as those that rejoice in iniquity, nor give credit to it as long as there remains any cause to question the truth of it. This is charity to our neighbour's good name, and doing as we would be done by.

2. The judges are here cautioned not to pervert judgment. (1.) They must not be overruled, either by might or multitude, to go against their consciences in giving judgment, *v.* 2. With the Jews causes were tried by a bench of justices, and judgment given according to the majority of votes, in which case every particular justice must go according to truth, as it appeared to him upon the strictest and most impartial enquiry, though the multitude of the people, and their outcries, or, the sentence of the *rabbim* (we translate it *many),* the more ancient and honourable of the justices, went the other way. Therefore (as with us), among the Jews, the junior upon the bench voted first, that he might not be swayed nor overruled by the authority of the senior. Judges must not respect the persons either of the parties or of their fellow-judges. The former part of this verse also gives a general rule for all, as well as judges, not *to follow a multitude to do evil.* General usage will never excuse us in a bad practice; nor is the broad way ever the better or safer for its being tracked and crowded. We must enquire what we ought to do, not what the majority do; because we must be judged by our Master, not by our fellow-servants, and it is too great a compliment to be willing to go to hell for company. (2.) They must not pervert judgment, no, not in

373

favour of a poor man, *v.* 3. Right must in all cases take place and wrong must be punished, and justice never biassed nor injury connived at under pretence of charity and compassion. If a poor man be a bad man, and do a bad thing, it is foolish pity to let him fare the better for his poverty, Deut. i. 16, 17. (3.) Neither must they pervert judgment in prejudice to a poor man, nor suffer him to be wronged because he had not wherewithal to right himself; in such cases the judges themselves must become advocates for the poor, as far as their cause was good and honest (*v.* 6): " *Thou shalt not wrest the judgment of the poor ;* remember they are thy poor, bone of thy bone, thy poor neighbours, thy poor brethren ; let them not therefore fare the worse for being poor." (4.) They must dread the thoughts of assisting or abetting a bad cause (*v.* 7): " *Keep thyself far from a false matter ;* do not only keep thyself free from it, nor think it enough to say thou art unconcerned in it, but keep far from it, dread it as a dangerous snare. The innocent and righteous thou wouldest not, for all the world, slay with thy own hands ; keep far therefore from a false matter, for thou knowest not but it may end in that, and the righteous God will not leave such wickedness unpunished : *I will not justify the wicked,*" that is, " I will condemn him that unjustly condemns others." Judges themselves are accountable to the great judge. (5.) They must not take bribes, *v.* 8. They must not only not be swayed by a gift to give an unjust judgment, to condemn the innocent, or acquit the guilty, or adjudge a man's right from him, but they must not so much as take a gift, lest it should have a bad influence upon them, and overrule them, contrary to their intentions ; for it has a strange tendency to blind those that otherwise would do well. (6.) They must not oppress a stranger, *v.* 9. Though aliens might not inherit lands among them, yet they must have justice done them, must peaceably enjoy their own, and be redressed if they were wronged, though they were strangers to the commonwealth of Israel. It is an instance of the equity and goodness of our law, that, if an alien be tried for any crime except treason, the one half of his jury, if he desire it, shall be foreigners ; they call it a trial *per medietatem linguæ,* a kind provision that strangers may not be oppressed. The reason here given is the same with that in *ch.* xxii. 21, *You were strangers,* which is here elegantly enforced, *You know the heart of a stranger ;* you know something of the griefs and fears of a stranger by sad experience, and therefore, being delivered, can the more easily put your souls into their souls' stead.

II. Commands concerning neighbourly kindnesses. We must be ready to do all good offices, as there is occasion, for any body, yea even for those that have done us ill offices, *v* 4, 5. The command of loving our enemies,

and doing good to those that hate us, is not only a *new.* but an *old* commandment, Prov. xxv. 21, 22. Infer hence, 1. If we must do this kindness for an enemy, much more for a friend, though an enemy only is mentioned, because it is supposed that a man would not be unneighbourly to any unless such as he had a particular spleen against. 2. If it be wrong not to prevent our enemy's loss and damage, how much worse is it to occasion harm and loss to him, or any thing he has. 3. If we must bring back our neighbours' cattle when they go astray, much more must we endeavour, by prudent admonitions and instructions, to bring back our neighbours themselves, when they go astray in any sinful path, see Jam. v. 19, 20. And, if we must endeavour to help up a fallen ass, much more should we endeavour, by comforts and encouragements, to help up a sinking spirit, *saying to those that are of a fearful heart, Be strong.* We must seek the relief and welfare of others *as our own,* Phil. ii. 4. *If thou sayest, Behold, we know it not, doth not he that pondereth the heart consider it?* See Prov. xxiv. 11, 12.

10 And six years thou shalt sow thy land, and shalt gather in the fruits thereof: 11 But the seventh *year* thou shalt let it rest and lie still; that the poor of thy people may eat: and what they leave the beasts of the field shall eat. In like manner thou shalt deal with thy vineyard, *and* with thy oliveyard. 12 Six days thou shalt do thy work, and on the seventh day thou shalt rest: that thine ox and thine ass may rest, and the son of thy handmaid, and the stranger, may be refreshed. 13 And in all *things* that I have said unto you be circumspect: and make no mention of the name of other gods, neither let it be heard out of thy mouth. 14 Three times thou shalt keep a feast unto me in the year. 15 Thou shalt keep the feast of unleavened bread : (thou shalt eat unleavened bread seven days, as I commanded thee, in the time appointed of the month Abib ; for in it thou camest out from Egypt : and none shall appear before me empty :) 16 And the feast of harvest, the firstfruits of thy labours, which thou hast sown in the field : and the feast of ingathering, *which is* in the end of the year, when thou hast gathered in thy labours out of the field. 17 Three times in the year all thy males shall appear before

the Lord God. 18 Thou shalt not offer the blood of my sacrifice with leavened bread; neither shall the fat of my sacrifice remain until the morning. 19 The first of the firstfruits of thy land thou shalt bring into the house of the Lord thy God. Thou shalt not seethe a kid in his mother's milk.

Here is, I. The institution of the sabbatical year, *v.* 10, 11. Every seventh year the land was to rest; they must not plough nor sow it at the beginning of the year, and then they could not expect any great harvest at the end of the year: but what the earth did produce of itself should be eaten from hand to mouth, and not laid up. Now this was designed, 1. To show what a plentiful land that was into which God was bringing them— that so numerous a people could have rich maintenance out of the produce of so small a country, without foreign trade, and yet could spare the increase of every seventh year. 2. To remind them of their dependence upon God their great landlord, and their obligation to use the fruit of their land as he should direct. Thus he would try their obedience in a matter that nearly touched their interest. Afterwards we find that their disobedience to this command was a forfeiture of the promises, 2 Chron. xxxvi. 21. 3. To teach them a confidence in the divine Providence, while they did their duty—that, as the sixth day's manna served for two days' meat, so the sixth year's increase should serve for two years' subsistence. Thus they must learn not to *take thought for their life,* Matt. vi. 25. If we are prudent and diligent in our affairs, we may trust Providence to furnish us with the bread of the day in its day.

II. The repetition of the law of the fourth commandment concerning the weekly sabbath, *v.* 12. Even in the year of rest they must not think that the sabbath day was laid in common with the other days, but, even that year, it must be religiously observed; yet thus some have endeavoured to take away the observance of the sabbath, by pretending that every day must be a sabbath day.

III. All manner of respect to the gods of the heathen is here strictly forbidden, *v.* 13. A general caution is prefixed to this, which has reference to all these precepts: *In all things that I have said unto you, be circumspect.* We are in danger of missing our way on the right hand and on the left, and it is at our peril if we do; therefore we have need to look about us, A man may ruin himself through mere carelessness, but he cannot save himself without great care and circumspection: particularly, since idolatry was a sin which they were much addicted to, and would be greatly tempted to, they must endeavour to blot out the remembrance of the gods of the heathen, and must disuse and forget all their superstitious forms of speech, and never mention

them but with detestation. In Christian schools and academies (for it is in vain to think of reforming the play-houses), it were to be wished that the names and stories of the heathen deities, or demons rather, were not so commonly and familiarly used as they are, even with intimations of respect, and sometimes with forms of invocation. Surely we have *not so learned Christ.*

IV. Their solemn religious attendance on God in the place which he should choose is here strictly required, *v.* 14—17. 1. Thrice a year all their males must come together in a holy convocation, that they might the better know and love one another, and keep up their communion as a dignified and peculiar people. 2. They must come together *before the Lord* (*v.* 17) to present themselves before him, looking towards the place where his honour dwelt, and to pay their homage to him as their great Lord, from and under whom they held all their enjoyments. 3. They must feast together before the Lord, eating and drinking together, in token of their joy in God and their grateful sense of his goodness to them; for *a feast is made for laughter,* Eccl. x. 19. O what a good Master do we serve, who has made it our duty to *rejoice before him,* who feasts his servants when they are in waiting! Never let religion be called a melancholy thing, when its solemn services are solemn feasts. 4. They must not *appear before God empty, v.* 15. Some free-will offering or other they must bring, in token of their respect and gratitude to their great benefactor; and, as they were not allowed to come empty-handed, so we must not come to worship God empty-hearted; our souls must be filled with grace, with pious and devout affections, holy desires towards him, and dedications of ourselves to him, for *with such sacrifices God is well-pleased.* 5. The passover, pentecost, and feast of tabernacles, in spring, summer, and autumn, were the three times appointed for their attendance: not in winter, because travelling was then uncomfortable; not in the midst of their harvest, because then they were otherwise employed; so that they had no reason to say that he *made them to serve with an offering,* or *wearied them with incense.*

V. Some particular directions are here given about the three feasts, though not so fully as afterwards. 1. As to the passover, it was not to be offered with leavened bread, for at that feast all leaven was to be cast out, nor was the fat of it to remain until the morning, lest it should become offensive, *v.* 18. 2. At the feast of pentecost, when they were to begin their harvest, they must bring *the first of their first-fruits* to God, by the pious presenting of which the whole harvest was sanctified, *v.* 19. 3. At the feast of *ingathering,* as it is called (*v.* 16), they must give God thanks for the harvest-mercies they had received, and must depend upon him for the next harvest, and must not think to receive benefit by that superstitious usage of some of the Gentiles, who, it is said, at the end of their harvest, *seethed a kid in its dam's milk,* and sprinkled that milk-pottage, in a magical way, upon their gardens and fields, to make them more fruitful next year. But Israel must abhor such foolish customs.

20 Behold, I send an Angel before thee, to keep thee in the way, and to bring thee into the place which I have prepared. 21 Beware of him, and obey his voice, provoke him not; for he will not pardon your transgressions: for my name *is* in him. 22 But if thou shalt indeed obey his voice, and do all that I speak; then I will be an enemy unto thine enemies, and an adversary unto thine adversaries. 23 For mine Angel shall go before thee, and bring thee in unto the Amorites, and the Hittites, and the Perizzites, and the Canaanites, the Hivites, and the Jebusites: and I will cut them off. 24 Thou shalt not bow down to their gods, nor serve them, nor do after their works: but thou shalt utterly overthrow them, and quite break down their images. 25 And ye shall serve the LORD your God, and he shall bless thy bread, and thy water; and I will take sickness away from the midst of thee. 26 There shall nothing cast their young, nor be barren, in thy land: the number of thy days I will fulfil. 27 I will send my fear before thee, and will destroy all the people to whom thou shalt come, and I will make all thine enemies turn their backs unto thee. 28 And I will send hornets before thee, which shall drive out the Hivite, the Canaanite, and the Hittite, from before thee. 29 I will not drive them out from before thee in one year; lest the land become desolate, and the beast of the field multiply against thee. 30 By little and little I will drive them out from before thee, until thou be increased, and inherit the land. 31 And I will set thy bounds from the Red sea even unto the sea of the Philistines, and from the desert unto the river: for I will deliver the inhabitants of the land into your hand; and thou shalt drive them out before thee. 32 Thou shalt make no covenant with them, nor with their gods.

33 They shall not dwell in thy land, lest they make thee sin against me: for if thou serve their gods, it will surely be a snare unto thee.

Three gracious promises are here made to Israel, to engage them to their duty and encourage them in it; and each of the promises has some needful precepts and cautions joined to it.

I. It is here promised that they should be guided and kept in their way through the wilderness to the land of promise: *Behold, I send an angel before thee* (v. 20), *my angel* (v. 23), a created angel, say some, a minister of God's providence, employed in conducting and protecting the camp of Israel; that it might appear that God took a particular care of them, he appointed one of his chief servants to make it his business to attend them, and see that they wanted for nothing. Others suppose it to be the Son of God, the angel of the covenant; for the Israelites in the wilderness are said to *tempt Christ;* and we may as well suppose him God's messenger, and the church's Redeemer, before his incarnation, as *the Lamb slain from the foundation of the world.* And we may the rather think he was pleased to undertake the deliverance and guidance of Israel because they were typical of his great undertaking. It is promised that this blessed angel should *keep them in the way,* though it lay through a wilderness first, and afterwards through their enemies' country; thus God's spiritual Israel shall be kept through the wilderness of this earth, and from the insults of the gates of hell. It is also promised that he should bring them into the place which God had not only designed but prepared for them: and thus Christ has prepared a place for his followers, and will preserve them to it, for he is faithful to him that appointed him. The precept joined with this promise is that they be observant of, and obedient to, this angel whom God would send before them (v. 21): *Beware of him, and obey his voice* in every thing; *provoke him not* in any thing, for it is at your peril if you do, he will *visit your iniquity."* Note, 1. Christ is the author of salvation to those only that obey him. The word of command is *Hear you him,* Matt. xvii. 5. *Observe what he hath commanded,* Matt. xxviii. 20. 2. Our necessary dependence upon the divine power and goodness should awe us into obedience. We do well to take heed of provoking our protector and benefactor, because if our defence depart from us, and the streams of his goodness be cut off, we are undone. Therefore, "*Beware of him,* and carry it towards him with all possible reverence and caution. Fear the *Lord, and his goodness."* 3. Christ will be faithful to those who are faithful to him, and will espouse their cause who adhere to his: *I will be an adversary to thine adversaries,* v. 22. The league shall be offensive and defensive, like that with Abraham, *I will bless him that blesseth thee, and curse him that curseth thee.* Thus is God pleased to twist his interests and friendships with his people's.

II. It is promised that they should have a comfortable settlement in the land of Canaan, which they hoped now (though it proved otherwise) within a few months to be in the possession of, v. 24—26. Observe, 1. How reasonable the conditions of this promise are—only that they should serve their own God, who was indeed the only true God, and not the gods of the nations, which were no gods at all, and which they had no reason at all to have any respect for. They must not only not worship their gods, but they must utterly overthrow them, in token of their great abhorrence of idolatry, their resolution never to worship idols themselves, and their care to prevent any other from worshipping them; as the converted conjurors *burnt their books,* Acts xix. 19. 2. How rich the particulars of this promise are. (1.) The comfort of their food. He shall *bless thy bread and thy water;* and God's blessing will make bread and water more refreshing and nourishing than a feast of fat things and wines on the lees without that blessing. (2.) The continuance of their health: "*I will take sickness away,* either prevent it or remove it. Thy land shall not be visited with epidemical diseases, which are very dreadful, and sometimes have laid countries waste." (3.) The increase of their wealth. Their cattle should not be barren, nor cast their young, which is mentioned as an instance of prosperity, Job xxi. 10. (4.) The prolonging of their lives to old age: "*The number of thy days I will fulfil,* and they shall not be cut off in the midst by untimely deaths." Thus hath godliness the *promise of the life that now is.*

III. It is promised that they should conquer and subdue their enemies, the present occupants of the land of Canaan, who must be driven out to make room for them. This God would do, 1. Effectually by his power (v. 27, 28); not so much by the sword and bow of Israel as by the terrors which he would strike into the Canaanites. Though they were so obstinate as not to be willing to submit to Israel, resign their country, and retire elsewhere, which they might have done, yet they were so dispirited that they were not able to stand before them. This completed their ruin; such power had the devil in them that they would resist, but such power had God over them that they could not. *I will send my fear before thee;* and those that fear will soon flee. Hosts of hornets made way for the hosts of Israel; such mean creatures can God make use of for the chastising of his people's enemies, as in the plagues of Egypt. When God pleases, hornets can drive out Canaanites, as well as lions could, Josh. xxiv. 12. 2. He would do it gradually, in wisdom (v. 29, 30), not all at once, but by little and little. As the Ca-

naanites had kept possession till Israel had grown into a people, so there should still be some remains of them till Israel should grow so numerous as to replenish the whole. Note, The wisdom of God is to be observed in the gradual advances of the church's interests. It is in real kindness to the church that its enemies are subdued by little and little; for thus we are kept upon our guard, and in a continual dependence upon God. Corruptions are thus driven out of the hearts of God's people; not all at once, but by little and little; the old man is crucified, and therefore dies slowly. God, in his providence, often delays mercies, because we are not ready for them. Canaan has room enough to receive Israel, but Israel is not numerous enough to occupy Canaan. We are not straitened in God; if we are straitened, it is in ourselves. The land of Canaan is promised them (v. 31) in its utmost extent, which yet they were not possessed of till the days of David; and by their sins they soon lost possession. The precept annexed to this promise is that they should not make any friendship, nor have any familiarity, with idolaters, v. 32, 33. Idolaters must not so much as sojourn in their land, unless they renounced their idolatry. Thus they must avoid the reproach of intimacy with the worshippers of false gods and the danger of being drawn to worship with them. By familiar converse with idolaters, their dread and detestation of the sin would wear off; they would think it no harm, in compliment to their friends, to pay some respect to their gods, and so by degrees would be drawn into the fatal snare. Note, Those that would be kept from bad courses must keep from bad company; it is dangerous living in a bad neighbourhood; others' sins will be our snares, if we look not well to ourselves. We must always look upon our greatest danger to be from those that would cause us to sin against God. Whatever friendship is pretended, that is really our worst enemy that draws us from our duty.

CHAP. XXIV.

Moses, as mediator between God and Israel, having received divers laws and ordinances from God privately in the three foregoing chapters, in this chapter, I. Comes down to the people, acquaints them with the laws he had received, and takes their consent to those laws (ver. 3), writes the laws, and reads them to the people, who repeat their consent (ver. 4—7), and then by sacrifice, and the sprinkling of blood, ratifies the covenant between them and God, ver. 5, 6, 8. II. He returns to God again, to receive further directions. When he was dismissed from his former attendance, he was ordered to attend again, ver. 1, 2. He did so with seventy of the elders, to whom God made a discovery of his glory, ver. 9—11. Moses is ordered up into the mount (ver. 12, 13); the rest are ordered down to the people, ver. 14. The cloud of glory is seen by all the people on the top of mount Sinai (ver. 15—17), and Moses is there with God forty days and forty nights, ver. 18.

AND he said unto Moses, Come up unto the LORD, thou, and Aaron, Nadab, and Abihu, and seventy of the elders of Israel; and worship ye afar off. 2 And Moses alone shall come near the LORD: but they shall not come nigh; neither shall the people go up with him. 3 And Moses came and told the people all the words of the LORD, and all the judgments : and all the people answered with one voice, and said, All the words which the LORD hath said will we do. 4 And Moses wrote all the words of the LORD, and rose up early in the morning, and builded an altar under the hill, and twelve pillars, according to the twelve tribes of Israel. 5 And he sent young men of the children of Israel, which offered burnt offerings, and sacrificed peace offerings of oxen unto the LORD. 6 And Moses took half of the blood, and put *it* in basons; and half of the blood he sprinkled on the altar. 7 And he took the book of the covenant, and read in the audience of the people : and they said, All that the LORD hath said will we do, and be obedient. 8 And Moses took the blood, and sprinkled *it* on the people, and said, Behold the blood of the covenant, which the LORD hath made with you concerning all these words.

The first two verses record the appointment of a second session upon mount Sinai, for the making of laws, when an end was put to the first. When a communion is begun between God and us, it shall never fail on his side, if it do not first fail on ours. Moses is directed to bring Aaron and his sons, and the seventy elders of Israel, that they might be witnesses of the glory of God, and that communion with him to which Moses was admitted; and that their testimony might confirm the people's faith. In this approach, 1. They must all be very reverent : *Worship you afar off*, v. 1. Before they came near, they must worship. Thus we must enter into God's gates with humble and solemn adorations, draw near as those that know our distance, and admire the condescensions of God's grace in admitting us to draw near. Are great princes approached with the profound reverences of the body? And shall not the soul that draws near to God be bowed before him ? 2. They must none of them come so near as Moses, *v. 2.* They must come up to the Lord (and those that would approach to God must *ascend*), but Moses alone must come near, being therein a type of Christ, who, as the high priest, entered alone into the most holy place.

In the following verses, we have the solemn covenant made between God and Israel, and the exchanging of the ratifications ; and a very solemn transaction it was, typifying the covenant of grace between God and believers through Christ.

I. Moses told the people the words of the

Lord, v. 3. He did not lead them blindfold into the covenant, nor teach them a devotion that was the daughter of ignorance; but laid before them all the precepts, general and particular, in the foregoing chapters ; and fairly put it to them whether they were willing to submit to these laws or no.

II. The people unanimously consented to the terms proposed, without reservation or exception : *All the words which the Lord hath said will we do.* They had before consented in general to be under God's government (*ch.* xix. 8); here they consent in particular to these laws now given. *O that there had been such a heart in them !* How well were it if people would but be always in the same good mind that sometimes they seem to be in! Many consent to the law, and yet do not live up to it; they have nothing to except against it, and yet will not persuade themselves to be ruled by it.

This is the tenour of the covenant, That, if they would observe the foregoing precepts, God would perform the foregoing promises. " Obey, and be happy." Here is the bargain made. Observe,

1. How it was engrossed in the book of the covenant : *Moses wrote the words of the Lord* (v. 4), that there might be no mistake ; probably he had written them as God dictated them on the mount. As soon as ever God had separated to himself a peculiar people in the world, he governed them by a written word, as he has done ever since, and will do while the world stands and the church in it. Moses, having engrossed the articles of agreement concluded upon between God and Israel, *read them in the audience of the people* (v. 7), that they might be perfectly apprised of the thing, and might try whether their second thoughts were the same with their first, upon the whole matter. And we may suppose they were so ; for their words (v. 7) are the same with what they were (v. 3), but something stronger : *All that the Lord hath said* (be it good, or be it evil, to flesh and blood, Jer. xlii. 6) *we will do ;* so they had said before, but now they add, " *And will be obedient ;* not only we will do what has been commanded, but in every thing which shall further be ordained *we will be obedient.*" Bravely resolved ! if they had but stuck to their resolution. See here that God's covenants and commands are so incontestably equitable in themselves, and so highly advantageous to us, that the more we think of them, and the more plainly and fully they are set before us, the more reason we shall see to comply with them.

2. How it was sealed by the blood of the covenant, that Israel might receive strong consolations from the ratifying of God's promises to them, and might lie under strong obligations from the ratifying of their promises to God. Thus has Infinite Wisdom devised means that we may be confirmed both in our faith and in our obedience, may

be both encouraged in our duty and engaged to it. The covenant must be made by sacrifice (Ps. l. 5), because, since man has sinned, and forfeited his Creator's favour, there can be no fellowship by covenant till there be first friendship and atonement by sacrifice.

(1.) In preparation therefore for the parties interchangeably putting their seals to this covenant, [1.] Moses builds an altar, to the honour of God, which was principally intended in all the altars that were built, and which was the first thing to be looked at in the covenant they were now to seal. No addition to the perfections of the divine nature can be made by any of God's dealings with the children of men, but in them his perfections are manifested and magnified, and his honour is shown forth; therefore he will now be represented by an altar, to signify that all he expected from them was that they should do him honour, and that, being his people, they should be to him for a name and a praise. [2.] He erects twelve pillars, according to the number of the tribes. These were to represent the people, the other party to the covenant; and we may suppose that they were set up against the altar, and that Moses, as mediator, passed to and fro between them. Probably each tribe set up and knew its own pillar, and their elders stood by it. [3.] He appointed sacrifices to be offered upon the altar (v. 5), burnt-offerings and peace-offerings, which yet were designed to be expiatory. We are not concerned to enquire who these young men were that were employed in offering these sacrifices; for Moses was himself the priest, and what they did was purely as his servants, by his order and appointment. No doubt they were men who by their bodily strength were qualified for the service, and by their station among the people were fittest for the honour.

(2.) Preparation being thus made, the ratifications were very solemnly exchanged. [1.] The blood of the sacrifice which the people offered was (part of it) sprinkled upon the altar (v. 6), which signifies the people's dedicating themselves, their lives, and beings, to God, and to his honour. In the blood (which is the life) of the dead sacrifices all the Israelites were presented unto God as living sacrifices, Rom. xii. 1. [2.] The blood of the sacrifice which God had owned and accepted was (the remainder of it) sprinkled either upon the people themselves (v. 8) or upon the pillars that represented them, which signified God's graciously conferring his favour upon them and all the fruits of that favour, and his giving them all the gifts they could expect or desire from a God reconciled to them and in covenant with them by sacrifice. This part of the ceremony was thus explained: "*Behold the blood of the covenant;* see here how God has sealed to you to be a God, and you seal to him to be to him a people; his promises to you, and yours to him, are both *yea and amen.*" Thus our

Lord Jesus, the Mediator of the new covenant (of whom Moses was a type), having offered up himself a sacrifice upon the cross, that his blood might be indeed the blood of the covenant, sprinkled it upon the altar in his intercession (Heb. ix. 12), and sprinkles it upon his church by his word and ordinances and the influences and operations of the Spirit of promise, by whom we are sealed. He himself seemed to allude to this solemnity when, in the institution of the Lord's supper, he said, *This cup is the New Testament* (or covenant) *in my blood.* Compare with this, Heb. ix. 19, 20.

9 Then went up Moses, and Aaron, Nadab, and Abihu, and seventy of the elders of Israel: 10 And they saw the God of Israel: and *there was* under his feet as it were a paved work of a sapphire stone, and as it were the body of heaven in *his* clearness. 11 And upon the nobles of the children of Israel he laid not his hand: also they saw God, and did eat and drink.

The people having, besides their submission to the ceremony of the sprinkling of blood, declared their well-pleasedness in their God and his law, again and again, God here gives to their representatives some special tokens of his favour to them (for God meets him that rejoices and works righteousness), and admits them nearer to him than they could, have expected. Thus, in the New-Testament church, we find the *four living creatures,* and the *four and twenty elders,* honoured with places round the throne, being *redeemed unto God* by the *blood of the Lamb* which is *in the midst of the throne,* Rev. iv. 4, 6; v. 8, 9. Observe, 1. They saw the God of Israel (v. 10), that is, they had some glimpse of his glory, in light and fire, though they saw *no manner of similitude,* and his being *no man hath seen nor can see,* 1 Tim. vi. 16. They saw the place where the God of Israel stood (so the LXX.), something that came near a similitude, but was not; whatever they saw, it was certainly something of which no image nor picture could be made, and yet enough to satisfy them that God was with them of a truth. Nothing is described but that which was under his feet; for our conceptions of God are all below him, and fall infinitely short of being adequate. They saw not so much as God's feet; but at the bottom of the brightness, and as the footstool or pedestal of it, they saw a most rich and splendid pavement, such as they never saw before nor after, as it had been of sapphires, azure or sky-coloured. The heavens themselves are the pavement of God's palace, and his throne is above the firmament. See how much better wisdom is than the precious onyx or the sapphires, for wisdom was from eternity God's delight (Prov. viii. 30), and lay in his bosom, but the sapphires are the pavement under his feet; there let us put all the wealth of this world, and not in our hearts. 2. *Upon the nobles* (or elders) *of Israel, he laid not his hand, v.* 11. Though they were men, the dazzling splendour of his glory did not overwhelm them; but it was so moderated (Job xxvi. 9), and they were so strengthened (Dan. x. 19), that they were able to bear it. Nay, though they were sinful men, and obnoxious to God's justice, yet he did not lay his punishing avenging hand upon them, as they feared he would. When we consider what a consuming fire God is, and what stubble we are before him, we shall have reason to say, in all our approaches to him, *It is of the Lord's mercies that we are not consumed.* 3. *They saw God, and did eat and drink.* They had not only their lives preserved, but their vigour, courage, and comfort; it cast no damp upon their joy, but rather increased and elevated it. They *feasted upon the sacrifice,* before God, in token of their cheerful consent to the covenant now made, their grateful acceptance of the benefits of it, and their communion with God, in pursuance of that covenant. Thus believers *eat and drink with Christ at his table,* Luke xxii. 30. Blessed are those that shall eat bread in the kingdom of our Father, and drink of the wine new there.

12 And the LORD said unto Moses, Come up to me into the mount, and be there: and I will give thee tables of stone, and a law, and commandments which I have written; that thou mayest teach them. 13 And Moses rose up, and his minister Joshua: and Moses went up into the mount of God. 14 And he said unto the elders, Tarry ye here for us, until we come again unto you: and, behold, Aaron and Hur *are* with you: if any man have any matters to do, let him come unto them. 15 And Moses went up into the mount, and a cloud covered the mount. 16 And the glory of the LORD abode upon mount Sinai, and the cloud covered it six days: and the seventh day he called unto Moses out of the midst of the cloud. 17 And the sight of the glory of the LORD *was* like devouring fire on the top of the mount in the eyes of the children of Israel. 18 And Moses went into the midst of the cloud, and gat him up into the mount: and Moses was in the mount forty days and forty nights.

The public ceremony of sealing the covenant being over, Moses is called up to re-

ceive further instructions, which we have in the following chapters.

I. He is called up into the mount, and there he remains six days at some distance. Orders are given him (*v.* 12): *Come up to the mount, and be there,* that is, "Expect to continue there for some considerable time." Those that would have communion with God must not only come to ordinances, but they must abide by them. Blessed are those that dwell in his house, not that merely call there. "Come up, and *I will give thee a law, that thou mayest teach them.*" Moses taught them nothing but what he had received from the Lord, and he received nothing from the Lord but what he taught them; for he was faithful both to God and Israel, and did neither add nor diminish, but kept close to his instructions. Having received these orders, 1. He appointed Aaron and Hur to be as lords-justices in his absence, to keep the peace and good order in the congregation, *v.* 14. The care of his government he would leave behind him when he went up into the mount, that he might not have that to distract his mind; and yet he would not leave the people as sheep having no shepherd, no, not for a few days. Good princes find their government a constant care, and their people find it a constant blessing. 2. He took Joshua up with him into the mount, *v.* 13. Joshua was his minister, and it would be a satisfaction to him to have him with him as a companion, during the six days that he tarried in the mount, before God called to him. Joshua was to be his successor, and therefore thus he was honoured before the people, above the rest of the elders, that they might afterwards the more readily take him for their governor; and thus he was prepared for service, by being trained up in communion with God. Joshua was a type of Christ, and (as the learned bishop Pearson well observes) Moses takes him with him into the mount, because without Jesus, in whom are hid all the treasures of wisdom and knowledge, there is no looking into the secrets of heaven, nor approaching the glorious presence of God. 3. A cloud covered the mount six days, a visible token of God's special presence there, for he so shows himself to us as at the same time to conceal himself from us. He lets us know so much as to assure us of his presence, power, and grace, but intimates to us that we cannot find him out to perfection. During these six days Moses staid waiting upon the mountain for a call into the presence-chamber, *v.* 15, 16. God thus tried the patience of Moses, and his obedience to that command (*v.* 12), *Be there.* If Moses had been tired before the seventh day (as Saul, 1 Sam. xiii. 8, 9), and had said, *What should I wait for the Lord any longer?* he would have lost the honour of entering into the cloud; but communion with God is worth waiting for. And it is fit we should address ourselves to solemn ordinances with a solemn pause, taking time to compose ourselves, Ps. cviii. 1.

II. He is called up into a cloud on the seventh day, probably on the sabbath day, *v.* 16. Now, 1. The thick cloud opened in the sight of all Israel, and the glory of the Lord broke forth *like devouring fire, v.* 17. God, even our God, is a consuming fire, and so he was pleased to manifest himself in the giving of the law, that, knowing the terrors of the Lord, we may be persuaded to obey, and may by them be prepared for the comforts of the gospel, and that the *grace and truth* which come by Jesus Christ may be the more acceptable. 2. The entrance of Moses into the cloud was very wonderful: *Moses went into the midst of the cloud, v.* 18. It was an extraordinary presence of mind which the grace of God furnished him with by his six days' preparation, else he durst not have ventured into the cloud, especially when it broke out in devouring fire. Moses was sure that he who called him would protect him; and even those glorious attributes of God which are most terrible to the wicked the saints with a humble reverence rejoice in. He that walks righteously, and speaks uprightly, is able to *dwell even with this devouring fire,* as we are told, Isa. xxxiii. 14, 15. There are persons and works that will abide the fire, 1 Cor. iii. 12, &c., and some that will have confidence before God. 3. His continuance in the cloud was no less wonderful; he was there *forty days and forty nights.* It should seem, the six days (*v.* 16) were not part of the forty; for, during those six days, Moses was with Joshua, who did eat of the manna, and drink of the brook, mentioned, Deut. ix. 21, and while they were together it is probable that Moses did eat and drink with him; but when Moses was called *into the midst of the cloud* he left Joshua without, who continued to eat and drink daily while he waited for Moses's return, but thenceforward Moses fasted. Doubtless God could have said what he had now to say to Moses in one day, but, for the greater solemnity of the thing, he kept him with him in the mount *forty days and forty nights.* We are hereby taught to spend much time in communion with God, and to think that time best spent which is so spent. Those that would get the knowledge of God's will must meditate *thereon day and night.*

CHAP. XXV.

At this chapter begins an account of the orders and instructions God gave to Moses upon the mount for the erecting and furnishing of a tabernacle to the honour of God. We have here, I. Orders given for a collection to be made among the people for this purpose, ver. 1–9. II. Particular instructions, 1. Concerning the ark of the covenant, ver. 10–22. 2. The table of shewbread, ver. 23–30. 3. The golden candlestick, ver. 31, &c.

AND the LORD spake unto Moses, saying, 2 Speak unto the children of Israel, that they bring me an offering; of every man that giveth it willingly with his heart ye shall take my offering. 3 And this *is* the offering which ye shall take of them; gold, and silver, and brass, 4 And blue, and purple, and scarlet, and fine linen, and goats' *hair,* 5 And rams' skins dyed red, and badgers' skins, and shittim wood, 6 Oil for the light, spices for anointing oil, and for sweet incense, 7 Onyx stones, and stones to be set in the ephod, and in the breastplate. 8 And let them make me a sanctuary; that I may dwell among them. 9 According to all that I show thee, *after* the pattern of the tabernacle, and the pattern of all the instruments thereof, even so shall ye make *it.*

We may suppose that when Moses went into the midst of the cloud, and abode there so long, where the holy angels attended the *shechinah,* or divine Majesty, he saw and heard very glorious things relating to the upper world, but they were things which it was not lawful nor possible to utter; and therefore, in the records he kept of the transactions there, he says nothing to satisfy the curiosity of those who would intrude into the things which they have not seen, but writes that only which he was to speak to the children of Israel. For the scripture is designed to direct us in our duty, not to fill our heads with speculations, nor to please our fancies.

In these verses God tells Moses his intention in general, that the children of Israel should build him a sanctuary, for he designed to *dwell among them* (*v.* 8); and some think that, though there were altars and groves used for religious worship before this, yet there never was any house, or temple, built for sacred uses in any nation before this tabernacle was erected by Moses, and that all the temples which were afterwards so much celebrated among the heathen took rise from this and pattern by it. God had chosen the people of Israel to be a peculiar people to himself (above all people), among whom divine revelation, and a religion according to it, should be lodged and established: he himself would be their King. As their King, he had already given them laws for the government of themselves, and their dealings one with another, with some general rules for religious worship, according to the light of reason and the law of nature, in the ten commandments and the following comments upon them. But this was not thought sufficient to distinguish them from other nations, or to answer to the extent of that covenant which God would make with them to be *their God;* and therefore,

I. He orders a royal palace to be set up among them for himself, here called a *sanctuary,* or *holy place,* or *habitation,* of which it is said (Jer. xvii. 12), *A glorious high* throne from the beginning is the place of our sanctuary. This sanctuary is to be considered,

1. As ceremonial, consonant to the other institutions of that dispensation, which consisted in carnal ordinances (Heb. ix. 10); hence it is called a *worldly sanctuary*, Heb. ix. 1. God in it kept his court, as Israel's King. (1.) There he manifested his presence among them, and it was intended for a sign or token of his presence, that, while they had that in the midst of them, they might never again ask, *Is the Lord among us or not?* And, because in the wilderness they dwelt in tents, even this royal palace was ordered to be a tabernacle too, that it might move with them, and might be an instance of the condescension of the divine favour. (2.) There he ordered his subjects to attend him with their homage and tribute. Thither they must come to consult his oracles, thither they must bring their sacrifices, and there all Israel must meet, to pay their joint respects to the God of Israel.

2. As typical; the holy places made with hands were the *figures of the true*, Heb. ix. 24. The gospel church is the true *tabernacle, which the Lord hath pitched, and not man*, Heb. viii. 2. The body of Christ, in and by which he made atonement, was the *greater and more perfect tabernacle*, Heb. ix. 11. *The Word was made flesh, and dwelt among us*, as in a tabernacle.

II. When Moses was to erect this palace, it was requisite that he should first be instructed where he must have the materials, and where he must have the model; for he could neither contrive it by his own ingenuity nor build it at his own charge; he is therefore directed here concerning both.

1. The people must furnish him with the materials, not by a tax imposed upon them, but by a voluntary contribution. This is the first thing concerning which orders are here given.

(1.) *Speak unto the children of Israel that they bring me an offering;* and there was all the reason in the world that they should, for (v. 1), [1.] It was God himself that had not only enlarged them, but enriched them with the spoils of the Egyptians. He had instructed them to borrow, and he had inclined the Egyptians to lend, so that from him they had their wealth, and therefore it was fit they should devote it to him and use it for him, and thus make a grateful acknowledgment of the favours they had received. Note, *First*, The best use we can make of our worldly wealth is to honour God with it in works of piety and charity. *Secondly*, When we have been blessed with some remarkable success in our affairs, and have had, as we say, a good turn, it may be justly expected that we should do something more than ordinary for the glory of God, consecrating our gain, in some reasonable proportion of it, to the Lord of the whole earth, Mic. iv. 13. [2.]

The sanctuary that was to be built was intended for their benefit and comfort, and therefore they must be at the expense of it. They had been unworthy of the privilege if they had grudged at the charge. They might well afford to offer liberally for the honour of God, while they lived at free quarters, having food for themselves and their families rained upon them daily from heaven. We also must own that we have our all from God's bounty, and therefore ought to use all for his glory. Since we live upon him, we must live to him.

(2.) This offering must be given willingly, and with the heart, that is, [1.] It was not prescribed to them what or how much they must give, but it was left to their generosity, that they might show their good-will to the house of God and the offices thereof, and might do it with a holy emulation, the zeal of a few *provoking many*, 2 Cor. ix. 2. We should ask, not only, "What must we do?" but, "What may we do for God?" [2.] Whatever they gave, they must give it cheerfully, not grudgingly and with reluctance, for *God loves a cheerful giver*, 2 Cor. ix. 7. What is laid out in the service of God we must reckon well bestowed.

(3.) The particulars are here mentioned which they must offer (*v.* 3—7), all of them things that there would be occasion for in the tabernacle, or the service of it. Some observe that here was gold, silver, and brass, provided, but no iron; that is the military metal, and this was to be a house of peace. Every thing that was provided was very rich and fine, and the best of the sort; for God, who is the best, should have the best.

2. God himself would furnish him with the model: *According to all that I show thee, v.* 9. God showed him an exact plan of it, in miniature, which he must conform to in all points. Thus Ezekiel saw in vision the form of the house and the fashion thereof, Ezek. xliii. 11. Note, Whatsoever is done in God's service must be done by his direction, and not otherwise. Yet God did not only show him the model, but gave him also particular directions how to frame the tabernacle according to that model, in all the parts of it, which he goes over distinctly in this and the following chapters. When Moses, in the beginning of Genesis, was to describe the creation of the world, though it is such a stately and curious fabric and made up of such a variety and vast number of particulars, yet he gave a very short and general account of it, and nothing compared with what the wisdom of this world would have desired and expected from one that wrote by divine revelation; but, when he comes to describe the tabernacle, he does it with the greatest niceness and accuracy imaginable. He that gave us no account of the lines and circles of the globe, the diameter of the earth, or the height and magnitude of the stars, has told us particularly the measure of every

board and curtain of the tabernacle; for God's church and instituted religion are more precious to him and more considerable than all the rest of the world. And the scriptures were written, not to describe to us the works of nature, a general view of which is sufficient to lead us to the knowledge and service of the Creator, but to acquaint us with the methods of grace, and those things which are purely matters of divine revelation. The blessedness of the future state is more fully represented under the notion of a new Jerusalem than under the notion of new heavens and a new earth.

10 And they shall make an ark *of* shittim wood: two cubits and a half *shall be* the length thereof, and a cubit and a half the breadth thereof, and a cubit and a half the height thereof. 11 And thou shalt overlay it with pure gold, within and without shalt thou overlay it, and shalt make upon it a crown of gold round about. 12 And thou shalt cast four rings of gold for it, and put *them* in the four corners thereof; and two rings *shall be* in the one side of it, and two rings in the other side of it. 13 And thou shalt make staves *of* shittim wood, and overlay them with gold. 14 And thou shalt put the staves into the rings by the sides of the ark, that the ark may be borne with them. 15 The staves shall be in the rings of the ark: they shall not be taken from it. 16 And thou shalt put into the ark the testimony which I shall give thee. 17 And thou shalt make a mercy seat *of* pure gold: two cubits and a half *shall be* the length thereof, and a cubit and a half the breadth thereof. 18 And thou shalt make two cherubims *of* gold, *of* beaten work shalt thou make them, in the two ends of the mercy seat. 19 And make one cherub on the one end, and the other cherub on the other end: *even* of the mercy seat shall ye make the cherubims on the two ends thereof. 20 And the cherubims shall stretch forth *their* wings on high, covering the mercy seat with their wings, and their faces *shall look* one to another; toward the mercy seat shall the faces of the cherubims be. 21 And thou shalt put the mercy seat above upon the ark; and in the ark thou shalt put the testimony that I

shall give thee. 22 And there I will meet with thee, and I will commune with thee from above the mercy seat, from between the two cherubims which *are* upon the ark of the testimony, of all *things* which I will give thee in commandment unto the children of Israel.

The first thing which is here ordered to be made is the ark with its appurtenances, the furniture of the most holy place, and the special token of God's presence, for which the tabernacle was erected to be the receptacle.

I. The ark itself was a chest, or coffer, in which the two tables of the law, written with the finger of God, were to be honourably deposited, and carefully kept. The dimensions of it are exactly ordered; if the Jewish cubit was, as some learned men compute, three inches longer than our half-yard (twenty-one inches in all), this chest or cabinet was about fifty-two inches long, thirty-one broad, and thirty-one deep. It was overlaid within and without with thin plates of gold. It had a crown, or cornice, of gold, round it, with rings and staves to carry it with; and in it he must put the testimony, *v.* 10—16. The tables of the law are called the *testimony* because God did in them testify his will: his giving them that law was in token of his favour to them; and their acceptance of it was in token of their subjection and obedience to him. This law was a testimony to them, to direct them in their duty, and would be a testimony against them if they transgressed. The ark is called the *ark of the testimony* (ch. xxx. 6), and the tabernacle *the tabernacle of the testimony* (Num. x. 11) or witness, Acts vii. 44. The gospel of Christ is also called a testimony or witness, Matt. xxiv. 14. It is observable, 1. That the tables of the law were carefully preserved in the ark for the purpose, to teach us to make much of the word of God, and to hide it in our hearts, in our innermost thoughts, as the ark was placed in the holy of holies. It intimates likewise the care which divine Providence ever did, and ever will, take to preserve the records of divine revelation in the church, so that even in the latter days there shall be seen in his temple the *ark of his testament.* See Rev. xi. 19. 2. That this ark was the chief token of God's presence, which teaches us that the first and great evidence and assurance of God's favour is the putting of his law in the heart. God dwells where that rules, Heb. viii. 10. 3. That provision was made for the carrying of this ark about with them in all their removals, which intimates to us that, wherever we go, we should take our religion along with us, always bearing about with us the love of the Lord Jesus, and his law.

II. The mercy-seat was the covering of the ark or chest, made of solid gold, exactly to fit the dimensions of the ark, *v.* 17, 21. This *propitiatory covering*, as it might well be translated, was a type of Christ, the great propitiation, whose satisfaction fully answers the demands of the law, covers our transgressions, and comes between us and the curse we deserve. Thus he is the *end of the law for righteousness.*

III. The cherubim of gold were fixed to the mercy-seat, and of a piece with it, and spread their wings over it, *v.* 18. It is supposed that these cherubim were designed to represent the holy angels, who always attended the *shechinah*, or divine Majesty, particularly at the giving of the law; not by any effigies of an angel, but some emblem of the angelical nature, probably some one of those four faces spoken of, Ezek. i. 10. Whatever the faces were, they looked one towards another, and both downward towards the ark, while their wings were stretched out so as to touch one another. The apostle calls them *cherubim of glory shadowing the mercy-seat*, Heb. ix. 5. It denotes their attendance upon the Redeemer, to whom they were ministering spirits, their readiness to do his will, their special presence in the assemblies of saints (Ps. lxviii. 17; 1 Cor. xi. 10), and their desire to look into the mysteries of the gospel which they diligently contemplate, 1 Pet. i. 12. God is said to dwell, or sit, *between the cherubim*, on the mercy-seat (Ps. lxxx. 1), and thence he here promises, for the future, to meet with Moses, and to *commune with him*, *v.* 22. There he would give law, and there he would give audience, as a prince on his throne; and thus he manifests himself willing to be reconciled to us, and keep up communion with us, in and by the mediation of Christ. In allusion to this mercy-seat, we are said to come boldly to *the throne of grace* (Heb. iv. 16); for we *are not under the law*, which is covered, *but under grace*, which is displayed; its wings are stretched out, and we are invited to come under the shadow of them, Ruth ii. 12.

23 Thou shalt also make a table *of* shittim wood: two cubits *shall be* the length thereof, and a cubit the breadth thereof, and a cubit and a half the height thereof. 24 And thou shalt overlay it with pure gold, and make thereto a crown of gold round about. 25 And thou shalt make unto it a border of a hand breadth round about, and thou shalt make a golden crown to the border thereof round about. 26 And thou shalt make for it four rings of gold, and put the rings in the four corners that *are* on the four feet thereof. 27 Over against the border shall the rings be for places of the staves to bear the table. 28 And thou

shalt make the staves *of* shittim wood, and overlay them with gold, that the table may be borne with them. 29 And thou shalt make the dishes thereof, and spoons thereof, and covers thereof, and bowls thereof, to cover withal : *of* pure gold shalt thou make them. 30 And thou shalt set upon the table showbread before me alway.

Here is, 1. A table ordered to be made of wood overlaid with gold, which was to stand, not in the holy of holies (nothing was in that but the ark with its appurtenances), but in the outer part of the tabernacle, called the *sanctuary*, or *holy place*, Heb. ix. 2, 23, &c. There must also be the usual furniture of the sideboard, dishes and spoons, &c., and all *of gold*, *v.* 29. 2. This table was to be always spread, and furnished with the show-bread (*v.* 30) or *bread of faces*, twelve loaves, one for each tribe, set in two rows, six in a row; see the law concerning them, Lev. xxiv. 5, &c. The tabernacle being God's house, in which he was pleased to say that he would dwell among them, he would show that he kept a good house. In the royal palace it was fit that there should be a royal table. Some make the twelve loaves to represent the twelve tribes, set before God as his people and *the corn of his floor*, as they are called, Isa. xxi. 10. As the ark signified God's being present with them, so the twelve loaves signified their being presented to God. This bread was designed to be, (1.) A thankful acknowledgment of God's goodness to them, in giving them their daily bread, manna in the wilderness, where he prepared a table for them, and, in Canaan, the corn of the land. Hereby they owned their dependence upon Providence, not only for the corn in the field, which they gave thanks for in offering the sheaf of first-fruits, but for the bread in their houses, that, when it was brought home, God did not *blow upon it*, Hag. i. 9. Christ has taught us to pray every day for the bread of the day. (2.) A token of their communion with God. This bread on God's table being made of the same corn with the bread on their own tables, God and Israel did, as it were, eat together, as a pledge of friendship and fellowship; he supped with them, and they with him. (3.) A type of the spiritual provision which is made in the church, by the gospel of Christ, for all that are made priests to our God. *In our Father's house there is bread enough and to spare*, a loaf for every tribe. All that attend in God's house shall be abundantly satisfied with the goodness of it, Ps. xxxvi. 8. Divine consolations are the continual feast of holy souls, notwithstanding there are those to whom *the table of the Lord*, and the *meat thereof* (because it is plain bread), are *contemptible*, Mal. i. 12. Christ has a table in his kingdom, at which all his saints shall for ever eat and drink with him, Luke xxii. 30.

31 And thou shalt make a candlestick *of* pure gold : *of* beaten work shall the candlestick be made : his shaft, and his branches, his bowls, his knops, and his flowers, shall be of the same. 32 And six branches shall come out of the sides of it ; three branches of the candlestick out of the one side, and three branches of the candlestick out of the other side : 33 Three bowls made like unto almonds, *with* a knop and a flower in one branch; and three bowls made like almonds in the other branch, *with* a knop and a flower : so in the six branches that come out of the candlestick. 34 And in the candlestick *shall be* four bowls made like unto almonds, *with* their knops and their flowers. 35 And *there shall be* a knop under two branches of the same, and a knop under two branches of the same, and a knop under two branches of the same, according to the six branches that proceed out of the candlestick. 36 Their knops and their branches shall be of the same : all of it *shall be* one beaten work *of* pure gold. 37 And thou shalt make the seven lamps thereof : and they shall light the lamps thereof, that they may give light over against it. 38 And the tongs thereof, and the snuffdishes thereof, *shall be of* pure gold. 39 *Of* a talent of pure gold shall he make it, with all these vessels. 40 And look that thou make *them* after their pattern, which was showed thee in the mount.

I. The next thing ordered to be made for the furnishing of God's palace was a rich stately candlestick, all of pure gold, not hollow, but solid. The particular directions here given concerning it show, 1. That it was very magnificent, and a great ornament to the place ; it had many branches drawn from the main shaft, which had not only their bowls (to put the oil and the kindled wick in) for necessity, but knops and flowers for ornament. 2. That it was very convenient, and admirably contrived both to scatter the light and to keep the tabernacle clean from smoke and snuffs. 3. That it was very significant. The tabernacle had no windows by which to let in the light of the day, all its light was candle-light, which intimates the comparative darkness of that dispensation, while the Sun of righteousness had not as yet risen, nor had the day-star from on high yet visited his

church. Yet God left not himself without witness, nor them without instruction ; the commandment was a lamp, and the law a light, and the prophets were branches from that lamp, which gave light in their several ages to the Old-Testament church. The church is still dark, as the tabernacle was, in comparison with what it will be in heaven ; but the word of God is the candlestick, *a light shining in a dark place* (2 Pet. i. 19), and a dark place indeed the world would be without it. The Spirit of God, in his various gifts and graces, is compared to the *seven lamps* which *burn before the throne*, Rev. iv. 5. The churches are golden candlesticks, the lights of the world, *holding forth the word of life* as the candlestick does the light, Phil. ii 15, 16. Ministers are to light the lamps, and snuff them (*v.* 37), by opening the scriptures. The treasure of this light is now put into *earthen vessels*, 2 Cor. iv. 6, 7. The branches of the candlestick spread every way, to denote the diffusing of the light of the gospel into all parts by the Christian ministry, Matt. v. 14, 15. There is a *diversity of gifts*, but the same Spirit gives to each to profit withal.

II. There is in the midst of these instructions an express caution given to Moses, to take heed of varying from his model : *Make them after the pattern shown thee, v.* 40. Nothing was left to his own invention, or the fancy of the workmen, or the people's humour; but the will of God must be religiously observed in every particular. Thus, 1. All God's providences are exactly according to his counsels, and the copy never varies from the original. Infinite Wisdom never changes its measures ; whatever is purposed shall undoubtedly be performed. 2. All his ordinances must be administered according to his institutions. Christ's instruction to his disciples (Matt. xxviii. 20) is similar to this · *Observe all things whatsoever I have commanded you.*

CHAP. XXVI.

Moses here receives instructions, I. Concerning the inner curtains of the tent or tabernacle, and the coupling of those curtains, ver. 1—6. II. Concerning the outer curtains which were of goats' hair, to strengthen the former, ver. 7—13. III. Concerning the case or cover which was to secure it from the weather, ver. 14. IV. Concerning the boards which were to be reared up to support the curtains, with their bars and sockets, ver. 15—30. V. The partition between the holy place and the most holy, ver. 31—35. VI. The veil for the door, ver. 36, 37. These particulars, thus largely recorded, seem of little use to us now ; yet, having been of great use to Moses and Israel, and God having thought fit to preserve down to us the remembrance of them, we ought not to overlook them. Even the antiquity renders this account venerable.

MOREOVER thou shalt make the tabernacle *with* ten curtains *of* fine twined linen, and blue, and purple, and scarlet : *with* cherubims of cunning work shalt thou make them. 2 The length of one curtain *shall be* eight and twenty cubits, and the breadth of one curtain four cubits : and every one of the curtains shall have one measure. 3 The five curtains shall be coupled together one to another; and *other* five curtains *shall be* coupled one to another. 4 And thou shalt make loops of blue upon the edge of the one curtain from the selvedge in the coupling; and likewise shalt thou make in the uttermost edge of *another* curtain, in the coupling of the second. 5 Fifty loops shalt thou make in the one curtain, and fifty loops shalt thou make in the edge of the curtain that *is* in the coupling of the second; that the loops may take hold one of another. 6 And thou shalt make fifty taches of gold, and couple the curtains together with the taches: and it shall be one tabernacle.

I. The house must be a *tabernacle* or *tent,* such as soldiers now use in the camp, which was both a mean dwelling and a movable one; and yet the ark of God had no better, till Solomon built the temple 480 years after this, 1 Kings vi. 1. God manifested his presence among them thus in a tabernacle, 1. In compliance with their present condition in the wilderness, that they might have him with them wherever they went. Note, God suits the tokens of his favour, and the gifts of his grace, to his people's wants and necessities, according as they are, accommodating his mercy to their state, prosperous or adverse, settled or unsettled. *When thou passest through the waters, I will be with thee,* Isa. xliii. 2. 2. That it might represent the state of God's church in this world, it is a *tabernacle-state,* Ps. xv. 1. *We have here no continuing city;* being strangers in this world, and travellers towards a better, we shall never be fixed till we come to heaven. Church-privileges are movable goods, from one place to another; the gospel is not tied to any place; the candlestick is in a tent, and may easily be taken away, Rev. ii. 5. If we make much of the tabernacle, and improve the privilege of it, wherever we go it will accompany us; but, if we neglect and disgrace it, wherever we stay it will forsake us. *What hath my beloved to do in my house?* Jer. xi. 15.

II. The curtains of the tabernacle must correspond to a divine pattern. 1. They were to be very rich, the best of the kind, *fine twined linen;* and colours very pleasing, *blue,* and *purple,* and *scarlet.* 2. They were to be embroidered with cherubim (*v.* 1), to intimate that the angels of God pitch their tents round about the church, Ps. xxxiv. 7. As there were cherubim over the mercy-seat, so there were round the tabernacle; for we find the angels compassing, not only the throne, but the elders; see Rev. v. 11. 3. There were to be two hangings, five breadths in each, sewed together, and the two hangings coupled

together with golden clasps, or tacks, so that it might be all one tabernacle, *v.* 6. Thus the churches of Christ and the saints, though they are many, are yet one, being *fitly joined together* in holy love, and by the *unity of the Spirit,* so growing into one *holy temple* in *the Lord,* Eph. ii. 21, 22; iv. 16. This tabernacle was very strait and narrow; but, at the preaching of the gospel, the church is bidden to *enlarge the place of her tent,* and to *stretch forth her curtains,* Isa. liv. 2.

7 And thou shalt make curtains *of* goats' *hair* to be a covering upon the tabernacle: eleven curtains shalt thou make. 8 The length of one curtain *shall be* thirty cubits, and the breadth of one curtain four cubits: and the eleven curtains *shall be all* of one measure. 9 And thou shalt couple five curtains by themselves, and six curtains by themselves, and shalt double the sixth curtain in the forefront of the tabernacle. 10 And thou shalt make fifty loops on the edge of the one curtain *that is* outmost in the coupling, and fifty loops in the edge of the curtain which coupleth the second. 11 And thou shalt make fifty taches of brass, and put the taches into the loops, and couple the tent together, that it may be one. 12 And the remnant that remaineth of the curtains of the tent, the half curtain that remaineth, shall hang over the backside of the tabernacle. 13 And a cubit on the one side, and a cubit on the other side of that which remaineth in the length of the curtains of the tent, it shall hang over the sides of the tabernacle on this side and on that side, to cover it. 14 And thou shalt make a covering for the tent *of* rams' skins dyed red, and a covering above *of* badgers' skins.

Moses is here ordered to make a double covering for the tabernacle, that it might not rain in, and that the beauty of those fine curtains might not be damaged. 1. There was to be a covering of hair camlet curtains, which were somewhat larger every way than the inner curtains, because they were to enclose them, and probably were stretched out at some little distance from them, *v.* 7, &c. These were coupled together with brass clasps. The stuff being less valuable, the tacks were so; but the brass tacks would answer the intention as effectually as the golden ones. The bonds of unity may be as strong between curtains of goats' hair as between those of purple and scarlet. 2. Over this there was to be another covering, and that a double one (*v.* 14), one of *rams' skins dyed red,* probably dressed with the wool on ; another of *badgers' skins,* so we translate it, but it should rather seem to have been some strong sort of leather (but very fine), for we read of the best sort of shoes being made of it, Ezek. xvi. 10. Now observe here, (1.) That the outside of the tabernacle was coarse and rough, the beauty of it was in the inner curtains. Those in whom God dwells must labour to be better than they seem to be. Hypocrites put the best side outwards, like *whited sepulchres ;* but *the king's daughter is all glorious within* (Ps. xlv. 13) ; in the eye of the world black as the tents of Kedar, but, in the eye of God, comely as the curtains of Solomon, Cant. i. 5. Let our adorning be that of the hidden man of the heart, which God values, 1 Pet. iii. 4. (2.) That where God places his glory he will create a defence upon it ; even upon the habitations of the righteous there shall be a covert, Isa. vi. 5, 6. The protection of Providence shall always be upon the beauty of holiness. God's tent will be a pavilion, Ps. xxvii. 5.

15 And thou shalt make boards for the tabernacle *of* shittim wood standing up. 16 Ten cubits *shall be* the length of a board, and a cubit and a half *shall be* the breadth of one board. 17 Two tenons *shall there be* in one board, set in order one against another : thus shalt thou make for all the boards of the tabernacle. 18 And thou shalt make the boards for the tabernacle, twenty boards on the south side southward. 19 And thou shalt make forty sockets of silver under the twenty boards ; two sockets under one board for his two tenons, and two sockets under another board for his two tenons. 20 And for the second side of the tabernacle on the north side *there shall be* twenty boards : 21 And their forty sockets *of* silver ; two sockets under one board, and two sockets under another board. 22 And for the sides of the tabernacle westward thou shalt make six boards. 23 And two boards shalt thou make for the corners of the tabernacle in the two sides. 24 And they shall be coupled together beneath, and they shall be coupled together above the head of it unto one ring : thus shall it be for them both ; they shall be for the two corners. 25 And they shall be eight boards, and their sockets *of* silver, sixteen sockets ; two sockets

under one board, and two sockets under another board. 26 And thou shalt make bars *of* shittim wood ; five for the boards of the one side of the tabernacle, 27 And five bars for the boards of the other side of the tabernacle, and five bars for the boards of the side of the tabernacle, for the two sides westward. 28 And the middle bar in the midst of the boards shall reach from end to end. 29 And thou shalt overlay the boards with gold, and make their rings *of* gold *for* places for the bars : and thou shalt overlay the bars with gold. 30 And thou shalt rear up the tabernacle according to the fashion thereof which was showed thee in the mount.

Very particular directions are here given about the boards of the tabernacle, which were to bear up the curtains, as the stakes of a tent which had need to be strong, Isa. liv. 2. These boards had tenons which fell into the mortises that were made for them in silver bases. God took care to have every thing strong, as well as fine, in his tabernacle. Curtains without boards would have been shaken by every wind ; but *it is a good thing* to have the *heart established with grace,* which is as the boards to support the curtains of profession, which otherwise will not hold out long. The boards were coupled together with gold rings at top and bottom (*v.* 24), and kept firm with bars that ran through golden staples in every board (*v.* 26), and the boards and bars were all richly gilded, *v.* 29. Thus every thing in the tabernacle was very splendid, agreeable to that infant state of the church, when such things were proper enough to please children, to possess the minds of the worshippers with a reverence of the divine glory, and to affect them with the greatness of that prince who said, *Here will I dwell ;* in allusion to this the new Jerusalem is said to be of *pure gold,* Rev. xxi. 18. But the builders of the gospel church said, *Silver and gold have we none ;* and yet the glory of their building far exceeded that of the tabernacle, 2 Cor. iii. 10, 11. *How much better is wisdom than gold !* No orders are given here about the floor of the tabernacle ; probably that also was boarded ; for we cannot think that within all these fine curtains they trod upon the cold or wet ground ; if it was so left, it may remind us of *ch.* xx. 24, *An altar of earth shalt thou make unto me.*

31 And thou shalt make a veil *of* blue, and purple, and scarlet, and fine twined linen of cunning work : with cherubims shall it be made : 32 And thou shalt hang it upon four pillars

of shittim *wood* overlaid with gold : their hooks *shall be of* gold, upon the four sockets of silver. 33 And thou shalt hang up the veil under the taches, that thou mayest bring in thither within the veil the ark of the testimony : and the veil shall divide unto you between the holy *place* and the most holy. 34 And thou shalt put the mercy seat upon the ark of the testimony in the most holy *place*. 35 And thou shalt set the table without the veil, and the candlestick over against the table on the side of the tabernacle toward the south: and thou shalt put the table on the north side. 26 And thou shalt make a hanging for the door of the tent, *of* blue, and purple, and scarlet, and fine twined linen, wrought with needlework. 37 And thou shalt make for the hanging five pillars *of* shittim *wood*, and overlay them with gold, *and* their hooks *shall be of* gold: and thou shalt cast five sockets of brass for them.

Two veils are here ordered to be made, 1. One for a partition between the holy place and the most holy, which not only forbade any to enter, but forbade them so much as to look into the holiest of all, *v.* 31, 33. Under that dispensation, divine grace was veiled, but now we behold it with open face, 2 Cor. iii. 18. The apostle tells us (Heb. ix. 8, 9) what was the meaning of this veil ; it intimated that the ceremonial law *could not make the comers thereunto perfect*, nor would the observance of it bring men to heaven ; the *way into the holiest of all was not made manifest while the first tabernacle was standing ; life and immortality* lay concealed till they were *brought to light by the gospel*, which was therefore signified by the rending of this veil at the death of Christ, Matt. xxvii. 51. We have now *boldness to enter into the holiest*, in all acts of devotion, *by the blood of Jesus*, yet such as obliges us to a holy reverence and a humble sense of our distance. 2. Another veil was for the outer door of the tabernacle, *v.* 36, 37. Through this first veil the priests went in every day to minister in the holy place, but not the people, Heb. ix. 6. This veil, which was all the defence the tabernacle had against thieves and robbers, might easily be broken through, for it could be neither locked nor barred, and the abundance of wealth in the tabernacle, one would think, might be a temptation ; but by leaving it thus exposed, (1.) The priests and Levites would be so much the more obliged to keep a strict watch upon it, and, (2.) God would show his care of his church on earth,

388

though it is weak and defenceless, and continually exposed. A curtain shall be (if God please to make it so) as strong a defence to his house as gates of brass and bars of iron.

CHAP. XXVII.

In this chapter directions are given, I. Concerning the brazen altar for burnt-offerings, ver. 1—8. II. Concerning the court of the tabernacle, with the hangings of it, ver. 9—19. III. Concerning oil for the lamp, ver. 20, 21.

AND thou shalt make an altar *of* shittim wood, five cubits long, and five cubits broad ; the altar shall be foursquare: and the height thereof *shall be* three cubits. 2 And thou shalt make the horns of it upon the four corners thereof: his horns shall be of the same : and thou shalt overlay it with brass. 3 And thou shalt make his pans to receive his ashes, and his shovels, and his basins, and his fleshhooks, and his fire-pans : all the vessels thereof thou shalt make *of* brass. 4 And thou shalt make for it a grate of net-work *of* brass; and upon the net shalt thou make four brazen rings in the four corners thereof. 5 And thou shalt put it under the compass of the altar beneath, that the net may be even to the midst of the altar. 6 And thou shalt make staves for the altar, staves *of* shittim wood, and overlay them with brass. 7 And the staves shall be put into the rings, and the staves shall be upon the two sides of the altar, to bear it. 8 Hollow with boards shalt thou make it : as it was showed thee in the mount, so shall they make *it*.

As God intended in the tabernacle to manifest his presence among his people, so there they were to pay their devotions to him, not in the tabernacle itself (into that only the priests entered as God's domestic servants), but in the court before the tabernacle, where, as common subjects, they attended. There an altar was ordered to be set up, to which they must bring their sacrifices, and on which their priests must offer them to God : and this altar was to sanctify their gifts. Here they were to present their services to God, as from the mercy-seat he gave his oracles to them ; and thus a communion was settled between God and Israel. Moses is here directed about, 1. The dimensions of it ; it was square, *v.* 1. 2. The horns of it (*v.* 2), which were for ornament and for use ; the sacrifices were *bound with cords to the horns of the altar*, and to them malefactors fled for refuge. 3. The materials ; it was of wood overlaid with brass, *v.* 1, 2. 4. The appurtenances of it (*v.* 3), which were all of brass. 5. The grate, which was let into the hollow of the altar, about the middle of it, in which the fire was kept, and the sacrifice burnt; it was made of network like a sieve, and hung hollow, that the fire might burn the better, and that the ashes might fall through into the hollow of the altar, *v.* 4, 5. 6. The staves with which it must be carried, *v.* 6, 7. And, *lastly*, he is referred to the pattern shown him, *v.* 8.

Now this brazen altar was a type of Christ dying to make atonement for our sins: the wood would have been consumed by the fire from heaven if it had not been secured by the brass; nor could the human nature of Christ have borne the wrath of God if it had not been supported by a divine power. Christ sanctified himself for his church, as their altar (John xvii. 19), and by his mediation sanctifies the daily services of his people, who have also *a right to eat of this altar* (Heb. xiii. 10), for they serve at it as spiritual priests. To the horns of this altar poor sinners fly for refuge when justice pursues them, and they are safe in virtue of the sacrifice there offered.

9 And thou shalt make the court of the tabernacle: for the south side southward *there shall be* hangings for the court *of* fine twined linen of a hundred cubits long for one side: 10 And the twenty pillars thereof and their twenty sockets *shall be of* brass; the hooks of the pillars and their fillets *shall be of* silver. 11 And likewise for the north side in length *there shall be* hangings of a hundred *cubits* long, and his twenty pillars and their twenty sockets *of* brass; the hooks of the pillars and their fillets *of* silver. 12 And *for* the breadth of the court on the west side *shall be* hangings of fifty cubits: their pillars ten, and their sockets ten. 13 And the breadth of the court on the east side eastward *shall be* fifty cubits. 14 The hangings of one side *of the gate shall be* fifteen cubits: their pillars three, and their sockets three. 15 And on the other side *shall be* hangings fifteen *cubits;* their pillars three, and their sockets three. 16 And for the gate of the court *shall be* a hanging of twenty cubits, *of* blue, and purple, and scarlet, and fine twined linen, wrought with needle-work: *and* their pillars *shall be* four, and their sockets four. 17 All the pillars round about the court *shall be* filleted with silver; their hooks *shall be of* silver, and their sockets *of* brass. 18 The length of the court *shall be* a hundred cubits, and the breadth fifty every where, and the height five cubits *of* fine twined linen, and their sockets *of* brass. 19 All the vessels of the tabernacle in all the service thereof, and all the pins thereof, and all the pins of the court, *shall be of* brass.

Before the tabernacle there was to be a court or yard, enclosed with hangings of the finest linen that was used for tents. This court, according to the common computation of cubits, was fifty yards long, and twenty-five broad. Pillars were set up at convenient distances, in sockets of brass, the pillars filleted with silver, and silver tenter-hooks in them, on which the linen hangings were fastened: the hanging which served for the gate was finer than the rest, *v.* 16. This court was a type of the church, enclosed and distinguished from the rest of the world, the enclosure supported by pillars, denoting the stability of the church, hung with the clean linen, which is said to be the *righteousness of saints*, Rev. xix. 8. These were the courts David longed for and coveted to reside in (Ps. lxxxiv. 2, 10), and into which the people of God entered with praise and thanksgiving (Ps. c. 4); yet this court would contain but a few worshippers. Thanks be to God, now, under the gospel, the enclosure is taken down. God's will is that men *pray every where;* and there is room for all that in every place call on the name of Jesus Christ.

20 And thou shalt command the children of Israel, that they bring thee pure oil olive beaten for the light, to cause the lamp to burn always. 21 In the tabernacle of the congregation without the veil, which *is* before the testimony, Aaron and his sons shall order it from evening to morning before the LORD: *it shall be* a statute for ever unto their generations on the behalf of the children of Israel.

We read of the candlestick in the twenty-fifth chapter; here is an order given for the keeping of the lamps constantly burning in it, else it was useless; in every candlestick there should be a burning and shining light; candlesticks without candles are as *wells without water* or as *clouds without rain.* Now, 1. The people were to provide the oil; from them the Lord's ministers must have their maintenance. Or, rather, the pure oil signified the gifts and graces of the Spirit, which are communicated to all believers from Christ the good olive, of whose fulness we receive (Zech. iv. 11, 12), and without which our light cannot shine before men. 2. The priests were to light the lamps, and to tend them; it was part of their daily service to *cause the lamp to burn always*, night and day; thus it is the work of ministers, by the preaching and expounding of the scriptures (which are as a lamp), to enlighten the church, God's tabernacle upon earth, and to direct the spiritual priests in his service. This is to be *a statute for ever,* that the lamps of the word be lighted as duly as the incense of prayer and praise is offered.

CHAP. XXVIII.

Orders being given for the fitting up of the place of worship, in this and the following chapter care is taken about the priests that were to minister in this holy place, as the menial servants of the God of Israel. He hired servants, as a token of his purpose to reside among them. In this chapter, I. He pitches upon the persons who should be his servants, ver. 1. II. He appoints their livery; their work was holy, and so must their garments be, and answerable to the glory of the house which was now to be erected, ver. 2–5. 1. He appoints the garments of the head-servant, the high priest, which were very rich. (1.) An ephod and girdle, ver. 6–14. (2.) A breast-plate of judgment (ver. 15—29), in which must be put the urim and thummim, ver. 30. (3.) The robe of the ephod, ver, 31—35. (4.) The mitre, ver. 36—39. 2. The garments of the inferior priests, ver. 40–43. And these also were shadows of good things to come.

AND take thou unto thee Aaron thy brother, and his sons with him, from among the children of Israel, that he may minister unto me in the priest's office, *even* Aaron, Nadab and Abihu, Eleazar and Ithamar, Aaron's sons. 2 And thou shalt make holy garments for Aaron thy brother for glory and for beauty. 3 And thou shalt speak unto all *that are* wise hearted, whom I have filled with the spirit of wisdom, that they may make Aaron's garments to consecrate him, that he may minister unto me in the priest's office. 4 And these *are* the garments which they shall make; a breastplate, and an ephod, and a robe, and a broidered coat, a mitre, and a girdle : and they shall make holy garments for Aaron thy brother, and his sons, that he may minister unto me in the priest's office. 5 And they shall take gold, and blue, and purple, and scarlet, and fine linen.

We have here,

I. The priests nominated : *Aaron and his sons, v.* 1. Hitherto every master of a family was priest to his own family, and offered, as he saw cause, upon altars of earth; but now that the families of Israel began to be incorporated into a nation, and a *tabernacle of the congregation* was to be erected, as a visible centre of their unity, it was requisite there should be a public priesthood instituted. Moses, who had hitherto officiated, and is therefore reckoned among the *priests of the Lord* (Ps. xcix. 6), had enough to do as their prophet to consult the oracle for them, and as their prince to judge among them ; nor was he desirous to engross all the honours to himself, or to entail that of the priesthood, which alone was hereditary, upon his own family, but was very well pleased to see his brother Aaron invested in this office, and his sons

after him, while (how great soever he was) his sons after him would be but common Levites. It is an instance of the humility of that great man, and an evidence of his sincere regard for the glory of God, that he had so little regard to the preferment of his own family. Aaron, who had humbly served as a prophet to his younger brother Moses, and did not decline the office (*ch.* vii. 1), is now advanced to be a priest, a high priest, to God; for he will exalt those that abase themselves. Nor could any man have *taken this honour to himself,* but he that was *called of God to it,* Heb. v. 4. God had said of Israel in general that they should be to him a *kingdom of priests, ch.* xix. 6. But because it was requisite that those who ministered at the altar should give themselves wholly to the service, and because that which is every body's work will soon come to be nobody's work, God here chose from among them one to be a family of priests, the father and his four sons; and from Aaron's loins descended all the priests of the Jewish church, of whom we read so often, both in the Old Testament and in the New. A blessed thing it is when real holiness goes, as the ceremonial holiness did, by succession in a family.

II. The priests' garments appointed, *for glory and beauty, v.* 2. Some of the richest materials were to be provided (*v.* 5), and the best artists employed in the making of them, whose skill God, by a *special gift* for this purpose, would improve to a very high degree, *v.* 3. Note, Eminence, even in common arts, is a gift of God, it comes from him, and, as there is occasion, it ought to be used for him. He that teaches the husbandman discretion teaches the tradesman also ; both therefore ought to honour God with their gain. Human learning ought particularly to be consecrated to the service of the priesthood, and employed for the adorning of those that minister about holy things. The garments appointed were, 1. Four, which both the high priest and the inferior priests wore, namely, the linen breeches, the linen coat, the linen girdle which fastened it to them, and the bonnet or turban ; that which the high priest wore is called *a mitre.* 2. Four more, which were peculiar to the high priest, namely, the ephod, with the curious girdle of it, the breast-plate of judgment, the long robe with the bells and pomegranates at the bottom of it, and the golden plate on his forehead. These glorious garments were appointed, (1.) That the priests themselves might be reminded of the dignity of their office, and might behave themselves with due decorum. (2.) That the people might thereby be possessed with a holy reverence of that God whose ministers appeared in such grandeur. (3.) That the priests might be types of Christ, who should offer himself without spot to God, and of all Christians, who have the beauty of holiness put upon them, in which they are consecrated to God. Our adorning, now under the gospel, both that of ministers and Christians, is not to be of gold, and pearl, and costly array, but the *garments of salvation, and the robe of righteousness*, Isa. lxi. 10; Ps. cxxxii. 9, 16. As the filthy garments wherewith Joshua the high priest was clothed signified the iniquity which cleaved to his priesthood, from which care was taken that it should be purged (Zech. iii. 3, 4), so those *holy garments* signified the perfect purity that there is in the priesthood of Christ; he is holy, harmless, and undefiled.

6 And they shall make the ephod *of* gold, *of* blue, and *of* purple, *of* scarlet, and fine twined linen, with cunning work. 7 It shall have the two shoulder pieces thereof joined at the two edges thereof; and *so* it shall be joined together. 8 And the curious girdle of the ephod, which *is* upon it, shall be of the same, according to the work thereof; *even of* gold, *of* blue, and purple, and scarlet, and fine twined linen. 9 And thou shalt take two onyx stones, and grave on them the names of the children of Israel: 10 Six of their names on one stone, and *the other* six names of the rest on the other stone, according to their birth. 11 With the work of an engraver in stone, *like* the engravings of a signet, shalt thou engrave the two stones with the names of the children of Israel: thou shalt make them to be set in ouches of gold. 12 And thou shalt put the two stones upon the shoulders of the ephod *for* stones of memorial unto the children of Israel: and Aaron shall bear their names before the LORD upon his two shoulders for a memorial. 13 And thou shalt make ouches *of* gold; 14 And two chains *of* pure gold at the ends; *of* wreathen work shalt thou make them, and fasten the wreathen chains to the ouches.

Directions are here given concerning the ephod, which was the outmost garment of the high priest. *Linen* ephods were worn by the inferior priests, 1 Sam. xxii. 18. Samuel wore one when he was a child (1 Sam. ii. 18), and David when he danced before the ark (2 Sam. vi. 14); but this which the high priest only wore was called a *golden ephod*, because there was a great deal of gold woven into it. It was a short coat without sleeves, buttoned closely to him, with a curious girdle of the same stuff (*v.* 6—8); the shoulder-pieces were buttoned together with two precious stones set in gold, one on each shoulder,

on which were engraven the names of the *children of Israel, v.* 9—12. In allusion to this, 1. Christ our high priest appeared to John *girt about the breast with a golden girdle*, such as was the curious girdle of the ephod, Rev. i. 13. Righteousness is the girdle of his loins (Isa. xi. 6), and should be of ours, Eph. vi. 14. He is girt with strength for the work of our salvation, and is ready for it. 2. The government is said to be *upon his shoulders* (Isa. ix. 6), as Aaron had the names of all Israel upon his shoulders in precious stones. He presents to himself and to his Father *a glorious church*, Eph. v. 27. He has power to support them, interest to recommend them, and it is in him that they are remembered with honour and favour. He bears them before the Lord *for a memorial* (*v.* 12), in token of his *appearing before God* as the representative of all Israel and an advocate for them.

15 And thou shalt make the breastplate of judgment with cunning work; after the work of the ephod thou shalt make it; *of* gold, *of* blue, and *of* purple, and *of* scarlet, and *of* fine twined linen, shalt thou make it. 16 Four-square it shall be *being* double; a span *shall be* the length thereof, and a span *shall be* the breadth thereof. 17 And thou shalt set in it settings of stones, *even* four rows of stones: *the first* row *shall be* a sardius, a topaz, and a carbuncle: *this shall be* the first row. 18 And the second row *shall be* an emerald, a sapphire, and a diamond. 19 And the third row a ligure, an agate, and an amethyst. 20 And the fourth row a beryl, and an onyx, and a jasper: they shall be set in gold in their inclosings. 21 And the stones shall be with the names of the children of Israel, twelve, according to their names, *like* the engravings of a signet; every one with his name shall they be according to the twelve tribes. 22 And thou shalt make upon the breastplate chains at the ends *of* wreathen work *of* pure gold. 23 And thou shalt make upon the breastplate two rings of gold, and shalt put the two rings on the two ends of the breastplate. 24 And thou shalt put the two wreathen *chains* of gold in the two rings *which are* on the ends of the breastplate. 25 And *the other* two ends of the two wreathen *chains* thou shalt fasten in the two ouches,

and put *them* on the shoulderpieces of the ephod before it. 26 And thou shalt make two rings of gold, and thou shalt put them upon the two ends of the breastplate in the border thereof, which *is* in the side of the ephod inward. 27 And two *other* rings of gold thou shalt make, and shalt put them on the two sides of the ephod, underneath, toward the forepart thereof, over against the *other* coupling thereof, above the curious girdle of the ephod. 28 And they shall bind the breastplate by the rings thereof unto the rings of the ephod with a lace of blue, that *it* may be above the curious girdle of the ephod, and that the breastplate be not loosed from the ephod. 29 And Aaron shall bear the names of the children of Israel in the breastplate of judgment upon his heart, when he goeth in unto the holy *place*, for a memorial before the LORD continually. 30 And thou shalt put in the breastplate of judgment the Urim and the Thummim; and they shall be upon Aaron's heart, when he goeth in before the LORD: and Aaron shall bear the judgment of the children of Israel upon his heart before the LORD continually.

The most considerable of the ornaments of the high priest was this breast-plate, a rich piece of cloth, curiously wrought with gold and purple, &c., two spans long and a span broad, so that, being doubled, it was a span square, *v.* 16. This was fastened to the ephod with wreathen chains of gold (*v.* 13, 14, 22, &c.) both at top and bottom, so that *the breast-plate might not be loosed from the ephod, v.* 28. The ephod was the garment of service; the breast-plate of judgment was an emblem of honour: these two must by no means be separated. If any man will *minister unto the Lord*, and *do his will*, he shall *know his doctrine*. In this breast-plate,

I. The tribes of Israel were recommended to God's favour in twelve precious stones, *v.* 17—21, 29. Some question whether Levi had a precious stone with his name or no. If not, Ephraim and Manasseh were reckoned distinct, as Jacob had said they should be, and the high priest himself, being head of the tribe of Levi, sufficiently represented that tribe. If there was a stone for Levi, as is intimated by this, that they were *engraven according to their birth* (*v.* 10), Ephraim and Manasseh were one in Joseph. Aaron was to bear their names for a *memorial before the Lord continually*, being *ordained for men*, to

represent them in things pertaining to God, herein typifying our great high priest, who always appears in the presence of God for us. 1. Though the people were forbidden to come near, and obliged to keep their distance, yet by the high priest, who had their names on his breast-plate, they entered into the holiest; so believers, even while they are here on this earth, not only *enter into the holiest*, but by faith are made to *sit with Christ in heavenly places*, Eph. ii. 6. 2. The name of each tribe was engraven in a precious stone, to signify how precious, in God's sight, believers are, and how honourable, Isa. xliii. 4. They shall be his in the day he *makes up his jewels*, Mal. iii. 17. How small and poor soever the tribe was, it was a precious stone in the breast-plate of the high priest; thus are all the saints dear to Christ, and his delight is in them as the excellent ones of the earth, however men may esteem them as *earthen pitchers*, Lam. iv. 2. 3. The high priest had the names of the tribes both on his shoulders and on his breast, intimating both the power and the love with which our Lord Jesus intercedes for those that are his. He not only bears them up in his arms with an almighty strength, but he bears them *upon his heart*, as the expression here is (*v.* 29), *carries them in his bosom* (Isa. xl. 11), with the most tender affection. How near should Christ's name be to our hearts, since he is pleased to lay our names so near his! and what a comfort it is to us, in all our addresses to God, that the great high priest of our profession has the names of all his Israel upon his breast before the Lord *for a memorial*, presenting them to God as the people of his choice, who were to be made *accepted in the beloved!* Let not any good Christians fear that God has forgotten them, nor question his being mindful of them upon all occasions, when they are not only engraven upon the *palms of his hands* (Isa. xlix. 16), but engraven upon the heart of the great intercessor. See Cant. viii. 6.

II. The urim and thummim, by which the will of God was made known in doubtful cases, were put in this breast-plate, which is therefore called the *breast-plate of judgment, v.* 30. *Urim* and *thummim* signify *light* and *integrity;* many conjectures there are among the learned what they were; we have no reason to think they were any thing that Moses was to make more than what was before ordered, so that either God made them himself, and gave them to Moses, for him to put into the breast-plate, when other things were prepared (Lev. viii. 8), or no more is meant than a declaration of the further use of what was already ordered to be made. I think the words may be read thus, *And thou shalt give*, or *add*, or *deliver, to the breast-plate of judgment, the illuminations and perfections, and they shall be upon the heart of Aaron;* that is, "He shall be endued with a power of knowing and making known the mind of God in all difficult doubtful cases, relating either to the civil or ecclesiastical state of the nation." Their government was a theocracy: God was their King, the high priest was, under God, their ruler, the urim and thummim were his cabinet-council; probably Moses wrote upon the breast-plate, or wove into it, these words, *Urim* and *Thummim*, to signify that the high priest, having on him this breast-plate, and asking counsel of God in any emergency relating to the public, should be directed to take those measures, and give that advice, which God would own. If he was standing before the ark (but without the veil) probably he received instructions from off the mercy-seat, as Moses did (*ch.* xxv. 22); thus, it should seem, Phinehas did, Judg. xx. 27, 28. If he was at a distance from the ark, as Abiathar was when he enquired of the Lord for David (1 Sam. xxiii. 6, &c.), then the answer was given either by a voice from heaven or rather by an impulse upon the mind of the high priest, which last is perhaps intimated in that expression, *He shall bear the judgment of the children of Israel upon his heart.* This oracle was of great use to Israel; Joshua consulted it (Num. xxvii. 21), and, it is likely, the judges after him. It was lost in the captivity, and never regained after, though, it should seem, it was expected, Ezra ii. 63. But it was a shadow of good things to come, and the substance is Christ. He is our oracle; by him God in these last days makes known himself and his mind to us, Heb. i. 2; John i. 18. Divine revelation centres in him, and comes to us through him; he is the light, the true light, the faithful witness, the truth itself, and from him we receive the Spirit of truth, who leads into all truth. The joining of the breast-plate to the ephod denotes that his prophetical office was founded in his priesthood; and it was by the merit of his death that he purchased this honour for himself and this favour for us. It was the *Lamb that had been slain* that was worthy to *take the book,* and to *open the seals,* Rev. v. 9.

31 And thou shalt make the robe of the ephod all *of* blue. 32 And there shall be a hole in the top of it, in the midst thereof: it shall have a binding of woven work round about the hole of it, as it were the hole of a habergeon, that it be not rent. 33 And *beneath* upon the hem of it thou shalt make pomegranates *of* blue, and *of* purple, and *of* scarlet, round about the hem thereof; and bells of gold between them round about: 34 A golden bell and a pomegranate, a golden bell and a pomegranate, upon the hem of the robe round about. 35 And it shall be upon Aaron to minister: and his sound shall be heard when he goeth

in unto the holy *place* before the LORD, and when he cometh out, that he die not. 36 And thou shalt make a plate *of* pure gold, and grave upon it, *like* the engravings of a signet, HOLINESS TO THE LORD. 37 And thou shalt put it on a blue lace, that it may be upon the mitre; upon the forefront of the mitre it shall be. 38 And it shall be upon Aaron's forehead, that Aaron may bear the iniquity of the holy things, which the children of Israel shall hallow in all their holy gifts; and it shall be always upon his forehead, that they may be accepted before the LORD. 39 And thou shalt embroider the coat of fine linen, and thou shalt make the mitre *of* fine linen, and thou shalt make the girdle *of* needlework.

Here is, 1. Direction given concerning *the robe of the ephod, v.* 31—35. This was next under the ephod, and reached down to the knees, was without sleeves, and was put on over their head, having holes on the sides to put the arms through, or, as Maimonides describes it, was not sewed together on the sides at all. The hole on the top, through which the head was put, was carefully bound about, that it might not tear in the putting on. In religious worship, care must be taken to prevent every thing that may distract the minds of the worshippers, or render the service despicable. Round the skirts of the robe were hung golden bells, and the representations of pomegranates made of yarn of divers colours. The pomegranates added to the beauty of the robe, and the sound of the bells gave notice to the people in the outer court when he went into the holy place to burn incense, that they might then apply themselves to their devotions at the same time (Luke i. 10), in token of their concurrence with him in his offering, and their hopes of the ascent of their prayers to God in virtue of the incense he offered. Aaron must come near to minister in the garments that were appointed him, *that he die not.* It is at his peril if he attend otherwise than according to the institution. This intimates that we must serve the Lord *with fear* and holy *trembling,* as those that know we deserve to die, and are in danger of making some fatal mistake. Some make the bells of the holy robe to typify the sound of the gospel of Christ in the world, giving notice of his entrance within the veil for us. *Blessed are those that hear this joyful sound,* Ps. lxxxix. 15. The adding of the pomegranates, which are a fragrant fruit, denotes the sweet savour of the gospel, as well as the joyful sound of it, for it is a *savour of life unto life.* The church is called an *orchard of pomegranates.* 2. Concerning the golden plate fixed upon Aaron's forehead, on which must be engraven, *Holiness to the Lord* (v. 36, 37), or *The holiness of Jehovah.* Aaron must hereby be reminded that God is holy, and that his priests must be holy. *Holiness becomes his house* and household. The high priest must be sequestered from all pollution, and consecrated to God and to his service and honour, and so must all his ministrations be. All that attend in God's house must have *Holiness to the Lord* engraven upon their foreheads, that is, they must be holy, devoted to the Lord, and designing his glory in all they do. This must appear in their forehead, in an open profession of their relation to God, as those that are not ashamed to own it, and in a conversation in the world answerable to it. It must likewise be engraven like the engravings of a signet, so deep, so durable, not painted to be washed off, but sincere and lasting; such must our *holiness to the Lord* be. Aaron must have this upon his forehead, that he may *bear the iniquity of the holy things* (v. 38), and that *they may be accepted before the Lord.* Herein he was a type of Christ, the great Mediator between God and man, through whom it is that we have to do with God. (1.) Through him what is amiss in our services is pardoned. The divine law is strict; in many things we come short of our duty, so that we cannot but be conscious to ourselves of much iniquity cleaving even to our holy things; when we would do good evil is present; even this would be our ruin if God should enter into judgment with us. But Christ, our high priest, bears this iniquity, bears it for us so as to bear it from us, and through him it is forgiven to us and not laid to our charge. (2.) Through him what is good is accepted; our persons, our performances, are pleasing to God upon the account of Christ's intercession, and not otherwise, 1 Pet. ii. 5. His being *holiness to the Lord* recommends all those to the divine favour that are interested in his righteousness, and clothed with his Spirit; and therefore he has said it was for our sakes that he *sanctified himself,* John xvii. 19. Having *such a high priest,* we come *boldly to the throne of grace,* Heb. iv. 14—16. 3. The rest of the garments are but named (v. 39), because there was nothing extraordinary in them. The embroidered coat of fine linen was the innermost of the priestly garments; it reached to the feet, and the sleeves to the wrists, and was bound to the body with a girdle or sash of needle-work. The mitre, or diadem, was of linen, such as kings anciently wore in the east, typifying the kingly office of Christ. He is a *priest upon a throne* (Zech. vi. 13), a priest with a crown. These two God has joined, and we must not think to separate them.

40 And for Aaron's sons thou shalt

make coats, and thou shalt make for them girdles, and bonnets shalt thou make for them, for glory and for beauty. 41 And thou shalt put them upon Aaron thy brother, and his sons with him; and shalt anoint them, and consecrate them, and sanctify them, that they may minister unto me in the priest's office. 42 And thou shalt make them linen breeches to cover their nakedness; from the loins even unto the thighs they shall reach: 43 And they shall be upon Aaron, and upon his sons, when they come in unto the tabernacle of the congregation, or when they come near unto the altar to minister in the holy *place;* that they bear not iniquity, and die: *it shall be* a statute for ever unto him and his seed after him.

We have here, 1. Particular orders about the vestments of the inferior priests. They were to have coats, and girdles, and bonnets, of the same materials with those of the high priest; but there was a difference in shape between their bonnets and his mitre. Theirs, as his, were to be *for glory and beauty* (v. 40), that they might look great in their ministration: yet all this glory was nothing compared with the glory of grace, this beauty nothing to the beauty of holiness, of which these holy garments were typical. They are particularly ordered, in their ministration, to wear *linen breeches, v.* 42. This teaches us modesty and decency of garb and gesture at all times, especially in public worship, in which a veil is becoming, 1 Cor. xi. 5, 6, 10. It also intimates what need our souls have of a covering, when we come before God, that the *shame of their nakedness may not appear.* 2. A general rule concerning the garments both of the high priest and of the inferior priests, that they were to be put upon them, at first, when they were consecrated, in token of their being invested in the office (v. 41), and then they were to wear them in all their ministrations, but not at other times (v. 43), and this at their peril, lest they *bear iniquity and die.* Those who are guilty of omissions in duty, as well as omissions of duty, shall *bear their iniquity.* If the priests perform the instituted service, and do not do it in the appointed garments, it is (say the Jewish doctors) as if a stranger did it, and the *stranger that comes nigh shall be put to death.* Nor will God connive at the presumptions and irreverences even of those whom he causes to draw most near to him; if Aaron himself put a slight upon the divine institution, he shall bear iniquity, and die. To us these garments typify, (1.) The righteousness of Christ; if we appear not before God in this, we shall *bear iniquity and die.* What have we to do at the wedding-feast without a wedding-garment, or at God's altar without the array of his priests? Matt. xxii. 12, 13. (2.) *The armour of God* prescribed Eph. vi. 13. If we venture without that armour, our spiritual enemies will be the death of our souls, and we shall bear the iniquity, our blood will be upon our own heads. Blessed is he therefore that watcheth, and keepeth his garments, Rev. xvi. 15. 3. This is said to be a *statute for ever,* that is, it is to continue as long as the priesthood continues. But it is to have its perpetuity in the substance of which these things were the shadows.

CHAP. XXIX.

Particular orders are given in this chapter, I. Concerning the consecration of the priests, and the sanctification of the altar, ver. 1—37. II. Concerning the daily sacrifice, ver. 38—41. To which gracious promises are annexed that God would own and bless them in all their services, ver. 42, &c.

AND this *is* the thing that thou shalt do unto them to hallow them, to minister unto me in the priest's office: Take one young bullock, and two rams without blemish, 2 And unleavened bread, and cakes unleavened tempered with oil, and wafers unleavened anointed with oil: *of* wheaten flour shalt thou make them. 3 And thou shalt put them into one basket, and bring them in the basket, with the bullock and the two rams. 4 And Aaron and his sons thou shalt bring unto the door of the tabernacle of the congregation, and shalt wash them with water. 5 And thou shalt take the garments, and put upon Aaron the coat, and the robe of the ephod, and the ephod, and the breastplate, and gird him with the curious girdle of the ephod: 6 And thou shalt put the mitre upon his head, and put the holy crown upon the mitre. 7 Then shalt thou take the anointing oil, and pour *it* upon his head, and anoint him. 8 And thou shalt bring his sons, and put coats upon them. 9 And thou shalt gird them with girdles, Aaron and his sons, and put the bonnets on them: and the priest's office shall be their's for a perpetual statute: and thou shalt consecrate Aaron and his sons. 10 And thou shalt cause a bullock to be brought before the tabernacle of the congregation: and Aaron and his sons shall put their hands upon the head of the bullock. 11 And thou shalt kill the bullock before

the LORD, *by* the door of the tabernacle of the congregation. 12 And thou shalt take of the blood of the bullock, and put *it* upon the horns of the altar with thy finger, and pour all the blood beside the bottom of the altar. 13 And thou shalt take all the fat that covereth the inwards, and the caul *that is* above the liver, and the two kidneys, and the fat that *is* upon them, and burn *them* upon the altar. 14 But the flesh of the bullock, and his skin, and his dung, shalt thou burn with fire without the camp: it *is* a sin offering. 15 Thou shalt also take one ram; and Aaron and his sons shall put their hands upon the head of the ram. 16 And thou shalt slay the ram, and thou shalt take his blood, and sprinkle *it* round about upon the altar. 17 And thou shalt cut the ram in pieces, and wash the inwards of him, and his legs, and put *them* unto his pieces, and unto his head. 18 And thou shalt burn the whole ram upon the altar: it *is* a burnt offering unto the LORD: it *is* a sweet savour, an offering made by fire unto the LORD. 19 And thou shalt take the other ram; and Aaron and his sons shall put their hands upon the head of the ram. 20 Then shalt thou kill the ram, and take of his blood, and put *it* upon the tip of the right ear of Aaron, and upon the tip of the right ear of his sons, and upon the thumb of their right hand, and upon the great toe of their right foot, and sprinkle the blood upon the altar round about. 21 And thou shalt take of the blood that *is* upon the altar, and of the anointing oil, and sprinkle *it* upon Aaron, and upon his garments, and upon his sons, and upon the garments of his sons with him: and he shall be hallowed, and his garments, and his sons, and his sons' garments with him. 22 Also thou shalt take of the ram the fat and the rump, and the fat that covereth the inwards, and the caul *above* the liver, and the two kidneys, and the fat that *is* upon them, and the right shoulder; for it *is* a ram of consecration: 23 And one loaf of bread, and one cake of oiled bread, and one wafer out of the basket of the unleavened bread that *is* before the LORD : 24 And thou shalt put all in the hands of Aaron, and in the hands of his sons ; and shalt wave them *for* a wave offering before the LORD. 25 And thou shalt receive them of their hands, and burn *them* upon the altar for a burnt offering, for a sweet savour before the LORD : it *is* an offering made by fire unto the LORD. 26 And thou shalt take the breast of the ram of Aaron's consecration, and wave it *for* a wave offering before the LORD : and it shall be thy part. 27 And thou shalt sanctify the breast of the wave offering, and the shoulder of the heave offering, which is waved, and which is heaved up, of the ram of the consecration, *even* of *that* which *is* for Aaron, and of *that* which is for his sons : 28 And it shall be Aaron's and his sons' by a statute for ever from the children of Israel : for it *is* a heave offering : and it shall be a heave offering from the children of Israel of the sacrifice of their peace offerings, *even* their heave offering unto the LORD. 29 And the holy garments of Aaron shall be his sons' after him, to be anointed therein, and to be consecrated in them. 30 *And* that son that is priest in his stead shall put them on seven days, when he cometh into the tabernacle of the congregation to minister in the holy *place.* 31 And thou shalt take the ram of the consecration, and seethe his flesh ·n the holy place. 32 And Aaron and his sons shall eat the flesh of the ram, and the bread that *is* in the basket, *by* the door of the tabernacle of the congregation. 33 And they shall eat those things wherewith the atonement was made, to consecrate *and* to sanctify them : but a stranger shall not eat *thereof*, because they *are* holy. 34 And if aught of the flesh of the consecrations, or of the bread, remain unto the morning, then thou shalt burn the remainder with fire: it shall not be eaten, because it *is* holy. 35 And thus shalt thou do unto Aaron, and to his sons, according to all *things* which I have commanded thee: seven

396

days shalt thou consecrate them. 36 And thou shalt offer every day a bullock *for* a sin offering for atonement : and thou shalt cleanse the altar, when thou hast made an atonement for it, and thou shalt anoint it, to sanctify it. 37 Seven days thou shalt make an atonement for the altar, and sanctify it; and it shall be an altar most holy: whatsoever toucheth the altar shall be holy.

Here is, I. The law concerning the consecration of Aaron and his sons to the priest's office, which was to be done with a great deal of ceremony and solemnity, that they themselves might be duly affected with the greatness of the work to which they were called, and that the people also might learn to magnify the office and none might dare to invade it.

1. The ceremonies wherewith it was to be done were very fully and particularly appointed, because nothing of this kind had been done before, and because it was to be a statute for ever that the high priest should be thus inaugurated. Now,

(1.) The work to be done was the consecrating of the persons whom God had chosen to be priests, by which they devoted and gave up themselves to the service of God and God declared his acceptance of them ; and the people were made to know that they *glorified not themselves* to be made priests, but were *called of God*, Heb. v. 4, 5. They were thus distinguished from common men, sequestered from common services, and set apart for God and an immediate attendance on him. Note, All that are to be employed for God are to be sanctified to him. The person must first be accepted, and then the performance. The Hebrew phrase for consecrating is *filling the hand* (v. 9): *Thou shalt fill the hand of Aaron and his sons*, and the *ram of consecration* is the *ram of fillings, v.* 22, 26. The consecrating of them was the perfecting of them ; Christ is said to be *perfect* or *consecrated for evermore*, Heb. vii. 28. Probably the phrase here is borrowed from the putting of the sacrifice into their hand, to be waved before the Lord, *v.* 24. But it intimates, [1.] That ministers have their hands full ; they have no time to trifle, so great, so copious, so constant is their work. [2.] That they must have their hands filled. Of necessity *they must have something to offer*, and they cannot find it in themselves, it must be given them from above. They cannot fill the people's hearts unless God fill their hands ; to him therefore they must go, and *receive from his fulness.*

(2.) The person to do it was Moses, by God's appointment. Though he was *ordained for men*, yet the people were not to consecrate him ; Moses the *servant of the Lord*, and his agent herein, must do i\ By God's special appointment he now did the priest's work, and therefore that which was the priest's part of the sacrifice was here ordered to be his, *v.* 26.

(3.) The place was at the *door of the tabernacle of meeting, v.* 4. God was pleased to dwell in the tabernacle, the people attending in the courts, so that the door between the court and the tabernacle was the fittest place for those to be consecrated in who were to mediate between God and man, and to stand between both, and *lay their hands* (as it were) *upon both.* They were consecrated at the door, for they were to be door-keepers.

(4.) It was done with many ceremonies. [1.] They were to be washed (*v.* 4), signifying that those must be clean who *bear the vessels of the Lord,* Isa. lii. 11. Those that would *perfect holiness* must *cleanse themselves from all filthiness of flesh and spirit,* 2 Cor. vii. 1; Isa i. 16—18. They were now washed all over; but afterwards, when they went into minister, they washed only their hands and feet (*ch.* xxx. 19); for *he that is washed needs* no more, John xiii. 10.

[2.] They were to be clothed with the holy garments (*v.* 5, 6, 8, 9), to signify that it was not sufficient for them to put away the pollutions of sin, but they must put on the graces of the Spirit, be *clothed with righteousness,* Ps. cxxxii. 9. They must be girded, as men prepared and strengthened for their work; and they must be robed and crowned, as men that counted their work and office their true honour.

[3.] The high priest was to be anointed with the *holy anointing oil* (*v.* 7), that the church might be filled and delighted with the sweet savour of his administrations (for *ointment and perfume rejoice the heart),* and in token of the pouring out of the Spirit upon him, to qualify him for his work. Brotherly love is compared to this oil with which Aaron was anointed, Ps. cxxxiii. 2. The inferior priests are said to be anointed (*ch.* xxx. 30), not on their heads, as the high priest (Lev. xxi. 10), the oil was only mingled with the blood that was sprinkled upon their garments.

[4.] Sacrifices were to be offered for them. The covenant of priesthood, as all other covenants, must be *made by sacrifice.*

First, There must be a sin-offering, to make atonement for them, *v.* 10—14. The law made those priests that had infirmity, and therefore they must first offer for their own sin, before they could make atonement *for the people,* Heb. vii. 27, 28. They were to put their hand on the head of their sacrifice (*v.* 10), confessing that they deserved to die for their own sin, and desiring that the killing of the beast might expiate their guilt, and be accepted as a vicarious satisfaction. It was used as other sin-offerings were; only, whereas the flesh of other sin-offerings was eaten by the priests (Lev. x. 18), in token of the priest's taking away the sin of the people, this was appointed to be all burnt without the camp (*v.* 14), to signify the imper-

fection of the legal dispensation (as the learned bishop Patrick notes); for the sins of the priests themselves could not be taken away by those sacrifices, but they must expect a better high priest and a better sacrifice.

Secondly, There must be a burnt-offering, a ram wholly burnt, to the honour of God, in token of the dedication of themselves wholly to God and to his service, as living sacrifices, kindled with the fire and ascending in the flame of holy love, *v.* 15—18. The sin-offering must first be offered and then the burnt-offering; for, till guilt be removed, no acceptable service can be performed, Isa. vi. 7.

Thirdly, There must be a peace-offering; it is called *the ram of consecration,* because there was more in this peculiar to the occasion than in the other two. In the burnt-offering God had the glory of their priesthood, in this they had the comfort of it; and, in token of a mutual covenant between God and them, 1. The blood of the sacrifice was divided between God and them (*v.* 20, 21); part of the blood was *sprinkled upon the altar round about,* and part put upon them, upon their bodies (*v.* 20), and upon their garments, *v.* 21. Thus the benefit of the expiation made by the sacrifice was applied and assured to them, and their whole selves from head to foot sanctified to the service of God. The blood was put upon the extreme parts of the body, to signify that it was all, as it were, enclosed and taken in for God, the tip of the ear and the great toe not excepted. We reckon that the blood and oil sprinkled upon garments spot and stain them; yet the holy oil, and the blood of the sacrifice, sprinkled upon their garments, must be looked upon as the greatest adorning imaginable to them, for they signified the blood of Christ, and the graces of the Spirit, which constitute and complete the beauty of holiness, and recommend us to God; we read of robes made *white with the blood of the Lamb.* 2. The *flesh of the sacrifice,* with the meat-offering annexed to it, was likewise divided between God and them, that (to speak with reverence) God and they might feast together, in token of friendship and fellowship. (1.) Part of it was to be first waved before the Lord, and then burnt upon the altar; part of the *flesh* (*v.* 22), part of the *bread,* for bread and flesh must go together (*v.* 23); these were first put into the hands of Aaron to be waved to and fro, in token of their being offered to God (who, though unseen, yet compasses us round on every side), and then they were to be burnt upon the altar (*v.* 24, 25), for the altar was to devour God's part of the sacrifice. Thus God admitted Aaron and his sons to be his servants, and wait at his table, taking the meat of his altar from their hands. Here, in a parenthesis, as it were, comes in the law concerning the priests' part of the peace-offerings afterwards, the breast and shoulder, which were now divided; Moses had the

397

breast, and the shoulder was burnt on the altar with God's part, *v.* 26—28. (2.) The other part, both of the flesh of the ram and of the bread, Aaron and his sons were to eat at the door of the tabernacle (*v.* 31—33), to signify that he called them not only *servants* but *friends,* John xv. 15. He *supped with them,* and *they with him.* Their eating of the things wherewith *the atonement was made* signified their *receiving the atonement,* as the expression is (Rom. v. 11), their thankful acceptance of the benefit of it, and their joyful communion with God thereupon, which was the true intent and meaning of a feast upon a sacrifice. If any of it was left, it must be burnt, that it might not be in any danger of putrefying, and to show that it was an extraordinary peace-offering.

2. The time that was to be spent in this consecration: *Seven days shalt thou consecrate them,* v. 35. Though all the ceremonies were performed on the first day, yet, (1.) They were not to look upon their consecration as completed till the seven days' end, which put a solemnity upon their admission, and a distance between this and their former state, and obliged them to enter upon their work with a pause, giving them time to consider the weight and seriousness of it. This was to be observed in after-ages, *v.* 30. He that was to succeed Aaron in the high-priesthood must put on the holy garments seven days together, in token of a deliberate and gradual advance into his office, and that one sabbath might pass over him in his consecration. (2.) Every day of the seven, in this first consecration, a bullock was to be offered for a sin-offering (*v.* 36), which was to intimate to them, [1.] That it was of very great concern to them to get their sins pardoned, and that though atonement was made, and they had the comfort of it, yet they must still keep up a penitent sense of sin and often repeat the confession of it. [2.] That those sacrifices which were thus offered day by day to make atonement could not make the *comers thereunto perfect,* for then they would have ceased to be offered, as the apostle argues, Heb. x. 1, 2. They must therefore expect the *bringing in of a better hope.*

3. This consecration of the priests was a *shadow of good things to come.* (1.) Our Lord Jesus is the great high-priest of our profession, called of God to be so, consecrated for evermore, anointed with the Spirit above his fellows (whence he is called *Messiah,* the *Christ*), clothed with the holy garments, even with glory and beauty, sanctified by his own blood, not that of bullocks and rams (Heb. ix. 12), *made perfect,* or consecrated, *through sufferings,* Heb. ii. 10. Thus in him this was a perpetual statute, *v.* 9. (2.) All believers are spiritual priests, to offer spiritual sacrifices (1 Pet. ii. 5), washed in the blood of Christ, and so *made to our God priests,* Rev. i. 5, 6. They also are clothed with the beauty of holiness, and have received the anointing,

1 John ii. 27. Their hands are filled with work, to which they must continually attend; and it is through Christ, the great sacrifice, that they are dedicated to this service. His blood *sprinkled upon the conscience purges it from dead works, that they may,* as priests, *serve the living God.* The Spirit of God (as Ainsworth notes) is called the *finger of God* (Luke xi. 20, compared with Matt. xii. 28), and by him the merit of Christ is effectually applied to our souls, as here Moses with his finger was to put the blood upon Aaron. It is likewise intimated that gospel ministers are to be solemnly set apart to the work of the ministry with great deliberation and seriousness both in the ordainers and in the ordained, as those that are to be employed in a great work and entrusted with a great charge.

II. The consecration of the altar, which seems to have been coincident with that of the priests, and the sin-offerings which were offered every day for seven days together had reference to the altar as well as the priests, *v.* 36, 37. An *atonement* was *made for the altar.* Though that was not a subject capable of sin, nor, having never yet been used, could it be said to be polluted with the sins of the people, yet, since the fall, there can be no sanctification to God but there must first be *an atonement for sin,* which renders us both unworthy and unfit to be employed for God. The altar was also *sanctified,* not only set apart itself to a sacred use, but made so holy as to *sanctify the gifts* that were offered upon it, Matt. xxiii. 19. Christ is our altar; for our sakes he sanctified himself, that we and our performances might be sanctified and recommended to God, John xvii. 19.

38 Now this *is that* which thou shalt offer upon the altar; two lambs of the first year day by day continually. 39 The one lamb thou shalt offer in the morning; and the other lamb thou shalt offer at even: 40 And with the one lamb a tenth deal of flour mingled with the fourth part of a hin of beaten oil; and the fourth part of a hin of wine *for* a drink offering. 41 And the other lamb thou shalt offer at even, and shalt do thereto according to the meat offering of the morning, and according to the drink offering thereof, for a sweet savour, an offering made by fire unto the Lord. 42 *This shall be* a continual burnt offering throughout your generations *at* the door of the tabernacle of the congregation before the Lord: where I will meet you, to speak there unto thee. 43 And there I will meet with the children of Israel, and *the taber-*

nacle shall be sanctified by my glory. 44 And I will sanctify the tabernacle of the congregation, and the altar: I will sanctify also both Aaron and his sons, to minister to me in the priest's office. 45 And I will dwell among the children of Israel, and will be their God. 46 And they shall know that I *am* the LORD their God, that brought them forth out of the land of Egypt, that I may dwell among them: I *am* the LORD their God.

In this paragraph we have,

I. The daily service appointed. A lamb was to be offered upon the altar every morning, and a lamb every evening, each with a meat-offering, both made by fire, as a *continual burnt-offering throughout their generations, v.* 38—41. Whether there were any other sacrifices to be offered or not, these were sure to be offered, at the public charge, for the benefit and comfort of all Israel, to make atonement for their daily sins, and to be an acknowledgment to God of their daily mercies. This was that which *the duty of every day required.* The taking away of this daily sacrifice by Antiochus, for so many evenings and mornings, was that great calamity of the church which was foretold, Dan. viii. 11. Now, 1. This typified the continual intercession which Christ ever lives to make, in virtue of his satisfaction, for the continual sanctification of his church: though he offered himself *once for all,* yet that one offering thus becomes a continual offering. 2. This teaches us to offer up to God the spiritual sacrifices of prayer and praise every day, morning and evening, in humble acknowledgment of our dependence upon him and our obligations to him. Our daily devotions must be looked upon as the most needful of our daily works and the most pleasant of our daily comforts. Whatever business we have, this must never be omitted, either morning or evening; prayer-time must be kept up as duly as meat-time. The daily sacrifices were as the daily meals in God's house, and therefore they were always attended with bread and wine. Those starve their own souls that keep not up a constant attendance on the throne of grace.

II. Great and precious promises made of God's favour to Israel, and the tokens of his special presence with them, while they thus kept up his institutions among them. He speaks as one well pleased with the appointment of the daily sacrifice; for, before he proceeds to the other appointments that follow, he interposes these promises. It is constancy in religion that brings in the comfort of it. He promises, 1. That he would keep up communion with them; that he would not only meet Moses, and speak to him, but that he would *meet the children of Israel (v.*

43), to accept the daily sacrifices offered up on their behalf. Note, God will not fail to give those the meeting who diligently and conscientiously attend upon him in the ordinances of his own appointment. 2. That he would own his own institutions, the tabernacle, the altar, the priesthood (*v.* 43, 44); he would take possession of that which was consecrated to him. Note, What is sanctified to the glory of God shall be sanctified by his glory. If we do our part, God will do his, and will mark and fit that for himself which is in sincerity given up to him. 3. That he would reside among them as a God in covenant with them, and would give them sure and comfortable tokens of his peculiar favour to them, and his special presence with them (*v.* 45, 46): *I will dwell among the children of Israel.* Note, Where God sets up the tabernacle of his ordinances he will himself dwell. *Lo, I am with you always,* Matt. xxviii. 20. Those that abide in God's house shall have God to abide with them. *I will be their God, and they shall know* that I am so. Note, Those are truly happy that have a covenant-interest in God as theirs and the comfortable evidence of that interest. If we have this, we have enough, and need no more to make us happy.

CHAP. XXX.

AND thou shalt make an altar to burn incense upon: *of* shittim wood shalt thou make it. 2 A cubit *shall be* the length thereof, and a cubit the breadth thereof; foursquare shall it be: and two cubits *shall be* the height thereof: the horns thereof *shall be* of the same. 3 And thou shalt overlay it with pure gold, the top thereof, and the sides thereof round about, and the horns thereof; and thou shalt make unto it a crown of gold round about. 4 And two golden rings shalt thou make to it under the crown of it, by the two corners thereof, upon the two sides of it shalt thou make *it ;* and they shall be for places for the staves to bear it withal. 5 And thou shalt make the staves *of* shittim wood, and overlay them with gold. 6 And thou shalt put it before the veil that *is* by the ark of the testimony, before the mercy seat that *is* over the testimony, where I will meet with thee. 7 And Aaron shall burn thereon sweet incense every morning: when he dresseth the lamps, he shall burn incense upon it. 8 And when Aaron lighteth the lamps at even, he shall burn incense upon it, a perpetual incense before the LORD throughout your generations. 9 Ye shall offer no strange incense thereon, nor burnt sacrifice, nor meat offering; neither shall ye pour drink offering thereon. 10 And Aaron shall make an atonement upon the horns of it once in a year with the blood of the sin offering of atonements: once in the year shall he make atonement upon it throughout your generations: it *is* most holy unto the LORD.

I. The orders given concerning the altar of incense are, 1. That it was to be made of wood, and covered with gold, pure gold, about a yard high and half a yard square, with horns at the corners, a golden cornice round it, with rings and staves of gold, for the convenience of carrying it, *v.* 1—5. It does not appear that there was any grate to this altar for the ashes to fall into, that they might be taken away; but, when they burnt incense, a golden censer was brought with coals in it, and placed upon the altar, and in that censer the incense was burnt, and with it all the coals were taken away, so that no coals nor ashes fell upon the altar. The measure of the altar of incense in Ezekiel's temple is double to what it is here (Ezek. xli. 22), and it is there called *an altar of wood*, and there is no mention of gold, to signify that the incense, in gospel times, should be spiritual, the worship plain, and the service of God enlarged, for *in every place incense should be offered*, Mal. i. 11. 2. That it was to be placed before the veil, on the outside of that partition, but before the mercy-seat, which was within the veil, *v.* 6. For though he that ministered at the altar could not see the mercy-seat, the veil interposing, yet he must look towards it, and direct his incense that way, to teach us that though we cannot with our bodily eyes see the throne of grace, that blessed mercy-seat (for it is such a throne of glory that God, in compassion to us, holds back the face of it, and spreads a cloud upon it), yet we must in prayer by faith set ourselves before it, direct our prayer, and look up. 3. That Aaron was to burn sweet incense upon this altar, every morning and every evening, about half a pound at a time, which was intended, not only to take away the ill smell of the flesh that was burnt daily on the brazen altar, but for the honour of God, and to show the acceptableness of his people's services to him, and the pleasure which they should take in ministering to him, *v.* 7, 8. As by the offerings on the brazen altar satisfaction was made for what

had been done displeasing to God, so, by the offering on this, what they did well was, as it were, recommended to the divine acceptance; for our two great concerns with God are to be acquitted from guilt and accepted as righteous in his sight. 4. That nothing was to be offered upon it but incense, nor any incense but that which was appointed, *v.* 9. God will have his own service done according to his own appointment, and not otherwise. 5. That this altar should be purified with the blood of the sin-offering put upon the *horns of it*, every year, upon *the day of atonement, v.* 10. See Lev. xvi. 18, 19. The high priest was to take this in his way, as he came out from the holy of holies. This was to intimate to them that the sins of the priests who ministered at this altar, and of the people for whom they ministered, put a ceremonial impurity upon it, from which it must be cleansed by the blood of atonement.

II. This incense-altar typified, 1. The mediation of Christ. The brazen altar in the court was a type of Christ dying on earth; the golden altar in the sanctuary was a type of Christ interceding in heaven, in virtue of his satisfaction. This altar was before the mercy-seat; for Christ always appears in the presence of God for us; he is our *advocate with the father* (1 John ii. 1), and his intercession is unto God of a sweet-smelling savour. This altar had a crown fixed to it; for Christ intercedes as a king. *Father, I will*, John xvii. 24. 2. The devotions of the saints, whose prayers are said to be set forth before God as incense, Ps. cxli. 2. As the smoke of the incense ascended, so must our desires towards God rise in prayer, being kindled with the fire of holy love and other pious affections. When the priest was burning incense the people were praying (Luke i. 10), to signify that prayer is the true incense. This incense was offered daily, it was a perpetual incense (*v.* 8); for we must pray always, that is, we must keep up stated times for prayer every day, morning and evening, at least, and never omit it, but thus pray without ceasing. The lamps were dressed or lighted at the same time that the incense was burnt, to teach us that the reading of the scriptures (which are our light and lamp) is a part of our daily work, and should ordinarily accompany our prayers and praises. When we speak to God we must hear what God says to us, and thus the communion is complete. The devotions of sanctified souls are well-pleasing to God, of a sweet-smelling savour; the prayers of saints are compared to sweet odours (Rev. v. 8), but it is the incense which Christ adds to them that makes them acceptable (Rev. viii. 3), and his blood that atones for the guilt which cleaves to our best services. And, if the heart and life be not holy, even *incense is an abomination* (Isa. i. 13), and he that offers it is *as if he blessed an idol*, Isa. lxvi. 3.

11 And the LORD spake unto Moses, saying, 12 When thou takest the sum of the children of Israel after their number, then shall they give every man a ransom for his soul unto the LORD, when thou numberest them; that there be no plague among them, when *thou* numberest them. 13 This they shall give, every one that passeth among them that are numbered, half a shekel after the shekel of the sanctuary: (a shekel *is* twenty gerahs:) a half shekel *shall be* the offering of the LORD. 14 Every one that passeth among them that are numbered, from twenty years old and above, shall give an offering unto the LORD. 15 The rich shall not give more, and the poor shall not give less than half a shekel, when *they* give an offering unto the LORD, to make an atonement for your souls. 16 And thou shalt take the atonement money of the children of Israel, and shalt appoint it for the service of the tabernacle of the congregation; that it may be a memorial unto the children of Israel before the LORD, to make an atonement for your souls.

Some observe that the repetition of those words, *The Lord spoke unto Moses*, here and afterwards (v. 17, 22, 34), intimates that God did not deliver these precepts to Moses in the mount, in a continued discourse, but with many intermissions, giving him time either to write what was said to him or at least to charge his memory with it. Christ gave instructions to his disciples as they were able to hear them. Moses is here ordered to levy money upon the people by way of poll, so much a head, for the service of the tabernacle. This he must do when he numbered the people. Some think that it refers only to the first numbering of them, now when the tabernacle was set up; and that this tax was to make up what was deficient in the voluntary contributions for the finishing of the work, or rather for the beginning of the service in the tabernacle. Others think that it was afterwards repeated upon any emergency and always when the people were numbered, and that David offended in not demanding it when he numbered the people. But many of the Jewish writers, and others from them, are of opinion that it was to be an annual tribute, only it was begun when Moses first numbered the people. This was that tribute-money which Christ paid, for fear of offending his adversaries (Matt. xvii. 27), when yet he showed good reason why

he should have been excused. Men were appointed in every city to receive this payment yearly. Now, 1. The tribute to be paid was *half a shekel*, about fifteen pence of our money. The rich were not to give more, nor the poor less (v. 15), to intimate that the souls of the rich and poor are alike precious, and that God is *no respecter of persons*, Acts x. 34; Job xxxiv. 19. In other offerings men were to give according to their ability; but this, which was the *ransom of the soul*, must be alike for all; for the rich have as much need of Christ as the poor, and the poor are as welcome to him as the rich. They both alike contributed to the maintenance of the temple-service, because both were to have a like interest in it and benefit by it. In Christ and his ordinances *rich and poor meet together; the Lord is the Maker*, the Lord Christ is the Redeemer of them both, Prov. xxii. 2. The Jews say, "If a man refused to pay this tribute, he was not comprehended in the expiation." 2. This tribute was to be paid as a *ransom of the soul, that there might be no plague among them.* Hereby they acknowledged that they received their lives from God, that they had forfeited their lives to him, and that they depended upon his power and patience for the continuance of them; and thus they did homage to the God of their lives, and deprecated those plagues which their sins had deserved. 3. This money that was raised was to be employed in the service of the tabernacle (v. 16); with it they bought sacrifices, flour, incense, wine, oil, fuel, salt, priests' garments, and all other things which the whole congregation was interested in. Note, Those that have the benefit of God's tabernacle among them must be willing to defray the expenses of it, and not grudge the necessary charges of God's public worship. Thus we must honour the Lord with our substance, and reckon that best laid out which is laid out in the service of God. Money indeed cannot make an *atonement for the soul*, but it may be used for the honour of him who has made the atonement, and for the maintenance of the gospel by which the atonement is applied.

17 And the LORD spake unto Moses, saying, 18 Thou shalt also make a laver *of* brass, and his foot *also of* brass, to wash *withal:* and thou shalt put it between the tabernacle of the congregation and the altar, and thou shalt put water therein. 19 For Aaron and his sons shall wash their hands and their feet thereat: 20 When they go into the tabernacle of the congregation, they shall wash with water, that they die not; or when they come near to the altar to minister, to burn an offering made by fire unto the LORD:

21 So they shall wash their hands and their feet, that they die not: and it shall be a statute for ever to them, *even* to him and to his seed throughout their generations.

Orders are here given, 1. For the making of a laver, or font, of brass, a large vessel, that would contain a good quantity of water, which was to be set near the door of the tabernacle, *v.* 18. The foot of brass, it is supposed, was so contrived as to receive the water, which was let into it out of the laver by spouts or cocks. They then had a laver for the priests only to wash in, but to us now there is a fountain open for Judah and Jerusalem to wash in (Zech. xiii. 1), an inexhaustible *fountain of living water,* so that it is our own fault if we remain in our pollution. 2. For the using of this laver. Aaron and his sons must wash their hands and feet at this laver every time they went in to minister, every morning, at least, *v.* 19—21. For this purpose clean water was put into the laver fresh every day. Though they washed themselves ever so clean at their own houses, that would not serve; they must wash at the laver, because that was appointed for washing, 2 Kings v. 12—14. This was designed, (1.) To teach them purity in all their ministrations, and to possess them with a reverence of God's holiness and a dread of the pollutions of sin. They must not only wash and be made clean when they were first consecrated, but they must wash and be kept clean whenever they went in to minister. He only shall *stand in God's holy place* that has *clean hands and a pure heart,* Ps. xxiv. 3, 4. And, (2.) It was to teach us, who are daily to attend upon God, daily to renew our repentance for sin and our believing application of the blood of Christ to our souls for remission; for in many things we daily offend and contract pollution, John xiii. 8, 10; Jam. iii. 2. This is the preparation we are to make for solemn ordinances. *Cleanse your hands and purify your hearts,* and then *draw nigh to God,* Jam. iv. 8. To this law David alludes in Ps. xxvi. 6, *I will wash my hands in innocency, so will I compass thine altar, O Lord.*

22 Moreover the LORD spake unto Moses, saying, 23 Take thou also unto thee principal spices, of pure myrrh five hundred *shekels,* and of sweet cinnamon half so much, *even* two hundred and fifty *shekels,* and of sweet calamus two hundred and fifty *shekels,* 24 And of cassia five hundred *shekels,* after the shekel of the sanctuary, and of oil olive a hin: 25 And thou shalt make it an oil of holy ointment, an ointment compound after the art of the apothecary: it shall be a holy anointing oil. 26 And thou shalt anoint the tabernacle of the congregation therewith, and the ark of the testimony, 27 And the table and all his vessels, and the candlestick and his vessels, and the altar of incense, 28 And the altar of burnt offering with all his vessels, and the laver and his foot. 29 And thou shalt sanctify them, that they may be most holy: whatsoever toucheth them shall be holy. 30 And thou shalt anoint Aaron and his sons, and consecrate them, that *they* may minister unto me in the priest's office. 31 And thou shalt speak unto the children of Israel, saying, This shall be a holy anointing oil unto me throughout your generations. 32 Upon man's flesh shall it not be poured, neither shall ye make *any other* like it, after the composition of it: it *is* holy, *and* it shall be holy unto you. 33 Whosoever compoundeth *any* like it, or whosoever putteth *any* of it upon a stranger, shall even be cut off from his people. 34 And the LORD said unto Moses, Take unto thee sweet spices, stacte, and onycha, and galbanum; *these* sweet spices with pure frankincense: of each shall there be a like *weight:* 35 And thou shalt make it a perfume, a confection after the art of the apothecary, tempered together, pure *and* holy: 36 And thou shall beat *some* of it very small, and put of it before the testimony in the tabernacle of the congregation, where I will meet with thee: it shall be unto you most holy. 37 And *as for* the perfume which thou shalt make, ye shall not make to yourselves according to the composition thereof: it shall be unto thee holy for the LORD. 38 Whosoever shall make like unto that, to smell thereto, shall even be cut off from his people.

Directions are here given for the composition of the holy anointing oil and the incense that were to be used in the service of the tabernacle; with these God was to be honoured, and therefore he would appoint the making of them; for nothing comes *to* God but what comes *from* him. 1. The holy anointing oil is here ordered to be made up: the ingredients, and their quantities, are prescribed, *v.* 23—25 Interpreters are not agreed concerning them; we are sure, in general, they were the best and fittest for the purpose; they must needs be so when the divine wisdom appointed them for the divine honour. It was to be compounded *secundum artem—after the art of the apothecary* (v. 25); the spices, which were in all nearly half a hundred weight, were to be infused in the oil, which was to be about five or six quarts, and then strained out, leaving an admirable sweet smell in the oil. With this oil God's tent and all the furniture of it were to be anointed; it was to be used also in the consecration of the priests, v. 26—30. It was to be continued *throughout their generations*, v. 31. The tradition of the Jews is that this very oil which was prepared by Moses himself lasted till near the captivity. But bishop Patrick shows the great improbability of the tradition, and supposes that it was repeated according to the prescription here, for Solomon was anointed with it (1 Kings i. 39), and some other of the kings; and all the high priests with such a quantity of it that it ran down to the skirts of the garments; and we read of the making up of this ointment (1 Chron. ix. 30): yet all agree that in the second temple there was none of this holy oil, which he supposes was owing to a notion they had that it was not lawful to make it up, Providence overruling that want as a presage of the better unction of the Holy Ghost in gospel times, the variety of whose gifts was typified by these several sweet ingredients. To show the excellency of holiness, there was that in the tabernacle which was in the highest degree grateful both to the sight and to the smell. Christ's name is said to be as *ointment poured forth* (Cant. i. 3), and the good name of Christians better than *precious ointment*, Eccl. vii. 1. 2. The incense which was burned upon the golden altar was prepared of sweet spices likewise, though not so rare and rich as those of which the anointing oil was compounded, v. 34, 35. This was prepared once a year (the Jews say), a pound for each day of the year, and three pounds over for the day of atonement. When it was used, it was to be beaten very small: thus it pleased the Lord to bruise the Redeemer when he offered himself for a sacrifice of a sweet-smelling savour. 3. Concerning both these preparations the same law is here given (v. 32, 33, 37, 38), that the like should not be made for any common use. Thus God would preserve in the people's minds a reverence for his own institutions, and teach us not to profane nor abuse any thing whereby God makes himself known, as those did who invented to themselves (for their common entertainments) instruments of music like David, Amos vi. 5. It is a great affront to God to jest with sacred things, particularly to make sport with the word and ordinances of God, or to treat them with lightness, Matt. xxii. 5. That which is God's peculiar must not be used as a common thing.

CHAP. XXXI.

God is here drawing towards a conclusion of what he had to say to Moses upon the mount, where he had now been with him forty days and forty nights; and yet no more is recorded of what was said to him in all that time than what we have read in the six chapters foregoing. In this, I. He appoints what workmen should be employed in the building and furnishing of the tabernacle, ver. 1—11. II. He repeats the law of the sabbath, and the religious observance of it, ver. 12—17. III. He delivers to him the two tables of the testimony at parting, ver. 18.

AND the LORD spake unto Moses, saying, 2 See, I have called by name Bezaleel the son of Uri, the son of Hur, of the tribe of Judah: 3 And I have filled him with the spirit of God, in wisdom, and in understanding, and in knowledge, and in all manner of workmanship, 4 To devise cunning works, to work in gold, and in silver, and in brass, 5 And in cutting of stones, to set *them*, and in carving of timber, to work in all manner of workmanship. 6 And I, behold, I have given with him Aholiab, the son of Ahisamach, of the tribe of Dan: and in the hearts of all that are wise hearted I have put wisdom, that they may make all that I have commanded thee; 7 The tabernacle of the congregation, and the ark of the testimony, and the mercy seat that *is* thereupon, and all the furniture of the tabernacle, 8 And the table and his furniture, and the pure candlestick with all his furniture, and the altar of incense, 9 And the altar of burnt offering with all his furniture, and the laver and his foot, 10 And the cloths of service, and the holy garments for Aaron the priest, and the garments of his sons, to minister in the priest's office, 11 And the anointing oil, and sweet incense for the holy *place:* according to all that I have commanded thee shall they do.

A great deal of fine work God had ordered to be done about the tabernacle; the materials the people were to provide, but who must put them into form? Moses himself was learned in all the learning of the Egyptians, nay, he was well acquainted with the words of God, and the visions of the Almighty; but he knew not how to engrave or embroider. We may suppose that there were some very ingenious men among the Israelites; but, having lived all their days in bondage in Egypt, we cannot think they were any of them instructed in these curious arts. They knew how to make brick and work in clay, but to work in gold and in cutting diamonds was what they had never been brought up to. How should the work be done with the neatness and exactness that were required when they had no goldsmiths or jewellers but what must be made out of masons and bricklayers? We may suppose that there were a sufficient number who would gladly be employed, and would do their best; but it would be hard to find out a proper person to preside in this work. *Who was sufficient for these things?* But God takes care of this matter also.

I. He nominates the persons that were to be employed, that there might be no contest about the preferment, nor envy at those that were preferred, God himself having made the choice. 1. Bezaleel was to be the architect, or master workman, *v.* 2. He was of the tribe of Judah, a tribe that God delighted to honour; the grandson of Hur, probably that Hur who had helped to hold up Moses's hands (*ch.* xvii.), and was at this time in commission with Aaron for the government of the people in the absence of Moses (*ch.* xxiv. 14); out of that family which was of note in Israel was the workman chosen, and it added no little honour to the family that a branch of it was employed, though but as a mechanic, or handicraft tradesman, for the service of the tabernacle. The Jews' tradition is that Hur was the husband of Miriam; and, if so, it was requisite that God should appoint him to this service, lest, if Moses himself had done it, he should be thought partial to his own kindred, his brother Aaron also being advanced to the priesthood. God will put honour upon Moses's relations, and yet will make it to appear that he takes not the honour to himself or his own family, but that it is purely the Lord's doing. 2. Aholiab, of the tribe of Dan, is appointed next to Bezaleel, and partner with him, *v.* 6. Two are better than one. Christ sent forth his disciples who were to rear the gospel tabernacle, two and two, and we read of his two witnesses. Aholiab was of the tribe of Dan, which was one of the less honourable tribes, that the tribes of Judah and Levi might not be lifted up, as if they were to engross all the preferments; to prevent a schism in the body, God gives honour to *that part which lacked,* 1 Cor. xii. 24. *The head cannot say to the foot, I have no need of thee.* Hiram, who was the head workman in the building of Solomon's temple, was also of the tribe of Dan, 2 Chron. ii. 14. 3. There were others that were employed by and under these in the several operations about the tabernacle, *v.* 6. Note, When God has work to do he will never want instruments to do it with, for all hearts and heads too are under his eye, and in his hand; and those may cheerfully go about any service for God, and go on in it, who have reason to think that, one way or other, he has called them to it; for whom he calls he will own and bear out.

II. He qualifies these persons for the service (*v.* 3): *I have filled him with the Spirit of God;* and (*v.* 6) *in the hearts of all that are wise-hearted I have put wisdom.* Note, 1.

Skill in common arts and employments is the gift of God; from him are derived both the faculty and the improvement of the faculty. It is he that puts even this *wisdom into the inward parts,* Job xxxviii. 36. He teaches the husbandman discretion (Isa. xxviii. 26), and the tradesman too; and he must have the praise of it. 2. God dispenses his gifts variously, one gift to one, another to another, and all for the good of the whole body, both of mankind and of the church. Moses was fittest of all to govern Israel, but Bezaleel was fitter than he to build the tabernacle. The common benefit is very much supported by the variety of men's faculties and inclinations; the genius of some leads them to be serviceable one way, of others another way, and *all these worketh that one and the self-same Spirit,* 1 Cor. xii. 11. This forbids pride, envy, contempt, and carnal emulation, and strengthens the bond of mutual love. 3. Those whom God calls to any service he will either find, or make, fit for it. If God give the commission, he will in some measure give the qualifications, according as the service is. The work that was to be done here was to make the tabernacle and the utensils of it, which are here particularly reckoned up, *v.* 7, &c. And for this the persons employed were enabled to *work in gold, and silver, and brass.* When Christ sent his apostles to rear the gospel tabernacle, he poured out his Spirit upon them, to enable them to speak with tongues the wonderful works of God; not to work upon metal, but to work upon men; so much more excellent were the gifts, as the tabernacle to be pitched was a *greater and more perfect tabernacle,* as the apostle calls it, Heb. ix. 11.

12 And the Lord spake unto Moses, saying, 13 Speak thou also unto the children of Israel, saying, Verily my sabbaths ye shall keep: for it *is* a sign between me and you throughout your generations; that *ye* may know that I *am* the Lord that doth sanctify you. 14 Ye shall keep the sabbath therefore; for it *is* holy unto you: every one that defileth it shall surely be put to death: for whosoever doeth *any* work therein, that soul shall be cut off from among his people. 15 Six days may work be done; but in the seventh *is* the sabbath of rest, holy to the Lord: whosoever doeth *any* work in the sabbath day, he shall surely be put to death. 16 Wherefore the children of Israel shall keep the sabbath, to observe the sabbath throughout their generations, *for* a perpetual covenant. 17 It *is* a sign between me and the children of Israel

for ever: for *in* six days the LORD made heaven and earth, and on the seventh day he rested, and was refreshed. 18 And he gave unto Moses, when he had made an end of communing with him upon mount Sinai, two tables of testimony, tables of stone, written with the finger of God.

Here is, I. A strict command for the sanctification of the sabbath day, *v.* 13—17. The law of the sabbath had been given them before any other law, by way of preparation (*ch.* xvi. 23); it had been inserted in the body of the moral law, in the fourth commandment; it had been annexed to the judicial law (*ch.* xxiii. 12); and here it is added to the first part of the ceremonial law, because the observance of the sabbath is indeed the hem and hedge of the whole law; where no conscience is made of that, farewell both godliness and honesty; for, in the moral law, it stands in the midst between the two tables. Some suggest that it comes in here upon another account. Orders were now given that a tabernacle should be set up and furnished for the service of God with all possible expedition; but lest they should think that the nature of the work, and the haste that was required, would justify them in working at it on sabbath days, that they might get it done the sooner, this caution is seasonably inserted, *Verily,* or *nevertheless, my sabbaths you shall keep.* Though they must hasten the work, yet they must not make more haste than good speed; they must not break the law of the sabbath in their haste: even tabernacle-work must give way to the sabbath-rest; so jealous is God for the honour of his sabbaths. Observe what is here said concerning the sabbath day.

1. The nature, meaning, and intention, of the sabbath, by the declaration of which God puts an honour upon it, and teaches us to value it. Divers things are here said of the sabbath. (1.) *It is a sign between me and you* (*v.* 13), and again, *v.* 17. The institution of the sabbath was a great instance of God's favour to them, and a sign that he had distinguished them from all other people; and their religious observance of the sabbath was a great instance of their duty and obedience to him. God, by sanctifying this day among them, let them know that he sanctified them, and set them apart for himself and his service; otherwise he would not have revealed to them his holy sabbaths, to be the support of religion among them. Or it may refer to the law concerning the sabbath, *Keep my sabbaths, that you may know that I the Lord do sanctify you.* Note, If God by his grace incline our hearts to keep the law of the fourth commandment, it will be an evidence of a good work wrought in us by his Spirit. If we sanctify God's day, it is a sign between him and us that he has sanctified our hearts:

hence it is the character of the blessed man that he *keepeth the sabbath from polluting it,* Isa. lvi. 2. The Jews, by observing one day in seven, after six days' labour, testified and declared that they worshipped the God who made the world in six days, and rested the seventh; and so distinguished themselves from other nations, who, having first lost the sabbath, which was instituted to be a memorial of the creation, by degrees lost the knowledge of the Creator, and gave that honour to the creature which was due to him alone. (2.) *It is holy unto you* (*v.* 14), that is, "It is designed for your benefit as well as for God's honour;" *the sabbath was made for man.* Or, "It shall be accounted holy by you, and shall so be observed, and you shall look upon it as sacrilege to profane it." (3.) It is the *sabbath of rest, holy to the Lord, v.* 15. It is separated from common use, and designed for the honour and service of God, and by the observance of it we are taught to rest from worldly pursuits and the service of the flesh, and to devote ourselves, and all we are, have, and can do, to God's glory. (4.) It was to be observed *throughout their generations,* in every age, *for a perpetual covenant, v.* 16. This was to be one of the most lasting tokens of that covenant which was between God and Israel.

2. The law of the sabbath. They must keep it (*v.* 13, 14, 16), keep it as a treasure, as a trust, observe it and preserve it, keep it from polluting it, keep it up as a sign between God and them, keep it and never part with it. The Gentiles had anniversary-feasts, to the honour of their gods; but it was peculiar to the Jews to have a weekly festival; this therefore they must carefully observe.

3. The reason of the sabbath; for God's laws are not only backed with the highest authority, but supported with the best reason. God's own example is the great reason, *v.* 17. As the work of creation is worthy to be thus commemorated, so the great Creator is worthy to be thus imitated, by a holy rest, the seventh day, after six days' labour, especially since we hope, in further conformity to the same example, shortly to rest with him from all our labours.

4. The penalty to be inflicted for the breach of this law: "Every one that *defileth the sabbath,* by doing *any work therein* but works of piety and mercy, *shall be cut off from among his people* (*v.* 14); *he shall surely be put to death, v.* 15. The magistrate must cut him off with the sword of justice if the crime can be proved; if it cannot, or if the magistrate be remiss, and do not do his duty, God will take the work into his own hands, and cut him off by a stroke from heaven, and his family shall be rooted out of Israel." Note, The contempt and profanation of the sabbath day is an iniquity to be punished by the judges; and, if men do not punish it, God will, here or hereafter, unless it be repented of.

II. The delivering of the two tables of testimony to Moses. God had promised him these tables when he called him up into the mount (*ch.* xxiv. 12), and now, when he was sending him down, he delivered them to him, to be carefully and honourably deposited in the ark, *v.* 18. 1. The ten commandments which God had spoken upon mount Sinai in the hearing of all the people were now written, *in perpetuam rei memoriam—for a perpetual memorial*, because that which is written remains. 2. They were written in *tables of stone*, prepared, not by Moses, as it should seem (for it is intimated, *ch.* xxiv. 12, that he found them ready written when he went up to the mount), but, as some think, by the ministry of angels. The law was written in *tables of stone*, to denote the perpetual duration of it (what can be supposed to last longer than that which is written in stone, and laid up ?), to denote likewise the hardness of our hearts; one might more easily write in stone than write any thing that is good in our corrupt and sinful hearts. 3. They were written *with the finger of God*, that is, by his will and power immediately, without the use of any instrument. It is God only that can write his law in the heart; he *gives a heart of flesh*, and then, by his Spirit, which is the *finger of God*, he writes his will in the *fleshly tables of the heart*, 2 Cor. iii. 3. 4. They were written in two tables, being designed to direct us in our duty both towards God and towards man. 5. They are called *tables of testimony*, because this written law testified both the will of God concerning them and his good-will towards them, and would be a testimony against them if they were disobedient. 6. They were delivered to Moses, probably with a charge, before he laid them up in the ark, to show them publicly, that they might be *seen and read of all men*, and so what they had heard with the hearing of the ear might now be brought to their remembrance. Thus *the law was given by Moses, but grace and truth came by Jesus Christ.*

CHAP XXXII.

It is a very lamentable interruption which the story of this chapter gives to the record of the establishment of the church, and of religion among the Jews. Things went on admirably well towards that happy settlement : God had shown himself very favourable, and the people also had seemed to be pretty tractable. Moses had now almost completed his forty days upon the mount, and, we may suppose, was pleasing himself with the thoughts of the very joyful welcome he should have to the camp of Israel at his return, and the speedy setting up of the tabernacle among them. But, behold, the measures are broken, the sin of Israel turns away those good things from them, and puts a stop to the current of God's favours ; the sin that did the mischief (would you think it ?) was worshipping a golden calf. The marriage was ready to be solemnized between God and Israel, but Israel plays the harlot, and so the match is broken, and it will be no easy matter to piece it again. Here is, I. The sin of Israel, and of Aaron particularly, in making the golden calf for a god (ver. 1—4), and worshipping it, ver. 5, 6. II. The notice which God gave of this to Moses, who was now in the mount with him (ver. 7, 8), and the sentence of his wrath against them, ver. 9, 10. III. The intercession which Moses immediately made for them in the mount (ver. 11—13), and the prevalency of that intercession, ver. 14. IV. His coming down from the mount, when he became an eye-witness of their idolatry (ver. 15—19), in abhorrence of which, and as an expression of just indignation, he broke the tables (ver. 19), and burnt the golden calf, ver 20. V. The examination of Aaron about it, ver. 21—24. VI. Execution done upon the ring-leaders in the idolatry, ver. 25—29. VII. The further intercession Moses made for them, to turn away the wrath of God from them (ver. 30—32), and a reprieve granted thereupon, reserving them for a further reckoning, ver. 33, &c.

AND when the people saw that Moses delayed to come down out of the mount, the people gathered themselves together unto Aaron, and said unto him, Up, make us gods, which shall go before us ; for *as for* this Moses, the man that brought us up out of the land of Egypt, we wot not what is become of him. 2 And Aaron said unto them, Break off the golden earrings, which *are* in the ears of your wives, of your sons, and of your daughters, and bring *them* unto me. 3 And all the people brake off the golden earrings which *were* in their ears, and brought *them* unto Aaron. 4 And he received *them* at their hand, and fashioned it with a graving tool, after he had made it a molten calf : and they said, These *be* thy gods, O Israel, which brought thee up out of the land of Egypt. 5 And when Aaron saw *it*, he built an altar before it ; and Aaron made proclamation, and said, To morrow *is* a feast to the LORD. 6 And they rose up early on the morrow, and offered burnt offerings, and brought peace offerings ; and the people sat down to eat and to drink, and rose up to play.

While Moses was in the mount, receiving the law from God, the people had time to meditate upon what had been delivered, and prepare themselves for what was further to be revealed, and forty days was little enough for that work ; but, instead of that, there were those among them that were contriving how to break the laws they had already received, and to anticipate those which they were in expectation of. On the thirty-ninth day of the forty, the plot broke out of rebellion against the Lord. Here is,

I. A tumultuous address which the people made to Aaron, who was entrusted with the government in the absence of Moses : *Up, make us gods, which shall go before us, v.* 1.

1. See the ill effect of Moses's absence from them ; if he had not had God's call both to go and stay, he would not have been altogether free from blame. Those that have the charge of others, as magistrates, ministers, and masters of families, ought not, without just cause, to absent themselves from their charge, *lest Satan get advantage* thereby.

2. See the fury and violence of a multitude when they are influenced and corrupted by such as lie in wait to deceive. Some few, it is likely, were at first possessed with this humour, while many, who would

never have thought of it if they had not put it into their hearts, were brought to follow their pernicious ways; and presently such a multitude were carried down the stream that the few who abhorred the proposal durst not so much as enter their protestation against it. *Behold how great a matter a little fire kindles!* Now what was the matter with this giddy multitude?

(1.) They were weary of waiting for the promised land. They thought themselves detained too long at mount Sinai; though there they lay very safe and very easy, well fed and well taught, yet they were impatient to be going forward. They had a God that staid with them, and manifested his presence with them by the cloud; but this would not serve. They must have a god to go before them; they are for hastening to the land *flowing with milk and honey*, and cannot stay to take their religion along with them. Note, Those that would anticipate God's counsels are commonly precipitate in their own. We must first wait for God's law before we catch at his promises. He that believeth doth not make haste, not more haste than good speed.

(2.) They were weary of waiting for the return of Moses. When he went up into the mount, he had not told them (for God had not told him) how long he must stay; and therefore, when he had outstaid their time, though they were every way well provided for in his absence, some bad people advanced I know not what surmises concerning his delay: *As for this Moses, the man that brought us up out of Egypt, we wot not what has become of him.* Observe, [1.] How slightly they speak of his person—*this Moses.* Thus ungrateful are they to Moses, who had shown such a tender concern for them, and thus do they walk contrary to God. While God delights to put honour upon him, they delight to put contempt upon him, and this to the face of Aaron his brother, and now his viceroy. Note, The greatest merits cannot secure men from the greatest indignities and affronts in this ungrateful world. [2.] How suspiciously they speak of his delay: *We wot not what has become of him.* They thought he was either consumed by the devouring fire or starved for want of food, as if that God who kept and fed them, who were so unworthy, would not take care for the protection and supply of Moses his favourite. Some of them, who were willing to think well of Moses, perhaps suggested that he was translated to heaven like Enoch; while others that cared not how ill they thought of him insinuated that he had deserted his undertaking, as unable to go on with it, and had returned to his father-in-law to keep his flock. All these suggestions were perfectly groundless and absurd, nothing could be more so; it was easy to tell *what had become of him:* he was seen to go into the cloud, and the cloud he went into was still seen by all Israel upon

the top of the mount; they had all the reason in the world to conclude that he was safe there; if the Lord had been pleased to kill him, he would not have shown him such favours as these. If he tarried long, it was because God had a great deal to say to him, for their good; he resided upon the mount as their ambassador, and he would certainly return as soon as he had finished the business he went upon; and yet they make this the colour for their wicked proposal: *We wot not what has become of him.* Note, *First,* Those that are resolved to think ill, when they have ever so much reason to think well, commonly pretend that they know not what to think. *Secondly,* Misinterpretations of our Redeemer's delays are the occasion of a great deal of wickedness. Our Lord Jesus has gone up into the mount of glory, where he is appearing in the presence of God for us, but out of our sight; the heavens must contain him, must conceal him, that we may live by faith. There he has been long; there he is yet. Hence unbelievers suggest that they know not what has become of him; and ask, *Where is the promise of his coming?* (2 Pet. iii. 4), as if, because he has not come yet, he would never come. The wicked servant emboldens himself in his impieties with this consideration, *My Lord delays his coming.* *Thirdly,* Weariness in waiting betrays us to a great many temptations. This began Saul's ruin; he staid for Samuel to the last hour of the time appointed, but had not patience to stay that hour (1 Sam. xiii. 8, &c.); so Israel here, if they could but have staid one day longer, would have seen what had become of Moses. *The Lord is a God of judgment,* and must be waited for till he comes, waited for though he tarry; and then we shall not lose our labour, for he that shall come will come, and will not tarry.

(3.) They were weary of waiting for a divine institution of religious worship among them for that was the thing they were now in expectation of. They were told that they must *serve God in this mountain,* and fond enough they would be of the pomp and ceremony of it; but, because that was not appointed them so soon as they wished, they would set their own wits on work to devise signs of God's presence with them, and would glory in them, and have a worship of their own invention, probably such as they had seen among the Egyptians; for Stephen says that when they said unto Aaron, *Make us gods,* they did, in heart, *turn back into Egypt,* Acts vii. 39, 40. This was a very strange motion, *Up, make us gods.* If they knew not what had become of Moses, and thought him lost, it would have been decent for them to have appointed a solemn mourning for him for certain days; but see how soon so great a benefactor is forgotten. If they had said, "Moses is lost, make us a governor," there would have been some sense in it, though a great deal of ingratitude

to the memory of Moses, and contempt of
Aaron and Hur who were left lords-justices
in his absence; but to say, *Moses is lost,
make us a god*, was the greatest absurdity
imaginable. Was Moses their god? Had
he ever pretended to be so? Whatever had
become of Moses, was it not evident, beyond contradiction, that God was still with
them? And had they any room to question
his leading their camp who victualled it so
well every day? Could they have any other
god that would provide so well for them as
he had done, nay as he now did? And yet,
*Make us gods, which shall go before us!
Gods!* How many would they have? Is
not one sufficient? *Make us gods!* and what
good would gods of their own making do
them? They must have such gods to go
before them as could not go themselves
further than they were carried. So wretchedly besotted and intoxicated are idolaters:
they are *mad upon their idols*, Jer. l. 38.

II. Here is the demand which Aaron
makes of their jewels thereupon: *Bring me
your golden ear-rings, v. 2.* We do not find
that he said one word to discountenance
their proposal; he did not reprove their insolence, did not reason with them to convince
them of the sin and folly of it, but seemed
to approve the motion, and showed himself
not unwilling to humour them in it. One
would hope he designed, at first, only to
make a jest of it, and, by setting up a ridiculous image among them, to expose the
motion, and show them the folly of it. But,
if so, it proved ill jesting with sin: it is of
dangerous consequence for the unwary fly
to play about the candle. Some charitably
suppose that when Aaron told them to break
off their ear-rings, and bring them to him,
he did it with design to crush the proposal,
believing that though their covetousness
would have let them *lavish gold out of the
bag* to make an idol of (Isa. xlvi. 6), yet their
pride would not have suffered them to part
with their golden ear-rings. But it is not
safe to try how far men's sinful lusts will
carry them in a sinful way, and what expense
they will be at; it proved here a dangerous
experiment.

III. Here is the making of the golden
calf, *v.* 3, 4 1. The people brought in their
ear-rings to Aaron, whose demand of them,
instead of discouraging the motion, perhaps
did rather gratify their superstition, and
beget in them a fancy that the gold taken
from their ears would be the most acceptable,
and would make the most valuable god.
Let their readiness to part with their rings to
make an idol of shame us out of our niggard-
liness in the service of the true God. Did
they not draw back from the charge of their
idolatry? And shall we grudge the expenses of our religion, or starve so good a
cause? 2. Aaron melted down their rings,
and, having a mould prepared for the purpose, poured the melted gold into it, and

then produced it in the shape of an ox or
calf, giving it some finishing strokes with a
graving tool. Some think that Aaron chose
this figure, for a sign or token of the divine
presence, because he thought the head and
horns of an ox a proper emblem of the divine
power, and yet, being so plain and common
a thing, he hoped the people would not be so
sottish as to worship it. But it is probable
that they had learnt of the Egyptians thus
to represent the Deity, for it is said (Ezek.
xx. 8), *They did not forsake the idols of
Egypt*, and (*ch.* xxiii. 8), *Neither left she her
whoredoms brought from Egypt. Thus they
changed their glory into the similitude of an
ox* (Ps. cvi. 20), and proclaimed their own
folly, beyond that of other idolaters, who
worshipped the host of heaven.

IV. Having made the calf in Horeb, they
worshipped the graven image, Ps. cvi. 19.
Aaron, seeing the people fond of their calf,
was willing yet further to humour them, and
he built an altar before it, and proclaimed a
feast to the honour of it (*v.* 5), a feast of dedication. Yet he calls it *a feast to Jehovah;*
for, brutish as they were, they did not
imagine that this image was itself a god,
nor did they design to terminate their
adoration in the image, but they made it
for a representation of the true God,
whom they intended to worship in and
through this image; and yet this did not
excuse them from gross idolatry, any more
than it will excuse the papists, whose plea it
is that they do not worship the image, but
God by the image, so making themselves
just such idolaters as the worshippers of the
golden calf, whose feast was a feast to Jehovah, and proclaimed to be so, that the
most ignorant and unthinking might not
mistake it. The people are forward enough
to celebrate this feast (*v.* 6): *They rose up
early on the morrow*, to show how well
pleased they were with the solemnity, and,
according to the ancient rites of worship,
they offered sacrifice to this new-made deity,
and then feasted upon the sacrifice; thus
having, at the expense of their ear-rings,
made their god, they endeavour, at the expense of their beasts, to make this god propitious. Had they offered these sacrifices
immediately to Jehovah, without the inter-
vention of an image, they might (for aught I
know) have been accepted (*ch.* xx. 24); but
having set up an image before them as a
symbol of God's presence, and so changed
the truth of God into a lie, these sacrifices
were an abomination, nothing could be more
so. When this idolatry of theirs is spoken
of in the New Testament the account of their
feast upon the sacrifice is quoted and referred
to (1 Cor. x. 7): *They sat down to eat and
drink* of the remainder of what was sacrificed, and then *rose up to play*, to play the
fool, to play the wanton. Like god, like
worship. They would not have made a calf
their god if they had not first made their

belly their god; but, when the god was a jest, no marvel that the service was sport. Being *vain in their imaginations*, they became vain in their worship, so great was this vanity. Now, 1. It was strange that any of the people, especially so great a number of them, should do such a thing. Had they not, but the other day, in this very place, heard the voice of the Lord God speaking to them out of the midst of the fire, *Thou shalt not make to thyself any graven image?* Had they not heard the thunder, seen the lightnings, and felt the earthquake, with the dreadful pomp of which this law was given? Had they not been particularly cautioned not to make *gods of gold? ch.* xx. 23. Nay, had they not themselves solemnly entered into covenant with God, and promised that all that which he had said unto them they *would do, and would be obedient? ch.* xxiv. 7. And yet, before they stirred from the place where this covenant had been solemnly ratified, and before the cloud was removed from the top of mount Sinai, thus to break an express command, in defiance of an express threatening that this *iniquity should be visited upon them and their children*—what shall we think of it? It is a plain indication that the law was no more able to sanctify than it was to justify; by it is the knowledge of sin, but not the cure of it. This is intimated in the emphasis laid upon the place where this sin was committed (Ps. cvi. 19)*; They made a calf in Horeb*, the very place where the law was given. It was otherwise with those that received the gospel; they immediately *turned from idols*, 1 Thess. i. 9. 2. It was especially strange that Aaron should be so deeply implicated in this sin, that he should make the calf, and proclaim the feast! Is this Aaron, the saint of the Lord, the brother of Moses his prophet, that could *speak so well* (*ch.* iv. 14), and yet speaks not one word against this idolatry? Is this he that had not only seen, but had been employed in summoning, the plagues of Egypt, and the judgments executed upon the gods of the Egyptians? What! and yet himself copying out the abandoned idolatries of Egypt? With what face could they say, *These are thy gods* that *brought thee up out of Egypt*, when they thus bring the idolatry of Egypt (the worst thing there) along with them? Is this Aaron, who had been with Moses in the mount (*ch.* xix. 24; xxiv. 9), and knew that there was no manner of similitude seen there, by which they might make an image? Is this Aaron who was entrusted with the care of the people in the absence of Moses? Is he aiding and abetting in this rebellion against the Lord? How was it possible that he should ever do so sinful a thing? Either he was strangely surprised into it, and did it when he was half asleep, or he was frightened into it by the outrages of the rabble. The Jews have a tradition that his colleague Hur opposing it the people fell upon him

and stoned him (and therefore we never read of him after) and that this frightened Aaron into a compliance. And God left him to himself, [1.] To teach us what the best of men are when they are so left, that we may *cease from man*, and that he who *thinks he stands may take heed lest he fall.* [2.] Aaron was, at this time, destined by the divine appointment to the great office of the priesthood; though he knew it not, Moses in the mount did. Now, lest he should be *lifted up, above measure*, with the honours that were to be put upon him, a messenger of Satan was suffered to prevail over him, that the remembrance thereof might keep him humble all his days. He who had once shamed himself so far as to build an altar to a golden calf must own himself altogether unworthy of the honour of attending at the altar of God, and purely indebted to free grace for it. Thus pride and boasting were for ever silenced, and a good effect brought out of a bad cause. By this likewise it was shown that *the law made those priests who had infirmity, and needed first to offer for their own sins.*

7 And the Lord said unto Moses, Go, get thee down; for thy people, which thou broughtest out of the land of Egypt, have corrupted *themselves:* 8 They have turned aside quickly out of the way which I commanded them: they have made them a molten calf, and have worshipped it, and have sacrificed thereunto, and said, These *be* thy gods, O Israel, which have brought thee up out of the land of Egypt. 9 And the Lord said unto Moses, I have seen this people, and, behold, it *is* a stiffnecked people: 10 Now therefore let me alone, that my wrath may wax hot against them, and that I may consume them: and I will make of thee a great nation.. 11 And Moses besought the Lord his God, and said, Lord, why doth thy wrath wax hot against thy people, which thou hast brought forth out of the land of Egypt with great power, and with a mighty hand? 12 Wherefore should the Egyptians speak, and say, For mischief did he bring them out, to slay them in the mountains, and to consume them from the face of the earth? Turn from thy fierce wrath, and repent of this evil against thy people. 13 Remember Abraham, Isaac, and Israel, thy servants, to whom thou swearest by thine own self, and saidst

unto them, I will multiply your seed as the stars of heaven, and all this land that I have spoken of will I give unto your seed, and they shall inherit *it* for ever. 14 And the LORD repented of the evil which he thought to do unto his people.

Here, I. God acquaints Moses with what was doing in the camp while he was absent, *v.* 7, 8. He could have told him sooner, as soon as the first step was taken towards it, and have hastened him down to prevent it; but he suffered it to come to this height, for wise and holy 'ends, and then sent him down to punish it. Note, It is no reproach to the holiness of God that he suffers sin to be committed, since he knows, not only how to restrain it when he pleases, but how to make it serviceable to the designs of his own glory. Observe what God here says to Moses concerning this sin. 1. That they had *corrupted themselves.* Sin is the corruption or depravation of the sinner, and it is a self-corruption ; *every man is tempted when he is drawn aside of his own lust.* 2. That they had *turned aside out of the way.* Sin is a deviation from the way of our duty into a by-path. When they promised to do all that God should command them, they set out as fair as could be ; but now they missed their way, and turned aside. 3. That they had turned aside quickly, quickly after the law was given them and they had promised to obey it, quickly after God had done such great things for them and declared his kind intentions to do greater. *They soon forgot his works.* To fall into sin quickly after we have renewed our covenants with God, or received special mercy from him, is very provoking. 4. He tells him particularly what they had done : *They have made a calf, and worshipped it.* Note, Those sins which are concealed from our governors are naked and open before God. He sees that which they cannot discover, nor is any of the wickedness in the world hidden from him. We could not bear to see the thousandth part of that provocation which God sees every day and yet keeps silence. 5. He seems to disown them, in saying to Moses, They are *thy people whom thou broughtest up out of the land of Egypt ;* as if he had said, "I will not own any relation to them, or concern for them ; let it never be said that they are my people, or that I brought them out of Egypt." Note, Those that corrupt themselves not only shame themselves, but even make God himself ashamed of them and of his kindness to them. 6. He sends him down to them with all speed : *Go, get thee down.* He must break off even his communion with God to go and do his duty as a magistrate among the people ; so must Joshua, *ch.* vii. 10. Every thing is beautiful in its season.

II. He expresses his displeasure against Israel for this sin, and the determination of his justice to cut them off, *v.* 9, 10. 1. He gives this people their true character : *" It is a stiff-necked people,* unapt to come under the yoke of the divine law, and governed as it were by a spirit of contradiction, averse to all good and prone to evil, obstinate against the methods employed for their cure." Note, The righteous God sees, not only what we do, but what we are, not only the actions of our lives, but the dispositions of our spirits, and has an eye to them in all his proceedings. 2. He declares what was their just desert—that his wrath should *wax hot against them,* so as to consume them at once, and *blot out their name from under heaven* (Deut. ix. 14) ; not only cast them out of covenant, but chase them out of the world. Note, Sin exposes us to the wrath of God ; and that wrath, if it be not allayed by divine mercy, will burn us up as stubble. It were just with God to let the law have its course against sinners, and to cut them off immediately in the very act of sin ; and, if he should do so, it would be neither loss nor dishonour to him. 3. He holds out inducements to Moses not to intercede for them : *Therefore, let me alone.* What did Moses, or what could he do, to hinder God from consuming them ? When God resolves to abandon a people, and the decree of ruin has gone forth, no intercession can prevent it, Ezek. xiv. 14 ; Jer. xv. 1. But God would thus express the greatness of his just displeasure against them, after the manner of men, who would have none to intercede for those they resolve to be severe with. Thus also he would put an honour upon prayer, intimating that nothing but the intercession of Moses could save them from ruin, that he might be a type of Christ, by whose mediation alone God would *reconcile the world unto himself.* That the intercession of Moses might appear the more illustrious, God fairly offers him that, if he would not interpose in this matter, he would *make of him a great nation,* that either, in process of time, he would raise up a people out of his loins, or that he would immediately, by some means or other, bring another great nation under his government and conduct, so that he should be no loser by their ruin. Had Moses been of a narrow selfish spirit, he would have closed with this offer ; but he prefers the salvation of Israel before the advancement of his own family. Here was a man fit to be a governor.

III. Moses earnestly intercedes with God on their behalf (*v.* 11—13) : he besought the Lord his God. If God would not be called *the God of Israel,* yet he hoped he might address him as *his own God.* What interest we have at the throne of grace we should improve for the church of God, and for our friends. Now Moses is standing in the gap to turn away the wrath of God, Ps. cvi. 23. He wisely took the hint which God gave him when he said, *Let me alone,* which, though it seemed to forbid his interceding, did really encourage it, by showing what power the prayer of faith has with God. In such a case, God *wonders if there be no intercessor,* Isa. lix. 16. Observe, 1. His prayer (*v.* 12): *Turn from thy fierce wrath;* not as if he thought God was not justly angry, but he begs that he would not be so greatly angry as to consume them. "Let mercy rejoice against judgment; *repent of this evil;* change the sentence of destruction into that of correction." 2. His pleas. He fills his mouth with arguments, not to move God, but to express his own faith and to excite his own fervency in prayer. He urges, (1.) God's interest in them, the great things he had already done for them, and the vast expense of favours and miracles he had been at upon them, *v.* 11. God had said to Moses (*v.* 7), They are *thy people, whom thou broughtest up out of Egypt;* but Moses humbly turns them back upon God again: "They are *thy people,* thou art their Lord and owner; I am but their servant. *Thou broughtest them forth out of Egypt;* I was but the instrument in thy hand; that was done in order to their deliverance which thou only couldest do." Though their being his people was a reason why he should be angry with them for setting up another god, yet it was a reason why he should not be so angry with them as to consume them. Nothing is more natural than for a father to correct his son, but nothing more unnatural than for a father to slay his son. And as the relation is a good plea ("they are *thy people*"), so is the experience they had had of his kindness to them: "Thou *broughtest them out of Egypt,* though they were unworthy, and had there served the gods of the Egyptians, Josh. xxiv. 15. If thou didst that for them, notwithstanding their sins in Egypt, wilt thou undo it for their sins of the same nature in the wilderness?" (2.) He pleads the concern of God's glory (*v.* 12): *Wherefore should the Egyptians say, For mischief did he bring them out?* Israel is dear to Moses as his kindred, as his charge; but it is the glory of God that he is most concerned for; this lies nearer his heart than any thing else. If Israel could perish without any reproach to God's name, Moses could persuade himself to sit down contented; but he cannot bear to hear God reflected on, and therefore this he insists upon, *Lord, what will the Egyptians say?* Their eyes, and the eyes of all the neighbouring nations, were now upon Israel; from the wondrous beginnings of that people, they raised their expectations of something great in their latter end; but, if a people so strangely saved should be suddenly ruined, what would the world say of it, especially the Egyptians, who have such an implacable hatred both to Israel and to the God of Israel? They would say, "God was either weak, and could not, or fickle, and would not, complete the salvation he began; he brought

them forth to that mountain, not to sacrifice (as was pretended), but to be sacrificed." They will not consider the provocation given by Israel, to justify the proceeding, but will think it cause enough for triumph that God and his people could not agree, but that their God had done that which they (the Egyptians) wished to see done. Note, The glorifying of God's name, as it ought to be our first petition (it is so in the Lord's prayer), so it ought to be our great plea, Ps. lxxix. 9 *Do not disgrace the throne of thy glory,* Jer. xiv. 21; and see Jer. xxxiii. 8, 9. And, if we would with comfort plead this with God as a reason why he should not destroy us, we ought to plead it with ourselves as a reason why we should not offend him: *What will the Egyptians say?* We ought always to be careful that the name of God and his doctrine be not blasphemed through us. (3.) He pleads God's promise to the patriarchs that he would multiply their seed, and give them the land of Canaan for an inheritance, and this promise confirmed by an oath, an oath by himself, since he could swear by no greater, *v.* 13. God's promises are to be our pleas in prayer; for what he has promised he is able to perform, and the honour of his truth is engaged for the performance of it. "Lord, if Israel be cut off, what will become of the promise? Shall their unbelief make that of no effect? God forbid." Thus we must take our encouragement in prayer from God only.

IV. God graciously abated the rigour of the sentence, and *repented of the evil he thought to do* (*v.* 14); though he designed to punish them, yet he would not ruin them. See here, 1. The power of prayer; God suffers himself to be prevailed with by the humble believing importunity of intercessors. 2. The compassion of God towards poor sinners, and how ready he is to forgive. Thus he has given other proofs besides his own oath that he has no pleasure in the death of those that die; for he not only pardons upon the repentance of sinners, but spares and reprieves upon the intercession of others for them.

15 And Moses turned, and went down from the mount, and the two tables of the testimony *were* in his hand: the tables *were* written on both their sides; on the one side and on the other *were* they written. 16 And the tables *were* the work of God, and the writing *was* the writing of God, graven upon the tables. 17 And when Joshua heard the noise of the people as they shouted, he said unto Moses, *There is* a noise of war in the camp. 18 And he said, *It is* not the voice of *them that* shout for mastery, neither *is it* the voice of *them that* cry for

being overcome: *but* the noise of *them that* sing do I hear. 19 And it came to pass, as soon as he came nigh unto the camp, that he saw the calf, and the dancing: and Moses' anger waxed hot, and he cast the tables out of his hands, and brake them beneath the mount. 20 And he took the calf which they had made, and burnt *it* in the fire, and ground *it* to powder, and strawed it upon the water, and made the children of Israel drink *of it.*

Here is, I. The favour of God to Moses, in trusting him with the two tables of the testimony, which, though of common stone, were far more valuable than all the precious stones that adorned the breast-plate of Aaron. The topaz of Ethiopia could not equal them, *v.* 15, 16. God himself, without the ministry either of man or angel (for aught that appears), wrote the ten commandments on these tables, *on both their sides,* some on one table and some on the other, so that they were folded together like a book, to be deposited in the ark.

II. The familiarity between Moses and Joshua. While Moses was in the cloud, as in the presence-chamber, Joshua continued as near as he might, in the anti-chamber (as it were), waiting till Moses came out, that he might be ready to attend him; and though he was all alone for forty days (fed, it is likely, with manna), yet he was not weary of waiting, as the people were, but when Moses came down he came with him, and not till then. And here we are told what constructions they put upon the noise that they heard in the camp, *v.* 17, 18. Though Moses had been so long in immediate converse with God, yet he did not disdain to talk freely with his servant Joshua. Those whom God advances he preserves from being puffed up. Nor did he disdain to talk of the affairs of the camp. Blessed Paul was not the less mindful of the church on earth for having been in the third heavens, where he heard unspeakable words. Joshua, who was a military man, and had the command of the train-bands, feared there was *a noise of war in the camp,* and then he would be missed; but Moses, having received notice of it from God, better distinguished the sound, and was aware that it was *the voice of those that sing.* It does not however appear that he told Joshua what he knew of the occasion of their singing; for we should not be forward to proclaim men's faults: they will be known too soon.

III. The great and just displeasure of Moses against Israel, for their idolatry. Knowing what to expect, he was presently aware of the golden calf, and the sport the people made with it. He saw how merry they could be in his absence, how soon he was forgotten among them, and what little thought

412

they had of him and his return. He might justly take this ill, as an affront to himself, but this was the least part of the grievance; he resented it as an offence to God, and the scandal of his people. See what a change it is to come down from the mount of communion with God to converse with a world that *lies in wickedness.* In God we see nothing but what is pure and pleasant, in the world nothing but pollution and provocation. Moses was the meekest man on the earth, and yet when he saw *the calf, and the dancing,* his *anger waxed hot.* Note, It is no breach of the law of meekness to show our displeasure at the wickedness of the wicked. Those are *angry and sin not* that are angry at sin only, not as against themselves, but as against God. Ephesus is famous for patience, and yet *cannot bear those that are evil,* Rev. ii. 2. It becomes us to be cool in our own cause, but warm in God's. Moses showed himself very angry, both by breaking the tables and burning the calf, that he might, by these expressions of strong indignation, awaken the people to a sense of the greatness of the sin they had been guilty of, which they would have been ready to make light of if he had not thus shown his resentment, as one in earnest for their conviction. 1. To convince them that they had forfeited and lost the favour of God, *he broke the tables, v.* 19. Though God knew of their sin, before Moses came down, yet he did not order him to leave the tables behind him, but gave them to him to take down in his hand, that the people might see how forward God was to take them into covenant with himself, and that nothing but their own sin prevented it; yet he put it into his heart, when the iniquity of Ephraim was discovered (as the expression is, Hos. vii. 1), to break the tables before their eyes (as it is Deut. ix. 17), that the sight of it might the more affect them, and fill them with confusion, when they saw what blessings they had lost. Thus, they being guilty of so notorious an infraction of the treaty now on foot, the writings were torn, even when they lay ready to be sealed. Note, The greatest sign of God's displeasure against any person or people is his taking his law from them. The breaking of the tables is the breaking of the *staff of beauty and band* (Zech. xi. 10, 14); it leaves a people unchurched and undone. Some think that Moses sinned in breaking the tables, and observe that, when men are angry, they are in danger of breaking all God's commandments; but it rather seems to be an act of justice than of passion, and we do not find that he himself speaks of it afterwards (Deut. ix. 17) with any regret 2. To convince them that they had betaken themselves to a God that could not help them, he *burnt the calf* (*v.* 20), melted it down, and then filed it to dust; and, that the powder to which it was reduced might be taken notice of throughout the camp, he strewed it upon that water of which they all drank. That it might appear that *an idol is nothing in the world* (1 Cor. viii. 4), he reduced this to atoms, that it might be as near nothing as could be. To show that false gods cannot help their worshippers, he here showed that this could not save itself, Isa. xlvi. 1, 2. And to teach us that all the relics of idolatry ought to be abolished, and that the names of Baalim should be taken away, the very dust to which it was ground was scattered. Filings of gold are precious (we say), and therefore are carefully gathered up; but the filings of the golden calf were odious, and must be scattered with detestation. Thus the idols of silver and gold must be cast to the moles and the bats (Isa. ii. 20; xxx. 22), and Ephraim shall say, *What have I to do any more with idols?* His mixing this powder with their drink signified to them that the curse they had thereby brought upon themselves would mingle itself with all their enjoyments, and embitter them; it would enter into their bowels like water, and like oil into their bones. *The backslider in heart shall be filled with his own ways;* he shall drink as he brews. These were indeed waters of Marah.

21 And Moses said·unto Aaron, What did this people unto thee, that thou hast brought so great a sin upon them? 22 And Aaron said, Let not the anger of my lord wax hot: thou knowest the people that they *are set* on mischief. 23 For they said unto me, Make us gods, which shall go before us: for *as for* this Moses, the man that brought us up out of the land of Egypt, we wot not what is become of him. 24 And I said unto them, Whosoever hath any gold, let them break *it* off. So they gave *it* me: then I cast it into the fire, and there came out this calf. 25 And when Moses saw that the people *were* naked; (for Aaron had made them naked unto *their* shame among their enemies :) 26 Then Moses stood in the gate of the camp, and said, Who *is* on the LORD's side? *let him come* unto me. And all the sons of Levi gathered themselves together unto him. 27 And he said unto them, Thus saith the LORD God of Israel, Put every man his sword by his side, *and* go in and out from gate to gate, throughout the camp, and slay every man his brother, and every man his companion, and every man his neighbour. 28 And the children of Levi did according to the word of Moses; and there fell

of the people that day about three thousand men. 29 For Moses had said, Consecrate yourselves to day to the LORD, even every man upon his son, and upon his brother; that he may bestow upon you a blessing this day.

Moses, having shown his just indignation against the sin of Israel by breaking the tables and burning the calf, now proceeds to reckon with the sinners and to call them to an account, herein acting as the representative of God, who is not only a holy God, and hates sin, but a just God, and is engaged in honour to punish it, Isa. lix. 18. Now,

I. He begins with Aaron, as God began with Adam, because he was the principal person, though not first in the transgression, but drawn into it. Observe here,

1. The just reproof Moses gives him, *v.* 21. He does not order him to be cut off, as those (*v.* 27) that had been the ring-leaders in the sin. Note, A great deal of difference will be made between those that presumptuously rush into sin and those that through infirmity are surprised into it, between those that overtake the fault that flees from them and those that are overtaken in the fault they flee from. See Gal. vi. 1. Not but that Aaron deserved to be cut off for this sin, and would have been so if Moses had not interceded particularly for him, as appears Deut. ix. 20. And having prevailed with God for him, to save him from ruin, he here expostulates with him, to bring him to repentance. He puts Aaron upon considering, (1.) What he had done to this people: *Thou hast brought so great a sin upon them.* The sin of idolatry is a great sin, so great a sin that the evil of it cannot be expressed; the people, as the first movers, might be said to bring the sin upon Aaron; but he being a magistrate, who should have suppressed it, and yet aiding and abetting it, might truly be said to bring it upon them, because he hardened their hearts and strengthened their hands in it. It is a shocking thing for governors to humour people in their sins, and give countenance to that to which they should be a terror. Observe, in general, Those who bring sin upon others, either by drawing them into it or encouraging them in it, do more mischief than they are aware of; we really hate those whom we either bring or suffer sin upon, Lev. xix. 17. Those that share in sin help to break their partners, and really ruin one another. (2.) What moved him to it: *What did this people unto thee?* He takes it for granted that it must needs be something more than ordinary that prevailed with Aaron to do such a thing, thus insinuating an excuse for him, because he knew that his heart was upright: " *What did they?* Did they accost thee fairly, and wheedle thee into it; and durst thou displease thy God, to please the people? Did they overcome thee by importunity; and hadst thou so little re-

413

solution left as to yield to the stream of a popular clamour? Did they threaten to stone thee; and couldest not thou have opposed God's threatenings to theirs, and frightened them worse than they could frighten thee?" Note, We must never be drawn into sin by any thing that man can say or do to us, for it will not justify us to say that we were so drawn in. Men can but tempt us to sin; they cannot force us. Men can but frighten us; if we do not comply, they cannot hurt us.

2. The frivolous excuse Aaron makes for himself. We will hope that he testified his repentance for the sin afterwards better than he did now; for what he says here has little in it of the language of a penitent. If a just man fall, he shall rise again, but perhaps not quickly. (1.) He deprecates the anger of Moses only, whereas he should have deprecated God's anger in the first place: *Let not the anger of my lord wax hot, v.* 22. (2.) He lays all the fault upon the people: *They are set on mischief, and they said, Make us gods.* It is natural to us to endeavour thus to transfer our guilt; we have it in our kind, Adam and Eve did so; sin is a brat that nobody is willing to own. Aaron was now the chief magistrate and had power over the people, and yet pleads that the people overpowered him; he that had authority to restrain them, yet had so little resolution as to yield to them. (3.) It is well if he did not intend a reflection upon Moses, as accessory to the sin, by staying so long on the mount, in repeating, without need, that invidious surmise of the people, *As for this Moses, we know not what has become of him, v.* 23. (4.) He extenuates and conceals his own share in the sin, as if he had only bidden them *break off their gold* that they had about them, intending to make a hasty assay for the present, and to try what he could make of the gold that was next hand: and childishly insinuates that when he cast the gold into the fire it came out, either by accident or by the magic art of some of the mixed multitude (as the Jewish writers dream), in this shape; but not a word of his graving and fashioning it, *v.* 24. But Moses relates to all ages what he did (*v.* 4), though he himself here would not own it. Note, *He that covers his sin shall not prosper,* for sooner or later it will be discovered. Well, this was all Aaron had to say for himself; and he had better have said nothing, for his defence did but aggravate his offence; and yet he is not only spared, but preferred; as sin did abound, grace did much more abound.

II. The people are next to be judged for this sin. The approach of Moses soon spoiled their sport and turned their dancing into trembling. Those that hectored Aaron into a compliance with them in their sin durst not look Moses in the face, nor make the least opposition to the severity which he thought fit to use both against the idol and against the idolaters. Note, It is not impossible

to make those sins which were committed with daring presumption appear contemptible, when the insolent perpetrators of them slink away overwhelmed in their own confusion. *The king that sits upon the throne of judgment scatters away all evil with his eyes.* Observe two things:—

1. How they were exposed to shame by their sin: *The people were naked (v.* 25), not so much because they had some of them lost their ear-rings (that was inconsiderable), but because they had lost their integrity, and lay under the reproach of ingratitude to their best benefactor, and a treacherous revolt from their rightful Lord. It was a shame to them, and a perpetual blot, that they *changed their glory into the similitude of an ox.* Other nations boasted that they were true to their false gods; well may Israel blush for being false to the true God. Thus were they made *naked,* stripped of their ornaments, and exposed to contempt; stripped of their armour, and liable to insults. Thus our first parents, when they had sinned, became *naked, to their shame.* Note, Those that do dishonour to God really bring the greatest dishonour upon themselves: so Israel here did, and Moses was concerned to see it, though they themselves were not; he *saw that they were naked.*

2. The course that Moses took to roll away this reproach, not by concealing the sin, or putting any false colour upon it, but by punishing it, and so bearing a public testimony against it. Whenever it should be cast in their teeth that they had *made a calf in Horeb,* they might have this to say, in answer to those that reproached them, that though it was true there were those that did so, yet justice was executed upon them. The government disallowed the sin, and suffered not the sinners to go unpunished. They did so, but they paid dearly for it. Thus (said God) thou shalt *put the evil away,* Deut. xiii. 5 Observe here,

(1.) By whom vengeance was taken—by the children of Levi (*v.* 26, 28); not by the immediate hand of God himself, as on Nadab and Abihu, but by the sword of man, to teach them that idolatry was an *iniquity to be punished by the judge,* being a *denial of the God that is above,* Job xxxi. 28; Deut. xiii. 9. It was to be done by the sword of their own brethren, that the execution of justice might redound more to the honour of the nation. And, if they must fall now into the hands of man, better so than flee before their enemies. The innocent must be culled out to be the executioners of the guilty, that it might be the more effectual warning to themselves, that they did not the like another time; and the putting of them upon such an unpleasant service, and so much against the grain as this must needs be, to kill their next neighbours, was a punishment to them too for not appearing sooner to prevent the sin, and make head against it. The Levites particularly were employed in doing this execution; for, it should seem, there were more of them than of any other tribe that had kept themselves free from the contagion, which was the more laudable because Aaron, the head of their tribe, was so deeply concerned in it. Now here we are told, [1.] How the Levites were called out to this service : *Moses stood in the gate of the camp,* the place of judgment ; there he *displayed a banner,* as it were, because of the truth, to enlist soldiers for God. He proclaimed, *Who is on the Lord's side ?* The idolaters had set up the golden calf for their standard, and now Moses set up his, in opposition to them. Now *Moses clad himself with zeal* as with a robe, and summoned all those to appear forthwith that were on God's side, against the golden calf. He does not proclaim, as Jehu, " *Who is on my side* (2 Kings ix. 32), to avenge the indignity done to me ?" but, *Who is on the Lord's side ?* It was God's cause that he espoused *against the evil-doers,* Ps. xciv. 16. Note, *First,* There are two great interests on foot in the world, with the one or the other of which all the children of men are siding. The interest of sin and wickedness is the devil's interest, and all wicked people side with that interest ; the interest of truth and holiness is God's interest, with which all godly people side ; and it is a case that will not admit a neutrality. *Secondly,* It concerns us all to enquire whether we are on the Lord's side or not. *Thirdly,* Those who are on his side are comparatively but few, and sometimes seem fewer than really they are. *Fourthly,* God does sometimes call out those that are on his side to appear for him, as witnesses, as soldiers, as intercessors. [2.] How they were commissioned for this service (*v.* 27): *Slay every man his brother,* that is, " Slay all those that you know to have been active for the making and worshipping of the golden calf, though they were your own nearest relations, or dearest friends." The crime was committed publicly, the Levites saw who of their acquaintance were concerned in it, and therefore needed no other direction than their own knowledge whom to slay. And probably the greatest part of those that were guilty were known, and known to be so, by some or other of the Levites who were employed in the execution. Yet, it should seem, they were to slay those only whom they found *abroad in the streets* of the camp ; for it might be hoped that those who had retired into their tents were ashamed of what they had done, and were upon their knees, repenting. Those are marked for ruin who persist in sin, and are not ashamed of the abominations they have committed, Jer. viii. 12. But how durst the Levites encounter so great a body, who probably were much enraged by the burning of their calf ? It is easy to account for this ; a sense of guilt disheartened the delinquents, and a divine commission animated the executioners. And one thing that put life into them was that Moses had said, *Consecrate*

yourselves to day to the Lord, that he may bestow a blessing upon you, thereby intimating to them that they now stood fair for preferment, and that, if they would but signalize themselves upon this occasion, it would be construed into such a consecration of themselves to God, and to his service, as would put upon their tribe a perpetual honour. Those that consecrate themselves to the Lord he will set apart for himself. Those that do the duty shall have the dignity ; and, if we do signal services for God, he will bestow especial blessings upon us. There was a blessing designed for the tribe of Levi ; now says Moses, " *Consecrate yourselves to the Lord,* that you may qualify yourselves to receive the blessing." The Levites were to assist in the offering of sacrifice to God ; and now they must begin with the offering of these sacrifices to the honour of divine justice. Those that are to minister about holy things must be not only sincere and serious, but warm and zealous, bold and courageous, for God and godliness. Thus all Christians, but especially ministers, must *forsake father and mother,* and prefer the service of Christ and his interest far before their nearest and dearest relations ; for if we love our relations better than Christ we are not *worthy of him.* See how this zeal of the Levites is applauded, Deut. xxxiii. 9.

(2.) On whom vengeance is taken : *There fell of the people that day about* 3000 *men, v.* 28. Probably these were but few, in comparison with the many that were guilty ; but these were the men that headed the rebellion, and were therefore picked out, to be made examples of, for terror to all others. Those that in the morning were shouting and dancing before night were dying in their own blood ; such a sudden change do the judgments of God sometimes make with sinners that are secure and jovial in their sin, as with Belshazzar by the hand-writing upon the wall. This is written for warning to us. 1 Cor. x. 7, *Neither be you idolaters, as were some of them.*

30 And it came to pass on the morrow, that Moses said unto the people, Ye have sinned a great sin : and now I will go up unto the Lord ; peradventure I shall make an atonement for your sin. 31 And Moses returned unto the Lord, and said, Oh, this people have sinned a great sin, and have made them gods of gold. 32 Yet now, if thou wilt forgive their sin— ; and if not, blot me, I pray thee, out of thy book which thou hast written. 33 And the Lord said unto Moses, Whosoever hath sinned against me, him will I blot out of my book. 34 Therefore now go, lead the people unto the

place of which I have spoken unto thee: behold, mine Angel shall go before thee: nevertheless in the day when I visit I will visit their sin upon them. 35 And the LORD plagued the people, because they made the calf, which Aaron made.

Moses, having executed justice upon the principal offenders, is here dealing both with the people and with God.

I. With the people, to bring them to repentance, *v.* 30.

1. When some were slain, lest the rest should imagine that, because they were exempt from the capital punishment, they were therefore looked upon as free from guilt, Moses here tells the survivors, *You have sinned a great sin*, and therefore, though you have escaped this time, *except you repent, you shall all likewise perish.* That they might not think lightly of the sin itself, he calls it *a great sin;* and that they might not think themselves innocent, because perhaps they were not all so deeply guilty as some of those that were put to death, he tells them all, *You have sinned a great sin.* The work of ministers is to show people their sins, and the greatness of their sins. " *You have sinned,* and therefore you are undone if your sins be not pardoned, for ever undone without a Saviour. It is a great sin, and therefore calls for great sorrow, for it puts you in great danger." To affect them with the greatness of their sin he intimates to them what a difficult thing it would be to make up the quarrel which God had with them for it. (1.) It would not be done, unless he himself *went up unto the Lord* on purpose, and gave as long and as solemn attendance as he had done for the receiving of the law. And yet, (2.) Even so it was but a peradventure that he should make atonement for them; the case was extremely hazardous. This should convince us of the great evil there is in sin, that he who undertook to make atonement found it no easy thing to do it; he must *go up to the Lord* with his own blood to *make atonement.* The malignity of sin appears in the price of pardons.

2. Yet it was some encouragement to the people (when they were told that they had *sinned a great sin)* to hear that Moses, who had so great an interest in heaven and so true an affection for them, would *go up unto the Lord to make atonement* for them. Consolation should go along with conviction: first wound, and then heal; first show people the greatness of their sin, and then make known to them the atonement, and give them hopes of mercy. *Moses will go up unto the Lord,* though it be but a *peradventure* that he should make atonement. Christ, the great Mediator, went upon greater certainty than this, for he had lain in the bosom of the Father, and perfectly knew all his counsels.

But to us poor supplicants it is encouragement enough in prayer for particular mercies that *peradventure* we may obtain them, though we have not an absolute promise. Zeph. ii. 3, *It may be, you shall be hid.* In our prayers for others, we should be humbly earnest with God, though it is but a *peradventure that God will give them repentance,* 2 Tim. ii. 25.

II. He intercedes with God for mercy. Observe,

1. How pathetic his address was. *Moses returned unto the Lord,* not to receive further instructions about the tabernacle: there were no more conferences now about that matter. Thus men's sins and follies make work for their friends and ministers, unpleasant work, many times, and give great interruptions to that work which they delight in. Moses in this address expresses, (1.) His great detestation of the people's sin, *v.* 31. He speaks as one overwhelmed with the horror of it: *Oh ! this people have sinned a great sin.* God had first told him of it (*v.* 7), and now he tells God of it, by way of lamentation. He does not call them God's people, he knew they were unworthy to be called so; but this people, this treacherous ungrateful people, they have made for themselves gods of gold. It is a great sin indeed to make gold our god, as those do that make it their hope, and set their heart on it. He does not go about to excuse or extenuate the sin; but what he had said to them by way of conviction he says to God by way of confession : *They have sinned a great sin;* he came not to make apologies, but to make atonement. "Lord, pardon the sin, *for it is great,*" Ps. xxv. 11. (2.) His great desire of the people's welfare (*v.* 32): *Yet now it is not too great a sin for* infinite mercy to pardon, and therefore *if thou wilt forgive their sin.* What then Moses? It is an abrupt expression, " *If thou wilt,* I desire no more ; *if thou wilt,* thou wilt be praised, I shall be pleased, and abundantly recompensed for my intercession." It is an expression like that of the dresser of the vineyard (Luke xiii. 9), *If it bear fruit ;* or, *If thou wilt forgive,* is as much as, " O that thou wouldest forgive !" as Luke xix. 42, *If thou hadst known* is, *O that thou hadst known.* "But *if not,* if the decree has gone forth, and there is no remedy, but they must be ruined ; if this punishment which has already been inflicted on many is not sufficient (2 Cor. ii. 6), but they must all be cut off, *blot me, I pray thee, out of the book which thou hast written ;*" that is, " If they must be cut off, let me be cut off with them, and cut short of Canaan ; if all Israel must perish, I am content to perish with them ; let not the land of promise be mine by survivorship." This expression may be illustrated from Ezek. xiii. 9, where this is threatened against the false prophets, *They shall not be written in the writing of the house of Israel, neither shall they enter into the land of Israel.* God had told Moses that, if he would not interpose

he would make of him a *great nation, v.* 10. "No," says Moses, "I am so far from desiring to see my name and family built up on the ruins of Israel, that I will choose rather to sink with them. If I cannot prevent their destruction, let me not see it (Num. xi. 15); let me not be *written among the living* (Isa. iv. 3), nor among those that are marked for preservation; even let me die in the last ditch." Thus he expresses his tender affection for the people, and is a type of the good Shepherd, that *lays down his life for the sheep* (John x. 11), who was to be *cut off from the land of the living for the transgression of my people,* Isa. liii. 8; Dan. ix. 26. He is also an example of public-spiritedness to all, especially to those in public stations. All private interests must be made subordinate to the good and welfare of communities. It is no great matter what becomes of us and our families in this world, so that it go well with the church of God, and there be peace upon Israel. Moses thus importunes for a pardon, and wrestles with God; not prescribing to him (" If thou wilt not forgive, thou art either unjust or unkind);" no, he is far from that; but, " If not, let me die with the Israelites, and the will of the Lord be done."

2. Observe how prevalent his address was. God would not take him at his word; no, he will not blot any out of his book but those that by their wilful disobedience have forfeited the honour of being enrolled in it (*v.* 33); the soul that sins shall die, and not the innocent for the guilty. This was also an intimation of mercy to the people, that they should not all be destroyed in a body, but those only that had a hand in the sin. Thus Moses gets ground by degrees. God would not at first give him full assurances of his being reconciled to them, lest, if the comfort of a pardon were too easily obtained, they should be emboldened to do the like again, and should not be made sensible enough of the evil of the sin. Comforts are suspended that convictions may be the deeper impressed: also God would hereby exercise the faith and zeal of Moses, their great intercessor. Further, in answer to the address of Moses, (1.) God promises, notwithstanding this, to go on with his kind intention of giving them the land of Canaan, the land he had *spoken to them of, v.* 34. Therefore he sends Moses back to them to lead them, though they were unworthy of him, and promises that his angel should go before them, some created angel that was employed in the common services of the kingdom of providence, which intimated that they were not to expect any thing for the future to be done for them out of the common road of providence, not any thing extraordinary. Moses afterwards obtained a promise of God's special presence with them (*ch.* xxxiii. 14, 17); but at present this was all he could prevail for. (2.) Yet he threatens to remember this sin against them when hereafter he should see cause to punish them for

other sins: " *When I visit, I will visit* for this among the rest. Next time I take the rod in hand, they shall have one stripe the more for this." The Jews have a saying, grounded on this, that henceforward no judgment fell upon Israel but there was in it an ounce of the powder of the golden calf. I see no ground in scripture for the opinion some are of, that God would not have burdened them with such a multitude of sacrifices and other ceremonial institutions if they had not provoked him by worshipping the golden calf. On the contrary, Stephen says that when they *made a calf, and offered sacrifice to the idol, God turned, and gave them up to worship the host of heaven* (Acts vii. 41, 42); so that the strange addictedness of that people to the sin of idolatry was a just judgment upon them for making and worshipping the golden calf, and a judgment they were never quite freed from till the captivity of Babylon. See Rom. i. 23—25. Note, Many that are not immediately cut off in their sins are reserved for a further day of reckoning: vengeance is slow, but sure. For the present, *the Lord plagued the people* (*v.* 35), probably by the pestilence, or some other infectious disease, which was a messenger of God's wrath, and an earnest of worse. Aaron made the calf, and yet it is said the people made it, because they worshipped it. *Deos qui rogat, ille facit* —He who asks for gods makes them. Aaron was not plagued, but the people; for his was a sin of infirmity, theirs a presumptuous sin, between which there is a great difference, not always discernible to us, but evident to God, whose judgment therefore, we are sure, is according to truth. Thus Moses prevailed for a reprieve and a mitigation of the punishment, but could not wholly turn away the wrath of God. This (some think) bespeaks the inability of the law of Moses to reconcile men to God and to perfect our peace with him, which was reserved for Christ to do, in whom alone it is that God so pardons sin as to *remember it no more.*

CHAP. XXXIII.

In this chapter we have a further account of the mediation of Moses between God and Israel, for the making up of the breach that sin had made between them. I. He brings a very humbling message from God to them (ver. 1—3, 5), which has a good effect upon them, and helps to prepare them for mercy, ver. 4, 6. II. He settles a correspondence between God and them, and both God and the people signify their approbation of that correspondence, God by descending in a cloudy pillar, and the people by worshipping at the tent doors, ver. 7—11. III. He is earnest with God in prayer, and prevails, 1. For a promise of his presence with the people, ver. 12—17. 2. For a sight of his glory for himself, ver. 18, &c.

AND the Lord said unto Moses, Depart, *and* go up hence, thou and the people which thou hast brought up out of the land of Egypt, unto the land which I sware unto Abraham, to Isaac, and to Jacob, saying, Unto thy seed will I give it: 2 And I will send an angel before thee; and I will drive out the Canaanite, the Amorite, and the Hittite, and the Perizzite, the

Hivite, and the Jebusite: 3 Unto a land flowing with milk and honey: for I will not go up in the midst of thee; for thou *art* a stiffnecked people: lest I consume thee in the way. 4 And when the people heard these evil tidings, they mourned: and no man did put on him his ornaments. 5 For the LORD had said unto Moses, Say unto the children of Israel, Ye *are* a stiffnecked people: I will come up into the midst of thee in a moment, and consume thee: therefore now put off thy ornaments from thee, .that I may know what to do unto thee. 6 And the children of Israel stripped themselves of their ornaments by the mount Horeb.

Here is, I. The message which God sent by Moses to the children of Israel, signifying the continuance of the displeasure against them, and the bad terms they yet stood upon with God. This he must let them know for their further mortification. 1. He applies to them a mortifying name, by giving them their just character—*a stiff-necked people, v.* 3, 5. " Go," says God to Moses, " go and tell them that they are so." He that knows them better than they know themselves says so of them. God would have brought them under the yoke of his law, and into the bond of his covenant, but their necks were too stiff to bow to them. God would have cured them of their corrupt and crooked dispositions, and have set them straight; but they were wilful and obstinate, and hated to be reformed, and would not have God to reign over them. Note, God judges of men by the temper of their minds. We know what man does; God knows what he is: we know what proceeds from man; God knows what is in man, and nothing is more displeasing to him than stiff-neckedness, as nothing in children is more offensive to their parents and teachers than stubbornness. 2. He tells them what they deserved, that he should *come into the midst of them in a moment, and consume them, v.* 5. Had he dealt with them according to their sins, he had taken them away with a swift destruction. Note, Those whom God pardons must be made to know what their sin deserved, and how miserable they would have been if they had been unpardoned, that God's mercy may be the more magnified. 3. He bids them *depart and go up hence* to the land of Canaan, *v.* 1. This mount Sinai, where they now were, was the place appointed for the setting up of God's tabernacle and solemn worship among them; this was not yet done, so that in bidding them depart hence God intimates that it should not be done—" Let them go forward as they are;" and so it was very expressive

of God's displeasure. 4. He turns them over to Moses, as the people whom he had brought up out of the land of Egypt, and leaves it to him to lead them to Canaan. 5. Though he promises to make good his covenant with Abraham, in giving them Canaan, yet he denies them the extraordinary tokens of his presence, such as they had hitherto been blessed with, and leaves them under the common conduct of Moses their prince, and the common convoy of a guardian angel: " *I will send an angel before thee,* for thy protector, otherwise the evil angels would soon destroy thee; but *I will not go up in the midst of thee, lest I consume thee*" (*v.* 2, 3); not as if an angel would be more patient and compassionate than God, but their affronts given to an angel would not be so provoking as those given to the *shechinah,* or divine Majesty itself. Note, The greater the privileges we enjoy the greater is our danger if we do not improve them and live up to them. 6. He speaks as one that was at a loss what course to take with them. Justice said, " Cut them off, and consume them." Mercy said, " *How shall I give thee up, Ephraim?*" Hos. xi. 8. Well, says God, *put off thy ornaments, that I may know what to do with thee;* that is, " Put thyself into the posture of a penitent, that the dispute may be determined in thy favour, and mercy may rejoice against judgment," *v.* 5. Note, Calls to repentance are plain indications of mercy designed. If the Lord were pleased to kill us, justice knows what to do with a stiffnecked people: but God has no pleasure in the death of those that die; let them return and repent, and then mercy, which otherwise is at a loss, knows what to do.

II. The people's melancholy reception of this message; it was evil tidings to them to hear that they should not have God's special presence with them, and therefore, 1. *They mourned* (*v.* 4), mourned for their sin which had provoked God to withdraw from them, and mourned for this as the sorest punishment of their sin. When 3000 of them were at one time laid dead upon the spot by the Levites' sword, we do not find that they mourned for this (hoping that it would help to expiate the guilt); but when God denied them his favourable presence then they mourned and were in bitterness. Note, Of all the bitter fruits and consequences of sin, that which true penitents most lament, and dread most, is God's departure from them. God had promised that, notwithstanding their sin, he would give them the *land flowing with milk and honey.* But they could have small joy of that if they had not God's presence with them. Canaan itself would be no pleasant land without that; therefore, if they want that, they mourn. 2. In token of great shame and humiliation, those that were undressed did *not put on their ornaments* (*v.* 4), and those that were dressed *stripped themselves of their ornaments, by the mount;* or, as some read it, *at a distance from the mount* (v. 6), standing afar off like the publican, Luke xviii. 13. God bade them *lay aside their ornaments* (v. 5), and they did so, both to show, in general, their deep mourning, and, in particular, to take a holy revenge upon themselves for giving their ear-rings to make the golden calf of. Those that would part with their ornaments for the maintenance of their sin could do no less than lay aside their ornaments in token of their sorrow and shame for it. When the *Lord God calls to weeping and mourning* we must comply with the call, and not only fast from pleasant bread (Dan. x. 3), but lay aside our ornaments; even those that are decent enough at other times are unseasonably worn on days of humiliation or in times of public calamity, Isa. iii. 18.

7 And Moses took the tabernacle, and pitched it without the camp, afar off from the camp, and called it the Tabernacle of the congregation. And it came to pass, *that* every one which sought the Lord went out unto the tabernacle of the congregation, which *was* without the camp. 8 And it came to pass, when Moses went out unto the tabernacle, *that* all the people rose up, and stood every man *at* his tent door, and looked after Moses, until he was gone into the tabernacle. 9 And it came to pass, as Moses entered into the tabernacle, the cloudy pillar descended, and stood *at* the door of the tabernacle, and *the LORD* talked with Moses. 10 And all the people saw the cloudy pillar stand *at* the tabernacle door: and all the people rose up and worshipped, every man *in* his tent door. 11 And the Lord spake unto Moses face to face, as a man speaketh unto his friend. And he turned again into the camp: but his servant Joshua, the son of Nun, a young man, departed not out of the tabernacle.

Here is, I. One mark of displeasure put upon them for their further humiliation : *Moses took the tabernacle*, not his own tent for his family, but the tent wherein he gave audience, heard causes, and enquired of God, the *guild-hall* (as it were) of their camp, and *pitched it without, afar off from the camp* (v. 7), to signify to them that they had rendered themselves unworthy of it, and that, unless peace was made, it would return to them no more. God would thus let them know that he was at variance with them : *The Lord is far from the wicked.* Thus the

glory of the Lord departed from the temple when it was polluted with sin, Ezek. x. 4; xi. 23. Note, It is a sign that God is angry when he removes his tabernacle, for his ordinances are fruits of his favour and tokens of his presence; while we have them with us we have him with us. Perhaps this tabernacle was a plan, or model rather, of the tabernacle that was afterwards to be erected, a hasty draught from the pattern shown him in the mount, designed for direction to the workmen, and used, in the mean time, as a tabernacle of meeting between God and Moses about public affairs. This was set up at a distance, to affect the people with the loss of that glorious structure which, if they had not forsaken their own mercies for lying vanities, was to have been set up in the midst of them. Let them see what they had forfeited.

II. Many encouragements given them, notwithstanding, to hope that God would yet be reconciled to them.

1. Though the tabernacle was removed, yet every one that was disposed to seek the Lord was welcome to follow it, v. 7. Private persons, as well as Moses, were invited and encouraged to apply to God, as intercessors upon this occasion. A place was appointed for them to go to *without the camp*, to solicit God's return to them. Thus when Ezra (a second Moses) interceded for Israel there were assembled to him many that *trembled at God's word*, Ezra ix. 4. When God designs mercy, he stirs up prayer. *He will be sought unto* (Ezek. xxxvi. 37); and, thanks be to his name, he may be sought unto, and will not reject the intercession of the poorest. Every Israelite that sought the Lord was welcome to this tabernacle, as well as Moses *the man of God*.

2. Moses undertook to mediate between God and Israel. He *went out to the tabernacle*, the place of treaty, probably pitched between them and the mount (v. 8), and he *entered into the tabernacle, v. 9.* That cause could not but speed well which had so good a manager; when their judge (under God) becomes their advocate, and he who was appointed to be their law-giver is an intercessor for them, there is *hope in Israel concerning this thing.*

3. The people seemed to be in a very good mind and well disposed towards a reconciliation. (1.) When Moses went out to go to the tabernacle, the people *looked after him* (v. 8), in token of their respect to him whom before they had slighted, and their entire dependence upon his mediation. By this it appeared that they were very solicitous about this matter, desirous to be at peace with God and concerned to know what would be the issue. Thus the disciples looked after our Lord Jesus, when he ascended on high to enter into the holy place not made with hands, till a *cloud received him out of their sight*, as Moses here. And we must with an eye of faith follow him likewise thither, where

he is appearing in the presence of God for us; then shall we have the benefit of his mediation. (2.) When they saw the cloudy pillar, that symbol of God's presence, give Moses the meeting, they all *worshipped, every man at his tent door, v.* 10. Thereby they signified, [1.] Their humble adoration of the divine Majesty, which they will ever worship, and not gods of gold any more. [2.] Their joyful thankfulness to God that he was pleased to show them this token for good, and give them hopes of a reconciliation; for, if he had been pleased to kill them, he would not have shown them such things as these, would not have raised them up such a mediator, nor given him such countenance. [3.] Their hearty concurrence with Moses as their advocate in every thing he should promise for them, and their expectation of a comfortable and happy issue of this treaty. Thus must we worship God in our tents with an eye to Christ as the Mediator. Their worshipping in their tent doors declared plainly that they were not ashamed publicly to own their respect to God and Moses, as they had publicly worshipped the calf.

4. God was, in Moses, reconciling Israel to himself, and manifested himself very willing to be at peace. (1.) God met Moses at the place of treaty, *v.* 9. The cloudy pillar, which had withdrawn itself from the camp when it was polluted with idolatry, now returned to this tabernacle at some distance, coming back gradually. If our hearts go forth towards God to meet him he will graciously come down to meet us. (2.) God *talked with Moses (v.* 9), *spoke to him face to face, as a man speaks to his friend (v.* 11), which intimates that God revealed himself to Moses, not only with greater clearness and evidence of divine light than to any other of the prophets, but also with greater expressions of particular kindness and grace. He spoke, not as a prince to a subject, but as a *man to his friend,* whom he loves, and with whom he takes sweet counsel. This was great encouragement to Israel, to see their advocate so great a favourite; and, that they might be encouraged by it, *Moses turned again into the camp,* to tell the people what hopes he had of bringing this business to a good issue, and that they might not despair if he should be long absent. But, because he intended speedily to return to the tabernacle of the congregation, he left Joshua there, for it was not fit that the place should be empty, so long as the cloud of glory *stood at the door (v.* 9); but, if God had any thing to say out of that cloud while Moses was absent, Joshua was there, ready to hear it.

12 And Moses said unto the LORD, See, thou sayest unto me, Bring up this people: and thou hast not let me know whom thou wilt send with me. Yet thou hast said, I know thee by name, and thou hast also found grace in my sight. 13 Now therefore, I pray thee, if I have found grace in thy sight, show me now thy way, that I may know thee, that I may find grace in thy sight: and consider that this nation *is* thy people. 14 And he said, My presence shall go *with thee,* and I will give thee rest. 15 And he said unto him, If thy presence go not *with me,* carry us not up hence. 16 For wherein shall it be known here that I and thy people have found grace in thy sight? *is it* not in that thou goest with us? so shall we be separated, I and thy people, from all the people that *are* upon the face of the earth. 17 And the LORD said unto Moses, I will do this thing also that thou hast spoken: for thou hast found grace in my sight, and I know thee by name. 18 And he said, I beseech thee, show me thy glory. 19 And he said, I will make all my goodness pass before thee, and I will proclaim the name of the LORD before thee; and will be gracious to whom I will be gracious, and will show mercy on whom I will show mercy. 20 And he said, Thou canst not see my face: for there shall no man see me, and live. 21 And the LORD said, Behold, *there is* a place by me, and thou shalt stand upon a rock: 22 And it shall come to pass, while my glory passeth by, that I will put thee in a clift of the rock, and will cover thee with my hand while I pass by: 23 And I will take away mine hand, and thou shalt see my back parts: but my face shall not be seen.

Moses, having returned to the door of the tabernacle, becomes a humble and importunate supplicant there for two very great favours, and as a prince he has power with God, and prevails for both: herein he was a type of Christ the great intercessor, *whom the Father heareth always.*

I. He is very earnest with God for a grant of his presence with Israel in the rest of their march to Canaan, notwithstanding their provocations. The people had by their sin deserved the wrath of God, and for the turning away of that Moses had already prevailed, *ch.* xxxii. 14. But they had likewise forfeited God's favourable presence, and all the benefit and comfort of that, and this Moses is here begging for the return of. Thus, by the intercession of Christ, we obtain not only the removal of the curse, but an assurance of the blessing; we are not only saved from ruin, but become entitled to everlasting happiness. Observe how admirably Moses orders this cause before God, and *fills his mouth with arguments.* What a value he expresses for God's favour, what a concern for God's glory and the welfare of Israel. How he pleads, and how he speeds.

1. How he pleads. (1.) He insists upon the commission God had given him to *bring up this people*, v. 12. This he begins with: "Lord, it is thou thyself that employest me; and wilt thou not own me? I am in the way of my duty; and shall I not have thy presence with me in that way?" Whom God calls out to any service he will be sure to furnish with necessary assistances. "Now, Lord, thou hast ordered me a great work, and yet left me at a loss how to go about it, and go through with it." Note, Those that sincerely design and endeavour to do their duty may in faith beg of God direction and strength for the doing of it. (2.) He improves the interest he himself had with God, and pleads God's gracious expressions of kindness to him: *Thou hast said, I know thee by name*, as a particular friend and confidant, *and thou hast also found grace in my sight*, above any other. *Now, therefore*, says Moses, if it be indeed so, that *I have found grace in thy sight, show me thy way*, v. 13. What favour God had expressed to the people they had forfeited the benefit of, there was no insisting upon that; and therefore Moses lays the stress of his plea upon what God had said to him, which, though he owns himself unworthy of, yet he hopes he has not thrown himself out of the benefit of. By this therefore he takes hold on God: "Lord, if ever thou wilt do any thing for me, do this for the people." Thus our Lord Jesus, in his intercession, presents himself to the Father, as one in whom he is always well pleased, and so obtains mercy for us with whom he is justly displeased; and we are *accepted in the beloved.* Thus also men of public spirit love to improve their interest both with God and man for the public good. Observe what it is he is thus earnest for: *Show me thy way*, that I may know that *I find grace in thy sight.* Note, Divine direction is one of the best evidences of divine favour. By this we may know that we *find grace in God's sight*, if we find grace in our hearts to guide and quicken us in the way of our duty. God's good work in us is the surest discovery of his good-will towards us. (3.) He insinuates that the people also, though most unworthy, yet were in some relation to God: "*Consider that this nation is thy people*, a people that thou hast done great things for, redeemed to thyself, and taken into covenant with thyself; Lord, they are thy own, do not leave them." The offended father considers this, "My child is foolish and froward, but he is my child, and I cannot abandon him." (4.) He expresses

the great value he had for the presence of God. When God said, *My presence shall go with thee*, he caught at that word, as that which he could not live and move without: *If thy presence go not with me, carry us not up hence*," v. 15. He speaks as one that dreaded the thought of going forward without God's presence, knowing that their marches could not be safe, nor their encampments easy, if they had not God with them. "Better lie down and die here in the wilderness than go forward to Canaan without God's presence." Note, Those who know how to value God's favours are best prepared to receive them. Observe how earnest Moses is in this matter; he begs as one that would take no denial. "Here we will stay till we obtain thy favour; like Jacob, *I will not let thee go except thou bless me.*" And observe how he advances upon God's concessions; the kind intimations given him make him yet more importunate. Thus God's gracious promises, and the advances of mercy towards us, should not only encourage our faith, but excite our fervency in prayer. (5.) He concludes with an argument taken from God's glory (v. 16): "*Wherein shall it be known* to the nations that have their eyes upon us that I *and thy people* (with whom my interests are all blended) *have found grace in thy sight*, distinguishing favour, so as to be *separated from all people upon earth?* How will it appear that we are indeed thus honoured? *Is it not in that thou goest with us?* Nothing short of this can answer these characters. Let it never be said that we are a peculiar people, and highly favoured, for we stand but upon a level with the rest of our neighbours unless thou go with us; sending an angel with us will not serve." He lays a stress upon the place—"*here* in this wilderness, whither thou hast led us, and where we shall be certainly lost if thou leave us." Note, God's special presence with us in this wilderness, by his Spirit and grace, to direct, defend, and comfort us, is the surest pledge of his special love to us and will redound to his glory as well as our benefit.

2. Observe how he speeds. He obtained an assurance of God's favour, (1.) To himself (v. 14): "*I will give thee rest*, I will take care to make thee easy in this matter; however it be, thou shalt have satisfaction." Moses never entered Canaan, and yet God made good his word that he would give him rest, Dan. xii. 13. (2.) To the people for his sake. Moses was not content with that answer which bespoke favour to himself only, he must gain a promise, an express promise, for the people too, or he is not at rest; gracious generous souls think it not enough to get to heaven themselves, but would have all their friends go thither too. And in this also Moses prevailed: *I will do this thing also that thou hast spoken*, v. 17. Moses is not checked as an unreasonable beggar, whom no saying would serve, but he is

encouraged. God grants as long as he asks, *gives liberally*, and *does not upbraid* him. See the power of prayer, and be quickened hereby to ask, and seek, and knock, and to *continue instant in prayer*, to *pray always and not to faint*. See the riches of God's goodness. When he has done much, yet he is willing to do more : *I will do this also—above what we are able to ask or think*. See, in type, the prevalency of Christ's intercession, which he ever lives to make for all those that come to God by him, and the ground of that prevalency. It is purely his own merit, not any thing in those for whom he intercedes; it is because *thou hast found grace in my sight*. And now the matter is settled, God is perfectly reconciled to them, his presence in the pillar of cloud returns to them and shall continue with them; all is well again, and henceforth we hear no more of the golden calf. *Lord, who is a God like unto thee, pardoning iniquity?*

II. Having gained this point, he next begs *a sight of God's glory*, and is heard in this matter also. Observe,

1. The humble request Moses makes : *I beseech thee, show me thy glory, v.* 18. Moses had lately been in the mount with God, had continued there a great while, and had enjoyed as intimate a communion with God as ever any man had on this side heaven; and yet he is still desiring a further acquaintance. All that are effectually called to the knowledge of God and fellowship with him, though they desire nothing more than God, are nevertheless still coveting more and more of him, till they come to see as they are seen. Moses had wonderfully prevailed with God for one favour after another, and the success of his prayers emboldened him to go on still to seek God; the more he had the more he asked : when we are in a good frame at the throne of grace, we should endeavour to preserve and improve it, and strike while the iron is hot : " *Show me thy glory ; make me to see* it (so the word is); " make it some way or other visible, and enable me to bear the sight of it." Not that he was so ignorant as to think God's essence could be seen with bodily eyes; but, having hitherto only heard a voice out of a pillar of cloud or fire, he desired to see some representation of the divine glory, such as God saw fit to gratify him with. It was not fit that the people should see any similitude when the Lord spoke unto them, *lest they should corrupt themselves ;* but he hoped that there was not that danger in his seeing some similitude. Something it was more than he had yet seen that Moses desired. If it was purely for the assisting of his faith and devotion, the desire was commendable; but perhaps there was in it a mixture of human infirmity. God will have us walk by faith, not by sight, in this world ; and *faith comes by hearing.* Some think that Moses desired a sight of God's glory as a token of his reconciliation,

and an earnest of that presence which he had promised them ; but he knew not what he asked.

2. The gracious reply God made to this request. (1.) He denied that which was not fit to be granted, and which Moses could not bear : *Thou canst not see my face, v.* 20. A full discovery of the glory of God would quite overpower the faculties of any mortal man in this present state, and overwhelm him, even Moses himself. Man is mean and unworthy of it, weak and could not bear it, guilty and could not but dread it. It is in compassion to our infirmity that God *holdeth back the face of his throne, and spreadeth a cloud upon it,* Job xxvi. 9. God has said that *here* (that is, in this world) his *face shall not be seen (v.* 23); that is an honour reserved for the future state, to be the eternal bliss of holy souls : should men in this state know what it is, they would not be content to live short of it. There is a knowledge and enjoyment of God which must be waited for in another world, when we shall *see him as he is,* 1 John iii. 2. In the mean time let us adore the height of what we do know of God, and the depth of what we do not. Long before this, Jacob had spoken of it with wonder that he had *seen God face to face,* and yet *his life was preserved,* Gen. xxxii. 30. Sinful man dreads the sight of God his Judge; but holy souls, being *by the Spirit of the Lord changed into the same image, behold with open face the glory of the Lord.* 2 Cor. iii. 18. (2.) He granted that which would be abundantly satisfying. [1.] He should hear what would please him (v. 19): *I'will make all my goodness pass before thee.* He had given him wonderful instances of his goodness in being reconciled to Israel : but that was only goodness in the stream ; he would show him goodness in the spring— *all his goodness.* This was a sufficient answer to his request. " Show me thy glory," says Moses. " I will show thee my goodness," says God. Note, God's goodness is his glory ; and he will have us to know him by the glory of his mercy more than by the glory of his majesty ; for we must fear even *the Lord and his goodness,* Hos. iii. 5. That especially which is the glory of God's goodness is the sovereignty of it, that he will be *gracious to whom he will be gracious,* that, as an absolute proprietor, he makes what difference he pleases in bestowing his gifts, and is not debtor to any, nor accountable to any *(may he not do what he will with his own ?) ;* also that all his reasons of mercy are fetched from within himself, not from any merit in his creatures : as he has mercy on whom he will, so, because he will. *Even so, Father, because it seemed good in thy sight.* It is never said, " I will be angry at whom I will be angry," for his wrath is always just and holy ; but *I will show mercy on whom I will show mercy,* for his grace is always free. He never damns by prerogative, but by preroga-

tive he saves. The apostle quotes this (Rom. ix. 15) in answer to those who charged God with unrighteousness in giving that grace freely to some which he withholds justly from others. [2.] He should see what he could bear, and what would suffice him. The matter is concerted so as that Moses might be safe and yet satisfied. *First*, Safe in a *cleft of the rock*, v. 21, 22. In this he was to be sheltered from the dazzling light and devouring fire of God's glory. This was the rock in Horeb out of which water was brought, of which it is said, *That rock was Christ*, 1 Cor. x. 4. It is in the clefts of this rock that we are secured from the wrath of God, which otherwise would consume us ; God himself will protect those that are thus hid. And it is only through Christ that we have *the knowledge of the glory of God*. None can see his glory to their comfort but those who stand upon this rock, and take shelter in it. *Secondly*, He was satisfied with a sight of his back-parts, v. 23. He should see more of God than any ever saw on earth, but not so much as those see who are in heaven. The face, in man, is the seat of majesty, and men are known by their faces ; in them we take a full view of men. That sight of God Moses might not have, but such a sight as we have of a man who has gone past us, so that we only see his back, and have (as we say) a blush of him. We cannot be said to look at God, but rather to look after him (Gen. xvi. 13) ; for we see *through a glass darkly*. When we see what God has done in his works, observe the goings of our God, our King, we see (as it were) his back-parts. The best thus *know but in part*, and we cannot order our speech concerning God, by reason of darkness, any more than we can describe a man whose face we never saw. Now Moses was allowed to see only the back-parts ; but long afterwards, when he was a witness to Christ's transfiguration, he saw *his face shine as the sun*. If we faithfully improve the discoveries God gives us of himself while we are here, a brighter and more glorious scene will shortly be opened to us ; for *to him that hath shall be given*.

CHAP. XXXIV.

God, having in the foregoing chapter intimated to Moses his reconciliation to Israel, here gives proofs of it, proceeding to settle his covenant and communion with them. Four instances of the return of his favour we have in this chapter :—I. The orders he gives to Moses to come up to the mount, the next morning, and bring two tables of stone with him, ver. 1—4. II. His meeting him there, and the proclamation of his name, ver. 5—9. III. The instructions he gave him there, and his converse with him for forty days together, without intermission, ver. 10—28. IV. The honour he put upon him when he sent him down with his face shining, ver. 29—35. In all this God dealt with Moses as a public person, and mediator between him and Israel, and a type of the great Mediator.

AND the LORD said unto Moses, Hew thee two tables of stone like unto the first : and I will write upon *these* tables the words that were in the first tables, which thou brakest. 2 And be ready in the morning, and come up in the morning unto mount Sinai, and present thyself there to me in the top of the mount. 3 And no man shall come up with thee, neither let any man be seen throughout all the mount ; neither let the flocks nor herds feed before that mount. 4 And he hewed two tables of stone like unto the first ; and Moses rose up early in the morning, and went up unto mount Sinai, as the LORD had commanded him, and took in his hand the two tables of stone.

The treaty that was on foot between God and Israel being broken off abruptly, by their worshipping the golden calf, when peace was made all must be begun anew, not where they left off, but from the beginning. Thus backsliders must *repent, and do their first works*, Rev. ii. 5.

I. Moses must prepare for the renewing of the tables, v. 1. Before, God himself provided the tables, and wrote on them ; now, Moses must *hew out the tables*, and God would only write upon them. Thus, in the first writing of the law upon the heart of man in innocency, both the tables and the writing were the work of God ; but when those were broken and defaced by sin, and the divine law was to be preserved in the scriptures, God therein made use of the ministry of man, and Moses first. But the prophets and apostles did only hew the tables, as it were ; the writing was God's still, for *all scripture is given by inspiration of God*. Observe, When God was reconciled to them, he ordered the tables to be renewed, and wrote his law in them, which plainly intimates to us, 1. That even under the gospel of peace and reconciliation by Christ (of which the intercession of Moses was typical) the moral law should continue to bind believers. Though Christ has redeemed us from the curse of the law, yet not from the command of it, but still we are *under the law to Christ ;* when our Saviour, in his sermon on the mount, expounded the moral law, and vindicated it from the corrupt glosses with which the scribes and Pharisees had broken it (Matt. v. 19), he did in effect renew the tables, and make them like the first, that is, reduce the law to its primitive sense and intention. 2. That the best evidence of the pardon of sin and peace with God is the writing of the law in the heart. The first token God gave of his reconciliation to Israel was the renewing of the tables of the law ; thus the first article of the new covenant is, *I will write my law in their heart* (Heb. viii. 10), and it follows (v. 12), *for I will be merciful to their unrighteousness.* 3. That, if we would have God to write the law in our hearts, we must prepare our hearts for the reception of it. The heart of stone must be hewn by conviction and humiliation for sin (Hos. vi. 5), the *superfluity of naughtiness* must be taken off (James i. 21), the heart made smooth, and laboured with, that the word may have a place in it. Moses did accordingly hew out the *tables of stone*, or slate, for they were so slight and thin that Moses carried them both in his hand; and, for their dimensions, they must have been somewhat less, and perhaps not much, than the ark in which they were deposited, which was a yard and quarter long, and three quarters broad. It should seem there was nothing particularly curious in the framing of them, for there was no great time taken; Moses had them ready presently, to take up with him, next morning. They were to receive their beauty, not from the art of man, but from the finger of God.

II. Moses must attend again on the top of mount Sinai, and present himself to God there, *v.* 2. Though the absence of Moses, and his continuance so long on the mount, had lately occasioned their making the golden calf, yet God did not therefore alter his measures, but he shall come up and tarry as long as he had done, to try whether they had learned to wait. To strike an awe upon the people, they are directed to keep their distance, none must come up with him, *v.* 3. They had said (*ch.* xxxii. 1), *We know not what has become of him,* and God will not let them know. Moses, accordingly, *rose up early* (*v.* 4), to go to the place appointed, to show how forward he was to present himself before God and loth to lose time. It is good to be early at our devotions. The morning is perhaps as good a friend to the graces as it is to the muses.

5 And the LORD descended in the cloud, and stood with him there, and proclaimed the name of the LORD. 6 And the LORD passed by before him, and proclaimed, The LORD, The LORD God, merciful and gracious, longsuffering, and abundant in goodness and truth, 7 Keeping mercy for thousands, forgiving iniquity and transgression and sin, and that will by no means clear *the guilty;* visiting the iniquity of the fathers upon the children, and upon the children's children, unto the third and to the fourth *generation.* 8 And Moses made haste, and bowed his head toward the earth, and worshipped. 9 And he said, If now I have found grace in thy sight, O Lord, let my Lord, I pray thee, go among us; for it *is* a stiffnecked people; and pardon our iniquity and our sin, and take us for thine inheritance.

No sooner had Moses got to the top of the mount than God gave him the meeting (*v.* 5): *The Lord descended,* by some sensible token of his presence, and manifestation of his glory. His descending bespeaks his condescension; he humbles himself to take cognizance of those that humble themselves to walk with him. Ps. cxiii. 6, *Lord, what is man, that he should be thus visited?* He descended *in the cloud,* probably that pillar of cloud which had hitherto gone before Israel, and had the day before met Moses at the door of the tabernacle. This cloud was to strike an awe upon Moses, that the familiarity he was admitted to might not breed contempt. The disciples *feared, when they entered into the cloud.* His making a cloud his pavilion intimated that, though he made known much of himself, yet there was much more concealed. Now observe,

I. How God proclaimed his name (*v.* 6, 7): he did it *in transitu—as he passed by him.* Fixed views of God are reserved for the future state; the best we have in this world are transient. God now was performing what he had promised Moses, the day before, that his glory should pass by, *ch.* xxxiii. 22. He *proclaimed the name of the Lord,* by which he would make himself known. He had made himself known to Moses in the glory of his self-existence and self-sufficiency when he proclaimed that name, *I am that I am;* now he makes himself known in the glory of his grace, and goodness, and all-sufficiency to us. Now that God is about to publish a second edition of the law he prefaces it with this proclamation; for it is God's grace or goodness that gives the law, especially the remedial law. The pardon of Israel's sin in worshipping the calf was now to pass the seals; and God, by this declaration, would let them know that he pardoned *ex mero motu—merely out of his own good pleasure,* not for their merits' sake, but from his own inclination to forgive. The proclaiming of it denotes the universal extent of God's mercy. He is not only good to Israel, but good to all; let all take notice of it. He that hath an ear, let him hear, and know, and believe,

1. That the God with whom we have to do is a great God. He is Jehovah, the Lord, who has his being of himself, and is the fountain of all being, *Jehovah-El, the Lord, the strong God,* a God of almighty power himself, and the original of all power. This is prefixed before the display of his mercy, to teach us to think and to speak even of God's grace and goodness with great seriousness and a holy awe, and to encourage us to depend upon these mercies; they are not the mercies of a man, that is frail and feeble, false and fickle, but the mercies of the Lord, the Lord God; therefore sure mercies, and sovereign mercies, mercies that may be trusted, but not tempted.

2. That he is a good God. His greatness

and goodness illustrate and set off each other. That the terror of his greatness may not make us afraid, we are told how good he is; and, that we may not presume upon his goodness, we are told how great he is. Many words are here heaped up, to acquaint us with, and convince us of, God's goodness, and to show how much his goodness is both his glory and his delight, yet without any tautology. (1.) He is *merciful.* This bespeaks his tender compassion, like that of a father to his children. This is put first, because it is the first wheel in all the instances of God's good-will to fallen man, whose misery makes him an object of pity, Judg. x. 16; Isa. lxiii. 9. Let us not then have either hard thoughts of God or hard hearts towards our brethren. (2.) He is *gracious.* This bespeaks both freeness and kindness; it intimates not only that he has a compassion to his creatures, but a complacency in them and in doing good to them, and this of his own good-will, and not for the sake of any thing in them. His mercy is grace, free grace; this teaches us to be not only pitiful, but courteous, 1 Pet. iii. 8. (3.) He is *long-suffering.* This is a branch of God's goodness which the wickedness of sinners gives occasion for; that of Israel had done so: they had tried his patience, and experienced it. He is long-suffering, that is, he is slow to anger, and delays the execution of his justice; he waits to be gracious, and lengthens out the offers of his mercy. (4.) He is *abundant in goodness and truth.* This bespeaks plentiful goodness, goodness abounding above our deserts, above our conception and expression. The springs of mercy are always full, the streams of mercy always flowing; there is mercy enough in God, enough for all, enough for each, enough for ever. It bespeaks promised goodness, goodness and truth put together, goodness engaged by promise, and his faithfulness pledged for the security of it. He not only does good, but by his promise he raises our expectation of it, and even binds himself to show mercy. (5.) He keepeth *mercy for thousands.* This denotes, [1.] Mercy extended to thousands of persons. When he gives to some, still he keeps for others, and is never exhausted; he has mercy enough for all the thousands of Israel, when they shall *multiply as the sand.* [2.] Mercy entailed upon thousands of generations, even those upon whom the ends of the world have come; nay, the line of it is drawn parallel with that of eternity itself. (6.) He *forgiveth iniquity, transgression, and sin.* Pardoning mercy is specified, because in this divine grace is most magnified, and because it is this which opens the door to all other gifts of his divine grace, and because of this he had lately given a very pregnant proof. He forgives offences of all sorts—*iniquity, transgression, and sin,* multiplies his pardons; and with him is *plenteous redemption.*

3. That he is a just and holy God. For, (1.) *He will by no means clear the guilty.* Some read it so as to express a mitigation of wrath, even when he does punish: *When he empties, he will not make quite desolate;* that is, "He does not proceed to the greatest extremity, till there be no remedy." As we read it, we must expound it that he will by no means connive at the guilty, as if he took no notice of their sin. Or, he will not clear the impenitently guilty, that go on still in their trespasses: he will not clear the guilty without some satisfaction to his justice, and necessary vindications of the honour of his government. (2.) *He visits the iniquity of the fathers upon the children.* He may justly do it, for all souls are his, and there is a malignity in sin that taints the blood. He sometimes will do it, especially for the punishment of idolaters. Thus he shows his hatred of sin, and displeasure against it; yet he *keepeth not his anger for ever,* but visits to the third and fourth generation only, while he *keepeth mercy for thousands.* Well, this is God's name for ever, and this is his memorial unto all generations.

II. How Moses received this declaration which God made of himself, and of his grace and mercy. It should seem as if Moses accepted this as a sufficient answer to his request that God would *show him his glory;* for we read not that he went into the cleft of the rock, whence to gain a sight of God's back parts. Perhaps this satisfied him, and he desired no more; as we read not that Thomas did *thrust his hand into Christ's side,* though Christ invited him to do it. God having thus proclaimed his name, Moses says, "It is enough, I expect no more till I come to heaven;" at least he did not think fit to relate what he saw. Now we are here told,

1. What impression it made upon him: *Moses made haste, and bowed his head, v. 8.* Thus he expressed, (1.) His humble reverence and adoration of God's glory, giving him *the honour due to that name* he had thus proclaimed. Even the goodness of God must be looked upon by us with a profound veneration and holy awe. (2.) His joy in this discovery which God had made of himself, and his thankfulness for it. We have reason gratefully to acknowledge God's goodness to us, not only in the real instances of it, but in the declarations he has made of it by his word; not only that he is, and will be, gracious to us, but that he is pleased to let us know it. (3.) His holy submission to the will of God, made known in this declaration, subscribing to his justice as well as mercy, and putting himself and his people Israel under the government and direction of such a God as Jehovah had now proclaimed himself to be. Let this God be our God for ever and ever.

2. What improvement he made of it. He immediately grounded a prayer upon it (v. 9); and a most earnest affectionate prayer it is,

(1.) For the presence of God with his people Israel in the wilderness: "*I pray thee, go among us,* for thy presence is all in all to our safety and success." (2.) For pardon of sin: " *O pardon our iniquity and our sin,* else we cannot expect thee to go among us." And, (3.) For the privileges of a peculiar people : "Take us for *thy inheritance,* which thou wilt have a particular eye to, and concern for, and delight in." These things God had already promised, and given Moses assurances of, and yet he prays for them, not as doubting the sincerity of God's grants, but as one solicitous for the ratification of them. God's promises are intended, not to supersede, but to direct and encourage, prayer. Those who have some good hopes, through grace, that their sins are pardoned, must yet continue to pray for pardon, for the renewing of their pardon, and the clearing of it more and more to their souls. The more we see of God's goodness the more ashamed we should be of our own sins, and the more earnest for an interest in it. God had said, in the close of the proclamation, that he would *visit the iniquity upon the children;* and Moses here deprecates that. " Lord, do not only pardon it to them, but to their children, and let our covenant-relation to thee be entailed upon our posterity, as an inheritance." Thus Moses, like a man of a truly public spirit, intercedes even for the children that should be born. But it is a strange plea he urges: *For it is a stiff-necked people.* God had given this as a reason why he would not go along with them, ch. xxxiii. 3. "Yea," says Moses, " the rather go along with us ; for the worse they are the more need they have of thy presence and grace to make them better." Moses sees them so stiff-necked that, for his part, he has neither patience nor power enough to deal with them.' " Therefore, Lord, do thou go among us, else they will never be kept in awe. Thou wilt spare, and bear with them, for thou art *God, and not man,*" Hos. xi. 9.

10 And he said, Behold, I make a covenant : before all thy people I will do marvels, such as have not been done in all the earth, nor in any nation: and all the people amongst which thou *art* shall see the work of the LORD: for it is a terrible thing that I will do with thee. 11 Observe thou that which I command thee this day : behold, I drive out before thee the Amorite, and the Canaanite, and the Hittite, and the Perizzite, and the Hivite, and the Jebusite. 12 Take heed to thyself, lest thou make a covenant with the inhabitants of the land whither thou goest, lest it be for a

snare in the midst of thee : 13 But ye shall destroy their altars, break their images, and cut down their groves : 14 For thou shalt worship no other god : for the LORD, whose name *is* Jealous, *is* a jealous God : 15 Lest thou make a covenant with the inhabitants of the earth, and they go a whoring after their gods, and do sacrifice unto their gods, and *one* call thee, and thou eat of his sacrifice ; 16 And thou take of their daughters unto thy sons, and their daughters go a whoring after their gods, and make thy sons go a whoring after their gods. 17 Thou shalt make thee no molten gods.

Reconciliation being made, a covenant of friendship is here settled between God and Israel. The traitors are not only pardoned, but preferred and made favourites again. Well may the assurances of this be ushered in with a *behold,* a word commanding attention and admiration: *Behold, I make a covenant.* When the covenant was broken, it was Israel that broke it ; now that it comes to be renewed, it is God that makes it. If there be quarrels, we must bear all the blame; if there be peace, God must have all the glory. Here is,

1. God's part of this covenant, what he would do for them, *v.* 10, 11. 1. In general: *Before all thy people, I will do marvels.* Note, Covenant-blessings are marvellous things (Ps. xcviii. 1), marvels in the kingdom of grace ; those mentioned here were marvels in the kingdom of nature, the drying up of Jordan, the standing still of the sun, &c. Marvels indeed, for they were without precedent, *such as have not been done in all the earth.* They were the joy of Israel, and the confirmation of their faith : *Thy people shall see,* and own *the work of the Lord.* And they were the terror of their enemies : *It is a terrible thing that I will do.* Nay, even God's own people should see them with astonishment. 2. In particular : *I drive out before thee the Amorite.* God, as King of nations, plucks up some, to plant others, as it pleases him ; as King of saints, he made room for the vine he brought out of Egypt, Ps. lxxx. 8, 9. Kingdoms are sacrificed to Israel's interests, Isa. xliii. 3, 4.

II. Their part of the covenant : *Observe that which I command thee.* We cannot expect the benefit of the promises unless we make conscience of the precepts.

1. The two great precepts are, (1.) *Thou shalt worship no other gods (v.* 14), not give divine honour to any creature, or any name whatsoever, the creature of fancy. A good reason is annexed. It is at thy peril if thou do: *For the Lord, whose name is Jealous, is a jealous God,* as tender in the matters of his

worship as the husband is of the honour of the marriage-bed. Jealousy is called the *rage of a man* (Prov vi. 34), but it is *God's holy and just displeasure.* Those cannot worship God aright who do not worship him alone. (2.) "*Thou shalt make thee no molten god* (*v.* 17); thou shalt not worship the true God by images." This was the sin they had lately fallen into, which therefore they are particularly cautioned against.

2 Fences are here erected about these two precepts by two others: (1.) That they might not be tempted to worship other gods, they must not join in affinity or friendship with those that did (*v.* 12): "*Take heed to thyself,* for thou art upon thy good behaviour. It is a sin that thou art prone to and that will easily beset thee, and therefore be very cautious, and carefully abstain from all appearances of it and advances towards it. *Make no covenant with the inhabitants of the land.*" If God, in kindness to them, drove out the Canaanites, they ought, in duty to God, not to harbour them. What could be insisted on more reasonable than this? If God make war with the Canaanites, let not Israel make peace with them. If God take care that the Canaanites be not their lords, let them take care that they be not their snares. It was for their civil interest to complete the conquest of the land; so much does God consult our benefit in the laws he gives us. They must particularly take heed of intermarrying with them, *v.* 15, 16. If they espoused their children, they would be in danger of espousing their gods; such is the corruption of nature that the bad are much more likely to debauch the good than the good to reform the bad. The way of sin is downhill: those that are in league with idolaters will come by degrees to be in love with idolatry; and those that are prevailed upon to eat of the idolatrous sacrifice will come at length to offer it, *Obsta principiis—Nip the mischief in the bud.* (2.) That they might not be tempted to make molten gods, they must utterly destroy those they found and all that belong to them, the altars and groves (*v.* 13), lest, if these were left standing, they should be brought, in process of time, either to use them or to take pattern by them, or to abate in their detestation and dread of idolatry. The relics of idolatry ought to be abolished as affronts to the holy God and a great reproach to human nature. Let it never be said that men who pretend to reason were ever guilty of such absurdities as to make gods of their own and worship them.

18 The feast of unleavened bread shalt thou keep. Seven days thou shalt eat unleavened bread, as I commanded thee, in the time of the month Abib: for in the month Abib thou camest out from Egypt. 19 All

that openeth the matrix *is* mine; and every firstling among the cattle, *whether* ox or sheep, *that is male.* 20 But the firstling of an ass thou shalt redeem with a lamb: and if thou redeem *him* not, then shalt thou break his neck. All the firstborn of thy sons thou shalt redeem. And none shall appear before me empty. 21 Six days thou shalt work, but on the seventh day thou shalt rest: in earing time and in harvest thou shalt rest. 22 And thou shalt observe the feast of weeks, of the firstfruits of wheat harvest, and the feast of ingathering at the year's end. 23 Thrice in the year shall all your menchildren appear before the Lord GOD, the God of Israel. 24 For I will cast out the nations before thee, and enlarge thy borders: neither shall any man desire thy land, when thou shalt go up to appear before the LORD thy God thrice in the year. 25 Thou shalt not offer the blood of my sacrifice with leaven; neither shall the sacrifice of the feast of the passover be left unto the morning. 26 The first of the firstfruits of thy land thou shalt bring unto the house of the LORD thy God. Thou shalt not seethe a kid in his mother's milk. 27 And the LORD said unto Moses, Write thou these words: for after the tenour of these words I have made a covenant with thee and with Israel.

Here is a repetition of several appointments made before, especially relating to their solemn feasts. When they had made the calf, they proclaimed a feast in honour of it; now, that they might never do so again, they are here charged with the observance of the feasts which God had instituted. Note, Men need not be drawn from their religion by the temptation of mirth, for we serve a Master that has abundantly provided for the joy of his servants: serious godliness is a continual feast, and joy in God always.

I. Once a week they must rest (*v.* 21), *even in earing time, and in harvest,* the most busy times of the year. All worldly business must give way to that holy rest; harvest-work will prosper the better for the religious observance of the sabbath-day in harvest-time. Hereby we must show that we prefer our communion with God, and our duty to him, before either the business or the joy of harvest.

II. Thrice a year they must feast (*v.* 23); they must then appear *before the Lord, God, the God of Israel.* In all our religious approaches to God, we must eye him as the Lord God, infinitely blessed, great, and glorious, that we may worship him with reverence and godly fear, as the God of Israel, a God in covenant with us, that we may be encouraged to trust in him, and to serve him cheerfully. We always are before God; but, in holy duties, we present ourselves before him, as servants to receive commands, as petitioners to sue for favours, and we have reason to do both with joy. But it might be suggested that, when all the males from every part of the country had gone up to worship in the place that God should choose, the country would be left exposed to the insults of their neighbours; and what would become of the poor women and children, and sick and aged, that were left at home? Trust God with them (*v.* 24): *Neither shall any man desire thy land ;* not only they shall not invade it, but they shall not so much as think of invading it. Note, 1. All hearts are in God's hands, and under his check; he can lay a restraint, not only upon men's actions, but upon their desires. Canaan was a desirable land, and the neighbouring nations were greedy enough; and yet God says, "They shall not desire it." Let us check all sinful desires in our own hearts against God and his glory, and then trust him to check all sinful desires in the hearts of others against us and our interest. 2. The way of duty is the way of safety. If we serve God, he will preserve us; and those that venture for him shall never lose by him. While we are employed in God's work, and are attending upon him, we are taken under special protection, as noblemen and members of parliament are privileged from arrests.

III. The three feasts are here mentioned, with their appendages. 1. The passover, and the feast of unleavened bread, in remembrance of their deliverance out of Egypt; and to this is annexed the law of the redemption of the first-born, *v.* 18—20. This feast was instituted, *ch.* xii. 13, and urged again, *ch.* xxiii. 15. 2. The feast of weeks, that is, that of pentecost, seven weeks after the passover; and to this is annexed the law of the first-fruits. 3. The feast of in-gathering at the year's end, which was the feast of tabernacles (*v.* 22): of these also he had spoken before, *ch.* xxiii. 16. As to those laws repeated here (*v.* 25, 26), that against leaven relates to the passover, that of the first-fruits to the feast of pentecost, and therefore that against seething the kid in his mother's milk in all probability relates to the feast of in-gathering, at which God would not have them use that superstitious ceremony, which probably they had seen the Egyptians, or some other of the neighbouring nations, bless their harvests with.

IV. With these laws, here repeated, it is probable all that was said to him when he

was before upon the mount was repeated likewise, and the model of the tabernacle shown him again, lest the ruffle and discomposure which the golden calf had put him into should have bereaved him of the ideas he had in his mind of what he had seen and heard; also in token of a complete reconciliation, and to show that *not one jot or tittle of the law should pass away,* but that all should be carefully preserved by the great Mediator, who came, not to destroy, but to fulfil, Matt. v. 17, 18. And in the close, 1. Moses is ordered to write these words (*v.* 27), that the people might be the better acquainted with them by a frequent perusal, and that they might be transmitted to the generations to come. We can never be enough thankful to God for the written word. 2. He is told that according to the tenour of these words God would make a covenant with Moses and Israel; not with Israel immediately, but with them in Moses as mediator. Thus the covenant of grace is made with believers through Christ, who is *given for a covenant to the people,* Isa. xlix. 8. And, as here the covenant was made according to the tenour of the command, so it is still; for we are by baptism brought into covenant, that we may be *taught to observe all things whatsoever Christ has commanded us,* Matt. xxviii. 19, 20.

28 And he was there with the Lord forty days and forty nights; he did neither eat bread, nor drink water. And he wrote upon the tables the words of the covenant, the ten commandments. 29 And it came to pass, when Moses came down from mount Sinai with the two tables of testimony in Moses' hand, when he came down from the mount, that Moses wist not that the skin of his face shone while he talked with him. 30 And when Aaron and all the children of Israel saw Moses, behold, the skin of his face shone; and they were afraid to come nigh him. 31 And Moses called unto them; and Aaron and all the rulers of the congregation returned unto him: and Moses talked with them. 32 And afterward all the children of Israel came nigh: and he gave them in commandment all that the Lord had spoken with him in mount Sinai. 33 And *till* Moses had done speaking with them, he put a veil on his face. 34 But when Moses went in before the Lord to speak with him, he took the veil off, until he came out. And he came out, and spake unto the children of Israel *that*

which he was commanded. 35 And the children of Israel saw the face of Moses, that the skin of Moses' face shone : and Moses put the veil upon nis face again, until he went in to speak with him.

Here is, I. The continuance of Moses in the mount, where he was miraculously sustained, *v.* 28. He was there in very intimate communion with God, without interruption, forty days and forty nights, and did not think it long. When we are weary of an hour or two spent in attendance upon God and adoration of him, we should think how many days and nights Moses spent with him, and of the eternal day we hope to spend in praising him. During all this time Moses did neither eat nor drink. Though he had before been kept so long fasting, yet he did not, this second time, take up so many days' provision along with him, but believed that *man lives not by bread alone,* and encouraged himself with the experience he had of the truth of it. So long he continued without meat and drink (and probably without sleep too), for, 1. The power of God supported him, that he did not need it. He who made the body can nourish it without ordinary means, which he uses, but is not tied to. *The life is more than meat.* 2. His communion with God entertained him, so that he did not desire it. He had meat to eat which the world knew not of, for it was his meat and drink to hear the word of God and pray. The abundant satisfaction his soul had in the word of God and the visions of the Almighty made him forget the body and the pleasures of it. When God would treat his favourite Moses, it was not with meat and drink, but with his light, law, and love, with the knowledge of himself and his will ; then man did indeed eat angels' food. See what we should value as the truest pleasure. *The kingdom of God is not meat and drink,* neither the abundance nor delicacy of food, but *righteousness and peace and joy in the Holy Ghost.* As Moses, so Elijah and Christ, fasted forty days and forty nights. The more dead we are to the delights of sense the better prepared we are for the pleasures of heaven.

II. The coming down of Moses from the mount, greatly enriched and miraculously adorned.

1. He came down enriched with the best treasure ; for he brought in his hands the two tables of the law, written with the finger of God, *v.* 28, 29. It is a great favour to have the law given us ; this favour was shown to Israel, Ps. cxlvii. 19, 20. It is a great honour to be employed in delivering God's law to others ; this honour was done to Moses.

2. He came down adorned with the best beauty ; for the *skin of his face shone, v.* 29. This time of his being in the mount he heard only what he had heard before, but he saw more

of the glory of God, which having with open face beheld, he was in some measure *changed into the same image from glory to glory,* 2 Cor. iii. 18. The last time he came down from the mount with the glory of a magistrate, to frown upon and chastise Israel's idolatry ; now with the glory of an angel, with tidings of peace and reconciliation. Then he came with a rod, now with the spirit of meekness Now,

(1.) This may be looked upon, [1.] As a great honour done to Moses, that the people might never again question his mission nor think nor speak lightly of him. He carried his credentials in his very countenance, which, some think, retained, as long as he lived, some remainders of this glory, which perhaps contributed, to the vigour of his old age ; that eye could not wax dim which had seen God, nor that face become wrinkled which had shone with his glory. The Israelites could not look him in the face but they must there read his commission. Thus it was done to the man whom the King of kings did delight to honour. Yet, after this, they murmured against him ; for the most sensible proofs will not of themselves conquer an obstinate infidelity. The shining of Moses's face was a great honour to him ; yet that was no glory, in comparison with the glory which excelled. We read of our Lord Jesus, not only that *his face shone* as the sun, but his whole body also, for his *raiment was white and glistering,* Luke ix. 29. But, when he came down from the mount, he quite laid aside that glory, it being his will that we should *walk by faith, not by sight.* [2.] It was also a great favour to the people, and an encouragement to them, that God put this glory upon him, who was their intercessor, thereby giving them assurance that he was accepted, and they through him. Thus the advancement of Christ, our advocate with the Father, is the great support of our faith. [3.] It was the effect of his sight of God. Communion with God, *First,* Makes the face to shine in true honour. Serious godliness puts a lustre upon a man's countenance, such as commands esteem and affection. *Secondly,* It should make the face to shine in universal holiness. When we have been in the mount with God, we should let our *light shine before men,* in humility, meekness, and all the instances of a heavenly conversation ; thus must the *beauty of the Lord our God be upon us,* even the *beauty of holiness,* that all we converse with may *take knowledge of us that we have been with Jesus,* Acts iv. 13.

(2.) Concerning the shining of Moses's face observe here, [1.] Moses was not aware of it himself : *He wist not that the skin of his face shone, v.* 29. Thus, *First,* It is the infelicity of some that, though their faces shine in true grace, yet they do not know it, to take the comfort of it. Their friends see much of God in them, but they themselves are ready to think they have no grace. *Secondly,* It is the humility of others that, though their faces shine in eminent gifts and usefulness, yet they do not know it, to be puffed up with it. Whatever beauty God puts upon us, we should still be filled with such a humble sense of our own unworthiness, and manifold infirmities, as will make us even overlook and forget that which makes our faces shine. [2.] Aaron and the children of Israel saw it, and *were afraid, v.* 30. The truth of it was attested by a multitude of witnesses, who were also conscious of the terror of it. It not only dazzled their eyes, but struck such an awe upon them as obliged them to retire. Probably they doubted whether it were a token of God's favour or of his displeasure; and, though it seemed most likely to be a good omen, yet, being conscious of guilt, they feared the worst, especially remembering the posture Moses found them in when he came last down from the mount. Holiness will command reverence; but the sense of sin makes men afraid of their friends, and even of that which really is a favour to them. [3.] Moses put a *veil upon his face,* when he perceived that it shone, *v.* 33, 35. *First,* This teaches us all a lesson of modesty and humility. We must be content to have our excellences obscured, and a veil drawn over them, not coveting to *make a fair show in the flesh.* Those that are truly desirous to be owned and accepted of God will likewise desire not to be taken notice of nor applauded by men. *Qui bene latuit, bene vixit—There is a laudable concealment. Secondly,* It teaches ministers to accommodate themselves to the capacities of people, and to preach to them as they are able to bear it. Let all that art and all that learning be veiled which tend to amusement rather than edification, and let the strong condescend to the infirmities of the weak. *Thirdly,* This veil signified the darkness of that dispensation. The ceremonial institutions had in them much of Christ, much of the grace of the gospel, but a veil was drawn over it, so that the children of Israel could not distinctly and *stedfastly see those good things to come which the law had the shadow of.* It was beauty veiled, gold in the mine, a pearl in the shell; but, thanks be to God, by the gospel life and immortality are brought to light, the veil is taken away from off the Old Testament; yet still it remains upon the hearts of those who shut their eyes against the light. Thus the apostle expounds this passage, 2 Cor. iii. 13—15. [4.] When Moses *went in before the Lord,* to speak with him in the tabernacle of meeting, he *put off the veil, v.* 34. Then there was no occasion for it, and, before God, every man does and must appear unveiled; for *all things are naked and open before the eyes of him with whom we have to do,* and it is folly for us to think of concealing or disguising any thing. Every veil must be thrown aside when we come to present ourselves unto the Lord. This signified also, as it is

430

explained (2 Cor. iii. 16), that when a soul turns to the Lord the veil shall be taken away, that with open face it may behold his glory. And when we shall come before the Lord in heaven, to be there for ever speaking with him, the veil shall not only be taken off from the divine glory, but from our hearts and eyes, that we may see as we are seen, and know as we are known.

CHAP. XXXV.

What should have been said and done upon Moses' coming down the first time from the mount, if the golden calf had not broken the measures and put all into disorder, now at last, when with great difficulty reconciliation was made, begins to be said and done; and that great affair of the setting up of God's worship is put into its former channel again, and goes on now without interruption. I. Moses gives Israel those instructions, received from God, which required immediate observance. 1. Concerning the sabbath, ver. 1—3. 2. Concerning the contribution that was to be made for the erecting of the tabernacle, ver. 4—9. 3. Concerning the framing of the tabernacle and the utensils of it, ver. 10—19. II. The people bring in their contributions, ver. 20—29. III. The head-workmen are nominated, ver. 30, &c.

AND Moses gathered all the congregation of the children of Israel together, and said unto them, These *are* the words which the LORD hath commanded, that *ye* should do them. 2 Six days shall work be done, but on the seventh day there shall be to you a holy day, a sabbath of rest to the LORD : whosoever doeth work therein shall be put to death. 3 Ye shall kindle no fire throughout your habitations upon the sabbath day. 4 And Moses spake unto all the congregation of the children of Israel, saying, This *is* the thing which the LORD commanded, saying, 5 Take ye from among you an offering unto the LORD : whosoever *is* of a willing heart, let him bring it, an offering of the LORD ; gold, and silver, and brass, 6 And blue, and purple, and scarlet, and fine linen, and goats' *hair,* 7 And rams' skins dyed red, and badgers' skins, and shittim wood, 8 And oil, for the light, and spices for anointing oil, and for the sweet incense, 9 And onyx stones, and stones to be set for the ephod, and for the breastplate. 10 And every wise hearted among you shall come, and make all that the LORD hath commanded ; 11 The tabernacle, his tent, and his covering, his taches, and his boards, his bars, his pillars, and his sockets. 12 The ark, and the staves thereof, *with* the mercy seat, and the veil of the covering, 13 The table, and his staves, and all his vessels, and the showbread, 14 The candlestick also for the light, and his furniture, and his lamps, with the oil for the light, 15 And the incense altar, and his staves, and the anointing oil, and the sweet incense, and the hanging for the door at the entering in of the tabernacle, 16 The altar of burnt offering, with his brazen grate, his staves, and all his vessels, the laver and his foot, 17 The hangings of the court, his pillars, and their sockets, and the hanging for the door of the court. 18 The pins of the tabernacle, and the pins of the court, and their cords, 19 The clothes of service, to do service in the holy *place*, the holy garments for Aaron the priest, and the garments of his sons, to minister in the priest's office.

It was said in general (*ch.* xxxiv. 32), *Moses gave them in commandment all that the Lord had spoken with him.* But, the erecting and furnishing of the tabernacle being the work to which they were now immediately to apply themselves, here is particular mention of the orders given concerning it.

I. All the congregation is summoned to attend (*v.* 1); that is, the heads and rulers of the congregation, the representatives of the several tribes, who must receive instructions from Moses as he had received them from the Lord, and must communicate them to the people. Thus John, being commanded to write to the seven churches what had been revealed to him, writes it to the angels, or ministers, of the churches.

II. Moses gave them in charge all that (and that only) which God had commanded him; thus he approved himself faithful both to God and Israel, between whom he was a messenger or mediator. If he had added, altered, or diminished, he would have been false to both. But, both sides having reposed a trust in him, he was true to the trust; yet he was faithful as a servant only, but *Christ as a Son,* Heb. iii. 5, 6.

III. He begins with the law of the sabbath, because that was much insisted on in the instructions he had received (*v.* 2, 3): *Six days shall work be done,* work for the tabernacle, the work of the day that was now to be done in its day; and they had little else to do here in the wilderness, where they had neither husbandry nor merchandise, neither food to get nor clothes to make: but *on the seventh day* you must not strike a stroke, no, not at the tabernacle-work; the honour of the sabbath was above that of the sanctuary, more ancient and more lasting; that must be to you a holy day, devoted to God, and not be spent in common business. It is a sabbath of rest. It is a *sabbath of sabbaths* (so some read it), more honourable and excellent than a.iy of the other feasts, and should survive

them all. A *sabbath of sabbatism,* so others read it, being typical of that sabbatism or rest, both spiritual and eternal, which *remains for the people of God,* Heb. iv. 9. It is a sabbath of rest, that is, in which a rest from all worldly labour must be very carefully and strictly observed. It is a sabbath and a little sabbath, so some of the Jews would have it read; not only observing the whole day as a sabbath, but an hour before the beginning of it, and an hour after the ending of it, which they throw in over and above out of their own time, and call *a little sabbath,* to show how glad they are of the approach of the sabbath and how loth to part with it. It is a sabbath of rest, but it is rest to the Lord, to whose honour it must be devoted. A penalty is here annexed to the breach of it: *Whosoever doeth work therein shall be put to death.* Also a particular prohibition of kindling fires on the sabbath day for any servile work, as smith's work, or plumbers, &c.

IV. He orders preparation to be made for the setting up of the tabernacle. Two things were to be done:—

1. All that were able must contribute: *Take you from among you an offering, v.* 5. The tabernacle was to be dedicated to the honour of God, and used in his service; and therefore what was brought for the setting up and furnishing of that was *an offering to the Lord.* Our goodness extends not to God, but what is laid out for the support of his kingdom and interest among men he is pleased to accept as an offering to himself; and he requires such acknowledgments of our receiving our all from him and such instances of our dedicating our all to him. The rule is, *Whosoever is of a willing heart let him bring.* It was not to be a tax imposed upon them, but a benevolence or voluntary contribution, to intimate to us, (1.) That God has not made our yoke heavy. He is a prince that does not burden his subjects with taxes, nor *make them to serve with an offering,* but *draws with the cords of a man,* and leaves it to ourselves to *judge what is right;* his is a government that there is no cause to complain of, for he does not rule with rigour. (2.) That God loves a cheerful giver, and is best pleased with the free-will offering. Those services are acceptable to him that come from the willing heart of a willing people, Ps. cx. 3.

2. All that were skilful must work: *Every wise-hearted among you shall come, and make, v.* 10. See how God dispenses his gifts variously; and, as *every man hath received the gift, so he must minister,* 1 Pet. iv. 10. Those that were rich must bring in materials to work on; those that were ingenious must serve the tabernacle with their ingenuity; as they needed one another, so the tabernacle needed them both, 1 Cor. xii. 7—21. The work was likely to go on when some helped with their purses, others with their hands, and both with a willing heart. Moses, as he had told them what must be given (*v.* 5—9),

so he gives them the general heads of what must be made (*v.* 11—19), that, seeing how much work was before them, they might apply themselves to it the more vigorously, and every hand might be busy; and it gave them such an idea of the fabric designed that they could not but long to see it finished.

20 And all the congregation of the children of Israel departed from the presence of Moses. 21 And they came, every one whose heart stirred him up, and every one whom his spirit made willing, *and* they brought the Lord's offering to the work of the tabernacle of the congregation, and for all his service, and for the holy garments. 22 And they came, both men and women, as many as were willing hearted, *and* brought bracelets, and earrings, and rings, and tablets, all jewels of gold : and every man that offered *offered* an offering of gold unto the Lord. 23 And every man, with whom was found blue, and purple, and scarlet, and fine linen, and goats' *hair*, and red skins of rams, and badgers' skins, brought *them*. 24 Every one that did offer an offering of silver and brass brought the Lord's offering : and every man, with whom was found shittim wood for any work of the service, brought *it*. 25 And all the women that were wise hearted did spin with their hands, and brought that which they had spun, *both* of blue, and of purple, *and* of scarlet, and of fine linen. 26 And all the women whose heart stirred them up in wisdom spun goats' *hair*. 27 And the rulers brought onyx stones, and stones to be set, for the ephod, and for the breastplate ; 28 And spice, and oil for the light, and for the anointing oil, and for the sweet incense. 29 The children of Israel brought a willing offering unto the Lord, every man and woman, whose heart made them willing to bring for all manner of work, which the Lord had commanded to be made by the hand of Moses.

Moses having made known to them the will of God, they went home and immediately put in practice what they had heard, *v.* 20. O that every congregation would thus depart from the hearing of the word of God, with a

432

full resolution to be *doers of the same !* Observe here,

I. The offerings that were brought for the service of the tabernacle (*v.* 21, &c.), concerning which many things may be noted. 1. It is intimated that they brought their offerings immediately ; they departed to their tents immediately to fetch their offering, and did not desire time to consider of it, lest their zeal should be cooled by delays. What duty God convinces us of, and calls us to, we should set about speedily. No season will be more convenient than the present season. 2. It is said that *their spirits made them willing* (*v.* 21), *and their hearts, v.* 29. What they did they did cheerfully, and from a good principle. They were willing, and it was not any external inducement that made them so, but their spirits. It was from a principle of love to God and his service, a desire of his presence with them in his ordinances, gratitude for the great things he had done for them, faith in his promise of what he would further do (or, at least, from the present consideration of these things), that they were willing to offer. What we give and do for God is then acceptable when it comes from a good principle in the heart and spirit. 3. When it is said that as many as were willing-hearted brought their offerings (*v.* 22), it should seem as if there were some who were not, who loved their gold better than their God, and would not part with it, no, not for the service of the tabernacle. Such there are, who will be called Israelites, and yet will not be moved by the equity of the thing, God's expectations from them, and the good examples of those about them, to part with any thing for the interests of God's kingdom : they are for the true religion, provided it be cheap and will cost them nothing. 4. The offerings were of divers kinds, according as they had ; those that had gold and precious stones brought them, not thinking any thing too good and too rich to part with for the honour of God. Those that had not precious stones to bring brought goats' hair, and rams' skins. If we cannot do as much as others for God, we must not therefore sit still and do nothing : if the meaner offerings which are according to our ability gain us not such a reputation among men, yet they shall not fail of acceptance with God, who requires *according to what a man hath, and not according to what he hath not,* 2 Cor. viii. 12 ; 2 Kings v. 23. Two mites from a pauper were more pleasing than so many talents from a Dives. God has an eye to the heart of the giver more than to the value of the gift. 5. Many of the things they offered were their ornaments, bracelets and rings, and tablets or lockets (*v.* 22) ; and even the women parted with these. *Can a maid forget her ornaments?* Thus far they forgot them that they preferred the beautifying of the sanctuary before their own adorning. Let this teach us, in general, to part with that for

God, when he calls for it, which is very dear to us, which we value, and value ourselves by; and particularly to lay aside our ornaments, and deny ourselves in them, when either they occasion offence to others or feed our own pride. If we think those gospel rules concerning our clothing too strict (1 Tim. ii. 9, 10; 1 Pet. iii. 3, 4), I fear we should scarcely have done as these Israelites did. If they thought their ornaments well bestowed upon the tabernacle, shall not we think the want of ornaments well made up by the graces of the Spirit? Prov. i. 9. 6. These rich things that they offered, we may suppose, were mostly the spoils of the Egyptians; for the Israelites in Egypt were kept poor, till they borrowed at parting. And we may suppose the rulers had better things (*v.* 27), because, having more influence among the Egyptians, they borrowed larger sums. Who would have thought that ever the wealth of Egypt should have been so well employed? but thus God has often made *the earth to help the woman,* Rev. xii. 16. It was by a special providence and promise of God that the Israelites got all that spoil, and therefore it was highly fit that they should devote a part of it to the service of that God to whom they owed it all. Let every man give *according as God hath prospered him,* 1 Cor. xvi. 2. Extraordinary successes should be acknowledged by extraordinary offerings. Apply it to human learning, arts and sciences, which are borrowed, as it were, from the Egyptians. Those that are enriched with these must devote them to the service of God and his tabernacle: they may be used as helps to understand the scriptures, as ornaments or handmaids to divinity. But then great care must be taken that Egypt's gods mingle not with Egypt's gold. Moses, though learned in all the learning of the Egyptians, did not therefore pretend, in the least instance, to correct the pattern shown him in the mount. The furnishing of the tabernacle with the riches of Egypt was perhaps a good omen to the Gentiles, who, in the fulness of time, should be brought into the gospel tabernacle, and their silver and their gold with them (Isa. lx. 9), and it should be said, *Blessed be Egypt my people,* Isa. xix. 25. 7. We may suppose that the remembrance of the offerings made for the golden calf made them the more forward in these offerings. Those that had then parted with their ear-rings would now testify their repentance by giving the rest of their jewels to the service of God: godly sorrow worketh such a revenge, 2 Cor. vii. 11. And those that had kept themselves pure from that idolatry yet argued with themselves, "Were they so forward in contributing to an idol, and shall we be backward or sneaking in our offerings to the Lord?" Thus some good was brought even out of that evil.

II. The work that was done for the service of the tabernacle (*v.* 25): *The women did spin with their hands.* Some spun fine work,

of blue and purple; others coarse work, of goats' hair, and yet theirs also is said to be done in wisdom, *v.* 26. As it is not only rich gifts, so it is not only fine work that God accepts. Notice is here taken of the good women's work for God, as well as of Bezaleel's and Aholiab's. The meanest hand employed, the meanest service performed, for the honour of God, shall have an honourable recompence. Mary's anointing of Christ's head shall be told for a memorial (Matt. xxvi. 13); and a record is kept of the women that laboured in the gospel tabernacle (Phil. iv. 3), and were helpers to Paul in Christ Jesus, Rom. xvi. 3. It is part of the character of the virtuous woman that she layeth *her hands to the spindle,* Prov. xxxi. 19. This employment was here turned to a pious use, as it may be still (though we have no hangings to make for the tabernacle) by the imitation of the charity of Dorcas, who made coats and garments for poor widows, Acts ix. 39. Even those that are not in a capacity to give in charity may yet work in charity; and thus the poor may relieve the poor, and those that have nothing but their limbs and senses may be very charitable in the labour of love.

30 And Moses said unto the children of Israel, See, the LORD hath called by name Bezaleel the son of Uri, the son of Hur, of the tribe of Judah; 31 And he hath filled him with the spirit of God, in wisdom, in understanding, and in knowledge, and in all manner of workmanship; 32 And to devise curious works, to work in gold, and in silver, and in brass, 33 And in the cutting of stones, to set *them,* and in carving of wood, to make any manner of cunning work. 34 And he hath put in his heart that he may teach, *both* he, and Aholiab, the son of Ahisamach, of the tribe of Dan. 35 Them hath he filled with wisdom of heart, to work all manner of work, of the engraver, and of the cunning workman, and of the embroiderer, in blue, and in purple, in scarlet, and in fine linen, and of the weaver, *even* of them that do any work, and of those that devise cunning work.

Here is the divine appointment of the master-workmen, that there might be no strife for the office, and that all who were employed in the work might take direction from, and give account to, these general inspectors; for God is the God of order and not of confusion. Observe, 1. Those whom God called by name to this service he *filled with the Spirit of God,* to qualify them for it, *v.* 30, 31. Skill in secular employments is God's gift, and comes from above, Jam. i. 17. From him the faculty is, and the improvement of it. To his honour therefore all knowledge must be devoted, and we must study how to serve him with it. The work was extraordinary which Bezaleel was designed for, and therefore he was qualified in an extraordinary manner for it; thus when the apostles were appointed to be masterbuilders in setting up the gospel tabernacle they were *filled with the Spirit of God in wisdom and understanding.* 2. They were appointed, not only to devise, but to work (*v.* 32), *to work all manner of work, v.* 35. Those of eminent gifts, that are capable of directing others, must not think that these will excuse them in idleness. Many are ingenious enough in cutting out work for other people, and can tell what this man and that man should do, but the burdens they bind on others they themselves *will not touch with one of their fingers.* These will fall under the character of slothful servants. 3. They were not only to devise and work themselves, but they were to teach others, *v.* 34. Not only had Bezaleel power to command, but he was to take pains to instruct. Those that rule should teach; and those to whom God has given knowledge should be willing to communicate it for the benefit of others, not coveting to monopolize it.

CHAP. XXXVI.

In this chapter, I. The work of the tabernacle is begun, ver. 1—4. II. A stop is put to the people's contributions, ver. 5—7. III. A particular account is given of the making of the tabernacle itself; the fine curtains of it, ver. 8—13. The coarse ones, ver. 14—19. The boards, ver. 20—30. The bars, ver. 31—34. The partition veil, ver. 35, 36. And the hanging for the door, ver. 37, &c.

THEN wrought Bezaleel and Aholiab, and every wise hearted man, in whom the LORD put wisdom and understanding to know how to work all manner of work for the service of the sanctuary, according to all that the LORD had commanded. 2 And Moses called Bezaleel and Aholiab, and every wise hearted man, in whose heart the LORD had put wisdom, *even* every one whose heart stirred him up to come unto the work to do it: 3 And they received of Moses all the offering, which the children of Israel had brought for the work of the service of the sanctuary, to make it *withal.* And they brought yet unto him free offerings every morning. 4 And all the wise men, that wrought all the work of the sanctuary, came every man from his work which they made; 5 And they spake unto Moses, saying, The people bring much more than enough for the service of the work,

434

which the LORD commanded to make. 6 And Moses gave commandment, and they caused it to be proclaimed throughout the camp, saying, Let neither man nor woman make any more work for the offering of the sanctuary. So the people were restrained from bringing. 7 For the stuff they had was sufficient for all the work to make it, and too much.

I. The workmen set in without delay. Then they wrought, *v.* 1. When God had qualified them for the work, then they applied themselves to it. Note, The talents we are entrusted with must not be laid up, but laid out; not hid in a napkin, but traded with. What have we all our gifts for, but to do good with them? They began when Moses called them, *v.* 2. Even those whom God has qualified for, and inclined to, the service of the tabernacle, yet must wait for a regular call to it, either extraordinary, as that of prophets and apostles, or ordinary, as that of pastors and teachers. And observe who they were that Moses called: Those *in whose heart God had put wisdom* for this purpose, beyond their natural capacity, and *whose heart stirred them up to come to the work* in good earnest. Note, Those are to be called to the building of the gospel tabernacle whom God has by his grace made in some measure fit for the work and free to engage in it. Ability and willingness (with resolution) are the two things to be regarded in the call of ministers. Has God given them not only knowledge, but wisdom? (for those that would win souls must be wise, and have their hearts stirred up to come to the work, and not to the honour only; to do it, and not to talk of it only), let them come to it with full purpose of heart to go through with it. The materials which the people had contributed were delivered by Moses to the workmen, *v.* 3. They could not create a tabernacle, that is, make it out of nothing, nor work, unless they had something to work upon; the people therefore brought the materials and Moses put them into their hands. Precious souls are the materials of the gospel tabernacle; they are *built up a spiritual house,* 1 Pet. ii. 5. To this end they are to offer themselves a freewill offering to the Lord, for his service (Rom. xv. 16), and they are then committed to the care of his ministers, as builders, to be framed and wrought upon by their edification and increase in holiness, till they all come, like the curtains of the tabernacle, *in the unity of the faith to be a holy temple,* Eph. ii. 21, 22; iv. 12, 13.

II. The contributions restrained. The people continued to bring *free offerings every morning, v.* 3. Note, We should always make it our morning's work to bring our offerings unto the Lord; even the spiritual offerings of prayer and praise, and a broken heart surrendered entirely to God. This is that which the duty of every day requires. God's compassions are new every morning, and so should our offerings be, our free offerings: God's grace to us is free, and so must our duty to him be. Probably there were some that were backward at first to bring their offering, but their neighbours' forwardness stirred them up and shamed them. The zeal of some provoked many. There are those who will be content to follow who yet do not care for leading in a good work. It is best to be forward, but better late than never. Or perhaps some who had offered at first, having pleasure in reflecting upon it, offered more; so far were they from grudging what they had contributed, that they doubled their contribution. Thus, in charity, *give a portion to seven, and also to eight;* having given much, give more. Now observe, 1. The honesty of the workmen. When they had cut out their work, and found how their stuff held out, and that the people were still forward to bring in more, they went in a body to Moses to tell him that there needed no more contributions, *v.* 4, 5. Had they sought their own things, they had now a fair opportunity of enriching themselves by the people's gifts; for they might have made up their work, and converted the overplus to their own use, as perquisites of their place. But they were men of integrity, that scorned to do so mean a thing as to sponge upon the people, and enrich themselves with that which was offered to the Lord. Those are the greatest cheats that cheat the public. If to murder many is worse than to murder one, by the same rule to defraud communities, and to rob the church or state, is a much greater crime than to pick the pocket of a single person. But these workmen were not only ready to account for all they received, but were not willing to receive more than they had occasion for, lest they should come either into the temptation or under the suspicion of taking it to themselves. These were men that knew when they had enough. 2. The liberality of the people. Though they saw what an abundance was contributed, yet they continued to offer, till they were forbidden by proclamation, *v.* 6, 7. A rare instance! Most need a spur to quicken their charity; few need a bridle to check it, yet these did. Had Moses aimed to enrich himself, he might have suffered them still to bring in their offerings; and when the work was finished might have taken the remainder to himself: but he also preferred the public before his own private interest, and was therein a good example to all in public trusts. It is said (*v.* 6), *The people were restrained from bringing;* they looked upon it as a restraint upon them not to be allowed to do more for the tabernacle; such was the zeal of those people, who gave *to their power, yea, and beyond their power, praying* the collectors *with much entreaty to*

receive the gift, 2 Cor. viii. 3, 4. These were the fruits of a first love; in these last days charity has grown too cold for us to expect such things from it.

8 And every wise hearted man among them that wrought the work of the tabernacle made ten curtains *of* fine twined linen, and blue, and purple, and scarlet: *with* cherubims of cunning work made he them. 9 The length of one curtain *was* twenty and eight cubits, and the breadth of one curtain four cubits: the curtains *were* all of one size. 10 And he coupled the five curtains one unto another: and *the other* five curtains he coupled one unto another. 11 And he made loops of blue on the edge of one curtain from the selvedge in the coupling; likewise he made in the uttermost side of *another* curtain, in the coupling of the second. 12 Fifty loops made he in one curtain, and fifty loops made he in the edge of the curtain which *was* in the coupling of the second: the loops held one *curtain* to another. 13 And he made fifty taches of gold, and coupled the curtains one unto another with the taches: so it became one tabernacle.

The first work they set about was the framing of the house, which must be done before the furniture of it was prepared. This house was not made of timber or stone, but of curtains curiously embroidered and coupled together. This served to typify the state of the church in this world, the palace of God's kingdom among men. 1. Though it is upon the earth, yet its foundation is not in the earth, as that of a house is; no, Christ's kingdom is not of this world, nor founded in it. 2. It is mean and mutable, and in a militant state; shepherds dwelt in tents, and God is the Shepherd of Israel; soldiers dwelt in tents, and the Lord is a man of war, and his church marches through an enemy's country, and must fight its way. The kings of the earth enclose themselves in cedar (Jer. xxii. 15), but the ark of God was lodged in curtains only. 3. Yet there is a beauty in holiness; the curtains were embroidered, so is the church adorned with the gifts and graces of the Spirit, that *raiment of needle-work,* Ps. xlv. 14. 4. The several societies of believers are united in one, and, as here, all *become one tabernacle; for there is one Lord, one faith, and one baptism.*

14 And he made curtains *of* goats' hair for the tent over the tabernacle: eleven curtains he made them. 15

The length of one curtain *was* thirty cubits, and four cubits *was* the breadth of one curtain: the eleven curtains *were* of one size. 16 And he coupled five curtains by themselves, and six curtains by themselves. 17 And he made fifty loops upon the uttermost edge of the curtain in the coupling, and fifty loops made he upon the edge of the curtain which coupleth the second. 18 And he made fifty taches *of* brass to couple the tent together, that it might be one. 19 And he made a covering for the tent *of* rams' skins dyed red, and a covering *of* badgers' skins above *that*. 20 And he made boards for the tabernacle *of* shittim wood, standing up. 21 The length of a board *was* ten cubits, and the breadth of a board one cubit and a half. 22 One board had two tenons, equally distant one from another: thus did he make for all the boards of the tabernacle. 23 And he made boards for the tabernacle; twenty boards for the south side southward: 24 And forty sockets of silver he made under the twenty boards; two sockets under one board for his two tenons, and two sockets under another board for his two tenons. 25 And for the other side of the tabernacle, *which is* toward the north corner, he made twenty boards, 26 And their forty sockets of silver; two sockets under one board, and two sockets under another board. 27 And for the sides of the tabernacle westward he made six boards. 28 And two boards made he for the corners of the tabernacle in the two sides. 29 And they were coupled beneath, and coupled together at the head thereof, to one ring: thus he did to both of them in both the corners. 30 And there were eight boards; and their sockets *were* sixteen sockets of silver, under every board two sockets. 31 And he made bars of shittim wood; five for the boards of the one side of the tabernacle, 32 And five bars for the boards of the other side of the tabernacle, and five bars for the boards of the tabernacle for the sides westward. 33 And he made the middle bar to shoot through the boards from the one end to the other. 34 And he overlaid the boards with gold, and made their rings *of* gold *to be* places for the bars, and overlaid the bars with gold.

Here, 1. The shelter and special protection that the church is under are signified by the curtains of hair-cloth, which were spread over the tabernacle, and the covering of rams' skins and badgers' skins over them, *v.* 14—19. God has provided for his people a *shadow from the heat, and a covert from storm and rain,* Isa. iv. 6. They are armed against all weathers; the sun and the moon shall not smite them: and they are protected from the storms of divine wrath, that hail which will *sweep away the refuge of lies,* Isa. xxviii. 17. Those that dwell in God's house shall find, be the tempest ever so violent, or the dropping ever so continual, it does not rain in. 2. The strength and stability of the church, though it is but a tabernacle, are signified by the boards and bars with which the curtains were borne up, *v.* 20—34. The boards were coupled together and joined by the bars which shot through them; for the union of the church, and the hearty agreement of those that are its stays and supporters, contribute abundantly to its strength and establishment.

35 And he made a veil *of* blue, and purple, and scarlet, and fine twined linen: *with* cherubims made he of it cunning work. 36 And he made thereunto four pillars *of* shittim *wood,* and overlaid them with gold: their hooks *were of* gold; and he cast for them four sockets of silver. 37 And he made a hanging for the tabernacle door *of* blue, and purple, and scarlet, and fine twined linen, of needlework; 38 And the five pillars of it with their hooks: and he overlaid their chapiters and their fillets with gold: but their five sockets *were of* brass.

In the building of a house there is a great deal of work about the doors and partitions. In the tabernacle these were answerable to the rest of the fabric; there were curtains for doors, and veils for partitions. 1. There was a veil made for a partition between the holy place, and the most holy, *v.* 35, 36. This signified the darkness and distance of that dispensation, compared with the New Testament, which shows us the glory of God more clearly and invites us to draw near to it; and the darkness and distance of our present state, in comparison with heaven, where we shall be *ever with the Lord* and *see him as he is.* 2. There was a veil made for the door of the tabernacle, *v.* 37, 38. At this door the people assembled, though forbidden to enter; for, while we are in this present state, we must get as near to God as we can

CHAP. XXXVII.

Bezaleel and his workmen are still busy, making, I. The ark with the mercy-seat and the cherubim, ver. 1—9. II. The table with its vessels, ver. 10—16. III. The candlestick with its appurtenances, ver. 17—24. IV. The golden altar for incense, ver. 25—28. V. The holy oil and incense, ver. 29. The particular appointment concerning each of which we had before in the 25th and 30th chapters.

AND Bezaleel made the ark *of* shittim wood : two cubits and a half *was* the length of it, and a cubit and a half the breadth of it, and a cubit and a half the height of it : 2 And he overlaid it with pure gold within and without, and made a crown of gold to it round about. 3 And he cast for it four rings of gold, *to be set* by the four corners of it ; even two rings upon the one side of it, and two rings upon the other side of it. 4 And he made staves *of* shittim wood, and overlaid them with gold. 5 And he put the staves into the rings by the sides of the ark, to bear the ark. 6 And he made the mercy seat *of* pure gold : two cubits and a half *was* the length thereof, and one cubit and a half the breadth thereof. 7 And he made two cherubims *of* gold, beaten out of one piece made he them, on the two ends of the mercy seat ; 8 One cherub on the end on this side, and another cherub on the *other* end on that side : out of the mercy seat made he the cherubims on the two ends thereof. 9 And the cherubims spread out *their* wings on high, *and* covered with their wings over the mercy seat, with their faces one to another ; *even* to the mercy seatward were the faces of the cherubims.

I. It may be thought strange that Moses, when he had recorded so fully the instructions given him upon the mount for the making of all these things, should here record as particularly the making of them, when it might have sufficed only to have said, in a few words, that each of these things was made exactly according to the directions before recited. We are sure that Moses, when he wrote by divine inspiration, used no vain repetitions ; there are no idle words in scripture. Why then are so many chapters taken up with this narrative, which we are tempted to think needless and tedious ? But we must consider, 1. That Moses wrote primarily for the people of Israel, to whom it would be of great use to read and hear often of these divine and sacred treasures with which they were entrusted. These several ornaments wherewith the tabernacle was furnished they were not admitted to see, but the

priests only, and therefore it was requisite that they should be thus largely described particularly to them. That which they ought to read again and again (lest they should fail of doing it) is written again and again : thus many of the same passages of the history of Christ are in the New Testament related by two or three, and some by four of the evangelists, for the same reason. The great things of God's law and gospel we need to have inculcated upon us again and again. To write the same (says St. Paul) to me *is not grievous, but for you it is safe*, Phil. iii. 1. 2. Moses would thus show the great care which he and his workmen took to make every thing exactly according to the pattern shown him in the mount. Having before given us the original, he here gives us the copy, that we may compare them, and observe how exactly they agree. Thus he appeals to every reader concerning his fidelity to him that appointed him, in all his house, and in all the particulars of it, Heb. iii. 5. And thus he teaches us to have respect to all God's commandments, even to every iota and tittle of them. 3. It is intimated hereby that God takes delight in the sincere obedience of his people, and keeps an exact account of it, which shall be produced to their honour in the resurrection of the just. None can be so punctual in their duty, but God will be as punctual in his notices of it. He is *not unrighteous to forget the work and labour of love*, in any instance of it, Heb. vi. 10. 4. The spiritual riches and beauties of the gospel tabernacle are hereby recommended to our frequent and serious consideration. Go walk about this Zion, view it and review it : the more you contemplate the glories of the church, the more you will admire them and be in love with them. The charter of its privileges, and the account of its constitution, will very well bear a second reading.

II. In these verses we have an account of the making of the ark, with its glorious and most significant appurtenances, the mercy-seat and the cherubim. Consider these three together, and they represent the glory of a holy God, the sincerity of a holy heart, and the communion that is between them, in and by a Mediator. 1. It is the glory of a holy God that he dwells between the cherubim ; that is, is continually attended and adored by the blessed angels, whose swiftness was signified by the wings of the cherubim, while their unanimity and joint concurrence in their services were signified by their faces being one towards another. 2. It is the character of an upright heart that, like the ark of the testimony, it has the law of God hid and kept in it. 3. By Jesus Christ, the great propitiation, there is reconciliation made, and a communion settled, between us and God : he interposes between us and God's displeasure ; and not only so, but through him we become entitled to God's favour. If he write his law in our heart, he will be to us a God and we

437

shall be to him a people. From the mercy-seat he will teach us, there he will accept us, and show himself merciful to our unrighteousnesses; and under the shadow of his wings we shall be safe and easy.

10 And he made the table *of* shittim wood: two cubits *was* the length thereof, and a cubit the breadth thereof, and a cubit and a half the height thereof: 11 And he overlaid it with pure gold, and made thereunto a crown of gold round about. 12 Also he made thereunto a border of a hand breadth round about; and made a crown of gold for the border thereof round about. 13 And he cast for it four rings of gold, and put the rings upon the four corners that *were* in the four feet thereof. 14 Over against the border were the rings, the places for the staves to bear the table. 15 And he made the staves *of* shittim wood, and overlaid them with gold, to bear the table. 16 And he made the vessels which *were* upon the table, his dishes, and his spoons, and his bowls, and his covers to cover withal, *of* pure gold. 17 And he made the candlestick *of* pure gold: *of* beaten work made he the candlestick; his shaft, and his branch, his bowls, his knops, and his flowers, were of the same: 18 And six branches going out of the sides thereof; three branches of the candlestick out of the one side thereof, and three branches of the candlestick out of the other side thereof: 19 Three bowls made after the fashion of almonds in one branch, a knop and a flower; and three bowls made like almonds in another branch, a knop and a flower: so throughout the six branches going out of the candlestick. 20 And in the candlestick *were* four bowls make like almonds, his knops, and his flowers: 21 And a knop under two branches of the same, and a knop under two branches of the same, and a knop under two branches of the same, according to the six branches going out of it. 22 Their knops and their branches were of the same: all of it *was* one beaten work *of* pure gold. 23 And he made his seven lamps, and his snuffers, and

his snuffdishes, *of* pure gold. 24 *Of* a talent of pure gold made he it, and all the vessels thereof.

Here is, 1. The making of the table on which the show-bread was to be continually placed. God is a good householder, that always keeps a plentiful table. Is the world his tabernacle? His providence in it spreads a table for all the creatures: he *provides food for all flesh.* Is the church his tabernacle? His grace in it spreads a table for all believers, furnished with the bread of life. But observe how much the dispensation of the gospel exceeds that of the law. Though here was a table furnished, it was only with *show-bread,* bread to be looked upon, not to be fed upon, while it was on this table, and afterwards only by the priests; but to the table which Christ has spread in the new covenant all real Christians are invited guests; and to them it is said, *Eat, O friends, come eat of my bread.* What the law gave but a sight of at a distance, the gospel gives the enjoyment of, and a hearty welcome to. 2. The making of the candlestick, which was not of wood overlaid with gold, but all beaten work of pure gold only, *v.* 17, 22. This signified that light of divine revelation with which God's church upon earth (which is his tabernacle among men) has always been enlightened, being always supplied with fresh oil from Christ the good Olive, Zech. iv. 2, 3. God's manifestations of himself in this world are but candle-light compared with the daylight of the future state. The Bible is a golden candlestick; it is of pure gold, Ps. xix. 10. From it light is diffused to every part of God's tabernacle, that by it his spiritual priests may see to minister unto the Lord, and to do the service of his sanctuary. This candlestick has not only its bowls for necessary use, but its knops and flowers for ornament; there are many things which God saw fit to beautify his word with which we can no more give a reason for than for these knops and flowers, and yet we are sure that they were added for a good purpose. Let us bless God for this candlestick, have an eye to it continually, and dread the removal of it out of its place.

25 And he made the incense altar *of* shittim wood: the length of it *was* a cubit, and the breadth of it a cubit; *it was* foursquare; and two cubits *was* the height of it; the horns thereof were of the same. 26 And he overlaid it with pure gold, *both* the top of it, and the sides thereof round about, and the horns of it: also he made unto it a crown of gold round about. 27 And he made two rings of gold for it under the crown thereof, by the two corners of it, upon the two sides

thereof, to be places for the staves to bear it withal. 28 And he made the staves *of* shittim wood, and overlaid them with gold. 29 And he made the holy anointing oil, and the 'pure incense of sweet spices, according to the work of the apothecary.

Here is, 1. The making of the golden altar, on which incense was to be burnt daily, which signified both the prayers of saints and the intercession of Christ, to which are owing the acceptableness and success of those prayers. The rings and staves, and all the appurtenances of this altar, were overlaid with gold, as all the vessels of the table and candlestick were of gold, for these were used in the holy place. God is the best, and we must serve him with the best we have; but the best we can serve him with in his courts on earth is but as brass, compared with the gold, the sinless and spotless perfection, with which his saints shall serve him in his holy place above. 2. The preparing of the incense which was to be burnt upon this altar, and with it the holy anointing oil (*v.* 29), according to that dispensatory, *ch.* xxx. 22, &c. God taught Bezaleel this art also; so that though he was not before acquainted with it yet he made up these things according to the work of the apothecary, as dexterously and exactly as if he had been bred up to the trade. Where God gives wisdom and grace, it will make the man of God *perfect, thoroughly furnished to every good work.*

CHAP. XXXVIII.

Here is an account, I. Of the making of the brazen altar (ver. 1—7), and the laver, ver. 8. II. The preparing of the hangings for the enclosing of the court in which the tabernacle was to stand, ver. 9—20. III. A summary of the gold, silver, and brass, that was contributed to, and used in, the preparing of the tabernacle, ver. 21, &c.

AND he made the altar of burnt offering *of* shittim wood: five cubits *was* the length thereof, and five cubits the breadth thereof; *it was* foursquare; and three cubits the height thereof. 2 And he made the horns thereof on the four corners of it; the horns thereof were of the same: and he overlaid it with brass. 3 And he made all the vessels of the altar, the pots, and the shovels, and the basins, *and* the fleshhooks, and the firepans: all the vessels thereof made he *of* brass. 4 And he made for the altar a brazen grate of network under the compass thereof beneath unto the midst of it. 5 And he cast four rings for the four ends of the grate of brass, *to be* places for the staves. 6 And he made the staves *of* shittim wood, and overlaid them with brass. 7 And he

put the staves into the rings on the sides of the altar, to bear it withal; he made the altar hollow with boards. 8 And he made the laver *of* brass, and the foot of it *of* brass, of the lookingglasses of *the women* assembling, which assembled *at* the door of the tabernacle of the congregation.

Bezaleel having finished the gold-work, which, though the richest, yet was ordered to lie most out of sight, in the tabernacle itself, here goes on to prepare the court, which lay open to the view of all. Two things the court was furnished with, and both made of brass:—

I. An altar of burnt-offering, *v.* 1—7. On this all their sacrifices were offered, and it was this which, being sanctified itself for this purpose by the divine appointment, sanctified the gift that was in faith offered on it. Christ was himself the altar to his own sacrifice of atonement, and so he is to all our sacrifices of acknowledgment. We must have an eye to him in offering them, as God has in accepting them.

II. A laver, to hold water for the priests to wash in when they went in to minister, *v.* 8. This signified the provision that is made in the gospel of Christ for the cleansing of our souls from the moral pollution of sin by the merit and grace of Christ, that we may be fit to serve the holy God in holy duties. This is here said to be made of the *looking-glasses* (or mirrors) of the women that assembled at the door of the tabernacle. 1. It should seem these women were eminent and exemplary for devotion, attending more frequently and seriously at the place of public worship than others did; and notice is here taken of it to their honour. Anna was such a one long afterwards, who *departed not from the temple, but served God with fastings and prayers night and day,* Luke ii. 37. It seems in every age of the church there have been some who have thus distinguished themselves by their serious zealous piety, and they have thereby distinguished themselves; for devout women are really honourable women (Acts xiii. 50), and not the less so for their being called, by the scoffers of the latter days, *silly women.* Probably these women were such as showed their zeal upon this occasion, by assisting in the work that was now going on for the service of the tabernacle. They assembled by *troops,* so the word is; a blessed sight, to see so many, and those so zealous and so unanimous, in this good work. 2. These women parted with their mirrors (which were of the finest brass, burnished for that purpose) for the use of the tabernacle. Those women that admire their own beauty, are in love with their own shadow, and make the putting on of apparel their chief adorning by which they value and recommend themselves, can but ill spare their *looking-glasses;* yet these women offered *them* to God, either, (1.) In token of their repentance for the former abuse of them, to the support of their pride and vanity; now that they were convinced of their folly, and had devoted themselves to the service of God at the door of the tabernacle, they thus threw away that which, though lawful and useful in itself, yet had been an occasion of sin to them. Thus Mary Magdalene, who had been a sinner, when she became a penitent wiped Christ's feet with her hair. Or, (2.) In token of their great zeal for the work of the tabernacle; rather than the workmen should want brass, or not have of the best, they would part with their mirrors, though they could not do well without them. God's service and glory must always be preferred by us before any satisfactions or accommodations of our own. Let us never complain of the want of that which we may honour God by parting with.

3. These mirrors were used for the making of the laver. Either they were artfully joined together, or else molten down and cast anew; but it is probable that the laver was so brightly burnished that the sides of it still served for mirrors, that the priests, when they came to wash, might there see their faces, and so discover the spots, to wash them clean. Note, In the washing of repentance, there is need of the looking-glass of self-examination. The word of God is a glass, in which we may see our own faces (see Jam. i. 23); and with it we must compare our own hearts and lives, that, finding out our blemishes, we may wash with particular sorrow, and application of the blood of Christ to our souls. Usually the more particular we are in the confession of sin the more comfort we have in the sense of the pardon.

9 And he made the court: on the south side southward the hangings of the court *were of* fine twined linen, a hundred cubits: 10 Their pillars *were* twenty, and their brazen sockets twenty; the hooks of the pillars and their fillets *were of* silver. 11 And for the north side *the hangings were* a hundred cubits, their pillars *were* twenty, and their sockets of brass twenty; the hooks of the pillars and their fillets *of* silver. 12 And for the west side *were* hangings of fifty cubits, their pillars ten, and their sockets ten; the hooks of the pillars and their fillets *of* silver. 13 And for the east side eastward fifty cubits. 14 The hangings of the one side *of the gate were* fifteen cubits; their pillars three, and their sockets three. 15 And for the other side of the court gate, on this hand and that hand, *were* hangings of fifteen cubits; their pillars three, and their sockets three. 16 All the hangings of the court round about *were* of fine twined linen. 17 And the sockets for the pillars *were of* brass; the hooks of the pillars and their fillets *of* silver; and the overlaying of their chapiters *of* silver; and all the pillars of the court *were* filleted with silver. 18 And the hanging for the gate of the court *was* needlework, *of* blue, and purple, and scarlet, and fined twined linen: and twenty cubits *was* the length, and the height in the breadth *was* five cubits, answerable to the hangings of the court. 19 And their pillars *were* four, and their sockets *of* brass four; their hooks *of* silver, and the overlaying of their chapiters and their fillets *of* silver. 20 And all the pins of the tabernacle, and of the court round about, *were of* brass.

The walls of the court, or church-yard, were like the rest curtains or hangings, made according to the appointment, *ch.* xxvii. 9, &c. This represented the state of the Old-Testament church: it was a garden enclosed; the worshippers were then confined to a little compass. But the enclosure being of curtains only intimated that the confinement of the church in one particular nation was not to be perpetual. The dispensation itself was a tabernacle-dispensation, movable and mutable, and in due time to be taken down and folded up, when the place of the tent should be enlarged and its cords lengthened, to make room for the Gentile world, as is foretold, Isa. liv. 2, 3. The church here on earth is but the court of God's house, and happy they that tread these courts and flourish in them; but through these courts we are passing to the holy place above. *Blessed are those that dwell in that house* of God: they will be *still praising him.* The enclosing of a court before the tabernacle teaches us a gradual approach to God. The priests that ministered must pass through the holy court, before they entered the holy house. Thus before solemn ordinances there ought to be the separated and enclosed court of a solemn preparation, in which we must wash our hands, and so draw near with a true heart.

21 This is the sum of the tabernacle, *even* of the tabernacle of testimony, as it was counted, according to the commandment of Moses, *for* the service of the Levites, by the hand of Ithamar, son to Aaron the priest. 22 And Bezaleel the son of Uri, the son of Hur, of the tribe of Judah, made

all that the LORD commanded Moses. 23 And with him *was* Aholiab, son of Ahisamach, of the tribe of Dan, an engraver, and a cunning workman, and an embroiderer in blue, and in purple, and in scarlet, and fine linen. 24 All the gold that was occupied for the work in all the work of the holy *place,* even the gold of the offering, was twenty and nine talents, and seven hundred and thirty shekels, after the shekel of the sanctuary: 25 And the silver of them that were numbered of the congregation *was* a hundred talents, and a thousand seven hundred and threescore and fifteen shekels, after the shekel of the sanctuary: 26 A bekah for every man, *that is,* half a shekel, after the shekel of the sanctuary for every one that went to be numbered, from twenty years old and upward, for six hundred thousand and three thousand and five hundred and fifty *men.* 27 And of the hundred talents of silver were cast the sockets of the sanctuary, and the sockets of the veil; a hundred sockets of the hundred talents, a talent for a socket. 28 And of the thousand seven hundred seventy and five *shekels* he made hooks for the pillars, and overlaid their chapiters, and filleted them. 29 And the brass of the offering *was* seventy talents, and two thousand and four hundred shekels. 30 And therewith he made the sockets to the door of the tabernacle of the congregation, and the brazen altar, and the brazen grate for it, and all the vessels of the altar, 31 And the sockets of the court round about, and the sockets of the court gate, and all the pins of the tabernacle, and all the pins of the court round about.

Here we have a breviat of the account which, by Moses's appointment, the Levites took and kept of the gold, silver, and brass, that was brought in for the tabernacle's use, and how it was employed. Ithamar the son of Aaron was appointed to draw up this account, and was thus by less services trained up and fitted for greater, *v.* 21. Bezaleel and Aholiab must bring in the account (*v.* 22, 23), and Ithamar must audit it, and give it in to Moses. And it was thus:—1. All the gold was a free-will offering; every man brought as he could and

would, and it amounted to twenty-nine talents, and 730 shekels over, which some compute to be about 150,000*l.* worth of gold, according to the present value of it. Of this were made all the golden furniture and vessels. 2. The silver was levied by way of tax; every man was assessed half a shekel, a kind of poll-money, which amounted in the whole to 100 talents, and 1775 shekels over, *v.* 25, 26. Of this they made the sockets into which the boards of the tabernacle were let, and on which they rested; so that they were as the foundation of the tabernacle, *v.* 27. The silver amounted to about 34,000*l.* of our money. The raising of the gold by voluntary contribution, and of the silver by way of tribute, shows that either way may be taken for the defraying of public expenses, provided that nothing be done with partiality. 3. The brass, though less valuable, was of use not only for the brazen altar, but for the sockets of the court, which probably in other tents were of wood: but it is promised (Isa. lx. 17), *For wood I will bring brass.* See how liberal the people were and how faithful the workmen were, in both which respects their good example ought to be followed.

CHAP. XXXIX.

This chapter gives us an account of the finishing of the work of the tabernacle. I. The last things prepared were the holy garments. The ephod and its curious girdle, ver. 1–5. The onyxstones for the shoulders, ver. 6, 7. The breastplate with the precious stones in it, ver. 8–21. The robe of the ephod, ver. 22–26. The coats, bonnets, and breeches, for the inferior priests, ver. 27—29. And the plate of the holy crown, ver. 30, 31. II. A summary account of the whole work, as it was presented to Moses when it was all finished, ver. 32, &c.

AND of the blue, and purple, and scarlet, they made clothes of service, to do service in the holy *place,* and made the holy garments for Aaron; as the LORD commanded Moses. 2 And he made the ephod *of* gold, blue, and purple, and scarlet, and fine twined linen. 3 And they did beat the gold into thin plates, and cut *it into* wires, to work *it* in the blue, and in the purple, and in the scarlet, and in the fine linen, *with* cunning work. 4 They made shoulderpieces for it, to couple *it* together: by the two edges was it coupled together. 5 And the curious girdle of his ephod, that *was* upon it, *was* of the same, according to the work thereof; *of* gold, blue, and purple, and scarlet, and fine twined linen; as the LORD commanded Moses. 6 And they wrought onyx stones inclosed in ouches of gold, graven, as signets are graven, with the names of the children of Israel. 7 And he put them on the shoulders of the ephod, *that they should be* stones for a memorial to the children of Israel; as the LORD commanded Moses. 8 And he made the breastplate *of* cunning work, like the work of the ephod; *of* gold, blue, and purple, and scarlet, and fine twined linen. 9 It was four-square; they made the breastplate double: a span *was* the length thereof, and a span the breadth thereof, *being* doubled. 10 And they set in it four rows of stones: *the first* row *was* a sardius, a topaz, and a carbuncle: this *was* the first row. 11 And the second row, an emerald, a sapphire, and a diamond. 12 And the third row, a ligure, an agate, an amethyst, 13 And the fourth row, a beryl, an onyx, and a jasper: *they were* inclosed in ouches of gold in their inclosings. 14 And the stones *were* according to the names of the children of Israel, twelve, according to their names, *like* the engravings of a signet, every one with his name, according to the twelve tribes. 15 And they made upon the breastplate chains at the ends, *of* wreathen work *of* pure gold. 16 And they made two ouches *of* gold, and two gold rings; and put the two rings in the two ends of the breastplate. 17 And they put the two wreathen chains of gold in the two rings on the ends of the breastplate. 18 And the two ends of the two wreathen chains they fastened in the two ouches, and put them on the shoulderpieces of the ephod, before it. 19 And they made two rings of gold, and put *them* on the two ends of the breastplate, upon the border of it, which *was* on the side of the ephod inward. 20 And they made two *other* golden rings, and put them on the two sides of the ephod underneath, toward the forepart of it, over against the *other* coupling thereof, above the curious girdle of the ephod. 21 And they did bind the breastplate by his rings unto the rings of the ephod with a lace of blue, that it might be above the curious girdle of the ephod, and that the breastplate might not be loosed from the ephod; as the LORD commanded Moses. 22 And he made the robe of the ephod *of* woven work, all *of* blue.

23 And *there was* a hole in the midst of the robe, as the hole of an habergeon, *with* a band round about the hole, that it should not rend. 24 And they made upon the hems of the robe pomegranates *of* blue, and purple, and scarlet, *and* twined *linen.* 25 And they made bells *of* pure gold, and put the bells between the pomegranates upon the hem of the robe, round about between the pomegranates; 26 A bell and a pomegranate, a bell and a pomegranate, round about the hem of the robe to minister *in; as the LORD commanded Moses. 27 And they made coats *of* fine linen *of* woven work for Aaron, and for his sons, 28 And a mitre *of* fine linen, and goodly bonnets *of* fine linen, and linen breeches *of* fine twined linen, 29 And a girdle *of* fine twined linen, and blue, and purple, and scarlet, *of* needlework; as the LORD commanded Moses. 30 And they made the plate of the holy crown *of* pure gold, and wrote upon it a writing, *like to* the engravings of a signet, HOLINESS TO THE LORD. 31 And they tied unto it a lace of blue, to fasten *it* on high upon the mitre; as the LORD commanded Moses.

In this account of the making of the priests' garments, according to the instructions given (*ch.* xxviii), we may observe, 1. That the priests' garments are called here *clothes of service, v.* 1. Note, Those that wear robes of honour must look upon them as clothes of service; for from those upon whom honour is put service is expected. It is said of those that are arrayed in white robes that they *are before the throne of God, and serve him day and night in his temple,* Rev. vii. 13, 15. Holy garments were not made for men to sleep in, or to strut in, but to do service in; and then they are indeed for glory and beauty. The Son of man himself *came not to be ministered unto, but to minister.* 2. That all the six paragraphs here, which give a distinct account of the making of these holy garments, conclude with those words, *as the Lord commanded Moses, v.* 5, 7, 21, 26, 29, 31. The like is not in any of the foregoing accounts, as if in these, more than any other of the appurtenances of the tabernacle, they had a particular regard to the divine appointment, both for warrant and for direction. It is an intimation to all the Lord's ministers to make the word of God their rule in all their ministrations, and to act in observance of and obedience to the command of God. 3. That

442

these garments, in conformity to the rest of the furniture of the tabernacle, were very rich and splendid; the church in its infancy was thus taught, thus pleased, with the rudiments of this world; but now under the gospel, which is the ministration of the Spirit, to affect and impose such pompous habits as the church of Rome does, under pretence of decency and instruction, is to betray *the liberty wherewith Christ has made us free*, and to entangle the church again in the bondage of those carnal ordinances which were imposed only till the time of reformation. 4. That they were all shadows of good things to come, but the substance is Christ, and the grace of the gospel; when therefore the substance has come, it is a jest to be fond of the shadow. (1.) Christ is our great high-priest; when he undertook the work of our redemption, he put on the clothes of service—he arrayed himself with the gifts and graces of the Spirit, which he received not by measure—girded himself with the curious girdle of resolution, to go through with his undertaking—charged himself with all God's spiritual Israel, bore them on his shoulders, carried them in his bosom, laid them near his heart, engraved them on the palms of his hands, and presented them in the breast-plate of judgment unto his Father. And (lastly) he crowned himself with *holiness to the Lord*, consecrating his whole undertaking to the honour of his Father's holiness: now consider how great this man is. (2.) True believers are spiritual priests. The clean linen with which all their clothes of service must be made is *the righteousness of saints* (Rev. xix. 8), and *Holiness to the Lord* must be so written upon their foreheads that all who converse with them may see, and say, that they bear the image of God's holiness, and are devoted to the praise of it.

32 Thus was all the work of the tabernacle of the tent of the congregation finished: and the children of Israel did according to all that the Lord commanded Moses, so did they. 33 And they brought the tabernacle unto Moses, the tent, and all his furniture, his taches, his boards, his bars, and his pillars, and his sockets, 34 And the covering of rams' skins dyed red, and the covering of badgers' skins, and the veil of the covering, 35 The ark of the testimony, and the staves thereof, and the mercy seat, 36 The table, *and* all the vessels thereof, and the showbread, 37 The pure candlestick, *with* the lamps thereof, *even with* the lamps to be set in order, and all the vessels thereof, and the oil for light, 38 And the golden

altar, and the anointing oil, and the sweet incense, and the hanging for the tabernacle door, 39 The brazen altar, and his grate of brass, his staves, and all his vessels, the laver and his foot, 40 The hangings of the court, his pillars, and his sockets, and the hanging for the court gate, his cords, and his pins, and all the vessels of the service of the tabernacle, for the tent of the congregation, 41 The clothes of service to do service in the holy *place*, and the holy garments for Aaron the priest, and his sons' garments, to minister in the priest's office. 42 According to all that the Lord commanded Moses, so the children of Israel made all the work. 43 And Moses did look upon all the work, and, behold, they had done it as the Lord had commanded, even so had they done it: and Moses blessed them.

Observe here, I. The builders of the tabernacle made very good despatch. It was not much more than five months from the beginning to the finishing of it. Though there was a great deal of fine work about it, such as is usually the work of time, embroidering and engraving, not only in gold, but in precious stones, yet they went through with it in a little time. Church-work is usually slow work, but they made quick work of this, and yet did it with the greatest exactness imaginable. For, 1. Many hands were employed, all unanimous, and not striving with each other. This expedited the business, and made it easy. 2. The workmen were taught of God, and so were kept from making blunders, which would have retarded them. 3. The people were hearty and zealous in the work, and impatient till it was finished. God had prepared their hearts, and then *the thing was done suddenly*, 2 Chron. xxix. 36. Resolution and industry, and a cheerful application of mind, will, by the grace of God, bring a great deal of good work to pass in a little time, in less than one would expect.

II. They punctually observed their orders, and did not in the least vary from them. They did it *according to all that the Lord commanded Moses, v.* 32, 42. Note, God's work must be done, in every thing, according to his own will. His institutions neither need nor admit men's inventions to make them either more beautiful or more likely to answer the intention of them. *Add thou not unto his words.* God is pleased with willing worship, but not with will-worship.

III. They brought all their work to Moses, and submitted it to his inspection and censure, *v.* 33. He knew what he had ordered them to make; and now the particulars were called over, and all produced, that Moses might see both that they had made all, omitting nothing, and that they had made all according to the instructions given them, and that, if they had made a mistake in any thing, it might be forthwith rectified. Thus they showed respect to Moses, who was set over them in the Lord; not objecting that Moses did not understand such work, and therefore that there was no reason for submitting it to his judgment. No, that God who gave them so much knowledge as to do the work gave them also so much humility as to be willing to have it examined and compared with the model. Moses was in authority, and they would pay a deference to his place. *The spirit of the prophets is subject to the prophets.* And besides, though they knew how to do the work better than Moses, Moses had a better and more exact idea of the model than they had, and therefore they could not be well pleased with their own work, unless they had his approbation. Thus in all the services of religion we should *labour to be accepted of the Lord.*

IV. Moses, upon search, found all done according to the rule, *v.* 43. Moses, both for their satisfaction and for his own, did look upon all the work, piece by piece, and behold they had done it according to the pattern shown him, for the same Being that showed him the pattern guided their hand in the work. All the copies of God's grace exactly agree with the original of his counsels: what God works in us, and by us, is the fulfilling of the good pleasure of his own goodness; and when the mystery of God shall be finished, and all his performances come to be compared with his purposes, it will appear that behold all is done according to the counsel of his own will, not one iota or tittle of which shall fall to the ground, or be varied from.

V. Moses blessed them. 1. He commended them, and signified his approbation of all they had done. He did not find fault where there was none, as some do, who think they disparage their own judgment if they do not find something amiss in the best and most accomplished performance. In all this work it is probable there might have been found here and there a stitch amiss, and a stroke awry, which would have served for an over-curious and censorious critic to animadvert upon; but Moses was too candid to notice small faults where there were no great ones. Note, All governors must be a praise to those that do well, as well as a terror to evil-doers. Why should any take a pride in being hard to be pleased? 2. He not only praised them, but prayed for them. He blessed them as one having authority, for the less is blessed of the better. We read not of any wages that Moses paid them for their work, but this blessing he gave them. For, though ordinarily the labourer be worthy of

444

his hire, yet in this case, 1. They wrought for themselves. The honour and comfort of God's tabernacle among them would be recompence enough. *If thou be wise, thou shalt be wise for thyself.* 2. They had their meat from heaven on free-cost, for themselves and their families, and their raiment waxed not old upon them; so that they neither needed wages nor had reason to expect any. *Freely you have received, freely give.* The obligations we lie under, both in duty and interest, to serve God, should be sufficient to quicken us to our work, though we had not a reward in prospect. But, 3. This blessing, in the name of the Lord, was wages enough for all their work. Those whom God employs he will bless, and those whom he blesses are blessed indeed. The blessing he commands is *life for evermore.*

CHAP. XL.

In this chapter, I. Orders are given for the setting up of the tabernacle and the fixing of all the appurtenances of it in their proper places (ver. 1—8), and the consecrating of it (ver. 9—11), and of the priests, ver. 12—15. II. Care is taken to do all this, and as it was appointed to be done, ver. 16—33. III. God takes possession of it by the cloud, ver. 34, &c.

AND the Lord spake unto Moses, saying, 2 On the first day of the first month shalt thou set up the tabernacle of the tent of the congregation. 3 And thou shalt put therein the ark of the testimony, and cover the ark with the veil. 4 And thou shalt bring in the table, and set in order the things that are to be set in order upon it; and thou shalt bring in the candlestick, and light the lamps thereof. 5 And thou shalt set the altar of gold for the incense before the ark of the testimony, and put the hanging of the door to the tabernacle. 6 And thou shalt set the altar of the burnt offering before the door of the tabernacle of the tent of the congregation. 7 And thou shalt set the laver between the tent of the congregation and the altar, and shalt put water therein. 8 And thou shalt set up the court round about, and hang up the hanging at the court gate. 9 And thou shalt take the anointing oil, and anoint the tabernacle, and all that *is* therein, and shalt hallow it, and all the vessels thereof: and it shall be holy. 10 And thou shalt anoint the altar of the burnt offering, and all his vessels, and sanctify the altar: and it shall be an altar most holy. 11 And thou shalt anoint the laver and his foot, and sanctify it. 12 And thou shalt bring Aaron and his sons unto the door of the tabernacle of the congregation, and wash them with water. 13 And thou shalt put upon Aaron the holy garments, and anoint him, and sanctify him ; that he may minister unto me in the priest's office. 14 And thou shalt bring his sons, and clothe them with coats : 15 And thou shalt anoint them, as thou didst anoint their father, that they may minister unto me in the priest's office: for their anointing shall surely be an everlasting priesthood throughout their generations.

The materials and furniture of the tabernacle had been viewed severally and approved, and now they must be put together. 1. God here directs Moses to set up the tabernacle and the utensils of it in their places. Though the work of the tabernacle was finished, and every thing ready for rearing, and the people, no doubt, were very desirous to see it up, yet Moses will not erect it till he has express orders for doing so. It is good to see God going before us in every step, Ps. xxxvii. 23. The time for doing this is fixed to *the first day of the first month* (v. 2), which wanted but fourteen days of a year since they came out of Egypt ; and a good year's work there was done in it. Probably the work was made ready but just at the end of the year, so that the appointing of this day gave no delay, or next to none, to this good work. We must not put off any necessary duty under pretence of waiting for some remarkable day ; the present season is the most convenient. But the tabernacle happening to be set up *on the first day of the first month* intimates that it is good to begin the year with some good work. Let him that is the first have the first ; and let the things of his kingdom be first sought. In Hezekiah's time we find they began to sanctify the temple *on the first day of the first month*, 2 Chron. xxix. 17. The new moon (which by their computation was the first day of every month) was observed by them with some solemnity ; and therefore this first new moon of the year was thus made remarkable. Note, When a new year begins, we should think of serving God more and better than we did the year before. Moses is particularly ordered to set up the tabernacle itself first, in which God would dwell and would be served (v. 2), then to put the ark in its place, and draw the veil before it (v. 3), then to fix the table, and the candlestick, and the altar of incense, without the veil (v. 4, 5), and to fix the hanging of the door before the door. Then in the court he must place the altar of burnt offering, and the laver (v. 6, 7) ; and, lastly, he must set up the curtains of the court, and a hanging for a court-gate. And all this would be easily done in one day, many hands no doubt being employed in it under the direction of Moses. 2. He directs Moses, when he had set up the tabernacle and all the furniture of it, to consecrate it and them, by anointing them with the oil which was prepared for the purpose, *ch.* xxx. 25, &c. It was there ordered that this should be done ; here it was ordered that it should be done now, v. 9—11. Observe, Every thing was sanctified when it was put in its proper place, and not till then, for till then it was not fit for the use to which it was to be sanctified. As every thing is beautiful in its season, so is every thing in its place. 3. He directs him to consecrate Aaron and his sons. When the goods were brought into God's house, they were marked first, and then servants were hired to bear the vessels of the Lord ; and those must be clean who were put into that office, v. 12—15. The law which was now ordered to be put in execution we had before, *ch.* xxix. Thus in the visible church, which is God's tabernacle among men, it is requisite that there be ministers to keep the charge of the sanctuary, and that they receive the anointing.

16 Thus did Moses : according to all that the LORD commanded him, so did he. 17 And it came to pass in the first month in the second year, on the first *day* of the month, *that* the tabernacle was reared up. 18 And Moses reared up the tabernacle, and fastened his sockets, and set up the boards thereof, and put in the bars thereof, and reared up his pillars. 19 And he spread abroad the tent over the tabernacle, and put the covering of the tent above upon it ; as the LORD commanded Moses. 20 And he took and put the testimony into the ark, and set the staves on the ark, and put the mercy seat above upon the ark : 21 And he brought the ark into the tabernacle, and set up the veil of the covering, and covered the ark of the testimony ; as the LORD commanded Moses. 22 And he put the table in the tent of the congregation, upon the side of the tabernacle northward, without the veil. 23 And he set the bread in order upon it before the LORD ; as the LORD had commanded Moses. 24 And he put the candlestick in the tent of the congregation, over against the table, on the side of the tabernacle southward. 25 And he lighted the lamps before the LORD, as the LORD commanded Moses. 26 And he put

445

the golden altar in the tent of the congregation before the veil: 27 And he burnt sweet incense thereon; as the LORD commanded Moses. 28 And he set up the hanging *at* the door of the tabernacle. 29 And he put the altar of burnt offering *by* the door of the tabernacle of the tent of the congregation, and offered upon it the burnt offering and the meat offering; as the LORD commanded Moses. 30 And he set the laver between the tent of the congregation and the altar, and put water there, to wash *withal.* 31 And Moses and Aaron and his sons washed their hands and their feet thereat: 32 When they went into the tent of the congregation, and when they came near unto the altar, they washed; as the LORD commanded Moses. 33 And he reared up the court round about the tabernacle and the altar, and set up the hanging of the court gate. So Moses finished the work.

When the tabernacle and the furniture of it were prepared, they did not put off the rearing of it till they came to Canaan, though they now hoped to be there very shortly; but, in obedience to the will of God, they set it up in the midst of their camp, while they were in the wilderness. Those that are unsettled in the world must not think that this will excuse them in their continued irreligion; as if it were enough to begin to serve God when they begin to be settled in the world. No; a tabernacle for God is a very needful and profitable companion even in a wilderness, especially considering that our carcases may fall in that wilderness, and we may be fixed in another world before we come to fix in this.

The rearing of the tabernacle was a good day's work; the consecrating of it, and of the priests, was attended to some days after. Here we have an account only of that newyear's-day's work. 1. Moses not only did all that God directed him to do, but in the order that God appointed; for God will be sought in the due order. 2. To each particular there is added an express reference to the divine appointment, which Moses governed himself by as carefully and conscientiously as the workmen did; and therefore, as before, so here it is repeated, *as the Lord commanded Moses,* seven times in less than fourteen verses. Moses himself, as great a man as he was, would not pretend to vary from the institution, neither to add to it nor diminish from it, in the least punctilio. Those that command others must remember that their Master also is in heaven, and they must do

446

as they are commanded. 3. That which was to be veiled he veiled (*v.* 21), and that which was to be used he used immediately, for the instruction of the priests, that by seeing him do the several offices they might learn to do them the more dexterously. Though Moses was not properly a priest, yet he is numbered among the priests (Ps. xcix. 6), and the Jewish writers call him *the priest of the priests;* what he did he did by special warrant and direction from God, rather as a prophet, or law-giver, than as a priest. He set the wheels a going, and then left the work in the hands of the appointed ministry. (1.) When he had placed the table, he set the show-bread in order upon it (*v.* 23); for God will never have his table unfurnished. (2.) As soon as he had fixed the candlestick, *he lighted the lamps before the Lord, v.* 25. Even that dark dispensation would not admit of unlighted candles. (3.) The golden altar being put in its place, immediately he *burnt sweet incense thereon* (*v.* 27); for God's altar must be a smoking altar. (4.) The altar of burnt-offering was no sooner set up in the court of the tabernacle than he had a *burntoffering, and a meat-offering, ready to offer upon it, v.* 29. Some think, though this is mentioned here, it was not done till some time after; but it seems to me that he immediately began the ceremony of its consecration, though it was not completed for seven days. (5.) At the laver likewise, when he had fixed that, Moses himself washed his hands and feet. Thus, in all these instances, he not only showed the priests how to do their duty, but has taught us that God's gifts are intended for use, and not barely for show. Though the altars, and table, and candlestick, were fresh and new, he did not say it was a pity to sully them; no, he handselled them immediately. Talents were given to be occupied, not to be buried.

34 Then a cloud covered the tent of the congregation, and the glory of the LORD filled the tabernacle. 35 And Moses was not able to enter into the tent of the congregation, because the cloud abode thereon, and the glory of the LORD filled the tabernacle. 36 And when the cloud was taken up from over the tabernacle, the children of Israel went onward in all their journeys: 37 But if the cloud were not taken up, then they journeyed not till the day that it was taken up. 38 For the cloud of the LORD *was* upon the tabernacle by day, and fire was on it by night, in the sight of all the house of Israel, throughout all their journeys.

As when, in the creation, God had finished this earth, which he designed for man's habitation, he made man, and put him in possession of it, so when Moses had finished the tabernacle, which was designed for God's dwelling-place among men, God came and took possession of it. The *shechinah,* the divine eternal Word, though not yet made flesh, yet, as a prelude to that event, came and dwelt among them, John i. 14. This was henceforward the *place of his throne,* and *the place of the soles of his feet* (Ezek. xliii. 7); here he resided, here he ruled. By the visible tokens of God's coming among them to take possession of the tabernacle he testified both the return of his favour to them, which they had forfeited by the golden calf (*ch.* xxxiii. 7), and his gracious acceptance of all the expense they had been at, and all the care and pains they had taken about the tabernacle. Thus God owned them, showed himself well pleased with what they had done, and abundantly rewarded them. Note, God will dwell with those that prepare him a habitation. The broken and contrite heart, the clean and holy heart, that is furnished for his service, and devoted to his honour, shall be his *rest for ever;* here will Christ dwell by faith, Eph. iii. 17. Where God has a throne and an altar in the soul, there is a living temple. And God will be sure to own and crown the operations of his own grace and the observance of his own appointments.

As God had manifested himself upon mount Sinai, so he did now in this newly-erected tabernacle. We read (*ch.* xxiv. 16) that *the glory of the Lord abode upon mount Sinai,* which is said to be like *devouring fire* (*v.* 17), and that the *cloud covered that glory.* Accordingly, when God descended to take possession of his house, the *cloud covered it* on the outside, and *the glory of the Lord filled it* within, to which, probably, there is an allusion in Zech. ii. 5, where God promises to be a *wall of fire round about Jerusalem* (and the pillar of cloud was by night a pillar of fire) *and the glory in the midst of her.*

I. *The cloud covered the tent.* That same cloud which, as the chariot or pavilion of the *shechinah,* had come up before them out of Egypt and led them hither, now settled upon the tabernacle and hovered over it, even in the hottest and clearest day; for it was none of those clouds which the sun scatters. This cloud was intended to be, 1. A token of God's presence constantly visible day and night (*v.* 38) to all Israel, even to those that lay in the remotest corners of the camp, that they might never again make a question of it, *Is the Lord among us, or is he not?* That very cloud which had already been so pregnant with wonders in the Red Sea, and on mount Sinai, sufficient to prove God in it of a truth, was continually *in sight of all the house of Israel throughout all their journeys;* so that they were inexcusable if they believed not their own eyes. 2. A concealment of the tabernacle, and the glory of God in it. God did indeed dwell among them, but he dwelt in a cloud: *Verily thou art a God that hidest*

thyself. Blessed be God for the gospel of Christ, in which *we all with open face behold as in a glass,* not in a cloud, *the glory of the Lord.* 3. A protection of the tabernacle. They had sheltered it with one covering upon another, but, after all, the cloud that covered it was its best guard. Those that dwell in the house of the Lord are hidden there, and are safe under the divine protection, Ps. xxvii. 4, 5. Yet this, which was then a peculiar favour to the tabernacle, is promised to every dwelling-place of mount Zion (Isa. iv. 5); for *upon all the glory shall be a defence.* 4. A guide to the camp of Israel in their march through the wilderness, *v.* 36, 37. While the cloud continued on the tabernacle, they rested; when it removed, they removed and followed it, as being purely under divine direction. This is spoken of more fully, Num. ix. 15, &c., and mentioned with thankfulness, to the glory of God, long afterwards, Neh. ix. 19; Ps. lxxviii. 14; cv. 39. As before the tabernacle was set up the Israelites had the cloud for their guide, which appeared sometimes in one place and sometimes in another, but henceforward rested on the tabernacle and was to be found there only, so the church had divine revelation for its guide from the first, before the making up of that canon it rests in that as its tabernacle, and there only it is to be found, as in the creation the light, which was made the first day, centred in the sun the fourth day. Blessed be God for the law and the testimony!

II. *The glory of the Lord filled the tabernacle, v.* 34, 35. The *shechinah* now made an awful and pompous entry into the tabernacle, through the outer part of which it passed into the most holy place, as the presence-chamber, and there seated itself between the cherubim. It was in light and fire, and (for aught we know) no otherwise, that the *shechinah* made itself visible; for *God is light; our God is a consuming fire.* With these the tabernacle was now filled, yet, as before the bush was not consumed, so now the curtains were not so much as singed by this fire; for to those that have received the anointing the terrible majesty of God is not destroying. Yet so dazzling was the light, and so dreadful was the fire, that Moses was *not able to enter into the tent of the congregation,* at the door of which he attended, till the splendour had a little abated, and the glory of the Lord retired within the veil, *v.* 35. This shows how terrible the glory and majesty of God are, and how unable the greatest and best of men are to stand before him. The divine light and fire, let forth in their full strength, will overpower the strongest heads and the purest hearts. But what Moses could not do, in that *he was weak through the flesh,* has been done by our Lord Jesus, whom God caused to draw near and approach, and who, as the forerunner, *has for us entered,* and has invited us to come boldly even to the mercy-seat

He was able to enter into the holy place not made with hands (Heb. ix. 24); nay, he is himself the true tabernacle, filled with the glory of God (John i. 14), even with the divine grace and truth prefigured by this fire and light. In him the shechinah took up its rest for ever, for in him *dwells all the fulness of the godhead bodily*, Blessed be God for Jesus Christ!

AN

EXPOSITION,

WITH PRACTICAL OBSERVATIONS,

OF THE THIRD BOOK OF MOSES, CALLED

LEVITICUS.

THERE is nothing historical in all this book of Leviticus except the account which it gives us of the consecration of the priesthood (*ch.* viii. ix.), of the punishment of Nadab and Abihu, by the hand of God, for offering strange fire (*ch.* x.), and of Shelomith's son, by the hand of the magistrate, for blasphemy, *ch.* xxiv. All the rest of the book is taken up with the laws, chiefly the ecclesiastical laws, which God gave to Israel by Moses, concerning their sacrifices and offerings, their meats and drinks, and divers washings, and the other peculiarities by which God set that people apart for himself, and distinguished them from other nations, all which were shadows of good things to come, which are realized and superseded by the gospel of Christ. We call the book *Leviticus*, from the Septuagint, because it contains the laws and ordinances of the *levitical priesthood* (as it is called, Heb. vii. 11), and the ministrations of it. The Levites were principally charged with these institutions, both to do their part and to teach the people theirs. We read, in the close of the foregoing book, of the setting up of the tabernacle, which was to be the place of worship; and, as that was framed according to the pattern, so must the ordinances of worship be, which were there to be administered. In these the divine appointment was as particular as in the former, and must be as punctually observed. The remaining record of these abrogated laws is of use to us, for the strengthening of our faith in Jesus Christ, as *the Lamb slain from the foundation of the world*, and for the increase of our thankfulness to God, that by him we are freed from the yoke of the ceremonial law, and live in the times of reformation.

CHAP. I.

This book begins with the laws concerning sacrifices, of which the most ancient were the burnt-offerings, about which God gives Moses instructions in this chapter. Orders are here given how that sort of sacrifice must be managed. I. If it was a bullock out of the herd, ver. 3—9. II. If it was a sheep or goat, a lamb or kid, out of the flock, ver. 10—13. III. If it was a turtle-dove or a young pigeon, ver. 14—17. And whether the offering was more or less valuable in itself, if it was offered with an upright heart, according to these laws, it was accepted of God.

AND the LORD called unto Moses, and spake unto him out of the tabernacle of the congregation, saying,

2 Speak unto the children of Israel, and say unto them, If any man of you bring an offering unto the LORD, ye shall bring your offering of the cattle, *even* of the herd, and of the flock.

Observe here, 1. It is taken for granted that people would be inclined to bring offerings to the Lord. The very light of nature directs man, some way or other, to do honour to his Maker, and pay him homage as his Lord. Revealed religion supposes natural religion to be an ancient and early institution, since the fall had directed men to glorify God by sacrifice, which was an implicit acknowledgment of their having received all from God as creatures, and their having forfeited all to him as sinners. A conscience thoroughly convinced of dependence and guilt would be willing to come before God with *thousands of rams*, Mic. vi. 6, 7. 2. Provision is made that men should not indulge their own fancies, nor become vain in their imaginations and inventions about their sacrifices, lest, while they pretended to honour God, they should really dishonour him, and do that which was unworthy of him. Every thing therefore is directed to be done with due decorum, by a certain rule, and so as that the sacrifices might be most significant both of the great sacrifice of atonement which Christ was to offer in the fulness of time and of the spiritual sacrifices of acknowledgment which believers should offer daily. 3. God gave those laws to Israel by Moses; nothing is more frequently repeated than this, *The Lord spoke unto Moses, saying, Speak unto the children of Israel.* God could have spoken it to the children of Israel himself, as he did the ten commandments; but he chose to deliver it to them by Moses, because they had desired he would no more speak to them himself, and he had designed that Moses should, above all the prophets, be a type of Christ, by whom God would in these last days speak to us, Heb. i. 2. By other prophets God sent messages to his people, but by Moses he gave them laws; and therefore he was fit to typify him to whom the Father has given all judgment. And, besides, the treasure of divine revelation was always to be put into earthen vessels, that our faith might be tried, and that the excellency of the power might be of God. 4. God spoke to him out of the tabernacle. As soon as ever the shechinah had taken possession of its new habitation, in token of the acceptance of what was done, God talked with Moses from the mercy-seat, while he attended without the veil, or rather at the door, hearing a voice only; and it is probable that he wrote what he heard at that time, to prevent any mistake, or slip of memory, in the rehearsal of it. The tabernacle was set up to be a place of communion between God and Israel; there, where they performed their services to God, God revealed his will to them. Thus, by the word and by prayer, we now have fellowship with the Father, and with his Son Jesus Christ, Acts vi. 4. When we speak to God we must desire to hear from him, and reckon it a great favour that he is pleased to speak to us. The Lord called to Moses, not to come near (under that dispensation, even Moses must keep his distance), but to attend and hearken to what should be said. A letter less than ordinary in the Hebrew word for *called*, the Jewish critics tell us, intimates that God spoke in a still small voice. The moral law was given with terror from a burning mountain in thunder and lightning; but the remedial law of sacrifice was given more gently from a mercy-seat, because that was typical of the grace of the gospel, which is the ministration of life and peace.

3 If his offering *be* a burnt sacrifice of the herd, let him offer a male without blemish: he shall offer it of his own voluntary will at the door of the tabernacle of the congregation before the LORD. 4 And he shall put his hand upon the head of the burnt offering; and it shall be accepted for him to make atonement for him. 5 And he shall kill the bullock before the LORD: and the priests, Aaron' sons, shall bring the blood, and sprinkle the blood round about upon the altar that *is by* the door of the tabernacle of the congregation. 6 And he shall flay the burnt offering, and cut it into his pieces. 7 And the sons of Aaron the priest shall put fire upon the altar, and lay the wood in order upon the fire: 8 And the priests, Aaron's sons, shall lay the parts, the head, and the fat, in order upon the wood that *is* on the fire which *is* upon the altar: 9 But his inwards and his legs shall he wash in water: and the priest shall burn all on the altar, *to be* a burnt sacrifice, an offering made by fire, of a sweet savour unto the LORD.

If a man were rich and could afford it, it is supposed that he would bring his burnt-sacrifice, with which he designed to honour God, out of his herd of larger cattle. He that considers that God is the best that is will resolve to give him the best he has, else he gives him not the glory due unto his name. Now if a man determined to kill a bullock, not for an entertainment for his family and friends, but for a sacrifice to his God, these rules must be religiously observed:—1. The beast to be offered must be a male, and without blemish, and the best he had in his pasture. Being designed purely for the honour of him that is infinitely perfect, it ought to be the most perfect in its kind. This signified the complete strength and purity that were in Christ the dying sacrifice, and the sincerity of heart and unblamableness of life that should be in Christians, who are presented to God as living sacrifices. But, literally, in Christ Jesus there is neither male nor female; nor is any natural blemish in the body a bar to our acceptance with God, but only the moral defects and deformities introduced by sin into the soul. 2. The owner must offer it voluntarily. What is done in religion, so as to please God, must be done by no other constraint than that of love. God accepts the willing people and the cheerful giver. Ainsworth and others read it, not as the principle, but as the end, of offering: " Let him offer it *for his favourable acceptation before the Lord.* Let him propose this to himself as his end in bringing his sacrifice, and let his eye be fixed steadily upon that end—that he may be accepted of the Lord. Those only shall find acceptance who sincerely desire and design it in all their religious services, 2 Cor. v. 9. 3. It must be offered at the door of the tabernacle, where the brazen altar of burnt-offerings stood, which sanctified the gift, and not elsewhere. He must offer it at the door, as one unworthy to enter, and acknowledging that there is no admission for a sinner into covenant and communion with God, but by sacrifice; but he must offer it at the tabernacle of the congregation, in token of his communion with the whole church of Israel even in this personal service. 4. The offerer must put his hand upon the head of his offering, *v.* 4. "He must put both his hands," say the Jewish doctors, "with all his might, between the horns of the beast," signifying thereby, (1.) The transfer of all his right to, and interest in, the beast, to God, actually, and by a manual delivery, resigning it to his service. (2.) An acknowledgment that he deserved to die, and would have been willing to die if God had required it, for the serving of his honour, and the obtaining of his favour. (3.) A dependence upon the sacrifice, as an instituted type of the great sacrifice on which the iniquity of us all was to be laid. The mystical signification of the sacrifices, and especially this rite, some think the apostle means by the doctrine of *laying on of hands* (Heb. vi. 2), which typified evangelical faith. The offerer's putting his hand on the head of the offering was to signify his desire and hope that it might *be accepted from him to make atonement for him.* Though the burnt-offerings had not respect to any particular sin, as the sin-offering had, yet they were to make atonement for sin in general; and he that laid his hand on the head of a burnt-offering was to confess that *he had left undone what he ought to have done and had done that which he ought not to have done*, and to pray that, though he deserved to die himself, the death of his sacrifice might be accepted for the expiating of his guilt. 5. The sacrifice was to be killed by the priests or Levites, before the Lord, that is, in a devout religious manner, and with an eye to God and his honour. This signified that our Lord Jesus was to make his soul, or life, an offering for sin. Messiah the prince must be cut off as a sacrifice, *but not for himself*, Dan. ix. 26. It signified also that in Christians, who are living sacrifices, the brutal part must be mortified or killed, the flesh crucified with its corrupt affections and lusts and all the appetites of the mere animal life. 6. The priests were to *sprinkle the blood upon the altar* (*v.* 5); for, the blood being the life, it was this that made atonement for the soul. This signified the direct and actual regard which our Lord Jesus had to the satisfaction of his Father's justice, and the securing of his injured honour, in the shedding of his blood; *he offered himself without spot to God.* It also signified the pacifying and purifying of our consciences by the sprinkling of the blood of Jesus Christ upon them by faith, 1 Pet. i. 2; Heb. x. 22. 7. The beast was to be flayed and decently cut up, and divided

450

into its several joints or pieces, according to the art of the butcher; and then all the pieces, with the head and the fat (the legs and inwards being first washed), were to be burnt together upon the altar, *v.* 6—9. "But to what purpose," would some say, "was this waste?" Why should all this good meat, which might have been given to the poor, and have served their hungry families for food a great while, be burnt together to ashes?" So was the will of God; and it is not for us to object or to find fault with it. When it was burnt for the honour of God, in obedience to his command, and to signify spiritual blessings, it was really better bestowed, and better answered the end of its creation, than when it was used as food for man. We must never reckon that lost which is laid out for God. The burning of the sacrifice signified the sharp sufferings of Christ, and the devout affections with which, as a holy fire, Christians must offer up themselves, their whole spirit, soul, and body, unto God. 8. This is said to be *an offering of a sweet savour*, or *savour of rest, unto the Lord.* The burning of flesh is unsavoury in itself; but this, as an act of obedience to a divine command, and a type of Christ, was well pleasing to God: he was reconciled to the offerer, and did himself take a complacency in that reconciliation. He rested, and was refreshed with these institutions of his grace, as, at first, with his works of creation (Exod. xxxi. 17), rejoicing therein, Ps. civ. 31. Christ's offering of himself to God is said to be of *a sweet-smelling savour* (Eph. v. 2), and the spiritual sacrifices of Christians are said to be *acceptable to God, through Christ*, 1 Pet. ii. 5.

10 And if his offering *be* of the flocks, *namely*, of the sheep, or of the goats, for a burnt sacrifice; he shall bring it a male without blemish. 11 And he shall kill it on the side of the altar northward before the Lord: and the priests, Aaron's sons, shall sprinkle his blood round about upon the altar. 12 And he shall cut it into his pieces, with his head and his fat: and the priest shall lay them in order on the wood that *is* on the fire which *is* upon the altar: 13 But he shall wash the inwards and the legs with water: and the priest shall bring *it* all, and burn *it* upon the altar: it *is* a burnt sacrifice, an offering made by fire, of a sweet savour unto the Lord. 14 And if the burnt sacrifice for his offering to the Lord *be* of fowls, then he shall bring his offering of turtledoves, or of young pigeons. 15 And the priest shall bring it unto the altar, and wring

off his head, and burn *it* on the altar; and the blood thereof shall be wrung out at the side of the altar: 16 And he shall pluck away his crop with his feathers, and cast it beside the altar on the east part, by the place of the ashes: 17 And he shall cleave it with the wings thereof, *but* shall not divide *it* asunder: and the priest shall burn it upon the altar, upon the wood that *is* upon the fire: it *is* a burnt sacrifice, an offering made by fire, of a sweet savour unto the LORD.

Here we have the laws concerning the burnt-offerings, which were of the flock or of the fowls. Those of the middle rank, that could not well afford to offer a bullock, would bring a sheep or a goat; and those that were not able to do that should be accepted of God if they brought a turtle-dove or a pigeon. For God, in his law and in his gospel, as well as in his providence, considers the poor. It is observable that those creatures were chosen for sacrifice which were most mild and gentle, harmless and inoffensive, to typify the innocence and meekness that were in Christ, and to teach the innocence and meekness that should be in Christians. Directions are here given, 1. Concerning the burnt-offerings of the flock, *v.* 10. The method of managing these is much the same with that of the bullocks; only it is ordered here that the sacrifice should be killed *on the side of the altar northward,* which, though mentioned here only, was probably to be observed concerning the former, and other sacrifices. Perhaps on that side of the altar there was the largest vacant space, and room for the priests to turn them in. It was of old observed that *fair weather comes out of the north,* and that *the north wind drives away rain;* and by these sacrifices the storms of God's wrath are scattered, and the light of God's countenance is obtained, which is more pleasant than the brightest fairest weather. 2. Concerning those of the fowls. They must be either turtle-doves (and, if so, "they must be *old* turtles," say the Jews), or *pigeons,* and, if so, they must be *young* pigeons. What was most acceptable at men's tables must be brought to God's altar. In the offering of these fowls, (1.) The head must be wrung off, "quite off," say some; others think only pinched, so as to kill the bird, and yet leave the head hanging to the body. But it seems more likely that it was to be quite separated, for it was to be burnt first. (2.) The blood was to be *wrung out at the side of the altar.* (3.) The garbages with the feathers were to be thrown by upon the dunghill. (4.) The body was to be opened, sprinkled with salt, and then burnt upon the altar. "This sacrifice of birds," the Jews say, " was one of the most

difficult services the priests had to do," to teach those that minister in holy things to be as solicitous for the salvation of the poor as for that of the rich, and that the services of the poor are as acceptable to God, if they come from an upright heart, as the services of the rich, for he accepts *according to what a man hath,* and not *according to what he hath not,* 2 Cor. viii. 12. The poor man's turtle-doves, or young pigeons, are here said to be *an offering of a sweet-smelling savour,* as much as that of an ox or bullock that hath horns or hoofs. Yet, after all, to *love God with all our heart, and to love our neighbour as ourselves, is better than all burnt-offerings and sacrifices,* Mark xii. 33.

CHAP. II.

In this chapter we have the law concerning the meat-offering. I. The matter of it; whether of raw flour with oil and incense (ver. 1), or baked in the oven (ver. 4), or upon a plate (ver. 5, 6), or in a frying pan, ver. 7. II. The management of it, of the flour (ver. 2, 3), of the cakes, ver. 8—10. III. Some particular rules concerning it, That leaven and honey must never be admitted (ver. 11, 12), and salt never omitted in the meat-offering, ver. 13. IV. The law concerning the offering of firstfruits in the ear, ver. 14, &c.

AND when any will offer a meat offering unto the LORD, his offering shall be *of* fine flour; and he shall pour oil upon it, and put frankincense thereon: 2 And he shall bring it to Aaron's sons the priests: and he shall take thereout his handful of the flour thereof, and of the oil thereof, with all the frankincense thereof; and the priest shall burn the memorial of it upon the altar, *to be* an offering made by fire, of a sweet savour unto the LORD: 3 And the remnant of the meat offering *shall be* Aaron's and his sons': *it is* a thing most holy of the offerings of the LORD made by fire. 4 And if thou bring an oblation of a meat offering baken in the oven, *it shall be* unleavened cakes of fine flour mingled with oil, or unleavened wafers anointed with oil. 5 And if thy oblation *be* a meat offering *baken* in a pan, it shall be *of* fine flour unleavened, mingled with oil. 6 Thou shalt part it in pieces, and pour oil thereon: it *is* a meat offering. 7 And if thy oblation *be* a meat offering *baken* in the fryingpan, it shall be made *of* fine flour with oil. 8 And thou shalt bring the meat offering that is made of these things unto the LORD: and when it is presented unto the priest he shall bring it unto the altar. 9 And the priest shall take from the meat offering a memorial thereof, and

451

shall burn *it* upon the altar: *it is* an offering made by fire, of a sweet savour unto the LORD. 10 And that which is left of the meat offering *shall be* Aaron's and his sons': *it is* a thing most holy of the offerings of the LORD made by fire.

There were some meat-offerings that were only appendices to the burnt-offerings, as that which was offered with the daily sacrifice (Exod. xxix. 38, 39) and with the peace-offerings ; these had drink-offerings joined with them (see Num. xv. 4, 7, 9, 10), and in these the quantity was appointed. But the law of this chapter concerns those meat-offerings that were offered by themselves, whenever a man saw cause thus to express his devotion. The first offering we read of in scripture was of this kind (Gen. iv. 3): *Cain brought of the fruit of the ground an offering.*

I. This sort of offerings was appointed, 1. In condescension to the poor, and their ability, that those who themselves lived only upon bread and cakes might offer an acceptable offering to God out of that which was their own coarse and homely fare, and by making for God's altar, as the widow of Sarepta for his prophet, a little cake first, might procure such a blessing upon the handful of meal in the barrel, and the oil in the cruse, as that it should not fail. 2. As a proper acknowledgment of the mercy of God to them in their food. This was like a quit-rent, by which they testified their dependence upon God, their thankfulness to him, and their expectations from him as their owner and bountiful benefactor, who giveth to all life, and breath, and food convenient. Thus must they honour the Lord with their substance, and, in token of their eating and drinking to his glory, must consecrate some of their meat and drink to his immediate service. Those that now, with a grateful charitable heart, deal out their bread to the hungry, and provide for the necessities of those that are destitute of daily food, and when they eat the fat and drink the sweet themselves send portions to those for whom nothing is prepared, offer unto God an acceptable meat-offering. The prophet laments it as one of the direful effects of famine that thereby the *meat-offering and drink-offering were cut off from the house of the Lord* (Joel i. 9), and reckoned it the greatest blessing of plenty that it would be the revival of them, Joel ii. 14.

II. The laws of the meat-offerings were these :—1. The ingredients must always be fine flour and oil, two staple commodities of the land of Canaan, Deut. viii. 8. Oil was to them then in their food what butter is now to us. If it was undressed, the oil must be poured upon the flour (*v.* 1); if cooked, it must be mingled with the flour, *v.* 4, &c.

452

2. If it was flour unbaked, besides the oil it must have frankincense put upon it, which was to be burnt with it (*v.* 1, 2), for the perfuming of the altar ; in allusion to this, gospel ministers are said to be *a sweet savour unto God*, 2 Cor. ii. 15. 3. If it was prepared, this might be done in various ways; the offerer might bake it, or fry it, or mix the flour and oil upon a plate, for the doing of which conveniences were provided about the tabernacle. The law was very exact even about those offerings that were least costly, to intimate the cognizance God takes of the religious services performed with a devout mind, even by the poor of his people. 4. It was to be presented by the offerer to the priest, which is called *bringing it to the Lord* (*v.* 8), for the priests were God's receivers, and were ordained to offer gifts. 5. Part of it was to be burnt upon the altar, for a memorial, that is, in token of their mindfulness of God's bounty to them, in giving them all things richly to enjoy. It was *an offering made by fire, v.* 2, 9. The consuming of it by fire might remind them that they deserved to have all the fruits of the earth thus burnt up, and that it was of the Lord's mercies that they were not. They might also learn that as *meats are for the belly, and the belly for meats, so God shall destroy both it and them* (1 Cor. vi. 13), and that *man lives not by bread alone.* This offering made by fire is here said to be *of a sweet savour unto the Lord ;* and so are our spiritual offerings, which are made by the fire of holy love, particularly that of almsgiving, which is said to be *an odour of a sweet smell, a sacrifice acceptable, well pleasing to God* (Phil. iv. 18), and *with such sacrifices God is well pleased,* Heb. xiii. 16. 6. The remainder of the meat-offering was to be given to the priests, *v.* 3, 10. *It is a thing most holy,* not to be eaten by the offerers, as the peace-offerings (which, though holy, were not most holy), but by the priests only, and their families. Thus God provided that those who served at the altar should live upon the altar, and live comfortably.

11 No meat offering, which ye shall bring unto the LORD, shall be made with leaven : for ye shall burn no leaven, nor any honey, in any offering of the LORD made by fire. 12 As for the oblation of the firstfruits, ye shall offer them unto the LORD : but they shall not be burnt on the altar for a sweet savour. 13 And every oblation of thy meat offering shalt thou season with salt ; neither shalt thou suffer the salt of the covenant of thy God to be lacking from thy meat offering : with all thine offerings thou shalt offer salt. 14 And if thou offer a meat of-

fering of thy firstfruits unto the LORD, thou shalt offer for the meat offering of thy firstfruits green ears of corn dried by the fire, *even* corn beaten out of full ears. 15 And thou shalt put oil upon it, and lay frankincense thereon : it *is* a meat offering. 16 And the priest shall burn the memorial of it, *part* of the beaten corn thereof, and *part* of the oil thereof, with all the frankincense thereof: *it is* an offering made by fire unto the LORD.

Here, I. Leaven and honey are forbidden to be put in any of their meat-offerings : *No leaven, nor any honey, in any offering made by fire, v.* 11. 1. The leaven was forbidden in remembrance of the unleavened bread they ate when they came out of Egypt. So much despatch was required in the offerings they made that it was not convenient they should stay for the leavening of them. The New Testament comparing pride and hypocrisy to leaven because they swell like leaven, comparing also malice and wickedness to leaven because they sour like leaven, we are to understand and improve this as a caution to take heed of those sins which will certainly spoil the acceptableness of our spiritual sacrifices. Pure hands must be lifted up without wrath, and all our gospel feasts kept with the unleavened bread of sincerity and truth. 2. Honey was forbidden, though Canaan flowed with it, because *to eat much honey is not good* (Prov. xxv. 16, 27); it turns to choler and bitterness in the stomach, though luscious to the taste. Some think the chief reason why these two things, leaven and honey, were forbidden, was because the Gentiles used them very much in their sacrifices, and God's people must not learn or use the way of the heathen, but his services must be the reverse of their idolatrous services; see Deut. xii. 30, 31. Some make this application of this double prohibition : leaven signifies grief and sadness of spirit (Ps. lxxiii. 21), *My heart was leavened ;* honey signifies sensual pleasure and mirth. In our service of God both these must be avoided, and a mean observed between those extremes ; for the sorrow of the world worketh death, and a love to the delights of sense is a great enemy to holy love.

II. Salt is required in all their offerings, *v.* 13. The altar was the table of the Lord ; and therefore, salt being always set on our tables, God would have it always used at his. It is called *the salt of the covenant,* because, as men confirmed their covenants with each other by eating and drinking together, at all which collations salt was used, so God, by accepting his people's gifts and feasting them upon his sacrifices, supping with them and they with him (Rev. iii. 20), did confirm his covenant with them. Among the ancients

salt was a symbol of friendship. The salt for the sacrifice was not brought by the offerers, but was provided at the public charge, as the wood was, Ezra vii. 20—22. And there was a chamber in the court of the temple called *the chamber of salt,* in which they laid it up. *Can that which is unsavoury be eaten without salt?* God would hereby intimate to them that their sacrifices in themselves were unsavoury. The saints, who are living sacrifices to God, must have salt in themselves, for *every sacrifice must be salted with salt* (Mark ix. 49, 50), and our speech must be *always with grace* (Col. iv. 6), so must all our religious performances be seasoned with that salt. Christianity is the salt of the earth.

III. Directions are given about the firstfruits. 1. The oblation of their first-fruits at harvest, of which we read, Deut. xxvi. 2. These were offered to the Lord, not to be burnt upon the altar, but to be given to the priests as perquisites of their office, *v.* 12. And *you shall offer them* (that is, leaven and honey) in the oblation of the first-fruits, though they were forbidden in other meat-offerings ; for they were proper enough to be eaten by the priests, though not to be burnt upon the altar. The loaves of the first-fruits are particularly ordered to be *baked with leaven,* Lev. xxiii. 17. And we read of the first-fruits of honey brought to the house of God, 2 Chron. xxxi. 5. 2. A meat-offering of their first-fruits. The former was required by the law; this was a free-will offering, *v.* 14—16. If a man, with a thankful sense of God's goodness to him in giving him hopes of a plentiful crop, was disposed to bring an offering in kind immediately out of his field, and present it to God, owning thereby his dependence upon God and obligations to him, (1.) Let him be sure to bring the first ripe and full ears, not such as were small and half-withered. Whatever was brought for an offering to God must be the best in its kind, though it were but green ears of corn. We mock God, and deceive ourselves, if we think to put him off with a corrupt thing while we have in our flock a male, Mal. i. 14. (2.) These green ears must be dried by the fire, that the corn, such as it was, might be beaten out of them. That is not expected from green ears which one may justly look for from those that have been left to grow fully ripe. If those that are young do God's work as well as they can, they shall be accepted, though they cannot do it so well as those that are aged and experienced. God makes the best of green ears of corn, and so must we. (3.) Oil and frankincense must be put upon it. Thus (as some allude to this) wisdom and humility must soften and sweeten the spirits and services of young people, and then their green ears of corn shall be acceptable. God takes a particular delight in the first ripe fruits of the Spirit and the expressions of early piety and devotion. Those that can but think and speak as children, yet, if they think and speak well, God will be well pleased with their buds and blossoms, and will never forget the kindness of their youth. (4.) It must be used as other meat-offerings, *v.* 16, compare *v.* 9. He shall *offer all the frankincense; it is an offering made by fire.* The fire and the frankincense seem to have had a special significancy. [1.] The fire denotes the fervency of spirit which ought to be in all our religious services. In every good thing we must be zealously affected. Holy love to God is the fire by which all our offerings must be made; else they are not of a sweet savour to God. [2.] The frankincense denotes the mediation and intercession of Christ, by which all our services are perfumed and recommended to God's gracious acceptance. Blessed be God that we have the substance of which all these observances were but shadows, the fruit that was hid under these leaves.

CHAP. III.

In this chapter we have the law concerning the peace-offerings, whether they were, I. Of the herd, a bullock or a heifer, ver. 1—5. Or, II. Of the flock, either a lamb (ver. 6—11) or a goat, ver. 12—17. The ordinances concerning each of these are much the same, yet they are repeated, to show the care we ought to take that all our services be done according to the appointment and the pleasure God takes in the services that are so performed. It is likewise to intimate what need we have of precept upon precept, and line upon line.

A ND if his oblation *be* a sacrifice of peace offering, if he offer *it* of the herd; whether *it be* a male or female, he shall offer it without blemish before the LORD. 2 And he shall lay his hand upon the head of his offering, and kill it *at* the door of the tabernacle of the congregation: and Aaron's sons the priests shall sprinkle the blood upon the altar round about. 3 And he shall offer of the sacrifice of the peace offering an offering made by fire unto the LORD; the fat that covereth the inwards, and all the fat that *is* upon the inwards, 4 And the two kidneys, and the fat that *is* on them, which *is* by the flanks, and the caul above the liver, with the kidneys, it shall he take away. 5 And Aaron's sons shall burn it on the altar upon the burnt sacrifice, which *is* upon the wood that *is* on the fire: it *is* an offering made by fire, of a sweet savour unto the LORD.

The burnt-offerings had regard to God as in himself the best of beings, most perfect and excellent; they were purely expressive of adoration, and therefore were wholly burnt. But the peace-offerings had regard to God as a benefactor to his creatures, and the giver of all good things to us; and therefore these were divided between the altar, the priest, and the owner. Peace signifies, 1. Recon-

ciliation, concord, and communion. And so these were called *peace-offerings,* because in them God and his people did, as it were, feast together, in token of friendship. The priest, who was ordained for men in things pertaining to God, gave part of this peace-offering to God (that part which he required, and it was fit he should be first served), burning it upon God's altar; part he gave to the offerer, to be eaten by him with his family and friends; and part he took to himself, as the days-man that laid his hand upon them both. They could not thus eat together unless they were agreed; so that it was a symbol of friendship and fellowship between God and man, and a confirmation of the covenant of peace. 2. It signifies prosperity and all happiness: *Peace be to you* was as much as, *All good* be to you; and so the peace-offerings were offered either, (1.) By way of supplication or request for some good that was wanted and desired. If a man was in the pursuit or expectation of any mercy, he would back his prayer for it with a peace-offering, and probably put up the prayer when he laid his hand upon the head of his offering. Christ is our peace, our peace-offering; for through him alone it is that we can expect to obtain mercy, and an answer of peace to our prayers; and in him an upright prayer shall be acceptable and successful, though we bring not a peace-offering. The less costly our devotions are the more lively and serious they should be. Or, (2.) By way of thanksgiving for some particular mercy received. It is called *a peace-offering of thanksgiving,* for so it was sometimes; as in other cases *a vow, ch.* vii. 15, 16. And some make the original word to signify *retribution.* When they had received any special mercy, and were enquiring what they should render, this they were directed to render to the God of their mercies as a grateful acknowledgment for the benefit done to them, Ps. cxvi. 12. And we must offer to God the sacrifice of praise continually, by Christ our peace; and then this shall please the Lord better than an ox or bullock. Observe,

I. As to the matter of the peace-offering, suppose it was of the herd, it must be *without blemish;* and, if it was so, it was indifferent whether it was male or female, *v.* 1. In our spiritual offerings, it is not the sex, but the heart, that God looks at, Gal. iii. 28.

II. As to the management of it. 1. The offerer was, by a solemn manumission, to transfer his interest in it to God (*v.* 2), and, with *his hand on the head* of the sacrifice, to acknowledge the particular mercies for which he designed this a thank-offering, or, if it was a vow, to make his prayer. 2. It must be killed; and, although this might be done in any part of the court, yet it is said to be *at the door of the tabernacle,* because the mercies received or expected were acknowledged to come from God, and the prayers or praises were directed to him, and both, as it were, through that door. Our Lord Jesus has said, *I am the door*, for he is indeed the door of the tabernacle. 3. The priest must *sprinkle the blood upon the altar*, for it was the blood that made atonement for the soul ; and, though this was not a sin-offering, yet we must be taught that in all our offerings we must have an eye to Christ as the propitiation for sin, as those who know that the best of their services cannot be accepted unless through him their sins be pardoned. Penitent confessions must always go along with our thankful acknowledgments ; and, whatever mercy we pray for, in order to it we must pray for the removal of guilt, as that which keeps good things from us. First *take away all iniquity*, and then *receive us graciously*, or *give good*, Hos. xiv. 2. 4. All the fat of the inwards, that which we call the tallow and suet, with the caul that encloses it and the kidneys in the midst of it, were to be taken away, and burnt upon the altar, as an offering *made by fire, v.* 3—5. And this was all that was sacrificed to the Lord out of the peace-offering ; how the rest was to be disposed of we shall find, *ch.* vii. 11, &c. It is ordered to be burnt upon the burnt-sacrifice, that is, the daily burnt-offering, the lamb which was offered every morning before any other sacrifice was offered ; so that the fat of the peace-offerings was an addition to that, and a continuation of it. The great sacrifice of peace, that of the Lamb of God which takes away the sins of the world, prepares the altar for our sacrifices of praise, which are not accepted till we are reconciled. Now the burning of this fat is supposed to signify, (1.) The offering up of our good affections to God in all our prayers and praises. God must have the inwards ; for we must pour out our souls, and lift up our hearts, in prayer, and must bless his name with all that is within us. It is required that we be inward with God in every thing wherein we have to do with him. The fat denotes the best and choicest, which must always be devoted to God, who has made for us a feast of fat things. (2.) The mortifying of our corrupt affections and lusts, and the burning up of them by the fire of divine grace, Col. iii. 5. Then we are truly thankful for former mercies, and prepared to receive further mercy, when we part with our sins, and have our minds cleared from all sensuality by the *spirit of judgment* and the *spirit of burning,* Isa. iv. 4.

6 And if his offering for a sacrifice of peace offering unto the Lord *be* ot the flock ; male or female, he shall offer it without blemish. 7 If he offer a lamb for his offering, then shall he offer it before the Lord. 8 And he shall lay his hand upon the head of his offering, and kill it before the tabernacle of the congregation : and

Aaron's sons shall sprinkle the blood thereof round about upon the altar. 9 And he shall offer of the sacrifice of the peace offering an offering made by fire unto the Lord ; the fat thereof, *and* the whole rump, it shall he take off hard by the backbone ; and the fat that covereth the inwards, and all the fat that *is* upon the inwards, 10 And the two kidneys, and the fat that *is* upon them, which *is* by the flanks, and the caul above the liver, with the kidneys, it shall he take away. 11 And the priest shall burn it upon the altar : *it is* the food of the offering made by fire unto the Lord. 12 And if his offering *be* a goat, then he shall offer it before the Lord. 13 And he shall lay his hand upon the head of it, and kill it before the tabernacle of the congregation : and the sons of Aaron shall sprinkle the blood thereof upon the altar round about. 14 And he shall offer thereof his offering, *even* an offering made by fire unto the Lord ; the fat that covereth the inwards, and all the fat that *is* upon the inwards, 15 And the two kidneys, and the fat that *is* upon them, which *is* by the flanks, and the caul above the liver, with the kidneys, it shall he take away. 16 And the priest shall burn them upon the altar : *it is* the food of the offering made by fire for a sweet savour : all the fat *is* the Lord's. 17 *It shall be* a perpetual statute for your generations throughout all your dwellings, that ye eat neither fat nor blood.

Directions are here given concerning the peace-offering, if it was a sheep or a goat. Turtle-doves or young pigeons, which might be brought for whole burnt offerings, were not allowed for peace-offerings, because they have no fat considerable enough to be burnt upon the altar ; and they would be next to nothing if they were to be divided according to the law of the peace-offerings. The laws concerning a lamb or goat offered for a peace offering are much the same with those concerning a bullock, and little now occurs here ; but, 1. The rump of the mutton was to be burnt with the fat of the inwards upon the altar, the *whole rump* (*v.* 9), because in those countries it was very fat and large. Some observe from this that, be a thing ever so contemptible, God can make it honourable, by applying it to his service. Thus

God is said to give more *abundant honour to that part which lacked*, 1 Cor. xii. 23, 24. 2. That which was burnt upon the altar is called the *food of the offering, v.* 11, 16. It fed the holy fire; it was acceptable to God as our food is to us; and since in the tabernacle God did, as it were, keep house among them, by the offerings on the altar he kept a good table, as Solomon in his court, 1 Kings iv. 22, &c. 3. Here is a general rule laid down, that *all the fat is the Lord's* (*v.* 16), and a law made thereupon, that they *should eat neither fat nor blood*, no, not in their private houses, *v.* 17. (1.) As for the *fat*, it is not meant of that which is interlarded with the meat (that they might eat, Neh. viii. 10), but the fat of the inwards, the suet, which was always God's part out of the sacrificed beasts; and therefore they must not eat of it, no, not out of the beasts that they killed for their common use. Thus would God preserve the honour of that which was sacred to himself. They must not only not feed upon that fat which was to be the food of the altar, but not upon any like it, lest the *table of the Lord* (as the altar is called), if something were not reserved peculiar to it, should become contemptible, and *the fruit thereof, even its meat, contemptible*, Mal. i. 7, 12. (2.) The blood was universally forbidden likewise, for the same reason that the fat was, because it was God's part of every sacrifice. The heathen drank the blood of their sacrifices; hence we read of their *drink-offerings of blood*, Ps. xvi. 4. But God would not permit the blood, that made atonement, to be used as a common thing (Heb. x. 29), nor will he allow us, though we have the comfort of the atonement made, to assume to ourselves any share in the honour of making it. He that glories, let him glory in the Lord, and to his praise let all the blood be poured out.

CHAP. IV.

This chapter is concerning the sin-offering, which was properly intended to make atonement for a sin committed through ignorance, I. By the priest himself, ver. 1—12. Or, II. By the whole congregation, ver. 13—21. Or, III. By a ruler, ver. 22—26. Or, IV. By a private person, ver. 27, &c.

A ND the LORD spake unto Moses, saying, 2 Speak unto the children of Israel, saying, If a soul shall sin through ignorance against any of the commandments of the LORD *concerning things* which ought not to be done, and shall do against any of them: 3 If the priest that is anointed do sin according to the sin of the people; then let him bring for his sin, which he hath sinned, a young bullock without blemish unto the LORD for a sin offering. 4 And he shall bring the bullock unto the door of the tabernacle of the congregation before the LORD; and shall lay his hand upon the bullock's head, and kill the bullock before the LORD. 5 And the priest that is anointed shall take of the bullock's blood, and bring it to the tabernacle of the congregation: 6 And the priest shall dip his finger in the blood, and sprinkle of the blood seven times before the LORD, before the veil of the sanctuary. 7 And the priest shall put *some* of the blood upon the horns of the altar of sweet incense before the LORD, which *is* in the tabernacle of the congregation; and shall pour all the blood of the bullock at the bottom of the altar of the burnt offering, which *is at* the door of the tabernacle of the congregation. 8 And he shall take off from it all the fat of the bullock for the sin offering; the fat that covereth the inwards, and all the fat that *is* upon the inwards, 9 And the two kidneys, and the fat that *is* upon them, which *is* by the flanks, and the caul above the liver, with the kidneys, it shall he take away, 10 As it was taken off from the bullock of the sacrifice of peace offerings: and the priest shall burn them upon the altar of the burnt offering. 11 And the skin of the bullock, and all his flesh, with his head, and with his legs, and his inwards, and his dung, 12 Even the whole bullock shall he carry forth without the camp unto a clean place, where the ashes are poured out, and burn him on the wood with fire: where the ashes are poured out shall he be burnt.

The laws contained in the first three chapters seem to have been delivered to Moses at one time. Here begin the statutes of another session, another day. From the throne of glory between the cherubim God delivered these orders. And he enters now upon a subject more strictly new than those before. Burnt-offerings, meat-offerings, and peace-offerings, it should seem, had been offered before the giving of the law upon mount Sinai; those sacrifices the patriarchs had not been altogether unacquainted with (Gen. viii. 20; Exod. xx. 24), and in them they had respect to sin, to make atonement for it, Job i. 5. But the law being now added *because of transgressions* (Gal. iii. 19), and havi entered, that eventually *the offence might abound* (Rom. v. 20), they were put into a way of making atonement for sin more particularly by sacrifice, which was (more than any of the ceremonial institutions) *a shadow of good things to come,* but the substance is Christ, and that one offering of himself by which he put away sin and *perfected for ever those who are sanctified.*

I. The general case supposed we have, *v.* 2. Here observe, 1. Concerning sin in general, that it is described to be against *any of the commandments of the Lord ;* for *sin is the transgression of the law,* the divine law. The wits or wills of men, their inventions or their injunctions, cannot make that to be sin which the law of God has not made to be so. It is said likewise, *if a soul sin,* for it is not sin if it be not some way or other the soul's act; hence it is called the *sin of the soul* (Mic. vi. 7), and it is the soul that is injured by it, Prov. viii. 36. 2. Concerning the sins for which those offerings were appointed. (1.) They are supposed to be overt acts; for, had they been required to bring a sacrifice for every sinful thought or word, the task had been endless. Atonement was made for those in the gross, on the day of expiation, once a year; but these are said to be done against the commandments. (2.) They are supposed to be sins of commission, things which ought not to be done. Omissions are sins, and must come into judgment; but what had been omitted at one time might be done at another, and so to obey was better than sacrifice : but a commission was past recal. (3.) They are supposed to be sins committed through ignorance. If they were done presumptuously, and with an avowed contempt of the law and the Law-maker, the offender was to be cut off, and there remained *no sacrifice for the sin,* Heb. x. 26, 27 ; Num. xv. 30. But if the offender were either ignorant of the law, as in divers instances we may suppose many were (so numerous and various were the prohibitions), or were surprised into the sin unawares, the circumstances being such as made it evident that his resolution against the sin was sincere, but that he was overtaken in it, as the expression is (Gal. vi. 1), in this case relief was provided by the remedial law of the sin-offering. And the Jews say, Those crimes only were to be expiated by sacrifice, if committed ignorantly, for which the criminal was to have been cut off if they had been committed presumptuously."

II. The law begins with the case of the anointed priest, that is, the high priest, provided he should sin through ignorance ; for *the law made men priests who had infirmity.* Though his ignorance was of all others least excusable, yet he was allowed to bring his offering. His office did not so far excuse his offence as that it should be forgiven him without a sacrifice ; yet it did not so far aggravate it but that it should be forgiven him when he did bring his sacrifice. If he sin *according to the sin of the people* (so the case is put, *v.* 3), which supposes him in this matter to stand upon the level with other Is-

raelites, and to have no benefit of his clergy at all. Now the law concerning the sin-offering for the high priest is, 1. That he must bring a bullock without blemish for a sin-offering (*v.* 3), as valuable an offering as that for the whole congregation (*v.* 14) ; whereas for any other ruler, or a common person, *a kid of the goats* should serve, *v.* 23, 28. This intimated the greatness of the guilt connected with the sin of a high priest. The eminency of his station, and his relation both to God and to the people, greatly aggravated his offences ; see Rom. ii. 21. 2. The hand of the offerer must be laid upon the head of the offering (*v.* 4), with a solemn penitent confession of the sin he had committed, putting it upon the head of the sin-offering, *ch.* xvi. 21. No remission without confession, Ps. xxxii. 5 ; Prov. xxviii. 13. It signified also a confidence in this instituted way of expiating guilt, as a figure of something better yet to come, which they could not stedfastly discern. He that laid his hand on the head of the beast thereby owned that he deserved to die himself, and that it was God's great mercy that he would please to accept the offering of this beast to die for him. The Jewish writers themselves say that neither the sin-offering nor the trespass-offering made atonement, except for those that repented and believed in their atonement. 3. The bullock must be killed, and a great deal of solemnity there must be in disposing of the blood ; for it was *the blood that made atonement,* and *without shedding of blood* there was *no remission, v.* 5—7. Some of the blood of the high-priest's sin-offering was to be *sprinkled seven times before the veil,* with an eye towards the mercy-seat, though it was veiled : some of it was to be put upon the horns of the golden altar, because at that altar the priest himself ministered ; and thus was signified the putting away of that pollution which from his sins did cleave to his services. It likewise serves to illustrate the influence which Christ's satisfaction has upon the prevalency of his intercession. The blood of his sacrifice is put upon the altar of his incense and sprinkled before the Lord. When this was done the remainder of the blood was poured at the foot of the brazen altar. By this rite, the sinner acknowledged that he deserved to have his blood thus poured out like water. It likewise signified the pouring out of the soul before God in true repentance, and typified our Saviour's *pouring out his soul unto death.* 4. The fat of the inwards was to be burnt upon the altar of burnt-offering, *v.* 8—10. By this the intention of the offering and of the atonement made by it was directed to the glory of God, who, having been dishonoured by the sin, was thus honoured by the sacrifice. It signified the sharp sufferings of our Lord Jesus, when he was made sin (that is, a sin-offering) for us, especially the sorrows of his soul and his inward agonies. It likewise teaches us, in conformity to the death of Christ, to crucify the flesh. 5. The head and body of the beast, skin and all, were to be carried *without the camp*, to a certain place appointed for that purpose, and there burnt to ashes, *v.* 11, 12. This was very significant, (1.) Of the duty of repentance, which is the putting away of sin as a detestable thing, which our soul hates. True penitents say to their idols, "Get you hence; what have we to do any more with idols?" The sin-offering is called *sin*. What they did to that we must do to our sins; the body of sin must be destroyed, Rom. vi. 6. (2.) Of the privilege of remission. When God pardons sin he quite abolishes it, casts it behind his back. *The iniquity of Judah shall be sought for and not found.* The apostle takes particular notice of this ceremony, and applies it to Christ (Heb. xiii. 11—13), who suffered without the gate, in the place of a skull, where the ashes of dead men, as those of the altar, were poured out.

13 And if the whole congregation of Israel sin through ignorance, and the thing be hid from the eyes of the assembly, and they have done *somewhat against* any of the commandments of the LORD *concerning things* which should not be done, and are guilty; 14 When the sin, which they have sinned against it, is known, then the congregation shall offer a young bullock for the sin, and bring him before the tabernacle of the congregation. 15 And the elders of the congregation shall lay their hands upon the head of the bullock before the LORD: and the bullock shall be killed before the LORD. 16 And the priest that is anointed shall bring of the bullock's blood to the tabernacle of the congregation: 17 And the priest shall dip his finger *in some* of the blood, and sprinkle *it* seven times before the LORD, *even* before the veil. 18 And he shall put *some* of the blood upon the horns of the altar which *is* before the LORD, that *is* in the tabernacle of the congregation, and shall pour out all the blood at the bottom of the altar of the burnt offering, which *is at* the door of the tabernacle of the congregation. 19 And he shall take all his fat from him, and burn *it* upon the altar. 20 And he shall do with the bullock as he did with the bullock for the sin offering, so shall he do with this: and the priest shall make an atonement for them, and it shall

be forgiven them. 21 And he shall carry forth the bullock without the camp, and burn him as he burned the first bullock: it *is* a sin offering for the congregation.

This is the law for expiating the guilt of a national sin, by a sin offering. If the leaders of the people, through mistake concerning the law, caused them to err, when the mistake was discovered an offering must be brought, that wrath might not come upon the whole congregation. Observe, 1. It is possible that the church may err, and that her guides may mislead her. It is here supposed that the whole congregation may sin, and sin through ignorance. God will always have a church on earth; but he never said it should be infallible, or perfectly pure from corruption on this side heaven. 2. When a sacrifice was to be offered for the whole congregation, the elders were to lay their hands upon the head of it (three of them at least), as representatives of the people and agents for them. The sin we suppose to have been some common custom, taken up and used by the generality of the people, upon presumption of its being lawful, which afterwards, upon search, appeared to be otherwise. In this case the commonness of the usage received perhaps by tradition from their fathers, and the vulgar opinion of its being lawful, would not so far excuse them from sin but that they must bring a sacrifice to make atonement for it. There are many bad customs and forms of speech which are thought to have no harm in them, and yet may bring guilt and wrath upon a land, which therefore it concerns the elders both to reform and to intercede with God for the pardon of, Joel ii. 16. 3. The blood of this sin-offering, as of the former, was to be *sprinkled seven times before the Lord, v.* 17. It was not to be poured out there, but sprinkled only; for the cleansing virtue of the blood of Christ was then and is still sufficiently signified and represented by sprinkling, Isa. lii. 15. It was to be sprinkled seven times. Seven is a number of perfection, because when God had made the world in six days he rested the seventh; so this signified the perfect satisfaction Christ made, and the complete cleansing of the souls of the faithful by it; see Heb. x. 14. The blood was likewise to be put upon the horns of the incense-altar, to which there seems to be an allusion in Jer. xvii. 1, where the sin of Judah is said to be *graven upon the horns of their altars.* If they did not forsake their sins, the putting of the blood of their sin-offerings upon the horns of their altars, instead of taking away their guilt, did but bind it on the faster, perpetuated the remembrance of it, and remained a witness against them. It is likewise alluded to in Rev. ix. 13, where a voice is heard *from the four horns of the golden altar;* that is, an answer of peace is given to the prayers of the saints, which are acceptable and prevalent only by virtue of the blood of the sin-offering put upon the horns of that altar; compare Rev. viii. 3. 4. When the offering is completed, it is said, *atonement is made, and the sin shall be forgiven,* *v.* 20. The promise of remission is founded upon the atonement. It is spoken here of the forgiveness of the sin of the whole congregation, that is, the turning away of those national judgments which the sin deserved. Note, The saving of churches and kingdoms from ruin is owing to the satisfaction and mediation of Christ.

22 When a ruler hath sinned, and done *somewhat* through ignorance *against* any of the commandments of the Lord his God *concerning things* which should not be done, and is guilty; 23 Or if his sin, wherein he hath sinned, come to his knowledge; he shall bring his offering, a kid of the goats, a male without blemish: 24 And he shall lay his hand upon the head of the goat, and kill it in the place where they kill the burnt offering before the Lord: it *is* a sin offering. 25 And the priest shall take of the blood of the sin offering with his finger, and put *it* upon the horns of the altar of burnt offering, and shall pour out his blood at the bottom of the altar of burnt offering. 26 And he shall burn all his fat upon the altar, as the fat of the sacrifice of peace offerings: and the priest shall make an atonement for him as concerning his sin, and it shall be forgiven him.

Observe here, 1. That God takes notice of and is displeased with the sins of rulers. Those who have power to call others to account are themselves accountable to the ruler of rulers; for, as high as they are, there is a higher than they. This is intimated in that the commandment transgressed is here said to be the *commandment of the Lord his God, v.* 22. He is a prince to others, but let him know the Lord is a God to him. 2. The sin of the ruler which he committed through ignorance is supposed afterwards to come to his knowledge (*v.* 23), which must be either by the check of his own conscience or by the reproof of his friends, both which we should all, even the best and greatest, not only submit to, but be thankful for. What we have done amiss we should be very desirous to come to the knowledge of. *That which I see not, teach thou me, and show me wherein I have erred,* are prayers we should put up to God every day, that though through ignorance we fall into sin we may not through ignorance lie still in it. 3. The sin-offering

for a ruler was to be *a kid of the goats,* not a bullock, as for the priest and the whole congregation; nor was the blood of his sin-offering to be brought into the tabernacle, as of the other two, but it was all bestowed upon the brazen altar (*v.* 25); nor was the flesh of it to be burnt, as that of the other two, without the camp, which intimated that the sin of a ruler, though worse than that of a common person, yet was not so heinous, nor of such pernicious consequence, as the sin of the high priest, or of the whole congregation. A kid of the goats was sufficient to be offered for a ruler, but a bullock for a tribe, to intimate that the ruler, though *major singulis—greater than each,* was *minor universis—less than the whole.* It is bad when great men give bad examples, but worse when all men follow them. 4, It is promised that the atonement shall be accepted and the sin forgiven (*v.* 26), that is, if he repent and reform; for otherwise God swore concerning Eli, a judge in Israel, that the iniquity of his house should not be purged with sacrifice nor offering for ever, 1 Sam. iii. 14.

27 And if any one of the common people sin through ignorance, while he doeth *somewhat against* any of the commandments of the Lord *concerning things* which ought not to be done, and be guilty; 28 Or if his sin, which he hath sinned, come to his knowledge: then he shall bring his offering, a kid of the goats, a female without blemish, for his sin which he hath sinned. 29 And he shall lay his hand upon the head of the sin offering, and slay the sin offering in the place of the burnt offering. 30 And the priest shall take of the blood thereof with his finger, and put *it* upon the horns of the altar of burnt offering, and shall pour out all the blood thereof at the bottom of the altar. 31 And he shall take away all the fat thereof, as the fat is taken away from off the sacrifice of peace offerings; and the priest shall burn *it* upon the altar for a sweet savour unto the Lord; and the priest shall make an atonement for him, and it shall be forgiven him. 32 And if he bring a lamb for a sin offering, he shall bring it a female without blemish. 33 And he shall lay his hand upon the head of the sin offering, and slay it for a sin offering in the place where they kill the burnt offering. 34 And the priest shall take of the blood of the sin offering with his finger, and

put *it* upon the horns of the altar of burnt offering, and shall pour out all the blood thereof at the bottom of the altar : 35 And he shall take away all the fat thereof, as the fat of the lamb is taken away from the sacrifice of the peace offerings; and the priest shall burn them upon the altar, according to the offerings made by fire unto the LORD : and the priest shall make an atonement for his sin that he hath committed, and it shall be forgiven him.

I. Here is the law of the sin-offering for a common person, which differs from that for a ruler only in this, that a private person might bring either a kid or a lamb, a ruler only a kid; and that for a ruler must be a male, for the other a female : in all the circumstances of the management of the offering they agreed. Observe, 1. The case supposed : *If any one of the common people sin through ignorance, v.* 27. The prophet supposes that they were not so likely as the great men to *know the way of the Lord, and the judgment of their God* (Jer. v. 4), and yet, if they sin through ignorance, they must bring a sin-offering. Note, Even sins of ignorance need to be atoned for by sacrifice. To be able to plead, when we are charged with sin, that we did it ignorantly, and through the surprise of temptation, will not bring us off if we be not interested in that great plea, *Christ hath died,* and entitled to the benefit of that. We have all need to pray with David (and he was a ruler) to be cleansed from *secret faults,* the errors which we ourselves do not understand or are not aware of, Ps. xix. 12. 2. That the sins of ignorance committed by a single person, a common obscure person, did require a sacrifice; for, as the greatest are not above the censure, so the meanest are not below the cognizance of the divine justice. None of the common people, if offenders, were overlooked in a crowd. 3. That a sin-offering was not only admitted, but accepted, even from one of the common people, and an atonement made by it, *v.* 31, 35. Here rich and poor, prince and peasant, meet together; they are both alike welcome to Christ, and to an interest in his sacrifice, upon the same terms. See Job xxxiv. 19.

II. From all these laws concerning the sin-offerings we may learn, 1. To hate sin, and to watch against it. That is certainly a very bad thing to make atonement for which so many innocent and useful creatures must be slain and mangled thus. 2. To value Christ, the great and true sin-offering, whose blood cleanses from all sin, which it was not possible that the *blood of bulls and of goats should take away.* Now, *if any man sin,* Christ is *the propitiation* (1 John ii. 1, 2), not for Jews only, but for Gentiles. And perhaps there was some allusion to this law concern-

460

ing sacrifices for sins of ignorance in that prayer of Christ's, just when he was offering up himself a sacrifice, *Father, forgive them, for they know not what they do.*

CHAP. V.

This chapter, and part of the next, concern the trespass-offering. The difference between this and the sin-offering lay not so much in the sacrifices themselves, and the management of them, as in the occasions of the offering of them. They were both intended to make atonement for sin; but the former was more general, this applied to some particular instances. Observe what is here said, I. Concerning the trespass. If a man sin, 1. In concealing his knowledge, when he is adjured, ver. 1. 2. In touching an unclean thing, ver. 2, 3. 3. In swearing, ver. 4. 4. In embezzling the holy things, ver. 14—16. 5. In any sin of infirmity, ver. 17—19. Some other cases there are, in which these offerings were to be offered, ch. vi. 2—4; xiv. 12; xix. 21; Num. vi. 12. II. Concerning the trespass-offerings, 1. Of the flock, ver. 5, 6. 2. Of fowls, ver. 7—10. 3. Of flour, ver. 11—13; but chiefly a ram without blemish, ver. 15, &c.

A ND if a soul sin, and hear the voice of swearing, and *is* a witness, whether he hath seen or known *of it ;* if he do not utter *it,* then he shall bear his iniquity. 2 Or if a soul touch any unclean thing, whether *it be* a carcase of any unclean beast, or a carcase of unclean cattle, or the carcase of unclean creeping things, and if it be hidden from him; he also shall be unclean, and guilty. 3 Or if he touch the uncleanness of man, whatsoever uncleanness *it be* that a man shall be defiled withal, and it be hid from him; when he knoweth *of it,* then he shall be guilty. 4 Or if a soul swear, pronouncing with *his* lips to do evil, or to do good, whatsoever *it be* that a man shall pronounce with an oath, and it be hid from him; when he knoweth *of it,* then he shall be guilty in one of these. 5 And it shall be, when he shall be guilty in one of these *things,* that he shall confess that he hath sinned in that *thing :* 6 And he shall bring his trespass offering unto the LORD for his sin which he hath sinned, a female from the flock, a lamb or a kid of the goats, for a sin offering; and the priest shall make an atonement for him concerning his sin.

I. The offences here supposed are, 1. A man's concealing the truth when he was sworn as a witness to speak the truth, the whole truth, and nothing but the truth. Judges among the Jews had power to adjure not only the witnesses, as with us, but the person suspected (contrary to a rule of our law, that no man is bound to accuse himself), as appears by the high priest adjuring our Saviour, who thereupon answered, though before he stood silent, Matt. xxvi. 63, 64. Now (*v.* 1), *If a soul sin* (that is, a person, for the soul is the man), if he *hear the voice of swearing* (that is, if he be adjured to testify what he knows, by an *oath* of the Lord upon him, 1 Kings viii. 31), if in such a case, for fear of offending one that either has been his friend or may be his enemy, he refuses to give evidence, or gives it but in part, *he shall bear his iniquity.* And that is a heavy burden, which, if some course be not taken to get it removed, will sink a man to the lowest hell. He that *heareth cursing* (that is, that is thus adjured) and betrayeth it not (that is, stifles his evidence, and does not utter it), he is a partner with the sinner, and *hateth his own soul;* see Prov. xxix. 24. Let all that are called out at any time to bear testimony think of this law, and be free and open in their evidence, and take heed of prevaricating. An oath of the Lord is a sacred thing, and not to be dallied with. 2. A man's touching any thing that was ceremonially unclean, *v.* 2, 3. If a man, polluted by such touch, came into the sanctuary inconsiderately, or if he neglected to wash himself according to the law, then he was to look upon himself as under guilt, and must bring his offering. Though his touching the unclean thing contracted only a ceremonial defilement, yet his neglect to wash himself according to the law was such an instance either of carelessness or contempt as contracted a moral guilt. If at first it be *hidden from him,* yet when he knows it he *shall be guilty.* Note, As soon as ever God by his Spirit convinces our consciences of any sin or duty we must immediately set in with the conviction, and prosecute it, as those that are not ashamed to own our former mistake. 3. Rash swearing. If a man binds himself by an oath that he will do or not do such a thing, and the performance of his oath afterwards proves either unlawful or impracticable, by which he is discharged from the obligation, yet he must bring an offering to atone for his folly in swearing so rashly, as David that he would kill Nabal. And then it was that he must *say before the angel* that it *was an error,* Eccl. v. 6. *He shall be guilty in one of these* (*ch.* v. 4), guilty if he do not perform his oath, and yet, if the matter of it were evil, guilty if he do. Such wretched dilemmas as these do some men bring themselves into by their own rashness and folly; go which way they will their consciences are wounded, sin stares them in the face, so sadly are they *snared in the words of their mouth.* A more sad dilemma this is than that of the lepers, "If we sit still, we die; if we stir, we die." Wisdom and watchfulness beforehand would prevent these straits.

II. Now in these cases, 1. The offender must confess his sin and bring his offering (*v.* 5, 6); and the offering was not accepted unless it was accompanied with a penitential confession and a humble prayer for pardon. Observe, The confession must be particular, *that he hath sinned in that thing;* such was David's confession (Ps. li. 4), *I have done this evil;* and Achan's (Josh. vii. 20), *Thus and thus have I done.* Deceit lies in generals;

many will own in general they have sinned, for that all must own, so that it is not any particular reproach to them; but that they have sinned *in this thing* they stand too much upon their honour to acknowledge: but the way to be well assured of pardon, and to be well armed against sin for the future, is to be particular in our penitent confessions. 2. The priest must *make an atonement for him.* As the atonement was not accepted without his repentance, so his repentance would not justify him without the atonement. Thus, in our reconciliation to God, Christ's part and ours are both needful.

7 And if he be not able to bring a lamb, then he shall bring for his trespass, which he hath committed, two turtledoves, or two young pigeons, unto the Lord; one for a sin offering, and the other for a burnt offering. 8 And he shall bring them unto the priest, who shall offer *that* which *is* for the sin offering first, and wring off his head from his neck, but shall not divide *it* asunder: 9 And he shall sprinkle of the blood of the sin offering upon the side of the altar; and the rest of the blood shall be wrung out at the bottom of the altar: it *is* a sin offering. 10 And he shall offer the second *for* a burnt offering, according to the manner: and the priest shall make an atonement for him for his sin which he hath sinned, and it shall be forgiven him. 11 But if he be not able to bring two turtledoves, or two young pigeons, then he that sinned shall bring for his offering the tenth part of an ephah of fine flour for a sin offering; he shall put no oil upon it, neither shall he put *any* frankincense thereon: for it *is* a sin offering. 12 Then shall he bring it to the priest, and the priest shall take his handful of it, *even* a memorial thereof, and burn *it* on the altar, according to the offerings made by fire unto the Lord: it *is* a sin offering. 13 And the priest shall make an atonement for him as touching his sin that he hath sinned in one of these, and it shall be forgiven him: and *the remnant* shall be the priest's, as a meat offering.

Provision is here made for the poor of God's people, and the pacifying of their consciences under the sense of guilt. Those that were not able to bring a lamb might bring for a sin-offering a pair of *turtle-doves* or *two young pigeons;* nay, if any were so extremely poor that they were not able to procure these so often as they would have occasion, they might bring a pottle of fine flour, and this should be accepted. Thus the expense of the sin-offering was brought lower than that of any other offering, to teach us that no man's poverty shall ever be a bar in the way of his pardon. The poorest of all may have atonement made for them, if it be not their own fault. Thus the poor are evangelized; and no man shall say that he had not wherewithal to bear the charges of a journey to heaven. Now,

I. If the sinner brought two doves, one was to be offered for a sin-offering and the other for a burnt-offering, *v.* 7. Observe, 1. Before he offered the burnt-offering, which was for the honour and praise of God, he must offer the sin-offering, to make atonement. We must first see to it that our peace be made with God, and then we may expect that our services for his glory will be accepted. The sin-offering must make way for the burnt-offering. 2. After the sin-offering, which made atonement, came the burnt-offering, as an acknowledgment of the great mercy of God in appointing and accepting the atonement.

II. If he brought fine flour, a handful of it was to be offered, but without either oil or frankincense (*v.* 11), not only because this would make it too costly for the poor, for whose comfort this sacrifice was appointed, but because it was a sin-offering, and therefore, to show the loathsomeness of the sin for which it was offered, it must not be made grateful either to the taste by oil or to the smell by frankincense. The unsavouriness of the offering was to intimate that the sinner must never relish his sin again as he had done. God by these sacrifices did speak, 1. Comfort to those that had offended, that they might not despair, nor pine away in their iniquity; but, peace being thus made for them with God, they might have peace in him. 2. Caution likewise not to offend any more, remembering what an expensive troublesome thing it was to make atonement.

14 And the Lord spake unto Moses, saying, 15 If a soul commit a trespass, and sin through ignorance, in the holy things of the Lord; then he shall bring for his trespass unto the Lord a ram without blemish out of the flocks, with thy estimation by shekels of silver, after the shekel of the sanctuary, for a trespass offering: 16 And he shall make amends for the harm that he hath done in the holy thing, and shall add the fifth part thereto, and give it unto the priest: and the priest shall make an atonement for him with the ram of the

462

trespass offering, and it shall be forgiven him. 17 And if a soul sin, and commit any of these things which are forbidden to be done by the commandments of the Lord; though he wist *it* not, yet is he guilty, and shall bear his iniquity. 18 And he shall bring a ram without blemish out of the flock, with thy estimation, for a trespass offering, unto the priest: and the priest shall make an atonement for him concerning his ignorance wherein he erred and wist *it* not, and it shall be forgiven him. 19 It *is* a trespass offering: he hath certainly trespassed against the Lord

Hitherto in this chapter orders were given concerning those sacrifices that were both sin-offerings and trespass-offerings, for they go by both names, *v.* 6. Here we have the law concerning those that were properly and peculiarly *trespass-offerings*, which were offered to atone for trespasses done against a neighbour, those sins we commonly call trespasses. Now injuries done to another may be either in holy things or in common things; of the former we have the law in these verses; of the latter in the beginning of the next chapter. If a man *did harm* (as it is *v.* 16) *in the holy things of the Lord*, he thereby committed a trespass against the priests, the Lord's ministers, who were entrusted with the care of these holy things, and had the benefit of them. Now if a man did alienate or convert to his own use any thing that was dedicated to God, unwittingly, he was to bring this sacrifice; as suppose he had ignorantly made use of the tithes, or first-fruits, or first-born of his cattle, or (which, it should seem by *ch.* xxii. 14—16, is principally meant here) had eaten any of those parts of the sacrifices which were appropriated to the priests; this was a trespass. It is supposed to be done through mistake, or forgetfulness, for want either of care or zeal; for if it was done presumptuously, and in contempt of the law, the offender died without mercy, Heb. x. 28. But in case of negligence and ignorance this sacrifice was appointed; and Moses is told, 1. What must be done in case the trespass appeared to be certain. The trespasser must bring an offering to the Lord, which, in all those that were purely trespass-offerings, must be a *ram without blemish,* "of the second year," say the Jewish doctors. He must likewise make restitution to the priest, according to a just estimation of the thing which he had so alienated, adding a fifth part to it, that he might learn to take more heed next time of embezzling what was sacred to God, finding to his cost that there was nothing got by it, and that he paid dearly for his oversights. 2. What must be done in case it were doubtful whether he had trespassed or no; he had cause to suspect it, but he *wist it not* (v. 17), that is, he was not very certain; in this case, because it is good to be sure, he must bring his trespass-offering, and the value of that which he feared he had embezzled, only he was not to add the fifth part to it. Now this was designed to show the very great evil there is in sacrilege. Achan, that was guilty of it presumptuously, died for it; so did Ananias and Sapphira. But this goes further to show the evil of it, that if a man had, through mere ignorance, and unwittingly, alienated the holy things, nay, if he did but suspect that he had done so, he must be at the expense, not only of a full restitution with interest, but of an offering, with the trouble of bringing it, and must take shame to himself, by making confession of it; so bad a thing is it to invade God's property, and so cautious should we be to abstain from all appearances of this evil. We are also taught here to be jealous over ourselves with a godly jealousy, to ask pardon for the sin, and make satisfaction for the wrong, which we do but suspect ourselves guilty of. In doubtful cases we should take and keep the safer side.

CHAP. VI.

The first seven verses of this chapter might fitly have been added to the foregoing chapter, being a continuation of the law of the trespass-offering, and the putting of other cases in which it was to be offered; and with this end the instructions God gave concerning the several kinds of sacrifices that should be offered: and then at ver. 8 (which in the original begins a new section of the law) he comes to appoint the several rites and ceremonies concerning these sacrifices which had not been mentioned before. I. The burnt-offering, ver. 8—13. II. The meat-offering (ver. 14—18), particularly that at the consecration of the priest, ver. 19—23. III. The sin-offering, ver. 24, &c.

AND the Lord spake unto Moses, saying, 2 If a soul sin, and commit a trespass against the Lord, and lie unto his neighbour in that which was delivered him to keep, or in fellowship, or in a thing taken away by violence, or hath deceived his neighbour; 3 Or have found that which was lost, and lieth concerning it, and sweareth falsely; in any of all these that a man doeth, sinning therein: 4 Then it shall be, because he hath sinned, and is guilty, that he shall restore that which he took violently away, or the thing which he hath deceitfully gotten, or that which was delivered him to keep, or the lost thing which he found, 5 Or all that about which he hath sworn falsely; he shall even restore it in the principal, and shall add the fifth part more thereto, *and* give it unto him to whom it appertaineth, in the day of his trespass offering. 6 And he shall bring his trespass offering unto the Lord, a

ram without blemish out of the flock, with thy estimation, for a trespass offering, unto the priest: 7 And the priest shall make an atonement for him before the Lord: and it shall be forgiven him for any thing of all that he hath done in trespassing therein.

This is the latter part of the law of the trespass-offering: the former part, which concerned trespasses about holy things, we had in the close of the foregoing chapter; this concerns trespasses in common things Observe here,

I. The trespass supposed, v. 2, 3. Though all the instances relate to our neighbour, yet it is called a *trespass against the Lord*, because, though the injury be done immediately to our neighbour, yet an affront is thereby given to his Maker and our Master. He that speaks evil of his brother is said to speak evil of the law, and consequently of the Law-maker, Jam. iv. 11. Though the person injured be ever so mean and despicable, and every way our inferior, yet the injury reflects upon that God who has made the command of loving our neighbour second to that of loving himself. The trespasses specified are, 1. Denying a trust: *If a man lie unto his neighbour in that which was delivered him to keep*, or, which is worse, which was lent him for his use. If we claim that as our own which is only borrowed, left in our custody, or committed to our care, this is a trespass *against the Lord*, who, for the benefit of human society, will have property and truth maintained. 2. Defrauding a partner: *If a man lie in fellowship*, claiming a sole interest in that wherein he has but a joint-interest. 3. Disowning a manifest wrong: *If a man* has the front to *lie in a thing taken away by violence*, which ordinarily cannot be hid. 4. Deceiving in commerce, or, as some think, by false accusation; if a man have *deceitfully oppressed* his neighbour, as some read it, either withholding what is due or extorting what is not. 5. Detaining what is found, and denying it (v. 3); if a man have *found that which was lost*, he must not call it his own presently, but endeavour to find out the owner, to whom it must be returned; this is doing as we would be done by: but he that *lies concerning it*, that falsely says he knows nothing of it, especially if he back this lie with a false oath, *trespasseth against the Lord*, who to every thing that is said is a witness, but in an oath he is the party appealed to, and highly affronted when he is called to witness to a lie.

II. The trespass-offering appointed. 1. *In the day of his trespass-offering* he must make satisfaction to his brother. This must be first done *if thy brother hath aught against thee: Because he hath sinned and is guilty*, (v. 4, 5), that is, is convicted of his guilt by his own conscience, and is touched with remorse for it; seeing himself guilty before God, let him faithfully restore all that he has got by fraud or oppression, with a fifth part added, to make amends to the owner for the loss and trouble he had sustained in the mean time; let him account both for debt and damages. Note, Where wrong has been done restitution must be made; and till it is made to the utmost of our power, or an equivalent accepted by the person wronged, we cannot have the comfort of the forgiveness of the sin; for the keeping of what is unjustly got avows the taking, and both together make but one continued act of unrighteousness. To repent is to undo what we have done amiss, which (whatever we pretend) we cannot be said to do till we restore what has been got by it, as Zaccheus (Luke xix. 8), and make satisfaction for the wrong done. 2. He must *then come and offer his gift*, must *bring his trespass-offering to the Lord* whom he had offended; and the priest must make an atonement for him, *v.* 6, 7. This trespass-offering could not, of itself, make satisfaction for sin, nor reconciliation between God and the sinner, but as it signified the atonement that was to be made by our Lord Jesus, when he should make his soul *an offering for sin*, a *trespass-offering;* it is the same word that is here used, Isa. liii. 10. The trespasses here mentioned are trespasses still against the law of Christ, which insists as much upon justice and truth as ever the law of nature or the law of Moses did; and though now we may have them pardoned without a trespass-offering, yet not without true repentance, restitution, reformation, and a humble faith in the righteousness of Christ: and, if any make the more bold with these sins because they are not now put to the expense of a trespass-offering for them, they turn the grace of God into wantonness, and so bring upon themselves a swift destruction. The Lord is the avenger of all such, 1 Thess. iv. 6.

8 And the LORD spake unto Moses, saying, 9 Command Aaron and his sons, saying, This *is* the law of the burnt offering: It *is* the burnt offering, because of the burning upon the altar all night unto the morning, and the fire of the altar shall be burning in it. 10 And the priest shall put on his linen garment, and his linen breeches shall he put upon his flesh, and take up the ashes which the fire hath consumed with the burnt offering on the altar, and he shall put them beside the altar. 11 And he shall put off his garments, and put on other garments, and carry forth the ashes without the camp unto a clean place. 12 And the fire upon the altar

464

shall be burning in it; it shall not be put out: and the priest shall burn wood on it every morning, and lay the burnt offering in order upon it; and he shall burn thereon the fat of the peace offerings. 13 The fire shall ever be burning upon the altar; it shall never go out.

Hitherto we have had the instructions which Moses was directed to give to the people concerning the sacrifices; but here begin the instructions he was to give to the priests; he must *command Aaron and his sons, v.* 9. The priests were rulers in the house of God, but these rulers must be ruled; and those that had the command of others must themselves be commanded. Let ministers remember that not only commissions, but commands, were given to Aaron and his sons, who must be in subjection to them.

In these verses we have the law of the burnt-offering, as far as it was the peculiar care of the priests. The daily sacrifice of a lamb, which was offered morning and evening for the whole congregation, is here chiefly referred to.

I. The priest must take care of the ashes of the burnt-offering, that they be decently disposed of, *v.* 10, 11. He must clear the altar of them every morning, and put them on the east side of the altar, which was furthest from the sanctuary; this he must do in his linen garment, which he always wore when he did any service at the altar; and then he must shift himself, and put on other garments, either such as were his common wear, or (as some think) other priestly garments less honourable, and must *carry the ashes into a clean place without the camp.* Now, 1. God would have this done, for the honour of his altar and the sacrifices that were burnt upon it. Even the ashes of the sacrifices must be preserved, to testify the regard God had to it; by the burnt-offering *he* was honoured, and therefore thus *it* was honoured. And some think that this care which was taken of the ashes of the sacrifice typified the burial of our Saviour; his dead body (the ashes of his sacrifice) was carefully laid up in a garden, in a new sepulchre, which was a *clean place.* It was also requisite that the altar should be kept as clean as might be; the fire upon it would burn the better, and it is decent in a house to have a clean fire-side. 2. God would have the priests themselves to keep it so, to teach them and us to stoop to the meanest services for the honour of God and of his altar. The priest himself must not only kindle the fire, but clean the hearth, and carry out the ashes. God's servants must think nothing below them but sin.

II. The priest must take care of the fire upon the altar, that it be kept *always burning.* This is much insisted on here (*v.* 9, 12), and this express law is given: *The fire shall ever be burning upon the altar, it shall never go out, v.* 13. We may suppose that no day passed without some extraordinary sacrifices, which were always offered between the morning and evening lamb; so that from morning to night the fire on the altar was kept up of course. But to preserve it *all night unto the morning* (*v.* 9) required some care. Those that keep good houses never let their kitchen fire go out; therefore God would thus give an instance of his good house-keeping. The first fire upon the altar came *from heaven* (*ch.* ix. 24), so that by keeping that up continually with a constant supply of fuel all their sacrifices throughout all their generations might be said to be consumed with that fire from heaven, in token of God's acceptance. If, through carelessness, they should ever let it go out, they could not expect to have it so kindled again. Accordingly the Jews tell us that the fire never did go out upon the altar, till the captivity in Babylon. This is referred to Isa. xxxi. 9, where God is said *to have his fire in Zion, and his furnace in Jerusalem.* By this law we are taught to keep up in our minds a constant disposition to all acts of piety and devotion, an habitual affection to divine things, so as to be always ready to every good word and work. We must not only not *quench the Spirit,* but we must *stir up the gift* that is in us. Though we be not always sacrificing, yet we must keep the fire of holy love always burning; and thus we must pray always.

14 And this *is* the law of the meat offering: the sons of Aaron shall offer it before the LORD, before the altar. 15 And he shall take of it his handful, of the flour of the meat offering, and of the oil thereof, and all the frankincense which *is* upon the meat offering, and shall burn *it* upon the altar *for* a sweet savour, *even* the memorial of it, unto the LORD. 16 And the remainder thereof shall Aaron and his sons eat: with unleavened bread shall it be eaten in the holy place; in the court of the tabernacle of the congregation they shall eat it. 17 It shall not be baken with leaven. I have given it *unto them for* their portion of my offerings made by fire; it *is* most holy, as *is* the sin offering, and as the trespass offering. 18 All the males among the children of Aaron shall eat of it. *It shall be* a statute for ever in your generations concerning the offerings of the LORD made by fire: every one that toucheth them shall be holy. 19 And the LORD spake unto Moses, saying, 20 This

is the offering of Aaron and of his sons, which they shall offer unto the LORD in the day when he is anointed; the tenth part of an ephah of fine flour for. a meat offering perpetual, half of it in the morning, and half thereof at night. 21 In a pan it shall be made with oil; *and when it is* baken, thou shalt bring it in: *and* the baken pieces of the meat offering shalt thou offer *for* a sweet savour unto the LORD. 22 And the priest of his sons that is anointed in his stead shall offer it: *it is* a statute for ever unto the LORD; it shall be wholly burnt. 23 For every meat offering for the priest shall be wholly burnt: it shall not be eaten.

The meat-offering was either that which was offered by the people or that by the priests at their consecration. Now,

I. As to the common meat-offering,

1. Only a handful of it was to be burnt upon the altar; all the rest was allowed to the priests for their food. The law of the burnt-offerings was such as imposed upon the priests a great deal of care and work, but allowed them little profit; for the flesh was wholly burnt, and the priests had nothing but the skin. But to make them amends the greatest part of the meat-offering was their own. The burning of a handful of it upon the altar (*v.* 15) was ordered before, *ch.* ii. 2, 9. Here the remainder of it is consigned to the priests, the servants of God's house: *I have given it unto them for their portion of my offerings, v.* 17. Note, (1.) It is the will of God that his ministers should be well provided for with food convenient; and what is given to them he accepts as offered to himself, if it be done with a single eye. (2.) All Christians, being spiritual priests, do themselves share in the spiritual sacrifices they offer. It is not God that is the gainer by them; the handful burnt upon the altar was not worth speaking of, in comparison with the priests' share; we ourselves are the gainers by our religious services. Let God have all the frankincense, and the priests shall have the flour and the oil; what we give to God the praise and glory of we may take to ourselves the comfort and benefit of.

2. The laws concerning the eating of it were, (1.) That it must be *eaten unleavened, v.* 16. What was offered to God must have no leaven in it, and the priests must have it as the altar had it, and no otherwise. Thus must we keep the feasts of the Lord with the *unleavened bread of sincerity and truth.* (2.) It must be eaten in *the court of the tabernacle* (here called the *holy place),* in some room prepared by the side of the court for this purpose. It was a great crime to carry any

of it out of the court. The very eating of it was a sacred rite, by which they were to honour God, and therefore it must be done in a religious manner, and with a holy reverence, which was preserved by confining it to the holy place. (3.) The males only must eat of it, *v.* 18. Of the less holy things, as the first-fruits and tithes, and the shoulder and breasts of the peace-offerings, the *daughters* of the priests might eat, for they might be carried out of the court; but this was of the most holy things, which being to be eaten only in the tabernacle, the *sons* of Aaron only might eat of it. (4.) The priests only that were clean might eat of it: *Every one that toucheth them shall be holy, v.* 18. Holy things for holy persons. Some read it, *Every thing that toucheth it shall be holy:* all the furniture of the table on which these holy things were eaten must be appropriated to that use only, and never after used as common things.

II. As to the consecration meat-offering, which was offered for the priests themselves, it was to be *wholly burnt, and none of it eaten, v.* 23. It comes in here as an exception to the foregoing law. It should seem that this law concerning the meat-offering of initiation did not only oblige the high priest to offer it, and on that day only that he was anointed, and so for his successors in the day they were anointed; but the Jewish writers say that by this law every priest, on the day he first entered upon his ministry, was bound to offer this meat-offering,—that the high priest was bound to offer it every day of his life, from the day in which he was anointed,—and that it was to be offered besides the meat-offering that attended the morning and evening sacrifice, because it is said here to be a *meat-offering perpetual, v.* 20. Josephus says, "The high priest sacrificed twice every day at his own charges, and this was his sacrifice." Note, Those whom God has advanced above others in dignity and power ought to consider that he expects more from them than from others, and should attend to every intimation of service to be done for him. The meat-offering of the priest was to be baked as if it were to be eaten, and yet it must be wholly burnt. Though the priest that ministered was to be paid for serving the people, yet there was no reason that he should be paid for serving the high priest, who was the father of the family of the priests, and whom therefore any priest should take a pleasure in serving gratis. Nor was it fit that the priests should eat of the offerings of a priest; for as the sins of the people were typically transferred to the priests, which was signified by their eating of their offerings (Hos. iv. 8), so the sins of the priests must be typically transferred to the altar, which therefore must eat up all their offerings. We are all undone, both ministers and people, if we must *bear our own iniquity ;* nor could we have had any comfort or hope if

God had not laid on his dear Son the iniquity of us all, and he is both the priest and the altar.

24 And the Lord spake unto Moses, saying, 25 Speak unto Aaron and to his sons, saying, This *is* the law of the sin offering: In the place where the burnt offering is killed shall the sin offering be killed before the Lord: it *is* most holy. 26 The priest that offereth it for sin shall eat it: in the holy place shall it be eaten, in the court of the tabernacle of the congregation. 27 Whatsoever shall touch the flesh thereof shall be holy: and when there is sprinkled of the blood thereof upon any garment, thou shalt wash that whereon it was sprinkled in the holy place. 28 But the earthen vessel wherein it is sodden shall be broken: and if it be sodden in a brazen pot, it shall be both scoured, and rinsed in water. 29 All the males among the priests shall eat thereof: it *is* most holy. 30 And no sin offering, whereof *any* of the blood is brought into the tabernacle of the congregation to reconcile *withal* in the holy *place,* shall be eaten : it shall be burnt in the fire.

We have here so much of the law of the sin-offering as did peculiarly concern the priests that offered it. As, 1. That it must be killed *in the place where the burnt-offering was killed* (*v.* 25), that is, on the north side of the altar (*ch.* i. 11), which, some think, typified the crucifying of Christ on mount Calvary, which was on the north side of Jerusalem. 2. That the priest who offered it for the sinner was (with his sons, or other priests, *v.* 29) to eat the flesh of it, after the blood and fat had been offered to God, in the *court of the tabernacle, v.* 26. Hereby they were to *bear the iniquity of the congregation,* as it is explained, *ch.* x. 17. 3. The blood of the sin-offering was with great reverence to be washed out of the clothes on which it happened to light (*v.* 27), which signified the awful regard we ought to have to the blood of Christ, not counting it a common thing; that blood must be sprinkled on the conscience, not on the raiment. 4. The vessel in which the flesh of the sin-offering was boiled must be broken if it were an earthen one, and, if a brazen one, well washed, *v.* 28. This intimated that the defilement was not wholly taken away by the offering, but did rather cleave to it, such was the weakness and deficiency of those sacrifices; but the blood of Christ thoroughly cleanses from all sin, and after it there needs no cleansing.

466

5. That all this must be understood of the common sin-offerings, not of those for the priest, or the body of the congregation, either occasional, or stated upon the day of atonement; for it had been before ordained, and was now ratified, that if the blood of the offering was brought into the holy place, as it was in those extraordinary cases, the flesh was not to be eaten, but burnt without the camp, *v.* 30. Hence the apostle infers the advantage we have under the gospel above what they had under the law; for though the blood of Christ was *brought into the tabernacle, to reconcile within the holy place,* yet we have a right by faith to *eat of the altar* (Heb. xiii. 10—12), and so to take the comfort of the great propitiation.

CHAP. VII.

Here is, I. The law of the trespass-offering (ver. 1—7), with some further directions concerning the burnt-offering and the meat-offering, ver. 8—10. II. The law of the peace-offering. The eating of it (ver. 11—21), on which occasion the prohibition of eating fat or blood is repeated (ver. 22—27), and the priests' share of it, ver. 28—34. III. The conclusion of those institutions, ver. 35, &c.

LIKEWISE this *is* the law of the trespass offering: it *is* most holy. 2 In the place where they kill the burnt offering shall they kill the trespass offering: and the blood thereof shall he sprinkle round about upon the altar. 3 And he shall offer of it all the fat thereof; the rump, and the fat that covereth the inwards, 4 And the two kidneys, and the fat that *is* on them, which *is* by the flanks, and the caul *that is* above the liver, with the kidneys, it shall he take away : 5 And the priest shall burn them upon the altar *for* an offering made by fire unto the LORD: it *is* a trespass offering. 6 Every male among the priests shall eat thereof: it shall be eaten in the holy place: it *is* most holy. 7 As the sin offering *is,* so *is* the trespass offering: *there is* one law for them : the priest that maketh atonement therewith shall have *it.* 8 And the priest that offereth any man's burnt offering, *even* the priest shall have to himself the skin of the burnt offering which he hath offered. 9 And all the meat offering that is baken in the oven, and all that is dressed in the fryingpan, and in the pan, shall be the priest's that offereth it. 10 And every meat offering, mingled with oil, and dry, shall all the sons of Aaron have, one *as much* as another.

Observe here, 1. Concerning the trespass-offering, that, being much of the same nature with the sin-offering, it was to be governed by the same rules, *v.* 6. When the blood and fat were offered to God to make atonement, the priests were to eat the flesh, as that of the sin-offering, in the holy place. The Jews have a tradition (as we have it from the learned bishop Patrick) concerning the sprinkling of the blood of the trespass-offering *round about upon the altar,* "That there was a scarlet line which went round about the altar exactly in the middle, and the blood of the burnt-offerings was sprinkled round about above the line, but that of the trespass-offerings and peace-offerings round about below the line." As to the flesh of the trespass-offering, the right to it belonged to the priest that offered it, *v.* 7. He that did the work must have the wages. this was an encouragement to the priests to give diligent attendance on the altar; the more ready and busy they were the more they got. Note, The more diligent we are in the services of religion the more we shall reap of the advantages of it. But any of the priests, and the males of their families, might be invited by him to whom it belonged to partake with him: *Every male among the priests shall eat thereof,* that is, may eat thereof, *in the holy place, v.* 6. And, no doubt, it was the usage to treat one another with those perquisites of their office, by which friendship and fellowship were kept up among the priests. Freely they had received, and must freely give. It seems the offerer was not himself to have any share of his trespass-offering, as he was to have of his peace-offering; but it was all divided between the altar and the priest. They offered peace-offerings in thankfulness for mercy, and then it was proper to feast; but they offered trespass-offerings in sorrow for sin, and then fasting was more proper, in token of holy mourning, and a resolution to abstain from sin. 2. Concerning the burnt-offering it is here appointed that the priest that offered it should have the skin (*v.* 8), which no doubt he might make money of. "This" (the Jews say) " is meant only for the burnt-offerings which were offered by particular persons; for the profit of the skins of the daily burnt-offerings for the congregation went to the repair of the sanctuary." Some suggest that this appointment will help us to understand God's clothing our first parents with *coats of skins,* Gen. iii. 21. It is probable that the beasts whose skins they were were offered in sacrifice as whole burnt-offerings, and that Adam was the priest that offered them; and then God gave him the skins, as his fee, to make clothes of for himself and his wife, in remembrance of which the skins ever after pertained to the priest; and see Gen. xxvii. 16. 3. Concerning the meat-offering, if it was dressed, it was fit to be eaten immediately; and therefore the priest that offered it was to have it, *v.* 9. If it was dry, there was not so much occasion for being in haste to use it; and therefore an equal dividend of it must be made among all the priests that were then in waiting, *v.* 10.

11 And this *is* the law of the sacrifice of peace offerings, which he shall offer unto the LORD. 12 If he offer it for a thanksgiving, then he shall offer with the sacrifice of thanksgiving unleavened cakes mingled with oil, and unleavened wafers anointed with oil, and cakes mingled with oil, of fine flour, fried. 13 Besides the cakes, he shall offer *for* his offering leavened bread with the sacrifice of thanksgiving of his peace offerings. 14 And of it he shall offer one out of the whole oblation *for* a heave offering unto the LORD, *and* it shall be the priest's that sprinkleth the blood of the peace offerings. 15 And the flesh of the sacrifice of his peace offerings for thanksgiving shall be eaten the same day that it is offered; he shall not leave any of it until the morning. 16 But if the sacrifice of his offering *be* a vow, or a voluntary offering, it shall be eaten the same day that he offereth his sacrifice: and on the morrow also the remainder of it shall be eaten: 17 But the remainder of the flesh of the sacrifice on the third day shall be burnt with fire. 18 And if *any* of the flesh of the sacrifice of his peace offerings be eaten at all on the third day, it shall not be accepted, neither shall it be imputed unto him that offereth it: it shall be an abomination, and the soul that eateth of it shall bear his iniquity. 19 And the flesh that toucheth any unclean *thing* shall not be eaten; it shall be burnt with fire: and as for the flesh, all that be clean shall eat thereof. 20 But the soul that eateth *of* the flesh of the sacrifice of peace offerings, that *pertain* unto the LORD, having his uncleanness upon him, even that soul shall be cut off from his people. 21 Moreover the soul that shall touch any unclean *thing, as* the uncleanness of man, or *any* unclean beast, or any abominable unclean *thing,* and eat of the flesh of the sacrifice of peace offerings, which *pertain* unto the LORD, even that soul shall be cut off from

his people. 22 And the LORD spake unto Moses, saying, 23 Speak unto the children of Israel, saying, Ye shall eat no manner of fat, of ox, or of sheep, or of goat. 24 And the fat of the beast that dieth of itself, and the fat of that which is torn with beasts, may be used in any other use: but ye shall in no wise eat of it. 25 For whosoever eateth the fat of the beast, of which men offer an offering made by fire unto the LORD, even the soul that eateth *it* shall be cut off from his people. 26 Moreover ye shall eat no manner of blood, *whether it be* of fowl or of beast, in any of your dwellings. 27 Whatsoever soul *it be* that eateth any manner of blood, even that soul shall be cut off from his people. 28 And the LORD spake unto Moses, saying, 29 Speak unto the children of Israel, saying, He that offereth the sacrifice of his peace offerings unto the LORD shall bring his oblation unto the LORD of the sacrifice of his peace offerings. 30 His own hands shall bring the offerings of the LORD made by fire, the fat with the breast, it shall he bring, that the breast may be waved *for* a wave offering before the LORD. 31 And the priest shall burn the fat upon the altar: but the breast shall be Aaron's and his sons'. 32 And the right shoulder shall ye give unto the priest *for* a heave offering of the sacrifices of your peace offerings. 33 He among the sons of Aaron, that offereth the blood of the peace offerings, and the fat, shall have the right shoulder for *his* part. 34 For the wave breast and the heave shoulder have I taken of the children of Israel from off the sacrifices of their peace offerings, and have given them unto Aaron the priest and unto his sons by a statute for ever from among the children of Israel.

All this relates to the peace-offerings: it is the repetition and explication of what we had before, with various additions.

I. The nature and intention of the peace-offerings are here more distinctly opened. They were offered either, 1. In thankfulness for some special mercy received, such as recovery from sickness, preservation in a journey, deliverance at sea, redemption out of captivity, all which are specified in Ps. cvii., and for them men are called upon to offer the sacrifice of thanksgiving, *v.* 22. Or, 2. In performance of some vow which a man made when he was in distress (*v.* 16), and this was less honourable than the former, though the omission of it would have been more culpable. Or, 3. In supplication for some special mercy which a man was in the pursuit and expectation of, here called a *voluntary offering.* This accompanied a man's prayers, as the former did his praises. We do not find that men were bound by the law, unless they had bound themselves by vow, to offer these peace-offerings upon such occasions, as they were to bring their sacrifices of atonement in case of sin committed. Not but that prayer and praise are as much our duty as repentance is; but here, in the expressions of their sense of mercy, God left them more to their liberty than in the expressions of their sense of sin—to try the generosity of their devotion, and that their sacrifices, being free-will offerings, might be the more laudable and acceptable; and, by obliging them to bring the sacrifices of atonement, God would show the necessity of the great propitiation.

II. The rites and ceremonies about the peace-offerings are enlarged upon.

1. If the peace-offering was offered for a thanksgiving, a meat-offering must be offered with it, cakes of several sorts, and wafers (*v.* 12), and (which was peculiar to the peace-offerings) leavened bread must be offered, not to be burnt upon the altar, that was forbidden (*ch.* ii. 11), but to be eaten with the flesh of the sacrifice, that nothing might be wanting to make it a complete and pleasant feast; for unleavened bread was less grateful to the taste, and therefore, though enjoined in the passover for a particular reason, yet in other festivals leavened bread, which was lighter and more pleasant, was appointed, that men might feast at God's table as well as at their own. And some think that a meat-offering is required to be brought with every peace-offering, as well as with that of thanksgiving, by that law (*v.* 29) which requires an oblation with it, that the table might be as well furnished as the altar.

2. The flesh of the peace-offerings, both that which was the priest's share and that which was the offerer's, must be eaten quickly, and not kept long, either raw, or dressed, cold. If it was a peace-offering for thanksgiving, it must be all eaten the same day (*v.* 15); if a vow, or voluntary offering, it must be eaten either the same day or the day after, *v.* 16. If any was left beyond the time limited, it was to be burnt (*v.* 17); and, if any person ate of what was so left their conduct should be animadverted upon as a very high misdemeanour, *v.* 18. Though they were not obliged to eat it in the holy place, as those offerings that are called most holy, but might take it to their own tents and feast upon it there, yet God would by this law make them to know a difference between that and other meat, and religiously to observe it, that whereas they might keep other meat cold in the house as long as they thought fit, and warm it again if they pleased, and eat it three or four days after, they might not do so with the flesh of their peace-offerings, but it must be eaten immediately. (1.) Because God would not have that holy flesh to be in danger of putrefying, or being fly-blown, to prevent which it must be salted with *fire* (as the expression is, Mark ix. 49) if it were kept; as, if it was used, it must be salted with salt. (2.) Because God would not have his people to be niggardly and sparing, and distrustful of providence, but cheerfully to enjoy what God gives them (Eccl. viii. 15), and to do good with it, and not to be anxiously solicitous for the morrow. (3.) The flesh of the peace-offerings was God's treat, and therefore God would have the disposal of it; and he orders it to be used generously for the entertainment of their friends, and charitably for the relief of the poor, to show that he is a bountiful benefactor, *giving us all things richly to enjoy*, the bread of the day in its day. If the sacrifice was a thanksgiving, they were especially obliged thus to testify their holy joy in God's goodness by their holy feasting. This law is made very strict (*v.* 18), that if the offerer did not take care to have all his offering eaten by himself or his family, his friends or the poor, within the time limited by the law, or, in the event of any part being left, to burn it (which was the most decent way of disposing of it, the sacrifices upon the altar being *consumed by fire*), then his offering should not be accepted, nor imputed to him. Note, All the benefit of our religious services is lost if we do not improve them, and conduct ourselves aright afterwards. They are not acceptable to God if they have not a due influence upon ourselves. If a man seemed generous in bringing a peace-offering, and yet afterwards proved sneaking and paltry in the using of it, it was as if he had never brought it; nay, *it shall be an abomination.* Note, There is no mean between God's acceptance and his abhorrence. If our persons and performances are sincere and upright, they are accepted; if not, they are an abomination, Prov. xv. 8. He that eats it after the time appointed shall *bear his iniquity*, that is, he shall be *cut off from his people*, as it is explained (*ch.* xix. 8), where this law is repeated. This law of eating the peace-offerings before the third day, that they might not putrefy, is applicable to the resurrection of Christ after two days, that, being God's *holy one*, he might not see corruption, Ps. xvi. 10. And some think that it instructs us speedily, and without delay, to partake of Christ and his grace, feeding and feasting thereon by faith to-day, *while it is*

called to-day (Heb. iii. 13, 14), for it will be too late shortly.

3. But the flesh, and those that eat it, must be pure. (1.) The flesh must *touch no unclean thing;* if it did, it must not be eaten, but burnt, *v.* 19. If, in carrying it from the altar to the place where it was eaten, a dog touched it, or it touched a dead body or any other unclean thing, it was then unfit to be used in a religious feast. Every thing we honour the holy God with must be pure and carefully kept from all pollution. It is a case adjudged (Hag. ii. 12) that the holy flesh could not by its touch communicate holiness to what was common; but by this law it is determined that by the touch of that which was unclean it received pollution from it, which intimates that the infection of sin is more easily and more frequently communicated than the savour of grace. (2.) It must not be eaten by any unclean person. When a person was upon any account ceremonially unclean it was at his peril if he presumed to eat of the flesh of the peace-offerings, *v.* 20, 21. Holy things are only for holy persons; the holiness of the food being ceremonial, those were incapacitated to partake of it who lay under any ceremonial uncleanness; but we are hereby taught to preserve ourselves pure from all the pollutions of sin, that we may have the benefit and comfort of Christ's sacrifice, 1 Pet. ii. 1, 2. Our consciences must be purged from dead works, that we may be fit to *serve the living God,* Heb. ix. 14. But if any dare to partake of the table of the Lord under the pollution of sin unrepented of, and so profane sacred things, they eat and drink *judgment to themselves,* as those did that ate of the peace-offerings in their uncleanness, 1 Cor. xi. 29. A good reason for the strictness of this law is intimated in the description given of the peace-offerings (*v.* 20) and again (*v.* 21), that they *pertain unto the Lord:* whatever pertains to the Lord is sacred, and must be used with great reverence and not with unhallowed hands. "*Be you holy,* for God is holy, and you pertain to him."

4. The eating of blood and the fat of the inwards is here again prohibited; and the prohibition is annexed as before to the law of the peace-offerings, *ch.* iii. 17. (1.) The prohibition of the fat seems to be confined to those beasts which were used for sacrifice, the bullocks, sheep, and goats: but of the roe-buck, the hart, and other clean beasts, they might eat the fat; for those only of which offerings were brought are mentioned here, *v.* 23—25. This was to preserve in their minds a reverence for God's altar, on which the fat of the inwards was burnt. The Jews say, "If a man eat so much as an olive of forbidden fat—if he do it presumptuously, he is in danger of being cut off by the hand of God—if ignorantly, he is to bring a sin-offering, and so to pay dearly for his carelessness." To eat of the flesh of that which died of itself, or was torn of beasts, was unlawful; but to eat of the fat of such was doubly unlawful, *v.* 24. (2.) The prohibition of blood is more general (*v.* 26, 27), because the fat was offered to God only by way of acknowledgment, but the blood *made atonement for the soul,* and so typified Christ's sacrifice much more than the burning of the fat did; to this therefore a greater reverence must be paid, till these types had their accomplishment in the offering up of the body of Christ once for all. The Jews rightly expound this law as forbidding only the *blood of the life,* as they express it, not that which we call the *gravy,* for of that they supposed it was lawful to eat.

5. The priest's share of the peace-offerings is here prescribed. Out of every beast that was offered for a peace-offering the priest that offered it was to have to himself the breast and the right shoulder, *v.* 30—34. Observe here, (1.) That when the sacrifice was killed the offerer himself must, with his own hands, present God's part of it, that he might signify thereby his cheerfully giving it up to God, and his desire that it might be accepted. He was with his own hands to *lift it up,* in token of his regard to God as the God of heaven, and then to *wave it to and fro,* in token of his regard to God as the Lord of the whole earth, to whom thus, as far as he could reach, he offered it, showing his readiness and wish to do him honour. Now that which was thus heaved and waved was the fat, and the breast, and the right shoulder, it was all offered to God; and then he ordered the fat to his altar, and the breast and shoulder to his priest, both being his receivers. (2.) That when the fat was burnt the priest took his part, on which he and his family were to feast, as well as the offerer and his family. In holy joy and thanksgiving, it is good to have our ministers to go before us, and to be our mouth to God. The melody is sweet when he that sows and those that reap rejoice together. Some observe a significancy in the parts assigned to the priests: the breast and the shoulder intimate the affections and the actions, which must be devoted to the honour of God by all his people and to the service also of the church by all his priests. Christ, our great peace-offering, feasts all his spiritual priests with the breast and shoulder, with the dearest love and the sweetest and strongest supports; for he is the wisdom of God and the power of God. When Saul was designed for a king Samuel ordered the shoulder of the peace-offering to be set before him (1 Sam. ix. 24), which gave him a hint of something great and sacred intended for him. Jesus Christ is our great peace-offering; for he made himself a sacrifice, not only to atone for sin, and so to save us from the curse, but to purchase a blessing for us, and all good. By our joyfully partaking of the benefits of redemption we *feast upon the sacrifice,* to signify which the Lord's supper was instituted.

35 This *is the portion* of the anointing of Aaron, and of the anointing of his sons, out of the offerings of the Lord made by fire, in the day *when* he presented them to minister unto the Lord in the priest's office; 36 Which the Lord commanded to be given them of the children of Israel, in the day that he anointed them, *by* a statute for ever throughout their generations. 37 This *is* the law of the burnt offering, of the meat offering, and of the sin offering, and of the trespass offering, and of the consecrations, and of the sacrifice of the peace offerings; 38 Which the Lord commanded Moses in mount Sinai, in the day that he commanded the children of Israel to offer their oblations unto the Lord, in the wilderness of Sinai.

Here is the conclusion of these laws concerning the sacrifices, though some of them are afterwards repeated and explained. They are to be considered, 1. As a grant to the priests, *v.* 35, 36. In the day they were ordained to that work and office this provision was made for their comfortable maintenance. Note, God will take care that those who are employed for him be well paid and well provided for. Those that receive the anointing of the Spirit to minister unto the Lord shall have their portion, and it shall be a worthy portion, out of the offerings of the Lord; for God's work is its own wages, and there is a present reward of obedience in obedience. 2. As a statute for ever to the people, that they should bring these offerings according to the rules prescribed, and cheerfully give the priests their share out of them. God *commanded the children of Israel to offer their oblations, v.* 38. Note, The solemn acts of religious worship are commanded. They are not things that we are left to our liberty in, and which we may do or not do at our pleasure; but we are under indispensable obligations to perform them in their season, and it is at our peril if we omit them. The observance of the laws of Christ cannot be less necessary than the observance of the laws of Moses was.

CHAP. VIII.

This chapter gives us an account of the solemn consecration of Aaron and his sons to the priest's office. I. It was done publicly, and the congregation was called together to be witnesses of it, ver. 1—4. II. It was done exactly according to God's appointment, ver. 5. 1. They were washed and dressed, ver. 6—9, 13. 2. The tabernacle and the utensils of it were anointed, and then the priests, ver. 10—12. 3. A sin-offering was offered for them, ver. 14—17. 4. A burnt-offering, ver. 18—21. 5. The ram of consecration, ver. 22—30. 6. The continuance of this solemnity for seven days, ver. 31, &c.

AND the Lord spake unto Moses, saying, 2 Take Aaron and his sons with him, and the garments, and the anointing oil, and a bullock for the sin offering, and two rams, and a basket of unleavened bread; 3 And gather thou all the congregation together unto the door of the tabernacle of the congregation. 4 And Moses did as the Lord commanded him; and the assembly was gathered together unto the door of the tabernacle of the congregation. 5 And Moses said unto the congregation, This *is* the thing which the Lord commanded to be done. 6 And Moses brought Aaron and his sons, and washed them with water. 7 And he put upon him the coat, and girded him with the girdle, and clothed him with the robe, and put the ephod upon him, and he girded him with the curious girdle of the ephod, and bound *it* unto him therewith. 8 And he put the breastplate upon him: also he put in the breastplate the Urim and the Thummim. 9 And he put the mitre upon his head; also upon the mitre, *even* upon his forefront, did he put the golden plate, the holy crown; as the Lord commanded Moses. 10 And Moses took the anointing oil, and anointed the tabernacle and all that *was* therein, and sanctified them. 11 And he sprinkled thereof upon the altar seven times, and anointed the altar and all his vessels, both the laver and his foot, to sanctify them. 12 And he poured of the anointing oil upon Aaron's head, and anointed him, to sanctify him. 13 And Moses brought Aaron's sons, and put coats upon them, and girded them with girdles, and put bonnets upon them; as the Lord commanded Moses.

God had given Moses orders to consecrate Aaron and his sons to the priests' office, when he was with him the first time upon mount Sinai, Exod. xxviii. and xxix., where we have also the particular instructions he had how to do it. Now here we have,

I. The orders repeated. What was there commanded to be done is here commanded to be done *now, v.* 2, 3. The tabernacle was newly set up, which, without the priests, would be as a candlestick without a candle; the law concerning sacrifices was newly given, but could not be observed without priests; for, though Aaron and his sons had been nominated to the office, they could not officiate, till they were consecrated, which yet must not be done till the place of their ministration was prepared, and the ordinances were instituted, that they might apply themselves to work as soon as ever they were consecrated, and might know that they were ordained, not only to the honour and profit, but to the business of the priesthood. Aaron and his sons were near relations to Moses, and therefore he would not consecrate them till he had further orders, lest he should seem too forward to bring honour into his family.

II. The congregation called together, *at the door*, that is, in the court *of the tabernacle*, *v.* 4. The elders and principal men of the congregation, who represented the body of the people, were summoned to attend; for the court would hold but a few of the many thousands of Israel. It was done thus publicly, 1. Because it was a solemn transaction between God and Israel; the priests were to be *ordained for men in things pertaining to God*, for the maintaining of a settled correspondence, and the negociating of all affairs between the people and God; and therefore it was fit that both sides should appear, to own the appointment, at the door of the tabernacle of meeting. 2. The spectators of the solemnity could not but be possessed, by the sight of it, with a great veneration for the priests and their office, which was necessary among a people so wretchedly prone as these were to envy and discontent. It was strange that any of those who were witnesses of what was here done should afterwards say, as some of them did, *You take too much upon you, you sons of Levi;* but what would they have said if it had been done clandestinely? Note, It is very fit, and of good use, that ministers should be ordained publicly, *plebe præsente—in the presence of the common people*, according to the usage of the primitive church.

III. The commission read, *v.* 5. Moses, who was God's representative in this solemnity, produced his orders before the congregation: *This is the thing which the Lord commanded to be done.* Though God had crowned him king in Jeshurun, when he made his face to shine in the sight of all Israel, yet he did not institute or appoint any thing in God's worship but what God himself had commanded. The priesthood he delivered to them was that which he had received from the Lord. Note, All that minister about holy things must have an eye to God's command as their rule and warrant; for it is only in the observance of this that they can expect to be owned and accepted of God. Thus we must be able to say, in all acts of religious worship, *This is the thing which the Lord commanded to be done.*

IV. The ceremony performed according to the divine ritual. 1. Aaron and his sons were *washed with water* (*v.* 6), to signify that they ought now to purify themselves from all sinful dispositions and inclinations, and ever after to keep themselves pure. Christ washes those from their sins in his own blood whom he makes to our God kings and priests

(Rev. i. 5, 6); and those that draw near to God must be washed in pure water, Heb. x. 22. Though they were ever so clean before, and no filth was to be seen upon them, yet they must be washed, to signify their purification from sin, with which their souls were polluted, how clean soever their bodies were. 2. They were clothed with the holy garments, Aaron with his (*v.* 7—9), which typified the dignity of Christ our great high priest, and his sons with theirs (*v.* 13), which typified the decency of Christians, who are spiritual priests. Christ wears the breast-plate of judgment and the holy crown; for the church's high priest is her prophet and king. All believers are clothed with the robe of righteousness, and girt with the girdle of truth, resolution, and close application; and their heads are *bound*, as the word here is, with the bonnet or diadem of beauty, the beauty of holiness. 3. The high priest was anointed, and, it should seem, the holy things were anointed at the same time; some think that they were anointed before, but that the anointing of them is mentioned here because Aaron was anointed with the same oil with which they were anointed; but the manner of relating it here makes it more than probable that it was done at the same time, and that the seven days employed in consecrating the altar were coincident with the seven days of the priests' consecration. The tabernacle, and all its utensils, had some of the anointing oil put upon them with Moses's finger (*v.* 10), so had the altar (*v.* 11); these were to sanctify the gold and the gift (Matt. xxiii. 17—19), and therefore must themselves be thus sanctified; but he poured it out more plentifully upon the head of Aaron (*v.* 12), so that it ran down to the *skirts of his garments*, because his unction was to typify the anointing of Christ with the Spirit, which was not given by measure to him. Yet all believers also have received the anointing, which puts an indelible character upon them, 1 John ii. 27.

14 And he brought the bullock for the sin offering: and Aaron and his sons laid their hands upon the head of the bullock for the sin offering. 15 And he slew *it;* and Moses took the blood, and put *it* upon the horns of the altar round about with his finger, and purified the altar, and poured the blood at the bottom of the altar, and sanctified it, to make reconciliation upon it. 16 And he took all the fat that *was* upon the inwards, and the caul *above* the liver, and the two kidneys, and their fat, and Moses burned *it* upon the altar, 17 But the bullock, and his hide, his flesh, and his dung, he burnt with fire without the camp; as the LORD commanded Mo-

ses. 18 And he brought the ram for the burnt offering : and Aaron and his sons laid their hands upon the head of the ram. 19 And he killed *it ;* and Moses sprinkled the blood upon the altar round about. 20 And he cut the ram into pieces; and Moses burnt the head, and the pieces, and the fat. 21 And he washed the inwards and the legs in water; and Moses burnt the whole ram upon the altar : it *was* a burnt sacrifice for a sweet savour, *and* an offering made by fire unto the Lord ; as the Lord commanded Moses. 22 And he brought the other ram, the ram of consecration : and Aaron and his sons laid their hands upon the head of the ram. 23 And he slew *it ;* and Moses took of the blood of it, and put *it* upon the tip of Aaron's right ear, and upon the thumb of his right hand, and upon the great toe of his right foot. 24 And he brought Aaron's sons, and Moses put of the blood upon the tip of their right ear, and upon the thumbs of their right hands, and upon the great toes of their right feet : and Moses sprinkled the blood upon the altar round about. 25 And he took the fat, and the rump, and all the fat that *was* upon the inwards, and the caul *above* the liver, and the two kidneys, and their fat, and the right shoulder : 26 And out of the basket of unleavened bread, that *was* before the Lord, he took one unleavened cake, and a cake of oiled bread, and one wafer, and put *them* on the fat, and upon the right shoulder : 27 And he put all upon Aaron's hands, and upon his sons' hands, and waved them *for* a wave offering before the Lord. 28 And Moses took them from off their hands, and burnt *them* on the altar upon the burnt offering : they *were* consecrations for a sweet savour; it *is* an offering made by fire unto the Lord. 29 And Moses took the breast, and waved it for a wave offering before the Lord : *for* of the ram of consecration it was Moses' part; as the Lord commanded Moses. 30 And Moses took of the anointing oil, and of the blood which *was* upon the altar, and sprinkled it upon Aaron, *and* upon

his garments, and upon his sons, and upon his sons' garments with him ; and sanctified Aaron, *and* his garments, and his sons, and his sons' garments with him.

The covenant of priesthood must be made by sacrifice, as well as other covenants, Ps. l. 5. And thus Christ was consecrated by the sacrifice of himself, once for all. Sacrifices of each kind must be offered for the priests, that they might with the more tenderness and concern offer the gifts and sacrifices of the people, with compassion on the ignorant, and on *those that were out of the way*, not insulting over those for whom sacrifices were offered, remembering that they themselves had had sacrifices offered for them, being *compassed with infirmity*. 1. A bullock, the largest sacrifice, was offered for a sin-offering (*v*. 14), that hereby atonement might be made, and they might not bring any of the guilt of the sins of their former state into the new character they were now to put on. When Isaiah was sent to be a prophet, he was told to his comfort, *Thy iniquity is taken away*, Isa. vi. 7. Ministers, that are to declare the remission of sins to others, should give diligence to get it made sure to themselves in the first place that their own sins are pardoned. Those to whom is committed *the ministry of reconciliation* must first be reconciled to God themselves, that they may deal for the souls of others as for their own. 2. A ram was offered for a burnt-offering, *v*. 18—21. By this they gave to God the glory of this great honour which was now put upon them, and returned him praise for it, as Paul thanked Christ Jesus for *putting him into the ministry*, 1 Tim. i. 12. They also signified the devoting of themselves and all their services to the honour of God. 3. Another ram, called the *ram of consecration*, was offered for a peace-offering, *v*. 22, &c. The blood of it was part put on the priests, on their ears, thumbs, and toes, and part sprinkled upon the altar ; and thus he did (as it were) marry them to the altar, upon which they must all their days give attendance. All the ceremonies about this offering, as those before, were appointed by the express command of God ; and, if we compare this chapter with Exod. xxix., we shall find that the performance of the solemnity exactly agrees with the precept there, and in nothing varies. Here, therefore, as in the account we had of the tabernacle and its vessels, it is again and again repeated, *As the Lord commanded Moses*. And thus Christ, when he sanctified himself with his own blood, had an eye to his Father's will in it. *As the Father gave me commandment so I do*, John xiv. 31; x. 18; vi. 38.

31 And Moses said unto Aaron and to his sons, Boil the flesh *at* the door of the tabernacle of the congregation :

and there eat it with the bread that *is* in the basket of consecrations, as I commanded, saying, Aaron and his sons shall eat it. 32 And that which remaineth of the flesh and of the bread shall ye burn with fire. 33 And ye shall not go out of the door of the tabernacle of the congregation *in* seven days, until the days of your consecration be at an end : for seven days shall he consecrate you. 34 As he hath done this day, *so* the LORD hath commanded to do, to make an atonement for you. 35 Therefore shall ye abide *at* the door of the tabernacle of the congregation day and night seven days, and keep the charge of the LORD, that ye die not: for so I am commanded. 36 So Aaron and his sons did all things which the LORD commanded by the hand of Moses.

Moses, having done his part of the ceremony, now leaves Aaron and his sons to do theirs.

I. They must boil the flesh of their peace-offering, and eat it in the court of the tabernacle, and what remained they must burn with fire, *v.* 31, 32. This signified their thankful consent to the consecration : when God gave Ezekiel his commission, he told him to eat the roll, Ezek. iii. 1, 2.

II. They must not stir out of the court of the tabernacle for seven days, *v.* 33. The priesthood being a good warfare, they must thus learn to endure hardness, and to disentangle themselves from the affairs of this life, 2 Tim. ii. 3, 4. Being consecrated to their service, they must *give themselves wholly to it*, and *attend continually to this very thing*. Thus Christ's apostles were appointed to *wait for the promise of the Father*, Acts i. 4. During this time appointed for their consecration, they were daily to repeat the same sacrifices which were offered the first day, *v.* 34. This shows the imperfection of the legal sacrifices, which, because they could not take away sin, were often repeated (Heb. x. 1, 2), but were here repeated seven times (a number of perfection), because they typified that *one offering, which perfected for ever those that were sanctified*. The work lasted seven days ; for it was a kind of creation : and this time was appointed in honour of the sabbath, which, probably, was the last day of the seven, for which they were to prepare during the six days. Thus the time of our life, like the six days, must be our preparation for the perfection of our consecration to God in the everlasting sabbath : they attended *day and night* (*v.* 35), and so constant should we be in our meditation on God's law, Ps. i. 2. They attended to *keep the charge of the Lord :* we have every one of us a charge to keep, an eternal God to glorify, an immortal soul to provide for, needful duty to be done, our generation to serve ; and it must be our daily care to keep this charge, for it is the charge of the Lord our Master, who will shortly call us to an account about it, and it is at our utmost peril if we neglect it. Keep it *that you die not :* it is death, eternal death, to betray the trust we are charged with ; by the consideration of this we must be kept in awe. *Lastly,* We are told (*v.* 36) that *Aaron and his sons did all that was commanded.* Thus their consecration was completed ; and thus they set an example before the people of an exact obedience to the laws of sacrifices now newly given, and then they could with the better grace teach them. Thus the *covenant of peace* (Num. xxv. 12), *of life and peace* (Mal. ii. 5), was made with Aaron and his sons ; but after all the ceremonies that were used in their consecration there was one point of ratification which was reserved to be the honour and establishment of Christ's priesthood, which was this, that they were *made priests without an oath, but Christ with an oath* (Heb. vii. 21), for neither such priests nor their priesthood could continue, but Christ's is a perpetual and unchangeable priesthood.

Gospel ministers are compared to those who served at the altar, for they *minister about holy things* (1 Cor. ix. 13), they are God's mouth to the people and the people's to God, the pastors and teachers Christ has appointed to continue in the church to the end of the world : they seem to be meant in that promise which points at gospel times (Isa. lxvi. 21), *I will take of them for priests and for Levites.* No man may take this honour to himself, but he who upon trial is found to be clothed and anointed by the Spirit of God with gifts and graces to qualify him for it, and who with purpose of heart devotes himself entirely to the service, and is then by the *word and prayer* (for so every thing is sanctified), and the imposition of the hands of those that *give themselves to the word and prayer*, set apart to the office, and recommended to Christ as a servant and to the church as a steward and guide. And those that are thus solemnly dedicated to God ought not to depart from his service, but faithfully to abide in it all their days; and those that do so, and continue *labouring in the word and doctrine*, are to be accounted *worthy of double honour*, double to that of the Old-Testament priests.

CHAP. IX.

Aaron and his sons, having been solemnly consecrated to the priest-hood, are in this chapter entering upon the execution of their office, the very next day after their consecration was completed. I. Moses (no doubt by direction from God) appoints a meeting between God and his priests, as the representatives of his people, ordering them to attend him, and assuring them that he would appear to them, ver. 1—7. II. The meeting is held according to the appointment. 1. Aaron attends on God by sacrifice, offering a sin-offering and a burnt-offering for himself (ver. 8—14), and then the offerings for the people, whom he blessed in the name of the Lord, ver. 15—22, 2. God signifies his acceptance, (1.) Of their persons, by showing them his glory, ver. 23. (2.) Of their sacrifices, by consuming them with fire from heaven, ver. 24.

AND it came to pass on the eighth day, *that* Moses called Aaron and his sons, and the elders of Israel; 2 And he said unto Aaron, Take thee a young calf for a sin offering, and a ram for a burnt offering, without blemish, and offer *them* before the LORD. 3 And unto the children of Israel thou shalt speak, saying, Take ye a kid of the goats for a sin offering; and a calf and a lamb, *both* of the first year, without blemish, for a burnt offering; 4 Also a bullock and a ram for pe ce offerings, to sacrifice before the LORD; and a meat offering mingled with oil: for to day the LORD will appear unto you. 5 And they brought *that* which Moses commanded before the tabernacle of the congregation: and all the congregation drew near and stood before the LORD. 6 And Moses said, This *is* the thing which the LORD commanded that ye should do: and the glory of the LORD shall appear unto you. 7 And Moses said unto Aaron, Go unto the altar, and offer thy sin offering, and thy burnt offering, and make an atonement for thyself, and for the people: and offer the offering of the people, and make an atonement for them; as the LORD commanded.

Orders are here given for another solemnity upon the eighth day; for the newly-ordained priests were set to work immediately after the days of their consecration were finished, to let them know that they were not ordained to be idle: *He that desires the office of a bishop desires a good work,* which must be looked at with desire, more than the honour and benefit. The priests had not so much as one day's respite from service allowed them, that they might divert themselves, and receive the compliments of their friends upon their elevation, but were busily employed the very next day; for their consecration was the *filling of their hands.* God's spiritual priests have constant work cut out for them, which the duty of every day requires; and those that would give up their account with joy must redeem time; see Ezek. xliii. 26, 27. Now, 1. Moses raises their expectation of a glorious appearance of God to them this day (*v.* 4): "*To day the Lord will appear to you* that are the priests." And when all the congregation are gathered together, and *stand before the Lord,* he tells them (*v.* 6), *The glory of the Lord shall appear to you.* Though they had reason enough to believe God's acceptance of all that they had done according to his appointment, upon the general assurance we have that he is the *rewarder of those*

that diligently seek him (even if he had not given them any sensible token of it), yet that if possible they and theirs might be effectually obliged to the service and worship of God, and might never turn aside to idols, the glory of God appeared to them, and visibly owned what they had done. We are not now to expect such appearances; we Christians walk more by faith, and less by sight, than they did. But we may be sure that God draws nigh to those who draw nigh to him, and that the offerings of faith are really acceptable to him, though, the sacrifices being spiritual, the tokens of the acceptance are, as it is fit they should be, spiritual likewise. To those who are duly consecrated to God he will undoubtedly manifest himself. 2. He puts both priests and people upon preparing to receive this favour which God designed them. *Aaron and his sons,* and *the elders of Israel,* are all summoned to attend, *v.* 1. Note, God will manifest himself in the solemn assemblies of his people and ministers; and those that would have the benefit and comfort of God's appearances must in them give their attendance. (1.) Aaron is ordered to prepare his offerings: *A young calf for a sin-offering, v.* 2. The Jewish writers suggest that a *calf* was appointed for a sin-offering to remind him of his sin in making the golden calf, by which he had rendered himself for ever unworthy of the honour of the priesthood, and which he had reason to reflect upon with sorrow and shame in all the atonements he made. (2.) Aaron must direct the people to get theirs ready. · Hitherto Moses had told the people what they must do; but now Aaron, as high priest over the house of God, must be their teacher, *in things pertaining to God: Unto the children of Israel thou shalt speak, v.* 3. Now that he was to speak from them to God in the sacrifices (the language of which he that appointed them very well understood) he must speak from God to them in the laws about the sacrifices. Thus Moses would engage the people's respect and obedience to him, as one that was set *over them in the Lord, to admonish them.* (3.) Aaron must offer his own first, and then the people's, *v.* 7. Aaron must now *go to the altar,* Moses having shown him the way to it; and there, [1.] He must *make an atonement for himself;* for the high priest, being *compassed with infirmity, ought, as for the people, so also for himself, to offer for sins* (Heb. v. 2, 3), and for himself first; for how can we expect to be accepted in our prayers for others, if we ourselves be not reconciled to God? Nor is any service pleasing to God till the guilt of sin be removed by our interest in the great propitiation. Those that have the care of the souls of others are also hereby taught to look to their own in the first place; this charity must begin at home, though it must not end there. It is the charge to Timothy, to take care to save himself first, and then those that heard him, 1 Tim. iv. 16.

The high priest made atonement for himself, as one that was joined with sinners; but we have a high priest that was separated from sinners, and needed no atonement. When Messiah the prince was cut off as a sacrifice, it was not for himself; for he knew no sin. [2.] He must *make an atonement for the people,* by offering their sacrifices. Now that he was made a high priest he must lay to heart the concerns of the people, and this as their great concern, their reconciliation to God, and the putting away of sin which had separated between them and God. He must *make atonement as the Lord commanded.* See here the wonderful condescension of the mercy of God, that he not only allows an atonement to be made, but commands it; not only admits, but requires us to be reconciled to him. No room therefore is left to doubt but that the atonement which is commanded will be accepted.

8 Aaron therefore went unto the altar, and slew the calf of the sin offering, which *was* for himself. 9 And the sons of Aaron brought the blood unto him: and he dipped his finger in the blood, and put *it* upon the horns of the altar, and poured out the blood at the bottom of the altar: 10 But the fat, and the kidneys, and the caul above the liver of the sin offering, he burnt upon the altar; as the Lord commanded Moses. 11 And the flesh and the hide he burnt with fire without the camp. 12 And he slew the burnt offering; and Aaron's sons presented unto him the blood, which he sprinkled round about upon the altar. 13 And they presented the burnt offering unto him, with the pieces thereof, and the head: and he burnt *them* upon the altar. 14 And he did wash the inwards and the legs, and burnt *them* upon the burnt offering on the altar. 15 And he brought the people's offering, and took the goat, which *was* the sin offering for the people, and slew it, and offered it for sin, as the first. 16 And he brought the burnt offering, and offered it according to the manner. 17 And he brought the meat offering, and took a handful thereof, and burnt *it* upon the altar, beside the burnt sacrifice of the morning. 18 He slew also the bullock and the ram *for* a sacrifice of peace offerings, which *was* for the people: and Aaron's sons presented unto him the blood, which he

sprinkled upon the altar round about, 19 And the fat of the bullock and of the ram, the rump, and that which covereth *the inwards,* and the kidneys, and the caul *above* the liver: 20 And they put the fat upon the breasts, and he burnt the fat upon the altar: 21 And the breasts and the right shoulder Aaron waved *for* a wave offering before the Lord; as Moses commanded. 22 And Aaron lifted up his hand toward the people, and blessed them, and came down from offering of the sin offering, and the burnt offering, and peace offerings.

These being the first offerings that ever were offered by the levitical priesthood, according to the newly-enacted law of sacrifices, the manner of offering them is particularly related, that it might appear how exactly they agreed with the institution. 1. Aaron with his own hands *slew the offering* (v. 8), and did the work of the inferior priests; for, great as he was, he must not think any service below him which he could do for the honour of God: and, as Moses had shown him how to do this work decently and dexterously, so he showed his sons, that they might do likewise; for this is the best way of teaching, and thus parents should instruct their children by example. Therefore as Moses before, so Aaron now offered some of each of the several sorts of sacrifices that were appointed, whose rites differed, that they might be *thoroughly furnished for every good work.* 2. He offered these *besides the burnt-sacrifice of the morning,* which was every day offered first, v. 17. Note, Our accustomed devotions morning and evening, alone and in our families, must not be omitted upon any pretence whatsoever, no, not when extraordinary services are to be performed; whatever is added, these must not be diminished. 3. It is not clear whether, when it is said that he burnt such and such parts of the sacrifices upon the altar (v. 10—20), the meaning is that he burnt them immediately with ordinary fire, as formerly, or that he laid them upon the altar ready to be burnt with the fire from heaven which they expected (v. 24), or whether, as bishop Patrick thinks, he burnt the offerings for himself with ordinary fire, but when they were burnt out he laid the people's sacrifices upon the altar, which were kindled and consumed by the fire of the Lord. I would rather conjecture, because it is said of all these sacrifices that *he burnt them* (except the burnt-offering for the people, of which it is said that he offered it *according to the manner* (v. 16), which seems to be equivalent), that he did not kindle the fire to burn them, but that then the fire from the Lord fastened upon

476

them, put out the fire that he had kindled (as we know a greater fire puts out a less), and suddenly consumed the remainder, which the fire he had kindled would have consumed slowly. 4. When Aaron had done all that on his part was to be done about the sacrifices he *lifted up his hand towards the people, and blessed them, v.* 22. This was one part of the priest's work, in which he was a type of Christ, who came into the world to bless us, and when he was parted from his disciples, at his ascension, *lifted up his hands and blessed them,* and in them his whole church, of which they were the elders and representatives, as the great high priest of our profession. Aaron *lifted up his hands* in blessing them, to intimate whence he desired and expected the blessing to come, even from heaven, which is God's throne. Aaron could but crave a blessing, it is God's prerogative to command it. Aaron, when he had blessed, came down; Christ, when he blessed, went up.

23 And Moses and Aaron went into the tabernacle of the congregation, and came out, and blessed the people: and the glory of the LORD appeared unto all the people. 24 And there came a fire out from before the LORD, and consumed upon the altar the burnt offering and the fat: *which* when all the people saw, they shouted, and fell on their faces.

We are not told what Moses and Aaron went into the tabernacle to do, *v.* 23. Some of the Jewish writers say, "They went in to pray for the appearance of the divine glory;" most probably they went in that Moses might instruct Aaron how to do the service that was to be done there—burn incense, light the lamps, set the show-bread, &c., that he might instruct his sons in it. But, when they came out, they both joined in blessing the people, who stood expecting the promised appearance of the divine glory; and it was now (when Moses and Aaron concurred in praying) that they had what they waited for. Note, God's manifestations of himself, of his glory and grace, are commonly given in answer to prayer. When Christ was praying the *heavens were opened,* Luke iii. 21. The glory of God appeared, not while the sacrifices were in offering, but when the priests prayed (as 2 Chron. v. 13), when they praised God, which intimates that the prayers and praises of God's spiritual priests are more pleasing to God than all burnt-offerings and sacrifices.

When the solemnity was finished, the blessing pronounced, and the congregation ready to be dismissed, in the close of the day, then God testified his acceptance, which gave them such satisfaction as was well worth waiting for.

I. *The glory of the Lord appeared unto all*

the people, v. 23. What the appearance of it was we are not told; no doubt it was such as carried its own evidence along with it. The glory which *filled the tabernacle* (Exod. xl. 34) now showed itself at the door of the tabernacle to those who attended there, as a prince shows himself to the expecting crowd, to gratify them. God hereby testified of their gifts, and showed them that he was worthy for whom they should do all this. Note, Those that diligently attend upon God in the way he has appointed shall have such a sight of his glory as shall be abundantly to their satisfaction. Those that dwell in God's house with an eye of faith may *behold the beauty of the Lord.*

II. *There came a fire out from before the Lord, and consumed the sacrifice, v.* 24. Here the learned bishop Patrick has a very probable conjecture, that Moses and Aaron staid in the tabernacle till it was time to offer the evening sacrifice, which Aaron did, but it is not mentioned, because it was done of course, and it was this which the *fire that came out from the Lord consumed.* Whether this fire came from heaven, or out of the most holy place, or from that visible appearance of the glory of God which all the people saw, it was a manifest token of God's acceptance of their service, as, afterwards, of Solomon's sacrifice, 2 Chron. vii. 1, and Elijah's, 1 Kings xviii. 38.

1. This fire did consume (or, as the word is, *eat up*) the present sacrifice. And two ways was this was a testimony of acceptance :—(1.) It signified the turning away of God's wrath from them. God's wrath is a consuming fire ; this fire might justly have fastened upon the people, and consumed them for their sins ; but its fastening upon the sacrifice, and consuming that, signified God's acceptance of that as an atonement for the sinner. (2.) It signified God's entering into covenant and communion with them : they ate their part of the sacrifice, and the fire of the Lord ate up his part; and thus he did, as it were, *sup with them, and they with him,* Rev. iii. 20.

2. This fire did, as it were, take possession of the altar. The fire was thus kindled in God's house, which was to continue as long as the house stood, as we read before, *ch.* vi. 13. This also was a figure of good things to come. The Spirit descended upon the apostles in *fire* (Acts ii. 3), so ratifying their commission, as this spoken of here did the priests'. And the descent of this holy fire into our souls to kindle in them pious and devout affections towards God, and such a holy zeal as burns up the flesh and the lusts of it, is a certain token of God's gracious acceptance of our persons and performances. That redounds to God's glory which is the work of his own grace in us. *Hereby we know that we dwell in God, and God in us, because he hath thus given us of his Spirit,* 1 John iv. 13. Now henceforward, (1.) All

their sacrifices and incense must be offered with this fire. Note, Nothing goes to God but what comes from him. We must have grace, that holy fire, from the God of grace, else we cannot *serve him acceptably*, Heb. xii. 28. (2.) The priests must keep it burning with a constant supply of fuel, and the fuel must be wood, the cleanest of fuel. Thus those to whom God has given grace must take heed of quenching the Spirit.

III. We are here told how the people were affected with this discovery of God's glory and grace; they received it, 1. With the highest joy: *They shouted;* so stirring up themselves and one another to a holy triumph, in the assurance now given them that they had God nigh unto them, which is spoken of the grandeur of their nation, Deut. iv. 7. 2. With the lowest reverence: *They fell on their faces*, humbly adoring the majesty of that God who vouchsafed thus to manifest himself to them. That is a sinful fear of God which drives us from him; a gracious fear makes us bow before him. Very good impressions were made upon their minds for the present, but they soon wore off, as those commonly do which are made by that which is only sensible; while the influences of faith are durable.

CHAP. X.

The story of this chapter is as sad an interruption to the institutions of the levitical law as that of the golden calf was to the account of the erecting of the tabernacle. Here is, I. The sin and death of Nadab and Abihu, the sons of Aaron, ver. 1, 2. II. The quieting of Aaron under this sore affliction, ver. 3. III. Orders given and observed about the funeral and mourning, ver. 4—7. IV. A command to the priests not to drink wine when they went in to minister, ver. 8—11. V. The care Moses took that they should go on with their work, notwithstanding the agitation produced by this event, ver. 12, &c.

AND Nadab and Abihu, the sons of Aaron, took either of them his censer, and put fire therein, and put incense thereon, and offered strange fire before the LORD, which he commanded them not. 2 And there went out fire from the LORD, and devoured them, and they died before the LORD.

Here is, I. The great sin that Nadab and Abihu were guilty of: and a great sin we must call it, how little soever it appears in our eye, because it is evident by the punishment of it that it was highly provoking to the God of heaven, whose judgment, we are sure, is according to truth. But what was their sin? All the account here given of it is that they *offered strange fire before the Lord, which he commanded them not* (v. 1), and the same Num. iii. 4. 1. It does not appear that they had any orders to burn incense at all at this time. It is true their consecration was completed the day before, and it was part of their work, as priests, to serve at the altar of incense; but, it should seem, the whole service of this solemn day of inauguration was to be performed by Aaron himself, for he *slew the sacrifices* (ch. ix. 8,

478

15, 18), and his sons were only to attend him (v. 9, 12, 18); therefore Moses and Aaron only *went into the tabernacle, v. 23.* But Nadab and Abihu were so proud of the honour they were newly advanced to, and so ambitious of doing the highest and most honourable part of their work immediately, that though the service of this day was extraordinary, and done by particular direction from Moses, yet without receiving orders, or so much as asking leave from him, they took their censers, and they would enter into the tabernacle, at the door of which they thought they had attended long enough, and would burn incense. And then their *offering strange fire* is the same with *offering strange incense*, which is expressly forbidden, Exod. xxx. 9. Moses, we may suppose, had the custody of the incense which was prepared for this purpose (Exod. xxxix. 38), and they, doing this without his leave, had none of the incense which should have been offered, but common incense, so that the smoke of their incense came from a *strange fire*. God had indeed required the priests to burn incense, but, at this time, it was what he commanded them not; and so their crime was like that of Uzziah the king, 2 Chron. xxvi. 16. The priests were to burn incense only when *it was their lot* (Luke i. 9), and, at this time, it was not theirs. 2. Presuming thus to burn incense of their own without order, no marvel that they made a further blunder, and instead of taking of the fire from the altar, which was newly kindled from before the Lord and which henceforward must be used in offering both sacrifice and incense (Rev. viii. 5), they took common fire, probably from that with which the flesh of the peace-offerings was boiled, and this they made use of in burning incense; not being holy fire, it is called *strange fire;* and, though not expressly forbidden, it was crime enough that God *commanded it not.* For (as bishop Hall well observes here) " It is a dangerous thing, in the service of God, to decline from his own institutions; we have to do with a God who is wise to prescribe his own worship, just to require what he has prescribed, and powerful to revenge what he has not prescribed." 3. Incense was always to be burned by only one priest at a time, but here they would both go in together to do it. 4. They did it rashly, and with precipitation. They *snatched* their censers, so some read it, in a light careless way, without due reverence and seriousness: when all the people *fell upon their faces*, before the *glory of the Lord*, they thought the dignity of their office was such as to exempt them from such abasements. The familiarity they were admitted to bred a contempt of the divine Majesty; and now that they were priests they thought they might do what they pleased. 5. There is reason to suspect that they were drunk when they did it, because of the law which was given upon this occasion, v. 8. They had been feasting upon the peace-offerings, and the drink-offerings that attended them, and so their heads were light, or, at least, their *hearts were merry with wine ;* they *drank and forgot the law* (Prov. xxxi. 5) and were guilty of this fatal miscarriage. 6. No doubt it was done presumptuously; for, if it had been done through ignorance, they would have been allowed the benefit of the law lately made, even for the priests, that they should bring a sin-offering, *ch.* iv. 2, 3. But *the soul that doth aught presumptuously,* and in contempt of God's majesty, authority, and justice, *that soul shall be cut off,* Num. xv. 30.

II. The dreadful punishment of this sin : *There went out fire from the Lord, and devoured them, v.* 2. This fire which consumed the sacrificers came the same way with that which had consumed the sacrifices (*ch.* ix. 24), which showed what justice would have done to all the guilty people if infinite mercy had not found and accepted a ransom ; and, if that fire struck such an awe upon the people, much more would this.

1. Observe the severity 'of their punishment. (1.) They *died.* Might it not have sufficed if they had been only struck with a leprosy, as Uzziah, or struck dumb, as Zechariah, and both by the altar of incense ? No; they were both struck dead. The wages of this sin was death. (2.) They died *suddenly,* in the very act of their sin, and had not time so much as to cry, " Lord, have mercy upon us !" Though God is longsuffering to us-ward, yet sometimes he makes quick work with sinners ; sentence is executed speedily : presumptuous sinners bring upon themselves a swift destruction, and are justly denied even space to repent. (3.) They died *before the Lord ;* that is, before the veil that covered the mercy-seat ; for even mercy itself will not suffer its own glory to be affronted. Those that sinned before the Lord died before him. Damned sinners are said to be tormented *in the presence of the Lamb,* intimating that he does not interpose on their behalf, Rev. xiv. 10. (4.) They died *by fire,* as by fire they sinned. They slighted the fire that came from before the Lord to consume the sacrifices, and thought other fire would do every jot as well ; and now God justly made them feel the power of that fire which they did not reverence. Thus those that hate to be refined by the fire of divine grace will undoubtedly be ruined by the fire of divine wrath. The fire did not burn them to ashes, as it had done the sacrifices, nor so much as singe their coats (*v.* 5), but, like lightning, struck them dead in an instant : by these different effects of the same fire God would show that it was no common fire, but kindled *by the breath of the Almighty,* Isa. xxx. 33. (5.) It is twice taken notice of in scripture that they *died childless,* Num. iii. 4, and 1 Chron. xxiv. 2. By their presumption they had reproached God's name, and God justly blotted out their names, and

laid that honour in the dust which they were proud of.

2. But why did the Lord deal thus severely with them ? Were they not the sons of Aaron, the saint of the Lord, nephews to Moses, the great favourite of heaven ? Was not the holy anointing oil sprinkled upon them, as men whom God had set apart for himself ? Had they not diligently attended during the seven days of their consecration, and *kept the charge of the Lord,* and might not that atone for this rashness ? Would it not excuse them that they were young men, as yet unexperienced in these services, that it was the first offence, and done in a transport of joy for their elevation ? And besides, never could men be worse spared : a great deal of work was now lately cut out for the priests to do, and the priesthood was confined to Aaron and his seed : he has but four sons ; if two of them die, there will not be hands enough to do the service of the tabernacle ; if they die childless, the house of Aaron will become weak and little, and the priesthood will be in danger of being lost for want of heirs. But none of all these considerations shall serve either to excuse the offence or bring off the offenders. For, (1.) The sin was greatly aggravated. It was a manifest contempt of Moses, and the divine law that was given by Moses. Hitherto it had been expressly observed concerning every thing that was done that they did it *as the Lord commanded Moses,* in opposition to which it is here said they did that *which the Lord commanded them not,* but they did it of their own heads. God was now teaching his people obedience, and to do every thing by rule, as becomes servants ; for priests therefore to break rules and disobey was such a provocation as must by no means go unpunished. Their character made their sin more exceedingly sinful. For the sons of Aaron, his eldest sons, whom God had chosen to be immediate attendants upon him, for them to be guilty of such a piece of presumption, it cannot, be suffered. There was in their sin a contempt of God's glory, which had now newly appeared in fire, as if that fire were needless, they had as good of their own before. (2.) Their punishment was a piece of necessary justice, now at the first settling of the ceremonial institutions. It is often threatened in the law that such and such offenders should be cut off from the people ; and here God explained the threatening with a witness. Now that the laws concerning sacrifices were newly made, lest any should be tempted to think lightly of them because they descended to many circumstances which seemed very minute, these that were the first transgressors were thus punished, for warning to others, and to show how jealous God is in the matters of his worship. Thus he *magnified the law and made it honourable ;* and let his priests know that the caution which so often occurs in the

laws concerning them, that they must do so *that they die not,* was not a mere bugbear, but fair warning of their danger, if they did the work of the Lord negligently. And no doubt this exemplary piece of justice at first prevented many irregularities afterwards. Thus Ananias and Sapphira were punished, when they presumed to lie to the Holy Ghost, that newly-descended fire. (3.) As the people's falling into idolatry, presently after the moral law was given, shows the weakness of the law and its insufficiency to take away sin, so the sin and punishment of these priests show the imperfection of that priesthood from the very beginning, and its inability to shelter any from the fire of God's wrath otherwise than as it was typical of Christ's priesthood, in the execution of which there never was, nor can be, any irregularity, or false step taken.

3 Then Moses said unto Aaron, This *is it* that the Lord spake, saying, I will be sanctified in them that come nigh me, and before all the people I will be glorified. And Aaron held his peace. 4 And Moses called Mishael and Elzaphan, the sons of Uzziel the uncle of Aaron, and said unto them, Come near, carry your brethren from before the sanctuary out of the camp. 5 So they went near, and carried them in their coats out of the camp; as Moses had said. 6 And Moses said unto Aaron, and unto Eleazar and unto Ithamar, his sons, Uncover not your heads, neither rend your clothes; lest ye die, and lest wrath come upon all the people: but let your brethren, the whole house of Israel, bewail the burning which the Lord hath kindled. 7 And ye shall not go out from the door of the tabernacle of the congregation, lest ye die: for the anointing oil of the Lord *is* upon you. And they did according to the word of Moses.

We may well think that when Nadab and Abihu were struck with death all about them were struck with horror, and every face, as well as theirs, gathered blackness. Great consternation, no doubt, seized them, and they were all full of confusion; but, whatever the rest were, Moses was composed, and knew what he said and did, not being displeased, as David was in a like case, 2 Sam. vi. 8. But though it touched him in a very tender part, and was a dreadful damp to one of the greatest joys he ever knew, yet he kept possession of his own soul, and took care to keep good order and a due decorum in the sanctuary.

480

I. He endeavours to pacify Aaron, and to keep him in a good frame under this sad dispensation, *v.* 3. Moses was a brother that was born for adversity, and has taught us, by his example, with seasonable counsels and comforts to *support the weak,* and *strengthen the feeble-minded.*· Observe here,

1. What it was that Moses suggested to his poor brother upon this occasion: *This is it that the Lord spake.* Note, The most quieting considerations under affliction are those that are fetched from the word of God. So and so *the Lord hath said,* and it is not for us to gainsay it. Note, also, In all God's providences it ·is good to observe the fulfilling of scripture, and to compare God's word and his works together, which if we do we shall find an admirable harmony and agreement between them, and that they mutually explain and illustrate each other. But, (1.) Where did God speak this? We do not find the very words; but to this purport he had said (Exod. xix. 22), *Let the priests who come near to the Lord sanctify themselves, lest the Lord break forth upon them.* Indeed the whole scope and tenour of his law spoke this, that being a holy God, and a sovereign Lord, he must always be worshipped with holiness and reverence, and exactly according to his own appointment; and, if any jest with him, it is at their peril. Much had been said to this purport, as Exod. xxix. 43, 44; xxxiv. 14; *ch.* viii. 35. (2.) What was it that God spoke? It was this (the Lord by his grace speak it to all our hearts!) *I will be sanctified in those that come nigh me,* whoever they are, and *before all the people I will be glorified.* Note, *First,* Whenever we worship God, we come nigh unto him, as spiritual priests. This consideration ought to make us very reverent and serious in all acts of devotion, that in them we approach to God, and present ourselves before him. *Secondly,* It concerns us all, when we come nigh to God, to sanctify him, that is, to give him the praise of his holiness, to perform every religious exercise as those who believe that the God with whom we have to do is a holy God, a God of spotless purity and transcendent perfection, Isa. viii. 13. *Thirdly,* When we sanctify God we glorify him, for his holiness is his glory; and, when we sanctify him in our solemn assemblies, we glorify him *before all the people,* confessing our own belief of his glory and desiring that others also may be affected with it. *Fourthly,* If God be not sanctified and glorified by us, he will be sanctified and glorified upon us. He will take vengeance on those that profane his sacred name by trifling with him. If his rent be not paid, it shall be distrained for. (3.) But what was this to the present case? What was there in this to quiet Aaron? Two things:—[1.] This must silence him, that his sons deserved their death; for they were thus cut off from their people because they did not sanctify and

glorify God. The acts of necessary justice, how hard soever they may seem to bear upon the persons concerned, are not to be complained of, but submitted to. [2.] This must satisfy him, that the death of his sons redounded to the honour of God, and his impartial justice would for it be adored throughout all ages.

2. What good effects this had upon him: *Aaron held his peace,* that is, he patiently submitted to the holy will of God in this sad providence, was *dumb, and opened not his mouth,* because God did it. Something he was ready to say by way of complaint (as losers think they may have leave to speak), but he wisely suppressed it, *laid his hand upon his mouth,* and said nothing, for fear lest he *should offend with his tongue,* now that his *heart was hot within him.* Note, (1.) When God corrects us or ours for sin, it is our duty to be silent under the correction, not to quarrel with God, arraign his justice, or charge him with folly, but to acquiesce in all that God does; not only bearing, but accepting, the punishment of iniquity, and saying, as Eli, in a case not much unlike this, *It is the Lord, let him do what seemeth him good,* 1 Sam. iii. 18. *If our children have sinned against God* (as Bildad puts the case, Job viii. 4), *and he have cast them away for their transgression,* though it must needs be grievous to think that the children of our love should be the children of God's wrath, yet we must awfully adore the divine justice, and make no exceptions against its processes. (2.) The most effectual arguments to quiet a gracious spirit under afflictions are those that are fetched from God's glory; this silenced Aaron. It is true he is a loser in his comforts by this severe execution, but Moses has shown him that God is a gainer in his glory, and therefore he has not a word to say against it: if God be sanctified, Aaron is satisfied. Far be it from him that he should honour his sons more than God, or wish that God's name, or house, or law, should be exposed to reproach or contempt for the preserving of the reputation of his family. No; now, as well as in the matter of the golden calf, Levi does not *acknowledge his brethren,* nor *know his own children;* and therefore *they shall teach Jacob thy judgments, and Israel thy law,* Deut. xxxiii. 9, 10. Ministers and their families are sometimes exercised with sore trials that they may be examples to the believers of patience and resignation to God, and they may comfort others with that with which they themselves have been comforted.

II. Moses gives orders about the dead bodies. It was not fit that they should be left to lie where they fell; yet their own father and brethren, the amazed spectators of this dismal tragedy, durst not offer to lift them up, no, not to see whether there was any life left in them; they must neither be diverted from nor unfitted for the great work

that was now upon their hands. *Let the dead bury their dead,* but they must go on with their service; that is, "Rather let the dead be unburied, if there be nobody else to do it, than that work for God should be left undone by those whom he has called to it." But Moses takes care of this matter, that though they died by the hand of justice in the act of sin, yet they should be decently buried, and they were so, *v.* 4, 5. 1. Some of their nearest relations were employed in it, who were cousins-german to their father, and are here named, who would perform this office with tenderness and respect. They were Levites only, and might not have come into the sanctuary, no, not upon such an occasion as this, if they had not had a special command for it. 2. They carried them out of the camp to be buried, so far were they from burying them in the place of worship, or the court of it, according to our modern usage, though they died there, that they did not bury them, nor any of their dead, within the lines of their camp; as afterwards their burying places were out of their cities. The tabernacle was pitched in the midst of the camp, so that they could not carry these dead priests to their graves without carrying them through one of the squadrons of the camp; and doubtless it was a very awful affecting sight to the people. The names of Nadab and Abihu had become very great and honourable among them; none more talked of, nor more expected to appear abroad after the days of their consecration, to receive the honours and caresses of the crowd, whose manner it is to adore the rising sun; and next to Moses and Aaron, who were old and going off, Nadab and Abihu (who had been in the mount with God, Exod. xxiv. 1) were looked upon as the great favourites of heaven, and the hopes of their people; and now on a sudden, when the tidings of the event had scarcely reached their ears, to see them both carried out dead, with the visible marks of divine vengeance upon them, as sacrifices to the justice of God, they could not choose but cry out, *Who is able to stand before this holy Lord God?* 1 Sam. vi. 20. 3. They carried them out (and probably buried them) in their coats, the garments of their priesthood, which they had lately put on, and perhaps were too proud of. Thus the impartiality of God's justice was proclaimed, and all the people were made to know that even priests' garments would not protect an offender from the wrath of God. And it was easy to argue, "If they escape not when they transgress, can we expect to go unpunished? And the priests' clothes being so soon made graveclothes might intimate both that *the law worketh death,* and that in process of time that priesthood itself should be abolished and buried in the grave of the Lord Jesus.

III. He gives directions about the mourning.

1. That the priests must not mourn. Aaron and his two surviving sons, though sad in spirit, must not use any outward expressions of sorrow upon this sad occasion, nor so much as follow the corpse one step from the door of the tabernacle, *v.* 7. It was afterwards forbidden to the high priest to use the ceremonies of mourning for the death of any friend whatsoever, though it were a father or mother (*ch.* xxi. 11); yet it was allowed at the same time to the inferior priests to mourn for their near relations, *v.* 2, 3. But here it was forbidden both to Aaron and his sons, because, (1.) They were now actually in waiting, doing a great work, which must by no means cease (Neh. vi. 3); and it was very much for the honour of God that their attendance on him should take place of their respects to their nearest relations, and that all services should give way to those of their ministry. By this they must make it to appear that they had a greater value and affection for their God and their work than for the best friend they had in the world; as Christ did, Matt. xii. 47, 48. And we are hereby taught, when we are serving God in holy duties, to keep our minds, as much as may be, intent and engaged, and not to suffer them to be diverted by any worldly thoughts, or cares, or passions. Let us always attend upon the Lord without distraction. (2.) Their brethren were cut off for their transgression by the immediate hand of God, and therefore they must not mourn for them lest they should seem to countenance the sin, or impeach the justice of God in the punishment. Instead of lamenting their own loss, they must be wholly taken up in applauding the sentence, and subscribing to the equity of it. Note, The public concerns of God's glory ought to lie nearer our hearts than any private affections of our own. Observe, How Moses frightens them into this submission, and holds the rod over them to still their crying (*v.* 6): "*Lest you die* likewise, and *lest wrath come upon all the people,* who may be in danger of suffering for your irreverence, and disobedience, and ungoverned passions;" and again (*v.* 7), *lest you die.* See here what use we are to make of the judgments of God upon others; we must double our guard over ourselves, *lest we likewise perish.* The death, especially the sudden death, of others, instead of moving our passion, should compose us into a holy reverence of God, a cautious separation from all sin, and a serious expectation of our own death. The reason given them is because *the anointing oil of your God is upon you,* the honour of which must be carefully preserved by your doing the duty of your office with cheerfulness. Note, Those that through grace have *received the anointing* ought not to disturb themselves with the *sorrow of the world,* which *worketh death.* It was very hard, no doubt, for Aaron and his sons to restrain themselves upon such an extraordinary occasion from inordinate grief, but reason and grace mastered the passion, and they bore the affliction with an obedient patience: *They did according to the word of Moses,* because they knew it to be the word of God. Happy those who thus are themselves under God's government, and have their passions under their own government.

2. The people must mourn: *Let the whole house of Israel bewail the burning which the Lord has kindled.* The congregation must lament, not only the loss of their priests, but especially the displeasure of God which appeared in it. They must bewail the burning that was kindled, that it might not burn further. Aaron and his sons were in danger of being too much affected with the providence, and therefore they are forbidden to mourn: the house of Israel were in danger of being too little affected with it, and therefore they are commanded to lament. Thus nature must always be governed by grace, according as it needs to be either constrained or restrained.

8 And the LORD spake unto Aaron, saying, 9 Do not drink wine nor strong drink, thou, nor thy sons with thee, when ye go into the tabernacle of the congregation, lest ye die: *it shall be* a statute for ever throughout your generations: 10 And that ye may put difference between holy and unholy, and between unclean and clean; 11 And that ye may teach the children of Israel all the statutes which the LORD hath spoken unto them by the hand of Moses.

Aaron having been very observant of what God said to him by Moses, now God does him the honour to speak to him immediately (*v.* 8): *The Lord spoke unto Aaron,* and the rather because what was now to be said Aaron might perhaps have taken amiss from Moses, as if he had suspected him to have been a gluttonous man and a wine-bibber, so apt are we to resent cautions as accusations; therefore God saith it himself to him, *Do not drink wine, nor strong drink, when you go into the tabernacle,* and this at their peril, *lest you die, v.* 9. Probably they had seen the ill effect of it in Nadab and Abihu, and therefore must take warning by them. Observe here, 1. The prohibition itself: *Do not drink wine nor strong drink.* At other times they were allowed it (it was not expected that every priest should be a Nazarite), but during the time of their ministration they were forbidden it. This was one of the laws in Ezekiel's temple (Ezek. xliv. 21), and so it is required of gospel ministers that they be *not given to wine,* 1 Tim. iii. 3. Note, Drunkenness is bad in any, but it is especially scandalous and pernicious in ministers, who of all men ought to have the clearest heads and the cleanest hearts. 2. The penalty annexed to the prohibition : *Lest you die ; lest you die* when you are in drink, *and so that day come upon you unawares,* Luke xxi. 34. Or, " Lest you do that which will make you liable to be cut off by the hand of God." The danger of death we are continually in should engage us to *be sober,* 1 Pet. iv. 7. It is a pity that it should ever be used for the support of licentiousness, as it is by those who argue, *Let us eat and drink, for to-morrow we die.* 3 The reasons assigned for this prohibition. They must needs be sober, else they could not duly discharge their office ; they will be in danger of *erring through wine,* Isa. xxviii. 7. They must be sure to keep sober, (1.) That they might themselves be able to distinguish, in their ministrations, between that which was sacred and that which was common, and might never confound them, *v.* 10. It concerns the Lord's ministers to put a difference between holy and unholy, both things and persons, that they may separate between *the precious and the vile,* Jer. xv. 19. (2.) That they might be able to teach the people (*v.* 11), for that was a part of the priests' work (Deut. xxxiii. 10) ; and those that are addicted to drunkenness are very unfit to teach people God's statutes, both because those that live after the flesh can have no experimental acquaintance with the things of the Spirit, and because such teachers pull down with one hand what they build up with the other.

12 And Moses spake unto Aaron, and unto Eleazar and unto Ithamar, his sons that were left, Take the meat offering that remaineth of the offerings of the Lord made by fire, and eat it without leaven beside the altar : for it *is* most holy : 13 And ye shall eat it in the holy place, because it *is* thy due, and thy sons' due, of the sacrifices of the Lord made by fire : for so I am commanded. 14 And the wave breast and heave shoulder shall ye eat in a clean place ; thou, and thy sons, and thy daughters with thee : for *they be* thy due, and thy sons' due, *which* are given out of the sacrifices of peace offerings of the children of Israel. 15 The heave shoulder and the wave breast shall they bring with the offerings made by fire of the fat, to wave *it for* a wave offering before the Lord ; and it shall be thine, and thy sons' with thee, by a statute for ever ; as the Lord hath commanded. 16 And Moses diligently sought the goat of the sin offering, and, behold, it was burnt : and he was angry with Eleazar and

Ithamar, the sons of Aaron *which were* left *alive,* saying, 17 Wherefore have ye not eaten the sin offering in the holy place, seeing it *is* most holy, and *God* hath given it you to bear the iniquity of the congregation, to make atonement for them before the Lord? 18 Behold, the blood of it was not brought in within the holy *place :* ye should indeed have eaten it in the holy *place,* as I commanded. 19 And Aaron said unto Moses, Behold, this day have they offered their sin offering and their burnt offering before the Lord ; and such things have befallen me : and *if* I had eaten the sin offering to day, should it have been accepted in the sight of the Lord? 20 And when Moses heard *that,* he was content.

Moses is here directing Aaron to go on with his service after this interruption. Afflictions should rather quicken us to our duty than take us off from it. Observe (*v.* 12), He spoke unto Aaron and to his sons *that were left.* The notice taken of their survivorship intimates, 1. That Aaron should take comfort under the loss of two of his sons, from this consideration, that God had graciously spared him the other two, and that he had reason to be thankful for the remnant that was left, that all his sons were not dead, and, in token of his thankfulness to God, to go on cheerfully in his work. 2. That God's sparing them should be an engagement upon them to proceed in his service, and not to fly off from it. Here were four priests consecrated together, two were taken away, and two left ; therefore the two that were left should endeavour to fill up the places of those that were gone, by double care and diligence in the services of the priesthood. Now,

I. Moses repeats the directions he had formerly given them about eating their share of the sacrifices, *v.* 12—14, 15. The priests must learn not only to *put a difference between the holy and the unholy,* as they had been taught (*v.* 10), but also to distinguish between that which was most holy and that which was only holy of the things that were to eat. That part of the meat-offering which remained to the priest was most holy, and therefore must be eaten in the courts of the tabernacle, and by Aaron's *sons* only (*v.* 12, 13) ; but the breast and shoulder of the peace-offerings might be eaten in any decent place out of the courts of the tabernacle, and by the daughters of their families. The meat-offerings, being annexed to the burnt-offerings, were intended only and wholly for the glory of God ; but the peace-offerings were ordained for the furtherance of men's joy and comfort ; the former therefore were the more sacred, and to be had more in veneration. This distinc-

483

tion the priests must carefully observe, and take heed of making any blunders. Moses does not pretend to give any reasons for this difference, but refers to his instructions : *For so am I commanded, v.* 13. This was reason enough ; he had *received of the Lord all that he delivered unto them,* 1 Cor. xi. 23.

II. He enquires concerning one deviation from the appointment, which it seems had happened upon this occasion, which was this: —There was a goat to be sacrificed as a *sin-offering for the people, ch.* ix. 15. Now the law of the sin-offerings was that if the blood of them was brought into the holy place, as that of the sin-offerings for the priest was, then the flesh was to be burnt without the camp; otherwise it was to be eaten by the priest in the holy place, *ch.* vi. 30. The meaning of this is here explained (*v.* 17), that the priests did hereby *bear the iniquity of the congregation,* that is, they were types of him who was to be made sin for us, and on whom God would *lay the iniquity of us all.* Now the blood of this goat was not brought into the holy place, and yet, it seems, it was burnt without the camp. Now observe here, 1. The gentle reproof Moses gives to Aaron and his sons for this irregularity. Here again Aaron's sons are said to be those *that were left alive* (*v.* 16), who therefore ought to have taken warning ; and Moses was *angry with them.* Though he was the meekest man in the world, it seems he could be angry ; and when he thought God was disobeyed and dishonoured, and the priesthood endangered, he would be angry. Yet observe how very mildly he deals with Aaron and his sons, considering their present affliction. He only tells them *they should indeed have eaten it in the holy place,* but is willing to hear what they have to say for themselves, being loth to speak to the grief of those whom God had wounded. 2. The plausible excuse which Aaron makes for this mistake. Moses charged the fault upon Eleazar and Ithamar (*v.* 16), but it is probable that what they did was by Aaron's direction, and therefore he apologized for it. He might have pleaded that this was a sin-offering for the congregation, and if it had been a bullock it must have been wholly burnt (*ch.* iv. 21), and therefore why not now that it was a goat ? But it seems it was otherwise ordered at this time, and therefore he makes his affliction his excuse, *v.* 19: Observe, (1.) How he speaks of affliction: *Such things have befallen me,* such sad things, which could not but go near his heart, and make it very heavy. He was a high priest *taken from among men,* and could not put off natural affection when he put on the holy garments. He held his peace (*v.* 3), yet his sorrow was stirred, as David's, Ps. xxxix. 2. Note, There may be a deep sense of affliction even where there is a sincere resignation to the will of God in the affliction. " *Such things* as never befel me before, and as I little expected now. My spirits cannot but sink,

when I see my family sinking ; I must needs be heavy, when God is angry :" thus it is easy to say a great deal to aggravate an affliction, but it is better to say little. (2.) How he makes this an excuse for his varying from the appointment about the sin-offering. He could not have eaten it but in his mourning, and with a sorrowful spirit ; and would this have been accepted ? He does not plead that his heart was so full of grief that he had no appetite for it, but that he feared it would not be accepted. Note, [1.] Acceptance with God is the great thing we should desire and aim at in all our religious services, particularly in the Lord's supper, which is our eating of the sin-offering. [2.] The sorrow of the world is a very great hindrance to our acceptable performance of holy duties, both as it is discomposing to ourselves, takes off our chariot-wheels and makes us drive heavily (1 Sam. i. 7, 8), and as it is displeasing to God, whose will it is that we should serve him cheerfully, Deut. xii. 7. Mourners' bread was polluted, Hos. ix. 4. See Mal. iii. 14. 3. The acquiescence of Moses in this excuse: *He was content, v.* 20. Perhaps he thought it justified what they had done. God had provided that what could not be eaten might be burnt. Our unfitness for duty, when it is natural and not sinful, will have great allowances made for it ; and God will have mercy and not sacrifice. At least he thought it did very much extenuate the fault ; *the spirit indeed was willing, but the flesh was weak.* God by Moses showed that he considered his frame. It appeared that Aaron sincerely aimed at God's acceptance ; and those that do so with an upright heart shall find he is not *extreme to mark what they do amiss.* Nor must we be severe in our animadversions upon every mistake, *considering ourselves, lest we also be tempted.*

CHAP. XI.

The ceremonial law is described by the apostle (Heb. ix. 9, 10) to consist, not only " in gifts and sacrifices," which hitherto have been treated of in this book, but " in meats, and drinks, and divers washings" from ceremonial uncleanness, the laws concerning which begin with this chapter, which puts a difference between some sorts of flesh-meat and others, allowing some to be eaten as clean and forbidding others as unclean. " There is one kind of flesh of men." Nature startles at the thought of eating this, and none do it but such as have arrived at the highest degree of barbarity, and become but one remove from brutes ; therefore there needed no law against it. But there is " another kind of flesh of beasts," concerning which the law directs here (ver. 1—8), " another of fishes" (ver. 9—12), " another of birds" (ver. 13—19), and " another of creeping things," which are distinguished into two sorts, flying creeping things (ver. 20—28) and creeping things upon the earth, ver. 29—43. And the law concludes with the general rule of holiness, and reasons for it, ver. 44, &c.

AND the LORD spake unto Moses and to Aaron, saying ˙ nto them, 2 Speak unto the children of Israel, saying, These *are* the beasts which ye shall eat among all the beasts that *are* on the earth. 3 Whatsoever parteth the hoof, and is clovenfooted, *and* cheweth the cud, among the beasts, that shall ye eat. 4 Nevertheless these shall ye not eat of them that chew the cud, or of them that divide the hoof: *as* the camel, because he cheweth the cud, but divideth not the hoof; he *is* unclean unto you. 5 And the coney, because he cheweth the cud, but divideth not the hoof; he *is* unclean unto you. 6 And the hare, because he cheweth the cud, but divideth not the hoof; he *is* unclean unto you. 7 And the swine, though he divide the hoof, and be clovenfooted, yet he cheweth not the cud; he *is* unclean to you. 8 Of their flesh shall ye not eat, and their carcase shall ye not touch; they *are* unclean to you.

Now that Aaron was consecrated a high priest over the house of God, God spoke to him with Moses, and appointed them both as joint-commissioners to deliver his will to the people. He spoke both to Moses and to Aaron about this matter; for it was particularly required of the priests that they should put a difference between clean and unclean, and teach the people to do so. After the flood, when God entered into covenant with Noah and his sons, he allowed them to eat flesh (Gen. ix. 13), whereas before they were confined to the productions of the earth. But the liberty allowed to the sons of Noah is here limited to the sons of Israel. They might eat flesh, but not all kinds of flesh; some they must look upon as unclean and forbidden to them, others as clean and allowed them. The law in this matter is both very particular and very strict. But what reason can be given for this law? Why may not God's people have as free a use of all the creatures as other people? 1. It is reason enough that God would have it so: his will, as it is law sufficient, so it is reason sufficient; for his will is his wisdom. He saw good thus to try and exercise the obedience of his people, not only in the solemnities of his altar, but in matters of daily occurrence at their own table, that they might remember they were under authority. Thus God had tried the obedience of man in innocency, by forbidding him to eat of one particular tree. 2. Most of the meats forbidden as unclean are such as were really unwholesome, and not fit to be eaten; and those of them that we think wholesome enough, and use accordingly, as the rabbit, the hare, and the swine, perhaps in those countries, and to their bodies, might be hurtful. And then God in this law did by them but as a wise and loving father does by his children, whom he restrains from eating that which he knows will make them sick. Note, The Lord is for the body, and it is not only folly, but sin against God, to prejudice our health for the pleasing of our appetite. 3. God would thus teach his people to distinguish themselves from other people, not only in their religious worship, but in the common actions of life. Thus he would show them that they must not be numbered among the nations. It should seem there had been, before this, some difference between the Hebrews and other nations in their food, kept up by tradition; for the Egyptians and they would not eat together, Gen. xliii. 32. And even before the flood there was a distinction of beasts into clean and not clean (Gen. vii. 2), which distinction was quite lost, with many other instances of religion, among the Gentiles. But by this law it is reduced to a certainty, and ordered to be kept up among the Jews, that thus, by having a diet peculiar to themselves, they might be kept from familiar conversation with their idolatrous neighbours, and might typify God's spiritual Israel, who not in these little things, but in the temper of their spirits, and the course of their lives, should be governed by a sober singularity, and not be conformed to this world. The learned observe further, That most of the creatures which by this law were to be abominated as unclean were such as were had in high veneration among the heathen, not so much for food as for divination and sacrifice to their gods; and therefore those are here mentioned as unclean, and an abomination, which yet they would not be in any temptation to eat, that they might keep up a religious loathing of that for which the Gentiles had a superstitious value. The swine, with the later Gentiles, was sacred to Venus, the owl to Minerva, the eagle to Jupiter, the dog to Hecate, &c., and all these are here made unclean. As to the beasts, there is a general rule laid down, that those which both part the hoof and chew the cud were clean, and those only: these are particularly mentioned in the repetition of this law (Deut. xiv. 4, 5), where it appears that the Israelites had variety enough allowed them, and needed not to complain of the confinement they were under. Those beasts that did not both *chew the cud and divide the hoof* were unclean, by which rule the flesh of swine, and of hares, and of rabbits, was prohibited to them, though commonly used among us. Therefore, particularly at the eating of any of these, we should give thanks for the liberty granted us in this matter by the gospel, which teaches us that *every creature of God is good,* and we are to *call nothing common or unclean.* Some observe a significancy in the rule here laid down for them to distinguish by, or at least think it may be alluded to. Meditation, and other acts of devotion done by the hidden man of the heart, may be signified by the chewing of the cud, digesting our spiritual food; justice and charity towards men, and the acts of a good conversation, may be signified by the *dividing of the hoof.* Now either of these without the other will not serve to recommend us to God, but both must go together, good affections in the heart and good works in the life: if either be wanting, we are not clean, surely we are not clean. Of all the creatures here forbidden as unclean, none has been more dreaded and detested by the pious Jews than swine's flesh. Many were put to death by Antiochus because they would not eat it. This, probably, they were most in danger of being tempted to, and therefore possessed themselves and their children with a particular antipathy to it, calling it not by its proper name, but *a strange thing*. It should seem the Gentiles used it superstitiously (Isa. lxv. 4), *they eat swine's flesh;* and therefore God forbids all use of it to his people, lest they should learn of their neighbours to make that ill use of it. Some suggest that the prohibition of these beasts as unclean was intended to be a caution to the people against the bad qualities of these creatures. We must not be filthy nor wallow in the mire as swine, nor be timorous and faint-hearted as hares, nor dwell in the earth as rabbits; let not man that is in honour make himself like these beasts that perish. The law forbade, not only the eating of them, but the very touching of them; for those that would be kept from any sin must be careful to avoid all temptations to it, and every thing that looks towards it or leads to it.

9 These shall ye eat of all that *are* in the waters: whatsoever hath fins and scales in the waters, in the seas, and in the rivers, them shall ye eat. 10 And all that have not fins and scales in the seas, and in the rivers, of all that move in the waters, and of any living thing which *is* in the waters, they *shall be* an abomination unto you: 11 They shall be even an abomination unto you; ye shall not eat of their flesh, but ye shall have their carcases in abomination. 12 Whatsoever hath no fins nor scales in the waters, that *shall be* an abomination unto you. 13 And these *are they which* ye shall have in abomination among the fowls; they shall not be eaten, they *are* an abomination: the eagle, and the ossifrage, and the ospray, 14 And the vulture, and the kite after his kind; 15 Every raven after his kind; 16 And the owl, and the night hawk, and the cuckow, and the hawk after his kind, 17 And the little owl, and the cormorant, and the great owl, 18 And the swan, and the pelican, and the gier eagle, 19 And the stork, the heron after her kind, and the lapwing, and the bat.

Here is, 1. A general rule concerning

fishes, which were clean and which not. All that had fins and scales they might eat, and only those odd sorts of water-animals that have not were forbidden, *v.* 9, 10. The ancients accounted fish the most delicate food (so far were they from allowing it on fasting-days, or making it an instance of mortification to eat fish); therefore God did not lay much restraint upon his people in them; for he is a Master that allows his servants not only for necessity but for delight. Concerning the prohibited fish it is said, *They shall be an abomination to you* (*v.* 10—12), that is, "You shall count them unclean, and not only not eat of them, but keep at a distance from them." Note, Whatever is unclean should be to us an abomination; *touch not the unclean thing*. But observe, It was to be an abomination only to Jews; the neighbouring nations were under none of these obligations, nor are these things to be an abomination to us Christians. The Jews were honoured with peculiar privileges, and therefore, lest they should be proud of those, *Transeunt cum onere—They were likewise laid under peculiar restraints*. Thus God's spiritual Israel, as they are dignified above others by the gospel-covenant of adoption and friendship, so they must be mortified more than others by the gospel-commands of self-denial and bearing the cross. 2. Concerning fowls here is no general rule given, but a particular enumeration of those fowls that they must abstain from as unclean, which implies an allowance of all others. The critics here have their hands full to find out what is the true signification of the Hebrew words here used, some of which still remain uncertain, some sorts of fowls being peculiar to some countries. Were the law in force now, we should be concerned to know with certainty what are prohibited by it; and perhaps if we did, and were better acquainted with the nature of the fowls here mentioned, we should admire the knowledge of Adam, in giving them names expressive of their natures, Gen. ii. 20. But the law being repealed, and the learning in a great measure lost, it is sufficient for us to observe that of the fowls here forbidden, (1.) Some are birds of prey, as the eagle, vulture, &c., and God would have his people to abhor every thing that is barbarous and cruel, and not to live by blood and rapine. Doves that are preyed upon were fit to be food for man and offerings to God; but kites and hawks that prey upon them must be looked upon as an abomination to God and man; for the condition of those that are persecuted for righteousness' sake appears to an eye of faith every way better than that of their persecutors. (2.) Others of them are solitary birds, that abide in dark and desolate places, as the owl and the pelican (Ps. cii. 6), and the cormorant and raven (Isa. xxxiv. 11); for God's Israel should not be a melancholy people, nor affect sadness and constant solitude. (3.) Others of them feed upon that which is impure, as the stork on serpents, others of them on worms; and we must not only abstain from all impurity ourselves, but from communion with those that allow themselves in it. (4.) Others of them were used by the Egyptians and other Gentiles in their divinations. Some birds were reckoned fortunate, others ominous; and their soothsayers had great regard to the flights of these birds, all which therefore must be an abomination to God's people, who must not learn the way of the heathen.

20 All fowls that creep, going upon *all* four, *shall be* an abomination unto you. 21 Yet these may ye eat of every flying creeping thing that goeth upon *all* four, which have legs above their feet, to leap withal upon the earth ; 22 *Even* these of them ye may eat ; the locust after his kind, and the bald locust after his kind, and the beetle after his kind, and the grasshopper after his kind. 23 But all *other* flying creeping things, which have four feet, *shall be* an abomination unto you. 24 And for these ye shall be unclean : whosoever toucheth the carcase of them shall be unclean until the even. 25 And whosoever beareth *aught* of the carcase of them shall wash his clothes, and be unclean until the even. 26 *The carcases* of every beast which divideth the hoof, and *is* not clovenfooted, nor cheweth the cud, *are* unclean unto you : every one that toucheth them shall be unclean. 27 And whatsoever goeth upon his paws, among all manner of beasts that go on *all* four, those *are* unclean unto you : whoso toucheth their carcase shall be unclean until the even. 28 And he that beareth the carcase of them shall wash his clothes, and be unclean until the even : they *are* unclean unto you. 29 These also *shall be* unclean unto you among the creeping things that creep upon the earth; the weasel, and the mouse, and the tortoise after his kind, 30 And the ferret, and the chameleon, and the lizard, and the snail, and the mole. 31 These *are* unclean to you among all that creep : whosoever doth touch them, when they be dead, shall be unclean until the even. 32 And upon whatsoever *any* of them, when they are dead, doth fall, it shall be unclean;

whether *it be* any vessel of wood, or raiment, or skin, or sack, whatsoever vessel *it be*, wherein *any* work is done, it must be put into water, and it shall be unclean until the even ; so it shall be cleansed. 33 And every earthen vessel, whereinto *any* of them falleth, whatsoever *is* in it shall be unclean ; and ye shall break it. 34 Of all meat which may be eaten, *that* on which *such* water cometh shall be unclean : and all drink that may be drunk in every *such* vessel shall be unclean. 35 And every *thing* whereupon *any* part of their carcase falleth shall be unclean ; *whether it be* oven, or ranges for pots, they shall be broken down : *for* they *are* unclean, and shall be unclean unto you. 36 Nevertheless a fountain or pit, *wherein there is* plenty of water, shall be clean : but that which toucheth their carcase shall be unclean. 37 And if *any part* of their carcase fall upon any sowing seed which is to be sown, it *shall be* clean. 38 But if *any* water be put upon the seed, and *any part* of their carcase fall thereon, it *shall be* unclean unto you. 39 And if any beast, of which ye may eat, die ; he that toucheth the carcase thereof shall be unclean until the even. 40 And he that eateth of the carcase of it shall wash his clothes, and be unclean until the even : he also that beareth the carcase of it shall wash his clothes, and be unclean until the even. 41 And every creeping thing that creepeth upon the earth *shall be* an abomination ; it shall not be eaten. 42 Whatsoever goeth upon the belly, and whatsoever goeth upon *all* four, or whatsoever hath more feet among all creeping things that creep upon the earth, them ye shall not eat; for they *are* an abomination.

Here is the law, 1. Concerning flying insects, as flies, wasps, bees, &c.; these they might not eat (*v.* 20), nor indeed are they fit to be eaten ; but there were several sorts of locusts which in those countries were very good meat, and much used : John Baptist lived upon them in the desert, and they are here allowed them, *v.* 21, 22. 2. Concerning the creeping things on the earth ; these were all forbidden (*v.* 29, 30, and again, *v.* 41, 42); for it was the curse of the serpent that *upon his belly he should go*, and therefore between him and man there was an enmity put (Gen. iii. 15), which was preserved by this law. Dust is the meat of the creeping things, and therefore they are not fit to be man's meat. 3. Concerning the dead carcases of all these unclean animals. (1.) Every one that touched them was to be unclean until the evening, *v.* 24—28. This law is often repeated, to possess them with a dread of every thing that was prohibited, though no particular reason for the prohibition did appear, but only the will of the Law-maker. Not that they were to be looked upon as defiling to the conscience, or that it was a sin against God to touch them, unless done in contempt of the law: in many cases, somebody must of necessity touch them, to remove them; but it was a *ceremonial* uncleanness they contracted, which for the time forbade them to come into the tabernacle, or to eat of any of the holy things, or so much as to converse familiarly with their neighbours. But the uncleanness continued only till the evening, to signify that all ceremonial pollutions were to come to an end by the death of Christ in the evening of the world. And we must learn, by daily renewing our repentance every night for the sins of the day, to cleanse ourselves from the pollution we contract by them, that we may not lie down in our uncleanness. Even unclean animals they might touch while they were alive without contracting any ceremonial uncleanness by it, as horses and dogs, because they were allowed to use them for service; but they might not touch them when they were dead, because they might not eat their flesh; and what must not be eaten must not be touched, Gen. iii. 3. (2.) Even the vessels, or other things they fell upon, were thereby made unclean until the evening (*v.* 32), and if they were earthen vessels they must be broken, *v.* 33. This taught them carefully to avoid every thing that was polluting, even in their common actions. Not only the vessels of the sanctuary, but every pot in Jerusalem and Judah, must be *holiness to the Lord,* Zech. xiv. 20, 21. The laws in these cases are very critical, and the observance of them would be difficult, we should think, if every thing that a dead mouse or rat, for instance, falls upon must be unclean; and if it were an oven, or ranges for pots, they must all be broken down, *v.* 35. The exceptions also are very nice, *v.* 36, &c. All this was designed to exercise them to a constant care and exactness in their obedience, and to teach us, who by Christ are delivered from these burdensome observances, not to be less circumspect in the more weighty matters of the law. We ought as industriously to preserve our precious souls from the pollutions of sin, and as speedily to cleanse them when they are polluted, as they were to preserve and cleanse their bodies and household goods from those ceremonial pollutions.

43 Ye shall not make yourselves abominable with any creeping thing that creepeth, neither shall ye make yourselves unclean with them, that ye should be defiled thereby. 44 For I *am* the Lord your God: ye shall therefore sanctify yourselves, and ye shall be holy; for I *am* holy: neither shall ye defile yourselves with any manner of creeping thing that creepeth upon the earth. 45 For I *am* the Lord that bringeth you up out of the land of Egypt, to be your God: ye shall therefore be holy, for I *am* holy. 46 This *is* the law of the beasts, and of the fowl, and of every living creature that moveth in the waters, and of every creature that creepeth upon the earth: 47 To make a difference between the unclean and the clean, and between the beast that may be eaten and the beast that may not be eaten.

Here is, I. The exposition of this law, or a key to let us into the meaning of it. It was not intended merely for a bill of fare, or as the directions of a physician about their diet, but God would hereby teach them to sanctify themselves and to be holy, *v.* 44. That is, 1. They must hereby learn to put a difference between good and evil, and to reckon that it could not be all alike what they did, when it was not all alike what they ate. 2. To maintain a constant observance of the divine law, and to govern themselves by that in all their actions, even those that are common, which ought to be performed *after a godly sort,* 3 John 6. Even eating and drinking must be by rule, and *to the glory of God,* 1 Cor. x. 31. 3. To distinguish themselves from all their neighbours, as a people set apart for God, and obliged not to walk as the Gentiles: and all this is holiness. Thus these *rudiments of the world* were their tutors and governors (Gal. iv. 2, 3), to bring them to that which is the revival of our first state in Adam and the earnest of our best state with Christ, that is, *holiness,* without which no man shall see the Lord. This is indeed the great design of all the ordinances, that by them we may sanctify ourselves and learn to be holy. Even this law concerning their food, which seemed to stoop so very low, aimed thus high, for it was the statute-law of heaven, under the Old Testament as well as the New, that *without holiness no man shall see the Lord.* The caution therefore (*v.* 43) is, *You shall not make yourselves abominable.* Note, By having fellowship with sin, which is abominable, we make ourselves abominable. That man is truly miserable who is in the sight of God abominable; and none are so but those that make themselves so. The Jewish writers themselves suggest that the intention of this law was to forbid them all communion by marriage, or otherwise, with the heathen, Deut. vii. 2, 3. And thus the moral of it is obligatory on us, forbidding us to *have fellowship with the unfruitful works of darkness ;* and, without this real holiness of the heart and life, *he that offereth an oblation* is *as if he offered swine's blood* (Isa. lxvi. 3) ; and, if it was such a provocation for a man to eat swine's flesh himself, much more it must be so to offer swine's blood at God's altar ; see Prov. xv. 8.

II. The reasons of this law ; and they are all taken from the Law-maker himself, to whom we must have respect in all acts of obedience. 1. *I am the Lord your God, v.* 44. "Therefore you are bound to do thus, in pure obedience." God's sovereignty over us, and propriety in us, oblige us to do whatever he commands us, how much soever it crosses our inclinations. 2. *I am holy, v.* 44, and again, *v.* 45. If God be holy, we must be so, else we cannot expect to be accepted of him. His holiness is his glory (Exod. xv. 11), and therefore it *becomes his house for ever,* Ps. xciii. 5. This great precept, thus enforced, though it comes in here in the midst of abrogated laws, is quoted and stamped for a gospel precept, 1 Pet. i. 16, where it is intimated that all these ceremonial restraints were designed to teach us that we must not *fashion ourselves according to our former lusts in our ignorance, v.* 14. 3. *I am the Lord that bringeth you out of the land of Egypt, v.* 45. This was a reason why they should cheerfully submit to distinguishing laws, having of late been so wonderfully dignified with distinguishing favours. He that had done more for them than for any other people might justly expect more from them.

III. The conclusion of this statute : *This is the law of the beasts, and of the fowl,* &c., *v.* 46, 47. This law was to them a statute for ever, that is, as long as that economy lasted ; but under the gospel we find it expressly repealed by a voice from heaven to Peter (Acts x. 15), as it had before been virtually set aside by the death of Christ, with the other ordinances that *perished in the using : Touch not, taste not, handle not,* Col. ii. 21, 22. And now we are sure that *meat commends us not to God* (1 Cor. viii. 8), and that *nothing is unclean of itself* (Rom. xiv. 14), nor does that defile a man which goes into his mouth, but that which comes out from the heart, Matt. xv. 11. Let us therefore, 1. Give thanks to God that we are not under this yoke, but that to us every creature of God is allowed as good, and nothing to be refused. 2. *Stand fast in the liberty wherewith Christ has made us free,* and take heed of those doctrines which *command to abstain from meats,* and so would revive Moses again, 1 Tim. iv. 3, 4. 3. Be strictly and conscientiously temperate in the use of the good creatures God has allowed us. If God's law has given us liberty, let us lay restraints upon ourselves,

and never feed ourselves without fear, lest our table be a snare. *Set a knife to thy throat, if thou be a man given to appetite ;* and *be not desirous of dainties* or varieties, Prov. xxiii. 2, 3. Nature is content with little, grace with less, but lust with nothing.

CHAP. XII.

AND the Lord spake unto Moses, saying, 2 Speak unto the children of Israel, saying, If a woman have conceived seed, and borne a man child : then she shall be unclean seven days ; according to the days of the separation for her infirmity shall she be unclean. 3 And in the eighth day the flesh of his foreskin shall be circumcised. 4 And she shall then continue in the blood of her purifying three and thirty days ; she shall touch no hallowed thing, nor come into the sanctuary, until the days of her purifying be fulfilled. 5 But if she bear a maid child, then she shall be unclean two weeks, as in her separation : and she shall continue in the blood of her purifying threescore and six days.

The law here pronounces women lying-in ceremonially unclean. The Jews say, "The law extended even to an abortion, if the child was so formed as that the sex was distinguishable." 1. There was some time of strict separation immediately after the birth, which continued seven days for a son and fourteen for a daughter, *v.* 2, 5. During these days she was separated from her husband and friends, and those that necessarily attended her were ceremonially unclean, which was one reason why the males were not circumcised till the eighth day, because they participated in the mother's pollution during the days of her separation. 2. There was also a longer time appointed for their purifying ; thirty-three days more (forty in all) if the birth were a male, and double that time if a female, *v.* 4, 5. During this time they were only separated from the sanctuary and forbidden to eat of the passover, or peace-offerings, or, if a priest's wife, to eat of any thing that was holy to the Lord. Why the time of both those was double for a female to what it was for a male I can assign no reason but the will of the Law-maker ; in Christ Jesus no difference is made of male and female, Gal. iii. 28 ; Col. iii. 11. But this ceremonial uncleanness which the law laid women in child-bed under was to signify the pollution of sin which we are all conceived and born in, Ps. li. 5. For, if the root be impure, so is the branch, *Who can bring a clean thing out of an unclean?* If sin had not entered, nothing but purity and honour had attended all the productions of that great blessing, *Be fruitful and multiply;* but now that the nature of man is degenerated the propagation of that nature is laid under these marks of disgrace, because of the sin and corruption that are propagated with it, and in remembrance of the curse upon the woman that was first in the transgression. That *in sorrow* (to which it is here further added *in shame)* she should *bring forth children.* And the exclusion of the woman for so many days from the sanctuary, and all participation of the holy things, signified that our original corruption (that sinning sin which we brought into the world with us) would have excluded us for ever from the enjoyment of God and his favours if he had not graciously provided for our purifying.

6 And when the days of her purifying are fulfilled, for a son, or for a daughter, she shall bring a lamb of the first year for a burnt offering, and a young pigeon, or a turtledove, for a sin offering, unto the door of the tabernacle of the congregation, unto the priest: 7 Who shall offer it before the Lord, and make an atonement for her; and she shall be cleansed from the issue of her blood. This *is* the law for her that hath borne a male or a female. 8 And if she be not able to bring a lamb, then she shall bring two turtles, or two young pigeons; the one for the burnt offering, and the other for a sin offering: and the priest shall make an atonement for her, and she shall be clean.

A woman that had lain in, when the time set for her return to the sanctuary had come, was not to attend there empty, but must bring her offerings, *v. 6.* 1. A *burnt-offering;* a lamb if she was able, if poor, a pigeon. This she was to offer in thankfulness to God for his mercy to her, in bringing her safely through the pains of child-bearing and all the perils of child-bed, and in desire and hopes of God's further favour both to her and to the child. When a child is born there is joy and there is hope, and therefore it was proper to bring this offering, which was of a general nature; for what we rejoice in we must give thanks for, and what we are in hopes of we must pray for. But, besides this, 2. She must offer a *sin-offering,* which must be the same for poor and rich, a turtle-dove or a young pigeon; for, whatever difference there may be between rich and poor in the sacrifices of acknowledgment, that of atonement is the same for both. This sin-offering was intended either, (1.) To complete her purification from that ceremonial uncleanness

which, though it was not in itself sinful, yet was typical of moral pollution; or, (2.) To make atonement for that which was really sin, either an inordinate desire of the blessing of children or discontent or impatience under the pains of child-bearing. It is only by Christ, the great sin-offering, that the corruption of our nature is done away, and to that it is owing that we are not for ever excluded by it from the sanctuary, and from eating of the holy things. According to this law, we find that the mother of our blessed Lord, though he was not conceived in sin as others, yet *accomplished the days of purification,* and then presented her son to the Lord, being a first-born, and brought her own offering, *a pair of turtle-doves,* Luke ii. 22—24. So poor were Christ's parents that they were not able to bring a lamb for a burnt-offering; and so early was Christ *made under the law, to redeem those that were under it.* The morality of this law obliges those women that have received mercy from God in child-bearing with all thankfulness to own God's goodness to them, acknowledging themselves unworthy of it, and (which is the best purification of women that have been saved in child-bearing, 1 Tim. ii. 15) to *continue in faith, and charity, and holiness, with sobriety;* for this shall please the Lord better than the turtle-doves or the young pigeons.

CHAP. XIII.

The next ceremonial uncleanness is that of the leprosy, concerning which the law was very large and particular; we have the discovery of it in this chapter, and the cleansing of the leper in the next. Scarcely any one thing in all the levitical law takes up so much room as this. I. Rules are here given by which the priest must judge whether the man had the leprosy or no, according as the symptom was that appeared. 1. If it was a swelling, a scab, or a bright spot, ver. 1—17. 2. If it was a bile, ver. 18—23. 3. If it was an inflammation, ver. 24—28. 4. If it was in the head or beard, ver. 29—37. 5. If it was a bright spot, ver. 38, 39. 6. If it was in a bald head, ver. 40—44. II. Direction is given how the leper must be disposed of, ver. 45, 46. III. Concerning the leprosy in garments, ver. 47, &c.

AND the Lord spake unto Moses and Aaron, saying, 2 When a man shall have in the skin of his flesh a rising, a scab, or bright spot, and it be in the skin of his flesh *like* the plague of leprosy; then he shall be brought unto Aaron the priest, or unto one of his sons the priests: 3 And the priest shall look on the plague in the skin of the flesh: and *when* the hair in the plague is turned white, and the plague in sight *be* deeper than the skin of his flesh, it *is* a plague of leprosy: and the priest shall look on him, and pronounce him unclean. 4 If the bright spot *be* white in the skin of his flesh, and in sight *be* not deeper than the skin, and the hair thereof be not turned white; then the priest shall shut up *him that hath* the plague seven days: 5 And the priest shall look on him the seventh day:

and, behold, *if* the plague in his sight be at a stay, *and* the plague spread not in the skin ; then the priest shall shut him up seven days more : 6 And the priest shall look on him again the seventh day : and, behold, *if* the plague *be* somewhat dark, *and* the plague spread not in the skin, the priest shall pronounce him clean : it *is but* a scab : and he shall wash his clothes, and be clean. 7 But if the scab spread much abroad in the skin, after that he hath been seen of the priest for his cleansing, he shall be seen of the priest again : 8 And *if* the priest see that, behold, the scab spreadeth in the skin, then the priest shall pronounce him unclean : it *is* a leprosy. 9 When the plague of leprosy is in a man, then he shall be brought unto the priest ; 10 And the priest shall see *him :* and, behold, *if* the rising *be* white in the skin, and it have turned the hair white, and *there be* quick raw flesh in the rising ; 11 It *is* an old leprosy in the skin of his flesh, and the priest shall pronounce him unclean, and shall not shut him up : for he *is* unclean. 12 And if a leprosy break out abroad in the skin, and the leprosy cover all the skin of *him that hath* the plague from his head even to his foot, wheresoever the priest looketh ; 13 Then the priest shall consider : and, behold, *if* the leprosy have covered all his flesh, he shall pronounce *him* clean *that hath* the plague : it is all turned white : he *is* clean. 14 But when raw flesh appeareth in him, he shall be unclean. 15 And the priest shall see the raw flesh, and pronounce him to be unclean : *for* the raw flesh *is* unclean : it *is* a leprosy. 16 Or if the raw flesh turn again, and be changed unto white, he shall come unto the priest ; 17 And the priest shall see him : and, behold, *if* the plague be turned into white ; then the priest shall pronounce *him* clean *that hath* the plague : he *is* clean.

I. Concerning the plague of leprosy we may observe in general, 1. That it was rather an uncleanness than a disease ; or, at least, so the law considered it, and therefore employed not the physicians but the priests about it. Christ is said to cleanse lepers, **not** to cure them. We do not read of any

that died of the leprosy, but it rather buried them alive, by rendering them unfit for conversation with any but such as were infected like themselves. Yet there is a tradition that Pharaoh, who sought to kill Moses, was the first that ever was struck with this disease, and that he died of it. It is said to have begun first in Egypt, whence it spread into Syria. It was very well known to Moses, when he put his own hand into his bosom and took it out leprous. 2. That it was a plague inflicted immediately by the hand of God, and came not from natural causes, as other diseases ; and therefore must be managed according to a divine law. Miriam's leprosy, and Gehazi's, and king Uzziah's, were all the punishments of particular sins : and, if generally it was so, no marvel there was so much care taken to distinguish it from a common distemper, that none might be looked upon as lying under this extraordinary token of divine displeasure but those that really were so. 3. That it is a plague not now known in the world ; what is commonly called the leprosy is of a quite different nature. This seems to have been reserved as a particular scourge for the sinners of those times and places. The Jews retained the idolatrous customs they had learnt in Egypt, and therefore God justly caused this with some others of the diseases of Egypt to follow them. Yet we read of Naaman the Syrian, who was a leper, 2 Kings v. 1. 4. That there were other breakings-out in the body which did very much resemble the leprosy, but were not it, which might make a man sore and loathsome and yet not ceremonially unclean. Justly are our bodies called vile bodies, which have in them the seeds of so many diseases, by which the lives of so many are made bitter to them. 5. That the judgment of it was referred to the priests. Lepers were looked upon as stigmatized by the justice of God, and therefore it was left to his servants the priests, who might be presumed to know his mark best, to pronounce who were lepers and who were not. And the Jews say, " Any priest, though disabled by a blemish to attend the sanctuary, might be a judge of the leprosy, provided the blemish were not in his eye. And he might" (they say) " take a common person to assist him in the search, but the priest only must pronounce the judgment." 6. That it was a figure of the moral pollution of men's minds by sin, which is the leprosy of the soul, defiling to the conscience, and from which Christ alone can cleanse us ; for herein the power of his grace infinitely transcends that of the legal priesthood, that the priest could only convict the leper (for by the law is the knowledge of sin), but Christ can cure the leper, he can take away sin. *Lord, if thou wilt, thou canst make me clean,* which was more than the priests could do, Matt. viii. 2. Some think that the leprosy signified, not so much sin in general as a state of sin, by which men are separated from God (their spot not being the spot of God's children), and scandalous sin, for which men are to be shut out from the communion of the faithful. It is a work of great importance, but of great difficulty, to judge of our spiritual state: we have all cause to suspect ourselves, being conscious to ourselves of sores and spots, but whether clean or unclean is the question. A man might have a scab (v. 6) and yet be clean: the best have their infirmities; but, as there were certain marks by which to know that it was a leprosy, so there are characters of such as are in the gall of bitterness, and the work of ministers is to declare the judgment of leprosy and to assist those that suspect themselves in the trial of their spiritual state, remitting or retaining sin. And hence the keys of the kingdom of heaven are said to be given to them, because they are to separate between the precious and the vile, and to judge who are fit as clean to partake of the holy things and who as unclean must be debarred from them.

II. Several rules are here laid down by which the judgment of the priest must be governed. 1. If the sore was but *skin-deep*, it was to be feared it was not the *leprosy*, v. 4. But, if it was *deeper than the skin*, the man must be pronounced unclean, v. 3. The infirmities that consist with grace do not sink deep into the soul, but *the mind* still *serves the law of God*, and the *inward man delights in it*, Rom. vii. 22, 25. But if the matter be really worse than it shows, and the inwards be infected, the case is dangerous. 2. If the sore *be at a stay*, and do not *spread*, it is no leprosy, v. 5, 6. But if it *spread much abroad*, and continue to do so after several inspections, the case is bad, v. 7, 8. If men do not grow worse, but a stop be put to the course of their sins and their corruptions be checked, it is to be hoped they will grow better; but if sin get ground, and they become worse every day, they are going downhill. 3. If there was *proud raw flesh* in the rising, the priest needed not to wait any longer, it was certainly a leprosy, v. 10, 11. Nor is there any surer indication of the badness of a man's spiritual state than the heart's rising in self-conceit, confidence in the flesh, and resistance of the reproofs of the word and strivings of the Spirit. 4. If the eruption, whatever it was, *covered all the skin* from head to foot, it was no leprosy (v. 12, 13); for it was an evidence that the vitals were sound and strong, and nature hereby helped itself, throwing out what was burdensome and pernicious. There is hope in the small-pox when they come out well: so if men freely confess their sins, and hide them not, there is no danger comparable to theirs that cover their sins. Some gather this from it, that there is more hope of the profane than of hypocrites. The publicans and harlots went into the kingdom of heaven before scribes and Pharisees. In one respect, the

sudden breakings-out of passion, though bad enough, are not so dangerous as malice concealed. Others gather this, that, if we judge ourselves, we shall not be judged; if we see and own that there is *no health in us, no soundness in our flesh*, by reason of sin, we shall *find grace in the eyes of the Lord.* 5. The priest must take time in making his judgment, and not give it rashly. If the matter looked suspicious, he must shut up the patient seven days, and then seven days more, that his judgment might be *according to truth*. This teaches all, both ministers and people, not to be hasty in their censures, nor to judge any thing *before the time.* If *some men's sins go before unto judgment*, the sins of others *follow after*, and so men's good works; therefore let nothing be done *suddenly*, 1 Tim. v. 22, 24, 25. 6. If the person suspected was found to be clean, yet he must *wash his clothes* (v. 6), because he had been under the suspicion, and there had been in him that which gave ground for the suspicion. Even the prisoner that is acquitted must go down on his knees. We have need to be washed in the blood of Christ from our spots, though they be not leprosy-spots; for who can say, *I am pure from sin?* though there are those who through grace are *innocent from the great transgression.*

18 The flesh also, in which, *even* in the skin thereof, was a boil, and is healed, 19 And in the place of the boil there be a white rising, or a bright spot, white, and somewhat reddish, and it be showed to the priest; 20 And if, when the priest seeth it, behold, it *be* in sight lower than the skin, and the hair thereof be turned white; the priest shall pronounce him unclean: it *is* a plague of leprosy broken out of the boil. 21 But if the priest look on it, and, behold, *there be* no white hairs therein, and *if* it *be* not lower than the skin, but *be* somewhat dark; then the priest shall shut him up seven days: 22 And if it spread much abroad in the skin, then the priest shall pronounce him unclean: it *is* a plague. 23 But if the bright spot stay in his place, *and* spread not, it *is* a burning boil; and the priest shall pronounce him clean. 24 Or if there be *any* flesh, in the skin whereof *there is* a hot burning, and the quick *flesh* that burneth have a white bright spot, somewhat reddish, or white; 25 Then the priest shall look upon it: and, behold, *if* the hair in the bright spot be turned white, and it *be in*

sight deeper than the skin; it *is* a leprosy broken out of the burning: wherefore the priest shall pronounce him unclean : it *is* the plague of leprosy. 26 But if the priest look on it, and, behold, *there be* no white hair on the bright spot, and it *be* no lower than the *other* skin, but *be* somewhat dark; then the priest shall shut him up seven days : 27 And the priest shall look upon him the seventh day: *and* if it be spread much abroad in the skin, then the priest shall pronounce him unclean : it *is* the plague of leprosy. 28 And if the bright spot stay in his place, *and* spread not in the skin, but it *be* somewhat dark; it *is* a rising of the burning, and the priest shall pronounce him clean : for it *is* an inflammation of the burning. 29 If a man or woman have a plague upon the head or the beard; 30 Then the priest shall see the plague : and, behold, if it *be* in sight deeper than the skin; *and there be* in it a yellow thin hair; then the priest shall pronounce him unclean : it *is* a dry scall, *even a* leprosy upon the head or beard. 31 And if the priest look on the plague of the scall, and, behold, it *be* not in sight deeper than the skin, and *that there is* no black hair in it; then the priest shall shut up *him that hath* the plague of the scall seven days : 32 And in the seventh day the priest shall look on the plague: and, behold, *if* the scall spread not, and there be in it no yellow hair, and the scall *be* not in sight deeper than the skin; 33 He shall be shaven, but the scall shall he not shave; and the priest shall shut up *him that hath* the scall seven days more : 34 And in the seventh day the priest shall look on the scall: and, behold, *if* the scall be not spread in the skin, nor *be* in sight deeper than the skin; then the priest shall pronounce him clean : and he shall wash his clothes, and be clean. 35 But if the scall spread much in the skin after his cleansing; 36 Then the priest shall look on him : and, behold, if the scall be spread in the skin, the priest shall not seek for yellow hair; he *is* unclean. 37 But if the scall be

in his sight at a stay, and *that* there is black hair grown up therein; the scall is healed, he *is* clean : and the priest shall pronounce him clean.

The priest is here instructed what judgment to make if there was any appearance of a leprosy, either, 1. In an old ulcer, or bile, that has been healed, *v.* 18, &c. When old sores, that seemed to be cured, break out again, it is to be feared there is a leprosy in them ; such is the danger of those who, having escaped the pollutions of the world, are again *entangled therein and overcome.* Or, 2. In a burn by accident, for this seems to be meant, *v.* 24, &c. The burning of strife and contention often proves the occasion of the rising up and breaking out of that corruption which witnesses to men's faces that they are unclean. 3. In a scall-head. And in this commonly the judgment turned upon a very small matter. If the hair in the scall was black, it was a sign of soundness; if yellow, it was an indication of a leprosy, *v.* 30—37. The other rules in these cases are the same with those mentioned before. In reading of these several sorts of ailments, it will be good for us, 1. To lament the calamitous state of human life, which lies exposed to so many grievances. What troops of diseases are we beset with on every side! and they all entered by sin. 2. To give thanks to God if he has never afflicted us with any of these sores : if the constitution is healthful, and the body lively and easy, we are bound to glorify God with our bodies.

38 If a man also or a woman have in the skin of their flesh bright spots, *even* white bright spots ; 39 Then the priest shall look : and, behold, *if* the bright spots in the skin of their flesh *be* darkish white ; it *is* a freckled spot *that* groweth in the skin ; he *is* clean. 40 And the man whose hair is fallen off his head, he *is* bald; *yet is* he clean. 41 And he that hath his hair fallen off from the part of his head toward his face, he *is* forehead bald : *yet is* he clean. 42 And if there be in the bald head, or bald forehead, a white reddish sore ; it *is* a leprosy sprung up in his bald head, or his bald forehead. 43 Then the priest shall look upon it : and, behold, *if* the rising of the sore *be* white reddish in his bald head, or in his bald forehead, as the leprosy appeareth in the skin of the flesh ; 44 He is a leprous man, he *is* unclean : the priest shall pronounce him utterly unclean; his plague *is* in his head.

45 And the leper in whom the plague *is*, his clothes shall be rent, and his head bare, and he shall put a covering upon his upper lip, and shall cry, Unclean, unclean. 46 All the days wherein the plague *shall be* in him he shall be defiled; he *is* unclean : he shall dwell alone; without the camp *shall* his habitation *be*.

We have here,

I. Provisos that neither a *freckled skin* nor a *bald head* should be mistaken for a leprosy, *v.* 38—41. Every deformity must not forthwith be made a ceremonial defilement. Elisha was jeered for his *bald head* (2 Kings ii. 23); but it was the children of Bethel, that knew not the judgments of their God, who turned it to his reproach.

II. A particular brand set upon the leprosy if at any time it did appear in a *bald head: The plague is in his head, he is utterly unclean, v.* 44. If the leprosy of sin have seized the head, if the judgment be corrupted, and wicked principles which countenance and support wicked practices, be embraced, it is an *utter uncleanness,* from which few are ever cleansed. Soundness in the faith keeps the leprosy from the head, and saves conscience from being shipwrecked.

III. Directions what must be done with the convicted leper. When the priest, upon mature deliberation, had solemnly pronounced him unclean,

1. He must pronounce himself so, *v.* 45. He must put himself into the posture of a mourner and cry, *Unclean, unclean.* The leprosy was not itself a sin, but it was a sad token of God's displeasure and a sore affliction to him that was under it. It was a reproach to his name, put a full stop to his business in the world, cut him off from conversation with his friends and relations, condemned him to banishment till he was cleansed, shut him out from the sanctuary, and was, in effect, the ruin of all the comfort he could have in this world. Heman, it would seem, either was a leper or alludes to the melancholy condition of a leper, Ps. lxxxviii. 8, &c. He must therefore, (1.) Humble himself under the mighty hand of God, not insisting upon his cleanness when the priest had pronounced him unclean, but justifying God and accepting the *punishment of his iniquity.* He must signify this by *rending his clothes, uncovering* his head, and *covering his upper lip,* all tokens of shame and confusion of face, and very significant of that self-loathing and self-abasement which should fill the hearts of penitents, the language of which is self-judging. Thus must we take to ourselves the shame that belongs to us, and with broken hearts call ourselves by our own name, *Unclean, unclean*—heart unclean, life unclean, unclean by original corruption, unclean by actual transgression—unclean, and

494

therefore worthy to be for ever excluded from communion with God, and all hope of happiness in him. *We are all as an unclean thing* (Isa. lxiv. 6)—unclean, and therefore undone, if infinite mercy do not interpose. (2.) He must give warning to others to take heed of coming near him. Wherever he went, he must cry to those he saw at a distance, " *I am unclean, unclean,* take heed of touching me.'' Not that the leprosy was catching, but by the touch of a leper ceremonial uncleanness was contracted. Every one therefore was concerned to avoid it; and the leper himself must give notice of the danger. And this was all that the law could do, in that it was weak through the flesh; it taught the leper to cry, *Unclean, unclean,* but the gospel has put another cry into the lepers' mouths, Luke xvii. 12, 13, where we find ten lepers crying with a loud voice, *Jesus, Master, have mercy on us.* The law only shows us our disease; the gospel shows us our help in Christ.

2. He must then be shut out of the camp, and afterwards, when they came to Canaan, out of the city, town, or village, where he lived, and *dwell alone* (*v.* 46), associating with none but those that were lepers like himself. When king Uzziah became a leper, he was banished from his palace, and *dwelt in a separate house,* 2 Chron. xxvi. 21. And see 2 Kings vii. 3. This typified the purity which ought to be preserved in the gospel church, by the solemn and authoritative exclusion of scandalous sinners, that hate to be reformed, from the communion of the faithful. *Put away from among yourselves that wicked person,* 1 Cor. v. 13.

47 The garment also that the plague of leprosy is in, *whether it be* a woollen garment, or a linen garment; 48 Whether *it be* in the warp, or woof; of linen, or of woollen; whether in a skin, or in any thing made of skin ; 49 And if the plague be greenish or reddish in the garment, or in the skin, either in the warp, or in the woof, or in any thing of skin; it *is* a plague of leprosy, and shall be showed unto the priest : 50 And the priest shall look upon the plague, and shut up *it that hath* the plague seven days; 51 And he shall look on the plague on the seventh day : if the plague be spread in the garment, either in the warp, or in the woof, or in a skin, *or* in any work that is made of skin ; the plague *is* a fretting leprosy, it *is* unclean. 52 He shall therefore burn that garment, whether warp or woof, in woollen or in- linen, or any thing of skin, wherein

the plague is: for it *is* a fretting leprosy; it shall be burnt in the fire. 53 And if the priest shall look, and, behold, the plague be not spread in the garment, either in the warp, or in the woof, or in any thing of skin; 54 Then the priest shall command that they wash *the thing* wherein the plague *is*, and he shall shut it up seven days more: 55 And the priest shall look on the plague, after that it is washed: and, behold, *if* the plague have not changed his colour, and the plague be not spread; it *is* unclean; thou shalt burn it in the fire; it *is* fret inward, *whether* it *be* bare within or without. 56 And if the priest look, and, behold, the plague *be* somewhat dark after the washing of it; then he shall rend it out of the garment, or out of the skin, or out of the warp, or out of the woof; 57 And if it appear still in the garment, either in the warp, or in the woof, or in any thing of skin; it *is* a spreading *plague:* thou shalt burn that wherein the plague *is* with fire. 58 And the garment, either warp, or woof, or whatsoever thing of skin *it be,* which thou shalt wash, if the plague be departed from them, then it shall be washed the second time, and shall be clean. 59 This *is* the law of the plague of leprosy in a garment of woollen or linen, either in the warp, or woof, or any thing of skins, to pronounce it clean, or to pronounce it unclean.

This is the law concerning the plague of leprosy in a garment, whether linen or woollen. A leprosy in a garment, with discernible indications of it, the colour changed by it, the garment fretted, the nap worn off, and this in some one particular part of the garment, and increasing when it was shut up, and not to be got out by washing, is a thing which to us now is altogether unaccountable. The learned confess that it was a sign and a miracle in Israel, an extraordinary punishment inflicted by the divine power, as a token of great displeasure against a person or family. 1. The process was much the same with that concerning a leprous person. The garment suspected to be tainted was not to be burnt immediately, though, it may be, there would have been no great loss of it; for in no case must sentence be given merely upon a surmise, but it must be *shown to the priest.* If, upon search, it was found that

there was a *leprous spot* (the Jews say no bigger than a bean), it must be *burnt,* or at least that part of the garment in which the spot was, *v.* 52, 57. If the cause of the suspicion was gone, it must be *washed,* and then might be used, *v.* 58. 2. The signification also was much the same, to intimate the great malignity there is in sin: it not only defiles the sinner's conscience, but it brings a stain upon all his employments and enjoyments, all he has and all he does. *To those that are defiled and unbelieving is nothing pure,* Tit. i. 15. And we are taught hereby to hate even *the garments spotted with the flesh,* Jude 23. Those that make their clothes servants to their pride and lust may see them thereby tainted with a leprosy, and doomed to the fire, Isa. iii. 18—24. But the ornament of *the hidden man of the heart is incorruptible,* 1 Pet. iii. 4. The robes of righteousness never fret nor are moth-eaten.

CHAP. XIV.

The former chapter directed the priests how to convict a leper of ceremonial uncleanness. No prescriptions are given for his cure; but, when God had cured him, the priests are in this chapter directed how to cleanse him. The remedy here is only adapted to the ceremonial part of his disease; but the authority Christ gave to his ministers was to cure the lepers, and so to cleanse them. We have here, I. The solemn declaration of the leper's being clean, with the significant ceremony attending it, ver. 1—9. II. The sacrifices which he was to offer to God eight days after, ver. 10—32. III. The management of a house in which appeared signs of a leprosy, ver. 33—53. And the conclusion and summary of this whole matter, ver. 54, &c.

AND the LORD spake unto Moses, saying, 2 This shall be the law of the leper in the day of his cleansing: He shall be brought unto the priest: 3 And the priest shall go forth out of the camp; and the priest shall look, and, behold, *if* the plague of leprosy be healed in the leper; 4 Then shall the priest command to take for him that is to be cleansed two birds alive *and* clean, and cedar wood, and scarlet, and hyssop: 5 And the priest shall command that one of the birds be killed in an earthen vessel over running water: 6 As for the living bird, he shall take it, and the cedar wood, and the scarlet, and the hyssop, and shall dip them and the living bird in the blood of the bird *that was* killed over the running water: 7 And he shall sprinkle upon him that is to be cleansed from the leprosy seven times, and shall pronounce him clean, and shall let the living bird loose into the open field. 8 And he that is to be cleansed shall wash his clothes, and shave off all his hair, and wash himself in water, that he may be clean: and after that he shall come into the camp, and shall tarry abroad out of his tent seven days. 9 But it shall be on the seventh day, that he shall shave all his hair off his head and his beard and his eyebrows, even all his hair he shall shave off: and he shall wash his clothes, also he shall wash his flesh in water, and he shall be clean.

Here, I. It is supposed that the plague of the leprosy was not an incurable disease. Uzziah's indeed continued to the day of his death, and Gehazi's was entailed upon his seed; but Miriam's lasted only seven days: we may suppose that it often wore off in process of time. Though God contend long, he will *not contend for ever.*

II. The judgment of the cure, as well as that of the disease, was referred to the priest. He must go out of the camp to the leper, to see whether his leprosy was healed, *v.* 3. And we may suppose the priest did not contract any ceremonial uncleanness by coming near the leper, as another person would. It was in mercy to the poor lepers that the priests particularly had orders to attend them, for *the priests' lips should keep knowledge;* and those in affliction have need to be instructed both how to bear their afflictions and how to reap benefit by them, have need of the word, in concurrence with the rod, to bring them to repentance; therefore it is well for those that are sick if they have these messengers of the Lord of hosts with them, these interpreters, to *show unto them God's uprightness,* Job xxxiii. 23. When the leper was shut out, and could not go to the priests, it was well that the priests might come to him. *Is any sick? Let him send for the elders,* the ministers, Jam. v. 14. If we apply it to the spiritual leprosy of sin, it intimates that when we withdraw from those who walk disorderly, that they may be ashamed, we must not count them as enemies, but admonish them as brethren, 2 Thess. iii. 15. And also that when God by his grace has brought those to repentance who were shut out of communion for scandal, they ought with tenderness, and joy, and sincere affection, to be received in again. Thus Paul orders concerning the excommunicated Corinthian that when he had given evidences of his repentance they should forgive him, and comfort him, and *confirm their love towards him,* 2 Cor. ii. 7, 8. And ministers are entrusted by our Master with the declarative power of loosing as well as binding: both must be done with great caution and deliberation, impartially and without respect of persons, with earnest prayer to God for directions, and a sincere regard to the edification of the body of Christ, due care being always taken that sinners may not be encouraged by an excess of lenity, nor penitents discouraged by an excess of severity. Wisdom and sincerity are profitable to direct in this case.

III. If it was found that the leprosy was

healed, the priest must declare it with a particular solemnity. The leper or his friends were to get ready two birds caught for this purpose (any sort of wild birds that were clean), and cedar-wood, and scarlet, and hyssop; for all these were to be used in the ceremony. 1. A preparation was to be made of blood and water, with which the leper must be sprinkled. One of the birds (and the Jews say, if there was any difference, it must be the larger and better of the two) was to be killed over an earthen cup of spring water, so that the blood of the bird might discolour the water. This (as some other types) had its accomplishment in the death of Christ, when out of his pierced side there came water and blood, John xix. 34. Thus Christ comes into the soul for its cure and cleansing, *not by water only, but by water and blood,* 1 John. v. 6. 2. The living bird, with a little scarlet wool, and a bunch of hyssop, must be fastened to a cedar stick, dipped in the water and blood, which must be so sprinkled upon him that was to be cleansed, *v.* 6, 7. The cedar-wood signified the restoring of the leper to his strength and soundness, for that is a sort of wood not apt to putrefy. The scarlet wool signified his recovering a florid colour again, for the leprosy made him white as snow. And the hyssop intimated the removing of the disagreeable scent which commonly attended the leprosy. The cedar the stateliest plant, and hyssop the meanest, are here used together in this service (see 1 Kings iv. 33); for those of the lowest rank in the church may be of use in their place, as well as those that are most eminent, 1 Cor. xii. 2. Some make the slain bird to typify Christ *dying for our sins,* and the living bird Christ *rising again for our justification.* The dipping of the living bird in the blood of the slain bird intimated that the merit of Christ's death was that which made his resurrection effectual for our justification. He took his blood with him into the holy place, and there appeared a lamb as it had been slain. The cedar, scarlet wool, and hyssop, must all be dipped in the blood; for the word and ordinances, and all the operations of the Spirit, receive their efficacy for our cleansing from the blood of Christ. The leper must be sprinkled *seven times,* to signify a complete purification, in allusion to which David prays, *Wash me thoroughly,* Ps. li. 2. Naaman was directed to wash *seven times,* 2 Kings v. 10. 3. The living bird was then to be let loose in the open field, to signify that the leper, being cleansed, was now no longer under restraint and confinement, but might take his liberty to go where he pleased. But this being signified by the flight of a bird towards heaven was an intimation to him henceforward to seek the things that are above, and not to spend this new life to which God had restored him merely in the pursuit of earthly things. This typified that glorious liberty of the children of God to which those are advanced who through grace are sprinkled from an evil conscience. Those whose souls before *bowed down to the dust* (Ps. xliv. 25), in grief and fear, now fly in the open firmament of heaven, and soar upwards upon the wings of faith and hope, and holy love and joy. 4. The priest must, upon this, pronounce him clean. It was requisite that this should be done with solemnity, that the leper might himself be the more affected with the mercy of God to him in his recovery, and that others might be satisfied to converse with him. Christ is our priest, to whom the Father has committed all judgment, and particularly the judgment of the leprosy. By his definitive sentence impenitent sinners will have their everlasting portion assigned them with the unclean (Job xxxvi. 14), out of the holy city; and all that by his grace are cured and cleansed shall be received into the camp of the saints, into which no unclean thing shall enter. Those are clean indeed whom Christ pronounces so, and they need not regard what men say of them. But, though Christ was the *end of this law for righteousness,* yet being in the days of his flesh *made under the law,* which as yet stood unrepealed, he ordered those lepers whom he had cured miraculously to go and *show themselves to the priest,* and *offer for their cleansing according to the law,* Matt. viii. 4; Luke xvii. 14. The type must be kept up till it was answered by its antitype. 5. When the leper was pronounced clean, he must wash his body and his clothes, and shave *off all his hair* (v. 8), must still tarry seven days out of the camp, and on the seventh day must do it again, *v.* 9. The priest having pronounced him clean from the disease, he must make himself as clean as ever he could from all the remains of it, and from all other defilements, and he must take time to do this. Thus those who have the comfort of the remission of their sins, by the sprinkling of the blood of Christ upon their consciences, must with the utmost care and caution *cleanse themselves from all filthiness both of flesh and spirit,* and thoroughly *purge themselves from their old sins;* for *every one that hath this hope in him will* be concerned to *purify himself.*

10 And on the eighth day he shall take two he lambs without blemish, and one ewe lamb of the first year without blemish, and three tenth deals of fine flour *for* a meat offering, mingled with oil, and one log of oil. 11 And the priest that maketh *him* clean shall present the man that is to be made clean, and those things, before the LORD, *at* the door of the tabernacle of the congregation: 12 And the priest shall take one he lamb, and offer him for a trespass offering, and the log of oil, and wave them *for* a

wave offering before the LORD: 13 And he shall slay the lamb in the place where he shall kill the sin offering and the burnt offering, in the holy place: for as the sin offering *is* the priest's, *so is* the trespass offering: it *is* most holy: 14 And the priest shall take *some* of the blood of the trespass offering, and the priest shall put *it* upon the tip of the right ear of him that is to be cleansed, and upon the thumb of his right hand, and upon the great toe of his right foot: 15 And the priest shall take *some* of the log of oil, and pour *it* into the palm of his own left hand: 16 And the priest shall dip his right finger in the oil that *is* in his left hand, and shall sprinkle of the oil with his finger seven times before the LORD: 17 And of the rest of the oil that *is* in his hand shall the priest put upon the tip of the right ear of him that is to be cleansed, and upon the thumb of his right hand, and upon the great toe of his right foot, upon the blood of the trespass offering: 18 And the remnant of the oil that *is* in the priest's hand he shall pour upon the head of him that is to be cleansed: and the priest shall make an atonement for him before the LORD. 19 And the priest shall offer the sin offering, and make an atonement for him that is to be cleansed from his uncleanness; and afterward he shall kill the burnt offering: 20 And the priest shall offer the burnt offering and the meat offering upon the altar: and the priest shall make an atonement for him, and he shall be clean.

Observe, I. To complete the purification of the leper, on the eighth day, after the former solemnity performed without the camp, and, as it should seem, before he returned to his own habitation, he was to attend *at the door of the tabernacle,* and was there to be *presented to the Lord,* with his offering, *v.* 11. Observe here, 1. That the mercies of God oblige us to present ourselves to him, Rom. xii. 1. 2. When God has restored us to the liberty of ordinances again, after restraint by sickness, distance, or otherwise, we should take the first opportunity of testifying our respect to God, and our affection to his sanctuary, by a diligent improvement of the liberty we are restored to. When Christ had healed the impotent man, he soon after *found him in the temple,* John. v. 14. When Hezekiah asks, *What is the sign that I shall go up to the house of the Lord?* he means, " What is the sign that I shall recover?" intimating that if God restored him his health, so that he should be able to go abroad, the house of the Lord should be the first place he would go to. 3. When we present ourselves before the Lord we must present our offerings, devoting to God with ourselves all we have and can do. 4. Both we and our offerings must be presented before the Lord by the priest that made us clean, even our Lord Jesus, else neither we nor they can be accepted.

II. Three lambs the cleansed leper was to bring, with a meat-offering, and a log of oil, which was about half a pint. Now, 1. Most of the ceremony peculiar to this case was about the trespass-offering, the lamb for which was offered first, *v.* 12. And, besides the usual rites with which the trespass-offering was offered, some of the blood was to be put upon the ear, and thumb, and great toe, of the leper that was to be cleansed (*v.* 14), the very same ceremony that was used in the consecration of the priests, *ch.* viii. 23, 24. It was a mortification to them to see the same purification necessary for them that was for a leper. The Jews say that the leper stood without the gate of the tabernacle, and the priest within, and thus the ceremony was performed through the gate, signifying that now he was admitted with other Israelites to attend in the courts of the Lord's house again, and was as welcome as ever; though he had been a leper, and though perhaps the name might stick by him as long as he lived (as we read of one who probably was cleansed by our Lord Jesus, who yet afterwards is called *Simon the leper*, Matt. xxvi. 6), yet he was as freely admitted as ever to communion with God and man. After the blood of the offering had been put with the priest's finger upon the extremities of the body, to include the whole, some of the oil that he brought, which was first waved and then sprinkled before the Lord, was in like manner put in the same places upon the blood. "The blood" (says the learned bishop Patrick) " seems to have been a token of forgiveness, the oil of healing," for God first *forgiveth our iniquities* and then *healeth our diseases*, Ps. ciii. 3. See Isa. xxxviii. 17. Wherever the blood of Christ is applied for justification the oil of the Spirit is applied for sanctification; for these two are inseparable and both necessary to our acceptance with God. Nor shall our former leprosy, if it be healed by repentance, be any bar to these glorious privileges. Cleansed lepers are as welcome to the blood and the oil as consecrated priests. *Such were some of you, but you are washed.* When the leper was sprinkled the water must have blood in it (*v.* 5), when he was anointed the oil must have blood under it, to signify that all the graces and comforts of the Spirit, all his purifying dignifying influences, are owing to the death of Christ: it is by his

blood alone that we are sanctified. 2. Besides this there must be a sin-offering and a burnt-offering, a lamb for each, *v.* 19, 20. By each of these offerings, it is said, the priests shall *make an atonement for him.* (1.) His moral guilt shall be removed; the sin for which the leprosy was sent shall be pardoned, and all the sins he had been guilty of in his afflicted state. Note, The removal of any outward trouble is then doubly comfortable to us when at the same time God gives us some assurance of the forgiveness of our sins. If we *receive the atonement*, we have reason to rejoice, Rom. v. 11. (2.) His ceremonial pollution shall be removed, which had kept him from the participation of the holy things. And this is called *making an atonement for him*, because our restoration to the privileges of God's children, typified hereby, is owing purely to the great propitiation. When the atonement is made for him he shall be clean, both to his own satisfaction and to his reputation among his neighbours; he shall retrieve both his credit and his comfort, and both these true penitents become entitled to, both ease and honour, by their interest in the atonement. The burnt-offering, besides the atonement that was made by it, was a thankful acknowledgment of God's mercy to him: and the more immediate the hand of God was both in the sickness and in the cure the more reason he had thus to give glory to him, and thus, as our Saviour speaks (Mark i. 44), to *offer for his cleansing* all *those things which Moses commanded for a testimony unto them.*

21 And if he *be* poor, and cannot get so much; then he shall take one lamb *for* a trespass offering to be waved, to make an atonement for him, and one tenth deal of fine flour mingled with oil for a meat offering, and a log of oil: 22 And two turtledoves, or two young pigeons, such as he is able to get; and the one shall be a sin offering, and the other a burnt offering. 23 And he shall bring them on the eighth day for his cleansing unto the priest, unto the door of the tabernacle of the congregation, before the LORD. 24 And the priest shall take the lamb of the trespass offering, and the log of oil, and the priest shall wave them *for* a wave offering before the LORD: 25 And he shall kill the lamb of the trespass offering, and the priest shall take *some* of the blood of the trespass offering, and put *it* upon the tip of the right ear of him that is to be cleansed, and upon the thumb of his right hand, and upon the great toe of

his right foot: 26 And the priest shall pour of the oil into the palm of his own left hand: 27 And the priest shall sprinkle with his right finger, *some* of the oil that *is* in his left hand seven times before the LORD: 28 And the priest shall put of the oil that *is* in his hand upon the tip of the right ear of him that is to be cleansed, and upon the thumb of his right hand and upon the great toe of his right foot, upon the place of the blood of the trespass offering: 29 And the rest of the oil that *is* in the priest's hand he shall put upon the head of him that is to be cleansed, to make an atonement for him before the LORD. 30 And he shall offer the one of the turtledoves, or of the young pigeons, such as he can get; 31 *Even* such as he is able to get, the one *for* a sin offering, and the other *for* a burnt offering, with the meat offering: and the priest shall make an atonement for him that is to be cleansed before the LORD. 32 This *is* the law *of him* in whom *is* the plague of leprosy, whose hand is not able to get *that which pertaineth* to his cleansing.

We have here the gracious provision which the law made for the cleansing of *poor lepers.* If they were not able to bring three lambs, and three tenth-deals of flour, they must bring one lamb, and one tenth-deal of flour, and, instead of the other two lambs, two turtle-doves or two young pigeons, *v.* 21, 22. Here see, 1. That the poverty of the person concerned would not excuse him if he brought no offering at all. Let none think that because they are poor God requires no service from them, since he has considered them, and demands that which it is in the power of the poorest to give. *"My son, give me thy heart,* and with that the *calves of thy lips* shall be accepted instead of the *calves of the stall."* 2. That God expected from those who were poor only according to their ability; *his commandments are not grievous,* nor does he make us to *serve with an offering.* The poor are as welcome to God's altar as the rich; and, if there be first a willing mind and an honest heart, two pigeons, when they are the utmost a man is able to get, are as acceptable to God as two lambs; for he requires *according to what a man has and not according to what he has not.* But it is observable that though a meaner sacrifice was accepted from the poor, yet the very same ceremony was used for them as was for the rich; for their souls are as precious and Christ and his gospel are the same to both. Let not us there-

fore have *the faith of our Lord Jesus Christ with respect of persons,* Jam. ii. 1.

33 And the LORD spake unto Moses and unto Aaron, saying, 34 When ye be come into the land of Canaan, which I give to you for a possession, and I put the plague of leprosy in a house of the land of your possession; 35 And he that owneth the house shall come and tell the priest, saying, It seemeth to me *there is* as it were a plague in the house: 36 Then the priest shall command that they empty the house, before the priest go *into it* to see the plague, that all that *is* in the house be not made unclean: and afterward the priest shall go in to see the house: 37 And he shall look on the plague, and, behold, *if* the plague *be* in the walls of the house with hollow strakes, greenish or reddish, which in sight *are* lower than the wall; 38 Then the priest shall go out of the house to the door of the house, and shut up the house seven days: 39 And the priest shall come again the seventh day, and shall look: and, behold, *if* the plague be spread in the walls of the house; 40 Then the priest shall command that they take away the stones in which the plague *is,* and they shall cast them into an unclean place without the city: 41 And he shall cause the house to be scraped within round about, and they shall pour out the dust that they scrape off without the city into an unclean place: 42 And they shall take other stones, and put *them* in the place of those stones; and he shall take other mortar, and shall plaster the house. 43 And if the plague come again, and break out in the house, after that he hath taken away the stones, and after he hath scraped the house, and after it is plastered; 44 Then the priest shall come and look, and, behold, *if* the plague be spread in the house, it *is* a fretting leprosy in the house: it *is* unclean. 45 And he shall break down the house, the stones of it, and the timber thereof, and all the mortar of the house; and he shall carry *them* forth out of the city into an unclean place. 46 More-

over he that goeth into the house all the while that it is shut up shall be unclean until the even. 47 And he that lieth in the house shall wash his clothes; and he that eateth in the house shall wash his clothes. 48 And if the priest shall come in, and look *upon it,* and, behold, the plague hath not spread in the house, after the house was plastered: then the priest shall pronounce the house clean, because the plague is healed. 49 And he shall take to cleanse the house two birds, and cedar wood, and scarlet, and hyssop: 50 And he shall kill the one of the birds in an earthen vessel over running water: 51 And he shall take the cedar wood, and the hyssop, and the scarlet, and the living bird, and dip them in the blood of the slain bird, and in the running water, and sprinkle the house seven times: 52 And he shall cleanse the house with the blood of the bird, and with the running water, and with the living bird, and with the cedar wood, and with the hyssop, and with the scarlet: 53 But he shall let go the living bird out of the city into the open fields, and make an atonement for the house: and it shall be clean.

This is the law concerning the leprosy in a house. Now that they were in the wilderness they dwelt in tents, and had no houses, and therefore the law is made only an appendix to the former laws concerning the leprosy, because it related, not to their present state, but to their future settlement. The leprosy in a house is as unaccountable as the leprosy in a garment; but, if we see not what natural causes of it can be assigned, we may resolve it into the power of the God of nature, who here says, *I put the leprosy in a house* (v. 34), as his curse is said to *enter into a house,* and *consume it with the timber and stones thereof,* Zech. v. 4. Now, 1. It is supposed that even in Canaan itself, the land of promise, their houses might be infected with a leprosy. Though it was a holy land, this would not secure them from this plague, while the inhabitants were many of them so unholy. Thus a place and a name in the visible church will not secure wicked people from God's judgments. 2. It is likewise taken for granted that the owner of the house will make the priest acquainted with it, as soon as he sees the least cause to suspect the leprosy in his house: *It seemeth to me there is as it were a plague in the house, v.* 35. Sin, where that reigns in a house, is a plague there, as it is in a heart.

500

And masters of families should be aware and afraid of the first appearance of gross sin in their families, and put away the iniquity, whatever it is, far from their tabernacles, Job xxii. 23. They should be jealous with a godly jealousy concerning those under their charge, lest they be drawn into sin, and take early advice, if it but seem that there is a plague in the house, lest the contagion spread, and many be by it defiled and destroyed. 3. If the priest, upon search, found that the leprosy had got into the house, he must try to cure it, by taking out that part of the building that was infected, v. 40, 41. This was like cutting off a gangrened limb, for the preservation of the rest of the body. Corruption should be purged out in time, before it spread; for *a little leaven leaveneth the whole lump. If thy right hand offend thee, cut it off.* 4. If yet it remained in the house, the whole house must be pulled down, and all the materials carried to the dunghill, v. 44, 45. The owner had better be without a dwelling than live in one that was infected. Note, The leprosy of sin, if it be obstinate under the methods of cure, will at last be the ruin of families and churches. If Babylon will not be healed, she shall be forsaken and abandoned, and (according to the law respecting the leprous house) they shall not *take of her a stone for a corner, nor a stone for foundations,* Jer. li. 9, 26. The remainders of sin and corruption in our mortal bodies are like this leprosy in the house; after all our pains in scraping and plastering, we shall never be quite clear of it, till the earthly house of this tabernacle be dissolved and taken down; when we are dead we shall be free from sin, and not till then, Rom. vi. 7. 5. If the taking out the infected stones cured the house, and the leprosy did not spread any further, then the house must be cleansed; not only aired, that it might be healthful, but purified from the ceremonial pollution, that it might be fit to be the habitation of an Israelite. The ceremony of its cleansing was much the same with that of cleansing a leprous person, v. 49, &c. This intimated that the house was smitten for the man's sake (as bishop Patrick expresses it), and he was to look upon himself as preserved by divine mercy. The houses of Israelites are said to be *dedicated* (Deut. xx. 5), for they were a holy nation, and therefore they ought to keep their houses pure from all ceremonial pollutions, that they might be fit for the service of that God to whom they were devoted. And the same care should we take to reform whatever is amiss in our families, that we and our houses may serve the Lord; see Gen. xxxv. 2. Some have thought the leprosy in the house was typical of the idolatry of the Jewish church, which did strangely cleave to it; for, though some of the reforming kings took away the infected stones, yet still it broke out again, till by the captivity of Babylon God took down the house, and carried it to an unclean land; and this proved an effectual cure of their inclination to idols and idolatrous worships.

54 This *is* the law for all manner of plague of leprosy and scall, 55 And for the leprosy of a garment, and of a house, 56 And for a rising, and for a scab, and for a bright spot: 57 To teach when *it is* unclean, and when *it is* clean: this *is* the law of leprosy.

This is the conclusion of this law concerning the leprosy. There is no repetition of it in Deuteronomy, only a general memorandum given (Deut. xxiv. 8), *Take heed in the plague of leprosy.* We may see in this law, 1. The gracious care God took of his people Israel, for to them only this law pertained, and not to the Gentiles. When Naaman the Syrian was cured of his leprosy he was not bidden to show himself to the priest, though he was cured in Jordan, as the Jews that were cured by our Saviour were. Thus those who are entrusted with the key of discipline in the church judge those only *that are within ;* but *those that are without God judgeth,* 1. Cor. v. 12, 13. 2. The religious care we ought to take of ourselves, to keep our minds from the dominion of all sinful affections and dispositions, which are both their disease and their defilement, that we may be fit for the service of God. We ought also to avoid all bad company, and, as much as may be, to avoid coming within the danger of being infected by it. *Touch not the unclean thing, saith the Lord, and I will receive you,* 2 Cor. vi. 17.

CHAP. XV.

In this chapter we have laws concerning other ceremonial uncleannesses contracted either by bodily disease like that of the leper, or some natural incidents, and this either, I. In men, ver. 1—18. Or, II. In women, ver. 19—33. We need not be at all curious in explaining these antiquated laws, it is enough if we observe the general intention ; but we have need to be very cautious lest sin take occasion by the commandment to become more exceedingly sinful ; and exceedingly sinful it is when lust is kindled by sparks of fire from God's altar. The case is bad with the soul when it is putrefied by that which should purify it.

AND the LORD spake unto Moses and to Aaron, saying, 2 Speak unto the children of Israel, and say unto them, When any man hath a running issue out of his flesh, *because of* his issue he *is* unclean. 3 And this shall be his uncleanness in his issue : whether his flesh run with his issue, or his flesh be stopped from his issue, *it is* his uncleanness. 4 Every bed, whereon he lieth that hath the issue, is unclean : and every thing, whereon he sitteth, shall be unclean. 5 And whosoever toucheth his bed shall wash his clothes, and bathe *himself* in water, and be unclean until the even. 6 And he that sitteth on *any* thing whereon he sat that hath the

issue shall wash his clothes, and bathe *himself* in water, and be unclean until the even. 7 And he that toucheth the flesh of him that hath the issue shall wash his clothes, and bathe *himself* in water, and be unclean until the even. 8 And if he that hath the issue spit upon him that is clean ; then he shall wash his clothes, and bathe *himself* in water, and be unclean until the even. 9 And what saddle soever he rideth upon that hath the issue shall be unclean. 10 And whosoever toucheth any thing that was under him shall be unclean until the even : and he that beareth *any of* those things shall wash his clothes, and bathe *himself* in water, and be unclean until the even. 11 And whomsoever he toucheth that hath the issue, and hath not rinsed his hands in water, he shall wash his clothes, and bathe *himself* in water, and be unclean until the even. 12 And the vessel of earth, that he toucheth which hath the issue, shall be broken : and every vessel of wood shall be rinsed in water. 13 And when he that hath an issue is cleansed of his issue ; then he shall number to himself seven days for his cleansing, and wash his clothes, and bathe his flesh in running water, and shall be clean. 14 And on the eighth day he shall take to him two turtledoves, or two young pigeons, and come before the LORD unto the door of the tabernacle of the congregation, and give them unto the priest : 15 And the priest shall offer them, the one *for* a sin offering, and the other *for* a burnt offering ; and the priest shall make an atonement for him before the LORD for his issue. 16 And if any man's seed of copulation go out from him, then he shall wash all his flesh in water, and be unclean until the even. 17 And every garment, and every skin, whereon is the seed of copulation, shall be washed with water, and be unclean until the even. 18 The woman also with whom man shall lie *with* seed of copulation, they shall *both* bathe *themselves* in water, and be unclean until the even.

We have here the law concerning the ceremonial uncleanness that was contracted by running issues in men. It is called in the margin (*v.* 2) the *running of the reins :* a very grievous and loathsome disease, which was, usually the effect and consequent of wantonness and uncleanness, and a dissolute course of life, filling men's bones with the sins of their youth, and leaving them to mourn at the last, when all the pleasures of their wickedness have vanished, and nothing remains but the pain and anguish of a rotten carcase and a wounded conscience. And what fruit has the sinner then of those things whereof he has so much reason to be ashamed? Rom. vi. 21. As modesty is *an ornament of grace to the head and chains about the neck,* so chastity is *health to the navel and marrow to the bones ;* but uncleanness is a *wound and dishonour,* the consumption of the flesh and the body, and a sin which is often its own punishment more than any other. It was also sometimes inflicted by the righteous hand of God for other sins, as appears by David's imprecation of a curse upon the family of Joab, for the murder of Abner. 2 Sam. iii. 29, *Let there not fail from the house of Joab one that hath an issue, or is a leper.* A vile disease for vile deserts. Now whoever had this disease upon him, 1. He was himself unclean, *v.* 2. He must not dare to come near the sanctuary, it was at his peril if he did, nor might he eat of the holy things. This signified the filthiness of sin, and of all the productions of our corrupt nature, which render us odious to God's holiness, and utterly unfit for communion with him. Out of a pure heart well kept are the issues of life (Prov. iv. 23), but out of an unclean heart comes that which is defiling, Matt. xii. 34, 35. 2. He made every person and thing unclean that he touched, or that touched him, *v.* 4—12. His bed, and his chair, and his saddle, and every thing that belonged to him, could not be touched without a ceremonial uncleanness contracted, which a man must remain conscious to himself of till sunset, and from which he could not be cleansed without washing his clothes, and bathing his flesh in water. This signified the contagion of sin, the danger we are in of being polluted by conversing with those that are polluted, and the need we have with the utmost circumspection to *save ourselves from this untoward generation.* 3. When he was cured of the disease, yet he could not be cleansed from the pollution without a sacrifice, for which he was to prepare himself by seven days' expectation after he was perfectly clear from his distemper, and by bathing in spring water, *v.* 13—15. This signified the great gospel duties of faith and repentance, and the great gospel privileges of the application of Christ's blood to our souls for our justification and his grace for our sanctification. God has promised to sprinkle clean water upon us, and to cleanse us from all our filthiness, and has appointed us by repentance to

502

wash and make ourselves clean: he has also provided a sacrifice of atonement, and requires us by faith to interest ourselves in that sacrifice ; for it is *the blood of Christ his Son that cleanses us from all sin,* and by which atonement is made for us, that we may have admission into God's presence and may partake of his favour.

19 And if a woman have an issue, *and* her issue in her flesh be blood, she shall be put apart seven days : and whosoever toucheth her shall be unclean until the even. 20 And every thing that she lieth upon in her separation shall be unclean : every thing also that she sitteth upon shall be unclean. 21 And whosoever toucheth her bed shall wash his clothes, and bathe *himself* in water, and be unclean until the even. 22 And whosoever toucheth any thing that she sat upon shall wash his clothes, and bathe *himself* in water, and be unclean until the even. 23 And if it *be* on *her* bed, or on any thing whereon she sitteth, when he toucheth it, he shall be unclean until the even. 24 And if any man lie with her at all, and her flowers be upon him, he shall be unclean seven days ; and all the bed whereon he lieth shall be unclean. 25 And if a woman have an issue of her blood many days out of the time of her separation, or if it run beyond the time of her separation ; all the days of the issue of her uncleanness shall be as the days of her separation : she *shall be* unclean. 26 Every bed whereon she lieth all the days of her issue shall be unto her as the bed of her separation : and whatsoever she sitteth upon shall be unclean, as the uncleanness of her separation. 27 And whosoever toucheth those things shall be unclean, and shall wash his clothes, and bathe *himself* in water, and be unclean until the even. 28 But if she be cleansed of her issue, then she shall number to herself seven days, and after that she shall be clean. 29 And on the eighth day she shall take unto her two turtles, or two young pigeons, and bring them unto the priest, to the door of the tabernacle of the congregation. 30 And the priest shall offer the one *for* a sin offering, and the

other *for* a burnt offering; and the priest shall make an atonement for her before the LORD for the issue of her uncleanness. 31 Thus shall ye separate the children of Israel from their uncleanness; that they die not in their uncleanness, when they defile my tabernacle that *is* among them. 32 This *is* the law of him that hath an issue, and *of him* whose seed goeth from him, and is defiled therewith; 33 And of her that is sick of her flowers, and of him that hath an issue, of the man, and of the woman, and of him that lieth with her that is unclean.

This is concerning the ceremonial uncleanness which women lay under from their issues, both those that were regular and healthful, and according to the course of nature (*v.* 19—24), and those that were unseasonable, excessive, and the disease of the body; such was the bloody issue of that poor woman who was suddenly cured by touching the hem of Christ's garment, after she had lain twelve years under her distemper, and had spent her estate upon physicians and physic in vain. This made the woman that was afflicted with it unclean (*v.* 25) and every thing she touched unclean, *v.* 26, 27. And if she was cured, and found by seven days' trial that she was perfectly free from her issue of blood, she was to be cleansed by the offering of two turtle-doves or two young pigeons, to make an atonement for her, *v.* 28, 29. All wicked courses, particularly idolatries, are compared to the uncleanness of a *removed woman* (Ezek. xxxvi. 17), and, in allusion to this, it is said of Jerusalem (Lam. i. 9), *Her filthiness is in her skirts,* so that (as it follows, *v.* 17) she was shunned as a menstruous woman.

I. The reasons given for all these laws (which we are ready to think might very well have been spared) we have, *v.* 31. 1. *Thus shall you separate the children of Israel* (for to them only and their servants and proselytes these laws pertained) *from their uncleanness;* that is, (1.) By these laws they were taught their privilege and honour, that they were *purified unto God a peculiar people,* and were intended by the holy God for a kingdom of priests, a holy nation; for that was a defilement to them which was not so to others. (2.) They were also taught their duty, which was to preserve the honour of their purity, and to keep themselves from all sinful pollutions. It was easy for them to argue that if those pollutions which were natural, unavoidable, involuntary, their affliction and not their sin, rendered them for the time so odious that they were not fit for communion either with God or man, much more abominable and filthy were they if they sinned against the light and law of nature, by drunkenness, adultery, fraud, and the like sins, which defile the very mind and conscience. And, if these ceremonial pollutions could not be done away but by sacrifice and offering, something greater and much more valuable must be expected and depended upon for the purifying of the soul from the uncleanness of sin. 2. Thus their dying in their uncleanness by the hand of God's justice, if while they were under any of these defilements they should come near the sanctuary, would be prevented. Note, It is a dangerous thing to die in our uncleanness; and it is our own fault if we do, since we have not only fair warning given us, by God's law, against those things that will defile us, but also such gracious provision made by his gospel for our cleansing if at any time we be defiled. 3. In all these laws there seems to be a special regard had to the honour of the tabernacle, to which none must approach in their uncleanness, that they *defile not my tabernacle.* Infinite Wisdom took this course to preserve in the minds of that careless people a continual dread of, and veneration for, the manifestations of God's glory and presence among them in his sanctuary. Now that the tabernacle of God was with men familiarity would be apt to breed contempt, and therefore the law made so many things of frequent incidence to be ceremonial pollutions, and to involve an incapacity of drawing near to the sanctuary (making death the penalty), that so they might not approach without great caution, and reverence, and serious preparation, and fear of being found unfit. Thus they were taught never to draw near to God but with an awful humble sense of their distance and danger, and an exact observance of every thing that was required in order to their safety and acceptance.

II. And what duty must we learn from all this? 1. Let us bless God that we are not under the yoke of these carnal ordinances, that, as nothing can destroy us, so nothing can defile us, but sin. Those may now partake of the Lord's supper who durst not then eat of the peace-offerings. And the defilement we contract by our sins of daily infirmity we may be cleansed from in secret by the renewed acts of repentance and faith, without bathing in water or bringing an offering to the door of the tabernacle. 2. Let us carefully abstain from all sin, as defiling to the conscience, and particularly from all fleshly lusts, *possessing our vessel in sanctification and honour, and not in the lusts of uncleanness,* which not only pollute the soul, but *war against it,* and threaten its ruin. 3. Let us all see how indispensably necessary real holiness is to our future happiness, and get our hearts purified by faith, that we may see God. Perhaps it is in allusion to these laws which forbade the unclean to approach the sanctuary that when it is asked, *Who shall stand in God's holy place?* it is answered, *He that hath clean hands and a pure heart* (Ps. xxiv. 3, 4); for *without holiness no man shall see the Lord.*

CHAP. XVI

In this chapter we have the institution of the annual solemnity of the day of atonement, or expiation, which had as much gospel in it as perhaps any of the appointments of the ceremonial law, as appears by the reference the apostle makes to it, Heb. ix. 7, &c. We had before divers laws concerning sin-offerings for particular persons, and to be offered upon particular occasions; but this is concerning the stated sacrifice, in which the whole nation was interested. The whole service of the day is committed to the high priest. I. He must never come into the most holy place but upon this day, ver. 1, 2. II. He must come dressed in linen garments, ver. 4. III. He must bring a sin-offering and a burnt-offering for himself (ver. 3), offer his sin-offering (ver. 6—11), then go within the veil with some of the blood of his sin-offering, burn incense, and sprinkle the blood before the mercy-seat, ver. 12—14. IV. Two goats must be provided for the people, lots cast upon them, and, 1. One of them must be a sin-offering for the people (ver. 5, 7—9), and the blood of it must be sprinkled before the mercy-seat (ver. 15—17), and then some of the blood of both the sin-offerings must be sprinkled upon the altar, ver. 18, 19. 2. The other must be a scape-goat (ver. 10), the sins of Israel must be confessed over him, and then he must be sent away into the wilderness (ver. 20—22), and he that brought him away must be ceremonially unclean, ver. 26. V. The burnt-offerings were then to be offered, the fat of the sin-offerings burnt on the altar, and their flesh burnt without the camp, ver. 23—25, 27, 28. VI. The people were to observe the day religiously by a holy rest and holy mourning for sin; and this was to be a statute for ever, ver. 29, &c.

AND the LORD spake unto Moses after the death of the two sons of Aaron, when they offered before the LORD, and died; 2 And the LORD said unto Moses, Speak unto Aaron thy brother, that he come not at all times into the holy *place,* within the veil before the mercy seat, which *is* upon the ark; that he die not: for I will appear in the cloud upon the mercy seat. 3 Thus shall Aaron come into the holy *place:* with a young bullock for a sin offering, and a ram for a burnt offering. 4 He shall put on the holy linen coat, and he shall have the linen breeches upon his flesh, and shall be girded with a linen girdle, and with the linen mitre shall he be attired: these *are* holy garments; therefore shall he wash his flesh in water, and *so* put them on.

Here is, I. The date of this law concerning the day of atonement: it was *after the death of the two sons of Aaron* (v. 1), which we read, *ch.* x. 1. 1. Lest Aaron should fear that any remaining guilt of that sin should cleave to his family, or (seeing the priests were so apt to offend) that some after-sin of his other sons should be the ruin of his family, he is directed how to make atonement for his house, that it might keep in with God; for the atonement for it would be the establishment of it, and preserve the entail of the blessing upon it. 2. The priests being warned by the death of Nadab and Abihu to approach to God with reverence and godly fear (without which they came at their peril), directions are here given how the nearest approach might be made, not only without peril, but to unspeakable advantage

504

and comfort, if the directions were observed. When they were cut off for an undue approach, the rest must not say, "Then we will not draw near at all," but, "Then we will do it by rule." They died for their sin, therefore God graciously provides for the rest, that they die not. Thus God's judgments on some should be instructions to others.

II. The design of this law. One intention of it was to preserve a veneration for the most holy place, within the veil, where the *Shechinah,* or divine glory, was pleased to dwell between the cherubim: *Speak unto Aaron, that he come not at all times into the holy place, v.* 2. Before the veil some of the priests came every day to burn incense upon the golden altar, but within the veil none must ever come but the high priest only, and he but on one day in the year, and with great ceremony and caution. That place where God manifested his special presence must not be made common. If none must come into the presence-chamber of an earthly king uncalled, no, not the queen herself, upon pain of death (Esth. iv. 11), was it not requisite that the same sacred respect should be paid to the King of kings? But see what a blessed change is made by the gospel of Christ; all good Christians have now *boldness to enter into the holiest,* through the veil, every day (Heb. x. 19, 20); and we *come boldly* (not as Aaron must, with fear and trembling) to the *throne of grace,* or mercy-seat, Heb. iv. 16. While the manifestations of God's presence and grace were sensible, it was requisite that they should thus be confined and upon the reserve, because the objects of sense the more familiar they are made the less awful or delightful they become; but now that they are purely spiritual it is otherwise, for the objects of faith the more they are conversed with the more do they manifest of their greatness and goodness: now therefore we are welcome to come at all times into the *holy place not made with hands,* for we are made to *sit together with Christ in heavenly places* by faith, Eph. ii. 6. Then Aaron must not come near at all times, *lest he die;* we now must come near at all times that we may live: it is distance only that is our death. Then God appeared in the cloud upon the mercy-seat, but now with open face we behold, not in a dark cloud, but in a clear glass, the glory of the Lord, 2 Cor. iii. 18.

III. The person to whom the work of this day was committed, and that was the high priest only: *Thus shall Aaron come into the holy place, v.* 3. He was to do all himself upon the day of atonement; only there was a second provided to be his substitute or supporter, in case any thing should befal him, either of sickness or ceremonial uncleanness, that he could not perform the service of the day. All Christians are spiritual priests, but Christ only is the high priest, and he alone it is that makes atonement, nor needed he either assistant or substitute.

IV. The attire of the high priest in this service. He was not to be dressed up in his rich garments that were peculiar to himself: he was not to put on the ephod, with the precious stones in it, but only the linen clothes which he wore in common with the inferior priests, v. 4. That meaner dress did best become him on this day of humiliation; and, being thinner and lighter, he would in it be more expedite for the work or service of the day, which was all to go through his hands. Christ, our high priest, made atonement for sin in our nature; not in the robes of his own peculiar glory, but the linen garments of our mortality, clean indeed, but mean.

5 And he shall take of the congregation of the children of Israel two kids of the goats for a sin offering, and one ram for a burnt offering. 6 And Aaron shall offer his bullock of the sin offering, which *is* for himself, and make an atonement for himself, and for his house. 7 And he shall take the two goats, and present them before the LORD *at* the door of the tabernacle of the congregation. 8 And Aaron shall cast lots upon the two goats; one lot for the LORD, and the other lot for the scapegoat. 9 And Aaron shall bring the goat upon which the LORD's lot fell, and offer him *for* a sin offering. 10 But the goat, on which the lot fell to be the scapegoat, shall be presented alive before the LORD, to make an atonement with him, *and* to let him go for a scapegoat into the wilderness. 11 And Aaron shall bring the bullock of the sin offering, which *is* for himself, and shall make an atonement for himself, and for his house, and shall kill the bullock of the sin offering which *is* for himself; 12 And he shall take a censer full of burning coals of fire from off the altar before the LORD, and his hands full of sweet incense beaten small, and bring *it* within the veil: 13 And he shall put the incense upon the fire before the LORD, that the cloud of the incense may cover the mercy seat that *is* upon the testimony, that he die not: 14 And he shall take of the blood of the bullock, and sprinkle *it* with his finger upon the mercy seat eastward; and before the mercy seat shall he sprinkle of the blood with his finger seven times.

The Jewish writers say that for seven days before the day of expiation the high priest was to retire from his own house, and to dwell in a chamber of the temple, that he might prepare himself for the service of this great day. During those seven days he himself did the work of the inferior priests about the sacrifices, incense, &c., that he might have his hand in for this day: he must have the institution read to him again and again, that he might be fully apprised of the whole method. 1. He was to begin the service of the day very early with the usual morning sacrifice, after he had first washed his whole body before he dressed himself, and his hands and feet again afterwards. He then burned the daily incense, dressed the lamps, and offered the extraordinary sacrifice appointed for this day (not here, but Num. xxix. 8), a bullock, a ram, and seven lambs, all for burnt-offerings. This he is supposed to have done in his high priest's garments. 2. He must now put off his rich robes, bathe himself, put on the linen garments, and present unto the Lord his own bullock, which was to be a sin-offering for himself and his house, v. 6. The bullock was set between the temple and the altar, and the offering of him mentioned in this verse was the making of a solemn confession of his sins and the sins of his house, earnestly praying for the forgiveness of them, and this with his hands on the head of the bullock. 3. He must then cast lots upon the two goats, which were to make (both together) one sin-offering for the congregation. One of these goats must be slain, in token of a satisfaction to be made to God's justice for sin, the other must be sent away, in token of the remission or dismission of sin by the mercy of God. Both must be presented together to God (v. 7) before the lot was cast upon them, and afterwards the scape-goat by itself, v. 10. Some think that goats were chosen for the sin-offering because, by the disagreeableness of their smell, the offensiveness of sin is represented: others think, because it was said that the demons which the heathens then worshipped often appeared to their worshippers in the form of goats, God therefore obliged his people to sacrifice goats, that they might never be tempted to sacrifice to goats. 4. The next thing to be done was to kill the bullock for the sin-offering for himself and his house, v. 11. "Now," say the Jews, "he must again put his hands on the head of the bullock, and repeat the confession and supplication he had before made, and kill the bullock with his own hands, to make atonement for himself first (for how could he make reconciliation for the sins of the people till he was himself first reconciled?) and for his house, not only his own family, but all the priests, who are called the *house of Aaron*," Ps. cxxxv. 19. This charity must begin at home, though it must not end there. The bullock being killed, he left one of the priests to stir the blood, that it might not thicken, and then, 5. He took a censer of burning coals (that would not smoke) in one hand, and a dish full of the sweet incense in the other, and then went into the holy of holies through the veil, went up towards the ark, set the coals down upon the floor, and scattered the incense upon them, so that the room was immediately filled with smoke. The Jews say that he was to go in *side-ways*, that he might not look directly upon the ark where the divine glory was, till it was covered with smoke; then he must come out *backwards*, out of reverence to the divine majesty; and, after a short prayer, he was to hasten out of the sanctuary, to show himself to the people, that they might not suspect that he had misbehaved himself and died before the Lord. 6. He then fetched the blood of the bullock from the priest whom he had left stirring it, and took that in with him the second time into the holy of holies, which was now filled with the smoke of the incense, and sprinkled with his finger of that blood upon, or rather towards, the mercy-seat, once over against the top of it and then seven times towards the lower part of it, *v.* 14. But the drops of blood (as the Jews expound it) all fell upon the ground, and none touched the mercy-seat. Having done this, he came out of the most holy place, set the basin of blood down in the sanctuary, and went out.

15 Then shall he kill the goat of the sin offering, that *is* for the people, and bring his blood within the veil, and do with that blood as he did with the blood of the bullock, and sprinkle it upon the mercy seat, and before the mercy seat: 16 And he shall make an atonement for the holy *place*, because of the uncleanness of the children of Israel, and because of their transgressions in all their sins: and so shall he do for the tabernacle of the congregation that remaineth among them in the midst of their uncleanness. 17 And there shall be no man in the tabernacle of the congregation when he goeth in to make an atonement in the holy *place*, until he come out, and have made an atonement for himself, and for his household, and for all the congregation of Israel. 18 And he shall go out unto the altar that *is* before the LORD, and make an atonement for it; and shall take of the blood of the bullock, and of the blood of the goat, and put *it* upon the horns of the altar round about. 19 And he shall sprinkle of the blood upon it with his finger seven times,

506

and cleanse it, and hallow it from the uncleanness of the children of Israel.

When the priest had come out from sprinkling the blood of the bullock before the mercy-seat, 1. He must next kill the goat which was the sin-offering for the people (*v.* 15) and go the third time into the holy of holies, to sprinkle the blood of the goat, as he had done that of the bullock; and thus he was to *make atonement for the holy place* (*v.* 16); that is, whereas the people by their sins had provoked God to take away those tokens of his favourable presence with them, and rendered even that holy place unfit to be the habitation of the holy God, atonement was hereby made for sin, that God, being reconciled to them, might continue with them. 2. He must then do the same for the outward part of the tabernacle that he had done for the inner room, by sprinkling the blood of the bullock first, and then that of the goat, without the veil, where the table and incense-altar stood, eight times each as before. The reason intimated is *because the tabernacle remained among them in the midst of their uncleanness*, *v.* 16. God would hereby show them how much their hearts needed to be purified, when even the tabernacle, only by standing in the midst of such an impure and sinful people, needed this expiation; and also that even their devotions and religious performances had much amiss in them, for which it was necessary that atonement should be made. During this solemnity, none of the inferior priests must come into the tabernacle (*v.* 17), but, by standing without, must own themselves unworthy and unfit to minister there, because their follies, and defects, and manifold impurities in their ministry, had made this expiation of the tabernacle necessary. 3. He must then put some of the blood, both of the bullock and of the goat mixed together, upon the horns of the altar that is before the Lord, *v.* 18, 19. It is certain that the altar of incense had this blood put upon it, for so it is expressly ordered (Exod. xxx. 10); but some think that this directs the high priest to the altar of burnt-offerings, for that also is here called the *altar before the Lord* (*v.* 12), because he is said to *go out* to it, and because it may be presumed that that also had need of an expiation; for to that the gifts and offerings of the children of Israel were all brought, from whose uncleanness the altar is here said to be hallowed.

20 And when he hath made an end of reconciling the holy *place*, and the tabernacle of the congregation, and the altar, he shall bring the live goat: 21 And Aaron shall lay both his hands upon the head of the live goat, and confess over him all the iniquities of the children of Israel, and all their

transgressions in all their sins, putting them upon the head of the goat, and shall send *him* away by the hand of a fit man into the wilderness : 22 And the goat shall bear upon him all their iniquities unto a land not inhabited : and he shall let go the goat in the wilderness. 23 And Aaron shall come into the tabernacle of the congregation, and shall put off the linen garments, which he put on when he went into the holy *place*, and shall leave them there : 24 And he shall wash his flesh with water in the holy place, and put on his garments, and come forth, and offer his burnt offering, and the burnt offering of the people, and make an atonement for himself, and for the people. 25 And the fat of the sin offering shall he burn upon the altar. 26 And he that let go the goat for the scapegoat shall wash his clothes, and bathe his flesh in water, and afterward come into the camp. 27 And the bullock *for* the sin offering, and the goat *for* the sin offering, whose blood was brought in to make atonement in the holy *place*, shall *one* carry forth without the camp ; and they shall burn in the fire their skins, and their flesh, and their dung. 28 And he that burneth them shall wash his clothes, and bathe his flesh in water, and afterward he shall come into the camp.

The high priest having presented unto the Lord the expiatory sacrifices, by the sprinkling of their blood, the remainder of which, it is probable, he poured out at the foot of the brazen altar, 1. He is next to confess the sins of Israel, with both his hands upon the head of the scape-goat (*v.* 20, 21); and whenever hands were imposed upon the head of any sacrifice it was always done with confession, according as the nature of the sacrifice was ; and, this being a sin-offering, it must be a confession of sin. In the latter and more degenerate ages of the Jewish church they had a set form of confession prepared for the high priest, but God here prescribed none ; for it might be supposed that the high priest was so well acquainted with the state of the people, and had such a tender concern for them, that he needed not any form. The confession must be as particular as he could make it, not only of *all the iniquities of the children of Israel*, but *all their transgressions in all their sins*. In one sin there may be many transgressions, from

the several aggravating circumstances of it ; and in our confessions we should take notice of them, and not only say, *I have sinned*, but, with Achan, "Thus and thus have I done." By this confession he must *put the sins of Israel upon the head of the goat ;* that is, exercising faith upon the divine appointment which constituted such a translation, he must transfer the punishment incurred from the sinners to the sacrifice, which would have been but a jest, nay, an affront to God, if he himself had not ordained it. 2. The goat was then to be sent away immediately by the hand of a fit person pitched upon for the purpose, into a wilderness, a land not inhabited ; and God allowed them to make this construction of it, that the sending away of the goat was the sending away of their sins, by a free and full remission : *He shall bear upon him all their iniquities, v.* 22. The losing of the goat was a sign to them that *the sins of Israel should be sought for, and not found,* Jer. l. 20. The later Jews had a custom to tie one shred of scarlet cloth to the horns of the goat and another to the gate of the temple, or to the top of the rock where the goat was lost, and they concluded that if it turned white, as they say it usually did, the sins of Israel were forgiven, as it is written, *Though your sins have been as scarlet, they shall be as wool :* and they add that for forty years before the destruction of Jerusalem by the Romans the scarlet cloth never changed colour at all, which is a fair confession that, having rejected the substance, the shadow stood them in no stead. 3. The high priest must then put off his linen garments in the tabernacle, and leave them there, the Jews say never to be worn again by himself or any other, for they made new ones every year ; and he must bathe himself in water, put on his rich clothes, and then offer both his own and the people's burnt-offerings, *v.* 23, 24. When we have the comfort of our pardon God must have the glory of it. If we have the benefit of the sacrifice of atonement, we must not grudge the sacrifices of acknowledgment. And, it should seem, the burning of the fat of the sin-offering was deferred till now (*v.* 25), that it might be consumed with the burnt-offerings. 4. The flesh of both those sin-offerings whose blood was taken within the veil was to be all burnt, not upon the altar, but at a distance without the camp, to signify both our putting away sin by true repentance, and the spirit of burning, and God's putting it away by a full remission, so that it shall never rise up in judgment against us. 5. He that took the scape-goat into the wilderness, and those that burned the sin-offering, were to be looked upon as ceremonially unclean, and must not come into the camp till they had washed their clothes and bathed their flesh in water, which signified the defiling nature of sin ; even the sacrifice which was but made sin was defiling :

also the imperfection of the legal sacrifices; they were so far from taking away sin that even *they* left some stain upon those that touched them.   6. When all this was done, the high priest went again into the most holy place to fetch his censer, and so returned to his own house with joy, because he had done his duty, and died not.

29 And *this* shall be a statute for ever unto you: *that* in the seventh month, on the tenth *day* of the month, ye shall afflict your souls, and do no work at all, *whether it be* one of your own country, or a stranger that sojourneth among you: 30 For on that day shall *the priest* make an atonement for you, to cleanse you, *that* ye may be clean from all your sins before the LORD. 31 It *shall be* a sabbath of rest unto you, and ye shall afflict your souls, by a statute for ever. 32 And the priest, whom he shall anoint, and whom he shall consecrate to minister in the priest's office in his father's stead, shall make the atonement, and shall put on the linen clothes, *even* the holy garments: 33 And he shall make an atonement for the holy sanctuary, and he shall make an atonement for the tabernacle of the congregation, and for the altar, and he shall make an atonement for the priests, and for all the people of the congregation. 34 And this shall be an everlasting statute unto you, to make an atonement for the children of Israel for all their sins once a year. And he did as the LORD commanded Moses.

I. We have here some additional directions in reference to this great solemnity, particularly,

1. The day appointed for this solemnity. It must be observed yearly on *the tenth day of the seventh month, v.* 29. The seventh had been reckoned the first month, till God appointed that the month in which the children of Israel came out of Egypt should thenceforward be accounted and called the first month. Some have fancied that this tenth day of the seventh month was the day of the year on which our first parents fell, and that it was kept as a fast in remembrance of their fall. Dr. Lightfoot computes that this was the day on which Moses came the last time down from the mount, when he brought with him the renewed tables, and the assurances of God's being reconciled to Israel, and his face shone: that day must be a day of atonement throughout their genera-
508

tions; for the remembrance of God's forgiving them their sin about the golden calf might encourage them to hope that, upon their repentance, he would forgive them all trespasses.

2. The duty of the people on this day. (1.) They must rest from all their labours: *It shall be a sabbath of rest, v.* 31. The work of the day was itself enough, and a good day's work if it was done well; therefore they must do no other work at all. The work of humiliation for sin requires such a close application of mind, and such a fixed engagement of the whole man; as will not allow us to turn aside to any other work. The day of atonement seems to be that sabbath spoken of by the prophet (Isa. lviii. 13), for it is the same with the fast spoken of in the verses before. (2.) They must afflict their souls. They must refrain from all bodily refreshments and delights, in token of inward humiliation and contrition of soul for their sins. They all fasted on this day from food (except the sick and children), and laid aside their ornaments, and did not anoint themselves, as Daniel, *ch.* x. 3, 12. *David chastened his soul with fasting,* Ps. xxxv. 13. And it signified the mortifying of sin and turning from it, *loosing the bands of wickedness,* Isa. lviii. 6, 7. The Jewish doctors advised that they should not on that day read those portions of scripture which were proper to affect them with delight and joy, because it was a day to afflict their souls.

3. The perpetuity of this institution: *It shall be a statute for ever, v.* 29, 34. It must not be intermitted any year, nor ever let fall till that constitution should be dissolved, and the type should be superseded by the antitype. As long as we are continually sinning, we must be continually repenting, and receiving the atonement. The law of afflicting our souls for sin is a statute for ever, which will continue in force till we arrive where all tears, even those of repentance, will be wiped from our eyes. The apostle observes it as an evidence of the insufficiency of the legal sacrifices to take away sin, and purge the conscience from it, that in them there was a *remembrance made of sin every year,* upon the day of atonement, Heb. x. 1—3. The annual repetition of the sacrifices showed that there was in them only a faint and feeble effort towards making atonement; it could be done effectually only by the *offering up of the body of Christ once for all,* and that once was sufficient; that sacrifice needed not to be repeated.

II. Let us see what there was of gospel in all this.

1. Here are typified the two great gospel privileges of the remission of sin and access to God, both which we owe to the mediation of our Lord Jesus. Here then let us see,

(1.) The expiation of guilt which Christ made for us. He is himself both the maker and the matter of the atonement; for he is,

[1.] The priest, the high priest, that *makes reconciliation for the sins of the people,* Heb. ii. 17. He, and he only, is *par negotio—fit for the work* and worthy of the honour: he is appointed by the Father to do it, who sanctified him, and sent him into the world for this purpose, that *God might in him reconcile the world to himself.* He undertook it, and for our sakes sanctified himself, and set himself apart for it, John xvii. 19. The high priest's frequently bathing himself on this day, and performing the service of it in fine linen clean and white, signified the holiness of the Lord Jesus, his perfect freedom from all sin, and his being beautified and adorned with all grace. No man was to be with the high priest when he made atonement (*v.* 17); for our Lord Jesus was to *tread the wine-press alone,* and of the people there must be *none with him* (Isa. lxiii. 3); therefore, when he entered upon his sufferings, *all his disciples forsook him and fled,* for if any of them had been taken and put to death with him it would have looked as if they had assisted in making the atonement; none but thieves, concerning whom there could be no such suspicion, must suffer with him. And observe what the extent of the atonement was which the high priest made : it was *for the holy sanctuary, for the tabernacle, for the altar, for the priests,* and *for all the people, v.* 33. Christ's satisfaction is that which atones for the sins both of ministers and people, the *iniquities of our holy* (and our unholy) *things;* the title we have to the privileges of ordinances, our comfort in them, and benefit by them, are all owing to the atonement Christ made. But, whereas the atonement which the high priest made pertained only to the congregation of Israel, Christ is the propitiation, not for their sins only, that are Jews, but for the sins of the whole Gentile world. And in this also Christ infinitely excelled Aaron, that Aaron needed to offer sacrifice for his own sin first, of which he was to make confession upon the head of his sin-offering; but our Lord Jesus had no sin of his own to answer for. *Such a high priest became us,* Heb. vii. 26. And therefore, when he was baptized in Jordan, whereas others stood in the water *confessing their sins* (Matt. iii. 6), he *went up straightway out of the water* (v. 16), having no sins to confess. [2.] As he is the high priest, so he is the sacrifice with which atonement is made ; for he is all in all in our reconciliation to God. Thus he was prefigured by the two goats, which both made one offering : the slain goat was a type of Christ dying for our sins, the scape-goat a type of Christ rising again for our justification. It was directed by lot, the disposal whereof was of the Lord, which goat should be slain; for Christ was delivered *by the determinate counsel and foreknowledge of God. First,* The atonement is said to be completed by putting the sins of Israel upon the head of the goat. They de-

served to have been abandoned and sent into a land of forgetfulness, but that punishment was here transferred to the goat that bore their sins, with reference to which God is said to have laid upon our Lord Jesus (the substance of all these shadows) *the iniquity of us all* (Isa. liii. 6), and he is said to have *borne our sins,* even the punishment of them, *in his own body upon the tree,* 1 Pet. ii. 24. Thus was he made sin for us, that is, a sacrifice for sin, 2 Cor. v. 21. He suffered and died, not only for our good, but in our stead, and was forsaken, and seemed to be forgotten for a time, that we might not be forsaken and forgotten for ever. Some learned men have computed that our Lord Jesus was baptized of John in Jordan upon the tenth day of the seventh month, which was the very day of atonement. Then he entered upon his office as Mediator, and was immediately *driven of the Spirit into the wilderness,* a land not inhabited. *Secondly,* The consequence of this was that all the iniquities of Israel were *carried into a land of forgetfulness.* Thus Christ, the Lamb of God, *takes away the sin of the world,* by taking it upon himself, John i. 29. And, when God forgives sin, he is said to remember it no more (Heb. viii. 12), *to cast it behind his back* (Isa. xxxviii. 17), *into the depths of the sea* (Mic. vii. 19), and to separate it *as far as the east is from the west,* Ps. ciii. 12.

(2.) The entrance into heaven which Christ made for us is here typified by the high priest's entrance into the most holy place. This the apostle has expounded (Heb. ix. 7, &c.), and he shows, [1.] That heaven is the holiest of all, but not of that building, and that the way into it by faith, hope, and prayer, through a Mediator, was not then so clearly manifested as it is to us now by the gospel. [2.] That Christ our high priest entered into heaven at his ascension once for all, and as a public person, in the name of all his spiritual Israel, and through the veil of his flesh, which was rent for that purpose, Heb. x. 20. [3.] That he entered *by his own blood* (Heb. ix. 12), taking with him to heaven the virtues of the sacrifice he offered on earth, and so sprinkling his blood, as it were, before the mercy-seat, where it speaks better things than the blood of bulls and goats could do. Hence he is said to appear in the midst of the throne as *a lamb that had been slain,* Rev. v. 6. And, though he had no sin of his own to expiate, yet it was by his own merit that he obtained for himself a restoration to his own ancient glory (John xvii. 4, 5), as well as an eternal redemption for us, Heb. ix. 12. [4.] The high priest in the holy place burned incense, which typified the intercession that Christ ever lives to make for us within the veil, in virtue of his satisfaction. And we could not expect to live, no, not before the mercy-seat, if it were not covered with the cloud of this incense. Mere mercy itself will not save us, without the interposition of a Mediator. The intercession of Christ is there set forth before God as incense, as *this incense.* And as the high priest interceded for himself first, then for his household, and then for all Israel, so our Lord Jesus, in the xviith of St. John (which was a specimen of the intercession he makes in heaven), recommended himself first to his Father, then his disciples who were his household, and then all that should believe on him through their word, as all Israel; and, having thus adverted to the uses and intentions of his offering, he was immediately seized and crucified, pursuant to these intentions. [5.] Herein the entry Christ made far exceeded Aaron's, that Aaron could not gain admission, no, not for his own sons, into the most holy place; but our Lord Jesus has consecrated for us also a *new and living way into the holiest,* so that we also have *boldness to enter,* Heb. x. 19, 20. [6.] The high priest was to come out again, but our Lord Jesus ever lives, making intercession, and always appears in the presence of God for us, whither as the forerunner he has for us entered, and where as agent he continues for us to reside.

2. Here are likewise typified the two great gospel duties of faith and repentance, by which we are qualified for the atonement, and come to be entitled to the benefit of it. (1.) By faith we must put our hands upon the head of the offering, relying on Christ as the Lord our Righteousness, pleading his satisfaction as that which was alone able to atone for our sins and procure us a pardon. " *Thou shalt answer, Lord, for me.* This is all I have to say for myself, *Christ has died, yea, rather has risen again;* to his grace and government I entirely submit myself, and in him I *receive the atonement,*" Rom. v. 11. (2.) By repentance we must afflict our souls; not only fasting for a time from the delights of the body, but inwardly sorrowing for our sins, and living a life of self-denial and mortification. We must also make a penitent confession of sin, and this with an eye to Christ, whom we have pierced, and mourning because of him; and with a hand of faith upon the atonement, assuring ourselves that, *if we confess our sins, God is faithful and just to forgive us our sins, and to cleanse us from all unrighteousness.*

Lastly, In the year of jubilee, the trumpet which proclaimed the liberty was ordered to be sounded in the close of the *day of atonement, ch.* xxv. 9. For the remission of our debt, release from our bondage, and our return to our inheritance, are all owing to the mediation and intercession of Jesus Christ. By the atonement we obtain rest for our souls, and all the glorious liberties of the children of God.

CHAP. XVII.

After the law concerning the atonement to be made for all Israel by the high priest, at the tabernacle, with the blood of bulls and goats, in this chapter we have two prohibitions necessary for the preservation of the honour of that atonement. I. That no sa-

crifice should be offered by any other than the priests, nor any where but at the door of the tabernacle, and this upon pain of death, ver. 1—9. II. That no blood should be eaten, and this under the same penalty, ver. 10, &c.

AND the Lord spake unto Moses, saying, 2 Speak unto Aaron, and unto his sons, and unto all the children of Israel, and say unto them; This *is* the thing which the Lord hath commanded, saying, 3 What man soever *there be* of the house of Israel, that killeth an ox, or lamb, or goat, in the camp, or that killeth *it* out of the camp, 4 And bringeth it not unto the door of the tabernacle of the congregation, to offer an offering unto the Lord before the tabernacle of the Lord; blood shall be imputed unto that man; he hath shed blood; and that man shall be cut off from among his people: 5 To the end that the children of Israel may bring their sacrifices, which they offer in the open field, even that they may bring them unto the Lord, unto the door of the tabernacle of the congregation, unto the priest, and offer them *for* peace offerings unto the Lord. 6 And the priest shall sprinkle the blood upon the altar of the Lord, *at* the door of the tabernacle of the congregation, and burn the fat for a sweet savour unto the Lord. 7 And they shall no more offer their sacrifices unto devils, after whom they have gone a whoring. This shall be a statute for ever unto them throughout their generations. 8 And thou shalt say unto them, Whatsoever man *there be* of the house of Israel, or of the strangers which sojourn among you, that offereth a burnt offering or sacrifice, 9 And bringeth it not unto the door of the tabernacle of the congregation, to offer it unto the Lord; even that man shall be cut off from among his people.

This statute obliged all the people of Israel to bring all their sacrifices to God's altar, to be offered there. And as to this matter we must consider,

I. How it stood before. 1. It was allowed to all people to build altars, and offer sacrifices to God, where they pleased. Wherever Abraham had a tent he built an altar, and every master of a family was a priest to his own family, as Job i. 5. 2. This liberty had been an occasion of idolatry. When every man was his own priest, and had an altar of his own, by degrees, as they became vain in their imaginations, they invented gods of their own, *and offered their sacrifices unto demons, v. 7.* The word signifies *rough* or *hairy goats*, because it is probable that in that shape the evil spirits often appeared to them, to invite their sacrifices and to signify their acceptance of them. For the devil, ever since he became a revolter from God and a rebel against him, has set up for a rival with him, and coveted to have divine honours paid him: he had the impudence to solicit our blessed Saviour to *fall down and worship him.* The Israelites themselves had learned in Egypt to sacrifice to demons. And some of them, it should seem, practised it even since the God of Israel had so gloriously appeared for them, and with them. They are said to *go a whoring after* these demons; for it was such a breach of their covenant with God as adultery is of the marriage covenant: and they were as strongly addicted to their idolatrous worships, and as hard to be reclaimed from them, as those that have given themselves over to fornication, to *work all uncleanness with greediness;* and therefore it is with reference to this that God calls himself *a jealous God.*

II. How this law settled it. 1. Some think that the children of Israel were by this law forbidden, while they were in the wilderness, to kill any beef, or mutton, or veal, or lamb, or goat, even for their common eating, but at the *door of the tabernacle,* where the blood and the fat were to be offered to God upon the altar, and the flesh to be returned back to the offerer to be eaten as a peace-offering, according to the law. And the statute is so worded (*v.* 3, 4) as to favour this opinion, for it speaks generally of killing any ox, or lamb, or goat. The learned Dr. Cudworth puts this sense upon it, and thinks that while they had their tabernacle so near them in the midst of their camp they ate no flesh but what had first been offered to God, but that when they were entering Canaan this constitution was altered (Deut. xii. 21), and they were allowed to kill their beasts of the flock and herd at home, as well as the roebuck and the hart; only thrice a year they were to see God at his tabernacle, and to eat and drink before him there. And it is probable that in the wilderness they did not eat much flesh but that of their peace-offerings, preserving what cattle they had, for breed, against they came to Canaan; therefore they murmured for flesh, being weary of manna; and Moses on that occasion speaks as if they were very sparing of the *flocks and the herds,* Num. xi. 4, 22. Yet it is hard to construe this as a temporary law, when it is expressly said to be a *statute for ever* (*v.* 7); and therefore, 2. It should seem rather to forbid only the killing of beasts for sacrifice any where but at God's altar. They must not offer sacrifice, as they had done, *in the open field*

(*v.* 5), no, not to the true God, but it must be brought to the priest, to be offered on the altar of the Lord: and the solemnity they had lately witnessed, of consecrating both the priests and the altar, would serve for a good reason why they should confine themselves to both these that God had so signally appointed and owned. This law obliged not only the Israelites themselves, but the proselytes or strangers that were circumcised and sojourned among them, who were in danger of retaining an affection to their old ways of worship. If any should transgress this law, and offer sacrifice any where but at the tabernacle, (1.) The guilt was great: *Blood shall be imputed to that man; he hath shed blood, v.* 4. Though it was but a beast he had killed, yet, killing it otherwise than God had appointed, he was looked upon as a murderer. It is by the divine grant that we have the liberty to kill the inferior creatures, to the benefit of which we are not entitled, unless we submit to the limitations of it, which are that it be not done either with cruelty or with superstition, Gen. ix. 3, 4. Nor was there ever any greater abuse done to the inferior creatures than when they were made either false gods or sacrifices to false gods, to which the apostle perhaps has special reference when he speaks of the vanity and bondage of corruption to which the creature was made subject, Rom. viii. 20, 21, compare *ch.* i. 23, 25. Idolatrous sacrifices were looked upon, not only as adultery, but as murder: he that *offereth them is as if he slew a man,* Isa. lxvi. 3. (2.) The punishment should be severe: *That man shall be cut off from among his people.* Either the magistrate must do it if it were manifest and notorious, or, if not, God would take the work into his own hands, and the offender should be cut off by some immediate stroke of divine justice. The reasons why God thus strictly ordered all their sacrifices to be offered at one place were, [1.] For the preventing of idolatry and superstition. That sacrifices might be offered to God, and according to the rule, and without innovations, they must always be offered by the hands of the priests, who were servants in God's house, and under the eye of the high priest, who was ruler of the house, and took care to see every thing done according to God's ordinance. [2.] For the securing of the honour of God's temple and altar, the peculiar dignity of which would be endangered if they might offer their sacrifices any where else as well as there. [3.] For the preserving of unity and brotherly love among the Israelites, that meeting all at one altar, as all the children of the family meet daily at one table, they might live and love as brethren, and be as one man, of one mind in the Lord.

III. How this law was observed. 1. While the Israelites kept their integrity they had a tender and very jealous regard to this law, as appears by their zeal against the altar which was erected by the two tribes and a half, which they would by no means have left standing if they had not been satisfied that it was never designed, nor should ever be used, for sacrifice or offering, Josh. xxii. 12, &c. 2. The breach of this law was for many ages the scandalous and incurable corruption of the Jewish church, witness that complaint which so often occurs in the history even of the good kings, *Howbeit the high places were not taken away;* and it was an inlet to the grossest idolatries. 3. Yet this law was, in extraordinary cases, dispensed with. Gideon's sacrifice (Judg. vi. 26), Manoah's (Judg. xiii. 19), Samuel's (1 Sam. vii. 9; ix. 13; xi. 15), David's (2 Sam. xxiv. 18), and Elijah's (1 Kings xviii. 23), were accepted, though not offered at the usual place: but these were all either ordered by angels or offered by prophets; and some think that after the desolation of Shiloh, and before the building of the temple, while the ark and altar were unsettled, it was more allowable to offer sacrifice elsewhere.

IV. How the matter stands now, and what use we are to make of this law. 1. It is certain that the spiritual sacrifices we are now to offer are not confined to any one place. Our Saviour has made this clear (John iv. 21), and the apostle (1 Tim. ii. 8), according to the prophecy, that *in every place incense should be offered,* Mal. i. 11. We have now no temple nor altar that sanctifies the gift, nor does the gospel unity lie in one place, but in one heart, and the *unity of the spirit.* 2. Christ is our altar, and the *true tabernacle* (Heb. viii. 2; xiii. 10); in him God dwells among us, and it is in him that our sacrifices are acceptable to God, and in him only, 1 Pet. ii. 5. To set up other mediators, or other altars, or other expiatory sacrifices, is, in effect, to set up other gods. He is the centre of unity, in whom all God's Israel meet. 3. Yet we are to have respect to the public worship of God, not *forsaking the assemblies* of his people, Heb. x. 25. The Lord loves *the gates of Zion more than all the dwellings of Jacob,* and so should we; see Ezek. xx. 40. Though God will graciously accept our family offerings, we must not therefore neglect the door of the tabernacle.

10 And whatsoever man *there be* of the house of Israel, or of the strangers that sojourn among you, that eateth any manner of blood; I will even set my face against that soul that eateth blood, and will cut him off from among his people. 11 For the life of the flesh *is* in the blood: and I have given it to you upon the altar to make an atonement for your souls: for it *is* the blood *that* maketh an atonement for the soul. 12 Therefore I said unto the children of Israel, No soul of you

shall eat blood, neither shall any stranger that sojourneth among you eat blood. 13 And whatsoever man *there be* of the children of Israel, or of the strangers that sojourn among you, which hunteth and catcheth any beast or fowl that may be eaten; he shall even pour out the blood thereof, and cover it with dust. 14 For *it is* the life of all flesh; the blood of it *is* for the life thereof: therefore I said unto the children of Israel, Ye shall eat the blood of no manner of flesh: for the life of all flesh *is* the blood thereof: whosoever eateth it shall be cut off. 15 And every soul that eateth that which died *of itself,* or that which was torn *with beasts, whether it be* one of your own country, or a stranger, he shall both wash his clothes, and bathe *himself* in water, and be unclean until the even: then shall he be clean. 16 But if he wash *them* not, nor bathe his flesh; then he shall bear his iniquity.

We have here, I. A repetition and confirmation of the law against eating blood. We have met with this prohibition twice before in the levitical law (*ch.* iii. 17; vii. 26), besides the place it had in the precepts of Noah, Gen. ix. 4. But here, 1. The prohibition is repeated again and again, and reference had to the former laws to this purport (*v.* 12): *I said to the children of Israel, No soul of you shall eat blood;* and again (*v.* 14), *You shall eat the blood of no manner of flesh.* A great stress is laid upon it, as a law which has more in it than at first view one would think. 2. It is made binding, not only on the *house of Israel,* but on *the strangers that sojourned among them* (*v.* 10), which perhaps was one reason why it was thought advisable, for a time, to forbid blood to the Gentile converts, Acts xv. 29. 3. The penalty annexed to this law is very severe (*v.* 10): *I will even set my face against that soul that eateth blood,* if he do it presumptuously, and *will cut him off;* and again (*v.* 14), *He shall be cut off.* Note, God's wrath will be the sinner's ruin. Write that man undone, for ever undone, against whom God sets his face; for 'what creature is able to confront the Creator? 4. A reason is given for this law (*v.* 11): because *it is the blood that makes atonement for the soul;* and *therefore* it was appointed to make atonement with, because *the life of the flesh is the blood.* The sinner deserved to die; therefore the sacrifice must die. Now, the blood being so the life that ordinarily beasts were killed for man's use by the drawing out of all their blood, God appointed the sprinkling or pouring out of the blood of the sacrifice upon the altar to signify that the life of the sacrifice was given to God instead of the sinner's life, and as a ransom or counter-price for it; therefore *without shedding of blood there was no remission,* Heb. ix. 22. For this reason they must eat no blood, and, (1.) It was then a very good reason; for God would by this means preserve the honour of that way of atonement which he had instituted, and keep up in the minds of the people a reverent regard to it. The blood of the covenant being then a sensible object, no blood must be either eaten or trodden under foot as a common thing, as they must have no ointment nor perfume like that which God ordered them to make for himself. But, (2.) This reason is now superseded, which intimates that the law itself was ceremonial, and is now no longer in force: the blood of Christ who has come (and we are to look for no other) is that alone which makes atonement for the soul, and of which the blood of the sacrifices was an imperfect type: the coming of the substance supersedes the shadow. The blood of beasts is no longer the ransom, but Christ's blood only; and therefore there is not now that reason for abstaining from blood which there was then, and we cannot suppose it was the will of God that the law should survive the reason of it. The blood, provided it be so prepared as not to be unwholesome, is now allowed for the nourishment of our bodies, because it is no longer appointed to make an atonement for the soul. (3.) Yet it has still a useful significancy. The life is in the blood; it is the vehicle of the animal spirits, and God would have his people to regard the life even of their beasts, and not to be cruel and hard-hearted, not to take delight in any thing that is barbarous. They must not be a blood-thirsty people. The blood then made atonement figuratively, now the blood of Christ makes atonement really and effectually; to this therefore we must have a reverent regard, and not use it as *a common thing,* for he will set his face against those that do so, and they shall be cut off, Heb. x. 29.

II. Some other precepts are here given as appendages to this law, and hedges about it. 1. They must cover the blood of that which they *took in hunting,* v. 13. They must not only not eat it, but must give it a decent burial, in token of some mystery which they must believe lay hidden in this constitution. The Jews look upon this as a very weighty precept and appoint that the blood should be covered with these words, *Blessed be he that hath sanctified us by his precepts, and commanded us to cover blood.* 2. They must not eat that which *died of itself* or was *torn of beasts* (v. 15), for the blood was either not at all, or not regularly, drawn out of them. God would have them to be curious in their diet, not with the curiosity that gratifies the

sensual appetite, but with that which checks and restrains it. God would not have his children to eat every thing that came in their way with greediness, but to consider diligently what was before them, that they might learn in other things to ask questions for conscience' sake. Those that *flew upon the spoil* sinned, 1 Sam. xiv. 32, 33. If a man did, through ignorance or inconsideration, eat the flesh of any beast not duly slain, he must *wash himself and his clothes,* else he bore his iniquity, v. 15, 16. The pollution was ceremonial, so was the purification from it; but if a man slighted the prescribed method of cleansing, or would not submit to it, he thereby contracted moral guilt. See the nature of a remedial law: he that obeys it has the benefit of it; he that does not, not only remains under his former guilt, but adds to that the guilt of contemning the provisions made by divine grace for his relief, and sins against the remedy.

CHAP. XVIII.

Here is, I. A general law against all conformity to the corrupt usages of the heathen, ver. 1—5. II. Particular laws, 1. Against incest, ver. 6—18. 2. Against beastly lusts, and barbarous idolatries, ver. 19—23. III. The enforcement of these laws from the ruin of the Canaanites, ver. 24—30.

AND the LORD spake unto Moses, saying, 2 Speak unto the children of Israel, and say unto them, I am the LORD your God. 3 After the doings of the land of Egypt, wherein ye dwelt, shall ye not do: and after the doings of the land of Canaan, whither I bring you, shall ye not do: neither shall ye walk in their ordinances. 4 Ye shall do my judgments, and keep mine ordinances, to walk therein: I *am* the LORD your God. 5 Ye shall therefore keep my statutes, and my judgments: which if a man do, he shall live in them: I *am* the LORD.

After divers ceremonial institutions, God here returns to the enforcement of moral precepts. The former are still of use to us as types, the latter still binding as laws. We have here, 1. The sacred authority by which these laws are enacted: *I am the Lord your God* (v. 1, 4, 30), and *I am the Lord,* v. 5, 6, 21. "The Lord, who has a right to rule all; your God, who has a peculiar right to rule you." Jehovah is the fountain of being, and therefore the fountain of power, whose we are, whom we are bound to serve, and who is able to punish all disobedience. "Your God to whom you have consented, in whom you are happy, to whom you lie under the highest obligations imaginable, and to whom you are accountable." 2. A strict caution to take heed of retaining the relics of the idolatries of Egypt, where they had dwelt, and of receiving the infection of the idolatries of Canaan, whither they were now going, v. 3. Now that God was by Moses teaching them his ordinances there was *aliquid dediscen-*

dum—something to be unlearned, which they had sucked in with their milk in Egypt, a country noted for idolatry : *You shall not do after the doings of the land of Egypt.* It would be the greatest absurdity in itself to retain such an affection for their house of bondage as to be governed in their devotions by the usages of it, and the greatest ingratitude to God, who had so wonderfully and graciously delivered them. Nay, as if governed by a spirit of contradiction, they would be in danger, even after they had received these ordinances of God, of admitting the wicked usages of the Canaanites and of inheriting their vices with their land. Of this danger they are here warned, *You shall not walk in their ordinances.* Such a tyrant is custom that their practices are called *ordinances,* and they became rivals even with God's ordinances, and God's professing people were in danger of receiving law from them. 3. A solemn charge to them to *keep God's judgments, statutes, and ordinances, v.* 4, 5. To this charge, and many similar ones, David seems to refer in the many prayers and professions he makes relating to God's laws in the 119th Psalm. Observe here, (1.) The great rule of our obedience—God's statutes and judgments. These we must *keep to walk therein.* We must keep them in our books, and keep them in our hands, that we may practise them in our hearts and lives. *Remember God's commandments to do them,* Ps. ciii. 18. We must keep in them as our way to travel in, keep to them as our rule to work by, keep them as our treasure, as the apple of our eye, with the utmost care and value. (2.) The great advantage of our obedience : *Which if a man do, he shall live in them,* that is, "he shall be happy here and hereafter." We have reason to thank God, [1.] That this is still in force as a promise, with a very favourable construction of the condition. If we keep God's commandments in sincerity, though we come short of sinless perfection, we shall find that the way of duty is the way of comfort, and will be the way to happiness. Godliness has the *promise of life,* 1 Tim. iv. 8. Wisdom has said, *Keep my commandments and live :* and *if through the Spirit we mortify the deeds of the body* (which are to us as the usages of Egypt were to Israel) *we shall live.* [2.] That it is not so in force in the nature of a covenant as that the least transgression shall for ever exclude us from this life. The apostle quotes this twice as opposite to the faith which the gospel reveals. It is the description of the *righteousness which is by the law, the man that doeth them shall live ἐν αὐτοῖς—in them* (Rom. x. 5), and is urged to prove that *the law is not of faith,* Gal. iii. 12. The alteration which the gospel has made is in the last word : still *the man that does them shall live,* but not live *in them ;* for the law could not give life, because we could not perfectly keep it ; it was *weak through the flesh,* not in itself ; but now *the man that does* 514

them shall *live by the faith of the Son of God.* He shall owe his life to the grace of Christ, and not to the merit of his own works ; see Gal. iii. 21, 22. *The just shall live,* but they shall live *by faith,* by virtue of their union with Christ, who is their life.

6 None of you shall approach to any that is near of kin to him, to uncover *their* nakedness : I *am* the LORD. 7 The nakedness of thy father, or the nakedness of thy mother, shalt thou not uncover : she *is* thy mother ; thou shalt not uncover her nakedness. 8 The nakedness of thy father's wife shalt thou not uncover : it *is* thy father's nakedness. 9 The nakedness of thy sister, the daughter of thy father, or daughter of thy mother, *whether she be* born at home, or born abroad, *even* their nakedness thou shalt not uncover. 10 The nakedness of thy son's daughter, or of thy daughter's daughter, *even* their nakedness thou shalt not uncover : for their's *is* thine own nakedness. 11 The nakedness of thy father's wife's daughter, begotten of thy father, she *is* thy sister, thou shalt not uncover her nakedness. 12 Thou shalt not uncover the nakedness of thy father's sister : she *is* thy father's near kinswoman. 13 Thou shalt not uncover the nakedness of thy mother's sister : for she *is* thy mother's near kinswoman. 14 Thou shalt not uncover the nakedness of thy father's brother, thou shalt not approach to his wife : she *is* thine aunt. 15 Thou shalt not uncover the nakedness of thy daughter in law : she *is* thy son's wife ; thou shalt not uncover her nakedness. 16 Thou shalt not uncover the nakedness of thy brother's wife : it *is* thy brother's nakedness. 17 Thou shalt not uncover the nakedness of a woman and her daughter, neither shalt thou take her son's daughter, or her daughter's daughter, to uncover her nakedness ; *for* they *are* her near kinswomen : it *is* wickedness. 18 Neither shalt thou take a wife to her sister, to vex *her,* to uncover her nakedness, beside the other in her life *time.*

These laws relate to the seventh commandment, and, no doubt, are obligatory on us under the gospel, for they are consonant to the very light and law of nature : one of the articles, that of a man's having his father's wife, the apostle speaks of as a sin *not so much as named among the Gentiles*, 1 Cor. v. 1. Though some of the incests here forbidden were practised by some particular persons among the heathen, yet they were disallowed and detested, unless among those nations who had become barbarous, and were quite given up to vile affections. Observe,

I. That which is forbidden as to the relations here specified is *approaching to them to uncover their nakedness, v.* 6.

1. It is chiefly intended to forbid the marrying of any of these relations. Marriage is a divine institution ; this and the sabbath, the eldest of all, of equal standing with man upon the earth : it is intended for the comfort of human life, and the decent and honourable propagation of the human race, such as became the dignity of man's nature above that of the beasts. It is *honourable in all*, and these laws are for the support of the honour of it. It was requisite that a divine ordinance should be subject to divine rules and restraints, especially because it concerns a thing wherein the corrupt nature of man is as apt as in any thing to be wilful and impetuous in its desires, and impatient of check. Yet these prohibitions, besides their being enacted by an incontestable authority, are in themselves highly reasonable and equitable. (1.) By marriage two were to become one flesh, therefore those that before were in a sense one flesh by nature could not, without the greatest absurdity, become one flesh by institution ; for the institution was designed to unite those who before were not united. (2.) Marriage puts an equality between husband and wife. "Is she not thy companion taken out of thy side?" Therefore, if those who before were superior and inferior should intermarry (which is the case in most of the instances here laid down), the order of nature would be taken away by a positive institution, which must by no means be allowed. The inequality between master and servant, noble and ignoble, is founded in consent and custom, and there is no harm done if that be taken away by the equality of marriage ; but the inequality between parents and children, uncles and nieces, aunts and nephews, either by blood or marriage, is founded in nature, and is therefore perpetual, and cannot without confusion be taken away by the equality of marriage, the institution of which, though ancient, is subsequent to the order of nature. (3.) No relations that are equals are forbidden, except brothers and sisters, by the whole blood or half blood, or by marriage ; and in this there is not the same natural absurdity as in the former, for Adam's sons must of necessity have married their own sisters ; but it was requisite that it should be made by a positive law unlawful and detestable, for the preventing of sinful familiarities between those that in the days of

their youth are supposed to live in a house together, and yet cannot intermarry without defeating one of the intentions of marriage, which is the enlargement of friendship and interest. If every man married his own sister (as they would be apt to do from generation to generation if it were lawful), each family would be a world to itself, and it would be forgotten that *we are members one of another*. It is certain that this has always been looked upon by the more sober heathen as a most infamous and abominable thing ; and those who had not this law yet were herein a law to themselves. The making use of the ordinance of marriage for the patronising of incestuous mixtures is so far from justifying them, or extenuating their guilt, that it adds the guilt of profaning an ordinance of God, and prostituting that to the vilest of purposes which was instituted for the noblest ends. But,

2. Uncleanness, committed with any of these relations out of marriage, is likewise, without doubt, forbidden here, and no less intended than the former : as also all lascivious carriage, wanton dalliance, and every thing that has the appearance of this evil Relations must love one another, and are to have free and familiar converse with each other, but it must be with all purity ; and the less it is suspected of evil by others the more care ought the persons themselves to take that *Satan do not get advantage against them*, for he is a very subtle enemy, and seeks all occasions against us.

II. The relations forbidden are most of them plainly described ; and it is generally laid down as a rule that what relations of a man's own he is bound up from marrying the same relations of his wife he is likewise forbidden to marry, for they two are one. That law which forbids marrying a brother's wife (*v.* 16) had an exception peculiar to the Jewish state, that, if a man died without issue, his brother or next of kin should marry the widow, and raise up seed to the deceased (Deut. xxv. 5), for reasons which held good only in that commonwealth ; and therefore now that those reasons have ceased the exception ceases, and the law is in force, that a man must in no case marry his brother's widow. That article (*v.* 18) which forbids a man to *take a wife to her sister* supposes a connivance at polygamy, as some other laws then did (Exod. xxi. 10 ; Deut. xxi. 15), but forbids a man's marrying two sisters, as Jacob did, because between those who had before been equal there would be apt to arise greater jealousies and animosities than between wives that were not so nearly related. If the sister of the wife be taken for the concubine, or secondary wife, nothing can be more vexing in her life, or as long as she lives.

19 Also thou shalt not approach unto a woman to uncover her nakedness, as long as she is put apart for

her uncleanness. 20 Moreover thou shalt not lie carnally with thy neighbour's wife, to defile thyself with her. 21 And thou shalt not let any of thy seed pass through *the fire* to Molech, neither shalt thou profane the name of thy God: I *am* the LORD. 22 Thou shalt not lie with mankind, as with womankind: it *is* abomination. 23 Neither shalt thou lie with any beast to defile thyself therewith: neither shall any woman stand before a beast to lie down thereto; it *is* confusion. 24 Defile not ye yourselves in any of these things: for in all these the nations are defiled which I cast out before you: 25 And the land is defiled: therefore I do visit the iniquity thereof upon it, and the land itself vomiteth out her inhabitants. 26 Ye shall therefore keep my statutes and my judgments, and shall not commit *any* of these abominations; *neither* any of your own nation, nor any stranger that sojourneth among you: 27 (For all these abominations have the men of the land done, which *were* before you, and the land is defiled;) 28 That the land spue not you out also, when ye defile it, as it spued out the nations that *were* before you. 29 For whosoever shall commit any of these abominations, even the souls that commit *them* shall be cut off from among their people. 30 Therefore shall ye keep mine ordinance, that *ye* commit not *any one* of these abominable customs, which were committed before you, and that ye defile not yourselves therein: I *am* the LORD your God.

Here is, I. A law to preserve the honour of the marriage-bed, that it should not be unseasonably used (*v.* 19), nor invaded by an adulterer, *v.* 20.

II. A law against that which was the most unnatural idolatry, causing their children to *pass through the fire to Moloch, v.* 21. Moloch (as some think) was the idol in and by which they worshipped the sun, that great fire of the world; and therefore in the worship of it they made their own children either sacrifices to this idol, burning them to death before it, or devotees to it, causing them to pass between two fires, as some think, or to be thrown through one, to the honour of this pretended deity, imagining that the
516

consecrating of but one of their children in this manner to Moloch would procure good fortune for all the rest of their children. Did idolaters thus give their own children to false gods, and shall we think any thing too dear to be dedicated to, or to be parted with for, the true God? See how this sin of Israel (which they were afterwards guilty of, notwithstanding this law) is aggravated by the relation which they and their children stood in to God. Ezek. xvi. 20, *Thou hast taken thy sons and thy daughters, whom thou hast borne unto me, and these thou hast sacrificed.* Therefore it is here called *profaning the name of their* God; for it looked as if they thought they were under greater obligations to Moloch than to Jehovah; for to him they offered their cattle only, but to Moloch their children.

III. A law against unnatural lusts, sodomy and bestiality, sins not to be named nor thought of without the utmost abhorrence imaginable, *v.* 22, 23. Other sins level men with the beasts, but these sink them much lower. That ever there should have been occasion for the making of these laws, and that since they are published they should ever have been broken, is the perpetual reproach and scandal of human nature; and the giving of men up to these vile affections was frequently the punishment of their idolatries; so the apostle shows, Rom. i. 24.

IV. Arguments against these and the like abominable wickednesses. He that has an indisputable right to command us, yet because he will deal with us as men, and *draw with the cords of a man,* condescends to reason with us. 1. Sinners defile themselves with these abominations: *Defile not yourselves in any of these things, v.* 24. All sin is defiling to the conscience, but these are sins that have a peculiar turpitude in them. Our heavenly Father, in kindness to us, requires of us that we keep ourselves clean, and do not wallow in the dirt. 2. *The souls that commit them shall be cut off, v.* 29. And justly; for, *if any man defile the temple of God, him shall God destroy,* 1 Cor. iii. 17. Fleshly lusts war against the soul, and will certainly be the ruin of it if God's mercy and grace prevent not. 3. *The land is defiled, v.* 25. If such wickednesses as these be practised and connived at, the land is thereby made unfit to have God's tabernacle in it, and the pure and holy God will withdraw the tokens of his gracious presence from it. It is also rendered unwholesome to the inhabitants, who are hereby infected with sin and exposed to plagues· and it is really nauseous and loathsome to all good men in it, as the wickedness of Sodom was to the soul of righteous Lot. 4. These have been the abominations of the former inhabitants, *v.* 24, 27. Therefore it was necessary that these laws should be made, as antidotes and preservatives from the plague are necessary when we go into an infected place. And therefore they should not practise any such things, because the nations that had practised them now lay under the curse of God, and were shortly to fall by the sword of Israel. They could not but be sensible how odious those people had made themselves who wallowed in this mire, and how they stank in the nostrils of all good men; and shall a people sanctified and dignified as Israel was make themselves thus vile? When we observe how ill sin looks in others we should use this as an argument with ourselves with the utmost care and caution to preserve our purity. 5. For these and the like sins the Canaanites were to be destroyed; these filled the measure of the Amorites' iniquity (Gen. xv. 16), and brought down that destruction of so many populous kingdoms which the Israelites were now shortly to be not only the spectators, but the instruments of: *Therefore I do visit the iniquity thereof upon it, v.* 25. Note, The tremendous judgments of God, executed on those that are daringly profane and atheistical, are intended as warnings to those who profess religion to take heed of every thing that has the least appearance of, or tendency towards, profaneness or atheism. Even the ruin of the Canaanites is an admonition to the Israelites not to do like them. Nay, to show that not only the Creator is provoked, but the creation burdened, by such abominations as these, it is added (*v.* 25), *The land itself vomiteth out her inhabitants.* The very ground they went upon did, as it were, groan under them, and was sick of them, and not easy till it had discharged itself of these *enemies of the Lord,* Isa. i. 24. This bespeaks the extreme loathsomeness of sin; sinful man indeed *drinks in iniquity like water,* but the harmless part of the creation even heaves at it, and rises against it. Many a house and many a town have spued out the wicked inhabitants, as it were, with abhorrence, Rev. iii. 16. Therefore take heed, saith God, *that the land spue not you out also, v.* 28. It was secured to them, and entailed upon them, and yet they must expect that, if they made the vices of the Canaanites their own, with their land their fate would be the same. Note, Wicked Israelites are as abominable to God as wicked Canaanites, and more so, and will be as soon spued out, or sooner. Such a warning as was here given to the Israelites is given by the apostle to the Gentile converts, with reference to the rejected Jews, in whose room they were substituted (Rom. xi. 19, &c.); they must take heed of falling *after the same example of unbelief,* Heb. iv. 11. Apply it more generally; and let it deter us effectually from all sinful courses to consider how many they have been the ruin of. Lay the ear of faith to the gates of the bottomless pit, and hear the doleful shrieks and outcries of damned sinners, whom earth has spued out and hell has swallowed, that find themselves undone, for ever undone, by sin; and tremble lest this be your portion at last. God's

threatenings and judgments should frighten us from sin. V. The chapter concludes with a sovereign antidote against this infection: *Therefore you shall keep my ordinance that you commit not any one of these abominable customs, v.* 30. This is the remedy prescribed. Note, 1. Sinful customs are abominable customs, and their being common and fashionable does not make them at all the less abominable nor should we the less abominate them, but the more; because the more customary they are the more dangerous they are. 2. It is of pernicious consequence to admit and allow of any one sinful custom, because one will make way for many. *Uno absurdo dato, mille sequuntur—Admit but a single absurdity, you invite a thousand.* The way of sin is downhill. 3. A close and constant adherence to God's ordinances is the most effectual preservative from the infection of gross sin. The more we taste of the sweetness and feel of the power of holy ordinances the less inclination we shall have to the forbidden pleasures of sinners' abominable customs. It is the grace of God only that will secure us, and that grace is to be expected only in the use of the means of grace. Nor does God ever leave any to their own hearts' lusts till they have first left him and his institutions.

CHAP. XIX.

Some ceremonial precepts there are in this chapter, but most of them are moral. One would wonder that when some of the lighter matters of the law are greatly enlarged upon (witness two long chapters concerning the leprosy) many of the weightier matters are put into a little compass: divers of the single verses of this chapter contain whole laws concerning judgment and mercy; for these are things which are manifest in every man's conscience; men's own thoughts are able to explain these, and to comment upon them. 1. The laws of this chapter, which were peculiar to the Jews, are, 1. Concerning their peace-offerings, ver. 5—8. 2. Concerning the gleanings of their fields, ver. 9, 10. 3. Against mixtures of their cattle, seed, and cloth, ver. 19. 4. Concerning their trees, ver. 23—25. 5. Against some superstitious usages, ver. 26—28. But, II. Most of these precepts are binding on us, for they are expositions of most of the ten commandments. 1. Here is the preface to the ten commandments, "I am the Lord," repeated fifteen times. 2. A sum of the ten commandments. All the first table in this, "Be you holy," ver. 2. All the second table in this, "Thou shalt love thy neighbour" (ver. 18), and an answer to the question, "Who is my neighbour?" ver. 33, 34. 3. Something of each commandment. (1.) The first commandment implied in that which is often repeated here, "I am your God." And here is a prohibition of enchantment (ver. 26) and witchcraft (ver. 31), which make a god of the devil. (2.) Idolatry, against the second commandment, is forbidden, ver. 4. (3.) Profanation of God's name, against the third, ver. 12. (4.) Sabbath-sanctification is pressed, ver. 3, 30. (5.) Children are required to honour their parents (ver. 3), and the aged, ver. 32. (6.) Hatred and revenge are here forbidden, against the sixth commandment, ver. 17, 18. (7.) Adultery (ver. 20—22), and whoredom, ver. 29. (8.) Justice is here required in judgment (ver. 15), theft forbidden (ver. 11), fraud and withholding dues (ver. 13), and false weights, ver. 35, 36. (9.) Lying, ver. 11. Slandering, ver. 14 Tale-bearing, and false-witness bearing, ver. 16. (10.) The tenth commandment laying a restraint upon the heart, so does that (ver. 17), "Thou shalt not hate thy brother in thy heart." And here is a solemn charge to observe all these statutes, ver. 37. Now these are things which need not much help for the understanding of them, but require constant care and watchfulness for the observing of them. "A good understanding have all they that do these commandments."

AND the LORD spake unto Moses, saying, 2 Speak unto all the congregation of the children of Israel, and say unto them, Ye shall be holy: for I the LORD your God *am* holy. 3 Ye shall fear every man his mother, and his father, and keep my sabbaths: I *am* the LORD your God. 4 Turn ye not unto idols, nor make to yourselves molten gods : I *am* the LORD your God. 5 And if ye offer a sacrifice of peace offerings unto the LORD, ye shall offer it at your own will. 6 It shall be eaten the same day ye offer it, and on the morrow : and if aught remain until the third day, it shall be burnt in the fire. 7 And if it be eaten at all on the third day, it *is* abominable ; it shall not be accepted. 8 Therefore *every* one that eateth it shall bear his iniquity, because he hath profaned the hallowed thing of the LORD : and that soul shall be cut off from among his people. 9 And when ye reap the harvest of your land, thou shalt not wholly reap the corners of thy field, neither shalt thou gather the gleanings of thy harvest. 10 And thou shalt not glean thy vineyard, neither shalt thou gather *every* grape of thy vineyard ; thou shalt leave them for the poor and stranger : I *am* the LORD your God.

Moses is ordered to deliver the summary of the laws *to all the congregation of the children of Israel* (*v.* 2); not to Aaron and his sons only, but to all the people, for they were all concerned to know their duty. Even in the darker ages of the law, that religion could not be of God which boasted of ignorance as its mother. Moses must make known God's statutes to all the congregation, and proclaim them through the camp. These laws, it is probable, he delivered himself to as many of the people as could be within hearing at once, and so by degrees at several times to them all. Many of the precepts here given they had received before, but it was requisite that they should be repeated, that they might be remembered. Precept must be upon precept, and line upon line, and all little enough. In these verses,

I. It is required that Israel be a holy people, because the God of Israel is a holy God, *v.* 2. Their being distinguished from all other people by peculiar laws and customs was intended to teach them a real separation from the world and the flesh, and an entire devotedness to God. And this is now the law of Christ (the Lord bring every thought within us into obedience to it!) *You shall be holy, for I am holy,* 1 Pet. i. 15, 16. We are the followers of the holy Jesus, and therefore must be, according to our capacity, consecrated to God's honour, and conformed to his nature and will. Israel was sanctified by the types and shadows (*ch.* xx. 8), but we are *sanctified by the truth,* or substance of all those shadows, John xvii. 17 ; Tit. ii. 14.
518

II. That children be obedient to their parents : " *You shall fear every man his mother and his father, v.* 3. 1. The fear here required is the same with the honour commanded by the fifth commandment ; see Mal. i. 6. It includes inward reverence and esteem, outward expressions of respect, obedience to the lawful commands of parents, care and endeavour to please them and make them easy, and to avoid every thing that may offend and grieve them, and incur their displeasure. The Jewish doctors ask, " What is this fear that is owing to a father ?" And they answer, " It is not to stand in his way nor to sit in his place, not to contradict what he says nor to carp at it, not to call him by his name, either living or dead, but 'My Father,' or ' Sir ;' it is to provide for him if he be poor, and the like." 2. Children, when they grow up to be men, must not think themselves discharged from this duty : every man, though he be a wise man, and a great man, yet must reverence his parents, because they are his parents. 3. The mother is put first, which is not usual, to show that the duty is equally owing to both ; if the mother survive the father, still she must be reverenced and obeyed. 4. It is added, *and keep my sabbaths.* If God provides by his law for the preserving of the honour of parents, parents must use their authority over their children for the preserving of the honour of God, particularly the honour of his sabbaths, the custody of which is very much committed to parents by the fourth commandment, *Thou, and thy son, and thy daughter.* The ruin of young people has often been observed to begin in the contempt of their parents and the profanation of the sabbath day. Fitly therefore are these two precepts here put together in the beginning of this abridgment of the statutes : " *You shall fear, every man, his mother and his father, and keep my sabbaths.* Those are hopeful children, and likely to do well, that make conscience of honouring their parents and keeping holy the sabbath day. 5. The reason added to both these precepts is, " *I am the Lord your God ;* the Lord of the sabbath and the God of your parents."

III. That God only be worshipped, and not by images (*v.* 4) : " *Turn you not to idols,* to *Elilim,* to vanities, things of no power, no value, gods that are no gods. Turn not from the true God to false ones, from the mighty God to impotent ones, from the God that will make you holy and happy to those that will deceive you, debauch you, ruin you, and make you for ever miserable. Turn not your eye to them, much less your heart. *Make not to yourselves gods,* the creatures of your own fancy, nor think to worship the Creator by molten gods. You are the work of God's hands, be not so absurd as to worship gods *the work of your own hands.*" Molten gods are specified for the sake of the molten calf.

IV. That the sacrifices of their peace-offerings should always be offered, and eaten, according to the law, *v.* 5—8. There was some particular reason, it is likely, for the repetition of this law rather than any other relating to the sacrifices. The eating of the peace-offerings was the people's part, and was done from under the eye of the priests, and perhaps some of them had kept the cold meat of their peace-offerings, as they had done the manna (Exod. xvi. 20), longer than was appointed, which occasioned this caution; see the law itself before, *ch.* vii. 16—18. God will have his own work done in his own time. Though the sacrifice was offered according to the law, if it was not eaten according to the law, it was not accepted. Though ministers do their part, what the better if people do not theirs? There is work to be done after our spiritual sacrifices, in a due improvement of them; and, if this be neglected, all is in vain.

V. That they should leave the gleanings of their harvest and vintage for the poor, *v.* 9, 10. Note, Works of piety must be always attended with works of charity, according as our ability is. When they gathered in their corn, they must leave some standing in the corner of the field; the Jewish doctors say, "It should be a sixtieth part of the field;" and they must also leave the gleanings and the small clusters of their grapes, which at first were overlooked. This law, though not binding now in the letter of it, yet teaches us, 1. That we must not be covetous and griping, and greedy of every thing we can lay any claim to; nor insist upon our right in things small and trivial. 2. That we must be well pleased to see the poor supplied and refreshed with the fruit of our labours. We must not think every thing lost that goes beside ourselves, nor any thing wasted that goes to the poor. 3. That times of joy, such as harvest-time is, are proper times for charity; that, when we rejoice, the poor may rejoice with us, and when our hearts are blessing God their loins may bless us.

11 Ye shall not steal, neither deal falsely, neither lie one to another. 12 And ye shall not swear by my name falsely, neither shalt thou profane the name of thy God: I *am* the LORD. 13 Thou shalt not defraud thy neighbour, neither rob *him:* the wages of him that is hired shall not abide with thee all night until the morning. 14 Thou shalt not curse the deaf, nor put a stumbling block before the blind, but shalt fear thy God: I *am* the LORD. 15 Ye shall do no unrighteousness in judgment: thou shalt not respect the person of the poor, nor honour the person of the mighty: *but* in righteousness shalt thou judge thy neighbour. 16 Thou shalt not go up

and down *as* a talebearer among thy people: neither shalt thou stand against the blood of thy neighbour: I *am* the LORD. 17 Thou shalt not hate thy brother in thine heart: thou shalt in any wise rebuke thy neighbour, and not suffer sin upon him. 18 Thou shalt not avenge, nor bear any grudge against the children of thy people, but thou shalt love thy neighbour as thyself: I *am* the LORD.

We are taught here,

I. To be honest and true in all our dealings, *v.* 11. God, who has appointed every man's property by his providence, forbids by his law the invading of that appointment, either by downright theft, *You shall not steal,* or by fraudulent dealing, " You shall not cheat, or deal falsely." Whatever we have in the world, we must see to it that it be honestly come by, for we cannot be truly rich, nor long rich, with that which is not. The God of truth, who requires truth in the heart (Ps. li. 6), requires it also in the tongue: *Neither lie one to another,* either in bargaining or common converse. This is one of the laws of Christianity (Col. iii. 9): *Lie not one to another.* Those that do not speak truth do not deserve to be told truth; those that sin by lying justly suffer by it; therefore we are forbidden to *lie one to another;* for, if we lie to others, we teach them to lie to us.

II. To maintain a very reverent regard to the sacred name of God (*v.* 12), and not to call him to be witness either, 1. To a lie: *You shall not swear falsely.* It is bad to tell a lie, but it is much worse to swear it. Or, 2. To a trifle, and every impertinence: *Neither shalt thou profane the name of thy God,* by alienating it to any other purpose than that for which it is to be religiously used.

III. Neither to take nor keep any one's right from him, *v.* 13. We must not take that which is none of our own, either by fraud or robbery; nor detain that which belongs to another, particularly the *wages of the hireling,* let it not *abide with thee all night.* Let the day-labourer have his wages as soon as he has done his day's work, if he desire it. It is a great sin to deny the payment of it, nay, to defer it, to his damage, a sin that cries to heaven for vengeance, Jam. v. 4.

IV. To be particularly tender of the credit and safety of those that cannot help themselves, *v.* 14. 1. The credit of the deaf: *Thou shalt not curse the deaf;* that is, not only those that are naturally deaf, that cannot hear at all, but also those that are absent, and at present out of hearing of the curse, and so cannot show their resentment, return the affront, nor right themselves, and those that are patient, that seem as if they heard not, and are not willing to take notice of it, as David, Ps. xxxviii. 13. Do not injure any because they are unwilling, or unable, to avenge themselves, for God sees and hears, though they do not. 2. The safety of the blind we must likewise be tender of, and not put a stumbling-block before them; for this is to add affliction to the afflicted, and to make God's providence a servant to our malice. This prohibition implies a precept to help the blind, and remove stumbling-blocks out of their way. The Jewish writers, thinking it impossible that any should be so barbarous as to put a *stumbling-block in the way of the blind,* understood it figuratively, that it forbids giving bad counsel to those that are simple and easily imposed upon, by which they may be led to do something to their own prejudice. We ought to take heed of doing any thing which may occasion our weak brother to fall, Rom. xiv. 13; 1 Cor. viii. 9. It is added, as a preservative from these sins, *but fear thou God.* "Thou dost not fear the deaf and blind, they cannot right themselves; but remember it is the glory of God to help the helpless, and he will plead their cause." Note, The fear of God will restrain us from doing that which will not expose us to men's resentments.

V. Judges and all in authority are here commanded to give verdict and judgment without partiality (v. 15); whether they were constituted judges by commission or made so in a particular case by the consent of both parties, as referees or arbitrators, they must do no wrong to either side, but, to the utmost of their skill, must go according to the rules of equity, having respect purely to the merits of the cause, and not to the characters of the person. Justice must never be perverted, either, 1. In pity to the poor: *Thou shalt not respect the person of the poor,* Exod. xxiii. 3. Whatever may be given to a poor man as an alms, yet let nothing be awarded him as his right but what he is legally entitled to, nor let his poverty excuse him from any just punishment for a fault. Or, 2. In veneration or fear of the mighty, in whose favour judges would be most frequently biassed. The Jews say, "Judges were obliged by this law to be so impartial as not to let one of the contending parties sit while the other stood, nor permit one to say what he pleased and bid the other be short; see James ii. 1—4.

VI. We are all forbidden to do any thing injurious to our neighbour's good name (v. 16), either, 1. In common conversation: *Thou shalt not go up and down as a tale-bearer.* It is as bad an office as a man can put himself into to be the publisher of every man's faults, divulging what was secret, aggravating crimes, and making the worst of every thing that was amiss, with design to blast and ruin men's reputation, and to sow discord among neighbours. The word used for a tale-bearer signifies a *pedlar,* or *petty chapman,* the interlopers of trade; for tale-bearers pick up ill-natured stories at one house and utter them at another, and commonly barter slanders

520

by way of exchange. See this sin condemned, Prov. xi. 13; xx. 19; Jer. ix. 4, 5; Ezek. xxii. 9. Or, 2, In witness-bearing: Neither *shalt thou stand* as a witness *against the blood of thy neighbour,* if his blood be innocent, nor join in confederacy with such bloody men as those described," Prov. i. 11, 12. The Jewish doctors put this further sense upon it: "Thou shalt not stand by and see thy brother in danger, but thou shalt come in to his relief and succour, though it be with the peril of thy own life or limb;" they add, "He that can by his testimony clear one that is accused is obliged by this law to do it;" see Prov. xxiv. 11, 12.

VII. We are commanded to rebuke our neighbour in love (v. 17): *Thou shalt in any wise rebuke thy neighbour.* 1. Rather rebuke him than hate him for an injury done to thyself. If we apprehend that our neighbour has any way wronged us, we must not conceive a secret grudge against him, and estrange ourselves from him, speaking to him neither bad nor good, as the manner of some is, who have the art of concealing their displeasure till they have an opportunity of a full revenge (2 Sam. xiii. 22); but we must rather give vent to our resentments with the meekness of wisdom, endeavour to convince our brother of the injury, reason the case fairly with him, and so put an end to the disgust conceived: this is the rule our Saviour gives in this case, Luke xvii. 3. 2. Therefore rebuke him for his sin against God, because thou lovest him; endeavour to bring him to repentance, that his sin may be pardoned, and he may turn from it, and it may not be suffered to lie upon him. Note, Friendly reproof is a duty we owe to one another, and we ought both to give it and take it in love. *Let the righteous smite me, and it shall be a kindness,* Ps. cxli. 5. Faithful and useful are those *wounds of a friend,* Prov. xxvii. 5, 6. It is here strictly commanded, "*Thou shalt in any wise* do it, and not omit it under any pretence." Consider, (1.) The guilt we incur by not reproving: it is construed here into a hating of our brother. We are ready to argue thus, "Such a one is a friend I love, therefore I will not make him uneasy by telling him of his faults;" but we should rather say, "therefore I will do him the kindness to tell him of them." Love covers sin from others, but not from the sinner himself. (2.) The mischief we do by not reproving: we *suffer sin upon him.* Must we help the ass of an enemy that has fallen under his burden, and shall we not help the soul of a friend? Exod. xxiii. 5. And by *suffering sin upon him* we are in danger of *bearing sin for him,* as the margin reads it. If we reprove not the *unfruitful works of darkness,* we have fellowship with them, and become accessaries *ex post facto—after the fact,* Eph. v. 11. It is thy brother, thy neighbour, that is concerned; and he was a Cain that said, *Am I my brother's keeper?*

VIII. We are here required to put off all

malice, and to put on brotherly love, *v.* 18. 1. We must be ill-affected to none: *Thou shalt not avenge, nor bear any grudge;* to the same purport with that *v.* 17, *Thou shalt not hate thy brother in thy heart;* for malice is murder begun. If our brother has done us an injury, we must not return it upon him, that is avenging ; we must not upon every occasion upbraid him with it, that is bearing a grudge ; but we must both forgive it and forget it, for thus we are forgiven of God. It is a most ill-natured thing, and the bane of friendship, to retain the resentment of affronts and injuries, and to let that *word devour for ever.* 2. We must be well-affected to all : *Thou shalt love thy neighbour as thyself.* We often wrong ourselves, but we soon forgive ourselves those wrongs, and they do not at all lessen our love to ourselves ; and in like manner we should love our neighbour. Our Saviour has made this the second great commandment of the law (Matt. **xxii.** 39), and the apostle shows how it is the summary of all the laws of the second table, Rom. xiii. 9, 10 ; Gal. v. 14. We must love our neighbour as truly as we love ourselves, and without dissimulation ; we must evidence our love to our neighbour in the same way as that by which we evidence our love to ourselves, preventing his hurt, and procuring his good, to the utmost of our power. We must do to our neighbour as we would be done to ourselves (Matt. vii. 12), putting *our souls into his soul's stead,* Job xvi. 4, 5. Nay, we must in many cases deny ourselves for the good of our neighbour, as Paul, 1 Cor. ix. 19, &c. Herein the gospel goes beyond even that excellent precept of the law ; for Christ, by laying down his life for us, has taught us even to *lay down our lives for the brethren,* in some cases (1 John iii. 16), and so to love our neighbour better than ourselves.

19 Ye shall keep my statutes. Thou shalt not let thy cattle gender with a diverse kind : thou shalt not sow thy field with mingled seed : neither shall a garment mingled of linen and woollen come upon thee. 20 And whosoever lieth carnally with a woman, that *is* a bondmaid, betrothed to a husband, and not at all redeemed, nor freedom given her ; she shall be scourged ; they shall not be put to death, because she was not free. 21 And he shall bring his trespass offering unto the LORD, unto the door of the tabernacle of the congregation, *even* a ram for a trespass offering. 22 And the priest shall make an atonement for him with the ram of the trespass offering before the LORD for his sin which he hath done : and the sin which he hath done

shall be forgiven him. 23 And when ye shall come into the land, and shall have planted all manner of trees for food, then ye shall count the fruit thereof as uncircumcised : three years shall it be as uncircumcised unto you : it shall not be eaten of. 24 But in the fourth year all the fruit thereof shall be holy to praise the LORD *withal.* 25 And in the fifth year shall ye eat of the fruit thereof, that it may yield unto you the increase thereof. I *am* the LORD your God. 26 Ye shall not eat *any thing* with the blood : neither shall ye use enchantment, nor observe times. 27 Ye shall not round the corners of your heads, neither shalt thou mar the corners of thy beard. 28 Ye shall not make any cuttings in your flesh for the dead, nor print any marks upon you : I *am* the LORD. 29 Do not prostitute thy daughter, to cause her to be a whore ; lest the land fall to whoredom, and the land become full of wickedness.

Here is, I. A law against mixtures, *v.* 19. God in the beginning made the cattle *after their kind* (Gen. i. 25), and we must acquiesce in the order of nature God hath established, believing that is best and sufficient, and not covet monsters. *Add thou not unto his works, lest he reprove thee;* for it is the excellency of the work of God that nothing can, without making it worse, be either put to it or taken from it, Eccl. iii. 14. As what God has joined we must not separate, so what he has separated we must not join. The sowing of mingled corn and the wearing of linsey-woolsey garments are forbidden, either as superstitious customs of the heathen or to intimate how careful they should be not to mingle themselves with the heathen nor to weave any of the usages of the Gentiles into God's ordinances. Ainsworth suggests that it was to lead Israel to the simplicity and sincerity of religion, and to all the parts and doctrines of the law and gospel in their distinct kinds. As faith is necessary, good works are necessary, but to mingle these together in the cause of our justification before God is forbidden, Gal. ii. 16.

II. A law for punishing adultery committed with one that was a bondmaid that was espoused, *v.* 20—22. If she had not been espoused, the law appointed no punishment at all ; being espoused, if she had not been a bondmaid, the punishment had been no less than death : but, being as yet a bondmaid (though before the completing of her espousals she must have been made free), the capital punishment is remitted, and they shall both be scourged; or, as some think, the woman only, and the man was to bring a sacrifice. It was for the honour of marriage, though but begun by betrothing, that the crime should be punished; but it was for the honour of freedom that it should not be punished as the debauching of a free woman was, so great was the difference then made between bond and free (Gal. iv. 30); but the gospel of Christ knows no such distinction, Col. iii. 11.

III. A law concerning fruit-trees, that for the first three years after they were planted, if they should happen to be so forward as to bear in that time, yet no use should be made of the fruit, *v.* 23—25. It was therefore the practice of the Jews to pluck off the fruit, as soon as they perceived it knit, from their young trees, as gardeners do sometimes, because their early bearing hinders their growing. If any did come to perfection, it was not to be used in the service either of God or man; but what they bore the fourth year was to be holy to the Lord, either given to the priests, or eaten before the Lord with joy, as their second tithe was, and thenceforward it was all their own. Now, 1. Some think this taught them not to follow the custom of the heathen, who, they say, consecrated the very first products of their fruit-trees to their idols, saying that otherwise all the fruits would be blasted. 2. This law in the case of fruit-trees seems to be parallel with that in the case of animals, that no creature should be accepted as an offering till it was past eight days old, nor till that day were children to be circumcised; see *ch.* xxii. 27. God would have the first-fruits of their trees, but, because for the first three years they were as inconsiderable as a lamb or a calf under eight days old, therefore God would not have them, for it is fit he should have every thing at its best; and yet he would not allow them to be used, because his first-fruits were not as yet offered: they must therefore be accounted as uncircumcised, that is, as an animal under eight days' old, not fit for any use. 3. We are hereby taught not to be over-hasty in catching at any comfort, but to be willing with patience to wait the time for the enjoyment of it, and particularly to acknowledge ourselves unworthy of the increase of the earth, our right to the fruits of which was forfeited by our first parents eating forbidden fruit, and we are restored to it only *by the word of God and prayer*, 1 Tim. iv. 5.

IV. A law against the superstitious usages of the heathen, *v.* 26—28. 1. Eating upon the blood, as the Gentiles did, who gathered the blood of their sacrifices into a vessel for their demons (as they fancied) to drink, and then sat about it, eating the flesh themselves, signifying their communion with devils by their feasting with them. Let not this custom be used, for the blood of God's sacrifices was to be sprinkled on the altar, and then poured

at the foot of it, and conveyed away. 2. Enchantment and divination, and a superstitious observation of the times, some days and hours lucky and others unlucky. Curious arts of this kind, it is likely, had been of late invented by the Egyptian priests, to amuse the people, and support their own credit. The Israelites had seen them practised, but must by no means imitate them. It would be unpardonable in those *to whom were committed the oracles of God* to ask counsel of the devil, and yet worse in Christians, to whom *the Son of God is manifested*, who has *destroyed the works of the devil*. For Christians to have their nativities cast, and their fortunes told them, to use spells and charms for the cure of diseases and the driving away of evil spirits, to be affected with the falling of the salt, a hare crossing the way, cross days, or the like, is an intolerable affront to the Lord Jesus, a support of paganism and idolatry, and a reproach both to themselves and to that worthy name by which they are called: and those must be grossly ignorant, both of the law and the gospel, that ask, " What harm is there in these things?" Is it no harm for those that have fellowship with Christ to have fellowship with devils, or to learn the ways of those that have? Surely *we have not so learned Christ*. 3. There was a superstition even in trimming themselves used by the heathen, which must not be imitated by the people of God: *You shall not round the corners of your heads.* Those that worshipped the hosts of heaven, in honour of them, cut their hair so as that their heads might resemble the celestial globe; but, as the custom was foolish in itself, so, being done with respect to their false gods, it was idolatrous. 4. The rites and ceremonies by which they expressed their sorrow at their funerals must not be imitated, *v.* 28. They must not make cuts or prints in their flesh for the dead; for the heathen did so to pacify the infernal deities they dreamt of, and to render them propitious to their deceased friends. Christ by his sufferings has altered the property of death, and made it a true friend to every true Israelite; and now, as there needs nothing to make death propitious to us (for, if God be so, death is so of course), so we sorrow not as those that have no hope. Those whom the God of Israel had set apart for himself must not receive the image and superscription of these dunghill deities. *Lastly,* The prostituting of their daughters to uncleanness, which is here forbidden (*v.* 29), seems to have been practised by the heathen in their idolatrous worships, for with such abominations those unclean spirits which they worshipped were well pleased. And when lewdness obtained as a religious rite, and was committed in their temples, no marvel that the land became full of that wickedness, which, when it entered at the temple-doors, overspread the land like **a** mighty torrent, and bore down all the fences of virtue and modesty. The devil himself could not have brought such abominations into their lives if he had not first brought them into their worships. And justly were those given up to vile affections who forsook the holy God, and gave divine honours to impure spirits. Those that dishonour God are thus suffered to dishonour themselves and their families.

30 Ye shall keep my sabbaths, and reverence my sanctuary: I *am* the LORD. 31 Regard not them that have familiar spirits, neither seek after wizards, to be defiled by them: I *am* the LORD your God. 32 Thou shalt rise up before the hoary head, and honour the face of the old man, and fear thy God: I *am* the LORD. 33 And if a stranger sojourn with thee in your land, ye shall not vex him. 34 But the stranger that dwelleth with you shall be unto you as one born among you, and thou shalt love him as thyself; for ye were strangers in the land of Egypt: I *am* the LORD your God. 35 Ye shall do no unrighteousness in judgment, in meteyard, in weight, or in measure. 36 Just balances, just weights, a just ephah, and a just hin, shall ye have: I *am* the LORD your God, which brought you out of the land of Egypt. 37 Therefore shall ye observe all my statutes, and all my judgments, and do them: I *am* the LORD.

Here is, I. A law for the preserving of the honour of the time and place appropriated to the service of God, *v.* 30. This would be a means to secure them both from the idolatries and superstitions of the heathen and from all immoralities in conversation. 1. Sabbaths must be religiously observed, and not those times mentioned (*v.* 26) to which the heathen had a superstitious regard. 2. The sanctuary must be reverenced; great care must be taken to approach the tabernacle with that purity and preparation which the law required, and to attend there with that humility, decency, and closeness of application which became them in the immediate presence of such an awful majesty. Though now there is no place holy by divine institution, as the tabernacle and temple then were, yet this law obliges us to respect the solemn assemblies of Christians for religious worship, as being held under a promise of Christ's special presence in them, and to carry ourselves with a due decorum while in those assemblies we attend the administration of holy ordinances, Eccl. v. 1.

II. A caution against all communion with witches, and those that were in league with familiar spirits: "*Regard them not, seek not after them*, be not in fear of any evil from them nor in hopes of any good from them. Regard not their threatenings, or promises, or predictions; seek not to them for discovery or advice, for, if you do, you are defiled by it, and rendered abominable both to God and your own consciences." This was the sin that completed Saul's wickedness, for which he was rejected of God, 1 Chron. x. 13.

III. A charge to young people to show respect to the aged: *Thou shalt rise up before the hoary head, v.* 32. Age is honourable, and he that is the Ancient of days requires that honour be paid to it. *The hoary head is a crown of glory.* Those whom God has honoured with the common blessing of long life we ought to honour with the distinguishing expressions of civility; and those who in age are wise and good are worthy of double honour: more respect is owing to such old men than merely to rise up before them; their credit and comfort must be carefully consulted, their experience and observations improved, and their counsels asked and hearkened to, Job xxxii. 6, 7. Some, by the old man whose face or presence is to be honoured, understand the elder in office, as by the hoary head the elder in age; both ought to be respected as fathers, and in the fear of God, who has put some of his honour upon both. Note, Religion teaches good manners, and obliges us to give honour to those to whom honour is due. It is an instance of great degeneracy and disorder in a land when *the child behaves himself proudly against the ancient, and the base against the honourable,* Isa. iii. 5; Job xxx. 1, 12. It becomes the aged to receive this honour, and the younger to give it; for it is the ornament as well as duty of their youth to *order themselves lowly and reverently to all their betters.*

IV. A charge to the Israelites to be very tender of strangers, *v.* 33, 34. Both the law of God and his providence had vastly dignified Israel above any other people, yet they must not therefore think themselves authorized to trample upon all mankind but those of their own nation, and to insult them at their pleasure; no, "*Thou shalt not vex a stranger,* but *love him as thyself,* and as one of thy own people." It is supposed that this stranger was not an idolater, but a worshipper of the God of Israel, though not circumcised, a proselyte of the gate at least, though not a proselyte of righteousness: if such a one sojourned among them, they must not vex him, nor oppress, nor over-reach him in a bargain, taking advantage of his ignorance of their laws and customs; they must reckon it as great a sin to cheat a stranger as to cheat an Israelite; "nay" (say the Jewish doctors) "they must not so much as upbraid him with his being a stranger, and his having been formerly an idolater." Strangers are God's particular care, as the widow and the fatherless are, because it is his honour to help the helpless, Ps. cxlvi. 9. It is therefore at our peril if we do them any wrong, or put any hardships upon them. Strangers shall be welcome to God's grace, and therefore we should do what we can to invite them to it, and to recommend religion to their good opinion. It argues a generous disposition, and a pious regard to God, as a common Father, to be kind to strangers; for those of different countries, customs, and languages, are all made of one blood. But here is a reason added peculiar to the Jews: " *For you were strangers in the land of Egypt.* God then favoured you, therefore do you now favour the strangers, and do to them as you then wished to be done to. You were strangers, and yet are now thus highly advanced; therefore you know not what these strangers may come to, whom you are apt to despise."

V. Justice in weights and measures is here commanded. That there should be no cheat in them, *v,* 35. That they should be very exact, *v.* 36. In weighing and measuring, we pretend a design to give all those their own whom we deal with; but, if the weights and measures be false, it is like a corruption in judgment, it cheats under colour of justice; and thus to deceive a man to his damage is worse than picking his pocket or robbing him on the highway. He that sells is bound to give the full of the commodity, and he that buys the full of the price agreed upon, which cannot be done without just balances, weights, and measures. *Let no man go beyond or defraud his brother,* for, though it be hidden from man, it will be found that *God is the avenger of all such.*

VI. The chapter concludes with a general command (*v.* 37): *You shall observe all my statutes, and do them.* Note, 1. We are not likely to do God's statutes, unless we observe them with great care and consideration. 2. Yet it is not enough barely to observe God's precepts, but we must make conscience of obeying them. What will it avail us to be critical in our notions, if we be not conscientious in our conversations? 3. An upright heart has respect to all God's commandments, Ps. cxix. 6. Though in many instances the hand fails in doing what should be done, yet the eye observes all God's statutes. We are not allowed to pick and choose our duty, but must aim at standing complete in all the will of God.

CHAP. XX.

The laws which before were made are in this chapter repeated and penalties annexed to them, that those who would not be deterred from sin by the fear of God might be deterred from it by the fear of punishment. If we will not avoid such and such practices because the law has made them sin (and it is most acceptable when we go on that principle of religion), surely we shall avoid them when the law has made them death, from a principle of self-preservation. In this chapter we have, I. Many particular crimes that are made capital. 1. Giving their children to Moloch, ver. 1—5. 2. Consulting witches, ver. 6, 27. 3. Cursing parents, ver. 9. 4. Adultery, ver. 10. 5. Incest, ver. 11, 12, 14, 17, 19—21. 6. Unnatural lusts, ver. 13, 15, 16, 18. II. General commands given to be holy, ver. 7, 8, 22—26.

AND the Lord spake unto Moses, saying, 2 Again, thou shalt say to the children of Israel, Whosoever

he be of the children of Israel, or of the strangers that sojourn in Israel, that giveth *any* of his seed unto Molech; he shall surely be put to death: the people of the land shall stone him with stones. 3 And I will set my face against that man, and will cut him off from among his people; because he hath given of his seed unto Molech, to defile my sanctuary, and to profane my holy name. 4 And if the people of the land do any ways hide their eyes from the man, when he giveth of his seed unto Molech, and kill him not: 5 Then I will set my face against that man, and against his family, and will cut him off, and all that go a whoring after him, to commit whoredom with Molech, from among their people. 6 And the soul that turneth after such as have familiar spirits, and after wizards, to go a whoring after them, I will even set my face against that soul, and will cut him off from among his people. 7 Sanctify yourselves therefore, and be ye holy: for I *am* the Lord your God. 8 And ye shall keep my statutes, and do them: I *am* the Lord which sanctify you. 9 For every one that curseth his father or his mother shall be surely put to death: he hath cursed his father or his mother; his blood *shall be* upon him.

Moses is here directed to say that again to the children of Israel which he had in effect said before, *v.* 2. We are sure it was no vain repetition, but very necessary, that they might *give the more earnest heed to the things that were spoken,* and might believe them to be of great consequence, being so often inculcated. *God speaketh once, yea, twice,* and what he orders to be said again we must be willing to hear again, because *for us it is safe,* Phil. iii. 1.

I. Three sins are in these verses threatened with death:—

1. Parents abusing their children, by sacrificing them to Moloch, *v.* 2, 3. There is the grossest absurdity that can be in all the rites of idolatry, and they are all a great reproach to men's reason; but none trampled upon all the honours of human nature as this did, the burning of children in the fire to the honour of a dunghill-god. It was a plain evidence that their gods were devils, who desired and delighted in the misery and ruin of mankind, and that the worshippers were worse than the beasts that perish, perfectly stripped, not only of reason, but of natural affection. Abraham's offering Isaac could

not give countenance, much less could it give rise to this barbarous practice, since, though that was commanded, it was immediately countermanded. Yet such was the power of the god of this world over the children of disobedience that this monstrous piece of inhumanity was generally practised; and even the Israelites were in danger of being drawn into it, which made it necessary that this severe law should be made against it. It was not enough to tell them they might spare their children (the fruit of their body should never be accepted for the sin of their soul), but they must be told, (1.) That the criminal himself should be put to death as a murderer: *The people of the land shall stone him with stones* (v. 2), which was looked upon as the worst of capital punishments among the Jews. If the children were sacrificed to the malice of the devil, the parents must be sacrificed to the justice of God. And, if either the fact could not be proved or the magistrates did not do their duty, God would take the work into his own hands: *I will cut him off*, v. 3. Note, Those that escape punishment from men, yet shall not escape the righteous judgments of God; so wretchedly do those deceive themselves that promise themselves impunity in sin. How can those escape against whom God sets his face, that is, whom he frowns upon, meets as an enemy, and fights against? The heinousness of the crime is here set forth to justify the doom: it *defiles the sanctuary*, and *profanes the holy name* of God, for the honour of both which he is jealous. Observe, The malignity of the sin is laid upon that in it which was peculiar to Israel. When the Gentiles sacrificed their children they were guilty of murder and idolatry; but, if the Israelites did it, they incurred the additional guilt of defiling the sanctuary (which they attended upon even when they lay under this guilt, as if there might be an agreement between the temple of God and idols), and of *profaning the holy name of God*, by which they were called, as if he allowed his worshippers to do such things, Rom. ii. 23, 24. (2.) That all his aiders and abetters should be cut off likewise by the righteous hand of God. If his neighbours concealed him, and would not come in as witnesses against him,—if the magistrates connived at him, and would not pass sentence upon him, rather pitying his folly than hating his impiety,—God himself would reckon with them, v. 4, 5. Misprision of idolatry is a crime cognizable in the court of heaven, and which shall not go unpunished: *I will set my face against that man* (that magistrate, Jer. v. 1) *and against his family*. Note, [1.] The wickedness of the master of a family often brings ruin upon a family; and he that should be the house-keeper proves the house-breaker. [2.] If magistrates will not do justice upon offenders, God will do justice upon them, because there is danger that many will *go a whoring after those* who do but countenance

sin by winking at it. And, if the sins of leaders be leading sins, it is fit that their punishments should be exemplary punishments.

2. Children's abusing their parents, by cursing them, v. 9. If children should speak ill of their parents, or wish ill to them, or carry it scornfully or spitefully towards them, it was an iniquity to be punished by the judges, who were employed as conservators both of God's honour and of the public peace, which were both attacked by this unnatural insolence. See Prov. xxx. 17, *The eye that mocks at his father the ravens of the valley shall pick out*, which intimates that such wicked children were in a fair way to be not only hanged, but hanged in chains. This law of Moses Christ quotes and confirms (Matt. xv. 4), for it is as direct a breach of the fifth commandment as wilful murder is of the sixth. The same law which requires parents to be tender of their children requires children to be respectful to their parents. He that despitefully uses his parents, the instruments of his being, flies in the face of God himself, the author of his being, who will not see the paternal dignity and authority insulted and trampled upon.

3. Persons abusing themselves by consulting such as have *familiar spirits*, v. 6. By this, as much as any thing, a man diminishes, disparages, and deceives himself, and so abuses himself. What greater madness can there be than for a man to go to a liar for information, and to an enemy for advice? Those do so who turn after those that deal in the black art, and know the depths of Satan. This is spiritual adultery as much as idolatry is, giving that honour to the devil which is due to God only; and the jealous God will give a bill of divorce to those that thus *go a whoring from him,* and will *cut them off*, they having first cut themselves off from him.

II. In the midst of these particular laws comes in that general charge, v. 7, 8, where we have,

1. The duties required; and they are two: —(1.) That in our principles, affections, and aims, we be holy: *Sanctify yourselves and be you holy.* We must cleanse ourselves from all the pollutions of sin, consecrate ourselves to the service and honour of God, and conform ourselves in every thing to his holy will and image: this is to *sanctify ourselves.* (2.) That in all our actions, and in the whole course of our conversation, we be obedient to the laws of God: *You shall keep my statutes.* By this only can we make it to appear that we have sanctified ourselves and are holy, even by our keeping God's commandments; *the tree is known by its fruit.* Nor can we keep God's statutes, as we ought, unless we first sanctify ourselves, and be holy. Make the tree good, and the fruit will be good.

2. The reasons to enforce these duties. (1.) "*I am the Lord your God;* therefore be holy, that you may resemble him whose peo-

ple you are, and may be pleasing to him. Holiness becomes his house and household.'' (2.) *I am the Lord who sanctifieth you.* God sanctified them by peculiar privileges, laws, and favours, which distinguished them from all other nations, and dignified them as a people set apart for God. He gave them his word and ordinances to be means of their sanctification, and his good Spirit to instruct them; therefore they must be holy, else they received the grace of God herein in vain. Note, [1.] God's people are, and must be, persons of distinction. God has distinguished them by his holy covenant, and therefore they ought to distinguish themselves by their holy conversation. [2.] God's sanctifying us is a good reason why we should sanctify ourselves, that we may comply with the designs of his grace, and not walk contrary to them. If it be the Lord that sanctifies us, we may hope the work shall be done, though it be difficult: the manner of expression is like that, 2 Cor. v. 5, *He that hath wrought us for the self-same thing is God.* And his grace is so far from superseding our care and endeavour that it most strongly engages and encourages them. *Work out your salvation, for it is God that worketh in you.*

10 And the man that committeth adultery with *another* man's wife, *even he* that committeth adultery with his neighbour's wife, the adulterer and the adulteress shall surely be put to death. 11 And the man that lieth with his father's wife hath uncovered his father's nakedness: both of them shall surely be put to death; their blood *shall be* upon them. 12 And if a man lie with his daughter in law, both of them shall surely be put to death: they have wrought confusion; their blood *shall be* upon them. 13 If a man also lie with mankind, as he lieth with a woman, both of them have committed an abomination: they shall surely be put to death; their blood *shall be* upon them. 14 And if a man take a wife and her mother, it *is* wickedness; they shall be burnt with fire, both he and they; that there be no wickedness among you. 15 And if a man lie with a beast, he shall surely be put to death: and ye shall slay the beast. 16 And if a woman approach unto any beast, and lie down thereto, thou shalt kill the woman, and the beast: they shall surely be put to death; their blood *shall be* upon them. 17 And if a man shall take his sister, his father's daughter, or his mother's

daughter, and see her nakedness, and she see his nakedness; it *is* a wicked thing; and they shall be cut off in the sight of their people: he hath uncovered his sister's nakedness; he shall bear his iniquity. 18 And if a man shall lie with a woman having her sickness, and shall uncover her nakedness; he hath discovered her fountain, and she hath uncovered the fountain of her blood: and both of them shall be cut off from among their people. 19 And thou shalt not uncover the nakedness of thy mother's sister, nor of thy father's sister: for he uncovereth his near kin: they shall bear their iniquity. 20 And if a man shall lie with his uncle's wife, he hath uncovered his uncle's nakedness: they shall bear their sin; they shall die childless. 21 And if a man shall take his brother's wife, it *is* an unclean thing: he hath uncovered his brother's nakedness; they shall be childless.

Sins against the seventh commandment are here ordered to be severely punished. These are sins which, of all others, fools are most apt to make a mock at; but God would teach those the heinousness of the guilt by the extremity of the punishment that would not otherwise be taught it.

I. Lying with another man's wife was made a capital crime. The adulterer and the adulteress that had joined in the sin must fall alike under the sentence: they shall both be *put to death, v.* 10. Long before this, even in Job's time, this was reputed a *heinous crime* and an *iniquity to be punished by the judges,* Job xxxi. 11. It is a presumptuous contempt of an ordinance of God, and a violation of his covenant, Prov. ii. 17. It is an irreparable wrong to the injured husband, and debauches the mind and conscience of both the offenders as much as any thing. It is a sin which headstrong and unbridled lusts hurry men violently to, and therefore it needs such a powerful restraint as this. It is a sin which defiles a land and brings down God's judgments upon it, which disquiets families, and tends to the ruin of all virtue and religion, and therefore is fit to be animadverted upon by the conservators of the public peace: but see John viii. 3—11.

II. Incestuous connections, whether by marriage or not. 1. Some of them were to be punished with death, as a man's *lying with his father's wife, v.* 11. Reuben would have been put to death for his crime (Gen. xxxv. 22) if this law had been then made. It was the sin of the incestuous Corinthian, for which he was to be *delivered unto Satan,* 1.

526

Cor. v. 1, 5. A man's debauching his daughter-in-law, or his mother-in-law, or his sister, was likewise to be punished with death, *v.* 12, 14, 17. 2. Others of them God would punish with the curse of barrenness, as a man's defiling his aunt, or his brother's wife (*v.* 19—21): *They shall die childless.* Those that keep not within the divine rules of marriage forfeit the blessings of marriage: *They shall commit whoredom, and shall not increase,* Hos. iv. 10. Nay it is said, *They shall bear their iniquity,* that is, though they be not immediately cut off by the hand either of God or man for this sin, yet the guilt of it shall lie upon them, to be reckoned for another day, and not be purged with sacrifice or offering.

III. The unnatural lusts of sodomy and bestiality (sins not to be mentioned without horror) were to be punished with death, as they are at this day by our law, *v.* 13, 15, 16. Even the beast that was thus abused was to be killed with the sinner, who was thereby openly put to the greater shame: and the villany was thus represented as in the highest degree execrable and abominable, all occasions of the remembrance or mention of it being to be taken away. Even the unseasonable use of the marriage bed, if presumptuous, and in contempt of the law, would expose the offenders to the just judgment of God: they *shall be cut off, v.* 18. For this is the will of God, that *every man should possess his vessel* (and the wife is called the weaker vessel) *in sanctification and honour,* as becomes saints.

22 Ye shall therefore keep all my statutes, and all my judgments, and do them: that the land, whither I bring you to dwell therein, spue you not out. 23 And ye shall not walk in the manners of the nation, which I cast out before you: for they committed all these things, and therefore I abhorred them. 24 But I have said unto you, Ye shall inherit their land, and I will give it unto you to possess it, a land that floweth with milk and honey: I *am* the LORD your God, which have separated you from *other* people. 25 Ye shall therefore put difference between clean beasts and unclean, and between unclean fowls and clean: and ye shall not make your souls abominable by beast, or by fowl, or by any manner of living thing that creepeth on the ground, which I have separated from you as unclean. 26 And ye shall be holy unto me: for I the LORD *am* holy, and have severed you from *other* people, that ye should be mine. 27 A

man also or woman that hath a familiar spirit, or that is a wizard, shall surely be put to death: they shall stone them with stones: their blood *shall be* upon them.

The last verse is a particular law, which comes in after the general conclusion, as if omitted in its proper place: it is for the putting of those to death that dealt with familiar spirits, *v.* 27. It would be an affront to God and to his lively oracles, a scandal to the country, and a temptation to ignorant bad people, to consult them, if such were known and suffered to live among them. Those that are in league with the devil have in effect made a covenant with death and an agreement with hell, and so shall their doom be.

The rest of these verses repeat and inculcate what had been said before; for to that unthinking forgetful people it was requisite that there should be line upon line, and that general rules, with their reasons, should be frequently insisted on, for the enforcement of particular laws, and making them more effectual. Three things we are here reminded of:—

I. Their dignity. 1. They had the *Lord for their God, v.* 24. They were his, his care, his choice, his treasure, his jewels, his kingdom of priests (*v.* 26): *That you should be mine.* Happy the people, and truly great, that are in such a case. 2. Their God was a holy God (*v.* 26), infinitely advanced above all others. His holiness is his glory, and it was their honour to be related to him, while their neighbours were the infamous worshippers of impure and filthy spirits. 3. The great God had separated them from other people (*v* 24), and again, *v.* 26. Other nations were the common; they were the enclosure, beautified and enriched with peculiar privileges, and designed for peculiar honours; let them therefore value themselves accordingly, preserve their honour, and not lay it in the dust, by walking in the way of the heathen.

II. Their duty; this is inferred from their dignity. God had done more for them than for others, and therefore expected more from them than from others. And what is it that the Lord their God requires, in consideration of the great things done and designed? 1. *You shall keep all my statutes* (*v.* 22); and there was all the reason in the world that they should, for the statutes were their honour, and obedience to them would be their lasting comfort. 2. *You shall not walk in the manners of the nations, v.* 23. Being separated from them, they must not associate with them, nor learn their ways. The manners of the nations were bad enough in them, but would be much worse in God's people. 3. You shall *put a difference between clean and unclean, v.* 25. This is holiness, to discern between things that differ, not to live at large, as if we might say and do any thing, but to speak and act with caution. 4. *You shall not make your souls abominable, v.* 25. Our constant care must be to preserve the honour, by preserving the purity, of our own souls, and never to do any thing to make them abominable to God and to our own consciences.

III. Their danger. 1. They were going into an infected place (*v.* 24): *You shall inherit their land,* a land *flowing indeed with milk and honey,* which they would have the comfort of if they kept their integrity; but, withal, it was a land full of idols, idolatries, and superstitious usages, which they would be apt to fall in love with, having brought from Egypt with them a strange disposition to take that infection. 2. If they took the infection, it would be of pernicious consequence to them. The Canaanites were to be expelled for these very sins: *They committed all these things, therefore I abhorred them, v.* 23. See what an evil thing sin is; it provokes God to abhor his own creatures, whereas otherwise he delights in the work of his hands. And, if the Israelites trod in the steps of their impiety, they must expect that the land would spue them out (*v.* 22), as he had told them before, *ch.* xviii. 28. If God spared not the natural branches, but broke them off, neither would he spare those who were grafted in, if they degenerated. Thus the rejection of the Jews stands for a warning to all Christian churches to take heed lest the kingdom of God be taken from them. Those that sin like others must expect to smart like them; and their profession of relation to God will be no security to them.

CHAP. XXI.

This chapter might borrow its title from Mal. ii. 1, "And now, O you priests, this commandment is for you." It is a law obliging priests with the utmost care and jealousy to preserve the dignity of their priesthood. I. The inferior priests are here charged both concerning their mourning and concerning their marriages and their children, ver. 1—9. II. The high priest is restrained more than any of them, ver. 10—15. III. Neither the one nor the other must have any blemish, ver. 16, &c.

AND the LORD said unto Moses, Speak unto the priests the sons of Aaron, and say unto them, There shall none be defiled for the dead among his people : 2 But for his kin, that is near unto him, *that is,* for his mother, and for his father, and for his son, and for his daughter, and for his brother, 3 And for his sister a virgin, that is nigh unto him, which hath had no husband ; for her may he be defiled. 4 *But* he shall not defile himself, *being* a chief man among his people, to profane himself. 5 They shall not make baldness upon their head, neither shall they shave off the corner of their beard, nor make any cuttings in their flesh. 6 They shall be holy unto their God, and not profane the name of their God : for the

offerings of the LORD made by fire, *and* the bread of their God, they do offer : therefore they shall be holy. 7 They shall not take a wife *that is* a whore, or profane ; neither shall they take a woman put away from her husband : for he *is* holy unto his God. 8 Thou shalt sanctify him therefore ; for he offereth the bread of thy God : he shall be holy unto thee : for I the LORD, which sanctify you, *am* holy. 9 And the daughter of any priest, if she profane herself by playing the whore, she profaneth her father : she shall be burnt with fire.

It was before appointed that the priests should teach the people the statutes God had given concerning the *difference between clean and unclean, ch.* x. 10, 11. Now here it is provided that they should themselves observe what they were to teach the people. Note, Those whose office it is to instruct must do it by example as well as precept, 1 Tim. iv. 12. The priests were to draw nearer to God than any of the people, and to be more intimately conversant with sacred things, and therefore it was required of them that they should keep at a greater distance than others from every thing that was defiling and might diminish the honour of their priesthood.

I. They must take care not to disparage themselves in their mourning for the dead. All that mourned for the dead were supposed to come near the body, if not to touch it : and the Jews say, "It made a man ceremonially unclean to come within six feet of a dead corpse ;" nay, it is declared (Num. xix. 14) that all who come into the tent where the dead body lies shall be unclean seven days. Therefore all the mourners that attended the funeral could not but defile themselves, so as not to be fit to come into the sanctuary for seven days : for this reason it is ordered, 1. That the priests should never put themselves under this incapacity of coming into the sanctuary, unless it were for one of their nearest relations, *v.* 1—3. A priest was permitted to do it for a parent or a child, for a brother or an unmarried sister, and therefore, no doubt (though this is not mentioned) for the wife of his bosom ; for Ezekiel, a priest, would have mourned for his wife if he had not been particularly prohibited, Ezek. xxiv. 17. By this allowance God put an honour upon natural affection, and favoured it so far as to dispense with the attendance of his servants for seven days, while they indulged themselves in their sorrow for the death of their dear relations ; but, beyond this period, weeping must not hinder sowing, nor their affection to their relations take them off from the service of the sanctuary. Nor was it at all allowed for the death of any other, no, not of a *chief man among the people*, as some read it, *v.* 4. They must not defile themselves, no, not for the high priest himself, unless thus akin to them. Though *there is a friend that is nearer than a brother*, yet the priests must not pay this respect to the best friend they had, except he were a relation, lest, if it were allowed for one, others should expect it, and so they should be frequently taken off from their work: and it is hereby intimated that there is a particular affection to be reserved for those that are thus near akin to us; and, when any such are removed by death, we ought to be affected with it, and lay it to heart, as the near approach of death to ourselves, and an alarm to us to prepare to follow. 2. That they must not be extravagant in the expressions of their mourning, no, not for their dearest relations, *v.* 5. Their mourning must not be either, (1.) Superstitious, according to the manner of the heathen, who cut off their hair, and let out their blood, in honour of the imaginary deities which presided (as they thought) in the congregation of the dead, that they might engage them to be propitious to their departed friends. Even the superstitious rites used of old at funerals are an indication of the ancient belief of the immortality of the soul, and its existence in a separate state: and though the rites themselves were forbidden by the divine law, because they were performed to false gods, yet the decent respect which nature teaches and which the law allows to be paid to the remains of our deceased friends, shows that we are not to look upon them as lost. Nor, (2.) Must it be passionate or immoderate. Note, God's ministers must be examples to others of patience under affliction, particularly that which touches in a very tender part, the death of their near relations. They are supposed to know more than others of the reasons why we must *not sorrow as those that have no hope* (1 Thess. iv. 13), and therefore they ought to be eminently calm and composed, that they may be able to comfort others with the same comforts wherewith they are themselves comforted of God. The people were forbidden to mourn for the dead with superstitious rites (*ch.* xix. 27, 28), and what was unlawful to them was much more unlawful to the priest. The reason given for their peculiar care not to defile themselves we have (*v.* 6): *Because* they offered *the bread of their God*, even *the offerings of the Lord made by fire*, which were the provisions of God's house and table. They are highly honoured, and therefore must not stain their honour by making themselves slaves to their passions; they are continually employed in sacred service, and therefore must not be either diverted from or disfitted fcr the services they were called to. If they pollute themselves, they profane the name of their God on whom they attend: if the servants are rude and of ill behaviour, it is a reflection upon the master, as if he kept a loose and disorderly house. Note, All that either offer or eat the bread of our God must be holy in all manner of conversation, or else they profane that name which they pretend to sanctify.

II. They must take care not to degrade themselves in their marriage, *v.* 7. A priest must not marry a woman of ill fame, that either had been guilty or was suspected to have been guilty of uncleanness. He must not only not marry a harlot, though ever so great a penitent for her former whoredoms, but he must not marry one that was profane, that is, of a light carriage or indecent behaviour. Nay, he must not marry one that was divorced, because there was reason to think it was for some fault she was divorced. The priests were forbidden to undervalue themselves by such marriages as these, which were allowed to others, 1. Lest it should bring a present reproach upon their ministry, harden the profane in their profaneness, and grieve the hearts of serious people: the New Testament gives laws to ministers' wives (1 Tim. iii. 11), that they be *grave and sober*, that *the ministry be not blamed*. 2. Lest it should entail a reproach upon their families; for the work and honour of the priesthood were to descend as an inheritance to their children after them. Those do not consult the good of their posterity as they ought who do not take care to marry such as are of good report and character. He that would seek *a godly seed* (as the expression is, Mal. ii. 15) must first seek a godly wife, and take heed of a corruption of blood. It is added here (*v.* 8), *Thou shalt sanctify him*, and *he shall be holy unto thee*. "Not only thou, O Moses, by taking care that these laws be observed, but thou, O Israel, by all endeavours possible to keep up the reputation of the priesthood, which the priests themselves must do nothing to expose or forfeit. *He is holy to his God* (*v.* 7), therefore *he shall be holy unto thee*." Note, We must honour those whom our God puts honour upon. Gospel ministers by this rule are to be *esteemed very highly in love for their works' sake* (1 Thess. v. 13), and every Christian must look upon himself as concerned to be the guardian of their honour.

III. Their children must be afraid of doing any thing to disparage them (*v.* 9): *If the daughter of any priest play the whore*, her crime is great; she not only polluteth but *profaneth herself*: other women have not that honour to lose that she has, who, as one of a priest's family, has eaten of the holy things, and is supposed to have been better educated than others. Nay, *she profaneth her father ;* he is reflected upon, and every body will be ready to ask, "Why did not he teach her better?" And the sinners in Zion will insult and say, "Here is your priest's daughter." Her punishment therefore must be peculiar: *She shall be burnt with fire*, for a terror to all priests' daughters. Note, The children of ministers ought, of all others, to take heed of doing any thing that is scandalous, because in them it is doubly scandalous, and will be punished accordingly by him whose name is *Jealous*.

10 And *he that is* the high priest among his brethren, upon whose head the anointing oil was poured, and that is consecrated to put on the garments, shall not uncover his head, nor rend his clothes; 11 Neither shall he go in to any dead body, nor defile himself for his father, or for his mother; 12 Neither shall he go out of the sanctuary, nor profane the sanctuary of his God; for the crown of the anointing oil of his God *is* upon him: I *am* the Lord. 13 And he shall take a wife in her virginity. 14 A widow, or a divorced woman, or profane, *or* a harlot, these shall he not take: but he shall take a virgin of his own people to wife. 15 Neither shall he profane his seed among his people: for I the Lord do sanctify him.

More was expected from a priest than from other people, but more from the high priest than from other priests, because upon his head the *anointing oil was poured*, and he was *consecrated to put on the garments* (v. 10), both which were typical of the anointing and adorning of the Lord Jesus, with all the gifts and graces of the Holy Spirit, which he received without measure. It is called *the crown of the anointing oil of his God* (v. 12); for the anointing of the Spirit is, to all that have it, a *crown of glory*, and a *diadem of beauty*. The high priest being thus dignified, I. He must not defile himself at all for the dead, no, not for his nearest relations, *his father or his mother*, much less his child or brother, *v.* 11. 1. He must not use the common expressions of sorrow on those occasions, such as *uncovering his head*, and *rending his clothes* (v. 10), so perfectly unconcerned must he show himself in all the crosses and comforts of this life: even his natural affection must be swallowed up in compassion to the ignorant, and a feeling of their infirmities, and a tender concern for the household of God, which he was made the ruler of. Thus being the holy one that was entrusted with the *thummim and the urim* he must not know *father or mother*, Deut. xxxiii. 8, 9. 2. He must not *go in to any dead body, v.* 11. If any of the inferior priests were under a ceremonial pollution, there were other priests that might supply their places; but, if the high priest were defiled, there would be a greater want of him.
530

And the forbidding of him to go to any house of mourning, or attend any funeral, would be an indication to the people of the greatness of that dignity to which he was advanced. Our Lord Jesus, the great high priest of our profession, touched the dead body of Jairus's daughter, the bier of the widow's son, and the grave of Lazarus, to show that he came to alter the property of death, and to take off the terror of it, by breaking the power of it. Now that it cannot destroy it does not defile. 3. He must *not go out of the sanctuary* (v. 12); that is, whenever he was attending or officiating in the sanctuary, where usually he tarried in his own apartment all day, he must not go out upon any occasion whatsoever, nor cut short his attendance on the living God, no, not to pay his last respects to a dying relation. It was a profanation of the sanctuary to leave it, while his presence was requisite there, upon any such occasion; for thereby he preferred some other business before the service of God and the business of his profession, to which he ought to make every thing else give place. Thus our Lord Jesus would not leave off preaching to *speak with his mother and brethren*, Matt. xii. 48.

II. He might not marry a widow (as other priests might), much less one divorced, or a harlot, *v.* 13, 14. The reason of this was to put a difference between him and other priests in this matter; and (as some suggest) that he might be a type of Christ, to whom the church was to be presented a *chaste virgin*, 2 Cor. xi. 2. See Ezek. xliv. 22. Christ must have our first love, our pure love, our entire love; thus the *virgins love thee* (Cant. i. 3), and such only are fit to *follow the Lamb*, Rev. xiv. 4.

III He might not profane his seed among his people, *v.* 15. Some understand it as forbidding him to marry any of an inferior rank, which would be a disparagement to his family. Jehoiada indeed married out of his own tribe, but then it was into the royal family, 2 Chron. xxii. 11. This was not to teach him to be proud, but to teach him to be pure, and to do nothing unbecoming his office and the worthy name by which he was called. Or it may be a caution to him in disposing of his children; he must not profane his seed by marrying them unsuitably Ministers' children are profaned if they be unequally yoked with unbelievers.

16 And the Lord spake unto Moses, saying, 17 Speak unto Aaron, saying, Whosoever *he be* of thy seed in their generations that hath *any* blemish, let him not approach to offer the bread of his God. 18 For whatsoever man *he be* that hath a blemish, he shall not approach: a blind man, or a lame, or he that hath a flat nose,

or any thing superfluous. 19 Or a man that is brokenfooted, or brokenhanded, 20 Or crookbackt, or a dwarf, or that hath a blemish in his eye, or be scurvy, or scabbed, or hath his stones broken; 21 No man that hath a blemish of the seed of Aaron the priest shall come nigh to offer the offerings of the LORD made by fire: he hath a blemish; he shall not come nigh to offer the bread of his God. 22 He shall eat the bread of his God, *both* of the most holy, and of the holy. 23 Only he shall not go in unto the veil, nor come nigh unto the altar, because he hath a blemish; that he profane not my sanctuaries: for I the LORD do sanctify them. 24 And Moses told *it* unto Aaron, and to his sons, and unto all the children of Israel.

The priesthood being confined to one particular family, and entailed upon all the male issue of that family throughout their generations, it was very likely that some or other in after-ages that were born to the priesthood would have natural blemishes and deformities: the honour of the priesthood would not secure them from any of those calamities which are common to men. Divers blemishes are here specified; some that were ordinarily for life, as blindness; others that might be for a time, as a scurf or scab, and, when they were gone, the disability ceased. Now,

I. The law concerning priests that had blemishes was, 1. That they might *live upon the altar* (v. 22): *He shall eat* of the sacrifices with the other priests, even the *most holy things*, such as the show-bread and the sin-offerings, as well as the *holy things*, such as the tithes and first-fruits, and the priests' share of the peace-offerings. The blemishes were such as they could not help, and therefore, though they might not work, they must not starve. Note, None must be abused for their natural infirmities. Even the deformed child in the family must have its child's part. 2. Yet they must not *serve at the altar*, at either of the altars, nor be admitted to attend or assist the other priests in offering sacrifice or burning incense, v. 17, 21, 23. Great men choose to have such servants about them as are sightly, and it was fit that the great God should have such in his house then, when he was pleased to manifest his glory in external indications of it. But it was especially requisite that comely men should be chosen to minister about holy things, for the sake of the people, who were apt to judge according to outward appearance, and to think meanly of the service, how honourable soever it was made by the divine institution, if those that performed it

looked despicably or went about it awkwardly. This provision God made for the preserving of the reputation of his altar, that it might not at any time fall under contempt. It was for the credit of the sanctuary that none should appear there who were any way disfigured, either by nature or accident.

II. Under the gospel, 1. Those that labour under any such blemishes as these have reason to thank God that they are not thereby excluded from offering spiritual sacrifices to God; nor, if otherwise qualified for it, from the office of the ministry. There is many a healthful beautiful soul lodged in a crazy deformed body. Yet, 2. We ought to infer hence how incapable those are to serve God acceptably whose minds are blemished and deformed by any reigning vice. Those are unworthy to be called Christians, and unfit to be employed as ministers, that are spiritually blind, and lame, and crooked, whose sins render them scandalous and deformed, so as that the offerings of the Lord are abhorred for their sakes. The deformities of Hophni and Phinehas were worse than any of the blemishes here mentioned. Let such therefore as are openly vicious be put out of the priesthood as polluted persons; and let all that are made to our God spiritual priests be before him *holy and without blemish,* and comfort themselves with this, that, though in this imperfect state they have spots that are the spots of God's children, yet they shall shortly appear before the throne of God *without spot, or wrinkle, or any such thing.*

CHAP. XXII.

In this chapter we have divers laws concerning the priests and sacrifices, all for the preserving of the honour of the sanctuary. I. That the priests should not eat of the holy things in their uncleanness, ver. 1—9. II. That no stranger who did not belong to some family of the priests should eat of the holy things (ver. 10—13), and, if he did it unwittingly, he must make restitution, ver. 14—16. III. That the sacrifices which were offered must be without blemish, ver. 17—25. IV. That they must be more than eight days old (ver. 26—28), and that the sacrifices of thanksgiving must be eaten the same day they were offered, ver. 29, &c.

AND the LORD spake unto Moses, saying, 2 Speak unto Aaron and to his sons, that they separate themselves from the holy things of the children of Israel, and that they profane not my holy name *in those things* which they hallow unto me: I *am* the LORD. 3 Say unto them, Whosoever *he be* of all your seed among your generations, that goeth unto the holy things, which the children of Israel hallow unto the LORD, having his uncleanness upon him, that soul shall be cut off from my presence: I *am* the LORD. 4 What man soever of the seed of Aaron *is* a leper, or hath a running issue; he shall not eat of the holy things, until he be clean. And whoso toucheth any thing *that is* unclean *by* the dead, or a man whose seed goeth from him; 5 Or whosoever toucheth any creeping thing, whereby he may be made unclean, or a man of whom he may take uncleanness, whatsoever uncleanness he hath; 6 The soul which hath touched any such shall be unclean until even, and shall not eat of the holy things, unless he wash his flesh with water. 7 And when the sun is down, he shall be clean, and shall afterward eat of the holy things; because it *is* his food. 8 That which dieth of itself, or is torn *with beasts,* he shall not eat to defile himself therewith: I *am* the LORD. 9 They shall therefore keep mine ordinance, lest they bear sin for it, and die therefore, if they profane it: I the LORD do sanctify them.

Those that had a natural blemish, though they were forbidden to do the priests' work, were yet allowed to eat of the holy things: and the Jewish writers say that "to keep them from idleness they were employed in the wood-room, to pick out that which was worm-eaten, that it might not be used in the fire upon the altar; they might also be employed in the judgment of leprosy:" but, I. Those that were under any ceremonial uncleanness, which possibly they contracted by their own fault, might not so much as eat of the holy things while they continued in their pollution. 1. Some pollutions were permanent, as a leprosy or a running issue, *v.* 4. These separated the people from the sanctuary, and God would show that they were so far from being more excusable that really they were more abominable in a priest. 2. Others were more transient, as the touching of a dead body, or any thing else that was unclean, from which, after a certain time, a man was cleansed by bathing his flesh in water, *v.* 6. But whoever was thus defiled might not *eat of the holy things,* under pain of God's highest displeasure, who said, and ratified the saying, *That soul shall be cut off from my presence, v.* 3. Our being in the presence of God, and attending upon him, will be so far from securing us that it will but the more expose us to God's wrath, if we dare to draw nigh to him in our uncleanness. The destruction shall come *from the presence of the Lord* (2 Thess. i. 9), as the fire by which Nadab and Abihu died came *from before the Lord.* Thus those who profane the holy word of God will be cut off by that word which they make so light of; it shall condemn them. They are again warned of their danger if they eat the holy thing in their uncleanness (*v.* 9), *lest they bear sin,*

and die therefore. Note, (1.) Those contract great guilt who profane sacred things, by touching them with unhallowed hands. Eating the holy things signified an interest in the atonement; but, if they ate of them in their uncleanness, they were so far from lessening their guilt that they increased it: They shall *bear sin.* (2.) Sin is a burden which, if infinite mercy prevent not, will certainly sink those that bear it: They shall *die therefore.* Even priests may be ruined by their pollutions and presumptions.

II. As to the design of this law we may observe, 1. This obliged the priests carefully to preserve their purity, and to dread every thing that would defile them. The holy things were their livelihood; if they might not eat of them, how must they subsist? The more we have to lose of comfort and honour by our defilement, the more careful we should be to preserve our purity. 2. This impressed the people with a reverence for the holy things, when they saw the priests themselves *separated from them* (as the expression is, *v.* 2) so long as they were in their uncleanness. He is doubtless a God of infinite purity who kept his immediate attendants under so strict a discipline. 3. This teaches us carefully to watch against all moral pollutions, because by them we are unfitted to receive the comfort of God's sanctuary. Though we labour not under habitual deformities, yet actual defilements deprive us of the pleasure of communion with God; and therefore *he that is washed needeth to wash his feet* (John xiii. 10), *to wash his hands,* and so to *compass the altar,* Ps. xxvi. 6. Herein we have need to be jealous over ourselves, lest (as it is observably expressed here) we *profane God's holy name in those things which we hallow unto him, v.* 2. If we affront God in those very performances wherein we pretend to honour him, and provoke him instead of pleasing him, we shall make up but a bad account shortly; yet thus we do if we profane God's name, by doing that in our uncleanness which pretends to be hallowed to him.

10 There shall no stranger eat *of* the holy thing: a sojourner of the priest, or a hired servant, shall not eat *of* the holy thing. 11 But if the priest buy *any* soul with his money, he shall eat of it, and he that is born in his house: they shall eat of his meat. 12 If the priest's daughter also be *married* unto a stranger, she may not eat of an offering of the holy things. 13 But if the priest's daughter be a widow, or divorced, and have no child, and is returned unto her father's house, as in her youth, she shall eat of her father's meat: but there shall

no stranger eat thereof. 14 And if a man eat *of* the holy thing unwittingly, then he shall put the fifth *part* thereof unto it, and shall give *it* unto the priest with the holy thing. 15 And they shall not profane the holy things of the children of Israel, which they offer unto the LORD; 16 Or suffer them to bear the iniquity of trespass, when they eat their holy things: for I the LORD do sanctify them.

The holy things were to be eaten by the priests and their families. Now,

I. Here is a law that no stranger should eat of them, that is, no person whatsoever but the priests only, and those that pertained to them, *v.* 10. The priests are charged with this care, not to *profane the holy things* by permitting the strangers to eat of them (*v.* 15) or *suffer them to bear the iniquity of trespass* (*v.* 16); that is, suffer them to bring guilt upon themselves, by meddling with that which they have no right to. Thus it is commonly understood. Note, We must not only be careful that we do not bear iniquity ourselves, but we must do what we can to prevent others bearing it. We must not only not suffer sin to *lie* upon our brother, but, if we can help it, we must not suffer it to *come* upon him. But perhaps there is another meaning of those words: the priests' eating the sin-offerings is said to signify their *bearing the iniquity of the congregation, to make an atonement for them,* ch. x. 17. Let not a stranger therefore eat of that holy thing particularly, and so pretend to *bear the iniquity of trespass;* for it is daring presumption for any to do that, but such as are appointed to do it. Those that set up other mediators besides Christ our priest, to *bear the iniquity of trespass,* sacrilegiously rob Christ of his honour, and invade his rights. When we warn people not to trust to their own righteousness, nor dare to appear before God in it, but to rely on Christ's righteousness only for peace and pardon, it is because we dare not *suffer them to bear the iniquity of trespass,* for we know it is too heavy for them.

II. Here is an explanation of the law, showing who were to be looked upon as belonging to the priest's family, and who not. 1. Sojourners and hired servants abode not in the house for ever; they were in the family, but not of it; and therefore they might not eat of the holy things (*v.* 10): but the servant that was born in the house or bought with money, being a heirloom to the family, though a servant, yet might eat of the holy things, *v.* 11. Note, Those only are entitled to the comforts of God's house who make it their *rest for ever,* and resolve to *dwell in it all the days of their life.* As for those who for a time only believe, to serve a present turn. they are looked upon but as sojourners and mercenaries, and have *no part nor lot in the matter.* 2. As to the children of the family, concerning the sons there could be no dispute, they were themselves priests, but concerning the daughters there was a distinction. While they continued in their father's house they might eat of the holy things; but, if they married such as were not priests, they lost their right (*v.* 12), for now they were cut off from the family of the priests. Yet if a priest's daughter became a widow, and had no children in whom she might preserve a distinct family, and returned to her father's house again, being neither wife nor mother, she should again be looked upon as a daughter, and might eat of the holy things. If those whom Providence has made sorrowful widows, and who are dislodged from the rest they had in the house of a husband, yet find it again in a father's house, they have reason to be thankful to the widows' God, who does not leave them comfortless. 3. Here is a demand of restitution to be made by him that had no right to the holy things, and yet should eat of them unwittingly, *v.* 14. If he did it presumptuously, and in contempt of the divine institution, he was liable to be cut off by the hand of God, and to be beaten by the magistrate; but, if he did it through weakness and inconsideration, he was to restore the value, adding a fifth part to it, besides which he was to bring an offering to atone for the trespass; see *ch.* v. 15, 16.

III. This law might be dispensed with in a case of necessity, as it was when David and his men ate of the show-bread, 1 Sam. xxi. 6. And our Saviour justifies them, and gives a reason for it, which furnishes us with a lasting rule in all such cases, that *God will have mercy and not sacrifice,* Matt. xii. 3, 4, 7. Rituals must give way to morals.

IV. It is an instruction to gospel ministers, who are *stewards of the mysteries of God,* not to admit all, without distinction, to *eat of the holy things,* but to take out the precious from the vile. Those that are scandalously ignorant or profane are strangers and aliens to the family of the Lord's priests; and it is not meet to take the children's bread and to cast it to such. Holy things are for holy persons, for those who are holy, at least, in profession, Matt. vii. 6.

17 And the LORD spake unto Moses, saying, 18 Speak unto Aaron, and to his sons, and unto all the children of Israel, and say unto them, Whatsoever *he be* of the house of Israel, or of the strangers in Israel, that will offer his oblation for all his vows, and for all his freewill offerings, which they will offer unto the LORD for a burnt offering; 19 *Ye shall offer* at

your own will a male without blemish, of the beeves, of the sheep, or of the goats. 20 *But* whatsoever hath a blemish, *that* shall ye not offer: for it shall not be acceptable for you. 21 And whosoever offereth a sacrifice of peace offerings unto the Lord to accomplish *his* vow, or a freewill offering in beeves or sheep, it shall be perfect to be accepted; there shall be no blemish therein. 22 Blind, or broken, or maimed, or having a wen, or scurvy, or scabbed, ye shall not offer these unto the Lord, nor make an offering by fire of them upon the altar unto the Lord. 23 Either a bullock or a lamb that hath any thing superfluous or lacking in his parts, that 'mayest thou offer *for* a freewill offering; but for a vow it shall not be accepted. 24 Ye shall not offer unto the Lord that which is bruised, or crushed, or broken, or cut; neither shall ye make *any offering thereof* in your land. 25 Neither from a stranger's hand shall ye offer the bread of your God of any of these; because their corruption *is* in them, *and* blemishes *be* in them: they shall not be accepted for you. 26 And the Lord spake unto Moses, saying, 27 When a bullock, or a sheep, or a goat, is brought forth, then it shall be seven days under the dam; and from the eighth day and thenceforth it shall be accepted for an offering made by fire unto the Lord. 28 And *whether it be* cow or ewe, ye shall not kill it and her young both in one day. 29 And when ye will offer a sacrifice of thanksgiving unto the Lord, offer *it* at your own will. 30 On the same day it shall be eaten up; ye shall leave none of it until the morrow: I *am* the Lord. 31 Therefore shall ye keep my commandments, and do them: I *am* the Lord. 32 Neither shall ye profane my holy name; but I will be hallowed among the children of Israel: I *am* the Lord which hallow you, 33 That brought you out of the land of Egypt, to be your God: I *am* the Lord.

Here are four laws concerning sacrifices:—
I. Whatever was offered in sacrifice to God

should be without blemish, otherwise it should not be accepted. This had often been mentioned in the particular institutions of the several sorts of offerings. Now here they are told what was to be accounted a blemish which rendered a beast unfit for sacrifice: if it was blind, or lame, had a wen, or the mange (*v.* 22),—if it was bruised, or crushed, or broken, or cut (*v.* 24), that is, as the Jewish writers understand it, if it was, in any of these ways, castrated, if bulls and rams were made into oxen and weathers, they might not be offered. Moreover a difference is made between what was brought as a free-will offering and what was brought as a vow, *v.* 23. And, though none that had any of the forementioned blemishes might be brought for either, yet if a beast had any thing superfluous or lacking (that is, as the Jews understand it, if there was a disproportion or inequality between those parts that are pairs, when one eye, or ear, or leg, was bigger than it should be, or less than it should be)—if there was no other blemish than this, it might be accepted for a free-will offering, to which a man had not before laid himself, nor had the divine law laid him, under any particular obligation; but for a vow it might not be accepted. Thus God would teach us to make conscience of performing our promises to him very exactly, and not afterwards to abate in quantity or value of what we had solemnly engaged to devote to him. What was, before the vow, in our own power, as in the case of a free-will offering, afterwards is not, Acts v. 4. It is again and again declared that no sacrifice should be accepted if it was thus blemished, *v.* 20, 21. According to this law great care was taken to search all the beasts that were brought to be sacrificed, that there might, to a certainty, be no blemish in them. A blemished sacrifice might not be accepted even *from the hand of a stranger,* though to such all possible encouragement should be given to do honour to the God of Israel, *v.* 25. By this it appears that strangers were expected to come to the house of God from a *far country* (1 Kings viii. 41, 42), and that they should be welcome, and their offerings accepted, as those of Darius, Ezra vi. 9, 10; Isa. lvi. 6, 7. The heathen priests were many of them not so strict in this matter, but would receive sacrifices for their gods that were ever so scandalous; but let strangers know that the God of Israel would not be so served. Now, 1. This law was then necessary for the preserving of the honour of the sanctuary, and of the God that was there worshipped. It was fit that every thing that was employed for his honour should be the best of the kind; for, as he is the greatest and brightest, so he is the best of beings; and he that is the best must have the best. See how greatly and justly displeasing the breach of this law was to the holy God, Mal. i. 8, 13, 14. 2. This law made all the legal sacrifices the fitter to be types of Christ, the great sacrifice from which all these derived their virtue. In allusion to this law, he is said to be *a Lamb without blemish* and *without spot,* 1 Pet. i. 19. As such a priest, so such a sacrifice, became us, who was harmless and undefiled. When Pilate declared, *I find no fault in this man,* he did thereby in effect pronounce the sacrifice without blemish. The Jews say it was the work of the sagan, or suffragan, high priest, to view the sacrifices, and see whether they were without blemish or no; when Christ suffered, Annas was in that office; but little did those who brought Christ to Annas first, by whom he was sent bound to Caiaphas, as a sacrifice fit to be offered (John xviii. 13, 24), think that they were answering the type of this law. 3. It is an instruction to us to offer to God the best we have in our spiritual sacrifices. If our devotions are ignorant, and cold, and trifling, and full of distractions, we offer *the blind, and the lame, and the sick, for sacrifice;* but cursed be the deceiver that does so, for, while he thinks to put a cheat upon God, he puts a damning cheat upon his own soul.

II. That no beast should be offered in sacrifice before it was eight days old, *v.* 26, 27. It was provided before that the firstlings of their cattle, which were to be dedicated to God, should not be brought to him till after the eighth day, Exod. xxii. 30. Here it is provided that no creature should be offered in sacrifice till it was eight days old complete. Sooner than that it was not fit to be used at men's tables, and therefore not at God's altar. The Jews say, "It was because the sabbath sanctifies all things, and nothing should be offered to God till at least one sabbath had passed over it." It was in conformity to the law of circumcision, which children were to receive on the eighth day. Christ was sacrificed for us, not in his infancy, though then Herod sought to slay him, but in the prime of his time.

III. That the dam and her young should not both be killed in one day, whether in sacrifice or for common use, *v.* 28. There is such a law as this concerning birds, Deut. xxii. 6. This was forbidden, not as evil in itself, but because it looked barbarous and cruel to the brute creatures; like the tyranny of the king of Babylon, that slew Zedekiah's sons before his eyes, and then put out his eyes. It looked ill-natured towards the species to kill two generations at once, as if one designed the ruin of the kind.

IV. That the flesh of their thank-offerings should be eaten on the same day that they were sacrificed, *v.* 29, 30. This is a repetition of what we had before, *ch.* vii. 15; xix. 6, 7. The chapter concludes with such a general charge as we have often met with, to *keep God's commandments,* and not to *profane his holy name, v.* 31, 32. Those that profess God's name, if they do not make conscience of keeping his commandments, do but profane his name. The general reasons are added: God's authority over them—*I am the Lord;* his interest in them—I am *your God;* the title he had to them by redemption—"*I brought you out of the land of Egypt,* on purpose that I might be your God;" the designs of his grace concerning them—*I am the Lord that hallow you;* and the resolutions of his justice, if he had not honour from them, to *get himself honour* upon them—I will be *hallowed among the children of Israel.* God will be a loser in his glory by no man at last; but sooner or later will recover his right, either in the repentance of sinners or in their ruin.

CHAP. XXIII.

Hitherto the levitical law has been chiefly conversant about holy persons, holy things, and holy places; in this chapter we have the institution of holy times, many of which had been mentioned occasionally before, but here they are all put together, only the new moons are not mentioned. All the rest of the feasts of the Lord are, I. The weekly feast of the sabbath, ver. 3. II. The yearly feasts, 1. The passover, and the feast of unleavened bread (ver. 4—8), to which was annexed the offering of the sheaf of firstfruits, ver. 9—14. 2. Pentecost, ver. 15—22. 3. The solemnities of the seventh month. The feast of trumpets on the first day (ver. 23—25), the day of atonement on the tenth day (ver. 26—32), and the feast of tabernacles on the fifteenth, ver. 33, &c.

AND the LORD spake unto Moses, saying, 2 Speak unto the children of Israel, and say unto them, *Concerning* the feasts of the LORD, which ye shall proclaim *to be* holy convocations, *even* these *are* my feasts. 3 Six days shall work be done: but the seventh day *is* the sabbath of rest, a holy convocation; ye shall do no work *therein:* it *is* the sabbath of the LORD in all your dwellings.

Here is, I. A general account of the holy times which God appointed (*v.* 2), and it is only his appointment that can make time holy; for he is the Lord of time, and as soon as ever he had set its wheels a-going it was he that sanctified and blessed one day above the rest, Gen. ii. 3. Man may by his appointment make a good day (Esth. ix. 19), but it is God's prerogative to make a holy day; nor is any thing sanctified but by the stamp of his institution. As all inherent holiness comes from his special grace, so all adherent holiness from his special appointment. Now, concerning the holy times here ordained, observe, 1. They are called *feasts.* The day of atonement, which was one of them, was a fast; yet, because most of them were appointed for joy and rejoicing, they are in the general called feasts. Some read it, *These are my assemblies,* but that is co-incident with *convocations.* I would rather read it, These are *my solemnities;* so the word here used is translated (Isa. xxxiii. 20), where Zion is called the *city of our solemnities:* and, reading it so here, the day of atonement was as great a solemnity as any of them. 2. They are the feasts of the Lord *(my feasts),* observed to the honour of his name, and in obedience to his command. 3. They were proclaimed; for they were not to be observed by the priests only that attended the sanctuary, but by all the people. And this proclamation was the joyful sound concerning which we read, *Blessed are the people that know it*, Ps. lxxxix. 15. 4. They were to be sanctified and solemnized with holy convocations, that the services of these feasts might appear the more honourable and august, and the people the more unanimous in the performance of them; it was for the honour of God and his institutions, which sought not corners and the purity of which would be best preserved by the public administration of them; it was also for the edification of the people in love that the feasts were to be observed as holy convocations.

II. A repetition of the law of the sabbath in the first place. Though the annual feasts were made more remarkable by the general attendance at the sanctuary, yet these must not eclipse the brightness of the sabbath, *v.* 3. They are here told, 1. That on that day they must withdraw themselves from all the affairs and business of the world. It is a *sabbath of rest*, typifying our spiritual rest from sin, and in God: *You shall do no work therein.* On other holy days they were forbidden to do any servile work (*v.* 7), but on the sabbath, and the day of atonement (which is also called a sabbath) they were to do no work at all, no, not the dressing of meat. 2. On that day they must employ themselves in the service of God. (1.) It is a *holy convocation ;* that is, "If it lie within your reach, you shall sanctify it in a religious assembly : let as many as can come to the door of the tabernacle, and let others meet elsewhere for prayer, and praise, and the reading of the law," as in the schools of the prophets, while prophecy continued, and afterwards in the synagogues. Christ appointed the New-Testament sabbath to be a holy convocation, by meeting his disciples once and again (and perhaps oftener) on the first day of the week. (2.) "Whether you have opportunity of sanctifying it in a holy convocation or not, yet let it be *the sabbath of the Lord in all your dwellings.* Put a difference between that day and other days in your families. It is the *sabbath of the Lord*, the day on which he rested from the work of creation, and on which he has appointed us to rest; let it be observed in all your dwellings, even now that you dwell in tents." Note, God's sabbaths are to be religiously observed in every private house, by every family apart, as well as by many families together in holy convocations. The sabbath of the Lord in our dwellings will be their beauty, strength, and safety; it will sanctify, edify, and glorify them.

4 These *are* the feasts of the LORD, *even* holy convocations, which ye shall proclaim in their seasons. 5 In the fourteenth *day* of the first month at even *is* the LORD's passover. 6 And on the fifteenth *day* of the same month *is* the feast of unleavened bread unto the LORD: seven days ye must eat unleavened bread. 7 In the first day ye shall have a holy convocation : ye shall do no servile work therein. 8 But ye shall offer an offering made by fire unto the LORD seven days : in the seventh day *is* a holy convocation : ye shall do no servile work *therein.* 9 And the LORD spake unto Moses, saying, 10 Speak unto the children of Israel, and say unto them, When ye be come into the land which I give unto you, and shall reap the harvest thereof, then ye shall bring a sheaf of the firstfruits of your harvest unto the priest : 11 And he shall wave the sheaf before the LORD, to be accepted for you : on the morrow after the sabbath the priest shall wave it. 12 And ye shall offer that day when ye wave the sheaf a he lamb without blemish of the first year for a burnt-offering unto the LORD. 13 And the meat offering thereof *shall be* two tenth deals of fine flour mingled with oil, an offering made by fire unto the LORD *for* a sweet savour : and the drink offering thereof *shall be* of wine, the fourth *part* of a hin. 14 And ye shall eat neither bread, nor parched corn, nor green ears, until the selfsame day that ye have brought an offering unto your God : *it shall be* a statute for ever throughout your generations in all your dwellings.

Here again the feasts are called the *feasts of the Lord*, because he appointed them. Jeroboam's feast, which he *devised of his own heart* (1 Kings xii. 33), was an affront to God, and a reproach upon the people. These feasts were to be proclaimed in their seasons (*v.* 4), and the seasons God chose for them were in March, May and September (according to our present computation), not in winter, because travelling would then be uncomfortable, when the days were short, and the ways foul; not in the middle of summer, because then in those countries they were gathering in their harvest and vintage, and could be ill spared from their country business. Thus graciously does God consult our comfort in his appointments, obliging us thereby religiously to regard his glory in our observance of them, and not to complain of them as a burden. The solemnities appointed them were, 1. Many and returned frequently, which was intended to preserve in them a deep sense of God and religion, and to prevent their inclining to the superstitions of the heathen. God kept them fully employed in his service, that they might not have time to hearken to the temptations of the idolatrous neighbourhood they lived in. 2. They were most of them times of joy and rejoicing. The weekly sabbath is so, and all their yearly solemnities, except the day of atonement. God would thus teach them that wisdom's ways are pleasantness, and engage them to his service by encouraging them to be cheerful in it and to sing at their work. Seven days were days of strict rest and holy convocations; the first day and the seventh of the feast of unleavened bread, the day of pentecost, the day of the feast of trumpets, the first day and the eighth of the feast of tabernacles, and the day of atonement : here were six for holy joy and one only for holy mourning. We are commanded to *rejoice evermore*, but not to be evermore weeping. Here is,

I. A repetition of the law of the passover, which was to be observed on the fourteenth day of the first month, in remembrance of their deliverance out of Egypt and the distinguishing preservation of their first-born, mercies never to be forgotten. This feast was to begin with the killing of the paschal lamb, *v.* 5. It was to continue seven days, during all which time they were to eat sad bread, that was unleavened (*v.* 6), and the first and last day of the seven were to be days of *holy rest* and *holy convocations*, *v.* 7, 8. They were not idle days spent in sport and recreation (as many that are called Christians spend their holy days), but offerings were *made by fire unto the Lord* at his altar ; and we have reason to think that the people were taught to employ their time in prayer, and praise, and godly meditation.

II. An order for the offering of a sheaf of the first-fruits, upon the second day of the feast of unleavened bread ; the first is called the *sabbath*, because it was observed as a sabbath (*v.* 11), and, on the morrow after, they had this solemnity. A sheaf or handful of new corn was brought to the priest, who was to heave it up, in token of his presenting it to the God of Heaven, and to wave it to and fro before the Lord, as the Lord of the whole earth, and this should be accepted for them as a thankful acknowledgment of God's mercy to them in clothing their fields with corn, and of their dependence upon God, and desire towards him, for the preserving of it to their use. For it was the expression both of prayer and praise, *v.* 11. A lamb for a burnt-offering was to be offered with it, *v.* 12. As the sacrifice of animals was generally attended with meat-offerings, so this sacrifice of corn was attended with a burnt-offering, that bread and flesh might be set together on God's table. They are forbidden to eat of their new corn till this handful was offered to God ; for it was fit, if God and Israel feast

together, that he should be served first. And the offering of this sheaf of first-fruits in the name of the whole congregation did, as it were, sanctify to them their whole harvest, and give them a comfortable use of all the rest ; for then we may *eat our bread with joy* when we have, in some measure, performed our duty to God, and God has accepted our works, for thus all our enjoyments become clean to us. Now, 1. This law was given now, though there was no occasion for putting it in execution till they came to Canaan : in the wilderness they sowed no corn ; but God's feeding them there with *bread from heaven* obliged them hereafter not to grudge him his share of their bread out of the earth. We find that when they came into Canaan the manna ceased upon the very day that the sheaf of first-fruits was offered ; they had eaten of the old corn the day before (Josh. v. 11), and then on this day they offered the first-fruits, by which they became entitled to the new corn too (*v.* 12), so that there was no more occasion for manna. 2. This sheaf of first-fruits was typical of our Lord Jesus, who has risen from the dead as the *first-fruits of those that slept*, 1 Cor. xv. 20. That *branch of the Lord* (Isa. iv. 2) was then presented to him, in virtue of the sacrifice of himself, the Lamb of God, and it was accepted for us. It is very observable that our Lord Jesus rose from the dead on the very day that the first-fruits were offered, to show that he was the substance of this shadow. 3. We are taught by this law to *honour the Lord with our substance, and with the first-fruits of all our increase*, Prov. iii. 9. They were not to eat of their new corn till God's part was offered to him out of it (*v.* 14), for we must always begin with God, begin our lives with him, begin every day with him, begin every meal with him, begin every affair and business with him ; *seek first the kingdom of God*.

15 And ye shall count unto you from the morrow after the sabbath, from the day that ye brought the sheaf of the wave offering ; seven sabbaths shall be complete : 16 Even unto the morrow after the seventh sabbath shall ye number fifty days ; and ye shall offer a new meat offering unto the LORD. 17 Ye shall bring out of your habitations two wave loaves of two tenth deals : they shall be of fine flour ; they shall be baken with leaven ; *they are* the firstfruits unto the LORD. 18 And ye shall offer with the bread seven lambs without blemish of the first year, and one young bullock, and two rams : they shall be *for* a burnt offering unto the LORD, with their meat offering, and their drink offerings, *even*

an offering made by fire, of sweet savour unto the LORD. 19 Then ye shall sacrifice one kid of the goats for a sin offering, and two lambs of the first year for a sacrifice of peace offerings. 20 And the priest shall wave them with the bread of the firstfruits *for* a wave offering before the LORD, with the two lambs: they shall be holy to the LORD for the priest. 21 And ye shall proclaim on the selfsame day, *that* it may be a holy convocation unto you: ye shall do no servile work *therein : it shall be* a statute for ever in all your dwellings throughout your generations. 22 And when ye reap the harvest of your land, thou shalt not make clean riddance of the corners of thy field when thou reapest, neither shalt thou gather any gleaning of thy harvest: thou shalt leave them unto the poor, and to the stranger: I *am* the LORD your God.

Here is the institution of the feast of *pentecost*, or *weeks*, as it is called (Deut. xvi. 9), because it was observed fifty days, or seven weeks, after the passover. It is also called the *feast of harvest*, Exod. xxiii. 16. For as the presenting of the sheaf of first-fruits was an introduction to the harvest, and gave them liberty to put in the sickle, so they solemnized the finishing of their corn-harvest at this feast. 1. Then they offered a handful of ears of barley, now they offered *two loaves of wheaten bread, v.* 17. This was leavened. At the passover they ate unleavened bread, because it was in remembrance of the bread they ate when they came out of Egypt, which was unleavened; but now at pentecost it was leavened, because it was an acknowledgment of God's goodness to them in their ordinary food, which was leavened. 2. With that sheaf of first-fruits they offered only one lamb for a burnt-offering, but with these loaves of first-fruits they offered seven lambs, two rams, and one bullock, all for a burnt-offering, so giving glory to God, as the Lord of their land and the Lord of their harvest, by whose favour they lived and to whose praise they ought to live. They offered likewise a kid for a sin-offering, so taking shame to themselves as unworthy of the bread they ate, and imploring pardon for their sins, by which they had forfeited their harvest-mercies, and which they had been guilty of in the receiving of them. And lastly, two lambs for a sacrifice of peace-offerings, to beg a blessing upon the corn they had gathered in, which would be neither sure nor sweet to them without that blessing, Hag. i. 9. These were the only peace-offerings that were offered on the behalf of the whole congregation, and

538

they were reckoned *most holy* offerings, whereas other peace-offerings were but *holy*. All these offerings are here appointed, v. 18— 20. 3. That one day was to be kept with a holy convocation, v. 21. It was one of the days on which all Israel was to meet God and one another, at the place which the Lord should choose. Some suggest that whereas seven days were to make up the feast of unleavened bread there was only one day appointed for the feast of pentecost, because this was a busy time of the year with them, and God allowed them speedily to return to their work in the country. This annual feast was instituted in remembrance of the giving of the law upon mount Sinai, the fiftieth day after they came out of Egypt. That was the feast which they were told in Egypt must be observed to God in the wilderness, as a memorial of which ever after they kept this feast. But the period and perfection of this feast was the pouring out of the Spirit upon the apostles on the day of this feast (Acts ii. 1), in which the law of faith was given, fifty days after Christ our passover was sacrificed for us. And on that day (as bishop Patrick well expresses it) the apostles, having themselves received the *first-fruits of the Spirit*, begat three thousand souls, through the word of truth, and presented them, as the first-fruits of the Christian church, to God and the Lamb.

To the institution of the feast of pentecost is annexed a repetition of that law which they had before (*ch.* xix. 9), by which they were required to leave the gleanings of their fields, and the corn that grew on the ends of the butts, for the poor, *v.* 22. Probably it comes in here as a thing which the priests must take occasion to remind the people of, when they brought their first-fruits, intimating to them that to obey even in this small matter was better than sacrifice, and that, unless they were obedient, their offerings should not be accepted. It also taught them that the joy of harvest should express itself in charity to the poor, who must have their due out of what we have, as well as God his. Those that are truly sensible of the mercy they receive from God will without grudging show mercy to the poor.

23 And the LORD spake unto Moses, saying, 24 Speak unto the children of Israel, saying, In the seventh month, in the first *day* of the month, shall ye have a sabbath, a memorial of blowing of trumpets, a holy convocation. 25 Ye shall do no servile work *therein :* but ye shall offer an offering made by fire unto the LORD. 26 And the LORD spake unto Moses, saying, 27 Also on the tenth *day* of this seventh month *there shall be* a day of atonement: it shall be a holy

convocation unto you; and ye shall afflict your souls, and offer an offering made by fire unto the Lord. 28 And ye shall do no work in that same day: for it *is* a day of atonement, to make an atonement for you before the Lord your God. 29 For whatsoever soul *it be* that shall not be afflicted in that same day, he shall be cut off from among his people. 30 And whatsoever soul *it be* that doeth any work in that same day, the same soul will I destroy from among his people. 31 Ye shall do no manner of work: *it shall be* a statute for ever throughout your generations in all your dwellings. 32 It *shall be* unto you a sabbath of rest, and ye shall afflict your souls: in the ninth *day* of the month at even, from even unto even, shall ye celebrate your sabbath.

Here is, I. The institution of the feast of trumpets, on the first day of the seventh month, *v.* 24, 25. That which was now the seventh month had been reckoned the first month, and the year of jubilee was still to begin with this month (*ch.* xxv. 8), so that this was their new year's day. It was to be as their other yearly sabbaths, a day of holy rest—*You shall do no servile work therein;* and a day of holy work—*You shall offer an offering to the Lord;* concerning these particular directions were afterwards given, Num. xxix. 1. That which is here made peculiar to this festival is that it was *a memorial of blowing of trumpets.* They blew the trumpet every new moon (Ps. lxxxi. 3), but in the new moon of the seventh month it was to be done with more than ordinary solemnity; for they began to blow at sun-rise and continued till sun-set. Now, 1. This is here said to be a *memorial,* perhaps of the sound of the trumpet upon mount Sinai when the law was given, which must never be forgotten. Some think that it was a memorial of the creation of the world, which is supposed to have been in autumn; for which reason this was, till now, the first month. The mighty word by which God made the world is called *the voice of his thunder* (Ps. civ. 7); fitly therefore was it commemorated by blowing of trumpets, or a memorial of *shouting,* as the Chaldee renders it; for, when the *foundations of the earth were fastened, all the sons of God shouted for joy,* Job xxxviii. 6, 7. 2. The Jewish writers suppose it to have a spiritual signification. Now at the beginning of the year they were called by this sound of trumpet to shake off their spiritual drowsiness, to search and try their ways, and to amend them: the day of atonement was the ninth day after this; and thus they were awakened to pre-

pare for that day, by sincere and serious repentance, that it might be indeed to them a day of atonement. And they say, "The devout Jews exercised themselves more in good works between the feast of trumpets and the day of expiation than at any other time of the year." 3. It was typical of the preaching of the gospel, by which joyful sound souls were to be called in to serve God and keep a spiritual feast to him. The conversion of the nations to the faith of Christ is said to be by the *blowing of a great trumpet,* Isa. xxvii. 13.

II. A repetition of the law of the day of atonement, that is, so much of it as concerned the people. 1. They must on this day rest from all manner of work, and not only from servile works as on other annual festivals; it must be as strict a rest as that of the weekly sabbath, *v.* 28, 30, 31. The reason is: *For it is a day of atonement.* Note, The humbling of our souls for sin, and the making of our peace with God, is work that requires the whole man, and the closest application of mind imaginable, and all little enough. He that would do the work of a day of atonement in its day, as it should be done, had need lay aside the thoughts of every thing else. On that day God *spoke peace unto his people, and unto his saints;* and therefore they must lay aside all their worldly business, that they might the more clearly and the more reverently hear that voice of joy and gladness. Fasting days should be days of rest. 2. They must afflict their souls, and this upon pain of being cut off by the hand of God, *v.* 27, 29, 32. They must mortify the body, and deny the appetites of it, in token of their sorrow for the sins they had committed, and the mortifying of their indwelling corruptions. Every soul must be afflicted, because every soul was polluted, and guilty before God; while none have fulfilled the law of innocency none are exempt from the law of repentance, besides that every man must sigh and cry for the *abominations of the land.* 3. The entire day must be observed: *From even to even you shall afflict your souls* (*v.* 32), that is, "You shall begin your fast, and the expressions of your humiliation, in the *ninth day of the month at even.*" They were to leave off all their worldly labour, and compose themselves to the work of the day approaching, some time before sun-set on the ninth day, and not to take any food (except children and sick people) till after sun-set on the tenth day. Note, The eves of solemn days ought to be employed in solemn preparation. When work for God and our souls is to be done, we should not straiten ourselves in time for the doing of it; for how can we spend our time better? Of this sabbath the rule here given is to be understood: *From even unto even shall you celebrate your sabbath.*

33 And the Lord spake unto Moses, saying, 34 Speak unto the children of Israel, saying, The fifteenth

day of this seventh month *shall be* the feast of tabernacles *for* seven days unto the LORD. 35 On the first day *shall be* a holy convocation: ye shall do no servile work *therein*. 36 Seven days ye shall offer an offering made by fire unto the LORD: on the eighth day shall be a holy convocation unto you; and ye shall offer an offering made by fire unto the LORD: it *is* a solemn assembly; *and* ye shall do no servile work *therein*. 37 These *are* the feasts of the LORD, which ye shall proclaim *to be* holy convocations, to offer an offering made by fire unto the LORD, a burnt offering, and a meat offering, a sacrifice, and drink offerings, every thing upon his day: 38 Beside the sabbaths of the LORD, and beside your gifts, and beside all your vows, and beside all your freewill offerings, which ye give unto the LORD. 39 Also in the fifteenth day of the seventh month, when ye have gathered in the fruit of the land, ye shall keep a feast unto the LORD seven days: on the first day *shall be* a sabbath, and on the eighth day *shall be* a sabbath. 40 And ye shall take you on the first day the boughs of goodly trees, branches of palm trees, and the boughs of thick trees, and willows of the brook; and ye shall rejoice before the LORD your God seven days. 41 And ye shall keep it a feast unto the LORD seven days in the year. *It shall be* a statute for ever in your generations: ye shall celebrate it in the seventh month. 42 Ye shall dwell in booths seven days; all that are Israelites born, shall dwell in booths: 43 That your generations may know that I made the children of Israel to dwell in booths, when I brought them out of the land of Egypt: I *am* the LORD your God. 44 And Moses declared unto the children of Israel the feasts of the LORD.

We have here, I. The institution of the feast of tabernacles, which was one of the three great feasts at which all the males were bound to attend, and celebrated with more expressions of joy than any of them.

1. As to the directions for regulating this feast, observe, (1.) It was to be observed on *the fifteenth day of the seventh month* (v. 34), but five days after the day of atonement.

540

We may suppose, though they were not all bound to attend on the day of atonement, as on the three great festivals, yet that many of the devout Jews came up so many days before the feast of tabernacles as to enjoy the opportunity of attending on the day of atonement. Now, [1.] The afflicting of their souls on the day of atonement prepared them for the joy of the feast of tabernacles. The more we are grieved and humbled for sin, the better qualified we are for the comforts of the Holy Ghost. [2.] The joy of this feast recompensed them for the sorrow of that fast; for those that *sow in tears* shall *reap in joy.* (2.) It was to continue eight days, the first and last of which were to be observed as sabbaths, days of holy rest and holy convocations, v. 35, 36, 39. The sacrifices to be offered on these eight days we have a very large appointment of, Num. xxix. 12, &c. (3.) During the first seven days of this feast all the people were to leave their houses, and the women and children in them, and to dwell in booths made of the boughs of thick trees, particularly palm-trees, v. 40, 42. The Jews make the taking of the branches to be a distinct ceremony from the making of the booths. It is said, indeed (Neh. viii. 15), that they *made their booths of the branches of trees,* which they might do, and yet use that further expression of joy, the carrying of palm-branches in their hands, which appears to have been a token of triumph upon other occasions (John xii. 13), and is alluded to, Rev. vii. 9. The eighth day some make a distinct feast of itself, but it is called (John vii. 37) *that great day of the feast;* it was the day on which they returned from their booths, to settle again in their own houses. (4.) They were to *rejoice before the Lord God* during all the time of this feast, v. 40. The tradition of the Jews is that they were to express their joy by dancing, and singing hymns of praise to God, with musical instruments: and not the common people only, but the wise men of Israel, and their elders, were to do it in the court of the sanctuary: for (say they) the joy with which a man rejoices in doing a commandment is really a great service.

2. As to the design of this feast,

(1.) It was to be kept in remembrance of their dwelling in tents in the wilderness. Thus it is expounded here (v. 43): *That your generations may know,* not only by the written history, but by this ocular tradition, *that I made the children of Israel to dwell in booths.* Thus it kept in perpetual remembrance, [1.] The meanness of their beginning, and the low and desolate state out of which God advanced that people. Note, Those that are comfortably fixed ought often to call to mind their former unsettled state, when they were but little in their own eyes. [2.] The mercy of God to them, that, when they dwelt in tabernacles, God not only set up a tabernacle for himself among them, but, with the utmost care and tenderness imaginable, hung a canopy over them, even the cloud that sheltered them from the heat of the sun. God's former mercies to us and our fathers ought to be kept in everlasting remembrance. The eighth day was the great day of this feast, because then they returned to their own houses again, and remembered how, after they had long dwelt in tents in the wilderness, at length they came to a happy settlement in the land of promise, where they dwelt in goodly houses. And they would the more sensibly value and be thankful for the comforts and conveniences of their houses when they had been seven days dwelling in booths. It is good for those that have ease and plenty sometimes to learn what it is to endure hardness.

(2.) It was a feast of in-gathering, so it is called, Exod. xxiii. 16. When they had gathered in the *fruit of their land* (*v.* 39), the vintage as well as the harvest, then they were to keep this feast in thankfulness to God for all the increase of the year; and some think that the eighth day of the feast had special reference to this ground of the institution. Note, The joy of harvest ought to be improved for the furtherance of our joy in God. *The earth is the Lord's and the fulness thereof*, and therefore whatever we have the comfort of he must have the glory of, especially when any mercy is perfected.

(3.) It was a typical feast. It is supposed by many that our blessed Saviour was born much about the time of this feast; then he left his mansions of light above to *tabernacle among us* (John i. 14), and he dwelt in booths. And the worship of God under the New Testament is prophesied of under the notion of keeping the *feast of tabernacles*, Zech. xiv. 16. For, [1.] The gospel of Christ teaches us to dwell in tabernacles, to sit loose to this world, as those that have here no continuing city, but by faith, and hope, and a holy contempt of present things, to *go out to Christ without the camp*, Heb. xiii. 13, 14. [2.] It teaches us to rejoice before the Lord our God. Those are the circumcision, Israelites indeed, that always *rejoice in Christ Jesus*, Phil. iii. 3. And the more we are taken off from this world the less liable we are to the interruption of our joys.

II. The summary and conclusion of these institutions.

1. God appointed these feasts (*v.* 37, 38), *besides the sabbaths and your free-will offerings.* This teaches us, (1.) That calls to extraordinary services will not excuse us from our constant stated performances. Within the days of the feast of tabernacles there must fall at least one sabbath, which must be as strictly observed as any other. (2.) That God's institutions leave room for free-will offerings. Not that we may invent what he never instituted, but we may repeat what he has instituted, ordinarily, the oftener the better. God is well pleased with a willing people.

2. Moses declared them to the children of Israel, *v.* 44. He let them know what God appointed, and neither more nor less. Thus Paul delivered to the churches what he had *received from the Lord.* We have reason to be thankful that the feasts of the Lord, declared unto us, are not so numerous, nor the observance of them so burdensome and costly, as theirs then were, but more spiritual and significant, and surer sweeter earnests of the everlasting feast, at the last in-gathering, which we hope to be celebrating to eternity

CHAP. XXIV.

In this chapter we have, I. A repetition of the laws concerning the lamps and the show-bread, ver. 1—9. II. A violation of the law against blasphemy, with the imprisonment, trial, condemnation, and execution, of the blasphemer, ver. 10—14, with ver. 23. III. The law against blasphemy reinforced (ver. 15, 16), with sundry other laws, ver. 17, &c.

AND the Lord spake unto Moses, saying, 2 Command the children of Israel, that they bring unto thee pure oil olive beaten for the light, to cause the lamps to burn continually. 3 Without the veil of the testimony, in the tabernacle of the congregation, shall Aaron order it from the evening unto the morning before the Lord continually: *it shall be* a statute for ever in your generations. 4 He shall order the lamps upon the pure candlestick before the Lord continually. 5 And thou shalt take fine flour, and bake twelve cakes thereof: two tenth deals shall be in one cake. 6 And thou shalt set them in two rows, six on a row, upon the pure table before the Lord. 7 And thou shalt put pure frankincense upon *each* row, that it may be on the bread for a memorial, *even* an offering made by fire unto the Lord. 8 Every sabbath he shall set it in order before the Lord continually, *being taken* from the children of Israel by an everlasting covenant. 9 And it shall be Aaron's and his sons'; and they shall eat it in the holy place: for it *is* most holy unto him of the offerings of the Lord made by fire by a perpetual statute.

Care is here taken, and orders are given, for he decent furnishing of the candlestick and table in God's house.

I. The lamps must always be kept burning. The law for this we had before, Exod. xxvii. 20, 21. It is here repeated, probably because it now began to be put in execution, when other things were settled. 1. The people were to provide oil (*v.* 2), and this, as every thing else that was to be used in God's service, must be of the best, *pure olive-oil, beaten,* probably it was double-strained. This was to *cause the lamps to burn;* all our English copies read it *lamps,* but in the original it is singular in *v.* 2—to *cause the lamp to burn;* but plural in *v.* 4—*he shall order the lamps.* The seven lamps made all one lamp, in allusion to which the blessed Spirit of grace is represented by *seven lamps of fire before the throne* (Rev. iv. 5), for there are *diversities of gifts, but one Spirit,* 1 Cor. xii. 4. Ministers are as burning and shining lights in Christ's church, but it is the duty of people to provide comfortably for them, as Israel for the lamps. Scandalous maintenance makes a scandalous ministry. 2. The priests were to tend the lamps; they must snuff them, clean the candlestick, and supply them with oil, morning and evening, *v.* 3, 4. Thus it is the work of the ministers of the gospel to *hold forth that word of life,* not to set up new lights, but, by expounding and preaching the word, to make the light of it more clear and extensive. This was the ordinary way of keeping the lamps burning; but, when the church was poor and in distress, we find its lamps fed constantly with *oil from the good olives* immediately, without the ministry of priest or people (Zech. iv. 2, 3); for, though God has tied us to means, he has not tied himself to them, but will take effectual care that his lamp never go out in the world for want of oil.

II. The table must always be kept spread. This was appointed before, Exod. xxv. 30. And here also, 1. The table was furnished with bread; not dainties nor varieties to gratify a luxurious palate, but twelve loaves or cakes of bread, *v.* 5, 6. Where there is plenty of bread there is no famine; and where bread is not there is no feast. There was a loaf for every tribe, for *in our Father's house there is bread enough.* They were all provided for by the divine bounty, and were all welcome to the divine grace. Even after the revolt of the ten tribes this number of loaves was continued (2 Chron. xiii. 11), for the sake of those few of each tribe that retained their affection to the temple and continued their attendance on it. 2. A handful of frankincense was put in a golden saucer, upon or by each row, *v.* 7. When the bread was removed, and given to the priests, this frankincense was burnt upon the golden altar (I suppose) over and above the daily incense: and this was for a memorial instead of the bread, an offering made by fire, as the handful of the meat-offering which was burnt upon the altar is called the *memorial thereof, ch.* ii. 2. Thus a little was accepted as a humble acknowledgment, and all the loaves were consigned to the priests. All God's spiritual Israel, typified by the twelve loaves, are made through Christ a sweet savour to him, and their prayers are said to come up before God *for a memorial,* Acts x. 4. The word is borrowed from the ceremonial law. 3. Every sabbath it was renewed. When the loaves had stood there a week, the priests had them to eat with other holy things that

were to be eaten in the holy place (*v.* 9), and new ones were provided at the public charge, and put in the room of them, *v.* 8. The Jews say, "The hands of those priests that put on were mixed with theirs that took off, that the table might be never empty, but the bread might be *before the Lord continually.*" God is never unprovided for the entertainment of those that visit him, as men often are, Luke xi. 5. Every one of those cakes contained two tenth-deals, that is, two omers of fine flour; just so much manna every Israelite gathered on the sixth day for the sabbath, Exod. xvi. 22. Hence some infer that this show-bread, which was set on the table on the sabbath, was intended as a memorial of the manna wherewith they were fed in the wilderness. Christ's ministers should provide new bread for his house every sabbath day, the production of their fresh studies in the scripture, that *their proficiency may appear to all,* 1 Tim. iv. 1, 5.

10 And the son of an Israelitish woman, whose father *was* an Egyptian, went out among the children of Israel: and this son of the Israelitish *woman* and a man of Israel strove together in the camp; 11 And the Israelitish woman's son blasphemed the name *of the LORD,* and cursed. And they brought him unto Moses: (and his mother's name *was* Shelomith, the daughter of Dibri, of the tribe of Dan:) 12 And they put him in ward, that the mind of the LORD might be showed them. 13 And the LORD spake unto Moses, saying, 14 Bring forth him that hath cursed without the camp; and let all that heard *him* lay their hands upon his head, and let all the congregation stone him. 15 And thou shalt speak unto the children of Israel, saying, Whosoever curseth his God shall bear his sin. 16 And he that blasphemeth the name of the LORD, he shall surely be put to death, *and* all the congregation shall certainly stone him: as well the stranger, as he that is born in the land, when he blasphemeth the name *of the LORD,* shall be put to death. 17 And he that killeth any man shall surely be put to death. 18 And he that killeth a beast shall make it good; beast for beast. 19 And if a man cause a blemish in his neighbour; as he hath done, so shall it be done to him; 20 Breach for breach, eye for

eye, tooth for tooth: as he hath caused a blemish in a man, so shall it be done to him *again*. 21 And he that killeth a beast, he shall restore it: and he that killeth a man, he shall be put to death. 22 Ye shall have one manner of law, as well for the stranger, as for one of your own country: for I *am* the LORD your God. 23 And Moses spake to the children of Israel, that they should bring forth him that had cursed out of the camp, and stone him with stones. And the children of Israel did as the LORD commanded Moses.

Evil manners, we say, beget good laws. We have here an account of the evil manners of a certain nameless mongrel Israelite, and the good laws occasioned thereby.

I. The offender was the son of an Egyptian father and an Israelitish mother (*v.* 10); his mother was of the tribe of Dan, *v.* 11. Neither he nor his father is named, but his mother only, who was an Israelite. This notice is taken of his parentage either, 1. To intimate what occasioned the quarrel he was engaged in. The Jews say, "He offered to set up his tent among the Danites in the right of his mother, but was justly opposed by some or other of that tribe, and informed that his father being an Egyptian he had no part nor lot in the matter, but must look upon himself as a stranger." Or, 2. To show the common ill effect of such mixed marriages. When a daughter of Israel would marry an idolatrous malignant Egyptian, what could be the fruit of such a marriage but a blasphemer? For the children will be apt to take after the worse side, whichsoever it is, and will sooner learn of an Egyptian father to blaspheme than of an Israelitish mother to pray and praise.

II. The occasion of the offence was contention: He *strove with a man of Israel.* The mixed multitude of Egyptians that came up with Israel (Exod. xii. 38) were in many ways hurtful to them, and this was one, they were often the authors of strife. The way to preserve the peace of the church is to preserve the purity of it. In this strife he broke out into ill language. Note, When quarrels begin we know not what mischief they will make before they end, nor how great a matter a little fire may kindle. When men's passion is up they are apt to forget both their reason and their religion, which is a good reason why we should not be apt either to give or to resent provocation, but leave off strife before it be meddled with, because the beginning of it is *as the letting forth of water.*

III. The offence itself was blasphemy and cursing, *v.* 11. It is supposed that his cause came to be heard before the judges, who de-

termined that he had no right to the privileges of an Israelite, his father being an Egyptian, and that, being enraged at the sentence, 1. He *blasphemed the name of the Lord.* He blasphemed *the name*, that is, he blasphemed God, who is known by his name only, not by his nature, or any similitude. Not as if God were a mere name, but his is a name above every name. The translators add *of the Lord*, which is implied, but not expressed, in the original, for the greater reverence of the divine Majesty: it is a shame that it should be found on record that the very name of Jehovah should be blasphemed; *tell it not in Gath.* It is a fond conceit of the superstitious Jews that his blasphemy was in pronouncing the name of *Jehovah*, which they call ineffable: he that made himself known by that name never forbade the calling of him by that name. It is probable that finding himself aggrieved by the divine appointment, which separated between the Israelites and strangers, he impudently reproached both the law and the Lawmaker, and set him at defiance. 2. He cursed either God himself (and then his cursing was the same with blaspheming) or the person with whom he strove. Imprecations of mischief are the hellish language of hasty passion, as well as of rooted malice. Or perhaps he cursed the judges that gave sentence against him; he flew in the face of the court, and ridiculed the processes of it; thus he added sin to sin.

IV. The caution with which he was proceeded against for this sin. The witnesses or inferior judges brought him and his case (which was somewhat extraordinary) unto Moses (*v.* 11), according to the order settled (Exod. xviii. 22), and Moses himself would not give judgment hastily, but committed the offender into custody, till he had consulted the oracle in this case. Note, Judges must deliberate; both those that give the verdict and those that give the sentence must consider diligently what they do, and do nothing rashly, for *the judgment is God's* (Deut. i. 17), and before him there will be a rehearing of the cause. They waited to know what was *the mind of the Lord*, whether he was to be put to death by the hand of the magistrate or to be left to the judgment of God: or, rather, they wanted to know whether he should be stoned, as those were to be that only cursed their *parents* (ch. xx. 9), or whether, the crime being so much greater, some sorer punishment should be inflicted on him. Note, Those that sit in judgment should sincerely desire, and by prayer and the use of all good means should endeavour to *know the mind of the Lord*, because they *judge for him* (2 Chron. xix. 6) and to him they are accountable.

V. Sentence passed upon this offender by the righteous Judge of heaven and earth himself: *Let all the congregation stone him, v.* 14. God could have cut him off by an immediate stroke from heaven, but he would put this honour upon the institution of magistracy to make use of it for the supporting and vindicating of his own glory in the world. Observe, 1. The place of execution appointed : *Bring him forth without the camp.* To signify their detestation of the crime, they must thus cast out the criminal as an abominable branch, and separate him from them as an unclean thing and unworthy a place in the camp of Israel. 2. The executioners : *Let all the congregation* do it, to show their zeal for the honour of God's name. Every man should have a stone to throw at him that blasphemes God, reckoning himself nearly concerned in the reproaches cast on God, Ps. lxix. 9. Thus also the greater terror would be cast upon the congregation ; those that once helped to stone a blasphemer would ever after dread every thing that bordered upon blasphemy, that looked like it or looked towards it. 3. The solemnity of the execution ; before the congregation stoned him, the witnesses were to *lay their hands upon his head.* The Jews say that this was used in the execution of no criminals but blasphemers ; and that it was done with words to this purport, " *Thy blood be upon thy own head, for thou thyself hast occasioned it.* Let no blame be laid on the law, judges, juries, or witnesses ; *if thou scornest, thou alone shalt bear it.*"

VI. A standing law made upon this occasion for the stoning of blasphemers, *v.* 15, 16. Magistrates are the guardians of both tables, and ought to be as jealous for the honour of God against those that speak contemptuously of his being and government as for the public peace and safety against the disturbers of them. 1. A great stress is laid upon this law, as in no case to be dispensed with : *He shall surely be put to death ; they shall certainly stone him.* Those that lightly esteemed God's honour might think it hard to make a man an offender for a word (words are but wind) ; but God would let them know that they must not make light of such words as these, which come from malice against God in the heart of him that speaks, and must occasion either great guilt or great grief to those that hear. 2. It is made to extend to the strangers that sojourned among them, as well as those that were born in the land. God never made any law to compel strangers to be circumcised and embrace the Jewish religion (proselytes made by force would be no honour to the God of Israel), but he made a law to restrain strangers from speaking evil of the God of Israel. 3. He that was put to death for blasphemy is said to *bear his sin,* in the punishment of it ; no sacrifice being appointed, on the head of which the sin might be transferred, he himself was to bear it upon his own head, as a sacrifice to divine justice. So *his own tongue fell upon him* (Ps. lxiv. 8), and the tongue of a blasphemer will fall heavily.

544

VII. A repetition of some other laws annexed to this new law. 1. That murder should be punished with death (*v.* 17, and again *v.* 21), according to an ancient law in Noah's time (Gen. ix. 6), and the very law of nature, Gen. iv. 10. 2. That maimers should in like manner be punished by the law of retaliation, *v.* 19, 20. Not that men might in these cases be their own avengers, but they might appeal to the civil magistrate, who should award suffering to the injurious and satisfaction to the injured as should be thought fit in proportion to the hurt done. This law we had before, Exod. xxii. 4, 5. And it was more agreeable to that dispensation, in which were revealed the rigour of the law and what sin deserved, than to the dispensation we are under, in which are revealed the grace of the gospel and the remission of sins : and therefore our Saviour has set aside this law (Matt. v. 38, 39), not to restrain magistrates from executing public justice, but to restrain us all from returning personal injuries and to oblige us to forgive as we are and hope to be forgiven. 3. That hurt done wilfully to a neighbour's cattle should be punished by making good the damage, *v.* 18, 21. Thus the divine law took not only their lives, but their goods also under its protection. Those beasts which belonged to no particular person, but were, as our law speaks, *feræ naturæ*—*of a wild nature,* it was lawful for them to kill ; but not those which any man had a property in. Does God take care for oxen ? Yes ; for our sakes he does. 4. That strangers, as well as native Israelites, should be both entitled to the benefit of this law, so as not to suffer wrong, and liable to the penalty of this law in case they did wrong. And, it should seem, this is it that brings in these laws here, to show how equitable it was that strangers as well as Israelites should be punished for blasphemy, because strangers as well as Israelites were punishable for other crimes. And there may be this further reason for the recognition of these laws here, God would hereby show what provision he had made for man's safety, in punishing those that were injurious to him, which should be an argument with magistrates to be jealous for his honour, and to punish those that blasphemed his name. If God took care for their comfort, they ought to take care for his glory.

VIII. The execution of the blasphemer. Moses did, as it were, sign the warrant for it : *He spoke unto the children of Israel* to do it, and they *did as the Lord commanded Moses, v.* 23. This teaches that death is the wages of sin, and that blasphemy in particular is an *iniquity to be punished by the judges.* But, if those who thus profane the name of God escape punishment from men, yet the Lord our God will not suffer them to escape his righteous judgments. This blasphemer was the first that died by the law of Moses. Stephen, the first that died for the gospel, died by the abuse of this law; the martyr and the malefactor suffered the same death: but how vast the difference between them!

CHAP. XXV.

The law of this chapter concerns the lands and estates of the Israelites in Canaan, the occupying and transferring of which were to be under the divine direction, as well as the management of religious worship; for, as the tabernacle was a holy house, so Canaan was a holy land; and upon that account, as much as any thing, it was the glory of all lands. In token of a peculiar title which God had to this land, and a right to dispose of it, he appointed, I. That every seventh year should be a year of rest from occupying the land, a sabbatical year, ver. 1—7. In this God expected from them extraordinary instances of faith and obedience, and they might expect from God extraordinary instances of power and goodness in providing for them, ver. 18—22. II. That every fiftieth year should be a year of jubilee, that is, 1. A year of release of debts and mortgages, and return to the possession of their alienated lands, ver. 8—17. Particular directions are given, (1.) Concerning the sale and redemption of lands, ver. 23—28. (2.) Of houses in cities and villages, with a proviso for Levite-cities, ver. 29—34. 2. A year of release of servants and bond-slaves. (1.) Here is inserted a law for the kind usage of poor debtors, ver. 35—38. (2.) Then comes the law for the discharge of all Israelites that were sold for servants, in the year of jubilee, if they were not redeemed before. [1.] If they were sold to Israelites, ver. 39—46. And, [2.] If sold to proselytes, ver. 47—55. All these appointments have something moral and of perpetual obligation in them, though in the letter of them they were not only peculiar to the Jews, but to them only while they were in Canaan.

AND the LORD spake unto Moses in mount Sinai, saying, 2 Speak unto the children of Israel, and say unto them, When ye come into the land which I give unto you, then shall the land keep a sabbath unto the LORD. 3 Six years thou shalt sow thy field, and six years thou shalt prune thy vineyard, and gather in the fruit thereof; 4 But in the seventh year shall be a sabbath of rest unto the land, a sabbath for the LORD: thou shalt neither sow thy field, nor prune thy vineyard. 5 That which groweth of its own accord of thy harvest thou shalt not reap, neither gather the grapes of thy vine undressed: *for* it is a year of rest unto the land. 6 And the sabbath of the land shall be meat for you; for thee, and for thy servant, and for thy maid, and for thy hired servant, and for thy stranger that sojourneth with thee, 7 And for thy cattle, and for the beast that *are* in thy land, shall all the increase thereof be meat.

The law of Moses laid a great deal of stress upon the sabbath, the sanctification of which was the earliest and most ancient of all divine institutions, designed for the keeping up of the knowledge and worship of the Creator among men; that law not only revived the observance of the weekly sabbath, but, for the further advancement of the honour of them, added the institution of a sabbatical year: *In the seventh year shall be a sabbath of rest unto the land, v.* 4. And hence the Jews collect that vulgar tradition that after the world has stood six thousand

years (a thousand years being to God as one day) it shall cease, and the eternal sabbath shall succeed—a weak foundation on which to build the fixing of that day and hour which it is God's prerogative to know. This sabbatical year began in September, at the end of harvest, the seventh month of their ecclesiastical year: and the law was, 1. That at the seed-time, which immediately followed the end of their in-gathering, they should sow no corn in their land, and that they should not in the spring dress their vineyards, and consequently that they should not expect either harvest or vintage the next year. 2. That what their ground did produce of itself they should not claim any property or use in, otherwise than from hand to mouth, but leave it for the poor, servants, strangers, and cattle, *v.* 5—7. It must be a sabbath of rest to the land; they must neither do any work about it, nor expect any fruit from it; all annual labours must be intermitted in the seventh year, as much as daily labours on the seventh day. The Jews say they "began not to reckon for the sabbatical year till they had completed the conquest of Canaan, which was in the eighth year of Joshua; the seventh year after that was the first sabbatical year, and so the fiftieth year was the jubilee." This year there was to be a general release of debts (Deut. xv. 1, 2), and a public reading of the law in the feast (Deut. xxxi. 10, 11), to make it the more solemn. Now, (1.) God would hereby show them that he was their landlord, and that they were tenants at will under him. Landlords are wont to stipulate with their tenants when they shall break up their ground, how long they shall till it, and when they shall let it rest: God would thus give, grant, and convey, that good land to them, under such provisos and limitations as should let them know that they were not proprietors, but dependents on their Lord. (2.) It was a kindness to their land to let it rest sometimes, and would keep it *in heart* (as our husbandmen express it) for posterity, whose satisfaction God would have them to consult, and not to use the ground as if it were designed only for one age. (3.) When they were thus for a whole year taken off from all country business, they would have the more leisure to attend the exercises of religion, and to get the knowledge of God and his law. (4.) They were hereby taught to be charitable and generous, and not to engross all to themselves, but to be willing that others should share with them in the gifts of God's bounty, which the earth brought forth of itself. (5.) They were brought to live in a constant dependence upon the divine providence, finding that, as man lives not by bread alone, so he has bread, not by his own industry alone, but, if God pleases, by the word of blessing from the mouth of God, without any care or pains of man, Matt. iv. 4. (6.) They were reminded of the easy life man lived in paradise, when he ate of every good thing, not, as since, in the sweat of his face. Labour and toil came in with sin. (7.) They were taught to consider how the poor lived, that did neither sow nor reap, even by the blessing of God upon a little. (8.) This year of rest typified the spiritual rest which all believers enter into through Christ, our true Noah, who giveth us comfort and rest *concerning our work, and the toil of our hands, because of the ground which the Lord hath cursed,* Gen. v. 29. Through him we are eased of the burden of worldly care and labour, both being sanctified and sweetened to us, and we are enabled and encouraged to live by faith. And, as the fruits of this sabbath of the land were enjoyed in common, so the salvation wrought out by Christ is a common salvation; and this sabbatical year seems to have been revived in the Christian church, when the believers had *all things common,* Acts ii. 44.

8 And thou shalt number seven sabbaths of years unto thee, seven times seven years; and the space of the seven sabbaths of years shall be unto thee forty and nine years. 9 Then shalt thou cause the trumpet of the jubilee to sound on the tenth *day* of the seventh month, in the day of atonement shall ye make the trumpet sound throughout all your land. 10 And ye shall hallow the fiftieth year, and proclaim liberty throughout *all* the land unto all the inhabitants thereof: it shall be a jubilee unto you; and ye shall return every man unto his possession, and ye shall return every man unto his family. 11 A jubilee shall that fiftieth year be unto you: ye shall not sow, neither reap that which groweth of itself in it, nor gather *the grapes* in it of thy vine undressed. 12 For it *is* the jubilee; it shall be holy unto you: ye shall eat the increase thereof out of the field. 13 In the year of this jubilee ye shall return every man unto his possession. 14 And if thou sell ought unto thy neighbour, or buyest *ought* of thy neighbour's hand, ye shall not oppress one another: 15 According to the number of years after the jubilee thou shalt buy of thy neighbour, *and* according unto the number of years of the fruits he shall sell unto thee: 16 According to the multitude of years thou shalt increase the price thereof, and according to the fewness of years

thou shalt diminish the price of it: for *according* to the number *of the years* of the fruits doth he sell unto thee. 17 Ye shall not therefore oppress one another; but thou shalt fear thy God: for I *am* the Lord your God. 18 Wherefore ye shall do my statutes, and keep my judgments, and do them; and ye shall dwell in the land in safety. 19 And the land shall yield her fruit, and ye shall eat your fill, and dwell therein in safety. 20 And if ye shall say, What shall we eat the seventh year? behold, we shall not sow, nor gather in our increase: 21 Then I will command my blessing upon you in the sixth year, and it shall bring forth fruit for three years. 22 And ye shall sow the eighth year, and eat *yet* of old fruit until the ninth year; until her fruits come in ye shall eat *of* the old *store.*

Here is, I. The general institution of the jubilee, *v.* 8, &c.

1. When it was to be observed: after *seven sabbaths of years* (*v.* 8), whether the forty-ninth or fiftieth is a great question among learned men: that it should be the seventh sabbatical year, that is, the forty-ninth (which by a very common form of speech is called the fiftieth), seems to me most probable, and is, I think, made pretty clear and the objections removed by that learned chronologer Calvisius; but this is not a place for arguing the question. Seven sabbaths of weeks were reckoned from the passover to the feast of pentecost (or fiftieth day, for so pentecost signifies), and so seven sabbaths of years from one jubilee to another, and the seventh is called the fiftieth; and all this honour is put upon the sevenths for the sake of God's resting the seventh day from the work of creation.

2. How it was to be proclaimed, with sound of trumpet in all parts of the country (*v.* 5), both to give notice to all persons of it, and to express their joy and triumph in it; and the word *jobel,* or *jubilee,* is supposed to signify some particular sound of the trumpet distinguishable from any other; for the trumpet that gives an uncertain sound is of little service, 1 Cor. xiv. 8. The trumpet was sounded in the close of the day of atonement; thence the jubilee commenced, and very fitly; when they had been humbling and afflicting their souls for sin, then they were made to hear this voice of *joy and gladness,* Ps. li. 8. When their peace was made with God, then liberty was proclaimed; for the removal of guilt is necessary to make way for the entrance of all true comfort, Rom. v. 1, 2. In allusion to this solemn proclamation of the jubilee, **it**

was foretold concerning our Lord Jesus that he should _preach the acceptable year of the Lord,_ Isa. lxi. 2. He sent his apostles to proclaim it with the trumpet of the everlasting gospel, which they were to preach to every creature. And it stands still foretold that at the last day the trumpet shall sound, which shall release the dead out of the bondage of the grave, and restore us to our possessions.

3. What was to be done in that year extraordinary; besides the common rest of the land, which was observed every sabbatical year (_v._ 11, 12), and the release of personal debts (Deut. xv. 2, 3), there was to be the legal restoration of every Israelite to all the property, and all the liberty, which had been alienated from him since the last jubilee; so that never was any people so secured in their liberty and property (those glories of a people) as Israel was. Effectual care was taken that while they kept close to God these should not only not be taken from them by the violence of others, but not thrown away by their own folly.

(1.) The property which every man had in his dividend of the land of Canaan could not be alienated any longer than till the year of jubilee, and then he or his should return to it, and have a title to it as undisturbed, as ever (_v._ 10, 13): "_You shall return every man to his possession;_ so that if a man had sold or mortgaged his estate, or any part of it, it should then return to him or his heirs, free of all charge and encumbrance. Now this was no wrong to the purchaser, because the year of jubilee was fixed, and every man knew when it would come, and made his bargain accordingly. By our law indeed, if lands be granted to a man and his heirs, upon condition that he should never sell or alienate them, the grant is good, but the condition is void and repugnant: _Iniquum est ingenuis hominibus_ (say the lawyers) _non esse liberam rerum suarum alienationem—It is unjust to prevent free men from alienating their own possessions._ Yet it is agreed in the books that if the king grant lands to a man in fee upon condition he shall not alienate, the condition is good. Now God would show his people Israel that their land was his, and they were his tenants; and therefore he ties them up that they shall not have power to sell, but only to make leases for any term of years, not going beyond the next jubilee. By this means it was provided, [1.] That their genealogies should be carefully preserved, which would be of use for clearing our Saviour's pedigree. [2.] That the distinction of tribes should be kept up; for, though a man might purchase lands in another tribe, yet he could not retain them longer than till the year of jubilee, and then they would revert of course. [3.] That none should grow exorbitantly rich, by laying _house to house, and field to field_ (Isa. v. 8),

but should rather apply themselves to the cultivating of what they had than the enlarging of their possessions. The wisdom of the Roman commonwealth sometimes provided that no man should be master of above 500 acres. [4.] That no family should be sunk and ruined, and condemned to perpetual poverty. This particular care God took for the support of the honour of that people, and the preserving, not only of that good land to the nation in general, but of every man's share to his family in particular, for a perpetual inheritance, that it might the better typify that good part which shall _never be taken away_ from those that have it.

(2.) The liberty which every man was born to, if it were sold or forfeited, should likewise return at the year of jubilee: _You shall return every man to his family,_ v. 10. Those that were sold into other families thereby became strangers to their own; but in this year of redemption they were to return. This was typical of our redemption by Christ from the slavery of sin and Satan, and our restoration to the glorious liberty of the children of God. Some compute that the very year in which Christ died was a year of jubilee, and the last that ever was kept. But, however that be, we are sure it is the Son that _makes us free,_ and then we are _free indeed._

II. A law upon this occasion against oppression in buying and selling of land; neither the buyer nor the seller must overreach, _v._ 14—17. In short, the buyer must not give less, nor the seller take more, than the just value of the thing, considered as necessarily returning at the year of jubilee. It must be settled what the clear yearly value of the land was, and then how many years' purchase it was worth till the year of jubilee. But they must reckon only _the years of the fruits_ (_v._ 15), and therefore must discount for the sabbatical years. It is easy to observe that the nearer the jubilee was the less must the value of the land be. _According to the fewness of the years thou shalt diminish the price._ But we do not find it so easy practically to infer thence that the nearer the world comes to its period the less value we should put upon the things of it: because _the time is short,_ and the _fashion of the world passeth away,_ let those that _buy be as though they possessed not._ One would put little value on an old house, that is ready to drop down. All bargains ought to be made by this rule, _You shall not oppress one another,_ nor take advantage of one another's ignorance or necessity, _but thou shalt fear thy God._ Note, The fear of God reigning in the heart would effectually restrain us from doing any wrong to our neighbour in word or deed; for, though man be not, God is the _avenger_ of those that _go beyond or defraud_ their brethren, 1 Thess. iv. 6. Perhaps Nehemiah refers to this very law (_ch._ v. 15), where he tells us that he did not oppress those he had under his power, _because of the fear of God._

III. Assurance given them that they should

be no losers, but great gainers, by observing these years of rest. It is promised, 1. That they should be safe: *You shall dwell in the land in safety*, v. 18, and again, v. 19. The word signifies both outward safety and inward security and confidence of spirit, that they should be quiet both from evil and from the fear of evil. 2. That they should be rich: *You shall eat your fill.* Note, If we be careful to do our duty, we may cheerfully trust God with our comfort. 3. That they should not want food convenient that year in which they did neither sow nor reap: *I will command my blessing in the sixth year, and it shall bring forth fruit for three years*, v. 21. This was, (1.) A standing miracle, that, whereas at other times one year did but serve to bring in another, the productions of the sixth year should serve to bring in the ninth. Note, The blessing of God upon our provision will make a little go a great way, and *satisfy* even *the poor with bread*, Ps. cxxxii. 15. (2.) A lasting memorial of the manna which was given double on the sixth day for two days. (3.) It was intended for an encouragement to all God's people, in all ages, to trust him in the way of duty, and to cast their care upon him. There is nothing lost by faith and self-denial in our obedience.

23 The land shall not be sold for ever: for the land *is* mine; for ye *are* strangers and sojourners with me. 24 And in all the land of your possession ye shall grant a redemption for the land. 25 If thy brother be waxen poor, and hath sold away *some* of his possession, and if any of his kin come to redeem it, then shall he redeem that which his brother sold. 26 And if the man have none to redeem it, and himself be able to redeem it; 27 Then let him count the years of the sale thereof, and restore the overplus unto the man to whom he sold it; that he may return unto his possession. 28 But if he be not able to restore *it* to him, then that which is sold shall remain in the hand of him that hath bought it until the year of jubilee: and in the jubilee it shall go out, and he shall return unto his possession. 29 And if a man sell a dwelling house in a walled city, then he may redeem it within a whole year after it is sold; *within* a full year may he redeem it. 30 And if it be not redeemed within the space of a full year, then the house that *is* in the walled city shall be established for ever to him that bought it throughout

his generations: it shall not go out in the jubilee. 31 But the houses of the villages which have no wall round about them shall be counted as the fields of the country: they may be redeemed, and they shall go out in the jubilee. 32 Notwithstanding the cities of the Levites, *and* the houses of the cities of their possession, may the Levites redeem at any time. 33 And if a man purchase of the Levites, then the house that was sold, and the city of his possession, shall go out in *the year of* jubilee: for the houses of the cities of the Levites *are* their possession among the children of Israel. 34 But the field of the suburbs of their cities may not be sold; for it *is* their perpetual possession. 35 And if thy brother be waxen poor, and fallen in decay with thee; then thou shalt relieve him: *yea, though he be a* stranger, or a sojourner; that he may live with thee. 36 Take thou no usury of him, or increase: but fear thy God; that thy brother may live with thee. 37 Thou shalt not give him thy money upon usury, nor lend him thy victuals for increase. 38 I *am* the LORD your God, which brought you forth out of the land of Egypt, to give you the land of Canaan, *and* to be your God.

Here is, I. A law concerning the real estates of the Israelites in the land of Canaan, and the transferring of them. 1. No land should be sold for ever from the family to whose lot it fell in the division of the land. And the reason given is, *The land is mine, and you are strangers and sojourners with me*, v. 23. (1.) God having a particular propriety in this land, he would by this restraint keep them sensible of it. The possessions of good people, who, having given up themselves to God, have therewith given up all they have to him, are in a particular manner at his disposal, and his disposal of them must be submitted to. (2.) They being *strangers and sojourners with him* in that land, and having his tabernacle among them, to alienate their part of that land would be in effect to cut themselves off from their fellowship and communion with God, of which that was a token and symbol, for which reason Naboth would rather incur the wrath of a king than part with the inheritance of his fathers, 1 Kings xxi. 3. 2. If a man was constrained through poverty to sell his land for the subsistence of his family, yet, if afterwards he was able, he might redeem it before the year of jubilee (v. 24, 26,

27), and the price must be settled according to the number of years since the sale and before the jubilee. 3. If the person himself was not able to redeem it, his next kinsman might (*v.* 25) : *The redeemer thereof, he that is near unto him, shall come and shall redeem,* so it might be read. The kinsman is called *Goel,* the redeemer (Num. v. 8; Ruth iii. 9), to whom belonged the right of redeeming the land. And this typified Christ, who assumed our nature, that he might be our *kinsman,* bone of our bone and flesh of our flesh, and, being the only kinsman we have that is able to do it, to him belonged the right of redemption. As for all our other kinsmen, their shoe must be plucked off (Ruth iv. 6, 7); they cannot redeem. But Christ can and hath redeemed the inheritance which we by sin had forfeited and alienated, and made a new settlement of it upon all that by faith become allied to him. We know that this *Redeemer liveth,* Job xix. 25. And some make this duty of the kinsman to signify the brotherly love that should be among Christians, inclining them to recover those that are fallen, and to restore them with the spirit of meekness. 4. If the land was not redeemed before the year of jubilee, then it should return of course to him that had sold or mortgaged it : *In the jubilee it shall go out,* *v.* 28. This was a figure of the free grace of God towards us in Christ, by which, and not by any price or merit of our own, we are restored to the favour of God, and become entitled to paradise, from which our first parents, and we in them, were expelled for disobedience. 5. A difference was made between houses in walled cities, and lands in the country, or houses in country villages. Houses in walled cities were more the fruits of their own industry than land in the country, which was the immediate gift of God's bounty; and therefore, if a man sold a house in a city, he might redeem it any time within a year after the sale, but otherwise it was confirmed to the purchaser for ever, and should not return, no, not at the year of the jubilee, *v.* 29, 30. This provision was made to encourage strangers and proselytes to come and settle among them. Though they could not purchase land in Canaan to them and their heirs, yet they might purchase houses in walled cities, which would be most convenient for those who were supposed to live by trade. But country houses could be disposed of no otherwise than as lands might. 6. A clause is added in favour of the Levites, by way of exception from these rules. (1.) Dwelling houses in the cities of the Levites might be redeemed at any time, and, if not redeemed, should revert in the year of jubilee (*v.* 32, 33), because the Levites had no other possessions than cities and their suburbs, and God would show that the Levites were his peculiar care; and it was for the interest of the public that they should not be impoverished, or wormed out of their inheritances. (2.) The fields

adjoining to their cities (Num. xxxv. 4, 5) might not be sold at any time, for they belonged, not to particular Levites, but to the city of the Levites, as a corporation, who could not alienate without a wrong to their tribe; therefore, if any of those fields were sold, the bargain was void, *v.* 34. Even the Egyptians took care to preserve the *land of the priests,* Gen. xlvii. 22. And there is no less reason for the taking of the maintenance of the gospel ministry under the special protection of Christian governments.

II. A law for the relief of the poor, and the tender usage of poor debtors, and these are of more general and perpetual obligation than the former.

1. The poor must be relieved, *v.* 35. Here is, (1.) Our brother's poverty and distress supposed : *If thy brother be waxen poor ;* not only thy brother by nation as a Jew, but thy brother by nature as a man, for it follows, *though he be a stranger or a sojourner.* All men are to be looked upon and treated as brethren, for *we have all one Father,* Mal. ii. 10. Though he be poor, yet still he is thy brother, and is to be loved and owned as a brother. Poverty does not destroy the relation. Though a son of Abraham, yet he may wax poor and fall into decay. Note, Poverty and decay are great grievances, and very common : *The poor you have always with you.* (2.) Our duty enjoined : *Thou shalt relieve him.* By sympathy, pitying the poor ; by service, doing for them ; and by supply, giving to them according to their necessity and thy ability.

2. Poor debtors must not be oppressed : *If thy brother be waxen poor,* and have occasion to borrow money of thee for the necessary support of his family, *take thou no usury of him,* either for money or victuals, *v.* 36, 37. And thus far this law binds still, but could never be thought binding where money is borrowed for purchase of lands, trade, or other improvements; for there it is reasonable that the lender share with the borrower in the profit. The law here is plainly intended for the relief of the poor, to whom it is sometimes as great a charity to lend freely as to give. Observe the arguments here used against extortion. (1.) God patronises the poor : " *Fear thy God,* who will reckon with thee for all injuries done to the poor : thou fearest not them, but fear him." (2.) Relieve the poor, *that they may live with thee,* and some way or other they may be serviceable to thee. The rich can as ill spare the hands of the poor as the poor can the purses of the rich. (3.) The same argument is used to enforce this precept that prefaces all the ten commandments : *I am the Lord your God which brought you out of Egypt, v.* 38. Note, It becomes those that have received mercy to show mercy. If God has been gracious to us, we ought not to be rigorous with our brethren.

39 And if thy brother *that dwelleth*

by thee be waxen poor, and be sold unto thee; thou shalt not compel him to serve as a bondservant: 40 *But* as a hired servant, *and* as a sojourner, he shall be with thee, *and* shall serve thee unto the year of jubilee: 41 And *then* shall he depart from thee, *both* he and his children with him, and shall return unto his own family, and unto the possession of his fathers shall he return. 42 For they *are* my servants, which I brought forth out of the land of Egypt: they shall not be sold as bondmen. 43 Thou shalt not rule over him with rigour; but shalt fear thy God. 44 Both thy bondmen, and thy bondmaids, which thou shalt have, *shall be* of the heathen that are round about you; of them shall ye buy bondmen and bondmaids. 45 Moreover of the children of the strangers that do sojourn among you, of them shall ye buy, and of their families that *are* with you, which they begat in your land: and they shall be your possession. 46 And ye shall take them as an inheritance for your children after you, to inherit *them for* a possession; they shall be your bondmen for ever: but over your brethren the children of Israel, ye shall not rule one over another with rigour. 47 And if a sojourner or stranger wax rich by thee, and thy brother *that dwelleth* by him wax poor, and sell himself unto the stranger *or* sojourner by thee, or to the stock of the stranger's family: 48 After that he is sold he may be redeemed again; one of his brethren may redeem him: 49 Either his uncle, or his uncle's son, may redeem him, or *any* that is nigh of kin unto him of his family may redeem him; or if he be able, he may redeem himself. 50 And he shall reckon with him that bought him from the year that he was sold to him unto the year of jubilee: and the price of his sale shall be according unto the number of years, according to the time of a hired servant shall it be with him. 51 If *there be* yet many years *behind,* according unto them he shall give again the price of his redemption out of the money that he was bought for. 52

And if there remain but few years unto the year of jubilee, then he shall count with him, *and* according unto his years shall he give him again the price of his redemption. 53 *And* as a yearly hired servant shall he be with him: *and the other* shall not rule with rigour over him in thy sight. 54 And if he be not redeemed in these *years,* then he shall go out in the year of jubilee, *both* he, and his children with him. 55 For unto me the children of Israel *are* servants; they *are* my servants whom I brought forth out of the land of Egypt: I *am* the LORD your God.

We have here the laws concerning servitude, designed to preserve the honour of the Jewish nation as a free people, and rescued by a divine power out of the house of bondage, into the glorious liberty of God's sons, his first-born. Now the law is,

I. That a native Israelite should never be made a bondman for perpetuity. If he was sold for debt, or for a crime, by the house of judgment, he was to serve but six years, and to go out the seventh; this was appointed, Exod. xxi. 2. But if he sold himself through extreme poverty, having nothing at all left him to preserve his life, and if it was to one of his own nation that he sold himself, in such a case it is here provided, 1. That he should not *serve as a bond-servant* (v. 39), nor be *sold with the sale of a bondman* (v. 42); that is, "it must not be looked upon that his master that bought him had as absolute a property in him as in a captive taken in war, that might be used, sold, and bequeathed, at pleasure, as much as a man's cattle; no, he shall serve thee as a *hired servant,* whom the master has the use of only, but not a despotic power over." And the reason is, *They are my servants,* v. 42. God does not make his servants slaves, and therefore their brethren must not. God had redeemed them out of Egypt, and therefore they must never be exposed to sale as bondmen. The apostle applies this spiritually (1 Cor. vii. 23), *You are bought with a price, be not the servants of men,* that is, "of the lusts of men, no, nor of your own lusts;" for, having *become the servants of God,* we must not *let sin reign in our mortal bodies,* Rom. vi. 12, 22. 2. That while he did serve he should not be ruled with rigour, as the Israelites were in Egypt, v. 43. Both his work and his usage must be such as were fitting for a son of Abraham. Masters are still required to *give to their servants that which is just and equal,* Col. iv. 1. They may be used, but must not be abused. Those masters that are always hectoring and domineering over their servants, taunting them and trampling upon them, that are unreasonable in exacting work and giving rebukes, and that rule them with a high hand, forget that their Master is in heaven; and what will they do when he rises up? as holy Job reasons with himself, Job xxxi. 13, 14. 3. That at the year of jubilee he should *go out free*, he *and his children*, and should *return to his own family, v.* 41. This typified our redemption from the service of sin and Satan by the grace of God in Christ, whose *truth makes us free*, John viii. 32. The Jewish writers say that, for ten days before the jubilee-trumpet sounded, the servants that were to be discharged by it did express their great joy by feasting, and wearing garlands on their heads : it is therefore called the *joyful sound*, Ps. lxxxix. 15. And we are thus to rejoice in the liberty we have by Christ.

II. That they might purchase bondmen of the heathen nations that were round about them, or of those strangers that sojourned among them (except of those seven nations that were to be destroyed); and might claim a dominion over them, and entail them upon their families as an inheritance, for the year of jubilee should give no discharge to them, *v.* 44, 46. Thus in our English plantations the *negroes* only are used as slaves; how much to the credit of Christianity I shall not say. Now, 1. This authority which they had over the bondmen whom they purchased from the neighbouring nations was in pursuance of the blessing of Jacob, Gen. xxvii. 29, *Let people serve thee.* 2. It prefigured the bringing in of the Gentiles to the service of Christ and his church. *Ask of me, and I will give thee the heathen for thy inheritance*, Ps. ii. 8. And it is promised (Isa. lxi. 5), *Strangers shall stand and feed your flocks, and the sons of the alien shall be your vine-dressers ;* see Rev. ii. 26, 27. *The upright shall have the dominion in the morning*, Ps. xlix. 14. 3. It intimates that none shall have the benefit of the gospel jubilee but those only that are Israelites indeed, and the children of Abraham by faith : as for those that continue heathenish, they continue bondmen. See this turned upon the unbelieving Jews themselves, Gal. iv. 25, where Jerusalem, when she had rejected Christ, is said to be *in bondage with her children.* Let me only add here that, though they are not forbidden to rule their bondmen with rigour, yet the Jewish doctors say, "It is the property of mercy, and way of wisdom, that a man should be compassionate, and not make his yoke heavy upon any servant that he has."

III. That if an Israelite sold himself for a servant to a wealthy proselyte that sojourned among them care should be taken that he should have the same advantages as if he had sold himself to an Israelite, and in some respects greater. 1. That he should not serve as a bondman, but as a hired servant, and not to be *ruled with rigour* (v. 53), *in thy sight*, which intimated that the Jewish magistrates should particularly have an eye to him, and, if he were abused, should take cognizance of it, and redress his grievances,

though the injured servant did not himself complain. Also he was to go free at the year of jubilee, *v.* 54. Though the sons of strangers might serve them for ever, yet the sons of Israel might not serve strangers for ever; yet the servant here, having made himself a slave by his own act and deed, should not go out in the seventh year of release, but in the jubilee only. 2. That he should have this further advantage that he might be redeemed again before the year of jubilee, *v.* 48, 49. He that had sold himself to an Israelite might, if ever he was able, redeem himself, but his relations had no right to redeem him. "But if a man sold himself to a stranger," the Jews say, "his relations were urged to redeem him; if they did not, it was fit that he should be redeemed at the public charge," which we find done, Neh. v. 8. The price of his ransom was to be computed according to the prospect of the year of jubilee (*v.* 50—52), as in the redemption of land, *v.* 15, 16. The learned bishop Patrick quotes one of the Jewish rabbin for an evangelical exposition of that appointment (*v.* 48), *One of his brethren shall redeem him.* "This Redeemer," says the rabbi, "*is the Messiah, the Son of David.*" They expected this Messiah to be their Redeemer out of their captivity, and to restore them to their own land again; but we welcome him as the Redeemer who shall come to Zion, and shall *turn away ungodliness from Jacob*, for he shall *save his people from their sins ;* and under this notion there were those that *looked for redemption in Jerusalem.*

CHAP. XXVI.

This chapter is a solemn conclusion of the main body of the levitical law. The precepts that follow in this and the following book either relate to some particular matters or are repetitions and explications of the foregoing institutions. Now this chapter contains a general enforcement of all those laws by promises of reward in case of obedience on the one hand, and threatenings of punishment for disobedience on the other hand, the former to work upon hope, the latter on fear, those two handles of the soul, by which it is taken hold of and managed. Here is, I. A repetition of two or three of the principal of the commandments, ver. 1, 2. II. An inviting promise of all good things, if they would but keep God's commandments, ver. 3—13. III. A terrible threatening of ruining judgments which would be brought upon them if they were refractory and disobedient, ver. 14—39. IV. A gracious promise of the return of mercy to those of them that would repent and reform, ver. 40, &c. Deut. xxviii. is paralle to this.

Y E shall make you no idols nor graven image, neither rear you up a standing image, neither shall ye set up *any* image of stone in your land, to bow down unto it : for I *am* the LORD your God. 2 Ye shall keep my sabbaths, and reverence my sanctuary : I *am* the LORD. 3 If ye walk in my statutes, and keep my commandments, and do them; 4 Then I will give you rain in due season, and the land shall yield her increase, and the trees of the field shall yield their fruit. 5 And your threshing shall reach unto the vintage, and the vintage shall reach unto the sowing time : and ye shall eat your bread to the full, and dwell in your land safely. 6 And I will give peace in the land, and ye shall lie down, and none shall make *you* afraid : and I will rid evil beasts out of the land, neither shall the sword go through your land. 7 And ye shall chase your enemies, and they shall fall before you by the sword. 8 And five of you shall chase a hundred, and a hundred of you shall put ten thousand to flight : and your enemies shall fall before you by the sword. 9 For I will have respect unto you, and make you fruitful, and multiply you, and establish my covenant with you. 10 And ye shall eat old store, and bring forth the old because of the new. 11 And I will set my tabernacle among you : and my soul shall not abhor you. 12 And I will walk among you, and will be your God, and ye shall be my people. 13 I *am* the LORD your God, which brought you forth out of the land of Egypt, that ye should not be their bondmen ; and I have broken the bands of your yoke, and made you go upright.

Here is, I. The inculcating of those precepts of the law which were of the greatest consequence, and by which especially their obedience would be tried, *v*. 1, 2. They are the abstract of the second and fourth commandments, which, as they are by much the largest in the decalogue, so they are most frequently insisted on in other parts of the law. As, when a master has given many things in charge to his servant, he concludes with the repetition of those things which were of the greatest importance, and which the servant was most in danger of neglecting, bidding him, whatever he did, be sure to remember those, so here God by Moses, after many precepts, closes all with a special charge to observe these two great commandments. 1. " Be sure you never worship images, nor ever make any sort of images or pictures for a religious use," *v*. 1. No sin was more provoking to God than this, and yet there was none that they were more addicted to, and which afterwards proved of more pernicious consequence to them. Next to God's being, unity, and universal influence, it is necessary that we know and believe that he is an infinite Spirit ; and therefore to represent him by an image in the making of it, to confine him to an image in the consecrating of it, and to worship him by an image in bowing down to it, *changes his truth into a lie* and *his glory into shame*, as

much as any thing. 2. " Be sure you keep up a great veneration for sabbaths and religious assemblies," *v*. 2. As nothing tends more to corrupt religion than the use of images in devotion, so nothing contributes more to the support of it than *keeping the sabbaths* and *reverencing the sanctuary*. These make up very much of the instrumental part of religion, by which the essentials of it are kept up. Therefore we find in the prophets that, next to the sin of idolatry, there is no sin for which the Jews are more frequently reproved and threatened than the profanation of the sabbath day.

II. Great encouragements given them to live in constant obedience to all God's commandments, largely and strongly assuring them that if they did so they should be a happy people, and should be blessed with all the good things they could desire. Human governments enforce their laws with penalties to be inflicted for the breach of them ; but God will be known as *the rewarder of those that seek and serve him*. Let us take a view of these great and precious promises, which, though they relate chiefly to the life which now is, and to the public national concerns of that people, were typical of the spiritual blessings entailed by the covenant of grace upon all believers through Christ. 1. Plenty and abundance of the fruits of the earth. They should have seasonable rain, neither too little nor too much, but what was requisite for their land, which was watered with the dew of heaven (Deut. xi. 10, 11), that it might *yield its increase, v*. 4. The dependence which the fruitfulness of the earth beneath has upon the influences of heaven above is a sensible intimation to us that every good and perfect gift must be expected *from above*, from the *Father of lights*. It is promised that the earth should produce its fruits in such great abundance that they would be kept in full employment, during both the harvest and the vintage, to gather it in, *v*. 5. Before they had reaped their corn and threshed it, the vintage would be ready ; and, before they had finished their vintage, it would be high time to begin their sowing. Long harvests are often with us the consequences of bad weather, but with them they should be the effects of a great increase. This signified the abundance of grace which should be poured out in gospel times, when the *ploughman should overtake the reaper* (Amos ix. 13), and a great harvest of souls should be gathered in to Christ. The plenty should be so great that they should *bring forth the old* to be given away to the poor *because of the new*, to make room for it in their barns, which yet they would not *pull down to build greater*, as that rich fool (Luke xii. 18), for God gave them this abundance to be laid out, not be hoarded up from one year to another. *He that withholdeth corn, the people shall curse him*, Prov. xi. 26. That promise (Mal. iii. 10), *I will pour you out a blessing, that there shall not be room enough to receive it*, explains this, *v.* 10. And that which crowns this blessing of plenty is (*v.* 5), You shall *eat your bread to the full*, which intimates that they should have, not only abundance, but content and satisfaction in it. They should have enough, and should know when they had enough. Thus *the meek shall eat and be satisfied*, Ps. xxii. 26. 2. Peace under the divine protection: " *You shall dwell in your land safely* (*v.* 5); both really safe, and safe in your own apprehensions; you shall lie down to rest in the power and promise of God, and not only none shall hurt you, but none shall so much as *make you afraid*," *v.* 6. See Ps. iv. 8. They should not be infested with wild beasts, these should be *rid out of the land*, or, as it is promised (Job v. 23), should *be at peace with them*. Nor should they be terrified with the alarms of war: *Neither shall the sword go through your land.* This holy security is promised to all the faithful, Ps. xci. 1, &c. Those must needs dwell in safety that *dwell in God*, Job ix. 18, 19. 3. Victory and success in their wars abroad, while they had peace and tranquillity at home, *v.* 7, 8. They are assured that the hand of God should so signally appear with them in their conquests that no disproportion of numbers should make against them : *Five of you shall have courage to attack, and strength to chase and defeat, a hundred*, as Jonathan did (1 Sam. xiv. 12), experiencing the truth of his own maxim (*v.* 6), that it is all one with the Lord to *save by many or by few.* 4. The increase of their people: *I will make you fruitful and multiply you, v.* 9. Thus the promise made to Abraham must be fulfilled, that his seed should be *as the dust of the earth ;* and much more numerous they would have been if they had not by their sin cut themselves short. It is promised to the gospel church that it shall be fruitful, John xv. 16. 5. The favour of God, which is the fountain of all good : *I will have respect unto you, v.* 9. If the eye of our faith be unto God, the eye of his favour will be unto us. More is implied than is expressed in that promise, *My soul shall not abhor you* (*v.* 11), as there is in that threatening, *My soul shall have no pleasure in him*, Heb. x. 38. Though there was that among them which might justly have alienated him from them, yet, if they would closely adhere to his institutions, he would not abhor them. 6. Tokens of his presence in and by his ordinances: *I will set my tabernacle among you, v.* 11. It was their honour and advantage that God's tabernacle was lately erected among them; but here he lets them know that the continuance and establishment of it depended upon their good behaviour. The tabernacle that was now set should be settled if they would be obedient, else not. Note, The way to have God's ordinances fixed among us, as a nail in a sure place, is to cleave closely to the institution of them. It is added (*v.* 12), " *I will walk among you*, with delight and satisfaction, as a man in his gar-

den ; I will keep up communion with you as a man walking with his friend." This seems to be alluded to, Rev. ii. 1, where Christ is said to *walk in the midst of the golden candlesticks.* 7 The grace of the covenant, as the fountain and foundation, the sweetness and security, of all these blessings : *I will establish my covenant with you, v.* 9. Let them perform their part of the covenant, and God would not fail to perform his. All covenant-blessings are summed up in the covenant-relation (*v.* 12): *I will be your God, and you shall be my people ;* and they are all grounded upon their redemption : *I am your God*, because *I brought you forth out of the land of Egypt, v.* 13. Having purchased them, he would own them, and never cast them off till they cast him off. He *broke their yoke*, and *made them go upright*, that is, their deliverance out of Egypt put them in a state both of ease and honour, that, being delivered out of the hands of their enemies, they might *serve God without fear*, each walking *in his uprightness.* When Israel rejected Christ, and was therefore rejected by him, their back is said to be *bowed down* always under the burden of their guilt, which was heavier than that of their bondage in Egypt, Rom. xi. 10.

14 But if ye will not hearken unto me, and will not do all these commandments ; 15 And if ye shall despise my statutes, or if your soul abhor my judgments, so that ye will not do all my commandments, *but* that ye break my covenant : 16 I also will do this unto you ; I will even appoint over you terror, consumption, and the burning ague, that shall consume the eyes, and cause sorrow of heart : and ye shall sow your seed in vain, for your enemies shall eat it. 17 And I will set my face against you, and ye shall be slain before your enemies : they that hate you shall reign over you ; and ye shall flee when none pursueth you. 18 And if ye will not yet for all this hearken unto me, then I will punish you seven times more for your sins. 19 And I will break the pride of your power ; and I will make your heaven as iron, and your earth as brass : 20 And your strength shall be spent in vain : for your land shall not yield her increase, neither shall the trees of the land yield their fruits. 21 And if ye walk contrary unto me, and will not hearken unto me ; I will bring seven times more plagues upon you accord-

ing to your sins. 22 I will also send wild beasts among you, which shall rob you of your children, and destroy your cattle, and make you few in number; and your *high* ways shall be desolate. 23 And if ye will not be reformed by me by these things, but will walk contrary unto me; 24 Then will I also walk contrary unto you, and will punish you yet seven times for sins. 25 And I will bring a sword upon you, that shall avenge the quarrel of *my* covenant: and when ye are gathered together within your cities, I will send the pestilence among you; and ye shall be delivered into the hand of the enemy. 26 *And* when I have broken the staff of your bread, ten women shall bake your bread in one oven, and they shall deliver *you* your bread again by weight: and ye shall eat, and not be satisfied. 27 And if ye will not for all this hearken unto me, but walk contrary unto me; 28 Then I will walk contrary unto you also in fury; and I, even I, will chastise you seven times for your sins. 29 And ye shall eat the flesh of your sons, and the flesh of your daughters shall ye eat. 30 And I will destroy your high places, and cut down your images, and cast your carcases upon the carcases of your idols, and my soul shall abhor you. 31 And I will make your cities waste, and bring your sanctuaries unto desolation, and I will not smell the savour of your sweet odours. 32 And I will bring the land into desolation: and your enemies which dwell therein shall be astonished at it. 33 And I will scatter you among the heathen, and will draw out a sword after you: and your land shall be desolate, and your cities waste. 34 Then shall the land enjoy her sabbaths, as long as it lieth desolate, and ye *be* in your enemies' land; *even* then shall the land rest, and enjoy her sabbaths. 35 As long as it lieth desolate it shall rest; because it did not rest in your sabbaths, when ye dwelt upon it. 36 And upon them that are left *alive* of you I will send a faintness into their hearts in the lands of their enemies; and the sound of a shaken leaf shall chase them; and they shall flee, as fleeing from a sword; and they shall fall when none pursueth. 37 And they shall fall one upon another, as it were before a sword, when none pursueth: and ye shall have no power to stand before your enemies. 38 And ye shall perish among the heathen, and the land of your enemies shall eat you up. 39 And they that are left of you shall pine away in their iniquity in your enemies' lands; and also in the iniquities of their families shall they pine away with them.

After God had set the blessing before them (the life and good which would make them a happy people if they would be obedient), he here sets the curse before them, the death and evil which would make them as miserable if they were disobedient. Let them not think themselves so deeply rooted as that God's power could not ruin them, nor so highly favoured as that his justice would not ruin them if they revolted from him and rebelled against him; no, *You only have I known, therefore I will punish you* soonest and sorest. Amos iii. 2. Observe,

I. How their sin is described, which would bring all this misery upon them. Not sins of ignorance and infirmity; God had provided sacrifices for those. Not the sins they repented of and forsook; but the sins that were presumptuously committed, and obstinately persisted in. Two things would certainly bring this ruin upon them:—

1. A contempt of God's commandments (*v.* 14): "*If you will not hearken to me* speaking to you by the law, nor *do all these commandments,* that is, desire and endeavour to do them, and, wherein you miss it, make use of the prescribed remedies." Thus their sin is supposed to begin in mere carelessness, and neglect, and omission. These are bad enough, but they make way for worse; for the people are brought in (*v.* 15) as, (1.) *Despising God's statutes,* both the duties enjoined and the authority enjoining them, thinking meanly of the law and the Law-maker. Note, Those are hastening apace to their own ruin who begin to think it below them to be religious. (2.) *Abhorring his judgments,* their very souls abhorring them. Note, Those that begin to despise religion will come by degrees to loathe it; and mean thoughts of it will ripen into ill thoughts of it; those that turn from it will turn against it, and their hearts will rise at it. (3.) *Breaking his covenant.* Though every breach of the commandment does not amount to a breach of the covenant (we were undone if it did), yet, when men have come to such a pitch of impiety as to despise and abhor the commandment, the next step will be to disown God, and all relation to him.

Those that reject the precept will come at last to renounce the covenant. Observe, It is God's covenant which they break : he made it, but they break it. Note, If a covenant be made and kept between God and man, God must have all the honour ; but, if ever it be broken, man must bear all the blame : on him shall this breach be.

2. A contempt of his corrections. Even their disobedience would not have been their destruction if they had not been obstinate and impenitent in it, notwithstanding the methods God took to reclaim them. Their contempt of God's word would not have brought them to ruin, if they had not added to that a contempt of his rod, which should have brought them to repentance. Three ways this is expressed:—(1.) *" If you will not for all this hearken to me,* v. 18, 21, 27. If you will not learn obedience by the things which you suffer, but be as deaf to the loud alarms of God's judgments as you have been to the close reasonings of his word and the secret whispers of your own consciences, you are obstinate indeed." (2.) *If you walk contrary to me,* v. 21, 23, 27. All sinners walk contrary to God, to his truths, laws, and counsels ; but those especially that are incorrigible under his judgments. The design of the rod is to humble them, and soften them, and bring them to repentance ; but, instead of this, their hearts are more hardened and exasperated against God, and *in their distress* they *trespass yet more against him,* 2 Chron. xxviii. 22. This is walking contrary to God. Some read it, " If you walk at all adventures with me, carelessly and presumptuously, as if you heeded not either what you do, whether it be right or wrong, or what God does with you, whether it be for you or against you, blundering on in wilful ignorance." (3.) *If you will not be reformed by these things.* God's design in punishing is to reform, by giving men sensible convictions of the evil of sin, and obliging them to seek unto him for relief : this is the primary intention ; but those that will not be reformed by the judgments of God must expect to be ruined by them. Those have a great deal to answer for that have been long and often under God's correcting hand, and yet go on frowardly in a sinful way ; sick and in pain, and yet not reformed ; crossed and impoverished, and yet not reformed ; broken with breach upon breach, yet *not returning to the Lord,* Amos iv. 6, &c.

II. How the misery is described which their sin would bring upon them, under two heads :—

1. God himself would be against them ; and this is the root and cause of all their misery. (1.) *I will set my face against you* (v. 17), that is, " I will set myself against you, set myself to ruin you." These proud sinners God will resist, and face those down that confront his authority. Or the face is put for the anger : " I will show myself

highly displeased at you." (2.) *I will walk contrary to you* (v. 24, 28) ; *with the froward he will wrestle,* Ps. xxviii. 26 [margin]. When God in his providence thwarts the designs of a people, which they thought well laid, crosses their purposes, breaks their measures, blasts their endeavours, and disappoints their expectations, then he walks contrary to them. Note, There is nothing got by striving with God Almighty, for he will break either the heart or the neck of those that contend with him, will bring them either to repentance or ruin. " I will walk at all adventures with you," so some read ; " all covenant loving-kindness shall be forgotten, and I will leave you to common providence." Note, Those that cast off God deserve that he should cast them off. (3.) As they continued obstinate, the judgments should increase yet more upon them. If the first sensible tokens of God's displeasure do not attain their end, to humble and reform them, then (v. 18), *I will punish you seven times more,* and again (v. 21), *I will bring seven times more plagues,* and (v. 24), *I will punish you yet seven times,* and (v. 28), *I, even I, will chastise you seven times for your sins.* Note, If less judgments do not do their work, God will send greater ; for, when he *judges, he will overcome.* If true repentance do not stay process, it will go on till execution be taken out. Those that are obstinate and incorrigible, when they have weathered one storm must expect another more violent ; and, how severely soever they are punished, till they are in hell they must still say, " There is worse behind," unless they repent. If the *founder have* hitherto *melted in vain* (Jer. vi. 29), the furnace will be heated *seven times hotter* (a proverbial expression, used Dan. iii. 19), and again and again *seven times hotter ;* and who among us can dwell with such devouring fire ? God does not begin with the sorest judgments, to show that he is patient, and delights not in the death of sinners ; but, if they repent not, he will proceed to the sorest, to show that he is righteous, and that he will not be mocked or set at defiance. (4.) Their misery is completed in that threatening : *My soul shall abhor you,* v. 30. That man is as miserable as he can be whom God abhors ; for his resentments are just and effective. Thus *if any man draw back,* as these are supposed to do, *God's soul shall have no pleasure in him* (Heb. x. 38), and he will *spue them out of his mouth,* Rev. iii. 16. It is spoken of as strange, and yet too true, *Hath thy soul loathed Zion ?* Jer. xiv. 19

2. The whole creation would be at war with them All God's sore judgments would be sent against them ; for he hath many arrows in his quiver. The threatenings here are very particular, because really they were prophecies, and he that foresaw all their rebellions knew they would prove so ; see Deut. xxxi. 16, 29. This long roll of threat-

ening shows that evil pursues sinners. We have here,

(1.) Temporal judgments threatened. [1.] Diseases of body, which should be epidemical: *I will appoint over you,* as task-masters, to rule you with rigour, *terror, consumption, and the burning ague, v.* 16. What we translate *terror,* some think, signifies a particular disease, probably (says the learned bishop Patrick) the *falling sickness,* which is terror indeed : all chronical diseases are included in the consumption, and all acute diseases in the burning ague or fever. These consume the eyes, and cause sorrow both to those that are visited with them and to their friends and relations. Note, All diseases are God's servants; they do what he appoints them, and are often used as scourges wherewith he chastises a provoking people. The pestilence is threatened (*v.* 25) to meet them, when they are gathered together in their cities for fear of the sword. The greater the concourse of people is, the greater desolation does the pestilence make; and, when it gets among the soldiers that should defend a place, it is of most fatal consequence. [2.] Famine and scarcity of bread, which should be brought upon them several ways; as, *First,* By plunder (*v.* 16): *Your enemies shall eat it* up, and carry it off as the Midianites did, Judg. vi. 5, 6. *Secondly,* By unseasonable weather, especially the want of rain (*v.* 19): *I will make your heaven as iron,* letting fall no rain, but reflecting heat, and then the earth would of course be as dry and hard *as brass,* and their labour in ploughing and sowing would *be in vain* (*v.* 20); for the increase of the earth depends upon God's good providence more than upon man's good husbandry. This should be the breaking of the *staff of bread* (*v.* 26), which life leans upon, and is supported by, on which perhaps they had leaned more than upon God's blessing. There should be so great a dearth of corn that, whereas every family used to fill an oven of their own with household bread, now ten families should have to fill but one oven, which would bring themselves and their children and servants to short allowance, so that they should *eat and not be satisfied.* The less they had the more craving should their appetites be. *Thirdly,* By the besieging of their cities, which would reduce them to such an extremity that they should *eat the flesh of their sons and daughters, v.* 29. [3.] War, and the prevailing of their enemies over them: " *You shall be slain before your enemies, v.* 17. Your choice men shall die in battle, and *those that hate you shall reign over you,* and justly, since you are not willing that the God that loved you should reign over you ;" 2 Chron. xii. 8. Miserable is that people whose enemies are their rulers and have got dominion over them, or whose rulers have become their enemies and under-hand seek the ruin of their interests. Thus God would *break the pride of their power, v.* 19. God had given

them power over the nations ; but when they, instead of being thankful for that power, and improving it for the service of God's kingdom, grew proud of it, and perverted the intentions of it, it was just with God to break it. Thus God would *bring a sword upon them to avenge the quarrel of his covenant, v.* 25. Note, God has a just quarrel with those that break covenant with him, for he will not be mocked by the treachery of perfidious men ; and one way or other he will avenge this quarrel upon those that play at fast and loose with him. [4.] Wild beasts, lions, bears, and wolves, which should increase upon them, and tear in pieces all that came in their way (*v.* 22), as we read of two bears that in an instant killed forty-two children, 2 Kings ii. 24. This is one of the four sore judgments threatened Ezek xiv. 21, which plainly refers to this chapter. Man was made to have dominion over the creatures, and, though many of them are stronger than he, yet none of them could have hurt him, nay, all of them would have served him, if he had not first shaken off God's dominion, and so lost his own ; and now the creatures are in rebellion against him that is in rebellion against his Maker, and, when the Lord of those hosts pleases, they are the executioners of his wrath and the ministers of his justice. [5.] Captivity, or dispersion: *I will scatter you among the heathen* (*v.* 33), *in your enemies' land, v.* 34. Never were any people so incorporated and united among themselves as they were; but for their sin God would scatter them, so that they should be lost among the heathen, from whom God had graciously distinguished them, but with whom they had wickedly mingled themselves. Yet, when they were scattered, divine justice had not done with them, but would draw out a sword after them, which would find them out, and follow them wherever they were. God's judgments, as they cannot be outfaced, so they cannot be outrun. [6.] The utter ruin and desolation of their land, which should be so remarkable that their very enemies themselves, who had helped it forward, should in the review be astonished at it, *v.* 32. *First,* Their cities should be waste, forsaken, uninhabited, and all the buildings destroyed ; those that escaped the desolations of war should fall to decay of themselves. *Secondly,* Their sanctuaries should be a desolation, that is, their synagogues where they met for religious worship every sabbath, as well as their tabernacle where they met thrice a year. *Thirdly,* The country itself should be desolate, not tilled or husbanded (*v.* 34, 35); then the land should enjoy its sabbaths, because they had not religiously observed the sabbatical years which God appointed them. They tilled their ground when God would have them let it rest; justly therefore were they driven out of it; and the expression intimates that the ground itself was pleased and easy when it was rid of the burden of such sinners, under which it had groaned, Rom. viii. 20, &c. The captivity in Babylon lasted seventy years, and so long the land *enjoyed her sabbaths,* as is said (2 Chron. xxxvi. 21) with reference to this. [7.] The destruction of their idols, though rather a mercy than a judgment, yet, being a necessary piece of justice, is here mentioned, to show what would be the sin that would bring all these miseries upon them: *I will destroy your high places, v.* 30. Those that will not be parted from their sins by the commands of God shall be parted from them by his judgments; since they would not destroy their high places, God would. And, to upbraid them with the unreasonable fondness they had shown for their idols, it is foretold that their *carcases should be cast upon the carcases of their idols.* Those that are wedded to their lusts will sooner or later have enough of them. Their idols would not be able to help either themselves or their worshippers; but, those that made them being like them, they should both perish alike, and fall together as blind into the ditch.

(2.) Spiritual judgments are here threatened. These should seize the mind; for he that made the mind can, when he pleases, make his sword approach to it. It is here threatened, [1.] That they should find no acceptance with God: *I will not smell the savour of your sweet odours, v.* 31. Though the judgments of God upon them did not separate them and their sins, yet they extorted incense from them; but in vain—even their incense was an abomination, Isa. i. 13. [2.] That they should have no courage in their wars, but should be quite dispirited and disheartened. They should not only fear and flee (*v.* 17), but fear and *fall, when none pursued, v.* 36. A guilty conscience would be their continual terror, so that not only the sound of a trumpet, but the very *sound of a leaf, should chase them.* Note, Those that cast off the fear of God expose themselves to the fear of every thing else, Prov. xxviii. 1. Their very fears should dash them *one against another, v.* 37, 38. And those that had increased one another's guilt would now increase one another's fears. [3.] That they should have no hope of the forgiveness of their sins (*v.* 39): *They shall pine away in their iniquity,* and *how should they then live?* Ezek. xxxiii. 10. Note, It is a righteous thing with God to leave those to despair of pardon that have presumed to sin; and it is owing to free grace if we are not abandoned to pine away in the iniquity we were born in and have lived in.

40 If they shall confess their iniquity, and the iniquities of their fathers, with their trespass which they trespassed against me, and that also they have walked contrary unto me; 41 And *that* I also have walked con-

trary unto them, and have brought them into the land of their enemies; if then their uncircumcised hearts be humbled, and they then accept of the punishment of their iniquity; 42 Then will I remember my covenant with Jacob, and also my covenant with Isaac, and also my covenant with Abraham will I remember; and I will remember the land. 43 The land also shall be left of them, and shall enjoy her sabbaths, while she lieth desolate without them: and they shall accept of the punishment of their iniquity: because, even because they despised my judgments, and because their soul abhorred my statutes. 44 And yet for all that, when they be in the land of their enemies, I will not cast them away, neither will I abhor them, to destroy them utterly, and to break my covenant with them: for I *am* the LORD their God. 45 But I will for their sakes remember the covenant of their ancestors, whom I brought forth out of the land of Egypt in the sight of the heathen, that I might be their God: I *am* the LORD. 46 These *are* the statutes and judgments and laws, which the LORD made between him and the children of Israel in mount Sinai by the hand of Moses.

Here the chapter concludes with gracious promises of the return of God's favour to them upon their repentance, that they might not (unless it were their own fault) *pine away in their iniquity.* Behold, with wonder, the riches of God's mercy to a people that had obstinately stood it out against the judgments of God, and would never think of surrendering till they were reduced to the last extremity. Yet *-turn to the strong-hold, you prisoners of hope,* Zech. ix. 12. As bad as things are, they may be mended. *Yet there is hope in Israel.* Observe,

I. How the repentance which would qualify them for this mercy is described, *v.* 40, 41. The instances of it are three:—1. Confession, by which they must give glory to God, and take shame to themselves. There must be a confession of sin, their own and their fathers', which they must lament the guilt of because they feel the smart of it; that thus they may cut off the entail of wrath. They must put in their confession put sin under its worst character, as *walking contrary to God;* this is the sinfulness of sin, the worst thing in it, and which in our repentance we should especially bewail. There must also be a confession of wrath; they must overlook the instruments of their trouble and the second causes, and confess that God has *walked contrary to them,* and so *dealt with them according to their sins.* Such a confession as this we find made by Daniel just before the dawning of the day of their deliverance (*ch.* ix.), and the like, Ezra ix. and Neh. ix. 2. Remorse and godly sorrow for sin: *If their uncircumcised heart be humbled.* An impenitent, unbelieving, unhumbled heart, is called an *uncircumcised* heart, the heart of a Gentile that is a stranger to God, rather than the heart of an Israelite in covenant with him. True circumcision is *of the heart* (Rom. ii. 29), without which the circumcision of the flesh avails nothing, Jer. ix. 26. Now in repentance this uncircumcised heart was humbled, that is, it was truly broken and contrite for sin. Note, A humble heart under humbling providences prepares for deliverance and true comfort. 3. Submission to the justice of God in all his dealings; if they then *accept of the punishment of their iniquity* (*v.* 41 and again *v.* 43), that is, if they justify God and condemn themselves, patiently bear the punishment as that which they have well deserved, and carefully answer the ends of it as that which God has well designed, accept it as a kindness, take it as physic, and improve it, then they are penitents indeed.

II. How the mercy which they should obtain upon their repentance is described. 1. They should not be abandoned: *Though they have despised my judgments, yet, for all that, I will not cast them away, v.* 43, 44. He speaks as a tender Father that cannot find in his heart to disinherit a son that has been very provoking. *How shall I do it?* Hos. xi. 8, 9. Till he had laid the foundations of a church for himself in the Gentile world, the Jewish church was not quite forsaken, nor cast away. 2. They should be remembered: *I will remember the land* with favour, which is grounded upon the promise before, *I will remember my covenant* (*v.* 42), which is repeated, *v.* 45. God is said *to remember the covenant* when he performs the promises of it, purely for his faithfulness' sake; not because there is any thing in us to recommend us to his favour, but because he will be as good as his word. This is the church's plea. Ps. lxxiv. 20, *Have respect unto the covenant.* He will remember the constitution of the covenant, which is such as leaves room for repentance, and promises pardon upon repentance; and the Mediator of the covenant, who was promised to Abraham, Isaac, and Jacob, and was sent, when the fulness of time came, in remembrance of that holy covenant. The word covenant is thrice repeated, to intimate that God is ever mindful of it and would have us to be so. The persons also with whom the covenant was made are mentioned in an unusual manner, *per modum ascensus—in the ascending line,* beginning with Jacob, to lead them gradually to the most ancient promise, which was made to the

father of the faithful: thus (Mic. vii. 20) he is said to perform the *truth to Jacob,* and the *mercy to Abraham.* He will for their sakes (*v.* 45), not their merit's sake, but their benefit's sake, remember the covenant of their ancestors, and upon that score show kindness to them, though most unworthy; they are therefore said to be, *as touching the election, beloved for the fathers' sake,* Rom. xi. 28. Note, When those that have walked contrary to God in a way of sin return to him by sincere repentance, though he has walked contrary to them in a way of judgment he will return to them in a way of special mercy, pursuant to the covenant of redemption and grace. None are so ready to repent as God is to forgive upon repentance, through Christ, who is given for a covenant.

Lastly, These are said to be *the laws which the Lord made between him and the children of Israel, v.* 46. His communion with his church is kept up by his law. He manifests not only his dominion over them, but his favour to them, by giving them his law; and they manifest not only their holy fear, but their holy love, by the observance of it; and thus it is made between them, rather as a covenant than a law; for he draws with the cords of a man.

CHAP. XXVII.

The last verse of the foregoing chapter seemed to close up the statute-book; yet this chapter is added as an appendix. Having given laws concerning instituted services, here he directs concerning vows and voluntary services, the free-will offerings of their mouth. Perhaps some devout serious people among them might be so affected with what Moses had delivered to them in the foregoing chapter as in a pang of zeal to consecrate themselves, or their children, or estates to him: this, because honestly meant, God would accept; but, because men are apt to repent of such vows, he leaves room for the redemption of what had been so consecrated, at a certain rate. Here is, I. The law concerning what was sanctified to God, persons (ver. 2—8), cattle, clean or unclean (ver. 9—13), houses and lands (ver. 14—25), with an exception of firstlings, ver. 26, 27. II. Concerning what was devoted, ver. 28, 29. III. Concerning tithes, ver. 30, &c.

AND the LORD spake unto Moses, saying, 2 Speak unto the children of Israel, and say unto them, When a man shall make a singular vow, the persons *shall be* for the LORD by thy estimation. 3 And thy estimation shall be of the male from twenty years old even unto sixty years old, even thy estimation shall be fifty shekels of silver, after the shekels of the sanctuary. 4 And if it *be* a female, then thy estimation shall be thirty shekels. 5 And if *it be* from five years old even unto twenty years old, then thy estimation shall be of the male twenty shekels, and for the female ten shekels. 6 And if *it be* from a month old even unto five years old, then thy estimation shall be of the male five shekels of silver, and for the female thy estimation *shall be* three shekels of silver. 7 And if *it be* from sixty years old and above; if *it be* a male, then thy estimation shall be fifteen shekels, and for the female ten shekels. 8 But if he be poorer than thy estimation, then he shall present himself before the priest, and the priest shall value him; according to his ability that vowed shall the priest value him. 9 And if *it be* a beast, whereof men bring an offering unto the LORD, all that *any* man giveth of such unto the LORD shall be holy. 10 He shall not alter it, nor change it, a good for a bad, or a bad for a good: and if he shall at all change beast for beast, then it and the exchange thereof shall be holy. 11 And if *it be* any unclean beast, of which they do not offer a sacrifice unto the LORD, then he shall present the beast before the priest: 12 And the priest shall value it, whether it be good or bad: as thou valuest it, *who art* the priest, so shall it be. 13 But if he will at all redeem it, then he shall add a fifth *part* thereof unto thy estimation.

This is part of the law concerning singular vows, extraordinary ones, which though God did not expressly insist on, yet, if they were consistent with and conformable to the general precepts, he would be well pleased with. Note, We should not only ask, What must we do, but, What may we do, for the glory and honour of God? As the *liberal devises liberal things* (Isa. xxxii. 8), so the pious devises pious things, and the enlarged heart would willingly do something extraordinary in the service of so good a Master as God is. When we receive or expect some singular mercy it is good to honour God with some singular vow.

I. The case is here put of persons vowed to God by a singular vow, *v.* 2. If a man consecrated himself, or a child, to the service of the tabernacle, to be employed therein in some inferior office, as sweeping the floor, carrying out ashes, running of errands, or the like, *the person* so consecrated *shall be for the Lord,* that is, "God will graciously accept the good-will." *Thou didst well that it was in thy heart,* 2 Chron. vi. 8. But forasmuch as he had no occasion to use their service about the tabernacle, a whole tribe being appropriated to the use of it, those that were thus vowed were to be redeemed, and the money paid for their redemption was employed for the repair of the sanctuary, or other uses of it, as appears by 2 Kings xii. 14, where it is called, in the margin, the *money of the souls of his estimation.* A book of rates is accordingly provided, by which the priests

were to go in their estimation. Here is, 1. The rate of the middle-aged, between twenty and threescore, these were valued highest, because most serviceable; a male fifty shekels, and a female thirty, *v.* 3, 4. The females were then less esteemed, but not so in Christ; for in *Christ Jesus there is neither male nor female,* Gal. iii. 28. Note, Those that are in the prime of their time must look upon themselves as obliged to do more in the service of God and their generation than can be expected either from minors, that have not yet arrived to their usefulness, or from the aged, that have survived it. 2. The rate of the youth between five years old and twenty was less, because they were then less capable of doing service, *v.* 5. 3. Infants under five years old were capable of being vowed to God by their parents, even before they were born, as Samuel was, but not to be presented and redeemed till a month old, that, as one sabbath passed over them before they were circumcised, so one new moon might pass over them before they were estimated; and their valuation was but small, *v.* 6. Samuel, who was thus vowed to God, was not redeemed, because he was a Levite, and a particular favourite, and therefore was employed in his childhood in the service of the tabernacle. 4. The aged are valued less than youth, but more than children, *v.* 7. And the Hebrews observe that the rate of an aged woman is two parts of three to that of an aged man, so that in that age the female came nearest to the value of the male, which occasioned (as bishop Patrick quotes it here) this saying among them, *That an old woman in a house is a treasure in a house.* Paul sets a great value upon the aged women, when he makes them *teachers of good things,* Tit. ii. 3. 5. The poor shall be valued according to their ability, *v.* 8. Something they must pay, that they might learn not to be rash in vowing to God, for *he hath no pleasure in fools,* Eccl. v. 4. Yet not more than their ability, but *secundum tenementum—according to their possessions,* that they might not ruin themselves and their families by their zeal. Note, God expects and requires from men according to what they have, and not according to what they have not, Luke xxi. 4.

II. The case is put of beasts vowed to God, 1. If it was a clean beast, such as was offered in sacrifice, it must not be redeemed, nor any equivalent given for it: *It shall be holy,* *v.* 9, 10. After it was vowed, it was not to be put to any common use, nor changed upon second thoughts; but it must be either offered upon the altar, or, if through any blemish it was not meet to be offered, he that vowed it should not take advantage of that, but the priests should have it for their own use (for they were God's receivers), or it should be sold for the service of the sanctuary. This teaches caution in making vows and constancy in keeping them when they are made; for *it is a snare to a man to devour* that which is holy, and after vows to make enquiry, Prov. xx. 25. And to this that rule of charity seems to allude (2 Cor. ix. 7), *Every man, according as he purposeth in his heart, so let him give.* 2. If it was an unclean beast, it should go to the use of the priest at such a value; but he that vowed it, upon paying that value in money, and adding a fifth part more to it, might redeem it if he pleased, *v.* 11—13. It was fit that men should smart for their inconstancy. God has let us know his mind concerning his service, and he is not pleased if we do not know our own. God expects that those that deal with him should be at a point, and say what they will stand to.

14 And when a man shall sanctify his house *to be* holy unto the LORD, then the priest shall estimate it, whether it be good or bad : as the priest shall estimate it, so shall it stand. 15 And if he that sanctified it will redeem his house, then he shall add the fifth *part* of the money of thy estimation unto it, and it shall be his. 16 And if a man shall sanctify unto the LORD *some part* of a field of his possession, then thy estimation shall be according to the seed thereof : a homer of barley seed *shall be valued* at fifty shekels of silver. 17 If he sanctify his field from the year of jubilee, according to thy estimation it shall stand. 18 But if he sanctify his field after the jubilee, then the priest shall reckon unto him the money according to the years that remain, even unto the year of the jubilee, and it shall be abated from thy estimation. 19 And if he that sanctified the field will in any wise redeem it, then he shall add the fifth *part* of the money of thy estimation unto it, and it shall be assured to him. 20 And if he will not redeem the field, or if he have sold the field to another man, it shall not be redeemed any more. 21 But the field, when it goeth out in the jubilee, shall be holy unto the LORD, as a field devoted; the possession thereof shall be the priest's. 22 And if *a man* sanctify unto the LORD a field which he hath bought, which *is* not of the fields of his possession ; 26 Then the priest shall reckon unto him the worth of thy estimation, *even* unto the year of the jubilee : and he shall give
560

thine estimation in that day, *as* a holy thing unto the LORD. 24 In the year of the jubilee the field shall return unto him of whom it was bought, *even* to him to whom the possession of the land *did belong.* 25 And all thy estimations shall be according to the shekel of the sanctuary : twenty gerahs shall be the shekel.

Here is the law concerning real estates dedicated to the service of God by a singular vow.

I. Suppose a man, in his zeal for the honour of God, should *sanctify his house to God (v.* 14), the house must be valued by the priest, and the money got by the sale of it was to be converted to the use of the sanctuary, which by degrees came to be greatly enriched with *dedicated things,* 1 Kings xv. 15 But, if the owner be inclined to redeem it himself, he must not have it so cheap as another, but must add a fifth part to the price, for he should have considered before he had vowed it, *v.* 15. To him that was necessitous God would abate the estimation (*v.* 8) ; but to him that was fickle and humoursome, and whose second thoughts inclined more to the world and his secular interest than his first, God would rise in the price. Blessed be God, there is a way of sanctifying our houses to be holy unto the Lord, without either selling them or buying them. If we and our houses serve the Lord, if religion rule in them, and we put away iniquity far from them, and have a church in our house, holiness to the Lord is written upon it, it is his, and he will dwell with us in it.

II. Suppose a man should sanctify some part of his land to the Lord, giving it to pious uses, then a difference must be made between land that came to the donor by descent and that which came by purchase, and accordingly the case altered.

1. If it was the inheritance of his fathers, here called the *field of his possession,* which pertained to his family from the first division of Canaan, he might not give it all, no, not to the sanctuary; God would not admit such a degree of zeal as ruined a man's family. But he might sanctify or dedicate only some part of it, *v.* 16. And in that case, (1.) The land was to be valued (as our countrymen commonly compute land) by so many measures' sowing of barley. So much land as would take a *homer,* or *chomer,* of barley, which contained ten ephahs, Ezek. xlv. 11 (not, as some have here mistaken it, an *omer,* which was but a tenth part of an ephah, Exod. xvi. 36), was valued at fifty shekels, a moderate price (*v.* 16), and that if it were sanctified immediately from the year of jubilee, *v.* 17. But, if some years after, there was to be a discount accordingly, even of that price, *v.* 18. And, (2.) When the value was fixed, the donor might, if he pleased, redeem it for

sixty shekels the homer's sowing, which was with the addition of a fifth part : the money then went to the sanctuary, and the land reverted to him that had sanctified it, *v.* 19. But if he would not redeem it, and the priest sold it to another, then at the year of jubilee, beyond which the sale could not go, the land came to the priests, and was theirs for ever, *v.* 20, 21. Note, What is given to the Lord ought not to be given with a power of revocation; what is devoted to the Lord must be his for ever, by a perpetual covenant.

2. If the land was his own purchase, and came not to him from his ancestors, then not the land itself, but the value of it was to be given to the priests for pious uses, *v.* 22, 24. It was supposed that those who, by the blessing of God, had grown so rich as to become purchasers would think themselves obliged in gratitude to sanctify some part of their purchase, at least (and here they are not limited, but they might, if they pleased, sanctify the whole), to the service of God. For we ought to give *as God prospers us,* 1 Cor. xvi. 2. Purchasers are in a special manner bound to be charitable. Now, forasmuch as purchased lands were by a former law to return at the year of jubilee to the family from which they were purchased, God would not have that law and the intentions of it defeated by making the lands *corban, a gift,* Mark vii. 11. But it was to be computed how much the land was worth for so many years as were from the vow to the jubilee; for only so long it was his own, and God *hates robbery for burnt-offerings.* We can never acceptably serve God with that of which we have wronged our neighbour. And so much money he was to give for the present, and keep the land in his own hands till the year of jubilee, when it was to return free of all encumbrances, even that of its being dedicated to him of whom it was bought. The value of the shekel by which all these estimations were to be made is here ascertained (*v.* 25); it shall be twenty gerahs, and every gerah was sixteen barley-corns. This was fixed before (Exod. xxx. 13); and, whereas there had been some alterations, it is again fixed in the laws of Ezekiel's visionary temple (Ezek. xlv. 12), to denote that the gospel should reduce things to their ancient standard.

26 Only the firstling of the beasts, which should be the LORD's firstling, no man shall sanctify it; whether *it be* ox, or sheep : it *is* the LORD's. 27 And if *it be* of an unclean beast, then he shall redeem *it* according to thine estimation, and shall add a fifth *part* of it thereto : or if it be not redeemed, then it shall be sold according to thy estimation. 28 Notwithstanding no devoted thing, that a man shall devote unto the LORD of all that he hath, *both* of man and beast, and of the field of his possession, shall be sold or redeemed : every devoted thing *is* most holy unto the LORD. 29 None devoted, which shall be devoted of men, shall be redeemed; *but* shall surely be put to death. 30 And all the tithe of the land, *whether* of the seed of the land, *or* of the fruit of the tree, *is* the LORD's : *it is* holy unto the LORD. 31 And if a man will at all redeem *aught* of his tithes, he shall add thereto the fifth *part* thereof. 32 And concerning the tithe of the herd, or of the flock, *even* of whatsoever passeth under the rod, the tenth shall be holy unto the LORD. 33 He shall not search whether it be good or bad, neither shall he change it : and if he change it at all, then both it and the change thereof shall be holy; it shall not be redeemed. 34 These *are* the commandments, which the LORD commanded Moses for the children of Israel in mount Sinai.

Here is, I. A caution given that no man should make such a jest of sanctifying things to the Lord as to sanctify any firstling to him, for that was his already by the law, *v.* 26. Though the matter of a general vow be that which we were before obliged to, as of our sacramental covenant, yet a singular vow should be of that which we were not, in such circumstances and proportions, antecedently bound to. The law concerning the firstlings of unclean beasts (*v.* 27) is the same with that before, *v.* 11, 12.

II. Things or persons devoted are here distinguished from things or persons that were only sanctified. 1. Devoted things were most holy to the Lord, and could neither revert nor be alienated, *v.* 28. They were of the same nature with those sacrifices which were called most holy, which none might touch but only the priests themselves. The difference between these and other sanctified things arose from the different expression of the vow. If a man dedicated any thing to God, binding himself with a solemn curse never to alienate it to any other purpose, then it was a thing devoted. 2. Devoted persons were to be put to death, *v.* 29. Not that it was in the power of any parent or master thus to devote a child or a servant to death; but it must be meant of the public enemies of Israel, who, either by the appointment of God or by the sentence of the congregation, were devoted, as the seven nations with which they must make no league. The city of Jericho in particular was thus devoted, Josh. vi. 17. The inhabitants of Jabesh-

Gilead were put to death for violating the curse pronounced upon those who came not up to Mizpeh, Judg. xxi. 9, 10. Some think it was for want of being rightly informed of the true intent and meaning of this law that Jephtha sacrificed his daughter as one devoted, who might not be redeemed.

III. A law concerning tithes, which were paid for the service of God before the law, as appears by Abraham's payment of them (Gen. xiv. 20), and Jacob's promise of them, Gen. xxviii. 22. It is here appointed, 1. That they should pay tithe of all their increase, their corn, trees, and cattle, *v.* 30, 32. Whatsoever productions they had the benefit of God must be honoured with the tithe of, if it were titheable. Thus they acknowledged God to be the owner of their land, the giver of its fruits, and themselves to be his tenants, and dependents upon him. Thus they gave him thanks for the plenty they enjoyed, and supplicated his favour in the continuance of it. And we are taught in general to *honour the Lord with our substance* (Prov. iii. 9), and in particular to support and maintain his ministers, and to be *ready to communicate* to them, Gal. vi. 6; 1 Cor. ix. 11. And how this may be done in a fitter and more equal proportion than that of the tenth, which God himself appointed of old, I cannot see. 2. That which was once marked for tithe should not be altered, no, not for a better (*v.* 33), for Providence directed the rod that marked it. God would accept it though it were not the best, and they must not grudge it though it were, for it was what passed under the rod. 3. That it should not be redeemed, unless the owner would give a fifth part more for its ransom, *v.* 31. If men had the curiosity to prefer what was marked for tithe before any other part of their increase, it was fit that they should pay for their curiosity.

IV. The last verse seems to have reference to this whole book, of which it is the conclusion: *These are the commandments which the* *Lord commanded Moses, for the children of Israel.* Many of these commandments are moral, and of perpetual obligation; others of them, which were ceremonial and peculiar to the Jewish economy, have notwithstanding a spiritual significancy, and are instructive to us who are furnished with a key to let us into the mysteries contained in them; for *unto us,* by those institutions, *is the gospel preached as well as unto them,* Heb. iv. 2. Upon the whole matter, we may see cause to bless God that *we have not come to mount Sinai,* Heb. xii. 18. 1. That we are not under the *dark shadows* of the law, but enjoy the clear light of the gospel, which shows us *Christ the end of the law for righteousness,* Rom. x. 4. The doctrine of our reconciliation to God by a Mediator is not clouded with the smoke of burning sacrifices, but cleared by the knowledge of *Christ and him crucified.* 2. That we are not under the *heavy yoke* of the law, and the carnal ordinances of it (as the apostle calls them, Heb. ix. 10), imposed till the time of reformation, a yoke which *neither they nor their fathers were able to bear* (Acts xv. 10), but under the sweet and easy institutions of the gospel, which pronounces those the *true worshippers that worship the Father in spirit and truth,* by Christ only, and in his name, who is our priest, temple, altar, sacrifice, purification, and all. Let us not therefore think that because we are not tied to the ceremonial cleansings, feasts, and oblations, a little care, time, and expense, will serve to honour God with. No, but rather have our hearts more enlarged with free-will offerings to his praise, more inflamed with holy love and joy, and more engaged in seriousness of thought and sincerity of intention. *Having boldness to enter into the holiest by the blood of Jesus, let us draw near with a true heart, and in full assurance of faith,* worshipping God with so much the more cheerfulness and humble confidence, still saying, *Blessed be God for Jesus Christ!*

AN

EXPOSITION,

WITH PRACTICAL OBSERVATIONS,

OF THE FOURTH BOOK OF MOSES, CALLED

NUMBERS.

THE titles of the five books of Moses, which we use in our Bibles, are all borrowed from the Greek translation of the Seventy, the most ancient version of the Old Testament that we know of. But the title of this book only we turn into English; in all the rest we retain the Greek word itself, for which difference I know no reason but that the Latin translators have generally done the same. Otherwise this book might as well have been called *Arithmoi*, the Greek title, as the first *Genesis*, and the second *Exodus ;* or these might as well have been translated, and called, the first the *Generation*, or *Original*, the second the *Out-let*, or *Escape*, as this *Numbers.—* This book was thus entitled because of the numbers of the children of Israel, so often mentioned in this book, and so well worthy to give a title to it, because it was the remarkable accomplishment of God's promise to Abraham that his seed should be as the stars of heaven for multitude. It also relates to two numberings of them, one at mount Sinai (*ch.* i.), the other in the plains of Moab, thirty-nine years after, *ch.* xxvi. And not three men the same in the last account that were in the first. The book is almost equally divided between histories and laws, intermixed.

We have here, I. The histories of the numbering and marshalling of the tribes (*ch.* i—iv.), the dedication of the altar and Levites (*ch.* vii. viii.), their march (*ch.* ix. x.), their murmuring and unbelief, for which they were sentenced to wander forty years in the wilderness (*ch.* xi—xiv.), the rebellion of Korah (*ch.* xvi. xvii.), the history of the last year of the forty (*ch.* xx—xxvi.), the conquest of Midian, and the settlement of the two tribes (*ch.* xxxi. xxxii.), with an account of their journeys, *ch.* xxxiii. II. Divers laws about the Nazarites, &c. (*ch.* v. vi.) ; and again about the priests' charge, &c. (*ch.* xviii. xix.), feasts (*ch.* xxviii. xxix.), and vows (*ch.* xxx.), and relating to their settlement in Canaan, *ch.* xxvii. xxxiv. xxxv. xxxvi. An abstract of much of this book we have in a few words in Ps. xcv. 10, *Forty years long was I grieved with this generation ;* and an application of it to ourselves in Heb. iv. 1, *Let us fear lest we seem to come short.* Many considerable nations there were now in being, that dwelt in cities and fortified towns, of which no notice is taken, no account kept, by the sacred history : but very exact records are kept of the affairs of a handful of people, that dwelt in tents, and wandered strangely in a wilderness, because they were the children of the covenant. *For the Lord's portion is his people, Jacob is the lot of his inheritance.*

CHAP. I.

Israel was now to be formed into a commonwealth, or rather a kingdom ; for "the Lord was their King" (1 Sam. xii. 12), their government a theocracy, and Moses under him was king in Jeshurun, Deut. xxxiii. 5. Now, for the right settlement of this holy state, next to the institution of good laws was necessary the institution of good order ; an account therefore must be taken of the subjects of this kingdom, which is done in this chapter, where we have, I. Orders given to Moses to number the people, ver. 1—4. II. Persons nominated to assist him herein, ver. 5—16. III. The particular number of each tribe, as it was given in to Moses, ver. 17—43. IV. The sum total of all together, ver. 44—46. V. An exception of the Levites, ver. 47, &c.

AND the Lord spake unto Moses in the wilderness of Sinai, in the tabernacle of the congregation, on the first *day* of the second month, in the second year after they were come out of the land of Egypt, saying, 2 Take ye the sum of all the congregation of the children of Israel, after their families, by the house of their fathers, with the number of *their* names, every male by their polls ; 3 From twenty years old and upward, all that are able to go forth to war in Israel : thou and Aaron shall number them by their armies. 4 And with you there shall be a man of every tribe ; every one head of the house of his fathers. 5 And these *are* the names of the men that shall stand with you : of *the tribe of* Reuben ; Elizur the son of Shedeur. 6 Of Simeon ; Shelumiel the son of Zurishaddai. 7 Of Judah ; Nahshon the son of Amminadab. 8 Of Issachar ; Nethaneel the son of Zuar. 9 Of Zebulun ; Eliab the son of Helon. 10 Of the children of Joseph : of Ephraim ; Elishama the son of Ammihud : of Manasseh ; Gamaliel the son of Pedahzur. 11 Of Benjamin ; Abidan the son of Gideoni. 12 Of Dan ; Ahiezer the son of Ammishaddai. 13 Of Asher ; Pagiel the son of Ocran. 14 Of Gad ; Eliasaph the son of Deuel. 15 Of Naphtali ; Ahira the son of Enan. 16 These *were* the renowned of the congregation, princes of the tribes of their fathers, heads of thousands in Israel.

I. We have here a commission issued out for the numbering of the people of Israel; and David, long after, paid dearly for doing it without a commission. Here is,

1. The date of this commission, *v.* 1. (1.) The place : it is given at God's court *in the wilderness of Sinai,* from his royal palace, *the tabernacle of the congregation.* (2.) The time : *In the second year* after they came up out of Egypt ; we may call it the second year of that reign. The laws in Leviticus were given in the first month of that year ; these orders were given in the beginning of the second month.

2. The directions given for the execution of it, *v.* 2, 3. (1.) None were to be numbered but the males, and those only such as were fit for war. None *under twenty years old :* for, though some such might have bulk and strength enough for military service, yet, in compassion to their tender years, God would not have them put upon it to bear arms. (2.) Nor were any to be numbered who through age, or bodily infirmity, blindness, lameness, or chronical diseases, were unfit for war. The church being militant, those only are reputed the true members of it that have enlisted

themselves soldiers of Jesus Christ; for our life, our Christian life, is a warfare. (3.) The account was to be taken *according to their families*, that it might not only be known how many they were, and what were their names, but of what tribe and family, or clan, nay, of what particular house every person was; or, reckoning it the muster of an army, to what regiment every man belonged, that he might know his place himself and the government might know where to find him. They were numbered a little before this, when their poll-money was paid for the service of the tabernacle, Exod. xxxviii. 25, 26. But it should seem they were not then registered *by the house of their fathers*, as now they were. Their number was the same then that it was now: 603,550 men; for as many as had died since then, and were lost in the account, so many had arrived to be twenty years old, and were added to the account. Note, As *one generation passeth away another generation cometh*. As vacancies are daily made, so recruits are daily raised to fill up the vacancies, and Providence takes care that, one time or other, in one place or other, the births shall balance the burials, that the race of mankind and the holy seed may not be cut off and become extinct.

3. Commissioners are named for the doing of this work. Moses and Aaron were to preside (*v.* 3), and one man of every tribe, that was renowned in his tribe, and was presumed to know it well, was to assist in it— *the princes of the tribes, v. 16.* Note, Those that are honourable should study to be serviceable; he that is great, let him be your minister, and show, by his knowing the public, that he deserves to be publicly known. The charge of this muster was committed to him who was the lord-lieutenant of that tribe. Now,

II. Why was this account ordered to be taken and kept? For several reasons. 1. To prove the accomplishment of the promise made to Abraham, that God would *multiply his seed exceedingly*, which promise was renewed to Jacob (Gen. xxviii. 14), that *his seed should be as the dust of the earth*. Now it appears that there did not fail one tittle of that good promise, which was an encouragement to hope that the other promise of the land of Canaan for an inheritance should also be fulfilled in its season. When the number of a body of men is only guessed at, upon the view, it is easy for one that is disposed to cavil to surmise that the conjecture is mistaken, and that, if they were to be counted, they would not be found half so many; therefore God would have Israel numbered, that it might be upon record how vastly they were increased in a little time, that the power of God's providence and the truth of his promise may be seen and acknowledged by all. It could not have been expected, in any ordinary course of nature, that seventy-five souls (which was the number of Jacob's family when he went down into

Egypt) should in 215 years (and it was no longer) multiply into so many hundred thousands. It is therefore to be attributed to an extraordinary virtue in the divine promise and blessing. 2. It was to intimate the particular care which God himself would take of his Israel, and which Moses and the inferior rulers were expected to take of them. God is called the *Shepherd of Israel*, Ps. lxxx. 1. Now the shepherds always kept count of their flocks, and delivered them by number to their under-shepherds, that they might know if any were missing; in like manner God numbers his flock, that of all which he took into his fold he might lose none but upon a valuable consideration, even those that were sacrificed to his justice. 3. It was to put a difference between the true-born Israelites and the mixed multitude that were among them; none were numbered but Israelites: all the world is but lumber in comparison with those jewels. Little account is made of others, but the saints God has a particular property in and concern for. *The Lord knows those that are his* (2 Tim. ii. 19), *knows them by name*, Phil. iv. 3. The hairs of their head are numbered; but he will say to others, "*I never knew you*, never made any account of you." 4. It was in order to their being marshalled into several districts, for the more easy administration of justice, and their more regular march through the wilderness. It is a rout and a rabble, not an army, that is not mustered and put in order.

17 And Moses and Aaron took these men which are expressed by *their* names: 18 And they assembled all the congregation together on the first *day* of the second month, and they declared their pedigrees after their families, by the house of their fathers, according to the number of the names, from twenty years old and upward, by their polls. 19 As the Lord commanded Moses, so he numbered them in the wilderness of Sinai. 20 And the children of Reuben, Israel's eldest son, by their generations, after their families, by the house of their fathers, according to the number of the names, by their polls, every male from twenty years old and upward, all that were able to go forth to war; 21 Those that were numbered of them, *even of* the tribe of Reuben, *were* forty and six thousand and five hundred. 22 Of the children of Simeon, by their generations, after their families, by the house of their fathers, those that were numbered of them, according to the number of the names, by their

polls, every male from twenty years old and upward, all that were able to go forth to war; 23 Those that were numbered of them, *even* of the tribe of Simeon, *were* fifty and nine thousand and three hundred. 24 Of the children of Gad, by their generations, after their families, by the house of their fathers, according to the number of the names, from twenty years old and upward, all that were able to go forth to war; 25 Those that were numbered of them, *even* of the tribe of Gad, *were* forty and five thousand six hundred and fifty. 26 Of the children of Judah, by their generations, after their families, by the house of their fathers, according to the number of the names, from twenty years old and upward, all that were able to go forth to war; 27 Those that were numbered of them, *even* of the tribe of Judah, *were* threescore and fourteen thousand and six hundred. 28 Of the children of Issachar, by their generations, after their families, by the house of their fathers, according to the number of the names, from twenty years old and upward, all that were able to go forth to war; 29 Those that were numbered of them, *even* of the tribe of Issachar, *were* fifty and four thousand and four hundred. 30 Of the children of Zebulun, by their generations, after their families, by the house of their fathers, according to the number of the names, from twenty years old and upward, all that were able to go forth to war; 31 Those that were numbered of them, *even* of the tribe of Zebulun, *were* fifty and seven thousand and four hundred. 32 Of the children of Joseph, *namely,* of the children of Ephraim, by their generations, after their families, by the house of their fathers, according to the number of the names, from twenty years old and upward, all that were able to go forth to war; 33 Those that were numbered of them, *even* of the tribe of Ephraim, *were* forty thousand and five hundred. 34 Of the children of Manasseh, by their generations, after their families, by the house of their fathers,

according to the number of the names, from twenty years old and upward, all that were able to go forth to war; 35 Those that were numbered of them, *even* of the tribe of Manasseh, *were* thirty and two thousand and two hundred. 36 Of the children of Benjamin, by their generations, after their families, by the house of their fathers, according to the number of the names, from twenty years old and upward, all that were able to go forth to war; 37 Those that were numbered of them, *even* of the tribe of Benjamin, *were* thirty and five thousand and four hundred. 38 Of the children of Dan, by their generations, after their families, by the house of their fathers, according to the number of the names, from twenty years old and upward, all that were able to go forth to war; 39 Those that were numbered of them, *even* of the tribe of Dan, *were* threescore and two thousand and seven hundred. 40 Of the children of Asher, by their generations, after their families, by the house of their fathers, according to the number of the names, from twenty years old and upward, all that were able to go forth to war; 41 Those that were numbered of them, *even* of the tribe of Asher, *were* forty and one thousand and five hundred. 42 Of the children of Naphtali, throughout their generations, after their families, by the house of their fathers, according to the number of the names, from twenty years old and upward, all that were able to go forth to war; 43 Those that were numbered of them, *even* of the tribe of Naphtali, *were* fifty and three thousand and four hundred.

We have here the speedy execution of the orders given for the numbering of the people. It was begun the same day that the orders were given, *The first day of the second month;* compare *v.* 18 with *v.* 1. Note, When any work is to be done for God it is good to set about it quickly, while the sense of duty is strong and pressing. And, for aught that appears, it was but one day's work, for many other things were done between this and the twentieth day of this month, when they removed their camp, *ch.* x. 11. Joab was almost ten months numbering the people in David's time (2 Sam. xxiv. 8); but then they were dispersed, now they lived closely together; then Satan proposed the doing of it, now God commanded it. It was the sooner and more easily done now because it had been done but a little while ago, and they needed but review the old books, with the alterations since made, which probably they had kept an account of as they occurred.

In the particulars here left upon record, we may observe, 1. That the numbers are registered in words at length (as I may say), and not in figures ; to every one of the twelve tribes it is repeated, for the greater ceremony and solemnity of the account, that they were numbered *by their generations, after their families, by the house of their fathers, according to the number of the names*, to show that every tribe took and gave in the account by the same rule and in the same method, though so many hands were employed in it, setting down the genealogy first, to show that their family descended from Israel, then the families themselves in their order, then dividing each family into the houses, or subordinate families, that branched from it, and under these the names of the particular persons, according to the rules of heraldry. Thus every man might know who were his relations or next of kin, on which some laws we have already met with did depend : besides that the nearer any are to us in relation the more ready we should be to do them good. 2. That they all end with hundreds, only Gad with fifty (*v.* 25), but none of the numbers descend to units or tens. Some think it was a special providence that ordered all the tribes just at this time to be even numbers, and no odd or broken numbers among them, to show them that there was something more than ordinary designed in their increase, there being this uncommon in the circumstance of it. It is rather probable that Moses having some time before appointed rulers of hundreds, and rulers of fifties (Exod. xviii. 25), they numbered the people by their respective rulers, which would bring the numbers to even hundreds or fifties. 3. That Judah is the most numerous of them all, more than double to Benjamin and Manasseh, and almost 12,000 more than any other tribe, *v.* 27. It was Judah whom *his brethren must praise* because from him Messiah the Prince was to descend ; but, because that was a thing at a distance, God did in many ways honour that tribe in the mean time, particularly by the great increase of it, for his sake who was to spring out of Judah (Heb. vii. 14) in the fulness of time. Judah was to lead the van through the wilderness, and therefore was furnished accordingly with greater strength than any other tribe. 4. Ephraim and Manasseh, the sons of Joseph, are numbered as distinct tribes, and both together made up almost as many as Judah ; this was in pursuance of Jacob's adoption of them, by which they were equalled with their uncles Reuben and Simeon, Gen. xlviii. 5. It was

also the effect of the blessing of Joseph, who was to be a *fruitful bough*, Gen. xlix. 22. And Ephraim the younger is put first, and is more numerous than Manasseh, for Jacob had crossed hands, and foreseen ten thousands of Ephraim and thousands of Manasseh. The fulfilling of this confirms our faith in the spirit of prophecy with which the patriarchs were endued. 5. When they came down into Egypt Dan had but one son (Gen. xlvi. 23), and so his tribe was but one family, *ch.* xxvi. 42. Benjamin had then ten sons (Gen. xlvi. 21), yet now the tribe of Dan is almost double in number to that of Benjamin. Note, The increasing and diminishing of families do not always go by probabilities. Some are multiplied greatly, and again are diminished, while others that were poor have families made them like a flock, Ps. cvii. 38, 39, 41 ; and see Job xii. 23. 6. It is said of each of the tribes that those were numbered who were able to go forth to war, to remind them that they had wars before them, though now they were in peace and met with no opposition. *Let not him that girdeth on the harness boast as though he had put it off.*

44 These *are* those that were numbered, which Moses and Aaron numbered, and the princes of Israel, *being* twelve men : each one was for the house of his fathers. 45 So were all those that were numbered of the children of Israel, by the house of their fathers, from twenty years old and upward, all that were able to go forth to war in Israel ; 46 Even all they that were numbered were six hundred thousand and three thousand and five hundred and fifty.

We have here the sum total at the foot of the account ; they were in all 600,000 fighting men, and 3550 over. Some think that when this was their number some months before (Exod. xxxviii. 26) the Levites were reckoned with them, but now that tribe was separated for the service of God, yet so many more had by this time attained to the age of twenty years as that still they were the same number, to show that whatever we part with for the honour and service of God it shall certainly be made up to us one way or other. Now we see what a vast body of men they were. Let us consider, 1. How much went to maintain all these (besides twice as many more, no question, of women and children, sick and aged, and the mixed multitude) for forty years together in the wilderness ; and they were all at God's finding every day, having their food from the dew of heaven, and not from the fatness of the earth. O what a great and good housekeeper is our God, that has such numbers depending on him and receiving from him every day ! 2. What work sin makes with a people ; within forty years most of them would indeed have died of course for the common sin of mankind ; for, when sin entered into the world, death came with it, and how great are the desolations which it makes in the earth ! But, for the particular sin of unbelief and murmuring, all those that were now numbered, except two, laid their bones under their iniquity, and perished in the wilderness. 3. What a great multitude God's spiritual Israel will amount to at last; though at one time, and in one place, they seem to be but a little flock, yet when they come all together they shall be a great multitude, innumerable, Rev. vii. 9. And, though the church's beginning be small, its latter end shall greatly increase. A little one shall become a thousand.

47 But the Levites after the tribe of their fathers were not numbered among them. 48 For the LORD had spoken unto Moses, saying, 49 Only thou shalt not number the tribe of Levi, neither take the sum of them among the children of Israel : 50 But thou shalt appoint the Levites over the tabernacle of testimony, and over all the vessels thereof, and over all things that *belong* to it : they shall bear the tabernacle, and all the vessels thereof ; and they shall minister unto it, and shall encamp round about the tabernacle. 51 And when the tabernacle setteth forward, the Levites shall take it down : and when the tabernacle is to be pitched, the Levites shall set it up : and the stranger that cometh nigh shall be put to death. 52 And the children of Israel shall pitch their tents, every man by his own camp, and every man by his own standard, throughout their hosts. 53 But the Levites shall pitch round about the tabernacle of testimony, that there be no wrath upon the congregation of the children of Israel : and the Levites shall keep the charge of the tabernacle of testimony. 54 And the children of Israel did according to all that the LORD commanded Moses, so did they.

Care is here taken to distinguish from the rest of the tribes the tribe of Levi, which, in the matter of the golden calf, had distinguished itself, Exod. xxxii. 26. Note, Singular services shall be recompensed with singular honours. Now,

I. It was the honour of the Levites that they were made guardians of the spiritualities; to them was committed the care of the tabernacle and the treasures thereof, both in their camps and in their marches. 1. When they moved the Levites were to take down the tabernacle, to carry it and all that belonged to it, and then to set it up again in the place appointed, v. 50, 51. It was for the honour of the holy things that none should be permitted to see them, or touch them, but those only who were called of God to the service. Thus we all are unfit and unworthy to have fellowship with God till we are first called by his grace *into the fellowship of his Son Jesus Christ our Lord,* and so, being the spiritual seed of that great high priest, are made *priests to our God ;* and it is promised that God would take Levites to himself, even from the Gentiles, Isa. lxvi. 21. 2. When they rested the Levites were to *encamp round about the tabernacle (v. 50, 53),* that they might be near their work, and resident upon their charge, always ready to attend, and that they might be a guard upon the tabernacle, to preserve it from being either plundered or profaned. They must pitch round about the tabernacle, *that there be no wrath upon the congregation,* as there would be if the tabernacle and the charge of it were neglected, or those crowded upon it that were not allowed to come near. Note, Great care must be taken to prevent sin, because the preventing of sin is the preventing of wrath.

II. It was their further honour that as Israel, being a holy people, was not *reckoned among the nations,* so they, being a holy tribe, were not reckoned among other Israelites, but numbered afterwards by themselves, v. 49. The service which the Levites were to do about the sanctuary is called (as we render it in the margin) a *warfare, ch.* iv. 23. And, being engaged in that warfare, they were discharged from military services, and therefore not numbered with those that were to *go out to war.* Note, Those that minister about holy things should neither entangle themselves, nor be entangled, in secular affairs. The ministry is itself work enough for a whole man, and all little enough to be employed in it. It is an admonition to ministers to distinguish themselves by their exemplary conversation from common Israelites, not affecting to seem greater, but aiming to be really better, every way better than others.

CHAP. II.

The thousands of Israel, having been mustered in the former chapter, in this are marshalled, and a regular disposition is made of their camp, by a divine appointment. Here is, I. A general order concerning it, ver. 1, 2. II. Particular directions for the posting of each of the tribes, in four distinct squadrons, three tribes in each squadron. 1. In the van-guard on the east were posted Judah, Issachar, and Zebulun, ver. 3–9. 2. In the right wing, southward, Reuben, Simeon, and Gad, ver. 10–16. 3. In the rear, westward, Ephraim, Manasseh, and Benjamin, ver. 18–24. 4. In the left wing, northward, Dan, Asher, and Naphtali, ver. 25–31. 5. The tabernacle in the centre, ver. 17. III. The conclusion of this appointment, ver. 32, &c.

AND the LORD spake unto Moses and unto Aaron, saying, 2 Every man of the children of Israel shall pitch by his own standard, with the ensign of their father's house : far off about the tabernacle of the congregation shall they pitch.

Here is the general appointment given both for their orderly encampment where they rested and their orderly march when they moved. Some order, it is probable, they had observed hitherto; they came out of Egypt in rank and file (Exod. xiii. 18), but now they were put into a better model. 1. They all dwelt in tents, and when they marched carried all their tents along with them, for *they found no city to dwell in*, Ps. cvii. 4. This represents to us our state in this world. It is a movable state (we are here to-day and gone to-morrow); and it is a military state: is not our life a warfare? We do but pitch our tents in this world, and have in it no continuing city. Let us, therefore, while we are pitching in this world, be pressing through it. 2. Those of a tribe were to pitch together, *every man by his own standard*. Note, It is the will of God that mutual love and affection, converse and communion, should be kept up among relations. Those that are of kin to each other should, as much as they can, be acquainted with each other; and the bonds of nature should be improved for the strengthening of the bonds of Christian communion. 3. Every one must know his place and keep in it; they were not allowed to fix where they pleased, nor to remove when they pleased, but God quarters them, with a charge to abide in their quarters. Note, It is God that *appoints us the bounds of our habitation*, and to him we must refer ourselves. *He shall choose our inheritance for us* (Ps. xlvii. 4), and in his choice we must acquiesce, and not love to flit, nor be *as the bird that wanders from her nest*. 4. Every tribe had its standard, flag, or ensign, and it should seem every family had some particular ensign of their father's house, which was carried as with us the colours of each troop or company in a regiment are. These were of use for the distinction of tribes and families, and the gathering and keeping of them together, in allusion to which the preaching of the gospel is said to *lift up an ensign, to which the Gentiles shall seek*, and by which they shall pitch, Isa. xi. 10, 12. Note, God is the God of order, and not of confusion. These standards made this mighty army seem more beautiful to its friends and more formidable to its enemies. The church of Christ is said to be as *terrible as an army with banners*, Cant. vi. 10. It is uncertain how these standards were distinguished: some conjecture that the standard of each tribe was of the same colour with the precious stone in which the name of that tribe was written in the high priest's ephod, and that this was all the difference. Many of the modern Jews think there was some coat of arms painted in each standard, which had reference to the blessing of that tribe by Jacob. Judah bore a lion, Dan a serpent, Naphtali a hind, Benjamin a wolf, &c. Some of them say the four principal standards were, Judah a lion, Reuben a man, Joseph an ox, and Dan an eagle, making the appearances in Ezekiel's

vision to allude to it. Others say the name of each tribe was written in its standard. Whatever it was, no doubt it gave a certain direction. 5. They were to pitch about the tabernacle, which was to be in the midst of them, as the tent or pavilion of a general in the centre of an army. They must encamp round the tabernacle, (1.) That it might be equally a comfort and joy to them all, as it was a token of God's gracious presence with them. Ps. xlvi. 5, *God is in the midst of her, she shall not be moved.* Their camp had reason to be hearty, when thus they had God in the heart of them. To have bread from heaven every day round about their camp, and fire from heaven, with other tokens of God's favour, in the midst of their camp, was abundantly sufficient to answer that question, *Is the Lord among us, or is he not? Happy art thou, O Israel!* It is probable that the doors of all their tents were made to look towards the tabernacle from all sides, for every Israelite should have his eyes always towards the Lord; therefore they worshipped at the tent-door. The tabernacle was in the midst of the camp, that it might be near to them; for it is a very desirable thing to have the solemn administrations of holy ordinances near us and within our reach. *The kingdom of God is among you.* (2.) That they might be a guard and defence upon the tabernacle and the Levites on every side. No invader could come near God's tabernacle without first penetrating the thickest of their squadrons. Note, If God undertake the protection of our comforts, we ought in our places to undertake the protection of his institutions, and stand up in defence of his honour, and interest, and ministers. 6. Yet they were to pitch afar off, in reverence to the sanctuary, that it might not seem crowded and thrust up among them, and that the common business of the camp might be no annoyance to it. They were also taught to keep their distance, lest too much familiarity should breed contempt. It is supposed (from Joshua iii. 4) that the distance between the nearest part of the camp and the tabernacle (or perhaps between them and the camp of the Levites, who pitched near the tabernacle) was 2000 cubits, that is, 1000 yards, little more than half a measured mile with us; but the outer parts of the camp must needs be much further off. Some compute that the extent of their camp could be no less than twelve miles square; for it was like a movable city, with streets and lanes, in which perhaps the manna fell, as well as on the outside of the camp, that they might have it at their doors. In the Christian church we read of a throne (as in the tabernacle there was a mercy-seat) which is called a *glorious high throne from the beginning* (Jer. xvii. 12), and that throne surrounded by spiritual Israelites, twenty-four elders, double to the number of the tribes, *clothed in white raiment* (Rev. iv. 4), and the banner over them is *Love;* but we are not ordered, as they were, to pitch afar off; no, we are invited to draw near, and come boldly. The saints of the Most High are said to be *round about him,* Ps. lxxvi. 11. God by his grace keep us close to him!

3 And on the east side toward the rising of the sun shall they of the standard of the camp of Judah pitch throughout their armies: and Nahshon the son of Amminadab *shall be* captain of the children of Judah. 4 And his host, and those that were numbered of them, *were* threescore and fourteen thousand and six hundred. 5 And those that do pitch next unto him *shall be* the tribe of Issachar: and Nethaneel the son of Zuar *shall be* captain of the children of Issachar. 6 And his host, and those that were numbered thereof, *were* fifty and four thousand and four hundred. 7 *Then* the tribe of Zebulun: and Eliab the son of Helon *shall be* captain of the children of Zebulun. 8 And his host, and those that were numbered thereof, *were* fifty and seven thousand and four hundred. 9 All that were numbered in the camp of Judah *were* a hundred thousand and fourscore thousand and six thousand and four hundred, throughout their armies. These shall first set forth. 10 On the south side *shall be* the standard of the camp of Reuben according to their armies: and the captain of the children of Reuben *shall be* Elizur the son of Shedeur. 11 And his host, and those that were numbered thereof, *were* forty and six thousand and five hundred. 12 And those which pitch by him *shall be* the tribe of Simeon: and the captain of the children of Simeon *shall be* Shelumiel the son of Zurishaddai. 13 And his host, and those that were numbered of them, *were* fifty and nine thousand and three hundred. 14 Then the tribe of Gad: and the captain of the sons of Gad *shall be* Eliasaph the son of Reuel. 15 And his host, and those that were numbered of them, *were* forty and five thousand and six hundred and fifty. 16 All that were numbered in the camp of Reuben *were* a hundred thousand and fifty and one thousand and four hundred and fifty, throughout their armies.

And they shall set forth in the second rank. 17 Then the tabernacle of the congregation shall set forward with the camp of the Levites in the midst of the camp: as they encamp, so shall they set forward, every man in his place by their standards. 18 On the west side *shall be* the standard of the camp of Ephraim according to their armies: and the captain of the sons of Ephraim *shall be* Elishama the son of Ammihud. 19 And his host, and those that were numbered of them, *were* forty thousand and five hundred. 20 And by him *shall be* the tribe of Manasseh: and the captain of the children of Manasseh *shall be* Gamaliel the son of Pedahzur. 21 And his host, and those that were numbered of them, *were* thirty and two thousand and two hundred. 22 Then the tribe of Benjamin: and the captain of the sons of Benjamin *shall be* Abidan the son of Gideoni. 23 And his host, and those that were numbered of them, *were* thirty and five thousand and four hundred. 24 All that were numbered of the camp of Ephraim *were* a hundred thousand and eight thousand and a hundred, throughout their armies. And they shall go forward in the third rank. 25 The standard of the camp of Dan *shall be* on the north side by their armies: and the captain of the children of Dan *shall be* Ahiezer the son of Ammishaddai. 26 And his host, and those that were numbered of them, *were* threescore and two thousand and seven hundred. 27 And those that encamp by him *shall be* the tribe of Asher: and the captain of the children of Asher *shall be* Pagiel the son of Ocran. 28 And his host, and those that were numbered of them, *were* forty and one thousand and five hundred. 29 Then the tribe of Naphtali: and the captain of the children of Naphtali *shall be* Ahira the son of Enan. 30 And his host, and those that were numbered of them, *were* fifty and three thousand and four hundred. 31 All they that were numbered in the camp of Dan *were* a hundred thousand and fifty and seven thousand and six hundred.

They shall go hindmost with their standards. 32 These *are* those which were numbered of the children of Israel by the house of their fathers: all those that were numbered of the camps throughout their hosts *were* six hundred thousand and three thousand and five hundred and fifty. 33 But the Levites were not numbered among the children of Israel; as the Lord commanded Moses. 34 And the children of Israel did according to all that the Lord commanded Moses: so they pitched by their standards, and so they set forward, every one after their families, according to the house of their fathers.

We have here the particular distribution of the twelve tribes into four squadrons, three tribes in a squadron, one of which was to lead the other two. Observe, 1. God himself appointed them their place, to prevent strife and envy among them. Had they been left to determine precedency among themselves, they would have been in danger of quarrelling with one another (as the disciples who strove *which should be greatest*); each would have had a pretence to be first, or at least not to be last. Had it been left to Moses to determine, they would have quarrelled with him, and charged him with partiality; therefore God does it, who is himself the fountain and judge of honour, and in his appointment all must acquiesce. If God in his providence advance others above us, and abase us, we ought to be as well satisfied in his doing it in that way as if he did it, as this was done here, by a voice out of the tabernacle; and this consideration, that it appears to be the will of God it should be so, should effectually silence all envies and discontents. And as far as our place comes to be our choice our Saviour has given us a rule in Luke xiv. 8, *Sit not down in the highest room;* and another in Matt. xx. 27, *He that will be chief, let him be your servant.* Those that are most humble and most serviceable are really most honourable. 2. Every tribe had a captain, a prince, or commander-in-chief, whom God himself nominated, the same that had been appointed to number them, *ch.* i. 5. Our being all the children of one Adam is so far from justifying the levellers, and taking away the distinction of place and honour, that even among the children of the same Abraham, the same Jacob, the same Judah, God himself appointed that one should be captain of all the rest. There are *powers ordained of God*, and those to whom honour and fear are due and must be paid. Some observe the significancy of the names of these princes, at least, in general, how much God was in the thoughts

of those that gave them their names, for most of them have *El, God,* at one end or other of their names. *Nethaneel, the gift of God; Eliab, my God a Father; Elizur, my God a rock; Shelumiel, God my peace; Eliasaph, God has added; Elishama, my God has heard: Gamaliel, God my reward; Pagiel, God has met me.* By this it appears that the Israelites in Egypt did not quite forget the name of their God, but, when they wanted other memorials, preserved the remembrance of it in the names of their children, and therewith comforted themselves in their affliction. 3. Those tribes were placed together under the same standard that were nearest of kin to each other; Judah, Issachar, and Zebulun, were the three younger sons of Leah, and they were put together; and Issachar and Zebulun would not grudge to be under Judah, since they were his younger brethren. Reuben and Simeon would not have been content in their place. Therefore Reuben, Jacob's eldest son, is made chief of the next squadron; Simeon, no doubt, is willing to be under him, and Gad, the son of Zilpah, Leah's handmaid, is fitly added to them in Levi's room: Ephraim, Manasseh, and Benjamin, are all the posterity of Rachel. Dan, the eldest son of Bilhah, is made a leading tribe, though the son of a concubine, that more abundant honour might be bestowed on that which lacked; and it was said, *Dan should judge his people,* and to him were added the two younger sons of the handmaids. Thus unexceptionable was the order in which they were placed. 4. The tribe of Judah was in the first post of honour, encamped towards the rising sun, and in their marches led the van, not only because it was the most numerous tribe, but chiefly because from that tribe Christ was to come, who is the *Lion of the tribe of Judah,* and was to descend from the loins of him who was now nominated chief captain of that tribe. Nahshon is reckoned among the ancestors of Christ, Matt. i. 4. So that, when he went before them, Christ himself went before them in effect, as their leader. Judah was the first of the twelve sons of Jacob that was blessed. Reuben, Simeon, and Levi, were censured by their dying father; he therefore being first in blessing, though not in birth, is put first, to teach children how to value the smiles of their godly parents and dread their frowns. 5. The tribe of Levi pitched closely about the tabernacle, within the rest of their tribes, *v.* 17. They must defend the sanctuary, and then the rest of the tribes must defend them. Thus, in the vision which John saw of the glory of heaven, between the elders and the throne were four *living creatures full of eyes,* Rev. iv. 6, 8. Civil powers should protect the religious interests of a nation, and be a defence upon that glory. 6. The camp of Dan (and so that tribe is called long after their settlement in Canaan (Judg. xiii. 25), because celebrated for their military prow-css), though posted in the left wing when they encamped, was ordered in their march to bring up the rear, *v.* 31. They were the most numerous, next to Judah, and therefore were ordered into a post which, next to the front, required the most strength, for as the strength is so shall the day be. *Lastly,* The children of Israel observed the orders given them, and did *as the Lord commanded Moses, v.* 34. They put themselves in the posts assigned them, without murmuring or disputing, and, as it was their safety, so it was their beauty; Balaam was charmed with the sight of it: *How goodly are thy tents, O Jacob! ch.* xxiv. 5. Thus the gospel church, called the *camp of saints,* ought to be compact according to the scripture model, every one knowing and keeping his place, and then all that wish well to the church rejoice, *beholding their order,* Col. ii. 5.

CHAP. III

This chapter and the next are concerning the tribe of Levi, which was to be mustered and marshalled by itself, and not in common with the other tribes, intimating the particular honour put upon them and the particular duty and service required from them. The Levites are in this chapter considered, I. As attendants on, and assistants to, the priests in the temple-service. And so we have an account, 1. Of the priests themselves (ver. 1—4) and their work, ver. 10. 2. Of the gift of the Levites to them (ver. 5—9), in order to which they are mustered (ver. 14—16), and the sum of them taken, ver. 39. Each particular family of them is mustered, has its place assigned and its charge, the Gershonites (ver. 17—26), the Kohathites (ver. 27—32), the Merarites, ver. 33—39. II. As equivalents for the first-born, ver. 11—13. 1. The first-born are numbered, and the Levites taken instead of them, as far as the number of the Levites went, ver. 40—45. 2. What first-born there were more than the Levites were redeemed, ver. 46, &c.

THESE also *are* the generations of Aaron and Moses in the day *that* the LORD spake with Moses in mount Sinai. 2 And these *are* the names of the sons of Aaron; Nadab the firstborn, and Abihu, Eleazar, and Ithamar. 3 These are the names of the sons of Aaron, the priests which were anointed, whom he consecrated to minister in the priest's office. 4 And Nadab and Abihu died before the LORD, when they offered strange fire before the LORD, in the wilderness of Sinai, and they had no children: and Eleazar and Ithamar ministered in the priest's office in the sight of Aaron their father. 5 And the LORD spake unto Moses, saying, 6 Bring the tribe of Levi near, and present them before Aaron the priest, that they may minister unto him. 7 And they shall keep his charge, and the charge of the whole congregation before the tabernacle of the congregation, to do the service of the tabernacle. 8 And they shall keep all the instruments of the tabernacle of the congregation, and the charge of the children of Is-

rael, to do the service of the tabernacle. 9 And thou shalt give the Levites unto Aaron and to his sons: they *are* wholly given unto him out of the children of Israel. 10 And thou shalt appoint Aaron and his sons, and they shall wait on their priest's office: and the stranger that cometh nigh shall be put to death. 11 And the LORD spake unto Moses, saying, 12 And I, behold, I have taken the Levites from among the children of Israel instead of all the firstborn that openeth the matrix among the children of Israel: therefore the Levites shall be mine; 13 Because all the firstborn *are* mine; *for* on the day that I smote all the firstborn in the land of Egypt I hallowed unto me all the firstborn in Israel, both man and beast: mine shall they be: I *am* the LORD.

Here, I. The family of Aaron is confirmed in the priests' office, *v.* 10. They had been called to it before, and consecrated; here they are appointed to *wait on their priests' office:* the apostle uses this phrase (Rom. xii. 7), *Let us wait on our ministry.* The office of the ministry requires a constant attendance and great diligence; so frequent are the returns of its work, and yet so transient its favourable opportunities, that it must be waited on. Here is repeated what was said before (*ch.* i. 51): *The stranger that cometh nigh shall be put to death,* which forbids the invading of the priest's office by any other person whatsoever; none must come nigh to minister but Aaron and his sons only, all others are strangers. It also lays a charge on the priests, as door-keepers in God's house, to take care that none should come near who were forbidden by the law; they must keep off all intruders, whose approach would be to the profanation of the holy things, telling them that if they came near it was at their peril, they would *die by the hand of God,* as Uzza did. The Jews say that afterwards there was hung over the door of the temple a golden sword (perhaps alluding to that flaming sword at the entrance of the garden of Eden), on which was engraven, *The stranger that cometh nigh shall be put to death.*

II. A particular account is given of this family of Aaron; what we have met with before concerning them is here repeated. 1. The consecration of the sons of Aaron, *v.* 3. They were all anointed to minister before the Lord, though it appeared afterwards, and God knew it, that two of them were wise and two were foolish. 2. The fall of the two elder (*v.* 4): they *offered strange fire,* and died for so doing, *before the Lord.* This is mentioned here in the preamble to the law concerning the priesthood, for a warning to all succeeding priests; let them know, by this example, that God is a jealous God, and will not be mocked; the holy anointing oil was an honour to the obedient, but not a shelter to the disobedient. It is here said, *They had no children,* Providence so ordering it, for their greater punishment, that none of their descendants should remain to be priests, and so bear up their name who had profaned God's name. 3. The continuance of the two younger: Eleazar and Ithamar ministered *in the sight of Aaron.* It intimates, (1.) The care they took about their ministration not to make any blunders; they kept under their father's eye, and took instruction from him in all they did, because, probably, Nadab and Abihu got out of their father's sight when they offered strange fire. Note, It is good for young people to act under the direction and inspection of those that are aged and experienced. (2.) The comfort Aaron took in it; it pleased him to see his younger sons behave themselves prudently and gravely, when his two elder had miscarried. Note, It is a great satisfaction to parents to *see their children walk in the truth,* 3 John 4.

III. A grant is made of the Levites to be assistants to the priests in their work: *Give the Levites to Aaron, v. 9.* Aaron was to have a greater propriety in, and power over, the tribe of Levi than any other of the princes had in and over their respective tribes. There was a great deal of work belonging to the priests' office, and there were now only three pairs of hands to do it all, Aaron's and his two sons'; for it does not appear that they had either of them any children at this time, at least not any that were of age to minister, therefore God appoints the Levites to attend upon them. Note, Those whom God finds work for he will find help for. Here is, 1. The service for which the Levites were designed: they were to *minister to the priests* in their ministration to the Lord (v. 6), and to *keep Aaron's charge* (v. 7), as the deacons to the bishops in the evangelical constitution, serving at tables, while the bishops waited on their ministry. The Levites killed the sacrifices, and then the priests needed only to sprinkle the blood and burn the fat: the Levites prepared the incense, the priests burnt it. They were to keep, not only Aaron's charge, but the *charge of the whole congregation.* Note, It is a great trust that is reposed in ministers, not only for the glory of Christ, but for the good of his church; so that they must not only keep the charge of the great high priest, but must also be faithful to the souls of men, in trust for whom a dispensation is committed to them. 2. The consideration upon which the Levites were demanded; they were taken instead of the first-born. The preservation of

the first-born of Israel, when all the first-born of the Egyptians (with whom they were many of them mingled) were destroyed, was looked upon by him who never makes any unreasonable demands as cause sufficient for the appropriating of all the first-born thenceforward to himself (v. 13): *All the first-born are mine.* That was sufficient to make them his, though he had given no reason for it, for he is the sole fountain and Lord of all beings and powers; but because all obedience must flow from love, and acts of duty must be acts of gratitude, before they were challenged into peculiar services they were crowned with peculiar favours. Note, When he that made us saves us we are thereby laid under further obligations to serve him and live to him. God's right to us by redemption corroborates the right he has to us by creation. Now because the first-born of a family are generally the favourites, and some would think it a disparagement to have their eldest sons servants to the priests, and attending before the door of the tabernacle, God took the tribe of Levi entire for his own, in lieu of the first-born, *v.* 12. Note, God's institutions put no hardships upon men in any of their just interests or reasonable affections. It was presumed that the Israelites would rather part with the Levites than with the first-born, and therefore God graciously ordered the exchange; yet for us he *spared not his own Son.*

14 And the LORD spake unto Moses in the wilderness of Sinai, saying, 15 Number the children of Levi after the house of their fathers, by their families: every male from a month old and upward shalt thou number them. 16 And Moses numbered them according to the word of the LORD, as he was commanded. 17 And these were the sons of Levi by their names; Gershon, and Kohath, and Merari. 18 And these *are* the names of the sons of Gershon by their families; Libni and Shimei. 19 And the sons of Kohath by their families; Amram, and Izehar, Hebron, and Uzziel. 20 And the sons of Merari by their families; Mahli, and Mushi. These *are* the families of the Levites according to the house of their fathers. 21 Of Gershon *was* the family of the Libnites, and the family of the Shimites: these *are* the families of the Gershonites. 22 Those that were numbered of them, according to the number of all the males, from a month old and upward, *even those*

that were numbered of them *were* seven thousand and five hundred. 23 The families of the Gershonites shall pitch behind the tabernacle westward. 24 And the chief of the house of the father of the Gershonites *shall be* Eliasaph the son of Lael. 25 And the charge of the sons of Gershon in the tabernacle of the congregation *shall be* the tabernacle, and the tent, the covering thereof, and the hanging for the door of the tabernacle of the congregation, 26 And the hangings of the court, and the curtain for the door of the court, which *is* by the tabernacle, and by the altar round about, and the cords of it for all the service thereof. 27 And of Kohath *was* the family of the Amramites, and the family of the Izeharites, and the family of the Hebronites, and the family of the Uzzielites: these *are* the families of the Kohathites. 28 In the number of all the males, from a month old and upward, *were* eight thousand and six hundred, keeping the charge of the sanctuary. 29 The families of the sons of Kohath shall pitch on the side of the tabernacle southward. 30 And the chief of the house of the father of the families of the Kohathites *shall be* Elizaphan the son of Uzziel. 31 And their charge *shall be* the ark, and the table, and the candlestick, and the altars, and the vessels of the sanctuary wherewith they minister, and the hanging, and all the service thereof. 32 And Eleazar the son of Aaron the priest *shall be* chief over the chief of the Levites, *and have* the oversight of them that keep the charge of the sanctuary. 33 Of Merari *was* the family of the Mahlites, and the family of the Mushites: these *are* the families of Merari. 34 And those that were numbered of them, according to the number of all the males, from a month old and upward, *were* six thousand and two hundred. 35 And the chief of the house of the father of the families of Merari *was* Zuriel the son of Abihail: *these* shall pitch on the side of the tabernacle northward. 36 And *under* the custody and charge of the sons of Merari

shall be the boards of the tabernacle, and the bars thereof, and the pillars thereof, and the sockets thereof, and all the vessels thereof, and all that serveth thereto, 37 And the pillars of the court round about, and their sockets, and their pins, and their cords. 38 But those that encamp before the tabernacle toward the east, *even* before the tabernacle of the congregation eastward, *shall be* Moses, and Aaron and his sons, keeping the charge of the sanctuary for the charge of the children of Israel; and the stranger that cometh nigh shall be put to death. 39 All that were numbered of the Levites, which Moses and Aaron numbered at the commandment of the LORD, throughout their families, all the males from a month old and upward, *were* twenty and two thousand.

The Levites being granted to Aaron to minister to him, they are here delivered to him by tale, that he might know what he had, and employ them accordingly. Observe,

I. By what rule they were numbered: *Every male from a month old and upward, v.* 15. The rest of the tribes were numbered only from twenty years old and upwards, and of them those only that were *able to go forth to war;* but into the number of the Levites they must take in both infants and infirm; being exempted from the war, it was not insisted upon that they should be of age and strength for the wars. Though it appears afterwards that little more than a third part of the Levites were fit to be employed in the service of the tabernacle (about 8000 out of 22,000, *ch.* iv. 47, 48), yet God would have them all numbered as retainers to his family; that none may think themselves disowned and rejected of God because they are not in a capacity of doing him that service which they see others do him. The Levites of a month old could not honour God and serve the tabernacle, as those that had grown up; yet out of the mouths of babes and sucklings the Levites' praise was perfected. Let not little children be hindered from being enrolled among the disciples of Christ, for such was the tribe of Levi, of such is the kingdom of heaven, that kingdom of priests. The redemption of the first-born was reckoned from a month old (*ch.* xviii. 15, 16), therefore from that age the Levites were numbered. They were numbered *after the house of their fathers,* not their *mothers,* for, if the daughter of a Levite married one of another tribe, her son was not a Levite; but we read of a spiritual priest to our God who inherited the unfeigned faith which dwelt in his mother and grandmother, 2 Tim. i. 5.

II. How they were distributed into three classes, according to the number of the sons of Levi, Gershon, Kohath, and Merari, and these subdivided into several families, v. 17—20.

1. Concerning each of these three classes we have an account, (1.) Of their number. The Gershonites were 7500. The Kohathites were 8600. The Merarites were 6200. The rest of the tribes had not their subordinate families numbered by themselves as those of Levi; this honour God put upon his own tribe. (2.) Of their post about the tabernacle on which they were to attend. The Gershonites pitched behind the tabernacle, westward, v. 23. The Kohathites on the right hand, southward, v. 29. The Merarites on the left hand, northward, v. 35. And, to complete the square, Moses and Aaron, with the priests, encamped in the front, eastward, v. 38. Thus was the tabernacle surrounded with its guards; and thus does the *angel of the Lord encamp round about those that fear him*, those living temples, Ps. xxxiv. 7. Every one knew his place, and must therein abide with God. (3.) Of their chief or head. As each class had its own place, so each had its own prince. The commander of the Gershonites was Eliasaph (v. 24); of the Kohathites Elizaphan (v. 30), of whom we read (Lev. x. 4) that he was one of the bearers at the funeral of Nadab and Abihu; of the Merarites Zuriel, v. 35. (4.) Of their charge, when the camp moved. Each class knew their own business; it was requisite they should, for that which is every body's work often proves nobody's work. The Gershonites were charged with the custody and carriage of all the curtains and hangings and coverings of the tabernacle and court (v. 25, 26), the Kohathites of all the furniture of the tabernacle—the ark, altar, table, &c. (v. 31, 32), the Merarites of the heavy carriage, boards, bars, pillars, &c., v. 36, 37.

2. Here we may observe, (1.) That the Kohathites, though they were the second house, yet were preferred before the elder family of the Gershonites. Besides that Aaron and the priests were of that family, they were more numerous, and their post and charge more honourable, which probably was ordered to put an honour upon Moses, who was of that family. Yet, (2.) The posterity of Moses were not at all dignified or privileged, but stood upon the level with other Levites, that it might appear he did not seek the advancement of his own family, nor to entail any honours upon it either in church or state; he that had honour enough himself coveted not to have his name shine by that borrowed light, but rather to have the Levites borrow honour from his name. Let none think contemptibly of the Levites, though inferior to the priests, for Moses himself thought it preferment enough for his sons to be Levites. Probably it was because

the family of Moses were Levites only that in the title of this chapter, which is concerning that tribe (v. 1), Aaron is put before Moses.

III. The sum total of the numbers of this tribe. They are computed in all 22,000, v. 39. The sum of the particular families amounts to 300 more; if this had been added to the sum total, the Levites, instead of being 273 fewer than the first-born, as they were (v. 43), would have been twenty-seven more, and so the balance would have fallen the other way; but it is supposed that the 300 which were struck off from the account when the exchange was to be made were the first-born of the Levites themselves, born since their coming out of Egypt, which could not be put into the exchange, because they were already sanctified to God. But that which is especially observable here is that the tribe of Levi was by much the least of all the tribes. Note, God's part in the world is too often the smallest part. His chosen are comparatively a little flock.

40 And the LORD said unto Moses, Number all the firstborn of the males of the children of Israel from a month old and upward, and take the number of their names. 41 And thou shalt take the Levites for me (I *am* the LORD) instead of all the firstborn among the children of Israel; and the cattle of the Levites instead of all the firstlings among the cattle of the children of Israel. 42 And Moses numbered, as the LORD commanded him, all the firstborn among the children of Israel. 43 And all the firstborn males by the number of names, from a month old and upward, of those that were numbered of them, were twenty and two thousand two hundred and threescore and thirteen. 44 And the LORD spake unto Moses, saying, 45 Take the Levites instead of all the firstborn among the children of Israel, and the cattle of the Levites instead of their cattle; and the Levites shall be mine: I *am* the LORD. 46 And for those that are to be redeemed of the two hundred and threescore and thirteen of the firstborn of the children of Israel, which are more than the Levites; 47 Thou shalt even take five shekels apiece by the poll, after the shekel of the sanctuary shalt thou take *them*: (the shekel *is* twenty gerahs:) 48 And thou shalt give the money, wherewith the odd number of them is to be redeemed,

unto Aaron and to his sons. 49 And Moses took the redemption money of them that were over and above them that were redeemed by the Levites: 50 Of the firstborn of the children of Israel took he the money; a thousand three hundred and threescore and five *shekels,* after the shekel of the sanctuary: 51 And Moses gave the money of them that were redeemed unto Aaron and to his sons, according to the word of the LORD, as the LORD commanded Moses.

Here is the exchange made of the Levites for the first-born. 1. The first-born were numbered from a month old, *v.* 42, 43. Those certainly were not reckoned who, though first-born, had become heads of families themselves, but those only that were under age; and the learned bishop Patrick is decidedly of opinion that none were numbered but those only that were born since their coming out of Egypt, when the first-born were sanctified, Exod. xiii. 2. If there were 22,000 first-born males, we may suppose as many females, and all these brought forth in the first year after they came out of Egypt, we must hence infer that in the last year of their servitude, even when it was in the greatest extremity, there were abundance of marriages made among the Israelites; they were not discouraged by the present distress, but married in faith, expecting that God would shortly visit them with mercy, and that their children, though born in bondage, should live in liberty and honour. And it was a token of good to them, an evidence that they were blessed of the Lord, that they were not only kept alive, but greatly increased, in a barren wilderness. 2. The number of the first-born, and that of the Levites, by a special providence, came pretty near to each other; thus, when he *divided the nations, he set the bounds of the people according to the number of the children of Israel,* Deut. xxxii. 8. Known unto God are all his works beforehand, and there is an exact proportion between them, and so it will appear when they come to be compared. The Levites' cattle are said to be taken instead of the firstlings *of the cattle of the children of Israel,* that is, the Levites, with all their possessions, were devoted to God instead of the first-born and all theirs; for, when we give ourselves to God, all we have passes as appurtenances with the premises. 3. The small number of first-born which exceeded the number of the Levites (273 in all) were to be redeemed, at five shekels apiece, and the redemption-money given to Aaron; for it would not do well to have them added to the Levites. It is probable that in the exchange they began with the eldest of the first-born, and so downward, so that those

were to be redeemed with money who were the 273 youngest of the first-born; more likely so than either that it was determined by lot or that the money was paid out of the public stock. The church is called the church of the *first-born,* which is redeemed, not as these were, with silver and gold, but, being devoted by sin to the justice of God, is ransomed with *the precious blood of the Son of God.*

<h2>CHAP. IV.</h2>

In the former chapter an account was taken of the whole tribe of Levi, in this we have an account of those of that tribe who were in the prime of their time for service, betwixt thirty and fifty years old. I. The serviceable men of the Kohathites are ordered to be numbered, and their charges are given them, ver. 2—20. II. Of the Gershonites, ver. 24—28. III. Of the Merarites, ver. 29—33. IV. The numbers of each, and the sum total at last, are recorded, ver. 34, &c.

AND the LORD spake unto Moses and unto Aaron, saying, 2 Take the sum of the sons of Kohath from among the sons of Levi, after their families, by the house of their fathers, 3 From thirty years old and upward even until fifty years old, all that enter into the host, to do the work in the tabernacle of the congregation. 4 This *shall be* the service of the sons of Kohath in the tabernacle of the congregation, *about* the most holy things: 5 And when the camp setteth forward, Aaron shall come, and his sons, and they shall take down the covering veil, and cover the ark of testimony with it: 6 And shall put thereon the covering of badgers' skins, and shall spread over *it* a cloth wholly of blue, and shall put in the staves thereof. 7 And upon the table of showbread they shall spread a cloth of blue, and put thereon the dishes, and the spoons, and the bowls, and covers to cover withal: and the continual bread shall be thereon: 8 And they shall spread upon them a cloth of scarlet, and cover the same with a covering of badgers' skins, and shall put in the staves thereof. 9 And they shall take a cloth of blue, and cover the candlestick of the light, and his lamps, and his tongs, and his snuffdishes, and all the oil vessels thereof, wherewith they minister unto it: 10 And they shall put it and all the vessels thereof within a covering of badgers' skins, and shall put *it* upon a bar. 11 And upon the golden altar they shall spread a cloth of blue, and cover it with a covering of badgers' skins, and shall put to the staves thereof: 12 And they shall take all the instruments of ministry, wherewith they minister in the sanctuary, and put *them* in a cloth of blue, and cover them with a covering of badgers' skins, and shall put *them* on a bar: 13 And they shall take away the ashes from the altar, and spread a purple cloth thereon: 14 And they shall put upon it all the vessels thereof, wherewith they minister about it, *even* the censers, the fleshhooks, and the shovels, and the basins, all the vessels of the altar; and they shall spread upon it a covering of badgers' skins, and put to the staves of it. 15 And when Aaron and his sons have made an end of covering the sanctuary, and all the vessels of the sanctuary, as the camp is to set forward; after that, the sons of Kohath shall come to bear *it*: but they shall not touch *any* holy thing, lest they die. These *things are* the burden of the sons of Kohath in the tabernacle of the congregation. 16 And to the office of Eleazar the son of Aaron the priest *pertaineth* the oil for the light, and the sweet incense, and the daily meat offering, and the anointing oil, *and* the oversight of all the tabernacle, and of all that therein *is*, in the sanctuary, and in the vessels thereof. 17 And the LORD spake unto Moses and unto Aaron, saying, 18 Cut ye not off the tribe of the families of the Kohathites from among the Levites: 19 But thus do unto them, that they may live, and not die, when they approach unto the most holy things: Aaron and his sons shall go in, and appoint them every one to his service and to his burden: 20 But they shall not go in to see when the holy things are covered, lest they die.

We have here a second muster of the tribe of Levi. As that tribe was taken out of all Israel to be God's peculiar, so the middle-aged men of that tribe were taken from among the rest to be actually employed in the service of the tabernacle. Now observe,

I. Who were to be taken into this number. All the males from thirty years old to fifty. Of the other tribes, those that were numbered to go forth to war were from twenty years old and upward, but of the Levites only from thirty to fifty; for the service of God requires

the best of our strength, and the prime of our time, which cannot be better spent than to the honour of him who is the first and best. And a man may make a good soldier much sooner than a good minister. Now,

1. They were not to be employed till they were thirty years old, because till then they were in danger of retaining something childish and youthful and had not gravity enough to do the service, and wear the honour, of a Levite. They were entered as probationers at twenty-five years old (*ch.* viii. 24), and in David's time, when there was more work to be done, at twenty (1 Chron. xxiii. 24, and so Ezra iii. 8); but they must be five years learning and waiting, and so fitting themselves for service; nay, in David's time they were ten years in preparation, from twenty to thirty. John Baptist began his public ministry, and Christ his, at thirty years old. This is not in the letter of it obligatory on gospel ministers now, as if they must either not begin their work till thirty years old or must leave off at fifty; but it gives us two good rules:—(1.) That ministers must not be novices, 1 Tim. iii. 6. It is a work that requires ripeness of judgment and great steadiness, and therefore those are very unfit for it who are but babes in knowledge and have not put away childish things. (2.) That they must learn before they teach, serve before they rule, and must *first be proved*, 1 Tim. iii. 10.

2. They were discharged at fifty years old from the toilsome part of the service, particularly that of carrying the tabernacle; for that is the special service to which they are here ordained, and which there was most occasion for while they were in the wilderness. When they began to enter upon old age, they were dismissed, (1.) In favour to them, that they might not be over-toiled when their strength began to decay. Twenty years' good service was thought pretty well for one man. (2.) In honour to the work, that it might not be done by those who, through the infirmities of age, were slow and heavy. The service of God should be done when we are in the most lively active frame. Those do not consider this who put off their repentance to old age, and so leave the best work to be done in the worst time.

II. How their work is described. They are said to *enter into the host*, or warfare, *to do the work in the tabernacle*. The ministry is *a good work* (1 Tim. iii. 1): ministers are not ordained to the honour only, but to the labour, not only to have the wages, but to do the work. It is also a *good warfare*, 1 Tim. i. 18. Those that enter into the ministry must look upon themselves as entered into the *host*, and approve themselves *good soldiers*, 2 Tim. ii. 3. Now, as to the sons of Kohath in particular, here is,

1. Their service appointed them, in the removes of the tabernacle. Afterwards, when the tabernacle was fixed, they had other work assigned them; but this was the work of the

day, which was to be done in its day. Observe, Wherever the camp of Israel went, the tabernacle of the Lord went with them, and care must be taken for the carriage of it. Note, Wherever we go, we must see to it that we take our religion along with us, and not forget that or any part of it. Now the Kohathites were to carry all the holy things of the tabernacle. They were charged with those things before (*ch.* iii. 31), but here they have more particular instructions given them. (1.) Aaron, and his sons the priests, must pack up the things which the Kohathites were to carry, as here directed, *v.* 5, &c. God had before appointed that none should come into the most holy place, but only Aaron once a year with a cloud of incense (Lev. xvi. 2); and yet, the necessity of their unsettled state requiring it, that law is here dispensed with; for every time they removed Aaron and his sons went in to take down the ark, and make it up for carriage; for (as the learned bishop Patrick suggests) the *shechinah*, or display of the divine majesty, which was over the mercy-seat, removed for the present in the pillar of cloud, which was taken up, and then the ark was not dangerous to be approached. (2.) All the holy things must be covered, the ark and table with three coverings, all the rest with two. Even the ashes of the altar, in which the holy fire was carefully preserved and raked up, must have a purple cloth spread over them, *v.* 13. Even the brazen altar, though in the court of the sanctuary it stood open to the view of all, yet was covered in the carriage of it. All these coverings were designed, [1.] For safety, that these holy things might not be ruffled with the wind, sullied with the rain, nor tarnished with the sun, but that they might be preserved in their beauty; for *on all the glory shall be a defence.* The coverings of badgers' skins, being thick and strong, would keep out wet; and, while we are in our passage through the wilderness of this world, it concerns us to be fenced *for all weathers,* Isa. iv. 5, 6. [2.] For decency and ornament. Most of these things had a cloth of blue, or purple, or scarlet, spread outmost; and the ark was covered with a cloth *wholly of blue* (*v.* 6), an emblem (say some) of the azure skies, which are spread like a curtain between us and the Majesty on high, Job xxvi. 9. Those that are faithful to God should endeavour likewise to appear beautiful before men, that they may *adorn the doctrine of God our Saviour.* [3.] For concealment. It signified the darkness of that dispensation. That which is now brought to light by the gospel, and revealed to babes, was then hidden from the wise and prudent. They saw only the coverings, not the holy things themselves (Heb. x. 1); but now Christ has *destroyed the face of the covering,* Isa. xxv. 7. (3.) When all the holy things were covered, then the Kohathites were to carry them on their shoulders. Those things that had staves were carried by their staves

(*v.* 6, 8, 11, 14); those that had not were carried upon a bar, or bier, or bearing barrow, *v.* 10, 12. See how the tokens of God's presence in this world are movable things; but we look for a kingdom that cannot be moved.

2. Eleazar, now the eldest son of Aaron, is appointed overseer of the Kohathites in this service (*v.* 16); he must take care that nothing was forgotten, left behind, or displaced. As a priest he had more honour than the Levites, but then he had more care; and that care was a heavier burden, no doubt, upon his heart, than all the burdens that were laid upon their shoulders. It is much easier to do the work of the tabernacle than to discharge the trusts of it, to obey than to rule.

3. Great care must be taken to preserve the lives of these Levites, by preventing their unseasonable irreverent approach to the most holy things: *Cut you not off the Kohathites,v.* 18. Note, Those who do not what they can to keep others from sin do what they can to cut them off. [1.] The Kohathites must not see the holy things till the priests had covered them, *v.* 20. Even those that bore the vessels of the Lord saw not what they bore, so much were even those in the dark concerning the gospel whose office it was to expound the law. And, [2.] When the holy things were covered, they might not touch them, at least not the ark, called here *the holy thing,* upon pain of death, *v.* 15. Uzza was struck dead for the breach of this law. Thus were the Lord's ministers themselves then kept in fear, and that was a dispensation of terror, as well as darkness; but now, through Christ, the case is altered; we have *seen with our eyes,* and our *hands have handled, the word of life* (1 John i. 1), and we are encouraged to *come boldly to the throne of grace.*

21 And the LORD spake unto Moses, saying, 22 Take also the sum of the sons of Gershon, throughout the houses of their fathers, by their families; 23 From thirty years old and upward until fifty years old shalt thou number them; all that enter in to perform the service, to do the work in the tabernacle of the congregation. 24 This *is* the service of the families of the Gershonites, to serve, and for burdens: 25 And they shall bear the curtains of the tabernacle, and the tabernacle of the congregation, his covering, and the covering of the badgers' skins that *is* above upon it, and the hanging for the door of the tabernacle of the congregation, 26 And the hangings of the court, and the hanging for the door of the gate of the court, which *is* by the tabernacle and by the altar round about,

and their cords, and all the instruments of their service, and all that is made for them : so shall they serve. 27 At the appointment of Aaron and his sons shall be all the service of the sons of the Gershonites, in all their burdens, and in all their service : and ye shall appoint unto them in charge all their burdens. 28 This *is* the service of the families of the sons of Gershon in the tabernacle of the congregation : and their charge *shall be* under the hand of Ithamar the son of Aaron the priest. 29 As for the sons of Merari, thou shalt number them after their families, by the house of their fathers ; 30 From thirty years old and upward even unto fifty years old shalt thou number them, every one that entereth into the service, to do the work of the tabernacle of the congregation. 31 And this *is* the charge of their burden, according to all their service in the tabernacle of the congregation ; the boards of the tabernacle, and the bars thereof, and the pillars thereof, and sockets thereof, 32 And the pillars of the court round about, and their sockets, and their pins, and their cords, with all their instruments, and with all their service : and by name ye shall reckon the instruments of the charge of their burden. 33 This *is* the service of the families of the sons of Merari, according to all their service, in the tabernacle of the congregation, under the hand of Ithamar the son of Aaron the priest.

We have here the charge of the other two families of the Levites, which, though not so honourable as the first, yet was necessary, and was to be done regularly. 1. The Gershonites were charged with all the drapery of the tabernacle, the curtains, and hangings, and the coverings of badgers' skins, *v.* 22—26. These they were to take down when the cloud removed, and the ark and the rest of the holy things were carried away, to pack up and bring with them, and then to set up again, where the cloud rested. Aaron and his sons allotted to them their respective charge : "You shall take care of such a curtain, and you of such a hanging, that every one may know his work, and there may be no confusion," *v.* 27. Ithamar particularly was to take the oversight of them, *v.* 28. 2. The Merarites were charged with the heavy carriage, the boards and bars, the pillars and
578

sockets, the pins and cords, and these were delivered to them by name, *v.* 31, 32. An inventory was given them of every particular, that it might be forthcoming, and nothing to seek, when the tabernacle was to be set up again. Though these seemed of less importance than the other things pertaining to the sanctuary, yet there was this care taken of them, to teach us with the greatest exactness to preserve pure and entire all divine institutions, and to take care that nothing be lost. It also intimates the care God takes of his church, and every member of it ; the good Shepherd *calls his own sheep by name,* John x. 3. Here were thousands of men employed about these services, though a much less number would have served for the bearing of those burdens ; but it was requisite that the tabernacle should be taken down, and set up, with great expedition, and many hands would make quick work, especially when every one knew his work. They had tents of their own to take care of, and to take along with them, but the young men under thirty, and the old men above fifty, might serve for them ; nor is there any mention of them, for God's house must always be preferred before our own. Their care was preposterous who built and ceiled their own houses while God's house lay waste, Hag. i. 4, 9. The death of the saints is represented as the taking down of the tabernacle (2 Cor. v. 1), and the putting of it off, 2 Pet. i. 14. The immortal soul, like the most holy things, is first covered and taken away, carried by angels, unseen, under the inspection of the Lord Jesus, our Eleazar. Care is also taken of the body—the skin and flesh, which are as the curtains, the bones and sinews which are as the bars and pillars ; none of these shall be lost ; commandment is given concerning the bones, a covenant made with the dust ; these are in safe custody, and shall all be produced in the great day, when this tabernacle shall be set up again, and these vile bodies made like the glorious body of Jesus Christ.

34 And Moses and Aaron and the chief of the congregation numbered the sons of the Kohathites after their families, and after the house of their fathers, 35 From thirty years old and upward even unto fifty years old, every one that entereth into the service, for the work in the tabernacle of the congregation : 36 And those that were numbered of them by their families were two thousand seven hundred and fifty. 37 These *were* they that were numbered of the families of the Kohathites, all that might do service in the tabernacle of the congregation, which Moses and Aaron did number according to the

commandment of the LORD by the hand of Moses. 38 And those that were numbered of the sons of Gershon, throughout their families, and by the house of their fathers, 39 From thirty years old and upward even unto fifty years old, every one that entereth into the service, for the work in the tabernacle of the congregation, 40 Even those that were numbered of them, throughout their families, by the house of their fathers, were two thousand and six hundred and thirty. 41 These *are* they that were numbered of the families of the sons of Gershon, of all that might do service in the tabernacle of the congregation, whom Moses and Aaron did number according to the commandment of the LORD. 42 And those that were numbered of the families of the sons of Merari, throughout their families, by the house of their fathers, 43 From thirty years old and upward even unto fifty years old, every one that entereth into the service, for the work in the tabernacle of the congregation, 44 Even those that were numbered of them after their families, were three thousand and two hundred. 45 These *be* those that were numbered of the families of the sons of Merari, whom Moses and Aaron numbered according to the word of the LORD by the hand of Moses. 46 All those that were numbered of the Levites, whom Moses and Aaron and the chief of Israel numbered, after their families, and after the house of their fathers, 47 From thirty years old and upward even unto fifty years old, every one that came to do the service of the ministry, and the service of the burden in the tabernacle of the congregation, 48 Even those that were numbered of them, were eight thousand and five hundred and fourscore. 49 According to the commandment of the LORD they were numbered by the hand of Moses, every one according to his service, and according to his burden: thus were they numbered of him: as the LORD commanded Moses.

We have here a particular account of the numbers of the three families of the Levites respectively, that is, of the effective men, between thirty years old and fifty. Observe, 1. The Kohathites were, in all, 8600 from a month old and upwards; but of these there were but 2750 serviceable men, not a third part. The Gershonites, in all, 7500, and of them but 2630 serviceable men, little more than a third part. Note, Of the many that add to the numbers of the church, there are comparatively but few that contribute to the service of it. So it has been, and so it is; many have a place in the tabernacle that do but little of the work of the tabernacle, Phil. ii. 20, 21. 2. That the Merarites were but 6200 in all, and yet of these there were 3200 serviceable men, that is, more than half. The greatest burden lay upon that family, the boards, and pillars, and sockets; and God so ordered it that, though they were the fewest in number, yet they should have the most able men among them; for whatever service God calls men to he will furnish them for it, and give strength in proportion to the work, grace sufficient. 3. The whole number of the able men of the tribe of Levi who entered into God's host to war his warfare was but 8580, whereas the able men of the other tribes that entered into the host of Israel to war their warfare were many more. The least of the tribes had almost four times as many able men as the Levites, and some of them more than eight times as many; for those that are engaged in the service of this world, and war after the flesh, are many more than those that are devoted to the service of God, and *fight the good fight of faith.*

CHAP. V.

In this chapter we have, I. An order, pursuant to the laws already made, for the removing of the unclean out of the camp, ver. 1—4. II. A repetition of the laws concerning restitution, in case of wrong done to a neighbour (ver. 5—8), and concerning the appropriating of the hallowed things to the priests, ver. 9, 10. III. A new law made concerning the trial of a wife suspected of adultery, by the waters of jealousy, ver. 11, &c.

AND the LORD spake unto Moses, saying, 2 Command the children of Israel, that they put out of the camp every leper, and every one that hath an issue, and whosoever is defiled by the dead: 3 Both male and female shall ye put out, without the camp shall ye put them; that they defile not their camps, in the midst whereof I dwell. 4 And the children of Israel did so, and put them out without the camp: as the LORD spake unto Moses, so did the children of Israel. 5 And the LORD spake unto Moses, saying, 6 Speak unto the children of Israel, When a man or woman shall commit any sin that men commit, to do a trespass against the LORD, and that person

579

be guilty; 7 Then they shall confess their sin which they have done: and he shall recompense his trespass with the principal thereof, and add unto it the fifth *part* thereof, and give *it* unto *him* against whom he hath trespassed. 8 But if the man have no kinsman to recompense the trespass unto, let the trespass be recompensed unto the LORD, *even* to the priest; beside the ram of the atonement, whereby an atonement shall be made for him. 9 And every offering of all the holy things of the children of Israel, which they bring unto the priest, shall be his. 10 And every man's hallowed things shall be his: whatsoever any man giveth the priest, it shall be his.

Here is, I. A command for the purifying of the camp, by turning out from within its lines all those that were ceremonially unclean, by issues, leprosies, or the touch of dead bodies, until they were cleansed according to the law, *v.* 2, 3.

1. These orders are executed immediately, *v.* 4. (1.) The camp was now newly-modelled and put in order, and therefore, to complete the reformation of it, it is next to be cleansed. Note, The purity of the church must be as carefully consulted and preserved as the peace and order of it. It is requisite, not only that every Israelite be confined to his own standard, but that every polluted Israelite be separated from it. *The wisdom from above is first pure, then peaceable.* (2.) God's tabernacle was now fixed in the midst of their camp, and therefore they must be careful to keep it clean. Note, The greater profession of religion any house or family make the more they are obliged to *put away iniquity far from their tabernacle,* Job xxii. 23. The person, the place, *in the midst of which God dwells,* must not be defiled; for, if it be, he will be affronted, offended, and provoked to withdraw, 1 Cor. iii. 16, 17.

2. This expulsion of the unclean out of the camp was to signify, (1.) What the governors of the church ought to do: they must *separate between the precious and the vile,* and purge out scandalous persons, as old leaven (1 Cor. v. 8, 13), lest others should be infected and defiled, Heb. xii. 15. It is for the glory of Christ and the edification of his church that those who are openly and incorrigibly profane and vicious should be put out and kept from Christian communion till they repent. (2.) What God himself will do in the great day: he will *thoroughly purge his floor,* and *gather out of his kingdom all things that offend.* As here the unclean were shut out of the camp, so into the new Jerusalem *no unclean thing shall enter,* Rev. xxi. 27.

II. A law concerning restitution, in case of wrong done to a neighbour. It is called *a sin that men commit* (v. 6), because it is common among men; *a sin of man,* that is, *a sin against man,* so it is thought it should be translated and understood. If a man overreach or defraud his brother in any matter, it is to be looked upon as a trespass against the Lord, who is the protector of right, the punisher of wrong, and who strictly charges and commands us to do justly. Now what is to be done when a man's awakened conscience charges him with guilt of this kind, and brings it to his remembrance though done long ago? 1. He must *confess his sin,* confess it to God, confess it to his neighbour, and so take shame to himself. If he have denied it before, though it go against the grain to own himself in a lie, yet he must do it; because his heart was hardened he denied it, therefore he has no other way of making it appear that his heart is now softened but by confessing it. 2. He must bring a sacrifice, a *ram of atonement, v.* 8. Satisfaction must be made for the offence done to God, whose law is broken, as well as for the loss sustained by our neighbour; restitution in this case is not sufficient without faith and repentance. 3. Yet the sacrifices would not be accepted till full amends were made to the party wronged, not only the principal, but a fifth part added to it, *v.* 7. It is certain that while that which is got by injustice is knowingly retained in the hands the guilt of the injustice remains upon the conscience, and is not purged by sacrifice nor offering, prayers nor tears, for it is one and the same continued act of sin persisted in. This law we had before (Lev. vi. 4), and it is here added that if the party wronged was dead, and he had no near kinsman who was entitled to the debt, or if it was any way uncertain to whom the restitution should be made, this should not serve for an excuse to detain what was unjustly gotten; to whomsoever it pertained, it was certainly none of his that got it by sin, and therefore it must be given to the priest, *v.* 8. If there were any that could make out a title to it, it must not be given to the priest (God hates robbery for burnt-offerings); but, if there were not, then it lapsed to the great Lord *(ob defectum sanguinis—for want of issue),* and the priests were his receivers. Note, Some work of piety or charity is a piece of necessary justice to be done by those who are conscious to themselves that they have done wrong, but know not how otherwise to make restitution; what is not our property will never be our profit.

III. A general rule concerning hallowed things given upon this occasion, that, whatever was given to the priest, *his it shall be, v.* 9, 10. 1. He that gave it was not to receive his gift again upon any pretence whatsoever. This law ratifies and confirms all grants for pious uses, that people might not give things to the priests in a fit of zeal, and then recal them in a fit of vexation. 2. The other priests should not come in sharers with that priest who then officiated, and to whom the hallowed thing, whatever it was, was given. Let him that was most ready and diligent in attending fare the better for it: if he do the work, let him have the pay, and much good may it do him.

11 And the LORD spake unto Moses, saying, 12 Speak unto the children of Israel, and say unto them, If any man's wife go aside, and commit a trespass against him, 13 And a man lie with her carnally, and it be hid from the eyes of her husband, and be kept close, and she be defiled, and *there be* no witness against her, neither she be taken *with the manner;* 14 And the spirit of jealousy come upon him, and he be jealous of his wife, and she be defiled: or if the spirit of jealousy come upon him, and he be jealous of his wife, and she be not defiled: 15 Then shall the man bring his wife unto the priest, and he shall bring her offering for her, the tenth *part* of an ephah of barley meal; he shall pour no oil upon it, nor put frankincense thereon; for it *is* an offering of jealousy, an offering of memorial, bringing iniquity to remembrance. 16 And the priest shall bring her near, and set her before the LORD: 17 And the priest shall take holy water in an earthen vessel; and of the dust that is in the floor of the tabernacle the priest shall take, and put *it* into the water: 18 And the priest shall set the woman before the LORD, and uncover the woman's head, and put the offering of memorial in her hands, which *is* the jealousy offering: and the priest shall have in his hand the bitter water that causeth the curse: 19 And the priest shall charge her by an oath, and say unto the woman, If no man have lain with thee, and if thou hast not gone aside to uncleanness *with another* instead of thy husband, be thou free from this bitter water that causeth the curse: 20 But if thou hast gone aside *to another* instead of thy husband, and if thou be defiled, and some man have lain with thee beside thine husband: 21 Then the priest shall charge the woman with an oath of cursing, and the priest shall say unto the woman, The LORD make thee a curse and an oath among thy people, when the LORD doth make thy thigh to rot, and thy belly to swell; 22 And this water that causeth the curse shall go into thy bowels, to make *thy* belly to swell, and *thy* thigh to rot: And the woman shall say, Amen, amen. 23 And the priest shall write these curses in a book, and he shall blot *them* out with the bitter water: 24 And he shall cause the woman to drink the bitter water that causeth the curse: and the water that causeth the curse shall enter into her, *and become* bitter. 25 Then the priest shall take the jealousy offering out of the woman's hand, and shall wave the offering before the LORD, and offer it upon the altar: 26 And the priest shall take a handful of the offering, *even* the memorial thereof, and burn *it* upon the altar, and afterward shall cause the woman to drink the water. 27 And when he hath made her to drink the water, then it shall come to pass, *that,* if she be defiled, and have done trespass against her husband, that the water that causeth the curse shall enter into her, *and become* bitter, and her belly shall swell, and her thigh shall rot: and the woman shall be a curse among her people. 28 And if the woman be not defiled, but be clean; then she shall be free, and shall conceive seed. 29 This *is* the law of jealousies, when a wife goeth aside *to another* instead of her husband, and is defiled; 30 Or when the spirit of jealousy cometh upon him, and he be jealous over his wife, and shall set the woman before the LORD, and the priest shall execute upon her all this law. 31 Then shall the man be guiltless from iniquity, and this woman shall bear her iniquity.

We have here the law concerning the solemn trial of a wife whose husband was jealous of her. Observe,

I. What was the case supposed: That a man had some reason to suspect his wife to have committed adultery, *v.* 12—14. Here, 1. The sin of adultery is justly represented as an exceedingly sinful sin; it is going aside from God, and virtue, and the good way, Prov. ii. 17. It is committing a trespass against the husband, robbing him of his honour, alienating his right, introducing a spurious breed into his family to share with his children in his estate, and violating her covenant with him. It is being defiled; for nothing pollutes the mind and conscience more than this sin does. 2. It is supposed to be a sin which great care is taken by the sinners to conceal, which there is no witness of. *The eye of the adulterer waits for the twilight*, Job xxiv. 15. And the adulteress takes her opportunity when *the good man is not at home*, Prov. vii. 19. It would not covet to be secret if it were not shameful; and the devil who draws sinners to this sin teaches them how to cover it. 3. The *spirit of jealousy* is supposed to come upon the husband, of which Solomon says, It is the *rage of a man* (Prov. vi. 34), and that it is *cruel as the grave*, Cant. viii. 6. 4. "Yet" (say the Jewish writers) "he must make it appear that he has some just cause for the suspicion." The rule they give is, " If the husband have said unto his wife before witnesses, 'Be not thou in secret with such a man;' and, notwithstanding that admonition, it is afterwards proved that she was in secret with that man, though her father or her brother, then he may compel her to drink the bitter water." But the law here does not tie him to that particular method of proving the just cause of his suspicion; it might be otherwise proved. In case it could be proved that she had committed adultery, she was to be put to death (Lev. xx. 10); but, if it was uncertain, then this law took place. Hence, (1.) Let all wives be admonished not to give any the least occasion for the suspicion of their chastity; it is not enough that they abstain from the evil of uncleanness, but they must abstain from all appearance of it, from every thing that looks like it, or leads to it, or may give the least umbrage to jealousy; for *how great a matter* may a *little fire kindle!* (2.) Let all husbands be admonished not to entertain any causeless or unjust suspicions of their wives. If charity in general, much more conjugal affection, teaches to *think no evil*, 1 Cor. xiii. 5. It is the happiness of the virtuous woman that *the heart of her husband does safely trust in her*, Prov. xxxi. 11.

II. What was the course prescribed in this case, that, if the suspected wife was innocent, she might not continue under the reproach and uneasiness of her husband's jealousy, and, if guilty, her sin might find her out, and others might hear, and fear, and take warning.

1. The process of the trial must be thus :— (1.) Her husband must *bring her to the priest*, with the witnesses that could prove the ground of his suspicion, and desire that she might be put upon her trial. The Jews say that the priest was first to endeavour to persuade her to confess the truth, saying to this purport, " Dear daughter, perhaps thou wast overtaken by drinking wine, or wast carried away by the heat of youth or the examples of bad neighbours ; come, confess the truth, for the sake of his great name which is described in the most sacred ceremony, and do not let it be blotted out with the bitter water." If she confessed, saying, " I am defiled," she was not put to death, but was divorced and lost her dowry ; if she said, " I am pure," then they proceeded. (2.) He must bring a coarse offering of barley-meal, without oil or frankincense, agreeably to the present afflicted state of his family; for a great affliction it was either to have cause to be jealous or to be jealous without cause. It is an *offering of memorial*, to signify that what was to be done was intended as a religious appeal to the omniscience and justice of God. (3.) The priest was to prepare the water of jealousy, the holy water out of the laver at which the priests were to wash when they ministered ; this must be brought in an *earthen vessel*, containing (they say) about a pint ; and it must be an *earthen* vessel, because the coarser and plainer every thing was the more agreeable it was to the occasion. *Dust* must be put into the water, to signify the reproach she lay under, and the shame she ought to take to herself, putting her mouth in the dust ; but dust from *the floor of the tabernacle*, to put an honour upon every thing that pertained to the place God had chosen to put his name there, and to keep up in the people a reverence for it ; see John viii. 6. (4.) The woman was to be *set before the Lord*, at the east gate of the temple-court (say the Jews), and her head was to be uncovered, in token of her sorrowful condition ; and there she stood for a spectacle to the world, that other women might learn not to do *after her lewdness*, Ezek. xxiii. 48. Only the Jews say, " Her own servants were not to be present, that she might not seem vile in their sight, who were to give honour to her ; her husband also must be dismissed." (5.) The priest was to adjure her to tell the truth, and to denounce the curse of God against her if she were guilty, and to declare what would be the effect of her drinking the water of jealousy, v. 19—22. He must assure her that, if she were innocent, the water would do her no harm, v. 19. None need fear the curse of the law if they have not broken the commands of the law. But, if she were guilty, this water would be poison to her, it would make her *belly to swell and her thigh to rot*, and she should be a curse or abomination among her people, v. 21, 22. To this she must say, *Amen*, as Israel must do to the curses pronounced on mount Ebal, Deut. xxvii. 15—26. Some think the *Amen*, being doubled, respects both parts of the adjuration, both that which freed her if innocent and that which condemned her if guilty. No woman, if she were guilty, could say *Amen* to this adjuration, and drink the water upon it, unless she dis-

believed the truth of God or defied his justice, and had come to such a pitch of impudence and hard-heartedness in sin as to challenge God Almighty to do his worst, and choose rather to venture upon his curse than to give him glory by making confession; thus has whoredom *taken away the heart.* (6.) The priest was to write this curse in a scrip or scroll of parchment, *verbatim—word for word,* as he had expressed it, and then to wipe or scrape out what he had written into the water (v. 23), to signify that it was that curse which impregnated the water, and gave it its strength to effect what was intended. It signified that, if she were innocent, the curse should be blotted out and never appear against her, as it is written, Isa. xliii. 25, *I am he that blotteth out thy transgression,* and Ps. li. 9, *Blot out my iniquities;* but that, if she were guilty, the curse, as it was written, being infused into the water, would enter into her bowels with the water, even *like oil into her bones* (Ps. cix. 18), as we read of a curse entering into a house, Zech. v. 4. (7.) The woman must then drink the water (v. 24); it is called *the bitter water,* some think because they put wormwood in it to make it bitter, or rather because it caused the curse. Thus sin is called *an evil thing and a bitter* for the same reason, because it *causeth the curse,* Jer. ii. 19. If she had been guilty (and otherwise it did not cause the curse), she was made to know that though her stolen waters had been sweet, and her *bread eaten in secret pleasant,* yet the end was *bitter as wormwood,* Prov. ix. 17, and *ch.* v. 4. Let all that meddle with forbidden pleasures know that they will be bitterness in the latter end. The Jews say that if, upon denouncing the curse, the woman was so terrified that she durst not drink the water, but confessed she was defiled, the priest flung down the water, and cast her offering among the ashes, and she was divorced without dowry: if she confessed not, and yet would not drink, they forced her to it; and, if she was ready to throw it up again, they hastened her away, that she might not pollute the holy place. (8.) Before she drank the water, the jealousy-offering was waved and offered upon the altar (v. 25, 26); a handful of it was burnt for a memorial, and the remainder of it eaten by the priest, unless the husband was a priest, and then it was scattered among the ashes. This offering in the midst of the transaction signified that the whole was an appeal to God, as a God that knows all things, and *from whom no secret is hid.* (9.) All things being thus performed according to the law, they were to wait the issue. The water, with a little dust put into it, and the scrapings of a written parchment, had no natural tendency at all to do either good or hurt; but if God was thus appealed to in the way of an instituted ordinance, though otherwise the innocent might have continued under suspicion and the guilty undiscovered, yet God would

so far own his own institution as that in a little time, by the miraculous operation of Providence, the innocency of the innocent should be cleared, and the sin of the guilty should find them out. [1.] If the suspected woman was really guilty, the water she drank would be poison to her (v. 37), her belly would swell and her thigh rot by a vile disease for vile deserts, and she would *mourn at the last when her flesh and body were consumed,* Prov. v. 11. Bishop Patrick says, from some of the Jewish writers, that the effect of these waters appeared immediately, she grew pale, and her eyes ready to start out of her head. Dr. Lightfoot says that sometimes it appeared not for two or three years, but she bore no children, was sickly, languished, and rotted at last; it is probable that some indications appeared immediately. The rabbin say that the adulterer also died in the same day and hour that the adulteress did, and in the same manner too, that his belly swelled, and his secret parts rotted: a disease perhaps not much unlike that which in these latter ages the avenging hand of a righteous God has made the scourge of uncleanness, and with which whores and whoremongers infect, and plague, and ruin one another, since they escape punishment from men. The Jewish doctors add that the waters had this effect upon the adulteress only in case the husband had never offended in the same kind; but that, if he had at any time defiled the marriage-bed, God did not thus right him against his injurious wife; and that therefore in the latter and degenerate ages of the Jewish church, when uncleanness did abound, this way of trial was generally disused and laid aside; men, knowing their own crimes, were content not to know their wives' crimes. And to this perhaps may refer the threatening (Hos. iv. 14), *I will not punish your spouses when they commit adultery, for you yourselves are separated with whores.* [2.] If she were innocent, the water she drank would be physic to her: *She shall be free, and shall conceive seed,* v. 28. The Jewish writers magnify the good effects of this water to the innocent woman, that, to recompense her for the wrong done to her by the suspicion, she should, after the drinking of these waters, be stronger and look better than ever; if she was sickly, she should become healthful, should bear a man-child, and have easy labour.

2. From the whole we may learn, (1.) That secret sins are known to God, and sometimes are strangely brought to light in this life; however, there is a day coming when God will, by Jesus Christ, as here by the priest, judge the *secrets of men according to the gospel,* Rom. ii. 16. (2.) That, in particular, *Whoremongers and adulterers God will judge.* The violation of conjugal faith and chastity is highly provoking to the God of heaven, and sooner or later it will be reckoned for. Though we have not now the waters of jealousy to be a sensible terror to the un-

583

clean, yet we have a word from God which ought to be as great a terror, that if *any man defile the temple of God, him shall God destroy,* 1 Cor. iii. 17. (3.) That God will find out some way or other to clear the innocency of the innocent, and to bring forth their righteousness as the light. (4.) That to *the pure all things are pure,* but *to the defiled nothing* is so, Tit. i. 15. The same word is to some a *savour of life unto life, to others a savour of death unto death,* like those waters of jealousy, according as they receive it; the same providence is for good to some and for hurt to others, Jer. xxiv. 5, 8, 9. And, whatsoever it is intended for, it *shall not return void.*

CHAP. VI.

In this chapter we have, I. The law concerning Nazarites, 1. What it was to which the vow of a Nazarite obliged him, ver. 1—8. 2. A remedial law in case a Nazarite happened to be polluted by the touch of a dead body, ver. 9—12. 3. The solemnity of his discharge when his time was up, ver. 13—21. II. Instructions given to the priests how they should bless the people, ver. 22, &c

AND the Lord spake unto Moses, saying, 2 Speak unto the children of Israel, and ·say unto them, When either man or woman shall separate *themselves* to vow a vow of a Nazarite, to separate *themselves* unto the Lord : 3 He shall separate *himself* from wine and strong drink, and shall drink no vinegar of wine, or vinegar of strong drink, neither shall he drink any liquor of grapes, nor eat moist grapes, or dried. 4 All the days of his separation shall he eat nothing that is made of the vine tree, from the kernels even to the husk. 5 All the days of the vow of his separation, there shall no razor come upon his head: until the days be fulfilled, in the which he separateth *himself* unto the Lord, he shall be holy, *and* shall let the locks of the hair of his head grow. 6 All the days that he separateth *himself* unto the Lord he shall come at no dead body. 7 He shall not make himself unclean for his father, or for his mother, for his brother, or for his sister, when they die: because the consecration of his God *is* upon his head. 8 All the days of his separation he *is* holy unto the Lord. 9 And if any man die very suddenly by him, and he hath defiled the head of his consecration; then he shall shave his head in the day of his cleansing, on the seventh day shall he shave it. 10 And on the eighth day he shall bring two turtles, or two young pigeons, to the priest,

to the door of the tabernacle of the congregation : 11 And the priest shall offer the one for a sin offering, and the other for a burnt offering, and make an atonement for him, for that he sinned by the dead, and shall hallow his head that same day. 12 And he shall consecrate unto the Lord the days of his separation, and shall bring a lamb of the first year for a trespass offering : but the days that were before shall be lost, because his separation was defiled. 13 And this *is* the law of the Nazarite, when the days of his separation are fulfilled : he shall be brought unto the door of the tabernacle of the congregation : 14 And he shall offer his offering unto the Lord, one he lamb of the first year without blemish for a burnt offering, and one ewe lamb of the first year without blemish for a sin offering, and one ram without blemish for peace offerings, 15 And a basket of unleavened bread, cakes of fine flour mingled with oil, and wafers of unleavened bread anointed with oil, and their meat offering, and their drink offerings. 16 And the priest shall bring *them* before the Lord, and shall offer his sin offering, and his burnt offering : 17 And he shall offer the ram *for* a sacrifice of peace offerings unto the Lord, with the basket of unleavened bread : the priest shall offer also his meat offering, and his drink offering. 18 And the Nazarite shall shave the head of his separation *at* the door of the tabernacle of the congregation, and shall take the hair of the head of his separation, and put *it* in the fire which *is* under the sacrifice of the peace offerings. 19 And the priest shall take the sodden shoulder of the ram, and one unleavened cake out of the basket, and one unleavened wafer, and shall put *them* upon the hands of the Nazarite, after *the hair of* his separation is shaven : 20 And the priest shall wave them *for* a wave offering before the Lord : this *is* holy for the priest, with the wave breast and heave shoulder : and after that the Nazarite may drink wine. 21 This *is* the law of the Nazarite who hath vowed, *and of* his offering unto the LORD for his separation, beside *that* that his hand shall get: according to the vow which he vowed, so he must do after the law of his separation.

After the law for the discovery and shame of those that by sin had made themselves vile, fitly follows this for the direction and encouragement of those who by their eminent piety and devotion had made themselves honourable, and distinguished themselves from their neighbours. It is very probable that there were those before the making of this law who went under the character of *Nazarites,* and were celebrated by that title as persons professing greater strictness and zeal in religion than other people; for the vow of a Nazarite is spoken of here as a thing already well known, but the obligation of it is reduced to a greater certainty than hitherto it had been. Joseph is called a Nazarite among his brethren (Gen. xlix. 26), not only because separate from them, but because eminent among them. Observe,

I. The general character of a Nazarite: it is a person *separated unto the Lord,* v. 2. Some were Nazarites for life, either by divine designation, as Samson (Judg. xiii. 5), and John Baptist (Luke i. 15), or by their parents' vow concerning them, as Samuel, 1 Sam. i. 11. Of these this law speaks not. Others were so for a certain time, and by their own voluntary engagement, and concerning them rules are given by this law. A woman might bind herself with the vow of a Nazarite, under the limitations we find, *ch.* xxx. 3, where the vow which the woman is supposed to vow unto the Lord seems to be meant especially of this vow. The Nazarites were, 1. Devoted to the Lord during the time of their Nazariteship, and, it is probable, spent much of their time in the study of the law, in acts of devotion, and instructing others. An air of piety was thereby put upon them, and upon their whole conversation. 2. They were separated from common persons and common things. Those that are consecrated to God must not be conformed to this world. They distinguished themselves, not only from others, but from what they themselves were before and after. 3. They separated themselves by vowing a vow. Every Israelite was bound by the divine law to love God with all his heart, but the Nazarites by their own act and deed bound themselves to some religious observances, as fruits and expressions of that love, which other Israelites were not bound to. Some such there were, whose spirits God stirred up to be in their day the ornaments of the church, the standard-bearers of religion, and patterns of piety. It is spoken of as a great favour to their nation that God *raised up of their young men for Nazarites,* Amos ii. 11. The Nazarites were known in the streets

and respected as *purer than snow, whiter than milk,* Lam. iv. 7. Christ was called in reproach a Nazarene, so were his followers: but he was no Nazarite according to this law; he drank wine, and touched dead bodies, yet in him this type had its accomplishment, for in him all purity and perfection met; and every true Christian is a spiritual Nazarite, separated by vow unto the Lord. We find St. Paul, by the persuasion of his friends, in complaisance to the Jews, submitting to this law of the Nazarites; but at the same time it is declared that the Gentiles should *observe no such thing,* Acts xxi. 24, 25. It was looked upon as a great honour to a man to be a Nazarite, and therefore if a man speak of it as a punishment, saying for instance, "I will be a Nazarite rather than do so or so," he is (say the Jews) a wicked man; but he that vows unto the Lord in the way of holiness to be a Nazarite, lo, *the crown of his God is upon his head.*

II. The particular obligations that the Nazarites lay under. That the fancies of superstitious men might not multiply their restraints endlessly, God himself lays down the law for them, and gives them the rule of their profession.

1. They must have nothing to do with *the fruit of the vine,* v. 3, 4. They must drink no wine nor strong drink, nor eat grapes, no, not the kernel nor the husk; they might not so much as eat a raisin. The learned Dr. Lightfoot has a conjecture (Hor. Heb. in Luc. i. 15), that, as the ceremonial pollutions by leprosy and otherwise represented the sinful state of fallen man, so the institution of the order of Nazarites was designed to represent the pure and perfect state of man in innocency, and that the tree of knowledge, forbidden to Adam, was the vine, and for that reason it was forbidden to the Nazarites, and all the produce of it. Those who gave the Nazarites wine to drink did the tempter's work (Amos ii. 12), persuading them to that forbidden fruit. That it was reckoned a perfection and praise not to drink wine appears from the instance of the Rechabites, Jer. xxxv. 6. They were to *drink no wine,* (1.) That they might be examples of temperance and mortification. Those that separate themselves to God and to his honour must not gratify the desires of the body, but keep it under and bring it into subjection. Drinking *a little wine for the stomach's sake* is allowed, to help that, 1 Tim. v. 23. But drinking much wine for the *palate's sake,* to please that, does by no means become those who profess to walk not *after the flesh, but after the Spirit.* (2.) That they might be qualified to employ themselves in the service of God. They must not drink, lest they should *forget the law* (Prov. xxxi. 5), lest they should *err through wine,* Isa. xxviii. 7. Let all Christians oblige themselves to be very moderate in the use of wine and strong drink; for, if the love of these once gets the mastery of a man, he

becomes a very easy prey to Satan. It is observable that because they were to drink no wine (which was the thing mainly intended) they were to eat nothing that came of the vine, to teach us with the utmost care and caution to avoid sin and every thing that borders upon it and leads to it, or may be a temptation to us. *Abstain from all appearance of evil*, 1 Thess. v. 22.

2. They must not *cut their hair, v.* 5. They must neither poll their heads nor shave their beards; this was that mark of Samson's Nazariteship which we often read of in his story. Now, (1.) This signified a noble neglect of the body and the ease and ornament of it, which became those who, being separated to God, ought to be wholly taken up with their souls, to secure their peace and beauty. It signified that they had, for the present, renounced all sorts of sensual pleasures and delights, and resolved to live a life of self-denial and mortification. Mephibosheth in sorrow *trimmed not his beard*, 2 Sam. xix. 24. (2.) Some observe that long hair is spoken of as a badge of subjection (1 Cor. xi. 5, &c.); so that the long hair of the Nazarites denoted their subjection to God, and their putting themselves under his dominion. (3.) By this they were known to all that met them to be Nazarites, and so it commanded respect. It made them look great without art; it was nature's crown to the head, and a testimony for them that they had preserved their purity. For, if they had been defiled, their hair must have been cut, *v.* 9. See Jer. vii. 29.

3. They must not come near any dead body, *v.* 6, 7. Others might touch dead bodies, and contracted only a ceremonial pollution by it for some time; some must do it, else the dead must be unburied; but the Nazarites must not do it, upon pain of forfeiting all the honour of their Nazariteship. They must not attend the funeral of any relation, no, not father nor mother, any more than the high priest himself, because *the consecration of his God is upon his head.* Those that separate themselves to God must learn, (1.) To distinguish themselves, and do more than others. (2.) To keep their consciences pure from dead works, and not to touch the unclean thing. The greater profession of religion we make, and the more eminent we appear, the greater care we must take to avoid all sin, for we have so much the more honour to lose by it. (3.) To moderate their affections even to their near relations, so as not to let their sorrow for the loss of them break in upon their joy in God and submission to his will. See Matt. viii. 21, 22.

4. All *the days of their separation* they must be *holy to the Lord, v.* 8. This was the meaning of those external observances, and without this they were of no account. The Nazarites must be devoted to God, employed for him, and their minds intent upon him; they must keep themselves pure in heart and life, and be in every thing conformable to the divine image and will; this is to be holy, this is to be a Nazarite indeed.

III. The provision that was made for the cleansing of a Nazarite, if he happened unavoidably to contract a ceremonial pollution by the touch of a dead body. No penalty is ordered by this law for the wilful breach of the foregoing laws; for it was not supposed that a man who had so much religion as to make that vow could have so little as to break it presumptuously: nor could it be supposed that he should drink wine, or have his hair cut, but by his own fault; but purely by the providence of God, without any fault of his own, he might be near a dead body, and that is the case put (*v.* 9): *If a man die very suddenly by him, he has defiled the head of his consecration.* Note, Death sometimes takes men away very suddenly, and without any previous warning. A man might be well and dead in so little a time that the most careful Nazarite could not avoid being polluted by the dead body; so short a step is it sometimes, and so soon taken, from time to eternity. God prepare us for sudden death! In this case, 1. He must be purified from the ceremonial pollution he had contracted, as others must, upon the seventh day, *v.* 9. Nay, more was required for the purifying of the Nazarite than of any other person that had touched a dead body; he must bring a sin-offering and a burnt-offering, and an atonement must be *made for him, v.* 10, 11. This teaches us that sins of infirmity, and the faults we are overtaken in by surprise, must be seriously repented of, and that an application must be made of the virtue of Christ's sacrifice to our souls for the forgiveness of them every day, 1 John ii. 1, 2. It teaches us also that, if those who make an eminent profession of religion do any thing to sully the reputation of their profession, more is expected from them than others, for the retrieving both of their peace and of their credit. 2. He must begin the days of his separation again; for all that were past before his pollution, though coming ever so near the period of his time set, were lost, and not reckoned to him, *v.* 12. This obliged them to be very careful not to defile themselves by the dead, for that was the only thing that made them lose their time, and it teaches us that *if a righteous man turn away from his righteousness,* and defile himself with dead works, all his righteousness that he has done shall be lost to him, Ezek. xxxiii. 13. It is all lost, all in vain, if he do not persevere, Gal. iii. 4. He must begin again, and do his first works.

IV. The law for the solemn discharge of a Nazarite from his vow, when he had completed the time he fixed to himself. Before the expiration of that term he could not be discharged; before he vowed, it was in his own power, but it was too late after the vow to make enquiry. The Jews say that the time of a Nazarite's vow could not be less than thirty days; and if a man said, "I will be a Nazarite but for two days," yet he was bound for thirty; but it should seem Paul's vow was for only seven days (Acts xxi. 27), or, rather, then he observed the ceremony of finishing that vow of Nazariteship from which, being at a distance from the temple, he had discharged himself some years before at Cenchrea only by the ceremony of cutting his hair, Acts xviii. 18. When the time of the vowed separation was out, he was to be made free, 1. Publicly, *at the door of the tabernacle* (*v.* 13), that all might take notice of the finishing of his vow, and none might be offended if they saw him now drink wine, who had so lately refused. 2. It was to be done with sacrifices, *v.* 14. Lest he should think that by this eminent piece of devotion he had made God a debtor to him, he is appointed, even when he had finished his vow, to bring an offering to God; for, when we have done our utmost in duty to God, still we must own ourselves behind-hand with him. He must bring one of each sort of the instituted offerings. (1.) A burnt-offering, as an acknowledgment of God's sovereign dominion over him and all he had still, notwithstanding his discharge from this particular vow. (2.) A sin-offering. This, though mentioned second (*v.* 14), yet seems to have been offered first (*v.* 16), for atonement must be made for our sins before any of our sacrifices can be accepted. And it is very observable that even the Nazarite, who in the eye of men was *purer than snow* and *whiter than milk*, yet durst not appear before the holy God without a sin-offering. Though he had fulfilled the vow of his separation without any pollution, yet he must bring a sacrifice for sin; for there is guilt insensibly contracted by the best of men, even in their best works—some good omitted, some ill admitted, which, if we were dealt with in strict justice, would be our ruin, and in consequence of which it is necessary for us to receive the atonement, and plead it as our righteousness before God. (3.) A peace-offering, in thankfulness to God who had enabled him to fulfil his vow, and in supplication to God for grace to preserve him from ever doing any thing unbecoming one that had been once a Nazarite, remembering that, though he was now freed from the bonds of his own vow, he still remained under the bonds of the divine law. (4.) To these were added the meat-offerings and drink-offerings, according to the manner (*v.* 15, 17), for these always accompanied the burnt-offerings and peace-offerings: and, besides these, a basket of unleavened cakes, and wafers. (5.) Part of the peace-offering, with a cake and wafer, was to be waved for a wave-offering (*v.* 19, 20); and this was a gratuity to the priest, who had it for his pains, after it had been first presented to God. (6.) Besides all this, he might bring his free-will offerings, *such as his hand shall get, v.* 21. More than this he might bring, but not less.

And, to grace the solemnity, it was common upon this occasion to have their friends to be at *charges with them,* Acts xxi. 24. *Lastly,* One ceremony more was appointed, which was like the cancelling of the bond when condition is performed, and that was the *cutting off of his hair,* which had been suffered to grow all the time of his being a Nazarite, and burning it in the fire over which the peace-offerings were boiling, *v.* 18. This intimated that his full performance of his vow was acceptable to God in Christ the great sacrifice, and not otherwise. Learn hence to *vow and pay to the Lord our God,* for *he has no pleasure in fools.*

22 And the LORD spake unto Moses, saying, 23 Speak unto Aaron and unto his sons, saying, On this wise ye shall bless the children of Israel, saying unto them, 24 The LORD bless thee, and keep thee: 25 The LORD make his face shine upon thee, and be gracious unto thee: 26 The LORD lift up his countenance upon thee, and give thee peace. 27 And they shall put my name upon the children of Israel; and I will bless them.

Here, I. The priests, among other good offices which they were to do, are appointed solemnly to bless the people in the *name of the Lord, v.* 23. It was part of their work, Deut. xxi. 5. Hereby God put an honour upon the priests, for *the less is blessed of the better;* and hereby he gave great comfort and satisfaction to the people, who looked upon the priest as God's mouth to them. Though the priest of himself could do no more than beg a blessing, yet being an intercessor by office, and doing that in his name who commands the blessing, the prayer carried with it a promise, and he pronounced it as one having authority with his hands lifted up and his face towards the people. Now, 1. This was a type of Christ's errand into the world, which was to *bless us* (Acts iii. 26), as the high priest of our profession. The last thing he did on earth was with uplifted hands to bless his disciples, Luke xxiv. 50, 51. The learned bishop Pearson observes it as a tradition of the Jews that the priests blessed the people only at the close of the morning sacrifice, not of the evening sacrifice, to show (says he) that in the last days, the days of the Messiah, which are (as it were) the evening of the world, the benediction of the law should cease, and the blessing of Christ should take place. 2. It was a pattern to gospel ministers, the masters of assemblies, who are in like manner to dismiss their solemn assemblies with a blessing. The same that are God's mouth to his people, to teach and command them, are his mouth likewise to bless them; and those that receive

587

the law shall receive the blessing. The Hebrew doctors warn the people that they say not, "What availeth the blessing of this poor simple priest? For," say they, "the receiving of the blessing depends, not on the priest, but on the holy blessed God."

II A form of blessing is here prescribed them. In their other devotions no form was prescribed, but this being God's command concerning benediction, that it might not look like any thing of their own, he puts the very words in their mouths, *v.* 24—26. Here observe, 1. That the blessing is commanded upon each particular person: *The Lord bless thee.* They must each of them prepare themselves to receive the blessing, and then they should find enough in it to make them every man happy. *Blessed shalt thou be,* Deut. xxviii. 3. If we take the law to ourselves, we may take the blessing to ourselves, as if our names were inserted. 2. That the name *Jehovah* is three times repeated in it, and (as the critics observe) each with a different accent in the original; the Jews themselves think there is some mystery in this, and we know what it is, the New Testament having explained it, which directs us to expect the blessing from *the grace of our Lord Jesus Christ, the love of the Father, and the communion of the Holy Ghost,* each of which persons is Jehovah, and yet they are "not three Lords, but one Lord," 2 Cor. xiii. 14. 3. That the favour of God is all in all in this blessing, for that is the fountain of all good. (1.) *The Lord bless thee!* Our blessing God is only our speaking well of him; his blessing us is doing well for us; those whom he blesses are blessed indeed. (2.) *The Lord make his face shine upon thee,* alluding to the shining of the sun upon the earth, to enlighten and comfort it, and to renew the face of it. "The Lord love thee and cause thee to know that he loves thee." We cannot but be happy if we have God's love; and we cannot but be easy if we know that we have it. (3.) *The Lord lift up his countenance upon thee.* This is to the same purport with the former, and it seems to allude to the smiles of a father upon his child, or of a man upon his friend whom he takes pleasure in. If God give us the assurances of his special favour and his acceptance of us, this will *put gladness into the heart,* Ps. iv. 7, 8. 4. That the fruits of this favour conveyed by this blessing are protection, pardon, and peace. (1.) Protection from evil, *v.* 24. The Lord *keep thee,* for it is he that keeps Israel, and neither *slumbers nor sleeps* (Ps. cxxi. 4), and all believers are *kept by the power of God.* (2.) Pardon of sin, *v.* 25. The Lord be *gracious,* or *merciful,* unto thee. (3.) Peace (*v.* 26), including all that good which goes to make up a complete happiness.

III. God here promises to ratify and confirm the blessing: *They shall put my name upon the children of Israel, v.* 27. God gives them

588

leave to make use of his name in blessing the people, and to bless them as his people, called by his name. This included all the blessings they could pronounce upon them, to mark them for God's peculiar, the people of his choice and love. God's name upon them was their honour, their comfort, their safety, their plea. *We are called by thy name, leave us not.* It is added, *and I will bless them.* Note, A divine blessing goes along with divine institutions, and puts virtue and efficacy into them. What Christ says of the peace is true of the blessing; when God's ministers pronounce the blessing, "Peace to this congregation," if the sons of peace and heirs of blessing be there, the peace, the blessing, shall rest upon them, Luke x. 5, 6. For in *every place where God records his name* he will *meet his people and bless them.*

CHAP. VII.

God having set up house (as it were) in the midst of the camp of Israel, the princes of Israel here come a visiting with their presents, as tenants to their landlord, in the name of their respective tribes. I. They brought presents, 1. Upon the dedication of the tabernacle, for the service of that, ver. 1—9. 2. Upon the dedication of the altar, for the use of that, ver. 10—88. And, II. God graciously signified his acceptance of them, ver. 89. The two foregoing chapters were the records of additional laws which God gave to Israel, this is the history of the additional services which Israel performed to God.

AND it came to pass on the day that Moses had fully set up the tabernacle, and had anointed it, and sanctified it, and all the instruments thereof, both the altar and all the vessels thereof, and had anointed them, and sanctified them; 2 That the princes of Israel, heads of the house of their fathers, who *were* the princes of the tribes, and were over them that were numbered, offered: 3 And they brought their offering before the LORD, six covered waggons, and twelve oxen; a waggon for two of the princes, and for each one an ox: and they brought them before the tabernacle. 4 And the LORD spake unto Moses, saying, 5 Take *it* of them, that they may be to do the service of the tabernacle of the congregation; and thou shalt give them unto the Levites, to every man according to his service. 6 And Moses took the waggons and the oxen, and gave them unto the Levites. 7 Two waggons and four oxen he gave unto the sons of Gershon, according to their service: 8 And four waggons and eight oxen he gave unto the sons of Merari, according unto their service, under the hand of Ithamar the son of Aaron the priest. 9 But unto the sons of Kohath he gave none: because the service of the sanctuary belonging unto them *was that* they should bear upon their shoulders.

Here is the offering of the princes to the service of the tabernacle. Observe,

I. When it was; not till it was *fully set up*, *v.* 1. When all things were done both about the tabernacle itself, and the camp of Israel which surrounded it, according to the directions given, then they began their presents, probably about the eighth day of the second month. Note, Necessary observances must always take place of free-will offerings: first those, and then these.

II. Who it was that offered: *The princes of Israel, heads of the house of their fathers*, *v.* 2. Note, Those that are above others in power and dignity ought to go before others, and endeavour to go beyond them, in every thing that is good. The more any are advanced the more is expected from them, on account of the greater opportunity they have of serving God and their generation. What are wealth and authority good for, but as they enable a man to do so much the more good in the world?

III. What was offered: six waggons, with each of them a yoke of oxen to draw them, *v.* 3. Doubtless these waggons were agreeable to the rest of the furniture of the tabernacle and its appurtenances, the best of the kind, like the carriages which great princes use when they go in procession. Some think that God, by Moses, intimated to them what they should bring, or their own consideration perhaps suggested to them to make this present. Though God's wisdom had ordained all the essentials of the tabernacle, yet it seems these accidental conveniences were left to be provided by their own discretion, which was to set in order that which was wanting (Tit. i. 5), and these waggons were not refused, though no pattern of them was shown to Moses in the mount. Note, It must not be expected that the divine institution of ordinances should descend to all those circumstances which are determinable, and are fit to be left alterable, by human prudence, that wisdom which is profitable to direct. Observe, No sooner is the tabernacle fully set up than this provision is made for the removal of it. Note, Even when we are but just settled in the world, and think we are beginning to take root, we must be preparing for changes and removes, especially for the great change. While we are here in this world, every thing must be accommodated to a militant and movable state. When the tabernacle was framing, the princes were very generous in their offerings, for then they brought *precious stones, and stones to be set* (Exod. xxxv. 27), yet now they bring more presents. Note, Those that have done good should study to abound therein yet more and more, and not be *weary of well-doing*.

IV. How the offering was disposed of, and what use was made of it: the waggons and oxen were given to the Levites, to be used in carrying the tabernacle, both for their ease (for God would not have any of his servants overburdened with work), and for the more safe and right conveyance of the several parts of the tabernacle, which would be best kept together, and sheltered from the weather, in waggons. 1. The Gershonites, that had the light carriage, the curtains and hangings, had but two waggons, and two yoke of oxen (*v.* 7); when they had loaded these, they must carry the rest, if any remained, upon their shoulders. 2. The Merarites, that had the heavy carriage, and that which was most unwieldy, the boards, pillars, sockets, &c., had four waggons, and four yoke of oxen allotted them (*v.* 8); and yet, if they had not more waggons of their own, they would be obliged to carry a great deal upon their backs too, for the silver sockets alone weighed 100 talents, which was above four tons, and that was enough to load four waggons that were drawn but by one yoke of oxen a-piece. But each socket being a talent weight, which is about a man's burden (as appears, 2 Kings v. 23) probably they carried those on their backs, and put the boards and pillars into the waggons. Observe here, How God wisely and graciously ordered the most strength to those that had the most work. Each had waggons *according to their service.* Whatever burden God in his providence lays upon us, he will by his sufficient grace proportion the strength to it, 1 Cor. x. 13. 3. The Kohathites, that had the most sacred carriage, had no waggons at all, because they were to carry their charge upon their shoulders (*v.* 9), with a particular care and veneration. When in David's time they carried the ark in a cart, God made them to know to their terror, by the death of Uzza, that they did not *seek him in the due order.* See 1 Chron. xv. 13.

10 And the princes offered for dedicating of the altar in the day that it was anointed, even the princes offered their offering before the altar. 11 And the Lᴏʀᴅ said unto Moses, They shall offer their offering, each prince on his day, for the dedicating of the altar. 12 And he that offered his offering the first day was Nahshon the son of Amminadab, of the tribe of Judah: 13 And his offering *was* one silver charger, the weight thereof *was* a hundred and thirty *shekels*, one silver bowl of seventy shekels, after the shekel of the sanctuary; both of them *were* full of fine flour mingled with oil for a meat offering: 14 One spoon of ten *shekels* of gold, full of

incense: 15 One young bullock, one ram, one lamb of the first year, for a burnt offering: 16 One kid of the goats for a sin offering: 17 And for a sacrifice of peace offerings, two oxen, five rams, five he goats, five lambs of the first year: this *was* the offering of Nahshon the son of Amminadab. 18 On the second day Nethaneel the son of Zuar, prince of Issachar, did offer: 19 He offered *for* his offering one silver charger, the weight whereof *was* a hundred and thirty *shekels*, one silver bowl of seventy shekels, after the shekel of the sanctuary; both of them full of fine flour mingled with oil for a meat offering: 20 One spoon of gold of ten *shekels*, full of incense: 21 One young bullock, one ram, one lamb of the first year, for a burnt offering: 22 One kid of the goats for a sin offering: 23 And for a sacrifice of peace offerings, two oxen, five rams, five he goats, five lambs of the first year: this *was* the offering of Nethaneel the son of Zuar. 24 On the third day Eliab the son of Helon, prince of the children of Zebulun, *did offer:* 25 His offering *was* one silver charger, the weight whereof *was* a hundred and thirty *shekels*, one silver bowl of seventy shekels, after the shekel of the sanctuary; both of them full of fine flour mingled with oil for a meat offering: 26 One golden spoon of ten *shekels*, full of incense: 27 One young bullock, one ram, one lamb of the first year, for a burnt offering: 28 One kid of the goats for a sin offering: 29 And for a sacrifice of peace offerings, two oxen, five rams, five he goats, five lambs of the first year: this *was* the offering of Eliab the son of Helon. 30 On the fourth day Elizur the son of Shedeur, prince of the children of Reuben, *did offer:* 31 His offering *was* one silver charger of the weight of a hundred and thirty *shekels*, one silver bowl of seventy shekels, after the shekel of the sanctuary; both of them full of fine flour mingled with oil for a meat offering: 32 One golden spoon of ten *shekels*, full of incense: 33 One young bullock, one ram, one lamb of the first

year, for a burnt offering: 34 One kid of the goats for a sin offering: 35 And for a sacrifice of peace offerings, two oxen, five rams, five he goats, five lambs of the first year: this *was* the offering of Elizur the son of Shedeur. 36 On the fifth day Shelumiel the son of Zurishaddai, prince of the children of Simeon, *did offer:* 37 His offering *was* one silver charger, the weight whereof *was* a hundred and thirty *shekels*, one silver bowl of seventy shekels, after the shekel of the sanctuary; both of them full of fine flour mingled with oil for a meat offering: 38 One golden spoon of ten *shekels*, full of incense: 39 One young bullock, one ram, one lamb of the first year, for a burnt offering: 40 One kid of the goats for a sin offering: 41 And for a sacrifice of peace offerings, two oxen, five rams, five he goats, five lambs of the first year: this *was* the offering of Shelumiel the son of Zurishaddai. 42 On the sixth day Eliasaph the son of Deuel, prince of the children of Gad, *offered:* 43 His offering *was* one silver charger of the weight of a hundred and thirty *shekels*, a silver bowl of seventy shekels, after the shekel of the sanctuary; both of them full of fine flour mingled with oil for a meat offering: 44 One golden spoon of ten *shekels*, full of incense: 45 One young bullock, one ram, one lamb of the first year, for a burnt offering: 46 One kid of the goats for a sin offering: 47 And for a sacrifice of peace offerings, two oxen, five rams, five he goats, five lambs of the first year: this *was* the offering of Eliasaph the son of Deuel. 48 On the seventh day Elishama the son of Ammihud, prince of the children of Ephraim, *offered:* 49 His offering *was* one silver charger, the weight whereof *was* a hundred and thirty *shekels*, one silver bowl of seventy shekels, after the shekel of the sanctuary; both of them full of fine flour mingled with oil for a meat offering: 50 One golden spoon of ten *shekels* full of incense: 51 One young bullock, one ram, one lamb of the first year, for a burnt offering: 52 One kid of the goats for a sin offering : 53 And for a sacrifice of peace offerings, two oxen, five rams, five he goats, five lambs of the first year : this *was* the offering of Elishama the son of Ammihud. 54 On the eighth day *offered* Gamaliel the son of Pedahzur, prince of the children of Manasseh : 55 His offering *was* one silver charger of the weight of a hundred and thirty *shekels*, one silver bowl of seventy shekels, after the shekel of the sanctuary ; both of them full of fine flour mingled with oil for a meat offering : 56 One golden spoon of ten *shekels*, full of incense : 57 One young bullock, one ram, one lamb of the first year, for a burnt offering : 58 One kid of the goats for a sin offering : 59 And for a sacrifice of peace offerings, two oxen, five rams, five he goats, five lambs of the first year : this *was* the offering of Gamaliel the son of Pedahzur. 60 On the ninth day Abidan the son of Gideoni, prince of the children of Benjamin, *offered* : 61 His offering *was* one silver charger, the weight whereof *was* a hundred and thirty *shekels*, one silver bowl of seventy shekels, after the shekel of the sanctuary ; both of them full of fine flour mingled with oil for a meat offering : 62 One golden spoon of ten *shekels*, full of incense : 63 One young bullock, one ram, one lamb of the first year, for a burnt offering : 64 One kid of the goats for a sin offering : 65 And for a sacrifice of peace offerings, two oxen, five rams, five he goats, five lambs of the first year : this *was* the offering of Abidan the son of Gideoni. 66 On the tenth day Ahiezer the son of Ammishaddai, prince of the children of Dan, *offered* : 67 His offering *was* one silver charger, the weight whereof *was* a hundred and thirty *shekels*, one silver bowl of seventy shekels, after the shekel of the sanctuary ; both of them full of fine flour mingled with oil for a meat offering : 68 One golden spoon of ten *shekels*, full of incense: 69 One young bullock, one ram, one lamb of the first year, for a burnt offering : 70 One kid of the goats for a sin offering : 71 And for a sacrifice of peace offerings, two oxen, five rams, five he goats, five lambs of the first year : this *was* the offering of Ahiezer the son of Ammishaddai. 72 On the eleventh day Pagiel the son of Ocran, prince of the children of Asher, *offered* : 73 His offering *was* one silver charger, the weight whereof *was* a hundred and thirty *shekels*, one silver bowl of seventy shekels, after the shekel of the sanctuary ; both of them full of fine flour mingled with oil for a meat offering : 74 One golden spoon of ten *shekels*, full of incense : 75 One young bullock, one ram, one lamb of the first year, for a burnt offering : 76 One kid of the goats for a sin offering : 77 And for a sacrifice of peace offerings, two oxen, five rams, five he goats, five lambs of the first year : this *was* the offering of Pagiel the son of Ocran. 78 On the twelfth day Ahira the son of Enan, prince of the children of Naphtali, *offered* : 79 His offering *was* one silver charger, the weight whereof *was* a hundred and thirty *shekels*, one silver bowl of seventy shekels, after the shekel of the sanctuary ; both of them full of fine flour mingled with oil for a meat offering : 80 One golden spoon of ten *shekels*, full of incense : 81 One young bullock, one ram, one lamb of the first year, for a burnt offering : 82 One kid of the goats for a sin offering : 83 And for a sacrifice of peace offerings, two oxen, five rams, five he goats, five lambs of the first year : this *was* the offering of Ahira the son of Enan. 84 This *was* the dedication of the altar, in the day when it was anointed, by the princes of Israel : twelve chargers of silver, twelve silver bowls, twelve spoons of gold : 85 Each charger of silver *weighing* a hundred and thirty *shekels*, each bowl seventy : all the silver vessels *weighed* two thousand and four hundred *shekels*, after the shekel of the sanctuary : 86 The golden spoons *were* twelve, full of incense, *weighing* ten *shekels* apiece, after the shekel of the sanctuary : all the gold of the spoons *was* a hundred and twenty *shekels*. 87 All the oxen for the burnt offering *were* twelve bullocks, the rams twelve, the lambs of the first year twelve, with their meat offering : and the kids of the goats for sin offering twelve. 88 And all the oxen for the sacrifice of the peace offerings *were* twenty and four bullocks, the rams sixty, the he goats sixty, the lambs of the first year sixty. This *was* the dedication of the altar, after that it was anointed. 89 And when Moses was gone into the tabernacle of the congregation to speak with him, then he heard the voice of one speaking unto him from off the mercy seat that *was* upon the ark of testimony, from between the two cherubims : and he spake unto him.

We have here an account of the great solemnity of dedicating the altars, both that of burnt-offerings and that of incense; they had been sanctified before, when they were anointed (Lev. viii. 10, 11), but now they were handselled, as it were, by the princes, with their free-will offerings. They began the use of them with rich presents, great expressions of joy and gladness, and extraordinary respect to those tokens of God's presence with them. Now observe here,

I. That the princes and great men were first and forwardest in the service of God. Those that are entitled to precedency should go before in good works, and that is true honour. Here is an example to the nobility and gentry, those that are in authority and of the first rank in their country; they ought to improve their honour and power, their estate and interest, for the promoting of religion, and the service of God, in the places where they live. It is justly expected that those who have more than others should do more good than others with what they have, else they are unfaithful stewards, and will not make up their *account with joy.* Nay, great men must not only with their wealth and power assist and protect those that serve God, but they must make conscience of being devout and religious themselves, and employing themselves in the exercises of piety, which will greatly redound to the honour of God (Ps. cxxxviii. 4, 5), and have a good influence upon others, who will be the more easily persuaded to acts of devotion when they see them thus brought into reputation. It is certain that the greatest of men is less than the least of the ordinances of God; nor are the meanest services of religion any disparagement to those that make the greatest figure in the world.

II. The offerings they brought were very rich and valuable, so rich that some think there was not so great a difference in estate between them and others as that they were able to bear the expense of them themselves,

but that the heads of each tribe contributed to the offering which their prince brought.

1. They brought some things to remain for standing service, twelve large silver dishes, each about sixty ounces weight, as many large silver cups, or bowls, of about thirty-five ounces—the former to be used for the meat-offerings, the latter for the drink-offerings—the former for the flesh of the sacrifices, the latter for the blood. The latter was God's table (as it were), and it was fit that so great a King should be served in plate. The golden spoons being filled with incense were intended, it is probable, for the service of the golden altar, for both the altars were anointed at the same time. Note, In works of piety and charity we ought to be generous according as our ability is. He that is the best should be served with the best we have. The Israelites indeed might well afford to part with their gold and silver in abundance to the service of the sanctuary, for they needed it not to buy meat and victual their camp, being daily fed with bread from heaven; nor did they need it to buy land, or pay their army, for they were shortly to be put in possession of Canaan.

2. They brought some things to be used immediately, offerings of each sort, burnt-offerings, sin-offerings, and a great many peace-offerings (on part of which they were to feast with their friends), and the meat-offerings that were to be annexed to them. Hereby they signified their thankful acceptance of, and cheerful submission to, all those laws concerning the sacrifices which God had lately by Moses delivered to them. And, though it was a time of joy and rejoicing, yet it is observable that still in the midst of their sacrifices we find a *sin-offering.* Since in our best services we are conscious to ourselves that there is a mixture of sin, it is fit that there should be even in our most joyful services a mixture of repentance. In all our approaches to God, we must by faith have an eye to Christ as the great sin-offering, and make mention of him.

3. They brought their offerings each on a separate day, in the order that they had been lately put into, so that the solemnity lasted twelve days. So God appointed (*v.* 11): *They shall bring their offering, each prince on his day,* and so they did. One sabbath must needs fall within the twelve days, if not two, but it should seem they did not intermit on the sabbath, for it was holy work, proper enough for a holy day. God appointed that it should thus be done on several days, (1.) That the solemnity might be prolonged, and so might be universally taken notice of by all Israel, and the remembrance of it more effectually preserved. (2.) That an equal honour might thereby be put upon each tribe respectively; in Aaron's breast-plate each had his precious stone, so in this offering each had his day. (3.) Thus it would be done more decently and in order ; God's

work should not be done confusedly, and in a hurry; take time, and we shall have done the sooner, or at least we shall have done the better. (4.) God hereby signified how much pleased he is, and how much pleased we should be, with the exercises of piety and devotion. The repetition of them should be a continual pleasure to us, and we must not be weary of well doing. If extraordinary service be required to be done for twelve days together, we must not shrink from it, nor call it a task and a burden. (5.) The priests and Levites, having this occasion to offer the same sacrifices, and those some of every sort, every day, for so many days together, would have their hands well set in, and would be well versed in the laws concerning them. (6.) The peace-offerings were all to be eaten the same day they were offered, and two oxen, five rams, five he-goats, and five lambs, were enough for one day's festival; had there been more, especially if all had been brought on one day, there might have been danger of excess. The virtue of temperance must not be left, under pretence of the religion of feasting.

4. All their offerings were exactly the same, without any variation, though it is probable that neither the princes nor the tribes were all alike rich; but thus it was intimated that all the tribes of Israel had an equal share in the altar, and an equal interest in the sacrifices that were offered upon it. Though one tribe was posted more honourably in the camp than another, yet they and their services were all alike acceptable to God. Nor must we have the faith of our Lord Jesus Christ *with respect to persons,* Jam. ii. 1.

5. Nahshon, the prince of the tribe of Judah, offered first, because God had given that tribe the first post of honour in the camp; and the rest of the tribes acquiesced, and offered in the same order in which God had appointed them to encamp. Judah, of which tribe Christ came, first, and then the rest; thus, in the dedication of souls to God, every man is presented in his own order, *Christ the first-fruits,* 1 Cor. xv. 23. Some observe that Nahshon is the only one that is not expressly called a prince (*v.* 12), which the Jews give this account of: he is not called a prince, that he might not be puffed up because he offered first; and all the others are called princes because they (though some of them of the elder house) submitted, and offered after him. Or, because the title of prince of Judah did more properly belong to Christ, for *unto him shall the gathering of the people be.*

6. Though the offerings were all the same, yet the account of them is repeated at large for each tribe, in the same words. We are sure there are no vain repetitions in scripture; what then shall we make of these repetitions? Might it not have served to say of this noble jury that the same offering

which their foreman brought each on his day brought likewise? No, God would have it specified for each tribe: and why so? (1.) It was for the encouragement of these princes, and of their respective tribes, that each of their offerings being recorded at large no slight might seem to be put upon them; for rich and poor meet together before God. (2.) It was for the encouragement of all generous acts of piety and charity, by letting us know that what is so given is lent to the Lord, and he carefully records it, with every one's name prefixed to his gift, because what is so given he will pay again, and even a *cup of cold water* shall have its *reward.* He is not unrighteous, to forget either the cost or the *labour of love,* Heb. vi. 10. We find Christ taking particular notice of what was cast into the treasury, Mark xii. 41. Though what is offered be but little, though it be a contribution to the charity of others, yet if it be according to our ability it shall be recorded, that it may be recompensed in the resurrection of the just.

7. The sum total is added at the foot of the account (*v.* 84—88), to show how much God was pleased with the mention of his freewill-offerings, and what a great deal they amounted to in the whole, when every prince brought in his quota! How greatly would the sanctuary of God be enriched and beautified if all would in their places do their part towards it, by exemplary purity and devotion, extensive charity, and universal usefulness!

8. God signified his gracious acceptance of these presents that were brought him, by speaking familiarly to Moses, as a man speaks to his friend, from off the mercy-seat (*v.* 89, *ch.* xii. 8); and in speaking to him he did in effect speak to all Israel, showing them this token for good, Ps. ciii. 7. Note. By this we may know that God hears and accepts our prayers if he gives us grace to hear and receive his word, for thus our communion with him is maintained and kept up. I know not why we may not suppose that upon each of the days on which these offerings were brought (probably while the priests and offerers were feasting upon the peace-offerings) Moses was in the tabernacle, receiving some of those laws and orders which we have already met with in this and the foregoing book. And here the excellent bishop Patrick observes that God's speaking to Moses thus by an audible articulate voice, as if he had been clothed with a body, might be looked upon as an earnest of the incarnation of the Son of God in the fulness of time, when the Word should be made flesh, and speak in the language of the sons of men. For, however *God at sundry times and in divers manners spoke unto the fathers, he has in these last days spoken unto us by his Son.* And that he who now spoke to Moses, as the *shechinah* or divine Majesty, from be-

tween the cherubim, was the eternal Word, the second person in the Trinity, was the pious conjecture of many of the ancients; for all God's communion with man is by his Son, by whom he made the world, and rules the church, and who *is the same yesterday, to-day, and for ever.*

CHAP. VIII.

This chapter is concerning the lamps or lights of the sanctuary. I. The burning lamps in the candlestick, which the priests were charged to tend, ver. 1—4. II. The living lamps (if I may so call them), the Levites, who as ministers were burning and shining lights. The ordination of the priests we had an account of, Lev. viii. Here we have an account of the ordination of the Levites, the inferior clergy. 1. How they were purified, ver. 5—8. 2. How they were parted with by the people, ver. 9, 10. 3. How they were presented to God in lieu of the firstborn, ver. 11—18. 4. How they were consigned to Aaron and his sons, to be ministers to them, ver. 19. 5. How all these orders were duly executed, ver. 20—22. And, lastly, The age appointed for their ministration, ver. 23, &c.

AND the Lord spake unto Moses, saying, 2 Speak unto Aaron, and say unto him, When thou lightest the lamps, the seven lamps shall give light over against the candlestick. 3 And Aaron did so; he lighted the lamps thereof over against the candlestick, as the Lord commanded Moses. 4 And this work of the candlestick *was of* beaten gold, unto the shaft thereof, unto the flowers thereof, *was* beaten work: according unto the pattern which the Lord had showed Moses, so he made the candlestick.

Directions were given long before this for the making of the golden candlestick (Exod. xxv. 31), and it was made according to the pattern shown to Moses in the mount, Exod. xxxvii. 17. But now it was that the lamps were first ordered to be lighted, when other things began to be used. Observe, 1. Who must light the lamps; Aaron himself, he *lighted the lamps, v.* 3. As the people's representative to God, he thus did the office of a servant in God's house, lighting his Master's candle; as the representative of God to the people, he thus gave them the intimations of God's will and favour, thus expressed (Ps. xviii. 28), *Thou wilt light my candle;* and thus Aaron himself was now lately directed to bless the people, *The Lord make his face to shine upon thee, ch.* vi. 25. The commandment is a *lamp,* Prov. vi. 23. The scripture is *a light shining in a dark place,* 2 Pet. 1. 19. And a dark place indeed even the church would be without it, as the tabernacle (which had no window in it) without the lamps. Now the work of ministers is to light these lamps, by expounding and applying the word of God. The priest lighted the middle lamp from the fire of the altar, and the rest of the lamps he lighted one from another, which (says Mr. Ainsworth) signifies that the fountain of all light and knowledge is in Christ, who has the *seven spirits of God* figured by the *seven lamps of fire* (Rev. iv. 5), but that in the expounding of scripture one

passage must borrow light from another. He also supposes that, *seven* being a number of perfection, by the seven branches of the candlestick is shown the full perfection of the scriptures, which are able to make us wise to salvation. 2. To what end the lamps were lighted, that they might give light *over against the candlestick,* that is, to that part of the tabernacle where the table stood, with the show-bread upon it, over against the candlestick. They were not lighted like tapers in an urn, to burn to themselves, but to give light to the other side of the tabernacle, for therefore candles are lighted, Matt. v. 15. Note, The lights of the world, the lights of the church, must shine as lights. Therefore we have light, that we may give light.

5 And the Lord spake unto Moses, saying, 6 Take the Levites from among the children of Israel, and cleanse them. 7 And thus shalt thou do unto them, to cleanse them: Sprinkle water of purifying upon them, and let them shave all their flesh, and let them wash their clothes, and *so* make themselves clean. 8 Then let them take a young bullock with his meat offering, *even* fine flour mingled with oil, and another young bullock shalt thou take for a sin offering. 9 And thou shalt bring the Levites before the tabernacle of the congregation: and thou shalt gather the whole assembly of the children of Israel together: 10 And thou shalt bring the Levites before the Lord: and the children of Israel shall put their hands upon the Levites: 11 And Aaron shall offer the Levites before the Lord *for* an offering of the children of Israel, that they may execute the service of the Lord. 12 And the Levites shall lay their hands upon the heads of the bullocks: and thou shalt offer the one *for* a sin offering, and the other *for* a burnt offering, unto the Lord, to make an atonement for the Levites. 13 And thou shalt set the Levites before Aaron, and before his sons, and offer them *for* an offering unto the Lord. 14 Thus shalt thou separate the Levites from among the children of Israel: and the Levites shall be mine. 15 And after that shall the Levites go in to do the service of the tabernacle of the congregation: and thou shalt

594

cleanse them, and offer them *for* an offering. 16 For they *are* wholly given unto me from among the children of Israel; instead of such as open every womb, *even instead of* the firstborn of all the children of Israel, have I taken them unto me. 17 For all the firstborn of the children of Israel *are* mine, *both* man and beast: on the day that I smote every firstborn in the land of Egypt I sanctified them for myself. 18 And I have taken the Levites for all the firstborn of the children of Israel. 19 And I have given the Levites *as* a gift to Aaron and to his sons from among the children of Israel, to do the service of the children of Israel in the tabernacle of the congregation, and to make an atonement for the children of Israel: that there be no plague among the children of Israel, when the children of Israel come nigh unto the sanctuary. 20 And Moses, and Aaron, and all the congregation of the children of Israel, did to the Levites according unto all that the LORD commanded Moses concerning the Levites, so did the children of Israel unto them. 21 And the Levites were purified, and they washed their clothes; and Aaron offered them *as* an offering before the LORD; and Aaron made an atonement for them to cleanse them. 22 And after that went the Levites in to do their service in the tabernacle of the congregation before Aaron, and before his sons: as the LORD had commanded Moses concerning the Levites, so did they unto them. 23 And the LORD spake unto Moses, saying, 24 This *is it* that *belongeth* unto the Levites: from twenty and five years old and upward they shall go in to wait upon the service of the tabernacle of the congregation: 25 And from the age of fifty years they shall cease waiting upon the service *thereof*, and shall serve no more: 26 But shall minister with their brethren in the tabernacle of the congregation, to keep the charge, and shall do no service. Thus shalt thou do unto the Levites touching their charge.

We read before of the separating of the Levites from among the children of Israel when they were numbered, and the numbering of them by themselves (*ch.* iii. 6, 15), that they might be employed in the service of the tabernacle. Now here we have directions given for their solemn ordination (*v.* 6), and the performance of it, *v.* 20. All Israel must know that they took not this honour to themselves, but were called of God to it; nor was it enough that they were distinguished from their neighbours, but they must be solemnly devoted to God. Note, All that are employed for God must be dedicated to him, according as the degree of the employment is. Christians must be baptized, ministers must be ordained; we must first give ourselves unto the Lord, and then our services. Observe in what method this was done:

I. The Levites must be cleansed, and were so. The rites and ceremonies of their cleansing were to be performed, 1. By themselves. They must *wash their clothes*, and not only bathe, but *shave all their flesh*, as the leper was to do when he was cleansed, Lev. xiv. 8. They must *cause a razor to pass over all their flesh*, to clear themselves from that defilement which would not wash off. Jacob, whom God loved, was a smooth man; it was Esau that was hairy. The great pains they were to take with themselves to make themselves clean teaches all Christians, and ministers particularly, by repentance and mortification, to *cleanse themselves from all filthiness of flesh and spirit*, that they may *perfect holiness*. Those must be clean that bear the vessels of the Lord. 2. By Moses. He must *sprinkle the water of purifying upon them*, which was prepared by divine direction. This signified the application of the blood of Christ to our souls by faith, to purify us from an evil conscience, that we may be fit to serve the living God. It is our duty to cleanse ourselves, and God's promise that he will cleanse us.

II. The Levites, being thus prepared, must be brought before the Lord in a solemn assembly of all Israel, and the *children of Israel* must *put their hands upon them* (*v.* 10), so transferring their interest in them and in their service (to which, as a part, the whole body of the people was entitled) to God and to his sanctuary. They presented them to God *as living sacrifices, holy and acceptable*, to perform a *reasonable service;* and therefore, as the offerers in all other cases did, *they laid their hands upon them*, desiring that their service might be accepted in lieu of the attendance of the whole congregation, particularly the first-born, which they acknowledge God might have insisted on. This will not serve to prove a power in the people to ordain ministers; for this imposition of hands by the children of Israel upon the Levites did not make them ministers of the sanctuary, but only signified the people's parting with that tribe out of their militia, and civil incorporations, in order to their being made ministers by Aaron, who was to offer them before the Lord. All the congregation of the children of Israel could not lay hands on them, but it is probable that the rulers and elders did it as the representative body of the people. Some think that the first-born did it because in their stead the Levites were consecrated to God. Whatever God calls for from us to serve his own glory by, we must cheerfully resign it, lay our hands upon it, not to detain it but to surrender it, and let it go to him that is entitled to it.

III. Sacrifices were to be offered for them, a sin-offering first (*v.* 12), and then a burnt-offering, to make an *atonement for the Levites,* who, as the parties concerned, were to lay their hands upon the head of the sacrifices. See here, 1. That we are all utterly unworthy and unfit to be admitted into and employed in the service of God, till atonement be made for sin, and thereby our peace made with God. That interposing cloud must be scattered before there can be any comfortable communion settled between God and our souls. 2. That it is by sacrifice, by Christ the great sacrifice, that we are reconciled to God, and made fit to be offered to him. It is by him that Christians are sanctified to the work of their Christianity, and ministers to the work of their ministry. The learned bishop Patrick's notion of the sacrifice offered by the Levites is that the Levites were themselves considered as an expiatory sacrifice, for they were given to *make atonement for the children of Israel* (*v.* 19), and yet not being devoted to death, any more than the first-born were, these two sacrifices were substituted in their stead, upon which therefore they were to lay their hands, that the sin which the children of Israel laid upon them (*v.* 10) might be transferred to these beasts.

IV. The Levites themselves were *offered before the Lord* for an *offering of the children of Israel, v.* 11. Aaron gave them up to God, as being first given up by themselves, and by the children of Israel. The original word signifies a *wave-offering,* not that they were actually waved, but they were presented to God as the God of heaven, and the Lord of the whole earth, as the wave-offerings were. And in calling them wave-offerings it was intimated to them that they must continually lift up themselves towards God in his service, lift up their eyes, lift up their hearts, and must move to and fro with readiness in the business of their profession. They were not ordained to be idle, but to be active and stirring.

V. God here declares his acceptance of them : *The Levites shall be mine, v.* 14. God took them instead of the first-born (*v.* 16—18), of which before, *ch.* iii. 41. Note, What is in sincerity offered to God shall be graciously owned and accepted by him. And his ministers who have obtained mercy of him to

596

be faithful have particular marks of favour and honour put upon them : *they shall be mine,* and then (*v.* 15) they shall *go in to do the service of the tabernacle.* God takes them for his own, that they may serve him. All that expect to share in the privileges of the tabernacle must resolve to do the service of the tabernacle. As, on the one hand, none of God's creatures are his necessary servants (he needs not the service of any of them), so, on the other hand, none are taken merely as honorary servants, to do nothing. All whom God owns he employs ; angels themselves have their services.

VI. They are then given as a gift to Aaron and his sons (*v.* 19), yet so as that the benefit accrued to the children of Israel. 1. The Levites must act under the priests as attendants on them, and assistants to them, in the service of the sanctuary. Aaron offers them to God (*v.* 11), and then God gives them back to Aaron, *v.* 19. Note, Whatever we give up to God, he will give back to us unspeakably to our advantage. Our hearts, our children, our estates, are never more ours, more truly, more comfortably ours, than when we have offered them up to God. 2. They must act for the people. They were taken to *do the service of the children of Israel,* that is, not only to do the service which they should do, but to serve their interests, and do that which would really redound to the honour, safety, and prosperity of the whole nation. Note, Those that faithfully perform the service of God do one of the best services that can be done to the public ; God's ministers, while they keep within the sphere of their office and conscientiously discharge the duty of it, must be looked upon as some of the most useful servants of their country. The children of Israel can as ill spare the tribe of Levi as any of their tribes. But what is the service they do the children of Israel ? It follows, it is to *make an atonement for them, that there be no plague among them.* It was the priests' work to make atonement by sacrifice, but the Levites made atonement by attendance, and preserved the peace with heaven which was made by sacrifice. If the service of the priests in the tabernacle had been left to all the first-born of Israel promiscuously, it would have been either neglected or done unskilfully and irreverently, being done by those that were not so closely tied to it, nor so diligently trained to it, nor so constantly used to it, as the Levites were ; and this would bring *a plague among the children of Israel*—meaning, perhaps, the death of the first-born themselves, which was the last and greatest of the plagues of Egypt. To prevent this, and to preserve the atonement, the Levites were appointed to do this service, who should be bred up to it under their parents from their infancy, and therefore would be well versed in it ; and so the children of Israel, that is, the first-born, should not need to come nigh to the sanctuary; or, when any Israelites had occasion, the Levites would be ready to instruct them, and introduce them, and so prevent any fatal miscarriage or mistake. Note, It is a very great kindness to the church that ministers are appointed to go before the people in the things of God, as guides, overseers, and rulers, in religious worship, and to make that their business. When Christ ascended on high, he *gave these gifts*, Eph. iv. 8, 11, 12.

VII. The time of their ministration is fixed. 1. They were to enter upon the service at twenty-five years old, *v.* 24. They were not charged with the carrying of the tabernacle and the utensils of it till they were thirty years old, *ch.* iv. 3. But they were entered to be otherwise serviceable at twenty-five years old, a very good age for ministers to begin their public work at. The work then required that strength of body and the work now requires that maturity of judgment and steadiness of behaviour which men rarely arrive at till about that age; and novices are in danger of being lifted up with pride. 2. They were to have a writ of ease at fifty years old; then they were to return from the warfare, as the phrase is (*v.* 25), not cashiered with disgrace, but preferred rather to the rest which their age required, to be loaded with the honours of their office, as hitherto they had been with the burdens of it. They shall *minister with their brethren in the tabernacle,* to direct the junior Levites, and set them in; and they shall *keep the charge,* as guards upon the avenues of the tabernacle, to see that no stranger intruded, nor any person in his uncleanness, but they shall not be put upon any service which may be a fatigue to them. If God's grace provide that men shall have ability according to their work, man's prudence should take care that men have work only according to their ability. The aged are most fit for trusts, and to keep the charge; the younger are most fit for work, and to do the service. Those that have *used the office of a servant well purchase to themselves a good degree,* 1 Tim. iii. 13. Yet indeed gifts are not tied to ages (Job xxxii. 9), but *all these worketh that one and the selfsame Spirit.* Thus was the affair of the Levites settled.

CHAP. IX.

This chapter is, I. Concerning the great ordinance of the passover; 1. Orders given for the observance of it, at the return of the year, ver. 1—5. 2. Provisos added in regard to such as should be ceremonially unclean, or otherwise disabled, at the time when the passover was to be kept, ver. 6—14. II. Concerning the great favour of the pillar of cloud, which was a guide to Israel through the wilderness, ver. 15, &c.

AND the LORD spake unto Moses in the wilderness of Sinai, in the first month of the second year after they were come out of the land of Egypt, saying,　2 Let the children of Israel also keep the passover at his appointed season. 3 In the fourteenth day of this month, at even, ye shall keep it in his appointed season: according to all the rites of it, and according to all the ceremonies thereof, shall ye keep it. 4 And Moses spake unto the children of Israel, that they should keep the passover. 5 And they kept the passover on the fourteenth day of the first month at even in the wilderness of Sinai: according to all that the LORD commanded Moses, so did the children of Israel. 6 And there were certain men, who were defiled by the dead body of a man, that they could not keep the passover on that day: and they came before Moses and before Aaron on that day: 7 And those men said unto him, We *are* defiled by the dead body of a man: wherefore are we kept back, that we may not offer an offering of the LORD in his appointed season among the children of Israel? 8 And Moses said unto them, Stand still, and I will hear what the LORD will command concerning you. 9 And the LORD spake unto Moses, saying, 10 Speak unto the children of Israel, saying, If any man of you or of your posterity shall be unclean by reason of a dead body, or *be* in a journey afar off, yet he shall keep the passover unto the LORD. 11 The fourteenth day of the second month at even they shall keep it, *and* eat it with unleavened bread and bitter *herbs*. 12 They shall leave none of it unto the morning, nor break any bone of it: according to all the ordinances of the passover they shall keep it. 13 But the man that *is* clean, and is not in a journey, and forbeareth to keep the passover, even the same soul shall be cut off from among his people: because he brought not the offering of the LORD in his appointed season, that man shall bear his sin. 14 And if a stranger shall sojourn among you, and will keep the passover unto the LORD; according to the ordinance of the passover, and according to the manner thereof, so shall he do: ye shall have one ordinance, both for the stranger, and for him that was born in the land.

Here we have,

I. An order given for the solemnization of the passover, the day twelvemonth after they came out of Egypt, on the fourteenth day of the first month of the second year, some days before they were numbered, for that was done in the beginning of the second month. Observe, 1. God gave particular orders for the keeping of this passover, otherwise (it should seem) they would not have kept it, for, in the first institution of this ordinance, it was appointed to be kept when they should *come into the land of promise*, Exod. xii. 25. And, for aught that appears, after this they kept no passover till they came to Canaan, Josh. v. 10. This was an early indication of the abolishing of the ceremonial institutions at last, that, so soon after they were first appointed, some of them were suffered to lie asleep for so many years. The ordinance of the Lord's supper (which came in the room of the passover) was not thus intermitted or set aside in the first days of the Christian church, though those were days of greater difficulty and distress than Israel knew in the wilderness; nay, in the times of persecution, the Lord's supper was celebrated more frequently than afterwards. The Israelites in the wilderness could not forget their deliverance out of Egypt, their present state was a constant memorandum of it to them. All the danger was when they came to Canaan; there therefore they had need to be reminded of the *rock out of which they were hewn*. However, because the first passover was celebrated in a hurry, and was rather the substance itself than the sign, it was the will of God that at the return of the year, when they were more composed, and better acquainted with the divine law, they should observe it again, that their children might more distinctly understand the solemnity and the better remember it hereafter. Calvin supposes that they were obliged to keep it now, and notes it as an instance of their carelessness that they had need to be reminded of an institution which they so lately received. 2. Moses faithfully transmitted to the people the orders given him, *v.* 4. Thus Paul delivered to the churches what he *received of the Lord* concerning the gospel passover, 1 Cor. xi. 23. Note, Magistrates must be monitors, and ministers must *stir up men's minds by way of remembrance* to that which is good. 3. The people observed the orders given them, *v.* 5. Though they had lately kept the feast of dedication (*ch.* vii.), yet they did not desire to excuse themselves with that from keeping this feast. Note, Extraordinary performances must not supersede or jostle out our stated services. They kept the passover even in the wilderness: though our condition be solitary and unsettled, yet we must keep up our attendance on God by holy ordinances as we have opportunity, for in them we may find the best conversation and the best repose. Thus is God's Israel provided for in a desert.

II. Instructions given concerning those that were ceremonially unclean when they were to eat the passover. The law of the passover required every Israelite to eat of it. Some subsequent laws had forbidden those that had contracted any ceremonial pollution to eat of the holy things; those whose minds and consciences are defiled by sin are utterly unfit for communion with God, and cannot partake, with any true comfort, of the gospel passover, till they are cleansed by true repentance and faith: and a sad dilemma they are in; if they come not to holy ordinances, they are guilty of a contempt of them; if they do come in their pollution, they are guilty of a profanation of them. They must therefore wash, and then *compass God's altar*. Now,

1. Here is the case that happened in Israel when this passover was to be kept: *Certain men were defiled by the dead body of a man* (*v.* 6), and they lay under that defilement seven days (*ch.* xix. 11), and in that time might not eat of the holy things, Lev. vii. 20. This was not their iniquity, but their infelicity: some persons must touch dead bodies, to bury them out of sight, and therefore they could, with the better grace, bring their complaint to Moses.

2. The application made to Moses by the persons concerned, *v.* 7. Note, It is people's wisdom, in difficult cases concerning sin and duty, to consult with their ministers whom God has set over them, and to *ask the law at their mouth*, Mal. ii. 7. These means we must use in pursuance of our prayers to God to lead us in a plain path. Observe with what trouble and concern these men complained that they were kept back from offering to the Lord. They did not complain of the law as unjust, but lamented their unhappiness that they fell under the restraint of it at this time, and desired some expedient might be found out for their relief. Note, It is a blessed thing to see people hungering and thirsting after God's ordinances, and to hear them complaining of that which prevents their enjoyment of them. It should be a trouble to us when by any occasion we are kept back from bringing our offering in the solemnities of a sabbath or a sacrament, as it was to David when he was banished from the altar, Ps. xlii. 1, 2.

3. The deliberation of Moses in resolving this case. Here seemed to be law against law; and, though it is a rule that the latter law must explain the former, yet he pitied these Israelites that were thus deprived of the privilege of the passover, and therefore took time to consult the oracles, and to know what was the mind of God in this case: *I will hear what the Lord will command concerning you*, *v.* 8. Ministers must take example hence in resolving cases of conscience. (1.) They must not determine rashly, but take time to consider, that every circumstance may be duly weighed, the case viewed in a true light, and spiritual things compared with spiritual. (2.) They must ask counsel at God's mouth, and not

determine according to the bias of their own fancy or affection, but impartially, according to the mind of God, to the best of their knowledge. We have no such oracle to consult as Moses had, but we must have recourse to *the law and the testimony*, and speak according to that rule; and if, in difficult cases, we take time to spread the matter in particular before God by humble believing prayer, we have reason to hope that the Spirit who is promised to *lead us into all truth* will enable us to direct others *in the good and right way.*

4. The directions which God gave in this case, and in other similar cases, explanatory of the law of the passover. This disagreeable accident produced good laws. (1.) Those that happened to be ceremonially unclean at the time when the passover should be eaten were allowed to eat it that day month, when they were clean; so were those that happened to be *in a journey afar off*, v. 10, 11. See here, [1.] That when we are to attend upon God in solemn ordinances it is very necessary both that we be clean and that we be composed. [2.] That that may excuse the deferring of a duty for a time which yet will 'not justify us in the total neglect and omission of it. He that is at variance with his brother may *leave his gift before the altar*, while he goes to be *reconciled to his brother;* but when he has done his part towards it, whether it be effected or no, he must *come again and offer his gift*, Matt. v. 23, 24. This secondary passover was to be kept on the same day of the month with the first, because the ordinance was a memorial of their deliverance on that day of the month. Once we find the whole congregation keeping the passover on this fourteenth day of the second month, in Hezekiah's time (2 Chron. xxx. 15), which perhaps may help to account for the admission of some that were not clean to the eating of it. Had the general passover been kept in the first month, the unclean might have been put off till the second; but, that being kept in the second month, they had no warrant to eat it in the third month, and therefore, rather than not eat of it at all, they were admitted, though not cleansed *according to the purification of the sanctuary*, v. 19, 20. (2.) Whenever the passover was kept in the second month, all the rites and ceremonies of it must be strictly observed, v. 12. They must not think that, because the time was dispensed with, any part of the solemnity of it might be abated; when we cannot do as we would we must do the utmost we can in the service of God. (3.) This allowance in a case of necessity would by no means countenance or indulge any in their neglect to keep the passover at the time appointed, when they were not under the necessity, v. 13. When a person is under no incapacity to eat the passover in the appointed time, if he neglects it then, upon the presumption of the liberty granted by this law, he puts an affront upon God, impiously abuses his kindness, and

he shall certainly *bear his sin*, and *be cut off from his people.* Note, As those who against their minds are forced to absent themselves from God's ordinances may comfortably expect the favours of God's grace under their affliction, so those who of choice absent themselves may justly expect the tokens of God's wrath for their sin. *Be not deceived, God is not mocked.* (4.) Here is a clause added in favour of strangers, v. 14. Though it was requisite that the stranger who would join with them in eating the passover should be circumcised as a proselyte to their religion (Exod. xii. 48, 49), yet this kind admission of those that were not native Israelites to eat the passover was an intimation of the favour designed for the poor Gentiles by Christ. As then there was one law, so in the days of the Messiah there should be one gospel, for the stranger and for him that was born in the land; for *in every nation he that fears God and works righteousness is accepted of him*, and this was a truth before Peter perceived it, Acts x. 34, 35.

15 And on the day that the tabernacle was reared up the cloud covered the tabernacle, *namely*, the tent of the testimony; and at even there was upon the tabernacle as it were the appearance of fire, until the morning. 16 So it was alway: the cloud covered it *by day*, and the appearance of fire by night. 17 And when the cloud was taken up from the tabernacle, then after that the children of Israel journeyed: and in the place where the cloud abode, there the children of Israel pitched their tents. 18 At the commandment of the LORD the children of Israel journeyed, and at the commandment of the LORD they pitched: as long as the cloud abode upon the tabernacle they rested in their tents. 19 And when the cloud tarried long upon the tabernacle many days, then the children of Israel kept the charge of the LORD, and journeyed not. 20 And *so* it was, when the cloud was a few days upon the tabernacle; according to the commandment of the LORD they abode in their tents, and according to the commandment of the LORD they journeyed. 21 And *so* it was, when the cloud abode from even unto the morning, and *that* the cloud was taken up in the morning, then they journeyed: whether *it was* by day or by night that the cloud was taken up, they

journeyed. 22 Or *whether it were* two days, or a month, or a year, that the' cloud tarried upon the tabernacle, remaining thereon, the children of Israel abode in their tents, and journeyed not: but when it was taken up, they journeyed. 23 At the commandment of the Lord they rested in the tents, and at the commandment of the Lord they journeyed: they kept the charge of the Lord, at the commandment of the Lord by the hand of Moses.

We have here the history of the cloud; not a natural history: *who knows the balancings of the clouds?* but a divine history of a cloud that was appointed to be the visible sign and symbol of God's presence with Israel.

I. When the tabernacle was finished this cloud, which before had hung on high over their camp, settled upon the tabernacle, and covered it, to show that God manifests his presence with his people in and by his ordinances; there he makes himself known, and to them we must look if we would *see the beauty of the Lord*, Ps. xxvii. 4; Ezek. xxxvii. 26, 27. Thus God glorified his own appointments, and signified his acceptance of his people's love and obedience.

II. That which appeared as a cloud by day appeared as a fire all night. Had it been a cloud only, it would not have been visible by night; and, had it been a fire only, it would have been scarcely discernible by day; but God would give them sensible demonstrations of the constancy of his presence with them, and his care of them, and that he *kept them night and day*, Isa. xxvii. 3; Ps. cxxi. 6. And thus we are taught to *set God always before us,* and to see him near us both night and day. Something of the nature of that divine revelation which the Old-Testament church was governed by might also be signified by these visible signs of God's presence, the cloud denoting the darkness and the fire the terror of that dispensation, in comparison with the more clear and comfortable discoveries God has made of his glory in the face of Jesus Christ.

III. This pillar of cloud and fire directed and determined all the motions, marches, and encampments, of Israel in the wilderness. 1. As long as the cloud rested upon the tabernacle, so long they continued in the same place, and never stirred; though no doubt they were very desirous to be pressing forward in their journey towards Canaan, where they longed to be and hoped to be quickly, yet as long as the cloud rested, if it was a month or a year, so long they rested, *v.* 22. Note, He that believeth doth not make haste. There is no time lost while we are waiting God's time. It is as acceptable a piece of submission to the will of God to sit still contentedly when our lot requires it as

600

to work for him when we are called to it. 2. When the cloud was taken up, they removed, how comfortably soever they were encamped, *v.* 17. Whether it moved by day or night, they delayed not to attend its motions (*v.* 21), and probably there were some appointed to stand sentinel day and night within sight of it, to give timely notice to the camp of its beginning to stir, and this is called *keeping the charge of the Lord.* The people, being thus kept at a constant uncertainty, and having no time fixed for stopping or removing, were obliged to hold themselves in constant readiness to march upon very short warning. And for the same reason we are kept at uncertainty concerning the time of our putting off the earthly house of this tabernacle, that we may be always ready to *remove at the commandment of the Lord.* 3. As long and as far as the cloud moved, so long and so far they marched, and just where it abode they pitched their tents about it, and God's tent under it, *v.* 17. Note, It is uncomfortable staying when God has departed, but very safe and pleasant going when we see God go before us and resting where he appoints us to rest. This is repeated again and again in these verses, because it was a constant miracle, and often repeated, and what never failed in all their travels, and because it is a matter which we should take particular notice of as very significant and instructive. It is mentioned long after by David (Ps. cv. 39), and by the people of God after their captivity, Neh. ix. 19. And the guidance of this cloud is spoken of as signifying the guidance of the blessed Spirit. Isa. lxiii. 14, *The Spirit of the Lord caused him to rest, and so didst thou lead thy people.* This teaches us, (1.) The particular care God takes of his people. Nothing could be more expressive and significant of God's tenderness of Israel than the guidance of this cloud was; it led them by the *right way* (Ps. cvii. 7), went on their pace: God did by it, as it were, cover them with his feathers. We are not now to expect such sensible tokens of the divine presence and guidance as this was, but the promise is sure to all God's spiritual Israel that he will *guide them by his counsel* (Ps. lxxiii. 24), *even unto death* (Ps. xlviii. 14), that all the children of God shall be *led by the Spirit of God* (Rom. viii. 14), that he will *direct the paths* of those who in *all their ways acknowledge him,* Prov. iii. 6. There is a particular providence conversant about all their affairs, to direct and overrule them for the best. *The steps of a good man are ordered by the Lord,* Ps. xxxvii. 23. (2.) The particular regard we ought to have to God in all our ways. In our affections and actions we must follow the direction of his word and Spirit; all the motions of our souls must be guided by the divine will; at the commandment of the Lord our hearts should always move and rest; in all our affairs we must follow Providence, reconciling ourselves to all its disposals, and bringing our mind to our condition, whatever it is. The people of Israel, having the cloud for their guide, were eased of the trouble of holding councils of war, to consider when and whither they should march, which might have occasioned strifes and debates among them : nor needed they to send spies before to inform them of the posture of the country, or pioneers to clear the way, or officers to mark out their camp; the pillar of cloud did all this for them : and those that by faith commit their works to the Lord, though they are bound to the prudent use of means, yet may in like manner be easy in the expectation of the event. "*Father, thy will be done;* dispose of me and mine as thou pleasest; here I am, desirous to be found *waiting on my God continually*, to journey and rest at *the commandment of the Lord*. What thou wilt, and where thou wilt, only let me be thine, and always in the way of my duty."

CHAP. X.

In this chapter we have, I. Orders given about the making and using of silver trumpets, which seems to have been the last of all the commandments God gave upon mount Sinai, and one of the least, yet not without its significancy, ver. 1–10. II. The history of the removal of Israel's camp from mount Sinai, and their orderly march into the wilderness of Paran, ver. 11–28. III. Moses's treaty with Hobab, his brother-in-law, ver. 29–32. IV. Moses's prayer at the removing and resting of the ark, ver. 33, &c.

AND the LORD spake unto Moses, saying, 2 Make thee two trumpets of silver; of a whole piece shalt thou make them : that thou mayest use them for the calling of the assembly, and for the journeying of the camps. 3 And when they shall blow with them, all the assembly shall assemble themselves to thee at the door of the tabernacle of the congregation. 4 And if they blow *but* with one *trumpet*, then the princes, *which are* heads of the thousands of Israel, shall gather themselves unto thee. 5 When ye blow an alarm, then the camps that lie on the east parts shall go forward. 6 When ye blow an alarm the second time, then the camps that lie on the south side shall take their journey : they shall blow an alarm for their journeys. 7 But when the congregation is to be gathered together, ye shall blow, but ye shall not sound an alarm. 8 And the sons of Aaron, the priests, shall blow with the trumpets; and they shall be to you for an ordinance for ever throughout your generations. 9 And if ye go to war in your land against the enemy that oppresseth you, then ye shall blow an alarm with the trumpets;

and ye shall be remembered before the LORD your God, and ye shall be saved from your enemies. 10 Also in the day of your gladness, and in your solemn days, and in the beginnings of your months, ye shall blow with the trumpets over your burnt offerings, and over the sacrifices of your peace offerings; that they may be to you for a memorial before your God: I *am* the LORD your God.

We have here directions concerning the public notices that were to be given to the people upon several occasions by sound of trumpet. In a thing of this nature, one would think, Moses needed not to have been taught of God : his own reason might teach him the conveniency of trumpets; but the constitution of Israel was to be in every thing divine, and therefore even in this matter, small as it seems. Moses is here directed, 1. About the making of them. They must be made of silver; not cast but of beaten work (as some read it), the matter and shape, no doubt, very fit for the purpose. He was now ordered to make but two, because there were but two priests to use them. But in Solomon's time we read of 120 *priests sounding with trumpets,* 2 Chron. v. 12. The form of these trumpets is supposed to have been much like ours at this day. 2. Who were to make use of them; not any inferior person, but the priests themselves, the *sons of Aaron, v.* 8. As great as they were, they must not think it a disparagement to them to be trumpeters in the house of God; the meanest office there was honourable. This signified that the Lord's ministers should *lift up their voice like a trumpet*, to show people their sins (Isa. lviii. 1), to call them to Christ, Isa. xxvii. 13. 3. Upon what occasions the trumpets were to be sounded. (1.) For the *calling of assemblies, v.* 2. Thus they are told to blow the trumpet in Zion for the calling of a solemn assembly together, to sanctify a fast, Joel ii. 15. Public notice ought to be given of the time and place of religious assemblies; for the invitation to the benefit of ordinances is general: *whoever will, let him come.* Wisdom cries in the chief places of concourse. But, that the trumpet might not *give an uncertain sound*, they are directed, if only the princes and elders were to meet, to blow but one of the trumpets; less should serve to call *them* together, who ought to be examples of forwardness in any thing that is good : but, if the body of the people were to be called together, both the trumpets must be sounded, that they might be heard at the greater distance. In allusion to this, they are said to be blessed that *hear the joyful sound* (Ps. lxxxix. 15), that is, that are invited and called upon to wait upon God in public ordinances, Ps. cxxii. 1. And the general

601

assembly at the great day will be summoned by *the sound of the archangel's trumpet*, Matt. xxiv. 31. (2.) For the *journeying of the camps*, to give notice when each squadron must move; for no man's voice could reach to give the word of command: soldiers with us that are well disciplined may be exercised by beat of drums. When the trumpets were blown for this purpose, they must *sound an alarm* (v. 5), a broken, quavering, interrupted sound, which was proper to excite and encourage the minds of people in their marches against their enemies; whereas a continued equal sound was more proper for the calling of the assembly together (v. 7): yet when the people were called together to deprecate God's judgments we find an alarm sounded, Joel ii. 1. At the first sounding, Judah's squadron marched, at the second Reuben's, at the third Ephraim's, at the fourth Dan's, v. 5, 6. And some think that this was intended to sanctify their marches, for thus were proclaimed by the priests, who were God's mouth to the people, not only the divine orders given them to move, but the divine blessing upon them in all their motions. He that hath ears, let him hear that *God is with them of a truth.* King Abijah valued himself and his army very much upon this (2 Chron. xiii. 12), *God himself is with us for our captain, and his priests with sounding trumpets.* (3.) For the animating and encouraging of their armies, when they went out in battle (v 9): "*If you go to war, blow with the trumpets*, signifying thereby your appeal to heaven for the decision of the controversy, and your prayer to God to give you victory; and God will own this his own institution, and *you shall be remembered before the Lord your God.*" God will take notice of this sound of the trumpet, and be engaged to fight their battles, and let all the people take notice of it, and be encouraged to fight his, as David, when he heard *a sound of a going upon the tops of the mulberry trees.* Not that God needed to be awaked by sound of trumpet any more than Christ needed to be awaked by his disciples in the storm, Matt. viii. 25. But where he intends mercy it is his will that we should solicit it; ministers must stir up the good soldiers of Jesus Christ to fight manfully against sin, the world, and the devil, by assuring them that Christ is the *captain of their salvation*, and will *tread Satan under their feet.* (4.) For the solemnizing of their sacred feasts, v. 10. One of their feasts was called *a memorial of the blowing of trumpets*, Lev. xxiii. 23, &c. And it should seem they were thus to grace the solemnity of all their feasts (Ps. lxxxi. 3), and their sacrifices (2 Chron. xxix. 27), to intimate with what joy and delight they performed their duty to God, and to raise the minds of those that attended the services to a holy triumph in the God they worshipped. And then their performances were for a *memorial before God;* for he takes pleasure in our

602

religious exercises when we take pleasure in them. Holy work should be done with holy joy.

11 And it came to pass on the twentieth *day* of the second month, in the second year, that the cloud was taken up from off the tabernacle of the testimony. 12 And the children of Israel took their journeys out of the wilderness of Sinai; and the cloud rested in the wilderness of Paran. 13 And they first took their journey according to the commandment of the Lord by the hand of Moses. 14 In the first *place* went the standard of the camp of the children of Judah according to their armies: and over his host *was* Nahshon the son of Amminadab. 15 And over the host of the tribe of the children of Issachar *was* Nethaneel the son of Zuar. 16 And over the host of the tribe of the children of Zebulun *was* Eliab the son of Helon. 17 And the tabernacle was taken down; and the sons of Gershon and the sons of Merari set forward, bearing the tabernacle. 18 And the standard of the camp of Reuben set forward according to their armies: and over his host *was* Elizur the son of Shedeur. 19 And over the host of the tribe of the children of Simeon *was* Shelumiel the son of Zurishaddai. 20 And over the host of the tribe of the children of Gad *was* Eliasaph the son of Deuel. 21 And the Kohathites set forward, bearing the sanctuary: and *the other* did set up the tabernacle against they came. 22 And the standard of the camp of the children of Ephraim set forward according to their armies: and over his host *was* Elishama the son of Ammihud. 23 And over the host of the tribe of the children of Manasseh *was* Gamaliel the son of Pedahzur. 24 And over the host of the tribe of the children of Benjamin *was* Abidan the son of Gideoni. 25 And the standard of the camp of the children of Dan set forward, *which was* the rereward of all the camps throughout their hosts: and over his host *was* Ahiezer the son of Ammishaddai. 26 And over the host of the tribe of the children of Asher *was* Pagiel the son of Ocran.

27 And over the host of the tribe of the children of Naphtali *was* Ahira the son of Enan. 28 Thus *were* the journeyings of the children of Israel according to their armies, when they set forward.

Here is, I. A general account of the removal of the camp of Israel from mount Sinai, before which mountain it had lain now about a year, in which time and place a great deal of memorable business was done. Of this removal, it should seem, God gave them notice some time before (Deut. i. 6, 7): *You have dwelt long enough in this mountain, turn you and take your journey towards the land of promise.* The apostle tells us that *mount Sinai genders to bondage* (Gal. iv. 24), and signifies the law there given, which is of use indeed as a schoolmaster to bring us to Christ, yet we must not rest in it, but advance towards the joys and liberties of the children of God, for our happiness is conferred not by the law, but by promise. Observe, 1. The signal given (*v.* 11): *The cloud was taken up,* and we may suppose it stood for some time, till they were ready to march; and a great deal of work it was to take down all those tents, and pack up all those goods that they had there; but every family being employed about its own, and all at the same time, many hands made quick work of it. 2. The march began: *They took their journey according to the commandment of the Lord,* and just as the cloud led them, *v.* 13. Some think that mention is thus frequently made in this and the foregoing chapter of the *commandment of the Lord,* guiding and governing them in all their travels, to obviate the calumny and reproach which were afterwards thrown upon Israel, that they tarried so long in the wilderness, because they had lost themselves there, and could not find the way out. No, the matter was not so; in every stage, in every step, they were under divine direction; and, if they knew not where they were, yet he that led them knew. Note, Those that have given up themselves to the direction of God's word and Spirit steer a steady course, even when they seem to be bewildered. While they are sure they cannot lose their God and guide, they need not fear losing their way. 3. The place they rested in, after three days' march: They went *out of the wilderness of Sinai,* and rested *in the wilderness of Paran.* Note, All our removals in this world are but from one wilderness to another. The changes which we think will be for the better do not always prove so; while we carry about with us, wherever we go, the common infirmities of human nature, we must expect, wherever we go, to meet with its common calamities; we shall never be at rest, never at home, till we come to heaven, and all will be well there.

II. A particular draught of the order of

their march, according to the late model. 1. Judah's squadron marched first, *v.* 14—16. The leading standard, now lodged with that tribe, was an earnest of the sceptre which in David's time should be committed to it, and looked further to the captain of our salvation, of whom it was likewise foretold that *unto him should the gathering of the people be.* 2. Then came those two families of the Levites which were entrusted to carry the tabernacle. As soon as ever the cloud was taken up, the tabernacle was taken down, and packed up for removing, *v.* 17. And here the six waggons came laden with the more bulky part of the tabernacle. This frequent removing of the tabernacle in all their journeys signified the movableness of that ceremonial dispensation. That which was so often shifted would at length vanish away, Heb. viii. 13. 3. Reuben's squadron marched forward next, taking place after Judah, *according to the commandment of the Lord, v.* 18—20. 4. Then the Kohathites followed with their charge, the sacred furniture of the tabernacle, *in the midst of the camp,* the safest and most honourable place, *v.* 21. And they (that is, says the margin, the Gershonites and Merarites) did *set up the tabernacle against they came;* and perhaps it is expressed thus generally because, if there was occasion, not those Levites only, but the other Israelites that were in the first squadron, lent a hand to the tabernacle to hasten the rearing of it up, even before they set up their own tents. 5. Ephraim's squadron followed next after the ark (*v.* 22—24), to which some think the psalmist alludes when he prays (Ps. lxxx. 2), *Before Ephraim, Benjamin, and Manasseh,* the three tribes that composed this squadron, *stir up thy strength* (and the ark is called his strength, Ps. lxxviii. 61), *and come and save us.* 6. Dan's squadron followed last, *v.* 25—27. It is called the *rearward,* or *gathering host,* of all the camps, because it gathered up all that were left behind; not the women and children (these we may suppose were taken care of by the heads of their families in their respective tribes), but all the unclean, the mixed multitude, and all that were weak and feeble, and cast behind in their march. Note, He that leadeth Joseph like a flock has a tender regard to the hindmost (Ezek. xxxiv. 16), that cannot keep pace with the rest, and *of all that are given him he will lose none,* John xvii. 11.

29 And Moses said unto Hobab, the son of Raguel the Midianite, Moses' father in law, We are journeying unto the place of which the Lord said, I will give it you: come thou with us, and we will do thee good: for the Lord hath spoken good concerning Israel. 30 And he said unto him, I will not go; but I will

depart to mine own land, and to my kindred. 31 And he said, Leave us not, I pray thee; forasmuch as thou knowest how we are to encamp in the wilderness, and thou mayest be to us instead of eyes. 32 And it shall be, if thou go with us, yea, it shall be, that what goodness the LORD shall do unto us, the same will we do unto thee. 33 And they departed from the mount of the LORD three days' journey: and the ark of the covenant of the LORD went before them in the three days' journey, to search out a resting place for them. 34 And the cloud of the LORD *was* upon them by day, when they went out of the camp. 35 And it came to pass, when the ark set forward, that Moses said, Rise up, LORD, and let thine enemies be scattered; and let them that hate thee flee before thee. 36 And when it rested, he said, Return, O LORD, unto the many thousands of Israel.

Here is, I. An account of what passed between Moses and Hobab, now upon this advance which the camp of Israel made towards Canaan. Some think that Hobab was the same with Jethro, Moses's father-in-law, and that the story, Exod. xviii., should come in here; it seems more probable that Hobab was the son of Jethro, *alias* Reuel, or Raguel (Exod. ii. 18), and that when the father, being aged, went to his own land (Exod. xviii. 27), he left his son Hobab with Moses, as Barzillai left Chimham with David; and the same word signifies both a *father-in-law* and a *brother-in-law*. Now this Hobab staid contentedly with Israel while they encamped at mount Sinai, near his own country; but, now that they were removing, he was for going back to his own country and kindred, and his father's house. Here is, 1. The kind invitation Moses gives him to go forward with them to Canaan, *v.* 29. He tempts him with a promise that they would certainly be kind to him, and puts God's word in for security: *The Lord hath spoken good concerning Israel.* As if he had said, "Come, cast in thy lot among us, and thou shalt fare as we fare; and we have the promise of God that we shall fare well." Note, Those that are bound for the heavenly Canaan should invite and encourage all their friends to go along with them, for we shall never the less of the treasures of the covenant, and the joys of heaven, for others coming in to share with us. And what argument can be more powerful with us to take God's people for our people than this, that God *hath spoken good concerning them?* It is good having fellow-

ship with those that have fellowship with God (1 John i. 3), and going with those with whom God is, Zech. viii. 23. 2. Hobab's inclination, and present resolution, to go back to his own country, *v.* 30. One would have thought that he who had seen so much of the special presence of God with Israel, and such surprising tokens of his favour to them, would not have needed much invitation to embark with them. But his refusal must be imputed to the affection he had for his native air and soil, which was not overpowered, as it ought to have been, by a believing regard to the promise of God and a value for covenant blessings. He was indeed a son of Abraham's loins (for the Midianites descended from Abraham by Keturah), but not an heir of Abraham's faith (Heb. xi. 8), else he would not have given Moses this answer. Note, The things of this world, which are seen, draw strongly from the pursuit of the things of the other world, which are not seen. The magnetic virtue of this earth prevails with most people above the attractives of heaven itself. 3. The great importunity Moses used with him to alter his resolution, *v.* 31, 32. He urges, (1.) That he might be serviceable to them: "*We are to encamp in the wilderness*" (a country well known to Hobab), "*and thou mayest be to us instead of eyes*, not to show us where we must encamp, nor what way we must march" (which the cloud was to direct), "but to show us the conveniences and inconveniences of the place we march through and encamp in, that we may make the best use we can of the conveniences, and the best fence we can against the inconveniences." Note, It will very well consist with our trust in God's providence to make use of the help of our friends in those things wherein they are capable of being serviceable to us. Even those that were led by miracle must not slight the ordinary means of direction. Some think that Moses suggests this to Hobab, not because he expected much benefit from his information, but to please him with the thought of being some way useful to so great a body, and so to draw him on with them, by inspiring him with an ambition to obtain that honour. Calvin gives quite another sense of this place, very agreeably with the original, which yet I do not find taken notice of by any since. "*Leave us not, I pray thee*, but come along, to share with us in the promised land, *for therefore hast thou known our encampment in the wilderness, and hast been to us instead of eyes; and we cannot make thee amends for sharing with us in our hardships, and doing us so many good offices, unless thou go with us to Canaan. Surely for this reason thou didst set out with us that thou mightest go on with us." Note, Those that have begun well should use that as a reason for their persevering, because otherwise they lose the benefit and recompence of all they have done and suffered. (2.) That they would be kind to him: *What* *goodness the Lord shall do to us, the same we will do to thee, v.* 32. Note, [1.] We can give only what we receive. We can do no more service and kindness to our friends than God is pleased to put it into the power of our hand to do. This is all we dare promise, to do good as God shall enable us. [2.] Those that share with God's Israel in their labours and hardships shall share with them in their comforts and honours. Those that are willing to take their lot with them in the wilderness shall have their lot with them in Canaan; *if we suffer with them we shall reign with them,* 2 Tim. ii. 12; Luke xxii. 28, 29.

We do not find any reply that Hobab here made to Moses, and therefore we hope that his silence gave consent, and he did not leave them, but that, when he perceived he might be useful, he preferred that before the gratifying of his own inclination; in this case he left us a good example. And we find (Judg. i. 16; 1 Sam. xv. 6) that his family was no loser by it.

II. An account of the communion between God and Israel in this removal. They left *the mount of the Lord* (*v.* 33), that Mount Sinai where they had seen his glory and heard his voice, and had been taken into covenant with him (they must not expect that such appearances of God to them as they had there been blessed with should be constant); they departed from that celebrated mountain, which we never read of in scripture any more, unless with reference to these past stories; now farewell, Sinai; *Zion* is the mountain of which God has said, *This is my rest for ever* (Ps. cxxxii. 14), and of which we must say so. But when they left the *mount of the Lord* they took with them the *ark of the covenant of the Lord,* by which their stated communion with God was to be kept up. For,

1. By it God did *direct their paths.* The ark of the covenant went before them, some think in *place,* at least in this removal; others think only in *influence;* though it was carried in the midst of the camp, yet the cloud that hovered over it directed all their motions. The ark (that is, the God of the ark) is said to *search out a resting place* for them; not that God's infinite wisdom and knowledge need to make searches, but every place they were directed to was as convenient for them as if the wisest man they had among them had been employed to go before them, and mark out their camp to the best advantage. Thus Canaan is said to be a land which God *spied out,* Ezek. xx. 6.

2. By it they did *in all their ways acknowledge God,* looking upon it as a token of God's presence; when that moved, or rested, they had their eye up unto God. Moses, as the mouth of the congregation, lifted up a prayer, both at the removing and at the resting of the ark; thus their going out and coming in were sanctified by prayer, and it is an example to

us to begin and end every day's journey, and every day's work, with prayer.

(1.) Here is his prayer when the ark set forward: *Rise up, Lord, and let thy enemies be scattered, v.* 35. They were now in a desolate country, but they were marching towards an enemy's country, and their dependence was upon God for success and victory in their wars, as well as for direction and supply in the wilderness. David used this prayer long after (Ps. lxviii. 1), for he also fought the Lord's battles. Note, [1.] There are those in the world that are enemies to God, and haters of him: secret and open enemies; enemies to his truths, his laws, his ordinances, his people. [2.] The scattering and defeating of God's enemies is a thing to be earnestly desired, and believingly expected, by all the Lord's people. This prayer is a prophecy. Those that persist in rebellion against God are hasting towards their own ruin. [3.] For the scattering and defeating of God's enemies, there needs no more but God's arising. *When God arose to judgment,* the work was soon done, Ps. lxxvi. 8, 9. "Rise, Lord, as the sun riseth to scatter the shadows of the night." Christ's rising from the dead scattered his enemies, Ps. lxviii. 18.

(2.) His prayer when the ark rested, *v.* 36. [1.] That God would cause his people to rest. So some read it, "*Return, O Lord, the many thousands of Israel,* return them to their rest again after this fatigue." Thus it is said (Isa. lxiii. 14), *The Spirit of the Lord caused him to rest.* Thus he prays that God would give Israel success and victory abroad, and peace and tranquillity at home. [2.] That God himself would take up his rest among them. So we read it: *Return to the thousands of Israel,* the *ten thousand thousand,* so the word is. Note, *First,* The church of God is a great body; there are many thousands belonging to God's Israel. *Secondly,* We ought in our prayers to concern ourselves for this body. *Thirdly,* The welfare and happiness of the Israel of God consist in the continual presence of God among them. Their safety consists not in their numbers, though they are thousands, many thousands, but in the favour of God, and his gracious return to them and residence with them. These thousands are cyphers; he is the figure: and upon this account, *Happy art thou, O Israel! who is like unto thee, O people!*

CHAP. XI.

Hitherto things had gone pretty well in Israel; little interruption had been given to the methods of God's favour to them since the matter of the golden calf; the people seemed teachable in marshalling and purifying the camp, the princes devout and generous in dedicating the altar, and there was good hope that they would be in Canaan presently. But at this chapter begins a melancholy scene; the measures are all broken, God has turned to be their enemy, and fights against them—and it is sin that makes all this mischief. I. Their murmurings kindled a fire among them, which yet was soon quenched by the prayer of Moses, ver. 1—3. II. No sooner was the fire of judgment quenched than the fire of sin breaks out again, and God takes occasion from it to magnify both his mercy and his justice. 1. The people fret for want of flesh, ver. 4—9. 2. Moses frets for want of help, ver. 10—15. Now, (1.) God promises to gratify them both, to appoint help for Moses (ver. 16, 17), and to give the people flesh, ver. 18—23. And, (2.) He presently makes good both these promises. For, [1.] The Spirit of God qualifies the seventy elders for the go-

AND when the people complained, it displeased the LORD: and the LORD heard *it;* and his anger was kindled; and the fire of the LORD burnt among them, and consumed *them that were* in the uttermost parts of the camp. 2 And the people cried unto Moses; and when Moses prayed unto the LORD, the fire was quenched. 3 And he called the name of the place Taberah: because the fire of the LORD burnt among them.

Here is, I. The people's sin. They *complained, v.* 1. *They were, as it were, complainers.* So it is in the margin. There were some secret grudgings and discontents among them, which as yet did not break out in an open mutiny. But how great a matter did this little fire kindle! They had received from God excellent laws and ordinances, and yet no sooner had they departed from the mount of the Lord than they began to quarrel with God himself. See in this, 1. The sinfulness of sin, which takes occasion from the commandment to be the more provoking. 2. The weakness of the law through the flesh, Rom. viii. 3. The law discovered sin, but could not destroy it; checked it, but could not conquer it. They *complained.* Interpreters enquire what they complained of; and truly, when they were furnished with so much matter for thanksgiving, one may justly wonder where they found any matter for complaint; it is probable that those who complained did not all agree in the cause. Some perhaps complained that they were removed from Mount Sinai, where they had been at rest so long, others that they did not remove sooner: some complained of the weather, others of the ways: some perhaps thought three days' journey was too long a march, others thought it not long enough, because it did not bring them into Canaan. When we consider how their camp was guided, guarded, graced, what good victuals they had and good company, and what care was taken of them in their marches that their feet should not swell nor their clothes wear (Deut. viii. 4), we may ask, "What could have been done more for a people to make them easy?" And yet they complained. Note, Those that are of a fretful discontented spirit will always find something or other to quarrel with, though the circumstances of their outward condition be ever so favourable.

II. God's just resentment of the affront given to him by this sin: *The Lord heard it,* though it does not appear that Moses did. Note, God is acquainted with the secret frettings and murmurings of the heart, though they are industriously concealed from men. What he took notice of he was much displeased with, and his *anger was kindled.* Note, Though God graciously gives us leave to complain to him when there is cause (Ps. cxlii. 2), yet he is justly provoked, and takes it very ill, if we complain of him when there is no cause: such conduct in our inferiors provokes us.

III. The judgment wherewith God chastised them for this sin: *The fire of the Lord burnt among them,* such flashes of fire from the cloud as had consumed Nadab and Abihu. The fire of their wrath against God burned in their minds (Ps. xxxix. 3), and justly does the fire of God's wrath fasten upon their bodies. We read of their murmurings several times, when they came first out of Egypt, Exod. xv., and xvi., and xvii. But we do not read of any plagues inflicted on them for their murmurings, as there were now; for now they had had great experience of God's care of them, and therefore now to distrust him was so much the more inexcusable. Now a *fire was kindled against Jacob* (Ps. lxxviii. 21), but, to show how unwilling God was to contend with them, it fastened on those only that were *in the uttermost parts of the camp.* Thus God's judgments came upon them gradually, that they might take warning.

IV. Their cry to Moses, who was their tried intercessor, *v.* 2. *When he slew them, then they sought him,* and made their application to Moses to stand their friend. Note, 1. When we complain without cause, it is just with God to give us cause to complain. 2. Those that slight God's friends when they are in prosperity would be glad to make them their friends when they are in distress. *Father Abraham, send Lazarus.*

V. The prevalency of, Moses's intercession for them: *When Moses prayed unto the Lord* (he was always ready to stand in the gap to turn away the wrath of God) God had respect to him and his offering, and *the fire was quenched.* By this it appears that God delights not in punishing, for, when he has begun his controversy, he is soon prevailed with to let it fall. Moses was one of those worthies who *by faith quenched the violence of fire.*

VI. A new name given hereupon to the place, to perpetuate the shame of a murmuring people and the honour of a righteous God; the place was called *Taberah,* a *burning* (*v.* 3), that others might hear, and fear, and take warning not to sin as they did, lest they should smart as they did, 1 Cor. x. 10.

4 And the mixt multitude that *was* among them fell a lusting: and the children of Israel also wept again, and said, Who shall give us flesh to eat? 5 We remember the fish, which we did eat in Egypt freely; the cucumbers, and the melons, and the leeks, and the onions, and the garlick: 6

But now our soul *is* dried away : *there is* nothing at all, beside this manna, *before* our eyes. 7 And the manna *was* as coriander seed, and the colour thereof as the colour of bdellium. 8 *And* the people went about, and gathered *it,* and ground *it* in mills, or beat *it* in a mortar, and baked *it* in pans, and made cakes of it : and the taste of it was as the taste of fresh oil. 9 And when the dew fell upon the camp in the night, the manna fell upon it. 10 Then Moses heard the people weep throughout their families, every man in the door of his tent : and the anger of the LORD was kindled greatly ; Moses also was displeased. 11 And Moses said unto the LORD, Wherefore hast thou afflicted thy servant ? and wherefore have I not found favour in thy sight, that thou layest the burden of all this people upon me ? 12 Have I conceived all this people ? have I begotten them, that thou shouldest say unto me, Carry them in thy bosom, as a nursing father beareth the sucking child, unto the land which thou swarest unto their fathers ? 13 Whence should I have flesh to give unto all this people ? for they weep unto me, saying, Give us flesh, that we may eat. 14 I am not able to bear all this people alone, because *it is* too heavy for me, 15 And if thou deal thus with me, kill me, I pray thee, out of hand, if I have found favour in thy sight ; and let me not see my wretchedness.

These verses represent things sadly unhinged and out of order in Israel, both the people and the prince uneasy.

I. Here is the people fretting, and speaking against God himself (as it is interpreted, Ps. lxxviii. 19), notwithstanding his glorious appearances both to them and for them. Observe;

1. Who were the criminals. (1.) The *mixed multitude* began, they *fell a lusting,* v. 4. The rabble that came with them out of Egypt, expecting only the land of promise, but not a state of probation in the way to it. They were hangers on, who took hold of the skirts of the Jews, and would go with them only because they knew not how to live at home, and were disposed to seek their fortunes (as we say) abroad. These were the scabbed sheep that infected the flock, the leaven that leavened the whole lump. Note,

A few factious, discontented, ill-natured people, may do a great deal of mischief in the best societies, if great care be not taken to discountenance them. Such as these are an *untoward generation,* from which it is our wisdom to *save ourselves,* Acts ii. 40. (2.) Even *the children of Israel* took the infection, as we are informed, v. 4. The holy seed joined themselves to the people of these abominations. The mixed multitude here spoken of were not numbered with the children of Israel, but were set aside as a people God made no account of ; and yet the children of Israel, forgetting their own character and distinction, herded themselves with them and learned their way, as if the scum and outcasts of the camp were to be the privy-counsellors of it. The children of Israel, a people near to God and highly privileged, yet drawn into rebellion against him ! O how little honour has God in the world, when even the people which he formed for himself, to show forth his praise, were so much a dishonour to him ! Therefore let none think that their external professions and privileges will be their security either against Satan's temptations to sin or God's judgments for sin. See 1 Cor. x. 1, 2, 12.

2. What was the crime : they lusted and murmured. Though they had been lately corrected for this sin, and many of them overthrown for it, as God overthrew Sodom and Gomorrah, and the smell of the fire was still in their nostrils, yet they returned to it. See Prov. xxvii. 22. (1.) They magnified the plenty and dainties they had had in Egypt (v. 5), as if God had done them a great deal of wrong in taking them thence. While they were in Egypt they sighed by reason of their burdens, for their lives were made bitter to them with hard bondage ; and yet now they talk of Egypt as if they had all lived like princes there, when this serves as a colour for their present discontent. But with what face can they talk of eating fish in Egypt freely, or for nought, as if it cost them nothing, when they paid so dearly for it with their hard service ? They *remember the cucumbers, and the melons, and the leeks, and the onions, and the garlick* (precious stuff indeed to be fond of !), but they do not remember the brick-kilns and the task-masters, the voice of the oppressor and the smart of the whip. No, these are forgotten by these ungrateful people. (2.) They were sick of the good provision God had made for them, v. 6. It was bread from heaven, angels' food. To show how unreasonable their complaint was, it is here described, v. 7—9. It was good for food, and pleasant to the eye, every grain like an orient pearl ; it was wholesome food and nourishing ; it was not to be called *dry bread,* for it tasted like fresh oil ; it was agreeable (the Jews say, Wisd. xvi. 20) to every man's palate, and tasted as he would have it ; and, though it was still the same, yet, by the

different ways of dressing it, it yielded them a grateful variety; it cost them no money, nor care, for it fell in the night, while they slept; and the labour of gathering it was not worth speaking of; they lived upon free quarter, and yet could talk of Egypt's cheapness and the fish they ate there freely. Nay, which was much more valuable than all this, the manna came from the immediate power and bounty of God, not from common providence, but from special favour. It was, as God's compassion, new every morning, always fresh, not as their food who live on shipboard. While they lived on manna, they seemed to be exempted from the curse which sin has brought on man, that in the *sweat of his face should he eat bread.* And yet they speak of the manna with such scorn, as if it were not good enough to be meat for swine: *Our soul is dried away.* They speak as if God dealt hardly with them in allowing them no better food. At first they admired it (Exod. xvi. 15): *What is this?* "What a curious precious thing is this!" But now they despised it. Note, Peevish discontented minds will find fault with that which has no fault in it but that it is too good for them. It is very provoking to God to undervalue his favours, and to put a *but* upon our common mercies. Nothing but manna! Those that might be very happy often make themselves very miserable by their discontents. (3.) They could not be satisfied unless they had flesh to eat. They brought flocks and herds with them in great abundance out of Egypt; but either they were covetous, and could not find in their hearts to kill them, lest they should lessen their flocks (they must have flesh as cheap as they had bread, or they would not be pleased), or else they were curious, beef and mutton would not please them; they must have something more nice and delicate, like the fish they did eat in Egypt. Food would not serve; they must be feasted. They had feasted with God upon the peace-offerings which they had their share of; but it seems God did not keep a table good enough for them, they must have daintier bits than any that came to his altar. Note, It is an evidence of the dominion of the carnal mind when we are solicitous to have all the delights and satisfactions of sense wound up to the height of pleasurableness. *Be not desirous of dainties,* Prov. xxiii. 1—3. If God give us food convenient, we ought to be thankful, though we do not eat the fat and drink the sweet. (4.) They distrusted the power and goodness of God as insufficient for their supply: *Who will give us flesh to eat?* taking it for granted that God could not. Thus this question is commented upon, Ps. lxxviii. 19, 20, *Can he provide flesh also?* though he had given them flesh with their bread once, when he saw fit (Exod. xvi. 13), and they might have expected that he would do it again, and in mercy, if, instead of murmuring, they had prayed. Note, It is an

offence to God to let our desires go beyond our faith. (5.) They were eager and importunate in their desires; they *lusted a lust,* so the word is, lusted greatly and greedily, till they wept again for vexation. So childish were the children of Israel, and so humoursome, that they cried because they had not what they would have and when they would have it. They did not offer up this desire to God, but would rather be beholden to any one else than to him. We should not indulge ourselves in any desire which we cannot in faith turn into prayer, as we cannot when we *ask meat for our lust,* Ps. lxxviii. 18. For this sin the *anger of the Lord was kindled greatly* against them, which is written for our admonition, that we should not *lust after evil things as they lusted,* 1 Cor. x. 6. (6.) Flesh is good food, and may lawfully be eaten; yet they are said to lust after evil things. What is lawful of itself becomes evil to us when it is what God does not allot to us and yet we eagerly desire it.

II. Moses himself, though so meek and good a man, is uneasy upon this occasion: *Moses also was displeased.* Now, 1. It must be confessed that the provocation was very great. These murmurings of theirs reflected great dishonour upon God, and Moses laid to heart the reproaches cast on him. They also created great vexation to himself; they knew that he did his utmost for their good, and that he neither did nor could do any thing without a divine appointment; and yet to be thus continually teased and clamoured against by an unreasonable ungrateful people would break in upon the temper even of Moses himself. God considered this, and therefore we do not find that he chided him for his uneasiness. 2. Yet Moses expressed himself otherwise than became him upon this provocation, and came short of his duty both to God and Israel in these expostulations. (1.) He undervalues the honour God had put upon him, in making him the illustrious minister of his power and grace, in the deliverance and guidance of that peculiar people, which might have been sufficient to balance the burden. (2.) He complains too much of a sensible grievance, and lays too near his heart a little noise and fatigue. If he could not bear the toil of government, which was but running with the footman, how would he bear the terrors of war, which was contending with horses? He might easily have furnished himself with considerations enough to enable him to slight their clamours, and make nothing of them. (3.) He magnifies his own performances, that *all the burden of the people lay upon him;* whereas God himself did in effect ease him of all the burden. Moses needed not to be in care to provide quarters for them, or victuals; God did all. And, if any difficult case happened, he needed not to be in any perplexity, while he had the oracle to consult, and in it the divine wisdom to direct him, the divine authority to back him and bear him out, and almighty power itself to dispense rewards and punishments. (4.) He is not so sensible as he ought to be of the obligation he lay under, by virtue of the divine commission and command, to do the utmost he could for his people, when he suggests that because they were not the children of his body therefore he was not concerned to take a fatherly care of them, though God himself, who might employ him as he pleased, had appointed him to be a father to them. (5.) He takes too much to himself when he asks, *Whence should I have flesh to give them* (v. 13), as if he were the housekeeper, and not God. *Moses gave them not the bread,* John vi. 32. Nor was it expected that he should give them the flesh, but as an instrument in God's hand; and if he meant, "Whence should God have it for them?" he too much limited the power of the Holy One of Israel. (6.) He speaks distrustfully of the divine grace when he despairs of being *able to bear all this people, v.* 14. Had the work been much less, he could not have gone through it in his own strength; but, had it been much greater, through God strengthening him, he might have done it. (7.) It was worst of all passionately to wish for death, and desire to be killed out of hand, because just at this time his life was made a little uneasy to him, *v.* 15. Is this Moses? Is this the meekest of all the men on the earth? The best have their infirmities, and fail sometimes in the exercise of that grace for which they are most eminent. But God graciously overlooked Moses's passion at this time, and therefore we must not be severe in our animadversions upon it, but pray, *Lord, lead us not into temptation.*

16 And the LORD said unto Moses, Gather unto me seventy men of the elders of Israel, whom thou knowest to be the elders of the people, and officers over them; and bring them unto the tabernacle of the congregation, that they may stand there with thee. 17 And I will come down and talk with thee there: and I will take of the spirit which *is* upon thee, and will put *it* upon them; and they shall bear the burden of the people with thee, that thou bear *it* not thyself alone. 18 And say thou unto the people, Sanctify yourselves against to morrow, and ye shall eat flesh: for ye have wept in the ears of the LORD, saying, Who shall give us flesh to eat? for *it was* well with us in Egypt: therefore the LORD will give you flesh, and ye shall eat. 19 Ye shall not eat one day, nor two days, nor five days,

neither ten days, nor twenty days; 20 *But* even a whole month, until it come out at your nostrils, and it be loathsome unto you : because that ye have despised the LORD which *is* among you, and have wept before him, saying, Why came we forth out of Egypt? 21 And Moses said, The people, among whom I *am, are* six hundred thousand footmen; and thou hast said, I will give them flesh, that they may eat a whole month. 22 Shall the flocks and the herds be slain for them, to suffice them? or shall all the fish of the sea be gathered together for them, to suffice them? 23 And the LORD said unto Moses, Is the LORD's hand waxed short? thou shalt see now whether my word shall come to pass unto thee or not.

We have here God's gracious answer to both the foregoing complaints, wherein his goodness takes occasion from man's badness to appear so much the more illustrious.

I. Provision is made for the redress of the grievances Moses complains of. If he find the weight of government lie too heavy upon him, though he was a little too passionate in his remonstrance, yet he shall be eased, not by being discarded from the government himself, as he justly might have been if God had been extreme to mark what he said amiss, but by having assistants appointed him, who should be, as the apostle speaks (1 Cor. xii. 28), *helps, governments* (that is, helps in government), not at all to lessen or eclipse his honour, but to make the work more easy to him, and to *bear the burden of the people with him.* And that this provision might be both agreeable and really serviceable,

1. Moses is directed to nominate the persons, *v.* 16. The people were too hot and heady and tumultuous to be entrusted with the election; Moses must please himself in the choice, that he may not afterwards complain. The number he is to choose is seventy men, according to the number of the souls that went down into Egypt. He must choose such as he knew to be elders, that is, wise and experienced men. Those that had acquitted themselves best, as *rulers of thousands and hundreds* (Exod. xviii. 25), purchase to themselves now this good degree. "Choose such as thou knowest to be elders indeed, and not in name only, officers that execute their office." We read of the same number of elders (Exod. xxiv. 1) that went up with Moses to Mount Sinai, but they were distinguished only for that occasion, these for a perpetuity; and, according to this constitution, the Sanhedrim, or great council of the Jews, which in after ages sat

at Jerusalem, and was the highest court of judgment among them, consisted of seventy men. Our Saviour seems to have had an eye to it in the choice of seventy disciples, who were to be assistants to the apostles, Luke x.

2. God promises to qualify them. If they were not found fit for the employ, they should be made fit, else they might prove more a hindrance than a help to Moses, *v.* 17. Though Moses had talked too boldly with God, yet God does not therefore break off communion with him; he bears a great deal with us, and we must with one another: *I will come down* (said God) *and talk with thee,* when thou art more calm and composed; *and I will take of the same spirit of* wisdom, and piety, and courage, *that is upon thee,* and *put it upon them.* Not that Moses had the less of the Spirit for their sharing, nor that they were hereby made equal with him; Moses was still unequalled (Deut. xxxiv. 10), but they were clothed with a spirit of government proportionable to their place, and with a spirit of prophecy to prove their divine call to it, the government being a Theocracy. Note, (1.) Those whom God employs in any service he qualifies for it, and those that are not in some measure qualified cannot think themselves duly called. (2.) All good qualifications are from God; every *perfect gift is from the Father of lights.*

II. Even the humour of the discontented people shall be gratified too, that every mouth may be stopped. They are ordered to *sanctify themselves* (*v.* 18), that is, to put themselves into a posture to receive such a proof of God's power as should be a token both of mercy and judgment. *Prepare to meet thy God, O Israel,* Amos iv. 12.

1. God promises (shall I say?)—he threatens rather, that they shall have their fill of flesh, that for a month together they shall not only be fed, but feasted, with flesh, besides their daily manna; and, if they have not a better government of their appetites than now it appears they have, they shall be surfeited with it (*v.* 19, 20): You shall eat *till it come out at your nostrils, and become loathsome to you.* See here, (1.) The vanity of all the delights of sense; they will cloy, but not satisfy: spiritual pleasures are the contrary. As the world passes away, so do the lusts of it, 1 John ii. 17. What was greedily coveted in a little time comes to be nauseated. (2.) What brutish sins (and worse than brutish) gluttony and drunkenness are; they put a force upon nature, and make that the sickness of the body which should be its health; they are sins that are their own punishments, and yet not the worst that attend them. (3.) What a righteous thing it is with God to make that loathsome to men which they have inordinately lusted after. God could make them despise flesh as much as they had despised manna.

2. Moses objects the improbability of

610

making good this word, *v.* 21, 22. It is an objection like that which the disciples made, Mark viii. 4, *Whence can a man satisfy these men?* Some excuse Moses here, and construe what he says as only a modest enquiry which way the supply must be expected; but it savours too much of diffidence and distrust of God to be justified. He objects the number of the people, as if he that provided bread for them all could not, by the same unlimited power, provide flesh too. He reckons it must be the flesh either of beasts or fishes, because they are the most bulky animals, little thinking that the flesh of birds, little birds, should serve the purpose. God sees not as man sees, but his thoughts are above ours. He objects the greediness of the people's desires in that word, *to suffice them.* Note, Even true and great believers sometimes find it hard to trust God under the discouragements of second causes, and *against hope to believe in hope.* Moses himself could scarcely forbear saying, *Can God furnish a table in the wilderness?* when this had become the common cry. No doubt this was his infirmity.

3. God gives a short but sufficient answer to the objection in that question, *Has the Lord's hand waxed short? v.* 23. If Moses had remembered *the years of the right hand of the Most High,* he would not have started all these difficulties; therefore God reminds him of them, intimating that this objection reflected upon the divine power, of which he himself had been so often, not only the witness, but the instrument. Had he forgotten what wonders the divine power had wrought for that people, when it inflicted the plagues of Egypt, divided the sea, broached the rock, and rained bread from heaven? Had that power abated? Was God weaker than he used to be? Or was he tired with what he had done? Whatever our unbelieving hearts may suggest to the contrary, it is certain, (1.) That God's hand is not short; his power cannot be restrained in the exerting of itself by any thing but his own will; with him nothing is impossible. That hand is not short which measures the waters, metes out the heavens (Isa. xl. 12), and grasps the winds, Prov. xxx. 4. (2.) That it has not waxed short. He is as strong as ever he was, *fainteth not, neither is weary.* And this is sufficient to silence all our distrusts when means fail us, *Is any thing too hard for the Lord?* God here brings Moses to this first principle, sets him back in his lesson, to learn the ancient name of God, *The Lord God Almighty,* and puts the proof upon the issue: *Thou shalt see whether my word shall come to pass or not.* This magnifies God's word above all his name, that his works never come short of it. If he speaks, it is done.

24 And Moses went out, and told the people the words of the LORD,

and gathered the seventy men of the elders of the people, and set them round about the tabernacle. 25 And the LORD came down in a cloud, and spake unto him, and took of the spirit that *was* upon him, and gave *it* unto the seventy elders : and it came to pass, *that,* when the spirit rested upon them, they prophesied, and did not cease. 26 But there remained two *of the* men in the camp, the name of the one *was* Eldad, and the name of the other Medad : and the spirit rested upon them ; and they *were* of them that were written, but went not out unto the tabernacle : and they prophesied in the camp. 27 And there ran a young man, and told Moses, and said, Eldad and Medad do prophesy in the camp. 28 And Joshua the son of Nun, the servant of Moses, *one* of his young men, answered and said, My lord Moses, forbid them. 29 And Moses said unto him, Enviest thou for my sake ? would God that all the LORD's people were prophets, *and* that the LORD would put his spirit upon them ! 30 And Moses gat him into the camp, he and the elders of Israel.

We have here the performance of God's word to Moses, that he should have help in the government of Israel.

I. Here is the case of the seventy privy-counsellors in general. Moses, though a little disturbed by the tumult of the people, yet was thoroughly composed by the communion he had with God, and soon came to himself again. And according as the matter was concerted, 1. He did his part ; he presented the seventy elders before the Lord, round the tabernacle (*v.* 24), that they might there stand ready to receive the grace of God, in the place where he manifested himself, and that the people also might be witnesses of their solemn call. Note, Those that expect favour from God must humbly offer themselves and their service to him. 2. God was not wanting to do his part. *He gave of his Spirit to the seventy elders* (*v.* 25), which enabled those whose capacities and education set them but on a level with their neighbours of a sudden to say and do that which was extraordinary, and which proved them to be actuated by divine inspiration : they prophesied, and did not cease all that day, and (some think) only that day. They discoursed to the people of the things of God, and perhaps commented upon the law they had lately received with admirable clearness,

and fulness, and readiness, and aptness of expression, so that all who heard them might see and say that *God was with them of a truth ;* see 1 Cor. xiv. 24, 25. Thus, long afterwards, Saul was marked for the government by the gift of prophecy, which came upon him for a day and a night, 1 Sam. x. 6, 11. When Moses was to fetch Israel out of Egypt, Aaron was appointed to be his prophet, Exod. vii. 1. But, now that God had called Aaron to other work, in his room Moses has seventy prophets to attend him. Note, Those are fittest to rule in God's Israel that are well acquainted with divine things and are apt to teach to edification.

II. Here is the particular case of two of them, *Eldad* and *Medad,* probably two brothers.

1. They were nominated by Moses to be assistants in the government, but they *went not out unto the tabernacle* as the rest did, *v.* 26. Calvin conjectures that the summons was sent them, but that it did not find them, they being somewhere out of the way ; so that, though they were written, yet they were not called. Most think that they declined coming to the tabernacle out of an excess of modesty and humility ; being sensible of their own weakness and unworthiness, they desired to be excused from coming into the government. Their principle was their praise, but their practice in not obeying orders was their fault.

2. The Spirit of God found them out in the camp, where they were hidden among the stuff, and there they prophesied, that is, they exercised their gift of praying, preaching, and praising God, in some private tent. Note, The Spirit of God is not tied to the tabernacle, but, *like the wind, blows where he listeth,* John iii. 8. *Whither can we go from that Spirit ?* There was a special providence in it that these two should be absent, for thus it appeared that it was indeed a divine Spirit which the elders were actuated by, and that Moses gave them not that Spirit, but God himself. They modestly declined preferment, but God forced it upon them ; nay, they have the honour of being *named,* which the rest have not : for those that humble themselves shall be exalted, and those are most fit for government who are least ambitious of it.

3. Information of this was given to Moses (*v.* 27) : " *Eldad and Medad do prophesy in the camp ;* there is a conventicle in such a tent, and Eldad and Medad are holding forth there, from under the inspection and presidency of Moses, and out of the communion of the rest of the elders." Whoever the person was that brought the tidings, he seems to have looked upon it as an irregularity.

4. Joshua moved to have them silenced : *My lord Moses, forbid them, v.* 28. It is probable that Joshua himself was one of the seventy, which made him the more jealous for the honour of their order. He takes it for granted that they were not under any neces-

sitating impulse, *for the spirit of the prophets is subject to the prophets*, and therefore he would have them either not to prophesy at all or to come to the tabernacle and prophesy in concert with the rest. He does not desire that they should be punished for what they had done, but only restrained for the future. This motion he made from a good principle, not out of any personal dislike to Eldad and Medad, but out of an honest zeal for that which he apprehended to be the unity of the church, and concern for the honour of God and Moses.

5. Moses rejected the motion, and reproved him that made it (*v.* 29): "*Enviest thou for my sake?* Thou knowest not what manner of spirit thou art of." Though Joshua was Moses's particular friend and confidant, though he said this out of a respect to Moses, whose honour he was very loth to see lessened by the call of those elders, yet Moses reproves him, and in him all that show such a spirit. (1.) We must not secretly grieve at the gifts, graces, and usefulness of others. It was the fault of John's disciples that they envied Christ's honour because it shaded their master's, John iii. 26, &c. (2.) We must not be transported into heats against the weaknesses and infirmities of others. Granting that Eldad and Medad were guilty of an irregularity, yet Joshua was too quick and too warm upon them. Our zeal must always be tempered with the meekness of wisdom: the righteousness of God needs not the wrath of man, Jam. i. 20. (3.) We must not make even the best and most useful men heads of a party. Paul would not have his name made use of to patronise a faction, 1 Cor. i. 12, 13. (4.) We must not be forward to condemn and silence those that differ from us, as if they did not follow Christ because they do not follow *him with us*, Mark ix. 38. Shall we reject those whom Christ has owned, or restrain any from doing good because they are not in every thing of our mind? Moses was of another spirit; so far from silencing these two, and quenching the Spirit in them, he wishes *all the Lord's people were prophets*, that is, that he would *put his Spirit upon them*. Not that he would have any set up for prophets that were not duly qualified, or that he expected that the Spirit of prophecy should be made thus common; but thus he expresses the love and esteem he had for *all the Lord's people*, the complacency he took in the gifts of others, and how far he was from being displeased at Eldad and Medad's prophesying from under his eye. Such an excellent spirit as this blessed Paul was of, rejoicing that Christ was preached, though it was by those who therein intended to *add affliction to his bonds*, Phil. i. 16. We ought to be pleased that God is served and glorified, and good done, though to the lessening of our credit and the credit of our way.

6. The elders, now newly ordained, immediately entered upon their administration (*v.*

30); when their call was sufficiently attested by their prophesying, they went with Moses to the camp, and applied themselves to business. Having received the gift, they *ministered the same as good stewards.* And now Moses was pleased that he had so many to share with him in his work and honour. And, (1.) Let the testimony of Moses be credited by those who desire to be in power, that government is a burden. It is a burden of care and trouble to those who make conscience of the duty of it; and to those who do not it will prove a heavier burden in the day of account, when they fall under the doom of the unprofitable servant that buried his talent. (2.) Let the example of Moses be imitated by those that are in power; let them not despise the advice and assistance of others, but desire it, and be thankful for it, not coveting to monopolize wisdom and power. In the multitude of counsellors there is safety.

31 And there went forth a wind from the LORD, and brought quails from the sea, and let *them* fall by the camp, as it were a day's journey on this side, and as it were a day's journey on the other side, round about the camp, and as it were two cubits *high* upon the face of the earth. 32 And the people stood up all that day, and all *that* night, and all the next day, and they gathered the quails: he that gathered least gathered ten homers: and they spread *them* all abroad for themselves round about the camp. 33 And while the flesh *was* yet between their teeth, ere it was chewed, the wrath of the LORD was kindled against the people, and the LORD smote the people with a very great plague. 34 And he called the name of that place Kibroth-hattaavah: because there they buried the people that lusted. 35 *And* the people journeyed from Kibroth-hattaavah unto Hazeroth; and abode at Hazeroth.

God, having performed his promise to Moses by giving him assessors in the government, thereby proving the power he has over the spirits of men by his Spirit, he here performs his promise to the people by giving them flesh, proving thereby his power over the inferior creatures and his dominion in the kingdom of nature. Observe, 1. How the people were gratified with flesh in abundance: *A wind* (a south-east wind, as appears, Ps. lxxviii. 26) *brought quails, v.* 31. It is uncertain what sort of animals they were; the psalmist calls them *feathered fowl*, or *fowl of wing.* The learned bishop Patrick inclines to agree with some modern writers, who think they were *locusts,* a delicious sort of food well known in those parts, the rather because they were brought with a wind, lay in heaps, and were dried in the sun for use. Whatever they were, they answered the intention, they served for a month's feast for Israel, such an indulgent Father was God to his froward family. Locusts, that had been a plague to fruitful Egypt, feeding upon the fruits, were a blessing to a barren wilderness, being themselves fed upon. 2. How greedy they were of this flesh that God sent them. They *flew upon the spoil* with an unsatiable appetite, not regarding what Moses had told them from God, that they would surfeit upon it, *v.* 32. Two days and a night they were at it, gathering flesh, till every master of a family had brought home ten homers (that is, ten ass-loads) at least. David longed for the water of the well of Bethlehem, but would not drink it when he had it, because it was obtained by venturing; much more reason these Israelites had to refuse this flesh, which was obtained by murmuring, and which, they might easily perceive, by what Moses said, was given them in anger; but those that are under the power of a carnal mind will have their lusts fulfilled, though it be to the certain damage and ruin of their precious souls. 3. How dearly they paid for their feasts, when it came into the reckoning: *The Lord smote them with a very great plague* (v. 33), some bodily disease, which probably was the effect of their surfeit, and was the death of many of them, and those, it is likely, the ring-leaders in the mutiny. Note, God often grants the desires of sinners in wrath, while he denies the desires of his own people in love. He *gave them their request,* but *sent leanness into their soul,* Ps. cvi. 15. By all that was said to them they *were not estranged from their lusts,* and therefore, *while the meat was in their mouths, the wrath of God came upon them,* Ps. lxxviii. 30, 31. What we inordinately desire, if we obtain it (we have reason to fear), will be some way or other a grief and cross to us. God satiated them first, and then plagued them, (1.) To save the reputation of his own power, that it might not be said, "He would not have cut them off had he been able to supply them." And, (2.) To show us the meaning of the prosperity of sinners; it is their preparation for ruin, they are fed as an ox for the slaughter. *Lastly,* The remembrance of this is preserved in the name given to the place, *v.* 34. Moses called it *Kibroth-hattaavah,* the *graves of lusters* or *of lust.* And well it had been if these graves of Israel's lusters had proved the graves of Israel's lust: the warning was designed to be so, but it had not its due effect, for it follows (Ps. lxxviii. 32), *For all this, they sinned still.*

CHAP. XII.

In the foregoing chapter we had the vexation which the people gave to Moses; in this we have his patience tried by his own relations. I. Miriam and Aaron, his own brother and sister, affronted him,

ver. 1--3. II. God called them to an account for it, ver. 4--9. III. Miriam was smitten with a leprosy for it, ver. 10. IV. Aaron submits, and Moses meekly intercedes for Miriam, ver. 11--13. V. She is healed, but put to shame for seven days, ver. 14--16. And this is recorded to show that the best persons and families have both their follies and their crosses.

AND Miriam and Aaron spake against Moses because of the Ethiopian woman whom he had married; for he had married an Ethiopian woman. 2 And they said, Hath the Lord indeed spoken only by Moses? hath he not spoken also by us? And the Lord heard *it.* 3 (Now the man Moses *was* very meek, above all the men which *were* upon the face of the earth.)

Here is, I. The unbecoming passion of Aaron and Miriam: they *spoke against Moses, v.* 1. If Moses, that received so much honour from God, yet received so many slights and affronts from men, shall any of us think such trials either strange or hard, and be either provoked or discouraged by them? But who would have thought that disturbance should be created to Moses, 1. From those that were themselves serious and good; nay, that were eminent in religion, Miriam a prophetess, Aaron the high priest, both of them joint-commissioners with Moses for the deliverance of Israel? Mic. vi. 4, *I sent before thee Moses, Aaron, and Miriam.* 2. From those that were his nearest relations, his own brother and sister, who shone so much by rays borrowed from him? Thus the spouse complains (Cant. i. 6), *My mother's children were angry with me;* and quarrels among relations are in a special manner grievous. *A brother offended is harder to be won than a strong city.* Yet this helps to confirm the call of Moses, and shows that his advancement was purely by the divine favour, and not by any compact or collusion with his kindred, who themselves grudged his advancement. Neither did many of our Saviour's kindred believe on him, John vii. 5. It should seem that Miriam began the quarrel, and Aaron, not having been employed or consulted in the choice of the seventy elders, was for the present somewhat disgusted, and so was the sooner drawn in to take his sister's part. It would grieve one to see the hand of Aaron in so many trespasses, but it shows that *the law made men priests who had infirmity.* Satan prevailed first with Eve, and by her with Adam; see what need we have to take heed of being drawn into quarrels by our relations, for we know not how great a matter a little fire may kindle. Aaron ought to have remembered how Moses stood his friend when God was angry with him for making the golden calf (Deut. ix. 20), and not to have rendered him evil for good. Two things they quarrelled with Moses about:—(1.) About his marriage: some think a late marriage with a Cushite or Arabian; others because of Zipporah, whom on this occasion they called, in scorn, an Ethiopian woman, and who, they insinuated, had too great an influence upon Moses in the choice of these seventy elders.   Perhaps there was some private falling out between Zipporah and Miriam, which occasioned some hot words, and one peevish reflection introduced another, till Moses and Aaron came to be interested.   (2.) About his government; not the mismanagement of it, but the monopolizing of it (*v.* 2): "*Hath the Lord spoken only by Moses?*   Must *he* alone have the choice of the persons on whom the spirit of prophecy shall come?   *Hath he not spoken also by us?*   Might not we have had a hand in that affair, and preferred our friends, as well as Moses his?"   They could not deny that God had spoken by Moses, but it was plain he had sometimes spoken also by them; and that which they intended was to make themselves equal with him, though God had so many ways distinguished him.   Note, Striving to be greatest is a sin which easily besets disciples themselves, and it is exceedingly sinful.   Even those that are well preferred are seldom pleased if others be better preferred.   Those that excel are commonly envied.

II. The wonderful patience of Moses under this provocation.   *The Lord heard it* (*v.* 2), but Moses himself took no notice of it, for (*v.* 3) he was very meek.   He had a great deal of reason to resent the affront; it was ill-natured and ill-timed, when the people were disposed to mutiny, and had lately given him a great deal of vexation with their murmurings, which would be in danger of breaking out again when thus headed and countenanced by Aaron and Miriam; but he, *as a deaf man, heard not.*   When God's honour was concerned, as in the case of the golden calf, no man more zealous than Moses; but, when his own honour was touched, no man more meek: as bold as a lion in the cause of God, but as mild as a lamb in his own cause.   God's people are the *meek of the earth* (Zeph. ii. 3), but some are more remarkable than others for this grace, as Moses, who was thus fitted for the work he was called to, which required all the meekness he had and sometimes more.   And sometimes the unkindness of our friends is a greater trial of our meekness than the malice of our enemies.   Christ himself records his own meekness (Matt. xi. 29, *I am meek and lowly in heart*), and the copy of meekness which Christ has set was without a blot, but that of Moses was not.

4 And the Lord spake suddenly unto Moses, and unto Aaron, and unto Miriam, Come out ye three unto the tabernacle of the congregation.   And they three came out.   5 And the

Lord came down in the pillar of the cloud, and stood *in* the door of the tabernacle, and called Aaron and Miriam: and they both came forth.   6 And he said, Hear now my words: If there be a prophet among you, *I* the Lord will make myself known unto him in a vision, *and* will speak unto him in a dream.   7 My servant Moses *is* not so, who *is* faithful in all mine house.   8 With him will I speak mouth to mouth, even apparently, and not in dark speeches; and the similitude of the Lord shall he behold: wherefore then were ye not afraid to speak against my servant Moses?   9 And the anger of the Lord was kindled against them; and he departed.

Moses did not resent the injury done him, nor complain of it to God, nor make any appeal to him; but God resented it.   He hears all we say in our passion, and is a swift witness of our hasty speeches, which is a reason why we should resolutely bridle our tongues, that we speak not ill of others, and why we should patiently stop our ears, and not take notice of it, if others speak ill of us.   *I heard not, for thou wilt hear*, Ps. xxxviii. 13—15.   The more silent we are in our own cause the more is God engaged to plead it.   The accused innocent needs to say little if he knows the judge himself will be his advocate.

I. The cause is called, and the parties are summoned forthwith to attend at the door of the tabernacle, *v.* 4, 5.   Moses had often shown himself jealous for God's honour, and now God showed himself jealous for his reputation; for *those that honour God he will honour*, nor will he ever be behind-hand with any that appear for him.   Judges of old sat in the gate of the city to try causes, and so on this occasion the *shechinah* in the cloud of glory stood *at the door of the tabernacle*, and Aaron and Miriam, as delinquents, were called to the bar.

II. Aaron and Miriam were made to know that great as they were they must not pretend to be equal to Moses, nor set up as rivals with him, *v.* 6—8.   Were they prophets of the Lord?   Of Moses it might be truly said, *He more.*   1. It was true that God put a great deal of honour upon the prophets.   However men mocked them and misused them, they were the favourites and intimates of heaven.   God *made himself known to them*, either by dreams when they were asleep or by visions when they were awake, and by them made himself known to others.   And those are happy, those are great, truly great, truly happy, to whom God *makes himself known.*   Now he does it not by dreams and visions, as of old, but by the *Spirit of wisdom and revelation*, who makes known those things to babes which *prophets and kings* desired to see and might not. Hence in the last days, the days of the Messiah, the *sons and daughters* are said to *prophesy* (Joel ii. 28), because they shall be better acquainted with the mysteries of the kingdom of grace than even the prophets themselves were; see Heb. i. 1, 2. 2. Yet the honour put upon Moses was far greater (*v.* 7): *My servant Moses is not so,* he excels them all. To recompense Moses for his meekly and patiently bearing the affronts which Miriam and Aaron gave him, God not only cleared him, but praised him; and took that occasion to give him an encomium which remains upon record to his immortal honour; and thus shall those that are reviled and persecuted for righteousness' sake have a *great reward in heaven,* Christ will confess them before his Father and the holy angels. (1.) Moses was a man of great integrity and tried fidelity. He is *faithful in all my house.* This is put first in his character, because grace excels gifts, love excels knowledge, and sincerity in the service of God puts a greater honour upon a man and recommends him to the divine favour more than learning, abstruse speculations, and an ability to *speak with tongues.* This is that part of Moses's character which the apostle quotes when he would show that Christ was greater than Moses, making it out that he was so in this chief instance of his greatness; for Moses was faithful only *as a servant,* but Christ *as a son,* Heb. iii. 2, 5, 6. God entrusted Moses to deliver his mind in all things to Israel; Israel entrusted him to treat for them with God; and he was faithful to both. He said and did every thing in the management of that great affair as became an honest good man, that aimed at nothing else but the honour of God and the welfare of Israel. (2.) Moses was therefore honoured with clearer discoveries of God's mind, and a more intimate communion with God, than any other prophet whatsoever. He shall, [1.] Hear more from God than any other prophet, more clearly and distinctly: *With him will I speak mouth to mouth,* or *face to face* (Exod. xxx. 11), *as a man speaks to his friend,* whom he discourses with freely and familiarly, and without any confusion or consternation, such as sometimes other prophets were under; as Ezekiel, and John himself, when God spoke to them. By other prophets God sent to his people reproofs, and predictions of good or evil, which were properly enough delivered in dark speeches, figures, types, and parables; but by Moses he gave laws to his people, and the institution of holy ordinances, which could by no means be delivered by dark speeches, but must be expressed in the plainest and most intelligible manner. [2.] He shall see more of God than any other prophet: *The similitude of the Lord shall he behold,* as he hath seen it in Horeb, when

God proclaimed his name before him. Yet he saw only the similitude of the Lord, angels and glorified saints always behold the face of our Father. Moses had the spirit of prophecy in a way peculiar to himself, and which set him far above all other prophets; yet *he that is least in the kingdom of heaven is greater than he,* much more does our Lord Jesus infinitely excel him, Heb. iii. 1, &c.

Now let Miriam and Aaron consider who it was that they insulted: *Were you not afraid to speak against my servant Moses? Against my servant, against Moses?* so it runs in the original. "How dare you abuse any servant of mine, especially such a servant as Moses, who is a friend, a confidant, and steward of the house?" How durst they speak to the grief and reproach of one whom God had so much to say in commendation of? Might they not expect that God would resent it, and take it as an affront to himself? Note, We have reason to be afraid of saying or doing any thing against the servants of God; it is at our peril if we do, for God will plead their cause, and reckon that what *touches them touches the apple of his eye.* It is a dangerous thing to *offend Christ's little ones,* Matt. xviii. 6. Those are presumptuous indeed that *are not afraid to speak evil of dignities,* 2 Pet. ii. 10.

III. God, having thus shown them their fault and folly, next shows them his displeasure (*v.* 9): *The anger of the Lord was kindled against them,* of which perhaps some sensible indications were given in the change of the colour of the cloud, or some flashes of lightning from it. But indeed it was indication enough of his displeasure that he departed, and would not so much as hear their excuse, for he needed not, *understanding their thoughts afar off;* and thus he would show that he was displeased. Note, The removal of God's presence from us is the surest and saddest token of God's displeasure against us. Woe unto us if he depart; and he never departs till we by our sin and folly drive him from us.

10 And the cloud departed from off the tabernacle; and, behold, Miriam *became* leprous, *white* as snow: and Aaron looked upon Miriam, and, behold, *she was* leprous. 11 And Aaron said unto Moses, Alas, my lord, I beseech thee, lay not the sin upon us, wherein we have done foolishly, and wherein we have sinned. 12 Let her not be as one dead, of whom the flesh is half consumed when he cometh out of his mother's womb. 13 And Moses cried unto the LORD, saying, Heal her now, O God, I beseech thee. 14 And the LORD said unto Moses, If her father had but spit in her face, should

she not be ashamed seven days? let her be shut out from the camp seven days, and after that let her be received in *again.* 15 And Miriam was shut out from the camp seven days: and the people journeyed not till Miriam was brought in *again.* 16 And afterward the people removed from Hazeroth, and pitched in the wilderness of Paran.

Here is, I. God's judgment upon Miriam (*v.* 10): *The cloud departed from off* that part of *the tabernacle,* in token of God's displeasure, and presently Miriam became leprous; when God goes, evil comes; expect no good when God departs. The leprosy was a disease often inflicted by the immediate hand of God as the punishment of some particular sin, as on Gehazi for lying, on Uzziah for invading the priest's office, and here on Miriam for scolding and making mischief among relations. The plague of the leprosy, it is likely, appeared in her face, so that it appeared to all that saw her that she was struck with it, with the worst of it, she was leprous as snow; not only so white, but so soft, the solid flesh losing its consistency, as that which putrefies does. Her foul tongue (says bishop Hall) is justly punished with a foul face, and her folly in pretending to be a rival with Moses is made manifest to all men, for every one sees his face to be glorious, and hers to be leprous. While Moses needs a veil to hide his glory, Miriam needs one to hide her shame. Note, Those distempers which any way deform us ought to be construed as a rebuke to our pride, and improved for the cure of it, and under such humbling providences we ought to be very humble. It is a sign that the heart is hard indeed if the flesh be mortified, and yet the lusts of the flesh remain unmortified. It should seem that this plague upon Miriam was designed for an exposition of the law concerning the leprosy (Lev. xiii.), for it is referred to upon the rehearsal of that law, Deut. xxiv. 8, 9. Miriam was struck with a leprosy, but not Aaron, because she was first in the transgression, and God would put a difference between those that mislead and those that are misled. Aaron's office, though it saved him not from God's displeasure, yet helped to secure him from this token of his displeasure, which would not only have suspended him for the present from officiating, when (there being no priests but himself and his two sons) he could ill be spared, but it would have rendered him and his office mean, and would have been a lasting blot upon his family. Aaron as priest was to be the judge of the leprosy, and his performing that part of his office upon this occasion, when he *looked upon Miriam, and behold she was leprous,* was a sufficient mortification to

him. He was struck through her side, and could not pronounce her leprous without blushing and trembling, knowing himself to be equally obnoxious. This judgment upon Miriam is improvable by us as a warning to take heed of putting any affront upon our Lord Jesus. If she was thus chastised for speaking against Moses, what will become of those that sin against Christ?

II. Aaron's submission hereupon (*v.* 11, 12); he humbles himself to Moses, confesses his fault, and begs pardon. He that but just now joined with his sister in speaking against Moses is here forced for himself and his sister to make a penitent address to him, and in the highest degree to magnify him (as if he had the power of God to forgive and heal) whom he had so lately vilified. Note, Those that trample upon the saints and servants of God will one day be glad to make court to them; at furthest, in the other world, as the foolish virgins to the wise for a little oil, and the rich man to Lazarus for a little water; and perhaps in this world, as Job's friend to him for his prayers, and here Aaron to Moses. Rev. iii. 9. In his submission, 1. He confesses his own and his sister's sin, *v.* 11. He speaks respectfully to Moses, of whom he had spoken slightly, calls him his lord, and now turns the reproach upon himself, speaks as one ashamed of what he had said: *We have sinned, we have done foolishly.* Those sin, and do foolishly, who revile and speak evil of any, especially of good people or of those in authority. Repentance is the unsaying of that which we have said amiss, and it had better be unsaid than that we be undone by it. 2. He begs Moses's pardon: *Lay not this sin upon us.* Aaron was to bring his gift to the altar, but, knowing that his brother had something against him, he of all men was concerned to reconcile himself to his brother, that he might be qualified to offer his gift. Some think that this speedy submission which God saw him ready to make was that which prevented his being struck with a leprosy as his sister was. 3. He recommends the deplorable condition of his sister to Moses's compassionate consideration (*v.* 12): *Let her not be as one dead,* that is, "Let her not continue so separated from conversation, defiling all she touches, and even to putrefy above ground as one dead." He eloquently describes the misery of her case, to move his pity.

III. The intercession made for Miriam (*v* 13): He *cried unto the Lord* with a loud voice, because the cloud, the symbol of his presence, was removed and stood at some distance, and to express his fervency in this request, *Heal her now, O Lord, I beseech thee.* By this he made it to appear that he did heartily forgive her the injury she had done him, that he had not accused her to God, nor called for justice against her; so far from this that, when God in tenderness to his honour had chastised her insolence, he was the first that moved for reversing the judgment. By this example we are taught to *pray for those that despitefully use us;* and not to take pleasure in the most righteous punishment inflicted either by God or man on those that have been injurious to us. Jeroboam's withered hand was restored at the special instance and request of the prophet against whom it had been stretched out, 1 Kings xiii. 6. So Miriam here was healed by the prayer of Moses, whom she had abused, and Abimelech by the prayer of Abraham, Gen. xx. 17. Moses might have stood off, and have said, " She is served well enough, let her govern her tongue better next time; but, not content with being able to say that he had not prayed for the inflicting of the judgment, he prays earnestly for the removal of it. This pattern of Moses, and that of our Saviour, *Father, forgive them,* we must study to conform to.

IV. The accommodating of this matter so as that mercy and justice might meet together. 1. Mercy takes place so far as that Miriam shall be healed; Moses forgives her, and God will. See 2 Cor. ii. 10. But, 2. Justice takes place so far as that Miriam shall be humbled (*v.* 14): *Let her be shut out from the camp seven days,* that she herself might be made more sensible of her fault and penitent for it, and that her punishment might be the more public, and all Israel might take notice of it and take warning by it not to mutiny. If Miriam the prophetess be put under such marks of humiliation for one hasty word spoken against Moses, what may we expect for our murmurings? *If this be done in a green tree, what shall be done in the dry?* See how people debase and diminish themselves by sin, stain their glory, and lay their honour in the dust. When Miriam praised God, we find her at the head of the congregation, and one of the brightest ornaments of it, Exod. xv. 20. Now that she quarrelled with God we find her expelled as the filth and off-scouring of it. A reason is given for her being put out of the camp for seven days, because thus she ought to *accept of the punishment of her iniquity.* If her father, her earthly father, had but spit in her face, and so signified his displeasure against her, would she not be so troubled and concerned at it, and so sorry that she had deserved it, as to shut herself up for some time in her room, and not come into his presence, or show her face in the family, being ashamed of her own folly and unhappiness? If such reverence as this be owing to the fathers of our flesh, when they correct us, much more ought we to humble ourselves under the mighty hand of the Father of spirits, Heb. xii. 9. Note, When we are under the tokens of God's displeasure for sin, it becomes us to take shame to ourselves, and to lie down in that shame, owning that *to us belongs confusion of face.* If by our own fault and folly we expose ourselves to the reproach and contempt of men, the just censures of the church, or the rebukes of the divine Providence, we must confess that our Father justly spits in our face, and be ashamed.

V. The hindrance that this gave to the people's progress : *The people journeyed not till Miriam was brought in again, v.* 15. God did not remove the cloud, and therefore they did not remove their camp. This was intended, 1. As a rebuke to the people, who were conscious to themselves of having sinned after the similitude of Miriam's transgression, in speaking against Moses : thus far therefore they shall share in her punishment, that it shall retard their march forward towards Canaan. Many things oppose us, but nothing hinders us in the way to heaven as sin does. 2. As a mark of respect to Miriam. If the camp had removed during the days of her suspension, her trouble and shame had been the greater ; therefore, in compassion to her, they shall stay till her excommunication be taken off, and she taken in again, it is probable with the usual ceremonies of the cleansing of lepers. Note, Those that are under censure and rebuke for sin ought to be treated with a great deal of tenderness, and not be over-loaded, no, not with the shame they have deserved, not *counted as enemies* (2 Thess. iii. 15), but *forgiven and comforted,* 2 Cor. ii. 7. Sinners must be cast out with grief, and penitents taken in with joy. When Miriam was absolved and re-admitted, the people went forward into the wilderness of Paran, which joined up to the south border of Canaan, and thither their next remove would have been if they had not put a bar in their own way.

CHAP. XIII.

It is a memorable and very melancholy story which is related in this and the following chapter, of the turning back of Israel from the borders of Canaan, when they were just ready to set foot in it, and the sentencing of them to wander and perish in the wilderness for their unbelief and murmuring. It is referred to Ps. xcv. 7, &c., and improved for warning to Christians, Heb. iii. 7, &c. In this chapter we have, I. The sending of twelve spies before them into Canaan, ver. 1—16. II. The instructions given to these spies, ver. 17—20. III. Their executing their commission according to their instructions, and their return from the search, ver. 21—25. IV. The report they brought back to the camp of Israel, ver. 26, &c.

AND the Lord spake unto Moses, saying, 2 Send thou men, that they may search the land of Canaan, which I give unto the children of Israel: of every tribe of their fathers shall ye send a man, every one a ruler among them. 3 And Moses by the commandment of the Lord sent them from the wilderness of Paran: all those men *were* heads of the children of Israel. 4 And these *were* their names: of the tribe of Reuben, Shammua the son of Zaccur. 5 Of the tribe of Simeon, Shaphat the son of Hori. 6 Of the tribe of Judah, Caleb the son of Jephunneh. 7 Of the tribe of Issachar, Igal the son of Joseph. 8 Of the tribe of Ephraim, Oshea the son of Nun. 9 Of the tribe of Benjamin, Palti the son of Raphu. 10 Of the tribe of Zebulun, Gaddiel the son of Sodi. 11 Of the tribe of Joseph, *namely*, of the tribe of Manasseh, Gaddi the son of Susi. 12 Of the tribe of Dan, Ammiel the son of Gemalli. 13 Of the tribe of Asher, Sethur the son of Michael. 14 Of the tribe of Naphtali, Nahbi the son of Vophsi. 15 Of the tribe of Gad, Geuel the son of Machi. 16 These *are* the names of the men which Moses sent to spy out the land. And Moses called Oshea the son of Nun Jehoshua. 17 And Moses sent them to spy out the land of Canaan, and said unto them, Get you up this *way* southward, and go up into the mountain: 18 And see the land, what it *is;* and the people that dwelleth therein, whether they *be* strong or weak, few or many; 19 And what the land *is* that they dwell in, whether it *be* good or bad; and what cities *they be* that they dwell in, whether in tents, or in strong holds; 20 And what the land *is*, whether it *be* fat or lean, whether there be wood therein, or not. And be ye of good courage, and bring of the fruit of the land. Now the time *was* the time of the firstripe grapes.

Here we have, I. Orders given to send spies to search out the land of Canaan. It is here said, God directed Moses to send them (*v.* 1, 2), but it appears by the repetition of the story afterwards (Deut. i. 22) that the motion came originally from the people; they came to Moses, and said, *We will send men before us;* and it was the fruit of their unbelief. They would not take God's word that it was a good land, and that he would, without fail, put them in possession of it. They could not trust the pillar of cloud and fire to show them the way to it, but had a better opinion of their own politics than of God's wisdom. How absurd was it for them to send to spy out a land which God himself had spied out for them, to enquire the way into it when God himself had undertaken to show them the way! But thus we ruin ourselves by giving more credit to the reports and representations of sense than to divine revelation; we walk by sight, not by faith; whereas, *if we* will *receive the witness of men,* without doubt *the witness of God is greater.* The people making this motion to Moses, he

(perhaps not aware of the unbelief at the bottom of it) consulted God in the case, who bade him gratify the people in this matter, and send spies before them : " Let them walk in their own counsels." Yet God was no way accessory to the sin that followed, for the sending of these spies was so far from being the cause of the sin that if the spies had done their duty, and the people theirs, it might have been the confirmation of their faith, and of good service to them.

II. The persons nominated that were to be employed in this service (*v.* 4, &c.), one of each tribe, that it might appear to be the act of the people in general ; and rulers, persons of figure in their respective tribes, some of the rulers of thousands or hundreds, to put the greater credit upon their embassy. This was designed for the best, but it proved to have this ill effect that the quality of the persons occasioned the evil report they brought up to be the more credited and the people to be the more influenced by it. Some think that they are all named for the sake of two good ones that were among them, Caleb and Joshua. Notice is taken of the change of Joshua's name upon this occasion, *v.* 16. He was Moses's minister, but had been employed, though of the tribe of Ephraim, as general of the forces that were sent out against Amalek. The name by which he was generally called and known in his own tribe was *Oshea*, but Moses called him *Joshua*, in token of his affection to him and power over him ; and now, it should seem, he ordered others to call him so, and fixed that to be his name henceforward. *Oshea* signifies a prayer for salvation, *Save thou ; Joshua* signifies a promise of salvation, *He will save*, in answer to that prayer : so near is the relation between prayers and promises. Prayers prevail for promises, and promises direct and encourage prayers. Some think that Moses designed, by taking the first syllable of the name Jehovah and prefixing it to his name, which turned *Hoshea* into *Jehoshua*, to put an honour upon him, and to encourage him in this and all his future services with the assurances of God's presence. Yet after this he is called *Hoshea*, Deut. xxxii. 44. *Jesus* is the same name with *Joshua*, and it is the name of our Lord Christ, of whom Joshua was a type as successor to Moses, Israel's captain, and conqueror of Canaan. There was another of the same name, who was also a type of Christ, Zech. vi. 11. Joshua was the saviour of God's people from the powers of Canaan, but Christ is their Saviour from the powers of hell.

III. The instructions given to those spies. They were sent into the land of Canaan the nearest way, to traverse the country, and to take account of its present state, *v.* 17. Two heads of enquiry were given them in charge, 1. Concerning the land itself : *See what that is* (*v.* 18, and again, *v.* 19), see whether it be *good or bad*, and (*v.* 20) *whether it be fat or lean.* All parts of the earth do not share alike in the blessing of fruitfulness; some countries are blessed with a richer soil than others. Moses himself was well satisfied that Canaan was a very good land, but he sent these spies to bring an account of it for the satisfaction of the people; as John Baptist sent to Jesus, to ask whether he was the Christ, not to inform himself, but to inform those he sent. They must take notice whether the air was healthful or no, what the soil was, and what the productions; and, for the better satisfaction of the people, they must bring with them some of the fruits. 2. Concerning the inhabitants—their number, few or many, —their size and stature, whether strong ablebodied men or weak,—their habitations, whether they lived in tents or houses, whether in open villages or in walled towns,—whether the woods were standing as in those countries that are uncultivated, through the unskilfulness and slothfulness of the inhabitants, or whether the woods were cut down, and the country made champaign, for the convenience of tillage. These were the things they were to enquire about. Perhaps there had not been of late years such commerce between Egypt and Canaan as there was in Jacob's time, else they might have informed themselves of these things without sending men on purpose to search. See the advantage we may derive from books and learning, which acquaint those that are curious and inquisitive with the state of foreign countries, at a much greater distance than Canaan was now from Israel, without this trouble and expense.

IV. Moses dismisses the spies with this charge, *Be of good courage,* intimating, not only that they should be themselves encouraged against the difficulties of this expedition, but that they should bring an encouraging account to the people and make the best of every thing. It was not only a great undertaking they were put upon, which required good management and resolution, but it was a great trust that was reposed in them, which required that they should be faithful.

21 So they went up, and searched the land from the wilderness of Zin unto Rehob, as men come to Hamath. 22 And they ascended by the south, and came unto Hebron; where Ahiman, Sheshai, and Talmai, the children of Anak, *were.* (Now Hebron was built seven years before Zoan in Egypt.) 23 And they came unto the brook of Eshcol, and cut down from thence a branch with one cluster of grapes, and they bare it between two upon a staff; and *they brought* of the pomegranates, and of the figs. 24

The place was called the brook Eshcol, because of the cluster of grapes which the children of Israel cut down from thence. 25 And they returned from searching of the land after forty days.

We have here a short account of the survey which the spies made of the promised land. 1. They went quite through it, from Zin in the south, to Rehob, near Hamath, in the north, *v.* 21. See *ch.* xxxiv. 3, 8. It is probable that they did not go altogether in a body, lest they should be suspected and taken up, which there would be the more danger of if the Canaanites knew (and one would think they could not but know) how near the Israelites were to them; but they divided themselves into several companies, and so passed unsuspected, as way-faring men. 2. They took particular notice of Hebron (*v.* 22), probably because near there was the field of Machpelah, where the patriarchs were buried (Gen. xxiii. 2), whose dead bodies did, as it were, keep possession of that land for their posterity. To this sepulchre they made a particular visit, and found the adjoining city in the possession of the sons of Anak, who are here named. In that place where they expected the greatest encouragements they met with the greatest discouragements. Where the bodies of their ancestors kept possession for them the giants kept possession against them. *They ascended by the south, and came to Hebron,* that is, " Caleb," say the Jews, " in particular," for to his being there we find express reference, Josh. xiv. 9, 12, 13. But that others of the spies were there too appears by their description of the Anakim, *v.* 33. 3. They brought a bunch of grapes with them, and some other of the fruits of the land, as a proof of the extraordinary goodness of the country. Probably they furnished themselves with these fruits when they were leaving the country and returning. The cluster of grapes was so large and so heavy that they hung it upon a bar, and carried it between two of them, *v.* 23, 24. The place whence they took it was, from this circumstance, called the *valley of the cluster,* that famous cluster which was to Israel both the earnest and the specimen of all the fruits of Canaan. Such are the present comforts which we have in communion with God, foretastes of the fulness of joy we expect in the heavenly Canaan. We may see by them what heaven is.

26 And they went and came to Moses, and to Aaron, and to all the congregation of the children of Israel, unto the wilderness of Paran, to Kadesh; and brought back word unto them, and unto all the congregation, and showed them the fruit of the land. 27 And they told him, and said, We came unto the land whither thou

sentest us, and surely it floweth with milk and honey; and this *is* the fruit of it. 28 Nevertheless the people *be* strong that dwell in the land, and the cities *are* walled, *and* very great: and moreover we saw the children of Anak there. 29 The Amalekites dwell in the land of the south: and the Hittites, and the Jebusites, and the Amorites, dwell in the mountains: and the Canaanites dwell by the sea, and by the coast of Jordan. 30 And Caleb stilled the people before Moses, and said, Let us go up at once, and possess it; for we are well able to overcome it. 31 But the men that went up with him said, We be not able to go up against the people; for they *are* stronger than we. 32 And they brought up an evil report of the land which they had searched unto the children of Israel, saying, The land, through which we have gone to search it, *is* a land that eateth up the inhabitants thereof; and all the people that we saw in it *are* men of a great stature. 33 And there we saw the giants, the sons of Anak, *which come* of the giants: and we were in our own sight as grasshoppers, and so we were in their sight.

It is a wonder how the people of Israel had patience to stay forty days for the return of their spies, when they were just ready to enter Canaan, under all the assurances of success they could have from the divine power, and a constant series of miracles that had hitherto attended them; but they distrusted God's power and promise, and were willing to be held in suspense by their own counsels, rather than be brought to a certainty by God's covenant. How much do we stand in our own light by our unbelief! Well, at length the messengers return, but they agree not in their report.

I. The major part discourage the people from going forward to Canaan; and justly are the Israelites left to this temptation, for putting so much confidence in the judgment of men, when they had the word of God to trust to. It is a righteous thing with God to give those up to strong delusions who will not receive his truth in the love of it.

1. Observe their report. (1.) They could not deny but that the land of Canaan was a very fruitful land; the bunch of grapes they brought with them was an ocular demonstration of it, *v.* 27. God had promised them a land flowing with milk and honey, and the evil spies themselves own that it is such a

land. Thus even out of the mouth of adversaries will God be glorified and the truth of his promise attested. And yet afterwards they contradict themselves, when they say (*v.* 32), *It is a land that eateth up the inhabitants thereof;* as if, though it had milk, and honey, and grapes, yet it wanted other necessary provisions; some think that there was a great plague in the country at the time they surveyed it, which they ought to have imputed to the wisdom of the divine Providence, which thus lessened the numbers of their enemies, to facilitate their conquests; but they invidiously imputed it to the unwholesomeness of the air, and thence took occasion to disparage the country. For this unreasonable fear of a plague in Canaan, they were justly cut off immediately by a *plague in the wilderness,* ch. xiv. 37. But, (2.) They represented the conquest of it as altogether impracticable, and that it was to no purpose to attempt it. The people are strong (*v.* 28), men of a *great stature* (*v.* 32), *stronger than we,* *v.* 31. The cities are represented as impregnable fortresses: they *are walled* and *very great, v.* 28. But nothing served their ill purpose more than a description of the giants, on whom they lay a great stress: *We saw the children of Anak there* (*v.* 28), and again, we *saw the giants,* those men of a prodigious size, the *sons of Anak,* who *come of the giants, v.* 33. They spoke as if they were ready to tremble at the mention of them, as they had done at the sight of them. " O these tremendous giants! when we were near them, *we were in our own sight as grasshoppers,* not only little and weak, but trembling and daunted." Compare Job xxxix. 20, *Canst thou make him afraid as a grasshopper?* " Nay, and *so we were in their sight;* they looked upon us with as much scorn and disdain as we did upon them with fear and trembling." So that upon the whole matter they gave it in as their judgment, *We are not able to go up against them* (*v* 31), and therefore must think of taking some other course.

2. Now, even if they had been to judge only by human probabilities, they could not have been excused from the imputation of cowardice. Were not the hosts of Israel very numerous? 600,000 effective men, well marshalled and modelled, closely embodied, and entirely united in interest and affection, constituted as formidable an army as perhaps was ever brought into the field; many a less has done more than perhaps the conquering of Canaan was, witness Alexander's army. Moses, their commander-in-chief, was wise and brave; and if the people had put on resolution, and behaved themselves valiantly, what could have stood before them? It is true the Canaanites were strong, but they were dispersed (*v.* 29): *Some dwell in the south and others in the mountains;* so that by reason of their distance they could not soon get together, and by reason of their

divided interests they could not long keep together, to oppose Israel. The country being plentiful would subsist an army, and, though the cities were walled, if they could beat them in the field the strong-holds would fall of course into their hands. And, lastly, as for the giants, their overgrown stature would but make them the better mark, and the bulkiest men have not always the best mettle.

3. But, though they deserved to be posted for cowards, this was not the worst, the scripture brands them for unbelievers. It was not any human probabilities they were required to depend upon, but, (1.) They had the manifest and sensible tokens of God's presence with them, and the engagement of his power for them. The Canaanites were stronger than Israel; suppose they were, but were they stronger than the God of Israel? We are not able to deal with them, but is not God Almighty able? Have we not him in the midst of us? Does not he go before us? And is any thing too hard for him? Were we as grasshoppers before the giants, and are not they less than grasshoppers before God? Their cities are walled against us, but can they be walled against heaven? Besides this, (2.) They had had very great experience of the length and strength of God's arm, lifted up and made bare on their behalf. Were not the Egyptians as much stronger than they as the Canaanites were? And yet, without a sword drawn by Israel or a stroke struck, the chariots and horsemen of Egypt were quite routed and ruined; the Amalekites took them at great disadvantages, and yet they were discomfited. Miracles were at this time their daily bread; were there nothing else, an army so well victualled as theirs was, so constantly, so plentifully, and all on free cost, would have a mighty advantage against any other force. Nay, (3.) They had particular promises made them of victory and success in their wars against the Canaanites. God had given Abraham all possible assurances that he would put his seed into possession of that land, Gen. xv. 18; xvii. 8. He had expressly promised them by Moses that he would *drive out the Canaanites from before them* (Exod. xxxiii. 2), and that he would do it *by little and little*, Exod. xxiii. 30. And, after all this, for them to say, *We are not able to go up against them*, was in effect to say, "God himself is not able to make his words good." It was in effect to give him the lie, and to tell him he had undertaken more than he could perform. We have a short account of their sin, with which they infected the whole congregation, Ps. cvi. 24. They *despised the land, they believed not his word*. Though, upon search, they had found it as good as he had said, *a land flowing with milk and honey*, yet they would not believe it as sure as he had said, but despaired of having it, though eternal truth itself had

engaged it to them. And now this is the representation of the evil spies.

II. Caleb encouraged them to go forward, though he was seconded by Joshua only (v. 30): *Caleb stilled the people*, whom he saw already put into a ferment, even *before Moses* himself, whose shining face could not daunt them, when they began to grow unruly. *Caleb* signifies *all heart*, and he answered his name, was hearty himself, and would have made the people so if they would have hearkened to him. If Joshua had begun to stem the tide, he would have been suspected of partiality to Moses, whose minister he was; and therefore he prudently left it to Caleb's management at first, who was of the tribe of Judah, the leading tribe, and therefore the fittest to be heard. Caleb had seen and observed the strength of the inhabitants as much as his fellows, and upon the whole matter, 1. He speaks very confidently of success: *We are well able to overcome them*, as strong as they are. 2. He animates the people to go on, and, his lot lying in the van, he speaks as one resolved to lead them on with bravery: " *Let us go up at once*, one bold step, one bold stroke more, will do our business; it is all our own if we have but courage to make it so: *Let us go up and possess it.*" He does not say, "Let us go up and conquer it;" he looks upon that to be as good as done already; but, "Let us go up and possess it; there is nothing to be done but to enter, and take the possession which God our great Lord is ready to give us." Note, *The righteous are bold as a lion*. Difficulties that lie in the way of salvation dwindle and vanish before a lively active faith in the power and promise of God. *All things are possible*, if they be but promised, to him that believes.

CHAP. XIV.

This chapter gives us an account of that fatal quarrel between God and Israel upon which, for their murmuring and unbelief, he swore in his wrath that they should not enter into his rest. Here is, I. The mutiny and rebellion of Israel against God, upon the report of the evil spies, ver. 1—4. II. The fruitless endeavour of Moses and Aaron, Caleb and Joshua, to still the tumult, ver. 5—10. III. Their utter ruin justly threatened by an offended God, ver. 11, 12. IV. The humble intercession of Moses for them, ver. 13—19. V. A mitigation of the sentence in answer to the prayer of Moses; they shall not all be cut off, but the decree goes forth ratified with an oath, published to the people, again and again repeated, that this whole congregation should perish in the wilderness, and none of them enter Canaan but Caleb and Joshua only, ver. 20—35. VI. The present death of the evil spies, ver. 36—39. VII. The rebuke given to those who attempted to go forward notwithstanding, ver. 40—45. And this is written for our admonition, that we "fall not after the same example of unbelief."

AND all the congregation lifted up their voice, and cried; and the people wept that night. 2 And all the children of Israel murmured against Moses and against Aaron: and the whole congregation said unto them, Would God that we had died in the land of Egypt! or would God we had died in the wilderness! 3 And wherefore hath the LORD brought us unto this land, to fall by the sword, that our wives and our children should be a prey? were it not better for us to return into Egypt? 4 And they said one to another, Let us make a captain, and let us return into Egypt.

Here we see what mischief the evil spies made by their unfair representation. We may suppose that these twelve that were impanelled to enquire concerning Canaan had talked it over among themselves before they brought it in their report in public; and Caleb and Joshua, it is likely, had done their utmost to bring the rest over to be of their mind, and if they would but have agreed that Caleb, according to his post, should have spoken for them all, as their foreman, all had been well; but the evil spies, it should seem, wilfully designed to raise this mutiny, purely in opposition to Moses and Aaron, though they could not propose any advantage to themselves by it, unless they hoped to be captains and commanders of the retreat into Egypt they were now meditating. But what came of it? Here in these verses we find those whom they studied to humour put into a vexation, and, before the end of the chapter, brought to ruin. Observe,

I. How the people fretted themselves: *They lifted up their voices and cried* (v. 1); giving credit to the report of the spies rather than to the word of God, and imagining their condition desperate, they laid the reins on the neck of their passions, and could keep no manner of temper. Like foolish froward children, they fall a crying, yet know not what they cry for. It would have been time enough to cry out when the enemy had beaten up their quarters, and they had seen the sons of Anak at the gate of their camp; but those that cried when nothing hurt them deserved to have something given them to cry for. And, as if all had been already gone, they sat down and *wept that night.* Note, Unbelief, or distrust of God, is a sin that is its own punishment. Those that do not trust God are continually vexing themselves. The world's mourners are more than God's, and the *sorrow of the world worketh death.*

II. How they flew in the face of their governors—*murmured against Moses and Aaron,* and in them reproached the Lord, v. 2, 3. The congregation of elders began the discontent (v. 1), but the contagion soon spread through the whole camp, for *the children of Israel murmured.* Jealousies and discontents spread like wildfire among the unthinking multitude, who are easily taught to *despise dominions, and to speak evil of dignities.* 1. They look back with a causeless discontent. They wish that they had died in Egypt with the first-born that were slain there, or in the wilderness with those that lately died of the plague for lusting. See the prodigious madness of unbridled passions, which make men prodigal even of that which nature accounts most dear, life itself. Never were so many

months spent so pleasantly as these which they had spent since they came out of Egypt, loaded with honours, compassed with favours, and continually entertained with something or other that was surprising; and yet, as if all these things had not made it worth their while to live, they wished they had died in Egypt. And such a light opinion they had of God's tremendous judgments executed on their neighbours for their sin that they wished they had shared with them in their plagues, rather than run the hazard of making a descent upon Canaan. They wish rather to die criminals under God's justice than live conquerors in his favour. Some read it, *O that we had died in Egypt, or in this wilderness! O that we might die!* They wish to die, for fear of dying; and have not sense enough to reason as the poor lepers, when rather than die upon the spot they ventured into an enemy's camp, *If they kill us, we shall but die,* 2 Kings vii. 4. How base were the spirits of these degenerate Israelites, who, rather than die (if it come to the worst) like soldiers in the bed of honour, with their swords in their hands, desire to die like rotten sheep in the wilderness. 2. They look forward with a groundless despair, taking it for granted (v. 3) that if they went on they must fall by the sword, and pretend to lay the cause of their fear upon the great care they had for their wives and children, who, they conclude, will be a prey to the Canaanites. And here is a most wicked blasphemous reflection upon God himself, as if he had brought them hither on purpose that they might fall by the sword, and that their wives and children, those poor innocents, should be a prey. Thus do they, in effect, charge that God who is love itself with the worst of malice, and eternal Truth with the basest hypocrisy, suggesting that all the kind things he had said to them, and done for them, hitherto, were intended only to decoy them into a snare, and to cover a secret design carried on all along to ruin them. Daring impudence! But what will not that tongue speak against heaven that is set on fire of hell? The devil keeps up his interest in the hearts of men by insinuating to them ill thoughts of God, as if he desired the death of sinners, and delighted in the hardships and sufferings of his own servants, whereas he knows his thoughts to us-ward (whether we know them so or no) to be *thoughts of good, and not of evil,* Jer. xxix. 11.

III. How they came at last to this desperate resolve, that, instead of going forward to Canaan, they would go back again to Egypt. The motion is first made by way of query only (v. 3): *Were it not better for us to return into Egypt?* But the ferment being high, and the spirits of the people being disposed to entertain any thing that was perverse, it soon ripened to a resolution, without a debate (v. 4): *Let us make a captain and return to Egypt;* and it is lamented long after (Neh ix. 17) that *in their rebellion they ap-*

pointed a captain to return to their bondage; for they knew Moses would not be their captain in this retreat. Now, 1. It was the greatest folly in the world to wish themselves in Egypt, or to think that if they were there it would be better with them than it was. If they durst not go forward to Canaan, yet better be as they were than go back to Egypt. What did they want? What had they to complain of? They had plenty, and peace, and rest, were under a good government, had good company, had the tokens of God's presence with them, and enough to make them easy even in the wilderness, if they had but hearts to be content. But whither were they thus eager to go to better themselves? To Egypt! Had they so soon forgotten the sore bondage they were in there? Would they be again under the tyranny of their taskmasters, and at the drudgery of making brick? And, after all the plagues which Egypt had suffered for their sakes, could they expect any better treatment there than they had formerly, and not rather much worse? In how little time (not a year and a half) have they forgotten all the sighs of their bondage, and all the songs of their deliverance! Like brute-beasts, they mind only what is present, and their memories, with the other powers of reason, are sacrificed to their passions. See Ps. cvi. 7. We find it threatened (Deut. xxviii. 68), as the completing of their misery, that they should be brought into Egypt again, and yet this is what they here wish for. Sinners are enemies to themselves; and those that walk not in God's counsels consult their own mischief and ruin. 2. It was a most senseless ridiculous thing to talk of returning thither through the wilderness. Could they expect that God's cloud would lead them or his manna attend them? And, if they did not, the thousands of Israel must unavoidably be lost and perish in the wilderness. Suppose the difficulties of conquering Canaan were as great as they imagined, those of returning to Egypt were much greater. In this let us see, (1.) The folly of discontent and impatience under the crosses of our outward condition. We are uneasy at that which is, complain of our place and lot, and we would shift; but is there any place or condition in this world that has not something in it to make us uneasy if we are disposed to be so? The way to better our condition is to get our spirits into a better frame; and instead of asking, "Were it not better to go to Egypt?" ask, "Were it not better to be content, and make the best of that which is?" (2.) The folly of apostasy from the ways of God. Heaven is the Canaan set before us, a land flowing with milk and honey; those that bring up ever so ill a report of it cannot but say that it is indeed a good land, only it is hard to get to it. Strict and serious godliness is looked upon as an impracticable thing, and this deters many who began well from going on; rather than undergo the imaginary hardships of a religious life, they run themselves upon the certain fatal consequences of a sinful course; and so they transcribe the folly of Israel, who, when they were within a step of Canaan, would make a captain, and return to Egypt.

5 Then Moses and Aaron fell on their faces before all the assembly of the congregation of the children of Israel. 6 And Joshua the son of Nun, and Caleb the son of Jephunneh, *which were* of them that searched the land, rent their clothes: 7 And they spake unto all the company of the children of Israel, saying, The land, which we passed through to search it, *is* an exceeding good land. 8 If the Lord delight in us, then he will bring us into this land, and give it us; a land which floweth with milk and honey. 9 Only rebel not ye against the Lord, neither fear ye the people of the land; for they *are* bread for us: their defence is departed from them, and the Lord *is* with us: fear them not. 10 But all the congregation bade stone them with stones. And the glory of the Lord appeared in the tabernacle of the congregation before all the children of Israel.

The friends of Israel here interpose to save them if possible from ruining themselves, but in vain. The physicians of their state would have healed them, but they would not be healed; their watchmen gave them warning, but they would not take the warning, and so their blood is upon their own heads.

I. The best endeavours were used to still the tumult, and, if now at last they would have understood the things that belonged to their peace, all the following mischief would have been prevented.

1. Moses and Aaron did their part, *v.* 5. Though it was against them that they murmured (*v.* 2), yet they bravely overlooked the affront and injury done them, and approved themselves faithful friends to those who were outrageous enemies to them. The clamour and noise of the people were so great that Moses and Aaron could not be heard; should they order any of their servants to proclaim silence, the angry multitude would perhaps be the more clamorous; and therefore, to gain audience in the sight of all the assembly, they fell on their faces, thus expressing, (1.) Their humble prayers to God to still the noise of this sea, the noise of its waves, even the tumult of the people. (2.) The great trouble and concern of their own spirits. They fell down as men astonished and even thunder-struck, amazed to see a people throw away

their own mercies: to see those so ill-humoured who were so well taught. And, (3.) Their great earnestness with the people to cease their murmurings; they hoped to work upon them by this humble posture, and to prevail with them not to persist in their rebellion; Moses and Aaron beseech them, as though by them God himself did beseech them, to be reconciled unto God. What they said to the people Moses relates in the repetition of this story. Deut. i. 29, 30, *Be not afraid; the Lord your God shall fight for you.* Note, Those that are zealous friends to precious souls will stoop to any thing for their salvation. Moses and Aaron, notwithstanding the posts of honour they are in, prostrate themselves to the people to beg of them not to ruin themselves.

2. Caleb and Joshua did their part: they rent their clothes in a holy indignation at the sin of the people, and a holy dread of the wrath of God, which they saw ready to break out against them. It was the greater trouble to these good men because the tumult was occasioned by those spies with whom they had been joined in commission; and therefore they thought themselves obliged to do what they could to still the storm which their fellows had raised. No reasoning could be more pertinent and pathetic than theirs was (*v.* 7—9), and they spoke as with authority.

(1.) They assured them of the goodness of the land they had surveyed, and that it was really worth venturing for, and not a land that *ate up the inhabitants*, as the evil spies had represented it. It is an *exceedingly good land* (*v.* 7); it is *very, very good*, so the word is; so that they had no reason to *despise this pleasant land.* Note, If men were but thoroughly convinced of the desirableness of the gains of religion, they would not stick at the services of it.

(2.) They made nothing of the difficulties that seemed to lie in the way of their gaining the possession of it: "*Fear not the people of the land, v.* 9. Whatever formidable ideas have been given you of them, the lion is not so fierce as he is painted. *They are bread for us*," that is, "they are set before us rather to be fed upon than to be fought with, so easily, so pleasantly, and with so much advantage to ourselves shall we master them." Pharaoh is said to have been given them for meat (Ps. lxxiv. 14), and the Canaanites will be so too. They show that, whatever was suggested to the contrary, the advantage was clear on Israel's side. For, [1.] Though the Canaanites dwell in walled cities, they are naked: *Their defence has departed from them;* that common providence which preserves the rights of nations has abandoned them, and will be no shelter nor protection to them. The other spies took notice of their strength, but these of their wickedness, and thence inferred that God had forsaken them, and therefore *their defence had departed.* No people can be safe when they have provoked

God to leave them. [2.] Though Israel dwell in tents they are fortified: *The Lord is with us*, and his name is a strong tower; *fear them not.* Note, While we have the presence of God with us, we need not fear the most powerful force against us.

(3.) They showed them plainly that all the danger they were in was from their own discontents, and that they would succeed against all their enemies if they did not make God their enemy. On this point alone the cause would turn (*v.* 8): "*If the Lord delight in us*, as certainly he does, and will if we do not provoke him, *he will bring us into this good land;* we shall without fail get it in possession by his favour, and the light of his countenance (Ps. xliv. 3), if we do not forfeit his favour and by our own follies turn away our own mercies." It has come to this issue (*v.* 9): *Only rebel not you against the Lord.* Note, Nothing can ruin sinners but their own rebellion. If God leave them, it is because they drive him from them; and they die because they will die. None are excluded the heavenly Canaan but those that exclude themselves. And, now, could the case have been made more plain? could it have been urged more closely? But what was the effect?

II. It was all to no purpose; they were deaf to this fair reasoning; nay, they were exasperated by it, and grew more outrageous: *All the congregation bade stone them with stones, v.* 10. The rulers of the congregation, and the great men (so bishop Patrick), ordered the common people to fall upon them, and knock their brains out. Their case was sad indeed when their leaders thus *caused them to err.* Note, It is common for those whose hearts are *fully set in them to do evil* to rage at those who give them good counsel. Those who hate to be reformed hate those that would reform them, and count them their enemies because they tell them the truth. Thus early did Israel begin to misuse the prophets, and *stone those that were sent to them*, and it was this that filled the measure of their sin, Matt. xxiii. 37. *Stone them with stones!* Why, what evil have they done? No crime can be laid to their charge; but the truth is *these two witnesses tormented those* that were obstinate in their infidelity, Rev. xi. 10. Caleb and Joshua had but just said, *The Lord is with us; fear them not* (*v.* 9): and, if Israel will not apply those encouraging words to their own fears, those that uttered them know how to encourage themselves with them against this enraged multitude that spoke of stoning them, as David in a like cause, 1 Sam. xxx. 6. Those that cannot prevail to edify others with their counsels and comforts should endeavour at least to edify themselves. Caleb and Joshua knew they appeared for God and his glory, and therefore doubted not but God would appear for them and their safety. And they were not disappointed, for immediately *the glory of the Lord appeared*, to the terror and confusion of those that were for stoning the servants of God. When they reflected upon God (*v.* 3), his glory appeared not to silence their blasphemies; but, when they threatened Caleb and Joshua, they touched the apple of his eye, and his glory appeared immediately. Note, Those who faithfully expose themselves for God are sure to be taken under his special protection, and shall be hidden from the rage of men, either under heaven or in heaven.

11 And the Lord said unto Moses, How long will this people provoke me? and how long will it be ere they believe me, for all the signs which I have showed among them? 12 I will smite them with the pestilence, and disinherit them, and will make of thee a greater nation and mightier than they. 13 And Moses said unto the Lord, Then the Egyptians shall hear *it,* (for thou broughtest up this people in thy might from among them;) 14 And they will tell *it* to the inhabitants of this land: *for* they have heard that thou Lord *art* among this people, that thou Lord art seen face to face, and *that* thy cloud standeth over them, and *that* thou goest before them, by day time in a pillar of a cloud, and in a pillar of fire by night. 15 Now *if* thou shalt kill *all* this people as one man, then the nations which have heard the fame of thee will speak, saying, 16 Because the Lord was not able to bring this people into the land which he sware unto them, therefore he hath slain them in the wilderness. 17 And now, I beseech thee, let the power of my Lord be great, according as thou hast spoken, saying, 18 The Lord *is* longsuffering, and of great mercy, forgiving iniquity and transgression, and by no means clearing *the guilty,* visiting the iniquity of the fathers upon the children unto the third and fourth *generation.* 19 Pardon, I beseech thee, the iniquity of this people according unto the greatness of thy mercy, and as thou hast forgiven this people, from Egypt even until now.

Here is, I. The righteous sentence which God gave against Israel for their murmuring and unbelief, which, though afterwards mitigated, showed what was the desert of their sin and the demand of injured justice, and

what would have been done if Moses had not interposed. When the glory of the Lord *appeared in the tabernacle* we may suppose that Moses took it for a call to him immediately to come and attend there, as before the tabernacle was erected he went up to the mount in a similar case, Exod. xxxii. 30. Thus, while the people were studying to disgrace him, God publicly put honour upon him, as the man of his counsel. Now here we are told what God said to him there.

1. He showed him the great evil of the people's sin, *v.* 11. What passed between God and Israel went through the hands of Moses: when they were displeased with God they told Moses of it (*v.* 2); when God was displeased with them he told Moses too, *revealing his secret to his servant the prophet,* Amos iii. 7. Two things God justly complains of to Moses:—(1.) Their sin. They *provoke me,* or (as the word signifies) they *reject, reproach, despise* me, for *they will not believe me.* This was the bitter root which bore the gall and wormwood. It was their unbelief that made this a day of provocation in the wilderness, Heb. iii. 8. Note, Distrust of God, of his power and promise, is itself a very great provocation, and at the bottom of many other provocations. Unbelief is a great sin (1 John v. 10), and a root sin, Heb. iii. 12. (2.) Their continuance in it: *How long will they do so?* Note, The God of heaven keeps an account how long sinners persist in their provocations; and the longer they persist the more he is displeased. The aggravations of their sin were, [1.] Their relation to God: *This people,* a peculiar people, a professing people. The nearer any are to God in name and profession, the more he is provoked by their sins, especially their unbelief. [2.] The experience they had had of God's power and goodness, in *all the signs* which he *had shown among them,* by which, one would think, he had effectually obliged them to trust him and follow him. The more God has done for us the greater is the provocation if we distrust him.

2. He showed him the sentence which justice passed upon them for it, *v.* 12. "What remains now but that I should make a full end of them? It will soon be done. *I will smite them with the pestilence,* not leave a man of them alive, but wholly blot out their name and race, and so disinherit them, and be no more troubled with them. *Ah, I will ease me of my adversaries.* They wish to die; and let them die, and neither root nor branch be left of them. Such rebellious children deserve to be disinherited." And if it be asked, "What will become of God's covenant with Abraham then?" here is an answer, "It shall be preserved in the family of Moses: *I will make of thee a greater nation.*" Thus, (1.) God would try Moses, whether he still continued that affection for Israel which he formerly expressed upon a

625

like occasion, in preferring their interests before the advancement of his own family; and it is proved that Moses was still of the same public spirit, and could not bear the thought of raising his own name upon the ruin of the name of Israel. (2.) God would teach us that he will not be a loser by the ruin of sinners. If Adam and Eve had been cut off and disinherited, he could have made another Adam and another Eve, and have glorified his mercy in them, as here he could have glorified his mercy in Moses, though Israel had been ruined.

II. The humble intercession Moses made for them. Their sin had made a fatal breach in the wall of their defence, at which destruction would certainly have entered if Moses had not seasonably stepped in and made it good. Here he was a type of Christ, who interceded for his persecutors, and *prayed for those* that *despitefully used* him, leaving us an example to his own rule, Matt. v. 44.

1. The prayer of his petition is, in one word, *Pardon, I beseech thee, the iniquity of this people* (v. 19), that is, "Do not bring upon them the ruin they deserve." This was Christ's prayer for those that crucified him, *Father forgive them.* The pardon of a national sin, as such, consists in the turning away of the national punishment; and that is it for which Moses is here so earnest.

2. The pleas are many, and strongly urged.

(1.) He insists most upon the plea that is taken from the glory of God, v. 13—16. With this he begins, and somewhat abruptly, taking occasion from that dreadful word, *I will disinherit them. Lord* (says he), *then the Egyptians shall hear it.* God's honour lay nearer to his heart than any interests of his own. Observe how he *orders this cause* before God. He pleads, [1.] That the eyes both of Egypt and Canaan were upon them, and great expectations were raised concerning them. They could not but have heard *that thou, Lord, art among this people,* v. 14. The neighbouring countries rang of it, how much this people were the particular care of heaven, so as never any people under the sun were. [2.] That if they should be cut off great notice would be taken of it. "The *Egyptians will hear it* (v. 13), for they have their spies among us, and they will *tell it to the inhabitants of the land*" (v. 14); for there was great correspondence between Egypt and Canaan, although not by the way of this wilderness. "If this people that have made so great a noise be all consumed, if their mighty pretensions come to nothing, and their light go out in a snuff, it will be told with pleasure in Gath, and published in the streets of Askelon; and what construction will the heathen put upon it? It will be impossible to make them understand it as an act of God's justice, and as such redounding to God's honour; *brutish men know not this* (Ps. xcii. 6): but they will impute it to the failing of God's power, and so turn it to his reproach, v 16.

626

They will say, He slew them in the wilderness because he was not able to bring them to Canaan, his arm being shortened, and his stock of miracles being spent. Now, Lord, let not one attribute be glorified at the expense of another; rather let mercy *rejoice against judgment* than that almighty power should be impeached." Note, The best pleas in prayer are those that are taken from God's honour; for they agree with the first petition of the Lord's Prayer, *Hallowed be thy name. Do not disgrace the throne of thy glory.* God pleads it with himself (Deut. xxxii. 27), *I feared the wrath of the enemy;* and we should use it as an argument with ourselves to walk so in every thing as to give no occasion to the enemies of the Lord to blaspheme, 1 Tim. vi. 1.

(2.) He pleads God's proclamation of his name at Horeb (v. 17, 18): *Let the power of the Lord be great.* Power is here put for pardoning mercy; it is his power over his own anger. If he should destroy them, God's power would be questioned; if he should continue and complete their salvation, notwithstanding the difficulties that arose, not only from the strength of their enemies, but from their own provocations, this would greatly magnify the divine power: what cannot he do who could make so weak a people conquerors and such an unworthy people favourites? The more danger there is of others reproaching God's power the more desirous we should be to see it glorified. To enforce this petition, he refers to the word which God had spoken: *The Lord is long-suffering and of great mercy.* God's goodness had there been spoken of as his glory; God gloried in it, Exod. xxxiv. 6, 7. Now here he prays that upon this occasion he would glorify it. Note, We must take our encouragement in prayer from the word of God, upon which he has *caused us to hope,* Ps. cxix. 49. "Lord, be and do *according as thou hast spoken*; for hast thou spoken, and wilt thou not make it good?" Three things God had solemnly made a declaration of, which Moses here fastens upon, and improves for the enforcing of his petition :—[1.] The goodness of God's nature in general, that he is long-suffering, or slow to anger, and of great mercy; not soon provoked, but tender and compassionate towards offenders. [2.] His readiness in particular to pardon sin: *Forgiving iniquity and transgression,* sins of all sorts. [3.] His unwillingness to proceed to extremity, even when he does punish. For in this sense the following words may be read: *That will by no means make quite desolate, in visiting the iniquity of the fathers upon the children.* God had indeed said in the second commandment that he would thus visit, but here he promises not to make a full end of families, churches, and nations, at once; and so it is very applicable to this occasion, for Moses cannot beg that God would not at all punish this sin (it would be too great an encouragement to rebellion if he should set no mark of his displeasure upon it), but that he would not *kill all this people as one man*, v. 15. He does not ask that they may not be corrected, but that they may not be disinherited. And this proclamation of God's name was the more apposite to his purpose because it was made upon occasion of the pardoning of their sin in making the golden calf. This sin which they had now fallen into was bad enough, but it was not idolatry.

(3.) He pleads past experience: *As thou hast forgiven this people from Egypt*, v. 19. This seemed to make against him. Why should those be forgiven any more who, after they had been so often forgiven, revolted yet more and more, and seemed hardened and encouraged in their rebellion by the lenity and patience of their God, and the frequent pardons they had obtained? Among men it would have been thought impolitic to take notice of such a circumstance in a request of this nature, as it might operate to the prejudice of the petitioner: but, as in other things so in pardoning sin, God's thoughts and ways are infinitely above ours, Isa. lv. 9. Moses looks upon it as a good plea, *Lord, forgive, as thou hast forgiven.* It will be no more a reproach to thy justice, nor any less the praise of thy mercy, to forgive now, than it has been formerly. Therefore the *sons of Jacob are not consumed*, because they have to do with a *God that changes not*, Mal. iii. 6.

20 And the LORD said, I have pardoned according to thy word: 21 But *as* truly *as* I live, all the earth shall be filled with the glory of the LORD. 22 Because all those men which have seen my glory, and my miracles, which I did in Egypt and in the wilderness, have tempted me now these ten times, and have not hearkened to my voice; 23 Surely they shall not see the land which I sware unto their fathers, neither shall any of them that provoked me see it: 24 But my servant Caleb, because he had another spirit with him, and hath followed me fully, him will I bring into the land whereinto he went; and his seed shall possess it. 25 (Now the Amalekites and the Canaanites dwelt in the valley.) To morrow turn you, and get you into the wilderness by the way of the Red sea. 26 And the LORD spake unto Moses and unto Aaron, saying, 27 How long *shall I bear with* this evil congregation, which murmur against me? I have heard the murmurings of the children of Israel, which they murmur against

me. 28 Say unto them, *As truly as* I live, saith the LORD, as ye have spoken in mine ears, so will I do to you: 29 Your carcases shall fall in this wilderness; and all that were numbered of you, according to your whole number, from twenty years old and upward, which have murmured against me, 30 Doubtless ye shall not come into the land, *concerning* which I sware to make you dwell therein, save Caleb the son of Jephunneh, and Joshua the son of Nun. 31 But your little ones, which ye said should be a prey, them will I bring in, and they shall know the land which ye have despised. 32 But *as for* you, your carcases, they shall fall in this wilderness. 33 And your children shall wander in the wilderness forty years, and bear your whoredoms, until your carcases be wasted in the wilderness. 34 After the number of the days in which ye searched the land, *even* forty days, each day for a year, shall ye bear your iniquities, *even* forty years, and ye shall know my breach of promise. 35 I the LORD have said, I will surely do it unto all this evil congregation, that are gathered together against me: in this wilderness they shall be consumed, and there they shall die.

We have here God's answer to the prayer of Moses, which sings both of mercy and judgment. It is given privately to Moses (*v.* 20—25), and then directed to be made public to the people, *v.* 26—35. The frequent repetitions of the same things in it speak these resolves to be unalterable. Let us see the particulars.

I. The extremity of the sentence is receded from (*v.* 20): "*I have pardoned*, so as not to cut them all off at once, and disinherit them." See the power of prayer, and the delight God takes in putting an honour upon it. He designed a pardon, but Moses shall have the praise of obtaining it by prayer: it shall be done *according to thy word;* thus, as a prince, he has power with God, and prevails. See what countenance and encouragement God gives to our intercessions for others, that we may be public-spirited in prayer. Here is a whole nation rescued from ruin by the effectual fervent prayer of one righteous man. See how ready God is to forgive sin, and how easy to be entreated: *Pardon*, says Moses (*v.* 19); *I have pardoned*, says God, *v.* 20. David found him thus swift to show mercy, Ps. xxxii. 5. *He deals not with us after our sins*, Ps. ciii. 10.

II. The glorifying of God's name is, in the general, resolved upon, *v.* 21. It is said, it is sworn, *All the earth shall be filled with the glory of the Lord.* Moses in his prayer had shown a great concern for the glory of God. "Let me alone," says God, "to secure that effectually, and to advance it, by this dispensation." All the world shall see how God hates sin even in his own people, and will reckon for it, and yet how gracious and merciful he is, and how slow to anger. Thus when our Saviour prayed, *Father, glorify thy name*, he was immediately answered, *I have glorified it, and will glorify it yet again*, John xii. 28. Note, Those that sincerely seek God's glory may be sure of what they seek. God having turned this prayer for the glorifying of himself into a promise, we may turn it into praise, in concert with the angels, Isa. vi. 3, *The earth is full of his glory.*

III. The sin of this people which provoked God to proceed against them is here aggravated, *v.* 22, 27. It is not made worse than really it was, but is shown to be exceedingly sinful. It was an evil congregation, each bad, but altogether in congregation very bad. 1. They tempted God—tempted his power, whether he could help them in their straits—his goodness, whether he would—and his faithfulness, whether his promise would be performed. They tempted his justice, whether he would resent their provocations and punish them or no. They dared him, and in effect challenged him, as God does the idols (Isa. xli. 23), to do *good*, or do *evil*. 2. They murmured against him. This is much insisted on, *v.* 27. As they questioned what he would do, so they quarrelled with him for every thing he did or had done, continually fretting and finding fault. It does not appear that they murmured at any of the laws or ordinances that God gave them (though they proved a heavy yoke), but they murmured at the conduct they were under, and the provision made for them. Note, It is much easier to bring ourselves to the external services of religion, and observe all the formalities of devotion, than to live a life of dependence upon, and submission to, the divine Providence in the course of our conversation. 3. They did this after they had seen God's miracles in Egypt and in the wilderness, *v.* 2. They would not believe their own eyes, which were witnesses for God that he was in the midst of them of a truth. 4. They had repeated the provocations ten times, that is, very often: the Jewish writers reckon this exactly the tenth time that the body of the congregation had provoked God. First, at the Red Sea, Exod. xiv. 11. In Marah, Exod. xv. 23, 24. In the wilderness of Sin, Exod. xvi. 2. Twice about manna, Exod. xvi. 20, 27. At Rephidim, Exod. xvii. 1, 2. The golden calf, Exod. xxxii. Then at Taberah. Then at

Kibroth-Hattaavah, *ch.* xi. And so this was the tenth. Note, God keeps an account how often we repeat our provocations, and will sooner or later set them in order before us. 5. They had not hearkened to his voice, though he had again and again admonished them of their sin.

IV. The sentence passed upon them for this sin. 1. That they should not see the promised land (*v.* 23), nor *come into it, v.* 30. *He swore in his wrath that they should not enter into his rest*, Ps. xcv. 11. Note, Disbelief of the promise is a forfeiture of the benefit of it. Those that despise the pleasant land shall be shut out of it. The promise of God should be fulfilled to their posterity, but not to them. 2. That they should immediately *turn back into the wilderness, v.* 25. Their next remove should be a retreat. They must face about, and instead of going forward to Canaan, on the very borders of which they now were, they must withdraw towards the Red Sea again. *To-morrow turn you;* that is, "Very shortly you shall be brought back to that vast howling wilderness which you are so weary of. And it is time to shift for your own safety, for *the Amalekites lie in wait in the valley*, ready to attack you if you march forward." Of them they had been distrustfully afraid (*ch.* xiii. 29), and now with them God justly frightened them. *The fear of the wicked shall come upon him.* 3. That all those who had now grown up to men's estate should die in the wilderness, not all at once, but by degrees. They wished that they might die in the wilderness, and God said *Amen* to their passionate wish, and made their sin their ruin, *snared them* in the *words of their mouth*, and *caused their own tongue to fall upon them*, took them at their word, and determined that their *carcases should fall in the wilderness, v.* 28, 29, and again, *v.* 32, 35. See with what contempt they are spoken of, now that they had by their sin made themselves vile; the mighty men of valour were but carcases, when the Spirit of the Lord had departed from them. They were all as dead men. Their fathers had such a value for Canaan that they desired to have their dead bodies carried thither to be buried, in token of their dependence upon God's promise that they should have that land for a possession: but these, having despised that good land and disbelieved the promise of it, shall not have the honour to be buried in it, but shall have their graves in the wilderness. 4. That in pursuance of this sentence they should wander to and fro in the wilderness, like travellers that have lost themselves, for forty years; that is, so long as to make it full forty years from their coming out of Egypt to their entrance into Canaan, *v.* 33, 34. Thus long they were kept wandering, (1.) To answer the number of the days in which the spies were searching the land. They were content to wait forty days for the testimony of men, because they could not take God's word; and therefore justly are they kept forty years waiting for the performance of God's promise. (2.) That hereby they might be brought to repentance, and find mercy with God in the other world, whatever became of them in this. Now they had time to bethink themselves, and to consider their ways; and the inconveniences of the wilderness would help to humble them and prove them, and *show them what was in their heart,* Deut. viii. 2. Thus long they *bore their iniquities,* feeling the weight of God's wrath in the punishment. They were made to groan under the burden of their own sin that brought it upon them, which was *too heavy for them to bear.* (3.) That they might sensibly feel what a dangerous thing it is for God's covenant-people to break with him: " *You shall know my breach of promise,* both the causes of it, that it is procured by your sin" (for God never leaves any till they first leave him), "and the consequences of it, that it will produce your ruin; you are quite undone when you are thrown out of covenant." (4) That a new generation might in this time be raised up, which could not be done all of a sudden. And the children, being brought up under the tokens of God's displeasure against their fathers, and so *bearing their whoredoms* (that is, the punishment of their sins, especially their idolatry about the golden calf, which God now remembered against them), might take warning not to tread in the steps of their fathers' disobedience. And their wandering so long in the wilderness would make Canaan at last the more welcome to them. It should seem that upon occasion of this sentence Moses penned the ninetieth Psalm, which is very apposite to the present state of Israel, and wherein they are taught to pray that since this sentence could not be reversed it might be sanctified, and they might learn to *apply their hearts unto wisdom.*

V. The mercy that was mixed with this severe sentence.

1. Mercy to Caleb and Joshua, that though they should wander with the rest in the wilderness, yet they, and they only of all that were now above twenty years old, should survive the years of banishment, and live to enter Canaan. Caleb only is spoken of (v. 24), and a particular mark of honour put upon him, both, (1.) In the character given of him: he had *another spirit,* different from the rest of the spies, an *after-spirit,* which furnished him with second thoughts, and he *followed the Lord fully,* kept close to his duty, and went through with it, though deserted and threatened; and, (2.) In the recompence promised to him: *Him will I bring in due time into the land whereinto he went.* Note, [1.] It ought to be the great care and endeavour of every one of us to follow the Lord fully. We must, in a course of obedience to God's will and of service to his honour, follow him universally, without

dividing,—uprightly, without dissembling,—cheerfully, without disputing,—and constantly, without declining; and this is following him fully. [2.] Those that would follow God fully must have another spirit, another from the spirit of the world, and another from what their own spirit has been. They must have the spirit of Caleb. [3.] Those that follow God fully in times of general apostasy God will own and honour by singular preservations in times of general calamity. The heavenly Canaan shall be the everlasting inheritance of those that follow the Lord fully. When Caleb is again mentioned (v. 30) Joshua stands with him, compassed with the same favours and crowned with the same honours, having stood with him in the same services.

2. Mercy to the children even of these rebels. They should have a seed preserved, and Canaan secured to that seed: *Your little ones,* now under twenty years old, *which you,* in your unbelief, *said should be a prey, them will I bring in,* v. 31. They had invidiously charged God with a design to ruin their children, v. 3. But God will let them know that he can put a difference between the guilty and the innocent, and cut them off without touching their children. Thus the promise made to Abraham, though it seemed to fail for a time, was kept from failing for evermore; and, though God chastened their transgressions with a rod, yet his *loving kindness he would not utterly take away.*

36 And the men which Moses sent to search the land, who returned, and made all the congregation to murmur against him, by bringing up a slander upon the land, 37 Even those men that did bring up the evil report upon the land, died by the plague before the LORD. 38 But Joshua the son of Nun, and Caleb the son of Jephunneh, *which were* of the men that went to search the land, lived *still.* 39 And Moses told these sayings unto all the children of Israel: and the people mourned greatly. 40 And they rose up early in the morning, and gat them up into the top of the mountain, saying, Lo, we *be here,* and will go up unto the place which the LORD hath promised: for we have sinned. 41 And Moses said, Wherefore now do ye transgress the commandment of the LORD? but it shall not prosper. 42 Go not up, for the LORD *is* not among you; that ye be not smitten before your enemies. 43 For the Amalekites and the Canaanites *are* there before you, and ye shall fall by

the sword: because ye are turned away from the LORD, therefore the LORD will not be with you. 44 But they presumed to go up unto the hill top: nevertheless the ark of the covenant of the LORD, and Moses, departed not out of the camp. 45 Then the Amalekites came down, and the Canaanites which dwelt in that hill, and smote them, and discomfited them, *even* unto Hormah.

Here is, I. The sudden death of the ten evil spies. While the sentence was passing upon the people, before it was published, they *died of the plague before the Lord, v. 36, 37.* Now,

1. God hereby showed his particular displeasure against those who *sinned and made Israel to sin.* (1.) They sinned themselves, in bringing up a slander upon the land of promise. Note, Those greatly provoke God who misrepresent religion, cast reproach upon it, and raise prejudices in men's minds against it, or give occasion to those to do so who seek occasion. Those that represent the service of God as mean and despicable, melancholy and uncomfortable, hard and impracticable, needless and unprofitable, bring up an *evil report* upon the good land, *pervert the right ways of the Lord,* and in effect give him the lie. (2.) They *made Israel to sin.* They designedly *made all the congregation murmur* against God. Note, Ring-leaders in sin may expect to fall under particular marks of the wrath of God, who will severely reckon for the blood of souls, which is thus spilt.

2. God hereby showed what he could have done with the whole congregation, and gave an earnest of the execution of the sentence now passed upon them. He that thus cut off one of a tribe could have cut off their whole tribes suddenly, and would do it gradually. Note, The remarkable deaths of notorious sinners are earnests of the final perdition of ungodly men, 2 Pet. ii. 5, 6. Thus the wrath of God is revealed, that sinners may hear and fear.

II. The special preservation of Caleb and Joshua: *They lived still, v.* 38. It is probable that all the twelve spies stood together, for the eyes of all Israel were now upon them; and therefore it is taken notice of as very remarkable, and which could not but be affecting to the whole congregation, that when the ten evil spies fell down dead of the plague, a malignant infectious distemper, yet these two that stood among them lived, and were well. God hereby confirmed their testimony, and put those to confusion that spoke of stoning them. He likewise gave them an assurance of their continued preservation in the wilderness, when thousands should fall on their right hand and on their

left, Ps. xci. 7. Death never misses his mark, nor takes any by oversight that were designed for life, though in the midst of those that were to die.

III. The publication of the sentence to all the people, *v.* 36. He told them all what the decree was which had gone forth concerning them, and which could not be reversed, that they must all die in the wilderness, and Canaan must be reserved for the next generation. It was a very great disappointment, we may well think, to Moses himself, who longed to be in Canaan, as well as to all the people; yet he acquiesced, but they wept and mourned greatly. The assurance which Moses had of God's being glorified by this sentence gave him satisfaction, while the consciousness of their own guilt, and their having procured it to themselves, gave them the greatest vexation. They wept for nothing (v. 1), and now they have cause given them to weep; so justly are murmurers made mourners. If they had mourned for the sin when they were faithfully reproved for it (v. 9), the sentence would have been prevented; but now that they mourned for the judgment only their grief came too late, and did them no service; they *found no place for repentance, though they sought it carefully with tears,* Heb. xii. 17. Such mourning as this there is in hell, but the tears will not quench the flames, no, nor cool the tongue.

IV. The foolish fruitless attempts of some of the Israelites to enter Canaan, notwithstanding the sentence.

1. They were now eager to go forward towards Canaan, *v.* 40. They were up early, mustered all their force, got together in a body, and begged of Moses to lead them on against the enemy, and now there is no more talk among them of making a captain to return into Egypt. They confess their fault: *We have sinned;* they profess reformation: *Lo, we be here, and will go up.* They now desire the land which they had despised, and put a confidence in the promise which they had distrusted. Thus when God judges he will overcome, and, first or last, will convince sinners of the evil of all their ungodly deeds, and hard speeches, and force them to recal their own words. But, though God was glorified by this recantation of theirs, they were not benefited by it, because it came too late. The decree had gone forth, the consumption was determined; they did not seek the Lord while he might be found, and now he would not be found. O, if men would but be as earnest for heaven while their day of grace lasts as they will be when it is over, would be as solicitous to provide themselves with oil while the bridegroom tarries as they will be when the bridegroom comes, how well were it for them!

2. Moses utterly disallows their motion, and forbids the expedition they were meditating: *Go not up, v.* 41—43. (1.) He gives them warning of the sin; it is *trans-*

gressing the commandment of the Lord, who had expressly ordered them, when they did move, to move back towards the Red Sea. Note, That which has been duty, in its season, when it comes to be mistimed may be turned into sin. It is true the command he refers to was in the nature of a punishment, but he that has not obeyed the law is obliged to submit to the penalty, for the Lord is our Judge as well as Lawgiver. (2.) He gives them warning of the danger: "*It shall not prosper,* never expect it." Note, It is folly to promise ourselves success in that which we undertake contrary to the mind of God. "*The Canaanites are before you* to attack you, and *the Lord is not among you* to protect you and fight for you, and therefore look to yourselves *that you be not smitten before your enemies.*" Those that are out of the way of their duty are from under God's protection, and go at their peril. It is dangerous going where we cannot expect God should go along with us. Nay, he plainly foresees and foretels their defeat: *You shall fall by the sword* of the Amalekites and Canaanites (who were to have fallen by their sword); *because you are turned away from the Lord,* from following the guidance of his precept and promise, *therefore the Lord will not be with you.* Note, God will certainly leave those that leave him ; and those that are left of him lie exposed to all misery.

3. They venture notwithstanding. Never was people so perverse and so desperately resolved in every thing to walk contrary to God. God bade them go, and they would not ; he forbade them, and they would. Thus is the *carnal mind enmity to God : They presumed to go up unto the hill-top, v.* 44. Here, (1.) They struggled against the sentence of divine justice, and would press on in defiance of it. (2.) They slighted the tokens of God's presence, for they would go though they left Moses and the ark of the covenant behind them. They had distrusted God's strength, and now they presume upon their own without his.

4. The expedition speeds accordingly, *v.* 45. The enemy had posted themselves upon the top of the hill, to make good that pass against the invaders, and, being informed by their scouts of their approach, sallied out upon them, and defeated them, and it is probable that many of the Israelites were killed. Now the sentence began to be executed that their *carcases should fall in the wilderness.* Note, That affair can never end well that begins with sin. The way to obtain peace with our friends, and success against our enemies, is to make God our friend, and keep ourselves in his love. The Jews, like these their ancestors, when they had rejected Christ's righteousness, attempted to establish their own, and it sped as this.

CHAP. XV.

This chapter, which is mostly concerning sacrifice and offering, comes in between the story of two rebellions (one ch. xiv. the other ch. xvi.), to signify that these legal institutions were typical of the gifts which Christ was to receive even for the rebellious, Ps. lxviii. 18. In the foregoing chapter, upon Israel's provocation, God had determined to destroy them, and in token of his wrath had sentenced them to perish in the wilderness. But, upon Moses's intercession, he said, "I have pardoned ;" and, in token of that mercy, in this chapter he repeats and explains some of the laws concerning offerings, to show that he was reconciled to them, notwithstanding the severe dispensation they were under, and would not unchurch them. Here is, I. The law concerning the meat-offerings and drink-offerings (ver. 1—12) both for Israelites and for strangers (ver. 13—16), and a law concerning the heave-offerings of the first of their dough, ver. 17—21. II. The law concerning sacrifices for sins of ignorance, ver. 22—29. III. The punishment of presumptuous sins (ver. 30, 31), and an instance given in the sabbath-breaker, ver. 32—36. IV. A law concerning fringes, for memorandums, upon the borders of their garments, ver. 37, &c.

AND the Lord spake unto Moses, saying, 2 Speak unto the children of Israel, and say unto them, When ye be come into the land of your habitations, which I give unto you, 3 And will make an offering by fire unto the Lord, a burnt offering, or a sacrifice in performing a vow, or in a freewill offering, or in your solemn feasts, to make a sweet savour unto the Lord, of the herd, or of the flock : 4 Then shall he that offereth his offering unto the Lord bring a meat offering of a tenth deal of flour mingled with the fourth *part* of a hin of oil. 5 And the fourth *part* of a hin of wine for a drink offering shalt thou prepare with the burnt offering or sacrifice, for one lamb. 6 Or for a ram, thou shalt prepare *for* a meat offering two tenth deals of flour mingled with the third *part* of a hin of oil. 7 And for a drink offering thou shalt offer the third *part* of a hin of wine, *for* a sweet savour unto the Lord. 8 And when thou preparest a bullock *for* a burnt offering, or *for* a sacrifice in performing a vow, or peace offerings unto the Lord : 9 Then shall he bring with a bullock a meat offering of three tenth deals of flour mingled with half a hin of oil. 10 And thou shalt bring for a drink offering half a hin of wine, *for* an offering made by fire, of a sweet savour unto the Lord. 11 Thus shall it be done for one bullock, or for one ram, or for a lamb, or a kid. 12 According to the number that ye shall prepare, so shall ye do to every one according to their number. 13 All that are born of the country shall do these things after this manner, in offering an offering made by fire, of a sweet savour unto the Lord. 14 And if a stranger sojourn

631

with you, or whosoever *be* among you in your generations, and will offer an offering made by fire, of a sweet savour unto the LORD; as ye do, so he shall do. 15 One ordinance *shall be both* for you of the congregation, and also for the stranger that sojourneth *with you*, an ordinance for ever in your generations: as ye *are*, so shall the stranger be before the LORD. 16 One law and one manner shall be for you, and for the stranger that sojourneth with you. 17 And the LORD spake unto Moses, saying, 18 Speak unto the children of Israel, and say unto them, When ye come into the land whither I bring you, 19 Then it shall be, that, when ye eat of the bread of the land, ye shall offer up a heave offering unto the LORD. 20 Ye shall offer up a cake of the first of your dough *for* a heave offering: as *ye do* the heave offering of the threshing-floor, so shall ye heave it. 21 Of the first of your dough ye shall give unto the LORD a heave offering in your generations.

Here we have,

I. Full instructions given concerning the meat-offerings and drink-offerings, which were appendages to all the sacrifices of animals. The beginning of this law is very encouraging: *When you come into the land of your habitation which I give unto you,* then you shall do so and so, *v.* 2 This was a plain intimation, not only that God was reconciled to them notwithstanding the sentence he had passed upon them, but that he would secure the promised land to their seed notwithstanding their proneness to rebel against him. They might think some time or other they should be guilty of a misdemeanour that would be fatal to them, and would exclude them for ever, as the last had done for one generation; but this intimates an assurance that they should be kept from provoking God to such a degree as would amount to a forfeiture; for this statute takes it for granted that there were some of them that should in due time come into Canaan. The meat-offerings were of two sorts; some were offered alone, and we have the law concerning those, Lev. ii. 1, &c. Others were added to the burnt-offerings and peace-offerings, and constantly attended them, and about these direction is here given. It was requisite, since the sacrifices of acknowledgment (specified in *v.* 3) were intended as the food of God's table, that there should be a constant provision of bread, oil, and wine, whatever the flesh-meat was. The caterers or purveyors for Solomon's temple provided
632

fine flour, 1 Kings iv. 22. And it was fit that God should keep a good house, that his table should be furnished with bread as well as flesh, and that his cup should run over. In my Father's house there is bread enough. Now the intent of this law is to direct what proportion the meat-offering and drink-offering should bear to the several sacrifices to which they were annexed. If the sacrifice was a lamb or a kid, then the meat-offering must be a tenth-deal of flour, that is, an omer, which contained about five pints; this must be mingled with oil, the fourth part of a hin (a hin contained about five quarts), and the drink-offering must be the same quantity of wine, about a quart and half a pint, *v.* 3—5. If it was a ram, the meat-offering was doubled, two tenth-deals of flour, about five quarts, and a third part of a hin of oil (which was to them as butter is to us) mingled with it; and the same quantity of wine for a drink-offering, *v.* 6, 7. If the sacrifice was a bullock, the meat-offering was to be trebled, three omers, with five pints of oil, and the same quantity of wine for a drink-offering, *v.* 8—10. And thus for each sacrifice, whether offered by a particular person or at the common charge. Note, Our religious services should be governed, as by other rules, so by the rule of proportion.

II. Natives and strangers are here set upon a level, in this as in other matters (*v.* 13—16): "One law shall be for you and for the stranger that is proselyted to the Jewish religion." Now, 1. This was an invitation to the Gentiles to become proselytes, and to embrace the faith and worship of the true God. In civil things there was a difference between strangers and true-born Israelites, but not in the things of God; *as you are, so shall the stranger be before the Lord,* for with him there is no respect of persons. See Isa. lvi. 3. 2. This was an obligation upon the Jews to be kind to strangers, and not to oppress them, because they saw them owned and accepted of God. Communion in religion is a great engagement to mutual affection, and should slay all enmities. 3. It was a mortification to the pride of the Jews, who are apt to be puffed up with their birthright privileges. "We are Abraham's seed." God let them know that the sons of the stranger were as welcome to him as the sons of Jacob; no man's birth or parentage shall turn either to his advantage or his prejudice in his acceptance with God. This likewise intimated that, as believing strangers should be accounted Israelites, so unbelieving Israelites should be accounted strangers. 4. It was a happy presage of the calling of the Gentiles, and of their admission into the church. If the law made so little difference between Jew and Gentile, much less would the gospel make, which broke down the partition-wall, and reconciled both to God in one sacrifice, without the observance of the legal ceremonies.

III. A law for the offering of the first of

their dough unto the Lord. This, as the former, goes upon the comfortable supposition of their having *come into the promised land*, v. 18. Now that they lived upon manna they needed not such an express acknowledgment of God's title to their daily bread, and their dependence upon him for it, the thing spoke for itself; but in Canaan, where they should eat the fruit of their own industry, God required that he should be owned as their landlord and their great benefactor. They must not only offer him the first-fruits and tenths of the corn in their fields (these had been already reserved); but when they had it in their houses, in their kneading troughs, when it was almost ready to be set upon their tables, God must have a further tribute of acknowledgment, part of their dough (the Jews say a fortieth part, at least, of the whole lump) must be heaved or offered up to God (v. 20, 21), and the priest must have it for the use of his family. Thus they must own their dependence upon God for their daily bread, even when they had it in the house with them; they must then wait on God for the comfortable use of it; for we read of that which was brought home, and yet God did blow upon it, and it came to little, Hag. i. 9. Christ has taught us to pray not, *Give us this year our yearly harvest*, but *Give us this day our daily bread.* God by this law said to the people, as the prophet long afterwards said to the widow of Sarepta (1 Kings xvii. 13), *Only make me thereof a little cake first.* This offering was expressly kept up by the laws of Ezekiel's visionary temple, and it is a commandment with promise of family-mercies (Ezek. xliv. 30): *You shall give unto the priest the first of your dough, that he may cause the blessing to rest in thy house:* for, when God has had his dues out of our estates, we may expect the comfort of what falls to our share.

22 And if ye have erred, and not observed all these commandments, which the LORD hath spoken unto Moses, 23 *Even* all that the LORD hath commanded you by the hand of Moses, from the day that the LORD commanded *Moses*, and henceforward among your generations; 24 Then it shall be, if *aught* be committed by ignorance without the knowledge of the congregation, that all the congregation shall offer one young bullock for a burnt offering, for a sweet savour unto the LORD, with his meat offering, and his drink offering, according to the manner, and one kid of the goats for a sin offering. 25 And the priest shall make an atonement for all the congregation of the children of

Israel, and it shall be forgiven them; for it *is* ignorance: and they shall bring their offering, a sacrifice made by fire unto the LORD, and their sin offering before the LORD, for their ignorance: 26 And it shall be forgiven all the congregation of the children of Israel, and the stranger that sojourneth among them; seeing all the people *were* in ignorance. 27 And if any soul sin through ignorance, then he shall bring a she goat of the first year for a sin offering. 28 And the priest shall make an atonement for the soul that sinneth ignorantly, when he sinneth by ignorance before the LORD, to make an atonement for him; and it shall be forgiven him. 29 Ye shall have one law for him that sinneth through ignorance, *both for* him that is born among the children of Israel, and for the stranger that sojourneth among them.

We have here the laws concerning sacrifices for sins of ignorance; the Jews understand it of idolatry, or false worship, through the error of their teachers. The case here supposed is that they *had not observed all these commandments*, v. 22, 23. If they had failed in the offerings of their acknowledgment, and had not brought them according to the law, then they must bring an offering of atonement, yea, though the omission had been through forgetfulness or mistake. If they failed in one part of the ceremony, they must make it up by the observance of another part, which was in the nature of a remedial law. 1. The case is put of a national sin, committed through ignorance, and become customary through a vulgar error (v. 24)—*the congregation*, that is, the body of the people, for so it is explained (v. 25): *All the congregation of the children of Israel.* The ceremonial observances were so numerous, and so various, that, it might easily be supposed, some of them by degrees would be forgotten and disused, as particularly that immediately before concerning the heave-offering of their dough: now if, in process of time, upon consulting the law, there should appear to have been a general neglect of that or any other appointment, then a sacrifice must be offered for the whole congregation, and the oversight shall be forgiven (v. 25, 26) and not punished, as it deserved, with some national judgment. The offering of the sacrifice *according to the manner*, or *ordinance*, plainly refers to a former statute, of which this is the repetition; and the same bullock which is there called *a sin-offering* (Lev. iv. 13, 21) is here called *a burnt-offering* (v. 24), because it was wholly burnt, though not upon the altar, yet without the camp. And here is the addition of a *kid of the goats for a sin-offering.* According to this law, we find that Hezekiah made atonement for the errors of his father's reign, by *seven bullocks, seven rams, seven lambs, and seven he-goats,* which he offered as a *sin-offering for the kingdom, and for the sanctuary, and for Judah* (2 Chron. xxix. 21), and *for all Israel, v.* 24. And we find the like done after the return out of captivity, Ezra viii. 35. 2. It is likewise supposed to be the case of a particular person: *If any soul sin through ignorance* (v. 27), neglecting any part of his duty, he must bring his offering, as was appointed,¹ Lev. iv. 27, &c. Thus atonement shall be made *for the soul that sins, when he sins through ignorance, v.* 28. Observe, (1.) Sins committed ignorantly need to have atonement made for them; for, though ignorance will in a degree excuse, it will not justify those that might have known their Lord's will and did it not. David prayed to be cleansed from his *secret faults,* that is, those sins which he himself was not aware of, the errors he did not understand, Ps. xix. 12. (2.) Sins committed ignorantly shall be forgiven, through Christ the great sacrifice, who, when he offered up himself once for all upon the cross, seemed to explain the intention of his offering in that prayer, *Father, forgive them, for they know not what they do.* And Paul seems to allude to this law concerning sins of ignorance (1 Tim. i. 13), *I obtained mercy, because I did it ignorantly and in unbelief.* And it looked favourably upon the Gentiles that this law of atoning for sins of ignorance is expressly made to extend to those who were strangers to the commonwealth of Israel (v. 29), but supposed to be *proselytes of righteousness.* Thus the blessing of Abraham comes upon the Gentiles.

30 But the soul that doeth *aught* presumptuously, *whether he be* born in the land, or a stranger, the same reproacheth the LORD; and that soul shall be cut off from among his people. 31 Because he hath despised the word of the LORD, and hath broken his commandment, that soul shall utterly be cut off; his iniquity *shall be* upon him. 32 And while the children of Israel were in the wilderness, they found a man that gathered sticks upon the sabbath day. 33 And they that found him gathering sticks brought him unto Moses and Aaron, and unto all the congregation. 34 And they put him in ward, because it was not declared what should be done to him. 35 And the LORD said unto

634

Moses, The man shall be surely put to death: all the congregation shall stone him with stones without the camp. 36 And all the congregation brought him without the camp, and stoned him with stones, and he died; as the LORD commanded Moses.

Here is, I. The general doom passed upon presumptuous sinners. 1. Those are to be reckoned presumptuous sinners that sin *with a high hand,* as the original phrase is (v. 30), that is, that avowedly confront God's authority, and set up their own lust in competition with it, that sin for sinning-sake, in contradiction to the precept of the law, and in defiance of the penalty, that fight against God, and dare him to do his worst; see Job xv. 25. It is not only to sin against knowledge, but to sin designedly against God's will and glory. 2. Sins thus committed are exceedingly sinful. He that thus breaks the commandment, (1.) *Reproaches the Lord* (v. 30); he says the worst he can of him, and most unjustly. The language of presumptuous sin is, "Eternal truth is not fit to be believed, the Lord of all not fit to be obeyed, and almighty power not fit to be either feared or trusted." It imputes folly to Infinite Wisdom, and iniquity to the righteous Judge of heaven and earth; such is the malignity of wilful sin. (2.) He *despises the word of the Lord, v.* 31. There are those who, in many instances, come short of fulfilling the word, and yet have a great value for it, and count the law honourable; but presumptuous sinners despise it, thinking themselves too great, too good, and too wise, to be ruled by it. *What is the Almighty that we should serve him?* Whatever the sin itself is, it is contumacy that incurs the anathema. It is rebellion added to the sin that is as witchcraft, and stubbornness as idolatry. 3. The sentence passed on such is dreadful. There remains no sacrifice for those sins; the law provided none: *That soul shall be cut off from among his people* (v. 30), *utterly cut off* (v. 31); and that God may be for ever justified, and the sinner for ever confounded, *his iniquity shall be upon him,* and there needs no more to sink him to the lowest hell. Thus the Jewish doctors understand it, that *the iniquity shall cleave to the soul, after it is cut off, and that man shall give an account of his sin at the great day of judgment.* Perhaps the kind of offence might be such as did not expose the offender to the censure of the civil magistrate, but, if it was done presumptuously, God himself would take the punishment of it into his own hands, and into them it is a fearful thing to fall. In the New Testament we find the like sentence of exclusion from all benefit by the great sacrifice passed upon the blasphemy against the Holy Ghost, and a total apostasy from Christianity.

See Matt. xii. 32, and Heb. x. 26, which refers to this.

II. A particular instance of presumption in the sin of sabbath-breaking. 1. The offence was the gathering of sticks on the sabbath day (*v.* 32), which, it is probable, were designed to make a fire of, whereas they were commanded to bake and seeth what they had occasion for the day before, Exod. xvi. 23. This seemed but a small offence, but it was a violation of the law of the sabbath, and so was a tacit contempt of the Creator, to whose honour the sabbath was dedicated, and an incursion upon the whole law, which the sabbath was intended as a hedge about. And it appears by the context to have been done presumptuously, and in affront both of the law and to the Lawmaker. 2. The offender was secured, *v.* 33, 34. Those that found him *gathering sticks,* in their zeal for the honour of the sabbath, *brought him to Moses and Aaron, and all the congregation,* which intimates that being the sabbath day the congregation was at that time gathered to Moses and Aaron, to receive instruction from them, and to join with them in religious worship. It seems, even common Israelites, though there was much amiss among them, yet would not contentedly see the sabbath profaned, which was a good sign that they had not quite forsaken God, nor were utterly forsaken of him. 3. God was consulted, *because it was not declared what should be done to him.* The law had already made the profanation of the sabbath a capital crime (Exod. xxxi. 14, *ch.* xxxv. 2); but they were in doubt, either concerning the offence (whether this that he had done should be deemed a profanation or no) or concerning the punishment, what death he should die. God was the Judge, and before him they brought this cause. 4. Sentence was passed; the prisoner was adjudged a sabbath-breaker, according to the intent of that law, and as such he must be put to death; and to show how great the crime was, and how displeasing to God, and that others might hear and fear and not do in like manner presumptuously, that death is appointed him which was looked upon as most terrible: He must be *stoned with stones,* *v.* 35. Note, God is jealous for the honour of his sabbaths, and will not hold those guiltless, whatever men do, that profane them. 5. Execution was done pursuant to the sentence, *v.* 36. He was *stoned* to death *by the congregation.* As many as could were employed in the execution, that those, at least, might be afraid of breaking the sabbath, who had thrown a stone at this sabbath-breaker. This intimates that the open profanation of the sabbath is a sin which ought to be punished and restrained by the civil magistrate, who, as far as overt acts go, is keeper of both tables. See Neh. xiii. 17. One would think there could be no great harm in gathering a few sticks, on what day

soever it was, but God intended the exemplary punishment of him that did so for a standing warning to us all, to make conscience of keeping holy the sabbath.

37 And the LORD spake unto Moses, saying, 38 Speak unto the children of Israel, and bid them that they make them fringes in the borders of their garments throughout their generations, and that they put upon the fringe of the borders a ribband of blue: 39 And it shall be unto you for a fringe, that ye may look upon it, and remember all the commandments of the LORD, and do them; and that ye seek not after your own heart and your own eyes, after which ye use to go a whoring: 40 That ye may remember, and do all my commandments, and be holy unto your God. 41 I *am* the LORD your God, which brought you out of the land of Egypt, to be your God: I *am* the LORD your God.

Provision had been just now made by the law for the pardon of sins of ignorance and infirmity; now here is an expedient provided for the preventing of such sins. They are ordered to make fringes upon the borders of their garments, which were to be memorandums to them of their duty, that they might not sin through forgetfulness. 1. The sign appointed is a fringe of silk, or thread, or worsted, or the garment itself ravelled at the bottom, and a blue riband bound on the top of it to keep it tight, *v.* 38. The Jews being a peculiar people, they were thus distinguished from their neighbours in their dress, as well as in their diet, and taught by such little instances of singularity not to be conformed to the way of the heathen in greater things. Thus likewise they proclaimed themselves Jews wherever they were, as those that were not ashamed of God and his law. Our Saviour, being made under the law, wore these fringes; hence we read of the hem or border. of his garment, Matt. ix. 20. These borders the Pharisees enlarged, that they might be thought more holy and devout than other people. The phylacteries were different things; these were their own invention, the fringes were a divine institution. The Jews at this day wear them, saying, when they put them on, *Blessed be he who has sanctified us unto himself, and commanded us to wear fringes.* 2. The intention of it was to remind them that they were a peculiar people. They were not appointed for the trimming and adorning of their clothes, but *to stir up their pure minds by way of remembrance* (2 Pet. iii. 1), that they might *look upon the fringe and remem-*

ber the commandments. Many look upon their ornaments to feed their pride, but they must look upon these ornaments to awaken their consciences to a sense of their duty, that their religion might constantly beset them, and that they might carry it about with them, as they did their clothes, wherever they went. If they were tempted to sin, the fringe would be a monitor to them not to break God's commandments: if a duty was forgotten to be done in its season, the fringe would remind them of it. This institution, though it is not an imposition upon us, is an instruction to us, always to *remember the commandments of the Lord our God,* that we *may do them,* to treasure them up in our memories, and to apply them to particular cases as there is occasion to use them. It was intended particularly to be a preservative from idolatry: that you *seek not after your own heart, and your own eyes,* in your religious worship. Yet it may extend also to the whole conversation, for nothing is more contrary to God's honour, and our own true interest, than to *walk in the way of our heart* and in *the sight of our eyes;* for the *imagination of the heart is evil,* and so is the *lust of the eyes.*

After the repetition of some ceremonial appointments, the chapter closes with that great and fundamental law of religion, *Be holy unto your God,* purged from sin, and sincerely devoted to his service; and that great reason for all the commandments is again and again inculcated, *I am the Lord your God.* Did we more firmly believe, and more frequently and seriously consider, that God is the Lord, and our God and Redeemer, we should see ourselves bound in duty, interest, and gratitude, to keep all his commandments.

CHAP. XVI.

The date of the history contained in this chapter is altogether uncertain. Probably these mutinies happened after their removal back again from Kadesh-barnea, when they were fixed (if I may so speak) for their wandering in the wilderness, and began to look upon that as their settlement. Presently after new laws given follows the story of a new rebellion, as if sin took occasion from the commandment to become more exceedingly sinful. Here is, I. A daring and dangerous rebellion raised against Moses and Aaron, by Korah, Dathan, and Abiram, ver. 1—15. 1. Korah and his accomplices contend for the priesthood against Aaron, ver. 3. Moses reasons with them, and appeals to God for a decision of the controversy, ver. 4—11. 2. Dathan and Abiram quarrel with Moses, and refuse to obey his summons, which greatly grieves him, ver. 12—15. II. A solemn appearance of the pretenders to the priesthood before God, according to order, and a public appearance of the glory of the Lord, which would have consumed the whole congregation if Moses and Aaron had not interceded, ver. 16—22. III. The deciding of the controversy, and the crushing of the rebellion, by the cutting off of the rebels. 1. Those in their tents were buried alive, ver. 23—34. 2. Those at the door of the tabernacle were consumed by fire (ver. 35), and their censers preserved for a memorial, ver. 37—40. IV. A new insurrection of the people, ver. 41—43. 1. God stayed the insurrection by a plague, ver. 45. 2. Aaron stayed the plague by offering incense, ver. 46—50. The manner and method of recording this story plainly show the ferment to have been very great.

NOW Korah, the son of Izhar, the son of Kohath, the son of Levi, and Dathan and Abiram, the sons of Eliab, and On, the son of Peleth, sons of Reuben, took *men:* 2 And they rose up before Moses, with certain of the children of Israel, two hundred

and fifty princes of the assembly, famous in the congregation, men of renown: 3 And they gathered themselves together against Moses and against Aaron, and said unto them, *Ye take* too much upon you, seeing all the congregation *are* holy, every one of them, and the Lord *is* among them: wherefore then lift ye up yourselves above the congregation of the Lord? 4 And when Moses heard *it,* he fell upon his face: 5 And he spake unto Korah and unto all his company, saying, Even to morrow the Lord will show who *are* his, and *who is* holy; and will cause *him* to come near unto him: even *him* whom he hath chosen will he cause to come near unto him. 6 This do; Take you censers, Korah, and all his company; 7 And put fire therein, and put incense in them before the Lord to morrow: and it shall be *that* the man whom the Lord doth choose, he *shall be* holy: ye *take* too much upon you, ye sons of Levi. 8 And Moses said unto Korah, Hear, I pray you, ye sons of Levi: 9 *Seemeth it but* a small thing unto you, that the God of Israel hath separated you from the congregation of Israel, to bring you near to himself to do the service of the tabernacle of the Lord, and to stand before the congregation to minister unto them? 10 And he hath brought thee near *to him,* and all thy brethren the sons of Levi with thee: and seek ye the priesthood also? 11 For which cause *both* thou and all thy company *are* gathered together against the Lord: and what *is* Aaron, that ye murmur against him?

Here is, I. An account of the rebels, who and what they were, not, as formerly, the mixed multitude and the dregs of the people, who are therefore never named, but men of distinction and quality, that made a figure. Korah was the ring-leader: he formed and headed the faction; therefore it is called *the gainsaying of Korah,* Jude 11. He was cousin-german to Moses, they were brothers' children, yet the nearness of the relation could not restrain him from being insolent and rude to Moses. Think it not strange if a man's foes be *those of his own house.* With him joined Dathan and Abiram, chief men of the tribe of Reuben, the eldest son of Jacob.

Probably Korah was disgusted both at the preferment of Aaron to the priesthood and the constituting of Elizaphan to the head of the Kohathites (*ch.* iii. 30); and perhaps the Reubenites were angry that the tribe of Judah had the first post of honour in the camp. *On* is mentioned (*v.* 1) as one of the heads of the faction, but never after in the whole story, either because, as some think, he repented and left them, or because he did not make himself so remarkable as Dathan and Abiram did. The Kohathites emcamped on the same side of the tabernacle that the Reubenites did, which perhaps gave Korah an opportunity of drawing them in, whence the Jews say, *Woe to the wicked man, and woe to his neighbour*, who is in danger of being infected by him. And, these being themselves *men of renown*, they seduced into the conspiracy *two hundred and fifty princes of the assembly* (*v.* 2); probably they were firstborn, or at least heads of families, who, before the elevation of Aaron, had themselves ministered in holy things. Note, The pride, ambition, and emulation, of great men, have always been the occasion of a great deal of mischief both in churches and states. God by his grace make great men humble, and so give peace in our time, O Lord! Famous men, and men of renown, as these are described to be, were the great sinners of the old world, Gen. vi. 4. The fame and renown which they had did not content them; they were high, but would be higher, and thus the famous men became infamous.

II. The rebels' remonstrance, *v.* 3. That which they quarrel with is the settlement of the priesthood upon Aaron and his family, which they think an honour too great for Moses to give and Aaron to accept, and so they are both charged with usurpation : *You take too much upon you ;* or, " Let it suffice you to be upon a level with your neighbours, who are all holy, all as good as you, and therefore ought to be as great." Or, " Let it suffice you to have domineered thus long, and now think of resigning your places to those who have as good a title to them and are as well able to manage them." 1. They proudly boast of the holiness of the congregation, and the presence of God in it. "They are *holy, every one of them*, and as fit to be employed in offering sacrifice as Aaron is, and as masters of families formerly were, and *the Lord is among them*, to direct and own them." Small reason they had to boast of the people's purity, or of God's favour, as the people had been so frequently and so lately polluted with sin, and were now under the marks of God's displeasure, which should have made them thankful for priests to mediate between them and God; but, instead of that, they envy them. 2. They unjustly charge Moses and Aaron with taking the honour they had to themselves, whereas it was evident, beyond contradiction, that they were called of God to it, Heb. v. 4. So that

they would either have no priests at all, nor any government, none to preside either in civil or sacred things, none over the congregation, none above it, or they would not acquiesce in that constitution of the government which God had appointed. See here, (1.) What spirit levellers are of, and those that despise dominions, and resist the powers that God has set over them; they are proud, envious, ambitious, turbulent, wicked, and unreasonable men. (2.) What usage even the best and most useful men may expect, even from those they have been serviceable to. If those be represented as usurpers that have the best titles, and those as tyrants that govern best, let them recollect that Moses and Aaron were thus abused.

III. Moses's conduct when this remonstrance was published against him. How did he take it?

1. He *fell on his face* (*v.* 4), as before, *ch.* xiv. 5. Thus he showed how willing he would have been to yield to them, and how gladly he would have resigned his government, if it would have consisted with his duty to God and his fidelity to the trust reposed in him. Thus also he applied to God, by prayer, for direction what to say and to do upon this sad occasion. He would not speak to them till he had thus humbled and composed his own spirit (which could not but begin to be heated), and had received instruction from God. The *heart of the wise* in such a case *studies to answer*, and asks counsel at God's mouth.

2. He agrees to refer the case to God, and leave it to him to decide it, as one well assured of the goodness of his title, and yet well content to resign, if God thought fit, to gratify this discontented people with another nomination. An honest cause fears not a trial, fears not a second trial, fears not a speedy trial; even to-morrow let it be brought on, *v.* 5—7. Let Korah and his partisans bring their censers, and offer incense before the Lord, and, if he testify his acceptance of them, well and good; Moses is now as willing that all the Lord's people should be priests, if God so pleased, as before that they should all be prophets, *ch* xi. 29. But if God, upon an appeal to him, determine (as no doubt he would) for Aaron, they would find it highly dangerous to make the experiment: and therefore he puts it off till to-morrow, to try whether, when they had slept upon it, they would desist, and let fall their pretensions.

3. He argues the case fairly with them, to still the mutiny with fair reasoning, if possible, before the appeal came to God's tribunal, for then he knew it would end in the confusion of the complainants.

(1.) He calls them *the sons of Levi, v.* 7, and again *v.* 8. They were of his own tribe, nay, they were of God's tribe; it was therefore the worse in them thus to mutiny both against God and against him. It was not long since the sons of Levi had bravely appeared on God's side, in the matter of the golden calf, and got immortal honour by it; and shall those that were then the only innocents now be the leading criminals, and lose all the honour they had won? Could there be such chaff on God's floor? Levites, and yet rebels?

(2.) He retorts their charge upon themselves. They had unjustly charged Moses and Aaron with taking too much upon them, though they had done no more than what God put upon them; nay, says Moses, *You take too much upon you, you sons of Levi.* Note, Those that take upon them to control and contradict God's appointment take too much upon them. It is enough for us to submit; it is too much to prescribe.

(3.) He shows them the privilege they had as Levites, which was sufficient for them, they needed not to aspire to the honour of the priesthood, v. 9, 10. He reminds them how great the honour was to which they were preferred, as Levites. [1.] They were *separated from the congregation of Israel,* distinguished from them, dignified above them; instead of complaining that Aaron's family was advanced above theirs, they ought to have been thankful that their tribe was advanced above the rest of the tribes, though they had been in all respects upon the level with them. Note, It will help to keep us from envying those that are above us duly to consider how many there are below us. Instead of fretting that any are preferred before us in honour, power, estate, or interest, in gifts, graces, or usefulness, we have reason to bless God if we, who are less than the least, are not put among the very last. Many perhaps who deserve better are not preferred so well. [2.] They were separated to very great and valuable honours, *First,* To *draw near to God,* nearer than the common Israelites, though they also were a people near unto him; the nearer any are to God the greater is their honour. *Secondly,* To *do the service of the tabernacle.* It is honour enough to bear the vessels of the sanctuary, and to be employed in any part of the service of the tabernacle. God's service is not only perfect freedom, but high preferment. *Thirdly,* To *stand before the congregation to minister unto them.* Note, Those are truly great that serve the public, and it is the honour of God's ministers to be the church's ministers; nay, which adds to the dignity put upon them, [3.] It was the God of Israel himself that separated them. It was his act and deed to put them into their place, and therefore they ought not to have been discontented: and he it was likewise that put Aaron into his place, and therefore they ought not to have envied him.

(4.) He convicts them of the sin of undervaluing those privileges: *Seemeth it a small thing unto you?* As if he had said, "It ill

becomes you of all men to grudge Aaron the priesthood, when at the same time that he was advanced to that honour you were designed for another honour dependent upon it, and shine with rays borrowed from him." Note, [1.] The privilege of drawing near to the God of Israel is not a small thing in itself, and therefore must not appear small to us. To those who neglect opportunities of drawing near to God, who are careless and formal in it, to whom it is a task and not a pleasure, we may properly put this question: "Seemeth it a small thing to you that God has made you a people near unto him?" [2.] Those who aspire after and usurp the honours forbidden them put a great contempt upon the honours allowed them. We have each of us as good a share of reputation as God sees fit for us, and sees us fit for, and much better than we deserve; and we ought to rest satisfied with it, and not, as these, *exercise ourselves in things too high for us: Seek you the priesthood also?* They would not *own* that they sought it, but Moses saw that they had this in their eye; the law had provided very well for those that served at the altar, and therefore they would put in for the office.

(5.) He interprets their mutiny to be a rebellion against God (v. 11); while they pretended to assert the holiness and liberty of the Israel of God, they really took up arms against the God of Israel: *You are gathered together against the Lord.* Note, Those that strive against God's ordinances and providences, whatever they pretend, and whether they are aware of it or no, do indeed strive with their Maker. Those resist the prince who resist those that are commissioned by him: for, alas! says Moses, *What is Aaron, that you murmur against him?* If murmurers and complainers would consider that the instruments they quarrel with are but instruments whom God employs, and that they are but what he makes them, and neither more nor less, better nor worse, they would not be so bold and free in their censures and reproaches as they are. Those that found the priesthood, as it was settled, a blessing, must give all the praise to God; but if any found it a burden they must not therefore quarrel with Aaron, who is but what he is made, and does but as he is bidden. Thus he interested God in the cause, and so might be sure of speeding well in his appeal.

12 And Moses sent to call Dathan and Abiram, the sons of Eliab: which said, We will not come up: 13 *Is it* a small thing that thou hast brought us up out of a land that floweth with milk and honey, to kill us in the wilderness, except thou make thyself altogether a prince over us? 14 Moreover thou hast not brought us into a

land that floweth with milk and honey, or given us inheritance of fields and vineyards : wilt thou put out the eyes of these men ? we will not come up. 15 And Moses was very wroth, and said unto the LORD, Respect not thou their offering : I have not taken one ass from them, neither have I hurt one of them. 16 And Moses said unto Korah, Be thou and all thy company before the LORD, thou, and they, and Aaron, to morrow : 17 And take every man his censer, and put incense in them, and bring ye before the LORD every man his censer, two hundred and fifty censers; thou also, and Aaron, each *of you* his censer. 18 And they took every man his censer, and put fire in them, and laid incense thereon, and stood in the door of the tabernacle of the congregation with Moses and Aaron. 19 And Korah gathered all the congregation against them unto the door of the tabernacle of the congregation : and the glory of the LORD appeared unto all the congregation. 20 And the LORD spake unto Moses and unto Aaron, saying, 21 Separate yourselves from among this congregation, that I may consume them in a moment. 22 And they fell upon their faces, and said, O God, the God of the spirits of all flesh, shall one man sin, and wilt thou be wroth with all the congregation?

Here is, I. The insolence of Dathan and Abiram, and their treasonable remonstrance. Moses had heard what Korah had to say, and had answered it; now he summons Dathan and Abiram to bring in their complaints (v. 12); but they would not obey his summons, either because they could not for shame say that to his face which they were resolved to say, and then it is an instance of some remains of modesty in them; or, rather, because they would not so far own his authority, and then it is an instance of the highest degree of impudence. They spoke the language of Pharaoh himself, who set Moses at defiance, but they forgot how dearly he paid for it. Had not their heads been wretchedly heated, and their hearts hardened, they might have considered that, if they regarded not these messengers, Moses could soon in God's name send messengers of death for them. But thus the God of this world *blinds the minds of those that believe not.* But by the same messengers they send their articles of impeachment against Moses;

and the charge runs very high. 1. They charge him with having done them a great deal of wrong in bringing them out of Egypt, invidiously calling that *a land flowing with milk and honey*, v. 13. Onions, and garlick, and fish, they had indeed plenty of in Egypt, but it never pretended to milk and honey; only they would thus banter the promise of Canaan. Ungrateful wretches, to represent that as an injury to them which was really the greatest favour that ever was bestowed upon any people! 2. They charge him with a design upon their lives, that he intended to *kill them in the wilderness*, though they were so well provided for. And, if they were sentenced to die in the wilderness, they must thank themselves. Moses would have healed them, and they would not be healed. 3. They charge him with a design upon their liberties, that he meant to enslave them, by *making himself a prince over them.* A prince over them! Was he not a tender father to them? nay, their devoted servant for the Lord's sake? Had they not their properties secured, their order preserved, and justice impartially administered? Did they not live in ease and honour? And yet they complain as if Moses's yoke were heavier than Pharaoh's. And did Moses make himself a prince? Far from it. How gladly would he have declined the office at first! How gladly would he have resigned it many a time since! And yet he is thus put under the blackest characters of a tyrant and a usurper. 4. They charge him with cheating them, raising their expectations of a good land, and then defeating them (v. 14): *Thou hast not brought us*, as thou promisedst us, *into a land that floweth with milk and honey;* and pray whose fault was that? He had brought them to the borders of it, and was just ready, under God, to put them in possession of it; but they thrust it away from them, and shut the door against themselves; so that it was purely their own fault that they were not now in Canaan, and yet Moses must bear the blame. Thus when the *foolishness of man perverteth his way his heart fretteth against the Lord*, Prov. xix. 3. 5. They charge him in the general with unfair dealing, that he put *out the eyes of these men*, and then meant to lead them blindfold as he pleased. The design of all he did for them was to open their eyes, and yet they insinuate that he intended to put out their eyes, that they might not see themselves imposed upon. Note, The wisest and best cannot please every body, nor gain the good word of all. Those often fall under the heaviest censures who have merited the highest applause. Many a good work Moses had shown them from the Father, and for which of these do they reproach him?

II. Moses's just resentment of their insolence, v. 15. Moses, though the meekest man, yet, finding God reproached in him, *was very wroth;* he could not bear to see a people ruining themselves for whose salvation he had done so much. In this discomposure,

1. He appeals to God concerning his own integrity; whereas they basely reflected upon him as ambitious, covetous, and oppressive, in making himself a prince over them, God was his witness, (1.) That he never got any thing by them: *I have not taken one ass from them*, not only not by way of bribery and extortion, but not by way of recompence or gratuity for all the good offices he had done them; he never took the pay of a general, or the salary of a judge, much less the tribute of a prince. He got more in his estate when he kept Jethro's flock than when he came to be king in Jeshurun. (2.) That they never lost any thing by him: *Neither have I hurt any one of them*, no, not the least, no, not the worst, no, not those that had been most peevish and provoking to him: he never abused his power to the support of wrong. Note, Those that have never blemished themselves need not fear being slurred by others: when men condemn us we may be easy, if our own hearts condemn us not.

2. He begs of God to plead his cause, and clear him, by showing his displeasure at the incense which Korah and his company were to offer, with whom Dathan and Abiram were in confederacy. Lord, says he, *Respect not thou their offering*. Herein he seems to refer to the history of Cain, lately written by his own hand, of whom it is said that to him and his offering God had not respect, Gen. iv. 5. These that *followed the gainsaying of Korah walked in the way of Cain* (these are put together, Jude 11), and therefore he prays that they might be frowned upon as Cain was, and put to the same confusion.

III. Issue joined between Moses and his accusers. 1. Moses challenges them to appear with Aaron next morning, at the time of offering up the morning incense, and refer the matter to God's judgment, *v.* 16, 17. Since he could not convince them by his calm and affectionate reasoning, he is ready to enter into bonds to stand God's award, not doubting but that God would appear, to decide the controversy. This reference he had agreed to before (*v.* 6, 7), and here adds only one clause, which bespeaks his great condescension to the plaintiffs, that Aaron, against whose advancement they excepted, though now advanced by the divine institution to the honour of burning incense within the tabernacle, yet, upon this trial, should put himself into the place of a probationer, and stand upon the level with Korah, at the door of the tabernacle; nay, and Moses would himself stand with them, so that the complainant shall have all the fair dealing he can desire; and thus *every mouth shall be stopped*. 2. Korah accepts the challenge, and makes his appearance with Moses and Aaron *at the door of the tabernacle*, to make good his pretensions, *v.* 18, 19. If he had not had a very great stock of impudence, he could

640

not have carried on the matter thus far. Had not he lately seen Nadab and Abihu, the consecrated priests, struck dead for daring to offer incense with unhallowed fire? and could he and his accomplices expect to fare any better in offering incense with unhallowed hands? Yet, to confront Moses and Aaron, in the height of his pride he thus bids defiance to Heaven, and pretends to demand divine acceptance without a divine warrant; thus wretchedly is the heart hardened through the deceitfulness of sin. They *took every man his censer*. Perhaps these were some of the censers which these heads of families had made use of at their family-altars, before this part of religious service was confined to the priesthood and the altar in the tabernacle (and they would bring them into use and reputation again); or they might be common chafing-dishes, which were for their ordinary use. Now to attend the solemn trial, and to be witness of the issue, one would have thought Moses should have *gathered the congregation against the rebels*, but it seems Korah gathered them against Moses (*v.* 19), which intimates that a great part of the congregation sided with Korah, were at his beck, and wished him success, and that Korah's hopes were very high of carrying the point against Aaron; for, had he suspected the event, he would not have coveted to make the trial thus public: but little did he think that he was now calling the congregation together to be the witnesses of his own confusion! Note, Proud and ambitious men, while they are projecting their own advancement, often prove to have been hurrying on their own shameful fall.

IV. The judgment set, and the Judge taking the tribunal, and threatening to give sentence against the whole congregation. 1. The *glory of the Lord appeared*, *v.* 19. The same glory that appeared to instal Aaron in his office at first (Lev. ix. 23) now appeared to confirm him in it, and to confound those that oppose him, and set up themselves in competition with him. The *Shechinah*, or divine Majesty, the glory of the eternal Word, which ordinarily dwelt between the cherubim within the veil, now was publicly seen over the door of the tabernacle, to the terror of the whole congregation; for, though they saw no manner of similitude, yet probably the appearances of the light and fire were such as plainly showed God to be angry with them; as when he appeared, *ch.* xiv. 10. Nothing is more terrible to those who are conscious of guilt than the appearances of divine glory; for such a glorious Being must needs be a formidable enemy. 2. God threatened to *consume them all in a moment*, and, in order to that, bade Moses and Aaron stand from among them, *v.* 21. God thus showed what their sin deserved, and how very provoking it was to him. See what a dangerous thing it is to have fellowship with sinners, and in the least to partake with them. **Many** of the congregation, it is likely, came only for company, following the crowd, or for curiosity, to see the issue, yet not coming, as they ought to have done, to bear their testimony against the rebels, and openly to declare for God and Moses, they had like to have been all consumed in a moment. If we follow the herd into which the devil has entered, it is at our peril.

V. The humble intercession of Moses and Aaron for the congregation, *v.* 22. 1. Their posture was importuning : they *fell on their faces,* prostrating themselves before God, as supplicants in good earnest, that they might prevail for sparing mercy. Though the people had treacherously deserted them, and struck in with those that were in arms against them, yet they approved themselves faithful to the trusts reposed in them, as shepherds of Israel, who were to stand in the breach when they saw the flock in danger. Note, If others fail in their duty to us, this does not discharge us from our duty to them, nor take off the obligations we lie under to seek their welfare. 2. Their prayer was a pleading prayer, and it proved a prevailing one. Now God would have *destroyed them* if Moses had not *turned away his wrath* (Ps. cvi. 23); yet far be it from us to imagine that Moses was more considerate or more compassionate than God in such a case as this : but God saw fit to show his just displeasure against the sin of sinners by the sentence, and at the same time to show his gracious condescension to the prayers of saints, by the revocation of the sentence at the intercession of Moses. Observe in the prayer, (1.) The title they give to God : *The God of the spirits of all flesh.* See what man is ; he is a spirit in flesh, a soul embodied, a creature wonderfully compounded of heaven and earth. See what God is ; he is the God of the spirits of all mankind. *He forms the spirit,* Zech. xii. 1. He *fathers it,* Heb. xii. 9. He has an ability to fashion it (Ps. xxxiii. 15), and authority to dispose of it, for he has said, *All souls are mine,* Ezek. xviii. 4. They insinuate hereby that though, as *the God of the spirits of all flesh,* he might in sovereignty consume this congregation in a moment, yet it was to be hoped that he would in mercy spare them, not only because they were the work of his own hands, and he had a propriety in them, but because, being the *God of spirits,* he knew their frame, and could distinguish between the leaders and the led, between those who sinned maliciously and those who were drawn in by their wiles, and would make a difference accordingly in his judgments. (2.) The argument they insist on ; it is much the same with that which Abraham urged in his intercession for Sodom (Gen. xviii. 23): *Will thou destroy the righteous with the wicked ?* Such is the plea here : *Shall one man sin and wilt thou be wroth with all the congregation ?* Not but that it was the sin of them all to join in this matter, but the

great transgression was his that first hatched the treason. Note, Whatever God may do in sovereignty and strict justice, we have reason to hope that he will not destroy a congregation for the sin of one, but that, *righteousness and peace* having *kissed each other* in the undertaking of the Redeemer, *mercy shall rejoice against judgment.* Moses knew that all the congregation must perish in the wilderness by degrees, yet he is thus earnest in prayer that they might not be consumed at once, and would reckon it a favour to obtain a reprieve. *Lord, let it alone this year.*

23 And the Lord spake unto Moses, saying, 24 Speak unto the congregation, saying, Get you up from about the tabernacle of Korah, Dathan, and Abiram. 25 And Moses rose up and went unto Dathan and Abiram ; and the elders of Israel followed him. 26 And he spake unto the congregation, saying, Depart, I pray you, from the tents of these wicked men, and touch nothing of their's, lest ye be consumed in all their sins. 27 So they gat up from the tabernacle of Korah, Dathan, and Abiram, on every side : and Dathan and Abiram came out, and stood in the door of their tents, and their wives, and their sons, and their little children. 28 And Moses said, Hereby ye shall know that the Lord hath sent me to do all these works ; for *I have* not *done them* of mine own mind. 29 If these men die the common death of all men, or if they be visited after the visitation of all men ; *then* the Lord hath not sent me. 30 But if the Lord make a new thing, and the earth open her mouth, and swallow them up, with all that *appertain* unto them, and they go down quick into the pit ; then ye shall understand that these men have provoked the Lord. 31 And it came to pass, as he had made an end of speaking all these words, that the ground clave asunder that *was* under them : 32 And the earth opened her mouth, and swallowed them up, and their houses, and all the men that *appertained* unto Korah, and all *their* goods. 33 They, and all that *appertained* to them, went down alive into the pit, and the earth closed upon them : and they perished from among the congregation. 34 And all Israel

that *were* round about them fled at the cry of them : for they said, Lest the earth swallow us up *also*.

We have here the determining of the controversy with Dathan and Abiram, who rebelled against Moses, as in the next paragraph the determining of the controversy with Korah and his company, who would be rivals with Aaron. It should seem that Dathan and Abiram had set up a spacious tabernacle in the midst of the tents of their families, where they kept court, met in council, and hung out their flag of defiance against Moses; it is here called *the tabernacle of Korah, Dathan, and Abiram, v.* 24, 27. There, as in the place of rendezvous, Dathan and Abiram staid, when Korah and his friends went up to the tabernacle of the Lord, waiting the issue of their trial; but here we are told how they had their business done, before that trial was over. For God will take what method he pleases in his judgments.

I. Public warning is given to the congregation to withdraw immediately from the tents of the rebels. 1. God bids Moses speak to this purport, *v.* 24. This was in answer to Moses's prayer. He had begged that God would not *destroy the whole congregation.* "Well," says God, "I will not, provided they be so wise as to shift for their own safety, and get out of the way of danger. If they will quit the rebels, well and good, they shall not perish with them; otherwise, let them take what follows." Note, We cannot expect to reap benefit by the prayers of our friends for our salvation, unless we ourselves be diligent and faithful in making use of the means of salvation; for God never promised to save by miracles those that would not save themselves by means. Moses that had prayed for them must preach this to them, and warn them to *flee from this wrath to come.* 2. Moses accordingly repairs to the head-quarters of the rebels, leaving Aaron at the door of the tabernacle, *v.* 25. Dathan and Abiram had contumaciously refused to come up to him (*v.* 12), yet he humbly condescends to go down to them, to try if he could yet convince and reclaim them. Ministers must thus with meekness instruct those that oppose themselves, and not think it below them to stoop to those that are most stubborn, for their good. Christ himself stretches out his hand to a rebellious and gainsaying people. The seventy elders of Israel attend Moses as his guard, to secure him from the insolence of the rabble, and by their presence to put an honour upon him, and if possible to strike an awe upon the rebels. It is our duty to contribute all we can to the countenance and support of injured innocency and honour. 3. Proclamation is made that all manner of persons, as they tendered their own safety, should forthwith *depart from the tents of these wicked men* (*v.* 26), and thus should signify that they de-

serted their cause and interest, detested their crimes and counsels, and dreaded the punishment coming upon them. Note, Those that would not perish with sinners must *come out from among them,* and be separate. In vain do we pray, *Gather not our souls with sinners,* if we save not ourselves from the *untoward generation.* God's people are called out of Babylon, lest they share both in her sins and in her plagues, Rev. xviii. 4.

II. The congregation takes the warning, but the rebels themselves continue obstinate, *v.* 27. 1. God, in mercy, inclined the people to forsake the rebels : *They got up from the tabernacle of Korah, Dathan, and Abiram,* both those whose lot it was to pitch near them (who doubtless with themselves removed their families, and all their effects) and those also who had come from all parts of their camp to see the issue. It was in answer to the prayer of Moses that God thus stirred up the hearts of the congregation to shift for their own preservation. Note, To those whom God will save he gives repentance, that they may *recover themselves out of the snare of the devil.* Grace to separate from evil doers is one of the things that accompany salvation. 2. God, in justice, left the rebels to the obstinacy and hardness of their own hearts. Though they saw themselves abandoned by all their neighbours, and set up as a mark to the arrows of God's justice, yet instead of falling down and humbling themselves before God and Moses, owning their crime and begging pardon, instead of fleeing and dispersing themselves to seek for shelter in the crowd, they impudently *stood in the doors of their tents,* as if they would out-face God himself, and dare him to his worst. Thus were their hearts hardened to their own destruction, and they were fearless when their case was most fearful. But what a pity was it that their little children, who were not capable of guilt or fear, should by the presumption of their parents be put in this audacious posture ! Happy they who are taught betimes to bow before God, and not as those unhappy little ones to stand it out against him !

III. Sentence is solemnly pronounced upon them by Moses in the name of the Lord, and the decision of the controversy is put upon the execution of that sentence by the almighty power of God. Moses, by divine instinct and direction, when the eyes of all Israel were fastened upon him, waiting the event, moved with a just and holy indignation at the impudence of the rebels, boldly puts the whole matter to a surprising issue, *v.* 28—30. 1. If the rebels die a common death, he will be content to be called and counted an impostor ; not only if they die a natural death, but if they die by any sort of judgment that has formerly been executed on other malefactors. " If they die by the plague, or by fire from heaven, or by the sword, then say, God has disowned Moses ;" but, 2. "If the earth open and swallow them up" (a punishment without precedent), "then let all the house of Israel know assuredly that I am God's servant, sent by him, and employed for him, and that those that fight against me fight against him." The judgment itself would have been proof enough of God's displeasure against the rebels, and would have given all men to *understand that they had provoked the Lord;* but when it was thus solemnly foretold and appealed to by Moses beforehand, when there was not the least previous indication of it from without, the convincing evidence of it was much the stronger, and it was put beyond dispute that he was not only a servant but a favourite of Heaven, who was so intimately acquainted with the divine counsels, and could obtain such extraordinary appearances of the divine power in his vindication.

IV. Execution is immediately done. It appeared that God and his servant Moses understood one another very well; for, as soon as ever Moses had spoken the word, God did the work, the earth *clave asunder (v. 31), opened her mouth, and swallowed them all up,* them and theirs (v. 32), and then *closed upon them, v. 33.* This judgment was, 1. Unparalleled. God, in it, *created a new thing,* did what he never did before; for he has many arrows in his quiver; and there are diversities of operations in wrath as well as mercy. Dathan and Abiram thought themselves safe because they were at a distance from the *shechinah,* whence the fire of the Lord had sometimes issued, *qui procul à Jove* (they say) *procul à fulmine—he who is far from Jove is far from the thunderbolt.* But God made them to know that he was not tied up to one way of punishing; the earth, when he pleases, shall serve his justice as effectually as the fire. 2. It was very terrible to the sinners themselves to go down alive into their own graves, to be dead and buried in an instant, to go down thus to the bars of the pit when they were in their *full strength wholly at ease and quiet.* 3. It was severe upon their poor children, who, for the greater terror of the judgment, and fuller indication of the divine wrath, perished as parts of their parents, in which, though we cannot particularly tell how bad they might be to deserve it or how good God might be otherwise to them to compensate it, yet of this we are sure in the general, that Infinite Justice did them no wrong. *Far be it from God that he should do iniquity.* 4. It was altogether miraculous. The cleaving of the earth was as wonderful, and as much above the power of nature, as the cleaving of the sea, and the closing of the earth again more so than the closing of the waters. God has all the creatures at his command, and can make any of them, when he pleases, instruments of his justice; nor will any of them be our friends if he be our enemy. God now confirmed to Israel what Moses had lately taught

them in that prayer of his, Ps. xc. 11, *Who knows the power of thy anger?* He has, when he pleases, *strange punishments for the workers of iniquity,* Job xxxi. 3. Let us therefore conclude, *Who is able to stand before this holy Lord God?* 5. It was very significant. They *set their mouths against the heavens,* and *their throat was an open sepulchre;* justly therefore does the earth open her mouth upon them and swallow them up. They made a rent in the congregation; justly therefore is the earth rent under them. Presumptuous sinners, that hate to be reformed, are a burden to the earth, the whole creation groans under them, which here was signified by this, that the earth sunk under these rebels, as weary of bearing them and being under them. And, considering how the earth is still in like manner loaded with the weight of iniquity, we have reason to wonder that this was the only time it ever sunk under its load. 6. It was typical of the eternal ruin of sinners who die impenitent, who, perhaps in allusion to this, are said to *sink down into the pit* (Ps. ix. 15) and to *go down quickly into hell,* Ps. lv. 15. But David, even when he *sinks in deep mire,* yet prays in faith, *Let not the pit shut her mouth upon me,* as it does on the damned, between whom and life there is a gulf fixed, Ps. lxix. 2—15. His case was bad, but not, like this, desperate.

V. All Israel is alarmed at the judgment: *They fled at the cry of them, v. 34.* They cried for help when it was too late. Their doleful shrieks, instead of fetching their neighbours in to their relief, drove them so much the further off; for knowing their own guilt, and one another's, they hastened one another, saying, *Lest the earth swallow us up also.* Note, Others' ruins should be our warnings. Could we by faith hear the outcries of those that have gone down to the bottomless pit, we should give more diligence than we do to escape for our lives, lest we also come into that condemnation.

35 And there came out a fire from the LORD, and consumed the two hundred and fifty men that offered incense. 36 And the LORD spake unto Moses, saying, 37 Speak unto Eleazar the son of Aaron the priest, that he take up the censers out of the burning, and scatter thou the fire yonder; for they are hallowed. 38 The censers of these sinners against their own souls, let them make them broad plates *for* a covering of the altar: for they offered them before the LORD, therefore they are hallowed: and they shall be a sign unto the children of Israel. 39 And Eleazar the priest took the brazen censers, wherewith they that were burnt had

offered ; and they were made broad *plates for* a covering of the altar; 40 *To be* a memorial unto the children of Israel, that no stranger, which *is* not of the seed of Aaron, come near to offer incense before the LORD; that he be not as Korah, and as his company : as the LORD said to him by the hand of Moses.

We must now look back to the door of the tabernacle, where we left the pretenders to the priesthood with their censers in their hands ready to offer incense ; and here we find,

I. Vengeance taken on them, *v.* 35. It is probable that when the earth opened in the camp to swallow up Dathan and Abiram *a fire went out from the Lord and consumed the* 250 *men that offered incense,* while Aaron that stood with them was preserved alive. This punishment was not indeed so new a thing as the former, for Nadab and Abihu thus died; but it was no less strange or dreadful, and in it it appeared, 1. That *our God is a consuming fire.* Is thunder a sensible indication of the terror of his voice? Lightning is also of the power of his hand. We must see in this his fiery indignation which devours the adversaries, and infer from it what a fearful thing it is to *fall into the hands of the living God,* Heb. x. 27—31. 2. That it is at our peril if we meddle with that which does not belong to us. God is jealous of the honour of his own institutions, and will not have them invaded. It is most probable that Korah himself was consumed with those 250 that presumed to offer incense ; for the priesthood was the thing he aimed at, and therefore we have reason to think that he would not quit his post at the door of the tabernacle. But, behold, those are made sacrifices to the justice of God who flattered themselves with the hopes of being priests. Had they been content with their office as Levites, which was sacred and honourable, and better than they deserved, they might have lived and died with joy and reputation; but, like the angels that sinned, *leaving their first estate,* and aiming at the honours that were not appointed them, they were thrust down to *Hades,* their censers struck out of their hands, and their breath out of their bodies, by a burning which typified *the vengeance of eternal fire.*

II. Care is taken to perpetuate the remembrance of this vengeance. No mention is made of the taking up of their carcases : the scripture leaves them as dung upon the face of the earth; but orders are given about their censers, 1. That they be secured, because they are hallowed. Eleazar is charged with this, *v.* 37. Those invaders of the priesthood had proceeded so far, by the divine patience and submission, as to kindle their incense with fire from off the altar, which they were suffered to use by way of

experiment : but, as soon as they had kindled their fire, God kindled another, which put a fatal final period to their pretensions ; now Eleazar is ordered to scatter the fire, with the incense that was kindled with it, in some unclean place without the camp, to signify God's abhorrence of their offering as a polluted thing : *The sacrifice of the wicked is an abomination to the Lord.* But he is to gather up the censers out of the mingled burning, God's fire and theirs, because *they are hallowed.* Having been once put to a holy use, and that by God's own order (though only for trial), they must not return to common service ; so some understand it : rather, *they are devoted,* they are an anathema ; and therefore, as all devoted things, they must be made some way or other serviceable to the glory of God. 2. That they be used in the service of the sanctuary, not as censers, which would rather have put honour upon the usurpers whose disgrace was intended ; nor was there occasion for brazen censers, the golden altar was served with golden ones ; but they must be beaten into *broad plates for a covering of the brazen altar, v.* 38—40. These pretenders thought to have ruined the altar, by laying the priesthood in common again ; but, to show that Aaron's office was so far from being shaken by their impotent malice that it was rather confirmed by it, their censers, which offered to rival his, were used both for the adorning and for the preserving of the altar at which he ministered. Yet this was not all ; this covering of the altar must be a *memorial to the children of Israel,* throughout their generations, of this great event. Though there was so much in it astonishing, and though Moses was to record it in his history, yet there was danger of its being forgotten in process of time ; impressions that seem deep are not always durable ; therefore it was necessary to appoint this record of the judgment, that the Levites who attended this altar, and had their inferior services appointed them, might learn to keep within their bounds, and be afraid of transgressing them, lest they should be made like Korah and his company, who were Levites, and would have been priests. These censers were preserved *in terrorem,* that others might hear and fear, and do no more presumptuously. Thus God has provided that his wonderful works, both in mercy and judgment, should be had in everlasting remembrance, that the end of them may be answered, and they may serve for instruction and admonition to those *on whom the ends of the world are come.*

41 But on the morrow all the congregation of the children of Israel murmured against Moses and against Aaron, saying, Ye have killed the people of the LORD. 42 And it came to pass, when the congregation was

gathered against Moses and against Aaron, that they looked toward the tabernacle of the congregation: and, behold, the cloud covered it, and the glory of the LORD appeared. 43 And Moses and Aaron came before the tabernacle of the congregation. 44 And the LORD spake unto Moses, saying, 45 Get you up from among this congregation, that I may consume them as in a moment. And they fell upon their faces. 46 And Moses said unto Aaron, Take a censer, and put fire therein from off the altar, and put on incense, and go quickly unto the congregation, and make an atonement for them: for there is wrath gone out from the LORD; the plague is begun. 47 And Aaron took as Moses commanded, and ran into the midst of the congregation; and, behold, the plague was begun among the people: and he put on incense, and made an atonement for the people. 48 And he stood between the dead and the living; and the plague was stayed. 49 Now they that died in the plague were fourteen thousand and seven hundred, beside them that died about the matter of Korah. 50 And Aaron returned unto Moses unto the door of the tabernacle of the congregation: and the plague was stayed.

Here is, I. A new rebellion raised the very next day against Moses and Aaron. Be astonished, O heavens, at this, and wonder, O earth! Was there ever such an instance of the incurable corruption of sinners? *On the morrow* (v. 41) the body of the people mutinied. 1. Though they were so lately terrified by the sight of the punishment of the rebels. The shrieks of those sinking sinners, those sinners against their own souls, were yet sounding in their ears, the smell of the fire yet remained, and the gaping earth was scarcely thoroughly closed, and yet the same sins were re-acted and all these warnings slighted. 2. Though they were so lately saved from sharing in the same punishment, and the survivors were *as brands plucked out of the burning*, yet they fly in the face of Moses and Aaron, to whose intercession they owed their preservation. Their charge runs very high: *You have killed the people of the Lord.* Could any thing have been said more unjustly and maliciously? They canonize the rebels, calling those the people of the Lord who died in arms against him. They

stigmatize divine justice itself. It was plain enough that Moses and Aaron had no hand in their death (they did what they could to save them), so that in charging them with murder they did in effect charge God himself with it. The continued obstinacy of this people, notwithstanding the terrors of God's law as it was given on Mount Sinai, and the terrors of his judgments as they were here executed on the disobedient, shows how necessary the grace of God is to the effectual change of men's hearts and lives, without which the most likely means will never attain the end. Love will do what fear could not.

II. God's speedy appearance against the rebels. When they had *gathered against Moses and Aaron,* perhaps with a design to depose or murder them, they *looked towards the tabernacle,* as if their misgiving consciences expected some frowns thence, and, *behold, the glory of the Lord appeared* (v. 42), for the protection of his servants, and the confusion of his and their accusers and adversaries. Moses and Aaron thereupon came before the tabernacle, partly for their own safety (there they took sanctuary from the strife of tongues, Ps. xxvii. 5; xxxi. 20), and partly for advice, to know what was the mind of God upon this occasion, *v.* 43. Justice hereupon declares that they deserve to be *consumed in a moment, v.* 45. Why should those live another day who hate to be reformed, and whose rebellions are their daily practices? Let just vengeance take place and do its work, and the trouble with them will soon be over; only Moses and Aaron must first be secured.

III. The intercession which Moses and Aaron made for them. Though they had as much reason, one would think, as Elias had to make intercession against Israel (Rom. xi. 2), yet they forgive and forget the indignities offered them, and are the best friends their enemies have. 1. They both *fell on their faces,* humbly to intercede with God for mercy, knowing how great the provocation was. This they had done several times before, upon similar occasions; and, though the people had basely requited them for it, yet, God having graciously accepted them, they still have recourse to the same method. This is praying always. 2. Moses, perceiving that the *plague had begun in the congregation* of the rebels (that is, that body of them which was gathered together against Moses), sent Aaron by an act of his priestly office to make atonement for them, *v.* 46. And Aaron readily went and burned incense between the living and the dead, not to purify the infected air, but to pacify an offended God, and so stayed the progress of the judgment. By this it appeared, (1.) That Aaron was a very good man, and a man that had a true love for the children of his people, though they hated and envied him. Though God was now avenging his quarrel and pleading the cause of his priesthood,

yet he interposes to turn away God's wrath.
Nay, forgetting his age and gravity, he ran
into the midst of the congregation to help
them. He did not say, "Let them smart
awhile, and then, when I come, I shall be
the more welcome;" but, as one tender of
the life of every Israelite, he makes all possible speed into the gap at which death was
entering. Moses and Aaron, who had been
charged with killing the people of the Lord,
might justly have upbraided them now;
could they expect those to be their saviours
whom they had so invidiously called their
murderers? But those good men have
taught us here by their example not to be
sullen towards those that are peevish with
us, nor to take the advantage which men
give us by their provoking language to deny
them any real kindness which it is in the
power of our hands to do them. We must
render good for evil. (2.) That Aaron was
a very bold man—bold to venture into the
midst of an enraged rabble that were gathered together against him, and who, for
aught he knew, might be the more exasperated by the plague that had begun—bold to
venture into the midst of the infection,
where the arrows of death flew thickest, and
hundreds, nay thousands, were falling on the
right hand and on the left. To save their lives
he put his own into his hand, not counting it
dear to him, so that he might but fulfil
his ministry. (3.) That Aaron was a man of
God, and *ordained for men, in things pertaining to God.* His call to the priesthood was
hereby abundantly confirmed and set above
all contradiction; God had not only saved
his life when the intruders were cut off, but
now made him an instrument for saving
Israel. Compare the censer of Aaron here
with the *censers of those sinners against their
own souls.* Those provoked God's anger,
this pacified it; those destroyed men's lives,
this saved them; no room therefore is left to
doubt of Aaron's call to the priesthood.
Note, Those make out the best title to public honours that lay out themselves the most
for the public good and obtain mercy of the
Lord to be faithful and useful. If any man
will be great, let him make himself the servant of all. (4.) That Aaron was a type of
Christ, who came into the world to make an
atonement for sin and to turn away the
wrath of God from us, and who, by his mediation and intercession, *stands between the
living and the dead,* to secure his chosen
Israel to himself, and save them out of the
midst of a world infected with sin and the
curse.

IV. The result and issue of the whole
matter. 1. God's justice was glorified in
the death of some. Great execution the
sword of the Lord did in a very little time.
Though Aaron made all the haste he could,
yet, before he could reach his post of service,
there were 14,700 men laid dead upon the spot,
v. 49. There were but few comparatively
646

that died about the matter of Koran, the
ring-leaders only were made examples; but,
the people not being led to repentance by
the patience and forbearance of God with
them, justice is not now so sparing of the
blood of Israelites. They complained of the
death of a few hundreds as an unmerciful
slaughter made among the *people of the
Lord,* but here God silences that complaint
by the slaughter of many thousands. Note,
Those that quarrel with less judgments prepare greater for themselves; for when God
judges he will overcome. 2. His mercy was
glorified in the preservation of the rest. God
showed them what he could do by his power,
and what he might do in justice, but then
showed them what he would do in his love
and pity: he would, notwithstanding all this,
preserve them a people to himself in and by
a mediator. The cloud of Aaron's incense
coming from his hand stayed the plague.
Note, It is much for the glory of God's
goodness that many a time even in wrath he
remembers mercy. And, even when judgments have been begun, prayer puts a stop
to them; so ready is he to forgive, and so
little pleasure does he take in the death of
sinners.

<h2 style="text-align:center">CHAP. XVII.</h2>

Enough had been done in the chapter before to quash all pretensions
of the families of the tribe of Levi that would set up in competition with Aaron, and to make it appear that Aaron was the head
of that tribe; but it seems, when that matter was settled, the
princes of the rest of the tribes began to murmur. If the head
of a tribe must be a priest, why not the head of some other
tribe than that of Levi? He that searches the heart knew
this thought to be in the breast of some of them, and before it
broke out into any overt act graciously anticipated it, to prevent
bloodshed; and it is done by miracle in this chapter, not a
miracle of wrath, as before, but of grace. I. The matter is put
upon trial by the bringing of twelve rods, one for each prince,
before the Lord, ver. 1—7. II. Upon trial, the matter is determined by the miraculous blossoming of Aaron's rod, ver. 8, 9.
III. The decision of the controversy is registered by the preservation of the rod, ver. 10, 11. IV. The people acquiesce in it with
some reluctance, ver. 12, 13.

AND the LORD spake unto Moses,
saying, 2 Speak unto the children of Israel, and take of every one
of them a rod according to the house
of *their* fathers, of all their princes
according to the house of their fathers
twelve rods: write thou every man's
name upon his rod. 3 And thou shalt
write Aaron's name upon the rod of
Levi: for one rod *shall be* for the
head of the house of their fathers. 4
And thou shalt lay them up in the
tabernacle of the congregation before
the testimony, where I will meet with
you. 5 And it shall come to pass,
that the man's rod, whom I shall
choose, shall blossom: and I will make
to cease from me the murmurings of
the children of Israel, whereby they
murmur against you. 6 And Moses
spake unto the children of Israel, and
every one of their princes gave him a

rod apiece, for each prince one, according to their fathers' houses, *even* twelve rods: and the rod of Aaron *was* among their rods. 7 And Moses laid up the rods before the LORD in the tabernacle of witness.

Here we have, I. Orders given for the bringing in of a rod for every tribe (which was peculiarly significant, for the word here used for a rod sometimes signifies a tribe, as particularly *ch.* xxxiv. 13), that God by a miracle, wrought on purpose, might make it known on whom he had conferred the honour of the priesthood. 1. It seems then the priesthood was a preferment worth seeking and striving for, even by the princes of the tribes. It is an honour to the greatest of men to be employed in the service of God. Yet perhaps these contended for it rather for the sake of the profit and power that attended the office than for the sake of that in it which was divine and sacred. 2. It seems likewise, after all that had been done to settle this matter, there were those who would be ready upon any occasion to contest it. They would not acquiesce in the divine appointment, but would make an interest in opposition to it. They strive with God for the dominion; and the question is whose will shall stand. God will rule, but Israel will not be ruled; and this is the quarrel. 3. It is an instance of the grace of God that, having wrought divers miracles to punish sin, he would work one more on purpose to prevent it. God has effectually provided that the obstinate shall be left inexcusable, and every mouth shall be stopped. Israel were very prone to murmur both against God and against their governors. "Now," said God, "*I will make to cease from me the murmurings of the children of Israel, v.* 5. If any thing will convince them, they shall be convinced; and, if this will not convince them, nothing will." This was to be to them, as Christ said the sign of the prophet Jonas (that is, his own resurrection) should be to the men of that generation, the highest proof of his mission that should be given them. The directions are, (1.) That twelve rods or staves should be brought in. It is probable that they were not now fresh cut out of a tree, for then the miracle would not have been so great; but that they were the staves which the princes ordinarily used as ensigns of their authority (of which we read *ch.* xxi. 18), old dry staves, that had no sap in them, and it is probable that they were all made of the almond-tree. It should seem they were but twelve in all, with Aaron's, for, when Levi comes into the account, Ephraim and Manasseh make but one, under the name of Joseph. (2.) That the name of each prince should be written upon his rod, that every man might know his own, and to prevent contests. Writing

is often a good preservative against strife, for what is written may be appealed to. (3.) That they should be laid up in the tabernacle, for one night, before the testimony, that is, before the ark, which, with its mercy-seat, was a symbol, token, or testimony, of God's presence with them. (4.) They were to expect, being told it before, that the rod of the tribe, or prince, whom God chose to the priesthood, should bud and blossom, *v.* 5. It was requisite that they should be told of it, that it might appear not to be casual, but according to the counsel and will of God.

II. The preparing of the rods accordingly. The princes brought them in, some of them perhaps fondly expecting that the choice would fall upon them, and all of them thinking it honour enough to be competitors with Aaron, and to stand candidates, even for the priesthood (*v.* 7); and *Moses laid them up before the Lord.* He did not object that the matter was sufficiently settled already, and enough done to convince those that were not invincibly hardened in their prejudices. He did not undertake to determine the controversy himself, though it might easily have been done; nor did he suggest that it would be to no purpose to offer satisfaction to a people that were willingly blind. But, since God will have it so, he did his part, and lodged the case before the Lord, to whom the appeal was made by consent, and left it with him.

8 And it came to pass, that on the morrow Moses went into the tabernacle of witness; and, behold, the rod of Aaron for the house of Levi was budded, and brought forth buds, and bloomed blossoms, and yielded almonds. 9 And Moses brought out all the rods from before the LORD unto all the children of Israel: and they looked, and took every man his rod. 10 And the LORD said unto Moses, Bring Aaron's rod again before the testimony, to be kept for a token against the rebels; and thou shalt quite take away their murmurings from me, that they die not. 11 And Moses did *so:* as the LORD commanded him, so did he. 12 And the children of Israel spake unto Moses, saying, Behold, we die, we perish, we all perish. 13 Whosoever cometh any thing near unto the tabernacle of the LORD shall die: shall we be consumed with dying?

Here is, I. The final determination of the controversy concerning the priesthood by a miracle, *v.* 8, 9. The rods or staves were brought out from the most holy place where they were laid up, and publicly produced before the people; and, while all the rest of the rods remained as they were, Aaron's rod only, of a dry stick, became a living branch, budded, and blossomed, and yielded almonds. In some places there were buds, in others blossoms, in others fruit, at the same time. This was miraculous, and took away all suspicion of a fraud, as if in the night Moses had taken away Aaron's rod, and put a living branch of an almond tree in the room of it; for no ordinary branch would have buds, blossoms, and fruits upon it, all at once. Now,

1. This was a plain indication to the people that Aaron was chosen to the priesthood, and not any other of the princes of the tribes. Thus he was distinguished from them and manifested to be under the special blessing of heaven, which sometimes yields increase where there is neither planting nor watering by the hand of man. Bishop Hall here observes that fruitfulness is the best evidence of a divine call, and that the plants of God's setting, and the boughs cut off from them, will flourish. See Ps. xcii. 12—14. The trees of the Lord, though they seem dry trees, are full of sap.

2. It was a very proper sign to represent the priesthood itself, which was hereby confirmed to Aaron. (1.) That it should be fruitful and serviceable to the church of God. It produced not only blossoms, but almonds; for the priesthood was designed, not only for an honour to Aaron, but for a blessing to Israel. Thus Christ ordained his apostles and ministers that they should go and bring forth fruit, and that their *fruit should remain*, John xv. 16. (2.) That there should be a succession of priests. Here were not only almonds for the present, but buds and blossoms promising more hereafter. Thus has Christ provided in his church that a seed should serve him from generation to generation. (3.) That yet this priesthood should not be perpetual, but in process of time, like the branches and blossoms of a tree, should fail and wither. The flourishing of the almond-tree is mentioned as one of the signs of old age, Eccl. xii. 5. This character was betimes put upon the Mosaic priesthood, which soon became old and *ready to vanish away*, Heb. viii. 13.

3. It was a type and figure of Christ and his priesthood: for he is *the man, the branch*, that is to be *a priest upon his throne*, as it follows (Zech. vi. 12); and he was to *grow up before God*, as this before the ark, *like a tender plant, and a root out of a dry ground*, Isa. liii. 2.

II. The record of this determination, by the preserving of the rod before the testimony, *in perpetuam rei memoriam—that it might be had in perpetual remembrance*, v. 10, 11. It is probable that the buds, and blossoms, and fruit, continued fresh; the same divine power that produced them in a night preserved them for ages, at least so long as it was necessary for a token against the

rebels. So it was a standing miracle, and the continuance of it was an undeniable proof of the truth of it. Even the leaf of God's trees shall not wither, Ps. i. 3. This rod was preserved, as the censers were, to *take away their murmurings, that they die not.* Note, 1. The design of God in all his providences, both mercies and judgments, and in the memorials of them, is to take away sin, and to prevent it. These things are done, these things written, *that we sin not*, 1 John ii. 1. Christ was *manifested to take away sin.* 2. What God does for the taking away of sin is done in real kindness to us, *that we die not.* All the bitter potions he gives, and all the sharp methods he uses with us, are for the cure of a disease which otherwise would certainly be fatal. Bishop Hall observes here that the tables of the law, the pot of manna, and Aaron's rod, were preserved together in or about the ark (the apostle takes notice of them all three together, Heb. ix. 4), to show to after-ages how the ancient church was taught, and fed, and ruled; and he infers how precious the doctrine, sacraments, and government, of the church are to God and should be to us. The rod of Moses was used in working many miracles, yet we do not find that this was preserved, for the keeping of it would serve only to gratify men's curiosity; but the rod of Aaron, which carried its miracle along with it, was carefully preserved, because that would be of standing use to convince men's consciences, to silence all disputes about the priesthood, and to confirm the faith of God's Israel in his institutions. Such is the difference between the sacraments which Christ has appointed for edification and the relics which men have devised for superstition.

III. The outcry of the people hereupon (v. 12, 13): *Behold, we die, we perish, we all perish. Shall we be consumed with dying?* This may be considered as the language either, 1. Of a repining people quarrelling with the judgments of God, which, by their own pride and obstinacy, they had brought upon themselves. They seem to speak despairingly, as if God was a hard Master, that sought advantage against them, and took all occasions to pick quarrels with them, so that if they trod ever so little awry, if they stepped ever so little beyond their bounds, they must die, they must perish, they must all perish, basely insinuating that God would never be satisfied with their blood and ruin, till he had made an end of them all and they were consumed with dying. Thus they seem to be like a *wild bull in a net, full of the fury of the Lord* (Isa. li. 20), fretting that God was too hard for them and that they were forced to submit, which they did only because they could not help it. Note, It is a very wicked thing to fret against God when we are in affliction, and in our distress thus to trespass yet more. If we die, if we perish, it is owing to ourselves, and the blame

648

will lie upon our own heads. Or, 2. Of a repenting people. Many interpreters take it as expressing their submission: "Now we see that it is the will of God we should keep our distance, and that it is at our peril if we draw nearer than is appointed. We submit to the divine will in this appointment; we will not contend any more, lest we all perish:" and they engage Moses to intercede for them, that they may not be all consumed with dying. Thus the point was gained, and in this matter God quite took away their murmurings, and henceforward they acquiesced. Note, When God judges he will overcome, and, one way or other, will oblige the most obstinate gainsayers to confess their folly sooner or later, and that wherein they dealt proudly he was above them. *Vicisti Galilæe—O Galilæan, thou hast conquered!*

CHAP. XVIII.

Aaron being now fully established in the priesthood abundantly to his own satisfaction, and to the satisfaction of the people (which was the good that God brought out of the evil opposition made to him), in this chapter God gives him full instructions concerning his office or rather repeats those which he had before given him. He tells him, I. What must be his work and the care and charge committed to him, and what assistance he should have from the Levites in that work, ver. 1–7. II. What should be his and the Levites' wages for this work. 1. The perquisites or fees peculiar to the priests, ver. 8–19. 2. The settled maintenance of the Levites, ver. 20–21. III. The portion which must be paid to the priests out of the Levites' maintenance, ver. 25–32. Thus every one knew what he had to do, and what he had to live upon.

AND the Lord said unto Aaron, Thou and thy sons and thy father's house with thee shall bear the iniquity of the sanctuary: and thou and thy sons with thee shall bear the iniquity of your priesthood. 2 And thy brethren also of the tribe of Levi, the tribe of thy father, bring thou with thee, that they may be joined unto thee, and minister unto thee: but thou and thy sons with thee *shall minister* before the tabernacle of witness. 3 And they shall keep thy charge, and the charge of all the tabernacle: only they shall not come nigh the vessels of the sanctuary and the altar, that neither they, nor ye also, die. 4 And they shall be joined unto thee, and keep the charge of the tabernacle of the congregation, for all the service of the tabernacle: and a stranger shall not come nigh unto you. 5 And ye shall keep the charge of the sanctuary, and the charge of the altar: that there be no wrath any more upon the children of Israel. 6 And I, behold, I have taken your brethren the Levites from among the children of Israel: to you *they are* given *as* a gift for the Lord, to do the service of the tabernacle of the congregation. 7 There-

fore thou and thy sons with thee shall keep your priest's office for every thing of the altar, and within the veil; and ye shall serve: I have given your priest's office *unto you as* a service of gift: and the stranger that cometh nigh shall be put to death.

The coherence of this chapter with that foregoing is very observable.

I. The people, in the close of that chapter, had complained of the difficulty and peril that there were in drawing near to God, which put them under some dreadful apprehensions that the tabernacle in the midst of them, which they hoped would have been their joy and glory, would rather be their terror and ruin. Now, in answer to this complaint, God here gives them to understand by Aaron that the priests should come near for them as their representatives; so that, though the people were obliged to keep their distance, yet that should not at all redound to their disgrace or prejudice, but their comfortable communion with God should be kept up by the interposition of the priests.

II. A great deal of honour God had now lately put upon Aaron; his rod had budded and blossomed, when the rods of the rest of the princes remained dry, and destitute both of fruit and ornament. Now lest Aaron should be puffed up with the abundance of the favours that were done him, and the miracles that were wrought for the support of him in his high station, God comes to him to remind him of the burden that was laid upon him, and the duty required from him as a priest. He would see reason not to be proud of his preferment, but to receive the honours of his office with reverence and holy trembling, when he considered how great was the charge committed to him, and how hard it would be for him to give a good account of it. *Be not high-minded, but fear.*

1. God tells him of the danger that attended his dignity, *v.* 1. (1.) That both the priests and Levites *(thou, and thy sons, and thy father's house)* should *bear the iniquity of the sanctuary;* that is, if the sanctuary were profaned by the intrusion of strangers, or persons in their uncleanness, the blame should lie upon the Levites and priests, who ought to have kept them off. Though the sinner that thrust in presumptuously should die in his iniquity, yet his blood should be required at the hands of the watchmen. Or it may be taken more generally: "If any of the duties or offices of the sanctuary be neglected, if any service be not done in its season or not according to the law, if any thing be lost or misplaced in the removal of the sanctuary, you shall be accountable for it, and answer it at your peril." (2.) That the priests should themselves *bear the iniquity of the priesthood;* that is, if they either neglected any part of their work or

649

permitted any other persons to invade their office, and take their work out of their hands, they should bear the blame of it. Note, The greater the trust is of work and power that is committed to us the greater is our danger of contracting guilt, by falsifying and betraying that trust. This is a good reason why we should neither be envious at others' honours nor ambitious ourselves of high places, because great dignity exposes us to great iniquity. Those that are entrusted with the charge of the sanctuary will have a great deal to answer for. Who would covet the care of souls who considers the account that must be given of that care?

2. He tells him of the duty that attended his dignity. (1.) That he and his sons must *minister before the tabernacle of witness* (v. 2); that is (as bishop Patrick explains it), *before the most holy place*, in which the ark was, on the outside of the veil of that tabernacle, but within the door of the tabernacle of the congregation. They were to attend the golden altar, the table, and candlestick, which no Levite might approach to. *You shall serve, v. 7.* Not, "You shall rule" (it was never intended that they should lord it over God's heritage), but "You shall serve God and the congregation." Note, The priesthood is a service. *If any desire the office of a bishop he desires a good work.* Ministers must remember that they are ministers, that is, servants, of whom it is required that they be humble, diligent, and faithful. (2.) That the Levites must assist him and his sons, and minister to them in all the *service of the tabernacle* (v. 2—4), though they must by no means come nigh the vessels of the sanctuary, nor at the altar meddle with the great services of burning the fat and sprinkling the blood. Aaron's family was very small, and, as it increased, the rest of the families of Israel would increase likewise, so that the hands of the priests neither were now nor were likely to be sufficient for all the service of the tabernacle; therefore (says God) *the Levites shall be joined to thee, v. 2,* and again *v. 4,* where there seems to be an allusion to the name of Levi, which signifies *joined.* Many of the Levites had of late set themselves against Aaron, but henceforward God promises that they should be heartily joined to him in interest and affection, and should no more contest with him. It was a good sign to Aaron that God owned him when he inclined the hearts of those concerned to own him too. The Levites are said to be given as a gift to the priests, *v. 6.* Note, We are to value it as a great gift of the divine bounty to have those joined to us that will be helpful and serviceable to us in the service of God. (3.) That both priests and Levites must carefully watch against the profanation of sacred things. The Levites must *keep the charge of the tabernacle,* that *no stranger* (that is, none who upon any account was forbidden to come) might *come nigh* (v. 4), and that upon

pain of death, *v. 7.* And the priests must *keep the charge of the sanctuary* (v. 5), must instruct the people, and admonish them concerning the due distance they were to keep, and not suffer them to break the bounds set them, as Korah's company had done, that there be *no wrath any more upon the children of Israel.* Note, The preventing of sin is the preventing of wrath; and the mischief sin has done should be a warning to us for the future to watch against it both in ourselves and others.

8 And the LORD spake unto Aaron, Behold, I also have given thee the charge of mine heave offerings of all the hallowed things of the children of Israel; unto thee have I given them by reason of the anointing, and to thy sons, by an ordinance for ever. 9 This shall be thine of the most holy things, *reserved* from the fire : every oblation of their's, every meat offering of their's, and every sin offering of their's, and every trespass offering of their's, which they shall render unto me, *shall be* most holy for thee and for thy sons. 10 In the most holy *place* shalt thou eat it; every male shall eat it : it shall be holy unto thee. 11 And this *is* thine; the heave offering of their gift, with all the wave offerings of the children of Israel : I have given them unto thee, and to thy sons and to thy daughters with thee, by a statute for ever : every one that is clean in thy house shall eat of it. 12 All the best of the oil, and all the best of the wine, and of the wheat, the firstfruits of them which they shall offer unto the LORD, them have I given thee. 13 *And* whatsoever is first ripe in the land, which they shall bring unto the LORD, shall be thine; every one that is clean in thine house shall eat *of* it. 14 Every thing devoted in Israel shall be thine. 15 Every thing that openeth the matrix in all flesh, which they bring unto the LORD, *whether it be* of men or beasts, shall be thine : nevertheless the firstborn of man shalt thou surely redeem, and the firstling of unclean beasts shalt thou redeem. 16 And those that are to be redeemed from a month old shalt thou redeem, according to thine estimation, for the money of five shekels,

after the shekel of the sanctuary, which *is* twenty gerahs. 17 But the firstling of a cow, or the firstling of a sheep, or the firstling of a goat, thou shalt not redeem; they *are* holy: thou shalt sprinkle their blood upon the altar, and shalt burn their fat *for* an offering made by fire, for a sweet savour unto the LORD. 18 And the flesh of them shall be thine, as the wave breast and as the right shoulder are thine. 19 All the heave offerings of the holy things, which the children of Israel offer unto the LORD, have I given thee, and thy sons and thy daughters with thee, by a statute for ever: it *is* a covenant of salt for ever before the LORD unto thee and to thy seed with thee.

The priest's service is called a *warfare;* and who goes a warfare at his own charges? As they were well employed, so they were well provided for, and well paid. None shall serve God for nought. All believers are spiritual priests, and God has promised to take care of them; they shall *dwell in the land,* and verily *they shall be fed,* and shall not *want any good thing.* Godliness has the *promise of the life that now is.* And from this plentiful provision here made for the priests the apostle infers that it is the duty of Christian churches to maintain their ministers; those that *served at the altar lived upon the altar.* So those that preach the gospel should *live upon the gospel,* and live comfortably, 1 Cor. ix. 13, 14. Scandalous maintenance makes scandalous ministers. Now observe, 1. That much of the provision that was made for them arose out of the sacrifices which they themselves were employed to offer. They had the skins of almost all the sacrifices, which they might sell, and they had a considerable share out of the meat-offerings, sin-offerings, &c. Those that had the charge of the offerings had the benefit, *v.* 8. Note, God's work is its own wages, and his service carries its recompence along with it. Even in keeping God's commandments there is great reward. The present pleasures of religion are part of its pay. 2. That they had not only a good table kept for them, but money likewise in their pockets for the redemption of the first-born, and those firstlings of cattle which might not be offered in sacrifice. Thus their maintenance was such as left them altogether *disentangled from the affairs of this life;* they had no grounds to occupy, no land to till, no vineyards to dress, no cattle to tend, no visible estate to take care of, and yet had a more plentiful income than any other families whatsoever. Thus God ordered it that they might be the

more entirely addicted to their ministry, and not diverted from it, nor disturbed in it, by any worldly care or business (the ministry requires a whole man); and that they might be examples of living by faith, not only in God's providence, but in his ordinance. They lived from hand to mouth, that they might learn to take no thought for the morrow; sufficient for the day would be the provision thereof: and they had no estates to leave their children, that they might by faith leave them to the care of that God who had *fed them all their lives long.* 3. Of the provision that was made for their tables some is said to be *most holy* (v. 9, 10), which was to be eaten by the priests themselves, and in the court of the tabernacle only; but other perquisites were less holy, of which their families might eat, at their own houses, provided they were clean, *v.* 11—13. See Lev. xxii. 10, &c. 4. It is commanded that the *best of the oil,* and *the best of the wine and wheat,* should be offered for the *first-fruits unto the Lord,* which the priests were to have, *v.* 12. Note, We must always serve and honour God with the best we have, for he is the best, and best deserves it; he is the first, and therefore must have the first ripe. Those that think to save charges by putting God off with the refuse do but deceive themselves, for *God is not mocked.* 5. All this is given to the priests *by reason of the anointing, v.* 8. It was not for the sake of their personal merits above other Israelites that they had these tributes paid to them, be it known unto them; but purely for the sake of the office to which they were anointed. Thus all the comforts that are given to the Lord's people are given them by reason of the anointing which they have received. It is said to be given them *by an ordinance for ever* (v. 8), and it is a *covenant of salt for ever, v.* 19. As long as the priesthood should continue this should continue to be the maintenance of it, that this lamp might not go out for want of oil to keep it burning. Thus provision is made that a gospel ministry should continue till Christ comes, by an ordinance for ever. *Lo, I am with you* (that is their maintenance and support) *always, even to the end of the world.* Thanks be to the Redeemer, it is the word which he has *commanded to a thousand generations.*

20 And the LORD spake unto Aaron, Thou shalt have no inheritance in their land, neither shalt thou have any part among them: I *am* thy part and thine inheritance among the children of Israel. 21 And, behold, I have given the children of Levi all the tenth in Israel for an inheritance, for their service which they serve, *even* the service of the tabernacle of the congregation. 22 Neither must the children of Israel henceforth come nigh

the tabernacle of the congregation, lest they bear sin, and die. 23 But the Levites shall do the service of the tabernacle of the congregation, and they shall bear their iniquity : *it shall be* a statute for ever throughout your generations, that among the children of Israel they have no inheritance. 24 But the tithes of the children of Israel, which they offer *as* a heave offering unto the LORD, I have given to the Levites to inherit : therefore I have said unto them, Among the children of Israel they shall have no inheritance. 25 And the LORD spake unto Moses, saying, 26 Thus speak unto the Levites, and say unto them, When ye take of the children of Israel the tithes which I have given you from them for your inheritance, then ye shall offer up a heave offering of it for the LORD, *even* a tenth *part* of the tithe. 27 And *this* your heave offering shall be reckoned unto you, as though *it were* the corn of the threshingfloor, and as the fulness of the winepress. 28 Thus ye also shall offer a heave offering unto the LORD of all your tithes, which ye receive of the children of Israel; and ye shall give thereof the LORD's heave offering to Aaron the priest. 29 Out of all your gifts ye shall offer every heave offering of the LORD, of all the best thereof, *even* the hallowed part thereof out of it. 30 Therefore thou shalt say unto them, When ye have heaved the best thereof from it, then it shall be counted unto the Levites as the increase of the threshingfloor, and as the increase of the winepress. 31 And ye shall eat it in every place, ye and your households : for it *is* your reward for your service in the tabernacle of the congregation. 32 And ye shall bear no sin by reason of it, when ye have heaved from it the best of it : neither shall ye pollute the holy things of the children of Israel, lest ye die.

Here is a further account of the provision that was made both for the Levites and for the priests, out of the country.

I They must have *no inheritance in the land;* only cities to dwell in were afterwards allowed them, but no ground to occupy :

Thou shalt not have any part among them, v. 20. It is repeated again v. 23, and again v. 24, *Among the children of Israel they shall have no inheritance,* either by purchase or descent. God would have them comfortably provided for, but would not have their families over-rich, lest they should think themselves above that work which their wages supposed and obliged them constantly to attend upon. As Israel was a peculiar people, and not to be numbered among the nations, so Levi was a peculiar tribe, and not to be settled as the rest of the tribes, but in all respects distinguished from them. A good reason is given why they must have *no inheritance in the land,* for, says God, *I am thy part, and thy inheritance.* Note, Those that have God for their inheritance and their portion for ever ought to look with a holy contempt and indifference upon the inheritances of this world, and not covet their portion in it. "*The Lord is my portion, therefore will I hope in him,* and not depend upon any thing I have on this earth," Lam. iii. 24. The Levites shall have no inheritance, and yet they shall live very comfortably and plentifully—to teach us that Providence has various ways of supporting those that live in a dependence upon it ; the fowls reap not, and yet are fed, the lilies spin not, and yet are clothed, the Levites have no inheritance in Israel, and yet live better than any other tribe. The repetition of that caution, that *no Israelite should approach the tabernacle,* comes in suitably, though somewhat abruptly, v. 22. It seems set in opposition to that order concerning the priests and Levites that they should have *no inheritance in Israel,* to show how God dispenses his favours variously. The Levites have the honour of attending the tabernacle, which is denied the Israelites; but then the Israelites have the honour of inheritances in Canaan, which is denied the Levites ; thus each is kept from either envying or despising the other, and both have reason to rejoice in their lot. The Israelites must not *come nigh the tabernacle,* but then the Levites must have *no inheritance in the land;* if ministers expect that people should keep in their sphere, and not intermeddle with sacred offices, let them keep in theirs, and not entangle themselves in secular affairs.

II. But they must both have tithes of the land. Besides the first-fruits which were appropriated to the priests, which, the Jews say, were to be a fiftieth part, or at least a sixtieth, the tithe also was appropriated. 1. The Levites had the tithes of the people's increase (v. 21): *I have given* (whose the whole is) *all the tenths in Israel,* of all the productions of the land, to *the children of Levi,* to be divided among them in just proportions, *for their service which they serve.* The Levites were the smallest tribe of the twelve, and yet, besides all other advantages, they had a tenth part of the yearly profits, without the trouble and expense of ploughing and sowing ; such care did God take of those that were devoted to his service; not only that they might be well maintained, but that they might be honoured with a national acknowledgment of the good services they did to the public, and owned as God's agents and receivers; for that which was a heave-offering, or an offering lifted heavenward unto the Lord, was by him consigned to the Levites. 2. The priests had the tenths of the Levites' tithes settled upon them. The order for this Moses is directed to give to the Levites, whom God would have to pay it with cheerfulness, rather than the priests to demand it with authority: *Speak to the Levites* that it be *offered by them,* rather than levied upon them. Now observe, (1.) The Levites were to give God his dues out of their tithes, as well as the Israelites out of their increase. They were God's tenants, and rent was expected from them, nor were they exempted by their office. Thus now, ministers must be charitable out of what they receive; and the more freely they have received the more freely they must give, and be examples of liberality. *You shall offer a heave-offering to the Lord, v.* 26. Those that are employed to assist the devotions of others must be sure to pay their own, as a heave-offering to the Lord. Prayers and praises lifted up to God, or rather the heart lifted up in them, are now our heave-offerings. This (says God) shall be *reckoned to you as though it were the corn of the threshing-floor ;* that is, though it was not the fruit of their ground, nor of their own labour, as the tithes of other Israelites were, yet being of such as they had it should be accepted, to the sanctifying of all the rest. (2.) This was to be given *to Aaron the priest* (*v.* 28), and to his successors the high priests, to be divided and disposed of in such proportions as they should think fit among the inferior priests. Most of the profits of the priests' office, which were appointed in the former part of the chapter, arising from the sacrifices, those priests had the benefit of who constantly attended at the altar; but, forasmuch as there were many priests employed in the country to teach and rule, those tithes taken by the Levites, it is probable, were directed by the high priest for their maintenance. It is the probable conjecture of the learned bishop Patrick that the tenth of this last tenth was reserved for the high priest himself, to support his state and dignity; for otherwise we read not of any peculiar provision made for him. (3.) When the Levites had thus paid the tenth of their income, as a heave-offering to the Lord, they had themselves the comfortable enjoyment of the other nine parts (*v.* 30): " When you have thus *heaved the best from it* (for still God's part must be the best) then you shall *eat the rest,* not as a holy thing, but with the same freedom that the other Israelites eat their part with, *in every place, you and your households,*" *v.* 31. See here what is the way to have the comfort of all our worldly pos-

sessions, so as to bear no sin by reason of them, as it follows, *v.* 32. [1.] We must be sure that what we have be got honestly and in the service of God. It is *your reward for your service :* that meat is the best eating that is first earned; but, if any *will not work, neither shall he eat,* 2 Thess. iii. 10. And that seems to be spoken of as having a particular comfort and satisfaction in it which is the reward of faithful service done in the tabernacle of the congregation. [2.] We must be sure that God has his dues out of it. Then we have the comfort of our substance when we have honoured the Lord with it. Then *you shall bear no sin by reason of it,* when *you have heaved the best from it.* This intimates that we must never feed ourselves without fear, lest our table become a snare, and we bear sin by reason of it; and that therefore we are concerned to *give alms of such things as we have,* that all may be clean and comfortable to us.

CHAP. XIX.

This chapter is only concerning the preparing and using of the ashes which were to impregnate the water of purification. The people had complained of the strictness of the law, which forbade their near approach to the tabernacle, ch. xvii. 13. In answer to this complaint, they are here directed to purify themselves, so as that they might come as far as they had occasion without fear. Here is, I. The method of preparing these ashes, by the burning of a red heifer, with a great deal of ceremony, ver. 1—10. II. The way of using them. 1. They were designed to purify persons from the pollution contracted by a dead body, ver. 11—16. 2. They were to be put into running water (a small quantity of them), with which the person to be cleansed must be purified, ver. 17—22. And that this ceremonial purification was a type and figure of the cleansing of the consciences of believers from the pollutions of sin appears by the apostle's discourse, Heb. ix. 13, 14, where he compares the efficacy of the blood of Christ with the sanctifying virtue that was in "the ashes of a heifer sprinkling the unclean."

AND the Lord spake unto Moses and unto Aaron, saying, 2 This *is* the ordinance of the law which the Lord hath commanded, saying, Speak unto the children of Israel, that they bring thee a red heifer without spot, wherein *is* no blemish, *and* upon which never came yoke: 3 And ye shall give her unto Eleazar the priest, that he may bring her forth without the camp, and *one* shall slay her before his face: 4 And Eleazar the priest shall take of her blood with his finger, and sprinkle of her blood directly before the tabernacle of the congregation seven times: 5 And *one* shall burn the heifer in his sight; her skin, and her flesh, and her blood, with her dung, shall he burn: 6 And the priest shall take cedar wood, and hyssop, and scarlet, and cast *it* into the midst of the burning of the heifer. 7 Then the priest shall wash his clothes, and he shall bathe his flesh in water, and afterward he shall come into the camp, and the priest shall be unclean until the even. 8 'And he that burneth her shall wash his clothes in water, and bathe his flesh in water, and shall be unclean until the even. 9 And a man *that is* clean shall gather up the ashes of the heifer, and lay *them* up without the camp in a clean place, and it shall be kept for the congregation of the children of Israel for a water of separation : it *is* a purification for sin. 10 And he that gathereth the ashes of the heifer shall wash his clothes, and be unclean until the even : and it shall be unto the children of Israel, and unto the stranger that sojourneth among them, for a statute for ever.

We have here the divine appointment concerning the solemn burning of a red heifer to ashes, and the preserving of the ashes, that of them might be made, not a beautifying, but a purifying, water, for that was the utmost the law reached to ; it offered not to adorn as the gospel does, but to cleanse only. This burning of the heifer, though it was not properly a sacrifice of expiation, being not performed at the altar, yet was typical of the death and sufferings of Christ, by which he intended, not only to satisfy God's justice, but to purify and pacify our consciences, that we may have peace with God and also peace in our own bosoms, to prepare for which Christ died, not only like the bulls and goats at the altar, but like the heifer without the camp.

I. There was a great deal of care employed in the choice of the heifer that was to be burnt, much more than in the choice of any other offering, *v.* 2. It must not only be without blemish, typifying the spotless purity and sinless perfection of the Lord Jesus, but it must be a red heifer, because of the rarity of the colour, that it might be the more remarkable : the Jews say, " If but two hairs were black or white, it was unlawful." Christ, as man, was the Son of Adam, *red earth,* and we find him red in his apparel, red with his own blood, and red with the blood of his enemies. And it must be one on which never came yoke, which was not insisted on in other sacrifices, but thus was typified the voluntary offer of the Lord Jesus, when he said, *Lo, I come.* He was bound and held with no other cords than those of his own love. This heifer was to be provided at the expense of the congregation, because they were all to have a joint interest in it ; and so all believers have in Christ.

II. There was to be a great deal of ceremony in the burning of it. The care of doing it was committed to Eleazar, not to Aaron himself, because it was not fit that he should do any thing to render himself ceremonially unclean, no, not so much as *till the*

654

evening (*v.* 8) ; yet it being an affair of great concern, especially in the significancy of it, it was to be performed by him that was next to Aaron in dignity. The chief priests of that time had the principal hand in the death of Christ. Now,

1. The heifer was to be slain without the camp, as an impure thing, which bespeaks the insufficiency of the methods prescribed by the ceremonial law to take away sin. So far were they from cleansing effectually that they were themselves unclean ; as if the pollution that was laid upon them continued to cleave to them. Yet, to answer this type, our Lord Jesus, being made sin and a curse for us, *suffered without the gate,* Heb. xiii. 12.

2. Eleazar was to *sprinkle the blood directly before the door of the tabernacle,* and looking stedfastly towards it, *v.* 4. This made it in some sort an expiation ; for the sprinkling of the blood before the Lord was the chief solemnity in all the sacrifices of atonement ; therefore, though this was not done at the altar, yet, being done towards the sanctuary, it was intimated that the virtue and validity of it depended upon the sanctuary, and were derived from it. This signified the satisfaction that was made to God by the death of Christ, our great high priest, who *by the eternal Spirit* (and the Spirit is called the finger of God, as Ainsworth observes, Luke xi. 20) *offered himself without spot unto God;* he did, as it were, sprinkle his own blood directly before the sanctuary, when he said, *Father, into thy hands I commit my spirit.* It also signifies how necessary it was to the purifying of our hearts that satisfaction should be made to divine justice. This sprinkling of the blood put virtue into the ashes.

3. The heifer was to be *wholly burnt, v.* 5. This typified the extreme sufferings of our Lord Jesus, both in soul and body, as a sacrifice made by fire. The priest was to cast into the fire, while it was burning, cedarwood, hyssop, and scarlet, which were used in the cleansing of lepers (Lev. xiv. 6, 7), that the ashes of these might be mingled with the ashes of the heifer, because they were designed for purification.

4. The ashes of the heifer (separated as well as they could from the ashes of the wood wherewith it was burnt) were to be carefully gathered up by the hand of a clean person, and (as the Jews say) pounded and sifted, and so laid up for the use of the congregation, as there was occasion (*v.* 9), not only for that generation, but for posterity ; for the ashes of this one heifer were sufficient to season as many vessels of water as the people of Israel would need for many ages. The Jews say that this one served till the captivity, nearly 1000 years, and that there was never another heifer burnt till Ezra's time, after their return, to which tradition of theirs, grounded (I suppose) only upon the silence of their old records, I see

no reason we have to give credit, since in the later times of their church, of which they had more full records, they find eight burnt between Ezra's time and the destruction of the second temple, which was about 500 years. These ashes are said to be laid up here as *a purification for sin,* because, **though** they were intended to purify only from ceremonial uncleanness, yet they were a type of that purification for sin which our Lord Jesus made by his death. Ashes mixed with water are used in scouring, but these had their virtue purely from the divine institution, and their accomplishment and perfection in Christ, who is *the end of this law for righteousness.* Now observe, (1.) That the water of purification was made so by the ashes of a heifer, whose blood was sprinkled before the sanctuary; so that which cleanses our consciences is the abiding virtue of the death of Christ; it is his blood that *cleanses from all sin,* 1 John i. 7. (2.) That the ashes were sufficient for all the people. There needed not to be a fresh heifer slain for every person or family that had occasion to be purified, but this one was enough for all, even for the strangers that sojourned among them (*v.* 10); so there is virtue enough in the blood of Christ for all that repent and believe the gospel, for every Israelite, and not for their sins only, but for *the sins of the whole world,* 1 John ii. 2. (3.) That these ashes were capable of being preserved without waste to many ages. No bodily substance is so incorruptible as ashes are, which (says bishop Patrick) made these a very fit emblem of the everlasting efficacy of the sacrifice of Christ. He is able to save, and, in order to that, able to cleanse, to the uttermost, both of persons and times. (4.) These ashes were laid up as a stock or treasure, for the constant purification of Israel from their pollutions; so the blood of Christ is laid up for us in the word and sacraments, as an inexhaustible fountain of merit, to which by faith we may have recourse daily 'or the purging of our consciences; see Zech. xiii. 1.

5. All those that were employed in this service were made ceremonially unclean by it; even Eleazar himself, though he did but sprinkle the blood, *v.* 7. He that *burned the heifer was unclean* (*v.* 8), and he that *gathered up the ashes* (*v.* 10); so all that had a hand in putting Christ to death contracted guilt by it: his betrayer, his prosecutors, his judge, his executioner, all did what they did with wicked hands, though it was *by the determinate counsel and foreknowledge of God* (Acts ii. 23); yet some of them were, and all might have been, cleansed by the virtue of that same blood which they had brought themselves under the guilt of. Some make this to signify the imperfection of the legal services, and their insufficiency to take away sin, inasmuch as those who prepared for the purifying of others were themselves polluted by the preparation. The Jews say, This is a mystery which Solomon himself did not understand, that the same thing should pollute those that were clean and purify those that were unclean. But (says bishop Patrick) it is not strange to those who consider that all the sacrifices which were offered for sin were therefore looked upon as impure, because the sins of men were laid upon them, as all our sins were upon Christ, who therefore is said to be *made sin for us,* 2 Cor. v. 21.

11 He that toucheth the dead body of any man shall be unclean seven days. 12 He shall purify himself with it on the third day, and on the seventh day he shall be clean: but if he purify not himself the third day, then the seventh day he shall not be clean. 13 Whosoever toucheth the dead body of any man that is dead, and purifieth not himself, defileth the tabernacle of the LORD; and that soul shall be cut off from Israel: because the water of separation was not sprinkled upon him, he shall be unclean; his uncleanness *is* yet upon him. 14 This *is* the law, when a man dieth in a tent: all that come into the tent, and all that *is* in the tent, shall be unclean seven days. 15 And every open vessel, which hath no covering bound upon it, *is* unclean. 16 And whosoever toucheth one that is slain with a sword in the open fields, or a dead body, or a bone of a man, or a grave, shall be unclean seven days. 17 And for an unclean *person* they shall take of the ashes of the burnt heifer of purification for sin, and running water shall be put thereto in a vessel: 18 And a clean person shall take hyssop, and dip *it* in the water, and sprinkle *it* upon the tent, and upon all the vessels, and upon the persons that were there, and upon him that touched a bone, or one slain, or one dead, or a grave: 19 And the clean *person* shall sprinkle upon the unclean on the third day, and on the seventh day: and on the seventh day he shall purify himself, and wash his clothes, and bathe himself in water, and shall be clean at even. 20 But the man that shall be unclean, and shall not purify himself, that soul shall be cut off from among the congregation, because he

hath defiled the sanctuary of the LORD: the water of separation hath not been sprinkled upon him; he *is* unclean. 21 And it shall be a perpetual statute unto them, that he that sprinkleth the water of separation shall wash his clothes; and he that toucheth the water of separation shall be unclean until even. 22 And whatsoever the unclean *person* toucheth shall be unclean; and the soul that toucheth *it* shall be unclean until even.

Directions are here given concerning the use and application of the ashes which were prepared for purification. They were laid up to be laid out; and therefore, though now one place would serve to keep them in, while all Israel lay so closely encamped, yet it is probable that afterwards, when they came to Canaan, some of these ashes were kept in every town, for there would be daily use for them. Observe,

I. In what cases there needed a purification with these ashes. No other is mentioned here than the ceremonial uncleanness that was contracted by the touch of a dead body, or of the bone or grave of a dead man, or being in the tent or house where a dead body lay, *v.* 11, 14—16. This I look upon to have been one of the greatest burdens of the ceremonial law, and one of the most unaccountable. He that touched the carcase of an unclean beast, or any living man under the greatest ceremonial uncleanness, was made unclean by it only *till the evening*, and needed only common water to purify himself with; but he that came near the dead body of man, woman, or child, must bear the reproach of his uncleanness seven days, must twice be purified with the water of separation, which he could not obtain without trouble and charge, and till he was purified must not come near the sanctuary upon pain of death.

1. This was strange, considering, (1.) That whenever any died (and we are in deaths oft) several persons must unavoidably contract this pollution, the body must be stripped, washed, wound up, carried out, and buried, and this could not be done without many hands, and yet all defiled, which signifies that in our corrupt and fallen state there is none that lives and sins not; we cannot avoid being polluted by the defiling world we pass through, and we offend daily, yet the impossibility of our being sinless does not make sin the less polluting. (2.) That taking care of the dead, to see them decently buried, is not only necessary, but a very good office, and an act of kindness, both to the honour of the dead and the comfort of the living, and yet uncleanness was contracted by it, which intimates that the pollutions of sin mix with and cleave to our best

services. *There is not a just man upon earth that doeth good and sinneth not;* we are apt some way or other to do amiss even in our doing good. (3.) That this pollution was contracted by what was done privately in their own houses, which intimates (as bishop Patrick observes) that God sees what is done in secret, and nothing can be concealed from the divine Majesty. (4.) This pollution might be contracted, and yet a man might never know it, as by the touch of a grave which appeared not, of which our Saviour says, Those that *walk over it are not aware of it* (Luke xi. 44), which intimates the defilement of the conscience by sins of ignorance, and the cause we have to cry out, " Who can understand his errors?" and to pray, " Cleanse us from secret faults, faults which we ourselves do not see ourselves guilty of."

2. But why did the law make a dead corpse such a defiling thing? (1.) Because death is the *wages of sin, entered into the world* by it, and reigns by the power of it. Death to mankind is another thing from what it is to other creatures: it is a curse, it is the execution of the law, and therefore the defilement of death signifies the defilement of sin. (2.) Because the law could not conquer death, nor abolish it and alter the property of it, as the gospel does by bringing life and immortality to light, and so introducing a better hope. Since our Redeemer was dead and buried, death is no more destroying to the Israel of God, and therefore dead bodies are no more defiling; but while the church was under the law, to show that it *made not the comers thereunto perfect,* the pollution contracted by dead bodies could not but form in their minds melancholy and uncomfortable notions concerning death, while believers now through Christ can triumph over it. *O grave! where is thy victory?* Where is thy pollution?

II. How the ashes were to be used and applied in these cases. 1. A small quantity of the ashes must be put into a cup of spring water, and mixed with the water, which thereby was made, as it is here called, a *water of separation,* because it was to be sprinkled on those who were separated or removed from the sanctuary by their uncleanness. As the ashes of the heifer signified the merit of Christ, so the running water signified the power and grace of the blessed Spirit, who is compared to rivers of living water; and it is by his operation that the righteousness of Christ is applied to us for our cleansing. Hence we are said to be washed, that is, sanctified and justified, not only in the name of the Lord Jesus, but by the *Spirit of our God,* 1 Cor. vi. 11; 1 Pet. i. 2. Those that promise themselves benefit by the righteousness of Christ, while they submit not to the grace and influence of the Spirit, do but deceive themselves, for we cannot put asunder what God has joined, nor be purified by the ashes otherwise than in the running water.

2. This water must be applied by a bunch of hyssop dipped in it, with which the person or thing to be cleansed must be sprinkled (*v.* 18), in allusion to which David prays, *Purge me with hyssop.* Faith is the bunch of hyssop wherewith the conscience is sprinkled and the heart purified. Many might be sprinkled at once, and the water with which the ashes were mingled might serve for many sprinklings, till it was all spent ; and a very little lighting upon a man served to purify him, if done with that intention. In allusion to this application of the water of separation by sprinkling, the blood of Christ is said to be the *blood of sprinkling* (Heb. xii. 24), and with it we are said to be *sprinkled from an evil conscience* (Heb. x. 22), that is, we are freed from the uneasiness that arises from a sense of our guilt. And it is foretold that Christ, by his baptism, shall *sprinkle many nations,* Isa. lii. 15. 3. The unclean person must be sprinkled with this water on *the third day* after his pollution, and on *the seventh day, v.* 12—19. The days were reckoned (we may suppose) from the last time of his touching or coming near the dead body ; for he would not begin the days of his cleansing while he was still under a necessity of repeating the pollution ; but when the dead body was buried, so that there was no further occasion of meddling with it, then he began to reckon his days. Then, and then only, we may with comfort apply Christ's merit to our souls, when we have forsaken sin, and cease all *fellowship with the unfruitful works of* death and *darkness.* The repetition of the sprinkling teaches us often to renew the actings of repentance and faith, wash as Naaman, *seven times ;* we need to do that often which is so necessary to be well done. 4. Though the pollution contracted was only ceremonial, yet the neglect of the purification prescribed would turn into moral guilt : *He that shall be unclean, and shall not purify himself, that soul shall be cut off, v.* 20. Note, It is a dangerous thing to contemn divine institutions, though they may seem minute. A slight wound, if neglected, may prove fatal ; a sin we call little, if not repented of, will be our ruin, when great sinners that repent shall find mercy. Our uncleanness separates us from God, but it is our being unclean and not purifying ourselves that will separate us for ever from him : it is not the wound that is fatal, so much as the contempt of the remedy. 5. Even he that *sprinkled the water of separation,* or *touched* it, or *touched the unclean person,* must be *unclean till the evening,* that is, must not come near the sanctuary on that day, *v.* 21, 22. Thus God would show them the imperfection of those services, and their insufficiency to purify the conscience, that they might look for the Messiah, who in the fulness of time should by the eternal Spirit offer himself without spot unto God, and so *purge our consciences from dead works* (that

is, from sin, which defiles like a dead body, and is therefore called a *body of death*), that we may have liberty of access to the sanctuary, to serve the living God with living sacrifices.

CHAP. XX.

At this chapter begins the history of the fortieth year (which was the last year) of the Israelites' wandering in the wilderness. And since the beginning of their second year, when they were sentenced to perform their quarantine in the desert, there to wear away the tedious revolution of forty years, there is little recorded concerning them till this last year, which brought them to the borders of Canaan, and the history of this year is almost as large as the history of the first year. This chapter gives an account of, I. The death of Miriam, ver. 1. II. The fetching of water out of the rock, in which observe, 1. The distress Israel was in, for want of water, ver. 2. 2. Their discontent and murmuring in that distress, ver. 3—5. 3. God's pity and power engaged for their supply with water out of the rock, ver. 6—9. 4. The infirmity of Moses and Aaron upon this occasion, ver. 10, 11. 5. God's displeasure against them, ver. 12, 13. III. The negociation with the Edomites. Israel's request (ver. 14—17), and the repulse the Edomites gave them, ver. 18—21. IV. The death of Aaron the high priest upon Mount Hor, the instalment of Eleazar in his room, and the people's mourning for him, ver. 22, &c.

THEN came the children of Israel, *even* the whole congregation, into the desert of Zin in the first month : and the people abode in Kadesh ; and Miriam died there, and was buried there. 2 And there was no water for the congregation : and they gathered themselves together against Moses and against Aaron. 3 And the people chode with Moses, and spake, saying, Would God that we had died when our brethren died before the LORD ! 4 And why have ye brought up the congregation of the LORD into this wilderness, that we and our cattle should die there ? 5 And wherefore have ye made us to come up out of Egypt, to bring us in unto this evil place ? it *is* no place of seed, or of figs, or of vines, or of pomegranates ; neither *is* there any water to drink. 6 And Moses and Aaron went from the presence of the assembly unto the door of the tabernacle of the congregation, and they fell upon their faces : and the glory of the LORD appeared unto them. 7 And the LORD spake unto Moses, saying, 8 Take the rod, and gather thou the assembly together, thou, and Aaron thy brother, and speak ye unto the rock before their eyes ; and it shall give forth his water, and thou shalt bring forth to them water out of the rock : so thou shalt give the congregation and their beasts drink. 9 And Moses took the rod from before the LORD, as he commanded him. 10 And Moses and Aaron gathered the congregation together before the rock, and he said unto them, Hear now, ye rebels; must we fetch you water out of this rock? 11 And Moses lifted up his hand, and with his rod he smote the rock twice: and the water came out abundantly, and the congregation drank, and their beasts *also.* 12 And the LORD spake unto Moses and Aaron, Because ye believed me not, to sanctify me in the eyes of the children of Israel, therefore ye shall not bring this congregation into the land which I have given them. 13 This *is* the water of Meribah; because the children of Israel strove with the LORD, and he was sanctified in them.

After thirty-eight years' tedious marches, or rather tedious rests, in the wilderness, backward towards the Red Sea, the armies of Israel now at length set their faces towards Canaan again, and had come not far off from the place where they were when, by the righteous sentence of divine Justice, they were made to begin their wanderings. Hitherto they had been led about as in a maze or labyrinth, while execution was doing upon the rebels that were sentenced; but they were now brought into the right way again: they abode in Kadesh (*v.* 1), not Kadesh-barnea, which was near the borders of Canaan, but another Kadesh on the confines of Edom, further off from the land of promise, yet in the way to it from the Red Sea, to which they had been hurried back. Now,

I. Here dies Miriam, the sister of Moses and Aaron, and as it should seem older than either of them. She must have been so if she was that sister that was set to watch Moses when he was put into the ark of bulrushes, Exod. ii. 4. *Miriam died there, v.* 1. She was a prophetess, and had been an instrument of much good to Israel, Mic. vi. 4. When Moses and Aaron with their rod went before them, to work wonders for them, Miriam with her timbrel went before them in praising God for these wondrous works (Exod. xv. 20), and therein did them real service; yet she had once been a murmurer (*ch.* xii. 1), and must not enter Canaan.

II. Here there is another Meribah. One place we met with before of that name, in the beginning of their march through the wilderness, which was so called *because of the chiding of the children of Israel*, Exod. xvii. 7. And now we have another place, at the latter end of their march, which bears the same name for the same reason: *This is the water of Meribah, v.* 13. What was there done was here re-acted.

1. *There was no water for the congregation, v.* 2. The water out of the rock of Rephidim had followed them while there was need of it; but it is probable that for some time they

had been in a country where they were supplied in an ordinary way, and when common providence supplied them it was fit that the miracle should cease. But in this place it fell out that there was no water, or not sufficient for the congregation. Note, We live in a wanting world, and, wherever we are, must expect to meet with some inconvenience or other. It is a great mercy to have plenty of water, a mercy which if we found the want of we should own the worth of.

2. Hereupon they murmured, mutinied (*v.* 2), *gathered themselves together*, and took up arms *against Moses and Aaron.* They chid with them (*v.* 3), spoke the same absurd and brutish language that their fathers had done before them. (1.) They wished they had died as malefactors by the hands of divine justice, rather than thus seem for a while neglected by the divine mercy: *Would God that we had died when our brethren died before the Lord!* Instead of giving God thanks, as they ought to have done, for sparing them, they not only despise the mercy of their reprieve, but quarrel with it, as if God had done them a great deal of wrong in giving them their lives for a prey, and snatching them as brands out of the burning. But they need not wish that they had died with their brethren, they are here taking the ready way to die like their brethren in a little while. *Woe unto those that desire the day of the Lord,* Amos v. 18. (2.) They were angry that they were brought out of Egypt, and led through this wilderness, *v.* 4, 5. They quarrelled with Moses for that which they knew was the Lord's doing; they represented that as an injury which was the greatest favour that ever was done to any people. They prefer slavery before liberty, the house of bondage before the land of promise; and though, the present want was of water only, yet, now that they are disposed to find fault, it shall be looked upon as an insufferable hardship put upon them that they have not vines and figs. It was an aggravation of their crime, [1.] That they had smarted so long for the discontents and distrusts of their fathers. *They had borne their whoredoms* now almost *forty years in the wilderness* (*ch.* xiv. 33); and yet they ventured in the same steps, and, as is charged upon Belshazzar, *humbled not their hearts, though they knew all this*, Dan. v. 22. [2.] That they had had such long and constant experience of God's goodness to them, and of the tenderness and faithfulness of Moses and Aaron. [3.] That Miriam was now lately dead; and, having lost one of their leaders, they ought to have been more respectful to those that were left; but, as if they were resolved to provoke God to leave them as sheep without any shepherd, they grow outrageous against them: instead of condoling with Moses and Aaron for the death of their sister, they add affliction to their grief.

3. Moses and Aaron made them no reply,

but retired to the door of the tabernacle to know God's mind in this case, *v.* 6. There they *fell on their faces*, as formerly on the like occasion, to deprecate the wrath of God and to entreat direction from him. Here is no mention of any thing they said; they knew that God heard the murmurings of the people, and before him they humbly prostrate themselves, making intercessions with *groanings that cannot be uttered.* There they lay waiting for orders. *Speak, Lord, for thy servants hear.*

4. God appeared, to determine the matter; not on his tribunal of justice, to sentence the rebels according to their deserts; no, he *will not return to destroy Ephraim* (Hosea xi. 9), will *not always chide;* see Gen. viii. 21. But he appeared, (1.) On his throne of glory, to silence their unjust murmuring (*v.* 6): The *glory of the Lord appeared*, to *still the tumult of the people*, by striking an awe upon them. Note, A believing sight of the glory of the Lord would be an effectual check to our lusts and passions, and would keep our mouths as with a bridle. (2.) On his throne of grace, to satisfy their just desires. It was requisite that they should have water, and therefore, though the manner of their petitioning for it was irregular and disorderly, yet God did not take that advantage against them to deny it to them, but gave immediate orders for their supply, *v.* 8. Moses must a second time in God's name command water out of a rock for them, to show that God is as able as ever to supply his people with good things, even in their greatest straits and in the utmost failure of second causes. Almighty power can bring water out of a rock, has done it, and can again, for his arm is not shortened. Lest it should be thought that there was something peculiar in the former rock itself, some secret spring which nature hid before in it, God here bids him broach another, and does not, as then, direct him which he must apply to, but lets him make use of which he pleased, or the first he came to; all alike to Omnipotence. [1.] God bids him take the rod, that famous rod with which he summoned the plagues of Egypt, and divided the sea, that, having that in his hand, both he and the people might be reminded of the great things God had formerly done for them, and might be encouraged to trust in him now. This rod, it seems, was kept in the tabernacle (*v.* 9), for it was the *rod of God*, the *rod of his strength*, as the gospel is called (Ps. cx. 2), perhaps in allusion to it. [2.] God bids him gather the assembly, not the elders only, but the people, to be witnesses of what was done, that by their own eyes they might be convinced and made ashamed of their unbelief. There is no fallacy in God's works of wonder, and therefore they shun not the light, nor the inspection and enquiry of many witnesses. [3.] He bids him speak to the rock, which would do as it was bidden, to

shame the people who had been so often spoken to, and would not hear nor obey. Their hearts were harder than this rock, not so tender, not so yielding, not so obedient. [4.] He promises that the rock should give forth water (*v.* 8), and it did so (*v.* 11): *The water came out abundantly.* This is an instance, not only of the power of God, that he could thus fetch *honey out of the rock,* and *oil out of the flinty rock,* but of his mercy and grace, that he would do it for such a provoking people. This was a new generation (most of the old stock were by this time worn off), yet they were as bad as those that went before them; murmuring ran in the blood, yet the entail of the divine favour was not cut off, but in this instance of it the divine patience shines as brightly as the divine power. He is God and not man, in sparing and pardoning; nay, he not only here gave them the drink which they drank of in common with their beasts (*v.* 8, 11), but in it he made them to drink spiritual drink, which typified spiritual blessings, *for that rock was Christ.*

5. Moses and Aaron acted improperly in the management of this matter, so much so that God in displeasure told them immediately that they should not have the honour of bringing Israel into Canaan, *v.* 10—12.

(1.) This is a strange passage of story, yet very instructive. [1.] It is certain that God was greatly offended, and justly, for he is never angry without cause. Though they were his servants, and had obtained mercy to be faithful, though they were his favourites, and such as he had highly honoured, yet for something they thought, or said, or did, upon this occasion, he put them under the disgrace and mortification of dying, as other unbelieving Israelites did, short of Canaan. And no doubt the crime deserved the punishment. [2.] Yet it is uncertain what it was in this management that was so provoking to God. The fault was complicated. *First,* They did not punctually observe their orders, but in some things varied from their commission; God bade them *speak to the rock,* and they spoke *to the people*, and *smote the rock,* which at this time they were not ordered to do, but they thought speaking would not do. When, in distrust of the power of the word, we have recourse to the secular power in matters of pure conscience, we do, as Moses here, smite the rock to which we should only speak, *Secondly,* They assumed too much of the glory of this work of wonder to themselves: *Must we fetch water?* as if it were done by some power or worthiness of theirs. Therefore it is charged upon them (*v.* 12) that *they did not sanctify God,* that is, they did not give him that glory of this miracle which was due unto his name. *Thirdly,* Unbelief was the great transgression (*v.* 12): *You believed me not;* nay, it is called *rebelling against God's commandment, ch.* xxvii. 14. The command was to bring water out of the rock, but they rebelled against this command, by distrusting it, and doubting whether it would take effect or no. They speak doubtfully : *Must we fetch water ?* And probably they did in some other ways discover an uncertainty in their own minds whether water would come or no for such a rebellious generation as this was. And perhaps they the rather questioned it, though God had promised it, because the glory of the Lord did not appear before them upon this rock, as it had done upon the rock in Rephidim, Exod. xvii. 6. They would not take God's word without a sign. Dr. Lightfoot's notion of their unbelief is that they doubted whether now at last, when the forty years had expired, they should enter Canaan, and whether they must not for the murmurings of the people be condemned to another period of toil, because a new rock was now opened for their supply, which they took for an indication of their longer stay. And, if so, justly were they kept out of Canaan themselves, while the people entered at the time appointed. *Fourthly*, They said and did all in heat and passion ; this is the account given of the sin (Ps. cvi. 33) : *They provoked his spirit, so that he spoke unadvisedly with his lips.* It was in his passion that he called them *rebels.* It is true they were so ; God had called them so ; and Moses afterwards, in the way of a just reproof (Deut. ix. 24), calls them so without offence ; but now it came from a provoked spirit, and was spoken unadvisedly : it was too much like *Raca*, and *Thou fool.* His smiting the rock twice (it should seem, not waiting at all for the eruption of the water upon the first stroke) shows that he was in a heat. The same thing said and done with meekness may be justifiable which when said and done in anger may be highly culpable ; see Jam. i. 20. *Fifthly*, That which aggravated all the rest, and made it the more provoking, was that it was public, *before the eyes of the children of Israel*, to whom they should have been examples of faith, and hope, and meekness. We find Moses guilty of sinful distrust, *ch.* xi. 22, 23. That was private between God and him, and therefore was only checked. But this was public ; it dishonoured God before Israel, as if he grudged them his favours, and discouraged the people's hope in God, and therefore this was severely punished, and the more because of the dignity and eminency of those that offended. (2.) From the whole we may learn, [1.] That the best of men have their failings, even in those graces that they are most eminent for. The man Moses was very meek, and yet here he sinned in passion ; wherefore *let him that thinks he stands take heed lest he fall.* [2.] That God judges not as man judges concerning sins ; we might think that there was not much amiss in what Moses said and did, yet God saw cause to animadvert severely upon it. He knows the frame of men's spirits, what temper they are of, and what temper they are in upon particular

occasions, and from what thoughts and intents words and actions do proceed ; and we are sure that therefore *his judgment is according to truth*, when it agrees not with ours. [3.] That God not only takes notice of, and is displeased with, the sins of his people, but that the nearer any are to him the more offensive are their sins, Amos iii. 2. It should seem, the Psalmist refers to this sin of Moses and Aaron (Ps. xcix. 8) : *Thou wast a God that forgavest them, though thou tookest vengeance on their inventions.* As many are spared in this life and punished in the other, so many are punished in this life and saved in the other. [4.] That, when our heart is hot within us, we are concerned to take heed that we offend not with our tongue. Yet, [5.] It is an evidence of the sincerity of Moses, and his impartiality in writing, that he himself left this upon record concerning himself, and drew not a veil over his own infirmity, by which it appeared that in what he wrote, as well as what he did, he sought God's glory more than his own.

Lastly, The place is hereupon called *Meribah, v.* 13. It is called *Meribah-Kadesh* (Deut. xxxii. 51), to distinguish it from the other Meribah. It is the *water of strife ;* to perpetuate the remembrance of the people's sin, and Moses's, and yet of God's mercy, who supplied them with water, and owned and honoured Moses notwithstanding. Thus he was sanctified in them, as the *Holy One of Israel*, so he is called when his mercy rejoices against judgment, Hos. xi. 9. Moses and Aaron did not sanctify God as they ought in the eyes of Israel (*v.* 12), but God was sanctified in them ; for he will not be a loser in his honour by any man. If he be not glorified by us, he will be glorified upon us.

14 And Moses sent messengers from Kadesh unto the king of Edom, Thus saith thy brother Israel, Thou knowest all the travel that hath befallen us : 15 How our fathers went down into Egypt, and we have dwelt in Egypt a long time ; and the Egyptians vexed us, and our fathers : 16 And when we cried unto the LORD, he heard our voice, and sent an angel, and hath brought us forth out of Egypt : and, behold, we *are* in Kadesh, a city in the uttermost of thy border : 17 Let us pass, I pray thee, through thy country : we will not pass through the fields, or through the vineyards, neither will we drink *of* the water of the wells : we will go by the king's *high* way, we will not turn to the right hand nor to the left, until we have passed thy borders. 18 And Edom said unto him, Thou shalt not

pass by me, lest I come out against thee with the sword. 19 And the children of Israel said unto him, We will go by the high way: and if I and my cattle drink of thy water, then I will pay for it: I will only, without *doing* any thing *else*, go through on my feet. 20 And he said, Thou shalt not go through. And Edom came out against him with much people, and with a strong hand. 21 Thus Edom refused to give Israel passage through his border: wherefore Israel turned away from him.

We have here the application made by Israel to the Edomites. The nearest way to Canaan from the place where Israel now lay encamped was through the country of Edom. Now,

I. Moses sends ambassadors to treat with the king of Edom for leave to pass through his country, and gives them instructions what to say, *v.* 14—17. 1. They are to claim kindred with the Edomites: *Thus saith thy brother Israel.* Both nations descended from Abraham and Isaac, their common ancestors; Esau and Jacob, the two fathers of their respective nations, were twin-brothers; and therefore, for relation-sake, they might reasonably expect this kindness from them; nor needed the Edomites to fear that their brother Israel had any ill design upon them, or would take any advantages against them. 2. They are to give a short account of the history and present state of Israel, which, they take it for granted, the Edomites were no strangers to. And in this there was a double plea:—(1.) Israel had been abused by the Egyptians, and therefore ought to be pitied and succoured by their relations: " *The Egyptians vexed us and our fathers,* but we may hope our brethren the Edomites will not be so vexatious." (2.) Israel had been wonderfully saved by the Lord, and therefore ought to be countenanced and favoured (*v.* 16): " *We cried unto the Lord, and he sent an angel,* the angel of his presence, the eternal Word, who has *brought us forth out of Egypt,* and led us hither." It was therefore the interest of the Edomites to ingratiate themselves with a people that had so great an interest in heaven and were so much its favourites, and it was at their peril if they offered them any injury. It is our wisdom and duty to be kind to those whom God is pleased to own, and to take his people for our people. *Come in, thou blessed of the Lord.* 3. They are humbly to beg a passport through their country. Though God himself, in the pillar of cloud and fire, was Israel's guide, in following which they might have justified their passing through any man's ground against all the world, yet God would have this respect paid to the Edomites, to show

that no man's property ought to be invaded under colour of religion. Dominion is founded in providence, not in grace. Thus when Christ was to pass through a village of the Samaritans, to whom his coming was likely to be offensive, he *sent messengers before his face* to ask leave, Luke ix. 52. Those that would receive kindness must not disdain to request it. 4. They are to give security for the good behaviour of the Israelites in this march, that they would keep in the king's high road, that they would commit no trespass upon any man's property, either in ground or water, that they would not so much as make use of a well without paying for it, and that they would make all convenient speed, as fast as they could well go on their feet, *v.* 17, 19. Nothing could be offered more fair and neighbourly.

II. The ambassadors returned with a denial, *v.* 18. Edom, that is, the king of Edom, as protector of his country, said, *Thou shalt not pass by me ;* and, when the ambassadors urged it further, he repeated the denial (*v.* 20) and threatened, if they offered to enter his country, it should be at their peril; he raised his trained bands to oppose them. *Thus Edom refused to give Israel passage.* This was owing, 1. To their jealousy of the Israelites; they feared they should receive damage by them, and would not trust their promises. And truly, had this numerous army been under any other discipline and command than that of the righteous God himself, who would no more suffer them to do wrong than to take wrong, there might have been cause for this jealousy; but what could they fear from a nation that had *statutes and judgments so righteous ?* 2. It was owing to the old enmity which Esau bore to Israel. If they had no reason to fear damage by them, yet they were not willing to show so much kindness to them. Esau hated Jacob because of the blessing, and now the hatred revived, when the blessing was ready to be inherited. God would hereby discover the ill-nature of the Edomites to their shame, and try the good-nature of the Israelites to their honour: they *turned away from him,* and did not take this occasion to quarrel with him. Note, We must not think it strange if the most reasonable requests be denied by unreasonable men, and if those be affronted by men whom God favours. *I as a deaf man heard not.* After this indignity which the Edomites offered to Israel God gave them a particular caution *not to abhor an Edomite* (Deut. xxiii. 7), though the Edomites had shown such an abhorrence of them, to teach us in such cases not to meditate revenge.

22 And the children of Israel, *even* the whole congregation, journeyed from Kadesh, and came unto mount Hor. 23 And the LORD spake unto Moses and Aaron in mount Hor, by

the coast of the land of Edom, saying, 24 Aaron shall be gathered unto his people: for he shall not enter into the land which I have given unto the children of Israel, because ye rebelled against my word at the waters of Meribah. 25 Take Aaron and Eleazar his son, and bring them up unto mount Hor: 26 And strip Aaron of his garments, and put them upon Eleazar his son: and Aaron shall be gathered *unto his people*, and shall die there. 27 And Moses did as the LORD commanded: and they went up into mount Hor in the sight of all the congregation. 28 And Moses stripped Aaron of his garments, and put them upon Eleazar his son; and Aaron died there in the top of the mount: and Moses and Eleazar came down from the mount. 29 And when all the congregation saw that Aaron was dead, they mourned for Aaron thirty days, *even* all the house of Israel.

The chapter began with the funeral of Miriam, and it ends with the funeral of her brother Aaron. When death comes into a family, it often strikes double. Israel had not improved the former affliction they were under, by the death of the prophetess, and therefore, soon after, God took away their priest, to try if they would lay that to heart. This happened at the very next stage, when they removed to Mount Hor, fetching a compass round the Edomites' country, leaving it on their left hand. Wherever we go, death attends us, and the graves are ready for us. I. God bids Aaron die, *v.* 24. God takes Moses and Aaron aside, and tells them, *Aaron shall be gathered to his people.* These two dear brothers are told that they must part. Aaron the elder must die first, but Moses is not likely to be long after him; so that it is but for a while, a little while, that they are parted. 1. There is something of displeasure in these orders. Aaron must not enter Canaan, because he had failed in his duty at the waters of strife. The mention of this, no doubt, went to the heart of Moses, who knew himself, perhaps, at that time, to be the guiltier of the two. 2. There is much of mercy in them. Aaron, though he dies for his transgression, is not put to death as a malefactor, by a plague, or fire from heaven, but dies with ease and in honour. He is not *cut off from his people*, as the expression usually is concerning those that die by the hand of divine justice, but he is *gathered to his people*, as one that died in the arms of divine grace. 3. There is much of type and significancy in them. Aaron must not enter

Canaan, to show that the Levitical priesthood could make nothing perfect: that must be done by the bringing in of a better hope. Those priests could not continue by reason of sin and death, but the priesthood of Christ, being undefiled, is unchangeable, and to this, which abides for ever, Aaron must resign all his honour, Heb. vii. 23—25.

II. Aaron submits, and dies in the method and manner appointed, and, for aught that appears, with as much cheerfulness as if he had been going to bed.

1. He puts on his holy garments to take his leave of them, and goes up with his brother and son to the top of Mount Hor, and probably some of the elders of Israel with him, *v.* 27. They went up *in the sight of all the congregation*, who, it is likely, were told on what errand they went up; by this solemn procession Aaron lets Israel know that he is neither afraid nor ashamed to die, but, when the bridegroom comes, can trim his lamp and go forth to meet him. His going up the hill to die signified that the death of saints (and Aaron is called *the saint of the Lord)* is their ascension; they rather go up than go down to death.

2. Moses, whose hands had first clothed Aaron with his priestly garments, now strips him of them; for, in reverence to the priesthood, it was not fit that he should die in them. Note, Death will strip us; naked we came into the world, and naked we must go out. We shall see little reason to be proud of our clothes, our ornaments, or marks of honour, if we consider how soon death will strip us of our glory, divest us of all our offices and honours, and take the crown off from our head.

3. Moses immediately puts the priestly garments upon Eleazar his son, clothes him with his father's robe, and *strengthens him with his girdle*, Isa. xxii. 21. Now, (1.) This was a great comfort to Moses, by whose hand the law of the priesthood was given. to see that it should be kept up in a succession, and that a lamp was ordained for the anointed, which should not be extinguished by death itself. This was a happy earnest and indication to the church of the care God would take that as one generation of ministers and Christians (spiritual priests) passes away another generation should come up instead of it. (2.) It was a great satisfaction to Aaron to see his son, who was dear to him, thus preferred, and his office, which was dearer, thus preserved and secured, and especially to see in this a figure of Christ's everlasting priesthood, in which alone his would be perpetuated. *Now, Lord, might Aaron say, let thy servant depart in peace, for my eyes have seen thy salvation.* (3.) It was a great kindness to the people. The installing of Eleazar before Aaron was dead would prevent those who bore ill-will to Aaron's family from attempting to set up another upon his death, in competition with his son. What could

they do when the matter was already settled? It would likewise encourage those among them that feared God, and be a token for good to them, that he would not leave them, nor suffer his faithfulness to fail.

4. *Aaron died there.* Quickly after he was stripped of his priestly garments, he laid himself down and died contentedly; for a good man would desire, if it were the will of God, not to outlive his usefulness. Why should we covet to continue any longer in this world than while we may do God and our generation some service in it?

5. Moses and Eleazar, with those that attended them, buried Aaron where he died, as appears by Deut. x. 6, and then *came down from the mount.* And now, when they came down, and had left Aaron behind, it might be proper for them to think that he had rather gone up to the better world and had left them behind.

6. All the congregation *mourned for Aaron thirty days, v.* 29. Though the loss was well made up in Eleazar, who, being in the prime of life, was fitter for public service than Aaron would have been if he had lived, yet it was a debt owing to their deceased high priest to mourn for him. While he lived, they were murmuring at him upon all occasions, but now that he was dead they mourned for him, Thus many are taught to lament the loss of those mercies which they would not learn to be thankful for the enjoyment of. Many good men have had more honour done to their memories than ever they had to their persons, witness those that were persecuted while they lived, but when they were dead had their sepulchres garnished.

CHAP. XXI.

The armies of Israel now begin to emerge out of the wilderness, and to come into a land inhabited, to enter upon action, and take possession of the frontiers of the land of promise. A glorious campaign this chapter gives us the history of, especially in the latter part of it. Here is, I. The defeat of Arad the Canaanite, ver. 1—3. II. The chastisement of the people with fiery serpents for their murmurings, and the relief granted them upon their submission by a brazen serpent, ver. 4—9. III. Several marches forward, and some occurrences by the way, ver. 10—20. IV. The celebrated conquest of Sihon king of the Amorites (ver. 21—32), and of Og king of Bashan (ver. 33—35), and possession taken of their land.

AND *when* king Arad the Canaanite, which dwelt in the south, heard tell that Israel came by the way of the spies; then he fought against Israel, and took *some* of them prisoners. 2 And Israel vowed a vow unto the Lord, and said, If thou wilt indeed deliver this people into my hand, then I will utterly destroy their cities. 3 And the Lord hearkened to the voice of Israel, and delivered up the Canaanites; and they utterly destroyed them and their cities: and he called the name of the place Hormah.

Here is, 1. The descent which Arad the Canaanite made upon the camp of Israel, hearing that they came *by the way of the*

spies; for, though the spies which Moses had sent thirty-eight years before then passed and repassed unobserved, yet their coming, and their errand, it is likely, were afterwards known to the Canaanites, gave them an alarm, and induced them to keep an eye upon Israel and get intelligence of all their motions. Now, when they understood that they were facing about towards Canaan, this Arad, thinking it policy to keep the war at a distance, made an onset upon them and fought with them. But it proved that he meddled to his own hurt; had he sat still, his people might have been last destroyed of all the Canaanites, but now they were the first. Thus those that are *overmuch wicked die before their time,* Eccl. vii. 17. 2. His success at first in this attempt. His advance-guards picked up some straggling Israelites, and took them prisoners, *v.* 1. This, no doubt, puffed him up, and he began to think that he should have the honour of crushing this formidable body, and saving his country from the ruin which it threatened. It was likewise a trial to the faith of the Israelites and a check to them for their distrusts and discontents. 3. Israel's humble address to God upon this occasion, *v.* 2. It was a temptation to them to murmur as their fathers did, and to despair of getting possession of Canaan; but God, who thus tried them by his providence, enabled them by his grace to quit themselves well in the trial, and to trust in him for relief against this fierce and powerful assailant. They, by their elders, in prayer for success, *vowed a vow.* Note, When we are desiring and expecting mercy from God we should bind our souls with a bond that we will faithfully do our duty to him, particularly that we will honour him with the mercy we are in the pursuit of. Thus Israel here promised to destroy the cities of these Canaanites, as devoted to God, and not to take the spoil of them to their own use. If God would give them victory, he should have all the praise, and they would not make a gain of it to themselves. When we are in this frame we are prepared to receive mercy. 4. The victory which the Israelites obtained over the Canaanites, *v.* 3. A strong party was sent out, probably under the command of Joshua, which not only drove back these Canaanites, but followed them to their cities, which probably lay on the edge of the wilderness, and utterly destroyed them, and so returned to the camp. *Vincimur in prælio, sed non in bello—We lose a battle, but we finally triumph.* What is said of the tribe of Gad is true of all God's Israel, a troop may overcome them, but they shall overcome at the last. The place was called *Hormah,* as a memorial of the destruction, for the terror of the Canaanites, and probably for warning to posterity not to attempt the rebuilding of these cities, which were destroyed as devoted to God and sacrifices to divine justice. And it appears from the instance of Jericho that the law concerning such cities was that they should never be re-built. There seems to be an allusion to this name in the prophecy of the fall of the New-Testament Babylon (Rev. xvi. 16), where its forces are said to be gathered together to a place called *Armageddon—the destruction of a troop.*

4 And they journeyed from mount Hor by the way of the Red Sea, to compass the land of Edom: and the soul of the people was much discouraged because of the way. 5 And the people spake against God, and against Moses, Wherefore have ye brought us up out of Egypt to die in the wilderness? for *there is* no bread, neither *is there any* water; and our soul loatheth this light bread. 6 And the Lord sent fiery serpents among the people, and they bit the people; and much people of Israel died. 7 Therefore the people came to Moses, and said, We have sinned, for we have spoken against the Lord, and against thee; pray unto the Lord, that he may take away the serpents from us. And Moses prayed for the people. 8 And the Lord said unto Moses, Make thee a fiery serpent, and set it upon a pole: and it shall come to pass, that every one that is bitten, when he looketh upon it, shall live. 9 And Moses made a serpent of brass, and put it upon a pole, and it came to pass, that if a serpent had bitten any man, when he beheld the serpent of brass, he lived.

Here is, I. The fatigue of Israel by a long march round the land of Edom, because they could not obtain passage through it the nearest way: *The soul of the people was much discouraged because of the way,* v. 4. Perhaps the way was rough and uneven, or foul and dirty; or it fretted them to go far about, and that they were not permitted to force their passage through the Edomites' country. Those that are of a fretful discontented spirit will always find something or other to make them uneasy.

II. Their unbelief and murmuring upon this occasion, v. 5. Though they had just now obtained a glorious victory over the Canaanites, and were going on conquering and to conquer, yet they speak very discontentedly of what God had done for them and distrustfully of what he would do, vexed that they were brought out of Egypt, that they had not bread and water as other people had by their own care and industry, but by miracle, they knew not how. They have *bread enough and to spare;* and yet they

complain *there is no bread,* because, though they eat angels' food, yet they are weary of it; manna itself is loathed, and called *light bread,* fit for children, not for men and soldiers. What will those be pleased with whom manna will not please? Those that are disposed to quarrel will find fault where there is no fault to be found. Thus those who have long enjoyed the means of grace are apt to surfeit even on the heavenly manna, and to call it light bread. But let not the contempt which some cast upon the word of God cause us to value it the less: it is the bread of life, substantial bread, and will nourish those who by faith feed upon it to eternal life, whoever calls it light bread.

III. The righteous judgment which God brought upon them for their murmuring, v. 6. He sent *fiery serpents among them,* which bit or stung many of them to death. The wilderness through which they had passed was all along infested with those fiery serpents, as appears, Deut. viii. 15. But hitherto God had wonderfully preserved his people from receiving hurt by them, till now that they murmured, to chastise them for which these animals, which hitherto had shunned their camp, now invade it. Justly are those made to feel God's judgments that are not thankful for his mercies. These serpents are called *fiery,* from their colour, or from their rage, or from the effects of their bitings, inflaming the body, putting it immediately into a high fever, scorching it with an insatiable thirst. They had unjustly complained for want of water (v. 5), to chastise them for which God sends upon them this thirst, which no water would quench. Those that cry without cause have justly cause given them to cry out. They distrustfully concluded that they must *die in the wilderness,* and God took them at their word, chose their delusions, and brought their unbelieving fears upon them; many of them did die. They had impudently flown in the face of God himself, and the *poison of asps was under their lips,* and now these fiery serpents (which, it should seem, were flying serpents, Isa. xiv. 29) flew in their faces and poisoned them. They in their pride had lifted themselves up against God and Moses, and now God humbled and mortified them, by making these despicable animals a plague to them. That artillery is now turned against them which had formerly been made use of in their defence against the Egyptians. He that brought quails to feast them let them know that he could bring serpents to bite them; the whole creation is at war with those that are in arms against God.

IV. Their repentance and supplication to God under this judgment, v. 7. They confess their fault: *We have sinned.* They are particular in their confession: *We have spoken against the Lord, and against thee.* It is to be feared that they would not have owned the sin if they had not felt the smart; but they relent under the rod; *when he slew them, then they sought him.* They beg the prayers of Moses for them, as conscious to themselves of their own unworthiness to be heard, and convinced of the great interest which Moses had in heaven. How soon is their tone altered! Those who had just before quarrelled with him as their worst enemy now make their court to him as their best friend, and choose him for their advocate with God. Afflictions often change men's sentiments concerning God's people, and teach them to value those prayers which, at a former period, they had scorned. Moses, to show that he had heartily forgiven them, blesses those who had cursed him, and *prays for those who had despitefully used him.* Herein he was a type of Christ, who interceded for his persecutors, and a pattern to us to go and do likewise, and thus to show that we *love our enemies.*

V. The wonderful provision which God made for their relief. He did not employ Moses in summoning the judgment, but, that he might recommend him to the good affection of the people, he made him instrumental in their relief, *v.* 8, 9. God ordered Moses to make the representation of a fiery serpent, which he did, in brass, and set it up on a very long pole, so that it might be seen from all parts of the camp, and every one that was stung with a fiery serpent was healed by looking up to this serpent of brass. The people prayed that God would *take away the serpents from them* (v. 7), but God saw fit not to do this : for he gives effectual relief in the best way, though not in our way. Thus those who did not die for their murmuring were yet made to smart for it, that they might the more feelingly repent and humble themselves for it ; they were likewise made to receive their cure from God, by the hand of Moses, that they might be taught, if possible, never again to speak against God and Moses. This method of cure was altogether miraculous, and the more wonderful if what some naturalists say be true, that looking upon bright and burnished brass is hurtful to those that are stung with fiery serpents. God can bring about his purposes by contrary means. The Jews themselves say that it was not the sight of the brazen serpent that cured them, but, in looking up to it, they looked up to God as the Lord that healed them. But there was much of gospel in this appointment. Our Saviour has told us so (John iii. 14, 15), that *as Moses lifted up the serpent in the wilderness so the Son of man must be lifted up, that whosoever believeth in him should not perish.* Observe then a resemblance,

1. Between their disease and ours. The devil is the old serpent, a fiery serpent, hence he appears (Rev. xii. 3) as a *great red dragon.* Sin is the biting of this fiery serpent ; it is painful to the startled conscience, and poisonous to the seared conscience. Satan's temptations are called his *fiery darts*, Eph. vi. 16. Lust and passion inflame the soul,

so do the terrors of the Almighty, when they *set themselves in array.* At the last, sin *bites like a serpent* and *stings like an adder ;* and even its sweets are turned into the gall of asps.

2. Between their remedy and ours. (1.) It was God himself that devised and prescribed this antidote against the fiery serpents ; so our salvation by Christ was the contrivance of Infinite Wisdom ; God himself has found the ransom. (2.) It was a very unlikely method of cure ; so our salvation by the death of Christ is *to the Jews a stumbling-block and to the Greeks foolishness.* It was Moses that *lifted up the serpent in the wilderness,* so the law is a schoolmaster to bring us to Christ, and Moses wrote of him, John v. 46. Christ was lifted up by the rulers of the Jews, who were the successors of Moses. (3.) That which cured was shaped in the likeness of that which wounded. So Christ, though perfectly free from sin himself, yet was *made in the likeness of sinful flesh* (Rom. viii. 3), so like that it was taken for granted that this man was a sinner, John ix. 24. (4.) The brazen serpent was lifted up ; so was Christ. He was lifted up upon the cross (John xii. 33, 34), for he was made a spectacle to the world. He was lifted up by the preaching of the gospel. The word here used for a *pole* signifies a *banner*, or *ensign*, for Christ crucified *stands for an ensign of the people,* Isa. xi. 10. Some make the lifting up of the serpent to be a figure of Christ's triumphing over Satan, the old serpent, whose head he bruised, when in his cross he made an open show of the principalities and powers which he had spoiled and destroyed, Col. ii. 15.

3. Between the application of their remedy and ours. They looked and lived, and we, if we believe, shall not perish ; it is by faith that we look unto Jesus, Heb. xii. 2. *Look unto me, and be you saved,* Isa. xlv. 22. We must be sensible of our wound and of our danger by it, receive the record which God has given concerning his Son, and rely upon the assurance he has given us that we shall be healed and saved by him if we resign ourselves to his direction. The brazen serpent's being lifted up would not cure if it was not looked upon. If any pored on their wound, and would not look up to the brazen serpent, they inevitably died. If they slighted this method of cure, and had recourse to natural medicines, and trusted to them, they justly perished ; so if sinners either despise Christ's righteousness or despair of benefit by it their wound will, without doubt, be fatal. But whoever looked up to this healing sign, though from the outmost part of the camp, though with a weak and weeping eye, was certainly healed ; so whosoever believes in Christ, though as yet but weak in faith, shall not perish. There are weak brethren *for whom Christ died.* Perhaps for some time after the serpent was set up the camp of Israel was molested by the fiery serpents ; and it is the probable conjecture of some

that they carried this brazen serpent along with them through the rest of their journey, and set it up wherever they encamped, and, when they settled in Canaan, fixed it somewhere within the borders of the land; for it is not likely that the children of Israel went so far off as this was into the wilderness to burn incense to it, as we find they did, 2 Kings xviii. 4. Even those that are delivered from the eternal death which is the wages of sin must expect to feel the pain and smart of it as long as they are here in this world; but, if it be not our own fault, we may have the brazen serpent to accompany us, to be still looked up to upon all occasions, by bearing about with us continually the dying of the Lord Jesus.

10 And the children of Israel set forward, and pitched in Oboth. 11 And they journeyed from Oboth, and pitched at Ije-abarim, in the wilderness which *is* before Moab, toward the sunrising. 12 From thence they removed, and pitched in the valley of Zared. 13 From thence they removed, and pitched on the other side of Arnon, which *is* in the wilderness that cometh out of the coasts of the Amorites: for Arnon *is* the border of Moab, between Moab and the Amorites. 14 Wherefore it is said in the book of the wars of the LORD, What he did in the Red Sea, and in the brooks of Arnon. 15 And at the stream of the brooks that goeth down to the dwelling of Ar, and lieth upon the border of Moab. 16 And from thence *they went* to Beer: that *is* the well whereof the LORD spake unto Moses, Gather the people together, and I will give them water. 17 Then Israel sang this song, Spring up, O well; sing ye unto it: 18 The princes digged the well, the nobles of the people digged it, by *the direction of* the lawgiver, with their staves. And from the wilderness *they went* to Mattanah: 19 And from Mattanah to Nahaliel: and from Nahaliel to Bamoth: 20 And from Bamoth *in* the valley, that *is* in the country of Moab, to the top of Pisgah, which looketh toward Jeshimon.

We have here an account of the several stages and removals of the children of Israel, till they came into the plains of Moab, out of which they at length passed over Jordan into Canaan, as we read in the beginning of

Joshua. Natural motions are quicker the nearer they are to their centre. The Israelites were now drawing near to the promised rest, and now they *set forward*, as the expression is, *v.* 10. It were well if we would do thus in our way to heaven, rid ground in the latter end of our journey, and the nearer we come to heaven be so much the more active and abundant in the work of the Lord. Two things especially are observable in the brief account here given of these removals:—

1. The wonderful success which God blessed his people with, near the brooks of Arnon, *v.* 13—15. They had now compassed the land of Edom (which they were not to invade, nor so much as to disturb, Deut. ii. 4, 5), and had come to the border of Moab. It is well that there are more ways than one to Canaan. The enemies of God's people may retard their passage, but cannot prevent their entrance into the promised rest. Care is taken to let us know that the Israelites in their march religiously observed the orders which God gave them to use no hostility against the Moabites (Deut. ii. 9), because they were the posterity of righteous Lot; therefore they pitched on the other side of Arnon (*v.* 13), that side which was now in the possession of the Amorites, one of the devoted nations, though formerly it had belonged to Moab, as appears here, *v.* 26, 27. This care of theirs not to offer violence to the Moabites is pleaded by Jephtha long afterwards, in his remonstrance against the Ammonites (Judg. xi. 15, &c.), and turned to them for a testimony. What their achievements were, now that they pitched on the banks of the river Arnon, we are not particularly told, but are referred to the *book of the wars of the Lord*, perhaps that book which was begun with the history of the war with the Amalekites, Exod. xvii. 14. *Write it* (said God) *for a memorial in a book*, to which were added all the other battles which Israel fought, in order, and, among the rest, their actions on the river Arnon, at *Vaheb* in *Suphah* (as our margin reads it) and other places on that river. Or, *it shall be said* (as some read it) *in the rehearsal*, or commemoration, *of the wars of the Lord, what he did in the Red Sea*, when he brought Israel out of Egypt, and what he did *in the brooks of Arnon*, just before he brought them into Canaan. Note, In celebrating the memorials of God's favours to us, it is good to observe the series of them, and how divine goodness and mercy have constantly followed us, even from the Red Sea to the brooks of Arnon. In every stage of our lives, nay, in every step, we should take notice of what God has wrought for us; what he did at such a time, and what in such a place, ought to be distinctly remembered.

2. The wonderful supply which God blessed his people with at *Beer* (*v.* 16), which signifies the *well* or *fountain*. It is said (*v.* 10) they pitched in *Oboth*, which signifies *bottles*, so called perhaps because there they filled their

bottles with water, which should last them for some time; but by this time, we may suppose, it was with them as it was with Hagar (Gen. xxi. 15), *The water was spent in the bottle;* yet we do not find that they murmured, and therefore God, in compassion to them, brought them to a well of water, to encourage them to wait on him in humble silence and expectation and to believe that he would graciously take cognizance of their wants, though they did not complain of them. In this world, we do at the best but pitch in *Oboth,* where our comforts lie in close and scanty vessels; when we come to heaven we shall remove to *Beer,* the well of life, the fountain of living waters. Hitherto we have found, when they were supplied with water, they asked it in unjust discontent, and God gave it in just displeasure; but here we find, (1.) That God gave it in love (v. 16): *Gather the people together,* to be witnesses of the wonder, and joint-sharers in the favour, *and I will give them water.* Before they prayed, God granted, and anticipated them with the blessings of his goodness. (2.) That they received it with joy and thankfulness, which made the mercy doubly sweet to them, v. 17. Then they sang this song, to the glory of God and the encouragement of one another, *Spring up, O well!* Thus they pray that it may spring up, for promised mercies must be fetched in by prayer; they triumph that it does spring up, and meet it with their joyful acclamations. With joy must we *draw water out of the wells of salvation,* Isa xi. 3. As the brazen serpent was a figure of Christ, who is lifted up for our cure, so is this well a figure of the Spirit, who is poured forth for our comfort, and from whom flow to us *rivers of living waters,* John vii. 38. Does this well spring up in our souls? We should sing to it; take the comfort to ourselves, and give the glory to God; stir up this gift, sing to it, *Spring up, O well!* thou *fountain of gardens,* to water my soul (Cant. iv. 15), plead the promise, which perhaps alludes to this story (Isa. xli. 17, 18), *I will make the wilderness wells of water.* (3.) That whereas before the remembrance of the miracle was perpetuated in the names given to the places, which signified the people's strife and murmuring, now it was perpetuated in a song of praise, which preserved on record the manner in which it was done (v. 18): *The princes digged the well,* the seventy elders, it is probable, *by direction of the lawgiver* (that is, Moses, under God) *with their staves;* that is, with their staves they made holes in the soft and sandy ground, and God caused the water miraculously to spring up in the holes which they made. Thus the pious Israelites long afterwards, *passing through the valley of Baca,* a dry and thirsty place, made wells, and God by rain from heaven filled the pools, Ps. lxxxiv. 6. Observe, [1.] God promised to give them water, but they must open the ground to receive it, and give it vent. God's favours must be expected in the use of such means as lie within our power, but still the excellency of the power is of God. [2.] The nobles of Israel were forward to set their hands to this work, and used their staves, probably those that were the ensigns of their honour and power, for the public service, and it is upon record to their honour. And we may suppose that it was a great confirmation to them in their offices, and a great comfort to the people, that they were made use of by the divine power as instruments to this miraculous supply. By this it appeared that the spirit of Moses, who must shortly die, rested in some measure upon the nobles of Israel. Moses did not strike the ground himself, as formerly the rock, but gave them direction to do it, that their staves might share in the honour of his rod, and they might comfortably hope that when he should leave them yet God would not, but that they also in their generation should be public blessings, and might expect the divine presence with them as long as they acted by the direction of the lawgiver. For comfort must be looked for only in the way of duty; and, if we would share in divine joys, we must carefully follow the divine direction.

21 And Israel sent messengers unto Sihon king of the Amorites, saying, 22 Let me pass through thy land: we will not turn into the fields, or into the vineyards; we will not drink *of* the waters of the well: *but* we will go along by the king's *high* way, until we be past thy borders. 23 And Sihon would not suffer Israel to pass through his border: but Sihon gathered all his people together, and went out against Israel into the wilderness: and he came to Jahaz, and fought against Israel. 24 And Israel smote him with the edge of the sword, and possessed his land from Arnon unto Jabbok, even unto the children of Ammon: for the border of the children of Ammon *was* strong. 25 And Israel took all these cities: and Israel dwelt in all the cities of the Amorites, in Heshbon, and in all the villages thereof. 26 For Heshbon *was* the city of Sihon the king of the Amorites, who had fought against the former king of Moab, and taken all his land out of his hand, even unto Arnon. 27 Wherefore they that speak in proverbs say, Come into Heshbon, let the city of Sihon be built and prepared: 28 For there is a fire gone out of Heshbon,

a flame from the city of Sihon : it hath consumed Ar of Moab, *and* the lords of the high places of Arnon. 29 Woe to thee, Moab ! thou art undone, O people of Chemosh : he hath given his sons that escaped, and his daughters, into captivity unto Sihon king of the Amorites. 30 We have shot at them; Heshbon is perished even unto Dibon, and we have laid them waste even unto Nophah, which *reacheth* unto Medeba. 31 Thus Israel dwelt in the land of the Amorites. 32 And Moses sent to spy out Jaazer, and they took the villages thereof, and drove out the Amorites that *were* there. 33 And they turned and went up by the way of Bashan : and Og the king of Bashan went out against them, he, and all his people, to the battle at Edrei. 34 And the LORD said unto Moses, Fear him not : for I have delivered him into thy hand, and all his people and his land ; and thou shalt do to him as thou didst unto Sihon king of the Amorites, which dwelt at Heshbon. 35 So they smote him, and his sons, and all his people, until there was none left him alive : and they possessed his land.

We have here an account of the victories obtained by Israel over Sihon and Og, which must be distinctly considered, not only because they are here distinctly related, but because long afterwards the memorial of them is distinctly celebrated, and they are severally assigned as instances of everlasting mercy. He slew *Sihon king of the Amorites, for his mercy endureth for ever, and Og the king of Bashan, for his mercy endureth for ever,* Ps. cxxxvi. 19, 20.

I. Israel sent a peaceable message to Sihon king of the Amorites (*v.* 21), but received an unpeaceable return, worse than that of the Edomites to the like message, *ch.* xx. 18, 20. For the Edomites only refused them a passage, and stood upon their own defence to keep them out ; but Sihon went out with his forces *against Israel in the wilderness,* out of his own borders, without any provocation given him (*v.* 23), and so ran himself upon his own ruin. Jephtha intimates that he was prompted by his politics to do this (Judg. xi. 20), *Sihon trusted not Israel to pass through his coast ;* but his politics deceived him, for Moses says, *God hardened his spirit and made his heart obstinate, that he might deliver him into the hand of Israel,* Deut. ii. 30. The enemies of God's church are often infatuated in those very counsels which they think most wisely

taken. Sihon's army was routed, and not only so, but all his country came into the possession of Israel, *v.* 24, 25. This seizure is justified, 1. Against the Amorites themselves, for they were the aggressors, and provoked the Israelites to battle ; and yet, perhaps, that would not have been sufficient to entitle Israel to their land, but that God himself, the King of nations, the Lord of the whole earth, had given them a grant of it. The Amorites formed one of the devoted nations whose land God had promised to Abraham and his seed, which promise should be performed when the iniquity of the Amorites should be full, Gen. xv. 16. Jephtha insists upon this grant as their title, Judg. xi. 23, 24. The victory which God gave them over the Amorites put them in possession, and then, the promise made to their fathers having given them a right, by virtue of that they kept possession. 2. Against the Moabites, who had formerly been the lords-proprietors of this country. If they should ever lay claim to it, and should plead that God himself had provided that *none of their land should be given to Israel for a possession* (Deut. ii. 9), Moses here furnishes posterity with a replication to their plea, and Jephtha makes use of it against the Amorites 260 years afterwards, when Israel's title to this country was questioned. (1.) The justification itself is that though it was true this country had belonged to the Moabites, yet the Amorites had taken it from them some time before, and were now in full and quiet possession of it, *v.* 26. The Israelites did not take it out of the hands of the Moabites, they had before lost it to the Amorites, and were constrained to give up their pretensions to it ; and, when Israel had taken it from the Amorites, they were under no obligation to restore it to the Moabites, whose title to it was long since extinguished. See here the uncertainty of worldly possessions, how often they change their owners, and how soon we may be deprived of them, even when we think ourselves most sure of them ; *they make themselves wings.* It is our wisdom therefore to secure the good part which cannot be taken away from us. See also the wisdom of the divine Providence and its perfect foresight, by which preparation is made long before for the accomplishment of all God's purposes in their season. This country being designed in due time for Israel, it is beforehand put into the hand of the Amorites, who little think that they have it but as trustees till Israel come of age, and then must surrender it. We understand not the vast reaches of Providence, but known unto God are all his works, as appears in this instance, that he *set the bounds of the people according to the number of the children of Israel,* Deut. xxxii. 8. All that land which he intended for his chosen people he put into the possession of the devoted nations, that were to be driven out. (2.) For proof of the allegation, he refers to the authentic records of the country, for so their proverbs or songs were, one of which he quotes some passages out of (*v.* 27—30), which sufficiently proves what is vouched for, namely, [1.] That such and such places that are here named, though they had been in the possession of the Moabites, had by right of war become the dominion of Sihon king of the Amorites. Heshbon had become his city, and he obtained such a quiet possession of it that it was built and prepared for him (*v.* 27), and the country to Dibon and Nophah was likewise subdued, and annexed to the kingdom of the Amorites, *v.* 30. [2.] That the Moabites were utterly disabled ever to regain the possession. Even Ar of Moab, though not taken or attempted by Sihon, but still remaining the metropolis of Moab, yet was so wasted by this loss that it would never be able to make head, *v.* 28. The Moabites were undone, and even Chemosh their god had given them up, as unable to rescue them out of the hands of Sihon, *v.* 29. By all this it appears that the Moabites' claim to this country was barred for ever. There may be a further reason for inserting this Amorite poem, namely, to show that the triumphing of the wicked is short. Those that had conquered the Moabites, and insulted over them, were now themselves conquered and insulted over by the Israel of God. It is very probable that the same Sihon, king of the Amorites, that had got this country from the Moabites, now lost it to the Israelites; for, though it is said to be taken from a former king of Moab (*v* 26), yet not by a former king of the Amorites; and then it shows how sometimes justice makes men to see the loss of that which they got by violence, and were puffed up with the gain of. They are *exalted but for a little while*, Job xxiv. 24.

II. Og king of Bashan, instead of being warned by the fate of his neighbours to make peace with Israel, is instigated by it to make war with them, which proves in like manner to be his destruction. Og was also an Amorite, and therefore perhaps thought himself better able to deal with Israel than his neighbours were, and more likely to prevail, because of his own gigantic strength and stature, which Moses takes notice of, Deut. iii. 11, where he gives a more full account of this story. Here observe, 1. That the Amorite begins the war (*v.* 33): He *went out to battle against Israel.* His country was very rich and pleasant. Bashan was famous for the best timber (witness the oaks of Bashan), and the best breed of cattle, witness the bulls and kine of Bashan, and the lambs and rams of that country, which are celebrated, Deut. xxxii. 14. Wicked men do their utmost to secure themselves and their possessions against the judgments of God, but all in vain, when their day comes, on which they must fall. 2. That God interests himself in the cause, bids Israel not to fear this threatening force, and promises

a complete victory: "*I have delivered him into thy hand* (*v.* 34); the thing is as good as done already, it is all thy own, enter and take possession." Giants are but worms before God's power. 3. That Israel is more than a conqueror, not only routs the enemies' army, but gains the enemies' country, which afterwards was part of the inheritance of the two tribes and a half that were first seated on the other side Jordan. God gave Israel these successes, while Moses was yet with them, both for his comfort (that he might see the beginning of that glorious work, which he must not live to see the finishing of) and for the encouragement of the people in the war of Canaan under Joshua. Though this was to them in comparison but as the day of small things, yet it was an earnest of great things.

CHAP. XXII.

At this chapter begins the famous story of Balak and Balaam, their attempt to curse Israel, and the baffling of that attempt; God's people are long afterwards told to remember what Balak the king of Moab consulted, and what Balaam the son of Beor answered him, that they might know the righteousness of the Lord, Mic. vi. 5. In this chapter we have, I. Balak's fear of Israel, and the plot he had to get them cursed, ver. 1—4. II. The embassy he sent to Balaam, a conjurer, to fetch him for that purpose, and the disappointment he met with in the first embassy, ver. 5—14. III. Balaam's coming to him upon his second message, ver. 15—21. IV. The opposition Balaam met with by the way, ver. 22—35. V. The interview at length between Balak and Balaam, ver. 36, &c.

AND the children of Israel set forward, and pitched in the plains of Moab on this side Jordan *by* Jericho. 2 And Balak the son of Zippor saw all that Israel had done to the Amorites. 3 And Moab was sore afraid of the people, because they *were* many: and Moab was distressed because of the children of Israel. 4 And Moab said unto the elders of Midian, Now shall this company lick up all *that are* round about us, as the ox licketh up the grass of the field. And Balak the son of Zippor *was* king of the Moabites at that time. 5 He sent messengers therefore unto Balaam the son of Beor to Pethor, which *is* by the river of the land of the children of his people, to call him, saying, Behold, there is a people come out from Egypt: behold, they cover the face of the earth, and they abide over against me: 6 Come now therefore, I pray thee, curse me this people; for they *are* too mighty for me: peradventure I shall prevail, *that* we may smite them, and *that* I may drive them out of the land: for I wot that he whom thou blessest *is* blessed, and he whom thou cursest is cursed. 7 And the elders of Moab and the elders of Midian departed with the rewards of divination in their hand; and they came unto Balaam, and spake unto him the words of Balak. 8 And he said unto them, Lodge here this night, and I will bring you word again, as the LORD shall speak unto me: and the princes of Moab abode with Balaam. 9 And God came unto Balaam, and said, What men *are* these with thee? 10 And Balaam said unto God, Balak, the son of Zippor, king of Moab, hath sent unto me, *saying*, 11 Behold, *there is* a people come out of Egypt, which covereth the face of the earth: come now, curse me them; peradventure I shall be able to overcome them, and drive them out. 12 And God said unto Balaam, Thou shalt not go with them; thou shalt not curse the people: for they *are* blessed. 13 And Balaam rose up in the morning, and said unto the princes of Balak, Get you into your land: for the LORD refuseth to give me leave to go with you. 14 And the princes of Moab rose up, and they went unto Balak, and said, Balaam refuseth to come with us.

The children of Israel have at length finished their wanderings in the wilderness, out of which they went up (*ch.* xxi. 18), and are now encamped in the plains of Moab near Jordan, where they continued till they passed through Jordan under Joshua, after the death of Moses. Now we have here,

I. The fright which the Moabites were in upon the approach of Israel, *v.* 2—4. They needed not to fear any harm from them if they knew (and it is probable that Moses let them know) the orders God had given to Israel not to contend with the Moabites, nor to use any hostility against them, Deut. ii. 9. But, if they had any notice of this, they were jealous that it was but a sham, to make them secure, that they might be the more easily conquered. Notwithstanding the old friendship between Abraham and Lot, the Moabites resolved to ruin Israel if they could, and therefore they will take it for granted, without any ground for the suspicion, that Israel resolves to ruin them. Thus it is common for those that design mischief to pretend that mischief is designed against them; and their groundless jealousies must be the colour of their causeless malice. They hear of their triumphs over the Amorites (*v.* 2), and think that their own house is in danger when their neighbour's is on fire. They observe their multitudes (*v.* 3): *They*

were many; and hence infer how easily they would conquer their country, and all about them, if some speedy and effectual course were not taken to stop the progress of their victorious arms: "They shall *lick up* or devour us, and *all that are round about us,* as speedily and irresistibly *as the ox eats up the grass*" (*v.*4), owning themselves to be an unequal match for so formidable an enemy. Therefore they were sorely afraid and distressed themselves; thus were the wicked *in great fear where no fear was,* Ps. liii. 5. These fears they communicated to their neighbours, the elders of Midian, that some measures might be concerted between them for their common safety; for, if the kingdom of Moab fall, the republic of Midian cannot stand long. The Moabites, if they had pleased, might have made a good use of the advances of Israel, and their successes against the Amorites. They had reason to rejoice, and give God and Israel thanks for freeing them from the threatening power of Sihon king of the Amorites, who had taken from them part of their country, and was likely to overrun the rest. They had reason likewise to court Israel's friendship, and to come in to their assistance; but having forsaken the religion of their father Lot, and being sunk into idolatry, they hated the people of the God of Abraham, and were justly infatuated in their counsels and given up to distress.

II. The project which the king of Moab formed to get the people of Israel cursed, that is, to set God against them, who, he perceived, hitherto fought for them. He trusted more to his arts than to his arms, and had a notion that if he could but get some prophet or other, with his powerful charms, to imprecate evil upon them, and to pronounce a blessing upon himself and his forces, then, though otherwise too weak, he should be able to deal with them. This notion arose, 1. Out of the remains of some religion; for it owns a dependence upon some visible sovereign powers that rule in the affairs of the children of men and determine them, and an obligation upon us to make application to these powers. 2. Out of the ruins of the true religion; for if the Midianites and Moabites had not wretchedly degenerated from the faith and worship of their pious ancestors, Abraham and Lot, they could not have imagined it possible to do any mischief with their curses to a people who alone adhered to the service of the true God, from whose service they had themselves revolted.

III. The court which he made to Balaam the son of Beor, a famous conjurer, to engage him to curse Israel. This Balaam lived a great way off, in that country whence Abraham came, and where Laban lived; but, though it was probable that there were many nearer home that were pretenders to divination, yet none had so great a reputation for success as Balaam, and Balak will employ the best he can hear of, though he send a great way for him, so much is his heart upon this project. And to gain him, 1. He makes him his friend, complaining to him, as his confidant, of the danger he was in from the numbers and neighbourhood of the camp of Israel : *They cover the face of the earth*, and they *abide over against me*, v. 5. 2. In effect he makes him his god, by the great power he attributes to his word : *He whom thou blessest is blessed*, and *he whom thou cursest is cursed*, v. 6. The learned bishop Patrick inclines to think, with many of the Jewish writers, that Balaam had been a great prophet, who, for the accomplishment of his predictions and the answers of his prayers, both for good and evil, had been looked upon justly as a man of great interest with God; but that, growing proud and covetous, God departed from him, and then, to support his sinking credit, he betook himself to diabolical arts. He is called a *prophet* (2 Pet. ii. 16), because he had been one, or perhaps he had raised his reputation from the first by his magical charms, as Simon Magus, who bewitched the people so far that he was called *the great power of God*, Acts viii. 10. Curses pronounced by God's prophets in the name of the Lord have wonderful effects, as Noah's (Gen. ix. 25), and Elisha's, 2 Kings ii. 24. But the curse *causeless shall not come* (Prov. xxvi. 2), no more than Goliath's, when he *cursed David by his gods*, 1 Sam. xvii. 43. Let us desire to have the prayers of God's ministers and people for us, and dread having them against us; for they are greatly regarded by him who blesseth indeed and curseth indeed. But Balak cannot rely upon these compliments as sufficient to prevail with Balaam, the main inducement is yet behind (v. 7): they took *the rewards of divination in their hand, the wages of unrighteousness*, which he *loved*, 2 Pet. ii. 15.

IV. The restraint God lays upon Balaam, forbidding him to curse Israel. It is very probable that Balaam, being a curious inquisitive man, was no stranger to Israel's case and character, but had heard that God was with them of a truth, so that he ought to have given the messengers their answer immediately, that he would never curse a people whom God had blessed; but he lodges the messengers, and takes a night's time to consider what he shall do, and to receive instructions from God, v. 8. When we enter into a parley with temptations we are in great danger of being overcome by them. In the night God comes to him, probably in a dream, and enquires what business those strangers had with him. He knows it, but he will know it from him. Balaam gives him an account of their errand (v. 9—11), and God thereupon charges him not to go with them, nor attempt to curse that blessed people, v. 12. Thus God sometimes, for the

preservation of his people, was pleased to speak to bad men, as to Abimelech (Gen. xx 3), and to Laban, Gen. xxxi. 24. And we read of some that were workers of iniquity, and yet in Christ's name prophesied, and *did many wondrous works*. Balaam is charged not only not to go to Balak, but not to offer to curse this people, which he might have attempted at a distance; and the reason is given : *They are blessed.* This was part of the blessing of Abraham (Gen. xii. 3), *I will curse him that curseth thee;* so that an attempt to curse them would be not only fruitless, but perilous. Israel had often provoked God in the wilderness, yet he will not suffer their enemies to curse them, for he *rewards them not according to their iniquities.* The blessedness of those whose sin is covered comes upon them, Rom. iv. 6, 7.

V. The return of the messengers without Balaam. 1. Balaam is not faithful in returning God's answer to the messengers, *v.* 13. He only tells them, *The Lord refuseth to give me leave to go with you.* He did not tell them, as he ought to have done, that Israel was a blessed people, and must by no means be cursed; for then the design would have been crushed, and the temptation would not have been renewed: but he, in effect, desired them to give his humble service to Balak, and let him know that he applauded his project, and would have been very glad to gratify him, but that truly he had the character of a prophet, and must not go without leave from God, which he had not yet obtained, and therefore for the present he must be excused. Note, Those are a fair mark for Satan's temptation that speak diminishingly of divine prohibitions, as if they amounted to no more than the denial of a permission, and as if to go against God's law were only to go without his leave 2. The messengers are not faithful in returning Balaam's answer to Balak. All the account they give of it is, *Balaam refuseth to come with us* (*v.* 14), intimating that he only wanted more courtship and higher proffers; but they are not willing Balak should know that God had signified his disallowance of the attempt. Thus are great men wretchedly abused by the flatteries of those about them, who do all they can to prevent their seeing their own faults and follies.

15 And Balak sent yet again princes, more, and more honourable than they. 16 And they came to Balaam, and said to him, Thus saith Balak the son of Zippor, Let nothing, I pray thee, hinder thee from coming unto me : 17 For I will promote thee unto very great honour, and I will do whatsoever thou sayest unto me : come therefore, I pray thee, curse me this people. 18 And Balaam answered

and said unto the servants of Balak, If Balak would give me his house full of silver and gold, I cannot go beyond the word of the LORD my God, to do less or more. 19 Now therefore, I pray you, tarry ye also here this night, that I may know what the LORD will say unto me more. 20 And God came unto Balaam at night, and said unto him, If the men come to call thee, rise up, *and* go with them; but yet the word which I shall say unto thee, that shalt thou do. 21 And Balaam rose up in the morning, and saddled his ass, and went with the princes of Moab.

We have here a second embassy sent to Balaam, to fetch him over to curse Israel. It were well for us if we were as earnest and constant in prosecuting a good work, notwithstanding disappointments, as Balak was in pursuing this ill design. The enemies of the church are restless and unwearied in their attempts against it; but he that sits in heaven laughs at them. Observe,

I. The temptation Balak laid before Balaam. He contrived to make this assault more vigorous than the former. It is very probable that he sent double money in the hands of his messengers; but, besides that, now he tempted him with honours, laid a bait not only for his covetousness, but for his pride and ambition. How earnestly should we beg of God daily to mortify in us these two limbs of the old man! Those that know how to look with a holy contempt upon worldly wealth and preferment will find it not so hard a matter as most men do to keep a good conscience. See how artfully Balak managed the temptation. 1. The messengers he sent were *more*, and *more honourable*, v. 15. He sent to this conjurer with as great respect and deference to his quality as if he had been a sovereign prince, apprehending perhaps that Balaam had thought himself slighted in the fewness and meanness of the former messengers. 2. The request was very urgent. This powerful prince becomes a suitor to him : " *Let nothing, I pray thee, hinder thee* (v. 16), no, not God, nor conscience, nor any fear either of sin or shame.*" 3. The proffers were high : " *I will promote thee to very great honour* among the princes of Moab;" nay, he gives him a blank, and he shall write his own terms: *I will do whatsoever thou sayest,* that is, " I will give thee whatever thou desirest, and observe whatever thou orderest; thy word shall be a law to me," v. 17. Thus sinners stick at no pains, spare no cost, and care not how low they stoop, for the gratifying either of their luxury or of their malice; shall we then be stiff and strait-

handed in our compliance with the laws of virtue ? God forbid.

II. Balaam's seeming resistance of, but real yielding to, this temptation. We may here discern in Balaam a struggle between his convictions and his corruptions. 1. His convictions charged him to adhere to the command of God, and he spoke their language, v. 18. Nor could any man have said better: " *If Balak would give me his house full of silver and gold,* and that is more than he can give or I can ask, *I cannot go beyond the word of the Lord my God.*" See how honourably he speaks of God; he is *Jehovah, my God.* Note, Many call God theirs that are not his, not *truly* because not *only* his; *they swear by the Lord, and by Malcham.* See how respectfully he speaks of the word of God, as one resolved to stick to it, and in nothing to vary from it, and how slightly of the wealth of this world, as if gold and silver were nothing to him in comparison with the favour of God; and yet, at the same time, the searcher of hearts knew that he loved the wages of unrighteousness. Note, It is an easy thing for bad men to speak very good words, and with their mouth to make a show of piety. There is no judging of men by their words. God knows the heart. 2. His corruptions at the same time strongly inclined him to go contrary to the command. He seemed to refuse the temptation, v. 18. But even then he expressed no abhorrence of it, as Christ did when he had the kingdoms of the world offered him *(Get thee hence Satan),* and as Peter did when Simon Magus offered him money: *Thy money perish with thee.* But it appears (v. 19) that he had a strong inclination to accept the proffer; for he would further attend, to know what God would say to him, hoping that he might alter his mind and give him leave to go. This was a vile reflection upon God Almighty, as if he could change his mind, and now at last suffer those to be cursed whom he had pronounced blessed, and as if he would be brought to allow what he had already declared to be evil. Surely he thought God *altogether such a one as himself.* He had already been told what the will of God was, in which he ought to have acquiesced, and not to have desired a re-hearing of that cause which was already so plainly determined. Note, It is a very great affront to God, and a certain evidence of the dominion of corruption in the heart, to beg leave to sin.

III. The permission God gave him to go, v. 20. God came to him, probably by an angel, and told him he might, if he pleased, go with Balak's messengers. *So he gave him up to his own heart's lust.* " Since thou hast such a mind to go, even go, yet know that *the journey thou undertakest shall not be for thy honour;* for, though thou hast leave to go, thou shalt not, as thou hopest, have leave to curse, *for the word which I shall say unto thee, that thou shalt do.*" Note, God has wicked men in a chain; *hitherto they shall come* by his permission, but no further than he does permit them. Thus he makes the wrath of man to praise him, yet, at the same time, restrains the remainder of it. It was in anger that God said to Balaam, "Go with them," and we have reason to think that Balaam himself so understood it, for we do not find him pleading this allowance when God reproved him for going. Note, As God sometimes denies the prayers of his people in love, so sometimes he grants the desires of the wicked in wrath.

IV. His setting out in the journey, *v.* 21. God gave him leave to go *if the men called him,* but he was so fond of the journey that we do not find he staid for their calling him, but he himself *rose up in the morning,* got every thing ready with all speed, and *went with the princes of Moab,* who were proud enough that they had carried their point. The apostle describes Balaam's sin here to be that he *ran greedily into an error for reward,* Jude 11. The love of money is the root of all evil.

22 And God's anger was kindled because he went: and the angel of the LORD stood in the way for an adversary against him. Now he was riding upon his ass, and his two servants *were* with him. 23 And the ass saw the angel of the LORD standing in the way, and his sword drawn in his hand: and the ass turned aside out of the way, and went into the field: and Balaam smote the ass, to turn her into the way. 24 But the angel of the LORD stood in a path of the vineyards, a wall *being* on this side, and a wall on that side. 25 And when the ass saw the angel of the LORD, she thrust herself unto the wall, and crushed Balaam's foot against the wall: and he smote her again. 26 And the angel of the LORD went further and stood in a narrow place, where *was* no way to turn either to the right hand or to the left. 27 And when the ass saw the angel of the LORD, she fell down under Balaam: and Balaam's anger was kindled, and he smote the ass with a staff. 28 And the LORD opened the mouth of the ass, and she said unto Balaam, What have I done unto thee, that thou hast smitten me these three times? 29 And Balaam said unto the ass, Because thou hast mocked me: I would there were a sword in mine hand, for now would I kill thee.

30 And the ass said unto Balaam, Am not I thine ass, upon which thou hast ridden ever since *I was* thine unto this day? was I ever wont to do so unto thee? And he said, Nay. 31 Then the LORD opened the eyes of Balaam, and he saw the angel of the LORD standing in the way, and his sword drawn in his hand: and he bowed down his head, and fell flat on his face. 32 And the angel of the LORD said unto him, Wherefore hast thou smitten thine ass these three times? behold, I went out to withstand thee, because *thy* way is perverse before me: 33 And the ass saw me, and turned from me these three times: unless she had turned from me, surely now also I had slain thee, and saved her alive. 34 And Balaam said unto the angel of the LORD, I have sinned; for I knew not that thou stoodest in the way against me: now therefore, if it displease thee, I will get me back again. 35 And the angel of the LORD said unto Balaam, Go with the men: but only the word that I shall speak unto thee, that thou shalt speak. So Balaam went with the princes of Balak.

We have here an account of the opposition God gave to Balaam in his journey towards Moab; probably the princes had gone before, or gone some other way, and Balaam had pointed out where he would meet them, or where they should stay for him, for we read nothing of them in this part of our narrative, only that Balaam, like a person of some quality, was attended with his two men—honour enough, one would think, for such a man, he needed not be beholden to Balak for promotion.

I. Here is God's displeasure against Balaam for undertaking this journey: God's *anger was kindled because he went, v.* 22. Note, 1. The sin of sinners is not to be thought the less provoking to God because he permits it. We must not think that, because God does not by his providence restrain men from sin, therefore he approves of it, or that it is therefore not hateful to him; he suffers sin, and yet is angry at it. 2. Nothing is more displeasing to God than malicious designs against his people; he that touches them touches the apple of his eye.

II. The way God took to let Balaam know his displeasure against him: *An angel stood in the way for an adversary.* Now God fulfilled his promise to Israel (Exod. xxiii. 22),

I will be an enemy to thy enemies. The holy angels are adversaries to sin, and perhaps are employed more than we are aware of in preventing it, particularly in opposing those that have any ill designs against God's church and people, for whom Michael our prince stands up, Dan. xii. 1 ; x. 21. What a comfort is this to all that wish well to the Israel of God, that he never suffers wicked men to form any attempt against them, without sending his holy angels forth to break the attempt and secure his little ones ! When the prophet saw the four horns that scattered Judah, at the same time he saw four carpenters that were to fray those horns, Zech. i. 18, &c. When the *enemy comes in like a flood the Spirit of the Lord will lift up a standard against him.* This angel was an adversary to Balaam, because Balaam counted him his adversary ; otherwise those are really our best friends, and we are so to reckon them, that stop our progress in a sinful way. The angel stood with his sword drawn (*v.* 23), *a flaming sword*, like that in the hands of the cherubim (Gen. iii. 24), *turning every way.* Note, The holy angels are at war with those with whom God is angry, for they are the ministers of his justice. Observe,

1. Balaam had notice given him of God's displeasure, by the ass, and this *did not startle him.* The *ass saw the angel, v.* 23. How vainly did Balaam boast that he was a man whose *eyes were open*, and that he *saw the visions of the Almighty* (*ch.* xxiv. 3, 4), when the ass he rode on saw more than he did, his eyes being blinded with covetousness and ambition and dazzled with the rewards of divination ! Note, Many have God against them, and his holy angels, but are not aware of it. The *ass knows his owner*, sees his danger, but Balaam does *not know, does not consider*, Isa. i. 3. *Lord, when thy hand is lifted up, they will not see*, Isa. xxvi. 11. Let none be puffed up with a conceit of visions and revelations, when even an ass saw an angel ; yet let those be ashamed of their own sottishness, worse than that of the beasts that perish, who, when they are told of the sword of God's wrath drawn against them, while they persist in wicked ways, yet will go on : the ass understood the law of self-preservation better than so ; for, to save both herself and her senseless rider, (1.) She *turned aside out of the way, v.* 23. Balaam should have taken the hint of this, and considered whether he was not out of the way of his duty ; but, instead of this, he *beat her into the way again.* Thus those who by wilful sin are running headlong into perdition are angry at those that would prevent their ruin. (2.) She had not gone much further before she saw the angel again, and then, to avoid him, *ran up to a wall*, and *crushed her rider's foot, v.* 24, 25. How many ill accidents are we liable to in travelling upon the road, from which if we are preserved we must own our obligations to the divine Providence, which by

the ministry of angels *keeps us in all our ways, lest we dash our foot against a stone ;* but, if we at any time meet with a disaster, it should put us upon enquiring whether our way be right in the sight of God or no. The crushing of Balaam's foot, though it was the saving of his life, provoked him so much that he smote his ass the second time, so angry are we apt to be at that which, though a present uneasiness, yet is a real kindness. (3.) Upon the next encounter with the angel, the ass fell down under Balaam, *v.* 26, 27. He ought to have considered that there was certainly something extraordinary in this ; for his ass was not restive, nor did she use to serve him thus : but it is common for those whose hearts are *fully set in them to do evil* to push on violently, and break through all the difficulties which Providence lays in their way to give check to them and to stop them in their career. Balaam the third time smote his ass, though she had now done him the best piece of service that ever she did him, saving him from the sword of the angel, and by her falling down teaching him to do likewise. (4.) When all this would not work upon him, God opened the mouth of the ass, and she spoke to him once and again ; and yet neither did this move him : *The Lord opened the mouth of the ass, v.* 28. This was a great miracle, quite above the power of nature, and wrought by the power of the God of nature, who made man's mouth, and taught him to speak, for otherwise (since we learn to speak purely by imitation, and therefore those that are born deaf are consequently dumb) the first man would never have spoken, nor any of his seed. He that made man speak could, when he pleased, make the ass to *speak with man's voice*, 2 Pet. ii. 16. Here Mr. Ainsworth observes that the devil, when he tempted our first parents to sin, employed a subtle serpent, but that God, when he would convince Balaam, employed a silly ass, a creature dull and sottish to a proverb ; for Satan corrupts men's minds by the *craftiness of those that lie in wait to deceive*, but Christ has *chosen the foolish things of the world to confound the wise.* By a dumb ass God rebukes the madness of the prophet, for he will never want reprovers, but when he pleases can make the stones cry out as witnesses to him, Luke xix. 40 ; Hab. ii. 11. [1.] The ass complained of Balaam's cruelty (*v.* 28) : *What have I done unto thee, that thou hast smitten me ?* Note, The righteous God will not see the meanest and weakest abused ; but either they shall be enabled to speak in their own defence or he will some way or other speak for them. If God would not suffer a beast to be wronged, much less a man, a Christian, a child of his own. We cannot *open the mouth of the dumb*, as God did here, but we may and must *open our mouth for the dumb*, Prov. xxxi. 8 ; Job xxxi. 13. The ass's complaint was just : *What have I done?* Note, When we are prompted to smite any with hand or tongue, we should consider what they have done unto us, and what provocation they have given us. We hear it not, but thus the whole creation groans, being burdened, Rom. viii. 22. It was much that Balaam was not astonished to hear his ass speak, and put to confusion: but some think that it was no new thing to him (being a conjurer) to be thus spoken to by his familiars; others rather think that his brutish head-strong passion so blinded him that he could not observe or consider the strangeness of the thing. Nothing besots men worse than unbridled anger. Balaam in his fury *wished he had a sword to kill his ass with, v.* 29. See his impotency; can he think by his curses to do mischief to Israel that has it not in his power to kill his own ass? This he cannot do, yet he fain would; and what would he get by that, but make himself so much the poorer (as many do), to gratify his passion and revenge? such was the madness of this false prophet. Here bishop Hall observes, It is ill falling into the hands of those whom the brute-creatures find unmerciful; for *a good man regardeth the life of his beast.* [2.] The ass reasoned with him, *v.* 30. God enabled not only a dumb creature to speak, but a dull creature to speak to the purpose. Three things she argues with him from:—*First,* His propriety in her: *Am not I thy ass?* Note, 1. God has given to man a dominion over the creatures: they are *delivered into his hand* to be used, and *put under his feet* to be ruled. 2. Even wicked people have a title to the possessions God gives to them, which they are not to be wronged of. 3. The dominion God has given us over the creatures is a good reason why we should not abuse them. We are their lords, and therefore must not be tyrants. *Secondly,* Her serviceableness to him: *On which thou hast ridden.* Note, It is good for us often to consider how useful the inferior creatures are, and have been, to us, that we may be thankful to God, and tender of them. *Thirdly,* That she was not wont to do so by him, and had never before crushed his foot, nor fallen down under him; he might therefore conclude there was something more than ordinary that made her do so now. Note, 1. The rare occurrence of an offence should moderate our displeasure against an offender. 2. When the creatures depart from their wonted obedience to us, we should enquire the cause within ourselves, and be humbled for our sin.

2. Balaam at length had notice of God's displeasure by the angel, and this did startle him. When God opened his eyes *he saw the angel* (*v.* 31), and then he himself *fell flat upon his face,* in reverence of that glorious messenger, and in fear of the sword he saw in his hand. God has many ways of breaking and bringing down the hard and un-humbled heart. (1.) The angel reproved

him for his outrageousness (*v.* 32, 33): *Wherefore hast thou smitten thy ass?* Whether we consider it or no, it is certain that God will call us to account for the abuses done to his creatures. Nay, he shows him how much more reason he had to smite upon his breast, and to condemn himself, than to fly out thus against his ass (*" Thy way is perverse before me,* and then how canst thou expect to prosper?"), and how much wiser his ass was than himself, and how much beholden he was to her that she turned aside; it was for his safety, and not for her own, for had she gone on he had been slain, and she had been saved alive. Note, When our eyes are opened we shall see what danger we are in in a sinful way, and how much it was for our advantage to be crossed in it, and what fools we were to quarrel with our crosses which helped to save our lives. (2.) Balaam then seemed to relent (*v.* 34): "*I have sinned,* sinned in undertaking this journey, sinned in pushing on so violently;" but he excused it with this, that he saw not the angel; yet, now that he did see him, he was willing to go back again. That which was displeasing to God was not so much his going as his going with a malicious design against Israel, and a secret hope that notwithstanding the proviso with which his permission was clogged he might prevail to curse them, and so gratify Balak, and get preferment under him. It does not appear that he was sensible of this wickedness of his heart, or willing to own it, but, when he finds he cannot go forward, he will be content (since there is no remedy) to go back. Here is no sign that his heart is turned, but, if his hands are tied, he cannot help it. Thus many leave their sins only because their sins have left them. There seems to be a reformation of the life, but what will this avail if there be no renovation of the heart? (3.) The angel however continued his permission: "*Go with the men, v.* 35. Go, if thou hast a mind to be made a fool of, and to be shamed before Balak, and all the princes of Moab. *Go, only the word that I shall speak unto thee, that thou shalt speak,* whether thou wilt or no," for this seems not to be a precept, but a prediction of the event, that he should not only not be able to curse Israel, but should be forced to bless them, which would be more for the glory of God and his own confusion than if he had turned back. Thus God gave him fair warning, but he would not take it; he *went with the princes of Balak.* For the iniquity of Balaam's covetousness God was wroth, and smote him, but he *went on frowardly,* Isa. lvii. 17.

36 And when Balak heard that Balaam was come, he went out to meet him unto a city of Moab, which *is* in the border of Arnon, which *is* in the utmost coast. 37 And Balak said unto Balaam, Did I not earnestly

send unto thee to call thee? wherefore camest thou not unto me? am I
not able indeed to promote thee to
honour? 38 And Balaam said unto
Balak, Lo, I am come unto thee:
have I now any power at all to say
any thing? the word that God putteth
in my mouth, that shall I speak. 39
And Balaam went with Balak, and
they came unto Kirjath-huzoth. 40
And Balak offered oxen and sheep,
and sent to Balaam, and to the princes
that *were* with him. 41 And it came to
pass on the morrow, that Balak took
Balaam, and brought him up into the
high places of Baal, that thence he
might see the utmost *part* of the people.

We have here the meeting between Balak
and Balaam, confederate enemies to God's
Israel; but here they seem to differ in their
expectations of the success. 1. Balak speaks
of it with confidence, not doubting but to
gain his point now that Balaam had come.
In expectation of this, he went out to meet
him, even to the utmost border of his country
(v. 36), partly to gratify his own impatient
desire to see one he had such great expectations from, and partly to do honour to Balaam, and so to engage him with his utmost
power to serve him. See what respect heathen
princes paid to those that had but the name
and face of prophets, and pretended to have
any interest in heaven; and how welcome
one was that came with his mouth full of
curses. What a shame is it then that the
ambassadors of Christ are so little respected
by most, so much despised by some, and that
those are so coldly entertained who bring
tidings of peace and a blessing! Balak has
now nothing to complain of but that Balaam
did not come sooner, v. 37. And he thinks
that he should have considered the importunity Balak had used, *Did I not earnestly
send to thee?* (and the importunity of people
inferior to kings has prevailed with many
against their inclinations), and that he should
also have considered Balak's intentions concerning him: *Am not I able to promote thee
to honour?* Balak, as king, was in his own
kingdom the fountain of honour, and Balaam
should have his choice of all the preferments
that were in his gift; he therefore thinks
himself affronted by Balaam's delays, which
looked as if he thought the honours he prepared not worthy his acceptance. Note,
Promotion to honour is a very tempting bait
to many people; and it were well if we would
be drawn into the service of God by the honour he sets before us. Why do we delay to
come unto him? Is *not he able to promote
us to honour?* 2. Balaam speaks doubtfully
of the issue, and bids Balak not depend too
much upon him (v. 38): "Have I now any
676

power at all to say any thing? I have come,
but what the nearer am I? Gladly would I
curse Israel; but I must not, I cannot, God
will not suffer me." He seems to speak with
vexation at the hook in his nose and the
bridle in his jaws, such as Sennacherib was
tied up with, Isa. xxxvii. 29. 3. They address themselves with all speed to the business. Balaam is nobly entertained over night,
a sacrifice of thanksgiving is offered to the
gods of Moab, for the safe arrival of this
welcome guest, and he is treated with a feast
upon the sacrifice, v. 40. And the next
morning, that no time might be lost, Balak
takes Balaam in his chariot to the high places
of his kingdom, not only because their holiness (such as it was), he thought, might give
some advantage to his divinations, but their
height might give him a convenient prospect
of the camp of Israel, which was to be the
butt or mark at which he must shoot his envenomed arrows. And now Balaam is really
as solicitous to please Balak as ever he had
pretended to be to please God. See what
need we have to pray every day, *Our Father
in heaven, lead us not into temptation.*

CHAP. XXIII.

In this chapter we have Balak and Balaam busy at work to do
Israel a mischief, and, for aught that appears, neither Moses nor
the elders of Israel know any thing of the matter, nor are in a
capacity to break the snare; but God, who keeps Israel, and
neither slumbers nor sleeps, baffles the attempt, without any
intercession or contrivance of theirs. Here is, I. The first
attempt to curse Israel. 1. The preparation made for it by
sacrifice, ver. 1—3. 2. The contrary instruction God gave
Balaam, ver. 4, 5. 3. The blessing Balaam was compelled to
pronounce upon Israel, instead of a curse, ver. 7—10. 4. The
great disappointment of Balak, ver. 11, 12. II. The second
attempt, in the same manner made, and in the same manner
frustrated, ver. 13—26. III. Preparations made for a third
attempt (ver. 27—30), the issue of which we have in the next
chapter.

AND Balaam said unto Balak,
Build me here seven altars, and
prepare me here seven oxen and seven
rams. 2 And Balak did as Balaam
had spoken; and Balak and Balaam
offered on *every* altar a bullock and a
ram. 3 And Balaam said unto Balak,
Stand by thy burnt offering, and I
will go: peradventure the LORD will
come to meet me: and whatsoever he
showeth me I will tell thee. And he
went to a high place. 4 And God
met Balaam: and he said unto him,
I have prepared seven altars, and I
have offered upon *every* altar a bullock and a ram. 5 And the LORD
put a word in Balaam's mouth, and
said, Return unto Balak, and thus
thou shalt speak. 6 And he returned
unto him, and, lo, he stood by his
burnt sacrifice, he, and all the princes
of Moab. 7 And he took up his parable and said, Balak the king of Moab
hath brought me from Aram, out of

the mountains of the east, *saying,* Come, curse me Jacob, and come, defy Israel. 8 How shall I curse, whom God hath not cursed? or how shall I defy, *whom* the Lord hath not defied? 9 For from the top of the rocks I see him, and from the hills I behold him: lo, the people shall dwell alone, and shall not be reckoned among the nations. 10 Who can count the dust of Jacob, and the number of the fourth *part* of Israel? Let me die the death of the righteous, and let my last end be like his! 11 And Balak said unto Balaam, What hast thou done unto me? I took thee to curse mine enemies, and, behold, thou hast blessed *them* altogether. 12 And he answered and said, Must I not take heed to speak that which the Lord hath put in my mouth?

Here is, I. Great preparation made for the cursing of Israel. That which was aimed at was to engage the God of Israel to forsake them, and either to be on Moab's side or to stand neuter. O the sottishness of superstition, to imagine that God will be at men's beck! Balaam and Balak think to bribe him with altars and sacrifices, offered without any warrant or institution of his: as if he would *eat the flesh of bulls or drink the blood of goats.* Ridiculous nonsense, to think that these would please God, and gain his favour, when there could be in them no exercise either of faith or obedience! Yet, it should seem, they offered these sacrifices to the God of heaven, the supreme *Numen—Divinity,* and not to any of their local deities. But the multiplying of altars was an instance of their degeneracy from the religion of their ancestors, and their apostasy to idolatry; for those that multiplied altars multiplied gods. *Ephraim made many altars to sin,* Hos. viii. 11. *Thus they liked not to retain God in their knowledge, but became vain in their imaginations;* and yet presumptuously expected hereby to gain God over to them from Israel, who had his sanctuary among them, and his anointed altar. Observe here, 1. How very imperious Balaam was, proud to have the command of a king and to give law to princes. Such is the spirit of that wicked one who exalts himself above all that is called God, or that is worshipped. With what authority does Balaam give orders! *Build me here* (in the place I have pitched upon) *seven altars,* of stone or turf. Thus he covers his malice against Israel with a show of devotion, but his sacrifice was an abomination, being brought with such a *wicked mind,* Prov. xxi. 27. That which he aimed at was not to honour God with the sacrifices of righteousness, but to

enrich himself with the wages of unrighteousness. 2. How very obsequious Balak was. The altars were presently built, and the sacrifices prepared, the best of the sort, *seven bullocks and seven rams.* Balak makes no objection to the charge, nor does he snuff at it, or think it either a weariness or a disparagement to *stand by his burnt-offering* as Balaam ordered him.

II. The turning of the curse into a blessing, by the overruling power of God, in love to Israel, which is the account Moses gives of it, Deut. xxiii. 5.

1. God puts the blessing into the mouth of Balaam. While the sacrifices were burning, Balaam retired; he *went solitary,* into some dark grove on the top of the high place, *v.* 3, *marg.* Thus much he knew, that solitude gives a good opportunity for communion with God; those that would meet with him must retire from the world, and the business and conversation of it, and love to be private, reckoning themselves never less alone than when alone, because the Father is with them. Enter therefore into thy closet, and shut the door, and be assured that God will meet thee if thou *seek him in the due order.* But Balaam retired with a peradventure only, having some thoughts that God might meet him; but being conscious to himself of guilt, and knowing that God had lately met him in anger, he had reason to speak doubtfully: *Peradventure the Lord will come to meet me,* v. 3. *But let not such a man think that he shall receive any* favour from God. Nay, it should seem, though he pretended to go and meet with God, he really designed to use enchantments; see *ch.* xxiv. 1. But, whatever he intended, God designed to serve his own glory by him, and therefore *met Balaam, v.* 4. *What communion has light with darkness?* No friendly communion, we may be sure. Balaam's way was still perverse, and God was still an adversary to him; but, Balak having chosen him for his oracle, God would constrain him to utter such a confession, to the honour of God and Israel, as should render those for ever inexcusable who should appear in arms against them. When Balaam was aware that God met him, probably by an angel, he boasted of his performances: *I have prepared seven altars, and offered upon every altar a bullock and a ram.* How had he done it? It cost him nothing; it was done at Balak's expense; yet, (1.) He boasts of it, as if he had done some mighty thing. The acts of devotion which are done in hypocrisy are commonly reflected upon with pride and vain glory. Thus the Pharisee went up to the temple to boast of his religion, Luke xviii. 11, 12. (2.) He insists upon it as a reason why God should gratify him in his desire to curse Israel, as if now he had made God his debtor, and might draw upon him for what he pleased. He thinks God is so much beholden to him for these sacrifices that the least he can do in recompence for them is to

sacrifice his Israel to the malice of the king of Moab. Note, It is a common cheat that wicked people put upon themselves, to think that by the shows of piety they may prevail with God to countenance them, and connive at them, in their greatest immoralities, especially in persecution, Isa. lxvi. 5. However, though the sacrifice was an abomination, God took the occasion of Balaam's expectation to *put a word into his mouth* (v. 5); *for the answer of the tongue is from the Lord,* and thus he would show how much those are mistaken who say, *With our tongue we will prevail, our lips are our own,* Ps. xii. 4. He that made man's mouth knows how to manage it, and to serve his own purposes by it. This speaks terror to daring sinners, that *set their mouth against the heavens. God can make their own tongues to fall upon them,* Ps. lxiv. 8. And it speaks comfort to God's witnesses, whom at any time he calls out to appear for him; if God put a word into the mouth of Balaam, who would have defied God and Israel, surely he will not be wanting to those who desire to glorify God and edify his people by their testimony, but it *shall be given them in that same hour what they should speak.*

2. Balaam pronounces the blessing in the ears of Balak. He found him *standing by his burnt-sacrifice* (v. 6), closely attending it, and earnestly expecting the success. Those that would have an answer of peace from God must abide by the sacrifice, and *attend on the Lord without distraction, not weary in well doing.* Balaam, having fixed himself in the place appointed for his denouncing curses against Israel, which perhaps he had drawn up in form ready to deliver, takes up his parable, and it proves a blessing, *v.* 7. He pronounces Israel safe and happy, and so blesses them.

(1.) He pronounces them safe, and out of the reach of his envenomed darts. [1.] He owns that the design was to curse them, that Balak sent for him out of his own country, and that he came, with that intent, *v.* 7. The message sent to him was, *Come, curse me Jacob, and come, defy Israel.* Balak intended to make war upon them, and he would have Balaam to bless his arms, and to prophesy and pray for the ruin of Israel. [2.] He owns the design defeated, and his own inability to accomplish it. He could not so much as give them an ill word or an ill wish: *How shall I curse those whom God has not cursed? v.* 8. Not that therefore he would not do it, but therefore he could not do it. This is a fair confession, *First,* Of the weakness and impotency of his own magic skill, for which others valued him so much, and doubtless he valued himself no less. He was the most celebrated man of that profession, and yet owns himself baffled. God had warned the Israelites not to use divination (Lev. xix. 31), and this providence gave them a reason for that law, by showing them the weakness and folly of it. As they had seen the magicians of Egypt befooled, so, here,

678

the great conjurer of the east. See Isa. xlvii. 12—14. *Secondly,* It is a confession of the sovereignty and dominion of the divine power. He owns that he could do no more than God would suffer him to do, for God could overrule all his purposes, and turn his counsels headlong. *Thirdly,* It is a confession of the inviolable security of the people of God. Note, 1. God's Israel are owned and blessed of him. He has not cursed them, for they are delivered from the curse of the law; he has not defied them, nor rejected or abandoned them, though mean and vile. 2. Those that have the good-will of Heaven have the ill-will of hell; the serpent and his seed have an enmity to them. 3. Though the enemies of God's people may prevail far against them, yet they cannot curse them; that is, they cannot do them any real mischief, much less a ruining michief, for they cannot *separate them from the love of God,* Rom. viii. 39.

(2.) He pronounces them happy in three things:—

[1.] Happy in their peculiarity, and distinction from the rest of the nations: *From the top of the rock I see him,* v. 9. And it seems to have been a great surprise to him that whereas, it is probable, they were represented to him as a rude and disorderly rabble, that infested the countries round about in rambling parties, he saw them a regular incorporated camp, in which appeared all the marks of discipline and good order; he saw them a people dwelling alone, and foresaw they would continue so, and their singularity would be their unspeakable honour. Persons of quality we call persons of *distinction ;* this was Israel's praise, though their enemies turned it to their reproach, that they differed from all the neighbouring nations, not only in their religion and sacred rites, but in their diet, and dress, and common usages, as a people called out of the world, and not to be conformed to it. They never lost their reputation till they *mingled among the heathen,* Ps. cvi. 35. Note, It is the duty and honour of those that are dedicated to God to be separated from the world, and not to walk according to the course and custom of it. Those who make conscience of peculiar duties may take the comfort of peculiar privileges, which it is probable Balaam has an eye to here. God's Israel shall not stand upon a level with other nations, but be dignified above them all, as a people near to God, and set apart for him.

[2.] Happy in their numbers, not so few and despicable as they were represented to him, but an innumerable company, which made them both honourable and formidable (v. 10): *Who can count the dust of Jacob?* The number of the people was the thing that Balak was vexed at (ch. xxii. 3): *Moab was afraid of them, because they were many ;* and God does here by Balaam promote that fear and vexation, foretelling their further increase. Balak would have him see *the utmost part of the people* (*ch.* xxii. 41), hoping the more he saw of them the more he would be exasperated against them, and throw about his curses with the more keenness and rage; but it proved quite contrary: instead of being angry at their numbers, he admired them. The better acquainted we are with God's people the better opinion we have of them. He takes notice of the number, *First*, Of the *dust of Jacob*; that is, the people of Jacob, concerning whom it was foretold that they should be as the dust for number, Gen. xxviii. 14. Thus he owns the fulfilling of the promise made to the fathers, and expects that it should be yet further accomplished. Perhaps it was part of David's fault in numbering the people that he offered to count the dust of Jacob, which God had said should be innumerable. *Secondly*, Of the *fourth part of Israel*, alluding to the form of their camp, which was cast into four squadrons, under four standards. Note, God's Israel are a very great body, his spiritual Israel are so, and they will appear to be so when they shall all be gathered together unto him in the great day, Rev. vii. 9.

[3.] Happy in their end: *Let me die the death of the righteous* Israelites, that are in covenant with God, and let my *last end, or future state, be like theirs*, or my recompence, namely, in the other world. Here, *First*, It is taken for granted that death is the end of all men; the righteous themselves must die: and it is good for us to think of this with application, as Balaam himself does here, speaking of his own death. *Secondly*, He goes upon the supposition of the soul's immortality, and a different state on the other side death, to which this is a noble testimony, and an evidence of its being anciently known and believed. For how could the death of the righteous be more desirable than the death of the wicked upon any other account than as it involved happiness in another world, since in the manner and circumstances of dying we see *all things come alike to all?* *Thirdly*, He pronounces the righteous truly blessed, not only while they live, but when they die, which makes their death not only more desirable than the death of others, but even more desirable than life itself; for in that sense his wish may be taken. Not only, "When I do die, let me die the death of the righteous;" but, "I could even now be willing to die, on condition that I might *die the death of the righteous*, and reach my end this moment, provided it might be like his." Very near the place where Balaam now was, on one of the mountains of Moab, not long after this, Moses died, and to that perhaps God, who put this word into his mouth, designed it should have a reference, that by it Moses might be encouraged to go up and die such a death as Balaam himself wished to die. *Fourthly*, He shows his opinion of religion to be better than his resolution; there are many who desire to die the death of the

righteous, but do not endeavour to live the life of the righteous. Gladly would they have their end like theirs, but not their way. They would be saints in heaven, but not saints on earth. This is the *desire of the slothful, which kills him, because his hands refuse to labour*. This of Balaam's is only a wish, not a prayer, and it is a vain wish, being only a wish for the end, without any care for the means. Thus far this blessing goes, even to death, and beyond it, as far as the last end. Now,

III. We are told, 1. How Balak fretted at it, *v.* 11. He pretended to honour the Lord with his sacrifices, and to wait for the answer God would send him; and yet, when it did not prove according to his mind, he forgot God, and flew into a great passion against Balaam, as if it had been purely his doing: "*What hast thou done unto me!* How hast thou disappointed me!" Sometimes God makes the enemies of his church a vexation one to another, while he that sits in heaven laughs at them, and the efforts of their impotent malice. 2. How Balaam was forced to acquiesce in it. He submits because he cannot help it, and yet humours the thing with no small address, as if he had been peculiarly conscientious, answering Balak with the gravity of a prophet: *Must I not take heed to speak that which the Lord has put in my mouth?* *v.* 12. Thus a confession of God's overruling power is extorted from a wicked prophet, to the further confusion of a wicked prince.

13 And Balak said unto him, Come, I pray thee, with me unto another place, from whence thou mayest see them: thou shalt see but the utmost part of them, and shalt not see them all: and curse me them from thence. 14 And he brought him into the field of Zophim, to the top of Pisgah, and built seven altars, and offered a bullock and a ram on *every* altar. 15 And he said unto Balak, Stand here by thy burnt offering, while I meet *the LORD* yonder. 16 And the LORD met Balaam, and put a word in his mouth, and said, Go again unto Balak, and say thus. 17 And when he came to him, behold, he stood by his burnt offering, and the princes of Moab with him. And Balak said unto him, What hath the LORD spoken? 18 And he took up his parable, and said, Rise up, Balak, and hear; hearken unto me, thou son of Zippor: 19 God *is* not a man, that he should lie; neither the son of man, that he should repent: hath he said, and shall he not do *it?* or hath he

spoken, and shall he not make it good? 20 Behold, I have received *commandment* to bless: and he hath blessed; and I cannot reverse it. 21 He hath not beheld iniquity in Jacob, neither hath he seen perverseness in Israel: the LORD his God *is* with him, and the shout of a king *is* among them. 22 God brought them out of Egypt; he hath as it were the strength of a unicorn. 23 Surely *there is* no enchantment against Jacob, neither *is there* any divination against Israel: according to this time it shall be said of Jacob and of Israel, What hath God wrought! 24 Behold, the people shall rise up as a great lion, and lift up himself as a young lion: he shall not lie down until he eat *of* the prey, and drink the blood of the slain. 25 And Balak said unto Balaam, Neither curse them at all, nor bless them at all. 26 But Balaam answered and said unto Balak, Told not I thee, saying, All that the LORD speaketh, that I must do? 27 And Balak said unto Balaam, Come, I pray thee, I will bring thee unto another place; peradventure it will please God that thou mayest curse me them from thence. 28 And Balak brought Balaam unto the top of Peor, that looketh toward Jeshimon. 29 And Balaam said unto Balak, Build me here seven altars, and prepare me here seven bullocks and seven rams. 30 And Balak did as Balaam had said, and offered a bullock and a ram on *every* altar.

Here is, I. Preparation made the second time, as before, for the cursing of Israel. 1. The place is changed, *v.* 13. Balak fancied that Balaam, having so full a prospect of the whole camp of Israel, *from the top of the rocks* (*v.* 9), was either so enamoured with the beauty of it that he would not curse them or so affrighted with the terror of it that he durst not; and therefore he would bring him to another place, from which he might see only some part of them, which would appear more despicable, and that part at least which would lie in view he hoped he might obtain leave to curse, and so by degrees he should get ground against them, intending, no doubt, if he had gained this point, to make his attack on that part of the camp of Israel which Balaam now had in his eye, and into which he was to throw the fireballs of his curses. See how restless and

unwearied the church's enemies are in their malicious attempts to ruin it; they leave no stone unturned, no project untried, to compass it. O that we were as full of contrivance and resolution in prosecuting good designs for the glory of God! 2. The sacrifices are repeated, new altars are built, a bullock and a ram offered on every altar, and Balak attends his sacrifice as closely as ever, *v.* 14, 15. Were we thus earnest to obtain the blessing as Balak was to procure a curse (designedly upon Israel, but really upon himself and his people), we should not grudge the return both of the charge and of the labour of religious exercises. 3. Balaam renews his attendance on God, and God meets him the second time, and puts another word into his mouth, not to reverse the former, but to ratify it, *v.* 16, 17. If God said not to Balaam, *Seek in vain,* much less shall he say so to *any of the seed of Jacob,* who shall surely find him, not only as Balaam, their instructor and oracle, but their bountiful rewarder. When Balaam returned Balak was impatient to know what message he had: " *What hath the Lord spoken?* Are there any better tidings yet, any hopes of speeding?" This should be our enquiry when we come to hear the word of God. See Jer. xxiii. 35.

II. A second conversion of the curse into a blessing by the overruling power of God; and this blessing is both larger and stronger than the former, and quite cuts off all hopes of altering it. Balak having been so forward to ask what the Lord had spoken (*v.* 17), Balaam now addresses himself particularly to him (*v.* 18): *Rise up, Balak, and hear.* It was a message from God that he had to deliver, and it is required of Balak, though a king, that he attend (*hear* and *hearken,* with a close application of mind, let not a word slip), and also that he attend with reverence: *Rise up, and hear.* His successor Eglon, when he was to receive a message from God, *rose out of his seat,* Judg. iii. 20.

1. Two things Balaam in this discourse informs Balak of, sorely to his grief and disappointment :—

(1.) That he had no reason to hope that he should ruin Israel.

[1.] It would be to no purpose to attempt to ruin them, and he would deceive himself if he expected it, for these reasons :—

First, Because God is unchangeable: *God is not a man that he should lie, v.* 19. Men change their minds, and therefore break their words; they lie, because they repent. But God does neither. He never changes his mind, and therefore never recals his promise. Balaam had owned (*v.* 8) that he could not alter God's counsel, and thence he infers here that God himself would not alter it; such is the imperfection of man, and such the perfection of God. It is impossible for God to lie, Heb. vi. 18. And, when in scripture he is said to *repent,* it is not meant of any change of his mind (for *he is in one mind, and who can turn him?*) but only of the change of his way. This is a great truth, that with God there is no *variableness nor shadow of turning.* Now here, 1. He appeals to Balak himself concerning it: "*Hath he said, and shall he not do it?*" Said it in his own purpose, and shall he not perform it in his providence, according to the counsel of his will? Hath he spoken in his word, in his promise, and shall he not make it good? Can we think otherwise of God than that he is unchangeably one with himself and true to his word? All his decrees are unalterable, and all his promises inviolable." 2. He applies this general truth to the case in hand (*v.* 20): *He hath blessed and I cannot reverse it,* that is, "I cannot prevail with him to reverse it." Israel were of old a blessed people, a seed that the Lord had blessed; the blessing of Abraham came upon them; they were born under the blessing of the covenant, and born to the blessing of Canaan, and therefore they could not be cursed, unless you could suppose that the God of eternal truth should break his word, and become false to himself and his people.

Secondly, Because Israel are at present unblamable: *He has not beheld iniquity in Jacob, v.* 21. Not but that there was iniquity in Jacob, and God saw it; but, 1. There was not such a degree of iniquity as might provoke God to abandon them and give them up to ruin. As bad as they were, they were not so bad as this. 2. There was no idolatry among them, which is in a particular manner called iniquity and perverseness; we have found nothing of that kind in Israel since the golden calf, and therefore, though they were in other instances very provoking, yet God would not cast them off. Balaam knew that nothing would separate between them and God but sin. While God saw no reigning sin among them, he would send no destroying curse among them; and therefore, as long as they kept in with God, he despaired of ever doing them any mischief. Note, While we keep from sin we keep from harm. Some give another sense of those words; they read it thus: *He has not beheld wrong offered to Jacob, nor will he see any grievance done to Israel,* that is, "He has not nor will he permit it, or allow it; he will not see Israel injured, but he will right them, and avenge their quarrel." Note, God will not bear to see any injury done to his church and people; for what is done against them he takes as done against himself, and will reckon for it accordingly.

Thirdly, Because the power of both was irresistible. He shows Balak that there was no contending with them, it was to no purpose to attempt it; for, 1. They had the presence of God with them: "*The Lord his God is with him,* in a particular manner, and not provoked to withdraw from him." 2. They had the joy of that presence, and were always made to triumph in it: *The shout* or alarm *of a king is among them.* They shout against their enemies, as sure of victory and success,

glorying continually in God as their King and conqueror for them. 3. They had had the experience of the benefit of God's presence with them, and his power engaged for them; for God *brought them out of Egypt, v.* 22. The power which had done that could never be restrained, never resisted; and, having begun so gloriously, he would no doubt finish gloriously. 4. While they had God's presence with them they had the strength of a unicorn, able to make head against all that opposed them. See *ch.* xxiv. 8. Such is the strength which the God of Israel gives unto his people.

[2.] From all this he infers that it was to no purpose for him to think of doing them a mischief by all the arts he could use, *v.* 23. *First,* He owns himself baffled. Surely there is no enchantment against Jacob so as to prevail. The curses of hell can never take place against the blessings of heaven. Not but that attempts of this kind would be made, but they would certainly be fruitless and ineffectual. Some observe that *Jacob* denotes the church low and afflicted, *Israel* denotes it prosperous and advanced; but be the church high or low, be her friends few or many, let second causes smile or frown, it comes all to one: no weapon formed against it shall prosper. Note, God easily can, and certainly will, baffle and disappoint all the devices and designs of the powers of darkness against his church, so that they shall not prevail to destroy it. *Secondly,* He foresees that this would be remembered in time to come. *According to this time,* that is, with reference to this we are now about, it shall be said concerning Jacob and Israel, and said by them, *What hath God wrought!* What great things hath God done for his people! It shall be said with wonder, joy, and thankfulness, and a challenge to the neighbouring nations to produce any similar instances of the care of their gods for them. Note, The defeating of the designs of the church's enemies ought to be had in everlasting remembrance to the glory of God. *There is none like unto the God of Jeshurun.* What Balaam says here concerning the pre-eminence of the God of Israel above all the gods of the Gentiles perhaps Moses refers to when he says (Deut. xxxii. 31), *Their rock is not as our rock, even our enemies themselves being judges,* Balaam particularly. Balak therefore has no hopes of ruining Israel. But,

(2.) Balaam shows him that he had more reason to fear being ruined by them, for they were likely to make bloody work among his neighbours; and, if he and his country escaped, it was not because he was too great for them to meddle with, but because he fell not within their commission, *v.* 24. Behold, and tremble; the people that now have lain for some time closely encamped do but repose themselves for a while like a lion couchant, but shortly they *shall rise up as a great lion,* a lion rampant, that *shall not lie down till he eat of the prey, and drink the blood of the slain.* This seems to point at the victories he foresaw they would obtain over the Canaanites, that they would never lay down their arms till they had made a complete conquest of the land they had now in view; and, when his neighbour's house was on fire, he had reason to think his own in danger.

2. Now what was the issue of this disappointment?

(1.) Balak and Balaam were both of them sick of the cause. [1.] Balak is now willing to have his conjurer silenced. Since he cannot say what he would have him, he wishes him to say nothing: "*Neither curse them at all nor bless them at all, v. 25.* If thou canst not curse them, I beseech thee not to bless them. If thou canst not assist and encourage my forces, yet do not oppose and dispirit them." Note, God can make those that depart from him weary of the *multitude of their counsels,* Isa. xlvii. 13; lvii. 10. [2.] Balaam is still willing to own himself overruled, and appeals to what he had said in the beginning of this enterprise (*ch.* xxii. 38): *All that the Lord speaketh, that I must do, v. 26.* This shows, *First,* In general, that the way of man is not in himself; there are many devices in man's heart, but God's counsels shall stand. *Secondly,* In particular, that, as no weapon formed against the church shall prosper, so every tongue that rises against her in judgment God will control and condemn, Isa. liv. 17.

(2.) Yet they resolve to make another attempt. They think it scorn to be baffled, and therefore pursue the design, though it be only to their further confusion. And now the third time, [1.] They change the place. Balak is at last convinced that it is not Balaam's fault, on whom, before, he had laid the blame, but that really he was under a divine check, and therefore now he hopes to bring him to a place whence God might at least permit him to curse them, *v. 27.* Probably he and Balaam were the more encouraged thus to repeat their attempt because God had the second time allowed Balaam to go, though he had forbidden him the first time. Since by repeated trials they had carried that point, they hope in like manner to carry this. Thus because sinners are borne with, and sentence against their evil works is not executed speedily, their hearts are the more fully set in them to do evil. The place to which Balak now took Balaam was the top of Peor, the most eminent high place in all his country, where, it is probable, Baal was worshipped, and it was thence called *Baal-peor.* He chose this place with a hope, either, *First,* That it being the residence (as he fancied) of Baal, the god of Moab, Jehovah the God of Israel would not, or could not, come hither to hinder the operation; or, *Secondly,* That, it being a place acceptable to his god, it would be so to the Lord, and there he would be brought into a good humour. Such idle conceits have foolish men of God, and so vain are their imaginations concerning him. Thus the Syrians

682

fancied the Lord to be God of the hills, but not of the valleys (1 Kings xx. 28), as if he were more powerful in one place than he is in every place. [2.] They repeat their sacrifice, seven bullocks and seven rams, upon seven altars, *v.* 29, 30. Thus do they persevere in their expensive oblations, though they had no promise on which to build their hopes of speeding. Let not us therefore, who have a promise that the vision at the end shall speak and not lie, be discouraged by delays, but continue instant in prayer, and not faint, Luke xviii. 1.

CHAP. XXIV.

This chapter continues and concludes the history of the defeat of the counsels of Balak and Balaam against Israel, not by might, nor by power, but by the Spirit of the Lord of hosts; and as great an instance it is of God's power over the children of men, and his favour towards his own children, as any of the victories recorded in the book of the wars of the Lord. What preparation was made the third time for the cursing of Israel we read of in the close of the foregoing chapter. In this chapter we are told, I. What the blessing was into which that intended curse was turned, ver. 1—9. II. How Balak dismissed Balaam from his service thereupon, ver. 10—13. III. The predictions Balaam left behind him concerning Israel, and some of the neighbouring nations, ver. 14, &c.

AND when Balaam saw that it pleased the LORD to bless Israel, he went not, as at other times, to seek for enchantments, but he set his face toward the wilderness. 2 And Balaam lifted up his eyes, and he saw Israel abiding *in his tents* according to their tribes; and the spirit of God came upon him. 3 And he took up his parable, and said, Balaam the son of Beor hath said, and the man whose eyes are open hath said: 4 He hath said, which heard the words of God, which saw the vision of the Almighty, falling *into a trance,* but having his eyes open: 5 How goodly are thy tents, O Jacob, *and* thy tabernacles, O Israel! 6 As the valleys are they spread forth, as gardens by the river's side, as the trees of lign aloes which the LORD hath planted, *and* as cedar trees beside the waters. 7 He shall pour the water out of his buckets, and his seed *shall be* in many waters, and his king shall be higher than Agag, and his kingdom shall be exalted. 8 God brought him forth out of Egypt; he hath as it were the strength of a unicorn: he shall eat up the nations his enemies, and shall break their bones, and pierce *them* through with his arrows. 9 He couched, he lay down as a lion, and as a great lion: who shall stir him up? Blessed *is* he that blesseth thee, and cursed *is* he that curseth thee.

The blessing itself which Balaam here pronounces upon Israel is much the same with the two we had in the foregoing chapter; but the introduction to it is different.

I. The method of proceeding here varies much in several instances. 1. Balaam laid aside the enchantments which he had hitherto depended on, used no spells, or charms, or magic arts, finding they did him no service; it was to no purpose to deal with the devil for a curse, when it was plain that God was determined immovably to bless, *v.* 1. Sooner or later God will convince men of their folly in seeking after lying vanities, which cannot profit. To what purpose should he seek for enchantment? He knew that God was out of the reach of them. 2. He did not now retire into a solitary place as before, but set his face directly towards the wilderness where Israel lay encamped; and, since there is no remedy, but they must be blessed, he will design nothing else, but will submit by compulsion. 3. Now *the Spirit of God came upon him*, that is, the Spirit of prophecy, as upon Saul to prevent him from taking David, 1 Sam. xix. 23. He spoke not his own sense, but the language of the Spirit that came upon him. 4. He used a different preface now from what he had used before (*v.* 3, 4), much like that of David (2 Sam. xxiii. 1—3), yet savouring very much (as some think) of pride and vain-glory, taking all the praise of this prophecy to himself, and magnifying himself as one of the cabinet-council of heaven. Two things he boasts of:—(1.) The favour God did him in making known himself to him. He *heard the words of God, and saw the vision of the Almighty.* God himself had met him and spoken to him (*ch.* xxiii. 16), and with this he was greatly puffed up. Paul speaks with humility of his visions and revelations (2 Cor. xii. 1), but Balaam speaks of his with pride. (2.) His own power to receive and bear those revelations. He fell into a trance indeed, as other prophets did, but he had his eyes open. This he mentions twice; but the words in the original are not the same. The *man whose eyes were shut*, some think it may be read so (*v.* 3), but now *having his eyes open*, *v.* 4. When he attempted to curse Israel, he owns, he was in a mistake, but now he began to see his error, and yet still he remained blinded by covetousness and ambition, those foolish and hurtful lusts. Note, [1.] Those that oppose God and his people will sooner or later be made to see themselves wretchedly deceived. [2.] Many have their eyes open that have not their hearts open, are enlightened, but not sanctified; and that knowledge which puffs men up with pride will but serve to light them to hell, whither many go with their eyes open.

II. Yet the blessing is for substance the same with those before. Several things he admires in Israel:—

1. Their beauty (*v.* 5): *How goodly are thy tents, O Jacob!* Though they dwelt not in stately palaces, but in coarse and homely tents, and these, no doubt, sadly weather-beaten, yet Balaam sees a beauty in those tents, because of their admirable order, according to their tribes, *v.* 2. Nothing recommends religion more to the good opinion of those that look upon it at a distance than the unity and harmony of its professors, Ps. cxxxiii. 1. The amiableness of this people, and the great reputation they should gain among their neighbours, are compared (*v.* 6) to the beauty and sweetness of fruitful valleys and fine gardens, flourishing trees and fragrant spices. Note, Those whose eyes are open see the saints on the earth to be excellent ones, and their delight is accordingly in them. *The righteous*, doubtless, *is more excellent than his neighbour.* They are *trees which the Lord has planted;* that is their excellency. The branches of righteousness are the planting of the Lord. See Hos. xiv. 5—7.

2. Their fruitfulness and increase. This may be intended by those similitudes (*v.* 6) of the valleys, gardens, and trees, as well as by those expressions (*v.* 7), *He shall pour the water out of his buckets;* that is, God shall water them with his blessing like rain from heaven, and then his *seed shall be in many waters.* Compare Hos. ii. 23, *I will sow her unto me in the earth.* And waters are in scripture put for *peoples, and multitudes, and nations.* This has been fulfilled in the wonderful increase of that nation and their vast multitude even in their dispersion.

3. Their honour and advancement. As the multitude of the people is the honour of the prince, so the magnificence of the prince is the honour of the people; Balaam therefore foretels that their *king shall be higher than Agag.* Agag, it is probable, was the most potent monarch in those parts; Balaam knew of none more considerable than he was; he rose above the rest of his neighbours. But Balaam foretels that Israel's chief commander, who, after Moses, was Joshua, should be more great and honourable than ever Agag was, and make a far better figure in history. Saul, their first king, triumphed over Agag, though, it is said, *he came delicately.*

4. Their power and victory, *v.* 8. (1.) He looks back upon what they had done, or rather what had been done for them: *God brought them forth out of Egypt;* this he had spoken of before, *ch.* xxiii. 22. The wonders that attended their deliverance out of Egypt contributed more to their honour, and the terror of their adversaries, than any thing else, Josh. ii. 10. He that brought them out of Egypt will not fail to bring them into Canaan, for, *as for God, his work is perfect.* (2.) He looks down upon their present strength. Israel hath, as it were, *the strength of a unicorn,* of which creature it is said (Job xxxix. 9, 10), *Will he be willing to serve thee, or abide by thy crib? Canst thou bind him with his band in the furrow?* "No, Israel is too powerful to be

checked or held in by my curses or thy armies." (3.) He looks forward to their future conquests: *He shall eat up the nations his enemies;* that is, "He shall not only destroy and devour them as easily and irresistibly as a lion does his prey, but he shall himself be strengthened, and fattened, and enriched, by their spoils."

5. Their courage and security: *He lay down as a lion, as a great lion, v.* 9. Now he does so in the plains of Moab, and asks no leave of the king of Moab, nor is he in fear of him; shortly will he do so in Canaan. When he has torn his prey, he will take his repose, *quiet from the fear of evil,* and bid defiance to all his neighbours; for who shall stir up a sleeping lion? It is observed of lions (as the learned bishop Patrick takes notice here) that they do not retire into places of shelter to sleep, but lie down any where, knowing that none dares meddle with them: thus secure were Israel in Canaan, chiefly in the days of David and Solomon; and thus is *the righteous bold as a lion* (Prov. xxviii. 1), not to assault others, but to repose themselves, because *God maketh them to dwell in safety,* Ps. iv. 8.

6. Their interest, and influence upon their neighbours. Their friends, and those in alliance with them, were happy: *Blessed is he that blesseth thee;* those that do them any kindness will certainly fare the better for it. But their enemies, and those in arms against them, were certainly miserable: *Cursed is he that curseth thee;* those that do them any injury do it at their peril; for God takes what is done to them, whether good or evil, as done to himself. Thus he confirms the blessing of Abraham (Gen. xii. 3), and speaks as if *therefore* he did at this time bless Israel, and not curse them, because he desired to share in the blessing of Israel's friends and dreaded the curse on Israel's enemies.

10 And Balak's anger was kindled against Balaam, and he smote his hands together: and Balak said unto Balaam, I called thee to curse mine enemies, and, behold, thou hast altogether blessed *them* these three times. 11 Therefore now flee thou to thy place: I thought to promote thee unto great honour; but, lo, the Lord hath kept thee back from honour. 12 And Balaam said unto Balak, Spake I not also to thy messengers which thou sentest unto me, saying, 13 If Balak would give me his house full of silver and gold, I cannot go beyond the commandment of the Lord, to do *either* good or bad of mine own mind; *but* what the Lord saith, that will I speak? 14 And now, behold, I go unto my people: come *therefore and*

I will advertise thee what this people shall do to thy people in the latter days.

We have here the conclusion of this vain attempt to curse Israel, and the total abandonment of it. 1. Balak made the worst of it. He broke out into a rage against Balaam (*v.* 10), expressed both in words and gesture the highest degree of vexation at the disappointment; he smote his hands together, for indignation, to see all his measures thus broken, and his project baffled. He charged Balaam with putting upon him the basest affront and cheat imaginable: " *I called thee to curse my enemies,* and thou hast shown thyself in league with them, and in their interests, for thou hast *blessed them these three times,* though, by appointing the altars to be built and sacrifices to be offered, thou madest me believe thou wouldest certainly curse them." Hereupon he forbade him his presence, expelled him his country, upbraided him with the preferments he had designed to bestow upon him, but now would not (*v.* 11): " *The Lord hath kept thee back from honour.* See what thou gettest by pleasing the Lord, instead of pleasing me; thou hast hindered thy preferment by it." Thus those who are any way losers by their duty are commonly upbraided with it, as fools, for preferring it before their interest in the world. Whereas, if Balaam had been voluntary and sincere in his adherence to the word of the Lord, though he lost the honour Balak designed him by it, God would have made that loss up to him abundantly to his advantage. 2. Balaam made the best of it. (1.) He endeavours to excuse the disappointment. And a very good excuse he has for it, that God restrained him from saying what he would have said, and constrained him to say what he would not; and that this was what Balak ought not to be displeased at, not only because he could not help it, but because he had told Balak before what he must depend upon, *v.* 12, 13. Balak could not say that he had cheated him, since he had given him fair notice of the check he found himself under. (2.) He endeavours to atone for it, *v.* 14. Though he cannot do what Balak would have him do, yet, [1.] He will gratify his curiosity with some predictions concerning the nations about him. It is natural to us to be pleased with prophecy, and with this he hopes to pacify the angry prince. [2.] He will satisfy him with an assurance that, whatever this formidable people should do to his people, it should not be till the latter days; so that he, for his part, needed not to fear any mischief or molestation from them; the *vision was for a great while to come,* but in his days there should be peace. [3.] He will put him into a method of doing Israel a mischief without the ceremonies of enchantment and execration. This seems to be implied in that word: *I will advertise thee;* for it properly signifies, *I will counsel thee.* What the counsel was is not set down here, because it was given privately, but we are told afterwards what it was, *ch.* xxxi. 16. He counselled him to entice the Israelites to idolatry, Rev. ii. 14. Since he could not have leave from God to curse them, he puts him in a way of getting help from the devil to tempt them. *Flectere si nequeo superos, Acheronta movebo—If I cannot move heaven, I will solicit hell.*

15 And he took up his parable, and said, Balaam the son of Beor hath said, and the man whose eyes are open hath said: 16 He hath said, which heard the words of God, and knew the knowledge of the most High, *which* saw the vision of the Almighty, falling *into a trance,* but having his eyes open: 17 I shall see him, but not now: I shall behold him, but not nigh: there shall come a Star out of Jacob, and a Sceptre shall rise out of Israel, and shall smite the corners of Moab, and destroy all the children of Sheth. 18 And Edom shall be a possession, Seir also shall be a possession for his enemies; and Israel shall do valiantly. 19 Out of Jacob shall come he that shall have dominion, and shall destroy him that remaineth of the city. 20 And when he looked on Amalek, he took up his parable, and said, Amalek *was* the first of the nations; but his latter end *shall be* that he perish for ever. 21 And he looked on the Kenites, and took up his parable, and said, Strong is thy dwellingplace, and thou puttest thy nest in a rock. 22 Nevertheless the Kenite shall be wasted, until Asshur shall carry thee away captive. 23 And he took up his parable, and said, Alas, who shall live when God doeth this! 24 And ships *shall come* from the coast of Chittim, and shall afflict Asshur, and shall afflict Eber, and he also shall perish for ever. 25 And Balaam rose up, and went and returned to his place: and Balak also went his way.

The office of prophets was both to bless and to prophesy in the name of the Lord. Balaam, as a prophet, per force had blessed Israel; here he foretels future events.

I. His preface is much the same as that, *v.* 3, 4. He personates a true prophet admirably well, God permitting and directing him to do so, because, whatever he was, the prophecy itself was a true prophecy. He

boasts, 1. That his *eyes are open* (*v.* 15), for prophets were *in old time called seers* (1 Sam. ix. 9), because they must speak what they had seen, and therefore, before they opened their lips, it was necessary that they should have their eyes open. 2. That he has *heard the words of God,* which many do that do not heed them, nor hear God in them. 3. That he *knew the knowledge of the Most High;* this is added here. A man may be full of the knowledge of God and yet utterly destitute of the grace of God, may receive the truth in the light of it and yet be a stranger to the love of it. 4. That *he saw the vision of the Almighty,* but not so as to be *changed into the same image.* He calls God the *Most High,* and the *Almighty;* no man could speak more honourably of him, nor seem to put a greater value upon his acquaintance with him, and yet he had no true fear of him, love to him, or faith in him, so far may a man go towards heaven, and yet come short.

II. Here is his prophecy concerning him that should be the crown and glory of his people Israel, who is, 1. David in the type, who *not now,* not quickly, but in process of time, should *smite the corners of Moab* (*v.* 17), and take possession of Mount Seir, and under whom the forces of Israel should *do valiantly,* v. 18. This was fulfilled when David smote Moab, and *measured them with a line,* so that *the Moabites became David's servants,* 2 Sam. viii. 2. And at the same time the Edomites likewise were brought into obedience to Israel, *v.* 14. But, 2. Our Lord Jesus, the promised Messiah, is chiefly pointed at in the antitype, and of him it is an illustrious prophecy; it was the will of God that notice should thus be given of his coming, a great while before, not only to the people of the Jews, but to other nations, because his gospel and kingdom were to extend themselves so far beyond the borders of the land of Israel. It is here foretold, (1.) That his coming should not be yet of a great while: "*I shall see him, but not now;* I do see him in vision, but at a very great distance, through the interposing space of 1500 years at least. Or understand it thus:—Balaam, a wicked man, shall see Christ, but shall not see him nigh, nor see him as Job, who saw him *as his Redeemer,* and saw him for himself, Job xix. 25, 27. When he comes in the clouds *every eye shall see him,* but many will see him (as the rich man in hell saw Abraham) *afar off.* (2.) That he shall come out of Jacob, and Israel, as a star and a sceptre, the former denoting his glory and lustre, as the *bright and morning star,* the latter his power and authority; it is *he that shall have dominion.* Perhaps this prophecy of Balaam (one of the children of the east) concerning a star that should arise out of Jacob, as the indication of a sceptre arising in Israel, being preserved by a tradition of that country, gave occasion to the

685

wise men, who were of the east too, upon the sight of an unusual star over the land of Judea, to enquire for him that was *born king of the Jews*, Matt. ii. 2. (3.) That his kingdom shall be universal, and victorious over all opposition, which was typified by David's victories over Moab and Edom. But the Messiah shall destroy, or, as some read it, *shall rule over, all the children of Seth* (*v.* 17), that is, all the children of men, who descend from Seth, the son of Adam, the descendants of the rest of Adam's sons being cut off by the deluge. Christ shall be king, not only of Jacob and Israel, but of all the world; so that all the children of Seth shall be either governed by his golden sceptre or dashed in pieces by his iron rod. He shall set up a universal rule, authority, and power, of his own, and shall put down all opposing rule, 1 Cor. xv. 24. He shall *unwall all the children of Seth;* so some read it. He shall take down all their defences and carnal confidences, so that they shall either admit his government or lie open to his judgments. (4.) That his Israel shall do valiantly; the subjects of Christ, animated by his might, shall maintain a spiritual war with the powers of darkness, and be more than conquerors. *The people that do know their God shall be strong, and do exploits,* Dan. xi. 32.

III. Here is his prophecy concerning the Amalekites and Kenites, part of whose country, it is probable, he had now in view. 1. The Amalekites were now the *chief of the nations* (*v.* 20), therefore Agag was spoken of (*v.* 7) as an eminent prince, and they were the first that engaged Israel when they came out of Egypt; but the time will come when that nation, as great as it looks now, will be totally ruined and rooted out: *His latter end shall be that he perish for ever.* Here Balaam confirms that doom of Amalek which Moses had read (Exod. xvii. 14, 16), where God had sworn that he would have *perpetual war with Amalek.* Note, Those whom God is at war with will certainly perish for ever; for when God judges he will overcome. 2. The Kenites were now the securest of the nations; their situation was such as that nature was their engineer, and had strongly fortified them: "*Thou puttest thy nest* (like the eagle) *in a rock, v.* 21. Thou thinkest thyself safe, and yet the *Kenites shall be wasted* (*v.* 22) and gradually brought to decay, till they be carried away captive by the Assyrians," which was done at the captivity of the ten tribes. Note, Bodies politic, like natural bodies, though of the strongest constitutions, will gradually decay, and come to ruin at last; even a nest in a rock will be no perpetual security.

IV. Here is a prophecy that looks as far forward as the Greeks and Romans, for theirs is supposed to be meant by the *coast of Chittim, v.* 24.

1. The introduction to this parable; this article of his prophecy is very observable

(*v.* 23): *Alas! who shall live when God doeth this?* Here he acknowledges all the revolutions of states and kingdoms to be the Lord's doing: *God doeth this;* whoever are the instruments, he is the supreme director. But he speaks mournfully concerning them, and has a very melancholy prospect of these events: *Who shall live?* Either, (1.) These events are so distant, and so far off to come, that it is hard to say *who shall live till they come;* but, whoever shall live to see them, there will be amazing turns. Or, (2.) They will be so dismal, and make such desolations, that scarcely any will escape or be left alive; who shall live when death rides in triumph? Rev. vi. 8. Those that live then will be as brands plucked out of the fire, and will have their lives given them as a prey. God fit us for the worst of times!

2. The prophecy itself is observable. Both Greece and Italy lie much upon the sea, and therefore their armies were sent forth mostly in ships. Now he seems here to foretel, (1.) That the forces of the Grecians should humble and bring down the Assyrians, who were united with the Persians, which was fulfilled when the eastern country was overcome, or overrun rather, by Alexander. (2.) That theirs and the Roman forces should afflict the Hebrews, or Jews, who were called *the children of Eber;* this was fulfilled in part when the Grecian empire was oppressive to the Jewish nation, but chiefly when the Roman empire ruined it and put a period to it. But, (3.) That Chittim, that is, the Roman empire, in which the Grecian was at length swallowed up, should itself perish for ever, when the stone cut out of the mountain without hands shall consume all these kingdoms, and particularly the *feet of iron and clay,* Dan. ii. 34. Thus (says Dr. Lightfoot) Balaam, instead of cursing the church, curses Amalek the first, and Rome the last, enemy of the church. And *so let all thy enemies perish, O Lord!*

CHAP. XXV.

Israel, having escaped the curse of Balaam, here sustains a great deal of damage and reproach by the counsel of Balaam, who, it seems, before he left Balak, put him into a more effectual way than that which Balak thought of to separate between the Israelites and their God. "The Lord will not be prevailed with by Balaam's charms to ruin them; try if they will not be prevailed with by the charms of the daughters of Moab to ruin themselves." None are more fatally bewitched than those that are bewitched by their own lusts. Here is, I. The sin of Israel; they were enticed by the daughters of Moab both to whoredom and to idolatry, ver. 1—3. II. The punishment of this sin by the hand of the magistrate (ver. 4, 5) and by the immediate hand of God, ver. 9. III. The pious zeal of Phinehas in slaying Zimri and Cozbi, two impudent sinners, ver. 6, 8, 14, 15. IV. God's commendation of the zeal of Phinehas, ver. 10—13. V. Enmity put between the Israelites and the Midianites, their tempters, as at first between the woman and the serpent, ver. 16, &c.

AND Israel abode in Shittim, and the people began to commit whoredom with the daughters of Moab.

2 And they called the people unto the sacrifices of their gods: and the people did eat, and bowed down to their gods. 3 And Israel joined himself unto Baal-peor: and the anger of the

LORD was kindled against Israel. 4 And the LORD said unto Moses, Take all the heads of the people, and hang them up before the LORD against the sun, that the fierce anger of the LORD may be turned away from Israel. 5 And Moses said unto the judges of Israel, Slay ye every one his men that were joined unto Baal-peor.

Here is, I. The sin of Israel, to which they were enticed by the daughters of Moab and Midian; they were guilty both of corporal and spiritual whoredoms, for *Israel joined himself unto Baal-peor, v.* 3. Not all, nor the most, but very many, were taken in this snare. Now concerning this observe, 1. That Balak, by the advice of Balaam, *cast this stumbling-block before the children of Israel,* Rev. ii. 14. Note, Those are our worst enemies that draw us to sin, for that is the greatest mischief any man can do us. If Balak had drawn out his armed men against them to fight them, Israel had bravely resisted, and no doubt had been more than conquerors; but now that he sends his beautiful women among them, and invites them to his idolatrous feasts, the Israelites basely yield, and are shamefully overcome: those are smitten with his harlots that could not be smitten with his sword. Note, We are more endangered by the charms of a smiling world than by the terrors of a frowning world. 2. That the daughters of Moab were their tempters and conquerors. Ever since Eve was first in the transgression the fairer sex, though the weaker, has been a snare to many; yea strong men have been wounded and slain by the lips of the strange woman (Prov. vii. 26), witness Solomon, whose wives were snares and nets to him, Eccl. vii. 26. 3. That whoredom and idolatry went together. They first defiled and debauched their consciences, by committing lewdness with the women, and then were easily drawn, in complaisance to them, and in contempt of the God of Israel, to bow down to their idols. And they were more likely to do so if, as it is commonly supposed, and seems probable by the joining of them together, the uncleanness committed was a part of the worship and service performed to Baal-peor. Those that have broken the fences of modesty will never be held by the bonds of piety, and those that have dishonoured themselves by fleshly lusts will not scruple to dishonour God by idolatrous worships, and for this they are justly given up yet further to vile affections. 4. That by eating of the idolatrous sacrifices they *joined themselves to Baal-peor* to whom they were offered, which the apostle urges as a reason why Christians should not *eat things offered to idols,* because thereby they had fellowship with the devils to whom they were offered, 1 Cor. x. 20. It is called *eating the sacrifices of the dead*

(Ps. cvi. 28), not only because the idol itself was a dead thing, but because the person represented by it was some great hero, who since his death was deified, as saints in the Roman church are canonized. 5. It was a great aggravation of the sin that *Israel abode in Shittim,* where they had the land of Canaan in view, and were just ready to enter and take possession of it. It was the highest degree of treachery and ingratitude to be false to their God, whom they had found so faithful to them, and to eat of idol-sacrifices when they were ready to be feasted so richly on God's favours.

II. God's just displeasure against them for this sin. Israel's whoredoms did that which all Balaam's enchantments could not do, they set God against them; now he was *turned to be their enemy, and fought against them.* So many of the people, nay, so many of the princes, were guilty, that the sin became national, and for it God was wroth with the whole congregation. 1. A plague immediately broke out, for we read of the staying of it (*v.* 8), and of the number that died of it (*v.* 9), but no mention of the beginning of it, which therefore must be implied in those words (*v.* 3), *The anger of the Lord was kindled against Israel.* It is said expressly (Ps. cvi. 29), *The plague broke in.* Note, Epidemical diseases are the fruits of God's anger, and the just punishments of epidemical sins; one infection follows the other. The plague, no doubt, fastened on those that were most guilty, who were soon made to pay dearly for their forbidden pleasures; and though now God does not always plague such sinners, as he did here, yet that word of God will be fulfilled, *If any man defile the temple of God, him shall God destroy,* 1 Cor. iii. 17. 2. The ringleaders are ordered to be put to death by the hand of public justice, which will be the only way to stay the plague (*v.* 4): *Take the heads of the people* (that is, of that part of the people that went out of the camp of Israel into the country of Moab, to join in their idolatries)—*take them and hang them up before the sun,* as sacrifices to God's justice, and for a terror to the rest of the people. The judges must first order them to be *slain with the sword* (*v.* 5), and their dead bodies must be hanged up, that the stupid Israelites, seeing their leaders and princes so severely punished for their whoredom and idolatry, without any regard to their quality, might be possessed with a sense of the evil of the sin and the terror of God's wrath against them. Ringleaders in sin ought to be made examples of justice.

6 And, behold, one of the children of Israel came and brought unto his brethren a Midianitish woman in the sight of Moses, and in the sight of all the congregation of the children of Israel, who *were* weeping *before* the

door of the tabernacle of the congregation. 7 And when Phinehas, the son of Eleazar, the son of Aaron the priest, saw *it,* he rose up from among the congregation, and took a javelin in his hand; 8 And he went after the man of Israel into the tent, and thrust both of them through, the man of Israel, and the woman through her belly. So the plague was stayed from the children of Israel. 9 And those that died in the plague were twenty and four thousand. 10 And the LORD spake unto Moses, saying, 11 Phinehas, the son of Eleazar, the son of Aaron the priest, hath turned my wrath away from the children of Israel, while he was zealous for my sake among them, that I consumed not the children of Israel in my jealousy. 12 Wherefore say, Behold, I give unto him my covenant of peace: 13 And he shall have it, and his seed after him, *even* the covenant of an everlasting priesthood; because he was 'zealous for his God, and made an atonement for the children of Israel. 14 Now the name of the Israelite that was slain, *even* that was slain with the Midianitish woman, *was* Zimri, the son of Salu, a prince of a chief house among the Simeonites. 15 And the name of the Midianitish woman that was slain *was* Cozbi the daughter of Zur; he *was* head over a people, *and* of a chief house in Midian.

Here is a remarkable contest between wickedness and righteousness, which shall be most bold and resolute; and righteousness carries the day, as no doubt it will at last.

I. Never was vice more daring than it was in Zimri, *a prince of a chief house* in the tribe of Simeon. Such a degree of impudence in wickedness had he arrived at that he publicly appeared leading a Midianitish harlot (and a harlot of quality too like himself, a *daughter of a chief house in Midian)* in the sight of Moses, and all the good people of Israel. He did not think it enough to go out with his harlot to worship the gods of Moab, but, when he had done that, he brought her with him to dishonour the God of Israel. He not only owned her publicly as his friend, and higher in his favour than any of the daughters of Israel, but openly went with her *into the tent, v.* 8. The word signifies such a booth or place of retirement as was designed and fitted up for lewdness. Thus he *declared his sin as Sodom,* and was so far

from blushing for it that he rather prided himself in it, and gloried in his shame. All the circumstances concurred to make it exceedingly sinful, exceedingly shameful. 1. It was an affront to the justice of the nation, and bade defiance to that. The judges were ordered to put the criminals to death, but he thought himself too great for them to meddle with, and, in effect, bade them touch him if they durst. He had certainly cast off all fear of God who stood in no awe of the powers which he had ordained to be *a terror to evil-doers.* 2. It was an affront to the religion of the nation, and put a contempt upon that. Moses, and the main body of the congregation, who kept their integrity, *were weeping at the door of the tabernacle,* lamenting the sin committed and deprecating the plague begun; they were *sanctifying a fast* in a solemn assembly, weeping *between the porch and the altar,* to turn away the wrath of God from the congregation. Then comes Zimri among them, with his harlot in his hand, to banter them, and, in effect, to tell them that he was resolved to fill the measure of sin as fast as they emptied it.

II. Never was virtue more daring than it was in Phinehas. Being aware of the insolence of Zimri, which, it is probable, all the congregation took notice of, in a holy indignation at the offenders he rises up from his prayers, takes his sword or half-pike, follows those impudent sinners into their tent, and stabs them both, *v.* 7, 8. It is not at all difficult to justify Phinehas in what he did; for, being now heir-apparent to the high-priesthood, no doubt he was one of those judges of Israel whom Moses had ordered, by the divine appointment, to slay all those whom they knew to have joined themselves to Baal-peor, so that this gives no countenance at all to private persons, under pretence of zeal against sin, to put offenders to death, who ought to be prosecuted by due course of law. The civil magistrate is the avenger, to *execute wrath upon him that doeth evil,* and no private person may take his work out of his hand. Two ways God testified his acceptance of the pious zeal of Phinehas:—1. He immediately put a stop to the plague, *v.* 8. Their weeping and praying prevailed not till this piece of necessary justice was done. If magistrates do not take care to punish sin, God will; but their justice will be the best prevention of his judgment, as in the case of Achan, Josh. vii. 13. 2. He put an honour upon Phinehas. Though he did no more than it was his duty to do as a judge, yet because he did it with extraordinary zeal against sin, and for the honour of God and Israel, and did it when the other judges, out of respect to Zimri's character as a prince, were afraid, and declined doing it, therefore God showed himself particularly well pleased with him, and it *was counted to him for righteousness,* Ps. cvi. 31. There is nothing lost by venturing for God. If Zimri's relations bore him a grudge for it, and his friends might censure him as indiscreet in this violent and hasty execution, what needed he care, while God accepted him ? In a good thing we should be zealously affected. (1.) Phinehas, upon this occasion, though a young man, is pronounced his country's patriot and best friend, *v.* 11. He has *turned away my wrath from the children of Israel.* So much does God delight in showing mercy that he is well pleased with those that are instrumental in turning away his wrath. This is the best service we can do to our people ; and we may contribute something towards it by our prayers, and by our endeavours in our places to *bring the wickedness of the wicked to an end.* (2.) The priesthood is entailed by covenant upon his family. It was designed him before, but now it was confirmed to him, and, which added much to the comfort and honour of it, it was made the recompence of his pious zeal, *v.* 12, 13. It is here called *an everlasting priesthood,* because it should continue to the period of the Old-Testament dispensation, and should then have its perfection and perpetuity in the unchangeable priesthood of Christ, who is *consecrated for evermore.* By the *covenant of peace* given him, some understand in general a promise of long life and prosperity, and all good ; it seems rather to be meant particularly of the covenant of priesthood, for that is called the *covenant of life and peace* (Mal. ii. 5), and was made for the preservation of peace between God and his people. Observe how the reward answered the service. By executing justice he had *made an atonement for the children of Israel* (*v.* 13), and therefore he and his shall henceforward be employed in making atonement by sacrifice. He *was zealous for his God,* and therefore he shall have the covenant of *an everlasting priesthood.* Note, It is requisite that ministers should be not only for God, but zealous for God. It is required of them that they do more than others for the support and advancement of the interests of God's kingdom among men.

16 And the LORD spake unto Moses, saying, 17 Vex the Midianites, and smite them : 18 For they vex you with their wiles, wherewith they have beguiled you in the matter of Peor, and in the matter of Cozbi, the daughter of a prince of Midian, their sister, which was slain in the day of the plague for Peor's sake.

God had punished the Israelites for their sin with a plague ; as a Father he corrected his own children with a rod. But we read not that any of the Midianites died of the plague ; God took another course with them, and punished them with the sword of an enemy, not with the rod of a father. 1. Moses,

though the meekest man, and far from a spirit of revenge, is ordered to *vex the Midianites and smite them,* v. 17. Note, We must set ourselves against that, whatever it is, which is an occasion of sin to us, though it be a right eye or a right hand that thus offends us, Matt. v. 29, 30. This is that holy indignation and revenge which godly sorrow worketh, 2 Cor. vii. 11. 2. The reason given for the meditating of this revenge is because they *vex you with their wiles,* v. 18. Note, Whatever draws us to sin should be a vexation to us, as a thorn in the flesh. The mischief which the Midianites did to Israel by enticing them to whoredom must be remembered and punished with as much severity as that which the Amalekites did in fighting with them when they came out of Egypt, Exod. xvii. 14. God will certainly reckon with those that do the devil's work in tempting men to sin, especially those that make Israel to sin. See further orders given in this matter, *ch.* xxxi. 2.

CHAP. XXVI.

This book is called Numbers, from the numberings of the children of Israel, of which it gives an account. Once they were numbered at Mount Sinai, in the first year after they came out of Egypt, which we had an account of, ch. i. and ii. And now a second time they were numbered in the plains of Moab, just before they entered Canaan, and of this we have an account in this chapter. We have, I. Orders given for the doing of it, ver. 1—4. II. A register of the families and numbers of each tribe (ver. 5—50), and the sum total, ver. 51. III. Direction given to divide the land among them, ver. 52—56. IV. The families and numbers of the Levites by themselves, ver. 57—62. V. Notice taken of the fulfilling of the threatening in the death of all those that were first numbered (ver. 63—65), and to this there seems to have been a special regard in the taking and keeping of this account.

AND it came to pass after the plague, that the LORD spake unto Moses and unto Eleazar the son of Aaron the priest, saying, 2 Take the sum of all the congregation of the children of Israel, from twenty years old and upward, throughout their fathers' house, all that are able to go to war in Israel. 3 And Moses and Eleazar the priest spake with them in the plains of Moab by Jordan *near* Jericho, saying, 4 *Take the sum of the people,* from twenty years old and upward ; as the LORD commanded Moses and the children of Israel, which went forth out of the land of Egypt.

Observe here, 1. That Moses did not number the people but when God commanded him. David in his time did it without a command, and paid dearly for it. God was Israel's king, and he would not have this act of authority done but by his express orders. Moses, perhaps, by this time, had heard of the blessing with which Balaam was constrained, sorely against his will, to bless Israel, and particularly the notice he took of their numbers ; and he was sufficiently pleased with that general testimony borne to this instance of their strength and honour by an adversary, though he knew not their numbers exactly, till God now appointed him to take the sum of them. 2. Eleazar was joined in commission with him, as Aaron had been before, by which God honoured Eleazar before the elders of his people, and confirmed his succession. 3. It was presently after the plague that this account was ordered to be taken, to show that though God had in justice contended with them by that sweeping pestilence, yet he had not made a full end, nor would he utterly cast them off. God's Israel shall not be ruined, though it be severely rebuked. 4. They were now to go by the same rule that they had gone by in the former numbering, counting those only that were able to go forth to war, for this was the service now before them.

5 Reuben, the eldest son of Israel: the children of Reuben; Hanoch, *of whom cometh* the family of the Hanochites: of Pallu, the family of the Palluites: 6 Of Hezron, the family of the Hezronites: of Carmi, the family of the Carmites. 7 These *are* the families of the Reubenites: and they that were numbered of them were forty and three thousand and seven hundred and thirty. 8 And the sons of Pallu; Eliab. 9 And the sons of Eliab; Nemuel, and Dathan and Abiram. This *is that* Dathan and Abiram, *which were* famous in the congregation, who strove against Moses and against Aaron in the company of Korah, when they strove against the LORD: 10 And the earth opened her mouth, and swallowed them up together with Korah, when that company died, what time the fire devoured two hundred and fifty men: and they became a sign. 11 Notwithstanding the children of Korah died not. 12 The sons of Simeon after their families: of Nemuel, the family of the Nemuelites: of Jamin, the family of the Jaminites: of Jachin, the family of the Jachinites: 13 Of Zerah, the family of the Zarhites: of Shaul, the family of the Shaulites. 14 These *are* the families of the Simeonites, twenty and two thousand and two hundred. 15 The children of Gad after their families: of Zephon, the family of the Zephonites: of Haggi, the family of the Haggites: of Shuni, the family of the Shunites: 16 Of Ozni, the family of

the Oznites: of Eri, the family of the Erites: 17 Of Arod, the family of the Arodites: of Areli, the family of the Arelites. 18 These *are* the families of the children of Gad according to those that were numbered of them, forty thousand and five hundred. 19 The sons of Judah *were* Er and Onan: and Er and Onan died in the land of Canaan. 20 And the sons of Judah after their families were; of Shelah, the family of the Shelanites: of Pharez, the family of the Parzites: of Zerah, the family of the Zarhites. 21 And the sons of Pharez were; of Hezron, the family of the Hezronites: of Hamul, the family of the Hamulites. 22 These *are* the families of Judah according to those that were numbered of them, threescore and sixteen thousand and five hundred. 23 *Of* the sons of Issachar after their families: *of* Tola, the family of the Tolaites: of Pua, the family of the Punites: 24 Of Jashub, the family of the Jashubites: of Shimron, the family of the Shimronites. 25 These *are* the families of Issachar according to those that were numbered of them, threescore and four thousand and three hundred. 26 *Of* the sons of Zebulun after their families: of Sered, the family of the Sardites: of Elon, the family of the Elonites: of Jahleel, the family of the Jahleelites. 27 These *are* the families of the Zebulunites according to those that were numbered of them, threescore thousand and five hundred. 28 The sons of Joseph after their families *were* Manasseh and Ephraim. 29 Of the sons of Manasseh: of Machir, the family of the Machirites: and Machir begat Gilead: of Gilead *come* the family of the Gileadites. 30 These *are* the sons of Gilead: *of* Jeezer, the family of the Jeezerites: of Helek, the family of the Helekites: 31 And *of* Asriel, the family of the Asrielites: and *of* Shechem, the family of the Shechemites: 32 And *of* Shemida, the family of the Shemidaites: and *of* Hepher, the family of the Hepherites. 33 And Zelophehad the son of Hepher had no sons, but daughters: and the names of the daughters of Zelophehad *were* Mahlah, and Noah, Hoglah, Milcah, and Tirzah. 34 These *are* the families of Manasseh, and those that were numbered of them, fifty and two thousand and seven hundred. 35 These *are* the sons of Ephraim after their families: of Shuthelah, the family of the Shuthelahites: of Becher, the family of the Bachrites: of Tahan, the family of the Tahanites. 36 And these *are* the sons of Shuthelah: of Eran, the family of the Eranites. 37 These *are* the families of the sons of Ephraim according to those that were numbered of them, thirty and two thousand and five hundred. These *are* the sons of Joseph after their families. 38 The sons of Benjamin after their families: of Bela, the family of the Belaites: of Ashbel, the family of the Ashbelites: of Ahiram, the family of the Ahiramites: 39 Of Shupham, the family of the Shuphamites: of Hupham, the family of the Huphamites. 40 And the sons of Bela were Ard and Naaman: *of Ard,* the family of the Ardites: *and* of Naaman, the family of the Naamites. 41 These *are* the sons of Benjamin after their families: and they that were numbered of them *were* forty and five thousand and six hundred. 42 These *are* the sons of Dan after their families: of Shuham, the family of the Shuhamites. These *are* the families of Dan after their families. 43 All the families of the Shuhamites, according to those that were numbered of them, *were* threescore and four thousand and four hundred. 44 *Of* the children of Asher after their families: of Jimna, the family of the Jimnites: of Jesui, the family of the Jesuites: of Beriah, the family of the Beriites. 45 Of the sons of Beriah: of Heber, the families of the Heberites: of Malchiel, the family of the Malchielites. 46 And the name of the daughter of Asher *was* Sarah. 47 These *are* the families of the sons of Asher according to those that were numbered of them; *who were* fifty and three thousand and four hundred. 48 *Of* the sons of Naphtali after their families: of Jahzeel, the family of the Jahzeelites: of Guni, the family of the Gunites: 49 Of Jezer, the family of the Jezerites: of Shillem, the family of the Shillemites. 50 These *are* the families of Naphtali according to their families: and they that were numbered of them *were* forty and five thousand and four hundred. 51 These *were* the number of the children of Israel, six hundred thousand and a thousand seven hundred and thirty.

This is the register of the tribes as they were now enrolled, in the same order that they were numbered in *ch.* i. Observe,

I. The account that is here kept of the families of each tribe, which must not be understood of such as we call families, those that live in a house together, but such as were the descendants of the several sons of the patriarchs, by whose names, in honour of them, their posterity distinguished themselves and one another. The families of the twelve tribes are thus numbered:—Of Dan but one, for Dan had but one son, and yet that tribe was the most numerous of all except Judah, *v.* 42, 43. Its beginning was small, but its latter end greatly increased. Zebulun was divided into three families, Ephraim into four, Issachar into four, Naphtali into four, and Reuben into four; Judah, Simeon, and Asher, had five families apiece, Gad and Benjamin seven apiece, and Manasseh eight Benjamin brought ten sons into Egypt (Gen. xlvi. 21), but three of them, it seems, either died childless or their families were extinct, for here we find seven only of those names preserved, and that whole tribe none of the most numerous; for Providence, in the building up of families and nations, does not tie itself to probabilities. *The barren hath borne seven, and she that hath many children has waxed feeble,* 1 Sam. ii. 5.

II. The numbers of each tribe. And here our best entertainment will be to compare these numbers with those when they were numbered at Mount Sinai. The sum total was nearly the same; they were now 1820 fewer than they were then; yet seven of the tribes had increased in number. Judah had increased 1900, Issachar 9900, Zebulun 3100, Manasseh 20,500, Benjamin 10,200, Dan 1700, and Asher 11,900. But the other five had decreased more than to balance that increase. Reuben had decreased 2770, Simeon 37,100, Gad 5150, Ephraim 8000, and Naphtali 8000. In this account we may observe, 1. That all the three tribes that were encamped under the standard of Judah, who was the ancestor of Christ, had increased, for his church shall be edified and multiplied 2. That none of the tribes had increased so much as that of Manasseh, which in the former account was the smallest of all the tribes, only 32,200, while here it is one of the most considerable ; and that of his brother Ephraim, which there was numerous, is here one of the least. Jacob had crossed hands upon their heads, and had preferred Ephraim before Manasseh, which perhaps the Ephraimites had prided themselves too much in, and had trampled upon their brethren the Manassites ; but, when the Lord saw that Manasseh was despised, he thus multiplied him exceedingly, for it is his glory to help the weakest, and raise up those that are cast down. 3. That none of the tribes decreased so much as Simeon did ; from 59,300, it sunk to 22,200, little more than a third part of what it was. One whole family of that tribe (namely Ohad, mentioned Exod. vi. 15) was extinct in the wilderness. Hence Simeon is not mentioned in Moses's blessing (Deut. xxxiii.), and the lot of that tribe in Canaan was inconsiderable, only a canton out of Judah's lot, Josh. xix. 9. Some conjecture that most of those 24,000 who were cut off by the plague for the iniquity of Peor were of that tribe ; for Zimri, who was a ringleader in that iniquity, was a prince of that tribe, many of whom therefore were influenced by his example to *follow his pernicious ways.*

III. In the account of the tribe of Reuben mention is made of the rebellion of Dathan and Abiram, who were of that tribe, in confederacy with Korah a Levite, *v.* 9—11. Though the story had been largely related but a few chapters before, yet here it comes in again, as fit to be had in remembrance and thought of by posterity, whenever they looked into their pedigree and pleased themselves with the antiquity of their families and the glory of their ancestors, that they might call themselves a seed of evil doers. Two things are here said of them :—1. That they had been *famous in the congregation, v.* 9. Probably they were remarkable for their ingenuity, activity, and fitness for business :—*That Dathan and Abiram* that might have been advanced in due time under God and Moses; but their ambitious spirits put them upon striving against God and Moses, and when they quarrelled with the one they quarrelled with the other. And what was the issue ? 2. Those that might have been famous were made infamous : they *became a sign, v.* 10. They were made monuments of divine justice ; God, in their ruin, showed himself glorious in holiness, and so they were set up for a warning to all others, in all ages, to take heed of treading in the steps of their pride and rebellion. Notice is here taken of the preservation of the *children of Korah* (*v.* 11); they *died not,* as the children of Dathan and Abiram did, doubtless because they kept themselves pure from the infection, and would not join, no, not with their own father, in rebellion. If we partake not of the sins of sinners, we shall not partake of their plagues. These sons of Korah were afterwards, in their posterity, eminently serviceable to the church, being em-

ployed by David as singers in the house of the Lord ; hence many psalms are said to be for *the sons of Korah :* and perhaps they were made to bear his name so long after, rather than the name of any other of their ancestors, for warning to themselves, and as an instance of the power of God, which brought those choice fruits even out of that bitter root. The children of families that have been stigmatized should endeavour, by their eminent virtues, to roll away the reproach of their fathers.

52 And the Lord spake unto Moses, saying, 53 Unto these the land shall be divided for an inheritance according to the number of names. 54 To many thou shalt give the more inheritance, and to few thou shalt give the less inheritance : to every one shall his inheritance be given according to those that were numbered of him. 55 Notwithstanding the land shall be divided by lot : according to the names of the tribes of their fathers they shall inherit. 56 According to the lot shall the possession thereof be divided between many and few.

If any ask why such a particular account is kept of the tribes, and families, and numbers, of the people of Israel, here is an answer for them ; as they were multiplied, so they were portioned, not by common providence, but by promise ; and, for the support of the honour of divine revelation, God will have the fulfilling of the promise taken notice of both in their increase and in their inheritance. When Moses had numbered the people God did not say, *By these shall the land be conquered :* but, taking that for granted, he tells him, *Unto these shall the land be divided.* "These that are now registered as the sons of Israel shall be admitted (as it were by copy of court-roll) heirs of the land of Canaan." Now, in the distributing, or quartering, of these tribes, 1. The general rule of equity is here prescribed to Moses, that to many he should give more, and to few he should give less (*v.* 54) ; yet, alas ! *he* was so far from giving any to others that he must not have any himself, but this direction given to him was intended for Joshua his successor. 2. The application of this general rule was to be determined *by lot* (*v.* 55) ; notwithstanding it seems thus to be left to the prudence of their prince, yet the matter must be finally reserved to the providence of their God, in which they must all acquiesce, how much soever it contradicted their policies or inclinations : *According to the lot shall the possession be divided.* ∴ As the God of nations, so the God of Israel in particular, reserves it to himself to *appoint the bounds of our habitation.* And thus Christ, our Joshua, when he was urged to appoint one of his disciples *to his right*

hand, and another *to his left* in his kingdom, acknowledged the sovereignty of his Father in the disposal: *It is not mine to give.* Joshua must not dispose of inheritances in Canaan according to his own mind. *But it shall be given to those for whom it is prepared of my Father.*

57 And these *are* they that were numbered of the Levites after their families: of Gershon, the family of the Gershonites: of Kohath, the family of the Kohathites: of Merari, the family of the Merarites. 58 These *are* the families of the Levites: the family of the Libnites, the family of the Hebronites, the family of the Mahlites, the family of the Mushites, the family of the Korathites. And Kohath begat Amram. 59 And the name of Amram's wife *was* Jochebed, the daughter of Levi, whom *her mother* bare to Levi in Egypt: and she bare unto Amram Aaron and Moses, and Miriam their sister. 60 And unto Aaron was born Nadab, and Abihu, Eleazar, and Ithamar. 61 And Nadab and Abihu died, when they offered strange fire before the LORD. 62 And those that were numbered of them were twenty and three thousand, all males from a month old and upward: for they were not numbered among the children of Israel, because there was no inheritance given them among the children of Israel.

Levi was God's tribe, a tribe that was to have no inheritance with the rest in the land of Canaan, and therefore was not numbered with the rest, but by itself; so it had been numbered in the beginning of this book at Mount Sinai, and therefore came not under the sentence passed upon all that were then numbered, that none of them should enter Canaan but Caleb and Joshua; for of the Levites that were not numbered with them, nor were to go forth to war, Eleazar and Ithamar, and perhaps others who were above twenty years old then (as appears, *ch.* iv. 16, 28), entered Canaan; and yet this tribe, now at its second numbering, had increased but 1000, and was still one of the smallest tribes. Mention is made here of the death of Nadab and Abihu for offering strange fire, as before of the sin and punishment of Korah, because *these things happened to them for ensamples.*

63 These *are* they that were numbered by Moses and Eleazar the priest, who numbered the children of Israel in the plains of Moab by Jordan *near*

Jericho. 64 But among these there was not a man of them whom Moses and Aaron the priest numbered, when they numbered the children of Israel in the wilderness of Sinai. 65 For the LORD had said of them, They shall surely die in the wilderness. And there was not left a man of them, save Caleb the son of Jephunneh, and Joshua the son of Nun.

That which is observable in this conclusion of the account is the execution of the sentence passed upon the murmurers (*ch.* xiv. 29), that not one of those who *were numbered from twenty years old and upwards* (and that the Levites were not, but either from a month old or from thirty years old to fifty) should enter Canaan, except Caleb and Joshua. In the muster now made particular directions, no doubt, were given to those of each tribe that were employed in taking the account, to compare these rolls with the former, and to observe whether there were any now left of those that were numbered at Mount Sinai, and it appeared that there was not one man numbered now that was numbered then except Caleb and Joshua, *v.* 64, 65. Herein appeared, 1. The righteousness of God, and his faithfulness to his threatenings, when once the *decree has gone forth.* He *swore in his wrath,* and what he had sworn he performed. Better all those carcases, had they been ten times as many, should fall to the ground, than the word of God. Though the rising generation was mixed with them, and many of the guilty and condemned criminals long survived the sentence, even to the last year of the forty, yet they were cut off by some means or other before this muster was made. Those whom God has condemned cannot escape either by losing themselves in a crowd or by the delay of execution. 2. The goodness of God to this people, notwithstanding their provocations. Though that murmuring race was cut off, yet God raised up another generation, which was as numerous as they, that, though they perished, yet the name of Israel might not be cut off, lest the inheritance of the promise should be lost for want of heirs. And, though the number fell a little short of what it was at Mount Sinai, yet those now numbered had this advantage, that they were all middle-aged men, between twenty and sixty, in the prime of their time for service; and during the thirty-eight years of their wandering and wasting in the wilderness they had an opportunity of acquainting themselves with the laws and ordinances of God, having no business, civil or military, to divert them from those sacred studies, and having Moses and Aaron to instruct them, and God's good Spirit, Neh. ix. 20. 3. The truth of God, in performing his promise made to Caleb and Joshua. They were to be preserved from falling in this common ruin, and they were so. The arrows of death, though they fly in the dark, do not fly at random, even when they fly thickest, but are directed to the mark intended, and no other. All that are written among the living shall have their lives given them for a prey, in the most dangerous times. Thousands may fall on their right hand, and ten thousands on their left, but they shall escape.

CHAP. XXVII.

Here is, I. The case of Zelophehad's daughters determined, ver. 1—11. II. Notice given to Moses of his death approaching, ver. 12—14. III. Provision made of a successor in the government, 1. By the prayer of Moses, ver. 15—17. 2. By the appointment of God, ver. 18, &c.

THEN came the daughters of Zelophehad, the son of Hepher, the son of Gilead, the son of Machir, the son of Manasseh, of the families of Manasseh the son of Joseph: and these *are* the names of his daughters; Mahlah, Noah, and Hoglah, and Milcah, and Tirzah. 2 And they stood before Moses, and before Eleazar the priest, and before the princes and all the congregation, *by* the door of the tabernacle of the congregation, saying, 3 Our father died in the wilderness, and he was not in the company of them that gathered themselves together against the LORD in the company of Korah; but died in his own sin, and had no sons. 4 Why should the name of our father be done away from among his family, because he hath no son? Give unto us *therefore* a possession among the brethren of our father. 5 And Moses brought their cause before the LORD. 6 And the LORD spake unto Moses, saying, 7 The daughters of Zelophehad speak right: thou shalt surely give them a possession of an inheritance among their father's brethren; and thou shalt cause the inheritance of their father to pass unto them. 8 And thou shalt speak unto the children of Israel, saying, If a man die, and have no son, then he shall cause his inheritance to pass unto his daughter. 9 And if he have no daughter, then ye shall give his inheritance unto his brethren. 10 And if he have no brethren, then ye shall give his inheritance unto his father's brethren. 11 And if his father have no brethren, then ye shall give his inheritance unto his kinsman that is next to him of his family, and he shall possess it: and it shall be unto the

694

children of Israel a statute of judgment, as the LORD commanded Moses.

Mention is made of the case of these daughters of Zelophehad in the chapter before, *v.* 33. It should seem, by the particular notice taken of it, that it was a singular case, and that the like did not at this time occur in all Israel, that the head of a family had no sons, but daughters only. Their case is again debated (*ch.* xxxvi.) upon another article of it; and, according to the judgments given in their case, we find them put in possession, Josh. xvii. 3, 4. One would suppose that their personal character was such as added weight to their case, and caused it to be so often taken notice of.

Here is, I. Their case stated by themselves, and their petition upon it presented to the highest court of judicature, which consisted of Moses as king, the princes as lords, and the congregation, or elders of the people who were chosen their representatives, as the commons, *v.* 2. This august assembly sat near the *door of the tabernacle,* that in difficult cases they might consult the oracle. To them these young ladies made their application; for it is the duty of magistrates to *defend the fatherless,* Ps. lxxxii. 3. We find not that they had any advocate to speak for them, but they managed their own cause ingeniously enough, which they could do the better because it was plain and honest, and spoke for itself. Now observe,

1. What it is they petition for: That they might have a possession in the land of *Canaan, among the brethren of their father,* v. 4. What God had said to Moses (*ch.* xxvi. 53) he had faithfully made known to the people, that the land of Canaan was to be divided among those that were now numbered; these daughters knew that they were not numbered, and therefore by this rule must expect no inheritance, and the family of their father must be looked upon as extinct, and written childless, though he had all these daughters: this they thought hard, and therefore prayed to be admitted heirs to their father, and to have an inheritance in his right. If they had had a brother, they would not have applied to Moses (as one did to Christ, Luke xii. 13) for an order to inherit with him. But, having no brother, they beg for a possession. Herein they discovered, (1.) A strong faith in the power and promise of God concerning the giving of the land of Canaan to Israel. Though it was yet unconquered, untouched, and in the full possession of the natives, yet they petition for their share in it as if it were all their own already. See Ps. lx. 6, 7, *God has spoken in his holiness,* and then *Gilead is mine, Manasseh is mine.* (2.) An earnest desire of a place and name in the land of promise, which was a type of heaven; and if they had, as some think, an eye to that, and by this claim laid hold on eternal life, they were five wise virgins indeed; and their ex-

ample should quicken us with all possible diligence to make sure our title to the heavenly inheritance, in the disposal of which, by the covenant of grace, no difference is made between male and female, Gal. iii. 28. (3.) A true respect and honour for their father, whose name was dear and precious to them now that he was gone, and they were therefore solicitous that it should not be *done away from among his family.* There is a debt which children owe to the memory of their parents, required by the fifth commandment: *Honour thy father and mother.*

2. What their plea is: That their father did not die under any attainder which might be thought to have corrupted his blood and forfeited his estate, but he *died in his own sin* (*v.* 3), not engaged in any mutiny or rebellion against Moses, particularly not in that of Korah and his company, nor in any way concerned in the sins of others, but chargeable only with the common iniquities of mankind, for which to his own Master he was to stand or fall, but laid not himself open to any judicial process before Moses and the princes. He was never convicted of any thing that might be a bar to his children's claim. It is a comfort to parents, when they come to die, if, though they smart themselves for their own sin, yet they are not conscious to themselves of any of those iniquities which God visits upon the children.

II. Their case determined by the divine oracle. Moses did not presume to give judgment himself, because, though their pretensions seemed just and reasonable, yet his express orders were to divide the land among those that were numbered, who were the males only; he therefore *brings their cause before the Lord,* and waits for his decision (*v.* 5), and God himself gives judgment upon it. He takes cognizance of the affairs, not only of nations, but of private families, and orders them in judgment, according to the counsel of his own will. 1. The petition is granted (*v.* 7): *They speak right, give them a possession.* Those that seek an inheritance in the land of promise shall have what they seek, and other things shall be added to them. These are claims which God will countenance and crown. 2. The point is settled for all future occasions. These daughters of Zelophehad consulted, not only their own comfort and the credit of their family, but the honour and happiness of their sex likewise; for on this particular occasion a general law was made that, in case a man had no son, his estate should go to his daughters (*v.* 8); not to the eldest, as the eldest son, but to them all in copartnership, share and share alike. Those that in such a case deprive their daughters of their right, purely to keep up the name of their family, unless a valuable consideration be allowed them, may make the entail of their lands surer than the entail of a blessing with them. Further directions are given for the disposal of inheritances, *v.* 9—11.

"If a man have no issue at all, his estate shall go to his brethren; if no brethren, then to his father's brethren; and, if there be no such, then to his next kinsman." With this the rules of our law exactly agree: and though the Jewish doctors here will have it understood that if a man have no children his estate shall go to his father, if living, before his brethren, yet there is nothing of that in the law, and our common law has an express rule against it, That an estate cannot ascend lineally; so that if a person purchase lands in fee-simple, and die without issue in the life-time of his father, his father cannot be his heir. See how God makes heirs, and in his disposal we must acquiesce.

12 And the LORD said unto Moses, Get thee up into this mount Abarim, and see the land which I have given unto the children of Israel. 13 And when thou hast seen it, thou also shalt be gathered unto thy people, as Aaron thy brother was gathered. 14 For ye rebelled against my commandment in the desert of Zin, in the strife of the congregation, to sanctify me at the water before their eyes: that *is* the water of Meribah in Kadesh in the wilderness of Zin.

Here, 1. God tells Moses of his fault, his speaking unadvisedly with his lips at the waters of strife, where he did not express, so carefully as he ought to have done, a regard to the honour both of God and Israel, *v.* 14. Though Moses was a servant of the Lord, a faithful servant, yet once he *rebelled against God's commandment,* and failed in his duty; and though a very honourable servant, and highly favoured, yet he shall hear of his miscarriage, and all the world shall hear of it too, again and again; for God will show his displeasure against sin, even in those that are nearest and dearest to him. Those that are *in reputation for wisdom and honour* have need to be constantly careful of their words and ways, lest at any time they say or do that which may be a diminution to their comfort, or to their credit, or both, a great while after. 2. He tells Moses of his death. His death was the punishment of his sin, and yet notice is given him of it in such a manner as might best serve to sweeten and mollify the sentence, and reconcile him to it. (1.) Moses must die, but he shall first have the satisfaction of seeing the land of promise, *v.* 12. God did not intend with this sight of Canaan to tantalize him, or upbraid him with his folly in doing that which cut him short of it, nor had it any impression of that kind upon him, but God appointed it and Moses accepted it as a favour, his sight (we have reason to think) being wonderfully strengthened and enlarged to take such a full and distinct view of it as did abundantly gratify his innocent curiosity.

This sight of Canaan signified his believing prospect of the better country, that is, the heavenly, which is very comfortable to dying saints. (2.) Moses must die, but death does not *cut him off;* it only gathers him to his people, brings him to rest with the holy patriarchs that had gone before him. Abraham, and Isaac, and Jacob, were *his people*, the people of his choice and love, and to them death gathered him. (3.) Moses must die, but only as Aaron died before him, *v.* 13. And Moses had seen how easily and cheerfully Aaron had put off the priesthood first and then the body; let not Moses therefore be afraid of dying; it was but to be *gathered to his people*, as Aaron was gathered. Thus the death of our near and dear relations should be improved by us, [1.] As an engagement to us to think often of dying. We are not better than our fathers or brethren; if they are gone, we are going; if they are gathered already, we must be gathered very shortly. [2.] As an encouragement to us to think of death without terror, and even to please ourselves with the thoughts of it. It is but to die as such and such died, if we live as they lived; and their *end was peace, they finished their course with joy;* why then should we fear any evil in that melancholy valley?

15 And Moses spake unto the LORD, saying, 16 Let the LORD, the God of the spirits of all flesh, set a man over the congregation, 17 Which may go out before them, and which may go in before them, and which may lead them out, and which may bring them in; that the congregation of the LORD be not as sheep which have no shepherd. 18 And the LORD said unto Moses, Take thee Joshua the son of Nun, a man in whom *is* the spirit, and lay thine hand upon him; 19 And set him before Eleazar the priest, and before all the congregation; and give him a charge in their sight. 20 And thou shalt put *some* of thine honour upon him, that all the congregation of the children of Israel may be obedient. 21 And he shall stand before Eleazar the priest, who shall ask *counsel* for him after the judgment of Urim before the LORD: at his word shall they go out, and at his word they shall come in, *both* he, and all the children of Israel with him, even all the congregation. 22 And Moses did as the LORD commanded him: and he took Joshua, and set him before Eleazar the priest, and before all the congregation: 23

And he laid his hands upon him, and gave him a charge as the LORD commanded by the hand of Moses.

Here, I. Moses prays for a successor. When God had told him that he must die, though it appears elsewhere that he solicited for a reprieve for himself (Deut. iii. 24, 25), yet, when this could not be obtained, he begged earnestly that the work of God might be carried on, though he might not have the honour of finishing it. Envious spirits do not love their successors, but Moses was not one of these. We should concern ourselves, both in our prayers and in our endeavours, for the rising generation, that religion may flourish, and the interests of God's kingdom among men may be maintained and advanced, when we are in our graves. In this prayer Moses expresses, 1. A tender concern for the people of Israel: *That the congregation of the Lord be not as sheep which have no shepherd.* Our Saviour uses this comparison in his compassions for the people when they wanted good ministers, Matt. ix. 36. Magistrates and ministers are the shepherds of a people; if these be wanting, or be not as they should be, people are apt to wander and be scattered abroad, are exposed to enemies, and in danger of wanting food and of hurting one another, *as sheep having no shepherd.* 2. A believing dependence upon God, as the *God of the spirits of all flesh.* He is both the former and the searcher of spirits, and therefore can either find men fit or make them fit to serve his purposes, for the good of his church. Moses prays to God, not to send an angel, but to *set a man over the congregation,* that is, to nominate and appoint one whom he would qualify and own as ruler of his people Israel. Before God gave this blessing to Israel, he stirred up Moses to pray for it: thus Christ, before he sent forth his apostles, called to those about him *to pray the Lord of the harvest that he would send forth labourers into his harvest,* Matt. ix. 38.

II. God, in answer to his prayer, appoints him a successor, even Joshua, who had long since signalized himself by his courage in fighting Amalek, his humility in ministering to Moses, and his faith and sincerity in witnessing against the report of the evil spies; this is the man whom God pitches upon to succeed Moses: *A man in whom is the Spirit,* the Spirit of grace (he is a good man, fearing God and hating covetousness, and acting from principle), the *spirit of government* (he is fit to do the work and discharge the trusts of his place), a spirit of conduct and courage; and he had also the *spirit of prophecy,* for the Lord often *spoke unto him,* Josh. iv. 1; vi. 2; vii. 10. Now here,

1. God directs Moses how to secure the succession to Joshua. (1.) He must ordain him: *Lay thy hand upon him, v.* 18. This was done in token of Moses's transferring the government to him, as the laying of hands

on the sacrifice put the offering in the place and stead of the offerer; also in token of God's conferring the blessing of the Spirit upon him, which Moses obtained by prayer. It is said (Deut. xxxiv. 9), *Joshua was full of the spirit of wisdom, for Moses had laid his hands on him.* This rite of imposing hands we find used in the New Testament in the setting apart of gospel ministers, denoting a solemn designation of them to the office and an earnest desire that God would qualify them for it and own them in it. It is the offering of them to Christ and his church for living sacrifices. (2.) He must present him to Eleazar and the people, set him before them, that they might know him to be designed of God for this great trust and consent to that designation. (3.) He must *give him a charge, v.* 19. He must be charged with the people of Israel, who were delivered into his hand as sheep into the hand of a shepherd, and for whom he must be accountable. He must be strictly charged to do his duty to them; though they were under his command, he was under God's command, and from him must receive charge. The highest must know that there is a higher than they. This charge must be given him *in their sight,* that it might be the more affecting to Joshua, and that the people, seeing the work and care of their prince, might be the more engaged to assist and encourage him. (4.) He must *put some of his honour upon him, v.* 20. Joshua at the most had but some of the honour of Moses, and in many instances came short of him; but this seems to be meant of his taking him now, while he lived, into partnership with him in the government and admitting him to act with authority as his assistant. It is an honour to be employed for God and his church; some of this honour must be put upon Joshua, that the people, being used to obey him while Moses lived, might the more cheerfully do it afterwards. (5.) He must appoint Eleazar the high priest, with his breast-plate of judgment, to be his privy-council (*v.* 21): *He shall stand before Eleazar,* by him to consult the oracle, ready to receive and observe all the instructions that should be given him by it. This was a direction to Joshua. Though he was full of the Spirit, and had all this honour put upon him, yet he must do nothing without asking counsel of God, not leaning to his own understanding. It was also a great encouragement to him. To govern Israel, and to conquer Canaan, were two hard tasks, but God assures him that in both he should be under a divine conduct; and in every difficult case God would advise him to that which should be for the best. Moses had recourse to the oracle of God himself, but Joshua and the succeeding judges must use the ministry of the high priest, and consult the judgment of urim, which, the Jews say, might not be enquired of but by the king or the head of the sanhedrim, or by the agent or representative

of the people, for them, and in their name. Thus the government of Israel was now purely divine, for both the designation and direction of their princes were entirely so. *At the word of the priest,* according to the *judgment of urim,* Joshua and all Israel must go out and come in; and no doubt God, who thus guided, would preserve both their going out and their coming in. Those are safe, and may be easy, that follow God, and in all their ways acknowledge him.

2. Moses does according to these directions, *v.* 22, 23. He cheerfully ordained Joshua, (1.) Though it was a present lessening to himself, and amounted almost to a resignation of the government. He was very willing that the people should look off from him, and gaze on the rising sun. (2.) Though it might appear a perpetual slur upon his family. It would not have been so much his praise if he had thus resigned his honour to a son of his own; but with his own hands first to ordain Eleazar high priest, and then Joshua, one of another tribe, chief ruler, while his own children had no preferment at all, but were left in the rank of common Levites, this was such an instance of self-denial and submission to the will of God as was more his glory than the highest advancement of his family could have been; for it confirms his character as the meekest man upon earth, and faithful to him that appointed him in all his house. This (says the excellent bishop Patrick) shows him to have had a principle which raised him above all other lawgivers, who always took care to establish their families in some share of that greatness which they themselves possessed; but hereby it appeared that Moses acted not from himself, because he acted not for himself.

CHAP. XXVIII.

Now that the people were numbered, orders given for the dividing of the land, and a general of the forces nominated and commissioned, one would have expected that the next chapter should begin the history of the campaign, or at least should give us an account of the ordinances of war; no, it contains the ordinances of worship, and provides that now, as they were on the point of entering Canaan, they should be sure to take their religion along with them, and not forget this, in the prosecution of their wars, ver. 1, 2. The laws are here repeated and summed up concerning the sacrifices that were to be offered, I Daily, ver. 3—8. II. Weekly, ver. 9, 10. III. Monthly, ver. 11—15. IV. Yearly. 1. At the passover, ver. 16—25. 2. At pentecost, ver. 26—31. And the next chapter is concerning the annual solemnities of the seventh month.

AND the LORD spake unto Moses, saying, 2 Command the children of Israel, and say unto them, My offering, *and* my bread for my sacrifices made by fire, *for* a sweet savour unto me, shall ye observe to offer unto me in their due season. 3 And thou shalt say unto them, This *is* the offering made by fire which ye shall offer unto the LORD; two lambs of the first year without spot day by day, *for* a continual burnt offering. 4 The one lamb shalt thou offer in the morning, and the other lamb shalt thou offer at even; 5 And a tenth *part* of an ephah of flour for a meat offering, mingled with the fourth *part* of a hin of beaten oil. 6 *It is* a continual burnt offering, which was ordained in mount Sinai for a sweet savour, a sacrifice made by fire unto the LORD. 7 And the drink offering thereof *shall be* the fourth *part* of a hin for the one lamb: in the holy *place* shalt thou cause the strong wine to be poured unto the LORD *for* a drink offering. 8 And the other lamb shalt thou offer at even: as the meat offering of the morning, and as the drink offering thereof, thou shalt offer *it*, a sacrifice made by fire, of a sweet savour unto the LORD.

Here is, I. A general order given concerning the offerings of the Lord, which were to be brought in their season, *v.* 2. These laws are here given afresh, not because the observance of them was wholly disused during their thirty-eight years' wandering in the wilderness (we cannot think that they were so long without any public worship, but that at least the daily lamb was offered morning and evening, and doubled on the sabbath day; so bishop Patrick conjectures); but that many of the sacrifices were then omitted is plainly intimated, Amos v. 25, quoted by Stephen, Acts vii. 42. *Did you offer unto me sacrifices and offerings in the wilderness forty years, O house of Israel?* It is implied, " No, you did not." But, whether the course of sacrifices had been interrupted or no, God saw fit now to repeat the law of sacrifices, 1. Because this was a new generation of men, that were most of them unborn when the former laws were given; therefore, that they might be left without excuse, they have not only these laws written, to be read to them, but again repeated from God himself, and put into a less compass and a plainer method. 2. Because they were now entering upon war, and might be tempted to think that while they were engaged in that they should be excused from offering sacrifices. *Inter arma silent leges—law is little regarded amidst the clash of arms.* No, says God, *my bread for my sacrifices* even now *shall you observe to offer,* and that *in the due season.* They were peculiarly concerned to keep their peace with God when they were at war with their enemies. In the wilderness they were solitary, and quite separate from all other people, and therefore there they needed not so much their distinguishing badges, nor would their omission of sacrifices be so scandalous as when they came into Canaan, when they mingled with other people. 3. Because possession was now to be given them of the land of promise, that land flowing with milk

and honey, where they would have plenty of all good things. "Now" (says God), "when you are feasting yourselves, forget not to offer the bread of your God." Canaan was given to them upon this condition, that they should *observe God's statutes,* Ps cv. 44, 45.

II. The particular law of the daily sacrifice, a lamb in the morning and a lamb in the evening, which, for the constancy of it as duly as the day came, is called a *continual burnt-offering* (*v.* 3), which intimates that when we are bidden to *pray always, and to pray without ceasing,* it is intended that at least every morning and every evening we offer up our solemn prayers and praises to God. This is said to be *ordained in Mount Sinai* (*v.* 6), when the other laws were given. The institution of it we have, Exod. xxix. 38. Nothing is here added in the repetition of the law, but that the wine to be poured out in the drink-offering is ordered to be *strong wine* (*v.* 7), the richest and most generous and best-bodied wine they could get. Though it was to be poured out upon the altar, and not drunk (they therefore might be ready to think the worst would serve to be so thrown away), yet God requires the strongest, to teach us to serve God with the best we have. The wine must be strong (says Ainsworth) because it was a figure of the blood of Christ, the memorial of which is still left to the church in wine, and of the blood of the martyrs, which was poured out as a drink-offering upon the *sacrifice and service of our faith,* Phil. ii. 17.

9 And on the sabbath day two lambs of the first year without spot, and two tenth deals of flour *for* a meat offering, mingled with oil, and the drink offering thereof: 10 *This is* the burnt offering of every sabbath, beside the continual burnt offering, and his drink offering. 11 And in the beginnings of your months ye shall offer a burnt offering unto the LORD; two young bullocks, and one ram, seven lambs of the first year without spot; 12 And three tenth deals of flour *for* a meat offering, mingled with oil, for one bullock; and two tenth deals of flour *for* a meat offering, mingled with oil, for one ram; 13 And a several tenth deal of flour mingled with oil *for* a meat offering unto one lamb; *for* a burnt offering of a sweet savour, a sacrifice made by fire unto the LORD. 14 And their drink offerings shall be half a hin of wine unto a bullock, and the third *part* of a hin unto a ram, and a fourth

part of a hin unto a lamb: this *is* the burnt offering of every month throughout the months of the year. 15 And one kid of the goats for a sin offering unto the LORD shall be offered, beside the continual burnt offering, and his drink offering.

The new moons and the sabbaths are often spoken of together, as great solemnities in the Jewish church, very comfortable to the saints then, and typical of gospel grace. Now we have here the sacrifices appointed, 1. For the sabbaths. Every sabbath day the offering must be doubled; besides the two lambs offered for the daily burnt-offering, there must be two more offered, one (it is probable) added to the morning sacrifice, and the other to the evening, *v.* 9, 10. This teaches us to double our devotions on sabbath days, for so the duty of the day requires. The sabbath rest is to be observed, in order to a more close application to the sabbath work, which ought to fill up sabbath time. In Ezekiel's temple-service, which points at gospel times, the sabbath offerings were to be six lambs and a ram, with their meat-offerings and drink-offerings (Ezek. xlvi. 4, 5), to intimate not only the continuance, but the advancement, of sabbath sanctification in the days of the Messiah. This is *the burnt-offering of the sabbath in his sabbath,* so it is in the original, *v.* 10. We must do every sabbath day's work in its day, studying to redeem every minute of sabbath time as those that believe it precious; and not thinking to put off one sabbath's work to another, for sufficient to every sabbath is the service thereof. 2. For the new moons. Some suggest that, as the sabbath was kept with an eye to the creation of the world, so the new moons were sanctified with an eye to the divine providence, which *appoints the moon for seasons,* guiding the revolutions of time by its changes, and governing sublunary bodies (as many think) by its influences. Though we observe not any feast of new moons, yet we must not forget to give God the glory of all the precious things put forth by the moon, which he has *established for ever, a faithful witness in heaven,* Ps. lxxxix. 37. The offerings in the new moons were very considerable, two bullocks, a ram, and seven lambs, with the meat-offerings and drink-offerings that were to attend them (*v.* 11, &c.), besides a sin-offering, *v.* 15. For, when we give glory to God by confessing his mercies, we must give glory to him likewise by confessing our own sins; and, when we rejoice in the gifts of common providence, we must make the sacrifice of Christ, that great gift of special grace, the fountain and spring-head of our joy. Some have questioned whether the new moons were to be reckoned among their feasts; but why should they not, when, besides the special

sacrifices which were then to be offered, they rested from servile works (Amos viii. 5), *blew the trumpets (ch.* x. 10), and went to the prophets *to hear the word?* 2 Kings iv. 23. And the worship performed in the new moons is made typical of gospel solemnities, Isa. lxvi. 23.

16 And in the fourteenth day of the first month *is* the passover of the LORD. 17 And in the fifteenth day of this month *is* the feast: seven days shall unleavened bread be eaten. 18 In the first day *shall be* a holy convocation; ye shall do no manner of servile work *therein:* 19 But ye shall offer a sacrifice made by fire *for* a burnt offering unto the LORD; two young bullocks, and one ram, and seven lambs of the first year: they shall be unto you without blemish: 20 And their meat offering *shall be of* flour mingled with oil: three tenth deals shall ye offer for a bullock, and two tenth deals for a ram; 21 A several tenth deal shalt thou offer for every lamb, throughout the seven lambs: 22 And one goat *for* a sin offering, to make an atonement for you. 23 Ye shall offer these beside the burnt offering in the morning, which *is* for a continual burnt offering. 24 After this manner ye shall offer daily, throughout the seven days, the meat of the sacrifice made by fire, of a sweet savour unto the LORD: it shall be offered beside the continual burnt offering, and his drink offering. 25 And on the seventh day ye shall have a holy convocation; ye shall do no servile work. 26 Also in the day of the firstfruits, when ye bring a new meat offering unto the LORD, after your weeks *be out,* ye shall have a holy convocation; ye shall do no servile work: 27 But ye shall offer the burnt offering for a sweet savour unto the LORD; two young bullocks, one ram, seven lambs of the first year; 28 And their meat offering of flour mingled with oil, three tenth deals unto one bullock, two tenth deals unto one ram. 29 A several tenth deal unto one lamb, throughout the seven lambs; 30 *And* one kid of the goats, to make an atonement for you. 31 Ye shall offer *them* beside the con-

tinual burnt offering, and his meat offering, (they shall be unto you without blemish) and their drink offerings.

Here is, I. The appointment of the passover sacrifices ; not that which was the chief, the paschal lamb (sufficient instructions had formerly been given concerning that), but those which were to be offered upon the seven days of unleavened bread, which followed it, *v.* 17—25. The first and last of those seven days were to be sanctified as sabbaths, by a holy rest and a holy convocation, and on each of the seven days they were to be liberal in their sacrifices, in token of their great and constant thankfulness for their deliverance out of Egypt: *Two bullocks, a ram, and seven lambs.* A gospel conversation, in gratitude for *Christ our passover* who was sacrificed, is called the *keeping of this feast* (1 Cor. v. 8) ; for it is not enough that we purge out the *leavened bread* of malice and wickedness, but we must *offer the bread of our God, even the sacrifice of praise, continually,* and continue herein unto the end. 2. The sacrifices are likewise appointed which were to be offered at the feast of pentecost, here called the *day of the first-fruits, v.* 26. In the feast of unleavened bread they offered a *sheaf of their first-fruits* of barley (which with them was first ripe) to the priest (Lev. xxiii. 10), as an introduction to the harvest ; but now, about seven weeks after, they were to bring a *new meat-offering to the Lord,* at the end of harvest, in thankfulness to God, who had not only given, *but preserved to their use, the kindly fruits of the earth, so as that in due time they did enjoy them.* It was at this feast that *the Spirit was poured out* (Acts ii. 1, &c.), and thousands were converted by the preaching of the apostles, and were presented to Christ, to be *a kind of first-fruits of his creatures.* The sacrifice that was to be offered with the loaves of the first-fruits was appointed, Lev. xxiii. 18. But over and above, besides that and besides the daily offerings, they were to offer *two bullocks, one ram, and seven lambs, with a kid for a sin-offering, v.* 27—30. When God sows plentifully upon us he expects to reap accordingly from us. Bishop Patrick observes that no *peace-offerings* are appointed in this chapter, which were chiefly for the benefit of the offerers, and therefore in them they were left more to themselves ; but *burnt-offerings* were purely for the honour of God, were confessions of his dominion, and typified evangelical piety and devotion, by which the soul is wholly offered up to God in the flames of holy love ; and *sin-offerings* were typical of Christ's sacrifice of himself, *by which we and our services are perfected and sanctified.*

CHAP. XXIX.

This chapter appoints the offerings that were to be made by fire unto the Lord in the three great solemnities of the seventh month. I. In the feast of trumpets on the first day of that month, ver. 1—6. II. In the day of atonement on the tenth day, ver. 7—11. III. In the feast of tabernacles on the fifteenth day

and the seven days following, ver. 12—38. And then the conclusion of these ordinances, ver. 39, 40.

AND in the seventh month, on the first *day* of the month, ye shall have a holy convocation ; ye shall do no servile work : it is a day of blowing the trumpets unto you. 2 And ye shall offer a burnt offering for a sweet savour unto the LORD ; one young bullock, one ram, *and* seven lambs of the first year without blemish : 3 And their meat offering *shall be of* flour mingled with oil, three tenth deals for a bullock, *and* two tenth deals for a ram, 4 And one tenth deal for one lamb, throughout the seven lambs : 5 And one kid of the goats *for* a sin offering, to make an atonement for you : 6 Beside the burnt offering of the month, and his meat offering, and the daily burnt offering, and his meat offering, and their drink offerings, according unto their manner, for a sweet savour, a sacrifice made by fire unto the LORD. 7 And ye shall have on the tenth *day* of this seventh month a holy convocation ; and ye shall afflict your souls : ye shall not do any work *therein :* 8 But ye shall offer a burnt offering unto the LORD *for* a sweet savour ; one young bullock, one ram, *and* seven lambs of the first year ; they shall be unto you without blemish : 9 And their meat offering *shall be of* flour mingled with oil, three tenth deals to a bullock, *and* two tenth deals to one ram, 10 A several tenth deal for one lamb, throughout the seven lambs : 11 One kid of the goats *for* a sin offering ; beside the sin offering of atonement, and the continual burnt offering, and the meat offering of it, and their drink offerings.

There were more sacred solemnities in the seventh month than in any other month of the year, not only because it had been the first month till the deliverance of Israel out of Egypt (which, falling in the month Abib, occasioned that to be thenceforth made the *beginning of the months* in all ecclesiastical computations), but because still it continued the first month in the civil reckonings of the jubilees and years of release, and also because it was the time of vacation between harvest and seedtime, when they had most leisure to attend the sanctuary, which intimates that, though God will dispense with sacrifices in consideration of works of necessity and mercy, yet the more leisure we have from the pressing occasions of this life the more time we should spend in the immediate service of God. 1. We have here the appointment of the sacrifices that were to be offered on the first day of the month, the day of *blowing the trumpets*, which was a preparative for the two great solemnities of holy mourning on the day of atonement and of holy joy in the feast of tabernacles. The intention of divine institutions is well answered when one religious service helps to fit us for another and all for heaven. The *blowing of the trumpets* was appointed, Lev. xxiii. 24. Here the people are directed what sacrifices to offer on that day, of which there was not then any mention made. Note, Those who would know the mind of God in the scripture must compare one part of the scripture with another, and put those parts together that have reference to the same thing, for the latter discoveries of divine light explain what was dark and supply what was defective in the former, *that the man of God may be perfect.* The sacrifices then to be offered are particularly ordered here (*v.* 2—6), and care taken that these should not supersede the daily oblation and that of the new moon. It is hereby intimated that we must not seek occasions to abate our zeal in God's service, nor be glad of an excuse to omit a good duty, but rather rejoice in an opportunity of accumulating and doing more than ordinary in religion. If we perform family-worship, we must not think that this will excuse us from our secret devotions; nor that on the days we go to church we need not worship God alone and with our families; but we should *always abound in the work of the Lord.* 2. On the *day of atonement.* Besides all the services of that day, which we had the institution of, Lev. xvi., and which, one would think, required trouble and charge enough, here are burnt-offerings ordered to be offered, *v.* 8—10. For in our faith and repentance, those two great gospel graces which were signified by that day's performances, we must have an eye to the glory and honour of God, which was purely intended in the burnt-offerings; there was likewise to be a *kid of the goats for a sin-offering, besides the great sin-offering of atonement* (*v.* 11), which intimates that there are so many defects and faults, even in the exercises and expressions of our repentance, that we have need of an interest in a sacrifice to expiate the guilt even of that part of our holy things. Though we must not repent that we have repented, yet we must repent that we have not repented better. It likewise intimated the imperfection of the legal sacrifices, and their insufficiency to take away sin, that on the very day the *sin-offering of atonement* was offered, yet there must be another sin-offering. But *what the law could not do, in that it was weak,* that Christ has done.

12 And on the fifteenth day of the seventh month ye shall have a holy convocation; ye shall do no servile work, and ye shall keep a feast unto the LORD seven days: 13 And ye shall offer a burnt offering, a sacrifice made by fire, of a sweet savour unto the LORD; thirteen young bullocks, two rams, *and* fourteen lambs of the first year; they shall be without blemish: 14 And their meat offering *shall be of* flour mingled with oil, three tenth deals unto every bullock of the thirteen bullocks, two tenth deals to each ram of the two rams, 15 And a several tenth deal to each lamb of the fourteen lambs: 16 And one kid of the goats *for* a sin offering; beside the continual burnt offering, his meat offering, and his drink offering. 17 And on the second day *ye shall offer* twelve young bullocks, two rams, fourteen lambs of the first year without spot: 18 And their meat offering and their drink offerings for the bullocks, for the rams, and for the lambs, *shall be* according to their number, after the manner: 19 And one kid of the goats *for* a sin offering; beside the continual burnt offering, and the meat offering thereof, and their drink offerings. 20 And on the third day eleven bullocks, two rams, fourteen lambs of the first year without blemish; 21 And their meat offering and their drink offerings for the bullocks, for the rams, and for the lambs, *shall be* according to their number, after the manner: 22 And one goat *for* a sin offering; beside the continual burnt offering, and his meat offering, and his drink offering. 23 And on the fourth day ten bullocks, two rams, *and* fourteen lambs of the first year without blemish: 24 Their meat offering and their drink offerings for the bullocks, for the rams, and for the lambs, *shall be* according to their number, after the manner: 25 And one kid of the goats *for* a sin offering; beside the continual burnt offering, his meat offering, and his drink offering. 26 And on the fifth day nine bullocks, two rams, *and* fourteen lambs of the first year without spot: 27 And their

meat offering and their drink offerings for the bullocks, for the rams, and for the lambs, *shall be* according to their number, after the manner : 28 And one goat *for* a sin offering ; beside the continual burnt offering, and his meat offering, and his drink offering. 29 And on the sixth day eight bullocks, two rams, *and* fourteen lambs of the first year without blemish : 30 And their meat offering and their drink offerings for the bullocks, for the rams, and for the lambs, *shall be* according to their number, after the manner : 31 And one goat *for* a sin offering ; beside the continual burnt offering, his meat offering, and his drink offering. 32 And on the seventh day seven bullocks, two rams, *and* fourteen lambs of the first year without blemish : 33 And their meat offering, and their drink offerings for the bullocks, for the rams, and for the lambs, *shall be* according to their number, after the manner : 34 And one goat *for* a sin offering ; beside the continual burnt offering, his meat offering, and his drink offering. 35 On the eighth day ye shall have a solemn assembly : ye shall do no servile work *therein :* 36 But ye shall offer a burnt offering, a sacrifice made by fire, of a sweet savour unto the LORD : one bullock, one ram, seven lambs of the first year without blemish : 37 Their meat offering and their drink offerings for the bullock, for the ram, and for the lambs, *shall be* according to their number, after the manner : 38 And one goat *for* a sin offering ; beside the continual burnt offering, and his meat offering, and his drink offering. 39 These *things* ye shall do unto the LORD in your set feasts, beside your vows, and your freewill offerings, for your burnt offerings, and for your meat offerings, and for your drink offerings, and for your peace offerings. 40 And Moses told the children of Israel according to all that the LORD commanded Moses.

Soon after the day of atonement, that day in which men were to afflict their souls, followed the feast of the tabernacles, in which they were to rejoice before the Lord ; for

702

those that *sow in tears* shall soon *reap in joy.* To the former laws about this feast, which we had, Lev. xxiii. 34, &c., here are added directions about the *offerings made by fire,* which they were to offer unto the Lord during the *seven days of that feast,* Lev. xxiii. 36. Observe here, 1. Their days of rejoicing were to be days of sacrifices. A disposition to be cheerful does us no harm, 'nor is any bad symptom, when it is so far from unfitting us for the duties of God's immediate service that it encourages and enlarges our hearts in them. 2. All the days of their dwelling in booths they must offer sacrifices. While we are here in a tabernacle-state, it is our interest as well as duty constantly to keep up communion with God ; nor will the unsettledness of our outward condition excuse us in our neglect of the duties of God's worship. 3. The sacrifices for each of the seven days, though differing in nothing but the number of the bullocks, are severally and particularly appointed, which yet is no vain repetition ; for God would thus teach them to be very exact in those observances, and to keep an eye of faith fixed upon the institution in every day's work. It likewise intimates that the repetition of the same services, if performed with an upright heart, and with a continued fire of pious and devout affection, is no weariness to God, and therefore we ought not to snuff at it, or to say, *Behold, what a weariness it is to us !* 4. The number of the bullocks (which were the most costly part of the sacrifice) decreased every day. On the first day of the feast they were to offer thirteen, on the second day but twelve, on the third day eleven, &c. So that on the seventh they offered seven ; and the last day, though it was the great day of the feast, and celebrated with a holy convocation, yet they were to offer but one bullock ; and, whereas on all the other days they offered two rams and fourteen lambs, on this they offered but one ram and seven lambs. Such was the will of the Law-maker, and that is reason enough for the law. Some suggest that God herein considered the infirmity of the flesh, which is apt to grudge the charge and expense of religion ; it is therefore ordered to grow less and less, that they might not complain as if God had *made them to serve with an offering,* Isa. xliii. 23. Or it is hereby intimated to them that the legal dispensation should wax old, and vanish away at last ; and the multitude of their sacrifices should end in one great sacrifice, infinitely more worthy than all of them. It was on the last day of the feast, after all these sacrifices had been offered, that our Lord Jesus stood and cried to those who still thirsted after righteousness (being sensible of the insufficiency of these sacrifices to justify them) *to come unto him and drink,* John vii. 37. 5. The meat-offerings and drink-offerings attended all the sacrifices, *according to their number, after the manner.* Be there ever so much flesh, it is no feast without bread and drink, therefore these must never be omitted at God's altar, which was his table. We must not think that doing much in religion will be accepted if we do not do it well, and after the manner that God has appointed. 6. Every day there must be a sin-offering presented, as we observed in the other feasts. Our burnt-offerings of praise cannot be accepted of God unless we have an interest in the great sacrifice of propitiation which Christ offered when for us he made himself a sin-offering. 7. Even when all these sacrifices were offered, yet the continual burnt-offering must not be omitted either morning or evening, but each day this must be offered first in the morning and last in the evening. No extraordinary services should jostle out our stated devotions. 8. Though all these sacrifices were required to be presented by the body of the congregation, at the common charge, yet, besides these, particular persons were to glorify God with their vows and their free-will offerings, *v.* 39. When God commanded that this *they must do,* he left room for the generosity of their devotion, a great deal more they *might do,* not inventing other worships, but abounding in these, as 2 Chron. xxx. 23, 24. Large directions had been given in Leviticus concerning the offerings of all sorts that should be brought by particular persons according to the providences of God concerning them and the graces of God in them. Though every Israelite had an interest in these common sacrifices, yet he must not think that these will serve instead of his vows and his free-will offerings. Thus our ministers' praying with us and for us will not excuse us from praying for ourselves.

CHAP. XXX.

In this chapter we have a law concerning vows, which had been mentioned in the close of the foregoing chapter. I. Here is a general rule laid down that all vows must be carefully performed, ver. 1, 2. II. Some particular exceptions to this rule. 1. That the vows of daughters should not be binding unless allowed by the father, ver. 3—5. Nor, 2. The vows of wives unless allowed by the husband, &c.

AND Moses spake unto the heads of the tribes concerning the children of Israel, saying, This *is* the thing which the LORD hath commanded. 2 If a man vow a vow unto the LORD, or swear an oath to bind his soul with a bond: he shall not break his word, he shall do according to all that proceedeth out of his mouth.

This law was delivered to the heads of the tribes that they might instruct those who were under their charge, explain the law to them, give them necessary cautions, and call them to account, if there were occasion, for the breach of their vows. Perhaps the heads of the tribes had, upon some emergency of this kind, consulted Moses, and desired by him to know the mind of God, and here they are told it: *This is the thing which the Lord has commanded* concerning vows, and it is a command still in force.

1. The case supposed is that a person vows

a vow unto the Lord, making God a party to the promise, and designing his honour and glory in it. The matter of the vow is supposed to be something lawful: no man can be by his own promise bound to do that which he is already by the divine precept prohibited from doing. Yet it is supposed to be something which, in such and such measures and degrees, was not a necessary duty antecedent to the vow. A person might vow to bring such and such sacrifices at certain times, to give such a sum or such a proportion in alms, to forbear such meats and drinks which the law allowed, to fast and afflict the soul (which is specified *v.* 13) at other times besides the day of atonement. And many similar vows might be made in an extraordinary heat of holy zeal, in humiliation for some sin committed or for the prevention of sin, in the pursuit of some mercy desired or in gratitude for some mercy received. It is of great use to make such vows as these, provided they be made in sincerity and with due caution. Vows (say the Jewish doctors) are *the hedge of separation,* that is, a fence to religion. He that vows is here said to *bind his soul with a bond.* It is a vow to God, who is a Spirit, and to him the soul, with all its powers, must be bound. A promise to man is a bond upon the estate, but a promise to God is a bond upon the soul. Our sacramental vows, by which we are bound to no more than what was before our duty, and which neither father nor husband can disannul, are bonds upon the soul, and by them we must feel ourselves bound out from all sin and bound up to the whole will of God. Our occasional vows concerning that which before was *in our own power* (Acts v. 4), when they are made, are bonds upon the soul likewise. 2. The command given is that these vows be conscientiously performed: *He shall not break his word,* though afterwards he may change his mind, but he shall do according to what he has said. *Margin, He shall not profane his word.* Vowing is an ordinance of God; if we vow in hypocrisy we profane that ordinance: it is plainly determined, *Better not vow than vow and not pay,* Eccl. v. 5. *Be not deceived, God is not mocked.* His promises to us are *yea and amen,* let not ours to him be *yea and nay.*

3 If a woman also vow a vow unto the LORD, and bind *herself* by a bond, *being* in her father's house in her youth; 4 And her father hear her vow, and her bond wherewith she hath bound her soul, and her father shall hold his peace at her: then all her vows shall stand, and every bond wherewith she hath bound her soul shall stand. 5 But if her father disallow her in the day that he heareth;

not any of her vows, or of her bonds wherewith she hath bound her soul, shall stand: and the LORD shall forgive her because her father disallowed her. 6 And if she had at all a husband, when she vowed, or uttered aught out of her lips, wherewith she bound her soul; 7 And her husband heard *it*, and held his peace at her in the day that he heard *it:* then her vows shall stand, and her bonds wherewith she bound her soul shall stand. 8 But if her husband disallowed her on the day that he heard *it;* then he shall make her vow which she vowed, and that which she uttered with her lips, wherewith she bound her soul, of none effect: and the LORD shall forgive her. 9 But every vow of a widow, and of her that is divorced, wherewith they have bound their souls, shall stand against her. 10 And if she vowed in her husband's house, or bound her soul by a bond with an oath; 11 And her husband heard *it*, and held his peace at her, *and* disallowed her not: then all her vows shall stand, and every bond wherewith she bound her soul shall stand. 12 But if her husband hath utterly made them void on the day he heard *them; then* whatsoever proceeded out of her lips concerning her vows, or concerning the bond of her soul, shall not stand: her husband hath made them void; and the LORD shall forgive her. 13 Every vow, and every binding oath to afflict the soul, her husband may establish it, or her husband may make it void. 14 But if her husband altogether hold his peace at her from day to day; then he establisheth all her vows, or all her bonds, which *are* upon her: he confirmeth them, because he held his peace at her in the day that he heard *them*. 15 But if he shall any ways make them void after that he hath heard *them;* then he shall bear her iniquity. 16 These *are* the statutes, which the LORD commanded Moses, between a man and his wife, between the father and his daughter, *being yet* in her youth in her father's house.

It is here taken for granted that all such persons as are *sui juris—at their own disposal,* and are likewise of sound understanding and memory, are bound to perform whatever they vow that is lawful and possible; but, if the person vowing be under the dominion and at the disposal of another, the case is different. Two cases much alike are here put and determined:—

I. The case of a daughter in her father's house: and some think, probably enough, that it extends to a son likewise, while he is at home with his father, and under tutors and governors. Whether the exception may thus be stretched I cannot say. *Non est distinguendum, ubi lex non distinguit—We are not allowed to make distinctions which the law does not.* The rule is general, If a man vow, he must pay. But for a daughter it is express: her vow is nugatory or in suspense till her father knows it, and (it is supposed) knows it from her; for, when it comes to his knowledge, it is in his power either to ratify or nullify it. But in favour of the vow, 1. Even his silence shall suffice to ratify it: If he *hold his peace, her vows shall stand, v.* 4. *Qui tacet, consentire videtur—Silence gives consent.* Hereby he allows his daughter the liberty she has assumed, and, as long as he says nothing against her vow, she shall be bound by it. But, 2. His protestation against it shall perfectly disannul it, because it is possible that such vow may be prejudicial to the affairs of the family, break the father's measures, perplex the provision made for his table if the vow related to meats, or lessen the provision made for his children if the vow would be more expensive than his estate would bear; however, it was certain that it was an infringement of his authority over his child, and therefore, if he disallow it, she is discharged, and *the Lord shall forgive her,* that is, she shall not be charged with the guilt of violating her vow; she showed her good-will in making the vow, and, if her intentions therein were sincere, she shall be accepted, and to obey her father shall be accounted better than sacrifice. This shows how great a deference children owe to their parents, and how much they ought to honour them and be obedient to them. It is for the interest of the public that the paternal authority be supported; for, when children are countenanced in their disobedience to their parents (as they were by the tradition of the elders, Matt. xv. 5, 6), they soon become in other things *children of Belial.* If this law be not to be extended to children's marrying without their parents' consent so far as to put it in parents' power to annul the marriage and dissolve the obligation (as some have thought it does), yet certainly it proves the sinfulness of it, and obliges the children that have thus done foolishly to repent and humble themselves before God and their parents.

II. The case of a wife is much the same. As for a woman that is a widow or divorced, she has neither father nor husband to control her, so that, whatever vows she binds her soul with, they shall *stand against her* (v. 9), it is at her peril if she run back ; but a wife, who has nothing that she can strictly call her own, but with her husband's allowance, cannot, without that, make any such vow.　1. The law is plain in case of a wife that continues so long after the vow. If her husband allow her vow, though only by silence, it must stand, v. 6, 7.　If he disallow it, since her obligation to that which she had vowed arose purely from her own act, and not from any prior command of God, her obligation to her husband shall take place of it, for to him she ought to be in subjection *as unto the Lord;* and now it is so far from being her duty to fulfil her vow that it would be her sin to disobey her husband, whose consent perhaps she ought to have asked before she made the vow; therefore she needs *forgiveness, v.* 8.　2. The law is the same in case of a wife that soon after becomes a widow, or is put away.　Though, if she return to her father's house, she does not therefore so come again under his authority as that he has power to disannul her vows (v. 9), yet if the vow was made while she was in the house of her husband, and her husband disallowed it, it was made void and of no effect for ever, and she does not return under the law of her vow when she is loosed from the law of her husband.　This seems to be the distinct meaning of v. 10—14, which otherwise would be but a repetition of v. 6—8.　But it is added (v. 15) that, if the husband make void the vows of his wife, he shall *bear her iniquity ;* that is, if the thing she had vowed was really good, for the honour of God and the prosperity of her own soul, and the husband disallowed it out of covetousness, or humour, or to show his authority, though she be discharged from the obligation of her vow, yet he will have a great deal to answer for.　Now here it is very observable how carefully the divine law consults the good order of families, and preserves the power of superior relations, and the duty and reverence of inferiors. It is fit that every man should *bear rule in his own house,* and have his wife and children in subjection with all gravity ; and rather than this great rule should be broken, or any encouragement given to inferior relations to break those bonds asunder, God himself would quit his right, and release the obligation even of a solemn vow ; so much does religion strengthen the ties of all relations, and secure the welfare of all societies, that in it the *families of the earth are blessed.*

CHAP. XXXI.

This chapter belongs to " the book of the wars of the Lord," in which it is probable it was inserted.　It is the history of a holy war, a war with Midian.　Here is, I. A divine command for the war, ver. 1, 2.　II. The undertaking of the war, ver. 3—6.　III. The glorious success of it, ver. 7—12.　IV. Their triumphant return from the war. 1. The respect Moses paid to the soldiers, ver. 13.　2. The rebuke he gave them for sparing the women, ver. 14—18.　3. The directions he gave them for the purifying of themselves and their effects, ver. 19—24.　4. The distribution of the spoil they had taken, one half to the soldiers, the other to

the congregation, and a tribute to the Lord out of each, ver. 25—47.　5. The free-will offering of the officers, ver. 48, &c.

ND the Lord spake unto Moses, saying,　2 Avenge the children of Israel of the Midianites : afterward shalt thou be gathered unto thy people.　3 And Moses spake unto the people, saying, Arm some of yourselves unto the war, and let them go against the Midianites, and avenge the Lord of Midian.　4 Of every tribe a thousand, throughout all the tribes of Israel, shall ye send to the war.　5 So there were delivered out of the thousands of Israel, a thousand of *every* tribe, twelve thousand armed for war.　6 And Moses sent them to the war, a thousand of *every* tribe, them and Phinehas the son of Eleazar the priest, to the war, with the holy instruments, and the trumpets to blow in his hand.

Here, I. The Lord of hosts gives orders to Moses to make war upon the Midianites, and his commission no doubt justified this war, though it will not serve to justify the like without such commission.　The Midianites were the posterity of Abraham by Keturah, Gen. xxv. 2.　Some of them settled south of Canaan, among whom Jethro lived, and they retained the worship of the true God; but these were settled east of Canaan, and had fallen into idolatry, neighbours to, and in confederacy with, the Moabites. Their land was not designed to be given to Israel, nor would Israel have meddled with them if they had not made themselves obnoxious to their resentment by sending their bad women among them to draw them to whoredom and idolatry.　This was the provocation, this was the quarrel.　For this (says God) *avenge Israel of the Midianites, v.* 2.　1. God would have the Midianites chastised, an inroad made upon that part of their country which lay next the camp of Israel, and which was probably more concerned in that mischief than the Moabites, who therefore were let alone.　God will have us to reckon those our worst enemies that draw us to sin, and to avoid them ; and since *every man is tempted when he is drawn aside of his own lusts,* and these are the Midianites which ensnare us with their wiles, on them we should avenge ourselves, not only make no league with them, but make war upon them by living a life of mortification.　God had taken vengeance on his own people for yielding to the Midianites' temptations; now the Midianites, that gave the temptation, must be reckoned with, for *the deceived and the deceiver are his* (Job xii. 16), both accountable to his tribunal; and, though *judgment begin at the house of* God, it shall not end there, 1 Pet. iv. 17.　There is a day coming when vengeance will be taken on those that have introduced errors and corruptions into the church, and the devil that deceived men will be *cast into the lake of fire.* Israel's quarrel with Amalek, that fought against them, was not avenged till long after: but their quarrel with Midian, that debauched them, was speedily avenged, for they were looked upon as much the more dangerous and malicious enemies　2. God would have it done by Moses, in his life-time, that he who had so deeply resented that injury might have the satisfaction of seeing it avenged.　" See this execution done upon the enemies of God and Israel, and *afterwards thou shalt be gathered to thy people."* This was the only piece of service of this kind that Moses must further do, and then he has accomplished, as a hireling, his day, and shall have his *quietus—enter into rest :* hitherto his usefulness must come, and no further ; the wars of Canaan must be carried on by another hand.　Note, God sometimes removes useful men when we think they can ill be spared ; but this ought to satisfy us, that they are never removed till they have done the work which was appointed them.

II. Moses gives orders to the people to prepare for this expedition, *v.* 3.　He would not have the whole body of the camp to stir, but they must *arm some of themselves to the war,* such as were either most fit or most forward, and *avenge the Lord of Midian.* God said, *Avenge Israel ;* Moses says, *Avenge the Lord ;* for the interests of God and Israel are united, and the cause of both is one and the same.　And if God, in what he does, shows himself jealous for the honour of Israel, surely Israel, in what they do, ought to show themselves jealous for the glory of God. Then only we can justify the avenging of ourselves when it is the vengeance of the Lord that we engage in.　Nay, for this reason we are forbidden to avenge ourselves, because God has said, *Vengeance is mine, I will repay.*

III. A detachment is drawn out accordingly for this service, 1000 *out of every tribe,* 12,000 in all, a small number in comparison with what they could have sent, and it is probable small in comparison with the number of the enemies they were sent against. But God would teach them that it is all one to him *to save by many or by few,* 1 Sam. xiv. 6.

IV. Phinehas the son of Eleazar is sent along with them.　It is strange that no mention is made of Joshua in this great action. If he was general of these forces, why do we not find him leading them out ? If he tarried at home, why do we not find him meeting them with Moses at their return ?　It is probable, each tribe having a captain of its own thousand, there was no general, but they proceeded in the order of their march through the wilderness, Judah first, and the rest in their posts, under the command of

their respective captains, spoken of *v.* 48. But, the war being a holy war, Phinehas was their common head, not to supply the place of a general, but, by the oracle of God, to determine the resolves of their councils of war, in which the captains of thousands would all acquiesce, and according to which they would act in conjunction. He therefore took with him the holy instruments or vessels, probably the breast-plate of judgment, by which God might be consulted in any emergency.　Though he was not yet the high priest, yet he might be delegated *pro hac vice —for this particular occasion,* to bear the urim and thummjm, as 1 Sam xxiii. 6.　And there was a particular reason for sending Phinehas to preside in this expedition ; he had already signalized himself for his zeal against the Midianites and their cursed arts to ensnare Israel when he slew Cozbi, a daughter of a chief house in Midian, for her impudence in the matter of Peor, *ch.* xxv. 15. He that had so well used the sword of justice against a particular criminal was best qualified to guide the sword of war against the whole nation.　*Thou hast been faithful over a few things, I will make thee ruler over many things.*

7 And they warred against the Midianites, as the LORD commanded Moses ; and they slew all the males. 8 And they slew the kings of Midian, beside the rest of them that were slain ; *namely*, Evi, and Rekem, and Zur, and Hur, and Reba, five kings of Midian : Balaam also the son of Beor they slew with the sword. 9 And the children of Israel took *all* the women of Midian captives, and their little ones, and took the spoil of all their cattle, and all their flocks, and all their goods.　10 And they burnt all their cities wherein they dwelt, and all their goodly castles, with fire.　11 And they took all the spoil, and all the prey, *both* of men and of beasts.　12 And they brought the captives, and the prey, and the spoil, unto Moses, and Eleazar the priest, and unto the congregation of the children of Israel, unto the camp at the plaiṇs of Moab, which *are* by Jordan *near* Jericho.

Here is, 1. The descent which this little army of Israelites made, under the divine commission, conduct, and command, upon the country of Midian. They *warred against the Midianites.*　It is very probable that they first published their manifesto, showing the reasons of the war, and requiring them to give up the ringleaders of the mischief to justice ; for such afterwards was the *law*

(Deut. xx. 10), and such the *practice*, Judg. xx. 12, 13. But the Midianites justifying what they had done, and standing by those that had done it, the Israelites attacked them with fire and sword, and all the pious fury with which their zeal for God and their people inspired them. 2. The execution (the military execution) they did in this descent. (1.) They *slew all the males* (v. 7), that is, all they met with as far as they went; they put them all to the sword, and gave no quarter. But that they did not slay all the males of the nation is certain, for we find the Midianites a powerful and formidable enemy to Israel in the days of Gideon; and they were the Midianites of this country, for they are reckoned with the *children of the east*, Judg. vi. 3. (2.) They *slew the kings of Midian*, the same that are called *elders of Midian* (ch. xxii. 4), and *dukes of Sihon*, Josh. xiii. 21. Five of these princes are here named, one of whom is *Zur*, probably the same Zur whose daughter Cosbi was, *ch.* xxv. 15. (3.) They slew Balaam. Many conjectures there are as to what brought Balaam among the Midianites at this time; it is probable that the Midianites, having intelligence of the march of this army of Israelites against them, hired Balaam to come and assist them with his enchantments, that if he could not prevail to act offensively in their favour, by cursing the armies of Israel, yet he might act defensively, by blessing the country of Midian. Whatever was the occasion of his being there, God's overruling providence brought him thither, and there his just vengeance found him. Had he himself believed what he said of the happy state of Israel, he would not have herded thus with the enemies of Israel; but justly does he die the death of the wicked (though he pretended to desire that of the righteous), and go *down slain to the pit with the uncircumcised*, who rebelled thus against the convictions of his own conscience. The Midianites' wiles were Balaam's projects, it was therefore just that he should perish with them, Hos. iv. 5. Now was *his* folly made manifest to all men, who foretold the fate of others, but foresaw not his own. (4.) They took all the *women and children captives, v.* 9. (5.) They *burnt their cities and goodly castles* (v. 10), not designing to inhabit them themselves (that country was out of their line), but they thus prevented those who had made their escape from sheltering themselves in their own country and settling there again. Some understand it of their idol-temples; it was fit that they should share in this vengeance. (6.) They plundered the country, and carried off all the cattle and valuable goods, and so returned to the camp of Israel laden with a very rich booty, *v.* 9, 11, 12. Thus (as when they came out of Egypt) they were enriched with the spoils of their enemies, and furnished with stock for the good land into which God was bringing them.

13 And Moses, and Eleazar the priest, and all the princes of the congregation, went forth to meet them without the camp. 14 And Moses was wroth with the officers of the host, *with* the captains over thousands, and captains over hundreds, which came from the battle. 15 And Moses said unto them, Have ye saved all the women alive? 16 Behold, these caused the children of Israel, through the counsel of Balaam, to commit trespass against the Lord in the matter of Peor, and there was a plague among the congregation of the Lord. 17 Now therefore kill every male among the little ones, and kill every woman that hath known man by lying with him. 18 But all the women children, that have not known a man by lying with him, keep alive for yourselves. 19 And do ye abide without the camp seven days: whosoever hath killed any person, and whosoever hath touched any slain, purify *both* yourselves and your captives on the third day, and on the seventh day. 20 And purify all *your* raiment, and all that is made of skins, and all work of goats' *hair*, and all things made of wood. 21 And Eleazar the priest said unto the men of war which went to the battle, This *is* the ordinance of the law which the Lord commanded Moses; 22 Only the gold, and the silver, the brass, the iron, the tin, and the lead, 23 Every thing that may abide the fire, ye shall make *it* go through the fire, and it shall be clean: nevertheless it shall be purified with the water of separation: and all that abideth not the fire ye shall make go through the water. 24 And ye shall wash your clothes on the seventh day, and ye shall be clean, and afterward ye shall come into the camp.

We have here the triumphant return of the army of Israel from the war with Midian, and here,

I. They were met with great respect, *v.* 13. Moses himself, notwithstanding his age and gravity, walked out of the camp to congratulate them on their victory, and to grace the solemnity of their triumphs. Public successes should be publicly acknowledged, to the glory of God, and the encouragement of those that have jeoparded their lives in their country's cause.

II. They were severely reproved for saving the women alive. It is very probable that Moses had commanded them to kill the women, at least this was implied in the general order to avenge Israel of the Midianites; the execution having reference to that crime, their drawing them in to the worship of Peor, it was easy to conclude that the women, who were the principal criminals, must not be spared. What! says Moses, *have you saved the women alive? v.* 15. He was moved with a holy indignation at the sight of them. *These were those that caused the children of Israel to commit this trespass;* and therefore, 1. It is just that they should die. The law in case of whoredom was, *The adulterer and adulteress shall surely be put to death.* God had put to death the adulterers of Israel by the plague, and now it was fit that the adulteresses of Midian, especially since they had been the tempters, should be put to death by the sword. 2. "It is dangerous to let them live; they will be still tempting the Israelites to uncleanness, and so your captives will be your conquerors and a second time your destroyers." Severe orders are therefore given that all the grown women should be slain in cold blood, and only the female children spared.

III. They were obliged to purify themselves, according to the ceremony of the law, and to abide without the camp seven days, till their purification was accomplished. For, 1. They had imbrued their hands in blood, by which, though they had not contracted any moral guilt, the war being just and lawful, yet they were brought under a ceremonial uncleanness, which rendered them unfit to come near the tabernacle till they were purified. Thus God would preserve in their minds a dread and detestation of murder. David must not build the temple because he had been a *man of war, and had shed blood,* 1 Chron. xxviii. 3. 2. They could not but have touched dead bodies, by which they were polluted, and that required they should be purified with the water of separation, *v.* 19, 20, 24.

IV. They must likewise purify the spoil they had taken, the captives (*v.* 19) and all the goods, *v.* 21—23. What would bear the fire must pass through the fire, and what would not must be washed with water. These things had been used by Midianites, and, having now come into the possession of Israelites, it was fit that they should be sanctified to the service of that holy nation and the honour of their holy God. To us now every thing is sanctified by the word and prayer, if we are sanctified by the Spirit, who is compared both to fire and water. *To the pure all things are pure.*

25 And the LORD spake unto Moses, saying, 26 Take the sum of the

708

prey that was taken, *both* of man and of beast, thou, and Eleazar the priest, and the chief fathers of the congregation: 27 And divide the prey into two parts; between them that took the war upon them, who went out to battle, and between all the congregation: 28 And levy a tribute unto the LORD of the men of war which went out to battle: one soul of five hundred, *both* of the persons, and of the beeves, and of the asses, and of the sheep: 29 Take *it* of their half, and give *it* unto Eleazar the priest, *for* a heave offering of the LORD. 30 And of the children of Israel's half, thou shalt take one portion of fifty, of the persons, of the beeves, of the asses, and of the flocks, of all manner of beasts, and give them unto the Levites, which keep the charge of the tabernacle of the LORD. 31 And Moses and Eleazar the priest did as the LORD commanded Moses. 32 And the booty, *being* the rest of the prey which the men of war had caught, was six hundred thousand and seventy thousand and five thousand sheep. 33 And threescore and twelve thousand beeves, 34 And threescore and one thousand asses, 35 And thirty and two thousand persons in all, of women that had not known man by lying with him. 36 And the half, *which was* the portion of them that went out to war, was in number three hundred thousand and seven and thirty thousand and five hundred sheep: 37 And the LORD's tribute of the sheep was six hundred and threescore and fifteen, 38 And the beeves *were* thirty and six thousand; of which the LORD's tribute *was* threescore and twelve. 39 And the asses *were* thirty thousand and five hundred; of which the LORD's tribute *was* threescore and one. 40 And the persons *were* sixteen thousand; of which the LORD's tribute *was* thirty and two persons. 41 And Moses gave the tribute, *which was* the LORD's heave offering, unto Eleazar the priest, as the LORD commanded Moses. 42 And of the children of Israel's half, which Moses divided from the men that warred, 43

(Now the half *that pertained unto* the congregation was three hundred thousand and thirty thousand *and* seven thousand and five hundred sheep, 44 And thirty and six thousand beeves, 45 And thirty thousand asses and five hundred, 46 And sixteen thousand persons ;) 47 Even of the children of Israel's half, Moses took one portion of fifty, *both* of man and of beast, and gave them unto the Levites, which kept the charge of the tabernacle of the LORD ; as the LORD commanded Moses.

We have here the distribution of the spoil which was taken in this expedition against Midian. God himself directed how it should be distributed, and Moses and Eleazar did according to the directions, and thus unhappy contests among themselves were prevented and the victory was made to turn to the common benefit. It was fit that he who gave them the prey should order the disposal of it. All we have is from God, and therefore must be subject to his will.

I. The prey is ordered to be divided into two parts, one for the 12,000 men that undertook the war, and the other for the congregation. The prey that was divided seems to have been only the captives and the cattle; as for the plate, and jewels, and other goods, every man kept what he took, as is intimated, *v.* 50—53. That only was distributed which would be of use for the stocking of that good land into which they were going. Now observe, 1. That the one half of the prey was given to the whole congregation, Moses allotting to each tribe its share, and then leaving it to the heads of the tribes to divide their respective shares among themselves, according to their families. The war was undertaken on the behalf of the whole congregation; they would all have been ready to go *to the help of the Lord against the mighty,* if they had been so ordered, and they did help, it is likely, by their prayers ; and therefore God appoints that those that *tarried at home should divide the spoil,* Ps. lxviii. 12. David, in his time, made it a *statute and an ordinance for Israel,* that, as his part is that *goes down to the battle, so shall his part be that tarrieth by the stuff,* 1 Sam. xxx. 24, 25. Those that are employed in public trusts must not think to benefit themselves only by their toils and hazards, but must aim at the advantage of the community. 2. That yet the 12,000 that went to the battle had as much for their share as the whole congregation (which were fifty times as many) had for theirs; so that the particular persons of the soldiery had a much better share than any of their brethren that tarried at home : and good reason they should. The greater pains we take, and the greater hazards we

run, in the service of God and our generation, the greater will our recompence be at last ; for *God is not unrighteous to forget the work and labour of love.*

II. God was to have a tribute out of it, as an acknowledgment of his sovereignty over them in general, and that he was their king to whom *tribute was due,* and particularly of his interest in this war and the gains of it, he having given them their success ; and that the priests, the Lord's receivers, might have something added to the provision made for their maintenance. Note, Whatever we have, God must have his dues out of it. And here (as before) the soldiers are favoured above the rest of the congregation, for out of the people's share God required one in fifty, but out of the soldiers' share only one in 500, because the people got theirs easily, without any peril or fatigue. The less opportunity we have of honouring God with our personal services the more it is expected we should honour him with our substance. The tribute out of the soldiers' half was given to the priests (*v.* 29), that out of the people's half was given to the Levites, *v.* 30. For the priests were taken from among the Levites, as these soldiers from among the people, for special and hazardous service, and their pay was proportioned accordingly.

48 And the officers which *were* over thousands of the host, the captains of thousands, and captains of hundreds, came near unto Moses : 49 And they said unto Moses, Thy servants have taken the sum of the men of war which *are* under our charge, and there lacketh not one man of us. 50 We have therefore brought an oblation for the LORD, what every man hath gotten, of jewels of gold, chains, and bracelets, rings, earrings, and tablets, to make an atonement for our souls before the LORD. 51 And Moses and Eleazar the priest took the gold of them, *even* all wrought jewels. 52 And all the gold of the offering that they offered up to the LORD, of the captains of thousands, and of the captains of hundreds, was sixteen thousand seven hundred and fifty shekels. 53 (*For* the men of war had taken spoil every man for himself.) 54 And Moses and Eleazar the priest took the gold of the captains of thousands and of hundreds, and brought it into the tabernacle of the congregation, *for* a memorial for the children of Israel before the LORD.

Here is a great example of piety and devotion in the officers of the army, the colonels, that are called *captains of thousands*, and the inferior officers that were *captains of hundreds;* they came to Moses as their general and commander-in-chief, and, though he was now going off the stage, they very humbly and respectfully addressed themselves to him, calling themselves his *servants;* the honours they had won did not puff them up, so as to make them forget their duty to him. Observe in their address to them, 1. The pious notice they take of God's wonderful goodness to them in this late expedition, in preserving not only their own lives, but the lives of all the men of war that they had under their charge; so that, upon the review of their muster-roll, it appeared there was not one missing, *v.* 49. This was very extraordinary, and perhaps cannot be paralleled in any history. So many thousands of lives jeoparded in the high places of the field, and not one lost, either by the sword of the enemy or by any disease or disaster. This was *the Lord's doing*, and cannot but be marvellous in the eyes of those that consider how the lives of all men, especially soldiers, are continually in their hands. It is an evidence of the tender feeling which these commanders had for their soldiers, and that their lives were very precious to them, that they looked upon it as a mercy to themselves that none of those under their charge miscarried. *Of all that were given them they had lost none;* so precious also is the blood of Christ's subjects and soldiers to him, Ps. lxxii. 14. 2. The pious acknowledgment they make for this favour: *Therefore we have brought an oblation to the Lord, v.* 50. The oblation they brought was out of that which *every man had gotten*, and it was gotten honestly by a divine warrant. Thus every man should lay by *according as God has prospered him*, 1 Cor. xvi. 2. For where God sows plentifully in the gifts of his bounty he expects to reap accordingly in the fruits of our piety and charity. The tabernacle first, and the temple afterwards, were beautified and enriched with the spoils taken from the enemies of Israel; as by David (2 Sam. viii. 11, 12), and his captains, 1 Chron. xxvi. 26, 27. We should never take any thing to ourselves, in war or trade, which we cannot in faith consecrate a part of to God, who *hates robbery for burnt-offerings;* but, when God has remarkably preserved and prospered us, he expects that we should make some particular return of gratitude to him. As to this oblation, (1.) The captains offered it to *make an atonement for their souls, v.* 50. Instead of coming to Moses to demand a recompence for the good service they had done in *avenging the Lord of Midian*, or to set up trophies of their victory for the immortalizing of their own names, they bring an oblation to *make atonement for their souls*, being conscious to themselves, as the best men must be even in their best services, that they had been defective

710

in their duty, not only in that instance for which they were reproved (*v.* 14), but in many others; *for there is not a just man upon earth that doeth good and sinneth not.* (2.) Moses accepted it, and laid it up in the tabernacle *as a memorial for the children of Israel* (*v.* 54), that is, a monument of God's goodness to them, that they might be encouraged to trust in him in their further wars, and a monument of their gratitude to God (sacrifices are said to be memorials), that he, being well pleased with this thankful acknowledgment of favours bestowed, might continue and repeat his mercies to them.

CHAP. XXXII.

In this chapter we have, I. The humble request of the tribes of Reuben and Gad for an inheritance on that side Jordan where Israel now lay encamped, ver. 1—5. II. Moses's misinterpretation of their request, ver. 6—15. III. Their explication of it, and stating it aright, ver. 16—19. IV. The grant of their petition under the provisos and limitations which they themselves proposed, ver. 20, &c.

NOW the children of Reuben and the children of Gad had a very great multitude of cattle: and when they saw the land of Jazer, and the land of Gilead, that, behold, the place *was* a place for cattle; 2 The children of Gad and the children of Reuben came and spake unto Moses, and to Eleazar the priest, and unto the princes of the congregation, saying, 3 Ataroth, and Dibon, and Jazer, and Nimrah, and Heshbon, and Elealeh, and Shebam, and Nebo, and Beon, 4 *Even* the country which the LORD smote before the congregation of Israel, *is* a land for cattle, and thy servants have cattle: 5 Wherefore, said they, if we have found grace in thy sight, let this land be given unto thy servants for a possession, *and* bring us not over Jordan. 6 And Moses said unto the children of Gad and to the children of Reuben, Shall your brethren go to war, and shall ye sit here? 7 And wherefore discourage ye the heart of the children of Israel from going over into the land which the LORD hath given them? 8 Thus did your fathers, when I sent them from Kadesh-barnea to see the land. 9 For when they went up unto the valley of Eshcol, and saw the land, they discouraged the heart of the children of Israel, that they should not go into the land which the LORD had given them. 10 And the LORD's anger was kindled the same time, and he sware, saying, 11 Surely none of the men that came up out of Egypt, from twenty years old and upward, shall see the land which I sware unto Abraham, unto Isaac, and unto Jacob; because they have not wholly followed me: 12 Save Caleb the son of Jephunneh the Kenezite, and Joshua the son of Nun: for they have wholly followed the LORD. 13 And the LORD's anger was kindled against Israel, and he made them wander in the wilderness forty years, until all the generation, that had done evil in the sight of the LORD, was consumed. 14 And, behold, ye are risen up in your fathers' stead, an increase of sinful men, to augment yet the fierce anger of the LORD toward Israel. 15 For if ye turn away from after him, he will yet again leave them in the wilderness; and ye shall destroy all this people.

Israel's tents were now pitched in the plains of Moab, where they continued many months, looking back upon the conquests they had already made of the land of Sihon and Og, and looking forward to Canaan, which they hoped in a little time to make themselves masters of. While they made this stand, and were at a pause, this great affair of the disposal of the conquests they had already made was here concerted and settled, not by any particular order or appointment of God, but at the special instance and request of two of the tribes, to which Moses, after a long debate that arose upon it, consented. For even *then*, when so much was done by the extraordinary appearances of divine Providence, many things were left to the direction of human prudence; for God, in governing both the world and the church, makes use of the reason of men, and serves his own purposes by it.

I. Here is a motion made by the Reubenites and Gadites, that the land which they had lately possessed themselves of, and which in the right of conquest belonged to Israel in common, might be assigned to them in particular for their inheritance: upon the general idea they had of the land of promise, they supposed this would be about their proportion. Reuben and Gad were encamped under the same standard, and so had the better opportunity of comparing notes, and settling this matter between themselves. In the first verse the children of Reuben are named first, but afterwards the children of Gad (v. 2, 25, 31), either because the Gadites made the first motion and were most forward for it, or because they were the better spokesmen and had more of the art of management, Reuben's tribe still lying under Jacob's sentence, *he shall not excel.* Two things common

in the world induced these tribes to make this choice and this motion upon it, the *lust of the eye* and the *pride of life*, 1 John ii. 16. 1. The *lust of the eye.* This land which they coveted was not only beautiful for situation, and pleasant to the eye, but it was good for food, food for cattle; and they had a great multitude of cattle, above the rest of the tribes, it is supposed because they brought more out of Egypt than the rest did; but that was forty years before, and stocks of cattle increase and decrease in less time than that; therefore I rather think they had been better husbands of their cattle in the wilderness, had tended them better, had taken more care of the breed, and not been so profuse as their neighbours in eating the *lambs out of the flock* and the *calves out of the midst of the stall.* Now they, having these large stocks, coveted land proportionable. Many scriptures speak of Bashan and Gilead as places famous for cattle; they had been so already, and therefore these tribes hoped they would be so to them, and, whatever comes of it, here they desire to take their lot. The judicious Calvin thinks there was much amiss in the principle they went upon, and that they consulted their own private convenience more than the public good, that they had not such regard to the honour and interest of Israel, and the promise made to Abraham of the land of Canaan (strictly so called), as they ought to have had. And still it is too true that many *seek their own things* more than the *things of Jesus Christ* (Phil. ii. 21), and that many are influenced by their secular interest and advantage to take up short of the heavenly Canaan. Their spirits agree too well with this world, and with the things that are seen, that are temporal; and they say, " It is good to be here," and so lose what is hereafter for want of seeking it. Lot thus chose *by the sight of the eye*, and smarted for his choice. Would we choose our portion aright we must look above the things that are seen. 2. Perhaps there was something of the *pride of life* in it. Reuben was the first-born of Israel, but he had lost his birthright. Several of the tribes, and Judah especially, had risen above him, so that he could not expect the best lot in Canaan; and therefore, to save the shadow of a birthright, when he had forfeited the substance, he here catches at the first lot, though it was out of Canaan, and far off from the tabernacle. Thus Esau sold his birthright, and yet got to be served first with an inheritance in Mount Seir. The tribe of Gad descended from the first-born of Zilpah, and were like pretenders with the Reubenites; and Manasseh too was a first-born, but knew he must be eclipsed by Ephraim his younger brother, and therefore he also coveted to get precedency.

II. Moses's dislike of this motion, and the severe rebuke he gives to it, as a faithful prince and prophet.

1. It must be confessed that, *prima facie—at first sight,* the thing looked ill, especially the closing words of their petition : *Bring us not over Jordan, v.* 5. (1.) It seemed to proceed from a bad principle, a contempt of the land of promise, which Moses himself was so desirous of a sight of, a distrust too of the power of God to dispossess the Canaanites, as if a lot in a land which they knew, and which was already conquered, was more desirable than a lot in a land they knew not, and which was yet to be conquered : one bird in the hand is worth two in the bush. There seemed also to be covetousness in it ; for that which they insisted on was that it was convenient for their cattle. It argued likewise a neglect of their brethren, as if they cared not what became of Israel, while they themselves were well provided for. (2.) It might have been of bad consequence. The people might have taken improper hints from it, and have suggested that they were few enough, when they had their whole number, to deal with the Canaanites, but how unequal would the match be if they should drop two tribes and a half (above a fifth part of their strength) on this side Jordan. It would likewise be a bad precedent ; if they must have the land thus granted them as soon as it was conquered, other tribes might make the same pretensions and claims, and so the regular disposition of the land by lot would be anticipated.

2. Moses is therefore very warm upon them, which is to be imputed to his pious zeal against sin, and not to any peevishness, the effect of old age, for his meekness abated not, any more than his natural force. (1.) He shows them what he apprehended to be evil in this motion, that it would discourage the heart of their brethren, *v.* 6, 7. " What !" (says he, with a holy indignation at their selfishness) " *shall your brethren go to war,* and expose themselves to all the hardships and hazards of the field, and *shall you sit here* at your ease ? No, do not deceive yourselves, you shall never be indulged by me in this sloth and cowardice." It ill becomes any of God's Israel to sit down unconcerned in the difficult and perilous concernments of their brethren, whether public or personal. (2.) He reminds them of the fatal consequences of the unbelief and faint-heartedness of their fathers, when they were just ready to enter Canaan, as they themselves now were. He recites the story very particularly (*v.* 8—13) : " *Thus did your fathers,* whose punishment should be a warning to you to take heed of sinning after the similitude of their transgression." (3.) He gives them fair warning of the mischief that would be likely to follow upon this separation which they were about to make from the camp of Israel ; they would be in danger of bringing wrath upon the whole congregation, and hurrying them all back again into the wilderness (*v.* 14, 15) : " *You have risen up in your fathers' stead*

to despise the pleasant land and reject it as they did, when we hoped you had risen up in their stead to possess it." It was an encouragement to Moses to see what an increase of men there was in these tribes, but a discouragement to see that it was withal an increase of sinful men, treading in the steps of their fathers' impiety. It is sad to see the rising generation in families and countries not only no better, but worse, than that which went before it ; and what comes of it ? Why, *it augments the fierce anger of the Lord ;* not only continues that fire, but increases it, and fills the measure, often till it overflows in a deluge of desolation. Note, If men did but consider, as they ought, what would be the end of sin, they would be afraid of the beginnings of it.

16 And they came near unto him, and said, We will build sheepfolds here for our cattle, and cities for our little ones : 17 But we ourselves will go ready armed before the children of Israel, until we have brought them unto their place : and our little ones shall dwell in the fenced cities because of the inhabitants of the land. 18 We will not return unto our houses, until the children of Israel have inherited every man his inheritance. 19 For we will not inherit with them on yonder side Jordan, or forward ; because our inheritance is fallen to us on this side Jordan eastward. 20 And Moses said unto them, If ye will do this thing, if ye will go armed before the Lord to war, 21 And will go all of you armed over Jordan before the Lord, until he hath driven out his enemies from before him, 22 And the land be subdued before the Lord : then afterward ye shall return, and be guiltless before the Lord, and before Israel ; and this land shall be your possession before the Lord. 23 But if ye will not do so, behold, ye have sinned against the Lord : and be sure your sin will find you out. 24 Build you cities for your little ones, and folds for your sheep ; and do that which hath proceeded out of your mouth. 25 And the children of Gad and the children of Reuben spake unto Moses, saying, Thy servants will do as my Lord commandeth. 26 Our little ones, our wives, our flocks, and all our cattle, shall be there in the cities of Gilead : 27 But thy servants

will pass over, every man armed for war, before the LORD to battle, as my LORD saith.

We have here the accommodating of the matter between Moses and the two tribes, about their settlement on this side Jordan. Probably the petitioners withdrew, and considered with themselves what answer they should return to the severe reproof Moses had given them; and, after some consultation, they return with this proposal, that their men of war should go and assist their brethren in the conquest of Canaan, and they would leave their families and flocks behind them in this land: and thus they might have their request, and no harm would be done. Now it is uncertain whether they designed this at first when they brought their petition or no. If they did, it is an instance how often that which is honestly meant is unhappily misinterpreted: yet Moses herein was excusable, for he had reason to suspect the worst of them, and the rebuke he gave them was from the abundance of his care to prevent sin. But, if they did not, it is an instance of the good effect of plain dealing; Moses, by showing them their sin, and the danger of it, brought them to their duty without murmuring or disputing. They object not that their brethren were able to contend with the Canaanites without their help, especially since they were sure of God's fighting for them; but engage themselves to stand by them.

I. Their proposal is very fair and generous, and such as, instead of disheartening, would rather encourage their brethren. 1. That their *men of war*, who were fit for service, would go *ready armed before the children of Israel* into the land of Canaan. So far would they be from deserting them that, if it were thought fit, they would lead them on, and be foremost in all dangerous enterprises. So far were they from either distrusting or despising the conquest of Canaan that they would assist in it with the utmost readiness and resolution. 2. That they would leave behind them their families and cattle (which would otherwise be but the incumbrance of their camp), and so they would be the more serviceable to their brethren, *v.* 16. 3. That they would not return to their possessions till the conquest of Canaan was completed, *v.* 18. Their brethren should have their best help as long as they needed it. 4. That yet they would not expect any share of the land that was yet to be conquered (*v.* 19): "*We will not desire to inherit with them*, nor, under colour of assisting them in the war, put in for a share with them in the land; no, we will be content with our inheritance on this side Jordan, and there will be so much the more on yonder side for them."

II. Moses thereupon grants their request, upon consideration that they would adhere to their proposals. 1. He insists much upon it that they should never lay down their arms

till their brethren laid down theirs. They promised to go armed *before the children of Israel, v.* 17. "Nay," says Moses, "you shall go armed *before the Lord, v.* 20, 21. It is God's cause more than your brethren's, and to him you must have an eye, and not to them only." *Before the Lord*, that is, before the ark of the Lord, the token of his presence, which, it should seem, they carried about with them in the wars of Canaan, and immediately before which these two tribes were posted, as we find in the order of their march, *ch.* ii. 10, 17. 2. Upon this condition he grants them this land for their possession, and tells them they shall be *guiltless before the Lord and before Israel, v.* 22. They should have the land, and neither sin nor blame should cleave to it, neither sin before God nor blame before Israel; and, whatever possessions we have, it is desirable thus to come guiltless to them. But, 3. He warns them of the danger of breaking their word: "If you fail, you *sin against the Lord* (*v.* 23), and not against your brethren only, and *be sure your sin will find you out:*" that is, "God will certainly reckon with you for it, though you may make a light matter of it." Note, Sin will, without doubt, find out the sinner sooner or later. It concerns us therefore to find our sins out, that we may repent of them and forsake them, lest our sins find us out to our ruin and confusion.

III. They unanimously agree to the provisos and conditions of the grant, and do, as it were, give bond for performance, by a solemn promise: *Thy servants will do as my lord commandeth, v.* 25. Their brethren had all contributed their assistance to the conquest of this country, which they desired for a possession, and therefore they owned themselves obliged in justice to help them in the conquest of that which was to be their possession. Having received kindness, we ought to return it, though it was not so conditioned when we received it. We may suppose that this promise was understood, on both sides, so as not to oblige all that were numbered of these tribes to go over armed, but those only that were fittest for the expedition, who would be most serviceable, while it was necessary that some should be left to till the ground and guard the country; and accordingly we find that about 40,000 of the two tribes and a half went over armed (Josh. iv. 13), whereas their whole number was about 100,000.

28 So concerning them Moses commanded Eleazar the priest, and Joshua the son of Nun, and the chief fathers of the tribes of the children of Israel: 29 And Moses said unto them, If the children of Gad and the children of Reuben will pass with you over Jordan, every man armed to battle, before the LORD, and the land shall be subdued before you;

then ye shall give them the land of Gilead for a possession : 30 But if they will not pass over with you armed, they shall have possessions among you in the land of Canaan. 31 And the children of Gad and the children of Reuben answered, saying, As the LORD hath said unto thy servants, so will we do. 32 We will pass over armed before the LORD into the land of Canaan, that the possession of our inheritance on this side Jordan *may be* our's. 33 And Moses gave unto them, *even* to the children of Gad, and to the children of Reuben, and unto half the tribe of Manasseh the son of Joseph, the kingdom of Sihon king of the Amorites, and the kingdom of Og king of Bashan, the land, with the cities thereof in the coasts, *even* the cities of the country round about. 34 And the children of Gad built Dibon, and Ataroth, and Aroer, 35 And Atroth, Shophan, and Jaazer, and Jogbehah, 36 And Beth-nimrah, and Beth-haran, fenced cities : and folds for sheep. 37 And the children of Reuben built Heshbon, and Elealeh, and Kirjathaim, 38 And Nebo, and Baal-meon, (their names being changed,) and Shibmah : and gave other names unto the cities which they builded. 39 And the children of Machir the son of Manasseh went to Gilead, and took it, and dispossessed the Amorite which *was* in it. 40 And Moses gave Gilead unto Machir the son of Manasseh; and he dwelt therein. 41 And Jair the son of Manasseh went and took the small towns thereof, and called them Havoth-jair. 42 And Nobah went and took Kenath, and the villages thereof, and called it Nobah, after his own name.

Here, 1. Moses settles this matter with Eleazar, and with Joshua who was to be his successor, knowing that he himself must not live to see it perfected, *v.* 28—30. He gives them an estate upon condition, leaving it to Joshua, if they fulfilled the condition, to declare the estate absolute : " If *they will not go over with you,*" he does not say, " you shall give them no inheritance at all," but "you shall not give them this inheritance which they covet. If their militia will not come over with you, compel the whole tribes to come over, and let them take their lot with their brethren, and fare as they fare ; *they shall have possessions in Canaan,* and let them not expect that the lot will favour them." Hereupon they repeat their promise to adhere to their brethren, *v.* 31, 32. 2. Moses settles them in the land they desired. He gave it to them for a possession, *v.* 33. Here is the first mention of the half tribe of Manasseh coming in with them for a share ; probably they had not joined with them in the petition, but, the land when it came to be apportioned proving to be too much for them, this half tribe had a lot among them, perhaps at their request, or by divine direction, or because they had signalized themselves in the conquest of this country : for the children of Machir, a stout and warlike family, had taken Gilead and dispossessed the Amorites, *v.* 39. " Let them win it and wear it, get it and take it." And, they being celebrated for their courage and bravery, it was for the common safety to put them in this frontier-country. Concerning the settlement of these tribes observe, (1.) They built the cities, that is, repaired them, because either they had been damaged by the war or the Amorites had suffered them to go to decay. (2.) They changed the names of them (*v.* 38), either to show their authority, that the change of the names might signify the change of their owners, or because their names were idolatrous, and carried in them a respect to the dunghill-deities that were there worshipped. Nebo and Baal were names of their gods, which they were forbidden to make mention of (Exod. xxiii. 13), and which, by changing the names of these cities, they endeavoured to bury in oblivion ; and God promises to take away the names of Baalim out of the mouths of his people, Hos. ii. 17.

Lastly, It is observable that, as these tribes were now first placed before the other tribes, so, long afterwards, they were displaced before the other tribes. We find that they were carried captive into Assyria some years before the other tribes, 2 Kings xv. 29. Such a proportion does Providence sometimes observe in balancing prosperity and adversity ; he sets the one over-against the other.

CHAP. XXXIII.

In this chapter we have, I. A particular account of the removals and encampments of the children of Israel, from their escape out of Egypt to their entrance into Canaan, forty-two in all, with some remarkable events that happened at some of those places, ver. 1—49. II. A strict command given them to drive out all the inhabitants of the land of Canaan, which they were now going to conquer and take possession of, ver. 50—56. So that the former part of the chapter looks back upon their march through the wilderness, the latter looks forward to their settlement in Canaan.

THESE *are* the journeys of the children of Israel, which went forth out of the land of Egypt with their armies under the hand of Moses and Aaron. 2 And Moses wrote their goings out according to their journeys by the commandment of the LORD : and these *are* their journeys according to their goings out. 3 And they departed from Rameses in the first month, on the fifteenth day of the first month; on the morrow after the passover the children of Israel went out with a high hand in the sight of all the Egyptians. 4 For the Egyptians buried all *their* firstborn, which the LORD had smitten among them: upon their gods also the LORD executed judgments. 5 And the children of Israel removed from Rameses, and pitched in Succoth. 6 And they departed from Succoth, and pitched in Etham, which *is* in the edge of the wilderness. 7 And they removed from Etham, and turned again unto Pihahiroth, which *is* before Baal-zephon: and they pitched before Migdol. 8 And they departed from before Pihahiroth, and passed through the midst of the sea into the wilderness, and went three days' journey in the wilderness of Etham, and pitched in Marah. 9 And they removed from Marah, and came unto Elim: and in Elim *were* twelve fountains of water, and threescore and ten palm trees; and they pitched there. 10 And they removed from Elim, and encamped by the Red sea. 11 And they removed from the Red sea, and encamped in the wilderness of Sin. 12 And they took their journey out of the wilderness of Sin, and encamped in Dophkah. 13 And they departed from Dophkah, and encamped in Alush. 14 And they removed from Alush, and encamped at Rephidim, where was no water for the people to drink. 15 And they departed from Rephidim, and pitched in the wilderness of Sinai. 16 And they removed from the desert of Sinai, and pitched at Kibroth-hattaavah. 17 And they departed from Kibroth-hattaavah, and encamped at Hazeroth. 18 And they departed from Hazeroth, and pitched in Rithmah. 19 And they departed from Rithmah, and pitched at Rimmon-parez. 20 And they departed from Rimmon-parez, and pitched in Libnah. 21 And they removed from Libnah, and pitched at Rissah. 22 And they journeyed from Rissah, and pitched in Kehelathah. 23 And they went from Kehelathah, and pitched in mount Shapher. 24 And they removed from mount Shapher, and encamped in Haradah. 25 And they removed from Haradah, and pitched in Makheloth. 26 And they removed from Makheloth, and encamped at Tahath. 27 And they departed from Tahath, and pitched at Tarah. 28 And they removed from Tarah, and pitched in Mithcah. 29 And they went from Mithcah, and pitched in Hashmonah. 30 And they departed from Hashmonah, and encamped at Moseroth. 31 And they departed from Moseroth, and pitched in Bene-jaakan. 32 And they removed from Bene-jaakan, and encamped at Hor-hagidgad. 33 And they went from Hor-hagidgad, and pitched in Jotbathah. 34 And they removed from Jotbathah, and encamped at Ebronah. 35 And they departed from Ebronah, and encamped at Ezion-gaber. 36 And they removed from Ezion-gaber, and pitched in the wilderness of Zin, which *is* Kadesh. 37 And they removed from Kadesh, and pitched in mount Hor, in the edge of the land of Edom. 38 And Aaron the priest went up into mount Hor at the commandment of the LORD, and died there, in the fortieth year after the children of Israel were come out of the land of Egypt, in the first *day* of the fifth month. 39 And Aaron *was* a hundred and twenty and three years old when he died in mount Hor. 40 And king Arad the Canaanite, which dwelt in the south in the land of Canaan, heard of the coming of the children of Israel. 41 And they departed from mount Hor, and pitched in Zalmonah. 42 And they departed from Zalmonah, and pitched in Punon. 43 And they departed from Punon, and pitched in Oboth. 44 And they departed from Oboth, and pitched in Ije-abarim, in the border of Moab. 45 And they departed from Iim, and pitched in Dibon-gad. 46 And they removed from Dibon-gad, and encamped in Almon-diblathaim. 47 And they removed from Almon-diblathaim, and pitched in the mountains of Abarim, before Nebo. 48 And they departed from the mountains of Abarim, and pitched in the plains of Moab by Jordan *near* Jericho. 49 And they pitched by Jordan, from Beth-jesimoth *even* unto Abel-shittim in the plains of Moab.

This is a review and brief rehearsal of the travels of the children of Israel through the wilderness. It was a memorable history and well worthy to be thus abridged, and the abridgment thus preserved, to the honour of God that led them and for the encouragement of the generations that followed. Observe here,

I. How the account was kept: *Moses wrote their goings out, v.* 2. When they began this tedious march, God ordered him to keep a journal or diary, and to insert in it all the remarkable occurrences of their way, that it might be a satisfaction to himself in the review and an instruction to others when it should be published. It may be of good use to private Christians, but especially to those in public stations, to preserve in writing an account of the providences of God concerning them, the constant series of mercies they have experienced, especially those turns and changes which have made some days of their lives more remarkable. Our memories are deceitful and need this help, that we may *remember all the way which the Lord our God has led us in this wilderness,* Deut. viii. 2.

II. What the account itself was. It began with their departure out of Egypt, continued with their march through the wilderness, and ended in the plains of Moab, where they now lay encamped.

1. Some things are observed here concerning their departure out of Egypt, which they are reminded of upon all occasions, as a work of wonder never to be forgotten. (1.) That they *went forth with their armies* (*v.* 1), rank and file, as an army with banners. (2.) Under the hand of Moses and Aaron, their guides, overseers, and rulers, under God. (3.) *With a high hand,* because God's hand was high that wrought for them, *and in the sight of all the Egyptians, v.* 3. They did not steal away clandestinely (Isa. lii. 12), but in defiance of their enemies, to whom God had made them such a burdensome stone that they neither could, nor would, nor durst, oppose them. (4.) They went forth while the Egyptians were burying, or at least preparing to bury, their first-born, *v.* 4. They had a mind good enough, or rather bad enough, still to have detained the Israelites their prisoners, but God found them other work to do. They would have God's first-born buried alive, but God set them a burying their own first-born. (5.) To all the plagues of Egypt it is added here that *on their gods also the Lord executed judgments.* Their idols which they wor-
716

shipped, it is probable, were broken down, as Dagon afterwards before the ark, so that they could not consult them about this great affair. To this perhaps there is reference, Isa. xix. 1, *The idols of Egypt shall be moved at his presence.*

2. Concerning their travels towards Canaan. Observe, (1.) They were continually upon the remove. When they had pitched a little while in one place they departed from that to another. Such is our state in this world; we have here no continuing city. (2.) Most of their way lay through a wilderness, uninhabited, untracked, unfurnished even with the necessaries of human life, which magnifies the wisdom and power of God, by whose wonderful conduct and bounty the thousands of Israel not only subsisted for forty years in that desolate place, but came out at least as numerous and vigorous as they went in. At first they pitched *in the edge of the wilderness* (*v.* 6), but afterwards in the heart of it; by less difficulties God prepares his people for greater. We find them in the wilderness of Etham (*v.* 8), of Sin (*v.* 11), of Sinai, *v.* 15. Our removals in this world are but from one wilderness to another. (3.) They were led to and fro, forward and backward, as in a maze or labyrinth, and yet were all the while under the direction of the pillar of cloud and fire. He led them about (Deut. xxxii. 10), and yet led them the right way, Ps. cvii. 7. The way which God takes in bringing his people to himself is always the best way, though it does not always seem to us the nearest way. (4.) Some events are mentioned in this journal, as their want of water at Rephidim (*v.* 14), the death of Aaron (*v.* 38, 39), the insult of Arad (*v.* 40); and the very name of *Kibroth-hattaavah—the graves of lusts* (*v.* 16), has a story depending upon it. Thus we ought to keep in mind the providences of God concerning us and our families, us and our land, and the many instances of that divine care which has led us, and fed us, and kept us, all our days hitherto. Shittim, the place where the people sinned in the matter of Peor (*ch.* xxv. 1), is here called *Abel-shittim. Abel* signifies *mourning* (as Gen. l. 11), and probably this place was so called from the mourning of the good people of Israel on account of that sin and of God's wrath against them for it. It was so great a mourning that it gave a name to the place.

50 And the Lord spake unto Moses in the plains of Moab by Jordan *near* Jericho, saying, 51 Speak unto the children of Israel, and say unto them, When ye are passed over Jordan into the land of Canaan; 52 Then ye shall drive out all the inhabitants of the land from before you, and destroy all their pictures, and destroy all their molten images, and quite

pluck down all their high places : 53
And ye shall dispossess *the inhabitants of* the land, and dwell therein:
for I have given you the land to possess it. 54 And ye shall divide the
land by lot for an inheritance among
your families : *and* to the more ye
shall give the more inheritance, and
to the fewer ye shall give the less inheritance : every man's *inheritance*
shall be in the place where his lot
falleth ; according to the tribes of your
fathers ye shall inherit. 55 But if ye
will not drive out the inhabitants of
the land from before you; then it
shall come to pass, that those which
ye let remain of them *shall be* pricks
in your eyes, and thorns in your sides,
and shall vex you in the land wherein
ye dwell. 56 Moreover it shall come
to pass, *that* I shall do unto you, as I
thought to do unto them.

While the children of Israel were in the
wilderness their total separation from all other
people kept them out of the way of temptation to idolatry, and perhaps this was one
thing intended by their long confinement in
the wilderness, that thereby the idols of
Egypt might be forgotten, and the people
aired (as it were) and purified from that infection, and the generation that entered Canaan might be such as never knew those
depths of Satan. But now that they were to
pass over Jordan they were entering again
into that temptation, and therefore, 1. They
are here strictly charged utterly to destroy
all the remnants of idolatry. They must not
only *drive out the inhabitants of the land,* that
they may possess their country, but they
must deface all their idolatrous pictures and
images, and *pull down all their high places, v.*
52. They must not preserve any of them,
no, not as monuments of antiquity to gratify
the curious, nor as ornaments of their houses,
nor toys for their children to play with, but
they must destroy all, both in token of their
abhorrence and detestation of idolatry and to
prevent their being tempted to worship those
images, and the false gods represented by
them, or to worship the God of Israel by such
images or representations. 2. They were
assured that, if they did so, God would by
degrees put them in full possession of the
land of promise, *v.* 53, 54. If they would
keep themselves pure from the idols of Canaan, God would enrich them with the wealth
of Canaan. Learn not their way, and then
fear not their power. 3. They were threatened that, if they spared either the idols or
the idolaters, they should be beaten with
their own rod and their sin would certainly
be their punishment. (1.) They would fos-

ter snakes in their own bosoms, *v.* 55. The
remnant of the Canaanites, if they made any
league with them, though it were but a cessation of arms, would be *pricks in their eyes
and thorns in their sides,* that is, they would
be upon all occasions vexatious to them, insulting them, robbing them, and, to the utmost of their power, making mischief among
them. We must expect trouble and affliction from that, whatever it is, which we sinfully indulge ; that which we are willing
should tempt us we shall find will vex us.
(2.) The righteous God would turn that
wheel upon the Israelites which was to have
crushed the Canaanites: *I shall do to you as
I thought to do unto them, v.* 56. It was intended that the Canaanites should be dispossessed ; but if the Israelites fell in with them,
and learned their way, they should be dispossessed, for God's displeasure would justly
be greater against them than against the Canaanites themselves. Let us hear this, and
fear. If we do not drive sin out, sin will
drive us out; if we be not the death of our
lusts, our lusts will be the death of our souls.

CHAP. XXXIV.

In this chapter God directs Moses, and he is to direct Israel, I.
Concerning the bounds and borders of the land of Canaan, ver.
1—15. II. Concerning the division and distribution of it to the
tribes of Israel, ver. 16, &c.

AND the LORD spake unto Moses,
saying, 2 Command the children of Israel, and say unto them,
When ye come into the land of Canaan ; (this *is* the land that shall fall
unto you for an inheritance, *even* the
land of Canaan with the coasts thereof:)
3 Then your south quarter shall be
from the wilderness of Zin along by
the coast of Edom, and your south
border shall be the outmost coast of
the salt sea eastward : 4 And your
border shall turn from the south to
the ascent of Akrabbim, and pass on
to Zin : and the going forth thereof
shall be from the south to Kadesh-
barnea, and shall go on to Hazar-addar,
and pass on to Azmon : 5 And the
border shall fetch a compass from
Azmon unto the river of Egypt, and
the goings out of it shall be at the
sea. 6 And *as for* the western border,
ye shall even have the great sea for a
border: this shall be your west border.
7 And this shall be your north border:
from the great sea ye shall point out
for you mount Hor : 8 From mount
Hor ye shall point out *your border*
unto the entrance of Hamath ; and
the goings forth of the border shall be
to Zedad : 9 And the border shall go

on to Ziphron, and the goings out of it shall be at Hazar-enan: this shall be your north border. 10 And ye shall point out your east border from Hazar-enan to Shepham: · 11 And the coast shall go down from Shepham to Riblah, on the east side of Ain; and the border shall descend, and shall reach unto the side of the sea of Chinnereth eastward: 12 And the border shall go down to Jordan, and the goings out of it shall be at the salt sea: this shall be your land with the coasts thereof round about. 13 And Moses commanded the children of Israel, saying, This *is* the land which ye shall inherit by lot, which the Lord commanded to give unto the nine tribes, and to the half tribe: 14 For the tribe of the children of Reuben according to the house of their fathers, and the tribe of the children of Gad according to the house of their fathers, have received *their inheritance;* and half the tribe of Manasseh have received their inheritance: 15 The two tribes and the half tribe have received their inheritance on this side Jordan *near* Jericho eastward, toward the sunrising.

We have here a particular draught of the line by which the land of Canaan was meted, and bounded, on all sides. God directs Moses to settle it here, not as a geographer in his map, merely to please the curious, but as a prince in his grant, that it may be certainly known what passes, and is conveyed, by the grant. There was a much larger possession promised them, which in due time they would have possessed if they had been obedient, reaching even to the river Euphrates, Deut. xi. 24. And even so far the dominion of Israel did extend in David's time and Solomon's, 2 Chron. ix. 26. But this which is here described is Canaan only, which was the lot of the nine tribes and a half, for the other two and a half were already settled, v. 14, 15. Now concerning the limits of Canaan observe,

I. That it was limited within certain bounds: for God *appoints the bounds of our habitation,* Acts xvii. 26. The borders are set them, 1. That they might know whom they were to dispossess, and how far the commission which was given them extended (ch. xxxiii. 53), that they should *drive out the inhabitants.* Those that lay within these borders, and those only, they must destroy; hitherto their bloody sword must go, and no further. 2. That they might know what to expect the

possession of themselves. God would not have his people to enlarge their desire of worldly possessions, but to know when they have enough, and to rest satisfied with it. The Israelites themselves must not be *placed alone in the midst of the earth,* but must leave room for their neighbours to live by them. God sets bounds to our lot; let us then set bounds to our desires, and bring our mind to our condition.

II. That it lay comparatively in a very little compass: as it is here bounded, it is reckoned to be but about 160 miles in length and about fifty in breadth; perhaps it did not contain more than half as much ground as England, and yet this is the country which was promised to the father of the faithful and was the possession of the seed of Israel. This was that little spot of ground in which only, for many ages, *God was known, and his name was great,* Ps. lxxvi. 1. This was the vineyard of the Lord, the garden enclosed; but, as it is with gardens and vineyards, the narrowness of the extent was abundantly compensated by the extraordinary fruitfulness of the soil, otherwise it could not have subsisted so numerous a nation as did inhabit it. See here then, 1. How small a part of the world God has for himself. Though the *earth is his, and the fulness thereof,* yet few have the knowledge of him and serve him; but those few are happy, very happy, because fruitful to God. 2. How small a share of the world God often gives to his own people. Those that have their portion in heaven have reason to be content with a small pittance of this earth; but, as here, what is wanting in quantity is made up in quality; *a little that a righteous man has,* having it from the love of God and with his blessing, is far better and more comfortable *than the riches of many wicked,* Ps. xxxvii. 16.

III. It is observable what the bounds and limits of it were. 1. Canaan was itself a *pleasant land* (so it is called Dan. viii. 9), and yet it bordered upon wildernesses and seas, and was surrounded with divers melancholy prospects. Thus the vineyard of the church is compassed on all hands with the desert of this world, which serves as a foil to it, to make it appear the more beautiful for situation. 2. Many of its borders were its defences and natural fortifications, to render the access of enemies the more difficult, and to intimate to Israel that the God of nature was their protector, and with his favour would *compass them as with a shield.* 3. The border reached to the *river of Egypt* (v. 5), that the sight of that country which they could look into out of their own might remind them of their bondage there, and their wonderful deliverance thence. 4. Their border is here made to begin at the *Salt Sea* (v. 3), and there it ends, v. 12. This was the remaining lasting monument of the destruction of Sodom and Gomorrah

That pleasant fruitful vale in which these cities stood became a lake, which was never stirred by any wind, bore no vessels, was replenished with no fish, no living creature of any sort being found in it, therefore called the *Dead Sea*. This was part of their border, that it might be a constant warning to them to take heed of those sins which had been the ruin of Sodom ; yet the iniquity of Sodom was afterwards found in Israel (Ezek. xvi. 49), for which Canaan was made, though not a salt sea as Sodom, yet a barren soil, and continues so to this day. 5. Their western border was the *Great Sea* (*v.* 6), which is now called the *Mediterranean*. Some consider this sea itself to have been a part of their possession, and that, by virtue of this grant, they had the dominion of it, and, if they had not forfeited it by sin, might have rode masters of it.

16 And the Lord spake unto Moses, saying, 17 These *are* the names of the men which shall divide the land unto you : Eleazar the priest, and Joshua the son of Nun. 18 And ye shall take one prince of every tribe, to divide the land by inheritance. 19 And the names of the men *are* these : Of the tribe of Judah, Caleb the son of Jephunneh. 20 And of the tribe of the children of Simeon, Shemuel the son of Ammihud. 21 Of the tribe of Benjamin, Elidad the son of Chislon. 22 And the prince of the tribe of the children of Dan, Bukki the son of Jogli. 23 The prince of the children of Joseph, for the tribe of the children of Manasseh, Hanniel the son of Ephod. 24 And the prince of the tribe of the children of Ephraim, Kemuel the son of Shiphtan. 25 And the prince of the tribe of the children of Zebulun, Elizaphan the son of Parnach. 26 And the prince of the tribe of the children of Issachar, Paltiel the son of Azzan. 27 And the prince of the tribe of the children of Asher, Ahihud the son of Shelomi. 28 And the prince of the tribe of the children of Naphtali, Pedahel the son of Ammihud. 29 These *are they* whom the Lord commanded to divide the inheritance unto the children of Israel in the land of Canaan.

God here appoints commissioners for the dividing of the land to them. The conquest of it is taken for granted, though as yet there was never a stroke struck towards it.

Here is no nomination of the generals and commanders-in-chief that should carry on the war ; for they were to get the land in possession, *not by their own sword or bow, but by the power and favour of God ;* and so confident must they be of victory and success while God fought for them that the persons must now be named who should be entrusted with the dividing of the land, that is, who should preside in casting the lots, and determine controversies that might arise, and see that all was done fairly. 1. The principal commissioners, who were of the *quorum*, were Eleazar and Joshua (*v.* 17), typifying Christ, who, as priest and king, divides the heavenly Canaan to the spiritual Israel ; yet, as they were to go by the lot, so Christ acknowledges the disposal must be by the will of the Father, Matt. xx. 23. Compare, Eph. i. 11. 2. Besides these, that there might be no suspicion of partiality, a prince of each tribe was appointed to inspect this matter, and to see that the tribe he served for was in no respect injured. Public affairs should be so managed as not only to give their right to all, but, if possible, to give satisfaction to all that they have justice done them. It is a happiness to a land to have the princes of their people meet together, some out of every tribe, to concert the affairs that are of common concern, a constitution which is the abundant honour, ease, and safety, of the nation that is blessed with it. 3. Some observe that the order of the tribes here very much differs from that in which they had hitherto, upon all occasions, been named, and agrees with the neighbourhood of their lots in the division of the land. Judah, Simeon, and Benjamin, the first three here named, lay close together ; the inheritance of Dan lay next them on one side, that of Ephraim and Manasseh on another side ; Zebulun and Issachar lay abreast more northerly, and, lastly, Asher and Naphtali most northward of all, as is easy to observe in looking over a map of Canaan ; this (says bishop Patrick) is an evidence that Moses was guided by a divine Spirit in his writings. Known unto God are all his works beforehand, and what is new and surprising to us he perfectly foresaw, without any confusion or uncertainty.

CHAP. XXXV.

Orders having been given before for the dividing of the land of Canaan among the lay-tribes (as I may call them), care is here taken for a competent provision for the clergy, the tribe of Levi, which ministered in holy things. I. Forty-eight cities were to be assigned them, with their suburbs, some in every tribe, ver. 1—8. II. Six cities out of these were to be for cities of refuge, for any man that killed another unawares, ver. 9—15. In the law concerning these observe, 1. In what case sanctuary was not allowed, namely, that of wilful murder, ver. 16—21. 2. In what cases it was allowed, ver. 22—24. 3. What was the law concerning those that took shelter in these cities of refuge, ver. 25, &c.

AND the Lord spake unto Moses in the plains of Moab by Jordan *near* Jericho, saying, 2 Command the children of Israel, that they give unto the Levites of the inheritance of their possession cities to dwell in; and ye shall give *also* unto the Levites suburbs for the cities round about them. 3 And the cities shall they have to dwell in; and the suburbs of them shall be for their cattle, and for their goods, and for all their beasts. 4 And the suburbs of the cities, which ye shall give unto the Levites, *shall reach* from the wall of the city and outward a thousand cubits round about. 5 And ye shall measure from without the city on the east side two thousand cubits, and on the south side two thousand cubits, and on the west side two thousand cubits, and on the north side two thousand cubits; and the city *shall be* in the midst: this shall be to them the suburbs of the cities. 6 And among the cities which ye shall give unto the Levites *there shall be* six cities for refuge, which ye shall appoint for the manslayer, that he may flee thither: and to them ye shall add forty and two cities. 7 *So* all the cities which ye shall give to the Levites *shall be* forty and eight cities: them *shall ye give* with their suburbs. 8 And the cities which ye shall give *shall be* of the possession of the children of Israel: from *them that have* many ye shall give many; but from *them that have* few ye shall give few: every one shall give of his cities unto the Levites according to his inheritance which he inheriteth.

The laws about the tithes and offerings had provided very plentifully for the maintenance of the Levites; but it was not to be thought, nor indeed was it for the public good, that when they came to Canaan they should all live about the tabernacle, as they had done in the wilderness, and therefore care must be taken to provide habitations for them, in which they might live comfortably and usefully. It is this which is here taken care of.

I. Cities were allotted them, with their suburbs, *v.* 2. They were not to have any ground for tillage; they needed not to *sow, nor reap, nor gather into barns,* for their heavenly Father fed them with the tithe of the increase of other people's labours, that they might the more closely attend to the study of the law, and might have more leisure to teach the people; for they were not fed thus easily that they might live in idleness, but that they might give themselves wholly to

720

the business of their profession, and not be entangled in the affairs of this life. 1. Cities were allotted them, that they might live near together, and converse with one another about the law, to their mutual edification; and that in doubtful cases they might consult one another, and in all cases strengthen one another's hands. 2. These cities had suburbs annexed to them for their cattle (*v.* 3), a thousand cubits from the wall was allowed them for out-houses to keep their cattle in, and then two thousand more for fields to graze their cattle in, *v.* 4, 5. Thus was care taken that they should not only live, but live plentifully, and have all desirable conveniences about them, that they might not be looked upon with contempt by their neighbours.

II. These cities were to be assigned them out of the possessions of each tribe, *v.* 8. 1. That each tribe might thus make a grateful acknowledgment to God out of their real as well as out of their personal estates (for what was given to the Levites was accepted as given to the Lord) and thus their possessions were sanctified to them. 2. That each tribe might have the benefit of the Levites' dwelling among them, to *teach them the good knowledge of the Lord;* thus that light was diffused through all parts of the country, and none were left to sit in darkness, Deut. xxxiii. 10, *They shall teach Jacob thy judgments.* Jacob's curse on Levi's anger was, *I will scatter them in Israel,* Gen. xlix. 7. But that curse was turned into a blessing, and the Levites, by being thus scattered, were put into a capacity of doing so much the more good. It is a great mercy to a country to be replenished in all parts with faithful ministers.

III. The number allotted them was forty-eight in all, four out of each of the twelve tribes, one with another. Out of the united tribes of Simeon and Judah nine, out of Naphtali three, and four apiece out of the rest, as appears, Josh. xxi. Thus were they blessed with a good ministry, and that ministry with a comfortable maintenance, not only in tithes, but in glebe-lands. And, though the gospel is not so particular as the law was in this matter, yet it expressly provides that he that is *taught in the word* should *communicate unto him that teaches in all good things,* Gal. vi. 6.

9 And the LORD spake unto Moses, saying, 10 Speak unto the children of Israel, and say unto them, When ye be come over Jordan into the land of Canaan; 11 Then ye shall appoint you cities to be cities of refuge for you; that the slayer may flee thither, which killeth any person at unawares. 12 And they shall be unto you cities for refuge

from the avenger; that the manslayer die not, until he stand before the congregation in judgment. 13 And of these cities which ye shall give six cities shall ye have for refuge. 14 Ye shall give three cities on this side Jordan, and three cities shall ye give in the land of Canaan, *which* shall be cities of refuge. 15 These six cities shall be a refuge, *both* for the children of Israel, and for the stranger, and for the sojourner among them: that every one that killeth any person unawares may flee thither. 16 And if he smite him with an instrument of iron, so that he die, he *is* a murderer: the murderer shall surely be put to death. 17 And if he smite him with throwing a stone, wherewith he may die, and he die, he *is* a murderer: the murderer shall surely be put to death. 18 Or *if* he smite him with a hand weapon of wood, wherewith he may die, and he die, he *is* a murderer: the murderer shall surely be put to death. 19 The revenger of blood himself shall slay the murderer: when he meeteth him, he shall slay him. 20 But if he thrust him of hatred, or hurl at him by laying of wait, that he die; 21 Or in enmity smite him with his hand, that he die: he that smote *him* shall surely be put to death; *for* he *is* a murderer: the revenger of blood shall slay the murderer, when he meeteth him. 22 But if he thrust him suddenly without enmity, or have cast upon him any thing without laying of wait, 23 Or with any stone, wherewith a man may die, seeing *him* not, and cast *it* upon him, that he die, and *was* not his enemy, neither sought his harm: 24 Then the congregation shall judge between the slayer and the revenger of blood according to these judgments: 25 And the congregation shall deliver the slayer out of the hand of the revenger of blood, and the congregation shall restore him to the city of his refuge, whither he was fled: and he shall abide in it unto the death of the high priest, which was anointed with the holy oil. 26 But if the slayer shall at any time come without the border of the city of his refuge,

whither he was fled; 27 And the revenger of blood find him without the borders of the city of his refuge, and the revenger of blood kill the slayer; he shall not be guilty of blood: 28 Because he should have remained in the city of his refuge until the death of the high priest: but after the death of the high priest the slayer shall return into the land of his possession. 29 So these *things* shall be for a statute of judgment unto you throughout your generations in all your dwellings. 30 Whoso killeth any person, the murderer shall be put to death by the mouth of witnesses: but one witness shall not testify against any person *to cause him* to die. 31 Moreover ye shall take no satisfaction for the life of a murderer, which *is* guilty of death: but he shall be surely put to death. 32 And ye shall take no satisfaction for him that is fled to the city of his refuge, that he should come again to dwell in the land, until the death of the priest. 33 So ye shall not pollute the land wherein ye *are*: for blood it defileth the land: and the land cannot be cleansed of the blood that is shed therein, but by the blood of him that shed it. 34 Defile not therefore the land which ye shall inhabit, wherein I dwell: for I the LORD dwell among the children of Israel.

We have here the orders given concerning the cities of refuge, fitly annexed to what goes before, because they were all Levites' cities. In this part of the constitution there is a great deal both of good law and pure gospel.

I. Here is a great deal of good law, in the case of murder and manslaughter, a case of which the laws of all nations have taken particular cognizance. It is here enacted and provided, consonant to natural equity,

1. That wilful murder should be punished with death, and in that case no sanctuary should be allowed, no ransom taken, nor any commutation of the punishment accepted: The *murderer shall surely be put to death*, *v.* 16. It is supposed to be done *of hatred* (*v.* 20), or *in enmity* (*v.* 21), upon a sudden provocation (for our Saviour makes rash anger, as well as malice prepense, to be murder, Matt. v. 21, 22), whether the person be murdered with an instrument of iron (*v.* 16) or wood (*v.* 18), or with a stone thrown at him (*v.* 17, 20); nay, if he smite him with

his hand in enmity, and death ensue, it is murder (*v.* 21); and it was an ancient law, consonant to the law of nature, that *whoso sheds man's blood, by man shall his blood be shed,* Gen. ix. 6. Where wrong has been done restitution must be made; and, since the murderer cannot restore the life he has wrongfully taken away, his own must be exacted from him in lieu of it, not (as some have fancied) to satisfy the manes or ghost of the person slain, but to satisfy the law and the justice of a nation; and to be a warning to all others not to do likewise. It is here said, and it is well worthy the consideration of all princes and states, *that blood defiles* not only the conscience of the murderer, who is thereby proved *not to have eternal life abiding in him* (1 John iii. 15), but also the land in which it is shed; so very offensive is it to God and all good men, and the worst of nuisances. And it is added that *the land cannot be cleansed* from the blood of the murdered, but by the blood of the murderer, *v.* 33. If murderers escape punishment from men, those that suffer them to escape will have a great deal to answer for, and God will nevertheless not suffer them to escape his righteous judgments. Upon the same principle it is provided that no satisfaction should be taken for the *life of a murderer* (*v.* 31): *If a man would give all the substance of his house* to the judges, to the country, or to the avenger of blood, to atone for his crime, it must *utterly be contemned.* The redemption of the life is so precious that it cannot be obtained by the *multitude of riches* (Ps. xlix. 6—8), which perhaps may allude to this law. A rule of law comes in here (which is a rule of our law in cases of treason only) that no man shall be put to death upon the testimony of one witness, but it was necessary there should be two (*v.* 30); this law is settled in all capital cases, Deut. xvii. 6; xix. 15. And, *lastly,* not only the prosecution, but the execution, of the murderer, is committed to the next of kin, who, as he was to be the redeemer of his kinsman's estate if it were mortgaged, so he was to be the *avenger of his blood if he were murdered* (*v.* 19): *The avenger of blood himself shall slay the murderer,* if he be convicted by the *notorious evidence of the fact,* and he needed not to have recourse by a judicial process to the court of judgment. But if it were uncertain who the murderer was, and the proof doubtful, we cannot think that his bare suspicion, or surmise, would empower him to do that which the judges themselves could not do but upon the testimony of two witnesses. Only if the fact were plain then the next heir of the person slain might himself, in a just indignation, slay the murderer wherever he met him. Some think this must be understood to be after the lawful judgment of the magistrate, and so the Chaldee says, "He shall slay him, *when he shall be condemned unto him by judgment;*" but it should seem,

by *v.* 24, that the judges interposed only in a doubtful case, and that if the person on whom he took vengeance was indeed the murderer, and a wilful murderer, the avenger was innocent (*v.* 27), only, if it proved otherwise, it was at his peril. Our law allows an appeal to be brought against a murderer by the widow, or next heir, of the person murdered, yea, though the murderer have been acquitted upon an indictment; and, if the murderer be found guilty upon that appeal, execution shall be awarded at the suit of the appellant, who may properly be called *the avenger of blood.*

2. But if the homicide was not voluntary, nor done designedly, if it was *without enmity, or lying in wait* (*v.* 22), not *seeing* the person or not *seeking his harm* (*v.* 23), which our law calls chance-medley, or homicide *per infortunium—through misfortune,* in this case there were cities of refuge appointed for the man-slayer to flee to. By our law this incurs a forfeiture of goods, but a pardon is granted of course upon the special matter found. Concerning the cities of refuge the law was, (1.) That, if a man killed another, in these cities he was safe, and under the protection of the law, till he had his trial *before the congregation,* that is, before the judges in open court. If he neglected thus to surrender himself, it was at his peril; if the avenger of blood met him elsewhere, or overtook him loitering in his way to the city of refuge, and slew him, his blood was upon his own head, because he did not make use of the security which God had provided for him. (2.) If, upon trial, it were found to be wilful murder, the city of refuge should no longer be a protection to him; it was already determined: *Thou shalt take him from my altar, that he may die,* Exod. xxi. 14. (3.) But if it were found to be by error or accident, and that the stroke was given without any design upon the life of the person slain or any other, then the man-slayer should continue safe in *the city of refuge,* and the avenger of blood might not meddle with him, *v.* 25. There he was to remain in banishment from his own house and patrimony *till the death of the high priest;* and, if at any time he went out of that city or the suburbs of it, he put himself out of the protection of this law, and the avenger of blood, if he met him, might slay him, *v.* 26—28. Now, [1.] By the preservation of the life of the man-slayer God would teach us that men ought not to suffer for that which is rather their unhappiness than their crime, rather the act of Providence than their own act, for *God delivered him into his hand,* Exod. xxi. 13. [2.] By the banishment of the man-slayer from his own city, and his confinement to the city of refuge, where he was in a manner a prisoner, God would teach us to conceive a dread and horror of the guilt of blood, and to be very careful of life, and always afraid lest by oversight or negligence we occasion the death of any

[3.] By the limiting of the time of the offender's banishment to the death of the high priest, an honour was put upon that sacred office. The high priest was to be looked upon as so great a blessing to his country that when he died their sorrow upon that occasion should swallow up all other resentments. The cities of refuge being all of them Levites' cities, and the high priest being the head of that tribe, and consequently having a peculiar dominion over these cities, those that were confined to them might properly be looked upon as his prisoners, and so his death must be their discharge; it was, as it were, at his suit that the delinquent was imprisoned, and therefore at his death it fell. *Actio moritur cum persona*—*The suit expires with the party.* Ainsworth has another notion of it, That as the high priests, while they lived, by their service and sacrificing made atonement for sin, wherein they prefigured Christ's satisfaction, so, at their death, those were released that had been exiled for casual murder, which typified redemption in Israel. [4.] By the abandoning of the prisoner to the avenger of blood, in case he at any time went out of the limits of the city of refuge, they were taught to adhere to the methods which Infinite Wisdom prescribed for their security. It was for the honour of a remedial law that it should be so strictly observed. How can we expect to be saved if we neglect the salvation, which is indeed a great salvation!

II. Here is a great deal of good gospel couched under the type and figure of the cities of refuge; and to them the apostle seems to allude when he speaks of our *fleeing for refuge to the hope set before us* (Heb. vi. 18), and being *found in Christ*, Phil. iii. 9. We never read in the history of the Old Testament of any use made of these cities of refuge, any more than of other such institutions, which yet, no doubt, were made use of upon the occasions intended; only we read of those that, in dangerous cases, took hold of *the horns of the altar* (1 Kings i. 50; ii. 28); for the altar, wherever that stood, was, as it were, the capital *city of refuge.* But the law concerning these cities was designed both to raise and to encourage the expectations of those who looked for redemption in Israel, which should be to those who were convinced of sin, and in terror by reason of it, as the cities of refuge were to the man-slayer. Observe, 1. There were several cities of refuge, and they were so appointed in several parts of the country that the man-slayer, wherever he dwelt in the land of Israel, might in half a day reach one or other of them; so, though there is but one Christ appointed for our refuge, yet, wherever we are, he is a refuge at hand, a very present help, for *the word is nigh us* and Christ in the word. 2. The man-slayer was safe in any of these cities; so in Christ believers that flee to him, and rest in him, are protected from the wrath of God and the curse of the law. *There is no con-*

demnation to those that are in Christ Jesus, Rom. viii. 1. Who shall condemn those that are thus sheltered? 3. They were all Levites' cities; it was a kindness to the poor prisoner that though he might not go up to the place where the ark was, yet he was in the midst of Levites, who would teach him the good knowledge of the Lord, and instruct him how to improve the providence he was now under. It might also be expected that the Levites would comfort and encourage him, and bid him welcome; so it is the work of gospel ministers to bid poor sinners welcome to Christ, and to assist and counsel those that through grace are in him. 4. Even strangers and sojourners, though they were not native Israelites, might take the benefit of these cities of refuge, *v.* 15. So in Christ Jesus no difference is made between Greek and Jew; even the *sons of the stranger* that by faith flee to Christ shall be safe in him. 5. Even the suburbs or borders of the city were a sufficient security to the offender, *v.* 26, 27. So there is virtue even in the hem of Christ's garment for the healing and saving of poor sinners. If we cannot reach to a full assurance, we may comfort ourselves in a good hope through grace. 6. The protection which the man-slayer found in the city of refuge was not owing to the strength of its walls, or gates, or bars, but purely to the divine appointment; so it is the word of the gospel that gives souls safety in Christ, *for him hath God the Father sealed.* 7. If the offender was ever caught straggling out of the borders of his city of refuge, or stealing home to his own house again, he lost the benefit of his protection, and lay exposed to the avenger of blood; so those that are in Christ must abide in Christ, for it is at their peril if they forsake him and wander from him. *Drawing back is to perdition.*

CHAP. XXXVI.

We have in this chapter the determination of another question that arose upon the case of the daughters of Zelophehad. God had appointed that they should inherit, ch. xxvii. 7. Now here, I. An inconvenience is suggested, in case they should marry into any other tribe, ver. 1—4. II. It is prevented by a divine appointment that they should marry in their own tribe and family (ver. 5—7), and this is settled for a rule in like cases (ver. 8, 9); and they did marry accordingly to some of their own relations (ver. 10—12), and with this the book concludes, ver. 13.

AND the chief fathers of the families of the children of Gilead, the son of Machir, the son of Manasseh, of the families of the sons of Joseph, came near, and spake before Moses, and before the princes, the chief fathers of the children of Israel: 2 And they said, The LORD commanded my lord to give the land for an inheritance by lot to the children of Israel: and my lord was commanded by the LORD to give the inheritance of Zelophehad our brother unto his daughters. 3 And if they be married to any of the sons of the *other* tribes of the children of Israel, then shall their inheritance be taken from the inheritance of our fathers, and shall be put to the inheritance of the tribe whereunto they are received: so shall it be taken from the lot of our inheritance. 4 And when the jubilee of the children of Israel shall be, then shall their inheritance be put unto the inheritance of the tribe whereunto they are received: so shall their inheritance be taken away from the inheritance of the tribe of our fathers.

We have here the humble address which the heads of the tribe of Manasseh made to Moses and the princes, on occasion of the order lately made concerning the daughters of Zelophehad. The family they belonged to was part of that half of the tribe of Manasseh which was yet to have their lot within Jordan, not that half that was already settled; and yet they speak of the land of their possession, and the inheritance of their fathers, with as great assurance as if they had it already in their hands, knowing whom they had trusted. In their appeal observe, 1. They fairly recite the former order made in this case, and do not move to have that set aside, but are very willing to acquiesce in it (v. 2): *The Lord commanded to give the inheritance of Zelophehad to his daughters ;* and they are very well pleased that it should be so, none of them knowing but that hereafter it might be the case of their own families, and then their daughters would have the benefit of this law. 2. They represent the inconvenience which might, possibly, follow hereupon, if the daughters of Zelophehad should see cause to marry into any other tribes, v. 3. And it is probable that this was not a bare surmise, or supposition, but that they knew, at this time, great court was made to them by some young gentlemen of other tribes, because they were heiresses, that they might get footing in this tribe, and so enlarge their own inheritance. This truly is often aimed at more than it should be in making marriages, not the meetness of the person, but the convenience of the estate, to *lay house to house, and field to field. Wisdom indeed is good with an inheritance ;* but what is an inheritance good for in that relation without wisdom? But here, we may presume, the personal merit of these daughters recommended them as well as their fortunes; however, the heads of their tribe foresaw the mischief that would follow, and brought the case to Moses, that he might consult the oracle of God concerning it The difficulty they start God could have obviated and provided against in the former order given in this case; but to teach us that we must, in our affairs, not only attend God's providence, but make use of our own prudence, God did not direct in it till they themselves that were concerned wisely foresaw the inconvenience, and piously applied to Moses for a rule in it. For though they were chief fathers in their families, and might have assumed a power to overrule these daughters of Zelophehad in disposing of themselves, especially their father being dead and the common interest of their tribe being concerned in it, yet they chose rather to refer the matter to Moses, and it issued well. We should not covet to be judges in our own case, for it is difficult to be so without being partial. It is easier in many cases to take good advice than to give it, and it is a satisfaction to be under direction. Two things they aimed at in their representation :—(1.) To preserve the divine appointment of inheritances. They urged the command (v. 2), that the land should be given by lot to the respective tribes, and urged that it would break in upon the divine appointment if such a considerable part of the lot of Manasseh should, by their marriage, be transferred to any other tribe; for the issue would be denominated from the father's tribe, not the mother's. This indeed would not lessen the lot of the particular persons of that tribe (they would have their own still), but it would lessen the lot of the tribe in general, and render it less strong and considerable; they therefore thought themselves concerned for the reputation of their tribe, and perhaps were the more jealous for it because it was already very much weakened by the sitting down of the one half of it on this side Jordan. (2.) To prevent contests and quarrels among posterity. If those of other tribes should come among them perhaps it might occasion some contests. They would be apt to give and receive disturbance, and their title might, in process of time, come to be questioned; and how great a matter would this fire kindle! It is the wisdom and duty of those that have estates in the world to settle them, and dispose of them, so as that no strife and contention may arise about them among posterity.

5 And Moses commanded the children of Israel according to the word of the LORD, saying, The tribe of the sons of Joseph hath said well. 6 This *is* the thing which the LORD doth command concerning the daughters of Zelophehad, saying, Let them marry to whom they think best; only to the family of the tribe of their father shall they marry. 7 So shall not the inheritance of the children of Israel remove from tribe to tribe : for every one of the children of Israel shall keep himself to the inheritance of the tribe of his fathers. 8 And every daughter, that possesseth an in-

heritance in any tribe of the children of Israel, shall be wife unto one of the family of the tribe of her father, that the children of Israel may enjoy every man the inheritance of his fathers. 9 Neither shall the inheritance remove from *one* tribe to another tribe; but every one of the tribes of the children of Israel shall keep himself to his own inheritance. 10 Even as the LORD commanded Moses, so did the daughters of Zelophehad: 11 For Mahlah, Tirzah, and Hoglah, and Milcah, and Noah, the daughters of Zelophehad, were married unto their father's brothers' sons: 12 *And* they were married into the families of the sons of Manasseh the son of Joseph, and their inheritance remained in the tribe of the family of their father. 13 These *are* the commandments and the judgments, which the LORD commanded by the hand of Moses unto the children of Israel in the plains of Moab by Jordan *near* Jericho.

Here is, I. The matter settled by express order from God between the daughters of Zelophehad and the rest of the tribe of Manasseh. The petition is assented to, and care taken to prevent the inconvenience feared: *The tribe of the sons of Joseph hath said well, v.* 5. Thus those that consult the oracles of God concerning the making of their heavenly inheritance sure shall not only be directed what to do, but their enquiries shall be graciously accepted, and they shall have not only their *well done*, but their *well said*, good and faithful servant. Now the matter is thus accommodated: these heiresses must be obliged to marry, not only within their own tribe of Manasseh, but within the particular family of the Hepherites, to which they did belong. 1. They are not determined to any particular persons; there was choice enough in the family of their father: *Let them marry to whom they think best.* As children must preserve the authority of their parents, and not marry against their minds, so parents must consult the affections of their children in disposing of them, and not compel them to marry such as they cannot love. Forced marriages are not likely to prove blessings. 2. Yet they

are confined to their own relations, that their inheritance may not go to another family. God would have them know that the land being to be divided by lot, the disposal whereof was of the Lord, they could not mend, and therefore should not alter, his appointment. The inheritances must not *remove from tribe to tribe (v.*7), lest there should be confusion among them, their estates entangled, and their genealogies perplexed. God would not have one tribe to be enriched by the straitening and impoverishing of another, since they were all alike the seed of Abraham his friend.

II. The law, in this particular case, was made perpetual, and to be observed whenever hereafter the like case should happen, *v.* 8. Those that were not heiresses might marry into what tribe they pleased (though we may suppose that, ordinarily, they kept within their own tribe), but those that were must either quit their claim to the inheritance or marry one of their own family, that each of the tribes might keep to its own inheritance, and one tribe might not encroach upon another, but throughout their generations there might remain immovable the ancient landmarks, set, not by their fathers, but by the *God of their fathers.*

III. The submission of the daughters of Zelophehad to this appointment. How could they but marry well, and to their satisfaction, when God himself directed them? They married their father's brothers' sons, *v.* 10—12. By this it appears, 1. That the marriage of cousin-germans is not in itself unlawful, nor within the degrees prohibited, for then God would not have countenanced these marriages. But, 2. That ordinarily it is not advisable; for, if there had not been a particular reason for it (which cannot hold in any case now, inheritances being not disposed of as then by the special designation of Heaven), they would not have married such near relations. The world is wide, and he that walks uprightly will endeavour to walk surely.

IV. The conclusion of this whole book, referring to the latter part of it: *These are the judgments which the Lord commanded in the plains of Moab (v.* 13), these foregoing, ever since *ch.* xxvi., most of which related to their settlement in Canaan, into which they were now entering. Whatever new condition God is by his providence bringing us into, we must beg of him to teach us the duty of it, and to enable us to do it, that we may do the work of the day in its day, of the place in its place.

AN

EXPOSITION,

WITH PRACTICAL OBSERVATIONS,

OF THE FIFTH BOOK OF MOSES, CALLED

DEUTERONOMY.

THIS book is a repetition of very much both of the history and of the laws contained in the three foregoing books, which repetition Moses delivered to Israel (both by word of mouth, that it might affect, and by writing, that it might abide) a little before his death. There is no new history in it but that of the death of Moses in the last chapter, nor any new revelation to Moses, for aught that appears, and therefore the style here is not, as before, *The Lord spoke unto Moses, saying.* But the former laws are repeated and commented upon, explained and enlarged, and some particular precepts added to them, with copious reasonings for the enforcing of them : in this Moses was divinely inspired and assisted, so that this is as truly the word of the Lord by Moses as that which was spoken to him with an audible voice *out of the tabernacle of the congregation,* Lev. i. 1. The Greek interpreters call it *Deuteronomy,* which signifies the *second law,* or a *second edition of the law,* not with amendments, for there needed none, but with additions, for the further direction of the people in divers cases not mentioned before. Now, I. It was much for the honour of the divine law that it should be thus repeated ; how great were the things of that law which was thus inculcated, and how inexcusable would those be by whom they were *counted as a strange thing !* Hos. viii. 12. II. There might be a particular reason for the repeating of it now ; the men of that generation to which the law was first given were all dead, and a new generation had sprung up, to whom God would have it repeated by Moses himself, that, if possible, it might make a lasting impression upon them. Now that they were just going to take possession of the land of Canaan, Moses must read the articles of agreement to them, that they might know upon what terms and conditions they were to hold and enjoy that land, and might understand that they were upon their good behaviour in it. III. It would be of great use to the people to have those parts of the law thus gathered up and put together which did more immediately concern them and their practice ; for the laws which concerned the priests and Levites, and the execution of their offices, are not repeated : it was enough for them that they were once delivered. But, in compassion to the infirmities of the people, the laws of more common concern are delivered a second time. *Precept must be upon precept, and line upon line,* Isa. xxviii. 10. The great and needful truths of the gospel should be often pressed upon people by the ministers of Christ. *To write the same things* (says Paul, Phil. iii. 1) *to me indeed is not grievous, but for you it is safe.* What God has spoken once we have need to hear twice, to hear many times, and it is well if, after all, it be duly perceived and regarded. In three ways this book of Deuteronomy was magnified and made honourable :—1. The king was to write a copy of it with his own hand, and to read therein all the days of his life, *ch.* xvii. xviii. xix. 2. It was to be written upon great stones plastered, at their passing over Jordan, *ch.* xxvii. 2, 3. 3. It was to be read pub-licly every seventh year, at the feast of tabernacles, by the priests, in the audience of all Israel, *ch.* xxxi. 9, &c. The gospel is a kind of Deuteronomy, a second law, a remedial law, a spiritual law, a law of faith ; by it we are under the law to Christ, and it is a law that *makes the comers thereunto perfect.*

This book of Deuteronomy begins with a brief rehearsal of the most remarkable events that had befallen the Israelites since they came from Mount Sinai. In the fourth chapter we have a most pathetic exhortation to obedience. In the twelfth chapter, and so on to the twenty-seventh, are repeated many particular laws, which are enforced (*ch.* xxvii. and xxviii.) with promises and threatenings, blessings and curses, formed into a covenant, *ch.* xxix. and xxx. Care is taken to perpetuate the remembrance of these things among them (*ch.* xxxi.), particularly by a song (*ch.* xxxii.), and so Moses concludes with a blessing, *ch.* xxxiii. All this was delivered by Moses to Israel in the last month of his life. The whole book contains the history but of two months ; compare *ch.* i. 3 with Josh. iv. 19, the latter of which was the thirty days of Israel's mourning for Moses ; see how busy that great and good man was to do good when he knew that his time was short, how quick his motion when he drew near his rest. Thus we have more recorded of what our blessed Saviour said and did in the last week of his life than in any other. The last words of eminent persons make or should make deep impressions. Observe, for the honour of this book, that when our Saviour would answer the devil's temptations with, *It is written,* he fetched all his quotations out of this book, Matt. iv. 4, 7, 10.

726

CHAP. I.

The first part of Moses's farewell sermon to Israel begins with this chapter, and is continued to the latter end of the fourth chapter. In the first five verses of this chapter we have the date of this sermon, the place where it was preached (ver. 1, 2, 5), and the time when, ver. 3, 4. The narrative in this chapter reminds them, I. Of the promise God made them of the land of Canaan, ver. 6—8. II. Of the provision made of judges for them, ver. 9—18. III. Of their unbelief and murmuring upon the report of the spies, ver. 19—33. IV. Of the sentence passed upon them for it, and the ratification of that sentence, ver. 34, &c.

THESE *be* the words which Moses spake unto all Israel on this side Jordan in the wilderness, in the plain over against the Red *sea*, between Paran, and Tophel, and Laban, and Hazeroth, and Dizahab. 2 (*There are* eleven days' *journey* from Horeb by the way of mount Seir unto Kadesh-barnea.) 3 And it came to pass in the fortieth year, in the eleventh month, on the first *day* of the month, *that* Moses spake unto the children of Israel, according unto all that the Lord had given him in commandment unto them; 4 After he had slain Sihon the king of the Amorites, which dwelt in Heshbon, and Og the king of Bashan, which dwelt at Astaroth in Edrei: 5 On this side Jordan, in the land of Moab, began Moses to declare this law, saying, 6 The Lord our God spake unto us in Horeb, saying, Ye have dwelt long enough in this mount: 7 Turn you, and take your journey, and go to the mount of the Amorites, and unto all *the places* nigh thereunto, in the plain, in the hills, and in the vale, and in the south, and by the sea side, to the land of the Canaanites, and unto Lebanon, unto the great river, the river Euphrates. 8 Behold, I have set the land before you: go in and possess the land which the Lord sware unto your fathers, Abraham, Isaac, and Jacob, to give unto them and to their seed after them.

We have here, I. The date of this sermon which Moses preached to the people of Israel. A great auditory, no question, he had, as many as could crowd within hearing, and particularly all the elders and officers, the representatives of the people; and, probably, it was on the sabbath day that he delivered this to them. 1. The place where they were now encamped was *in the plain, in the land of Moab* (*v.* 1, 5), where they were just ready to enter Canaan, and engage in a war with the Canaanites. Yet he discourses not to them concerning military affairs, the arts and stratagems of war, but concerning their duty to

God; for, if they kept themselves in his fear and favour, he would secure to them the conquest of the land : their religion would be their best policy. 2. The time was near the end of the fortieth year since they came out of Egypt. So long God had *borne their manners,* and they had *borne their own iniquity* (Num. xiv. 34), and now that a new and more pleasant scene was to be introduced, as a token for good, Moses repeats the law to them Thus, after God's controversy with them on account of the golden calf, the first and surest sign of God's being reconciled to them was the *renewing of the tables.* There is no better evidence and earnest of God's favour than his putting his law in our hearts, Ps. cxlvii. 19, 20.

II. The discourse itself. In general, Moses spoke unto them *all that the Lord had given him in commandment* (*v.* 3), which intimates, not only that what he now delivered was for substance the same with what had formerly been commanded, but that it was what God now commanded him to repeat. He gave them this rehearsal and exhortation purely by divine direction; God appointed him to leave this legacy to the church. He begins his narrative with their removal from Mount Sinai (*v.* 6), and relates here, 1. The orders which God gave them to decamp, and proceed in their march (*v.* 6, 7) : *You have dwelt long enough in this mount.* This was the mount *that burned with fire* (Heb. xii. 18), and *gendered to bondage,* Gal. iv. 24. Thither God brought them to humble them, and by the terrors of the law to prepare them for the land of promise. There he kept them about a year, and then told them they had *dwelt long enough* there, they must go forward. Though God brings his people into trouble and affliction, into spiritual trouble and affliction of mind, he knows when they have dwelt long enough in it, and will certainly find a time, the fittest time, to advance them from the terrors of the spirit of bondage to the comforts of the spirit of adoption. See Rom. viii. 15. 2. The prospect which he gave them of a happy and early settlement in Canaan : *Go to the land of the Canaanites* (*v.* 7); enter and take possession, it is all your own. *Behold I have set the land before you, v.* 8. When God commands us to go forward in our Christian course he sets the heavenly Canaan before us for our encouragement.

9 And I spake unto you at that time, saying, I am not able to bear you myself alone : 10 The Lord your God hath multiplied you, and, behold, ye *are* this day as the stars of heaven for multitude. 11 (The Lord God of your fathers make you a thousand times so many more as ye *are,* and bless you, as he hath promised you!) 12 How can I myself alone bear your cumbrance, and your burden, and your

strife? 13 Take you wise men, and understanding, and known among your tribes, and I will make them rulers over you. 14 And ye answered me, and said, The thing which thou hast spoken *is* good *for us* to do. 15 So I took the chief of your tribes, wise men, and known, and made them heads over you, captains over thousands, and captains over hundreds, and captains over fifties, and captains over tens, and officers among your tribes. 16 And I charged your judges at that time, saying, Hear *the causes* between your brethren, and judge righteously between *every* man and his brother, and the stranger *that is* with him. 17 Ye shall not respect persons in judgment; *but* ye shall hear the small as well as the great; ye shall not be afraid of the face of man; for the judgment *is* God's: and the cause that is too hard for you, bring *it* unto me, and I will hear it. 18 And I commanded you at that time all the things which ye should do.

Moses here reminds them of the happy constitution of their government, which was such as might make them all safe and easy if it was not their own fault. When good laws were given them good men were entrusted with the execution of them, which, as it was an instance of God's goodness to them, so it was of the care of Moses concerning them; and, it should seem, he mentions it here to recommend himself to them as a man that sincerely sought their welfare, and so to make way for what he was about to say to them, wherein he aimed at nothing but their good. In this part of his narrative he insinuates to them,

I. That he greatly rejoiced in the increase of their numbers. He owns the accomplishment of God's promise to Abraham (*v.* 10): *You are as the stars of heaven for multitude;* and prays for the further accomplishment of it (*v.* 11): *God make you a thousand times more.* This prayer comes in in a parenthesis, and a good prayer prudently put in cannot be impertinent in any discourse of divine things, nor will a pious ejaculation break the coherence, but rather strengthen and adorn it. But how greatly are his desires enlarged when he prays that they might be made a thousand times more than they were! We are not straitened in the power and goodness of God, why should we be straitened in our own faith and hope, which ought to be as large as the promise? larger they need not be. It is from the promise that Moses here takes the measures of his prayer: *The Lord bless*
728

you as he hath promised you. And why might he not hope that they might become a thousand times more than they were now when they were now ten thousand times more than they were when they went down into Egypt, about 250 years ago? Observe, When they were under the government of Pharaoh the increase of their numbers was envied, and complained of as a grievance (Exod. i. 9); but now, under the government of Moses, it was rejoiced in, and prayed for as a blessing. The consideration of this might give them occasion to reflect with shame upon their own folly when they had talked of making a captain and returning to Egypt.

II. That he was not ambitious of monopolizing the honour of the government, and ruling them himself alone, as an absolute monarch, *v.* 9. Though he was a man as well worthy of that honour, and as well qualified for the business, as ever any man was, yet he was desirous that others might be taken in as assistants to him in the business and consequently sharers with him in the honour: *I cannot myself alone bear the burden, v.* 12. Magistracy is a burden. Moses himself, though eminently gifted for it, found it lay heavy on his shoulders; nay, the best magistrates complain most of the burden, and are most desirous of help, and most afraid of undertaking more than they can perform.

III. That he was not desirous to prefer his own creatures, or such as should underhand have a dependence upon him; for he leaves it to the people to choose their own judges, to whom he would grant commissions, not *durante bene placito—to be turned out when he pleased;* but *quam diu se bene gesserint—to continue so long as they approved themselves faithful. Take you wise men, that are known to be so among your tribes, and I will make them rulers, v.* 13. Thus the apostles directed the multitude to choose overseers of the poor, and then they ordained them, Acts vi. 3, 6. He directs them to *take wise men and understanding,* whose personal merit would recommend them. The rise and origin of this nation were so late that none of them could pretend to antiquity of race, and nobility of birth, above their brethren; and, having all lately come out of slavery in Egypt, it is probable that one family was not much richer than another; so that their choice must be directed purely by the qualifications of wisdom, experience, and integrity. "Choose those," says Moses, "whose praise is in your tribes, and with all my heart *I will make them rulers.*" We must not grudge that God's work be done by other hands than ours, provided it be done by good hands.

IV. That he was in this matter very willing to please the people; and, though he did not in any thing aim at their applause, yet in a thing of this nature he would not act without their approbation. And they agreed to the proposal: *The thing which thou hast spoken is good, v.* 14. This he mentions to aggravate the sin of their mutinies and discontents after this, that the government they quarrelled with was what they themselves had consented to; Moses would have pleased them if they would have been pleased.

V. That he aimed to edify them as well as to gratify them; for,

1. He appointed men of good characters (*v.* 15), *wise men and men known,* men that would be faithful to their trust and to the public interest.

2. He gave them a good charge, *v.* 16, 17. Those that are advanced to honour must know that they are charged with business, and must give account another day of their charge. (1.) He charges them to be diligent and patient: *Hear the causes.* Hear both sides, hear them fully, hear them carefully; for nature has provided us with two ears, and *he that answereth a matter before he heareth it, it is folly and shame to him.* The ear of the learner is necessary to the tongue of the learned, Isa. l. 4. (2.) To be just and impartial: *Judge righteously.* Judgment must be given according to the merits of the cause, without regard to the quality of the parties. The natives must not be suffered to abuse the strangers any more than the strangers to insult the natives or to encroach upon them; the great must not be suffered to oppress the small, nor to crush them, any more than the small to rob the great, or to affront them. No faces must be known in judgment, but unbribed unbiassed equity must always pass sentence. (3.) To be resolute and courageous: "*You shall not be afraid of the face of man;* be not overawed to do an ill thing, either by the clamours of the crowd or by the menaces of those that have power in their hands." And he gave them a good reason to enforce this charge: "*For the judgment is God's.* You are God's vicegerents, you act for him, and therefore must act like him; you are his representatives, but, if you judge unrighteously, you misrepresent him. The judgment is his, and therefore he will protect you in doing right, and will certainly call you to account if you do wrong."

3. He allowed them to bring all difficult cases to him, and he would always be ready to hear and determine, and to make both the judges and the people easy. *Happy art thou, O Israel!* in such a prince as Moses was.

19 And when we departed from Horeb, we went through all that great and terrible wilderness, which ye saw by the way of the mountain of the Amorites, as the LORD our God commanded us; and we came to Kadesh-barnea. 20 And I said unto you, Ye are come unto the mountain of the Amorites, which the LORD our God doth give unto us. 21 Behold, the LORD thy God hath set the land before thee: go up *and* possess *it,* as the LORD God of thy fathers hath said unto thee; fear not, neither be discouraged. 22 And ye came near unto me every one of you, and said, We will send men before us, and they shall search us out the land, and bring us word again by what way we must go up, and into what cities we shall come. 23 And the saying pleased me well: and I took twelve men of you, one of a tribe: 24 And they turned and went up into the mountain, and came unto the valley of Eshcol, and searched it out. 25 And they took of the fruit of the land in their hands, and brought *it* down unto us, and brought us word again, and said, *It is* a good land which the LORD our God doth give us. 26 Notwithstanding ye would not go up, but rebelled against the commandment of the LORD your God: 27 And ye murmured in your tents, and said, Because the LORD hated us, he hath brought us forth out of the land of Egypt, to deliver us into the hand of the Amorites, to destroy us. 28 Whither shall we go up? our brethren have discouraged our heart, saying, The people *is* greater and taller than we; the cities *are* great and walled up to heaven; and moreover we have seen the sons of the Anakims there. 29 Then I said unto you, Dread not, neither be afraid of them. 30 The LORD your God which goeth before you, he shall fight for you, according to all that he did for you in Egypt before your eyes; 31 And in the wilderness, where thou hast seen how that the LORD thy God bare thee, as a man doth bear his son, in all the way that ye went, until ye came into this place. 32 Yet in this thing ye did not believe the LORD your God, 33 Who went in the way before you, to search you out a place to pitch your tents *in,* in fire by night, to show you by what way ye should go, and in a cloud by day. 34 And the LORD heard the voice of your words, and was wroth, and sware, saying, 35 Surely there shall not one of these men of this evil generation see that

good land, which I sware to give unto your fathers, 36 Save Caleb the son of Jephunneh ; he shall see it, and to him will I give the land that he hath trodden upon, and to his children, because he hath wholly followed the LORD. 37 Also the LORD was angry with me for your sakes, saying, Thou also shalt not go in thither. 38 *But* Joshua the son of Nun, which standeth before thee, he shall go in thither : encourage him : for he shall cause Israel to inherit it. 39 Moreover your little ones, which ye said should be a prey, and your children, which in that day had no knowledge between good and evil, they shall go in thither, and unto them will I give it, and they shall possess it. 40 But *as for* you, turn you, and take your journey into the wilderness by the way of the Red sea. 41 Then ye answered and said unto me, We have sinned against the LORD, we will go up and fight, according to all that the LORD our God commanded us. And when ye had girded on every man his weapons of war, ye were ready to go up into the hill. 42 And the LORD said unto me, Say unto them, Go not up, neither fight; for I *am* not among you; lest ye be smitten before your enemies. 43 So I spake unto you; and ye would not hear, but rebelled against the commandment of the LORD, and went presumptuously up into the hill. 44 And the Amorites, which dwelt in that mountain, came out against you, and chased you, as bees do, and destroyed you in Seir, *even* unto Hormar. 45 And ye returned and wept before the LORD; but the LORD would not hearken to your voice, nor give ear unto you. 46 So ye abode in Kadesh many days, according unto the days that ye abode *there.*

Moses here makes a large rehearsal of the fatal turn which was given to their affairs by their own sins, and God's wrath, when, from the very borders of Canaan, the honour of conquering it, and the pleasure of possessing it, the whole generation was hurried back into the wilderness, and their carcases fell there. It was a memorable story; we read it Num. xiii. and xiv., but divers circumstances are found here which are not related there.

I. He reminds them of their march from Horeb to Kadesh-barnea (*v.* 19), through *that great and terrible wilderness.* This he takes notice of, 1. To make them sensible of the great goodness of God to them, in guiding them through so great a wilderness, and protecting them from the mischiefs they were surrounded with in such a terrible wilderness. The remembrance of our dangers should make us thankful for our deliverances. 2. To aggravate the folly of those who, in their discontent, would have gone back to Egypt through the wilderness, though they had forfeited, and had no reason to expect, the divine guidance, in such a retrograde motion.

II. He shows them how fair they stood for Canaan at that time, *v.* 20, 21. He told them with triumph, the land is *set before you, go up and possess it.* He lets them see how near they were to a happy settlement when they put a bar in their own door, that their sin might appear the more exceedingly sinful. It will aggravate the eternal ruin of hypocrites that they were *not far from the kingdom of God* and yet came short, Mark xii. 34.

III. He lays the blame of sending the spies upon them, which did not appear in Numbers; there it is said (*ch.* xiii. 1, 2) that the Lord directed the sending of them, but here we find that the people first desired it, and God, in permitting it, gave them up to their counsels: *You said, We will send men before us, v.* 22. Moses had given them God's word (*v.* 20, 21), but they could not find in their hearts to rely upon that : human policy goes further with them than divine wisdom, and they will needs light a candle to the sun. As if it were not enough that they were sure of a God before them, they must send men before them.

IV. He repeats the report which the spies brought of the goodness of the land which they were sent to survey, *v.* 24, 25. The blessings which God has promised are truly valuable and desirable, even the unbelievers themselves being judges : never any looked into the holy land, but they must own it a good land. Yet they represented the difficulties of conquering it as insuperable (*v.* 28); as if it were in vain to think of attacking them either by battle, "for the people are taller than we," or by siege, "for the cities are walled up to heaven," an hyperbole which they made use of to serve their ill purpose, which was to dishearten the people, and perhaps they intended to reflect on the God of heaven himself, as if they were able to defy him, like the Babel-builders, the top of whose tower must reach to heaven, Gen. xi. 4. Those places only are walled up to heaven that are compassed with God's favour as with a shield.

V. He tells them what pains he took with them to encourage them, when their brethren had said so much to discourage them (*v.* 29): *Then I said unto you, Dread not.* Moses suggested enough to have stilled the tumult, and to have kept them with their faces towards Canaan. He assured them that God was present with them, and president among them, and would certainly *fight for them*, v. 30. And for proof of his power over their enemies he refers them to what they had seen done in Egypt, where their enemies had all possible advantages against them and yet were humbled and forced to yield, v. 30. And for proof of God's goodwill to them, and the real kindness which he intended them, he refers them to what *they had seen in the wilderness* (v. 31, 33), through which they had been guided by the eye of divine wisdom in a pillar of cloud and fire (which guided both their motions and their rests), and had been carried in the arms of divine grace with as much care and tenderness as were ever shown to any child borne in the arms of a nursing father. And was there any room left to distrust this God? Or were they not the most ungrateful people in the world, who, after such sensible proofs of the divine goodness, *hardened their hearts in the day of temptation?* Moses had complained once that God had charged him to carry this people *as a nursing father doth the sucking child* (Num. xi. 12); but here he owns that it was God that so carried them, and perhaps this is alluded to (Acts xiii. 18), where he is said to *bear them*, or to *suffer their manners*.

VI. He charges them with the sin which they were guilty of upon this occasion. Though those to whom he was now speaking were a new generation, yet he lays it upon them: *You rebelled, and you murmured;* for many of these were then in being, though under twenty years old, and perhaps were engaged in the riot; and the rest inherited their fathers' vices, and smarted for them. Observe what he lays to their charge. 1. Disobedience, and rebellion against God's law: *You would not go up, but rebelled*, v. 26. The rejecting of God's favours is really a rebelling against his authority. 2. Invidious reflections upon God's goodness. They basely suggested: *Because the Lord hated us, he brought us out of Egypt*, v. 27. What could have been more absurd, more disingenuous, and more reproachful to God? 3. An unbelieving heart at the bottom of all this: *You did not believe the Lord your God*, v. 32. All your disobedience to God's laws, and distrust of his power and goodness, flow from a disbelief of his word. A sad pass it has come to with us when the God of eternal truth cannot be believed.

VII. He repeats the sentence passed upon them for this sin, which now they had seen the execution of. 1. They were all condemned to die in the wilderness, and none of them must be suffered to enter Canaan except Caleb and Joshua, v. 34—38. So long they must continue their wanderings in the wilderness that most of them would drop off of course, and the youngest of them should be cut off. Thus *they could not enter in be-*

cause of unbelief. It was not the breach of any of the commands of the law that shut them out of Canaan, no, not the golden calf, but their disbelief of that promise which was typical of gospel grace, to signify that no sin will ruin us but unbelief, which is a sin against the remedy. 2. Moses himself afterwards fell under God's displeasure for a hasty word which they provoked him to speak: *The Lord was angry with me for your sakes*, v. 37. Because all the old stock must go off, Moses himself must not stay behind. Their unbelief let death into the camp, and, having entered, even Moses falls within his commission. 3. Yet here is mercy mixed with wrath. (1.) That, though Moses might not bring them into Canaan, Joshua should (v. 38): *Encourage him;* for he would be discouraged from taking up a government which he saw Moses himself fall under the weight of; but let him be assured that he shall accomplish that for which he is raised up: *He shall cause Israel to inherit it.* Thus *what the law could not do, in that it was weak*, Jesus, our Joshua, does by bringing in the better hope. (2.) That, though this generation should not enter into Canaan, the next should, v. 39. As they had been chosen for their fathers' sakes, so their children might justly have been rejected for their sakes. But *mercy rejoiceth against judgment.*

VIII. He reminds them of their foolish and fruitless attempt to get this sentence reversed when it was too late. 1. They tried it by their reformation in this particular; whereas they had refused to go up against the Canaanites, now they would go up, aye, that they would, in all haste, and they girded on their weapons of war for that purpose, v. 41. Thus, when the door is shut, and the day of grace is over, there will be found those that stand without and knock. But this, which looked like a reformation, proved but a further rebellion. God, by Moses, prohibited the attempt (v. 42); *yet they went presumptuously up to the hill* (v. 43), acting now in contempt of the threatening, as before in contempt of the promise, as if they were governed by a spirit of contradiction; and it sped accordingly (v. 44): they were chased and destroyed; and, by this defeat which they suffered when they had provoked God to leave them, they were taught what success they might have had if they had kept themselves in his love. 2. They tried by their prayers and tears to get the sentence reversed: *They returned and wept before the Lord*, v. 45. While they were fretting and quarrelling, it is said (Num. xiv. 1): *They wept that night;* those were tears of rebellion against God, these were tears of repentance and humiliation *before* God. Note, Tears of discontent must be wept over again; the sorrow of the world worketh death, and is to be repented of; it is not so with godly sorrow, *that* will end in joy. But their weeping was all to no purpose *The Lord would not hearken to your voice,* because you would not hearken to his; the decree had gone forth, and, like Esau, they found no place of repentance, though they sought it carefully with tears.

CHAP. II.

.moses, in this chapter, proceeds in the rehearsal of God's providences concerning Israel in their way to Canaan, yet preserves not the record of any thing that happened during their tedious march back to the Red Sea, in which they wore out almost thirty-eight years, but passes that over in silence as a dark time, and makes his narrative to begin again when they faced about towards Canaan (ver. 1–3), and drew towards the countries that were inhabited, concerning which God here gives them direction, I. What nations they must not give any disturbance to. 1. Not to the Edomites, ver. 4–8. 2. Not to the Moabites (ver. 9), of the antiquities of whose country, with that of the Edomites, he gives some account, ver. 10–12. And here comes in an account of their passing the river Zered, ver. 13–16. 3. Not to the Ammonites, of whose country here is some account given, ver. 17–23. II. What nations they should attack and conquer. They must begin with Sihon, king of the Amorites, ver. 24, 25. And accordingly, 1. They had a fair occasion of quarrelling with him, ver. 26–32. 2. God gave them a complete victory over him, ver. 33, &c.

THEN we turned, and took our journey into the wilderness by the way of the Red sea, as the LORD spake unto me: and we compassed mount Seir many days. 2 And the LORD spake unto me, saying, 3 Ye have compassed this mountain long enough: turn you northward. 4 And command thou the people, saying, Ye *are* to pass through the coast of your brethren the children of Esau, which dwell in Seir; and they shall be afraid of you: take ye good heed unto yourselves therefore: 5 Meddle not with them; for I will not give you of their land, no, not so much as a foot breadth; because I have given mount Seir unto Esau *for* a possession. 6 Ye shall buy meat of them for money, that ye may eat; and ye shall also buy water of them for money, that ye may drink. 7 For the LORD thy God hath blessed thee in all the works of thy hand: he knoweth thy walking through this great wilderness: these forty years the LORD thy God *hath been* with thee; thou hast lacked nothing.

Here is, I. A short account of the long stay of Israel in the wilderness: *We compassed Mount Seir many days, v.* 1. Nearly *thirty-eight* years they wandered in the deserts of Seir; probably in some of their rests they staid several years, and never stirred; God by this not only chastised them for their murmuring and unbelief, but, 1. Prepared them for Canaan, by humbling them for sin, teaching them to mortify their lusts, to follow God, and to comfort themselves in him. It is a work of time to make souls meet for heaven, and it must be done by a long train of exercises. 2. He prepared the Canaanites

732

for destruction. All this time the measure of their iniquity was filling up; and, though it might have been improved by them as a space to repent in, it was abused by them to the hardening of their hearts. Now that the host of Israel was once repulsed, and after that was so long entangled and seemingly lost in the wilderness, they were secure, and thought the danger was over from that quarter, which would make the next attempt of Israel upon them the more dreadful.

II. Orders given them to turn towards Canaan. Though God contend long, he will not contend for ever. Though Israel may be long kept waiting for deliverance or enlargement, it will come at last: *The vision is for an appointed time, and at the end it shall speak, and not lie.*

III. A charge given them not to annoy the Edomites.

1. They must not offer any hostility to them as enemies: *Meddle not with them, v.* 4, 5. (1.) They must not improve the advantage they had against them, by the fright they would be put into upon Israel's approach: " *They shall be afraid of you,* knowing your strength and numbers, and the power of God engaged for you; but think not that, because their fears make them an easy prey, you may therefore prey upon them; no, *take heed to yourselves.*" There is need of great caution and a strict government of our own spirits, to keep ourselves from injuring those against whom we have an advantage. Or this caution is given to the princes; they must not only not meddle with the Edomites themselves, but not permit any of the soldiers to meddle with them. (2.) They must not avenge upon the Edomites the affront they gave them in refusing them passage through their country, Num. xx. 21. Thus, before God brought Israel to destroy their enemies in Canaan, he taught them to forgive their enemies in Edom. (3.) They must not expect to have any part of their land given them for a possession; Mount Seir was already settled upon the Edomites, and they must not, under pretence of God's covenant and conduct, think to seize for themselves all they could lay hands on. Dominion is not founded in grace. God's Israel shall be well placed, but must not expect to be *placed alone in the midst of the earth,* Isa. v. 8.

2. They must trade with them as neighbours, buy meat and water of them, and pay for what they bought, *v.* 6. Religion must never be made a cloak for injustice. The reason given (*v.* 7) is, " God hath blessed thee, and hitherto thou hast lacked nothing; and therefore, (1.) " Thou needest not beg; scorn to be beholden to Edomites, when thou hast a God all-sufficient to depend upon. Thou hast wherewithal to pay for what thou callest for (thanks to the divine blessing!); use therefore what thou hast, use it cheerfully, and do not sponge upon

the Edomites." (2.) "Therefore thou must not steal. Thou hast experienced the care of the divine providence concerning thee, in confidence of which for the future, and in a firm belief of its sufficiency, never use any indirect methods for thy supply. Live by thy faith and not by thy sword,"

8 And when we passed by from our brethren the children of Esau, which dwelt in Seir, through the way of the plain from Elath, and from Ezion-gaber, we turned and passed by the way of the wilderness of Moab. 9 And the LORD said unto me, Distress not the Moabites, neither contend with them in battle: for I will not give thee of their land *for* a possession; because I have given Ar unto the children of Lot *for* a possession. 10 The Emims dwelt therein in times past, a people great, and many, and tall, as the Anakims; 11 Which also were accounted giants, as the Anakims; but the Moabites call them Emims. 12 The Horims also dwelt in Seir beforetime; but the children of Esau succeeded them, when they had destroyed them from before them, and dwelt in their stead; as Israel did unto the land of his possession, which the LORD gave unto them. 13 Now rise up, *said I*, and get you over the brook Zered. And we went over the brook Zered. 14. And the space in which we came from Kadesh-barnea, until we were come over the brook Zered, *was* thirty and eight years; until all the generation of the men of war were wasted out from among the host, as the LORD sware unto them. 15 For indeed the hand of the LORD was against them, to destroy them from among the host, until they were consumed. 16 So it came to pass, when all the men of war were consumed and dead from among the people, 17 That the LORD spake unto me, saying, 18 Thou art to pass over through Ar, the coast of Moab, this day: 19 And *when* thou comest nigh over against the children of Ammon, distress them not, nor meddle with them: for I will not give thee of the land of the children of Ammon *any* possession: because I have given it unto the children of Lot *for* a pos-

session. 20 (That also was accounted a land of giants: giants dwelt therein in old time; and the Ammonites call them Zamzummims; 21 A people great, and many, and tall, as the Anakims; but the LORD destroyed them before them; and they succeeded them, and dwelt in their stead: 22 As he did to the children of Esau, which dwelt in Seir, when he destroyed the Horims from before them; and they succeeded them, and dwelt in their stead even unto this day: 23 And the Avims which dwelt in Hazerim, *even* unto Azzah, the Caphtorims, which came forth out of Caphtor, destroyed them, and dwelt in their stead.)

It is observable here that Moses, speaking of the Edomites (*v.* 8), calls them "*our brethren, the children of Esau.*" Though they had been unkind to Israel, in refusing them a peaceable passage through their country, yet he calls them brethren. For, though our relations fail in their duty to us, we must retain a sense of the relation, and not be wanting in our duty to them, as there is occasion. Now in these verses we have,

I. The account which Moses gives of the origin of the nations of which he had here occasion to speak, the Moabites, Edomites, and Ammonites. We know very well, from other parts of his history, whose posterity they were; but here he tells us how they came to those countries in which Israel found them; they were not the *aborigines*, or first planters. But, 1. The Moabites dwelt in a country which had belonged to a numerous race of giants, called *Emim* (that is, *terrible ones*), as tall as the Anakim, and perhaps more fierce, *v.* 10, 11.　2. The Edomites in like manner dispossessed the Horim from Mount Seir, and took their country (*v.* 12. and again *v.* 22), of which we read, Gen. xxxvi. 20.　3. The Ammonites likewise got possession of a country that had formerly been inhabited by giants, called *Zamzummim*, *crafty men*, or *wicked men* (*v.* 20, 21), probably the same that are called *Zuzim*, Gen. xiv. 5. He illustrates these remarks by an instance older than any of these; the Caphtorim (who were akin to the Philistines, Gen. x. 14) drove the Avim out of their country, and took possession of it, *v.* 23.　The learned bishop Patrick supposes these Avites, being expelled hence, to have settled in Assyria, and to be the same people we read of under that name, 2 Kings xvii. 31.　Now these revolutions are recorded, (1.) To show how soon the world was peopled after the flood, so well peopled that, when a family grew numerous, they could not find a place to settle in, at least in that part of the world, but they must drive out those that were already settled. (2.) To

733

show that the race is not to the swift, nor the battle to the strong. Giants were expelled by those of ordinary stature; for probably these giants, like those before the flood (Gen. vi. 4), were notorious for impiety and oppression, which brought the judgments of God upon them, against which their great strength would be no defence. (3.) To show what uncertain things worldly possessions are, and how often they change their owners; it was so of old, and ever will be so. Families decline, and from them estates are transferred to families that increase; so little constancy or continuance is there in these things. (4.) To encourage the children of Israel, who were now going to take possession of Canaan, against the difficulties they would meet with, and to show the unbelief of those that were afraid of the sons of Anak, to whom the giants, here said to be conquered, are compared, v. 11, 21. If the providence of God had done this for Moabites and Ammonites, much more would his promise do it for Israel his peculiar people.

II. The advances which Israel made towards Canaan. They *passed by the way of the wilderness of Moab* (v. 8), and then went over the brook or vale of Zered (v. 13), and there Moses takes notice of the fulfilling of the word which God had spoken concerning them, that none of those that were numbered at Mount Sinai should see the land that God had promised, Num. xiv. 23. According to that sentence, now that they began to set their faces towards Canaan, and to have it in their eye, notice is taken of their being all destroyed and consumed, and not a man of them left, v. 14. Common providence, we may observe, in about thirty-eight years, ordinarily raises a new generation, so that in that time few remain of the old one; but here it was entirely new, and none at all remained but Caleb and Joshua: *for indeed the hand of the Lord was against them,* v. 15. Those cannot but waste, until they are consumed, who have the hand of God against them. Observe, Israel is not called to engage with the Canaanites till all the men of war, the veteran regiments, that had been used to hardship, and had learned the art of war from the Egyptians, *were consumed and dead from among the people* (v. 16), that the conquest of Canaan, being effected by a host of new-raised men, trained up in a wilderness, the excellency of the power might the more plainly appear to be *of God and not of men.*

III. The caution given them not to meddle with the Moabites or Ammonites, whom they must not disseize, nor so much as disturb in their possessions: *Distress them not, nor contend with them,* v. 9. Though the Moabites aimed to ruin Israel (Num. xxii. 6), yet Israel must not aim to ruin them. If others design us a mischief, this will not justify us in designing them a mischief. But why must not the Moabites and Ammonites be meddled with? 1. Because they were the

734

children of Lot (v. 9, 19), righteous Lot, who kept his integrity in Sodom. Note, Children often fare the better in this world for the piety of their ancestors: the seed of the upright, though they degenerate, yet are blessed with temporal good things. 2. Because the land they were possessed of was what God had given them, and he did not design it for Israel. Even wicked men have a right to their worldly possessions, and must not be wronged. The tares are allowed their place in the field, and must not be rooted out until the harvest. God gives and preserves outward blessings to wicked men, to show that these are not the best things, but he has better in store for his own children.

24 Rise ye up, take your journey, and pass over the river Arnon: behold, I have given into thine hand Sihon the Amorite, king of Heshbon, and his land: begin to possess *it*, and contend with him in battle. 25 This day will I begin to put the dread of thee and the fear of thee upon the nations *that are* under the whole heaven, who shall hear report of thee, and shall tremble, and be in anguish because of thee. 26 And I sent messengers out of the wilderness of Kedemoth unto Sihon king of Heshbon with words of peace, saying, 27 Let me pass through thy land: I will go along by the high way, I will neither turn unto the right hand nor to the left. 28 Thou shalt sell me meat for money, that I may eat; and give me water for money, that I may drink: only I will pass through on my feet; 29 (As the children of Esau which dwell in Seir, and the Moabites which dwell in Ar, did unto me;) until I shall pass over Jordan into the land which the LORD our God giveth us. 30 But Sihon king of Heshbon would not let us pass by him: for the LORD thy God hardened his spirit, and made his heart obstinate, that he might deliver him into thy hand, as *appeareth* this day. 31 And the LORD said unto me, Behold, I have begun to give Sihon and his land before thee: begin to possess, that thou mayest inherit his land. 32 Then Sihon came out against us, he and all his people, to fight at Jahaz. 33 And the LORD our God delivered him before us; and we smote him, and his sons, and all his people. 34

And we took all his cities at that time, and utterly destroyed the men, and the women, and the little ones, of every city, we left none to remain: 35 Only the cattle we took for a prey unto ourselves, and the spoil of the cities which we took. 36 From Aroer, which *is* by the brink of the river of Arnon, and *from* the city that *is* by the river, even unto Gilead, there was not one city too strong for us: the Lord our God delivered all unto us: 37 Only unto the land of the children of Ammon thou camest not, *nor* unto any place of the river Jabbok, nor unto the cities in the mountains, nor unto whatsoever the Lord our God forbad us.

God having tried the self-denial of his people in forbidding them to meddle with the Moabites and Ammonites, and they having quietly passed by those rich countries, and, though superior in number, not made any attack upon them, here he recompenses them for their obedience by giving them possession of the country of Sihon king of the Amorites. If we forbear what God forbids, we shall receive what he promises, and shall be no losers at last by our obedience, though it may seem for the present to be to our loss. Wrong not others, and God shall right thee.

I. God gives them commission to seize upon the country of Sihon king of Heshbon, *v.* 24, 25. This was then God's way of disposing of kingdoms, but such particular grants are not now either to be expected or pretended. In this commission observe, 1. Though God assured them that the land should be their own, yet they must bestir themselves, and contend in battle with the enemy. What God gives we must endeavour to get. 2. God promises that when they fight he will fight for them. Do you *begin to possess it, and I will begin to put the dread of you* upon them. God would dispirit the enemy and so destroy them, would magnify Israel and so terrify all those against whom they were commissioned. See Exod. xv. 14.

II. Moses sends to Sihon a message of peace, and only begs a passage through his land, with a promise to give his country no disturbance, but the advantage of trading for ready money with so great a body, *v.* 26—29. Moses herein did neither disobey God, who bade him contend with Sihon, nor dissemble with Sihon; but doubtless it was by divine direction that he did it, that Sihon might be left inexcusable, though God hardened his heart. This may illustrate the method of God's dealing with those to whom he gives his gospel, but does not give grace to believe it.

III. Sihon began the war (*v.* 32), God

having *made his heart obstinate*, and hidden from his eyes the things that belonged to his peace (*v.* 30), that he might deliver him into the hand of Israel. Those that meddle with the people of God meddle to their own hurt; and God sometimes ruins his enemies by their own resolves. See Mic. iv. 11—13; Rev. xvi. 14.

IV. Israel was victorious. 1. They put all the Amorites to the sword, men, women, and children (*v.* 33, 34); this they did as the executioners of God's wrath; now the measure of the Amorites' iniquity was full (Gen. xv. 16), and the longer it was in the filling the sorer was the reckoning at last. This was one of the devoted nations. They died, not as Israel's enemies, but as sacrifices to divine justice, in the offering of which sacrifices Israel was employed, as a kingdom of priests. The case being therefore extraordinary, it ought not to be drawn into a precedent for military executions, which make no distinction and give no quarter: those will have *judgment without mercy that show no mercy.* 2. They took possession of all they had; their cities (*v.* 34), their goods (*v.* 35), and their land, *v.* 36. The wealth of the sinner is laid up for the just. What a new world did Israel now come into! Most of them were born, and had lived all their days, in a vast howling wilderness, where they knew not what either fields or cities were, had no houses to dwell in, and neither sowed nor reaped; and now of a sudden to become masters of a country so well built, so well husbanded, this made them amends for their long waiting, and yet it was but the earnest of a great deal more. Much more joyful will the change be which holy souls will experience when they remove out of the wilderness of this world to the *better country, that is, the heavenly, to the city that has foundations.*

CHAP. III.

Moses, in this chapter, relates, I. The conquest of Og, king of Bashan, and the seizing of his country, ver. 1—11. II. The distribution of these new conquests to the two tribes and a half, ver. 12—17. Under certain provisos and limitations, ver. 18—20. III. The encouragement given to Joshua to carry on the war which was so gloriously begun, ver. 21, 22. IV. Moses's request to go over into Canaan (ver. 23—25), with the denial of that request, but the grant of an equivalent, ver. 26, &c.

THEN we turned, and went up the way to Bashan: and Og the king of Bashan came out against us, he and all his people, to battle at Edrei. 2 And the Lord said unto me, Fear him not: for I will deliver him, and all his people, and his land, into thy hand; and thou shalt do unto him as thou didst unto Sihon king of the Amorites, which dwelt at Heshbon. 3 So the Lord our God delivered into our hands Og also, the king of Bashan, and all his people: and we smote him until none was left to him remaining. 4 And we took all his cities at that time, there was not a city which we took not from them, threescore cities, all the region of Argob, the kingdom of Og in Bashan. 5 All these cities *were* fenced with high walls, gates, and bars; beside unwalled towns a great many. 6 And we utterly destroyed them, as we did unto Sihon king of Heshbon, utterly destroying the men, women, and children, of every city. 7 But all the cattle, and the spoil of the cities, we took for a prey to ourselves. 8 And we took at that time out of the hand of the two kings of the Amorites the land that *was* on this side Jordan, from the river of Arnon unto mount Hermon; 9 (*Which* Hermon the Sidonians call Sirion; and the Amorites call it Shenir;) 10 All the cities of the plain, and all Gilead, and all Bashan, unto Salchah and Edrei, cities of the kingdom of Og in Bashan. 11 For only Og king of Bashan remained of the remnant of giants; behold, his bedstead *was* a bedstead of iron; *is* it not in Rabbath of the children of Ammon? nine cubits *was* the length thereof, and four cubits the breadth of it, after the cubit of a man.

We have here another brave country delivered into the hand of Israel, that of Bashan; the conquest of Sihon is often mentioned together with that of Og, to the praise of God, the rather because in these Israel's triumphs began, Ps. cxxxv. 11; cxxxvi. 19, 20. See,

I. How they got the mastery of Og, a very formidable prince, 1. Very strong, for he was of the remnant of the giants (*v.* 11); his personal strength was extraordinary, a monument of which was preserved by the Ammonites in his bedstead, which was shown as a rarity in their chief city. You might guess at his weight by the materials of his bedstead; it was iron, as if a bedstead of wood were too weak for him to trust to: and you might guess at his stature by the dimensions of it; it was nine cubits long and four cubits broad, which, supposing a cubit to be but half a yard (and some learned men have made it appear to be somewhat more), was four yards and a half long, and two yards broad; and if we allow his bedstead to be two cubits longer than himself, and that is as much as we need allow, he was three yards and a half high, double the stature of an ordinary man, and every way proportionable, yet they smote him, *v.* 3.

736

Note, When God pleads his people's cause he can deal with giants as with grasshoppers. No man's might can secure him against the Almighty. The army of Og was very powerful, for he had the command of sixty fortified cities, besides unwalled towns, *v.* 5. Yet all this was nothing before God's Israel, when they came with commission to destroy him. 2. He was very bold and daring: He *came out against Israel to battle, v.* 1. It was wonderful that he did not take warning by the ruin of Sihon, and send to desire conditions of peace; but he trusted to his own strength, and so was hardened to his destruction. Note, Those that are not awakened by the judgments of God upon others, but persist in their defiance of heaven, are ripening apace for the like judgments upon themselves, Jer. iii. 8. God bade Moses not fear him, *v.* 2. If Moses himself was so strong in faith as not to need the caution, yet it is probable that the people needed it, and for them these fresh assurances are designed: "*I will deliver him into thy hand;* not only deliver thee out of his hand, that he shall not be thy ruin, but deliver him *into thy hand,* that thou shalt be his ruin, and make him pay dearly for his attempt." He adds, *Thou shalt do to him as thou didst to Sihon,* intimating that they ought to be encouraged by their former victory to trust in God for another victory, for he is God, and changeth not.

II. How they got possession of Bashan, a very desirable country. They took all the cities (*v.* 4), and all the spoil of them, *v.* 7. They made them all their own, *v.* 10. So that now they had in their hands all that fruitful country which lay east of Jordan, from *the river Arnon unto Hermon, v.* 8. Their conquering and possessing these countries was intended, not only for the encouragement of Israel in the wars of Canaan, but for the satisfaction of Moses before his death. Since he must not live to see the completing of their victory and settlement, God thus gives him a specimen of it. Thus the Spirit is given to those that believe as the *earnest of their inheritance,* until the redemption of the purchased possession.

12 And this land, *which* we possessed at that time, from Aroer, which *is* by the river Arnon, and half mount Gilead, and the cities thereof, gave I unto the Reubenites and to the Gadites. 13 And the rest of Gilead, and all Bashan, *being* the kingdom of Og, gave I unto the half tribe of Manasseh; all the region of Argob, with all Bashan, which was called the land of giants. 14 Jair the son of Manasseh took all the country of Argob unto the coasts of Geshuri and Maa-

chathi; and called them after his own name, Bashan-havoth-jair, unto this day. 15 And I gave Gilead unto Machir. 16 And unto the Reubenites and unto the Gadites I gave from Gilead even unto the river Arnon half the valley, and the border even unto the river Jabbok, *which is* the border of the children of Ammon; 17 The plain also, and Jordan, and the coast *thereof*, from Chinnereth even unto the sea of the plain, *even* the salt sea, under Ashdoth-pisgah eastward. 18 And I commanded you at that time, saying, The LORD your God hath given you this land to possess it: ye shall pass over armed before your brethren the children of Israel, all *that are* meet for the war. 19 But your wives, and your little ones, and your cattle, *(for* I know that ye have much cattle,) shall abide in your cities which I have given you; 20 Until the LORD have given rest unto your brethren, as well as unto you, and *until* they also possess the land which the LORD your God hath given them beyond Jordan: and *then* shall ye return every man unto his possession, which I have given you.

Having shown how this country which they were now in was conquered, in these verses he shows how it was settled upon the Reubenites, Gadites, and half tribe of Manasseh, which we had the story of before, Num. xxxii. Here is the rehearsal. 1. Moses specifies the particular parts of the country that were allotted to each tribe, especially the distribution of the lot to the half tribe of Manasseh, the subdividing of which tribe is observable. Joseph was divided into Ephraim and Manasseh; Manasseh was divided into one half on the one side Jordan and the other half on the other side: that on the east side Jordan was again divided into two great families, which had their several allotments: Jair, *v.* 14, Machir, *v.* 15. And perhaps Jacob's prediction of the smallness of that tribe was now accomplished in these divisions and subdivisions. Observe that Bashan is here called *the land of the giants,* because it had been in their possession, but Og was the last of them. These giants, it seems, had lost their country, and were rooted out of it sooner than any of their neighbours; for those who, presuming upon their strength and stature, had their hand against every man, had every man's hand against them, and went down slain to the pit, though they were the terror of the mighty in

the land of the living. 2. He repeats the condition of the grant which they had already agreed to, *v.* 18—20. That they should send a strong detachment over Jordan to lead the van in the conquest of Canaan, who should not return to their families, at least not to settle (though for a time they might retire thither into winter quarters, at the end of a campaign), till they had seen their brethren in as full possession of their respective allotments as they themselves were now in of theirs. They must hereby be taught not to *look at their own things only, but at the things of others,* Phil. ii. 4. It ill becomes an Israelite to be selfish, and to prefer any private interest before the public welfare. When we are at rest we should desire to see our brethren at rest too, and should be ready to do what we can towards it; for we are not born for ourselves, but are members one of another. A good man cannot rejoice much in the comforts of his family unless withal he sees *peace upon Israel,* Ps. cxxviii. 6.

21 And I commanded Joshua at that time, saying, Thine eyes have seen all that the LORD your God hath done unto these two kings: so shall the LORD do unto all the kingdoms whither thou passest. 22 Ye shall not fear them: for the LORD your God he shall fight for you. 23 And I besought the LORD at that time, saying, 24 O Lord GOD, thou hast begun to show thy servant thy greatness, and thy mighty hand: for what God *is there* in heaven or in earth, that can do according to thy works, and according to thy might? 25 I pray thee, let me go over, and see the good land that *is* beyond Jordan, that goodly mountain, and Lebanon. 26 But the LORD was wroth with me for your sakes, and would not hear me: and the LORD said unto me, Let it suffice thee; speak no more unto me of this matter. 27 Get thee up into the top of Pisgah, and lift up thine eyes westward, and northward, and southward, and eastward, and behold *it* with thine eyes: for thou shalt not go over this Jordan. 28 But charge Joshua, and encourage him, and strengthen him: for he shall go over before this people, and he shall cause them to inherit the land which thou shalt see. 29 So we abode in the valley over against Beth-peor.

Here is, I. The encouragement which Moses gave to Joshua, who was to succeed

737

him in the government, *v.* 21, 22. He commanded him not to fear. Thus those that are aged and experienced in the service of God should do all they can to strengthen the hands of those that are young, and setting out in religion. Two things he would have him consider for his encouragement:—1. What God had done. Joshua had seen what a total defeat God had given by the forces of Israel to these two kings, and thence he might easily infer, *so shall the Lord do to all the rest of the kingdoms* upon which we are to make war. He must not only infer thence that thus the Lord can do with them all, for his arm is not shortened, but thus he will do, for his purpose is not changed; he that has begun will finish; *as for God, his work is perfect.* Joshua had seen it with his own eyes. And the more we have seen of the instances of divine wisdom, power, and goodness, the more inexcusable we are if we *fear what flesh can do unto us.* 2. What God had promised. The *Lord your God he shall fight for you;* and that cause cannot but be victorious which the Lord of hosts fights for. *If God be for us, who can be against us* so as to prevail? We reproach our leader if we follow him trembling.

II. The prayer which Moses made for himself, and the answer which God gave to that prayer.

1. His prayer was that, if it were God's will, he might go before Israel over Jordan into Canaan. At that time, when he had been encouraging Joshua to fight Israel's battles, taking it for granted that he must be their leader, he was touched with an earnest desire to go over himself, which expresses itself not in any passionate and impatient complaints, or reflections upon the sentence he was under, but in humble prayers to God for a gracious reversing of it. *I besought the Lord.* Note, We should never allow any desires in our hearts which we cannot in faith offer up to God by prayer; and what desires are innocent, let them be presented to God. We have not, because we ask not. Observe,

(1.) What he pleads here. Two things:— [1.] The great experience which he had had of God's goodness to him in what he had done for Israel: *"Thou hast begun to show thy servant thy greatness.* Lord, perfect what thou hast begun. Thou hast given me to see thy glory in the conquest of these two kings, and the sight has affected me with wonder and thankfulness. O let me see more of the outgoings of my God, my King! This great work, no doubt, will be carried on and completed; let me have the satisfaction of seeing it." Note, The more we see of God's glory in his works the more we shall desire to see. *The works of the Lord are great,* and therefore are sought out more and more *of all those that have pleasure therein.* [2.] The good impressions that had been made upon his heart by what he had seen: *For what God is there in heaven or earth that*

can do according to thy works? The more we are affected with what we have seen of God, of his wisdom, power, and goodness, the better we are prepared for further discoveries. Those shall see the works of God that admire him in them. Moses had thus expressed himself concerning God and his works long before (Exod. xv. 11), and he still continues of the same mind, that there are no works worthy to be compared with God's works, Ps. lxxxvi. 8.

(2.) What he begs: *I pray thee let me go over, v.* 25. God had said he should not go over; yet he prays that he might, not knowing but that the threatening was conditional, for it was not ratified with an oath, as that concerning the people was, that they should not enter. Thus Hezekiah prayed for his own life, and David for the life of his child, after both had been expressly threatened; and the former prevailed, though the latter did not. Moses remembered the time when he had by prayer prevailed with God to recede from the declarations which he had made of his wrath against Israel, Exod. xxxii. 14. And why might he not hope in like manner to prevail for himself? *Let me go over and see the good land.* Not, "Let me go over and be a prince and a ruler there;" he seeks not his own honour, is content to resign the government to Joshua; but, "Let me go to be a spectator of thy kindness to Israel, to see what I believe concerning the goodness of the land of promise." How pathetically does he speak of Canaan, that *good land,* that *goodly mountain!* Note, Those may hope to obtain and enjoy God's favours that know how to value them. What he means by *that goodly mountain* we may learn from Ps. lxxviii. 54, where it is said of God's Israel that *he brought them to the border of his sanctuary, even to this mountain which his right hand had purchased,* where it is plainly to be understood of the whole land of Canaan, yet with an eye to the sanctuary, the glory of it.

2. God's answer to this prayer had in it a mixture of mercy and judgment, that he might sing unto God of both.

(1.) There was judgment in the denial of his request, and that in something of anger too: *The Lord was wroth with me for your sakes, v.* 26. God not only sees sin in his people, but is much displeased with it; and even those that are delivered from the wrath to come may yet lie under the tokens of God's wrath in this world, and may be denied some particular favour which their hearts are much set upon. God is a gracious, tender, loving Father; but he is angry with his children when they do amiss, and denies them many a thing that they desire and are ready to cry for. But how was he wroth with Moses *for the sake of Israel?* Either, [1.] For that sin which they provoked him to; see Ps. cvi. 32, 33. Or, [2.] The removal of Moses at that time, when he could so ill be spared, was a rebuke to all Israel, and a punishment of their sin. Or, [3.] It was for their sakes, that it might be a warning to them to take heed of offending God by passionate and unbelieving speeches at any time, after the similitude of his transgression; for, if *this were done to such a green tree, what should be done to the dry ?* He acknowledges that God would not hear him. God had often heard him for Israel, yet he would not hear him for himself. It was the prerogative of Christ, the great Intercessor, to be heard always; yet of him his enemies said, *He saved others, himself he could not save,* which the Jews would not have upbraided him with had they considered that Moses, their great prophet, prevailed for others, but for himself he could not prevail. Though Moses, being one of the wrestling seed of Jacob, did not seek in vain, yet he had not the thing itself which he sought for. God may accept our prayers, and yet not grant us the very thing we pray for.

(2.) Here is mercy mixed with this wrath in several things :—[1.] God quieted the spirit of Moses under the decree that had gone forth by that word (*v.* 26), *Let it suffice thee.* With this word, no doubt, a divine power went to reconcile Moses to the will of God, and to bring him to acquiesce in it. If God does not by his providence give us what we desire, yet, if by his grace he makes us content without it, it comes much to one. *" Let it suffice thee* to have God for thy Father, and heaven for thy portion, though thou hast not every thing thou wouldest have in this world. Be satisfied with this, *God is all-sufficient."* [2.] He put an honour upon his prayer in directing him not to insist upon this request: *Speak no more to me of this matter.* It intimates that what God does not think fit to grant we should not think fit to ask, and that God takes such a pleasure in the prayer of the upright that it is no pleasure to him, no, not in any particular instance, to give a denial to it. [3.] He promised him a sight of Canaan *from the top of Pisgah, v.* 27. Though he should not have the possession of it, he should have the prospect of it; not to tantalize him, but such a sight of it as would yield him true satisfaction, and would enable him to form a very clear and pleasing idea of that promised land. Probably Moses had not only his sight preserved for other purposes, but greatly enlarged for this purpose; for, if he had not had such a sight of it as others could not have from the same place, it would have been no particular favour to Moses, nor the matter of a promise. Even great believers, in this present state, see heaven but at a distance. [4.] He provided him a successor, one who should support the honour of Moses and carry on and complete that glorious work which the heart of Moses was so much upon, the bringing of Israel to Canaan, and settling them there

(*v.* 28): *Charge Joshua and encourage him* in this work. Those to whom God gives a charge, he will be sure to give encouragement to. And it is a comfort to the church's friends (when they are dying and going off) to see God's work likely to be carried on by other hands, when they are silent in the dust.

CHAP. IV.

In this chapter we have, I. A most earnest and pathetic exhortation to obedience, both in general, and in some particular instances, backed with a great variety of very pressing arguments, repeated again and again, and set before them in the most moving and affectionate manner imaginable, ver. 1–40. II. The appointing of the cities of refuge on that side Jordan, ver. 41–43. III. The particular description of the place where Moses delivered the following repetition of the law, ver. 44, &c.

NOW therefore hearken, O Israel, unto the statutes and unto the judgments, which I teach you, for to do *them,* that ye may live, and go in and possess the land which the LORD God of your fathers giveth you. 2 Ye shall not add unto the word which I command you, neither shall ye diminish *aught* from it, that ye may keep the commandments of the LORD your God which I command you. 3 Your eyes have seen what the LORD did because of Baal-peor : for all the men that followed Baal-peor, the LORD thy God hath destroyed them from among you. 4 But ye that did cleave unto the LORD your God *are* alive every one of you this day. 5 Behold, I have taught you statutes and judgments, even as the LORD my God commanded me, that ye should do so in the land whither ye go to possess it. 6 Keep therefore and do *them ;* for this *is* your wisdom and your understanding in the sight of the nations, which shall hear all these statutes, and say, Surely this great nation *is* a wise and understanding people. 7 For what nation *is there so* great who *hath* God *so* nigh unto them, as the LORD our God *is* in all *things that* we call upon him *for ?* 8 And what nation *is there so* great, that hath statutes and judgments *so* righteous as all this law, which I set before you this day ? 9 Only take heed to thyself, and keep thy soul diligently, lest thou forget the things which thine eyes have seen, and lest they depart from thy heart all the days of thy life : but teach them thy sons, and thy sons' sons ; 10 *Specially* the day that thou stoodest before the LORD thy God in Horeb, when the

LORD said unto me, Gather me the people together, and I will make them hear my words, that they may learn to fear me all the days that they shall live upon the earth, and *that* they may teach their children. 11 And ye came near and stood under the mountain; and the mountain burned with fire unto the midst of heaven, with darkness, clouds, and thick darkness. 12 And the LORD spake unto you out of the midst of the fire: ye heard the voice of the words, but saw no similitude; only *ye heard* a voice. 13 And he declared unto you his covenant, which he commanded you to perform, *even* ten commandments; and he wrote them upon two tables of stone. 14 And the LORD commanded me at that time to teach you statutes and judgments, that ye might do them in the land whither ye go over to possess it. 15 Take ye therefore good heed unto yourselves; for ye saw no manner of similitude on the day *that* the LORD spake unto you in Horeb out of the midst of the fire: 16 Lest ye corrupt *yourselves*, and make you a graven image, the similitude of any figure, the likeness of male or female, 17 The likeness of any beast that *is* on the earth, the likeness of any winged fowl that flieth in the air, 18 The likeness of any thing that creepeth on the ground, the likeness of any fish that *is* in the waters beneath the earth: 19 And lest thou lift up thine eyes unto heaven, and when thou seest the sun, and the moon, and the stars, *even* all the host of heaven, shouldest be driven to worship them, and serve them, which the LORD thy God hath divided unto all nations under the whole heaven. 20 But the LORD hath taken you, and brought you forth out of the iron furnace, *even* out of Egypt, to be unto him a people of inheritance, as *ye are* this day. 21 Furthermore the LORD was angry with me for your sakes, and sware that I should not go over Jordan, and that I should not go in unto that good land, which the LORD thy God giveth thee *for* an inheritance: 22 But I must die in this land, I must not go over Jordan but

ye shall go over, and possess that good land. 23 Take heed unto yourselves, lest ye forget the covenant of the LORD your God, which he made with you, and make you a graven image, *or* the likeness of any *thing,* which the LORD thy God hath forbidden thee. 24 For the LORD thy God *is* a consuming fire, *even* a jealous God. 25 When thou shalt beget children, and children's children, and ye shall have remained long in the land, and shall corrupt *yourselves,* and make a graven image, *or* the likeness of any *thing,* and shall do evil in the sight of the LORD thy God, to provoke him to anger: 26 I call heaven and earth to witness against you this day, that ye shall soon utterly perish from off the land whereunto ye go over Jordan to possess it; ye shall not prolong *your* days upon it, but shall utterly be destroyed. 27 And the LORD shall scatter you among the nations, and ye shall be left few in number among the heathen, whither the LORD shall lead you. 28 And there ye shall serve gods, the work of men's hands, wood and stone, which neither see, nor hear, nor eat, nor smell. 29 But if from thence thou shalt seek the LORD thy God, thou shalt find *him,* if thou seek him with all thy heart and with all thy soul. 30 When thou art in tribulation, and all these things are come upon thee, *even* in the latter days, if thou turn to the LORD thy God, and shalt be obedient unto his voice; 31 (For the LORD thy God *is* a merciful God;) he will not forsake thee, neither destroy thee, nor forget the covenant of thy fathers which he sware unto them. 32 For ask now of the days that are past, which were before thee, since the day that God created man upon the earth, and *ask* from the one side of heaven unto the other, whether there hath been *any such thing* as this great thing *is,* or hath been heard like it? 33 Did *ever* people hear the voice of God speaking out of the midst of the fire, as thou hast heard, and live? 34 Or hath God assayed to go *and* take him a nation from the midst of *an-*

other nation, by temptations, by signs, and by wonders, and by war, and by a mighty hand, and by a stretched out arm, and by great terrors, according to all that the LORD your God did for you in Egypt before your eyes? 35 Unto thee it was showed, that thou mightest know that the LORD he *is* God; *there is* none else beside him. 36 Out of heaven he made thee to hear his voice, that he might instruct thee : and upon earth he showed thee his great fire; and thou heardest his words out of the midst of the fire. 37 And because he loved thy fathers, therefore he chose their seed after them, and brought thee out in his sight with his mighty power out of Egypt; 38 To drive out nations from before thee greater and mightier than thou *art*, to bring thee in, to give thee their land *for* an inheritance, as *it is* this day. 39 Know therefore this day, and consider *it* in thine heart, that the LORD he *is* God in heaven above, and upon the earth beneath : *there is* none else. 40 Thou shalt keep therefore his statutes, and his commandments, which I command thee this day, that it may go well with thee, and with thy children after thee, and that thou mayest prolong *thy* days upon the earth, which the LORD thy God giveth thee, for ever.

This most lively and excellent discourse is so entire, and the particulars of it are so often repeated, that we must take it altogether in the exposition of it, and endeavour to digest it into proper heads, for we cannot divide it into paragraphs.

I. In general, it is the use and application of the foregoing history; it comes in by way of inference from it : *Now therefore hearken, O Israel, v.* 1. This use we should make of the review of God's providences concerning us, we should by them be quickened and engaged to duty and obedience. The histories of the years of ancient times should in like manner be improved by us.

II. The scope and drift of his discourse is to persuade them to keep close to God and to his service, and not to forsake him for any other god, nor in any instance to decline from their duty to him. Now observe what he says to them, with a great deal of divine rhetoric, both by way of exhortation and direction, and also by way of motive and argument to enforce his exhortations.

1. See here how he charges and commands

them, and shows them *what is good, and what the Lord requires of them.*

(1.) He demands their diligent attention to the word of God, and to the statutes and judgments that were taught them : *Hearken, O Israel.* He means, not only that they must now give him the hearing, but that whenever the book of the law was read to them, or read by them, they should be attentive to it. "Hearken to the statutes, as containing the great commands of God and the great concerns of your own souls, and therefore challenging your utmost attention." At Horeb God had *made them hear his words* (*v.* 10), hear them with a witness; the attention which was then constrained by the circumstances of the delivery ought ever after to be engaged by the excellency of the things themselves. What God so *spoke once*, we should *hear twice*, hear often.

(2.) He charges them to preserve the divine law pure and entire among them, *v.* 2. Keep it pure, and do not add to it; keep it entire, and do not diminish from it. Not in practice, so some : "You shall not add by committing the evil which the law forbids, nor diminish by omitting the good which the law requires." Not in opinion, so others : "You shall not add your own inventions, as if the divine institutions were defective, nor introduce, much less impose, any rites of religious worship other than what God has appointed; nor shall you diminish, or set aside, any thing that is appointed, as needless or superfluous." God's work is perfect, nothing can be put to it, nor taken from it, without making it the worse. See Eccl. iii. 14. The Jews understand it as prohibiting the alteration of the text or letter of the law, even in the least jot or tittle; and to their great care and exactness herein we are very much indebted, under God, for the purity and integrity of the Hebrew code. We find a fence like this made about the New Testament in the close of it, Rev. xxii. 18, 19.

(3.) He charges them to keep God's *commandments* (*v.* 2), to *do them* (*v.* 5, 14), to *keep and do them* (*v.* 6), to *perform the covenant, v.* 13. Hearing must be in order to doing, knowledge in order to practice. God's commandments were the way they must keep in, the rule they must keep to; they must govern themselves by the moral precepts, perform their devotion according to the divine ritual, and administer justice according to the judicial law. He concludes his discourse (*v.* 40) with this repeated charge : *Thou shalt keep his statutes and his commandments which I command thee.* What are laws made for but to be observed and obeyed?

(4.) He charges them to be very strict and careful in their observance of the law (*v.* 9) : *Only take heed to thyself, and keep thy soul diligently ;* and (*v.* 15), *Take you therefore good heed unto yourselves ;* and again (*v.* 23), *Take heed to yourselves.* Those that would be religious must be very cautious, and walk circumspectly. Considering how many temptations we are compassed about with, and what corrupt inclinations we have in our own bosoms, we have great need to look about us and to keep our hearts with all diligence. Those cannot walk aright that walk carelessly and at all adventures.

(5.) He charges them particularly to take heed of the sin of idolatry, that sin which of all others they would be most tempted to by the customs of the nations, which they were most addicted to by the corruption of their hearts, and which would be most provoking to God and of the most pernicious consequences to themselves : *Take good heed,* lest in this matter *you corrupt yourselves, v.* 15, 16. Two sorts of idolatry he cautions them against :— [1.] The worship of images, however by them they might intend to worship the true God, as they had done in the golden calf, so changing the *truth of God into a lie* and his *glory into shame.* The second commandment is expressly directed against this, and is here enlarged upon, *v.* 15—18. "Take heed *lest you corrupt yourselves,*" that is, "lest you debauch yourselves ;" for those that think to make images of God form in their minds such notions of him as must needs be an inlet to all impieties ; and it is intimated that it is a spiritual adultery. "And take heed lest you destroy yourselves. If any thing ruin you, this will be it. Whatever you do, make no similitude of God, either in a human shape, *male or female,* or in the shape of any *beast or fowl, serpent or fish ;*" for the heathen worshipped their gods by images of all these kinds, being either not able to form, or not willing to admit, that plain demonstration which we find, Hos. viii. 6 : *The workman made it, therefore it is not God.* To represent an infinite Spirit by an image, and the great Creator by the image of a creature, is the greatest affront we can put upon God and the greatest cheat we can put upon ourselves. As an argument against their making images of God, he urges it very much upon them that when God made himself known to them at Horeb he did it by a voice of words which sounded in their ears, to teach them that *faith comes by hearing,* and God in the word is nigh us ; but no image was presented to their eye, for to see God as he is is reserved for our happiness in the other world, and to see him as he is not will do us hurt and no good in this world. You saw *no similitude (v.* 12), *no manner of similitude, v.* 15. Probably they expected to have seen some similitude, for they were ready to *break through unto the Lord to gaze,* Exod. xix. 21. But all they saw was *light* and *fire,* and nothing that they could make an image of, God in infinite wisdom so ordering his manifestation of himself because of the *peril of idolatry.* It is said indeed of Moses that he *beheld the similitude of the Lord* (Num. xii. 8), God allowing him that favour because he was above the temptation of idolatry ; but for the people

742

who had lately come from admiring the idols of Egypt, they must see no resemblance of God, lest they should have pretended to copy it, and so should have received the second commandment in vain ; "for" (says bishop Patrick) "they would have thought that this forbade them only to make any representation of God besides that wherein he showed himself to them, in which they would have concluded it lawful to represent him." Let this be a caution to us to take heed of making images of God in our fancy and imagination when we are worshipping him, lest thereby we corrupt ourselves. There may be idols in the heart, where there are none in the sanctuary. [2.] The worship of the sun, moon, and stars, is another sort of idolatry which they are here cautioned against, *v.* 19. This was the most ancient species of idolatry and the most plausible, drawing the adoration to those creatures that not only are in a situation above us, but are most sensibly glorious in themselves and most generally serviceable to the world. And the plausibleness of it made it the more dangerous. It is intimated here, *First,* How strong the temptation is to sense ; for the caution is, *Lest thou shouldest be driven to worship them* by the strong impulse of a vain imagination and the impetuous torrent of the customs of the nations. The heart is supposed to *walk after the eye,* which, in our corrupt and degenerate state, it is very apt to do. " *When thou seest the sun, moon, and stars,* thou wilt so admire their height and brightness, their regular motion and powerful influence, that thou wilt be strongly tempted to give that glory to them which is due to him that made them, and made them what they are to us—gave them their beings, and made them blessings to the world." It seems there was need of a great deal of resolution to arm them against this temptation, so weak was their faith in an invisible God and an invisible world. *Secondly,* Yet he shows how weak the temptation would be to those that would use their reason ; for these pretended deities, the *sun, moon, and stars,* were only blessings which the Lord their God, whom they were obliged to worship, had imparted to all nations. It is absurd to worship them, for they are man's servants, were made and ordained to give light on earth ; and shall we serve those that were made to serve us ? The sun, in Hebrew, is called *shemesh,* which signifies a *servant,* for it is the minister-general of this visible world, and holds the candle to all mankind ; let it not then be worshipped as a lord. Moreover, they are God's gifts ; he has imparted them ; whatever benefit we have by them, we owe it to him ; it is therefore highly injurious to him to give that honour and praise to them which is due to him only.

(6.) He charges them to teach their children to observe the laws of God : *Teach to thy sons, and thy sons' sons (v.* 9), *that they may teach their children, v.* 10. [1.] Care must be taken in general to preserve the entail of religion among them, and to transmit the knowledge and worship of God to posterity; for the kingdom of God in Israel was designed to be perpetual, if they did not forfeit the privilege of it. [2.] Parents must, in order hereunto, particularly take care to teach their own children the fear of God, and to train them up in an observance of all his commandments.

(7.) He charges them never to forget their duty: *Take heed lest you forget the covenant of the Lord your God, v. 23.* Though God is ever mindful of the covenant, we are apt to forget it; and this is at the bottom of all our departures from God. We have need therefore to watch against all those things which would put the covenant out of our minds, and to watch over our own hearts, lest at any time we let it slip; and so we must take heed lest at any time we forget our religion, lest we lose it or leave it off. Care and caution, and holy watchfulness, are the best helps against a bad memory. These are the directions and commands he gives them.

2. Let us see now what are the motives or arguments with which he backs these exhortations. How does he order the cause before them, and fill his mouth with arguments! He has a great deal to say on God's behalf. Some of his topics are indeed peculiar to that people, yet applicable to us. But, upon the whole, it is evident that religion has reason on its side, the powerful charms of which all that are irreligious wilfully stop their ears against.

(1.) He urges the greatness, glory, and goodness, of God. Did we consider what a God he is with whom we have to do, we should surely make conscience of our duty to him and not dare to sin against him. He reminds them here, [1.] That the Lord Jehovah is the *one only living and true God.* This they must *know and consider, v. 39.* There are many things which we know, but are not the better for, because we do not consider them, we do not apply them to ourselves, nor draw proper inferences from them. This is a truth so evident that it cannot but be known, and so influential that, if it were duly considered, it would effectually reform the world, *That the Lord Jehovah he is God,* an infinite and eternal Being, self-existent and self-sufficient, and the fountain of all being, power, and motion—that he is *God in heaven above,* clothed with all the glory and Lord of all the hosts of the upper world, and that he is God *upon earth beneath,* which, though distant from the throne of his glory, is not out of the reach of his sight or power, and though despicable and mean is not below his care and cognizance. And *there is none else,* no true and living God but himself. All the deities of the heathen were counterfeits and usurpers; nor did any of them so much as pretend to be universal

monarchs in heaven and earth, but only local deities. The Israelites, who worshipped no other than the supreme *Numen—Divinity,* were for ever inexcusable if they either changed their God or neglected him. [2.] That he is a *consuming fire, a jealous God, v. 24.* Take heed of offending him, for, *First,* He has a jealous eye to discern an affront; he must have your entire affection and adoration, and will by no means endure a rival. God's jealousy over us is a good reason for our godly jealousy over ourselves. *Secondly,* He has a heavy hand to punish an affront, especially in his worship, for therein he is in a special manner jealous. He is a *consuming fire:* his wrath against sinners is so: it is dreadful and destroying, it is a *fiery indignation* which will *devour the adversaries,* Heb. x. 27. Fire consumes that only which is fuel for it, so the wrath of God fastens upon those only who, by their own sin, have fitted themselves for destruction, 1 Cor iii. 13; Isa. xxvii. 4. Even in the New Testament we find the same argument urged upon us as a reason why we should serve *God with reverence* (Heb. xii. 28, 29), because though he is our God, and a rejoicing light to those that serve him faithfully, yet he is a consuming fire to those that trifle with him. *Thirdly,* That yet he is *a merciful God, v. 31.* It comes in here as an encouragement to repentance, but might serve as an inducement to obedience, and a consideration proper to prevent their apostasy. Shall we forsake a merciful God, who will never forsake us, as it follows here, if we be faithful unto him? Whither can we go to better ourselves? Shall we forget the covenant of our God, who will not *forget the covenant of our fathers?* Let us be held to our duty by the bonds of love, and prevailed with by the mercies of God to cleave to him.

(2.) He urges their relation to this God, his authority over them and their obligations to him. "The commandments you are to keep and do are not mine," says Moses, "not my inventions, not my injunctions, but they are the commandments of the Lord, framed by infinite wisdom, enacted by sovereign power. He is the *Lord God of your fathers* (v. 1), so that you are his by inheritance: your fathers were his, and you were born in his house. He is the *Lord your God* (v. 2), so that you are his by your own consent. He is the *Lord my God* (v. 5), so that I treat with you as his agent and ambassador;" and in his name Moses delivered unto them all that, and that only, which he had received from the Lord.

(3.) He urges the wisdom of being religious: *For this is your wisdom in the sight of the nations, v. 6.* In keeping God's commandments, [1.] They would act wisely for themselves: *This is your wisdom.* It is not only agreeable to right reason, but highly conducive to our true interest; this is one of the first and most ancient maxims of divine revelation, *The fear of the Lord, that is wisdom,* Job xxviii. 28. [2.] They would answer the expectations of their neighbours, who, upon reading or hearing the precepts of the law that was given them, would conclude that certainly the people that were governed by this law were a wise and understanding people. Great things may justly be looked for from those who are guided by divine revelation, and unto whom are committed the oracles of God. They must needs be wiser and better than other people; and so they are if they are ruled by the rules that are given them; and if they are not, though reproach may for their sakes be cast upon the religion they profess, yet it will in the end certainly return upon themselves to their eternal confusion. Those that enjoy the benefit of divine light and laws ought to conduct themselves so as to support their own reputation for wisdom and honour (see Eccl. x. 1), that God may be glorified thereby.

(4.) He urges the singular advantages which they enjoyed by virtue of the happy establishment they were under, *v.* 7, 8. Our communion with God (which is the highest honour and happiness we are capable of in this world) is kept up by the word and prayer; in both these Israel were happy above any people under heaven. [1.] Never were any people so privileged in speaking to God, *v.* 7. He was nigh unto them in all that they called upon him for, ready to answer their enquiries and resolve them by his oracle, ready to answer their requests and to grant them by a particular providence. When they had cried unto God for bread, for water, for healing, they had found him near them, to succour and relieve them, a very present help, and in the midst of them (Ps. xlvi. 1, 5), his ear open to their prayers. Observe, *First,* It is the character of God's Israel that on all occasions they call upon him, in every thing they make their requests known to God. They do nothing but what they consult him in, they desire nothing but what they come to him for. *Secondly,* Those that call upon God shall certainly find him within call, and ready to give an answer of peace to every prayer of faith; see Isa. lviii. 9, " Thou shalt cry, as the child for the nurse, *and he shall say, Here I am,* what does my dear child cry for?" *Thirdly,* This is a privilege which makes the Israel of God truly great and honourable. What can go further than this to magnify a people or person? Is any name more illustrious than that of Israel, *a prince with God? What nation is there so great?* Other nations might boast of greater numbers, larger territories, and more ancient incorporations; but none could boast of such an interest in heaven as Israel had. They had their gods, but not so nigh to them as Israel's God was; they could not help them in a time of need, as 1 Kings xviii. 27. [2.] Never were any people so privileged in hearing from God, by the statutes and judgments

744

which were set before them, *v.* 8. This also was the grandeur of Israel above any people. *What nation is there so great, that hath statutes and judgments so righteous?* Observe, *First,* That all these statutes and judgments of the divine law are infinitely just and righteous, above the statutes and judgments of any of the nations. The law of God is far more excellent than the law of nations. No law so consonant to natural equity and the unprejudiced dictates of right reason, so consistent with itself in all the parts of it, and so conducive to the welfare and interest of mankind, as the scripture-law is, Ps. cxix. 128. *Secondly,* The having of these statutes and judgments set before them is the true and trancendent greatness of any nation or people. See Ps. cxlvii. 19, 20. It is an honour to us that we have the Bible in reputation and power among us. It is an evidence of a people's being high in the favour of God, and a means of making them high among the nations. Those that magnify the law shall be magnified by it.

(5.) He urges God's glorious appearances to them at Mount Sinai, when he gave them this law. This he insists much upon. Take heed *lest thou forget the day that thou stoodest before the Lord thy God in Horeb, v.* 10. Some of them were now alive that could remember it, though they were then under twenty years of age, and the rest of them might be said to stand there in the loins of their fathers, who received the law and entered into covenant there, not for themselves only, but for their children, to whom God had an eye particularly in giving the law, that they might teach it to their children. Two things they must remember, and, one would think, they could never forget them:—[1.] What they saw at Mount Sinai, *v.* 11. They saw a strange composition of fire and darkness, both dreadful and very awful; and they must needs be a striking foil to each other; the darkness made the fire in the midst of it look the more dreadful. Fires in the night are most frightful, and the fire made the darkness that surrounded it look the more awful; for it must needs be a strong darkness which such a fire did not disperse. In allusion to this appearance upon Mount Sinai, God is said to show himself for his people, and against his and their enemies, in fire and darkness together, Ps. xviii. 8, 9. He tells them again (*v.* 36) what they saw, for he would have them never to forget it: *He showed thee his great fire.* One flash of lightning, that fire from heaven, strikes an awe upon us; and some have observed that most creatures naturally turn their face towards the lightning, as ready to receive the impressions of it; but how dreadful then must a constant fire from heaven be! It gave an earnest of the day of judgment, in which *the Lord Jesus shall be revealed in flaming fire.* As he reminds them of what they saw, so he tells them what they saw not; no manner of similitude, from which they might form either an idea of God in their fancies or an image of God in their high places. By what we see of God sufficient ground is given us to believe him to be a Being of infinite power and perfection, but no occasion given us to suspect him to have a body such as we have. [2.] What they heard at Mount Sinai (*v.* 12): " *The Lord spoke unto you* with an intelligible voice, in your own language, and you heard it." This he enlarges upon towards the close of his discourse, *v.* 32, 33, 36. *First, They heard the voice of God, speaking out of heaven.* God manifests himself to all the world in the works of creation, without speech or language, and yet their voice is heard (Ps. xix. 1—3); but to Israel he made himself known by speech and language, condescending to the weakness of the church's infant state. Here was the *voice of one crying in the wilderness, to prepare the way of the Lord. Secondly,* They heard it *out of the midst of the fire,* which showed that it was God himself that spoke to them, for who else could dwell with devouring fire? God spoke to Job out of the whirlwind, which was terrible; but to Israel out of the fire, which was more terrible. We have reason to be thankful that he does not thus speak to us, but by men like ourselves, *whose terror shall not make us afraid,* Job xxxiii. 6, 7. *Thirdly,* They heard it and yet lived, *v.* 33. It was a wonder of mercy that the fire did not devour them, or that they did not die for fear, when Moses himself trembled. *Fourthly,* Never any people heard the like. He bids them enquire of former days and distant places, and they would find this favour of God to Israel without precedent or parallel, *v.* 32. This singular honour done them called for singular obedience from them. It might justly be expected that they should do more for God than other people, since God had done so much more for them.

(6.) He urges God's gracious appearances for them, in bringing them out of Egypt, from the iron furnace, where they laboured in the fire, forming them into a people, and then taking them to be his own people, a *people of inheritance* (*v.* 20); this he mentions again, *v.* 34, 37, 38. Never did God do such a thing for any people: the rise of this nation was quite different from that of all other nations. [1.] They were thus dignified and distinguished, not for any thing in them that was deserving or inviting, but because God had a kindness for their fathers: he chose them. See the reasons of free grace; we are not beloved for our own sakes, but for his sake who is the great trustee of the covenant. [2.] They were delivered out of Egypt by miracles and signs, in mercy to them and in judgment upon the Egyptians, against whom God stretched out his arm, which was signified by Moses's stretching out his hand in summoning the plagues. [3.] They were designed for a happy settle-

ment in Canaan, *v.* 38. Nations must be driven out from before them, to make room for them, to show how much dearer they were to God than any other people were. Egyptians and Canaanites must both be sacrificed to Israel's honour and interest. Those that stand in Israel's light, in Israel's way, shall find that it is at their peril.

(7.) He urges God's righteous appearance against them sometimes for their sins. He specifies particularly the matter of Peor, *v.* 3, 4. This had happened very lately: their eyes had seen but the other day the sudden destruction of those that joined themselves to Baal-peor and the preservation of those that clave to the Lord, from which they might easily infer the danger of apostasy from God and the benefit of adherence to him. He also takes notice again of God's displeasure against himself: *The Lord was angry with me for your sakes, v.* 21, 22. He mentions this to try their ingenuousness, whether they would really be troubled for the great prejudice which they had occasioned to their faithful friend and leader. Others' sufferings for our sakes should grieve us more than our own.

(8.) He urges the certain advantage of obedience. This argument he begins with (*v.* 1): *That you may live, and go in and possess the land;* and this he concludes with (*v.* 40): *That it may go well with thee, and with thy children after thee.* He reminds them that they were upon their good behaviour, that their prosperity would depend upon their piety. If they kept God's precepts, he would undoubtedly fulfil his promises.

(9.) He urges the fatal consequences of their apostasy from God, that it would undoubtedly be the ruin of their nation. This he enlarges upon, *v.* 25—31. Here, [1.] He foresees their revolt from God to idols, that in process of time, when they had remained long in the land and were settled upon their lees, they *would corrupt themselves, and make a graven image;* this was the sin that would most easily beset them, *v.* 25. [2.] He foretels the judgments of God upon them for this: *You shall utterly be destroyed* (*v.* 26), *scattered among the nations, v.* 27. And their sin should be made their punishment (*v.* 28): " *There shall you serve gods, the work of men's hands,* be compelled to serve them, whether you will or no, or, through your own sottishness and stupidity, you will find no better succours to apply yourselves to in your captivity." Those that cast off the duties of religion in their prosperity cannot expect the comforts of it when they come to be in distress. Justly are they then sent to the *gods whom they have served,* Judg. x. 14. [3.] Yet he encourages them to hope that God would reserve mercy for them in the latter days, that he would by his judgments upon them bring them to repentance, and take them again into covenant with himself, *v.* 29—31. Here observe, *First*, That whatever place we are in we may *thence seek the Lord our God*, though ever so remote from our own land or from his holy temple. There is no part of this earth that has a gulf fixed between it and heaven. *Secondly*, Those, and those only, shall find God to their comfort, who seek him with all their heart, that is, who are entirely devoted to him, earnestly desirous of his favour and solicitous to obtain it. *Thirdly*, Afflictions are sent to engage and quicken us to see God, and, by the grace of God working with them, many are thus reduced to their right mind. " When these things shall come upon thee, it is to be hoped that thou wilt *turn to the Lord thy God*, for thou seest what comes of turning from him; see Dan. ix. 11, 12. *Fourthly*, God's faithfulness to his covenant encourages us to hope that he will not reject us, though we be driven to him by affliction. If we at length remember the covenant, we shall find that he has not forgotten it.

Now let all these arguments be laid together, and then say whether religion has not reason on its side. None cast off the government of their God but those that have first abandoned the understanding of a man.

41 Then Moses severed three cities on this side Jordan toward the sunrising; 42 That the slayer might flee thither, which should kill his neighbour unawares, and hated him not in times past; and that fleeing unto one of these cities he might live: 43 *Namely*, Bezer in the wilderness, in the plain country, of the Reubenites; and Ramoth in Gilead, of the Gadites; and Golan in Bashan, of the Manassites. 44 And this *is* the law which Moses set before the children of Israel: 45 These *are* the testimonies, and the statutes, and the judgments, which Moses spake unto the children of Israel, after they came forth out of Egypt, 46 On this side Jordan, in the valley over against Beth-peor, in the land of Sihon king of the Amorites, who dwelt at Heshbon, whom Moses and the children of Israel smote, after they were come forth out of Egypt: 47 And they possessed his land, and the land of Og king of Bashan, two kings of the Amorites, which *were* on this side Jordan toward the sun rising; 48 From Aroer, which *is* by the bank of the river Arnon, even unto mount Sihon, which *is* Hermon, 49 And all the plain on this

side Jordan eastward, even unto the sea of the plain, under the springs of Pisgah.

Here is, 1. The nomination of the cities of refuge on that side Jordan where Israel now lay encamped. Three cities were appointed for that purpose, one in the lot of Reuben, another in that of Gad, and another in that of the half tribe of Manasseh, *v.* 41—43. What Moses could do for that people while he was yet with them he did, to give example to the rulers who were settled that they might observe them the better when he was gone. 2. The introduction to another sermon that Moses preached to Israel, which we have in the following chapters. Probably it was preached the next sabbath day after, when the congregation attended to receive instruction. He had in general exhorted them to obedience in the former chapter; here he comes to repeat the law which they were to observe, for he demands a universal but not an implicit obedience. How can we do our duty if we do not know it? Here therefore he sets the law before them as the rule they were to work by, the way they were to walk in, sets it before them as the glass in which they were to see their natural face, that, looking into this perfect law of liberty, they might continue therein. *These are the testimonies, the statutes, and the judgments*, the moral, ceremonial, and judicial laws, which had been enacted before, when Israel had newly come out of Egypt, and were now repeated, *on this side Jordan, v.* 44—46. The place where Moses gave them these laws in charge is here particularly described. (1.) It was over-against Beth-peor, an idol-temple of the Moabites, which perhaps Moses sometimes looked towards, with a particular caution to them against the infection of that and other such like dangerous places. (2.) It was upon their new conquests, in the very land which they had got out of the hands of Sihon and Og, and were now actually in possession of, *v.* 47. Their present triumphs herein were a powerful argument for obedience.

CHAP. V.

In this chapter we have the second edition of the ten commandments. I. The general intent of them; they were in the nature of a covenant between God and Israel, ver. 1—5. II. The particular precepts are repeated (ver. 6—21), with the double delivery of them, both by word and writing, ver. 22. III. The settling of the correspondence thenceforward between God and Israel, by the mediation and ministry of Moses. 1. It was Israel's humble petition that it might be so, ver. 23—27. 2. It was God's gracious grant that it should be so, ver. 28—31. And hence he infers the obligation they were under to obedience, ver. 32, 33.

AND Moses called all Israel, and said unto them, Hear, O Israel, the statutes and judgments which I speak in your ears this day, that ye may learn them, and keep, and do them. 2 The LORD our God made a covenant with us in Horeb. 3 The LORD made not this covenant with our fathers, but with us, *even* us, who *are* all of us here alive this day. 4 The LORD talked with you face to face in the mount out of the midst of the fire, 5 (I stood between the LORD and you at that time, to show you the word of the LORD: for ye were afraid by reason of the fire, and went not up into the mount;) saying,

Here, 1. Moses summons the assembly. He *called all Israel;* not only the elders, but, it is likely, as many of the people as could come within hearing, *v.* 1. The greatest of them were not above God's command, nor the meanest of them below his cognizance; but they were all concerned to hear what they were all bound to do. 2. He demands attention: " *Hear, O Israel;* hear and heed, hear and remember, hear, that you may learn, and keep, and do; else your hearing is to no purpose." When we hear the word of God we must set ourselves to learn it, that we may have it ready to us upon all occasions, and what we have learned we must put in practice, for that is the end of hearing and learning; not to fill our heads with notions, or our mouths with talk, but to rectify and direct our affections and conversations. 3. He refers them to the covenant made with them in Horeb, as that which they must govern themselves by. See the wonderful condescension of divine grace in turning the command into a covenant, that we might be the more strongly bound to obedience by our own consent and the more encouraged in it by the divine promise, both which are supposed in the covenant. The promises and threatenings annexed to some of the precepts, as to the second, third, and fifth, make them amount to a covenant. Observe, (1.) The parties to this covenant. God made it, *not with our fathers,* not with Abraham, Isaac, and Jacob; to them God gave the *covenant of circumcision* (Acts vii. 8), but not that of the ten commandments. The light of divine revelation shone gradually, and the children were made to know more of God's mind than their fathers had done. "The covenant was made with us, or our immediate parents that represented us, before Mount Sinai, and transacted for us." (2.) The publication of this covenant. God himself did, as it were, read the articles to them (*v.* 4): He *talked with you face to face; word to word,* so the Chaldee. Not in dark visions, as of old he spoke to the fathers (Job iv. 12, 13), but openly and clearly, and so that all the thousands of Israel might hear and understand. He spoke to them, and then received the answer they returned to him: thus was it transacted *face to face.* (3.) The mediator of the covenant: *Moses stood between God and them,* at the foot of the mount (*v.* 5), and carried messages between them both for the settling of the pre-liminaries (Exod. xix.) and for the exchanging of the ratifications, Exod. xxiv. Herein Moses was a type of Christ, who *stands between God and man, to show us the word of the Lord,* a blessed days-man, that has laid his hand upon us both, so that we may both hear from God and speak to him without trembling.

6 I *am* the LORD thy God, which brought thee out of the land of Egypt, from the house of bondage. 7 Thou shalt have none other gods before me. 8 Thou shalt not make thee *any* graven image, *or* any likeness *of any thing* that *is* in heaven above, or that *is* in the earth beneath, or that *is* in the waters beneath the earth: 9 Thou shalt not bow down thyself unto them, nor serve them: for I the LORD thy God *am* a jealous God, visiting the iniquity of the fathers upon the children unto the third and fourth *generation* of them that hate me, 10 And showing mercy unto thousands of them that love me and keep my commandments. 11 Thou shalt not take the name of the LORD thy God in vain: for the LORD will not hold *him* guiltless that taketh his name in vain. 12 Keep the sabbath day to sanctify it, as the LORD thy God hath commanded thee. 13 Six days thou shalt labour, and do all thy work: 14 But the seventh day *is* the sabbath of the LORD thy God: *in it* thou shalt not do any work, thou, nor thy son, nor thy daughter, nor thy manservant, nor thy maidservant, nor thine ox, nor thine ass, nor any of thy cattle, nor thy stranger that *is* within thy gates; that thy manservant and thy maidservant may rest as well as thou. 15 And remember that thou wast a servant in the land of Egypt, and *that* the LORD thy God brought thee out thence through a mighty hand and by a stretched out arm: therefore the LORD thy God commanded thee to keep the sabbath day. 16 Honour thy father and thy mother, as the LORD thy God hath commanded thee; that thy days may be prolonged, and that it may go well with thee, in the land which the LORD thy God giveth thee. 17 Thou shalt not kill. 18 Neither shalt thou commit adultery. 19

Neither shalt thou steal. 20 Neither shalt thou bear false witness against thy neighbour. 21 Neither shalt thou desire thy neighbour's wife, neither shalt thou covet thy neighbour's house, his field, or his manservant, or his maidservant, his ox, or his ass, or any *thing* that *is* thy neighbour's. 22 These words the LORD spake unto all your assembly in the mount out of the midst of the fire, of the cloud, and of the thick darkness, with a great voice : and he added no more. And he wrote them in two tables of stone, and delivered them unto me.

Here is the repetition of the ten commandments, in which observe, 1. Though they had been spoken before, and written, yet they are again rehearsed ; for precept must be upon precept, and line upon line, and all little enough to keep the word of God in our minds and to preserve and renew the impressions of it. We have need to have the same things often inculcated upon us. See Phil. iii. 1. 2. There is some variation here from that record (Exod. xx.), as there is between the Lord's prayer as it is in Matt. vi. and as it is Luke xi. In both it is more necessary that we tie ourselves to the things than to the words unalterably. 3. The most considerable variation is in the fourth commandment. In Exod. xx. the reason annexed is taken from the creation of the world ; here it is taken from their deliverance out of Egypt, because that was typical of our redemption by Jesus Christ, in remembrance of which the Christian sabbath was to be observed : *Remember that thou wast a servant, and God brought thee out, v.* 15. And therefore, (1.) " It is fit that thy servants should be favoured by the sabbath-rest ; for thou knowest the heart of a servant, and how welcome one day's ease will be after six days' labour." (2.) " It is fit that thy God should be honoured by the sabbath-work, and the religious services of the day, in consideration of the great things he has done for thee." In the resurrection of Christ we were brought into the glorious liberty of the children of God, *with a mighty hand and an outstretched arm:* therefore, by the gospel-edition of the law, we are directed to observe the first day of the week, in remembrance of that glorious work of power and grace. 4. It is added in the fifth commandment, *That it may go well with thee,* which addition the apostle quotes, and puts first (Eph. vi. 3), *that it may be well with thee, and that thou mayest live long.* If there be instances of some that have been very dutiful to their parents, and yet have not lived long upon earth, we may reconcile it to the promise by this explication of it, Whether they live long

748

or no, it shall go well with them, either in this world or in a better. See Eccl. viii. 12. 5. The last five commandments are connected or coupled together, which they are not in Exodus : *Neither shalt thou commit adultery, neither shalt thou steal,* &c., which intimates that God's commands are all of a piece : the same authority that obliges us to one obliges us to another ; and we must not be partial in the law, but have respect to all God's commandments, for he that *offends in one point is guilty of all,* Jam. ii. 10, 11. 6. That these commandments were given with a great deal of awful solemnity, *v.* 22. (1.) They were spoken with *a great voice out of the fire and thick darkness.* That was a dispensation of terror, designed to make the gospel of grace the more welcome, and to be a specimen of the terrors of the judgment-day, Ps. l. 3, 4. (2.) *He added no more.* What other laws he gave them were sent by Moses, but no more were spoken in the same manner that the ten commandments were. *He added no more,* therefore we must not add : the law of the Lord is perfect. (3.) *He wrote them in two tables of stone,* that they might be preserved from corruption, and might be transmitted pure and entire to posterity, for whose use they were intended, as well as for the present generation. These being the heads of the covenant, the chest in which the written tables were deposited was called the *ark of the covenant.* See Rev. xi. 19.

23 And it came to pass, when ye heard the voice out of the midst of the darkness, (for the mountain did burn with fire,) that ye came near unto me, *even* all the heads of your tribes, and your elders ; 24 And ye said, Behold, the LORD our God hath showed us his glory and his greatness, and we have heard his voice out of the midst of the fire : we have seen this day that God doth talk with man, and he liveth. 25 Now therefore why should we die ? for this great fire will consume us : if we hear the voice of the LORD our God any more, then we shall die. 26 For who *is there of* all flesh, that hath heard the voice of the living God, speaking out of the midst of the fire, as we *have,* and lived ? 27 Go thou near, and hear all that the LORD our God shall say : and speak thou unto us all that the LORD our God shall speak unto thee ; and we will hear *it,* and do *it.* 28 And the LORD heard the voice of your words, when ye spake unto me ; and the LORD said unto me, I have heard

the voice of the words of this people, which they have spoken unto thee: they have well said all that they have spoken. 29 O that there were such a heart in them, that they would fear me, and keep all my commandments always, that it might be well with them, and with their children for ever! 30 Go say to them, Get you into your tents again. 31 But as for thee, stand thou here by me, and I will speak unto thee all the commandments, and the statutes, and the judgments, which thou shalt teach them, that they may do *them* in the land which I give them to possess it. 32 Ye shall observe to do therefore as the LORD your God hath commanded you: ye shall not turn aside to the right hand or to the left. 33 Ye shall walk in all the ways which the LORD your God hath commanded you, that ye may live, and *that it may be* well with you, and *that* ye may prolong *your* days in the land which ye shall possess.

Here, I. Moses reminds them of the agreement of both the parties that were now treating, in the mediation of Moses.

1. Here is the consternation that the people were put into by that extreme terror with which the law was given. They owned that they could not bear it any more: *"This great fire will consume us;* this dreadful voice will be fatal to us; we shall certainly die if we hear it any more," *v.* 25. They wondered that they were not already struck dead with it, and took it for an extraordinary instance of the divine power and goodness, not only that they were thus spoken to, but that they were enabled to bear it. For *who ever heard the voice of the living God, as we have, and lived?* God's appearances have always been terrible to man, ever since the fall: but Christ, having taken away sin, invites us to come boldly to the throne of grace.

2. Their earnest request that God would henceforward speak to them by Moses, with a promise that they would hear what he said as from God himself, and do it, *v.* 27. It seems by this, (1.) That they expected to receive further commands from God and were willing to hear more from him. (2.) That they thought Moses able to bear those discoveries of the divine glory which they by reason of guilt were sensible of their inability to stand up under. They believed him to be a favourite of Heaven, and also one that would be faithful to them; yet at other times they murmured at him, and but a little before this were ready to stone him, Exod. xvii.

4. See how men's convictions correct their

passions. (3.) That now they were in a good mind, under the strong convictions of the word they heard. Many have their consciences startled by the law that have them not purified; fair promises are extorted from them, but no good principles fixed and rooted in them.

3. God's approbation of their request. (1.) He commends what they said, *v.* 28. They spoke it to Moses, but God took notice of it; for there is not a word in our tongue but he knows it. He acknowledges, *They have well said.* Their owning the necessity of a mediator to deal between them and God was well said. Their desire to receive further directions from God by Moses, and their promise to observe what directions should be given them, were well said. And what is well said shall have its praise with God, and should have with us. What is good, as far as it goes, let it be commended. (2.) He wishes they were but sincere in it: *O that there were such a heart in them! v.* 29. [1.] Such a heart as they should have, a heart to fear God, and keep his commandments for ever. Note, The God of heaven is truly and earnestly desirous of the welfare and salvation of poor sinners. He has given abundant proof that he is so: he gives us time and space to repent, by his mercies invites us to repentance, and waits to be gracious; he has sent his Son to redeem us, published a general offer of pardon and life, promised his Spirit to those that pray for him, and has said and sworn that he has no pleasure in the ruin of sinners. [2.] Such a heart as they now had, or one would think they had. Note, It would be well with many if there were always such a heart in them as there seems to be sometimes, when they are under conviction of sin, or the rebukes of Providence, or when they come to look death in the face: *How gracious will they be when these pangs come upon them!* O that there were always such a heart in them! (3.) He appoints Moses to be his messenger to them, to receive the law from his mouth and to communicate it to them, *v.* 31. Here the matter was settled by consent of both parties that God should henceforward speak to us by men like ourselves, by Moses and the prophets, by the apostles and the evangelists, and, if we believe not these, neither should we be persuaded though God should speak to us as he did to Israel at Mount Sinai, or send expresses from heaven or hell.

II. Hence he infers a charge to them to observe and do all that God had commanded them, *v.* 32, 33. Seeing God had shown himself so tender of them, and so willing to consider their frame and gratify them in what they desired, and withal so ready to make the best of them,—seeing they themselves had desired to have Moses for their teacher, who was now teaching them,—and seeing they had promised so solemnly, and under the influence of so many good causes and considerations, that they would hear and do, he charges them to *walk in all the ways that God had commanded them,* assuring them that it would be highly for their advantage to do so. The only way to be happy is to be holy. *Say to the righteous, It shall be well with them.*

CHAP. VI.

Moses, in this chapter, goes on with his charge to Israel, to be sure to keep up their religion in Canaan. It is much the same with ch. iv. I. His preface is a persuasive to obedience, ver. 1—3. II. He lays down the great principles of obedience. The first truth to be believed, That God is one, ver. 4. The first duty to be done, To love him with all our heart, ver. 5. III. He prescribes the means for keeping up religion, ver. 6—9. IV. He cautions them against those things which would be the ruin of religion—abuse of plenty (ver. 10—12), inclination to idolatry (ver. 14, 15), and gives them some general precepts, ver. 13, 16—18. V. He directs them what instructions to give their children, ver. 20, &c.

NOW these *are* the commandments, the statutes, and the judgments, which the LORD your God commanded to teach you, that ye might do *them* in the land whither ye go to possess it: 2 That thou mightest fear the LORD thy God, to keep all his statutes and his commandments, which I command thee, thou, and thy son, and thy son's son, all the days of thy life; and that thy days may be prolonged. 3 Hear therefore, O Israel, and observe to do *it;* that it may be well with thee, and that ye may increase mightily, as the LORD God of thy fathers hath promised thee, in the land that floweth with milk and honey.

Observe here, 1. That Moses taught the people all that, and that only, which God commanded him to teach them, *v.* 1. Thus Christ's ministers are to teach his churches *all that he has commanded,* and neither more nor less, Matt. xxviii. 20. 2. That the end of their being taught was that they might do as they were taught (*v.* 1), might *keep God's statutes* (*v.* 2), and *observe to do them, v.* 3. Good instructions from parents and ministers will but aggravate our condemnation if we do not live up to them. 3. That Moses carefully endeavoured to fix them for God and godliness, now that they were entering upon the land of Canaan, that they might be prepared for the comforts of that land, and fortified against the snares of it, and now that they were setting out in the world might set out well. 4. That the fear of God in the heart will be the most powerful principle of obedience: *That thou mightest fear the Lord thy God, to keep all his statutes, v.* 2. 5. The entail of religion in a family, or country, is the best entail: it is highly desirable that not we only, but our children, and our children's children, may fear the Lord. 6. Religion and righteousness advance and secure the prosperity of any people. Fear God, and it shall be well with thee. Those that are well taught, if they do what they are taught, shall
750

be well fed too, as Israel in the *land flowing with milk and honey, v.* 3.

4 Hear, O Israel: The LORD our God *is* one LORD: 5 And thou shalt love the LORD thy God with all thine heart, and with all thy soul, and with all thy might. 6 And these words, which I command thee this day, shall be in thine heart: 7 And thou shalt teach them diligently unto thy children, and shalt talk of them when thou sittest in thine house, and when thou walkest by the way, and when thou liest down, and when thou risest up. 8 And thou shalt bind them for a sign upon thine hand, and they shall be as frontlets between thine eyes. 9 And thou shalt write them upon the posts of thy house, and on thy gates. 10 And it shall be, when the LORD thy God shall have brought thee into the land which he sware unto thy fathers, to Abraham, to Isaac, and to Jacob, to give thee great and goodly cities, which thou buildedst not, 11 And houses full of all good *things,* which thou filledst not, and wells digged, which thou diggedst not, vineyards and olive trees, which thou plantedst not; when thou shalt have eaten and be full; 12 *Then* beware lest thou forget the LORD, which brought thee forth out of the land of Egypt, from the house of bondage. 13 Thou shalt fear the LORD thy God, and serve him, and shalt swear by his name. 14 Ye shall not go after other gods, of the gods of the people which *are* round about you; 15 (For the LORD thy God *is* a jealous God among you) lest the anger of the LORD thy God be kindled against thee, and destroy thee from off the face of the earth. 16 Ye shall not tempt the LORD your God, as ye tempted *him* in Massah.

Here is, I. A brief summary of religion, containing the first principles of faith and obedience, *v.* 4, 5. These two verses the Jews reckon one of the choicest portions of scripture: they write it in their phylacteries, and think themselves not only obliged to say it at least twice every day, but very happy in being so obliged, having this saying among them, *Blessed are we, who every morning and evening say, Hear, O Israel, the*

Lord our God is one Lord. But more blessed are we if we duly consider and improve,

1. What we are here taught to believe concerning God : That *Jehovah our God is one Jehovah.* (1.) That the God whom we serve is Jehovah, a Being infinitely and eternally perfect, self-existent, and self-sufficient. (2.) That he is the one only living and true God; he only is God, and he is but one. The firm belief of this self-evident truth would effectually arm them against all idolatry, which was introduced by that fundamental error, that there are gods many. It is past dispute that there is one God, and there *is no other but he,* Mark xii. 32. Let us therefore have no other, nor desire to have any other. Some have thought there is here a plain intimation of the trinity of persons in the unity of the Godhead; for here is the name of God three times, and yet all declared to be one. Happy they that have this one Lord for their God; for they have but one master to please, but one benefactor to seek to. It is better to have one fountain than a thousand cisterns, one all-sufficient God than a thousand insufficient ones.

2. What we are here taught concerning the duty which God requires of man. It is all summed up in this as its principle, *Thou shalt love the Lord thy God with all thy heart.* He had undertaken (*v.* 2) to teach them to fear God; and, in pursuance of his undertaking, he here teaches them to love him, for the warmer our affection to him the greater will be our veneration for him: the child that honours his parents no doubt loves them. Did ever any prince make a law that his subjects should love him? Yet such is the condescension of the divine grace that this is made the first and great commandment of God's law, that we love him, and that we perform all other parts of our duty to him from a principle of love. *My son, give me thy heart.* We must highly esteem him, be well pleased that there is such a Being, well pleased in all his attributes, and relations to us: our desire must be towards him, our delight in him, our dependence upon him, and to him we must be entirely devoted. It must be a constant pleasure to us to think of him, hear from him, speak to him, and serve him. We must love him, (1.) As the Lord, the best of beings, most excellent and amiable in himself. (2.) As our God, a God in covenant with us, our Father, and the most kind and bountiful of friends and benefactors. We are also commanded to love God *with all our heart, and soul, and might ;* that is, we must love him, [1.] With a sincere love; not in word and tongue only, saying we love him when our hearts are not with him, but inwardly, and in truth, solacing ourselves in him. [2] With a strong love; the heart must be carried out towards him with great ardour and fervency of affection. Some have hence thought that we should avoid saying (as we commonly express ourselves) that we will do this or that

with all our heart, for we must not do any thing with all our heart but love God; and that this phrase, being here used concerning that sacred fire, should not be unhallowed. He that is our all must have our all, and none but he. [3.] With a superlative love; we must love God above any creature whatsoever, and love nothing besides him but what we love for him and in subordination to him. [4.] With an intelligent love; for so it is explained, Mark xii. 33. To love him with all the heart, and with all the understanding, we must know him, and therefore love him as those that see good cause to love him. [5.] With an entire love; he is one, and therefore our hearts must be united in this love, and the whole stream of our affections must run towards him. O that this love of God may be shed abroad in our hearts !

II. Means are here prescribed for the maintaining and keeping up of religion in our hearts and houses, that it might not wither and go to decay. And they are these :—1. Meditation : *These words which I command thee shall be in thy heart, v.* 6. Though the words alone without the things will do us no good, yet we are in danger of losing the things if we neglect the words, by which ordinarily divine light and power are conveyed to the heart. God's words must be laid up in our heart, that our thoughts may be daily conversant with them and employed about them, and thereby the whole soul may be brought to abide and act under the influence and impression of them. This immediately follows upon the law of loving God with all your heart; for those that do so will lay up his word in their hearts both as an evidence and effect of that love and as a means to preserve and increase it. He that loves God loves his Bible. 2. The religious education of children (*v.* 7): " *Thou shalt teach them diligently to thy children ;* and by communicating thy knowledge thou wilt increase it." Those that love the Lord God themselves should do what they can to engage the affections of their children to him, and so to preserve the entail of religion in their families from being cut off. *Thou shalt whet them diligently upon thy children,* so some read it ; frequently repeat these things to them, try all ways of instilling them into their minds, and making them pierce into their hearts ; as, in whetting a knife, it is turned first on this side, then on that. "Be careful and exact in teaching thy children; and aim, as by whetting, to sharpen them, and put an edge upon them. Teach them to thy children, not only those of thy own body" (say the Jews) "but all those that are any way under thy care and tuition." Bishop Patrick well observes here that Moses thought his law so very plain and easy that every father might be able to instruct his sons in it and every mother her daughters. Thus that good thing which is committed to us we must carefully transmit to those that come after us, that it may be perpetuated. 3. Pious discourse. "Thou shalt talk of these things, with due reverence and seriousness, for the benefit not only of thy children, but of thy other domestics, thy friends and companions, as thou sittest in thy house at work, or at meat, or at rest, or to receive visits, and when thou walkest by the way for diversion, or for conversation, or in journeys, when at night thou art retiring from thy family to lie down for sleep, and when in the morning thou hast risen up and returnest to thy family again. Take all occasions to discourse with those about thee of divine things ; not of unrevealed mysteries, or matters of doubtful disputation, but of the plain truths and laws of God, and the things that belong to our peace." So far is it from being reckoned a diminution to the honour of sacred things to make them the subject of our familiar discourse that they are recommended to us to be talked of ; for the more conversant we are with them the more we shall admire them and be affected with them, and may thereby be instrumental to communicate divine light and heat. 4. Frequent reading of the word : *They shall be as frontlets between thy eyes, and thou shalt write them upon the posts of thy house, v.* 8, 9. It is probable that at that time there were few written copies of the whole law, only at the feasts of tabernacles the people had it read to them ; and therefore God appointed them, at least for the present, to write some select sentences of the law, that were most weighty and comprehensive, upon their walls, or in scrolls of parchment to be worn about their wrists ; and some think that hence the phylacteries so much used among the Jews took rise. Christ blames the Pharisees, not for wearing them, but for affecting to have them broader than other people's, Matt. xxiii. 5. But when Bibles came to be common among them there was less occasion for this expedient. It was prudently and piously provided by the first reformers of the English church that then, when Bibles were scarce, some select portions of scripture should be written on the walls and pillars of the churches, which the people might make familiar to them, in conformity to this direction, which seems to have been binding in the letter of it to the Jews as it is to us in the intent of it, which is that we should endeavour by all means possible to make the word of God familiar to us, that we may have it ready to us upon all occasions, for our restraint from sin and our direction and excitement to our duty. It must be as that which is *graven on the palms of our hands,* always before our eyes. See Prov. vii. 1—3. It is also intimated that we must never be ashamed to own our religion, nor to own ourselves under the check and government of it. Let it be written on our gates, and let every one that goes by our door read it, that we believe Je-

752

hovah to be God alone, and believe ourselves bound to *love him with all our hearts.*

III. A caution is here given not to forget God in a day of prosperity and plenty, *v.* 10—12. Here, 1. He raises their expectations of the goodness of their God, taking it for granted that he would bring them into the good land that he had promised (*v.* 10), that they should no longer dwell in tents as shepherds and poor travellers, but should settle in great and goodly cities, should no longer wander in a barren wilderness, but should enjoy houses well furnished and gardens well planted (*v.* 11), and all this without any care and expense of their own, which he here lays a great stress upon—*Cities which thou buildedst not, houses which thou filledst not, &c.,* both because it made the mercy really much more valuable that what they had came to them so cheaply, and yet, if they did not actually consider it, the mercy would be the less esteemed, for we are most sensible of the value of that which has cost us dear. When they came so easily by the gift they would be apt to grow secure, and unmindful of the giver. 2. He engages their watchfulness against the badness of their own hearts : *Then beware,* when thou liest safe and soft, *lest thou forget the Lord, v.* 12. Note, (1.) In a day of prosperity we are in great danger of forgetting God, our dependence upon him, our need of him, and our obligations to him. When the world smiles we are apt to make our court to it, and expect our happiness in it, and so we forget him that is our only portion and rest. Agur prays against this temptation (Prov. xxx. 9) : *Lest I be full and deny thee.* (2.) There is therefore need of great care and caution at such a time, and a strict watch over our own hearts. " *Then beware ;* being warned of your danger, stand upon your guard against it. *Bind the words of God for a sign upon thy hand,* for this end, to prevent thy forgetting God. When thou art settled in Canaan forget not thy deliverance out of Egypt ; but look to the *rock out of which thou wast hewn.* When thy latter end has greatly increased, remember the smallness of thy beginnings."

IV. Some special precepts and prohibitions are here given, which are of great consequence. 1. They must upon all occasions give honour to God (*v.* 13) : *Fear him and serve him* (for, if he be a Master, we must both reverence him and do his work); *and swear by his name,* that is, they must not upon any occasion appeal to any other, as the discerner of truth and avenger of wrong. Swear by him only, and not by any idol, or any other creature. Swear by his name in all treaties and covenants with the neighbouring nations, and do not compliment them so far as to swear by their gods. Swearing by his name is sometimes put for an open profession of his name. Isa. xlv. 23, *Every tongue shall swear,* is expounded (Rom. xiv. 11), *Every tongue shall confess to God.*

2. They must not upon any occasion give that honour to other gods (*v.* 14): *You shall not go after other gods,* that is, "You shall not serve nor worship them;" for therein they went astray, they went a whoring from the true God, who in this, more than in any thing, is a *jealous God* (*v.* 15): and the learned bishop Patrick observes here, out of Maimonides, that we never find, either in the law or the prophets, *anger,* or *fury,* or *jealousy,* or *indignation,* attributed to God but upon occasion of idolatry. 3. They must take heed of dishonouring God by *tempting him* (*v.* 16): *You shall not tempt the Lord your God,* that is, "You shall not in any exigence distrust the power, presence, and providence of God, nor quarrel with him, which, if they indulged an evil heart of unbelief, they would take occasion to do in Canaan as well as in the wilderness. No change of condition will cure a disposition to murmur and fret. Our Saviour uses this caution as an answer to one of Satan's temptations, with application to himself, Matt. iv. 7, *Thou shalt not tempt the Lord thy God,* either by despairing of his power and goodness while we keep in the way of our duty, or by presuming upon it when we turn aside out of that way.

17 Ye shall diligently keep the commandments of the Lord your God, and his testimonies, and his statutes, which he hath commanded thee. 18 And thou shalt do *that which is* right and good in the sight of the Lord: that it may be well with thee, and that thou mayest go in and possess the good land which the Lord sware unto thy fathers, 19 To cast out all thine enemies from before thee, as the Lord hath spoken. 20 *And* when thy son asketh thee in time to come, saying, What *mean* the testimonies, and the statutes, and the judgments, which the Lord our God hath commanded you? 21 Then thou shalt say unto thy son, We were Pharaoh's bondmen in Egypt; and the Lord brought us out of Egypt with a mighty hand: 22 And the Lord showed signs and wonders, great and sore, upon Egypt, upon Pharaoh, and upon all his household, before our eyes: 23 And he brought us out from thence, that he might bring us in, to give us the land which he sware unto our fathers. 24 And the Lord commanded us to do all these statutes, to fear the Lord our God, for our good always, that he might preserve us alive, as *it is* at this day. 25 And it

shall be our righteousness, if we observe to do all these commandments before the Lord our God, as he hath commanded us.

Here, I. Moses charges them to keep God's commandments themselves: *You shall diligently keep God's commandments,* v. 17—19. Note, It requires a great deal of care and pains to keep up religion in the power of it in our hearts and lives. Negligence will ruin us; but we cannot be saved without diligence. To induce them to this, he here shows them, 1. That this would be very acceptable to God: it is *right and good in the sight of the Lord;* and that is right and good indeed that is so in *God's sight.* If we have any regard to the favour of our Creator as our felicity, and the law of our creation as our rule, we shall be religious. 2. That it would be very advantageous and profitable to themselves. It would secure to them the possession of the land of Canaan, prosperity there, and constant victory over those that stood in their way. In short, "Do well, and it shall be *well with thee.*"

II. He charges them to instruct their children in the commands of God, not only that they might in their tender years intelligently and affectionately join in religious services, but that afterwards they might in their day keep up religion, and convey it to those that should come after them. Now,

1. Here is a proper question which it is supposed the children would ask (*v.* 20): "*What mean the testimonies and the statutes?* What is the meaning of the feasts we observe, the sacrifices we offer, and the many peculiar customs we keep up?" Observe, (1.) All divine institutions have a certain meaning, and there is something great designed in them. (2.) It concerns us to know and understand the meaning of them, that we may perform a reasonable service and may not *offer the blind for sacrifice.* (3.) It is good for children betimes to enquire into the true intent and meaning of the religious observances they are trained up in. If any are thus inquisitive in divine things it is a good sign that they are concerned about them, and a good means of their attaining to a great acquaintance with them. *Then shall we know* if thus we *follow on to know.*

2. Here is a full answer put into the parents' mouths to be given to this good question. Parents and teachers must give instruction to those under their charge, though they do not ask it, nay, though they have an aversion to it; much more must they be ready to answer questions, and to give instruction when it is desired; for it may be hoped that those who ask it will be willing to receive it. Did the children ask the meaning of God's laws? Let them be told that they were to be observed, (1.) In a grateful remembrance of God's former favours to them, especially their deliverance out of

753

Egypt, v. 21—23. The children must be often told of the deplorable state their ancestors were in when they were bondmen in Egypt, the great salvation God wrought for them in fetching them out thence, and that God, in giving them these peculiar statutes, meant to perpetuate the memorial of that work of wonder, by which they were formed into a peculiar people. (2.) As the prescribed condition of his further favours (v. 24): *The Lord commanded us all these statutes for our good.* Note, God commands us nothing but what is really for our good. It is our interest as well as our duty to be religious. [1.] It will be our life: *That he might preserve us alive,* which is a great favour, and more than we could expect, considering how often we have forfeited life itself. Godliness has the promise of the continuance and comfort of the life that now is as far as it is for God's glory. [2.] It will be our righteousness. Could we perfectly fulfil but that one command of loving God with all our heart, soul, and might, and could we say, "We have never done otherwise," this would be so our righteousness as to entitle us to the benefits of the covenant of innocency; had we continued in every thing that is written in the book of the law to do it, the law would have justified us. But this we cannot pretend to, therefore our sincere obedience shall be accepted through a Mediator to denominate us, as Noah was, *righteous before God,* Gen. vii. 1; Luke i. 6; and 1 John iii. 7. The Chaldee reads it, *There shall be a reward to us if we observe to do these commandments;* for, without doubt, in keeping God's commandments there is great reward.

CHAP. VII.

Moses in this chapter exhorts Israel, I. In general, to keep God's commandments, ver. 11, 12. II. In particular, and in order to that, to keep themselves pure from all communion with idolaters. 1. They must utterly destroy the seven devoted nations, and not spare them, or make leagues with them, ver. 1, 2, 16, 24. 2. They must by no means marry with the remainders of them, ver. 3, 4. 3. They must deface and consume their altars and images, and not so much as take the silver and gold of them to their own use, ver. 5, 25, 26. To enforce this charge, he shows that they were bound to do so, (1.) in duty. Considering [1.] Their election to God, ver. 6. [2.] The reason of that election, ver. 7, 8. [3.] The terms they stood upon with God, ver. 9, 10. (2.) In interest. It is here promised, [1.] In general, that, if they would serve God, he would bless and prosper them, ver. 12—15. [2.] In particular, that if they would drive out the nations, that they might not be a temptation to them, God would drive them out, that they should not be any vexation to them, ver. 17, &c.

WHEN the Lord thy God shall bring thee into the land whither thou goest to possess it, and hath cast out many nations before thee, the Hittites, and the Girgashites, and the Amorites, and the Canaanites, and the Perizzites, and the Hivites, and the Jebusites, seven nations greater and mightier than thou; 2 And when the Lord thy God shall deliver them before thee; thou shalt smite them, *and* utterly destroy them; thou shalt make no covenant with them, nor show mercy unto them: 3 Neither

shalt thou make marriages with them; thy daughter thou shalt not give unto his son, nor his daughter shalt thou take unto thy son. 4 For they will turn away thy son from following me, that they may serve other gods: so will the anger of the Lord be kindled against you, and destroy thee suddenly. 5 But thus shall ye deal with them; ye shall destroy their altars, and break down their images, and cut down their groves, and burn their graven images with fire. 6 For thou *art* a holy people unto the Lord thy God: the Lord thy God hath chosen thee to be a special people unto himself, above all people that *are* upon the face of the earth. 7 The Lord did not set his love upon you, nor choose you, because ye were more in number than any people; for ye *were* the fewest of all people: 8 But because the Lord loved you, and because he would keep the oath which he had sworn unto your fathers, hath the Lord brought you out with a mighty hand, and redeemed you out of the house of bondmen, from the hand of Pharaoh king of Egypt. 9 Know therefore that the Lord thy God, he *is* God, the faithful God, which keepeth covenant and mercy with them that love him and keep his commandments to a thousand generations; 10 And repayeth them that hate him to their face, to destroy them: he will not be slack to him that hateth him, he will repay him to his face. 11 Thou shalt therefore keep the commandments, and the statutes, and the judgments, which I command thee this day, to do them.

Here is, I. A very strict caution against all friendship and fellowship with idols and idolaters. Those that are taken into communion with God must have no communication with the unfruitful works of darkness. These things they are charged about for the preventing of this snare now before them.

1. They must *show them no mercy,* v. 1, 2. Bloody work is here appointed them, and yet it is God's work, and good work, and in its time and place needful, acceptable, and honourable.

(1.) God here engages to do his part. It is spoken of as a thing taken for granted that God would *bring them into the land of promise,* that he would cast out the nations before them, who were the present occupants of that land; no room was left to doubt of that. His power is irresistible, and therefore he can do it; his promise is inviolable, and therefore he will do it. Now, [1.] These devoted nations are here named and numbered (v 1), *seven* in all, and seven to one are great odds. They are specified, that Israel might know the bounds and limits of their commission: hitherto their severity must come, but no further; nor must they, under colour of this commission, kill all that came in their way; no, here must its waves be stayed. The confining of this commission to the nations here mentioned plainly intimates that after-ages were not to draw this into a precedent; this will not serve to justify those barbarous laws which give no quarter. How agreeable soever this method might be, when God himself prescribed it, to that dispensation under which such multitudes of beasts were killed and burned in sacrifice, now that all sacrifices of atonement are perfected in, and superseded by, the great propitiation made by the blood of Christ, human blood has become perhaps more precious than it was, and those that have most power yet must not be prodigal of it. [2.] They are here owned to be greater and mightier than Israel. They had been long rooted in this land, to which Israel came strangers; they were more numerous, had men much more bulky and more expert in war than Israel had; yet all this shall not prevent their being cast out before Israel. The strength of Israel's enemies magnifies the power of Israel's God, who will certainly be too hard for them.

(2.) He engages them to do their part. Thou shalt *smite them, and utterly destroy them, v.* 2. If God cast them out, Israel must not take them in, no, not as tenants, nor tributaries, nor servants. No covenant of any kind must be made with them, no mercy must be shown them. This severity was appointed, [1.] By way of punishment for the wickedness they and their fathers had been guilty of. The iniquity of the Amorites was now full, and the longer it had been in the filling the sorer was the vengeance when it came at last. [2.] In order to prevent the mischiefs they would do to God's Israel if they were left alive. The people of these abominations must not be mingled with the holy seed, lest they corrupt them. Better that all these lives should be lost from the earth than that religion and the true worship of God should be lost in Israel. Thus we must deal with our lusts that war against our souls; God has delivered them into our hands by that promise, *Sin shall not have dominion over you,* unless it be your own faults; let not us then make covenants with them, nor show them any mercy, but mortify and crucify them, and utterly destroy them.

2. They must make no marriages with those of them that escaped the sword, v. 3, 4. The families of the Canaanites were an-

cient, and it is probable that some of them were called *honourable*, which might be a temptation to the Israelites, especially those of them that were of least note in their tribes, to court an alliance with them, to ennoble their blood; and the rather because their acquaintance with the country might be serviceable to them in the improvement of it: but religion, and the fear of God, must overrule all these considerations. To intermarry with them was *therefore* unlawful, because it was dangerous; this very thing had proved of fatal consequence to the old world (Gen. vi. 2), and thousands in the world that now is have been undone by irreligious ungodly marriages; for there is more ground of fear in mixed marriages that the good will be perverted than of hope that the bad will be converted. The event proved the reasonableness of this warning: *They will turn away thy son from following me.* Solomon paid dearly for his folly herein. We find a national repentance for this sin of marrying strange wives, and care taken to reform (Ezra ix. x., and Neh. xiii.), and a New-Testament caution not to be *unequally yoked with unbelievers,* 2 Cor. vi. 14. Those that in choosing yokefellows keep not at least within the bounds of a justifiable profession of religion cannot promise themselves helps meet for them. One of the Chaldee paraphrases adds here, as a reason of this command (v. 3), *For he that marries with idolaters does in effect marry with their idols.*

3. They must destroy all the relics of their idolatry, v. 5. Their altars and pillars, their groves and graven images, all must be destroyed, both in a holy indignation against idolatry and to prevent infection. This command was given before, Exod. xxiii. 24; xxxiv. 13. A great deal of good work of this kind was done by the people, in their pious zeal (2 Chron. xxxi. 1), and by good Josiah (2 Chron. xxxiv. 3, 7), and with this may be compared the burning of the conjuring books, Acts xix. 19.

II. Here are very good reasons to enforce this caution.

1. The choice which God had made of this people for his own, v. 6. There was such a covenant and communion established between God and Israel as was not between him and any other people in the world. Shall they by their idolatries dishonour him who had thus honoured them? Shall they slight him who had thus testified his kindness for them? Shall they put themselves upon the level with other people, when God had thus dignified and advanced them above all people? Had God taken them to be a special people to him, and no other but them, and will not they take God to be a special God to them, and no other but him?

2. The freeness of that grace which made this choice. (1.) There was nothing in them to recommend or entitle them to this favour. *In the multitude of the people is the king's*

honour, Prov. xiv. 28. But their number was inconsiderable; they were only seventy souls when they went down into Egypt, and, though greatly increased there, yet there were many other nations more numerous: *You were the fewest of all people, v. 7.* The author of the Jerusalem Targum passes too great a compliment upon his nation in his reading this, *You were humble in spirit, and meek above all people;* quite contrary: they were rather stiff-necked and ill-natured above all people. (2.) God fetched the reason of it purely from himself, *v.* 8. [1.] He loved you *because he would love you.* Even so, Father, because it seemed good in thy eyes. All that God loves he loves freely, Hos. xiv. 4. Those that perish perish by their own merits, but all that are saved are saved by prerogative. [2.] He has done his work because he would keep his word. "He has brought you out of Egypt in pursuance of the oath sworn to your fathers." Nothing in them, or done by them, did or could make God a debtor to them; but he had made himself a debtor to his own promise, which he would perform notwithstanding their unworthiness.

3. The tenour of the covenant into which they were taken; it was in short this, That as they were to God so God would be to them. They should certainly find him, (1.) Kind to his friends, *v.* 9. "The Lord thy God is not like the gods of the nations, the creatures of fancy, subjects fit enough for loose poetry, but no proper objects of serious devotion; no, he is God, God indeed, God alone, the faithful God, able and ready not only to fulfil his own promises, but to answer all the just expectations of his worshippers, and he will certainly keep covenant and mercy," that is, "show mercy according to covenant, to *those that love him and keep his commandments*" (and in vain do we pretend to love him if we do not make conscience of his commandments); "and this" (as is here added for the explication of the promise in the second commandment) "not only to thousands of persons, but to thousands of generations—so inexhaustible is the fountain, so constant are the streams!" (2.) Just to his enemies: He *repays those that hate him, v.* 10. Note, [1.] Wilful sinners are haters of God; for the carnal mind is enmity against him. Idolaters are so in a special manner, for they are in league with his rivals. [2.] Those that hate God cannot hurt him, but certainly ruin themselves. He will repay them to their face, in defiance of them and all their impotent malice. His arrows are said to be *made ready against the face of them,* Ps. xxi. 12. Or, He will bring those judgments upon them which shall appear to themselves to be the just punishment of their idolatry. Compare Job xxi. 19, *He rewardeth him, and he shall know it.* Though vengeance seem to be slow, yet it is not slack. The wicked and sinner shall be *recompensed*

in the earth, Prov. xi. 31. I cannot pass the gloss of the Jerusalem Targum upon this place, because it speaks the faith of the Jewish church concerning a future state: *He recompenses to those that hate him the reward of their good works in this world, that he may destroy them in the world to come.*

12 Wherefore it shall come to pass, if ye hearken to these judgments, and keep, and do them, that the Lord thy God shall keep unto thee the covenant and the mercy which he sware unto thy fathers: 13 And he will love thee, and bless thee, and multiply thee: he will also bless the fruit of thy womb, and the fruit of thy land, thy corn, and thy wine, and thine oil, the increase of thy kine, and the flocks of thy sheep, in the land which he sware unto thy fathers to give thee. 14 Thou shalt be blessed above all people: there shall not be male or female barren among you, or among your cattle. 15 And the Lord will take away from thee all sickness, and will put none of the evil diseases of Egypt, which thou knowest, upon thee; but will lay them upon all *them* that hate thee. 16 And thou shalt consume all the people which the Lord thy God shall deliver thee; thine eye shall have no pity upon them: neither shalt thou serve their gods; for that *will be* a snare unto thee. 17 If thou shalt say in thine heart, These nations *are* more than I; how can I dispossess them? 18 Thou shalt not be afraid of them: *but* shalt well remember what the Lord thy God did unto Pharaoh, and unto all Egypt; 19 The great temptations which thine eyes saw, and the signs, and the wonders, and the mighty hand, and the stretched out arm, whereby the Lord thy God brought thee out: so shall the Lord thy God do unto all the people of whom thou art afraid. 20 Moreover the Lord thy God will send the hornet among them, until they that are left, and hide themselves from thee, be destroyed. 21 Thou shalt not be affrighted at them: for the Lord thy God *is* among you, a mighty God and terrible. 22 And the Lord thy God will put out those nations before thee by little and little:

thou mayest not consume them at once, lest the beasts of the field increase upon thee. 23 But the LORD thy God shall deliver them unto thee, and shall destroy them with a mighty destruction, until they be destroyed. 24 And he shall deliver their kings into thine hand, and thou shalt destroy their name from under heaven: there shall no man be able to stand before thee, until thou have destroyed them. 25 The graven images of their gods shall ye burn with fire: thou shalt not desire the silver or gold *that is* on them, nor take *it* unto thee, lest thou be snared therein: for it *is* an abomination to the LORD thy God. 26 Neither shalt thou bring an abomination into thine house lest thou be a cursed thing like it: *but* thou shalt utterly detest it, and thou shalt utterly abhor it; for it *is* a cursed thing.

Here, I. The caution against idolatry is repeated, and against communion with idolaters: "*Thou shalt consume the people, and not serve their gods,*" v. 16. We are in danger of having fellowship with the works of darkness if we take pleasure in fellowship with those that do those works. Here is also a repetition of the charge to destroy the images, v. 25, 26. The idols which the heathen had worshipped were an abomination to God, and therefore must be so to them: all that truly love God hate what he hates. Observe how this is urged upon them: *Thou shalt utterly detest it, and thou shalt utterly abhor it;* such a holy indignation as this must we conceive against sin, that *abominable thing which the Lord hates.* They must not retain the images to gratify their covetousness: *Thou shalt not desire the silver nor gold that is on them,* nor think it a pity to have that destroyed. Achan paid dearly for converting that to his own use which was an anathema. Nor must they retain them to gratify their curiosity: "Neither shalt thou bring it into thy house, to be hung up as an ornament, or preserved as a monument of antiquity. No, to the fire with it, that is the fittest place for it." Two reasons are given for this caution:—1. Lest *thou be snared therein* (v. 25), that is, "Lest thou be drawn, ere thou art aware, to like it and love it, to fancy it and pay respect to it" 2. *Lest thou be a cursed thing like it,* v. 26. Those that make images are said to be like them, stupid and senseless; here they are said to be in a worse sense like them, accursed of God and devoted to destruction. Compare these two reasons together, and observe that whatever brings us into a snare brings us under a curse.

II. The promise of God's favour to them,

if they would be obedient, is enlarged upon with a most affecting copiousness and fluency of expression, which intimates how much it is both God's desire and our own interest that we be religious. All possible assurance is here given them,

1. That, if they would sincerely endeavour to do their part of the covenant, God would certainly perform his part. He shall *keep the mercy which he swore to thy fathers, v.* 12. Let us be constant in our duty, and we cannot question the constancy of God's mercy.

2. That if they would love God and serve him, and devote themselves and theirs to him, he would love them, and bless them, and multiply them greatly, v. 13, 14. What could they desire more to make them happy? (1.) "*He will love thee.*" He began in love to us (1 John iv. 10), and, if we return his love in filial duty, then, and then only, we may expect the continuance of it, John xiv. 21. (2.) "He will bless thee with the tokens of his love above all people." If they would distinguish themselves from their neighbours by singular services, God would dignify them above their neighbours by singular blessings. (3.) "He will *multiply thee.*" Increase was the ancient blessing for the peopling of the world, once and again (Gen. i. 28; ix. 1), and here for the peopling of Canaan, that little world by itself. The increase both of their families and of their stock is promised: they should neither have estates without heirs nor heirs without estates, but should have the complete satisfaction of having many children and plentiful provisions and portions for them.

3. That, if they would keep themselves pure from the idolatries of Egypt, God would keep them clear from the *diseases of Egypt, v.* 15. It seems to refer not only to those plagues of Egypt by the force of which they were delivered, but to some other epidemical country disease (as we call it), which they remembered the prevalency of among the Egyptians, and by which God had chastised them for their national sins. Diseases are God's servants; they go where he sends them, and do what he bids them. It is therefore good for the health of our bodies to mortify the sin of our souls.

4. That, if they *would* cut off the devoted nations, they *should* cut them off, and none should be able to stand before them. Their duty in this matter would itself be advantage: *Thou shalt consume all the people which the Lord thy God shall deliver thee*—this is the precept (v. 16); and then *the Lord thy God shall deliver them unto thee, and shall destroy them*—this is the promise, v. 23. Thus we are commanded not to let sin reign, not to indulge ourselves in it nor give countenance to it, but to hate it and strive against it; and then God has promised that *sin shall not have dominion over us* (Rom. vi. 12, 14), but that we shall be more than conquerors over it. The difficulty and doubtfulness of

the conquest of Canaan having been a stone of stumbling to their fathers, Moses here animates them against those things which were most likely to discourage them, bidding them not to be *afraid of them, v.* 18, and again *v.* 21. (1.) Let them not be disheartened by the number and strength of their enemies : *Say not, They are more than I, how can I dispossess them ? v.* 17. We are apt to think that the most numerous must needs be victorious: but, to fortify Israel against this temptation, Moses reminds them of the destruction of Pharaoh and all the power of Egypt, *v.* 18, 19. They had seen the great *temptations,* or *miracles* (so the Chaldee reads it), the signs and wonders, wherewith God had brought them out of Egypt, in order to his bringing them into Canaan, and thence might easily infer that God *could* dispossess the Canaanites (who, though formidable enough, had not such advantages against Israel as the Egyptians had; he that had done the greater could do the less), and that he *would* dispossess them, otherwise his bringing Israel out of Egypt had been no kindness to them. He that begun would finish. Thou shalt therefore *well remember* this, *v.* 18. The word and works of God are well remembered when they are improved as helps to our faith and obedience. That is well laid up which is ready to us when we have occasion to use it. (2.) Let them not be disheartened by the weakness and deficiency of their own forces; for God will send them in auxiliary troops of *hornets,* or *wasps,* as some read it (*v.* 20), probably larger than ordinary, which would so terrify and molest their enemies (and perhaps be the death of many of them) that their most numerous armies would become an easy prey to Israel. God plagued the Egyptians with flies, but the Canaanites with hornets. Those who take not warning by less judgments on others may expect greater on themselves. But the great encouragement of Israel was that they had God among them, a *mighty God and terrible, v.* 21. And if God be for us, if God be with us, we need not fear the power of any creature against us. (3.) Let them not be disheartened by the slow progress of their arms, nor think that the Canaanites would never be subdued if they were not expelled the first year; no, they must be *put out by little and little,* and not *all at once, v.* 22. Note, We must not think that, because the deliverance of the church and the destruction of its enemies are not effected immediately, therefore they will never be effected. God will do his own work in his own method and time, and we may be sure that they are always the best. Thus corruption is driven out of the hearts of believers *by little and little.* The work of sanctification is carried on gradually; but that judgment will at length be brought forth into a complete victory. The reason here given (as before, Exod. xxiii. 29, 30) is, *Lest the beast of the*

field increase upon thee. The earth God has given to the children of men ; and therefore there shall rather be a remainder of Canaanites to keep possession till Israel become numerous enough to replenish it than that it should be a habitation of dragons, and a court for *the wild beasts of the desert,* Isa. xxxiv. 13, 14. Yet God could have prevented this mischief from the beasts, Lev. xxvi. 6. But pride and security, and other sins that are the common effects of a settled prosperity, were enemies more dangerous than the beasts of the field, and these would be apt to increase upon them. See Judges iii. 1, 4.

CHAP. VIII.

Moses had charged parents in teaching their children to whet the word of God upon them (ch. vi. 7) by frequent repetition of the same things over and over again ; and here he himself takes the same method of instructing the Israelites as his children, frequently inculcating the same precepts and cautious, with the same motives or arguments to enforce them, that what they heard so often might abide with them. In this chapter Moses gives them, 1. General exhortations to obedience, ver. 1, 6. II. A review of the great things God had done for them in the wilderness, as a good argument for obedience, ver. 2—5, and ver. 15, 16. III. A prospect of the good land into which God would now bring them, ver. 7—9. IV. A necessary caution against the temptations of a prosperous condition, ver. 10 –14, and 17, 18. V. A fair warning of the fatal consequences of apostasy from God, ver. 19, 20.

ALL the commandments which I command thee this day shall ye observe to do, that ye may live, and multiply, and go in and possess the land which the LORD sware unto your fathers. 2 And thou shalt remember all the way which the LORD thy God led thee these forty years in the wilderness, to humble thee, *and* to prove thee, to know what *was* in thine heart, whether thou wouldest keep his commandments, or no. 3 And he humbled thee, and suffered thee to hunger, and fed thee with manna, which thou knewest not, neither did thy fathers know ; that he might make thee know that man doth not live by bread only, but by every *word* that proceedeth out of the mouth of the LORD doth man live. 4 Thy raiment waxed not old upon thee, neither did thy foot swell, these forty years. 5 Thou shalt also consider in thine heart, that, as a man chasteneth his son, *so* the LORD thy God chasteneth thee. 6 Therefore thou shalt keep the commandments of the LORD thy God, to walk in his ways, and to fear him. 7 For the LORD thy God bringeth thee into a good land, a land of brooks of water, of fountains and depths that spring out of valleys and hills ; 8 A land of wheat, and barley, and vines, and fig trees, and pomegranates; a land of oil olive, and honey; 9 A land wherein thou shalt eat bread without scarceness, thou shalt not lack any *thing* in it; a land whose stones *are* iron, and out of whose hills thou mayest dig brass.

The charge here given them is the same as before, to keep and do all God's commandments. Their obedience must be, 1. Careful: *Observe to do.* 2. Universal: To *do all the commandments, v.* 1. And, 3. From a good principle, with a regard to God as the Lord, and their God, and particularly with a holy fear of him (*v.* 6), from a reverence of his majesty, a submission to his authority, and a dread of his wrath. To engage them to this obedience, besides the great advantages of it, which he sets before them (that they should *live and multiply,* and all should be well with them, *v.* 1), he directs them,

I. To look back upon the wilderness through which God had now brought them: *Thou shalt remember all the way which the Lord thy God led thee these forty years in the wilderness, v.* 2. Now that they had come of age, and were entering upon their inheritance, they must be reminded of the discipline they had been under during their minority and the method God had taken to train them up for himself. The wilderness was the school in which they had been for forty years boarded and taught, under tutors and governors; and this was a time to bring it all to remembrance. The occurrences of these last forty years were very memorable and well worthy to be remembered, very useful and profitable to be remembered, as yielding a complication of arguments for obedience; and they were recorded on purpose that they might be remembered. As the feast of the passover was a memorial of their deliverance out of Egypt, so was the feast of tabernacles of their passage through the wilderness. Note, It is very good for us to remember all the ways both of God's providence and grace, by which he has led us hitherto through this wilderness, that we may be prevailed with cheerfully to serve him and trust in him. Here let us set up our Ebenezer.

1. They must remember the straits they were sometimes brought into, (1.) For the mortifying of their pride; it was to *humble* them, that they might not be exalted above measure with the abundance of miracles that were wrought in their favour, and that they might not be secure, and confident of being in Canaan immediately. (2.) For the manifesting of their perverseness: to *prove* them, that they and others might know (for God himself perfectly knew it before) all that was in their heart, and might see that God chose them not for any thing in them that might recommend them to his favour, for their whole carriage was untoward and provoking. Many

commandments God gave them which there would have been no occasion for if they had not been led through the wilderness, as those relating to the manna (Exod. xvi. 28); and God thereby tried them, as our first parents were tried by the trees of the garden, whether they would keep God's commandments or not. Or God thereby proved them whether they would trust his promises, the word which he commanded to a thousand generations, and, in dependence on his promises, obey his precepts.

2. They must remember the supplies which were always granted them.

(1.) God himself took particular care of their food, raiment, and health; and what would they have more? [1.] They had manna for food (*v.* 3): *God suffered them to hunger,* and then *fed them with manna,* that the extremity of their want might make the supply the more acceptable, and God's goodness to them therein the more remarkable. God often brings his people low, that he may have the honour of helping them. And thus the manna of heavenly comforts is given to those that *hunger and thirst after righteousness,* Matt. v. 6. *To the hungry soul every bitter thing is sweet.* It is said of the manna that it was a sort of food which neither *they nor their fathers knew.* And again, *v.* 16. If they knew there was such a thing that fell sometimes with the dew in those countries, as some think they did, yet it was never known to fall in such vast quantities, so constantly, and at all seasons of the year, so long, and only about a certain place. These things were altogether miraculous, and without precedent; *the Lord created a new thing* for their supply. And hereby he taught them that *man liveth not by bread alone.* Though God has appointed bread for the strengthening of man's heart, and that is ordinarily made the staff of life, yet God can, when he pleases, command support and nourishment without it, and make something else, very unlikely, to answer the intention as well. We might live upon air if it were sanctified for that use by *the word of God;* for the means God ordinarily uses he is not tied to, but can perform his kind purposes to his people without them. Our Saviour quotes this scripture in answer to that temptation of Satan, *Command that these stones be made bread.* "What need of that?" says Christ; "my heavenly Father can keep me alive without bread," Matt. iv. 3, 4. Let none of God's children distrust their Father, nor take any sinful indirect course for the supply of their own necessities; some way or other, God will provide for them in the way of duty and honest diligence, *and verily they shall be fed.* It may be applied spiritually; the *word of God,* as it is the revelation of God's will and grace duly received and entertained by faith, is the food of the soul, the life which is supported by that is the life of the man, and not only that life which is supported by bread. The manna typified Christ, *the bread of life.* He is *the Word of God;* by him we live. The Lord evermore give us that bread which endures to eternal life, and let us not be put off with the *meat that perisheth!* [2.] The same clothes served them from Egypt to Canaan, at least the generality of them. Though they had no change of raiment, yet it was always new, and waxed not old upon them, *v.* 4. This was a standing miracle, and the greater if, as the Jews say, they grew with them, so as to be always fit for them. But it is plain that they brought out of Egypt bundles of clothes on their shoulders (Exod. xii. 34), which they might barter with each other as there was occasion; and these, with what they wore, sufficed till they came into a country where they could furnish themselves with new clothes.

(2.) By the method God took of providing food and raiment for them, [1.] He humbled them. It was a mortification to them to be tied for forty years. together to the same meat, without any varieties, and to the same clothes, in the same fashion. Thus he taught them that the good things he designed for them were figures of better things, and that the happiness of man consists not in being clothed in *purple or fine linen,* and in *faring sumptuously every day,* but in being taken into covenant and communion with God, and in *learning his righteous judgments.* God's law, which was given to Israel in the wilderness, must be to them instead of food and raiment. [2.] He proved them, whether they could trust him to provide for them when means and second causes failed. Thus he taught them to live in a dependence upon Providence, and not to perplex themselves with care *what they should eat and drink,* and *wherewithal they should be clothed.* Christ would have his disciples learn the same lesson (Matt. vi. 25), and took a like method to teach it to them, when he *sent them out without purse or scrip,* and yet took care that they *lacked nothing,* Luke xxii. 35. [3.] God took care of their health and ease. Though they travelled on foot in a dry country, the way rough and untrodden, yet their *feet swelled not.* God preserved them from taking hurt by the inconveniences of their journey; and mercies of this kind we ought to acknowledge. Note, Those that follow God's conduct are not only safe but easy. Our feet swell not while we keep in the way of duty; it is the *way of transgression* that *is hard,* Prov. xiii. 15. God has promised to *keep the feet of his saints,* 1 Sam. ii. 9.

3. They must also remember the rebukes they had been under, *v.* 5. During these years of their education they had been kept under a strict discipline, and not without need. *As a man chasteneth his son,* for his good, and because he loves him, *so the Lord thy God chasteneth thee.* God is a loving tender Father to all his children, yet when

there is occasion they shall feel the smart of the rod. Israel did so: they were chastened that they might not be condemned, chastened with the rod of men. Not as a man wounds and slays his enemies whose destruction he aims at, but as a man chastens his son whose happiness and welfare he designs: so did their God chasten them; he chastened and taught them, Ps. xciv. 12. This they must *consider in their heart,* that is, they must own it from their own experience that God had corrected them with a fatherly love, for which they must return to him a filial reverence and compliance. Because God has chastened thee as a father, *therefore (v.* 6) *thou shalt keep his commandments.* This use we should make of all our afflictions; by them let us be engaged and quickened to our duty. Thus they are directed to look back upon the wilderness.

II. He directs them to look forward to Canaan, into which God was now bringing them. Look which way we will, both our reviews and our prospects will furnish us with arguments for obedience. Observe,

1. The land which they were now going to take possession of is here described to be a very good land, having every thing in it that was desirable, *v.* 7—9. (1) It was *well-watered, like Eden, the garden of the Lord.* It was *a land of brooks of water, of fountains and depths,* which contributed to the fruitfulness of the soil. Perhaps there was a greater plenty of water there now than in Abraham's time, the Canaanites having found and digged wells; so that Israel reaped the fruit of their industry as well as of God's bounty. (2.) The ground produced great plenty of all good things, not only for the necessary support, but for the convenience and comfort of human life. In their fathers' land they had bread enough; it was corn land, a land of wheat and barley, where, with the common care and labour of the husbandman, they might eat bread without scarceness. It was a fruitful land, that was never turned into barrenness but for the iniquity of those that dwelt therein. They had not only water enough to quench their thirst, but vines, the fruit whereof was ordained to make glad the heart. And, if they were desirous of dainties, they needed not to send to far countries for them, when their own was so well stocked with fig-trees, and pomegranates, olives of the best kind, and honey, or *date-trees,* as some think it should be read. (3.) Even the bowels of its earth were very rich, though it should seem that *silver and gold they had none;* of these the princes of Sheba should bring presents (Ps. lxxii. 10, 15); yet they had plenty of those more serviceable metals, iron and brass. Iron-stone and mines of brass were found in their hills. See Job xxviii. 2.

2. These things are mentioned, (1.) To show the great difference between that wilderness through which God had led them and the good land into which he was bring-

ing them. Note, Those that bear the inconveniences of an afflicted state with patience and submission, are humbled by them and prove well under them, are best prepared for better circumstances. (2.) To show what obligations they lay under to keep God's commandments, both in gratitude for his favours to them and from a regard to their own interest, that the favours might be continued. The only way to keep possession of this good land would be to keep in the way of their duty. (3.) To show what a figure it was of good things to come. Whatever others saw, it is probable that Moses in it saw a type of the better country: the gospel church is the New-Testament Canaan, watered with the Spirit in his gifts and graces, planted with the trees of righteousness, bearing the fruits of righteousness. Heaven is the good land, in which there is nothing wanting, and where there is a fulness of joy.

10 When thou hast eaten and art full, then thou shalt bless the LORD thy God for the good land which he hath given thee. 11 Beware that thou forget not the LORD thy God, in not keeping his commandments, and his judgments, and his statutes, which I command thee this day: 12 Lest *when* thou hast eaten and art full, and hast built goodly houses, and dwelt *therein;* 13 And *when* thy herds and thy flocks multiply, and thy silver and thy gold is multiplied, and all that thou hast is multiplied; 14 Then thine heart be lifted up, and thou forget the LORD thy God, which brought thee forth out of the land of Egypt, from the house of bondage; 15 Who led thee through that great and terrible wilderness, *wherein were* fiery serpents, and scorpions, and drought, where *there was* no water; who brought thee forth water out of the rock of flint; 16 Who fed thee in the wilderness with manna, which thy fathers knew not, that he might humble thee, and that he might prove thee, to do thee good at thy latter end; 17 And thou say in thine heart, My power and the might of *mine* hand hath gotten me this wealth. 18 But thou shalt remember the LORD thy God: for *it is* he that giveth thee power to get wealth, that he may establish his covenant which he sware unto thy fathers, as *it is* this day. 19 And it shall be, if thou do at all forget the LORD thy

God, and walk after other gods, and serve them, and worship them, I testify against you this day that ye shall surely perish. 20 As the nations which the LORD destroyeth before your face, so shall ye perish; because ye would not be obedient unto the voice of the LORD your God.

Moses, having mentioned the great plenty they would find in the land of Canaan, finds it necessary to caution them against the abuse of that plenty, which was a sin they would be the more prone to now that they came into that vineyard of the Lord, immediately out of a barren desert.

I. He directs them to the duty of a prosperous condition, v. 10. They are allowed to eat even to fulness, not to surfeiting nor excess; but let them always remember their benefactor, the founder of their feast, and never fail to give thanks after meat: *Then thou shalt bless the Lord thy God.* 1. They must take heed of eating or drinking so much as to indispose themselves for this duty of blessing God, rather aiming to serve God therein with so much the more cheerfulness and enlargement. 2. They must not have any fellowship with those that, when they had eaten and were full, blessed false gods, as the Israelites themselves had done in their worship of the golden calf, Exod. xxxii. 6. 3. Whatever they had the comfort of God must have the glory of. As our Saviour has taught us to bless before we eat (Matt. xiv. 19, 20), so we are here taught to bless after meat. That is our *Hosannah—God bless ;* this is our *Hallelujah—Blessed be God. In every thing we must give thanks.* From this law the religious Jews took up a laudable usage of blessing God, not only at their solemn meals, but upon other occasions; if they drank a cup of wine they lifted up their hands and said, *Blessed be he that created the fruit of the vine to make glad the heart.* If they did but smell at a flower, they said, *Blessed be he that made this flower sweet.* 4. When they gave thanks for the fruits of the land they must give thanks for the good land itself, which was given them by promise. From all our comfortable enjoyments we must take occasion to thank God for our comfortable settlements; and I know not but we of this nation have as much reason as they had to give thanks for a good land.

II. He arms them against the temptations of a prosperous condition, and charges them to stand upon their guard against them: "When thou art settled in goodly houses of thy own building," v. 12 (for though God gave them houses which they builded not, ch. vi. 10, these would not serve them, they must have larger and finer),—and when thou hast grown *rich in cattle, in silver, and in gold* (v. 13), as Abraham (Gen. xiii. 2),—when *all thou hast is multiplied,*" 1. "Then

761

take heed of pride. Beware *lest then thy heart be lifted up,*" v. 14. When the estate rises, the mind is apt to rise with it, in self-conceit, self-complacency, and self-confidence. Let us therefore strive to keep the spirit low in a high condition; humility is both the ease and the ornament of prosperity. Take heed of saying, so much as in thy heart, that proud word, *My power, even the might of my hand, hath gotten me this wealth, v.* 17. Note, We must never take the praise of our prosperity to ourselves, nor attribute it to our ingenuity or industry; for bread is not always *to the wise,* nor *riches to men of understanding,* Eccl. ix. 11. It is spiritual idolatry thus to *sacrifice to our own net,* Hab. i. 16. 2. "Then take heed of forgetting God." This follows upon the *lifting up of the heart;* for it is *through the pride of the countenance* that the *wicked seek not after God,* Ps. x. 4. Those that admire themselves despise God. (1.) "Forget not thy duty to God," v. 11. We forget God if we keep not his commandments; we forget his authority over us, and our obligations to him and expectations from him, if we are not obedient to his laws. When men grow rich they are tempted to think religion a needless thing. They are happy without it, think it a thing below them and too hard upon them. Their dignity forbids them to stoop, and their liberty forbids them to serve. But we are basely ungrateful if the better God is to us the worse we are to him. (2.) "Forget not God's former dealings with thee. Thy deliverance out of Egypt, v. 14. The provision he made for thee in the wilderness, that great and terrible wilderness." They must never forget the impressions which the horror of that wilderness made upon them; see Jer. ii. 6, where it is called the very *shadow of death.* There God preserved them from being destroyed by the fiery serpents and scorpions, though sometimes he made use of them for their correction: there he kept them from perishing for want of water, following them with water out of a rock of flint (v. 15), out of which (says bishop Patrick) one would rather have expected fire than water. There he fed them with manna, of which before (v. 3), taking care to keep them alive, that he might *do them good at their latter end, v.* 16. Note, God reserves the best till the last for his Israel. However he may seem to deal hardly with them by the way, he will not fail to do them good at their latter end. (3.) "Forget not God's hand in thy present prosperity, v. 18. Remember it is he that giveth thee wealth; for he *giveth thee power to get wealth.*" See here how God's giving and our getting are reconciled, and apply it to spiritual wealth. It is our duty to get wisdom, and above all our gettings to get understanding; and yet it is God's grace that gives wisdom, and when we have got it we must not say, It was the might of our hand

762

that got it, but must own it was God that gave us power to get it, and therefore to him we must give the praise and consecrate the use of it. The *blessing of the Lord* on the *hand of the diligent* makes rich both for this world and for the other. He *giveth thee power to get wealth,* not so much to gratify thee, and make thee easy, as that he may establish his covenant. All God's gifts are in pursuance of his promises.

III. He repeats the fair warning he had often given them of the fatal consequences of their apostasy from God, v. 19, 20. Observe, 1. How he describes the sin; it is forgetting God, and then worshipping other gods. What wickedness will not those fall into that have bad thoughts of God out of their minds? And, when once the affections are displaced from God, they will soon be misplaced upon lying vanities. 2. How he denounces wrath and ruin against them for it: "If you do so, *you shall surely perish,* and the power and might of your hands, which you are so proud of, cannot help you. Nay, you shall perish as the nations that are driven out before you. God will make no more account of you, notwithstanding his covenant with you and your relation to him, than he does of them, if you will not be obedient and faithful to him." Those that follow others in sin will certainly follow them to destruction. If we do as sinners do, we must expect to fare as sinners fare.

CHAP. IX.

The design of Moses in this chapter is to convince the people of Israel of their utter unworthiness to receive from God those great favours that were now to be conferred upon them, writing this, as it were, in capital letters at the head of their charter, "Not for your sake, be it known unto you," Ezek. xxxvi. 32. I. He assures them of victory over their enemies, ver. 1—3. II. He cautions them not to attribute their successes to their own merit, but to God's justice, which was engaged against their enemies, and his faithfulness, which was engaged to their fathers, ver. 4—6. III. To make it evident that they had no reason to boast of their own righteousness, he mentions their faults, shows Israel their transgressions, and the house of Jacob their sins. In general, they had been all along a provoking people, ver. 7—24. In particular, 1. In the matter of the golden calf, the story of which he largely relates, ver. 8—21. 2. He mentions some other instances of their rebellion, ver. 22, 23. And, 3. Returns, at ver. 25, to speak of the intercession he had made for them at Horeb, to prevent their being ruined for the golden calf.

HEAR, O Israel: Thou *art* to pass over Jordan this day, to go in to possess nations greater and mightier than thyself, cities great and fenced up to heaven, 2 A people great and tall, the children of the Anakims, whom thou knowest, and *of whom* thou hast heard *say,* Who can stand before the children of Anak! 3 Understand therefore this day, that the Lord thy God *is* he which goeth over before thee; *as* a consuming fire he shall destroy them, and he shall bring them down before thy face: so shalt thou drive them out, and destroy them quickly, as the Lord hath said unto thee. 4 Speak not thou in thine heart, after that the LORD thy God hath cast them out from before thee, saying, For my righteousness the LORD hath brought me in to possess this land: but for the wickedness of these nations the LORD doth drive them out from before thee. 5 Not for thy righteousness, or for the uprightness of thine heart, dost thou go to possess their land: but for the wickedness of these nations the LORD thy God doth drive them out from before thee, and that he may perform the word which the LORD sware unto thy fathers, Abraham, Isaac, and Jacob. 6 Understand therefore, that the LORD thy God giveth thee not this good land to possess it for thy righteousness; for thou *art* a stiff-necked people.

The call to attention (*v.* 1), *Hear, O Israel,* intimates that this was a new discourse, delivered at some distance of time after the former, probably the next sabbath day.

I. Moses represents to the people the formidable strength of the enemies which they were now to encounter, *v.* 1. The nations they were to dispossess were mightier than themselves, not a rude and undisciplined rout, like the natives of America, that were easily made a prey of. But, should they besiege them, they would find their cities well fortified, according as the art of fortification then was; should they engage them in the field, they would find the people great and tall, of whom common fame had reported that there was no standing before them, *v.* 2. This representation is much the same with that which the evil spies had made (Num. xiii. 28, 33), but made with a very different intention: that was designed to drive them from God and to discourage their hope in him; this to drive them to God and to engage their hope in him, since no power less than that which is almighty could secure and prosper them.

II. He assures them of victory, by the presence of God with them, notwithstanding the strength of the enemy, *v.* 3. "Understand therefore what thou must trust to for success, and which way thou must look; it is the Lord thy God that goes before thee, not only as thy captain, or commander-in-chief, to give direction, but as a consuming fire, to do execution among them. Observe, He shall destroy them, and then thou shalt drive them out. Thou canst not drive them out, unless he destroy them and bring them down. But he will not destroy them and bring them down, unless thou set thyself in good earnest to drive them out." We must do our endeavour in dependence upon God's

grace, and we shall have that grace if we do our endeavour

III. He cautions them not to entertain the least thought of their own righteousness, as if that had procured them this favour at God's hand: "Say not, *For my righteousness* (either with regard to my good character or in recompence for any good service) *the Lord hath brought me in to possess this land* (*v.* 4); never think it is for thy righteousness or the uprightness of thy heart, that it is in consideration either of thy good conversation or of thy good disposition," *v.* 5. And again (*v.* 6) it is insisted on, because it is hard to bring people from a conceit of their own merit, and yet very necessary that it be done: "*Understand* (know it, and believe it, and consider it) that *the Lord thy God giveth thee not this land for thy righteousness.* Hadst thou been to come to it upon that condition, thou wouldst have been for ever shut out of it, *for thou art a stiff-necked people.*" Note, Our gaining possession of the heavenly Canaan, as it must be attributed to God's power and not to our own might, so it must be ascribed to God's grace and not to our own merit: in Christ we have both righteousness and strength; in him therefore we must glory, and not in ourselves, or any sufficiency of our own.

IV. He intimates to them the true reasons why God would take this good land out of the hands of the Canaanites, and settle it upon Israel, and they are borrowed from his own honour, not from Israel's deserts. 1. He will be honoured in the destruction of idolaters; they are justly looked upon as haters of him, and therefore he will visit their iniquity upon them. It is *for the wickedness of these nations* that God *drives them out, v.* 4, and again, *v.* 5. All those whom God rejects are rejected for their own wickedness: but none of those whom he accepts are accepted for their own righteousness. 2. He will be honoured in the performance of his promise to those that are in covenant with him: God swore to the patriarchs, who loved him and left all to follow him, that he would give this land to their seed; and therefore he would *keep that promised mercy for thousands of those that loved him and kept his commandments;* he would not suffer his promise to fail. It was for their fathers' sakes that they were beloved, Rom. xi. 28. Thus boasting is for ever excluded. See Eph. i. 9, 11.

7 Remember, *and* forget not, how thou provokedst the LORD thy God to wrath in the wilderness: from the day that thou didst depart out of the land of Egypt, until ye came unto this place, ye have been rebellious against the LORD. 8 Also in Horeb ye provoked the LORD to wrath, so that the LORD was angry with you to have

destroyed you. 9 When I was gone up into the mount to receive the tables of stone, *even* the tables of the covenant which the LORD made with you, then I abode in the mount forty days and forty nights, I neither did eat bread nor drink water: 10 And the LORD delivered unto me two tables of stone written with the finger of God; and on them *was written* according to all the words, which the LORD spake with you in the mount out of the midst of the fire in the day of the assembly. 11 And it came to pass at the end of forty days and forty nights, *that* the LORD gave me the two tables of stone, *even* the tables of the covenant. 12 And the LORD said unto me, Arise, get thee down quickly from hence; for thy people which thou hast brought forth out of Egypt have corrupted *themselves;* they are quickly turned aside out of the way which I commanded them; they have made them a molten image. 13 Furthermore the LORD spake unto me, saying, I have seen this people, and, behold, it *is* a stiffnecked people: 14 Let me alone, that I may destroy them, and blot out their name from under heaven: and I will make of thee a nation mightier and greater than they. 15 So I turned and came down from the mount, and the mount burned with fire: and the two tables of the covenant *were* in my two hands. 16 And I looked, and, behold, ye had sinned against the LORD your God, *and* had made you a molten calf: ye had turned aside quickly out of the way which the LORD had commanded you. 17 And I took the two tables, and cast them out of my two hands, and brake them before your eyes. 18 And I fell down before the LORD, as at the first, forty days and forty nights: I did neither eat bread nor drink water, because of all your sins which ye sinned, in doing wickedly in the sight of the LORD, to provoke him to anger. 19 For I was afraid of the anger and hot displeasure, wherewith the LORD was wroth against you to destroy you. But the LORD hearkened unto me at that time also. 20 And the LORD was very angry with Aaron to have destroyed him: and I prayed for Aaron also the same time. 21 And I took your sin, the calf which ye had made, and burnt it with fire, and stamped *it*, and ground *it* very small, *even* until it was as small as dust: and I cast the dust thereof into the brook that descended out of the mount. 22 And at Taberah, and at Massah, and at Kibroth-hattaavah, ye provoked the LORD to wrath. 23 Likewise when the LORD sent you from Kadesh-barnea, saying, Go up and possess the land which I have given you; then ye rebelled against the commandment of the LORD your God, and ye believed him not, nor hearkened to his voice. 24 Ye have been rebellious against the LORD from the day that I knew you. 25 Thus I fell down before the LORD forty days and forty nights, as I fell down *at the first;* because the LORD had said he would destroy you. 26 I prayed therefore unto the LORD, and said, O Lord GOD, destroy not thy people and thine inheritance, which thou hast redeemed through thy greatness, which thou hast brought forth out of Egypt with a mighty hand. 27 Remember thy servants, Abraham, Isaac, and Jacob; look not unto the stubbornness of this people, nor to their wickedness, nor to their sin: 28 Lest the land whence thou broughtest us out say, Because the LORD was not able to bring them into the land which he promised them, and because he hated them, he hath brought them out to slay them in the wilderness. 29 Yet they *are* thy people and thine inheritance, which thou broughtest out by thy mighty power and by thy stretched out arm.

That they might have no pretence to think that God brought them to Canaan *for their righteousness,* Moses here shows them what a miracle of mercy it was that they had not long ere this been destroyed in the wilderness: " *Remember, and forget not, how thou provokedst the Lord thy God* (*v.* 7); so far from purchasing his favour, thou hast many a time laid thyself open to his displeasure." Their fathers' provocations are here charged upon them; for, if God had dealt with their fathers according to their deserts, this generation would never have been, much less would they have entered Canaan. We are apt to forget our provocations, especially when the smart of the rod is over, and have need to be often put in mind of them, that we may never entertain any conceit of our own righteousness. Paul argues from the guilt which all mankind is under to prove that we cannot be *justified before God* by our own works, Rom. iii. 19, 20. If our works condemn us, they will not justify us. Observe, 1. They had been a provoking people ever since they came out of Egypt, *v.* 7. *Forty years long,* from first to last, were God and Moses grieved with them. It is a very sad character Moses now at parting leaves of them : *You have been rebellious since the day I knew you, v.* 24. No sooner were they formed into a people than there was a faction formed among them, which upon all occasions made head against God and his government. Though the Mosaic history records little more than the occurrences of the first and last year of the forty, yet it seems by this general account that the rest of the years were not much better, but one continued provocation. 2. Even in Horeb they made a calf and worshipped it, *v.* 8, &c. That was a sin so heinous, and by several aggravations made so exceedingly sinful, that they deserved upon all occasions to be upbraided with it. It was done in the very place where the law was given by which they were expressly forbidden to worship God by images, and while the mountain was yet burning before their eyes, and Moses had gone up to fetch them the law in writing. They *turned aside quickly, v.* 16. 3. God was very angry with them for their sin. Let them not think that God overlooked what they did amiss, and gave them Canaan for what was good among them. No, God had determined to destroy them (*v.* 8), could easily have done it, and would have been no loser by it; he even desired Moses to let him alone that he might do it, *v.* 13, 14. By this it appeared how heinous their sin was, for God is never angry with any above what there is cause for, as men often are. Moses himself, though a friend and favourite, trembled at the revelation of God's wrath from heaven against their ungodliness and unrighteousness (*v.* 19): *I was afraid of the anger of the Lord,* afraid perhaps not for them only, but for himself, Ps. cxix. 120. 4. They had by their sin broken covenant with God, and forfeited all the privileges of the covenant, which Moses signified to them by *breaking the tables, v.* 17. A bill of divorce was given them, and thenceforward they might justly have been abandoned for ever, so that their mouth was certainly stopped from pleading any righteousness of their own. God had, in effect, disowned them, when he said to Moses (*v.* 12), "They are thy people, they are none of mine, nor shall they be dealt with as mine." 5. Aaron

himself fell under God's displeasure for it, though he was the saint of the Lord, and was only brought by surprise or terror to be confederate with them in the sin : *The Lord was very angry with Aaron, v.* 20. No man's place or character can shelter him from the wrath of God if he have *fellowship with the unfruitful works of darkness.* Aaron, that should have made atonement for them if the iniquity could have been purged away by sacrifice and offering, did himself fall under the wrath of God : so little did they consider what they did when they drew him in. 6. It was with great difficulty and very long attendance that Moses himself prevailed to turn away the wrath of God, and prevent their utter ruin. He fasted and prayed full forty days and forty nights before he could obtain their pardon, *v.* 18. And some think twice forty days (*v.* 25), because it is said, *as I fell down before,* whereas his errand in the first forty was not of that nature. Others think it was but one forty, though twice mentioned (as also in *ch.* x. 10); but this was enough to make them sensible how great God's displeasure was against them, and what a narrow escape they had for their lives. And in this appears the greatness of God's anger against all mankind that no less a person than his Son, and no less a price than his own blood, would serve to turn it away. Moses here tells them the substance of his intercession for them. He was obliged to own their stubbornness, and their wickedness, and their sin, *v.* 27. Their character was bad indeed when he that appeared an advocate for them could not give them a good word, and had nothing else to say in their behalf but that God had done great things for them, which really did but aggravate their crime (*v.* 26),—that they were the posterity of good ancestors (*v.* 27), which might also have been turned upon him, as making the matter worse and not better,— and that the Egyptians would reproach God, if he should destroy them, as unable to perfect what he had wrought for them (*v.* 28), a plea which might easily enough have been answered : no matter what the Egyptians say, while the heavens declare God's righteousness ; so that the saving of them from ruin at that time was owing purely to the mercy of God, and the importunity of Moses, and not to any merit of theirs, that could be offered so much as in mitigation of their offence. 7. To affect them the more with the destruction they were then at the brink of, he describes very particularly the destruction of the calf they had made, *v.* 21. He calls it their *sin :* perhaps not only because it had been the matter of their sin, but because the destroying of it was intended for a testimony against their sin, and an indication to them what the sinners themselves did deserve. Those that made it were like unto it, and would have had no wrong done them if they had been thus stamped to dust, and consumed, and scattered, and no remains of them left. It was infinite mercy that accepted the destruction of the idol instead of the destruction of the idolaters. 8. Even after this fair escape that they had, in many other instances they provoked the Lord again and again. He needed only to name the places, for they carried the memorials either of the sin or of the punishment in their names (v. 22): at *Taberah, burning,* where God set fire to them for their murmuring,—at *Massah, the temptation,* where they challenged almighty power to help them,—and at *Kibroth-hattaavah, the graves of lusters,* where the dainties they coveted were their poison; and, after these, their unbelief and distrust at Kadesh-barnea, of which he had already told them (*ch.* i.), and which he here mentions again (*v.* 23), would certainly have completed their ruin if they had been dealt with according to their own merits.

Now let them lay all this together, and it will appear that whatever favour God should hereafter show them, in subduing their enemies and putting them in possession of the land of Canaan, it was not for their righteousness. It is good for us often to remember against ourselves, with sorrow and shame, our former sins, and to review the records conscience keeps of them, that we may see how much we are indebted to free grace, and may humbly own that we never merited at God's hand any thing but wrath and the curse.

CHAP. X.

Moses having, in the foregoing chapter, reminded them of their own sin, as a reason why they should not depend upon their own righteousness, in this chapter he sets before them God's great mercy to them, notwithstanding their provocations, as a reason why they should be more obedient for the future. I. He mentions divers tokens of God's favour and reconciliation to them, never to be forgotten. (1.) The renewing of the tables of the covenant, ver. 1—5. (2.) Giving orders for their progress towards Canaan, ver. 6, 7. (3.) Choosing the tribe of Levi for his own, ver. 8, 9. (4.) And continuing the priesthood after the death of Aaron, ver. 6. (5.) Owning and accepting the intercession of Moses for them, ver. 10, 11. II. Hence he infers what obligations they lay under to fear, and love, and serve God, which he presses upon them with many motives, ver. 12, &c.

AT that time the Lord said unto me, Hew thee two tables of stone like unto the first, and come up unto me into the mount, and make thee an ark of wood. 2 And I will write on the tables the words that were in the first tables which thou brakedst, and thou shalt put them in the ark. 3 And I made an ark *of* shittim wood, and hewed two tables of stone like unto the first, and went up into the mount, having the two tables in mine hand. 4 And he wrote on the tables, according to the first writing, the ten commandments, which the Lord spake unto you in the mount out of the midst of the fire in the day of the assembly: and the Lord gave them unto me. 5 And I turned myself and came down from the mount, and put the tables

in the ark which I had made; and there they be, as the Lord commanded me. 6 And the children of Israel took their journey from Beeroth of the children of Jaakan to Mosera: there Aaron died, and there he was buried; and Eleazar his son ministered in the priest's office in his stead. 7 From thence they journeyed unto Gudgodah; and from Gudgodah to Jotbath, a land of rivers of waters. 8 At that time the Lord separated the tribe of Levi, to bear the ark of the covenant of the Lord, to stand before the Lord to minister unto him, and to bless in his name, unto this day. 9 Wherefore Levi hath no part nor inheritance with his brethren; the Lord *is* his inheritance, according as the Lord thy God promised him. 10 And I stayed in the mount, according to the first time, forty days and forty nights; and the Lord hearkened unto me at that time also, *and* the Lord would not destroy thee. 11 And the Lord said unto me, Arise, take *thy* journey before the people, that they may go in and possess the land, which I sware unto their fathers to give unto them.

There were four things in and by which God showed himself reconciled to Israel and made them truly great and happy, and in which God's goodness took occasion from their badness to make him the more illustrious:—

I. He gave them his law, gave it to them in writing, as a standing pledge of his favour. Though the tables that were first written were broken, because Israel had broken the commandments, and God might justly break the covenant, yet when his anger was turned away the tables were renewed, *v.* 1, 2. Note, God's putting his law in our hearts, and writing it in our inward parts, furnish the surest evidence of our reconciliation to God and the best earnest of our happiness in him. Moses is told to hew the tables; for the law prepares the heart by conviction and humiliation for the grace of God, but it is only that grace that then writes the law in it. Moses made *an ark of shittim-wood* (*v.* 3), a plain chest, the same, I suppose, in which the tables were afterwards preserved: but Bezaleel is said to make it (Exod. xxxvii. 1), because he afterwards finished it up and overlaid it with gold. Or Moses is said to make it because, when he went up the second time into the mount, he ordered it to be made by Bezaleel against he came down. And it is observable that for this reason the ark was the first thing that God gave orders about, Exod. xxv. 10. And this left an earnest to the congregation that the tables should not miscarry this second time, as they had done the first. God will send his law and gospel to those whose hearts are prepared as arks to receive them. Christ is the ark in which now our salvation is kept safely, that it may not be lost as it was in the first Adam, when he had it in his own hand. Observe, 1. What it was that God wrote on the two tables, the ten commandments (*v.* 4), or *ten words*, intimating in how little a compass they were contained : they were not ten volumes, but ten words : it was the same with the first writing, and both the same that he spoke in the mount. The second edition needed no correction nor amendment, nor did what he wrote differ from what he spoke. The written word is as truly the word of God as that which he spoke to his servants the prophets. 2. What care was taken of it. These two tables, thus engraven, were faithfully laid up in the ark. *And there they be*, said Moses, pointing it is probable towards the sanctuary, *v.* 5. That good thing which was committed to him he transmitted to them, and left it pure and entire in their hands ; now let them look to it at their peril. Thus we may say to the rising generation, "God has entrusted us with Bibles, sabbaths, sacraments, &c., as tokens of his presence and favour, and there they be ; we lodge them with you," 2 Tim. i. 13, 14.

II. He led them forward towards Canaan, though they in their hearts turned back towards Egypt, and he might justly have chosen their delusions, *v.* 6, 7. He brought them to a land of *rivers of waters*, out of a dry and barren wilderness. Sometimes God supplied their wants by the ordinary course of nature : when that failed, then by miracles ; and yet after this, when they were brought into a little distress, we find them distrusting God and murmuring, Num. xx. 3, 4.

III. He appointed a standing ministry among them, to deal for them in holy things. At that time when Moses went up a second time to the mount, or soon after, he had orders to separate the tribe of Levi to God, and to his immediate service, they having distinguished themselves by their zeal against the worshippers of the golden calf, *v.* 8, 9. The Kohathites carried the ark ; they and the other Levites stood *before the Lord*, to minister to him in all the offices of the tabernacle ; and the priests, who were of that tribe, were to bless the people. This was a standing ordinance, which had now continued almost forty years, even unto this day ; and provision was made for the perpetuating of it by the settled maintenance of that tribe, which was such as gave them great encouragement in their work, and no diversion from it. *The Lord is his inheritance.* Note, A settled ministry is a great blessing to a people, and a special token of God's favour. And, since the particular priests could not

continue by reason of death, God showed his care of the people in securing a succession, which Moses takes notice of here, *v.* 6. When *Aaron died*, the priesthood did not die with him, but *Eleazar his son ministered in his stead*, and took care of the ark, in which the tables of stone, those precious stones, were deposited, that they should suffer no damage ; there they be, and he has the custody of them. Under the law, a succession in the ministry was kept up, by an entail of the office on a certain tribe and family. But now, under the gospel, when the effusion of the Spirit is more plentiful and powerful, the succession is kept up by the Spirit's operation on men's hearts, qualifying men for, and inclining men to, that work, some in every age, that the name of Israel may not be blotted out.

IV. He accepted Moses as an advocate or intercessor for them, and therefore constituted him their prince and leader (*v.* 10, 11): *The Lord hearkened to me and said, Arise, go before the people.* It was a mercy to them that they had such a friend, so faithful both to him that appointed him and to those for whom he was appointed. It was fit that he who had saved them from ruin, by his intercession with heaven, should have the conduct and command of them. And herein he was a type of Christ, who, as he ever lives making intercession for us, so he has *all power both in heaven and in earth.*

12 And now, Israel, what doth the LORD thy God require of thee, but to fear the LORD thy God, to walk in all his ways, and to love him, and to serve the LORD thy God with all thy heart, and with all thy soul, 13 To keep the commandments of the LORD, and his statutes, which I command thee this day for thy good? 14 Behold, the heaven and the heaven of heavens *is* the LORD's thy God, the earth *also*, with all that therein *is*. 15 Only the LORD had a delight in thy fathers to love them, and he chose their seed after them, *even* you above all people, as *it is* this day. 16 Circumcise therefore the foreskin of your heart, and be no more stiffnecked. 17 For the LORD your God *is* God of gods, and Lord of lords, a great God, a mighty, and a terrible, which regardeth not persons, nor taketh reward : 18 He doth execute the judgment of the fatherless and widow, and loveth the stranger, in giving him food and raiment. 19 Love ye therefore the stranger : for ye were strangers in the land of Egypt. 20 Thou shalt

fear the LORD thy God; him shalt
thou serve, and to him shalt thou
cleave, and swear by his name.　21
He *is* thy praise, and he *is* thy God,
that hath done for thee these great
and terrible things, which thine eyes
have seen.　22 Thy fathers went down
into Egypt with threescore and ten
persons; and now the LORD thy God
hath made thee as the stars of heaven
for multitude.

Here is a most pathetic exhortation to
obedience, inferred from the premises, and
urged with very powerful arguments and a
great deal of persuasive rhetoric.　Moses
brings it in like an orator, with an appeal to
his auditors · *And now, Israel, what doth the
Lord thy God require of thee? v.* 12.　Ask
what he requires; as David (Ps. cxvi. 12),
What shall I render? When we have received mercy from God it becomes us to enquire what returns we shall make to him.
Consider what he requires, and you will find
it is nothing but what is highly just and reasonable in itself and of unspeakable benefit
and advantage to you.　Let us see here what
he does require, and what abundant reason
there is why we should do what he requires.

I. We are here most plainly directed in
our duty to God, to our neighbour, and to
ourselves.

1. We are here taught our duty to God,
both in the dispositions and affections of our
souls and in the actions of our lives, our
principles and our practices.　(1.) We must
fear the Lord our God, v. 12, and again *v.* 20.
We must adore his majesty, acknowledge his
authority, stand in awe of his power, and
dread his wrath.　This is gospel duty, Rev.
xiv. 6, 7.　(2.) We must love him, be well
pleased that he is, desire that he may be ours,
and delight in the contemplation of him and
in communion with him.　Fear him as a
great God, and our Lord, love him as a good
God, and our Father and benefactor.　(3.)
We must walk in his ways, that is, the ways
which he has appointed us to walk in.　The
whole course of our conversation must be
conformable to his holy will.　(4.) We must
serve him (*v.* 20), *serve him with all our heart
and soul* (*v.* 12), devote ourselves to his honour, put ourselves under his government,
and lay out ourselves to advance all the interests of his kingdom among men.　And
we must be hearty and zealous in his service, engage and employ our inward man in
his work, and what we do for him we must
do cheerfully and with a good will.　(5.) We
must *keep his commandments and his statutes,
v.* 13.　Having given up ourselves to his service, we must make his revealed will our rule
in every thing, perform all he prescribes, forbear all he forbids, firmly believing that all
the statutes he commands us are for our

good.　Besides the reward of obedience,
which will be our unspeakable gain, there are
true honour and pleasure in obedience.　It
is really for our present good to be meek and
humble, chaste and sober, just and charitable,
patient and contented; these make us easy,
and safe, and pleasant, and truly great.　(6.)
We must give honour to God, in swearing
by *his name* (*v.* 20); so give him the honour
of his omniscience, his sovereignty, his justice, as well as of his necessary existence.
Swear by his name, and not by the name of
any creature, or false god, whenever an oath
for confirmation is called for.　(7.) To him
we must cleave, *v.* 20.　Having chosen him
for our God, we must faithfully and constantly abide with him and never forsake him.
Cleave to him as one we love and delight in,
trust and confide in, and from whom we have
great expectations.

2. We are here taught our duty to our
neighbour (*v.* 19): *Love the stranger;* and,
if the stranger, much more our brethren,
as ourselves.　If the Israelites that were such
a peculiar people, so particularly distinguished
from all people, must be kind to strangers,
much more must we, that are not enclosed
in such a pale; we must have a tender concern for all that share with us in the human
nature, and *as we have opportunity* (that is,
according to their necessities and our abili-
ties) we must *do good to all men.*　Two arguments are here urged to enforce this duty:—
(1.) God's common providence, which extends itself to all nations of men, they being
all *made of one blood.* God *loveth the stranger*
(*v.* 18), that is, he gives to all life, and breath,
and all things, even to those that are Gentiles, and *strangers to the commonwealth of Israel* and to Israel's God.　He knows those
perfectly whom we know nothing of.　He
gives *food and raiment* even to those to
whom he has not shown his word and statutes.　God's common gifts to mankind oblige
us to honour all men.　Or the expression
denotes the particular care which Providence
takes of strangers in distress, which we
ought to praise him for (Ps. cxlvi. 9, The
Lord preserveth the strangers), and to imitate him, to serve him, and concur with him
therein, being forward to make ourselves
instruments in his hand of kindness to
strangers.　(2.) The afflicted condition which
the Israelites themselves had been in, when
they were strangers in Egypt.　Those that
have themselves been in distress, and have
found mercy with God, should sympathize
most feelingly with those that are in the like
distress and be ready to show kindness to
them.　The people of the Jews, notwithstanding these repeated commands given them
to be kind to strangers, conceived a rooted
antipathy to the Gentiles, whom they looked
upon with the utmost disdain, which made
them envy the grace of God and the gospel
of Christ, and this brought a final ruin upon
themselves.

3. We are here taught our duty to ourselves (*v.* 16): *Circumcise the foreskin of your hearts*, that is, " Cast away from you all corrupt affections and inclinations, which hinder you from fearing and loving God. *Mortify the flesh* with the lusts of it. Away with all filthiness and superfluity of naughtiness, which obstruct the free course of the word of God to your hearts. Rest not in the circumcision of the body, which was only the sign, but be circumcised in heart, which is the thing signified." See Rom. ii. 29. The command of Christ goes further than this, and obliges us not only to cut off the foreskin of the heart, which may easily be spared, but to cut off the right hand and to pluck out the right eye that is an offence to us ; the more spiritual the dispensation is the more spiritual we are obliged to be, and to go the closer in mortifying sin. And *be no more stiff-necked*, as they had been hitherto, *ch.* ix. 24. " Be not any longer obstinate against divine commands and corrections, but ready to comply with the will of God in both." The circumcision of the heart makes it ready to yield to God, and draw in his yoke.

II. We are here most pathetically persuaded to our duty. Let but reason rule us, and religion will.

1. Consider the greatness and glory of God, and therefore fear him, and from that principle serve and obey him. What is it that is thought to make a man great, but great honour, power, and possessions ? Think then how great the Lord our God is, and greatly to be feared. (1.) He has great honour, a name above every name. He is *God of gods*, and *Lord of lords*, *v.* 17. Angels are called *gods*, so are magistrates, and the Gentiles had *gods many, and lords many*, the creatures of their own fancy ; but God is infinitely above all these nominal deities. What an absurdity would it be for them to worship other gods when the God to whom they had sworn allegiance was the God of gods ! (2.) He has great power. He is a *mighty God and terrible* (*v.* 17), *who regardeth not persons.* He has the power of a conqueror, and so he is terrible to those that resist him and rebel against him. He has the power of a judge, and so he is just to all those that appeal to him or appear before him. And it is as much the greatness and honour of a judge to be impartial in his justice, without respect to persons or bribes, as it is to a general to be terrible to the enemy. Our God is both. (3.) He has great possessions. Heaven and earth are his (*v.* 14), and all the hosts of both. Therefore he is able to bear us out in his service, and to make up the losses we sustain in discharging our duty to him. And yet therefore he has no need of us, nor any thing we have or can do ; we are undone without him, but he is happy without us, which makes the condescensions of his grace, in accepting us and our services, truly admirable. Heaven and earth are his

possession, and yet *the Lord's portion is his people.*

2. Consider the goodness and grace of God, and therefore love him, and from that principle serve and obey him. His goodness is his glory as much as his greatness. (1.) He is good to all. Whomsoever he finds miserable, to them he will be found merciful : He *executes the judgment of the fatherless and widow*, *v.* 18. It is his honour to help the helpless, and to succour those that most need relief and that men are apt to do injury to, or at least to put a slight upon. See Ps. lxviii. 4, 5 ; cxlvi. 7, 9. (2.) But *truly God is good to Israel* in a special manner, and therefore they are under special obligations to him : " *He is thy praise, and he is thy God*, *v.* 21. *Therefore* love him and serve him, because of the relation wherein he stands to thee. He is thy God, a God in covenant with thee, and as such he is thy praise," that is, [1.] " He puts honour upon thee ; he is the God in whom, all the day long, thou mayest boast that thou knowest him, and art known of him. If he is thy God, he is thy glory." [2.] " He expects honour from thee. *He is thy praise*," that is, " he is the God whom thou art bound to praise ; if he has not praise from thee, whence may he expect it ?" He *inhabits the praises of Israel.* Consider, *First*, The gracious choice he made of Israel, *v.* 15. " He had a delight in thy fathers, and therefore chose their seed." Not that there was any thing in them to merit his favour, or to recommend them to it, but so it seemed good in his eyes. He would be kind to them, though he had no need of them. *Secondly*, The great things he had done for Israel, *v.* 21, 22. He reminds them not only of what they had heard with their ears, and which their fathers had told them of, but of what they had seen with their eyes, and which they must tell their children of, particularly that within a few generations seventy souls (for they were no more when Jacob went down into Egypt) increased to a great nation, *as the stars of heaven for multitude.* And the more they were in number the more praise and service God expected from them ; yet it proved, as in the old world, that when they began to multiply they corrupted themselves.

CHAP. XI.

<small>With this chapter Moses concludes his preface to the repetition of the statutes and judgments which they must observe to do. He repeats the general charge (ver. 1), and, having in the close of the foregoing chapter begun to mention the great things God had done among them, in this, I. He specifies several of the great works God had done before their eyes, ver. 2—7. II. He sets before them, for the future, life and death, the blessing and the curse, according as they did, or did not, keep God's commandments, that they should certainly prosper if they were obedient, should be blessed with plenty of all good things (ver. 8—15), and with victory over their enemies, and the enlargement of their coast thereby, ver. 22—25. But their disobedience would undoubtedly be their ruin, ver. 16, 17. III. He directs them what means to use that they might keep in mind the law of God, ver. 18—21. And, IV. Concludes all with solemnly charging them to choose which they would have, the blessing or the curse, ver. 26, &c.</small>

THEREFORE thou shalt love the
　Lord thy God, and keep his

charge, and his statutes, and his judgments, and his commandments, alway.
2 And know ye this day: for I *speak*
not with your children which have
not known, and which have not seen
the chastisement of the LORD your
God, his greatness, his mighty hand,
and his stretched out arm, 3 And
his miracles, and his acts, which he
did in the midst of Egypt unto Pharaoh the king of Egypt, and unto all
his land; 4 And what he did unto
the army of Egypt, unto their horses,
and to their chariots; how he made
the water of the Red sea to overflow
them as they pursued after you, and
how the LORD hath destroyed them
unto this day; 5 And what he did
unto you in the wilderness, until ye
came into this place; 6 And what
he did unto Dathan and Abiram, the
sons of Eliab, the son of Reuben:
how the earth opened her mouth, and
swallowed them up, and their households, and their tents, and all the
substance that *was* in their possession, in the midst of all Israel; 7
But your eyes have seen all the great
acts of the LORD which he did.

Because *God has made thee as the stars of
heaven for multitude* (so the preceding chapter
concludes), *therefore thou shalt love the Lord
thy God* (so this begins). Those whom God
has built up into families, whose beginning
was small, but whose latter end greatly increases, should use that as an argument with
themselves why they should serve God.
Thou shalt *keep his charge,* that is, the oracles
of his word and ordinances of his worship,
with which they were entrusted and for
which they were accountable. It is a phrase
often used concerning the office of the priests
and Levites, for all Israel was a kingdom of
priests, a holy nation. Observe the connection of these two: *Thou shalt love the Lord,*
and *keep his charge,* since love will work in
obedience, and that only is acceptable obedience which flows from a principle of love.
1 John v. 3.
Mention is made of the great and terrible
works of God which their *eyes had seen, v.* 7.
This part of his discourse Moses addresses
to the *seniors* among the people, the elders in
age; and probably the elders in office were
so, and were now his immediate auditors:
there were some among them that could remember their deliverance out of Egypt, all
above fifty, and to them he speaks this, not
to the children, who knew it by hearsay only,
v 2. Note, God's mercies to us when we

were young we should remember and retain
the impressions of when we are old; what
our eyes have seen, especially in our early
days, has affected us, and should be improved
by us long after. They had seen what terrible judgments God had executed upon the
enemies of Israel's peace, 1. Upon Pharaoh
and the Egyptians that enslaved them. What
a fine country was ruined and laid waste by
one plague after another, to force Israel's
enlargement! *v.* 3. What a fine army was
entirely drowned in the Red Sea, to prevent
Israel's being re-enslaved! *v.* 4. Thus did
he give *Egypt for their ransom,* Isa. xliii. 3.
Rather shall that famous kingdom be destroyed than that Israel shall not be delivered.
2. Upon Dathan and Abiram that embroiled
them. Remember *what he did in the wilderness (v.* 5), by how many necessary *chastisements* (as they are called, *v.* 2) they were kept
from ruining themselves, particularly when
those daring Reubenites defied the authority
of Moses and headed a dangerous rebellion
against God himself, which threatened the
ruin of a whole nation, and might have ended
in that if the divine power had not immediately crushed the rebellion by burying the
rebels alive, them and *all that was in their
possession, v.* 6. What was done against
them, though misinterpreted by the disaf-
fected party (Num. xvi. 41), was really done
in mercy to Israel. To be saved from the
mischiefs of insurrections at home is as great
a kindness to a people, and therefore lays
them under as strong obligations, as protection from the invasion of enemies abroad.

8 Therefore shall ye keep all the
commandments which I command you
this day, that ye may be strong, and
go in and possess the land, whither
ye go to possess it; 9 And that ye
may prolong *your* days in the land,
which the LORD sware unto your fathers to give unto them and to their
seed, a land that floweth with milk
and honey. 10 For the land, whither
thou goest in to possess it, *is* not as
the land of Egypt, from whence ye
came out, where thou sowedst thy
seed, and wateredst *it* with thy foot,
as a garden of herbs: 11 But the
land, whither ye go to possess it, *is* a
land of hills and valleys, *and* drinketh
water of the rain of heaven: 12 A
land which the LORD thy God careth
for: the eyes of the LORD thy God
are always upon it, from the beginning of the year even unto the end of
the year. 13 And it shall come to pass,
if ye shall hearken diligently unto my
commandments which I command

you this day, to love the LORD your God, and to serve him with all your heart and with all your soul, 14 That I will give *you* the rain of your land in his due season, the first rain and the latter rain, that thou mayest gather in thy corn, and thy wine, and thine oil. 15 And I will send grass in thy fields for thy cattle, that thou mayest eat and be full. 16 Take heed to yourselves, that your heart be not deceived, and ye turn aside, and serve other gods, and worship them; 17 And *then* the LORD's wrath be kindled against you, and he shut up the heaven, that there be no rain, and that the land yield not her fruit; and *lest* ye perish quickly from off the good land which the LORD giveth you.

Still Moses urges the same subject, as loth to conclude till he had gained his point. " *If thou wilt enter into life,* if thou wilt enter into Canaan, a type of that life, and find it a good land indeed to thee, *keep the commandments: Keep all the commandments which I command you this day;* love God, and serve him with all your heart."

I. Because this was the way to get and keep possession of the promised land. 1. It was the way to get possession (*v.* 8): *That you may be strong* for war, and so *go in and possess it.* So little did they know either of hardship or hazard in the wars of Canaan that he does not say they should go in and fight for it; no, they had nothing in effect to do but go in and possess it. He does not go about to teach them the art of war, how to draw the bow, and use the sword, and keep ranks, that they might be strong, and go in and possess the land; no, but let them keep God's commandments, and their religion, while they are true to it, will be their strength, and secure their success. (2.) It was the way to keep possession (*v.* 9): *That you may prolong your days in this land* that your eye is upon. Sin tends to the shortening of the days of particular persons and to the shortening of the days of a people's prosperity; but obedience will be a lengthening out of their tranquillity.

II. Because the land of Canaan, into which they were going, had a more sensible dependence upon the blessing of heaven than the land of Egypt had, *v.* 10—12. Egypt was a country fruitful enough, but it was all flat, and was watered, not as other countries with rain (it is said of Egypt, Zech. xiv. 18, that it *has no rain*), but by the overflowing of the river Nile at a certain season of the year, to the improving of which there was necessary a great deal of the art and labour

of the husbandman, so that in Egypt a man must bestow as much cost and pains upon a field as upon a garden of herbs. And this made them the more apt to imagine that the power of their own hands got them this wealth. But the land of Canaan was an uneven country, a land of hills and valleys, which not only gave a more pleasing prospect to the eye, but yielded a greater variety of soils for the several purposes of the husbandman. It was a land that had no great rivers in it, except Jordan, but *drank water of the rain of heaven,* and so, 1. Saved them a great deal of labour. While the Egyptians were ditching and guttering in the fields, up to the knees in mud, to bring water to their land, which otherwise would soon become like the heath in the wilderness, the Israelites could sit in their houses, warm and easy, and leave it to God to water their land with the former and the latter rain, which is called *the river of God* (Ps. lxv. 9), perhaps in allusion to, and contempt of, the river of Egypt, which that nation was so proud of. Note, The better God has provided, by our outward condition, for our ease and convenience, the more we should abound in his service: the less we have to do for our bodies the more we should do for God and our souls. 2. So he directed them to look upwards to God, who *giveth us rain from heaven and fruitful seasons* (Acts xiv. 17), and promised to be himself as *the dew unto Israel,* Hos. xiv. 5. Note, (1.) Mercies bring with them the greatest comfort and sweetness when we see them coming from heaven, the immediate gifts of divine Providence. (2.) The closer dependence we have upon God the more cheerful we should be in our obedience to him. See how Moses here magnifies the land of Canaan above all other lands, that the eyes of God were always upon it, that is, they should be so, to see that nothing was wanting, while they kept close to God and duty; its fruitfulness should be not so much the happy effect of its soil as the immediate fruit of the divine blessing; this may be inferred from its present state, for it is said to be at this day, now that God has departed from it, as barren a spot of ground as perhaps any under heaven. Call it not *Naomi:* call it *Marah.*

III. Because God would certainly bless them with an abundance of all good things if they would love him and serve him (*v.* 13—15): *I will give you the rain of your land in due season,* so that they should neither want it when the ground called for it nor have it in excess; but they should have the former rain, which fell at seed-time, and the latter rain, which fell before the harvest, Amos iv. 7. This represented all the seasonable blessings which God would bestow upon them, especially spiritual comforts, which should come *as the latter and former rain,* Hos. vi. 3. And the earth thus watered produced, 1. Fruits for the service of man, *corn and wine, and oil*, Ps. civ. 13—15. 2. Grass for the cattle, that they also might be serviceable to them, that *he might eat of them and be full, v.* 15. Godliness hath here the *promise of the life that now is ;* but the favour of God shall put gladness into the heart, more than the increase of corn, and wine, and oil will.

IV. Because their revolt from God to idols would certainly be their ruin : *Take heed that your hearts be not deceived, v.* 16, 17. All that forsake God to set their affection upon, or pay their devotion to, any creature, will find themselves wretchedly deceived to their own destruction ; and this will aggravate it that it was purely for want of taking heed. A little care would have prevented their being imposed upon by the great deceiver. To awaken them to take heed, Moses here tells them plainly that if they should *turn aside to other gods*, 1. They would provoke the wrath of God against them ; and *who knows the power of that anger ?* 2. Good things would be turned away from them ; the heaven would withhold its rain, and then of course the earth would not yield its fruit. 3. Evil things would come upon them ; they would perish quickly from off this good land. And the better the land was the more grievous it would be to perish from it. The goodness of the land would not be their security, when the badness of the inhabitants had made them ripe for ruin.

18 Therefore shall ye lay up these my words in your heart and in your soul, and bind them for a sign upon your hand, that they may be as frontlets between your eyes. 19 And ye shall teach them your children, speaking of them when thou sittest in thine house, and when thou walkest by the way, when thou liest down, and when thou risest up. 20 And thou shalt write them upon the door posts of thine house, and upon thy gates : 21 That your days may be multiplied, and the days of your children, in the land which the LORD sware unto your fathers to give them, as the days of heaven upon the earth. 22 For if ye shall diligently keep all these commandments which I command you, to do them, to love the LORD your God, to walk in all his ways, and to cleave unto him ; 23 Then will the LORD drive out all these nations from before you, and ye shall possess greater nations and mightier than yourselves. 24 Every place whereon the soles of your feet shall tread shall be your's : from the wilderness and Lebanon,

from the river, the river Euphrates, even unto the uttermost sea shall your coast be. 25 There shall no man be able to stand before you : *for* the LORD your God shall lay the fear of you and the dread of you upon all the land that ye shall tread upon, as he hath said unto you.

Here, I. Moses repeats the directions he had given for the guidance and assistance of the people in their obedience, and for the keeping up of religion among them (*v.* 18—20), which is much to the same purport with what we had before, *ch.* vi. 6, &c. Let us all be directed by the three rules here given :— 1. Let our hearts be filled with the word of God : *Lay up these words in your heart and in your soul.* The heart must be the treasury or store-house in which the word of God must be laid up, to be used upon all occasions. We cannot expect good practices in the conversation, unless there be good thoughts, good affections, and good principles, in the heart. 2. Let our eyes be fixed upon the word of God. " Bind these words for a sign *upon your hand*, which is always in view (Isa. xlix. 16), *and as frontlets between your eyes*, which you cannot avoid the sight of ; let them be as ready and familiar to you, and have your eye as constantly upon them, as if they were *written upon your door-posts*, and could not be overlooked either when you go out or when you come in." Thus we must *lay God's judgments before us*, having a constant regard to them, as the guide of our way, as the rule of our work, Ps. cxix. 30. 3. Let our tongues be employed about the word of God. Let it be the subject of our familiar discourse, wherever we are ; especially with our children, who must be taught the service of God, as the one thing needful, much more needful than either the rules of decency or the calling they must live by in this world. Great care and pains must be taken to acquaint children betimes, and to affect them, with the word of God and the wondrous things of his law. Nor will any thing contribute more to the prosperity and perpetuity of religion in a nation than the good education of children : if the seed be holy, it is the substance of a land.

II. He repeats the assurances he had before given them, in God's name, of prosperity and success if they were obedient. 1. They should have a happy settlement, *v.* 21. Their days should be multiplied ; and, when they were fulfilled, the days of their children likewise should be many, as the days of heaven, that is, Canaan should be sure to them and their heirs for ever, as long as the world stands, if they did not by their own sin throw themselves out of it. 2. It should not be in the power of their enemies to give them any disturbance, nor make them upon any account uneasy. " If you will *keep God's command-*

ments, and be careful to do your duty (*v.* 22), God will not only crown the labours of the husbandman with plenty of the fruits of the earth, but he will own and succeed the more glorious undertakings of the men of war. Victory shall attend your arms; which way soever they turn, God will drive out these nations, and put you in possession of their land," *v.* 23, 24. Their territories should be enlarged to the utmost extent of the promise, Gen. xv. 18. And all their neighbours should stand in awe of them, *v.* 25. Nothing contributes more to the making of a nation considerable abroad, valuable to its friends and formidable to its enemies, than religion reigning in it; for who can be against those that have God for them? And he is certainly for those that are sincerely for him, Prov. xiv. 34.

26 Behold, I set before you this day a blessing and a curse; 27 A blessing, if ye obey the commandments of the LORD your God, which I command you this day: 28 And a curse, if ye will not obey the commandments of the LORD your God, but turn aside out of the way which I command you this day, to go after other gods, which ye have not known. 29 And it shall come to pass, when the LORD thy God hath brought thee in unto the land whither thou goest to possess it, that thou shalt put the blessing upon mount Gerizim, and the curse upon mount Ebal. 30 *Are* they not on the other side Jordan, by the way where the sun goeth down, in the land of the Canaanites, which dwell in the champaign over against Gilgal, beside the plains of Moreh? 31 For ye shall pass over Jordan to go in to possess the land which the LORD your God giveth you, and ye shall possess it, and dwell therein. 32 And ye shall observe to do all the statutes and judgments which I set before you this day.

Here Moses concludes his general exhortation to obedience; and his management is very affecting, and such as, one would think, should have engaged them for ever to God, and should have left impressions upon them never to be worn out.

I. He sums up all his arguments for obedience in two words, *the blessing and the curse* (*v.* 26), that is, the rewards and the punishments, as they stand in the promises and the threatenings, which are the great sanctions of the law, taking hold of hope and fear, those two handles of the soul, by which it is caught, held, and managed. These two, the blessing

and the curse, he set before them, that is, 1. He explained them, that they might know them; he enumerated the particulars contained both in the blessing and in the curse, that they might see the more fully how desirable the blessing was, and how dreadful the curse. 2. He confirmed them, that they might believe them, made it evident to them, by the proofs he produced of his own commission, that the blessing was not a fool's paradise, nor the curse a bugbear, but that both were real declarations of the purpose of God concerning them. 3. He charged them to choose which of these they would have, so fairly does he deal with them, and so far is he from *putting out the eyes of these men,* as he was charged, Num. xvi. 14. They and we are plainly told on what terms we stand with Almighty God. (1.) If we be obedient to his laws, we may be sure of a blessing, *v.* 27. But, (2.) If we be disobedient, we may be as sure of a curse, *v.* 28. *Say you to the righteous* (for God has said it, and all the world cannot unsay it) that *it shall be well with them: but woe to the wicked, it shall be ill with them.*

II. He appoints a public and solemn proclamation to be made of the blessing and curse which he had set before them, upon the two mountains of Gerizim and Ebal, *v.* 29, 30. We have more particular directions for this solemnity in *ch.* xxvii. 11, &c., and an account of the performance of it, Josh. viii. 33, &c. It was to be done, and was done, immediately upon their coming into Canaan, that when they first took possession of that land they might know upon what terms they stood. The place where this was to be done is particularly described by Moses, though he never saw it, which is one circumstance among many that evidences his divine instructions. It is said to be near the *plain,* or *oaks,* or *meadows,* of *Moreh,* which was one of the first places that Abraham came to in Canaan; so that in sending them thither, to hear the blessing and the curse, God reminded them of the promise he made to Abraham in that very place, Gen. xii. 6, 7. The mention of this appointment here serves, 1. For the encouragement of their faith in the promise of God, that they should be masters of Canaan quickly. Do it (says Moses) on the other side Jordan (*v.* 30), for you may be confident *you shall pass over Jordan,* *v.* 31. The institution of this service to be done in Canaan was an assurance to them that they should be brought into possession of it, and a token like that which God gave to Moses (Exod. iii. 12): *You shall serve God upon this mountain.* And, 2. It serves for an engagement upon them to be obedient, that they might escape that curse, and obtain that blessing, which, besides what they had already heard, they must shortly be witnesses to the solemn publication of (*v.* 32): " *You shall observe to do the statutes and judgments,* that you may not in that solemnity be witnesses against yourselves."

CHAP. XII.

Moses at this chapter comes to the particular statutes which he had to give in charge to Israel, and he begins with those which relate to the worship of God, and particularly those which explain the second commandment, about which God is in a special manner jealous. 1. They must utterly destroy all relics and remains of idolatry, ver. 1--3. II. They must keep close to the tabernacle, ver. 4, 5. The former precept was intended to prevent all false worship, the latter to preserve the worship God had instituted. By this latter law, 1. They are commanded to bring all their offerings to the altar of God, and all their holy things to the place which he should choose, ver. 6, 7, 11, 12, 14, 18, 26—28. 2. They are forbidden, in general, to do as they now did in the wilderness (ver. 8—11), and as the Canaanites had done (ver. 29—32), and, in particular, to eat the hallowed things at their own houses (ver. 13, 17, 18), or to forsake the instituted ministry, ver. 19. 3. They are permitted to eat flesh as common food at their own houses, provided they do not eat the blood, ver. 15, 16, and again, ver. 20—26.

THESE *are* the statutes and judgments, which ye shall observe to do in the land, which the LORD God of thy fathers giveth thee to possess it, all the days that ye live upon the earth. 2 Ye shall utterly destroy all the places, wherein the nations which ye shall possess served their gods, upon the high mountains, and upon the hills, and under every green tree : 3 And ye shall overthrow their altars, and break their pillars, and burn their groves with fire ; and ye shall hew down the graven images of their gods, and destroy the names of them out of that place. 4 Ye shall not do so unto the LORD your God.

From those great original truths, That there is a God, and that there is but one God, arise those great fundamental laws, That that God is to be worshipped, and he only, and that therefore we are to have no other God before him : this is the first commandment, and the second is a guard upon it, or a hedge about it. To prevent a revolt to false gods, we are forbidden to worship the true God in such a way and manner as the false gods were worshipped in, and are commanded to observe the instituted ordinances of worship that we may adhere to the proper object of worship. For this reason Moses is very large in his exposition of the second commandment. What is contained in this and the four following chapters mostly refers to that. *These are statutes and judgments* which they must *observe to do* (v. 1), 1. In the days of their rest and prosperity, when they should be masters of Canaan. We must not think that our religion is instituted only to be our work in the years of our servitude, our entertainment in the places of our solitude, and our consolation in affliction ; no, when we come to possess a good land, still we must keep up the worship of God in Canaan as well as in a wilderness, when we have grown up as well as when we are children, when we are full of business as well as when we have nothing else to do. 2. *All the days*, as long as you *live upon the earth.* While we are here in our state of trial,

we must continue in our obedience, even to the end, and never leave our duty, nor grow weary of well-doing. Now,

I. They are here charged to abolish and extirpate all those things that the Canaanites had served their idol-gods with, *v.* 2, 3. Here is no mention of idol-temples, which countenances the opinion some have, that the tabernacle Moses reared in the wilderness was the first habitation that ever was made for religious uses, and that from it temples took their rise. But the places that had been used, and were now to be levelled, were enclosures for their worship on *mountains and hills* (as if the height of the ground would give advantage to the ascent of their devotions), and under green trees, either because pleasant or because awful : whatever makes the mind easy and reverent, contracts and composes it, was thought to befriend devotion. The solemn shade and silence of a grove are still admired by those that are disposed to contemplation. But the advantages which these retirements gave to the Gentiles in the worship of their idols was that they concealed those works of darkness which could not bear the light ; and therefore they must all be destroyed, with the altars, pillars, and images, that had been used by the natives in the worship of their gods, so as that the very names of them might be buried in oblivion, and not only not be remembered with respect, but not remembered at all. They must thus consult, 1. The reputation of their land ; let it never be said of this holy land that it had been thus polluted, but let all these dunghills be carried away, as things they were ashamed of. 2. The safety of their religion ; let none be left remaining, lest profane unthinking people, especially in degenerate ages, should make use of them in the service of the God of Israel. Let these pest-houses be demolished, as things they were afraid of. He begins the statutes that relate to divine worship with this, because there must first be an abhorrence of that which is evil before there can be a steady adherence to that which is good, Rom. xii. 9. The kingdom of God must be set up, both in persons and places, upon the ruins of the devil's kingdom ; for they cannot stand together, nor can there be any communion between Christ and Belial.

II. They are charged not to transfer the rites and usages of idolaters into the worship of God ; no, not under colour of beautifying and improving it (*v.* 4) : *You shall not do so to the Lord your God,* that is, "you must not think to do honour to him by offering sacrifices on mountains and hills, erecting pillars, planting groves, and setting up images ; no, you must not indulge a luxurious fancy in your worship, nor think that whatever pleases that will please God : *he is above all gods,* and will not be worshipped as other gods are."

5 But unto the place which the

LORD your God shall choose out of all your tribes to put his name there, *even* unto his habitation shall ye seek, and thither thou shalt come : 6 And thither ye shall bring your burnt offerings, and your sacrifices, and your tithes, and heave offerings of your hand, and your vows, and your freewill offerings, and the firstlings of your herds and of your flocks : 7 And there ye shall eat before the LORD your God, and ye shall rejoice in all that ye put your hand unto, ye and your households, wherein the LORD thy God hath blessed thee. 8 Ye shall not do after all *the things* that we do here this day, every man whatsoever *is* right in his own eyes. 9 For ye are not as yet come to the rest and to the inheritance, which the LORD your God giveth you. 10 But *when* ye go over Jordan, and dwell in the land which the LORD your God giveth you to inherit, and *when* he giveth you rest from all your enemies round about, so that ye dwell in safety; 11 Then there shall be a place which the LORD your God shall choose to cause his name to dwell there ; thither shall ye bring all that I command you; your burnt offerings, and your sacrifices, your tithes, and the heave offering of your hand, and all your choice vows which ye vow unto the LORD : 12 And ye shall rejoice before the LORD your God, ye, and your sons, and your daughters, and your menservants, and your maidservants, and the Levite that *is* within your gates ; forasmuch as he hath no part nor inheritance with you. 13 Take heed to thyself that thou offer not thy burnt offerings in every place that thou seest : 14 But in the place which the LORD shall choose in one of thy tribes, there thou shalt offer thy burnt offerings, and there thou shalt do all that I command thee. 15 Notwithstanding thou mayest kill and eat flesh in all thy gates, whatsoever thy soul lusteth after, according to the blessing of the LORD thy God which he hath given thee : the unclean and the clean may eat thereof, as of the roebuck, and as of the hart. 16 Only ye shall not eat the blood; ye shall pour it upon the earth as water. 17 Thou mayest not eat within thy gates the tithe of thy corn, or of thy wine, or of thy oil, or the firstlings of thy herds or of thy flock, nor any of thy vows which thou vowest, nor thy freewill offerings, or heave offering of thine hand : 18 But thou must eat them before the LORD thy God in the place which the LORD thy God shall choose, thou, and thy son, and thy daughter, and thy manservant, and thy maidservant, and the Levite that *is* within thy gates : and thou shalt rejoice before the LORD thy God in all that thou puttest thine hands unto. 19 Take heed to thyself that thou forsake not the Levite as long as thou livest upon the earth. 20 When the LORD thy God shall enlarge thy border, as he hath promised thee, and thou shalt say, I will eat flesh, because thy soul longeth to eat flesh ; thou mayest eat flesh, whatsoever thy soul lusteth after. 21 If the place which the LORD thy God hath chosen to put his name there be too far from thee, then thou shalt kill of thy herd and of thy flock, which the LORD hath given thee, as I have commanded thee, and thou shalt eat in thy gates whatsoever thy soul lusteth after. 22 Even as the roebuck and the hart is eaten, so thou shalt eat them : the unclean and the clean shall eat *of* them alike. 23 Only be sure that thou eat not the blood : for the blood *is* the life ; and thou mayest not eat the life with the flesh. 24 Thou shalt not eat it ; thou shalt pour it upon the earth as water. 25 Thou shalt not eat it ; that it may go well with thee, and with thy children after thee, when thou shalt do *that which is* right in the sight of the LORD. 26 Only thy holy things which thou hast, and thy vows, thou shalt take, and go unto the place which the LORD shall choose : 27 And thou shalt offer thy burnt offerings, the flesh and the blood, upon the altar of the LORD thy God : and the blood of thy sacrifices shall be poured out upon the altar of the LORD thy God, and thou shalt eat the flesh. 28 Observe and hear all these words which I command thee, that it may go well with thee, and with thy children after thee for ever, when thou doest *that which is* good and right in the sight of the LORD thy God. 29 When the LORD thy God shall cut off the nations from before thee, whither thou goest to possess them, and thou succeedest them, and dwellest in their land; 30 Take heed to thyself that thou be not snared by following them, after that they be destroyed from before thee; and that thou enquire not after their gods, saying, How did these nations serve their gods? even so will I do likewise. 31 Thou shalt not do so unto the LORD thy God: for every abomination to the LORD, which he hateth, have they done unto their gods; for even their sons and their daughters they have burnt in the fire to their gods. 32 What thing soever I command you, observe to do it: thou shalt not add thereto, nor diminish from it.

There is not any one particular precept (as I remember) in all the law of Moses so largely pressed and inculcated as this, by which they are all tied to bring their sacrifices to that one altar which was set up in the court of the tabernacle, and there to perform all the rituals of their religion; for, as to moral services, then, no doubt, as now, men might pray every where, as they did in their synagogues. The command to do this, and the prohibition of the contrary, are here repeated again and again, as we teach children: and yet we are sure that there is in scripture no vain repetition; but all this stress is laid upon it, 1. Because of the strange proneness there was in the hearts of the people to idolatry and superstition, and the danger of their being seduced by the many temptations which they would be surrounded with. 2. Because of the great use which the observance of this appointment would be of to them, both to prevent the introducing of corrupt customs into their worship and to preserve among them unity and brotherly love, that, meeting all in one place, they might continue both of one way and of one heart. 3. Because of the significancy of this appointment. They must keep to one place, in token of their belief of those two great truths, which we find together (1 Tim. ii. 5), That *there is one God*, and *one Mediator between God and man.* It not only served to keep up the notion of the unity of the Godhead, but was an intimation to them (though they could not stedfastly discern it)

of the one only way of approach to God and communion with him, in and by the Messiah.

Let us now reduce this long charge to its proper heads.

I. It is here promised that when they were settled in Canaan, when they had *rest from their enemies, and dwelt in safety,* God would choose a certain place, which he would appoint to be the centre of their unity, to which they should bring all their offerings, *v.* 10, 11. Observe, 1. If they must be tied to one place, they should not be left in doubt concerning it, but should certainly know what place it was. Had Christ intended, under the gospel, to make any one place such a seat of power as Rome pretends to be, we should not have been left so destitute of instruction as we are concerning the appointed place. 2. God does not leave it to them to choose the place, lest the tribes should have quarrelled about it, each striving, for their secular advantage, to have it among them; but he reserves the choice to himself, as he does the designation of the Redeemer and the institution of holy ordinances. 3. He does not appoint the place now, as he had appointed mounts Gerizim and Ebal, for the pronouncing of the blessings and curses (*ch.* xi. 29), but reserves the doing of it till hereafter, that hereby they might be made to expect further directions from heaven, and a divine conduct, after Moses should be removed. The place which God would choose is said to be the place where he would put his name, that is, which he would have to be called his, where his honour should dwell, where he would manifest himself to his people, and make himself known, as men do by their names, and where he would receive addresses, by which his name is both praised and called upon. It was to be his habitation, where, as King of Israel, he would keep court, and be found by all those that reverently sought him. The ark was the token of God's presence, and where that was put there God put his name, and that was his habitation. It contained the tables of the law; for none must expect to receive favours from God's hand but those that are willing to *receive the law from his mouth.* The place which God first chose for the ark to reside in was Shiloh; and, after that place had sinned away its honours, we find the ark at Kirjath-jearim and other places; but at length, in David's time, it was fixed at Jerusalem, and God said concerning Solomon's temple, more expressly than ever he had said concerning any other place, *This I have chosen for a house of sacrifice,* 2 Chron. vii. 12. Compare 2 Chron. vi. 5. Now, under the gospel, we have no temple that sanctifies the gold, no altar that sanctifies the gift, but Christ only; and, as to the places of worship, the prophets foretold that *in every place* the spiritual *incense should be offered,* Mal. i. 11. And our Saviour has declared that those are accepted as true worshippers who worship God in sincerity and truth, without regard either to this mountain or Jerusalem, John iv. 23.

II. They are commanded to bring all their burnt-offerings and sacrifices to this place that God would choose (*v.* 6 and again *v.* 11): *Thither shall you bring all that I command you*; and (*v.* 14), *There thou shalt offer thy burnt offerings*; and (*v.* 27), *The flesh and the blood must be offered upon the altar of the Lord thy God.* And of their peace-offerings, here called their *sacrifices*, though they were to *eat the flesh*, yet *the blood* was to be *poured out upon the altar.* By this they were taught that sacrifices and offerings God did not desire, nor accept, for their own sake, nor for any intrinsic worth in them, as natural expressions of homage and adoration; but that they received their virtue purely from the altar on which they were offered, as it typified Christ; whereas prayers and praises, as much more necessary and valuable, were to be offered every day by the people of God wherever they were. A devout Israelite might honour God, and keep up communion with him, and obtain mercy from him, though he had not an opportunity, perhaps, for many months together, of bringing a sacrifice to his altar. But this signified the obligation we Christians are under to offer up all our spiritual sacrifices to God in the name of Jesus Christ, hoping for acceptance only upon the score of his mediation, 1 Pet. ii. 5.

III. They are commanded to feast upon their hallowed things before the Lord, with holy joy. They must not only bring to the altar the sacrifices which were to be offered to God, but they must bring to the place of the altar all those things which they were appointed by the law to eat and drink, to the honour of God, in token of their communion with him, *v.* 6. Their *tithes, and heave-offerings of their hand*, that is, their first-fruits, their vows, and *free-will-offerings*, and firstlings, all those things which were to be religiously made use of either by themselves or by the priests and Levites, must be brought to the place which God would choose; as all the revenues of the crown, from all parts of the kingdom, are brought into the exchequer. And (*v.* 7): *There you shall eat before the Lord, and rejoice in all that you put your hands unto;* and again (*v.* 12), *You shall rejoice before the Lord, you, and your sons, and your daughters.* Observe here, 1. That what we do in the service of God and to his glory redounds to our benefit, if it be not our own fault. Those that sacrifice to God are welcome to eat before him, and to feast upon their sacrifices: he *sups with us*, and *we with him*, Rev. iii. 20. If we glorify God, we edify ourselves, and cultivate our own minds, through the grace of God, by the increase of our knowledge and faith, the enlivening of devout affections, and the confirming of gracious habits and resolutions: thus is the soul nourished. 2. That work for God

should be done with holy joy and cheerfulness. You shall *eat and rejoice*, *v.* 7, and again, *v.* 12 and *v.* 18. (1.) Now while they were before the Lord they must rejoice, *v.* 12. It is the will of God that we should serve him with gladness; none displeased him more than those that *covered his altar with tears*, Mal. ii. 13. See what a good Master we serve, who has made it our duty to sing at our work. Even the children and servants must rejoice with them before God, that the services of religion might be a pleasure to them, and not a task or drudgery. (2.) They must *carry away with them* the grateful relish of that delight which they found in communion with God; they must rejoice in all that they *put their hands unto*, *v.* 7. Some of the comfort which they had had in the business of religion they must take with them into their common employments; and, being thus strengthened in soul, whatever they did they must do it heartily and cheerfully. And this holy pious joy in God and his goodness, with which we are to rejoice evermore, would be the best preservative against the sin and snare of *vain and carnal mirth* and a relief against the *sorrows of the world.*

IV. They are commanded to be kind to the Levites. Did they feast with joy? The Levites must feast with them, and rejoice with them, *v.* 12, and again, *v.* 18; and a general caution (*v.* 19), *Take heed that thou forsake not the Levite as long as thou livest.* There were Levites that attended the altar as assistants to the priests, and these must not be forsaken, that is, the service they performed must be constantly adhered to; no other altar must be set up than that which God appointed; for that would be to forsake the Levites. But this seems to be spoken of the Levites that were dispersed in the country to instruct the people in the law of God, and to assist them in their devotions; for it is *the Levite within their gates* that they are here commanded to make much of. It is a great mercy to have Levites near us, within our gates, that we may ask the law at their mouth, and at our feasts to be a check upon us, to restrain excesses. And it is the duty of people to be kind to their ministers that give them good instructions and set them good examples. As long as we live we shall need their assistance, till we come to that world where ordinances will be superseded; and therefore *as long as we live* we must not forsake the Levites. The reason given (*v.* 12) is because *the Levite has no part nor inheritance with you*, so that he cannot grow rich by husbandry or trade; let him therefore share with you in the comfort of your riches. They must give the Levites their tithes and offerings, settled on them by the law, because they had no other maintenance.

V. They are allowed to eat common flesh, but not the flesh of their offerings, in their own houses, wherever they dwelt. What was any way devoted to God they must not eat at home, *v.* 13, 17. But what was not so devoted they might kill and eat of at their pleasure, *v.* 15. And this permission is again repeated, *v.* 20—·22. It should seem that while they were in the wilderness they did not eat the flesh of any of those kinds of beasts that were used in sacrifice, but what was killed at the door of the tabernacle, and part of it presented to God as a peace-offering, Lev. xvii. 3, 4. But when they came to Canaan, where they must live at a great distance from the tabernacle, they might kill what they pleased for their own use of their flocks and herds, without bringing part to the altar. This allowance is very express, and repeated, lest Satan should take occasion from that law which forbade the eating of their sacrifices at their own houses to suggest to them, as he did to our first parents, hard thoughts of God, as if he grudged them the enjoyment of what he had given them : *Thou mayest eat whatsoever thy soul lusteth after.* There is a natural regular appetite, which it is lawful to gratify with temperance and sobriety, not taking too great a pleasure in the gratification, nor being uneasy if it be crossed. The unclean, who might not eat of the holy things, yet might eat of the same sort of flesh when it was only used as common food. The distinction between clean persons and unclean was sacred, and designed for the preserving of the honour of their holy feasts, and therefore must not be brought into their ordinary meals. This permission has a double restriction :—1. They must eat according to the blessing which God had given them, *v.* 15. Note, It is not only our wisdom, but our duty, to live according to our estates, and not to spend above what we have. As it is unjust on the one hand to hoard what should be laid out, so it is much more unjust to lay out more than we have ; for what is not our own must needs be another's, who is thereby robbed and defrauded. And this, I say, is much more unjust, because it is easier afterwards to distribute what has been unduly spared, and so to make a sort of restitution for the wrong, than it is to repay to wife, and children, and creditors, what has been unduly spent. Between these two extremes let wisdom find the mean, and then let watchfulness and resolution keep it. 2. They must not eat blood (*v.* 16, and again, *v.* 23): *Only be sure that thou eat not the blood* (*v.* 24), *Thou shalt not eat it ;* and (*v.* 25), *Thou shalt not eat it, that it may go well with thee.* When they could not bring the blood to the altar, to pour it out there before the Lord, as belonging to him, they must pour it out upon the earth, as not belonging to them, because it was the life, and therefore, as an acknowledgment, belonged to him who gives life, and, as an atonement, belonged to him to whom life is forfeited. Bishop Patrick thinks one reason why they were forbidden thus

strictly the eating of blood was to prevent the superstitions of the old idolaters about the blood of their sacrifices, which they thought their demons delighted in, and by eating of which they imagined that they had communion with them.

VI. They are forbidden to keep up either their own corrupt usages in the wilderness or the corrupt usages of their predecessors in the land of Canaan.

1. They must not keep up those improper customs which they had got into in the wilderness, and which were connived at in consideration of the present unsettledness of their condition (*v.* 8, 9): *You shall not do after all the things that we do here this day.* Never was there a better governor than Moses, and one would think never a better opportunity of keeping up good order and discipline than now among the people of Israel, when they lay so closely encamped under the eye of their governor ; and yet it seems there was much amiss and many irregularities had crept in among them. We must never expect to see any society perfectly pure and right, and as it should be, till we come to the heavenly Canaan. They had sacrifices and religious worship, courts of justice and civil government, and, by the stoning of the man that *gathered sticks on the sabbath day,* it appears there was great strictness used in guarding the most weighty matters of the law ; but being frequently upon the remove, and always at uncertainty, (1.) They could none of them observe the solemn feasts, and the rites of cleansing, with the exactness that the law required. And, (2.) Those among them that were disposed to do amiss had opportunity given them to do it unobserved by the frequent interruptions which their removals gave to the administration of justice. But (says Moses) when you come to Canaan, you *shall not do as we do here.* Note, When the people of God are in an unsettled condition, that may be tolerated and dispensed with which would by no means be allowed at another time. Cases of necessity are to be considered while the necessity continues ; but that must not be done in Canaan which was done in the wilderness. While a house is in the building a great deal of dirt and rubbish are suffered to lie by it, which must all be taken away when the house is built. Moses was now about to lay down his life and government, and it was a comfort to him to foresee that Israel would be better in the next reign than they had been in his.

2. They must not worship the Lord by any of those rites or ceremonies which the nations of Canaan had made use of in the service of their gods, *v.* 29—32. They must not so much as enquire into the modes and forms of idolatrous worship. What good would it do to them to *know those depths of Satan?* Rev. ii. 24. It is best to be ignorant of that which there is danger of being

infected by. They must not introduce the customs of idolaters, (1.) Because it would be absurd to make those their patterns whom God had made their slaves and captives, cut off, and destroyed from before them. The Canaanites had not flourished and prospered so much in the service of their gods as that the Israelites should be invited to take up their customs. Those are wretchedly besotted indeed who will walk in the way of sinners, after they have seen their end. (2.) Because some of their customs were most barbarous and inhuman, and such as trampled, not only upon the light and law of nature, but upon natural affection itself, as *burning their sons and their daughters in the fire to their gods* (v. 31), the very mention of which is sufficient to make it odious, and possess us with a horror of it. (3.) Because their idolatrous customs were an abomination to the Lord, and the translating of them into his worship would make even that an abomination and an affront to him by which they should give him honour, and by which they hoped to obtain his favour. The case is bad indeed when the sacrifice itself has become an abomination, Prov. xv. 8. He therefore concludes (v. 32) with the same caution concerning the worship of God which he had before given concerning the word of God (ch. iv. 2): " *You shall not add thereto* any inventions of your own, under pretence of making the ordinance either more significant or more magnificent, *nor diminish from it*, under pretence of making it more easy and practicable, or of setting aside that which may be spared; but observe to do all that, and that only, which God has commanded." We may then hope in our religious worship to obtain the divine acceptance when we observe the divine appointment. God will have his own work done in his own way.

CHAP. XIII.

Moses is still upon that necessary subject concerning the peril of idolatry. In the close of the foregoing chapter he had cautioned them against the peril that might arise from their predecessors the Canaanites. In this chapter he cautions them against the rise of idolatry from among themselves; they must take heed lest any should draw them to idolatry, I. By the pretence of prophecy, ver. 1–5. II. By the pretence of friendship and relation, ver. 6–11. III. By the pretence of numbers, ver. 12–18. But in all these cases the temptation must be resolutely resisted and the tempters punished and cut off.

IF there arise among you a prophet, or a dreamer of dreams, and giveth thee a sign or a wonder, 2 And the sign or the wonder come to pass, whereof he spake unto thee, saying, Let us go after other gods, which thou hast not known, and let us serve them; 3 Thou shalt not hearken unto the words of that prophet, or that dreamer of dreams: for the LORD your God proveth you, to know whether ye love the LORD your God with all your heart and with all your soul. 4 Ye shall walk after the LORD your

God, and fear him, and keep his commandments, and obey his voice, and ye shall serve him, and cleave unto him. 5 And that prophet, or that dreamer of dreams, shall be put to death; because he hath spoken to turn *you* away from the LORD your God, which brought you out of the land of Egypt, and redeemed you out of the house of bondage, to thrust thee out of the way which the LORD thy God commanded thee to walk in. So shalt thou put the evil away from the midst of thee.

Here is, I. A very strange supposition, v. 1, 2. 1. It is strange that there should arise any among themselves, especially any pretending to vision and prophecy, who should instigate them to *go and serve other gods*. Was it possible that any who had so much knowledge of the methods of divine revelation as to be able to personate a prophet should yet have so little knowledge of the divine nature and will as to go himself and entice his neighbours *after other gods?* Could an Israelite ever be guilty of such impiety? Could a man of sense ever be guilty of such absurdity? We see it in our own day, and therefore may think it the less strange; multitudes that profess both learning and religion, yet exciting both themselves and others, not only to worship God by images, but to give divine honour to saints and angels, which is no better than *going after other gods to serve them;* such is the power of strong delusions. 2. It is yet more strange that the sign or wonder given for the confirmation of this false doctrine should come to pass. Can it be thought that God himself should give any countenance to such a vile proceeding? Did ever a false prophet work a true miracle? It is only supposed here for two reasons :—(1.) To strengthen the caution here given against hearkening to such a one. " Though it were possible that he should work a true miracle, yet you must not believe him if he tell you that you must serve other gods, for the divine law against that is certainly perpetual and unalterable." The supposition is like that in Gal. i. 8, *If we, or an angel from heaven, preach any other gospel to you*—which does not prove it possible that an angel should preach another gospel, but strongly expresses the certainty and perpetuity of that which we have received. So here, (2.) It is to fortify them against the danger of impostures and lying wonders (2 Thess. ii. 9): " Suppose the credentials he produces be so artfully counterfeited that you cannot discern the cheat, nor disprove them, yet, if they are intended to draw you to the service of other gods, that alone is sufficient to disprove them; no evidence can be admitted against so clear a truth as that of the unity of the Godhead, and so plain a law as that of worshipping the *one only living and true God."* We cannot suppose that the God of truth should set his seal of miracles to a lie, to so gross a lie as is supposed in that temptation, *Let us go after other gods.* But if it be asked, Why is this false prophet permitted to counterfeit this broad seal? It is answered here (*v.* 3): *"The Lord your God proveth you.* He suffers you to be set upon by such a temptation to try your constancy, that both those that are perfect and those that are false and corrupt may be made manifest. It is to prove you; therefore see that you acquit yourselves well in the trial, and stand your ground.

II. Here is a very necessary charge given in this case,

1. Not to yield to the temptation: *" Thou shalt not hearken to the words of that prophet, v.* 3. Not only thou shalt not do the thing he tempts thee to, but thou shalt not so much as patiently hear the temptation, but reject it with the utmost disdain and detestation. Such a suggestion as this is not to be so much as parleyed with, but the ear must be stopped against it. *Get thee behind me, Satan."* Some temptations are so grossly vile that they will not bear a debate, nor may we so much as give them the hearing. What follows (*v.* 4), *You shall walk after the Lord,* may be looked upon, (1.) As prescribing a preservative from the temptation: " Keep close to your duty, and you keep out of harm's way. God never leaves us till we leave him. Or, (2.) As furnishing us with an answer to the temptation; say, "It is written, *Thou shalt walk after the Lord,* and *cleave unto him ;* and therefore what have I to do with idols?"

2. Not to spare the tempter, *v.* 5. That prophet shall be *put to death,* both to punish him for the attempt he has made (the seducer must die, though none were seduced by him— a design upon the crown is treason) and to prevent his doing further mischief. This is called *putting away the evil.* There is no way of removing the guilt but by removing the guilty; if such a criminal be not punished, those that should punish him make themselves responsible. And thus the *mischief must be put away ;* the infection must be kept from spreading by cutting off the gangrened limb, and putting away the mischief-makers. Such dangerous diseases as these must be taken in time.

6 If thy brother, the son of thy mother, or thy son, or thy daughter, or the wife of thy bosom, or thy friend, which *is* as thine own soul, entice thee secretly, saying, Let us go and serve other gods, which thou hast not known, thou, nor thy fathers; 7 *Namely,* of the gods of the people which *are* round about you, nigh unto thee, or far off from thee, from the

780

one end of the earth even unto the *other* end of the earth; 8 Thou shalt not consent unto him, nor hearken unto him; neither shall thine eye pity him, neither shalt thou spare, neither shalt thou conceal him: 9 But thou shalt surely kill him; thine hand shall be first upon him to put him to death, and afterwards the hand of all the people. 10 And thou shalt stone him with stones, that he die; because he hath sought to thrust thee away from the LORD thy God, which brought thee out of the land of Egypt, from the house of bondage. 11 And all Israel shall hear, and fear, and shall do no more any such wickedness as this is among you.

Further provision is made by this branch of the statute against receiving the infection of idolatry from those that are near and dear to us.

I. It is the policy of the tempter to send his solicitations by the hand of those whom we love, whom we least suspect of any ill design upon us, and whom we are desirous to please and apt to conform ourselves to. The enticement here is supposed to come from a brother or child that are near by nature, from a wife or friend that are near by choice, and are to us *as our own souls, v.* 6. Satan tempted Adam by Eve and Christ by Peter. We are therefore concerned to stand upon our guard against a bad proposal when the person that makes it can pretend to an interest in us, that we may never sin against God in compliment to the best friend we have in the world. The temptation is supposed to be private: he will *entice thee secretly,* implying that idolatry is a work of darkness, which dreads the light and covets to be concealed, and in which the sinner promises himself, and the tempter promises him, secrecy and security. Concerning the false gods proposed to be served, 1. The tempter suggests that the worshipping of these gods was the common practice of the world; and, if they limited their adorations to an invisible Deity, they were singular, and like nobody, for these gods were the *gods of the people round about them,* and indeed of all the nations of the earth, *v.* 7. This suggestion draws many away from religion and godliness, that it is an unfashionable thing; and they make their court to the world and the flesh because these are the *gods of the people that are round about them.* 2. Moses suggests, in opposition to this, that it had not been the practice of their ancestors; they are gods which *thou hast not known, thou nor thy fathers.* Those that are born of godly parents, and have been educated in pious exercises, when they are enticed to a vain, loose, careless way of living should remember that those are ways which *they have not known, they nor their fathers.* And will they thus degenerate?

II. It is our duty to prefer God and religion before the best friends we have in the world. 1. We must not, in complaisance to our friends, break God's law (*v.* 8): "*Thou shalt not consent to him,* nor go with him to his idolatrous worship, no, not for company, or curiosity, or to gain a better interest in his affections." It is a general rule, *If sinners entice thee, consent thou not,* Prov. i. 10. 2. We must not, in compassion to our friends, obstruct the course of God's justice. He that attempts such a thing must not only be looked upon as an enemy, or dangerous person, whom one should be afraid of, and swear the peace against, but as a criminal or traitor, whom, in zeal for our sovereign Lord, his crown and dignity, we are bound to inform against, and cannot conceal without incurring the guilt of a great misprision (*v.* 9): *Thou shalt surely kill him.* By this law the persons enticed were bound to prosecute the seducer, and to give evidence against him before the proper judges, that he might suffer the penalty of the law, and that without delay, which the Jews say is here intended in that phrase, as it is in the Hebrew, *killing thou shalt kill him.* Neither the prosecution nor the execution must be deferred; and he that was first in the former must be first in the latter, to show that he stood to his testimony: "*Thy hand shall be first upon him,* to mark him out as an anathema, and then the hands of all the people, to put him away as an accursed thing." The death he must die was that which was looked upon among the Jews as the severest of all deaths. He must be stoned: and his accusation written is that he has sought to thrust thee away, by a kind of violence, *from the Lord thy God, v.* 10. Those are certainly our worst enemies that would *thrust us from God,* our best friend; and whatever draws us to sin, separates between us and God, is a design upon our life, and to be resented accordingly. And, lastly, here is the good effect of this necessary execution (*v.* 11): *All Israel shall hear and fear.* They *ought to hear and fear;* for the punishment of crimes committed is designed *in terrorem—to terrify,* and so to prevent their repetition. And it is to be hoped they will hear and fear, and by the severity of the punishment, especially when it is at the prosecution of a father, a brother, or a friend, will be made to conceive a horror of the sin, as exceedingly sinful, and to be afraid of incurring the like punishment themselves. *Smite the scorner* that sins presumptuously, *and the simple,* that is in danger of sinning carelessly, *will beware.*

12 If thou shalt hear *say* in one of thy cities, which the LORD thy God hath given thee to dwell there, saying, 13 *Certain* men, the children of Belial, are gone out from among you,

and have withdrawn the inhabitants of their city, saying, Let us go and serve other gods, which ye have not known; 14 Then shalt thou enquire, and make search, and ask diligently; and, behold, *if it be* truth, *and* the thing certain, *that* such abomination is wrought among you; 15 Thou shalt surely smite the inhabitants of that city with the edge of the sword, destroying it utterly, and all that *is* therein, and the cattle thereof, with the edge of the sword. 16 And thou shalt gather all the spoil of it into the midst of the street thereof, and shalt burn with fire the city, and all the spoil thereof every whit, for the LORD thy God: and it shall be a heap for ever; it shall not be built again. 17 And there shall cleave nought of the cursed thing to thine hand: that the LORD may turn from the fierceness of his anger, and show thee mercy, and have compassion upon thee, and multiply thee, as he hath sworn unto thy fathers; 18 When thou shalt hearken to the voice of the LORD thy God, to keep all his commandments which I command thee this day, to do *that which is* right in the eyes of the LORD thy God.

Here the case is put of a city revolting from its allegiance to the God of Israel, *and serving other gods.*

I. The crime is supposed to be committed, 1. By one of the cities of Israel, that lay within the jurisdiction of their courts. The church then *judged those only that were within,* 1 Cor. v. 12, 13. And, even when they were ordered to preserve their religion in the first principles of it by fire and sword, yet they were not allowed by fire and sword to propagate it. Those that are born within the allegiance of a prince, if they take up arms against him, are dealt with as traitors, but foreign invaders are not so. The city that is here supposed to have become idolatrous is one that formerly worshipped the true God, but had now withdrawn to other gods, which intimates how great the crime is, and how sore the punishment will be, of those that, *after they have known the way of righteousness, turn aside from it,* 2 Pet. ii. 21. 2. It is supposed to be committed by the generality of the inhabitants of the city, for we may conclude that, if a considerable number did retain their integrity, those only that were guilty were to be destroyed, and the city was to be spared for the sake of the righteous in it; for *will not the Judge of all the earth do right ?* No doubt he will. 3. They are supposed to be drawn to idolatry by *certain men, the children of Belial,* men that would endure no yoke (so it signifies), that neither fear God nor regard man, but shake off all restraints of law and conscience, and are perfectly lost to all manner of virtue; these are those that say, "Let us serve other gods," that will not only allow, but will countenance and encourage, our immoralities. Belial is put for *the devil* (2 Cor. vi. 15), and the children of Belial are his children. These withdraw the inhabitants of the city; for a little of this old leaven, when it is entertained, soon leavens the whole lump.

II. The cause is ordered to be tried with a great deal of care (*v.* 14): *Thou shalt enquire and make search.* They must not proceed upon common fame, or take the information by hearsay, but must examine the proofs, and not give judgment against them unless the evidence was clear and the charge fully made out. God himself, before he destroyed Sodom, is said to have come down to see whether its crimes were according to the clamour, Gen. xviii. 21. In judicial processes it is requisite that time, and care, and pains, be taken to find out the truth, and that search be made without any passion, prejudice, or partiality. The Jewish writers say that, though particular persons who were idolaters might be judged by the inferior courts, the defection of a city was to be tried by the great Sanhedrim; and, if it appeared that they were thrust away to idolatry, two learned men were sent to them to admonish and reclaim them. If they repented, all would be well; if not, then all Israel must go up to war against them, to testify their indignation against idolatry and to stop the spreading of the contagion.

III. If the crime were proved, and the criminals were incorrigible, the city was to be wholly destroyed. If there were a few righteous men in it, no doubt they would remove themselves and their families out of such a dangerous place, and then all the inhabitants, men, women, and children, must be put to the sword (*v.* 15), all the spoil of the city, both shop-goods and the furniture of houses, must be brought into the market-place and burned, and the city itself must be laid in ashes and never built again, *v.* 16. The soldiers are forbidden, upon pain of death, to convert any of the plunder to their own use, *v.* 17. It was a devoted thing, and dangerous to meddle with, as we find in the case of Achan. Now, 1. God enjoins this severity to show what a jealous God he is in the matters of his worship, and how great a crime it is to serve other gods. Let men know that God will not give his glory to another, nor his praise to graven images. 2. He expects that magistrates, having their honour and power from him, should be concerned for his honour, and use their power for *terror to evil doers,* else they bear the

sword in vain. 3. The faithful worshippers of the true God must take all occasions to show their just indignation against idolatry, much more against atheism, infidelity, and irreligion. 4. It is here intimated that the best expedient for the turning away of God's anger from a land is to execute justice upon the *wicked of the land* (*v.* 17), that the Lord may *turn from the fierceness of his anger,* which was ready to break out against the whole nation, for the wickedness of that one apostate city. It is promised that, if they would thus root wickedness out of their land, God would multiply them. They might think it impolitic, and against the interest of their nation, to ruin a whole city for a crime relating purely to religion, and that they should be more sparing of the blood of Israelites: "Fear not that" (says Moses), "God will multiply you the more; the body of your nation will lose nothing by the letting out of this corrupt blood." *Lastly,* Though we do not find this law put in execution in all the history of the Jewish church (Gibeah was destroyed, not for idolatry, but immorality), yet for the neglect of the execution of it upon the inferior cities that served idols God himself, by the army of the Chaldeans, put it in execution upon Jerusalem, the head city, which, for its apostasy from God, was utterly destroyed and laid waste, and lay in ruins seventy years. Though idolaters may escape punishment from men (nor is this law in the letter of it binding now, under the gospel), yet the Lord our God will not suffer them to escape his righteous judgments. The New Testament speaks of communion with idolaters as a sin which, above any other, *provokes the Lord to jealousy,* and dares him as if we were *stronger than he,* 1 Cor. x. 21, 22.

CHAP. XIV.

Moses in this chapter teaches them, I. To distinguish themselves from their neighbours by a singularity, 1. In their mourning, ver. 1, 2. 2. In their meat, ver. 3–21. II. To devote themselves unto God, and, in token of that, to give him his dues out of their estates, the yearly tithe, and that every third year, for the maintenance of their religious feasts, the Levites, and the poor, ver. 22, &c.

YE *are* the children of the LORD your God: ye shall not cut yourselves, nor make any baldness between your eyes for the dead. 2 For thou *art* a holy people unto the LORD thy God, and the LORD hath chosen thee to be a peculiar people unto himself, above all the nations that *are* upon the earth. 3 Thou shalt not eat any abominable thing. 4 These *are* the beasts which ye shall eat: the ox, the sheep, and the goat, 5 The hart, and the roebuck, and the fallow deer, and the wild goat, and the pygarg, and the wild ox, and the chamois. 6 And every beast that parteth the hoof, and cleaveth the cleft into two claws, *and* cheweth the cud among the beasts, that ye shall eat. 7 Nevertheless these ye shall not eat of them that chew the cud, or of them that divide the cloven hoof; *as* the camel, and the hare, and the coney: for they chew the cud, but divide not the hoof; *therefore* they *are* unclean unto you. 8 And the swine, because it divideth the hoof, yet cheweth not the cud, it *is* unclean unto you: ye shall not eat of their flesh, nor touch their dead carcase. 9 These ye shall eat of all that *are* in the waters: all that have fins and scales shall ye eat: 10 And whatsoever hath not fins and scales ye may not eat; it *is* unclean unto you. 11 *Of* all clean birds ye shall eat. 12 But these *are they* of which ye shall not eat: the eagle, and the ossifrage, and the ospray, 13 And the glede, and the kite, and the vulture after his kind, 14 And every raven after his kind, 15 And the owl, and the night hawk, and the cuckow, and the hawk after his kind, 16 The little owl, and the great owl, and the swan, 17 And the pelican, and the gier eagle, and the cormorant, 18 And the stork, and the heron after her kind, and the lapwing, and the bat. 19 And every creeping thing that flieth *is* unclean unto you: they shall not be eaten. 20 *But of* all clean fowls ye may eat. 21 Ye shall not eat *of* any thing that dieth of itself: thou shalt give it unto the stranger that *is* in thy gates, that he may eat it; or thou mayest sell it unto an alien: for thou *art* a holy people unto the LORD thy God. Thou shalt not seethe a kid in his mother's milk.

Moses here tells the people of Israel,

I. How God had dignified them, as a peculiar people, with three distinguishing privileges, which were their honour, and figures of those spiritual blessings in heavenly things with which God has in Christ blessed us. 1. Here is election: *The Lord hath chosen thee, v.* 2. Not for their own merit, nor for any good works foreseen, but because he would magnify the riches of his power and grace among them. He did not choose them because they were by their own dedication and subjection a peculiar people to him above other nations, but he chose them that they might be so by his grace; and thus were be-

lievers chosen, Eph. i. 4. 2. Here is adoption (*v.* 1): " *You are the children of the Lord your God,* formed by him into a people, owned by him as his people, nay, his family, *a people near unto him,* nearer than any other." *Israel is my son, my first-born;* not because he needed children, but because they were orphans, and needed a father. Every Israelite is indeed a child of God, a partaker of his nature and favour, his love and blessing· *Behold what manner of love the Father has bestowed upon us!* 3. Here is sanctification (*v.* 2): " *Thou art a holy people,* separated and set apart for God, devoted to his service, designed for his praise, governed by a holy law, graced by a holy tabernacle, and the holy ordinances relating to it." God's people are under the strongest obligations to be holy, and, if they are holy, are indebted to the grace of God that makes them so. The Lord has set them apart for himself, and qualified them for his service and the enjoyment of him, and so has made them holy to himself.

II. How they ought to distinguish themselves by a sober singularity from all the nations that were about them. And, God having thus advanced them, let not them debase themselves by admitting the superstitious customs of idolaters, and, by making themselves like them, put themselves upon the level with them. *Be you the children of the Lord your God;* so the Seventy read it, as a command, that is, " Carry yourselves as becomes the children of God, and do nothing to disgrace the honour and forfeit the privileges of the relation." In two things particularly they must distinguish themselves:—

1. In their mourning: *You shall not cut yourselves, v.* 1. This forbids (as some think), not only their cutting themselves at their funerals, either to express their grief or with their own blood to appease the infernal deities, but their wounding and mangling themselves in the worship of their gods, as Baal's prophets did (1 Kings xviii. 28), or their marking themselves by incisions in their flesh for such and such deities, which in them, above any, would be an inexcusable crime, who in the sign of circumcision bore about with them in their bodies the marks of the Lord Jehovah. So that, (1.) They are forbidden to deform or hurt their own bodies upon any account. Methinks this is like a parent's charge to his little children, that are foolish, careless, and wilful, and are apt to play with knives: *Children, you shall not cut yourselves.* This is the intention of those commands which oblige us to deny ourselves; the true meaning of them, if we understood them aright, would appear to be, *Do yourselves no harm.* And this also is the design of those providences which most cross us, to remove from us those things by which we are in danger of doing ourselves harm. Knives are taken from us, lest we should cut ourselves. Those that are dedicated to God as a holy people must do nothing to disfigure them-

selves; the body is for the Lord, and is to be used accordingly. (2.) They are forbidden to disturb and afflict their own minds with inordinate grief for the loss of near and dear relations: "You shall not express or exasperate your sorrow, even upon the most mournful occasions, by cutting yourselves, and making baldness between your eyes, like men enraged, or resolvedly hardened in sorrow for the dead, as those that have no hope," 1 Thess. iv. 13. It is an excellent passage which Mr. Ainsworth here quotes from one of the Jewish writers, who understands this as a law against immoderate grief for the death of our relations. *If your father* (for instance) *die, you shall not cut yourselves*, that is, *you shall not sorrow more than is meet, for you are not fatherless, you have a Father, who is great, living, and permanent, even the holy blessed God*, whose children you are, *v.* 1. *But an infidel* (says he), *when his father dies, hath no father that can help him in time of need; for he hath said to a stock, Thou art my father, and to a stone, Thou hast brought me forth* (Jer. ii. 27); *therefore he weeps, cuts himself, and makes himself bald.* We that have a God to hope in, and a heaven to hope for, must bear up ourselves with that hope under every burden of this kind.

2. They must be singular in their 'meat. Observe,

(1.) Many sorts of flesh which were wholesome enough, and which other people did commonly eat, they must religiously abstain from as unclean. This law we had before Lev. xi. 2, where it was largely opened. It seems plainly, by the connection here, to be intended as a mark of peculiarity; for their observance of it would cause them to be taken notice of in all mixed companies as a separate people, and would preserve them from mingling themselves with, and conforming themselves to, their idolatrous neighbours. [1.] Concerning beasts, here is a more particular enumeration of those which they were allowed to eat than was in Leviticus, to show that they had no reason to complain of their being restrained from eating swines' flesh, and hares, and rabbits (which were all that were then forbidden, but are now commonly used), when they were allowed so great a variety, not only of that which we call butcher's meat (*v.* 4), which alone was offered in sacrifice, but of venison, which they had great plenty of in Canaan, *the hart, and the roe-buck, and the fallow deer* (*v.* 5), which, though never brought to God's altar, was allowed them at their own table. See *ch.* xii. 22. When of all these (as Adam of *every tree of the garden)* they might freely eat, those were inexcusable who, to gratify a perverse appetite, or (as should seem) in honour of their idols, and in participation of their idolatrous sacrifices, *ate swines' flesh, and had broth of abominable things* (made so by this law) *in their vessels*, Isa. lxv. 4. [2.] Concerning fish there is only one general

784

rule given, that whatsoever had not fins and scales (as shell-fish and eels, besides leeches and other animals in the water that are not proper food) was *unclean and forbidden, v.* 9, 10. [3.] No general rule is given concerning fowl, but those are particularly mentioned that were to be unclean to them, and there are few or none of them which are here forbidden that are now commonly eaten; and whatsoever is not expressly forbidden is allowed, *v.* 11—20. *Of all clean fowls you may eat.* [4.] They are further forbidden, *First*, To eat the flesh of any creature that died of itself, because the blood was not separated from it, and, besides the ceremonial uncleanness which it lay under (from Lev. xi. 39), it is not wholesome food, nor ordinarily used among us, except by the poor. *Secondly*, To *seethe a kid in its mother's milk*, either to gratify their own luxury, supposing it a dainty bit, or in conformity to some superstitious custom of the heathen. The Chaldee paraphrasts read it, *Thou shalt not eat flesh-meats and milk-meats together;* and so it would forbid the use of butter as sauce to any flesh.

(2.) Now as to all these precepts concerning their food, [1.] It is plain in the law itself that they belonged only to the Jews, and were not moral, nor of perpetual use, because not of universal obligation; for what they might not eat themselves they might give to a stranger, a proselyte of the gate, that had renounced idolatry, and therefore was permitted to live among them, though not circumcised; or they might sell it to an alien, a mere Gentile, that came into their country for trade, but might not settle in it, *v.* 21. They might feed upon that which an Israelite might not touch, which is a plain instance of their peculiarity, and their being a holy people. [2.] It is plain in the gospel that they are now antiquated and repealed. For *every creature of God is good, and nothing now to be refused*, or *called common and unclean*, 1 Tim. iv. 4.

22 Thou shalt truly tithe all the increase of thy seed, that the field bringeth forth year by year. 23 And thou shalt eat before the LORD thy God, in the place which he shall choose to place his name there, the tithe of thy corn, of thy wine, and of thine oil, and the firstlings of thy herds and of thy flocks; that thou mayest learn to fear the LORD thy God always. 24 And if the way be too long for thee, so that thou art not able to carry it; *or* if the place be too far from thee, which the LORD thy God shall choose to set his name there, when the LORD thy God hath blessed thee: 25 Then shalt thou

turn *it* into money, and bind up the money in thine hand, and shalt go unto the place which the LORD thy God shall choose: 26 And thou shalt bestow that money for whatsoever thy soul lusteth after, for oxen, or for sheep, or for wine, or for strong drink, or for whatsoever thy soul desireth : and thou shalt eat there before the LORD thy God, and thou shalt rejoice, thou, and thy household, 27 And the Levite that *is* within thy gates; thou shalt not forsake him; for he hath no part nor inheritance with thee. 28 At the end of three years thou shalt bring forth all the tithe of thine increase the same year, and shalt lay *it* up within thy gates : 29 And the Levite, (because he hath no part nor inheritance with thee,) and the stranger, and the fatherless, and the widow, which *are* within thy gates, shall come, and shall eat and be satisfied; that the LORD thy God may bless thee in all the work of thine hand which thou doest.

We have here a part of the statute concerning tithes. The productions of the ground were twice tithed, so that, putting both together, a fifth part was devoted to God out of their increase, and only four parts of five were for their own common use; and they could not but own they paid an easy rent, especially since God's part was disposed of to their own benefit and advantage. The first tithe was for the maintenance of their Levites, who taught them the good knowledge of God, and ministered to them in holy things; this is supposed as anciently due, and is entailed upon the Levites as an inheritance, by that law, Num. xviii. 24, &c. But it is the second tithe that is here spoken of, which was to be taken out of the remainder when the Levites had had theirs.

I. They are here charged to separate it, and set it apart for God: *Thou shalt truly tithe all the increase of thy seed,* v. 22. The Levites took care of their own, but the separating of this was left to the owners themselves, the law encouraging them to be honest by reposing a confidence in them, and so trying their fear of God. They are commanded to tithe *truly,* that is, to be sure to do it, and to do it faithfully and carefully, that God's part might not be diminished either with design or by oversight. Note, We must be sure to give God his full dues out of our estates; for, being but stewards of them, it is required that we be faithful, as those that must give account.

II. They are here directed how to dispose of it when they had separated it. Let every man lay by as God prospers him and gives him success, and then let him lay out in pious uses as God gives him opportunity; and it will be the easier to lay out, and the proportion will be more satisfying, when first we have laid by. This second tithe may be disposed of,

1. In works of piety, for the first two years after the year of release. They must bring it up, either in kind or in the full value of it, to the place of the sanctuary, and there must spend it in holy feasting before the Lord. If they could do it with any convenience, they must bring it in kind (*v.* 23); but, if not, they might turn it into money (*v.* 24, 25), and that money must be laid out in something to feast upon before the Lord. The comfortable cheerful using of what God has given us, with temperance and sobriety, is really the honouring of God with it. Contentment, holy joy, and thankfulness, make every meal a religious feast. The end of this law we have (*v.* 23): *That thou mayest learn to fear the Lord thy God always ;* it was to keep them right and firm to their religion, (1.) By acquainting them with the sanctuary, the holy things, and the solemn services that were there performed. What they read the appointment of in their Bibles, it would do them good to see the observance of in the tabernacle; it would make a deeper impression upon them, which would keep them out of the snares of the idolatrous customs. Note, It will have a good influence upon our constancy in religion *never to forsake the assembling of ourselves together,* Heb. x. 25. By the comfort of the communion of saints, we may be kept to our communion with God. (2.) By using them to the most pleasant and delightful services of religion. Let them *rejoice before the Lord, that they may learn to fear him always.* The more pleasure we find in the ways of religion the more likely we shall be to persevere in those ways. One thing they must remember in their pious entertainments—to bid their Levites welcome to them. Thou shalt not *forsake the Levites* (*v.* 27): "Let him never be a stranger to thy table, especially when thou eatest before the Lord."

2. Every third year this tithe must be disposed of at home in works of charity (*v.* 28, 29): *Lay it up within thy own gates,* and let it be given to the poor, who, knowing the provision this law had made for them, no doubt would come to seek it; and, that they might make the poor familiar to them and not disdain their company, they are here directed to welcome them to their houses. "Thither let them come, and eat and be satisfied." In this charitable distribution of the second tithe they must have an eye to the poor ministers and add to their encouragement by entertaining them, then to poor strangers (not only for the supply of their necessities,

but to put a respect upon them, and so to invite them to turn proselytes), and then to the fatherless and widow, who, though perhaps they might have a competent maintenance left them, yet could not be supposed to live so plentifully and comfortably as they had done in months past, and therefore they were to countenance them, and help to make them easy by inviting them to this entertainment. God has a particular care for widows and fatherless, and he requires that we should have the same. It is his honour, and will be ours, to help the helpless. And if we thus serve God, and do good with what we have, it is promised here that the Lord our God will *bless us in all the work of our hand.* Note, (1.) The blessing of God is all in all to our outward prosperity, and, without that blessing, the work of our hands which we do will bring nothing to pass. (2.) The way to obtain that blessing is to be diligent and charitable. The blessing descends upon the working hand: " Expect not that God should bless thee in thy idleness and love of ease, but in all the work of thy hand." It is the hand of the diligent, with the blessing of God upon it, that makes rich, Prov. x. 4, 22. And it descends upon the giving hand; he that thus scatters certainly increases, and the liberal soul will be made fat. It is an undoubted truth, though little believed, that to be charitable to the poor, and to be free and generous in the support of religion and any good work, is the surest and safest way of thriving. What is lent to the Lord will be repaid with abundant interest. See Ezek. xliv. 30.

CHAP. XV.

In this chapter Moses gives orders, I. Concerning the release of debts, every seventh year (ver. 1—6), with a caution that this should be no hindrance to charitable lending, ver. 7—11. II. Concerning the release of servants after seven years' service, ver. 12—18. III. Concerning the sanctification of the firstlings of cattle to God, ver. 19, &c.

A T the end of *every* seven years thou shalt make a release. 2 And this *is* the manner of the release : Every creditor that lendeth *aught* unto his neighbour shall release *it ;* he shall not exact *it* of his neighbour, or of his brother; because it is called the Lord's release. 3 Of a foreigner thou mayest exact *it again :* but *that* which is thine with thy brother thine hand shall release; 4 Save when there shall be no poor among you; for the Lord shall greatly bless thee in the land which the Lord thy God giveth thee *for* an inheritance to possess it : 5 Only if thou carefully hearken unto the voice of the Lord thy God, to observe to do all these commandments which I command thee this day. 6 For the Lord thy

God blesseth thee, as he promised thee : and thou shalt lend unto many nations, but thou shalt not borrow; and thou shalt reign over many nations, but they shall not reign over thee. 7 If there be among you a poor man of one of thy brethren within any of thy gates in thy land which the Lord thy God giveth thee, thou shalt not harden thine heart, nor shut thine hand from thy poor brother : 8 But thou shalt open thine hand wide unto him, and shalt surely lend him sufficient for his need, *in that* which he wanteth. 9 Beware that there be not a thought in thy wicked heart, saying, The seventh year, the year of release, is at hand; and thine eye be evil against thy poor brother, and thou givest him not; and he cry unto the Lord against thee, and it be sin unto thee. 10 Thou shalt surely give him, and thine heart shall not be grieved when thou givest unto him : because that for this thing the Lord thy God shall bless thee in all thy works, and in all that thou puttest thine hand unto. 11 For the poor shall never cease out of the land : therefore I command thee, saying, Thou shalt open thine hand wide unto thy brother, to thy poor, and to thy needy, in thy land.

Here is, I. A law for the relief of poor debtors, such (we may suppose) as were insolvent. Every seventh year was a year of release, in which the ground rested from being tilled and servants were discharged from their services; and, among other acts of grace, this was one, that those who had borrowed money, and had not been able to pay it before, should this year be released from it; and though, if they were able, they were afterwards bound in conscience to repay it, yet thenceforth the creditor should never recover it by law. Many good expositors think it only forbids the exacting of the debt in the year of release, because, no harvest being gathered in that year, it could not be expected that men should pay their debts then, but that afterwards it might be sued for and recovered : so that the release did not extinguish the debt, but only stayed the process for a time. But others think it was a release of the debt for ever, and this seems more probable, yet under certain limitations expressed or implied. It is supposed (*v.* 3) that the debtor was an Israelite (an alien could not take the benefit of this law) and that he was poor (*v.* 4), that he did not borrow for trade or purchase, but for the subsistence of his family, and that now he could not pay it without reducing himself to poverty and coming under a necessity of seeking relief in other countries, which might be his temptation to revolt from God. The law is not that the creditor shall not receive the debt if the debtor, or his friends for him, can pay it; but he shall not exact it by a legal process. The reasons of this law are, 1. To put an honour upon the sabbatical year: *Because it is called the Lord's release, v.* 2. That was God's year for their land, as the weekly sabbath was God's day for themselves, their servants, and cattle; and, as by the resting of their ground, so by the release of their debts, God would teach them to depend upon his providence. This year of release typified the grace of the gospel, in which is proclaimed the acceptable year of the Lord, and by which we obtain the release of our debts, that is, the pardon of our sins, and we are taught to forgive injuries, as we are and hope to be forgiven of God. 2. It was to prevent the falling of any Israelite into extreme poverty: so the margin reads (*v.* 4), *To the end there shall be no poor among you,* none miserably and scandalously poor, to the reproach of their nation and religion, the reputation of which they ought to preserve. 3. God's security is here given by a divine promise that, whatever they lost by their poor debtors, it should be made up to them in the blessing of God upon all they had and did, *v.* 4—6. Let them take care to do their duty, and then God would bless them with such great increase that what they might lose by bad debts, if they generously remitted them, should not be missed out of their stock at the year's end. Not only, *the Lord shall bless thee* (*v.* 4), but he *doth bless thee, v.* 6. It is altogether inexcusable if, though God has given us abundance, so that we have not only enough but to spare, yet we are rigorous and severe in our demands from our poor brethren; for our abundance should be the supply of their wants, that at least there may not be such an inequality as is between two extremes, 2 Cor. viii. 14. They must also consider that their land was God's gift to them, that all their increase was the fruit of God's blessing upon them, and therefore they were bound in duty to him to use and dispose of their estates as he should order and direct them. And, *lastly,* If they would remit what little sums they had lent to their poor brethren, it is promised that they should be able to lend great sums to their rich neighbours, *even to many nations* (*v.* 6), and should be enriched by those loans. Thus the nations should become subject to them, and dependent on them, as *the borrower is servant to the lender,* Prov. xxii. 7. To be able to lend, and not to have need to borrow, we must look upon as a great mercy, and a good reason why we should do good with what we have, lest we provoke God to turn the scales.

II. Here is a law in favour of poor borrowers, that they might not suffer damage by the former law. Men would be apt to argue, *If the case of a man be so with his debtor* that if the debt be not paid before the year of release it shall be lost, it were better not to lend. "No," says this branch of the statute, "thou shalt not think such a thought." 1. It is taken for granted that there would be poor among them, who would have occasion to borrow (*v.* 7), and that there would never cease to be some such objects of charity (*v.* 11): *The poor shall never cease out of thy land,* though not such as were reduced to extreme poverty, yet such as would be behind-hand, and would have occasion to borrow; of such poor he here speaks, and such we have always with us, so that a charitable disposition may soon find a charitable occasion. 2. In such a case we are here commanded to lend or give, according to our ability and the necessity of the case: *Thou shalt not harden thy heart, nor shut thy hand, v.* 7. If the hand be shut, it is a sign the heart is hardened; for, *if the clouds were full of rain, they would empty themselves,* Eccl. xi. 3. Bowels of compassion would produce liberal distributions, Jam. ii. 15, 16. Thou shalt not only stretch out thy hand to him to reach him something, but thou shalt *open thy hand wide unto him,* to *lend him sufficient, v.* 8. Sometimes there is as much charity in prudent lending as in giving, as it obliges the borrower to industry and honesty and may put him into a way of helping himself. We are sometimes tempted to think, when an object of charity presents itself, we may choose whether we will give any thing or nothing, little or much; whereas it is here an express precept (*v.* 11), *I command thee,* not only to give, but to *open thy hand wide,* to give liberally. 3. Here is a caveat against that objection which might arise against charitable lending from the foregoing law for the release of debts (*v.* 9): *Beware that there be not a thought,* a covetous ill-natured thought, *in thy Belial heart,* "The year of release is at hand, and therefore I will not lend what I must then be sure to lose;" lest thy poor brother, whom thou refusest to lend to, complain to God, and it will be a sin, a great sin, to thee. Note, (1.) The law is spiritual, and lays a restraint upon the thoughts of the heart. We mistake if we think thoughts are free from the divine cognizance and check. (2.) That is a wicked heart indeed that raises evil thoughts from the good law of God, as theirs did who, because God had obliged them to the charity of forgiving, denied the charity of giving. (3.) We must carefully watch against all those secret suggestions which would divert us from our duty or discourage us in it. Those that would keep from the act of sin must keep out of their minds the very thought of sin. (4.) When we have an occasion of charitable lending, if we cannot trust the borrower, we must trust God, and lend, hoping for nothing again in this world, but expecting it will be recompensed in the resurrection of the just, Luke vi. 35; xiv. 14. (5.) It is a dreadful thing to have the cry of the poor against us, for God has his ear open to that cry, and, in compassion to them, will be sure to reckon with those that deal hardly with them. (6.) That which we think is our prudence often proves sin to us; he that refused to lend because the year of release was at hand thought he did wisely, and that men should *praise him as doing well for himself,* Ps. xlix. 18. But he is here told that he did wickedly, and that God would condemn him as doing ill to his brother; and we are sure that the *judgment of God is according to truth,* and that what he says is sin to us will certainly be ruin to us if it be not repented of.

III. Here is a command to give cheerfully whatever we give in charity: *Thy heart shall not be grieved when thou givest, v.* 10. Be not loth to part with thy money on so good an account, nor think it lost; grudge not a kindness to thy brother; and distrust not the providence of God, as if thou shouldest want that thyself which thou givest in charity; but, on the contrary, let it be a pleasure and a satisfaction of soul to thee to think that thou art honouring God with thy substance, doing good, making thy brother easy, and laying up for thyself a good security for the time to come. What thou doest do freely, for God *loves a cheerful giver,"* 2 Cor. ix. 7.

IV. Here is a promise of a recompence in this life: "*For this thing the Lord thy God shall bless thee.* Covetous people say, "Giving undoes us;" no, giving cheerfully in charity will enrich us, it will *fill the barns with plenty* (Prov. iii. 10) and the soul with true comfort, Isa. lviii. 10, 11.

12 *And* if thy brother, a Hebrew man, or a Hebrew woman, be sold unto thee, and serve thee six years; then in the seventh year thou shalt let him go free from thee. 13 And when thou sendest him out free from thee, thou shalt not let him go away empty: 14 Thou shalt furnish him liberally out of thy flock, and out of thy floor, and out of thy winepress: *of that* wherewith the LORD thy God hath blessed thee thou shalt give unto him. 15 And thou shalt remember that thou wast a bondman in the land of Egypt, and the LORD thy God redeemed thee: therefore I command thee this thing to day. 16 And it shall be, if he say unto thee, I will not go away from thee; because he

loveth thee and thine house, because he is well with thee; 17 Then thou shalt take an awl, and thrust *it* through his ear unto the door, and he shall be thy servant for ever. And also unto thy maidservant thou shalt do likewise. 18 It shall not seem hard unto thee, when thou sendest him away free from thee; for he hath been worth a double hired servant *to thee,* in serving thee six years: and the LORD thy God shall bless thee in all that thou doest.

Here is, I. A repetition of the law that had been given concerning Hebrew servants who had sold themselves for servants, or were sold by their parents through extreme poverty, or were sold by the court of judgment for some crime committed. The law was, 1. That they should serve but six years, and in the seventh should go out free, *v.* 12. Compare Exod. xxi. 2. And, if the year of jubilee happened before they served out their time, that would be their discharge. God's Israel were a free people, and must not be compelled to perpetual slavery; thus are God's spiritual Israel called unto liberty. 2. That if, when their six years' service had expired, they had no mind to go out free, but would rather continue in service, as having less care, though taking more pains, than their masters, in this case they must lay themselves under an obligation to serve for ever, that is, for life, by having *their ears bored to the door-posts, v.* 16, 17. Compare Exod. xxi. 6. If hereby a man disgraced himself with some, as of a mean and servile spirit, that had not a due sense of the honour and pleasure of liberty, yet, we may suppose, with others he got reputation, as of a quiet contented spirit, humble, and diligent, and loving, and not *given to change.*

II. Here is an addition to this law, requiring them to put some small stock into their servants' hands to set up with for themselves, when they sent them out of their service, *v.* 13, 14. It was to be supposed that they had nothing of their own, and that their friends had little or nothing for them, else they would have been redeemed before they were discharged by law; they had no wages for their service, and all they got by their labour was their masters', so that their liberty would do them little good, having nothing to begin the world with; therefore their masters are here commanded to furnish them liberally with corn and cattle. No certain measure is prescribed: that is left to the generosity of the master, who probably would have respect to the servant's merit and necessity; but the Jewish writers say, "He could not give less than the value of thirty shekels of silver, but as much more as he pleased " The maid-servants, though they were not to have their ears bored if they were disposed to stay, yet, if they went out free, they were to have a gratuity given them; for to this those words refer, *Unto thy maid-servant thou shalt do likewise, v.* 17. The reasons for this are taken from the law of gratitude. They must do it, 1. In gratitude to God, who had not only brought them out of Egypt (*v.* 15), but brought them out greatly enriched with the spoils of the Egyptians. Let them not send their servants out empty, for they were not sent empty out of the house of bondage. God's tender care of us and kindness to us oblige us to be careful of, and kind to, those that have a dependence upon us. Thus we must *render according to the benefit done unto us.* 2. In gratitude to their servants, *v.* 18. "Grudge not to give him a little out of thy abundance, for *he has been worth a double hired servant unto thee.* The days of the hireling at most were but three years (Isa. xvi. 14), but he has served thee six years, and, unlike the hired servant, without any wages." Masters and landlords ought to consider what need they have of, and what ease and advantage they have by, their servants and tenants, and should not only be just but kind to them. To these reasons it is added, as before in this chapter (*v.* 4, 6, 10), *The Lord thy God shall bless thee.* Then we may expect family blessings, the springs of family-prosperity, when we make conscience of our duty to our family-relations.

19 All the firstling males that come of thy herd and of thy flock thou shalt sanctify unto the Lord thy God: thou shalt do no work with the firstling of thy bullock, nor shear the firstling of thy sheep. 20 Thou shalt eat *it* before the Lord thy God year by year in the place which the Lord shall choose, thou and thy household. 21 And if there be *any* blemish therein, *as if it be* lame, or blind, *or* have any ill blemish, thou shalt not sacrifice it unto the Lord thy God. 22 Thou shalt eat it within thy gates: the unclean and the clean *person shall eat it* alike, as the roebuck, and as the hart. 23 Only thou shalt not eat the blood thereof; thou shalt pour it upon the ground as water.

Here is, 1. A repetition of the law concerning the firstlings of their cattle, that, if they were males, they were to be *sanctified to the Lord* (*v.* 19), in remembrance of, and in thankfulness for, the sparing of the first-born of Israel, when the first-born of the Egyptians, both of man and beast, were slain by the destroying angel (Exod. xiii. 2, 15); on the eighth day it was to be given to God (Exod. xxii. 30), and to be divided between the priest and the altar, Num. xviii. 17, 18.

2. An addition to that law, for the further explication of it, directing them what to do with the firstlings, (1.) That were females: "Thou shalt *do no work with the* female *firstlings of the cow,* nor shear those of the sheep" (*v.* 19); of them the learned bishop Patrick understands it. Though the female firstlings were not so entirely sanctified to God as the males, nor so early as at eight days old, yet they were not to be converted by the owners to their own use as the other cattle, but must be offered to God as peace-offerings, or used in a religious feast, at the year's end, *v.* 20. *Thou shalt eat it before the Lord thy God,* as directed *ch.* xii. 18. (2.) But what must they do with that which was blemished, ill-blemished? *v.* 21. Were it male or female, it must not be brought near the sanctuary, nor used either for sacrifice or for holy feasting, for it would not be fit to honour God with, nor to typify Christ, who is a *Lamb without blemish;* yet it must not be reared, but killed and eaten at their own houses as common food (*v.* 22), only they must be sure *not to eat it with the blood, v.* 23. The frequent repetition of this caution intimates what need the people had of it, and what stress God laid upon it. What a mercy it is that we are not under this yoke! We are not dieted as they were; we make no difference between a first calf, or lamb, and the rest that follow. Let us therefore realize the gospel meaning of this law, devoting ourselves and the first of our time and strength to God, as a kind of first-fruits of his creatures, and using all our comforts and enjoyments to his praise and under the direction of his law, as we have them all by his gift.

CHAP. XVI.

In this chapter we have, I. A repetition of the laws concerning the three yearly feasts; in particular, that of the passover, ver. 1–8. That of pentecost, ver. 9–12. That of tabernacles, ver. 13–15. And the general law concerning the people's attendance on them, ver. 16, 17. II. The institution of an inferior magistracy, and general rules of justice given to those that were called into office, ver. 18–20. III. A caveat against groves and images, ver. 21, 22.

OBSERVE the month of Abib, and keep the passover unto the Lord thy God: for in the month of Abib the Lord thy God brought thee forth out of Egypt by night. 2 Thou shalt therefore sacrifice the passover unto the Lord thy God, of the flock and the herd, in the place which the Lord shall choose to place his name there. 3 Thou shalt eat no leavened bread with it; seven days shalt thou eat unleavened bread therewith, *even* the bread of affliction; for thou camest forth out of the land of Egypt in haste: that thou mayest remember the day when thou camest forth out of the land of Egypt all the days of thy life. 4 And there shall be no leavened bread seen with thee in all thy coast seven days; neither shall there *any thing* of the flesh, which thou sacrificedst the first day at even, remain all night until the morning. 5 Thou mayest not sacrifice the passover within any of thy gates, which the LORD thy God giveth thee: 6 But at the place which the LORD thy God shall choose to place his name in, there thou shalt sacrifice the passover at even, at the going down of the sun, at the season that thou camest forth out of Egypt. 7 And thou shalt roast and eat *it* in the place which the LORD thy God shall choose: and thou shalt turn in the morning, and go unto thy tents. 8 Six days thou shalt eat unleavened bread: and on the seventh day *shall be* a solemn assembly to the LORD thy God: thou shalt do no work *therein.* 9 Seven weeks shalt thou number unto thee: begin to number the seven weeks from *such time as* thou beginnest *to put* the sickle to the corn. 10 And thou shalt keep the feast of weeks unto the LORD thy God with a tribute of a freewill offering of thine hand, which thou shalt give *unto the LORD thy God,* according as the LORD thy God hath blessed thee: 11 And thou shalt rejoice before the LORD thy God, thou, and thy son, and thy daughter, and thy manservant, and thy maidservant, and the Levite that *is* within thy gates, and the stranger, and the fatherless, and the widow, that *are* among you, in the place which the LORD thy God hath chosen to place his name there. 12 And thou shalt remember that thou wast a bondman in Egypt: and thou shalt observe and do these statutes. 13 Thou shalt observe the feast of tabernacles seven days, after that thou hast gathered in thy corn and thy wine: 14 And thou shalt rejoice in thy feast, thou, and thy son, and thy daughter, and thy manservant, and thy maidservant, and the Levite, the stranger, and the fatherless, and the widow, that *are* within thy gates. 15 Seven days shalt thou keep a solemn feast unto the LORD thy God in the place which the LORD shall choose: because the LORD

thy God shall bless thee in all thine increase, and in all the works of thine hands, therefore thou shalt surely rejoice. 16 Three times in a year shall all thy males appear before the LORD thy God in the place which he shall choose; in the feast of unleavened bread, and in the feast of weeks, and in the feast of tabernacles: and they shall not appear before the LORD empty: 17 Every man *shall give* as he is able, according to the blessing of the LORD thy God which he hath given thee.

Much of the communion between God and his people Israel was kept up, and a face of religion preserved in the nation, by the three yearly feasts, the institution of which, and the laws concerning them, we have several times met with already; and here they are repeated.

I. The law of the passover, so great a solemnity that it made the whole month, in the midst of which it was placed, considerable: *Observe the month Abib,* v. 1. Though one week only of this month was to be kept as a festival, yet their preparations before must be so solemn, and their reflections upon it and improvements of it afterwards so serious, as to amount to an observance of the whole month. The month of Abib, or of *new fruits,* as the Chaldee translates it, answers to our March (or part of March and part of April), and was by a special order from God, in remembrance of the deliverance of Israel out of Egypt, made the *beginning of their year* (Exod. xii. 2), which before was reckoned to begin in September. This month they were to keep the passover, in remembrance of their being *brought out of Egypt by night,* v. 1. The Chaldee paraphrasts expound it, "Because they came out of Egypt by daylight," there being an express order that they should not stir out of their doors till morning, Exod. xii. 22. One of them expounds it thus: "*He brought thee out of Egypt,* and did wonders *by night.*" The other, "and thou shalt eat the passover *by night.*" The laws concerning it are, 1. That they must be sure to sacrifice the passover in the place that God should choose (v. 2), and in no other place, v. 5—7. The passover was itself a sacrifice; hence Christ, as our passover, is said to be *sacrificed for us* (1 Cor. v. 7), and many other sacrifices were offered during the seven days of the feast (Num. xxviii. 19, &c.), which are included here, for they are said to be sacrificed *of the flock and the herd,* whereas the passover itself was only of the flock, either a lamb or a kid: now no sacrifice was accepted but from the altar that sanctified it; it was therefore necessary that they should go up to the place of the altar, for, though the paschal lamb was entirely eaten by the owners, yet it must be killed in the court, the blood sprinkled, and the inwards burned upon the altar. By confining them to the appointed place, he kept them to the appointed rule, from which they would have been apt to vary, and to introduce foolish inventions of their own, had they been permitted to offer these sacrifices within their own gates, from under the inspection of the priests. They were also hereby directed to have their eye up unto God in the solemnity, and the *desire of their hearts towards the remembrance of his name,* being appointed to attend where he had chosen *to place his name, v.* 2 and 6. But, when the solemnity was over, they might *turn and go unto their tents, v.* 7. Some think that they might, if they pleased, return the very morning after the paschal lamb was killed and eaten, the priests and Levites being sufficient to carry on the rest of the week's work; but the first day of the seven is so far from being the day of their dispersion that it is expressly appointed for a *holy convocation* (Lev. xxiii. 7; Num. xxviii. 18); therefore we must take it as Jonathan's paraphrase expounds it, *in the morning after the end of the feast thou shalt go to thy cities.* And it was the practice to keep together the whole week, 2 Chron. xxxv. 17. 2. That they must eat unleavened bread for seven days, and no leavened bread must be seen in all their coasts, *v.* 3, 4, 8. The bread they were confined to is here called *bread of affliction,* because neither grateful to the taste nor easy of digestion, and therefore proper to signify the heaviness of their spirits in their bondage and to keep in remembrance the haste in which they came out, the case being so urgent that they could not stay for the leavening of the bread they took with them for their march. The Jewish writers tell us that the custom at the passover supper was that the master of the family broke this unleavened bread, and gave to every one a piece of it, saying, *This is* (that is, this signifies, represents, or commemorates, which explains that saying of our Saviour, *This is my body) the bread of affliction which your fathers did eat in the land of Egypt.* The gospel meaning of this feast of unleavened bread the apostle gives us, 1 Cor. v. 7. *Christ our passover being sacrificed for us,* and we having participated in the blessed fruits of that sacrifice to our comfort, *let us keep the feast* in a holy conversation, free from *the leaven of malice* towards our brethren and hypocrisy towards God, and *with the unleavened bread of sincerity* and love. *Lastly,* Observe, concerning the passover, for what end it was instituted: " *That thou mayest remember the day when thou camest forth out of Egypt,* not only on the day of the passover, or during the seven days of the feast, but *all the days of thy life* (*v.* 3), as a constant induement to obedience." Thus we celebrate the memorial of Christ's death at certain times, that we may remember it at all times, as a reason why we should *live to him that died for us and rose again.*

II. Seven weeks after the passover the feast of pentecost was to be observed, concerning which they are here directed, 1. Whence to number their seven weeks, *from the time thou beginnest to put the sickle to the corn* (*v.* 9), that is, from the morrow after the first day of the feast of unleavened bread, for on that day (though it is probable the people did not begin their harvest till the feast was ended) messengers were sent to reap a sheaf of barley, which was to be offered to God as the first-fruits, Lev. xxiii. 10. Some think it implies a particular care which Providence would take of their land with respect to the weather, that their harvest should be always ripe and ready for the sickle just at the same time. 2. How they were to keep this feast. (1.) They must *bring an offering unto God, v.* 10. It is here called a *tribute of a free-will-offering.* It was required of them as a tribute to their Sovereign Lord and owner, under whom they held all they had; and yet because the law did not determine the *quantum,* but it was left to every man's generosity to bring what he chose, and whatever he brought he must give cheerfully, it is therefore called a *free-will offering.* It was a grateful acknowledgment of the goodness of God to them in the mercies of these corn-harvests now finished, and therefore must be *according as God had blessed them.* Where God sows plentifully he expects to reap accordingly. (2.) They must rejoice before God, *v.* 11. Holy joy is the heart and soul of thankful praises, which are as the language and expression of holy joy. They must rejoice in their receivings from God, and in their returns of service and sacrifice to him; our duty must be our delight as well as our enjoyments. They must have their very servants to rejoice with them, " for remember (*v.* 12) that *thou wast a bond-man,* and wouldest have been very thankful if thy taskmasters would have given thee some time and cause for rejoicing; and thy God did bring thee out to keep a feast with gladness; therefore be pleasant with thy servants, and make them easy." And, it should seem, those general words, *thou shalt observe and do these statutes,* are added here for a particular reason, because this feast was kept in remembrance of the giving of the law upon Mount Sinai, fifty days after they came out of Egypt; now the best way of expressing our thankfulness to God for his favour to us in giving us his law is to *observe and do according to the precepts* of it.

III. They must keep the feast of tabernacles, *v.* 13—15. Here is no repetition of the law concerning the sacrifices that were to be offered in great abundance at this feast (which we had at large, Num. xxix. 12, &c.), because the care of these belonged to the priests and Levites, who had not so much need of a repetition as the people had, and because the spiritual part of the service, which consisted in holy joy, was most pleasing to God, and was to be the perpetual duty of a gospel conversation, of which this feast was typical. Observe what stress is laid upon it here: *Thou shalt rejoice in thy feast* (*v.* 14), *and, because the Lord shall bless thee, thou shalt surely rejoice, v.* 15. Note, 1. It is the will of God that his people should be a cheerful people. If those that were under the law must rejoice before God, much more must we that are under the grace of the gospel, which makes it our duty, not only as here to rejoice in our feasts, but to *rejoice evermore, to rejoice in the Lord always.* 2. When we rejoice in God ourselves we should do what we can to assist others also to rejoice in him, by comforting the mourners and supplying the necessitous, that even *the stranger, the fatherless, and the widow may rejoice with us.* See Job xxix. 13. 3. We must rejoice in God, not only because of what we have received and are receiving from him daily, but because of what he has promised, and we expect to receive yet further from him: because *he shall bless thee,* therefore *thou shalt rejoice.* Those that make God their joy may *rejoice in hope,* for he is faithful that has promised.

IV. The laws concerning the three solemn feasts are summed up (*v.* 16, 17), as often before, Exod. xxiii. 16, 17; xxxiv. 23. The general commands concerning them are, 1. That all the males must then make their personal appearance before God, that by their frequent meeting to worship God, at the same place, and by the same rule, they might be kept faithful and constant to that holy religion which was established among them. 2. That none must appear before God empty, but every man must bring some offering or other, in token of a dependence upon God and gratitude to him. And God was not unreasonable in his demands; let every man but give as he was able, and no more was expected. The same is still the rule of charity, 1 Cor. xvi. 2. Those that give to their power shall be accepted, but those that give beyond their power are accounted worthy of double honour (2 Cor. viii. 3), as the poor widow that gave *all she had,* Luke xxi. 4.

18 Judges and officers shalt thou make thee in all thy gates, which the Lord thy God giveth thee, throughout thy tribes: and they shall judge the people with just judgment. 19 Thou shalt not wrest judgment; thou shalt not respect persons, neither take a gift: for a gift doth blind the eyes of the wise, and pervert the words of the righteous. 20 That which is altogether just shalt thou follow, that thou mayest live, and inherit the land

which the Lord thy God giveth thee. 21 Thou shalt not plant thee a grove of any trees near unto the altar of the Lord thy God, which thou shalt make thee. 22 Neither shalt thou set thee up *any* image; which the Lord thy God hateth.

Here is, I. Care taken for the due administration of justice among them, that controversies might be determined, matters in variance adjusted, the injured redressed, and the injurious punished. While they were encamped in the wilderness, they had *judges and officers* according to their numbers, rulers of thousands and hundreds, Exod. xviii. 25. When they came to Canaan, they must have them according to their towns and cities, in all their gates; for the courts of judgment sat in the gates. Now, 1. Here is a commission given to these inferior magistrates: "Judges to try and pass sentence, and officers to execute their sentences, shalt thou make thee." However the persons were pitched upon, whether by the nomination of their sovereign or by the election of the people, *the powers were ordained of God,* Rom. xiii. 1. And it was a great mercy to the people thus to have justice brought to their doors, that it might be more expeditious and less expensive, a blessing which we of this nation ought to be very thankful for. Pursuant to this law, besides the great sanhedrim that sat at the sanctuary, consisting of seventy elders and a president, there was in the larger cities, such as had in them above 120 families, a court of twenty-three judges, in the smaller cities a court of three judges. See this law revived by Jehoshaphat, 2 Chron. xix. 5, 8. 2. Here is a command given to these magistrates to do justice in the execution of the trust reposed in them. Better not judge at all than not judge with just judgment, according to the direction of the law and the evidence of the fact. (1.) The judges are here cautioned not to do wrong to any (*v.* 19), nor to take any gifts, which would tempt them to do wrong. This law had been given before, Exod. xxiii. 8. (2.) They are charged to do justice to all: "*That which is altogether just shalt thou follow, v.* 20. Adhere to the principles of justice, act by the rules of justice, countenance the demands of justice, imitate the patterns of justice, and pursue with resolution that which appears to be just. *Justice, justice, shalt thou follow.*" This is that which the magistrate is to have in his eye, on this he must be intent, and to this all personal regards must be sacrificed, to do *right to all* and *wrong to none.*

II. Care taken for the preventing of all conformity to the idolatrous customs of the heathen, *v.* 21, 22. They must not only not join with the idolaters in their worships, not visit their groves, nor bow before the images which they had set up, but, 1. They must not plant a grove, nor so much as a tree, near God's altar, lest they should make it look like the altars of the false gods. They made groves the places of their worship either to make it secret (but that which is true and good desires the light rather), or to make it solemn, but the worship of the true God has enough in itself to make it so and needs not the advantage of such a circumstance. 2. They must not set up any image, statue, or pillar, to the honour of God, for it is a thing which the Lord hates ; nothing belies or reproaches him more, or tends more to corrupt and debauch the minds of men, than representing and worshipping by an image that God who is an infinite and eternal Spirit.

CHAP. XVII.

The charge of this chapter is, I. Concerning the purity and perfection of all those animals that were offered in sacrifice, ver. 1. II. Concerning the punishment of those that worshipped idols, ver. 2—7. III. Concerning appeals from the inferior courts to the great sanhedrim, ver. 8—13. IV. Concerning the choice and duty of a king, ver. 14, &c.

THOU shalt not sacrifice unto the Lord thy God *any* bullock, or sheep, wherein is blemish, *or* any evilfavouredness : for that *is* an abomination unto the Lord thy God. 2 If there be found among you, within any of thy gates which the Lord thy God giveth thee, man or woman, that hath wrought wickedness in the sight of the Lord thy God, in transgressing his covenant, 3 And hath gone and served other gods, and worshipped them, either the sun, or moon, or any of the host of heaven, which I have not commanded ; 4 And it be told thee, and thou hast heard *of it,* and enquired diligently, and, behold, *it be* true, *and* the thing certain, *that* such abomination is wrought in Israel : 5 Then shalt thou bring forth that man or that woman, which have committed that wicked thing, unto thy gates, *even* that man or that woman, and shalt stone them with stones, till they die. 6 At the mouth of two witnesses, or three witnesses, shall he that is worthy of death be put to death ; *but* at the mouth of one witness he shall not be put to death. 7 The hands of the witnesses shall be first upon him to put him to death, and afterward the hands of all the people. So thou shalt put the evil away from among you.

Here is, I. A law for preserving the honour of God's worship, by providing that no crea-

ture that had any blemish should be offered in sacrifice to him, *v.* 1. This caveat we have often met with : *Thou shalt not sacrifice that which has any blemish,* which renders it unsightly, or *any evil matter or thing* (as the following word might better be rendered), any sickness or weakness, though not discernible at first view ; it is an abomination to God. God is the best of beings, and therefore whatsoever he is served with ought to be the best in its kind. And the Old-Testament sacrifices in a special manner must be so, because they were types of Christ, who is a *Lamb without blemish or spot* (1 Pet. i. 19), perfectly pure from all sin and all appearance of it. In the latter times of the Jewish church, when by the captivity in Babylon they were cured of idolatry, yet they were charged with profaneness in the breach of this law, with *offering the blind, and the lame, and the sick for sacrifice,* Mal. i. 8.

II. A law for the punishing of those that worshipped false gods. It was made a capital crime to seduce others to idolatry (*ch.* xiii.), here it is made no less to be seduced. If the *blind thus mislead the blind, both must fall into the ditch.* Thus God would possess them with a dread of that sin, which they must conclude exceedingly sinful when so many sanguinary laws were made against it, and would deter those from it that would not otherwise be persuaded against it ; and yet the law, which works death, proved ineffectual. See here,

1. What the crime was against which this law was levelled, serving or worshipping other gods, *v.* 3. That which was the most ancient and plausible idolatry is specified, worshipping the sun, moon, and stars ; and, if that was so detestable a thing, much more was it so to worship stocks and stones, or the representations of mean and contemptible animals. Of this it is said, (1.) That it is what God had not commanded. He had again and again forbidden it ; but it is thus expressed to intimate that, if there had been no more against it, this had been enough (for in the worship of God his institution and appointment must be our rule and warrant), and that God never commanded his worshippers to debase themselves so far as to do homage to their fellow-creatures : had God commanded them to do it, they might justly have complained of it as a reproach and disparagement to them ; yet, when he has forbidden it, they will, from a spirit of contradiction, put this indignity upon themselves. (2.) That it is *wickedness in the sight of God, v.* 2. Be it ever so industriously concealed, he sees it, and, be it ever so ingeniously palliated, he hates it : it is a sin in itself exceedingly heinous, and the highest affront that can be offered to Almighty God. (3.) That it is a transgression of the covenant. It was on this condition that God took them to be his peculiar people, that they should serve and worship him only as their God, so

that if they gave to any other the honour which was due to him alone the covenant was void, and all the benefit of it forfeited. Other sins were transgressions of the command, but this was a transgression of the covenant. It was spiritual adultery, which breaks the marriage bond. (4.) That it is abomination in Israel, *v.* 4. Idolatry was bad enough in any, but it was particularly abominable in Israel, a people so blessed with peculiar discoveries of the will and favour of the only true and living God.

2. How it must be tried. Upon information given of it, or any ground of suspicion that any person whatsoever, man or woman, had served other gods, (1.) Enquiry must be made, *v.* 4. Though it appears not certain at first, it may afterwards upon search appear so; and, if it can possibly be discovered, it must not be unpunished; if not, yet the very enquiry concerning it would possess the country with a dread of it. (2.) Evidence must be given in, *v.* 6. How heinous and dangerous soever the crime is, yet they must not punish any for it, unless there were good proof against them, by two witnesses at least. They must not, under pretence of honouring God, wrong an innocent man. This law, which requires two witnesses in case of life, we had before, Num. xxxv. 30; it is quoted, Matth. xviii. 16.

3. What sentence must be passed and executed. So great a punishment as death, so great a death as stoning, must be inflicted on the idolater, whether man or woman, for the infirmity of the weaker sex would be no excuse, *v.* 5. The place of execution must be the gate of the city, that the shame might be the greater to the criminal and the warning the more public to all others. The hands of the witnesses, in this as in other cases, must be first upon him, that is, they must cast the first stone at him, thereby avowing their testimony, and solemnly imprecating the guilt of his blood upon themselves if their evidence were false. This custom might be of use to deter men from false-witness bearing. The witnesses are really, and therefore it was required that they should be actually, the death of the malefactor. But they must be followed, and the execution completed, by the hands of all the people, who were thus to testify their detestation of the crime and to *put the evil away from among them*, as before, *ch.* xiii. 9.

8 If there arise a matter too hard for thee in judgment, between blood and blood, between plea and plea, and between stroke and stroke, *being* matters of controversy within thy gates: then shalt thou arise, and get thee up into the place which the Lord thy God shall choose; 9 And thou shalt come unto the priests the Levites, and unto the judge that shall be in those days, and enquire; and they shall show thee the sentence of judgment: 10 And thou shalt do according to the sentence, which they of that place which the Lord shall choose shall show thee; and thou shalt observe to do according to all that they inform thee: 11 According to the sentence of the law which they shall teach thee, and according to the judgment which they shall tell thee, thou shalt do: thou shalt not decline from the sentence which they shall show thee, *to* the right hand, nor *to* the left. 12 And the man that will do presumptuously, and will not hearken unto the priest that standeth to minister there before the Lord thy God, or unto the judge, even that man shall die: and thou shalt put away the evil from Israel. 13 And all the people shall hear, and fear, and do no more presumptuously.

Courts of judgment were ordered to be erected in every city (*ch.* xvi. 18), and they were empowered to hear and determine causes according to law, both those which we call pleas of the crown and those between party and party; and we may suppose that ordinarily they ended the matters that were brought before them, and their sentence was definitive; but, 1. It is here taken for granted that sometimes a case might come into their court too difficult for those inferior judges to determine, who could not be thought to be so learned in the laws as those that presided in the higher courts; so that (to speak in the language of our law) they must find a special verdict, and take time to advise before the giving of judgment (*v.* 8): *If there arise a matter too hard for thee in judgment*, which it would be no dishonour to the judges to own the difficulty of,—suppose it between *blood and blood*, the blood of a person which cried and the blood of him that was charged with the murder which was demanded, when it was doubtful upon the evidence whether it was wilful or casual,—or between *plea and plea*, the plea (that is, the bill or declaration) of the plaintiff and the plea of the defendant, —or between *stroke and stroke*, in actions of assault and battery; in these and similar cases, though the evidence were plain, yet doubts might arise about the sense and meaning of the law and the application of it to the particular case. 2. These difficult cases, which hitherto had been brought to Moses, according to Jethro's advice, were, after his death, to be brought to the supreme power, wherever it was lodged, whether in a judge (when there was such an extraordinary person raised up and qualified for that great service, as Othniel, Deborah, Gideon, &c.) or in the high-priest (when he was by the eminency of his gifts called of God to preside in public affairs, as Eli), or, if no single person were marked by heaven for this honour, then in the priests-and Levites (or in the priests, who were Levites of course), who not only attended the sanctuary, but met in council to receive appeals from the inferior courts, who might reasonably be supposed, not only to be best qualified by their learning and experience, but to have the best assistance of the divine Spirit for the deciding of doubts, *v.* 9, 11, 12. They are not appointed to consult the urim and thummim, for it is supposed that these were to be consulted only in cases relating to the public, either the body of the people or the prince; but in ordinary cases the wisdom and integrity of those that sat at the stern must be relied on, their judgment concerning the meaning of the law must be acquiesced in, and the sentence must be passed accordingly: and, though their judgment had not the divine authority of an oracle, yet besides the moral certainty it had, as the judgment of knowing, prudent, and experienced men, it had the advantage of a divine promise, implied in those words (*v.* 9), *They shall show thee the sentence of judgment;* it had also the support of a divine institution, by which they were made the supreme judicature of the nation. 3. The definitive sentence given by the judge, priest, or great council, must be obeyed by the parties concerned, upon pain of death: *Thou shalt do according to their sentence* (*v.* 10); thou shalt observe to do it, thou shalt not *decline from it* (*v.* 11), *to the right hand nor to the left.* Note, It is for the honour of God and the welfare of a people that the authority of the higher power be supported and the due order of government observed, that those be obeyed who are appointed to rule, and that every soul be subject to them in all those things that fall within their commission. Though the party thought himself injured by the sentence (as every man is apt to be partial in his own cause), yet he must needs be subject, must stand to the award, how unpleasing soever, and bear, or lose, or pay, according to it, not only for wrath, but also for conscience' sake. But if an inferior judge contradict the sentence of the higher court and will not execute the orders of it, or a private person refuse to conform to their sentence, the contumacy must be punished with death, though the matter were ever so small in which the opposition was made: *That man shall die, and all the people shall hear and fear, v.* 12, 13. See here, (1.) The evil of disobedience. Rebellion and stubbornness, from a spirit of contradiction and opposition to God, or those in authority under him, from a principle of contempt and self-willedness, are as witchcraft and idolatry. To differ in opinion from weakness and infirmity may be excused and must be borne with; but to do so presumptuously, in pride and wickedness (as the ancient translations explain it), this is to take up arms against the government, and is an affront to him by whom the powers that be are ordained. (2.) The design of punishment: that others may hear and fear, and not do the like. Some would be so considerate as to infer the heinousness of the offence from the grievousness of the penalty, and therefore would detest it; and others would so far consult their own safety as to cross their humours by conforming to the sentence rather than to sin against their own heads, and forfeit their lives by going contrary to it. From this law the apostle infers the greatness of the punishment of which those will be thought worthy that trample on the authority of the Son of God, Heb. x. 28, 29.

14 When thou art come unto the land which the LORD thy God giveth thee, and shalt possess it, and shalt dwell therein, and shalt say, I will set a king over me, like as all the nations that *are* about me; 15 Thou shalt in any wise set *him* king over thee, whom the LORD thy God shall choose: *one* from among thy brethren shalt thou set king over thee: thou mayest not set a stranger over thee, which *is* not thy brother. 16 But he shall not multiply horses to himself, nor cause the people to return to Egypt, to the end that he should multiply horses: forasmuch as the LORD hath said unto you, Ye shall henceforth return no more that way. 17 Neither shall he multiply wives to himself, that his heart turn not away: neither shall he greatly multiply to himself silver and gold. 18 And it shall be, when he sitteth upon the throne of his kingdom, that he shall write him a copy of this law in a book out of *that which is* before the priests the Levites: 19 And it shall be with him, and he shall read therein all the days of his life: that he may learn to fear the LORD his God, to keep all the words of this law and these statutes, to do them: 20 That his heart be not lifted up above his brethren, and that he turn not aside from the commandment, *to* the right hand, or *to* the left: to the end that he may prolong *his* days in his kingdom, he, and his children, in the midst of Israel.

After the laws which concerned subjects
795

fitly followed the laws which concern kings; for those that rule others must themselves remember that they are under command. Here are laws given,

I. To the electors of the empire, what rules they must go by in making their choice, v. 14, 15. 1. It is here supposed that the people would, in process of time, be desirous of a king, whose royal pomp and power would be thought to make their nation look great among their neighbours. Their having a king is neither promised as a mercy nor commanded as a duty (nothing could be better for them than the divine regimen they were under), but it is permitted them if they desired it. If they would but take care to have the ends of government answered, and God's laws duly observed and put in execution, they should not be tied to any one form of government, but should be welcome to have a king. Though something irregular is supposed to be the principle of the desire, that they might be like the nations (whereas God in many ways distinguished them from the nations), yet God would indulge them in it, because he intended to serve his own purposes by it, in making the regal government typical of the kingdom of the Messiah. 2. They are directed in their choice. If they will have a king over them, as God foresaw they would (though it does not appear that ever the motion was made till almost 400 years after), then they must, (1.) Ask counsel at God's mouth, and make him king whom God shall choose; and happy it was for them that they had an oracle to consult in so weighty an affair, and a God to choose for them who knows infallibly what every man is and will be. Kings are God's vicegerents, and therefore it is fit that he should have the choosing of them: God had himself been in a particular manner Israel's King, and if they set another over them, under him, it was necessary that he should nominate the person. Accordingly, when the people desired a king, they applied to Samuel a prophet of the Lord; and afterwards David, Solomon, Jeroboam, Jehu, and others, were chosen by the prophets; and the people are reproved for not observing this law, Hos. viii. 4 : *They have set up kings but not by me.* In all cases God's choice, if we can but know it, should direct, determine, and overrule ours. (2.) They must not choose a foreigner under pretence of strengthening their alliances, or of the extraordinary fitness of the person, lest a strange king should introduce strange customs or usages, contrary to those that were established by the divine law; but he must be *one from among thy brethren*, that he may be a type of Christ, who is bone of our bone, Heb. ii. 14.

II. Laws are here given to the prince that should be elected for the due administration of the government.

1. He must carefully avoid every thing that would divert him from God and religion.

796

Riches, honours, and pleasures are the three great hindrances of godliness *(the lusts of the flesh, the lusts of the eye, and the pride of life)*, especially to those in high stations : against these therefore the king is here warned. (1.) He must not gratify the love of honour by multiplying horses, v. 16. He that rode upon a horse (a stately creature) in a country where asses and mules were generally used looked very great; and therefore though he might have horses for his own saddle, and chariots, yet he must not set *servants on horseback* (Eccl. x. 7) nor have many horses for his officers and guards (when God was their King, his judges rode on asses, Judg. v. 10 ; xii. 14), nor must he multiply horses for war, lest he should trust too much to them, Ps. xx. 7 ; xxxiii. 17 ; Hos. xiv. 3. The reason here given against his multiplying horses is because it would produce a greater correspondence with Egypt (which furnished Canaan with horses, 1 Kings x. 28, 29) than it was fit the Israel of God should have, who were brought thence with such a high hand: *You shall return no more that way*, for fear of being infected with the idolatries of Egypt (Lev. xviii. 3), to which they were very prone. Note, We should take heed of that commerce or conversation by which we are in danger of being drawn into sin. If Israel must not return to Egypt, they must not trade with Egypt; Solomon got no good by it. (2.) He must not gratify the love of pleasure by multiplying wives (v. 17), as Solomon did to his undoing (1 Kings xi. 1), that his heart, being set upon them, turn not away from business, and every thing that is serious, and especially from the exercise of piety and devotion, to which nothing is a greater enemy than the indulgence of the flesh. (3.) He must not gratify the love of riches by greatly multiplying silver and gold. A competent treasure is allowed him, and he is not forbidden to be a good husband of it, but, [1.] He must not greatly multiply money, so as to oppress his people by raising it (as Solomon seems to have done, 1 Kings xii. 4), nor so as to deceive himself, by trusting to it, and setting his heart upon it, Ps. lxii. 10. [2.] He must not multiply it to himself. David multiplied silver and gold, but it was for the service of God (1 Chron. xxix. 4), not for himself; for his people, not for his own family.

2. He must carefully apply himself to the law of God, and make that his rule. This must be to him better than all riches, honours, and pleasures, than many horses or many wives, better than thousands of gold and silver.

(1.) He must write himself a copy of the law out of the original, which was in the custody of the priests that attended the sanctuary, v. 18. Some think that he was to write only this book of Deuteronomy, which is an abstract of the law, and the precepts of which, being mostly moral and judicial, concerned the king more than the laws in Leviticus and Numbers, which, being ceremonial, concerned chiefly the priests. Others think that he was to transcribe all the five books of Moses, which are called *the law,* and which were preserved together as the foundation of their religion. Now, [1.] Though the king might be presumed to have very fair copies by him from his ancestors, yet, besides those, he must have one of his own : it might be presumed that theirs were worn with constant use ; he must have a fresh one to begin the world with. [2.] Though he had secretaries about him whom he might employ to write this copy, and who perhaps could write a better hand than he, yet he must do it himself, with his own hand, for the honour of the law, and that he might think no act of religion below him, to inure himself to labour and study, and especially that he might thereby be obliged to take particular notice of every part of the law and by writing it might imprint it in his mind. Note, It is of great use for each of us to write down what we observe as most affecting and edifying to us, out of the scriptures and good books, and out of the sermons we hear. A prudent pen may go far towards making up the deficiencies of the memory, and the furnishing of the treasures of the good householder with things new and old. [3.] He must do this even when he sits upon the throne of his kingdom, provided that he had not done it before. When he begins to apply himself to business, he must apply himself to this in the first place. He that sits upon the throne of a kingdom cannot but have his hands full. The affairs of his kingdom both at home and abroad call for a large share of his time and thoughts, and yet he must write himself a copy of the law. Let not those who call themselves men of business think that this will excuse them from making religion their business ; nor let great men think it any disparagement to them to write for themselves those *great things of God's law which he hath written to them,* Hos. viii. 12.

(2.) Having a Bible by him of his own writing, he must not think it enough to keep it in his cabinet, but he must *read therein all the days of his life, v.* 19. It is not enough to have Bibles, but we must use them, use them daily, as the duty and necessity of every day require : our souls must have their constant meals of that manna ; and, if well digested, it will be true nourishment and strength to them. As the body is receiving benefit by its food continually, and not only when it is eating, so is the soul, by the word of God, if it *meditate therein day and night,* Ps. i. 2. And we must persevere in the use of the written word of God as long as we live. Christ's scholars never learn above their Bibles, but will have a constant occasion for them till they come to that world where knowledge and love will both be made perfect.

(3.) His writing and reading were all no-

thing if he did not reduce to practice what he wrote and read, *v.* 19, 20. The word of God is not designed merely to be an entertaining subject of speculation, but to be a commanding rule of conversation. Let him know, [1.] What dominion his religion must have over him, and what influence it must have upon him. *First,* It must possess him with a very reverent and awful regard to the divine majesty and authority. He must learn (and thus the most learned must be ever learning) *to fear the Lord his God;* and, as high as he is, he must remember that God is above him, and, whatever fear his subjects owe to him, that, and much more, he owes to God as his King. *Secondly,* It must engage him to a constant observance of the law of God, and a conscientious obedience to it, as the effect of that fear. He must keep *all the words of this law* (he is *custos utriusque tabulæ*—*the keeper of both tables*), not only take care that others do them, but do them himself as a humble servant to the God of heaven and a good example to his inferiors. *Thirdly,* It must keep him humble. How much soever he is advanced, let him keep his spirit low, and let the *fear of his God prevent the contempt of his brethren;* and let not his heart *be lifted up above them,* so as to carry himself haughtily or disdainfully towards them, and to trample upon them. Let him not conceit himself better than they because he is greater and makes a fairer show ; but let him remember that he is the *minister of God to them for good (major singulis,* but *minor universis*—*greater than any one,* but *less than the whole).* It must prevent his errors, either *on the right hand or on the left* (for there are errors on both hands), and keep him right, in all instances, to his God and to his duty. [2.] What advantage his religion would be of to him. Those that fear God and keep his commandments will certainly fare the better for it in this world. The greatest monarch in the world may receive more benefit by religion than by all the wealth and power of his monarchy. It will be of advantage, *First,* To his person: *He shall prolong his days in his kingdom.* We find in the history of the kings of Judah that, generally, the best reigns were the longest, except when God shortened them for the punishment of the people, as Josiah's. *Secondly,* To his family : his children shall also prosper. Entail religion upon posterity, and God will entail a blessing upon it.

CHAP. XVIII.

In this chapter, I. The rights and revenues of the church are settled, and rules given concerning the Levites' ministration and maintenance, ver. 1—8. II. The caution against the idolatrous abominable customs of the heathen is repeated, ver. 9—14. III. A promise is given them of the spirit of prophecy to continue among them, and to centre at last in Christ the great prophet, ver. 15—18. IV. Wrath threatened against those that despise prophecy (ver. 19) or counterfeit it (ver. 20), and a rule given for the trial of it, ver. 21, 22.

THE priests the Levites, *and* all the tribe of Levi, shall have no part nor inheritance with Israel : they shall eat the offerings of the LORD made by fire, and his inheritance. 2 Therefore shall they have no inheritance among their brethren : the LORD *is* their inheritance, as he hath said unto them. 3 And this shall be the priest's due from the people, from them that offer a sacrifice, whether *it be* ox or sheep ; and they shall give unto the priest the shoulder, and the two cheeks, and the maw. 4 The firstfruits *also* of thy corn, of thy wine, and of thine oil, and the first of the fleece of thy sheep, shalt thou give him. 5 For the LORD thy God hath chosen him out of all thy tribes, to stand to minister in the name of the LORD, him and his sons for ever. 6 And if a Levite come from any of thy gates out of all Israel, where he sojourned, and come with all the desire of his mind unto the place which the LORD shall choose ; 7 Then he shall minister in the name of the LORD his God, as all his brethren the Levites *do,* which stand there before the LORD. 8 They shall have like portions to eat, beside that which cometh of the sale of his patrimony.

Magistracy and ministry are two divine institutions of admirable use for the support and advancement of the *kingdom of God among men.* Laws concerning the former we had in the close of the foregoing chapter, directions are in this given concerning the latter. Land-marks are here set between the estates of the priests and those of the people.

I. Care is taken that the priests entangle not themselves with the affairs of this life, nor enrich themselves with the wealth of this world ; they have better things to mind. They *shall have no part nor inheritance with Israel,* that is, no share either in the spoils taken in war or in the land that was to be divided by lot, *v.* 1. Their warfare and husbandry are both spiritual, and enough to fill their hands both with work and profit and to content them. *The Lord is their inheritance, v.* 2. Note, Those that have God for their inheritance, according to the new covenant, should not be greedy of great things in the world, neither gripe what they have nor grasp at more, but look upon all present things with the indifference which becomes those that believe God to be all-sufficient.

II. Care is likewise taken that they want not any of the comforts and conveniences of this life. Though God, who is a Spirit, is their inheritance, it does not therefore follow that they must live upon the air ; no, 798

1. The people must provide for them. They must have their *due from the people, v.* 3. Their maintenance must not depend upon the generosity of the people, but they must be by law entitled to it. He that is taught in the word ought in justice to communicate to him that teaches him ; and he that has the benefit of solemn religious assemblies ought to contribute to the comfortable support of those that preside in such assemblies. (1.) The priests who in their courses served at the altar had their share of the sacrifices, namely, the peace-offerings, that were brought while they were in waiting : besides the breast and shoulder, which were appointed them before (Lev. vii. 32—34), the cheeks and maw are here ordered to be given them ; so far was the law from diminishing what was already granted that it gave them an augmentation. (2.) The first-fruits which arose within such a precinct were brought in, as it should seem, to the priests that resided among them, for their maintenance in the country ; the first of their corn and wine for food, and the first of their fleece for clothing (*v.* 4) ; for the priests who were employed to teach others ought themselves to learn, having food and raiment, to be therewith content. The first-fruits were devoted to God, and he constituted the priests his receivers ; and if God reckons what is, in general, given to the poor, lent to him, to be repaid with interest, much more what is, in particular, given to poor ministers. There is a good reason given for this constant charge upon their estates (*v.* 5), because the Levites were *chosen of God,* and his choice must be owned and countenanced, and those honoured by us whom he honours ; and *because they stood to minister,* and ought to be recompensed for their attendance and labour, especially since it was *in the name of the Lord,* by his warrant, in his service, and for his praise, and this charge entailed upon their seed for ever ; those who were thus engaged and thus employed ought to have all due encouragement given them, as some of the most needful useful members of their commonwealth.

2. The priests must not themselves stand in one another's light. If a priest that by the law was obliged to serve at the altar only in his turn, and was paid for that, should, out of his great affection to the sanctuary, devote himself to a constant attendance there, and quit the ease and pleasure of the city in which he had his lot for the satisfaction of serving the altar, the priests whose turn it was to attend must admit him both to join in the work and to share in the wages, and not grudge him either the honour of the one or the profit of the other, though it might seem to break in upon them, *v.* 6—8. Note, A hearty pious zeal to serve God and his church, though it may a little encroach upon a settled order, and there may be somewhat in it that looks irregular, yet ought to be gratified and not discouraged. He that ap-

pears to have a hearty affection to the sanctuary, and loves dearly to be employed in the service of it, *in God's name let him minister ;* he shall be as welcome to God as the Levites whose course it was to minister, and should be so to them. The settling of the courses was intended rather to secure those to the work that were not willing to do so much than to exclude any that were willing to do more. And he that thus serves as a volunteer shall have as good pay as the pressed men, *besides that which comes of the sale of his patrimony.* The church of Rome obliges those who leave their estates to go into a monastery to bring the produce of their estates with them into the common stock of the monastery, for gain is their godliness ; but here it is ordered that the pious devotee should reserve to himself the produce of his patrimony, for religion and the ministry were never appointed of God, however they have been abused by men, to serve a secular interest.

9 When thou art come into the land which the LORD thy God giveth thee, thou shalt not learn to do after the abominations of those nations. 10 There shall not be found among you *any one* that maketh his son or his daughter to pass through the fire, *or* that useth divination, *or* an observer of times, or an enchanter, or a witch, 11 Or a charmer, or a consulter with familiar spirits, or a wizard, or a necromancer. 12 For all that do these things *are* an abomination unto the LORD : and because of these abominations the LORD thy God doth drive them out from before thee. 13 Thou shalt be perfect with the LORD thy God. 14 For these nations, which thou shalt possess, hearkened unto observers of times, and unto diviners : but as for thee, the LORD thy God hath not suffered thee so *to do.*

One would not think there had been so much need as it seems there was to arm the people of Israel against the infection of the idolatrous customs of the Canaanites. Was it possible that a people so blessed with divine institutions should ever admit the brutish and barbarous inventions of men and devils ? Were they in any danger of making those their tutors and directors in religion whom God had made their captives and tributaries ? It seems they were in danger, and therefore, after many similar cautions, they are here charged not to do after the abominations of those nations, *v.* 9.

I. Some particulars are specified ; as, 1. The consecrating of their children to Moloch, an idol that represented the sun, by making

them to *pass through the fire,* and sometimes consuming them as sacrifices in the fire, *v.* 10. See the law against this before, Lev. xviii. 21. 2. Using arts of divination, to get the unnecessary knowledge of things to come, *enchantments, witchcrafts, charms,* &c., by which the power and knowledge peculiar to God were attributed to the devil, to the great reproach both of God's counsels and of his providence, *v.* 10, 11. One would wonder that such arts and works of darkness, so senseless and absurd, so impious and profane, could be found in a country where divine revelation shone so clearly ; yet we find remains of them even where Christ's holy religion is known and professed ; such are the powers and policies of the *rulers of the darkness of this world.* But let those that give heed to fortune-tellers, or go to wizards for the discovery of things secret, that use spells for the cure of diseases, are in any league or acquaintance with familiar spirits, or form a confederacy with those that are—let them know that they can have no fellowship with God while thus they have fellowship with devils. It is amazing to think that there should be any pretenders of this kind in such a land and day of light as we live in.

II. Some reasons are given against their conformity to the customs of the Gentiles. 1. Because it would make them abominable to God. The things themselves being hateful to him, those that do them are an abomination ; and miserable is that creature that has become odious to its Creator, *v.* 12. See the malignity and mischievousness of sin ; that must needs be an evil thing indeed which provokes the God of mercy to detest the work of his own hands. 2. Because these abominable practices had been the ruin of the Canaanites, of which ruin they were not only the witnesses but the instruments. It would be the most inexcusable folly, as well as the most unpardonable impiety, for them to practise themselves those very things for which they had been employed so severely to chastise others. Did the land spue out the abominations of the Canaanites, and shall Israel lick up the vomit ? 3. Because they were *better taught, v.* 13, 14. It is an argument like that of the apostle against Christians walking as the Gentiles walked (Eph. iv. 17, 18, 20) : *You have not so learned Christ.* "It is true these nations, whom God *gave up to their own hearts' lusts, and suffered to walk in their own ways* (Acts xiv. 16), did thus corrupt themselves ; but thou art not thus abandoned by the grace of God : *the Lord thy God has not suffered thee to do so ;* thou art instructed in divine things, and hast fair warning given thee of the evil of those practices ; and therefore, whatever others do, it is expected that thou shouldest be *perfect with the Lord thy God,"* that is, "that thou shouldest give divine honours to him, to him only, and to no other, and not mix any of the superstitious customs of the heathen with his institutions." One of the Chaldee para- phrasts here takes notice of God's furnishing them with the oracle of urim and thummim, as a preservative from all unlawful arts of divination. Those were fools indeed who would go to consult the father of lies when they had such a ready way of consulting the God of truth.

15 The Lᴏʀᴅ thy God will raise up unto thee a Prophet from the midst of thee, of thy brethren, like unto me ; unto him ye shall hearken ; 16 According to all that thou desiredst of the Lᴏʀᴅ thy God in Horeb in the day of the assembly, saying, Let me not hear again the voice of the Lᴏʀᴅ my God, neither let me see this great fire any more, that I die not. 17 And the Lᴏʀᴅ said unto me, They have well *spoken that* which they have spoken. 18 I will raise them up a Prophet from among their brethren, like unto thee, and will put my words in his mouth ; and he shall speak unto them all that I shall command him. 19 And it shall come to pass, *that* whosoever will not hearken unto my words which he shall speak in my name, I will require *it* of him. 20 But the prophet, which shall presume to speak a word in my name, which I have not commanded him to speak, or that shall speak in the name of other gods, even that prophet shall die. 21 And if thou say in thine heart, How shall we know the word which the Lᴏʀᴅ hath not spoken ? 22 When a prophet speaketh in the name of the Lᴏʀᴅ, if the thing follow not, nor come to pass, that *is* the thing which the Lᴏʀᴅ hath not spoken, *but* the prophet hath spoken it presumptuously : thou shalt not be afraid of him.

Here is, I. The promise of the great prophet, with a command to receive him, and hearken to him. Now,

1. Some think it is the promise of a succession of prophets, that should for many ages be kept up in Israel. Besides the priests and Levites, their ordinary ministers, whose office it was to teach Jacob God's law, they should have prophets, extraordinary ministers, to reprove them for their faults, remind them of their duty, and foretel things to come, judgments for warning and deliverances for their comfort. Having these prophets, (1.) They need·not use divinations, nor consult with familiar spirits, for they might en-

quire of God's prophets even concerning their private affairs, as Saul did when he was in quest of his father's asses, 1 Sam. ix. 6. (2.) They could not miss the way of their duty through ignorance or mistake, nor differ in their opinions about it, having prophets among them, whom, in every difficult doubtful case, they might advise with and appeal to. These prophets were like unto Moses in some respects, though far inferior to him, Deut. xxxiv. 10.

2. Whether a succession of prophets be included in this promise or not, we are sure that it is primarily intended as a promise of Christ, and it is the clearest promise of him that is in all the law of Moses. It is expressly applied to our Lord Jesus as the Messiah promised (Acts iii. 22 ; vii. 37), and the people had an eye to this promise when they said concerning him, *This is of a truth that prophet that should come into the world* (John vi. 14); and it was his Spirit that spoke in all the other prophets, 1 Pet. i. 11. Observe,

(1.) What it is that is here promised concerning Christ. What God promised Moses at Mount Sinai (which he relates, *v.* 18), he promised the people (*v.* 15) in God's name. [1.] That there should come a prophet, great above all the prophets, by whom God would make known himself and his will to the children of men more fully and clearly than ever he had done before. He is the *light of the world,* as prophecy was of the Jewish church, John viii. 12. He is the Word, by whom God speaks to us, John i. 1; Heb. i. 2. [2.] That God would *raise him up from the midst of them.* In his birth he should be one of that nation, should live among them and be sent to them. In his resurrection he should be *raised up at Jerusalem,* and thence his doctrine should go forth to all the world : thus God, having raised up his Son Christ Jesus, sent him to bless us. [3.] That he should be like unto Moses, only as much above him as the other prophets came short of him. Moses was such a prophet as was a law-giver to Israel and their deliverer out of Egypt, and so was Christ : he not only teaches, but rules and saves. Moses was the founder of a new dispensation by signs and wonders and mighty deeds, and so was Christ, by which he proved himself a teacher come from God. Was Moses faithful ? So was Christ ; Moses as a servant, but Christ as a Son. [4.] That God would put his words in his mouth, *v.* 18. What messages God had to send to the children of men he would send them by him, and give him full instructions what to say and do as a prophet. Hence our Saviour says, *My doctrine is not mine* originally, *but his that sent me,* John vii. 16. So that this great promise is performed ; this Prophet has come, even Jesus ; it is he that should come, and we are to look for no other

(2.) The agreeableness of this designed dispensation to the people's avowed choice and desire at Mount Sinai, *v.* 16, 17. There God had spoken to them in thunder and lightning, out of the midst of the fire and thick darkness. Every word made their ears tingle and their hearts tremble, so that the whole congregation was ready to die with fear. In this fright, they begged hard that God would not speak to them in this manner any more (they could not bear it, it would overwhelm and distract them), but that he would speak to them by men like themselves, by Moses now, and afterwards by other prophets like unto him. "Well," says God, "it shall be so; they shall be spoken to by men, whose *terrors shall not make them afraid;*" and, to crown the favour beyond what they were able to ask or think, in the fulness of time the Word itself was made flesh, and they saw his glory as of the *only-begotten of the Father*, not, as at Mount Sinai, full of majesty and terror, *but full of grace and truth*, John i. 14. Thus, in answer to the request of those who were struck with amazement by the law, God promised the incarnation of his Son, though we may suppose it far from the thoughts of those that made that request.

(3.) A charge and command given to all people to hear and believe, hear and obey, this great prophet here promised: *Unto him you shall hearken* (*v.* 15); and whoever will not hearken to him shall be surely and severely reckoned with for his contempt (*v.* 19): *I will require it of him.* God himself applied this to our Lord Jesus in the *voice that came out of the excellent glory*, Matt. xvii. 5, *Hear you him*, that is, this is he concerning whom it was said by Moses of old, *Unto him you shall hearken;* and Moses and Elias then stood by and assented to it. The sentence here passed on those that hearken not to this prophet is repeated and ratified in the New Testament. *He that believeth not the Son, the wrath of God abideth on him*, John iii. 36. *And how shall we escape if we turn away from him that speaketh from heaven?* Heb. xii. 25. The Chaldee paraphrase here reads it, *My Word shall require it of him*, which can be no other than a divine person, Christ the eternal Word, to whom the Father has committed all judgment, and by whom he will at the last day judge the world. Whoever turns a deaf ear to Jesus Christ shall find that it is at his peril; the same that is the prophet is to be his judge, John xii. 48.

II. Here is a caution against false prophets, 1. By way of threatening against the pretenders themselves, *v.* 20. Whoever sets up for a prophet, and produces either a commission from a false god, as the prophets of Baal, or a false and counterfeit commission from the true God, shall be deemed and adjudged guilty of high treason against the crown and dignity of the King of kings, and that traitor shall be put to death (*v.* 20), namely, by the judgment of the great sanhedrim, which, in process of time, sat at Jerusalem; and therefore our Saviour says that a prophet could not perish but at Jerusalem, and lays the blood of the prophets at Jerusalem's door (Luke xiii. 33, 34), whom therefore God himself would punish; yet *there* false prophets were supported. 2. By way of direction to the people, that they might not be imposed upon by pretenders, of which there were many, as appears, Jer. xxiii. 25; Ezek. xiii. 6; 1 Kings xxii. 6. It is a very proper question which they are supposed to ask, *v.* 21. Since it is so great a duty to hearken to the true prophets, and yet there is so much danger of being misled by false prophets, *how shall we know the word which the Lord has not spoken?* By what marks may we discover a cheat? Note, It highly concerns us to have a right touchstone wherewith to try the word we hear, that we may know what that word is which the Lord has not spoken. Whatever is directly repugnant to sense, to the light and law of nature, and to the plain meaning of the written word, we may be sure is not that which the Lord has spoken; nor that which gives countenance and encouragement to sin, or has a manifest tendency to the destruction of piety or charity: far be it from God that he should contradict himself. The rule here given in answer to this enquiry was adapted chiefly to that state, *v.* 22. If there was any cause to suspect the sincerity of a prophet, let them observe that if he gave them any sign, or foretold something to come, and the event was not according to his prediction, they might be sure he was not sent of God. This does not refer so much to the foretelling of mercies and judgments (though as to these, and the difference between the predictions of mercies and judgments, there is a rule of discerning between truth and falsehood laid down by the prophet, Jer. xxviii. 8, 9), but rather to the giving of signs on purpose to confirm their mission. Though the sign did come to pass, yet this would not serve to prove their mission if they called them to serve other gods; this point had been already settled, Deut. xiii. 1—3. But, if the sign did not come to pass, this would serve to disprove their mission. "When Moses cast his rod upon the ground (it is bishop Patrick's explanation of this), and said it would become a serpent, if it had not accordingly been turned into a serpent, Moses had been a false prophet: if, when Elijah called for fire from heaven to consume the sacrifice, none had come, he had been no better than the prophets of Baal." Samuel's mission was proved by this, that *God let none of his words fall to the ground*, 1 Sam. iii. 19, 20. And by the miracles Christ wrought, especially by that great sign he gave of his resurrection the third day, which came to pass as he foretold, it appeared that he was a teacher come from God. *Lastly,* They are directed not to be afraid of a false prophet; that is, not to be afraid of the judgments such a one might denounce to amuse people and strike terror upon them; nor to be afraid of executing the law upon him when, upon a strict and impartial scrutiny, it appeared that he was a false prophet. This command not to fear a false prophet implies that a true prophet, who proved his commission by clear and undeniable proofs, was to be feared, and it was at their peril if they offered him any violence or put any slight upon him.

CHAP. XIX.

The laws which Moses had hitherto been repeating and urging mostly concerned the acts of religion and devotion towards God; but here he comes more fully to press the duties of righteousness between man and man. This chapter relates, I. To the sixth commandment, "Thou shalt not kill," ver. 1—13. II. To the eighth commandment, "Thou shalt not steal," ver. 14. III. To the ninth commandment, "Thou shalt not bear false witness," ver. 15, &c.

WHEN the LORD thy God hath cut off the nations, whose land the LORD thy God giveth thee, and thou succeedest them, and dwellest in their cities, and in their houses; 2 Thou shalt separate three cities for thee in the midst of thy land, which the LORD thy God giveth thee to possess it. 3 Thou shalt prepare thee a way, and divide the coasts of thy land, which the LORD thy God giveth thee to inherit, into three parts, that every slayer may flee thither. 4 And this *is* the case of the slayer, which shall flee thither, that he may live : Whoso killeth his neighbour ignorantly, whom he hated not in time past ; 5 As when a man goeth into the wood with his neighbour to hew wood, and his hand fetcheth a stroke with the ax to cut down the tree, and the head slippeth from the helve, and lighteth upon his neighbour, that he die; he shall flee unto one of those cities, and live : 6 Lest the avenger of the blood pursue the slayer, while his heart is hot, and overtake him, because the way is long, and slay him; whereas he *was* not worthy of death, inasmuch as he hated him not in time past. 7 Wherefore I command thee, saying, Thou shalt separate three cities for thee. 8 And if the LORD thy God enlarge thy coast, as he hath sworn unto thy fathers, and give thee all the land which he promised to give unto thy fathers ; 9 If thou shalt keep all these commandments to do them, which I command thee this day, to love the LORD thy God, and to walk ever in his ways;

then shalt thou add three cities more for thee, beside these three : 10 That innocent blood be not shed in thy land, which the LORD thy God giveth thee *for* an inheritance, and *so* blood be upon thee. 11 But if any man hate his neighbour, and lie in wait for him, and rise up against him, and smite him mortally that he die, and fleeth into one of these cities : 12 Then the elders of his city shall send and fetch him thence, and deliver him into the hand of the avenger of blood, that he may die. 13 Thine eye shall not pity him, but thou shalt put away *the guilt of* innocent blood from Israel, that it may go well with thee.

It was one of the precepts given to the sons of Noah that *whoso sheddeth man's blood by man shall his blood be shed,* that is, by the avenger of blood, Gen. ix. 6. Now here we have the law settled between blood and blood, between the blood of the murdered and the blood of the murderer, and effectual provision made,

I. That the cities of refuge should be a protection to him that slew another casually, so that he should not die for that as a crime which was not his voluntary act, but only his unhappiness. The appointment of these cities of refuge we had before (Exod. xxi. 13), and the law laid down concerning them at large, Num. xxxv. 10, &c. It is here repeated, and direction is given concerning three things :—

1. The appointing of three cities in Canaan for this purpose. Moses had already appointed three on that side Jordan which he saw the conquest of; and now he bids them, when they should be settled in the other part of the country, to appoint three more, *v.* 1—3, 7. The country was to be divided into three districts, as near by as might be equal, and a city of refuge in the centre of each, so that every corner of the land might have one within reach. Thus Christ is not a refuge at a distance, which we must ascend to heaven or go down to the deep for, but the word is nigh us, and Christ in the word, Rom. x. 8. The gospel brings salvation *to our door,* and there it knocks for admission. To make the flight of the delinquent the more easy, the way must be prepared that led to the city of refuge. Probably they had causeways or street-ways leading to those cities, and the Jews say that the magistrates of Israel, upon one certain day in the year, sent out messengers to see that those roads were in good repair, and they were to remove stumbling-blocks, mend bridges that were broken, and, where two ways met, they were to set up a Mercurial post, with a finger to point the right way,

on which was engraven in great letters, *Miklat, Miklat—Refuge, Refuge.* In allusion to this, gospel ministers are to show people the way to Christ, and to assist and direct them in flying by faith to him for refuge. They must be ready to remove their prejudices, and help them over their difficulties. And, blessed be God, *the way of holiness,* to all that seek it faithfully, is a highway so plain that *the wayfaring men, though fools, shall not err therein.*

2. The use to be made of these cities, *v.* 4—6. (1.) It is supposed that it might so happen that a man might be the death of his neighbour without any design upon him either from a sudden passion or malice prepense, but purely by accident, as by the flying off of an axe-head, which is the instance here given, with which every case of this kind was to be compared, and by it adjudged. See how human life lies exposed daily, and what deaths we are often in, and what need therefore we have to be always ready, our souls being continually in our hands. How are the sons of men *snared in an evil time, when it falls suddenly upon them!* Eccl. ix. 12. An evil time indeed it is when this happens not only to the slain but to the slayer. (2.) It is supposed that the relations of the person slain would be forward to avenge the blood, in affection to their friend and in zeal for public justice. Though the law did not allow the avenging of any other affront or injury with death, yet the avenger of blood, the blood of a relation, shall have great allowances made for the heat of his heart upon such a provocation as that, and his killing the manslayer, though he was so by accident only, should not be accounted murder if he did it before he got to the city of refuge, though it is owned he was not worthy of death. Thus would God possess people with a great horror and dread of the sin of murder: if mere chance-medley did thus expose a man, surely he that wilfully does violence to the blood of any person, whether from an old grudge or upon a sudden provocation, must flee to the pit, and *let no man stay him* (Prov. xxviii. 17); yet the New Testament represents the sin of murder as more heinous and more dangerous than even this law does. 1 John iii. 15, *You know that no murderer has eternal life abiding in him.* (3.) It is provided that, if an avenger of blood should be so unreasonable as to demand satisfaction for blood shed by accident only, then the city of refuge should protect the slayer. Sins of ignorance indeed do expose us to the wrath of God, but there is relief provided, if by faith and repentance we make use of it. Paul that had been a persecutor obtained mercy, because he did it ignorantly; and Christ prayed for his crucifiers, *Father, forgive them, for they know not what they do.*

3. The appointing of three cities more for this use in case God should hereafter enlarge their territories and the dominion of their religion, that all those places which came under the government of the law of Moses in other instances might enjoy the benefit of that law in this instance, *v.* 8—10. Here is, (1.) An intimation of God's gracious intention to enlarge their coast, as he had promised to their fathers, if they did not by their disobedience forfeit the promise, the condition of which is here carefully repeated, that, if it were not performed, the reproach might lie upon them, and not on God. He promised to give it, *if thou shalt keep all these commandments;* not otherwise. (2.) A direction to them to appoint three cities more in their new conquests, which, the number intimates, should be as large as their first conquests were; wherever the border of Israel went this privilege must attend it, that *innocent blood be not shed, v.* 10. Though God is the saviour and preserver of all men, and has a tender regard to all lives, yet the blood of Israelites is in a particular manner precious to him, Ps. lxxii. 14. The learned Ainsworth observes that the Jewish writers themselves own that, the condition not being performed, the promise of the enlarging of their coast was never fulfilled; so that there was no occasion for ever adding these three cities of refuge; yet the holy blessed God (say they) *did not command it in vain, for in the days of Messiah the prince* three other cities shall be added to these six : they expect it to be fulfilled in the letter, but we know that in Christ it has its spiritual accomplishment, for the borders of the gospel Israel are enlarged according to the promise, and in Christ, *the Lord our righteousness,* refuge is provided for those that by faith flee to him.

II. It is provided that the cities of refuge should be no sanctuary or shelter to a wilful murderer, but even thence he should be fetched, and delivered to the avenger of blood, *v.* 11—13. 1. This shows that wilful murder must never be protected by the civil magistrate; he bears the sword of justice in vain if he suffers those to escape the edge of it that lie under the guilt of blood, which he by office is the avenger of. During the dominion of the papacy in our own land, before the Reformation, there were some churches and religious houses (as they called them) that were made sanctuaries for the protection of all sorts of criminals that fled to them, wilful murderers not excepted, so that (as Stamford says, in his *Pleas of the Crown, lib.* II. c. xxxviii.) the government follows not Moses but Romulus, and it was not till about the latter end of Henry VIII.'s time that this privilege of sanctuary for wilful murder was taken away, when in that, as in other cases, the word of God came to be regarded more than the dictates of the see of Rome. And some have thought it would be a completing of that instance of reformation if the benefit of clergy were taken away for man-slaughter, that is, the killing of a man upon a small provocation, since this law allowed refuge only in case of that which our law calls chance-medley. 2. It may be alluded to to show that in Jesus Christ there is no refuge for presumptuous sinners, that *go on still in their trespasses.* If we thus *sin wilfully,* sin and go on in it, there *remains no sacrifice,* Heb. x. 26. Those that flee to Christ from their sins shall be safe in him, but not those that expect to be sheltered by him in their sins. Salvation itself cannot save such: divine justice will fetch them even from the city of refuge, the protection of which they are not entitled to.

14 Thou shalt not remove thy eighbour's landmark, which they of old time have set in thine inheritance, which thou shalt inherit in the land that the LORD thy God giveth thee to possess it. 15 One witness shall not rise up against a man for any iniquity, or for any sin, in any sin that he sinneth: at the mouth of two witnesses, or at the mouth of three witnesses, shall the matter be established. 16 If a false witness rise up against any man to testify against him *that which is* wrong; 17 Then both the men, between whom the controversy *is,* shall stand before the LORD, before the priests and the judges, which shall be in those days; 18 And the judges shall make diligent inquisition: and, behold, *if* the witness *be* a false witness, *and* hath testified falsely against his brother; 19 Then shall ye do unto him, as he had thought to have done unto his brother: so shalt thou put the evil away from among you. 20 And those which remain shall hear, and fear, and shall henceforth commit no more any such evil among you. 21 And thine eye shall not pity; *but* life *shall go* for life, eye for eye, tooth for tooth, hand for hand, foot for foot.

Here is a statute for the preventing of frauds and perjuries; for the divine law takes care of men's rights and properties, and has made a hedge about them. Such a friend is it to human society and men's civil interest.

I. A law against frauds, *v.* 14. 1. Here is an implicit direction given to the first planters of Canaan to fix land-marks, according to the distribution of the land to the several tribes and families by lot. Note, It is the will of God that every one should know his own, and that all good means should be used to prevent encroachments and the doing and
804

suffering of wrong. When right is settled, care must be taken that it be not afterwards unsettled, and that, if possible, no occasion of dispute may arise. 2. An express law to posterity not to remove those land-marks which were thus fixed at first, by which a man secretly got that to himself which was his neighbour's. This, without doubt, is a moral precept, and still binding, and to us it forbids, (1.) The invading of any man's right, and taking to ourselves that which is not our own, by any fraudulent arts or practices, as by forging, concealing, destroying, or altering deeds and writings (which are our land-marks, to which appeals are made), or by shifting hedges, meer-stones, and boundaries. Though the land-marks were set by the hand of man, yet he was a thief and a robber by the law of God that removed them. Let every man be content with his own lot, and just to his neighbours, and then we shall have no land-marks removed. (2.) It forbids the sowing of discord among neighbours, and doing any thing to occasion strife and law-suits, which is done (and it is very ill done) by confounding those things which should determine disputes and decide controversies. And, (3.) It forbids breaking in upon the settled order and constitution of civil government, and the altering of ancient usages without just cause. This law supports the honour of prescriptions. *Consuetudo facit jus—Custom is to be held as law.*

II. A law against perjuries, which enacts two things:—1. That a single witness should never be admitted to give evidence in a criminal cause, so as that sentence should be passed upon his testimony, *v.* 15. This law we had before, Num. xxxv. 30, and in this book, *ch.* xvii. 6. This was enacted in favour to the prisoner, whose life and honour should not lie at the mercy of a particular person that had a pique against him, and for caution to the accuser not to say that which he could not corroborate by the testimony of another. It is a just shame which this law puts upon mankind as false and not to be trusted; every man is by it suspected: and it is the honour of God's grace that the record he has given concerning his Son is confirmed both in heaven and in earth by *three witnesses,* 1 John v. 7. *Let God be true and every man a liar,* Rom. iii. 4. 2. That a false witness should incur the same punishment which was to have been inflicted upon the person he accused, *v.* 16—21. (1.) The criminal here is a false witness, who is said to *rise up* against a man, not only because all witnesses stood up when they gave in their evidence, but because a false witness did indeed rise up as an enemy and an assailant against him whom he accused. *If two, or three,* or many witnesses, concurred in a false testimony, they were all liable to be prosecuted upon this law. (2.) The person wronged or brought into peril by the false testimony is supposed to be the appellant, *v.* 17. And yet if the person were put to death upon the evidence, and afterwards it appeared to be false, any other person, or the judges themselves, *ex officio—by virtue of their office,* might call the false witness to account. (3.) Causes of this kind, having more than ordinary difficulty in them, were to be brought before the supreme court, *The priests and judges,* who are said to be *before the Lord,* because, as other judges sat in the gates of their cities, so these at the gate of the sanctuary, *ch.* xvii. 12. (4.) There must be great care in the trial, *v.* 18. A diligent inquisition must be made into the characters of the persons, and all the circumstances of the case, which must be compared, that the truth might be found out, which, where it is thus faithfully and impartially enquired into, Providence, it may be hoped, will particularly advance the discovery of. (5.) If it appeared that a man had knowingly and maliciously borne false witness against his neighbour, though the mischief he designed him thereby was not effected, he must undergo the same penalty which his evidence would have brought his neighbour under, *v.* 19. *Nec lex est justior ulla—Nor could any law be more just.* If the crime he accused his neighbour of was to be punished with death, the false witness must be put to death; if with stripes, he must be beaten; if with a pecuniary mulct, he was to be fined the same sum. And because to those who considered not the heinousness of the crime, and the necessity of making this provision against it, it might seem hard to punish a man so severely for a few words' speaking, especially when no mischief did actually follow, it is added: *Thy eye shall not pity, v.* 21. No man needs to be more merciful than God. The benefit that will accrue to the public from this severity will abundantly recompense it: *Those that remain shall hear and fear, v.* 20. Such exemplary punishments will be warnings to others not to attempt any such mischief, when they see how he that *made the pit and digged it has fallen into the ditch which he made.*

CHAP. XX.

This chapter settles the militia, and establishes the laws and ordinances of war, I. Relating to the soldiers. 1. Those must be encouraged that were drawn up to battle, ver. 1—4. 2. Those must be dismissed and sent back again whose private affairs called for their attendance at home (ver. 5—7), or whose weakness and timidity unfitted them for service in the field, ver. 8, 9. II. Relating to the enemies they made war with. 1. The treaties they must make with the cities that were far off, ver. 10—15. 2. The destruction they must make of the people into whose land they were going, ver. 16—18. 3. The care they must take, in besieging cities, not to destroy the fruit-trees, ver. 19, 20.

WHEN thou goest out to battle against thine enemies, and seest horses, and chariots, *and* a people more than thou, be not afraid of them: for the LORD thy God *is* with thee, which brought thee up out of the land of Egypt. 2 And it shall be, when ye are come nigh unto the battle, that the priest shall approach and speak unto the people, 3 And shall say unto them, Hear, O Israel, ye approach this day unto battle against your enemies: let not your hearts faint, fear not, and do not tremble, neither be ye terrified because of them; 4 For the LORD your God *is* he that goeth with you, to fight for you against your enemies, to save you. 5 And the officers shall speak unto the people, saying, What man *is there* that hath built a new house, and hath not dedicated it? let him go and return to his house, lest he die in the battle, and another man dedicate it. 6 And what man *is he* that hath planted a vineyard, and hath not *yet* eaten of it? let him *also* go and return unto his house, lest he die in the battle, and another man eat of it. 7 And what man *is there* that hath betrothed a wife, and hath not taken her? let him go and return unto his house, lest he die in the battle, and another man take her. 8 And the officers shall speak further unto the people, and they shall say, What man *is there that is* fearful and fainthearted? let him go and return unto his house, lest his brethren's heart faint as well as his heart. 9 And it shall be, when the officers have made an end of speaking unto the people, that they shall make captains of the armies to lead the people.

Israel was at this time to be considered rather as a camp than as a kingdom, entering upon an enemy's country, and not yet settled in a country of their own; and, besides the war they were now entering upon in order to their settlement, even after their settlement they could neither protect nor enlarge their coast without hearing the alarms of war. It was therefore needful that they should have directions given them in their military affairs; and in these verses they are directed in managing, marshalling, and drawing up their own forces. And it is observable that the discipline of war here prescribed is so far from having any thing in it harsh or severe, as is usual in martial law, that the intent of the whole is, on the contrary, to encourage the soldiers, and to make their service easy to them.

I. Those that were disposed to fight must be encouraged and animated against their fears.

1. Moses here gives a general encouragement, which the leaders and commanders in the war must take to themselves: "*Be not*

afraid of them, v. 1. Though the enemy have ever so much the advantage by their numbers (being more than thou), and by their cavalry (their armies being much made up of horses and chariots, which thou art not allowed to multiply), yet decline not coming to a battle with them, dread not the issue, nor aoubt of success." Two things they must encourage themselves with in their wars, provided they kept close to their God and their religion, otherwise they forfeited these encouragements :—(1.) The presence of God with them : *" The Lord thy God is with thee,* and therefore thou art not in danger, nor needest thou be afraid." See Isa. xli. 10. (2.) The experience they and their fathers had had of God's power and goodness in *bringing them out of the land of Egypt,* in defiance of Pharaoh and all his hosts, which was not only in general a proof of the divine omnipotence, but to them in particular a pledge of what God would do further for them. He that saved them from those greater enemies would not suffer them to be run down by those that were every way less considerable, and thus to have all he had done for them undone again.

2. This encouragement must be particularly addressed to the common soldiers by a priest appointed, and, the Jews say, anointed, for that purpose, whom they call *the anointed of the war,* a very proper title for our anointed Redeemer, the captain of our salvation. This priest, in God's name, was to animate the people; and who so fit to do that as he whose office it was as priest to pray for them ? For the best encouragements arise from the precious promises made to the prayer of faith. This priest must, (1.) Charge them not to be afraid (*v.* 3), for nothing weakens the hands so much as that which makes the heart tremble, *v.* 3. There is need of precept upon precept to this purport, as there is here: *Let not your hearts be tender* (so the word is), to receive all the impressions of fear, but let a believing confidence in the power and promise of God harden them. *Fear not, and do not make haste* (so the word is), for he that believeth doth not make more haste than good speed. " Do not make haste either rashly to anticipate your advantages or basely to fly off upon every disadvantage." (2.) He must assure them of the presence of God with them, to own and plead their righteous cause, and not only to save them from their enemies, but to give them victory over them, *v.* 4. Note, Those have no reason to fear that have God with them. The giving of this encouragement by a priest, one of the Lord's ministers, intimates, [1.] That it is very fit that armies should have chaplains, not only to pray for them, but to preach to them, both to reprove that which would hinder their success and to raise their hopes of it. [2.] That it is the work of Christ's ministers to encourage his good soldiers in their spiritual conflicts with the world and the flesh,

and to assure them of a conquest, yea, more than a conquest, through Christ that loved us.

II. Those that were indisposed to fight must be discharged, whether the indisposition did arise,

1. From the circumstances of a man's outward condition ; as, (1.) If he had lately built or purchased a new house, and had not taken possession of it, had not dedicated it (*v.* 5), that is, made a solemn festival for the entertainment of his friends, that came to him to welcome him to his house ; let him go home and take the comfort of that which God had blessed him with, till, by enjoying it for some time, he become less fond of it, and consequently less disturbed in the war by the thoughts of it, and more willing to die and leave it. For this is the nature of all our worldly enjoyments, that they please us best at first; after a while we see the vanity of them. Some think that this dedication of their houses was a religious act, and that they took possession of them with prayers and praises, with a solemn devoting of themselves and all their enjoyments to the service and honour of God. David penned the 30th Psalm on such an occasion, as appears by the title. Note, He that has a house of his own should dedicate it to God by setting up and keeping up the fear and worship of God in it, that he may have a church in his house ; and nothing should be suffered to divert a man from this. Or, (2.) If a man had been at a great expense to *plant a vineyard,* and longed to *eat of the fruit* of it, which for the first three years he was forbidden to do by the law (Lev. xix. 23, &c.), let him go home, if he has a mind, and gratify his own humour with the fruits of it, *v.* 6. See how indulgent God is to his people in innocent things, and how far from being a hard Master. Since we naturally covet to eat the labour of our hands, rather than an Israelite should be crossed therein, his service in war shall be dispensed with. Or, (3.) If a man had made up his mind to be married, and the marriage were not solemnized, he was at liberty to return (*v.* 7), as also to tarry at home for one year after marriage (*ch.* xxiv. 5), for the terrors of war would be disagreeable to a man who had just welcomed the soft scene of domestic attachment. And God would not be served in his wars by pressed men, that were forced into the army against their will, but they must all be perfectly volunteers. Ps. cx. 3, *Thy people shall be willing.* In running the Christian race, and fighting the good fight of faith, we must *lay aside every weight,* and all that which would clog and divert our minds and make us unwilling. The Jewish writers agree that this liberty to return was allowed only in those wars which they made voluntarily (as bishop Patrick expresses it), not those which were made by the divine command against Amalek and the Canaanites, in which every man was bound to fight.

2. If a man's indisposition to fight arose from the weakness and timidity of his own spirit, he had leave to return from the war, *v.* 8. This proclamation Gideon made to his army, and it detached above two-thirds of them, Judg. vii. 3. Some make the fearfulness and faintheartedness here supposed to arise from the terrors of an evil conscience, which would make a man afraid to look death and danger in the face. It was then thought that men of loose and profligate lives would not be good soldiers, but must needs be both cowards in an army and curses to it, the shame and trouble of the camp; and therefore those who were conscious to themselves of notorious guilt were shaken off. But it seems rather to be meant of a natural fearfulness. It was partly in kindness to them that they had their discharge (for, though shamed, they were eased); but much more in kindness to the rest of the army, who were hereby freed from the incumbrance of such as were useless and unserviceable, while the danger of infection from their cowardice and flight was prevented. This is the reason here given: *Lest his brethren's heart fail as well as his heart.* Fear is catching, and in an army is of most pernicious consequence. We must take heed that we *fear not the fear of those that are afraid,* Isa. viii. 12.

III. It is here ordered that, when all the cowards were dismissed, then captains should be nominated (*v.* 9), for it was in a special manner necessary that the leaders and commanders should be men of courage. That reform therefore must be made when the army was first mustered and marshalled. The soldiers of Christ have need of courage, that they may quit themselves like men, and endure hardness like good soldiers, especially the officers of his army.

10 When thou comest nigh unto a city to fight against it, then proclaim peace unto it. 11 And it shall be, if it make thee answer of peace, and open unto thee, then it shall be, *that* all the people *that is* found therein shall be tributaries unto thee, and they shall serve thee. 12 And if it will make no peace with thee, but will make war against thee, then thou shalt besiege it: 13 And when the Lord thy God hath delivered it into thine hands, thou shalt smite every male thereof with the edge of the sword: 14 But the women, and the little ones, and the cattle, and all that is in the city, *even* all the spoil thereof, shalt thou take unto thyself; and thou shalt eat the spoil of thine enemies, which the Lord thy God hath given thee. 15 Thus shalt thou do unto all the cities

which are very far off from thee, which *are* not of the cities of these nations. 16 But of the cities of these people, which the Lord thy God doth give thee *for* an inheritance, thou shalt save alive nothing that breatheth: 17 But thou shalt utterly destroy them; *namely,* the Hittites, and the Amorites, the Canaanites, and the Perizzites, the Hivites, and the Jebusites; as the Lord thy God hath commanded thee: 18 That they teach you not to do after all their abominations, which they have done unto their gods; so should ye sin against the Lord your God. 19 When thou shalt besiege a city a long time, in making war against it to take it, thou shalt not destroy the trees thereof by forcing an ax against them: for thou mayest eat of them, and thou shalt not cut them down (for the tree of the field *is* man's *life*) to employ *them* in the siege: 20 Only the trees which thou knowest that they *be* not trees for meat, thou shalt destroy and cut them down; and thou shalt build bulwarks against the city that maketh war with thee, until it be subdued.

They are here directed what method to take in dealing with the cities (these only are mentioned, *v.* 10, but doubtless the armies in the field, and the nations they had occasion to deal with, are likewise intended) upon which they made war. They must not make a descent upon any of their neighbours till they had first given them fair notice, by a public manifesto, or remonstrance, stating the ground of their quarrel with them. In dealing with the worst of enemies, the laws of justice and honour must be observed; and, as the sword must never be taken in hand without cause, so not without cause shown. War is an appeal, in which the merits of the cause must be set forth.

I. Even to the proclamation of war must be subjoined a tender of peace, if they would accept of it upon reasonable terms. That is (say the Jewish writers), "upon condition that they renounce idolatry, worship the God of Israel, as proselytes of the gate that were not circumcised, pay to their new masters a yearly tribute, and submit to their government:" on these terms the process of war should be stayed, and their conquerors, upon this submission, were to be their protectors, *v.* 10, 11. Some think that even the seven nations of Canaan were to have this offer of peace made to them; and the offer was no jest or mockery, though *it was of the Lord* to harden their hearts that they should not accept it, Josh. xi. 20. Others think that they are excluded (*v.* 16) not only from the benefit of that law (*v.* 13) which confines military execution to the males only, but from the benefit of this also, which allows not to make war till peace was refused. And I see not how they could proclaim peace to those who by the law were to be utterly rooted out, and to whom they were to show no mercy, *ch.* vii. 2. But for any other nation which they made war upon, for the enlarging of their coast, the avenging of any wrong done, or the recovery of any right denied, they must first proclaim peace to them. Let this show, 1. God's grace in dealing with sinners: though he might most justly and easily destroy them, yet, having no pleasure in their ruin, he proclaims peace, and beseeches them to be reconciled; so that those who lie most obnoxious to his justice, and ready to fall as sacrifices to it, if they make him an answer of peace, and open to him, upon condition that they will be tributaries and servants to him, shall not only be saved from ruin but incorporated with his Israel, as fellow-citizens with the saints. 2. Let it show us our duty in dealing with our brethren: if any quarrel happen, let us not only be ready to hearken to the proposals of peace, but forward to make such proposals. We should never make use of the law till we have first tried to accommodate matters in variance amicably, and without expense and vexation. *We* must be for peace, whoever are for war.

II. If the offers of peace were not accepted, then they must proceed to push on the war. And let those to whom God offers peace know that if they reject the offer, and take not the benefit of it within the time limited, judgment will rejoice against mercy in the execution as much as now mercy rejoices against judgment in the reprieve. In this case, 1. There is a promise implied that they should be victorious. It is taken for granted that *the Lord their God would deliver it into their hands, v.* 13. Note, Those enterprises which we undertake by a divine warrant, and prosecute by divine direction, we may expect to succeed in. If we take God's method, we shall have his blessing. 2. They are ordered, in honour to the public justice, to put all the soldiers to the sword, for them I understand by *every male* (*v.* 13), all that bore arms (as all then did that were able); but the spoil they are allowed to take to themselves (*v.* 14), in which were reckoned the women and children. Note, A justifiable property is acquired in that which is won in lawful war. God himself owns the title: *The Lord thy God gives it thee;* and therefore he must be owned in it, Ps. xliv. 3.

III. The nations of Canaan are excepted from the merciful provisions made by this law. Remnants might be left of the cities

that were very far off (*v.* 15), because by them they were not in so much danger of being infected with idolatry, nor was their country so directly and immediately intended in the promise; but of the cities which were given to Israel for an inheritance no remnants must be left of their inhabitants (*v.* 16), for it put a slight upon the promise to admit Canaanites to share with them in the peculiar land of promise; and for another reason they must be utterly destroyed (*v.* 17), because, since it could not be expected that they should be cured of their idolatry, if they were left with that plague-sore upon them they would be in danger of infecting God's Israel, who were too apt to take the infection: *They will teach you to do after their abominations* (*v.* 18), to introduce their customs into the worship of the God of Israel, and by degrees to forsake him and to worship false gods; for those that dare violate the second commandment will not long keep to the first. Strange worships open the door to strange deities.

IV. Care is here taken that in the besieging of cities there should not be any destruction made of fruit-trees, *v.* 19, 20. In those times, when besiegers forced their way, not as now with bombs and cannon-ball, but with battering rams, they had occasion for much timber in carrying on their sieges: now because, in the heat of war, men are not apt to consider, as they ought, the public good, it is expressly provided that fruit-trees should not be used as timber-trees. That reason, *for the tree of the field is man's* (the word *life* we supply), all the ancient versions, the Septuagint, Targums, &c., read, *For is the tree of the field a man?* Or *the tree of the field is not a man, that it should come against thee in the siege,* or *retire from thee into the bulwark.* "Do not brutishly vent thy rage against the trees that can do thee no harm." But our translation seems most agreeable to the intent of the law, and it teaches us, 1. That God is a better friend to man than man is to himself; and God's law, which we are apt to complain of as a heavy yoke, consults our interest and comfort, while our own appetites and passions, of which we are so indulgent, are really enemies to our welfare. The intent of many of the divine precepts is to restrain us from destroying that which is our life and food. 2. That armies and their commanders are not allowed to make what desolation they please in the countries that are the seat of war. Military rage must always be checked and ruled with reason. War, though carried on with ever so much caution, is destructive enough, and should not be made more so than is absolutely necessary. Generous spirits will show themselves tender, not only of men's lives, but of their livelihoods; for, though *the life is more than meat,* yet it will soon be nothing without meat. 3. The Jews understand this as a prohibition of all wilful waste upon any account whatsoever. No fruit-tree is to be destroyed unless it be barren, and cumber the ground. "Nay," they maintain, "whoso wilfully breaks vessels, tears clothes, stops wells, pulls down buildings, or destroys meat, transgresses this law: *Thou shalt not destroy.*" Christ took care that the broken meat should be gathered up, that nothing might be lost. Every creature of God is good, and, as nothing is to be refused, so nothing is to be abused. We may live to want what we carelessly waste.

CHAP. XXI.

In this chapter provision is made, I. For the putting away of the guilt of blood from the land, when he that shed it had fled from justice, ver. 1—9. II. For the preserving of the honour of a captive maid, ver. 10—14. III. For the securing of the right of a first-born son, though he were not a favourite, ver. 15—17. IV. For the restraining and punishing of a rebellious son, ver. 18—21. V. For the maintaining of the honour of human bodies, which must not be hanged in chains, but decently buried, even the bodies of the worst malefactors, ver. 22, 23.

IF one be found slain in the land which the Lord thy God giveth thee to possess it, lying in the field, *and* it be not known who hath slain him: 2 Then thy elders and thy judges shall come forth, and they shall measure unto the cities which *are* round about him that is slain: 3 And it shall be, *that* the city *which is* next unto the slain man, even the elders of that city shall take a heifer, which hath not been wrought with, *and* which hath not drawn in the yoke; 4 And the elders of that city shall bring down the heifer unto a rough valley, which is neither eared nor sown, and shall strike off the heifer's neck there in the valley: 5 And the priests the sons of Levi shall come near; for them the Lord thy God hath chosen to minister unto him, and to bless in the name of the Lord; and by their word shall every controversy and every stroke be *tried:* 6 And all the elders of that city, *that are* next unto the slain *man*, shall wash their hands over the heifer that is beheaded in the valley: 7 And they shall answer and say, Our hands have not shed this blood, neither have our eyes seen *it*. 8 Be merciful, O Lord, unto thy people Israel, whom thou hast redeemed, and lay not innocent blood unto thy people of Israel's charge. And the blood shall be forgiven them. 9 So shalt thou put away the *guilt of* innocent blood from among you, when thou shalt do *that which is* right in the sight of the Lord.

Care had been taken by some preceding laws for the vigorous and effectual prosecution of a wilful murderer (*ch.* xix. 11, &c.), the putting of whom to death was the putting away of the guilt of blood from the land; but if this could not be done, the murderer not being discovered, they must not think that the land was in no danger of contracting any pollution because it was not through any neglect of theirs that the murderer was unpunished; no, a great solemnity is here provided for the putting away of the guilt, as an expression of their dread and detestation of that sin.

I. The case supposed is that *one is found slain, and it is not known who slew him*, v. 1. The providence of God has sometimes wonderfully brought to light these hidden works of darkness, and by strange occurrences the sin of the guilty has found them out, insomuch that it has become a proverb, *Murder will out*. But it is not always so; now and then the devil's promises of secrecy and impunity in this world are made good; yet it is but for a while: there is a time coming when secret murders will be discovered; the *earth shall disclose her blood* (Isa. xxvi. 21), upon the inquisition which justice makes for it; and there is an eternity coming when those that escaped punishment from men will lie under the righteous judgment of God. And the impunity with which so many murders and other wickednesses are committed in this world makes it necessary that there should be a day of judgment, to *require that which is past*, Eccl. iii. 15.

II. Directions are given concerning what is to be done in this case. Observe,

1. It is taken for granted that a diligent search had been made for the murderer, witnesses examined, and circumstances strictly enquired into, that if possible they might find out the guilty person; but if, after all, they could not trace it out, nor fasten the charge upon any, then, (1.) The *elders of the next city* (that had a court of three and twenty in it) were to concern themselves about this matter. If it were doubtful which city was next, the great sanhedrim were to send commissioners to determine that matter by an exact measure, v. 2, 3. Note, Public persons must be solicitous about the public good; and those that are in power and reputation in cities must lay out themselves to redress grievances, and reform what is amiss in the country and neighbourhood that lie about them. Those that are next to them should have the largest share of their good influence, as ministers of God for good. (2.) The priests and Levites must assist and preside in this solemnity (v. 5), that they might direct the management of it in all points according to the law, and particularly might be the people's mouth to God in the prayer that was to be put up on this sad occasion, v. 8. God being Israel's King, his ministers must be their magistrates, and by their word, as the mouth of the court and learned in the laws, every

controversy must be tried. It was Israel's privilege that they had such guides, overseers, and rulers, and their duty to make use of them upon all occasions, especially in sacred things, as this was. (3.) They were to bring a heifer down into a rough and unoccupied valley, and to kill it there, *v.* 3, 4. This was not a sacrifice (for it was not brought to the altar), but a solemn protestation that thus they would put the murderer to death if they had him in their hands. The heifer must be one that had not drawn in the yoke, to signify (say some) that the murderer was a son of Belial; it must be brought into a rough valley, to signify the horror of the fact, and that the defilement which blood brings upon a land turns it into barrenness. And the Jews say that unless, after this, the murderer was found out, this valley where the heifer was killed was never to be tilled nor sown. (4.) The elders were to *wash their hands in water* over the heifer that was killed, and to profess, not only that they had not shed this innocent blood themselves, but that they knew not who had (*v.* 6, 7), nor had knowingly concealed the murderer, helped him to make his escape, or been any way aiding or abetting. To this custom David alludes, Ps. xxvi. 6, *I will wash my hands in innocency:* but if Pilate had any eye to it (Matt. xxvii. 24) he wretchedly misapplied it when he condemned Christ, knowing him to be innocent, and yet acquitted himself from the guilt of innocent blood. *Protestatio non valet contra factum—Protestations are of no avail when contradicted by fact.* (5.) The priests were to pray to God for the country and nation, that God would be merciful to them, and not bring upon them the judgments which the connivance at the sin of murder would deserve. It might be presumed that the murderer was either one of their city or was now harboured in their city; and therefore they must pray that they might not fare the worse for his being among them, Num. xvi. 22. *Be merciful, O Lord, to thy people Israel, v.* 8. Note, When we hear of the wickedness of the wicked we have need to cry earnestly to God for mercy for our land, which groans and trembles under it. We must empty the measure by our prayers which others are filling by their sins. Now,

2. This solemnity was appointed, (1.) That it might give occasion to common and public discourse concerning the murder, which perhaps might some way or other occasion the discovery of it. (2.) That it might possess people with a dread of the guilt of blood, which defiles not only the conscience of him that sheds it (this should engage us all to pray with David, *Deliver me from blood-guiltiness*), but the land in which it is shed; it cries to the magistrate for justice on the criminal, and, if that cry be not heard, it cries to heaven for judgment on the land. If there must be so much care employed to save the land from guilt when the murderer was not

known, it was certainly impossible to secure it from guilt if the murderer was known and yet protected. All would be taught, by this solemnity, to use their utmost care and diligence to prevent, discover, and punish murder. Even the heathen mariners dreaded the guilt of blood, Jon. i. 14. (3.) That we might all learn to take heed of partaking in other men's sins, and making ourselves accessory to them *ex post facto—after the fact*, by countenancing the sin or sinner, and not witnessing against it in our places. We have *fellowship with the unfruitful works of darkness* if we do not reprove them rather, and bear our testimony against them. The repentance of the church of Corinth for the sin of one of their members produced such a carefulness, such a clearing of themselves, such a holy indignation, fear, and revenge (2 Cor. vii. 11), as were signified by the solemnity here appointed.

10 When thou goest forth to war against thine enemies, and the LORD thy God hath delivered them into thine hands, and thou hast taken them captive, 11 And seest among the captives a beautiful woman, and hast a desire unto her, that thou wouldest have her to thy wife; 12 Then thou shalt bring her home to thine house; and she shall shave her head, and pare her nails; 13 And she shall put the raiment of her captivity from off her, and shall remain in thine house, and bewail her father and her mother a full month: and after that, thou shalt go in unto her, and be her husband, and she shall be thy wife. 14 And it shall be, if thou have no delight in her, then thou shalt let her go whither she will; but thou shalt not sell her at all for money, thou shalt not make merchandise of her, because thou hast humbled her.

By this law a soldier is allowed to marry his captive if he pleased. For the hardness of their hearts Moses gave them this permission, lest, if they had not had liberty given them to marry such, they should have taken liberty to defile themselves with them, and by such wickedness the camp would have been troubled. The man is supposed to have a wife already, and to take this wife for a secondary wife, as the Jews called them. This indulgence of men's inordinate desires, in which their hearts walked after their eyes, is by no means agreeable to the law of Christ, which therefore in this respect, among others, far exceeds in glory the law of Moses. The gospel permits not him that has one wife to take another, for *from the beginning it was not so.* The gospel forbids looking upon a woman, though a beautiful one, to lust after her, and commands the mortifying and denying of all irregular desires, though it be as uneasy as the cutting off of a right hand; so much does our holy religion, more than that of the Jews, advance the honour and support the dominion of the soul over the body, the spirit over the flesh, consonant to the glorious discovery it makes of life and immortality, and the better hope.

But, though military men were allowed this liberty, yet care is here taken that they should not abuse it, that is,

I. That they should not abuse themselves by doing it too hastily, though the captive was ever so desirable: "*If thou wouldest have her to thy wife* (v. 10, 11), it is true thou needest not ask her parents' consent, for she is thy captive, and is at thy disposal. But, 1. Thou shalt have no familiar intercourse till thou hast married her." This allowance was designed to gratify, not a filthy brutish lust, in the heat and fury of its rebellion against reason and virtue, but an honourable and generous affection to a comely and amiable person, though in distress; therefore he may make her his wife if he will, but he must not *deal with her as with a harlot.* 2. "Thou shalt not marry her of a sudden, but keep her a full month in thy house," v. 12, 13. This he must do either, (1.) That he may try to take his affection off from her; for he must know that, though in marrying her he does not do ill (so the law then stood), yet in letting her alone he does much better. Let her therefore shave her head, that he might not be enamoured with her locks, and *let her nails grow* (so the margin reads it), to spoil the beauty of her hand. *Quicquid amas cupias non placuisse nimis—We should moderate our affection for those things which we are tempted to love inordinately.* Or rather, (2.) This was done in token of her renouncing idolatry, and becoming a proselyte to the Jewish religion. The shaving of her head, the paring of her nails, and the changing of her apparel, signified her putting off her former conversation, which was corrupt in her ignorance, that she might become a new creature. She must remain in his house to be taught the good knowledge of the Lord and the worship of him: and the Jews say that if she refused, and continued obstinate in idolatry, he must not marry her. Note, The professors of religion must not be unequally yoked with unbelievers, 2 Cor. vi. 14.

II. That they should not abuse the poor captive. 1. She must have time to *bewail her father and mother,* from whom she was separated, and without whose consent and blessing she is now likely to be married, and perhaps to a common soldier of Israel, though in her country ever so nobly born and bred. To force a marriage till these sorrows were digested, and in some measure got over, and she was better reconciled to the land of her captivity by being better acquainted with it, would be very unkind. She must not bewail her idols, but be glad to part with them; to her near and dear relations only her affection must be thus indulged. 2. If, upon second thoughts, he that had brought her to his house with a purpose to marry her changed his mind and would not marry her, he might not make merchandise of her, as of his other prisoners, but must give her liberty to return, if she pleased, to her own country, because he had humbled her and afflicted her, by raising expectations and then disappointing them (v. 14); having made a fool of her, he might not make a prey of her. This intimates how binding the laws of justice and honour are, particularly in the pretensions of love, the courting of affections, and the promises of marriage, which are to be looked upon as solemn things, that have something sacred in them, and therefore are not to be jested with.

15 If a man have two wives, one beloved, and another hated, and they have borne him children, *both* the beloved and the hated; and *if* the firstborn son be her's that was hated: 16 Then it shall be, when he maketh his sons to inherit *that* which he hath, *that* he may not make the son of the beloved firstborn before the son of the hated, *which is indeed* the firstborn: 17 But he shall acknowledge the son of the hated *for* the firstborn, by giving him a double portion of all that he hath: for he *is* the beginning of his strength; the right of the firstborn *is* his.

This law restrains men from disinheriting their eldest sons out of mere caprice, and without just provocation.

I. The case here put (v. 15) is very instructive. 1. It shows the great mischief of having more wives than one, which the law of Moses did not restrain, probably in hopes that men's own experience of the great inconvenience of it in families would at last put an end to it and make them a law to themselves. Observe the supposition here: If a man have two wives, it is a thousand to one but one of them is beloved and the other hated (that is, manifestly loved less) as Leah was by Jacob, and the effect of this cannot but be strifes and jealousies, envy, confusion, and every evil work, which could not but create a constant uneasiness and vexation to the husband, and involve him both in sin and trouble. Those do much better consult their own ease and satisfaction who adhere to God's law than those who indulge their own lusts. 2. It shows how Providence commonly sides with the weakest, and *gives more abundant honour to that part which lacked;* for the first-born son is here supposed to be *hers that was hated;* it was so in Jacob's family: because *the Lord saw that Leah was hated,* Gen. xxix. 31. The great householder wisely gives to each his dividend of comfort; if one had the honour to be the beloved wife, it often proved that the other had the honour to be the mother of the first-born.

II. The law in this case is still binding on parents; they must give their children their right without partiality. In the case supposed, the eldest son, though the son of the less-beloved wife, must have his birthright privilege, which was a double portion of the father's estate, because he was the beginning of his strength that is, in him his family began to be strengthened, and his quiver began to be filled with the *arrows of a mighty man* (Ps. cxxvii. 4), and therefore the right of the first-born is his, *v.* 16, 17. Jacob had indeed deprived Reuben of his birthright, and given it to Joseph, but it was because Reuben had forfeited the birthright by his incest, not because he was the *son of the hated;* now, lest that which Jacob did justly should be drawn into a precedent for others to do the same thing unjustly, it is here provided that when the father makes his will, or otherwise settles his estate, the child shall not fare the worse for the mother's unhappiness in having less of her husband's love, for that was not the child's fault. Note, (1.) Parents ought to make no other difference in dispensing their affections among their children than what they see plainly God makes in dispensing his grace among them. (2.) Since it is the providence of God that makes heirs, the disposal of providence in that matter must be acquiesced in and not opposed. No son should be abandoned by his father till he manifestly appear to be abandoned of God, which is hard to say of any while there is life.

18 If a man have a stubborn and rebellious son, which will not obey the voice of his father, or the voice of his mother, and *that,* when they have chastened him, will not hearken unto them: 19 Then shall his father and his mother lay hold on him, and bring him out unto the elders of his city, and unto the gate of his place; 20 And they shall say unto the elders of his city, This our son *is* stubborn and rebellious, he will not obey our voice; *he is* a glutton, and a drunkard. 21 And all the men of his city shall stone him with stones, that he die: so shalt thou put evil away from among you; and all Israel shall hear, and fear. 22 And if a man have committed a sin worthy of death, and he be to be put

812

to death, and thou hang him on a tree: 23 His body shall not remain all night upon the tree, but thou shalt in any wise bury him that day; (for he that is hanged *is* accursed of God;) that thy land be not defiled, which the LORD thy God giveth thee *for* an inheritance.

Here is, I. A law for the punishing of a rebellious son. Having in the former law provided that parents should not deprive their children of their right, it was fit that it should next be provided that children withdraw not the honour and duty which are owing to their parents, for there is no partiality in the divine law. Observe,

1. How the criminal is here described. He is a *stubborn and rebellious son, v.* 18. No child was to fare the worse for the weakness of his capacity, the slowness or dulness of his understanding, but for his wilfulness and obstinacy. If he carry himself proudly and insolently towards his parents, contemn their authority, slight their reproofs and admonitions, disobey the express commands they give him for his own good, hate to be reformed by the correction they give him, shame their family, grieve their hearts, waste their substance, and threaten to ruin their estate by riotous living—this is a *stubborn and rebellious son.* He is particularly supposed (*v.* 20) to be a *glutton or a drunkard.* This intimates either, (1.) That these were sins which his parents did in a particular manner warn him against, and therefore that in these instances there was a plain evidence that he did not obey their voice. Lemuel had this charge from his mother, Prov. xxxi. 4. Note, In the education of children, great care should be taken to suppress all inclinations to drunkenness, and to keep them out of the way of temptations to it; in order hereunto they should be possessed betimes with a dread and detestation of that beastly sin, and taught betimes to deny themselves. Or, (2.) That his being a *glutton and a drunkard* was the cause of his insolence and obstinacy towards his parents. Note, There is nothing that draws men into all manner of wickedness, and hardens them in it, more certainly and fatally than drunkenness does. When men take to drink they forget the law, they forget all law (Prov. xxxi. 5), even that fundamental law of honouring parents.

2. How this criminal is to be proceeded against. His own father and mother are to be his prosecutors, *v.* 19, 20. They might not put him to death themselves, but they must complain of him to the elders of the city, and the complaint must needs be made with a sad heart: *This our son is stubborn and rebellious.* Note, Those that give up themselves to vice and wickedness, and will not be reclaimed, forfeit their interest in the natural affections of their nearest relations;

the instruments of their being justly become the instruments of their destruction. The children that forget their duty must thank themselves and not blame their parents if they are regarded with less and less affection. And, how difficult soever tender parents now find it to reconcile themselves to the just punishment of their rebellious children, in the day of the revelation of the righteous judgment of God all natural affection will be so entirely swallowed up in divine love that they will acquiesce even in the condemnation of those children, because God will be therein for ever glorified.

3. What judgment is to be executed upon him: he must be publicly *stoned to death by the men of his city*, v. 21. And thus, (1.) The paternal authority was supported, and God, our common Father, showed himself jealous for it, it being one of the first and most ancient streams derived from him that is the fountain of all power. (2.) This law, if duly executed, would *early destroy the wicked of the land* (Ps. ci. 8), and prevent the spreading of the gangrene, by cutting off the corrupt part betimes; for those that were bad members of families would never make good members of the commonwealth. (3.) It would strike an awe upon children, and frighten them into obedience to their parents, if they would not otherwise be brought to their duty and kept in it: *All Israel shall hear.* The Jews say, "The elders that condemned him were to send notice of it in writing all the nation over, *In such a court, such a day, we stoned such a one, because he was a stubborn and rebellious son.*" And I have sometimes wished that as in all our courts there is an exact record kept of the condemnation of criminals, *in perpetuam rei memoriam—that the memorial may never be lost,* so there might be public and authentic notice given in print to the kingdom of such condemnations, and the executions upon them, by the elders themselves, *in terrorem—that all may hear and fear.*

II. A law for the burying of the bodies of malefactors that were hanged, v. 22. The hanging of them by the neck till the body was dead was not used at all among the Jews, as with us; but of such as were stoned to death, if it were for blasphemy, or some other very execrable crime, it was usual, by order of the judges, to hang up the dead bodies upon a post for some time, as a spectacle to the world, to express the ignominy of the crime, and to strike the greater terror upon others, that they might not only hear and fear, but see and fear. Now it is here provided that, whatever time of the day they were thus hanged up, at sun-set they should be taken down and buried, and not left to hang out all night; sufficient (says the law) *to such a man is this punishment;* hitherto let it go, but no further. Let the malefactor and his crime be hidden in the grave. Now, 1. God would thus preserve the honour of

human bodies and tenderness towards the worst of criminals. The time of exposing dead bodies thus is limited for the same reason that the number of stripes was limited by another law: *Lest thy brother seem vile unto thee.* Punishing beyond death God reserves to himself; as for man, there is no more that he can do. Whether therefore the hanging of malefactors in chains, and setting up their heads and quarters, be decent among Christians that look for the resurrection of the body, may perhaps be worth considering. 2. Yet it is plain there was something ceremonial in it; by the law of Moses the touch of a dead body was defiling, and therefore dead bodies must not be left hanging up in the country, because, by the same rule, this would defile the land. But, 3. There is one reason here given which has reference to Christ. *He that is hanged is accursed of God,* that is, it is the highest degree of disgrace and reproach that can be done to a man, and proclaims him under the curse of God as much as any external punishment can. Those that see him thus hang between heaven and earth will conclude him abandoned of both and unworthy of either; and therefore let him not hang all night, for that would carry it too far. Now the apostle, showing how Christ has redeemed us from the curse of the law by being himself made a curse for us, illustrates it by comparing the brand here put on him that was hanged on a tree with the death of Christ, Gal. iii. 13. Moses, by the Spirit, uses this phrase of being *accursed of God,* when he means no more than being treated most ignominiously, that it might afterwards be applied to the death of Christ, and might show that in it he underwent the curse of the law for us, which is a great enhancement of his love and a great encouragement to our faith in him. And (as the excellent bishop Patrick well observes) this passage is applied to the death of Christ, not only because he bore our sins and was exposed to shame, as these malefactors were that were accursed of God, but because he was in the evening taken down from the cursed tree and buried (and that by the particular care of the Jews, with an eye to this law, John xix. 31), in token that now, the guilt being removed, the law was satisfied, as it was when the malefactor had hanged till sun-set; it demanded no more. Then he ceased to be a curse, and those that were his. And, as the land of Israel was pure and clean when the dead body was buried, so the church is washed and cleansed by the complete satisfaction which thus Christ made.

CHAP. XXII.

the chastity of wives, ver. 22. Virgins betrothed (ver. 23—27), or not betrothed, ver. 28, 29. And, lastly, against incest, ver. 30.

THOU shalt not see thy brother's ox or his sheep' go astray, and hide thyself from them : thou shalt in any case bring them again unto thy brother. 2 And if thy brother *be* not nigh unto thee, or if thou know him not, then thou shalt bring it unto thine own house, and it shall be with thee until thy brother seek after it, and thou shalt restore it to him again. 3 In like manner shalt thou do with his ass ; and so shalt thou do with his raiment ; and with all lost thing of thy brother's, which he hath lost, and thou hast found, shalt thou do likewise : thou mayest not hide thyself. 4 Thou shalt not see thy brother's ass or his ox fall down by the way, and hide thyself from them : thou shalt surely help him to lift *them* up again.

The kindness that was commanded to be shown in reference to an enemy (Exod. xxiii. 4, &c.) is here required to be much more done for a neighbour, though he were not an Israelite, for the law is consonant to natural equity. 1. That strayed cattle should be brought back, either to the owner or to the pasture out of which they had gone astray, *v.* 1, 2. This must be done in pity to the very cattle, which, while they wandered, were exposed ; and in civility and respect to the owner, nay, and in justice to him, for it was doing as we would be done by, which is one of the fundamental laws of equity. Note, Religion teaches us to be neighbourly, and to be ready to do all good offices, as we have opportunity, to all men. In doing this, (1.) They must not mind trouble, but, if they knew who the owner was, must take it back themselves ; for, if they should only send notice to the owner to come and look after it himself, some mischief might befal it ere he could reach it. (2.) They must not mind expense, but, if they knew not who the owner was, must take it home and feed it till the owner was found. If such care must be taken of a neighbour's ox or ass going astray, much more of himself going astray from God and his duty ; we should do our utmost to convert him (Jam. v. 19), and restore him, considering ourselves, Gal. vi. 1. 2. That lost goods should be brought to the owner, *v.* 3. The Jews say, " He that found the lost goods was to give public notice of them by the common crier three or four times," according to the usage with us ; if the owner could not be found, he that found the goods might convert them to his own use ; but (say some learned writers in this case) he would do very well to give the value of the goods to the poor. 3. That cattle in distress should

be helped, *v.* 4. This must be done both in compassion to the brute-creatures (for a *merciful man regardeth the life of a beast*, though it be not his own) and in love and friendship to our neighbour, not knowing how soon we may have occasion for his help. If one member may say to another, " I have at present no need of thee," it cannot say, " I never shall."

5 The woman shall not wear that which pertaineth unto a man, neither shall a man put on a woman's garment : for all that do so *are* abomination unto the LORD thy God. 6 If a bird's nest chance to be before thee in the way in any tree, or on the ground, *whether they be* young ones, or eggs, and the dam sitting upon the young, or upon the eggs, thou shalt not take the dam with the young : 7 *But* thou shalt in any wise let the dam go, and take the young to thee ; that it may be well with thee, and *that* thou mayest prolong *thy* days. 8 When thou buildest a new house, then thou shalt make a battlement for thy roof, that thou bring not blood upon thine house, if any man fall from thence. 9 Thou shalt not sow thy vineyard with divers seeds : lest the fruit of thy seed which thou hast sown, and the fruit of thy vineyard, be defiled. '10 Thou shalt not plough with an ox and an ass together. 11 Thou shalt not wear a garment of divers sorts, *as* of woollen and linen together. 12 Thou shalt make thee fringes upon the four quarters of thy vesture, wherewith thou coverest *thyself.*

Here are several laws in these verses which seem to stoop very low, and to take cognizance of things mean and minute. Men's laws commonly do not so : *De minimis non curat lex—The law takes no cognizance of little things ;* but, because God's providence extends itself to the smallest affairs, his precepts do so, that even in them we may be *in the fear of the Lord,* as we are under his eye and care. And yet the significancy and tendency of these statutes, which seem little, are such that, notwithstanding their minuteness, being found among the things of God's law, which he has written to us, they are to be accounted great things.

I. The distinction of sexes by the apparel is to be kept up, for the preservation of our own and our neighbour's chastity, *v.* 5. *Nature itself teaches* that a difference be made between them in *their hair* (1 Cor. xi. 14), and by the same rule in their clothes, which therefore ought not to be confounded, either in ordinary wear or occasionally. To befriend a lawful escape or concealment it may be done, but whether for sport or in the acting of plays is justly questionable. 1. Some think it refers to the idolatrous custom of the Gentiles: in the worship of Venus, women appeared in armour, and men in women's clothes; this, as other such superstitious usages, is here said to be *an abomination to the Lord.* 2. It forbids the confounding of the dispositions and affairs of the sexes: men must not be effeminate, nor do the women's work in the house, nor must women be viragos, pretend to *teach, or usurp authority,* 1 Tim. ii. 11, 12. 3. Probably this confounding of garments had been used to gain opportunity of committing uncleanness, and is therefore forbidden; for those that would be kept from sin must keep themselves from all occasions of it and approaches to it.

II. In taking a bird's-nest, the dam must be let go, *v.* 6, 7. The Jews say, " This is the least of all the commandments of the law of Moses," and yet the same promise is here made to the observance of it that is made to the keeping of the fifth commandment, which is one of the greatest, *that it may be well with thee, and that thou mayest prolong thy days;* for, as disobedience in a small matter shows a very great contempt of the law, so obedience in a small matter shows a very great regard to it. He that let go a bird out of his hand (which was worth two in the bush) purely because God bade him, in that made it to appear that he *esteemed all God's precepts concerning all things to be right,* and that he could deny himself rather than sin against God. But *doth God take care* for birds? 1 Cor. ix. 9. Yes, certainly; and perhaps to this law our Saviour alludes. Luke xii. 6, *Are not five sparrows sold for two farthings, and not one of them is forgotten before God?* This law, 1. Forbids us to be cruel to the brute-creatures, or to take a pleasure in destroying them. Though God has made us *wiser than the fowls of heaven,* and given us *dominion over them,* yet we must not abuse them nor rule them with rigour. *Let go the dam* to breed again; *destroy it not, for a blessing is in it,* Isa. lxv. 8. 2. It teaches us compassion to those of our own kind, and to abhor the thought of every thing that looks barbarous, and cruel, and ill-natured, especially towards those of the weaker and tender sex, which always ought to be treated with the utmost respect, in consideration of the sorrows wherein they bring forth children. It is spoken of as an instance of the most inhuman cruelty that *the mother was dashed to pieces upon her children* (Hos. x. 14), and that the *women with child were ripped open,* Amos i. 13 3. It further intimates that we must not take advantage against any, from their natural affection and the tenderness of their disposition, to do

them an injury. The dam could not have been taken if her concern for her eggs or young (unlike to the ostrich) had not detained her upon the nest when otherwise she could easily have secured herself by flight. Now, since it is a thousand pities that she should fare the worse for that which is her praise, the law takes care that she shall be let go. The remembrance of this may perhaps, some time or other, keep us from doing a hard or unkind thing to those whom we have at our mercy.

III. In building a house, care must be taken to make it safe, that none might receive mischief by falling from it, *v.* 8. The roofs of their houses were flat for people to walk on, as appears by many scriptures; now lest any, through carelessness, should fall off them, they must compass them with battlements, which (the Jews say) must be three feet and a half high; if this were not done, and mischief followed, the owner, by his neglect, brought the guilt of blood upon his house. See here, 1. How precious men's lives are to God, who protects them, not only by his providence, but by his law. 2. How precious, therefore, they ought to be to us, and what care we should take to prevent hurt from coming to any person. The Jews say that by the equity of this law they were obliged (and so are we too) to fence, or remove, every thing by which life may be endangered, as to cover draw-wells, keep bridges in repair, and the like, lest, if any perish through our omission, their blood be required at our hand.

IV. Odd mixtures are here forbidden, *v.* 9, 10. Much of this we met with before, Lev. xix. 19. There appears not any thing at all of moral evil in these things, and therefore we now make no conscience of sowing wheat and rye together, ploughing with horses and oxen together, and of wearing linsey-woolsey garments; but hereby is forbidden either, 1. A conformity to some idolatrous customs of the heathen. Or, 2. That which is contrary to the plainness and purity of an Israelite. They must not gratify their own vanity and curiosity by putting these things together which the Creator in infinite wisdom had made asunder: they must not be unequally yoked with unbelievers, nor mingle themselves with the unclean, as an ox with an ass. Nor must their profession and appearance in the world be motley, or party-coloured, but all of a piece, all of a kind.

V. The law concerning fringes upon their garments, and memorandums of the commandments, which we had before (Num. xv. 38, 39), is here repeated, *v.* 12. By these they were distinguished from other people, so that it might be said, upon the first sight, There goes an Israelite, which taught them not to be ashamed of their country, nor the peculiarities of their religion, how much soever their neighbours looked upon them and it with contempt: and they were also put in mind of the precepts upon the particular occasions to which they had reference ; and perhaps this law is repeated here because the precepts immediately foregoing seemed so minute that they were in danger of being overlooked and forgotten. The fringes will remind you not to make your garments of linen and woollen, *v.* 11.

13 If any man take a wife, and go in unto her, and hate her. 14 And give occasions of speech against her, and bring up an evil name upon her, and say, I took this woman, and when I came to her, I found her not a maid : 15 Then shall the father of the damsel, and her mother, take and bring forth *the tokens of* the damsel's virginity unto the elders of the city in the gate : 16 And the damsel's father shall say unto the elders, I gave my daughter unto this man to wife, and he hateth her ; 17 And, lo, he hath given occasions of speech *against her*, saying, I found not thy daughter a maid ; and yet these *are the tokens of* my daughter's virginity. And they shall spread the cloth before the elders of the city. 18 And the elders of that city shall take that man and chastise him ; 19 And they shall amerce him in a hundred *shekels* of silver, and give *them* unto the father of the damsel, because he hath brought up an evil name upon a virgin of Israel : and she shall be his wife ; he may not put her away all his days. 20 But if this thing be true, *and the tokens of* virginity be not found for the damsel : 21 Then they shall bring out the damsel to the door of her father's house, and the men of her city shall stone her with stones that she die : because she hath wrought folly in Israel, to play the whore in her father's house : so shalt thou put evil away from among you. 22 If a man be found lying with a woman married to a husband, then they shall both of them die, *both* the man that lay with the woman, and the woman : so shalt thou put away evil from Israel. 23 If a damsel *that is* a virgin be betrothed unto a husband, and a man find her in the city, and lie with her ; 24 Then ye shall bring them both out unto the gate of that city, and ye shall stone them with stones that they

816

die ; the damsel, because she cried not, *being* in the city ; and the man, because he hath humbled his neighbour's wife : so thou shalt put away evil from among you. 25 But if a man find a betrothed damsel in the field, and the man force her, and lie with her : then the man only that lay with her shall die : 26 But unto the damsel thou shalt do nothing ; *there is* in the damsel no sin *worthy* of death : for as when a man riseth against his neighbour, and slayeth him, even so *is* this matter : 27 For he found her in the field, *and* the betrothed damsel cried, and *there was* none to save her. 28 If a man find a damsel *that is* a virgin, which is not betrothed, and lay hold on her, and lie with her, and they be found ; 29 Then the man that lay with her shall give unto the damsel's father fifty *shekels* of silver, and she shall be his wife ; because he hath humbled her, he may not put her away all his days. 30 A man shall not take his father's wife, nor discover his father's skirt.

These laws relate to the seventh commandment, laying a restraint by laying a penalty upon those fleshly lusts which war against the soul.

I. If a man, lusting after another woman, to get rid of his wife slander her and falsely accuse her, as not having the virginity she pretended to when he married her, upon the disproof of his slander he must be punished, *v.* 13—19. What the meaning of that evidence is by which the husband's accusation was to be proved false the learned are not agreed, nor is it at all necessary to enquire—those for whom this law was intended, no doubt, understood it : it is sufficient for us to know that this wicked husband, who had thus endeavoured to ruin the reputation of his own wife, was to be scourged, and fined, and bound out from ever divorcing the wife he had thus abused, *v.* 18, 19. Upon his dislike of her he might have divorced her if he had pleased, by the permission of the law (ch. xxiv. 1), but then he must have given her her dowry : if therefore to save that, and to do her the greater mischief, he would thus destroy her good name, it was fit that he should be severely punished for it, and for ever after forfeit the permission to divorce her. Observe, 1. The nearer any are in relation to us the greater sin it is to belie them and blemish their reputation. It is spoken of as a crime of the highest nature to *slander thy own mother's son* (Ps. l. 20), who is next to thyself, much more to slander thy own wife, or thy own husband, that is thyself : it is an ill bird indeed that defiles its own nest. 2. Chastity is honour as well as virtue, and that which gives occasion for the suspicion of it is as great a reproach and disgrace as any whatsoever : in this matter therefore, above any thing, we should be highly tender both of our own good name and that of others. 3. Parents must look upon themselves as concerned to vindicate the reputation of their children, for it is a branch of their own.

II. If the woman that was married as a virgin was not found to be one she was to be stoned to death at her father's door, v. 20, 21. If the uncleanness had been committed before she was betrothed it would not have been punished as a capital crime ; but she must die for the abuse she put upon him whom she married, being conscious to herself of being defiled, while she made him believe her to be a chaste and modest woman. But some think that her uncleanness was punished with death only in case it was committed after she was betrothed, supposing there were few come to maturity but what were betrothed, though not yet married. Now, 1. This gave a powerful caution to young women to flee fornication, since, however concealed before, so as not to mar their marriage, it would very likely be discovered afterwards, to their perpetual infamy and utter ruin. 2. It is intimated to parents that they must by all means possible preserve their children's chastity, by giving them good advice and admonition, setting them good examples, keeping them from bad company, praying for them, and laying them under needful restraints, because, if the children committed lewdness, the parents must have the grief and shame of the execution at their own door. That phrase of *folly wrought in Israel* was used concerning this very crime in the case of Dinah, Gen. xxxiv. 7. All sin is folly, uncleanness especially ; but, above all, uncleanness in Israel, by profession a holy people.

III. If any man, single or married, lay with a married woman, they were both to be put to death, v. 22. This law we had before, Lev. xx. 10. For a married man to lie with a single woman was not a crime of so high a nature, nor was it punished with death, because not introducing a spurious brood into families under the character of legitimate children.

IV. If a damsel were betrothed and not married, she was from under the eye of her intended husband, and therefore she and her chastity were taken under the special protection of the law. 1. If her chastity were violated by her own consent, she was to be put to death, and her adulterer with her, v. 23, 24. And it shall be presumed that she consented if it were done in the city, or in any place where, had she cried out, help might speedily have come in to prevent the injury offered her. *Qui tacet, consentire videtur—Silence implies consent.* Note, It may be presumed that those willingly yield to a tempta-

tion (whatever they pretend) who will not use the means and helps they might be furnished with to avoid and overcome it. Nay, her being found in the city, a place of company and diversion, when she should have kept under the protection of her father's house, was an evidence against her that she had not that dread of the sin and the danger of it which became a modest woman. Note, Those that needlessly expose themselves to temptation justly suffer for the same, if, ere they are aware, they be surprised and caught by it. Dinah lost her honour to gratify her curiosity with a sight of the *daughters of the land.* By this law the Virgin Mary was in danger of being made a public example, that is, of being stoned to death, but that God, by an angel, cleared the matter to Joseph. 2. If she were forced, and never consented, he that committed the rape was to be put to death, but the damsel was to be acquitted, v. 25—27. Now if it were done in the field, out of the hearing of neighbours, it shall be presumed that she cried out, but there was none to save her ; and, besides, her going into the field, a place of solitude, did not so much expose her. Now by this law it is intimated to us, (1.) That we shall suffer only for the wickedness we do, not for that which is done to us. That is no sin which has not more or less of the will in it. (2.) That we must presume the best concerning all persons, unless the contrary do appear ; not only charity, but equity teaches us to do so. Though none heard her cry, yet, because none could hear it if she did, it shall be taken for granted that she did. This rule we should go by in judging of persons and actions : *believe all things, and hope all things.* (3.) That our chastity should be as dear to us as our life when that is assaulted, it is not at all improper to cry *murder, murder,* for, *as when a man riseth against his neighbour and slayeth him, even so is this matter.* (4.) By way of allusion to this, see what we are to do when Satan sets upon us with his temptations : wherever we are, let us cry aloud to heaven for help *(Succurre, Domine, vim patior—Help me, O Lord, for I suffer violence),* and there we may be sure to be heard, and answered, as Paul was, *My grace is sufficient for thee.*

V. If a damsel not betrothed were thus abused by violence, he that abused her should be fined, the father should have the fine, and, if he and the damsel did consent, he should be bound to marry her, and never to divorce her, how much soever she was below him, and how unpleasing soever she might afterwards be to him, as Tamar was to Amnon after he had forced her, v. 28, 29. This was to deter men from such vicious practices, which it is a shame that we are necessitated to read and write of.

VI. The law against a man's marrying his father's widow, or having any undue familiarity with his father's wife, is here repeated (v. 30) from Lev. xviii. 8. And, probably, it is intended (as bishop Patrick notes) for a short memorandum to them carefully to observe all the laws there made against incestuous marriages, that being specified which is the most detestable of all; it is that of which the apostle says, *It is not so much as named among the Gentiles,* 1 Cor. v. 1.

CHAP. XXIII.

The laws of this chapter provide, I. For the preserving of the purity and honour of the families of Israel, by excluding such as would be a disgrace to them, ver. 1—8. II. For the preserving of the purity and honour of the camp of Israel when it was abroad, ver. 9—14. III. For the encouraging and entertaining of slaves who fled to them, ver. 15, 16. IV. Against whoredom, ver. 17, 18. V. Against usury, ver. 19, 20. VI. Against the breach of vows, ver. 21—23. VII. What liberty a man might take in his neighbour's field and vineyard, and what not, ver. 24, 25.

HE that is wounded in the stones, or hath his privy member cut off, shall not enter into the congregation of the LORD. 2 A bastard shall not enter into the congregation of the LORD; even to his tenth generation shall he not enter into the congregation of the LORD. 3 An Ammonite or Moabite shall not enter into the congregation of the LORD; even to their tenth generation shall they not enter into the congregation of the LORD for ever: 4 Because they met you not with bread and with water in the way, when ye came forth out of Egypt; and because they hired against thee Balaam the son of Beor of Pethor of Mesopotamia, to curse thee. 5 Nevertheless the LORD thy God would not hearken unto Balaam; but the LORD thy God turned the curse into a blessing unto thee, because the LORD thy God loved thee. 6 Thou shalt not seek their peace nor their prosperity all thy days for ever. 7 Thou shalt not abhor an Edomite; for he *is* thy brother: thou shalt not abhor an Egyptian; because thou wast· a stranger in his land. 8 The children that are begotten of them shall enter into the congregation of the LORD in their third generation.

Interpreters are not agreed what is here meant by *entering into the congregation of the Lord,* which is here forbidden to eunuchs and to bastards, Ammonites and Moabites, for ever, but to Edomites and Egyptians only till the third generation. 1. Some think they are hereby excluded from communicating with the people of God in their religious services. Though eunuchs and bastards were owned as members of the church, and the Ammonites and Moabites might be circumcised and proselyted to the Jewish religion, yet they and their families must lie for some time under marks of disgrace, remembering

the rock whence they were hewn, and must not come so near the sanctuary as others might, nor have so free a communion with Israelites. 2. Others think they are hereby excluded from bearing office in the congregation: none of these must be elders or judges, lest the honour of the magistracy should thereby be stained. 3. Others think they are excluded only from marrying with Israelites. Thus the learned bishop Patrick inclines to understand it; yet we find that when this law was put in execution after the captivity they separated from Israel, not only the strange wives, but all the mixed multitude, see Neh. xiii. 1—3. With the daughters of these nations (though out of the nations of Canaan), it should seem, the men of Israel might marry, if they were completely proselyted to the Jewish religion; but with the men of these nations the daughters of Israel might not marry, nor could the men be naturalized otherwise than as here provided.

It is plain, in general, that disgrace is here put,

I. Upon bastards and eunuchs, *v.* 1, 2. By bastards here the Jewish writers understand, not all that were born of fornication, or out of marriage, but all the issue of those incestuous mixtures which are forbidden, Lev. xviii. And, though it was not the fault of the issue, yet, to deter people from those unlawful marriages and unlawful lusts, it was very convenient that their posterity should thus be made infamous. By this rule Jephthah, though the son of a harlot, a strange woman (Judg. xi. 1, 2), yet was not a bastard in the sense of this law. And as for the eunuchs, though by this law they seemed to be cast out of the vineyard as dry trees, which they complain of (Isa. lvi. 3), yet it is here promised (*v.* 5) that if they took care of their duty to God, as far as they were admitted, by keeping his sabbaths and choosing the things that pleased him, the want of this privilege should be made up to them with such spiritual blessings as would entitle them to an everlasting name.

II. Upon Ammonites and Moabites, the posterity of Lot, who, for his outward convenience, had separated himself from Abraham, Gen. xiii. 11. And we do not find that he or his ever joined themselves again to the children of the covenant. They are here cut off *to the tenth generation,* that is (as some think it is explained), for ever. Compare Neh. xiii. 1. The reason of this quarrel which Israel must have with them, so as not to *seek their peace* (*v.* 6), is because of the unkindness they had now lately done to the camp of Israel, notwithstanding the orders God had given not to distress or vex them, *ch.* ii. 9, 19. 1. It was bad enough that they did not *meet them with bread and water in the way* (*v.* 4), that they did not as allies, or at least as neutral states, bring victuals into their camp, which they should have been duly paid for. It was well that God's Israel did not need their kindness, God himself following them with bread and water. However this omission of the Ammonites should be remembered against their nation in future ages. Note, God will certainly reckon, not only with those that oppose his people, but with those that do not help and further them, when it is in the power of their hand to do it. The charge at the great day is for an omission : *I was hungry, and you gave me no meat.* 2. The Moabites had done worse, they hired Balaam to curse Israel, *v.* 4. It is true *God turned the curse into a blessing* (*v.* 5), not only changing the word in Balaam's mouth, but making that really turn to the honour and advantage of Israel which was designed for their ruin. But though the design was defeated, and overruled for good, the Moabites' wickedness was not the less provoking. God will deal with sinners, not only according to their deeds, but according to their endeavours, Ps. xxviii. 4.

III. The Edomites and Egyptians had not so deep a mark of displeasure put upon them as the Moabites and Ammonites had. If an Edomite or Egyptian turned proselyte, his grand-children should be looked upon as members of the congregation of the Lord to all intents and purposes, *v.* 7, 8. We should think that the Edomites had been more injurious to the Israelites than the Ammonites, and deserved as little favour from them (Num. xx. 20), and yet " *Thou shalt not abhor an Edomite,* as thou must an Ammonite, for he is thy brother." Note, The unkindness of near relations, though by many worst taken, yet should with us, for that reason, because of the relation, be first forgiven. And then, as to the Egyptians, here is a strange reason given why they must not be abhorred : "*Thou wast a stranger in their land,* and therefore, though hardly used there, be civil to them, for old acquaintance' sake." They must not remember their bondage in Egypt for the keeping up of any ill will to the Egyptians, but only for the magnifying of God's power and goodness in their deliverance.

9 When the host goeth forth against thine enemies, then keep thee from every wicked thing. 10 If there be among you any man, that is not clean by reason of uncleanness that chanceth him by night, then shall he go abroad out of the camp, he shall not come within the camp : 11 But it shall be, when evening cometh on, he shall wash *himself* with water : and when the sun is down, he shall come into the camp *again.* 12 Thou shalt have a place also without the camp, whither thou shalt go forth abroad : 13 And thou shalt have a paddle upon thy weapon ; and it shall be, when thou

wilt ease thyself abroad, thou shalt dig therewith, and shalt turn back and cover that which cometh from thee : 14 For the LORD thy God walketh in the midst of thy camp, to deliver thee, and to give up thine enemies before thee ; therefore shall thy camp be holy : that he see no unclean thing in thee, and turn away from thee.

Israel was now encamped, and this vast army was just entering upon action, which was likely to keep them together for a long time, and therefore it was fit to give them particular directions for the good ordering of their camp. And the charge is in one word to be *clean.* They must take care to keep their camp pure from moral, ceremonial, and natural pollution.

I. From moral pollution (*v.* 9) : *When the host goes forth against thy enemy* then look upon thyself as in a special manner engaged to *keep thyself from every evil thing.* 1. The soldiers themselves must take heed of sin, for sin takes off the edge of valour ; guilt makes men cowards. Those that put their lives in their hands are concerned to make and keep their peace with God, and preserve a conscience void of offence ; then may they look death in the face without terror. Soldiers, in executing their commission, must keep themselves from gratifying the lusts of malice, covetousness, or uncleanness, for these are wicked things—must keep themselves from the idols, or accursed things, they found in the camps they plundered. 2. Even those that tarried at home, the body of the people, and every particular person, must at that time especially keep from every wicked thing, lest by sin they provoke God to withdraw his presence from the host, and give victory to the enemy for the correcting of his own people. Times of war should be times of reformation, else how can we expect God should hear and answer our prayers for success ? Ps. lxvi. 18. See 1 Sam. vii. 3.

II. From ceremonial pollution, which might befal a person when unconscious of it, for which he was bound to wash his flesh in water, and look upon himself as *unclean until the evening,* Lev. xv. 16. A soldier, notwithstanding the constant service and duty he had to do in the camp, must be so far from looking upon himself as discharged from the observance of this ceremony that more was required from him than at another time ; had he been at his own house, he needed only to wash his flesh, but, being in the army, he must go abroad out of the camp, as one concerned to keep it pure and ashamed of his own impurity, and not return till after sun-set, *v.* 10, 11. By this trouble and reproach, which even involuntary pollutions exposed men to, they were taught to keep up a very great dread of all fleshly lusts. It were well if military men would consider this.

819

III. From natural pollution; the camp of the Lord must have nothing offensive in it, *v.* 12—14. It is strange that the divine law, or at least the solemn order and direction of Moses, should extend to a thing of this nature; but the design of it was to teach them, 1. Modesty and decorum; nature itself teaches them thus to distinguish themselves from beasts that know no shame. 2. Cleanliness, and, though not niceness, yet neatness, even in their camp. Filthiness is offensive to the senses God has endued us with, prejudicial to the health, a wrong to the comfort of human life, and an evidence of a careless slothful temper of mind. 3. Purity from the pollutions of sin; if there must be this care taken to preserve the body clean and sweet, much more should we be solicitous to keep the mind so. 4. A reverence of the divine majesty. This is the reason here given: *For the Lord thy God walketh by his ark, the special token of his presence, in the midst of thy camp;* with respect to that external symbol this external purity is required, which (though not insisted on in the letter when that reason ceases) teaches us to preserve inward purity of soul, in consideration of the eye of God, which is always upon us. By this expression of respect to the presence of God among them, they were taught both to fortify themselves against sin and to encourage themselves against their enemies with the consideration of that presence. 5. A regard one to another. The filthiness of one is noisome to many; this law of cleanliness therefore teaches us not to do that which will be justly offensive to our brethren and grieve them. It is a law against nuisances.

15 Thou shalt not deliver unto his master the servant which is escaped from his master unto thee: 16 He shall dwell with thee, *even* among you, in that place which he shall choose in one of thy gates, where it liketh him best: thou shalt not oppress him. 17 There shall be no whore of the daughters of Israel, nor a sodomite of the sons of Israel. 18 Thou shalt not bring the hire of a whore, or the price of a dog, into the house of the LORD thy God for any vow: for even both these *are* abomination unto the LORD thy God. 19 Thou shalt not lend upon usury to thy brother; usury of money, usury of victuals, usury of any thing that is lent upon usury: 20 Unto a stranger thou mayest lend upon usury; but unto thy brother thou shalt not lend upon usury: that the LORD thy God may bless thee in

all that thou settest thine hand to in the land whither thou goest to possess it. 21 When thou shalt vow a vow unto the LORD thy God, thou shalt not slack to pay it: for the LORD thy God will surely require it of thee; and it would be sin in thee. 22 But if thou shalt forbear to vow, it shall be no sin in thee. 23 That which is gone out of thy lips thou shalt keep and perform; *even* a freewill offering, according as thou hast vowed unto the LORD thy God, which thou hast promised with thy mouth. 24 When thou comest into thy neighbour's vineyard, then thou mayest eat grapes thy fill at thine own pleasure; but thou shalt not put *any* in thy vessel. 25 When thou comest into the standing corn of thy neighbour, then thou mayest pluck the ears with thine hand; but thou shalt not move a sickle unto thy neighbour's standing corn.

Orders are here given about five several things which have no relation one to another:—

I. The land of Israel is here made a sanctuary, or city of refuge, for servants that were wronged and abused by their masters, and fled thither for shelter from the neighbouring countries, *v.* 15, 16. We cannot suppose that they were hereby obliged to give entertainment to all the unprincipled men that ran from service; Israel needed not (as Rome at first did) to be thus peopled. But, 1. They must not deliver up the trembling servant to his enraged master, till upon trial it appeared that the servant had wronged his master and was justly liable to punishment. Note, It is an honourable thing to shelter and protect the weak, provided they be not wicked. God allows his people to patronise the oppressed. The angel bid Hagar return to her mistress, and Paul sent Onesimus back to his master Philemon, because they had neither of them any cause to go away, nor was either of them exposed to any danger in returning. But the servant here is supposed to escape, that is, to run for his life, to the people of Israel, of whom he had heard (as Benhadad of the kings of Israel, 1 Kings xx. 31) that they were a merciful people, to save himself from the fury of a tyrant; and in that case to deliver him up is to throw a lamb into the mouth of a lion. 2. If it appeared that the servant was abused, they must not only protect him, but, supposing him willing to embrace their religion, they must give him all the encouragement that might be to settle among them. Care is taken both that he should not be imposed upon in the place of his settlement—let it be *that which he shall choose and where it liketh him best,* and that he should not exchange one hard master for many—*thou shalt not oppress him.* Thus would he soon find a comfortable difference between the land of Israel and other lands, and would choose it to be his rest for ever. Note, Proselytes and converts to the truth should be treated with particular tenderness, that they may have no temptation to return.

II. The land of Israel must be no shelter for the unclean; no whore, no Sodomite, must be suffered to live among them (v. 17, 18), neither a whore nor a whoremonger. No houses of uncleanness must be kept either by men or women. Here is, 1. A good reason intimated why there should be no such wickedness tolerated among them: they were Israelites. This seems to have an emphasis laid upon it. For a daughter of Israel to be a whore, or a son of Israel a whoremaster, is to reproach the stock they are come of, the people they belong to, and the God they worship. It is bad in any, but worst in Israelites, a holy nation, 2 Sam. xiii. 12. 2. A just mark of displeasure put upon this wickedness, that the hire of a whore, that is, the money she gets by her whoring, and the price of a dog, that is, of the Sodomite, pimp, or whoremaster (so I incline to understand it, for such are called *dogs,* Rev. xxii. 15), the money he gets by his lewd and villanous practices, no part of it shall be *brought into the house of the Lord* (as the hire of prostitutes among the Gentiles was into their temples) *for any vow.* This intimates, (1.) That God would not accept of any offering at all from such wicked people; they had nothing to bring an offering of but what they got by their wickedness, and therefore their sacrifice could not but be *an abomination to the Lord,* Prov. xv. 8. (2.) That they should not think, by making and paying vows, and bringing offerings to the Lord, to obtain leave to go on in this sin, as (it should seem) some that followed that trade suggested to themselves, when their offerings were admitted. Prov. vii. 14, 15, *This day have I paid my vows, therefore came I forth to meet thee.* Nothing should be accepted in commutation of penance. (3.) That we cannot honour God with our substance unless it be honestly and honourably come by. It must not only be considered what we give, but how we got it; God hates robbery for burnt-offerings, and uncleanness too.

III. The matter of usury is here settled, *v.* 19, 20. (1.) They must not lend upon usury to an Israelite. They had and held their estates immediately from and under God, who, while he distinguished them from all other people, might have ordered, had he so pleased, that they should have all things in common among themselves; but instead of that, and in token of their joint interest in the good land he had given them, he only

appointed them, as there was occasion, to lend to one another without interest, which among them would be little or no loss to the lender, because their land was so divided, their estates were so settled, and there was so little of merchandise among them, that it was seldom or never that they had occasion to borrow any great sums, only what was necessary for the subsistence of their families when the fruits of their ground had met with any disaster, or the like; and, in such a case, for a small matter to insist upon usury would have been very barbarous. Where the borrower gets, or hopes to get, it is just that the lender should share in the gain; but to him that borrows for his necessary food pity must be shown, and we must lend, hoping for nothing again, if we have wherewithal to do it, Luke vi. 35. (2.) They might lend upon usury to a stranger, who was supposed to live by trade, and (as we say) by turning the penny, and therefore got by what he borrowed, and came among them in hopes to do so. By this it appears that usury is not in itself oppressive; for they must not oppress a stranger, and yet might exact usury from him.

IV. The performance of the vows wherewith we have bound our souls is here required; and it is a branch of the law of nature, *v.* 21—23. (1.) We are here left at our liberty whether we will make vows or no: *If thou shalt forbear to vow* (some particular sacrifice and offering, more than was commanded by the law), *it shall be no sin to thee.* God had already signified his readiness to accept a free-will-offering thus vowed, though it were but a little fine flour (Lev. ii. 4, &c.), which was encouragement enough to those who were so inclined. But lest the priests, who had the largest share of those vows and voluntary offerings, should sponge upon the people, by pressing it upon them as their duty to make such vows, beyond their ability and inclination, they are here expressly told that it should not be reckoned a sin in them if they did not make any such vows, as it would be if they omitted any of the sacrifices that God had particularly required. For (as bishop Patrick well expresses it) God would have men to be easy in his service, and all their offerings to be free and cheerful. (2.) We are here laid under the highest obligations, when we have made a vow, to perform it, and to perform it speedily: *"Thou shalt not be slack to pay it,* lest if it be delayed beyond the first opportunity the zeal abate, the vow be forgotten, or something happen to disable thee for the performance of it. *That which has gone out of thy lips* as a solemn and deliberate vow must not be recalled, but *thou shalt keep and perform it,* punctually and fully.'' The rule of the gospel goes somewhat further than this. 2 Cor. ix. 7, *Every one, according as he purposeth in his heart,* though it have not gone out of his lips, *so let him give.* Here is a good reason why we should pay our vows, that if we do not *God will require it of us,* will surely and severely reckon with us, not only for lying, but for going about to mock him, who cannot be mocked. See Eccl. v. 4.

V. Allowance is here given, when they passed through a cornfield or vineyard, to pluck and eat of the corn or grapes that grew by the road-side, whether it was done for necessity or delight, only they must carry none away with them, *v.* 24, 25. Therefore the disciples were not censured for plucking the ears of corn (it was well enough known that the law allowed it), but for doing it on the sabbath day, which the tradition of the elders had forbidden. Now, 1. This law intimated to them what great plenty of corn and wine they should have in Canaan, so much that a little would not be missed out of their fruits ; they should have enough for themselves and all their friends. 2. It provided for the support of poor travellers, to relieve the fatigue of their journey, and teaches us to be kind to such. The Jews say, "This law was chiefly intended in favour of labourers, who were employed in gathering in their harvest and vintage ; their mouths must not be muzzled any more than that of the ox when he treads out the corn." 3. It teaches us not to insist upon property in a small matter, of which it is easy to say, *What is that between me and thee ?* It was true the grapes which the passenger ate were none of his own, nor did the proprietor give them to him ; but the thing was of so small value that he had reason to think, were he present, he would not deny them to him, any more than he himself would grudge the like courtesy, and therefore it was no theft to take them. 4. It used them to hospitality, and teaches us to be ready to distribute, willing to communicate, and not to think every thing lost that is given away. Yet, 4. It forbids us to abuse the kindness of our friends, and to take the advantage of fair concessions to make unreasonable encroachments: we must not draw an ell from those that give but an inch. They may eat of their neighbour's grapes ; but it does not therefore follow that they may carry away.

CHAP. XXIV.

In this chapter we have, I. The toleration of divorce, ver. 1—4. II. A discharge of new-married men from the war, ver. 5. III. Laws concerning pledges, ver. 6, 10—13, 17. IV. Against man-stealing, ver. 7. V. Concerning the leprosy, ver. 8, 9. VI. Against the injustice of masters towards their servants, ver. 14, 15. Judges in capital causes (ver. 16), and civil concerns, ver. 17, 18. VII. Of charity to the poor, ver. 19, &c.

WHEN a man hath taken a wife, and married her, and it come to pass that she find no favour in his eyes, because he hath found some uncleanness in her : then let him write her a bill of divorcement, and give *it* in her hand, and send her out of his house. 2 And when she is departed out of his house, she may go and be

another man's *wife.* 3 And if the latter husband hate her, and write her a bill of divorcement, and giveth *it* in her hand, and sendeth her out of his house ; or if the latter husband die, which took her *to be* his wife ; 4 Her former husband, which sent her away, may not take her again to be his wife, after that she is defiled ; for that *is* abomination before the Lord : and thou shalt not cause the land to sin, which the Lord thy God giveth thee *for* an inheritance.

This is that permission which the Pharisees erroneously referred to as a precept, Matt. xix. 7, *Moses commanded to give a writing of divorcement.* It was not so ; our Saviour told them that he only suffered it because of the hardness of their hearts, lest, if they had not had liberty to divorce their wives, they should have ruled them with rigour, and, it may be, have been the death of them. It is probable that divorces were in use before (they are taken for granted, Lev. xxi. 14), and Moses thought it needful here to give some rules concerning them. 1. That a man might not divorce his wife unless he *found some uncleanness in her, v.* 1. It was not sufficient to say that he did not like her, or that he liked another better, but he must show cause for his dislike ; something that made her disagreeable and unpleasant to him, though it might not make her so to another. This uncleanness must mean something less than adultery ; for, for that, she was to die ; and less than the suspicion of it, for in that case he might give her the waters of jealousy ; but it means either a light carriage, or a cross froward disposition, or some loathsome sore or disease ; nay, some of the Jewish writers suppose that an offensive breath might be a just ground for divorce. Whatever is meant by it, doubtless it was something considerable ; so that their modern doctors erred who allowed divorce for every cause, though ever so trivial, Matt. xix. 3. 2. That it must be done, not by word of mouth, for that might be spoken hastily, but by writing, and that put in due form, and solemnly declared, before witnesses, to be his own act and deed, which was a work of time, and left room for consideration, that it might not be done rashly. 3. That the husband must give it into the hand of his wife, and send her away, which some think obliged him to endow her and make provision for her, according to her quality and such as might help to marry her again ; and good reason he should do this, since the cause of quarrel was not her fault, but her infelicity. 4. That being divorced it was lawful for her to marry another husband, *v.* 2. The divorce had dissolved the bond of marriage as effectually as death could dissolve it ; so that she was as free to marry again as if her first husband had been naturally dead. 5. That if her second husband died, or divorced her, then still she might marry a third, but her first husband should never take her again (*v.* 3, 4), which he might have done if she had not married another; for by that act of her own she had perfectly renounced him for ever, and, as to him, was looked upon as defiled, though not as to another person. The Jewish writers say that this was to prevent a most vile and wicked practice which the Egyptians had of changing wives; or perhaps it was intended to prevent men's rashness in putting away their wives; for the wife that was divorced would be apt, in revenge, to marry another immediately, and perhaps the husband that divorced her, how much soever he thought to better himself by another choice, would find the next worse, and something in her more disagreeable, so that he would wish for his first wife again. "No" (says this law) "you shall not have her, you should have kept her when you had her." Note, It is best to be content with such things as we have, since changes made by discontent often prove for the worse. The uneasiness we know is commonly better, though we are apt to think it worse, than that which we do not know. By the strictness of this law God illustrates the riches of his grace in his willingness to be reconciled to his people that had gone a whoring from him. Jer. iii. 1, *Thou hast played the harlot with many lovers, yet return again to me.* For his thoughts and ways are above ours.

5 When a man hath taken a new wife, he shall not go out to war, neither shall he be charged with any business: *but* he shall be free at home one year, and shall cheer up his wife which he hath taken. 6 No man shall take the nether or the upper millstone to pledge: for he taketh *a man's* life to pledge. 7 If a man be found stealing any of his brethren of the children of Israel, and maketh merchandise of him, or selleth him; then that thief shall die; and thou shalt put evil away from among you. 8 Take heed in the plague of leprosy, that thou observe diligently, and do according to all that the priests the Levites shall teach you: as I commanded them, *so* ye shall observe to do. 9 Remember what the LORD thy God did unto Miriam by the way, after that ye were come forth out of Egypt. 10 When thou dost lend thy brother any thing, thou shalt not go into his house to fetch his pledge. 11 Thou shalt stand abroad,

and the man to whom thou dost lend shall bring out the pledge abroad unto thee. 12 And if the man *be* poor, thou shalt not sleep with his pledge: 13 In any case thou shalt deliver him the pledge again when the sun goeth down, that he may sleep in his own raiment, and bless thee: and it shall be righteousness unto thee before the LORD thy God.

Here is, I. Provision made for the preservation and confirmation of love between new-married people, *v.* 5. This fitly follows upon the laws concerning divorce, which would be prevented if their affection to each other were well settled at first. If the husband were much abroad from his wife the first year, his love to her would be in danger of cooling, and of being drawn aside to others whom he would meet with abroad; therefore his service to his country in war, embassies, or other public business that would call him from home, shall be dispensed with, *that he may cheer up the wife that he has taken.* Note, 1. It is of great consequence that love be kept up between husband and wife, and that every thing be very carefully avoided which might make them strange one to another, especially at first; for in that relation, where there is not the love that should be, there is an inlet ready to abundance of guilt and grief. 2. One of the duties of that relation is to cheer up one another under the cares and crosses that happen, as helpers of each other's joy; for a cheerful heart does good like a medicine.

II. A law against man-stealing, *v.* 7. It was not death by the law of Moses to steal cattle or goods; but to steal a child, or a weak and simple man, or one that a man had in his power, and to make merchandize of him, this was a capital crime, and could not be expiated, as other thefts, by restitution— so much is *a man better than a sheep,* Matt. xii. 12. It was a very heinous offence, for, 1. It was robbing the public of one of its members. 2. It was taking away a man's liberty, the liberty of a free-born Israelite, which was next in value to his life. 3. It was driving a man out from the inheritance of the land, to the privileges of which he was entitled, and bidding him go serve other gods, as David complains against Saul, 1 Sam. xxvi. 19.

III. A memorandum concerning the leprosy, *v.* 8, 9. 1. The laws concerning it must be carefully observed. The laws concerning it we had, Lev. xiii. 14. They are here said to be commanded to the *priests and Levites,* and therefore are not repeated in a discourse to the people; but the people are here charged, in case of leprosy, to apply to the priest according to the law, and to abide by his judgment, so far as it agreed with the law and the plain matter of fact. The plague of leprosy being usually a particular mark of God's displeasure for sin, he in whom the signs of it did appear ought not to conceal it, nor cut out the signs of it, nor apply to the physician for relief; but he must go to the priest, and follow his directions. Thus those that feel their consciences under guilt and wrath must not cover it, nor endeavour to shake off their convictions, but by repentance, and prayer, and humble confession, take the appointed way to peace and pardon. 2. The particular case of Miriam, who was smitten with leprosy for quarrelling with Moses, must not be forgotten. It was an explication of the law concerning the leprosy. Remember that, and, (1.) "Take heed of sinning after the similitude of her transgression, by despising dominions and speaking evil of dignities, lest you thereby bring upon yourselves the same judgment." (2.) "If any of you be smitten with a leprosy, expect not that the law should be dispensed with, nor think it hard to be shut out of the camp and so made a spectacle; there is no remedy: Miriam herself, though a prophetess and the sister of Moses, was not exempted, but was forced to submit to this severe discipline when she was under this divine rebuke." Thus David, Hezekiah, Peter, and other great men, when they had sinned, humbled themselves, and took to themselves shame and grief; let us not expect to be reconciled upon easier terms.

IV. Some necessary orders given about pledges for the security of money lent. They are not forbidden to take such securities as would save the lender from loss, and oblige the borrower to be honest; but, 1. They must not take the millstone for a pledge (v. 6), for with that they ground the corn that was to be bread for their families, or, if it were a public mill, with it the miller got his livelihood; and so it forbids the taking of any thing for a pledge by the want of which a man was in danger of being undone. Consonant to this is the ancient common law of England, which provides that no man be distrained of the utensils or instruments of his trade or profession, as the axe of a carpenter, or the books of a scholar, or beasts belonging to the plough, as long as there are other beasts of which distress may be made (*Coke, 1 Inst. fol.* 47). This teaches us to consult the comfort and subsistence of others as much as our own advantage. That creditor who cares not though his debtor and his family starve, nor is at all concerned what becomes of them, so he may but get his money or secure it, goes contrary, not only to the law of Christ, but even to the law of Moses too. 2. They must not go into the borrower's house to fetch the pledge, but must stand without, and he must bring it, *v.* 10, 11. *The borrower* (says Solomon) *is servant to the lender;* therefore lest the lender should abuse the advantage he has against him, and improve it for his own interest, it is
824

provided that he shall take not what he pleases, but what the borrower can best spare. A man's house is his castle, even the poor man's house is so, and is here taken under the protection of the law. 3. That a poor man's bed-clothes should never be taken for a pledge, *v.* 12, 13. This we had before, Exod. xxii. 26, 27. If they were taken in the morning, they must be brought back again at night, which is in effect to say that they must not be taken at all. "Let the poor debtor sleep in his own raiment, and bless thee," that is, "pray for thee, and praise God for thy kindness to him." Note, Poor debtors ought to be sensible (more sensible than commonly they are) of the goodness of those creditors that do not take all the advantage of the law against them, and to repay their kindnesses by their prayers for them, when they are not in a capacity to repay it in any other way. "Nay, thou shalt not only have the prayers and good wishes of thy poor brother, but *it shall be righteousness to thee before the Lord thy God*," that is, "It shall be accepted and rewarded as an act of mercy to thy brother and obedience to thy God, and an evidence of thy sincere conformity to the law. Though it may be looked upon by men as an act of weakness to deliver up the securities thou hast for thy debt, yet it shall be looked upon by thy God as an act of goodness, which shall in no wise lose its reward."

14 Thou shalt not oppress a hired servant *that is* poor and needy, *whether he be* of thy brethren, or of thy strangers that *are* in thy land within thy gates: 15 At his day thou shalt give *him* his hire, neither shall the sun go down upon it; for he *is* poor, and setteth his heart upon it: lest he cry against thee unto the LORD, and it be sin unto thee. 16 The fathers shall not be put to death for the children, neither shall the children be put to death for the fathers: every man shall be put to death for his own sin. 17 Thou shalt not pervert the judgment of the stranger, *nor* of the fatherless; nor take the widow's raiment to pledge: 18 But thou shalt remember that thou wast a bondman in Egypt, and the LORD thy God redeemed thee thence: therefore I command thee to do this thing. 19 When thou cuttest down thine harvest in thy field, and hast forgot a sheaf in the field, thou shalt not go again to fetch it: it shall be for the stranger, for the fatherless, and for the widow: that

the LORD thy God may bless thee in all the work of thine hands. 20 When thou beatest thine olive tree, thou shalt not go over the boughs again: it shall be for the stranger, for the fatherless, and for the widow. 21 When thou gatherest the grapes of thy vineyard, thou shalt not glean *it* afterward: it shall be for the stranger, for the fatherless, and for the widow. 22 And thou shalt remember that thou wast a bondman in the land of Egypt: therefore I command thee to do this thing.

Here, I. Masters are commanded to be just to their poor servants, *v.* 14, 15. 1. They must not oppress them, by overloading them with work, by giving them undue and unreasonable rebukes, or by withholding from them proper maintenance. A servant, though a stranger to the commonwealth of Israel, must not be abused: "For *thou wast a bondman* in the land where thou wast a stranger (*v.* 18), and thou knowest what a grievous thing it is to be oppressed by a task-master, and therefore, in tenderness to those that are servants and strangers, and in gratitude to that God who set thee at liberty and settled thee in a country of thy own, *thou shalt not oppress a servant.*" Let not masters be tyrants to their servants, for their Master is in heaven. See Job xxxi. 13. 2. They must be faithful and punctual in paying them their wages: "*At his day thou shalt give him his hire,* not only pay it to him in full, without fraud, but pay it in time, without further delay. As soon as he has done his day's work, if he desire it, let him have his day's wages," as those labourers (Matt. xx. 8), *when evening had come.* He that works by day-wages is supposed to live from hand to mouth, and cannot have to-morrow's bread for his family till he is paid for this day's labour. If the wages be withheld, (1.) It will be grief to the servant, for, poor man, he *sets his heart upon it,* or, as the word is, he *lifts up his soul to it,* he is earnestly desirous of it, as the reward of his work (Job vii. 2), and depends upon it as the gift of God's providence for the maintenance of his family. A compassionate master, though it should be somewhat inconvenient to himself, would not disappoint the expectation of a poor servant that was so fond to think of receiving his wages. But that is not the worst. (2.) It will be guilt to the master. "The injured servant will cry against thee to the Lord; since he has no one else to appeal to, he will lodge his appeal in the court of heaven, and it will be sin to thee." Or, if he do not complain, the cause will speak for itself, the *hire of the labourers which is kept back by fraud* will itself *cry,*" Jam. v. 4. It is a greater sin

than most people think it is, and will be found so in the great day, to put hardships upon poor servants, labourers, and workmen, that we employ. God will do them right if men do not.

II. Magistrates and judges are commanded to be just in their administrations. 1. In those which we call *pleas of the crown* a standing rule is here given, that *the fathers shall not be put to death for the children, nor the children for the fathers, v.* 16. If the children make themselves obnoxious to the law, let them suffer for it, but let not the parents suffer either for them or with them; it is grief enough to them to see their children suffer: if the parents be guilty, let them die for their own sin; but though God, the sovereign Lord of life, sometimes visits the iniquity of the fathers upon the children, especially the sin of idolatry, and when he deals with nations in their national capacity, yet he does not allow men to do so. Accordingly, we find Amaziah sparing the children, even when the fathers were put to death for killing the king, 2 Kings xiv. 6. It was in an extraordinary case, and no doubt by special direction from heaven, that Saul's sons were put to death for his offence, and they died rather as sacrifices than as malefactors, 2 Sam. xxi. 9, 14. 2. In common pleas between party and party, great care must be taken that none whose cause was just should fare the worse for their weakness, nor for their being destitute of friends, as strangers, fatherless, and widows (*v.* 17): "*Thou shalt not pervert their judgment,* nor force them to give their very raiment for a pledge, by defrauding them of their right." Judges must be advocates for those that cannot speak for themselves and have no friends to speak for them.

III. The rich are commanded to be kind and charitable to the poor. Many ways they are ordered to be so by the law of Moses. The particular instance of charity here prescribed is that they should not be greedy in gathering in their corn, and grapes, and olives, so as to be afraid of leaving any behind them, but be willing to overlook some, and let the poor have the gleanings, *v.* 19—22. 1. "Say not, 'It is all my own, and why should not I have it?' But learn a generous contempt of property in small matters. One sheaf or two forgotten will make thee never the poorer at the year's end, and it will do somebody good, if thou have it not." 2. "Say not, '*What I give I will give,* and know whom I give it to, why should I leave it to be gathered by I know not whom, that will never thank me.' But trust God's providence with the disposal of thy charity, perhaps that will direct it to the most necessitous." Or, "Thou mayest reasonably think it will come to the hands of the most industrious, that are forward to seek and gather that which this law provides for them." 3. "Say not, 'What should the poor do with grapes and olives? It is enough for them to have bread and water;' for, since they have the same senses that the rich have, why should not they have some little share of the delights of sense?" Boaz ordered handfuls of corn to be left on purpose for Ruth, and God blessed him. All that is left is not lost.

CHAP. XXV.

Here is, I. A law to moderate the scourging of malefactors, ver. 1—3. II. A law in favour of the ox that treads out the corn, ver. 4. III. For the disgracing of him that refused to marry his brother's widow, ver. 5—10. IV. For the punishment of an immodest woman, ver. 11, 12. V. For just weights and measures, ver. 13—16. VI. For the destroying of Amalek, ver. 17, &c.

IF there be a controversy between men, and they come unto judgment, that *the judges* may judge them; then they shall justify the righteous, and condemn the wicked. 2 And it shall be, if the wicked man *be* worthy to be beaten, that the judge shall cause him to lie down, and to be beaten before his face, according to his fault, by a certain number. 3 Forty stripes he may give him, *and* not exceed: lest, *if* he should exceed, and beat him above these with many stripes, then thy brother should seem vile unto thee. 4 Thou shalt not muzzle the ox when he treadeth out *the corn.*

Here is, I. A direction to the judges in scourging malefactors, *v.* 1—3. 1. It is here supposed that, if a man be charged with a crime, the accuser and the accused *(Actor* and *Reus)* should be brought face to face before the judges, that the controversy may be determined. 2. If a man were accused of a crime, and the proof fell short, so that the charge could not be made out against him by the evidence, then he was to be acquitted: "*Thou shalt justify the righteous,*" that is, "him that appears to the court to be so." If the accusation be proved, then the conviction of the accused is a justification of the accuser, as righteous in the prosecution. 3. If the accused were found guilty, judgment must be given against him: "Thou shalt *condemn the wicked;*" for to justify the wicked is as much an abomination to the Lord as it is to condemn the righteous, Prov. xvii. 15. 4. If the crime were not made capital by the law, then the criminal must be beaten. A great many precepts we have met with which have not any particular penalty annexed to them, the violation of most of which, according to the constant practice of the Jews, was punished by scourging, from which no person's rank or quality did exempt him if he were a delinquent, but with this proviso, that he should never be upbraided with it, nor should it be looked upon as leaving any mark of infamy or disgrace upon him. The directions here given for the

826

scourging of criminals are, (1.) That it be done solemnly; not tumultuously through the streets, but in open court before the judge's face, and with so much deliberation as that the stripes might be numbered. The Jews say that while execution was in doing the chief justice of the court read with a loud voice Deut. xxviii. 58, 59, and xxix. 9, and concluded with those words (Ps. lxxviii. 38), *But he, being full of compassion, forgave their iniquity.* Thus it was made a sort of religious act, and so much the more likely to reform the offender himself and to be a warning to others. (2.) That it be done in proportion to the crime, *according to his fault,* that some crimes might appear, as they are, more heinous than others, the criminal being *beaten with many stripes,* to which perhaps there is an allusion, Luke xii. 47, 48. (3.) That how great soever the crime were the number of stripes should never exceed *forty, v.* 3. Forty *save one* was the common usage, as appears, 2 Cor. xi. 24. It seems, they always gave Paul as many stripes as ever they gave to any malefactor whatsoever. They abated one for fear of having miscounted (though one of the judges was appointed to number the stripes), or because they would never go to the utmost rigour, or because the execution was usually done with a whip of three lashes, so that thirteen stripes (each one being counted for three) made up thirty-nine, but one more by that reckoning would have been forty-two. The reason given for this is, *lest thy brother should seem vile unto thee.* He must still be looked upon as *a brother* (2 Thess. iii. 15), and his reputation as such was preserved by this merciful limitation of his punishment. It saves him from seeming vile to his brethren, when God himself by his law takes this care of him. Men must not be treated as dogs; nor must those seem vile in our sight to whom, for aught we know, God may yet give grace to make them precious in his sight.

II. A charge to husbandmen not to hinder their cattle from eating when they were working, if meat were within their reach, *v.* 4. This instance of the beast that trod out the corn (to which there is an allusion in that of the prophet, Hos. x. 11) is put for all similar instances. That which makes this law very remarkable above its fellows (and which countenances the like application of other such laws) is that it is twice quoted in the New Testament to show that it is the duty of the people to give their ministers a comfortable maintenance, 1 Cor. ix. 9, 10, and 1 Tim. v. 17, 18. It teaches us in the letter of it to make much of the brute-creatures that serve us, and to allow them not only the necessary supports for their life, but the advantages of their labour; and thus we must learn not only to be just, but kind, to all that are employed for our good, not only to maintain but to encourage them, especially those that labour among us in the word and doctrine, and so are employed for the good of our better part.

5 If brethren dwell together, and one of them die, and have no child, the wife of the dead shall not marry without unto a stranger: her husband's brother shall go in unto her, and take her to him to wife, and perform the duty of a husband's brother unto her. 6 And it shall be, *that* the firstborn which she beareth shall succeed in the name of his brother *which is* dead, that his name be not put out of Israel. 7 And if the man like not to take his brother's wife, then let his brother's wife go up to the gate unto the elders, and say, My husband's brother refuseth to raise up unto his brother a name in Israel, he will not perform the duty of my husband's brother. 8 Then the elders of his city shall call him, and speak unto him: and if he stand *to it*, and say, I like not to take her; 9 Then shall his brother's wife come unto him in the presence of the elders, and loose his shoe from off his foot, and spit in his face, and shall answer and say, So shall it be done unto that man that will not build up his brother's house. 10 And his name shall be called in Israel, The house of him that hath his shoe loosed. 11 When men strive together one with another, and the wife of the one draweth near for to deliver her husband out of the hand of him that smiteth him, and putteth forth her hand, and taketh him by the secrets: 12 Then thou shalt cut off her hand, thine eye shall not pity *her*.

Here is, I. The law settled concerning the marrying of a brother's widow. It appears from the story of Judah's family that this had been an ancient usage (Gen. xxxviii. 8), for the keeping up of distinct families. The case put is a case that often happens, of a man's dying without issue, it may be in the prime of his time, soon after his marriage, and while his brethren were yet so young as to be unmarried. Now in this case, 1. The widow was not to marry again into any other family, unless all the relations of her husband did refuse her, that the estate she was endowed with might not be alienated. 2. The husband's brother, or next of kin, must marry her, partly out of respect to her, who, having forgotten her own people and her father's house, should have all possible kindness shown her by the family into which she was married; and partly out of respect to the deceased husband, that though he was dead and gone he might not be forgotten, nor lost out of the genealogies of his tribe; for the first-born child, which the brother or next kinsman should have by the widow, should be denominated from him that was dead, and entered in the genealogy as his child, v. 5, 6. Under that dispensation we have reason to think men had not so clear and certain a prospect of living themselves on the other side death as we have now, to whom *life and immortality are brought to light by the gospel;* and therefore they could not but be the more desirous to live in their posterity, which innocent desire was in some measure gratified by this law, an expedient being found out that, though a man had no child by his wife, yet *his name should not be put out of Israel,* that is, out of the pedigree, or, which is equivalent, remain there under the brand of childlessness. The Sadducees put a case to our Saviour upon this law, with a design to perplex the doctrine of the resurrection by it (Matt. xxii. 24, &c.), perhaps insinuating that there was no need of maintaining the immortality of the soul and a future state, since the law had so well provided for the perpetuating of men's names and families in the world. But, 3. If the brother, or next of kin, declined to do this good office to the memory of him that was gone, what must be done in that case? Why, (1.) He shall not be compelled to do it, v. 7. If he like her not, he is at liberty to refuse her, which, some think, was not permitted in this case before this law of Moses. Affection is all in all to the comfort of the conjugal relation; this is a thing which cannot be forced, and therefore the relation should not be forced without it. (2.) Yet he shall be publicly disgraced for not doing it. The widow, as the person most concerned for the name and honour of the deceased, was to complain to the elders of his refusal; if he persist in it, she must *pluck off his shoe, and spit in his face,* in open court (or, as the Jewish doctors moderate it, spit *before* his face), thus to fasten a mark of infamy upon him, which was to remain with his family after him, v. 8—10. Note, Those justly suffer in their own reputation who do not do what they ought to preserve the name and honour of others. He that would not build up his brother's house deserved to have this blemish put upon his own, that it should be called *the house of him that had his shoe loosed,* in token that he deserved to go barefoot. In the case of Ruth we find this law executed (Ruth iv. 7), but because, upon the refusal of the next kinsman, there was another ready to perform the duty of a husband's brother, it was that other that plucked off the shoe, and not the widow—Boaz, and not Ruth.

II. A law for the punishing of an immodest

woman, *v.* 11, 12. The woman that by the foregoing law was to complain against her husband's brother for not marrying her, and to spit in his face before the elders, needed a good measure of assurance; but, lest the confidence which that law supported should grow to an excess unbecoming the sex, here is a very severe but just law to punish impudence and immodesty. 1. The instance of it is confessedly scandalous to the highest degree. A woman could not do it unless she were perfectly lost to all virtue and honour. 2. The occasion is such as might in part excuse it; it was to help her husband out of the hands of one that was too hard for him. Now if the doing of it in a passion, and with such a good intention, was to be so severely punished, much more when it was done wantonly and in lust. 3. The punishment was that her hand should be cut off; and the magistrates must not pretend to be more merciful than God: *Thy eye shall not pity her.* Perhaps our Saviour alludes to this law when he commands us to *cut off the right hand* that *offends us,* or is an occasion of sin to us. Better put the greatest hardships that can be upon the body than ruin the soul for ever. Modesty is the hedge of chastity, and therefore ought to be very carefully preserved and kept up by both sexes.

13 Thou shalt not have in thy bag divers weights, a great and a small. 14 Thou shalt not have in thine house divers measures, a great and a small. 15 *But* thou shalt have a perfect and just weight, a perfect and just measure shalt thou have: that thy days may be lengthened in the land which the Lord thy God giveth thee. 16 For all that do such things, *and* all that do unrighteously, *are* an abomination unto the Lord thy God. 17 Remember what Amalek did unto thee by the way, when ye were come forth out of Egypt; 18 How he met thee by the way, and smote the hindmost of thee, *even* all *that were* feeble behind thee, when thou *wast* faint and weary; and he feared not God. 19 Therefore it shall be, when the Lord thy God hath given thee rest from all thine enemies round about, in the land which the Lord thy God giveth thee *for* an inheritance to possess it, *that* thou shalt blot out the remembrance of Amalek from under heaven; thou shalt not forget *it.*

Here is, I. A law against deceitful weights and measures: they must not only not use them, but they must not have them, not have them in the bag, not have them in the house

(*v.* 13, 14); for, if they had them, they would be strongly tempted to use them. They must not have a great weight and measure to buy by and a small one to sell by, for that was to cheat both ways, when either was bad enough; as we read of those that made the *ephah* small, in which they measured the corn they sold, and the *shekel* great, by which they weighed the money they received for it, Amos viii. 5. But *thou shalt have a perfect and just weight, v.* 15. That which is the rule of justice must itself be just; if that be otherwise, it is a constant cheat. This had been taken care of before, Lev. xix. 35, 36. This law is enforced with two very good reasons:—1. That justice and equity will bring down upon us the blessing of God. The way to have our days lengthened, and to prosper, is to be just and fair in all our dealings. *Honesty is the best policy.* 2. That fraud and injustice will expose us to the curse of God, *v.* 16. Not only unrighteousness itself, but all that do unrighteously, are an *abomination to the Lord.* And miserable is that man who is abhorred by his Maker. How hateful, particularly, all the arts of deceit are to God, Solomon several times observes, Prov. xi. 1; xx. 10, 23; and the apostle tells us *that the Lord is the avenger of all such* as overreach and *defraud in any matter,* 1 Thess. iv. 6.

II. A law for the rooting out of Amalek. Here is a *just weight* and a *just measure,* that, as Amalek had *measured* to Israel, so it should be measured to Amalek again.

1. The mischief Amalek did to Israel must be here remembered, *v.* 17, 18. When it was first done it was ordered to be recorded (Exod. xvii. 14—16), and here the remembrance of it is ordered to be preserved, not in personal revenge (for that generation which suffered by the Amalekites was gone, so that those who now lived, and their posterity, could not have any personal resentment of the injury), but in a zeal for the glory of God (which was insulted by the Amalekites), that *throne of the Lord* against which the hand of Amalek was stretched out. The carriage of the Amalekites towards Israel is here represented, (1.) As very base and disingenuous. They had no occasion at all to quarrel with Israel, nor did they give them any notice, by a manifesto or declaration of war; but took them at an advantage, when they had just come out of the house of bondage, and, for aught that appeared to them, were only going to *sacrifice to God in the wilderness.* (2.) As very barbarous and cruel; for they smote those that were more feeble, whom they should have succoured. The greatest cowards are commonly the most cruel; while those that have the courage of a man will have the compassion of a man. (3.) As very impious and profane: they feared not God. If they had had any reverence for the majesty of the God of Israel, which they saw a token of in the cloud, or any dread of his

wrath, which they lately heard of the power of over Pharaoh, they durst not have made this assault upon Israel. Well, here was the ground of the quarrel : and it shows how God takes what is done against his people as done against himself, and that he will particularly reckon with those that discourage and hinder young beginners in religion, that (as Satan's agents) set upon the weak and feeble, either to divert them or to disquiet them, and offend his little ones.

2. This mischief must in due time be revenged, *v.* 19. When their wars were finished, by which they were to settle their kingdom and enlarge their coast, then they must *make war upon Amalek* (*v.* 19), not merely to chase them, but to consume them, to *blot out the remembrance of Amalek.* It was an instance of God's patience that he deferred the vengeance so long, which should have led the Amalekites to repentance ; yet an instance of fearful retribution that the posterity of Amalek, so long after, were destroyed for the mischief done by their ancestors to the Israel of God, that all the world might see, and say, that he who *toucheth them toucheth the apple of his eye.* It was nearly 400 years after this' that Saul was ordered to put this sentence in execution (1 Sam. xv.), and was rejected of God because he did not do it effectually, but spared some of that devoted nation, in contempt, not only of the particular orders he received from Samuel, but of this general command here given by Moses, which he could not be ignorant of. David afterwards made some destruction of them ; and the Simeonites, in Hezekiah's time, smote the rest that remained (1 Chron. iv. 43) ; for when God judges he will overcome.

CHAP. XXVI.

With this chapter Moses concludes the particular statutes which he thought fit to give Israel in charge at his parting with them ; what follows is by way of sanction and ratification. In this chapter, I. Moses gives them a form of confession to be made by him that offered the basket of his first-fruits, ver. 1–11. II. The protestation and prayer to be made after the disposal of the third year's tithe, ver. 12 15. III. He binds on all the precepts he had given them, 1. By the divine authority: "Not I, but the Lord thy God has commanded thee to do these statutes," ver. 16. 2. By the mutual covenant between God and them, ver. 17, &c.

AND it shall be, when thou *art* come in unto the land which the Lord thy God giveth thee *for* an inheritance, and possessest it, and dwellest therein ; 2 That thou shalt take of the first of all the fruit of the earth, which thou shalt bring of thy land that the Lord thy God giveth thee, and shalt put *it* in a basket, and shalt go unto the place which the Lord thy God shall choose to place his name there. 3 And thou shalt go unto the priest that shall be in those days, and say unto him, I profess this day unto the Lord thy God, that I am come unto the country which the

Lord sware unto our fathers for to give us. 4 And the priest shall take the basket out of thine hand, and set it down before the altar of the Lord thy God. 5 And thou shalt speak and say before the Lord thy God, A Syrian ready to perish *was* my father, and he went down into Egypt, and sojourned there with a few, and became there a nation, great, mighty, and populous : 6 And the Egyptians evil entreated us, and afflicted us, and laid upon us hard bondage : 7 And when we cried unto the Lord God of our fathers, the Lord heard our voice, and looked on our affliction, and our labour, and our oppression : 8 And the Lord brought us forth out of Egypt with a mighty hand, and with an outstretched arm, and with great terribleness, and with signs, and with wonders : 9 And he hath brought us into this place, and hath given us this land, *even* a land that floweth with milk and honey. 10 And now, behold, I have brought the firstfruits of the land, which thou, O Lord, hast given me. And thou shalt set it before the Lord thy God, and worship before the Lord thy God : 11 And thou shalt rejoice in every good *thing* which the Lord thy God hath given unto thee, and unto thine house, thou, and the Levite, and the stranger that *is* among you.

Here is, I. A good work ordered to be done, and that is the presenting of a basket of their first-fruits to God every year, *v.* 1, 2. Besides the *sheaf of first-fruits,* which was offered for the whole land, on the morrow after the passover (Lev. xxiii. 10), every man was to bring for himself a basket of first-fruits at the feast of pentecost, when the harvest was ended, which is therefore called the *feast of first-fruits* (Exod. xxxiv. 22), and is said to be kept with a *tribute of free-will-offering,* Deut. xvi. 10. But the Jews say, "The first-fruits, if not brought then, might be brought any time after, between that and winter." When a man went into the field or vineyard at the time when the fruits were ripening, he was to mark that which he observed most forward, and to lay it by for first-fruits, wheat, barley, grapes, figs, pomegranates, olives, and dates, some of each sort must be put in the same basket, with leaves between them, and presented to God in the place which he should choose. Now from this law we may learn, 1. To acknowledge

829

God as the giver of all those good things which are the support and comfort of our natural life, and therefore to serve and honour him with them. 2. To deny ourselves. What is first ripe we are most fond of; those that are nice and curious expect to be served with each fruit at its first coming in. *My soul desired the first ripe fruits,* Micah vii. 1. When therefore God appointed them to lay those by for him he taught them to prefer the glorifying of his name before the gratifying of their own appetites and desires. 3. To give to God the first and best we have, as those that believe him to be the first and best of beings. Those that consecrate the days of their youth, and the prime of their time, to the service and honour of God, bring him their first-fruits, and with such offerings he is well pleased. *I remember the kindness of thy youth.*

II. Good words put into their mouths be said in the doing of this good work, as an explication of the meaning of this ceremony, that it might be a reasonable service. The offerer must begin his acknowledgment before he delivered his basket to the priest, and then must go on with it, when the priest had set down the basket before the altar, as a present to God their great landlord, v. 3, 4.

1. He must begin with a receipt in full for the good land which God had given them (v. 3): *I profess that I have come* now at last, after forty years' wandering, *unto the country which the Lord swore to give us.* This was most proper to be said when they came first into Canaan; probably when they had been long settled there they varied from this form. Note, When God has made good his promises to us he expects that we should own it, to the honour of his faithfulness; this is like giving up the bond, as Solomon does, 1 Kings viii. 56, *There has not failed one word of all his good promise.* And our creature-comforts are doubly sweet to us when we see them flowing from the fountain of the promise.

2. He must remember and own the mean origin of that nation of which he was a member. How great soever they were now, and he himself with them, their beginning was very small, which ought thus to be kept in mind throughout all the ages of their church by this public confession, that they might not be proud of their privileges and advantages, but might for ever be thankful to that God whose grace chose them when they were so low and raised them so high. Two things they must own for this purpose:—(1.) The meanness of their common ancestor : *A Syrian ready to perish was my father, v. 5.* Jacob is here called an *Aramite,* or *Syrian,* because he lived twenty years in Padan-Aram; his wives were of that country, and his children were all born there, except Benjamin; and perhaps the confessor means not Jacob himself, but that son of Jacob who was the father of his tribe. However it be, both father and sons were more than once ready to

830

perish, by Laban's severity, Esau's cruelty, and the famine in the land, which last was the occasion of their going down into Egypt. *Laban the Syrian sought to destroy my father* (so the Chaldee), *had almost destroyed him,* so the Arabic. (2.) The miserable condition of their nation in its infancy. They sojourned in Egypt as strangers, they served there as slaves (v. 6), and that a great while : as their father was called a *Syrian,* they might be called *Egyptians;* so that their possession of Canaan being so long discontinued they could not pretend any tenant-right to it. A poor, despised, oppressed people they were in Egypt, and therefore, though now rich and great, had no reason to be proud, or secure, or forgetful of God.

3. He must thankfully acknowledge God's great goodness, not only to himself in particular, but to Israel in general. (1.) In bringing them out of Egypt, v. 7, 8. It is spoken of here as an act of pity—*he looked on our affliction,* and an act of power—he *brought us forth with a mighty hand.* This was a great salvation, fit to be remembered upon all occasions, and particularly upon this; they need not grudge to bring a basket of first-fruits to God, for to him they owed it that they were not now bringing in the tale of bricks to their cruel task-masters. (2.) In settling them in Canaan: *He hath given us this land, v. 9.* Observe, He must not only give thanks for his own lot, but for the land in general which was given to Israel; not only for this year's profits, but for the ground itself which produced them, which God had graciously granted to his ancestors and entailed upon his posterity. Note, The comfort we have in particular enjoyments should lead us to be thankful for our share in public peace and plenty; and with present mercies we should bless God for the former mercies we remember and the further mercies we expect and hope for.

4. He must offer to God his basket of first-fruits (v. 10): " I have *brought the first-fruits of the land* (like a pepper-corn), as a quit-rent *for the land which thou hast given me."* Note, Whatever we give to God, it is but of his own that we give him, 1 Chron. xxix. 14. And it becomes us, who receive so much from him, to study what we shall render to him. The basket he set before God; and the priests, as God's receivers, had the first-fruits, as perquisites of their place and fees for attending, Num. xviii. 12.

III. The offerer is here appointed, when he has finished the service, 1. To give glory to God : *Thou shalt worship the Lord thy God.* His first-fruits were not accepted without further acts of adoration. A humble, reverent, thankful heart is that which God looks at and requires, and, without this, all we can put in a basket will not avail. *If a man would give all the substance of his house* to be excused from this, or in lieu of it, *it would utterly be contemned.* 2. To take the comfort of it to himself and family : *Thou shalt rejoice in every good thing, v.* 11. It is the will of God that we should be cheerful, not only in our attendance upon his holy ordinances, but in our enjoyments of the gifts of his providence. Whatever good thing God gives us, it is his will that we should make the most comfortable use we can of it, yet still tracing the streams to the fountain of all comfort and consolation.

12 When thou hast made an end of tithing all the tithes of thine increase the third year, *which is* the year of tithing, and hast given *it* unto the Levite, the stranger, the fatherless, and the widow, that they may eat within thy gates, and be filled ; 13 Then thou shalt say before the LORD thy God, I have brought away the hallowed things out of *mine* house, and also have given them unto the Levite, and unto the stranger, to the fatherless, and to the widow, according to all thy commandments which thou hast commanded me : I have not transgressed thy commandments, neither have I forgotten *them :* 14 I have not eaten thereof in my mourning, neither have I taken away *aught* thereof for *any* unclean *use,* nor given *aught* thereof for the dead : *but* I have hearkened to the voice of the LORD my God, *and* have done according to all that thou hast commanded me. 15 Look down from thy holy habitation, from heaven, and bless thy people Israel, and the land which thou hast given us, as thou swarest unto our fathers, a land that floweth with milk and honey.

Concerning the disposal of their tithe the third year we had the law before, *ch.* xiv. 28, 29. The second tithe, which in the other two years was to be spent in extraordinaries at the feasts, was to be spent the third year at home, in entertaining the poor. Now because this was done from under the eye of the priests, and a great confidence was put in the people's honesty, that they would dispose of it according to the law, to *the Levite, the stranger, and the fatherless (v.* 12), it is therefore required that when at the next feast after they appeared *before the Lord* they should there testify (as it were) upon oath, in a religious manner, that they had fully administered, and been true to their trust.

I. They must make a solemn protestation to this purport, *v.* 13, 14. 1. That no hallowed things were hoarded up : " *I have brought them away out of my house,* nothing now remains there but my own part." 2.

That the poor, and particularly poor ministers, poor strangers, and poor widows, had had their part according to the commandment. It is fit that God, who by his providence gives us all we have, should by his law direct the using of it, and, though we are not now under such particular appropriations of our revenue as they then were, yet, in general, we are commanded to give alms of such things as we have ; and then, and not otherwise, all things are clean to us. *Then* we may take the comfort of our enjoyments, when God has thus had his dues out of them. This is a commandment which must not be transgressed, no, not with an excuse of its being forgotten, *v.* 13. 3. That none of this tithe had been misapplied to any common use, much less to any ill use. This seems to refer to the tithe of the other two years, which was to be eaten by the owners themselves ; they must profess, (1.) That they had not eaten of it in their mourning, when, by their mourning for the dead, they were commonly unclean ; or they had not eaten of it grudgingly, as those that all their days eat in darkness. (2.) That they had not sacrilegiously alienated it to any common use, for it was not their own. And, (3.) That they had not given it for the dead, for the honour of their dead gods, or in hope of making it beneficial to their dead friends. Now the obliging of them to make this solemn protestation at the three years' end would be an obligation upon them to deal faithfully, knowing that they must be called upon thus to purge themselves. It is our wisdom to keep conscience clear at all times, that when we come to give up our account we may lift up our face without spot. The Jews say that this protestation of their integrity was to be made with a low voice, because it looked like a self-commendation, but that the foregoing confession of God's goodness was to be made with a loud voice to his glory. He that durst not make this protestation must bring his *trespass-offering,* Lev. v. 15.

II. To this solemn protestation they must add a *solemn prayer (v.* 15), not particularly for themselves, but for *God's people Israel ;* for in the common peace and prosperity every particular person prospers and has peace. We must learn hence to be public-spirited in prayer, and to wrestle with God for blessings for the land and nation, our English Israel, and for the universal church, which we are directed to have an eye to in our prayers, as the *Israel of God,* Gal. vi. 16. In this prayer we are taught, 1. To look up to God as in a holy habitation, and thence to infer that holiness becomes his house, and that he will be sanctified in those that are about him. 2. To depend upon the favour of God, and his gracious cognizance, as sufficient to make us and our people happy. 3. To reckon it wonderful condescension in God to cast an eye even upon so great and honourable a body as Israel was. It is looking down. 4. To be earnest with God for a blessing upon his people Israel, and upon the *land which he has given us.* For how should the earth yield its increase, or, if it does, what comfort can we take in it, unless therewith *God, even our own God, gives us his blessing?* Ps. lxvii. 6.

16 This day the LORD thy God hath commanded thee to do these statutes and judgments: thou shalt therefore keep and do them with all thine heart, and with all thy soul. 17 Thou hast avouched the LORD this day to be thy God, and to walk in his ways, and to keep his statutes, and his commandments, and his judgments, and to hearken unto his voice: 18 And the LORD hath avouched thee this day to be his peculiar people, as he hath promised thee, and that *thou* shouldest keep all his commandments; 19 And to make thee high above all nations which he hath made, in praise, and in name, and in honour; and that thou mayest be a holy people unto the LORD thy God, as he hath spoken.

Two things Moses here urges to enforce all these precepts:—1. That they were the commands of God, *v.* 16. They were not the dictates of his own wisdom, nor were they enacted by any authority of his own, but infinite wisdom framed them, and the power of the King of kings made them binding to them: "*The Lord thy God commands thee,* therefore thou art bound in duty and gratitude to obey him, and it is at thy peril if thou disobey. They are his laws, therefore thou shalt do them, for to that end were they given thee: do them and not dispute them, do them and not draw back from them; do them not carelessly and hypocritically, but with thy heart and soul, thy whole heart and thy whole soul." 2. That their covenant with God obliged them to keep these commands. He insists not only upon God's sovereignty over them, but his propriety in them, and the relation wherein they stood to him. The covenant is mutual, and it binds to obedience both ways. (1.) That we may perform our part of the covenant, and answer the intentions of that (*v.* 17): "*Thou hast avouched* and solemnly owned and confessed the *Lord Jehovah to be thy God,* thy Prince and Ruler. As he is so by an incontestable right, so he is by thy own consent." They did this implicitly by their attendance on his word, had done it expressly (Exod. xxiv.), and were now to do it again before they parted, *ch.* xxix. 1. Now this obliges us, in fidelity to our word, as well as in duty to our Sovereign, to *keep his statutes and his commandments.* We really forswear ourselves, and perfidiously violate the most sacred engagements, if, when we have taken the Lord to be our God, we do not make conscience of obeying his commands. (2.) That God's part of the covenant also may be made good, and the intentions of that answered (*v.* 18, 19): The *Lord has avouched,* not only taken, but publicly owned thee to be his *segullah,* his *peculiar people, as he has promised thee,* that is, according to the true intent and meaning of the promise. Now their obedience was not only the condition of this favour, and of the continuance of it (if they were not obedient, God would disown them, and cast them off), but it was also the principal design of this favour. "He has avouched thee on purpose *that thou shouldest keep his commandments,* that thou mightest have both the best directions and the best encouragements in religion." Thus we are *elected to obedience* (1 Pet. i. 2), *chosen that we should be holy* (Eph. i. 4), purified, a peculiar people, that we might not only do good works, but be zealous in them, Tit. ii. 14. Two things God is here said to design in avouching them to be his peculiar people (*v.* 19), to make them high, and, in order to that, to make them holy; for holiness is true honour, and the only way to everlasting honour. [1.] To make them high above all nations. The greatest honour we are capable of in this world is to be taken into covenant with God, and to live in his service. They should be, *First,* High *in praise;* for God would accept them, which is true praise, Rom. ii. 29. Their friends would admire them, Ps. xlviii. 2. Their enemies would envy them, Zeph. iii. 19, 20. *Secondly,* High *in name,* which, some think, denotes the continuance and perpetuity of that praise, *a name that shall not be cut off. Thirdly,* High *in honour,* that is, in all the advantages of wealth and power, which would make them great above their neighbours. See Jer. xiii. 11. [2.] That they might be a holy people, separated for God, devoted to him, and employed continually in his service. This God aimed at in taking them to be his people; so that, if they did not keep his commandments, they received all this grace in vain.

CHAP. XXVII.

Moses having very largely and fully set before the people their duty, both to God and one another, in general and in particular instances, —having shown them plainly what is good, and what the law requires of them,—and having in the close of the foregoing chapter laid them under the obligation both of the command and the covenant, he comes in this chapter to prescribe outward means, I. For the helping of their memories, that they might not forget the law as a strange thing. They must write all the words of this law upon stones, ver. 1—10. II. For the moving of their affections, that they might not be indifferent to the law as a light thing. When they came into Canaan, the blessings and curses which were the sanctions of the law, were to be solemnly pronounced in the hearing of all Israel, who were to say Amen to them, ver. 11—26. And if such a solemnity as this would not make a deep impression upon them, and affect them with the great things of God's law, nothing would.

AND Moses with the elders of Israel commanded the people, saying, Keep all the commandments which I command you this day. 2 And it shall be on the day when ye shall pass over Jordan unto the land which the LORD thy God giveth thee, that thou

832

shalt set thee up great stones, and plaster them with plaster: 3 And thou shalt write upon them all the words of this law, when thou art passed over, that thou mayest go in unto the land which the LORD thy God giveth thee, a land that floweth with milk and honey; as the LORD God of thy fathers hath promised thee. 4 Therefore it shall be when ye be gone over Jordan, *that* ye shall set up these stones, which I command you this day, in mount Ebal, and thou shalt plaster them with plaster. 5 And there shalt thou build an altar unto the LORD thy God, an altar of stones: thou shalt not lift up *any* iron *tool* upon them. 6 Thou shalt build the altar of the LORD thy God of whole stones: and thou shalt offer burnt offerings thereon unto the LORD thy God: 7 And thou shalt offer peace offerings, and shalt eat there, and rejoice before the LORD thy God. 8 And thou shalt write upon the stones all the words of this law very plainly. 9 And Moses and the priests the Levites spake unto all Israel, saying, take heed, and hearken, O Israel; this day thou art become the people of the LORD thy God. 10 Thou shalt therefore obey the voice of the LORD thy God, and do his commandments and his statutes, which I command thee this day.

Here is, I. A general charge to the people to keep God's commandments; for in vain did they know them, unless they would do them. This is pressed upon them, 1. With all authority. *Moses with the elders of Israel,* the rulers of each tribe (*v.* 1), and again, *Moses and the priests the Levites* (*v.* 9); so that the charge is given by Moses who was king in Jeshurun, and by their lords, both spiritual and temporal, in concurrence with him. Lest they should think that it was Moses only, an old and dying man, that made such ado about religion, or the priests and Levites only, whose trade it was to attend religion and who had their maintenance out of it, the elders of Israel, whom God had placed in honour and power over them, and who were men of business in the world and likely to be long so when Moses was gone, *they* commanded their people to *keep God's law.* Moses, having put some of his honour upon them, joins them in commission with himself, in giving this charge, as Paul sometimes in his epistles joins with himself Sil-

vanus and Timotheus. Note, All that have any interest in others, or power over them, should use it for the support and furtherance of religion among them. Though the supreme power of a nation provide ever so good laws for this purpose, if inferior magistrates in their places, and ministers in theirs, and masters of families in theirs, do not execute their offices, it will all be to little effect. 2. With all importunity. They press it upon them with the utmost earnestness (*v.* 9, 10): *Take heed and hearken, O Israel.* It is a thing that requires and deserves the highest degree of caution and attention. They tell them of their privilege and honour: " *This day thou hast become the people of the Lord thy God,* the Lord having avouched thee to be his own, and being now about to put thee in possession of Canaan which he had long promised as *thy God* (Gen. xvii. 7, 8), and which if he had failed to do in due time, he would have been ashamed to be called thy God, Heb. xi. 16. Now thou art more than ever his people, therefore *obey his voice.*" Privileges should be improved as engagements to duty. Should not a people be ruled by their God?

II. A particular direction to them with great solemnity to register *the words of this law,* as soon as they came into Canaan. It was to be done but once, and at their entrance into the land of promise, in token of their taking possession of it under the several provisos and conditions contained in this law. There was a solemn ratification of the covenant between God and Israel at Mount Sinai, when an altar was erected, with twelve pillars, and the book of the covenant was produced, Exod. xxiv. 4. That which is here appointed is a somewhat similar solemnity.

1. They must set up a monument on which they must *write the words of this law.* (1.) The monument itself was to be very mean, only rough unhewn stone plastered over; not polished marble or alabaster, nor brass tables, but common plaster upon stone, *v.* 2. The command is repeated (*v.* 4), and orders are given that it be written, not very finely, to be admired by the curious, but very plainly, that he who runs may read it, Hab ii. 2. The word of God needs not to be set off by the art of man, nor embellished with the *enticing words of man's wisdom.* But, (2.) The inscription was to be very great· *All the words of this law, v.* 3, and again, *v.* 8. Some understand it only of the covenant between God and Israel, mentioned *ch.* xxvi. 17, 18. Let this heap be set up for a witness, like that memorial of the covenant between Laban and Jacob, which was nothing but a heap of stones thrown hastily together, upon which they did eat together in token of friendship (Gen. xxxi. 46, 47), and that stone which Joshua set up, Josh. xxiv. 26. Others think that the curses of the covenant in this chapter were written upon this monument, the rather because it was set up in Mount

Ebal, *v.* 4. Others think that the whole book of Deuteronomy was written upon this monument, or at least the statutes and judgments from *ch.* xii. to the end of *ch.* xxvi. And it is not improbable that the heap might be so large as, taking in all the sides of it, to contain so copious an inscription, unless we will suppose (as some do) that the ten commandments only were here written, as an authentic copy of the close rolls which were laid up in the ark. They must write this when they had gone into Canaan, and yet Moses says (*v.* 3), " *Write it that thou mayest go in,*" that is, "that thou mayest go in with comfort, and assurance of success and settlement, otherwise it were well for thee not to go in at all. Write it as the conditions of thy entry, and own that thou comest in upon these terms and no other: since Canaan is given by promise, it must be held by obedience."

2. They must also set up an altar. By the words of the law which were written upon the plaster, God *spoke to them ;* by the altar, and the sacrifices offered upon it, they spoke to God; and thus was communion kept up between them and God. The word and prayer must go together. Though they might not, of their own heads, set up any altar besides that at the tabernacle, yet, by the appointment of God, they might upon a special occasion. Elijah built a temporary altar of twelve unhewn stones, similar to this, when he brought Israel back to the covenant which was now made, 1 Kings xviii. 31, 32. Now, (1.) This altar must be made of such stones as they found ready upon the field, not newly cut out of the rock, much less squared artificially : *Thou shalt not lift up any iron tool upon them, v.* 5. Christ, our altar, is a *stone cut out of the mountain without hands* (Dan. ii. 34, 35), and therefore *refused by the builders,* as having no form or comeliness, but accepted of God the Father, and made the head of the corner. (2.) Burnt-offerings and peace-offerings must be offered upon this altar (*v.* 6, 7), that by them they might give glory to God and obtain favour. Where the law was written, an altar was set up close by it, to signify that we could not look with any comfort upon the law, being conscious to ourselves of the violation of it, if it were not for the great sacrifice by which atonement is made for sin ; and the altar was set up on Mount Ebal, the mount on which those tribes stood that said *Amen* to the curses, to intimate that through Christ we are *redeemed from the curse of the law.* In the Old Testament the words of the law are written, with the curse annexed, which would fill us with horror and amazement if we had not in the New Testament (which is bound up with it) an altar erected close by it, which gives us everlasting consolation. (3.) They must eat there, and *rejoice before the Lord their God, v.* 7. This signified, [1.] The consent they gave to the covenant; for the

parties to a covenant ratified the covenant by feasting together. They were partakers of the altar, which was God's table, as his servants and tenants, and such they acknowledged themselves, and, being put in possession of this good land, bound themselves to pay the rent and to do the services reserved by the royal grant. [2.] The comfort they took in the covenant ; they had reason to rejoice in the law, when they had an altar, a remedial law, so near it. It was a great favour to them, and a token for good, that God *gave them his statutes ;* and that they were owned as the people of God, and the *children of the promise,* was what they had reason to rejoice'in, though, when this solemnity was to be performed, they were not put in full possession of Canaan ; but God has *spoken in his holiness,* and then *I will rejoice, Gilead is mine, Manasseh is mine ;* all my own.

11 And Moses charged the people the same day, saying, 12 These shall stand upon mount Gerizim to bless the people, when ye are come over Jordan ; Simeon, and Levi, and Judah, and Issachar, and Joseph, and Benjamin : 13 And these shall stand upon mount Ebal to curse ; Reuben, Gad, and Asher, and Zebulun, Dan, and Naphtali. 14 And the Levites shall speak, and say unto all the men of Israel with a loud voice, 15 Cursed *be* the man that maketh *any* graven or molten image, an abomination unto the LORD, the work of the hands of the craftsman, and putteth *it* in *a* secret *place.* And all the people shall answer and say, Amen. 16 Cursed *be* he that setteth light by his father or his mother. And all the people shall say, Amen. 17 Cursed *be* he that removeth his neighbour's landmark. And all the people shall say, Amen. 18 Cursed *be* he that maketh the blind to wander out of the way. And all the people shall say, Amen. 19 Cursed *be* he that perverteth the judgment of the stranger, fatherless, and widow. And all the people shall say, Amen. 20 Cursed *be* he that lieth with his father's wife ; because he uncovereth his father's skirt. And all the people shall say, Amen. 21 Cursed *be* he that lieth with any manner of beast. And all the people shall say, Amen. 22 Cursed *be* he that lieth with his sister, the daughter of his

father, or the daughter of his mother. And all the people shall say, Amen. 23 Cursed *be* he that lieth with his mother in law. And all the people shall say, Amen. 24 Cursed *be* he that smiteth his neighbour secretly. And all the people shall say, Amen. 25 Cursed *be* he that taketh reward to slay an innocent person. And all the people shall say, Amen. 26 Cursed *be* he that confirmeth not *all* the words of this law to do them. And all the people shall say, Amen.

When the law was written, to be *seen and read by all men*, the sanctions of it were to be published, which, to complete the solemnity of their covenanting with God, they were deliberately to declare their approbation of. This they were before directed to do (*ch.* xi. 29, 30), and therefore the appointment here begins somewhat abruptly, *v.* 12. There were, it seems, in Canaan, that part of it which afterwards fell to the lot of Ephraim (Joshua's tribe), two mountains that lay near together, with a valley between, one called *Gerizim* and the other *Ebal*. On the sides of these two mountains, which faced one another, all the tribes were to be drawn up, six on one side and six on the other, so that in the valley, at the foot of each mountain, they came pretty near together, so near as that the priests standing betwixt them might be heard by those that were next them on both sides; then when silence was proclaimed, and attention commanded, one of the priests, or perhaps more at some distance from each other, pronounced with a loud voice one of the curses here following, and all the people that stood on the side and foot of Mount Ebal (those that stood further off taking the signal from those that stood nearer and within hearing) said *Amen;* then the contrary blessing was pronounced, "Blessed is he that doth not so or so," and then those that stood on the side, and at the foot, of Mount Gerizim, said *Amen*. This could not but affect them very much with the blessings and curses, the promises and threatenings, of the law, and not only acquaint all the people with them, but teach them to apply them to themselves.

I. Something is to be observed, in general, concerning this solemnity, which was to be done but once and not repeated, but would be talked of to posterity. 1. God appointed which tribes should stand upon Mount Gerizim and which on Mount Ebal (*v.* 12, 13), to prevent the disputes that might have arisen if they had been left to dispose of themselves. The six tribes that were appointed for blessing were all the children of the free women, for to such the promise belongs, Gal. iv. 31. Levi is here put among the rest, to teach ministers to apply to them-

selves the blessing and curse which they preach to others, and by faith to set their own *Amen* to it. 2. Of those tribes that were to say *Amen* to the blessings it is said, *They stood to bless the people*, but of the other, *They stood to curse*, not mentioning the people, as loth to suppose that any of this people whom God had taken for his own should lay themselves under the curse. Or, perhaps, the different mode of expression intimates that there was to be but one blessing pronounced in general upon the people of Israel, as a happy people, and that should ever be so, *if they were obedient;* and to this blessing the tribes on Mount Gerizim were to say *Amen*— "Happy art thou, O Israel, and mayest thou ever be so;" but then the curses come in as exceptions from the general rule, and we know *exceptio firmat regulam—the exception confirms the rule*. Israel is a blessed people, but, if there be any particular persons even among them that do such and such things as are mentioned, let them know that they have no part nor lot in the matter, but are under a curse. This shows how ready God is to bestow the blessing; if any fall under the curse, they may thank themselves, they bring it upon their own heads. 3. The Levites or priests, such of them as were appointed for that purpose, were to pronounce the curses as well as the blessings. They were ordained to bless (*ch.* x. 8), the priests did it daily, Num. vi. 23. But they *must separate between the precious and the vile;* they must not give that blessing promiscuously, but must declare to whom it did not belong, lest those who had no right to it themselves should think to share in it by being in the crowd. Note, Ministers must preach the terrors of the law as well as the comforts of the gospel; must not only allure people to their duty with the promises of a blessing, but awe them to it with the threatenings of a curse. 4. The curses are here expressed, but not the blessings; for as many as were under the law were under the curse, but it was an honour reserved for Christ to bless us, and so to do that for us which *the law could not do, in that it was weak*. In Christ's sermon upon the mount, which was the true Mount Gerizim, we have blessings only, Matt. v. 3, &c. 5. To each of the curses the people were to say *Amen*. It is easy to understand the meaning of *Amen* to the blessings. The Jews have a saying to encourage people to say *Amen* to the public prayers, *Whosoever answereth* Amen, *after him that blesseth, he is as he that blesseth*. But how could they say *Amen* to the curses? (1.) It was a profession of their faith in the truth of them, that these and the like curses were not bug-bears to frighten children and fools, but the real declarations of the wrath of God against the ungodliness and unrighteousness of men, not one *iota* of which shall fall to the ground. (2.) It was an acknowledgment of the equity of these curses; when they said

Amen, they did in effect say, not only, *It is certain it shall be so,* but, *It is just it should be so.* Those who do such things deserve to fall and lie under the curse. (3.) It was such an imprecation upon themselves as strongly obliged them to have nothing to do with those evil practices upon which the curse is here entailed. " Let God's wrath fall upon us if ever we do such things." We read of those that entered into a curse (and with us that is the usual form of a solemn oath) to *walk in God's law,* Neh. x. 29. Nay, the Jews say (as the learned bishop Patrick quotes them), " All the people, by saying this *Amen,* became bound for one another, that they would observe God's laws, by which every man was obliged, as far as he could, to prevent his neighbour from breaking these laws, and to reprove those that had offended, lest they should bear sin and the curse for them."

II. Let us now observe what are the particular sins against which the curses are here denounced.

1. Sins against the second commandment. This flaming sword is set to keep that commandment first, *v.* 15. Those are here cursed, not only that worship images, but that make them or keep them, if they be such (or like such) as idolaters used in the service of their gods. Whether it be a graven image or a molten image, it comes all to one, *it is an abomination to the Lord,* even though it be not set up in public, but in a secret place,—though it be not actually worshipped, nor is it said to be designed for worship, but reserved there with respect and a constant temptation. He that does this may perhaps escape punishment from men, but he cannot escape the curse of God.

2. Against the fifth commandment, *v.* 16. The contempt of parents is a sin so heinous that it is put next to the contempt of God himself. If a man abused his parents, either in word or deed, he fell under the sentence of the magistrate, and must be *put to death,* Exod. xxi. 15, 17. But to set light by them in his heart was a thing which the magistrate could not take cognizance of, and therefore it is here laid under the curse of God, who knows the heart. Those are cursed children that carry themselves scornfully and insolently towards their parents.

3. Against the eighth commandment. The curse of God is here fastened, (1.) Upon an unjust neighbour that *removes the land-marks, v.* 17. See *ch.* xix. 14. (2.) Upon an unjust counsellor, who, when his advice is asked, maliciously directs his friend to that which he knows will be to his prejudice, which is *making the blind to wander out of the way,* under pretence of directing him in the way, than which nothing can be either more barbarous or more treacherous, *v.* 18. Those that seduce others from the way of God's commandments, and entice them to sin, bring this curse upon themselves, which our Saviour has explained, Matt. xv. 14, *The*

blind lead the blind, and both shall fall into the ditch. (3.) Upon an unjust judge, that *perverteth the judgment of the stranger, fatherless, and widow,* whom he should protect and vindicate, *v.* 19. These are supposed to be poor and friendless (nothing to be got by doing them a kindness, nor any thing lost by disobliging them), and therefore judges may be tempted to side with their adversaries against right and equity ; but cursed are such judges.

4. Against the seventh commandment. Incest is a cursed sin, with a *sister, a father's wife, or a mother-in-law, v.* 20, 22, 23. These crimes not only exposed men to the sword of the magistrate (Lev. xx. 11), but, which is more dreadful, to the wrath of God; bestiality likewise, *v.* 21.

5. Against the sixth commandment. Two of the worst kinds of murder are here specified :—(1.) Murder unseen, when a man does not set upon his neighbour as a fair adversary, giving him an opportunity to defend himself, but *smites him secretly (v.* 24), as by poison or otherwise, when he sees not who hurts him. See Ps. x. 8, 9. Though such secret murders may go undiscovered and unpunished, yet the curse of God will follow them. (2.) Murder under colour of law, which is the greatest affront to God, for it makes an ordinance of his to patronise the worst of villains, and the greatest wrong to our neighbour, for it ruins his honour as well as his life : cursed therefore is he that will be hired, or bribed, to accuse, or to convict, or to condemn, and so *to slay, an innocent person, v.* 25. See Ps. xv. 5.

6. The solemnity concludes with a general curse upon him *that confirmeth not,* or, as it might be read, that *performeth not, all the words of this law to do them, v.* 26. By our obedience to the law we set our seal to it, and so confirm it, as by our disobedience we do what lies in us to disannul it, Ps. cxix. 126. The apostle, following all the ancient versions, reads it, *Cursed is every one that continues not,* Gal. iii. 10. Lest those who were guilty of other sins, not mentioned in this commination, should think themselves safe from the curse, this last reaches all ; not only those who do the evil which the law forbids, but those also who omit the good which the law requires : to this we must all say *Amen,* owning ourselves under the curse, justly to have deserved it, and that we must certainly have perished for ever under it, if Christ had not *redeemed us from the curse of the law, by being made a curse for us.*

CHAP. XXVIII.

This chapter is a very large exposition of two words in the foregoing chapter, the blessing and the curse. Those were pronounced blessed in general that were obedient, and those cursed that were disobedient; but, because generals are not so affecting, Moses here descends to particulars, and describes the blessing and the curse, not in their fountains (these are out of sight, and therefore the most considerable, yet least considered, the favour of God the spring of all the blessings, and the wrath of God the spring of all the curses), but in their streams, the sensible effects of the blessing and the curse, for they are real things and have real effects. I. He describes the blessings that should come upon them if they were obedient; personal, family, and especially national, for in that capacity especially they are here treated with, ver. 1.—14. II. He more largely describes the curses which would come upon them if they were disobedient; such as would be, 1. Their extreme vexation, ver. 15—44. 2. Their utter ruin and destruction at last, ver. 45 – 68. This chapter is much to the same purport with Lev. xxvi., setting before them life and death, good and evil; and the promise, in the close of that chapter, of their restoration, upon their repentance, is here likewise more largely repeated, ch. xxx. Thus, as they had line upon line in the repetition of the law, so they had line upon line in the repetition of the promises and threatenings. And these are both there and here delivered, not only as sanctions of the law, what should be conditionally, but as predictions of the event, what would be certainly, that for a while the people of Israel would be happy in their obedience, but that at length they would be undone by their disobedience; and therefore it is said (ch. xxx. 1) that all those things would come upon them, both the blessing and the curse.

AND it shall come to pass, if thou shalt hearken diligently unto the voice of the LORD thy God, to observe *and* to do all his commandments which I command thee this day, that the LORD thy God will set thee on high above all nations of the earth: 2 And all these blessings shall come on thee, and overtake thee, if thou shalt hearken unto the voice of the LORD thy God. 3 Blessed *shalt* thou *be* in the city, and blessed *shalt* thou *be* in the field. 4 Blessed *shall be* the fruit of thy body, and the fruit of thy ground, and the fruit of thy cattle, the increase of thy kine, and the flocks of thy sheep. 5 Blessed *shall be* thy basket and thy store. 6 Blessed *shalt* thou *be* when thou comest in, and blessed *shalt* thou *be* when thou goest out. 7 The LORD shall cause thine enemies that rise up against thee to be smitten before thy face: they shall come out against thee one way, and flee before thee seven ways. 8 The LORD shall command the blessing upon thee in thy storehouses, and in all that thou settest thine hand unto; and he shall bless thee in the land which the LORD thy God giveth thee. 9 The LORD shall establish thee a holy people unto himself, as he hath sworn unto thee, if thou shalt keep the commandments of the LORD thy God, and walk in his ways. 10 And all people of the earth shall see that thou art called by the name of the LORD; and they shall be afraid of thee. 11 And the LORD shall make thee plenteous in goods, in the fruit of thy body, and in the fruit of thy cattle, and in the fruit of thy ground, in the land which the LORD sware unto thy fathers to give thee. 12 The LORD shall open unto thee his good treasure, the hea-

ven to give the rain unto thy land in his season, and to bless all the work of thine hand: and thou shalt lend unto many nations, and thou shalt not borrow. 13 And the LORD shall make thee the head, and not the tail; and thou shalt be above only, and thou shalt not be beneath; if that thou hearken unto the commandments of the LORD thy God, which I command thee this day, to observe and to do *them :* 14 And thou shalt not go aside from any of the words which I command thee this day, *to* the right hand, or *to* the left, to go after other gods to serve them.

The blessings are here put before the curses, to intimate, 1. That God is slow to anger, but swift to show mercy: he has said it, and sworn, that he would much rather we would obey and live than sin and die. It is his delight to bless. 2. That though both the promises and the threatenings are designed to bring and hold us to our duty, yet it is better that we be allured to that which is good by a filial hope of God's favour than that we be frightened to it by a servile fear of his wrath. That obedience pleases best which comes from a principle of delight in God's goodness. Now,

I. We have here the conditions upon which the blessing is promised. 1. It is upon condition that they *diligently hearken to the voice of God (v. 1, 2)*, that they hear God speaking to them by his word, and use their utmost endeavours to acquaint themselves with his will, v. 13. 2. Upon condition that they *observe and do all his commandments* (and in order to obedience there is need of observation) and that they *keep the commandments of God (v. 9) and walk in his ways*. Not only do them for once, but keep them for ever; not only set out in his ways, but walk in them to the end. 3. Upon condition that they should not *go aside either to the right hand or to the left,* either to superstition on the one hand or profaneness on the other; and particularly that they should not go after other gods (v. 14), which was the sin that of all others they were most prone to, and God would be most displeased with. Let them take care to keep up religion, both the form and power of it, in their families and nation, and God would not fail to bless them.

II. The particulars of this blessing. 1. It is promised that the providence of God should prosper them in all their outward concerns. These blessings are said to *overtake them, v. 2.* Good people sometimes, under the sense of their unworthiness, are ready to fly from the blessing and to conclude that it belongs not to them; but the blessing shall find them out and follow them notwithstanding.

Thus in the great day the blessing will overtake the righteous that say, Lord, *when saw we thee hungry and fed thee?* Matt. xxv. 37. Observe, (1.) Several things are enumerated in which God by his providence would bless them:— [1.] They should be safe and easy; a blessing should rest upon their persons wherever they were, *in the city* or *in the field, v.* 3. Whether their habitation was in town or country, whether they were husbandmen or tradesmen, whether their business called them into the city or into the field, they should be preserved from the dangers and have the comforts of their condition. This blessing should attend them in their journeys, going out and coming in, *v.* 6. Their persons should be protected, and the affair they went about should succeed well. Observe here, What a necessary and constant dependence we have upon God both for the continuance and comfort of this life. We need him at every turn, in all the various movements of life; we cannot be safe if he withdraw his protection, nor easy if he suspend his favour; but, if he bless us, go where we will it is well with us. [2.] Their families should be built up in a numerous issue: blessed *shall be the fruit of thy body* (*v.* 4), and in that the Lord shall *make thee plenteous* (*v.* 11), in pursuance of the promise made to Abraham, that his seed should be *as the stars of heaven* for multitude, and that God would be a God to them, than which a greater blessing, and more comprehensive, could not be entailed upon the fruit of their body. See Isa. lxi. 9. [3.] They should be rich, and have an abundance of all the good things of this life, which are promised them, not merely that they might have the pleasure of enjoying them, but (as bishop Patrick observes out of one of the Jewish writers) that they might have wherewithal to honour God, and might be helped and encouraged to serve him cheerfully and to proceed and persevere in their obedience to him. A blessing is promised, *First,* On all they had without doors, corn and cattle in the field (*v.* 4, 11), their cows and sheep particularly, which should be blessed for the owners' sakes, and made blessings to them. In order to this, it is promised that God would give them *rain in due season,* which is called his *good treasure* (*v.* 12), because with this river of God the earth is enriched, Ps. lxv. 9. Our constant supplies we must see coming from God's good treasure, and own our obligations to him for them; if he withhold his rain, the fruits both of the ground and of the cattle soon perish. *Secondly,* On all they had within doors, the basket and the store (*v.* 5), the store-houses or barns, *v.* 8. When it is brought home, God will bless it, and not blow upon it as sometimes he does, Hag. i. 6, 9. We depend upon God and his blessing, not only for our yearly corn out of the field, but for our daily bread out of our basket and store, and therefore are taught to pray for it every day. [4.] They should have success in all their employments, which would be a constant satisfaction to them: " *The Lord shall command the blessing* (and it is he only that can command it) upon thee, not only in all thou hast, but in all thou doest, all *that thou settest thy hand to,*" *v.* 8. This intimated that even when they were rich they must not be idle, but must find some good employment or other to set their hand to, and God would own their industry, and *bless the work of their hand* (*v.* 12); for that which *makes rich,* and keeps so, is *the blessing of the Lord* upon *the hand of the diligent,* Prov. x. 4, 22. [5.] They should have honour among their neighbours (*v.* 1): *The Lord thy God will set thee on high above all nations.* He made them so, by taking them into covenant with himself, *ch.* xxvi. 19. And he would make them more and more so by their outward prosperity, if they would not by sin disparage themselves. Two things should help to make them great among the nations:— *First,* Their wealth (*v.* 12): " *Thou shalt lend to many nations* upon interest " (which they were allowed to take from the neighbouring nations), but thou shalt not have occasion to borrow." This would give them great influence with all about them; for the borrower is servant to the lender. It may be meant of trade and commerce, that they should export abundantly more than they should import, which would keep the balance on their side. *Secondly,* Their power (*v.* 13): " *The Lord shall make thee the head,* to give law to all about thee, to exact tribute, and to arbitrate all controversies." Every sheaf should bow to theirs, which would make them so considerable that *all the people of the earth* would be *afraid of them* (*v.* 10), that is, would reverence their true grandeur, and dread making them their enemies. The flourishing of religion among them, and the blessing of God upon them, would make them formidable to all their neighbours, terrible as an army with banners. [6.] They should be victorious over their enemies, and prosper in all their wars. If any were so daring as to rise up against them to oppress them, or encroach upon them, it should be at their peril, they should certainly fall before them, *v.* 7. The forces of the enemy, though entirely drawn up to come against them one way, should be entirely routed, and flee before them seven ways, each making the best of his way.

(2.) From the whole we learn (though it were well if men would believe it) that religion and piety are the best friends to outward prosperity. Though temporal blessings do not take up so much room in the promises of the New Testament as they do in those of the Old, yet it is enough that our Lord Jesus has given us his word (and surely we may take his word) that if we *seek first the kingdom of God, and the righteousness thereof, all other things* shall be added to us, as far as Infinite Wisdom sees good; and who can desire them further? Matt. vi. 33.

2. It is likewise promised that the grace of God should *establish them a holy people, v.* 9. Having taken them into covenant with himself, he would keep them in covenant; and, provided they used the means of stedfastness, he would give them the grace of steadfastness, that they should not depart from him. Note, Those that are sincere in holiness God will establish in holiness; and he is *of power to do it,* Rom. xvi. 25. He that is holy shall be holy still; and those whom God establishes in holiness he thereby establishes a people to himself, for as long as we keep close to God he will never forsake us. This establishment of their religion would be the establishment of their reputation (*v.* 10): *All the people of the earth shall see,* and own, *that thou art called by the name of the Lord,* that is, "that thou art a most excellent and glorious people, under the particular care and countenance of the great God. They shall be made to know that a people called by the name of Jehovah are without doubt the happiest people under the sun, even their enemies themselves being judges." The favourites of Heaven are truly great, and, first or last, it will be made to appear that they are so, if not in this world, yet at that day when those who confess Christ now shall be confessed by him before men and angels, as those whom he delights to honour.

15 But it shall come to pass, if thou wilt not hearken unto the voice of the LORD thy God, to observe to do all his commandments and his statutes which I command thee this day; that all these curses shall come upon thee, and overtake thee: 16 Cursed *shalt* thou *be* in the city, and cursed *shalt* thou *be* in the field. 17 Cursed *shall be* thy basket and thy store. 18 Cursed *shall be* the fruit of thy body, and the fruit of thy land, the increase of thy kine, and the flocks of thy sheep. 19 Cursed *shalt* thou *be* when thou comest in, and cursed *shalt* thou *be* when thou goest out. 20 The LORD shall send upon thee cursing, vexation, and rebuke, in all that thou settest thine hand unto for to do, until thou be destroyed, and until thou perish quickly; because of the wickedness of thy doings, whereby thou hast forsaken me. 21 The LORD shall make the pestilence cleave unto thee, until he have consumed thee from off the land, whither thou goest to possess it. 22 The LORD shall smite thee with a consumption,. and with a fever, and with an inflamma-

tion, and with an extreme burning, and with the sword, and with blasting, and with mildew; and they shall pursue thee until thou perish. 23 And thy heaven that *is* over thy head shall be brass, and the earth that *is* under thee *shall be* iron. 24 The LORD shall make the rain of thy land powder and dust: from heaven shall it come down upon thee, until thou be destroyed. 25 The LORD shall cause thee to be smitten before thine enemies: thou shalt go out one way against them, and flee seven ways before them: and shalt be removed into all the kingdoms of the earth. 26 And thy carcase shall be meat unto all fowls of the air, and unto the beasts of the earth, and no man shall fray *them* away. 27 The LORD will smite thee with the botch of Egypt, and with the emerods, and with the scab, and with the itch, whereof thou canst not be healed. 28 The LORD shall smite thee with madness, and blindness, and astonishment of heart: 29 And thou shalt grope at noonday, as the blind gropeth in darkness, and thou shalt not prosper in thy ways: and thou shalt be only oppressed and spoiled evermore, and no man shall save *thee.* 30 Thou shalt betroth a wife, and another man shall lie with her: thou shalt build a house, and thou shalt not dwell therein: thou shalt plant a vineyard, and shalt not gather the grapes thereof. 31 Thine ox *shall be* slain before thine eyes, and thou shalt not eat thereof: thine ass *shall be* violently taken away from before thy face, and shall not be restored to thee: thy sheep *shall be* given unto thine enemies, and thou shalt have none to rescue *them.* 32 Thy sons and thy daughters *shall be* given unto another people, and thine eyes shall look, and fail *with longing* for them all the day long; and *there shall be* no might in thine hand. 33 The fruit of thy land, and all thy labours, shall a nation which thou knowest not eat up; and thou shalt be only oppressed and crushed alway: 34 So that thou shalt be mad for the sight of thine eyes which thou shalt see. 35 The LORD shall smite thee in the knees, and in the legs, with a sore botch that cannot be healed, from the sole of thy foot unto the top of thy head. 36 The LORD shall bring thee, and thy king which thou shalt set over thee, unto a nation which neither thou nor thy fathers have known; and there shalt thou serve other gods, wood and stone. 37 And thou shalt become an astonishment, a proverb, and a byword, among all nations whither the LORD shall lead thee. 38 Thou shalt carry much seed out into the field, and shalt gather *but* little in; for the locust shall consume it. 39 Thou shalt plant vineyards, and dress *them*, but shalt neither drink *of* the wine, nor gather *the grapes;* for the worms shall eat them. 40 Thou shalt have olive trees throughout all thy coasts, but thou shalt not anoint *thyself* with the oil; for thine olive shall cast *his fruit.* 41 Thou shalt beget sons and daughters, but thou shalt not enjoy them; for they shall go into captivity. 42 All thy trees and fruit of thy land shall the locust consume. 43 The stranger that *is* within thee shall get up above thee very high; and thou shalt come down very low. 44 He shall lend to thee, and thou shalt not lend to him : he shall be the head, and thou shalt be the tail.

Having viewed the bright side of the cloud, which is towards the obedient, we have now presented to us the dark side, which is towards the disobedient. If we do not keep God's commandments, we not only come short of the blessing promised, but we lay ourselves under the curse, which is as comprehensive of all misery as the blessing is of all happiness. Observe,

I. The equity of this curse. It is not a curse causeless, nor for some light cause; God seeks not occasion against us, nor is he apt to quarrel with us. That which is here mentioned as bringing the curse is, 1. Despising God, refusing to *hearken to his voice* (*v.* 15), which bespeaks the highest contempt imaginable, as if what he said were not worth the heeding, or we were not under any obligation to him. 2. Disobeying him, *not doing his commandments*, or not observing to do them. None fall under his curse but those that rebel against his command. 3. Deserting him. "It is because of *the wickedness of thy doings*, not only whereby thou hast
840

slighted me, but *whereby thou hast forsaken me*," *v.* 20. God never casts us off till we first cast him off. It intimates that their idolatry, by which they forsook the true God for false gods, would be their destroying sin more than any other.

II. The extent and efficacy of this curse.

1. In general, it is declared, "*All these curses shall come upon thee* from above, *and shall overtake thee;* though thou endeavour to escape them, it is to no purpose to attempt it, they shall follow thee whithersoever thou goest, and seize thee, overtake thee, and overcome thee," *v.* 15. It is said of the sinner, when God's wrath is in pursuit of him, that he *would fain flee out of his hand* (Job xxvii. 22), but he cannot; if he *flee from the iron weapon, yet the bow of steel shall* reach him and *strike him through.* There is no running from God but by running to him, no fleeing from his justice but by fleeing to his mercy. See Ps. xxi. 7, 8. (1.) Wherever the sinner goes, the curse of God follows him; wherever he is, it rests upon him. He is cursed *in the city* and *in the field, v.* 16. The strength of the city cannot shelter him from it, the pleasant air of the country is no fence against these pestilential steams. He is cursed (*v.* 19) when he comes in, for the curse is *upon the house of the wicked* (Prov. iii. 33), and he is cursed when he goes out, for he cannot leave that curse behind him, nor get rid of it, which has entered into his bowels like water and like oil into his bones. (2.) Whatever he has is under a curse: *Cursed is the ground for his sake*, and all that is on it, or comes out of it, and so he is cursed from the ground, as Cain, Gen. iv 11. The *basket and store* are cursed, *v.* 17, 18. All his enjoyments being forfeited by him are in a manner forbidden to him, as cursed things, which he has no title to. To those whose *mind and conscience are defiled* every thing else is so, Tit. i. 15. They are all embittered to him; he cannot take any true comfort in them, for the wrath of God mixes itself with them, and he is so far from having any security of the continuance of them that, if his eyes be open, he may see them all condemned and ready to be confiscated, and with them all his joys and all his hopes gone for ever. (3.) Whatever he does is under a curse too. It is a curse in all that *he sets his hand to* (*v.* 20), a constant disappointment, which those are subject to that set their hearts upon the world, and expect their happiness in it, and which cannot but be a constant vexation. This curse is just the reverse of the blessing in the former part of the chapter. Thus whatever bliss there is in heaven there is not only the want of it, but the contrary to it, in hell. Isa. lxv. 13, *My servants shall eat, but you shall be hungry.*

2. Many particular judgments are here enumerated, which would be the fruits of the curse, and with which God would punish

the people of the Jews for their apostasy and disobedience. These judgments threatened are of divers kinds, for God has many arrows in his quiver, *four sore judgments* (Ezek. xiv. 21), and many more. They are represented as very terrible, and the descriptions of them are exceedingly lively and affecting, that men, knowing these terrors of the Lord, might, if possible, be persuaded. The threatenings of the same judgment are several times repeated, that they might make the more deep and lasting impressions, and that, if men persisted in their disobedience, the judgment which they thought was over, and of which they said, "Surely the bitterness of it is past," would return with double force; for when God judges he will overcome. (1.) Bodily diseases are here threatened, that they should be epidemical in their land. These God sometimes makes use of for the chastisement and improvement of his own people. *Lord, behold, he whom thou lovest is sick.* But here they are threatened to be brought upon his enemies as tokens of his wrath, and designed for their ruin. So that according to the temper of our spirits, under sickness, accordingly it is to us a blessing or a curse. But, whatever sickness may be to particular persons, it is certain that epidemical diseases raging among a people are national judgments, and are so to be accounted. He here threatens, [1.] Painful diseases (v. 35), a sore botch, beginning in the legs and knees, but spreading, like Job's boils, from head to foot. [2.] Shameful diseases (v. 27), the botch of Egypt (such boils and blains as the Egyptians had been plagued with, when God brought Israel from among them), and the emerods and scab, vile diseases, the just punishment of those who by sin had made themselves vile. [3.] Mortal diseases, the pestilence (v. 21), the consumption (put for all chronical diseases), and the fever (for all acute diseases), v. 22. See Lev. xxvi. 16. And all incurable, v. 27. (2.) Famine, and scarcity of provisions; and this, [1.] For want of rain (v. 23, 24): *Thy heaven over thy head,* that part that is over thy land, *shall be as dry as brass,* while the heavens over other countries shall distil their dews; and, when the heaven is as brass, the earth of course will be as iron, so hard and unfruitful. Instead of rain, the dust shall be blown out of the highways into the field, and spoil the little that there is of the fruits of the earth. [2.] By destroying insects. The locust should destroy the corn, so that they should not have so much as their *seed again,* v. 38, 42. And the fruit of the vine, which should make glad their hearts, should all be worm-eaten, v. 39. And the olive, some way or other, should be made to *cast its fruit,* v. 40. The heathen use many superstitious customs in honour of their idol-gods for preserving the fruits of the earth; but Moses tells Israel that the only way they had to preserve them was to keep God's command-

ments; for he is a God that will not be sported with, like their idols, but will be served in spirit and truth. This threatening we find fulfilled in Israel, 1 Kings xvii. 1; Jer. xiv. 1, &c.; Joel i. 4. (3.) That they should be smitten before their enemies in war, who, it is likely, would be the more cruel to them, when they had them at their mercy, for the severity they had used against the nations of Canaan, which their neighbours in after-ages would be apt to remember against them, v. 25. It would make their flight the more shameful, and the more grievous, that they might have triumphed over their enemies if they had but been faithful to their God. The carcases of those that were slain in war, or died in captivity among strangers, should be *meat for the fowls* (v. 26); and an Israelite, having forfeited the favour of his God, should have so little humanity shown him as that *no man should drive them away,* so odious would God's curse make him to all mankind. (4.) That they should be infatuated in all their counsels, so as not to discern their own interest, nor bring any thing to pass for the public good: *The Lord shall smite thee with madness and blindness,* v. 28, 29. Note, God's judgments can reach the minds of men, to fill them with darkness and horror, as well as their bodies and estates; and those are the sorest of all judgments which make men a terror to themselves, and their own destroyers. That which they contrived to secure themselves by should still turn to their prejudice. Thus we often find that the allies they confided in *distressed them* and *strengthened them not,* 2 Chron. xxviii. 20. Those that will not walk in God's counsels are justly left to be ruined by their own; and those that are wilfully blind to their duty deserve to be made blind to their interest, and, seeing they *loved darkness rather than light,* let them *grope at noon-day* as in the dark. (5.) That they should be plundered of all their enjoyments, stripped of all by the proud and imperious conqueror, such as Benhadad was to Ahab, 1 Kings xx. 5, 6. Not only their houses and vineyards should be taken from them, but their wives and children, v. 30, 32. Their dearest comforts, which they took most pleasure in, and promised themselves most from, should be the entertainment and triumph of their enemies. As they had dwelt in houses which they built not, and eaten of vineyards which they planted not (ch. vi. 10, 11), so others should do by them. Their oxen, asses, and sheep, like Job's, should be taken away before their eyes, and they should not be able to recover them, v. 31. And all the fruit of their land and labours should be devoured and eaten up by the enemy; so that they and theirs would want necessaries, while their enemies were revelling with that which they had laboured for. (6.) That they should be carried captives into a far country; nay, into *all the kingdoms of the earth,* v. 25. Their sons and daughters, whom they promised themselves comfort in, should go into captivity (*v.* 41), and they themselves at length, and their king in whom they promised themselves safety and settlement, *v.* 36. This was fully accomplished when the ten tribes first were carried captive into Assyria (2 Kings xvii. 6), and not long after the two tribes into Babylon, and two of their kings, 2 Kings xxiv. 14, 15; xxv. 7, 21. That which is mentioned as an aggravation of their captivity is that they should go into an unknown country, the language and customs of which would be very uncouth, and their treatment among them barbarous, and there they should *serve other gods*, that is, be compelled to do so by their enemies, as they were in Babylon, Dan. iii. 6. Note, God often makes men's sin their punishment, and chooses their delusions. You shall *serve other gods*, that is, "You shall serve those that do serve them;" a nation is often in scripture called by the name of its gods, as Jer. xlviii. 7. They had made idolaters their associates, and now God made idolaters their oppressors. (7.) That those who remained should be insulted and tyrannized over by strangers, *v.* 43, 44. So the ten tribes were by the colonies which the king of Assyria sent to take possession of their land, 2 Kings xvii. 24. Or this may be meant of the gradual encroachments which the strangers within their gates should make upon them, so as insensibly to worm them out of their estates. We read of the fulfilling of this, Hos. vii. 9, *Strangers have devoured his strength.* Foreigners ate the bread out of the mouths of trueborn Israelites, by which they were justly chastised for introducing strange gods. (8.) That their reputation among their neighbours should be quite sunk, and those that had been a name, and a praise, should be an astonishment, a proverb, and a by-word, *v.* 37. Some have observed the fulfilling of this threatening in their present state; for, when we would express the most perfidious and barbarous treatment, we say, *None but a Jew would have done so.* Thus is sin a reproach to any people. (9.) To complete their misery, it is threatened that they should be put quite out of the possession of their minds by all these troubles (*v.* 34): *Thou shalt be mad for the sight of thy eyes,* that is, quite bereaved of all comfort and hope, and abandoned to utter despair. Those that walk by sight, and not by faith, are in danger of losing reason itself, when every thing about them looks frightful; and their condition is woeful indeed that are *mad for the sight of their eyes.*

45 Moreover all these curses shall come upon thee, and shall pursue thee, and overtake thee, till thou be destroyed; because thou harkenedst not unto the voice of the LORD thy God, to keep his commandments and his statutes which he commanded

thee: 46 And they shall be upon thee for a sign and for a wonder, and upon thy seed for ever. 47 Because thou servedst not the LORD thy God with joyfulness, and with gladness of heart, for the abundance of all *things;* 48 Therefore shalt thou serve thine enemies which the LORD shall send against thee, in hunger, and in thirst, and in nakedness, and in want of all *things:* and he shall put a yoke of iron upon thy neck, until he have destroyed thee. 49 The LORD shall bring a nation against thee from far, from the end of the earth, *as swift* as the eagle flieth; a nation whose tongue thou shalt not understand; 50 A nation of fierce countenance, which shall not regard the person of the old, nor show favour to the young: 51 And he shall eat the fruit of thy cattle, and the fruit of thy land, until thou be destroyed: which *also* shall not leave thee *either* corn, wine, or oil, *or* the increase of thy kine, or flocks of thy sheep, until he have destroyed thee. 52 And he shall besiege thee in all thy gates, until thy high and fenced walls come down, wherein thou trustedst, throughout all thy land: and he shall besiege thee in all thy gates throughout all thy land, which the LORD thy God hath given thee. 53 And thou shalt eat the fruit of thine own body, the flesh of thy sons and of thy daughters, which the LORD thy God hath given thee, in the siege, and in the straitness, wherewith thine enemies shall distress thee: 54 *So that* the man *that is* tender among you, and very delicate, his eye shall be evil toward his brother, and toward the wife of his bosom, and toward the remnant of his children which he shall leave: 55 So that he will not give to any of them of the flesh of his children whom he shall eat: because he hath nothing left him in the siege, and in the straitness, wherewith thine enemies shall distress thee in all thy gates. 56 The tender and delicate woman among you, which would not adventure to set the sole of her foot upon the ground for delicateness and tenderness. her eye shall be evil toward the husband of her bosom, and toward her son, and toward her daughter, 57 And toward her young one that cometh out from between her feet, and toward her children which she shall bear : for she shall eat them for want of all *things* secretly in the siege and straitness, wherewith thine enemy shall distress thee in thy gates. 58 If thou wilt not observe to do all the words of this law that are written in this book, that thou mayest fear this glorious and fearful name, THE LORD THY GOD ; 59 Then the LORD will make thy plagues wonderful, and the plagues of thy seed, *even* great plagues, and of long continuance, and sore sicknesses, and of long continuance. 60 Moreover he will bring upon thee all the diseases of Egypt, which thou wast afraid of; and they shall cleave unto thee. 61 Also every sickness, and every plague, which *is* not written in the book of this law, them will the LORD bring upon thee, until thou be destroyed. 62 And ye shall be left few in number, whereas ye were as the stars of heaven for multitude; because thou wouldest not obey the voice of the LORD thy God. 63 And it shall come to pass, *that* as the LORD rejoiced over you to do you good, and to multiply you; so the LORD will rejoice over you to destroy you, and to bring you to nought; and ye shall be plucked from off the land whither thou goest to possess it. 64 And the LORD shall scatter thee among all people, from the one end of the earth even unto the other; and there thou shalt serve other gods, which neither thou nor thy fathers have known, *even* wood and stone. 65 And among these nations shalt thou find no ease, neither shall the sole of thy foot have rest : but the LORD shall give thee there a trembling heart, and failing of eyes, and sorrow of mind : 66 And thy life shall hang in doubt before thee ; and thou shalt fear day and night, and shalt have none assurance of thy life : 67 In the morning thou shalt say, Would God it were even ! and at even thou

shalt say, Would God it were morning ! for the fear of thine heart wherewith thou shalt fear, and for the sight of thine eyes which thou shalt see. 68 And the LORD shall bring thee into Egypt again with ships, by the way whereof I spake unto thee, Thou shalt see it no more again : and there ye shall be sold unto your enemies for bondmen and bondwomen, and no man shall buy *you.*

One would have thought that enough had been said to possess them with a dread of that *wrath of God* which is *revealed from heaven against the ungodliness and unrighteousness of men.* But to show how deep the treasures of that wrath are, and that still there is more and worse behind, Moses, when one would have thought that he had concluded this dismal subject, begins again, and adds to this roll of curses many similar words ; as Jeremiah did to his, Jer. xxxvi. 32. It should seem that in the former part of this commination Moses fortels their captivity in Babylon, and the calamities which introduced and attended that, by which, even after their return, they were brought to that low and poor condition which is described, *v.* 44. That their enemies should be *the head,* and they *the tail :* but here, in this latter part, he foretels their last destruction by the Romans and their dispersion thereupon. And the present deplorable state of the Jewish nation, and of all that have incorporated themselves with them, by embracing their religion, does so fully and exactly answer to the prediction in these verses that it serves for an incontestable proof of the truth of prophecy, and consequently of the divine authority of the scripture. And, this last destruction being here represented as more dreadful than the former, it shows that their sin, in rejecting Christ and his gospel, was more heinous and more provoking to God than idolatry itself, and left them more under the power of Satan ; for their captivity in Babylon cured them effectually of their idolatry in seventy years' time ; but under this last destruction now for above 1600 years they continue incurably averse to the Lord Jesus. Observe,

I. What is here said in general of the wrath of God, which should light and lie upon them for their sins.

1. That, if they would not be *ruled by the commands of God,* they should certainly be *ruined by his curse, v.* 45, 46. Because thou didst not *keep his commandments* (especially that of hearing and obeying the great prophet), *these curses shall come upon thee,* as upon a people appointed to destruction, the generation of God's wrath : and they shall be *for a sign* and *for a wonder.* It is amazing to think that a people so long the favourites of

Heaven should be so perfectly abandoned and cast off, that a people so closely incorporated should be so universally dispersed, and yet that a people so scattered in all nations should preserve themselves distinct and not mix with any, but like Cain be fugitives and vagabonds, and yet marked to be known.

2. That, if they would not serve God with cheerfulness, they should be compelled to *serve their enemies* (v. 47, 48), that they might know the difference (2 Chron. xii. 8), which, some think, is the meaning of Ezek. xx. 24, 25, *Because they despised my statutes, I gave them statutes that were not good.* Observe here, (1.) It is justly expected from those to whom God gives an abundance of the good things of this life that they should serve him. What does he maintain us for but that we may do his work, and be some way serviceable to his honour? (2.) The more God gives us the more cheerfully we should serve him; our abundance should be oil to the wheels of our obedience. God is a Master that will be served with gladness, and delights to hear us sing at our work. (3.) If, when we receive the gifts of God's bounty, we either do not serve him at all or serve him with reluctance, it is a righteous thing with him to make us know the hardships of want and servitude. Those deserve to have cause given them to complain who complain without a cause. *Tristis es et felix—Happy, and yet not easy!* Blush at thy own folly and ingratitude.

3. That, if they would not *give glory to God* by a reverential obedience, he would get *him honour upon them* by *wonderful* plagues, v. 58, 59. Note, (1.) God justly expects from us that we should fear his fearful name; and, which is strange, that name which is here proposed as the object of our fear is, THE LORD THY GOD, which is very fitly here put in our Bibles in capital letters; for nothing can sound more truly august. As nothing is more comfortable, so nothing more awful, than this, that he with whom we have to do is Jehovah, a being infinitely perfect and blessed, and the author of all being; and that he is our God, our rightful Lord and owner, from whom we are to receive laws and to whom we are to give account: this is great, and greatly to be feared. (2.) We may justly expect from God that, if we do not fear his fearful name, we shall feel his fearful plagues; for one way or other God will be feared. All God's plagues are dreadful, but some are wonderful, carrying in them extraordinary signatures of divine power and justice, so that a man, upon the first view of them, may say, *Verily, there is a God that judgeth in the earth.*

II. How the destruction threatened is described. Moses is here upon the same melancholy subject that our Saviour is discoursing of to his disciples in his farewell sermon (Matt. xxiv.), namely, The destruc-

tion of Jerusalem and the Jewish nation. Observe,

1. Five things are here foretold as steps to their ruin :—

(1.) That they should be invaded by a foreign enemy (v. 49, 50): A *nation from far,* namely, the Romans, *as swift as the eagle* hastening to the prey. Our Saviour makes use of this similitude, in foretelling this destruction, that *where the carcase is there will the eagles be gathered together,* Matt. xxiv. 28. And bishop Patrick observes (to make the accomplishment the more remarkable) that the ensign of the Roman armies was an eagle. This nation is said to be of a fierce countenance, an indication of a fierce nature, stern and severe, that would not pity the weakness and infirmity either of little children or of old people.

(2.) That the country should be laid waste, and all the fruits of it eaten up by this army of foreigners, which is the natural consequence of an invasion, especially when it is made, as that by the Romans was, for the chastisement of rebels: He *shall eat the fruits of thy cattle and land* (v. 51), so that the inhabitants should be starved, while the invaders were fed to the full.

(3.) That their cities should be besieged, and that such would be the obstinacy of the besieged, and such the vigour of the besiegers, that they would be reduced to the last extremity, and at length fall into the hands of the enemy, v. 52. No place, though ever so well fortified, no, not Jerusalem itself, though it held out long, would escape. Two of the common consequences of a long siege are here foretold :—[1.] A miserable famine, which would prevail to such a degree that, for want of food, they should *kill and eat their own children,* v. 53. Men should do so, notwithstanding their hardiness, and ability to bear hunger; and, though obliged by the law of nature to provide for their own families, yet should refuse to give to the wife and children that were starving any of the child that was barbarously butchered, v. 54, 55. Nay, women, ladies of quality, notwithstanding their natural niceness about their food, and their natural affection to their children, yet, for want of food, should so far forget all humanity as to kill and eat them, v. 56, 57. Let us observe, by the way, how hard this fate must needs be to the tender and delicate women, and learn not to indulge ourselves in tenderness and delicacy, because we know not what we may be reduced to before we die; the more nice we are, the harder it will be to us to bear want, and the more danger we shall be in of sacrificing reason, and religion, and natural affection itself, to the clamours and cravings of an unmortified and ungoverned appetite. This threatening was fulfilled in the letter of it, more than once, to the perpetual reproach of the Jewish nation: never was the like done either by Greek or barbarian, but in the siege of Samaria, a woman *boiled her own son*, 2 Kings vi. 28, 29. And it is spoken of as commonly done among them in the siege of Jerusalem by the Babylonians, Lam. iv. 10. And, in the last siege by the Romans, Josephus tells us of a noble woman that killed and ate her own child, through the extremity of the famine, and when she had eaten one half secretly (*v.* 57), that she might have it to herself, the mob, smelling meat, got into the house, to whom she showed the other half, which she had kept till another time, inviting them to share with her. What is too barbarous for those to do that are abandoned of God! [2.] Sickness is another common effect of a strait and long siege, and that is here threatened: *Sore sickness, and of long continuance, v.* 59. These should attend the Jews wherever they went afterwards, the diseases of Egypt, leprosies, botches, and foul ulcers, *v.* 60. Nay, as if the particular miseries here threatened were not enough, he concludes with an *et cetera, v.* 61. The Lord will bring upon thee every sickness, and every plague, though it be *not written in , the book of this law.* Those that fall under the curse of God will find that the one half was not told them of the weight and terror of that curse.

(4.) That multitudes of them should perish, so that they should become *few in number, v.* 62. It was a nation that God had wonderfully increased, so that they were *as the stars of heaven for multitude;* but, for their sin, they were *diminished and brought low,* Ps. cvii. 38, 39. It is computed that in the destruction of the Jewish nation by the Romans, as appears by the account Josephus gives of it, above two millions fell by the sword at several places, besides what perished by famine and pestilence; so that the whole country was laid waste and turned into a wilderness. That is a terrible word (*v.* 63), *As the Lord rejoiced over you to do you good, so he will rejoice over you to destroy you.* Behold here *the goodness and severity of God :* mercy here shines brightly in the pleasure God takes in doing good—he rejoices in it; yet justice here appears no less illustrious in the pleasure he takes in destroying the impenitent; not as it is the making of his creatures miserable, but as it is the asserting of his own honour and the securing of the ends of his government. See what a malignant mischievous thing sin is, which (as I may say) makes it necessary for the God of infinite goodness to rejoice in the destruction of his own creatures, even those that had been favourites.

(5.) That the remnant should be scattered throughout the nations. This completes their woe : *The Lord shall scatter thee among all people, v.* 64. This is remarkably fulfilled in their present dispersion, for there are Jews to be found almost in all countries that are possessed either by Christians or Mahometans, and in such numbers that it has been said,

If they could unite in one common interest, they would be a very formidable body, and able to deal with the most powerful states and princes ; but they abide under the power of this curse, and are so scattered that they are not able to incorporate. It is here foretold that in this dispersion, [1.] They should have no religion, or none to any purpose, should have no temple, nor altar, nor priesthood, for they should *serve other gods.* Some think this has been fulfilled in the force put upon the Jews in popish countries to worship the images that are used in the Romish church, to their great vexation. [2.] They should have no rest, no rest of body : *The sole of thy foot shall not have rest* (*v.* 65), but be continually upon the remove, either in hope of gain or fear of persecution ; all wandering Jews : no rest of the mind (which is much worse), but a *trembling heart* (*v.* 65); *no assurance of life* (*v.* 66); weary both of light and darkness, which are, in their turns, both welcome to a quiet mind, but to them both day and night would be a terror, *v.* 67. Such was once the condition of Job (Job vii. 4), but to them this should be constant and perpetual ; that blindness and darkness which the apostle speaks of as having happened to Israel, and that guilt which *bowed down their back always* (Rom. xi. 8—10), must needs occasion a constant restlessness and amazement. Those are a torment to themselves, and to all about them, that fear day and night and are always uneasy. Let good people strive against it, and not give way to that fear which has torment ; and let wicked people not be secure in their wickedness, for their hearts cannot endure, nor can their hands be strong, when the terrors of God set themselves in array against them. Those that say *in the morning, O that it were evening,* and *in the evening, O that it were morning,* show, *First,* A constant fret and vexation, chiding the hours for lingering and complaining of the length of every minute. Let time be precious to us when we are in prosperity, and then it will not be so tedious to us when we are in afflictions as otherwise it would. *Secondly,* A constant fright and terror, afraid in the morning of the *arrow that flieth by day,* and therefore wishing the day over ; but what will this do for them ? When evening comes, the trembling heart is no less apprehensive of the *terror by night,* Ps. 91. 5, 6. Happy they whose minds, being stayed on God, are *quiet from the fear of evil !* Observe here, The terror arises not only from the sight of the eyes, but from the fear of the heart, not only from real dangers, but from imaginary ones ; the causes of fear, when they come to be enquired into, often prove to be only the creatures of the fancy.

2. In the close, God threatens to leave them as he found them, in a *house of bondage* (*v.* 68) : *The Lord shall bring thee into Egypt again,* that is into such a miserable state as

they were in when they were slaves to the Egyptians, and ruled by them with rigour. God had brought them out of Egypt, and had said, *They shall see it no more again* (ch. xvii. 16); but now they should be reduced to the same state of slavery that they had been in there. To be sold to strangers would be bad enough, but much worse to be sold to their enemies. Even slaves may be valued as such, but a Jew should have so ill a name for all that is base that when he was exposed to sale no man would buy him, which would make his master that had him to sell the more severe with him. Thirty Jews (they say) have been sold for one small piece of money, as they sold our Saviour for thirty pieces.

3. Upon the whole matter, (1.) The accomplishment of these predictions upon the Jewish nation shows that Moses spoke by the Spirit of God, who certainly foresees the ruin of sinners, and gives them warning of it, that they may prevent it by a true and timely repentance, or else be left inexcusable. (2.) Let us all hence learn to stand in awe and not to sin. I have heard of a wicked man, who, upon reading the threatenings of this chapter, was so enraged that he tore the leaf out of the Bible, as Jehoiakim cut Jeremiah's roll; but to what purpose is it to deface a copy, while the original remains upon record in the divine counsels, by which it is unalterably determined that *the wages of sin is death*, whether men will hear or whether they will forbear?

CHAP. XXIX.

The first words of this chapter are the contents of it, "These are the words of the covenant" (ver. 1), that is, these that follow. Here is, I. A recital of God's dealings with them, in order to the bringing of them into this covenant, ver. 2—8. II. A solemn charge to them to keep the covenant, ver. 9. III. An abstract of the covenant itself, ver. 12, 13. IV. A specification of the persons taken into the covenant, ver. 10, 11, 14, 15. V. An intimation of the great design of this covenant against idolatry, in a parenthesis, ver. 16, 17. VI. A most solemn and dreadful denunciation of the wrath of God against such persons as promise themselves peace in a sinful way, ver. 18—28. VII. The conclusion of this treaty, with a distinction between things secret and things revealed, ver. 29.

THESE *are* the words of the covenant, which the LORD commanded Moses to make with the children of Israel in the land of Moab, beside the covenant which he made with them in Horeb. 2 And Moses called unto all Israel, and said unto them, Ye have seen all that the LORD did before your eyes in the land of Egypt unto Pharaoh, and unto all his servants, and unto all his land; 3 The great temptations which thine eyes have seen, the signs, and those great miracles: 4 Yet the LORD hath not given you a heart to perceive, and eyes to see, and ears to hear, unto this day. 5 And I have led you forty years in the wilderness: your clothes

are not waxen old upon you, and thy shoe is not waxen old upon thy foot. 6 Ye have not eaten bread, neither have ye drunk wine or strong drink: that ye might know that I *am* the LORD your God. 7 And when ye came unto this place, Sihon the king of Heshbon, and Og the king of Bashan, came out against us unto battle, and we smote them: 8 And we took their land, and gave it for an inheritance unto the Reubenites, and to the Gadites, and to the half tribe of Manasseh. 9 Keep therefore the words of this covenant, and do them, that ye may prosper in all that ye do.

Now that Moses had largely repeated the commands which the people were to observe as their part of the covenant, and the promises and threatenings which God would make good (according as they behaved themselves) as his part of the covenant, the whole is here summed up in a federal transaction. The covenant formerly made is here renewed, and Moses, who was before, is still, the mediator of it (v. 1): *The Lord commanded Moses to make it.* Moses himself, though king in Jeshurun, could not make the covenant any otherwise than as God gave him instructions. It does not lie in the power of ministers to fix the terms of the covenant; they are only to dispense the seals of it. This is said to be *besides the covenant made in Horeb;* for, though the covenant was the same, yet it was a new promulgation and ratification of it. It is probable that some now living, though not of age to be mustered, were of age to consent for themselves to the covenant made at Horeb, and yet it is here renewed. Note, Those that have solemnly covenanted with God should take all opportunities to do it again, as those that like their choice too well to change. But the far greater part were a new generation, and therefore the covenant must be made afresh with them, for it is fit that the covenant should be renewed to the children of the covenant.

I. It is usual for indentures to begin with a recital; this does so, with a rehearsal of the great things God had done for them, 1. As an encouragement to them to believe that God would indeed be to them a God, for he would not have done so much for them if he had not designed more, to which all he had hitherto done was but a preface (as it were) or introduction; nay, he had shown himself a God in what he had hitherto done for them, which might raise their expectations of something great and answering the vast extent and compass of that pregnant promise, that God would be to them a God. 2. As an engagement upon them to be to him an obedient people, in consideration of what he had done for them.

II. For the proof of what he here advances he appeals to their own eyes (*v.* 2): *You have seen all that the Lord did.* Their own senses were incontestable evidence of the matter of fact, that God had done great things for them; and then their own reason was a no less competent judge of the equity of his inference from it: *Keep therefore the words of this covenant, v.* 9.

III. These things he specifies, to show the power and goodness of God in his appearances for them. 1. Their deliverance out of Egypt, *v.* 2, 3. The amazing signs and miracles by which Pharaoh was plagued and compelled to dismiss them, and Israel was tried (for they are called *temptations)* whether they would trust God to secure them from, and save them by, those plagues. 2. Their conduct through the wilderness for forty years, *v.* 5, 6. There they were led, and clad, and fed, by miracles; though the paths of the wilderness were not only unknown but untrodden, yet God kept them from being lost there; and (as bishop Patrick observes) those very shoes which by the appointment of God they put on in Egypt, at the passover, when they were ready to march (Exod. xii. 11), never wore out, but served them to Canaan: and though they lived not upon bread which strengthens the heart, and wine which rejoices it, but upon manna and rock-water, yet they were men of strength and courage, mighty men, and able to go forth to war. By these miracles they were made to know that the Lord was God, and by these mercies that he was their God. 3. The victory they had lately obtained over Sihon and Og, and that good land which they had taken possession of, *v.* 7, 8. Both former mercies and fresh mercies should be improved by us as inducements to obedience.

IV. By way of inference from these memoirs, 1. Moses laments their stupidity: *Yet the Lord has not given you a heart to perceive, v.* 4. This does not lay the blame of their senselessness, and sottishness, and unbelief, upon God, as if they had stood ready to receive his grace and had begged for it, but he had denied them; no, but it fastens the guilt upon themselves. "The Lord, who is the Father of spirits, a God in covenant with you, and who had always been so rich in mercy to you, no doubt would have crowned all his other gifts with this, he would have given you a heart to perceive and eyes to see if you had not by your own frowardness and perverseness frustrated his kind intentions, and received his grace in vain." Note, (1.) The hearing ear, the seeing eye, and the understanding heart, are the gift of God. All that have them have them from him. (2.) God gives not only food and raiment, but wealth and large possessions, to many to whom he does not give grace. Many enjoy the gifts who have not hearts to perceive the giver,

nor the true intention and use of the gifts. (3.) God's readiness to do us good in other things is a plain evidence that if we have not grace, that best of gifts, it is our own fault and not his; he would have gathered us and we would not.

2. Moses charges them to be obedient: *Keep therefore, and do, v.* 9. Note, We are bound in gratitude and interest, as well as duty and faithfulness, to *keep the words of the covenant.*

10 Ye stand this day all of you before the LORD your God; your captains of your tribes, your elders, and your officers, *with* all the men of Israel, 11 Your little ones, your wives, and thy stranger that *is* in thy camp, from the hewer of thy wood unto the drawer of thy water: 12 That thou shouldest enter into covenant with the LORD thy God, and into his oath, which the LORD thy God maketh with thee this day: 13 That he may establish thee to-day for a people unto himself, and *that* he may be unto thee a God, as he hath said unto thee, and as he hath sworn unto thy fathers, to Abraham, to Isaac, and to Jacob. 14 Neither with you only do I make this covenant and this oath; 15 But with *him* that standeth here with us this day before the LORD our God, and also with *him* that *is* not here with us this day: 16 (For ye know how we have dwelt in the land of Egypt; and how we came through the nations which ye passed by; 17 And ye have seen their abominations, and their idols, wood and stone, silver and gold, which *were* among them:) 18 Lest there should be among you man, or woman, or family, or tribe, whose heart turneth away this day from the LORD our God, to go *and* serve the gods of these nations; lest there should be among you a root that beareth gall and wormwood; 19 And it come to pass, when he heareth the words of this curse, that he bless himself in his heart, saying, I shall have peace, though I walk in the imagination of mine heart, to add drunkenness to thirst: 20 The LORD will not spare him, but then the anger of the LORD and his jealousy shall smoke against that man,

847

and all the curses that are written in this book shall lie upon him, and the LORD shall blot out his name from under heaven. 21 And the LORD shall separate him unto evil out of all the tribes of Israel, according to all the curses of the covenant that are written in this book of the law : 22 So that the generation to come of your children that shall rise up after you, and the stranger that shall come from a far land, shall say, when they see the plagues of that land, and the sicknesses which the LORD hath laid upon it ; 23 *And that* the whole land thereof *is* brimstone, and salt, *and* burning, *that* it is not sown, nor beareth, nor any grass groweth therein, like the overthrow of Sodom, and Gomorrah, Admah, and Zeboim, which the LORD overthrew in his anger, and in his wrath : 24 Even all nations shall say, Wherefore hath the LORD done thus unto this land ? what *meaneth* the heat of this great anger ? 25 Then men shall say, Because they have forsaken the covenant of the LORD God of their fathers, which he made with them when he brought them forth out of the land of Egypt : 26 For they went and served other gods, and worshipped them, gods whom they knew not, and *whom* he had not given unto them : 27 And the anger of the LORD was kindled against this land, to bring upon it all the curses that are written in this book : 28 And the LORD rooted them out of their land in anger, and in wrath, and in great indignation, and cast them into another land, as *it is* this day. 29 The secret *things* belong unto the LORD our God : but those *things which are* revealed *belong* unto us and to our children for ever, that *we* may do all the words of this law.

It appears by the length of the sentences here, and by the copiousness and pungency of the expressions, that Moses, now that he was drawing near to the close of his discourse, was very warm and zealous, and very desirous to impress what he said upon the minds of this unthinking people. To bind them the faster to God and duty, he here, with great solemnity of expression (to make up the want of the external ceremony that was used Exod.

xxiv. 4, &c.), concludes a bargain (as it were) between them and God, an everlasting covenant, which God would not forget and they must not. He requires not their explicit consent, but lays the matter plainly before them, and then leaves it between God and their own consciences. Observe,

I. The parties to this covenant. 1. It is the Lord their God they are to covenant with, *v.* 12. To him they must give up themselves, to him they must join themselves. " It is his oath ; he has drawn up the covenant and settled it ; he requires your consent to it ; he has sworn to you, and to him you must be sworn." This requires us to be sincere and serious, humble and reverent, in our covenant-transactions with God, remembering how great a God he is with whom we are covenanting, who has a perfect knowledge of us and an absolute dominion over us. 2. They are all to be taken into covenant with him. They were all summoned to attend (*v.* 2), and did accordingly, and are told (*v.* 10) what was the design of their appearing before God now in a body— they were to enter into covenant with him. (1.) Even their great men, the captains of their tribes, their elders and officers, must not think it any disparagement to their honour, or any diminution of their power, to put their necks under the yoke of this covenant, and to draw in it. They must rather enter into the covenant first, to set a good example to their inferiors. (2.) Not the men only, but their wives and children, must come into this covenant; though they were not numbered and mustered, yet they must be *joined to the Lord, v.* 11. Observe, Even little ones are capable of being taken into covenant with God, and are to be admitted with their parents. Little children, so little as to be carried in arms, must be brought to Christ, and shall be blessed by him, for *of such* was and *is the kingdom of God.* (3.) Not the men of Israel only, but the stranger that was in their camp, provided he was so far proselyted to their religion as to renounce all false gods, was taken into this covenant with the God of Israel, forasmuch as he also, though a stranger, was to be looked upon in this matter as a *son of Abraham*, Luke xix. 9. This was an early indication of favour to the Gentiles, and of the kindness God had in store for them. (4.) Not the freemen only, but the hewers of wood and drawers of water, the meanest drudge they had among them. Note, As none are too great to come under the bonds of the covenant, so none are too mean to inherit the blessings of the covenant. In Christ no difference is made between *bond and free*, Col. iii. 11. *Art thou called being a servant?* *Care not for it*, 1 Cor. vii. 21. (5.) Not only those that were now present before God in this solemn assembly, but those also that were not here with them were taken into covenant (*v.* 15) : *As with him that standeth here with us* (so bishop Patrick thinks it should be rendered) *so also with him that is not here with us this day;* that is, [1.] Those that tarried at home were included; though detained either by sickness or necessary business, they must not therefore think themselves disengaged; no, every Israelite shares in the common blessings. Those that tarry at home divide the spoil, and therefore every Israelite must own himself bound by the consent of the representative body. Those who cannot go up to the house of the Lord must keep up a spiritual communion with those that do, and be present in spirit when they are absent in body. [2.] The generations to come are included. Nay, one of the Chaldee paraphrasts reads it, *All the generations that have been from the first days of the world, and all that shall arise to the end of the whole world, stand with us here this day.* And so, taking this covenant as a typical dispensation of the covenant of grace, it is a noble testimony to the Mediator of that covenant, who is *the same yesterday, to-day, and for ever.*

II. The summary of this covenant. All the precepts and all the promises of the covenant are included in the covenant-relation between God and them, *v.* 13. That they should be appointed, raised up, *established, for a people to him,* to observe and obey him, to be devoted to him and dependent on him, and that he should be to them a God, according to the tenour of the covenant made with their fathers, to make them holy, high, and happy. Their fathers are here named, *Abraham, Isaac,* and *Jacob,* as examples of piety, which those were to set themselves to imitate who expected any benefit from the covenant made with them. Note, A due consideration of the relation we stand in to God as our God, and of the obligation we lie under as a people to him, is enough to bring us to all the duties and all the comforts of the covenant.

III. The principal design of the renewing of this covenant at this time was to fortify them against temptations to idolatry. Though other sins will be the sinner's ruin, yet this was the sin that was likely to be *their* ruin. Now concerning this he shows,

1. The danger they were in of being tempted to it (*v.* 16, 17): " *You know we have dwelt in the land of Egypt,* a country addicted to idolatry; and it were well if there were not among you some remains of the infection of that idolatry; we have *passed by other nations, the Edomites, Moabites,* &c., and have *seen their abominations* and *their idols,* and some among you, it may be, have liked them too well, and still hanker after them, and would rather worship a wooden god that they can see than an infinite Spirit whom they never saw." It is to be hoped that there were those among them who, the more they saw of these abominations and idols, the more they hated them; but there were those that were smitten with the sight of them, saw the accursed things and coveted them.

2. The danger they were in if they yielded to the temptation. He gives them fair warning: it was at their peril if they forsook God to serve idols. If they would not be bound and held by the precepts of the covenant, they would find that the curses of the covenant would be strong enough to bind and hold them.

(1.) Idolatry would be the ruin of particular persons and their families, *v.* 18—21, where observe,

[1.] The sinner described, *v.* 18. *First,* He is one whose *heart turns away from his God;* there the mischief begins, in the *evil heart of unbelief,* which inclines men to *depart from the living God* to dead idols. Even to this sin men are tempted when they are drawn aside by their own lusts and fancies. Those that begin to turn from God, by neglecting their duty to him, are easily drawn to other gods: and those that serve other gods do certainly turn away from the true God; for he will admit of no rivals: he will be all or nothing. *Secondly,* He is *a root that bears gall and wormwood;* that is, he is a dangerous man, who, being himself poisoned with bad principles and inclinations, with a secret contempt of the God of Israel and his institutions and a veneration for the gods of the nations, endeavours, by all arts possible, to corrupt and poison others and draw them to idolatry: this is a man whose fruit is *hemlock* (so the word is translated, Hos. x. 4) and *wormwood;* it is very displeasing to God, and will be, to all that are seduced by him, *bitterness in the latter end.* This is referred to by the apostle, Heb. xii. 15, where he is in like manner cautioning us to take heed of those that would seduce us from the Christian faith; they are the weeds or tares in a field, which, if let alone, will overspread the whole field. A little of this leaven will be in danger of infecting the whole lump.

[2.] His security in the sin. He promises himself impunity, though he persists in his impiety, *v.* 19. Though he *hears the words of the curse,* so that he cannot plead ignorance of the danger, as other idolaters, yet even then he *blesses himself in his own heart,* thinks himself safe from the wrath of the God of Israel, under the protection of his idol-gods, and *therefore says,* " *I shall have peace,* though I be governed in my religion, not by God's institution, but by my own imagination, to add drunkenness to thirst, one act of wickedness to another." Idolaters were like drunkards, violently set upon their idols themselves and industrious to draw others in with them. Revellings commonly accompanied their idolatries (1 Pet. iv. 3), so that this speaks a woe to drunkards (especially the drunkards of Ephraim), who, when they are awake, being thirsty, *seek it yet again,* Prov. xxiii. 35. And those that made themselves drunk in honour of their idols were the worst of drunkards. Note, *First,* There are many who are under the curse of God and yet bless themselves; but it will soon be found that in blessing themselves they do but deceive themselves. *Secondly,* Those are ripe for ruin, and there is little hope of their repentance, who have made themselves believe that they shall have peace though they go on in a sinful way. *Thirdly,* Drunkenness is a sin that hardens the heart, and debauches the conscience, as much as any other, a sin to which men are strangely tempted themselves even when they have lately felt the mischiefs of it, and to which they are strangely fond of drawing others, Hab. ii. 15. And such an ensnaring sin is idolatry.

[3.] God's just severity against him for the sin, and for the impious affront he put upon God in saying he should have peace though he went on, so giving the lie to eternal truth, Gen. iii. 4. There is scarcely a threatening in all the book of God that sounds more dreadful than this. O that presumptuous sinners would read it and tremble! For it is not a bug-bear to frighten children and fools, but a real declaration of the wrath of God against the ungodliness and the unrighteousness of men, *v.* 20, 21. *First, The Lord shall not spare him.* The days of his reprieve, which he abuses, will be shortened, and no mercy remembered in the midst of judgment. *Secondly,* The *anger of the Lord, and his jealousy,* which is the fiercest anger, *shall smoke against him,* like the smoke of a furnace. *Thirdly,* The *curses written* shall *lie upon him,* not only light upon him to terrify him, but abide upon him, to sink him to the lowest hell, John iii. 36. *Fourthly, His name shall be blotted out,* that is, he himself shall be cut off, and his memory shall rot and perish with him. *Fifthly,* He shall be *separated unto evil,* which is the most proper notion of a curse; he shall be cut off from all happiness and all hope of it, and marked out for misery without remedy. And *(lastly)* All this *according to the curses of the covenant,* which are the most fearful curses, being the just revenges of abused grace.

(2.) Idolatry would be the ruin of their nation; it would bring plagues upon the land that connived at this root of bitterness and received the infection; as far as the sin spread, the judgment should spread likewise. [1.] The ruin is described. It begins with plagues and sicknesses (*v.* 22), to try if they will be reclaimed by less judgments; but, if not, it ends in a total overthrow, like that of Sodom, *v.* 23. As that valley, which had been like the garden of the Lord for fruitfulness, was turned into a lake of salt and sulphur, so should the land of Canaan be made desolate and barren, as it has been ever since the last destruction of it by the Romans. The lake of Sodom bordered closely upon

the land of Israel, that by it they might be warned against the iniquity of Sodom; but, not taking the warning, they were made as like to Sodom in ruin as they had been in sin. [2.] The reason of it is enquired into, and assigned. *First,* It would be enquired into by the *generations to come* (*v.* 22), who would find the state of their nation in all respects the reverse of what it had been, and, when they read both the history and the promise, would be astonished at the change. The stranger likewise, and the nations about them, as well as particular persons, would ask, *Wherefore hath the Lord done thus unto this land?* *v.* 24. Great desolations are thus represented elsewhere as striking the spectators with amazement, 1 Kings ix. 8, 9; Jer. xxii. 8, 9. It was time for the neighbours to tremble when judgment thus *began at the house of God,* 1 Pet. iv. 17. The emphasis of the question is to be laid upon *this land,* the land of Canaan, this good land, the glory of all lands, this land flowing with milk and honey. A thousand pities that such a good land as this should be made desolate. but this is not all; it is this *holy* land, the land of Israel, a people in covenant with God; it is Immanuel's land, a land where God was known and worshipped, and yet thus wasted. Note, 1. It is no new thing for God to bring desolating judgments upon a people that in profession are near to him, Amos. iii. 2. 2. He never does this without a good reason. 3. It concerns us to enquire into the reason, that we may give glory to God and take warning to ourselves. *Secondly,* The reason is here assigned, in answer to that enquiry. The matter would be so plain that all men would say, It was because they *forsook the covenant of the Lord God of their fathers,* *v.* 25. Note, God never forsakes any till they first forsake him. But those that desert the God of their fathers are justly cast out of the inheritance of their fathers. They went and *served other gods* (*v.* 26), gods that they had no acquaintance with, nor lay under any obligation to either in duty or gratitude; for God has not given the creatures to be served by us, but to serve us; nor have they done any good to u; ('as some read it), more than what God has enabled them to do; to the Creator therefore we are debtors, and not to the creatures. It was for this that God was angry with them (*v.* 27), and *rooted them out in anger,* *v.* 28. So that, how dreadful soever the desolation was, the Lord was righteous in it, which is acknowledged, Dan. ix. 11—14. "Thus" (says Mr. Ainsworth) " the law of Moses leaves sinners under the curse, and *rooted out of the Lord's land;* but the grace of Christ towards penitent believing sinners plants them again *upon their land, and they shall no more be pulled up,* being kept by the power of God," Amos. ix. 15.

[3.] He concludes his prophecy of the Jews' rejection just as St. Paul concludes his discourse on the same subject, when it began to be fulfilled (Rom. xi. 33), *How unsearchable are God's judgments, and his ways past finding out!* So here (*v.* 29), *Secret things belong to the Lord our God.* Some make it to be one sentence, *The secret things of the Lord our God are revealed to us and to our children,* as far as we are concerned to know them, and *he hath not dealt so with other nations :* but we make it two sentences, by which, *First,* We are forbidden curiously to enquire into the secret counsels of God and to determine concerning them. A full answer is given to that question, *Wherefore has the Lord done thus to this land?* sufficient to justify God and admonish us. But if any ask further why God would be at such a vast expense of miracles to form such a people, whose apostasy and ruin he plainly foresaw, why he did not by his almighty grace prevent it, or what he intends yet to do with them, let such know that these are questions which cannot be answered, and therefore are not fit to be asked. It is presumption in us to pry into the *Arcana imperii—the mysteries of government,* and to enquire into the reasons of state which *it is not for us to know.* See Acts i. 7 ; John xxi. 22 ; Col. ii. 18. *Secondly,* We are directed and encouraged diligently to enquire into that which God has made known : things *revealed belong to us and to our children.* Note, 1. Though God has kept much of his counsel secret, yet there is enough revealed to satisfy and save us. He has *kept back nothing that is profitable for us,* but that only which it is good for us to be ignorant of. 2. We ought to acquaint ourselves, and our children too, with the things of God that are revealed. We are not only allowed to search into them, but are concerned to do so. They are things which we and ours are nearly interested in. They are the rules we are to live by, the grants we are to live upon ; and therefore we are to learn them diligently ourselves, and to teach them diligently to our children. 3. All our knowledge must be in order to practice, for this is the end of all divine revelation, not to furnish us with curious subjects of speculation and discourse, with which to entertain ourselves and our friends, *but that we may do all the words of this law,* and be blessed in our deed.

CHAP. XXX.

One would have thought that the threatenings in the close of the foregoing chapter had made a full end of the people of Israel, and had left their case for ever desperate ; but in this chapter we have a plain intimation of the mercy God had in store for them in the latter days, so that mercy at length rejoices against judgment, and has the last word. Here we have, I. Exceedingly great and precious promises made to them, upon their repentance and return to God, ver. 1—10. II. The righteousness of faith set before them in the plainness and easiness of the commandment that was now given them, ver. 11—14. III. A fair reference of the whole matter to their choice, ver. 15, &c.

AND it shall come to pass, when all these things are come upon thee, the blessing and the curse, which I have set before thee, and thou shalt call *them* to mind among all the nations, whither the LORD thy God

hath driven thee, 2 And shalt return unto the LORD thy God, and shalt obey his voice according to all that I command thee this day, thou and thy children, with all thine heart, and with all thy soul ; 3 That then the LORD thy God will turn thy captivity, and have compassion upon thee, and will return and gather thee from all the nations, whither the LORD thy God hath scattered thee. 4 If *any* of thine be driven out unto the outmost *parts* of heaven, from thence will the LORD thy God gather thee, and from thence will he fetch thee : 5 And the LORD thy God will bring thee into the land which thy fathers possessed, and thou shalt possess it ; and he will do thee good, and multiply thee by thy fathers. 6 And the LORD thy God will circumcise thine heart, and the heart of thy seed, to love the LORD thy God with all thine heart, and with all thy soul, that thou mayest live. 7 And the LORD thy God will put all these curses upon thine enemies, and on them that hate thee, which persecuted thee. 8 And thou shalt return and obey the voice of the LORD, and do all his commandments which I command thee this day. 9 And the LORD thy God will make thee plenteous in every work of thine hand, in the fruit of thy body, and in the fruit of thy cattle, and in the fruit of thy land, for good : for the LORD will again rejoice over thee for good, as he rejoiced over thy fathers : 10 If thou shalt hearken unto the voice of the LORD thy God to keep his commandments and his statutes which are written in this book of the law, *and* if thou turn unto the LORD thy God with all thine heart, and with all thy soul.

These verses may be considered either as a conditional promise or as an absolute prediction.

I. They are chiefly to be considered as a conditional promise, and so they belong to all persons and all people, and not to Israel only ; and the design of them is to assure us that the greatest sinners, if they repent and be converted, shall have their sins pardoned, and be restored to God's favour. This is the purport of the covenant of grace, it leaves room for repentance in case of misdemeanour, and promises pardon upon repentance, which the covenant of innocency did not. Now observe here,

1. How the repentance is described which is the condition of these promises. (1.) It begins in *serious consideration, v* 1. "Thou shalt call to mind that which thou hadst forgotten or not regarded." Note, Consideration is the first step towards conversion. Isa. xlvi. 8, *Bring to mind, O you transgressors.* The prodigal son came to himself first, and then to his father. That which they should call to mind is the blessing and the curse. If sinners would but seriously consider the happiness they have lost by sin and the misery they have brought themselves into, and that by repentance they may escape that misery and recover that happiness, they would not delay to *return to the Lord their God.* The prodigal *called to mind the blessing and the curse* when he considered his present poverty and the plenty of bread *in his father's house,* Luke xv. 17. (2.) It consists in sincere conversion. The effect of the consideration cannot but be godly sorrow and shame, Ezek. vi. 9 ; vii. 16. But that which is the life and soul of repentance, and without which the most passionate expressions are but a jest, is *returning to the Lord our God, v.* 2. If thou turn (*v.* 10) *with all thy heart and with all thy soul.* We must return to our allegiance to God as our Lord and ruler, our dependence upon him as our Father and benefactor, our devotedness to him as our highest end, and our communion with him as our God in covenant. We must return to God from all that which stands in opposition to him or competition with him. In this return to God we must be upright—with the heart and soul, and universal—with all the heart and all the soul. (3.) It is evidenced by a constant obedience to the holy will of God : If thou shalt *obey his voice* (*v.* 2), *thou and thy children ;* for it is not enough that we do our duty ourselves, but we must train up and engage our children to do it. Or this comes in as the condition of the entail of the blessing upon their children, provided their children kept close to their duty. [1.] This obedience must be with an eye to God : Thou shalt *obey his voice* (*v.* 8), and hearken to it, *v.* 10. [2.] It must be sincere, and cheerful, and entire : *With all thy heart, and with all thy soul, v.* 2. [3.] It must be from a principle of love, and that love must be *with all thy heart and with all thy soul, v.* 6. It is the heart and soul that God looks at and requires ; he will have these or nothing, and these entire or not at all. [4.] It must be universal : *According to all that I command thee, v.* 2, and again *v.* 8, *to do all his commandments ;* for he that allows himself in the breach of one commandment involves himself in the guilt of contemning them all, James ii. 10. An upright heart has *respect to all God's commandments,* Ps. cxix. 6.

2. What the favour is which is promised upon this repentance. Though they are

brought to God by their trouble and distress, in the nations whither they were driven (*v.* 1), yet God will graciously accept of them notwithstanding ; for on this errand afflictions are sent, to bring us to repentance. Though they are *driven out to the utmost parts of heaven,* yet thence their penitent prayers shall reach God's gracious ear, and there his favour shall find them out, *v.* 4. *Undique ad cœlos tantundem est viæ—From every place there is the same way to heaven.* This promise Nehemiah pleads in his prayer for dispersed Israel, Neh. i. 9. It is here promised, (1.) That God would have compassion upon them, as proper objects of his pity, *v.* 3. Against sinners that go on in sin God has indignation (*ch.* xxix. 20), but on those that repent and bemoan themselves he has compassion, Jer. xxxi. 18, 20. True penitents may take great encouragement from the compassions and tender mercies of our God, which never fail, but overflow. (2.) That he would *turn their captivity, and gather them from the nations whither they were scattered* (*v.* 3), though ever so remote, *v.* 4. One of the Chaldee paraphrasts applies this to the Messiah, explaining it thus · *The word of the Lord shall gather you by the hand of Elias the great priest, and shall bring you by the hand of the king Messiah ;* for this was God's covenant with him, that he should *restore the preserved of Israel,* Isa. xlix. 6. And this was the design of his death, to *gather into one the children of God that were scattered abroad,* John xi. 51, 52. *To him shall the gathering of the people be.* (3.) That he would *bring them into their land again, v.* 5. Note, Penitent sinners are not only delivered out of their misery, but restored to true happiness in the favour of God. The land they are brought into to possess it is, though not the same, yet in some respects better than that which our first father Adam possessed, and out of which he was expelled. (4.) That he would *do them good* (*v.* 5), and *rejoice over them for good, v.* 9. For there is joy in heaven upon the repentance and conversion of sinners : the father of the prodigal *rejoiced over him for good.* (5.) That he would multiply them (*v.* 5), and that, when they grew numerous, every mouth might have meat : he would *make them plenteous in every work of their hand, v.* 9. National repentance and reformation bring national plenty, peace, and prosperity. It is promised, *The Lord will make thee plenteous* in the fruit of thy cattle and land, for good. Many have plenty for hurt ; the prosperity of fools destroys them. Then it is for good when with it God gives us grace to use it for his glory. (6.) That he would transfer the curses they had been under to their enemies, *v.* 7. When God was gathering them in to re-establish them they would meet with much opposition ; but the same curses that had been a burden upon them should become a defence to them, by being turned upon their adversaries. The cup of trembling should be taken out of their hand, and put into the hand of those that afflicted them, Isa. li. 22, 23. (7.) That he would give them his grace to change their hearts, and rule there (v. 6): *The Lord thy God will circumcise thy heart, to love the Lord.* Note, [1.] The heart must be circumcised to love God. The filth of the flesh must be put away; and the foolishness of the heart, as the Chaldee paraphrase expounds it. See Col. ii. 11, 12; Rom. ii. 29. Circumcision was a seal of the covenant; the heart is then *circumcised to love God* when it is strongly engaged and held by that bond to this duty. [2.] It is the work of God's grace to circumcise the heart, and to shed abroad the love of God there; and this grace is given to all that repent and seek it carefully. Nay, that seems to be rather a promise than a precept (v. 8): *Thou shalt return and obey the voice of the Lord.* He that requires us to return promises grace to enable us to return: and it is our fault if that grace be not effectual. Herein the covenant of grace is well ordered, that whatsoever is required in the covenant is promised. *Turn you at my reproof: behold, I will pour out my Spirit,* Prov. i. 23.

3. It is observable how Moses here calls God *the Lord thy God* twelve times in these ten verses, intimating, (1.) That penitents may take direction and encouragement in their return to God from their relation to him. Jer. iii. 22, " *Behold, we come unto thee, for thou art the Lord our God;* therefore to thee we are bound to come, whither else should we go? And therefore we hope to find favour with thee." (2.) That those who have revolted from God, if they return to him and do their first works, shall be restored to their former state of honour and happiness. *Bring hither the first robe.* In the threatenings of the former chapter he is all along called the *Lord,* a God of power and the Judge of all: but, in the promises of this chapter, *the Lord thy God,* a God of grace, and in covenant with thee.

II. This may also be considered as a prediction of the repentance and restoration of the Jews: *When all these things shall have come upon thee* (v. 1), the blessing first, and after that the curse, then the mercy in reserve shall take place. Though their hearts were wretchedly hardened, yet the grace of God could soften and change them; and then, though their case was deplorably miserable, the providence of God would redress all their grievances. Now, 1. It is certain that this was fulfilled in their return from their captivity in Babylon. It was a wonderful instance of their repentance and reformation that Ephraim, who had been joined to idols, renounced them, and said, *What have I to do any more with idols?* That captivity effectually cured them of idolatry; and then God planted them again in their own land and did them good. But, 2. Some think that it is yet further to be accomplished in the conver-

sion of the Jews who are now dispersed, their repentance for the sin of their fathers in crucifying Christ, their return to God through him, and their accession to the Christian church. But, *alas! who shall live when God doth this?*

11 For this commandment which I command thee this day, it *is* not hidden from thee, neither *is* it far off. 12 It *is* not in heaven, that thou shouldest say, Who shall go up for us to heaven, and bring it unto us, that we may hear it, and do it? 13 Neither *is* it beyond the sea, that thou shouldest say, Who shall go over the sea for us, and bring it unto us, that we may hear it, and do it? 14 But the word *is* very nigh unto thee, in thy mouth, and in thy heart, that thou mayest do it.

Moses here urges them to obedience from the consideration of the plainness and easiness of the command.

I. This is true of the law of Moses. They could never plead in excuse of their disobedience that God had enjoined them that which 'was either unintelligible or impracticable, impossible to be known or to be done (v. 11): *It is not hidden from thee.* That is, 1. " It is not too high for thee; thou needest not send messengers to heaven (v. 12), to enquire what thou must do to please God; nor needest thou go *beyond sea* (v. 13), as the philosophers did, that travelled through many and distant regions in pursuit of learning; no, thou art not put to that labour and expense; nor is the commandment within the reach of those only that have a great estate or a refined genius, but it is *very nigh unto thee, v.* 14. It is written in thy books, made plain upon tables, so that he that runs may read it; thy priests' lips keep this knowledge, and, when any difficulty arises, thou mayest *ask the law at their mouth,* Mal. ii. 7. It is not communicated in a strange language; but it is in thy mouth, that is, in the vulgar tongue that is commonly used by thee, in which thou mayest hear it read, and talk of it familiarly among thy children. It is not wrapped up in obscure phrases or figures to puzzle and amuse thee, or in hieroglyphics, but it is in thy heart; it is delivered in such a manner as that it is level to thy capacity, even to the capacity of the meanest." 2. " It is not too *hard* nor *heavy* for thee:" so the Septuagint reads it, *v.* 11. Thou needest not say, " As good attempt to climb to heaven, or flee upon the wings of the morning to the uttermost part of the sea, as go about to do all the words of this law:" no, the matter is not so; it is no such intolerable yoke as some ill-minded people represent it. It was indeed a heavy yoke in comparison with that of Christ (Acts xv. 10), but not in

853

comparison with the idolatrous services of the neighbouring nations. God appeals to themselves that he had not *made them to serve with an offering, nor wearied them with incense,* Isa. xliii. 23 ; Mic. vi. 3. But he speaks especially of the moral law, and its precepts : " That is very nigh thee, consonant to the law of nature, which would have been found in every man's heart, and every man's mouth, if he would but have attended to it. There is that in thee which *consents to the law that it is good,* Rom. vii. 16. Thou hast therefore no reason to complain of any insuperable difficulty in the observance of it." II. This is true of the gospel of Christ, to which the apostle applies it, and makes it the language of the *righteousness which is of faith,* Rom. x. 6—8. And many think this is principally intended by Moses here ; for he *wrote of Christ,* John v. 46. This is God's commandment now under the gospel that we *believe in the name of his Son Jesus Christ,* 1 John iii. 23. If we ask, as the blind man did, *Lord, who is he ?* or where is he, that we may believe on him ? (John ix. 36), this scripture gives an answer, We need not go up to heaven, to fetch him thence, for he has come down thence in his incarnation ; nor down to the deep, to fetch him thence, for thence he has come up in his resurrection. But the word is nigh us, and Christ in that word ; so that if we believe with the heart that the promises of the incarnation and resurrection of the Messiah are fulfilled in our Lord Jesus, and receive him accordingly, and confess him with our mouth, we have then Christ with us, and we shall be saved. He is near, very near, that justifies us. The law was plain and easy, but the gospel much more so.

15 See, I have set before thee this day life and good, and death and evil; 16 In that I command thee this day to love the LORD thy God, to walk in his ways, and to keep his commandments and his statutes and his judgments, that thou mayest live and multiply: and the LORD thy God shall bless thee in the land whither thou goest to possess it. 17 But if thine heart turn away, so that thou wilt not hear, but shalt be drawn away, and worship other gods, and serve them ; 18 I denounce unto you this day, that ye shall surely perish, *and that* ye shall not prolong *your* days upon the land, whither thou passest over Jordan to go to possess it. 19 I call heaven and earth to record this day against you, *that* I have set before you life and death, blessing and cursing : therefore choose life, that both

thou and thy seed may live : 20 That thou mayest love the LORD thy God, *and* that thou mayest obey his voice, and that thou mayest cleave unto him : for he *is* thy life, and the length of thy days : that thou mayest dwell in the land which the LORD sware unto thy fathers, to Abraham, to Isaac, and to Jacob, to give them.

Moses here concludes with a very bright light, and a very strong fire, that, if possible, what he had been preaching of might find entrance into the understanding and affections of this unthinking people. What could be said more moving, and more likely to make deep and lasting impressions ? The manner of his treating with them is so rational, so prudent, so affectionate, and every way so apt to gain the point, that it abundantly shows him to be in earnest, and leaves them inexcusable in their disobedience.

I. He states the case very fairly. He appeals to themselves concerning it whether he had not laid the matter as plainly as they could wish before them. 1. Every man covets to obtain life and good, and to escape death and evil, desires happiness and dreads misery. " Well," says he, " I have shown you the way to obtain all the happiness you can desire and to avoid all misery. Be obedient, and all shall be well, and nothing amiss." Our first parents ate the forbidden fruit, in hopes of getting thereby the knowledge of good and evil; but it was a miserable knowledge they got, of good by the loss of it, and of evil by the sense of it ; yet such is the compassion of God towards man that, instead of giving him up to his own delusion, he has favoured him by his word with such a knowledge of good and evil as will make him for ever happy if it be not his own fault. 2. Every man is moved and governed in his actions by hope and fear, hope of good and fear of evil, real or apparent. " Now," says Moses, " I have tried both ways; if you will be either drawn to obedience by the certain prospect of advantage by it, or driven to obedience by the no less certain prospect of ruin in case you be disobedient— if you will be wrought upon either way, you will be kept close to God and your duty; but, if you will not, you are utterly inexcusable." Let us, then, hear the conclusion of the whole matter. (1.) If they and theirs would love God and serve him, they should live and be happy, *v.* 16. If they would love God, and evidence the sincerity of their love by keeping his commandments—if they would make conscience of keeping his commandments, and do it from a principle of love—then God would do them good, and they should be as happy as his love and blessing could make them. (2.) If they or theirs should at any time turn from God, desert his service, and worship other gods.

this would certainly be their ruin, *v.* 17, 18. Observe, It is not for every failure in the particulars of their duty that ruin is threatened, but for apostasy and idolatry : though every violation of the command deserved the curse, yet the nation would be destroyed by that only which is the violation of the marriage covenant. The purport of the New Testament is much the same; this, in like manner, sets before us life and death, good and evil : *He that believes shall be saved ; he that believes not shall be damned,* Mark xvi. 16. And this faith includes love and obedience. *To those who by patient continuance in well doing seek for glory, honour, and immortality,* God will give *eternal life. But to those that are contentious, and do not obey the truth, but obey unrighteousness* (and so, in effect, worship other gods and serve them), will be rendered the indignation and wrath of an immortal God, the consequence of which must needs be the tribulation and anguish of an immortal soul, Rom. ii. 7—9.

II. Having thus stated the case, he fairly puts them to their choice, with a direction to them to choose well. He appeals to heaven and earth concerning his fair and faithful dealing with them, *v.* 19. They could not but own that whatever was the issue he had delivered his soul ; therefore, that they might deliver theirs, he bids them choose life, that is, choose to do their duty, which would be their life. Note, 1. Those shall have life that choose it : those that choose the favour of God and communion with him for their felicity, and prosecute their choice as they ought, shall have what they choose. 2. Those that come short of life and happiness must thank themselves ; they would have had it if they had chosen it when it was put to their choice : but they die because they *will* die ; that is, because they do not like the life promised upon the terms proposed.

III. In the last verse, 1. He shows them, in short, what their duty is, *to love God,* and to love him as *the Lord,* a Being most amiable, and as *their God,* a God in covenant with them ; and, as an evidence of this love, to *obey his voice* in every thing, and by a constancy in this love and obedience to *cleave to him,* and never to forsake him in affection or practice. 2. He shows them what reason there was for this duty, in consideration, (1.) Of their dependence upon God: *He is thy life, and the length of thy days.* He gives life, preserves life, restores life, and prolongs it by his power though it is a frail life, and by his patience though it is a forfeited life : he sweetens life with his comforts, and is the sovereign Lord of life ; *in his hand our breath is.* Therefore we are concerned to keep ourselves in his love ; for it is good having him our friend, and bad having him our enemy. (2.) Of their obligation to him for the promise of Canaan made to their fathers and ratified with an oath. And, (3.) Of their expectations from him in performance of that

promise : " Love God, and serve him, that thou mayest dwell in that land of promise which thou mayest be sure he can give, and uphold to thee who is *thy life and the length of thy days.*" All these are arguments to us to continue in love and obedience to the God of our mercies.

CHAP. XXXI.

In this chapter Moses, having finished his sermon, I. Encourages both the people who were now to enter Canaan (ver. 1—6,) and Joshua who was to lead them, ver. 7, 8, 23. And, II. He takes care for the keeping of these things always in their remembrance after his decease, 1. By the book of the law which was, (1.) Written. (2.) Delivered into the custody of the priests, ver. 9, and 24—27. (3.) Ordered to be publicly read every seventh year, ver. 10—13. 2. By a song which God orders Moses to prepare for their instruction and admonition. (1.) He calls Moses and Joshua to the door of the tabernacle, ver. 14, 15. (2.) He foretels the apostasy of Israel in process of time, and the judgments they would thereby bring upon themselves, ver. 16—18. (3.) He prescribes the following song to be a witness against them, ver. 19—21. (4.) Moses wrote it, ver. 22. And delivered it to Israel, with an intimation of the design of it, as he had received it from the Lord, ver. 28, &c.

AND Moses went and spake these words unto all Israel. 2 And he said unto them, I *am* a hundred and twenty years old this day ; I can no more go out and come in : also the Lord hath said unto me, Thou shalt not go over this Jordan. 3 The Lord thy God, he will go over before thee, *and* he will destroy these nations from before thee, and thou shalt possess them : *and* Joshua, he shall go over before thee, as the Lord hath said. 4 And the Lord shall do unto them as he did to Sihon and to Og, kings of the Amorites, and unto the land of them, whom he destroyed. 5 And the Lord shall give them up before your face, that ye may do unto them according unto all the commandments which I have commanded you. 6 Be strong and of a good courage, fear not, nor be afraid of them : for the Lord thy God, he *it is* that doth go with thee ; he will not fail thee, nor forsake thee. 7 And Moses called unto Joshua, and said unto him in the sight of all Israel, Be strong and of a good courage : for thou must go with this people unto the land which the Lord hath sworn unto their fathers to give them ; and thou shalt cause them to inherit it. 8 And the Lord, he *it is* that doth go before thee ; he will be with thee, he will not fail thee, neither forsake thee : fear not, neither be dismayed.

Loth to part (we say) *bids oft farewell.* Moses does so to the children of Israel : not because he was loth to go to God, but because he was loth to leave them, fearing that when he had left them they would leave God. He had finished what he had to say to them by way of counsel and exhortation: here he calls them together to give them a word of encouragement, especially with reference to the wars of Canaan, in which they were now to engage. It was a discouragement to them that Moses was to be removed at a time when he could so ill be spared: though Joshua was continued to fight for them in the valley, they would want Moses to intercede for them on the hill, as he did, Exod. xvii. 10. But there is no remedy: *Moses can no more go out and come in, v. 2.* Not that he was disabled by any decay either of body or mind; for his *natural force was not abated, ch.* xxxiv. 7. But he cannot any longer discharge his office; for, 1. He is 120 *years old,* and it is time for him to think of resigning his honour and returning to his rest. He that had arrived at so great an age then, when seventy or eighty was the ordinary stint, as appears by the prayer of Moses (Ps. xc. 10), might well think that he had accomplished as a hireling his day. 2. He is under a divine sentence: *Thou shalt not go over Jordan.* Thus a full stop was put to his usefulness; hitherto he must go, hitherto he must serve, but no further. So God had appointed it and Moses acquiesces: for I know not why we should any of us desire to live a day longer than while God has work for us to do; nor shall we be accountable for more time than is allotted us. But, though Moses must not go over himself, he is anxious to encourage those that must.

I. He encourages the people; and never could any general animate his soldiers upon such good grounds as those on which Moses here encourages Israel. 1. He assures them of the constant presence of God with them (*v.* 3): *The Lord thy God* that has led thee and kept thee hitherto *will go over before thee;* and those might follow boldly who were sure that they had God for their leader. He repeats it again (*v.* 6) with an emphasis: "*The Lord thy God,* the great Jehovah, who is thine in covenant, *he it is,* he and no less, he and no other, *that goes before thee:* not only who by his promise has assured thee that he *will go before thee;* but by his ark, the visible token of his presence, shows thee that he *does* actually *go before thee.*" And he repeats it with enlargement: "Not only he goes over before thee at first, to bring thee in, but he will continue with thee all along, with thee and thine; *he will not fail thee nor forsake thee;* he will not disappoint thy expectations in any strait, nor will he ever desert thy interest; be constant to him, and he will be so to thee." This is applied by the apostle to all God's spiritual Israel, for the encouragement of their faith and hope; unto us is this gospel preached, as well as unto them. *He will never fail thee, nor forsake thee,* Heb. xiii. 5. 2. He commends Joshua to them for a leader: *Joshua, he shall go over before thee,*

v. 3. One whose conduct, and courage, and sincere affection to their interest, they had had long experience of; and one whom God had ordained and appointed to be their leader, and therefore, no doubt, would own and bless, and make a blessing to them. See Num. xxvii. 18. Note, It is a great encouragement to a people when, instead of some useful instruments that are removed, God raises up others to carry on his work. 3. He ensures their success. The greatest generals, supported with the greatest advantages, must yet own the issues of war to be doubtful and uncertain; the battle is not always to the strong nor to the bold; an ill accident unthought of may turn the scale against the highest hopes. But Moses had warrant from God to assure Israel that, notwithstanding the disadvantages they laboured under, they should certainly be victorious. A coward will fight when he is sure to be a conqueror. God undertakes to do the work—*he will destroy these nations;* and Israel shall do little else than divide the spoil—*thou shalt possess them, v.* 3. Two things might encourage their hopes of this:—(1.) The victories they had already obtained over Sihon and Og (*v.* 4), from which they might infer both the power of God, that he could do what he had done, and the purpose of God, that he would finish what he had begun to do. Thus must we improve our experience. (2.) The command God had given them to destroy the Canaanites (*ch.* vii. 2; xii. 2), to which he refers here (*v.* 5, that you *may do unto them according to all which I have commanded you*), and from which they might infer that, if God had commanded them to destroy the Canaanites, no doubt he would put it into the power of their hands to do it. Note, What God has made our duty we have reason to expect opportunity and assistance from him for the doing of. So that from all this he had reason enough to bid them *be strong and of a good courage, v.* 6. While they had the power of God engaged for them they had no reason to fear all the powers of Canaan engaged against them.

II. He encourages Joshua, *v.* 7, 8. Observe, 1. Though Joshua was an experienced general, and a man of approved gallantry and resolution, who had already signalized himself in many brave actions, yet Moses saw cause to bid him *be of good courage,* now that he was entering upon a new scene of action; and Joshua was far from taking it as an affront, or as a tacit questioning of his courage, to be thus charged, as sometimes we find proud and peevish spirits invidiously taking exhortations and admonitions for reproaches and reflections. Joshua himself is very well pleased to be admonished by Moses to be strong and of good courage. 2. He gives him this charge *in the sight of all Israel,* that they might be the more observant of him whom they saw thus solemnly inaugurated, and that he might set himself the more to be an example of courage to the people who were witnesses to this charge here given to him as well as to themselves. 3. He gives him the same assurances of the divine presence, and consequently of a glorious success, that he had given the people. God would be with him, would not forsake him, and therefore he should certainly accomplish the glorious enterprise to which he was called and commissioned: *Thou shalt cause them to inherit the land* of promise. Note, Those shall speed well that have God with them; and therefore they ought to *be of good courage.* Through God let us do valiantly, for through him we shall do victoriously; if we resist the devil, he shall flee, and God shall *shortly* *tread him under our feet.*

9 And Moses wrote this law, and delivered it unto the priests the sons of Levi, which bare the ark of the covenant of the LORD, and unto all the elders of Israel. 10 And Moses commanded them, saying, At the end of *every* seven years, in the solemnity of the year of release, in the feast of tabernacles, 11 When all Israel is come to appear before the LORD thy God in the place which he shall choose, thou shalt read this law before all Israel in their hearing. 12 Gather the people together, men, and women, and children, and thy stranger that *is* within thy gates, that they may hear, and that they may learn, and fear the LORD your God, and observe to do all the words of this law: 13 And *that* their children, which have not known *any thing*, may hear, and learn to fear the LORD your God, as long as ye live in the land whither ye go over Jordan to possess it.

The law was given by Moses; so it is said, John i. 17. He was not only entrusted to deliver it to that generation, but to transmit it to the generations to come; and here it appears that he was faithful to that trust.

I. *Moses wrote this law, v.* 9. The learned bishop Patrick understands this of all the five books of Moses, which are often called the *law;* he supposes that though Moses had written most of the Pentateuch before, yet he did not finish it till now; now he put his last hand to that sacred volume. Many think that the law here (especially since it is called *this law*, this grand abridgment of the law) is to be understood of this book of Deuteronomy; all those discourses to the people which have taken up this whole book, he, being in them divinely inspired, wrote them as the word of God. He wrote this law, 1. That those who had heard it might

often review it themselves, and call it to mind. 2. That it might be the more safely handed down to posterity. Note, The church has received abundance of advantage from the writing, as well as from the preaching, of divine things; faith comes not only by hearing, but by reading. The same care that was taken of the law, thanks be to God, is taken of the gospel too; soon after it was preached it was written, that it might reach to those on whom the ends of the world shall come.

II. Having written it, he committed it to the care and custody of the priests and elders. He delivered one authentic copy to the priests, to be laid up by the ark (*v.* 26), there to remain as a standard by which all other copies must be tried. And it is supposed that he gave another copy to the elders of each tribe, to be transcribed by all of that tribe that were so disposed. Some observe that the elders, as well as the priests, were entrusted with the law, to intimate that magistrates by their power, as well as ministers by their doctrine, are to maintain religion, and to take care that the law be not broken nor lost.

III. He appointed the public reading of this law in a general assembly of all Israel every seventh year. The pious Jews (it is very probable) read the law daily in their families, and *Moses of old time was read in the synagogue every sabbath day,* Acts xv. 21. But once in seven years, that the law might be the more magnified and made honourable, it must be read in a general assembly. Though we read the word in private, we must not think it needless to hear it read in public. Now here he gives direction,

1. When this solemn reading of the law must be, that the time might add to the solemnity; it must be done, (1.) In the year of release. In that year the land rested, so that they could the better spare time to attend this service. Servants who were then discharged, and poor debtors who were then acquitted from their debts, must know that, having the benefit of the law, it was justly expected they should yield obedience to it, and therefore give up themselves to be God's servants, because he had loosed their bonds. The year of release was typical of gospel grace, which therefore is called the *acceptable* *year of the Lord;* for our remission and liberty by Christ engage us to keep his commandments, Luke i. 74, 75. (2.) At the feast of tabernacles in that year. In that feast they were particularly required to *rejoice before God*, Lev. xxiii. 40. Therefore then they must read the law, both to qualify their mirth and keep it in due bounds, and to sanctify their mirth, that they might make the law of God the matter of their rejoicing, and might read it with pleasure and not as a task.

2. To whom it must be read: To *all Israel* (*v.* 11), *men, women, and children, and the strangers, v.* 12. The women and children were not obliged to go up to the other feasts,

but to this only in which the law was read. Note, It is the will of God that all people should acquaint themselves with his word. It is a rule to all, and therefore should be read to all. It is supposed that, since all Israel could not possibly meet in one place, nor could one man's voice reach them all, as many as the courts of the Lord's house would hold met there, and the rest at the same time in their synagogues. The Jewish doctors say that the hearers were bound to *prepare their hearts,* and to hear *with fear and reverence, and with joy and trembling,* as in the day *when the law was given on Mount Sinai;* and, though there were *great and wise men who knew the whole law very well,* yet they were bound to *hear with great attention;* for he that *reads is the messenger of the congregation to cause the words of God to be heard.* I wish those that hear the gospel read and preached would consider this.

3. By whom it must be read: *Thou shalt read it* (v. 11), "Thou, O Israel," by a proper person appointed for that purpose; or, "Thou, O Joshua," their chief ruler; accordingly we find that he did read the law himself, Josh. viii. 34, 35. So did Josiah, 2 Chron. xxxiv. 30, and Ezra, Neh. viii. 3. And the Jews say that the king himself (when they had one) was the person that read in the courts of the temple, that a pulpit was set up for that purpose in the midst of the court, in which the king stood, that the book of the law was delivered to him by the high priest, that he stood up to receive it, uttered a prayer (as every one did that was to read the law in public) before he read; and then, if he pleased, he might sit down and read. But if he read standing it was thought the more commendable, as (they say) king Agrippa did. Here let me offer it as a conjecture that Solomon is called the *preacher,* in his Ecclesiastes, because he delivered the substance of that book in a discourse to the people, after his public reading of the law in the feast of tabernacles, according to this appointment here.

4. For what end it must be thus solemnly read. (1.) That the present generation might hereby keep up their acquaintance with the law of God, v. 12. They must hear, that they may learn, and *fear God, and observe to do their duty.* See here what we are to aim at in hearing the word; we must hear, that we may learn and grow in knowledge; and every time we read the scriptures we shall find that there is still more and more to be learned out of them. We must learn, that we may fear God, that is, that we may be duly affected with divine things; and must fear God, that we may *observe and do the words of his law;* for in vain do we pretend to fear him if we do not obey him. (2.) That the rising generation might betimes be leavened with religion (v. 13); not only that those who know something may thus know more, but that *the children who have not known any thing* may betimes know this, how

858

much it is their interest as well as duty to fear God.

14 And the LORD said unto Moses, Behold, thy days approach that thou must die: call Joshua, and present yourselves in the tabernacle of the congregation, that I may give him a charge. And Moses and Joshua went, and presented themselves in the tabernacle of the congregation. 15 And the LORD appeared in the tabernacle in a pillar of a cloud: and the pillar of the cloud stood over the door of the tabernacle. 16 And the LORD said unto Moses, Behold, thou shalt sleep with thy fathers; and this people will rise up, and go a whoring after the gods of the strangers of the land, whither they go *to be* among them, and will forsake me, and break my covenant which I have made with them. 17 Then my anger shall be kindled against them in that day, and I will forsake them, and I will hide my face from them, and they shall be devoured, and many evils and troubles shall befal them; so that they will say in that day, Are not these evils come upon us, because our God *is* not among us? 18 And I will surely hide my face in that day for all the evils which they shall have wrought, in that they are turned unto other gods. 19 Now therefore write ye this song for you, and teach it the children of Israel: put it in their mouths, that this song may be a witness for me against the children of Israel. 20 For when I shall have brought them into the land which I sware unto their fathers, that floweth with milk and honey; and they shall have eaten and filled themselves, and waxen fat; then will they turn unto other gods, and serve them, and provoke me, and break my covenant. 21 And it shall come to pass, when many evils and troubles are befallen them, that this song shall testify against them as a witness; for it shall not be forgotten out of the mouths of their seed: for I know their imagination which they go about, even now, before I have brought them into the land which I sware.

Here, I. Moses and Joshua are summoned

to attend the divine majesty at the door of the tabernacle, *v.* 14. Moses is told again that he must shortly die; even those that are most ready and willing to die have need to be often reminded of the approach of death. In consideration of this, he must come himself to meet God; for whatever improves our communion with God furthers our preparation for death. He must also bring Joshua with him to be presented to God for a successor, and to receive his commission and charge. Moses readily obeys the summons, for he was not one of those that look with an evil eye upon their successors, but, on the contrary, rejoiced in him.

II. God graciously gives them the meeting: *He appeared in the tabernacle* (as the shechinah used to appear) *in a pillar of a cloud, v.* 15. This is the only time in all this book that we read of the glory of God appearing, whereas we often read of it in the three foregoing books, which perhaps signifies that in the latter days, under the evangelical law, such visible appearances as these of the divine glory are not to be expected, but we must take heed to the more sure word of prophecy.

III. He tells Moses that, after his death, the covenant which he had taken so much pains to make between Israel and their God would certainly be broken. 1. That Israel would *forsake* God, *v.* 16. And we may be sure that if the covenant between God and man be broken the blame must lie on man, it is he that breaks it; we have often observed it, That God never leaves any till they first leave him. Worshipping the gods of the Canaanites (who had been the natives, but henceforward were to be looked upon as the strangers of that land) would undoubtedly be counted a deserting of God, and, like adultery, a violation of the covenant. Thus still those are revolters from Christ, and will be so adjudged, who either make a god of their money by reigning covetousness or a god of their belly by reigning sensuality. Those that *turn to other gods* (*v.* 18) forsake their own mercies. This apostasy of theirs is foretold to be the effect of their prosperity (*v.* 20): *They shall have eaten and filled themselves;* this is all they will aim at in eating, to gratify their own appetites, and then they will wax fat, grow secure and sensual; their security will take off their dread of God and his judgments; and their sensuality will incline them to the idolatries of the heathen, which *made provision for the flesh to fulfil the lusts of it.* Note, God has a clear and infallible foresight of all the wickedness of the wicked, and has often covenanted with those who *he knew would deal very treacherously* (Isa. xlviii. 8), and conferred many favours on those who he knew would deal very ungratefully. 2. That then God would forsake Israel; and justly does he cast those off who had so unjustly cast him off (*v.* 17): *My anger shall be kindled against them, and I will forsake them.* His providence would forsake

them, no longer to protect and prosper them, and then they would become a prey to all their neighbours. His spirit and grace would forsake them, no longer to teach and guide them, and then they would be more and more bigoted, besotted, and hardened in their idolatries. Thus *many evils and troubles would befal them* (*v.* 17, 21), which would be such manifest indications of God's displeasure against them that they themselves would be constrained to own it: *Have not these evils come upon us because our God is not among us?* Those that have sinned away their God will find that thereby they pull all mischiefs upon their own heads. But that which completed their misery was that God would *hide his face from them in that day*, that day of their trouble and distress, *v.* 18. Whatever outward troubles we are in, if we have but the light of God's countenance, we may be easy. But, if God hide his face from us and our prayers, we are undone.

IV. He directs Moses to deliver them a song, in the composing of which he should be divinely inspired, and which should remain a standing testimony for God as faithful to them in giving them warning, and against them as persons false to themselves in not taking the warning, *v.* 19. The written word in general, as well as this song in particular, is a witness for God against all those that break covenant with him. It shall be for a testimony, Matt. xxiv. 14. The wisdom of man has devised many ways of conveying the knowledge of good and evil, by laws, histories, prophecies, proverbs, and, among the rest, by songs; each has its advantages. And the wisdom of God has in the scripture made use of them all, that ignorant and careless men might be left inexcusable. 1. This song, if rightly improved, might be a means to prevent their apostasy; for in the inditing of it God had an eye to their present imagination, now, *before they were brought into the land of promise, v.* 21. God knew very well that there were in their hearts such gross conceits of the deity, and such inclinations to idolatry, that they would be tinder to the sparks of that temptation; and therefore in this song he gives them warning of their danger that way. Note, The word of God is a *discerner of the thoughts and intents of men's hearts*, and meets with them strangely by its reproofs and corrections, Heb. iv. 12. Compare 1 Cor. xiv. 25. Ministers who preach the word know not the imaginations men go about, but God, whose word it is, knows perfectly. 2. If this song did not prevent their apostasy, yet it might help to bring them to repentance, and to recover them from their apostasy. When their troubles come upon them, this *song shall not be forgotten*, but may serve as a glass to show them their own faces, that they may humble themselves, and return to him from whom they have revolted. Note, Those for whom God has mercy in store he may leave to fall, yet he will provide means for their recovery. Medicines are prepared before-hand for their cure.

22 Moses therefore wrote this song the same day, and taught it the children of Israel. 23 And he gave Joshua the son of Nun a charge, and said, Be strong and of a good courage : for thou shalt bring the children of Israel into the land which I sware unto them : and I will be with thee. 24 And it came to pass, when Moses had made an end of writing the words of this law in a book, until they were finished, 25 That Moses commanded the Levites, which bare the ark of the covenant of the LORD, saying, 26 Take this book of the law, and put it in the side of the ark of the covenant of the LORD your God, that it may be there for a witness against thee. 27 For I know thy rebellion, and thy stiff neck : behold, while I am yet alive with you this day, ye have been rebellious against the LORD ; and how much more after my death ? 28 Gather unto me all the elders of your tribes, and your officers, that I may speak these words in their ears, and call heaven and earth to record against them. 29 For I know that after my death ye will utterly corrupt *yourselves,* and turn aside from the way which I have commanded you; and evil will befal you in the latter days ; because ye will do evil in the sight of the LORD, to provoke him to anger through the work of your hands. 30 And Moses spake in the ears of all the congregation of Israel the words of this song, until they were ended.

Here, I. The charge is given to Joshua, which God had said (*v.* 14) he would give him. The same in effect that Moses had given him (*v.* 7) : *Be strong and of a good courage, v.* 23. Joshua had now heard from God so much of the wickedness of the people whom he was to have the conduct of as could not but be a discouragement to him : "Nay," says God, "how bad soever they are, thou shalt go through thy undertaking, for *I will be with thee.* Thou shalt put them into possession of Canaan. If they afterwards by their sin throw themselves out of it again, that will be no fault of thine, nor any dishonour to thee, therefore *be of good courage.*"

II. The solemn delivery of the book of the law to the Levites, to be deposited in the side

of the ark, is here again related (*v.* 24—26), of which before, *v.* 9. Only they are here directed where to treasure up this precious original, not in the ark (there only the two tables were preserved), but in another box *by the side of the ark.* It is probable that this was the very book that was found in the house of the Lord (having been somehow or other misplaced) in the days of Josiah (2 Chron. xxxiv. 14), and so perhaps the following words here, *that it may be a witness against thee,* may particularly point at that event, which happened so long after ; for the finding of this very book occasioned the public reading of it by Josiah himself, for a witness against a people who were then almost ripe for their ruin by the Babylonians.

III. The song which follows in the next chapter is here delivered to Moses, and by him to the people. He wrote it first (*v.* 22), as the Spirit of God indited it, and then *spoke it in the ears of all the congregation* (*v.* 30), and taught it to them (*v.* 22), that is, gave out copies of it, and ordered the people to learn it by heart. It was delivered by word of mouth first, and afterwards in writing, to the elders and officers, as the representatives of their respective tribes (*v.* 28), by them to be transmitted to their several families and households. It was delivered to them with a solemn appeal to heaven and earth concerning the fair warning which was given them by it of the fatal consequences of their apostasy from God, and with a declaration of the little joy and little hope Moses had in and concerning them. 1. He declares what little joy he had had of them while he was with them, *v.* 27. It is not in a passion that he says, *I know thy rebellion* (as once he said unadvisedly, *Hear now, you rebels),* but it is the result of a long acquaintance with them : *you have been rebellious against the Lord.* Their rebellions against himself he makes no mention of : these he had long since forgiven and forgotten ; but they must be made to hear of their rebellions against God, that they may be ever repented of and never repeated. 2. What little hopes he had of them now that he was leaving them. From what God had now said to him (*v.* 16) more than from his own experience of them, though that was discouraging enough, he tells them (*v.* 29), *I know that after my death you will utterly corrupt yourselves.* Many a sad thought, no doubt, it occasioned to this good man, to foresee the apostasy and ruin of a people he had taken so much pains with, in order to do them good and make them happy ; but this was his comfort, that he had done his duty, and that God would be glorified, if not in their settlement, yet in their dispersion. Thus our Lord Jesus, a little before his death, foretold the rise of false Christs and false prophets (Matt. xxiv. 24), notwithstanding which, and all the apostasies of the latter times, we may be confident that *the gates of hell shall not prevail against the church,* for the *foundation of God stands sure.*

CHAP. XXXII.

In this chapter we have, I. The song which Moses, by the appointment of God, delivered to the children of Israel, for a standing admonition to them, to take heed of forsaking God. This takes up most of the chapter, in which we have, 1. The preface, ver. 1, 2. 2. A high character of God, and, in opposition to that, a bad character of the people of Israel, ver. 3 – 6. 3. A rehearsal of the great things God had done for them, and in opposition to that an account of their ill carriage towards him, ver. 7 – 18. 4. A prediction of the wasting destroying judgments which God would bring upon them for their sins, in which God is here justified by the many aggravations of their impieties, ver. 19—33. 5. A promise of the destruction of their enemies and oppressors at last, and the glorious deliverance of a remnant of Israel, ver. 36—43. II. The exhortation with which Moses delivered this song to them, ver. 44 –47. III. The orders God gives to Moses to go up to Mount Nebo and die, ver. 48, &c.

GIVE ear, O ye heavens, and I will speak; and hear, O earth, the words of my mouth. 2 My doctrine shall drop as the rain, my speech shall distil as the dew, as the small rain upon the tender herb, and as the showers upon the grass: 3 Because I will publish the name of the LORD: ascribe ye greatness unto our God. 4 *He is* the Rock, his work *is* perfect: for all his ways *are* judgment: a God of truth and without iniquity, just and right *is* he. 5 They have corrupted themselves, their spot *is* not *the spot* of his children: *they are* a perverse and crooked generation. 6 Do ye thus requite the LORD, O foolish people and unwise; *is* not he thy father *that* hath bought thee? hath he not made thee, and established thee?

Here is, I. A commanding preface or introduction to this song of Moses, *v.* 1, 2. He begins, 1. With a solemn appeal to heaven and earth concerning the truth and importance of what he was about to say, and the justice of the divine proceedings against a rebellious and backsliding people, for he had said (*ch.* xxxi. 28) that he would in this song call heaven and earth to record against them. Heaven and earth would sooner hear than this perverse and unthinking people; for they revolt not from their obedience to their Creator, but *continue to this day, according to his ordinances, as his servants* (Ps. cxix. 89—91), and therefore will rise up in judgment against rebellious Israel. Heaven and earth will be witnesses against sinners, witnesses of the warning given them and of their refusal to take the warning (see Job xx. 27); the *heaven shall reveal his iniquity, and the earth shall rise up against him.* Or heaven and earth are here put for the inhabitants of both, angels and men; both shall agree to justify God in his proceedings against Israel, and to *declare his righteousness,* Ps. l. 6; see Rev. xix. 1, 2. He begins with a solemn application of what he was about to say to the people (*v.* 2): *My doctrine shall drop as the rain.* " It shall be a beating sweeping rain to the

rebellious;" so one of the Chaldee paraphrasts expounds the first clause. Rain is sometimes sent for judgment, witness that with which the world was deluged; and so the word of God, while to some it is reviving and refreshing—a *savour of life unto life,* is to others terrifying and killing—a *savour of death unto death.* It shall be as a sweet and comfortable dew to those who are rightly prepared to receive it. Observe, (1.) The subject of this song is doctrine; he had given them a song of praise and thanksgiving (Exod. xv.), but this is a song of instruction, for in psalms, and hymns, and spiritual songs, we are not only to give glory to God, but to *teach and admonish one another,* Col. iii. 16. Hence many of David's psalms are entitled *Maschil—to give instruction.* (2.) This doctrine is fitly compared to rain and showers which come from above, to make the earth fruitful, and *accomplish that for which they are sent* (Isa. lv. 10, 11), and depend not upon the wisdom or will of man, Mic. v. 7. It is a mercy to have this rain come often upon us, and our duty to *drink it in,* Heb. vi. 7. (3.) He promises that his doctrine shall drop and distil as the dew, and the small rain, which descend silently and without noise. The word preached is likely to profit when it comes gently, and sweetly insinuates itself into the hearts and affections of the hearers. (4.) He bespeaks their acceptance and entertainment of it, and that it might be as sweet, and pleasant, and welcome to them as rain to the *thirsty earth,* Ps. lxxii. 6. And the word of God is likely to do us good when it is thus acceptable. (5.) The learned bishop Patrick understands it as a prayer that his words which were sent from heaven to them might sink into their hearts and soften them, as the rain softens the earth, and so make them fruitful in obedience.

II. An awful declaration of the greatness and righteousness of God, *v.* 3, 4. 1. He begins with this, and lays it down as his first principle, (1.) To preserve the honour of God, that no reproach might be cast upon him for the sake of the wickedness of his people Israel; how wicked and corrupt soever those are who, are called by his name, he is just, and right, and all that is good, and is not to be thought the worse of for their badness. (2.) To aggravate the wickedness of Israel, who knew and worshipped such a holy God, and yet were themselves so unholy. And, (3.) To justify God in his dealings with them; we must abide by it, that God is righteous, even when his *judgments are a great deep,* Jer. xii. 1 ; Ps. xxxvi. 6. 2. Moses here sets himself to *publish the name of the Lord* (*v.* 3), that Israel, knowing what a God he is *whom* they had avouched for theirs, might never be such fools as to exchange him for a false god, a dunghill god. He calls upon them therefore to ascribe greatness to him. It will be of great use to us for the preventing of sin, and the preserv-

861

ing of us in the way of our duty, always to keep up high and honourable thoughts of God, and to take all occasions to express them : *Ascribe greatness to our God.* We cannot add to his greatness, for it is infinite ; but we must acknowledge it, and give him the glory of it. Now, when Moses would set forth the greatness of God, he does it, not by explaining his eternity and immensity, or describing the brightness of his glory in the upper world, but by showing the faithfulness of his word, the perfection of his works, and the wisdom and equity of all the administrations of his government; for in these his glory shines most clearly to us, and these are the things revealed concerning him, which *belong to us and our children, v.* 4. (1.) *He is the rock.* So he is called six times in this chapter, and the LXX. all along translate it Θεὸς, *God.* The learned Mr. Hugh Broughton reckons that God is called the *rock* eighteen times (besides in this chapter) in the Old Testament (though in some places we translate it *strength),* and charges it therefore upon the papists that they make St. Peter a god when they make him the rock on which the church is built. God is the rock, for he is in himself immutable immovable, and he is to all that seek him and fly to him an impenetrable shelter, and to all that trust in him an everlasting foundation. (2.) *His work is perfect.* His work of creation was so, *all very good ;* his works of providence are so, or will be so in due time, and when the mystery of God shall be finished the perfection of his works will appear to all the world. Nothing that God does can be mended, Eccl. iii. 14 God was now perfecting what he had promised and begun for his people Israel, and from the perfection of this work they must take occasion to give him the glory of the perfection of all his works. The best of men's works are imperfect, they have their flaws and defects, and are left unfinished ; but, *as for God, his work is perfect ;* if he begin, he will make an end. (3.) *All his ways are judgment.* The ends of his ways are all righteous, and he is wise in the choice of the means in order to those ends. *Judgment* signifies both *prudence* and *justice. The ways of the Lord are right,* Hos. xiv. 9. (4.) He is *a God of truth,* whose word we may take and rely upon, for he cannot lie who is faithful to all his promises, nor shall his threatenings fall to the ground. (5.) He is *without iniquity,* one who never cheated any that trusted in him, never wronged any that appealed to his justice, nor ever was hard upon any that cast themselves upon his mercy. (6.) *Just and right is he.* As he will not wrong any by punishing them more than they deserve, so he will not fail to recompense all those that serve him or suffer for him. He is indeed just and right ; for he will effectually take care that none shall lose by him. Now what a bright and amiable idea does this one verse give us of the God

whom we worship ; and what reason have we then to love him and fear him, to live a life of delight in him, dependence on him, and devotedness to him ! This is *our rock, and there is no unrighteousness in him ;* nor can there be, Ps. xcii. 15.

III. A high charge exhibited against the Israel of God, whose character was in all respects the reverse of that of the *God of Israel, v.* 5. 1. *They have corrupted themselves.* Or, *It has corrupted itself ;* the body of the people has : *the whole head sick, and the whole heart faint.* God did not corrupt them, for *just and right is he ;* but they are themselves the sole authors of their own sin and ruin ; and both are included in this word. *They have debauched themselves ;* for every man is tempted when he is drawn away of his own lust. And *they have destroyed themselves,* Hos. xiii. 9. If thou scornest, thou alone shalt bear the guilt and grief, Prov. ix. 12. 2. *Their spot is not the spot of his children.* Even God's children have their spots, while they are in this imperfect state ; for if we say we have no sin, no spot, we deceive ourselves. But the sin of Israel was none of those ; it was not an infirmity which they strove against, watched and prayed against, but an evil which their hearts were fully set in them to do. For, 3. They were a *perverse and crooked generation,* that were actuated by a spirit of contradiction, and therefore would do what was forbidden because it was forbidden, would set up their own humour and fancy in opposition to the will of God, were impatient of reproof, hated to be reformed, and *went on frowardly in the way of their heart.* The Chaldee paraphrase reads this verse thus : *They have scattered* or changed *themselves, and not him, even the children that served idols, a generation that has depraved its own works, and alienated itself.* Idolaters cannot hurt God, nor do any damage to his works, nor make him a stranger to this world. See Job xxxv. 6. No, all the hurt they do is to themselves and their own works. The learned bishop Patrick gives another reading of it : *Did he do him any hurt ?* That is, " Is God the rock to be blamed for the evils that should befal Israel ? No, *His children are their blot,*" that is, " All the evil that comes upon them is the fruit of their children's wickedness ; for the whole generation of them is crooked and perverse." All that are ruined ruin themselves ; they die because they will die.

IV. A pathetic expostulation with this provoking people for their ingratitude (*v.* 6) : " *Do you thus requite the Lord ?* Surely you will not hereafter be so base and disingenuous in your carriage towards him as you have been." 1. He reminds them of the obligations God had laid upon them to serve him, and to cleave to him. He had been a Father to them, had begotten them, fed them, carried them, nursed them, and borne their manners ; and would they spurn at the bowels of a Father ? He had bought them, had been at a vast expense of miracles to bring them out of Egypt, had given *men for them*, and *people for their life*, Isa. xliii. 4. *" Is not he thy Father, thy owner* (so some), that has an incontestable propriety in thee ?" and *the ox knoweth his owner.* " He has made thee, and brought thee into being, established thee and kept thee in being; has he not done so ? Can you deny the engagements you lie under to him, in consideration of the great things he has done and designed for you ?" And are not our obligations, as baptized Christians, equally great and strong to our Creator that made us, our Redeemer that bought us, and our Sanctifier that has established us. 2. Hence he infers the evil of deserting him and rebelling against him. For, (1.) It was base ingratitude : *" Do you thus requite the Lord ?* Are these the returns you make him for all his favours to you ? The powers you have from him will you employ them against him ?" See Mic. vi. 3, 4 ; John x. 32. This is such monstrous villany as all the world will cry shame of : call a man ungrateful, and you can call him no worse. (2.) It was prodigious madness : *O foolish people and unwise !* Fools, and double fools ! *who has bewitched you ?* Gal. iii. 1. " Fools indeed, to disoblige one on whom you have such a necessary dependence ! To forsake your own mercies for lying vanities !" Note, All wilful sinners, especially sinners in Israel, are the most unwise and the most ungrateful people in the world.

7 Remember the days of old, consider the years of many generations: ask thy father, and he will show thee; thy elders, and they will tell thee. 8 When the Most High divided to the nations their inheritance, when he separated the sons of Adam, he set the bounds of the people according to the number of the children of Israel. 9 For the LORD's portion *is* his people; Jacob *is* the lot of his inheritance. 10 He found him in a desert land, and in the waste howling wilderness; he led him about, he instructed him, he kept him as the apple of his eye. 11 As an eagle stirreth up her nest, fluttereth over her young, spreadeth abroad her wings, taketh them, beareth them on her wings: 12 *So* the LORD alone did lead him, and *there was* no strange god with him. 13 He made him ride on the high places of the earth, that he might eat the increase of the fields; and he made him to suck honey out of the rock, and oil out of the flinty rock; 14 Butter of kine, and milk of sheep, with fat of

lambs, and rams of the breed of Bashan, and goats, with the fat of kidneys of wheat; and thou didst drink the pure blood of the grape.

Moses, having in general represented God to them as their great benefactor, whom they were bound in gratitude to observe and obey, in these verses gives particular instances of God's kindness to them and concern for them. 1. Some instances were ancient, and for proof of them he appeals to the records (*v.* 7) : *Remember the days of old;* that is, " Keep in remembrance the history of those days, and of the wonderful providences of God concerning the old world, and concerning your ancestors Abraham, Isaac, and Jacob ; you will find a constant series of mercies attending them, and how long since things were working towards that which has now come to pass." Note, The authentic histories of ancient times are of singular use, and especially the history of the church in its infancy, both the Old-Testament and the New-Testament church. 2. Others were more modern, and for proof of them he appeals to their fathers and elders that were now alive and with them. Parents must diligently teach their children, 'not only the word of God, his laws (*ch.* vi. 7), and the meaning of his ordinances (Exod. xii. 26, 27), but his works also, and the methods of his providence. See Ps. lxxviii. 3, 4, 6, 7. And children should desire the knowledge of those things which will be of use to engage them to their duty and to direct them in it.

Three things are here enlarged upon as instances of God's kindness to his people Israel, and strong obligations upon them never to forsake him :—

I. The early designation of the land of Canaan for their inheritance ; for herein it was a type and figure of our heavenly inheritance, that it was of old ordained and prepared in the divine counsels, *v.* 8. Observe, 1. When the earth was divided among the sons of men, in the days of Peleg, after the flood, and each family had its lot, in which it must settle, and by degrees grow up into a nation, then God had Israel in his thoughts and in his eye ; for, designing this good land into which they were now going to be in due time an inheritance for them, he ordered that the posterity of Canaan, rather than any other of the families then in being, should be planted there in the mean time, to keep possession, as it were, till Israel was ready for it, because those families were under the curse of Noah, by which they were condemned to servitude and ruin (Gen. ix. 25), and therefore would be the more justly, honourably, easily, and effectually, rooted out, when the fulness of time should come that Israel should take possession. Thus he set the bounds of that people with an eye to the designed number of the children of Israel, that they might have just as much as would serve

863

their turn. And some observe that Canaan himself, and his eleven sons (Gen. x. 15, &c.), make up just the number of the twelve tribes of Israel. Note, (1.) The wisdom of God has appointed the bounds of men's habitation, and determined both the place and time of our living in the world, Acts xvii. 26. When he *gave the earth to the children of men* (Ps. cxv. 16), it was not that every man might catch as he could; no, he divides to nations their inheritance, and will have every one to know his own, and not to invade another's property. (2.) Infinite wisdom has a vast reach, and designs beforehand what is brought to pass long after. *Known unto God are all his works* from the beginning to the end (Acts xv. 18), but they are not so to us, Eccl. iii. 11. (3.) The great God, in governing the world, and ordering the affairs of states and kingdoms, has a special regard to his church and people, and consults their good in all. See 2 Chron. xvi. 9, and Isa. xlv. 4. The Canaanites thought they had as good and sure a title to their land as any of their neighbours had to theirs; but God intended that they should only be tenants, till the Israelites, their landlords, came. Thus God serves his own purposes of kindness to his people, by those that neither know him nor love him, *who mean not so, neither doth their heart think so,* Isa. x. 7; Mic. iv. 12.

2. The reason given for the particular care God took for this people, so long before they were either born or thought of (as I may say), in our world, does yet more magnify the kindness, and make it obliging beyond expression (*v.* 9): *For the Lord's portion is his people.* All the world is his. He is owner and possessor of heaven and earth, but his church is his in a peculiar manner. It is his demesne, his vineyard, his garden enclosed. He has a particular delight in it: it is the beloved of his soul, in it he walks, he dwells, it is his rest for ever. He has a particular concern for it, keeps it as the apple of his eye. He has particular expectations from it, as a man has from his portion, has a much greater rent of honour, glory, and worship, from that distinguished remnant, than from all the world besides. That God should be his people's portion is easy to be accounted for, for he is their joy and felicity; but how they should be his portion, who neither needs them nor can be benefited by them, must be resolved into the wondrous condescensions of free grace. *Even so, Father, because it seemed good in thy eyes* so to call and to account them.

II. The forming of them into a people, that they might be fit to enter upon this inheritance, like an heir of age, at the time appointed of the Father. And herein also Canaan was a figure of the heavenly inheritance; for, as it was from eternity proposed and designed for all God's spiritual Israel, so they are, in time (and it is a work of time), fitted and made meet for it, Col. i. 12. The

deliverance of Israel out of slavery, by the destruction of their oppressors, was attended with so many wonders obvious to sense, and had been so often spoken of, that it needed not to be mentioned in this song; but the gracious works God wrought upon them would be less taken notice of than the glorious works he had wrought for them, and therefore he chooses rather to advert to them. A great deal was done to model this people, to cast them into some shape, and to fit them for the great things designed for them in the land of promise; and it is here most elegantly described.

1. *He found him in a desert land, v.* 10. This refers, no doubt, to the wilderness through which God brought them to Canaan, and in which he took so much pains with them; it is called *the church in the wilderness,* Acts vii. 38. There it was born, and nursed, and educated, that all might appear to be divine and from heaven, since they had there no communication with any part of this earth either for food or learning But, because he is said to *find* them there, it seems designed also to represent both the bad state and the bad character of that people when God began first to appear for them. (1.) Their condition was forlorn. Egypt was to them a desert land, and a waste howling wilderness, for they were bond-slaves in it, and cried by reason of their oppression, and were perfectly bewildered and at a loss for relief; there God found them, and thence he fetched them. And, (2.) Their disposition was very unpromising. So ignorant were the generality of them in divine things, so stupid and unapt to receive the impressions of them, so peevish and humoursome, so froward and quarrelsome, and withal so strangely addicted to the idolatries of Egypt, that they might well be said to be found in a desert land; for one might as reasonably expect a crop of corn from a barren wilderness as any good fruit of service to God from a people of such a character. Those that are renewed and sanctified by grace should often remember what they were by nature.

2. *He led him about and instructed him.* When God had them in the wilderness he did not bring them directly to Canaan, but made them go a great way about, and so he instructed them; that is, (1.) By this means he took time to instruct them, and gave them commandments as they were able to receive them. Those whose business it is to instruct others must not expect it will be done of a sudden; learners must have time to learn. (2.) By this means he tried their faith, and patience, and dependence upon God, and inured them to the hardships of the wilderness, and so instructed them. Every stage had something in it that was instructive; even when he chastened them, he thereby *taught them out of his law.* It is said (Ps. cvii. 7) that he *led them forth by the right way;* and yet here that he *led them about:*

for God always leads his people the right way, however to us it may seem circuitous : so that the furthest way about proves, if not the nearest way, yet the best way home to Canaan. How God instructed them is explained long after (Neh. ix. 13), *Thou gavest them right judgments and true laws, good statutes and commandments ;* and especially (*v.* 20), *Thou gavest them also thy good Spirit to instruct them ;* and he instructs effectually. We may well imagine how unfit that people would have been for Canaan had they not first gone through the discipline of the wilderness.

3. *He kept him as the apple of his eye,* with all the care and tenderness that could be, from the malignant influences of an open sky and air, and all the perils of an inhospitable desert. The pillar of cloud and fire was both a guide and a guard to them.

4. He did that for them which the eagle does for her nest of young ones, *v.* 11, 12. The similitude was touched, Exod. xix. 4, *I bore you on eagles' wings ;* here it is enlarged upon. The eagle is observed to have a strong affection for her young, and to show it, not only as other creatures by protecting them and making provision for them, but by educating them and teaching them to fly. For this purpose she stirs them out of the nest where they lie dozing, flutters over them, to show them how they must use their wings, and then accustoms them to fly upon her wings till they have learnt to fly upon their own. This, by the way, is an example to parents to train up their children to business, and not to indulge them in idleness and the love of ease. God did thus by Israel ; when they were in love with their slavery, and loth to leave it, God, by Moses, stirred them up to aspire after liberty, and many a time kept them from returning to the house of bondage. He carried them out of Egypt, led them into the wilderness, and now at length had led them through it. *The Lord alone did lead him,* he needed not any assistance, nor did he take any to be partner with him in the achievement, which was a good reason why they should serve the Lord only and no other, so much as in partnership, much less in rivalship with him. There was no strange god with him to contribute to Israel's salvation, and therefore there should be none to share in Israel's homage and adoration, Ps. lxxxi. 9.

III. The settling of them in a good land. This was done in part already, in the happy planting of the two tribes and a half, an earnest of what would speedily and certainly be done for the rest of the tribes. 1. They were blessed with glorious victories over their enemies (*v.* 13): *He made him ride on the high places of the earth,* that is, he brought him on with conquest, and brought him home with triumph. He rode over the high places or strong holds that were kept against him, sat in ease and honour upon the fruitful hills of Canaan. In Egypt they looked mean, and

were so, in poverty and disgrace ; but in Canaan they looked great, and were so, advanced and enriched ; they rode in state, as a people whom the King of kings delighted to honour. 2. With great plenty of all good things. Not only the ordinary increase of the field, but, which was uncommon, *Honey out of the rock, and oil out of the flinty rock,* which may refer either, (1.) To their miraculous supply of fresh water out of the rock that followed them in the wilderness, which is called *honey and oil,* because the necessity they were reduced to made it as sweet and acceptable as honey and oil at another time. Or, (2.) To the great abundance of honey and oil they should find in Canaan, even in those parts that were least fertile. The rocks in Canaan should yield a better increase than the fields and meadows of other countries. Other productions of Canaan are mentioned, *v.* 14. Such abundance and such variety of wholesome food (and every thing the best in its kind) that every meal might be a feast if they pleased : excellent bread made of the best corn, here called the *kidneys of the wheat* (for a grain of wheat is not unlike a kidney), butter and milk in abundance, the flesh of cattle well fed, and for their drink, no worse than the *pure blood of the grape ;* so indulgent a Father was God to them, and so kind a benefactor. Ainsworth makes the plenty of good things in Canaan to be a figure of the fruitfulness of Christ's kingdom, and the heavenly comforts of his word and Spirit : for the children of his kingdom he has butter and milk, the sincere milk of the word ; and strong meat for strong men, with the wine that makes glad the heart.

15 But Jeshurun waxed fat, and kicked : thou art waxen fat, thou art grown thick, thou art covered *with fatness ;* then he forsook God *which* made him, and lightly esteemed the Rock of his salvation. 16 They provoked him to jealousy with strange *gods,* with abominations provoked they him to anger. 17 They sacrificed unto devils, not to God ; to gods whom they knew not, to new *gods that* came newly up, whom your fathers feared not. 18 Of the Rock *that* begat thee thou art unmindful, and hast forgotten God that formed thee.

We have here a description of the apostasy of Israel from God, which would shortly come to pass, and to which already they had a disposition. One would have thought that a people under so many obligations to their God, in duty, gratitude, and interest, would never have turned from him ; but, alas ! they *turned aside quickly.* Here are two great instances of their wickedness, and each of them amounted to an apostasy from God :—

I. Security and sensuality, pride and insolence, and the other common abuses of plenty and prosperity, *v.* 15. These people were called *Jeshurun—an upright people* (so some),*a seeing people,* so others: but they soon lost the reputation both of their knowledge and of their righteousness; for, being well-fed, 1. They *waxed fat,* and *grew thick,* that is, they indulged themselves in all manner of luxury and gratifications of their appetites, as if they had nothing to do but to *make provision for the flesh, to fulfil the lusts of it.* They *grew fat,* that is, they grew big and unwieldy, unmindful of business, and unfit for it; dull and stupid, careless and senseless; and this was the effect of their plenty. Thus *the prosperity of fools destroys them,* Prov. i. 32. Yet this was not the worst of it. 2. They *kicked;* they grew proud and insolent, and *lifted up the heel* even against God himself. If God rebuked them, either by his prophets or by his providence, they *kicked against the goad,* as an *untamed heifer,* or a *bullock unaccustomed to the yoke,* and in their rage persecuted the prophets, and flew in the face of providence itself. And thus he *forsook God that made him* (not paying due respect to his Creator, nor answering the ends of his creation), and put an intolerable contempt upon *the rock of his salvation,* as if he were not indebted to him for any past favours, nor had any dependence upon him for the future. Those that make a god of themselves and a god of their bellies, in pride and wantonness, and cannot bear to be told of it, certainly thereby forsake God and show how lightly they esteem him.

II. Idolatry was the great instance of their apostasy, and which the former led them to, as it made them sick of their religion, self-willed, and fond of changes. Observe,

1. What sort of gods they chose and offered sacrifice to, when they forsook the God that made them, *v.* 16, 17. This aggravated their sin that those very services which they should have done to the true God they did, (1.) To *strange gods,* that could not pretend to have done them any kindness, or laid them under any obligation to them, gods that they had no knowledge of, nor could expect any benefit by, for they were strangers. Or they are called *strange gods,* because they were other than the one only true God, to whom they were betrothed and ought to have been faithful. (2.) To *new gods, that came newly up;* for even in religion, the antiquity of which is one of its honours, vain minds have strangely affected novelty, and, in contempt of the Ancient of days, have been fond of new gods. A new god! can there be a more monstrous absurdity? Would we find the right way to rest, we must ask for the *good old way,* Jer. vi. 16. It was true their fathers had worshipped *other gods* (Josh. xxiv. 2), and perhaps it had been some little excuse if the children had returned to them; but to serve *new gods whom their fathers feared not,*

and to like them the better for being new, was to open a door to endless idolatries. (3.) They were such as were no gods at all, but mere counterfeits and pretenders; their names the invention of men's fancies, and their images the work of men's hands. Nay, (4.) They were devils. So far from being *gods, fathers* and *benefactors* to mankind, they really were *destroyers* (so the word signifies), such as aimed to do mischief. If there were any spirits or invisible powers that possessed their idol-temples and images, they were evil spirits and malignant powers, whom yet they did not need to worship for fear they should hurt them, as they say the Indians do; for those that faithfully worship God are out of the devil's reach: nay, the devil can destroy those only that sacrifice to him. How mad are idolaters, who forsake the *rock of salvation* to run themselves upon the *rock of perdition!*

2. What a great affront this was to Jehovah their God. (1.) It was justly interpreted a forgetting of him (*v.* 18): *Of the Rock that begat thee thou art unmindful.* Mindfulness of God would prevent sin, but, when the world is served and the flesh indulged, God is forgotten; and can any thing be more base and unworthy than to forget the God that is the author of our being, by whom we subsist, and in whom we live and move? And see what comes of it, Isa. xvii. 10, 11, *Because thou hast forgotten the God of thy salvation, and hast not been mindful of the Rock of thy strength,* though the strange slips be pleasant plants at first, yet the harvest at last *will be a heap in the day of grief and of desperate sorrow.* There is nothing got by forgetting God. (2.) It was justly resented as an inexcusable offence: *They provoked him to jealousy and to anger* (*v.* 16), for their idols were abominations to him. See here God's displeasure against idols, whether they be set up in the heart or in the sanctuary. [1.] He is jealous of them, as rivals with him for the throne in the heart. [2.] He hates them, as enemies to his crown and government. [3.] He is, and will be, very angry with those that have any respect or affection for them. Those consider not what they do that provoke God; for *who knows the power of his anger?*

19 And when the LORD saw *it,* he abhorred *them,* because of the provoking of his sons, and of his daughters. 20 And he said, I will hide my face from them, I will see what their end *shall be:* for they *are* a very froward generation, children in whom *is* no faith. 21 They have moved me to jealousy with *that which is* not God; they have provoked me to anger with their vanities: and I will move them to jealousy with *those which are* not a people; I will provoke them to

anger with a foolish nation. 22 For a fire is kindled in mine anger, and shall burn unto the lowest hell, and shall consume the earth with her increase, and set on fire the foundations of the mountains. 23 I will heap mischiefs upon them; I will spend mine arrows upon them. 24 *They shall be* burnt with hunger, and devoured with burning heat, and with bitter destruction: I will also send the teeth of beasts upon them, with the poison of serpents of the dust. 25 The sword without, and terror within, shall destroy both the young man and the virgin, the suckling *also* with the man of gray hairs.

The method of this song follows the method of the predictions in the foregoing chapter, and therefore, after the revolt of Israel from God, described in the foregoing verses, here follow immediately the resolves of divine Justice concerning them; we deceive ourselves if we think that God will be thus mocked by a foolish faithless people, that play fast and loose with him.

I. He had delighted in them, but now he would reject them with detestation and disdain, *v.* 19. When the Lord saw their treachery, and folly, and base ingratitude, he abhorred them, he despised them, so some read it. Sin makes us odious in the sight of the holy God; and no sinners are so loathsome to him as those that he has called, and that have called themselves, his sons and his daughters, and yet have been provoking to him. Note, The nearer any are to God in profession the more noisome are they to him if they are defiled in a sinful way, Ps. cvi. 39, 40.

II. He had given them the tokens of his presence with them and his favour to them; but now he would withdraw and *hide his face from them, v.* 20. His *hiding his face* signifies his great displeasure; they had *turned their back* upon God, and now God would turn his back upon them (compare Jer. xviii. 17 with Jer. ii. 27); but here it denotes also the slowness of God's proceedings against them in a way of judgment. They began in their apostasy with omissions of good, and so proceeded to commissions of evil. In like manner God will first suspend his favours, and let them see what the issue of that will be, what a friend they lose when they provoke God to depart, and will try whether this will bring them to repentance. Thus we find God hiding himself, as it were, in expectation of the event, Isa. lvii. 17. To justify himself in leaving them he shows that they were such as there was no dealing with; for, 1. They were froward and a people that could not be pleased, or obstinate in sin, and

that could not be convinced and reclaimed. 2. They were faithless, and a people that could not be trusted. When he saved them, and took them into covenant, he said, *Surely they are children that will not lie* (Isa. lxiii. 8); but when they proved otherwise, *children in whom is no faith,* they deserved to be abandoned, and that the God of truth should have no more to do with them.

III. He had done every thing to make them easy and to please them, but now he would do that against them which should be most vexatious to them. The punishment here answers the sin, *v.* 21. 1. They had provoked God with despicable deities which were not gods at all, but vanities, creatures of their own imagination, that could not pretend either to merit or to repay the respects of their worshippers; the more vain and vile the gods were after which they went a whoring the greater was the offence to that great and good God whom they set them up in competition with and contradiction to. This put two great evils into their idolatry, Jer. ii. 13. 2. God would therefore plague them with despicable enemies, that were worthless, weak, and inconsiderable, and not deserving the name of a people, which was a great mortification to them, and aggravated the oppressions they groaned under. The more base the people were that tyrannised over them the more barbarous they would be (none so insolent as a beggar on horseback), besides that it would be infamous to Israel, who had so often triumphed over great and mighty nations, to be themselves trampled upon by the weak and foolish, and to come under the curse of Canaan, who was to be a servant of servants. But God can make the weakest instrument a scourge to the strongest sinner; and those that by sin insult their mighty Creator are justly insulted by the meanest of their fellow-creatures. This was remarkably fulfilled in the days of the judges, when they were sometimes oppressed by the very Canaanites themselves, whom they had subdued, Jud. iv. 2. But the apostle applies it to the conversion of the Gentiles, who had been a people not in covenant with God, and foolish in divine things, yet were brought into the church, sorely to the grief of the Jews, who upon all occasions showed a great indignation at it, which was both their sin and their punishment, as envy always is, Rom. x. 19.

IV. He had planted them in a good land, and replenished them with all good things; but now he would strip them of all their comforts, and bring them to ruin. The judgments threatened are very terrible, *v.* 22—25. 1. The fire of God's anger shall consume them, *v.* 22. Are they proud of their plenty? It shall burn up the increase of the earth. Are they confident of their strength? It shall destroy the very foundations of their mountains: there is no fence against the judgments of God when they
867

come with commission to lay all waste. It shall burn to the lowest hell, that is, it shall bring them to the very depth of misery in this world, which yet would be but a faint resemblance of the complete and endless misery of sinners in the other world. The damnation of hell (as our Saviour calls it) is the fire of God's anger, fastening upon the guilty conscience of a sinner, to its inexpressible and everlasting torment, Isa. xxx. 33. 2. The arrows of God's judgments shall be spent upon them, till his quiver is quite exhausted, *v.* 23. The judgments of God, like arrows, fly swiftly (Ps. lxiv. 7), reaching those at a distance who flatter themselves with hopes of escaping them, Ps. xxi. 8, 12. They come from an unseen hand, but wound mortally, for God never misses his mark, 1 Kings. xxii. 34. The particular judgments here threatened are, (1.) Famine : *they shall be burnt,* or *parched, with hunger.* (2.) Pestilence and other diseases, here called *burning heat and bitter destruction.* (3.) The insults of the inferior creatures : *the teeth of beasts and the poison of serpents, v.* 24. (4.) War and the fatal consequences of it, *v.* 25. [1.] Perpetual frights. When the *sword is without,* there cannot but be *terror within.* 2 Cor. vii. 5, *Without were fightings, within were fears.* Those who cast off the fear of God are justly exposed to the fear of enemies. [2.] Universal deaths. The sword of the Lord, when it is sent to lay all waste, will destroy without distinction; neither the strength of the young man nor the beauty of the virgin, neither the innocency of the suckling nor the gravity or infirmity of the man of gray hairs, will be their security from the sword when it devours one as well as another. Such devastation does war make, especially when it is pushed on by men as ravenous as wild beasts and as venomous as serpents, *v.* 24. See here what mischief sin does, and reckon those fools that make a mock at it.

26 I said, I would scatter them into corners, I would make the remembrance of them to cease from among men : 27 Were it not that I feared the wrath of the enemy, lest their adversaries should behave themselves strangely, *and* lest they should say, Our hand *is* high, and the LORD hath not done all this. 28 For they *are* a nation void of counsel, neither *is there any* understanding in them. 29 O that they were wise, *that* they understood this, *that* they would consider their latter end ! 30 How should one chase a thousand, and two put ten thousand to flight, except their Rock had sold them, and the LORD had shut them up ? 31 For their rock *is* not as our Rock, even our enemies

themselves *being* judges. 32 For their vine *is* of the vine of Sodom, and of the fields of Gomorrah : their grapes *are* grapes of gall, their clusters *are* bitter : 33 Their wine *is* the poison of dragons, and the cruel venom of asps. 34 *Is* not this laid up in store with me, *and* sealed up among my treasures ? 35 To me *belongeth* vengeance, and recompence ; their foot shall slide in *due* time : for the day of their calamity *is* at hand, and the things that shall come upon them make haste. 36 For the LORD shall judge his people, and repent himself for his servants, when he seeth that *their* power is gone, and *there is* none shut up, or left. 37 And he shall say, Where *are* their gods, *their* rock in whom they trusted, 38 Which did eat the fat of their sacrifices, *and* drank the wine of their drink offerings ? let them rise up and help you, *and* be your protection.

After many terrible threatenings of deserved wrath and vengeance, we have here surprising intimations of mercy, undeserved mercy, which rejoices against judgment, and by which it appears that God has *no pleasure in the death of sinners,* but would rather they should *turn and live.*

I. In jealousy for his own honour, he will not *make a full end* of them, *v.* 26—28. 1. It cannot be denied but that they deserved to be utterly ruined, and that their *remembrance should be made to cease from among men,* so that the name of an Israelite should never be known but in history ; *for they were a nation void of counsel* (*v.* 28), the most sottish inconsiderate people that ever were, that would not believe the glory of God, though they saw it, nor understand his loving kindness, though they tasted it and lived upon it. Of those who could cast off such a God, such a law, such a covenant, for vain and dunghill-deities, it might truly be said, There is *no understanding in them.* 2. It would have been an easy thing with God to ruin them and blot out the remembrance of them; when the greatest part of them were cut off by the sword, it was but scattering the remnant into some remote obscure corners of the earth, where they should never have been heard of any more, and the thing had been done. See Ezek. v. 12. God can destroy those that are most strongly fortified, disperse those that are most closely united, and bury those names in perpetual oblivion that have been most celebrated. 3. Justice demanded it : *I said I would scatter them.* It is fit those should be cut off from the earth that have cut themselves off from their God ; why should they not be dealt with according to their deserts? 4. Wisdom considered the pride and insolence of the enemy, which would take occasion from the ruin of a people that had been so dear to God, and for whom he had done such great things, to reflect upon God and to imagine that because they had got the better of Israel they had carried the day against the God of Israel: The *adversaries will say, Our hand is high*, high indeed, when it has been too high for those whom God himself fought for; nor will they consider that *the Lord has done all this*, but will dream that they have done it in despite of him, as if the God of Israel were as weak and impotent, and as easily run down, as the pretended deities of other nations. 5. In consideration of this, Mercy prevails for the sparing of a remnant and the saving of that unworthy people from utter ruin: *I feared the wrath of the enemy.* It is an expression after the manner of men; it is certain that God fears no man's wrath, but he acted in this matter as if he had feared it. Those few good people in Israel that had a concern for the honour of God's name *feared the wrath of the enemy* in this instance more than in any other, as Joshua (Josh. vii. 9), and David often; and, because they feared it, God himself is said to fear it. He needed not Moses to plead it with him, but reminded himself of it: *What will the Egyptians say?* Let all those whose hearts tremble for the ark of God and his Israel comfort themselves with this, that God will *work for his own name*, and will not suffer it to be profaned and polluted: how much soever we deserve to be disgraced, God will never *disgrace the throne of his glory*.

II. In concern for their welfare, he earnestly desires their conversion; and, in order to that, their serious consideration of their latter end, v. 29. Observe, 1. Though God had pronounced them a foolish people and of no understanding, yet he wishes they were wise, as Deut. v. 29, *O that there were such a heart in them!* and Ps. xciv. 8, *You fools, when will you be wise?* God delights not to see sinners ruin themselves, but desires they will help themselves; and, if they will, he is ready to help them. 2. It is a great piece of wisdom, and will contribute much to the return of sinners to God, seriously to consider the latter end, or the future state. It is here meant particularly of that which God by Moses had foretold concerning this people in the latter days: but it may be applied more generally. We ought to understand and consider, (1.) The latter end of life, and the future state of the soul. To think of death as our removal from a world of sense to a world of spirits, the final period of our state of trial and probation, and our entrance upon an unchangeable state of recompence and re-bution. (2.) The latter end of sin, and the future state of those that live and die in it. O that men would consider the happiness they will lose, and the misery they will certainly

plunge themselves into, if they *go on still in their trespasses, what will be in the end thereof*, Jer. v. 31. Jerusalem forgot this, and therefore *came down wonderfully*, Lam. i. 9.

III. He calls to mind the great things he had done for them formerly, as a reason why he should not quite cast them off. This seems to be the meaning of that (v. 30, 31), "How should one Israelite have been too hard for a thousand Canaanites, as they have been many a time, but that God, who is greater than all gods, fought for them!" And so it corresponds with that, Isa. lxiii. 10, 11. When he was *turned to be their enemy*, as here, *and fought against them* for their sins, *then he remembered the days of old*, saying, *Where is he that brought them out of the sea?* So here, his arm begins to awake as in the days of old *against the wrath of the enemy*, Ps. cxxxviii. 7. There was a time when the enemies of Israel were sold by their own rock, that is, their own idol-gods, who could not help them, but betrayed them, because Jehovah, the God of Israel, had shut them up as sheep for the slaughter. For the enemies themselves must own that their gods were a very unequal match for the God of Israel. *For their vine is of the vine of Sodom*, v. 32, 33. This must be meant of the enemies of Israel, who fell so easily before the sword of Israel because they were ripe for ruin, and the measure of their iniquity was full. Yet these verses may be understood of the strange prevalency of the enemies of Israel against them, when God made use of them as the *rod of his anger*, Isa. x. 5, 6. "How should one Canaanite chase a thousand Israelites" (as it is threatened against those that trust to Egypt for help, Isa. xxx. 17, *One thousand shall flee at the rebuke of one*) "unless Israel's rock had deserted them and given them up?" For otherwise, however they may impute their power *to their gods* (Hab. i. 11), as the Philistines imputed their victory to Dagon, it is certain the enemies' rock could not have prevailed against the rock of Israel; God would soon have subdued their enemies (Ps. lxxxi. 14), but that the wickedness of Israel delivered them into their hands. For their vine, that is, Israel's, is of the *vine of Sodom*, v. 32, 33. They were planted a choice vine, wholly a right seed, but by sin had become the *degenerate plant of a strange vine* (Jer. ii. 21), and not only transcribed the iniquity of Sodom, but outdid it, Ezek. xvi. 48. God called them his *vineyard*, his *pleasant plant*, Isa. v. 7. But their fruits were, 1. Very offensive, and displeasing to God, bitter as gall. 2. Very malignant, and pernicious one to another, *like the cruel venom of asps.* Some understand this of their punishment; their sin would be *bitterness in the latter end* (2 Sam. ii. 26), it would *bite like a serpent and sting like an adder*, Job xx. 14; Prov. xxiii. 32.

IV. He resolves upon the destruction of those at last that had been their persecutors and oppressors. When the cup of trembling goes round, the king of Babel shall pledge it at last, Jer. xxv. 26, and see Isa. li. 22, 23. The day is coming when the judgment that began at the house of God shall end with the sinner and ungodly, 1 Pet. iv. 17, 18. God will in due time bring down the church's enemies,

1. In displeasure against their wickedness, which he takes notice of, and keeps an account of, v. 34, 35. " Is not this implacable fury of theirs against Israel *laid up in store with me*, to be reckoned for hereafter, when it shall be made to appear that *to me belongs vengeance ?*" Some understand it of the sin of Israel, especially their persecuting the prophets, which was laid up in store against them from the *blood of righteous Abel*, Matt. xxiii. 35. However, it teaches us that the wickedness of the wicked is all laid up in store with God. (1.) He observes it, Ps. xc. 8. He knows both what the vine is and what the grapes are, what is the temper of the mind and what are the actions of life. (2.) He keeps a record of it both in his own omniscience and in the sinner's conscience ; and this is *sealed up among his treasures*, which denotes both safety and secresy : these books cannot be lost, nor will they be opened till the great day. See Hos. xiii. 12. (3.) He often delays the punishment of sin for a great while ; it is laid up in store, till the measure be full, and the day of divine patience has expired. See Job. xxi. 28—30. (4.) There is a day of reckoning coming, when all the treasures of guilt and wrath will be broken up, and the sin of sinners shall surely find them out. [1.] The thing itself will certainly be done, for the Lord is a *God to whom vengeance belongs*, and therefore he will repay, Isa. lix. 18. This is quoted by the apostle to show the severity of God's wrath against those that revolt from the faith of Christ, Heb. x. 30. [2.] It will be done in due time, in the best time ; nay, it will be done in a short time. The *day of their calamity is at hand ;* and, though it may seem to tarry, it lingers not, it slumbers not, but makes haste. *In one hour* shall the judgment of Babylon come.

2. He will do it in compassion to his own people, who, though they had greatly provoked him, yet stood in relation to him, and their misery appealed to his mercy (v. 36): *The Lord shall judge his people*, that is, judge for them against their enemies, plead their cause, and break the yoke of oppression under which they had long groaned, *repenting himself for his servants ;* not changing his mind, but changing his way, and fighting for them, as he had fought against them, *when he sees that their power is gone.* This plainly points at the deliverances God wrought for Israel by the judges out of the hands of those to whom he had sold them for their sins (see Judg. ii. 11—18), and how *his soul was grieved for the misery of Israel* (Judg. x. 16),

and this when they were reduced to the last extremity. God helped them when they could not help themselves ; for there was *none shut up or left ;* that is, none that dwelt either in cities or walled towns, in which they were shut up, nor any that dwelt in scattered houses in the country, in which they were left at a distance from neighbours. Note, God's time to appear for the deliverance of his people is when things are at the worst with them. God tries his people's faith, and stirs up prayer, by letting things go to the worst, and then magnifies his own power, and fills the faces of his enemies with shame and the hearts of his people with so much the greater joy, by rescuing them out of extremity as *brands out of the burning.*

3. He will do it in contempt and to the reproach of the idol-gods, v. 37, 38. *Where are their gods ?* Two ways it may be understood :—(1.) That God would do that for his people which the idols they had served could not do for them. They had forsaken God, and been very liberal in their sacrifices to idols, had brought to their altars the *fat of their sacrifices* and the *wine of their drink-offerings*, which they supposed their deities to feed upon and on which they feasted with them. " Now," says God, " will these gods you have made your court to, at so great an expense, help you in your distress, and so repay you for all your charges in their service? *Go get you to the gods you have served, and let them deliver you*, Judg. x. 14. This is intended to convince them of their folly in forsaking a God that could help them for gods that could not, and so to bring them to repentance and qualify them for deliverance. When the adulteress shall *follow after her lovers* and *not overtake them*, pray to her idols and receive no kindness from them, *then she shall say, I will go and return to my first husband*, Hos. ii. 7. See Isa. xvi. 12 ; Jer. ii. 27, 28. Or, (2.) That God would do that against his enemies which the idols they had served could not save them from. Sennacherib and Nebuchadnezzar boldly challenged the God of Israel to deliver his worshippers (Isa. xxxvii. 10 ; Dan. iii. 15), and he did deliver them, to the confusion of their enemies. But the God of Israel challenged Bel and Nebo to deliver their worshippers, to rise up and help them, and to be their protection (Isa. xlvii. 12, 13) ; but they were so far from helping them that they themselves, that is, their images, which was all that was of them, *went into captivity*, Isa. xlvi. 1, 2. Note, Those who trust to any rock but God will find it sand in the day of their distress ; it will fail them when they most need it.

39 See now that I, *even* I, *am* he, and *there is* no god with me : I kill, and I make alive ; I wound, and I heal : neither *is there any* that can deliver out of my hand. 40 For I

lift up my hand to heaven, and say, I live for ever. 41 If I whet my glittering sword, and mine hand take hold on judgment; I will render vengeance to mine enemies, and will reward them that hate me. 42 I will make mine arrows drunk with blood, and my sword shall devour flesh ; *and that* with the blood of the slain and of the captives, from the beginning of revenges upon the enemy. 43 Rejoice, O ye nations, *with* his people : for he will avenge the blood of his servants, and will render vengeance to his adversaries, and will be merciful unto his land, *and* to his people.

This conclusion of the song speaks three things :—

I. Glory to God, *v.* 39. " See now upon the whole matter, *that I, even I, am he.* Learn this from the destruction of idolaters, and the inability of their idols to help them." The great God here demands the glory, 1. Of a self-existence : *I, even I, am he.* Thus Moses concludes with that name of God by which he was first made to know him (Exod. iii. 14), " *I am that I am.* I am he that I have been, that I will be, that I have promised to be, that I have threatened to be ; all shall find me true to my word." The Targum of Uzzielides paraphrases it thus : *When the Word of the Lord shall reveal himself to redeem his people, he shall say to all people, See that I now am what I am, and have been, and I am what I will be,* which we know very well how to apply to him who said to John, *I am he who is, and was, and is to come,* Rev. i. 8. These words, *I, even I, am he,* we meet with often in those chapters of Isaiah where God is encouraging his people to hope for their deliverance out of Babylon, Isa. xli. 4 ; xliii. 11, 13, 25 ; xlvi. 4. 2. Of a sole supremacy. " There *is no god with me.* None to help with me, none to cope with me." See Isa. xliii. 10, 11. 3. Of an absolute sovereignty, a universal agency : *I kill, and I make alive ;* that is, all evil and all good come from his hand of providence ; he forms both the light of life and the darkness of death, Isa. xlv. 7 ; Lam. iii. 37, 38. Or, He kills and wounds his enemies, but heals and makes alive his own people, kills and wounds with his judgments those that revolt from him and rebel against him ; but, when they return and repent, he heals them, and makes them alive with his mercy and grace. Or it denotes his incontestable authority to dispose of all his creatures, and the beings he has given them, so as to serve his own purposes by them : *Whom he will he slays, and whom he will he keeps alive,* when his judgments are abroad. Or thus, Though he kill, yet he makes alive

again : *though he cause grief, yet will he have compassion,* Lam. iii. 32. Though he have torn, he will *heal us,* Hos. vi. 1, 2. The Jerusalem Targum reads it, *I kill those that are alive in this world, and make those alive in the other world that are dead.* And some of the Jewish doctors themselves have observed that death, and a life after it, that is, eternal life, is intimated in these words. 4. Of an irresistible power, which cannot be controlled : *Neither is there any that can deliver out of my hand* those that I have marked for destruction. As no exception can be made against the sentence of God's justice, so no escape can be made from the executions of his power.

II. Terror to his enemies, *v.* 40—42. Terror indeed to those that hate him, as all those do that serve other gods, that persist in wilful disobedience to the divine law, and that malign and persecute his faithful servants. These are those to whom God will render vengeance, those his enemies that will not have him to reign over them. In order to alarm such in time to repent and return to their allegiance, the wrath of God is here revealed from heaven against them. 1. The divine sentence is ratified with an oath (*v.* 40): He *lifts up his hand to heaven,* the habitation of his holiness ; this was an ancient and very significant sign used in swearing, Gen. xiv. 22. And, since he could swear by no greater, he swears by himself and his own life. Those are miserable without remedy that have the word and oath of God against them. The Lord hath sworn, and will not repent, that the sin of sinners shall be their ruin if they go on in it. 2. Preparation is made for the execution : The *glittering sword is whet.* See Ps. vii. 12. It is a sword *bathed in heaven,* Isa. xxxiv. 5. While the sword is in whetting, space is given to the sinner to repent and make his peace, which, if he neglects, will render the wound the deeper. And, as the sword is whet, so the hand that is to wield it takes hold on judgment with a resolution to go through with it. 3. The execution itself will be very terrible : The *sword shall devour flesh* in abundance, and the *arrows* be made *drunk with blood,* such vast quantities of it shall be shed, the blood of the slain in battle, and of the captives, to whom no quarter shall be given, but who shall be put under military execution. When he begins revenge he will make an end ; for in this also his work is perfect. The critics are much perplexed with the last clause, *From the beginning of revenges upon the enemy.* The learned bishop Patrick (that great master) thinks it may admit this reading, *From the king to the slave of the enemies,* Jer. l. 35—37. When the sword of God's wrath is drawn it will make bloody work, blood to the horse-bridles, Rev. xiv. 20.

III. Comfort to his own people (*v.* 43): *Rejoice, O you nations, with his people.* He concludes the song with words of joy ; for in God's Israel there is a remnant whose end will be peace. God's people will rejoice at last, will rejoice everlastingly. Three things are here mentioned as matter of joy :—1. The enlarging of the church's bounds. The apostle applies the first words of this verse to the conversion of the Gentiles. Rom. xv. 10, *Rejoice you Gentiles with his people.* See what the grace of God does in the conversion of souls, it brings them to rejoice with the people of God ; for true religion brings us acquainted with true joy, so great a mistake are those under that think it tends to make men melancholy. 2. The avenging of the church's controversies upon her adversaries. He will make inquisition for *the blood of his servants,* and it shall appear how precious it is to him; for those that spilt it shall have blood given them to drink. 3. The mercy God has in store for his church, and for all that belong to it : He will be *merciful to his land, and to his people,* that is, to all every where that fear and serve him. Whatever judgments are brought upon sinners, it shall go well with the people of God ; in this let Jews and Gentiles rejoice together.

44 And Moses came and spake all the words of this song in the ears of the people, he, and Hoshea the son of Nun. 45 And Moses made an end of speaking all these words to all Israel : 46 And he said unto them, Set your hearts unto all the words which I testify among you this day, which ye shall command your children to observe to do, all the words of this law. 47 For it *is* not a vain thing for you; because it *is* your life : and through this thing ye shall prolong *your* days in the land, whither ye go over Jordan to possess it. 48 And the LORD spake unto Moses that selfsame day, saying, 49 Get thee up into this mountain Abarim, *unto* mount Nebo, which *is* in the land of Moab, that *is* over against Jericho ; and behold the land of Canaan, which I give unto the children of Israel for a possession : 50 And die in the mount whither thou goest up, and be gathered unto thy people ; as Aaron thy brother died in mount Hor, and was gathered unto his people : 51 Because ye trespassed against me among the children of Israel at the waters of Meribah-Kadesh, in the wilderness of Zin ; because ye sanctified me not in the midst of the children of Israel. 52 Yet thou shalt see the land before *thee ;* but thou shalt
872

not go thither unto the land which I give the children of Israel.

Here is, I. The solemn delivery of this song to the children of Israel, *v.* 44, 45. Moses spoke it to as many as could hear him, while Joshua, in another assembly, at the same time, delivered it to as many as his voice would reach. Thus coming to them from the mouth of both their governors, Moses who was laying down the government, and Joshua who was taking it up, they would see they were both in the same mind, and that, though they changed their commander, there was no change in the divine command ; Joshua, as well as Moses, would be a witness against them if ever they forsook God.

II. An earnest charge to them to mind these and all the rest of the good words that Moses had said to them. How earnestly does he long after them all, how very desirous that the word of God might make deep and lasting impressions upon them, how jealous over them with a godly jealousy, lest they should at any time let slip these great things !

1. The duties he charges upon them are, (1.) Carefully to attend to these themselves: " Set your hearts both to the laws, and to the promises and threatenings, the blessings and curses, and now at last to this song. Let the mind be closely applied to the consideration of these things; be affected with them ; be intent upon your duty, and cleave to it with full purpose of heart." (2.) Faithfully to transmit these things to those that should come after them: " What interest you have in your children, or influence upon them, use it for this purpose ; and *command them* (as your father Abraham did, Gen. xviii. 19) *to observe to do all the words of this law.*" Those that are good themselves cannot but desire that their children may be so likewise, and that posterity may keep up religion in their day and the entail of it may not be cut off.

2. The arguments he uses to persuade them to make religion their business and to persevere in it are, (1.) The vast importance of the things themselves which he had charged upon them (*v.* 47): "*It is not a vain thing, because it is your life.* It is not an indifferent thing, but of absolute necessity; it is not a trifle, but a matter of consequence, a matter of life and death ; mind it, and you are made for ever; neglect it, and you are for ever undone." O that men were but fully persuaded of this, that religion is their life, even the life of their souls ! (2.) The vast advantage it would be of to them : *Through this thing you shall prolong your days* in Canaan, which is a typical promise of that eternal life which Christ has assured us those shall enter into that keep the commandments of God, Matt. xix. 17.

III. Orders given to Moses concerning his

death. Now that this renowned witness for God had finished his testimony, he must go up to Mount Nebo and die; in the prophecy of Christ's two witnesses there is a plain allusion to Moses and Elias (Rev. xi. 6), and perhaps their removal, being by martyrdom, is no less glorious than the removal either of Moses or Elias. Orders were given to Moses that self-same day, v. 48. Now that he had done his work, why should he desire to live a day longer? He had indeed formerly prayed that he might go over Jordan, but now he is entirely satisfied, and, as God had bidden him, *saith no more of that matter.* 1. God here reminds him of the sin he had been guilty of, for which he was excluded Canaan (v. 51), that he might the more patiently bear the rebuke because he had sinned, and that now he might renew his sorrow for that unadvised word, for it is good for the best of men to die repenting of the infirmities they are conscious to themselves of. It was an omission that was thus displeasing to God; he did *not sanctify God,* as he ought to have done, *before the children of Israel,* he did not carry himself with a due decorum in executing the orders he had then received. 2. He reminds him of the death of his brother Aaron (v. 50), to make his own the more familiar and the less formidable. Note, It is a great encouragement to us, when we die, to think of our friends that have gone before us through that darksome valley, especially of Christ, our elder brother and great high priest. 3. He sends him up to a high hill, thence to take a view of the land of Canaan and then die, v. 49, 50. The remembrance of his sin might make death terrible, but the sight God gave him of Canaan took off the terror of it, as it was a token of God's being reconciled to him, and a plain indication to him that though his sin shut him out of the earthly Canaan, yet it should not deprive him of that better country which in this world can only be seen, and that with an eye of faith. Note, Those may die with comfort and ease whenever God calls for them (notwithstanding the sins they remember against themselves) who have a believing prospect and a well-grounded hope of eternal life beyond death.

CHAP. XXXIII.

Yet Moses has not done with the children of Israel; he seemed to have taken final leave of them in the close of the foregoing chapter, but still he has something more to say. He had preached them a farewell sermon, a very copious and pathetic discourse. After sermon he had given out a psalm, a long psalm; and now nothing remains but to dismiss them with a blessing; that blessing he pronounces in this chapter in the name of the Lord, and so leaves them. I. He pronounces them all blessed in what God had done for them already, especially in giving them his law, ver. 2–5. II. He pronounces a blessing upon each tribe, which is both a prayer for and a prophecy of their felicity. 1. Reuben, ver. 6. 2. Judah, ver. 7. 3. Levi, ver. 8–11. 4. Benjamin, ver. 12. 5. Joseph, ver. 13–17. 6. Zebulun and Issachar, ver. 18, 19. 7. Gad, ver. 20, 21. 8. Dan, ver. 22. 9. Naphtali, ver. 23. 10. Asher, ver. 24, 25. III. He pronounces them all in general blessed upon the account of what God would be to them, and do for them, if they were obedient, ver. 26, &c.

AND this *is* the blessing, wherewith Moses the man of God blessed the children of Israel before

his death. 2 And he said, The LORD came from Sinai, and rose up from Seir unto them: he shined forth from mount Paran, and he came with ten thousands of saints: from his right hand *went* a fiery law for them. 3 Yea, he loved the people; all his saints *are* in thy hand: and they sat down at thy feet; *every one* shall receive of thy words. 4 Moses commanded us a law, *even* the inheritance of the congregation of Jacob. 5 And he was king in Jeshurun, when the heads of the people *and* the tribes of Israel were gathered together.

The first verse is the title of the chapter: it is a blessing. In the foregoing chapter he had thundered out the terrors of the Lord against Israel for their sin; it was a chapter like Ezekiel's roll, full of lamentation, and mourning, and woe. Now to soften that, and that he might not seem to part in anger, he here subjoins a blessing, and leaves his peace, which should descend and rest upon all those among them that were the sons of peace. Thus Christ's last work on earth was to bless his disciples (Luke xxiv. 50), like Moses here, in token of parting as friends. Moses blessed them, 1. As a prophet—a *man of God.* Note, It is a very desirable thing to have an interest in the prayers of those that have an interest in heaven; it is a *prophet's reward.* In this blessing Moses not only expresses his good wishes to this people, but by the spirit of prophecy foretels things to come concerning them. 2. As a parent to Israel; for so good princes are to their subjects. Jacob upon his death-bed blessed his sons (Gen. xlix. 1), in conformity to whose example Moses here blesses the tribes that were descended from them, to show that though they had been very provoking yet the entail of the blessing was not cut off. The doing of this immediately before his death would not only be the more likely to bless his disciples them, but would be an indication of the great good-will of Moses to them, that he desired their happiness, though he must die and not share in it.

He begins his blessing with a lofty description of the glorious appearances of God to them in giving them the law, and the great advantage they had by it.

I. There was a visible and illustrious discovery of the divine majesty, enough to convince and for ever silence atheists and infidels, to awaken and affect those that were most stupid and careless, and to put to shame all secret inclinations to other gods, v. 2. 1. His appearance was glorious: he shone forth like the sun when he goes forth in his strength. Even Seir and Paran, two mountains at some distance, were illuminated by the divine glory which appeared on Mount Sinai, and reflected some of the rays of it, so bright was the appearance, and so much taken notice of by the adjacent countries. To this the prophet alludes, to set forth the wonders of the divine providence, Hab. iii. 3, 4; Ps. xviii. 7—9. The Jerusalem Targum has a strange gloss upon this, that, "when God came down to give the law, he offered it on Mount Seir to the Edomites, but they refused it, because they found in it, *Thou shalt not kill.* Then he offered it on Mount Paran to the Ishmaelites, but they also refused it, because they found in it, *Thou shalt not steal;* and then he came to Mount Sinai, and offered it to Israel, and they said, *All that the Lord shall say we will do.*" I would not have transcribed so groundless a conceit but for the antiquity of it. 2. His retinue was glorious; he came with his holy myriads, as Enoch had long since foretold he should come in the last day to judge the world, Jude 14. These were the angels, those *chariots of God in the midst of which* the Lord was, on *that holy place,* Ps. lxviii. 17. They attended the divine majesty, and were employed as his ministers in the solemnities of the day. Hence the law is said to *be given by the disposition of angels,* Acts vii. 53; Heb. ii. 2.

II. He gave them his law, which is, 1. Called a *fiery law,* because it was given them *out of the midst of the fire* (Deut. iv. 33), and because it works like fire; if it be received, it is melting, warming, purifying, and burns up the dross of corruption; if it be rejected, it hardens, sears, torments, and destroys. The Spirit descended in cloven tongues as of fire; for the gospel also is a fiery law. 2. It is said to *go from his right hand,* either because he wrote it on tables of stone, or to denote the power and energy of the law and the divine strength that goes along with it, that it may not return void. Or it came as a gift to them, and a precious gift it was, a right-hand blessing. 3. It was an instance of the special kindness he had for them: *Yea, he loved the people* (v. 3), and therefore, though it was a fiery law, yet it is said to *go for them* (v. 2), that is, in favour to them. Note, The law of God written in the heart is a certain evidence of the love of God shed abroad there: we must reckon God's law one of the gifts of his grace. Yea, he embraced the people, or *laid them in his bosom;* so the word signifies, which denotes not only the dearest love, but the most tender and careful protection. *All his saints are in his hand.* Some understand it particularly of his supporting them and preserving them alive at Mount Sinai, when the terror was so great that Moses himself quaked; they heard the voice of God and lived, ch. iv. 33. Or it denotes his forming them into a people by his law; he moulded and fashioned them as a potter does the clay. Or they were in his 874

hand to be covered and protected, used and disposed of, as the seven stars were in the hand of Christ, Rev. i. 16. Note, God has all his saints in his hand; and, though there are *ten thousands of his saints* (v. 2), yet his hand, with which he measures the waters, is large enough, and strong enough, to hold them all, and we may be sure that *none can pluck them out of his hand,* John x. 28.

III. He disposed them to receive the law which he gave them: *They sat down at thy feet,* as scholars at the feet of their master, in token of reverence, in attendance and humble submission to what is taught; so Israel sat at the foot of Mount Sinai, and promised to hear and do whatever God should say. They were *struck to thy feet,* so some read it; namely, by the terrors of Mount Sinai, which greatly humbled them for the present, Exod. xx. 19. Every one then stood ready to receive God's words, and did so again when the law was publicly read to them, as Josh. viii. 34. It is a great privilege when we have heard the words of God, to have opportunity of hearing them again. John xvii. 26, *I have declared thy name, and will declare it.* So Israel not only had received the law, but should still receive it by their prayers, and other lively oracles. The people are taught (v. 4, 5), in gratitude for the law of God, always to keep up an honourable remembrance both of the law itself and of Moses by whom it was given. Two of the Chaldee paraphrasts read it, *The children of Israel said, Moses commanded us a law.* And the Jews say that as soon as a child was able to speak his father was obliged to teach him these words: *Moses commanded us a law, even the inheritance of the congregation of Jacob.*

1. They are taught to speak with great respect of the law, and to call it *the inheritance of the congregation of Jacob.* They looked upon it, (1.) As peculiar to them, and that by which they were distinguished from other nations, who neither had the knowledge of it (Ps. cxlvii. 20), nor, if they had, were under those obligations to observe it that Israel were under: and therefore (says bishop Patrick), "when the Jews conquered any country, they did not force any to embrace the law of Moses, but only to submit to the seven precepts of Noah." (2.) As entailed upon them; for so inheritances are to be transmitted to their posterity. And, (3.) As their wealth and true treasure. Those that enjoy the word of God and the means of grace have reason to say, We have a goodly heritage. He is indeed a rich man in whom the word of Christ dwells richly. Perhaps the law is called their *inheritance* because it was given them with their inheritance, and was so annexed to it that the forsaking of the law would be a forfeiture of the inheritance. See Ps. cxix. 111.

2. They are taught to speak with great respect of Moses; and they were the more obliged to keep up his name because he had not provided for the keeping of it up in his·

family; his posterity were never called the sons of Moses, as the priests were the sons of Aaron. (1.) They must own Moses a great benefactor to their nation, in that he *commanded them the law;* for, though it came from the hand of God, it went through the hand of Moses. (2.) *He was king in Jeshurun. Having commanded them the law,* as long as he lived he took care to see it observed and put in execution; and they were very happy in having such a king, who ruled them, and went in and out before them at all times, but did in a special manner look great when the *heads of the people were gathered together* in parliament, as it were, and Moses was president among them. Some understand this of God himself; he did then declare himself their King when he gave them the law, and he continued so as long as they were *Jeshurun,* an upright people, and till they rejected him, 1 Sam. xii. 12. But it seems rather to be understood of Moses. A good government is a great blessing to any people, and what they have reason to be very thankful for; and that constitution is very happy which as Israel's, which as ours, divides the power between the king in Jeshurun and the heads of the tribes, when they are gathered together.

6 Let Reuben live, and not die; and let *not* his men be few. 7 And this *is the blessing* of Judah: and he said, Hear, Lord, the voice of Judah, and bring him unto his people: let his hands be sufficient for him; and be thou a help *to him* from his enemies.

Here is, I. The blessing of Reuben. Though Reuben had lost the honour of his birthright, yet Moses begins with him; for we should not insult over those that are disgraced, nor desire to perpetuate marks of infamy upon any, though ever so justly fastened at first, *v.* 6. Moses desires and foretels, 1. The preserving of this tribe. Though a frontier tribe on the other side Jordan, yet, "*Let it live,* and not be either ruined by its neighbours or lost among them." And perhaps he refers to those chosen men of that tribe who, having had their lot assigned them already, left their families in it, and were now ready to *go over armed before their brethren,* Num. xxxii. 27. "Let them be protected in this noble expedition, and have their heads covered in the day of battle." 2. The increase of this tribe: *Let not his men be few;* or, *Let his men be a number,* that is, "Let it be a numerous tribe; though their other honours be lost, so that they shall not excel, yet let them multiply." *Let Reuben live and not die, though his men be few;* so bishop Patrick thinks it may be rendered. "Though he must not expect to flourish (Gen. xlix. 4), yet let him not perish." All the Chaldee paraphrasts refer this to the other world: *Let Reuben live in life eternal, and not die the*

second death, so Onkelos. *Let Reuben live in this world, and not die that death which the wicked die in the world to come,* so Jonathan and the Jerusalem Targum.

II. The blessing of Judah, which is put before Levi because our Lord *sprang out of Judah,* and (as Dr. Lightfoot says) because of the dignity of the kingdom above the priesthood. The blessing (*v.* 7) may refer either, 1. To the whole tribe in general. Moses prays for, and prophesics, the great prosperity of that tribe. That God would hear his prayers (see an instance, 2 Chron. xiii. 14, 15), settle him in his lot, prosper him in all his affairs, and give him victory over his enemies. It is taken for granted that the tribe of Judah would be both a praying tribe and an active tribe. "Lord," says Moses, "hear his prayers, and give success to all his undertakings: *let his hands be sufficient for him* both in husbandry and in war." The voice of prayer should always be attended with the hand of endeavour, and then we may expect prosperity. Or, 2. It may refer in particular to David, as a type of Christ, that God *would hear his prayers,* Ps. xx. 1 (and Christ was *heard always,* John xi. 42), that he would give him victory over his enemies, and success in his great undertakings. See Ps. lxxxix. 20, &c. And that prayer that God would *bring him to his people* seems to refer to Jacob's prophecy concerning Shiloh, That *to him should the gathering of the people be,* Gen. xlix. 10. The tribe of Simeon is omitted in the blessing, because Jacob had left it under a brand, and it had never done any thing, as Levi had done, to retrieve its honour. It was lessened in the wilderness more than any other of the tribes; and Zimri, who was so notoriously guilty in the matter of Peor but the other day, was of that tribe. Or, because the lot of Simeon was an appendage to that of Judah, that tribe is included in the blessing of Judah. Some copies of the LXX. join Simeon with Reuben: *Let Reuben live and not die; and let Simeon be many in number.*

8 And of Levi he said, *Let* thy Thummim and thy Urim *be* with thy holy one, whom thou didst prove at Massah, *and with* whom thou didst strive at the waters of Meribah; 9 Who said unto his father and to his mother, I have not seen him; neither did he acknowledge his brethren, nor knew his own children: for they have observed thy word, and kept thy covenant. 10 They shall teach Jacob thy judgments, and Israel thy law: they shall put incense before thee, and whole burnt sacrifice upon thine altar. 11 Bless, Lord, his substance, and accept the work of his hands: smite

875

through the loins of them that rise against him, and of them that hate him, that they rise not again.

In blessing the tribe of Levi, Moses expresses himself more at large, not so much because it was his own tribe (for he takes no notice of his relation to it) as because it was God's tribe. The blessing of Levi has reference,

I. To the high priest, here called God's *holy one (v.* 8), because his office was holy, in token of which, *Holiness to the Lord* was written upon his forehead. 1. He seems to acknowledge that God might justly have displaced Aaron and his seed, for his sin at Meribah, Num. xx. 12. So many understand it. It seems rather probable to me that, on the contrary, he pleads with God the zeal and faithfulness of Aaron, and his boldness in stemming the tide of the people's murmurings at the other Meribah (Exod. xvii. 7), which might be very remarkable, and which God might have an eye to in conferring the priesthood upon him, though no mention is made of it there. All the Chaldee paraphrasts agree that it was a trial in which he was *found perfect and faithful,* and *stood in the trial;* therefore not that, Num. xx. 2. He prays that the office of the high priest might ever remain : *Let thy thummim and thy urim be with him.* It was given him for some eminent piece of service, as appears, Mal. ii. 5. " Lord, let it never be taken from him." Notwithstanding this blessing, the urim and thummim were lost in the captivity, and never restored under the second temple. But this prayer has its full accomplishment in Jesus Christ, God's Holy One, and our great high priest, of whom Aaron was a type: with him who had lain in the Father's bosom from eternity the urim and thummim shall remain ; for he is the wonderful and everlasting counsellor. Some translate the thummim and urim appellatively, the rather because the usual order is here inverted, here only. *Thummim* signifies *integrity,* and *Urim illumination:* Let these be with thy holy one, that is, " Lord, let the high priest ever be both an upright man and an understanding man." A good prayer to be put up for the ministers of the gospel, that they may have clear heads and honest hearts ; light and sincerity make a complete minister.

II. To the inferior priests and Levites, *v.* 9—11.

1. He commends the zeal of this tribe for God when they sided with Moses (and so with God) against the worshippers of the golden calf (Exod. xxxii. 26, &c.), and, being employed in cutting off the ring-leaders in that wickedness, they did it impartially : the best friends they had in the world, though as dear to them as their next relations, they did not spare if they were idolaters. Note, Our regard to God and to his glory ought always to prevail above our regard to any creature

876

whatsoever. And those who not only keep themselves pure from the common iniquities of the times and places in which they live, but, as they are capable, bear testimony against them, and *stand up for God against the evil-doers,* shall have special marks of honour put upon them. Perhaps Moses may have an eye to the sons of Korah, who refused to join with their father in his gainsaying, Num. xxvi. 11. Also to Phinehas, who *executed judgment,* and *stayed the plague.* And indeed the office of the priests and Levites, which engaged their constant attendance, at least in their turns, at God's altar, laid them under a necessity of being frequently absent from their families, which they could not take such care of, nor make such provision for, as other Israelites might. This was the constant self-denial they submitted to, that they might *observe God's word,* and keep the *covenant of priesthood.* Note, Those that are called to minister in holy things must sit loose to the relations and interests that are dearest to them in this world, and prefer the fulfilling of their ministry before the gratifying of the best friend they have, Acts xxi. 13 ; xx. 24. Our Lord Jesus knew not his mother and his brethren when they would have taken him off from his work, Matt. xii. 48.

2. He confirms the commission granted to this tribe to minister in holy things, which was the recompence of their zeal and fidelity, *v.* 10. (1.) They were to deal for God with the people : " *They shall teach Jacob thy judgments and Israel thy laws,* both as preachers in thy religious assemblies, reading and expounding the law (Neh. viii. 7, 8), and as judges, determining doubtful and difficult cases that were brought before them," 2 Chron. xvii. 8, 9. The priests' lips kept this knowledge for the use of the people, who were to ask the law at their mouth, Mal. ii. 7. Even Haggai, a prophet, consulted the priests in a case of conscience, Hag. ii. 11, &c. Note, Preaching is necessary, not only for the first planting of churches, but for the preserving and edifying of churches when they are planted. See Ezek. xliv. 23, 24. (2.) They were to deal for the people with God, in burning incense to the praise and glory of God, and offering sacrifices to make atonement for sin and to obtain the divine favour. This was the work of the priests, but the Levites attended and assisted in it. Those that would have benefit by their incense and offerings must diligently and faithfully observe their instructions.

3. He prays for them, *v.* 11. (1.) That God would prosper them in their estates, and make that which was allotted them for their maintenance comfortable to them. *Bless, Lord, his substance.* The provision made for them was very plentiful, and came to them easily, and yet they could have no joy of it unless God blessed it to them ; and, since God himself was their portion, a par-

ticular blessing might be expected to attend this portion. *Bless, Lord, his virtue;* so some read it. *" Lord, increase thy graces in them, and make them more and more fit for their work."* (2.) That he would accept them in their services: *" Accept the work of his hands,* both for himself and for the people for whom he ministers." Acceptance with God is that which we should all aim at, and be ambitious of, in all our devotions, whether men accept us or no (2 Cor. v. 9), and it is the most valuable blessing we can desire either for ourselves or others. (3.) That he would take his part against all his enemies: *Smite through the loins of those that rise against him.* He supposes that God's ministers would have many enemies: some would hate their persons for their faithfulness, and would endeavour to do them a mischief; others would envy them their maintenance, and endeavour sacrilegiously to deprive them of it; others would oppose them in the execution of their office, and not submit to the sentence of the priests; and some would aim to overthrow the office itself. Now he prays that God would blast all such attempts, and return the mischief upon the heads of the authors. This prayer is a prophecy that God will certainly reckon with those that are enemies to his ministers, and will keep up a ministry in his church to the end of time, in spite of all the designs of the gates of hell against it. Saul rose up against the Lord's priests (1 Sam. xxii. 18), and this filled the measure of his sin.

12 *And* of Benjamin he said, The beloved of the LORD shall dwell in safety by him ; *and the LORD* shall cover him all the day long, and he shall dwell between his shoulders. 13 And of Joseph he said, Blessed of the LORD *be* his land, for the precious things of heaven, for the dew, and for the deep that coucheth beneath, 14 And for the precious fruits *brought forth* by the sun, and for the precious things put forth by the moon, 15 And for the chief things of the ancient mountains, and for the precious things of the lasting hills, 16 And for the precious things of the earth and fulness thereof, and *for* the good will of him that dwelt in the bush : let *the blessing* come upon the head of Joseph, and upon the top of the head of him *that was* separated from his brethren. 17 His glory *is like* the firstling of his bullock, and his horns *are like* the horns of unicorns : with them he shall push the people together to the ends of the earth :

and they *are* the ten thousands of Ephraim, and they *are* the thousands of Manasseh.

Here is, I. The blessing of Benjamin, *v.* 12. Benjamin is put next to Levi, because the temple, where the priests' work lay, was just upon the edge of the lot of this tribe ; and it is put before Joseph because of the dignity of Jerusalem (part of which was in this tribe) above Samaria, which was in the tribe of Ephraim, and because Benjamin adhered to the house of David, and to the temple of the Lord, when the rest of the tribes deserted both with Jeroboam. 1. Benjamin is here called the *beloved of the Lord,* as the father of this tribe was Jacob's beloved son, the *son of his right hand.* Note, Those are blessed indeed that are beloved of the Lord. Saul the first king, and Paul the great apostle, were both of this tribe. 2. He is here assured of the divine protection : he shall *dwell safely.* Note, Those are safe whom God loves, Ps. xci. 1. 3. It is here intimated that the temple in which God would dwell should be built in the borders of this tribe. Jerusalem the holy city was in the lot of this tribe (Josh. xviii. 28) ; and though Zion, the city of David, is supposed to belong to Judah, yet Mount Moriah, on which the temple was built, was in Benjamin's lot. God is *therefore* said to dwell *between his shoulders,* because the temple stood on that mount, as the head of a man upon his shoulders. And by this means Benjamin was *covered all the day long* under the protection of the sanctuary (Ps. cxxv. 2), which is often spoken of as a place of refuge, Ps. xxvii. 4, 5; Neh. vi. 10. Benjamin, dwelling by the temple of God, *dwelt in safety by him.* Note, It is a happy thing to be in the neighbourhood of the temple. This situation of Benjamin, it is likely, was the only thing that kept that tribe in adherence with Judah to the divine institutions, when the other ten tribes apostatized. Those have corrupt and wicked hearts indeed who, the nearer they are to the church, are so much the further from God.

II. The blessing of Joseph, including both Manasseh and Ephraim. In Jacob's blessing (Gen. xlix.) that of Joseph is the largest, and so it is here ; and thence Moses here borrows the title he gives to Joseph (*v.* 16), that he was *separated from his brethren,* or, as it might be read, *a Nazarite among them,* both in regard of his piety, wherein it appears, by many instances, he excelled them all, and of his dignity in Egypt, where he was both their ruler and benefactor. His brethren separated him from them by making him a slave, but God distinguished him from them by making him a prince. Now the blessings here prayed for, and prophesied of, for this tribe, are great plenty and great power. 1. Great plenty, *v.* 13—16. In general : *Blessed of the Lord be his land.* Those were very fruitful countries that fell into the lot of Ephraim and Manasseh, yet Moses prays they might be watered with the blessing of God, which makes rich, and on which all fruitfulness depends. Now,

(1.) He enumerates many particulars which he prays may contribute to the wealth and abundance of those two tribes, looking up to the Creator for the benefit and serviceableness of all the inferior creatures, for they are all that to us which he makes them to be. He prays, [1.] For seasonable rains and dews, *the precious things of heaven;* and so precious they are, though but pure water, that without them the fruits of the earth would all fail and be cut off. [2.] For plentiful springs, which help to make the earth fruitful, called here *the deep that coucheth beneath;* both are the *rivers of God* (Ps. lxv. 9), for he is the Father of the rain (Job xxxviii. 28), and he made particularly the *fountains of waters,* Rev. xiv. 7. [3.] For the benign influences of the heavenly bodies (*v.* 14), *for the precious fruits* (the word signifies that which is most excellent, and the best in its kind) put forth by the quickening heat of the sun, and the cooling moisture of the moon. "Let them have the yearly fruits in their several months, according to the course of nature, in one month olives, in another dates," &c. So some understand it. [4.] For the fruitfulness even of their hills and mountains, which in other countries used to be barren (*v.* 15): Let them have *the chief things of the ancient mountains;* and, if the mountains be fruitful, the fruits on them will be first and best ripened. They are called ancient mountains, not because prior in time to other mountains, but because, like the first-born, they were superior in worth and excellency; and lasting hills, not only because as other mountains they were immovable (Hab. iii. 6), but because the fruitfulness of them should continue. [5.] For the productions of the lower grounds (*v.* 16): *For the precious things of the earth.* Though the earth itself seems a useless worthless lump of matter, yet there are precious things produced out of it, for the support and comfort of human life. Job xxviii. 5, *Out of it cometh bread,* because out of it came our bodies, and to it they must return. But what are the *precious things of the earth* to a soul that came from God and must return to him? Or what is its fulness to the fulness that is in Christ, whence we receive grace for grace? Some make these precious things here prayed for to be figures of *spiritual blessings in heavenly things by Christ,* the gifts, graces, and comforts of the Spirit.

(2.) He crowns all with the good-will, or favourable acceptance, of him that *dwelt in the bush* (*v.* 16), that is, of God, that God who appeared to Moses in the bush that burned and was not consumed (Exod. iii. 2), to give him his commission for the bringing of Israel out of Egypt. Though God's glory ap-
878

peared there but for a while, yet it is said to dwell there, because it continued as long as there was occasion for it : *the good-will of the shechinah in the bush;* so it might be read, for *shechinah* signifies *that which dwelleth;* and, though it was but a little while a dweller in the bush, yet it continued to dwell with the people of Israel. *My dweller in the bush;* so it should be rendered; that was an appearance of the divine Majesty to Moses only, in token of the particular interest he had in God, which he desires to improve for the good of this tribe. Many a time God had appeared to Moses, but now that he is just dying he seems to have the most pleasing remembrance of that which was the first time, when his acquaintance with the visions of the Almighty first began, and his correspondence with heaven was first settled : that was a time of love never to be forgotten. It was at the bush that God declared himself *the God of Abraham, Isaac, and Jacob,* and so confirmed the promise made to the fathers, that promise which reached as far as the resurrection of the body and eternal life, as appears by our Saviour's argument from it, Luke xx. 37. So that, when he prays for the good-will of him that *dwelt in the bush,* he has an eye to the covenant then and there renewed, on which all our hopes of God's favour must be bottomed. Now he concludes this large blessing with a prayer for the favour or good-will of God, [1.] Because that is the fountain and spring-head of all these blessings; they are the gifts of God's good-will; they are so to his own people, whatever they are to others. Indeed when Ephraim (a descendant from Joseph) slid back from God, *as a backsliding heifer,* those fruits of his country were so far from being the gifts of God's good-will that they were intended but to fatten him for the slaughter, *as a lamb in a large place,* Hos. iv. 16, 17. [2.] Because that is the comfort and sweetness of all these blessings; then we have joy of them when we taste God's good-will in them. [3.] Because that is better than all these, infinitely better; for if we have but the favour and good-will of God we are happy, and may be easy in the want of all these things, and may rejoice in the God of our salvation *though the fig-tree do not blossom, and there be no fruit in the vine,* Hab. iii. 17, 18.

2. Great power Joseph is here blessed with, *v.* 17. Here are three instances of his power foretold :—(1.) His authority among his brethren : *His glory is like the firstling of his bullock,* or young bull, which is a stately creature, and therefore was formerly used as an emblem of royal majesty. Joshua, who was to succeed Moses, was of the tribe of Ephraim the son of Joseph, and his glory was indeed illustrious, and he was an honour to his tribe. In Ephraim was the royal city of the ten tribes afterwards. And of Manasseh were Gideon, Jephthah, and Jair, who were all ornaments and blessings to their

country. Some think he is compared to the firstling of the bullock because the birthright which Reuben lost devolved upon Joseph (1 Chron. v. 1, 2), and to the firstling of *his* bullock, because Bashan, which was in the lot of Manasseh, was famous for bulls and cows, Ps. xxii. 12; Amos iv. 1. (2.) His force against his enemies and victory over them: *His horns are like the horn of a unicorn*, that is, "The forces he shall bring into the field shall be very strong and formidable, and *with them he shall push the people*," that is, "He shall overcome all that stand in his way." It appears from the Ephraimites' contests, both with Gideon (Judg. viii. 1) and with Jephthah (Judg. xii. 1), that they were a warlike tribe and fierce. Yet we find the children of Ephraim, when they had forsaken the covenant of God, though they were *armed, turning back in the day of battle* (Ps. lxxviii. 9, 10); for, though here pronounced *strong and bold as unicorns*, when God had departed from them they became as weak as other men. (3.) The numbers of his people, in which Ephraim, though the younger house, exceeded, Jacob having, in the foresight of the same thing, crossed hands, Gen. xlviii. 19. *They are the ten thousands of Ephraim, and the thousands of Manasseh.* Jonathan's Targum applies it to the ten thousands of Canaanites conquered by Joshua, who was of the tribe of Ephraim, and the thousands of Midianites conquered by Gideon, who was of the tribe of Manasseh. And the gloss of the Jerusalem Targum upon the former part of this verse is observable, that "as the firstlings of the bullock were never to be worked, nor could the unicorn ever be tamed, so Joseph should ever continue free; and they would have continued free if they had not by sin sold themselves."

18 And of Zebulun he said, Rejoice, Zebulun, in thy going out; and, Issachar, in thy tents. 19 They shall call the people unto the mountain; there they shall offer sacrifices of righteousness: for they shall suck *of* the abundance of the seas, and *of* treasures hid in the sand. 20 And of Gad he said, Blessed *be* he that enlargeth Gad: he dwelleth as a lion, and teareth the arm with the crown of the head. 21 And he provided the first part for himself, because there, *in* a portion of the lawgiver, *was he* seated; and he came with the heads of the people, he executed the justice of the LORD, and his judgments with Israel.

Here we have, I. The blessings of Zebulun and Issachar put together, for they were both the sons of Jacob by Leah, and by their lot in Canaan they were neighbours; it is foretold,

1. That they should both have a comfortable settlement and employment, v. 18. Zebulun must rejoice, for he shall have cause to rejoice; and Moses prays that he may have cause in his going out, either to war (for *Zebulun jeoparded their lives in the high places of the field*, Judg. v. 18), or rather to sea, for Zebulun was a *haven of ships*, Gen. xlix. 13. And Issachar must rejoice in his tents, that is, in his business at home, his husbandry, to which the men of that tribe generally confined themselves, because they saw that rest was good, and when the sea was rough the land was pleasant, Gen. xlix. 14, 15. Observe here, (1.) That the providence of God, as it variously appoints the bounds of men's habitation, some in the city and some in the country, some in the sea-ports and some in the inland towns, so it wisely disposes men's inclinations to different employments for the good of the public, as each member of the body is situated and qualified for the service of the whole. The genius of some men leads them to a book, of others to the sea, of others to the sword; some are inclined to rural affairs, others to trade, and some have a turn for mechanics; and it is well it is so. *If the whole body were an eye, where were the hearing?* 1 Cor. xii. 17. It was for the common good of Israel that the men of Zebulun were merchants and that the men of Issachar were husbandmen. (2.) That whatever our place and business are it is our wisdom and duty to accommodate ourselves to them, and it is a great happiness to be well pleased with them. Let Zebulun rejoice in his going out; let him thank God for the gains and make the best of the losses and inconveniences of his merchandise, and not despise the meanness, nor envy the quietness, of Issachar's tents. Let *Issachar rejoice in his tents*, let him be well pleased with the retirements and content with the small profits of his country seats, and not grudge that he has not Zebulun's pleasure of travelling and profit of trading. Every business has both its conveniences and inconveniences, and therefore whatever Providence has made our business we ought to bring our minds to it; and it is really a great happiness, whatever our lot is, to be easy with it. This is the gift of God, Eccl. v. 19.

2. That they should both be serviceable in their places to the honour of God and the interests of religion in the nation (v. 19): *They shall call the people to the mountain*, that is, to the *temple*, which Moses foresaw should be built upon a mountain. I see not why this should be confined (as it is by most interpreters) to Zebulun; if both Zebulun and Issachar received the comforts of their respective employments, why may we not suppose that they both took care to give God the glory of them? Two things they shall do for God:—

(1.) They shall invite others to his service.

Call the people to the mountain. [1.] Zebulun shall improve his acquaintance and commerce with the neighbouring nations, to whom he goes out, for this noble purpose, to propagate religion among them, and to invite them into the service of the God of Israel. Note, Men of great business, or large conversation, should wisely and zealously endeavour to recommend the practice of serious godliness to those with whom they converse and among whom their business lies. Such are blessed, for they are blessings. It were well if the enlargement of trade with foreign countries might be made to contribute to the spreading of the gospel. This prophecy concerning Zebulun perhaps looks as far as the preaching of Christ and his apostles, which began in the land of Zebulun (Matt. iv. 14, 15); then they *called the people to the mountain,* that is, to the kingdom of the Messiah, which is called the *mountain of the Lord's house,* Isa. ii. 2. [2.] Issachar that tarries at home, and dwells in tents, shall call upon his neighbours to go up to the sanctuary at the times appointed for their solemn feasts, either because they should be more zealous and forward than their neighbours (and it has been often observed that though those that with Zebulun dwell in the haven of ships, which are places of concourse, have commonly more of the *light* of religion, those that with Issachar dwell in tents in the country have more of the *life* and *heat* of it), and may therefore with their zeal provoke those to a holy emulation that have more knowledge (Ps. cxxii. 1); or because they were more observant of the times appointed for their feasts than others were. One of the Chaldee paraphrasts reads the foregoing verse, *Rejoice, Issachar, in the tents of thy schools,* supposing they would many of them be scholars, and would use their learning for that purpose, according to the revolutions of the year, to give notice of the times of the feasts; for almanacs were not then so common as they are now. And Onkelos more particularly, *Rejoice, Issachar, when thou goest to compute the times of the solemnities at Jerusalem;* for then *the tribes of Israel shall be gathered to the mountain of the house of the sanctuary.* So he reads the beginning of this verse; and many think this the meaning of that character of the men of Issachar in David's time, That *they had understanding of the times to know what Israel ought to do,* 1 Chron. xii. 32. And the character which follows (v. 33) of the men of Zebulun, that they were such as *went forth to battle, expert in war,* perhaps may explain the blessing of that tribe here. Note, Those that have not opportunity as Zebulun had of bringing into the church those that are without may yet be very serviceable to its interest by helping to quicken, encourage, and build up, those that are within. And it is good work to call people to God's ordinances, to put those in remembrance that are forgetful, and to stir up those that are

880

slothful, who will follow, but care not to lead.

(2.) They shall not only invite others to the service of God, but they shall abound in it themselves: *There they shall offer sacrifices of righteousness.* They shall not send others to the temple and stay at home themselves, under pretence that they cannot leave their business; but, when they stir up others to *go speedily to pray before the Lord,* they shall say, *We will go also,* as it is Zech. viii. 21. Note, The good we exhort others to we should ourselves be examples of. And, when they come to the temple, they shall not appear before the Lord empty, but shall bring for the honour and service of God according as he has prospered them, 1 Cor. xvi. 2. [1.] It is here foretold that both these tribes should grow rich. Zebulun that goes abroad shall *suck of the abundance of the seas,* which are full breasts to the merchants, while Issachar, that tarries at home, shall enrich himself with *treasures hid in the sands,* either the fruits of the earth or the underground treasures of metals and minerals, or (because the word for sand here signifies properly the sand of the sea) the rich things thrown up by the sea, for the lot of Issachar reached to the sea-side. Perhaps their success in *calling the people to the mount* is intimated by their *sucking of the abundance of the seas,* for we have a like phrase used for the bringing in of the nations to the church (Isa. lx. 5), *The abundance of the sea shall be converted unto thee,* and (v. 16), *Thou shalt suck the milk of the Gentiles.* It is foretold, [2.] That these tribes, being thus enriched, should *consecrate their gain unto the Lord, and their substance unto the Lord of the whole earth,* Mic. iv. 13. The *merchandise* of Zebulun, and the *hire* of Issachar, shall be *holiness to the Lord* (Isa. xxiii. 18), for thereof they shall *offer sacrifices of righteousness,* that is, sacrifices according to the law. Note, We must serve and honour God with what we have; and where he sows plentifully he expects to reap accordingly. Those that *suck of the abundance of the seas, and of the treasures hid in the sand,* ought to offer sacrifices of righteousness proportionable.

II. The blessing of the tribe of Gad comes next, v. 20, 21. This was one of the tribes that was already seated on that side Jordan where Moses now was. Now,

1. He foretels what this tribe would be, v. 20. (1.) That it would be enlarged, as at present it had a spacious allotment; and he gives God the glory both of its present and of its future extent: *Blessed be he that enlargeth Gad.* We find how this tribe was enlarged by their success in a war which it seems they carried on very religiously against the Hagarites, 1 Chron. v. 19, 20, 22. Note, God is to have the glory of all our enlargements. (2.) That it would be a valiant and victorious tribe, would, if let alone, dwell secure and fearless as a lion; but, if provoked,

would, like a lion, *tear the arm with the crown of the head;* that is, would pull in pieces all that stood in his way, both the arm (that is, the strength) and the crown of the head (that is, the policy and authority) of his enemies. In David's time there were Gadites whose faces were *as the faces of lions,* 1 Chron. xii. 8. Some reckon Jehu to be of this tribe, because the first mention we have of him is at Ramoth Gilead, which belonged to Gad, and they think this may refer to his valiant acts. 2. He commends this tribe for what they had done and were now doing, v. 21. (1.) They had done very wisely for themselves, when they chose their lot with the first, in a country already conquered: *He provided the first part for himself;* though he had a concern for his brethren, yet his charity began at home, and he was willing to see himself first served, first settled. The Gadites were the first and most active movers for an allotment on that side Jordan, and therefore are still mentioned before the Reubenites in the history of that affair, Num. xxxii. 2. And thus, while the other tribes had their portion assigned them by Joshua the conqueror, Gad and his companions had theirs from Moses the law-giver, and in it they were seated by law; or (as the word is) *covered* or protected by a special providence which watched over those that were left behind, while the men of war went forward with their brethren. Note, *Men will praise thee when thou doest well for thyself* (when thou providest first for thyself, as Gad did), Ps. xlix. 18. And God will praise thee when thou doest well for thy soul, which is indeed thyself, and providest the first part for that in a portion from the lawgiver. (2.) They were now doing honestly and bravely for their brethren; for they *came with the heads of the people,* before whom they went armed over Jordan, to *execute the justice of the Lord* upon the Canaanites, under the conduct of Joshua, to whom we afterwards find they solemnly vowed obedience, Josh. i. 12, 16. This was what they undertook to do when they had their lot assigned them, Num. xxxii. 27. This they did, Josh. iv. 12. And, when the wars of Canaan were ended, Joshua dismissed them with a blessing, Josh. xxii. 7. Note, It is a blessed and honourable thing to be helpful to our brethren in their affairs, and particularly to assist in executing the justice of the Lord by suppressing that which is provoking to him: it was this that was counted to Phinehas for righteousness.

22 And of Dan he said, Dan *is* a lion's whelp: he shall leap from Bashan. 23 And of Naphtali he said, O Naphtali, satisfied with favour, and full with the blessing of the LORD: possess thou the west and the south. 24 And of Asher he said, *Let* Asher *be* blessed with children; let him

be acceptable to his brethren, and let him dip his foot in oil. 25 Thy shoes *shall be* iron and brass; and as thy days, *so shall* thy strength *be.*

Here is, I. The blessing of Dan, *v.* 22. Jacob in his blessing had compared him to a serpent for subtlety; Moses compares him to a lion for courage and resolution: and what could stand before those that had the head of a serpent and the heart of a lion? He is compared to the lions that leaped from Bashan, a mountain noted for fierce lions, whence they came down to leap upon their prey in the plains. This may refer either, 1. To the particular victories obtained by Samson (who was of this tribe) over the Philistines. *The Spirit of the Lord began to move him in the camp of Dan* when he was very young, as *a lion's whelp,* so that in his attacks upon the Philistines he surprised them, and overpowered them by main strength, as a lion does his prey; and one of his first exploits was the rending of a lion. Or, 2. To a more general achievement of that tribe, when a party of them, upon information brought them of the security of Laish, which lay in the furthest part of the land of Canaan from them, surprised it, and soon made themselves masters of it. See Judg. xviii. 27. And, the mountains of Bashan lying not far from that city, probably thence they made their descent upon it; and therefore are here said to *leap from Bashan.*

II. The blessing of Naphtali, *v.* 23. He looks upon this tribe with wonder, and applauds it: "O Naphtali, thou art happy, thou shalt be so, mayest thou be ever so!" Three things make up the happiness of this tribe:—1. Be thou *satisfied with favour.* Some understand it of the favour of men, their good-will and good word. Jacob had described this tribe to be, generally, courteous obliging people, giving goodly words, as the loving hind, Gen. xlix. 21. Now what should they get by being so? Moses here tells them they should have an interest in the affections of their neighbours, and be satisfied with favour. Those that are loving shall be beloved. But others understand it of the favour of God, and with good reason; for that only is the favour that is satisfying to the soul and puts true gladness into the heart. Those are happy indeed that have the favour of God; and those shall have it that place their satisfaction in it, and reckon that, in having that, they have enough and desire no more. 2. Be thou *full with the blessing of the Lord,* that is, not only with those good things that are the fruits of the blessing (corn, and wine, and oil), but with the blessing itself; that is, the grace of God, according to his promise and covenant. Those who have that blessing may well reckon themselves full: they need nothing else to make them happy. "The portion of the tribe of Naphtali" (the Jews say) "was so fruitful, and the productions so forward, though it lay north, that those of that tribe were generally the first that brought their first-fruits to the temple ; and so they had first the blessing from the priest, which was the blessing of the Lord." Capernaum, in which Christ chiefly resided, lay in this tribe. 3. Be thou *in possession of the sea and the south ;* so it may be read, that is, of that sea which shall lie south of thy lot, that was the sea of Galilee, which we so often read of in the gospels, directly north of which the lot of this tribe lay, and which was of great advantage to this tribe, witness the wealth of Capernaum and Bethsaida, which lay within this tribe, and upon the shore of that sea. See how Moses was guided by a spirit of prophesy in these blessings ; for before the lot was cast into the lap he foresaw and foretold how the disposal of it would be.

III. The blessing of Asher, v. 24, 25. Four things he prays for and prophecies concerning this tribe, which carries blessedness in its name ; for Leah called the father of it *Asher,* saying, *Happy am I,* Gen. xxx. 13. 1. The increase of their numbers. They were now a numerous tribe, Num. xxvi. 47. "Let it be more so : *Let Asher be blessed with children.*" Note, Children, especially children of the covenant, are blessings, not burdens. 2. Their interest in their neighbours : *Let him be acceptable to his brethren.* Note, It is a very desirable thing to have the love and good-will of those we live among : it is what we should pray to God for, who has all hearts in his hand ; and what we should endeavour to gain by meekness and humility, and a readiness, as we have ability and opportunity, to do good to all men. 3. The richness of their land. (1.) Above ground : *Let him dip his foot in oil,* that is, "Let him have such plenty of it in his lot that he may not only anoint his head with it, but, if he please, wash his feet in it," which was not commonly done ; yet we find our blessed Saviour so acceptable to his brethren that his feet were anointed with the most precious ointment, Luke vii. 46. (2.) Under ground : *Thy shoes shall be iron and brass,* that is, "Thou shalt have great plenty of these metals (mines of them) in thy own ground, which by an uncommon blessing shall have both its surface and its bowels rich :" or, if they had them not as the productions of their own country, they should have them imported from abroad ; for the lot of this tribe lay on the sea-coast. The Chaldee paraphrasts understand this figuratively : "Thou shalt be strong and bright, as iron and brass." 4. The continuance of their strength and vigour : *As thy days, so shall thy strength be.* Many paraphrase it thus, "The strength of thy old age shall be like that of thy youth ; thou shalt not feel a decay, nor be the worse for the wearing, but shalt renew thy youth ; as if not thy shoes only, but thy bones, were iron and brass." The day is often in scripture put for the events of the day ; and, taking

it so here, it is a promise that God would graciously support them under their trials and troubles, whatever they were. And so it is a promise sure to all the spiritual seed of Abraham, that God will wisely proportion their graces and comforts to the services and sufferings he calls them out to. Have they work appointed them ? They shall have strength to do it. Have they burdens appointed them ? They shall have strength to bear them ; and never be *tempted above that they are able.* Faithful is he that has thus promised, and hath caused us to hope in this promise.

26 *There is* none like unto the God of Jeshurun, *who* rideth upon the heaven in thy help, and in his excellency on the sky. 27 The eternal God *is thy* refuge, and underneath *are* the everlasting arms : and he shall thrust out the enemy from before thee ; and shall say, Destroy *them.* 28 Israel then shall dwell in safety alone : the fountain of Jacob *shall be* upon a land of corn and wine ; also his heavens shall drop down dew. 29 Happy *art* thou, O Israel : who *is* like unto thee, O people saved by the LORD, the shield of thy help, and who *is* the sword of thy excellency ! and thine enemies shall be found liars unto thee ; and thou shalt tread upon their high places.

These are the last words of all that ever Moses, that great writer, that great dictator, either wrote himself or had written from his dictation ; they are therefore very remarkable, and no doubt we shall find them very improving. Moses, the man of God (who had as much reason as ever any mere man had to know both), with his last breath magnifies both the God of Israel and the Israel of God. They are both incomparable in his eye ; and we are sure that in this his judgment of both his eye did not wax dim.

I. No God like the God of Israel. None of the gods of the nations were capable of doing that for their worshippers which Jehovah did for his : *There is none like unto the God of Jeshurun, v.* 26. Note, When we are expecting that God should bless us in doing well for us we must bless him by speaking well of him : and one of the most solemn ways of praising God is by acknowledging that there is none like him. Now, 1. This was the honour of Israel. Every nation boasted of its god ; but none had such a God to boast of as Israel had. 2. It was their happiness that they were taken into covenant with such a God. Two things he takes notice of as proofs of the incontestable pre-eminence of the God of Jeshurun above all other gods :

(1.) His sovereign power and authority: *He rides upon the heavens,* and with the greatest state and magnificence on the skies. Riding on the heavens denotes his greatness and glory, in which he manifests himself to the upper world, and the use he makes of the influences of heaven, and the productions of the clouds, in bringing to pass his own counsels in this lower world: he manages and directs them as a man does the horse he rides on. When he has any thing to do for his people he *rides upon the heavens* to do it; for he does it swiftly and strongly: no enemy can either anticipate or obstruct the progress of him that rides on the heavens. (2.) His boundless eternity; he is the eternal God, and his arms are *everlasting,* v. 27. The gods of the heathen were but lately invented, and would shortly perish; but the God of Jeshurun is eternal: he was before all worlds, and will be when time and days shall be no more. See Hab. i. 12.

II. No people like the Israel of God. Having pronounced each tribe happy, in the close he pronounces all together very happy, so happy in all respects that there was no nation under the sun comparable to them (v. 29): *Happy art thou, O Israel,* a people whose God is the Lord, on that account truly happy, and *none like unto thee.* If Israel honour God as a non-such God, he will favour them so as to make them a non-such people, the envy of all their neighbours and the joy of all their well-wishers. *Who is like unto thee, O°people? Behold, thou art fair, my love,* says Christ of his spouse. To which she presently returns, *Behold, thou art fair, my beloved. What one nation* (no, not all the nations together) is *like thy people Israel?* 2 Sam. vii. 23. What is here said of the church of Israel and the honours and privileges of it is certainly to be applied to *the church of the first-born,* that are written in heaven. The Christian church is the Israel of God, as the apostle calls it (Gal. vi. 16), on which there shall be peace, and which is dignified above all societies in the world, as Israel was.

1. Never were people so well seated and sheltered (v. 27): *The eternal God is thy refuge.* Or, as the word signifies, "thy habitation, or *mansion-house,* in which thou art safe, and easy, and at rest, as a man in his own house." Every Israelite indeed is at home in God; the soul returns to him, and reposes in him as its resting-place (Ps. cxvi. 7), its hiding-place, Ps. xxxii. 7. And those that make him their habitation shall have all the comforts and benefits of a habitation in him, Ps. xci. 1. Moses had an eye to God as the habitation of Israel when they were wandering in the wilderness (Ps. xc. 1): *Lord, thou hast been our dwelling-place in all generations.* And now that they were going to settle in Canaan they must not change their habitation; still they will need, and still they shall have, the eternal God for their

dwelling-place; without him Canaan itself would be a wilderness, and a land of darkness.

2. Never were people so well supported and borne up: *Underneath are the everlasting arms;* that is, the almighty power of God is engaged for the protection and consolation of all that trust in him, in their greatest straits and distresses, and under their heaviest burdens. The everlasting arms shall support, (1.) The interests of the church in general, that they shall not sink, or be run down; underneath the church is that rock of ages on which it is built, and against which the gates of hell shall never prevail, Matt. xvi. 18. (2.) The spirits of particular believers, so that, though they may be oppressed, they shall not be overwhelmed by any trouble. How low soever the people of God are at any time brought, everlasting arms are underneath them to keep the spirit from sinking, from fainting, and the faith from failing, even when they are pressed above measure. The everlasting covenant, and the everlasting consolations that flow from it, are indeed everlasting arms, with which believers have been wonderfully sustained, and kept·cheerful in the worst of times; divine grace is sufficient for them, 2 Cor. xii. 9.

3. Never were people so well commanded and led on to battle: " *He shall thrust out the enemy from before thee* by his almighty power, which will make room for thee; and by a commission which will bear thee out by which he shall say, *Destroy them.*" They were now entering upon a land that was in the full possession of a strong and formidable people, and who, being its first planters, looked upon themselves as its rightful owners; how shall Israel justify, and how shall they accomplish, the expulsion of them? (1.) God will give them a commission to destroy the Canaanites, and that will justify them, and bear them out in it, against all the world. He that is sovereign Lord of all lives and all lands not only allowed and permitted, but expressly commanded and appointed the children of Israel both to take possession of the land of Canaan and to put to the sword the people of Canaan, which, being thus authorized, they might not only lawfully but honourably do, without incurring the least stain or imputation of theft by the one or murder by the other. (2.) God will give them power and ability to destroy them; nay, he will in effect do it to their hands: he will *thrust out the enemy from before them;* for the very fear of Israel shall put them to flight. God *drove out the heathen to plant his people,* Ps. xliv. 2. Thus believers are more than conquerors over their spiritual enemies, through Christ that loved them. The captain of our salvation *thrust· out the enemy from before us* when he overcame the world and spoiled principalities and powers on the cross: and the word of command to us is,

"*Destroy them;* pursue the victory, and you shall divide the spoil."

4. Never were people so well secured and protected (*v.* 28): *Israel shall then dwell in safety alone.* Those that dwell in God, and make his name their strong tower, *dwell in safety;* the *place of their defence is the munitions of rocks,* Isa. xxxiii. 16. They shall dwell in safety alone. (1.) Though alone. Though they contract no alliances with their neighbours, nor have any reason to expect help or succour from any of them, yet they shall dwell in safety; they shall really be safe, and they shall think themselves so. (2.) Because alone. They shall dwell in safety as long as they continue pure, and unmixed with the heathen, a singular and peculiar people. Their distinction from other nations, though it made them *like a speckled bird* (Jer. xii. 9), and exposed them to the ill-will of those about them, yet was really their preservation from the mischief their neighbours wished them, as it kept them under the divine protection. All that keep close to God shall be kept safely by him. It is promised that in the kingdom of Christ *Israel shall dwell safely,* Jer. xxiii. 6.

5. Never were people so well provided for: *The fountain of Jacob* (that is, the present generation of that people, which is as the fountain to all the streams that shall hereafter descend and be derived from it) shall now presently be fixed upon a good land. *The eye of Jacob* (so it might be read, for the same word signifies a fountain and an eye) *is upon the land of corn and wine,* that is, where they now lay encamped they had Canaan in their eye, it was just before their faces, on the other side the river, and they would have it in their hands and under their feet quickly. This land upon which they had set their eye was blessed both with the fatness of the earth and the dew of heaven; it was a *land of corn and wine,* substantial and useful productions: also his heavens (as if the heavens were particularly designed to be blessings to that land) *shall drop down dew,* without which, though the soil were ever so good, the corn and wine would soon fail. Every Israelite indeed has his eye, the eye of faith, upon the better country, the heavenly Canaan, which is richly replenished with better things than corn and wine.

6. Never were people so well helped. If they were in any strait, God himself rode upon the heavens for *their help, v.* 26. And they were *a people saved by the Lord, v.* 29. If they were in danger of any harm, or in want of any good, they had an eternal God to go to, an almighty power to trust to; nothing could hurt those whom God helped, nor was it possible that that people should perish which *was saved by the Lord.* Those that are added to the gospel Israel are *such as shall be saved,* Acts ii. 47.

7. Never were people so well armed. God himself was the shield of their help by whom

they were armed defensively, and sufficiently guarded against all assailants: and he was the *sword of their excellency,* by whom they were armed offensively, and made both formidable and successful in all their wars. God is called the *sword of their excellency* because, in fighting for them, he made them to excel other people, or because in all he did for them he had an eye to his sanctuary among them, which is called the *excellency of Jacob,* Ps. xlvii. 4; Ezek. xxiv. 21; Amos vi. 8. Those in whose hearts is the excellency of holiness have God himself for their shield and sword—are defended by the whole armour of God; his word is their sword, and faith in it is their shield, Eph. vi. 16, 17.

8. Never were people so well assured of victory over their enemies: *They shall be found liars unto thee;* that is, "shall be forced to submit to thee sorely against their will, so that it will be but a counterfeit submission; yet the point shall be gained, for thou shalt *tread upon their necks"* (so the LXX.), which we find done, Josh. x. 24. "Thou shalt tread down their strong-holds, be they ever so high, and trample upon their palaces and temples, though esteemed ever so sacred. *If thy enemies be found liars to thee"* (so some read it), *"thou shalt tread upon their high places;* if they will not be held by the bonds of leagues and treaties, they shall be broken by the force of war." Thus shall the God of peace tread Satan under the feet of all believers, and shall *do it shortly,* Rom. xvi. 20.

Now lay all this together, and then you will say, *Happy art thou, O Israel! Who is like unto thee, O people!* Thrice happy the people whose God is the Lord.

CHAP. XXXIV.

Having read how Moses finished his testimony, we are told here how he immediately after finished his life. This chapter could not be written by Moses himself, but was added by Joshua or Eleazar, or, as bishop Patrick conjectures, by Samuel, who was a prophet, and wrote by divine authority what he found in the records of Joshua, and his successors the judges. We have had an account of his dying words, here we have an account of his dying work, and that is work we must all do shortly, and it had need be well done. Here is, I. The view Moses had of the land of Canaan just before he died, ver. 1—4. II. His death and burial, ver. 5, 6. III. His age, ver. 7. IV. Israel's mourning for him, ver. 8. V. His successor, ver. 9. VI. His character, ver. 10, &c.

AND Moses went up from the plains of Moab unto the mountain of Nebo, to the top of Pisgah, that *is* over against Jericho. And the LORD showed him all the land of Gilead, unto Dan, 2 And all Naphtali, and the land of Ephraim, and Manasseh, and all the land of Judah, unto the utmost sea, 3 And the south, and the plain of the valley of Jericho, the city of palm trees, unto Zoar. 4 And the LORD said unto him, This *is* the land which I sware unto Abraham, unto Isaac, and unto Jacob, saying, I will give it unto thy seed: I have caused thee to see *it* with thine eyes, but thou shalt not go over thither. Here is, I. Moses climbing upwards towards heaven, as high as the top of Pisgah, there to die; for that was the place appointed, *ch.* xxxii. 49, 50. Israel lay encamped upon the flat grounds in the plains of Moab, and thence he went up, according to order, to the mountain of Nebo, to the highest point or ridge of that mountain, which was called *Pisgah, v.* 1. Pisgah is an appellative name for all such eminences. It should seem, Moses went up alone to the top of Pisgah, *alone without help*—a sign that his natural force was not abated when on the last day of his life he could walk up to the top of a high hill without such supporters as once he had when his hands were heavy (Exod. xvii. 12), *alone without company.* When he had made an end of blessing Israel, we may suppose, he solemnly took leave of Joshua, and Eleazar, and the rest of his friends, who probably brought him to the foot of the hill; but then he gave them such a charge as Abraham gave to his servants at the foot of another hill: *Tarry you here while I go yonder and die:* they must not see him die, because they must not know of his sepulchre. But, whether this were so or not, he went up to the top of Pisgah, 1. To show that he was willing to die. When he knew the place of his death, he was so far from avoiding it that he cheerfully mounted a steep hill to come at it. Note, Those that through grace are well acquainted with another world, and have been much conversant with it, need not be afraid to leave this. 2. To show that he looked upon death as his ascension. The soul of a man, of a good man, when it leaves the body, *goes upwards* (Eccl. iii. 21), in conformity to which motion of the soul, the body of Moses shall go along with it as far upwards as its earth will carry it. When God's servants are sent for out of the world, the summons runs thus, *Go up and die.*

II. Moses looking downward again towards this earth, to see the earthly Canaan into which he must never enter, but therein by faith looking forwards to the heavenly Canaan into which he should now immediately enter. God had threatened that he should not come into the possession of Canaan, and the threatening is fulfilled. But he had also promised that he should have a prospect of it, and the promise is here performed: *The Lord showed him* all that good land, *v.* 1. 1. If he went up alone to the top of Pisgah, yet he *was not alone, for the Father was with him,* John xvi. 32. If a man has any friends, he will have them about him when he lies a dying. But if, either through God's providence or their unkindness, it should so happen that we should then be alone, we need *fear no evil* if the great and good Shepherd

be with us, Ps. xxiii. 4. 2. Though his sight was very good, and he had all the advantage of high ground that he could desire for the prospect, yet he could not have seen what he now saw, all Canaan from end to end (reckoned about 160 miles), and from side to side (reckoned about fifty or sixty miles), if his sight had not been miraculously assisted and enlarged, and therefore it is said, *The Lord showed it to him.* Note, All the pleasant prospects we have of the better country we are beholden to the grace of God for; it is he that gives the *spirit of wisdom* as well as the *spirit of revelation,* the eye as well as the object. This sight which God here gave Moses of Canaan, probably, the devil designed to mimic, and pretended to out-do, when in an airy phantom he showed to our Saviour, whom he had placed like Moses upon an *exceedingly high mountain,* all the kingdoms of the world and the glory of them, not gradually, as here, first one country and then another, but all in a moment of time. 3. He saw it at a distance. Such a sight the Old-Testament saints had of the kingdom of the Messiah; they *saw it afar off.* Thus Abraham, long before this, saw Christ's day; and, being fully persuaded of it, embraced it in the promise, leaving others to embrace it in the performance, Heb. xi. 13. Such a sight believers now have, through grace, of the bliss and glory of their future state. The word and ordinances are to them what Mount Pisgah was to Moses; from them they have comfortable prospects of the glory to be revealed, and rejoice in hope of it. 4. He saw it, but must never enjoy it. As God sometimes takes his people away from the evil to come, so at other times he takes them away from the good to come, that is, the good which shall be enjoyed by the church in the present world. Glorious things are spoken of the kingdom of Christ in the latter days, its advancement, enlargement, and flourishing state; we foresee it, but we are not likely to live to see it. Those that shall come after us, we hope, will enter that promised land, which is a comfort to us when we find our own carcases falling in this wilderness. See 2 Kings vii. 2. 5. He saw all this just before his death. Sometimes God reserves the brightest discoveries of his grace to his people to be the support of their dying moments. Canaan was *Immanuel's land* (Isa. viii. 8), so that in viewing it he had a view of the blessings we enjoy by Christ. It was a type of heaven (Heb. xi. 16), which faith is the substance and evidence of. Note, Those may leave this world with a great deal of cheerfulness that die in the faith of Christ, and in the hope of heaven, and with Canaan in their eye. Having thus seen the salvation of God, we may well say, *Lord, now let thou thy servant depart in peace.*

5 So Moses the servant of the Lord died there in the land of Moab, ac-

cording to the word of the LORD. 6 And he buried him in a valley in the land of Moab, over against Beth-peor: but no man knoweth of his sepulchre unto this day. 7 And Moses *was* a hundred and twenty years old when he died: his eye was not dim, nor his natural force abated. 8 And the children of Israel wept for Moses in the plains of Moab thirty days: so the days of weeping *and* mourning for Moses were ended.

Here is, I. The death of Moses (*v.* 5): *Moses the servant of the Lord died.* God told him he must not go over Jordan, and, though at first he prayed earnestly for the reversing of the sentence, yet God's answer to his prayer sufficed him, and now he *spoke no more of that matter,* ch. iii. 26. Thus our blessed Saviour prayed that the cup might pass from him, yet, since it might not, he acquiesced with, *Father, thy will be done.* Moses had reason to desire to live a while longer in the world. He was old, it is true, but he had not yet *attained to the years of the life of his fathers ;* his father Amram lived to be 137 ; his grandfather Kohath 133 ; his great grandfather Levi 137 ; Exod. vi. 16—20. And why must Moses, whose life was more serviceable than any of theirs, die at 120, especially since he felt not the decays of age, but was as fit for service as ever ? Israel could ill spare him at this time ; his conduct and his converse with God would be as great a happiness to them in the conquest of Canaan as the courage of Joshua. It bore hard upon Moses himself, when he had gone through all the fatigues of the wilderness, to be prevented from enjoying the pleasures of Canaan; when he had borne the burden and heat of the day, to resign the honour of finishing the work to another, and that not his son, but his servant, who must enter into his labours. We may suppose that this was not pleasant to flesh and blood. But *the man Moses was very meek ;* God will have it so, and he cheerfully submits. 1. He is here called *the servant of the Lord,* not only as a good man (all the saints are God's servants), but as a useful man, eminently useful, who had served God's counsels in bringing Israel out of Egypt, and leading them through the wilderness. It was more his honour to be the *servant of the Lord* than to be king in Jeshurun. 2. Yet he dies. Neither his piety nor his usefulness would exempt him from the stroke of death. God's servants must die that they may rest from their labours, receive their recompence, and make room for others. When God's servants are removed, and must serve him no longer on earth, they go to serve him better, to serve him *day and night in his temple.* 3. He dies in the land of Moab, short of Canaan, while as yet he

and his people were in an unsettled condition and had not entered into their rest. In the heavenly Canaan there will be no more death. 4. He dies *according to the word of the Lord. At the mouth of the Lord ;* so the word is. The Jews say, " with a kiss from the mouth of God." No doubt, he died very easily (it was an *ευθανασία—a delightful death),* there were no bands in his death ; and he had in his death a most pleasing taste of the love of God to him : but that he *died at the mouth of the Lord* means no more but that he died in compliance with the will of God. Note, The servants of the Lord, when they have done all their other work, must die at last, in obedience to their Master, and be freely willing to go home whenever he sends for them, Acts xxi. 13.

II. His burial, *v.* 6. It is a groundless conceit of some of the Jews that Moses was translated to heaven as Elijah was, for it is expressly said he *died and was buried ;* yet probably he was raised to meet Elias, to grace the solemnity of Christ's transfiguration. ˙1. God himself buried him, namely, by the ministry of angels, which made this funeral, though very private, yet very magnificent. Note, God takes care of the dead bodies of his servants ; as their death is precious, so is their dust, not a grain of it shall be lost, but the covenant with it shall be remembered. When Moses was dead, God buried him ; when Christ was dead, God raised him, for the law of Moses was to have an end, but not the gospel of Christ. Believers are dead to the law that they might be married to another, even *to him who is raised from the dead,* Rom. vii. 4. It should seem Michael, that is, Christ (as some think), had the burying of Moses, for by him the Mosaical ordinances were abolished and taken out of the way, *nailed to his cross,* and buried in his grave, Col. ii. 14. 2. He was buried in a valley *over against Beth-peor.* How easily could the angels that buried him have conveyed him over Jordan and buried him with tne patriarchs in the cave of Machpelah ! But we must learn not to be over-solicitous about the place of our burial. If the soul be at rest with God, the matter is not great where the body rests. One of the Chaldee paraphrasts says, " He was buried over against Beth-peor, that, whenever Baal-peor boasted of the Israelites being joined to him, the grave of Moses over against his temple might be a check to him." 3. The particular place was not known, lest the children of Israel, who were so very prone to idolatry, should have enshrined and worshipped the dead body of Moses, that great founder and benefactor of their nation. It is true we read not, among all the instances of their idolatry, that they worshipped relics, the reason of which perhaps was because they were thus prevented from worshipping Moses, and so could not for shame worship any other. Some of the Jewish writers say that the body of Moses was concealed, that necromancers, who enquired of the dead, might not disquiet him, as the witch of Endor did Samuel, to *bring him up.* God would not have the name and memory of his servant Moses thus abused. Many think this was the contest between Michael and the devil about the body of Moses, mentioned Jude 9. The devil would make the place known that it might be a snare to the people, and Michael would not let him. Those therefore who are for giving divine honours to the relics of departed saints side with the devil against Michael our prince.

III. His age, *v.* 7. His life was prolonged, 1. To old age. He was 120 years old, which, though far short of the years of the patriarchs, yet much exceeded the years of most of his contemporaries, for the ordinary age of man had been lately reduced to seventy, Ps. xc. 10. The years of the life of Moses were three forties. The first forty he lived a courtier, at ease and in honour in Pharaoh's court; the second forty he lived a poor desolate shepherd in Midian; the third forty he lived a king in Jeshurun, in honour and power, but encumbered with a great deal of care and toil: so changeable is the world we live in, and alloyed with such mixtures; but the world before us is unmixed and unchangeable. 2. To a good old age: *His eye was not dim* (as Isaac's, Gen. xxvii. 1, and Jacob's, Gen. xlviii. 10), *nor was his natural force abated;* there was no decay either of the strength of his body or of the vigour and activity of his mind, but he could still speak, and write, and walk as well as ever. His understanding was as clear, and his memory as strong, as ever. " His visage was not wrinkled," say some of the Jewish writers; " he had lost never a tooth," say others; and many of them expound it of the shining of his face (Exod. xxxiv. 30), that that continued to the last. This was the general reward of his services; and it was in particular the effect of his extraordinary meekness, for that is a grace which is, as much as any other, *health to the navel and marrow to the bones.* Of the moral law which was given by Moses, though the condemning power be vacated to true believers, yet the commands are still binding, and will be to the end of the world; the eye of them is not waxen dim, for they shall discern the thoughts and intents of the heart, nor is their natural force or obligation abated, but still we are *under the law to Christ.*

IV. The solemn mourning that there was for him, *v.* 8. It is a debt owing to the surviving honour of deceased worthies to follow them with our tears, as those who loved and valued them, are sensible of our loss of them, and are truly humbled for those sins which have provoked God to deprive us of them; for penitential tears very fitly mix with these. Observe, 1. Who the mourners were: *The children of Israel.* They all conformed to the ceremony, whatever it was, though some of them perhaps, who were ill-affected to

his government, were but mock-mourners; yet we may suppose there were those among them who had formerly quarrelled with him and his government, and perhaps had been of those who spoke of stoning him, who now were sensible of their loss, and heartily lamented him when he was removed from them, though they knew not how to value him when he was with them. Thus those who had murmured were made to learn doctrine, Isa. xxix. 24. Note, The loss of good men, especially good governers, is to be much lamented and laid to heart: those are stupid who do not consider it. 2. How long they mourned: *Thirty days.* So long the formality lasted, and we may suppose there were some in whom the mourning continued much longer. Yet the *ending of the days of weeping and mourning* for Moses is an intimation that, how great soever our losses have been, we must not abandon ourselves to perpetual grief; we must suffer the wound at least to heal up in time. If we hope to go to heaven rejoicing, why should we resolve to go to the grave mourning? The ceremonial law of Moses is dead and buried in the grave of Christ; but the Jews have not yet ended the days of their mourning for it.

9 And Joshua the son of Nun was full of the spirit of wisdom; for Moses had laid his hands upon him : and the children of Israel hearkened unto him, and did as the LORD commanded Moses. 10 And there arose not a prophet since in Israel like unto Moses, whom the LORD knew face to face, 11 In all the signs and the wonders, which the LORD sent him to do in the land of Egypt to Pharaoh, and to all his servants, and to all his land, 12 And in all that mighty hand, and in all the great terror which Moses showed in the sight of all Israel.

We have here a very honourable encomium passed both on Moses and Joshua; each has his praise, and should have. It is ungrateful so to magnify our living friends as to forget the merits of those that are gone, to whose memories there is a debt of honour due : all the respect must not be paid to the rising sun; and, on the other hand, it is unjust so to cry up the merits of those that are gone as to despise the benefit we have in those that survive and succeed them. Let God be glorified in both, as here.

I. Joshua is praised as a man admirably qualified for the work to which he was called, *v.* 9. Moses brought Israel to the borders of Canaan and then died and left them, to signify that *the law made nothing perfect,* Heb. vii. 19. It brings men into a wilderness of conviction, but not into the Canaan of rest and settled peace. It is an honour reserved for Joshua (our Lord Jesus, of whom Joshua was a type) to do that for us which *the law could not do, in that it was weak through the flesh,* Rom. viii. 3. Through him we enter into rest, the spiritual rest of conscience and eternal rest in heaven. Three things concurred to clear Joshua's call to this great undertaking:—1. God fitted him for it: *He was full of the spirit of wisdom;* and so he had need who had such a peevish people to rule, and such a politic people to conquer. Conduct is as requisite in a general as courage. Herein Joshua was a type of Christ, in whom are hidden the treasures of wisdom. 2. Moses, by the divine appointment, had ordained him to it: *He had laid his hands upon him,* so substituting him to be his successor, and praying to God to qualify him for the service to which he had called him; and this comes in as a reason why God gave him a more than ordinary *spirit of wisdom,* because his designation to the government was God's own act (those whom God employs he will in some measure make fit for the employment) and because this was the thing that Moses had asked of God for him when he laid his hands on him. When the bodily presence of Christ withdrew from his church, he prayed the Father to send another Comforter, and obtained what he prayed for. 3. The people cheerfully owned him and submitted to him. Note, An interest in the affections of people is a great advantage, and a great encouragement to those that are called to public trusts of what kind soever. It was also a great mercy to the people that when Moses was dead they were not as sheep having no shepherd, but had one ready among them in whom they did unanimously, and might with the highest satisfaction, acquiesce.

II. Moses is praised (*v.* 10—12), and with good reason.

1. He was indeed a very great man, especially upon two accounts:—(1.) His intimacy with the God of nature: *God knew him face to face,* and so he knew God. See Num. xii. 8. He saw more of the glory of God than any (at least of the Old-Testament saints) ever did. He had more free and frequent access to God, and was spoken to not in dreams, and visions, and slumberings on the bed, but when he was awake and standing before the cherubim. Other prophets, when God appeared and spoke to them, were struck with terror (Dan. x. 7), but Moses, whenever he received a divine revelation, preserved his tranquillity. (2.) His interest and power in the kingdom of nature. The miracles of judgment he wrought in Egypt

before Pharaoh, and the miracles of mercy he wrought in the wilderness before Israel, served to demonstrate that he was a particular favourite of Heaven, and had an extraordinary commission to act as he did on this earth. Never was there any man whom Israel had more reason to love, or whom the enemies of Israel had more reason to fear. Observe, The historian calls the miracles Moses wrought *signs and wonders,* done with *a mighty hand and great terror,* which may refer to the terrors of Mount Sinai, by which God fully ratified Moses's commission and demonstrated it beyond exception to be divine, and this *in the sight of all Israel.*

2. He was greater than any other of the prophets of the Old Testament. Though they were men of great interest in heaven and great influence upon earth, yet they were none of them to be compared with this great man; none of them either so evidenced or executed a commission from heaven as Moses did. This encomium of Moses seems to have been written long after his death, yet then there had not arisen any prophet *like unto Moses,* nor did there arise any such between that period and the *sealing up of the vision and prophecy.* By Moses God gave the law, and moulded and formed the Jewish church; by the other prophets he only sent particular reproofs, directions, and predictions. The last of the prophets concludes with a charge *to remember the law of Moses,* Mal. iv. 4. Christ himself often appealed to the writings of Moses, and vouched him for a witness, as one that *saw his day* at a distance *and spoke of him.* But, as far as the other prophets came short of him, our Lord Jesus went beyond him. His doctrine was more excellent, his miracles were more illustrious, and his communion with his Father was more intimate, for he *had lain in his bosom from eternity,* and by him God does now in these last days speak to us. Moses was faithful as a servant, but Christ as a Son. The history of Moses leaves him buried in the plains of Moab, and concludes with the period of his government; but the history of our Saviour leaves him sitting *at the right hand of the Majesty on high,* and we are assured that *of the increase of his government and peace there shall be no end.* The apostle, in his epistle to the Hebrews, largely proves the pre-eminence of Christ above Moses, as a good reason why we that are Christians should be obedient, faithful, and constant, to that holy religion which we make profession of. God, by his grace, make us all so!

888